The Gun Digest® Book of
Modern
15th Edition
GUN VALUES
The Shooter's Guide to Guns 1900–Present

Edited by Dan Shideler

©2009 Krause Publications, Inc., a subsidiary of F+W Media, Inc.

Published by

Gun Digest® Books
An imprint of F+W Media, Inc.
700 East State Street • Iola, WI 54990-0001
715-445-2214 • 888-457-2873
www.gundigestbooks.com

Our toll-free number to place an order or obtain
a free catalog is (800) 258-0929.

Library of Congress Control Number: 2008937698

ISBN 13: 978-0-89689-824-0
ISBN 10: 0-89689-824-5

Designed by Kara Grundman
Edited by Dan Shideler

Printed in the United States of America

The **Gun Digest**® Book Of
Modern
GUN VALUES
15th Edition

Table of Contents

Arms Pricing & Reference

Introduction

This 14th edition of *Modern Gun Values* continues its established role as an ongoing research project within the field of modern arms collecting and valuing. It is as much a firearm identification guide – providing over 3000 photographs of 20th- and 21st-century handguns, rifles, shotguns and commemoratives – as it is a guide to current used firearm values.

As a basic reference work, it provides specifications for most of the world's small arms manufactured in or imported into the United States since 1900. Over 7000 firearms are documented and valued in these pages.

For some of the more widely collected firearms – such as Colt Single Action Armies, High Standards, Lugers and Mausers – our coverage includes most if not all of the most commonly encountered variations as well as some rarely found in even advanced collections. We also include selected military firearms such as Nambus and Tokarevs, but our focus is on commercial firearms.

Because of its historical base, *Modern Gun Values* does include some prototypes, experimental pieces and one-of-a-kind developmental or evolutionary models which are very rare and seldom, if ever, seen on the used firearm market. These rarities are important and interesting to document but, as non-production firearms, next to impossible to price since they have little history on the used gun market.

Modern Gun Values is not 100 percent comprehensive – nor can it be, given that manufacturers have their own product development cycles that may or may not coincide with our production schedules. Also, many manufacturers provide private or "boutique" models for large distributors that virtually defy categorization. Any attempt to include data on every firearm manufacturer over the last century would result in a book twice the size of the collected US Tax Code, and twice as burdensome. However, we are quite confident that this 14th edition of *Modern Gun Values* will prove of inestimable value in identifying and assigning realistic dollar values to 99 percent of the used firearms most frequently encountered. For those readers seeking more comprehensive treatment, to the extent that it is possible, or for those seeking data on pre-1900 firearms, we recommend *Standard Catalog of Firearms* or *Flayderman's Guide To Antique American Firearms and Their Values*, both published by Krause Publications.

HOW TO USE THIS EDITION

Modern Gun Values is divided into four major sections – Handguns, Rifles, Shotguns and Commemoratives. Within each of these sections the individual firearms entries are listed in numerical model, then alphabetical, order. (A valuable reference section is also included in the back pages of this book.)

Readers can locate a particular gun in three ways: by browsing through the sections and alphabetical manufacturers' listings; by consulting the comprehensive "GUNDEX" index section; or by consulting the "Manufacturers' Directory" that precedes each respective section of the book. We have attempted to improve the illustrations shown in this book wherever possible and especially in those cases in which illustrations help the reader to differentiate between similar models.

We have established a three-tiered pricing approach for each firearm based on the six NRA Modern Condition Pricing Standards: New, Perfect, Excellent, Very Good, Good and Fair. Each firearm has been evaluated to determine which three NRA standards most accurately reflect the condition in which the particular firearm is most likely to be found on the used market; the firearm is priced accordingly. For example, firearms currently on the retail market, or manufactured in the last four years, will most always be found in New or Perfect condition on the used market, while most older firearms will rarely be found in any condition exceeding Very Good. The three pricing levels we provide reflect current observations of prices seen at gun shows, in the gun shops or in the various periodicals, dealer's catalogs or at auction sales.

KEYS TO DETERMINING VALUE

There are three primary factors that are key to establishing a firearm's value. These are demand, availability and condition.

Demand and Availability

One of the factors driving demand – and thus the value of a particular firearm – is availability. When demand exceeds availability, the price of the firearm increases. This pertains not only to collectibles but to shooting guns as well. For example, it is not unusual for a current-production firearm in limited supply to sell in the marketplace for prices considerably above the manufacturer's suggested list price. Even some Colt and Smith & Wesson models have enjoyed such run-ups. However, realize that in this case when supply finally catches up with demand, prices will dip. This was the case, to cite one example among thousands, in 2001 when Browning released its High Grade Model 1895 lever-action rifle in the legendary 405 Winchester chambering.

For collectibles, although the supply is fixed, demand plays a similar role in establishing value. In the used firearms markets, demand seems to come in instinctive waves, much as a school of minnows will wheel and change direction in perfect synchronicity, as though by telepathy. Believe it or not, there was a day when Webley commercial revolvers in excellent condition could be had for well under $100, even adjusted for inflation. Then one day Webleys caught on for some reason, and values doubled and tripled seemingly overnight. The same process is occurring now, although at a slower rate, in regard to Great Western single action revolvers, the scarcer variants of the Remington Nylon 66 rifle family, Merwin-Hulbert revolvers, and many other former "sleepers."

Some older firearms may be in scarce supply, yet are not in demand by collectors. Without demand, regardless of availability, the dollar value of the firearm will be low.

Condition

Of the three factors used to establish value, condition is perhaps the most important and certainly the factor most frequently used by shooters as well as collectors for determining the price of a firearm. A "like new" example of a relatively common older Colt, Smith & Wesson, Luger or other arm popular with collectors can bring up to twice the price of another that easily ranks as "Excellent." On the other end of the scale, a scarce, popular collectible in "Poor" or even "Fair" condition often will go begging at a fraction of its value in more acceptable shape.

Of course, neither condition nor pricing is ever absolute. There is no such thing as a fixed price. It's an axiom among gun enthusiasts that there are only two conditions any two collectors can agree upon and those are "New" and "Junk"; everything in between is highly subjective and subject to debate. For example, a shooter looking at a potential acquisition might rate a gun with little finish but mechanically tight and with a fine bore, "Excellent"; to the collector that same firearm would rate only a "Good" or possibly "Very Good." An old Luger with most of its original blue but with the bore badly pitted from corrosive ammunition would rate an "Excellent" from most collectors but only a "Fair" from a shooter. Collectors and shooters alike find the line between "Good" and "Very Good" or "Very Good" and "Excellent" a fuzzy one. When angels tire of dancing on the heads of pins, they discuss firearms condition.

WHAT? NO MSRP?

We have deleted MSRPs (manufacturer's suggested retail prices) from this edition of *Modern Gun Values* because they are meaningless. In this internet age, guns sell for whatever the market will bear, and discounting is rampant. When a new model is introduced on the market, it may sell for more than MSRP because of consumer demand. As the gun in question is produced in greater numbers, discounters reduce the street price below MSRP. The result? MSRP means nothing.

Federal courts have found that manufacturers cannot dictate street pricing to their distributors and retailers. (They can *control* their own channels of distribution, but that's another matter.) However, manufacturers can assign an MSRP to their products to be used "for comparison purposes only." The difference between MSRP and street pricing is well-known to anyone who has ever bought a new car. All prices in this book are street prices.

THE INTERNET – AND WHY WE SHOULD LOVE IT

In the past, firearms street pricing was established at retail gunshops and gun shows. Today, the internet has made everyone with an FFL an internet retailer, or e-tailer.

In assigning values to new firearms for this book, I found an enormous range of prices offered by internet retails operating through one of the web's firearms auction sites.

On this particular day, I can go to an internet firearms auction site and search for a Remington Model 673 Guide Rifle (alas, lately discontinued by Remington). Now, MSRP on the Model 673 was around $929. Yet I find new in-the-box Model 673s being offered for as much as $725 and for as little as $524.99. So what is the value of a new Model 673? One thing's for certain: it sure isn't MSRP!

The internet makes everyone a seller and everyone a buyer. It has infused an enormous volume of fresh blood into the hobby. In the past, a shooter or collector had to comb the classifieds, drive to every retail shop in the county, and attend gun shows to find a rare or scarce model. Nowadays virtually any gun can be found after a few minutes' searching online. The result? For newer guns, it's a buyer's market. For scarce vintage or antique models, it's a seller's market, at least as far as the internet is concerned.

At any rate, the effect of the internet on firearms pricing can neither be ignored nor overestimated. The worldwide web is the single greatest influence on modern gun values, and we can all use it to our advantage, either as buyers or sellers.

A REMINDER

Remember that the values shown here should be taken as guidelines, not absolutes. When a rarely seen gun that you've been wanting for a long time shows up at a price somewhat higher than we indicate, it still may be worth buying because the pleasure of ownership is often well worth the higher price. Many collectors freely admit they rarely regret the firearms they buy, but all too often regret the ones they didn't buy. On the other hand, don't be too quick to buy a common gun that you'd like to have when you see it at market price, since one will likely show up sooner or later at a lower price.

From the buyer's standpoint, pricing at the extreme ends of the condition scale (New to Poor) generally reflects the most you might consider paying for a particular firearm in a particular condition. From the seller's standpoint, these values reflect ballpark figures where you might start your pricing, leaving yourself ample room for negotiation. In a bidding or other competitive situation, however, all bets are off. Whoever wants the item the most, and can reinforce his sentiments with his checkbook, will ultimately obtain it. The sky's the limit.

With any luck, however, the buyer's and the seller's comfort zones will overlap at a certain point, and that will be the figure for which the firearm is sold.

RESTORATION

For collectors in particular, there's another important aspect of condition that needs to be addressed and that is restoration. As the demand for many collectible arms has exceeded the supply of those in "acceptable" condition, many rare, and even not so rare, firearms have been restored. Pitted areas built up by welding, missing or damaged parts remade, obliterated markings re-rolled, grips and stocks with re-cut checkering, or the metal polished and refinished using the techniques of the original maker are some examples of the restoration work possible. A first-class restoration is an expensive proposition, but if properly done is often difficult to tell from original factory work.

But how does the value of a restored firearm compare with that of an original in like condition? A truly first-class job can bring close to the price of an original-condition example; however, very few restorations are that good. Generally, a very good restoration is usually worth at best half as much as a nice original. Two warnings: First, beware of restorations passed off as original. Second, be extra aware of a common model that's "restored" into a rare variation by modifying markings, barrel length or the like. When in

doubt, ask an expert and refer to the NRA's Code of Ethics. Misrepresentation can be fraud.

NRA CODE OF ETHICS

A listing of practices considered unethical and injurious to the best interests of the collecting fraternity.

1. The manufacture or sale of a spurious copy of a valuable firearm. This shall include the production of full-scale replicas of historic models and accessories, regardless of easily effaced modern markings, and it also shall include the rebuilding of any authentic weapon into a rarer and more valuable model. It shall not include the manufacture or sale of firearms or accessories which cannot be easily confused with the rare models of famous makers. Such items are: plastic or pottery products, miniatures, firearms of original design, or other examples of individual skill, plainly stamped with the maker's name and date, made up as examples of utility and craftsmanship, and not representative of the designs or models of any old-time arms maker.

2. The alteration of any marking or serial number, or the assembling and artificially aging of unrelated parts for the purpose of creating a more valuable or unique firearm with or without immediate intent to defraud. This shall not include the legitimate restoration or completion of missing parts with those of original type, provided that such completions or restorations are indicated to a prospective buyer.

3. The refinishing (bluing, browning, or plating) or engraving of any collector's weapons, unless the weapons may be clearly marked under the stocks or elsewhere to indicate the date and nature of the work, and provided the seller unequivocally shall describe such non-original treatment to a buyer.*

4. The direct or indirect efforts of a seller to attach a spurious historical associatizon to a firearm in an effort to inflate its fair value; efforts to "plant" a firearm under circumstances which are designed to inflate the fair value.

5. The employment of unfair or shady practices in buying, selling, or trading at the expense of young and inexperienced collectors or anyone else; the devious use of false appraisals, collusion and other sharp practices for personal gain.

6. The use of inaccurate, misleading, or falsified representations in direct sales or in selling by sales list, catalog, periodical advertisement and other media; the failure to make prompt refunds, adjustments or other proper restitution on all just claims which may arise from arms sales, direct or by mail.

*When the NRA formulated this Code of Ethics many years ago restoration was rarer than it is today and some restoration was indeed marked. However, such marking is rarely if ever done today and restoration is not only considered ethical but desirable when appropriate. Furthermore, for many, a restorer's mark in even the most inconspicuous internal location would detract from originality.

Fortunately, many knowledgeable collectors and dealers are able to distinguish even the best restoration work from "factory original." In addition, in the current marketplace it is not at all unusual for an owner or seller to not only admit restoration, but to state with pride that

a certain arm was restored by a specific well-known restorer.

Ethically, of course, the fact that restoration work has been done and to what extent should always be disclosed to a prospective purchaser. Not to do so has, in the case of some very valuable collectibles, resulted in expensive and embarrassing legal actions.

NRA MODERN CONDITION STANDARDS

To give a firm foundation for the pricing structure of the 14th Edition, it is essential to establish a set of condition standards by which a firearm can be judged. We have adopted the well-respected and popular National Rifle Association's Modern Condition Standards as a guideline to the various grades of condition but have made slight modifications (italics) to further help readers determine condition degrees.

New: In same condition as current factory production, with original box and accessories.

Perfect: In new condition in every respect, but may be lacking box and/or accessories.

Excellent: Near new condition, used but little, no noticeable marring of wood or metal, bluing perfect (except at muzzle or sharp edges).

Very Good: In perfect working condition, no appreciable wear on working surfaces, visible finish wear but no corrosion or pitting, only minor surface dents or scratches.

Good: In safe working condition, minor wear on working surfaces, no corrosion or pitting that will interfere with proper functioning.

Fair: In safe working condition, but well worn, perhaps requiring replacement of minor parts or adjustments, no rust, but may have corrosion pits which do not render article unsafe or inoperable.

****

A final word: May your firearms collecting experience be rewarding and enjoyable, and may you be the lucky soul who finds that one-in-a-thousand "diamond in the rough" that was passed over by less fortunate bargain-hunters who did not have this book!

Cordially,
Dan Shideler, Editor
And the past editors of *Modern Gun Values*

****

Appeal to Our Readers

Because *Modern Gun Values* is an ongoing research project, we welcome input from our readers. No one can hope to know everything about the more than 7000 firearms found here. Thus, we ask any collector or enthusiast who wishes to contribute information on the firearms found here or other firearms not found in these pages, but known to be manufactured or imported into the U.S. in the last 100 years, to please contact DBI Books in writing. This includes historical insights to firearms that played a role in U.S. and world events. Submissions made on "all rights, non-returnable" basis, subject to our evaluation. Unusable submissions returned if accompanied by SASE.

Write to:
Modern Gun Values
Krause Publications
700 East State Street
Iola WI 54990

Inspection Guide To Used Guns

by Patrick Sweeney

WHILE THE SATISFACTION of buying a new firearm, from the standpoint of warranty and features, appeals to many shooters and collectors, sometimes "used" is the only route. After all, how many new-in-the-box Winchester pre-64s still exist? Sometimes the only way to acquire the firearm model, or the firearm with the features you desire, is by buying it used. We all have budgets, and purchasing a used gun is much easier on them! Read on and learn how to buy "used" – safely.

If at all possible buy from an established dealer, with a track record and reputation. Even better, a dealer who has an in-house gunsmith who inspects all their used firearms and makes sure no lemons slip through. In the event one does, a reputable dealer will take it back or make it right.

What should the dealer warranty? The normal and expected performance and durability of that model firearm, and that he presented it correctly as to its features and performance. If you buy a plain old used 30-30 and find it shoots three- to four-inch groups at 100 yards, don't expect to be able to return it. If, however, it shoots those groups four feet to the left or right, you have every right to return it. An as-new benchrest rifle

better do well under an inch with its provided ammo, or you may have cause to return it (assuming you can shoot that well). If the dealer doesn't have a written warranty, ask what the return policy is.

If you are not buying from a dealer, you have the standard business-school Latin to guide you – Caveat Emptor: "Let the buyer beware." One approach that some of my customers took – and more should have – was to have their purchase inspected by a pro. If you have any doubts about an attractive purchase, take it to a gunsmith and explain things. Don't just drop it off for a "strip and clean" and count on him (or her) uncovering hidden problems.

Come right out and explain: You just bought it, and you want it inspected for safety, durability, function and headspace. If there is a limited return time, the gunsmith needs to know in order to inspect it within the allotted time. Many gunsmiths are booked solid for months and may not get it back to you in time if you leave your purchase for what the 'smith understands is just a "regular cleaning." By explaining your inspection period time constraint you can get your new purchase back in time to meet the refund terms of the sale, should you need to return the gun.

General Inspection of a Used Firearm

To start, give the firearm in question a quick visual inspection. I call it the "tire tracks and hammer marks" look, and it is the same regardless of the type you are thinking of buying. The inspection of a firearm to determine the percentage of finish remaining is covered elsewhere. The purpose of this initial inspection is to uncover damage, repairs or abuse. Is the stock straight and clean? Is the barrel straight? Are the sights centered? Are there dents, scratches, cracks or repairs to be seen? Does the bluing have the right color? Are the barrel markings clean and crisp, or are they blurry or smeared? Is the barrel, the correct

length? Is the muzzle uniform? Does the chambering marked on, the barrel match what the seller tells you it shoots? Try to get a "feel" for the history and typical condition of the gun you are looking at. Does it match the description of the one the seller is trying to sell you? A firearm that doesn't match what the seller describes is probably best left on the table.

Just because you are looking at a worn, used-to-gray rifle the seller describes as "the best he's seen" doesn't mean he's fibbing. If you are holding a Remington 700 in 308 Winchester – yes, he is. On the other hand, if you are holding a pre-'64 M-70 in 300 Savage – no, he isn't.

RIFLES

Open the action. With a light or reflector – and with the action open and bolt removed if appropriate – look down the bore. Clean, shiny and clear of obstructions, right? If not, let the bargaining begin!

While many rifles will shoot accurately with a slightly pitted bore, some won't – and all will require more frequent cleaning. Work the action and see if there are any binding spots or if the action is

rough. Ask if you can dry fire it to check the safety.

Some people do not like to have any gun in their possession dry-fired; others don't care. If you cannot, you may have to pass on the deal. Or, you can assure the owner that you will restrain the cocking piece to keep the striker from falling.

Close the action and dry-fire it. How much is the trigger pull? Close the action, push the safety to *ON*, and pull the trigger. It should stay cocked. Let go of the trigger and push the safety *OFF*. It should stay cocked. Now, dry-fire it. Is the trigger pull different than it was before? If the pull is now lighter, the safety is not fully engaging the cocking piece, and you'll have to have someone work on it to make it safe. If the rifle fires at any time while manipulating the safety (even without your having touched the trigger) it is unsafe until a gunsmith repairs it.

While you were checking the safety, just what was the trigger pull? A very light trigger pull is not always bad, but may need adjustment. As an example, if you are handling a Remington 700 or Winchester 70, and the trigger pull is one pound, someone may have adjusted the trigger mechanism. If you are handling a Winchester '94 and the trigger pull is a pound, someone has been stoning the hammer or sear. On the first two, you or your gunsmith can adjust the weight back to normal ranges. On the '94 you may have to buy a new hammer or sear – or both – to get the pull back into the normal range.

Inspect the action and barrel channel. Is the gap between the barrel and the channel uniform? Ordoes the forearm bend right or left? Changes in humidity can warp aforearm and, if the wood touches the barrel, alter accuracy. The owner may be selling it because the accuracy has "*gone south,*" and not know that some simple bedding work can cure it.

Look at the action where it meets the stock. Is the wood/metal edge clean and uniform? Or do you see traces of epoxy bedding compound? Epoxy could mean a bedding job,and it could mean a repair of a cracked stock. Closely inspect the wrist of the stock, right behind the tang. Look for cracks and repairs.

Turn the rifle over and look at the action screws. Are the slots clean, or are they chewed up? Mangled slots indicates a rifle that has been taken apart many times – and at least a few of those times with a poorly-fitting screwdriver.

A rifle fired with a poorly-fitted stock, or one dried out from decades of storage, will often crack light behind the tang. Look closely for cracks or repairs.

Are the screw slots clean, or are they chewed up? This screw is just tolerable. Any worse and it would indicate abuse instead of 59 years of indifferent attention.

Check the edges of the stock where the action rests for signs of glass bedding. Bedding is not bad; in fact, it can be good. But don't pay collectors' prices for a working tool that has been modified.

Be sure of the chambering, and be sure it is clearly marked. This Marlin was not a 38-55 when it left the factory; but is now and is clearly so marked.

Consider rarity when assessing condition. A 30-06 with signs of honest use and hunting wear is a tool. This same rifle, were the barrel marked "300 Savage" or "35 Remington," would be a collector's dream.

Remove the bolt if you can. If not, use a reflector or light to illuminate the bore. Is the bore clean and bright? Look at the bore near the muzzle. Do you see jacket fouling or lead deposits? Many an "*inaccurate*" rifle can be made accurate again simply by cleaning the jacket fouling out of the bore. While looking down the bore, hold the barrel so a vertical or horizontal bar in a window reflects down the bore. If the reflection of the bar has a 'break' in it, the barrel is bent. Sight down the outside of the barrel and see if you can spot it. A slightly bent barrel can still be accurate, but will walk its shots when it heats up. A severely bent barrel must be replaced.

SHOTGUNS

Pump-Action & Autoloading Shotguns

Pumps and autoloaders require the same safety check as rifles do, with a few additions. Safety on, pull the trigger, let go, safety off. Dry fire and see if the weight of the trigger pull changes.

When inspecting the barrel, look for dents or creases. Also,

inspect the rib (if there is one) to see if it has been dented. While a dented barrel or rib can be repaired so the damage is almost unnoticeable, you can still see evidence of the repair.

Remove the barrel to inspect the bore. Is the bore clean of plastic? Is the choke clean? If not, swab them clean. If there are screw-in chokes, do they unscrew easily and smoothly? While you have the forearm off an autoloader, look at the gas system. Is it clean? Or is it crusty from powder residue? Powder residue can be wiped off, but rust requires more a vigorous remedy, and may leave the shotgun as a non-cycling autoloader.

Double-Barrel Shotguns

Doubles require a different inspection. While looking over the barrels, look to see that the side or bottom ribs are smoothly attached along their length. A lifted rib that has been repaired will have a different appearance at the repair.

Open and close the action. Does the lever move smoothly into place, or do you have to push it the last fraction to fully close it? How far does the lever move? Levers are initially positioned to not go fully to the centerline. As the action wears, the lever moves further and further, taking up the wear. A shotgun with a lever too far past the centerline may have been shot a great deal, or been taken apart and put back together with the lever mis-timed.

Next, check to see the barrels are tight. Often, the forearm will put enough pressure on the action to make it seem tight. Remove the forearm and then check barrel

Are screw-in chokes easy to remove? Or do you have to wrestle with them? A bulged choke may mean a ruined barrel. Always unscrew the chokes to make sure they work as intended.

The screw-in chokes in this barrel, while functional, doom the barrel for resale. The wall was cut too thin on one side and chipped out. The owner will never be able to sell the barrel, for who would buy it? You might, if you neglected to check.

tightness. Does the barrel assembly move or wobble when closed? Can you see the joint at the action changing size when you try to move the barrel? A loose barrel is an expensive repair, so be sure to check. Pull or twist the barrel in all three axes; attempt to move the rear side to side, lift as if you were opening the action (but not pushing the lever), and pull the barrels forward. The action should be as tight as a bank vault.

Next, the triggers. You'll need snap caps and the owner's permission. Insert the snap caps and close the action. Put the safety on. If the double is a twin trigger, check to make sure the safety blocks both triggers. If it is a single trigger, make sure the safety blocks the trigger when the barrel selector is set to each barrel in turn.

Push the safety to *OFF* and snap one of the barrels. Open the action *(keep your hand over the action to stop the snap cap from being launched across the room)* then close it and select the other barrel. Snap that barrel and open the action again, stopping the snap cap from being ejected. Both barrels work? Good. Close the action, snap one of the barrels, and then slap the butt of the shotgun with your hand. If the shotgun has a non-inertial trigger – like the Ruger Red Label – you can forego the slapping. Does the second barrel now fire when you pull the trigger? If so, the inertial trigger is working. If not, you may have to slap it harder, or the inertia weight needs adjusting.

HANDGUNS

Handguns come in two types: revolvers and autoloading pistols,

and each has sub-types with their own peculiarities. The four types we'll cover are the **single-action revolver** and **double-action revolver**, **single-action autoloading pistol** and **double-action autoloading pistol**.

Single-Action Revolvers

The single-action revolver is known by many as the *cowboy* revolver. Your quick visual inspection of the exterior should start with the sights, to make sure they are straight, and the grips to make sure they are without cracks or dents. Also look at the exterior edge of the muzzle, and the corners of the frame, for signs of dropping. Bent sights and cracked grips indicate a dropped handgun. Dropping can bend the barrel, warp the frame or throw off the timing.

Hold the revolver up to the light, sideways, and look at the cylinder gap. There should be daylight, but not too much of it. The SA comes in the Colt pattern, old Ruger, and the new Ruger.

In Colts and old Rugers, open the loading gate, cock the hammer back to the *(half-cock)* notch that frees the cylinder, and rotate the cylinder. Look to see that it isn't loaded. On new Rugers, opening the loading gate frees the cylinder to rotate. To close up both action "systems," close the loading gate, cock the hammer and, with your thumb on the hammer spur, pull the trigger and ease the hammer forward while holding the trigger back. Check the cylinder for play.

For those who may not know, spinning the cylinder at high speed, or fanning the hammer are both considered abusive handling, and will likely end the sale before it starts. Don't do either!

Does the cylinder move back and forth? Called *endshake*, it can be easily fixed, but if there is too much it indicates a revolver that has seen a lot of use. On a Colt-pattern revolver it could mean that the cylinder has been replaced and not properly fitted, or the bushing is worn – or peened – from heavy loads.

The wood on this shotgun can be repaired, but what caused it? If a previous owner used magnum shells in a non-magnum-capable gun, the action may be loose. Check the tightness of the barrels to the receiver.

On doubles, check to see if the top lever is easy to move and the action easy to open.

You must remove the forearm before checking a double for tightness. If you don't, the forearm's support may mask any looseness present in the action.

Does the top lever go past center? As the locking surfaces wear the lever moves farther and farther. When it reaches the far side of the top strap, it needs to be refitted.

Does it wobble from side to side? The cylinder stop may be worn, or the slots may be worn or too large. Look at the slots. If they have been abused, the edges will be chewed up. If they appear sharp and clean, the cylinder stop may be worn or its spring weak. A worn or abused cylinder is expensive, while a new cylinder stop or spring is relatively cheap.

Slowly cock the revolver, watching the cylinder. Does it come fully into position? Or do you have to push the cylinder around the last fraction of an inch to get it to lock? A cylinder failing to carry up will require a new hand – or require that the old one be "stretched."

Check each chamber. It isn't unusual for a revolver to have one chamber that has a slightly different timing on the *carry up* than the others do. Once you've checked *carry-up*, test the trigger pull. If the owner is leery of letting you dry fire, catch the hammer with your other hand each time you cock it and pull the trigger. Is the pull within normal limits? A heavy pull may indicate someone has fussed with the trigger – as would a very light pull.

While a trigger is relatively cheap, they can be salvaged only sometimes. The hammer is expensive, but you can often have the notch re-stoned (properly, of course) or in extreme cases, welded and re-cut. If the trigger pull has been "messed with," what was done? You can't tell without getting out a screwdriver set and disassembling the revolver there and then. You will have to either take the risk, or insist on a return/refund option if your gunsmith finds something too expensive to fix.

To continue inspecting the Single Action, open the loading gate, release and pull the center pin, roll the freed-up cylinder out of the frame *(to the right)* and inspect the front and rear of the cylinder. On the rear, is the bluing of the ratchet that the hand pushes against evenly worn white? *(A difficult inspection on a stainless or nickel gun, but you can see the wear if you look closely.)* Each chamber should be clean, their edges unmarred. On the front face of the cylinder, check to see if there are marks from the cylinder face rubbing against the rear of the barrel. A cylinder with *endshake* may rub. The rubbing may even be only partial. Don't worry unless the rubbing has been hard or extensive enough to have marred the face of the cylinder.

When doubles loosen their ribs and plates, the damage often starts at the muzzle. Check there first, and then work your way down the barrels.

Hammer clearance on a revolver in single action mode is important. You can see here the hammer may bind on the frame if the spur is bent.

Look at the rear of the barrel. Is the end even and square to the bore? Or has someone been stoning or filing the rear face for some reason? Is the forcing cone clean and smooth?

A revolver that has been fired with lead alloy bullets will often have a forcing cone crusted with lead, even when the rest of the barrel is clean.

A revolver that has seen a lot of jacketed magnum-level loads will show the wear in the forcing cone, the edges of which will be slightly rounded from the heat and abrasion.

Look down the bore. Is it clean and are the lands and grooves smooth and shiny? A pitted bore means the barrel must be replaced. If you see a dark ring (or *donut*) that indicates a "ringed barrel," the barrel may still be accurate but will probably lead quickly. A bullet stopping partway down the bore, and then being jolted out by the next round fired, causes a "ringed" barrel. The bulge may not show on the outside.

Double-Action Revolvers

The quick exterior inspection should include the hammer spur. Dropping a DA revolver can bend the spur, keeping the hammer from being cocked. Your inspection will reveal this, so be prepared when you get there.

Push the cylinder latch and open the cylinder. Does the latch move smoothly? Does the cylinder move without binding or catching?

Check by opening the cylinder at each of its six (or five, seven or eight) positions. A dropped DA revolver can have a bent center pin, and the bend will interfere with opening at only one chamber. On a DA revolver, opening and closing it Hollywood-style, by flicking the wrist, is flagrant handling abuse which will get it snatched out of your hands by many owners.

Check *carry-up*, both in single action and double action modes. You may have to ride your offhand thumb on the hammer as you slowly do the double-action check, to keep the hammer (and the trigger) from jerking to the end of the DA stroke and thus hiding improper carry-up. If the revolver has been dropped and the hammer spur bent, this is when you'll find out. A bent spur can still work fine in double action, but the hammer goes back farther in cocking for single action. A bent spur may bind against the frame and not allow the revolver to be cocked. With the hammer cocked, put your thumb behind it and give it a gentle push... no more than ten pounds worth. The hammer should stay cocked.

Years ago I had a run-in with a desk sergeant at a local police department about proper testing for push-off (*my home state of Michigan*

To check single action engagement, cock the hammer and push the hammer forward with one thumb. Again, ten pounds is all you need.

requires a safety inspection for the sale of a handgun). He was pushing for all he was worth, with both thumbs, and rejecting every revolver my customers came in

Does the cylinder unlatch smoothly and easily? Binding or requiring force to move is a bad sign, usually indicating a bent crane or bent center pin.

Close the cylinder, dry fire and hold the trigger back. Check the cylinder for wobble: front-to-back and side-to-side. Then release the trigger and try again. The cylinder shouldn't move at all when the trigger is held back, and only a little when released.

A peened cylinder locking slot indicates heavy use, either many rounds or magnum loads. Peened slots can't be fixed, and require a new cylinder, a major cost.

Endshake is a sign of use with heavy or magnum loads.

Endshake is easy and inexpensive to fix by stretching the crane or installing shims, but both increase cylinder gap at the rear of the barrel. If removing *endshake* increases the gap beyond tolerances, you'll have to have the barrel set back, a moderately expensive fix.

Open the action and look at the front and rear of the cylinder. The front of the cylinder should not show rub marks from the rear of barrel. If it does, it is a sign of excessive *endshake*, which must be fixed. The rear of the chambers

should have clean ninety-degree edges. Some shooters bevel the rear opening of the chambers to make speedloading faster and easier. Properly done, beveling does speed reloads but, improperly done, it can cause improper ejection.

If you see beveling, look closely at the ejector star. Has the star been beveled, too? A proper job bevels the cylinder but not the ejector. A beveled ejector that improperly ejects (the empties will not be fully ejected) is a moderately expensive repair.

Inspect the forcing cone. Is it clean, with sharp edges? A revolver that has seen a lot of magnum loads, especially jacketed ones, will have an eroded forcing cone. A worn forcing cone can cause *spitting* and a loss of accuracy. A worn forcing cone can be fixed, but only by setting the barrel back and cutting a new cone in fresh steel. The gunsmith will also have to shorten the ejector rod and center pin, and will have to remove *endshake* to do the job properly and the cost will be moderate to moderately high.

Look down the bore. Clean, shiny and straight? Good. If it is pitted, or ringed from a bullet having been lodged in the bore, you'll need a new barrel.

The last check concerns the crane. The swing-out crane makes loading and unloading easier, but it is relatively fragile and can be bent by being dropped, or being flipped open Hollywood-style.

Gently close the cylinder, and see how much thumb pressure it takes to lock up. Does the cylinder swing

with. I finally had to bring in the S&W Armorers Manual, and show him and his supervisor what the factory-accepted test was. If the revolver you are testing pushes off at ten pounds or less, the single-action notch is worn – or has been worked on. Depending on theremedy required, it may be expensive to fix; sometimes requiring a new hammer.

Check cylinder tightness with the trigger held back, as with the SA revolver, checking for play side-to-side and front-to-back. As on the SA revolver, side-to-side play can be caused by peened locking slots in the cylinder, which is expensive to repair. Or, it can be caused by a worn cylinder stop (less expensive), or a tired cylinder stop spring (cheap to fix).

The crane on a DA revolver is easily bent from abuse, dropping or incorrect gunsmithing.

into place and click shut without force? Great. Try it on all chambers, as a bent crane can be offset by other tolerances, and may be hidden on one or more chambers. If you find you need moderate thumb pressure to get the cylinder to lock in place, the crane may be bent.

A bent crane and its repair are brand-dependent. Rugers are so stoutly built that you need a ball-peen hammer to bend the crane. You also need one to straighten it. A S&W crane is more fragile and more sensitive to misalignment, but a simple job to straighten. The Colt system is less sensitive than the S&W, not as stout as the Ruger, and a more involved job to fix.

Autoloading Pistols, Single-Action

The icon of single-action autoloading pistols is the 1911 pistol. Of all handguns, this one is the most likely to be assembled from parts, played with, experimented upon – and had parts swapped in and out. Any used pistol requires a close inspection to ensure you don't end up with a pig in a poke.

On your exterior visual inspection, don't be put off by parts of different colors. The government never cared about matching the color of Parkerized parts on military-issue 45s, and many shooters through the years

A dropped revolver can bend the center pin where it protudes into the frame. It cannot be straightened and must be replaced.

have come to favor deliberately two-toned pistols. It is not at all unusual to find a 1911 with a blued slide and nickeled or stainless frame, or blued or Parkerized parts on a hard-chromed gun.

Check the muzzle end of the slide for dings and gouges indicating it has been dropped. Look at the magazine well. A dropped pistol can crack at the magazine well if the well has been beveled for fast magazine insertion. You may see a crack on the frame forward of the slide stop lever. Pay it no mind. A cracked dustcover on high-mileage auto-pistols is not rare. If you see the crack and the owner says it has never been shot, be suspicious. *Any crack in a slide is grounds for immediate rejection.* Cracked slides cannot be repaired, cannot be trusted, and must be replaced.

Give the pistol a brief visual check for signs of dropping, or tool marks from previous experimenting. Work the slide. Does it move smoothly? It should move its full travel without catching, binding or hesitating. A binding slide could be a bent slide, dented frame rails, or a mis-fit replacement barrel. All will be moderately expensive to fix. Or, it could simply be a replacement slide that was not fully lapped to fit – which is cheap to fix.

Flip the thumb safety up and down. It should move smoothly and snap from one setting to another. Check the grip safety. It should move in and out without binding, and its spring should snap it back out when released. A grip safety that doesn't move should set off alarm bells in your head. It was popular in competition circles a decade or more ago to pin down grip safeties so they would not move. A pistol with a pinned grip safety is probably a high-mileage

Some home gunsmithing is beyond the pale. These home-drilled "ports" on this revolver have ruined the barrel. If the seller won't subtract the cost of a new barrel and installation from the cost, pass it up.

A revolver with a cylinder that won't fully "carry up" into position behind the barrel is dangerous. If it fires unlocked, the bullet won't be centered in the bore, and will split fragments out through the gap.

competition gun that has seen tens of thousands of rounds. Even if it has seen only light use, you will have to have the grip safety unpinned and properly tuned.

Now check the function of the safeties. Happily, owners of the 1911 are much less prone to the *"don't dry fire"* attitude. Check to

The grip safety on the left has been pinned down, and doesn't work. Don't buy a 1911 with a pinned grip safety unless it can be unpinned and tested for function.

make sure the pistol isn't loaded, then cycle the slide and dry fire it. Hold the trigger back and work the slide. It should move smoothly. A pistol that is hard to cycle with the trigger held back could have disconnector problems – or an improperly adjusted trigger binding the disconnector. With the slide cycled back and forth, does the hammer stay cocked *(It better, or you will be facing expensive repairs)?* Next, push the thumb safety *ON*. Pull the trigger (using no more than ten pounds pressure), release the trigger and push the safety *OFF*. If the hammer falls, the safety isn't blocking the sear's movement. I've seen pistols that would fire when the safety was ON and the trigger was pulled. Not very safe and, potentially, an expensive repair.

If the hammer stays back, you now listen. Lift the pistol to

Does the thumb safety move smoothly, or do you need to force it? Forcing is bad, and indicates a poorly fitted thumb safety.

Once the safety is on, pull the trigger with about 10 pounds of force. Then push the safety off and listen to the sear.

your ear, and gently thumb back the hammer. If you hear nothing *(assuming you have properly worn hearing protection during all those years of shooting)* then the thumb safety is fine. If you hear a little metallic *"tink"* then the safety needs adjustment. If the safety blocks the sear – but not entirely – the sear can move minutely when you pull the trigger. The *"tink"* is the sear tip snapping back into the bottom of the hammer hooks when the spring pressure is released. If the thumb safety passes the "listen" test, you're on to the grip safety.

Cock the hammer and hold the pistol so you don't grip the grip safety. Pull the trigger. The test, and "listen," are the same as the thumb safety test, looking for the same problems. Now start looking for signs of abuse or experimentation.

Hold the slide partway back and look at the feed ramp. It should be clean and shiny. There should be a gap between the ramp on the frame and the ramp on the barrel. If someone has polished them to be an uninterrupted surface, they have decreased feeding reliability. An improperly polished or ground ramp is expensive to fix.

Should you check barrel fit? Checking won't tell you much.

To check the grip safety's function you have to hold the pistol so you don't depress the safety. Then pull the trigger.

The customary check is to press down on the chamber area to see if it moves, and having moved, if it springs back. The problem is, it doesn't tell you much. I've seen apparently loose pistols that shot quite accurately, and tight pistols that wouldn't shoot worth a darn.

There are some indications that something is amiss. If you are

looking at a custom competition gun with a name-brand barrel fitted, and the fit is loose, be suspicious. The barrel may have been simply dropped in (with no attempt at properly fitting it), or it may have been shot tens of thousands of rounds until it wore loose.

If you have a pistol with a plain barrel, tightly fitted, and the front

To check the disconnector: dry fire, hold the trigger down and slowly cycle the slide.

sight is very short, something is up. The barrel may be tight simply because the owner has fitted a long link to the barrel. In which case the link is propping the barrel up to be tight, and the front sight had to be shortened to get the sights to line up with the groups.

Lock the slide open and look down the bore. More so than many other pistols, the 1911 can be a high-mileage survivor. Is the bore clean, or fouled with lead or copper? Is the muzzle worn from cleaning? Is there heavy brass "marking" behind the ejection port? Signs of high mileage are not a reason to pass, but if the pistol is offered as "new" or "like new" and you see signs of bore wear, hold on to your money.

On the subject of the cost of repairs to a 1911, the same symptoms can be cheap – or expensive – depending whether the parts involved merely need adjustment, or must be replaced. Accept a dysfunctional 1911 into your home only after careful consideration and acceptance of potentially high repair costs.

Autoloading Pistols, Double-Action

Your visual inspection for the DAs will be the same as with the 1911, except that more of the DAs will have alloy frames. You must

The bulge in this barrel remains hidden by the slide when cycled, and can only be seen by removing the barrel from the slide, or carefully looking down the bore.

take a closer look, especially at a police trade-in, to check for signs of dropping. If you have a pistol with worn bluing, but new grips, look closely. New grips go on only when the old ones are too far gone to be presentable. Police guns get dropped, whacked into car doors and frames, door jambs, light poles, vending machines and seat belt buckles – and that is just when holstered!

Check the frame closely for cracks and signs of dropping, and pass on cracked frames. Glocks get an automatic "passing grade" here, as you can't do more than cosmetic damage, even by throwing one into a cement mixer. Do the dry fire and slide cycle test just as you would with the 1911. Hammerless guns, or DA-only guns, where the hammer follows the slide down, obviously won't show you a cocked hammer to manually manipulate.

Dry fire them, cycle the slide, and dry fire again.

The safety check is less involved than with the 1911, and is dependent on design. On Glocks, cycle the action and attempt to press the trigger back without depressing the centrally-mounted trigger safety. On DA guns, drop a pencil down the muzzle, eraser end first, and point up.

Push the safety lever to *SAFE*, or use the de-cocking lever. The pencil shouldn't move. Don't pay attention to vibrations. If the safety isn't blocking the firing pin, the pencil will get launched out and upwards.

Buying a used firearm can be rewarding, fun and educational. By taking a few precautions, and using the inspection procedures outlined, you can avoid buying a walnut and blue steel lemon. Have fun and stay safe! ★

A pistol should not "smokestack," or trap the empties in the ejection port, as shown in this simulated malfunction. The cause can be ammo, the pistol – or the shooter. Take the pistol to an independent gunsmith for inspection before returning to the seller, so you know the problem's source.

Guide to Evaluating Arms Condition

Before a firearm-pricing guide can be effectively used, the condition of the given firearm must be properly evaluated. The following examples provide perspective on establishing a realistic condition assessment of a firearm. MODERN GUN VALUES uses the widely accepted grading criteria developed by the National Rifle Association for modern firearms. For more information, read the Introduction that begins on page 4.

NRA Modern Condition Standards

Here are the NRA guidelines; we have made slight modifications (italics) to further help readers determine degrees of condition.

New: In same condition as current factory production, *with original box and accessories.*

Perfect: In new condition in every respect, *but may be lacking box and/or accessories.*

Excellent: Near new condition, used but little, no noticeable marring of wood or metal. Bluing perfect (except at muzzle or sharp edges).

Very Good: In perfect working condition, no appreciable wear on working surfaces, *visible finish wear* but no corrosion or pitting, only minor surface dents or scratches.

Good: In safe working condition, minor wear on working surfaces, no corrosion or pitting that will interfere with proper functioning.

Fair: In safe working condition, but well worn, perhaps requiring replacement of minor parts, or adjustments; no rust, but may have corrosion pits which do not render article unsafe or inoperable.

S&W Highway Patrolman, Model 28

Smith & Wesson Highway Patrolman, Model 28, in 357 Magnum with a 6-inch barrel. Factory target grips exhibit some wear, but no chipping or gouges. Bore and chambers are slick. The exterior shows typical, but modest, wear. NRA VERY GOOD-plus

Colt Police Positive Special

Colt Police Positive Special, 38 Special. This revolver has been buffed and reblued, and a Pachmayr grip-filler added. There is occasional light pitting in the bore and chambers. A collector would pass on this specimen, but the excellent mechanics & reliable function make it a perfectly good utility gun. NRA GOOD

Winchester Model 94 XTR Big Bore

Winchester Model 94 XTR Big Bore, chambered for the 375 Winchester. Used but well-maintained. Only faint wear visible in the usual places on both metal and wood. A slightly modified Lyman receiver sight has been installed; using the factory drilled and tapped mounting holes. The bore is bright and the mechanics are excellent. NRA EXCELLENT

Stevens Favorite No. 26 Crack Shot

Stevens Favorite No. 26 Crack Shot with a 22-inch barrel chambered for the 22LR. Well-used, with obvious wear–but mechanically sound. **NRA GOOD**

BSA Model 12/15 Match

BSA Model 12/15 Match, a British WWII-era shooting club target rifle chambered for the 22LR rimfire cartridge. There were a number of these, and other Martini-actioned target rifles, imported in the late 1990s and into 2000. This rifle was obviously well used, but maintained. The stock retains about 60 percent of the factory finish, with an old repair – and a ragged hole *(likely from a sling swivel stud that took a bit too much stress)* – at the rear of the forearm. The barrel, receiver and trigger/lever assembly are worn but retain about 80 percent of the original bluing that is thinning in places and turning brown in others. There are no mechanical problems; the reliable Martini action cycles and extracts flawlessly and the trigger breaks cleanly and consistently. The bore is bright, with strong rifling. The Parker-Hale micrometer rear sight is interesting in that the base is drilled through, matching a hole in the receiver that is in alignment with the rifle's bore. Remove the breechblock assembly and the bore can be cleaned from the breech-end, with the sight base serving as the cleaning rod guide. **NRA GOOD**

Colt Buntline Scout

Colt Frontier Buntline Scout, chambered for the 22LR rimfire cartridge. This model was produced only a dozen or so years, and then discontinued. This particular specimen is mechanically sound, although exhibiting a bit of looseness in the cylinder lockup. Bore and chambers are bright, with no pitting. Bluing on the cylinder and barrel shows distinct holster wear, and the scrapes and scratches accumulated during the 40-odd years since it left the Colt factory. The anodized aluminum frame, trigger guard and backstrap are in good shape, as are the factory walnut two-piece grips. **NRA GOOD-plus**

S&W Highway Patrolman, Model 28

Smith & Wesson Highway Patrolman, Model 28. This revolver wears a 6-inch barrel and, like all M28s, is chambered for the 357 Magnum. Bore and chambers are bright, and the mechanical function is excellent. The exterior shows some holster wear, as well as a few other wear marks. The original factory Magna grips were replaced by a set of Pachmayr rubber grips. **NRA VERY GOOD**

Winchester Model 70 Deluxe

Winchester Model 70 Deluxe. This is obviously a hunting rifle, with a handy trajectory and wind drift table taped on the left side of the stock. No pitting or corrosion anywhere, and the bore is bright. The bluing is a bit scratched and worn as might be expected on a field rifle and the stock shows field use as well, although in nice overall condition. NRA VERY GOOD

High Standard Sentinel Mark IV

High Standard Sentinel Mark IV, 22WMR with a 2-inch barrel. There is external wear, and the common bolt drag ring around the cylinder. Excellent function. NRA VERY GOOD

Winchester Model 52A

Winchester Model 52A. A nice rifle with most finish remaining on the action and barrel, with few scratches or wear spots. The stock has a few dents and dings, but the factory finish is still strong & unworn. Bore is bright, and function is excellent. **NRA VERY GOOD-plus**

Remington Model 14

Remington Model 14. This particular specimen, fitted with a Williams receiver sight, is chambered for the 30 Remington cartridge and exhibits the wear typical of a well-used but well-maintained hunting rifle. **NRA GOOD**

Remington Model 11A

Remington Model 11A, in 20-gauge with a Modified choke. The gun has been buffed and reblued. The stock is refinished and shows an amateurish attempt to expand upon the factory wrist checkering. The front sight has been replaced with a white bead. Bore is bright and function is excellent. Not much collector value here, but a good find for a hunter. **NRA GOOD**

Sturm, Ruger Blackhawk New Model

Sturm, Ruger Blackhawk New Model, 45 Colt, with 7 1/2-inch barrel. The gun has been fired a fair amount, but is well-maintained. The grips are intact and retain the factory finish. The exterior shows light wear only, and the typical bolt drag ring on the cylinder. Excellent function. **NRA VERY GOOD-plus**

Savage Model 99C

Savage Model 99C. Half-round, half-octagon barrel, chambered for the 303 Savage cartridge. Fitted with a tang sight and combination front sight. This is a well-used rifle with worn stock and metal finish. The action works smoothly and this rifle still has plenty of hunts in it. **NRA FAIR**

Lefever Nitro Special

Lefever Nitro Special, in 20-gauge with 26-inch barrels. Bores are bright. The frame retains much of the original case-color and the barrels have at least 90 percent of the bluing remaining. The wood shows no cracks, but there are scratches, and a distinct gouge on the forend. All in all, a tight lightly-used specimen with the wear appropriate for its age. **NRA VERY GOOD-plus**

An Illustrated Guide To Condition

by Joseph Schroeder

To further clarify the standard classifications of "Excellent" through "Fair," we present the following photographs. Since "New" means just that—new, in the original box with all papers and accessories and perfect means the gun is new but the original box and/or accessories may be missing, we do not show those classifications. All other classifications are subjective, and subject to argument!

Excellent

A Mauser 1930 "Broomhandle" in "Excellent" condition; the original finish is bright and shiny, showing wear only on the high points, while the grips are clean and sharp with little wear and no dents.

The left side of the "Excellent" Mauser 1930; note the tight fit of the magazine bottom. The Chinese characters translate to "Made In Germany" and add 5 to 10 percent to the value as compared to the same model without markings.

Very Good

A Mauser Model 1930, this one about "Very Good." Note the finish, though almost all there, has dull areas with some light rust "freckling," and shows more high point wear.

Though the grip grooves are still deep and sharp on this "Very Good" Model 1930, the wood does show the nicks and scratches that come from use.

Excellent

A Colt "Cobra" that rates a solid "Excellent." Its finish is bright and clean with only slight edge wear, and the light original checkering on the grips shows only slight wear on the high spots.

Very Good

A Colt Cobra in "Very Good" condition. The blue, though mostly there, shows more wear and some discoloration. The aftermarket wraparound grips could be considered a plus for some buyers.

Two examples of the import markings now required on all firearms imported into the U.S. The OBI OBNY under the Mauser chamber (right) indicates the importer was Oyster Bay Industries in Oyster Bay, New York. Oyster Bay also marked some Mausers by rolling their marking around the barrel (above). Guns without import markings such as those brought back by GIs bring a premium from collectors.

Good

A Model 1930, this one about "Good." The finish is mostly gone, and there is pitting on the muzzle and around the grips. The grips themselves have some bad scars, with much wear.

The muzzle of the "Good" Mauser; in addition to the deep pitting, the muzzle crown is also worn almost flat.

Fair

A Mauser Model 1930 in "Fair" condition. Not only is there no original finish but there is extensive pitting on the frame, barrel and barrel extension. The push-button on the rear sight latch is missing, and the magazine bottom is a poor fit with a mismatched serial number. The grips are worn almost smooth, and the grip screw is scarred from a slipping screwdriver.

The underside of the "Fair" Mauser; the magazine bottom is a poor fit in the gun, showing an irregular gap between parts. The scratch is from careless use of a screwdriver during removal.

Good

A Colt Cobra that would rate a high "Good." There is a good deal of blue wear with some light rust freckling, and the frame has been drilled just above the hammer for a hammer shroud (missing). The grips are so worn that the original checkering is entirely gone.

The cylinder of the "Good" condition Colt Cobra. Note the fingerprint etched into the cylinder by perspiration and the pits on the adjacent chamber.

Firearms Restoration

by Peter Koppmann

What is firearms restoration – making old guns look new? That definition is close, but not completely accurate. Restoration of anything (cars, boats, paintings, furniture – even airplanes) is the careful re-construction of that particular item to as close to new condition as possible.

The most important factors in any type of restoration project are time, price, and the skill and resources of the restorer. The factor that surprises most people is the cost of a full, high-quality restoration project. High-quality restoration takes a great deal of skill and knowledge; the ability of the restorer to deliver the highest quality restoration possible should be the foremost concern.

Refinishing vs. Restoration

The terms **refinishing** and **restoration** are sometimes used interchangeably, although there is considerable difference between the two. **Refinishing** is just what the name implies, applying a new finish to an existing piece with little or no concern for the underlying surface or internal condition. Think of refinishing as what you do when you repaint a room; you are basically putting a new finish over the old. **Restoration** is refinishing taken to the highest level.

When restoring firearms, the gun must not only look good but it must be safe to shoot. Any mechanical problems should be corrected before any other work is started. If the mechanical problems cannot be fixed at a reasonable cost, this a good time to decide whether to proceed with the restoration. Once the mechanical issues have been addressed, work on the outside of the gun can begin.

The key to any restoration project is the surface preparation of either the wood or the metal – or both. One of the most overlooked details of modern firearms manufacturing is the fit and finish of the final product. The degree to which most early firearms were finished is one of the reasons they are so desirable. In a restoration project, however, the aspects that generally receive the most attention are the preparation of both the wood and metal surfaces.

Value of Restored Firearms

For whatever reason, firearms restoration has long been looked upon as an undesirable practice. The commonly-held view is that a restored gun is not worth as much as an untouched original gun. That view would be accurate only if you could find an original gun in "as-new condition." In most cases restoration of a firearm will improve the condition and value of the firearm – providing the restoration is done correctly.

Reasons for Restoration

Restoration offers the shooter the opportunity to own a firearm (often historical) that is as close to factory original as possible. Firearms have played an important role in shaping and protecting this country and certain models are important pieces of history that should be preserved.

In some instances, the costs involved in restoration greatly exceed the value of the finished gun. Remember, the value of the gun is what you would expect to pay for the same gun–if and when you could find it. In some cases the gun may have belonged to a family member—or hold some other sentimental value. A sentimental restoration can return a piece of family history to the current generation or fulfill a desire to own a firearm with particular significance.

These two photos are great examples of "before & after" images of a restoration project to return a Colt Single Action Army to original condition. The original gun (left) was chrome-plated and fitted with a set of plastic imitation stag grips. Notice the gap where the grips meet the frame, and the rounded edges on the cylinder. The completed gun (right) has undergone a complete restoration, including a complete metal polish & new period-correct grips. Notice the crisp lines of the frame and the crisp edges on the cylinder.

Notice the crisp, straight edges on this Colt 1911. This gun has been completely restored and looks just the way it did when it was made in 1917.

Metal Polishing

The degree and direction of polish on metal parts in a restoration is one of the things that differentiate a restored gun from a refinished gun. Remember, a **restoration** is trying to return that firearm to as close to original condition as possible. A **refinished** gun may receive only a minimal amount of metal polishing before the final finishes are applied. In contrast, some restorations may require as many as 40 or 50 hours of polish time to prepare the surface for final finishing. Metal polishing, if done correctly, will never be noticed; if done incorrectly, however, the deficiency will stick out like a sore thumb.

True metal polishing is a lost art. Most people think of polishing as machine-buffing the part until you can see your reflection. Polishing is not just about making the metal shiny. The order, direction and degree of the polish are just as important as (in most cases, more important than) getting the

metal bright and shiny. One of the most critical areas in the polishing sequence is the restoration of the edges. The transition between flat and round surfaces should be sharp and crisp, with the correct direction and degree of polish. The early gunmakers were masters at keeping the edges sharp, crisp and straight.

Another area where the early gunmakers excelled was the polishing of large flat areas leaving few, if any, flaws in the surface. Remember, the surface has to be completely flat, with no ripples or flaws; it's not as easy as it may sound. The skill and talent required to correctly polish these areas cannot be understated.

Stock Work

The marriage of wood to metal is one of the most complex and sometimes frustrating aspects of gunmaking. A restoration may involve only the refinishing of the wood to return it to the correct color. It may also involve the repair of dents, scratches, cracks or splits in the wood. Some restorations may require the complete restocking of the gun, starting with a blank that must be cut and shaped to duplicate the original piece. The type of wood, direction of the grain and the color of the wood are just a few of the variables in constructing a stock from scratch.

Restocking is the last resort in the restoration of a firearm. If the original wood can be saved it can significantly reduce the cost of the project.

The new stock must be cut and shaped from a block of wood, then married to the action in a process known as inletting. Once the inletting is complete, shaping the stock – an art – to final dimensions can begin.

Once the stock has been shaped, sanded and finished, the process of checkering can begin. Checkering is the cutting of lines into the wood to form small diamonds so the shooter has a textured stock surface to grip. Checking comes in many shapes and styles,

from basic to elaborate patterns with carving; in some cases ebony, brass, and gold – even ivory – may be inletted in and around the checkering. Checkering can add great beauty to the stock as well as being a truly functional part of the gun.

Metal Finishing

Metal finishing comes in many different variations. We are all familiar with the bluing on a gun. But did

Checkering patterns come in many forms. This Parker A1 Special is an example of a very elaborate checkering pattern that combines standard checkering with woodcarving. This type of work takes a keen eye for detail, and a very steady hand.

This Winchester 1873 features a color case-hardened receiver, one of the most beautiful of the old-time firearm finishes. Due to the varying composition of steel, no two guns ever have the same pattern.

you know that bluing comes in many different varieties and color shades and is specific to certain parts of the gun? For example, Winchester rifles used three different types of bluing on rifle and shotgun barrels throughout the years. The original gunmakers, to harden steel, used color case-hardening. Today we use its vivid colors and unique patterns on the frames of shotguns, rifles and handguns.

Without going into the specifics of each process, the biggest mistake do-it-yourself gun restorers make is using the wrong finish for a particular firearm. For example, one of the simplest methods of bluing is hot bluing, also referred to as salt bluing. Hot bluing is used by almost every modern gunmaker because it is very easy to do and requires only a small amount of specialized equipment. If you can read a thermometer, you can hot blue! The problem is that hot bluing was not used until the mid-1940s. One of the most common mistakes

we see as professional gun restorers is the incorrect use of finishes on vintage firearms. That said, some guns were reblued before they became so highly collectible.

Do-It-Yourself vs. Professional Restoration

Most firearm owners do some form of gunsmithing at some point. One of the most important things to remember about working on your own firearm is to know your limitations and to be careful. The last thing you want to do is something detrimental to you or the firearm.

aIf you decide to restore your own firearm, pay attention to such details as wood-to-metal fit, direction and degree of the metal polish, barrel and frame markings (these may need to be re-cut or re-applied) and, of course, the correct final finishes. The restoration of a firearm can be a very satisfying and rewarding undertaking, whether you chose to do the work yourself or have it done by a professional. The reasons for restoring firearms vary greatly. Maybe you want to restore your father's old gun, or you just like the look and feel of a classic firearm.

Whatever the reason, firearms restoration is a great way to preserve these important pieces of history for future generations.

★

This Colt SAA is a current production 3rd Generation gun that has been completely re-worked by Turnbull Restoration to 1st Generation specifications. The gun is chambered in 45 Colt and has a 5 1/2-inch barrel. The 1st Generation conversion includes: enlarging the cylinder flutes, beveling the front of the cylinder, re-knurling the hammer and beveling the front of the ejector housing. The gun has also undergone a complete metal polish to true and crisp all the edges. The frame and hammer are finished with original style bone color case-hardening and the blued parts are finished in traditional Carbona blue. The grips are two-piece amber stag.

Author Peter Koppmann is the shop manager at Turnbull Restorations, which specializes in the refurbishment of American firearms made from 1870 to 1940; to include Colt, Winchester, Marlin, Parker, Fox, L.C. Smith and Ithaca. Specializing in historically-correct metal finishes, including bone color case-hardening, charcoal bluing, rust bluing, nitre bluing and hot bluing, Turnbull Restoration also offers complete metal polishing services and has a complete wood department for restocking and repairs – all under one roof.

Better than Book:

Factors that Add to the Value of a Firearm

By Phillip Peterson

We all know that non-factory alterations can reduce the value of a collectible firearm. Aftermarket chokes, cutdown stocks, recoil pads and other "improvements" may have looked good in their day, but for the most part they leave today's collectors cold. (How many Winchester Model 12s have you seen with those hideous adjustable chokes hanging off them?)

Recently, however, it was suggested to me that there might also be items or features that could add value to a given firearm. So true.

There are many factors that can be used to arrive at a price for a gun. Some reduce the price, some add to it. In fact, almost any of the factors I just mentioned that can lower the price can add to it as well. It really depends on the intended use for the firearm. Certainly, if you repair a broken gun to make it usable again, that will add to the value of that gun. It might hurt the value in the eyes of a collector or investor but not the hunter who wants a functional tool to use in the field. The collector probably would not have wanted that particular firearm anyway. If it was in need of repair it likely was not in good enough condition to appeal to discriminating collectors or investors. Thus it still comes down to the seller and potential buyer agreeing on a price.

Here, the, are just a few of the factors that can add to the value of a firearm:

Scopes & Sights

Many add-on accessories and customizations found on firearms are there to make aiming the piece easier and increase the chance of hitting the target. After all, that is the ultimate use for any firearm. So, the holes that are drilled in the receiver of, say, a Winchester Model 75 bolt action .22 to allow the mounting of a scope might not hurt its value at all. In fact, if a hunter wants that model with a scope he will likely be more interested in it. Yes, it is still reduced in value to a collector, but the hunter's cash

is just as spendable. Of course, if a "gunsmith" drilled seven off-center holes in the receiver before he got four to match the mounts he had, the gun just looks bad. You can take a good thing too far.

When a rifle or shotgun is offered with a scope already installed, the value of the scope should be included in the overall value of the gun. How much are used scopes worth? I figure current production optics at about one third to one half of retail price when attached to a gun. That way, if the buyer does not want the particular scope they can negotiate a price reduction with the scope removed. Or they can sell it themselves and buy the scope that suits their needs. Older, out of production scopes have become collectibles in their own right. The long target scopes as made by Unertl, Fecker, Winchester and others can be worth hundreds of dollars. Some firearms manufacturers, such as Marlin and Mossberg, actually used to make their own scopes or had scopes made for them that had their name on it.

Many times I have bought a used Stevens or Mossberg .22 rifle with an old scope on it that is worth more than the gun. I suggest consulting the book *Old Rifle Scopes* by Nick Stroebel when attempting to price older optics. Always check the scope for damage if it is adding to the price of the gun. Make sure the optics are clear, glass lenses have no chips or scratches, crosshairs are intact, and adjusting knobs are working. Getting a broken scope fixed is possible but expensive. Original replacement parts are hard to come by.

In addition to scopes, metallic sights of several configurations will be found. The most popular of these is the tang sight. This is a peep sight that mounts on the tang or back of the receiver of many guns. These were frequently found on Winchester, Sharps, Remington, and other quality sporting rifles. The tang sights made by a gun manufacturer are especially desirable. Winchester-made sights

are among the most valuable as collectibles. Other tang sight makers include Marble and Lyman.

Besides tang sights, there are peep sights that mount on the side of a firearm. These were offered by companies like Mossberg, Redfield, Williams, and Lyman. When a firearm is offered that has an older metallic sight, I refer the reader to the book *Old Gunsights*, also by Nick Stroebel. This fine book lists the metallic sights by maker and model number.

Some of the old aftermarket tang or peep sights required the gun to be drilled and tapped to install the sight. This sort of modification usually reduces the price of a firearm. On the other hand, a Winchester Model 1886 that has had its receiver drilled to install a newer Marbles sight might be worth less to some buyers, but if a period, i.e., vintage, sight is present it could add to the value. Depends on the buyer.

All Scratched Up

Fine engraving on a firearm definitely adds to its value. The amount of coverage can range from a fine highlight on the edges all the way to fully engraved hunting scenes complete with gold inlay. If the work is done by a known engraver, pricing the firearm becomes more akin to pricing a piece of art than a useful tool. As with a fine painting or sculpture, when a known engraver dies, examples of his or her work will skyrocket in price. Some gun makers offered engraving as a special order option on their products. The factory engraved Colts and Winchesters done in the late 1800s by artists such as Nimschke and Ulrich will bring several times their book value. Indeed, many books are devoted solely to this subject.

Engraving done by an amateur or unknown craftsman will be judged solely on its attractiveness on a particular firearm. If you are contemplating the purchase of an engraved firearm, look closely at the work. Some engraving I have seen was cut too deep and really did not look pleasing. Or there were errors in the pattern that the engraver tried to blend in. After all, an apprentice engraver had to perfect his craft somewhere. The "practice" pieces frequently were sold to buyers who did not spot the defects.

Sometimes the style of engraving may make a gun more (or less) attractive to a given buyer. For example, Germanic-style engraving, with its deep-cut oak-leaf patterns and dramatic portraiture, may turn off some buyers but attract others.

Got Wood?

Walnut was the primary type of wood used to make factory gunstocks in America through the WW II era. The massive production of rifles for military use reduced the stands of available walnut trees and set the industry on a quest to find acceptable substitutes that cost less. In the 1950s, many of the less expensive firearms began being equipped with birch, ash or particle wood stocks. When a model that was once offered with a walnut stock is then sold with a cheaper kind of wood, the older walnut stocked models can bring a higher price. A good example of this is the Ruger 10-22 semi automatic rifle. When introduced in 1964, it sported a walnut stock. In the early 1980s a birch stock replaced the walnut. So a 10-22 with a walnut stock can be worth as much as $75 more than a recent birch stocked rifle.

The grain structure or pattern in nice walnut stocks can add a lot to the price of a long gun. When walnut stock blanks are sold to gun makers there is a grading system based on the attractiveness of the wood. They use terms like AAA or AA Fancy down to field or utility grade. Very desirable is a striped pattern in the buttstock. This can look like the stripes on a tiger or it might be a pattern of wavy lines of coloration. The finest grade AAA walnut stock blanks can be priced at over $1000 just for an unshaped wood blank. Imagine how much that finished stock would add to the value of a pre 1964 Winchester Model 70. It could quickly make that $750 rifle in to a $4500 rifle.

I have seen many mid-grade stocks on field-grade shotguns and rifles. Mid-grade walnut might have some tiger stripe pattern near the butt end but standard grain in the rest. These are fairly common so they don't attract the high rollers who want the AAA fancy wood. There is no set way to calculate the additional value in stock appearance. It is a very subjective thing, attractiveness of a piece of wood. But it can add to the price of a gun for someone who likes it.

Any discussion of stock materials must also consider synthetics. Some synthetics can add significantly to the value of a gun. A Remington Nylon 66 .22 rifle with Seneca Green stock can bring twice as much as an otherwise identical model in Mohawk Brown.

Get a Grip

Grip materials can also add to the value of a handgun. A S&W First Model .32 Hand Ejector with factory pearl grips can bring 50 percent more than an otherwise identical gun with hard rubber grips. In fact, in some cases factory pearls are worth more than the gun itself! None-factory aftermarket grips, no matter how nice, do not generally add to the value of a gun. Quite the contrary.

Previous Ownership

Previous ownership of a gun can also add significantly to its value. One of John Wayne's Great Western revolvers, for example, can bring many times as much as a similar model owned by Joe Blow. But such enhanced value depends on the celebrity status of the previous owner. A Colt SAA owned by Mel Torme might not be particularly attractive to a younger buyer ("Mel *Who*?").

Note that previous ownership of a gun always depends on provenance, i.e., the paper trail that proves such ownership. Without provenance, claims of previous ownership are merely talk, and worth about just as much.

Potential Historical Association

Sometimes a gun is worth more merely because it was produced during a historically-relevant era. A Colt SAA whose serial number places it in the range of those used by the U.S. Army at the Battle of Little Big Horn, for example, is automatically more valuable than one outside that range. It doesn't matter if it can't be proven that the gun in question was carried during the battle–although that would be nice. The mere fact that it *might* have been significantly adds to its value.

Wrapping It Up

Another item that will add to the price of an older gun is the original box and paperwork that came with a gun when sold new. On vintage Colts or Smith & Wessons a box and papers could almost double the price of the gun. Of course, the Commemorative guns as made by Colt and Winchester in the 1960s and 70s have to be unfired and have their boxes and literature to be worth full book price. Even utility grade firearms sold as recently as five or 10 years ago can be enhanced by having the box with them.

Finally, there are any number of add-on accessories that might come with a used gun that can add to the value for a prospective buyer: Slings, holsters, extra magazines, boxes of ammunition or brass, scope covers, bi-pods, cases, or any other accessory that was purchased and installed by the owner. All of these cost money. I frequently buy guns, then the owner brings in another $50 or 100 worth of stuff and says "here, these were with that gun." Every little bit helps.

When acquiring or selling firearms, it pays to remember that not everyone wants a museum-quality collectible. Some want hunting guns, some want shooters. Some want guns from a specific period in history. Any factor that caters to any of these interests can add to the value of a gun – sometimes a little, sometimes a lot. ★

GUNDEX®

BERGMANN

BERNARDELLI

GUNDEX

IVER JOHNSON

JAEGER

MARLIN-GLENFIELD

MAROCCHI

MAUSER

MODERN GUN VALUES
HANDGUNS
DIRECTORY OF MANUFACTURERS

A.A. Arms AP9

Accu-Tek AT-9SS

Accu-Tek BL-9

Accu-Tek AT-380SS

Accu-Tek HC-380SS

A.A. ARMS AP9

Semi-automatic; 9mm Para.; 20-shot magazine; 5-inch barrel; 11-13/16-inch overall length; weighs 3-1/2 lbs.; adjustable post front sight in ring, open fixed rear; vented barrel shroud; checkered plastic grips; lever safety; fires from closed bolt; 3-inch barrel available; matte blue-black or nickel finish. Introduced 1988; dropped 1999.

| **Perf.:** $425 | **Exc.:** $375 | **VGood:** $250 |

Nickel finish

| **Perf.:** $500 | **Exc.:** $450 | **VGood:** $325 |

A.A. ARMS AP9 TARGET

Same specs as the AP9 except 12-inch barrel; grooved forend; blue finish. No longer in production. Was marketed by Kimel Industries.

| **Perf.:** $425 | **Exc.:** $375 | **VGood:** $250 |

ACCU-TEK MODEL AT-9SS

Semi-automatic; double-action-only; 9mm Para.; 8-shot magazine; 3-1/4-inch barrel; 6-1/4-inch overall length; weighs 28 oz.; black checkered nylon grips; blade front sight, windage-adjustable rear; three-dot system; stainless steel construction; firing pin block with no external safeties. Made in U.S. by Accu-Tek. Introduced 1992, dropped 1996.

| **New:** $295 | **Perf.:** $205 | **Exc.:** $175 |

ACCU-TEK MODEL AT-25SS

Semi-automatic; single action; 25 ACP; 7-shot magazine; 2-3/4-inch barrel; 6-inch overall length; weighs 28 oz.; blade front sight, windage-adjustable rear; checkered black composition grips; external hammer; manual thumb safety; firing pin block; trigger disconnect; satin stainless steel finish. Made in U.S. by Accu-Tek. Introduced 1991; dropped 1995.

| **Perf.:** $165 | **Exc.:** $125 | **VGood:** $105 |

ACCU-TEK MODEL AT-25AL

Same specs as AT-25SS except aluminum frame and slide with 11-oz. weight. Made in U.S. by Accu-Tek. Introduced 1991; dropped 1995.

| **Perf.:** $175 | **Exc.:** $135 | **VGood:** $115 |

ACCU-TEK MODEL AT-25SSB

Same specs as Model AT-25SS except matte black finish over stainless steel. Introduced 1991; dropped 1995.

| **Perf.:** $200 | **Exc.:** $160 | **VGood:** $135 |

ACCU-TEK MODEL AT-32SS

Semi-automatic; single action; 32 ACP; 5-shot magazine; 2-3/4-inch barrel; 6-inch overall length; weighs 28 oz.; blade front sight, windage-adjustable rear; checkered black composition grips; external hammer; manual thumb safety; firing pin block; trigger disconnect. Satin stainless steel finish. Made in U.S. by Accu-Tek. Introduced 1991; dropped 2003.

| **Perf.:** $245 | **Exc.:** $225 | **VGood:** $200 |

ACCU-TEK MODEL AT-32SSB

Same specs as Model AT-32SS except matte black finish over stainless steel. Introduced 1991; dropped 2003.

| **Perf.:** $195 | **Exc.:** $160 | **VGood:** $135 |

ACCU-TEK MODEL AT-40SS

Semi-automatic; double-action-only; 40 S&W; 7-shot magazine; 3-1/4-inch barrel; 6-1/4-inch overall length; weighs 28 oz.; black checkered nylon grips; blade front sight, windage-adjustable rear; three-dot system; stainless steel construction; firing pin block with no external safeties. Similar to Model CP-9SS. Made in U.S. by Accu-Tek. Introduced 1992; dropped 1996.

| **New:** $295 | **Perf.:** $205 | **Exc.:** $175 |

ACCU-TEK MODEL AT-45SS

Semi-automatic; double-action-only; 45 ACP; 6-shot magazine; 3-1/4-inch barrel; 6-1/4-inch overall length; weighs 28 oz.; blade front sight, windage-adjustable rear; three-dot sight system; stainless steel construction; firing pin block with no external safeties. Similar to Model AT-40SS. Made in U.S. by Accu-Tek. Introduced 1995; dropped 1996.

| **New:** $295 | **Perf.:** $205 | **Exc.:** $175 |

ACCU-TEK MODEL AT-380SS/SSB

Semi-automatic; single action; .380 ACP; 5-shot magazine; 2-3/4-inch barrel; 5-5/8-inch overall length; weighs 16 oz.; blade front sight, windage-adjustable rear; black combat or wood stocks; external hammer; manual safety with firing pin block, trigger disconnect; black (discontinued 1999), chrome or chrome with black slide. Alloy (discontinued 1991) or stainless steel construction. Made in U.S. by Accu-Tek. Introduced 1990.

| **Perf.:** $195 | **Exc.:** $160 | **VGood:** $120 |

ACCU-TEK MODEL AT-380 LADY

Same specs as Accu-Tek 380 except 380 ACP only; chrome finish; gray bleached oak stocks. Introduced 1990; dropped 1991.

| **Perf.:** $195 | **Exc.:** $160 | **VGood:** $120 |

ACCU-TEK BL-9 AUTO PISTOL

Caliber: 9mm Para., 5-shot magazine. Barrel: 3-inch. Weight: 22 oz. Length: 5.6-inch overall. Carbon steel construction. Stocks: Black composition. Sights: Fixed. Features: Double action only; black finish. Was furnished with lockable case. Introduced 1997; dropped 2002.

| **New:** $295 | **Perf.:** $205 | **Exc.:** $175 |

ACCU-TEK BL-380

Same as the BL-9 except chambered for 380 ACP. Introduced 1997. Made in U.S. by Accu-Tek; dropped 1999.

| **Perf.:** $195 | **Exc.:** $160 | **VGood:** $120 |

ACCU-TEK MODEL CP-9SS AUTO PISTOL

Caliber: 9mm Para., 8-shot magazine. Barrel: 3.2-inch. Weight: 28 oz. Length: 6.25-inch overall. Stocks: Black checkered nylon. Sights: Blade front, rear adjustable for windage; three-dot system. Features: Stainless steel construction. Double action only. Firing pin block with no external safeties. Lifetime warranty. Introduced 1992. Made in U.S. by Accu-Tek; dropped 1999.

| **New:** $295 | **Perf.:** $205 | **Exc.:** $175 |

Action Arms AT-84

Agner Model 80

Alkartasuna Ruby

Action Arms Uzi Pistol

Advantage Arms Model 442

ACCU-TEK CP-40SS AUTO PISTOL
Same as the Model CP-9SS except chambered for 40 S&W, 7-shot magazine. Introduced 1992; dropped 1999.

New: $250   **Perf.:** $200   **Exc.:** $165

ACCU-TEK CP-45SS AUTO PISTOL
Same as the Model CP-9SS except chambered for 45 ACP, 6-shot magazine. Introduced 1995; dropped 1999. Made in U.S. by Accu-Tek.

New: $295   **Perf.:** $205   **Exc.:** $175

ACCU-TEK MODEL HC-380SS
Semi-automatic; single action; 380 ACP, 10-shot magazine; 2-3/4-inch barrel; 6-inch overall length; weighs 28 oz.; checkered black composition grips; blade front sight, windage-adjustable rear; external hammer; manual thumb safety with firing pin and trigger disconnect; bottom magazine release; stainless finish. Made in U.S. by Accu-Tek. Introduced 1993; dropped 2003.

New: $210   **Perf.:** $175   **Exc.:** $155

ACTION ARMS AT-84
Semi-automatic; double action; 9mm Para., 41 Action Express; 15-shot magazine (9mm), 10-shot (41 AE): 4-3/4-inch barrel; 8-1/16-inch overall length; weighs 35-1/2 oz.; drift-adjustable rear sight, blade front; polished blued finish. Made in Switzerland. Introduced 1987; dropped 1989.

Perf.: $500   **Exc.:** $465   **VGood:** $395

ACTION ARMS AT-84P
Same specs as Model AT-84 except 13-shot (9mm Para.), 8-shot (41 AE); 3-11/16-inch barrel; weighs 32 oz. Prototype only.

ACTION ARMS AT-88S
Semi-automatic; double action; 9mm Para., 41 Action Express; 10-shot magazine; 4-3/4-inch barrel; 8-1/8-inch overall length; weighs 35-1/2 oz.; blade front sight, drift-adjustable rear; checkered walnut grips; polished blue finish; originally marketed with both barrels. Made in Switzerland. Introduced 1987; importation dropped 1990.

Perf.: $550   **Exc.:** $500   **VGood:** $475

ACTION ARMS AT-88H
Same specs as AT-88S except 10-shot (9mm Para.), 7-shot (41 Action Express) magazine; 3-1/2-inch barrel; 6-7/8-inch overall length; weighs 30-1/2 oz. Introduced 1989; importation dropped 1990.

Perf.: $550   **Exc.:** $500   **VGood:** $475

ACTION ARMS AT-88P
Same specs as AT-88S except 13-shot (9mm Para.), 8-shot (41 Action Express) magazine; 3-11/16-inch barrel; 7-5/16-inch overall length; weighs 32 oz. Introduced 1989; importation dropped 1990.

Perf.: $550   **Exc.:** $500   **VGood:** $475

ACTION ARMS UZI PISTOL
Semi-automatic; single action; 9mm Para., 45 ACP; 20-shot magazine; 4-1/2-inch barrel; 9-1/2-inch overall length; weighs 3-1/2 lbs.; black plastic grip; post front sight with white dot, open fully click-adjustable rear, two white dots; semi-auto blowback action; fires from closed bolt; floating firing pin; comes in molded plastic case. Imported from Israel by Action Arms. Introduced 1984; dropped 1993.

Perf.: $1300   **Exc.:** $1100   **VGood:** $895

ADVANTAGE ARMS MODEL 442
Derringer; break-top action; 22 LR, 22 WMR; 4-shot; 2-1/2-inch barrel; 4-1/2-inch overall length; weighs 15 oz.; smooth walnut stocks; fixed sights; double-action trigger; rotating firing pin; spring-loaded extractors; nickel, blued or black finish. Introduced 1983; dropped 1987. Reintroduced 1989 by New Advantage Arms Corp.; no longer in production.

Perf.: $150   **Exc.:** $125   **VGood:** $115
Add $10 to above prices for .22 WMR chambering.

AGNER MODEL 80
Semi-automatic; 22 LR; 5-shot magazine; 5-15/16-inch barrel; 9-1/2-inch overall length; weighs 36 oz.; adjustable French walnut stocks; fixed blade front sight, adjustable rear; safety key locks trigger, slide, magazine; dry fire button; right- or left-hand models. Made in Denmark. Introduced 1984; dropped 1987; was imported by Beeman.

Perf.: $1,125   **Exc.:** $1,040   **VGood:** $950
Add $100 to above prices for left-hand action.

AIR MATCH 500
Single-shot; 22 LR; 10-7/16-inch barrel; weighs 28 oz.; match grip of stippled hardwood; left- or right-hand; match post front sight, adjustable match rear; adjustable sight radius; marketed in case with tools, spare sights. Made in Italy. Introduced 1984; dropped 1987; was imported by Kendall International Arms.

Perf.: $550   **Exc.:** $495   **VGood:** $450

A.J. ORDNANCE THOMAS 45
Semi-automatic; double action; 45 ACP; 6-shot magazine; 3-1/2-inch barrel; 6-1/2-inch overall length; windage-adjustable rear sight, blade front; checkered plastic grips; blued finish; matte sighting surface. Introduced 1977; discontinued 1978.

Perf.: $1100   **Exc.:** $975   **VGood:** $675

Chrome finish
Perf.: $1175   **Exc.:** $1050   **VGood:** $750

AJAX ARMY
Single action revolver; solid frame; spur trigger; .44 Rimfire. Sold by E.C. Meacham Co. of St. Louis, MO, in mid-1880s.

Perf.: $500   **Exc.:** $440   **VGood:** $300

ALAMO RANGER
Double-action revolver formerly manufactured in Spain; resembles Colt SAA; .38 Spl.

Perf.: $295   **Exc.:** $275   **VGood:** $200

ALASKA
Single action revolver; made by Hood Firearms Co., Norwich, CT, from 1873 to 1884; .22 rimfire; 7-shot; spur trigger; solid frame.

Perf.: $275   **Exc.:** $220   **VGood:** $190

ALKARTASUNA RUBY
Semi-automatic; 32 ACP; 9-shot magazine; 3-3/8-inch barrel; 6-3/8-inch overall length; checkered hard rubber or wooden stocks; blued finish; fixed sights. Manufactured in Spain, 1917 to 1922; distributed primarily in Europe; some used by French army in World Wars I, II.

Exc.: $165   **VGood:** $100   **Good:** $85

Allen Buckhorn Target

Allen 1875 Army Outlaw

Allen Cattleman

American Arms Escort

American Arms CX-22

ALCHEMY ARMS SPECTRE STANDARD ISSUE

Semi-automatic; 9mm Para., .40 S&W, .45 CP; 10-shot double column magazine; 4-1/2-inch barrel; single-action; 32 oz.; linear action trigger; aluminum receiver; keyed internal locking device; tactical rail; lowered ejection port. Introduced 2000.

Exc.: $675   **VGood:** $585   **Good:** $525

ALCHEMY ARMS SPECTRE SERVICE GRADE (SG & SGC)

Similar to Spectre Standard Issue, except does not have tactical rail or rounded trigger guard. SGC is designed as a Colt Commander-style pistol with 4-inch barrel, weighing 27 oz. SG introduced 2000; SGC introduced 2001.

Exc.: 675   **VGood:** $585
Good: $525

ALCHEMY ARMS SPECTRE TITANIUM EDITION

Another in the Spectre series with difference being a titanium lide with an aluminum receiver. Introduced 2000.

Exc.: $895   **VGood:** $775   **Good:** $675

ALLEN 1875 ARMY OUTLAW

Revolver; single action; 357 Mag., 44-40, 45 Colt; 6-shot cylinder; 7-1/2-inch barrel; 13-3/4-inch overall length; weighs 44 oz.; notch rear sight, blade front; uncheckered walnut stocks; brass triggerguard; color case-hardened frame, rest blued. Copy of Model 1875 Remington. Made in Italy by Uberti. Introduced 1986; importation dropped 1987. Importaton resumed 2001 by Uberti USA, Inc.; dropped 2002.

Perf.: $395   **Exc.:** $295   **VGood:** $225
Add $45 to above prices for models with convertible cylinder (.45LC/.45ACP).

ALLEN BUCKHORN

Revolver; single-action; 44 Mag., 44 Spl., 44-40; 6-shot cylinder; 4-3/4-inch, 6-inch, 7-1/2-inch barrel; grooved rear sight, blade front; one-piece uncheckered walnut stocks; steel or brass backstrap, triggerguard; color case-hardened frame; blued cylinder, barrel. Made in Italy by Uberti. Formerly

imported by Iver Johnson. Reintroduced 1986; importation dropped by Allen Fire Arms 1987. Importation resumed by Uberti USA, Inc. but dropped in 2002.

Perf.: $350   **Exc.:** $300   **VGood:** $275
Add $70 to above prices for converticle cylinder; add $40 for Target Model.

ALLEN BUCKHORN BUNTLINE MODEL

Same specs as Buckhorn except 18-inch barrel. Was imported by Allen up to 1989; resume by Uberti USA, Inc. in 2001; dropped 2002.

Perf.: $400   **Exc.:** $350   **VGood:** $325
Add $40 to above prices for target sights; add $40 for extra .44-40 WCF cylinder combo; add $125 for detachable shoulder stock; subtract $50 for brass frame.

ALLEN BUCKHORN TARGET MODEL

Same specs as Buckhorn except flat-top frame; adjustable rear sight ramp front. No longer imported by Allen.

Perf.: $425   **Exc.:** $375   **VGood:** $350
Convertible cylinder model
Perf.: $475   **Exc.:** $425   **VGood:** $400

ALLEN CATTLEMAN

Revolver; single action; 22 LR, 22 WMR, 38 Spl., 357 Mag., 44-40, 45 Colt; 6-shot cylinder; 4-3/4-inch, 5-1/2-inch, 7-1/2-inch barrel; fixed groove rear sight, blade front; one-piece uncheckered walnut stocks; brass or steel backstrap and triggerguard; blued barrel, cylinder; case-hardened frame; polished hammer flats. Made in Italy by Uberti. Formerly imported by Iver Johnson. Reintroduced 1986; no longer imported by Allen Fire Arms. Reintroduced by A. Uberti USA 2001; dropped 2002.

Perf.: $335   **Exc.:** $295   **VGood:** $255
Add $50 to above prices for convertible cylinder (.45LC/45ACP).
Add $10 for chambering in 44 Spl. or 44-40 WCF.
Add $75 for nickel finish (New Model) or Old West (Old Model) finish.

ALLEN CATTLEMAN BUNTLINE MODEL

Same specs as Cattleman except 18-inch barrel; 22 LR/22WMR combo, 357, 44-40, 45 Colt only. No longer imported by Allen.

Perf.: $425   **Exc.:** $375   **VGood:** $325

ALLEN CATTLEMAN SHERIFF'S MODEL

Same specs as Cattleman except 3-inch or 4-inch barrel; 44-40, 45 Colt only. No longer imported by Allen. Importation discontinued 2002.

Perf.: $350   **Exc.:** $300   **VGood:** $275

ALLEN CATTLEMAN TARGET MODEL

Same specs as Cattleman except flat-top frame; fully-adjustable rear sight. No longer imported by Allen. Importation discontinued 1990.

Perf.: $315   **Exc.:** $275   **VGood:** $250
Add $25 to above prices for steel backstrap and trigger guard.
Add $60 for stainless steel construction.

ALLEN 1871 ROLLING BLOCK TARGET PISTOL

Single shot; 22 LR, 22 WMR, 22 Hornet, 357 Mag., 45 Colt (Navy Model with open sights manufactured from 1992 to 1995); 9-7/8-inch half-round, half-octagon barrel; 14-inch overall length; weighs 44 oz.; fully-adjustable rear sight, blade front; walnut stocks, forend; brass triggerguard; color case-hardened frame, blued barrel. Replica of 1871 target rolling block. Made in Italy by Uberti. Introduced 1986; no longer imported by Allen Fire Arms; importation resumed by Uberti USA in 2002; dropped 2002. Add 10% for centerfires.

Perf.: $350   **Exc.:** $300   **VGood:** $275

AMERICAN ARMS BUCKHORN

Revolver; single action; 44 Mag.; 4-3/4-inch, 6-inch, 7-1/2-inch barrel; 11-inch overall length; weighs 44 oz. (6-inch barrel); smooth walnut grips; blade front sight, groove rear; blued barrel and cylinder; brass triggerguard and backstrap. Imported from Italy by American Arms, Inc. from 1993; dropped 1996.

Perf.: $350   **Exc.:** $300   **VGood:** $275

American Arms PK-22

American Arms Regulator

American Arms PX-22

American Arms ZC-380

American Arms P-98

AMERICAN ARMS CX-22

Semi-automatic; double action; 22 LR; 8-shot magazine; 3-5/16-inch barrel; 6-5/16-inch overall length; weighs 22 oz.; blade front sight, windage-adjustable rear; checkered black polymer grips; manual hammer-block safety; firing pin safety; alloy frame; blue-black finish. Resembles Walther PPK externally. Introduced 1990; dropped 1995.

Perf.: $175   **Exc.:** $145   **VGood:** $125

AMERICAN ARMS CXC-22

Same specs as CX-22 except chromed slide. Introduced 1990; dropped 1990.

Perf.: $170   **Exc.:** $150   **VGood:** $125

AMERICAN ARMS EP-380

Semi-automatic; double action; 380 ACP; 7-shot magazine; 3-1/2-inch barrel; 5-1/2-inch overall length; weighs 25 oz.; checkered wood stocks; fixed sights; slide-mounted safety; made of stainless steel. Manufactured in West Germany. Introduced 1988; dropped 1990.

Perf.: $375   **Exc.:** $325   **VGood:** $300

AMERICAN ARMS ESCORT

Semi-automatic; double-action-only; 380 ACP; 7-shot magazine; 3-3/8-inch barrel; 6-1/8-inch overall length; weighs 19 oz.; soft polymer grips; blade front sight, windage-adjustable rear; stainless steel construction; chamber-loaded indicator. Marketed by American Arms, Inc. Introduced 1995; dropped 1997.

New: $285   **Perf.:** $230   **Exc.:** $220

AMERICAN ARMS MATEBA AUTO/REVOLVER

Caliber: 357 Mag., 44 mag., 6-shot. Barrel: 4-inch. Weight: 2.75 lbs. Length: 8.77-inch overall. Stocks: Smooth walnut. Sights: Blade on ramp front, adjustable rear. Features: Double or single action. Cylinder and slide recoil together upon firing. All-steel construction with polished blue finish. Introduced 1997. Imported from Italy by American Arms, Inc.

New: $1300   **Perf.:** $1100   **Exc.:** $925

AMERICAN ARMS MODEL P-98

Semi-automatic; double action; 22 LR; 8-shot magazine; 5-inch barrel; 8-1/8-inch overall length; weighs 25 oz.; blade front sight, windage-adjustable rear; grooved black polymer grips; magazine disconnect safety; hammer-block safety; alloy frame; blue-black finish. Has external appearance of Walther P.38. Introduced 1989; dropped 1996.

Perf.: $175   **Exc.:** $150   **VGood:** $135

AMERICAN ARMS PK-22

Semi-automatic; double action; 22 LR; 8-shot magazine; 3-5/16-inch barrel; 6-5/16-inch overall length; weighs 22 oz.; fixed rear sight; checkered plastic grips; slide-mounted safety; polished blue finish. From American Arms, Inc. Introduced 1989; dropped 1996.

Perf.: $175   **Exc.:** $150   **VGood:** $135

AMERICAN ARMS PX-22

Semi-automatic; double action; 22 LR; 7-shot magazine; 2-15/16-inch barrel; 5-3/8-inch overall length; weighs 15 oz.; checkered black plastic stocks; fixed sights; polished blued finish. From American Arms, Inc. Introduced 1989; dropped 1995.

Perf.: $175   **Exc.:** $150   **VGood:** $135

AMERICAN ARMS PX-25

Semi-automatic; double action; 25 ACP; 7-shot magazine; 2-3/4-inch barrel; 5-3/8-inch overall length; weighs 15 oz.; checkered black plastic stocks; fixed sights; blued finish. Introduced 1990; dropped 1991.

Perf.: $175   **Exc.:** $150   **VGood:** $135

AMERICAN ARMS REGULATOR

Revolver; single action; 357 Mag., 44-40, 45 Colt; 4-3/4-inch, 5-1/2-inch, 7-1/2-inch barrel; 8-1/6-inch overall length (4-3/4-inch barrel); weighs 32 oz. (4-3/4-inch barrel); smooth walnut grips; blade front sight, groove rear; blued barrel and cylinder, brass triggerguard and backstrap. Imported from Italy by American Arms, Inc. Introduced 1992; dropped 2000.

New: $345   **Perf.:** $295   **Exc.:** $250

Dual cylinder (44-40/44 Spl. or 45 Colt/45 ACP), or DLX all-steel model

Perf.: $355   **Exc.:** $340   **VGood:** $275

AMERICAN ARMS REGULATOR DELUXE

Similar to Regulator except 45 LC only; all blue charcoal finish (mfd. 1996 to 1997); or color case hardened frame (introduced 1998); steel trigger guard and back strap. Importation dropped in 1992; resumed from 1994 to 2000.

Perf.: $325   **Exc.:** $300   **VGood:** $280

AMERICAN ARMS BISLEY SINGLE-ACTION REVOLVER

Similar to the Regulator except has Bisley-style grip with steel backstrap and trigger guard, Bisley-style hammer. Color case-hardened steel frame. Hammer block safety. Available with 4-3/4-inch, 5-1/2-inch, 7-1/2-inch barrel, 45 Colt only. Imported from Italy by American Arms, Inc.; introduced 1997; dropped 1998.

New: $395   **Perf.:** $375   **Exc.:** $350

AMERICAN ARMS SPECTRE

Semi-automatic; double action; 9mm Para., .40 S&W (1991 only), 45 ACP; 30-shot magazine; 6-inch barrel; 13-3/4-inch overall length; weighs 4 lbs. 8 oz.; black nylon grip; fully-adjustable post front sight, fixed U-notch rear; blowback action fires from closed bolt; ambidextrous safety and decocking levers; matte black finish; comes with magazine loading tool. For standard velocity ammunition only. Was marketed by American Arms, Inc.; Introduced 1990; dropped 1993.

9mm & .40 S&W calibers

Perf.: $450   **Exc.:** $350   **VGood:** $300

45 ACP caliber

Perf.: $475   **Exc.:** $375   **VGood:** $325

AMERICAN ARMS TT-9MM TOKAREV

Semi-automatic; single action; 9mm Para.; 9-shot magazine; 4-1/2-inch barrel; 8-inch overall length; weighs 32 oz.; grooved plastic stocks; fixed sights; blued finish. Copy of Russian Tokarev, made in Yugoslavia. Introduced 1988; dropped 1990.

Perf.: $350   **Exc.:** $300   **VGood:** $275

American Arms
TT-9mm Tokarev

American Derringer
High Standard
Derringer

American Derringer
Lady Derringer

American Derringer
COP

American
Derringer DA 38

American Derringer
Model 1 Texas
Commemorative

AMERICAN ARMS ZC-380

Semi-automatic; single action; 380 ACP; 7-shot magazine; 3-3/4-inch barrel; 6-1/2-inch overall length; weighs 26 oz.; checkered plastic stocks; fixed sights; polished, blued finish. Made in Yugoslavia. Introduced 1988; dropped 1990.

Perf.: $250   **Exc.:** $225   **VGood:** $200

AMERICAN DERRINGER COP 357

Derringer; double-action-only; 4-shot; 38 Spl., 357 Mag.; 3-1/8-inch barrel; 5-1/2-inch overall length; weighs 16 oz.; rosewood grips; fixed sights; stainless steel construction. Made in U.S. by American Derringer Corp. Introduced 1990; no longer in production. Add 15 percent for Cop, Inc./Torrance, CA production.

Perf.: $900   **Exc.:** $725   **VGood:** $400

AMERICAN DERRINGER COP MINI

Same specs as COP 357 except 22 WMR; 2-7/8-inch barrel; 4-15/16-inch overall length; double action; automatic hammer-block safety; rosewood, walnut or other hardwood grips. Made in U.S. by American Derringer Corp. Introduced 1990; dropped 1994.

Perf.: $800   **Exc.:** $625   **VGood:** $300

AMERICAN DERRINGER DA 38

Derringer; double action; 22 LR, 38 Spl., 357 Mag., 9mm Para., 40 S&W; 3-inch over/under barrels; 4-13/16-inch overall length; weighs 14-1/2 oz.; rosewood, walnut or other hardwood grips; fixed sights; manual safety; made of satin-finished stainless steel, aluminum. Introduced 1989; still in production.

Perf.: $360   **Exc.:** $250   **VGood:** $200
Add $10 to above prices for 9mm Para., $15 for 357 Mag., and $40 for 40 S&W.

AMERICAN DERRINGER STANDARD DERRINGER

Derringer; double action; 22 LR, 22 WMR; 2-shot; 3-1/2-inch barrel; 5-1/8-inch overall length; weighs 11 oz.; hammer-block safety; blued finish. Direct copy of

original High Standard derringer. Reintroduced 1990; dropped 1995. Reintroduced 1998; dropped 2002.

Perf.: $320   **Exc.:** $245   **VGood:** $185

AMERICAN DERRINGER LADY DERRINGER

Derringer; over/under; 32 H&R Mag., 38 Spl., 22 LR, 22 WMR, 380 ACP, 357 Mag., 9mm Para., 45 ACP, 45 Colt/.410 shotshell; 2-shot; tuned action; scrimshawed synthetic ivory grips; deluxe grade polished; also deluxe engraved version with 1880s-style engraving. Marketed in fitted box. Introduced 1991; still in production on limited basis.

Perf.: $325   **Exc.:** $300   **VGood:** $255

Deluxe grade		
Perf.: $350	**Exc.:** $275	**VGood:** $200
Deluxe engraved		
Perf.: $650	**Exc.:** $500	**VGood:** $400

AMERICAN DERRINGER MODEL 1

Derringer; over/under; 22 LR, 22 WMR, 22 Hornet, 223 Rem., 30 Luger, 30-30, 32 ACP, 38 Super, 380 ACP, 38 Spl., 9x18, 9mm Para., 357 Mag., 41 Mag., 44-40, 44 Spl., 44 Mag., 45-70 Govt., 45 Colt/.410; 2-shot; break action; 3-inch barrel; 4-13/16-inch overall length; weighs 15-1/2 oz. (38 Spl.); rosewood, zebra wood stocks; blade front sight; stainless steel with high-polish or satin finish; manual hammer-block safety. Made in U.S. by American Derringer Corp. Introduced 1980; still in production on limited basis.

Regular calibers		
Perf.: $295	**Exc.:** $235	**VGood:** $185
Large caliber		
Perf.: $345	**Exc.:** $285	**VGood:** $205

Add $30 to above prices for high polish finish.

AMERICAN DERRINGER MODEL 1 TEXAS COMMEMORATIVE

Same specs as Model 1 except solid brass frame; stainless steel barrel; rosewood grips; 38 Spl., 44-40 Win., 45 Colt. Made in U.S. by American Derringer

Corp. Introduced 1987; still in production on limited basis.

38 Special caliber		
Perf.: $385	**Exc.:** $340	**VGood:** $250
44-40 or 45 Colt caliber		
Perf.: $470	**Exc.:** $415	**VGood:** $250
32 Mag caliber		
Perf.: $265	**Exc.:** $245	**VGood:** $220

AMERICAN DERRINGER MODEL 3

Derringer; single shot; 32 Mag. 38 Spl.; 2-1/2-inch barrel; 4-15/16-inch overall length; weighs 8-1/2 oz.; rosewood grips; blade front sight; stainless steel construction; manual hammer-block safety. Made in U.S. by American Derringer Corp. Introduced 1985; dropped 1994.

Perf.: $250   **Exc.:** $225   **VGood:** $200

AMERICAN DERRINGER MODEL 4

Derringer; over/under; 357 Mag., 357 Max., 45-70/.410/3-inch, 45 Colt/.410/3-inch, 45 ACP, 44 Mag.; 2-shot; break-action; 4-1/8-inch barrel; 6-inch overall length; weighs 16-1/2 oz.; stainless steel construction. Made in U.S. by American Derringer Corp. Introduced 1985; still in production.

Perf.: $375   **Exc.:** $290   **VGood:** $230

AMERICAN DERRINGER MODEL 4 ALASKAN SURVIVAL MODEL

Same specs as Model 4 except upper barrel chambered for 45-70 or 44 Mag. Made in U.S. by American Derringer Corp. Introduced 1980; still in limited production.

Perf.: $525   **Exc.:** $450   **VGood:** $400

AMERICAN DERRINGER MODEL 6

Derringer; over/under; 45 LC/410 3-inch, 22 WMR, 357 Mag., 45 ACP; 2-shot; 6-inch barrels; 8-1/4-inch overall length; weighs 21 oz.; rosewood stocks; manual hammer-block safety. Made in U.S. by

American Derringer Model 4

American Firearms 25

American Firearms 380

American Derringer Semmerling LM-4

American Derringer Model 6

American Frontier 1851 Navy Richards & Mason Conversion

American Derringer Corp. Introduced 1986; still in limited production.

Perf.: $355   **Exc.:** $250   **VGood:** $200
Add $10 to above prices for 45 LC/410 shotshell chambering.
Add $15 for satin finish (discontinued in 1994).
Add $40 for high polish finish.
Add $50 for oversized grips (discontinued in 1994 but reinstated 1998-99).

AMERICAN DERRINGER MODEL 7 ULTRA LIGHTWEIGHT

Derringer; over/under; 22 LR, 22 WMR, 32 H&R Mag., 380 ACP, 38 Spl., 44 Spl.; 2-shot; break-action; 3-inch barrel; 4-7/8-inch overall length; weighs 7-1/2 oz.; high strength aircraft aluminum construction; rosewood, zebra wood stocks; blade front sight; stainless steel; manual hammer-block safety. Made in U.S. by American Derringer Corp. Introduced 1986; still in production.

Perf.: $275   **Exc.:** $185   **VGood:** $145

44 Spl. caliber		
Perf.: $450	**Exc.:** $395	**VGood:** $300

AMERICAN DERRINGER MODEL 10 LIGHTWEIGHT

Derringer; over/under; 38 Special, 45 ACP, 45 Colt; 2-shot; break-action; 3-inch barrels; 4-13/16-inch overall length; weighs 10 oz.; aluminum frame; matte gray finish. Introduced 1990; still in production.

45 Colt		
Perf.: $3850	**Exc.:** $315	**VGood:** $280
38 Special		
Perf.: $300	**Exc.:** $250	**VGood:** $200
45 ACP		
Perf.: $325	**Exc.:** $275	**VGood:** $225

AMERICAN DERRINGER MODEL 11

Derringer; over/under; 22 LR, 22 WMR, 32 H&R Mag., .380 ACP, 38 Spl.; 2-shot; break-action; 3-inch barrel; 4-13/16-inch overall length; weighs 11 oz.; aluminum barrels; matte gray frame. Introduced 1990.

Perf.: $300   **Exc.:** $230   **VGood:** $195

AMERICAN DERRINGER SEMMERLING LM-4

Derringer; manually-operated repeater; 9mm Para., 45 ACP; 7-shot (9mm), 5-shot (45 ACP) magazine; 3-inch barrel; 5-1/4-inch overall length; weighs 24 oz.; height 3-3/4-inch; width 1 inch; checkered plastic grips (blued finish), rosewood (stainless finish); open fixed sights. Was sold with manual, leather carrying case, spare stock screws, wrench. Limited manufacture in U.S. by American Derringer Corp.; dropped 2003.

Perf.: $2390   **Exc.:** $2045   **VGood:** $1876

Stainless steel		
Perf.: $2450	**Exc.:** $2250	**VGood:** $2050

AMERICAN FIREARMS 25

Semi-automatic; 25 ACP; 8-shot magazine; 2-1/8-inch barrel; 4-7/16-inch overall length; fixed sights; walnut grips; blued ordnance steel or stainless steel. Manufactured by American Firearms Co., Inc. Introduced 1966; dropped 1974.

Perf.: $225   **Exc.:** $175   **VGood:** $150

Stainless steel		
Perf.: $275	**Exc.:** $225	**VGood:** $200

AMERICAN FIREARMS 380

Semi-automatic; 380 ACP; 8-shot magazine; 3-1/2-inch barrel; 5-1/2-inch overall; stainless steel; smooth walnut stocks. Limited manufacture 1972.

Perf.: $395   **Exc.:** $325   **VGood:** $225

AMERICAN FIREARMS DERRINGER

Derringer; over/under; 38 Spl., 22 LR, 22 WMR; 2-shot; 3-inch barrel; fixed open sights; checkered plastic grips; stainless steel construction; spur trigger, half-cock safety. Introduced 1972; dropped 1974.

Perf.: $225   **Exc.:** $175   **VGood:** $135

AMERICAN FRONTIER 1851 NAVY CONVERSION

Revolver; single action; 38, 44. Barrel: 4-3/4-inch, 5-1/2-inch, 7-1/2-inch, octagon. Weight: NA. Length: NA. Stocks: Varnished walnut, Navy size. Sights: Blade front, fixed rear. Features: Shoots metallic cartridge ammunition. Non-rebated cylinder; blued steel backstrap and trigger guard; color case-hardened hammer, trigger, ramrod, plunger; no ejector rod assembly. Introduced 1996; discontinued 2000. Imported from Italy by American Frontier Firearms Mfg.

Perf.: $575   **Exc.:** $400   **VGood:** $275

AMERICAN FRONTIER 1851 NAVY RICHARDS & MASON CONVERSION

Similar to the 1851 Navy Conversion except has Mason ejector assembly. Introduced 1996; discontinued 2000. Imported from Italy by American Frontier Firearms Mfg.

Perf.: $575   **Exc.:** $400   **VGood:** $275

AMERICAN FRONTIER REMINGTON NEW ARMY CAVALRY

Revolver; single action; 38, 44, 45. Barrel: 5-1/2-inch, 7-1/2-inch, 8-inch. Weight: NA. Length: NA. Stocks: Varnished walnut Sights: Blade front, fixed rear. Features: High polish blue finish; color case-hardened hammer. Has ejector assembly, loading gate. Government inspector's cartouche on left grip, sub-inspector's initials on various parts. Introduced 1997; discontinued 2000. Imported from Italy by American Frontier Firearms Mfg.

Perf.: $575   **Exc.:** $400   **VGood:** $275

AMERICAN FRONTIER RICHARDS 1860 ARMY

Revolver; single action; 38 Spl., 44 Spl. Barrel: 4-3/4-inch, 5-1/2-inch, 7-1/2-inch, round. Weight: NA. Length: NA. Stocks: Varnished walnut, Army size. Sights: Blade front, fixed rear. Features: Shoots metallic cartridge ammunition. Rebated cylinder; available with or without ejector assembly; high-polish blue including backstrap; silver-plated trigger guard; color case-hardened hammer and trigger. Introduced 1996; discontinued 2000. Imported from Italy by American Frontier Firearms Mfg.

Perf.: $575   **Exc.:** $400   **VGood:** $275

American Frontier 1871-1872, Open-Top Revolvers

AMT Automag II

AMT Backup Double-Action-Only

AMT Automag III

AMT Backup

AMERICAN FRONTIER 1871-1872 POCKET MODEL REVOLVER

Revolver; single action; 32, 5-shot cylinder. Barrel: 4-3/4-inch, 5-1/2-inch round. Weight: NA. Length: NA. Stocks: Varnished walnut or Tiffany. Sights: Blade front, fixed rear. Features: Based on the 1862 Police percussion revolver converted to metallic cartridge. High polish blue finish with silver-plated brass backstrap and trigger guard, color case-hardened hammer. Introduced 1996; discontinued 2000. Imported from Italy by American Frontier Firearms Mfg.

Perf.: $395   **Exc.:** $295   **VGood:** $205

AMERICAN FRONTIER REMINGTON NEW MODEL REVOLVER

Revolver; single action; 38, 44.; 5-1/2-inch, 7-1/2-inch barrel; varnished walnut grips; blade front, fixed rear sights; replica of the factory conversions by Remington between 1863 and 1875; high polish blue or silver finish with color case-hardened hammer; has original loading lever and no gate or ejector assembly. Introduced 1996; discontinued 2000. Imported from Italy by American Frontier Firearms Mfg.

Perf.: $400   **Exc.:** $300   **VGood:** $275

AMERICAN FRONTIER POCKET RICHARDS & MASON NAVY

Revolver; single action; 32; 5-shot cylinder; 4-3/4-inch, 5-1/2-inch barrel; varnished walnut stocks; blade front, fixed rear sights; shoots metallic-cartridge ammunition; non-rebated cylinder; high-polish blue; silver-plated brass backstrap and trigger guard; ejector assembly; color case-hardened hammer and trigger. Introduced 1996; discontinued 2000. Imported from Italy by American Frontier Firearms Mfg.

Perf.: $400   **Exc.:** $300   **VGood:** $275

AMERICAN FRONTIER 1871-1872 OPEN-TOP REVOLVERS

Revolver; single action; 38 Spl., 44 Spl.; 4-3/4-inch, 5-1/2-inch, 7-1/2-inch, 8-inch round barrel; varnished walnut grips; blade front, fixed rear sights; reproduction of the early cartridge conversions from percussion; made for metallic cartridges; high polish blued steel; silver-plated brass backstrap and trigger guard; color case-hardened hammer; straight non-rebated cylinder with naval engagement engraving; stamped with original patent dates; does not have conversion breechplate. Introduced 1996; discontinued 2000. Imported from Italy by American Frontier Firearms Mfg.

Perf.: $575   **Exc.:** $400   **VGood:** $275

Tiffany model with Tiffany grips, silver and gold finish with engraving

Perf.: $895   **Exc.:** $695   **VGood:** $450

AMT AUTOMAG II

Semi-automatic; 22 WMR; 9-shot magazine, 7-shot (3-3/8-inch barrel); 3-3/8-inch, 4-1/2-inch, 6-inch barrel; 9-3/4-inch overall length; weighs 23 oz.; Millett adjustable rear sight, blade front; grooved black composition stocks; squared triggerguard; stainless steel construction; gas-assisted action; brushed finish on slide flats, rest sandblasted. Introduced 1987; discontinued 2001.

Perf.: $405   **Exc.:** $300   **VGood:** $250

AMT AUTOMAG III

Semi-automatic; single action; 30 Carbine, 9mm Win. Mag.; 8-shot magazine; 6-3/8-inch barrel; 10-1/2-inch overall length; weighs 43 oz.; carbon fiber grips; blade front sight, adjustable rear; stainless steel construction; hammer-drop safety; brushed finish on slide flats, rest sandblasted. Made in U.S. by AMT. Introduced 1989; discontinued 2001.

Perf.: $600   **Exc.:** $550   **VGood:** $475

AMT AUTOMAG IV

Semi-automatic; single action; 10mm (discontinued 1993) or 45 Winchester Mag.; 7-shot magazine; 6-1/2-inch barrel; 10-1/2-inch overall length; weighs 46 oz.; carbon fiber grips; blade front sight, adjustable rear; stainless steel construction with brushed finish. Made in U.S. by AMT. Introduced 1990; discontinued 2001.

Perf.: $600   **Exc.:** $550   **VGood:** $475

AMT AUTOMAG V

Semi-automatic; single action; 50 AE; 5-shot magazine; 6-1/2-inch barrel; 10-1/2-inch overall length; weighs 46 oz.; carbon fiber grips; blade front sight, adjustable rear; stainless steel construction with brushed finish. Made in U.S. by AMT. Introduced 1990; dropped 1995.

Perf.: $850   **Exc.:** $775   **VGood:** $695

AMT BACKUP

Semi-automatic; double action; 22 LR (discontinued 1987), 357 SIG (from 1996), 380 ACP, 38 Super (from 1995), 9mm Para. (from 1995), 40 S&W (from 1995), 400 Cor-Bon (from 1997); 8-shot (22 LR), 5-shot (380 ACP & 40S&W) magazine; 2-1/2-inch barrel; 5-inch overall length; weighs 17 oz.; smooth wood stocks; fixed open sights; concealed hammer; manual grip safeties; blowback operated; stainless steel. 380 ACP introduced 1974; 22 introduced 1982. No longer in production. (22 LR & 380 ACP), $349 (9mm Para., 40 S&W & 45 ACP), $389 (357 SIG, 38 Super, 400 Cor-Bon).

22 LR		
Perf.: $250	**Exc.:** $190	**VGood:** $145
380 ACP		
Perf.: $250	**Exc.:** $190	**VGood:** $145
9mm Para., 40 S&W & 45 ACP		
Perf.: $250	**Exc.:** $190	**VGood:** $145
357 SIG, 38 Super & 400 Cor-Bon		
Perf.: $375	**Exc.:** $320	**VGood:** $275

AMT BACKUP II

Same specs as standard Backup except single action; 380 ACP only with 5-shot magazine; carbon fiber grips; weighs 18 oz. Introduced 1993; dropped 1998.

Perf.: $260   **Exc.:** $200   **VGood:** $175

AMT Hardballer

AMT On Duty

AMT Skipper

AMT Hardballer Long Slide

Anschutz Exemplar

AMT Lightning

AMT Javelina

AMT BACKUP DOUBLE-ACTION-ONLY

Same specs as standard Backup except 9mm Para., 38 Super, 40 S&W, 45 ACP; double-action-only; enlarged triggerguard; slide rounded at rear; 5-shot magazine. Made in U.S. by AMT. Introduced 1992. No longer in production.

Perf.: $260   **Exc.:** $200   **VGood:** $175

AMT BULL'S-EYE TARGET

Semi-automatic; 40 S&W; 8-shot magazine; 5-inch barrel; 8-1/2-inch overall length; weighs 38 oz.; Millett adjustable rear sight; neoprene wrap-around grips; stainless steel construction; long grip safety; wide adjustable trigger; beveled magazine well. Introduced 1991; dropped 1992.

Perf.: $400   **Exc.:** $340   **VGood:** $295

AMT BULL'S-EYE TARGET REGULATION

Same specs as Bull's-Eye Target except 22 LR; 5-inch, 6-1/2-inch, 8-1/2-inch, 10-1/2-inch, 12-1/2-inch bull or tapered barrel; adjustable sights; vent rib; wooden target grips. Manufactured 1986 only.

Perf.: $425   **Exc.:** $350   **VGood:** $285

AMT COMBAT GOVERNMENT

Semi-automatic; single action; 45 ACP; 5-inch barrel; 8-1/2-inch overall length; stainless steel construction; extended combat safety; adjustable target-type trigger; flat mainspring housing; custom-fitted barrel bushing; fixed combat sights; checkered walnut grips. Introduced 1978; dropped 1980.

Perf.: $450   **Exc.:** $365   **VGood:** $295

AMT HARDBALLER

Semi-automatic; 45 ACP; 5-inch barrel; 8-1/2-inch overall length; weighs 39 oz.; stainless steel construction; extended combat safety; serrated matted slide rib; long grip safety; beveled magazine well; grooved front, back straps; adjustable trigger; custom barrel bushing; adjustable combat sights; checkered walnut or wrap-around rubber grips. Introduced 1978; dropped 2001.

New.: $525   **Exc.:** $425   **VGood:** $300

AMT HARDBALLER LONG SLIDE

Same specs as Hardballer except 7-inch barrel; was available in 400 Cor-Bon; 10-1/2-inch overall length; fully-adjustable micro rear sight. Introduced 1977; discontinued in 2001. Add 125% for Arcadia, California, address.

Perf.: $800   **Exc.:** $625   **VGood:** $425
Add $50 to above prices for 400 Cor-Bon chambering.
Add $300 for 5-inch Longslide conversion kit (discontinued 1997).

AMT JAVELINA

Semi-automatic; single action; 10mm Auto; 8-shot magazine; 7-inch barrel; 10-1/2-inch overall length; weighs 40 oz.; wrap-around rubber grips; blade front sight, Millett adjustable rear; all stainless construction, brushed finish. Made in U.S. by AMT. Introduced 1989; dropped 1992.

Perf.: $560   **Exc.:** $460   **VGood:** $400

AMT LIGHTNING

Semi-automatic; 22 LR; 10-shot magazine; 6-1/2-inch, 8-1/2-inch, 10-1/2-inch, 12-1/2-inch tapered barrels; 5-inch, 6-1/2-inch, 8-1/2-inch, 10-1/2-inch, 12-1/2-inch bull barrels; 10-3/4-inch overall length 6-1/2-inch barrel); weighs 45 oz.; checkered wrap-around rubber stocks; blade front sight, fixed rear; adjustable rear at extra cost; stainless steel; Clark trigger with adjustable stops; receiver grooved for scope; interchangeable barrels. Introduced 1984; dropped 1989.

Perf.: $350   **Exc.:** $250   **VGood:** $175
Adjustable Sights
Perf.: $375   **Exc.:** $350   **VGood:** $285

AMT ON DUTY

Semi-automatic; double action; 9mm Para., 40 S&W, 45 ACP; 15-shot (9mm), 11-shot (40 S&W), 9-shot (45 ACP) magazine; 4-1/2-inch barrel; 7 3/4-inch overall length; weighs 32 oz.; smooth carbon fiber grips; blade front sight, windage-adjustable rear; three-dot system; choice of DA with decocker or double-action-only; inertia firing pin, trigger disconnector safety; aluminum frame with steel recoil

shoulder, stainless steel slide and barrel. Made in U.S. by AMT. Introduced 1991; dropped 1994.

Perf.: $385   **Exc.:** $300   **VGood:** $275
45 ACP caliber
Perf.: $445   **Exc.:** $360   **VGood:** $335

AMT SKIPPER

Semi-automatic; 45 ACP, 40 S&W; 7-shot magazine; 4-1/4-inch barrel; 7-inch overall length; weighs 33 oz.; Millet adjustable rear sight; checkered walnut grips; matte stainless steel construction. Introduced 1978; dropped 1984.

Perf.: $500   **Exc.:** $400   **VGood:** $300

AMT SKIPPER COMBAT

Same specs as standard Skipper except fixed sights. Discontinued 1984.

Perf.: $500   **Exc.:** $400   **VGood:** $300

ANSCHUTZ EXEMPLAR

Bolt action; 22 LR, 22 Hornet; 5-shot magazine; 10-inch, 14-inch barrel; 17-inch overall length; weighs 56 oz.; open-notch adjustable rear sight, hooded front on ramp; European walnut stock, stippled grip, forend; built on Anschutz Match 64 rifle action with left-hand bolt; Anschutz #5091 two-stage trigger; receiver grooved for scope mount. Made in Germany. Introduced 1987; dropped 1997.

Perf.: $600   **Exc.:** $525   **VGood:** $300
22 Hornet
Perf.: $835   **Exc.:** $685   **VGood:** $575

ANSCHUTZ MODEL 64P SPORT/TARGET

Bolt action; 22 LR, 22 WMR, 5-shot magazine. Barrel: 10-inch. Weight: 3 lbs., 8 oz. Length: 18-1/2-inch overall. Stock: Choate Rynite. Sights: None furnished; grooved for scope mounting. Features: Right-hand bolt; polished blue finish. Introduced 1998; dropped 2003. Imported from Germany by AcuSport.

Perf.: $700   **Exc.:** $585   **VGood:** $400

ANSCHUTZ MODEL 17 LP

Similar to Model 64LP except 17 HMR; 4-shot magazine. Importation began 2003.

Perf.: $700   **Exc.:** $585   **VGood:** $400

Argentine Hi-Power 9mm

Arcus 94 Auto Pistol

Anschutz Model 64P Sport Target

Armalite AR-24

Armalite AR-24 Tactical Custom

Arcus Model 94C Compact

Arminex Tri-Fire

ARCUS-94 AUTO PISTOL

Caliber: 9mm Para., 10-shot magazine. Barrel: 5.24-inch. Weight: 32 oz. Length: 8 inches overall. Stocks: Textured rubber. Sights: Blade front, rear adjustable for windage. Features: Single-action trigger. Available in blued, brushed chrome and two-tone finishes. Compact and double-action versions also available. Introduced 1998. Previously imported from Bulgaria by Miltex, Inc. (from 1998 to 2000).

Perf.: $285   **Exc.:** $250   **VGood:** $225

ARCUS-94C COMPACT AUTO PISTOL

Similar to Arcus-94 except compact version with overall length 7-1/2-inch; Barrel length 4-3/4-inch; weight 2 lbs.

Perf.: $285   **Exc.:** $250   **VGood:** $225

ARGENTINE FM HI-POWER 9MM

Semi-automatic; single action; 9mm Para.; 10-shot magazine; 4-21/32-inch barrel; 7-3/4-inch overall length; weighs 32 oz.; blade front sight, adjustable rear; checkered walnut grips; licensed copy of Browning Hi-Power made by FM Fray Luis Beltrain. Previously imported from Argentina by Century International Arms, Inc. Introduced 1990; imported by Sarco, Inc. and Pacific Armament Corp.

Perf.: $300   **Exc.:** $250   **VGood:** $200
Add $150 to above price for Detective Model conversion kit.

ARGENTINE FM HI-POWER DETECTIVE MODEL

Same specs as standard model except 3-13/16-inch barrel; 6-15/16-inch overall length; weighs 33 oz.; finger-groove, checkered soft rubber grips; matte black finish. Formerly imported by Century International Arms, Inc., Sarco, Inc. and Pacific Armament Corp.

New: $275   **Perf.:** $250   **Exc.:** $200

ARMALITE AR-24 PISTOL

Single-/double-action semi-auto pistol chambered in 9mm Parabellum; based on CZ-75 design. Steel slide and frame; 5.26" (Full-Size) and 3.89" (Compact) barrel lengths. Blue-black finish. Fixed-and adjustable-sight models available. Introduced in 2007. Deduct 15 percent for Compact model.

NIB: $425   **Exc.:** $395   **VGood:** $300

ARMALITE AR-24 TACTICAL CUSTOM

Similar to above with tactical refinements including stippled front and back straps, 3-dot luminous sights, etc. Also available inW compact version (shown).

NIB: $475   **Exc.:** $445   **VGood:** $350

ARMINEX TRI-FIRE

Semi-automatic; single action; 9mm Para., 38 Super, 45 ACP; 9-shot (9mm), 7-shot (45 ACP) magazine; 5-inch, 6-inch, 7-inch barrel; 8-inch overall length; weighs 38 oz.; smooth contoured walnut stocks; interchangeable post front sight, adjustable rear; slide-mounted firing pin safety; contoured backstrap; blued or electroless nickel finish; convertible by changing barrel, magazine, recoil spring. Introduced 1982; dropped 1987.

Perf.: $750   **Exc.:** $650   **VGood:** $475

Presentation cased
Perf.: $800   **Exc.:** $700   **VGood:** $525

With conversion unit
Perf.: $880   **Exc.:** $780   **VGood:** $605

ARMINEX TRI-FIRE TARGET MODEL

Same specs as Tri-Fire except 1-inch longer slide; 6-inch or 7-inch barrel. Introduced 1982; dropped 1987.

Perf.: $850   **Exc.:** $725   **VGood:** $550

ARMINIUS MODEL 3

Revolver; double action; 25 ACP; 5-shot; 2-inch barrel; hammerless; safety catch; folding trigger. Produced by Friedrick Pickert, Arminius Waffenwerk. Not currently imported into U.S.

Perf.: $175   **Exc.:** $135   **VGood:** $125

ARMINIUS MODEL 8

Revolver; double action; 320, 32 ACP; 5-shot; 2-inch, 5-1/2-inch barrel; hammerless; safety catch; folding trigger. Produced by Friedrick Pickert, Arminius Waffenwerk. Not currently imported into U.S.

Perf.: $175   **Exc.:** $135   **VGood:** $125

ARMINIUS MODEL 9

Revolver; double action; 320, 32 ACP; 5-shot; 2-5/16-inch barrel; hammer model. Produced by Friedrick Pickert, Arminius Waffenwerk. Not currently imported into U.S.

Perf.: $185   **Exc.:** $140   **VGood:** $130

ARMINIUS MODEL 9A

Same specs as Model 9 except 3-1/8-inch barrel.

Perf.: $185   **Exc.:** $135   **VGood:** $110

ARMINIUS MODEL 10

Revolver; double action; 320, 32 ACP; 5-shot; 2-5/16-inch barrel; hammerless; safety catch; folding trigger. Produced by Friedrick Pickert, Arminius Waffenwerk. Not currently imported into U.S.

Perf.: $165   **Exc.:** $145   **VGood:** $125

ARMINIUS MODEL TP1

Single shot; 22 LR; adjustable sights; drop-down action; hammer fired. Target pistol produced by Friedrick Pickert, Arminius Waffenwerk. Not currently imported into U.S.

Perf.: $400   **Exc.:** $325   **VGood:** $275

ARMINIUS MODEL TP2

Similiar to Model TP1 except double-set trigger; concealed hammer. Target pistol produced by Friedrick Pickert, Arminius Waffenwerk. Not currently imported into U.S.

Perf.: $500   **Exc.:** $425   **VGood:** $325

ARMSCOR MODEL 38

Revolver; double action; 38 Spl.; 6-shot cylinder; 4-inch barrel; weighs 32 oz.; windage-adjustable rear sight, ramp front; checkered Philippine mahogany stocks; vent rib; polished blue finish. Made in the Philippines. Introduced 1986; dropped 1999; reintroduced 2001.

Perf.: $175   **Exc.:** $135   **VGood:** $110

ARMSCOR MODEL 200P

Revolver; double action; 38 Spl.; 6-shot cylinder; 2-1/2-inch, 4-inch barrel; 8-7/8-inch overall length (4-inch barrel); weighs 26 oz.; ramp front sight, fixed rear; checkered mahogany or rubber grips; blued

Armscor Model 38

Armscor Model 200SE

Astra A-100

Astra A-70

Astra A-80

Astra Constable

finish. Made in the Philippines. Introduced 1990; dropped 1999; reintroduced 2001.

Perf.: $175   **Exc.:** $135   **VGood:** $110A

ARMSCOR MODEL 200SE

Same specs as Model 200P except 22 LR, 22 WMR, 38 Spl.; 2-inch, 3-inch, 6-inch barrel; overall length 9-1/4 inches (4-inch barrel); weighs 36 oz.; Introduced 1989; dropped 1999; reintroduced 2001.

Perf.: $200   **Exc.:** $175   **VGood:** $150

ARMSCOR MODEL 200TC

Same specs as Model 200P except 22 LR, 22 WMR, 38 Spl.; full shroud barrel; adjustable rear sight; checkered wood grips. Introduced 1990; dropped 1999; reintroduced 2001.

Perf.: $225   **Exc.:** $200   **VGood:** $175

ARMSCOR MODEL 202

Similar to Model 200, except does not have barrel shroud. Imported from 2001.

Perf.: $175   **Exc.:** $150   **VGood:** $125

ARMSCOR MODEL 206

Similar to Model 200, except has 2-inch barrel, weighs 24 oz. Imported from 2001.

Perf.: $175   **Exc.:** $150   **VGood:** $125

ARMSCOR MODEL 210

Similar to Model 200, except has 4-inch vent-rib barrel, and adjustable rear sight. Weight: 28 oz. Imported from 2001.

Perf.: $175   **Exc.:** $150   **VGood:** $125

ARMSCOR MAP1 FS

Single/double-action 9mm semi-auto with 16+1 capacity. Fixed sights, 4.45-inch barrel, 40.5 oz. nickel alloy steel frame and slide. (Shorter, lighter MS model has 3.66-inch barrel.) Introduced 2006.

NIB: $425   **Exc.:** $350   **VGood:** $275

ARMSCOR MAPP1 FS

Single/double-action 9mm semi-auto with 16+1 capacity. Fixed sights, 4.45-inch barrel, 40.5 oz. polymer frame with integrated accessory rail, and

nickel alloy steel slide. (Shorter, lighter MS model has 3.66-inch barrel.)

NIB: $435   **Exc.:** $365   **VGood:** $285

ARM TECH DERRINGER

Derringer; double-action-only; 22 LR, 22 WMR; 2-5/8-inch barrel; 4-5/8-inch overall length; weighs 19 oz.; fixed sights; hard rubber or walnut stocks; stainless steel; blued model available. Introduced 1983; no longer in production.

Perf.: $175   **Exc.:** $150   **VGood:** $125

ASTRA A-70

Semi-automatic; double action; 9mm Para., 40 S&W; 8-shot (9 mm), 7-shot (40 S&W) magazine; 3-1/2-inch barrel; 6-1/2-inch overall length; checkered black plastic grips; blade front sight, windage-adjustable rear; all steel frame and slide; checkered grip straps and trigger guard; nickel or blue finish. Imported from Spain by European American Armory. Introduced 1992; dropped 1996.

New: $300	**Perf.:** $250	**Exc.:** $225	
Nickel finish			
New: $325	**Perf.:** $300	**Exc.:** $250	
Stainless steel			
New: $350	**Perf.:** $325	**Exc.:** $275	

ASTRA A-75 DECOCKER

Semi-automatic; double action; 9mm Para., 40 S&W, 45 ACP (9mm), 7-shot (40 S&W) magazine; 3-1/2-inch barrel; 6-1/2-inch overall length; weighs 29 oz. (Featherweight, 23-1/2 oz.); contoured pebble-grain grips; blade front sight, windage-adjustable rear; all steel frame and slide; checkered grip straps, triggerguard; nickel or blue finish; ambidextrous decocker system. Imported from Spain by European American Armory. Introduced 1993; dropped 1997.

Blue finish			
New: $300	**Perf.:** $265	**Exc.:** $240	
Nickel finish			
New: $325	**Perf.:** $275	**Exc.:** $255	
Stainless finish MSR $485			
New: $400	**Perf.:** $350	**Exc.:** $325	
Featherweight, 9mm Para.			
New: $420	**Perf.:** $370	**Exc.:** $345	

ASTRA A-80

Semi-automatic; double action; 9mm Para., 38 Super, 45 ACP; 15-shot (9mm, 38 Super), 9-shot (45 ACP); 3-3/4-inch barrel; 7-inch overall length; weighs 40 oz.; checkered black plastic stocks; square blade front sight, drift-adjustable square notch rear; loaded-chamber indicator; combat-style triggerguard; optional right-side slide release; automatic internal safety; decocking lever; blued or chrome finish. Imported from Spain by Interarms. Introduced 1982; dropped 1989.

Blue finish			
Perf.: $350	**Exc.:** $300	**VGood:** $285	
Chrome finish			
Perf.: $385	**Exc.:** $335	**VGood:** $325	

ASTRA A-90

Semi-automatic; double action; 9mm Para., 45 ACP; 14-shot (9mm), 8-shot (45 ACP); 3-3/4-inch barrel; 7-inch overall length; weighs 48 oz.; checkered black plastic stocks; square blade front sight, square notch windage-adjustable rear; double or single action; loaded chamber indicator; optional right- or left-side slide release; combat-type triggerguard; auto internal safety; decocking lever. Made in Spain. Introduced 1985; dropped 1990. Replaced by Model A-100.

Perf.: $375   **Exc.:** $325   **VGood:** $300

ASTRA A-100

Semi-automatic; double action; 9mm Para., 40 S&W, 45 ACP; 10-shot (9mm, 40 S&W), 9-shot (45 ACP) magazine; 3-15/16-inch barrel; 7-1/16-inch overall length; weighs 29 oz.; checkered black plastic grips; blade front sight, interchangeable rear blades for elevation, screw-adjustable for windage; decocking lever permits lowering hammer onto locked firing pin; automatic firing pin block; side button magazine release. Imported from Spain by European American Armory. Introduced 1993; dropped 1997.

Blue finish		
New: $375	**Perf.:** $325	**Exc.:** $300
Nickel finish		
New: $400	**Perf.:** $350	**Exc.:** $325

For pistols made for the Turkish police add 50 percent.

Astra Cadix

Astra A-60

Astra Model 44

Astra Model 357

Astra Cub (2000)

Astra Model 600

ASTRA CADIX

Revolver; double action; 22 LR, 38 Spl.; 9-shot (22), 5-shot (38 Spl.); 4-inch, 6-inch barrel; blued finish; adjustable rear sight, ramp front; checkered plastic stocks. Manufactured 1960 to 1968.

Perf.: $195   **Exc.:** $165   **VGood:** $140

ASTRA CONSTABLE

Semi-automatic; double action; 22 LR, 32 ACP, 380 ACP; 10-shot (22 LR), 8-shot (32 ACP), 7-shot (380 ACP) magazine; 3-1/2-inch barrel; adjustable rear sight, fixed front; molded plastic grips; exposed hammer; non-glare rib on slide; quick, no-tool take-down feature; blued or chrome finish except 32. Was imported by Interarms. Introduced 1969; dropped 1990.

Perf.: $295   **Exc.:** $250   **VGood:** $210

Chrome finish or wood grips

Perf.: $305   **Exc.:** $260   **VGood:** $220

Blue, engraved

Perf.: $350   **Exc.:** $325   **VGood:** $275

Chrome, engraved

Perf.: $395   **Exc.:** $325   **VGood:** $300

Add $20 to above prices for 22 LR chambering or checkered wood grips.

ASTRA A-60 CONSTABLE

Semi-automatic; double action; 380 ACP; 13-shot magazine; 3-1/2-inch barrel; adjustable rear sight, fixed front; molded plastic grips; slide mounted ambidextrous safety; blued steel only. Made in Spain. Introduced 1986; dropped 1991.

Perf.: $395   **Exc.:** $325   **VGood:** $280

ASTRA CONSTABLE STAINLESS

Same specs as Constable except 380 ACP only; stainless steel finish. Manufactured 1986.

Perf.: $350   **Exc.:** $300   **VGood:** $250

ASTRA CONSTABLE SPORT

Same specs as Constable except 6-inch barrel; blue finish; weighs 35 oz. Manufactured 1986-1987.

Perf.: $325   **Exc.:** $250   **VGood:** $225

ASTRA CUB (2000)

Semi-automatic; 22 Short, 25 ACP; 6-shot magazine; 2-1/2-inch barrel; 4-7/16-inch overall length; fixed sights; blued or chrome finish; plastic grips. Introduced 1957; still in production, but U.S. importation dropped 1968.

Perf.: $250   **Exc.:** $190   **VGood:** $140

Chrome finish

Perf.: $315   **Exc.:** $235   **VGood:** $175

Engraved

Perf.: $375   **Exc.:** $290   **VGood:** $225

ASTRA CAMPER (2000)

Semi-automatic; 22 Short; 4-inch barrel; 6-1/4-inch overall length; fixed sights; blued or chrome finish; plastic grips. Manufactured 1953 to 1960.

Perf.: $350   **Exc.:** $275   **VGood:** $200

ASTRA MODEL 41

Revolver; double action; 41 Mag.; 6-shot; 6-inch barrel only; 11-3/8-inch overall length; weighs 2-3/4 lbs. Introduced 1980; no longer manufactured.

Perf.: $275   **Exc.:** $250   **VGood:** $200

ASTRA MODEL 44

Revolver; double action; 44 Mag.; 8-1/2-inch barrel. Introduced 1980; importation dropped 1990.

Perf.: $300   **Exc.:** $275   **VGood:** $250

Stainless, 6-inch barrel

Perf.: $350   **Exc.:** $300   **VGood:** $275

ASTRA MODEL 45

Revolver; double action; 45 Colt; 6-shot; 6-inch barrel. Manufactured in Spain. Introduced 1980; dropped 1987.

Perf.: $325   **Exc.:** $275   **VGood:** $220

ASTRA MODEL 200 FIRECAT

Semi-automatic; 25 ACP, 6-shot magazine; 2-1/4-inch barrel; 4-3/8-inch overall length; fixed sights; blued finish; plastic grips. Introduced in 1920; U.S. importation dropped 1968.

Perf.: $250   **Exc.:** $190   **VGood:** $165

Engraved Model 200 Firecat

Perf.: $375   **Exc.:** $285   **VGood:** $250

ASTRA MODEL 300

Semi-automatic; 32 ACP, 380 ACP; 4-inch barrel; 5-3/8-inch overall length; hard rubber grips. Introduced 1922; dropped 1947.

Perf.: $850   **Exc.:** $650   **VGood:** $450

With Nazi proofmarks

Perf.: $1000   **Exc.:** $950   **VGood:** $700

Lightly engraved Astra Model 300

Perf.: $1700   **Exc.:** $1300   **VGood:** $900

Deeply engraved Astra Model 300

Perf.: $2550   **Exc.:** $1950   **VGood:** $1350

ASTRA MODEL 357

Revolver; 357 Mag.; 6-shot swing-out cylinder; 3-inch, 4-inch, 6-inch, 8-1/2-inch barrel; integral rib, ejector rod; click-adjustable rear sight, ramp front; target hammer; checkered walnut grips; blued. Imported by Interarms. Introduced 1972; importation dropped 1990.

Perf.: $250   **Exc.:** $215   **VGood:** $185

Stainless, 4-inch barrel

Perf.: $370   **Exc.:** $300   **VGood:** $265

ASTRA MODEL 400

Semi-automatic; 9mm Bergmann-Bayard/9mm Largo; 9-shot magazine; 6-inch barrel; 10-inch overall length; fixed sights; blowback action; some will also chamber and fire 9mm Para. and 38 ACP but it isn't recommended; blued finish; hard rubber or walnut grips. Introduced 1921; dropped 1946.

Exc.: $425   **VGood:** $325   **Good:** $230

Navy Model

Exc.: $1275   **VGood:** $975   **Good:** $690

With Nazi proof marks

Exc.: $850   **VGood:** $650   **Good:** $460

ASTRA MODEL 600

Semi-automatic; 9mm Luger; 8-shot; 5-1/4-inch barrel, 8-inch overall length; fixed sights; blued finish; hard rubber or walnut grips. Military, police issue. Introduced 1942; dropped 1946.

Exc.: $600   **VGood:** $495   **Good:** $350

With Nazi proofmarks

Exc.: $900   **VGood:** $750   **Good:** $550

Astra Model 800 Condor

Astra Model 900

Auto Mag

Astra Model 1915

Auto-Ordnance Model 1911TC

Auto-Ordnance Model 1911A1

ASTRA MODEL 800 CONDOR

Semi-automatic; 9mm Para.; 8-shot magazine; 5-5/16-inch barrel; 8-1/4-inch overall length; fixed sights; blued finish; grooved plastic grips; tubular-type design. Based on Model 400 design. Introduced 1958; dropped 1968. Few imported; produced primarily for European police, military use.

Exc.: $1200   **VGood:** $950   **Good:** $650

ASTRA MODEL 900

Semi-automatic; 7.63mm Mauser; 10-shot fixed magazine; 5-1/2-inch barrel; 11-1/2-inch overall length; adjustable rear sight, fixed front; small ring hammer on early models, larger hammer on later; grooved walnut grips; lanyard ring. Resembles design of "broomhandle" Mauser, but has barrel, barrel extension as two parts rather than one as in German Mauser, different lockwork, etc. Introduced 1927; dropped 1940. Originally priced at $37; has collector value. Add $600 for proper Astra holster-stock. Add 50 percent for early Bolo grips. Add 20 percent for those marked with Japanese characters.

Exc.: $2500   **VGood:** $1850   **Good:** $1350

ASTRA MODEL 1911 25

Semi-automatic; 25 ACP; 6-shot; 2-inch barrel; 4-1/8-inch overall length; fixed sights; horn grips; external hammer, loaded indicator on top; marked "Victoria Patent." Rare.

Exc.: $365   **VGood:** $265   **Good:** $175

ASTRA MODEL 1911 32

Semi-automatic; 32 ACP; 7-shot; 3-3/16-inch barrel; 5-1/2-inch overall length; weighs 21 oz.; black horn grips; blued finish. Similar to the Browning Model 1903 with internal hammer; marked "Victoria Patent." Manufactured until 1916.

Exc.: $365   **VGood:** $265   **Good:** $175

ASTRA MODEL 1915/1916

Semi-automatic; 32 ACP; 9-shot magazine; 3-1/4-inch barrel; 5-3/4-inch overall length; fixed sights; checkered wood or horn grips. Actually introduced in 1911 as the "Victoria," first marked "Astra" in 1915; dropped after WWI.

Exc.: $350   **VGood:** $265   **Good:** $175

ASTRA MODEL 3000

Semi-automatic; 32 ACP; 380 ACP; 6-shot, 7-shot magazine; 4-inch barrel; fixed sights; plastic grips; blued finish. Introduced 1948; dropped 1956.

Perf.: $550   **Exc.:** $425   **VGood:** $350

Engraved

Perf.: $1300   **Exc.:** $1000   **VGood:** $610

ASTRA MODEL 4000 FALCON

Semi-automatic; 22 LR, 32 ACP, 380 ACP; 10-shot (22 LR), 8-shot (32 ACP), 7-shot (380 ACP) magazine; 3-1/2-inch barrel; 6-1/2-inch overall length; thumb safety; exposed hammer; fixed sights; checkered black plastic grips; blued. Introduced 1956; U.S. importation dropped 1968.

Perf.: $550   **Exc.:** $425   **VGood:** $350

22 LR

Perf.: $825   **Exc.:** $637   **VGood:** $495

With caliber conversion kit in factory box

Perf.: $1250   **Exc.:** $950   **VGood:** $750

AUTAUGA MK II

Semi-automatic; double action only; 32 ACP, 6-shot magazine. Barrel: 2-inch. Weight: 11.3 oz. Length: 4.3-inch overall. Stocks: Black polymer. Sights: Fixed. Features: Double-action-only mechanism. Stainless steel construction. Uses Winchester Silver Tip ammunition. Introduced in 1996; dropped 2000. Clone of the Seecamp.

Perf.: $225   **Exc.:** $200   **VGood:** $150

AUTO MAG

Semi-automatic; 357 Auto Mag., 44 Auto Mag.; 7-shot magazine; 6-1/2-inch barrel; 11-1/2-inch overall length; short recoil; rotary bolt system; stainless steel construction; checkered plastic grips; fully-adjustable rear sight, ramp front. Manufactured by Auto Mag. Corp. and TDE Corp. 1970 to 1982.

Original Pasadena manufacture

Perf.: $2500   **Exc.:** $2300   **VGood:** $1995

TDE North Hollywood marked

Perf.: $2275   **Exc.:** $1850   **VGood:** $1700

AUTO-ORDNANCE MODEL 1911C

.45 ACP semi-auto with fixed sights and 7+1 capacity. Stainless frame and slide. 5-inch barrel, 39 oz. Laminate grips.

NIB: $400   **Exc.:** $350   **VGood:** $295

AUTO-ORDNANCE MODEL 1911CAF

.45 ACP semi-auto with fixed sights and 7+1 capacity. Aluminum frame and stainless slide. 5-inch barrel, 31.5 oz. Laminate grips.

NIB: $400   **Exc.:** $350   **VGood:** $295

AUTO-ORDNANCE 1911A1

Semi-automatic; 9mm Para., 38 Super, 10mm, 41 AE, 45 ACP; 7- shot (45 ACP), 8-shot (41 AE), 9-shot (others); 5-inch barrel; 8-1/2-inch overall length; weighs 39 oz.; blade front sight, windage-adjustable rear; parts interchangeable with original Colt Gov't. Model; blued, non-glare finish. Made in U.S. by Auto-Ordnance Corp. Introduced 1983; still in production except for 10mm and 41 AE.

Perf.: $445   **Exc.:** $365   **VGood:** $29

AUTO-ORDNANCE 1911A1 40 S&W

Same specs as standard Auto-Ordnance 1911A1, except 4-1/2-inch barrel; 7-3/4-inch overall length; weighs 37 oz.; 40 S&W; 8-shot magazine; black rubber wrap-around grips; 3-dot sight system. Introduced 1991; no longer in production.

Perf.: $445   **Exc.:** $365   **VGood:** $295

AUTO-ORDNANCE 1911A1 COMPETITION MODEL

Same specs as 1911A1 except 45 ACP (38 Super version produced in 1996 only); black textured, rubber wrap-around grips; fully-adjustable rear sight with three-dot system; machined compensator; Commander combat hammer; flat mainspring housing; low-profile magazine funnel; magazine bumper; high-ride beavertail grip safety; full-length recoil spring guide system; extended slide stop, safety and magazine catch; Videcki adjustable speed trigger; extended combat ejector. Made in

Auto-Ordnance
Thompson Custom 1911

Azul

Baer Concept
Series V

Auto-Ordnance
ZG-51 Pit Bull

Baer 1911 Bullseye
Wadcutter

Baer Concept
Series IX

U.S. by Auto-Ordnance Corp. Introduced 1994; dropped 1996.

New: $525   **Perf.:** $450   **Exc.:** $425

AUTO-ORDNANCE 1911A1 CUSTOM HIGH POLISH

Similar to the standard 1911A1 except has a Videcki speed trigger, extended thumb safety, flat mainspring housing, Acurod recoil spring guide system, osewood grips, custom combat hammer, beavertail grip safety. High-polish blue finish. Introduced 1998. Made in U.S. by Auto-Ordnance Corp.; dropped 1999.

New: $485   **Perf.:** $395   **Exc.:** $300

AUTO-ORDNANCE 1911A1 GENERAL MODEL

Same specs as 1911A1 except 45 ACP (38 Super version produced in 1996 only); 4-1/2-inch barrel; 7-3/4-inch overall length; weighs 37 oz.; three-dot sight system; black textured, rubber wrap-around grips with medallion; full-length recoil guide; blue finish.

New: $385   **Perf.:** $325   **Exc.:** $300

AUTO-ORDNANCE ZG-51 PIT BULL

Semi-automatic; single action; 45 ACP; 7-shot magazine; 3-1/2-inch barrel; 7-1/4-inch overall length; weighs 36 oz. Introduced 1989; dropped 1999.

Perf.: $385   **Exc.:** $310   **VGood:** $275

AUTO-ORDNANCE THOMPSON CUSTOM 1911

Semi-automatic; single action; 45 ACP; stainless steel construction; Series 80 design; barrel; 7-shot; grip safety; checkered laminate grips with medallion; skeletonized trigger; combat hammer; low profile sights; 39 oz.; Thompson bullet logo on left side of double serrated slide.

Perf.: $625   **Exc.:** $525   **VGood:** $450

AZUL

Semi-automatic; 7.63mm Mauser; 10-shot magazine; 5-1/2-inch barrel; 12-inch overall length; grooved wood grips. Close Spanish copy of Mauser Model 1896. Introduced 1930, dropped about 1935.

Warning: Some Azuls have selector switches for full-auto fire and are illegal unless registered with the U.S. Treasury.

Exc.: $1,700   **VGood:** $1250   **Good:** $900

BAER 1911 BULLSEYE WADCUTTER

Semi-automatic; single action; 45 ACP; 7-shot magazine; 5-inch barrel; 8-1/2-inch overall length; weighs 37 oz.; Baer dovetail front sight with undercut post, low-mount Bo-Mar rear with hidden leaf rear; checkered walnut grips; polished feed ramp and barrel throat; Bo-Mar rib on slide; full-length recoil rod; Baer speed trigger; Baer deluxe hammer and sear; Baer beavertail grip safety with pad; flat mainspring housing checkered 20 lpi; blue finish. Made in U.S. by Les Baer Custom, Inc.

New: $1500   **Perf.:** $1200   **Exc.:** $1100

BAER 1911 CONCEPT SERIES I-X PISTOLS

Semi-automatic; single action; 45 ACP; 7-shot magazine; 5-inch barrel; 8-1/2-inch overall length; weighs 37 oz.; checkered rosewood grips; Baer dovetail front sight, Bo-Mar deluxe low-mount rear with hidden leaf; Baer forged steel frame, slide and barrel with Baer stainless bushing; slide fitted to frame; double serrated slide; Baer beavertail grip safety; checkered walnut grips; tuned extractor; extended ejector; deluxe hammer and sear; match disconnector; lowered and flared ejection port; fitted recoil link; polished feed ramp, throated barrel; Baer fitted speed trigger; flat serrated mainspring housing; blue finish. Aluminum frame, stainless slide, BoMar and Novak sights and smaller Commanche frame sizes compose the Series I-X.

New: $1800   **Perf.:** $1475   **Exc.:** $1000

BAER 1911 CUSTOM CARRY

Semi-automatic; single action; 45 ACP; 7- or 10-shot magazine; 5-inch barrel; 8-1/2-inch overall length; weighs 37 oz.; checkered walnut grips; Baer improved ramp-style dovetailed front sight, Novak low-mount rear; Baer forged NM frame, slide and barrel with stainless bushing; fitted slide to frame; double serrated slide (full-size only); Baer speed trigger with 4-lb. pull; Baer deluxe hammer and sear;

tactical-style extended ambidextrous safety; beveled magazine well; polished feed ramp and throated barrel; tuned extractor; Baer extended ejector; checkered slide stop; lowered and flared ejection port; full-length recoil guide rod; recoil buff. Made in U.S. by Les Baer Custom, Inc.

Standard size, blued		
New: $1400	**Perf.:** $1100	**Exc.:** $1000
Standard size, stainless		
New: $1500	**Perf.:** $1200	**Exc.:** $1100
Commanche size, blued		
New: $1600	**Perf.:** $1100	**Exc.:** $1000
Commanche size, stainless		
New: $1700	**Perf.:** $1200	**Exc.:** $1100
Commanche size, aluminum frame, blued slide		
New: $1700	**Perf.:** $1200	**Exc.:** $1100
Commanche size, aluminum frame, stainless slide		
New: $1800	**Perf.:** $1300	**Exc.:** $1200

BAER 1911 NATIONAL MATCH HARDBALL

Semi-automatic; single action; 45 ACP; 7-shot magazine; 5-inch barrel; 8-1/2-inch overall length; weighs 37 oz.; Baer dovetail front sight with undercut post, low-mount Bo-Mar rear with hidden leaf rear; checkered walnut grips; Baer NM forged steel frame, double serrated slide and barrel with stainless steel bushing; slide fitted to frame; Baer match trigger with 4-lb. pull; polished feed ramp; throated barrel; checkered frontstrap; arched mainspring housing; Baer beveled magazine well; lowered, flared ejection port; tuned extractor; Baer extended ejector; checkered slide stop; recoil buff. Made in U.S. by Les Baer Custom, Inc.

New: $1100   **Perf.:** $875   **Exc.:** $725

BAER 1911 PREMIER II

Semi-automatic; single action; 45 ACP; 7-shot magazine; 5-inch barrel; 8-1/2-inch overall length; weighs 37 oz.; Baer dovetail front sight with undercut post, low-mount Bo-Mar rear with hidden leaf rear; checkered rosewood grips with double diamond pattern; Baer NM forged steel frame and barrel with stainless steel bushing; slide fitted to frame; double

Baer Ultimate Master Combat

Baer Custom Carry

Baer 1911 National Match Hardball

Baer 1911 Premier II

Baer 1911 Prowler III

Baford Arms Thunder Derringer

serrated slide; aluminum speed trigger with 4-lb. pull; deluxe Commander hammer and sear; polished feed ramp; throated barrel; checkered frontstrap; flat mainspring housing; Baer beveled magazine well; lowered, flared ejection port; tuned, polished extractor; Baer extended ejector; checkered slide stop. Made in U.S. by Les Baer Custom, Inc.

Blued		
New: $1800	**Perf.:** $1200	**Exc.:** $975
Stainless stee4		
New: $2000	**Perf.:** $1395	**Exc.:** $1100

BAER 1911 PROWLER III

Semi-automatic; single action; 45 ACP, 7- or 10-shot magazine; 5-inch barrel; 8-1/2-inch overall length; weighs 37 oz.; checkered rosewood grips with double diamond pattern; Baer dovetailed front sight, low-mount Bo-Mar rear with hidden leaf; Baer NM forged steel frame and barrel with stainless bushing; slide fitted to frame; double serrated slide; lowered, flared ejection port; tuned, polished extractor; Baer extended ejector; checkered slide stop; aluminum speed trigger with 4-lb. pull; deluxe Commander hammer and sear; beavertail grip safety with pad; beveled magazine well; extended ambidextrous safety; flat mainspring housing; polished feed ramp and throated barrel; 30 lpi checkered frontstrap; tapered cone stub weight and reverse recoil plug. Made in U.S. by Les Baer Custom, Inc. Still in production.

Standard or Commanche size, blued		
New: $1700	**Perf.:** $1625	**Exc.:** $1500
Standard or Commanche size, stainless		
New: $1800	**Perf.:** $1725	**Exc.:** $1600

BAER 1911 TARGET MASTER

Semi-automatic; single action; 45 ACP; 7-shot magazine; 5-inch barrel; 8-1/2-inch overall length; weighs 37 oz.; checkered walnut grips; Baer post-style dovetail front sight, low-mount Bo-Mar rear with hidden leaf; Baer NM forged steel frame; double serrated slide and barrel with stainless bushing; slide fitted to frame; standard trigger; polished feed ramp; throated barrel; checkered frontstrap; flat serrated mainspring housing; Baer beveled magazine well; lowered, flared ejection port; tuned extractor;

Baer extended ejector; checkered slide stop; recoil buff. Made in U.S. by Les Baer Custom, Inc. Still in production.

New: $1850	**Perf.:** $1495	**Exc.:** $1000

BAER 1911 ULTIMATE MASTER COMBAT

Semi-automatic; single action; 45 ACP (others available); 10-shot magazine; 5-inch Baer NM barrel; 8-1/2-inch overall length; weighs 37 oz.; checkered rosewood grips; Baer dovetail front sight, low-mount Bo-Mar rear with hidden leaf; Baer forged NM blued steel frame and double serrated slide; Baer triple port, tapered cone compensator; fitted slide to frame; lowered, flared ejection port; Baer reverse recoil plug; full-length guide rod; recoil buff; beveled magazine well; Baer Commander hammer and sear; Baer extended ambidextrous safety, extended ejector; checkered slide stop; beavertail grip safety with pad; extended magazine release button; Baer speed trigger. Made in U.S. by Les Baer Custom, Inc. Still in production.

Compensated, open sights		
New: $1900	**Perf.:** $1795	**Exc.:** $1650
Uncompensated "Limited" Model		
New: $1800	**Perf.:** $1695	**Exc.:** $1550
Compensated, with Baer optics mount		
New: $2300	**Perf.:** $2250	**Exc.:** $2100

BAER 1911 ULTIMATE MASTER "STEEL SPECIAL"

Same specs as Ultimate Master except scope and Baer scope mount; bushing-type compensator; fitted slide to frame; lowered, flared ejection port; Baer reverse recoil plug; two-piece guide rod. Designed for maximum 150 Power Factor; hard chrome finish. Still in production.

New: $2500	**Perf.:** $2425	**Exc.:** $2350

BAER MODEL 1911 TWENTY-FIFTH ANNIVERSARY

Custom-engraved limited collector edition .45 ACP semi-auto. Built on fully functional, fully equipped Baer Premier II. Hand engraved, both sides of slide

and frame. Les Baer signature. Inlaid with white gold. Ivory grips. Deep blue finish. Presentation box.

NIB: $6100	**Exc.:** $5200	**VGood:** $3950

BAER ULTIMATE RECO

Semi-auto with integral Picatinny rail, 5-inch barrel, .45 ACP. Blue or chrome. Comes with SureFire X-200 light. Fixed sights. 4-pound trigger. Two 8-round magazines. Cocobolo grips.

NIB: $2700	**Exc.:** $1850	**VGood:** $1450

BAFORD ARMS THUNDER DERRINGER

Derringer; .410 2-1/2-inch shotshell/44 Spl.; insert sleeves available for 22 Short, 22 LR, 25 ACP, 32 ACP, 32 H&R Mag., 30 Luger, 380 ACP, 38 Super, 38 Spl., 38 S&W, 9mm Para.; barrel lengths vary with caliber inserts; weighs 8-1/2 oz., sans inserts; no sights; uncheckered walnut stocks; blued steel barrel, frame; polished steel hammer, trigger; side-swinging barrel; positive lock, half-cock safety; roll block safety. Introduced 1986; dropped 1991.

Perf.: $130	**Exc.:** $110	**VGood:** $100
Extra barrel inserts		
Perf.: $75	**Exc.:** $65	**VGood:** $50

BAIKAL IZH-35M

Semi-automatic 22 target pistol with fully adjustable walnut target grip; 6-inch hammer forged barrel; adjustable trigger; integral grip safety; 5-shot; weighs 2.3 lbs.; cocking indicator; detachable scope mount. Imported from Russia.

Perf.: $325	**Exc.:** $305	**VGood:** $275

BAIKAL IJ-70

Semi-automatic; double action; 9x18mm Makarov; 8-shot magazine; 4-inch barrel; 6-1/4-inch overall length; weighs 25 oz.; checkered composition grips; blade front sight, fully-adjustable rear; all-steel construction; frame-mounted safety with decocker. Comes with two magazines, cleaning rod, universal tool. Imported from Russia by Century International Arms, K.B.I., Inc. Introduced 1994; dropped 1996. Add 20% for nicke4l finish.

New: $275	**Perf.:** $235	**Exc.:** $175

Bauer 25

Beeman P-08

Bayard Model 1908
Pocket Automatic

Benelli B76

Beeman SP Deluxe

Bayard Model 1923
(Large Model)

Beholla
Pocket Auto

BAIKAL IJ-70HC
Same specs as IJ-70 except 10-shot magazine.
Introduced 1994; dropped 1996.

New: $285   **Perf.:** $245   **Exc.:** $185

BAIKAL IJ-70HC, 380 ACP
Same specs as IJ-70HC except 380 ACP. Importation
ceased in 1996.

New: $275   **Perf.:** $235   **Exc.:** $175

BAUER 25
Semi-automatic; 25 ACP; 6-shot magazine; 2-1/8-
inch barrel; 4-inch overall length; stainless steel
construction; fixed sights; plastic pearl or checkered
walnut grips; manual, magazine safeties. Identical
to Baby Browning except for stainless construction.
Introduced 1973; dropped 1984.

Perf.: $240   **Exc.:** $185   **VGood:** $150

BAUER 25 ACP BICENTENNIAL MODEL
Identical to standard Bauer 25 except with engraving
and packaged with buckle in display case.

Perf.: $300   **Exc.:** $200   **VGood:** $150

BAUER RABBIT DERRINGER
Over/under derringer in 22 LR and 410 bore
shotshell; all metal construction. Introduced 1982;
dropped 1984.

Perf.: $300   **Exc.:** $250   **VGood:** $190

BAYARD MODEL 1908 POCKET AUTOMATIC
Semi-automatic; 25 ACP, 32 ACP, 380 ACP; 6-shot
magazine; 2-1/4-inch barrel; 4-7/8-inch overall
length; fixed sights, blued finish; hard rubber grips.
Introduced 1908; dropped 1923.

25-caliber		
Exc.: $385	**VGood:** $220	**Good:** $175
32-caliber		
Exc.: $350	**VGood:** $250	**Good:** $165
380-caliber		
Exc.: $350	**VGood:** $250	**Good:** $165

Note: Model marked with an Imperial Eagle
command 25 percent additional; factory engraved
specimens command 200 percent more.

BAYARD MODEL 1923 POCKET AUTOMATIC (LARGE MODEL)
Semi-automatic; 32 ACP, 380 ACP; 6-shot magazine;
3 -5/16-inch barrel; 4-5/16-inch overall length; fixed
sights; blued finish; checkered grips of hard rubber.
Introduced 1923; dropped 1940.

32 cal.		
Exc.: $375	**VGood:** $295	**Good:** $225
380 ACP Model		
Exc.: $750	**VGood:** $590	**Good:** $450

BAYARD MODEL 1923 POCKET AUTOMATIC (SMALL MODEL)
Semi-automatic; 25 ACP only; 2-1/2-inch barrel;
4-5/16-inch overall length; fixed sights, blued finish;
checkered grips of hard rubber. Scaled-down model
of large Model 1923. Introduced 1923; dropped 1930.

Exc.: $350   **VGood:** $295   **Good:** $225

BAYARD MODEL 1930 POCKET AUTOMATIC
Semi-automatic; 25 ACP; 6-shot; 2-1/8-inch barrel;
5-15/16-inch overall length; fixed sights; blued finish;
checkered hard rubber grips. Similar to small Model
1923 auto pistol with improvements in finish, internal
mechanism. Introduced 1930; dropped 1940.

Exc.: $350   **VGood:** $250   **Good:** $200

BEEMAN P-08
Semi-automatic; 22 LR; 8-shot magazine; 4-inch
barrel; 7 3/4-inch overal length; weighs 25 oz.;
checkered hardwood stocks; fixed sights; based on
original Luger design; Luger-type toggle action. Made
in Germany. Introduced 1989; importation dropped
1990.

Perf.: $325   **Exc.:** $295   **VGood:** $245

BEEMAN P-08 MINI
Same specs as P-08 except 380 ACP or .32 ACP;
5-shot magazine; 3-1/2-inch barrel; weighs 22-1/2
oz.; magazine and sear disconnect safeties. Made

in Germany. Introduced 1989; importation dropped
1990.

Exc.: $350   **VGood:** $250   **Good:** $200

BEEMAN SP DELUXE
Single shot; 22 LR; 8-inch, 10-inch, 11-3/16-inch,
15-inch barrel; European walnut stocks; adjustable
palm rest; blade front sight, adjustable notch rear;
detachable forend, barrel weight; standard version
has no forend or weight. Imported by Beeman.
Introduced 1984; dropped 1987.

Perf.: $600   **Exc.:** $550   **VGood:** $500

BEEMAN SP STANDARD
Single shot; 22 LR; sidelever action; 8-inch, 10-inch,
12-inch, or 15-inch barrel; adjustable sights; walnut
grips. Made in West Germany. Imported 1985-1986
only.

Perf.: $300   **Exc.:** $250   **VGood:** $220

BEEMAN SP/SPX
Single shot; 22 LR; made for silhouette shooting;
10-inch bull barrel; blued metal parts; burwood stock
and forearm; aperture sights; 3.9 lbs. Dropped 1994.

Perf.: $625   **Exc.:** $550   **VGood:** $475

BEEMAN MODEL SPX DELUXE
Similar to Model SPX, except has matte chrome
metal finish; hand stippled walnut grips; Anshutz rear
sight. Introduced 1993; dropped 1994.

Perf.: $800   **Exc.:** $725   **VGood:** $650

BEHOLLA POCKET AUTO
Semi-automatic; 32 ACP; 7-shot magazine; 3-inch
barrel; 5-1/2-inch overall length; fixed sights; grooved
hard rubber or wooden stocks; blued finish. German-
made. Manufactured 1915 to 1925.

Exc.: $225   **VGood:** $170   **Good:** $150

BENELLI B76
Semi-automatic; 9mm Para.; 8-shot magazine;
4-1/4-inch chrome-lined barrel; 8-1/16-inch overall
length; weighs 34 oz. (empty); walnut stocks with cut
checkering and high gloss finish; blade front sight
with white face, windage-adjustable; fixed barrel,
locked breech; stainless steel inertia firing pin and
loaded chamber indicator; blued finish with internal

Benelli B76

Benelli MP90S Match

Beretta Model 20

Beretta Model 21A Bobcat

Beretta Model 70

Beretta Model 70S

parts hard chrome plated; all steel construction. Introduced 1979; dropped 1990.

Perf.: $700   **Exc.:** $575   **VGood:** $400

BENELLI B-76S TARGET
Similar to B-76 except has 5-1/2-inch barrel; target grips; adjustable rear sight; 9mm Para. Importation dropped 1990.

Perf.: $725   **Exc.:** $600   **VGood:** $450

BENELLI MODEL B-77
Semi-automatic; selective double action; 32 ACP; all steel construction; 4-1/4-inch barrel; 8-shot magazine. Importation dropped 1995.

Perf.: $395   **Exc.:** $350   **VGood:** $295

BENELLI MODEL B-80
Semi-automatic; selective double action; 32 ACP; all steel construction; 4-1/4-inch barrel; 8-shot magazine; 34 oz. Importation dropped 1995.

Perf.: $395   **Exc.:** $350   **VGood:** $295

BENELLI MODEL B-80S TARGET
Similar to B-80 except has 5-1/2-inch barrel; target grips; adjustable rear sight. Importation dropped 1995.

Perf.: $500   **Exc.:** $450   **VGood:** $375

BENELLI MP90S MATCH
Semi-automatic; single action; 22 Short, 22 LR, 32 S&W wadcutter; 5-shot magazine; 4-3/8-inch barrel; 11-7/8-inch overall length; weighs 39 oz.; stippled walnut match-type grips with fully-adjustable palm shelf, anatomically shaped; match type, blade front sight, fully click-adjustable rear; removable trigger fully-adjustable for pull and position; special internal weight box on sub-frame below barrel; comes with loading tool, cleaning rod. Imported from Italy by European American Armory. Introduced 1993; still imported.

Perf.: $1050   **Exc.:** $900   **VGood:** $850
Add $105 to above prices for 32 S&W Wadcutter chambering.

BENELLI MP95E MATCH
Semi-automatic; single action; 22 LR, 32 S&W WC; 9-shot magazine; 4-3/8-inch barrel; 11-7/8-inch

overall length; weighs 39 oz.; checkered walnut match-type grips, anatomically shaped; blade front sight, fully click-adjustable match-type rear; removable, adjustable trigger; special internal weight box on sub-frame below barrel; cut for scope rails. Imported from Italy by European American Armory. Introduced 1993; still imported.

Blue finish		
New: $645	**Perf.:** $575	**Exc.:** $495
Chrome finish		
New: $700	**Perf.:** $625	**Exc.:** $550

Add $120 to above prices for 32 S&W Wadcutter chambering.

BERETTA MODEL 20
Semi-automatic; double action; 25 ACP; 8-shot magazine; 2-1/2-inch barrel; 4-1/2-inch overall length; weighs 11 oz.; fixed sights; plastic or walnut stocks. Made in Italy. Introduced 1984; dropped 1986.

Perf.: $275   **Exc.:** $200   **VGood:** $150

BERETTA MODEL 21A BOBCAT
Semi-automatic; double action; 22 LR, 25 ACP; 7-shot (22 LR), 8-shot (25 ACP); 2-1/2-inch barrel; 4-15/16-inch overall length; weighs 11-1/2 oz.; fixed sights; thumb safety; half-cock safety; hinged tip-up barrel; blued, nickel or matte finish; checkered walnut or plastic grips. Introduced 1985; still in production. Made in the U.S.

New: $300	**Exc.:** $190	**VGood:** $145
Nickel finish		
New: $310	**Exc.:** $215	**VGood:** $165
Matte finish		
New: $300	**Exc.:** $175	**VGood:** $140
Engraved		
New: $400	**Exc.:** $225	**VGood:** $200

BERETTA LADY BERETTA
Semi-automatic; double action; 22 LR; 7-shot; 2-1/2-inch barrel; 4-15/16-inch overall length; weighs 11-1/2 oz.; fixed sights; thumb safety; half-cock safety; hinged tip-up barrel; similar to Model 21A

except gold etching on top of frame and side of slide. Introduced 1990; dropped 1990.

Perf.: $295   **Exc.:** $215   **VGood:** $160

BERETTA MODEL 70
Semi-automatic; double action; 32 ACP; 8-shot magazine; 3-1/2-inch barrel; 6-5/16-inch overall length; 23-1/2 oz.; fixed sights; plastic grips; crossbolt safety; blue or chrome finish. Replaced Model 948; has hold-open device and push-button magazine release. Alloy frame 32 ACP marketed in U.S. as the New Puma. Introduced 1958; dropped 1968.

Perf.: $385   **Exc.:** $325   **VGood:** $275

Chrome finish		
Perf.: $395	**Exc.:** $335	**VGood:** $285

BERETTA MODEL 70S
Same specs as Beretta Model 70 except 380 ACP, 22 LR; weighs 18 oz. (22 LR), magazine safety; steel frame; fixed sights (380 ACP); adjustable rear (22 LR); checkered plastic wrap-around grips with thumbrest; blued. Steel frame 380 ACP marketed in U.S. as the Cougar. Introduced 1977; dropped 1985.

Perf.: $385   **Exc.:** $325   **VGood:** $275

BERETTA MODEL 70T
Same specs as Beretta Model 70 except 9-shot magazine; 32 ACP; 6-inch barrel; 8-1/2-inch overall length; adjustable rear sight, fixed front; slide stays open after last shot; checkered plastic wrap-around grips. Introduced 1969; dropped 1975.

Perf.: $385   **Exc.:** $325   **VGood:** $275

BERETTA MODEL 71
Semi-automatic; single action; 22 LR; 8-shot magazine; 6-inch barrel only; 8-3/4-inch overall length; adjustable rear sight; wrap-around checkered plastic grips; lever thumb safety. Imported 1987 only.

Perf.: $385   **Exc.:** $325   **VGood:** $275

BERETTA MODEL 71 JAGUAR
Semi-automatic; 22 LR; 8-shot magazine; 3-1/2-inch barrel; windage-adjustable rear sight, fixed front; checkered plastic grips; blued. Marketed in U.S. as Jaguar. Introduced 1956; dropped 1968.

Perf.: $385   **Exc.:** $325   **VGood:** $275

Beretta Model 76

Beretta Model 84
Cheetah

Beretta Model 85F

Beretta Model 89

Beretta Model 84F

Beretta Model 89 Gold
Standard Pistol

BERETTA MODEL 72 JAGUAR
Semi-automatic; 22 LR; 8-shot magazine; 3-1/2-inch, 6-inch interchangeable barrels; windage-adjustable rear sight, fixed front; checkered plastic grips; blued finish. Introduced 1956; dropped 1968.

Perf.: $325	**Exc.:** $250	**VGood:** $200

BERETTA MODEL 76
Semi-automatic; single action; 22 LR only; 10-shot magazine; 6-inch barrel; 9-1/2-inch overall length; adjustable rear sight, interchangeable blade front; non-glare, ribbed slide; heavy barrel; external hammer; checkered wrap-around plastic (76P) or wood (76W) grips; blued. Also known as New Sable. Introduced 1971; dropped 1985.

Perf.: $350	**Exc.:** $300	**VGood:** $275
With wood grips		
Perf.: $400	**Exc.:** $350	**VGood:** $325

BERETTA MODEL 81
Semi-automatic; double action; 32 ACP; 12-shot magazine; 3-13/16-inch barrel; 6-13/16-inch overall length; blued finish; fixed sights; plastic or wood stocks. Introduced 1976; dropped 1981.

Perf.: $375	**Exc.:** $250	**VGood:** $200
Nickel finish		
Perf.: $425	**Exc.:** $340	**VGood:** $290
With wood grips		
Perf.: $395	**Exc.:** $275	**VGood:** $225
Beretta Model 81BB		
Perf.: $300	**Exc.:** $275	**VGood:** $225

BERETTA MODEL 82
Semi-automatic; double action; 32 ACP; 9-shot straightline magazine; 3-13/16-inch barrel; 6-13/16-inch overall length; weighs 17 oz.; non-reversible magazine release; blued finish; fixed sights; wood grips. Introduced 1977; dropped 1984.

Perf.: $295	**Exc.:** $250	**VGood:** $225
Nickel finish		
Perf.: $355	**Exc.:** $325	**VGood:** $300

BERETTA MODEL 84 CHEETAH
Semi-automatic; double action; 380 ACP; 10-shot magazine; 3-7/8-inch barrel; 6-13/16-inch overall length; weighs 23 oz.; black plastic (84P) or wood (84W) grips; fixed front sight, drift-adjustable rear; blue finish; squared trigger guard; exposed hammer. Imported from Italy by Beretta U.S.A. Introduced 1977.

Perf.: $400	**Exc.:** $325	**VGood:** $275
Blue, wood grips		
Perf.: $375	**Exc.:** $350	**VGood:** $300
Nickel, wood grips		
Perf.: $475	**Exc.:** $400	**VGood:** $325

BERETTA MODEL 84F
Same specs as Model 84 except combat-style frame; grooved triggerguard; plastic grips; manual safety; decocking device; matte finish. Made in Italy. Introduced 1990; still in production.

Perf.: $395	**Exc.:** $330	**VGood:** $300

BERETTA MODEL 85 CHEETAH
Semi-automatic; double action; 380 ACP; 8-shot straightline magazine; 3-7/8-inch barrel; 6-13/16-inch overall length; weighs 23 oz.; black plastic (85P) or wood (85W) grips; fixed front sight, drift-adjustable rear; non-reversible magazine release; blue finish; squared triggerguard; exposed hammer. Imported from Italy by Beretta U.S.A. Introduced 1977; still imported.

Perf.: $450	**Exc.:** $350	**VGood:** $295
Blue, wood grips		
Perf.: $485	**Exc.:** $385	**VGood:** $330
Nickel, wood grips		
Perf.: $530	**Exc.:** $430	**VGood:** $375

BERETTA MODEL 85F
Same specs as Model 85 except combat-type frame; grooved triggerguard; plastic grips; matte black finish; manual safety; decocking device. Made in Italy. Introduced 1990; dropped 1990.

Perf.: $375	**Exc.:** $325	**VGood:** $275

BERETTA MODEL 86 CHEETAH
Semi-automatic; double action; 22 LR; 8-shot magazine; 4-7/16-inch barrel; 7-5/16-inch overall length; weighs 23-1/2 oz.; fixed sights; tip-up barrel; checkered walnut grips; matte finish; gold trigger. Importation began 1991.

Perf.: $450	**Exc.:** $375	**VGood:** $300

BERETTA MODEL 87 CHEETAH
Semi-automatic; double action; 22 LR; 7-shot magazine; 3-7/8-inch barrel; 6-13/16-inch overall length; weighs 21 oz.; black plastic grips; fixed front sight, drift-adjustable rear; blue finish; squared trigger guard; exposed hammer. Imported from Italy by Beretta U.S.A. Introduced 1977; dropped 1990.

Perf.: $450	**Exc.:** $375	**VGood:** $300

BERETTA MODEL 87 TARGET
Same specs as Model 87 except single action; 6-inch barrel with counterweight; wood grips. Made in Italy. Introduced 1977; importation began in 1986; dropped 1994; importation resumed 2000.

Perf.: $600	**Exc.:** $465	**VGood:** $380

BERETTA MODEL 89
Semi-automatic; single-action only; 22 LR; 8-shot magazine; 6-inch barrel; 9-1/2-inch overall length; weighs 41 oz.; interchangeable front sight, fully-adjustable rear; semi-anatomical walnut grips; fixed monoblock barrel machined from forged steel block; aluminum alloy frame; manual safety on either side. Made in Italy. Introduced 1977. Importation began 1986; still imported.

Perf.: $600	**Exc.:** $500	**VGood:** $400

BERETTA MODEL 89 GOLD STANDARD PISTOL
Caliber: 22 LR, 8-shot magazine. Barrel: 6. Weight: 41 oz. Length: 9-1/2-inch overall. Stocks: Target-type walnut with thumbrest. Sights: Interchangeable blade front, fully adjustable rear. Features: Single action target pistol. Matte black, Bruniton finish. Imported from Italy by Beretta U.S.A.

Perf.: $650	**Exc.:** $510	**VGood:** $410

Beretta Model 90

Beretta M9 Special Edition Pistol

Beretta Model 92FS

Beretta Model 92

Beretta Model 92F Compact

Beretta Model 92F Centurion

BERETTA MODEL 90
Semi-automatic; double action; 32 ACP; 8-shot magazine; 3-5/8-inch barrel; 6-3/4-inch overall length; fixed sights, matted rib on slide; chamber-loaded indicator; external hammer; stainless steel barrel; molded plastic wrap-around grips; blued. Introduced 1969; dropped 1982.

Perf.: $275 **Exc.:** $200 **VGood:** $175

BERETTA 90-TWO
Wrap-around polymer grip, standard or slim. Single/double-action semi-auto in 9mm (10+1, 15+1 or 17+1 capacity) or .40 S&W (10+1 or 12+1 capacity). Types D, F or G. Fixed sights. 4.9-inch barrel, 32.5 oz.

NIB: $685 **Exc.:** $575 **VGood:** $400

BERETTA MODEL 92
Semi-automatic, double action; 9mm Para.; 15-shot magazine; 5-inch barrel; 8-1/2-inch overall length; blued finish; fixed sights; plastic grips. Updated version of the Model 951. Introduced 1976; dropped 1981.

Perf.: $750 **Exc.:** $600 **VGood:** $450

BERETTA MODEL 92S (SECOND ISSUE)
Semi-automatic; double action; 9mm Para.; 15-shot magazine; 5-inch barrel; 8-1/2-inch overall length; fixed sights; plastic grips; blued finish. Variant of Model 92 with safety catch on side. Discontinued.

Perf.: $575 **Exc.:** $475 **VGood:** $400

BERETTA MODEL 92SB-P (THIRD ISSUE)
Automatic; double action; 9mm Para.; 16-shot magazine; 5-inch barrel; 8-1/2-inch overall length; weighs 34-1/2 oz.; blade front sight, windage-adjustable rear; black plastic or wood grips. Developed for U.S. Army pistol trials of 1979-1980. Introduced 1979; dropped 1985.

Perf.: $525 **Exc.:** $425 **VGood:** $395

Wood grips

Perf.: $550 **Exc.:** $450 **VGood:** $400

BERETTA MODEL 92SB-P COMPACT
Same specs as Model 92SB-P except 4-5/16-inch barrel, 14-shot magazine; plastic grips. Introduced 1977; dropped 1985.

Perf.: $500 **Exc.:** $450 **VGood:** $400

Wood grips

Perf.: $525 **Exc.:** $475 **VGood:** $425

BERETTA MODEL 92D
Semi-automatic; double-action only; 9mm Para.; 10-shot magazine; 5-inch barrel; 8-1/2-inch overall length; weighs 34 oz.; bobbed hammer; no external safety; plastic grips; three-dot sights. Also offered with Trijicon sights. From Beretta U.S.A. Introduced 1992; dropped 1998.

New: $475 **Perf.:** $400 **Exc.:** $350

BERETTA MODEL 92FS
Semi-automatic; double action; 9mm Para.; 15-shot magazine; 5-inch barrel; 8-1/2-inch overall length; matte black finish; squared triggerguard; grooved front backstraps; inertia firing pin; extractor acts as chamber loaded indicator; wood or plastic grips. Adopted 1985 as official U.S. military sidearm. Introduced 1984; still produced by Beretta USA.

Perf.: $595 **Exc.:** $500 **VGood:** $450
Add $25 to above prices for olive drab finish
Add $465 for 22 LR conversion kit
Add $395 for 9mm Competition Conversion kit

Stainless steel barrel and slide (92F)

Perf.: $635 **Exc.:** $550 **VGood:** $400

BERETTA M9 SPECIAL EDITION PISTOL
Copy of the U.S. M9 military pistol. Similar to the Model 92FS except has special M9 serial number range; one 15-round (pre-ban) magazine; dot-and-post sight system; special M9 military packaging; Army TM 9-1005-317-10 operator's manual; M9 Special Edition patch; certificate of authenticity; Bianchi M12 holster, M1025 magazine pouch, and M1015 web pistol belt. Introduced 1998; dropped 2000. From Beretta U.S.A.

Perf.: $850 **Exc.:** $700 **VGood:** $550

BERETTA MODEL 92F COMPACT
Same specs as Beretta Model 92FS except cut down frame; 4-3/8-inch barrel; 7-7/8-inch overall length; 13-shot magazine; weighs 3-1/2 oz.; Trijicon sights and wood grips optionally available. From Beretta U.S.A. Introduced 1989; no longer in production.

Perf.: $500 **Exc.:** $450 **VGood:** $400

Wood grips

Perf.: $525 **Exc.:** $475 **VGood:** $425

BERETTA MODEL 92F STAINLESS PISTOL
Same as the Model 92FS except has stainless steel barrel and slide, and frame of aluminum-zirconium alloy. Has three-dot sight system. Introduced 1992.

Perf.: $635 **Exc.:** $500 **VGood:** $400
Add $90 for specimens with Tritium or Trijicon night sight system

BERETTA MODEL 92FCM
Same specs as Model 92F Compact except thinner grip; straightline 8-shot magazine; weighs 31 oz.; 1-1/4-inch overall width; plastic grips. From Beretta U.S.A. Introduced 1989; no longer in production.

Perf.: $575 **Exc.:** $465 **VGood:** $415

BERETTA MODEL 92FS CENTURION
Same specs as Model 92FS except 4-3/8-inch barrel shorter slide; Trijicon or three-dot sights; plastic or wood grips; 9mm Para. only. From Beretta U.S.A. Introduced 1992.

With plastic grips, three-dot sights

New: $550 **Perf.:** $500 **Exc.:** $450

With wood grips

New: $575 **Perf.:** $525 **Exc.:** $475
Add $90 to above prices for Tritium sight system (available 1994-1998)

BERETTA MODEL 92FS STAINLESS
Same specs as Model 92FS except for stainless steel satin finish; groove in slide rail; larger hammer pin head; modified to meet special-use military specs. Introduced 1990.

Perf.: $620 **Exc.:** $500 **VGood:** $450

Beretta M9A1

Beretta Model 96D

Beretta Model 96 Brigadier

Beretta Model 949 Tipo Olimpionico

Beretta 950B Jetfire

Beretta Model 418

Beretta Model 950BS (2½" barrel)

BERETTA MODEL 92F-EL

Same specs as Model 92FS Stainless except gold trim on safety levers, magazine release, trigger and grip screws; gold inlaid Beretta logo top of barrel; P. Beretta signature inlaid in gold on slide; contoured walnut grips with Beretta logo engraved; high-polish blued finish on barrel, frame, slide. Introduced 1991; dropped 1994.

Perf.: $685 **Exc.:** $600 **VGood:** $500

BERETTA 92 STEEL-I

Steel-frame semi-auto in 9mm or .40 S&W. Single- or single/double-action. 15+1 capacity, 4.7-inch barrel, 42.3 oz. IDPA certified. Fixed, 3-dot sights.

NIB: $950 **Exc.:** $825 **VGood:** $675

BERETTA M9A1

Semi-auto, single/double-action in 9mm developed for U.S. Marine Corps. Capacity 10+1 or 15+1. Fixed sights.

NIB: $800 **Exc.:** $695 **VGood:** $525

BERETTA MODEL 96

Semi-automatic; double action; 40 S&W; 10-shot magazine; 5-inch barrel; 8-1/2-inch overall length; weighs 34 oz.; ambidextrous triple safety with passive firing pin catch; slide safety/decocking lever; trigger bar disconnect; plastic grips; blued finish. Introduced 1992. Add 40 percent for Steel Target version.

New: $595 **Perf.:** $500 **Exc.:** $430

BERETTA MODEL 96 BRIGADIER

Same specs as Model 96 except removable front sight; reconfigured high slide wall profile; 10-shot magazine; three-dot sights system; 4-15/16-inch barrel; matte black Bruniton finish. From Beretta U.S.A. Introduced 1995; still in production.

New: $645 **Perf.:** $550 **Exc.:** $450

BERETTA MODEL 96 CENTURION

Same specs as Model 96 except 4-3/8-inch barrel; shorter slide; Trijicon or three-dot sights; plastic or wood grips; 40 S&W only. From Beretta U.S.A. Introduced 1992.

New: $550 **Perf.:** $500 **Exc.:** $400

With three-dot sights, plastic grips
New: $650 **Perf.:** $600 **Exc.:** $500

BERETTA MODEL 96D

Same specs as Model 96 except double-action-only; three-dot sights. From Beretta U.S.A. Introduced 1992.

New: $600 **Perf.:** $550 **Exc.:** $450

BERETTA MODEL 318

Semi-automatic; 25 ACP; 8-shot magazine; 2-1/2-inch barrel; 4-1/2-inch overall length; weighs 14 oz.; blued finish, fixed sights; plastic grips. Sold in the U.S. as the Panther. Manufactured 1934 to 1946.

Exc.: $275 **VGood:** $225 **Good:** $175

BERETTA MODEL 418

Semi-automatic; 25 ACP; 8-shot magazine; 3-1/2-inch barrel; 5-3/4-inch overall length; fixed sights; plastic grips; blued finish; grip safety redesigned to match contour of backstrap. Introduced 1946; dropped 1958.

Exc.: $250 **VGood:** $175 **Good:** $150

BERETTA MODEL 420

Semi-automatic; 25 ACP; 8-shot magazine; 3-1/2-inch barrel; 5-inch overall length; fixed sights; plastic grips; chrome-plated, engraved version of the Model 418.

Exc.: $250 **VGood:** $200 **Good:** $150

BERETTA MODEL 421

Semi-automatic; 25 ACP; 8-shot magazine; 3-1/2-inch barrel; 5-inch overall length; fixed sights; plastic grips; gold-plated, elaborately engraved version of the Model 418.

Exc.: $500 **VGood:** $350 **Good:** $250

BERETTA MODEL 948

Semi-automatic; double action; 22 LR; 3-5/16-inch, 6-inch barrel; fixed sights; hammer; grip displays "BERETTA" across top instead of earlier "PB" monogram. Sold in U.S. as Featherweight or Plinker.

Exc.: $250 **VGood:** $225 **Good:** $195

BERETTA MODEL 949 TIPO OLIMPIONICO

Semi-automatic; 22 Short; 6-shot magazine; 8-3/4-inch barrel; 12-1/2-inch overall length; target sights; adjustable barrel weight; muzzle brake; hand-checkered walnut thumbrest grips; blued. Introduced 1949; dropped 1968.

Exc.: $575 **VGood:** $400 **Good:** $300

BERETTA MODEL 950B JETFIRE

Semi-automatic; single action; 22 Short (discontinued 1992); 25 ACP; 7-shot magazine; 2-3/8-inch barrel; 4-1/2-inch overall length; weighs 9-1/2 oz.; tip-up barrel; rear sight milled in slide, fixed front; black plastic or wood grips; blue or nickel finish. Introduced 1950; imported from Italy until 1968, made in U.S. from 1968; dropped 2002.

Exc.: $225 **VGood:** $185 **Good:** $165

BERETTA MODEL 950B MINX M2

Semi-automatic; 22 Short; 6-shot magazine; 2-3/8-inch barrel; 4-1/2-inch overall length; rear sight milled in slide, fixed front; black plastic grips; blued. Introduced 1950; importation dropped 1968.

Exc.: $145 **VGood:** $115 **Good:** $100

BERETTA MODEL 950CC MINX M4

Same specs as Model M2 except 3-3/4-inch barrel. Introduced 1956. Not imported since 1968.

Exc.: $145 **VGood:** $115 **Good:** $100

BERETTA MODEL 950BS

Semi-automatic; single action; 22 Short, 25 ACP; 8-shot magazine; 2-1/2-inch, 4-inch (22) barrel; 4-1/2-inch overall length; weighs 10 oz. (25 ACP); checkered plastic or walnut grips; fixed sights; thumb safety, half-cock safety; hinged barrel for single loading, cleaning; blued, nickel or matte finish. Made by Beretta USA. Introduced 1982; dropped 2002.

Perf.: $180 **Exc.:** $145 **VGood:** $125

Beretta Model 951 Brigadier

Beretta Model 1931

Beretta Model 950BS
(4″ barrel)

Beretta Model 1923

Beretta Model 3032 Tomcat

Beretta Model 8000 Cougar

Beretta Stampede Blued

BERETTA MODEL 951 BRIGADIER

Semi-automatic; 9mm Para.; 8-shot magazine; 4-1/2-inch barrel; 8-inch overall length; external hammer; crossbolt safety; slide stays open after last shot; fixed sights; molded grooved plastic grips; blued. Advertised originally as Brigadier model. Introduced 1951; no longer in production.

Exc.: $450   **VGood:** $325   **Good:** $275

BERETTA MODEL 1915

Semi-automatic; 32 ACP, 9mm Glisenti; 8-shot magazine; 6-inch overall length; 3-5/16-inch barrel; blued finish; fixed sights; grooved wooden grips. Smaller caliber manufactured 1915 to 1930; 9mm Glisenti, 1915 to 1918.

32 ACP		
Exc.: $325	**VGood:** $250	**Good:** $175
9mm Glisenti		
Exc.: $600	**VGood:** $450	**Good:** $300

BERETTA MODEL 1919

Semi-automatic; 25 ACP; 8-shot magazine; 3-1/2-inch barrel; 5-3/4-inch overall length; hammerless; grip safety on frame backstrap; fixed sights; wood (early models), pressed sheet steel or plastic grips; blued finish. Introduced in 1919, went through several modifications to be designated as Model 318; dropped 1939.

Exc.: $295   **VGood:** $195   **Good:** $150

BERETTA MODEL 1923

Semi-automatic; 9mm Glisenti; 8-shot magazine; 4-inch barrel; 6-1/2-inch overall length; 28 oz.; ring-type external hammer; blued finish; fixed sights; pressed steel or wood grips. Manufactured 1923 to 1936.

Exc.: $550   **VGood:** $375   **Good:** $275

BERETTA MODEL 1931

Semi-automatic; double-action; 32 ACP; 8-shot magazine; 6-inch overall length; weighs 22-1/2 oz.; fixed sights; walnut grips; blued finish. Italian Navy issue bears medallion with "R/

Anchor/M" emblem. Commercial issue has standard "PB" embossed black plastic grips.

Exc.: $650   **VGood:** $575   **Good:** $400

BERETTA MODEL 1934

Semi-automatic; 380 ACP; 7-shot magazine; 3-3/8-inch barrel; 5-7/8-inch overall length; weighs 28-1/8 oz.; fixed sights; plastic grips; thumb safety; blued or chrome finish. Official Italian service sidearm in WWII; military versions marked "RE," "RA" or "RM" for the army, air force and navy respectively. Police versions marked "PS" on rear of frame. Wartime version lacks quality of commercial model. Introduced 1934.

Exc.: $350   **VGood:** $300   **Good:** $200

BERETTA MODEL 1935

Semi-automatic; double action; 32 ACP; 7-shot magazine; 3-3/8-inch barrel; 5-7/8-inch overall length; fixed sights; plastic grips; thumb safety; blued or chrome finish. Italian service pistol during WWII; frame markings "RA" or "RM" on frame for the air force and navy respectively. Commercial version after 1945 known as Model 935.

Exc.: $300   **VGood:** $275   **Good:** $200

BERETTA MODEL 3032 TOMCAT

Semi-automatic; 32 ACP, 7-shot magazine. Barrel: 2.45-inch. Weight: 14.5 oz. Length: 5 inches overall. Stocks: Checkered black plastic. Sights: Blade front, drift-adjustable rear. Features: Double action with exposed hammer; tip-up barrel for direct loading/unloading; thumb safety; polished or matte blue finish. Made by Beretta U.S.A. Introduced 1996.

Perf.: $300   **Exc.:** $245   **VGood:** $165

BERETTA MODEL 8000 COUGAR

Semi-automatic; double action; 9mm Para.; 10-shot magazine; 3-1/2-inch barrel; 7-inch overall length; weighs 33-1/2 oz.; textured composition grips; blade front sight, drift-adjustable rear; slide-mounted safety; exposed hammer; matte black Bruniton finish. Imported from Italy by Beretta U.S.A. Introduced 1994. A Turkish-made version under the

Stoeger name was introduced c. 2008 and is worth approximately 35% less.

New: $615   **Perf.:** $555   **Exc.:** $420

BERETTA MODEL 8000/8040 MINI COUGAR

Similar to the Model 8000/8040 Cougar except has shorter grip frame and weighs 27.6 oz. Introduced 1998. Imported from Italy by Beretta U.S.A.

Perf.: $600   **Exc.:** $550   **VGood:** $400

BERETTA MODEL 8000D COUGAR

Same specs as Model 8000 except double-action-only trigger mechanism. Imported from Italy by Beretta U.S.A. Introduced 1994.

New: $550   **Perf.:** $500   **Exc.:** $400

BERETTA MODEL 8040 COUGAR

Semi-automatic; double action; 40 S&W; 10-shot magazine; 3-1/2-inch barrel; 7-inch overall length; weighs 33-1/2 oz.; textured composition grips; blade front sight, drift-adjustable rear; slide-mounted safety; exposed hammer; matte black Bruniton finish. Imported from Italy by Beretta U.S.A. Introduced 1994.

Exc.: $615   **Perf.:** $555   **Exc.:** $525

BERETTA MODEL 8040D COUGAR

Same specs as Model 8040 except double-action-only trigger mechanism. Imported from Italy by Beretta U.S.A. Introduced 1994.

Exc.: $615   **Perf.:** $555   **Exc.:** $525

BERETTA STAMPEDE

Single action revolver patterned after the Colt Single Action Army; 357 Mag; 44-40 (mfd. in 2003), 45 LC; transfer bar; half cock safety; 6-shot; 4-3/4-inch, 5-1/2-inch, 7-1/2-inch barrel; 37 oz. Made by Aldo Uberti in Italy, which is owned by Beretta.

Stampede Blue		
Exc.: $395	**Perf.:** $345	**VGood:** $300
Stampede Brushed Nickel		
Exc.: $415	**Perf.:** $365	**VGood:** $330
Stampede Stainless (Inox)		
Exc.: $510	**Perf.:** $460	**VGood:** $400

Bergmann-Bayard Model 1908

Bergmann Model 1903 "Mars"

Bergmann Vest Pocket

Bergmann Special

Bernardelli Model 68

Bernardelli Model 69

Bernardelli Model 80

Stampede Marshal		
Exc.: $415	**Perf.:** $365	**VGood:** $330
Stampede Deluxe		
Exc.: $510	**Perf.:** $460	**VGood:** $400

BERETTA STAMPEDE BISLEY
Single action 6-shot Bisley replica revolver in .45 Colt or .357 Magnum. Blued with 4-3/4-inch, 5-1/2-inch or 7-1/2-inch barrel.

NIB: $425 **Exc.:** $385 **VGood:** $350

BERETTA LARAMIE
Break-open single-action revolver reminiscent of S&W #3 chambered for.45 LC or .38 Special. Six-shot cylinder. Adjustable rear sight. 5-inch or 6-1/2-inch barrels.

NIB: $800 **Exc.:** $700 **VGood:** $595

BERGMANN MODEL 1903 "MARS"
Semi-automatic; 9mm Bergmann-Bayard; 6-, 10-shot magazine; 4-inch barrel; 10-inch overall length; checkered wood grips. Marked "Bergmann Mars Pat. Brev. S.G.D.G." on locking block top. About 1,000 made in Germany before rights were sold to Pieper in Belgium where, with a few minor changes, it was made as the Bergmann-Bayard.

Exc.: $5500 **VGood:** $4250 **Good:** $3000

BERGMANN SPECIAL
Semi-automatic; double action; 32 ACP; 8-shot magazine; 3-7/16-inch barrel; 6-3/16-inch overall length; checkered plastic wrap-around grips. Rare double-action competitor to Walther's Model PP, actually made by Menz but sold under Bergmann's name.

Exc.: $1200 **VGood:** $850 **Good:** $500

BERGMANN VEST POCKET MODELS
Semi-automatic; 25 ACP; 6-, 9-shot magazine; 2-1/8-inch barrel; 4-3/4-inch overall length; checkered hard rubber or wood (rare) grips. Both conventional and one-hand-cocked ("Einhand") models later marketed under the Lignose name (see Lignose).

Conventional		
Exc.: $300	**VGood:** $200	**Good:** $125
Einhand		
Exc.: $500	**VGood:** $400	**Good:** $250
32 or 380 Einhand		

Cataloged but apparently never made.

BERGMANN-BAYARD MODEL 1908
Semi-automatic; 9mm Bergmann-Bayard; 6-shot magazine; 4-inch barrel; 10-inch overall length; checkered wood or hard rubber (rare) grips. Marked "ANCIENS ESTABLISSEMENTS PIEPER" on side. Made under contract for the Spanish and Danish armies as well as commercial sale.

Exc.: $2300 **VGood:** $1900 **Good:** $1500

Spanish contract (tiny circle with three-line proofmark)		
Exc.: $1500	**VGood:** $1250	**Good:** $750
Shoulder stock slot in backstrap		
Exc.: $2400	**VGood:** $1800	**Good:** $1450

BERGMANN-BAYARD MODEL 1910/21 TOJHUS
Semi-automatic; 9mm Bergmann-Bayard; 6-shot magazine; 4-inch barrel; 10-inch overall length. Made under contract for Danish army but reworked post-WWI models with oversize wood or plastic grips; screw-retained instead of latched sideplate; stamped "1910/21" on side. After WWI when Pieper could no longer supply pistols to Denmark, the Danes produced about 2200 Model 1910/21 pistols in their own arsenals.

Exc.: $2150 **VGood:** $1800 **Good:** $1450

BERNARDELLI MODEL 60
Semi-automatic; 22 LR, 32 ACP, 380 ACP; 10-shot (22 LR), 9-shot (32 ACP), 7-shot (380 ACP); 3-1/2-inch barrel; 6-1/2-inch overall length; weighs 26-1/2 oz.; ramp front sight, adjustable white-outlined rear; checkered plastic grips, thumbrest; hammer-block slide safety; loaded chamber indicator; dual recoil buffer springs; serrated trigger, inertia-type firing pin. Made in Italy. Introduced 1978; no longer imported.

Perf.: $250 **Exc.:** $195 **VGood:** $180

BERNARDELLI MODEL 68
Semi-automatic; 22 Short, 22 LR; 6-shot; 2-inch barrel; 4-1/8-inch overall length; weighs 8-1/2 oz.; plastic grips; blued finish. A replacement for the Vest Pocket Model with rounded slide, loaded chamber indicator, optional extended magazine. Discontinued 1970.

Perf.: $195 **Exc.:** $150 **VGood:** $125

BERNARDELLI MODEL 69 TARGET
Semi-automatic; 22 LR; 10-shot magazine; 5-15/16-inch barrel; 9-inch overall length; weighs 38 oz.; interchangeable target sights; wrap-around hand-checkered walnut stocks; thumbrest; meets UIT requirements; manual thumb safety, magazine safety; grooved trigger. Made in Italy. Introduced 1987.

Perf.: $575 **Exc.:** $475 **VGood:** $400

BERNARDELLI MODEL 80
Semi-automatic; 22 LR, 32 ACP, 380 ACP; 10-shot (22 LR), 8-shot (32 ACP, 380 ACP); 3-1/2-inch barrel; 6-1/2-inch overall length; adjustable rear sight, white dot front; plastic thumbrest stocks; blued finish;. Introduced 1968 as modification of Model 60 to meet U.S. import requirements; dropped 1988.

Perf.: $185 **Exc.:** $160 **VGood:** $150

BERNARDELLI MODEL 90
Semi-automatic; 22 LR, 32 ACP; 10-shot (22 LR), 8-shot (32 ACP); 6-inch barrel; 9-inch overall length; adjustable rear sight, white dot front; plastic thumbrest stocks; blued finish. Introduced 1968; dropped 1988.

Perf.: $210 **Exc.:** $185 **VGood:** $170

BERNARDELLI MODEL 100 TARGET
Semi-automatic; 22 LR; 10-shot magazine; 6-inch barrel; 9-inch overall length; adjustable rear sight, interchangeable front; checkered walnut thumbrest stocks; blued finish. Introduced in 1969 as Model 68; dropped 1983.

Perf.: $395 **Exc.:** $325 **VGood:** $295

Bernardelli Model AMR

Bernardelli Model PO10

Bernardelli Model Baby

Bernardelli Model PO18

Bernardelli Model USA

Bernardelli Vest Pocket Model

Bersa Model 23

BERNARDELLI MODEL AMR

Semi-automatic; single action; 22 LR, 32, 380 ACP; 6-inch barrel; target sights. Similar to the Model USA. Introduced 1989; dropped 1991. Was imported by Magnum Research.

Perf.: $395   **Exc.:** $325   **VGood:** $275

BERNARDELLI MODEL BABY

Semi-automatic; 22 Short; 22 LR; 2-1/8-inch barrel; fixed sights; plastic grips; blued finish. This was the first of Bernardelli's 22 pistols and was largely the Vest Pocket Model altered to handle rimfire cartridges. Introduced 1949; discontinued 1968.

Perf.: $295   **Exc.:** $225   **VGood:** $175

BERNARDELLI MODEL PO10 TARGET

Semi-automatic; single action; 22 LR; 5- or 10-shot magazine; 6-inch barrel; weighs 40-1/2 oz.; walnut thumbrest stocks; fully-adjustable target-type sights; external hammer with safety notch; pivoted adjustable trigger; matte black finish. Made in Italy. Introduced 1989; importation dropped 1990.

Perf.: $475   **Exc.:** $405   **VGood:** $355

BERNARDELLI MODEL PO18

Semi-automatic; double action; 9mm Para; 16-shot magazine; 4-7/8-inch barrel; 6-3/16-inch overall length; weighs 36-1/3 oz.; low-profile combat sights; checkered, contoured plastic or optional walnut stocks; manual thumb safety, half-cock, magazine safeties; ambidextrous magazine release; auto-locking firing pin block safety. Made in Italy. Introduced 1987; was imported by Armsport and by Magnum Research, Inc.; no longer imported.

Perf.: $485   **Exc.:** $400   **VGood:** $350

Walnut grips

Perf.: $525   **Exc.:** $450   **VGood:** $375
Add $60 to above prices for chrome finish

BERNARDELLI MODEL PO18 COMPACT

Same specs as standard PO18 except 4-1/8-inch barrel; 14-shot magazine. Introduced 1987; was imported by Armsport and by Magnum Research, Inc.; no longer imported.

Perf.: $545   **Exc.:** $450   **VGood:** $400

Walnut stocks

Perf.: $550   **Exc.:** $500   **VGood:** $450
Add $55 to above prices for chrome finish

BERNARDELLI MODEL USA

Semi-automatic; 22 LR, 380 ACP; 10-shot (22 LR), 7-shot (380 ACP) magazine; 3-1/2-inch barrel, 6-1/2-inch overall length; weighs 26-1/2 oz.; ramp front sight; fully-adjustable white-outline rear; checkered plastic stocks, thumbrest; serrated trigger; inertia-type firing pin; hammer-block safety; loaded chamber indicator. Made in Italy. Introduced 1989; was imported by Armsport and by Magnum Research, Inc.; no longer imported.

Perf.: $380   **Exc.:** $300   **VGood:** $275

BERNARDELLI P. ONE

Semi-automatic; double action; 9mm Para., 40 S&W; 16-shot (9mm), 10-shot (40 S&W) magazine; 4-7/8-inch barrel; 8-3/8-inch overall length; weighs 34 oz.; checkered black plastic grips; blade front sight, fully adjustable rear; three-dot system; forged steel frame and slide; full-length slide rails; reversible magazine release; thumb safety/decocker; squared triggerguard; blue/black finish. Imported from Italy by Armsport. Introduced 1994; no longer imported.

Perf.: $580   **Exc.:** $495   **VGood:** $400

Chrome finish

Perf.: $575   **Exc.:** $500   **VGood:** $450
Add $40 to above prices for wood grips

BERNARDELLI P. ONE PRACTICAL VB PISTOL

Same specs as P. One except 9x21mm; two- or four-port compensator; straight trigger; micro-adjustable rear sight. Imported from Italy by Armsport. Introduced 1994; dropped 1997.

New: 900   **Perf.:** $850   **Exc.:** $750
Add $60 to above price for 4-port compensator.
Add $60 to above price for chrome finish

BERNARDELLI STANDARD

Semi-automatic; 22 LR; 10-shot magazine; 6-inch, 8-inch, 10-inch barrel; 13-inch overall length (10-inch barrel); target sights; adjustable sight ramp; walnut target grips; blued. Simply the Pocket Model adapted for 22 LR cartridge. Introduced 1949; no longer imported. Smallest 25 Auto ever mfd.

Perf.: $225   **Exc.:** $200   **VGood:** $175

BERNARDELLI VEST POCKET MODEL

Semi-automatic; 25 ACP; 5-shot; 8-shot extension magazine also available; 2-1/8-inch barrel; 4-1/8-inch overall length; no sights, but sighting groove milled in slide; plastic grips; blued finish. Introduced 1948; U.S. importation dropped 1968.

Exc.: $250   **VGood:** $195   **Good:** $165

BERSA MODEL 23

Semi-automatic; double action; 22 LR; 10-shot magazine; 3-1/2-inch barrel; 6-1/2-inch overall length; weighs 24-1/2 oz.; walnut grips with stippled panels; blade front sight, notch windage-adjustable rear; three-dot system; firing pin, magazine safeties; blue or nickel finish. Made in Argentina; distributed by Eagle Imports, Inc. Introduced 1989; dropped 1994.

Blue finish

Perf.: $230   **Exc.:** $195   **VGood:** $155

Nickel finish

Perf.: $250   **Exc.:** $215   **VGood:** $175

BERSA MODEL 83

Semi-automatic; double action; 380 ACP; 7-shot magazine; 3-1/2-inch barrel; 6-1/2-inch overall length; weighs 25-3/4 oz.; stippled walnut grips; blade front sight, notch windage-adjustable rear; three-dot system; firing pin, magazine safety systems; blue or nickel finish. Imported from Argentina; distributed by Eagle Imports, Inc. Introduced 1989; dropped 1994.

Blue finish

Perf.: $235   **Exc.:** $180   **VGood:** $150

Nickel finish

Perf.: $270   **Exc.:** $235   **VGood:** $185

Bersa Model 83

Bersa Model 95 Series

Bersa Model 223

Bersa Model 225

Bersa Model 383

Bersa Thunder 380

BERSA MODEL 85

Semi-automatic; double action; 380 ACP; 13-shot magazine; 3-1/2-inch barrel; 6-1/2-inch overall length; weighs 25-3/4 oz.; stippled walnut grips; blade front sight, notch windage-adjustable rear; three-dot system; firing pin, magazine safety systems; blue or nickel finish. Imported from Argentina; distributed by Eagle Imports, Inc. Introduced 1989; dropped 1994.

Blue finish		
Perf.: $285	**Exc.:** $245	**VGood:** $220
Nickel finish		
Perf.: $340	**Exc.:** $295	**VGood:** $270

BERSA MODEL 86

Semi-automatic; double action; 380 ACP; 13-shot magazine; 3-1/2-inch barrel; 6-1/2-inch overall length; weighs 22 oz.; wrap-around textured rubber grips; blade front sight, windage-adjustable rear; three-dot system; firing pin, magazine safeties; combat-style triggerguard; matte blue or satin nickel finish. Imported from Argentina; distributed by Eagle Imports, Inc. Introduced 1992; dropped 1994.

Blue finish		
Perf.: $315	**Exc.:** $265	**VGood:** $225
Nickel finish		
Perf.: $345	**Exc.:** $295	**VGood:** $255

BERSA MODEL 95 SERIES

Semi-automatic; double action; 380 ACP; 7-shot magazine; 3-1/2-inch barrel; 6-1/2-inch overall length; weighs 22 oz.; blade front sight, windage-adjustable rear; three-dot system; firing pin and magazine safeties; combat-style triggerguard; wrap-around textured rubber grips; matte blue or satin nickel. Imported from Argentina; distributed by Eagle Imports, Inc. Introduced 1992.

Matte blue finish		
New: $225	**Perf.:** $185	**Exc.:** $150
Satin nickel finish		
New: $250	**Perf.:** $240	**Exc.:** $175

BERSA MODEL 223

Semi-automatic; double action; 22 LR; 11-shot magazine; 3-1/2-inch barrel; weighs 24-1/2 oz; blade front sight, square-notch windage-adjustable rear; checkered target-type nylon stocks; thumbrest; blowback action; squared-off triggerguard; magazine safety; blued finish. Made in Argentina. Introduced 1984; dropped 1987.

Perf.: $200	**Exc.:** $175	**VGood:** $150

BERSA MODEL 224

Semi-automatic; single action; 22 LR; 11-shot magazine; 4-inch barrel; weighs 26 oz; blade front sight, square-notch windage-adjustable rear; checkered target-type nylon stocks; thumbrest; blowback action; combat-type triggerguard; magazine safety; blued finish. Made in Argentina. Introduced 1984; dropped 1987.

Perf.: $200	**Exc.:** $175	**VGood:** $150

BERSA MODEL 225

Semi-automatic; single action; 22 LR; 10-shot magazine; 5-inch barrel; weighs 26 oz.; blade front sight, square-notch windage-adjustable rear; checkered target-type nylon stocks; thumbrest; blowback action; combat-type triggerguard; magazine safety; blued finish. Made in Argentina. Introduced 1984; dropped 1987.

Perf.: $175	**Exc.:** $150	**VGood:** $135

BERSA MODEL 226

Semi-automatic; single action; 22 LR; 10-shot magazine; 6-inch barrel; weighs 26 oz; blade front sight, square-notch windage-adjustable rear; checkered target-type nylon stocks; thumbrest; blowback action; combat-type triggerguard; magazine safety; blued finish. Made in Argentina. Introduced 1984; dropped 1987.

Perf.: $200	**Exc.:** $170	**VGood:** $150

BERSA MODEL 383

Semi-automatic; single action; 380 ACP; 9-shot magazine; 3-1/2-inch barrel; weighs 25 oz.; square-notch windage-adjustable rear sight, blade front; target-type black nylon stocks; blowback action; combat-type trigger guard; magazine safety; blued finish. Made in Argentina. Introduced 1984; dropped 1987.

Perf.: $200	**Exc.:** $175	**VGood:** $150

BERSA MODEL 383DA

Same specs as Model 383 except double action.

Perf.: $150	**Exc.:** $135	**VGood:** $125

BERSA THUNDER 9

Semi-automatic; double action; 9mm; barrel length 3.6"; alloy frame; weight 23 oz; 6.53" overall length; polymer grips; capacity 10+1; fixed sights. Imported from Argentina. Still in production as Bersa Mini Thunder Nine.

New: $300	**Perf.:** $265	**Exc.:** $250

BERSA THUNDER 9 ULTRA COMPACT

Available blued or stainless with 10- or 13-round capacity. Double-action chambered for 9mm. 3.5-inch barrel, 25 oz., fixed sights and polymer grips.

New: $300	**Perf.:** $265	**Exc.:** $250

BERSA THUNDER 9/40 HIGH CAPACITY SERIES

Double-action semi-autos available chambered for 9mm (17-rd.) or .40 S&W (13-rd.) and in matte blued or satin nickel-plate. Fixed sights and polymer grips. LOA 7 1/2-inch, 4 1/4-inch barrel, 26 oz.

New: $300	**Perf.:** $265	**Exc.:** $250

BERSA THUNDER 22

Semi-automatic; double action; 22 LR; 10+1 capacity; 3-1/2" barrel; alloy frame; polymer grips; 6-1/2" overall length. Introduced 1995; dropped 1996.

New: $230	**Perf.:** $200	**Exc.:** $175
Nickel finish		
New: $250	**Perf.:** $225	**Exc.:** $200

BERSA THUNDER 380

Semi-automatic; double action; 380 ACP; 7-shot magazine; 3-1/2-inch barrel; 6-1/2-inch overall length; weighs 25-3/4 oz.; black rubber grips; blade front sight, notch windage-adjustable rear; three-dot system; firing pin and magazine safeties; blue, nickel or duo-tone finish. Imported from Argentina; distributed by Eagle Imports, Inc. Introduced 1995; dropped 1998.

New: $235	**Perf.:** $200	**Exc.:** $175

BF Single Shot

Bersa Thunder 9

Bond Arms Snake Slayer IV

Bren Ten

BRNO Drulov 75 Target (Right-handed)

Bond Arms Texas Defender

Bren Ten Special Forces Model

Nickel finish

New: $255	**Perf.:** $225	**Exc.:** $200

Duo-tone finish

New: $255	**Perf.:** $220	**Exc.:** $200

BERSA THUNDER 380 PLUS

Same specs as Thunder 380 except 10-shot magazine. Imported from Argentina; distributed by Eagle Imports, Inc. Introduced 1995; dropped 1998.

New: $265	**Perf.:** $210	**Exc.:** $175

Nickel finish

New: $300	**Perf.:** $250	**Exc.:** $225

Duo-tone finish

New: $275	**Perf.:** $225	**Exc.:** $200

BF SINGLE SHOT (E. A. BROWN)

Single shot; 22 LR, 357 Mag., 44 Mag., 7-30 Waters, 30-30 Win., 375 Win., 45-70; custom chamberings from 17 Rem. through 45-cal.; 10-inch, 10-3/4-inch, 12-inch, 15+-inch barrel lengths; weighs about 52 oz.; custom Herrett finger-groove grip, forend; undercut Patridge front sight, 1/2-MOA match-quality fully-adjustable RPM Iron Sight rear; barrel or receiver mounting; drilled and tapped for scope mounting; rigid barrel/receiver; falling block action with short lock time; automatic ejection; air-gauged match barrels by Wilson or Douglas; matte black oxide finish standard, electroless nickel optional. Guns with RPM sights worth slightly more. Made in U.S. by E.A. Brown Mfg. Introduced 1988;.

New: $700	**Exc.:** $600	**VGood:** $450

BF SINGLE SHOT ULTIMATE SILHOUETTE

Same specs as standard model except 10-3/4-inch heavy barrel; special forend; RPM rear sight; hooded front; gold-plated trigger. Made in U.S. by E.A. Brown Mfg. Introduced 1988; still in production.

New: $750	**Exc.:** $650	**VGood:** $500

BOND ARMS TEXAS DEFENDER

Over-Under; 9mm Para, 38 Spec./357 Mag., 44 Spec./44 Mag., 45 Colt/410 shotshell. Barrel: 3-1/2-inch. Weight: 21 oz. Length: 5-inch overall. Stocks:

Laminated black ash or rosewood. Sights: Blade front, fixed rear. Features: Interchangeable barrels; retracting firing pins; rebounding firing pins; cross-bolt safety; removable trigger guard; automatic extractor for rimmed calibers. Stainless steel construction with blasted/polished and ground combination finish. Introduced 1997. Made in U.S. by Bond Arms, Inc.

New: $400	**Perf.:** $345	**Exc.:** $260

BOND ARMS COWBOY DEFENDER

Similar to Texas Defender except designed for Cowboy Action Shooting without trigger guard. Introduced 2000.

New: $400	**Perf.:** $345	**Exc.:** $260

Add $20 to above prices for left-hand model

BOND ARMS SNAKE SLAYER IV

Modern variation of the Remington over/under derringer. Interchangeable 4.5-inch barrel assemblies, rosewood grip panels, stainless finish, fixed sights. Chambered for .410-bore shotshell/.45 LC, 9mm, 10mm, .40 S&W, .45 ACP.

NIB: $435	**Exc.:** $395	**VGood:** $295

BREN TEN

Semi-automatic; 10mm Auto; 11-shot magazine; 5-inch barrel; 8-3/4-inch overall length; textured black nylon stocks; adjustable, replaceable combat sights; double- or single-action; stainless steel frame; blued slide; reversible thumb safety, firing pin block. Made by Dornaus & Dixon. Introduced 1983; dropped 1986. Deduct 25 percent if missing magazine or with non-factory magzine.

Perf.: $1675	**Exc.:** $1200	**VGood:** $1000

Military/Police black matte finish model

Perf.: $1600	**Exc.:** $1200	**VGood:** $1000

Dual presentation 10mm and 45 ACP

Perf.: $3900	**Exc.:** $3000	**VGood:** $2200

BREN TEN POCKET MODEL

Same specs as Bren Ten except 4-inch barrel; 7-3/8-inch overall length; weighs 28 oz.; 9-shot magazine; chrome slide.

Perf.: $1475	**Exc.:** $1100	**VGood:** $900

BREN TEN SPECIAL FORCES MODEL

Same specs as Pocket Model except standard grip frame; 11-shot magazine; weighs 33 oz.; black or natural light finish. Introduced 1984; dropped 1986.

Perf.: $2400	**Exc.:** $1800	**VGood:** $1400

Light finish

Perf.: $2400	**Exc.:** $1800	**VGood:** $1400

BRNO CZ 75

Semi-automatic; double action; 9mm Para., 40 S&W; 15-shot magazine; 4-11/16-inch barrel; 8-inch overall length; weighs 35 oz.; windage-adjustable rear sight, blade front; checkered wood stocks; blued finish. Made in Czechoslovokia. Introduced 1986; no longer imported.

Perf.: $420	**Exc.:** $350	**VGood:** $300

BRNO CZ 83

Semi-automatic; double action; 32 ACP, 380 ACP; 15-shot magazine (32), 13-shot (380); 3-11/16-inch barrel; 6-11/16-inch overall length; weighs 26-1/2 oz.; windage-adjustable rear sight, blade front; checkered black plastic stocks; ambidextrous magazine release, safety; matte blue or polished. Made in Czechoslovakia. Introduced 1987; no longer imported.

Perf.: $335	**Exc.:** $275	**VGood:** $225

BRNO CZ 85

Semi-automatic; double action; 9mm Para., 40 S&W; 15-shot; 4-11/16-inch barrel; 8-inch overall length; weighs 35 oz.; ambidextrous slide release; safety lever; contoured composition stocks; matte finish on top of slide. Made in Czechoslovakia. Introduced 1986; formerly imported by Action Arms Ltd.

Perf.: $435	**Exc.:** $375	**VGood:** $325

BRNO DRULOV 75 TARGET

Bolt-action; single shot; 22 LR; 10-inch barrel; 14-3/4-inch overall length; weighs 44 oz.; interchangeable blade front sight, micro-click fully adjustable rear; European walnut grips; all-steel construction; adjustable set trigger; blued finish. Made in Czechoslovakia. Introduced 1991; importation dropped 1992.

Perf.: $250	**Exc.:** $200	**VGood:** $175

Brolin Legend
L45C Compact

Brolin L45T Compact

Bronco Model 1918

Brown Executive Elite

Brown Executive Carry

BRNO ZBP 99

Semi-automatic; 9mm. Para., 40 S&W, 10-shot magazine. Barrel: 4-inch. Weight: 27.5 oz. Length: 7.2-inch overall. Stocks: Black composition. Sights: Blade front, rear adjustable for elevation; three-dot system. Features: Double action mechanism; polymer frame; chamber loaded indicator. Announced 1998. Was to be imported from The Czech Republic by Euro-Imports.

BROLIN LEGEND L45 STANDARD

Semi-automatic; 45 ACP, 7-shot magazine. Barrel: 5-inch. Weight: 35.9 oz. Length: 8-1/2 inches overall. Stocks: Checkered walnut. Sights: Millett High Visibility front, white outline fixed rear. Features: Throated match barrel; polished feed ramp; lowered and flared ejection port; beveled magazine well; flat top slide; flat mainspring housing; lightened aluminum match trigger; slotted Commander hammer; matte blue finish. Introduced 1996; dropped 1998.

New: $425   **Perf.:** $365   **Exc.:** $325

BROLIN LEGEND L45C COMPACT

Similar to the L45 Standard pistol except has 4-inch barrel with conical lock up; overall length 7-1/2 inches; weighs 32 oz. Matte blue finish. Introduced 1996; dropped 1998.

New: $440   **Perf.:** $380   **Exc.:** $330

BROLIN L45T COMPACT

Same as the L45 Legend except uses compact slide on the standard-size frame. Has 4-inch barrel, weighs 33.9 oz., and is 7-1/2 inches overall. Introduced 1996; dropped 1998.

New: $440   **Perf.:** $380   **Exc.:** $330

BROLIN TAC SERIES SERVICE MODEL

Semi-automatic; double action; 45 ACP, 8-shot magazine. Barrel: 5-inch. Weight: 23 oz. Length: 8-inch overall. Stocks: Checkered black plastic. Sights: Blade front, drift adjustable rear. Features: Skeletonized hammer; low-profile three-dot sight

system. Introduced 1998; dropped 1998. By Brolin Industries.

New: $360   **Perf.:** $315   **Exc.:** $285

BROLIN TAC SERIES FULL SIZE

Similar to the Service Model except available in 9mm Para. 40 S&W (10- shot), and 45 ACP (8-shot). Checkered walnut or plastic grips, checkered full-length slide rib. Introduced 1998; dropped 1998. By Brolin Industries.

New: $360   **Perf.:** $315   **Exc.:** $285

Add $90 to above prices for specimens with Tritium sights

BROLIN TAC SERIES COMPACT DA

Similar to the Service Model except has 3-1/2-inch barrel, 6-1/2-inch overall length, and weighs 19 oz. Available in 9mm Para. or 40 S&W only. Introduced 1998; dropped 1998. By Brolin Industries.

New: $360   **Perf.:** $315   **Exc.:** $285

BROLIN TAC SERIES BANTAM DA

Similar to the Compact pistol except has shorter grip frame for 4-inch overall height. Has 3-1/2-inch barrel, 6-1/4-inch overall length, and weighs 17 oz. Chambered for the 9mm Para. and 40 S&W; 6-shot magazine; concealed hammer. Introduced 1998; dropped 1998. By Brolin Industries.

New: $375   **Perf.:** $325   **Exc.:** $275

BROLIN TAC SERIES MODEL TAC-11

Semi-automatic; 45 ACP, 8-shot magazine. Barrel: 5-inch; conical match design. Weight: 35.1 oz. Length: 8.5 inches overall. Stocks: Black rubber contour. Sights: Ramp front, Novak Low Profile Combat Sight or Novak tritium. Features: Throated Conical barrel; polished feed ramp; lowered and flared ejection port; beveled magazine well; flat-top slide; flat mainspring housing; front strap high relief cut; lightened aluminum match trigger; slotted commander hammer; custom beavertail grip safety; Brolin "Iron Claw" extractor. Introduced 1997; dropped 1998. Made in the U.S. by Brolin Industries.

New: $595   **Perf.:** $465   **Exc.:** $425

BRONCO MODEL 1918

Semi-automatic; 32 ACP; 6-shot magazine; 2-1/2-inch barrel; 5-inch overall length; blued finish; fixed sights; hard rubber stocks. Manufactured in Spain 1918 to 1925.

Exc.: $175   **VGood:** $125   **Good:** $100

BRONCO VEST POCKET AUTOMATIC

Semi-automatic; 6.35; small frame. Discontinued.

Exc.: $160   **VGood:** $125   **Good:** $110

BROWN CLASSIC

Single-shot; 17 Ackley Hornet through 45-70 Govt. Barrel: 15-inch air gauged match grade. Weight: About 3 lbs., 7 oz. Stocks: Walnut; thumbrest target style. Sights: None furnished; drilled and tapped for scope mounting. Features: Falling block action gives rigid barrel-receiver mating; hand-fitted and headspaced. Introduced 1998. Made in U.S. by E.A. Brown Mfg.

New: $525   **Perf.:** $450   **Exc.:** $300

BROWN EXECUTIVE TARGET

1911 Executive Elite modified for target/range with adjustable BoMar rear sight, ambidextrous safety. 38 oz. 5-inch barrel chambered for .45 ACP. 7-round magazine.

NIB: $2200   **Exc.:** $1800   **VGood:** $1350

BROWN EXECUTIVE ELITE

Government model 5-inch barrel, 38 oz., chambered for .45 ACP. 7-round magazine. Fixed sights. Blue/blue, stainless/blue or all-stainless.

NIB: $2050   **Exc.:** $1650   **VGood:** $1225

BROWN EXECUTIVE CARRY

A 4.25-inch commander model .45 ACP with Ed Brown Bobtail. 38 oz. 7-round magazine, fixed sights. Blue/blue, stainless/blue or all-stainless.

NIB: $2200   **Exc.:** $1800   **VGood:** $1350

Brown Special Forces

Browning BDM

Browning Buck Mark Target 5.5

Browning 380 Standard

Browning Buck Mark Bullseye

Browning BDA 380

Browning Buck Mark Micro

Browning Buck Mark Unlimited Silhouette

BROWN SPECIAL FORCES
Blue/blue 1911 semi-auto with 5-inch barrel and fixed 3-dot night sights. Chambered for .45 ACP. 38 oz.; 7-round magazine. Cocobolo grips.

NIB: $1900   **Exc.:** $1575   **VGood:** $1150

BROWNING 25 BABY
Semi-automatic; 25 ACP; 6-shot magazine; 2-1/8-inch barrel; 4-inch overall length; fixed sights, hard rubber grips; blued finish. Introduced ca. 1936; dropped 1968, not currently importable.

Browning Arms Co. marked		
Perf.: $475	**Exc.:** $375	**VGood:** $250
FN marked		
Perf.: $500	**Exc.:** $440	**VGood:** $375
Built-up model marketed by Iver Johnson 2007		
Perf.: $425	**Exc.:** $395	**VGood:** $300

BROWNING 25 LIGHTWEIGHT
Same specs as Browning 25 except chrome-plated; polymer pearl grips; alloy frame. Introduced 1954; dropped 1968.

Perf.: $450   **Exc.:** $365   **VGood:** $325

BROWNING 25 RENAISSANCE MODEL
Same specs as standard Browning 25 except chrome-plated finish; polyester pearl grips; full engraving. Introduced 1954; dropped 1968.

Perf.: $975   **Exc.:** $750   **VGood:** $550

BROWNING 380 STANDARD
Semi-automatic; 380 ACP, 32 ACP; 9-shot magazine; 3-7/16-inch barrel; 6-inch overall length; pre-'68 models have fixed sights, later adjustable; hard rubber grips; blued finish. Redesigned 1968; dropped 1974. Last models had 4-1/2-inch barrel; 7-inch overall length.

Perf.: $300   **Exc.:** $250   **VGood:** $200

BROWNING 380 RENAISSANCE
Same specs as standard Browning 380 Standard except chrome-plated finish; full engraving; polyester pearl grips. Introduced 1954; dropped 1981.

Perf.: $900   **Exc.:** $800   **VGood:** $700

BROWNING BDA
Semi-automatic; 9mm Para., 38 Super, 45 ACP; 9-shot magazine (9mm, 38 Super), 7-shot (45 ACP); 4-7/16-inch barrel; 7-13/16-inch overall length; fixed sights; plastic stocks; blued finish. Manufactured by Sauer; same as SIG-Sauer P220. Imported 1977 to 1981.

9mm, 45 ACP		
Perf.: $550	**Exc.:** $450	**VGood:** $375
38 Super		
Perf.: $650	**Exc.:** $575	**VGood:** $495

BROWNING BDA 380
Semi-automatic; 380 Auto; 12-shot magazine; 3-13/16-inch barrel; 6-3/4-inch overall length; blade front sight, windage-adjustable rear; combination safety; de-cocking lever; inertia firing pin; uncheckered walnut grips. Manufactured in Italy by Beretta. Introduced 1978; dropped 1997.

Perf.: $450   **Exc.:** $350   **VGood:** $300
Add $30 to above prices for nickel finish

BROWNING BDM
Semi-automatic; double action; 9mm Para.; 15-shot magazine; 4-3/4-inch barrel; weighs 31 oz; low-profile removable blade front sight, windage-adjustable rear; checkered black molded composition grips, thumbrest on both sides; all-steel frame; matte black finish; two safety systems; mode selector for switching from DA auto to revolver mode. Introduced 1991; dropped 1997.

Perf.: $500   **Exc.:** $400   **VGood:** $365

BROWNING BUCK MARK
Semi-automatic; 22 LR; 10-shot magazine; 5-1/2-inch barrel; 9-inch overall length; weighs 32 oz.; adjustable rear sight, ramp front; skip-line checkered molded black composition stocks; all-steel construction; gold-colored trigger; matte blue finish. Introduced 1985; still in production.

Perf.: $245   **Exc.:** $195   **VGood:** $160
Add $60 to above prices for nickel finish

BROWNING BUCK MARK FIELD 5.5
Same specs as Buck Mark except 9-7/8-inch barrel; matte blue finish only; hoodless ramp-type front

sight, low profile rear; contoured or finger-groove walnut stocks. Introduced 1991; still in production.

Perf.: $400   **Exc.:** $295   **VGood:** $240

BROWNING BUCK MARK MICRO
Same specs as Buck Mark except 4-inch barrel; 16-click Pro Target rear sight; blue or nickel finish. From Browning. Introduced 1992.

Perf.: $295   **Exc.:** $245   **VGood:** $195
Nickel finish		
Perf.: $325	**Exc.:** $275	**VGood:** $230

BROWNING BUCK MARK MICRO PLUS
Same specs as Buck Mark Micro except laminated wood grips. From Browning. Introduced 1992; still in production.

New: $300   **Perf.:** $250   **Exc.:** $175

BROWNING BUCK MARK PLUS
Same specs as Buck Mark except laminated wood stocks. Introduced 1985; still in production.

Perf.: $325   **Exc.:** $275   **VGood:** $230

BROWNING BUCK MARK SILHOUETTE
Same specs as Buck Mark except 9-7/8-inch heavy barrel; hooded sights; interchangeable posts; black, laminated wood grip and forend. Introduced 1987; dropped 1999.

Perf.: $450   **Exc.:** $350   **VGood:** $300

BROWNING BUCK MARK BULLSEYE
Similar to the Buck Mark Silhouette except has 7-1/4-inch heavy barrel with three flutes per side; trigger is adjustable from 2-1/2 to 5 lbs.; specially designed rosewood target or three-finger-groove stocks with competition-style heel rest, or with contoured rubber grip. Overall length is 11-5/16-inch, weighs 36 oz. Introduced 1996. Made in U.S. From Browning.

Perf.: $450   **Exc.:** $350   **VGood:** $300

BROWNING BUCK MARK TARGET 5.5
Same specs as Buck Mark except 5-1/2-inch barrel with .900-inch diameter hooded sights; adjustable post front; contoured walnut target grips; matte

Browning Buck Mark Varmint

Buck Mark Camper Cocobola UD

Browning Challenger Gold Model

Browning Buck Mark Bullseye Target

Browning Buck Mark Lite Splash

Browning Buck Mark Plus UDX

Browning Buck Mark Micro Standard URX

Browning Buck Mark Stainless Black Laminted UDX

Browning Full Line Dealer Buck Mark Plus Rosewood UDX

blue or gold anodized finish; 10-shot magazine. Introduced 1990; still in production.

Perf.: $370   **Exc.:** $300   **VGood:** $250

Gold anodized

Perf.: $355   **Exc.:** $325   **VGood:** $300

Add $55 to above prices for nickel finish

BROWNING BUCK MARK UNLIMITED MATCH

Same specs as Buck Mark except 14-inch heavy barrel; 15-inch sight radius. Introduced 1991; dropped 1999.

Perf.: $425   **Exc.:** $350   **VGood:** $300

BROWNING BUCK MARK UNLIMITED SILHOUETTE

Same as the Buck Mark Silhouette except has 14-inch heavy barrel. Conforms to IHMSA 15 maximum sight radius rule. Introduced 1991; dropped 1999.

New: $450   **Per.:** $400   **Exc.:** $350

BROWNING BUCK MARK VARMINT

Same specs as Buck Mark except 9-7/8-inch heavy barrel; full-length scope base; no sights; black laminated wood stocks, optional forend; weighs 48 oz. Introduced 1987; dropped 1999.

Perf.: $365   **Exc.:** $310   **VGood:** $250

BROWNING BUCK MARK BULLSEYE TARGET STAINLESS

Blowback, single action .22 LR semi-auto. Matte blued, heavy 7.25-inch round and fluted stainless bull barrel. Laminated rosewood grip, adjustable sights.

NIB: $575   **Exc.:** $515   **VGood:** $495

BROWNING BUCK MARK BULLSEYE TARGET URX

Blowback, single-action semi-auto in .22LR. Matte blued, heavy 7.25-inch round and fluted bull barrel. Grooved, rubberized grip, 39 oz., adjustable sights.

NIB: $470   **Exc.:** $425   **VGood:** $315

BROWNING BUCK MARK CONTOUR 5.5 URX

Blowback, single-action .222 semi-auto. Matte blued, contoured 5.5-inch barrel. Full-length scope base,

36 oz., adjustable sights. (Multiple barrel lengths and options.)

NIB: $460   **Exc.:** $410   **VGood:** $300

BROWNING BUCK MARK CONTOUR LITE 5.5 URX

.22 LR blowback, single-action semi-auto. Matte blued, contoured 5.5-inch barrel. Full-length scope base, 28 oz. Adjustable sights. (Multiple barrel lengths and options.)

NIB: $425   **Exc.:** $400   **VGood:** $300

BROWNING BUCK MARK FLD PLUS ROSEWOOD UDX

.22 LR blowback single-action semi-auto. "FLD" sculpted grip with rosewood panels. Blued, contoured 5.5-inch barrel, 34 oz., adjustable rear sight, fiber optic front sight. (Multiple barrel lengths and options.)

NIB: $425   **Exc.:** $400   **VGood:** $300

BROWNING BUCK MARK LITE SPLASH 5.5 URX

Blowback single-action semi-auto. Matte blued finish, gold splash anodizing. Chambered for .22 LR, 5.5-inch barrel. Rubberized ambidextrous grip. Adjustable sights; fiber optic front sight. (Also available with 7 1/2-inch barrel.)

NIB: $400   **Exc.:** $375   **VGood:** $285

BROWNING BUCK MARK MICRO STANDARD STAINLESS URX

With a 4-inch stainless barrel, this .22 LR weighs 32 oz. Ambidextrous rubberized grip and adjustable sights. (Also available in alloy steel.)

NIB: $375   **Exc.:** $350   **VGood:** $275

BROWNING BUCK MARK MICRO BULL

4-inch stainless bull barrel; .22 LR; weight 33 oz. Plastic grip panels and adjustable sights.

NIB: $250   **Exc.:** N/A   **VGood:** N/A

BROWNING BUCK MARK PLUS STAINLESS UDX

.22 LR semi-auto with finger-grooved wood grips. 5.5-inch barrel, 34 oz. Adjustable sights, fiber optic front sight. (Also available blued alloy steel.)

NIB: $425   **Exc.:** $375   **VGood:** $295

BROWNING BUCK MARK STANDARD STAINLESS URX

.22 LR semi-auto. 5.5-inch stainless bull barrel; 34 oz. Ambidextrous rubberized grip and adjustable sights. (Also available in alloy steel.)

NIB: $375   **Exc.:** $335   **VGood:** $295

BROWNING BUCK MARK PLUS STAINLESS BLACK LAMINATED UDX

Similar to Buck Mark Standard Stainless UDX but with ambidextrous grips.

NIB: $450   **Exc.:** $395   **VGood:** $310

BROWNING BUCK MARK PLUS UDX

Similar to Buck Mark FLD Plus but with ambidextrous walnut grips.

NIB: $400   **Exc.:** $335   **VGood:** $285

BROWNING FULL LINE DEALER BUCK MARK PLUS ROSEWOOD UDX

Similar to Buck Mark Plus UDX but with ambidextrous rosewood grips. Available only to full-line and Medallion-level Browning dealers.

NIB: $400   **Exc.:** $350   **VGood:** $285

BUCK MARK CAMPER

This model is fitted with a heavy 5.5" barrel and has a matte blue finish. Ten-round magazine capacity. Weight is about 34 oz. Introduced in 1999. Add $50 for stainless.

NIB: $300   **Exc.:** $265   **VGood:** $225

Similar to above but with cocobolo Ultra DX grips and TruGlo front sight. Introduced 2008.

NIB: $360   **Exc.:** $310   **VGood:** $285

BUCK MARK PRACTICAL URX FIBER OPTIC

Matte grey finish, 5.5-inch tapered bull barrel, Ultragrip RX ambi grips, adjustable ProTarget rear

Browning Challenger II

Browning Hi-Power

Buck Mark Practical URX Fiber Optic

Browning Challenger III

Browning Hi-Power Capitan

Browning Hi-Power Louis XVI

Browning Hi-Power 40 S&W Mark III

Browning Nomad

Browning Medalist International

sight with TruGlo fiber optic front sight. Introduced 2008.

NIB: $350   **Exc.:** $300   **VGood:** $2755

BROWNING CHALLENGER

Semi-automatic; 22 LR; 10-shot magazine; 4-1/2-inch, 6 3/4-inch barrels; overall length 11-7/16 inches (6-3/4-inch barrel); screw-adjustable rear sight, removable blade front; hand-checkered walnut grips; gold-plated trigger; blued finish. Introduced 1962; dropped 1974.

Perf.: $375   **Exc.:** $315   **VGood:** $275

BROWNING CHALLENGER II

Same specs as Challenger except changed grip angle; impregnated hardwood stocks. Introduced 1975; replaced by Challenger III, 1982.

Perf.: $275   **Exc.:** $225   **VGood:** $195

BROWNING CHALLENGER III

Same specs as Challenger except 5-1/2-inch heavy bull barrel; 9-1/2-inch overall length; weighs 35 oz.; lightweight alloy frame; improved sights; smooth impregnated hardwood grips; gold-plated trigger. Introduced 1982; dropped 1985.

Perf.: $350   **Exc.:** $295   **VGood:** $225

BROWNING CHALLENGER III SPORTER

Same specs as Challenger III except 6-3/4-inch barrel; 10-7/8-inch overall length; weighs 29 oz.; all-steel construction; blade ramped front sight, screw-adjustable rear, drift-adjustable front. Introduced 1982; dropped 1985.

Perf.: $300   **Exc.:** $190   **VGood:** $170

BROWNING CHALLENGER GOLD MODEL

Same specs as Challenger except gold wire inlays in metal; figured hand-carved, checkered walnut grips. Introduced 1971; dropped 1974.

Perf.: $1450   **Exc.:** $1250   **VGood:** $850

BROWNING CHALLENGER RENAISSANCE MODEL

Same specs as Challenger except satin nickel finish; full engraving; top-grade hand-carved, figured walnut grips. Introduced 1971; dropped 1974.

Perf.: $1450   **Exc.:** $1250   **VGood:** $850

BROWNING HI-POWER

Semi-automatic; 9mm para.; 13-shot magazine; 4 5/8" barrel; fixed sights; checkered walnut (pre-1986) or moulded grips; ambidextrous safety added in '80s; blued finish. Introduced 1954; still in production.

Perf.: $600   **Exc.:** $525   **Vgood:** $395

BROWNING HI-POWER 40 S&W MARK III

Same specs as standard Hi-Power except 40 S&W; 10-shot magazine; weighs 35 oz.; 4-3/4-inch barrel; matte blue finish; low profile front sight blade, drift-adjustable rear; ambidextrous safety; molded polyamide grips with thumbrest. Imported from Belgium by Browning. Introduced 1993; still imported.

New: $600   **Perf.:** $525   **Exc.:** $395

BROWNING HI-POWER CAPITAN

Same specs as standard Hi-Power except adjustable tangent rear sight authentic to early-production model; Commander-style hammer; checkered walnut grips; polished blue finish. Imported from Belgium by Browning. Reintroduced 1993; dropped 2000.

New: $650   **Perf.:** $575   **Exc.:** $450

BROWNING HI-POWER HP-PRACTICAL

Same specs as standard Hi-Power except silver-chromed frame, blued slide; wrap-around Pachmayr rubber grips; round-style serrated hammer; removable front sight, windage-adjustable rear. Introduced 1981; still in production.

Perf.: $650   **Exc.:** $575   **VGood:** $450

BROWNING HI-POWER LOUIS XVI

Same specs as standard Hi-Power 9mm except fully engraved silver-gray frame, slide; gold-plated trigger; hand checkered walnut grips; issued in deluxe walnut case. Introduced 1981; dropped 1984.

Perf.: $2300   **Exc.:** $1770   **VGood:** $1050

BROWNING HI-POWER RENAISSANCE

Same specs as standard Hi-Power except chrome-plated finish; full engraving; polyester pearl grips. Introduced 1954; dropped 1982.

Perf.: $2500   **Exc.:** $2200   **VGood:** 1675

Add $200 to above prices for internal extractor
Add $300-$500 for coin finish

BROWNING MEDALIST

Semi-automatic; 22 LR only; 10-shot magazine; 6-3/4-inch barrel; 11-1/8-inch overall length; vent rib; full wrap-around grips of select walnut, checkered with thumbrest; matching walnut forend; left-hand model available; screw-adjustable rear sight, removable blade front; dry-firing mechanism; blued finish. Introduced 1962; dropped 1974.

Perf.: $900   **Exc.:** $750   **VGood:** $595

BROWNING MEDALIST GOLD MODEL

Same general specs as Browning Medalist except gold wire inlays; better wood in grip. Introduced 1963; dropped 1974.

Perf.: $1950   **Exc.:** $1400   **VGood:** $1000

BROWNING MEDALIST INTERNATIONAL

Same specs as Medalist except sans forend; 5-15/16-inch barrel; 10-15/16-inch overall length; meets qualifications for International Shooting Union regulations. Introduced 1964; dropped 1974.

Perf.: $615   **Exc.:** $550   **VGood:** $500

Browning Medalist International (early model)

Perf.: $850   **Exc.:** $700   **VGood:** $550

BROWNING MEDALIST RENAISSANCE MODEL

Same specs as Medalist except finely figured, hand-carved grips; chrome plating; full engraving. Introduced 1964; dropped 1974.

Perf.: $2350   **Exc.:** $1750   **VGood:** $1250

BROWNING NOMAD

Semi-automatic; 22 LR; 10-shot magazine; 4-1/2-inch, 6 3/4-inch barrel; 8-15/16-inch overall length (4-1/2-inch barrel); screw-adjustable rear sight, removable blade front; brown plastic grips; blued finish. Introduced 1962; dropped 1973.

Perf.: $325   **Exc.:** $295   **VGood:** $250
Add 10 percent to above prices for alloy frame

Browning Renaissance Cased Set

Browning (FN) Hi-Power 9mm

Browning (FN) Hi-Power 9mm

Browning (FN) Model 1910

Browning (FN) Model 1903

Browning (FN) Model 1900

Bryco Model 25

Bryco Model 48

Bryco Model 38

BROWNING RENAISSANCE CASED SET

Includes Renaissance versions of Hi-Power 9mm, 380 Automatic, 25 ACP in a specially fitted walnut case. Oddly, value depends to a degree upon condition of the case. Introduced 1954; dropped 1968.

Perf.: $4000   **Exc.:** $3300   **VGood:** $2500
Add 20 percent to above prices for coin finish and early walnut case
Add $100 to above prices for "St. Louis" slide address
Add $100 for old style extractor

BROWNING (FN) HI-POWER 9MM

Semi-automatic; 9mm Para.; 13-shot magazine; 4-5/8-inch barrel; 7-3/4-inch overall length; based on Browning-Colt 45 ACP; adjustable or fixed rear sight; checkered walnut grips; thumb, magazine safeties; external hammer with half-cock safety feature; blued finish. Pre-WWII-made and Nazi occupation marked models have collector value. Introduced 1935; still in production.

Pre-War Commercial Adjustable Sight		
Exc.: $950	**VGood:** $750	**Good:** $450
Pre-War Military Contact		
Exc.: $1000	**VGood:** $850	**Good:** $700
WWII Production (Fixed sights, Nazi proofed)		
Exc.: $500	**VGood:** $400	**Good:** $300
Post-War Production (Adjustable sights)		
Exc.: $750	**VGood:** $600	**Good:** $500
Post-War Production (Fixed sights)		
Exc.: $600	**VGood:** $465	**Good:** $395

BROWNING (FN) MODEL 1900

Semi-automatic; 32 ACP; 7-shot magazine; 4-inch barrel; 6-3/4-inch overall length; checkered hard rubber stocks; fixed sights; blued finish. Manufactured in Belgium, 1899 to 1910.

Exc.: $450   **VGood:** $375   **Good:** $300
Add about 50 percent to above prices for factory nickel finish

BROWNING (FN) MODEL 1903

Semi-automatic; 9mm Browning Long; 7-shot magazine; 5-inch barrel; 8-inch overall length; hard rubber checkered stocks; fixed sights; blued finish. Designed primarily for military use. Manufactured 1903 to 1939.

Exc.: $500   **VGood:** $400   **Good:** $325

BROWNING (FN) MODEL 1906

Semi-automatic; 25 ACP; 6-shot magazine; 2-inch barrel; 4-1/2-inch overall length; weighs 12-1/2 oz.; fixed sights; blued or nickel finish; hard rubber grips. At about production number 100,000, a safety lever was fitted to left rear of frame. Almost identical to Colt Vest Pocket 25 semi-auto. Introduced 1906; dropped 1940.

Exc.: $325   **VGood:** $295   **Good:** $225

BROWNING (FN) MODEL 1910

Semi-automatic; 32 ACP, 380 ACP; 7-shot magazine (32), 6-shot (380); 3-1/2-inch barrel; 6-inch overall length; weighs 20-1/2 oz.; hard rubber stocks; fixed sights; blued finish. Made in Belgium. Introduced 1910; dropped 1983.

Exc.: $350   **VGood:** $325   **Good:** $300

BROWNING (FN) MODEL 1922

Semi-automatic; 32 ACP, 380 ACP; 9-shot magazine (32), 8-shot (380); 4-1/2-inch barrel; 7-inch overall; checkered hard rubber stocks; fixed sights; blued finish. Modified 1910 with longer barrel and slide and deeper grip to fulfill military contracts. Introduced 1922; dropped 1945. Nazi proofed pistols bring a premium.

Exc.: $300   **VGood:** $275   **Good:** $250

BRYCO MODEL J-25

Semi-automatic; 25 ACP; 6-shot magazine; 2-1/2-inch barrel; 5-inch overall length; weighs 11 oz.; resin-impregnated wood stocks; fixed sights; safety locks sear and slide; satin nickel, chrome or black Teflon finish. Introduced 1988; dropped 2004. Briefly resurfaced under the name "Jimenex Arms" c. 2005.

Perf.: $65   **Exc.:** $55   **VGood:** $45

BRYCO MODEL M-38

Semi-automatic; 22 LR, 32 ACP, 380 ACP; 6-shot magazine; 2-13/16-inch barrel; 5-5/16-inch overall length; weighs 15 oz.; resin-impregnated wood stocks; fixed sights; safety locks sear and slide; satin nickel, chrome or black Teflon finish. Introduced 1988; dropped 2004. Briefly resurfaced under the name "Jimenez Arms" c. 2005.

Perf.: $85   **Exc.:** $75   **VGood:** $65

BRYCO MODEL M-48

Semi-automatic; 22 LR, 32 ACP, 380 ACP; 6-shot magazine; 4-inch barrel; 6-11/16-inch overall length; weighs 19 oz.; resin-impregnated wood stocks; fixed sights; safety locks sear and slide; satin nickel, chrome or black Teflon finish. Introduced 1988; dropped 1995.

Perf.: $100   **Exc.:** $85   **VGood:** $65

BRYCO MODEL 58

Semi-automatic; single action; 9mm Para.; 10-shot magazine; 4-inch barrel; 5-1/2-inch overall length; weighs 30 oz.; black composition grips; blade front sight, fixed rear; striker-fired action; manual thumb safety; polished blue finish. Made in U.S. by Jennings Firearms. Introduced 1994; dropped 1995.

Perf.: $100   **Exc.:** $85   **VGood:** $75

BRYCO MODEL M-59

Semi-automatic; single action; 9mm Para.; 10-shot magazine; 4-inch barrel; 6-1/2-inch overall length; weighs 33 oz.; black composition grips; blade front sight, fixed rear; striker-fired action; manual thumb safety; polished blue finish. Made in U.S. by Jennings Firearms. Introduced 1994; dropped 1995.

New: $100   **Perf.:** $85   **Exc.:** $65
Add $15 to above prices for 9mm chambering

BUDISCHOWSKY TP-70

Semi-automatic; double action; 22 LR, 25 ACP; 6-shot magazine; 2-7/16-inch barrel; 4-11/16-inch overall length; fixed sights; all stainless steel construction; manual, magazine safeties. Introduced 1973; dropped 1977.

Exc.: $540   **VGood:** $485   **Good:** $390

Bushmaster Carbon-15 Type 21 Pistol

Century Model 100

Budischowsky TP-70

Cabanas Single-Shot

Charles Daly M911-A1P

Calico M-100

Carbon-15

Campo-Giro Model 1913-16

BUSHMASTER CARBON-15 TYPE 21 PISTOL

Semi-automatic; 223 Rem.; tool steel side bolt operation; ultra light carbon fiber upper and lower receivers; 7-1/4-inch stainless steel barrel; quick detachable muzzle compensator; ghost ring sights; A2 pistol grip; uses standard AR-15 magazines; 40 oz. Formerly made by Professional Ordnance. Bushmaster production began 2003.

Perf.: $750   **Exc.:** $675   **VGood:** $600

BUSHMASTER CARBON-15 TYPE 97 PISTOL

Similar to Carbon-15 Type 21, execept has fluted barrel; Hogue overmolded pistol grip and chrome plated bolt carrier; 46 oz. Formerly made by Professional Ordnance. Bushmaster production began 2003.

Perf.: $795   **Exc.:** $725   **VGood:** 625

BUTLER DERRINGER

Derringer; single shot; 22 Short; 2-1/2-inch barrel; blade front sight, no rear; smooth walnut or pearlite grips; spur trigger; blued, gold, chrome finish. Introduced 1978; dropped 1980.

Exc.: $85   **VGood:** $65   **Good:** $50

CABANAS SINGLE-SHOT

Single shot; 177 pellet or round ball; 9-inch barrel; 19-inch overall length; weighs 51 oz.; smooth wood stocks, thumbrest; ramped blade front sight, open adjustable rear; automatic safety; muzzle brake. Fires pellet or ball with 22 blank cartridge. Made in Mexico. Introduced 1987; last imported by Mandall Shooting Supplies, which closed in late 2004.

Exc.: $125   **VGood:** $75   **Good:** $65

CALICO MODEL M-100

Semi-automatic; single action; 22 LR; 100-shot magazine; 6-inch barrel; 17-15/16-inch overall length; weighs 3-3/4 lbs. (loaded); molded composition grip; adjustable post front sight, notch rear; aluminum alloy frame; flash suppressor; pistol grip compartment; ambidextrous safety. Uses same helical-feed magazine as M-100 Carbine. Made in U.S. by Calico.

Introduced 1986 as Model 100-P; no longer in production.

Perf.: $495   **Exc.:** $455   **VGood:** $365

CALICO MODEL M-950

Semi-automatic; single action; 9mm Para.; 50- or 100-shot helical-feed magazine; 7-3/4-inch barrel; 14-inch overall length with 50-shot magazine; weighs 2-1/4 lbs. (empty); glass-filled polymer grip; fully-adjustable post front sight, fixed notch rear; ambidextrous safety; static cocking handle; retarded blowback action. Made in U.S. by Calico. Introduced 1989; dropped 1994.

Perf.: $455   **Exc.:** $410   **VGood:** $385

CAMPO-GIRO MODEL 1913

Semi-automatic; 9mm Largo (Bergmann-Bayard); 8-shot magazine; 6-1/2-inch barrel; 9-1/4-inch overall length; weighs 32 oz.; fixed sights; checkered black horn grips; blued finish. Distinguished by magazine release lever behind triggerguard. Adopted by Spanish Army in 1913, superseded by 1913-16 Model after only 1300 made.

Exc.: $3000   **VGood:** $2500   **Good:** $1900

CAMPO-GIRO MODEL 1913-16

Semi-automatic; 9mm Largo; 8-shot magazine; 6-1/2-inch barrel; 9-1/4-inch overall length; weighs 35 oz.; fixed sights; checkered black horn or wood grips; blued finish. Magazine release at bottom of left grip. Total production 13,625.

Exc.: $2800   **VGood:** $2250   **Good:** $1550

CARBON-15

Semi-automatic; 223, Barrel: 7.25". Weight: 46 oz. Length: 20" overall. Stock: Checkered composite. Sights: Ghost ring. Features: gas-operated, rotary bolt action. Carbon fiber upper and lower receiver; chrome-moly bolt carrier; fluted stainless match barrel; uses AR-15-type magazines. Introduced 1992. From Professional Ordnance, Inc.

Perf.: $875   **Exc.:** $795   **VGood:** $650

CENTURY FEG P9R

Semi-automatic; double action; 9mm Para.; 10-shot magazine; 4-5/8-inch barrel; 8-inch overall length; weighs 35 oz.; checkered walnut grips; blade front sight, windage drift-adjustable rear; hammer-drop safety; polished blue finish; comes with spare magazine; blue or chrome finish. Imported from Hungary by Century International Arms.

New: $250   **Perf.:** $200   **Exc.:** $150

Chrome finish

New: $250   **Perf.:** $200   **Exc.:** $150

CENTURY FEG P9R PISTOL

Caliber: 9mm Para., 10-shot magazine. Barrel: 4.6-inch. Weight: 35 oz. Length: 8 inches overall. Stocks: Checkered walnut. Sights: Blade front, rear drift adjustable for windage. Features: Double action with hammer-drop safety. Polished blue finish. Comes with spare magazine. Imported from Hungary by Century International Arms.

Price: About $263.00

CENTURY FEG P9RK

Same specs as the P9R except 4-1/8-inch barrel; 7-1/2-inch overall length; weighs 33-1/2 oz.; checkered walnut grips; fixed sights; 10-shot magazine. Imported from Hungary by Century International Arms, Inc. Introduced 1994.

New: $225   **Perf.:** $200   **Exc.:** $150

CENTURY MODEL 100

Revolver; single action; 375 Winchester, 30-30 Win., 50-70 Gov't., 444 Marlin, 45-70; 6-1/2-inch, 8-inch, 12-inch barrel; 15-inch overall length (8-inch barrel); weighs 6 lbs.; Millett adjustable square notch rear, ramp front sights; uncheckered walnut stocks; manganese bronze frame; blued cylinder, barrel; coil spring trigger mechanism. Imported by Century Gun Distributors. Introduced 1975.

Perf.: $2000   **Exc.:** $1650   **VGood:** $1250

CHARLES DALY M-1911-A1P

Semi-automatic; 45 ACP, 7- or 10-shot magazine. Barrel: 5-inch. Weight: 38 oz. Length: 8-3/4 inches overall. Stocks: Checkered. Sights: Blade front, rear drift adjustable for windage; three-dot system. Features: Skeletonized combat hammer and trigger; beavertail grip safety; extended slide release; oversize thumb safety; Parkerized finish. Introduced 1996. Imported from the Philippines by K.B.I., Inc.

Perf.: $380   **Exc.:** $330   **VGood:** $255

Charles Daly Field EFS1911

Charles Daly Field ECS1911 Compact

Charles Daly Empire EFS1911

Charles Daly Empire HP

Charles Daly M-5

Charles Daly Model 1873 Stainless

Charles Daly Model 1873 Steel Frame

Charter Arms Bulldog

Charter Arms Magnum Pug

Charter Arms Mag Pug (2006)

CHARLES DALY 1911-A1 FIELD EFS

Semi-automatic; 45 ACP, 8-shot capacity. Barrel: 5-inch. Weight: 39.5 oz. Length: 8-3/4 inches overall. Stocks: Checkered. Sights: Blade front, rear drift adjustable for windage; three-dot system. Features: Skeletonized combat hammer and trigger; beavertail grip safety; extended slide release; oversize thumb safety; matte blue finish; flared and lowered ejection port.

Perf.: $400   **Exc.:** $350   **VGood:** $300

CHARLES DALY 1911-A1 FIELD ECS COMPACT

Similar to 1911-A1 Field EFS but with 3.5-inch barrel, 7-1/4-inch overall length and 6-shot capacity. Values similar.

CHARLES DALY 1911-A1 EMPIRE EFS

Similar to 1911-A1 Field EFS but in stainless steel. Add 10 percent to above values.

CHARLES DALY 1911-A1 EMPIRE ECS COMPACT

Similar to 1911-A1 Field ECS Compact but in stainless steel. Values similar.

CHARLES DALY HP

Semi-automatic; 9mm Parabellum, 10-shot magazine. Barrel: 4-5/8 inches. Weight: 34.5 oz. Length: 7-3/8 inches overall. Matte blue finish. Copy of Browning Hi Power/P35.

Perf.: $475   **Exc.:** $395   **VGood:** $275

CHARLES DALY EMPIRE HP

Same as Charles Daly HP but in stainless steel.

CHARLES DALY M-5

Semi-automatic; 9mm Parabellum, 40 S&W, 45 ACP; 10-shot magazine; polymer frame. Based on 1911 design. Made in Israel by BUL.

CHARLES DALY MODEL 1873

Single action revolver; 357 Mag or 45 LC; 4-3/4-inch, 4-1/2-inch, or 7-1/2-inch barrel; case-hardened frame; blue finish; brass or steel backstrap and triggerguard. Importation began 2004.

Perf.: $395   **Exc.:** $350   **VGood:** $300

CHARLES DALY MODEL 1873 STAINLESS

Similar to Model 1873, except has matte finish, stainless construction with steel backstrap and triggerguard. Importation began 2004.

Perf.: $595   **Exc.:** $525   **VGood:** $450

CHARTER ARMS BONNIE & CLYDE SET

Revolvers; double action; 32 H&R Mag. (Bonnie) and 38 Spl. (Clyde); 6-shot magazine; 2-1/2-inch barrels, fully shrouded; fixed rear sight, serrated ramp front; laminated grips; various colors; marked as "Bonnie" or "Clyde" on barrels; blued finish. Introduced 1989; dropped 1991.

Perf.: $425   **Exc.:** $365   **VGood:** $335

CHARTER ARMS BULLDOG

Revolver; double action; 44 Spl.; 5-shot cylinder; 2-1/2-inch, 3-inch barrel; 7-1/2-inch overall length; weighs 19 oz.; square notch fixed rear sight, Patridge-type front; checkered walnut or neoprene grips; chrome-moly steel frame; wide trigger and hammer, or spurless pocket hammer; blued or stainless finish. Introduced 1973; dropped 1996.

Perf.: $325   **Exc.:** $285   **VGood:** $200

Stainless Bulldog (discontinued 1991)

Perf.: $345   **Exc.:** $305   **VGood:** $195

CHARTER ARMS BULLDOG PUG

Same specs as Bulldog except 2-1/2-inch shrouded barrel; 7-1/4-inch overall length; weighs 19 oz.; notch rear sight, ramp front; wide trigger and hammer spur; shrouded ejector rod; blued or stainless steel finish. Introduced 1986; reintroduced 1993; dropped 1993.

Perf.: $325   **Exc.:** $285   **VGood:** $200

Stainless Bulldog Pug

Perf.: $345   **Exc.:** $305   **VGood:** $195

CHARTER ARMS MAG PUG (2006)

A 5-shot revolver chambered for .357 Magnum. Stainless or blue. Ported 2.2-inch barrel. 23 oz. Fixed sights, rubber grips. Stainless or black.

NIB: $325   **Exc.:** $285   **VGood:** $245

CHARTER ARMS EXPLORER II

Semi-automatic; 22 LR; 8-shot magazine; 6-inch, 8-inch or 10-inch barrel; 15-1/2-inch overall length; blade front sight, open elevation-adjustable rear; serrated simulated walnut stocks; action adapted from Explorer AR-7 carbine; black, camo, gold or silver finish. Introduced 1980; discontinued 1986.

Perf.: $100   **Exc.:** $85   **VGood:** $75

CHARTER ARMS LADY ON DUTY

Revolver; double action; 22 LR, 22 WMR, 38 Spl.; 6-shot (22LR, 22 WMR), 5-shot (38 Spl.) cylinder; 2-inch barrel; 6-1/4-inch overall length; weighs 17 oz.; rosewood-color checkered plastic grips; ramp-style front sight, fixed rear; comes with lockable plastic case, trigger lock; choice of spur, pocket or double-action hammer; blue or nickel finish. Made in U.S. by Charco, Inc. Introduced 1995; dropped 1996.

New: $225   **Perf.:** $165   **Exc.:** $150

CHARTER ARMS MAGNUM PUG

Revolver; double action; 357 Mag.; 5-shot magazine; 2-1/4-inch barrel; weighs 18 oz.; Bulldog or neoprene combat grips; ramp-style front sight, fixed rear; fully shrouded barrel; pocket or spur hammer; blue finish. Made in U.S. by Charco, Inc. Introduced 1995; dropped 1996.

New: $265   **Perf.:** $195   **Exc.:** $165
Production resumed in 2001 by Charter 2000, Inc.

CHARTER ARMS MODEL 40

Semi-automatic; double action; 22 LR; 8-shot magazine; 3-5/16-inch barrel; weighs 2-11/2 oz.; fixed sights; stainless steel finish. Introduced 1984; discontinued 1986.

Perf.: $265   **Exc.:** $240   **VGood:** $220

Charter Arms
Model 40

Charter Arms
Off-Duty

Charter Arms
Pathfinder

Charter Arms
Pit Bull

Charter Arms
Police Bulldog

Charter Arms
Undercover

Charter Arms
Target Bulldog

Charter Arms
Dixie Derringer

Charter Arms
Pink Lady

Charter Arms
Goldfinger

Charter Arms
Patriot with Ker-
shaw Knife

CHARTER ARMS MODEL 79K

Semi-automatic; double action; 32 ACP, 380 ACP; 7-shot magazine; 3-5/8-inch barrel; 6-1/2-inch overall length; weighs 24-1/2 oz.; fixed sights; hammer block; firing pin, magazine safeties; stainless steel finish. Imported from West Germany. Introduced 1984; no longer imported.

Perf.: $325   **Exc.:** $300   **VGood:** $280

CHARTER ARMS OFF-DUTY

Revolver; double action; 22 LR, 38 Spl.; 5-shot magazine (38 Spl.); 2-inch barrel; 6-3/4-inch overall length; fixed sights; choice of smooth or checkered walnut, neoprene grips; all steel; matte black finish. Introduced 1984; reintroduced 1993; dropped 1996. Production resumed in 2002 by Charter 2000, Inc.

Perf.: $275   **Exc.:** $250   **VGood:** $135

Stainless Off-Duty

Perf.: $295   **Exc.:** $275   **VGood:** $175

CHARTER ARMS PATHFINDER

Revolver; double action; 22 LR, 22 WMR; 6-shot magazine; 2-inch, 3-inch, 6-inch barrels; 7-3/8-inch overall length; weighs 18-1/2 oz.; adjustable rear sight, ramp front; round butt; wide hammer spur and trigger; blued finish. Introduced 1971; dropped 1990. Later reintroduced. Prices shown are for reintroduced version.

NIB: $325   **Exc.:** $285   **VGood:** $245

STAINLESS PATHFINDER WITH 3-1/2-INCH SHROUDED BARREL

Values shown are for Charter 2000 version.

Perf.: $185   **Exc.:** $165   **VGood:** $150

CHARTER ARMS PIT BULL

Revolver; double action; 9mm Federal, 38 Spl., 357 Mag.; 5-shot magazine; 2-1/2-inch, 3-1/2-inch, 4-inch barrels; 7-1/4-inch overall length; weighs 24-1/2 oz. (2-1/2-inch barrel); blade front sight, fixed rear on 2-1/2-inch, adjustable on others; checkered neoprene grips; blued finish. Introduced 1989; discontinued 1991.

Perf.: $235   **Exc.:** $200   **VGood:** $165

Stainless Pit Bull

Perf.: $310   **Exc.:** $275   **VGood:** $235

CHARTER ARMS POLICE BULLDOG

Revolver; double action; 32 H&R, 38 Spl., 44 Spl.; 5-shot magazine (44) or 6-shot; 3-1/2-inch, 4-inch barrel; fixed sights; neoprene grips; square butt (44 Spl.); blued finish. Introduced 1976; dropped 1991. Production resumed in 2002 by Charter, 2000, Inc. Values shown are for original version.

Perf.: $345   **Exc.:** $295   **VGood:** $185

CHARTER ARMS POLICE BULLDOG STAINLESS

Same specs as Police Bulldog except also offered in 357 Mag. (5-shot); shrouded barrel; square butt; stainless finish.

Perf.: $360   **Exc.:** $310   **VGood:** $195

CHARTER ARMS UNDERCOVER

Revolver; double action; 32 H&R Mag., 38 Spl.; 6-shot magazine; 2-inch barrel, shrouded; Patridge front sight, fixed square-notch rear; checkered walnut grips; pocket or spur hammer; blued finish. Introduced 1984; dropped 1989. Reintroduced c. 2007.

Perf.: $295   **Exc.:** $275   **VGood:** $175

Police Undercover Stainless

Perf.: $325   **Exc.:** $300   **VGood:** $280

CHARTER ARMS TARGET BULLDOG

Revolver; double action; 357 Mag., 44 Spl.; 5-shot magazine; 4-inch barrel; 9-inch overall length; weighs 21 oz.; adjustable rear sight, blade front; square-butt walnut stocks; all-steel frame; shrouded barrel, ejector rod. Introduced 1986; discontinued 1988. Reintrodeuced c. 2007.

Perf.: $325   **Exc.:** $300   **VGood:** $280

CHARTER ARMS TARGET BULLDOG STAINLESS

Same specs as Target Bulldog except also in 9mm Federal; 5-1/2-inch barrel, fully shrouded; adjustable sights; square butt target grips; stainless finish. Discontinued 1991. Reintroduced c. 2007.

Perf.: $325   **Exc.:** $300   **VGood:** $280

CHARTER ARMS UNDERCOVER

Revolver; double action; 22 LR, 22 WMR, 32 S&W Long, 38 Spl.; 6-shot magazine (32), 5-shot (38 Spl.); 2-inch (32), 3-inch barrels; 6 3/4-inch overall length; weighs 16 oz.; fixed rear sight, serrated ramp front; walnut standard or Bulldog grips; wide spur hammer and trigger, or pocket hammer (38 Spl.); blued. Introduced 1965; dropped 1991. Production resumed in 1998 by Charter 2000, Inc., which itself went kablooey some years later. Production resumed c. 2007.

Perf.: $285   **Exc.:** $250   **VGood:** $200

Stainless with 2-inch barrel only

Perf.: $295   **Exc.:** $260   **VGood:** $210

CHARTER ARMS UNDERCOVERETTE

Same specs as Undercover except 32 S&W Long; 6-shot magazine; 2-inch barrel; blued finish. Introduced 1969; discontinued 1981.

Perf.: $285   **Exc.:** $250   **VGood:** $200

CHARTER ARMS PINK LADY

Similar to Undercover Lite but with pink anodized frame. .38 Special only.

Perf.: $300   **Exc.:** $250   **VGood:** $200

CHARTER ARMS GOLDFINGER

Similar to above but with gold anodized frame. .38 Special only.

Perf.: $300   **Exc.:** $250   **VGood:** $200

CHARTER ARMS PATRIOT

Built on Bulldog frame but chambered in .327 Federal Magnum (six-shot). Rubber grips, 2.2- or 4-inch barrel. Comes with Kershar "327" knife.

Perf.: $375   **Exc.:** $325   **VGood:** $275

CHARTER ARMS DIXIE DERRINGER

Stainless mini-revolver chambered for .22 LR (5 oz.) or .22 Mag (6 oz.). 5-shot, 1.175-inch barrel.

NIB: $175   **Exc.:** $140   **VGood:** $110

Chipmunk Silhouette Model

Cimarron Peacekeeper

Cimarron Artillery Model

Cimarron New Thunderer

Cimarron U.S. Cavalry Model

Claridge Hi-Tec Model L-9

CHARTER 2000, INC. DIXIE DERRINGER

Similar to above. Single action revolver; 22 LR or 22 WMR; 5-shot; 1-1/8-inch barrel; stainless construction; spur trigger; hardwood grips; 5 oz. Introduced 2002.

Perf.: $165   **Exc.:** $130   **VGood:** $110

CHIPMUNK SILHOUETTE MODEL

Bolt action; single shot; 22 LR; 14 -7/8-inch barrel; 20-inch overall length; weighs 32 oz.; American walnut stock; post ramp front sight, peep rear; meets IHMSA 22 Unlimited competition rules. Introduced 1985; dropped 1990.

Perf.: $135   **Exc.:** $115   **VGood:** $100

CIMARRON 1873 PEACEMAKER

Revolver; single action; 22 LR, 22 WMR, 38 Spl., 357 Mag., 44-40, 45 Colt; 3-inch, 4-inch, 4-3/4-inch, 5-1/2-inch, 7-1/2-inch barrel; 10-inch overall length (4-inch barrel); weighs 39 oz.; blade front, fixed or adjustable rear sight; walnut stocks; reproduction of original Colt design; various grades of engraving; old model blackpowder frame with "bullseye" ejector or New Model frame. Made in Europe. Introduced 1989; no longer imported by Cimarron Arms.

Perf.: $495   **Exc.:** $300   **VGood:** $250

Engraved

Perf.: $800   **Exc.:** $700   **VGood:** $500

CIMARRON 1873 PEACEMAKER SHERIFF'S MODEL

Same specs as 1873 Peacemaker except 44-40, 45 Colt; 3-inch, 4-inch barrels. Introduced 1989; importation dropped 1990; reintroduced 2000-2001.

Perf.: $495   **Exc.:** $325   **VGood:** $250

CIMARRON 1875 REMINGTON

Revolver; single action; 357 Mag., 44-40, 45 Colt; 6-shot cylinder; 7-1/2-inch barrel; 13-3/4-inch overall length; weighs 44 oz.; blade front, notch rear sight; smooth walnut stocks; replica of 1875 Remington Single Action Army model; brass triggerguard; color case-hardened frame; rest blued or nickel finished. Made in Europe. Introduced 1989; dropped 1993.

Perf.: $440   **Exc.:** $350   **VGood:** $225

CIMARRON 1890 REMINGTON

Revolver; single action; 357 Mag., 44-40, 45 Colt; 6-shot cylinder; 5-1/2-inch barrel; 12-1/2-inch overall length; weighs 37 oz; blade front, groove-type rear sight; American walnut stocks; replica of 1890 Remington Single Action; brass trigger guard; rest blued or nickel finished; lanyard ring. Made in Europe. Introduced 1989; dropped 1993.

Perf.: $440   **Exc.:** $350   **VGood:** $225

CIMARRON NEW THUNDERER

Revolver; single action; 357 Mag., 44 WCF, 44 Spl., 45 Colt; 6-shot; 3-1/2-inch, 4-3/4-inch barrel, with ejector; weighs 38 oz. (3-1/2-inch barrel); hand-checkered walnut grips; blade front, notch rear sight; Thunderer grip; color case-hardened frame with balance blued, or nickel finish. Imported by Cimarron Arms. Introduced 1993; still in production.

New: $430   **Perf.:** $350   **Exc.:** $300
Add $45 to above prices for checkered walnut grips

CIMARRON PEACEKEEPER

Revolver; single action; 357 Mag., 44 WCF, 44 Spl., 45 Colt; 6-shot; 3-1/2-inch, 4-3/4-inch barrel, with ejector; weighs 38 oz. (3-1/2-inch barrel); hand-checkered walnut grips; blade front, notch rear sight; Thunderer grip; color case-hardened frame with balance blued, or nickel finish. Imported by Cimarron Arms. Introduced 1993; no longer imported.

Perf.: $450   **Exc.:** $350   **VGood:** $325

CIMARRON U.S. ARTILLERY MODEL

Revolver; single action; 45 Colt; 5-1/2-inch barrel; 11-1/2-inch overall length; weighs 39 oz.; fixed sights; walnut stocks; Rinaldo A. Carr Commemorative Edition. Made in Europe. Introduced 1989; still imported.

Perf.: $450   **Exc.:** $365   **VGood:** $315

CIMARRON U.S. CAVALRY MODEL

Revolver; single action; 45 Colt; 7-1/2-inch barrel; 13-1/2-inch overall length; weighs 42 oz.; fixed sights; walnut stocks; original-type inspector and martial markings; color case-hardened frame and hammer; charcoal blued; exact copy of original. Made in Europe. Introduced 1989; still in production.

Perf.: $465   **Exc.:** $385   **VGood:** $335

CIMARRON 8TH ARTILLERY CASED SET

U.S. Cavalry Model in case with accessories. Discontinued 1990.

Perf.: $695   **Exc.:** $625   **VGood:** $550

CIMARRON ROUGH RIDER ARTILLERY MODEL SINGLE-ACTION

Similar to the U.S. Cavalry model except has 5-1/2-inch barrel, weighs 39 oz., and is 11-1/2-inch overall. U.S. markings and cartouche, case-hardened frame and hammer; 45 Colt only.

Perf.: $465   **Exc.:** $385   **VGood:** $335

CLARIDGE HI-TEC MODEL L-9

Semi-automatic; single action; 9mm Para., 40 S&W, 45 ACP; 18-shot magazine; 7-1/2-inch barrel; 12-3/4-inch overall length (5-inch barrel); weighs about 3 lbs.; aluminum or stainless frame; telescoping bolt; floating firing pin locked by the safety; molded composition grip; post elevation-adjustable front sight, open windage-adjustable rear. Made in U.S. by Claridge Hi-Tec, Inc. No longer produced.

Perf.: $500   **Exc.:** $400   **VGood:** $275

CLARIDGE HI-TEC S-9

Similar to L-9, except has 5-inch non-shrouded threaded barrel; weighs 3 lbs. 9 oz. Discontinued 1993.

Perf.: $425   **Exc.:** $425   **VGood:** $350

CLARIDGE HI-TEC T-9

Similar to L-9, except has 9-inch barrel. Introduced 1992; dropped 1993.

Perf.: $550   **Exc.:** $495   **VGood:** $375

CLARIDGE M

Similar to L-9, except has 7-1/2-inch barrel; weighs 3 lbs. Discontinued 1991.

Perf.: $550   **Exc.:** $495   **VGood:** $375

CLASSIC ARMS SOUTHERN DERRINGER

Single shot; 22 LR, 41 rimfire; 2-1/2-inch barrel; 5-inch overall length; weighs 12 oz.; blade front sight; white plastic stocks; steel barrel; brass frame. Introduced 1982; dropped 1984.

Perf.: $75   **Exc.:** $60   **VGood:** $50

Clerke First Model

Colt Ace

Colt All American Model 2000

Classic Arms Twister

Colt Combat Commander MKIV Series 70

Colt Challenger

Colt Combat Elite MKIV Series 80

CLASSIC ARMS TWISTER

Derringer; over/under; 22 LR, 9mm rimfire; 3-1/4-inch barrel; no sights; pearlite grips; rotating barrels; spur trigger. Originally marketed by Navy Arms. Introduced 1980; dropped 1984.

Perf.: $85   **Exc.:** $75
VGood: $60

CLERKE FIRST MODEL

Revolver; double action; 32 S&W, 22 LR, 22 Long, 22 Short; 5-shot swing-out cylinder (32), 6-shot (22); 2-1/4-inch barrel; 6-1/4-inch overall length; fixed sights; checkered plastic grips; blued, nickel finish.

Perf.: $50   **Exc.:** $35
VGood: $25

COLT 22 AUTOMATIC PISTOL

Semi-automatic; single action; 22 LR; 10-shot magazine; 4-1/2-inch barrel; weighs 33 oz.; 8-5/8-inch overall length; textured black polymer grip; blade front sight, rear drift-adjustable for windage; stainless steel construction; ventilated barrel rib; single-action mechanism; cocked striker indicator; push-button safety. Introduced 1994; no longer produced. Also known as Cadet.

New: $425   **Perf.:** $325   **Exc.:** $295

COLT 22 TARGET PISTOL

Same specs as the Colt 22 except 6-inch bull barrel; full-length sighting rib with lightening cuts and mounting rail for optical sights; fully-adjustable rear sight; removable sights for optics mounting; two-point factory adjusted trigger travel; stainless steel frame. Introduced 1995; no longer produced.

New: $450   **Perf.:** $415   **Exc.:** $355

COLT ACE

Semi-automatic; 22 LR only, standard or high velocity; 4-3/4-inch barrel; 8-1/4-inch overall length; no floating chamber; adjustable rear, fixed front sight; target barrel; hand-honed action. Built on same frame as Government Model 45 automatic. Introduced 1931; dropped 1947.

Exc.: $2400   **VGood:** $1500   **Good:** $1000

COLT ACE SERVICE MODEL

Semi-automatic; 22 LR, standard or high velocity; 10-shot magazine; identical to Colt National Match.

Specially designed chamber increases recoil four-fold to approximate that of 45 auto. Introduced 1937; dropped 1945; reintroduced 1978; dropped 1982.

Old model
Exc.: $3000   **VGood:** $2250   **Good:** $1500

New model
Perf.: $600   **Exc.:** $500   **VGood:** $450

COLT ALL AMERICAN MODEL 2000

Semi-automatic; double-action-only; 9mm Para.; 15-shot magazine; 4-1/2-inch barrel; 7-1/2-inch overall length; weighs 29 oz. (polymer frame), 33 oz. (aluminum frame); checkered polymer grips; ramped blade front sight, drift-adjustable rear; three-dot system; molded polymer or aluminum frame; blued steel slide; internal striker block safety. Made in U.S. by Colt's Mfg. Co., Inc. Introduced 1991; dropped 1993.

Polymer frame
Perf.: $550   **Exc.:** $450   **VGood:** $375

Aluminum frame
Perf.: $850   **Exc.:** $700   **VGood:** $550

COLT CHALLENGER

Semi-automatic; 22 LR; 4-1/2-inch, 6-inch barrel; 9-inch overall length (4-1/2-inch barrel); fixed sights; checkered plastic grips; blued finish. Same basic specs as Target Woodsman, with fewer features; slide does not stay open after last shot. Introduced 1950; dropped 1955.

Perf.: $500   **Exc.:** $375   **VGood:** $275

COLT COMBAT COMMANDER (PRE-1970)

Semi-automatic; single action; 45 ACP, 38 Super, 9mm Para.; 7-shot (45 ACP), 9-shot (38 Super, 9mm); 4-1/2-inch barrel; 7 7/8-inch overall length; weighs 35 oz.; fixed sights; thumb grip safties; steel or alloy frame; grooved trigger; walnut grips; blue or satin nickel finish. Introduced 1950; dropped 1976.

45 ACP, 38 Super
Exc.: $800   **VGood:** $600   **Good:** $400
9mm
Exc.: $600   **VGood:** $450   **Good:** $300

COLT COMBAT COMMANDER MKIV SERIES 70

Semi-automatic; single action; 45 ACP, 38 Super, 9mm Para.; 7-shot (45 ACP), 9-shot (38 Super, 9mm); 4-1/4-inch barrel; 7-7/8-inchoverall length; weighs 36 oz.; fixed blade front sight; square notch rear; all steel frame; grooved trigger; lanyard-style hammer; checkered walnut grips; blue or nickel finish. Introduced, 1970; dropped 1983.

Perf.: $750   **Exc.:** $600   **VGood:** $400

Nickel finish
Perf.: $800   **Exc.:** $650   **VGood:** $450

COLT COMBAT COMMANDER LIGHTWEIGHT MKIV SERIES 70

Same specs as Combat Commander MKIV Series 70 except 45 ACP; weighs 27 oz.; aluminum alloy frame; Introduced 1970; dropped 1983.

Perf.: $750   **Exc.:** $650   **VGood:** $500

COLT COMBAT COMMANDER MKIV SERIES 80

Semi-automatic; 45 ACP, 38 Super Auto, 9mm Para.; 7-shot (45 ACP), 9-shot (38 Super, 9mm); 4-1/4-inch barrel; 8-inch overall length; weighs 36 oz.; fixed blade front sight; grooved trigger, hammer spur; arched housing, grip and thumb safeties; steel frame; rubber combat grips; blued finish, except for satin nickel (no longer offered) and stainless steel 45 version. Introduced, 1979; called Commander until 1981; discontinued.

Perf.: $750   **Exc.:** $600   **VGood:** $450

Stainless steel finish
Perf.: $800   **Exc.:** $650   **VGood:** $500

Satin nickel finish
Perf.: $850   **Exc.:** $700   **VGood:** $550

COLT COMBAT ELITE MKIV SERIES 80

Semi-automatic; single action; 38 Super, 45 ACP; 7-, 8-shot magazine; 5-inch barrel; 8-1/2-inch overall length; weighs 39 oz.; high profile sights with 3-dot system; checkered rubber combat grips; stainless steel frame; ordnance steel slide, internal parts; beveled magazine well; extended grip safety. Introduced, 1986; still in production.

Perf.: $750   **Exc.:** $600   **VGood:** $500

Colt Combat Government MKIV Series 80

Colt Double Eagle Combat Commander MKII Series 90

Colt Defender

Colt Delta Elite

Colt Gold Cup National Match MKIII

COLT COMBAT GOVERNMENT MKIV SERIES 70

Semi-automatic; single action; 45 ACP; 8-shot magazine; 5-inch barrel; 8-3/8-inch overall length; weighs 40 oz. Similar to Government Model except higher undercut front sight, white outlined rear; flat mainspring housing; longer trigger; beveled magazine well; angled ejection port; Colt/Pachmayr wrap-around grips; internal firing pin safety. Introduced 1973; dropped 1983.

Perf.: $650   **Exc.:** $550   **VGood:** $450

COLT COMBAT GOVERNMENT MKIV SERIES 80

Semi-automatic; single action; 45 ACP; 5-shot magazine; 5-inch barrel; 8-1/2-inch overall length; weighs 39 oz. Similar to Combat Government MKIV Series 70 with higher undercut front sight, white outlined rear; flat mainspring housing; longer trigger beveled magazine well; angled ejection port; Colt/Pachmayr wrap-around grips; internal firing pin safety; 45 with blue, satin or stainless finish; 9mm, 38 blue only. Introduced 1983; dropped 1996.

Perf.: $600   **Exc.:** $500   **VGood:** $400

COLT COMMANDER LIGHTWEIGHT MKIV SERIES 80

Semi-automatic; 45 ACP, 38 Super, 9mm Para.; 4-1/4-inch barrel, 8-inch overall length; 7-shot magazine (45 ACP), 9-shot (38 Super, 9mm); weighs 26-1/2 oz.; basic design of Government Model auto, but of lightweight alloy, reducing weight; checkered walnut grips; fixed sights; rounded hammer spur; blued, nickel finish. Introduced 1983; dropped 1997.

Perf.: $695   **Exc.:** $585   **VGood:** $495

COLT DEFENDER

Semi-automatic; 45 ACP, 7-shot magazine. Barrel: 3-inch. Weight: 22-1/2 oz. Length: 6-3/4-inch overall. Stocks: Pebble-finish rubber wraparound with finger grooves. Sights: White dot front, snag-free Colt competition rear. Features: Stainless finish; aluminum frame; combat-style hammer; Hi Ride grip safety,

extended manual safety, magazine disconnect safety. Introduced 1998.

Perf.: $895   **Exc.:** $775   **VGood:** $575

COLT DELTA ELITE

Semi-automatic; 10mm Auto; 8-shot; 5-inch barrel; 8-1/2-inch overall length; weighs 38 oz.; same general design as Government Model; 3-dot high profile combat sights; rubber combat stocks; internal firing pin safety; new recoil spring/buffer system; blued or matte stainless finish. Introduced 1987; dropped 1996.

Perf.: $950   **Exc.:** $825   **VGood:** $650

Matte stainless		
Perf.: $975	**Exc.:** $850	**VGood:** $675

COLT DELTA GOLD CUP

Same specs as Delta Elite except Accro adjustable rear sight; adjustable trigger; wrap-around grips; stainless steel finish. Introduced 1989; dropped 1991.

Perf.: $1200   **Exc.:** $1050   **VGood:** $8950

COLT DOUBLE EAGLE COMBAT COMMANDER MKII SERIES 90

Semi-automatic; double action; 40 S&W, 45 ACP; 8-shot magazine; 4-1/4-inch barrel; 7-3/4-inch overall length; weighs 36 oz.; blade front sight, windage-adjustable rear; 3-dot system; Colt Accro adjustable sight optional; stainless steel; checkered, curved extended triggerguard; wide steel trigger; decocking lever; traditional magazine release; beveled magazine well; grooved frontstrap; extended grip guard; combat-type hammer. Introduced 1991; dropped 1996.

Perf.: $850   **Exc.:** $650   **VGood:** $500

Accro sight		
Perf.: $650	**Exc.:** $550	**VGood:** $450

COLT DOUBLE EAGLE MKII SERIES 90

Semi-automatic; double action; 45 ACP; 8-shot magazine; 4-1/2-inch, 5-inch barrel; 8-1/2-inch overall length; weighs 39 oz.; blade front sight, windage-adjustable rear; black checkered thermoplastic grips; stainless steel construction;

matte finish; extended triggerguard; decocking lever; grooved frontstrap; beveled magazine well; rounded hammer; extended grip guard. Introduced 1989; dropped 1996.

Perf.: $850   **Exc.:** $650   **VGood:** $500

COLT DOUBLE EAGLE OFFICER'S MODEL MKIV SERIES 90

Semi-automatic; double action; 45 ACP; 8-shot magazine; 3-1/2-inch barrel; 7-1/4-inch overall length; weighs 35 oz.; stainless steel construction; blade front, windage-adjustable rear sight with 3-dot system; black checkered thermoplastic grips; matte finish; extended trigger guard; decocking lever; grooved frontstrap; beveled magazine well; rounded hammer; extended grip guard. Introduced 1989; dropped 1996.

Perf.: $850   **Exc.:** $650   **VGood:** $500

Lightweight model (25 oz.)		
Perf.: $900	**Exc.:** $700	**VGood:** $500

COLT GOLD CUP NATIONAL MATCH MKIII

Semi-automatic; 45 ACP, 38 Spl.; 5-inch match barrel; 8-1/2-inch overall length; weighs 37 oz.; Patridge front sight, Colt Elliason adjustable rear; arched or flat housing; wide, grooved trigger with adjustable stop; ribbed top slide; hand-fitted with improved ejection port. Introduced 1959; dropped 1970.

45 ACP		
Exc.: $1000	**VGood:** $800	**Good:** $650
38 Spl.		
Exc.: $1200	**VGood:** $950	**Good:** $800

COLT GOLD CUP NATIONAL MATCH MKIV SERIES 70

Semi-automatic; 45 ACP; 7-shot magazine; 5-inch barrel; 8-3/8-inch overall length; weighs 38-1/2 oz; undercut front sight, Colt Elliason adjustable rear; match-grade barrel, bushing; long, wide grooved trigger; flat grip housing; hand-fitted slide; checkered walnut grips; blued finish. Introduced 1970; dropped 1983.

Exc.: $1300   **VGood:** $995   **Good:** $700

Colt Gold Cup National Match MKIV Series 80

Colt Gold Cup Trophy

Colt Government Model 380 MKIV Series 80

Colt Government Model MKIV Series 80

Colt Huntsman

Colt Junior

Colt Model 1900

COLT GOLD CUP NATIONAL MATCH MKIV SERIES 80

Semi-automatic; single action; 45 ACP; 8-shot magazine; 5-inch barrel; 8-1/2-inch overall length; weighs 39 oz.; Patridge front sight, Colt-Elliason adjustable rear; match-grade barrel, bushing; long, wide trigger adjustable trigger stop; flat mainspring housing; hand-fitted slide; wider ejection port; checkered walnut grips; blue, stainless, bright stainless finish. Introduced 1983; dropped 1996.

Perf.: $950	**Exc.:** $775	**VGood:** $600
Stainless finish		
Perf.: $950	**Exc.:** $775	**VGood:** $600
Bright stainless		
Perf.: $1020	**Exc.:** $850	**VGood:** $675

COLT GOLD CUP TROPHY

Semi-automatic: 45 ACP, 8-shot magazine. Barrel: 5, with new design bushing. Weight: 39 oz. Length: 8-1/2. Stocks: Checkered rubber composite with silver-plated medallion. Sights: Patridge-style front, Colt-Elliason rear adjustable for windage and elevation, sight radius 6-3/4-inch. Features: Arched or flat housing; wide, grooved trigger with adjustable stop; ribbed-top slide, hand fitted, with improved ejection port. Available only from the Colt Custom Shop.

Perf.: $1250	**Exc.:** $1000	**VGood:** $800

COLT GOVERNMENT MODEL MKIV SERIES 70

Semi-automatic; single action; 45 ACP, 38 Super, 9mm Para.; 7-shot magazine; 5-inch barrel; 8-3/8-inch overall length; weighs 40 oz; ramp front sight, fixed square notch rear; grip, thumb safeties; grooved trigger; accurizor barrel, bushing; blue or nickel (45 only) finish. Redesigned, redesignated Colt Model 1911A1. Introduced 1970; dropped 1983.

Perf.: $925	**Exc.:** $700	**VGood:** $525
Nickel finish		
Perf.: $1000	**Exc.:** $750	**VGood:** $550

COLT GOVERNMENT MODEL MKIV SERIES 80

Semi-automatic; single action; 45 ACP, 38 Super, 9mm Para.; 7-, 8-shot magazine; 5-inch barrel; 8-1/2-inch overall length; weighs 38 oz.; ramp front sight,

fixed square notch rear; grip and thumb safeties; internal firing pin safety; grooved trigger; accurizor barrel bushing; checkered walnut grips; blue, nickel, satin nickel, bright stainless, stainless steel finish. Introduced 1983; still in production.

Blue, nickel, satin nickel finish		
Perf.: $775	**Exc.:** $650	**VGood:** $525
Stainless steel, bright stainless finish		
Perf.: $725	**Exc.:** $600	**VGood:** $475

COLT GOVERNMENT MODEL 380 MKIV SERIES 80

Semi-automatic; 380 ACP; 7-shot magazine; 3-inch barrel; 6-inch overall length; weighs 21-3/4 oz.; checkered composition stocks; ramp front sight, fixed square-notch rear; thumb and internal firing pin safeties; blue, nickel, satin nickel or stainless steel finish. Introduced 1983; dropped 1997.

Perf.: $750	**Exc.:** $650	**VGood:** $495
Nickel, satin nickel finish		
Perf.: $795	**Exc.:** $695	**VGood:** $525
Stainless steel finish		
Perf.: $595	**Exc.:** $495	**VGood:** $425

COLT HUNTSMAN, TARGETSMAN

Semi-automatic; 22 LR; 4-1/2-inch, 6-inch barrel; 9-inch overall length; checkered plastic grips; no hold-open device; fixed sights (Huntsman), adjustable sights and 6-inch barrel only (Targetsman). Introduced 1955; dropped 1977.

Huntsman		
Exc.: $595	**VGood:** $495	**Good:** $350
Targetsman		
Exc.: $650	**VGood:** $495	**Good:** $350

COLT JUNIOR

Semi-automatic; 22 Short, 25 ACP; 6-shot magazine; 2-1/4-inch barrel; 4-3/8-inch overall length; exposed hammer with round spur; checkered walnut stocks; fixed sights; blued. Initially produced in Spain by Astra, with early versions having Spanish markings as well as Colt identity; parts were assembled in U.S., sans Spanish identification after GCA '68 import ban. Introduced 1968; dropped 1973.

Spanish model		
Exc.: $305	**VGood:** $275	**Good:** $225
U.S.-made model		
Exc.: $425	**VGood:** $375	**Good:** $250

COLT MODEL 1900

Semi-automatic; 38 ACP; 7-shot magazine; 6-inch barrel; 9-inch overall length; spur hammer; plain walnut stocks; blued finish. Dangerous to fire modern high-velocity ammo. Was made in several variations. Introduced 1900; dropped 1903. Collector value.

Standard model		
Exc.: $7500	**VGood:** $5650	**Good:** $4150
Altered sight safety		
Exc.: $10500	**VGood:** $7900	**Good:** $5100

COLT MODEL 1900 ARMY

Same specs as Model 1900. Marked U.S. on left side of triggerguard bow, with inspector markings.

Exc.: $7500	**VGood:** $5500	**Good:** $450

COLT MODEL 1900 USN

Same specs as Model 1900. Marked USN and Navy serial number on left side of frame, Colt serial number on right.

Exc.: $10,000	**VGood:** $8500	**Good:** $7000

COLT MODEL 1902 MILITARY

Semi-automatic; 38 ACP; 8-shot magazine; 9-inch overall length; 6-inch barrel; fixed blade front, notched V rear sight; checkered hard rubber stocks; round-back hammer (changed to spur type in 1908); blued finish. Dangerous to fire modern high-velocity loads. Early production with serrations on front area of slide. U.S. Army marked pistols between serial numbers 15,001 and 15,200 have inspector stampings, slide serrations at front. Introduced 1902; dropped 1929.

Early production		
Exc.: $4500	**VGood:** $3750	**Good:** $2500
Standard production		
Exc.: $4225	**VGood:** $3500	**Good:** $2000
U.S. Army test pistols		
Exc.: $8500	**VGood:** $6500	**Good:** $5500

Colt Model 1902 Military

Colt Model 1902 Sporting

Colt Model 1903 Pocket Hammerless (Early Model)

Colt Model 1903 Pocket Hammerless (Fourth Issue) U.S. Property marked

Colt Model 1905

Colt Model 1911 Military (Springfield Armory)

Colt Vest Pocket Model 1908 Hammerless

COLT MODEL 1902 SPORTING

Semi-automatic; 38 ACP; 8-shot magazine; 6-inch barrel; 9-inch overall length; sans safety; checkered hard rubber grips; blade front sight, fixed notch V rear; round hammer. Not safe with modern loads. Manufactured 1902 to 1908.

Exc.: $4500   **VGood:** $3250   **Good:** $2500

COLT MODEL 1903 POCKET HAMMER

Semi-automatic; 38 ACP; 4-1/2-inch barrel; 7-1/2-inch overall length; round back hammer changed to spur type in 1908; checkered hard rubber grips; blued finish. Not safe with modern ammo. Manufactured 1903 to 1929.

Exc.: $1850   **VGood:** $1550   **Good:** $850

COLT MODEL 1903 POCKET HAMMERLESS (FIRST ISSUE)

Semi-automatic; 32 ACP; 8-shot magazine; 4-inch barrel; 7-inch overall length; fixed sights; internal hammer; slidelock; grip safety; hard rubber stocks; blued or nickel finish; barrel takedown bushing. Manufactured from 1903 until 1908.

Exc.: $1850   **VGood:** $1550   **Good:** $1250

COLT MODEL 1903 POCKET HAMMERLESS (SECOND ISSUE)

Same specs as First Issue except 3 3/4-inch barrel. Made from 1908 until 1910.

Exc.: $800   **VGood:** $600   **Good:** $450

COLT MODEL 1903 POCKET HAMMERLESS (THIRD ISSUE)

Same specs as First Issue except no barrel bushing. Introduced 1910; dropped 1926.

Exc.: $800   **VGood:** $600   **Good:** $450

COLT MODEL 1903 POCKET HAMMERLESS (FOURTH ISSUE)

Same specs as First Model except magazine safety. On all guns above serial number 468,097, safety disconnector prevents firing cartridge in chamber if magazine is removed. Manufactured from 1926 to 1945.

Exc.: $775   **VGood:** $595   **Good:** $400

U.S. Property marked
Exc.: $1000   **VGood:** $850   **Good:** $750

COLT MODEL 1905

Semi-automatic; single action; 45 ACP; 7-shot magazine; 5-inch barrel; snub-type and spur hammers; checkered, varnished walnut stocks; case-hardened hammer; blued finish; forerunner of the Model 1911 45 Auto; produced in standard, military test (with loaded chamber indicator, separate serial range 1-200) and shoulder-stocked models. Introduced 1905; dropped 1911.

Early production (s/n below 700)
Exc.: $5500   **VGood:** $3250   **Good:** $2150
Standard production
Exc.: $3500   **VGood:** $2250   **Good:** $1300
Military test model
Exc.: $8500   **VGood:** $6500   **Good:** $4500
With shoulder stock
Exc.: $12,500   **VGood:** $10,000   **Good:** $8500

COLT MODEL 1908 POCKET HAMMERLESS (FIRST ISSUE)

Semi-automatic; 380 ACP; 7-shot magazine; 3-3/4-inch barrel; 7-inch overall length; fixed sights; hammerless; slidelock; grip safety; hard rubber stocks; blued finish. Same general design, specs as Model 1903 Pocket Hammerless. Manufactured from 1908 to 1911.

Exc.: $1000   **VGood:** $800   **Good:** $650

COLT MODEL 1908 POCKET HAMMERLESS (SECOND ISSUE)

Same specs as First Issue sans barrel bushing. Manufactured from 1911 to 1926.

Exc.: $550   **VGood:** $450   **Good:** $375

COLT MODEL 1908 POCKET HAMMERLESS (THIRD ISSUE)

Same specs as Second Issue except safety disconnector installed on guns with serial numbers above 92,894. Introduced 1926; dropped 1945.

Exc.: $550   **VGood:** $350   **Good:** $295
U.S. Property marked3
Exc.: $1500   **VGood:** $1250   **Good:** $1000

COLT MODEL 1911 COMMERCIAL

Semi-automatic; also known as Government Model; 45 ACP; 7-shot magazine; 5-inch barrel; weighs 39 oz.; checkered walnut grips; fixed sights; blued finish; commercial variations with letter "C-inch preceding serial number. Introduced 1912; dropped 1923 to be replaced by Model 1911A1.

Early production High Polish Blue (through s/n 4500)
Exc.: $12,000   **VGood:** $10,000   **Good:** $7500
Standard model
Exc.: $4500   **VGood:** $3000   **Good:** $1750

COLT MODEL 1911 BRITISH 455

Same specs as standard model but carries "Calibre 455" on right side of slide and may have broad arrow British ordnance stamp; made 1915 to 1916; 11,000 manufactured.

Exc.: $3500   **VGood:** $2750   **Good:** $2100

COLT MODEL 1911 MILITARY

Same specs as the civilian version except serial numbers not preceded by the letter C; produced from 1912 to 1924; bright blue finish, early production; duller blue during war. Parkerized finish indicates post-war reworking and commands lesser value than original blue finish. Navy issue marked "Model of 1911 U.S. Navy" on slide.

Standard
Exc.: $2000   **VGood:** $1400   **Good:** $850
U.S. Navy marked
Exc.: $6000   **VGood:** $4800   **Good:** $3600
Remington-UMC (21,676)
Exc.: $2200   **VGood:** $1700   **Good:** $950
Springfield Armory (25,767)
Exc.: $2500   **VGood:** $2000   **Good:** $950

COLT MODEL 1911 RUSSIAN

Same specs as the standard version except Russian characters ANGLOZAKAZIVAT stamped on the slide. All were in 45 ACP, carrying serial numbers C-50000 through C-85000. This is an exceedingly rare collector item.

Exc.: $5000   **VGood:** $4250   **Good:** $3750

Colt 1911A1

Colt National Match

Colt Model 1991A1 Compact

Colt Super 38 National Match

Colt Mustang

Colt Mustang Plus II

.38 SUPER (2007)

1911-style (not 1911A1-style) single-action semi-auto chambered in .38 Super. Nine-shot magazine, double-diamond walnut or checkered hard rubber stocks, fixed 3-dot sights, 5" barrel. Stainless, bright stainless or blued finish.

Exc.: $900   **VGood:** $675   **Good:** $425

COLT MODEL 1911A1

Semi-automatic; single action; 45 ACP, 7-shot magazine; 5-inch barrel; 8-1/2-inch overall length; weighs 38 oz.; checkered walnut (early production) or brown composition (military version) grips; ramped blade front sight, fixed high-profile square notch rear; Parkerized finish. Same specs as Model 1911 except longer grip safety spur; arched mainspring housing; finger relief cuts in frame behind trigger; plastic grips. During WWII other firms produced the 1911A1 under Colt license, including Remington-Rand, Ithaca Gun Co., and Union Switch & Signal Co. These government models bear imprint of licensee on slide. In 1970, this model was redesigned and redesignated as Government Model MKIV Series 70; approximately 850 1911A1 guns were equipped with split-collet barrel bushing and BB prefix serial number which adds to the value. Modern version (marked "Colt M1911A1™") continues serial number range used on original GI 1911A1 guns and comes with one magazine and molded carrying case. Introduced 1923; still produced.

Commercial model (C s/n)		
Exc.: $1250	**VGood:** $1000	**Good:** $850
BB s/n prefix		
Exc.: $950	**VGood:** $800	**Good:** $600
Military model		
Exc.: $950	**VGood:** $650	**Good:** $500
Singer Mfg. Co. (500)		
Exc.: $24,000	**VGood:** $18,500	**Good:** $15,000
Union Switch & Signal (55,000)		
Exc.: $2650	**VGood:** $2250	**Good:** $1750
Remington-Rand (1,000,000)		
Exc.: $1200	**VGood:** $975	**Good:** $775
Ithaca Gun Co. (370,000)		
Exc.: $1250	**VGood:** $1050	**Good:** $850
45/22 conversion unit		
Exc.: $650	**VGood:** $550	**Good:** $400
22/45 conversion unit		
Exc.: $1500	**VGood:** $1000	**Good:** $800

COLT NATIONAL MATCH

Semi-automatic; 45 ACP; 7-shot; 5-inch barrel; 8-1/2-inch overall length; weighs 37 oz.; adjustable rear, ramp front target sight; match-grade barrel; hand-honed action. Also available with fixed sights. Introduced 1933; dropped 1941.

Fixed sights		
Exc.: $2750	**VGood:** $2000	**Good:** $1600
Target sights		
Exc.: $3250	**VGood:** $2500	**Good:** $1850

COLT SUPER 38

Semi-automatic; double action; 38 Colt Super; 9-shot magazine; fixed sights standard, adjustable rear sights available. Same frame as 1911 commercial until 1970. Introduced in 1929. In 1937, the design of the firing pin, safety, hammer, etc. were changed and the model renamed the New Style Super 38. Still in production as Government Model Mark IV/Series 80.

Exc.: $1400	**VGood:** $1100	**Good:** $700
Pre-WWI		
Exc.: $2500	**VGood:** $2000	**Good:** $1500

COLT SUPER 38 NATIONAL MATCH

Same specs as Colt Super 38 except hand-honed action; adjustable target sights; match-grade barrel. Manufactured from 1935 to 1941.

Exc.: $4500   **VGood:** $3500   **Good:** $2500

COLT MODEL 1991A1

Semi-automatic; 45 ACP; 7-shot magazine; 5-inch barrel; 8-1/2-inch overall length; weighs 38 oz.; ramped blade front sight, fixed square notch high-profile rear; checkered black composition grips; Parkerized finish; continuation of serial number range used on original GI 1911A1 guns. Introduced 1991; still in production.

New: $700   **Perf.:** $650   **Exc.:** $525

COLT MODEL 1991A1 COMMANDER

Same specs as the Model 1991A1 except 4-1/4-inch barrel; Parkerized finish. Comes in molded case. Made in U.S. by Colt's Mfg. Co. Introduced 1993.

New: $700   **Perf.:** $650   **Exc.:** $525

COLT MODEL 1991A1 COMPACT

Same specs as the Model 1991A1 except 3-1/2-inch barrel; 7-inch overall length; 3/8-inch shorter height. Comes with one 6-shot magazine, molded case. Made in U.S. by Colt's Mfg. Co. Introduced 1993.

New: $700   **Perf.:** $650   **Exc.:** $525

COLT MUSTANG

Semi-automatic; 380 ACP; 5-, 6-shot magazine; 2-3/4-inch barrel; 5-1/2-inch overall length; weighs 18-1/2 oz.; steel frame; stainless, blued or nickel finish. Similar to Colt Government Model 380. Introduced 1987; dropped 1997.

Perf.: $550	**Exc.:** $475	**VGood:** $400
Nickel finish		
Perf.: $595	**Exc.:** $495	**VGood:** $425
Stainless finish		
Perf.: $595	**Exc.:** $495	**VGood:** $425

COLT MUSTANG PLUS II

Same specs as Mustang except 7-shot magazine; weighs 20 oz.; composition grips; blued or stainless finish. Introduced 1988; dropped 1997.

Perf.: $550   **Exc.:** $475   **VGood:** $400

COLT MUSTANG POCKET LITE

Same specs as Mustang except aluminum alloy frame; 2-3/4-inch barrel; weighs 12-1/2 oz; blue or stainless finish. Introduced 1987; no longer produced.

Perf.: $550	**Exc.:** $475	**VGood:** $400
Stainless finish		
Perf.: $595	**Exc.:** $495	**VGood:** $425

COLT CZ40

Semi-automatic; double action only; 40 S&W, 10-shot magazine. Barrel: 4-inch. Weight: 34 oz. Length: 7-3/4-inch overall. Stock: Textured black polymer. Sights: Dovetailed white dot front, No-Snag rear with two white dots. Features: Double-action-only mechanism; alloy frame, carbon steel slide; matte blue finish. Introduced 1998. Made under license for Colt; imported from the Czech Republic; no longer in production.

New: $795   **Perf.:** $625   **Exc.:** $475

Colt Officer's ACP
MKIV Series 80

Colt 1911 – WWI Replica

Colt Woodsman
(First Issue)

Colt Pony

Colt Woodsman
(Second Issue)

COLT OFFICER'S ACP MKIV SERIES 80

Semi-automatic; single action; 45 ACP; 6-shot magazine; 3-1/2-inch barrel; 7-1/4-inch overall length; weighs 34 oz. (steel frame), 24 oz. (alloy frame); checkered walnut or rubber composite grips; blade front sight, square notch rear; 3-dot sight system; grooved trigger; flat mainspring housing; blued, matte, stainless or bright stainless finishes. Introduced 1985; discontinued 1997.

Perf.: $625	**Exc.:** $525	**VGood:** $435
Matte finish		
Perf.: $575	**Exc.:** $490	**VGood:** $420
Stainless steel finish		
Perf.: $640	**Exc.:** $525	**VGood:** $450
Bright stainless finish		
Perf.: $715	**Exc.:** $600	**VGood:** $525
Alloy frame		
Perf.: $550	**Exc.:** $450	**VGood:** $40

COLT PONY AUTOMATIC PISTOL

Caliber: 380 ACP. Barrel: 2-3/4-inch. Weight: 19 oz. Length: 5-1/2-inch. Stocks: Black composition. Sights: Ramp front, fixed rear. Features: Stainless steel construction. Double-action-only mechanism; recoil-reducing locked breech. Produced in 1997 only.

Perf.: $595	**Exc.:** $525	**VGood:** $455

COLT PONY POCKETLITE LIGHTWEIGHT

Similar to Colt Pony, except has aluminum and stainless steel construction; brushed finish; 380 ACP; 13 oz. Produced from 1997 to 1999.

Perf.: $595	**Exc.:** $525	**VGood:** $455

COLT 1911 – WWI REPLICA

Single-action semi-auto chambered in .45 ACP. Faithful external reproduction of the WWI-era service pistol with original-style rollmarks, grips, sights, etc. Series 70 lockwork.

NIB: $900	**Exc.:** $795	**VGood:** $650

COLT CONCEALED CARRY

Chopped, lightweight 1911-style semi-auto chambered in .45 ACP. Weighs 25 oz. unloaded; overall length 6.75"; 7+1 capacity; Series 80 lockwork; black anodized aluminum frame with double-diamond wood grips.

NIB: $850	**Exc.:** $775	**VGood:** $615

COLT .38 SUPER (2006)

1911-style single-action semi-auto chambered in .38 Super. Nine-shot magazine, double-diamond walnut or checkered hard rubber stocks, fixed 3-dot sights, 5" barrel. Stainless, bright stainless or blued finish.

NIB: $835	**Exc.:** $695	**VGood:** $525

COLT WOODSMAN (FIRST ISSUE)

Semi-automatic; 22 LR standard velocity; 10-shot magazine; 6-1/2-inch barrel; 10-1/2-inch overall length. Designation, "The Woodsman," added after serial number 34,000; adjustable sights; checkered walnut grips. Introduced 1915; replaced 1943.

Exc.: $1295	**VGood:** $995	**Good:** $650

COLT WOODSMAN (FIRST ISSUE) SPORT MODEL

Same specs as First Issue Woodsman except adjustable rear sight; adjustable or fixed front; 4-1/2-inch barrel; 8-1/2-inch overall length; fires standard- or high-velocity 22 LR ammo. Introduced 1933; dropped 1943.

Exc.: $1295	**VGood:** $995	**Good:** $650

COLT WOODSMAN (FIRST ISSUE) MATCH TARGET

Same specs as Woodsman First Issue except 6-1/2-inch flat-sided barrel; 11-inch overall length; adjustable rear sight, blade front; checkered walnut one-piece extension grips; blued. Introduced 1938; dropped 1943.

Exc.: $2495	**VGood:** $1895	**Good:** $1095
U.S. Property marked		
Exc.: $2700	**VGood:** $2200	**Good:** $1500

COLT WOODSMAN (SECOND ISSUE)

Semi-automatic; 22 LR; 10-shot magazine; 6-1/2-inch barrel; 10-1/2-inch overall length; slide stop; hold-open device; heat-treated mainspring housing for use with high-velocity cartridges; heavier barrel; push-button magazine release on top side of frame. Introduced in 1932; dropped 1948.

Exc.: $895	**VGood:** $695	**Good:** $495

COLT WOODSMAN (SECOND ISSUE) SPORT MODEL

Same specs as the Second Issue Woodsman except 4-1/2-inch barrel; 9-inch overall length; plastic grips. Introduced 1947; dropped 1955.

Exc.: $895	**VGood:** $695	**Good:** $495

COLT WOODSMAN (SECOND ISSUE) MATCH TARGET 4-1/2-INCH

Same specs as Second Issue Woodsman except 4-1/2-inch heavy barrel. Introduced 1947; dropped 1955.

Exc.: $1295	**VGood:** $995	**Good:** $695

COLT WOODSMAN (SECOND ISSUE) MATCH TARGET 6-INCH

Same specs as Second Issue Woodsman except flat-sided 6-inch heavy barrel; 10-1/2-inch overall length; 22 LR, standard- or high-velocity; checkered walnut or plastic grips; click-adjustable rear sight, ramp front; blued. Introduced 1947; dropped 1955.

Exc.: $1095	**VGood:** $895	**Good:** $600

COLT WOODSMAN (THIRD ISSUE)

Semi-automatic; 22 LR; 10-shot; 6-1/2-inch barrel; longer grip; larger thumb safety; slide stop magazine disconnector; thumbrest; plastic or walnut grips; magazine catch on bottom of grip; click-adjustable rear sight, ramp front. Introduced 1955; dropped 1977.

Exc.: $750	**VGood:** $650	**Good:** $450

Colt Woodsman (Third Issue) Match Target 6"

Colt 3rd Model Derringer

Colt Python Elite

Colt 357 Magnum

Colt 38 SF-VI

Colt Anaconda

Colt Agent (Second Issue)

Colt Army Special

COLT WOODSMAN (THIRD ISSUE) SPORT MODEL

Same specs as Third Issue Woodsman except 4-1/2-inch barrel. Introduced 1955; dropped 1977.

Exc.: $750   **VGood:** $650   **Good:** $450

COLT WOODSMAN (THIRD ISSUE) MATCH TARGET 4-1/2-INCH

Same specs as Third Issue Woodsman except 4-1/2-inch heavy barrel. Introduced 1955; dropped 1977.

Perf.: $600   **Exc.:** $550   **VGood:** $500

COLT WOODSMAN (THIRD ISSUE) MATCH TARGET 6-INCH

Same specs as Third Issue Woodsman except 6-inch heavy barrel. Introduced 1955; dropped 1977.

Perf.: $950   **Exc.:** $850   **VGood:** $600

COLT 3RD MODEL DERRINGER

Derringer; single shot; 41 rimfire; 2-1/2-inch pivoting barrel; varnished walnut grips; bronze frame, nickel- or sliver-plated; blued or plated barrels. Introduced 1875; dropped 1912. (Note: Since 1959, Colt has produced this model intermittently in 22 caliber; it should not be confused with the 41 version.)

Exc.: $1200   **VGood:** $850   **Good:** $725

S/N under 2000

Exc.: $2500   **VGood:** $2000   **Good:** $1200

COLT 38 SF-VI

Revolver; double action; 38 Spl.; 6-shot cylinder; 2-inch barrel; 7-inch overall length; weighs 21 oz.; checkered black composition grips; ramp front sight, fixed rear; new (for Colt) lockwork; made of stainless steel. Made in U.S. by Colt's Mfg. Introduced 1995; dropped 1996.

New: $525   **Perf.:** $400   **Exc.:** $350

COLT PYTHON ELITE REVOLVER

Revolver; double action; 357 Magnum (handles all 38 Spec.), 6-shot. Barrel: 6-inch, with ventilated

rib. Weight: 43-1/2 oz. Length: 11-1/2-inch overall. Stocks: Walnut. Sights: 1/8-inch ramp front, adjustable notch rear. Features: Ventilated rib; grooved, crisp trigger; swing-out cylinder; target hammer. Introduced 2001.

New: $1500   **Perf.:** $1150   **Exc.:** $900

COLT 357 MAGNUM

Revolver; double action; 357 Mag.; 6-shot swing-out cylinder; 4-inch, 6-inch barrel; 9-1/4-inch overall length (4-inch barrel); available as service revolver or in target version; latter with wide hammer spur, target grips; checkered walnut grips; Accro rear sight, ramp front; blued finish. Introduced 1953; dropped 1961.

Perf.: $625   **Exc.:** $550   **VGood:** $475

Target Model

Perf.: $700   **Exc.:** $575   **VGood:** $4500

COLT AGENT (FIRST ISSUE)

Revolver; double action; 38 Spl.; 6-shot swing-out cylinder; 2-inch barrel; 6-3/4-inch overall length; weighs 14 oz.; minor variation of Colt Cobra with shorter stub grip for maximum concealment; Colt alloy frame, sideplate; steel cylinder, barrel; no housing around ejector rod; square butt; blued finish. Introduced 1955; dropped 1972.

Perf.: $600   **Exc.:** $550   **VGood:** $420

COLT AGENT (SECOND ISSUE)

Same specs as Agent First Issue except 6-5/8-inch overall length; weighs 16 oz; ramp front sight, square notch rear; checkered walnut grips; grip design extends just below bottom of frame. Introduced 1973; dropped 1981.

Perf.: $495   **Exc.:** $375   **VGood:** $300

COLT AGENT (THIRD ISSUE)

Same specs as Agent First Issue except shrouded ejector rod; alloy frame; Parkerized-type finish. Introduced 1982; dropped 1986.

Perf.: $395   **Exc.:** $325   **VGood:** $285

COLT ANACONDA

Revolver; double action; 44 Rem. Mag., 45 LC; 6-shot cylinder; 4-inch, 6-inch, 8-inch barrel; 11-5/8-inch overall length; weighs 53 oz.; red insert front sight, white-outline adjustable rear; finger-grooved

black neoprene combat grips; stainless steel construction; ventilated barrel rib; offset bolt notches in cylinder; full-length ejector rod housing; wide spur hammer. Introduced 1990. Add 25 percent for camo finish; add 15 percent for factory ported barrel.

New: $1250   **Perf.:** $1000   **Exc.:** $900

COLT ARMY SPECIAL

Revolver; double action; 32-20, 38 Spl., 41 Colt; 6-shot cylinder; 4-inch, 4-1/2-inch, 5-inch, 6-inch barrels; 9-1/4-inch overall length (4-inch barrel); 41-caliber frame; hard rubber grips; fixed sights; blued or nickel finish. Not safe for modern 38 Special high-velocity loads in guns chambered for that caliber. Introduced 1908; dropped 1927.

Exc.: $750   **VGood:** $675   **Good:** $500

COLT BANKER'S SPECIAL

Revolver; double action; 22 LR (with countersunk chambers after 1932), 38 New Police, 38 S&W; 6-shot swing-out cylinder; 2-inch barrel; 6-1/2-inch overall length; essentially the same as pre-1972 Detective Special, but with shorter cylinder of Police Positive rather than that of Police Positive Special; a few produced with Fitzgerald cutaway triggerguard; checkered hammer spur, trigger; blued or nickel finish. Low production run on 22 gives it collector value. Introduced 1926; dropped 1940.

22 blue finish		
Exc.: $1750	**VGood:** $1250	**Good:** $800
22 nickel finish		
Exc.: $2250	**VGood:** $1600	**Good:** $1000
38 blue finish		
Exc.: $850	**VGood:** $650	**Good:** $400
38 nickel finish		
Exc.: $1200	**VGood:** $800	**Good:** $500

COLT BISLEY

Revolver; single action; 455 Eley, 45, 44-40, 41, 38-40, 32-20; with trigger, hammer and grips redesigned for target shooting. Target model features target sights, flat-top frame. Bisley version of Colt SAA revolver first offered in flat-top target version in 1896 for use in target matches held at Bisley Common in England. The revolver's good performance encouraged Colt to offer it both in target and standard sighted versions until 1912. Bisley version featured

Colt Bisley

Colt Buntline Special

Colt Camp Perry Model (Second Issue)

Colt Cobra (First Issue)

Colt Cobra (Second Issue)

Colt Commando Special

Colt Detective Special (First Issue)

Colt Detective Special (Second Issue)

Colt Detective Special (Third Issue)

a longer, more angled grip frame that placed the hand at almost a 90-degree angle to the bore. Parts, except for triggerguard, backstrap, grips, mainspring, hammer, and trigger, are totally interchangeable with standard Colt SAA. Standard calibers, barrel lengths, and finishes same as 1st Generation Colt SAA. Manufactured from 1894 to 1913.

Standard model		
Exc.: $7000	**VGood:** $4500	**Good:** $2500
Target model		
Exc.: $12,000	**VGood:** $7500	**Good:** $4000

COLT BUNTLINE SPECIAL

Revolver; single action; 45 Colt; 12-inch barrel; case-hardened frame; hard rubber or walnut grips; designed after guns made as presentation pieces for author Ned Buntline. Introduced 1957; dropped 1992.

2nd Generation (1957-1975)		
Perf.: $1695	**Exc.:** $1275	**VGood:** $1000
3rd Generation (1976-1992)		
Perf.: $1250	**Exc.:** $850	**VGood:** $700

COLT CAMP PERRY MODEL (FIRST ISSUE)

Single shot; 22 LR, with countersunk chamber for high-velocity ammo after 1930; 10-inch barrel; 13-3/4-inch overall length; built on frame of Colt Officers Model; checkered walnut grips; hand-finished action; adjustable target sights; trigger, backstrap, hammer spur checkered; blued finish, with top, back of frame stippled to reduce glare. Chamber, barrel are single unit, pivoting to side for loading and extraction. Introduced 1926; dropped 1934.

Exc.: $2000	**VGood:** $1600	**Good:** $1000

COLT CAMP PERRY MODEL (SECOND ISSUE)

Same specs as First Issue except 8-inch barrel; 12-inch overall length; shorter hammer fall. Only 440 produced. Collector value. Introduced 1934; dropped 1941.

Perf.: $3000	**Exc.:** $2000	**VGood:** $1500

COLT COBRA (FIRST ISSUE)

Revolver; double action; 22 LR, 32 New Police, 38 New Police, 38 Spl.; 6-shot swing-out cylinder; 2-inch, 3-inch, 4-inch, 5-inch barrels; 3-inch, 4-inch, 5-inch barrel styles special order; based on pre-1972 Detective Special, except frame, sideplate of high-tensile aluminum alloy; Coltwood plastic grips on later guns, checkered wood on early issues; square butt, early issue, replaced by round butt; optional hammer shroud; blue finish, matted on top, rear of frame; shrouded ejector rod (later issue). Introduced 1951; dropped 1972.

Perf.: $445	**Exc.:** $325	**VGood:** $250
Nickel finish		
Perf.: $475	**Exc.:** $355	**VGood:** $295
22 LR		
Perf.: $575	**Exc.:** $425	**VGood:** $300

COLT COBRA (SECOND ISSUE)

Same specs as Cobra First Issue except integral protective shroud enclosing ejector rod. Introduced 1973; dropped 1981.

Perf.: $485	**Exc.:** $375	**VGood:** $295

COLT COMMANDO

Revolver; double action; 38 Spl.; 6-shot cylinder; 2-inch, 4-inch, 6-inch barrels; plastic grips; sand-blasted blue finish. Government contract issue made to military specs; a downgraded version of the Colt Official Police. Introduced 1942; dropped 1945.

Exc.: $450	**VGood:** $325	**Good:** $250

COLT COMMANDO SPECIAL

Revolver; 38 Spl.; 6-shot cylinder; 2-inch barrel; 6-5/8-inch overall length; weighs 22 oz.; steel frame; combat grade finish; rubber grips. Identical to Detective Special. Introduced 1984; dropped 1987.

Perf.: $475	**Exc.:** $375	**VGood:** $325

COLT DETECTIVE SPECIAL (FIRST ISSUE)

Revolver; double action; 38 Spl.; 6-shot swing-out cylinder; 2-inch, 3-inch barrels; 6-3/4-inch overall length; rounded butt introduced in 1934; blue or nickel finish. Introduced 1927; dropped 1936.

Exc.: $850	**VGood:** $725	**Good:** $650
Nickel finish		
Exc.: $900	**VGood:** $800	**Good:** $725

COLT DETECTIVE SPECIAL (SECOND ISSUE)

Same specs as First Issue except 32 New Police, 38 New Police; heavier barrel; integral protective shroud enclosing ejector rod; frame, sideplate, cylinder, barrel, internal parts of high-tensile alloy steel; plastic or walnut Bulldog-type grips; fixed rear sight; notch milled in topstrap, serrated ramp front; checkered hammer spur; blue or nickel finish. Introduced 1947; dropped 1972.

Perf.: $535	**Exc.:** $450	**VGood:** $350
Nickel finish		
Perf.: $600	**Exc.:** $475	**VGood:** $395

COLT DETECTIVE SPECIAL (THIRD ISSUE)

Same specs as Second Issue except 38 Spl.; shrouded ejector rod; wrap-around walnut grips. Introduced 1973; dropped 1986.

Perf.: $475	**Exc.:** $325	**VGood:** $275

COLT DETECTIVE SPECIAL (FOURTH ISSUE)

Same specs as Third Issue except 2-inch barrel only; weighs 22 oz.; 6-5/8-inch overall length; black composition grips; ramp front sight, fixed square notch rear; glare-proof sights; grooved trigger; Colt blue finish. Made in U.S. by Colt's Mfg. Reintroduced 1993; no longer produced.

New: $425	**Perf.:** $375	**Exc.:** $325

COLT DIAMONDBACK

Revolver; double action; 38 Spl., 22 LR; 6-shot swing-out cylinder; 2-1/2-inch, 4-inch (22 LR), 6-inch barrel; vent-rib barrel; scaled-down version of Python; target-type adjustable rear sight, ramp front; full checkered walnut grips; integral rounded rib beneath barrel shrouds, ejector rod; broad checkered hammer spur. Introduced 1966; dropped 1986.

Perf.: $1000	**Exc.:** $750	**VGood:** $475
Nickel finish		
Perf.: $1200	**Exc.:** $850	**VGood:** $550
22 LR		
Perf.: $800	**Exc.:** $900	**VGood:** $650

Colt Detective Special (Fourth Issue)

Colt Diamondback

Colt Frontier Scout

Colt Lawman MKIII

Colt Navy Model 1889 (First Issue)

Colt Model 1905 Marine Corps

Colt Model 1878 Frontier

Colt Navy Model 1892-1903 (Second Issue)

COLT FRONTIER SCOUT

Revolver; single action; 22 LR, 22 Long, 22 Short; interchangeable cylinder for 22 WMR; 4-1/2-inch barrel; 9-15/16-inch overall length; originally introduced with alloy frame; steel frame, blue finish introduced in 1959; fixed sights; plastic or wooden grips. Introduced 1958; dropped 1971.

Alloy frame		
Perf.: $600	**Exc.:** $425	**VGood:** $325
Blue finish, plastic grips		
Perf.: $600	**Exc.:** $400	**VGood:** $300
Nickel finish, wood grips		
Perf.: $650	**Exc.:** $475	**VGood:** $350
With 22 WMR cylinder		
Perf.: $650	**Exc.:** $475	**VGood:** $375

COLT FRONTIER SCOUT BUNTLINE

Same specs as Frontier Scout except 9-1/2-inch barrel. Introduced 1959; dropped 1971.

Perf.: $600   **Exc.:** $425   **VGood:** $325

COLT KING COBRA

Revolver; double action; 357 Mag.; 6-shot cylinder; 2-1/2-inch, 4-inch, 6-inch barrels; 9-inch overall length (4-inch barrel); weighs 42 oz.; adjustable white outline rear sight, red insert ramp front; full-length contoured ejector rod housing, barrel rib; matte finish; stainless steel construction. Introduced 1986; dropped 1992.

Perf.: $500   **Exc.:** $425   **VGood:** $375

COLT MAGNUM CARRY REVOLVER

Caliber: 357 Mag., 6-shot. Barrel: 2-inch. Weight: 21 oz. Length: NA. Stocks: Combat-style rubber. Sights: Ramp front, fixed notch rear. Features: Stainless steel construction. Smooth combat trigger. Introduced 1998. No longer produced.

New: $525   **Perf.:** $475   **Exc.:** $400

COLT LAWMAN MKIII

Revolver; double action; 357 Mag.; also chambers 38 Spl.; 2-inch, 4-inch barrels; 9-3/8-inch overall length (4-inch barrel); choice of square, round butt walnut

grips; fixed sights; blued, nickel finish. Introduced 1969; dropped 1983.

Perf.: $400   **Exc.:** $300   **VGood:** $250

Nickel finish		
Perf.: $425	**Exc.:** $325	**VGood:** $275

COLT LAWMAN MKV

Same specs as Lawman MKIII except redesigned lockwork to reduce double-action trigger pull; faster lock time; redesigned grips; shrouded ejector rod (2-inch barrel); fixed sights; solid rib. Introduced 1984; dropped 1985.

Perf.: $375   **Exc.:** $275   **VGood:** $225

Nickel finish		
Perf.: $395	**Exc.:** $295	**VGood:** $250

COLT METROPOLITAN MKIII

Revolver; double action; 38 Spl.; 6-shot swing-out cylinder; 4-inch barrel; designed for urban law enforcement; fixed sights; choice of service, target grips of checkered walnut; blued finish, standard; nickel, optional. Introduced 1969; dropped 1972.

Perf.: $350   **Exc.:** $300   **VGood:** $200

COLT MODEL 1877 LIGHTNING

Revolver; double action; 32 Colt, 38 Colt; 6-shot cylinder; 4-1/2-inch to 10-inch barrels with ejector; 1-1/2-inch, 2-1/2-inch, 3-1/2-inch, 4-1/2-inch, 6-inch sans ejector; fixed sights; blued or nickel finish; hard rubber grips. Manufactured 1877 to 1909.

Exc.: $2000   **VGood:** $1500   **Good:** $750

COLT MODEL 1877 THUNDERER

Revolver; double action; 41 Colt; 6-shot cylinder; 4-1/2-inch to 10-inch barrels with ejector; 1-1/2-inch, 2-1/2-inch, 3-1/2-inch, 4-1/2-inch, 6-inch sans ejector; fixed sights; blued or nickel finish; hard rubber grips. Manufactured 1877 to 1909.

Exc.: $2000   **VGood:** $1500   **Good:** $750

COLT MODEL 1878 FRONTIER

Revolver; double action; 32-20, 38-40, 44-40, 45 Colt, 450, 455, 476 Eley; 6-shot cylinder; 4-3/4-inch, 5-1/2-inch, 7-1/2-inch barrels with ejector; 3-1/2-inch, 4-inch without ejector; similar to Lightning

model but with heavier frame; lanyard ring in butt; hard rubber grips; fixed sights; blued or nickel finish. Manufactured 1878 to 1905.

Exc.: $4750   **VGood:** $2500   **Good:** $1500

COLT MODEL 1905 MARINE CORPS

Revolver; double action; 38 Spl., 38 Short, 38 Long; 6-inch barrel; round butt; double cylinder notches; shorter flutes; double locking butt. Manufactured 1905 to 1909.

Exc.: $4000   **VGood:** $2000   **Good:** $1000

COLT MODEL 1917 ARMY

Revolver; double action; 6-shot swing-out cylinder; 45 Auto Rim cartridge can be fired in conventional manner; based upon New Service revolver to fire 45 ACP cartridge with steel half-moon clips; 10-13/16-inch overall length; 5-1/2-inch barrel; smooth walnut grips; fixed sights; dull finish. Should be checked for damage by corrosive primers before purchase. Introduced 1917; dropped 1925.

Exc.: $1550   **VGood:** $900   **Good:** $695

COLT NAVY MODEL 1889 (FIRST ISSUE)

Revolver; double action; 38 Short Colt, 38 Long Colt, 41 Short Colt, 41 Long Colt; 6-shot left-revolving cylinder; 3-inch, 4-1/2-inch, 6-inch barrels; fixed blade front sight, V-notched rear; Colt's first solid-frame, swing-out cylinder model; blued or nickel finish; hard rubber or walnut grips; blued or nickel finish. Manufactured 1889 to 1894. In demand by collectors.

Exc.: $5000   **VGood:** $4000   **Good:** $2500

COLT NAVY MODEL 1892-1903 (SECOND ISSUE)

Same specs as First Issue except double cylinder notches, double locking bolt; lanyard loop on butt; added calibers; 38 Spl., 32-20; does not fire modern high-velocity loads safely. Also known as New Army, adopted by both Army and Navy. Manufactured 1892 to 1905.

Exc.: $2750   **VGood:** $1500   **Good:** $600

Colt New Frontier

Colt New Police

Colt Officer's Model Match

Colt New Service Shooting Master

Colt New Frontier 22

Colt New Service

COLT NEW FRONTIER

Revolver; flat-top target version of Colt Single Action Army first introduced in 1962 during 2nd Generation production and continued until 1974. Serial numbers began at 3000NF and ended in 1974 with 7288NF. Calibers offered during 2nd Generation were 45 Colt, 44 Spl., 357 Mag., and 38 Spl. Standard barrel lengths 4-3/4-inch, 5-1/2-inch, 7-1/2-inch; a total of seventy-two 45 Colt Buntline New Frontiers manufactured with 12-inch barrels. Finish was Colt's royal blue with color case-hardened frame. Two-piece walnut grips were standard. Manufacture of New Frontiers resumed in 1978 during 3rd Generation production and continued until 1985. Serial numbers began again at 01001NF and ran to approximately 17000NF by 1985. During 3rd Generation production, calibers offered were 45 Colt, 44 Spl., and 357 Mag., with 44-40 being added in 1981. Finishes were Colt's royal blue with color case-hardened frame, with fully nickel-plated, and fully-blued being rarely-found options. Barrel lengths were the standard 4-3/4-inch, 5-1/2-inch, and 7-1/2-inch.

2nd Generation		
Perf.: $1500	Exc.: $1200	VGood: $700
3rd Generation		
Perf.: $1000	Exc.: $900	VGood: $695

COLT NEW FRONTIER BUNTLINE SPECIAL

Same specs as New Frontier except 45 Colt; 12-inch barrel; flat-top frame; adjustable rear sight.

2nd Generation		
Perf.: $2500	Exc.: $1850	VGood: $1250
3rd Generation		
Perf.: $2000	Exc.: $1500	VGood: $1000

COLT NEW FRONTIER 22

Revolver; single action; 6-shot cylinder; furnished with dual cylinders for 22 LR, 22 WMR; 4-3/8-inch, 6-inch, 7-1/2-inch barrels; 11-1/2-inch overall length (6-inch barrel); scaled-down version of New Frontier 45; target-type fully-adjustable rear sight, ramp front; checkered black plastic grips; flat topstrap; color case-hardened frame, rest blued. Introduced 1973; dropped 1975; reintroduced 1981; dropped 1982.

Perf.: $600	Exc.: $450	VGood: $300

7-1/2-inch barrel		
Perf.: $650	Exc.: $475	VGood: $325

COLT NEW POCKET MODEL

Revolver; double action; 32 Colt, 32 S&W; 6-shot cylinder; 2-1/2-inch, 3-1/2-inch, 5-inch, 6-inch barrels; checkered hard rubber stocks; blued or nickel finish. Introduced 1893; dropped 1905. Collector value.

Exc.: $550	VGood: $400	Good: $350

COLT NEW POLICE

Revolver; double action; 32 Colt, 32 Colt New Police; 2-1/2-inch, 4-inch, 6-inch barrels; built on New Pocket Model frame, with larger hard rubber grips; same sights as New Pocket Colt; blued or nickel finish. Manufactured 1896 to 1907.

Exc.: $550	VGood: $425	Good: $350

COLT NEW POLICE TARGET

Same specs as New Police model except target sights; 6-inch barrel only. Manufactured 1896 to 1905.

Exc.: $1500	VGood: $1250	Good: $750

COLT NEW SERVICE

Revolver; double action; 38 Spl., 357 Mag., 38-40, 38-44, 44 Russian, 44 Spl., 44-40, 45 Colt, 45 ACP, 450 Eley, 455 Eley, 476 Eley; 2-inch, 3-1/2-inch 4-inch, 4-1/2-inch, 5-inch, 5-1/2-inch, 6-inch, 7-1/2-inch barrels; 6-shot swing-out cylinder; large frame. Special run in 45 ACP. During WWI was designated as Model 1917 Revolver under government contract. Fixed open notch rear sight milled in topstrap, fixed front; checkered hard rubber grips on commercial New Service; lanyard loop on most variations; blued, nickel finish. Introduced 1897; dropped 1944.

Commercial model		
Exc.: $1675	VGood: $1250	Good: $750
Military model		
Exc.: $1575	VGood: $1350	Good: $850
357 Mag.		
Exc.: $1550	VGood: $1400	Good: $875

COLT NEW SERVICE SHOOTING MASTER

Same specs as New Service except 38 Spl., 357 Mag., 44 Spl., 45 ACP/Auto Rim, 45 Colt; 6-inch barrel; 11-1/4-inch overall length; deluxe target version; checkered walnut grips, rounded butt; windage-adjustable rear sight, elevation-adjustable front; blued. Introduced 1932; dropped 1941.

38 Special		
Exc.: $1750	VGood: $1325	Good: $900
44 Spl., 45 ACP, 45 Colt		
Exc.: $3500	VGood: $2500	Good: $1500

COLT NEW SERVICE TARGET

Same specs as standard New Service model except windage-adjustable rear sight, elevation-adjustable front; 44 Spl., 44 Russian, 45 Colt, 45 ACP, 450 Eley, 455 Eley, 476 Eley; 5-inch, 6-inch, 7-1/2-inch barrels; flat topstrap; finished action; blued finish; hand-checkered walnut grips. Introduced 1900; dropped 1940.

Exc.: $2850	VGood: $2575	Good: $2100

COLT OFFICER'S MODEL TARGET (FIRST, SECOND, THIRD ISSUES)

Revolver; double action; 38 Spl. (First Issue); 32 Colt, 38 Spl. (Second Issue); 22 LR (Third Issue); 6-shot cylinder; 6-inch barrel (38 Spl.); 4-inch, 4-1/2-inch, 5-inch, 6-inch, 7-1/2-inch barrels (32 Colt, 38 Spl., 22 LR); hand-finished action; adjustable rear target, blade front sight; blued finish. First Issue manufactured 1904-1908; Second Issue, 1908-1926; Third Issue, 1927-1949.

First Issue		
Exc.: $1500	VGood: $1250	Good: $950
Second Issue		
Exc.: $1150	VGood: $1000	Good: $850
Third Issue		
Exc.: $825	VGood: $750	Good: $650

COLT OFFICER'S MODEL MATCH

Same specs as Officer's Model Special, which it replaced, except checkered walnut target grips; tapered heavy barrel; wide hammer spur. Introduced 1953; dropped 1970.

Perf.: $425	Exc.: $375	VGood: $300

Colt Official Police

Colt Official Police MKIII

Colt Peacekeeper

Colt Peacemaker 22

Colt Police Positive

Colt Pocket Positive

Colt Police Positive Special

Colt Police Positive (1995)

Colt Python

COLT OFFICER'S MODEL SPECIAL
Same specs as Second Issue Officer's Model Target except heavier barrel; ramp front, Coltmaster adjustable rear sight; redesigned hammer; checkered plastic stocks; 6-inch barrel; 22 LR, 38 Spl.; blued finish. Introduced 1949; dropped 1955.

Exc.: $550   **VGood:** $425   **Good:** $375

COLT OFFICIAL POLICE
Revolver; double action; 22 LR, 32-20, 38 Spl., 41 Long Colt; 6-shot cylinder; 2-inch, 6-inch heavy barrels (38 Spl. only); 4-inch, 6-inch barrels (22 LR only); 4-inch, 5-inch, 6-inch (other calibers); checkered walnut grips, plastic grips on post-WWII models. Version made to military specs in WWII was called Commando model, had sand-blasted blue finish. Introduced 1927 as a replacement for Army Special; dropped 1970. Collector value.

Perf.: $525   **Exc.:** $425   **VGood:** $350

Military model

Perf.: $550   **Exc.:** $460   **VGood:** $375

COLT OFFICIAL POLICE MKIII
Revolver; double action; 38 Spl.; 4-inch, 5-inch, 6-inch barrels; 9-3/8-inch overall length; an old name, but a renewed design, incorporating coil mainspring in place of leaf spring; square butt, checkered walnut grips; fixed rear sight notch milled in topstrap, fixed ramp front; grooved front surface on trigger; checkered hammer spur. Introduced 1969; dropped 1975.

Perf.: $450   **Exc.:** $375   **VGood:** $295

COLT PEACEKEEPER
Revolver; double action; 357 Mag.; 6-shot cylinder; 4-inch, 6-inch barrel; weighs 42 oz. (6-inch barrel); red insert ramp front sight, white outline adjustable rear; rubber round-bottom combat grips; matte blue finish. Introduced 1985; dropped 1987.

Perf.: $525   **Exc.:** $450   **VGood:** $300

COLT PEACEMAKER 22
Revolver; single action; dual cylinders for 22 LR, 22 WMR; 6-shot cylinder; 4-3/8-inch, 6-inch, 7-1/2-inch barrels; 11-1/4-inch overall length (6-inch barrel); scaled-down version of century-old Model 1873; rear sight notch milled into rounded topstrap; fixed blade front; color case-hardened frame, rest blued; black plastic grips. Introduced 1973; dropped 1975.

Perf.: $475   **Exc.:** $375   **VGood:** $300

7-1/2-inch barrel

Perf.: $510   **Exc.:** $425   **VGood:** $325

COLT POCKET POSITIVE
Revolver; double action; 32 Short Colt, 32 Long Colt, 32 Colt New Police (interchangeable with 32 S&W Long, S&W Short cartridges); 6-shot cylinder; 2-inch, 2-1/2-inch, 3-1/2-inch, 4-inch, 5-inch, 6-inch barrels; 7-1/2-inch overall length (3-1/2-inch barrel); rear sight groove milled in topstrap, rounded front sight; positive lock feature; hard rubber grips; blued or nickel finish. Based upon New Pocket Model dropped in 1905. Introduced 1905; dropped 1940. Subtract 5% for 32 SC and .32 LC chamberings.

Exc.: $595   **VGood:** $450   **Good:** $385

Nickel finish

Exc.: $650   **VGood:** $550   **Good:** $475

COLT POLICE POSITIVE
Revolver; double action; 32 Short Colt, 32 Long Colt, 32 Colt New Police, 38 S&W; 6-shot swing-out cylinder; 2-1/2-inch, 4-inch, 5-inch, 6-inch barrels; 8-1/2-inch overall length (4-inch barrel); fixed sights; checkered walnut, plastic or hard rubber grips; top of frame matted to reduce glare; blue or nickel finish; replaced New Police model. Introduced 1905; dropped 1943. Reintroduced 1995.

Exc.: $450   **VGood:** $395   **Good:** $335

Nickel finish

Exc.: $550   **VGood:** $450   **Good:** $375

COLT POLICE POSITIVE SPECIAL (FIRST, SECOND, THIRD ISSUES)
Same specs as standard Police Positive except lengthened frame to accommodate longer cylinder for 38 Spl., 32-20; also made in 32 and 38 Colt New Police; 4-inch, 5-inch, 6-inch barrels; 8-3/4-inch overall length (4-inch barrel); blued or nickel. Introduced 1908; dropped 1970. Reintroduced 1995; no longer produced.

Perf.: $495   **Exc.:** $450   **VGood:** $395

COLT POLICE POSITIVE TARGET
Same specs as standard Police Positive except 32 Short Colt, 32 Long Colt, 32 New Police, 32 S&W Short, 32 S&W Long, 22 LR. In 1932, cylinder was modified by countersinking chambers for safety with high-velocity 22 ammo; those with non-countersunk chambers should be fired only with standard-velocity 22 ammo. Has 6-inch barrel; 10-1/2-inch overall length, windage-adjustable rear sight, elevation-adjustable front; checkered walnut grips; blued; backstrap, hammer spur, trigger checkered. Introduced 1905; dropped 1941.

Exc.: $795   **VGood:** $550   **Good:** $350

COLT PYTHON
Revolver; double action; 357 Mag., but will handle 38 Spl.; 6-shot swing-out cylinder; made first appearance in 6-inch barrel later with 2-1/2-inch, 3-inch, 8-inch; checkered walnut grips contoured for support for middle finger of shooting hand; vent-rib barrel; ramp front sight, fully-adjustable rear; full-length ejector rod shroud; wide-spur hammer; grooved trigger; blued, nickel finish; hand-finished action. Introduced 1955. **Discontinued.**

Perf.: $1000   **Exc.:** $875   **VGood:** $775

Nickel finish

Perf.: $1150   **Exc.:** $925   **VGood:** $775

COLT PYTHON STAINLESS
Same specs as standard Python except stainless steel construction; 4-inch, 6-inch barrel lengths only. Introduced 1983.

Perf.: $1150   **Exc.:** $900   **VGood:** $800

COLT SINGLE ACTION ARMY
Colt Single Action Army also known as Peacemaker, or Frontier Six Shooter (44-40 caliber only). Originally introduced in 1873 and produced continuously until 1941. This production run is known as "1st Generation." The production run resumed in 1956 and stopped again in 1974 is known as "2nd Generation." Production known as "3rd Generation" began in 1976 and is still being manufactured. 1st Generation serial numbers began in 1873 with #1 and ended in 1941 with serial number 357859. The first Generation production included two frame styles: From 1873 until 1892, frames had screw

Colt Python Stainless

Colt Single Action Army (1st Generation)

Colt Python (1995)

Colt Single Action Army (2nd Generation)

Colt Trooper MKV

Colt Trooper

Colt Cowboy

Colt Viper

angling in from front of frame to secure cylinder base pin; starting in 1892, and becoming standard by 1896, cylinder pin is secured by spring-loaded transverse catch. These frames are mistakenly called "blackpowder" and "smokeless powder" frames respectively, but it should be noted that Colt did not warranty any SAA revolvers for smokeless powder until 1900 at about serial number 192000. Rarer calibers and barrel lengths bring considerable premium over prices shown. When 2nd Generation production began in 1956, serial numbers started at #0001SA, and continued until approximately #74000SA. 3rd Generation production started in 1976 and serial numbers resumed at #80000SA. When #99999SA was reached in 1978, the SA was made a prefix and numbers started once more at #SA00001. When #SA99999 was reached about 1993, the SA was split and numbers started once more at #S0001A. Standard barrel lengths for all three generations have been 4-3/4-inch (introduced 1879), 5-1/2-inch (introduced 1875), and 7-1/2-inch (introductory length offered in 1873). During 1st Generation production, any barrel length could be special ordered. Examples are known ranging from 2-1/2-inch to 16-inch. During 2nd and 3rd Generation production, special runs were made as Sheriff's Model with 3-inch barrels and no ejector rod housings. During 2nd and 3rd Generation, Buntline Special versions with 12-inch barrels were cataloged. A 3rd Generation Storekeeper's Model was also cataloged with 4-inch barrel and no ejector rod housing. Standard finishes for all three generations have been color case-hardened frame with remainder blued, or fully nickel-plated. Some fully-blued SAAs have been offered by Colt from time to time. For 1st Generation, standard grips were one-piece walnut in early production and two-piece hard rubber in later production. Standard grips in 2nd Generation were hard rubber, and both hard rubber and two-piece walnut in 3rd Generation. Standard sights were groove down revolver's topstrap and blade front. However, a rare flattop target model was also offered during 1st Generation run. Caliber options for 1st Generation revolvers numbered approximately thirty, ranging from 22 rimfire to 476 Eley. However, the top five in terms of numbers produced were 45 Colt, 44-40, 38-40, 32-20 and 41 Colt. 2nd Generation calibers in order of numbers produced were 45 Colt, 357 Magnum, 38 Special, 44 Spl. 3rd Generation calibers started in 1976 with 45 Colt and 357 Mag.

In 1978, 44 Spl. was added, and in 1980 44-40 was included once more. In 1993, 38-40 was made an option again. 2nd Generation Buntline and Sheriff's Models made only in 45 Colt from 1957 until 1974. 3rd Generation Buntline and Sheriff's Models made in 45 Colt, 44-40, and 44 Spl. calibers from 1980 until 1985. So-called "blackpowder frame" model with screw angling in from front of frame to secure cylinder base pin re-introduced in 1984 and offered as custom feature until early 1990s. During period 1984 to 1994, Colt SAAs could be ordered from Colt Custom Shop with almost any combination of features listed above.

1st Generation (s/n up to 357859, common models)		
Exc.: $8500	**VGood:** $4500	**Good:** $3000
2nd Generation (s/n #0001SA to #74000SA)		
Exc.: $1600	**VGood:** $1200	**Good:** $800
3rd Generation (s/n #80000SA to present)		
Perf.: $1200	**Exc.:** $800	**VGood:** $700

COLT SINGLE ACTION (CURRENT PRODUCTION)

Revolver; single action; 32-20, .357, 38 Special, 44-40, 45 Colt, .38-40 6-shot. Barrel: 4-3/4-inch, 5-1/2-inch, 7-1/2-inch. Weight: 40 oz. (4-3/4-inch barrel). Length: 10-1/4-inch overall (4-3/4 inch barrel). Stocks: Black Eagle composite. Sights: Blade front, notch rear. Features: Available in full nickel finish with nickel grip medallions, or Royal Blue with color case-hardened frame, gold grip medallions. Reintroduced 1992.

New: $1200   **Perf.:** $1000   **Exc.:** $850

COLT COWBOY SINGLE-ACTION REVOLVER

Caliber: 45 Colt, 6-shot. Barrel: 5-1/2-inch. Weight: 42 oz. Stocks: Black composition, first generation style. Sights: Blade front, notch rear. Features: Dimensional replica of Colt's original Peacemaker with medium-size color case-hardened frame; transfer bar safety system; half-cock loading. Introduced 1998. Assembled in USA from parts made in Canada.

New: $675   **Perf.:** $575   **Exc.:** $495

COLT TROOPER

Revolver; double action; 22 LR, 38 Spl., 357 Mag.; 6-shot swing-out cylinder; ramp front sight; choice of standard hammer, service grips, wide hammer spur, target grips. Has the same specs as Officer's Match model except 4-inch barrel. Introduced 1953; dropped 1969.

Exc.: $450	**VGood:** $300	**Good:** $275
Target model		
Exc.: $475	**VGood:** $325	**Good:** $300

COLT TROOPER MKIII

Revolver; double action; 22 LR, 22 WMR, 38 Spl., 357 Mag.; 4-inch, 6-inch, 8-inch barrels; 9-1/2-inch overall length (4-inch barrel); rear sight fully-adjustable, ramp front; shrouded ejector rod; checkered walnut target grips; target hammer; wide target trigger; blued, nickel finish. Introduced 1969; dropped 1983.

Perf.: $525	**Exc.:** $425	**VGood:** $375
Nickel finish		
Perf.: $600	**Exc.:** $500	**VGood:** $425

COLT TROOPER MKV

Same specs as Trooper MKIII with redesigned lock work to reduce double-action trigger pull; faster lock time; redesigned grips; adjustable rear sight, red insert front; 4-inch, 6-inch, 8-inch vent-rib barrel; blued or nickel finish. Introduced 1984; dropped 1988.

Perf.: $425	**Exc.:** $350	**VGood:** $275
Nickel finish		
Perf.: $475	**Exc.:** $400	**VGood:** $300

COLT VIPER

Revolver; double action; 38 Spl.; 6-shot cylinder; 4-inch barrel; 9-inch overall length; weighs 20 oz.; ramp front, fixed square-notch rear sights; checkered walnut wrap-around grips; lightweight aluminum alloy frame; blue or nickel finish. Uses Colt Cobra frame. Introduced 1977; no longer produced.

Perf.: $525	**Exc.:** $475	**VGood:** $425
Nickel finish		
Perf.: $495	**Exc.:** $475	**VGood:** $430

Commanche I

Commanche II

Competition Arms
Competitor

Commanche III

Commanche Super
Comanche

Competitor
Single Shot

Coonan 357
Magnum

CZ Model 27

CZ Model 38

COMANCHE I

Single-/double-action revolver chambered in .22 LR.
Nine-shot cylinder, 6" barrel, adjustable sights, blued
or stainless steel construction with rubber grips.

NIB: $165   **Exc.:** $130   **VGood:** $90

COMANCHE II

Similar to above but in .38 Special with 2", 3" or 4"
barrel.

NIB: $175   **Exc.:** $140   **VGood:** $100

COMANCHE III

Similar to above but in .357 Magnum and additional
6" barrel option.

NIB: $195   **Exc.:** $160   **VGood:** $120

COMANCHE SUPER COMANCHE

Single-shot break-action pistol chambered in.410/.45
Colt. Matte black finish, rubber grips.

NIB: $165   **Exc.:** $140   **VGood:** $100

COMPETITION ARMS COMPETITOR

Single shot; 22 LR, 223, 7mm TCU, 7mm
International, 30 Herrett, 357 Mag., 41 Mag., 454
Casull, 375 Super Mag.; other calibers on special
order; 10-inch, 14-inch barrels; adjustable open rear
sight, ramp front; interchangeable barrels of blued
ordnance or stainless steel; vent barrel shroud;
integral scope mount. Introduced 1987; no longer in
production.

Perf.: $395   **Exc.:** $365   **VGood:** $315

COMPETITOR SINGLE SHOT

Single shot; 22 LR through 50 Action Express,
including belted magnums; 14-inch barrel (standard),
10-1/2-inch silhouette, 16-inch (optional); weights
about 59 oz. (14-inch barrel); 15-1/8-inch overall
length; rotary cannon-type action; ambidextrous
synthetic grip (standard) or laminated or natural wood;
ramp front sight, adjustable rear; actions cocks on
opening; cammed ejector; interchangeable barrels,
ejectors; adjustable single-stage trigger; sliding thumb
safety and trigger safety; matte blue finish. Made

in U.S. by Competitor Corp. Introduced 1988; still
produced.

14-inch barrel, standard calibers, synthetic grips		
Perf.: $395	**Exc.:** $365	**VGood:** $315
Extra barrels		
Perf.: $175	**Exc.:** $165	**VGood:** $150

COONAN 357 MAGNUM

Semi-automatic; 357 Mag.; 7-shot magazine; 5-inch
barrel; 8-5/16-inch overall length; weighs 42 oz.;
smooth walnut stocks; open adjustable sights; barrel
hood; many parts interchangeable with Colt autos;
grip, hammer, half-cock safeties. Introduced 1983;
dropped 1999.

New: $1500   **Perf.:** $1200   **Exc.:** $900

COONAN 357 MAGNUM CLASSIC

Same specs as 357 Magnum except 8-shot
magazine; Teflon black two-tone or Kal-Gard finish;
fully-adjustable rear sight; integral compensated
barrel. Introduced 1983; dropped 1999.

New: $1550   **Perf.:** $1250   **Exc.:** $950

COONAN 357 MAGNUM COMPACT CADET

Semi-automatic; single action; 357 Mag.; 6-shot
magazine; 3-15/16-inch barrel; weighs 39 oz.;
7-7/8-inch overall length; smooth walnut grips;
interchangeable ramp front sight, windage-adjustable
rear; linkless bull barrel; full-length recoil spring guide
rod; extended slide latch. Introduced 1993; dropped
1999.

New: $1575   **Perf.:** $1300   **Exc.:** $975

COONAN 357 MAGNUM COMPENSATED MODEL

Same specs as 357 Magnum except 6-inch barrel
with compensator. Introduced 1990; dropped 1999.

New: $1550   **Perf.:** $1250   **Exc.:** $950

CUMBERLAND MOUNTAIN ARMS THE JUDGE SINGLE SHOT

Single shot; 22 Hornet, 22 K-Hornet, 218 Bee, 7-30
Waters, 30-30; 10-inch, 16-inch barrel; walnut grip;
bead on ramp front sight, open adjustable rear;

break-open design; made of 17-4 stainless steel.
Also available as a kit. Made in U.S. by Cumberland
Mountain Arms. Introduced 1995; dropped 1999.

Perf.: $395   **Exc.:** $365   **VGood:** $315

CZ MODEL 22

Semi-automatic; 380 ACP; 8-shot magazine; 3-5/16-
inch barrel; 6-inch overall length; weighs 21-7/8 oz.;
made under license from Mauser; external hammer;
rotating barrel lock system. About 20,000 made 1921
to 1923.

Exc.: $600   **VGood:** $425   **Good:** $300

CZ MODEL 24

Semi-automatic; 380 ACP; 8-shot magazine; 3-1/2-
inch barrel; 6-inch overall length; weighs 24 oz.;
same general design as Model 22 except addition of
magazine safety; about 190,000 made. Manufactured
from 1924 to 1939.

Exc.: $350   **VGood:** $320   **Good:** $290

CZ MODEL 27

Semi-automatic; 32 ACP; 8-shot magazine; 3-
13/16-inch barrel; 6-1/2-inch overall length; weighs
25 oz.; vertical retracting grooves on slide; fixed
sights; plastic grips; blued finish. Commercial and
non-commercial models made until 1939 marked on
top rib and left side of frame; post-1941 omit top rib
marking; post-war models made until 1951 marked
on slide. Manufactured from 1927 to 1951.

Pre-war		
Exc.: $550	**VGood:** $450	**Good:** $350
Post-1941		
Exc.: $325	**VGood:** $275	**Good:** $225
Post-war		
Exc.: $300	**VGood:** $250	**Good:** $200

CZ MODEL 38

Semi-automatic; double-action-only; 380 ACP; 8-
shot magazine; 4-5/8-inch barrel; 8 1/8-inch overall
length; weighs 32 oz.; plastic grips; fixed sights;
blued finish. Also listed as CZ Pistole 39(t) during
German occupation. Manufactured 1939 to 1945.

Exc.: $450   **VGood:** $350   **Good:** $275

CZ Model 75

CZ Model 83

CZ 100

CZ 75 Stainless

CZ75 SP-01 Shadow

CZ Model 1945

CZ Pocket Duo

CZ MODEL 50

Semi-automatic; double action; 32 ACP; 8-shot; 3-3/4-inch barrel; 6-1/2-inch overall length; weighs 24-3/4 oz.; frame mounted safety catch; loaded chamber indicator. Issued to Czech police as Model VZ50. Manufactured from 1951 to approximately 1967.

Exc.: $135 **VGood:** $110 **Good:** $100

CZ MODEL 52

Semi-automatic; 7.62 Tokarev; 8-shot; 4-3/4-inch barrel; 8 1/4-inch overall length; weighs 40 oz.; complex roller locking breech system. Manufactured from 1952 to approximately 1956.

Exc.: $300 **VGood:** $275 **Good:** $195

CZ MODEL 75

Semi-automatic; double action or double-action-only; 9mm Para., 40 S&W; 15-shot magazine; 4-3/4-inch barrel; 8-inch overall length; weighs 35 oz.; all-steel frame; adjustable rear sight, square post front; checkered plastic; black polymer, matte or high-polish blued finish. Imported from the Czech Republic by CZ-USA.

Perf.: $420 **Exc.:** $350 **VGood:** $300

CZ MODEL 75 COMPACT

Same specs as Model 75 except 10-shot magazine; 3-15/16-inch barrel; weighs 32 oz.; removable front sight; non-glare ribbed slide top; squared and serrated triggerguard; combat hammer. Introduced 1993; imported from the Czech Republic by CZ-USA.

Perf.: $430 **Exc.:** $365 **VGood:** $340

CZ MODEL 75 SEMI-COMPACT

Same specs as Model 75 Compact with shorter slide and barrel on full-size CZ 75 frame; 10-shot magazine; 9mm Para. only. Introduced 1994; imported from the Czech Republic by CZ-USA.

Perf.: $400 **Exc.:** $350 **VGood:** $300

CZ MODEL 83

Semi-automatic; double action; 32 ACP, 380 ACP; 3-13/16-inch barrel; 6-15/16-inch overall length; weighs 26 1/4 oz; adjustable rear, removable square post front sight; ambidextrous magazine release and safety; non-glare ribbed slide top; high-impact

checkered plastic grips; blue finish. Imported from the Czech Republic by CZ-USA.

Perf.: $395 **Exc.:** $325 **VGood:** $275

CZ MODEL 85

Semi-automatic; double action or double-action-only; 9mm Para., 40 S&W; 15-shot magazine; 4-3/4-inch barrel; 8-inch overall length; weighs 35 oz.; all-steel frame; ambidextrous slide release and safety levers; non-glare ribbed slide top; squared, serrated trigger-guard; trigger stop to prevent overtravel; adjustable rear sight, square post front; checkered plastic; black polymer, matte or high-polish blued finish. Introduced 1986; imported from the Czech Republic by CZ-USA.

Perf.: $475 **Exc.:** $400 **VGood:** $350

CZ MODEL 85 COMBAT

Same specs as the Model 85 except walnut grips; round combat hammer; fully-adjustable rear sight; extended magazine release; trigger parts coated with friction-free beryllium copper. Introduced 1992; imported from the Czech Republic by CZ-USA.

Perf.: $500 **Exc.:** $450 **VGood:** $400

CZ 100 AUTO PISTOL

Caliber: 9mm Para., 40 S&W, 10-shot magazine. Barrel: 3.7-inch. Weight: 24 oz. Length: 6.9-inch overall. Stocks: Grooved polymer. Sights: Blade front with dot, white outline rear drift adjustable for windage. Features: Double action only with firing pin block; polymer frame, steel slide; has laser sight mount. Introduced 1996. Imported from the Czech Republic by CZ-USA.

Perf.: $425 **Exc.:** $365 **VGood:** $295

CZ MODEL 1945

Semi-automatic; double action; 25 ACP; 8-shot magazine; 2-inch barrel; 5-inch overall length; plastic grips; fixed sights; blued finish. Manufactured from 1945 to approximately 1960.

Exc.: $250 **VGood:** $200 **Good:** $165

CZ POCKET DUO

Semi-automatic; 25 ACP; 6-shot magazine; 2-1/8-inch barrel; 4-1/2-inch overall length; fixed sights;

plastic grips; manufactured in Czechoslovakia; blue or nickel finish. Manufactured 1926 to 1960.

Exc.: $295 **VGood:** $240 **Good:** $170

CZ (STRAKONICE)

Manufacturer established in 1919 and situated in Strakonice, Czech Republic. Currently imported by ADCO Sales Inc. of Woburn, MA.

CZ-75

Semi-automatic; 9mm Para.; 10-shot magazine; single/double action; 4-3/4-inch barrel; steel frame; blue finish only. Importation began 2004.

Perf.: $475 **Exc.:** $425 **VGood:** $375

CZ 75 STAINLESS

All steel construction, double-stack magazines, 3-dot fixed sights and chambered for 9mm. 16+1 or 10+1 capacity with 4.72-inch barrel. The first stainless from CZ. Introduced 2006.

NIB: $550 **Exc.:** $485 **VGood:** $395

CZ 75 TACTICAL SPORT

Single-action for IPSC competition. Chambered in 9mm and .40 S&W. Dual tone (nickel/blued). Capacity 20+1 (9mm) or 16+1 (.40 S&W). 5.4-inch barrel; 45 oz.

NIB: $725 **Exc.:** $625 **VGood:** $500

CZ 75 SP-01 SHADOW

Chambered 9mm for IPSC "Production" Division competition. 19+1 capacity, 4.72-inch barrel. 41 oz., wood grip.

NIB: $600 **Exc.:** $525 **VGood:** $425

CZ-TT

Semi-automatic; 9mm Para., 40 S&W, 45 ACP; 10-shot magazine; single/double action; polymer frame; 3.77-inch ported or unported barrel; matte finish; 26.1 oz. Importation by ADCO began 2004.

Perf.: $450 **Exc.:** $415 **VGood:** $375

Add $30 to above prices for ported barrel
Add $40 to above prices for ported barrel and slide serrations
Add $399 for caliber conversion kit with one magazine

Daewoo DH40

Dakota 1890 Remington
Police Model

Daewoo DP51C

Dakota New Model
Single Action

CZ-T POLYMER COMPACT

Similar to CZ-TT, except has shorter barrel.
Importation by ADCO began 2004.

Perf.: $475   **Exc.:** $425   **VGood:** $375

CZ/ADCO 1911-A1

Semi-automatic; 38 Super or 45 ACP; standard size
Government model; 5-inch barrel; black matte finish.
Importation by ADCO began 2004.

Perf.: $475   **Exc.:** $425   **VGood:** $375
Add $10 to above price for 38 Super chambering

DAEWOO DH40

Semi-automatic; double action; 40 S&W; 10-shot
magazine; 4-1/8-inch barrel; 7-1/2-inch overall
length; weighs 28-1/4 oz.; checkered composition
grips; 1/8-inch blade front sight, adjustable rear;
three-dot system; fast-fire mechanism; ambidextrous
manual safety with internal firing pin lock; no
magazine safety; alloy frame; squared triggerguard;
matte black finish. Formerly imported from Korea by
Nationwide Sports Distributors. Introduced 1991;
Now imported by Century International Arms, Inc.

Perf.: $395   **Exc.:** $350   **VGood:** $275

DAEWOO DH380

Semi-automatic; double action; 380 ACP; 8-shot
magazine; 3-7/8-inch barrel; 6-3/4-inch overall
length; weighs 23 oz.; checkered black composition
thumbrest grips; 1/8-inch blade front sight,
drift-adjustable rear; three-dot system; all-steel
construction; blue finish; dual safety system with
hammer block. Formerly imported from Korea by
Kimber of America; distributed by Nationwide Sports
Dist. Imported by Century International Arms, Inc.
Introduced 1994.

Perf.: $395   **Exc.:** $350   **VGood:** $275

DAEWOO DP51

Semi-automatic; 9mm Para., 40 S&W; 12-shot (40
S&W), 13-shot (9mm) magazine; 4-1/8-inch barrel;
7-1/2-inch overall length; weighs 28-1/4 oz.; blade
front, drift-adjustable square-notch rear sight;
checkered composition grips; tri-action mechanism;
ambidextrous manual safety, magazine catch;
half-cock and firing pin block; alloy frame; matte

black finish; square triggerguard. Made in Korea.
Introduced 1991.

Perf.: $395   **Exc.:** $350   **VGood:** $275

DAEWOO DP51C

Same specs as the DP51 except 3-5/8-inch barrel;
1/4-inch shorter grip frame; flat mainspring housing;
weighs 26 oz. Formerly imported from Korea by by
Kimber of America, Inc.. Introduced 1995.

Perf.: $395   **Exc.:** $350   **VGood:** $275

DAEWOO DP51S

Same specs as the DP51 except 3-5/8-inch barrel;
weighs 27 oz. Formerly imported from Korea by
Kimber of America, Inc. Introduced 1995.

Perf.: $395   **Exc.:** $350   **VGood:** $275

DAEWOO DP52

Semi-automatic; double action; 22 LR; 10-shot
magazine; 3-7/8-inch barrel; 6-3/4-inch overall
length; weighs 23 oz.; checkered black composition
thumbrest grips; 1/8-inch blade front sight,
drift-adjustable rear; three-dot system; all-steel
construction; blue finish; dual safety system with
hammer block. Formerly imported from Korea by
Kimber of America; distributed by Nationwide Sports
Dist. Now imported and distributed by Century
International Arms, Inc. Introduced 1994.

Perf.: $395   **Exc.:** $350   **VGood:** $275

DAKOTA 1873 PREMIER

Revolver; single action; 45 Colt; 6-shot cylinder; 4-
5/8-inch, 5-1/2-inch barrel; 10-inch overall length
(4-5/8-inch barrel); weighs 39 oz.; blade front, fixed
rear sight; smooth walnut grips; reproduction of the
1873 Colt revolver with set-screw for the cylinder pin
release; most parts said to interchange with the early
Colts; blue finish, color case-hardened frame. Was
imported by E.M.F.; no longer imported.

Perf.: $525   **Exc.:** $450   **VGood:** $275

DAKOTA 1875 REMINGTON OUTLAW MODEL

Revolver; single action; 357 Mag., 44-40, 45 Colt; 7-
1/2-inch barrel; 13-1/2-inch overall length; weighs 46
oz.; blade front, fixed groove rear sight; uncheckered
walnut stocks; authentic copy of 1875 Remington;

color case-hardened frame; blued cylinder, barrel;
steel backstrap; brass triggerguard; also made
with nickel finish; factory engraving. Made in Italy.
Introduced 1986; still imported by EMF.

	Perf.:	Exc.:	VGood:
	$400	$350	$300
Nickel finish			
	$450	$400	$350
Engraved			
	$500	$450	$400

DAKOTA 1890 REMINGTON POLICE MODEL

Revolver; single action; 357 Mag., 44-40, 45 Colt;
5-1/2-inch barrel; 12-inch overall length; weighs 40
oz.; blade front, fixed groove rear sight; uncheckered
walnut stocks; color case-hardened frame; blued
cylinder, barrel; steel backstrap; brass trigger guard;
lanyard ring in butt; also available in nickel finish,
factory engraving. Made in Italy. Introduced 1986;
currently imported by EMF.

	Perf.:	Exc.:	VGood:
	$400	$350	$300
Nickel finish			
	$450	$400	$350
Engraved			
	$500	$450	$400

DAKOTA BISLEY MODEL

Revolver; single action; 22 LR, 22 WMR, 32-20,
32 H&R Mag., 357 Mag., 38-40, 44 Spl., 44-40, 45
Colt, 45 ACP; 4-3/4-inch, 5-1/2-inch, 7-1/2-inch
barrels; 10-1/2-inch overall length (5-1/2-inch barrel);
weighs 37 oz.; blade front, fixed groove rear sight;
uncheckered walnut stocks; color case-hardened
frame; blued barrel, cylinder; steel trigger guard,
backstrap; Colt-type firing pin on hammer. Also
available with nickel finish, factory engraving. Made in
Italy. Introduced 1985; dropped 1991; reintroduced,
1993.

	Perf.:	Exc.:	VGood:
	$400	$325	$275
Nickel finish			
	$425	$350	$300
Engraved			
	$600	$550	$500

Dakota Hartford Model

Dan Wesson VH8

Davis P-32

Dan Wesson RZ-10

Davis D-Series
D-38 Derringer

DAKOTA HARTFORD MODEL
Revolver; single action; 22 LR, 32-20, 357 Mag., 38-40, 44 Spl., 45 Colt; 4-3/4-inch, 5-1/2-inch, 7-1/2-inch barrel; blade front, fixed rear sight; one-piece walnut stock; identical to original Colts; all major parts serial numbered with original Colt-type lettering, numbers; color case-hardened frame, hammer; various options. Made in Italy. Introduced 1990; still imported by EMF.

Perf.: $400	Exc.: $350	VGood: $300
Nickel plated		
Perf.: $500	Exc.: $450	VGood: $400
Calvary or Artillery models		
Perf.: $400	Exc.: $350	VGood: $300
Cattlebrand engraved		
Perf.: $500	Exc.: $450	VGood: $400
Engraved nickel		
Perf.: $600	Exc.: $550	VGood: $500

DAKOTA HARTFORD MODEL PINKERTON
Same specs as Hartford Model except 4-inch barrel; 45 Colt; bird's-head walnut grips; ejector tube. Introduced 1994; still in production.

Perf.: $350	Exc.: $300	VGood: $250

DAKOTA NEW MODEL SINGLE ACTION
Revolver; single action; 357 Mag., 44-40, 45 Colt; 6-shot; 4-3/4-inch, 5-1/2-inch, 7-1/2-inch barrel; blade front, fixed rear sight; one-piece walnut stock; Colt-type hammer, firing pin; nickel or color case-hardened forged frame; black nickel backstrap, triggerguard; also available in nickel finish. Made in Italy. Introduced 1991; currently imported by EMF.

Perf.: $300	Exc.: $250	VGood: $200
Nickel finish		
Perf.: $350	Exc.: $300	VGood: $250
Engraved, nickel-plated		
Perf.: $400	Exc.: $350	VGood: $300

DAKOTA OLD MODEL SINGLE ACTION
Revolver; single action; 22 LR, 32-20, 357 Mag., 38-40, 44 Spl., 44-40, 45 Colt; 6-shot cylinder; 4-5/8-inch, 5-1/2-inch, 7-1/2-inch barrel; blade front, fixed rear sight; one-piece walnut stocks; color case-hardened frame; brass grip frame, triggerguard; blued barrel cylinder; also available in nickel finish. Made in Italy. Introduced 1967; sporadic production. Was imported by EMF.

Perf.: $375	Exc.: $325	VGood: $250
Nickel finish		
Perf.: $395	Exc.: $295	VGood: $225

DAKOTA SHERIFF'S MODEL
Revolver; single action; 32-20, 357 Mag., 38-40, 44 Spl., 44-40, 45 Colt; 6-shot; 3-1/2-inch barrel; blade front, fixed rear sight; one-piece walnut stock; blued finish. Made in Italy. Introduced 1994; was imported by EMF.

Perf.: $415	Exc.: $335	VGood: $300

DAN WESSON VH8
.445 SuperMag revolver designed for barrel interchangeability. Also fires standard .44-caliber rounds. Stainless, 6-shot; 8-inch barrel, 4.1 lb. Single/double action. Other chamberings offered; demand for these varies.

NIB: $1300	Exc.: $1000	VGood: $775

DAN WESSON RZ-10
10mm single-action semi-auto with 8+1 capacity. 5-inch barrel, 2.4 lb. Fixed sights.

NIB: $1010	Exc.: $910	VGood: $785

DAVIS BIG-BORE DERRINGERS
Derringer; over/under; 22 WMR, 32 H&R Mag., 38 Spl., 9mm Para.; 2-shot; 2-3/4-inch barrels; 4-9/16-inch overall length; weighs about 14 oz.; textured black synthetic grips; fixed sights; chrome or black teflon finish. Larger than the Davis D-Series models. Formerly made in U.S. by Davis Industries. Introduced 1995; still produced by Cobra Enterprises of Salt Lake City, UT.

Perf.: $90	Exc.: $65	VGood: $55

DAVIS D-SERIES DERRINGERS
Derringer over/under; 22 WMR, 32 H&R, 38 Spl; 2-shot; 2-3/8-inch barrels; 4-inch overall length; weighs about 11-1/2 oz.; textured black synthetic grips; blade front, fixed notch rear sight; alloy frame; steel-lined barrels; steel breechblock; plunger-type safety with integral hammer block; chrome or black Teflon finish. Formerly made in U.S. by Davis Industries. Introduced 1992; still produced by Cobra Enterprises of Salt Lake City, UT.

Perf.: $95	Exc.: $75	VGood: $55

DAVIS LONG-BORE DERRINGERS
Derringer over/under; 22 WMR, 32 H&R Mag., 38 Spl., 9mm Para.; 2-shot; 3-1/2-inch barrels; 5-3/8-inch overall length; weighs 16 oz.; textured black synthetic grips; fixed sights; chrome or black teflon finish. Larger than the Davis D-Series models. Formerly made in U.S. by Davis Industries. Introduced 1995; still produced by Cobra Enterprises of Salt Lake City, UT.

Perf.: $95	Exc.: $75	VGood: $65

DAVIS P-32
Semi-automatic; double action; 32 ACP; 6-shot magazine; 2-13/16-inch barrel; 5-3/8-inch overall length; weighs 22 oz.; laminated wood stocks; fixed sights; chrome or black Teflon finish. Introduced 1986; still in production by Cobra Enterprises of Salt Lake City, UT.

Perf.: $105	Exc.: $85	VGood: $65

DAVIS P-380
Semi-automatic; double action; 380 ACP; 5-shot magazine; 2-13/16-inch barrel; 5-7/16-inch overall length; weighs 22 oz.; fixed sights; black composition grips; chrome or black Teflon finish. Introduced 1991; still in production by Cobra Enterprises of Salt Lake City, UT.

Perf.: $85	Exc.: $75	VGood: $65

Desert Industries War Eagle

Desert Industries Double Deuce

Detonics Pocket 9LS

Detonics Combat Master Mark V

Detonics Scoremaster

DESERT INDUSTRIES DOUBLE DEUCE

Semi-automatic; double action; 22 LR; 6-shot; 2-1/2-inch barrel; 5-1/2-inch overall length; weighs 15 oz.; fixed groove sights; smooth rosewood grips; ambidextrous slide-mounted safety; stainless steel construction; matte finish. Introduced 1991; still in production by Steel City Arms.

Perf.: $350   **Exc.:** $295   **VGood:** $275

DESERT INDUSTRIES TWO-BIT SPECIAL

Semi-automatic; double action; 25 ACP; 5-shot; 2-1/2-inch barrel; 5-1/2-inch overall length; weighs 15 oz.; fixed groove sights; smooth rosewood grips; ambidextrous slide-mounted safety; stainless steel construction; matte finish. Introduced 1991; only about 12 prototypes were produced.

Perf.: $375   **Exc.:** $350   **VGood:** $295

DESERT INDUSTRIES WAR EAGLE

Semi-automatic; double action; 380 ACP, 9mm Para., 40 S&W, 10mm Auto, 45 ACP; 10-shot, 14-shot (9mm), 8-shot (380 ACP); 4-inch barrel; fixed sights; rosewood grips; stainless steel construction; matte finish. Introduced 1991. No longer produced.

Perf.: $700   **Exc.:** $650   **VGood:** $550

DETONICS COMBAT MASTER MARK I

Semi-automatic; 9mm Para., 38 Super, 45 ACP; 6-shot magazine (45 ACP); 3-1/2-inch barrel; 6-3/4-inch overall length; weighs 28 oz.; fixed or adjustable combat-type sights; checkered walnut stocks; throated barrel; polished feed ramp; self-adjusting cone barrel centering system; beveled magazine inlet; full-clip indicator; two-tone matte blue and stainless finish. Introduced 1977; discontinued 1992.

Perf.: $850   **Exc.:** $700   **VGood:** $600

DETONICS COMBAT MASTER MARK V

Same specs as Combat Master I except all matte stainless finish. Introduced 1977; discontinued 1985.

Perf.: $800   **Exc.:** $650   **VGood:** $600

DETONICS COMBAT MASTER MARK VI

Same specs as Combat Master Mark I except 451 Detonics Mag.; adjustable sights; polished stainless steel slide. Introduced 1977; discontinued 1989.

Perf.: $995   **Exc.:** $750   **VGood:** $600

DETONICS COMBAT MASTER MARK VII

Same specs as Combat Master Mark VI except no sights as special order option. Introduced 1977; discontinued 1982.

Perf.: $895   **Exc.:** $750   **VGood:** $650

DETONICS COMPMASTER

Semi-automatic; 45 ACP; 7-, 8-shot magazine; 5-inch, 6-inch barrel; Millet adjustable sights; checkered Pachmayr stocks; matching mainspring housing; Detonics recoil system; extended grip safety; ambidextrous safety; extended magazine release; stainless steel. Introduced 1988; discontinued 1992.

Perf.: $1895   **Exc.:** $1400   **VGood:** $1200

DETONICS MARK I

Semi-automatic; 45 ACP; 6-shot magazine; 3-1/2-inch barrel; 6-3/4-inch overall length; weighs 29 oz.; fixed sights; adjustable rear sights available; checkered walnut stocks; compact based on Model 1911; blued finish. Introduced 1977; discontinued 1981.

Perf.: $595   **Exc.:** $500   **VGood:** $450

DETONICS MARK II

Same specs as Mark I except satin nickel plated. Introduced 1977; discontinued 1979.

Perf.: $675   **Exc.:** $550   **VGood:** $500

DETONICS MARK III

Same specs as Mark I except hard chrome plated. Introduced 1977; discontinued 1979.

Perf.: $675   **Exc.:** $500   **VGood:** $425

DETONICS MARK IV

Same specs as Mark I except polished blue finish. Introduced 1977; discontinued 1981.

Perf.: $695   **Exc.:** $525   **VGood:** $450

DETONICS MILITARY COMBAT MC2

Semi-automatic; 38 Super, 9mm Para., 45 ACP; 6-shot magazine; 3-1/2-inch barrel; 6-3/4-inch overall length; weighs 29 oz.; fixed sights; Pachmayr grips; camo pistol rug; matte finish. Introduced 1977; discontinued 1984.

Perf.: $675   **Exc.:** $550   **VGood:** $475

DETONICS POCKET 9

Semi-automatic; double action; 9mm Para.; 6-shot; 3-inch barrel; 5-11/16-inch overall length; weighs 26 oz.; fixed sights; black Micarta stocks; triggerguard hook; snag-free hammer; captive recoil spring; matte stainless steel finish. Introduced 1985; dropped 1986.

Perf.: $400   **Exc.:** $300   **VGood:** $250

DETONICS POCKET 9LS

Same specs as Pocket 9 except 4-inch barrel; weighs 28 oz. Introduced 1986; discontinued 1986.

Perf.: $450   **Exc.:** $375   **VGood:** $300

DETONICS POCKET 380

Same specs as Pocket 9 except in 380 ACP; weighs 23 oz. Introduced 1986; discontinued 1986.

Perf.: $400   **Exc.:** $350   **VGood:** $300

DETONICS POWER 9

Semi-automatic; double-action; 9mm Para.; 6-shot; 4-inch barrel; weighs 28 oz.; polished slide flats; fixed sights; black Micarta stocks; triggerguard hook; snag-free hammer; captive recoil spring; matte stainless steel finish. Introduced 1985; dropped 1986.

Perf.: $525   **Exc.:** $450   **VGood:** $400

DETONICS SCOREMASTER

Semi-automatic; 45 ACP, 451 Detonics Mag.; 7-, 8-shot; 5-inch, 6-inch barrel; 8-3/4-inch overall length (5-inch barrel); weighs 41 oz.; Millet adjustable sights; checkered Pachmayr stocks, matching mainspring housing; Detonics recoil system; extended grip safety; ambidextrous safety; extended magazine release; stainless steel. Introduced 1983; discontinued, 1992.

Perf.: $950   **Exc.:** $800   **VGood:** $700

D-Max Sidewinder

Downsizer WSP

Dreyse Model 1907 (Early model)

DWM Pocket Model

Dreyse Vest Pocket Model

E.A.A. Big Bore Bounty Hunter

DETONICS SERVICEMASTER

Semi-automatic; 45 ACP; 8-shot magazine; 4-1/4-inch barrel; 7-7/8-inch overall length; weighs 39 oz.; adjustable combat sights; Pachmayr rubber stocks; extended grip safety; thumb and grip safeties; stainless steel construction; matte finish. Introduced 1977; discontinued 1986.

Perf.: $875   **Exc.:** $700   **VGood:** $600

DETONICS SERVICEMASTER II

Same specs as Servicemaster except polished slide flats. Introduced 1986; discontinued 1992.

Perf.: $800   **Exc.:** $650   **VGood:** $550

DOWNSIZER WSP

Single shot; 22 WMR, 32 H&R Mag., 380 ACP, 9mm Para, 357 Magnum, 40 S&W, 45 ACP. Barrel: 2.10-inch. Weight: 11 oz. Length: 3.25-inch overall. Stocks: Black polymer. Sights: None. Features: Single shot, tip-up barrel. Double action only. Stainless steel construction. Measures .900-inch thick. Introduced 1997. From Downsizer Corp.

Perf.: $435   **Exc.:** $350   **VGood:** $300

D-MAX SIDEWINDER

Revolver; single action; 45 Colt/410 shotshell; 6-shot cylinder; 6-1/2-inch, 7-1/2-inch and 14-1/8-inch overall length (6-1/2-inch barrel); weighs 57 oz. (6-1/2-inch barrel); Hogue black rubber grips with finger grooves; blade on ramp front sight, fully-adjustable rear; stainless steel construction; removable choke for firing shotshells; grooved, wide-spur hammer; transfer bar ignition; satin finish. Made in U.S. by D-Max, Inc. Introduced 1992; still produced.

Perf.: $700   **Exc.:** $650   **VGood:** $600

DREYSE MODEL 1907

Semi-automatic; 32 ACP; 8-shot magazine; 3-1/2-inch barrel; 6-1/4-inch overall length; fixed sights; hard rubber checkered stocks; blued finish. Manufactured in Germany, 1907 to 1920. Very early model shown brings a premium.

Exc.: $250   **VGood:** $185   **Good:** $150

DREYSE VEST POCKET MODEL

Semi-automatic; 25 ACP; 6-shot magazine; 2-inch barrel; 4-1/2-inch overall length; fixed sights; checkered hard rubber grips; blued finish. Manufactured 1909 to 1914.

Exc.: $325   **VGood:** $235   **Good:** $150

DREYSE MODEL 1910

Manufactured 1912-1915; 9mm Para.; about 1,000 pieces were produced; very rare.

Perf.: $6500   **Exc.:** $5500   **VGood:** $4500

DWM POCKET MODEL

Semi-automatic; 32 ACP; 3-1/2-inch barrel; 6-inch overall length; hard rubber checkered stocks; blued finish. Design resembles Browning FN Model 1910. Manufactured in Germany, 1920 to 1931.

Exc.: $600   **VGood:** $500   **Good:** $425

DSA B&T TP9 TACTICAL PISTOL

Swiss made recoil-operated, rotating-bolt semi-auto chambered in 9mm Parabellum. Semi-auto, civilian-legal version of B&T TP9SF select-fire submachine gun. Planned to be imported in 2007.

New.: $2200   **Exc:** $2000   **Good:** $1750

E.A.A. BIG BORE BOUNTY HUNTER

Revolver; single action; 357 Mag., 44 Mag., 45 Colt; 6-shot cylinder; 4-1/2-inch, 7-1/2-inch barrel; 11-inch overall length (4-5/8-inch barrel); weighs 2-1/2 lbs.; smooth walnut grips; blade front sight, grooved topstrap rear; transfer bar safety; three-position hammer; hammer-forged barrel; blue, nickel or case-hardened frame. Imported by European American Armory. Introduced 1992; still imported.

Blue or case-hardened frame		
Perf.: $315	**Exc.:** $255	**VGood:** $205
Nickel finish		
Perf.: $345	**Exc.:** $285	**VGood:** $235

E.A.A. BOUNTY HUNTER

Revolver; single action; 22 LR, 22 WMR; 6-shot cylinder; 4-3/4-inch, 6-inch, 9-inch barrel; 10-inch overall length (4-3/4-inch barrel); weighs 32 oz.; European hardwood grips; blade front sight, adjustable rear; blue finish only. From European American Armory Corp. Introduced 1991; no longer available.

Perf.: $160	**Exc.:** $145	**VGood:** $135
4-3/4-inch, 9-inch barrel; 22 LR/22 WMR combo		
Perf.: $210	**Exc.:** $175	**VGood:** $150

E.A.A. EA22T TARGET

Semi-automatic; 22 LR; 12-shot magazine; 6-inch barrel; 9-1/8-inch overall length; weighs 40 oz.; ramped blade front sight, fully-adjustable rear;

checkered walnut grips; thumbrest; blued finish. Made in Italy. Introduced 1991; no longer imported.

Perf.: $375   **Exc.:** $295   **VGood:** $260

E.A.A. EUROPEAN 320

Semi-automatic; 22 LR, 32 ACP, 380 ACP, 10-shot (22), 7-shot (32 ACP, 380 ACP); 3-7/8-inch barrel; 7-3/8-inch overall length; weighs 26 oz.; fixed blade front sight, windage-adjustable rear; European hardwood grips; magazine, thumb and firing pin safeties; external hammer; safety-lever; chrome or blued finish. Made in Italy. Introduced 1991; dropped 1995. Formerly imported by European American Armory Corp.

Perf.: $130   **Exc.:** $110   **VGood:** $95

E.A.A. EUROPEAN 380/DA

Revolver; double action; 380 ACP; 7-shot; 3-7/8-inch barrel; 7-3/8-inch overall length; 26 oz.; double-action trigger mechanism; steel construction; blue, chrome or blue/chrome finish. From European American Armory Corp. Introduced 1992; dropped 2001. Blue finish.

Perf.: $145	**Exc.:** $115	**VGood:** $95
Chrome finish or blue/chrome finish		
Perf.: $160	**Exc.:** $130	**VGood:** $110

E.A.A. EUROPEAN 380 LADIES

Same specs as European 380/DA except blue or gold finish; ivory polymer grips. From European American Armory Corp.

Perf.: $200   **Exc.:** $175   **VGood:** $150v

E.A.A. WINDICATOR STANDARD GRADE

Revolver; double action; 22 LR, 22 LR/22 WMR combo, 38 Spl.; 8-shot cylinder (22 LR, 22 LR/22 WMR); 6-shot cylinder (38 Spl.); 4-inch, 6-inch barrel (22); 2-inch, 4-inch barrel (38 Spl.); 8-13/16-inch overall length (4-inch barrel); weighs 38 oz. (22, 4-inch barrel); rubber grips with finger grooves; blade front sight, fixed or adjustable (22); fixed sights (32, 38 Spl. only); swing-out cylinder; hammer-block safety; blue finish. Imported from Germany by European American Armory Corp. Introduced 1991.

38 Special, 2-inch barrel		
Perf.: $205	**Exc.:** $170	**VGood:** $145
22 LR, 6-inch barrel, 38 Special, 4-inch barrel		
Perf.: $140	**Exc.:** $120	**VGood:** $110

E.A.A. Windicator
Standard Grade

E.A.A. Witness
Gold Team

E.A.A. Witness

EntrEprise Elite P500

EntrEprise Tactical P500

22 LR/22 WMR combo, 4-inch or 6-inch barrel		
Perf.: $280	**Exc.:** $245	**VGood:** $225

E.A.A. WINDICATOR TACTICAL GRADE

Revolver; double action; 38 Spl.; 2-inch, 4-inch barrel; fixed sights; compensator on 4-inch; bobbed hammer (DA only) on 2-inch model. Imported from Germany by European American Armory Corp. Introduced 1991; no longer imported.

2-inch barrel, bobbed hammer		
Perf.: $200	**Exc.:** $175	**VGood:** $150
4-inch barrel, compensator		
Perf.: $250	**Exc.:** $225	**VGood:** $200

E.A.A. WINDICATOR TARGET GRADE

Revolver; double action; 22 LR, 38 Spl., 357 Mag.; 8-shot cylinder (22 LR); 6-shot (38 Spl., 357 Mag.); 6-inch barrel; 11-13/16-inch overall length; weighs 50 oz.; walnut competition-style grips; blade front sight with three interchangeable blades, fully-adjustable rear; adjustable trigger with trigger stop and trigger shoe; frame drilled and tapped for scope mount; target hammer; comes with barrel weights, plastic carrying box. Imported from Germany by European American Armory Corp. Introduced 1991; dropped 1993.

Perf.: $350	**Exc.:** $300	**VGood:** $250

E.A.A. WITNESS

Semi-automatic; 9mm Para., 40 S&W, 41 AE, 45 ACP; 16-shot (9mm), 12-shot (40 S&W), 11-shot (41 AE), 10-shot (45 ACP); 4-11/16-inch barrel; 8-1/8-inch overall length; weighs 35-3/8 oz.; undercut blade front, open adjustable rear sight; squared-off triggerguard; frame mounted safety; checkered rubber grips; blue, satin chrome finish.

9mm, blue finish		
Perf.: $475	**Exc.:** $250	**VGood:** $200
9mm, satin finis3		
Perf.: $485	**Exc.:** $275	**VGood:** $225
40 S&W, blue finish		
Perf.: $495	**Exc.:** $315	**VGood:** $250
40 S&W, satin finish		
Perf.: $500	**Exc.:** $325	**VGood:** $275

45 ACP, blue finish		
Perf.: $500	**Exc.:** $325	**VGood:** $275
45 ACP, satin finish		
Perf.: $525	**Exc.:** $350	**VGood:** $300
41 AE		
Perf.: $525	**Exc.:** $350	**VGood:** $300

E.A.A. WITNESS COMPACT

Same specs as Witness except 9mm, 40 S&W, 45 ACP; 10-shot (9mm), 9-shot (40 S&W), 8-shot (45 ACP); 3-5/8-inch barrel; 7-1/4-inch overall length; weighs 30 oz.; blue or hard chrome finish. Introduced 1995; still in production.

New: $300	**Perf.:** $275	**Exc.:** $250
45 ACP		
New: $350	**Perf.:** $300	**Exc.:** $275

E.A.A. WITNESS GOLD TEAM

Semi-automatic; single action; 9mm Para., 9x21, 38 Super, 10mm, 40 S&W, 45 ACP; 10-shot magazine; 5-1/8-inch barrel; 9-5/8-inch overall length; weighs 41-1/2 oz.; checkered walnut competition-style grips; square post front sight, fully-adjustable rear; triple-chamber cone compensator; competition SA trigger; extended safety and magazine release; competition hammer; beveled magazine well; beavertail grip; hand-fitted major components; match-grade barrel; hard chrome finish. From E.A.A. Custom Shop. Marketed by European American Armory Corp. Introduced 1992; still offered.

Perf.: $1500	**Exc.:** $1225	**VGood:** $995

E.A.A. WITNESS SILVER TEAM

Semi-automatic; single action; 9mm Para., 9x21, 38 Super, 10mm, 40 S&W, 45 ACP; 10-shot magazine; 5-1/8-inch barrel; 9-5/8-inch overall length; weighs 41-1/2 oz.; black rubber grips; square post front sight, fully-adjustable rear; double-chamber compensator; competition SA trigger; extended safety; oval magazine release; competition hammer; beveled magazine well; beavertail grip; hand-fitted major components; match-grade barrel; double-dip blue finish. Comes with Super Sight and drilled and tapped for scope mount. Built for the intermediate competition shooter. From E.A.A. Custom Shop. Marketed by European American Armory Corp. Introduced 1992; still offered.

Perf.: $895	**Exc.:** $750	**VGood:** $655

E.A.A. WITNESS ELITE MATCH

Single action semi-auto featuring 4.5-inch polygonal rifled steel barrel, adjustable rear sights, rubber grips. Two-tone finish. Chambered for 9 mm (18+1), 10 mm (15+1), 38 Super (15+1), .40 S&W (15+1) and .45 ACP (10+1). 33 oz.

NIB: $560	**Exc.:** $495	**VGood:** $375

WITNESS FCP

Novel semi-auto pistol that uses reusable tubular chambers that encase each cartridge. Chambered in .45 ACP, .38 Special, .380 ACP, 9mm Parabellum, .40 S&W, and .38 Super. Six-shot capacity. Built on EAA Witness polymer frame. Introduced 2007. As of this writing, this gun seems not to be generally available, and, like so many things in the gun business, it's unknown whether it ever will be.

New: $300	**Perf.:** $275	**Exc.:** $250

E.A.A. ZASTAVA EZ PISTOL

CZ75 clone. Single-/double-action pistol with four-inch (Full Size) or 3.5-inch (Compact) barrel, polymer frame. Chambered in 9mm, .40 S&W or .45 ACP. Magazine capacity varies from 7 rounds (.45 ACP) to 15 (9mm).

New: $425	**Perf.:** $375	**Exc.:** $300

ENTREPRISE ELITE P500

Semi-automatic; 45 ACP, 10-shot magazine. Barrel: 5-inch. Weight: 40 oz. Length: 8-1/2-inch overall. Stocks: Black ultra-slim, double diamond, checkered synthetic. Sights: Dovetailed blade front, rear adjustable for windage; three-dot system. Features: Reinforced dust cover; lowered and flared ejection port; squared trigger guard; adjustable match trigger; bolstered front strap; high grip cut; high ride beavertail grip safety; steel flat mainspring housing; extended thumb lock; skeletonized hammer, match grade sear, disconnector; Wolff springs. Introduced 1998. Made in U.S. by Entreprise Arms. Apparently discontinued.

Perf.: $625	**Exc.:** $565	**VGood:** $500

ENTREPRISE TACTICAL P500 AUTO PISTOL

Similar to the Elite model except has Tactical2 Ghost Ring sight or Novak lo-mount sight; ambidextrous thumb safety; front and rear slide serrations; full-length guide rod; throated barrel, polished ramp; tuned match extractor; fitted barrel and bushing; stainless firing pin; slide lapped to frame; dehorned. Introduced 1998. Made in U.S. by Entreprise Arms. Apparently discontinued.

Perf.: $875	**Exc.:** $750	**VGood:** $650

EntrEprise Boxer P500

Erma ESP-85A Junior Match

Erma ER 773

Erma ESP-85A Target

Erma ER 777

ENTREPRISE MEDALIST P500 AUTO PISTOL

Similar to the Elite model except has adjustable Competizione "melded" rear sight with dovetailed Patridge front; machined slide parallel rails with polished breech face and barrel channel; front and rear slide serrations; lowered and flared ejection port; full-length one-piece guide rod with plug; National Match barrel and bushing; stainless firing pin; tuned match extractor; oversize firing pin stop; throated barrel and polished ramp; slide lapped to frame. Introduced 1998. Made in U.S. by Entreprise Arms. Apparently discontinued.

Perf.: $875   **Exc.:** $750   **VGood:** $675

ENTREPRISE BOXER P500 AUTO PISTOL

Similar to the Medalist model except has adjustable Competizione "melded" rear sight with dovetailed Patridge front; high mass chiseled slide with sweep cut; machined slide parallel rails; polished breech face and barrel channel. Introduced 1998. Made in U.S. by Entréprise Arms. Apparently discontinued.

Perf.: $875   **Exc.:** $750   **VGood:** $650

ENTREPRISE TOURNAMENT SHOOTER MODEL I

Semi-automatic; 45 ACP, 10-shot magazine. Barrel: 5-inch. Weight: 40 oz. Length: 8-1/2-inch overall. Stocks: Black ultra-slim double diamond checkered synthetic. Sights: Dovetailed Patridge front, adjustable Competizione "melded" rear. Features: Oversized magazine release button; flared magazine well; fully machined parallel slide rails; polished barrel channel and breech face; front and rear slide serrations; serrated top of slide; stainless ramped bull barrel with fully supported chamber; full-length guide rod with plug; stainless firing pin; match extractor; polished ramp; tuned match extractor; hard chrome finish. Introduced 1998. Made in U.S. by Entreprise Arms. Apparently discontinued.

Perf.: $1850   **Exc.:** $1600   **VGood:** $1450

ERMA ER 772

Revolver; double action; 22 LR; 6-shot; 6-inch shrouded barrel; 11-3/16-inch overall length; blade front, adjustable micro rear sight; sporting or adjustable match-type walnut stocks; solid rib; blued finish. Made in Germany. Introduced 1989.

Perf.: $550   **Exc.:** $450   **VGood:** $350

ERMA ER 773

Revolver; double action; 32 S&W Long; 6-shot; 6-inch shrouded barrel; 11-3/16-inch overall length; weighs 46 oz.; blade front, adjustable micro rear sight; sporting or adjustable match-type walnut stocks; solid rib; blued finish. Made in Germany. Introduced 1989; dropped 1995.

Perf.: $1100   **Exc.:** $825   **VGood:** $695

ERMA ER 777

Revolver; double action; 357 Mag.; 6-shot; 4-inch, 5-1/2-inch shrouded barrel; 9-1/2-inch overall length (4-inch barrel); weighs 44 oz.; blade front, adjustable micro rear sight; checkered sport grips; solid rear; blued finish. Made in Germany. Introduced 1989; dropped 1995.

Perf.: $875   **Exc.:** $775   **VGood:** $650

ERMA ESP-85A SPORTING/MATCH TARGET

Semi-automatic; single action; 22 LR, 32 S&W Long; 8-shot (22 LR), 5-shot (32 S&W Long); 6-inch barrel; 10-inch overall length; weighs 40 oz.; checkered walnut thumbrest grips; adjustable target stocks optional; interchangeable blade front sight, micrometer fully-adjustable rear; interchangeable caliber conversion kit available; adjustable trigger, trigger stop. Imported from Germany by Precision Sales Int'l. Introduced 1988; all importation ceased by 1994.

22 LR		
Perf.: $1225	**Exc.:** $925	**VGood:** $800
32 S&W Long		
Perf.: $1225	**Exc.:** $1000	**VGood:** $850
22 LR, chrome finish		
Perf.: $1450	**Exc.:** $1225	**VGood:** $975
22 LR conversion unit		
Perf.: $1300	**Exc.:** $1100	**VGood:** $975
32 S&W conversion unit		
Perf.: $1300	**Exc.:** $1100	**VGood:** $975

ERMA ESP-85A GOLDEN TARGET

Same specs as the ESP-85A except high-polish gold finish on the slide; adjustable match stocks with finger grooves; comes with fully interchangeable 6-inch barrels for 22 LR and 32 S&W. Imported from Germany by Precision Sales International. Introduced 1994; no longer imported.

Perf.: $1600   **Exc.:** $1350   **VGood:** $1000

ERMA ESP-85A JUNIOR MATCH

Same specs as the ESP-85A except 22 LR; blue finish only; stippled non-adjustable walnut match grips (adjustable grips optional). Imported from Germany by Precision Sales International. Introduced 1995; no longer imported.

Perf.: $750   **Exc.:** $650   **VGood:** $600

ERMA KGP68A

Semi-automatic; 32 ACP, 380 ACP; 6-shot; 3-1/2-inch, 4-inch barrel; 6-3/4-inch overall length; weighs 20 oz.; adjustable blade front, fixed rear sight; checkered plastic or walnut grips; Luger look-alike; blued finish. Later models designated KGP32, KGP38. Introduced 1968.

Perf.: $450   **Exc.:** $350   **VGood:** $300

ERMA KGP69

Semi-automatic; 22 LR; 8-shot magazine; 3-3/4-inch barrel; 7-3/4-inch overall length; weighs 22 oz.; fixed sights; checkered plastic or walnut grips; Luger look-alike; blued finish. Later models designated KGP22. Introduced 1969.

Perf.: $295   **Exc.:** $275   **VGood:** $250

ERMA LA 22

Semi-automatic; 22 LR; 10-shot magazine; 8-3/16-inch, 11-3/4-inch barrel; adjustable target sights; checkered plastic grips; Luger look-alike; blued finish. Introduced 1964; discontinued 1967.

Exc.: $350   **VGood:** $275   **Good:** $175

ERMA RX 22

Semi-automatic; double action; 22 LR; 8-shot magazine; 3-1/4-inch barrel, 5-9/16-inch overall length; fixed sights; plastic wrap-around grips; thumb safety; patented ignition safety system; polished blued finish. Assembled in USA. Introduced 1980; discontinued 1986.

Perf.: $125   **Exc.:** $110   **VGood:** $100

Falcon Portsider

ESFAC Little Ace Derringer

FAS Model 607 Match

ESFAC Pocket Pony

ESFAC Four Aces Model 1

Federal Ordnance Ranger G.I. Model

ESFAC FOUR ACES MODEL 1

Derringer; 22 Short; 4-shot; 1-11/16-inch barrels (4); black plastic grips; round butt; post front sight; manganese bronze frame; spur trigger; barrel selector on hammer; blued steel barrels. Introduced 1973; maker ceased business 1974.

Exc.: $175   **VGood:** $135   **Good:** $100

ESFAC FOUR ACES MODEL 2

Same specs as Model 1 except square-butt frame.

Exc.: $175   **VGood:** $135   **Good:** $100

ESFAC FOUR ACES MODEL 3

Same specs as Model 2 except 2-inch barrels; 22 LR.

Exc.: $160   **VGood:** $135   **Good:** $100

ESFAC FOUR ACES MODEL 4

Same specs as Model 3 except slightly longer overall length.

Exc.: $160   **VGood:** $135   **Good:** $100

ESFAC LITTLE ACE DERRINGER

Derringer; single shot; 22 Short; 2-inch barrel; black plastic grips; no sights; manganese bronze frame; blued barrel; color case-hardened spur trigger, hammer. Introduced 1973; maker ceased business 1974.

Exc.: $120   **VGood:** $95   **Good:** $80

ESFAC POCKET PONY

Revolver; single action; 22 LR; 6-shot; 1-3/8-inch barrel; fixed sights; black plastic grips; manganese bronze frame; blued barrel; color case-hardened trigger, hammer; non-fluted cylinder. Introduced 1973; maker ceased business 1974.

Exc.: $150   **VGood:** $125   **Good:** $100

FALCON PORTSIDER

Semi-automatic; 45 ACP; 7-shot magazine; 5-inch barrel; 8-1/2-inch overall length; weighs 38 oz.; fixed combat sights; checkered walnut stocks; stainless steel construction; extended safety; wide grip safety; enlarged left-hand ejection port; extended ejector. Introduced 1986; dropped about 1989. Scarce.

Perf.: $595   **Exc.:** $450   **VGood:** $400

Portsider Set with right and left hand models with matching serial numbers. Only 100 sets were manufactured from 1986-87.

Perf.: $1300   **Exc.:** $1100   **VGood:** $895

FAS MODEL 601 MATCH

Semi-automatic; 22 Short; 5-shot magazine; 5-1/2-inch barrel; 11-inch overall length; weighs 41 oz.; gas ported barrel; wrap-around adjustable walnut stocks; match blade front sight, fully-adjustable open notch rear; magazine inserts from top; adjustable, removable trigger group; single-lever take-down. Made in Italy. Introduced 1984; formerly imported by Nygord Precision Products.

Perf.: $1325   **Exc.:** $975   **VGood:** $695

FAS MODEL 602 MATCH

Semi-automatic; single action; 22 LR; 5-shot magazine; 5-5/8-inch barrel; 11-inch overall length; weighs 37 oz.; walnut wrap-around grips in small, medium or large, or adjustable; match blade front, open notch fully-adjustable rear sight; magazine inserted from top; adjustable and removable trigger mechanism; single-lever takedown. Formerly imported from Italy by Nygord Precision Products; no longer imported.

Perf.: $1195   **Exc.:** $800   **VGood:** $625

FAS MODEL 603 MATCH

Semi-automatic; 32 S&W; 5-shot magazine; 5-5/8-inch barrel; 11-inch overall length; weighs 37 oz.; walnut wrap-around grips in sizes small, medium or large, or adjustable; blade front, open notch fully-adjustable rear match sight; magazine inserted from top; adjustable and removable trigger mechanism; single-lever takedown. Formerly imported from Italy by Nygord Precision Products.

Perf.: $1075   **Exc.:** $875   **VGood:** $755

FAS MODEL 607 MATCH

Semi-automatic; single action; 22 LR; 5-shot magazine; 5-5/8-inch barrel; 11-inch overall length; weighs 37 oz.; walnut wrap-around grips in small, medium or large, or adjustable; blade front, open notch fully-adjustable rear match sight; magazine inserted from top; adjustable and removable trigger

mechanism; single-lever takedown. Formerly imported from Italy by Nygord Precision Products.

Perf.: $1075   **Exc.:** $875   **VGood:** $755

FEATHER GUARDIAN ANGEL

Derringer; 9mm Para., 38 Spl.; 3-inch barrel; 5-1/2-inch overall length; weighs 17 oz.; black composition stocks; fixed sights; stainless steel; matte finish; two-shot drop-in magazine. Introduced 1988; dropped 1989. New 22 LR/22 WMR model introduced 1990 with 2-inch barrels; no longer in production. Was also offered for a time by Mitchell Arms.

Perf.: $175   **Exc.:** $125   **VGood:** $95

22 LR or 22 WMR version

Perf.: $100   **Exc.:** $75   **VGood:** $60

FEDERAL ORDNANCE RANGER ALPHA

Semi-automatic; single action; 38 Super, 10mm Auto, 45 ACP; 9-shot (38 Super), 8-shot (10mm Auto), 7-shot (45 ACP); 5-inch, 6-inch barrel, ported or unported; 8-1/2-inch overall length; weighs 42 oz.; wrap-around rubber grips; interchangeable front sight, fully-adjustable Peters Stahl rear; Peters Stahl linkless barrel system; polygonal rifling; extended grip safety, thumb safety, slide release, magazine release; high polish blue finish. Imported by Federal Ordnance. Introduced 1990; no longer imported.

5-inch unported barrel, 38 Super, 45 ACP		
Perf.: $895	**Exc.:** $775	**VGood:** $675
5-inch ported barrel, 38 Super 45 ACP or unported 10mm		
Perf.: $920	**Exc.:** $795	**VGood:** $695
5-inch, 6-inch ported barrel, 10mm, 38 Super, 45 ACP		
Perf.: $950	**Exc.:** $750	**VGood:** $700
6-inch ported barrel, 10mm		
Perf.: $950	**Exc.:** $750	**VGood:** $700

Federal Ordnance Ranger
G.I. Model, Ambo

Federal Ordnance
Ranger Supercomp

FEG FP9

FEG B9R

FEG GKK-45C

FEDERAL ORDNANCE RANGER G.I. MODEL

Semi-automatic; single action; 45 ACP; 7-shot magazine; 5-inch barrel; 8-1/2-inch overall length; weighs 38 oz.; checkered plastic grips; blade front sight, drift-adjustable rear; made in U.S. from 4140 steel and other high-strength alloys; barrel machined from a forged billet. From Federal Ordnance, Inc. Introduced 1988; no longer produced.

Perf.: $485   **Exc.:** $450   **VGood:** $410

FEDERAL ORDNANCE RANGER G.I. MODEL, AMBO

Same specs as Ranger G.I. Model except ambidextrous slide release, safety; extended grip safety, thumb safety; slide and magazine releases; weighs 40 oz. Introduced 1990; discontinued 1992.

Perf.: $485   **Exc.:** $450   **VGood:** $410

FEDERAL ORDNANCE RANGER G.I. MODEL, EXTENDED

Same specs as Ranger G.I. Model except extended grip safety, thumb safety; slide and magazine releases; weighs 40 oz. Introduced 1990; discontinued 1992.

Perf.: $485   **Exc.:** $450   **VGood:** $410

FEDERAL ORDNANCE RANGER G.I. MODEL, LITE

Same specs as Ranger G.I. Model except aluminum alloy frame; Millet fixed sights; rubber wrap-around grips; lightened speed trigger; black anodized frame; blued steel slide. Introduced 1990; discontinued 1992.

Perf.: $485   **Exc.:** $450   **VGood:** $410

FEDERAL ORDNANCE RANGER G.I. MODEL, TEN AUTO

Same specs as Ranger G.I. Model except 10mm Auto chambering. Introduced 1990; discontinued 1991.

Perf.: $695   **Exc.:** $575   **VGood:** $475

FEDERAL ORDNANCE RANGER SUPERCOMP

Semi-automatic; single action; 10mm Auto, 45 ACP; 8-shot (10mm Auto), 7-shot (45 ACP); 6-inch barrel; 9-1/2-inch overall length; weighs 42 oz.; wrap-around rubber grips; ramped blade front sight, fully-adjustable, low-profile Ranger rear; Peters Stahl linkless barrel system with polygonal rifling and integral competition compensator; lightened speed trigger; beveled magazine well; ramped and throated barrel; blued slide, electroless nickel frame. From Federal Ordnance. Introduced 1990; dropped 1991.

Perf.: $895   **Exc.:** $775   **VGood:** $625

FEG B9R

Semi-automatic; 380 ACP; 10-shot magazine; 4-inch barrel; 7-inch overall length; weighs 25 oz.; blade front, drift-adjustable rear sight; hand-checkered walnut grips; hammer drop safety; grooved backstrap; squared trigger guard. Introduced 1993; still imported.

New: $290   **Perf.:** $250   **Exc.:** $200

FEG FP9

Semi-automatic; single action; 9mm Para.; 10-shot magazine; 5-inch barrel; 7-7/8-inch overall length; weighs 35 oz.; checkered walnut grips; blade front sight, windage-adjustable rear; full-length ventilated rib; polished blue finish; comes with extra magazine. Imported from Hungary by Century International Arms. Introduced 1993; still imported.

New: $225   **Perf.:** $200   **Exc.:** $175

FEG GKK-40C

Semi-automatic; double action; 40 S&W; 9-shot magazine; 4-1/8-inch barrel; 7-3/4-inch overall length; weighs 36 oz.; hand-checkered walnut grips; blade front sight, windage-adjustable rear; three-dot system; combat-type trigger guard; polished blue finish; comes with two magazines, cleaning rod. Imported from Hungary by K.B.I., Inc. Introduced 1995; no longer imported.

New: $300   **Perf.:** $250   **Exc.:** $200

FEG GKK-45C

Semi-automatic; double action; 45 ACP; 8-shot magazine; 4-1/8-inch barrel; 7-3/4-inch overall length; weighs 36 oz.; hand-checkered walnut grips; blade front sight, windage-adjustable rear; three-dot system; combat-type trigger guard; polished blue finish; comes with two magazines, cleaning rod.

Imported from Hungary by K.B.I., Inc. Introduced 1995; no longer imported.

New: $300   **Perf.:** $250   **Exc.:** $200

FEG GKK-92C

Semi-automatic; double action; 9mm Para.; 14-shot magazine; 4-inch barrel; 7-3/8-inch overall length; weighs 34 oz.; hand-checkered walnut grips; blade front sight, windage-adjustable rear; slide-mounted safety; hooked trigger guard; finger-grooved frontstrap; polished blue finish. Imported from Hungary by K.B.I., Inc. Introduced 1992; no longer imported.

Perf.: $315   **Exc.:** $280   **VGood:** $250

FEG MARK II AP PISTOL

Semi-automatic; double action; 380 ACP, 7-shot magazine. Barrel: 3.9-inch. Weight: 27 oz. Length: 6.9-inch overall. Stocks: Checkered black composition. Sights: Blade front, rear adjustable for windage. Features: Double action. All-steel construction. Polished blue finish. Comes with two magazines. Introduced 1997. Imported from Hungary by Interarms. No longer imported.

Perf.: $235   **Exc.:** $200   **VGood:** $1755

FEG MARK II AP22 PISTOL

Semi-automatic; double action; 22 LR, 8-shot magazine. Barrel: 3.4-inch. Weight: 23 oz. Length: 6.3-inch overall. Stocks: Checkered black composition. Sights: Blade front, rear adjustable for windage. Features: Double action. All-steel construction. Polished blue finish. Introduced 1997. Formerly imported from Hungary by Interarms.

Perf.: $275   **Exc.:** $250   **VGood:** $225

FEG MBK-9HP

Semi-automatic; double action; 9mm Para.; 14-shot magazine; 4-5/8-inch barrel; 7-3/8-inch overall length; weighs 34 oz.; hand-checkered walnut grips; blade front sight, windage-adjustable rear; slide-mounted safety; hooked trigger guard; smooth frontstrap; polished blue finish. Imported from Hungary by K.B.I., Inc. Introduced 1992; no longer imported.

Perf.: $315   **Exc.:** $270   **VGood:** $250

FEG P9R

Felk MTF450
Auto Pistol

FEG PJK-9HP

F.I.E. Arminus
N-38

F.I.E. Arminus
384TB

FEG MBK-9HPC

Semi-automatic; double action; 9mm Para.; 14-shot magazine; 4-inch barrel; 7-1/4-inch overall length; weighs 34 oz.; hand-checkered walnut grips; blade front sight, windage-adjustable rear; slide-mounted safety; hooked trigger guard; smooth frontstrap; polished blue finish. Imported from Hungary by K.B.I., Inc. Introduced 1992; no longer imported.

Perf.: $325 **Exc.:** $275 **VGood:** $250

FEG P9R

Semi-automatic; double action; 9mm Para.; 10-shot magazine; 4-5/8-inch barrel; 7-15/16-inch overall length; weighs 35 oz.; checkered walnut grips; blade front sight, windage-adjustable rear; slide-mounted safety; all-steel construction with polished blue finish; comes with extra magazine. Imported from Hungary by Century International Arms. Introduced 1993; still imported.

New: $225 **Perf.:** $200 **Exc.:** $185

FEG PJK-9HP

Semi-automatic; single action; 9mm Para.; 10-shot magazine; 4-3/4-inch barrel; 8-inch overall length; weighs 32 oz.; hand-checkered walnut grips; blade front sight, windage-adjustable rear; three-dot system; polished blue or hard chrome finish; rounded combat-style serrated hammer; comes with two magazines and cleaning rod. Formerly imported from Hungary by K.B.I., Inc. Introduced 1992.

New: $250 **Perf.:** $225 **Exc.:** $195

FEG PMK-380

Semi-automatic; double action; 380 ACP; 7-shot magazine; 4-inch barrel; 7-inch overall length; weighs 21 oz.; checkered black nylon thumbrest grips; blade front sight, windage-adjustable rear; anodized aluminum frame; polished blue slide; comes with two magazines, cleaning rod. Imported from Hungary by K.B.I., Inc. Introduced 1992; no longer imported.

Perf.: $225 **Exc.:** $180 **VGood:** $160

FEG SMC-22

Semi-automatic; double action; 22 LR; 8-shot magazine; 3-1/2-inch barrel; 6-1/8-inch overall length; weighs 18-1/2 oz.; checkered composition thumbrest grips; blade front sight, windage-

adjustable rear; alloy frame, steel slide; blue finish; comes with two magazines, cleaning rod. Patterned after the PPK pistol. Formerly imported from Hungary by K.B.I., Inc. Introduced 1994.

New: $210 **Perf.:** $195 **Exc.:** $180

FEG SMC-380

Semi-automatic; double action; 380 ACP; 6-shot magazine; 3-1/2-inch barrel; 6-1/8-inch overall length; weighs 18-1/2 oz.; checkered composition thumbrest grips; blade front sight, windage-adjustable rear; alloy frame, steel slide; blue finish; comes with two magazines, cleaning rod. Patterned after the PPK pistol. Imported from Hungary by K.B.I. Introduced 1994; no longer imported.

New: $205 **Perf.:** $180 **Exc.:** $160

FEG SMC-918

Semi-automatic; double action; 9x18 Makarov; 6-shot magazine; 3-1/2-inch barrel; 6-1/8-inch overall length; weighs 18-1/2 oz.; checkered composition thumbrest grips; blade front sight, rear adjustable for windage; alloy frame, steel slide; blue finish; comes with two magazines, cleaning rod. Patterned after the PPK pistol. Formerly imported from Hungary by K.B.I. Introduced 1995.

New: $250 **Perf.:** $225 **Exc.:** $200

FELK MTF 450 AUTO PISTOL

Semi-automatic; double action only; 9mm Para. (10-shot); 40 S&W (8-shot); 45 ACP (9-shot magazine). Barrel: 3.5-inch. Weight: 19.9 oz. Length: 6.4-inch overall. Stocks: Checkered. Sights: Blade front; adjustable rear. Features: Double-action-only trigger, striker fired; polymer frame; trigger safety, firing pin safety, trigger bar safety; adjustable trigger weight; fully interchangeable slide/barrel to change calibers. Introduced 1998. Imported from Australia by Felk Inc.

Perf.: $350 **Exc.:** $300 **VGood:** $250

45 ACP pistol with 9mm and 40 S&W slide/barrel assemblies

Perf.: $850 **Exc.:** $750 **VGood:** $650

F.I.E. ARMINIUS MODEL 222

Revolver; double action; 22 LR, 22 WMR; 8-shot; 2-inch barrel; plastic or walnut grips; swing-out cylinder; blued or chrome finish. Discontinued 1985;

reintroduced as F.I.E. Arminius Model 222B 1987; discontinued 1989.

Perf.: $145 **Exc.:** $115 **VGood:** $100

F.I.E. ARMINIUS MODEL 232

Revolver; double action; 32 S&W; 7-shot; 2-inch barrel; fixed or adjustable sights; plastic or walnut grips; swing-out cylinder; blued finish. Discontinued 1985; reintroduced as F.I.E. Arminius Model 232B 1987; discontinued 1989.

Perf.: $120 **Exc.:** $105 **VGood:** $95

F.I.E. ARMINIUS MODEL 357

Revolver; double action; 357 Mag.; 6-shot; 3-inch, 4-inch, 6-inch barrel; plastic or walnut grips; blued or chrome finish. Discontinued 1990.

Perf.: $200 **Exc.:** $170 **VGood:** $135

Chrome finish

Perf.: $235 **Exc.:** $205 **VGood:** $170

F.I.E. ARMINIUS MODEL 357T

Revolver; double action; 357 Mag.; 6-shot; 2-inch barrel; plastic or walnut grips; blued or chrome finish. Discontinued 1984.

Perf.: $175 **Exc.:** $155 **VGood:** $135

Chrome finish

Perf.: $185 **Exc.:** $175 **VGood:** $150

F.I.E. ARMINIUS MODEL 382TB

Revolver; double action; 38 Spl.; 6-shot; 2-inch barrel; plastic or walnut grips; blued or chrome finish. Discontinued 1985.

Perf.: $120 **Exc.:** $95 **VGood:** $85

Chrome finish

Perf.: $135 **Exc.:** $105 **VGood:** $95

F.I.E. ARMINIUS MODEL 384TB

Revolver; double action; 38 Spl.; 6-shot; 4-inch barrel; plastic or walnut grips; blued or chrome finish. Discontinued 1990.

Perf.: $155 **Exc.:** $135 **VGood:** $105

Chrome finish

Perf.: $185 **Exc.:** $175 **VGood:** $140

F.I.E. Cowboy

F.I.E. Buffalo Scout E15

F.I.E. Super Titan II E32

F.I.E. Hombre

F.I.E. Little Ranger

F.I.E. ARMINIUS MODEL 386TB
Revolver; double action; 38 Spl.; 6-shot; 6-inch barrel; plastic or walnut grips; blued or chrome finish. Discontinued 1990.

Perf.: $150   **Exc.:** $125   **VGood:** $105

Chrome finish
Perf.: $175   **Exc.:** $150   **VGood:** $140

F.I.E. ARMINIUS MODEL 522TB
Revolver; double action; 22 LR; 8-shot cylinder; 4-inch barrel; fixed sights; plastic or walnut grips; swing-out cylinder; blued finish. Discontinued 1990.

Perf.: $135   **Exc.:** $105   **VGood:** $95

F.I.E. ARMINIUS MODEL 532TB
Revolver; double action; 32 S&W; 7-shot cylinder; 4-inch barrel; adjustable sights; plastic or walnut grips; blued or chrome finish. Discontinued 1985.

Perf.: $145   **Exc.:** $120   **VGood:** $100

Chrome finish
Perf.: $160   **Exc.:** $140   **VGood:** $120

F.I.E. ARMINIUS MODEL 722
Revolver; double action; 22 LR; 8-shot cylinder; 6-inch barrel; fixed sights; plastic or walnut grips; swing-out cylinder; blued or chrome finish. Discontinued 1985.

Perf.: $125   **Exc.:** $100   **VGood:** $90

Chrome finish
Perf.: $145   **Exc.:** $125   **VGood:** $120

F.I.E. ARMINIUS MODEL 732B
Revolver; double action; 32 S&W; 7-shot cylinder; 6-inch barrel; fixed sights; blued finish. Discontinued 1988.

Perf.: $130   **Exc.:** $100   **VGood:** $95

F.I.E. ARMINIUS MODEL N-38
Revolver; double action; 38 Spl.; 6-shot cylinder; 2-inch, 4-inch barrel; ramp front sight, fixed rear; Bulldog-style checkered plastic or walnut grips; swing-out cylinder; one-stroke ejection; blued or chrome finish. Marketed as Titan Tiger. Introduced 1978; discontinued 1990.

Perf.: $130   **Exc.:** $110   **VGood:** $95

Chrome finish
Perf.: $150   **Exc.:** $130   **VGood:** $115

F.I.E. ARMINIUS STANDARD MODEL
Revolver; double action; 22 LR, 22 WMR, 32 H&R Mag., 38 Spl.; 8-shot cylinder (rimfire), 6-shot swing-out cylinder (centerfire); 2-inch, 4-inch barrel; 6-1/4-inch overall length (2-inch barrel); weighs 27 oz.; fixed sights; Bulldog-style checkered plastic or walnut grips; swing-out cylinder; one-stroke ejection; blued, chrome finish or gold-plated. Introduced 1989; discontinued 1990.

Perf.: $100   **Exc.:** $80   **VGood:** $75

Chrome finish
Perf.: $120   **Exc.:** $110   **VGood:** $95

Gold plated
Perf.: $140   **Exc.:** $130   **VGood:** $115

F.I.E. ARMINIUS ZEPHYR
Revolver; double action; 38 Spl.; 5-shot cylinder; 2-inch barrel; weighs 14 oz.; checkered grips; aluminum frame; blued finish. Introduced 1990; discontinued 1990.

Perf.: $150   **Exc.:** $125   **VGood:** $110

F.I.E. ARMINIUS ZEPHYR LADY
Same specs as Zephyr except polymer ivory grips with scrimshaw; gold trim; gold case. Introduced 1990; discontinued 1990.

Perf.: $250   **Exc.:** $210   **VGood:** $180

F.I.E. BUFFALO SCOUT E15
Revolver; single action; 22 LR, 22 WMR; 6-shot cylinder; 4-3/4-inch barrel; 10-inch overall length; adjustable sights; black checkered plastic or uncheckered red walnut grips; sliding spring ejector; blued, chromed or blue/brass finish. Introduced 1978; discontinued 1990.

Perf.: $95   **Exc.:** $65   **VGood:** $55

Chrome finish
Perf.: $115   **Exc.:** $75   **VGood:** $65

Blue/brass finish
Perf.: $130   **Exc.:** $115   **VGood:** $95

F.I.E. COWBOY
Revolver; single action; 22 LR, 22 WMR; 6-shot cylinder; 3-1/4-inch, 6-1/2-inch barrel; weighs 28 oz. (3-1/4-inch barrel); blade front sight, fixed rear; smooth nylon square butt grips; hammer-block safety; floating firing pin; blued finish. Introduced 1989; discontinued 1990.

Perf.: $95   **Exc.:** $75   **VGood:** $55

With combo cylinders
Perf.: $115   **Exc.:** $95   **VGood:** $65

F.I.E. GOLD RUSH
Revolver; single action; 22 LR, 22 WMR, 22 LR/22 WMR combo; 6-shot cylinder; 3-1/4-inch, 4-3/4-inch, 6-1/2-inch barrel; blade front, fixed rear sight; ivory-styled grips; gold band on barrel and cylinder; round or square butt; blue finish. Introduced 1989; discontinued 1990.

Perf.: $155   **Exc.:** $135   **VGood:** $125

With combo cylinders
Perf.: $200   **Exc.:** $175   **VGood:** $160

F.I.E. HOMBRE
Revolver; single action; 357 Mag., 44 Mag., 45 Colt; 5-1/2-inch, 6-inch, 7-1/2-inch barrels; 45 oz.; blade front, grooved backstrap rear sight; smooth walnut grips, medallion; color case-hardened frame; blue finish. Introduced 1970; discontinued 1990.

Perf.: $250   **Exc.:** $195   **VGood:** $150

Gold plated
Perf.: $300   **Exc.:** $210   **VGood:** $175

F.I.E. KG-99 PISTOL
Semi-automatic; 9mm Para.; 20-, 36-shot magazine; 3-inch, 5-inch barrel; 12-1/2-inch overall length; weighs 46 oz.; fixed sights; military-type configuration. Introduced 1982; discontinued 1984.

Perf.: $400   **Exc.:** $325   **VGood:** $250

F.I.E. LEGEND
Revolver; single action; 22 LR, 22 LR/22 WMR combo; 6-shot cylinder; 4-3/4-inch, 5-1/2-inch barrel; fixed sights; black checkered plastic or walnut grips; brass backstrap, trigger guard; case-hardened steel

F.I.E. Titan E27

F.I.E. Model D38

F.I.E. TZ-75 Series 88

F.I.E. Model D86

F.I.E. Model 722 TP Silhouette Pistol

frame; blue finish. Introduced 1978; discontinued 1984.

Perf.: $120	**Exc.:** $100	**VGood:** $85
With combo cylinder		
Perf.: $140	**Exc.:** $120	**VGood:** $105

F.I.E. LITTLE RANGER
Revolver; single action; 22 LR, 22LR/22WMR combo; 6-shot cylinder; 3-1/4-inch barrel; blade front, notch rear sight; American hardwood bird's-head grips; blue/black finish. Introduced 1986; discontinued 1990.

Perf.: $90	**Exc.:** $80	**VGood:** $70
With combo cylinders		
Perf.: $110	**Exc.:** $95	**VGood:** $85

F.I.E. MODEL 722 TP SILHOUETTE PISTOL
Repeater; bolt action; 22 LR; 6-, 10-shot magazine; 10-inch barrel; 19-inch overall length; weighs 54 oz.; hooded front sight, micro-adjustable target rear; walnut-finished hardwood stock with stippled grip, forend; fully-adjustable match trigger; receiver grooved for scope mounting; marketed with two-piece high-base mount, both magazines. Made in Brazil. Introduced 1990; importation dropped 1990.

Perf.: $220	**Exc.:** $190	**VGood:** $16

F.I.E. MODEL D38
Derringer; over/under; 38 Spl.; 2-shot cylinder; 2-inch barrel; fixed sights; checkered plastic or walnut grips; spur trigger; chrome finish. Introduced 1979; discontinued 1985.

Perf.: $100	**Exc.:** $70	**VGood:** $55

F.I.E. MODEL D86
Derringer; single shot; 38 Spl.; 3-inch barrel; weighs 14 oz.; fixed sights; checkered black nylon or walnut grips; spur trigger; tip-up barrel; extractors; chrome or blued finish. Introduced 1986; dropped 1990.

Perf.: $100	**Exc.:** $75	**VGood:** $65
Chrome finish		
Perf.: $110	**Exc.:** $85	**VGood:** $75

F.I.E. SPECTRE PISTOL
Semi-automatic; double action; 9mm Para., 45 ACP; 30-, 50-shot magazine; 6-inch barrel; weighs 76 oz.; adjustable sights; military-type configuration. Introduced 1989; discontinued 1990.

Perf.: $675	**Exc.:** $600	**VGood:** $525

F.I.E. SSP MODEL
Semi-automatic; single action; 32 ACP, 380 ACP; 3-1/8-inch barrel; 6-1/4-inch overall length; weighs 25 oz.; blade front, windage-adjustable rear sight; smooth European walnut grips; external hammer, magazine safety; blued, satin chrome finish. Introduced 1990; dropped 1990.

Perf.: $120	**Exc.:** $95	**VGood:** $85
Satin chrome finish		
Perf.: $140	**Exc.:** $115	**VGood:** $115

F.I.E. SSP MODEL LADY
Same specs as SSP except scrimshawed polymer ivory grips; gold trimmed; gold case. Introduced 1990; discontinued 1990.

Perf.: $210	**Exc.:** $180	**VGood:** $155

F.I.E. SUPER TITAN II E32
Semi-automatic; single action; 32 ACP, 380 ACP; 12-shot magazine (32 ACP), 11-shot (380 ACP); 3-7/8-inch barrel; 6-3/4-inch overall length; adjustable sights; walnut grips; blue finish. Introduced 1981; discontinued 1990.

Perf.: $195	**Exc.:** $160	**VGood:** $135

F.I.E. TITAN A27
Semi-automatic; single action; 25 ACP; 6-shot magazine; 2-1/2-inch barrel; 4-3/8-inch overall length; fixed sights; checkered walnut stocks; all-steel construction; thumb, magazine safeties; exposed hammer; blued finish. Introduced 1978; discontinued 1988.

Perf.: $125	**Exc.:** $105	**VGood:** $90

F.I.E. TITAN E27
Semi-automatic; single action; 25 ACP; 6-shot magazine; 4-inch barrel; fixed sights; checkered walnut stocks; wide trigger; blue or chrome finish. Introduced 1977; dropped 1990.

Perf.: $90		**Exc.:** $70
VGood: $65		
Chrome finish		
Perf.: $110	**Exc.:** $80	**VGood:** $75

F.I.E. TITAN E38
Semi-automatic; single action; 25 ACP; 6-shot magazine; 4-inch, 6-inch barrel; fixed sights; checkered walnut stocks; wide trigger; blue or chrome finish. Introduced 1990; dropped 1990.

Perf.: $100	**Exc.:** $60	**VGood:** $45

F.I.E. TITAN II E22
Semi-automatic; single action; 22 LR; 10-shot; 3-7/8-inch barrel; 6-3/4-inch overall length; adjustable sights; walnut grips; magazine disconnector; firing pin block; standard slide safety; blued finish. Introduced 1978; discontined 1990.

Perf.: $130	**Exc.:** $105	**VGood:** $90

F.I.E. TITAN II E22 LADY
Same specs as Titan II E22 except scrimshaw polymer ivory grips; blue/gold finish. Introduced 1990; discontinued 1990.

Perf.: $185	**Exc.:** $155	**VGood:** $130

F.I.E. TITAN II E32
Semi-automatic; single action; 32 ACP, 380 ACP; 6-shot magazine; 3-7/8-inch barrel; 6-3/4-inch overall length; adjustable sights; checkered nylon thumbrest or walnut grips; magazine disconnector; firing pin block; standard slide safety; blue or chrome finish. Introduced 1978; discontinued 1990.

Perf.: $195	**Exc.:** $160	**VGood:** $135
Chrome finish		
Perf.: $205	**Exc.:** $170	**VGood:** $145

F.I.E. TZ-75
Semi-automatic; double action; 9mm Para.; 15-shot magazine; 4-3/4-inch barrel; 8-1/4-inch overall length; weighs 35 oz.; undercut blade front, windage-adjustable open rear sight; walnut stocks or rubber grips; squared-off trigger guard; rotating slide-mounted safety; steel frame, slide; blue or chrome finish. Introduced 1983; dropped 1990.

Perf.: $400	**Exc.:** $350	**VGood:** $275
Chrome finish		
Perf.: $425	**Exc.:** $375	**VGood:** $300

F.I.E. Yellow Rose

F.I.E. Texas Ranger

Freedom Arms Boot Gun

Freedom Arms 454 Casull

Firestorm Government

F.I.E. TZ-75 SERIES 88

Semi-automatic; double action; 9mm Para., 41 AE; 17-shot magazine (9mm Para.), 11-shot (41 AE); 4-3/4-inch barrel; 8-1/4-inch overall length; weighs 35 oz.; undercut blade front, removable rear sight; walnut or rubber grips; re-engineered version of the TZ-75 with frame mounted safety; matte blue, chrome finish or with blue slide/chrome frame. Introduced 1988; discontinued 1990.

Perf.: $435	**Exc.:** $360	**VGood:** $330
Chrome finish		
Perf.: $460	**Exc.:** $385	**VGood:** $355
With blue slide/chrome frame		
Perf.: $400	**Exc.:** $375	**VGood:** $350

F.I.E. TZ-75 SERIES 88 COMPENSATED

Same specs as TZ-75 Series 88 except 5-3/4-inch compensated barrel; weighs 42 oz. Introduced 1990; discontinued 1990.

Perf.: $700	**Exc.:** $615	**VGood:** $535
Chrome finish		
Perf.: $750	**Exc.:** $665	**VGood:** $600
With blue slide/chrome frame		
Perf.: $675	**Exc.:** $635	**VGood:** $565

F.I.E. TZ-75 SERIES 88 GOVERNMENT MODEL

Same specs as TZ-75 Series 88 except 9mm Para.; 12-shot magazine; 3-1/2-inch barrel; 6-7/8-inch overall length; weighs 33-1/2 oz.; walnut grips; compact version of TZ-75 Series 88; blue, chrome or with blue slide/chrome frame. Introduced 1990; discontinued 1990.

Perf.: $435	**Exc.:** $360	**VGood:** $330
Chrome finish		
Perf.: $455	**Exc.:** $380	**VGood:** $350
With blue slide/chrome frame		
Perf.: $455	**Exc.:** $380	**VGood:** $350

F.I.E. TZ-75 SERIES 88 PORTED

Same specs as TZ-75 Series 88 except 5-inch barrel and slide. Introduced 1990; discontinued 1990.

Perf.: $615	**Exc.:** $535	**VGood:** $475
Chrome finish		
Perf.: $645	**Exc.:** $575	**VGood:** $495
Blue slide/chrome frame finish		
Perf.: $645	**Exc.:** $575	**VGood:** $495

F.I.E. TEXAS RANGER

Revolver; single action; 22 LR, 22 LR/22 WMR combo; 6-shot cylinder; 3-1/4-inch, 4-3/4-inch, 6-1/2-inch, 7-inch, 9-inch barrels; blade front, notch rear sight; American hardwood stocks; blue/black finish. Introduced 1983; discontinued 1990.

Perf.: $100	**Exc.:** $75	**VGood:** $60
With combo cylinders		
Perf.: $125	**Exc.:** $100	**VGood:** $85

F.I.E. YELLOW ROSE

Revolver; single action; 22 LR, 22 WMR; 6-shot cylinder; 4-3/4-inch barrel; 10-inch overall length; adjustable sights; walnut grips; sliding spring ejector; 24-karat gold plated. Introduced 1986; discontinued 1990.

Perf.: $150	**Exc.:** $135	**VGood:** $110
With scrimshawed ivory grips and walnut case		
Perf.: $275	**Exc.:** $225	**VGood:** $200

FIRESTORM .32

Double-action semi-auto chambered for .32 with 10+1 capacity. Blued, 3.5-inch barrel, 23 oz. Fixed sights and rubber grips.

NIB: $250	**Exc.:** $200	**VGood:** $165

FIRESTORM 1911 MIL-SPEC STANDARD GOVERNMENT

1911A1-style single-action semi-auto chambered in .45 ACP; 5.125" barrel, steel frame, 7- or 8-round magazine, steel frame, plastic or wood grips, matte blue or deluxe polished blue finish.

NIB: $315	**Exc.:** $275	**VGood:** $225

FNH MODEL FORTY-NINE

This pistol is built by FN Manufacturing, Inc. in Columbia, S.C. It has a polymer frame and stainless steel slide. Chambered for 9mm or .40 S&W cartridge. Barrel length is 4.25". Magazine capacity is 16 rounds for law enforcement and 10 rounds for commercial sales. It features a repeatable secure striker trigger system. Offered in stainless steel slide or black coated slide. Weight is about 26 oz. Offered primarly for sale to law enforcement agencies. Introduced in 2000.

NIB: $550	**Exc.:** $495	**VGood:** $400

FORT WORTH HSO

Semi-automatic; 22 Short: 10-shot magazine: 6-3/4-inch round tapered barrel, with stabilizer and built-in muzzlebrake; 40 oz.; 11-1/4-inch overall; checkered walnut grips with thumbrest; undercut ramp front, frame-mounted click adjustable square notch rear; drilled and tapped for scope mount; integral stabilizer with two removable weights; trigger adjustable for pull and length of travel; stippled front and backstraps; push-button barrel takedown. Introduced 1995; production ceased 2000.

Perf.: $475	**Exc.:** $425	**VGood:** $3500

FORT WORTH HSS

Semi-automatic; 22 LR, 10-shot magazine; 5-1/2-inch bull barrel; 45 oz.; 10.25-inch overall; checkered walnut grips; ramp front, slide-mounted square notch rear sight adjustable for windage and elevation; stainless steel construction; military grip; slide lock; smooth grip straps; push-button takedown; drilled and tapped for barrel weights. Introduced 1995; production ceased 2000.

Perf.: $325	**Exc.:** $275	**VGood:** $225

FORT WORTH HSSK

Semi-automatic; 22 LR; 10-shot magazine; 4-1/2-inch or 6-3/4-inch barrel; 39 oz. (with 4-1/2-inch barrel); 9-inch overall (4-1/2-inch barrel); checkered black plastic; side-mounted rear adjustable for windage; stainless steel construction; military grip; standard trigger; push-button barrel takedown. Introduced 1995; production ceased 2000.

Perf.: $295	**Exc.:** $265	**VGood:** $250

FORT WORTH HST TARGET PISTOL

Semi-automatic; 22 LR; 10-shot magazine; 5-1/2 bull or 7-1/4 fluted barrel; 44 oz.; 9.5-inch overall; checkered hardwood with thumbrest; undercut ramp front, frame-mounted micro-click rear sight adjustable for windage and elevation; drilled and tapped for scope mounting; gold-plated trigger; slide lock; safety-lever and magazine release; stippled front grip and backstrap; adjustable trigger and sear. Barrel weights optional. Introduced 1995; production ceased 2000.

Perf.: $375	**Exc.:** $325	**VGood:** $275
Left hand		
Perf.: $400	**Exc.:** $350	**VGood:** $300

Fraser Automatic

Freedom Arms Model 83
Field Grade

Freedom Arms Model 83
Premier Grade

Freedom Arms Model 83
Wyoming Express

FORT WORTH HSC TARGET PISTOL
Same as the HST model except has nickel-plated trigger; slide lock; safety lever; magazine release; has slightly heavier trigger pull; stippled front-grip and backstrap; checkered walnut thumbrest grips; adjustable trigger and sear; matte finish; drilled and tapped for scope mount and barrel weight. Introduced 1995; production ceased 2000.

Perf.: $375   **Exc.:** $295   **VGood:** $255

FORT WORTH HSV TARGET PISTOL
Semi-automatic; 22 LR; 10-shot magazine; 4-1/2 or 5-1/2 barrel; push-button takedown; 46 oz.; 9.5-inch overall; checkered hardwood with thumbrest; undercut ramp front, micro-click rear sight adjustable for windage and elevation; also available with scope mount, rings; no sights; stainless steel construction; full-length vent rib; gold-plated trigger; slide lock; safety-lever and magazine release; stippled front grip and backstrap; polished slide; adjustable trigger and sear; barrel weight. Introduced 1995; production ceased 2000.

Perf.: $455   **Exc.:** $395   **VGood:** $330

With Weaver rib		
Perf.: $495	**Exc.:** $425	**VGood:** $375

With 8-inch barrel, Weaver rib, custom grips, sights		
Perf.: $575	**Exc.:** $525	**VGood:** $450

FORT WORTH MATCHMASTER STANDARD PISTOL
Semi-automatic; 22 LR; 3-7/8-inch, 4-1/2-inch, 5-1/2-inch, 7-1/2-inch, 10-inch; checkered walnut grips; ramp front, slide-mounted adjustable rear sights; stainless steel construction; double extractors; trigger finger magazine release button and standard button; beveled magazine well; grip angle equivalent to M1911; low-profile frame. Introduced 1997; production ceased 2000.

Perf.: $395   **Exc.:** $325   **VGood:** $295

FORT WORTH MATCHMASTER DELUXE PISTOL
Same as the Matchmaster Standard except comes with Weaver-style rib mount and integral adjustable rear sight system. Introduced 1997; production ceased 2000.

Perf.: $475   **Exc.:** $425   **VGood:** $375

FORT WORTH MATCHMASTER DOVETAIL PISTOL
Same as the Matchmaster Standard except has a dovetail-style mount and integral rear sight system. Available with 3-7/8-inch, 4-1/2-inch or 5-1/2-inch barrel only. Introduced 1997; production ceased 2000.

Perf.: $435   **Exc.:** $395   **VGood:** $325

FRASER AUTOMATIC
Semi-automatic; 25 ACP; 6-shot magazine; 2-1/4-inch barrel; 4-inch overall length; weighs 10 oz.; recessed fixed sights; checkered walnut or plastic pearl stocks; stainless steel construction; positive manual and magazine safeties; satin stainless, gold-plated or black QPQ finish. Introduced 1983; dropped 1986.

Exc.: $195   **VGood:** $175   **Good:** $110

Gold plated		
Exc.: $250	**Vgood:** $235	**Good:** $200

FREEDOM ARMS MODEL 83
Revolver; single action; 357 Mag., 41 Mag., 45 LC, 454 Casull, 44 Mag., 475 Linebaugh, 50 AE; 5-shot cylinder; 4-3/4-inch, 6-inch, 7-1/2-inch, 10-inch barrel; 14-inch overall length (7-1/2-inch barrel); weighs about 59 oz.; blade front sight on ramp, fully-adjustable rear; Pachmayr rubber grips; Field Grade with matte stainless finish; Premier Grade with brushed stainless finish; impregnated hardwood grips, Premier Grade sights. Made in U.S. by Freedom Arms. Introduced 1992; still in production. Add 20% for octagonal barrel.

Field Grade		
New: $1325	**Perf.:** $995	**Exc.:** $825
Premier Grade		
New: $1500	**Perf.:** $1200	**Exc.:** $900

MODEL 83 .500 WYOMING EXPRESS
Similar to Model 83 but chambered in .500 Wyoming Express. Introduced 2007.

New: $2125   **Perf.:** $1850   **Exc.:** $1650

FREEDOM ARMS 44 MAGNUM SILHOUETTE
Same specs as the Model 83 except 10-inch barrel only; silhouette competition sights; Field Grade finish

only; trigger over-travel screw; front sight hood. Made in U.S. by Freedom Arms. Introduced 1992; no longer produced.

New: $1400   **Perf.:** $1100   **Exc.:** $950

FREEDOM ARMS 454 CASULL
Revolver; single action; 454 Casull; 5-shot cylinder; 4-3/4-inch, 6-inch, 7-1/2-inch, 10-inch, barrels; weighs 50 oz. (7-1/2-inch barrel); impregnated hardwood stocks; blade front sight, notch or adjustable rear; stainless steel; sliding bar safety. Introduced 1983; still in production.

Fixed sights		
Perf.: $1250	**Exc.:** $950	**VGood:** $800
Adjustable sights		
Perf.: $1300	**Exc.:** $1000	**VGood:** $850

FREEDOM ARMS 454 CASULL SILHOUETTE MODEL
Same specs as 454 Casull except competition sights and trigger overtravel screw.

Perf.: $1350   **Exc.:** $1100   **VGood:** $950

FREEDOM ARMS MODEL 83 .500 WYOMING EXPRESS
Similar to Model 83 but chambered in .500 Wyoming Express.

NIB: $2100   **Exc.:** $1850   **VGood:** $1500

FREEDOM ARMS BOOT GUN
Revolver; single action; 22 LR, 22 WMR; 3-inch barrel; 5-7/8-inch overall length; weighs 5 oz.; oversize grips; floating firing pin; stainless steel construction. Introduced 1982; dropped 1990.

Perf.: $335   **Exc.:** $295   **VGood:** $210

22 WMR		
Perf.: $375	**Exc.:** $315	**VGood:** $225

FREEDOM ARMS FA-S-22LR
Revolver; 22 LR; 5-shot; 1-inch, 1-3/4-inch, 3-inch barrels; blade front, notched rear sights; black ebonite grips; stainless steel construction; partial high polish finish; simulated ivory or ebony grips. No longer produced.

Perf.: $295   **Exc.:** $225   **VGood:** $200

Galesi Model 9

Gamba SAB G91

FTL Auto Nine

Frommer Baby
Pocket Model

Frommer Liliput
Pocket Model

Galesi Model 6

FREEDOM ARMS FA-S-22M

Revolver; 22 WMR; 4-shot; 1-inch, 1-3/4-inch, 3-inch barrels; stainless steel construction; blade front, notched rear sights; simulated ivory or ebony grips. No longer produced.

Perf.: $295 **Exc.:** $225 **VGood:** $200

FREEDOM ARMS MINI REVOLVER

Revolver; single action; 22 LR, 22 WMR; 5-shot; 4-inch (22 WMR), 1-inch, 1-3/4-inch barrel (22 LR); 4-inch overall length; blade front sight, notched rear; black ebonite grips; stainless steel construction; marketed in presentation case. Introduced 1978; dropped 1990.

Perf.: $295 **Exc.:** $275 **VGood:** $210

FREEDOM ARMS MODEL 97 MID FRAME REVOLVER

Caliber: 357 Mag., 6-shot cylinder. Barrel: 5-1/2-inch, 7-1/2-inch. Weight: 40 oz. (5-1/2-inch barrel). Length: 10-3/4-inch overall (5-1/2-inch barrel). Stocks: Wine wood. Sights: Blade on ramp front, fixed or fully adjustable rear. Features: Made of stainless steel; polished cylinder, matte frame. Introduced 1997.

New: $1350 **Perf.:** $1000 **Exc.:** $850

FREEDOM ARMS MODEL 252 VARMINT

Same specs as Model 252 Silhouette except 7-1/2-inch barrel; weighs 59 oz.; black/green laminated hardwood grips; brass bead front sight, fully-adjustable rear; extra 22 WMR cylinder available. Introduced 1991; still produced.

Perf.: $1100 **Exc.:** $800 **VGood:** $700

FREEDOM ARMS MODEL 353

Revolver; single action; 5-shot; 4-3/4-inch, 6-inch, 7-1/2-inch, 9-inch barrel; 14-inch overall length (7-1/2-inch barrel); weighs about 59 oz.; blade front sight on ramp, fully-adjustable rear; Pachmayr rubber grips (Field Grade), impregnated hardwood grips (Premier Grade); Field Grade with matte stainless finish; Premier Grade with brush stainless finish. Introduced 1992; still in production.

Field Grade
New: $1200 **Perf.:** $1050 **Exc.:** $800

Premier Grade
New: $1600 **Perf.:** $1200 **Exc.:** $950

FREEDOM ARMS MODEL 353 SILHOUETTE

Same specs as Model 353 except 9-inch barrel; silhouette competition sights; Field Grade finish and grips; trigger over-travel screw; front sight hood. Introduced 1992; still in production.

New: $1100 **Perf.:** $1000 **Exc.:** $850

FREEDOM ARMS MODEL 555

Revolver; single action; 50 AE; 5-shot cylinder; 4-3/4-inch, 6-inch, 7-1/2-inch, 10-inch barrel; 14-inch overall length (7-1/2-inch barrel); weighs 50 oz.; removable blade front sight on ramp, adjustable rear; Pachmayr rubber grips on Field Grade; impregnated hardwood on Premier Grade; Field Grade with matte stainless finish; Premier Grade with brushed stainless finish. Introduced 1994; still produced.

Field Grade
New: $1100 **Perf.:** $1000 **Exc.:** $850

Premier Grade
New: $1400 **Perf.:** $1250 **Exc.:** $1000

FROMMER BABY POCKET MODEL

Semi-automatic; 32 ACP; 6-shot magazine; smaller version of Stop Pocket Model with 2-inch barrel; 4-3/4-inch overall length. Manufactured from 1919 to approximately 1922.

Exc.: $350 **VGood:** $275 **Good:** $200

FROMMER LILIPUT POCKET MODEL

Semi-automatic; blowback action; 25 ACP; 6-shot magazine; 2-1/8-inch barrel; 4-5/16-inch overall length; hard rubber stocks; fixed sights; blued finish. Manufactured 1921 to 1924.

Exc.: $400 **VGood:** $300 **Good:** $200

FROMMER STOP POCKET MODEL

Semi-automatic; 32 ACP, 380 ACP; 6-shot (380 ACP), 7-shot (32 ACP) magazine; 3-7/8-inch barrel; 6-1/2-inch overall length; external hammer; grooved wood or checkered hard rubber stocks; fixed sights; blued finish. Manufactured in Hungary, 1912 to 1920.

Exc.: $325 **VGood:** $250 **Good:** $175

FTL AUTO NINE

Semi-automatic; single action; 22 LR; 8-shot magazine; 2-1/8-inch barrel; 4-5/16-inch overall length; weighs 9 1/4 oz.; blade front sight, fixed notch rear; checkered black plastic grips; manual push-button safety; alloy frame; hard chromed slide and magazine; barrel support bushing. Made by Auto Nine Corp. Marketed by FTL Marketing Corp. Introduced 1985; no longer in production.

Perf.: $200 **Exc.:** $160 **VGood:** $125

FTL POCKET PARTNER

Semi-automatic; 22 LR; 8-shot magazine; 2-1/4-inch barrel; 4-3/4-inch overall length; weighs 10 oz.; internal hammer; fixed sights; checkered plastic stocks; all-steel construction; brushed blue finish. Introduced 1985; no longer in production.

Perf.: $145 **Exc.:** $110 **VGood:** $95

GAL COMPACT AUTO PISTOL

Semi-automatic; 45 ACP; 8-shot magazine; 4-1/4-inch barrel; 36 oz.; 7-3/4-inch overall; rubberized wrap-around grip; low profile, fixed, three-dot sight system; forged steel frame and slide; competition trigger, hammer; slide stop magazine release; beavertail grip safety; front and rear slide grooves; two-tone finish. Introduced 1996. Imported from Israel by J.O. Arms, Inc.; dropped 1997.

Perf.: $425 **Exc.:** $375 **VGood:** $300

GALESI MODEL 6

Semi-automatic; 25 ACP; 6-shot magazine; 2-1/2-inch barrel; 4-3/8-inch overall length; plastic stocks; slide-top groove sights; blued finish. Manufactured in Italy. Introduced 1930; no longer in production.

Exc.: $250 **VGood:** $150 **Good:** $125

GALESI MODEL 9

Semi-automatic; 22 LR, 32 ACP, 380 ACP; 7-shot magazine; 3-1/4-inch barrel; plastic stocks; fixed sights; blued finish. Introduced 1930; no longer in production.

Exc.: $300 **VGood:** $250 **Good:** $175

Freedom Arms Model 97

Glock Model 20

Gaucher GN1 Silhouette

Glock Model 17

Gamba Trident Fast Action

Garcia/FI Model D

Gamba Trident Match 900

GAMBA SAB G90 STANDARD

Semi-automatic; double-action; 32 ACP, 9x18 Ultra, 9mm Para.; 15-shot magazine; 4-3/4-inch barrel; weighs 33 oz.; windage-adjustable rear sight, undercut blade front; uncheckered European walnut stocks; squared trigger guard; blue or chrome finish. Made in Italy. Introduced 1986; discontinued 1990.

Perf.: $625 **Exc.:** $450 **VGood:** $375

Chrome finish

Perf.: $700 **Exc.:** $515 **VGood:** $435

GAMBA SAB G90 COMPETITION

Same specs as SAB G90 Standard except 9mm Para. only; cocked-and-locked operation; checkered walnut grips. Introduced 1990; discontinued 1990.

Perf.: $1175 **Exc.:** $800 **VGood:** $600

GAMBA SAB G91 COMPACT

Semi-automatic; double action; 32 ACP, 9x18 Ultra, 9mm Para.; 12-shot magazine; 3-9/16-inch barrel; 30 oz.; windage-adjustable rear sight, undercut blade front; squared trigger guard; blued or chrome finish. Introduced 1986; discontinued 1990.

Perf.: $625 **Exc.:** $450 **VGood:** $375

Chrome finish

Perf.: $690 **Exc.:** $515 **VGood:** $435

GAMBA SAB G91 COMPETITION

Same specs as SAB G91 Compact except 9mm Para.; cocked-and-locked operation; checkered walnut grips. Introduced 1990; discontinued 1990.

Perf.: $450 **Exc.:** $400 **VGood:** $300

GAMBA TRIDENT FAST ACTION

Revolver; double action; 32 S&W, 38 Spl.; 6-shot; 2-1/2-inch, 3-inch barrel; 23 oz.; fixed sights; checkered walnut grips; blued finish. Discontinued 1986.

Perf.: $595 **Exc.:** $425 **VGood:** $365

GAMBA TRIDENT MATCH 900

Same specs as Trident Fast Action except 6-inch heavy barrel; 35 oz.; adjustable sights; checkered walnut target grips; blued finish. Discontinued 1986.

Perf.: $795 **Exc.:** $650 **VGood:** $595

GAMBA TRIDENT SUPER

Same specs as Trident Fast Action except 4-inch vent-rib barrel; 25 oz. Discontinued 1986.

Perf.: $595 **Exc.:** $425 **VGood:** $365

GARCIA REGENT

Revolver; 22 LR; 3-inch, 4-inch, 6-inch barrel; 8-shot swing-out cylinder; fixed rear sight, ramp front; checkered plastic grips; blued. Introduced 1972; dropped, 1977.

Exc.: $100 **VGood:** $85 **Good:** $65

GARCIA/FI MODEL D

Semi-automatic; 380 ACP; 6-shot magazine; 3-1/8-inch barrel; 6-1/8-inch overall length; checkered American walnut stocks; windage-adjustable rear sight, blade front; blued finish; lanyard ring. Imported by Firearms International 1977 to 1979.

Perf.: $200 **Exc.:** $150 **VGood:** $125

GAUCHER GN1 SILHOUETTE

Single shot; bolt action; 22 LR; 10-inch barrel; 15-1/2-inch overall length; weighs 2-1/2 lbs.; blade front, open adjustable rear sight; Euopean hardwood stock; adjustable trigger. Made in France. Introduced 1990; formerly imported by Mandall Shooting Supplies.

Perf.: $360 **Exc.:** $325 **VGood:** $290

GAUCHER GP SILHOUETTE

Single shot; bolt action; 22 LR; 10-inch barrel; 15-1/2-inch overall length; weighs 2-1/2 lbs.; hooded ramp front, open adjustable rear sight; stained harwood grips; matte chrome barrel; blued bolt, sights. Made in France. Introduced 1991; formerly imported by Mandall Shooting Supplies.

Perf.: $300 **Exc.:** $275 **VGood:** $250

GAUCHER RANDALL SINGLESHOT

Bolt action; 9mm Para.; 16-1/2-inch overall length; weighs 36 oz.; bead front sight; European hardwood stock; blued finish. Made in France. Introduced 1990; discontinued 1992. Reportedly formerly imported by Mandall Shooting Supplies.

GLOCK MODEL 17

Semi-automatic; double action; 9mm Para.; 17-, 19-shot magazine; 4-1/2-inch barrel; 7-7/16-inch overall length; weighs 24 oz.; white outline adjustable rear sight, dot on front blade; polymer frame; steel slide;

trigger safety; recoil-operated action; firing pin safety; drop safety. Made in Austria. Introduced, 1986; still imported.

Perf.: $495 **Exc.:** $425 **VGood:** $345

GLOCK MODEL 17L COMPETITION

Same specs as Model 17 except compensated 6-inch barrel; lighter trigger pull; 26 oz. Made in Austria. Introduced 1988; still imported.

Perf.: $650 **Exc.:** $545 **VGood:** $425

GLOCK MODEL 19 COMPACT

Semi-automatic; double action; 9mm Para.; 15-, 17-shot magazine; 4-inch barrel; 6-7/8-inch overall length; 22 oz.; white outline adjustable rear sight, dot on front blade; polymer frame; steel slide; trigger safety; recoil-operated action; firing pin safety; drop safety. Made in Austria. Introduced 1988.

Perf.: $495 **Exc.:** $425 **VGood:** $345

Add $35 to above prices for Model 19C with adjustable rear sight

Add $30 for Model 19 with adjustable rear sight

Add $80 for fixed Meprolight sight

Add $105 for fixed Trijicon sight

GLOCK MODEL 20

Semi-automatic; double action; 10mm Auto; 15-shot magazine; 4-5/8-inch barrel; 28 oz.; white outline adjustable rear sight, dot on front blade; polymer frame; steel slide; trigger safety; recoil-operated action; firing pin safety; drop safety. Made in Austria. Introduced 1990; still imported.

Perf.: $600 **Exc.:** $525 **VGood:** $450

GLOCK MODEL 21

Semi-automatic; double action; 45 ACP; 13-shot magazine; 4-5/8-inch barrel; 27 oz.; white outline adjustable rear sight, dot on front blade; polymer frame; steel slide; trigger safety; recoil-operated action; firing pin safety; drop safety. Made in Austria. Introduced 1991; still imported.

Perf.: $600 **Exc.:** $500 **VGood:** $425

GLOCK 21 SF

Slenderized version of Model 21 with slimmer frame and ambidextrous magazine catch. Introduced 2007.

NIB: $525 **Exc.:** $485 **VGood:** $400

Glock Model 24 Competition

Glock Model 22

Great Western Frontier

Glock Model 23

GLOCK MODEL 22

Semi-automatic; double action; 40 S&W; 15-shot magazine; 4-1/2-inch barrel; 7-7/16-inch overall length; 24 oz.; white outline adjustable rear sight, dot on front blade; polymer frame; steel slide; trigger safety; recoil-operated action; firing pin safety; drop safety. Made in Austria. Introduced 1990; still imported.

    Perf.: $495   **Exc.:** $425   **VGood:** $350
Add $35 to above prices for Model 22C with adjustable rear sight
Add $30 for Model 22 with adjustable rear sight
Add $80 for fixed Meprolight sight
Add $105 for fixed Trijicon sight
Add $35 for Model 22C with compensated barrel

GLOCK MODEL 23 COMPACT

Semi-automatic; double action; 40 S&W; 13-shot magazine; 4-inch barrel; 6-7/8-inch overall length; 22 oz.; white outline adjustable rear sight, dot on front blade; polymer frame; steel slide; trigger safety; recoil-operated action; firing pin safety; drop safety. Made in Austria. Introduced 1991; still imported.

    Perf.: $500   **Exc.:** $450   **VGood:** $400
Add $30 to above prices for adjustable rear sight
Add $80 for fixed Meprolight sight
Add $105 for fixed Trijicon sight

GLOCK MODEL 24 COMPETITION

Semi-automatic; double action; 40 S&W; 10-shot magazine; 6-inch barrel; 8-1/2-inch overall length; weighs 29-1/2 oz.; black polymer grips; blade front sight with dot, white outline windage-adjustable rear; long-slide competition model available as compensated or non-compensated; factory-installed competition trigger; drop-free magazine. Imported from Austria by Glock, Inc. Introduced 1994; dropped 1999.

    New: $665   **Perf.:** $525   **Exc.:** $450
Compensated barrel
    New: $700   **Perf.:** $575   **Exc.:** $500

GLOCK 26, 27 AUTO PISTOLS

Semi-automatic; 9mm Para (M26) 10-shot magazine; 40 S&W (M27) 9-shot magazine; 3.47-inch barrel; 21.75 oz.; 6.3-inch overall; integral stippled polymer grips; dot on front blade, fixed or fully adjustable white outline rear sight; subcompact size; polymer frame; steel slide; double-action trigger with "Safe Action" system composing three safeties; matte black Tenifer finish; hammer-forged barrel. Imported from Austria by Glock, Inc. Introduced 1996.

    Perf.: $500   **Exc.:** $450   **VGood:** $400
Adjustable sight
    Perf.: $525   **Exc.:** $475   **VGood:** $425

GLOCK MODEL 28

Similar to Models 26/27, except scaled down smaller size; 380 ACP; 3.46-inch barrel; 20 oz. Available to law enforcement only. Pricing unavailable.

GLOCK 29, 30 AUTO PISTOLS

Caliber: 10mm (M29); 45 ACP (M30); 10-shot magazine; 3.78-inch barrel; 24 oz.; 6.7-inch overall; integral stippled polymer grips; dot on front, fixed or fully adjustable white outline rear sights; compact size; polymer frame; steel slide; double-recoil spring reduces recoil; Safe Action system with three safeties; Tenifer finish; two magazines supplied. Introduced 1997. Imported from Austria by Glock, Inc.

    Perf.: $585   **Exc.:** $490   **VGood:** $425
Adjustable sight
    Perf.: $625   **Exc.:** $530   **VGood:** $480

GLOCK 31

Chambered for the .357 SIG cartridge this pistol is fitted with a 4.5" barrel and a magazine capacity of 10 rounds (15 rounds law enforcement). Overall length is 7.3" and the height is 5.4". Weight is about 23.3 oz. Introduced in 1998. Also available with OD green frame.

    NIB.: $500   **Exc.:** $450   **VGood:** $400

GLOCK 31C

Same as the Model 31 but with an integral compensator. Also available with OD green frame.

    NIB: $550   **Exc.:** $500   **VGood:** $450

GLOCK 32

Similar to the Glock 31 except fitted with a 4" barrel. Overall length is 6.85" and height is 5". Magazine capacity is 10 rounds (13 rounds law enforcement). Weight is approximately 21.5 oz. Introduced in 1998. Also available with OD green frame.

    NIB: $550   **Exc.:** $500   **VGood:** $450

GLOCK 32C

Same as above but fitted with integral ported barrel and slide. Also available with OD green frame.

    NIB: $700   **Exc.:** $600   **VGood:** $500

GLOCK 33

This .357 SIG model has a 3.5" barrel and an overall length of 6.3". Height is 4.2" and weight is about 17.7 oz. Introduced in 1998. Also available with OD green frame.

    NIB: $500   **Exc.:** $450   **VGood:** $400

GLOCK 34

This model is chambered for the 9x19 cartridge and has a 5.3" barrel, overall length of 8.2", and a magazine capacity of 10 rounds. Empty weight is approximately 23 oz. Also available with OD green frame.

    NIB: $575   **Exc.:** $500   **VGood:** $450

GLOCK 35

The Glock 35 is chambered for the .40 S&W cartridge. It has the same dimensions as the Glock 34 except for weight, which is 24.5 oz. Also available with OD green frame.

    NIB: $600   **Exc.:** $500   **VGood:** $450

GLOCK MODEL 37

This semi-automatic pistol is chambered for the .45 G.A.P. cartridge, which is slightly shorter than the .45 ACP cartridge. This cartridge has a muzzle speed of 951 fps and muzzle energy of 405 ft. lbs. Fitted with a 4.49" barrel. Height is 5.5". Overall length is 7.3". Weight is about 26 oz. Also available with OD green frame.

    NIB: $500   **Exc.:** $425   **VGood:** $375

GLOCK MODEL 38

This .45 G.A.P. pistol is fitted with a 4" barrel. Height is 5" and overall length is 6.85". Magazine capacity is 8 rounds. Weight is about 24 oz. Introduced in 2005. Also available with OD green frame.

    NIB: $425   **Exc.:** $375   **VGood:** $350

GLOCK MODEL 39

Introduced in 2005 this sub-compact .45 G.A.P. pistol has a 3.46" barrel. Height is 4.17" and overall length is 6.3". Magazine capacity is 6 rounds. Weight is about 19.3 oz. Also available with OD green frame.

    NIB: $425   **Exc.:** $375   **VGood:** $350

Grendel P-10

Grendel P-12

Grendel P-30

Hammerli Model 104 Match

Hammerli Model 33MP

GOLAN

Semi-automatic; 9mm Para., 40 S&W; 10-shot magazine; 3.9-inch barrel; 34 oz.; 7-inch overall; textured composition grips; fixed sights; fully ambidextrous double/single action; forged steel slide; alloy frame; matte blue finish. Introduced 1994. Imported from Israel by KSN Industries, Ltd.

Perf.: $565   **Exc.:** $515   **VGood:** $460

GREAT WESTERN DERRINGER

Derringer; over/under; 38 S&W, 38 S&W Special; 2-shot; 3-inch barrels; 5-inch overall length; checkered black plastic grips; fixed sights; blued finish. Replica of Remington Double Derringer. Manufactured 1953 to 1962.

Exc.: $400   **VGood:** $375   **Good:** $300

GREAT WESTERN FRONTIER

Revolver; single action; 22 LR, 22 Hornet, 38 Spl., 357 Mag., 44 Spl., 44 Mag., 45 Colt; 6-shot cylinder; 4-3/4-inch, 5-1/2-inch, 7-1/2-inch barrel lengths; grooved rear sight, fixed blade front; imitation stag grips; blued finish. Was sold primarily by mail order. Manufactured 1951 to 1962. Add 10% for .44 Special. Deduct 25% for rimfire. Deduct 30% for kit guns, except if new in original kit, unassembled. Note that values shown are for unmodified factory specimens.

Exc.: $595   **VGood:** $475   **Good:** $400

GRENDEL P-10

Semi-automatic; double action; 380 ACP; 10-shot magazine; 3-inch barrel; 5-5/16-inch overall length; weighs 15 oz.; checkered polycarbonate metal composite grips; fixed sights; inertia safety hammer system; magazine loads from top; matte black, electroless nickel or green finish. Made in U.S. by Grendel, Inc. Introduced 1987; discontinued 1991.

Perf.: $160   **Exc.:** $135   **VGood:** $125

GRENDEL P-12

Semi-automatic; double action; 380 ACP; 10-shot magazine; 3-inch barrel; 5-5/16-inch overall length; weighs 13 oz.; checkered DuPont ST-800 polymer grips; fixed sights; inertia safety hammer system; all-steel frame; grip forms magazine well and trigger guard; blue finish. Made in U.S. by Grendel, Inc.

Introduced 1992; dropped 1995.

New: $155   **Perf.:** $135   **Exc.:** $120

Electroless nickel finish

New: $175   **Perf.:** $155   **Exc.:** $140

GRENDEL P-30

Semi-automatic; double action; 22 WMR; 30-shot magazine; 5-inch, 8-inch barrel; 8-1/2-inch overall length (5-inch barrel); weighs 21 oz. (5-inch barrel); checkered Zytel grips; blade front sight, fixed rear; blowback action with fluted chamber; ambidextrous safety; reversible magazine catch. Made in U.S. by Grendel, Inc. Introduced 1990; dropped 1994.

Perf.: $240   **Exc.:** $200   **VGood:** $175

GRENDEL P-30L

Same specs as the P-30 except 8-inch barrel only. Made in U.S. by Grendel, Inc. Introduced 1990; dropped 1994.

Perf.: $275   **Exc.:** $235   **VGood:** $200

GRENDEL P-30M

Same specs as the P-30 except removable muzzlebrake. Made in U.S. by Grendel, Inc. Introduced 1990; dropped 1994.

Perf.: $250   **Exc.:** $210   **VGood:** $180

GRENDEL P-31

Semi-automatic; 22 WMR; 30-shot magazine; 11-inch barrel; 17-1/2-inch overall length; 48 oz.; adjustable blade front, fixed rear; blowback action with fluted chamber; ambidextrous safety; muzzlebrake; scope mount optional; checkered black Zytel grip and forend; matte black finish. Made in U.S. by Grendel, Inc. Introduced 1991; dropped 1995.

Perf.: $350   **Exc.:** $315   **VGood:** $275

GUARDIAN-SS

Semi-automatic; double action; 380 ACP; 6-shot magazine; 3-1/4-inch barrel; 6-inch overall length; weighs 20 oz.; checkered walnut stocks; ramp front sight, windage-adjustable combat rear; narrow polished trigger; Pachmayr grips; blue slide; hand-fitted barrel; polished feed ramp; funneled magazine well; stainless steel. Introduced 1982; dropped 1985. Marketed by Michigan Armament, Inc.

Exc.: $375   **VGood:** $295   **Good:** $225

GUNWORKS MODEL 9 DERRINGER

Derringer; over/under; 38/357 Mag., 9mm/9mm Mag.; bottom-hinged action; 3-inch barrel; weighs 15 oz.; smooth wood stocks; Millett orange bar front sight, fixed rear; all steel; half-cock, through-frame safety; dual extraction; electroless nickel finish; marketed with in-pants holster. Introduced 1984, dropped 1986.

Exc.: $135   **VGood:** $120   **Good:** $105

HAMMERLI MODEL 33MP

Single shot; 22 LR; 11-1/2-inch octagonal barrel; 16-1/2-inch overall length; competition free pistol; micrometer rear sight, interchangeable front; European walnut stocks, forearm; Martini-type action; set trigger; blued finish. Manufactured in Switzerland 1933 to 1949.

Exc.: $1200   **VGood:** $925   **Good:** $650

HAMMERLI MODEL 100 FREE PISTOL

Single shot; 22 LR; 11-1/2-inch octagon barrel; micrometer rear sight, interchangeable post or bead front; European walnut grips, forearm; adjustable set trigger; blued finish. Introduced 1933; discontinued 1949.

Exc.: $975   **VGood:** $700   **Good:** $605

Deluxe model

Exc.: $1050   **VGood:** $800   **Good:** $715

HAMMERLI MODEL 101

Single shot; 22 LR; 11-1/2-inch heavy round barrel; adjustable sights; European walnut grip, forearm; adjustable set trigger; same general specs as Model 100 Free Pistol with improved action; matte blue finish. Introduced 1956; discontinued 1960.

Exc.: $1080   **VGood:** $700   **Good:** $605

HAMMERLI MODEL 102

Single shot; 22 LR; 11-1/2-inch heavy round barrel; adjustable sights; European walnut grip, forearm; adjustable set trigger; same general specs as Model 101 with high gloss blued finish. Introduced 1956; discontinued 1960.

Exc.: $980   **VGood:** $660   **Good:** $605

Deluxe model

Exc.: $1090   **VGood:** $770   **Good:** $715

Hammerli Model 106

Hammerli Model 120

Hammerli Model 120-2

Hammerli Model 150
Free Pistol

Hammerli Model 160
Free Pistol

Hammerli Model 206
International

HAMMERLI MODEL 103 FREE PISTOL

Single shot; 22 LR; 11-1/2-inch lightweight octagon barrel; adjustable sights; European walnut grip, forearm; adjustable set trigger; same general specs as Model 101 with high gloss blued finish. Introduced 1956; discontinued 1960.

Exc.: $1035 **VGood:** $715 **Good:** $660

With inlaid ivory carvings

Exc.: $1200 **VGood:** $900 **Good:** $690

HAMMERLI MODEL 104 MATCH

Single shot; 22 LR; 11-1/2-inch lightweight round barrel; adjustable sights; redesigned adjustable walnut grip; adjustable set trigger; action similar to Model 103; high gloss blued finish. Introduced 1961; discontinued 1965.

Exc.: $860 **VGood:** $660 **Good:** $550

HAMMERLI MODEL 105 MATCH

Single shot; 22 LR; 11-1/2-inch octagon barrel; adjustable sights; redesigned adjustable walnut grip; adjustable set trigger; redesigned action; high gloss blued finish. Introduced 1962; discontinued 1965.

Exc.: $1035 **VGood:** $715 **Good:** $660

HAMMERLI MODEL 106 MATCH

Single shot; 22 LR; 11-1/2-inch octagon barrel; adjustable sights; same general specs as Model 105 Match except redesigned trigger; replaced Model 104; matte blue finish. Introduced 1966; discontinued 1972.

Exc.: $1010 **VGood:** $690 **Good:** $580

HAMMERLI MODEL 107

Single shot; 22 LR; 11-5/16-inch barrel; 16-3/4-inch overall length; weighs 49-1/2 oz.; octagonal barrel; adjustable five-lever set trigger. Introduced 1965; discontinued 1971.

Exc.: $1090 **VGood:** $770 **Good:** $660

Deluxe model

Exc.: $1400 **VGood:** $990 **Good:** $880

HAMMERLI MODEL 120

Single shot; 22 Short; 10-inch barrel; 15-3/4 inch overall length; weighs 43-1/4 oz.; side-lever operation; micrometer sight; plain butt and trigger guard.

Exc.: 7600 **VGood:** $540 **Good:** $475

HAMMERLI MODEL 120-1 FREE PISTOL

Single shot; bolt action; 22 LR; 10-inch barrel; 14-3/4-inch overall length; micrometer rear sight, post front; hand-checkered walnut target grips; adjustable trigger for single- or two-stage pull; aluminum construction; blued finish. Introduced 1972; discontinued 1985.

Exc.: $700 **VGood:** $540 **Good:** $475

HAMMERLI MODEL 120-2

Same specs as Model 120-1 Free Pistol except special contoured walnut hand rest; movable sights; blued finish. Introduced 1973; discontinued 1985.

Exc.: $700 **VGood:** $540 **Good:** $475

HAMMERLI MODEL 120 HEAVY BARREL

Same specs as Model 120-1 Free Pistol except 5-3/4-inch bull barrel; designed to conform to existing laws governing sporting handgun sales in Great Britain. Introduced 1973; discontinued 1985.

Exc.: $700 **VGood:** $540 **Good:** $475

HAMMERLI MODEL 150 FREE PISTOL

Single shot; 22 LR; 11-3/8-inch barrel; 15-3/8-inch overall length; movable front sight on collar, micrometer rear; adjustable palm-shelf grip; Martini-type action; straight-line firing pin, no hammer; adjustable set trigger; blued finish. Introduced 1973; discontinued 1989.

Perf.: $1950 **Exc.:** $1495 **VGood:** $1275

Left-hand

Perf.: $2065 **Exc.:** $1650 **VGood:** $1425

HAMMERLI MODEL 151 FREE PISTOL

Single shot; 22 LR; 11-3/8-inch barrel; 15-3/8-inch overall length; movable front sight on collar, micrometer rear; uncheckered adjustable palm-shelf grip; Martini-type action; straight-line firing pin; no hammer; adjustable set trigger; blued finish. Replaced Model 150 Free Pistol. Introduced 1990; discontinued 1993.

Perf.: $1950 **Exc.:** $1495 **VGood:** $1275

HAMMERLI MODEL 152 MATCH

Single shot; 22 LR; 11-5/16-inch barrel; 16-7/8-inch

overall length; weighs 46-5/8 oz.; changeable post-type front sight, micrometer rear; match stocks; electronic trigger; improved Martini-style action; blued action. Introduced 1990; discontinued 1992.

Perf.: $2095 **Exc.:** $1600 **VGood:** $1350

Left-hand

Perf.: $2060 **Exc.:** $1660 **VGood:** $1410

HAMMERLI MODEL 160 FREE PISTOL

Single shot; 22 LR; 11-1/4-inch barrel; 17-1/2-inch overall length; weighs 47 oz.; walnut grip; full match-style with adjustable palm shelf, stippled surfaces; changeable blade front sight, open, fully-adjustable match rear; mechanical set trigger, fully adjustable with provision for dry firing. Imported from Switzerland by Hammerli Pistols USA. Introduced 1993; dropped 2002.

New: $1900 **Perf.:** $1700 **Exc.:** $1450

HAMMERLI MODEL 162 FREE PISTOL

Single shot; 22 LR; 11-1/4-inch barrel; 17-1/2-inch overall length; weighs 47 oz.; walnut grip; full match-style with adjustable palm shelf, stippled surfaces; changeable blade front sight, open, fully-adjustable match rear; electronic trigger, fully adjustable with provision for dry firing. Imported from Switzerland by Hammerli Pistols USA. Introduced 1993; dropped 2000.

New: $2250 **Perf.:** $1850 **Exc.:** $1500

HAMMERLI MODEL 206 INTERNATIONAL

Semi-automatic; single action; 22 LR, 22 Short; 8-shot magazine; 7-1/16-inch barrel; adjustable sights; checkered walnut thumbrest grips; muzzlebrake; slide stop; adjustable trigger; blued finish. Introduced 1964; discontinued 1967.

Exc.: $775 **VGood:** $625 **Good:** $525

HAMMERLI MODEL 207 INTERNATIONAL

Semi-automatic; single action; 22 LR, 22 Short; 8-shot magazine; 7-1/16-inch barrel; adjustable sights; smooth walnut grips with adjustable grip plates; muzzlebrake; slide stop; adjustable trigger; blued finish. Introduced 1964; discontinued 1969.

Exc.: $825 **VGood:** $650 **Good:** $550

Hammerli Model 208 International

Hammerli Model 208S International

Hammerli Model 211

Hammerli Model 230-1

Hammerli Model 280 Target

Hammerli Model 212 Hunter

Hammerli SP 20 Target

HAMMERLI MODEL 208 INTERNATIONAL

Semi-automatic; single action; 22 LR; 8-shot magazine; 6-inch barrel; 10-inch overall length; weighs 37-1/2 oz.; adjustable sights; smooth walnut grips with adjustable grip plates; adjustable trigger; blued finish. Introduced 1966; discontinued 1988.

Perf.: $2100   **Exc.:** $1700   **VGood:** $1450

HAMMERLI MODEL 208S INTERNATIONAL

Same specs as International Model 208 except interchangeable rear sight; restyled trigger guard. Introduced 1988; dropped 2000.

New: $2550   **Perf.:** $2150   **Exc.:** $1750

HAMMERLI MODEL 209 INTERNATIONAL

Semi-automatic; single action; 22 Short; 5-shot magazine; 4-3/4-inch barrel; adjustable sights; walnut grips; adjustable muzzlebrake, barrel vents, gas-escape ports; lightweight bolt; blued finish. Introduced 1967; discontinued 1970.

Exc.: $900   **VGood:** $690   **Good:** $635

HAMMERLI MODEL 210 INTERNATIONAL

Semi-automatic; single action; 22 Short; 5-shot magazine; 4-3/4-inch barrel; adjustable sights; adjustable walnut grip plates; adjustable muzzlebrake, barrel vents, gas-escape ports; lightweight bolt; blued finish. Introduced 1967; discontinued 1970.

Exc.: $900   **VGood:** $715   **Good:** $660

HAMMERLI MODEL 211

Semi-automatic; single action; 22 LR; 9-shot magazine; 6-inch barrel; 10-inch overall length; weighs 37 oz.; walnut stocks with adjustable palm rest; fully-adjustable match sights; interchangeable front and rear blades; fully-adjustable trigger. Imported from Switzerland by Mandall Shooting Supplies, and also Beeman. Introduced 1973; discontinued 1990.

Perf.: $1650   **Exc.:** $1275   **VGood:** $1050

HAMMERLI MODEL 212 HUNTER

Semi-automatic; single action; 22 LR; 8-shot magazine; 5-inch barrel; 8-1/2-inch overall length; weighs 31 oz.; adjustable sights; checkered walnut stocks; adjustable trigger; blued finish. Made in Switzerland. Introduced 1984; no longer imported.

Perf.: $1350   **Exc.:** $1000   **VGood:** $950

HAMMERLI MODEL 215

Semi-automatic; single action; target model; 22 LR; 8-shot magazine; 5-inch barrel; adjustable sights; walnut grip with plates; adjustable trigger; blued finish. Made in Switzerland. Importation discontinued 1991.

Perf.: $1495   **Exc.:** $1050   **VGood:** $850

HAMMERLI MODEL 230-1

Semi-automatic; 22 Short; 5-shot magazine; 6-5/16-inch barrel; 11-5/8-inch overall length; micrometer rear sight, post front; uncheckered European walnut thumbrest grips; blued finish. Designed for rapid-fire International competition. Introduced 1970; discontinued 1983.

Exc.: $800   **VGood:** $635   **Good:** $585

HAMMERLI MODEL 230-2

Same specs as Model 230-1 except partially checkered stocks; adjustable heel plate. Introduced 1970; discontinued 1983.

Exc.: $835   **VGood:** $655   **Good:** $605

HAMMERLI MODEL 232-1

Semi-automatic; 22 Short; 6-shot magazine; 5-inch barrel with six exhaust ports; 10-3/8-inch overall length; weighs 44 oz.; rear blades, adjustable micrometer rear sight; walnut grips; recoil-operated; adjustable trigger; blued finish. Made in Switzerland. Introduced 1984; importation discontinued 1993.

Perf.: $1495   **Exc.:** $1125   **VGood:** $950

HAMMERLI MODEL 232-2

Same specs as Model 232-1 except wrap-around grips. Introduced 1984; importation discontinued 1993.

Perf.: $1400   **Exc.:** $1150   **VGood:** $950

HAMMERLI MODEL 280 TARGET

Semi-automatic; 22 LR; 32 S&W Long WC; 6-shot magazine (22 LR), 5-shot (32 S&W); 4-1/2-inch barrel; 11-13/16-inch overall length; weighs 39 oz.; micro-adjustable match sights; stippled match-type walnut stocks; adjustable palm shelf carbon-reinforced synthetic frame and bolt/barrel housing; fully-adjustable, interchangeable trigger. Made in Switzerland. Introduced, 1990; importation dropped 2000.

Perf.: $1550   **Exc.:** $1125   **VGood:** $900

HAMMERLI SP 20 TARGET

Semi-automatic; 22 LR, 32 S&W; 4.6-inch barrel; 34.6-41.8 oz.; 11.8-inch overall; anatomically shaped synthetic Hi-Grip available in five sizes; integral front sight in three widths, adjustable rear with changeable notch widths; extremely low-level sight line; anatomically shaped trigger; adjustable JPS buffer system for different recoil characteristics; receiver available in red, blue, gold, violet or black. Introduced 1998. Imported from Switzerland by SIGARMS, Inc.

Perf.: $1425   **Exc.:** $1075   **VGood:** $925

HAMMERLI VIRGINIAN

Revolver; single action; 357 Mag., 45 Colt; 6-shot cylinder; 4-5/8-inch, 5-1/2-inch, 7-1/2-inch barrels; grooved rear sight, blade front; one-piece European walnut grips; case-hardened; chrome grip frame, triggerguard; blued frame cylinder; same general design as Colt SAA except for base pin safety feature. Manufactured in Europe, 1973 to 1976, for exclusive Interarms importation.

Exc.: $575   **VGood:** $450   **Good:** $325

HAMMERLI-WALTHER MODEL 200 OLYMPIA

Semi-automatic; 22 LR, 22 Short; 8-shot magazine; 7-1/2-inch barrel; micrometer rear sight, ramp front; walnut thumbrest grip; muzzle brake; adjustable barrel weights; blued finish. Also known as Quickfire. Based on 1936 Olympia with some parts interchangeable. Introduced 1950. In 1958, muzzle brake was redesigned. Discontinued 1963.

Exc.: $825   **VGood:** $605   **Good:** $550

HAMMERLI-WALTHER MODEL 201

Semi-automatic; 22 LR, 22 Short; 8-shot magazine; 9-1/2-inch barrel; micrometer rear sight, ramp front; adjustable custom walnut grip; muzzle brake; adjustable barrel weights; blued finish. Introduced 1955; discontinued 1957.

Exc.: $750   **VGood:** $600   **Good:** $550

Hammerli Virginian

H&R Model 4

H&R 22 Special

H&R Automatic Ejecting Model

H&R Expert

H&R Model 5

H&R Hunter

HAMMERLI-WALTHER MODEL 202

Semi-automatic; 22 LR, 22 Short; 8-shot magazine; 9-1/2-inch barrel; micrometer rear sight, ramp front; adjustable walnut thumbrest grip; muzzle brake; adjustable barrel weights; blued finish. Introduced 1955; discontinued 1957.

Exc.: $775   **VGood:** $605   **Good:** $550

HAMMERLI-WALTHER MODEL 203

Semi-automatic; 22 LR, 22 Short; 8-shot magazine; 7-1/2-inch barrel; micrometer rear sight, ramp front; adjustable walnut thumbrest grip; optional muzzle brake (1958 model); slide stop; adjustable barrel weights; blued finish. Called the American Model. Introduced 1955; discontinued 1959.

Exc.: $775   **VGood:** $605   **Good:** $550

With muzzle brake

Exc.: $850   **VGood:** $660   **Good:** $605

HAMMERLI-WALTHER MODEL 204

Semi-automatic; 22 LR; 8-shot magazine; 7-1/2-inch barrel; micrometer rear sight, ramp front; walnut thumbrest grip; optional muzzle brake; slide stop; adjustable barrel weights; blued finish. Introduced 1956; discontinued 1963.

Exc.: $775   **VGood:** $635   **Good:** $580

With muzzle brake

Exc.: $875   **VGood:** $690   **Good:** $635

HAMMERLI-WALTHER MODEL 205

Semi-automatic; 22 LR; 8-shot magazine; 7-1/2-inch barrel; micrometer rear sight, ramp front; checkered French walnut thumbrest grip; detachable muzzle brake; slide stop; adjustable barrel weights; blued finish. Introduced 1956; discontinued 1963.

Exc.: $900   **VGood:** $690   **Good:** $635

With muzzle brake

Exc.: $955   **VGood:** $745   **Good:** $715

HARRINGTON & RICHARDSON 22 SPECIAL

Revolver; double action; 22 Short, 22 Long, 22 LR, 22 WMR; 9-shot cylinder; 6-inch barrel; 11-inch overall length; weighs 23 oz.; heavy hinged-frame; fixed notch rear sight, gold-plated front; checkered walnut grips; blued. Originally introduced as Model 944; later version with recessed cylinder for high-speed ammo was listed as Model 945. Introduced 1925; dropped 1941.

Exc.: $165   **VGood:** $140   **Good:** $120

HARRINGTON & RICHARDSON YOUNG AMERICAN

Revolver; double action; 32 S&W Long, 32 S&W, 32 Colt New Police; 6-shot (32), 5-shot (38); 2-1/2-inch, 4-1/2-inch, 6-inch barrel; weighs 16 oz.; solid frame; fixed sights; hard rubber grips; blued, nickel finish. Introduced 1883; dropped during WWII.

Exc.: $100   **VGood:** $75   **Good:** $50

HARRINGTON & RICHARDSON AUTOMATIC EJECTING MODEL

Revolver; double action; 32 S&W Long, 38 S&W; 6-shot cylinder (32), 5-shot (38); 3-1/4-inch, 4-inch, 5-inch, 6-inch barrel; weighs 16 oz.; hinged-frame; fixed sights; hard rubber or checkered walnut target grips; blued, nickel finish. Introduced 1891; dropped 1941.

Exc.: $160   **VGood:** $150   **Good:** $105

HARRINGTON & RICHARDSON BOBBY MODEL

Revolver; double action; 32 S&W Long, 38 S&W; 6-shot cylinder (32), 5-shot (38); 4-inch barrel; 9-inch overall length; hinged-frame; fixed sights; checkered walnut grips; blued finish. Also listed as the Model 15. Designed for use by London police during WWII. Introduced 1941; dropped 1943. Collector value.

Exc.: $200   **VGood:** $150   **Good:** $125

HARRINGTON & RICHARDSON EXPERT

Revolver; double action; 22 LR, 22 WMR; 9-shot; 10-inch barrel; heavy hinged frame; fixed rear sight; gold-plated front; checkered walnut grips; blued

finish. Listed as the Model 955. Introduced 1929; dropped 1941.

Exc.: $150   **VGood:** $140   **Good:** $120

HARRINGTON & RICHARDSON HUNTER MODEL

Revolver; double action; 22 LR; 9-shot cylinder; 10-inch octagon barrel; solid-frame; fixed sights; checkered walnut grips; blued finish. Introduced 1926; dropped 1941.

Exc.: $200   **VGood:** $170   **Good:** $100

HARRINGTON & RICHARDSON MODEL 4

Revolver; double action; 32 S&W Long, 38 S&W, 38 Colt New Police; 6-shot cylinder (32), 5-shot (38); 21/2-inch, 41/2-inch, 6-inch barrels; solid frame; fixed sights; hard rubber grips; blued or nickel finish. Introduced 1905; dropped 1941.

Exc.: $95   **VGood:** $85   **Good:** $75

HARRINGTON & RICHARDSON MODEL 5

Revolver; double action; 32 S&W Short; 5-shot cylinder; 2-1/2-inch, 4-1/2-inch, 6-inch barrels; light frame; fixed sights; hard rubber grips; blued or nickel finish. Introduced 1905; dropped 1941.

Exc.: $95   **VGood:** $85   **Good:** $7

HARRINGTON & RICHARDSON MODEL 6

Revolver; double action; 22 Short, 22 Long, 22 LR; 7-shot cylinder; 2-1/2-inch, 4-1/2-inch, 6-inch barrels; solid frame; fixed sights; blued or nickel finish. Introduced 1906; dropped 1941.

Exc.: $95   **VGood:** $85   **Good:** $70

HARRINGTON & RICHARDSON MODEL 40 HAMMERLESS

Revolver; double action; 22 LR, 32 S&W Short; 7-shot cylinder (22), 5-shot (32); 2-inch, 3-inch, 4-inch, 5-inch, 6-inch barrels; fixed sights; small hinged-frame; hard rubber stocks; blued or nickel finish. Also listed during late production as Model 45. Introduced

H&R Model 40 Hammerless

H&R Model 504

H&R Model 532

H&R Model 622

H&R Model 586

H&R Model 650

H&R Model 649

H&R Model 686

1899; dropped 1941.
Exc.: $150   **VGood:** $85   **Good:** $65

HARRINGTON & RICHARDSON MODEL 50 HAMMERLESS
Revolver; double action; 32 S&W Long, 38 S&W; 6-shot cylinder (32), 5-shot (38); 3-1/4-inch, 4-inch, 5-inch, 6-inch barrels; fixed sights; small hinged-frame; hard rubber stocks; blued or nickel finish. Also listed during late production as Model 55. Introduced 1899; dropped 1941.
Exc.: $135   **VGood:** $80   **Good:** $60

HARRINGTON & RICHARDSON MODEL 504
Revolver; 32 H&R Mag.; 5-shot cylinder; 3-inch, 4-inch, 6-inch barrel; blued finish. Introduced 1984; dropped 1985.
Perf.: $165   **Exc.:** $145   **VGood:** $135

HARRINGTON & RICHARDSON MODEL 532
Revolver; 32 H&R Mag.; 5-shot cylinder: 2-1/2-inch, 4-inch barrel; solid frame; round butt; wood grips; blued finish. Introduced 1984; dropped 1985.
Perf.: $200   **Exc.:** $150   **VGood:** $85

HARRINGTON & RICHARDSON MODEL 586
Revolver; double action; 32 H&R Mag.; 5-shot cylinder; 4-1/2-inch, 5-1/2-inch, 7-1/2-inch, 10-inch barrel; adjustable rear sight; fixed cylinder; plastic or wood grips. Introduced 1984; dropped 1985.
Perf.: $250   **Exc.:** $225   **VGood:** $195

HARRINGTON & RICHARDSON MODEL 603
Revolver; double action; 22 WMR; 6-shot cylinder; 6-inch flat-sided barrel; blade front sight, fully-adjustable rear; smooth walnut grips; swing-out cylinder; coil spring construction; blued finish. Introduced 1981; dropped 1983.
Exc.: $159   **VGood:** $120   **Good:** $110

HARRINGTON & RICHARDSON MODEL 604
Revolver; double action; 22 WMR; 6-shot cylinder; 6-inch bull barrel with raised solid rib; blade front, fully-adjustable rear sight; smooth walnut grips; swing-out cylinder; coil spring construction; blued finish. Introduced 1981; dropped 1985.
Exc.: $170   **VGood:** $130   **Good:** $115

HARRINGTON & RICHARDSON MODEL 622
Revolver; double action; 22 LR, 22 Short, 22 Long; 6-shot cylinder; 2-1/2-inch, 4-inch, 6-inch barrels; solid frame; fixed sights; checkered black plastic grips; satin blued finish. Introduced 1957; dropped 1963.
Exc.: $150   **VGood:** $110   **Good:** $75

HARRINGTON & RICHARDSON MODEL 623
Revolver; double action; 22 LR, 22 Short; 6-shot cylinder; 2-1/2-inch, 4-inch, 6-inch barrels; solid frame; fixed sights; checkered plastic grips; chrome finish. Introduced 1957; dropped 1963.
Exc.: $135   **VGood:** $105   **Good:** $85

HARRINGTON & RICHARDSON MODEL 632 GUARDSMAN
Revolver; double action; 32 S&W, 32 S&W Long; 6-shot cylinder; 2-1/2-inch, 4-inch barrels; weighs 20 oz.; solid frame; fixed sights; checkered Tenite grips; blued finish. Introduced 1946; dropped 1957.
Exc.: $140   **VGood:** $95   **Good:** $75

HARRINGTON & RICHARDSON MODEL 633
Revolver; double action; 32 S&W, 32 S&W Long; 6-shot cylinder; 2-1/2-inch, 4-inch barrels; weighs 20 oz.; solid frame; fixed sights; checkered Tenite grips; nickel finish. Introduced 1946; dropped 1957.
Exc.: $135   **VGood:** $95   **Good:** $75

HARRINGTON & RICHARDSON MODEL 649
Revolver; double action; two 6-shot cylinders; 22 LR, 22 WMR; 5-1/2-inch, 7-1/2-inch barrel; solid frame;

blade front, adjustable rear sight; one-piece walnut grip; blued finish. Introduced in 1976; dropped 1980.
Exc.: $140   **VGood:** $120   **Good:** $110

HARRINGTON & RICHARDSON MODEL 650
Revolver; double action; 22 LR, 22 WMR; 6-shot cylinder; 5-1/2-inch barrel; solid frame; blade front, adjustable rear sight; one-piece walnut grip; nickel finished. Introduced 1976; dropped 1980.
Exc.: $150   **VGood:** $130   **Good:** $115

HARRINGTON & RICHARDSON MODEL 666
Revolver; double action; 22 LR, 22 WMR; two 6-shot cylinders; 6-inch barrel; solid frame; fixed sights; plastic stocks; blued finish. Introduced 1976; dropped 1980.
Exc.: $130   **VGood:** $110   **Good:** $95

HARRINGTON & RICHARDSON MODEL 676
Revolver; double action; 22 LR, 22 WMR; two 6-shot cylinders; 4-1/2-inch, 5-1/2-inch, 7-1/2-inch, 12-inch barrel; solid frame; blade front, adjustable rear sight; one-piece walnut grip; color case-hardened frame; blued finish. Introduced 1976; dropped 1985.
Exc.: $140   **VGood:** $120   **Good:** $100

HARRINGTON & RICHARDSON MODEL 686
Revolver; double action; 22 LR, 22 WMR; two 6-shot cylinders; 5-1/2-inch, 7-1/2-inch, 10-inch, 12-inch barrel; ramp and blade front sight, fully-adjustable rear; one-piece walnut grip; color case-hardened frame; blued finish. Introduced 1981; dropped 1985.
Exc.: $185   **VGood:** $160   **Good:** $140

H&R Model 732

H&R Model 939

H&R Model 766

H&R Model 904

H&R Model 830

H&R Model 905

HARRINGTON & RICHARDSON MODEL 732

Revolver; double action; 32 S&W, 32 S&W Long, 32 H&R Mag.; 6-shot swing-out cylinder; 2-1/2-inch, 4-inch barrels; solid frame; windage-adjustable rear sight (4-inch model), fixed on shorter barrel, ramp front; black plastic checkered grips; blued finish. Introduced 1958; dropped 1985.

Exc.: $150   **VGood:** $110   **Good:** $95

32 H&R Mag.

Exc.: $175   **VGood:** $120   **Good:** $105

HARRINGTON & RICHARDSON MODEL 733

Revolver; double action; 32 S&W, 32 S&W Long, 32 H&R Mag.; 6-shot swing-out cylinder; 2-1/2-inch barrel; solid frame; Windage-adjustable rear sight (4-inch model), fixed on shorter barrel; ramp front; plastic checkered grips; same as Model 932 except nickel finish. Introduced 1958; dropped 1985.

Exc.: $140   **VGood:** $125   **Good:** $110

32 H&R Mag.

Exc.: $150   **VGood:** $135   **Good:** $120

HARRINGTON & RICHARDSON MODEL 766

Revolver; double action; 22 LR; 7-shot cylinder; 6-inch barrel; target; hinged frame; fixed sights; checkered walnut grips; blued finish. Introduced 1926; dropped 1936.

Exc.: $125   **VGood:** $110   **Good:** $100

HARRINGTON & RICHARDSON MODEL 826

Revolver; double action; 22 LR, 22 WMR; 9-shot; 3-inch bull barrel; weighs 27 oz.; ramp blade front, adjustable rear sight; uncheckered American walnut stocks; recessed muzzle; swing-out cylinder; blued finish. Introduced 1982; dropped 1984.

Exc.: $120   **VGood:** $105   **Good:** $95

HARRINGTON & RICHARDSON MODEL 829

Revolver; double action; 22 LR; 9-shot cylinder; 3-inch bull barrel; weighs 27 oz.; uncheckered American walnut stocks; ramp/blade front sight, adjustable rear; blued finish; recessed muzzle; swing-out cylinder. Introduced 1982; dropped 1984.

Exc.: $120   **VGood:** $90   **Good:** $75

HARRINGTON & RICHARDSON MODEL 830

Revolver; double action; 22 LR, 22 WMR; 9-shot; 3-inch bull barrel; weighs 27 oz.; ramp blade front, adjustable rear sight; uncheckered American walnut stocks; recessed muzzle; swing-out cylinder; nickel finish. Introduced 1982; dropped 1984.

Exc.: $120   **VGood:** $95   **Good:** $75

HARRINGTON & RICHARDSON MODEL 832

Revolver; double action; 32 S&W Long; 9-shot; 3-inch bull barrel; weighs 27 oz.; ramp blade front, adjustable rear sight; uncheckered American walnut stocks; recessed muzzle; swing-out cylinder; blued finish. Introduced 1982; dropped 1984.

Exc.: $120   **VGood:** $75   **Good:** $70

HARRINGTON & RICHARDSON MODEL 833

Revolver; double action; 32 S&W Long; 9-shot; 3-inch bull barrel; weighs 27 oz.; ramp blade front, adjustable rear sight; uncheckered American walnut stocks; recessed muzzle; swing-out cylinder; nickel finish. Introduced 1982; dropped 1984.

Exc.: $130   **VGood:** $95   **Good:** $75

HARRINGTON & RICHARDSON MODEL 900

Revolver; double action; 22 LR, 22 Short, 22 Long; 9-shot swing-out cylinder; 2-1/2-inch, 4-inch, 6-inch barrels; solid frame; blade front sight; high-impact black plastic grips; blued finish. Introduced 1962; dropped 1973.

Exc.: $120   **VGood:** $95   **Good:** $75

HARRINGTON & RICHARDSON MODEL 901

Revolver; double action; 22 LR, 22 Short, 22 Long; 9-shot swing-out cylinder; 2-1/2-inch, 4-inch, 6-inch barrels; solid frame; high-impact white plastic grips; chrome finish. Introduced 1962; dropped 1963.

Exc.: $150   **VGood:** $125   **Good:** $90

HARRINGTON & RICHARDSON MODEL 903

Revolver; double action; 22 LR; 9-shot cylinder; 6-inch flat-sided barrel; blade front sight, fully-adjustable rear; smooth walnut grips; swing-out cylinder; coil spring construction; blued finish. Introduced 1981; dropped 1985.

Exc.: $100   **VGood:** $85   **Good:** $75

HARRINGTON & RICHARDSON MODEL 904

Revolver; double action; 22 LR; 9-shot cylinder; 6-inch bull barrel with raised solid rib; blade front, fully-adjustable rear sight; smooth walnut grips; swing-out cylinder; coil spring construction; blued finish. Introduced 1981; dropped 1985.

Exc.: $150   **VGood:** $135   **Good:** $120

HARRINGTON & RICHARDSON MODEL 905

Revolver; double action; 22 LR; 9-shot cylinder; 4-inch bull barrel with raised solid rib; blade front, fully-adjustable rear sight; smooth walnut grips; swing-out cylinder; coil spring construction; H&R Hard-Guard finish. Introduced 1981; dropped 1985.

Exc.: $160   **VGood:** $140   **Good:** $125

HARRINGTON & RICHARDSON MODEL 922

Revolver; double action; 22 Short, 22 Long, 22 LR; 9-shot cylinder; 4-inch, 6-inch, 10-inch barrel; 10-1/2-inch overall length (6-inch barrel); weighs 21-3/4 oz.; solid frame; fixed sights; checkered walnut or Tenite grips; blued finish.

H&R Model 926

H&R Model 925
(Early Model)

H&R Model 929

H&R Model 925
(1960s model)

H&R Model 939
Premier

H&R Model 940

H&R Model 949

Introduced in 1919. Early production had 10-inch octagonal barrel, later dropped.

Exc.: $150   **VGood:** $115   **Good:** $100

HARRINGTON & RICHARDSON MODEL 922 BANTAMWEIGHT

Same specs as Model 922 except 2-1/2-inch barrel; weighs 20 oz.; rounded butt. Introduced 1951; no longer produced.

Exc.: $150   **VGood:** $115   **Good:** $100

HARRINGTON & RICHARDSON MODEL 922 CAMPER

Same specs as Model 922 except 4-inch barrel; weighs 21 oz.; special small Tenite grips. Introduced 1952.

Exc.: $150   **VGood:** $115   **Good:** $100

HARRINGTON & RICHARDSON MODEL 923

Revolver; double action; 22 Short, 22 Long, 22 LR; 9-shot cylinder; 4-inch, 6-inch, 10-inch barrel; 10-1/2-inch overall length (6-inch barrel); weighs 21-3/4 oz.; solid frame; fixed sights; checkered walnut or Tenite grips; chrome finish. Introduced in 1919. Early production had 10-inch octagonal barrel, later dropped.

Exc.: $120   **VGood:** $85   **Good:** $75

HARRINGTON & RICHARDSON MODEL 925

Revolver; double action; 38 S&W; 5-shot cylinder; 2-1/2-inch, 4-inch, 6-inch barrel; weighs 25 oz. (4-inch barrel); hinged frame; fixed front, adjustable rear sight; one-piece smooth or checkered plastic grip; blued finish. Advertised as the Defender Model; originally introduced as Model 25. Introduced 1964; dropped 1981.

Exc.: $250   **VGood:** $200   **Good:** $125

HARRINGTON & RICHARDSON MODEL 926

Revolver; double action; 22 LR, 22 Short, 22 Long, 38 S&W; 9-shot cylinder (22), 5-shot (38 S&W); 4-inch barrel; weighs 31 oz.; hinged frame; fixed front, adjustable rear sight; checkered walnut stocks; blued finish. Introduced 1968; dropped 1980.

Exc.: $250   **VGood:** $200   **Good:** $125

HARRINGTON & RICHARDSON MODEL 929

Revolver; double action; 22 LR, 22 Short, 22 Long; 9-shot cylinder; 2-1/2-inch, 4-inch, 6-inch barrels; weighs 23 oz. (2-1/2-inch barrel); solid frame; swing-out cylinder; auto extractor; fixed sights; checkered plastic grips; blued finish. Advertised as Sidekick Model. Introduced 1956; dropped 1985. Reintroduced 1996 by H&R 1871, Inc.; no longer produced.

Exc.: $225   **VGood:** $165   **Good:** $100

HARRINGTON & RICHARDSON MODEL 930

Revolver; double action; 22 LR, 22 Short, 22 Long; 9-shot cylinder; 2-1/2-inch, 4-inch, 6-inch barrels; solid frame; swing-out cylinder; fixed sights; checkered plastic grips; same as Model 929 except nickel finish. Introduced 1956; dropped 1985.

Exc.: $125   **VGood:** $110   **Good:** $80

HARRINGTON & RICHARDSON MODEL 939

Revolver; double action; 22 LR; 9-shot cylinder; 6-inch barrel with vent rib; solid-frame; swing-out cylinder; ramp front, adjustable rear sight; checkered walnut grips; blued finish. Advertised as the Ultra Sidekick Model. Introduced 1958; dropped 1981. Reintroduced in 1995 by H&R 1871, Inc.; no longer in production.

Exc.: $150   **VGood:** $125   **Good:** $85

HARRINGTON & RICHARDSON MODEL 939 PREMIER

Revolver; double action; 22 LR; 9-shot cylinder; 6-inch heavy barrel; weighs 36 oz.; walnut-finished hardwood grips; blade front sight, fully-adjustable rear; swing-out cylinder; plunger-type ejection; solid barrel rib; high-polish blue finish; Western-style grip. Made in U.S. by H&R 1871, Inc. Introduced 1995; no longer produced.

New: $150   **Perf.:** $135   **Exc.:** $115

HARRINGTON & RICHARDSON MODEL 940

Revolver; double action; 22 Short, 22 Long, 22 LR; 9-shot; 6-inch barrel; ramp front sight, adjustable rear; checkered hardwood grips; thumbrest; swingout cylinder; blued finish. Advertised as Ultra Sidekick. Introduced 1978; dropped 1982.

Exc.: $105   **VGood:** $95   **Good:** $75

HARRINGTON & RICHARDSON MODEL 949

Revolver; double action; 22 LR, Long, Short; 9-shot cylinder; 5-1/2-inch barrel; solid-frame; side-loading, ejection; adjustable rear sight; blade front; one-piece plain walnut grip; blued, nickel finish. Advertised as Forty-Niner Model. Introduced in 1960; dropped, 1985.

Exc.: $115   **VGood:** $100   **Good:** $85

HARRINGTON & RICHARDSON MODEL 949 WESTERN

Revolver; double action; 22 LR; 9-shot cylinder; 5-1/2-inch, 7-1/2-inch barrel; weighs 36 oz.; walnut-stained hardwood grips; blade front sight, adjustable rear; color case-hardened frame and backstrap; traditional loading gate and ejector rod. Made in U.S. by Harrington & Richardson. Introduced 1994; no longer produced.

New: $140   **Perf.:** $125   **Exc.:** $110

H&R Model 999
Sportsman

H&R Trapper Model

H&R Vest
Pocket Model

H&R Self-Loading 32

H&R USRA Model

H&R No. 199

HARRINGTON & RICHARDSON MODEL 950

Revolver; double action; 22 LR, 22 Long, 22 Short; 9-shot cylinder; 5-1/2-inch barrel; solid-frame; side-loading, ejection; adjustable rear sight, blade front; one-piece plain walnut grip; nickel finish. Introduced 1960; dropped 1985.

Exc.: $125   **VGood:** $105   **Good:** $90

HARRINGTON & RICHARDSON MODEL 976

Revolver; double action; 22 LR, 38 S&W; 9-shot cylinder (22 LR), 5-shot (38 S&W); 4-inch barrel; hinged frame; fixed front, adjustable rear sight; checkered walnut stocks; blued finish. Introduced 1968; dropped 1981.

Exc.: $110   **VGood:** $90   **Good:** $85

HARRINGTON & RICHARDSON MODEL 999

Revolver; double action; 22 Short, 22 Long, 22 LR; 9-shot cylinder; 4-inch, 6-inch top-break barrel; weighs 34 oz.; checkered hardwood grips; elevation-adjustable front sight, windage-adjustable rear; automatic ejection; triggerguard extension; blued finish; optional engraving. Marketed as Sportsman Model. Introduced 1936; dropped 1985.

Exc.: $300   **VGood:** $270   **Good:** $225

Engraved

Exc.: $425   **VGood:** $375   **Good:** $300

HARRINGTON & RICHARDSON MODEL 999 SPORTSMAN

Revolver; double action; 22 LR; 9-shot cylinder; 4-inch, 6-inch barrel; 8-1/2-inch overall length; weighs 30 oz.; walnut-finished hardwood grips; elevation-adjustable blade front sight, windage-adjustable rear; top-break loading; automatic shell ejection; polished blue finish. Made in U.S. by Harrington & Richardson. Reintroduced 1992; no longer in production. Add 25% for scarce nickel variant.

Perf.: $360   **Exc.:** $295   **VGood:** $175

HARRINGTON & RICHARDSON NEW DEFENDER

Revolver; double action; 22 LR; 2-inch barrel; 6-1/4-inch overall length; checkered hard rubber grips; adjustable front and rear sights; automatic ejector; triggerguard extention; blued finish. Also listed as Model 299. Introduced 1936; dropped 1941.

Exc.: $220   **VGood:** $200   **Good:** $180

HARRINGTON & RICHARDSON NO. 196

Revolver; 22 Short, 22 Long, 22 LR; 6-1/4-inch barrel; 11-inch overall length; weighs 32 oz.; adjustable Patridge front, adjustable rear; wide hammer; blue finish. Called the "Eureka" Sportsman.

Exc.: $175   **VGood:** $150   **Good:** $100

HARRINGTON & RICHARDSON NO. 199

Revolver; single action; 22 LR; 9-shot cylinder; 6-inch barrel; 11-inch overall length; weighs 30 oz.; hinged frame; adjustable target sights; checkered walnut grips; blued finish. Single action version of the double-action Model 999 Sportsman. Introduced 1933; dropped 1951.

Exc.: $195   **VGood:** $110   **Good:** $85

HARRINGTON & RICHARDSON PREMIER MODEL

Revolver; double action; hinged-frame; 22 LR, 32 S&W Short; 7-shot (22), 5-shot (32); 2-inch, 3-inch, 4-inch, 5-inch, 6-inch barrel; weighs 13 oz.; fixed sights; hard rubber grips; blued nickel finish. Introduced 1895; dropped 1941.

Exc.: $195   **VGood:** $85   **Good:** $65

HARRINGTON & RICHARDSON SELF-LOADING 25

Semi-automatic; 25 ACP; 6-shot magazine; 2-inch barrel, 4-1/2-inch overall; hammerless checkered hard rubber stocks; fixed sights; blued finish. Based on Webley & Scott design. Approximately 16,000 manufactured from 1912 to 1916.

Exc.: $375   **VGood:** $330   **Good:** $305

HARRINGTON & RICHARDSON SELF-LOADING 32

Semi-automatic; 32 ACP; 8-shot magazine; 3-1/2-inch barrel; 6-1/2-inch overall length; weighs 22 oz.; grip safety; magazine disconnector; hammerless; checkered hard rubber stocks; fixed sights; blued finish. Based on Webley & Scott design. Approximately 40,000 manufactured from 1916 to 1924.

Exc.: $330   **VGood:** $305   **Good:** $250

HARRINGTON & RICHARDSON TRAPPER MODEL

Revolver; double action; 22 Short, 22 Long, 22 LR; 7-shot cylinder; 6-inch octagonal barrel; weighs 12-1/4 oz.; solid frame; gold front sight; checkered walnut stocks; blued finish. Introduced 1924; dropped during WWII. 15% premium for longer barrel.

Exc.: $150   **VGood:** $90   **Good:** $75

HARRINGTON & RICHARDSON USRA MODEL

Single shot; 22 LR; 7-inch, 8-inch, 10-inch barrel; weighs 31 oz. (10-inch barrel); hinged frame target pistol; adjustable trigger pull; checkered walnut grips; blued finish. Introduced 1928; dropped 1943.

Exc.: $650   **VGood:** $450   **Good:** $250

HARRINGTON & RICHARDSON VEST POCKET MODEL

Revolver; double action; 22 Long, 32 S&W Short; 5-shot cylinder (32), 7-shot (22); 1-1/8-inch barrel; weighs 8-1/2 oz.; solid frame; spurless hammer; no sights except for milled slot in top frame; hard rubber grips; blued or nickel finish. Introduced 1891; dropped during WWII.

Exc.: $150   **VGood:** $85   **Good:** $75

HARRIS-MCMILLAN SIGNATURE JR. LONG RANGE

Bolt action; single shot or repeater; chambered for any suitable caliber; custom barrel length to customer specs.; weighs about 5 lbs.; fiberglass stock; no sights; scope rings; right- or left-hand

Hartford Target Auto

Hartford Target Single Shot

Hawes Favorite

Hawes Deputy Marshal, Texas Model

Hawes Deputy Marshal, Silver City Model

Hawes Marshal, Federal Model

Hawes Marshal, Montana Model

benchrest action of titanium or stainless steel; bipod. All parts and components made in U.S. by Harris Gunworks, Inc. Introduced 1992; dropped 1995.

New: $2200   **Perf.:** $1750   **Exc.:** $1500

HARRIS-MCMILLAN WOLVERINE

Semi-automatic; single action; 9mm Para., 10mm Auto, 38 Wadcutter, 38 Super, 45 Italian, 45 ACP; 6-inch barrel; 9-1/2-inch overall length; weighs 45 oz.; Pachmayr rubber grips; blade front sight, fully-adjustable low profile rear; integral compensator; round burr-style hammer; extended grip safety; checkered backstrap; skeletonized aluminum match trigger. Many finish options offered. Combat or Competition Match styles. All parts and components were made in U.S. by Harris Gunworks, Inc. Introduced 1992.

New: $1600   **Perf.:** $1350   **Exc.:** $1200

HARTFORD REPEATING PISTOL

Repeater; 22 LR; 10-shot magazine; 6-3/4-inch barrel; 10-3/4-inch overall length; hand-operated repeater; slide manually moved rearward to eject cartridge case, forward to chamber new round; same general outward design characteristics as Target Automatic; checkered, black rubber grips; target sights; blued finish. Very similar to Fiala.

Exc.: $450   **VGood:** $350   **Good:** $200

HARTFORD TARGET AUTOMATIC

Semi-automatic; 22 LR; 10-shot magazine; 6-3/4-inch barrel; 10-3/4-inch overall length; checkered black rubber grips; target sights; blued finish. Hartford was the predecessor of High Standard. Introduced 1929; dropped 1932. Has more collector than shooter value.

Exc.: $550   **VGood:** $500   **Good:** $450

HARTFORD TARGET SINGLE SHOT

Single shot; 22 LR; 5-3/4-inch barrel; 10-3/4 overall length; same general outward appearance as Hartford Target Auto; black rubber or walnut grips;

target sights; color case-hardened frame; blued barrel. Introduced 1929; dropped 1932.

Exc.: $550   **VGood:** $500   **Good:** $450

HASKELL JS-45

Semi-automatic; single action; 45 ACP; 7-shot magazine; 4-1/2-inch barrel; 8-inch overall length; weighs 44 oz.; checkered acetal resin grips; fixed low profile sights; internal drop-safe mechanism; all aluminum frame; matte black finish. From MKS Supply, Inc. Introduced 1991; still produced as Hi-Point JS-45.

Perf.: $125   **Exc.:** $110   **VGood:** $100

Brushed nickel finish

Perf.: $135   **Exc.:** $125   **VGood:** $110

HAWES DEPUTY MARSHAL

Revolver; single action; 22 LR, 22 WMR; 6-shot; 5-1/2-inch barrel; 11-inch overall length; blade front sight, adjustable rear; plastic or walnut grips; blued finish. Introduced 1973; dropped 1980.

Exc.: $85   **VGood:** $65   **Good:** $50

HAWES DEPUTY MARSHAL, DENVER MODEL

Same specs as Deputy Marshal except brass frame. Introduced 1973; dropped 1980.

Exc.: $85   **VGood:** $65   **Good:** $50

HAWES DEPUTY MARSHAL, MONTANA MODEL

Same specs as Deputy Marshal except walnut grips only; brass grip frame. Introduced 1973; dropped 1980.

Exc.: $95   **VGood:** $75   **Good:** $55

HAWES DEPUTY MARSHAL, SILVER CITY MODEL

Same specs as Deputy Marshal except brass grip frame; chromed frame; blued barrel and cylinder. Introduced 1973; discontinued 1980.

Exc.: $95   **VGood:** $75   **Good:** $55

HAWES DEPUTY MARSHAL, TEXAS MODEL

Same specs as Deputy Marshal except for chrome finish. Introduced 1973; discontinued 1980.

Exc.: $95   **VGood:** $75   **Good:** $55

HAWES FAVORITE

Break-action single shot; 22 LR; 8-inch barrel; 12-inch overall length; tip-up action; target sights; plastic or rosewood stocks; blued barrel; chromed frame. Replica of Stevens No. 35 Target Model. Manufactured 1968 to 1976.

Exc.: $195   **VGood:** $175   **Good:** $155

HAWES MARSHAL, CHIEF MODEL

Revolver; single action; 357 Mag., 9mm, 44-40, 44 Mag., 45 Colt, 45 ACP; 6-inch barrel; target-type front sight, adjustable rear; oversize rosewood stocks; available with interchangeable cylinder combos; blued finish. Manufactured in West Germany by Sauer & Sohn exclusively for Hawes. Introduced 1968; discontinued 1980.

Exc.: $200   **VGood:** $165   **Good:** $135

HAWES MARSHAL, FEDERAL MODEL

Same specs as Hawes Marshal, Chief Model except color case-hardened frame; one-piece European walnut grip; brass grip frame; fixed sights. Introduced 1969; discontinued 1980.

Exc.: $200   **VGood:** $165   **Good:** $135

HAWES MARSHAL, MONTANA MODEL

Same specs as Hawes Marshal, Chief Model except also 22 LR, 22 WMR chamberings; 5-inch barrel (rimfires); fixed sights; plastic stag (rimfires) or rosewood (centerfire) grips; brass stag frame. Introduced 1968; discontinued 1980.

Exc.: $200   **VGood:** $165   **Good:** $135

HAWES MARSHAL, SILVER CITY MODEL

Same specs as Hawes Marshal, Chief Model except fixed sights; pearlite grips; brass frame. Introduced 1969; discontinued 1980.

Exc.: $200   **VGood:** $165   **Good:** $135

Hawes/Sig-Sauer P220

H&K HK4

Heckler & Koch Mark 23

H&K P7 M8

H&K P9S

H&K USP45 Tactical

H&K P7 M13

H&K P7 PSP

H&K P9S Competition Kit

HAWES MARSHAL, TEXAS MODEL

Same specs as Hawes Marshal, Chief Model except also 22 LR, 22 WMR chamberings; 5-inch barrel (rimfires); fixed sights; pearlite grips; nickel finish. Introduced 1969; discontinued 1980.

Exc.: $200   **VGood:** $165   **Good:** $135

HAWES MARSHAL, WESTERN MODEL

Same specs as Hawes Marshal, Chief Model except also 22 LR, 22 WMR chamberings; 5-inch barrel (rimfire); fixed sights; plastic stag (rimfire) or rosewood (centerfire) grips. Introduced 1968; discontinued 1980.

Exc.: $200   **VGood:** $165   **Good:** $135

HAWES MEDALLION MODEL

Revolver; double action; 22 LR, 38 Spl.; 6-shot; 3-inch, 4-inch, 6-inch barrel; fixed sights; swing-out cylinder; blued finish. No longer in production.

Exc.: $135   **VGood:** $125   **Good:** $100

HAWES TROPHY MODEL

Revolver; double action; 22 LR, 38 Spl.; 6-shot; 6-inch barrel; adjustable sights; swing-out cylinder; blued finish. No longer in production.

Exc.: $135   **VGood:** $125   **Good:** $100

HAWES/SIG-SAUER P220

Semi-automatic; 9mm Para., 38 Super, 45 ACP; 7-shot magazine (45 ACP), 9-shot (9mm, 38); 4-3/8-inch barrel; 7-3/4-inch overall length; checkered European walnut or black plastic stocks; windage-adjustable rear sight, blade front; square combat triggerguard. Manufactured in Germany. Introduced 1977; still in production; dropped by Hawes in 1980. Also known as Browning BDA, SIG/Sauer P220.

Exc.: $450   **VGood:** $400   **Good:** $350

HECKLER & KOCH HK4

Semi-automatic; double action; 22 LR, 25 ACP, 32 ACP, 380 ACP; 8-shot magazine; 3-1/2-inch barrel; 6-inch overall length; windage-adjustable rear sight, fixed front; checkered black plastic grips; blued finish. Early version available with interchangeable barrels, magazines for four calibers. Imported from

Germany originally by Harrington & Richardson, then by Heckler & Koch; importation dropped 1984.

Single caliber		
Exc.: $350	**VGood:** $275	**Good:** $200
Four caliber set		
Exc.: $750	**VGood:** $650	**Good:** $500

HECKLER & KOCH MARK 23

Semi-automatic; 45 ACP; 10-shot magazine; 5.87-inch barrel; 43 oz.; 9.65-inch overall; grips integral with frame, black polymer; blade front sight; rear drift adjustable for windage, three-dot; polymer frame; double action; exposed hammer; short recoil, modified Browning action. Civilian version of the SOCOM pistol. Introduced 1996. Imported from Germany by Heckler & Koch, Inc.

Exc.: $1995   **VGood:** $1750   **Good:** $1550

HECKLER & KOCH P7 K3

Semi-automatic; single action; 22 LR, 380 ACP; 8-shot magazine; 3-13/16-inch barrel; 26-1/2 oz.; fixed sights; black plastic grips; cocked by pressure on frontstrap; large triggerguard with heat shield; oil-filled buffer to decrease recoil; blue or nickel finish. Introduced 1988; no longer imported.

Exc.: $1295   **VGood:** $850   **Good:** $715

22 LR conversion unit		
Exc.: $600	**VGood:** $500	**Good:** $400
32 ACP conversion unit		
Exc.: $300	**VGood:** $200	**Good:** $150

Add $85 to above prices for Tritium sights

HECKLER & KOCH P7 M8

Semi-automatic; 9mm Para.; 8-shot magazine; 4-1/8-inch barrel; 6 3/4-inch overall length; weighs 29 oz.; blade front, adjustable rear sight with three-dot system; unique squeeze-cocker system in frontstrap; gas-retarded action; squared combat-type triggerguard; stippled black plastic grips; blue finish. Imported from Germany by Heckler & Koch, Inc.

Perf.: $1125   **Exc.:** $950   **VGood:** $775

Add $105 to above prices for pistols fitted with Tritium sights
Add $575 for 22 LR conversion kit
(barrel, slide and two magazines)

HECKLER & KOCH P7 M10

Semi-automatic; 40 S&W; 10-shot magazine; 4-1/8-inch barrel; 7-inch overall length; weighs 43 oz.; blade front, adjustable rear sight with three-dot system; unique "squeeze-cocker" system in frontstrap; gas-retarded action; squared combat-type triggerguard; stippled black plastic grips; blue finish. Imported from Germany by Heckler & Koch, Inc. Introduced 1992; no longer in production.

Perf.: $1125   **Exc.:** $950   **VGood:** $775

Add $85 to above prices for pistols with Tritium sights

HECKLER & KOCH P7 M13

Semi-automatic; single action; 9mm Para.; 13-shot magazine; 4-1/8-inch barrel; 6-1/2-inch overall length; 30 oz.; fixed sights; black plastic grips; cocked by pressure on frontstrap; large triggerguard with heat shield; ambidextrous magazine release; blue or nickel finish. Introduced 1986; importation discontinued 1994.

Perf.: $1575   **Exc.:** $1250   **VGood:** $1050

Nickel finish		
Perf.: $1650	**Exc.:** $1350	**VGood:** $1150

Add $85 to above prices for pistols with Tritium sights

HECKLER & KOCH P7 PSP

Semi-automatic; single action; 9mm Para; 8-shot magazine; 4-1/8-inch barrel; 6-1/2-inch overall length; weighs 29 oz.; fixed sights; black plastic grips; cocked by pressure on frontstrap; squared combat triggerguard; blued finish. Imported from West Germany. Introduced 1982; discontinued 1986.

Perf.: $700   **Exc.:** $700   **VGood:** $600

HECKLER & KOCH P9S

Semi-automatic; double action; 9mm Para., 45 ACP; 9-shot magazine (9mm), 7-shot (45 ACP); 4-inch barrel; 5-7/16-inch overall length; fixed sights; checkered plastic grips; loaded/cocked indicators; hammer cocking lever; phosphated finish. Originally imported from Germany by Gold Rush Gun Shop in 1977, then by Heckler & Koch, Inc.; importation dropped 1984.

Exc.: $800   **VGood:** $700   **Good:** $500

H&K SP 89

H&K USP 9mm

H&K USP Compact
Auto Pistol

H&K USPExpert

H&K HK45

H&K USP45
Compact

H&K USP Elite

H&K VP 70Z

H&K P2000

HECKLER & KOCH P9S COMPETITION KIT

Same specs as P9S except 9mm Para.; additional 5-1/2-inch barrel with weight; additional slide; adjustable sights, trigger; walnut stock. Introduced 1977; discontinued 1984.

Exc.: $1300   **VGood:** $950   **Good:** $750

HECKLER & KOCH P9S TARGET

Same specs as P9S except adjustable sights, trigger. Introduced 1977; discontinued 1984.

Exc.: $1000   **VGood:** $800   **Good:** $650

HECKLER & KOCH SP 89

Semi-automatic; single action; 9mm Para.; 15-, 30-shot magazine; 4-1/2-inch barrel; 12-7/8-inch overall length; weighs 4-1/2 lbs.; black high-impact plastic grip; post front sight, fully-adjustable diopter rear; design inspired by the HK94 rifle; has special flash-hider forend. Imported from Germany by Heckler & Koch, Inc. Introduced 1989; no longer imported.

Perf.: $3750   **Exc.:** $3400   **VGood:** $3100

HECKLER & KOCH USP

Semi-automatic; single action/double action or double-action-only; 9mm Para., 40 S&W, 45 ACP; 15-shot magazine (9mm), 13-shot (40 S&W), 12-shot (45 ACP); 4-1/4-inch barrel; 6-15/16-inch overall length; weighs 28 oz.; non-slip stippled black polymer grips; blade front sight, windage-adjustable rear; polymer frame; modified Browning action with recoil reduction system; single control lever; special "hostile environment" finish on all metal parts; available in SA/DA, DAO, left- and right-hand versions. Imported from Germany by Heckler & Koch, Inc. Introduced 1993; still imported.

Right-hand		
New: $670	**Perf.:** $540	**Exc.:** $485
Left-hand		
New: $750	**Perf.:** $650	**Exc.:** $560

HECKLER & KOCH USP COMPACT AUTO PISTOL

Similar to the USP except has 3.58-inch barrel, measures 6.81-inch overall, and weighs 1.60 lbs. (9mm). Available in 9mm Para. or 40 S&W with 10-shot magazine. Introduced 1996. Imported from Germany by Heckler & Koch, Inc.

Right-hand		
New: $680	**Perf.:** $550	**Exc.:** $475
Left-hand		
New: $705	**Perf.:** $650	**Exc.:** $550

HECKLER & KOCH USP45 COMPACT

Similar to the USP45 except has stainless slide; 8-shot magazine; modified and contoured slide and frame; extended slide release; 3.80-inch barrel, 7.09-inch overall length, weighs 1.75 lbs.; adjustable three-dot sights. Introduced 1998. Imported from Germany by Heckler & Koch, Inc.

New: $760   **Perf.:** $595   **Exc.:** $500

HECKLER & KOCH USP45 COMPACT TACTICAL

Blued semi-auto .45 ACP. Double-action with 4.46-inch barrel, 8-round capacity. 27.5 oz. Polymer grip.

NIB: $1050   **Exc.:** $975   **VGood:** $825

HECKLER & KOCH USP45 MATCH

Semi-automatic; 45 ACP; 10-shot magazine; 6.02 barrel; 9.45-inch overall; textured polymer grips; high profile target front sight; fully adjustable target rear; adjustable trigger stop; polymer frame; blue or stainless steel slide. Introduced 1997. Imported from Germany by Heckler & Koch, Inc.

Blue		
New: $1275	**Perf.:** $1025	**Exc.:** $825
Stainless		
New: $1300	**Perf.:** $1100	**Exc.:** $900

HECKLER & KOCH USP45 TACTICAL

Semi-automatic; 45 ACP; 10-shot magazine; 4.92-inch barrel; 2.24 lbs.; 8.64-inch overall; non-slip stippled polymer grips; blade front sight, fully adjustable target rear; has extended threaded barrel with rubber O-ring; adjustable trigger; extended magazine floorplate; adjustable trigger stop; polymer frame. Introduced 1998. Imported from Germany by

Heckler & Koch, Inc.

New: $995   **Perf.:** $875   **Exc.:** $775

HECKLER & KOCH USP EXPERT

Similar to H&K USP but meets IPSC specifications. Add 20 percent to above values.

HECKLER & KOCH USP ELITE

Similar to H&K USP but with long (6.2-inch) barrel. Add 5 percent to above values.

HECKLER & KOCH VP 70Z

Semi-automatic; double-action-only; 9mm Para.; 18-shot magazine; 4-1/2-inch barrel; 8-inch overall length; ramp front sight, channeled rear on slide; stippled black plastic stocks; recoil-operated; only four moving parts; double-column magazine; phosphated finish. Manufactured in West Germany. Introduced 1976; importation dropped 1989.

Perf.: $750   **Exc.:** $675   **VGood:** $500

Add 125 percent to above prices if frame is cut for shoulder stock. Note: Such pistols are subject to provisions of the NFA.

HECKLER & KOCH P2000

Semi-automatic; 40 S&W, 357 SIG, 9mm Parabellum; 3.62-inch barrel; weight 1.5 lbs; overall length 7 inches. corrosion proof fiber-reinforced polymer frame; Polygonal bore profile for increased velocity, easier cleaning, and longer barrel life; Low profile slide and slimline, compact dimensions; Ambidextrous slide release (located on both sides of the frame); Corrosion resistant "Hostile Environment" Nitro Carburized finish.

Perf.: $775   **Exc.:** $700   **VGood:** $600

HECKLER & KOCH HK45

Full-size autoloader chambered in .45 ACP. Features include polygonal bore, front and rear slide serrations, integrated picatinny rail, amibi mag release levers, interchangeable backstrap panels, polymer frame, modular action design allowing for double action, singlke action or double action-only operation. Measures 7.52 inches overall length. 10+1 capacity.

New: $995   **Perf.:** $875   **Exc.:** $775

Helwan 9mm

Heritage H25S Auto Pistol

Heritage Rough Rider

H&K HK45 Compact

Heritage Sentry

Heritage Stealth Auto

H2758 H&K P30

Hi-Point .40 Compact with laser

Hi-Point 9mm Compact with laser

HECKLER & KOCH HK45 COMPACT

Similar to above but with 8-round capacity; overall length 7.2 inches.

New: $995   **Perf.:** $875   **Exc.:** $775

HECKLER & KOCH P30

Polymer-frame 9mm autoloader. Features include loaded chamber indicator, integral picatinny rail, oversized trigger guard, doible or single action fiurting mode with decocker, "Hostile Environment" black finish, ambidextrous, oversized controls.

New: $800   **Perf.:** $700   **Exc.:** $695

HELWAN 9MM

Semi-automatic; 9mm Para.; 8-shot magazine; 4-1/2-inch barrel; 8 1/4-inch overall length; weighs 33 oz; blade front sight, drift-adjustable rear; grooved black plastic stocks; updated version of Beretta Model 951. Imported from Egypt by Steyr Daimler Puch of America, Navy Arms and Interarms.Introduced 1982; dropped 1983. Reintroduced recently by Century International Arms, Inc.

Exc.: $285   **VGood:** $225   **Good:** $175

HERITAGE MODEL HA25

Semi-automatic; single action; 25 ACP; 6-shot magazine; 2-1/2-inch barrel; 4-5/8-inch overall length; weighs 12 oz.; smooth or checkered walnut grips; fixed sights; exposed hammer; manual safety; open-top slide; polished blue or blue/gold finish. Made in U.S. by Heritage Mfg., Inc. Introduced 1993; no longer produced.

Perf.: $125   **Exc.:** $95   **VGood:** $80

Blue/gold finish		
Perf.: $135	**Exc.:** $105	**VGood:** $90

HERITAGE H25S AUTO PISTOL

Semi-automatic; 25 ACP; 6-shot magazine; 2.25-inch barrel; 13.5 oz.; 4.5-inch overall; smooth hardwood grips; fixed sights; frame-mounted trigger safety; magazine disconnect safety. Introduced 1995; dropped 1999.

New: $135   **Perf.:** $95   **Exc.:** $80

HERITAGE ROUGH RIDER

Revolver; single action; 22 LR, 22 LR/22 WMR combo; 6-shot cylinder; 4-3/4-inch, 6-1/2-inch, 9-inch barrel; weighs 31 to 38 oz.; Goncolo Alves grips; blade front sight, fixed rear; hammer-block safety; high polish blue or nickel finish. Made in U.S. by Heritage Mfg., Inc. Introduced 1993; still produced.

New: $130   **Perf.:** $110   **Exc.:** $95

2-inch, 3-inch, 4-inch, barrel, birdshead grip		
New: $135	**Perf.:** $110	**Exc.:** $95
Steel frame series		
News: $160	**Perf.:** $125	**Exc.:** $95

HERITAGE ROUGH RIDER .32

Six-shot revolver chambered for .32 H&R Magnum centerfire (interchangeably .32 S&W, .32 S&W Long). Black satin finish. Offered with 3.5-inch, 4.75-inch or 6.5-inch barrels. 35 oz. (6.5-inch bbl.). 11.785-inch LOA.) Fixed sights. Bird's head grip available.

NIB: $215   **Exc.:** $180   **VGood:** $150

HERITAGE ROUGH RIDER BIG-BORE SERIES

Six-shot revolver chambered for .357, .44-40 or .45 Long Colt. Barrel lengths 4.75-inch, 5.5-inch or 7.5-inch. 36 oz. Fixed sights.

NIB: $375   **Exc.:** $325   **VGood:** $295

HERITAGE SENTRY

Revolver; double action; 22 LR, 22 WMR, 9mm Para., 38 Spl.; 8-shot cylinder (22 LR), 6-shot (22 WMR, 9mm, 38 Spl.); 2-inch, 4-inch barrel; 6-1/4-inch overall length (2-inch barrel); weighs 23 oz.; magnum-style round butt grips of checkered plastic; ramp front sight, fixed rear; pull-pin-type ejection; serrated hammer and trigger; polished blue or nickel finish. Made in U.S. by Heritage Mfg., Inc. Introduced 1993; dropped 1997.

New: $110   **Perf.:** $90   **Exc.:** $75

HERITAGE STEALTH AUTO PISTOL

Semi-automatic; 9mm Para., 40 S&W; 10-shot magazine; 3.9-inch barrel; 20.2 oz.; 6.3-inch overall; black polymer integral grips; blade front sight, rear drift adjustable for windage; gas retarded blowback action; polymer frame; 17-4 stainless slide; frame mounted ambidextrous trigger safety, magazine safety. Introduced 1996. Made in U.S. by Heritage

Mfg., Inc.

Blue		
New: $255	**Perf.:** $220	**Exc.:** $190
Stainless		
New: $275	**Perf.:** $235	**Exc.:** $220

HI-POINT FIREARMS JS-9MM

Semi-automatic; single action; 9mm Para.; 9-shot magazine; 4-1/2-inch barrel; 7-3/4-inch overall length; weighs 41 oz.; textured acetal plastic grips; fixed low profile sights; scratch-resistant, non-glare blue finish. From MKS Supply, Inc. Introduced 1990; still produced.

New: $140   **Perf.:** $110   **Exc.:** $95

HI-POINT FIREARMS JS-9MM COMPACT

Same specs as JS-9mm except 380 ACP, 9mm Para.; 8-shot magazine; 3-1/2-inch barrel; 6-3/4-inch overall length; weighs 35 oz.; textured acetal plastic grips; low profile, combat-style, fixed three-dot sight system; frame-mounted magazine release; scratch-resistant matte finish. From MKS Supply, Inc. Introduced 1993; still produced.

9mm Para.		
New: $110	**Perf.:** $90	**Exc.:** $75
9mm Para., polymer frame, non-slip grips		
New: $120	**Perf.:** $110	**Exc.:** $95
380 ACP		
New: $80	**Perf.:** $60	**Exc.:** $50

HI-POINT FIREARMS JS-40 S&W

Semi-automatic; 40 S&W; 8-shot magazine; 4-1/2-inch barrel; 7-3/4-inch overall length; weighs 42 oz.; checkered acetal resin grips; fixed, low profile sights; optional laser sight; internal drop-safe mechansim; all aluminum frame; matte black finish. From MKS Supply, Inc. Introduced 1991; still produced.

New: $135   **Perf.:** $125   **Exc.:** $110

HI-POINT FIREARMS JS-45

Semi-automatic; single action; 45 ACP; 7-shot magazine; 4-1/2-inch barrel; 8-inch overall length; weighs 44 oz.; checkered acetal resin grips; fixed low profile sights; internal drop-safe mechanism; all aluminum frame. From MKS Supply, Inc. Introduced

High Standard Citation (106 Series)

High Standard Citation II (SH Series)

Hi-Point Firearms Model JS-9mm Compact

High Standard Citation (106 Series)

Hi-Point Firearms JS45

Hi-Point Firearms JS-40 S&W

High Standard Custom 10-X

1991; still produced.

New: $135 **Perf.:** $125 **Exc.:** $110

HI-POINT FIREARMS MODEL 9MM COMPACT PISTOL

Caliber: 9mm Para.; 8-shot magazine; 3.5-inch barrel; 29 oz.; 6.7-inch overall; textured acetal plastic grips; combat-style fixed three-dot sight system, low profile; single-action design; frame-mounted magazine release; polymer or alloy frame; scratch-resistant matte finish. Introduced 1993. From MKS Supply, Inc. Price: Black or chrome/black $124.95 Price: With polymer frame (29 oz.), non-slip grips.

New: $110 **Perf.:** $90 **Exc.:** $80

With compensator and optional laser

Perf.: $250 **Exc.:** $225 **VGood:** $150

HI-POINT FIREARMS MODEL 380 POLYMER PISTOL

Similar to the 9mm Compact model except chambered for 380 ACP, 8-shot magazine, adjustable three-dot sights. Weighs 29 oz. Polymer frame. Introduced 1998. Made in U.S. From MKS Supply.

New: $90 **Perf.:** $70 **Exc.:** $65

HI-POINT .380 ACP

Compensated Semi-auto with fully-adjustable 3-dot sights, muzzle compensator, 4-inch barrel, 31 oz, polymer frame. Two magazines: one 10-round, one 8-round. Add 50 percent for laser sight.

NIB: $110 **Exc.:** $95 **VGood:** $85

HIGH STANDARD SEMI-AUTOMATIC PISTOLS HIGH STANDARD CITATION (FIRST MODEL 102 SERIES)

Semi-automatic; 22 LR; 10-shot; 6-3/4-inch, 8-inch, 10-inch interchangeable tapered barrels; hammerless; push-button takedown; ramp front, click-adjustable rear sights; trigger pull and backlash adjustment screws; new rakish-looking barrels with grooves for weight attachment and knob on end for removable stabilizer; plastic grips, walnut optional; two removable weights; blued finish. Marked "SUPERMATIC" top line; "CITATION" in smaller letters underneath on left side of frame. Introduced

1958; dropped 1963.

Two barrels		
Exc.: 7800	**VGood:** $600	**Good:** $500
One barrel		
Exc.: $550	**VGood:** $450	**Good:** $375

HIGH STANDARD CITATION (103 SERIES)

Same specs as First Model except 5-1/2-inch bull barrel; tapped and notched for optional weights and stabilizer. Marked "Model 103" on right side of slide. Introduced 1962; dropped 1963.

Exc.: $600 **VGood:** $500 **Good:** $400

HIGH STANDARD CITATION (104 SERIES)

Same specs as 103 Series Citation except marked "Model 104" on right side of slide. Introduced 1963; dropped 1966.

Exc.: $550 **VGood:** $450 **Good:** $400

HIGH STANDARD CITATION (106 SERIES)

Same specs as 103 Series Citation except also offered in 7-1/4-inch barrel; positive magazine latch; military-style grips; stippled front, backstraps, saddle-type rear sight. Introduced 1965; dropped 1967.

Exc.: $500 **VGood:** $400 **Good:** $325

HIGH STANDARD CITATION (107 SERIES)

Same specs as 106 Series Citation except marked "Model 107" on right side of slide. Introduced 1968; dropped 1968.

Exc.: $500 **VGood:** $400 **Good:** $300

HIGH STANDARD CITATION (ML SERIES)

Same specs as 107 Series except "ML" prefixed serial number.

Exc.: $425 **VGood:** $350 **Good:** $295

HIGH STANDARD CITATION (SEVEN NUMBER SERIES)

Same specs as 107 Series except seven-digit serial number appears alone on right side of frame.

Exc.: $500 **VGood:** $425 **Good:** $325

HIGH STANDARD CITATION II (SH SERIES)

Semi-automatic; 22 LR; 10-shot magazine; 5-1/2-inch, 7-1/4-inch slab-sided bull barrel; weighs 45 oz.; adjustable sights; Allen-screw takedown; checkered walnut grips. Replaced Sharpshooter in High Standard line and early models inscribed "Sharpshooter" on frame with "Citation II" inscribed on barrel. Serial numbers prefixed with the letters "SH" Introduced 1982; dropped 1984.

Exc.: $400 **VGood:** $325 **Good:** $240

HIGH STANDARD CITATION II SURVIVAL PACK

Same specs as Citation II except 5-1/2-inch barrel only; electroless nickel finish; padded canvas carry case; extra magazine. Introduced 1982; dropped 1984.

Exc.: $425 **VGood:** $350 **Good:** $295

HIGH STANDARD CUSTOM 10-X

Semi-automatic; 22 LR; 10-shot magazine; 5-1/2-inch bull barrel, some with Victor barrel and vent rib with rear sight on rib; 9-3/4-inch overall length; weighs 44-1/2 oz.; black, ambidextrous, checkered walnut grips; undercut ramp front sight, frame-mounted adjustable rear; custom-made, fitted; fully-adjustable target trigger; stippled front, backstraps; slide lock; marketed with two extra magazines; non-reflective black/gray Parkerizing; stamped with maker's initials on frame under left grip. Approximately 600 produced. Introduced 1981; dropped 1984.

Perf.: $1800 **Exc.:** $1450 **VGood:** $900

HIGH STANDARD CUSTOM 10-X TARGET

Semi-automatic; single action; 22 LR; 10-shot magazine; 5-1/2-inch barrel; 9-1/2-inch overall length; weighs 44 oz.; ambidextrous, checkered black epoxied walnut grips; undercut ramp front sight, fully-adjustable, micrometer-click rear; hand built with select parts; adjustable trigger and sear; push-button takedown; Parkerized finish; stippled front grip and backstrap; barrel weights optional; comes with test target. Made in U.S. by High Standard Mfg. Co., Inc. Reintroduced 1994; still produced.

New: $750 **Perf.:** $650 **Exc.:** $550

High Standard
Dura-Matic (M-101)

High Standard Model A

High Standard Model B

High Standard Field King
(First Model)

High Standard Model G-B

High Standard Model D

High Standard
Model G-E

High Standard Model C

HIGH STANDARD DURA-MATIC

Semi-automatic; 22 LR; 4-1/2-inch, 6-1/2-inch interchangeable barrels; 10-7/8-inch overall length (6-1/2-inch barrel); hammerless; screw take-down; fixed sights; modified magazine with small rectangular recession on top left side to fit clip release; plastic grips; blued finish. Marked "DURA-MATIC" on left side of frame. Introduced 1954; dropped 1970.

Exc.: $295   **VGood:** $225   **Good:** $200

HIGH STANDARD FIELD KING (FIRST MODEL)

Semi-automatic; 22 LR; 10-shot magazine; 4-1/2-inch, 6-3/4-inch medium weight barrels; 11-1/2-inch overall length (6-3/4-inch barrel); hammerless; lever take-down; fixed front, adjustable rear sights. Similar to Supermatic First Model except no notch groove for weight attachment; no raised rib atop barrel. Introduced 1951; dropped 1953.

Exc.: $600   **VGood:** $500   **Good:** $375

HIGH STANDARD FIELD KING (101 SERIES)

Same specs as First Model except push-button takedown; optional slotted stabilizer (6-3/4-inch barrel). Marked "FK-101" on right side of slide. Introduced 1954; dropped 1957.

Exc.: $550   **VGood:** $520   **Good:** $450

HIGH STANDARD FLITE KING (FIRST MODEL)

Semi-automatic; 22 Short; 10-shot magazine; 4-1/2-inch, 6-3/4-inch interchangeable lightweight barrels; hammerless; push-button takedown; aluminum alloy frame and slide; fixed sights; automatic slide lock; blue finish. Marked "LW 100" or "LW 101" on right side of frame. Introduced 1954; dropped 1960.

Two barrels		
Exc.: $525	**VGood:** $450	**Good:** $350
One barrel		
Exc.: $450	**VGood:** $375	**Good:** $300

HIGH STANDARD FLITE KING (102 SERIES)

Same specs as First Model except all-steel construction; weighs 36 oz. (6-3/4-inch barrel); improved push-button takedown; heavier weight tapered barrels. Marked "FLITE KING" in block letters on left side of frame, "Model 102" on right side. Introduced 1958; dropped 1965.

Exc.: $425   **VGood:** $375   **Good:** $325

HIGH STANDARD FLITE KING (103 SERIES)

Same specs as 102 Series Flite King except marked "Model 103" on right side of frame.

Exc.: $400   **VGood:** $350   **Good:** $300

HIGH STANDARD MODEL A

Semi-automatic; 22 LR; 10-shot magazine; 4-1/2-inch, 6-3/4-inch barrel; 11-1/2-inch overall length (6-3/4-inch barrel); hammerless; adjustable target-type sights; new longer grip frame with checkered walnut grips. Model A had both 1B and Type II takedowns. The new grip frame style caught Colt by surprise and prompted Colt to extend grips on the 2nd Model Woodsman. Introduced 1938; dropped 1942. Approximately 7,300 produced.

Exc.: $650   **VGood:** $500   **Good:** $350

HIGH STANDARD MODEL B

Semi-automatic; 22 LR; 10-shot magazine; 4-1/2-inch, 6-3/4-inch barrels; 10-3/4-inch overall length (6-3/4-inch barrel); small frame; fixed sights; blued finish. Early Model B had checkered hard rubber grips. At S/N 31508 on Feb. 18, 1938, a new borderless grip with "HS" monogram in circle at center of grip was introduced. Approximately 65,000 produced. Introduced 1932; dropped 1942.

Exc.: $500   **VGood:** $350   **Good:** $250

HIGH STANDARD MODEL C

Semi-automatic; 22 Short; 10-shot magazine; 4-1/2-inch, 6-3/4-inch barrels; 10-3/4-inch overall length (6-3/4-inch barrel); small frame; hammerless; fixed sights; checkered hard rubber grips; blued finish. Approximately 4700 produced. Introduced 1936; dropped 1942.

Exc.: $800   **VGood:** $500   **Good:** $400

HIGH STANDARD MODEL D

Semi-automatic; 22 LR only; 10-shot magazine; 4-1/2-inch, 6-3/4-inch barrel; 11-1/2-inch overall length (6-3/4-inch barrel); hammerless; adjustable target-type sights; checkered walnut grips; blued finish. The Model D had both 1B and Type II takedowns with 1B type the rarest. Introduced 1938; dropped, 1942. Approximately 2500 produced.

Exc.: $750   **VGood:** $450   **Good:** $300

HIGH STANDARD MODEL E

Semi-automatic; 22 LR; 10-shot; 4-1/2-inch, 6-3/4-inch barrels; 11-1/2-inch overall length (6-3/4-inch barrel); hammerless; adjustable target-type sights; bull barrel and deluxe walnut grips with thumbrest (known as Roper grips); deluxe blued finish. Introduced 1937; dropped 1942. Approximately 2600 produced.

Exc.: $950   **VGood:** $600   **Good:** $450

HIGH STANDARD MODEL G-380

Semi-automatic; 380 ACP; 5-inch barrel; visible hammer; thumb safety; first lever take-down model; fixed sights; checkered plastic grips; blued finish. Introduced 1947; dropped 1950. Approximately 7400 produced.

Exc.: $550   **VGood:** $450   **Good:** $400

HIGH STANDARD MODEL G-B

Semi-automatic; 22 LR; 4-1/2-inch, 6-3/4-inch interchangeable barrels; 10-3/4-inch overall length (6-3/4-inch barrel); hammerless; small frame; fixed sights; brown checkered plastic grip with "HS" medallion; blued finish. Introduced 1949; dropped 1951.

Two barrels		
Exc.: $750	**VGood:** $650	**Good:** $550
One barrel		
Exc.: $550	**VGood:** $475	**Good:** $375

HIGH STANDARD MODEL G-D

Semi-automatic; 22 LR; 10-shot; 4-1/2-inch, 6-3/4-inch interchangeable barrels; 11-1/2-inch overall length (6-3/4-inch barrel); lever take-down; large frame; heavy barrel; adjustable target sights; checkered walnut grips; blued finish. Introduced 1949; dropped 1951. Approximately 3300 produced.

Two barrels		
Exc.: $1050	**VGood:** $800	**Good:** $550

High Standard Model
H-B (First Model)

High Standard Model
H-B (Second Model)

High Standard Olympic
(Second Model)

High Standard
Model G-D

High Standard Model
H-D U.S.A.

High Standard
H-D
U.S.A. Military

High Standard Model H-A

High Standard Olympic
(102-103 Series)

High Standard Olympic
(Third Model)

One barrel
Exc.: $800   **VGood:** $500   **Good:** $350

HIGH STANDARD MODEL G-E

Semi-automatic; 22 LR; 10-shot; 4-1/2-inch, 6-3/4-inch bull barrel; 11-1/2-inch overall length (6-3/4-inch barrel); large frame; lever take-down; adjustable sights; deluxe checkered walnut grips; high polish blued finish. Introduced 1949; dropped 1951. Approximately 3000 produced.

Two barrels
Exc.: $1500   **VGood:** $1100   **Good:** $800

One barrel
Exc.: $1250   **VGood:** $800   **Good:** $500

HIGH STANDARD MODEL H-A

Semi-automatic; 22 LR; 10-shot magazine; 4-1/2-inch, 6-3/4-inch barrels; 11-1/2-inch overall length (6-3/4-inch barrel); visible hammer; no thumb safety; small diameter barrel; checkered walnut grips. Introduced 1940; dropped 1942. Approximately 1042 produced.

Exc.: $900   **VGood:** $500   **Good:** $300

HIGH STANDARD MODEL H-B (FIRST MODEL)

Semi-automatic; 22 LR; 10-shot magazine; 4-1/2-inch, 6-3/4-inch barrels; 10-3/4-inch overall length (6-3/4-inch barrel); fixed sights; checkered hard rubber grips. Same as Model B except visible hammer and no thumb safety. Marked "H-B." Introduced 1940; dropped 1942. Reintroduced 1949; dropped 1950. Approximately 2100 produced.

Exc.: $700   **VGood:** $550   **Good:** $350

HIGH STANDARD MODEL H-B (2ND MODEL)

Same specs as Model H-B (1st Model) except presence of thumb safety. Marked "HB." Approximately 25,000 produced.

Exc.: $550   **VGood:** $450   **Good:** $375

HIGH STANDARD MODEL H-D

Semi-automatic; 22 LR; 10-shot magazine; 4-1/2-inch, 6-3/4-inch barrel; 11-1/2-inch overall length (6-3/4-inch barrel); adjustable target-type sights;

deluxe checkered walnut grips with thumbrest. Same as the Model D except visible hammer and no thumb safety. Introduced 1940; dropped 1942. Approximately 6900 produced.

Exc.: $700   **VGood:** $500   **Good:** $350

HIGH STANDARD MODEL H-D U.S.A.

Semi-automatic; 22 LR; 10-shot magazine; 4-1/2-inch, 6-3/4-inch barrels; adjustable target-type sights; medium weight barrel; thumb safety; black or checkered hard rubber grips; high polish blue (early models), Parkerized finish. U.S. military training pistol. Introduced 1943; dropped 1946. Approximately 44,000 produced.

Exc.: $850   **VGood:** $500   **Good:** $400

HIGH STANDARD H-D U.S.A. MILITARY

Same specs as Model H-D U.S.A. except adjustable sights. Introduced 1946; dropped 1955. Approximately 150,000 produced.

Exc.: $700   **VGood:** $500   **Good:** $350

HIGH STANDARD MODEL H-E

Semi-automatic; 22 LR; 10-shot; 4-1/2-inch, 6-3/4-inch bull barrels; 11-1/2-inch overall length (6-3/4-inch barrel); large frame; adjustable target-type sights. Same specs as the Model E except visible hammer, no thumb safety, high polished blue finish and deluxe walnut grips. Introduced 1941; dropped 1942. Approximately 1006 produced.

Exc.: $1400   **VGood:** $900   **Good:** $600

HIGH STANDARD MODEL S-B

Semi-automatic; 22 shot cartridge; 6-3/4-inch barrel; 10-3/4-inch overall length; smoothbore; checkered rubber grips. Introduced 1939; dropped 1940. Only 12 produced.

Exc.: $2500   **VGood:** $2000   **Good:** $1500

HIGH STANDARD OLYMPIC (FIRST MODEL)

Semi-automatic; 22 Short; 4-1/2-inch, 6-3/4-inch interchangeable bull barrels; hammerless; first use of light alloy slide; adjustable rear sight; deluxe

checkered walnut grips with thumbrest; lever takedown; special banana-shaped magazine. Also known as Model G-O. Introduced 1950; dropped 1951. Approximately 1200 produced.

Two barrels
Exc.: $1000   **VGood:** $1150   **Good:** $800

One barrel
Exc.: $900   **VGood:** $800   **Good:** $600

HIGH STANDARD OLYMPIC (SECOND MODEL)

Same specs as First Model except medium barrel; interchangeable 2 oz. and 3 oz. weights attached by dovetail on bottom of barrel plus filler strip for dovetail when weights not in use; standard magazine with filler in front to fit 22 Short cartridges. Introduced 1951; dropped 1953.

Two barrels
Exc.: $1300   **VGood:** $1100   **Good:** $850

One barrel
Exc.: $1000   **VGood:** $800   **Good:** $650

HIGH STANDARD OLYMPIC (THIRD MODEL)

Same specs as First Model except push button takedown; optional slotted stabilizer for 6-3/4-inch barrel. Marked "0-101-inch on right side of slide. Introduced 1954; dropped 1958.

Exc.: $800   **VGood:** $600   **Good:** $500

HIGH STANDARD OLYMPIC (102 SERIES)

Same specs as First Model except 6-3/4-inch, 8-inch, 10-inch barrel; same as Citation 102 except 22 Short with alloy slide; adjustable and removable barrel weights; removable stabilizer; aluminum slide. Marked "Model 102" on right side of slide. Introduced 1958; dropped 1965.

Exc.: $900   **VGood:** $700   **Good:** $600

HIGH STANDARD OLYMPIC (103 SERIES)

Same specs as 102 Series Olympic except plastic grips standard, walnut optional. Introduced 1963; dropped 1965.

Exc.: $900   **VGood:** $700   **Good:** $600

High Standard Olympic
ISU (104 Series)

High Standard Olympic
ISU Standard

High Standard Olympic
(104 Series)

High Standard
Sharpshooter

High Standard Plinker

HIGH STANDARD OLYMPIC (104 SERIES)

Same specs as 102/103 Series Olympic except new Allen screw backlash adjustor in trigger which carried over to all future models. Introduced 1964; dropped 1972.

Exc.: $900   **VGood:** $750   **Good:** $550

HIGH STANDARD OLYMPIC (106 SERIES MILITARY)

Same specs as the 104 Series except 5-1/2-inch bull barrel, 6-3/4-inch space gun barrel; new frame with military Colt 1911-style grips; fitted magazine extension foot; new magazine release. Introduced 1965; dropped 1966.

Exc.: $950   **VGood:** $800   **Good:** $550

HIGH STANDARD OLYMPIC ISU (102 SERIES)

Semi-automatic; 22 Short; 10-shot magazine; ported 6-3/4-inch barrel; 11-1/2-inch overall length; larger push-button takedown; alloy slide; new rear target sight; high polished finish. Marked "Model 102" on right side of slide. Unlike Olympic 102 Series, the ISU has integral stabilizer and comes standard with checkered walnut grips. Introduced 1957; dropped 1960.

Exc.: $1000   **VGood:** $800   **Good:** $650

HIGH STANDARD OLYMPIC ISU (103 SERIES)

Same specs as ISU Model 102 except 5-1/2-inch, 6-3/4-inch bull barrel. Introduced 1960; dropped 1963.

Exc.: $1000   **VGood:** $800   **Good:** $650

HIGH STANDARD OLYMPIC ISU (104 SERIES)

Same specs as ISU Model 102 except bull barrel with removable stabilizer (5-1/2-inch barrel); integral stabilizer (6-3/4-inch barrel); barrel weights and new Allen screw backlash adjuster in trigger. Introduced 1964; dropped 1964.

Exc.: $950   **VGood:** $800   **Good:** $650

HIGH STANDARD OLYMPIC ISU (106 SERIES MILITARY)

Same specs as the 102 Series except military Colt 1911-style grips; integral barrel stabilizer. Introduced

1965; dropped 1967.

Exc.: $1050   **VGood:** $850   **Good:** $700

HIGH STANDARD OLYMPIC ISU MILITARY

Same specs as the Olympic ISU Standard model except 5-1/2-inch bull barrel with removable stabilizer; high strength aluminum slide; carbon steel frame; adjustable trigger and sear; overall blue finish. From High Standard Mfg. Co., Inc. Reintroduced 1994; still produced.

Perf.: $500   **Exc.:** $400   **VGood:** $300

HIGH STANDARD OLYMPIC ISU STANDARD

Semi-automatic; 22 Short; 5-shot magazine; 6-3/4-inch tapered barrel with intergral stabilizer; 10 3/4-inch overall length; weighs 45 oz.; push-button takedown; undercut ramp front sight, micro-click adjustable rear; checkered walnut grips; adjustable trigger and sear; stippled front grip and backstrap; comes with weights and brackets. Reintroduced 1994; still in production.

Perf.: $550   **Exc.:** $450   **VGood:** $375

HIGH STANDARD PLINKER

Semi-automatic; 22 LR; 10-shot magazine; interchangeable 4-1/2-inch, 6-3/4-inch barrels; 9-inch overall length (4-1/2-inch barrel); hammerless; same gun as Duramatic; grooved trigger; checkered plastic target grips; fixed square-notch rear sight, ramp front; blued finish. Introduced 1962; dropped 1973.

Exc.: $300   **VGood:** $250   **Good:** $200

HIGH STANDARD SHARPSHOOTER

Semi-automatic; 22 LR; 9-shot magazine; 5-1/2-inch bull barrel; 10-1/4-inch overall length; weighs 42 oz.; push-button take-down; hammerless; scored trigger; adjustable square-notch rear, ramp front sight; slidelock; checkered laminated plastic grips with medallion or walnut with medallion; blued finish. Marked "The Sharpshooter" in block letters on barrel flat. Introduced 1972; dropped 1982.

Exc.: $550   **VGood:** $450   **Good:** $300

HIGH STANDARD SPORT KING (FIRST MODEL)

Semi-automatic; 22 LR; 10-shot magazine; 4-1/2-inch, 6-3/4-inch lightweight interchangeable barrels;

11-1/2-inch overall length (6-3/4-inch barrel); lever takedown; fixed sights; optional adjustable sight; checkered thumbrest plastic grips; blue finish. Introduced 1950; dropped 1953.

Two barrels		
Exc.: $600	**VGood:** $500	**Good:** $400
One barrel		
Exc.: $400	**VGood:** $300	**Good:** $250

HIGH STANDARD SPORT KING (101 SERIES)

Same specs as First Model except push-button takedown; all-steel frame and slide. Marked "SK-100" or "SK-101" on right side of slide. Introduced 1954; dropped 1984.

Two barrels		
Exc.: $600	**VGood:** $500	**Good:** $400
One barrel		
Exc.: $400	**VGood:** $300	**Good:** $250

HIGH STANDARD SPORT KING LIGHTWEIGHT (101 SERIES)

Same specs as 101 Series Sport King except forged aluminum alloy frame; weighs 30 oz. (6-3/4-inch barrel). Marked "Lightweight" on left side of frame. Introduced 1954; dropped 1964.

Two barrels		
Exc.: $675	**VGood:** $575	**Good:** $525
One barrel		
Exc.: $500	**VGood:** $425	**Good:** $375

HIGH STANDARD SPORT KING (102 SERIES)

Same specs as 101 Series Sport King except brown plastic grips (black plastic grips on nickel-plated guns); new optional nickel-plated finish. Late Sport King 102s had "G" in front of serial number. Introduced 1958; dropped 1963.

Exc.: $350   **VGood:** $300   **Good:** $250

HIGH STANDARD SPORT KING (103 SERIES)

Same specs as 102 Series Sport King except marked "Model 103" on right side of slide.

Exc.: $350   **VGood:** $300   **Good:** $250

High Standard Supermatic Tournament
(102 Series)

High Standard Supermatic Trophy
(102 Series)

High Standard Sport
King (101 Series)

High Standard Supermatic Trophy
(107 Series)

High Standard Supermatic Trophy
(SH Series)

HIGH STANDARD SPORT KING
(106 SERIES MILITARY MODEL)
Same specs as 102 Series Sport King except military-style grips. Introduced 1977; dropped 1983.

Exc.: $300   VGood: $250   Good: $200

HIGH STANDARD SUPERMATIC
(FIRST MODEL)
Semi-automatic; 22 LR; 10-shot magazine; 4-1/2-inch, 6-3/4-inch interchangeable barrels; 11-1/2-inch overall length (6-3/4-inch barrel); hammerless; lever takedown; adjustable ramp front, click-adjustable rear target sights; automatic slidelock; 2-, 3-oz. adjustable barrel weights; adjustable ramp front; click-adjustable rear; automatic slidelock; checkered plastic thumbrest grips; blue-black finish with Parkerized slide top and barrel chamber. Introduced 1951; dropped 1958.

Two barrels		
Exc.: $750	**VGood: $550**	**Good: $375**
One barrel		
Exc.: $550	**VGood: $450**	**Good: $250**

HIGH STANDARD SUPERMATIC
(101 SERIES 2ND MODEL)
Same specs as First Model except push-button takedown; fixed front sight; integral stabilizer (6-3/4-inch barrel). Marked "S100" or "S101" on right side of slide. Introduced, 1954; dropped, 1958.

Exc.: $350   VGood: $275   Good: $225

HIGH STANDARD
SUPERMATIC CITATION
Semi-automatic; 22 LR; 10-shot magazine; 5-1/2-inch, 7-1/4-inch barrel; 9-1/2-inch overall length; weighs 44 oz.; under-cut ramp front, micro-click adjustable rear sight; checkered walnut grip with thumbrest; nickel-plated trigger, slidelock, safety lever, magazine release; blue finish. Reintroduced 1994; still in production.

New: $375   Perf.: $325   Exc.: $275

HIGH STANDARD
SUPERMATIC TROPHY
Semi-automatic; single action; 22 LR; 10-shot magazine; 5-1/2-inch, 7-1/4-inch barrel; 9-1/2-inch overall length; weighs 44 oz.; checkered walnut thumbrest grips; undercut ramp front sight, fully-adjustable, micrometer-click rear; push-button takedown; removable muzzle stabilizer; gold-plated trigger, slidelock, safety-lever and magazine release; stippled front grip and backstrap; adjustable trigger and sear; drilled and tapped for scope mount; barrel weights optional. Reintroduced 1994; still produced.

New: $400   Perf.: $350   Exc.: $275

HIGH STANDARD
SUPERMATIC TOURNAMENT
Semi-automatic; 22 LR; 10-shot magazine; 4-1/2-inch, 5-1/2-inch barrel; 8-1/2-inch overall length; weighs 43 oz.; push-button takedown; undercut ramp front, micro-click adjustable rear sight; black rubber ambidextrous grips; drilled and tapped for scope mount; blue finish. Reintroduced 1994.

New: $375   Perf.: $350   Exc.: $325

HIGH STANDARD
TOURNAMENT (102 SERIES)
Semi-automatic; 22 LR; 10-shot magazine; 6-3/4-inch medium weight, 4-1/2-inch bull barrel; 1/4-inch high base front sight, click-adjustable rear on slide; push-button takedown; backlash adjustable screw; plastic grips; no grooving atop slide; dull black finish. Marked "SUPERMATIC" top line; "Tournament" in smaller letters underneath on left side of frame. Introduced 1958; dropped 1963.

Exc.: $600   VGood: $500   Good: $375

HIGH STANDARD TOURNAMENT
(103 SERIES)
Same specs as 102 Series Tournament except 5-1/2-inch bull barrel offering. Introduced 1958; dropped 1963.

Exc.: $550   VGood: $450   Good: $350

HIGH STANDARD TOURNAMENT
(106 SERIES MILITARY)
Same specs as 103 Series Tournament except military-style grips. Introduced 1965; dropped 1966.

Exc.: $550   VGood: $450   Good: $375

HIGH STANDARD TROPHY
(102 SERIES)
Semi-automatic; 22 LR; 10-shot; 6-3/4-inch, 8-inch, 10-inch tapered "space gun" barrels; push-button takedown; 2-, 3-oz. adjustable barrel weights; detachable stabilizer; trigger pull adjustment screw at rear of frame; overtravel adjustment screw on right side of frame; adjustable sights (barrel mounted on 8-inch, 10-inch); gold trigger safety; checkered walnut thumbrest grips; blue/black finish. Marked "Model 102" on right side of frame; "Supermatic Trophy" on left side. Introduced 1961; dropped 1966.

Exc.: $950   VGood: $750   Good: $625

HIGH STANDARD TROPHY
(103/104 SERIES)
Same specs as the 102 Series except 5-1/2-inch, 7-1/4-inch bull barrels; recessed bore at muzzle. Marked "Supermatic Trophy" on left side of frame; "Model 103" or "Model 104" on right side of frame. Introduced 1960; dropped 1965.

Exc.: $900   VGood: $700   Good: $50

HIGH STANDARD TROPHY
(106/107 SERIES)
Same specs as the 102 Series except military-style grips; saddle-type rear sight; new slide with angled gripping ribs. Marked "Supermatic Trophy" and "HIGH STANDARD" on left side of slide; "Model 106" or "Model 107" above triggerguard on right side. Introduced 1965; dropped 1967.

Exc.: $950   VGood: $800   Good: $650

HIGH STANDARD TROPHY
(ML SERIES)
Same specs as 106/107 Series except "ML" prefixed serial number.

Exc.: $675   VGood: $525   Good: $425

HIGH STANDARD TROPHY
(SEVEN NUMBER SERIES)
Same specs as 106/107 Series except seven-digit serial number appears alone on right side of frame.

Exc.: $800   VGood: $625   Good: $400

HIGH STANDARD TROPHY
(SH SERIES)
Same specs as 106/107 Series except "SH" prefixed serial number.

Exc.: $550   VGood: $450   Good: $325

High Standard Victor
Target Pistol

High Standard Victor
First Model 107 Series

High Standard Camp Model

High Standard
Derringer

High Standard Crusader

High Standard Double-
Nine Convertible

HIGH STANDARD VICTOR (FIRST MODEL 107 SERIES)

Semi-automatic; 22 LR only; 10-shot magazine; 4-1/2-inch, 5-1/2-inch barrels; 8-3/4-inch overall length (4-1/2-inch barrel); 48 oz. (4-1/2-inch barrel), 52 oz. (5-1/2-inch barrel); hammerless; solid steel rib, later guns with aluminum vented rib; interchangeable barrel feature; rib-mounted click-adjustable rear sight, undercut ramp front; checkered walnut grips with thumbrest; blued finish. Marked "The Victor" on left side of barrel. Introduced 1963; dropped 1984.

Solid rib		
Exc.: $750	**VGood:** $650	**Good:** $450
Vent rib		
Exc.: $800	**VGood:** $700	**Good:** $475

HIGH STANDARD VICTOR (ML SERIES)

Same specs as standard Victor except marked "Victor" above triggerguard. Serial number prefixed with letters "ML."

Exc.: $550	**VGood:** $450	**Good:** $350

HIGH STANDARD VICTOR (SEVEN NUMBER SERIES)

Same specs as Model 107 except seven-digit serial number appears alone on right side of frame.

Exc.: $525	**VGood:** $325	**Good:** $300

HIGH STANDARD VICTOR (SH SERIES)

Same specs as standard Victor except Allen-screw takedown; small grip thumbrest; rib cut-out for shell ejection. Serial number prefixed with letters "SH."

Exc.: $500	**VGood:** $450	**Good:** $350

HIGH STANDARD VICTOR TARGET PISTOL

Semi-automatic; single action; 22 LR; 10-shot magazine; 4-1/2-inch, 5-1/2-inch barrel; 9-1/2-inch overall length; weighs 46 oz.; checkered walnut thumbrest grips; undercut ramp front sight, fully-adjustable, micrometer-click rear; push-button takedown; full-length aluminum vent rib (steel optional); gold-plated trigger, slidelock, safety-lever and magazine release; stippled front grip and backstrap; adjustable trigger and sear; comes with barrel weight; blue or Parkerized finish. Reintroduced 1994; still produced. Add 200% for Hamden-marked 4-1/2-inch barrel model with solid steel rib.

New: $500	**Perf.:** $450	**Exc.:** $400

HIGH STANDARD CAMP GUN

Revolver; double action; 22 LR, 22 WMR; 9-shot cylinder; 6-inch barrel; 11-1/8-inch overall length; weighs 28 oz.; steel frame; adjustable rear sight; target-type checkered walnut grips; blued finish. Introduced 1976; dropped 1979.

Exc.: $200	**VGood:** $160	**Good:** $120

HIGH STANDARD CRUSADER

Revolver; double action; 357 Mag., 44 Mag., 45 Colt; 6-shot swing-out cylinder; 4-inch, 6-inch, 8-inch barrel (medium frame), 4-inch, 6-inch, 8-inch (large frame); weighs 38 oz. (med. frame), 48 oz. (large frame); unique internal gear mechanism which allows hammer to rest on frame when trigger is disengaged and brings hammer in direct line with firing pin when trigger is engaged; lack of transfer bar safety and trigger spring account for light weight; ramp front sight, adjustable rear; solid ribbed barrel; shrouded ejector rod; one-piece grip; blued finish. Introduced 1976; discontinued 1979. Limited production; slight premium for anniversary edition..

Exc.: $1100	**VGood:** $900	**Good:** $600

HIGH STANDARD DERRINGER

Derringer; double action; 22 LR, 22 Short, 22 WMR; 2-shot; hammerless; over/under 3-1/2-inch barrels; 5-1/8-inch overall length; weighs 11 oz.; plastic grips; fixed sights; standard model has blue, nickel finish. Early derringers marked "Hamden Conn." on barrel; later models marked "E. Hartford" on barrel. Presentation model gold-plated, introduced in 1965; dropped 1966. Presentation model has some collector value. Standard model introduced in 1963; dropped 1984.

Early model, blue finish		
Exc.: $250	**VGood:** $185	**Good:** $140
Early model, nickel finish		
Exc.: $275	**VGood:** $225	**Good:** $150
Late model, blue finish		
Exc.: $250	**VGood:** $185	**Good:** $140
Late model, nickel finish		
Exc.: $275	**VGood:** $225	**Good:** $150
Presentation model		
Exc.: $400	**VGood:** $350	**Good:** $300

HIGH STANDARD DOUBLE-NINE

Revolver; double action; 22 Short, 22 LR; 9-shot swing-out cylinder; 5-1/2-inch barrel; 11-inch overall length; dummy ejection rod housing; spring-loaded ejection; rebounding hammer; movable notch rear sight, blade front; plastic simulated stag, ebony or ivory grips; blued or nickel finish. Introduced 1959; dropped 1971.

Exc.: $175	**VGood:** $150	**Good:** $125
Nickel finish		
Exc.: $185	**VGood:** $160	**Good:** $135

HIGH STANDARD DOUBLE-NINE CONVERTIBLE

Same specs as Double-Nine except two cylinders, one for 22 LR, 22 Long, 22 Short; other for 22 WMR; smooth frontier-type walnut grips; movable notched rear sight, blade front; blued, nickel finish. Introduced 1972; dropped 1984.

Exc.: $200	**VGood:** $175	**Good:** $150
Nickel finish		
Exc.: $225	**VGood:** $220	**Good:** $175

HIGH STANDARD DURANGO

Revolver; double action; 22 LR, 22 Long, 22 Short; 4-1/2-inch, 5-1/2-inch barrels; 10-inch overall length (4-1/2-inch barrel); brass-finished triggerguard, backstrap; uncheckered walnut grips; blued only in shorter barrel length; blued, nickel (5-1/2-inch barrel). Introduced 1972; dropped 1975.

Exc.: $300	**VGood:** $225	**Good:** $175
Nickel finish		
Exc.: $375	**VGood:** $295	**Good:** $200

High Standard Durango

High Standard High Sierra

High Standard Kit Gun

High Standard Longhorn

High Standard Natchez

High Standard Sentinel Mark IV

HJS Frontier Four Derringer

HIGH STANDARD HIGH SIERRA

Revolver; double action; 22 LR, 22 WMR; 9-shot; 7-inch octagonal barrel; 12-1/2-inch overall length; blade front, adjustable rear sight; smooth walnut grips; swing-out cylinder; gold-plated backstrap, triggerguard. Introduced 1978; dropped 1984. Add 50% premium for convertible model with both cylinder assemblies.

    Exc.: $400   **VGood:** $300   **Good:** $195

HIGH STANDARD KIT GUN

Revolver; double action; 22 LR, 22 Long, 22 Short; 9-shot swing-out cylinder; 4-inch barrel; 9-inch overall length; micro-adjustable rear, target ramp front sight; checkered walnut grips; blued finish.

    Exc.: $175   **VGood:** $125   **Good:** $100

HIGH STANDARD LONGHORN

Revolver; double action; 22 LR; 4-1/2-inch, 5-1/2-inch barrels; pearl-like plastic grips; 5-1/2-inch barrel model with plastic staghorn grips; later model with walnut grips. Introduced 1961; dropped 1966.

    Exc.: $300   **VGood:** $225   **Good:** $175

HIGH STANDARD LONGHORN CONVERTIBLE

Same specs as standard Longhorn but with 9-1/2-inch barrel only; aluminum alloy frame; smooth walnut grips; dual cylinder to fire 22 WMR cartridge. Introduced 1971; dropped 1984.

    Exc.: $400   **VGood:** $300   **Good:** $195

HIGH STANDARD MARSHALL

Revolver; 22 LR; 9-shot swing-out cylinder; 5-1/2-inch barrel; fixed sights; Staglite western-style grips with gold medallion inset; blued finish; comes complete with leather holster. Introduced 1973; discontinued 1974. Limited production precludes pricing.

HIGH STANDARD NATCHEZ

Revolver; double action; 22 LR, 22 Short; 4-1/2-inch barrel; 10-inch overall length; fluted cylinder; ivory-like plastic bird's-head grips; blued. Introduced 1961; dropped 1966.

    Exc.: $500   **VGood:** $400   **Good:** $300

HIGH STANDARD POSSE

Revolver; double action; 22 LR; 3-1/2-inch barrel; 9-inch overall length; no ejector rod housing; uncheckered walnut grips; brass grip frame, triggerguard; blued. Introduced 1961; dropped 1966.

    Exc.: $500   **VGood:** $400   **Good:** $300

HIGH STANDARD SENTINEL

Revolver; double action; 22 Short, 22 LR; 9-shot swing-out cylinder; 3-inch, 4-inch, 6-inch barrels; 9-inch overall length (4-inch barrel); weighs 23 oz.; solid aluminum alloy frame; fixed sights; checkered plastic grips; blued or nickel finish. Introduced 1955; dropped 1974.

    Exc.: $235   **VGood:** $200   **Good:** $165

Nickel finish		
Exc.: $250	**VGood:** $215	**Good:** $175

HIGH STANDARD SENTINEL DELUXE

Same specs as the standard Sentinel except for movable rear sight; two-piece square-butt checkered walnut grips; wide triggers; 4-inch, 6-inch barrels only. Introduced 1957; dropped 1974.

Blue finish		
Exc.: $250	**VGood:** $215	**Good:** $180
Nickel finish		
Exc.: $265	**VGood:** $230	**Good:** $185

HIGH STANDARD SENTINEL IMPERIAL

Same specs as standard Sentinel model except blade ramp front sight; two-piece checkered walnut grips; onyx-black or nickel finish. Introduced 1962; dropped 1965.

Blue finish		
Exc.: $250	**VGood:** $215	**Good:** $180
Nickel finish		
Exc.: $265	**VGood:** $230	**Good:** $185

HIGH STANDARD SENTINEL MARK I

Revolver; double action; 22 LR; 9-shot cylinder; 2-inch, 3-inch, 4-inch barrel; ramp front, fixed or adjustable rear sight; uncheckered walnut stocks; blued or nickel finish. Introduced 1974; dropped 1984.

Blue finish		
Exc.: $180	**VGood:** $165	**Good:** $150
Nickel finish		
Exc.: $205	**VGood:** $190	**Good:** $170

HIGH STANDARD SENTINEL MARK II

Same specs as Sentinel Mark I except 357 Mag.; 6-shot cylinder; 2-1/2-inch, 4-inch, 6-inch barrel lengths; walnut combat grips; fixed sights; blued finish. Manufactured 1973 to 1975.

    Exc.: $200   **VGood:** $160   **Good:** $120

HIGH STANDARD SENTINEL MARK III

Same specs as Sentinel Mark II except ramp front sight, adjustable rear. Manufactured 1973 to 1975.

    Exc.: $275   **VGood:** $235   **Good:** $200

HIGH STANDARD SENTINEL MARK IV

Same specs as Sentinel Mark I except 22 WMR. Introduced 1974; dropped 1979.

Blue finish		
Exc.: $210	**VGood:** $190	**Good:** $170
Nickel finish		
Exc.: $235	**VGood:** $210	**Good:** $190

HIGH STANDARD SENTINEL SNUB

Revolver; double action; 22 LR; 9-shot swing-out cylinder; 2-3/8-inch barrel; solid aluminum alloy frame; quick draw sights and hammer; checkered bird's-head-type grips; blued or nickel finish. Introduced 1957; dropped 1974.

Blue finish		
Exc.: $235	**VGood:** $210	**Good:** $180
Nickel finish		
Exc.: $245	**VGood:** $220	**Good:** $190

IAR Model 1872
Derringer

IAI Automag III

Interarms Virginian
Dragoon

IAR Model 1873

Indian Arms
Stainless

HJS ANTIGUA DERRINGER

Derringer; four-shot; 22 LR; 2-inch barrels; 3-15/16-inch overall length; weighs 5-1/2 oz.; brown plastic grips; no sights; four barrel fire with rotating firing pin; blued barrels; brass frame; brass pivot pins. Made in U.S. by HJS Arms, Inc. Introduced 1994.

New: $160 **Perf.:** $135 **Exc.:** $125

HJS FRONTIER FOUR DERRINGER

Derringer; four-shot; 22 LR; 2-inch barrel; 3-15/16-inch overall length; weighs 5-1/2 oz.; brown plastic grips; no sights; four barrels fire with rotating firing pin; stainless steel construction. Made in U.S. by HJS Arms, Inc. Introduced 1993.

New: $135 **Perf.:** $115 **Exc.:** $100

HJS LONE STAR DERRINGER

Derringer; single shot; 32 S&W, 380 ACP; 2-inch barrel; 3-15/16-inch overall length; weighs 6 oz.; brown plastic grips; groove sight; stainless steel construction; beryllium copper firing pin; button-rifled barrel. Made in U.S. by HJS Arms, Inc. Introduced 1993.

New: $165 **Perf.:** $135 **Exc.:** $120

HUNGARIAN T-58

Semi-automatic; single action; 7.62mm, 9mm Para.; 8-shot magazine; 4-1/2-inch barrel; 7-11/16-inch overall length; weighs 31 oz.; grooved composition grips; blade front sight, windage-adjustable rear; comes with both barrels and magazines; blue finish. Imported by Century International Arms.

Perf.: $160 **Exc.:** $145 **VGood:** $125

IAI AUTOMAG III

Semi-automatic; single action; 30 Carbine, 9mm Win. Mag.; 8-shot magazine; 6-3/8-inch barrel; 10-1/2-inch overall length; weighs 43 oz.; blade front sight, Millett adjustable rear; wrap-around rubber grips; hammer-drop safety; sandblasted finish; stainless steel construction. Introduced 1989; discontinued 1992.

Perf.: $550 **Exc.:** $475 **VGood:** $400

IAI AUTOMAG IV

Semi-automatic; single-action; 45 Mag., 10mm Auto.; 7-shot magazine; 6-1/2-inch, 8-5/8-inch barrel; 10-1/2-inch overall length; weighs 46 oz; blade front sight, Millett adjustable rear; black carbon fiber grips; stainless steel construction; brushed finish. Introduced 1990; discontinued 1991.

Perf.: $775 **Exc.:** $625 **VGood:** $500

IAI BACKUP

Semi-automatic; 380 ACP; 5-shot magazine; 2-1/2-inch barrel; 4-1/2-inch overall length; weighs 18 oz.; fixed sights; wrap-around rubber or walnut grips; stainless steel construction. Introduced 1988; discontinued 1989.

Perf.: $295 **Exc.:** $195 **VGood:** $135

IAI JAVELINA

Semi-automatic; 10mm Auto; 8-shot magazine; 5-inch, 7-inch barrel; 10-1/2-inch overall length; weighs 40 oz.; blade front sight, Millett adjustable rear; wrap-around rubber stocks; brushed finish; stainless steel construction. Introduced 1990; discontinued 1991.

Exc.: $700 **VGood:** $595 **Good:** $375

IAR MODEL 1873

Revolver; single action; 22 LR, 22 LR/22 WMR; 4-3/4-inch barrel; 45 oz. 10-1/2-inch overall; one-piece walnut stocks with inspector's cartouche; blade front, notch rear sights; color case-hardened frame; blued barrel; black nickel-plated brass trigger guard and backstrap; bright nickel and engraved versions available. Introduced 1997. Imported from Italy by IAR, Inc.

Perf.: $300 **Exc.:** $250 **VGood:** $200

Nickel-plated

Perf.: $350 **Exc.:** $300 **VGood:** $250

22 LR/22WMR combo

Perf.: $350 **Exc.:** $300 **VGood:** $250

IAR MODEL 1872 DERRINGER

Single shot; 22 Short; 2-3/8-inch barrel; 7 oz.; 5-1/8-inch overall; smooth walnut grips; blade front, notch rear sights; gold or nickel frame with blue barrel. Reintroduced 1996 using original Colt designs and tooling for the Colt Model 4 Derringer. Made in U.S. by IAR, Inc.

Perf.: $95 **Exc.:** $75 **VGood:** $60

Single cased gun

Perf.: $110 **Exc.:** $85 **VGood:** $75

Double cased set

Perf.: $195 **Exc.:** $165 **VGood:** $135

IAR MODEL 1888 DOUBLE DERRINGER

Over under; 38 Special; 2-3/4-inch barrel; 16 oz.; smooth walnut grips; blade front, notch rear sights; all steel construction; blue barrel; color case-hardened frame. Uses original designs and tooling for the Uberti New Maverick Derringer. Introduced 1997. Made in U.S. by IAR, Inc.

Perf.: $175 **Exc.:** $150 **VGood:** $125

IBERIA FIREARMS JS-40 S&W

Semi-automatic; single action; 40 S&W; 8-shot magazine; 4-1/2-inch barrel; 8-inch overall length; weighs 44 oz.; checkered acetal resin grips; fixed low profile sights; internal drop-safe mechanism; all aluminum frame; matte black finish. Marketed by MKS Supply, Inc. Introduced 1991; now marketed as Hi-Point JS-40 S&W.

Perf.: $115 **Exc.:** $100 **VGood:** $85

Brushed nickel finish

Perf.: $125 **Exc.:** $110 **VGood:** $100

INDIAN ARMS STAINLESS

Semi-automatic; double action; 380 ACP; 6-shot magazine; 3-1/2-inch barrel; 6-1/16-inch overall length; checkered walnut stocks; adjustable rear sight, blade front; made of stainless steel, with natural or blued finish; optional safety lock. Introduced 1977; dropped 1978.

Exc.: $395 **VGood:** $300 **Good:** $250

INTERARMS VIRGINIAN DRAGOON

Revolver; single action; 357 Mag., 44 Mag., 45 Colt; 6-shot; 6-inch, 7-1/2-inch, 8-3/8-inch barrel; 12-inch buntline on special order; ramp-type Partridge front sight; micro-adjustable target rear; smooth walnut grips; spring-loaded firing pin; color case-hardened frame; blued finish. Introduced 1977; dropped 1986.

Exc.: $375 **VGood:** $325 **Good:** $250

Buntline barrel

Exc.: $400 **VGood:** $350 **Good:** $275

Interarms Virginian 22 Convertible

Intratec TEC-9C

Intratec Category 9

Intratec TEC-DC9

Intratec TEC-DC9M

INTERARMS VIRGINIAN DRAGOON DEPUTY MODEL

Same specs as standard model except fixed sights; 5-inch barrel (357), 6-inch (44 Mag.). Introduced 1983; dropped 1986.

Exc.: $325   **VGood:** $295   **Good:** $275

INTERARMS VIRGINIAN DRAGOON ENGRAVED

Same specs as standard Dragoon except 44 Mag.; 6-inch, 7-inch barrel; fluted or unfluted cylinders; stainless or blued; hand-engraved frame, cylinder, barrel; marketed in felt-lined walnut case. Introduced 1983; dropped 1986.

Exc.: $545   **VGood:** $470   **Good:** $430

INTERARMS VIRGINIAN DRAGOON SILHOUETTE

Same specs as standard model except stainless steel; 357 Mag., 41 Mag., 44 Mag.; 7-1/2-inch, 8-3/8-inch, 10-1/2-inch barrels; smooth walnut and Pachmayr rubber grips; undercut blade front sight, adjustable square notch rear; meets IHMSA standards. Made by Interarms. Introduced 1982; dropped 1986.

Exc.: $365   **VGood:** $320   **Good:** $275

INTERARMS VIRGINIAN 22 CONVERTIBLE

Revolver; 22 LR, 22 WMR; 5-1/2-inch barrel; 10-3/4-inch overall length; weighs 38 oz.; smaller version of standard Dragoon; comes with both cylinders; case-hardened frame, rest blued or stainless steel. Made in Italy. Introduced 1983; dropped 1987; was imported by Interarms.

Exc.: $185   **VGood:** $155   **Good:** $145

Stainless finish		
Exc.: $200	**VGood:** $170	**Good:** $155

INTRATEC CATEGORY 9

Semi-automatic; double action; 380 ACP, 9mm Para.; 7-shot magazine; 3-inch barrel; 5-1/2-inch overall length; weighs 21 oz.; textured black polymer grips; fixed channel sights; black polymer frame. Made in U.S. by Intratec. Introduced 1993; dropped 2000.

New: $215   **Perf.:** $180   **Exc.:** $155

INTRATEC CAT 45

Semi-automatic; double action; 40 S&W, 45 ACP; 6-shot magazine. Barrel: 3.25-inch. Weight: 19 oz. Length: 6.35-inch overall. Stocks: Molded composition. Sights: Fixed, channel. Features: Black polymer frame. Introduced 1996; dropped 2000.

New: $225   **Perf.:** $200   **Exc.:** $150

INTRATEC PROTEC-22

Semi-automatic; double-action-only; 22 LR; 10-shot magazine; 2-1/2-inch barrel; 5-inch overall length; weighs 14 oz.; wrap-around composition grips in gray, black or driftwood color; fixed sights; choice of black, satin or Tec-Kote finishes. Introduced 1991; dropped 1993.

Black finish		
Perf.: $85	**Exc.:** $75	**VGood:** $65
Satin or Tec-Kote finish		
Perf.: $90	**Exc.:** $80	**VGood:** $70

INTRATEC PROTEC-25

Semi-automatic; double-action-only; 25 ACP; 8-shot magazine; 2-1/2-inch barrel; 5-inch overall length; weighs 14 oz.; wrap-around composition grips in gray, black or driftwood color; fixed sights; choice of black, satin or Tec-Kote finishes. Introduced 1991; dropped 2000.

Black finish		
Perf.: $110	**Exc.:** $80	**VGood:** $65
Satin or Tec-Kote finish		
Perf.: $120	**Exc.:** $95	**VGood:** $85

INTRATEC TEC-9C

Semi-automatic; 9mm Para.; 36-shot magazine; 5-inch barrel; weighs 50 oz.; fixed sights; molded composition stocks; matte blue finish. Introduced 1987; no longer in production.

Perf.: $700   **Exc.:** $545   **VGood:** $325

INTRATEC TEC-22T

Semi-automatic; single action; 22 LR; 10-shot magazine; 4-inch barrel; 11-3/16-inch overall length; weighs 30 oz.; molded composition grip; protected post front, fully-adjustable front and rear sights; ambidextrous cocking knobs and safety; matte black finish; accepts any 10/22-type magazine.

Made in U.S. by Intratec. Introduced 1988; no longer produced.

Perf.: $300   **Exc.:** $255   **VGood:** $215

INTRATEC TEC-22TK

Same specs as the TEC-22T except Tec-Kote finish. Made in U.S. by Intratec. Introduced 1988; no longer produced.

Perf.: $300   **Exc.:** $255   **VGood:** $215

INTRATEC TEC-DC9

Semi-automatic; single action; 9mm Para.; 10-shot magazine; 5-inch barrel; 12-1/2-inch overall length; weighs 50 oz.; molded composition grip; fixed sights; fires from closed bolt; firing pin block safety; matte blue finish. Made in U.S. by Intratec. Introduced 1985; dropped 1994.

Perf.: $310   **Exc.:** $265   **VGood:** $250

INTRATEC TEC-DC9S

Same specs as TEC-DC9 except stainless steel construction. Made in U.S. by Intratec. Introduced 1985; dropped 1994.

Perf.: $350   **Exc.:** $275   **VGood:** $200

INTRATEC TEC-DC9K

Same specs as TEC-DC9 except Tec-Kote finish. Made in U.S. by Intratec. Introduced 1985; dropped 1994.

Perf.: $295   **Exc.:** $250   **VGood:** $185

INTRATEC TEC-DC9M

Same specs as TEC-DC9 except 3-inch barrel; weighs 44 oz.; 20-shot magazine. Made in U.S. by Intratec. Introduced 1985; dropped 1994.

Perf.: $325   **Exc.:** $245   **VGood:** $185

INTRATEC TEC-DC9MK

Same specs as the TEC-DC9 except Tec-Kote finish. Made in U.S. by Intratec. Introduced 1985; dropped 1994.

Perf.: $325   **Exc.:** $275   **VGood:** $200

INTRATEC TEC-DC9MS

Same specs as TEC-DC9 except made of stainless steel. Made in U.S. by Intratec. Introduced 1985; dropped 1994.

Perf.: $375   **Exc.:** $295   **VGood:** $225

Ithaca X-Caliber

Iver Johnson 22 Supershot Sealed Eight (Second Model)

Iver Johnson 22 Supershot Sealed Eight (First Model)

Iver Johnson 22 Supershot Sealed Eight (Third Model 844)

Iver Johnson Cattleman

Iver Johnson Bulldog

Iver Johnson Armsworth Model 855

ITHACA MODEL 20

Single shot; 22 LR, 44 Mag.; 10-inch, 12-inch barrel; 15-inch overall length (10-inch barrel); weighs 3-1/4 lbs.; American walnut stock with satin finish; Ithaca Gun Raybar Deerslayer sights or drilled and tapped for scope mounting; single firing pin for RF/CF use; comes with both barrels matched to one frame; matte blue finish. Made in U.S. by Ithaca Acquisition Corp. Introduced 1994; no longer produced.

Perf.: $695   **Exc.:** $625   **VGood:** $550

ITHACA X-CALIBER

Single shot; 22 LR, 44 Mag.; 10-inch, 15-inch barrel; 15-inch overall length (10-inch barrel); weighs 3-1/4 lbs.; Goncalo Alves grip and forend; blade on ramp front sight, adjustable, removable target-type rear; drilled and tapped for scope mounting; polished blue finish. Made in U.S. by Ithaca Acquisition Corp. Made only in 1988. Deduct slightly for .22 rimfire.

Perf.: $695   **Exc.:** $625   **VGood:** $550

IVER JOHNSON 22 SUPERSHOT

Revolver; double action; 22 LR; 7-shot; 6-inch barrel; 10-3/4-inch overall length; weighs 24 oz.; top-break; automatic cartridge extraction; fixed sights; front sight and lettering gold-plated; one-piece saw-handle checkered walnut grips; has "Hammer the Hammer" action; blued finish. Marked 22 SUPERSHOT in script. Introduced 1928; dropped 1931.

VGood: $125   **Good:** $100   **Fair:** $75

IVER JOHNSON 22 SUPERSHOT MODEL 90

Revolver; double action; 22 LR; 9-shot; 6-inch barrel; 10-3/4-inch overall length; weighs 24 oz.; top-break; automatic cartridge extraction; fixed sights; front sight and lettering gold-plated; one-piece saw-handle shaped checkered walnut oversize grips; has "Hammer the Hammer" action; blued finish. Marked 22 SUPERSHOT in script on left side of barrel. Pre-WWII model has adjustable finger rest. Introduced 1929; dropped 1949.

VGood: $135   **Good:** $110   **Fair:** $85

IVER JOHNSON 22 SUPERSHOT SEALED EIGHT (FIRST MODEL)

Revolver; double action; 22 LR; 8-shot; 6-inch barrel; 10-3/4-inch overall length; weighs 24 oz.; large frame; top-break; recessed cylinder chambers; oversize target-type one-piece checkered walnut grips called Hi-Hold by the factory; has "Hammer the Hammer" action; blue finish. Three models: Model 88, fixed sights; Model 833, adjustable sights; Model 834, adjustable sights and adjustable finger rest. Marked 22 SUPERSHOT SEALED EIGHT on left side of barrel. Introduced 1932; dropped 1941.

VGood: $150   **Good:** $125   **Fair:** $100

IVER JOHNSON 22 SUPERSHOT SEALED EIGHT (SECOND MODEL)

Same specs as First Model except weighs 28 oz.; grip frame modified for ease of manufacture. Two models: Model 88, fixed sights; Model 833, adjustable sights. Marked 22 SUPERSHOT SEALED EIGHT on left side of barrel. Introduced 1946; dropped 1954.

VGood: $150   **Good:** $125   **Fair:** $100

IVER JOHNSON 22 SUPERSHOT SEALED EIGHT (THIRD MODEL 844)

Same specs as First Model except 4-1/2-inch, 6-inch barrel; 9-1/4-inch (4-1/2-inch barrel), 10-3/4-inch (6-inch barrel) overall length; weighs 27 oz. (4-1/2-inch), 29 oz. (6-inch); unfluted cylinder; flat-sided barrel with full-length rib; recessed cylinder chambers with flash control front rim. Introduced 1955; dropped 1957.

VGood: $175   **Good:** $150   **Fair:** $125

IVER JOHNSON ARMSWORTH MODEL 855

Revolver; single action; 22 LR; 6-inch barrel; 10-3/4-inch overall length; weighs 30 oz.; top-break; large frame; trigger pull factory set at 2-1/2 lbs.; recessed cylinder chambers with flash control front rim; flat-sided barrel with full-length rib; adjustable sights; adjustable finger rest; one-piece oversize target-type checkered walnut grip; does not have "Hammer the Hammer" action; blued finish. Limited production; rare. Introduced 1955; dropped 1957.

VGood: $300   **Good:** $250   **Fair:** $225

IVER JOHNSON BULLDOG

Revolver; double action; 22 LR, 22 WMR, 38 Spl.; 6-shot (22), 5-shot (38); 2-1/2-inch, 4-inch barrel; 6-1/2-inch overall length (2-1/2-inch barrel); 9-inch overall length (4-inch barrel); weighs 26 oz. (2-1/2-inch), 30 oz. (4-inch); large solid frame; pull pin cylinder release; adjustable sights; one-piece oversize molded Tenite plastic target grips (4-inch), two-piece pocket size plastic (2-1/2-inch); full-length barrel rib; does not have "Hammer the Hammer" action; blue or nickel finish. Introduced 1974; dropped 1979.

VGood: $135   **Good:** $110   **Fair:** $75

IVER JOHNSON CATTLEMAN MAGNUM

Revolver; single action; 357 Mag., 45 LC, 44 Mag.; 6-shot; 4-3/4-inch, 5-1/2-inch, 7-1/4-inch (357, 45); 4-3/4-inch, 6-inch, 7-1/4-inch (44) barrel; 10-1/4-inch (4-3/4-inch), 11-inch (5-1/2-inch), 11-1/2-inch (6-inch), 12-3/4-inch (7-1/4-inch) overall length; 40 oz. (4-3/4-inch), 41 oz. (5-1/2-inch), 44 oz. (7-1/4-inch); large solid frame; rod ejection; automatic hammer-block safety; fixed sights; one-piece European walnut grips; brass grip frame; color case-hardened frame; blue barrel and cylinder. A limited number chambered in 44-40 caliber; add 20 percent. Introduced 1973; dropped 1979.

VGood: $275   **Good:** $215   **Fair:** $165

44 Magnum
VGood: $300   **Good:** $250   **Fair:** $190

IVER JOHNSON CATTLEMAN BUCKHORN MAGNUM

Same specs as Cattleman Magnum except 5-3/4-inch, 7-1/2-inch (357, 45) barrel; 4-3/4-inch, 6-inch, 7-1/2-inch (44) barrel; 12-3/4-inch (7-1/2-inch barrel), 11-1/2-inch (6-inch barrel), 11-inch (5-3/4-inch barrel), 10-3/4-inch (4-3/4-inch barrel) overall length; 44 oz. (7-1/2-inch), 42-1/2 oz. (6-inch), 41 oz. (5-3/4-inch), 41 oz. (4-3/4-inch). A limited number manufactured with 12-inch barrel with shoulder stock lugs; add 20 percent. Introduced 1973; dropped 1979.

VGood: $250   **Good:** $210   **Fair:** $185

Iver Johnson Cattleman
Buckhorn Magnum

Iver Johnson
Compact

Iver Johnson
Champion Model 822

Iver Johnson Enforcer
Model 3000

Iver Johnson
Model 55 Target

Iver Johnson Hijo
Quickbreak 1961

Iver Johnson
Model 55A

Iver Johnson Model 50
Sidewinder

IVER JOHNSON CATTLEMAN BUCKHORN BUNTLINE

Same specs as Cattleman Magnum except 18-inch barrel; 23-1/4-inch overall length; weighs 56 oz.; detachable shoulder stock; adjustable sights. Introduced 1973; dropped 1979.

VGood: $300   **Good:** $250   **Fair:** $175

IVER JOHNSON CATTLEMAN TRAILBLAZER

Same specs as Cattleman Magnum except 22 LR, 22 WMR; 5-1/2-inch, 6-1/2-inch barrel; 10-3/4-inch (5-1/2-inch), 11-3/4-inch (6-1/2-inch) overall length; weighs 38 oz. (5-1/2-inch), 40 oz. (6-1/2-inch); adjustable sights. Introduced 1973; dropped 1979.

VGood: $175   **Good:** $145   **Fair:** $110

IVER JOHNSON CHAMPION MODEL 822

Revolver; single-action; 22 LR; 6-inch barrel; 8-shot; 10-3/4-inch overall length; weighs 24 oz.; recessed cylinder chambers; adjustable finger rest; adjustable target-type sights; oversize one-piece target-type checkered walnut grips; does not have "Hammer the Hammer" action; blued finish. Marked CHAMPION SINGLE ACTION on left side of barrel. Cataloged several years after WWII but none manufactured after 1941. Very rare; very collectible. Introduced 1939; dropped 1941.

VGood: $300   **Good:** $250   **Fair:** $200

IVER JOHNSON COMPACT

Semi-automatic; single action; 25 ACP; 6-shot; 3-inch barrel; 4-1/4-inch overall length; weighs 9-5/16-inch oz.; checkered composite grips; trigger block safety; matte blue frame; bright blue slide. Introduced 1991; dropped 1993.

VGood: $165   **Good:** $135   **Fair:** $115

IVER JOHNSON COMPACT ELITE

Same specs as Compact except 24K gold finish; Ivorex grips. Introduced 1991; dropped 1993.

VGood: $550   **Good:** $450   **Fair:** $295

IVER JOHNSON DELUXE STARTER MODEL 69

Revolver; double action; 22, 32 blanks; 8-shot (22), 5-shot (32); 2-3/4-inch solid barrel; 7-inch overall length; weighs 22 oz.; top-break; recessed cylinder chambers; built on 66S Trailsman frame; fixed sights; two-piece small pocket-size plastic grips; does not have "Hammer the Hammer" action; matte blue finish. Introduced 1964; dropped 1974.

VGood: $65   **Good:** $45   **Fair:** $30

IVER JOHNSON ENFORCER MODEL 3000/IVER JOHNSON SUPER ENFORCER MODEL PP30

Semi-automatic; single action; 30 Carbine; 15-, 30-shot; 9-1/2-inch barrel; 17-inch overall length; weighs 4 lbs.; gas-operated; fires from closed bolt; American walnut stock; blue finish. Pistol version of Universal M1 Carbine; Iver Johnson purchased Universal in 1985. Manufactured 1986.

VGood: $400   **Good:** $325   **Fair:** $275

IVER JOHNSON HIJO QUICKBREAK 1961

Revolver; double action; 22 LR, 32 S&W, 38 S&W; 8-shot (22), 5-shot (32, 38); 7-inch overall length; weighs 25 oz.; recessed cylinder chambers; rimfire model with flash control front rim; two-piece pocket-size plastic grips; adjustable sights; does not have "Hammer the Hammer" action; nickel finish only. Same as the Model 66S made to be sold by several mail-order companies in New York City area.

VGood: $100   **Good:** $75   **Fair:** $50

IVER JOHNSON MODEL 50 SIDEWINDER

Revolver; double action; 22 LR; 8-shot; 6-inch barrel (1961-1978/1979); 4-3/4-inch barrel (1974-1978/1979); 10-inch (4-3/4-inch barrel), 11-1/4-inch (6-inch barrel) overall length; 30 oz. (4-3/4-inch), 31 oz. (6-inch); large solid frame; rod ejection; recessed chambers with flash control front rim; 22 LR/22 WMR combo available after 1974; fixed sights; adjustable

after 1974; Western-style walnut grips; stag plastic grips standard after 1968; several model numbers for different finish and sight combinations after 1974; matte blue and satin nickel finish. Introduced 1961; dropped 1979.

VGood: $110   **Good:** $85   **Fair:** $60

IVER JOHNSON MODEL 55 TARGET

Revolver; double action; 22 LR; 8-shot; 4-1/2-inch, 6-inch barrels; 10-3/4-inch (4-1/4-inch), 9-1/4-inch (6-inch) overall length; weighs 24 oz. (4-1/2-inch), 26 oz. (6-inch); large solid frame; pull pin cylinder release with flash control front rim; recessed cylinder chambers; fixed sights; oversize molded one-piece Tenite plastic target-type grips; does not have "Hammer the Hammer" action; matte blue finish. After 1958 cylinder fluted; hard chrome lined barrel. Introduced 1955; dropped 1960.

VGood: $100   **Good:** $70   **Fair:** $50

IVER JOHNSON MODEL 55A

Same specs as Model 55 except incorporation of loading gate; weighs 28-1/2 oz. (4-1/2-inch barrel), 30-1/2 oz. (6-inch barrel). After 1974/1975 this model called the "I J SPORTSMAN." Introduced 1961; dropped 1979.

VGood: $90   **Good:** $70   **Fair:** $50

IVER JOHNSON MODEL 55S CADET

Same specs as Model 55 except 2-1/2-inch barrel; 7-inch overall length; weighs 27 oz.; two-piece small pocket-size grips; fluted cylinder after 1958. Introduced 1955; dropped 1960.

VGood: $145   **Good:** $100   **Fair:** $75

IVER JOHNSON MODEL 55S-A CADET

Same specs as Model 55 except 22 LR, 32 S&W, 38 S&W; 8-shot (22), 5-shot (32, 38); 7-inch overall length; loading gate on right side of frame. After 1974/1975 this model called "I J CADET." Introduced 1961; dropped 1979.

VGood: $145   **Good:** $100   **Fair:** $75

Iver Johnson
Model 55S Cadet

Iver Johnson
Model 55S-A Cadet

Iver Johnson Model 56A IJ
Starter Revolver

Iver Johnson
Model 57 Target

Iver Johnson
Model 57A Target

Iver Johnson
Model 1900

Iver Johnson
Protector Sealed Eight
Model 84

Iver Johnson
Rookie

IVER JOHNSON MODEL 56 I J STARTER REVOLVER

Revolver; double action; 22 blank; 8-shot; 2-1/2-inch solid barrel; 6-3/4-inch overall length; weighs 10 oz.; large solid frame; pull pin cylinder release; recessed cylinder chambers; cylinder half-length; hard rubber or walnut pocket-size grips; built on Model 1900 large frame; blue finish. Introduced 1956; dropped 1960.

VGood: $75   **Good:** $55   **Fair:** $35

IVER JOHNSON MODEL 56A I J STARTER REVOLVER

Same specs as Model 56 except 22, 32 rimfire blank; 8-shot (22), 5-shot (32); 22 oz.; plastic grips; loading gate on right side of frame; matte blue finish; built on Model 55S-A frame. Introduced 1961; dropped 1974.

VGood: $60   **Good:** $40   **Fair:** $20

IVER JOHNSON MODEL 57 TARGET

Revolver; double action; 22 LR; 8-shot; 2-1/2-inch, 4-1/2-inch, 6-inch barrel; 7-1/2-inch (2-1/2-inch barrel), 9-1/2-inch (4-1/2-inch barrel), 10-3/4-inch (6-inch barrel) overall length; 27 oz. (2-1/2-inch), 29 oz. (4-1/2-inch), 30-1/2 oz. (6-inch); large solid frame; pull pin cylinder release; unfluted cylinder; recessed cylinder chambers with flash control front rim; scored trigger; music wire springs; checkered thumbrest; half-cock safety; adjustable front and rear sight; one-piece molded Tenite plastic target-type grips; does not have "Hammer the Hammer" action; matte blue finish. Introduced 1955; dropped 1960.

VGood: $100   **Good:** $80   **Fair:** $55

IVER JOHNSON MODEL 57A TARGET

Same specs as Model 57 except 4-1/2-inch, 6-inch barrel only; loading gate on right side of frame; adjustable sights. After 1974 this model called "I J TARGET DELUXE." Introduced 1961; dropped 1979.

VGood: $105   **Good:** $75   **Fair:** $55

IVER JOHNSON MODEL 1900

Revolver; double action; solid frame; pull pin cylinder release; 2-1/2-inch (standard), 4-1/2-inch, 6-inch octagon barrel; standard finish nickel, blue optional;

three frame sizes. Small frame: 22 LR; 7-shot; 6-inch overall length (2-1/2-inch barrel); weighs 11 oz. Medium frame: 32 S&W; 5-shot; 6-1/8-inch overall length (2-1/2-inch barrel); weighs 12 oz. Large frame: 32 S&W Long, 38 S&W; 6-shot (32), 5-shot (38); 6-3/4-inch overall length; weighs 18 oz. Small pocket-size hard rubber grips, oversize target-type hard rubber optional. Introduced 1900; dropped 1941.

VGood: $100   **Good:** $75   **Fair:** $50

IVER JOHNSON MODEL 1900 TARGET

Same specs as Model 1900 except blue finish only; 6-inch, 9-inch octagon barrel; 9-1/4-inch overall length (6-inch barrel), 14-3/8-inch (9-inch barrel); weighs 12-7/8 oz. (6-inch barrel), 14-3/8 oz. (9-inch barrel); built on Model 1900 small frame. Two-piece oversize walnut grips. Introduced 1925; dropped 1928. Add 20 percent for 9-inch barrel.

VGood: $135   **Good:** $110   **Fair:** $100

IVER JOHNSON MODEL 1900 TARGET MODELS 69 & 79

Same specs as Model 1900 except blue finish only; 6-inch (Model 69), 10-inch (Model 79) octagon barrel; 9-shot; built on Model 1900 large frame; 10-3/4-inch overall length (6-inch barrel), 14-3/8-inch (10-inch barrel); weighs 24 oz. (6-inch), 27 oz. (10-inch); one-piece oversize target-type walnut grips. Introduced 1929; dropped 1941. Add 20 percent for 10-inch barrel.

VGood: $145   **Good:** $135   **Fair:** $110

IVER JOHNSON MODEL 1908 PETITE HAMMERLESS

Revolver; double action; 22 LR; 1-1/4-inch barrel; 3-15/16-inch overall length; weighs 4-7/8 oz.; solid frame; folding trigger; pull pin cylinder release; small pocket-size hard rubber grips. One of the smallest revolvers built in U.S. Fewer than 1000 manufactured. Manufactured 1908 only. Rare and collectible.

VGood: $450   **Good:** $300   **Fair:** $150

IVER JOHNSON PROTECTOR SEALED EIGHT MODEL 84

Revolver; double action; 22 LR; 8-shot; 2-1/2-inch barrel; 10-3/4-inch overall length; weighs 20 oz.; large

frame; top-break; automatic extraction; recessed cylinder chambers; pocket-size one-piece checkered walnut grips; fixed sights, adjustable optional; has "Hammer the Hammer" action; blue finish. Marked PROTECTOR SEALED EIGHT on left side of barrel. Rare model. Introduced 1933; dropped 1941.

VGood: $200   **Good:** $175   **Fair:** $150

IVER JOHNSON ROOKIE

Revolver; double action; 38 Spl.; 5-shot; 4-inch barrel; 9-inch overall length; weighs 29 oz.; pull pin cylinder release; fixed sights; one-piece oversize molded Tenite plastic target-type grips; does not have "Hammer the Hammer" action; blue finish. Introduced 1974; dropped 1979.

VGood: $225   **Good:** $160   **Fair:** $85

IVER JOHNSON SAFETY AUTOMATIC HAMMER (SECOND MODEL)

Revolver; double action; hinged frame top-break; double top post barrel latch; "Hammer the Hammer" action; flat springs; two frame sizes; standard finish, nickel; blue finish optional. Small frame: 22 LR, 32 S&W; 7-shot (22), 5-shot (32); 3-inch (standard), 4-inch, 5-inch, 6-inch barrel; 6-3/4-inch overall length; weighs 12 oz. (3-inch 22 LR), 12-1/4 oz. (32 S&W). Large frame: 38 S&W (blackpowder cartridges only); 3-1/4-inch (standard), 2-inch, 4-inch, 5-inch, 6-inch barrels; 7-3/8-inch overall length; weighs 17-1/4 oz. Fixed sights; small pocket size hard rubber grips. Introduced 1897; dropped 1908. For rimfire models add 20 percent.

VGood: $100   **Good:** $75   **Fair:** $50

IVER JOHNSON SAFETY AUTOMATIC HAMMER (THIRD MODEL)

Same specs as Second Model except coil springs; small frame comes in 3-inch (standard), 2-inch, 4-inch, 5-inch, 6-inch barrel; large frame model in 32 S&W Long, 38 S&W for smokeless powder. Cataloged until 1948. Introduced 1909; dropped 1941. For rimfire models add 20 percent.

VGood: $125   **Good:** $100   **Fair:** $75

Iver Johnson Safety Automatic Hammer (Third Model)

Iver Johnson Sealed 8 Snub Model 68S

Iver Johnson Target Sealed 8 (Second Model)

Iver Johnson Trailsman

Iver Johnson Safety Hammerless (Third Model)

Iver Johnson Trailsman Snub Model 66S

Iver Johnson Trailsman Model 66

IVER JOHNSON SAFETY HAMMERLESS (SECOND MODEL)

Revolver; double action; hinged frame top-break; double top post barrel latch; "Hammer the Hammer" action; flat springs; basic design comparable to Safety Hammer model; two frame sizes; standard finish, nickel; blue finish optional. Small frame: 22 LR, 32 S&W; 7-shot (22), 5-shot (32); 3-inch (standard), 2-inch, 4-inch, 5-inch, 6-inch barrel; 6-3/8-inch overall length (3-inch barrel); weighs 12-1/2 oz. (3-inch 22 LR), 13-1/2 oz. (32). Large frame: 38 S&W (blackpowder cartridges only); 5-shot (38); 3-1/4-inch (standard), 2-inch, 4-inch, 5-inch, 6-inch barrels; 7-3/8-inch overall length; weighs 18-1/4 oz. (32), 19 oz. (38). Fixed sights; small pocket size hard rubber grips. Introduced 1897; dropped 1908. For rimfire models add 20 percent.

VGood: $100   **Good:** $75   **Fair:** $50

IVER JOHNSON SAFETY HAMMERLESS (THIRD MODEL)

Same specs as Second Model except small frame weighs 13-1/2 oz. (3-inch 22 LR), 14 oz. (32); large frame weighs 19 oz. (38 S&W); 38 S&W, 32 S&W Long (smokeless cartridge); oversize target hard rubber or walnut grips optional. Cataloged until 1948. Introduced 1909; dropped 1941. For rimfire models add 20 percent.

VGood: $125   **Good:** $100   **Fair:** $75

IVER JOHNSON SEALED 8 SNUB MODEL 68S

Revolver; double action; 22 LR; 8-shot; 2-1/2-inch barrel; 6-3/4-inch overall length; weighs 20-1/2 oz.; large solid frame; pull pin cylinder release; recessed cylinder chambers; round barrel; small pocket-size two-piece walnut grips; does not have "Hammer the Hammer" action. Introduced 1952; dropped 1954. Rare and limited production.

VGood: $200   **Good:** $175   **Fair:** $150

IVER JOHNSON SECRET SERVICE SPECIAL MODELS 1917 & 1923

Revolver; double action; top break; hammer and hammerless versions; two frame sizes. Small frame: 32 S&W; 5-shot; 3-inch (standard), 5-inch barrel; 6-3/8-inch overall length; weighs 12 oz. (hammer model), 13 oz. (hammerless model). Large frame: 38 S&W; 5-shot; 3-1/4-inch (standard), 5-inch barrel; 7-3/8-inch overall length; weighs 18 oz. (hammer model), 19 oz. (hammerless); blue finish, nickel optional; hard rubber pocket-size grips; oversize target grips optional. Marked on left side of barrel SECRET SERVICE SPECIAL; on top of barrel "for .32 [or .38] SMITH & WESSON CARTRIDGES." Note: Not all revolvers so marked were manufactured by Iver Johnson. The name "Secret Service Special" was owned by the Fred Biffar Co. of Chicago, IL. For models with hammer-block safety add 20 percent.

VGood: $135   **Good:** $100   **Fair:** $50

IVER JOHNSON TARGET SEALED 8 (FIRST MODEL)

Revolver; double action; 22 LR; 8-shot; 6-inch (Model 68), 10-inch (Model 78) barrel; 10-3/4-inch (M68), 14-3/4-inch (M78) overall length; weighs 24 oz. (M68), 27 oz. (M78); large solid frame; pull pin cylinder release; recessed cylinder chambers; fixed sights, front blade gold-plated; one-piece oversized checkered walnut grips; octagon barrel; does not have "Hammer the Hammer" action. Introduced 1932; dropped 1941.

VGood: $125   **Good:** $100   **Fair:** $75

IVER JOHNSON TARGET SEALED 8 (SECOND MODEL)

Same specs as First Model except 4-1/2-inch, 6-inch barrel; 9-1/4-inch (4-1/2-inch barrel), 10-3/4-inch (6-inch barrel) overall length; weighs 22-1/2 oz. (4-inch), 24 oz. (6-inch); round barrel. Introduced 1946; dropped 1954.

VGood: $125   **Good:** $100   **Fair:** $75

IVER JOHNSON TP22

Semi-automatic; double action; 22 LR; 2 7/8-inch barrel; 5-3/8-inch overall length; weighs 14-1/2 oz.; hammer-block safety; no magazine safety; no slide stop; fixed sights; black plastic wrap-around grips;

designed by ERMA WERKES Germany; blue and nickel finish; features patented passive firing pin block safety. Introduced 1982; dropped 1988.

VGood: $175   **Good:** $125   **Fair:** $100

IVER JOHNSON TP25

Semi-automatic; double action; 25 ACP; 2-7/8-inch barrel; 5-3/8-inch overall length; weighs 14-1/2 oz.; hammer-block safety; no magazine safety; no slide stop; fixed sights; black plastic wrap-around grips; designed by ERMA WERKES Germany; blue finish. Introduced 1981; dropped 1988.

VGood: $175   **Good:** $110   **Fair:** $95

IVER JOHNSON TRAILSMAN

Semi-automatic; single action; 22 LR; 4-1/2-inch, 6-inch barrel; 8-3/4-inch (4-1/2-inch barrel) overall length; weighs 46 oz. (4-1/2-inch), 64 oz. (6-inch); checkered black plastic grips; slide hold-open latch; push button magazine release; sear block safety; fixed sights; blue finish. First 500+ actually manufactured in Argentina; worth a premium. Introduced 1984; dropped 1988.

VGood: $195   **Good:** $175   **Fair:** $145

IVER JOHNSON TRAILSMAN MODEL 66

Revolver; double action; 22 LR; 8-shot; 4-1/2-inch (added in 1962; dropped 1964), 6-inch barrel; 9-1/2-inch (4-1/2-inch barrel), 11-inch (6-inch barrel) overall length; weighs 31 oz. (4-1/2-inch), 34 oz. (6-inch); large frame; top-break; recessed cylinder chambers with flash control front rim; manual extraction; adjustable sights; one-piece molded Tenite plastic target-type grips; does not have "Hammer the Hammer" action; matte blue finish. Introduced 1958; dropped 1974.

VGood: $120   **Good:** $95   **Fair:** $75

IVER JOHNSON TRAILSMAN SNUB MODEL 66S

Same specs as Model 66 except 22 LR, 32 S&W, 38 S&W; 8-shot (22), 5-shot (32, 38); centerfire calibers not added until 1962; 2-3/4-inch barrel; 7-inch overall length; weighs 25 oz.; two-piece pocket-size plastic grips. Introduced 1959; dropped 1963.

VGood: $110   **Good:** $85   **Fair:** $65

Iver Johnson Trigger
Cocking Model 36T

Iver Johnson
U.S. Revolver Co.
Automatic Hammer Model

Iver Johnson Viking
Snub Model 67S

Iver Johnson Viking
Model 67

Iver Johnson
X300 Pony

Jennings
Model J-22

IVER JOHNSON TRIGGER COCKING MODEL 36T

Revolver; single action; 22 LR; 8-shot; 6-inch barrel; 10-3/4-inch overall length; weighs 24 oz.; large frame; top-break; recessed cylinder chambers; adjustable sights; one-piece oversize target-type checkered walnut grips; adjustable finger rest; does not have "Hammer the Hammer" action; first pull of the trigger cocks the hammer; second pull releases it; blue finish. Marked "I J TRIGGER COCKING 22 SINGLE ACTION TARGET" in two lines on left side of barrel. Limited production; considered rare and collectible. Introduced 1936; dropped 1941.

> **VGood:** $300 **Good:** $250 **Fair:** $200

IVER JOHNSON U.S. REVOLVER CO. AUTOMATIC HAMMER MODEL

Revolver; double action; top-break; automatic cartridge extraction; two frame sizes; blue finish, nickel optional. Small frame: 22 LR, 32 S&W; 7-shot (22), 5-shot (32); 3-inch (standard), 5-inch barrel; 6-3/8-inch overall length (3-inch barrel); 12 oz. (22), 12-1/2 oz. (32). Large frame: 38 S&W; 5-shot; 7-3/8-inch overall length; weighs 17-3/4 oz.; small hard rubber pocket-size grips, oversize grips optional. Marked on barrel top rib: "U.S. REVOLVER Co." Introduced 1910; dropped 1935.

> **VGood:** $85 **Good:** $65 **Fair:** $45

IVER JOHNSON U.S. REVOLVER CO. AUTOMATIC HAMMERLESS MODEL

Revolver; double action; top-break; automatic cartridge extraction; two frame sizes; blue finish, nickel optional. Small frame: 32 S&W; 5-shot; 3-inch (standard), 5-inch barrel; 6-3/8-inch overall length (3-inch barrel); 12-1/2 oz. Large frame: 38 S&W; 5-shot; 7-3/8-inch overall length; weighs 18 oz.; small hard rubber pocket-size grips, oversize grips optional. Marked on barrel top rib: "U.S. REVOLVER Co." Introduced 1910; dropped 1935.

> **VGood:** $85 **Good:** $65 **Fair:** $45

IVER JOHNSON U.S. REVOLVER CO. DOUBLE ACTION

Revolver; double action; solid frame; pull pin cylinder release; two frame sizes; round barrel; unfluted cylinder. Small frame: 22 LR, 32 S&W; 7-shot (22), 5-shot (32); 2-1/2-inch barrel (standard), 4-1/2-inch optional; 6-inch overall length (22), 6-1/8-inch (32); weighs 10-1/2 oz. (22), 12 oz. (32). Large frame: 32 S&W Long, 38 S&W; 6-shot (32), 5-shot (38); 6-3/4-inch overall length; weighs 17 oz.; small pocket-size hard rubber grips. Marked on frame topstrap: "U.S. REVOLVER Co." Introduced 1911; dropped 1935.

> **VGood:** $105 **Good:** $70 **Fair:** $55

IVER JOHNSON VIKING MODEL 67

Revolver; double action; 22 LR; 8-shot; 4-1/2-inch, 6-inch barrel; 9-1/2-inch (4-1/4-inch barrel), 11-inch (6-inch barrel) overall length; weighs 31 oz. (4-1/2-inch), 34 oz. (6-inch); chrome-lined barrel; large frame; top-break; recessed cylinder chambers and flash control front rim; one-piece molded oversize target-type Tenite grip; adjustable sights; matte blue finish. Introduced 1964; dropped 1974.

> **VGood:** $125 **Good:** $100 **Fair:** $75

IVER JOHNSON VIKING SNUB MODEL 67S

Same specs as Model 67 except 22 LR, 32 S&W, 38 S&W; 8-shot (22), 5-shot (32, 38); centerfire calibers not added until 1962; 2-3/4-inch barrel; 7-inch overall length; weighs 25 oz.; two-piece pocket-size plastic grips. Introduced 1964; dropped 1974.

> **VGood:** $135 **Good:** $110 **Fair:** $85

IVER JOHNSON X300 PONY

Semi-automatic; single action; 380 ACP; 6-shot; 3-inch barrel; 6-1/4-inch overall length; weighs 20 oz.; all steel construction; inertia firing pin; loaded chamber indicator; lanyard ring; no magazine safety; adjustable rear sight; matte blue, bright blue or nickel finish. Three production periods: Middlesex, NJ 1978 to 1982; Jacksonville, AR 1983 to 1988; Jacksonville, AR by AMAC 1989 to 1991.

> **VGood:** $225 **Good:** $200 **Fair:** $150

IVER-JOHNSON FRONTIER FOUR DERRINGER

Four-barrel, stainless .22 LR single-action derringer with unique rotating firing pin. Based on old Sharps derringer. 5.5 oz.

> **NIB:** $165 **Exc.:** $125 **VGood:** $85

IVER-JOHNSON 1911 .45

All-steel 7+1 capacity 1911 .45 ACP with 5-inch Government or 4.5-inch Commander barrel. Adjustable white outline rear sight. Adjustable trigger. Polished blue.

> **NIB:** $625 **Exc.:** $565 **VGood:** $485

IVER-JOHNSON 1911 .22 LR

Aluminum slide and frame, 15+1 capacity 1911 .22 LR with 5-inch Government or 4.5-inch Commander barrel. 19 oz. Adjustable white outline rear sight. Adjustable trigger. Blued or stainless.

> **NIB:** $585 **Exc.:** $545 **VGood:** $475

JANA BISON

Revolver; single action; 22 LR, 22 WMR; 4-3/4-inch barrel; fixed front sight, adjustable rear; imitation stag grips; blued finish. Introduced 1978; imported from West Germany; dropped 1980.

> **Exc.:** $100 **VGood:** $85 **Good:** $60

JANZ JTL-S

Revolver; double action; 22 LR; 38 Spl./357 Mag.; 44 Mag.; 45 Win. Mag.; 454 Casull/45 LC; 6 or 7 shot; .500 S&W added 2006. unique interchangeable barrel and cylinder system allows calibers to be rapidly changed; 4 - 10-inch barrel with full lug; ergonomic stippled wood grips; target sights. Introduced in 2003. Made in Germany; limited importation. Prices start at about $10,000 Euros.
Add $500 for 44 Magnum chambering
Add $800 for 45 Win. Mag., 45 LC or 454 Casull chambering

Jennings Model J-25

Jennings/Bryce
Model J-38

Jennings/Bryce
Model J-48

Jericho Model 941

Kahr K9

Kahr K9

Kahr MK9 Micro
Compact Pistol

Kahr CW40

Kahr TP40

JENNINGS/BRYCO MODEL J-22

Semi-automatic; 22 LR; 6-shot magazine; 2-1/2-inch barrel; weighs 12 oz.; 4-15/16-inch overall length; fixed sights; walnut stocks. Introduced 1981; dropped 2004.

Perf.: $70   **Exc.:** $55   **VGood:** $45

JENNINGS/BRYCO MODEL J-25

Semi-automatic; 25 ACP; 6-shot magazine; 2-1/2-inch barrel; weighs 12 oz.; 4-15/16-inch overall length; fixed sights; synthetic walnut or black combat-style grips. Introduced 1981; dropped 2004.

Perf.: $65   **Exc.:** $50   **VGood:** $40

JENNINGS/BRYCO MODEL M-38

Semi-automatic; 22 LR, 32 ACP, 380 ACP; 2-13/16-inch barrel; weighs 16 oz.; non-ferrous alloy construction; black grips; chrome or blue finish. Production ceased in 2004 but reportedly resumed in late 2004 under the name "Jimenez Arms," a new corporate entity.

Perf.: $75   **Exc.:** $60   **VGood:** $50

JENNINGS MODEL M-48

Semi-automatic; 22 LR, 32 ACP, 380 ACP; 4-inch barrel; weighs 24 oz.; non-ferrous alloy construction; black grips; chrome or blue finish. dropped 1995.

Perf.: $75   **Exc.:** $60   **VGood:** $50

JERICHO MODEL 941

Semi-automatic; double action; 9mm Para.; 16-shot magazine; 4-3/8-inch barrel; 8-1/8-inch overall length; weighs 33 oz.; high impact black polymer grips; blade front sight, windage-adjustable rear; three tritium dots; all steel construction; polygonal rifling; ambidextrous safety. Produced in Israel by Israel Military Industries; distributed by K.B.I., Inc. Introduced 1990; dropped 1991.

Perf.: $550   **Exc.:** $475   **VGood:** $425

JSL SPITFIRE

Semi-automatic; double action; 9mm Para.; 15-shot magazine; 4-3/8-inch barrel; 8-7/8-inch overall length; weighs 40 oz.; textured composition grips; blade front sight, fully-adjustable rear; stainless steel construction; ambidextrous safety. Imported from England by Rogers Ltd. International. Introduced 1992; importation dropped 1993.

Perf.: $1335   **Exc.:** $1100   **VGood:** $925
Add $80 to above prices for adjustable rear sight

KAHR K9, K40

Semi-automatic; double action; 9mm Para.; 7-shot magazine; 40 S&W; 6-shot magazine; 3-1/2-inch barrel; 6-inch overall length; weighs 25 oz.; wrap-around textured soft polymer grips; blade front sight, windage drift-adjustable rear; bar-dot combat style; passive firing pin block; made of 4140 ordnance steel; matte black finish. Made in U.S. by Kahr Arms. Many sight, finish options. Introduced 1994; dropped 2003.

New: $550   **Perf.:** $475   **Exc.:** $395

KAHR KS40 SMALL FRAME PISTOL

Same as standard K40 except 1/2-inch shorter grip. Comes with one 5-shot, one 6-shot magazine. Introduced 1998. Made in U.S. by Kahr Arms.

New: $550   **Perf.:** $475   **Exc.:** $400

With night sights $677.00

New: $600   **Perf.:** $525   **Exc.:** $450

KAHR MK9 MICRO-COMPACT PISTOL

Similar to the K9 except is 5.5-inch overall, 4-inch high, has a 3-inch barrel. Weighs 22 oz. Has snag-free bar-dot sights, polished feed ramp, dual recoil spring system, DA-only trigger. Comes with 6- and 7-shot magazines. Introduced 1998.

Matte stainless		
New: $595	**Perf.:** $495	**Exc.:** $425
Matte stainless, tritium night sights		
New: $650	**Perf.:** $575	**Exc.:** $500
Duo-Tone (stainless frame, Black-T slide)		$749.00
New: $700	**Perf.:** $600	**Exc.:** $500
Duo-Tone with tritium night sights $$836.00		
New: $775	**Perf.:** $675	**Exc.:** $600

KAHR ARMS CW40

Semi-auto with textured polymer grip chambered for .40 S&W and 6+1 capacity. Double-action with 3.6-inch barrel, 16.8 oz. Adjustable rear sights.

NIB: $515   **Exc.:** $475   **VGood:** $375

KAHR ARMS TP40

Double-action-only semi-auto pistol chambered in .40 S&W. Black polymer frame, matte stainless slide, 4" barrel, textured polymer grips, 6- or 7-round capacity depending on magazine. Drift-adjustable white bar-dot sights or Novak two-dot tritium sights.

NIB: $575   **Exc.:** $515   **VGood:** $465

KAHR E9

Semi-automatic; double action; 9mm Para.; economized version of the K9; matte black or duotone finish; supplied with one magazine. Produced during 1997 and 2003 only.

Perf.: $425   **Exc.:** $365   **VGood:** $335

Kareen MKII Auto Pistol

KBI PSP-25

Kassnar PJK-9HP

Kassnar M-100D

Kel-Tec P-32

Kel-Tec P-3AT

Kimber Classic 45 Custom

Kel-Tec P-11

KAHR MODEL 1911 STANDARD

This model features a blued finish, plastic grips with Thompson medallion and bullet logo on the slide. Seven-round magazine. Introduced in 2001.

New: $500   **Exc.:** $400   **VGood:** $275

KAHR MODEL 1911C

Similar to the Standard Model but with a 4.25" barrel.

New: $500   **Exc.:** $400   **VGood:** $275

KAHR MODEL 1911WGS DELUXE

This model has a blued finish, rubber wrap-around grips with Thompson medallion, high profile white dot sights, and Thompson bullet logo on the slide. Seven-round magazine. Introduced in 2001.

New: $600   **Exc.:** $500   **VGood:** $275400

KAREEN MKII AUTO PISTOL

Semi-automatic; single action; 9mm Para.; 13 (now 10)-shot magazine; 4-3/4-inch barrel; 8-inch overall length; weighs 32 oz.; blade front sight, windage-adjustable rear; checkered European walnut grips (early model), rubberized grips (later versions); blued finish, two-tone or matte black finish, optional. Made in Israel. Introduced 1969 by Century International Arms, Inc.; later imported by J.O. Arms until 1997.

Perf.: $350   **Exc.:** $275   **VGood:** $225

KAREEN MKII COMPACT

Same specs as MKII except 3-1/4-inch barrel; 6-1/2-inch overall length; weighs 28 oz.; rubber grips. Introduced 1995; still in production.

New: $350   **Exc.:** $300   **VGood:** $275

KASSNAR M-100D

Revolver; double action; 22 LR, 22 WMR, 38 Spl.; 6-shot cylinder; 3-inch, 4-inch, 6-inch barrels; target-style checkered hardwood stocks; elevation-adjustable rear sight, ramp front; vent-rib barrel.

Manufactured in the Philippines by Squires Bingham; imported by Kassnar. Introduced 1977; no longer imported.

Exc.: $125   **VGood:** $110   **Good:** $100

KASSNAR MODEL M-100TC

Revolver; double action; 22 LR, 22 WMR, 38 Spl.; 6-shot cylinder; 3-inch, 4-inch, 6-inch barrels; full ejector rod shroud; target-style checkered hardwood stocks; elevation-adjustable rear sight, ramp front; vent-rib barrel. Manufactured in the Philippines by Squires Bingham; imported by Kassnar. Introduced 1977; no longer imported.

Exc.: $135   **VGood:** $125   **Good:** $110

KASSNAR PJK-9HP

Semi-automatic; single action; 9mm Para.; 13-shot magazine; 4-3/4-inch barrel; 8-inch overall length; weighs 32 oz.; adjustable rear sight, ramp front; checkered European walnut stocks; with or without full-length vent rib. Made in Hungary. Introduced 1986; no longer imported.

Perf.: $225   **Exc.:** $200   **VGood:** $165

KBI PSP-25

Semi-automatic; single action; 25 ACP; 6-shot magazine; 2-1/8-inch barrel; 4-1/8-inch overall length; weighs 9-1/2 oz.; fixed sights; checkered black plastic grips; all-steel construction; polished blue or chrome finish. Close copy of Browning Baby 25 made under F.N. license. Introduced 1990; no longer in production.

Perf.: $195   **Exc.:** $175   **VGood:** $145

KEL-TEC P-11

Semi-automatic; double-action-only; 9mm Para.; 10-shot magazine; 3-1/8-inch barrel; 5-9/16-inch overall length; weighs 14 oz.; checkered black polymer grips; blade front sight, windage-adjustable rear; ordnance steel slide, aluminum frame; blue finish. Made in U.S. by Kel-Tec CNC Industries, Inc. Introduced 1995.

New: $265   **Perf.:** $225   **Exc.:** $200

Electroless nickel finish

New: $350   **Perf.:** $300   **Exc.:** $235

Gray finish

New: $280   **Perf.:** $250   **Exc.:** $200

KEL-TEC P-32

Semi-automatic; 32 ACP; double action only with internal hammer block safety; composite frame with steel slide; 2.68-inch barrel; blue, parkerized or hard chrome finish; light blue, dark blue, grey, green or ivory finished grips; 6.6 oz.

Perf.: $255   **Exc.:** $200   **VGood:** $175

KEL-TEC P-3AT

Similar to the P-32. except 380 ACP; 2.76-inch barrel; 6-shot magazine; black composite frame; parkerized steel slide; 7.3 oz. Introduced 2003.

Perf.: $$255   **Exc.:** $200   **VGood:** $175
Add $40 to above prices for parkerized finish
Add $55 for hard chrome finish

KEL-TEC P-40

Semi-automatic, 40 S&W; double action only with internal hammer block safety; composite frame; steel slide; 3.3-inch barrel; parkerized, blue, or hard chrome finish; 9 or 10-shot magazine; 15.8 oz. Introduced 1999; dropped 2001.

Perf.: $275   **Exc.:** $225   **VGood:** $190

KEL-TEC PLR-16

A 5.56 mm NATO gas-operated, semi-automatic AR-15-style long-range pistol. Windage-adjustable rear sight. Picatinny rail. Muzzle threaded for muzzle-brake. 9.2-inch barrel, 51 oz. 10-round or M-16 magazine. Blued finish, polymer construction.

NIB: $625   **Exc.:** $585   **VGood:** $475

KIMBER CLASSIC 45 CUSTOM

Semi-automatic; single action; 45 ACP; 8-shot magazine; 5-inch barrel; 8-1/2-inch overall length; weighs 38 oz.; checkered hard synthetic grips; McCormick dovetailed front sight, low combat rear; Chip McCormick Corp. forged frame and slide; match barrel; extended combat thumb safety; high beavertail grip safety; skeletonized lightweight composite trigger; skeletonized Commander-type hammer; elongated Commander ejector; bead-blasted black oxide finish; flat mainspring housing; short guide rod; lowered and flared ejection port; serrated front and rear of slide; relief cut under trigger guard; Wolff spring set; beveled magazine well. Made in U.S. by Kimber of America, Inc. Introduced 1995.

Kimber Classic 45 Gold Match

Kimber Classic 45 Polymer Frame

Kimber Custom Target

Kimber Gold Match Target Pistol

Kimber KPD 40

Kimber Pro Covert II

Kimber Compact 45

Kimber Custom Covert II

New: $620	Perf.: $550	Exc.: $475
Custom stainless		
New: $700	Perf.: $650	Exc.: $500

KIMBER CLASSIC 45 GOLD MATCH

Same specs as Custom except long guide rod; polished blue finish; Bo-Mar BMCS low-mount adjustable rear sight; fancy walnut grips; tighter tolerances; comes with one 10-shot and one 8-shot magazine, factory proof target. Made in U.S. by Kimber of America, Inc. Introduced 1995.

New: $1000	Perf.: $850	Exc.: $750

KIMBER CLASSIC 45 POLYMER FRAME

Similar to the Classic 45 Custom except has black polymer frame with stainless steel insert, hooked trigger guard, checkered front strap. Weighs 34.4 oz., overall length 8.75-inch. Introduced 1997.

New: $750	Perf.: $675	Exc.: $600
Polymer Stainless		
New: $850	Perf.: $675	Exc.: $650
Polymer Target		
New: $850	Perf.: $675	Exc.: $650
Polymer Stainless Target		
New: $900	Perf.: $800	Exc.: $700

KIMBER CLASSIC 45 ROYAL

Same specs as the Custom model except has checkered diamond-pattern walnut grips; long guide rod; polished blue finish; comes with two 8-shot magazines. Made in U.S. by Kimber of America, Inc. Introduced 1995; still produced.

New: $750	Perf.: $670	Exc.: $575

KIMBER COMPACT 45 AUTO PISTOL

Similar to the Classic Custom except has 4-inch barrel fitted directly to the slide with no bushing; full-length guide rod; 7-shot magazine; grip is .400-inch shorter than full-size guns. Weighs 34 oz.; Compact Aluminum weighs 28 oz. Introduced 1998.

New: $635	Perf.: $530	Exc.: $435
Compact Stainless		
New: $740	Perf.: $650	Exc.: $525
Compact Aluminum		
New: $700	Perf.: $550	Exc.: $450

KIMBER CUSTOM TARGET AUTO PISTOL

Caliber: 45 ACP, 7-shot magazine. Barrel: 5 inches. Weight: 38 oz. Length: 8.7 inches. overall. Stocks: Black synthetic. Sights: Blade front, Kimber fully adjustable rear; dovetailed. Features: Match trigger; beveled front and rear slide serrations; lowered, flared ejection port; full-length guide rod; Wolff springs. Introduced 1996.

Custom Target		
New: $675	Perf.: $625	Exc.: $530
Stainless Target		
New: $800	Perf.: $700	Exc.: $625

KIMBER GOLD MATCH TARGET PISTOL

Similar to the Custom Target except has highly polished blue finish; hand-fitted stainless steel barrel, bushing, slide and frame; ambidextrous thumb safety; hand-checkered rosewood grips with double diamond pattern; and skeletonized aluminum match-grade trigger. Has 8-shot magazine. Introduced 1998.

Gold Match		
New: $1050	Perf.: $850	Exc.: $725
Stainless Target		
New: $1150	Perf.: $985	Exc.: $800

KIMBER KPD 40

Kimber Pro Defense double-action .40 S&W semi-auto. Comes with two 12-round magazines for 12+1 capacity. 4.1-inch barrel, 25 oz. Fixed white dot sights.

NIB: $545	Exc.: $500	VGood: $475

KIMBER SUPER AMERICA

Billed as Kimber's ultimate top-of-the-line custom 1911. Polished/matte blue finish, scroll engraving, mammoth ivory grips, presentation case with matching sheath knife.

NIB: $2300	Exc.: $2000	VGood: $1750

KIMBER CUSTOM COVERT II

1911-style semiauto carry gun chambered in .45 ACP. Aluminum frame, steel slide. Frame finished in Desert Tan; slide finished in matte black. Five-inch

barrel with 3-dot sights.

NIB: $1100	Exc.: $975	VGood: $825

KIMBER PRO COVERT II

Similar to Custom Covert II but with four-inch barrel.

NIB: $1100	Exc.: $975	VGood: $825

KIMBER ULTRA COVERT II

Similar to Pro Covert II but with three-inch barrel. Introduced 2007.

NIB: $1150	Exc.: $1000	VGood: $850

KIMBER PRO AEGIS II

1911-style semiauto carry gun chambered in 9mm Parabellum. Aluminum frame, steel slide. Frame finished in matte aluminum; slide finished in matte black. Four-inch bull barrel with 3-dot sights.

NIB: $975	Exc.: $900	VGood: $800

KIMBER CUSTOM AEGIS II

Full-size 1911-style semiauto carry gun chambered in 9mm Parabellum. Aluminum frame, steel slide. Frame finished in matte aluminum; slide finished in matte black. Five-inch bull barrel with 3-dot sights.

NIB: $995	Exc.: $900	VGood: $800

KIMBER ULTRA AEGIS II

Similar to Pro Aegis II but with four-inch barrel. Introduced 2007.

NIB: $975	Exc.: $900	VGood: $800

KIMBER PREDATOR HUNTER

Single-shot; 221 Fireball, 223 Rem., 6mm TCU, 6x45, 7mm TCU; 15-3/4-inch barrel; weighs 88 oz.; no sights; accepts Kimber scope mount system; AA Claro walnut stock; uses Kimber Model 84 mini-Mauser action. Introduced 1987; dropped 1989.

Perf.: $1500	VGood: $1250	Good: $950

KIMBER PREDATOR SUPERGRADE

Same specs as Predator Hunter except French walnut stock; ebony forend tip; 22-line hand checkering. Introduced 1987; dropped 1989.

Perf.: $2200	VGood: $1800	Good: $1300

Kimber Ultra Covert II

Kimber Pro Aegis II

Kimber Custom Aegis II

Korriphila HSP 701

Kimel AP9

Kimber Predator Supergrade

Korth Revolver

Korth Sport

Korth Match Model

KIMEL AP9
Semi-automatic; single action; 9mm Para.; 20-shot magazine; 5-inch barrel; 11-7/8-inch overall length; weighs 3-1/2 lbs.; checkered plastic grip; adjustable post front sight in ring, fixed open rear; matte blue/black or nickel finish; fires from closed bolt. Made in U.S. Was available from Kimel Industries. Introduced 1988; dropped 1994.

Perf.: $425   Exc.: $365   VGood: $325

KIMEL AP9 MINI
Same specs as the AP9 except 3-inch barrel. Made in U.S. Was available from Kimel Industries. Introduced 1988; dropped 1994.

Perf.: $475   Exc.: $425   VGood: $350

KIMEL AP9 TARGET
Same specs as the AP9 except 12-inch barrel; grooved forend. Made in U.S. Was available from Kimel Industries. Introduced 1988; dropped 1994.

Perf.: $495   Exc.: $462   VGood: $375

KLEINGUENTHER R-15
Revolver; double action; 22 LR, 22 WMR, 32 S&W; 6-shot cylinder; 6-inch barrel; 11-inch overall length; checkered thumbrest walnut stocks; adjustable rear sight, fixed front; full-length solid barrel rib; adjustable trigger; blued finish. Manufactured in Germany. Introduced 1976; dropped 1978.

Exc.: $200   VGood: $175   Good: $150

KORRIPHILA HSP 701
Semi-automatic; double action; 9mm Para., 38 Wadcutter, 38 Super, 45 ACP; 9-shot magazine (9mm), 7-shot (45 ACP); 4-inch, 5-inch barrel; weighs 35 oz.; adjustable rear sight, ramp or target front; checkered walnut stocks; delayed roller lock action; limited production. Made in West Germany. Introduced 1986; importation dropped 1989. Importation resumed for a brief period but not currently imported.

Perf.: $6500   Exc.: $5500   VGood: $3700

KORRIPHILA HSP 701 ODIN'S EYE (DAMASCUS)
Similar to HSP 701, except is made entirely from one block of Damascus stainless steel; rosewood grips with Manta skin inlays. Built on custom order basis only. Not currently imported into U.S.

Perf.: $12,500   Exc.: $10,5000   VGood: $8500

KORTH COMBAT MODEL REVOLVER
Double action. Caliber: 357 Magnum. Barrel: 3", 4", 5-14", 6". Stocks: Checkered walnut, round butt. Sights: Baughman ramp front, fully adjustable rear. Features: Forged steel construction; trigger adjustable for slack, pull, and overtravel; hammer-forged barrel; removable cylinder. Imported from Germany by Korth U.S.A.

High polish blued finish		
New: $4700	**Perf.: $4200**	**Exc.: $3700**
Plasma-coated matte silver finish		
New: $5000	**Perf.: $4700**	**Exc.: $4200**
Plasma-coated high polish silver finish		
New: $5700	**Perf.: $5200**	**Exc.: $4400**

KORTH SPORT MODEL REVOLVER
Similar to Combat model but has square-butt stocks, fully adjustable target rear sight and undercut Patridge front. Imported from Germany by Korth U.S.A.

High polish blued finish		
New: $5700	**Perf.: $5500**	**Exc.: $4500**

Plasma-coated matte silver finish		
New: $6200	**Perf.: $5700**	**Exc.: $5200**
Plasma-coated high polish silver finish		
New: $6700	**Perf.: $6200**	**Exc.: $5700**

KORTH MATCH MODEL REVOLVER
Double action. Caliber: 22 LR, 32 S&W Long.. Barrel: 5-14", 6". Stocks: Adjustable stippled target match type. Sights: undercut Patridge front, fully adjustable rear with interchangeable blades. Features: Forged steel construction; trigger adjustable for slack, pull, and overtravel; hammer-forged barrel; removable cylinder. Imported from Germany by Korth U.S.A.

High polish blued finish		
New: $5700	**Perf.: $5200**	**Exc.: $4700**
Plasma-coated matte silver finish		
New: $6200	**Perf.: $6000**	**Exc.: $5700**
Plasma-coated high polish silver finish		
New: $6700	**Perf.: $6200**	**Exc.: $5700**

KORTH REVOLVER
Double action. Caliber: 22 LR, 22 Mag., 32 H&R Mag., 32 S&W Long, 9mm Para., 357 Magnum. Barrel: 3", 4", 6". Stocks: Checkered walnut sport or combat grips. Sights: Blade front, fully adjustable rear. Four interchangeable cylinders available; comes with two per caliber. High polish blue; presentation models have gold trim. Formerly imported from Germany by Mandall Shooting Supplies. No longer produced.

Perf.: $2700   Exc.: $2200   VGood: $1900

Korth Semi-Automatic

Lahti Finnish
Model L-35

Lahti Swedish
Model 40

L.A.R. Grizzly 50 Mark V

L.A.R. Grizzly Win.
Mag. Mark IV

Laseraim Arms
Series I

KORTH SEMI-AUTOMATIC (OLD MODEL)

Semi-automatic; double action; 9mm Para., 9x21mm; 10-shot capacity. Barrel: 4", 5", 6". Weight: 35 oz. Features: Forged steel frame and slide, adjustable combat sights, checkered walnut grips, matte or polished blue finish. Introduced 1985, discontinued 1989. Seldom encountered.

Perf.: $3000   **Perf.:** $2700   **Exc.:** $2200

KORTH SEMI-AUTOMATIC (NEW MODEL)

Semi-automatic; double action; 9mm Para., 40 S&W. Barrel: 4", 5". Grips: Checkered walnut. Sights: Ramp front, fully adjustable rear. Features: Forged steel construction, locked breech, recoil operated. Imported from Germany by Korth USA.

New: $6300   **Perf.:** $6000   **Exc.:** $5500

Plasma-coated matte silver finish

New: $7200   **Perf.:** $6500   **Exc.:** $6000

Plasma-coated high polish silver finish

New: $7700   **Perf.:** $7200   **Exc.:** $6700

LAHTI FINNISH MODEL L-35

Semi-automatic; 9mm Para.; 8-shot magazine; 4-3/4-inch barrel; fixed sights; checkered plastic stocks; blued finish. Manufactured on a limited basis in Finland from 1935 to 1954.

1st Variation serial number range 1001-3700

Perf.: $2500   **Exc.:** $2250   **VGood:** $1650

2nd Variation serial number range 3701-4700

Perf.: $2500   **Exc.:** $2250   **VGood:** $2000

3rd Variation serial number range 4701-6800

Perf.: $1350   **Exc.:** $1100   **VGood:** $850

4th Variation serial number range 6801-9100

Perf.: $1100   **Exc.:** $900   **VGood:** $850

Add $3000-$3500 to above prices for original shoulder stock
Add $1800-$2250 for more recent manufacture shoulder stock

LAHTI SWEDISH MODEL 40

Semi-automatic; 9mm Para.; 8-shot magazine; 4-3/4-inch barrel; fixed sights; checkered plastic stocks;

blued finish. Manufactured in Sweden by Husqvarna. Manufactured 1942 to 1946.

Exc.: $550   **VGood:** $400   **Good:** $300

L.A.R. GRIZZLY WIN. MAG. MARK I

Semi-automatic; single action; 30 Mauser, 357 Mag., 357/45 Grizzly Win. Mag., 10mm, 45 ACP, 45 Win. Mag.; 7-shot magazine; 5-1/2-inch, 6-1/2-inch barrel; 10-5/8-inch overall length; weighs 51 oz.; ramped blade front, adjustable rear sight; no-slip rubber combat grips; ambidextrous safeties; conversion units 45 to 357 Mag., 45 ACP, 10mm, 45 Win. Mag. available; phosphated finish. Introduced 1984; dropped 1999.

Perf.: $1175   **Exc.:** $950   **VGood:** $775

L.A.R. GRIZZLY WIN. MAG. MARK I, 8-INCH, 10-INCH

Same specs as Mark I standard except 8-inch, 10-inch barrel; lengthened slide. Introduced 1984; dropped 1999.

Perf.: $1200   **Exc.:** $1000   **VGood:** $900

10-inch barrel

Perf.: $1250   **Exc.:** $1100   **VGood:** $950

L.A.R. GRIZZLY WIN. MAG. MARK II

Same specs as the Grizzly Win. Mag. Mark I except fixed sights; standard safeties. Introduced 1986; discontinued 1986.

Perf.: $1150   **Exc.:** $975   **VGood:** $875

L.A.R. GRIZZLY 44 MAG. MARK IV

Semi-automatic; single action; 44 Mag.; 7-shot magazine; 5-1/2-inch, 6-1/2-inch barrel; 10-5/8-inch overall length; weighs 51 oz.; ramped blade front, adjustable rear sight; no-slip rubber combat grips; beavertail grip safety; matte blue, hard chrome, chrome or nickel finish. Introduced 1991; dropped 1999.

Perf.: $1200   **Exc.:** $1000   **VGood:** $900

Hand chrome, chrome or nickel finish

Perf.: $1350   **Exc.:** $1150   **VGood:** $1050

L.A.R. GRIZZLY 50 MARK V

Semi-automatic; single action; 50 AE; 6-shot magazine; 5-1/2-inch, 6-1/2-inch barrel; 10-5/8-inch

overall length; weighs 56 oz.; ramped blade front, adjustable rear sight; no-slip rubber combat grips; ambidextrous safeties; conversion units available; phosphated finish. Made in U.S. by L.A.R. Mfg., Inc. Introduced, 1993; dropped 1999.

New: $1400   **Perf.:** $1300   **Exc.:** $1200

LASERAIM ARMS SERIES I

Semi-automatic; single action; 10mm Auto, 45 ACP; 8-shot magazine (10mm), 7-shot (45 ACP); 4-3/8-inch, 6-inch barrel, with compensator; 9-3/4-inch overall length (6-inch barrel); weighs 46 oz.; pebble-grained black composite grips; blade front sight, fully-adjustable rear; barrel compensator; stainless steel construction; ambidextrous safety-levers; extended slide release; integral mount for laser sight; matte black Teflon finish. Made in U.S. by Emerging Technologies, Inc. Introduced 1993; dropped 1999.

New: $500   **Perf.:** $450   **Exc.:** $400

With adjustable sight

New: $550   **Perf.:** $500   **Exc.:** $450

With fixed sight and Auto Illusion red dot sight system

New: $650   **Perf.:** $600   **Exc.:** $550

With fixed sight and Laseraim Laser with Hotdot

New: $750   **Perf.:** $700   **Exc.:** $650

LASERAIM ARMS SERIES II

Semi-automatic; single action; 10mm Auto, 45 ACP, 40 S&W; 8-shot magazine (10mm), 7-shot (45 ACP); 3-3/8-inch, 5-inch barrel without compensator; weighs 43 oz. (5-inch), 37 oz. (3-3/8-inch); pebble-grained black composite grips; blade front sight, fixed or windage-adjustable rear; stainless steel construction; ambidextrous safety-levers; extended slide release; integral mount for laser sight; matte stainless finish. Made in U.S. by Emerging Technologies, Inc. Introduced 1993; dropped 1999.

New: $550   **Perf.:** $500   **Exc.:** $450

With adjustable sight (5-inch barrel)

New: $575   **Perf.:** $525   **Exc.:** $475

With fixed sight and Auto Illusion red dot sight

New: $600   **Perf.:** $525   **Exc.:** $500

With fixed sight and Laseraim Laser with Hotdot

New: $650   **Perf.:** $575   **Exc.:** $550

Laseraim Arms
Series III

Le Francais
Pocket Model

Les Incorporated
Rogak P-18

Le Francais
Army Model

Liberty
Mustang

Le Francais
Policeman Model

Lignose Model
3A Einhand

LASERAIM ARMS SERIES III

Semi-automatic; single action; 10mm Auto, 45
ACP; 8-shot magazine (10mm), 7-shot (45 ACP);
5-inch barrel with dual-port compensator; 7-5/8-
inch overall length; weighs 43 oz.; pebble-grained
black composite grips; blade front sight, fixed or
windage-adjustable rear; stainless steel construction;
ambidextrous safety-levers; extended slide release;
integral mount for laser sight; matte stainless
finish. Made in U.S. by Emerging Technologies, Inc.
Introduced 1994; dropped 1999.

With fixed sight		
New: $600	**Perf.:** $550	**Exc.:** $500
With adjustable sight		
New: $625	**Perf.:** $575	**Exc.:** $525
With fixed sight and Dream Team Laseraim laser sight		
New: $700	**Perf.:** $650	**Exc.:** $600

LASERAIM ARMS SERIES IV

Semi-automatic; 45 ACP; 7-shot magazine; 3-3/8-
inch, 5-inch barrel; weighs 37 oz.; full serrated slide;
diamond wood grips; stainless steel construction;
blade front, fully-adjustable rear sight; ambidextrous
safety levers; integral mount for laser sight. Made
in U.S. by Emerging Technologies, Inc. Introduced
1996; dropped 1999.

New: $675	**Perf.:** $625	**Exc.:** $575

LE FRANCAIS ARMY MODEL

Semi-automatic; double action; 9mm Browning Long;
8-shot magazine; 5-inch flip up barrel; 7-3/4-inch
overall length; fixed sights; checkered European
walnut stocks; blued finish. Manufactured 1928 to
1938.

Exc.: $1500	**VGood:** $1100	**Good:** $850

Add 10 percent to above prices for finned barrel
Add 50 percent-100 percent for engraved examples,
depending on amount of coverage

LE FRANCAIS POCKET MODEL

Semi-automatic; double action; 32 ACP; 7-shot
magazine; 3-1/2-inch flip-up barrel; 6-inch overall
length; fixed sights; checkered hard rubber stocks;
blued finish. Manufactured in France. Introduced
1950; discontinued 1965. Rare in the U.S.

Exc.: $750	**VGood:** $600	**Good:** $450

LE FRANCAIS POLICEMAN MODEL

Semi-automatic; double action; 25 ACP; 7-shot
magazine; 2-1/2-inch, 3-1/2-inch flip up barrel; fixed
sights; hard rubber stocks; blued finish. Some are
marked "FRANCO." Introduced 1914; discontinued
about 1960.

Exc.: $375	**VGood:** $300	**Good:** $260

LES INCORPORATED ROGAK P-18

Semi-automatic; double action; 9mm Para.; 18-shot
magazine; 5-1/2-inch barrel; post front sight, V-notch
rear, drift adjustable for windage; checkered resin
stocks; stainless steel; matte or deluxe high gloss
finishes. Introduced 1977; discontinued 1981.

Exc.: $525	**VGood:** $400	**Good:** $300
Deluxe high gloss finish		
Exc.: $550	**VGood:** $425	**Good:** $325

LIBERTY MUSTANG

Revolver; single action; 22 LR, 22 WMR or combo;
8-shot cylinder; 5-inch barrel; 10-1/2-inch overall
length; weighs 34 oz.; blade front, adjustable rear
sight; smooth rosewood grips; side ejector rod; blued
finish. Imported from Italy by Liberty. Introduced
1976; discontinued 1980.

Exc.: $150	**VGood:** $135	**Good:** $110

LIGNOSE MODEL 2 POCKET

Semi-automatic; 25 ACP; 6-shot magazine; 2-
inch barrel; 4-1/2-inch overall length; checkered
hard rubber stocks; blued finish. Manufactured in
Germany from 1920 first under Bergmann name, then
Lignose to late 1920s.

Exc.: $325	**VGood:** $265	**Good:** $215

LIGNOSE MODEL 2A EINHAND

Same specs as Model 2 Pocket except sliding trigger
guard allows slide retraction with trigger finger.

Exc.: $550	**VGood:** $450	**Good:** $325

LIGNOSE MODEL 3 POCKET

Semi-automatic; 25 ACP; 9-shot magazine; 2-
inch barrel; 4-1/2-inch overall length; checkered
hard rubber stocks; blued finish. Manufactured in
Germany.

Exc.: $250	**VGood:** $220	**Good:** $195

LIGNOSE MODEL 3A EINHAND

Same specs as Model 3 Pocket except sliding trigger
guard allows slide retraction with trigger finger.

Exc.: $495	**VGood:** $425	**Good:** $350

LILIPUT 4.25

Semi-automatic; 4.25mm; 6-shot; 1-13/16-inch
barrel; 3-1/2-inch overall length; weighs 8 oz.; blue or
nickel finish. Made by August Menz, Suhl, Germany.
Introduced 1920.

Exc.: $1500	**VGood:** $950	**Good:** $675

LILIPUT 25 ACP

Semi-automatic; 25 ACP; 6-shot; 2-inch barrel;
4-1/8-inch overall length; weighs 10 oz.; blue or
nickel finish. Made by August Menz, Suhl Germany.
Introduced 1925. Manufactured in large quantities
prior to onset of World War Two. Served as the later
design basis for the Lorcin line in the U.S.

Exc.: $350	**VGood:** $300	**Good:** $250

LJUTIC LJ II

Derringer; double action; 22 WMR; 2-shot; 2-3/4-
inch side-by-side barrels; fixed sights; checkered
walnut stocks; vent rib; positive safety; stainless steel
construction. Introduced 1981; dropped 1989. About
1000 produced.

Perf.: $1500	**Exc.:** $1200	**VGood:** $1000

LLAMA IIIA SMALL FRAME

Semi-automatic; single action; 380 ACP, 32 ACP
(disc. 1993); 7-shot magazine; 3-11/16-inch barrel;
6-1/2-inch overall length; weighs 23 oz.; adjustable
target sights; checkered thumbrest plastic grips; vent
rib; grip safety; loaded chamber indicator; blued,
chrome engraved, blue engraved or gold engraved
finishes. Early versions were sans vent rib, had
lanyard ring, no thumbrest on grips. Introduced 1951;
no longer in production.

Blued finish		
Perf.: $250	**Exc.:** $200	**VGood:** $175

Liliput 4.25

Ljutic LJII

Llama IIIA
Small Frame

Llama IX-C
New Generation
Large Model

Llama XI
Large Frame

Llama VIII

Llama XV
Small Frame

Chrome engraved		
Perf.: $275	**Exc.:** $225	**VGood:** $200
Blue engraved		
Perf.: $275	**Exc.:** $225	**VGood:** $200
Gold engraved		
Perf.: $500	**Exc.:** $450	**VGood:** $400

LLAMA VIII

Semi-automatic; 38 Super; 9-shot magazine; 5-inch barrel; 8-1/2-inch overall length; fixed sights; hand-checkered walnut grips; vent rib; grip safety; blued, chrome, chrome engraved or blued engraved finishes. Imported by Stoeger. Introduced 1952; no longer in production.

Perf.: $375	**Exc.:** $350	**VGood:** $325
Chrome finish		
Perf.: $395	**Exc.:** $370	**VGood:** $270
Chrome engraved		
Perf.: $425	**Exc.:** $400	**VGood:** $375
Blue engraved		
Perf.: $400	**Exc.:** $350	**VGood:** $325

LLAMA IX LARGE FRAME

Semi-automatic; single action; 9mm, 38 Super, 45 ACP; 9-shot magazine (9mm, 38 Super), 7-shot (45 ACP); 5-1/8-inch barrel; 41 oz.; adjustable sights; black plastic grips; blued or satin chrome finish. Introduced 1936; no longer imported.

Perf.: $325	**Exc.:** $275	**VGood:** $225
Satin chrome finish		
Perf.: $350	**Exc.:** $300	**VGood:** $250

LLAMA IX-A LARGE FRAME

Semi-automatic; 45 ACP; 7-shot magazine; 5-1/8-inch barrel; 8-1/2-inch overall length; weighs 36 oz.; hand-checkered walnut grips; vent rib; fixed sights; grip safety; loaded chamber indicator; blue, chrome, chrome engraved or blue engraved finishes. Introduced 1952; no longer imported.

Perf.: $375	**Exc.:** $325	**VGood:** $275
Chrome finish		
Perf.: $400	**Exc.:** $350	**VGood:** $300
Chrome engraved		
Perf.: $450	**Exc.:** $400	**VGood:** $350

Blue engraved		
Perf.: $400	**Exc.:** $350	**VGood:** $300

LLAMA IX-B COMPACT FRAME

Semi-automatic; single action; 45 ACP; 7-shot magazine; 4-1/4-inch barrel; 7-7/8-inch overall length; weighs 34 oz.; checkered polymer grips; blade front sight, fully-adjustable rear; scaled-down version of Llama Large Frame; locked breech mechanism; manual and grip safeties; blue or chrome finish. Formerly imported from Spain by SGS Importers Int'l., Inc. Introduced 1985.

Perf.: $300	**Exc.:** $250	**VGood:** $225
Chrome finish		
Perf.: $325	**Exc.:** $275	**VGood:** $250

LLAMA IX-C NEW GENERATION LARGE FRAME

Semi-automatic; single action; 45 ACP; 13-shot magazine; 5-1/8-inch barrel; 8-1/2-inch overall length; 41 oz.; three-dot combat sights; military-style hammer; loaded chamber indicator; anatomically designed rubber grips; non-glare matte finish. Introduced 1994; Converted to 10-shot magazine 1995; no longer imported.

New: $350	**Perf.:** $300	**Exc.:** $250

LLAMA IX-D NEW GENERATION COMPACT FRAME

Semi-automatic; single action; 45 ACP; 13-shot; 4-1/4-inch barrel; 7-7/8-inch overall length; weighs 39 oz.; three-dot combat sights; rubber grips; non-glare matte finish. Converted to 10-shot 1995; no longer imported.

New: $350	**Perf.:** $300	**Exc.:** $250

LLAMA XA SMALL FRAME

Semi-automatic; 32 ACP; 7-shot magazine; 3-11/16-inch barrel; 6-1/2-inch overall length; adjustable target sights; checkered thumbrest plastic grips; grip safety; blued, chrome engraved or blue engraved finishes; successor to Llama X, which had no grip safety. Imported by Stoeger. Introduced 1951; no longer in production.

Exc.: $200	**VGood:** $175	**Good:** $150

Chrome engraved		
Exc.: $225	**VGood:** $200	**Good:** $150
Blue engraved		
Exc.: $225	**VGood:** $200	**Good:** $175

LLAMA XI

Semi-automatic; 9mm Para.; 8-shot magazine; 5-inch barrel; 8-1/2-inch overall length; adjustable sights; checkered thumbrest; plastic grips; vent rib; blued, chrome, chrome engraved or blued engraved finishes. Imported by Stoeger Arms. Introduced 1954; no longer in production.

Perf.: $275	**Exc.:** $250	**VGood:** $200
Chrome finish		
Perf.: $300	**Exc.:** $275	**VGood:** $250
Chrome engraved		
Perf.: $325	**Exc.:** $300	**VGood:** $275
Blue engraved		
Perf.: $325	**Exc.:** $300	**VGood:** $275

LLAMA XV SMALL FRAME

Semi-automatic; 22 LR; 8-shot magazine; 3-11/16-inch barrel; 6-1/2-inch overall length; weighs 23 oz.; adjustable target sights; checkered thumbrest plastic grips; vent rib; grip safety; blued, chrome engraved or blue engraved finishes. Introduced 1951; no longer in production.

Perf.: $225	**Exc.:** $200	**VGood:** $175
Chrome engraved		
Perf.: $250	**Exc.:** $225	**VGood:** $200
Blue engraved		
Perf.: $250	**Exc.:** $225	**VGood:** $200

LLAMA COMANCHE

Revolver; double action; 22 LR, 357 Mag.; 6-shot cylinder; 4-inch, 6-inch barrel; 9-1/4-inch overall length (4-inch barrel); weighs 28 oz.; blade front sight, fully-adjustable rear; checkered walnut stocks; ventilated rib; wide spur hammer; blue finish. Was imported from Spain by SGS Importers International, Inc. No longer imported.

Exc.: $245	**VGood:** $175	**Good:** $150

Llama Comanche

Llama Martial

Llama Martial Deluxe

Llama Max-I

Llama Max-I New Generation Large Frame

Llama Micromax 380

Llama Minimax Series

Llama Model 82

LLAMA COMANCHE I

Revolver; double action; 22 LR; 6-shot cylinder; 6-inch barrel; 11-1/4-inch overall length; target-type sights; checkered walnut stocks; blued finish. Introduced in 1977, replacing Martial 22 model; discontinued 1982.

Exc.: $200   **VGood:** $175   **Good:** $150

LLAMA COMANCHE II

Same specs as Comanche I except 38 Spl.; 4-inch barrel. Introduced 1977; discontinued 1982.

Exc.: $175   **VGood:** $150   **Good:** $135

LLAMA COMANCHE III

Same specs as Comanche I except 22 LR, 357 Mag.; 4-inch, 6-inch, 8-1/2-inch barrel; 9-1/4-inch overall length; ramp front, adjustable rear sight; blued, satin chrome or gold finish. Introduced 1977 as "Comanche"; renamed 1977; no longer in production.

Perf.: $295   **Exc.:** $225   **VGood:** $200

Satin chrome finish

Perf.: $300   **Exc.:** $250   **VGood:** $225

Gold finish

Perf.: $750   **Exc.:** $650   **VGood:** $500

LLAMA MARTIAL

Revolver; double action; 22 LR, 38 Spl.; 6-shot cylinder; 4-inch barrel (38 Spl.), 6-inch (22 LR); 11-1/4-inch overall length (6-inch barrel); target sights; hand-checkered walnut stocks; blued finish. Imported by Stoeger. Introduced 1969; discontinued 1976.

Exc.: $250   **VGood:** $205   **Good:** $180

LLAMA MARTIAL DELUXE

Same specs as Martial model except choice of satin chrome, chrome engraved, blued engraved, gold engraved finishes; simulated pearl stocks.

Satin chrome finish

Exc.: $275   **VGood:** $250   **Good:** $220

Chrome engraved

Exc.: $305   **VGood:** $275   **Good:** $250

Blue engraved

Exc.: $290   **VGood:** $265   **Good:** $235

Gold engraved

Exc.: $750   **VGood:** $600   **Good:** $500

Gold damascened

Exc.: $1430   **VGood:** $880   **Good:** $660

LLAMA MAX-I AUTO PISTOLS

Semi-automatic; 45 ACP; 7-shot; 5-1/8-inch barrel; 36 oz.; 8-1/2-inch overall; black rubber grips; blade front, rear sight adjustable for windage, three-dot system; single-action trigger; skeletonized combat-style hammer; steel frame; extended manual and grip safeties. Introduced 1995. Imported from Spain by Import Sports, Inc.

Price: 45 ACP, 7-shot, Government model $291.95
Price: As above, satin chrome finish $314.95

LLAMA MAX-I NEW GENERATION LARGE FRAME

Semi-automatic; single action; 9mm Para., 45 ACP; 9-shot magazine (9mm), 7-shot (45 ACP); 5-1/8-inch barrel; 8-1/2-inch overall length; weighs 36 oz.; blade front sight, windage-adjustable rear; black rubber grips; three-dot system; skeletonized combat-style hammer; steel frame; extended manual and grip safeties; blue or duo-tone finish. Formerly imported from Spain by Import Sports, Inc. Introduced 1995.

New: $265   **Perf.:** $220   **Exc.:** $175

Duo-tone finish

New: $325   **Perf.:** $300   **Exc.:** $250

LLAMA MAX-I NEW GENERATION COMPACT FRAME

Same specs as the Max-I except 7-shot; 4-1/4-inch barrel; 7-7/8-inch overall length; weighs 34 oz. Imported from Spain by Import Sports, Inc. Introduced 1995; no longer imported.

New: $300   **Perf.:** $275   **Exc.:** $225

Duo-tone finish

New: $350   **Perf.:** $325   **Exc.:** $300

LLAMA MICROMAX 380 AUTO PISTOL

Semi-automatic; 380 ACP; 7-shot magazine; 3-11/16-inch barrel; 23 oz.; 6-1/2-inch overall; checkered grips made of high impact polymer; 3-dot combat sights; single action design; mini custom extended slide release; mini custom extended beavertail grip safety; combat-style hammer.

Introduced 1997. Imported from Spain by Import Sports, Inc.

New: $260   **Perf.:** $225   **Exc.:** $200

Satin chrome

New: $225   **Perf.:** $250   **Exc.:** $225

LLAMA MINIMAX SERIES

Semi-automatic; 9mm Para., 8-shot; 40 S&W, 7-shot; 45 ACP, 6-shot magazine. Barrel: 3-1/2-inch. Weight: 35 oz. Length: 7-1/3-inch overall. Stocks: Checkered rubber. Sights: Three-dot combat. Features: Single action, skeletonized combat-style hammer, extended slide release, cone-style barrel, flared ejection port. Introduced 1996. Imported from Spain by Import Sports, Inc.

New: $300   **Perf.:** $255   **Exc.:** $205

Duo-tone finish (45 only) or satin chrome

New: $320   **Perf.:** $275   **Exc.:** $225

LLAMA MINIMAX-II AUTO PISTOL

Same as the Minimax except in 45 ACP only, with 10-shot staggered magazine. Introduced 1997. Imported from Spain by Import Sports, Inc.

New: $300   **Perf.:** $275   **Exc.:** $225

Satin chrome

New: $325   **Perf.:** $300   **Exc.:** $250

LLAMA MODEL 82

Semi-automatic; double action; 9mm Para.; 15-shot magazine; 4-1/4-inch barrel; 8-inch overall length; weighs 39 oz.; blade-type front sight, drift-adjustable rear; 3-dot system; matte black polymer stocks; ambidextrous safety; blued finish. Made in Spain. Introduced 1987; discontinued 1993.

Perf.: $650   **Exc.:** $600   **VGood:** $550

LLAMA MODEL 87 COMPETITION MODEL

Semi-automatic; 9mm Para.; 14-shot magazine; 6-inch barrel; 9-1/2-inch overall length; weighs 47 oz.; Patridge-type front sight, fully-adjustable rear; Polymer composition stocks; built-in ported compensator; oversize magazine, safety releases; fixed barrel bushing; extended triggerguard; beveled magazine well. Made in Spain. Introduced 1989; discontinued 1993.

Perf.: $995   **Exc.:** $850   **VGood:** $750

Llama Omni

Llama Super Comanche IV

Lorcin L-9mm

Lorcin L-25

Lorcin L-22

Lorcin L-380

Luger Model 1900 Commercial

LLAMA OMNI

Semi-automatic; double action; 9mm Para., 45 ACP; 13-shot magazine (9mm), 7-shot (45 ACP); 4-1/4-inch barrel; 7-3/4-inch overall length (45 ACP), 8-inch (9mm); weighs 40 oz.; adjustable sights; checkered plastic stocks; ball-bearing action; double sear bars; articulated firing pin; low-friction rifling; blued finish. Made in Spain. Introduced 1982; dropped 1986.

9mm version
Exc.: $440   **VGood:** $380   **Good:** $330

45 ACP version
Exc.: $395   **VGood:** $360   **Good:** $320

LLAMA SUPER COMANCHE IV

Revolver; double action; 44 Mag.; 6-shot cylinder; 6-inch, 8-1/2-inch barrel; adjustable sights; oversize walnut grips; wide hammer, trigger; blued finish. No longer imported.

Perf.: $325   **Exc.:** $275   **VGood:** $250

LLAMA SUPER COMANCHE V

Same specs as Super Comanche IV except 357 Mag. only; 4-inch barrel also available. Discontinued 1988.

Perf.: $300   **Exc.:** $250   **VGood:** $200

LORCIN L-9MM

Semi-automatic; single action; 9mm Para.; 10- or 13-shot magazine; 4-1/2-inch barrel; 7-1/2-inch overall length; weighs 31 oz.; grooved black composition grips; fixed sights with three-dot system; matte black finish; hooked triggerguard; grip safety. Made in U.S. by Lorcin Engineering. Introduced 1994; dropped 1999.

New: $125   **Perf.:** $110   **Exc.:** $90

LORCIN L-22

Semi-automatic; single action; 22 LR; 9-shot magazine; 2-1/2-inch barrel; 5-1/4-inch overall length; weighs 16 oz.; black combat, or pink or pearl grips; fixed three-dot sight system; chrome or black Teflon finish. From Lorcin Engineering. Introduced 1989; dropped 1999

Perf.: $75   **Exc.:** $60   **VGood:** $50

Pink grips
Perf.: $80   **Exc.:** $65   **VGood:** $55

LORCIN L-25

Semi-automatic; single action; 25 ACP; 7-shot magazine; 2-5/16-inch barrel; 4-5/8-inch overall length; weighs 14-1/2 oz.; fixed sights; smooth composition stocks; black/gold, chrome/satin chrome, black finish. Made in U.S. by Lorcin Engineering. Introduced 1989; dropped 1999.

Perf.: $65   **Exc.:** $50   **VGood:** $45

LORCIN LADY LORCIN

Same specifications as above except with pink grips. Introduced 1990; dropped 1999.

Perf.: $70   **Exc.:** $60   **VGood:** $50

LORCIN L-32

Semi-automatic; single action; 32 ACP; 7-shot magazine; 3-1/2-inch barrel; 6-5/8-inch overall length; weighs 23 oz.; fixed sights; grooved composition grips; black Teflon or chrome finish with black grips. Made in U.S. by Lorcin Engineering. Introduced 1992; dropped 1999.

New: $80   **Perf.:** $70   **Exc.:** $60

LORCIN L-380

Semi-automatic; single action; 380 ACP; 7-shot magazine; 3-1/2-inch barrel; 6 5/8-inch overall length; weighs 23 oz.; fixed sights; grooved composition grips; black Teflon or chrome finish with black grips. Made in U.S. by Lorcin Engineering. Introduced 1992; dropped 1999.

New: $85   **Perf.:** $75   **Exc.:** $65

LORCIN LH-380

Semi-automatic; 380 ACP; 10-shot magazine; 4-1/2-inch barrel; 7-1/2-inch overall length; weighs 31 oz.; grooved black compostion grips; fixed sights with three-dot system; matte black finish; hooked triggerguard; grip safety. Similar to Model L9MM. Made in U.S. by Lorcin Engineering. Introduced 1994; dropped 1999.

New: $125   **Perf.:** $115   **Exc.:** $100

LORCIN LT-25

Semi-automatic; single action; 25 ACP; 7-shot magazine; 2-1/3-inch barrel; 4-2/3-inch overall length; weighs 14-1/2 oz.; fixed sights; smooth composition grips; available in chrome, black Teflon or camouflage. Made in U.S. by Lorcin Engineering. Introduced 1989; dropped 1999.

New: $60   **Perf.:** $50   **Exc.:** $40

LORCIN O/U DERRINGER

Stainless steel construction, .357 Mag. Or .45 LC; 2-shot over/under 3-1/2-inch barrels; synthetic grips; rebounding hammer; fixed sights. Made in U.S. by Lorcin Engineering. Introduced 1996; dropped 1998.

New: $95   **Perf.:** $80   **Exc.:** $65

LUGER MODEL 1900 COMMERCIAL

Semi-automatic; 7.65mm Para.; 7-shot magazine; 4-3/4-inch barrel; 9-1/4-inch overall length; fixed sights; toggle-joint action; grip safety; checkered wood grips; blued finish. Toggle marked in script "DWM" for Deutsche Waffen und Munitionsfabrik. Distinguished by dished toggle knobs with a lock, recessed breechblock.

Exc.: $3500   **VGood:** $2750   **Good:** $2000

LUGER MODEL 1900 SWISS

Same specs as Model 1900 Commercial except Swiss cross on chamber.

Exc.: $4000   **VGood:** $3250   **Good:** $2500

LUGER MODEL 1900 EAGLE

Same specs as Model 1900 Commercial except American eagle on chamber.

Exc.: $3500   **VGood:** $2750   **Good:** $1500

U.S. Army test guns s/n 6000-7000 distinguished by no proof marks
Exc.: $5000   **VGood:** $4250   **Good:** $2750

LUGER MODEL 1902

Semi-automatic; 9mm Para.; 7-shot magazine; 4-inch fat barrel; fixed sights; toggle-joint action; grip safety; checkered walnut grips; blued finish. Made with or without American eagle. Toggle marked in script "DWM" for Deutsche Waffen und Munitionsfabrik. Distinguished by fat 9mm barrel, dished toggle knobs with a lock, recessed breechblock.

Exc.: $9500   **VGood:** $7500   **Good:** $5500

Luger Model 1902 Carbine

Luger Model 1906 9mm

Luger Model 1906 Dutch Contract

Luger 1908 Bulgarian Contract

Luger 1906 Navy

LUGER MODEL 1902 CARBINE

Same specs as Model 1902 except 7.65mm Para.; 11-3/4-inch barrel with adjustable rear sight and checkered wood forend; contoured detachable wood stock.

Exc.: $14,500 **VGood:** $11,000 **Good:** $7500

Without stock

Exc.: $9500 **VGood:** $7000 **Good:** $5000

LUGER MODEL 1906 NAVY

Semi-automatic; 9mm Para.; 6-inch barrel; flat checkered toggle knobs; exposed breechblock with extractor that protrudes when chamber is loaded and exposes German word "GELADEN" (LOADED); adjustable rear sight on rear toggle link; coil instead of leaf recoil spring; grip safety; stock lug on rear of frame. Usually called "Model 1906 Navy" by collectors but was officially designated Model 1904 by the German navy. Note: Original 1904 Navies that have a toggle lock cut into right toggle knob like Model 1900 are very rare and valuable but beware of fakes.

Exc.: $3000 **VGood:** $2500 **Good:** $1500

With proper Navy stock

Exc.: $4050 **VGood:** $3550 **Good:** $2500

LUGER MODEL 1906

Semi-automatic; 7.65mm Para., 9mm Para.; 4-3/4-inch (7.65), 4-inch (9mm) barrel; flat checkered toggle knobs; exposed breechblock with extractor that protrudes when chamber is loaded and exposes German word "GELADEN" (LOADED); fixed rear sight on rear toggle link; coil instead of leaf recoil spring; no stock lug on rear frame. Note: 1906 Russian (crossed rifles on chamber) and Bulgarian (Bulgarian crest on chamber) very rare, very valuable.

With or without American Eagle, 7.65mm

Exc.: $2500 **VGood:** $2000 **Good:** $1090

With or without American Eagle, 9mm

Exc.: $2750 **VGood:** $2000 **Good:** $1250

With Swiss cross, 7.65mm only

Exc.: $3000 **VGood:** $2500 **Good:** $1500

Portuguese contract with M2 on chamber, 7.65mm only

Exc.: $2200 **VGood:** $1650 **Good:** $1050

Brazilian contract with no chamber marking, extractor marked "CARREGADA," 7.65mm only

Exc.: $2500 **VGood:** $1800 **Good:** $1000

Dutch contract with safety marked "RUST" with arrow, 9mm only.

Exc.: $2000 **VGood:** $1400 **Good:** $1200

Dutch Vickers made for the Dutch after WWI by Vickers in England.

Exc.: $2750 **VGood:** $2200 **Good:** $1700

LUGER MODEL 1908

Semi-automatic; 9mm Para.; 4-inch barrel; flat checkered toggle knobs; no grip safety; no hold-open device on early models, added later to many 1908 militaries; fixed rear sight on rear toggle link; coil instead of leaf recoil spring; no stock lug on rear frame.

COMMERCIAL

5-digit s/n and commercial proofs

Exc.: $1100 **VGood:** $850 **Good:** $600

ARMY

(Military proofs, chamber date from 1910 on, "DWM" or "Erfurt" on toggle)

Exc.: $1250 **VGood:** $800 **Good:** $500

BULGARIAN CONTRACT

("DWM" over chamber, Bulgarian crest on toggle, cyrillic safety markings. Rarely found in better than Good condition.)

VGood: $1500 **Good:** $950 **Fair:** $750

NAVY

(6-inch barrel, stock lug, adjustable rear sight, no chamber date)

Exc.: $2500 **VGood:** $1750 **Good:** $1250

LUGER MODEL 1914 MILITARY

Semi-automatic; 9mm Para.; 4-inch barrel; flat checkered toggle knobs; fixed rear sight; stock lug on frame; hold-open device; chamber dated 1914 to 1918.

DWM

Exc.: $850 **VGood:** $600 **Good:** $350

Erfurt

Exc.: $1250 **VGood:** $850 **Good:** $750

LUGER MODEL 1914 ARTILLERY

Same specs as the 1914 Military model except 8-inch barrel; adjustable sight on barrel. Add $300 for stock; $250 for holster (beware of fakes); $750 for 32-shot drum magazine.

DWM or Erfurt

Exc.: $2750 **VGood:** $1900 **Good:** $1200

LUGER MODEL 1914 NAVY

Same specs as 1914 Military except 6-inch barrel; adjustable sight on rear toggle link. DWM only.

Exc.: $3750 **VGood:** $2650 **Good:** $1850

LUGER MODEL 1920 MILITARY

Semi-automatic; 9mm Para.; 4-inch barrel. The Model 1914 Military Luger dated 1920, often in addition to the original date, to indicate compliance with the Treaty of Versailles for issue to the 100,000-man post-war German army.

Exc.: $900 **VGood:** $700 **Good:** $600

LUGER MODEL 1920 COMMERCIAL

Same specs as Military model except 7.65mm Para. or 9mm Para. Mostly reworked wartime DWM and Erfurt handguns or made up from surplus parts in every possible variation for commercial sale outside Germany. Marked GERMANY or MADE IN GERMANY. Note: Original Stoeger or Abercrombie & Fitch markings will add $2000 to any variation.

7.65mm Para.

Exc.: $900 **VGood:** $650 **Good:** $500

9mm Para.

Exc.: $900 **VGood:** $650 **Good:** $500

Navy, either caliber

Exc.: $2650 **VGood:** $1950 **Good:** $1250

Artillery, either caliber

Exc.: $2400 **VGood:** $1950 **Good:** $1250

Carbine, either caliber

Exc.: $7500 **VGood:** $6000 **Good:** $4000

Luger 1914 Artillery

Luger Model 1923 Commercial

Luna Model 300 Free Pistol

Luger Mauser Military (P.08)

Luger "Mauser Parabellum" Commemorative

LUGER MODEL 1923 COMMERCIAL

Semi-automatic; 7.65mm Para., 9mm Para.; 4-inch barrel. New manufacture by DWM and serial numbers continued from pre-war commercials starting about 73,000. Note: Original Stoeger or Abercrombie & Fitch markings will add $2000.

Exc.: $900   **VGood:** $600   **Good:** $450

Marked SAFE and LOADED

Exc.: $1500   **VGood:** $1075   **Good:** $875

LUGER SIMSON & CO.

Semi-automatic; 9mm Para.; 4-inch barrel. Made by Simson from surplus parts for military and limited commercial sale.

Undated

Exc.: $1250   **VGood:** $1000   **Good:** $750

Dated 1925 through 1928

Exc.: $2500   **VGood:** $2000   **Good:** $1500

LUGER SWISS MANUFACTURE

Semi-automatic; 7.65mm Para.; 4-3/4-inch barrel. Made at Waffenfabrik Bern for Swiss army, police and commercial sale. Model 1906 (sometimes called Model 1924) marked "Waffenfabrik Bern" with small Swiss cross on front of toggle and is mechanically same as DWM; Model 1929 has large Swiss cross in shield on front toggle; no checkering on toggle knobs; longer grip safety; other minor cosmetic differences.

Model 1906

Exc.: $2375   **VGood:** $1750   **Good:** $1250

Model 1929 Commercial ("P" before s/n)

Exc.: $2250   **VGood:** $1750   **Good:** $1250

Model 1929 Military

Exc.: $2500   **VGood:** $1850   **Good:** $1250

LUGER MAUSER COMMERCIAL

Semi-automatic; 7.65mm Para., 9mm Para. Distinguished by Mauser banner on toggle; for commercial or contract sale outside Germany, German police issue.

4-inch barrel, 9mm

Exc.: $2000   **VGood:** $1500   **Good:** $900

Nazi police proofs

Exc.: $2800   **VGood:** $2150   **Good:** $1550

4-inch barrel, 7.65mm

Exc.: $2250   **VGood:** $1750   **Good:** $1250

Artillery model

Exc.: $3500   **VGood:** $2500   **Good:** $1750

Luger Mauser Persian (4-inch barrel)

Exc.: $4000   **VGood:** $3500   **Good:** $2500

Portuguese Contract "GNR" (7.65mm, 4-3/4-inch barrel)

Exc.: $2250   **VGood:** $1750   **Good:** $1250

LUGER MAUSER MILITARY (P.08)

Semi-automatic; 9mm Para.; 4-inch barrel; front toggle marked with "S/42," "42" or "byf" Nazi manufacturer's codes. Date of manufacture on chamber ("K" for 1934; "G" for 1935 or four, or later two, digits for actual year).

Exc.: $1000   **VGood:** $750   **Good:** $400

"K" date

Exc.: $1500   **VGood:** $1100   **Good:** $800

"G" date

Exc.: $1250   **VGood:** $950   **Good:** $550

LUGER KRIEGHOFF

Semi-automatic; 9mm Para.; 4-inch barrel. Front toggle marked with anchor "HK" trademark over "KRIEGHOFF SUHL" and date of manufacture on chamber. A few from 1935 have "S" over chamber and only "SUHL."

Military

Exc.: $3250   **VGood:** $2750   **Good:** $1900

Commercial, "P" before s/n, usually undated chamber

Exc.: $3500   **VGood:** $2500   **Good:** $2000

LUGER MAUSER POST-WAR MANUFACTURE

In 1970 Mauser resumed limited production of the Luger using tooling purchased from the Swiss. Chambered in 7.65mm Para., 9mm Para.; 4-inch, 4-3/4-inch, 6-inch barrel; front toggle marked "Original MAUSER."

Perf.: $800   **Exc.:** $600   **VGood:** $500

With original box

New: $850   **Perf.:** $670   **Exc.:** $550

LUGER "MAUSER PARABELLUM" COMMEMORATIVES

A very limited number (250 each) of replica 1900 Swiss and Bulgarian, 1906 Russian and Navy as well as the 1902 carbine were produced by Mauser. Front toggles marked with gold inlaid "DWM" with appropriate gold inlaid inscription on side panel, cased in fitted leather case with accessories.

As new pistols

Exc.: $2500

As new carbines

Exc.: $4500

LUNA MODEL 200 FREE PISTOL

Single shot; falling block; 22 LR; 11-inch barrel; target sights; checkered, carved walnut stock, forearm; adjustable palm rest; set trigger; blued finish. Manufactured in Germany approximately 1929 to 1939.

Exc.: $1100   **VGood:** $950   **Good:** $850

LUNA MODEL 300 FREE PISTOL

Single shot; 22 Short; 11-inch barrel; target sights; set trigger; checkered, carved walnut stock, forearm; adjustable palm rest; blued finish. Manufactured in Germany approximately 1929 to 1939.

Exc.: $850   **VGood:** $750   **Good:** $500

MAB Model A

MAB Model B

MAB Model C

MAB Model D

MAB PA-15

MAB Model E

Magnum Research
Baby Eagle 9mm

Magnum Research
Desert Eagle

MAB MODEL A

Semi-automatic; 25 ACP; 6-shot magazine; 2-1/2-inch barrel; 4-1/2-inch overall length; no rear sight, fixed front; checkered plastic or hard rubber grips; based on Browning design; blued finish. Introduced in 1921; production suspended in 1942; production resumed in 1945 for importation into U.S. as WAC Model A or Le Defendeur; importation dropped in 1968. Manufactured by Manufacture d'Armes de Bayonne, France.

Exc.: $275   **VGood:** $225   **Good:** $180

MAB MODEL B

Semi-automatic; 25 ACP; 6-shot magazine; 2-inch barrel; 4-1/2-inch overall length; no rear sight, fixed front; hard rubber grips; blued finish. Introduced 1932; dropped 1949.

Exc.: $250   **VGood:** $235   **Good:** $200

MAB MODEL C

Semi-automatic; 32 ACP, 380 ACP; 7-shot magazine (32 ACP), 6-shot (380 ACP); 3-3/4-inch barrel; 6-inch overall length; fixed sights; black checkered hard rubber grips; push-button magazine release behind trigger; blued finish. Introduced 1933; made under German supervision during WWII. Importation discontinued 1968.

Exc.: $250   **VGood:** $235   **Good:** $200

MAB MODEL D

Semi-automatic; 32 ACP, 380 ACP; 9-shot magazine (32 ACP), 8-shot (380 ACP); 4-inch barrel; 7-inch overall length; fixed sights; black checkered hard rubber grips; push-button magazine release; blued finish. Introduced 1933; made under German supervision in WWII. Imported to U.S. as WAC Model D or MAB Le Gendarme. Importation discontinued 1968.

Exc.: $250   **VGood:** $235   **Good:** $200

MAB MODEL E

Semi-automatic; 25 ACP; 10-shot magazine; 3-1/4-inch barrel; 6-1/8-inch overall length; fixed sights; plastic grips; blued finish. Introduced 1949; imported into U.S. as WAC Model E. Importation discontinued 1968.

Exc.: $225   **VGood:** $210   **Good:** $150

MAB MODEL F

Semi-automatic; 22 LR; 10-shot magazine; 3-1/4-inch, 6-inch, 7-1/4-inch barrel; 10-3/4-inch overall length; windage-adjustable rear sight, ramp front; plastic thumbrest grips; blued finish. Introduced 1950; variation imported into U.S. as Le Chasseur. Importation discontinued 1968.

Exc.: $200   **VGood:** $165   **Good:** $135

MAB MODEL PA-15

Semi-automatic; 9mm Para.; 15-shot magazine; 4-1/2-inch barrel; 8-inch overall length; fixed sights; checkered plastic grips; blued finish. Still in production; not currently imported.

Perf.: $500   **Exc.:** $400   **VGood:** $325

MAGNUM RESEARCH BABY EAGLE 9MM

Semi-automatic; double action; 9mm Para.; 40 S&W, 41 A.E.; 4-3/8-inch barrel; 8-1/16-inch overall length; weighs 35 oz.; high-impact polymer grips; combat sights; polygonal rifling; ambidextrous safety; matte black or chrome finish. Imported by Magnum Research. Introduced 1992.

Perf.: $400   **Exc.:** $350   **VGood:** $300

Chrome finish

Perf.: $450   **Exc.:** $400   **VGood:** $325

MAGNUM RESEARCH BABY EAGLE 9MM MODEL F

Same specs as the standard model except has frame-mounted safety on left side.

Perf.: $425   **Exc.:** $375   **VGood:** $325

MAGNUM RESEARCH DESERT EAGLE

Semi-automatic; 357 Mag., 41 Mag., 44 Mag., 50 Mag.; 9-shot (357), 8-shot (41 Mag., 44 Mag.), 7-shot (50 Mag.); 6-inch, 10-inch, 14-inch interchangeable barrels; 10-1/4-inch overall length; weighs 62 oz. (357), 69 oz. (41,44), 72 oz. (50); wrap-around plastic stocks; blade on ramp front, combat-style rear sight; rotating three-lug bolt; ambidextrous safety; combat-style trigger guard; military epoxy finish; satin, bright nickel, hard chrome, polished and blued finishes available. Imported from Israel by Magnum Research, Inc.

Perf.: $1200   **Exc.:** $950   **VGood:** $775

50 Mag.

Perf.: $1300   **Exc.:** $1150   **VGood:** $950

MAGNUM RESEARCH LITTLE MAX REVOLVER

Caliber: 22 Hornet, 45 Colt, 454 Casull, 50 A.E. Barrel: 6-1/2-inch, 7-1/2-inch, 10-inch. Weight: 45 oz. Length: 13-inch overall (7-1/2-inch barrel). Stocks: Rubber. Sights: Ramp front, adjustable rear. Features: Single action; stainless steel construction. Announced 1998.

Perf.: $1000   **Exc. $850**   **VGood:** $600

Maxline model
(7-1/2-inch, 10-inch, 45 Colt, 45-70, 444 Marlin)

Perf.: $1000   **Exc. $850**   **VGood:** $600

MAGNUM RESEARCH LONE EAGLE

Single shot; 22 Hornet, 223, 22-250, 243, 7mm BR, 7mm-08, 30-30, 308, 30-06, 357 Max., 35 Rem., 358 Win., 44 Mag., 444 Marlin; 14-inch interchangeable barrel; 15-inch overall length; weighs 4 lbs. to 4 lbs. 7 oz.; composition thumbrest stock; no sights furnished; drilled and tapped for scope mounting and optional open sights; cannon-type rotating breech with spring-activated ejector; external cocking lever on left side of gun; ordnance steel with matte blue finish. Made in U.S.; marketed by Magnum Research, Inc. Introduced 1991.

New: $450   **Perf.:** $350   **Exc.:** $300

Magnum Research
Lone Eagle

Magnum Research
Mountain Eagle
Compact Edition

Magnum Research
Mountain Eagle

Manurhin Model
MR 32 Match

Manurhin Model
73 Sport

Manurhin
Model PP

Manurhin
Model PPK/S

MAGNUM RESEARCH MOUNTAIN EAGLE

Semi-automatic; single action; 22 LR; 10-shot magazine; 6-1/2-inch, 8-inch barrel; 10-5/8-inch overall length (6-1/2-inch barrel); weighs 21 oz.; serrated ramp front sight with interchangeable blades, fully-adjustable rear; one-piece impact-resistant polymer grip with checkered panels; interchangeable blades; injection molded grip frame; alloy receiver; hybrid composite barrel replicates shape of the Desert Eagle pistol; flat, smooth trigger. Made in U.S. Marketed by Magnum Research. Introduced 1992.

Perf.: $200   **Excc.:** $175   **Exc.:** $150

MAGNUM RESEARCH MOUNTAIN EAGLE COMPACT EDITION

Same specs as Mountain Eagle except 4-1/2-inch barrel; shorter grip; windage-adjustable rear sight; weighs 19-1/4 oz. Introduced 1995.

Perf.: $200   **Excc.:** $175   **Exc.:** $150

MAGNUM RESEARCH MOUNTAIN EAGLE TARGET EDITION

Same specs as the Mountain Eagle except 8-inch barrel; two-stage trigger. Made in U.S. Marketed by Magnum Research. Introduced 1992.

New: $200   **Perf.:** $175   **Exc.:** $150

MANDALL/CABANAS PISTOL

Caliber: 177, pellet or round ball; single shot. Barrel: 9-inch. Weight: 51 oz. Length: 19-inch overall. Stock: Smooth wood with thumbrest. Sights: Blade front on ramp, open adjustable rear. Features: Fires round ball or pellets with 22 blank cartridge. Automatic safety; muzzlebrake. Imported from Mexico by Mandall Shooting Supplies.

Perf.:$125   **Exc.:** $100   **VGood:** $85

MAKAROV SPECIAL EDITION PISTOL

Caliber: 9x18 Makarov, 8-shot magazine. Barrel: 3.68-inch. Weight: 24 oz. Length: 6.3-inch overall. Stocks: Textured composition. Sights: Blade front, rear drift-adjustable for windage; three-dot system. Features:

Available in polished blue and brushed chrome finishes. Extended magazine floorplate. Introduced 1998. Imported from Bulgaria by Miltex, Inc.

Perf.: $250   **Exc.:** $200   **VGood:** $110

MANURHIN MODEL 73 CONVERTIBLE

Revolver; single action; 22 LR/38 Spl., 22 LR/32 ACP; 6-shot cylinder; 5-3/4-inch barrel (38), 6-inch (32); interchangeable blade front sight, adjustable micrometer rear; checkered walnut stocks; blued finish. Made in France. Introduced 1988 by Manurhin International.

Perf.: $2000   **Exc.:** $1750   **VGood:** $1250

MANURHIN MODEL 73 DEFENSE

Revolver; single action; 357 Mag./38 Spl.; 6-shot cylinder; 2-1/2-inch, 3-inch, 4-inch barrel; fixed sights; checkered walnut stocks; blued finish. Made in France. Introduced 1988 by Manurhin International.

Perf.: $1100   **Exc.:** $950   **VGood:** $700

MANURHIN MODEL 73 GENDARMERIE

Same specs as Model 73 Defense except also offered with 5-1/4-inch, 6-inch, 8-inch barrel; distinguished by prominent ramped front sight, adjustable rear with rounded edge. Used by French police forces and government agencies.

Perf.: $1250   **Exc.:** $1000   **VGood:** $850

MANURHIN MODEL 73 SILHOUETTE

Same specs as Model 73 Defense except also offered in 22 LR; 10-inch, 10-3/4-inch heavy barrel with shroud; adjustable sights; contoured walnut stocks.

Perf.: $1750   **Exc.:** $1500   **VGood:** $1000

MANURHIN MODEL 73 SPORT

Same specs as Model 73 Defense except 6-inch barrel; 11-inch overall length; weighs 37 oz.; fully-adjustable rear sight; adjustable trigger; reduced hammer travel. Imported from France by Century International Arms. Introduced 1988; still in production.

Perf.: $1250   **Exc.:** $1000   **VGood:** $850

MANURHIN MODEL MR .32 MATCH

Revolver; 32 S&W Long; 6-shot cylinder; 6-inch barrel; 11-/4-inch overall length; weighs 42 oz.; interchangeable blade front sight, adjustable micrometer rear; anatomical target shaped but unfinished grips; externally adjustable trigger; trigger shoe. Made in France. Introduced 1984; discontinued 1986; was imported by Manurhin International.

Perf.: $750   **Exc.:** $600   **VGood:** $500

MANURHIN MODEL MR .38

Revolver; 38 Spl.; 6-shot cylinder; 5-3/4-inch barrel; interchangeable blade front sight, adjustable micrometer rear; anatomical target shaped but unfinished grips; externally adjustable trigger; trigger shoe. Made in France. Introduced 1984; discontinued 1986; was imported by Manurhin International.

Perf.: $750   **Exc.:** $600   **VGood:** $500

MANURHIN MODEL PP

Semi-automatic; double action; 22 LR, 32 ACP, 380 ACP; 10-shot magazine (22 LR), 8-shot (32 ACP), 7-shot (380 ACP); 3-7/8-inch barrel; 7-3/4-inch overall length; weighs 23 oz.; white-outline front, rear sights; checkered compostion stocks; hammer drop safety; all-steel construction; supplied with two magazines; blued finish. Made in France. 22 or 380 caliber worth 50 percent more than prices shown. Importation began in 1950s; dropped 1960s.

Perf.: $300   **Exc.:** $225   **VGood:** $20

MANURHIN MODEL PPK/S

Same specs as Model PP except 3-1/4-inch barrel; 6-1/8-inch overall length.

Perf.: $300   **Exc.:** $250   **VGood:** $225

With brushed chrome finish

Perf.: $350   **Exc.:** $300   **VGood:** $250

MAUSER MODEL 1896 CONEHAMMER

Semi-automatic; 7.63mm Mauser; 10-shot magazine; 5-1/2-inch barrel; 11-1/2-inch overall length; tangent rear sight; locked breech action; grooved wood or (rarely) hard rubber grips; blued finish. The first model, made from 1896-1898 and considered

Mauser Model 1896 Conehammer (fixed rear sight)

Mauser Model 1896 Conehammer 6-shot

Mauser Model 1896 Conehammer 20-Shot

Mauser Model 1896 "Flatside"

Mauser Model 1896 6-Shot (fixed rear sight)

Mauser Model 1896 "Pre-War" Bolo

Mauser Model 1896 6-Shot (tangent sight)

Mauser Model 1896 "Pre-War" Commercial

Mauser Model 1896 Carbine

antique under federal law, is distinguished by a "beehive" or cone-shaped hammer (though some have a much larger open ring hammer), wide trigger and milled frame panels. Serial numbers run up to 15000. Note: First few hundred had SYSTEM MAUSER engraved on top of chamber and bring a very high premium. Add $500 for matching stock holster; $100 for engraved dealer's name.

Exc.: $2000   **VGood:** $1500   **Good:** $950

Turkish contract with Turkish crest in side panel and serial/sight numbering in Cyrillic

Exc.: $5000   **VGood:** $3500   **Good:** $2000

With fixed rear sight, 4-5/8-inch barrel

Exc.: $2500   **VGood:** $2000   **Good:** $1500

MAUSER MODEL 1896 CONEHAMMER 6-SHOT

Same specs as standard model except shortened 6-shot magazine; may have fixed or adjustable rear sight.

Exc.: $6000   **VGood:** $4000   **Good:** $2500

MAUSER MODEL 1896 CONEHAMMER 20-SHOT

Same specs as standard model except fixed 20-shot magazine extending well below trigger guard; milled out or flat frame panels. Very high collector value.

Exc.: $35,000   **VGood:** $20,000 **Good:** $15,000

With original 20-shot stock holster

Exc.: $40,000 **VGood:** $25,000 **Good:** $20,000

MAUSER MODEL 1896 "FLATSIDE"

Semi-automatic; 7.63mm Mauser; 10-shot magazine; 5-1/2-inch barrel; 11-1/2-inch overall length; flat frame sides; narrow trigger; large ring hammer; tangent rear sight; locked breech action; grooved wood or (rarely) hard rubber grips; blued finish. The 6-shot flatsides are very rare and very valuable.

Exc.: $2000   **VGood:** $1500   **Good:** $1000

MAUSER MODEL 1899 "FLATSIDE" ITALIAN NAVY

Semi-automatic; 7.63mm Mauser; 10-shot magazine; 5-1/2-inch barrel; 11-1/2-inch overall length; flat frame sides; narrow trigger; large ring hammer;

tangent rear sight; locked breech action; grooved wood grips; blued finish. 5,000 flatsides made for Italian navy and distinguished by small "DV" on chamber side and crown over "AV" under barrel; serial numbered 1 to 5000.

Exc.: $2500   **VGood:** $2000   **Good:** $1000

MAUSER MODEL 1896 LARGE RING HAMMER

Semi-automatic; 7.63mm Mauser; 10-shot magazine; 5-1/2-inch barrel; 11-1/2-inch overall length; paneled frame sides like the Conehammer; narrow trigger; large ring hammer; tangent rear sight; locked breech action; grooved wood or (rarely) hard rubber grips; blued finish.

Exc.: $1750   **VGood:** $1350   **Good:** $950

MAUSER MODEL 1896 PRE-WAR BOLO

Semi-automatic; 7.63mm Mauser; 10-shot magazine; 3-15/16-inch barrel; 10-inch overall length; paneled frame sides; narrow trigger; large or small ring hammer; tangent rear sight; locked breech action; small grip frame with wood or hard rubber grips; blued finish.

Exc.: $2250   **VGood:** $1500   **Good:** $950

With original Bolo (short) stock-holster

Exc.: $3500   **VGood:** $2750   **Good:** $1750

MAUSER MODEL 1896 6-SHOT

Semi-automatic; 7.63mm Mauser; 6-shot magazine; 3-15/16-inch barrel; large or small-ring hammer; fixed or tangent rear sight.

Exc.: $4500   **VGood:** $3500   **Good:** $2000

MAUSER MODEL 1896 PRE-WAR COMMERCIAL

Semi-automatic; 7.63mm Mauser; 10-shot magazine; 5-1/2-inch barrel; 11-1/2-inch overall length; paneled frame sides like the Conehammer; narrow trigger; small ring hammer; tangent rear sight; locked breech action; grooved wood or (rarely) hard rubber grips; blued finish. Made 1905-1918. Higher serial numbered examples usually have German military proofs.

Exc.: $1000   **VGood:** $850   **Good:** $500

With Mauser banner over chamber

Exc.: $1500   **VGood:** $1250   **Good:** $1000

With Persian Lion crest on side s/n in 154000 range

Exc.: $2750   **VGood:** $2000   **Good:** $1500

MAUSER MODEL 1896 9MM EXPORT

Semi-automatic; 9mm Mauser; 10-shot magazine; 5-1/2-inch barrel; 11 1/2-inch overall length; paneled frame sides like the Conehammer; narrow trigger; small ring hammer; tangent rear sight; locked breech action; grooved wood or (rarely) hard rubber grips; blued finish.

Exc.: $1750   **VGood:** $1250   **Good:** $950

MAUSER MODEL 1896 CARBINE

Semi-automatic; 7.63mm; 10-shot; 11 3/4-inch, 16-inch barrel; take-down sporting carbine made on Mauser pistol action. Made in limited numbers from 1896 to about 1906 with paneled or smooth sides and with all three hammer styles. Very high collector value. Note: Very early cone-hammer and a few very late carbines chambered for 9mm Para. or 9mm Export bring a premium.

Exc.: $15,000 **VGood:** $12,500 **Good:** $9000

MAUSER MODEL 1916 "RED 9"

Semi-automatic; 9mm Para.; 10-shot; 5-1/2-inch barrel. Made under contract for the German army. Called by collectors "Red 9" because most (but not all) have large figure "9" cut into the wood grips and painted red to distinguish them from 7.63mm pistols also in use by army.

Exc.: $1350   **VGood:** $750   **Good:** $650

MAUSER MODEL 1896 WEIMAR REWORK

Many WWI Red 9 military pistols were reworked 1920-1921 to conform with the Treaty of Versailles by cutting barrels to 4-inch, replacing tangent sight with fixed rear sight. Usually identified by "1920" stamped on side.

Exc.: $850   **VGood:** $600   **Good:** $500

With Weimar navy markings

Exc.: $1250   **VGood:** $900   **Good:** $750

Mauser Model 1896
"French Gendarme"

Mauser Model
1896 Postwar Bolo

Mauser
Model 1930

Mauser Small Ring
Hammer Chinese Copy

Mauser
Shansei 45
Copy

Mauser Model
1910 Early

Mauser Model
1910/1934

Mauser Model
1914 Humpback

Mauser HSc Early

MAUSER MODEL 1896 "FRENCH GENDARME"

Semi-automatic; 7.63mm; 10-shot magazine; supposedly made for French occupation forces with 3-15/16-inch Bolo barrel but full-size grip frame; checkered hard rubber grips.

Exc.: $1000 **VGood:** $850 **Good:** $600

MAUSER MODEL 1896 POSTWAR BOLO

Semi-automatic; 7.63mm; 10-shot; 3-15/16-inch barrel; small grip frame with grooved wood grips. Made about 1920 through 1930.

Exc.: $950 **VGood:** $700 **Good:** $450

MAUSER MODEL 1930

Semi-automatic; 7.63mm; 10-shot; 5-1/4-inch barrel (early), 5-1/2-inch barrel. Slightly updated version of Model 1896 distinguished by small step in barrel, wide grip straps with 12-groove wood grips, high polish bright acid blue finish instead of duller rust blue. Note: A few 1930-type Mausers were made with detachable 10- or 20-shot magazines and are very rare and valuable. Beware of fakes made by welding up switch holes of a Model 1932.

Exc.: $1500 **VGood:** $1250 **Good:** $500

With proper stock-holster with Mauser banner, no serial number

Exc.: $2000 **VGood:** $1500 **Good:** $1100

Warning: Model 1932 (also called Model 712) pistols have a selector switch for full-auto fire as well as detachable magazine. They are illegal to own unless registered with the BATF.

MAUSER CHINESE COPIES OF THE MODEL 1896
TAKU NAVAL DOCKYARD

Semi-automatic; 7.63mm; 10-shot; 5-1/2-inch barrel; flat frame panel sides; large ring hammer; grooved wood grips. Marked "TAKU NAVAL DOCKYARD" on top of chamber.

Exc.: $1250 **VGood:** $850 **Good:** $500

With unmarked chamber

Exc.: $750 **VGood:** $500 **Good:** $300

MAUSER CHINESE SMALL RING HAMMER COPIES

Same specs as above except paneled frame sides; small ring hammer. Quality varies from quite good to simply awful. May be unmarked except for serial numbers with spurious Mauser markings (often misspelled) or with markings in Chinese.

Exc.: $450 **VGood:** $300 **Good:** $200

MAUSER SHANSEI 45 COPY

Semi-automatic; 45 ACP; 10-shot; 6-1/4-inch barrel; 12-1/2-inch overall length; weighs 3 lbs., 7 oz. Oversize version of the Model 1896 built in the 1930s for a Chinese warlord who liked the 45 cartridge. Note: A copy of this copy, recently made in China, has been imported and sold at $1000-$1500. If the condition of a Shansei seems too good, it is.

Exc.: $4500 **VGood:** $3000 **Good:** $2000

MAUSER MODEL 1910

Semi-automatic; 25 ACP; 9-shot; 3-1/8-inch barrel; 5-3/8-inch overall length; fixed sights; checkered walnut or (rarely) hard rubber wrap-around grips. Introduced 1910; dropped 1934.

Exc.: $250 **VGood:** $185 **Good:** $135

Early model with takedown latch above trigger (s/n below about 60000)

Exc.: $350 **VGood:** $250 **Good:** $185

MAUSER MODEL 1914

Semi-automatic; 32 ACP; 8-shot; 3-1/4-inch barrel; 6-1/8-inch overall length; fixed sights; checkered walnut or (rarely) hard rubber wrap-around grip. Introduced 1914; dropped 1934.

Exc.: $235 **VGood:** $185 **Good:** $135

Early model with hump on top of slide (s/n below about 3000)

Exc.: $2200 **VGood:** $1800 **Good:** $1250

MAUSER MODEL 1910/1934

Semi-automatic; 25 ACP; 9-shot; 3-1/8-inch barrel; 5-3/8-inch overall length. Like the Model 1910 except for swept-back grip of walnut or plastic, bright high polish blue or nickel (rare) instead of rust blue finish.

Exc.: $350 **VGood:** $250 **Good:** $175

MAUSER MODEL 1914

Semi-automatic; 32 ACP; 8-shot; 3-1/2-inch barrel; 6-1/8-inch overall length; fixed sights; swept-back grip of walnut or plastic; bright high polish blue instead of rust blue finish. Made from 1934 to 1940.

Exc.: $400 **VGood:** $300 **Good:** $175

With Nazi Navy eagle over M marking

Exc.: $700 **VGood:** $500 **Good:** $400

MAUSER WTP

Semi-automatic; 25 ACP; 6-shot; 2-1/2-inch barrel; 4-1/2-inch overall length; checkered wrap-around hard rubber grips; blue finish. Made from 1922 to 1938.

Exc.: $275 **VGood:** $150 **Good:** $125

MAUSER WTP II

Semi-automatic; 25 ACP; 6-shot; 2-inch barrel; 4-3/16-inch overall length; checkered plastic grips; blue finish. Made from 1938 to 1944.

Exc.: $350 **VGood:** $250 **Good:** $175

MAUSER HSC

Semi-automatic; double action; 32 ACP; 8-shot; 3-1/2-inch barrel; 6-1/2-inch overall length; checkered wood or plastic grips; blue finish. Made 1940 to 1946. Last production was during French occupation.

Exc.: $350 **VGood:** $275 **Good:** $200

With Nazi navy eagle over M marking

Exc.: $700 **VGood:** $500 **Good:** $400

Very early model with grip screws near bottom of grips

Exc.: $2200 **VGood:** $1800 **Good:** $1300

MAUSER HSC POST-WAR

Same specs as above except also made in 380 ACP; 7-shot. Made from 1962 to 1976.

Exc.: $300 **VGood:** $200 **Good:** $150

MAUSER HSC SUPER (GAMBA)

Semi-automatic; 32 ACP, 380, 3-1/2-inch barrel; 6-1/2-inch overall length; 13-shot magazine; checkered wood grips; double action; blue. Made for Mauser by Gamba in Italy; imported 1968-1981.

Exc.: $275 **VGood:** $225 **Good:** $175

Mauser HSc Super

Mauser WTP II

Medusa Model 47

Merrill Sportsman

Mitchell Arms 45 Gold Series

Mitchell Arms Alpha

MAUSER MODEL 80

Semi-automatic; single action; 9mm Para.; 13-shot magazine; 4-11/16-inch barrel; 8-inch overall length; weighs 32 oz.; checkered beechwood grips; blade front sight, windage-adjustable rear; uses basic Hi-Power design; polished blue finish. Made in Hungary for Mauser and imported from Germany by Precision Imports, Inc. Introduced 1992; importation dropped 1993.

Perf.: $450   **Exc.:** $400   **VGood:** $350

MAUSER MODEL 90

Semi-automatic; double action; 9mm Para.; 14-shot magazine; 4-11/16-inch barrel; 8-inch overall length; weighs 35 oz.; checkered beechwood grips; blade front sight, windage-adjustable rear; uses basic Hi-Power design; polished blue finish. Made in Hungary for Mauser and imported from Germany by Precision Imports, Inc. Introduced 1992; importation dropped 1993.

Perf.: $450   **Exc.:** $400   **VGood:** $350

MAUSER MODEL 90 COMPACT

Same specs as the Model 90 except 4-1/8-inch barrel; 7-1/2-inch overall length; weighs 33-1/2-inch. Imported from Germany by Precision Imports, Inc. Introduced 1992; importation dropped 1993.

Perf.: $500   **Exc.:** $450   **VGood:** $400

MEDUSA MODEL 47 REVOLVER

For most 9mm, 38 and 357 caliber cartridges; 6-shot cylinder. Barrel: 2-1/2-inch, 3-inch, 4-inch, 5-inch, 6-inch; fluted. Weight: 39 oz. Length: 10-inch overall (4-inch barrel). Stocks: Gripper-style rubber. Sights: Changeable front blades, fully adjustable rear. Patented extractor allows gun to chamber, fire and extract over 25 different cartridges in the .355- to .357 range, without half-moon clips. Steel frame and cylinder; match quality barrel. Matte blue finish. Introduced 1996. Made in U.S. by Phillips & Rogers, Inc.

Perf.: $950   **Exc.:** $800   **VGood:** $700

MERRILL SPORTSMAN

Single shot; 22 Short, 22 Long, 22 LR, 22 WMR, 22 Rem. Jet, 22 Hornet, 30 Herrett, 38 Spl. 45-70, 357

Mag., 256 Win. Mag., 45 Colt, 44 Mag., 30-30; 9-inch, 12-inch, 14-inch semi-octagon hinged barrel; adjustable rear sight, fixed front; uncheckered walnut grips with thumb, heel rest; hammerless; top rib grooved for scope mounts. Introduced 1972.

Perf.: $775   **Exc.:** $700   **VGood:** $550

MITCHELL ARMS 45 GOLD SERIES (HIGH STANDARD/SIGNATURE SERIES)

Semi-automatic; single action; 45 ACP; 8-, 10-shot magazine; 5-inch barrel; 8-3/4-inch overall length; weighs 39 oz.; interchangeable blade front sight, drift adjustable combat rear or fully-adjustable rear; smooth American walnut or checkered black rubber grips; bull barrel/slide lockup (no bushing design); full-length guide rod; extended ambidextrous safety; adjustable trigger; beveled magazine well; royal blue or stainless steel. Guns are marked with "High Standard" or "Signature Series" depending on date of manufacture. Made in U.S. From Mitchell Arms, Inc. Introduced 1994; still produced.

New: $550	**Perf.:** $475	**Exc.:** $400
Stainless finish, fixed sights.		
New: $675	**Perf.:** $525	**Exc.:** $450
Blue finish, adjustable sights		
New: $575	**Perf.:** $500	**Exc.:** $450
Stainless finish, adjustable sights		
New: $650	**Perf.:** $525	**Exc.:** $475

MITCHELL ARMS 45 GOLD SERIES (HIGH-STANDARD/SIGNATURE SERIES) WIDE-BODY

Same specs as 45 Gold except 10-shot magazine (accepts 8- and 13-shot magazines); fixed combat sights; black rubber grips; blue or stainless steel. Guns are marked with "High Standard" or "Signature Series" depending on date of manufacture. Made in U.S. From Mitchell Arms, Inc. Introduced 1994; still produced.

New: $600	**Perf.:** $550	**Exc.:** $500
Stainless finish, fixed sights.		
New: $675	**Perf.:** $650	**Exc.:** $500

Blue finish, fixed sights		
New: $700	**Perf.:** $675	**Exc.:** $525
Stainless finish, adjustable sights		
New: $725	**Perf.:** $700	**Exc.:** $575

MITCHELL ARMS ALPHA

Semi-automatic; double-action-only, single-action-only or SA/DA; 45 ACP; 8-, 10-shot magazine; 5-inch barrel; 8-1/2-inch overall length; weighs 41 oz.; interchangeable blade front sight, fully-adjustable rear or drift-adjustable rear; smooth polymer grips; accepts any single-column, 8-shot 1911-style magazine; frame-mounted decocker/safety; extended ambidextrous safety; extended slide latch; serrated combat hammer; beveled magazine well; heavy bull barrel (no bushing design); extended slide underlug; full-length recoil spring guide system. Also available as Alpha X with 14-shot magazine for police, military and export only. Made in U.S. From Mitchell Arms, Inc. Introduced 1995; still in production.

New: $600	**Perf.:** $550	**Exc.:** $500
Stainless finish		
New: $650	**Perf.:** $600	**Exc.:** $550
With adjustable sights		
New: $650	**Perf.:** $600	**Exc.:** $550

MITCHELL ARMS AMERICAN EAGLE

Semi-automatic; single action; 9mm Para.; 7-shot magazine; 4-inch barrel; 9-5/8-inch overall length; weighs 30 oz.; blade front sight, fixed rear; checkered walnut grips; recreation of the American Eagle Parabellum pistol in stainless steel. Made in U.S. Marketed by Mitchell Arms, Inc. Introduced 1992.

New: $550   **Perf.:** $475   **Exc.:** $400

MITCHELL ARMS BAT MASTERSON MODEL

Revolver; single action; 45 Colt; 6-shot cylinder; 4-3/4-inch, 5-1/2-inch, 7-1/2-inch barrel; fixed sights; one-piece walnut grip; hammer-block safety; nickel-plated. Introduced 1989; no longer imported.

Perf.: $325   **Exc.:** $250   **VGood:** $175

Mitchell Arms
American Eagle

Mitchell Arms
Sharpshooter II

Mitchell Arms
Citation II

Mitchell Arms Guardian II

Mitchell Arms Single
Action Army

Mitchell Arms
Olympic II I.S.U.

MITCHELL ARMS CITATION II

Semi-automatic; single action; 22 LR; 10-shot magazine; 5-1/2-inch bull, 7-1/4-inch fluted barrel; weighs 44-1/2 oz. (5-1/2-inch barrel); 9-3/4-inch overall length; undercut ramp front sight, click-adjustable frame-mounted rear; checkered walnut thumbrest grips; grips duplicate feel of military 45 auto; positive action magazine latch; front- and backstraps stippled; adjustable nickel-plated trigger, safety and magazine release; silver-filled roll marks; push-button barrel takedown; made of stainless steel; satin stainless or blue finish. Guns are marked with "High Standard" depending on date of manufacture. Made in U.S. Marketed by Mitchell Arms, Inc. Introduced 1992; still produced.

New: $400   **Perf.:** $350   **Exc.:** $300

MITCHELL ARMS DERRINGER

Derringer; over/under; 38 Spl.; 2-shot; 2 3/4-inch barrel; 5-1/4-inch overall length; weighs 11 oz.; fixed sights; checkered walnut grips; has same basic design as original Remington except for ramp front sight; polished blue finish. Introduced 1981; no longer imported.

Perf.: $100   **Exc.:** $90   **VGood:** $75

Stainless steel

Perf.: $110   **Exc.:** $100   **VGood:** $85

MITCHELL ARMS GUARDIAN II

Revolver; double action; 38 Spl.; 6-shot cylinder; 3-inch, 4-inch barrel; 8-1/2-inch overall length (3-inch barrel); weighs 32 oz.; combat or target grips of checkered black rubber or walnut; blade on ramp front sight, fixed rear; target hammer; shrouded ejector rod; smooth trigger; blue finish. Made in U.S. Marketed by Mitchell Arms, Inc. Introduced 1995.

Perf.: $200   **Exc.:** $175   **VGood:** $135

MITCHELL ARMS GUARDIAN III

Same specs as Guardian II except 3-inch, 4-inch, 6-inch barrel; adjustable rear sight. Made in U.S. Marketed by Mitchell Arms. Introduced 1995.

Perf.: $250   **Exc.:** $225   **VGood:** $200

MITCHELL ARMS MODEL 57A

Semi-automatic; single action; 30 Mauser; 9-shot magazine; all-steel construction; magazine safety;

hammer-block safety. Made in Yugoslavia. Introduced 1990; discontinued 1990.

Perf.: $175   **Exc.:** $150   **VGood:** $125

MITCHELL ARMS MODEL 70A

Semi-automatic; single action; 9mm Para.; 9-shot magazine; all-steel construction; magazine safety; hammer-block safety. Made in Yugoslavia. Introduced 1990; discontinued 1990.

Perf.: $175   **Exc.:** $135   **VGood:** $125

MITCHELL ARMS MODEL 1875 REMINGTON

Revolver; single action; 357 Mag., 45 Colt; 6-shot cylinder; fixed sights; walnut stock; color case-hardened frame; blued finish. Introduced 1990; discontinued 1991.

Perf.: $325   **Exc.:** $250   **VGood:** $225

MITCHELL ARMS OFFICERS MODEL 88A

Semi-automatic; single action; 9mm Para.; 9-shot magazine; all-steel construction; slenderized version of Model 70A; finger extension magazine. Made in Yugoslavia. Introduced 1990; discontinued 1990.

Perf.: $250   **Exc.:** $225   **VGood:** $175

MITCHELL ARMS OLYMPIC II I.S.U.

Semi-automatic; single action; 22 Short, 22 LR; 10-shot magazine; 6-3/4-inch round tapered barrel with stabilizer; 11-1/4-inch overall length; weighs 40 oz.; checkered walnut thumbrest grips; undercut ramp front sight, frame-mounted click-adjustable square notch rear; integral stabilizer with two removable weights; trigger adjustable for pull and over-travel; stippled front and backstraps; push-button barrel takedown; blue finish or stainless or combo. Some guns are marked with "High-Standard" depending on date of manufacture. Introduced 1992; still produced.

New: $550   **Perf.:** $475   **Exc.:** $400

MITCHELL ARMS ROLLING BLOCK TARGET

Single shot; 22 LR, 22 WMR, 357 Mag., 45 Colt, 223 Rem.; 9-7/8-inch half-round, half-octagon barrel;

14-inch overall length; weighs 44 oz.; walnut grip and forend; blade front sight, fully-adjustable rear; replica of the 1871 rolling block target pistol; brass trigger guard; color case-hardened frame; blue barrel. Imported from Italy by Mitchell Arms, Inc. Introduced 1992; dropped 1993.

Perf.: $350   **Exc.:** $300   **VGood:** $225

MITCHELL ARMS SHARPSHOOTER II

Semi-automatic; single action; 22 LR; 10-shot magazine; 5-1/2-inch bull barrel; 10-1/4-inch overall length; weighs 45 oz.; checkered walnut thumbrest grips; ramp front sight, slide-mounted square notch fully-adjustable rear; military grip; slide lock; smooth gripstraps; push-button takedown; drilled and tapped for barrel weights; stainless steel, blue or combo. Made in U.S. Marketed by Mitchell Arms, Inc. Introduced 1992.

New: $300   **Perf.:** $250   **Exc.:** $200

MITCHELL ARMS SINGLE ACTION ARMY

Revolver; single action; 22 LR, 357 Mag., 44 Mag., 45 ACP, 45 Colt; 6-shot cylinder; 4-3/4-inch, 5-1/2-inch, 6-inch, 7-1/2-inch, 10-inch, 12-inch, 18-inch barrel; ramp front, adjustable rear sight; one-piece walnut grips; brass grip frame; color case-hardened frame; hammer-block safety; blued finish. Introduced 1986.

Perf.: $250   **Exc.:** $225   **VGood:** $200

MITCHELL ARMS SINGLE ACTION ARMY, U.S. ARMY MODEL

Same specs as Single Action Army except 357 Mag., 45 ACP, 45 Colt; 5-1/2-inch barrel; serrated ramp front sight, fixed or adjustable rear; brass or steel backstrap/trigger guard; bright nickel-plated model and dual cylinder models available. Was imported by Mitchell Arms, Inc. No longer imported.

Perf.: $350   **Exc.:** $275   **VGood:** $200

Nickel finish

Perf.: $375   **Exc.:** $300   **VGood:** $225

With 45 Colt/45 ACP dual cylinder

Perf.: $425   **Exc.:** $375   **VGood:** $300

Mitchell Arms Sport King II

Mitchell Arms Trophy II

Mitchell Arms Victor II

MKE Kirikkale

MOA Maximum

Mitchell Arms Titan II

Morini CM-80

MITCHELL ARMS SINGLE ACTION ARMY, CAVALRY MODEL

Same specs as Single Action Army except 357 Mag., 45 ACP, 45 Colt; 7-1/2-inch barrel; serrated ramp front sight, fixed or adjustable rear; brass or steel backstrap/trigger guard; bright nickel-plated model and dual cylinder models available. Was imported by Mitchell Arms, Inc. No longer imported.

Perf.: $350	**Exc.:** $275	**VGood:** $200
Nickel finish		
Perf.: $375	**Exc.:** $300	**VGood:** $225
With 45 Colt/45 ACP dual cylinder		
Perf.: $425	**Exc.:** $375	**VGood:** $300

MITCHELL ARMS SINGLE ACTION ARMY, COWBOY MODEL

Same specs as Single Action Army except 357 Mag., 45 ACP, 45 Colt; 4-3/4-inch barrel; serrated ramp front sight, fixed or adjustable rear; brass or steel backstrap/trigger guard; bright nickel-plated model and dual cylinder models available. Was imported by Mitchell Arms, Inc. No longer imported.

Perf.: $350	**Exc.:** $275	**VGood:** $200
Nickel finish		
Perf.: $375	**Exc.:** $300	**VGood:** $225
With 45 Colt/45 ACP dual cylinder		
Perf.: $425	**Exc.:** $375	**VGood:** $30

MITCHELL ARMS SKORPION

Semi-automatic; single action; 32 ACP; 20-, 30-shot magazine; 4-5/8-inch barrel; blued finish. Made in Yugoslavia. Apparently never imported.

MITCHELL ARMS SPECTRE

Semi-automatic; single action; 9mm Para.; 30-, 50-shot magazine; 8-inch barrel, shrouded; weighs 64 oz.; blued finish. Made in Yugoslavia. Apparently never imported.

MITCHELL ARMS SPORT KING II

Semi-automatic; single action; 22 LR; 10-shot magazine; 4-1/2-inch, 6-3/4-inch barrel; 9-inch overall length (4-1/2-inch barrel); weighs 39 oz.; checkered walnut or black plastic grips; blade front

sight, windage-adjustable rear; military grip; standard trigger; push-button barrel takedown; stainless steel or blue. Guns are marked with "High Standard" depending on date of manufacture. Introduced 1992; still produced.

New: $250	**Perf.:** $225	**Exc.:** $200

MITCHELL ARMS TITAN II

Revolver; double action; 357 Mag.; 6-shot cylinder; 2-inch, 4-inch, 6-inch barrel; 7-3/4-inch overall length (2-inch barrel); weighs 38 oz.; Pachmayr black rubber grips, combat or target; blade front, fixed rear sight; crane-mounted cylinder release; shrouded ejector rod; blue or stainless steel. Introduced 1995; still produced.

New: $250	**Perf.:** $225	**Exc.:** $200

MITCHELL ARMS TITAN III

Same specs as the Titan II except adjustable rear sight. Made in U.S. Marketed by Mitchell Arms, Inc. Introduced 1995; still produced.

New: $325	**Perf.:** $300	**Exc.:** $250

MITCHELL ARMS LUGER

Stainless steel replica of P-08.

New: $675	**Perf.:** $600	**Exc.:** $500

MITCHELL ARMS TROPHY II

Semi-automatic; single action; 22 LR; 10-shot magazine; 5-1/2-inch bull, 7-1/4-inch fluted barrel; 9 3/4-inch overall length (5-1/2-inch barrel); weighs 44-1/2 oz.; checkered walnut thumbrest grips; undercut ramp front sight, click-adjustable frame-mounted rear; grip duplicates feel of military 45; positive action magazine latch; front and backstraps stippled; trigger adjustable for pull, over-travel; gold-filled roll marks, gold-plated trigger, safety, magazine release; push-button barrel takedown; stainless or blue finish. Made 1992 only.

New: $400	**Perf.:** $350	**Exc.:** $275

MITCHELL ARMS VICTOR II

Semi-automatic; single action; 22 LR; 10-shot magazine; 4-1/2-inch vent rib, 5-1/2-inch vent, dovetail or Weaver rib barrels; 9-3/4-inch overall length; weighs 44 oz.; military-type checkered walnut thumbrest or rubber grips; blade front sight,

fully-adjustable rear mounted on rib; push-button takedown for barrel interchangeability; bright stainless steel combo or royal blue finish. Introduced 1994; still produced.

With 4-1/2-inch vent rib barrel		
New: $500	**Perf.:** $450	**Exc.:** $400
With 5-1/2-inch dovetail rib barrel		
New: $550	**Perf.:** $500	**Exc.:** $450
With 5-1/2-inch Weaver rib barrel		
New: $550	**Perf.:** $500	**Exc.:** $450

MKE KIRIKKALE

Semi-automatic; double action; 32 ACP, 380 ACP; 8-shot magazine (32 ACP), 7-shot (380 ACP); 4-inch barrel; 6-1/2-inch overall length; adjustable notch rear sight, fixed front; checkered plastic grips; exposed hammer; safety blocks firing pin, drops hammer; chamber-loaded indicator pin; blued finish. Copy of Walther PP. Imported from Turkey by Firearms Center, Inc., then by Mandall Shooting Supplies; no longer imported.

Exc.: $250	**VGood:** $200	**Good:** $175

MOA MAXIMUM

Single shot; falling block action; 28 standard chamberings from 22 to 44 caliber; 8-3/4-inch, 10-3/4-inch, 14-inch interchangeable barrel; ramp front sight, fully-adjustable open rear; drilled and tapped for scope mounts; integral grip frame/receiver; smooth walnut stocks, forend; adjustable trigger; Armaloy finish. Introduced 1983.

New: $650	**Perf.:** $550	**Exc.:** $475

MORINI MODEL CM-80

Single shot; 22 LR; 10-inch free-floating barrel; 21-1/4-inch overall length; weighs 30 oz.; adjustable or wrap-around stocks; adjustable match sights; adjustable grip/frame angle; adjustable barrel alignment; adjustable trigger weight, sight radius. Made in Switzerland. Introduced 1985; importation discontinued 1989.

Perf.: $850	**Exc.:** $750	**VGood:** $700

Mossberg Abilene

Mossberg Brownie

Nagant Model 1895

Nagant Model 1895 Training Model

Nambu Model 1902 First Type ("Grandpa")

Nambu Model 1902 Second Type ("Papa")

Nambu Model 1902 7mm ("Baby")

Nambu Type 14 (1925)

Nambu Type 26 Revolver

MORINI MODEL CM-80 SUPER COMPETITION

Same specs as Model CM-80 except deluxe finish; plexiglass front sighting system.

Perf.: $1000   **Exc.:** $850   **VGood:** $750

MORINI MODEL 84E FREE PISTOL

Single shot; 22 LR; 11-7/16-inch barrel; 19-1/2-inch overall length; weighs 44 oz.; adjustable match-type grip with stippled surfaces; interchangeable blade front sight, match-type fully-adjustable rear; fully-adjustable electronic trigger. Imported from Switzerland by Nygord Precision Products. Introduced 1995; still imported.

New: $1250   **Perf.:** $1100   **Exc.:** $1000

MOSSBERG ABILENE

Revolver; single action; 357 Mag., 44 Mag., 45 Colt; 6-shot cylinder; 4-5/8-inch, 6-inch, 7-1/2-inch barrel; serrated ramp front sight, click-adjustable rear; smooth walnut grips; wide hammer spur; transfer bar ignition; blued or Magnaloy finish. Introduced 1978 by United States Arms; taken over by Mossberg; not currently in production.

Exc.: $250   **VGood:** $200   **Good:** $175

Magnaloy finish

Exc.: $275   **VGood:** $225   **Good:** $200

MOSSBERG BROWNIE

Pocket pistol; top-break; double action; 22 LR, 22 Short; 4-shot; four 2-1/2-inch barrels; revolving firing pin; steel extractor. Introduced in 1919; discontinued 1932. Most found with well-worn finish; premium for VGood+ specimens.

Exc.: $475   **VGood:** $370   **Good:** $300

NAGANT MODEL 1895

Revolver; 7.62mm Nagant; 4-1/4-inch barrel; 9-3/16-inch overall length; 7-shot cylinder; checkered wood grips. Unique gas-seal action cams the cylinder forward to mate with end of barrel before firing. Russian military issue from 1895 to 1944.

Exc.: $225   **VGood:** $195   **Good:** $150

NAGANT MODEL 1895 TRAINING MODEL

Same specs as Model 1895 except 22 LR for training purposes. Conversions from 7.62mm revolver (scarce) or arsenal manufactured in 1937 on 7.62mm frames (rare).

Exc.: $600   **VGood:** $500   **Good:** $400

NAMBU MODEL 1902 FIRST TYPE ("GRANDPA")

Semi-automatic; 8mm Nambu; 8-shot magazine; 4-3/4-inch barrel; 9-inch overall lengh; adjustable rear (tangent) and front sights; blued finish; checkered wood grips and magazine bottom; grip safety; rear of frame slotted for shoulder-stock holster. Introduced 1903; discontinued 1906. Add $3500 for original (beware of reproductions!) shoulder-stock holster.

Exc.: $4500   **VGood:** $3500   **Good:** $2500

NAMBU MODEL 1902 SECOND TYPE ("PAPA")

Semi-automatic; same specs as first type except not slotted (except first few hundred) for or supplied with shoulder-stock holster; aluminum bottom instead of wood bottom magazine; flexible instead of fixed lanyard ring. Introduced 1906; discontinued 1928.

Exc.: $1500   **VGood:** $1000   **Good:** $700

NAMBU MODEL 1902 7MM ("BABY")

Semi-automatic; 7mm Nambu; 7-shot magazine; 3-1/4-inch barrel; 6-3/4-inch overall length; fixed rear, adjustable front sights; blued finish; checkered wood grips; grip safety. Introduced 1903; dropped 1929.

Exc.: $2500   **VGood:** $1750   **Good:** $1250

NAMBU TYPE 14 (1925)

Semi-automatic; 8mm Nambu; 8-shot magazine; 4-5/8-inch barrel; 9-inch overall length; fixed rear, adjustable front sights; blued finish; grooved wood grips. Introduced 1926; discontinued 1945. Very early production brings a small premium price.

Exc.: $350   **VGood:** $250   **Good:** $150

NAMBU TYPE 26 REVOLVER

Revolver; 9mm Japanese; 6-shot; 4-3/4-inch barrel; 9-inch overall length; fixed sights; blued finish; checkered or grooved (rare late production) wood grips. Introduced 1893; discontinued 1935.

Exc.: $325   **VGood:** $250   **Good:** $185

NAMBU TYPE 94

Semi-automatic; 8mm Nambu; 6-shot magazine; 3-3/4-inch barrel; 7-5/16-inch overall length; fixed rear, adjustable front sights; blued finish; checkered plastic or smooth wood (late war) grips. Introduced 1935; discontinued 1945.

Exc.: $500   **VGood:** $375   **Good:** $250

NAVY ARMS 1873 SINGLE-ACTION REVOLVER

Caliber: 357 Mag., 44-40, 45 Colt, 6-shot cylinder. Barrel: 3-inch, 4-3/4-inch, 5-1/2-inch, 7-1/2-inch. Weight: 36 oz. Length: 10-3/4-inch overall (5-1/2-inch barrel). Stocks: Smooth walnut. Sights: Blade front, groove in topstrap rear. Features: Blue with color case-hardened frame, or nickel. Introduced 1991. Imported by Navy Arms.

Perf.: $350   **Exc.:** $275   **VGood:** $200

Nickel finish

Perf.: $375   **Exc.:** $300   **VGood:** $225

1873 U.S. Cavalry Model (7-1/2-inch, 45 Colt, arsenal markings) or Artillery Model, 5-1/2-inch).

Perf.: $350   **Exc.:** $275   **VGood:** $200

NAVY ARMS BISLEY MODEL SINGLE-ACTION REVOLVER

Caliber: 44-40 or 45 Colt, 6-shot cylinder. Barrel: 4-3/4-inch, 5-1/2-inch, 7-1/2-inch Weight: 40 oz. Length: 12-1/2-inch overall (7-1/2-inch barrel). Stocks: Smooth walnut. Sights: Blade front, notch rear. Polished blue finish, color case-hardened frame. Introduced 1997. Imported by Navy Arms.

Perf.: $350   **Exc.:** $275   **VGood:** $200

Navy Arms Model 1873

Navy Arms Bisley Model
Single-Action Revolver

Navy Arms Frontier,
Target Model

Navy Arms Model 1873
Economy Model

Navy Arms Model
1875 Remington

Navy Arms Model 1875
Schofield Wells Fargo Model

NAVY ARMS FLAT TOP TARGET MODEL REVOLVER

Caliber: 45 Colt, 6-shot cylinder. Barrel: 7-1/2-inch. Weight: 40 oz. Length: 13-1/4-inch overall. Stocks: Smooth walnut. Sights: Spring-loaded German silver front, rear adjustable for windage. Blue with color case-hardened frame. Introduced 1997. Imported by Navy Arms.

Perf.: $350   **Exc.:** $275   **VGood:** $200

NAVY ARMS FRONTIER MODEL

Revolver; single action; 357 Mag., 45 Colt; 6-shot cylinder; 4-1/2-inch, 5-1/2-inch, 7-1/2-inch barrel; fixed sights; uncheckered one-piece walnut grip; brass grip frame; color case-hardened frame; blued barrel and cylinder. Manufactured in Italy. Introduced 1976; discontinued 1978.

Exc.: $300   **VGood:** $225   **Good:** $175

NAVY ARMS FRONTIER, BUNTLINE MODEL

Same specs as Frontier except 16-1/2-inch barrel; detachable shoulder stock.

Exc.: $450   **VGood:** $375   **Good:** $300

NAVY ARMS GRAND PRIX

Single shot; rolling block; 44 Mag., 30-30, 7mm Spl., 45-70; 13-3/4-inch barrel; weighs 64 oz.; adjustable target sights; walnut forend, thumbrest grip; adjustable aluminum barrel rib; matte blue finish. Introduced 1983; discontinued 1985.

Exc.: $275   **VGood:** $225   **Good:** $185

NAVY ARMS HIGH POWER

Semi-automatic; single action; 9mm Para.; 13-shot magazine; 4-5/8-inch barrel; fixed sights; black plastic grips; similar to older FN manufacture; blued finish. Introduced 1993; no longer in production.

New: $350   **Perf.:** $275   **Exc.:** $200

NAVY ARMS LUGER

Semi-automatic; 22 LR; 10-shot magazine; 4-inch, 6-inch, 8-inch barrel; 9-inch overall length; weighs 44 oz.; fixed sights; checkered walnut stocks; all-steel

construction; blowback toggle action; blued finish. Made in U.S. Introduced 1986; discontinued 1987.

Exc.: $375   **VGood:** $300   **Good:** $200

NAVY ARMS MODEL 1873

Revolver; single action; 44-40, 45 Colt; 6-shot cylinder; 3-inch, 4-3/4-inch, 5-1/2-inch, 7-1/2-inch barrels; 10-3/4-inch overall length (5-1/2-inch barrel); weighs 47 oz.; blade front sight, grooved rear; uncheckered walnut grips; nickel or blued finish with color case-hardened frame. Made in Italy. Introduced 1991; still imported.

New: $325   **Perf.:** $275   **Exc.:** $225

Nickel

New: $375   **Perf.:** $325   **Exc.:** $275

NAVY ARMS MODEL 1873, ECONOMY MODEL

Same specs as standard Model 1873 single action except brass trigger guard, backstrap; two piece walnut grip. Introduced 1993; dropped 1996.

New: $250   **Perf.:** $200   **Exc.:** $175

NAVY ARMS MODEL 1875 REMINGTON

Revolver; single action; 44-40, 45 Colt; 6-shot cylinder; 7-1/2-inch barrel; 13-inch overall length; weighs 41 oz.; blade front sight, grooved rear; uncheckered walnut grips; color case-hardened frame; brass trigger guard; balance blued finish. Made in Italy. Introduced 1991; discontinued 1992; resumed 1994; discontinued 1995.

New: $350   **Perf.:** $275   **Exc.:** $225

NAVY ARMS MODEL 1875 SCHOFIELD WELLS FARGO MODEL

Revolver; single action; 44-40, 45 Colt; 6-shot cylinder; 5-inch barrel; 10-3/4-inch overall length; weighs 39 oz.; smooth walnut grips; blade front sight, notch rear; replica of Smith & Wesson Model 3 Schofield; top-break action with automatic ejection; polished blue finish. Imported by Navy Arms. Introduced 1994; still imported.

New: $600   **Perf.:** $500   **Exc.:** $400

NAVY ARMS MODEL 1875 SCHOFIELD U.S. CAVALRY MODEL

Same specs as the Wells Fargo model except 7-inch barrel; original-type military markings. Imported by Navy Arms. Introduced 1994; still imported.

New: $600   **Perf.:** $500   **Exc.:** $400

NAVY ARMS MODEL 1890 REMINGTON

Revolver; single action; 44-40, 6-shot cylinder; 5-1/2-inch barrel; 10-3/4-inch overall length; weighs 39 oz.; blade front, grooved rear sight; walnut grip; brass trigger guard; lanyard loop; blued finish. Made in Italy. Introduced 1991; discontinued 1992; resumed 1994; discontinued 1995.

New: $350   **Perf.:** $275   **Exc.:** $225

NAVY ARMS "PINCHED FRAME" SINGLE-ACTION REVOLVER

Caliber: 45 Colt. Barrel: 7-1/2-inch. Weight: 37 oz. Length: 13-inch overall. Stocks: Smooth walnut Sights: German silver blade, notch rear. Features: Replica of Colt's original Peacemaker. Color case-hardened frame, hammer, rest charcoal blued. Introduced 1997.

Perf.: $350   **Exc.:** $275   **VGood:** $20

NAVY ARMS ROLLING BLOCK

Single shot; 22 LR, 22 Hornet, 357 Mag.; 8-inch barrel; 12-inch overall length; adjustable sights; uncheckered walnut stocks, forearm; color case-hardened frame; brass trigger guard; blued barrel. Manufactured in Italy. Introduced 1965; Hornet chambering discontinued 1975; 22 LR discontinued 1979. No longer imported.

Exc.: $350   **VGood:** $300   **Good:** $175

NAVY ARMS TT-OLYMPIA

Semi-automatic; single action; 22 LR; 4-5/8-inch barrel; 8-inch overall length; weighs 28 oz.; checkered hardwood grips; blade front sight, windage-adjustable rear; reproduction of the Walther Olympia pistol; polished blue finish. Imported by Navy Arms. Introduced 1992; no longer imported.

New: $200   **Perf.:** $150   **Exc.:** $125

Navy Arms Model 1890 Remington

Navy Arms Rolling Block

Navy Arms TT-Olympia

New Advantage Derringer

New England Firearms Lady Ultra

New England Firearms Model R92

Nighthawk Custom Talon

Nighthawk Custom Predator

NAVY ARMS TU-90

Semi-automatic; single action; 30 Tokarev, 9mm Para.; 8-shot magazine; 4-1/2-inch barrel; weighs 30 oz.; wrap-around synthetic grip; similar to TT-33 Tokarev. Made in China. Introduced 1992; no longer imported.

    New: $305   **Perf.:** $275   **Exc.:** $250

NAVY ARMS TU-711 MAUSER

Semi-automatic; 9mm Para.; 10-, 20-shot magazine; 5-1/4-inch barrel; weighs 43 oz.; similar to Mauser 711. Introduced 1992; discontinued 1992.

    Perf.: $550   **Exc.:** $500   **VGood:** $450

NAVY ARMS U.S. GOVERNMENT MODEL

Semi-automatic; 45 ACP; 7-shot; 5-inch barrel; fixed sights; checkered walnut grips; standard G.I. 1911 issue pistol; blue finish. Introduced 1993; no longer in production.

    New: $325   **Perf.:** $275   **Exc.:** $200

NEW ADVANTAGE DERRINGER

Double action; 22 LR, 22 WMR; 4-shot; four 2-1/2-inch barrels; 4-1/2-inch overall length; weighs 15 oz.; fixed sights; smooth walnut stocks; revolving firing pin; rebounding hammer; polished blue finish. Reintroduced, 1989 by New Advantage Arms Corp.

    Perf.: $175   **Exc.:** $150   **VGood:** $135

NEW DETONICS LADIES ESCORT

Semi-automatic; single action; 45 ACP; 6-shot magazine; 3-1/2-inch barrel; 4-1/2-inch overall length; weighs 26 oz.; checkered walnut grips; rubber mainspring housing; ramp front sight, adjustable rear; reduced grip frame size; color polymer finish. Made in U.S. by New Detonics Corp. Introduced 1990; dropped 1991. Very few made.

    Royal Escort, iridescent purple slide, blackened stainless frame, gold-plated hammer and trigger

    Perf.: $750   **Exc.:** $650   **VGood:** $500

    Jade Escort, jade-colored slide, satin stainless frame

    Perf.: $750   **Exc.:** $650   **VGood:** $500

    Midnight Escort, black slide, satin stainless frame

    Perf.: $800   **Exc.:** $700   **VGood:** $600

NEW ENGLAND FIREARMS LADY ULTRA

Revolver; double action; 32 H&R Mag.; 5-shot cylinder; 3-inch barrel; 7-1/4-inch overall length; weighs 31 oz.; walnut-finished hardwood grips with NEF medallion; blade front sight, fully-adjustable rear; swing-out cylinder; polished blue finish; comes with lockable storage case. From New England Firearms Co. Introduced 1992; dropped 1999.

    New: $135   **Perf.:** $115   **Exc.:** $100

NEW ENGLAND FIREARMS MODEL R73

Revolver; double action; 32 H&R Mag.; 5-shot cylinder; 3-inch barrel; 7-1/4-inch overall length; weighs 31 oz.; walnut finished American hardwood grips with NEF medallion; fixed sights; blue or nickel finish. From New England Firearms Co. Introduced 1988; dropped 1999.

    New: $120   **Perf.:** $100   **Exc.:** $75

NEW ENGLAND FIREARMS MODEL R92

Revolver; double action; 22 LR; 9-shot cylinder; 2-1/2-inch barrel, 8-1/2-inch overall length (4-inch barrel); weighs 26 oz.; walnut-finished American hardwood grips with NEF medallion; fixed sights; blue or nickel finish. From New England Firearms Co. Introduced 1988; dropped 1999.

    New: $110   **Perf.:** $100   **Exc.:** $85

NEW ENGLAND FIREARMS SINGLE SHOT

Single shot; rotary cannon-type action; 357 Mag., 357 Rem. Maximum, 44 Mag., 223, 30-30, 7-30 Waters, 35 Rem.; 14-inch barrel; 15-1/8-inch overall length; weighs 49 oz. (synthetic stock), 70 oz. (laminated wood); ramp front sight, adjustable rear; action cocks on opening; single stage trigger; trigger and sliding thumb safeties; matte blue finish. Made by Competitor Corp. Marketed by New England Firearms. Introduced 1995; still produced.

    New: $350   **Perf.:** $300   **Exc.:** $275

NEW ENGLAND FIREARMS TOP BREAK

Revolver; double action; 22 LR; 9-shot cylinder; 4-inch, 6-inch barrel; weighs 30 oz. (4-inch barrel); walnut-finished hardwood grips; elevation-adjustable front sight, windage-adjustable rear; ventilated barrel rib; automatic ejection; blue finish. Made in U.S. by New England Firearms. Introduced 1991; dropped 1999.

    Perf.: $125   **Exc.:** $115   **VGood:** $100

NEW ENGLAND FIREARMS ULTRA

Revolver; double action; 22 LR, 22 WMR; 9-shot (22 LR), 6-shot (22 WMR); 4-inch, 6-inch barrel; 10 5/8-inch overall length (6-inch barrel); weighs 36 oz.; walnut-finished hardwood grips with NEF medallion; blade front sight, fully-adjustable rear; bull-style barrel with recessed muzzle; high "Lustre" blue/black finish. Made in U.S. by New England Firearms. Introduced 1989; dropped 1999.

    New: $135   **Perf.:** $115   **Exc.:** $100

NIGHTHAWK CUSTOM TALON

1911-style .45 ACP semi-auto with 5-inch or 4.25-inch barrel and fixed or adjustable sights. Several other barrel lengths/finishes available.

    NIB: $2100   **Exc.:** $1750   **VGood:** $1475

NIGHTHAWK CUSTOM PREDATOR

1911-style .45 ACP semi-auto with 5-inch barrel or 4.25-inch and fixed or adjustable sights. Several other barrel lengths/finishes available.

    NIB: $2500   **Exc.:** $2150   **VGood:** $1775

NIGHTHAWK GRP

Global Response Pistol. 1911-style .45 ACP semi-auto with 5-inch or 4.25-inch barrel and fixed or adjustable sights. Several other barrel lengths/finishes available.

    NIB: $2400   **Exc.:** $1950   **VGood:** $1550

Norinco Type 54-1 Tokarev

Norinco Type 59 Makarov

North American Arms Guardian

North American Arms Mini-Master Black Widow

North American Arms Mini-Master Target

North American Arms Model 22 LR

North American Arms Single Action

NORINCO MODEL 1911A1
Semi-automatic; single action; 45 ACP; 7-shot magazine; 5-inch barrel; 8-1/2-inch overall length; weighs 39 oz.; checkered wood grips; blade front sight, windage-adjustable rear; matte blue finish. Comes with two magazines. Imported from China by China Sports, Inc.; dropped 1995.

   New: $250   **Perf.:** $200   **Exc.:** $175

NORINCO MODEL 77B
Semi-automatic; single action; 9mm Para.; 8-shot magazine; 5-inch barrel; 7-1/2-inch overall length; weighs 34 oz.; checkered wood grips; blade front sight, adjustable rear; gas-retarded recoil action; front of trigger guard able to cock the action with the trigger finger. Imported from China as the NP-20. Introduced 1989; dropped 1995; few imported.

   Perf.: $350   **Exc.:** $275   **VGood:** $200

NORINCO TYPE 54-1 TOKAREV
Semi-automatic; single action; 7.62x25mm, 9mm Para.; 8-shot magazine; 4-1/2-inch barrel; 7-3/4-inch overall length; weighs 29 oz.; grooved black plastic grips; fixed sights; matte blue finish. Imported from China; dropped 1995.

   Perf.: $295   **Exc.:** $250   **VGood:** $200

NORINCO TYPE 59 MAKAROV
Semi-automatic; double action; 9x18mm, 380 ACP; 8-shot magazine; 3-1/2-inch barrel; weighs 21 oz.; 6-3/8-inch overall length; checkered plastic grips; blade front sight, adjustable rear; blue finish. Direct copy of Russian-made pistol. Imported from China. Introduced 1990; dropped 1995.

   Perf.: $250   **Exc.:** $200   **VGood:** $150

NORTH AMERICAN ARMS GUARDIAN PISTOL
Caliber: 380, 32 NAA, 32 ACP or 25 NAA, 6-shot magazine. Barrel: 2.1-inch. Weight: 13.5 oz. Length: 4.36-inch overall. Stocks: Black polymer. Sights: Fixed. Features: Doube-action-only mechanism. All stainless steel construction; snag-free. Introduced 1998. Made in U.S. by North American Arms.

   Perf.: $300   **Exc.:** $250   **VGood:** $200

NORTH AMERICAN ARMS MINI-MASTER BLACK WIDOW
Revolver; single action; 22 LR, 22 WMR; 5-shot cylinder; 2-inch heavy vent barrel; 5-7/8-inch overall length; weighs 8-7/8 oz.; black rubber grips; Millett Low Profile fixed sights or Millett sight adjustable for elevation only; built on the 22 WMR frame; non-fluted cylinder. Made in U.S. by North American Arms. Introduced 1989; still produced.

With adjustable sight		
New: $225	**Perf.:** $185	**Exc.:** $150
With adjustable sight, extra LR/WMR cylinder		
New: $250	**Perf.:** $235	**Exc.:** $200
With fixed sight		
New: $185	**Perf.:** $175	**Exc.:** $150
With fixed sight, extra LR/WMR cylinder		
New: $275	**Perf.:** $250	**Exc.:** $200

NORTH AMERICAN ARMS MINI-MASTER TARGET
Revolver; single action; 22 LR, 22 WMR; 5-shot; heavy vent-rib 4-inch barrel; 7-3/4-inch overall length; weighs 10-3/4 oz.; blade-type front sight, elevation-adjustable white-outline rear; checkered hard black rubber stocks. Introduced 1989; still in production.

   New: $235   **Perf.:** $210   **Exc.:** $190

NORTH AMERICAN ARMS MODEL 22 LR
Revolver; single action; 22 Short, 22 LR; 5-shot; 1-1/8-inch, 1-5/8-inch, 2-1/2-inch barrel; 3-7/8-inch overall length; weighs 4-1/2 oz.; fixed sights; plastic or rosewood grips; stainless steel construction. Introduced 1976; still in production.

   New: $135   **Perf.:** $115   **Exc.:** $100

NORTH AMERICAN ARMS MODEL 22 MAGNUM
Revolver; single action; 22 WMR; 5-shot; 1-1/8-inch, 1-5/8-inch, 2-1/2-inch barrel; 3-7/8-inch overall length; weighs 4-1/2 oz.; fixed sights; plastic or rosewood grips; stainless steel construction. Introduced 1976; still in production.

   New: $150   **Perf.:** $135   **Exc.:** $125

NORTH AMERICAN ARMS MODEL 22 MAGNUM CONVERTIBLE
Same specs as 22 Magnum, except supplied with extra 22 LR cylinder.

   New: $185   **Perf.:** $170   **Exc.:** $150

NORTH AMERICAN ARMS SINGLE ACTION REVOLVER
Revolver; single action; 45 Win. Mag., 450 Mag. Express; 5-shot; 7-1/2-inch, 10-1/2-inch barrel; weighs 52 oz.; adjustable rear sight, blade front; uncheckered walnut stocks; stainless steel construction; matte finish. Introduced 1984; discontinued 1985.

   Perf.: $1100   **Exc.:** $850   **VGood:** $750

High polish finish		
Perf.: $1350	**Exc.:** $1000	**VGood:** $850

NORTH AMERICAN ARMS VIPER BELT BUCKLE
Revolver; single action; 22 LR; 5-shot; 1-1/8-inch, 1-5/8-inch barrel; weighs 4-1/2 oz.; fixed sights; plastic or rosewood grips; belt buckle with built-in revolver; stainless steel construction. Introduced 1976; discontinued 1990; reintroduced 1993; no longer in production.

   New: $175   **Perf.:** $150   **Exc.:** $135

ODI Viking

Olympic Arms/Schuetzen
Pistol Works Griffon

Olympic Arms/Schuetzen
Pistol Works Big Deuce

Olympic Arms
Constable

Olympic Arms
Street Deuce

Olympic Arms
Journeyman

Olympic Arms
Trail Boss

Olympic Arms
Westerner

ODI VIKING

Semi-automatic; double action; 45 ACP; 7-shot;
5-inch barrel; weighs 39 oz.; fixed notched rear sight,
blade front; smooth teak stocks; Seecamp double-
action system; spur-type hammer; stainless steel
construction; brushed satin finish. Introduced 1982;
discontinued 1985.

> **Perf.:** $450   **Exc.:** $400   **VGood:** $350

OLYMPIC ARMS
OA-96 AR PISTOL

Caliber: 223. Barrel: 6-inch, 4140 chromemoly steel.
Weight: 5 lbs. Length: 15-3/4-inch overall. Stocks: A2
stowaway pistol grip; no buttstock or receiver tube.
Sights: Flat-top upper receiver, cut-down front sight
base. Features: AR-15-type receivers with special
bolt carrier; short aluminum hand guard; Vortex flash
hider. Introduced 1996.

> **Perf.:** $850   **Exc.:** $675   **VGood:** $500

OLYMPIC ARMS
SCHUETZEN PISTOL WORKS
BIG DEUCE

Semi-automatic; single action; 45 ACP; 7-shot
magazine; 6-inch barrel; 9-1/2-inch overall length;
weighs 40 oz.; smooth walnut grips; ramped blade
front sight, LPA adjustable rear; stainless steel barrel;
beavertail grip safety; extended thumb safety and
slide release; Commander-style hammer; throated,
polished and tuned; Parkerized matte black slide with
satin stainless steel frame. Made in U.S. by Olympic
Arms, Inc.'s specialty shop Schuetzen Pistol Works.
Marked "Schuetzen Pistol Works" on the slide;
"Safari Arms" on the frame. Introduced 1995; still
produced.

> **New:** $700   **Perf.:** $600   **Exc.:** $500

OLYMPIC ARMS
SCHUETZEN PISTOL WORKS
CREST SERIES

Semi-automatic; single action; 45 ACP; 6-, 7-shot
magazine; 4-1/2-inch (4-star), 5-inch, 5-1/2-inch
barrel; 8-1/2-inch overall length; weighs 39 oz.;
checkered walnut grips; ramped blade front sight,
LPA adjustable rear; stainless steel barrel; right- or
left-hand models available; long aluminum trigger;

full-length recoil spring guide; throated, polished,
tuned; satin stainless steel. Made in U.S. by Olympic
Arms, Inc.'s specialty shop Schuetzen Pistol Works.
Marked "Schuetzen Pistol Works" on the slide;
"Safari Arms" on the frame. Introduced 1993; still
produced.

Right-hand		
Perf.: $650	**Exc.:** $600	**VGood:** $550
Left-hand		
Perf.: $750	**Exc.:** $700	**VGood:** $650

OLYMPIC ARMS
SCHUETZEN PISTOL WORKS
GRIFFON

Semi-automatic; single action; 45 ACP; 10-shot
magazine; 5-inch barrel; 8-1/2-inch overall length;
smooth walnut grips; ramped blade front sight, LPA
adjustable rear; stainless barrel; beavertail grip safety;
long aluminum trigger; full-length recoil spring guide;
Commander-style hammer; throated, polished and
tuned; grip size comparable to standard 1911; satin
stainless steel finish. Made in U.S. by Olympic Arms,
Inc.'s specialty shop Schuetzen Pistol Works. Marked
"Schuetzen Pistol Works" on the slide; "Safari Arms"
on the frame. Introduced 1995; still produced.

> **Perf.:** $750   **Exc.:** $625   **VGood:** $500

OLYMPIC ARMS BLACK-TAC

Semi-auto .45 ACP pistol treated with "black-tac"
process – advantages of hard chrome without its
drawbacks such as embrittlement.

> **NIB:** $800   **Exc.:** $700   **VGood:** $575

OLYMPIC ARMS CONSTABLE

Semi-auto pistol chambered for .45 ACP with 4-inch
barrel, 5.75-inch sight radius, 7+1 capacity, 35 oz.

> **NIB:** $900   **Exc.:** $800   **VGood:** $675

OLYMPIC ARMS CUSTOM
STREET DEUCE

Semi-auto chambered for .45 ACP with 5.2-inch bull
barrel, 7-inch sight radius, 7+1 capacity, 38 oz. Many
options.

> **NIB:** $1200   **Exc.:** $1100   **VGood:** $775

OLYMPIC ARMS CUSTOM
JOURNEYMAN

Semi-auto chambered for .45 ACP with 4-inch bull
barrel, 6-inch sight radius, 6+1 capacity, 35 oz. Many
options.

> **NIB:** $1200   **Exc.:** $1100   **VGood:** $775

OLYMPIC ARMS TRAIL BOSS

Semi-auto pistol in the Westerner line chambered
for .45 ACP. 6-inch barrel, 8-inch sight radius, 7+1
capacity, 43 oz.

> **NIB:** $895   **Exc.:** $775   **VGood:** $600

OLYMPIC ARMS WESTERNER

Semi-auto pistol chambered for .45 ACP with 5-inch
barrel, 7-inch sight radius, 7+1 capacity, 39 oz.

> **NIB:** $800   **Exc.:** $675   **VGood:** $545

OLYMPIC ARMS WOLVERINE

Polymer-frame, vent-rib replica of the old "ray gun"
.22 Whitney Wolverine semi-auto pistol. Cool, baby!

> **New:** $275   **Perf.:** $250   **Exc.:** $225

ONE PRO .45 AUTO

Semi-automatic; double action; 45 ACP or 400
Corbon, 10-shot magazine. Barrel: 3.75-inch Weight:
31.1 oz. Length: 7.04-inch overall. Stocks: Textured
composition. Sights: Blade front, drift-adjustable rear;
three-dot system. Features: All-steel construction;
decocking lever and automatic firing pin lock; DA

Ortgies Pocket Pistol

Pachmayr Dominator

Para-Ordnance P-12.45

Para-Ordnance P-13.45

Para-Ordnance P-14.45

Para-Ordnance P-16.40

Para Ordnance Wart Hog

Para-Ordnance Nite Hawg

or DAO operation. Introduced 1997. Imported from Switzerland by Magnum Research, Inc.

New: $550	**Perf.:** $450	**Exc.:** $400
Conversion kit, 45 ACP/400, 400/45 ACP		
New: $200	**Perf.:** $175	**Exc.:** $150

ONE PRO 9 AUTO

Semi-automatic; double action; 9mm Para., 10-shot magazine. Barrel: 3.01-inch. Weight: 25.1 oz. Length: 6 inches overall. Stocks: Smooth wood. Sights: Blade front, rear adjustable for windage. Features: Rotating barrel; short slide; double recoil springs; double-action mechanism; decocking lever. Introduced 1998. Imported from Switzerland by Magnum Research. Price: NA

ORTGIES POCKET PISTOL

Semi-automatic; blowback action; 32 ACP, 380 ACP; 8-shot (32), 7-shot (380); 3-1/4-inch barrel; 6-1/2-inch overall length; fixed sights; uncheckered walnut grips; constructed without screws, uses pins and spring-loaded catches; grip safety protrudes only when firing pin is cocked; blued finish. Introduced about 1919; discontinued 1926.

Exc.: $200	**VGood:** $175	**Good:** $135
Nickel finish		
Exc.: $300	**VGood:** $250	**Good:** $150

ORTGIES VEST POCKET PISTOL

Semi-automatic; blowback action; 25 ACP; 6-shot; 2-3/4-inch barrel; 5-3/16-inch overall length; fixed sights; uncheckered walnut grips; blued finish. Introduced 1920; discontinued 1926.

Exc.: $225	**VGood:** $200	**Good:** $175
Nickel finish		
Exc.: $275	**VGood:** $250	**Good:** $200

PACHMAYR DOMINATOR

Single shot; bolt action on 1911A1 frame; 22 Hornet, 223, 7mm-06, 308, 35 Rem., 44 Mag.; 10-1/2-inch barrel in 44 Mag., 14-inch all other calibers; weighs 4 lbs. (14-inch barrel); 16-inch overall length; Pachmayr Signature system grips; optional adjustable sights

or drilled and tapped for scope mounting. From Pachmayr. Introduced 1988; discontinued 1994.

New: $450	**Perf.:** $375	**Exc.:** $325

PARA-ORDNANCE P-12.45

Semi-automatic; single action; 45 ACP; 10-shot magazine (pre-1994 guns have 12-shot); 3-1/2-inch barrel; 7-1/8-inch overall length; weighs 34 oz. (steel and stainless frame), 26 oz. (alloy frame); textured composition grips; blade front sight, adjustable rear; high visibility three-dot system; matte black finish; grooved match trigger; rounded combat-style hammer; beveled magazine well; manual thumb, grip and firing pin safeties; solid barrel bushing. Made in Canada by Para-Ordnance. Introduced 1990; still produced. Steel frame, matte black

New: $650	**Perf.:** $600	**Exc.:** $500
Alloy frame, matte black		
New: $600	**Perf.:** $550	**Exc.:** $450
Stainless frame, stainless		
New: $700	**Perf.:** $650	**Exc.:** $550
Stainless frame, Duotone		
New: $685	**Perf.:** $635	**Exc.:** $575

PARA-ORDNANCE P-13.45

Semi-automatic; single action; 45 ACP; 10-shot magazine (pre-1994 guns have 13-shot); 4-1/4-inch barrel; 7-3/4-inch overall length; weighs 36 oz. (steel and stainless frame), 28 oz. (alloy frame); textured composition grips; blade front sight, adjustable rear; high visibility three-dot system; grooved match trigger; rounded combat-style hammer; beveled magazine well; manual thumb, grip and firing pin safeties; solid barrel bushing. Made in Canada by Para-Ordnance. Introduced 1993; still produced.

Steel frame		
New: $650	**Perf.:** $600	**Exc.:** $500
Alloy frame		
New: $600	**Perf.:** $550	**Exc.:** $450
Stainless frame, stainless		
New: $700	**Perf.:** $650	**Exc.:** $550
Stainless frame, Duotone		
New: $685	**Perf.:** $635	**Exc.:** $575

PARA-ORDNANCE P-14.40

Semi-automatic; single action; 40 S&W; 10-shot magazine; 3-1/2-inch barrel; 7-1/8-inch overall length; weighs 34 oz. (steel frame), 26 oz. (alloy frame); all the rest same as 14.45.

Steel frame		
New: $600	**Perf.:** $550	**Exc.:** $500
Alloy frame		
New: $600	**Perf.:** $550	**Exc.:** $450
Stainless frame, stainless		
New: $625	**Perf.:** $575	**Exc.:** $500
Stainless frame, Duotone		
New: $685	**Perf.:** $635	**Exc.:** $575

PARA-ORDNANCE P-14.45

Semi-automatic; single action; 45 ACP; 10-shot magazine (pre-1994 guns have 14-shot); 5-inch barrel; 8-1/2-inch overall length; weighs 40 oz. (steel frame), 31 oz. (alloy frame); textured composition grips; blade front sight, adjustable rear; high visibility three-dot system; matte black finish; grooved match trigger; rounded combat-style hammer; beveled magazine well; manual thumb, grip and firing pin safeties; solid barrel bushing. Made in Canada by Para-Ordnance. Introduced 1990; still produced.

Steel frame		
New: $650	**Perf.:** $600	**Exc.:** $500
Alloy frame		
New: $600	**Perf.:** $550	**Exc.:** $450
Stainless frame, stainless		
New: $700	**Perf.:** $650	**Exc.:** $550
Stainless frame, Duotone		
New: $685	**Perf.:** $635	**Exc.:** $575

PARA-ORDNANCE P-15.40

Semi-automatic; single action; 40 S&W; 10-shot magazine; 4-1/4-inch barrel; 7-3/4-inch overalllength; weighs 36 oz. (steel frame), 28 oz. (alloy frame); textured composition grips; blade front sight, adjustable rear; high visibility three-dot system; matte black finish; grooved match trigger; rounded combat-style hammer; beveled magazine well; manual thumb, grip and firing pin safeties; solid barrel bushing. Made

Para-Ordnance 1911 SSP

Para-Ordnance Slim Hawg

Para-Ordnance Stainless Warthog

Para-Ordnance Lite Hawg 9

Para-Ordnance Midnight Blue

Para-Ordnance Todd Jarrett .45 USPSA

Para-Ordnance Tac-Five

Para-Ordnance Nite-Tac .40

Para-Ordnance Nite-Tac 9

in Canada by Para-Ordnance. Introduced 1990; still produced.

Steel frame		
New: $650	**Perf.:** $600	**Exc.:** $500
Alloy frame		
New: $600	**Perf.:** $550	**Exc.:** $450
Stainless frame, stainless		
New: $700	**Perf.:** $650	**Exc.:** $550
Stainless frame, Duotone		
New: $685	**Perf.:** $635	**Exc.:** $575

PARA-ORDNANCE P-16.40

Semi-automatic; single action; 40 S&W; 10-shot magazine (pre-1994 guns have 16-shot); 5-inch barrel; 8-1/2-inch overall length; weighs 40 oz. (steel frame); textured composition grips; blade front sight, windage-adjustable rear; high visibility three-dot system; matte black finish; grooved match trigger; rounded combat-style hammer; beveled magazine well; manual thumb, grip and firing pin safeties; solid barrel bushing. Made in Canada by Para-Ordnance. Introduced 1994; still produced.

Steel frame		
New: $625	**Perf.:** $575	**Exc.:** $500
Stainless frame, stainless		
New: $650	**Perf.:** $600	**Exc.:** $525
Stainless frame, Duotone		
New: $685	**Perf.:** $635	**Exc.:** $575

PARA-ORDNANCE S-SERIES LIMITED PISTOLS

Similar to the P-Series pistols except with full-length recoil guide system; fully adjustable rear sight; tuned trigger with overtravel stop; beavertail grip safety; competition hammer; front and rear slide serrations; ambidextrous safety; lowered ejection port; ramped match-grade barrel; dovetailed front sight. Introduced

1998. Made in Canada by Para-Ordnance. Add 20 percent to price of comparable P-Series Model.

PARA-ORDNANCE WARTHOG

Semi-automatic; single action; 45ACP; 10+1 capacity; 3-inch barrel; weighs 24 oz.; 6.5-inch overall length; spurred hammer; 3-dot sights; Regal finish.

New: $725	**Perf.:** $675	**Exc.:** $600

PARA-ORDNANCE NITEHAWG

Similar to Warthog but with non-reflective black finish and tritium sights.

New: $725	**Perf.:** $675	**Exc.:** $600

PARA-ORDNANCE 1911 SSP

7+1 capacity .45 ACP 1911-style semi-auto with 5-inch barrel. 39 oz. Competition triggers and hammers. Fixed sights. Cocobolo grip panels.

NIB: $1000	**Exc.:** $895	**VGood:** $725

PARA-ORDNANCE SLIM HAWG

A .45 ACP pistol with 6+1 capacity. Single-stack, single-action 1911. Barrel 3-inch, 30 oz. Stainless construction, checkered wood grips. Fixed, 3-dot sights.

NIB: $100	**Exc.:** $895	**VGood:** $725

PARA-ORDNANCE STAINLESS WARTHOG

Stainless .45 ACP with 10+1 capacity. Single-stack, single-action 1911. Barrel 3-inch, 31 oz. Fixed, 3-dot sights and plastic grips.

NIB: $950	**Exc.:** $850	**VGood:** $695

PARA-ORDNANCE LITE HAWG 9

Double-stack, 12+1 single-action 9mm Parabellum in non-reflective black finish. Barrel 3-inch, 31.5 oz and capacity. Fixed, 3-dot sights.

NIB: $1000	**Exc.:** $895	**VGood:** $725

PARA-ORDNANCE MIDNIGHT BLUE P14-45

Double-stack, 14+1 single-action 45 ACP in non-reflective black. 5-inch barrel, fixed, 3-dot sights and black plastic grips.

NIB: $850	**Exc.:** $775	**VGood:** $650

PARA-ORDNANCE TODD JARRETT .40 USPSA

A limited edition 16+1 (or 10+1) .40 S&W custom competition pistol with adjustable rear sight and fiber optic front sight. 5-inch barrel, 40 oz., covert non-reflective black or sterling.

NIB: $1525	**Exc.:** $1395	**VGood:** $1125

PARA-ORDNANCE TODD JARRETT .45 USPSA

Limited edition 8+1 .45 ACP caliber custom competition pistol with adjustable rear sight and fiber optic front sight. 5-inch barrel, 39 oz.; covert non-reflective black or stainless finish.

NIB: $995	**Exc.:** $895	**VGood:** $675

PARA-ORDNANCE TAC-FIVE

Light double-action 9mm with 18+1 capacity. 5-inch barrel, 37.5 oz., stainless finish, adjustable rear sight, plastic grips.

NIB: $1100	**Exc.:** $975	**VGood:** $795

Para-Ordnance
LTC

Phelps Heritage I

Phoenix Arms
HP22

Phoenix Arms
Model Raven

Plainfield Model 71

PARA-ORDNANCE NITE-TAC .40

A .40 S&W 16+1 capacity double-action duty pistol with fixed sights. 5-inch barrel, 40 oz., stainless finish.

NIB: $1075　　**Exc.:** $975　　**VGood:** $800

PARA-ORDNANCE NITE-TAC 9

A 9mm 18+1 double-action duty pistol with fixed sights. 5-inch barrel, 40 oz., stainless finish.

NIB: $1075　　**Exc.:** $975　　**VGood:** $800

PARA-ORDNANCE LTC

Semi-auto; single action; .45ACP; 7+1 capacity; 4.25-inch barrel; 35 oz. weight; 7.75 inches overall; 3-dot sights; steel frame; Regal finish.

New: $725　　**Perf.:** $675　　**Exc.:** $600

PARDINI GP RAPID FIRE MATCH

Semi-automatic; single action; 22 Short; 5-shot magazine; 4-5/8-inch barrel; 11-5/8-inch overall length; weighs 43 oz.; wrap-around stippled walnut grips; interchangeable post front sight, fully-adjustable match rear. Imported from Italy by Nygord Precision Products. Introduced 1995.

Perf.: $850　　**Exc.:** $750　　**VGood:** $650

PARDINI GP RAPID FIRE MATCH SCHUMAN

Same specs as the GP model except extended rear sight for longer sight radius. Imported from Italy by Nygord Precision Products. Introduced 1995; still imported.

New: $1500　　**Perf.:** $1350　　**Exc.:** $1100

PARDINI K50 FREE PISTOL

Single shot; 22 LR; 9-7/8-inch barrel; 18-3/4-inch overall length; weighs 35 oz.; adjustable match-type wrap-around walnut grips; interchangeable post front sight, fully-adjustable match rear; removable, adjustable match trigger; barrel weights mount above the barrel. Imported from Italy by Nygord Precision Products. Introduced 1995; dropped 1999.

Perf.: $850　　**Exc.:** $750　　**VGood:** $650

PARDINI MODEL HP TARGET

Semi-automatic; single action; 32 S&W; 5-shot magazine; 4-3/4-inch barrel; 11-5/8-inch overall length; weighs 40 oz.; adjustable, stippled walnut, match-type grips; interchangeable blade front sight, interchangeable, fully-adjustable rear; fully-adjustable match trigger. Imported from Italy by Nygord Precision Products. Introduced 1995; still imported.

New: $1000　　**Perf.:** $900　　**Exc.:** $800

PARDINI MODEL SP LADIES

Semi-automatic; single action; 22 LR; 5-shot magazine; 4-3/4-inch barrel; 11-5/8-inch overall length; weighs 40 oz.; adjustable, stippled walnut, small match-type grips for smaller hands; interchangeable blade front sight, fully-adjustable rear; fully-adjustable match trigger. Imported from Italy by Nygord Precision Products. Introduced 1986; discontinued 1990.

Perf.: $850　　**Exc.:** $750　　**VGood:** $650

PARDINI MODEL SP TARGET

Semi-automatic; single action; 22 LR; 5-shot magazine; 4-3/4-inch barrel; 11-5/8-inch overall length; weighs 40 oz.; adjustable, stippled walnut,

match-type grips; interchangeable blade front sight, interchangeable, fully-adjustable rear; fully-adjustable match trigger. Imported from Italy by Nygord Precision Products. Introduced 1995; still imported.

New: $1150　　**Perf.:** $950　　**Exc.:** $650

PETERS STAHL PS-07 COMBAT COMPENSATOR

Semi-automatic; single action; 45 ACP, 10mm; 7-shot (45 ACP), 8-shot (10mm); 6-inch barrel; 10-inch overall length; weighs 45 oz.; Pachmayr Presentation rubber grips; interchangeable blade front sight, fully-adjustable Peters Stahl rear; linkless barrel with polygonal rifling and integral PS competition compensator; semi-extended PS slide stop and thumb safety; rearward extended magazine release; adjustable Videcki trigger; Wilson stainless beavertail grip safety; Pachmayr rubber mainspring housing. Imported from Germany by Federal Ordnance. Introduced 1989; dropped 1991.

45 ACP		
Perf.: $2200	**Exc.:** $1800	**VGood:** $1350
10mm Auto		
Perf.: $2100	**Exc.:** $1600	**VGood:** $1100

PHELPS EAGLE I

Revolver; single action; 444 Marlin; 6-shot cylinder; 8-inch barrel, others to customer specifications; 15-1/2-inch overall length (8-inch barrel); weighs 5-1/2 lbs.; smooth walnut grips; ramp front sight, adjustable rear; polished blue finish; transfer bar safety. Made in U.S. by Phelps Mfg. Co. Introduced 1978; dropped 1996.

Perf.: $2000　　**Exc.:** $1750　　**VGood:** $1500

PHELPS GRIZZLY

Revolver; single action; 50-70; 6-shot cylinder; 8-inch barrel, others to customer specifications; 15-1/2-inch overall length (8-inch barrel); weighs 5-1/2 lbs.; smooth walnut grips; ramp front sight, adjustable rear; polished blue finish; transfer bar safety. Made in U.S. by Phelps Mfg. Co. Introduced 1978; dropped 1996.

Perf.: $2200　　**Exc.:** $1850　　**VGood:** $1600

PHELPS HERITAGE I

Revolver; single action; 45-70; 6-shot cylinder; 8-inch barrel, others to customer specifications; 15-1/2-inch overall length (8-inch barrel); weighs 5-1/2 lbs.; smooth walnut grips; ramp front sight, adjustable rear; polished blue finish; transfer bar safety. Made in U.S. by Phelps Mfg. Co. Introduced 1978; dropped 1996.

Perf.: $2000　　**Exc.:** $1750　　**VGood:** $1500

PHELPS PATRIOT

Revolver; single action; 375 Win.; 6-shot; 8-inch barrel, others on special order; adjustable sights;

blued finish. Introduced 1993; discontinued 1995.

New: $1850　　**Perf.:** $1600　　**Exc.:** $1350

PHOENIX ARMS HP22

Semi-automatic; single action; 22 LR; 10-shot magazine; 3-inch barrel; 5-1/2-inch overall length; weighs 20 oz.; checkered composition grips; blade front sight, adjustable rear; exposed hammer; manual hold-open; button magazine release; available in satin nickel, polished blue finish. Made in U.S. by Phoenix Arms. Introduced 1993; still produced.

New: $85　　**Perf.:** $75　　**Exc.:** $60

PHOENIX ARMS HP25

Semi-automatic; single action; 25 ACP; 10-shot magazine; 3-inch barrel; 5-1/2-inch overall length; weighs 20 oz.; checkered composition grips; blade front sight, adjustable rear; exposed hammer; manual hold-open; button magazine release; satin nickel or polished blue finish. Made in U.S. by Phoenix Arms. Introduced 1994; still produced.

New: $80　　**Perf.:** $70　　**Exc.:** $50

PHOENIX ARMS MODEL RAVEN

Semi-automatic; single action; 25 ACP; 6-shot magazine; 2-7/16-inch barrel; 4-3/4-inch overall length; weighs 15 oz.; ivory-colored or black slotted plastic grips; ramped front sight, fixed rear; available in blue, nickel or chrome finish. Made in U.S. by Phoenix Arms. Introduced 1992; no longer produced.

New: $65　　**Perf.:** $50　　**Exc.:** $40

PLAINFIELD MODEL 71

Semi-automatic; 22 LR, 25 ACP; 10-shot (22 LR), 8-shot (25 ACP); 1-inch barrel; 5-1/8-inch overall length; fixed sights; checkered walnut stocks; stainless steel slide frame. Also made with caliber conversion kit. Introduced 1970; discontinued approximately 1980.

Exc.: $200	**VGood:** $165	**Good:** $125
With conversion kit		
Exc.: $250	**VGood:** $225	**Good:** $175

PLAINFIELD MODEL 72

Semi-automatic; 22 LR, 25 ACP; 10-shot (22 LR), 8-shot (25 ACP); 3-1/2-inch barrel; 6-inch overall length; fixed sights; checkered walnut stocks; aluminum slide. Introduced 1970; discontinued 1978.

Exc.: $200	**VGood:** $175	**Good:** $125
With conversion kit		
Exc.: $250	**VGood:** $200	**Good:** $150

PSA-25 AUTO POCKET PISTOL

Caliber: 25 ACP, 6-shot magazine. Barrel: 2-1/8-inch. Weight: 9.5 oz. Length: 4-1/8-inch overall. Stocks: Checkered black polymer, ivory, checkered

PSA-25 Auto Pocket Pistol

RG 14

RG 23

RG 31

RG 26

transparent carbon fiber-filled polymer. Sights: Fixed. Features: All steel construction; striker fired; single action only; magazine disconnector; cocking indicator. Introduced 1987. Made in U.S. by Precision Small Arms, Inc.

Traditional (polished black oxide) or Nouveau - Satin (brushed nickel)		
Perf.: $225	**Exc.:** $180	**VGood:** $150
Nouveau - Mirror (highly polished nickel)		
Perf.: $300	**Exc.:** $250	**VGood:** $200
Featherweight (aluminum frame, nickel slide)		
Perf.: $325	**Exc.:** $275	**VGood:** $225
Diplomat (black oxide with gold highlights, ivory grips)		
Perf.: $525	**Exc.:** $400	**VGood:** $300
Montreaux (gold plated, ivory grips)		
Perf.: $550	**Exc.:** $475	**VGood:** $350
Renaissance (hand engraved nickel, ivory grips)		
Perf.: $900	**Exc.:** $750	**VGood:** $600

QFI DARK HORSEMAN

Revolver; single action; 44 Mag., 45 Colt; 6-1/2-inch, 7-1/2-inch barrel; adjustable sights; black composition stocks; extended grip frame; blued finish. Introduced 1991; discontinued 1992.

Perf.: $200   **Exc.:** $175   **VGood:** $125

QFI HORSEMAN

Revolver; single action; 357 Mag., 44 Mag., 45 Colt; 6-1/2-inch, 7-1/2-inch barrel; weighs 45 oz. (6-1/2-inch barrel); blade front sight, grooved rear; uncheckered walnut grips; color case-hardened frame; bright blue finish. Assembled in U.S. Introduced 1991; discontinued 1992.

Perf.: $250   **Exc.:** $200   **VGood:** $175

QFI MODEL LA380

Semi-automatic; single action; 380 ACP; 6-shot; 3-1/8-inch barrel; 6-1/4-inch overall length; weighs 25 oz.; blade front sight, windage-adjustable rear; uncheckered European walnut grips; external hammer; magazine safety; hammer, trigger, firing pin block; blued finish. Introduced 1991; discontinued 1992.

Perf.: $100	**Exc.:** $90	**VGood:** $75
Chrome finish		
Perf.: $125	**Exc.:** $110	**VGood:** $100
Stainless steel		
Perf.: $165	**Exc.:** $145	**VGood:** $135

QFI MODEL LA380 TIGRESS

Same specs as Model LA380 except scrimshawed white polymer grips; blue frame with gold-plated slide. Introduced 1991; discontinued 1991.

Perf.: $125   **Exc.:** $110   **VGood:** $100

QFI MODEL SA25

Semi-automatic; single action; 25 ACP; 6-shot; 2-1/2-inch barrel; 4-5/8-inch overall length; weighs 12 oz.; fixed sights; smooth walnut or pearlite grips; external hammer; blued finish. Introduced 1991; discontinued 1991.

Perf.: $60   **Exc.:** $45   **VGood:** $35

QFI MODEL SA25 TIGRESS

Same specs as Model SA25 except scrimshawed white polymer grips; blue frame with gold-plated slide. Introduced 1991; discontinued 1991.

Perf.: $125   **Exc.:** $100   **VGood:** $85

QFI MODEL SO38

Revolver; double action; 38 Spl.; 6-shot; 2-inch solid, 4-inch vent-rib barrel; weighs 27 oz. (2-inch barrel); fixed sights; bulldog-type checkered plastic or walnut grips; one-stroke ejection. Introduced 1991; discontinued 1992.

Perf.: $165   **Exc.:** $145   **VGood:** $120

QFI PLAINS RIDER

Revolver; single action; 22 LR, 22 LR/22 WMR; 6-shot cylinder; 3-inch, 4-3/4-inch, 6-1/2-inch, 9-inch, 11-inch overall length (6-1/2-inch barrel); weighs 35 oz. (6-1/2-inch barrel); black composition grips; blade front sight, fixed rear; blue/black finish; available with extra cylinder. From QFI. Introduced 1991; dropped 1992.

22 LR, 3-inch, 4-3/4-inch, 6-1/2-inch barrel		
Perf.: $110	**Exc.:** $75	**VGood:** $60
22 LR, 3-inch, 4-3/4-inch, 6-1/2-inch barrel, dual cylinder		
Perf.: $135	**Exc.:** $90	**VGood:** $85
22 LR, 9-inch barrel		
Perf.: $105	**Exc.:** $80	**VGood:** $65
22 LR, 9-inch barrel, dual cylinder		
Perf.: $110	**Exc.:** $100	**VGood:** $90

QFI RP SERIES

Revolver; double action; 22 LR, 22 WMR, 22 LR/WMR combo, 32 S&W, 32 S&W Long, 32 H&R Mag., 38 Spl.; 6-shot cylinder; 2-inch, 4-inch barrel; 6-1/4-inch overall length (2-inch barrel); weighs 23 oz.; magnum-style round butt grips of checkered plastic; ramp front sight, fixed square notch rear; one-piece solid frame; checkered hammer spur; serrated trigger; blue finish. Made in U.S. by QFI. Introduced 1991; dropped 1992.

Perf.: $100   **Exc.:** $65   **VGood:** $50

QFI WESTERN RANGER

Revolver; single action; 22 LR, 22 LR/22 WMR combo; 3-inch, 4-inch, 4-3/4-inch, 6-inch, 6-1/2-inch, 7-inch, 9-inch barrel; 10-inch overall length (4-3/4-inch barrel); weighs 31 oz.; blade front sight, notch rear; American walnut grips; blue/black finish. dropped 1992.

Perf.: $100   **Exc.:** $75   **VGood:** $60

RG 14

Revolver; double action; 22 LR; 6-shot; 1 3/4-inch, 3-inch barrel; 5-1/2-inch overall length (13/4 inch barrel); fixed sights; checkered plastic grips;

cylinder swings out when pin removed; blued finish. Introduced 1978; discontinued 1986.

Exc.: $65   **VGood:** $50   **Good:** $40

RG 16

Derringer; over/under; 22 WMR; 2-shot; 3-inch barrel; 5-inch overall length; weighs 15 oz.; fixed sights; blue or nickel finish. Introduced 1975; no longer in production.

Exc.: $60   **VGood:** $50   **Good:** $35

RG 17

Derringer; over/under; 38 Spl.; 2-shot; 3-inch barrel; 5-inch overall length; weighs 15 oz.; fixed sights; blue or nickel finish. Introduced 1975; no longer in production.

Exc.: $60   **VGood:** $50   **Good:** $35

RG 23

Revolver; double action; 22 LR; 6-shot; 1-3/4-inch, 3-inch barrel; 5-1/2-inch overall length (1-3/4-inch barrel); fixed sights; checkered plasticgrips; central ejector system; blued finish. Introduced 1978; discontinued 1986.

Exc.: $70   **VGood:** $60   **Good:** $45

RG 25

Semi-automatic; 25 ACP; 6-shot; 2-1/2-inch barrel; 4-3/4-inch overall length; weighs 12 oz.; fixed sights; thumb safety; blue or nickel finish. Introduced 1975; no longer in production.

Exc.: $75   **VGood:** $60   **Good:** $50

RG 26

Semi-automatic; single action; 25 ACP; 6-shot; 2-1/2-inch barrel; 4-3/4-inch overall length; 12 oz.; fixed sights; checkered plastic stocks; thumb safety; blued finish. Introduced 1977; discontinued 1986.

Exc.: $75   **VGood:** $60   **Good:** $50

RG 30

Revolver; double action; 22 LR, 22 WMR; 6-shot swing-out cylinder; 4-inch barrel; 9-inch overall length; windage-adjustable rear sight, fixed front; checkered plastic stocks; blued finish. Introduced 1977; discontinued 1986.

Exc.: $65	**VGood:** $60	**Good:** $50
Nickel finish		
Exc.: $70	**VGood:** $65	**Good:** $55

RG 31

Revolver; double action; 32 S&W, 38 Spl.; 6-shot (32 S&W), 5-shot (38 Spl.); 2-inch barrel; 6-3/4-inch overall length; fixed sights; checkered plastic grips; cylinder swings out when pin removed; blued finish. Introduced 1978; discontinued 1986.

Exc.: $110   **VGood:** $100   **Good:** $85

RG 38S   RG 39   RG 57

RG 63   RG 66   RG 88

RG 38S

Revolver; double action; 38 Spl.; 6-shot swing-out cylinder; 3-inch, 4-inch, 6-inch (38T) barrel; 9-1/4-inch overall length (4-inch barrel); weighs 35 oz.; windage-adjustable rear sight, fixed front; checkered plastic stocks; blued finish. Introduced 1977; discontinued 1986.

Exc.: $125	VGood: $110	Good: $100
Nickel finish		
Exc.: $135	VGood: $120	Good: $110

RG 39

Revolver; 38 Spl., 32 S&W; 6-shot; 2-inch barrel; 7-inch overall length; weighs 21 oz.; fixed sights; American walnut grips; blue finish. Introduced 1981; no longer in production.

Exc.: $125	VGood: $110	Good: $85

RG 40

Revolver; double action; 38 Spl., 32 S&W; 6-shot; 2-inch barrel; 7-inch overall length; fixed sights; checkered plastic grips; swing-out cylinder; spring ejector; blued finish. Introduced 1980; discontinued 1986.

Exc.: $110	VGood: $100	Good: $75

RG 42

Semi-automatic; 25 ACP; 7-shot; 2-3/4-inch barrel; 5-5/16-inch overall length; fixed sights; thumb and magazine safety; blue finish.

Exc.: $75	VGood: $60	Good: $50

RG 57

Revolver; double action; 357 Mag., 44 Mag.; 6-shot swing-out cylinder; 4-inch barrel; 9-1/2-inch overall length; fixed sights; checkered plastic stocks; steel frame; blued finish. Manufactured in Germany, imported by RG Industries. Introduced 1977; discontinued 1986.

Exc.: $125	VGood: $110	Good: $85

RG 63

Revolver; double action; 22 LR; 8-shot; 5-inch barrel; 10-1/4-inch overall length; fixed sights; checkered plastic stocks; Western configuration with slide ejector rod; blued finish. Introduced 1976; discontinued 1986.

Exc.: $100	VGood: $85	Good: $65
Nickel finish		
Exc.: $110	VGood: $90	Good: $70

RG 66

Revolver; single action; 22 LR, 22 WMR; 6-shot; 4-3/4-inch barrel; 10-inch overall length; adjustable rear sight, fixed front; checkered plastic stocks;

Ram-Line
Exactor Target

slide ejector rod; blued finish. Introduced 1977; discontinued 1986.

Exc.: $90	VGood: $75	Good: $60
Nickel finish		
Exc.: $95	VGood: $80	Good: $65

RG 74

Revolver; double action; 22 LR; 6-shot; 3-inch barrel; 7-3/4-inch overall length; fixed sights; checkered plastic stocks; swing-out cylinder with spring ejector; blued finish. Introduced 1978; discontinued 1986.

Exc.: $65	VGood: $50	Good: $40

RG 88

Revolver; double action; 38 Spl., 357 Mag.; 6-shot swing-out cylinder; 4-inch barrel; 9-inch overall length; fixed sights; checkered walnut stocks; wide spur hammer, trigger; blued finish. Introduced 1977; dropped 1986.

Exc.: $135	VGood: $110	Good: $90

RADOM P-35

Semi-automatic; 9mm Para; 8-shot; 4-3/4-inch barrel; 7-3/4-inch overall length; fixed sights; checkered plastic stocks; blued finish. Design based on Colt Model 1911A1. Manufactured in Poland 1936 to 1945.

Pre-War, dated 1936 to 1939		
Exc.: $1500	VGood: $1100	Good: $800
Wartime manufacture		
Exc.: $425	VGood: $325	Good: $250

RAM-LINE EXACTOR TARGET

Semi-automatic; single action; 22 LR; 15-shot magazine; 8-inch barrel; 12-5/16-inch overall length; weighs 23 oz.; one-piece injection molded grips in conventional contour; checkered side panels; ridged front and backstraps; ramp front sight, adjustable

Randall
Raider/Service
Model C

rear; injection molded grip frame, alloy receiver; hybrid composite barrel; constant force sear spring gives 2-1/2-lb. trigger pull; Adapt-A-Barrel for mounting weights, flashlight; drilled and tapped receiver for scope mounting; jeweled bolt; comes with carrying case, test target. Made in U.S. by Ram-Line, Inc. Introduced 1990; no longer in production.

Perf.: $200	Exc.: $250	VGood: $175

RAM-LINE RAM-TECH

Semi-automatic; single action; 22 LR; 15-shot magazine; 4-1/2-inch barrel; weighs 19 oz.; one-piece injection molded grips with checkered panels; ramp front sight, adjustable rear; compact frame; injection molded grip frame, alloy receiver; hybrid composite barrel; constant force sear spring gives 3-lb. trigger pull; comes with carrying case. Made in U.S. by Ram-Line, Inc. Introduced 1994; no longer produced.

Perf.: $175	Exc.: $150	VGood: $135

RANDALL CURTIS E. LEMAY FOUR-STAR MODEL

Semi-automatic; 9mm Para., 45 ACP; 7-shot (9mm), 6-shot (45 ACP); 4-1/4-inch barrel; 7-3/4-inch overall length; weighs 35 oz.; fixed or adjustable sights; checkered walnut stocks; squared trigger guard; stainless steel construction. Introduced 1984; discontinued 1984. Add 400% for 9mm.

Exc.: $1000	VGood: $850	Good: $700

RANDALL RAIDER/SERVICE MODEL-C

Semi-automatic; 9mm Para., 45 ACP; 6-shot; 4-1/4-inch barrel; 7-3/4-inch overall length; weighs 36 oz.; fixed or adjustable sights; checkered walnut stocks; squared trigger guard; extended magazine baseplate; stainless steel construction. Introduced 1983; discontinued 1984. Add 400% for 9mm.

Exc.: $600	VGood: $500	Good: $450

Raven MP-25

Reising Target Model

Remington Model 95

Record Match Model 200 Free Pistol

Remington Model 1901 Target

Remington Model 51

Remington XP-100 Hunter

RANDALL SERVICE MODEL
Semi-automatic; 38 Super, 9mm Para., 45 ACP; 5-inch barrel; 8-1/2-inch overall length; weighs 38 oz.; blade front sight, fixed or adjustable rear; checkered walnut stocks; round-top or ribbed slide; all stainless steel construction. Introduced 1983; discontinued 1984.

   Exc.: $850   VGood: $650   Good: $500

RAVEN MP-25
Semi-automatic; single action; 25 ACP; 6-shot; 2-7/16-inch barrel; 5-1/2-inch overall length; weighs 15 oz.; uncheckered pearlite stocks; die-cast slide serrations; blued, nickel or satin nickel finish. Manufactured in U.S. Introduced 1984; discontinued 1992.

   Exc.: $50   VGood: $40   Good: $30

RAVEN P-25
Semi-automatic; single action; 25 ACP; 6-shot; 2-7/16-inch barrel; 5-1/2-inch overall length; weighs 15 oz.; fixed sights; uncheckered walnut; blued, nickel or satin nickel finish. Manufactured in U.S. Introduced 1977; discontinued 1984.

   Exc.: $50   VGood: $40   Good: $25

RECORD-MATCH MODEL 200 FREE PISTOL
Single shot; Martini action; 22 LR; 11-inch barrel; micrometer rear sight, target-type front; carved, checkered European walnut stock, forearm, with adjustable hand base; set trigger, spur trigger guard; blued finish. Manufactured in Germany prior to WWII.

   Exc.: $1050   VGood: $950   Good: $600

RECORD-MATCH MODEL 210 FREE PISTOL
Single shot; Martini action; 22 LR; 11-inch barrel; micrometer rear sight, target-type front; carved, checkered deluxe European walnut stock, forearm with adjustable hand base; button release set trigger; blued finish. Manufactured in Germany prior to WWII.

   Exc.: $1200   VGood: $1050   Good: $700

RECORD-MATCH MODEL 210A FREE PISTOL
Same specs as Model 210 except alloy frame. Manufactured in Germany prior to WWII.

   Exc.: $1300   VGood: $1100   Good: $700

REISING TARGET MODEL
Semi-automatic; hinged frame; 22 LR; 12-shot; 6-1/2-inch barrel; fixed sights; hard rubber checkered stocks; external hammers; blued finish. Manufactured 1921 to 1924.

   Exc.: $400   VGood: $350   Good: $205

REMINGTON MODEL 51
Semi-automatic; 32 ACP, 380 ACP; 8-shot; 3-1/2-inch barrel; 6-5/8-inch overall length; weighs 21 oz.; fixed sights; hard rubber grips; blued finish. Introduced 1918; discontinued 1943. .32 is somewhat scarce; add 10 percent.

   Exc.: $500   VGood: $375   Good: $250

REMINGTON MODEL 95
Derringer; over/under; single action; 41 Short Rimfire; 3-inch barrels; 4-7/8-inch overall length. Introduced 1866; discontinued 1935. Prior to 1888 the model was stamped "E Remington & Sons"; from 1888 to 1910 the derringers were marked "Remington Arms Co."; from 1910 to 1935 guns were marked "Remington Arms-U.M.C. Co." The early styles have a two-armed extractor, long hammer spur. In later models a few have no extractor, majority have sliding extractor, short hammer spur. Available with all-blued finish, full nickel plate or blued barrels with nickel-plated frame; factory engraving; choice of checkered hard rubber, walnut, mother-of-pearl, ivory grips; fixed rear groove sight, front blade integral with top barrel. Values shown are for early issues. Beware of cracked barrel hinge.

   Exc.: $1300   VGood: $950   Good: $600

Nickel finish

   Exc.: $1500   VGood: $1150   Good: $750

Engraved with mother-of-pearl or ivory grips

   Exc.: $2300   VGood: $1850   Good: $1050

REMINGTON MODEL 1901 TARGET
Single shot; rolling block action; 22 Short, 22 LR, 25 Rimfire, 32 Centerfire, 44 S&W Russian; 10-inch barrel; 14-inch overall length; target sights; checkered walnut grips, forearm; blued finish. Manufactured 1901 to 1909.

   Exc.: $1500   VGood: $1250   Good: $1000

REMINGTON MODEL 1911 MILITARY
Semi-automatic; single action; 45 ACP; 8-shot; fixed sight; checkered walnut grip; Colt Model 1911 made under U.S. contract by Remington UMC; blued finish. Introduced 1918; discontinued 1919.

   Exc.: $1000   VGood: $850   Good: $600

REMINGTON XP-22R
Single shot; bolt-action; 22 LR; 5-shot; 14-1/2-inch barrel; weighs 68 oz.; no sights; drilled, tapped for scope mounts or iron sights; rear-handled stock of fiberglass-reinforced Kevlar built on Remington Model 541-7 rifle action. Available on special order from Remington Custom Shop. Introduced 1991; discontinued 1992.

   Exc.: $650   VGood: $550   Good: $350

REMINGTON XP-100 HUNTER PISTOL
Single shot; bolt action; 223 Rem., 7mm BR Rem., 7mm-08 Rem., 35 Rem.; 14-1/2-inch barrel; 21-1/4-inch overall length; weighs 4-1/2 lbs.; laminated wood stock with contoured grip; no sights furnished; drilled and tapped for scope mounting; mid-handle grip design with scalloped contours for right- or left-handed use; two-position safety; matte blue finish. Introduced 1993; dropped 1995.

   New: $650   Perf.: $500   Exc.: $300

REMINGTON XP-100 CUSTOM HB LONG RANGE PISTOL
Single shot; bolt-action; 221 Rem. Fireball; 10-1/2-inch barrel; 16-3/4-inch overall length; vent rib; blade front sight, adjustable rear; receiver drilled, tapped for scope mounts; one-piece brown nylon stock; blued finish. Introduced 1963; dropped 1985.

   Exc.: $850   VGood: $700   Good: $575

Remington XP-100
Varmint Special

Remington XP-100
Silhouette

Republic Patriot

Rocky Mountain
Arms Patriot

Rocky Mountain
Arms 1911A1-LH

Rossi Cyclops Revolver

Rossi Lady Rossi

REMINGTON XP-100 SILHOUETTE

Single shot; bolt action; 7mm BR Rem.; 10-1/2-inch barrel; 17-1/4-inch overall length; weighs 3-7/8 lbs.; American walnut stock; blade front sight, fully-adjustable square-notch rear; mid-handle grip with scalloped contours for left- or right-handed use; match-type trigger; two-position thumb safety; matte blue finish. Dropped 1995.

    Perf.: $600   **Exc.:** $500   **VGood:** $300

REMINGTON XP-100 VARMINT SPECIAL

Single shot; bolt action; 221 Rem. Fireball, 223 Rem.; 10-1/2-inch barrel (221), 14-1/2-inch barrel (223); weighs 70 oz.; adjustable sights, drilled, tapped for scope; one-piece nylon grip; forend weights for balance; matte blue finish. Introduced 1963; discontinued 1992.

    Perf.: $700   **Exc.:** $595   **VGood:** $350

REMINGTON XP-100R

Repeater; bolt action; 223 Rem., 22-250, 7mm-08 Rem., 250 Savage, 308, 350 Rem. Mag., 35 Rem.; blind magazine; 5-shot (7mm-08, 35), 6-shot (223 Rem.); 14-1/2-inch standard-weight barrel; weighs about 4-1/2 lbs; rear-handle, synthetic Du Pont Kevlar stock to eliminate transfer bar between forward trigger and rear trigger assembly; front and rear sling swivel studs; adjustable leaf rear sight, bead front; receiver drilled and tapped for scope mounts. From Remington Custom Shop. Introduced 1990; dropped 1995.

    New: $850   **Perf.:** $700   **Exc.:** $600

REPUBLIC PATRIOT PISTOL

Caliber: 45 ACP, 6-shot magazine. Barrel: 3-inch. Weight: 20 oz. Length: 6-inch overall. Stocks: Checkered. Sights: Blade front, drift-adjustable rear. Features: Black polymer frame; stainless steel slide; double-action-only trigger system; squared trigger guard. Introduced 1997. Made in U.S. by Republic Arms, Inc.

    Perf.: $275   **Exc.:** $225   **VGood:** $175

REXIO PUCARA M224 REVOLVER

Caliber: 22 LR, 9-shot cylinder. Barrel: 4-inch. Weight: 33 oz. Length: 9-inch overall. Stocks: Checkered hardwood. Sights:• Blade front, square notch rear adjustable for windage. Features: Alloy frame; hammer block safety; polished blue finish. Introduced 1997. Imported from Argentina by Century International Arms.

    Perf.: $150   **Exc.:** $125   **VGood:** $95

REXIO PUCARA M324 REVOLVER

Caliber: 32 S&W Long, 7-shot cylinder. Barrel: 4-inch. Weight: 31 oz. Length: 9-inch overall. Stocks: Checkered hardwood. Sights: Blade front, square notch rear adjustable for windage. Features: Alloy frame; polished blue finish; hammer block safety. Introduced 1997. Imported from Argentina by Century International Arms.

    Perf.: $150   **Exc.:** $110   **VGood:** $100

REXIO PUCARA M384 REVOLVER

Caliber: 38 Spec., 6-shot. Barrel: 4-inch. Weight: 30 oz. Length: 9-inch overall. Stocks: Checkered hardwood. Sights: Blade front, rear adjustable for windage. Features: Alloy frame. Polished blue finish. Imported from Argentina by Century International Arms.

    Perf.: $150   **Exc.:** $110   **VGood:** $100

ROCK RIVER ARMS PRO CARRY

4.25", 5" or 6" barrel and choice of Heinie or Novak tritium sights and polished finish; guaranteed to shoot 2.5" group at 50 yards with select ammunition. Other options available.

    NIB: $1895   **Exc.:** $1500   **VGood:** $1100

ROCKY MOUNTAIN ARMS 1911A1-LH

Semi-automatic; single action; 40 S&W, 45 ACP; 7-shot magazine; 5-1/4-inch barrel; 8-13/16-inch overall length; weighs 37 oz.; checkered walnut grips; red insert Patridge front sight, white outline click-adjustable rear; fully left-handed pistol; slide, frame, barrel made from stainless steel; working parts coated with Teflon-S; single-stage trigger with 3-1/2-lb. pull. Made in U.S. by Rocky Mountain Arms, Inc. Introduced 1993; dropped 1993.

    Perf.: $1200   **Exc.:** $950   **VGood:** $750

ROCKY MOUNTAIN ARMS PATRIOT

Semi-automatic; single action; 223 Rem.; 10-shot magazine; 7-inch barrel with muzzlebrake; 20 1/2-inch overall length; weighs 5 lbs.; black composition grips; no sights; milled upper receiver with enhanced Weaver base; milled lower receiver from billet plate; machined aluminum National Match handguard; finished in DuPont Teflon-S matte black or NATO green; comes with black nylon case, one magazine. Made in U.S. by Rocky Mountain Arms, Inc. Introduced 1993; still in production.

With A-2 handle top		
New: $2250	**Perf.:** $2000	**Exc.:** $1850
Flat top model		
New: $2400	**Perf.:** $2200	**Exc.:** $1950

ROSSI CYCLOPS REVOLVER

Caliber: 357 Magnum, 6-shot. Barrel: 6-inch, 8-inch. Weight: 44 oz. (6-inch barrel). Length: 11-3/4-inch overall (6-inch barrel). Stocks: Checkered rubber. Sights: Blade front, fully adjustable rear. Features: Extra-heavy barrel with four recessed compensator ports on each side of the muzzle. Stainless steel construction. Comes with scope mount and rings. Polished finish. Introduced 1997. Imported from Brazil by Interarms.

    Exc.: $400   **VGood:** $350   **Good:** $205

ROSSI LADY ROSSI

Revolver; double action; 38 Spl.; 5-shot cylinder; 2-inch, 3-inch barrel; 6-1/2-inch overall length (2-inch barrel); weighs 21 oz.; smooth rosewood grips; fixed sights; high-polish stainless steel with "Rossi" engraved on frame; comes with velvet carry bag. Imported from Brazil by Interarms. Introduced 1995; no longer imported.

    New: $200   **Perf.:** $160   **Exc.:** $135

Rossi Model 68

Rossi Model 68S

Rossi Model 70

Rossi Model 84

Rossi Model 88 Stainless

Rossi Model 511 Sportsman

Rossi Model 518

Rossi Model 720

Rossi Model 720C

ROSSI MODEL 31

Revolver; double action; 38 Spl.; 5-shot; 4-inch barrel; weighs 22 oz.; ramp front sight, low-profile adjustable rear; checkered wood stocks; all-steel frame; blue or nickel finish. Introduced 1978; discontinued 1985.

Exc.: $125   **VGood:** $110   **Good:** $100

ROSSI MODEL 51

Revolver; double action; 22 LR; 6-shot; 6-inch barrel; adjustable sights; checkered wood stocks; blued finish. Discontinued 1985.

Exc.: $125   **VGood:** $110   **Good:** $100

ROSSI MODEL 68

Revolver; double action; 38 Spl.; 5-shot; 2-inch, 3-inch barrel; weighs 22 oz.; ramp front sight, low-profile adjustable rear; checkered rubber or wood stocks; all-steel frame; swing-out cylinder; blue or nickel finish. Made in Brazil. Introduced 1978; discontinued 1985. Reintroduced in 1993 as the Model 68S. No longer imported

Exc.: $150   **VGood:** $125   **Good:** $110

ROSSI MODEL 68S

Same specs as Model 68 except weighs 23 oz.; fixed sights. Introduced 1993; no longer in production.

New: $175   **Perf.:** $150   **Exc.:** $125

ROSSI MODEL 69

Revolver; double action; 32 S&W; 6-shot; 3-inch barrel; ramp front sight, low-profile adjustable rear; checkered wood stocks; all-steel frame; swing-out cylinder; blue or nickel finish. Made in Brazil. Introduced 1978; discontinued 1985.

Exc.: $110   **VGood:** $90   **Good:** $80

ROSSI MODEL 70

Revolver; double action; 22 LR; 6-shot; 3-inch barrel; ramp front sight, low-profile adjustable rear; checkered wood stocks; all-steel frame; swing-out cylinder; blue or nickel finish. Made in Brazil. Introduced 1978; discontinued 1985.

Exc.: $125   **VGood:** $100   **Good:** $75

ROSSI MODEL 84 STAINLESS

Revolver; double action; 38 Spl.; 6-shot; 3-inch, 4-inch barrel; 8-inch overall length; weighs 27½ oz.; fixed sights; checkered wood grips; solid raised rib; stainless steel. Made in Brazil. Introduced 1984; discontinued 1986.

Exc.: $200   **VGood:** $175   **Good:** $150

ROSSI MODEL 88 STAINLESS

Revolver; double action; 38 Spl.; 5-shot; 2-inch, 3-inch barrel; 8-3/4-inch overall length; weighs 21 oz.; ramp front sight, drift-adjustable square-notch rear; checkered wood or rubber stocks; small frame; stainless steel construction; matte finish. Introduced 1993; no longer imported

New: $200   **Perf.:** $175   **Exc.:** $150

ROSSI MODEL 89 STAINLESS

Revolver; double action; 32 S&W; 6-shot; 3-inch barrel; 8-3/4-inch overall length; weighs 21 oz.; ramp front sight, drift-adjustable square notch rear; checkered wood or rubber stocks; stainless steel; matte finish. Introduced 1985; discontinued 1986; reintroduced 1989; no longer imported.

Exc.: $160   **VGood:** $150   **Good:** $125

ROSSI MODEL 94

Revolver; double action; 38 Spl.; 6-shot; 3-inch, 4-inch barrel; 27-1/2 oz.; ramp front sight; adjustable rear; checkered wood stocks; blued finish. Introduced 1985; discontinued 1988.

Exc.: $175   **VGood:** $150   **Good:** $135

ROSSI MODEL 511 SPORTSMAN

Revolver; double action; 22 LR; 6-shot; 4-inch barrel; 9-inch overall length; weighs 30 oz.; adjustable square-notch rear sight, orange-insert ramp front; checkered wood stocks; heavy barrel; integral sight rib; shrouded ejector rod; stainless steel construction. Made in Brazil. Introduced 1986; discontinued 1990.

Exc.: $150   **VGood:** $135   **Good:** $125

ROSSI MODEL 515

Revolver; double action; 22 WMR; 6-shot cylinder; 4-inch barrel; 9-inch overall length; weighs 30 oz.; checkered wood and finger-groove wrap-around rubber grips; blade front sight with red insert, fully-adjustable rear; small frame; stainless steel construction; solid integral barrel rib. Imported from Brazil by Interarms. Introduced 1994; still imported.

New: $200   **Perf.:** $175   **Exc.:** $150

ROSSI MODEL 518

Revolver; double action; 22 LR; 6-shot cylinder; 4-inch barrel; 9-inch overall length; weighs 30 oz.; checkered wood and finger-groove wrap-around rubber grips; blade front sight with red insert, fully-adjustable rear; small frame; stainless steel construction; solid integral barrel rib. Imported from Brazil by Interarms. Introduced 1994; no longer imported.

New: $200   **Perf.:** $185   **Exc.:** $160

ROSSI MODEL 720

Revolver; double action; 44 Spl.; 5-shot cylinder; 3-inch barrel; 8-inch overall length; weighs 27-1/2 oz.; checkered rubber, combat-style grips; red insert front sight on ramp, fully-adjustable rear; all stainless steel construction; solid barrel rib; full ejector rod shroud. Imported from Brazil by Interarms. Introduced 1992.

New: $375   **Perf.:** $315   **Exc.:** $250

ROSSI MODEL 720C

Same specs as the Model 720 except spurless hammer; double-action only. Imported from Brazil by Interarms. Introduced 1992; no longer imported.

New: $375   **Perf.:** $315   **Exc.:** $250

Rossi Model 851

Rossi Model 877

Rossi Model 951

Rossi Model 971 Comp Gun

Safari Arms Enforcer

RPM XL Single Shot

ROSSI MODEL 851

Revolver; double action; 38 Spl.; 6-shot; 3-inch, 4-inch barrel; 8-inch overall length (3-inch barrel); weighs 27-1/2 oz.; red-insert blade front sight, windage-adjustable rear; checkered Brazilian hardwood grips; medium-size frame; stainless steel construction; vent rib. Introduced 1991; no longer imported.

New: $200   **Perf.:** $175   **Exc.:** $135

ROSSI MODEL 877 REVOLVER

Caliber: 357 Mag., 6-shot cylinder. Barrel: 2-inch. Weight: 26 oz. Length: NA. Stocks: Stippled synthetic. Sights: Blade front, fixed groove rear. Features: Stainless steel construction; fully enclosed ejector rod. Introduced 1996. no longer imported.

Perf.: $200   **Exc.:** $165   **VGood:** $140

ROSSI MODEL 941

Revolver; double action; 38 Spl.; 6-shot; 4-inch solid rib barrel; 9-inch overall length; weighs 30 oz.; colored insert front sight, adjustable rear; checkered hardwood combat stocks; shrouded ejector rod; blued finish. Made in Brazil. Introduced 1985; discontinued 1990.

Exc.: $175   **VGood:** $150   **Good:** $125

ROSSI MODEL 951

Revolver; double action; 38 Spl.; 6-shot; 4-inch vent-rib barrel; 9-inch overall length; weighs 30 oz.; colored insert front sight, adjustable rear; checkered hardwood combat stocks; shrouded ejector rod; blued finish. Made in Brazil. Introduced 1985; discontinued 1990.

Exc.: $175   **VGood:** $150   **Good:** $125

ROSSI MODEL 971

Revolver; double action; 357 Mag.; 6-shot; 2-1/2-inch, 4-inch, 6-inch heavy barrel; 9-inch overall length; weighs 36 oz.; blade front sight, fully-adjustable rear; checkered Brazilian hardwood grips; matted sight rib; target trigger; wide checkered hammer spur; full-length ejector rod shroud; blued (4-inch only) or stainless finish. Made in Brazil. Introduced 1988; no longer imported.

New: $200   **Perf.:** $175   **Exc.:** $150

ROSSI MODEL 971 COMP GUN

Same specs as Model 971 except stainless finish; 3-1/4-inch barrel with integral compensator; overall length 9-inch; weighs 32 oz.; red insert front sight, fully-adjustable rear; checkered, contoured rubber grips. Imported from Brazil by Interarms. Introduced 1993; no longer imported

New: $225   **Perf.:** $200   **Exc.:** $175

ROSSI MODEL 971 STAINLESS

Same general specs as Model 971 except 2-1/2-inch, 4-inch, 6-inch barrel; rubber grips; stainless steel construction. Introduced 1989; no longer imported.

New: $225   **Perf.:** $200   **Exc.:** $175

ROSSI MODEL 971 VRC REVOLVER

Similar to the Model 971 except has Rossi's 8-port Vented Rib Compensator; checkered finger-groove rubber grips; stainless steel construction. Available with 2.5-inch, 4-inch, 6-inch barrel; weighs 30 oz. with 2-5/8-inch barrel. Introduced 1996. No longer imported.

Perf.: $275   **Exc.:** $235   **VGood:** $200

ROSSI MODEL 972

Revolver; 6-shot polished stainless double-action .357 Magnum. Adjustable rear sight and red insert on front sight. 6-inch barrel, rubber grip, 35 oz. Uses Taurus security system.

NIB: $375   **Exc.:** $325   **VGood:** $275

ROYAL

Semi-automatic; 7.63mm Mauser; 5-1/2-inch barrel; 11-3/4-inch overall length; 10-shot magazine; grooved wood grips. Spanish copy of Mauser Model 1896 but with different internal mechanism, round bolt. Introduced 1926; dropped 1930 when the maker replaced it with the Azul, an almost identical copy of the Mauser.

Exc.: $1800   **VGood:** $1250   **Good:** $850

RPM XL SINGLE SHOT

Single shot; 22 LR through 45-70; 8-inch, 10-3/4-inch, 12-inch, 14-inch barrel; weighs about 60 oz.; smooth Goncalo Alves stock with thumb and heel rest; hooded front sight with interchangeable post, ISGW fully-adjustable rear; barrel tapped and drilled for scope mount; cocking indicator; spring-loaded barrel lock; positive hammer-block safety.

New: $750   **Perf.:** $600   **Exc.:** $500

RPM XL HUNTER SINGLE SHOT

Same specs as RPM XL except stainless frame; 5/16-inch underlug; latch lever; positive extractor.

New: $1000   **Perf.:** $850   **Exc.:** $750

SAFARI ARMS BLACK WIDOW

Semi-automatic; 45 ACP; 6-shot; 3-3/4-inch barrel; 7-11/16-inch overall length; weighs 28 oz.; adjustable sights; scrimshawed Micarta grip with black widow ensignia; nickel finish. Discontinued 1987.

Exc.: $500   **VGood:** $450   **Good:** $400

SAFARI ARMS COHORT PISTOL

Caliber: 45 ACP, 7-shot magazine. Barrel: 3.8-inch, 416 stainless. Weight: 37 oz. Length: 8.5-inch overall. Stocks: Smooth walnut with laser-etched black widow logo. Sights: Ramped blade front, LPA adjustable rear. Features: Combines the Enforcer model, slide and MatchMaster frame. Beavertail grip safety; extended thumb safety and slide release; Commander-style hammer. Throated, polished and tuned. Satin stainless finish. Introduced 1996.

New: $650   **Perf.:** $600   **Exc.:** $550

SAFARI ARMS ENFORCER

Semi-automatic; single action; 45 ACP; 6-shot magazine; 3-13/16-inch barrel; 7-5/16-inch overall length; weighs 36 oz.; smooth walnut grips with etched black widow spider logo; ramped blade front sight, LPA adjustable rear; stainless barrel; extended safety and slide release; Commander-style hammer; beavertail grip safety; throated, polished, tuned; Parkerized matte black or satin stainless steel finishes. In 1988 Olympic Arms bought M-S Safari Arms of Phoenix, Arizona. Some guns will be marked M-S Safari; some Safari Arms. Current production guns are still being stamped "Safari Arms." Made in U.S. by Olympic Arms, Inc.'s specialty shop Schuetzen Pistol Works. Still produced.

New: $600   **Perf.:** $500   **Exc.:** $450

Safari Arms Matchmaster

Safari Arms
Model 81L

Sarsilmaz Professional

SAFARI ARMS ENFORCER CARRYCOMP II

Same specs as the Enforcer except Wil Schueman-designed hybrid compensator system. In 1988 Olympic Arms bought M-S Safari Arms of Phoenix, Arizona. Some guns will be marked M-S Safari; some Safari Arms. Current production guns are still being stamped "Safari Arms." Made in U.S. by Olympic Arms, Inc.'s specialty shop Schuetzen Pistol Works. Introduced 1993.

New: $1100   **Perf.:** $900   **Exc.:** $750

SAFARI ARMS G.I. SAFARI

Semi-automatic; single action; 45 ACP; 7-shot magazine; 5-inch barrel; 8-1/2-inch overall length; weighs 40 oz.; checkered walnut grips; blade front sight, fixed rear; beavertail grip safety; extended safety and slide release; Commander-style hammer; chrome-lined 4140 steel barrel; National Match 416 stainless optional; Parkerized matte black finish. Made in U.S. by Safari Arms, Inc. Introduced 1991.

New: $450   **Perf.:** $350   **Exc.:** $225

SAFARI ARMS MATCHMASTER

Semi-automatic; single action; 45 ACP; 7-shot magazine; 5-inch, 6-inch barrel; 8-1/2-inch overall length; weighs 38 oz.; smooth walnut grips with etched scorpion logo; ramped blade front sight, LPA adjustable rear; stainless steel barrel; beavertail grip safety; extended safety; extended slide release; Commander-style hammer; throated, polished, tuned; Parkerized matte black or satin stainless steel. In 1988 Olympic Arms bought M-S Safari Arms of Phoenix, Arizona. Some guns will be marked M-S Safari; some Safari Arms. Current production guns are still being stamped "Safari Arms." Made in U.S. by Olympic Arms, Inc.'s specialty shop Schuetzen Pistol Works. Introduced 1995; still produced.

New: $600   **Perf.:** $550   **Exc.:** $475

SAFARI ARMS MATCHMASTER CARRYCOMP I

Same specs as Matchmaster except Wil Schueman-designed hybrid compensator system. Made in U.S. by Olympic Arms, Inc. Introduced 1993.

New: $1000   **Perf.:** $850   **Exc.:** $750

SAFARI ARMS MODEL 81

Semi-automatic; 45 ACP, 38 Spl.; 5-inch barrel; weighs 42 oz.; adjustable sights; fixed or adjustable walnut target grips; optional Aristocrat rib with extended front sight optional; nickel finish. Introduced 1983; discontinued 1987.

Exc.: $750   **VGood:** $550   **Good:** $450

SAFARI ARMS MODEL 81BP

Same specs as Model 81 except contoured front grip strap; quicker slide cycle time; designed for bowling pin matches. Introduced 1983; discontinued 1987.

Exc.: $850   **VGood:** $650   **Good:** $500

SAFARI ARMS MODEL 81L

Same specs as Model 81 except 6-inch barrel; long slide; weighs 45 oz. Introduced 1983; discontinued 1987.

Exc.: $750   **VGood:** $550   **Good:** $400

SAFARI ARMS MODEL 81NM

Same specs as Model 81 except flat front grip strap. Introduced 1983; discontinued 1987.

Exc.: $750   **VGood:** $600   **Good:** $500

SAFARI ARMS MODEL 81 SILUETA

Same specs as Model 81 except 38-45 wildcat, 45 ACP; 10-inch barrel; designed for silhouette competition. Introduced 1983; discontinued 1987.

Exc.: $850   **VGood:** $650   **Good:** $500

SAFARI ARMS OA-93

Semi-automatic; single action; 223, 7.62x39mm; 20-, 30-shot magazine (223), 5-, 30-shot magazine (7.62x39mm); 6-inch, 9-inch, 14-inch 4140 steel or 416 stainless barrel; 15 oz.; 15-3/4-inch overall length (6-inch barrel); weighs 4 lbs.; A2 stowaway pistol grip; no sights; cut-off carrying handle with attached scope rail; AR-15 receiver with special bolt carrier; short slotted aluminum handguard; button-cut or broach-cut barrel; Vortex flash suppressor. Made in U.S. by Olympic Arms, Inc. Introduced 1993; dropped 1994.

New: $2500   **Perf.:** $2250   **Exc.:** $2000

SAFARI ARMS RELIABLE PISTOL

Caliber: 45 ACP, 7-shot magazine. Barrel: 5-inch, 416 stainless steel. Weight: 39 oz. Length: 8.5-inch overall. Stocks: Checkered walnut. Sights: Ramped blade front, LPA adjustable rear. Features: Beavertail grip safety; long full-length recoil spring guide; Commander-style hammer. Throated, polished and tuned. Satin stainless steel finish. Introduced 1996; dropped 1998.

New: $650   **Perf.:** $600   **Exc.:** $550

SAFARI ARMS RELIABLE 4-STAR PISTOL

Similar to the Reliable except has 4.5-inch barrel, 7.5-inch overall length, and weighs 35.7 oz. Introduced 1996.

New: $700   **Perf.:** $600   **Exc.:** $550

SAFARI ARMS RENEGADE

Caliber: 45 ACP, 7-shot magazine. Barrel: 5-inch, 416 stainless steel. Weight: 39 oz. Length: 8.5-inch overall. Stocks: Checkered walnut. Sights: Ramped blade, LPA adjustable rear. Features: True left-hand pistol. Beavertail grip safety; long aluminum trigger;

full-length recoil spring guide; Commander-style hammer; satin stainless finish. Throated, polished and tuned. Introduced 1996; dropped 1998.

New: $950   **Perf.:** $800   **Exc.:** $650

SAFARI ARMS UNLIMITED

Single shot; bolt action; 308 or smaller; 14-15/16-inch barrel; 21-1/2-inch overall length; weighs 72 oz.; open iron sights; fiberglass stock; electronic trigger; black finish. Introduced 1983; discontinued 1987.

Exc.: $800   **VGood:** $700   **Good:** $575

SAKO TRIACE MATCH

Semi-automatic; 22 Short, 22 LR, 32 S&W Long; 6-shot; 5-7/8-inch barrel; 11-inch overall length; weighs 44 to 48 oz.; adjustable trigger for weight of pull, free travel and sear engagement; marketed in case with tool/cleaning kit, two magazines. Made in Finland. Introduced 1988; discontinued 1989.

Exc.: $1200   **VGood:** $1000   **Good:** $750

SARSILMAZ PROFESSIONAL

CZ-75-style compensated semi-auto in white chrome finish chambered for 9mm. Single-action with adjustable trigger, laser engraving. 16 or 18 round capacity. 42.3 oz.; 5.1-inch barrel.

NIB: $400   **Exc.:** $375   **VGood:** $300

SARSILMAZ K2

CZ-75-style double-action semi-auto in white chrome or blued. Chambered for 9mm. 16 or 18 round capacity. 35.3 oz.; 4.6-inch barrel. Plastic grips.

NIB: $300   **Exc.:** $275   **VGood:** $235

SARSILMAZ KAMA SPORT

CZ-75-style semi-auto 9mm in white chrome or blued. Double-action with 3.9-inch compensated barrel, laser engraving. 15+1 or 17+1 capacity. 35.4 oz. Plastic grips.

NIB: $350   **Exc.:** $295   **VGood:** $250

SARSILMAZ KAMA

CZ-75-style semi-auto 9mm in white chrome or blued. Double-action with 4.3-inch compensated barrel, laser engraving. 15+1 or 17+1 capacity. 35.4 oz.; 7.7-inch. Plastic grips.

NIB: $350   **Exc.:** $295   **VGood:** $250

SARSILMAZ KILINC 2000 MEGA

CZ-75-style semi-auto 9mm in white chrome or blued. Double-action with 4.7-inch barrel. 16 or 18 capacity. 35 oz. Plastic grips. Fixed sights.

NIB: $225   **Exc.:** $200   **VGood:** $150

SARSILMAZ KILINC 2000 LIGHT

CZ-75-style semi-auto 9mm in white chrome, blued or camo. Double-action with 4.7-inch barrel, laser engraving. 15+1 or 17+1 capacity. 35.4 oz. Plastic grips.

NIB: $225   **Exc.:** $200   **VGood:** $150

Sarsilmaz Hancer 2000

Sauer Model 38H

Sauer Model 1913

Sauer WTM

Sauer Model 1930
(Behorden Model)

Savage Model 101

Savage
Model 1907

Savage Model 1917

SARSILMAZ HANCER 2000/2000 LIGHT

CZ-75-style semi-auto 9mm in white chrome or blued. Double-action with 3.9-inch barrel, laser engraving. 13+1 capacity. 33.5 oz. (25.4 oz. Light model). Plastic grips.

NIB: $225   **Exc.:** $200   **VGood:** $150

SARSILMAZ BERNARDELLI

CZ-75-style double-action semi-auto in 9mm. Black/white or blued finish. The 15+1 model has a 4.7-inch barrel, 27 oz., Plastic grips. The 13+1 model has a 3.9-inch barrel; 26.7 oz. Plastic grips, fixed sights.

NIB: $235   **Exc.:** $225   **VGood:** $175

SAUER MODEL 28

Semi-automatic; 25 ACP; 6-shot; 3-inch overall length; slanted serrations on slide; top ejection; checkered black rubber grips with Sauer imprint; blued finish. Introduced about 1928; discontinued 1938.

Exc.: $200   **VGood:** $165   **Good:** $135

SAUER MODEL 38H

Semi-automatic; double action; 32 ACP; 7-shot; 3-1/4-inch barrel; 6-1/4-inch overall length; fixed sights; black plastic grips; blued finish. Introduced 1938; discontinued 1944.

Exc.: $325   **VGood:** $275   **Good:** $200

SAUER MODEL 1913

Semi-automatic; 32 ACP; 7-shot; 3-inch barrel; 5-7/8-inch overall length; fixed sights; checkered rubber black grips; blued finish. Introduced 1913; discontinued 1930.

Exc.: $200   **VGood:** $150   **Good:** $125

SAUER MODEL 1913 POCKET

Same specs as Model 1913 except smaller in size; 25 ACP; 2-1/2-inch barrel; 4-1/4-inch overall length; improved grip, safety features. Introduced 1920; discontinued 1930.

Exc.: $250   **VGood:** $200   **Good:** $150

SAUER MODEL 1930 (BEHORDEN MODEL)

Semi-automatic; 32 ACP; 7-shot; 3-inch barrel; fixed sights; black plastic grips; blued finish. Has grip safety on front of trigger. Introduced 1930; discontinued 1938.

Exc.: $350   **VGood:** $300   **Good:** $225

SAUER WTM

Semi-automatic; 25 ACP; 6-shot; 2-1/2-inch barrel; 4-1/8-inch overall length; fixed sights; checkered hard rubber grips; top ejector; fluted slide; blued finish. Introduced 1924; discontinued 1927.

Exc.: $250   **VGood:** $200   **Good:** $150

SAVAGE AUTOMATIC PISTOL

Semi-automatic; 25 ACP; 6-shot; 2-3/8-inch barrel; weighs 12 oz.; hammerless; wide or narrow slide serrations. Experimental only pre-WWI. Only 50-100 produced. Extremely rare; extremely valuable.

SAVAGE MODEL 101

Single shot; single action; 22 Short, 22 LR; 5-1/2-inch barrel integral with chamber; 9-inch overall length; adjustable slotted rear sight, blade front; compressed, plastic-impregnated wood grips; fake cylinder swings out for loading, ejection; manual ejection with spring-rod ejector; blued finish. Introduced 1959; discontinued 1968.

Exc.: $295   **VGood:** $200   **Good:** $135

SAVAGE MODEL 1907

Semi-automatic; 32 ACP, 380 ACP; 10-shot (32), 9-shot (380); 3 3/4-inch barrel, 6-1/2-inch overall length (32 ACP); 4-1/2-inch barrel, 7-inch overall length (380 ACP); fixed sights; checkered hard rubber stocks; exposed hammer; blued finish. The 380-caliber serial number followed by letter "B". Manufactured 1910 to 1917.

32 ACP		
Exc.: $350	**VGood:** $300	**Good:** $250
380 ACP		
Exc.: $450	**VGood:** $375	**Good:** $325

SAVAGE MODEL 1907 U.S. ARMY TEST TRIAL

Same specs as Model 1907 except enlarged model for 45 ACP only; exposed hammer; approximately 300 made for test trials from 1907 to 1911.

Exc.: $7000   **VGood:** $5500   **Good:** $3500

SAVAGE MODEL 1915 HAMMERLESS

Semi-automatic; 32 ACP, 380 ACP; 10-shot (32), 9-shot (380); 3-3/4-inch barrel, 6-1/2-inch overall length (32 ACP); 4-1/2-inch barrel, 7-inch overall (380 ACP); fixed sights; checkered hard rubber stocks; hammerless; grip safety; blued finish. Manufactured 1915 to 1917.

32 caliber		
Exc.: $350	**VGood:** $300	**Good:** $200
380 caliber		
Exc.: $450	**VGood:** $350	**Good:** $250

SAVAGE MODEL 1917

Semi-automatic; 32 ACP, 380 ACP; 10-shot (32), 9-shot (380); 3-3/4-inch barrel, 6-1/2-inch overall length (32 ACP); 4-1/2-inch barrel, 7-inch overall length (380 ACP); fixed sights; hard rubber grips; spurred hammer; blued finish. Marked "Savage Model 1917" on left side. Introduced 1920; discontinued 1928.

32 caliber		
Exc.: $350	**VGood:** $300	**Good:** $225
380 caliber		
Exc.: $400	**VGood:** $350	**Good:** $250

Savage Striker

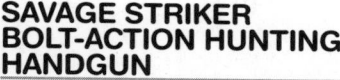

Sedco Model SP-22

Seecamp LWS 32

Security Industries
Model PSS38

SIG Sauer P220
"American"

SIGARMS P220R
SAO

SAVAGE STRIKER BOLT-ACTION HUNTING HANDGUN

Caliber: 22-250, 243, 308, 2-shot magazine. Barrel: 14-inch. Weight: About 5 lbs. Length: 22-1/2-inch overall. Stock: Black composite ambidextrous mid-grip; grooved forend; "Dual Pillar" bedding. Sights: None furnished; drilled and tapped for scope mounting. Features: Short left-hand bolt with right-hand ejection; free-floated barrel; uses Savage Model 110 rifle scope rings/bases. Introduced 1998. Made in U.S. by Savage Arms, Inc.

New: $500   **Perf.:** $395   **Exc.:** $300

SECURITY INDUSTRIES MODEL PM357

Revolver; double action; 357 Mag.; 5-shot; 2-1/2-inch barrel; 7-1/2-inch overall length; fixed sights; uncheckered American walnut target stocks; stainless steel. Introduced 1973; discontinued 1977.

Exc.: $225   **VGood:** $175   **Good:** $150

SECURITY INDUSTRIES MODEL PPM357

Revolver; double action; 357 Mag.; 5-shot; 2-inch barrel; 6-1/8-inch overall length; fixed sights; checkered American walnut target stocks; stainless steel. Introduced 1976 with spurless hammer, converted to conventional hammer 1977; discontinued 1977.

Exc.: $225   **VGood:** $175   **Good:** $150

SECURITY INDUSTRIES MODEL PSS38

Revolver; double action; 38 Spl.; 5-shot; 2-inch barrel; 6-1/2-inch overall length; fixed sights; checkered or smooth American walnut stocks; stainless steel. Introduced 1973; discontinued 1977.

Exc.: $150   **VGood:** $125   **Good:** $110

SEDCO MODEL SP-22

Semi-automatic; single action; 22 LR; 6-shot; 2-1/2-inch barrel; 5-inch overall length; weighs 11 oz.; fixed sights; simulated pearl stocks; rotary safety blocks sear, slide; chrome or black Teflon finish. Introduced 1988; discontinued 1990.

Exc.: $65   **VGood:** $50   **Good:** $40

SEDGELY BABY HAMMERLESS MODEL

Revolver; double action; 22 LR; 6-shot; 4-inch overall length; solid frame; hard rubber stocks; fixed sights; folding trigger; blued or nickel finish. Manufactured 1930 to 1939.

Exc.: $300   **VGood:** $225   **Good:** $175

SEECAMP LWS 25 ACP MODEL

Semi-automatic; double action; 25 ACP; 7-shot; 2-inch barrel; 4-1/8-inch overall length; weighs 12 oz.; fixed sights; plastic grips; stainless steel; matte finish. Introduced 1982; discontinued 1985.

Exc.: $400   **VGood:** $300   **Good:** $225

SEECAMP LWS 32

Semi-automatic; double-action-only; 32 ACP Win. Silvertip; 6-shot magazine; 2-inch barrel; 4-1/8-inch overall length; weighs 10-1/2 oz.; glass-filled nylon grips; smooth, no-snag, contoured slide and barrel top serve as sights; aircraft quality 17-4 PH stainless steel; inertia-operated firing pin; magazine safety disconnector; polished stainless. Made in U.S. by L.W. Seecamp. Introduced 1985.

New: $500   **Perf.:** $450   **Exc.:** $400

SHERIDAN KNOCABOUT

Single; tip-up action; 22 Short, 22 LR; 5-inch barrel; 8-3/4-inch overall length; fixed sights; checkered plastic grips; blued finish. Introduced 1953; discontinued 1960. Note that the correct spelling is "Knocabout" (without the "k"). It was also referred to by the factory as the Model D.

Exc.: $295   **VGood:** $225   **Good:** $175

SIG P210-2

Semi-automatic; single action; 9mm Para., 7.65mm Luger; 8-shot; 4-3/4-inch barrel; 8-1/2-inch overall length; weighs 32 oz.; fixed sights; black plastic grips; standard-issue Swiss army sidearm; blued finish. Manufactured in Switzerland. Introduced 1947; still in production.

Exc.: $2000   **VGood:** $1650   **Good:** $1400

SIG P210-1

Same specs as P210-2 except; walnut grips; polished blued finish. Discontinued 1986.

Exc.: $2250   **VGood:** $2000   **Good:** $1750

SIG P210-5

Same specs as P210-2 except 6-inch barrel; micrometer sights; target trigger special hammer; hard rubber grips; matte finish.

Exc.: $2250   **VGood:** $1950   **Good:** $1500

SIG P210-6

Same specs as P210-2 except fixed rear sight, target front; target trigger. Still in production.

New: $2000   **Perf.:** $1750   **Exc.:** $1500

SIG-HAMMERLI MODEL P240

Semi-automatic; single action; 32 S&W Long, 38 Spl.; 5-shot; 6-inch barrel; 10-inch overall length; micrometer rear sight, post front; uncheckered European walnut stocks with target thumbrest;

adjustable triggers; blued finish. Manufactured in Switzerland. Introduced 1975; discontinued 1988.

Exc.: $1350   **VGood:** $1000   **Good:** $850

SIG SAUER P220 "AMERICAN"

Semi-automatic; double action; 38 Super, 45 ACP; 9-shot (38 Super), 7-shot (45 ACP) magazine; 4-3/8-inch barrel; 7-3/4-inch overall length; weighs 28-1/4 oz. (9mm); checkered black plastic grips; blade front sight, drift-adjustable rear; squared combat-type trigger guard; side-button magazine release. Imported from Germany by SIGARMS, Inc. Still imported but only in 45 ACP.

New: $650   **Perf.:** $600   **Exc.:** $500

With Siglite night sights
New: $750   **Perf.:** $700   **Exc.:** $575

With K-Kote finish
New: $675   **Perf.:** $625   **Exc.:** $525

With K-Kote finish, Siglite night sights
New: $800   **Perf.:** $750   **Exc.:** $600

SIGARMS P220R SAO

An 8+1 or 10+1 capacity single-action semi-auto chambered for .45 ACP. Polymer grip and Nitron finish, 4.4-inch barrel, 30.4 oz., 5-lb. trigger. Picatinny rail.

NIB: $800   **Exc.:** $725   **VGood:** $625

SIGARMS P220R DAK

Semi-auto with 8+1 or 10+1 capacity chambered for .45 ACP. Polymer grip and Nitron finish, 4.4-inch barrel, 30.4 oz., 7.5-lb. trigger. Picatinny rail.

NIB: $800   **Exc.:** $725   **VGood:** $625

SIGARMS P220 SAS

An 8+1 capacity double-action semi-auto chambered for .45 ACP. Fixed sights, wood grips, 4.4-inch barrel, 30.4 oz., 6.5-lb. trigger.

NIB: $1000   **Exc.:** $900   **HGood:** $750

SIGARMS P220 ELITE

SIGARMS P220 Platinum Elite

SIGARMS P226 SCT

SIGARMS P226 Elite Stainless

SIGARMS P220 Elite Stainless

SIGARMS P226 Elite

SIGARMS P220 Carry Elite Stainless

SIGARMS P226 Platinum Elite

SIGARMS P220R Carry Equinox

SIGARMS P2225

SIG Sauer P226

SIG Sauer P228

SIGARMS P220 CARRY SAS

An 8+1 capacity double-action semi-auto chambered for .45 ACP. Fixed sights, wood grips, 3.9-inch barrel, 30.4 oz., 6.5-lb. trigger.

NIB: $1000   **Exc.:** $900   **VGood:** $750

SIGARMS P220 CARRY

An 8+1 or 10+1 capacity single/double-action semi-auto chambered for .45 ACP. Fixed sights, polymer grips, 3.9-inch barrel, 30.4 oz.

NIB: $800   **Exc.:** $725   **VGood:** $625

SIGARMS P220R EQUINOX

An 8+1 or 10+1 capacity single/double-action semi-auto chambered for .45 ACP. Fixed sights, wood grips, 4.4-inch barrel, 30.4 oz.

NIB: $1000   **Exc.:**900   **VGood:** $750

SIGARMS P220R CARRY EQUINOX

An 8+1 or 10+1 capacity single/double-action semi-auto chambered for .45 ACP. Fixed sights, wood grips, 3.9-inch barrel, 30.4 oz.

NIB: $1000   **Exc.:** $900   **VGood:** $750

SIGARMS P220 COMBAT

Similar to P220 but with sand-colored alloy slide and steel frame. Capacity 8+1 or 10+1. Designed for SOCOM sidearm trials.

NIB: $950   **Exc.:** $850   **VGood:** $700

SIGARMS P220 MATCH

Similar to P220 but with 5-inch barrel and adjustable sights.

NIB: $910   **Exc.:** $825   **VGood:** $675

SIGARMS P220 SUPER MATCH

Super-accurized version of P220 Match with single-action-only trigger and custom wood grips. Limited edition.

NIB: $1795   **Exc.:** $1200   **VGood:** $975

SIGARMS P220 COMPACT

Similar to P220 but with 3.9-inch barrel and 6+1 capacity. Single-action-only or single-/double-action. Various finish, grip and sight options.

NIB: $825   **Exc.:** $775   **VGood:** $600

SIGARMS P220 ELITE

Similar to P220 but with SIG's new Short Reset Trigger or SRT. Beavertail safety, front cocking serrations, front strap checkering, SIGLITE® Night

Sights and custom wood grips. Introduced in 2008. Also available in single action-only model.

NIB: $1140   **Exc.:** $925   **VGood:** $700

SIGARMS P220 ELITE STAINLESS

Similar to above but in stainless. Introduced 2008.

NIB: $1240   **Exc.:** $1000   **VGood:** $800

SIGARMS P220 CARRY ELITE STAINLESS

Compact version of above with 3.9-inch barrel; chambered in .45 ACP with 8-round capacity. Introduced 2008.

NIB: $1250   **Exc.:** $1050   **VGood:** $850

SIGARMS P220 PLATINUM ELITE

Fine-tuned, enhanced version of P220 Elite with front cocking serrations, front strap checkering, SIGLITE® Adjustable Combat Night Sights and custom aluminum grips.

NIB: $1200   **Exc.:** $1000   **VGood:** $800

SIG SAUER P225

Semi-automatic; double action, DA-only; 9mm Para.; 8-shot; 3-7/8-inch barrel; 7-3/32-inch overall length; weighs 26 oz.; blade-type front sight, windage-adjustable rear; checkered black plastic stocks; squared combat-type trigger guard; shorter, lighter version of P220; blued finish. Made in Germany. Introduced 1985, dropped 1998.

New: $600	**Perf.:** $550	**Exc.:** $450
K-Kote finish		
New: $650	**Perf.:** $600	**Exc.:** $500
Nickel finish		
New: $650	**Perf.:** $600	**Exc.:** $500
Siglite night sights		
New: $700	**Perf.:** $650	**Exc.:** $525

SIG SAUER P226

Semi-automatic; double action, DA-only; 9mm Para.; 15-, 20-shot; 4-3/8-inch barrel; weighs 26-1/2 oz.; high contrast sights; black plastic checkered stocks; blued finish. Made in Germany. Introduced 1983; still imported.

New: $700	**Perf.:** $600	**Exc.:** $500
K-Kote finish		
New: $750	**Perf.:** $650	**Exc.:** $550
Nickel finish		
New: $750	**Perf.:** $650	**Exc.:** $550
Siglite night sights		
New: $800	**Perf.:** $700	**Exc.:** $575

SIGARMS P226 SAS

Double-action semi-auto with 12+1 capacity chambered for .40 S&W. Fixed sights, wood grips, 4.4-inch barrel, 34 oz., 6.5-lb. trigger.

NIB: $1000   **Exc.:** $900   **VGood:** $750

SIGARMS P226R EQUINOX

An 10+1 or 12+1 capacity single/double-action semi-auto chambered for .40 S&W. Fixed sights, wood grips, 4.4-inch barrel, 34 oz.

NIB: $1000   **Exc.:** $900   **VGood:** $750

SIGARMS P226 SCT

An all black, Nitron® finished P226 featuring front cocking serrations, a SIGLITE® rear night sight, a TRUGLO® tritium fiber optic front sight and comes with four newly designed 20-round magazines for the 9mm version or four 15-round magazines for the .40S&W version.

NIB: $1100   **Exc.:** $900   **VGood:** $650

SIGARMS P226 ELITE

Introduced 2008. Similar to P226 but with redesigned shoprt-reset trigger and improved ergonomics. Chambered in 9mm, .40 S&W and .357 SIG.

NIB: $1140   **Exc.:** $925   **VGood:** $700

SIGARMS P226 ELITE STAINLESS

Similar to above but in stainless steel.

NIB: $1200 Exc.: $975 VGood: $750

SIGARMS P226 PLATINUM ELITE

Fine-tuned, enhanced version of P226 Elite with front cocking serrations, front strap checkering, SIGLITE® Adjustable Combat Night Sights and custom aluminum grips.

NIB: $1215   **Exc.:** $925   **VGood:** $700

SIG SAUER P228

Semi-automatic; double action, DA-only; 9mm Para.; 10-shot; 3-7/8-inch barrel; 7-inch overall length; weighs 29 oz.; three-dot sights; black plastic grips; blued finish. Made in Germany. Introduced 1989; dropped 1997.

New: $650	**Perf.:** $550	**Exc.:** $475
K-Kote finish		
New: $700	**Perf.:** $600	**Exc.:** $500
Nickel finish		
New: $700	**Perf.:** $600	**Exc.:** $500
Siglite night sights		
New: $750	**Perf.:** $650	**Exc.:** $550

SIGARMS P229 Elite

SIGARMS P229 Platinuim Elite

SIGARMS 1911 C3

SIGARMS 1911 Platinum Elite

SIGARMS 1911 Platinum Carry Elite

SIGARMS P250 Compact

SIG Sauer P232

SIG Sauer P230

SIG Sauer P239

SIGARMS Revolution Compact

SIGARMS Revolution TTT

SIGARMS Revolution

SIG SAUER P229

Semi-automatic; double action, DA-only; 9mm Para., 40 S&W, 357 SIG; 12-shot; 3-7/8-inch barrel; 7-inch overall length; 30-1/2 oz.; three-dot sights; checkered black plastic grips; aluminum alloy frame; blued slide. Made in Germany. Introduced 1991; still produced.

New: $700   **Perf.:** $600   **Exc.:** $500

Siglite night sights

New: $800   **Perf.:** $700   **Exc.:** $575

Nickel

New: $850   **Perf.:** $750   **Exc.:** $650

SIG SAUER P229 S AUTO PISTOL

Similar to the P229 except available in 357 SIG only; 4.8-inch heavy barrel; 8.6-inch overall length; weighs 40.6 oz.; vented compensator; adjustable target sights; rubber grips; extended slide latch and magazine release. Made of stainless steel. Introduced 1998.

New: $1100   **Perf.:** $950   **Exc.:** $750

SIGARMS P229 ELITE

The P229 Elite features an ergonomic beavertail grip, front cocking serrations, front strap checkering, SIGLITE Night Sights, custom wood grips and the new Short Reset Trigger or SRT. Available in 9mm and .40 S&W.

New: $1100   **Perf.:** $950   **Exc.:** $750

SIGARMS P229 PLATINUM ELITE

Fine-tuned, enhanced version of P229 Elite with front cocking serrations, front strap checkering, SIGLITE® Adjustable Combat Night Sights and custom aluminum grips.

New: $1200   **Perf.:** $950   **Exc.:** $750

SIGARMS 1911 C3

!911-style 6+1 autoloader in .45 ACP. 4-2/4-inch barrel, alloy frame. Introduced in 2008.

New: $1100   **Perf.:** $950   **Exc.:** $750

SIGARMS 1911 PLATINUM ELITE

!911-style 8+1 autoloader in .45 ACP. 5-inch barrel, Nitron frame, aluminum grips. Introduced in 2008.

New: $1200   **Perf.:** $950   **Exc.:** $750

SIGARMS 1911 PLATINUM ELITE CARRY

Compact version of the above with 4.5-inch barrel. Introduced in 2008.

New: $1200   **Perf.:** $950   **Exc.:** $750

SIG SAUER P230

Semi-automatic; double action; 22 LR, 32 ACP, 380 ACP, 9mm Ultra; 10-shot (22 LR), 8-shot (32 ACP), 7-shot (380 ACP, 9mm); 3-3/4-inch barrel; 6-1/2-inch overall length; weighs 16 oz.; fixed sights; checkered black plastic stocks; blued finish. Introduced 1977; dropped 1996. Manufactured in Germany.

New: $400   **Perf.:** $350   **Exc.:** $300

SIG SAUER P230 SL STAINLESS

Same specs as P230 except stainless steel; 22 oz.

New: $450   **Perf.:** $400   **Exc.:** $350

SIG SAUER P232 PERSONAL SIZE PISTOL

Semi-automatic; double action. Improved version of P230; 32 ACP, 380 ACP, 8-shot (32 ACP), 7-shot (380 ACP); 3-3/4-inch barrel; 6-1/2-inch overall length; weighs 16 oz.; fixed sights; checkered black plastic stocks; blued finish. Introduced 1997. Imported from Germany by SIGARMS, Inc.

New: $500   **Perf.:** $600   **Exc.:** $500

SIG SAUER P239 PISTOL

Semi-automatic; double action; 9mm Para., 8-shot, 357 SIG, 40 S&W, 7-shot magazine. Barrel: 3.6-inch Weight: 25.2 oz. Length: 6.6-inch overall. Stocks: Checkered black composite. Sights: Blade front, rear adjustable for windage. Optional Siglite night sights. Features: SA/DA or DAO; blackened stainless steel slide, aluminum alloy frame. Introduced 1996.

New: $600   **Perf.:** $500   **Exc.:** $450

With Siglite night sights

New: $675   **Perf.:** $550   **Exc.:** $500

SIGARMS P250 COMPACT

Introduced in 2008. A 9mm semiauto pistol of so-called "modular design" that enables the shooter to quickly remove the functional mechanism and place it into the polymer grip of his choice. This allows an immediate change in caliber and size;(subcompact, compact and full). And after any change the pistol delivers both outstanding accuracy and reliable functionality. Its modularity not only provides incredible ease of maintenance, but also provides a solution for accommodating different hand sizes - there are 6 different ergonomic combinations for each size, accomplished by changes in grip circumference and trigger style. Matte or duotone finish.

New: $700   **Perf.:** $600   **Exc.:** $500

SIGARMS REVOLUTION

All-stainless frames and slides in four configurations. Novak Night Sights, Roswood- or DiamondWood custom grips. Stainless or Nitron finish. 8+1 capacity, 45 ACP, single-action, 5-inch barrel, 40.3 oz.

NIB: $1000   **Exc.:** $900   **VGood:** $750

SIGARMS REVOLUTION CUSTOM STX

Single-action .45 ACP stainless semi-auto with 8+1 capacity. Adjustable combat night sights and custom wood grip panels, 5-inch barrel, 40.6 oz.

NIB: $1250   **Exc.:** $1100   **VGood:** $800

SIGARMS REVOLUTION TTT

Stainless semi-auto with 8+1 capacity. Single-action .45 ACP. Adjustable combat night sights and custom wood grip panels, 5-inch barrel, 40.3 oz.

NIB: $1250   **Exc.:** $1100   **VGood:** $800

SIGARMS REVOLUTION XO

Single-action .45 ACP stainless semi-auto with 8+1 capacity. Polymer grip panels. 8.65-inch LOA, 5-inch barrel, 40.3 oz.

NIB: $850   **Exc.:** $795   **VGood:** $650

SIGARMS REVOLUTION TARGET

Single-action .45 ACP stainless semi-auto with 8+1 capacity. Adjustable target night sights. Custom wood grip panels, 5-inch barrel, 40.3 oz. Stainless or Nitron finish.

NIB: $1050   **Exc.:** $950   **VGood:** $825

SIGARMS REVOLUTION CARRY

Single-action .45 ACP stainless semi-auto with 8+1 capacity. Fixed sights. Custom wood grip panels, 4-inch barrel, 35.4 oz. Stainless or Nitron finish.

NIB: $1000   **Exc.:** $900   **VGood:** $750

SIGARMS REVOLUTION COMPACT

Stainless semi-auto single-action .45 ACP with 6+1 capacity. Fixed sights. Custom wood grip panels, 4-inch barrel, 30.3 oz. Stainless or Nitron finish.

NIB: $1000   **Exc.:** $900   **VGood:** $750

Smith & Wesson
44 Double Action
First Model

Smith & Wesson New
Model No. 3 Target

Smith & Wesson
New Model No. 3

Smith & Wesson 22 Straight Line

Smith & Wesson 38
Safety Hammerless
(New Departure)

Smith & Wesson
Single Shot First Model

SIGARMS REVOLUTION COMPACT SAS

Dehorned version of Revolution Compact. "SAS" stands for "SIG Anti Snag."

NIB: $1000   **Exc.:** $900   **VGood:** $750

SIGARMS REVOLUTION CUSTOM COMPACT RCS

Stainless semi-auto single-action .45 ACP with 6+1 capacity. Fixed sights. Custom wood grip panels, 4-inch barrel, 30.3 oz. Stainless or Nitron finish.

NIB: $1000   **Exc.:** $900   **VGood:** $750

SIGARMS REVOLUTION COMPACT C3

Similar to Revolution Compact but with black anodized alloy frame and stainless or Nitron-finished slide.

NIB: $900   **Exc.:** $850   **VGood:** $725

SMITH & WESSON 22 STRAIGHT LINE

Single shot; 22 LR; 10-inch barrel; pivoted frame; has the appearance of a single-action semi-automatic; smooth walnut grips; target sights; blued finish only; came in green felt-lined blued steel case with cleaning rod and screwdriver. Manufactured 1925 to 1936 with a total of 1870 produced.

Exc.: $1200   **VGood:** $850   **Good:** $500

With case		
Exc.: $1600	**VGood:** $1100	**Good:** $700

SMITH & WESSON 32 DOUBLE ACTION

Revolver; double action; 32 S&W; 5-shot cylinder; 3-inch, 3-1/2-inch, 6-inch, 8-inch, 10-inch barrels; hard rubber stocks; fixed sights; blued or nickel finish. Manufactured 1880 to 1919. Early serial numbers have great collector significance, with numbers through 50 bringing as high as $6500.

Exc.: $350   **VGood:** $225   **Good:** $150

SMITH & WESSON 32 SAFETY HAMMERLESS

Revolver; double action; 32 S&W; 5-shot; 2-inch, 3-inch, 3-1/2-inch, 6-inch barrels; black, hard rubber or walnut grips; blue or nickel finish. Numbered in separate serial number series. The 2-inch barrel models called "Bicycle Model" and demand premium prices. 249,981 produced. Manufactured from 1887 to 1937.

Exc.: $400   **VGood:** $325   **Good:** $200

2-inch barrel Bicycle Model		
Exc.: $450	**VGood:** $300	**Good:** $175

SMITH & WESSON 38 DOUBLE ACTION

Revolver; double action; 38 S&W; 5-shot cylinder; 4-inch, 4-1/2-inch, 5-inch, 6-inch, 8-inch, 10-inch barrel; hinged frame; hard rubber checkered stocks; fixed sights; blued or nickel finish. Several design variations. Manufactured 1880 to 1911; some collector value.

S/N through 4000		
Exc.: $800	**VGood:** $650	**Good:** $375
S/N over 4000		
Exc.: $325	**VGood:** $225	**Good:** $150
8-inch, 10-inch barrels		
Exc.: $2500	**VGood:** $1750	**Good:** $1200

SMITH & WESSON 38 DOUBLE ACTION PERFECTED MODEL

Revolver; double action; 38 S&W; 5-shot; 3-1/4-inch to 6-inch barrels; hard black rubber grips; blue or nickel finish. Distinguishing features include: manufactured on a modified 32 Hand Ejector frame; incorporates both a top barrel latch and frame-mounted side latch. The last top-break revolver introduced by S&W, the Perfected model was introduced in 1909 and produced until 1920 with a total production run of 59,400.

Exc.: $500   **VGood:** $300   **Good:** $200

SMITH & WESSON 38 SAFETY HAMMERLESS (NEW DEPARTURE)

Revolver; double action; 38 S&W; 5-shot; 3-1/4-inch, 4-inch, 5-inch, 6-inch barrel; checkered hard rubber or walnut grips; blue or nickel finish. Numbered in separate serial number series. Total production run of 261,493. Manufactured from 1887 to 1937.

Exc.: $450   **VGood:** $275   **Good:** $200

SMITH & WESSON 38 SINGLE ACTION THIRD MODEL (MODEL 1891)

Revolver; single action; 38 S&W; 5-shot; 3-1/4-inch, 4-inch, 5-inch, 6-inch barrel; checkered hard rubber or walnut grips; blued or nickel finish. A special variation was manufactured with a spur trigger assembly inserted in place of the standard trigger and trigger guard. This was called the Mexican Model (100 percent premium) and is very rare; beware of fakes.

Conventional trigger guard		
Exc.: $1600	**VGood:** $1250	**Good:** $750

SMITH & WESSON 44 DOUBLE ACTION FIRST MODEL

Revolver; double action; 44 Russian, 38-40; 6-shot cylinder; 4-inch, 5-inch, 6-inch, 6-1/2-inch barrel; hard rubber or walnut grips; fixed sights; blued or nickel finish. Manufactured 1881 to 1913. 53,668 manufactured.

Exc.: $1800   **VGood:** $950   **Good:** $700

SMITH & WESSON 44 DOUBLE ACTION FAVORITE

Same specs as the First Model except 5-inch barrel. Approximately 1000 manufactured between 1882 to 1883.

Exc.: $6000   **VGood:** $4000   **Good:** $2500

SMITH & WESSON NEW MODEL NO. 3

Revolver; single action; hinged frame; 44 Russian; 3-1/2-inch, 4-inch, 5-inch, 6-inch, 6-1/2-inch, 7-inch, 7-1/2-inch, 8-inch barrel; rounded hard rubber or walnut stocks; fixed or target sights; blued or nickel finish; manufactured 1878 to 1908; broad collector value.

Exc.: $2000   **VGood:** $1600   **Good:** $800

SMITH & WESSON NEW MODEL NO. 3 FRONTIER

Same specs as New Model No. 3 except 44-40 Win.; 4-inch, 5-inch, 6-3/4-inch barrel; longer 19/16-inch cylinder. Manufactured 1885 to 1908; great collector interest.

Exc.: $3000   **VGood:** $2250   **Good:** $1600

SMITH & WESSON NEW MODEL NO. 3 TARGET

Same specs as New Model No. 3 except 32-44 S&W, 38-44 S&W; 6-inch, 61/2-inch barrel; adjustable sights. Manufactured 1887 to 1910; collector interest.

Exc.: $2250   **VGood:** $1600   **Good:** $1000

SMITH & WESSON NEW MODEL NO. 3 WINCHESTER

Same specs as New Model No. 3 Frontier except 38-40. Manufactured 1900 to 1907; extremely rare; only 74 manufactured.

Exc.: $10,000   **VGood:** $7500   **Good:** $4000

SMITH & WESSON SINGLE SHOT FIRST MODEL

Single shot; 22 LR, 32 S&W, 38 S&W; 6-inch, 8-inch, 10-inch barrels; target sights; square-butt, hard rubber grips; blued or nickel finish; built on same frame as 38 Single Action Third Model. Also furnished with 38 S&W barrel, cylinder to convert to single action. 1200 manufactured between 1893 and 1905; collector interest.

22 LR		
Exc.: $650	**VGood:** $450	**Good:** $300
32 S&W		
Exc.: $950	**VGood:** $650	**Good:** $350
38 S&W		
Exc.: $900	**VGood:** $600	**Good:** $350

Smith & Wesson 22/32 Kit Gun (Model 34)

Smith & Wesson Single Shot Third Model

Smith & Wesson 38 Regulation Police (Model 33)

Smith & Wesson 1977 22/32 Kit Gun M.R.F. (Model 63)

Smith & Wesson 32 Hand Ejector First Model

Smith & Wesson 32 Hand Ejector (Model 30)

Smith & Wesson Bodyguard (Model 49)

SMITH & WESSON SINGLE SHOT SECOND MODEL

Same specs as First Model except 22 LR only; 10-inch barrel; cannot be converted to revolver configuration; serial numbered in separate series.

Exc.: $600   VGood: $450   Good: $275

SMITH & WESSON SINGLE SHOT THIRD MODEL (PERFECTED SINGLE SHOT)

Same specs as First Model except 22 LR; hinged frame; target model; redesigned to incorporate new frame design developed for the 38 Double Action Perfected Model; checkered walnut target grips. Manufactured from 1909 to 1923. A special group featuring a short chamber was manufactured in 1910 and called the Olympic Model; the 22 LR cartridge must be forced into the rifling.

Perfected Single Shot
Exc.: $600   VGood: $450   Good: $300

SMITH & WESSON 22 WMR SERVICE KIT GUN (MODEL 650)

Revolver; double action; 22 WMR; 6-shot cylinder; 3-inch heavy barrel; 7-1/4-inch overall length; weighs 23 oz.; stainless steel construction; fixed 1/10-inch serrated front ramp, micro-click adjustable rear; checkered walnut round butt stocks with medallion; satin finish. Introduced 1983; dropped 1987.

Exc.: $250   VGood: $200   Good: $150

SMITH & WESSON 22/32 KIT GUN

Revolver; 22 LR; 6-shot; 4-inch barrel; 8-inch overall length; weighs 21 oz.; 1/10-inch Patridge or pocket revolver front sight, with rear sight adjustable for elevation and windage; checkered round-butt Circassian walnut or hard rubber stocks; (small or special oversized target square-butt stocks were offered on special order); blued or nickel finish; a compact outdoorsman's revolver based on the 22/32 Target. Introduced in 1935; replaced in 1953 by the Model 34.

Exc.: $750   VGood: $500   Good: $400

SMITH & WESSON 22/32 KIT GUN (MODEL 34)

Revolver; 22 LR; 6-shot; 2-inch, 4-inch barrels; 8-inch overall length (4-inch barrel); weighs 22-1/2 oz.; fixed 1/10-inch serrated front ramp, micro-click adjustable rear; checkered walnut round or square-butt grips with medallion; blued finish. Originally introduced in 1936; pre-war variations feature round barrel and bring premium prices. Discontinued in 1991.

Exc.: $375   VGood: $295   Good: $200

SMITH & WESSON 22/32 TARGET

Revolver; 22 LR; 6-shot; 6-inch barrel; 10-1/2-inch overall length; sights, 1/10-inch or 1/8-inch Patridge front, fully-adjustable square notch rear sight; stocks, special, oversize, square-butt pattern in checkered Circassian walnut with S&W monogram; chambers countersunk at the heads around 1935 for the higher-velocity cartridges; blued finish only. A forerunner of the Model 35. Introduced in 1911; superseded by the Model 35 in 1953.

Exc.: $800   VGood: $650   Good: $400

SMITH & WESSON 32 HAND EJECTOR FIRST MODEL (MODEL OF 1896)

Revolver; double action, hand ejector; 32 S&W Long; 3-1/4-inch, 4-1/4-inch, 6-inch barrel; fixed sights; hard rubber stocks; blued or nickel finish. First S&W solid-frame revolver with swing-out cylinder. Company name and patent dates marked on cylinder rather than barrel. Total production run of 19,712. Manufactured 1896 to 1903. Significant premium for factory-0engraved presentation models.

Exc.: $600   VGood: $450   Good: $225

SMITH & WESSON 32 HAND EJECTOR (MODEL 30)

Revolver; double action; 32 S&W Long; will accept 32 S&W and 32 S&W Long wadcutter; 6-shot; 2-inch, 3-inch, 4-inch barrels; 6-inch available at one time; 8-inch overall length (4-inch barrel); weighs 18 oz.; checkered walnut grips with medallion; formerly hard rubber; serrated ramp front and square notch rear; blue or nickel finish. Introduced 1908; dropped 1972. Values are for later production.

Exc.: $375   VGood: $295   Good: $175

SMITH & WESSON 38 REGULATION POLICE (MODEL 31)

Revolver; 32 S&W Long; accepts 32 S&W, 32 Colt New Police; 6-shot; 2-inch, 3-inch, 3-1/4-inch, 4-inch, 4-1/4-inch, 6-inch barrels; 8-1/2-inch overall length (4-inch barrel); weighs 18-3/4 oz.; fixed sights with 1/10-inch serrated ramp front and square notch rear; checkered walnut stocks with medallion; blue or nickel finish. Introducted 1917; dropped 1991.

Exc.: $350   VGood: $295   Good: $150

SMITH & WESSON 38 REGULATION POLICE TARGET MODEL

Same specs as Model 31 except target model with 6-inch barrel; 10-1/4-inch overall length; weighs 20 oz.; adjustable target sights. Introduced 1917; dropped 1941.

Exc.: $600   VGood: $450   Good: $300

SMITH & WESSON 38 REGULATION POLICE (MODEL 33)

Revolver; 38 S&W; accepts 38 Colt New Police; 5-shot; 4-inch barrel; 8-1/2-inch overall length; weighs 18 oz.; fixed sights, with 1/10-inch serrated ramp front and square notch rear; checkered walnut stocks with medallion; blue or nickel finish. Introduced in 1917; dropped 1974.

Exc.: $350   VGood: $275   Good: $195

SMITH & WESSON 1960 22/32 KIT GUN WMR (MODEL 51)

Revolver; 22 WMR; 3-1/2-inch barrel; 8-inch overall length; weighs 24 oz.; all steel frame and cylinder; fixed 1/10-inch serrated front ramp, micro-click adjustable rear; checkered walnut, round or square-butt stocks; blue or nickel finish. Introduced 1960; dropped 1974.

Exc.: $350   VGood: $300   Good: $225

Nickel finish
Exc.: $400   VGood: $350   Good: $250

SMITH & WESSON 1977 22/32 KIT GUN WMR (MODEL 63)

Revolver; 22 LR; 6-shot; 2-inch, 4-inch barrel; 8-inch overall length (4-inch barrel); weighs 24-1/4 oz.; stainless steel construction; fixed 1/10-inch serrated front ramp sight, micro-click adjustable rear; round butt soft rubber or checkered walnut square-butt stocks with medallion; satin finish. Introduced 1977; still in production.

New: $375   Perf.: $325   Exc.: $250

SMITH & WESSON AIRWEIGHT KIT GUN (MODEL 43)

Revolver; 22 LR; 3-1/2-inch barrel; 8-inch overall length; weighs 14-1/4-inch oz.; alloy aluminum frame and cylinder; fixed 1/10-inch serrated front ramp, micro-click adjustable rear; checkered walnut, round or square-butt stocks; blue or nickel finish. Introduced 1955; dropped 1974.

Exc.: $350   VGood: $300   Good: $250

SMITH & WESSON BODYGUARD (MODEL 49)

Revolver; double action; 38 Spl.; 5-shot; 2-inch barrel; 6-5/16-inch overall length; steel construction; weighs 20-1/2 oz.; fixed 1/10-inch serrated front ramp, square notch rear; blue or nickel finish; features shrouded hammer that can be cocked manually for single-action firing. Introduced 1955; dropped 1996. Later reintroduced.

Perf.: $500   Exc.: $400   VGood: $275

Smith & Wesson Bodyguard (Model 649)

Smith & Wesson Model 642 PowerPort Pro Series

Smith & Wesson Centennial (Model 40)

Smith & Wesson Centennial (Model 640)

Smith & Wesson Centennial (Model 940)

Smith & Wesson Centennial Airweight (Model 442)

Smith & Wesson Centennial Airweight (Model 642)

Smith & Wesson Chief's Special (Model 36)

Smith & Wesson Chief's Special Airweight (Model 37)

SMITH & WESSON BODYGUARD (MODEL 649)

Revolver; double action; 38 Spl.; 5-shot; 2-inch barrel; 6-5/16-inch overall length; weighs 20 1/2 oz.; stainless steel construction; fixed 1/10-inch serrated front ramp, square notch rear; satin finish; features shrouded hammer that can be cocked manually for single-action firing. Introduced 1955; still in production.

Perf.: $375   **Exc.:** $325   **VGood:** $250

SMITH & WESSON BODYGUARD AIRWEIGHT (MODEL 38)

Revolver; double action; 38 Spl.; 5-shot; 2-inch barrel; 6 5/16-inch overall length; weighs 14-1/2 oz.; fixed 1/10-inch serrated front ramp, square notch rear; blue or nickel finish; features shrouded hammer that can be cocked manually for single-action firing. Introduced 1955; dropped 1998.

Perf.: $350   **Exc.:** $250   **VGood:** $200

SMITH & WESSON CENTENNIAL (MODEL 40)

Revolver; double action; 38 Spl; 5-shot; 2-inch barrel; 6-1/2-inch overall length; weighs 19 oz.; concealed hammer; fixed 1/10-inch serrated front ramp, square notch rear. Swing-out version of earlier top-break design with grip safety. Introduced 1953; dropped 1974. Collector value.

Exc.: $475   **VGood:** $425   **Good:** $300

SMITH & WESSON CENTENNIAL (MODEL 640)

Revolver; double action; 38 Spl.; 5-shot; 2-inch, 3-inch barrel; 6-5/16-inch overall length; weighs 20 oz.; serrated ramp front, fixed notch rear sight; Goncalo Alves round-butt grips; stainless steel version of the Model 40 sans grip safety; concealed hammer; smoothed edges. Introduced 1990; still in production.

Perf.: $375   **Exc.:** $325   **VGood.:** $275

SMITH & WESSON CENTENNIAL (MODEL 940)

Revolver; double action; 9mm Para.; 5-shot; 2-inch, 3-inch barrel; 6-5/16-inch overall length; weighs 20 oz.; serrated ramp front, fixed notch rear sight; rubber grips; stainless steel version of the Model 40 sans grip safety; concealed hammer; smoothed edges. Introduced 1990; dropped 1998.

New: $375   **Perf.:** $325   **Exc.:** $275

SMITH & WESSON CENTENNIAL AIRWEIGHT (MODEL 42)

Revolver; double action; 38 Spl; 5-shot; 2-inch barrel; 6-1/2-inch overall length; concealed hammer; aluminum alloy frame and cylinder; fixed 1/10-inch serrated front ramp, square notch rear. Lightweight version of Model 40. Introduced 1953; dropped 1974. Collector value.

Blue		
Exc.: $400	**VGood:** $350	**Good:** $250
Nickel		
Exc.: $800	**VGood:** $650	**Good:** $450

SMITH & WESSON CENTENNIAL AIRWEIGHT (MODEL 442)

Revolver; double action; 38 Spl.; 5-shot cylinder; 2-inch barrel; weighs 15-3/4 oz.; 6-5/8-inch overall length; Uncle Mike's Custom Grade Santoprene grips; serrated ramp front sight, fixed notch rear; alloy frame; carbon steel barrel and cylinder; concealed hammer. Made in U.S. by Smith & Wesson. Introduced 1993; still produced.

Perf.: $350	**Exc.:** $300	**VGood.:** $250
Nickel finish		
Perf.: $375	**Exc..:** $325	**VGood.:** $275

SMITH & WESSON CENTENNIAL AIRWEIGHT (MODEL 642)

Revolver; double action; 38 Spl.; 5-shot; 2-inch carbon steel barrel; 6-5/16-inch overall length; anodized alloy frame; weighs 16 oz.; serrated ramp front, fixed notch rear sight; Uncle Mike's Custom Grade Santoprene grips; same as the Model 40 sans grip safety; concealed hammer; smoothed edges. Introduced 1990; still in production.

Perf.: $400   **Exc.:** $350   **VGood:** $250

SMITH & WESSON MODEL 642 POWERPORT PRO SERIES

Similar to Model 642 buit with gray aluminum frame and black stainless ported barrel. Dealer sets pricing. Introduced 2008.

New: $695   **Perf.:** $525   **Exc.:** $375

SMITH & WESSON CHIEF'S SPECIAL (MODEL 36)

Revolver; double action; 38 Spl.; 5-shot; 2-inch, 3-inch barrel; 7-3/8-inch overall length (3-inch barrel); weighs 21-1/2 oz.; fixed 1/10-inch serrated front ramp, square notch rear; all steel frame and cylinder; checkered round butt soft rubber grips most common; square-butt available; blue or nickel finish. Dropped 1999.

New: $365   **Perf.:** $325   **Exc.:** $295

SMITH & WESSON CHIEF'S SPECIAL AIRWEIGHT (MODEL 37)

Revolver; double action; 38 Spl.; 5-shot; 2-inch barrel; 6-1/2-inch overall length; weighs 19-1/2 oz.; lightweight version of Model 36, incorporating aluminum alloy frame; weighs 14-1/2 oz.; fixed 1/10-inch serrated front ramp, square notch rear; all steel frame and cylinder; checkered round butt grips most common; square-butt available; blue or nickel finish. Still in production.

New: $350   **Perf.:** $275   **Exc.:** $225

Smith & Wesson Model 637
Airweight Revolver

Smith & Wesson
Ladysmith (Model 36-LS)

Smith & Wesson Model 60
357 Magnum Chiefs Special

Smith & Wesson
Ladysmith (Model 60-LS)

Smith & Wesson
Model 60 3" Full Lug

Smith & Wesson
Model 651

Smith & Wesson
Model 60 Pro Series

Smith & Wesson Target
Model 1953 (Model 35)

SMITH & WESSON MODEL 637 AIRWEIGHT REVOLVER

Similar to the Model 37 Airweight except has alloy frame, stainless steel barrel, cylinder and yoke; rated for 38 Spec. +P; Uncle Mike's Boot Grip. Weighs 15 oz. Introduced 1996.

New: $375   **Perf.:** $300   **Exc.:** $225

SMITH & WESSON CHIEF'S SPECIAL STAINLESS (MODEL 60)

Revolver; double action; 38 Spl.; 5-shot; 2-inch barrel; 6-1/2-inch overall length; weighs 19 oz.; stainless steel construction; fixed 1/10-inch serrated front ramp, square notch rear; checkered walnut round butt grips. Dropped 1996.

New: $355   **Perf.:** $335   **Exc.:** $300

SMITH & WESSON MODEL 60 .357 MAGNUM CHIEFS SPECIAL

Similar to the Model 60 in 38 Special except is 357 Magnum; 2-1/8-inch or 3-inch barrel. Weighs 24 oz.; 7-1/2-inch overall length (3-inch barrel). Has Uncle Mike's Combat grips.

New: $400   **Perf.:** $350   **Exc.:** $275

SMITH & WESSON MODEL 60 PRO SERIES

Similar to Model 60 but in .38/.357 with night front sights, "high-hold" enforcing walnut grips, 3-inch battel and matte stainless finish. Introduced 2008.

New: $750   **Perf.:** $550   **Exc.:** $475

SMITH & WESSON LADYSMITH (MODEL 36-LS)

Revolver; double action; 38 Spl.; 5-shot; 2-inch barrel; 6-5/16-inch overall length; weighs 20 oz.; carbon steel construction; serrated front ramp, square notch rear; rosewood laminate grips; comes in fitted carry/storage case; blue finish. Introduced 1989; still in production.

New: $350   **Perf.:** $300   **Exc.:** $225

SMITH & WESSON LADYSMITH (MODEL 60-LS)

Revolver; double action; 38 Spl.; 5-shot; 2-inch barrel; 6-5/16-inch overall length; weighs 20 oz.; stainless steel construction; serrated front ramp, square notch rear; rosewood laminate grips; stainless satin finish. Introduced 1989; still in production.

New: $350   **Perf.:** $300   **Exc.:** $250

SMITH & WESSON MODEL 60 3-INCH FULL LUG

Revolver; double action; 38 Spl.; 5-shot; 3-inch full lug barrel; 7-1/2-inch overall length; weighs 24-1/2 oz.; stainless steel construction; fixed pinned black ramp front sight, adjustable black blade rear; rubber combat grips. Introduced 1991; Still in production.

New: $350   **Perf.:** $300   **Exc.:** $250

SMITH & WESSON MODEL 651

Revolver; double action; 22 WMR; 6-shot cylinder; 4-inch heavy barrel; 8-11/16-inch overall length; weighs 24-1/2 oz.; stainless steel construction; ramp front, adjustable micrometer-click rear; semi-target hammer; combat trigger; soft rubber or checkered walnut square-butt stocks with medallion; satin finish. Introduced 1983; dropped 1998.

Exc.: $300   **VGood:** $250   **Good:** $150

SMITH & WESSON TARGET MODEL 1953 (MODEL 35)

Revolver; 22 LR; 6-shot; 6-inch barrel; 10-1/2-inch overall length; weighs 25 oz.; ribbed barrel; micrometer rear sight; Magna-type stocks; flattened cylinder latch; blue finish. A redesign of the 22/32 Target model. Introduced 1953; dropped 1974.

Exc.: $300   **VGood:** $200   **Good:** $175

SMITH & WESSON TERRIER (MODEL 32)

Revolver; 38 S&W, 38 Colt New Police; 5-shot; 2-inch barrel; 6-1/4-inch overall length; weighs 17 oz.; fixed sights with 1/10-inch serrated ramp front, square notch rear; round butt checkered walnut stocks with medallion; blue or nickel finish. Introduced 1936; dropped 1974.

Exc.: $325   **VGood:** $275   **Good:** $225

SMITH & WESSON K AND L MEDIUM FRAME REVOLVERS

Smith & Wesson's original medium-frame revolver was the "K" frame introduced in 1899. In 1980, S&W offered an improved medium frame revolver for the 357 Magnum cartridge and this new frame was called the "L" frame.

SMITH & WESSON 32-20 HAND EJECTOR

Revolver; 32 Winchester; 6-shot; 4-inch, 5-inch, 6-inch, 6-1/2-inch barrels; fixed or adjustable sights (rare); hard black rubber round or checkered walnut square-butt grips; caliber marking on early models, 32 Winchester; late models, 32 W.C.F., marked 32/20.

Exc.: $400   **VGood:** $325   **Good:** $175

SMITH & WESSON 38 MILITARY & POLICE

Revolver; double action; 38 Spl.; 6-shot; 4-inch, 5-inch, 6-inch, 6-1/2-inch barrels; hard rubber round butt (early models) or checkered walnut square-butt grips; blue or nickel finish. The first S&W K-frame was the 38 Hand Ejector which later became known as the 38 Military & Police. This model was introduced in 1899 and has been in continuous production. During the last 96 years, S&W has produced over 5 million of these revolvers, resulting in numerous variations which affect values only slightly. The most collectable of these, the 38 Hand Ejector First Model, can be easily recognized by the lack of a locking lug located on the underside of the barrel and the serial number 1 through 20,975. Between 1899 and 1940 this model was available with both fixed sights and an adjustable target sight. The target model, referred to as the 38 Military and Police Target Model, brings a premium price and was the predecessor to all K-frame target models.

38 Hand Ejector First Model		
Exc.: $450	**VGood:** $300	**Good:** $150
Standard models		
Exc.: $300	**VGood:** $225	**Good:** $135

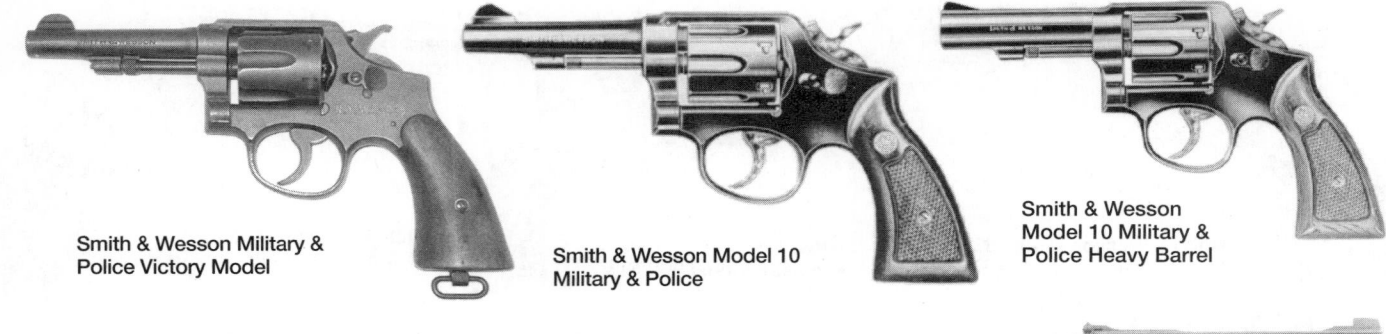

Smith & Wesson Military &
Police Victory Model

Smith & Wesson Model 10
Military & Police

Smith & Wesson
Model 10 Military &
Police Heavy Barrel

Smith & Wesson Model 10
Military & Police (1995 model)

Smith & Wesson Model 13
H.B. Military & Police

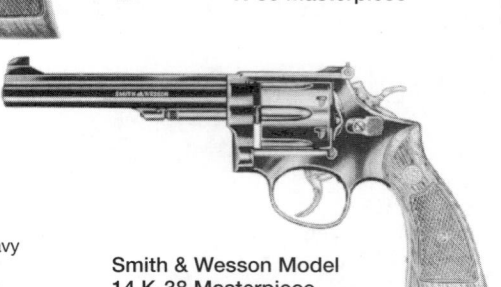

Smith & Wesson Model 14
K-38 Masterpiece

Smith & Wesson Model
14 K-38 Masterpiece
Single Action

SMITH & WESSON 38 MILITARY & POLICE VICTORY MODEL

Revolver; 38 Spl., 38 S&W; 2-inch, 4-inch, 5-inch barrels; smooth walnut grips; midnight black finish. The Victory Model is the WWII production variation of the 38 Military & Police Model. Its name was derived from the serial number prefix "V," a symbol for "Victory." The revolvers provided the U.S. government were in 38 Special; those provided to the U.S. Allied Forces in 38 S&W. At the end of WWII the "V" serial number prefix was changed to "S," which was continued to 1948 when the series again reached 1,000,000. Add 50 percent for U.S. military markings (beware of fakes!).

Exc.: $375   **VGood: $265**   **Good: $125**

SMITH & WESSON K-22 OUTDOORSMAN

Revolver; 22 LR; 6-shot; 6-inch round barrel; adjustable rear sight; square-butt checkered walnut grips; blue finish. Also known as the K-22 First Model, this was the first in a long line of K-frame 22 rimfire target revolvers. Introduced 1931.

Exc.: $500   **VGood: $350**   **Good: $200**

SMITH & WESSON K-22 SECOND MODEL

Revolver; 22 LR; 6-shot; 6-inch round barrel; checkered walnut square-butt grips; blue finish. This revolver was the first to be called the "Masterpiece." It was introduced in 1940 and, because of the factory shift to wartime production, it was manufactured for only a limited time. Total production was 1067 revolvers in serial number range 682,420 to 696,952 without a letter prefix.

Exc.: $1000   **VGood: $850**   **Good: $500**

SMITH & WESSON K-32 FIRST MODEL

Revolver; 32 S&W Long; 6-inch round barrel; checkered walnut square-butt grips; blue finish. The K-32 First Model was a companion model to both the 38 M&P and K-22 Outdoorsman. It was introduced in 1938 and only produced until 1940 with approximately 125 handguns manufactured. It is the rarest of the early target models.

Exc.: $3000   **VGood: $2500**   **Good: $1800**

SMITH & WESSON MODEL 10 MILITARY & POLICE

Revolver; double action; 38 Spl.; 6-shot; 2-inch, 3-inch, 4-inch, 5-inch, 6-1/2-inch barrel; 11-1/8-inch overall length with square butt, 1/4-inch less for round butt; weighs 31 oz.; 1/10-inch service-type front sight and square notch non-adjustable rear; square-butt checkered walnut stocks, round butt pattern with choice of hard rubber or checkered walnut; blued or nickel finish. In 1957 a 4-inch heavy barrel became available and is the 4-inch barrel configuration still available. The 38 M&P has been the true workhorse of the Smith & Wesson line of revolvers. The basic frame is termed S&'s K-frame, the derivative source of the K-38, et al. It is, quite possibly, the most popular, widely accepted police duty revolver ever made. Introduced about 1902. Reintroduced 1995.

Perf.: $350   **Exc.: $300**   **VGood: $235**

Nickel finish

Perf.: $375   **Exc.: $325**   **VGood: $275**

SMITH & WESSON MODEL 10 MILITARY & POLICE HEAVY BARREL

Same specs as standard Model 10 except 4-inch heavy ribbed barrel; ramp front sight, square notch rear; square-butt; blued or nickel finish. Introduced 1957.

Perf.: $350   **Exc.: $300**   **VGood: $250**

SMITH & WESSON MODEL 12 MILITARY & POLICE AIRWEIGHT

Revolver; double action; 38 Spl.; 6-shot; 2-inch, 4-inch barrel; overall length, 6-7/8-inch (2-inch, round butt); weighs 18 oz.; aluminum alloy frame; fixed 1/8-inch serrated ramp front sight, square-notch rear; checkered walnut Magna-type, round or square-butt. Introduced about 1952; dropped 1986.

Exc.: $350   **VGood: $300**   **Good: $250**

SMITH & WESSON MODEL 13 H.B. MILITARY & POLICE

Revolver; double action; 357 Mag.; 6-shot cylinder; 3-inch, 4-inch heavy barrel; 9-5/16-inch overall length (4-inch barrel); serrated ramp front sight, fixed square notch rear; square or round butt; blued finish. Introduced 1974; dropped 1998.

New: $350   **Perf.: $300**   **Exc.: $250**

SMITH & WESSON MODEL 14 K-38 MASTERPIECE

Revolver; double action; 38 Spl.; 6-shot; 6-inch, 8-3/8-inch barrel; 11-1/8-inch overall length (6-inch barrel); swing-out cylinder; micrometer rear sight, 1/8-inch Patridge-type front; hand-checkered service-type walnut grips; blued. Introduced 1947; dropped 1983.

Exc.: $425   **VGood: $365**   **Good: $270**

SMITH & WESSON MODEL 14 K-38 MASTERPIECE FULL LUG

Same specs as standard Model 14 except 6-inch full-lug barrel; weighs 47 oz.; pinned Patridge-type front sight, micrometer click-adjustable rear; square-butt combat grips; combat trigger, hammer; polished blue finish. Reintroduced 1991.

New: $400   **Perf.: $375**   **Exc.: $350**

SMITH & WESSON MODEL 14 K-38 MASTERPIECE SINGLE ACTION

Same specs as standard Model 14 except 6-inch barrel only; single-action only; target hammer; target trigger.

Exc.: $425   **VGood: $365**   **Good: $270**

SMITH & WESSON MODEL 15 38 COMBAT MASTERPIECE

Revolver; double action; 38 Spl.; 6-shot; 2-inch, 4-inch, 6-inch, 8-3/8-inch barrel; 9-1/8-inch overall length; weighs 34 oz.; blue or nickel finish. It took some years after WWII to re-establish commercial production and begin catching up with civilian demands at S&W. By the early '50s the situation was bright enough to warrant introducing a 4-inch version of the K-38, which was designated the 38 Combat Masterpiece. Its only nominal companion was the 22 Combat Masterpiece and no attempt was made to match loaded weights, as in the K-series-the 38 weighing 34 oz. empty, compared to 36-1/2 oz. for the 22 version. Barrel ribs were narrower than the K-series and front sights were of the Baughman, quick-draw ramp pattern, replacing the vertical surface of the K-series Patridge-type. No longer in production.

New: $350   **Perf.: $275**   **Exc.: $200**

Nickel finish

New: $375   **Perf.: $300**   **Exc.: $250**

Smith & Wesson Model 16 K-32 Masterpiece Full Lug

Smith & Wesson Model 17 K-22 Masterpiece

Smith & Wesson Model 15 38 Combat Masterpiece

Smith & Wesson Model 48 K-22 Masterpiece WMR

Smith & Wesson Model 18 22 Combat Masterpiece

Smith & Wesson Model 19 Combat Magnum

Smith & Wesson Model 53 22 Magnum

SMITH & WESSON MODEL 16 K-32 MASTERPIECE

Revolver; double action; 32 S&W Long; 6-shot; 6-inch barrel; target hammer; target trigger; red-insert front sight, white-outline rear; optional Patridge or Baughman front sights; walnut, Magna-pattern stocks with medallions standard; optional factory target stocks in exotic woods; blued finish. Originated as target version of the hand-ejector in 32 S&W Long about 1935, and dropped at the beginning of WWII. Appeared in its present form in the late '40s and designated the K-32 as a companion to the K-22 and K-38. Introduced 1947; dropped 1983.

Exc.: $2000　**VGood:** $900　**Good:** $675

SMITH & WESSON MODEL 16 K-32 MASTERPIECE FULL LUG

Same specs as standard Model 16 except 32 Mag.; 4-inch, 6-inch, 8-3/8-inch full-lug barrel; Patridge-type front sight, click-adjustable micrometer rear; combat-style Goncalo Alves grips; polished blue finish. Introduced 1990; dropped 1992.

Semi-target 4-inch barrel		
Perf.: $900	**Exc.:** $650	**VGood:** $450
Target 6-inch barrel		
Perf.: $1000	**Exc.:** $725	**VGood:** $495
Target 8-3/8-inch barrel		
Perf.: $1050	**Exc.:** $800	**VGood:** $3525

SMITH & WESSON MODEL 17 K-22 MASTERPIECE

Revolver; double action; 22 LR; 6-shot; 6-inch barrel standard, 8-3/8-inch available; 11-1/8-inch overall length (6-inch barrel); weighs 38-1/2 oz. (6-inch), 42-1/2 oz. (8-3/8-inch) loaded; blue finish. Redesigned version of Model 16. Postwar production added the refinement of a broad barrel rib, intended to compensate for weight variations between the three Masterpiece models. Likewise added were the redesigned hammer with its broad spur and thumb tip relief notch, an adjustable anti-backlash stop for the trigger and the Magna-type grips developed in the mid-'30s to help cushion the recoil of the 357 Magnum. Introduced around 1947; dropped 1998.

6-inch barrel		
Perf.: $350	**Exc.:** $300	**VGood:** $250
8-3/8-inch barrel		
Perf.: $500	**Exc.:** $400	**VGood:** $325

SMITH & WESSON MODEL 17 K-22 MASTERPIECE FULL LUG

Same specs as standard Model 17 except 4-inch, 6-inch, 8-3/8-inch barrel; Patridge-type front sight on two longer barrel lengths (serrated type on 4-inch version), S&W click-adjustable micrometer rear; grooved tang; polished blue finish. Introduced 1990; dropped 1998.

4-inch, 6-inch barrel		
Perf.: $425	**Exc.:** $375	**VGood:** $325
8-3/8-inch barrel		
Perf.: $800	**Exc.:** $575	**VGood:** $425

SMITH & WESSON MODEL 18 22 COMBAT MASTERPIECE

Revolver; double action; 22 LR, 22 Long, 22 Short; 6-shot; 4-inch barrel; 9-1/8-inch overall length; weighs 36-1/2 oz. (loaded); Baughman 1/8-inch quick-draw front sight on plain ramp, fully-adjustable S&W micrometer-click rear; checkered walnut, Magna-type grips with S&W medallion; options include broad-spur target hammer, wide target trigger, hand-filling target stocks, red front sight insert and white outlined rear sight notch; finish, blue only. Dropped 1985.

Exc.: $425　**VGood:** $300　**Good:** $250

SMITH & WESSON MODEL 19 COMBAT MAGNUM

Revolver; double action; 357 Mag.; 6-shot; 2-1/2-inch, 4-inch, 6-inch barrel; available with 4-inch barrel; 9-1/2-inch overall length; weighs 35 oz.; 1/8-inch Baughman quick-draw front plain ramp, fully-adjustable S&W micrometer-click rear; checkered Goncalo Alves grips with S&W medallion; S&W bright blue or nickel finish; built on the lighter S&W K-frame as used on the K-38, et al., rather than on the heavier N-frame used for the Model 27 and 28. Introduced about 1956; dropped 1999.

Perf.: $500　**Exc.:** $395　**VGood:** $345

SMITH & WESSON MODEL 48 K-22 MASTERPIECE WMR

Revolver; double action; 22 WMR; 4-inch, 6-inch, 8-3/8-inch barrel; weighs 39 oz. (6-inch barrel). A modification of the K-22 Model 17 without being distinctly designated as a Combat Masterpiece in 4-inch barrel configuration; auxiliary cylinder offered to permit the use with 22 LR cartridge with 1969 quoted price of $35.50. Dropped 1986.

Exc.: $400　**VGood:** $300　**Good:** $275

With 22 LR and 22 WMR cylinder		
Exc.: $450	**VGood:** $350	**Good:** $300

SMITH & WESSON MODEL 53

Revolver; double action; 22 Jet; 6-shot; 4-inch, 6-inch, 8-3/8-inch barrel; 11-1/4-inch overall length (6-inch barrel); weighs 40 oz.; 1/8-inch Baughman ramp front, adjustable S&W micrometer-click rear; checkered walnut grips with S&W medallion; blued finish only. Starting in the late '50s, there was considerable interest in converting K-22s to centerfire wildcat (i.e., nonstandard cartridge) configurations usually being chambered for a shortened version of the 22 Hornet, known as the 22 Harvey K-Chuck. With the intent of capitalizing on this interest, S&W introduced the 22 Remington CFM or centerfire magnum cartridge – also termed the 22 Jet – and the Model 53 chambered for it. The 22 Jet was a necked-down 357 case, designed to use a bullet of .222-inch to .223-inch diameter. The Model 53 was supplied with six chamber bushings, adapting it for firing 22 rimfire ammo, by means of repositioning the striker on the hammer. Alternatively, a standard 22 LR cylinder was offered as a factory-fitted accessory at about $35.30 for interchanging with the 22 Jet cylinder. Introduced 1960; dropped 1974.

Exc.: $650　**VGood:** $500　**Good:** $400

With chamber inserts		
Exc.: $700	**VGood:** $600	**Good:** $500
With 22 LR cylinder		
Exc.: $700	**VGood:** $600	**Good:** $500
With 8-3/8-inch barrel.		
Exc.: $750	**VGood:** $650	**Good:** $550

Smith & Wesson Model 64

Smith & Wesson Model 65

Smith & Wesson Model 65LS LadySmith

Smith & Wesson Model 66 Combat Magnum

Smith & Wesson Model 67 K-38 Combat Masterpiece

Smith & Wesson Model 547

Smith & Wesson Model 317 Airlite, 317 Ladysmith Revolvers

Smith & Wesson Model 586 Distinguished Combat Magnum

Smith & Wesson Model 610 Classic Hunter Revolver

SMITH & WESSON MODEL 64

Revolver; double action; 38 Spl.; 6-shot cylinder; 4-inch barrel; 9-1/2-inch overall length; weighs 30-1/2 oz.; Military & Police design; stainless steel construction; fixed, serrated front ramp sight, square-notch rear; service-style checkered American walnut square-butt stocks; satin finish. Introduced 1981.

Perf.: $400 **Exc.:** $350 **VGood:** $200

SMITH & WESSON MODEL 65

Revolver; double action; 357 Mag.; 6-shot cylinder; 3-inch, 4-inch, 6-inch barrel; 9-5/16-inch length (4-inch barrel); weighs 34 oz.; stainless steel construction; serrated ramp front sight, fixed square notch rear; square or round butt; blued finish. Introduced 1974; still in production.

Perf.: $400 **Exc.:** $350 **VGood:** $200

SMITH & WESSON MODEL 65LS LADYSMITH

Same specs as the Model 65 except 3-inch barrel; weighs 31 oz.; rosewood round-butt grips; stainless steel construction with frosted finish; smooth combat trigger; service hammer; shrouded ejector rod; comes with soft case. Made in U.S. by Smith & Wesson. Introduced 1992.

Perf.: $400 **Exc.:** $350 **VGood:** $200

SMITH & WESSON MODEL 66 COMBAT MAGNUM

Revolver; double action; 357 Mag., 38 Spl.; 6-shot cylinder; 2-1/2-inch, 4-inch, 6-inch barrel; 9-1/2-inch overall length (4-inch barrel); weighs 36 oz.; stainless steel construction; checkered Goncalo Alves target stocks; Baughman Quick Draw front sight on plain ramp, micro-click adjustable rear; grooved trigger, adjustable stop; satin finish. Introduced 1971.

Perf.: $400 **Exc.:** $350 **VGood:** $200

SMITH & WESSON MODEL 67 K-38 COMBAT MASTERPIECE

Revolver; double action; 38 Spl.; 6-shot cylinder; 4-inch barrel; 9-1/2-inch overall length; weighs 32 oz.; stainless steel construction; marketed as Combat Masterpiece; soft rubber or service-style checkered

American walnut stocks; Baughman Quick Draw front sight on ramp, micro-click adjustable rear; square-butt with grooved tangs; grooved trigger, adjustable stop. Introduced 1972; reintroduced 1994.

Perf.: $400 **Exc.:** $325 **VGood:** $275

SMITH & WESSON MODEL 547

Revolver; double action; 9mm Para.; 3-inch, 4-inch heavy barrel; 9-1/8-inch overall length (4-inch barrel); half-spur hammer; special extractor system; serrated ramp front sight, fixed square notch rear; checkered square-butt Magna Service stocks with 4-inch barrel; checkered round butt target stocks with 3-inch; blued finish. Introduced 1981; dropped 1985.

Exc.: $825 **VGood:** $525 **Good:** $375

SMITH & WESSON MODEL 317 AIRLITE, 317 LADYSMITH

Revolver; single action; 22 LR, 8-shot. Barrel: 1-7/8-inch. Weight: 9.9 oz. Length: 6-3/16-inch overall. Stocks: Dymondwood Boot or Uncle Mike's Boot. Sights: Serrated ramp front, fixed notch rear. Features: Aluminum alloy, carbon and stainless steels, and titanium construction. Short spur hammer, smooth combat trigger. Clear Cote finish. Introduced 1997.

New: $500 **Perf.:** $375 **Exc.:** $295

Model 317 LadySmith (DymondWood only, comes with display case).

New: $450 **Perf.:** $400 **Exc.:** $350

SMITH & WESSON MODEL 317 AIRLITE KIT GUN

Similar to the Model 317 Airlite except has 3-inch barrel, pinned black front sight, micro-click rear adjustable for windage and elevation. Weighs 11 oz. Introduced 1998.

New: $550 **Perf.:** $450 **Exc.:** $295

SMITH & WESSON MODEL 586 DISTINGUISHED COMBAT MAGNUM

Revolver; double action; 357 Mag.; 4-inch, 6-inch heavy barrel; weighs 46 oz. (6-inch barrel), 41 oz. (4-inch barrel); L-frame design; ejector rod shroud;

combat-type trigger; semi-target hammer; Baughman red ramp front sight, micrometer-click rear; soft rubber or Goncalo Alves target stocks; blued or nickel finish. Introduced 1981; dropped 1999.

Perf.: $450 **Exc..:** $300 **VGood:** $275

SMITH & WESSON MODEL 610 CLASSIC HUNTER REVOLVER

Revolver; double action; 10mm, 6-shot cylinder. Barrel: 6-1/2-inch full lug. Weight: 52 oz. Length: 12-inch overall. Stocks: Hogue rubber combat. Sights: Interchangeable blade front, micro-click rear adjustable for windage and elevation. Features: Stainless steel construction; target hammer, target trigger; unfluted cylinder; drilled and tapped for scope mounting. Introduced 1998.

Perf.: $650 **Exc.:** $450 **VGood:** $375

SMITH & WESSON MODEL 617 K-22 MASTERPIECE FULL LUG

Revolver; double action; 22 LR; 6-shot; 4-inch, 6-inch, 8-3/8-inch barrel; weighs 42 oz. (4-inch barrel); Patridge-type front sight on two longer barrel lengths, serrated type on 4-inch version, S&W click-adjustable micrometer rear; grooved tang; polished blue finish. Has same general specs as Model 17 Full Lug version except made of stainless steel; semi-target hammer (4-inch barrel); smooth combat trigger standard; smooth or serrated trigger or target hammer (6-inch barrel) optional; target hammer, serrated trigger (8-3/8-inch barrel). Introduced 1990; still in production.

4-inch barrel

New: $450 **Perf.:** $375 **Exc.:** $325

8-3/8-inch barrel with target hammer, trigger

New: $500 **Perf.:** $425 **Exc.:** $375

SMITH & WESSON MODEL 651

Revolver; double action; 22 WMR, 6-shot cylinder. Barrel: 4-inch. Weight: 24-1/2 oz. Length: 8-11/16-inch overall. Stocks: Soft rubber; wood optional. Sights: Red ramp front, adjustable micrometer click rear. Features: Stainless steel construction with semi-target hammer, smooth combat trigger. Reintroduced 1991. Limited production.

New: $400 **Perf.:** $350 **Exc.:** $300

Smith & Wesson Model
396 Night Guard

Smith & Wesson
Model 657

Smith & Wesson
Model 696

Smith & Wesson 640
Centennial

Smith & Wesson
Model 442

Smith & Wesson
Model 642
Airweight Revolver

Smith & Wesson
642LS LadySmith

Smith & Wesson
Model 686

Smith &
Wesson
Model 686
Magnum PLUS

SMITH & WESSON MODEL 657

Revolver; double action; 41 Mag., 6-shot. Barrel: 6-inch. Weight: 48 oz. Length: 11-3/8-inch overall. Stocks: Soft rubber; wood optional. Sights: Pinned 1/8-inch red ramp front, micro-click rear adjustable for windage and elevation. Features: Stainless steel construction.

New: $450   **Perf.:** $375   **Exc.:** $325

SMITH & WESSON MODEL 696

Revolver; double action; 44 Spec., 5-shot. Barrel: 3-inch. Weight: 35.5 oz. Length: 8-1/4-inch overall. Stocks: Uncle Mike's Combat. Sights: Red ramp front, click adjustable white outline rear. Features: Stainless steel construction; round butt frame; satin finish. Introduced 1997.

New: $450   **Perf.:** $375   **Exc.:** $325

MODEL 396 NIGHT GUARD

A 2-1/2-inch snubbie chambered for .44 Special. 5-shot cylinder. Tritium sights, scandium alloy frame, matte black finish overll. Neoprene grips. Introduced 2008.

New: $750   **Perf.:** $575   **Exc.:** $350

SMITH & WESSON MODEL 640 CENTENNIAL

Revolver; double action; 357 Mag., 38 Spec., 5-shot. Barrel: 1-7/8-inch (38 Spec.), 2-1/8-inch (357 Magnum). Weight: 25 oz. Length: 6-3/4-inch overall. Stocks: Uncle Mike's Boot Grip. Sights: Serrated ramp front, fixed notch rear. Features: Stainless steel version of the original Model 40 but without the grip safety. Fully concealed hammer, snag-proof smooth edges. Introduced 1995 in 357 Magnum.

New: $400   **Perf.:** $350   **Exc.:** $300

Model 940 (9mm Para.)

New: $425   **Perf.:** $375   **Exc.:** $325

SMITH & WESSON MODEL 442 CENTENNIAL AIRWEIGHT

Similar to the Model 640 Centennial except has alloy frame giving weight of 15.8 oz. Chambered for 38 Special, 2-inch carbon steel barrel; carbon steel cylinder; concealed hammer; Uncle Mike's Custom Grade Santoprene grips. Fixed square notch rear sight, serrated ramp front. Introduced 1993.

New: $375   **Perf.:** $325   **Exc.:** $275

SMITH & WESSON MODEL 642 AIRWEIGHT REVOLVER

Similar to the Model 442 Centennial Airweight except has stainless steel barrel, cylinder and yoke with matte finish; Uncle Mike's Boot Grip; weights 15.8 oz. Introduced 1996.

New: $400   **Perf.:** $350   **Exc.:** $300

SMITH & WESSON MODEL 642LS LADYSMITH REVOLVER

Same as the Model 642 except has smooth combat wood grips, and comes with case; aluminum alloy frame, stainless cylinder, barrel and yoke; frosted matte finish. Weighs 15.8 oz. Introduced 1996.

New: $425   **Perf.:** $375   **Exc.:** $325

SMITH & WESSON MODEL 648 K-22 MASTERPIECE WMR

Revolver; double action; 22 WMR; 6-shot; 6-inch full lug barrel; 11-1/8-inch overall length; weighs 38-1/2 oz. loaded; stainless steel construction; combat trigger; semi-target hammer; square-butt combat-style grips; satin finish. Introduced 1991; dropped 1994.

Exc.: $325   **VGood:** $250   **Good:** $200

SMITH & WESSON MODEL 681

Revolver; double action; 357 Mag.; 4-inch, 6-inch heavy barrels; L-frame design; stainless steel construction; ejector rod shroud; combat-type trigger; semi-target hammer; fixed sights; Goncalo Alves target stocks; satin finish. Introduced 1981.

Perf.: $450   **Exc.:** $400   **VGood:** $350

SMITH & WESSON MODEL 686

Revolver; double action; 357 Mag.; 2-1/2-inch, 4-inch, 6-inch heavy barrels; weighs 46 oz. (6-inch barrel); L-frame design; stainless steel construction; ejector rod shroud; combat-type trigger; semi-target hammer; Baughman red ramp front sight, micrometer-click rear; soft rubber or Goncalo Alves target stocks; satin finish. Introduced 1981.

Perf.: $495   **Exc.:** $445   **VGood:** $375

SMITH & WESSON MODEL 686 MAGNUM PLUS REVOLVER

Similar to the Model 686 except has 7-shot cylinder, 2-1/2-inch, 4-inch or 6-inch barrel. Weighs 34-1/2 oz., overall length 7-1/2-inch (2-1/2-inch barrel). Hogue rubber grips. Introduced 1996.

New: $650   **Perf.:** $600   **Exc.:** $500

SMITH & WESSON MODEL 686 MIDNIGHT BLACK

Same specs as Model 686 except black finish; semi-target hammer; red ramp front sight, plain or white-outline micro rear; speedloader cut-out; full lug barrel; Goncalo Alves target stocks. Introduced 1989; no longer in production.

Exc.: $600   **VGood:** $550   **Good:** $450

SMITH & WESSON 38/44 HEAVY DUTY (MODEL 20)

Revolver; 38 Spl.; 6-shot; 4-inch, 5-inch, 6-1/2-inch barrel; 10-3/8-inch overall length (5-inch barrel); weighs 40 oz.; built on the S&W 44 frame, often termed N-frame, hence the 38/44 designation; designed to handle high-velocity 38 Special ammunition; fixed sights, with 1/10-inch service-type (semi-circle) front and square notch rear; checkered walnut Magna-type grips with S&W medallion; blued or nickel finish. Introduced 1930; discontinued 1967.

Pre-War		
Exc.: $1000	**VGood:** $750	**Good:** $450
Post-War		
Exc.: $775	**VGood:** $525	**Good:** $375

Smith & Wesson 38/44
Heavy Duty (Model 20)

Smith & Wesson 44
Magnum (Model 629)

Smith & Wesson 44
Hand Ejector, 1st Model
(Triple Lock)

Smith & Wesson Model
627 Pro Series

Smith & Wesson 41
Magnum (Model 58)

Smith & Wesson 44
Hand Ejector, 2nd Model

Smith & Wesson 44
Hand Ejector, 3rd Model

Smith & Wesson 44
Magnum (Model 29)

SMITH & WESSON 38/44 OUTDOORSMAN (MODEL 23)

Revolver; 38 Spl.; 6-shot; 6-1/2-inch barrel; 11-3/4-inch overall length; weighs, 41-3/4 oz.; plain Patridge 1/8-inch front sight, S&W micro-adjustable rear; blue finish. Introduced in 1930 as a companion to the Model 20; reintroduced about 1950 with ribbed barrel and Magna-type stocks. Discontinued 1967.

Pre-War		
Exc.: $1000	**VGood:** $800	**Good:** $600
Post-War		
Exc.: $950	**VGood:** $675	**Good:** $500

SMITH & WESSON MODEL 57

Revolver; 41 Mag.; 6-shot; 4-inch, 6-inch, 8-3/8-inch barrel; 11-3/8-inch overall length (6-inch barrel); weighs 48 oz.; wide, grooved target trigger and broad-spur target hammer; 1/8-inch red ramp front, S&W micro-adjustable rear with white-outline notch; special oversize target-type of Goncalo Alves grips with S&W medallion; bright blue or nickel finish. Introduced as a deluxe companion to the Model 58, both being chambered for a new cartridge developed especially for them at that time, carrying a bullet of .410-inch diameter. The old 41 Long Colt cartridge cannot be fired in guns chambered for the 41 Magnum, nor can any other standard cartridge. Introduced 1964; dropped 1993.

4-inch and 6-inch barrels		
Perf.: $575	**Exc.:** $535	**VGood:** $450
8-3/8-inch barrel		
Perf.: $600	**Exc.:** $550	**VGood:** $475

SMITH & WESSON MODEL 58

Revolver; 41 Mag.; 6-shot; 4-inch barrel; 9-1/4-inch overall length; weighs 41 oz.; 1/8-inch serrated ramp front, square notch rear sight; checkered Magna-type walnut grips with S&W medallion; blue or nickel finish. Also known as the 41 Military & Police, this is a fixed-sight version of the Model 57. No longer in production.

Perf.: $850	**Exc.:** $650	**VGood:** $450
Nickel finish		
Perf.: $900	**Exc.:** $675	**VGood:** $475

SMITH & WESSON 44 HAND EJECTOR 1ST MODEL (TRIPLE LOCK, NEW CENTURY)

Revolver; 44 S&W Spl., 44 S&W Russian, 44-40, 45 Colt, 45 S&W Spl., 450 Eley, 455 Mark II; 6-shot cylinder; 4-inch, 5-inch, 6-1/2-inch, 7-1/2-inch barrel; also known as 44 Triple Lock and 44 New Century; square-butt checkered walnut grips; fixed or factory-fitted target sights. Introduced 1908; dropped 1915.

44 Russian, 44-40, 45 Colt, 45 S&W Spl., 450 Eley		
Exc.: $1900	**VGood:** $1200	**Good:** $800
44 S&W Special		
Exc.: $1950	**VGood:** $1250	**Good:** $850
455 Mark II		
Exc.: $1000	**VGood:** $700	**Good:** $400

SMITH & WESSON 44 HAND EJECTOR 2ND MODEL

Revolver; 44 S&W Special, 38-40, 44-40, 45 Colt; 4-inch, 5-inch, 6-inch, 6-1/2-inch barrel; internal changes; on exterior, heavy barrel lug was dropped; cylinder size and frame cut enlarged; fixed or factory target sights. Introduced 1915; dropped 1937. Collector value.

44 S&W Special		
Exc.: $1100	**VGood:** $750	**Good:** $495
Other calibers		
Exc.: $1500	**VGood:** $1200	**Good:** $600

SMITH & WESSON 44 HAND EJECTOR 3RD MODEL

Revolver; 44 S&W, 44-40, 45 LC; 6-shot cylinder; 4-inch, 5-inch, 6-1/2-inch barrel; also known as Model 1926; fixed or factory target sights; checkered walnut square-butt grips; blue or nickel finish. Introduced 1925; dropped 1949.

44 S&W Special		
Exc.: $1250	**VGood:** $1050	**Good:** $675
Other calibers		
Exc.: $1700	**VGood:** $1200	**Good:** $950

SMITH & WESSON 44 MAGNUM (MODEL 29)

Revolver; 44 Mag.; also handles 44 Spl., 44 Russian; 6-shot; 4-inch, 5-inch, 6-1/2-inch, 8-3/8-inch; 11-7/8-inch overall length (6-1/2-inch barrel); weighs 43 oz. (4-inch barrel), 47 oz. (6-1/2-inch barrel), 51-1/2 oz. (8-3/8-inch barrel); 1/8-inch red ramp front sight, S&W micro-adjustable rear; target-type Goncalo Alves grips with S&W medallion; broad, grooved target trigger; wide-spur target hammer; bright blue or nickel finish. As with the Model 27, the Model 29 was developed to take a new cartridge developed by lengthening the 44 Special case by 0.125-inch to prevent use of 44 Magnum ammo in guns chambered for the 44 Special. The 44 Magnum is loaded to pressures approximately twice that of the 44 Special. Introduced in 1956. Premium of 30 percent for 1956 production; 75 percent premium for Model 29-2.

Exc.: $725	**VGood:** $650	**Good:** $485

SMITH & WESSON 44 MAGNUM MODEL 29 CLASSIC

Same specs as standard model except 5", 6-1/2", 8-3/8" barrel; chamfered cylinder front; interchangeable red ramp front, adjustable white outline rear sights; Hogue square-butt Santoprene grips; D&T for scope mount. Introduced 1990; no longer in production.

Exc.: $650	**VGood:** $500	**Good:** $375

SMITH & WESSON 44 MAGNUM MODEL 29 CLASSIC DX

Same specs as Model 29 Classic except 6-1/2", 8-3/8" barrel with full-length lug; Morado combat-type grips. Five different front sight options and Hogue combat-style square butt conversion grip. Introduced 1991; no longer in production.

Exc.: $575	**VGood:** $475	**Good:** $375

Smith & Wesson 357 Magnum (Pre-War Registered)

Smith & Wesson 1950 44 Military (Model 21)

Smith & Wesson 1950 Army (Model 22)

Smith & Wesson 41 Magnum (Model 57)

Smith & Wesson 357 Magnum (Model 27)

Smith & Wesson 38/44 Outdoorsman (Model 23)

Smith & Wesson 1950/1955 45 Target (Model 25 and 26)

SMITH & WESSON 44 MAGNUM MODEL 29 SILHOUETTE

Same specs as Model 29 except 10-5/8"; oversize target-type checkered Goncalo Alves grips; four click-adjustable front sight positions. Introduced 1983; dropped 1991. Not successful; a scarce model.

Exc.: $675 **VGood:** $575 **Good:** $435

SMITH & WESSON 44 MAGNUM MODEL 629

Same specs as Model 29 except in stainless steel.

Exc.: $600 **VGood:** $575 **Good:** $375

SMITH & WESSON 44 MAGNUM MODEL 629 CLASSIC

Same specs as Model 29 Classic except in stainless steel.

Exc.: $600 **VGood:** $575 **Good:** $375

SMITH & WESSON 44 MAGNUM MODEL 629 CLASSIC DX

Same specs as Model 29 Classic DX except in stainless steel.

Exc.: $650 **VGood:** $575 **Good:** $375

SMITH & WESSON 357 MAGNUM (PRE-WAR REGISTERED)

Revolver; 357 Magnum; 3-1/2", 5", 6", 6-1/2", and 8-3/8" barrel with custom lengths up to 8-3/8" available; variety of optional target sights; 3-1/2" version ("FBI model") usually had Baughman quick-draw sight on a King ramp; finely-checkered topstrap and barrel rib; bright blue or nickel finish; square or Magna walnut grips. Introduced 1935 for the new 357 S&W Magnum cartridge. Guns made 1935-1938 were registered to original owner (approximately 6,000). Later reintroduced as Model 27-8.

Exc.: $4750 **VGood:** $1900 **Good:** $1200

1938-1941 (Unregistered)

Exc.: $1200 **VGood:** $800 **Good:** $500

SMITH & WESSON 357 MAGNUM (POST-WAR/MODEL 27)

Revolver, .357 Magnum. Similar to pre-war unregistered model except for short action (post-1950) and minor differences. Known as Model 27 after 1957. Nickeled examples increasingly command a premium.

Exc.: $650 **VGood:** $450 **Good:** $350

SMITH & WESSON 1950 44 MILITARY (MODEL 21)

Revolver; 44 Special; 5-1/2" barrel; 10-1/2" overall length; semi-circular front sight and fixed groove rear. Blued or nickel finish; checkered walnut Magna grips. Post-WWII version of the Model of 1926 with new short action, and other improvements. Remained in the S&W lineup until 1967. A Target version with adjustable sights was also available.

Exc.: $1200 **VGood:** $750 **Good:** $550

SMITH & WESSON MODEL 27 (1991 REINTRODUCTION)

Same specs as Model 27 but with 3-1/2" or 5" barrel lengths only. Reintroduced in 1991 in limited edition; dropped 1992.

Exc.: $550 **VGood:** $375 **Good:** $300

MODEL 627 PRO SERIES

Introduced in 2008. This is an eight-shot .357 revolver with stainless steel frame, adjustable sights, 4-inch barrel and various accurizing refinements.

Exc.: $950 **VGood:** $750 **Good:** $550

SMITH & WESSON 455 HAND EJECTOR 1ST MODEL

Revolver; .455 Mark II cartridge (British); 6-1/2" barrel; fized sights; checkered walnut square-butt grips; blue finish. Designed in 1914 for the British war effort in 1916. Discontinued 1918. Usually have British proof marks. As war surplus, many were rechambered to 45 Colt (deduct 30 percent).

Exc.: $750 **VGood:** $575 **Good:** $300

SMITH & WESSON 455 HAND EJECTOR 2ND MODEL

Similar to 455 Hand Ejector First Model but lacks ejector rod housing/barrel lug. Introduced 1915; discontinued 1916. Usually have British proof marks. As war surplus, many were rechambered to 45 Colt (deduct 30 percent).

Exc.: $700 **VGood:** $550 **Good:** $300

SMITH & WESSON 1950 ARMY (MODEL 22)

Revolver; 45 ACP, 45 Auto Rim; 5-1/2" barrel; 10-1/2" overall length; semi-circular front sight and fixed groove rear. Post-WWII version of the Model of 1917 with redesigned grips, short action, and other improvements. Remained in the S&W lineup until 1967. A Target version with adjustable sights was also available.

44 S&W Special		
Exc.: $1050	**VGood:** $750	**Good:** $600
Other calibers		
Exc.: $1000	**VGood:** $725	**Good:** $575

SMITH & WESSON 1950 44 TARGET (MODEL 24)

Revolver; 44 Special; 6-shot; 4", 6" barrel. Introduced in 1950 as an updated version of the Model 1926 Target Model. Post-1957 models known as Model 24. Patridge-type front sight with perpendicular leading edge, S&W Micro rear sights. 4" version had Baughman quick-draw front sight on serrated ramp. Blued or nickel finish. 4" vesions command 20 percent premium; nickel finish add 25 percent.

Exc.: $1050 **VGood:** $750 **Good:** $500

SMITH & WESSON MODEL 24 TARGET (1983 REINTRODUCTION)

Same specs as earlier Model 24 except offered in 4" and 6-1/2" barrel lengths; grooved topstrap; barrel rib. 7500 produced in 1983.

Exc.: $775 **VGood:** $550 **Good:** $300

SMITH & WESSON 1950/1955 45 TARGET (MODEL 25 & 26)

Revolver; 45 ACP, 45 Auto Rim; 6-1/2" barrel; 11-7/8" overall length. Sights: Patridge front and S&W Micro rear. Checkered walnut grips. Blued finish. Introduced in 1950 as a companion to the Model 1950 44 Target. Redesigned in 1955 and released as the Model of 1955, known post-1957 as the Model 25, while the 1950 Model became known as the Model 26.

1950/Model 26		
Exc.: $1100	**VGood:** $750	**Good:** $500
1955/Model 25		
Exc.: $1050	**VGood:** $700	**Good:** $500

Smith & Wesson Highway Patrolman (Model 28)

Smith & Wesson Military Model of 1917

Smith & Wesson Model 22 Classic

Smith & Wesson Model 610

Smith & Wesson Model 625-2

Smith & Wesson Model 21 Classic

Smith & Wesson Model 624

Smith & Wesson Model 1926 44 Military

Smith & Wesson Model 460V

Smith & Wesson Model 36 Classic

SMITH & WESSON HIGHWAY PATROLMAN (MODEL 28)
Similar to Model 27 except offered in 4" and 6" barrel lengths only; has uncheckered topstrap and matte finish overall. Known as Model 28 after 1957. Introduced 1954. Once a dog on the market; now increasingly desirable.

Exc.: $450   **VGood:** $300   **Good:** $250

SMITH & WESSON MILITARY MODEL OF 1917
Revolver; 45 ACP, 45 Auto Rim. Entry of the U.S. into WWI found facilities unable to produce sufficient quantities of the recently adopted Colt Government Model auto pistol, so approximately 175,000 Smith & Wesson revolvers were manufactured, being chambered to fire the 45 ACP cartridge by means of the two 3-shot steel clips; also fires the 45 Auto Rim round. The wartime units had a duller blued finish and smooth walnut grips, with 5-1/2-inch barrel; overall length, 10-1/4-inch; weighs 36-1/4 oz. with lanyard ring in the butt. A commercial version remained in production after the end of WWI to the start of WWII, distinguished by a bright blue finish and checkered walnut stocks.

Military model
Exc.: $750   **VGood:** $595   **Good:** $450
Commercial model
Exc.: $1000   **VGood:** $700   **Good:** $495

SMITH & WESSON MODEL 25
Revolver; double action; 45 Colt; 6-shot cylinder; 4-inch, 6-inch, 8-3/8-inch barrel; 11-3/8-inch overall length (6-inch barrel); weighs about 46 oz.; target-type checkered Goncalo Alves grips; S&W red ramp front sight, S&W micrometer-click rear with white outline; available in bright blue or nickel finish; target trigger; target hammer. Dropped 1994. Model 25-2 chambered in 45 ACP.

4-inch or 6-inch barrel, blue
Perf.: $600   **Exc.:** $550   **VGood:** $450
8-3/8-inch barrel, blue or nickel
Perf.: $550   **Exc.:** $500   **VGood:** $400

SMITH & WESSON MODEL 625
Revolver; double action; 45 ACP, 6-shot. Barrel: 5-inch. Weight: 46 oz. Length: 11-3/8-inch overall. Stocks: Soft rubber; wood optional. Sights: Patridge front on ramp, S&W micrometer click rear adjustable for windage and elevation. Features: Stainless steel construction with .400-inch semi-target hammer, .312-inch smooth combat trigger; full lug barrel. Introduced 1989.

New: $675   **Perf.:** $595   **Exc.:** $400

SMITH & WESSON MODEL 25-5
Revolver; 45 Colt; 6-shot; 4-inch, 6-inch, 8-3/8-inch barrel; adjustable sights; square-butt, checkered, target-type Goncalo Alves grips; blue or nickel finish. Introduced in 1978 and called the 25-5 to distinguish it from the Model 25-2 in 45 ACP. Available with presentation case. Discontinued 1987.

Exc.: $350   **VGood:** $300   **Good:** $250

SMITH & WESSON MODEL 610
Revolver; 10mm; 5-inch, 6-1/2-inch barrel; .500-inch target hammer; .400-inch smooth combat trigger; round-butt frame with smooth Goncalo Alves finger groove grips; stainless steel construction; satin finish. Introduced April 1990.

Perf.: $650   **Exc.:** $450   **VGood:** $375

SMITH & WESSON MODEL 624
Revolver; 44 Spl.; 6-shot cylinder; 4-inch, 6-inch barrel; 9-1/2-inch overall length (4-inch barrel); weighs 41-1/2 oz.; target-type checkered Goncalo Alves stocks; black ramp front sight, adjustable micrometer-click rear; stainless steel version of Model 24. Dropped 1986.

Exc.: $625   **VGood:** $550   **Good:** $375

SMITH & WESSON MODEL 625-2
Revolver; double-action; 45 ACP; 3-inch full-lug barrel; same general specs as S&W Model 25, but is made of stainless steel; black pinned ramp front sight, micrometer rear; semi-target hammer; combat trigger; full lug barrel; round butt Pachmayr stocks. Introduced 1989.

New: $600   **Perf.:** $550   **Exc.:** $500

SMITH & WESSON MODEL 1926 44 MILITARY
Revolver; primarily produced in 44 Spl., sometimes encountered in 45 Colt, 455 Webley or 455 Eley; 6-shot; 4-inch, 5-inch, 6-1/2-inch barrel; 11-3/4-inch overall length (6-1/2-inch barrel); weighs 39-1/2 oz.; 1/10-inch service-type front sight, fixed square-notch rear; checkered walnut, square or Magna-type grips with S&W medallion; blued or nickel finish. Modified version of S&W's earlier 44 Hand Ejector First Model, minus the triple-lock feature, but retaining the heavy shroud around the ejector rod. Discontinued at the start of WWII; replaced after the war by the 1950 model.

Exc.: $900   **VGood:** $700   **Good:** $400
Nickel finish
Exc.: $800   **VGood:** $600   **Good:** $350

SMITH & WESSON MODEL 1926 44 TARGET
Same specs as 1926 44 Military except target version with rear sight adjustable for windage and elevation; produced from 1926 to the beginning of WWII; replaced after the war by the 1950 Target Model 24.

Exc.: $1100   **VGood:** $950   **Good:** $700

SMITH & WESSON MODEL 500
Monstrous extra-large-frame (X frame) single/double action revolver chambered in .500 S&W. Stainless finish, sorbothane grips. Adjustable sights, 5-shot cylinder.

Exc.: $1000   **VGood:** $895   **Good:** $700

SMITH & WESSON MODEL 460V
X-frame double-action trigger and 5-inch barrel in .460 S&W Magnum caliber. Also accepts .454 Casull and .45 Colt. Sorbothane recoil-reducing grip, interchangeable muzzle compensator. 5-shot, stainless with satin finish. 62.5 oz.

New: $1100   **Exc.:** $975   **VGood:** $800

Smith & Wesson M&P340

Smith & Wesson M&P340CT

Smith & Wesson M&P360

Smith & Wesson M&PR8

Smith & Wesson Model 60 Hi-Viz

Smith & Wesson Model 386 SC/S

Smith & Wesson Model 325 Night Guard

Smith & Wesson Model 686 Plus

Smith & Wesson Model 327 Night Guard

Smith & Wesson Model 22 Classic

Smith & Wesson 35

SMITH & WESSON MODEL 22 – THUNDER RANCH .45 ACP

Limited edition six-shot single/double-action chambered for .45 ACP. Blued with 4-inch tapered barrel, 37.5 oz. Cocobolo grips engraved with Thunder Ranch insignia. Fixed sights. SNs begin with TRR0000.

New: $725   **Exc.:** $625   **VGood:** $500

SMITH & WESSON FIFTIETH ANNIVERSARY MODEL 29

A commemorative edition of the classic .44 Magnum. Carbon steel with polished blue finish. Double-action 6-shot. LOA 12-inch, 6.5-inch barrel, 48.5 oz. Cocobolo wood grips with 24kt gold anniversary logo.

New: $1050   **Exc.:** $875   **VGood:** $695

SMITH & WESSON M&P340

Double-action-only revolver built on Centennial (hammerless J) frame. .357 Magnum/.38 Special; five-shot cylinder; 1.87" barrel with fixed night sights. Matte black finish on scandium/alloy frame.

New: $675   **Exc.:** $600   **VGood:** $525

SMITH & WESSON MODEL 325 NIGHT GUARD

A 2-1/2-inch snubbie chambered for .45 ACP. Tritium sights, scandium alloy frame, matte black finish overll. Neoprene grips. Introduced 2008.

New: $1050   **Exc.:** $895   **VGood:** $600

SMITH & WESSON MODEL 327 NIGHT GUARD

A 2-1/2-inch snubbie chambered for .357 Magnum. 8-shot cylinder. Tritium sights, scandium alloy frame, matte black finish overll. Neoprene grips. Introduced 2008.

New: $1050   **Exc.:** $895   **VGood:** $600

SMITH & WESSON MODEL 329 NIGHT GUARD

A 2-1/2-inch snuibbie chambered for .44 Magnum. Scandium frame, fixed sights, matte black finish overall. Introduced 2008.

New: $1050   **Exc.:** $895   **VGood:** $600

SMITH & WESSON M&P340CT

Similar to above but with Crimson Trace lasergrips.

New: $725   **Exc.:** $650   **VGood:** $575

SMITH & WESSON M&P360

Double-action-only revolver built on Chief's Special (hammered J) frame. .357 Magnum/.38 Special; five-shot cylinder; 1.87" barrel with fixed night sights. Matte black finish on scandium/alloy frame.

New: $795   **Exc.:** $725   **VGood:** $595

SMITH & WESSON MODEL 315 NIGHT GUARD .38

Scandium-framed, 5-shot .38 snubbie with 2.5-inch barrel. Finished overall in matte black. Tritium sights. Introduced 2008.

New: $795   **Exc.:** $725   **VGood:** $595

SMITH & WESSON MODEL 637 POWER PORT PRO SERIES

Aluminum J-frame 5-shot revolver with stainless steel cylinder chambered for .38 Special (5 shots). 2-1/8-inch ported black stainless barrel. Introduced 2008.

New: $795   **Exc.:** $725   **VGood:** $595

SMITH & WESSON M&PR8

Double-action-only revolver built on large (N) frame. .357 Magnum/.38 Special; eight-shot cylinder; 5" barrel with adjustable Patridge sights with interchangeable inserts. Matte black finish on scandium/alloy frame.

New: $1250   **Exc.:** $1150   **VGood:** $1025

SMITH & WESSON MODEL 60 WITH HI-VIZ SIGHT

Similar to Model 60 but with light-gathering HI-VIZ red dot front sight and adjustable rear sight.

New: $650   **Exc.:** $595   **VGood:** $435

SMITH & WESSON MODEL 386 SC/S

Single-/double-action L-frame revolver in .38/.357 Magnum. 7-shot cylinder, 2.5" barrel, Patridge front sight, adjustable rear, scandium/alloy frame, matte black finish, rubber grips.

New: $800   **Exc.:** $725   **VGood:** $635

SMITH & WESSON MODEL 686 PLUS

Single-/double-action L-frame revolver in .38/.357 Magnum. 7-shot cylinder, 3" barrel, Patridge front sight, adjustable rear, stainless finish, rubber grips. Introduced 2007.

New: $600   **Exc.:** $525   **VGood:** $400

SMITH & WESSON MODEL 36 CLASSIC

Replica of vintage Model 36 Chief's Special in .38 Special. Five-shot cylinder. Carbon steel frame, 1-7/8" or 3" barrel, fixed sights. Blued, case colored, or nickel finish with Altamont wood grips.

New: $625   **Exc.:** $550   **VGood:** $425

SMITH & WESSON MODEL 21 CLASSIC

Replica of vintage Model 21 N-frame revolver in .44 Special. Six-shot cylinder. Carbon steel frame, 4" barrel, fixed sights. Blued, case colored, or nickel finish with Altamont wood grips.

New: $950   **Exc.:** $825   **VGood:** $500

SMITH & WESSON MODEL 22 CLASSIC

Replica of vintage Model 22 N-frame revolver in .45 ACP. Six-shot cylinder. Carbon steel frame, 4" barrel, fixed sights. Blued, case colored, or nickel finish with Altamont wood grips.

New: $950   **Exc.:** $825   **VGood:** $500

SMITH & WESSON MODEL 22 OF 1917 CLASSIC

Similar to Model 22 Classic but without ejector rod shroud and with lanyard ring on butt. Replica of U.S. Army WWI-era revolver.

New: $950   **Exc.:** $825   **VGood:** $500

SMITH & WESSON MODEL 29 CLASSIC

Replica of original (1956) Model 29 N-frame revolver in .44 Magnum. Six-shot cylinder. Carbon steel frame, 6.5" barrel, fixed sights. Blued or nickel finish with or without engraving. Altamont wood grips.

New: $975   **Exc.:** $850   **VGood:** $575

SMITH & WESSON MODEL 32 AUTO

Semi-automatic; 32 ACP, 7.65mm; 8-shot; 4-inch barrel; 7-inch overall length; weighs 28 oz.; unusual grip safety just below the trigger guard; successor to S&W's original auto pistol; walnut, uncheckered grips; blue or nickel finish. Introduced 1924; discontinued 1937. Collector interest.

Exc.: $2500   **VGood:** $2000   **Good:** $1500

SMITH & WESSON MODEL 35

Semi-automatic; 35 S&W Auto; 7-shot magazine; 3-1/2-inch barrel; 6-1/2-inch overall length; uncheckered walnut stocks; fixed sights; blued or nickel finish. Manufactured 1913 to 1921. Collector interest.

Exc.: $700   **VGood:** $375   **Good:** $250

Smith & Wesson 38
Target Auto (Model 52)

Smith & Wesson
Model 439

Smith & Wesson
Model 39 9mm Auto

Smith & Wesson
Model 457

Smith & Wesson
Model 645

Smith & Wesson
Model 59 9mm Auto

Smith & Wesson
Model 469

Smith & Wesson
Model 669

SMITH & WESSON 38 TARGET AUTO (MODEL 52)

Semi-automatic; 38 Spl.; 5-shot; 5-inch barrel; 8-5/8-inch overall length; weighs 41 oz.; Patridge-type front on ramp, S&W micro-adjustable rear; checkered walnut grips with S&W medallion; blue finish only. Designed to fire a mid-range loading of the 38 Special, requiring a wadcutter bullet seated flush with the case mouth; action is straight blowback, thus not suited for firing of high-velocity 38 Special ammo. Introduced 1961. Considerable premium for early issues.

> Exc.: $750   VGood: $600   Good: $400

SMITH & WESSON MODEL 39 9MM AUTO

Semi-automatic; 9mm; 8-shot magazine; 4-inch barrel; 7-7/16-inch overall length; weighs 26-1/2 oz.; 1/8-inch serrated ramp front, windage-adjustable square notch rear; checkered walnut grips with S&W medallion; bright blue or nickel finish. During the first dozen years of production, a limited number were made with steel frames rather than the standard aluminum alloy and command premium price. Introduced 1954. Collector value.

> Exc.: $400   VGood: $350   Good: $275

Nickel finis3

> Exc.: $375   VGood: $325   Good: $225

Steel frame model

> Exc.: $1100   VGood: $850   Good: $750

SMITH & WESSON MODEL 59 9MM AUTO

Semi-automatic; 9mm; 14-shot staggered column magazine; 4-inch barrel; 7-7/16-inch overall length; weighs 27-1/2 oz. sans magazine; 1/8-inch serrated ramp front, windage-adjustable square notch rear; checkered high-impact molded nylon; bright blue or nickel finish. Similar to the Model 39. Like the Model 39, the 59 offers the option of carrying a round in the chamber, with hammer down, available for firing via a double-action pull of the trigger. Introduced 1971; dropped 1981.

> Exc.: $450   VGood: $350   Good: $250

Nickel finish

> Exc.: $575   VGood: $425   Good: $315

SMITH & WESSON MODEL 439

Semi-automatic; double-action; 9mm Para.; 8-shot magazine; 4-inch barrel; 7-7/16-inch overall length; weighs 27-1/2 oz. sans magazine; same specs as Model 39 except new trigger-actuated firing pin lock; magazine disconnector; new extractor design; 1/8-inch serrated ramp front, windage-adjustable square notch rear and protective shield on both sides of blade; checkered high-impact molded nylon; bright blue or nickel finish. Introduced 1980; dropped 1988.

> Exc.: $300   VGood: $250   Good: $200

Nickel finish

> Exc.: $325   VGood: $275   Good: $225

SMITH & WESSON MODEL 457

Semi-automatic; double-action; 45 ACP, 7-shot magazine. Barrel: 3-3/4-inch. Weight: 29 oz. Length: 7-1/4-inch overall. Stocks: One-piece Xenoy, wrap-around with straight backstrap. Sights: Post front, fixed rear, three-dot system. Features: Aluminum alloy frame, matte blue carbon steel slide; bobbed hammer; smooth trigger. Introduced 1996.

> New: $375   Perf.: $325   Exc.: $275

SMITH & WESSON MODEL 459

Semi-automatic; double-action; 9mm Para.; 14-shot magazine; 4-inch barrel; 7-7/16-inch overall length; weighs 27-1/2 oz. sans magazine; has same general specs as Model 439, except for increased magazine capacity, straighter, longer grip frame; blued or nickel finish. Introduced 1980; dropped 1989.

Blue finish

> Exc.: $350   VGood: $300   Good: $250

Nickel finish

> Exc.: $375   VGood: $325   Good: $275

SMITH & WESSON MODEL 469

Semi-automatic; 9mm Para.; 3-1/2-inch barrel; 12-shot magazine; accepts 14-shot 459 magazine; 6-7/8-inch overall length; weighs 26 oz.; cut-down version of Model 459; cross-hatching on front of trigger guard, backstrap; plastic pebble-grain grips; curved finger-extension magazine; bobbed hammer; sandblasted blued finish. Introduced 1983; dropped 1988.

> Exc.: $300   VGood: $250   Good: $225

SMITH & WESSON MODEL 539

Semi-automatic; double action; 9mm Para.; 8-shot magazine; 4-inch barrel; 7-7/16-inch overall length; weighs 36 oz.; carbon steel construction; trigger-actuated firing pin lock; magazine disconnector; 1/8-inch serrated ramp front, windage-adjustable square notch rear and protective shield on both sides of blade; checkered high-impact molded nylon; bright blue or nickel finish. Approximately 10,000 manufactured. Introduced 1981; dropped 1984.

> Exc.: $400   VGood: $350   Good: $300

SMITH & WESSON MODEL 559

Semi-automatic; double action; 9mm Para.; 14-shot magazine; 4-inch barrel; 7-7/16-inch overall length; weighs 40 oz. sans magazine; has same general specs as Model 459, except carbon steel construction; blue or nickel finish. Approximately 10,000 manufactured. Introduced 1981; dropped 1984.

> Exc.: $450   VGood: $400   Good: $350

SMITH & WESSON MODEL 639

Semi-automatic; double action; 9mm Para.; 8-shot magazine; 4-inch barrel; 7-7/16-inch overall length; weighs 27-1/2 oz. sans magazine; stainless steel construction; trigger-actuated firing pin lock; magazine disconnector; 1/8-inch serrated ramp front, windage-adjustable square notch rear with protective shield on both sides of blade; checkered high-impact molded nylon; bright blue or nickel finish. Introduced 1981; dropped 1988.

> Exc.: $350   VGood: $300   Good: $250

SMITH & WESSON MODEL 645

Semi-automatic; double action; 45 ACP; 8-shot magazine; 5-inch barrel; 8-3/4-inch overall length; weighs 37-5/8 oz.; red ramp front sight, drift-adjustable rear; checkered nylon stocks; stainless steel construction; cross-hatch knurling on recurved front trigger guard, backstrap; beveled magazine well. Introduced 1985; dropped 1988.

> Exc.: $450   VGood: $400   Good: $350

SMITH & WESSON MODEL 659

Semi-automatic; double action; 9mm Para.; 14-shot magazine; 4-inch barrel; 7-7/16-inch overall length; weighs 27-1/2 oz. sans magazine; has same general specs as Model 439, except stainless steel construction. Introduced 1981; dropped 1988.

> Exc.: $350   VGood: $300   Good: $225

SMITH & WESSON MODEL 669

Semi-automatic; 9mm Para.; 3-1/2-inch barrel; 12-shot magazine; accepts 14-shot 459 magazine; 6-7/8-inch overall length; weighs 26 oz.; same specs

Smith & Wesson
Model 745

Smith & Wesson
Model 410 DA

Smith & Wesson
Model 908

Smith & Wesson
Model 909

Smith & Wesson
Model 910

Smith & Wesson
Model 915

Smith & Wesson
Model 1006

Smith & Wesson
Model 1026

as Model 469 except slide and barrel manufactured of stainless steel; aluminum alloy frame finished in natural finish. Introduced 1985; dropped 1988.

Exc.: $350   **VGood:** $300   **Good:** $250

SMITH & WESSON MODEL 745

Semi-automatic; 45 ACP; 8-shot magazine; 5-inch barrel; 8-5/8-inch overall length; weighs 38-3/4 oz.; fixed Novak rear sight, serrated ramp front; blued slide, trigger, hammer, sights. Marketed with two magazines. Introduced 1987; dropped 1990.

Exc.: $450   **VGood:** $400   **Good:** $350

SMITH & WESSON MODEL 356 TSW LIMITED

Semi-automatic; single action; 356 TSW; 15-shot magazine; 5-inch barrel; weighs 44 oz.; 8-1/2-inch overall length; checkered black composition grips; blade front sight drift adjustable for windage, fully-adjustable Bo-Mar rear; stainless steel frame and slide; hand-fitted titanium-coated stainless steel bushing; match grade barrel; extended magazine well and oversize release; magazine pads; extended safety. Checkered front strap. Made in U.S. by Smith & Wesson; available through Lew Horton Dist. Introduced 1993; no longer in production.

Exc.: $1200   **VGood:** $850   **Good:** $750

SMITH & WESSON MODEL 356 TSW COMPACT

Same specs as the 356 TSW Limited except has 3-1/2-inch barrel; 12-shot magazine; Novak LoMount combat sights; 7-inch overall length; weighs 37 oz. Made in U.S. by Smith & Wesson; available from Lew Horton Dist. Introduced 1993; no longer in production.

Exc.: $850   **VGood:** $725   **Good:** $550

SMITH & WESSON MODEL 410 DA

Semi-automatic; double action; 40 S&W, 10-shot magazine. Barrel: 4-inch. Weight: 28.5 oz. Length: 7.5 oz. Stocks: One-piece Xenoy, wrap-around with straight backstrap. Sights: Post front, fixed rear; three-dot system. Features: Aluminum alloy frame; blued carbon steel slide; traditional double action with left-side slide-mountd decocking lever. Introduced 1996.

New: $425   **Perf.:** $375   **Exc.:** $300

SMITH & WESSON MODEL 411

Semi-automatic; double action; 40 S&W; 10-shot magazine; 4-inch barrel; weighs 28 oz.; 7-3/8-inch overall length; one-piece Xenoy wrap-around grips with straight backstrap; post front sight with white dot, fixed two-dot rear; alloy frame, blue carbon steel slide; slide-mounted decocking lever. Made in U.S. by Smith & Wesson. Introduced 1994; still produced.

New: $450   **Perf.:** $400   **Exc.:** $325

SMITH & WESSON MODEL 908

Caliber: 9mm Para., 8-shot magazine. Barrel: 3-1/2-inch. Weight: 26 oz. Length: 6-13/16-inch. Stocks: One-piece Xenoy, wrap-around with straight backstrap. Sights: Post front, fixed rear, three-dot system. Features: Aluminum alloy frame, matte blue carbon steel slide; bobbed hammer; smooth trigger. Introduced 1996.

New: $425   **Perf.:** $375   **Exc.:** $300

SMITH & WESSON MODEL 909

Semi-automatic; double action; 9mm Para.; 9-shot magazine; 4-inch barrel; weighs 27 oz.; 7-3/8-inch overall length; one-piece Xenoy wrap-around grips with curved backstrap; post front sight with white dot, fixed two-dot rear; alloy frame, blue carbon steel slide; slide mounted decocking lever. Made in U.S. by Smith & Wesson. Introduced 1995; still produced.

New: $350   **Perf.:** $300   **Exc.:** $250

SMITH & WESSON MODEL 910

Semi-automatic; double action; 9mm Para.; 10-shot magazine; 4-inch barrel; weighs 27 oz.; 7-3/8-inch overall length; one-piece Xenoy wrap-around grips with curved backstrap; post front sight with white dot, fixed two-dot rear; alloy frame, blue carbon steel slide; slide mounted decocking lever. Introduced 1995; still produced.

New: $375   **Perf.:** $325   **Exc.:** $275

SMITH & WESSON MODEL 915

Semi-automatic; double action; 9mm Para.; 15-shot magazine; 4-inch barrel; 7-1/2-inch overall length; weighs 28-1/2 oz.; one-piece Xenoy wrap-around grips with straight backstrap; post front sight with white dot, fixed rear; alloy frame, blue carbon steel slide; slide-mounted decocking lever. Made in U.S. by Smith & Wesson. Introduced 1992; dropped 1995.

New: $350   **Perf.:** $300   **Exc.:** $250

SMITH & WESSON MODEL 1006

Semi-automatic; double action; 10mm auto; 9-shot magazine; 5-inch barrel; weighs 38 oz.; one-piece Xenoy wrap-around grips with straight backstrap; rounded trigger guard; choice of Novak LoMount Carry fixed rear sight with two white dots or adjustable micro-click rear with two white dots; stainless steel construction; satin stainless finish. Introduced 1990; dropped 1993.

Perf.: $750   **Exc.:** $575   **VGood:** $450

SMITH & WESSON MODEL 1026

Semi-automatic; double action; 10mm auto; 9-shot magazine; 5-inch barrel; weighs 38 oz.; frame mounted decocking lever, fixed sights; one-piece Delrin grips; rounded trigger guard. Introduced 1990; dropped 1992.

Exc.: $700   **VGood:** $550   **Good:** $420

Smith & Wesson
Model 1066

Smith & Wesson
Model 1086

Smith & Wesson
Model 3904

Smith & Wesson
Model 3906

Smith & Wesson
Model 3913

Smith & Wesson
Model 3913 LadySmith

Smith & Wesson
Model 3914

Smith & Wesson
Model 3914 LadySmith

SMITH & WESSON MODEL 1046

Semi-automatic; double-action-only; 10mm auto; 9-shot magazine; 5-inch barrel; weighs 38 oz.; rounded trigger guard; fixed sights; wrap-around grips with straight backstrap; stainless steel with satin finish. Introduced 1990; dropped 1992.

Exc.: $700   **VGood:** $495   **Good:** $375

SMITH & WESSON MODEL 1066

Semi-automatic; double action; 10mm auto; 9-shot magazine; 4-1/4-inch barrel; fixed sights; wrap-around grips with straight backstrap; ambidextrous safety. Introduced 1990; dropped 1992.

Exc.: $725   **VGood:** $550   **Good:** $375

SMITH & WESSON MODEL 1066-NS

Same specs as Model 1066 except Tritium night sights.

Exc.: $750   **VGood:** $600   **Good:** $400

SMITH & WESSON MODEL 1076

Semi-automatic; double action; 10mm auto; 9-shot magazine; 4-1/4-inch barrel; frame mounted decocking lever; wrap-around grips with straight backstrap; fixed sights. Introduced 1990; dropped 1993.

Exc.: $700   **VGood:** $600   **Good:** $395

SMITH & WESSON MODEL 1086

Semi-automatic; double-action-only; 10mm auto; 9-shot magazine; 4-1/4-inch barrel; wrap-around grips with straight backstrap; fixed sights; ambidextrous safety. Introduced 1990; dropped 1993.

Perf.: $700   **Exc.:** $600   **VGood:** $450

SMITH & WESSON MODEL 3904

Semi-automatic; double action; 9mm Para.; 8-shot magazine; 4-inch barrel; 7-1/2-inch overall length; weighs 28 oz.; one-piece wrap-around Delrin stocks; post front sight with white dot, fixed or fully-adjustable two-dot rear; blued finish; smooth trigger; serrated hammer. Introduced 1989; dropped 1991.

Exc.: $400   **VGood:** $350   **Good:** $300

SMITH & WESSON MODEL 3906

Semi-automatic; double action; 9mm Para.; 8-shot magazine; 4-inch barrel; 7-5/8-inch overall length; weighs 28 oz.; stainless steel construction; one-piece wrap-around Delrin stocks; post front sight with white dot, fixed or fully-adjustable two-dot rear; blued finish; smooth trigger; serrated hammer. Introduced 1989; dropped 1991.

Exc.: $450   **VGood:** $400   **Good:** $350

SMITH & WESSON MODEL 3913

Semi-automatic; double action; 9mm Para.; 8-shot magazine; 3-1/2-inch barrel; 6-13/16-inch overall length; weighs 26 oz.; post white-dot front sight, two-dot windage-adjustable Novak LoMount Carry rear; aluminum alloy frame; stainless steel slide; bobbed hammer; no half-cock notch; smooth trigger; straight backstrap. Introduced 1990; dropped 1999.

New: $500   **Perf.:** $450   **Exc.:** $350

SMITH & WESSON MODEL 3913 LADYSMITH

Semi-automatic; double action; 9mm Para.; 8-shot magazine; 3-1/2-inch barrel; 6-13/16-inch overall length; weighs 26 oz.; post white-dot front sight, two-dot windage-adjustable Novak LoMount Carry rear; upswept frame at front; rounded trigger guard; frosted stainless steel finish; gray ergonomic grips designed for smaller hands. Introduced 1990.

New: $575   **Perf.:** $500   **Exc.:** $400

SMITH & WESSON MODEL 3913-NL

Same specs as Model 3913 except without LadySmith logo; slightly modified frame design; right-hand safety only; stainless slide in alloy frame. Introduced 1990; dropped 1994.

Perf.: $450   **Exc.:** $350   **VGood:** $275

SMITH & WESSON MODEL 3913TSW/ 3953TSW AUTO PISTOLS

Similar to the Model 3913 and 3953 except TSW guns have tighter tolerances, ambidextrous manual safety/decocking lever, flush-fit magazine, delayed-unlock firing system. DAO Model 3953 has magazine disconnector. Compact alloy frame, stainless steel slide. Straight backstrap. Introduced 1998.

New: $600   **Perf.:** $525   **Exc.:** $450

SMITH & WESSON MODEL 3914

Semi-automatic; double action; 9mm Para.; 8-shot magazine; 3-1/2-inch barrel; 6-13/16-inch overall length; weighs 26 oz.; post white-dot front sight, two-dot windage-adjustable Novak LoMount Carry rear; aluminum alloy frame; blued steel slide; bobbed hammer; no half-cock notch; smooth trigger straight backstrap. Introduced 1990; dropped 1995.

New: $400   **Perf.:** $325   **Exc.:** $250

SMITH & WESSON MODEL 3914 LADYSMITH

Semi-automatic; double action; 9mm Para.; 8-shot magazine; 3-1/2-inch barrel; 6-13/16-inch overall length; weighs 26 oz.; post white-dot front sight, two-dot windage-adjustable Novak LoMount Carry rear; same specs as standard 3913, except slide is of blued steel. Introduced 1990; dropped 1992.

Perf.: $450   **Exc.:** $375   **VGood:** $275

SMITH & WESSON MODEL 3914-NL

Same specs as 3914 except without LadySmith logo; slightly modified frame design; right-hand safety only; blued finish, black grips. Introduced 1990; dropped 1991.

Perf.: $400   **Exc.:** $300   **VGood:** $250

SMITH & WESSON MODEL 3953

Semi-automatic; double-action-only; 9mm Para.; 8-shot magazine; 3-1/2-inch barrel; 7-inch overall length; weighs 25-1/2 oz.; post white-dot front sight, two-dot windage-adjustable Novak LoMount Carry rear; aluminum alloy frame; stainless steel slide; bobbed hammer; no half-cock notch; smooth trigger straight backstrap. Introduced 1990; dropped 1999.

New: $500   **Perf.:** $450   **Exc.:** $350

Smith & Wesson
Model 3954

Smith & Wesson
Model 4006

Smith & Wesson
Model 4013

Smith & Wesson
Model 4014

Smith & Wesson
Model 4046

Smith & Wesson
Model 4053

Smith & Wesson
Model 4053

Smith & Wesson
Model 4054

Smith & Wesson
Model 4506

SMITH & WESSON MODEL 3954

Semi-automatic; double-action-only; 9mm Para.; 8-shot magazine; 3-1/2-inch barrel; 7-inch overall length; weighs 25-1/2 oz.; post white-dot front sight, two-dot windage-adjustable Novak LoMount Carry rear; aluminum alloy frame; blued steel slide; alloy frame; bobbed hammer; no half-cock notch; smooth trigger straight backstrap. Introduced 1990; dropped 1992.

Perf.: $400   **Exc.:** $350   **VGood:** $275

SMITH & WESSON MODEL 4006

Semi-automatic; 40 S&W; 11-shot magazine; 4-inch barrel; 7-1/2-inch overall length; weighs 38 oz.; replaceable white-dot post front sight, Novak two-dot fixed rear or two-dot micro-click adjustable rear; Xenoy wrap-around grips, checkered panels; straight backstrap; made of stainless steel; non-reflective finish. Introduced 1991.

New: $650   **Perf.:** $600   **Exc.:** $500

Tritium night sights

New: $725   **Perf.:** $675   **Exc.:** $575

SMITH & WESSON MODEL 4043

Similar to the Model 4006 except is double-action-only. Has a semi-bobbed hammer, smooth trigger, 4-inch barrel; Novak LoMount Carry rear sight, post front with white dot. Overall length is 7-1/2-inch, weighs 28 oz. Alloy frame. Extra magazine included. Introduced 1991; dropped 1999.

New: $700   **Perf.:** $600   **Exc.:** $500

SMITH & WESSON MODEL 4013

Semi-automatic; double action; 40 S&W; 7-shot magazine; 3-1/2-inch barrel; 7-inch overall length; weighs 26 oz.; white-dot post front sight, two-dot Novak LoMount Carry rear; one-piece Xenoy wrap-around grip; straight backstrap; alloy frame; stainless steel slide. Introduced 1991; dropped 1996.

New: $550   **Perf.:** $475   **Exc.:** $425

SMITH & WESSON MODEL 4053 TSW

Semi-automatic; double action; 40 S&W, 9-shot magazine. Barrel: 3-1/2-inch. Weight: 26.4 oz. Length: 6-7/8-inch overall. Stocks: Checkered black polymer. Sights: Novak three-dot system. Features: double-action only system; stainless slide, alloy frame; fixed barrel bushing; ambidextrous decocker; reversible magazine catch. Introduced 1997.

New: $725   **Perf.:** $625   **Exc.:** $550

SMITH & WESSON MODEL 4014

Semi-automatic; double action; 40 S&W; 7-shot magazine; 3-1/2-inch barrel; 7-inch overall length; weighs 26 oz.; blued steel slide; white-dot post front sight, two-dot Novak LoMount Carry rear; one-piece Xenoy wrap-around grip; straight backstrap; alloy frame; stainless steel slide. Introduced 1991; dropped 1993

Perf.: $500   **Exc.:** $450   **VGood:** $350

SMITH & WESSON MODEL 4046

Semi-automatic; double-action-only; 40 S&W; 11-shot; 4-inch barrel; 7-1/2-inch overall length; weighs 38 oz.; smooth trigger; semi-bobbed hammer; post white-dot front sight, Novak LoMount Carry rear. Introduced 1991; dropped 1999.

Perf.: $550   **Exc.:** $475   **VGood:** $350

SMITH & WESSON MODEL 4053

Semi-automatic; double-action-only; 40 S&W; 7-shot magazine; 3-1/2-inch barrel; 7-inch overall length; weighs 26 oz.; white-dot post front sight, two-dot

Novak LoMount Carry rear; one-piece Xenoy wrap-around grip; straight backstrap; alloy frame; stainless steel slide. Introduced 1991; dropped 1997.

New: $600   **Perf.:** $550   **Exc.:** $450

SMITH & WESSON MODEL 4054

Semi-automatic; double-action-only; 40 S&W; 7-shot magazine; 3-1/2-inch barrel; 7-inch overall length; weighs 26 oz.; blued steel slide; white-dot post front sight, two-dot Novak LoMount Carry rear; one-piece Xenoy wrap-around grip; straight backstrap; alloy frame; stainless steel slide. Introduced 1991; dropped 1992.

Perf.: $475   **Exc.:** $400   **VGood:** $300

SMITH & WESSON MODEL 4505

Semi-automatic; 45 ACP; 8-shot magazine; 5-inch barrel; one-piece wrap-around Delrin stock; arched or straight backstrap; post front sight with white dot, fixed or adjustable rear; blued finish. Introduced 1990; dropped 1991.

Perf.: $500   **Exc.:** $400   **VGood:** $295

SMITH & WESSON MODEL 4506

Semi-automatic; 45 ACP; 8-shot magazine; 5-inch barrel; one-piece, wrap-around Xenoy stocks; arched or straight backstrap; post front sight with white dot, fixed or adjustable Novak LoMount Carry rear; serrated hammer spur; stainless steel construction. Introduced 1989; dropped 1999.

Perf.: $500   **Exc.:** $400   **VGood:** $295

SMITH & WESSON MODEL 4513TSW/4553TSW

Semi-automatic; double action; 45 ACP, 6-shot magazine. Barrel: 3-3/4-inch. Weight: 28 oz. (M4513TSW). Length: 6-7/8 overall. Stocks: Checkered Xenoy; straight backstrap. Sights: White

Smith & Wesson
Model 4516

Smith & Wesson
Model 4536

Smith & Wesson
Model 4546

Smith & Wesson
Model 4586

Smith & Wesson
Model 5903

Smith & Wesson
Model 5904

dot front, Novak Lo Mount Carry 2-Dot rear. Features: Model 4513TSW is traditional double action, Model 4553TSW is double action only. TSW series has tighter tolerances, ambidextrous manual safety/decocking lever, flush-fit magazine, delayed-unlock firing system. DAO has magazine disconnector. Compact alloy frame, stainless steel slide. Introduced 1998.

Model 4513TSW
Perf.: $500   **Exc.:** $400   **VGood:** $295

Model 4553TSW
Perf.: $500   **Exc.:** $400   **VGood:** $295

SMITH & WESSON MODEL 4516

Semi-automatic; 45 ACP; 7-shot magazine; 3-3/4-inch barrel; one-piece wrap-around Xenoy stock; straight backstrap; post front sight with white dot; fixed Novak rear sight; bobbed hammer. Introduced 1989; dropped 1997.

Perf.: $500   **Exc.:** $400   **VGood:** $295

SMITH & WESSON MODEL 4526

Semi-automatic; 45 ACP; 8-shot magazine; 5-inch barrel; one-piece wrap-around Delrin stock; arched or straight backstrap; post front sight with white dot, fixed or adjustable rear; serrated hammer spur; stainless steel construction. Introduced 1991; dropped 1993.

Perf.: $500   **Exc.:** $400   **VGood:** $295

SMITH & WESSON MODEL 4536

Semi-automatic; 45 ACP; 8-shot magazine; 3-3/4-inch barrel; decocking lever; one-piece wrap-around Delrin stock; arched or straight backstrap; post front sight with white dot, fixed or adjustable rear; serrated hammer spur; stainless steel construction. Introduced 1990; dropped 1991.

Perf.: $500   **Exc.:** $400   **VGood:** $295

SMITH & WESSON MODEL 4546

Semi-automatic; double-action-only; 45 ACP; 8-shot magazine; 5-inch barrel; decocking lever;

stainless steel construction; one-piece wrap-around Delrin stock; arched or straight backstrap; post front sight with white dot, fixed or adjustable rear; serrated hammer spur; stainless steel construction. Introduced 1990; dropped 1991.

Perf.: $500   **Exc.:** $400   **VGood:** $295

SMITH & WESSON MODEL 4556

Semi-automatic; double-action-only; 45 ACP; 8-shot magazine; 3-3/4-inch barrel; decocking lever; stainless steel construction; one-piece wrap-around Delrin stock; arched or straight backstrap; post front sight with white dot, fixed or adjustable rear; serrated hammer spur; stainless steel construction. Introduced 1990; dropped 1991.

Perf.: $500   **Exc.:** $400   **VGood:** $295

SMITH & WESSON MODEL 4566

Semi-automatic; double-action-only; 45 ACP; 8-shot magazine; 4-1/4-inch barrel; ambidextrous safety; decocking lever; stainless steel construction; one-piece wrap-around Delrin stocks; arched or straight backstrap; fixed sights; serrated hammer spur; stainless steel construction. Introduced 1990; dropped 1999.

Perf.: $500   **Exc.:** $400   **VGood:** $295

SMITH & WESSON MODEL 4567-NS

Semi-automatic; 45 ACP; 4-1/4-inch barrel; stainless steel slide; blued steel frame; bobbed hammer; one-piece wrap-around grip; straight, blued backstrap; rounded edges; Novak sights with tritium inserts. Introduced 1991; dropped 1991.

Perf.: $550   **Exc.:** $450   **VGood:** $350

SMITH & WESSON MODEL 4576

Semi-automatic; double action; 45 ACP; 8-shot magazine; 4-1/4-inch barrel; ambidextrous safety; decocking lever; stainless steel construction; one-piece wrap-around Delrin stocks; arched or straight backstrap; fixed sights; serrated hammer spur

made of stainless steel. Introduced 1990; no longer produced.

Perf.: $500   **Exc.:** $400   **VGood:** $295

SMITH & WESSON MODEL 4586

Semi-automatic; double-action-only; 45 ACP; 8-shot magazine; 4-1/4-inch barrel; ambidextrous safety; decocking lever; stainless steel construction; one-piece wrap-around Xenoy stock; arched or straight backstrap; fixed sights; serrated hammer spur. Introduced 1990; dropped 1999.

Perf.: $500   **Exc.:** $400   **VGood:** $295

SMITH & WESSON MODEL 5903

Semi-automatic; double action; 9mm Para.; 14-, 10-shot magazine; 7-1/2-inch overall length; weighs 28-37 oz.; stainless steel alloy frame; ambidextrous safety; one-piece wrap-around Xenoy stocks; fixed sights; blued finish; smooth trigger; serrated hammer. Introduced 1989; dropped 1997.

New: $550   **Perf.:** $500   **Exc.:** $425

SMITH & WESSON MODEL 5904

Semi-automatic; double action; 9mm Para.; 14-, 10-shot magazine; 4-inch barrel; 7-1/2-inch overall length; weighs 28 to 37 oz.; one-piece wrap-around Xenoy stocks; fixed or adjustable sights; blued finish; smooth trigger; serrated hammer. Introduced 1989; dropped 1998.

New: $550   **Perf.:** $500   **Exc.:** $400

SMITH & WESSON MODEL 5905

Semi-automatic; double action; 9mm Para.; 14-shot magazine; 4-inch barrel; 7-5/8-inch overall length; weighs 30 oz.; blued frame, slide; ambidextrous safety; one-piece wrap-around Delrin stocks; adjustable sights; blued finish; smooth trigger; serrated hammer. Introduced 1989; dropped 1992.

Perf.: $650   **Exc.:** $600   **VGood:** $550

Smith & Wesson
Model 5906

Smith & Wesson
Model 5926

Smith & Wesson
Model 5946

Smith & Wesson
Model 6904

Smith & Wesson
Model 6906

Smith & Wesson
Model 6946

SMITH & WESSON MODEL 5906

Semi-automatic; double action; 9mm Para.; 14-, 10-shot magazine; 4-inch barrel; 7-1/2-inch overall length; weighs 28-38 oz.; stainless steel construction; ambidextrous safety; one-piece wrap-around Xenoy stock; fixed or adjustable sights; blued finish; smooth trigger; serrated hammer. Introduced 1989; dropped 1999.

New: $600   **Perf.:** $525   **Exc.:** $425

SMITH & WESSON MODEL 5924

Semi-automatic; double action; 9mm Para.; 14-shot magazine; 4-inch barrel; 7-1/2-inch overall length; weighs 30 oz.; blue frame; frame mounted decocking lever; ambidextrous safety; one-piece wrap-around Delrin stocks; fixed sights; blued finish; smooth trigger; serrated hammer. Introduced 1989; dropped 1992.

Perf.: $450   **Exc.:** $350   **VGood:** $300

SMITH & WESSON MODEL 5926

Semi-automatic; double action; 9mm Para.; 14-shot magazine; 4-inch barrel; 7-1/2-inch overall length; weighs 30 oz.; stainless steel construction; frame mounted decocking lever; ambidextrous safety; one-piece wrap-around Delrin stocks; fixed sights; blued finish; smooth trigger; serrated hammer. Introduced 1989; dropped 1992.

Perf.: $550   **Exc.:** $450   **VGood:** $375

SMITH & WESSON MODEL 5943

Semi-automatic; double-action-only; 9mm Para.; 14-shot magazine; 4-inch barrel; 7-1/2-inch overall length; weighs 30 oz.; stainless alloy frame; frame mounted decocking lever; ambidextrous safety; one-piece wrap-around Delrin stocks; fixed sights; blued finish; smooth trigger; serrated hammer. Introduced 1989; dropped 1992.

Perf.: $500   **Exc.:** $450   **VGood:** $350

SMITH & WESSON MODEL 5943-SSV

Same specs as 5943 except 3-1/2-inch barrel; bobbed hammer; short slide; double-action-only;

alloy frame; blued slide, slide stop, magazine release, trigger, hammer; black post front sight, Novak fixed rear tritium inserts; black curved backstrap grips. Introduced 1990; dropped 1992.

Perf.: $525   **Exc.:** $475   **VGood:** $350

SMITH & WESSON MODEL 5944

Semi-automatic; double-action-only; 9mm Para.; 14-shot magazine; 4-inch barrel; 7-1/2-inch overall length; weighs 30 oz.; blue alloy frame; frame mounted decocking lever; ambidextrous safety; one-piece wrap-around Delrin stocks; fixed sights; blued finish; smooth trigger; serrated hammer. Introduced 1989; dropped 1992.

Perf.: $450   **Exc.:** $400   **VGood:** $325

SMITH & WESSON MODEL 5946

Semi-automatic; double-action-only; 9mm Para.; 14-shot magazine; 4-inch barrel; 7-5/8-inch overall length; weighs 30 oz.; stainless steel construction; frame mounted decocking lever; ambidextrous safety; one-piece wrap-around Delrin stocks; fixed sights; blued finish; smooth trigger; serrated hammer. Introduced 1989; dropped 1999.

New: $500   **Perf.:** $450   **Exc.:** $450

SMITH & WESSON MODEL 6904

Semi-automatic; double action; 9mm Para.; 12-, 10-shot magazine; 3-1/2-inch barrel; weighs 26-1/2 oz.; fixed rear sight; .260-inch bobbed hammer; blue finish. Introduced 1989; dropped 1997.

New: $500   **Perf.:** $450   **Exc.:** $375

SMITH & WESSON MODEL 6906

Semi-automatic; double action; 9mm Para.; 12-, 10-shot magazine; 3-1/2-inch barrel; weighs 26-1/2 oz.; stainless steel construction; fixed rear sight; .260-inch bobbed hammer. Introduced 1989; dropped 1999.

New: $500   **Perf.:** $400   **Exc.:** $350

With night sights

New: $600   **Perf.:** $500   **Exc.:** $450

SMITH & WESSON MODEL 6926

Semi-automatic; double action; 9mm Para.; 12-shot magazine; 3-1/2-inch barrel; weighs 26-1/2 oz.; aluminum alloy frame; stainless slide; decocking lever; fixed sights; bobbed hammer. Introduced 1990; dropped 1992.

Perf.: $400   **Exc.:** $350   **VGood:** $300

SMITH & WESSON MODEL 6944

Semi-automatic; double-action-only; 9mm Para.; 12-shot magazine; 3-1/2-inch barrel; weighs 26-1/2 oz.; aluminum alloy frame; blued steel slide; decocking lever; fixed sights; bobbed hammer. Introduced 1990; dropped 1992.

Perf.: $450   **Exc.:** $400   **VGood:** $300

SMITH & WESSON MODEL 6946

Semi-automatic; double-action-only; 9mm Para.; 12-, 10-shot magazine; 3-1/2-inch barrel; weighs 26-1/2 oz.; aluminum alloy frame; stainless steel slide; decocking lever; fixed sights or night sights; .260-inch bobbed hammer. Introduced 1990; dropped 1999.

New: $400   **Perf.:** $300   **Exc.:** $295

With night sights

New: $550   **Perf.:** $500   **Exc.:** $400

SMITH & WESSON SIGMA SW9F

Semi-automatic; double action; 9mm Para.; 10-shot magazine; 4-1/2-inch barrel; 7-1/2-inch overall length; weighs 26 oz.; integral polymer grips; post front sight with white dot, fixed rear with two dots; tritium night sights optional; ergonomic polymer frame; internal striker firing system; corrosion-resistant slide; Teflon-filled, electroless-nickel coated magazine. Introduced 1994; dropped 1996.

New: $400   **Perf.:** $350   **Exc.:** $300

With fixed tritium night sights

New: $425   **Perf.:** $375   **Exc.:** $425

Smith & Wesson
Sigma SW40F

Smith & Wesson
Sigma SW380

Smith & Wesson 22
Auto Target (Model 41)

Smith & Wesson
Escort Model 61

Smith & Wesson 22
Auto Match (Model 41)

Smith & Wesson 22
Auto Target (Model 46)

Smith & Wesson Model 41
Fiftieth Anniversary Edition

Smith & Wesson
Model 422

Smith & Wesson
Model 2206

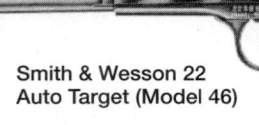

SMITH & WESSON SIGMA SW9C
Same specs as the SW9F except 4-inch barrel; weighs 24-1/2 oz. Introduced 1995; dropped 1998.

New: $400 **Perf.:** $350 **Exc.:** $300

With fixed tritium night sights

New: $425 **Perf.:** $375 **Exc.:** $425

SMITH & WESSON SIGMA SW40F
Semi-automatic; double action; 40 S&W; 10-shot magazine; 4-1/2-inch barrel; weighs 26 oz.; 7-1/2-inch overall length; integral polymer grips; post front sight with white dot, fixed rear with two dots; tritium night sights optional; ergonomic polymer frame; internal striker firing system; corrosion-resistant slide; Teflon-filled, electroless-nickel coated magazine. Made in U.S. by Smith & Wesson. Introduced 1994; dropped 1998.

New: $400 **Perf.:** $350 **Exc.:** $300

With fixed tritium night sights

New: $425 **Perf.:** $375 **Exc.:** $425

SMITH & WESSON SIGMA SW40C
Same specs as the SW40F except 4-inch barrel; weighs 24-1/2 oz. Introduced 1995; dropped 1998.

New: $400 **Perf.:** $350 **Exc.:** $300

With fixed tritium night sights

New: $425 **Perf.:** $375 **Exc.:** $425

SMITH & WESSON SIGMA SW380
Semi-automatic; double-action-only; 380 ACP; 6-shot magazine; 3-inch barrel; 5-13/16-inch overall length; weighs 14 oz.; integral polymer grips; fixed groove in the slide sights; polymer frame; grooved/serrated front and rear grip straps; two passive safeties. Introduced 1995; dropped 1996.

New: $275 **Perf.:** $225 **Exc.:** $200

SMITH & WESSON 22 AUTO TARGET (MODEL 41)
Semi-automatic; 22 LR; 10-shot clip magazine; 5-inch, 7-3/8-inch overall length (7 3/8-inch barrel); weighs 43-1/2 oz.; 3/8-inch wide trigger, grooved, with adjustable stop; detachable muzzle brake supplied with 7-3/8-inch barrel only (muzzle brake recently dropped); 1/8-inch undercut Patridge-type front sight, fully-adjustable S&W micrometer-click rear; checkered walnut grips with modified thumbrest for right- or left-handed shooters; S&W bright blue finish. The Model 41 was at one time also available in 22 Short for international competition. Introduced about 1957; still in production.

New: $750 **Perf.:** $650 **Exc.:** $550

SMITH & WESSON 22 AUTO MATCH (MODEL 41)
Same specs as Model 41 except 5-1/2-inch heavy barrel; 9-inch overall length; weighs 44-1/2 oz.; checkered walnut stocks; modified thumbrest; 1/8-inch Patridge front sight on ramp base, S&W micro-click adjustable rear; grooved trigger; adjustable trigger stop; bright blued finish; matted top area. Extension front sight added 1965. Introduced 1963; dropped 1989.

Exc.: $700 **VGood:** $600 **Good:** $500

SMITH & WESSON MODEL 41 FIFTIETH ANNIVERSARY EDITION
Similar to original Model 41 but machine-engraved with Class A+ coverage, gold plated borders, and glass-topped presentation case. Introduced 2008. Serial Number Range: FYA0001 - FYA0500.

New: $1350 **Perf.:** $1100 **Exc.:** $650

SMITH & WESSON 22 AUTO TARGET (MODEL 46)
Semi-automatic; 22 LR; 10-shot; 5-inch, 5-1/2-inch, 7-inch heavy barrel; same as the Model 41 except with or without extendable front sight; less elaborate; molded nylon stocks. Approximately 4000 manufactured.

Exc.: $675 **VGood:** $550 **Good:** $450

SMITH & WESSON ESCORT MODEL 61
Semi-automatic; 22 LR; 5-shot magazine; 2-1/4-inch barrel; 4-13/16-inch overall length; hammerless; thumb safety on left side of grip; fixed sights; cocking indicator; checkered plastic grips; blued or nickel finish. Introduced in 1970; dropped 1973. Collector value.

Exc.: $225 **VGood:** $175 **Good:** $135

Nickel finish

Exc.: $250 **VGood:** $200 **Good:** $150

SMITH & WESSON MODEL 422
Semi-automatic; 22 LR; 10-shot magazine; 4-1/2-inch, 6-inch barrel; 7-1/2-inch overall length (4-1/2-inch barrel); weighs 22 oz.; serrated ramp front, fixed rear field sights; serrated ramp front, adjustable rear target sights; checkered plastic stocks on field model, checkered walnut on target version; aluminum frame, steel slide; brushed blued finish; internal hammer. Introduced 1987.

Adjustable sights

Perf.: $200 **Exc.:** $175 **VGood:** $150

Fixed sights

New: $175 **Perf.:** $150 **Exc.:** $125

SMITH & WESSON MODEL 622
Semi-automatic; 22 LR; 10-shot magazine; 4-1/2-inch, 6-inch barrel; 7-1/2-inch overall length (4-1/2-inch barrel); weighs 22 oz.; serrated ramp front, fixed rear field sight or serrated ramp front, adjustable rear target sights; checkered plastic stocks on field model, checkered walnut on target version; stainless steel construction; satin finish; internal hammer. Introduced 1990; dropped 1996.

Adjustable sights

Perf.: $250 **Exc.:** $225 **VGood:** $175

Fixed sights

Perf.: $200 **Exc.:** $150 **VGood:** $135

SMITH & WESSON MODEL 2206
Semi-automatic; single action; 22 LR; 10-shot magazine; 4-1/2-inch, 6-inch barrel; weighs 35 oz. (4-1/2-inch barrel); fixed or adjustable sights; checkered black plastic stocks; stainless steel construction with non-reflective finish; internal hammer. Introduced 1990; dropped 1996.

Adjustable sights

New: $300 **Perf.:** $250 **Exc.:** $200

Fixed sights

New: $275 **Perf.:** $225 **Exc.:** $175

SMITH & WESSON MODEL 2206 TARGET
Same specs as Model 2206 except 6-inch barrel; Millett Series adjustable sight system; Patridge front sight; Herett walnut target grips with thumbrest; serrated trigger with adjustable stop; bead blasted sight plane; drilled, tapped for scope mounts. Introduced 1994; dropped 1996.

New: $375 **Perf.:** $300 **Exc.:** $250

SMITH & WESSON MODEL 2213
Semi-automatic; 22 LR; 8-shot magazine; 3-inch barrel 6-1/8-inch overall length; weighs 18 oz.; dovetailed Patridge front sight with white dot,

Smith & Wesson Model 2214 Sportsman

Smith & Wesson Model 2213

Smith & Wesson Model 22A Target

Smith & Wesson Model 22A Sport

Smith & Wesson Model 22S Sport

Smith & Wesson M&P 40

Smith & Wesson M&P 357

Smith & Wesson M&P9C

Smith & Wesson M&P 45

Smith & Wesson M&P9 Pro Series

Smith & Wesson M&P40C

Smith & Wesson Model M&P9-JG

Smith & Wesson Model M&P9L

two-dot fixed rear; black composition grips with checkered panels; stainless steel slide and alloy frame with satin stainless finish. Comes with holster and softside carry case. Introduced 1990; dropped 1999.

Perf.: $250   **Exc.:** $200   **VGood:** $175

SMITH & WESSON MODEL 2214 SPORTSMAN

Semi-automatic; 22 LR; 8-shot magazine; 3-inch barrel; 6-1/4-inch overall length; weighs 18 oz.; dovetail Patridge front sight with white dot, two-dot fixed rear; black composition grips with checkered panels; matte blue finish. Introduced 1990; dropped 1999.

Adjustable sights

New: $225   **Perf.:** $175   **Exc.:** $150

SMITH & WESSON MODEL 22A SPORT

Semi-automatic; 22 LR, 10-shot magazine. Barrel: 4-inch, 5-1/2-inch, 7-inch. Weight: 29 oz. Length: 8-inch overall. Stocks: Two-piece polymer. Sights: Patridge front, fully adjustable rear. Features: Comes with a sight bridge with Weaver-style integral optics mount; alloy frame; .312-inch serrated trigger; stainless steel slide and barrel with matte blue finish. Introduced 1997.

New: $175   **Perf.:** $150   **Exc.:** $135

7-inch barrel

New: $200   **Perf.:** $175   **Exc.:** $150

SMITH & WESSON MODEL 22S SPORT

Similar to the Model 22A Sport except with stainless steel frame. Available only with 5-1/2-inch or 7-inch barrel. Introduced 1997.

New: $250   **Perf.:** $225   **Exc.:** $175

5-1/2-inch bull barrel, wood target stocks with thumbrest

New: $300   **Perf.:** $275   **Exc.:** $250

5-1/2-inch bull barrel, two-piece target stocks with thumbrest

New: $275   **Perf.:** $250   **Exc.:** $200

SMITH & WESSON MODEL 22A TARGET

Semi-automatic; 22 LR, 10-shot magazine. Barrel: 5-1/2 bull. Weight: 38.5 oz. Length: 9-1/2 overall. Stocks: Dymondwood with ambidextrous thumbrests and flared bottom. Sights: Patridge front, fully adjustable rear. Features: Sight bridge with Weaver-

style integral optics mount; alloy frame, stainless barrel and slide; matte blue finish. Introduced 1997.

New: $275   **Perf.:** $250   **Exc.:** $200

SMITH & WESSON MODEL 22S TARGET PISTOL

Similar to the Model 22A except has stainless steel frame. Introduced 1997.

New: $300   **Perf.:** $275   **Exc.:** $225

SMITH & WESSON M&P 9

Full-size Military and Police semi-auto chambered in 9mm. Capacity 17+1, 4.25-inch barrel, 6 1/2 lb. trigger, 24.25 oz. Picatinny rail and polymer frame. Optional tritium low-light sights.

New: $675   **Exc.:** $615   **VGood:** $525

SMITH & WESSON MODEL M&P9-JG

Similar to above but with interchangeable palmswell grip panels, including two pink ones. Dealer sets pricing. Inroduced 2008.

New: $675   **Exc.:** $615   **VGood:** $525

SMITH & WESSON MODEL M&P9 PRO SERIES

Similar to M&P9 but with green fiber optic sights and interchangeable palmswell grip panels. Black Melonite finish. Introduced 2008.

New: $675   **Exc.:** $615   **VGood:** $525

SMITH & WESSON MODEL M&P9L

Similar to M&P9 but with 5-inch barrel. Introduced 2008.

New: $675   **Exc.:** $615   **VGood:** $525

SMITH & WESSON M&P 40

Full-size semi-auto chambered in .40 S&W; this is the first of the new Military and Police series. Capacity 15+1, 4.25-inch barrel, .5 lb. trigger, 24.25

oz. Polymer frame and Picatinny rail. Optional tritium low-light sights.

New: $675   **Exc.:** $615   **VGood:** $525

SMITH & WESSON M&P .357 SIG

Full-size Military and Police semi-auto chambered in .357 SIG. Capacity 15+1, 4.25-inch barrel, 6.5 lb. trigger, 24.25 oz. Polymer frame and Picatinny rail. Optional tritium low-light sights.

New: $685   **Exc.:** $625   **VGood:** $535

SMITH & WESSON M&P45

Semi-auto; similar to M&P40 but in .45 ACP. Black or Dark Earth Brown finish.

New: $685   **Exc.:** $625   **VGood:** $535

SMITH & WESSON M&P9C

Semi-auto; compact model; similar to M&P9 but with 3.5" barrel, short grip frameM&P and 10+1 or 12+1 capacity. Black Melonite finish.

New: $685   **Exc.:** $725   **VGood:** $535

SMITH & WESSON M&P40C

Semi-auto; compact model; similar to M&P9C but in .40 S&W. Black Melonite finish.

New: $685   **Exc.:** $725   **VGood:** $535

SMITH & WESSON M&P357C

Semi-auto; compact model; similar to M&P40c but in .357 SIG. Black Melonite finish.

New: $685   **Exc.:** $725   **VGood:** $535

Smith & Wesson
SW9VE

Sokolovsky 45
Automaster

Smith & Wesson
SW40VE

Smith & Wesson
Model SW1911
Pro Series

Sphinx AT-2000C
Competitor

Smith & Wesson
SW1911 PD Gunsite
Commemorative

Smith & Wesson SW1911
Rolling Thunder
Commemorative

Sphinx
AT-2000GM
Grand Master

SMITH & WESSON SW9VE ALLIED FORCES

Similar to SW9VE but with black Melonite slide. Adopted by Afghanistan internal security and border forces. Add 75 percent for "Disaster Ready Kit" (case and emergency supplies).

New: $400 **Exc.:** $350 **VGood:** $295

SMITH & WESSON SW40VE ALLIED FORCES

Similar to SW9VE Allied Forces but in .40 S&W. Add 75 percent for "Disaster Ready Kit" (case and emergency supplies).

New: $400 **Exc.:** $350 **VGood:** $295

SMITH & WESSON MODEL SW1911

1911-style semiauto pistol in .45 ACP. 5" barrel; blued, stainless, or two-tone finish; carbon steel frame and slide with polished flats on slide; standard GI recoil guide; external extractor; laminated double diamond walnut grips with silver S&W medallions, adjustable target sight.

New: $900 **Exc.:** $795 **VGood:** $650

SMITH & WESSON MODEL SW1911 PD

Part of Tactical Rail Series developed for SWAT Teams and tactical operations. Picatinny rail. Scandium alloy, single-action .45 ACP with 5-inch barrel and 8+1 capacity. Fixed sights. 32 oz.

New: $1100 **Exc.:** $950 **VGood:** $695

SMITH & WESSON MODEL SW1911 PD GUNSITE COMMEMORATIVE

Honors Lt. Col. Jeff Cooper's Gunsite Training Academy. Scandium alloy, single-action .45 ACP with 4.25-inch barrel and 8+1 capacity. Fixed sights. 28 oz.

New: $1150 **Exc.:** $1000 **VGood:** $725

SMITH & WESSON SW1911 TACTICAL RAIL

One of Tactical Rail Series for SWAT Teams and tactical applications. Picatinny rail and fixed sights. Blued or stainless, single-action .45 ACP with 5-inch barrel and 8+1 capacity. 39 oz.

New: $1000 **Exc.:** $895 **VGood:** $700

SMITH & WESSON MODEL SW1911 – ROLLING THUNDER COMMEMORATIVE

Limited edition commemorating American POW-MIAs. Rolling Thunder and POW-MIA logos in imitation bonded ivory grips. Chambered for .45 ACP. Blued, 8+1 capacity, 5-inch barrel, 38.5 oz.

New: $1550 **Exc.:** $1200 **VGood:** $875

SMITH & WESSON MODEL SW1911 PRO SERIES

Similar to Model SW1911 but with Novak fiber optic sights, skeletonized trigger and various tactical/performance enhancements. Introduced 2008.

New: $975 **Exc.:** $825 **VGood:** $650

SOKOLOVSKY 45 AUTOMASTER

Semi-automatic; single action; 45 ACP; 6-shot; 6-inch barrel; 9-1/2-inch overall length; weighs 55 oz.; ramp front sight, Millett adjustable rear; smooth walnut stocks; semi-custom built with precise tolerances for target shooting; special safety trigger; primarily stainless steel. Introduced 1985; dropped 1990.

Exc.: $2500 **VGood:** $2000 **Good:** $1750

SPECIALIZED WEAPONS SPECTRE FIVE

Revolver; double action; 45 Colt/410 2-inch, 3-inch shotshell; 5-shot; 2-inch barrel; 9-inch overall length; weighs 48 oz.; fixed sights; Pachmayr checkered rubber grips; ambidextrous hammer-block safety; draw bar safety; squared triggerguard; steel construction; matte blue finish. Introduced 1991; discontinued 1992. Limited production; lack of information precludes pricing.

SPHINX AT-380

Semi-automatic; double-action-only; 380 ACP; 10-shot magazine; 3-1/4-inch barrel; 6-inch overall length; weighs 25 oz.; checkered plastic grips; fixed sights; chamber loaded indicator; ambidextrous magazine release and slide latch; blued slide, bright Palladium frame, or bright Palladium finish overall. Imported from Switzerland by Sphinx U.S.A., Inc. Introduced 1993.

New: $450 **Perf.:** $350 **Exc.:** $300

SPHINX AT-2000S

Semi-automatic; double action; 9mm Para., 9x21mm, 40 S&W; 10-shot magazine; 4-1/2-inch barrel; 8-inch overall length; weighs 36 oz.; checkered neoprene grips; blade front sight, fixed rear; three-dot system; double-action mechanism changeable to double-action-only; stainless frame, blued slide; ambidextrous safety, magazine release, slide latch.

Imported from Switzerland by Sphinx U.S.A., Inc. Introduced 1993; still imported.

9mm, two-tone finish		
New: $900	**Perf.:** $850	**Exc.:** $750
9mm, Palladium finish		
New: $1000	**Perf.:** $900	**Exc.:** $800
40 S&W, two-tone finish		
New: $1000	**Perf.:** $900	**Exc.:** $800
40 S&W, Palladium finish		
New: $1100	**Perf.:** $1000	**Exc.:** $900

SPHINX AT-2000C COMPETITOR

Same specs as AT-2000S except 5-5/16-inch barrel; 9-7/8-inch overall length; weighs 40-1/2 oz.; fully-adjustable Bo-Mar open sights or Tasco Pro-Point dot sight in Sphinx mount; extended magazine release; competition slide with dual-port compensated barrel; two-tone finish only. Imported from Switzerland by Sphinx U.S.A., Inc. Introduced 1993.

With Bo-Mar sights		
New: $1750	**Perf.:** $1200	**Exc.:** $850
With Tasco Pro-Point and mount		
New: $1900	**Perf.:** $1450	**Exc.:** $1250

SPHINX AT-2000GM GRAND MASTER

Same specs as the AT-2000S except single-action-only trigger mechanism; squared triggerguard; extended beavertail grip, safety and magazine release; notched competition slide for easier cocking; two-tone finish; dual-port compensated barrel; fully-adjustable Bo-Mar open sights or Tasco Pro-Point and Sphinx mount. Imported from Switzerland by Sphinx U.S.A., Inc. Introduced 1993; still imported.

With Bo-Mar sights		
New: $2500	**Perf.:** $1750	**Exc.:** $1250
With Tasco Pro-Point and mount		
New: $2650	**Perf.:** $1850	**Exc.:** $1350

Sphinx AT-2000P

Sphinx 3000

Sphinx AT-2000PS

Sportarms
Model HS38S

Sportarms
Model HS21S

Sportarms Tokarev
Model 213

Springfield Armory
Model 1911-A1

Springfield Amory
Model 1911-A1
Basic Competition

SPHINX AT-2000H

Same specs as the AT-2000S except shorter slide with 3-1/2-inch barrel; shorter frame; 7-inch overall length; weighs 32 oz. Imported from Switzerland by Sphinx U.S.A., Inc. Introduced 1993.

9mm, two-tone finish		
New: $800	**Perf.:** $750	**Exc.:** $650
9mm, Palladium finish		
New: $850	**Perf.:** $800	**Exc.:** $700
40 S&W, two-tone finish		
New: $850	**Perf.:** $800	**Exc.:** $700
40 S&W, Palladium finish		
New: $900	**Perf.:** $850	**Exc.:** $750

SPHINX AT-2000P

Same specs as AT-2000S except 13-shot magazine; 3-3/4-inch barrel; 7-1/4-inch overall length; weighs 34 oz.; double-action mechanism changeable to double-action-only; stainless steel frame, blued slide, or bright Palladium overall finish; ambidextrous safety magazine release and slide latch. Imported from Switzerland by Sphinx U.S.A., Inc. Introduced 1993.

9mm, two-tone finish		
New: $800	**Perf.:** $750	**Exc.:** $650
9mm, Paladium finish		
New: $850	**Perf.:** $800	**Exc.:** $700
40 S&W, two-tone finish		
New: $850	**Perf.:** $800	**Exc.:** $700
40 S&W, Paladium finish		
New: $900	**Perf.:** $850	**Exc.:** $750

SPHINX AT-2000PS

Same specs as the AT-2000S except 3-3/4-inch barrel; 7-1/4-inch overall length; full-size frame; weighs 34 oz. Imported from Switzerland by Sphinx U.S.A., Inc. Introduced 1993.

9mm, two-tone finish		
New: $800	**Perf.:** $750	**Exc.:** $650
9mm, Palladium finish		
New: $850	**Perf.:** $800	**Exc.:** $700
40 S&W, two-tone finish		
New: $850	**Perf.:** $800	**Exc.:** $700
40 S&W, Palladium finish		
New: $900	**Perf.:** $850	**Exc.:** $750

SPHINX 3000

16+1 autoloader chambered in 9mm or .45 ACP. Stainless steel frame and slide, manual safety, single/

double/decocking action, weight 40.56 oz. Also available in compact version.

New: $1800   **Perf.:** $1350   **Exc.:** $850

SPORTARMS MODEL HS21S

Revolver; single action; 22 LR, 22 LR/22 WMR combo; 6-shot cylinder; 5-1/2-inch barrel; 11-inch overall length; weighs 33-1/2 oz.; smooth hardwood or imitation stag grips; blade front sight, windage-adjustable rear; blue finish. Made in Germany by Herbert Schmidt; imported by Sportarms of Florida. Dropped 1994.

22 LR, blue, stag grips		
Perf.: $125	**Exc.:** $110	**VGood:** $100
22 LR/22 WMR combo, blue, wood grips		
Perf.: $150	**Exc.:** $135	**VGood:** $125

SPORTARMS MODEL HS38S

Revolver; double action; 38 Spl.; 6-shot cylinder; 3-inch, 4-inch barrel; 8-inch overall length (3-inch barrel); weighs 31 oz.; checkered hardwood grips, round butt on 3-inch model, target-style on 4-inch; blade front sight, adjustable rear; polished blue finish; ventilated rib on 4-inch barrel. Made in Germany by Herbert Schmidt; imported by Sportarms of Florida. Dropped 1994.

Perf.: $135   **Exc.:** $100   **VGood:** $85

SPORTARMS TOKAREV MODEL 213

Semi-automatic; single action; 9mm Para.; 8-shot magazine; 4-1/2-inch barrel; 7-1/2-inch overall length; weighs 31 oz.; grooved plastic grips; fixed sights; blue finish, hard chrome optional; 9mm version of the famous Russian Tokarev pistol. Made in China by Norinco. Imported by Sportarms of Florida. Introduced 1988; dropped 1994.

Perf.: $125   **Exc.:** $100   **VGood:** $85

SPRINGFIELD ARMORY M6

Single shot; 22 rimfire/45 Colt; 16-inch barrel; weighs 3 lbs.; rubberized wrap-around grips; blade front sight, adjustable rear; pistol version of the M6 rifle; matte blue/black finish. From Springfield Armory; now Springfield, Inc. Introduced 1991; dropped 1992.

Perf.: $175   **Exc.:** $135   **VGood:** $125

SPRINGFIELD ARMORY MODEL 1911-A1

Semi-automatic; 38 Super, 9mm Para., 10mm Auto, 45 ACP; 10-shot (38 Super, 9mm), 9-shot (10mm), 8-shot (45 ACP); 4-inch, 5-inch barrel; 8-1/2-inch overall length (5-inch barrel); weighs 35-1/2 oz.; blade front, windage drift-adjustable rear; walnut grips; reproduction of original Colt model; all new forged parts; phosphated finish. Introduced 1985; replaced by '90s Edition, 1990.

	Perf.: $350	**Exc.:** $300	**VGood:** $275
Blued finish			
	Perf.: $375	**Exc.:** $325	**VGood:** $300
Duotone finish			
	Perf.: $400	**Exc.:** $350	**VGood:** $325

SPRINGFIELD ARMORY MODEL 1911-A1 BASIC COMPETITION

Same specs as the standard 1911-A1 except low-mounted Bo-Mar adjustable rear sight, undercut blade front; match throated barrel and bushing; polished feed ramp; lowered and flared ejection port; fitted Videcki speed trigger with tuned 3-1/2-lb. pull; fitted slide to frame; recoil buffer system; Pachmayr mainspring housing; Pachmayr grips; comes with two magazines with slam pads, plastic carrying case. From Springfield, Inc. Introduced 1992; still produced.

New: $1200   **Perf.:** $1000   **Exc.:** $850

Springfield Armory
Model 1911-A1
Bullseye Wadcutter

Springfield Armory
Model 1911-A1
Champion

Springfield Armory
Model 1911-A1
Combat Commander

Springfield Amory
Model 1911-A1
Compact

Springfield Armory
Model 1911-A1
Compact V10 Ultra

Springfield Amory
Model 1911-A1
Custom Carry

SPRINGFIELD ARMORY MODEL 1911-A1 BULLSEYE WADCUTTER

Same specs as Model 1911-A1 except 45 ACP; 7-shot magazine; weighs 45 oz.; checkered walnut grips; Bo-Mar rib with undercut blade front sight, fully-adjustable rear; built for wadcutter loads only; full-length recoil spring guide rod; fitted Videcki speed trigger with 3-1/2-lb. pull; match Commander hammer and sear; beavertail grip safety; lowered and flared ejection port; tuned extractor; fitted slide to frame; recoil buffer system; beveled and polished magazine well; checkered frontstrap and steel mainspring housing (flat housing standard); polished and throated National Match barrel and bushing. From Springfield, Inc. Introduced 1992.

Perf.: $1250   **Exc.:** $1000   **VGood:** $850

SPRINGFIELD ARMORY MODEL 1911-A1 WADCUTTER ENTRY LEVEL

Same specs as the 1911-A1 Bullseye Wadcutter except low-mounted Bo-Mar adjustable rear sight, undercut blade front; match throated barrel and bushing; polished feed ramp; lowered and flared ejection port; fitted Videcki speed trigger with tuned 3-1/2-lb. pull; fitted slide to frame; Shok Buff; Pachmayr mainspring housing; Pachmayr grips; comes with two magazines with slam pads, plastic carrying case, test target. From Springfield, Inc. Introduced 1992; dropped 1993.

Perf.: $800   **Exc.:** $700   **VGood:** $600

SPRINGFIELD ARMORY MODEL 1911-A1 CHAMPION

Same specs as the standard 1911-A1 except 4-1/4-inch slide; low-profile three-dot sight system; skeletonized hammer; walnut stocks; available in 45 ACP only; blue or stainless. From Springfield, Inc. Introduced 1989; still produced.

Blue finish		
New: $450	**Perf.:** $350	**Exc.:** $275
Stainless steel		
New: $500	**Perf.:** $400	**Exc.:** $300
Blue, with compensator		
New: $700	**Perf.:** $600	**Exc.:** $500

SPRINGFIELD ARMORY MODEL 1911A1 DEFENDER PISTOL

Similar to the 1911A1 Champion except has tapered cone dual-port compensator system, rubberized grips. Has reverse recoil plug, full-length recoil spring guide, serrated frontstrap, extended thumb safety, skeletonized hammer with modified grip safety to match and a Videki speed trigger. Bi-Tone finish. Introduced 1991.

New: $800   **Perf.:** $700   **Exc.:** $600

SPRINGFIELD ARMORY MODEL 1911-A1 CHAMPION MD-1

Same specs as the 1911-A1 Champion except chambered for 380 ACP; 7-shot magazine; 3-1/2-inch barrel; 7-1/8-inch overall length; weighs 30 oz.; three-dot "hi-viz" sights; blued or Parkerized finish. From Springfield, Inc. Introduced 1995.

New: $450   **Perf.:** $350   **Exc.:** $250

SPRINGFIELD ARMORY MODEL 1911-A1 COMMANDER

Same general specs as Model 1911-A1 except 45 ACP only; 3-5/8-inch barrel; shortened slide; Commander hammer; three-dot sight system; walnut stocks; phosphated finish. Introduced 1989; discontinued 1990.

Perf.: $400	**Exc.:** $350	**VGood:** $300
Blued finish		
Perf.: $425	**Exc.:** $375	**VGood:** $300
Duotone finish		
Perf.: $450	**Exc.:** $400	**VGood:** $350

SPRINGFIELD ARMORY MODEL 1911-A1 COMBAT COMMANDER

Same general as Model 1911-A1 except 45 ACP only; 4-1/2-inch barrel; bobbed hammer; walnut grips. Introduced 1988; discontinued 1989.

Perf.: $425	**Exc.:** $375	**VGood:** $325
Blued finish		
Perf.: $450	**Exc.:** $400	**VGood:** $350

SPRINGFIELD ARMORY MODEL 1911-A1 COMPACT

Same general specs as Model 1911-A1 except 45 ACP only; 6-shot; 4-1/2-inch barrel, 7-1/4-inch overall length; three-dot sight system; checkered walnut stocks. Introduced 1989; discontinued 1990.

Perf.: $375	**Exc.:** $325	**VGood:** $275
Blued finish		
Perf.: $400	**Exc.:** $350	**VGood:** $300
Duotone finish		
Perf.: $425	**Exc.:** $375	**VGood:** $350

SPRINGFIELD ARMORY MODEL 1911-A1 COMPACT V10 ULTRA

Same specs as the 1911-A1 Compact except recoil reducing compensator built into the barrel and slide; beavertail grip safety; beveled magazine well; "hi-viz" combat sights; Videcki speed trigger; flared ejection port; stainless steel frame, blued slide; match-grade barrel; walnut grips. From Springfield, Inc. Introduced 1995; still produced.

New: $500	**Perf.:** $450	**Exc.:** $375
Without compensator		
New: $450	**Perf.:** $375	**Exc.:** $300

SPRINGFIELD ARMORY MODEL 1911-A1 COMPETITION

Same specs as Model 1911-A1 except low-mounted Bo-Mar adjustable rear, brazed serrated improved ramp front sight; extended ambidextrous thumb safety; match Commander hammer and sear; serrated rear slide; Pachmayr flat mainspring housing; extended magazine release; beavertail grip safety; full-length recoil spring guide; Pachmayr wrap-around grips; 45 ACP; blue finish; comes with two magazines with slam pads, plastic carrying case. From Springfield, Inc. Introduced 1992; still produced.

New: $1250   **Perf.:** $1000   **Exc.:** $850

SPRINGFIELD ARMORY MODEL 1911-A1 CUSTOM CARRY

Same specs as the standard 1911-A1 except fixed, three-dot low profile sights; Videcki speed trigger; match barrel and bushing; extended thumb and beavertail grip safeties; beveled, polished magazine well; polished feed ramp; throated barrel; match Commander hammer and sear; tuned extractor; lowered and flared ejection port; recoil buffer system; full-length spring guide rod; walnut grips; comes with two magazines with slam pads, plastic carrying case. Available in all popular calibers. From Springfield, Inc. Introduced 1992.

New: $800   **Perf.:** $650   **Exc.:** $500

SPRINGFIELD ARMORY MODEL 1911-A1 CUSTOM COMPACT

Same specs as Model 1911-A1 except 45 ACP; 4-inch barrel with compensator; Videcki speed trigger; match barrel and bushing; extended thumb and beavertail grip safeties; beveled, polished magazine well; polished feed ramp; throated barrel; match Commander hammer and sear; tuned extractor; lowered and flared ejection port; recoil buffer system; full-length spring guide rod; shortened slide; fixed three-dot sights; walnut grips; blued finish. Introduced 1991; no longer in production.

Perf.: $1400   **Exc.:** $1100   **VGood:** $850

Springfield Amory
Model 1911-A1
Defender

Springfield Amory
Model 1911-A1
Expert

Springfield Armory
P9 Factory Comp

Springfield Armory
Model 1911-A1
High Capacity

Springfield Armory
Model V10 Ultra
Compact Pistol

Springfield Armory
TRP

Springfield Armory
1911-A1 N.R.A. PPC

SPRINGFIELD ARMORY MODEL 1911-A1 DEFENDER

Same specs as Model 1911-A1 except 45 ACP only; fixed combat-type sights; beveled magazine well; bobbed hammer; extended thumb safety; serrated frontstrap; walnut stocks; marketed with two stainless steel magazines; phosphated finish. Introduced 1988; discontinued 1990.

Perf.: $450	Exc.: $400	VGood: $325
Blued finish		
Perf.: $475	Exc.: $425	VGood: $350

SPRINGFIELD ARMORY MODEL 1911-A1 DISTINGUISHED

Same specs as the 1911-A1 except full-house pistol with match barrel with match trigger; Bo-Mar low-mounted adjustable rear sight; full-length recoil spring guide rod and recoil spring retainer; beveled and polished magazine well; walnut grips; hard chrome finish; 45 ACP; comes with two magazines with slam pads, plastic carrying case. From Springfield, Inc. Introduced 1992.

New: $2200	Perf.: $1850	Exc.: $1500

SPRINGFIELD ARMORY MODEL 1911-A1 EXPERT PISTOL

Same specs as Model 1911-A1 except triple-chamber tapered cone compensator on match barrel with dovetailed front sight; lowered and flared ejection port; fully tuned for reliability; bobbed hammer; match trigger; Duotone finish; comes with two magazines, plastic carrying case. From Springfield, Inc. Introduced 1992.

New: $1600	Perf.: $1250	Exc.: $1000

SPRINGFIELD ARMORY MODEL 1911-A1 FACTORY COMP

Same specs as the standard 1911-A1 except bushing-type dual-port compensator; adjustable rear sight; extended thumb safety; Videcki speed trigger; beveled magazine well; checkered walnut grips standard. Available in 38 Super or 45 ACP, blue only. From Springfield, Inc. Introduced 1992.

New: $750	Perf.: $650	Exc.: $500

SPRINGFIELD ARMORY MODEL 1911-A1 HIGH CAPACITY

Same specs as the Model 1911-A1 except 45 ACP, 9mm; 10-shot magazine; Commander-style hammer; walnut grips; ambidextrous thumb safety;

beveled magazine well; plastic carrying case. From Springfield, Inc. Introduced 1993; still produced.

45 ACP		
New: $600	Perf.: $500	Exc.: $350
9mm Para.		
New: $500	Perf.: $450	Exc.: $375
45 ACP Factory Comp		
New: $700	Perf.: $600	Exc.: $500
45 ACP Comp Lightweight, matte finish		
New: $700	Perf.: $600	Exc.: $500
45 ACP Compact, blued		
New: $550	Perf.: $475	Exc.: $350
45 ACP Compact, stainless steel		
New: $650	Perf.: $550	Exc.: $450

SPRINGFIELD ARMORY MODEL V10 ULTRA COMPACT PISTOL

Similar to the 1911A1 Compact except has shorter slide, 3.5-inch barrel, recoil reducing compensator built into the barrel and slide. Beavertail grip safety, beveled magazine well, "hi-viz" combat sights, Videcki speed trigger, flared ejection port, stainless steel frame, blued slide, match grade barrel, walnut grips. Introduced 1996. From Springfield, Inc.

New: $550	Perf.: $475	Exc.: $400

SPRINGFIELD ARMORY TRP PISTOLS

Similar to the 1911A1 except 45 ACP only; has checkered front strap and mainspring housing; Novak combat rear sight and matching dovetailed front sight; tuned, polished extractor; oversize barrel link; lightweight speed trigger and combat action job; match barrel and bushing; extended thumb safety and fitted beavertail grip safety; carry bevel on entire pistol; checkered cocobolo wood grips; comes with two Wilson 8-shot magazines. Frame is engraved "Tactical," both sides of frame "TRP." Introduced 1998.

Standard with Armory Kote finish		
New: $950	Perf.: $800	Exc.: $700
Standard, stainless steel		
New: $1000	Perf.: $850	Exc.: $750
Price: Champion, Armory Kote		
New: $1100	Perf.: $950	Exc.: $800

SPRINGFIELD ARMORY MODEL 1911-A1 N.M. HARDBALL

Same specs as Model 1911-A1 except Bo-Mar adjustable rear sight with undercut front blade; fitted match Videcki trigger with 4-lb. pull; fitted slide to frame; throated National Match barrel and bushing; polished feed ramp; recoil buffer system; tuned extractor; Herrett walnut grips; comes with two magazines, plastic carrying case, test target. From Springfield, Inc. Introduced 1992.

New: $1000	Perf.: $850	Exc.: $650

SPRINGFIELD ARMORY MODEL 1911-A1 N.R.A. PPC

Specifically designed to comply with NRA rules for PPC competition; custom slide-to-frame fit; polished feed ramp; throated barrel; total internal honing; tuned extractor; recoil buffer system; fully checkered walnut grips; two fitted magazines; factory test target; custom carrying case. From Springfield, Inc. Introduced 1995; still produced.

New: $1350	Perf.: $1100	Exc.: $900

SPRINGFIELD ARMORY MODEL 1911-A1 PRODUCT IMPROVED DEFENDER

Same specs as Model 1911-A1 except 4-1/4-inch slide; low-profile three-dot sight system; tapered cone dual-port compensator system; rubberized grips; reverse recoil plug; full-length recoil spring guide; serrated frontstrap; extended thumb safety; skeletonized hammer with modified grip safety to match; Videcki speed trigger; Bi-Tone finish. From Springfield, Inc. Introduced 1991.

New: $800	Perf.: $700	Exc.: $600

Springfield Armory
Model 1911-A1
'90s Edition

SPRINGFIELD ARMORY MODEL 1911-A1 TROPHY MASTER COMPETITION PISTOL

Same specs as Model 1911-A1 except combat-type sights; Pachmayr wrap-around grips; ambidextrous safety; match trigger; bobbed hammer. Introduced 1988; discontinued 1990.

Perf.: $1450　　**Exc.:** $1200　　**VGood:** $950

SPRINGFIELD ARMORY MODEL 1911-A1 TROPHY MASTER COMPETITION EXPERT PISTOL

Same specs as Model 1911-A1 except match barrel with compensator; wrap-around Pachmayer grips; ambidextrous thumb safety; lowered, flared ejection port; blued finish. Introduced 1988; discontinued 1990.

Perf.: $1600　　**Exc.:** $1350　　**VGood:** $1000

SPRINGFIELD ARMORY MODEL 1911-A1 TROPHY MATCH

Same specs as Model 1911-A1 except factory accurized; 4- to 5-1/2-lb. trigger pull; click-adjustable rear sight; match-grade barrel and bushing; checkered walnut grips. From Springfield, Inc. Introduced 1994; still produced.

Blue finish		
New: $800	**Perf.:** $700	**Exc.:** $600
Stainless steel		
New: $825	**Perf.:** $725	**Exc.:** $650
High Capacity (stainless steel, 10-shot magazine, front slide serrations, checkered slide serrations)		
New: $950	**Perf.:** $800	**Exc.:** $700

SPRINGFIELD ARMORY MODEL 1911-A1 '90S EDITION

Semi-automatic; single action; 38 Super, 9mm Para., 10mm Auto, 40 S&W, 45 ACP; 10-shot (38 Super), 9-shot (9mm, 10mm), 8-shot (40 S&W, 45 ACP); 5-inch barrel; 8-1/2-inch overall length; weighs 36 oz.; fixed low-profile combat sights; checkered walnut grips; beveled magazine well; linkless operation; all parts forged; phosphated finish. Introduced 1990; still in production.

Perf.: $450　　**Exc.:** $375　　**VGood:** $325

SPRINGFIELD ARMORY MODEL 1911-A1 '90S EDITION CHAMPION COMP

Same specs as Model 1911-A1 '90s Edition except 45 ACP only; 4-inch barrel with compensator; three-dot sights; blued finish. Introduced 1993.

New: $750　　**Perf.:** $650　　**Exc.:** $550

SPRINGFIELD ARMORY MODEL 1911-A1 '90S EDITION CHAMPION XM4 HIGH CAPACITY

Same specs as Model 1911-A1 '90s Edition except 9mm, 45 ACP only; high-capacity variant. Introduced 1994; discontinued 1994.

Perf.: $575　　**Exc.:** $500　　**VGood:** $425

SPRINGFIELD ARMORY MODEL 1911-A1 '90S EDITION COMBAT COMMANDER

Same specs as Model 1911-A1 '90s Edition except 45 ACP only; 4-1/2-inch barrel; walnut grips; bobbed hammer. Introduced 1991; discontinued 1991.

Perf.: $400　　**Exc.:** $350　　**VGood:** $300

Springfield Armory
Bobcat

Springfield Armory
Firecat

SPRINGFIELD ARMORY MODEL 1911-A1 '90S EDITION COMMANDER

Same specs as Model 1911-A1 '90s Edition except 45 ACP only; 3-5/8-inch barrel; shortened slide; three-dot sights; walnut grips; commander hammer. Introduced 1991; discontinued 1992.

Perf.: $400　　**Exc.:** $350　　**VGood:** $300

SPRINGFIELD ARMORY MODEL 1911-A1 '90S EDITION COMPACT

Same specs as Model 1911-A1 '90s Edition except 45 ACP only; 7-shot; 4-inch barrel; shortened slide; three-dot sights; combat hammer; standard or lightweight alloy frame; phosphated finish. Introduced 1991.

New: $350	**Perf.:** $300	**Exc.:** $275
Blued finish		
New: $400	**Perf.:** $350	**Exc.:** $250
Stainless steel finish		
New: $475	**Perf.:** $425	**Exc.:** $375

SPRINGFIELD ARMORY MODEL 1911-A1 '90S EDITION COMPACT COMP

Same specs as Model 1911-A1 '90s Edition except 45 ACP only; 7-shot; 4-inch barrel with compensator; shortened slide; three-dot sights; combat hammer; standard or lightweight alloy frame; duotone finish. Introduced 1993.

Perf.: $750　　**Exc.:** $650　　**VGood:** $500

SPRINGFIELD ARMORY MODEL 1911-A1 '90S EDITION STAINLESS

Same specs as Model 1911-A1 '90s Edition except 9mm Para., 45 ACP only; 8-shot; rubber grips; stainless steel construction. Introduced 1991; still in production.

New: $500　　**Perf.:** $400　　**Exc.:** $350

SPRINGFIELD ARMORY MODEL 1911-A2 S.A.S.S.

Single shot; break-open action; 22 LR, 223, 7mm BR, 7mm-08, 308, 357 Mag., 358 Win., 44 Mag.; 10-3/4-inch, 14-15/16-inch barrel; 17-1/4-inch overall length (14-15/16-inch barrel); weighs 66 oz.; ramped blade front sight, fully adjustable open rear; drilled, tapped for scope mounts; rubberized wrap-around stock; built on standard 1911-A1 frame. Introduced 1989; discontinued 1992.

Perf.: $600　　**Exc.:** $500　　**VGood:** $400

Springfield Armory
1911-A2 S.A.S.S.

Springfield Armory
Model P9 Factory
Comp

Star Firestar

SPRINGFIELD ARMORY BOBCAT

Semi-automatic; 380 ACP; 13-shot magazine; 3-1/2-inch barrel; 6-1/2-inch overall length; weighs 22 oz.; blade front sight, windage-adjustable rear; textured composition stocks; slide-mounted ambidextrous decocker; frame-mounted slide stop; button magazine release; Commander hammer; matte blue finish. Announced 1991; never manufactured.

SPRINGFIELD ARMORY FIRECAT

Semi-automatic; single action; 9mm Para., 40 S&W; 8-shot (9mm), 7-shot (40 S&W) magazine; 3-1/2-inch barrel; 6-1/2-inch overall length; weighs 25-3/4 oz.; checkered walnut grips; low profile blade front sight, fixed rear; three-dot system; all-steel construction; firing pin block safety and frame-mounted thumb safety; frame-mounted slide stop; button magazine release; checkered front and rear straps; checkered and squared triggerguard; Commander hammer; matte blue only. From Springfield, Inc. Introduced 1991; dropped 1993.

Perf.: $450　　**Exc.:** $350　　**VGood:** $30

SPRINGFIELD ARMORY LYNX

Semi-automatic; 25 ACP; 7-shot magazine; 2-1/4-inch barrel; 4-3/8-inch overall length; weighs 10-1/2 oz.; blade front sight, windage-adjustable rear with three-dot system; all steel construction; frame-mounted thumb safety/ slide stop; Commander hammer; magazine safety; matte blue finish. Announced 1991; never manufactured.

SPRINGFIELD ARMORY MODEL P9

Semi-automatic; double action; 9mm Para., 9x21mm, 40 S&W, 45 ACP; 15-shot (9mm, 9x21), 11-shot (40 S&W, 45 ACP); 4-3/4-inch barrel; 8-inch overall length; weighs 35.3 oz.; blade front sight; three-dot windage-adjustable sight system; checkered walnut stocks; based upon CZ-75 design; firing pin safety block; thumb safety on frame; interchangeable magazine catch; Commander hammer; blued finish. Introduced 1990; dropped 1993.

Perf.: $400　　**Exc.:** $325　　**VGood:** $225

Star Firestar Plus

Star Megastar

Star Model 28

Star Model 30M

Star Model A

Star Model B

Star Model BKM

Phosphated finish
Perf.: $450   **Exc.:** $375   **VGood:** $250
Stainless steel
Perf.: $475   **Exc.:** $375   **VGood:** $325

SPRINGFIELD ARMORY MODEL P9 COMPACT
Same specs as Model P9 except 9mm Para., 40 S&W; 13-shot (9mm), 10-shot (40 S&W); 3-7/8-inch barrel; 7-1/4-inch overall length; weighs 32 oz.; compact slide frame; round triggerguard. Introduced 1990; discontinued 1992.
    Perf.: $350   **Exc.:** $300   **VGood:** $250

SPRINGFIELD ARMORY MODEL P9 FACTORY COMP
Same specs as the standard P9 except comes with dual-port compensator system; extended sear safety; extended magazine release; fully-adjustable rear sight; extra-slim competition wood grips; stainless or bi-tone (stainless and blue) finish; overall length is 9-1/2-inch with 5-1/2-inch barrel; weighs 34 oz. From Springfield, Inc. Introduced 1992; dropped 1993.
9mm Para., bi-tone finish or stainless
Perf.: $550   **Exc.:** $450   **VGood:** $350
40 S&W, bi-tone finish
Perf.: $575   **Exc.:** $475   **VGood:** $375
40 S&W, stainless, 45 ACP bi-tone finish
Perf.: $600   **Exc.:** $500   **VGood:** $400
45 ACP, stainless
Perf.: $550   **Exc.:** $500   **VGood:** $450

STALLARD JS-9
Semi-automatic; single action; 9mm Para.; 8-shot; 4-1/2-inch barrel; 7-3/4-inch overall length; weighs 48 oz.; low-profile fixed sights; textured plastic grips; non-glare blued finish. Introduced 1990; still in production.
    New: $120   **Perf.:** $100   **Exc.:** $80

STAR FIRESTAR
Semi-automatic; single action; 9mm Para., 40 S&W; 7-shot (9mm), 6-shot (40 S&W); 3-3/8-inch barrel; 6-1/2-inch overall length; weighs 30 oz.; blade front sight, fully-adjustable three-dot rear; ambidextrous safety; blued or Starvel finish. Introduced 1990. Dropped 1993.
    New: $275   **Perf.:** $250   **Exc.:** $200

STAR FIRESTAR M45
Same specs as Firestar except 45 ACP; 6-shot magazine; 3-1/2-inch barrel; 6-13/16-inch overall length; weighs 35 oz.; reverse-taper Acculine barrel. Imported from Spain by Interarms. Introduced 1992. Production ended when Star went out of business in 1997.
Blue finish
New: $300   **Perf.:** $250   **Exc.:** $200
Starvel finish
New: $325   **Perf.:** $275   **Exc.:** $225

STAR FIRESTAR PLUS
Same specs as Firestar except 10-shot (9mm) magazine; also available in 40 S&W and 45 ACP. Imported from Spain by Interarms. Introduced 1994. Production ended 1997.

Blue finish, 9mm		
New: $300	**Perf.:** $250	**Exc.:** $200
Starvel finish, 9mm		
New: $325	**Perf.:** $275	**Exc.:** $225
Blue finish, 40 S&W		
New: $350	**Perf.:** $300	**Exc.:** $250
Starvel finish, 40 S&W		
New: $375	**Perf.:** $325	**Exc.:** $300
Blue finish, 45 ACP		
New: $375	**Perf.:** $325	**Exc.:** $300
Starvel finish, 45 ACP		
New: $400	**Perf.:** $350	**Exc.:** $375

STAR MEGASTAR
Semi-automatic; double action; 10mm, 45 ACP; 14-shot (10mm), 12-shot (45 ACP) magazine; 4-9/16-inch barrel; 8-1/2-inch overall length; weighs 47-1/2 oz.; checkered composition grips; blade front sight, adjustable rear; steel frame and slide; reverse-taper Acculine barrel. Imported from Spain by Interarms. Introduced 1992. Production ended 1997.
Blue finish, 10mm, 45 ACP
Perf.: $400   **Exc.:** $350   **VGood:** $275
Starvel finish, 10mm, 45 ACP
Perf.: $425   **Exc.:** $375   **VGood:** $30

STAR MODEL 28
Semi-automatic; double action; 9mm Para.; 15-shot; 4-1/4-inch barrel; 8-inch overall length; weighs 40 oz.; square blade front sight, square-notch click-adjustable rear; grooved triggerguard face, front and backstraps; checkered black plastic stocks; ambidextrous safety; blued finish. Introduced 1983; discontinued 1984; replaced by Model 30M.
    Exc.: $400   **VGood:** $350   **Good:** $300

STAR MODEL 30M
Semi-automatic; double action; 9mm Para.; 15-shot; 4-5/16-inch barrel; 8-inch overall length; weighs 40 oz.; square blade front sight, click-adjustable rear; grooved front, backstraps, triggerguard face; checkered black plastic stocks; ambidextrous safety; steel frame; blued finish. Introduced 1985; discontinued 1991.
    Perf.: $350   **Exc.:** $300   **VGood:** $250

STAR MODEL 31P
Semi-automatic; double action; 9mm Para.; 15-shot magazine; 3-7/8-inch barrel; 7-5/8-inch overall length; weighs 30 oz.; checkered black plastic grips; square blade front sight, square notch click-adjustable rear; grooved front- and backstraps and triggerguard face; ambidextrous safety cams firing pin forward; removable backstrap houses the firing mechanism. Imported from Spain by Interarms. Introduced 1984; last imported 1991.
9mm or 40 S&W, blue finish
Perf.: $350   **Exc.:** $300   **VGood:** $250
9mm or 40 S&W, Starvel finish
Perf.: $375   **Exc.:** $325   **VGood:** $275

STAR MODEL 31PK
Same specs as the Model 31P except alloy frame with blue finish. Imported from Spain by Interarms. Introduced 1984; last imported 1991.
    Perf.: $350   **Exc.:** $300   **VGood:** $250

STAR MODEL A
Semi-automatic; 7.63 Mauser, 9mm Largo, 38 Super, 45 ACP; 8-shot; 5-inch barrel; 8-1/2-inch overall length; fixed or adjustable sights; checkered walnut grips; modified version of Colt 1911; blued finish. Introduced 1921; no longer produced.
    Exc.: $550   **VGood:** $400   **Good:** $250

STAR MODEL B
Semi-automatic; 9mm Para.; 9-shot; 4-1/8-inch, 4-3/16-inch, 6-5/16-inch barrel; fixed sights; checkered walnut grips; blued finish. Introduced 1928; no longer produced.
    Exc.: $400   **VGood:** $300   **Good:** $150

STAR MODEL BKM
Semi-automatic; single action; 9mm Para.; 8-shot; 4-inch barrel; weighs 25 oz.; fixed sights; checkered walnut or plastic grips; lightweight duraluminum frame; blued finish. Introduced 1976; importation discontinued 1991.
    Perf.: $275   **Exc.:** $225   **VGood:** $200

STAR MODEL BKS STARLIGHT
Semi-automatic; 9mm Para.; 8-shot; 4-1/4-inch barrel; fixed sights; checkered plastic grips; magazine; manual safeties; blued, chrome finish. Introduced in 1970; discontinued 1981.
    Exc.: $200   **VGood:** $175   **Good:** $150

Star Model BM

Star Model F Target

Star Model HK Lancer

Star Model M

Star Model CO Pocket

Star Model F

Star Model Olympic

Star Model PD

Star Model I

STAR MODEL BM

Semi-automatic; single action; 9mm Para.; 8-shot; 4-inch barrel; 25 oz.; fixed sights; checkered walnut or plastic grips; blued or Starvel finish. Importation discontinued 1991.

Perf.: $225   **Exc.:** $200   **VGood:** $175

Starvel or Chrome finish

Perf.: $250   **Exc.:** $225   **VGood:** $20

STAR MODEL CO POCKET

Semi-automatic; 25 ACP; 6-shot; 2-3/4-inch barrel; 4-1/2-inch overall length; fixed sights; checkered plastic grips; blued finish. Introduced 1934; discontinued 1957.

Exc.: $165   **VGood:** $135   **Good:** $110

STAR MODEL CU STARLET

Semi-automatic; 25 ACP; 5-shot; 2 3/8-inch barrel; fixed sights; plastic grips; aluminum alloy frame; blue, chrome slide; number of color finish options. Introduced 1957; discontinued 1968.

Exc.: $200   **VGood:** $165   **Good:** $135

STAR MODEL DK

Semi-automatic; 380 ACP; 3-1/8-inch barrel; 5-11/16-inch overall length; fixed sights; plastic stocks; aluminum alloy frame; blue, chrome slide; number color finish options. Introduced 1957; discontinued 1968.

Exc.: $300   **VGood:** $250   **Good:** $200

STAR MODEL F

Semi-automatic; 22 LR; 10-shot; 4-inch barrel; 7-1/4-inch overall length; fixed sights; checkered thumbrest plastic grips; blued finish. Introduced 1942; discontinued 1969.

Exc.: $250   **VGood:** $200   **Good:** $150

STAR MODEL F SPORT

Same specs as Model F except 6-inch barrel; adjustable target-type rear sight. Introduced 1942; dropped 1969.

Exc.: $325   **VGood:** $250   **Good:** $185

STAR MODEL F TARGET

Same specs as Model F except adjustable target sights; 7-inch barrel; weights. Introduced 1942; dropped 1969.

Exc.: $325   **VGood:** $250   **Good:** $18

STAR MODEL FM

Semi-automatic; 22 LR; 10-shot; 4-1/2-inch barrel; adjustable sights; checkered plastic grips; heavy frame; triggerguard web; blued frame. Introduced 1972; no longer in production.

Perf.: $250   **Exc.:** $200   **VGood:** $165

STAR MODEL FR

Semi-automatic; 22 LR; 10-shot; 4-inch barrel; adjustable sights; checkered plastic grips; slide stop; blued finish. Introduced 1967; discontinued 1972.

Exc.: $200   **VGood:** $185   **Good:** $165

STAR MODEL FRS

Semi-automatic; 22 LR; 10-shot; 6-inch barrel; adjustable sights; checkered plastic grips; blued or chrome finish. Introduced 1967; no longer in production.

Perf.: $225   **Exc.:** $200   **VGood:** $175

STAR MODEL FS

Semi-automatic; 22 LR; 10-shot; 6-inch barrel; adjustable sights; checkered plastic grips; blued finish. Introduced 1942; discontinued 1967.

Exc.: $200   **VGood:** $185   **Good:** $165

STAR MODEL H

Semi-automatic; 32 ACP; 7-shot; 2-3/4-inch barrel; fixed sights; plastic grips; blued finish. Introduced 1934; discontinued 1941.

Exc.: $225   **VGood:** $185   **Good:** $165

STAR MODEL HK LANCER

Semi-automatic; 22 LR; 10-shot; 3-1/8-inch barrel; fixed sights; plastic grips; blued finish. Introduced 1955; discontinued 1968.

Exc.: $200   **VGood:** $185   **Good:** $165

STAR MODEL HN

Semi-automatic; 380 ACP; 6-shot; 2-3/4-inch barrel; fixed sights; plastic grips; blued finish. Introduced 1934; discontinued 1941.

Exc.: $250   **VGood:** $225   **Good:** $185

STAR MODEL I

Semi-automatic; 32 ACP; 9-shot; 4-3/4-inch barrel; 7-1/2-inch overall length; fixed sights; checkered plastic grips: blued finish. Introduced 1934; discontinued 1945.

Exc.: $200   **VGood:** $175   **Good:** $150

STAR MODEL IN

Semi-automatic; 380 ACP; 8-shot; 4-3/4-inch barrel; 7-1/2-inch overall length; fixed sights; checkered plastic grips; blued finish. Introduced 1934; discontinued 1945.

Exc.: $225   **VGood:** $185   **Good:** $165

STAR MODEL M

Semi-automatic; 9mm Bergman, 9mm Para., 38 Super, 45 ACP; 8-shot (9mm, 38), 7-shot (45 ACP); 5-inch barrel; 8-1/2-inch overall length; fixed sights; checkered walnut grips; blued finish. Not imported into U.S. Introduced 1935.

Exc.: $375   **VGood:** $325   **Good:** $250

STAR MODEL OLYMPIC

Semi-automatic; 22 Short; 9-shot; 7-inch barrel; 11-1/16-inch overall length; adjustable rear target sight; checkered plastic grips; alloy slide; muzzle brake; blued finish. Introduced 1942; discontinued 1967.

Exc.: $350   **VGood:** $300   **Good:** $200

STAR MODEL P

Semi-automatic; 45 ACP; 7-shot; 5-inch barrel; 8-1/2-inch overall length; fixed sights; checkered walnut grips; blued finish. Introduced 1934; discontinued 1975.

Exc.: $350   **VGood:** $300   **Good:** $225

STAR MODEL PD

Semi-automatic; single action; 45 ACP; 6-shot; 4-inch barrel; 7-inch overall length; weighs 25 oz.; adjustable rear sight, ramp front; checkered walnut stocks; blued finish. Introduced 1975; discontinued 1991.

Exc.: $300   **VGood:** $250   **Good:** $200

STAR MODEL S

Semi-automatic; 380 ACP; 9-shot; 4-inch barrel; 6-1/2-inch overall length; fixed sights; checkered plastic grips; no grip safety; blued finish. Scaled-down modification of Colt 1911. Introduced 1941; discontinued 1965.

Exc.: $250   **VGood:** $200   **Good:** $150

Starvel finish

Exc.: $225   **VGood:** $200   **Good:** $175

Star Ultrastar

Star Model Super P

Sterling Model 286

Sterling Model 284

Sterling Model 300

Sterling Model 400

Sterling Model 302

Star Super SM

STAR MODEL SI
Semi-automatic; 32 ACP; 8-shot; 4-inch barrel; 6-1/2-inch overall length; fixed sights; checkered plastic grips; no grip safety; blued finish. Scaled-down modification of Colt 1911. Introduced 1941; discontinued 1965.

Exc.: $225   **VGood:** $175   **Good:** $150

STAR MODEL SUPER A
Semi-automatic; 38 Super; 8-shot; 5-inch barrel; luminous sights; checkered plastic grips; magazine safety; disarming bolt; loaded chamber indicator; blued finish. Introduced 1946; discontinued 1989.

Exc.: $225   **VGood:** $185   **Good:** $165

STAR MODEL SUPER B
Semi-automatic; 9mm Para.; 8-shot; 5-inch barrel; luminous sights; checkered walnut grips; magazine safety; disarming bolt; loaded chamber indicator; blued finish. Discontinued 1990.

Exc.: $200   **VGood:** $175   **Good:** $150

Starvel finish

Exc.: $225   **VGood:** $200   **Good:** $175

STAR MODEL SUPER M
Semi-automatic; 9mm Bergman, 9mm Para., 38 Super, 45 ACP; 8-shot (9mm, 38), 7-shot (45); 5-inch barrel; luminous sights; checkered walnut grips; magazine safety; disarming bolt; loaded chamber indicator; blued finish. Introduced 1946; discontinued 1989.

Exc.: $375   **VGood:** $275   **Good:** $200

STAR MODEL SUPER P
Semi-automatic; 45 ACP; 7-shot; 5-inch barrel; luminous sights; checkered walnut grips; magazine safety; disarming bolt; loaded chamber indicator; blued finish. Introduced 1946; discontinued 1989.

Exc.: $650   **VGood:** $550   **Good:** $450

STAR MODEL SUPER S
Semi-automatic; 380 ACP; 9-shot; 4-inch barrel; 6-1/2-inch overall length; luminous sights; checkered plastic grips; magazine safety; disarming bolt; loaded chamber indicator; blued finish. Introduced 1946; discontinued 1972.

Exc.: $250   **VGood:** $200   **Good:** $185

STAR MODEL SUPER SI
Semi-automatic; 32 ACP; 8-shot; 4-inch barrel; 6-1/2-inch overall length; luminous sights; checkered plastic grips; magazine safety; disarming bolt; loaded chamber indicator; blued finish. Introduced 1946; discontinued 1972.

Exc.: $200   **VGood:** $175   **Good:** $165

STAR SUPER SM
Semi-automatic; 380 ACP; 9-shot; 4-inch barrel; 6-5/8-inch overall length; adjustable luminous sights; walnut grips; magazine safety; disarming bolt; loaded chamber indicator; blued finish. Introduced 1973; discontinued 1981.

Exc.: $200   **VGood:** $165   **Good:** $135

STAR MODEL SUPER TARGET
Semi-automatic; 9mm Para., 38 Super, 45 ACP; 8-shot (9mm, 38), 7-shot (45); 5-inch barrel; adjustable target sights; wood grips; blue finish. Introduced 1942; discontinued 1954.

Exc.: $450   **VGood:** $350   **Good:** $275

STAR ULTRASTAR
Semi-automatic; double action; 9mm Para.; 9-shot magazine; 3-1/2-inch barrel; 7-inch overall length; weighs 26 oz.; checkered black polymer grips; blade front sight, windage-adjustable rear; three-dot system; polymer frame with inside steel slide rails; ambidextrous two-position safety (Safe and Decock). Imported from Spain by Interarms. Introduced 1994. Production ended 1997.

New: $300   **Perf.:** $250   **Exc.:** $200

STERLING MODEL 283
Semi-automatic; 22 LR; 10-shot; 4-1/2-inch, 6-inch, 8-inch barrel; 9-inch overall length (4-1/2-inch barrel); micrometer rear sight, blade front; checkered plastic grips; external hammer; adjustable trigger; all-steel construction; blued finish. Also designated Model 300 Target. Introduced 1970; discontinued 1972.

Exc.: $175   **VGood:** $150   **Good:** $135

STERLING MODEL 284
Semi-automatic; 22 LR; 10-shot; 4-1/2-inch, 6-inch tapered barrel; 9-inch overall length (4-1/2-inch barrel); micrometer rear sight, blade front; checkered plastic grips; adjustable trigger; all-steel construction; blued finish. Also designated Model 300L Target. Introduced 1970; discontinued 1972.

Exc.: $185   **VGood:** $165   **Good:** $135

STERLING MODEL 285
Semi-automatic; 22 LR; 10-shot; 4-1/2-inch barrel; 9-inch overall length; fixed sights; checkered plastic grips; external hammer; adjustable trigger; all-steel construction; blued finish. Also designated Husky. Introduced 1970; discontinued 1971.

Exc.: $165   **VGood:** $135   **Good:** $110

STERLING MODEL 286
Semi-automatic; 22 LR; 10-shot; 4-1/2-inch, 6-inch tapered barrel; 9-inch overall length (4-1/2-inch barrel); fixed rear sight, serrated ramp front; checkered plastic grips; external hammer; target-type trigger; all-steel construction; blued finish. Also designated Trapper. Introduced 1970; discontinued 1972.

Exc.: $165   **VGood:** $135   **Good:** $110

STERLING MODEL 295
Semi-automatic; 22 LR; 10-shot; 4-1/2-inch heavy barrel; 9-inch overall length; fixed rear sight, serrated ramp front; checkered plastic grips; external hammer; target-type trigger; all-steel construction; blued finish. Also designated Husky Heavy Barrel. Introduced 1970; discontinued 1972.

Exc.: $175   **VGood:** $150   **Good:** $135

STERLING MODEL 300
Semi-automatic; blowback action; 25 ACP; 6-shot; 2-1/2-inch barrel; 4-1/2-inch overall length; no sights; black, white plastic grips; all-steel construction; blued finish. Introduced 1971; discontinued 1984.

Exc.: $125   **VGood:** $100   **Good:** $85

Satin nickel finish

Exc.: $135   **VGood:** $110   **Good:** $85

Stainless steel

Exc.: $135   **VGood:** $110   **Good:** $100

STERLING MODEL 302
Semi-automatic; blowback action; 22 LR; 6-shot; 2-1/2-inch barrel; 4-1/2-inch overall length; no sights; black plastic grips; all-steel construction; blued finish. Introduced 1972; discontinued 1984.

Exc.: $125   **VGood:** $110   **Good:** $100

Satin nickel finish

Exc.: $135   **VGood:** $115   **Good:** $100

Stainless steel

Exc.: $135   **VGood:** $115   **Good:** $100

STERLING MODEL 400
Semi-automatic; double action; 380 ACP; 3-1/2-inch barrel; 6-1/2-inch overall length; micrometer rear sight, fixed ramp front; checkered rosewood grips; thumb-roll safety; all-steel construction; blued finish. Introduced 1973; discontinued 1984.

Exc.: $165   **VGood:** $135   **Good:** $110

Sterling Model 450

Stevens Diamond No. 43

STI GP6

Steyr Mannlicher Model 1901

Stevens No. 35 Autoshot

STI Sentinel Premier

Steyr Model SP

Steyr Mannlicher Model 1905

Satin nickel finish
Exc.: $175   **VGood:** $150   **Good:** $125

Stainless steel
Exc.: $175   **VGood:** $165   **Good:** $135

STERLING MODEL 402

Semi-automatic; double action; 22 LR; 3-1/2-inch barrel; 6-1/2-inch overall length; micrometer rear sight, fixed ramp front; checkered rosewood grips; thumb-roll safety; all-steel construction; blued finish. Introduced 1973; discontinued 1974.

Exc.: $125   **VGood:** $115   **Good:** $100

Satin nickel finish
Exc.: $135   **VGood:** $125   **Good:** $115

Stainless steel
Exc.: $150   **VGood:** $135   **Good:** $125

STERLING MODEL 450

Semi-automatic; double action; 45 ACP; 8-shot; 4-inch barrel; 7-1/2-inch overall length; adjustable rear sight; uncheckered walnut stocks; blued finish. Introduced 1977; discontinued 1984.

Exc.: $350   **VGood:** $300   **Good:** $250

STERLING X-CALIBER

Single shot; 22 LR, 22 WMR, 357 Mag., 44 Mag.; interchangeable 8-inch, 10-inch barrel; 13-inch overall length (8-inch barrel); Patridge front sight, fully-adjustable rear; drilled/tapped for scope mounts; Goncalo Alves stocks; notched hammer for easy cocking; finger-grooved grips. Introduced 1980; discontinued 1984.

Exc.: 325   **VGood:** $250   **Good:** $215

STEVENS CONLIN NO. 38

Single shot; 22 Short, 22 LR, 22 WMR, 25 Stevens, 32 Long, 32 Short Colt; finger-rest grip; tip-down barrel; conventional trigger and guard with spur; peep rear, globe front sight. Manufactured from 1884 to 1903.

Exc.: $750   **VGood:** $600   **Good:** $450

STEVENS DIAMOND NO. 43

Single shot; 22 Short, 22 LR; 6-inch, 10-inch barrel; weighs 10 oz. (6-inch barrel), 12 oz. (10-inch barrel); round barrel; octagon breech; plain walnut grips; open or peep rear, globe front sights; spur trigger; nickel-plated finish. Manufactured from 1886 to early 1900s.

Exc.: $250   **VGood:** $175   **Good:** $125

STEVENS GOULD NO. 37

Single shot; 22 Short, 22 LR, 22 WMR, 25 Stevens, 32 Long, 32 Short Colt; tip-down barrel; conventional trigger and guard without spur; peep rear, globe front sight. Manufactured from 1889 to 1903.

Exc.: $800   **VGood:** $600   **Good:** $400

STEVENS LORD NO. 36

Single shot; 22 Short, 22 LR, 22 WMR, 25 Stevens, 32 Short Colt, 38 Long Colt, 44 Russian Centerfire; 10-inch heavy tip-down barrel; weighs 2-3/4 lbs. (10-inch barrel); octagon breech; triggerguard with spur; sporting rear and bead front sights; checkered walnut grips; nickel-plated finish. Manufactured from 1880 to 1911.

Exc.: $850   **VGood:** $700   **Good:** $500

STEVENS NO. 10

Single shot; tip-up action; 22 LR; 8-inch barrel; 11-1/2-inch overall length; target sights; hard rubber stocks; blued finish. Manufactured 1919 to 1933.

Exc.: $300   **VGood:** $225   **Good:** $175

STEVENS NO. 35 OFF-HAND TARGET

Single shot; tip-up action; 22 LR; 6-inch, 8-inch, 10-inch barrel; weighs 27-1/2 oz.; external hammer; triggerguard without spur; target sights; walnut grips; nickel-plated, case-hardened or blued finish. Introduced 1907; discontinued 1939.

Exc.: $300   **VGood:** $250   **Good:** $150

STEVENS NO. 35 AUTOSHOT

Single shot; tip-up action; 410 shotshell; 8-inch, 12-1/4-inch barrel; walnut grips; blued finish. Manufactured from 1929 to 1934. Illegal unless registered with BATF.

Exc.: $300   **VGood:** $250   **Good:** $150

STEVENS TIP-UP NO. 41

Single shot; 22 Short, 30 Short; 3-1/2-inch barrel; weighs 7 oz.; round barrel; octagon breech; open sights; plain walnut grips; nickel-plated finish. Early manufacture with brass frame; later with iron. Manufactured from 1886 to 1916.

Exc.: $225   **VGood:** $175   **Good:** $125

STEYR GB

Semi-automatic; double action; 9mm Para.; 18-shot; 5-1/4-inch barrel; 8-3/8-inch overall length; weighs 53 oz.; post front sight, fixed rear; checkered European walnut stocks; matte finish. Imported from Germany by Gun South, Inc. Introduced 1981; discontinued 1988.

Exc.: $550   **VGood:** $450   **Good:** $300

STEYR MODEL SP

Semi-automatic; double action; 32 ACP; 7-shot; adjustable rear sight, fixed front; checkered black plastic grips; revolver-type trigger; blued finish. Very few made; collector value. Introduced 1957; discontinued 1959.

Exc.: $900   **VGood:** $750   **Good:** $500

STEYR SSP

Semi-automatic; single action; 9mm Para.; 15- or 30-shot magazine; 5-15/16-inch barrel; 12-3/4-inch overall length; weighs 42 oz.; grooved synthetic grips; post elevation-adjustable front sight, open windage-adjustable rear; delayed blowback, rotating barrel operating system; synthetic upper and lower receivers; drop and cross-bolt safeties; rail mount for optics. Imported from Austria by GSI, Inc. Introduced 1993; dropped 1994.

Perf.: $700   **Exc.:** $600   **VGood:** $500

STEYR MANNLICHER MODEL 1901

Semi-automatic; 7.63mm Mannlicher; 5-1/2 inch barrel; 8-3/4-inch overall length; 8-shot; fine checkered wood or hard rubber (rare) grips; marked WAFFENFABRIK STEYR and SYSTEM MANNLICHER on sides.

Exc.: $2400   **VGood:** $1850   **Good:** $1100

STEYR MANNLICHER MODEL 1905

Semi-automatic; 7.63mm Mannlicher; 6-inch barrel; 9-1/2-inch overall length; 10-shot; grooved wood grips; Marked WAFFENFABRIK STEYR and SYSTEM MANNLICHER on sides. Also marked "Md. 1905" on side.

Exc.: $1750   **VGood:** $1100   **Good:** $700

Steyr 1907 (Roth Steyr)

Steyr 1911 (Steyr Hahn)

STI Eagle 5.1

Sturm Ruger Bearcat

Sturm Ruger Super Bearcat

Sturm Ruger Bearcat (Third Issue) New Super Bearcat

Stoeger American Eagle Luger

STI International Duty CT

STEYR 1907 (ROTH STEYR)

Semi-automatic; 8mm Roth Steyr; 5-1/8-inch barrel; 8-13/16-inch overall length; grooved wood grips. Slight premium for Budapest manufacture.

Exc.: $1000   **VGood:** $800   **Good:** $450

STEYR 1911 (STEYR HAHN)

Semi-automatic; 9mm Steyr; 5-1/8-inch barrel; 8-5/8-inch overall length; checkered wood grips.

Exc.: $475   **VGood:** $400   **Good:** $350

STI EAGLE 5.1 PISTOL

Semi-automatic. 9mm Para., 38 Super, 40 S&W, 45 ACP, 10-ACP, 10-shot magazine. Barrel:5, bull. Weight: 34 oz. Length: 8.62 overall. Stocks: Checkered polymer. Sights: Bo-Mar blade front, Bo-Mar fully adjustable rear. Features: Modular frame design; adjustable match trigger; skeletonized hammer; extended grip safety with locator pad; match-grade fit of all parts. Many options available. Introduced 1994.

New: $1400   **Perf.:** $1200   **Exc.:** $1000

STI TRUSIGHT

Chambered for 9mm, .40 S&W, .45 ACP double-stack. Steel frame, GFN grips and 4.15-inch slide/barrel. Dawson fiber optic front sight, adjustable rear sight. LOA 8.6-inch and 36.1 oz. Blue with multiple options. IPSC, USPSA approved.

New: $1875   **Exc.:** $1750   **VGood:** $1350

STI DUTY CT

1911 steel frame single-stack with integral tactical rail and rosewood grips. 5-inch slide/barrel, fixed 2-dot tritium rear sight. LOA 7.75-inch and 36.6 oz. Also available in 4.15-inch commander size. Blue.

New: $1575   **Exc.:** $1450   **VGood:** $1000

STI LEGACY

Chambered for .45 ACP single-stack. 5-inch slide/barrel, LOA 8.5-inch, 38 oz. with adjustable rear sight. Cocobola smooth grips. IDPA, USPSA approved.

New: $1875   **Exc.:** $1750   **VGood:** $1350

STI RANGEMASTER II

Single-stack blued variation of Rangemaster. Chambered for 9mm, .40 S&W, .45 ACP. 5-inch slide/barrel, LOA 8.5-inch, 37 oz.

New: $1295   **Exc.:** $1100   **VGood:** $895

STI GP6

Polymer-framed single/double action pistol with ambidextrous safeties and fized three-dot sight system. Chambered in 9mm Parabellum.

New: $675   **Exc.:** $595   **VGood:** $395

STI SENTINEL PREMIER

Top-of-the-line ISPC and IDPAcompetition 1911 with Dawson Precision/STI "Perfect Impact" style white outline tritium adjustable sights and the STI Tritium competition front; forged steel, government length, standard-width frame; and many other refinements. The Sentinel Premier comes standard with case, owner's manual, and one Wilson Combat ® Elite Tactical magazine.

New: $2295   **Exc.:** $1925   **VGood:** $1375

STOEGER AMERICAN EAGLE LUGER

Semi-automatic; single action; 9mm Para.; 7-shot magazine; 4-inch barrel; 9-5/8-inch overall length; weighs 32 oz.; checkered walnut grips; blade front sight, fixed rear; recreation of the American Eagle Luger pistol in stainless steel; chamber loaded indicator. Made in U.S. From Stoeger Industries. Introduced 1994.

New: $500   **Perf.:** $450   **Exc.:** $400

With matte black finish $789.00

New: $550   **Perf.:** $475   **Exc.:** $400

STOEGER AMERICAN EAGLE LUGER NAVY MODEL

Same general specs as the American Eagle except has 6-inch barrel. Made in U.S. From Stoeger Industries. Introduced 1994.

New: $550   **Perf.:** $475   **Exc.:** $425

STOEGER LUGER

Semi-automatic; 22 LR; 11-shot; 4-1/2-inch, 5-1/2-inch barrel; blade front sight, fixed rear; checkered or smooth wooden grips; blued finish. Based on original Luger design. Introduced 1970; discontinued 1978; all-steel model reintroduced 1980; discontinued 1985.

Exc.: $225   **VGood:** $205   **Good:** $185

STOEGER LUGER TARGET

Same general specs as Stoeger Luger, except target sights; checkered hardwood stocks. Introduced 1975; all-steel model reintroduced 1980; discontinued 1985.

Exc.: $260   **VGood:** $240   **Good:** $205

STURM RUGER BEARCAT (FIRST ISSUE)

Revolver; single action; 22 LR, 22 Long, 22 Short; 6-shot cylinder; 4-inch barrel; 8-7/8-inch overall length; weighs 17 oz.; non-fluted cylinder; fixed Patridge front, square notch rear sights; alloy solid frame; uncheckered walnut grips; blued. Introduced 1958; dropped 1973.

Exc.: $350   **VGood:** $300   **Good:** $250

STURM RUGER BEARCAT (SECOND ISSUE) SUPER BEARCAT

Revolver; single action; 22 LR, 22 Long, 22 Short; improved version of Bearcat except all-steel construction; weighs 22-1/2 oz.; music wire coil springs; non-fluted engraved cylinder. Introduced 1971; dropped 1975.

Exc.: $300   **VGood:** $275   **Good:** $225

STURM RUGER BEARCAT (THIRD ISSUE) NEW SUPER BEARCAT

Revolver; single action; 22 LR/22 WMR; 6-shot cylinder; 4-inch barrel; weighs 23 oz.; 8-7/8-inch overall length; smooth rosewood grips with Ruger medallion; blade front sight, fixed notch rear; reintroduction of the Ruger Super Bearcat with slightly lengthened frame; Ruger patented transfer bar safety system; comes with two cylinders; available in blue or stainless steel. Made in U.S. by Sturm, Ruger & Co. Introduced 1993; still produced.

New: $350   **Perf.:** $300   **Exc.:** $245

Stainless

New: $375   **Perf.:** $325   **Exc.:** $275

Sturm Ruger Blackhawk

Sturm Ruger Bisley

Sturm Ruger Blackhawk
Flat-Top 44 Magnum

Sturm Ruger
Blackhawk
Convertible

Sturm Ruger Fiftieth
Anniversary

Sturm Ruger Redhawk
4-Inch .45 Colt

Sturm Ruger GP-100

STURM RUGER BISLEY

Revolver; single action; 22, 32 H&R Mag., 357, 41 Mag., 44 Mag., 45 Colt; 7-1/2-inch barrel; 13-inch overall length; flat-top frame; low hammer with deeply checkered wide spur; wide, smooth trigger; longer grip frame; unfluted cylinder; roll engraved with Bisley marksman, trophy. Introduced 1985.

New: $425   **Perf.:** $375   **Exc.:** $325

STURM RUGER BISLEY SMALL FRAME

Same specs as Bisley except 22 LR, 32 H&R; 6-1/2-inch barrel; weighs 41 oz.; 11-1/2-inch overall length; American walnut grips; front sight base accepts interchangeable square blades of various heights and fully-adjustable dovetailed rear; large oval trigger guard. Made in U.S. by Sturm, Ruger. Introduced 1985; still produced.

New: $350   **Perf.:** $325   **Exc.:** $225

STURM RUGER BLACKHAWK

Revolver; single action; 357 Mag., 41 Mag., 45 LC; 6-shot; 4-5/8-inch, 6-1/2-inch (357, 41 Mag.) barrel; 12-inch overall length (6-1/2-inch barrel); large frame; checkered hard rubber or uncheckered walnut grips; hooded adjustable rear sight, ramp front; blued. Introduced 1956; dropped 1972.

New: $400   **Perf.:** $350   **Exc.:** $275

STURM RUGER BLACKHAWK CONVERTIBLE

Same specs as standard Blackhawk except interchangeable cylinders for 9mm Para., 357 Mag. or 45 Colt/45 ACP. Introduced 1967; dropped 1985.

Exc.: $425   **VGood:** $375   **Good:** $295

STURM RUGER BLACKHAWK FLAT-TOP

Revolver; single action; 357 Mag.; 6-shot; 4-5/8-inch, 6-1/2-inch, 10-inch barrel; 12-inch overall length (6-1/2-inch barrel); checkered hard rubber or uncheckered walnut grips; click-adjustable rear sight, ramp front; blued. Introduced 1955; dropped 1963.

Exc.: $900	**VGood:** $600	**Good:** $400
6-1/2-inch barrel		
Exc.: $975	**VGood:** $650	**Good:** $475
10-inch barrel		
Exc.: $1500	**VGood:** $1275	**Good:** $800

STURM RUGER BLACKHAWK FLAT-TOP 44 MAGNUM

Same specs as Blackhawk Flat-Top except 44 Mag.; 6-1/2-inch, 7-1/2-inch, 10-inch barrel; 121/8-inch overall length; uncheckered walnut grips; blued. Introduced 1956; dropped 1963.

Exc.: $1675	**VGood:** $1050	**Good:** $775
7-1/2-inch, 10-inch barrel		
Exc.: $1700	**VGood:** $1075	**Good:** $800

STURM RUGER BLACKHAWK NEW MODEL

Revolver; single action; 30 Carbine, 357 Mag./38 Spl., 41 Mag., 45 LC; 6-shot cylinder; 4-5/8-inch, 6-1/2-inch barrel; 7-1/2-inch barrel (30 Carbine, 45 LC); 12-1/2-inch overall length (6-1/2-inch barrel); weighs 42 oz.; new Ruger interlocked mechanism; transfer bar ignition; hardened chrome-moly steel frame; wide trigger music wire springs; independent firing pin; blue, stainless or high-gloss stainless finish. Introduced 1973; still in production. As of 2005

New: $470	**Perf.:** $375	**Exc.:** $325
Stainless finish		
New: $490	**Perf.:** $400	**Exc.:** $230
High-gloss stainless finish		
New: $3510	**Perf.:** $300	**Exc.:** $250

STURM RUGER BLACKHAWK NEW MODEL 357 MAXIMUM

Same specs as Blackhawk New Model except 357 Maximum; 7-1/2-inch, 10-inch bull barrel; 16-7/8-inch overall length (10-1/2-inch barrel). Introduced 1983; dropped 1984.

Exc.: $650   **VGood:** $475   **Good:** $300

STURM RUGER BLACKHAWK NEW MODEL CONVERTIBLE

Same specs as Blackhawk New Model except interchangeable cylinders for 357 Mag./9mm, 44 Mag./44-40, 45 LC/45 ACP; 4-5/8-inch, 6-1/2-inch barrel. Add 10 percent to above pricing.

STURM RUGER FIFTIETH ANNIVERSARY .44 MAGNUM FLATTOP NEW MODEL BLACKHAWK

Six-shot, single-action .44 Magnum (also accepts .44 Special) with 6.5-inch barrel and adjustable rear sight, 47 oz. Recreation of original .44 Flat-Top Blackhawk. Blued with checkered rubber grips. Gold, color-filled rollmark on top of barrel. Introduced 2006.

New: $595   **Exc.:** $515   **VGood:** $395

STURM RUGER GP-100

Revolver; double action; 357 Mag., 38 Spl.; 6-shot cylinder; 3-inch, 4-inch, 6-inch standard or heavy barrel; weighs 40 oz.; fully-adjustable rear sight, interchangeable grip; Ruger cushioned grip with Goncalo Alves inserts; new design action, frame; full-length ejector shroud; satin blue finish or stainless steel. Introduced 1986; still in production.

New: $450   **Perf.:** $400   **Exc.:** $350

Sturm Ruger Hawkeye

Sturm Ruger Police Service-Six Model 107

Sturm Ruger Redhawk

Sturm Ruger SP101

Sturm Ruger Police Service-Six Model 708

STURM RUGER HAWKEYE

Single shot; single action; 256 Mag.; 8-1/2-inch barrel; 14-1/2-inch overall length; standard frame with cylinder replaced with rotating breech block; uncheckered walnut grips; click-adjustable rear sight, ramp front; barrel drilled, tapped for scope mounts; blued. Introduced 1963; dropped 1964.

Exc.: $1600   **VGood:** $1100   **Good:** $900

STURM RUGER POLICE SERVICE-SIX MODEL 107

Revolver; double action; 357 Mag.; 6-shot cylinder; 2-3/4-inch, 4-inch, 6-inch barrel; 6-inch barrel dropped in 1973; 9-1/4-inch overall length (4-inch barrel); integral ejector rod shroud and sight rib; fixed sights; semi-target-type checkered walnut grips; blued. Introduced 1972; dropped 1987.

Exc.: $325   **VGood:** $250   **Good:** $195

STURM RUGER POLICE SERVICE-SIX MODEL 108

Same specs as Model 107 except 38 Spl.; 4-inch barrel. Introduced 1972; dropped 1987.

Exc.: $275   **VGood:** $200   **Good:** $150

STURM RUGER POLICE SERVICE-SIX MODEL 109

Same specs as Model 107 except 9mm Para.; 4-inch barrel. Introduced 1976; dropped 1984.

Exc.: $500   **VGood:** $400   **Good:** $295

STURM RUGER POLICE SERVICE-SIX MODEL 707

Same specs as Model 107 except 357 Mag.; stainless steel construction; 4-inch standard or heavy barrel. Introduced 1973; dropped 1987.

Exc.: $300   **VGood:** $285   **Good:** $265

STURM RUGER POLICE SERVICE-SIX MODEL 708

Same specs as Model 107 except 38 Spl.; stainless steel construction; 4-inch standard or heavy barrel; square butt grips. Introduced 1973; dropped 1987.

Exc.: $275   **VGood:** $200   **Good:** $150

STURM RUGER REDHAWK

Revolver; double action, 357 Mag., 41 Mag., 44 Mag.; 6-shot; 5-1/2-inch, 7-1/2-inch barrel; 5-1/2-inch barrel added 1984; 13-inch overall length (7-1/2-inch barrel); weighs 54 oz.; stainless steel brushed satin or blued finish; Patridge-type front sight, fully-adjustable rear; square-butt Goncalo Alves grips. Introduced 1979; still in production. Add 15 percent for .357, 20 percent for .41. Four-inch barrel introduced 2007. .45 Colt introduced 2008.

Blue		
New: $500	**Perf.:** $375	**Exc.:** $300
Stainless		
New: $525	**Perf.:** $400	**Exc.:** $350

STURM RUGER REDHAWK 4-INCH .45 COLT

Similar to original stainless Redhawk but in .45 Colt only and with a 4-inch barrel. Hogue molded grips.

New: $600   **Perf.:** $525   **Exc.:** $425

STURM RUGER SECURITY-SIX MODEL 117

Revolver; double action; 357 Mag.; 6-shot cylinder; 2 -/4-inch, 4-inch, 6-inch barrel; 9-1/4-inch overall length (4-inch barrel); hand-checkered semi-target walnut grips; adjustable rear sight, Patridge type front on ramp; music wire coil springs throughout. Introduced 1974; dropped 1985.

Exc.: $300   **VGood:** $285   **Good:** $265

STURM RUGER SECURITY-SIX MODEL 717

Same specs as Model 117 except 357 Mag.; all metal parts except sights of stainless steel; black alloy sights for visibility. Introduced 1974; dropped 1985.

Exc.: $300   **VGood:** $285   **Good:** $265

STURM RUGER SINGLE-SIX

Revolver; single action; 22 LR, 22 WMR; 6-shot; 4-5/8-inch, 5-1/2-inch, 6-1/2-inch, 9-1/2-inch barrel; 10-inch overall length (4-inch barrel); checkered hard rubber grips on early production, uncheckered walnut on later versions; windage-adjustable rear sight; blued. Introduced 1953; dropped 1972.

Exc.: $300   **VGood:** $285   **Good:** $265

STURM RUGER SINGLE-SIX CONVERTIBLE

Same general specs as standard Single-Six except interchangeable cylinders, 22 LR, Long, Short/22 WRM; 5-1/2-inch, 6-1/2-inch, 91/2-inch barrel. Introduced 1962; dropped 1972.

Exc.: $300   **VGood:** $285   **Good:** $265

STURM RUGER SUPER SINGLE SIX

Same specs as Single Six except Ruger "Interlocked" mechanism, transfer bar ignition; gate-controlled loading; hardened chrome-moly steel frame; wide trigger; music wire springs; independent firing pin. Introduced 1973; still in production.

New: $325   **Perf.:** $295   **Exc.:** $225

STURM RUGER SINGLE SIX SSM

Same specs as Super Single Six except 32 H&R Mag. Introduced 1985; still in production.

New: $350   **Perf.:** $300   **Exc.:** $250

STURM RUGER SP101

Revolver; double action; 22 LR, 32 H&R Mag., 9mm Para., 38 Spl. +P, 357 Mag.; 6-shot (22 LR, 32 H&R Mag.), 5-shot (9mm, 38 Spl. +P, 357 Mag.); 2-1/4-inch, 3-1/16-inch, 4-inch barrel; weighs 25 oz. (2-1/4-inch), 27 oz. (3-1/16-inch); adjustable sights (22, 32), fixed (others); Ruger Santoprene cushioned grips with Xenoy inserts; incorporates improvements and features found in the GP-100 revolvers into a compact, small frame, double-action revolver; full-length ejector shroud; stainless steel only; available with high-polish finish. Introduced 1988; still in production. .327 Federal added in 2008.

New: $375   **Perf.:** $275   **Exc.:** $200

STURM RUGER SP101 DOUBLE-ACTION-ONLY REVOLVER

Similar to the standard SP101 except is double-action-only with no single-action sear notch. Has spurless hammer for snag-free handling, floating firing pin and Ruger's patented transfer bar safety system. Available with 2-1/4-inch barrel in 38 Special +P and 357 Magnum only. Weighs 25-1/2 oz., overall length 7.06-inch. Natural brushed satin or high-polish stainless steel. Introduced 1993.

New: $395   **Perf.:** $325   **Exc.:** $300

Sturm Ruger Super Blackhawk Hunter

Sturm Ruger Redhawk

Sturm Ruger Bisley Vaquero

Sturm Ruger Vaquero

Sturm Ruger 50th Anniversary Matched Set

Sturm Ruger 22/45 KP4 Mark II

STURM RUGER SUPER BLACKHAWK

Revolver; 44 Mag.; 5-1/2-inch, 7-1/2-inch, 10-1/2-inch barrel; 13-3/8-inch overall length (7-1/2-inch barrel); weighs 48 oz.; 1/8-inch ramp front, micro-click fully-adjustable rear; American walnut grips; interlock mechanism; non-fluted cylinder; steel grip and cylinder frame; square back trigger guard; wide serrated trigger; wide spur hammer.

New: $450   **Perf.:** $400   **Exc.:** $350

Stainless

New: $500   **Perf.:** $450   **Exc.:** $400

STURM RUGER BLACKHAWK HUNTER

Same specs as Super Blackhawk except stainless finish; 7-1/2-inch; scope rings. Introduced 1992; still in prduction.

New: $450   **Perf.:** $400   **Exc.:** $325

STURM RUGER SUPER REDHAWK

Revolver; double action; 44 Mag.; 6-shot; 7-1/2-inch, 9-1/2-inch barrel; 13-inch overall length (7-1/2-inch barrel); weighs 54 oz.; heavy extended frame with Ruger Integral Scope Mounting System; wide topstrap; ramp front with interchangeable sight blades, adjustable rear; Santoprene grips with Goncalo Alves panels; satin polished stainless steel finish. Introduced 1987; still in production.

New: $575   **Perf.:** $500   **Exc.:** $400

STURM RUGER SUPER REDHAWK ALASKAN

Snubby version of Super Redhawk with 2-1/2-inch barrel.. Chambered in .480 Ruger (discontinued), .454 Casual/.45 Colt, and .44 Magnum.

New: $650   **Perf.:** $525   **Exc.:** $450

STURM RUGER VAQUERO

Revolver; single action; 44-40, 44 Mag., 45 Colt; 6-shot; 4-5/8-inch, 5-1/2-inch, 7-1/2-inch barrel; 13-3/8-inch overall length (7-1/2-inch barrel); weighs 41 oz.; blade front, fixed notch rear sight; transfer bar safety system; loading gate interlock; color case-hardened frame on blue model; blue or high-polish stainless finish. Introduced 1993; still in production. with new, smaller frame.

New: $450   **Perf.:** $425   **Exc.:** $375

STURM RUGER BISLEY VAQUERO

Similar to the Vaquero except has Bisley-style hammer, grip and trigger and is available in 44 Magnum and 45 Colt only, with 5-1/2-inch barrel. Has smooth rosewood grips with Ruger medallion. Introduced 1997. Discontinued.

Color case-hardened frame, blue grip frame, barrel and cylinder

New: $500   **Perf.:** $450   **Exc.:** $375

High-gloss stainless steel

New: $525   **Perf.:** $475   **Exc.:** $400

STURM RUGER "COWBOY PAIR"

Matched pair of engraved and consecutively serial-numbered New Vaquero revolvers in .45 Colt. Includes lined wood collector case. Production limited to 500 sets.

New: $3700   **Exc.:** $2000   **VGood:** $995

STURM RUGER 50TH ANNIVERSARY MATCHED SET .357 AND .44 MAGNUM

Matched pair of Ruger New Blackhawks, one in .44 and the other in .357, commemorating 50th anniversary of Ruger Blackhawk revolver. Gold-filled rollmarked 6-1/2" and 4-5/8" barrels, respectively. Includes presentation case. Limited production.

New: $1250   **Exc.:** $975   **VGood:** $575

STURM RUGER 22/45 KP4 MARK II

Semi-automatic; single action; 22 LR; 10-shot magazine; 4-3/4-inch stainless steel barrel; 8-7/8-inch overall length; weighs 28 oz.; Zytel grip frame matches angle and magazine latch of Model 1911 45 ACP pistol; Patridge front sight, square notch windage-adjustable rear; brushed stainless steel. Introduced 1992; still produced.

New: $345   **Perf.:** $315   **Exc.:** $275

STURM RUGER 22/45 KP512 MARK II

Same specs as P4 except 5-1/2-inch stainless steel bull barrel; weighs 35 oz. Made in U.S. by Sturm, Ruger & Company. Introduced 1992; still produced

New: $345   **Perf.:** $315   **Exc.:** $275

STURM RUGER 22/45 P512 BULL BARREL MARK II

Same specs as P4 except 5-1/2-inch steel bull barrel; 9-5/8-inch overall length; weighs 36 oz.; fully-adjustable rear sight; brushed satin blue finish. Introduced 1995; still produced.

New: $345   **Perf.:** $315   **Exc.:** $275

STURM RUGER MARK I STANDARD MODEL

Semi-automatic; 22 LR only; 9-shot magazine 4-3/4-inch, 6-inch barrel (4-3/4-inch barrel), 8-3/4-inch overall length (6-inch barrel); checkered hard rubber grips walnut optional; windage-adjustable square-notch rear, fixed wide blade front sight; blued. Introduced 1949; dropped 1982 in favor of Mark II. Until 1951 featured red eagle insignia in grips; changed to black upon death of Alex Sturm. This type has considerable collector value.

Exc.: $250   **VGood:** $225   **Good:** $195

Red eagle model (pre-1951)

Exc.: $650   **VGood:** $300   **Good:** $250

Sturm Ruger 22/45 KP512 Mark II

Sturm Ruger Mark II Standard Model

Sturm Ruger MK-4B Compact

Sturm Ruger Mark I Standard Model

Sturm Ruger Cowboy Pair

Sturm Ruger Mark II Government Model Target

Sturm Ruger 22/45 Mark III Hunter

STURM RUGER MARK I TARGET MODEL

Same specs as Standard Model except 5-1/2-inch heavy barrel, 5-3/4-inch tapered barrel, 6-7/8-inch heavy tapered barrel; adjustable rear, target front sight. Introduced 1951; dropped 1982.

New: $345　　**Perf.: $315**　　**Exc.: $275**

STURM RUGER MARK II STANDARD MODEL

Semi-automatic; 22 LR; 10-shot magazine; 4-3/4-inch, 6-inch barrel; checkered hard rubber stocks; fixed blade front sight, square-notch windage-adjustable rear; new bolt hold-open device, magazine catch; new receiver contours; stainless steel or blued. Introduced 1982; still in production.

Exc.: $175　　**VGood: $150**　　**Good: $135**

Stainless steel finish

Exc.: $225　　**VGood: $200**　　**Good: $175**

STURM RUGER MARK II BULL BARREL

Same specs as standard model except 5-1/2-inch, 10-inch heavy barrel. Introduced 1982; still in production.

Perf.: $275　　**Exc.: $225**　　**VGood: $200**

Stainless finish

Exc.: $300　　**VGood: $275**　　**Good: $225**

STURM RUGER MARK II GOVERNMENT MODEL TARGET

Same specs as Mark II Standard except 6-7/8-inch bull barrel; adjustable rear sight; black plastic grips; roll-stamped "Government Target Model" on right side of receiver; blued finish. Introduced 1987; still in production.

New: $300　　**Perf.: $250**　　**Exc.: $200**

STURM RUGER MARK II GOVERNMENT MODEL STAINLESS

Same specs as Model Target except 6-7/8-inch slab-sided barrel; receiver drilled, tapped for Ruger scope base adaptor; checkered walnut grip panels; right-hand thumb rest; blued open sights. Marketed with 1-inch stainless scope rings, integral base. Introduced 1991; still in production.

New: $350　　**Perf.: $300**　　**Exc.: $250**

STURM RUGER MARK II TARGET

Same specs as standard model except 5-1/4-inch, 6-7/8-inch barrel; 11-1/8-inch overall length; weighs 42 oz.; .125-inch blade front sight, adjustable micro-click rear; sight radius 9-3/8-inch. Introduced 1982; still in production.

New: $250　　**Perf.: $200**　　**Exc.: $165**

Stainless steel finish

New: $300　　**Perf.: $250**　　**Exc.: $200**

STURM RUGER MK-4B COMPACT PISTOL

Similar to the Mark II Standard pistol except has 4-inch bull barrel, Patridge-type front sight, fully adjustable rear, and smooth laminated hardwood thumbrest stocks. Weighs 38 oz., overall length of 8-3/16-inch. Comes with extra magazine, plastic case, lock. Introduced 1996.

New: $300　　**Perf.: $250**　　**Exc.: $200**

STURM RUGER MARK III STANDARD PISTOL

Introduced in 2005 this .22 caliber pistol is fitted with a 4.75" or 6" barrel. Fixed rear sight. Blued finish. Magazine capacity is 10 rounds. Black checkered grips. Weight is about 35 oz. depending on barrel length.

New: $300　　**Perf.: $250**　　**Exc.: $200**

STURM RUGER MARK III HUNTER

This .22 caliber pistol is fitted with a 6.88" target crowned fluted stainless steel barrel. Adjustable rear sight with Hi-Viz front sight. Checkered Cocobolo grips. Drilled and tapped for scope mount. Supplied with green case, scope base adapter, and 6 interchangeable LitePipes for front sight. Weight is about 41 oz. Introduced in 2005. Add 50 percent for Crimson Trace lasergrips (limited edition for 2008).

New: $350　　**Perf.: $275**　　**Exc.: $225**

STURM RUGER MARK III COMPETITION

This .22 caliber model features a 6.88" flat sided heavy barrel with adjustable rear sight and Patridge front sight. Stainless steel finish. Checkered wood grips. Weight is about 45 oz. Introduced in 2005.

New: $425　　**Perf.: $350**　　**Exc.: $295**

STURM RUGER MARK III 512 PISTOL

This .22 LR pistol has a 5.5" bull barrel and adjustable rear sight. Steel frame is blued. Checkered black synthetic grips. Weaver-style scope base adapter included. Magazine capacity is 10 rounds. Weight is about 41 oz.

New: $375　　**Perf.: $225**　　**Exc.: $200**

STURM RUGER 22/45 MARK III HUNTER

Similar to 22/45 .22 pistol but with Mark III-style improvements. 6-7/8" or 4-1/2" fluted barrel, HiViz front sight with six interchangeable inserts. Blued or stainless finish. Pricing is for stainless model. Introduced in 2007.

New: $375　　**Perf.: $225**　　**Exc.: $200**

STURM RUGER 22/45 MARK III HUNTER

Similar to 22/45 .22 pistol but with Mark III-style improvements. 6-7/8" or 4-1/2" fluted barrel, HI-VIZ front sight with six interchangeable inserts. Blued or stainless finish. Pricing is for stainless model.

New: $435　　**Exc.: $395**　　**VGood: $300**

Sturm Ruger
Charger

Sturm Ruger P85 Mark II

Sturm Ruger P89

Sturm Ruger P89
Decocker Model

Sturm Ruger P93
Compact
Decocker Model

Sturm Ruger P90
Decocker Model

Sturm Ruger P94

STURM RUGER CHARGER

Introduced in 2008. A 10-inch-barrel pistol version of the 10/22 .22 LR rifle. Black matte finish, black laminated stock, bipod, and Weaver-style mounts. Include one 10-round magazine.

New: $350   **Perf.:** $300   **Exc.:** $250

STURM RUGER P85 MARK II

Semi-automatic; double action, DAO; 9mm Para.; 15-shot magazine; 4-1/2-inch barrel; 7-13/16-inch overall length; weighs 32 oz.; windage-adjustable square-notch rear sight, square post front; ambidextrous slide-mounted safety levers; 4140 chrome-moly steel slide; aluminum alloy frame; grooved Xenoy composition stocks; ambidextrous magazine release; blue or stainless finish. Decocker version also available. Introduced 1986; dropped 1992.

New: $325   **Perf.:** $300   **Exc.:** $250

Stainless finish

New: $375   **Perf.:** $325   **Exc.:** $275

STURM RUGER P89

Semi-automatic; double action; 9mm Para., 10-shot magazine. Barrel: 4.50-inch. Weight: 32 oz. Length: 7.84-inch overall. Stocks: Grooved black Xenoy composition. Sights: Square post front, square notch rear adjustable for windage, both with white dot inserts. Features: Double action with ambidextrous slide-mounted safety. Slide is 4140 chrome-moly steel or 400-series stainless steel, frame is a lightweight aluminum alloy. Ambidextrous magazine release. Blue or stainless steel. Introduced 1986; stainless introduced 1990.

New: $325   **Perf.:** $300   **Exc.:** $250

Stainless finish

New: $375   **Perf.:** $325   **Exc.:** $275

STURM RUGER P89D DECOCKER

Similar to the standard P89 except has ambidextrous decocking levers in place of the regular slide-mounted safety. The decocking levers move the firing pin inside the slide where the hammer can not reach it, while simultaneously blocking the firing pin from forward movement-allows shooter to decock a cocked pistol without manipulating the trigger. Conventional thumb decocking procedures

are therefore unnecessary. Blue or stainless steel. Introduced 1990.

New: $325   **Perf.:** $300   **Exc.:** $250

Stainless finish

New: $375   **Perf.:** $325   **Exc.:** $275

STURM RUGER P89/DAO

Semi-automatic; double action, double-action-only; 9mm Para.; 15-shot magazine; 4-1/2-inch barrel; 7-13/16-inch overall length; weighs 32 oz.; improved version of P85 Mark II; windage-adjustable square-notch rear sight, square post front; internal safety; bobbed, spurless hammer; gripping grooves on rear of slide; stainless steel construction. Decocker model also available at no extra cost; blue or stainless (DAO) finish. Marketed with plastic case, extra magazine, loading tool. Introduced 1991; still in production.

New: $325   **Perf.:** $300   **Exc.:** $250

Stainless

New: $400   **Perf.:** $350   **Exc.:** $300

STURM RUGER P90

Semi-automatic; double action; 45 ACP; 7-shot magazine; 4-1/2-inch barrel; 7-15/16-inch overall length; weighs 33-1/2 oz.; aluminum frame; stainless steel slide; ambidextrous slide-mounted safety levers; square post front, square notch windage-adjustable rear; stainless steel only. Decocker model also available at no extra cost. Introduced 1991; still in production.

New: $400   **Perf.:** $350   **Exc.:** $300

STURM RUGER P91 DC DECOCKER

Semi-automatic; double action, double-action-only; 40 S&W; 11-shot magazine; 4-1/2-inch barrel; 7-15/16-inch overall length; weighs 33 oz.; ambidextrous slide-mounted safety levers; square post front, windage-adjustable square notch rear with white dot inserts; grooved black Xenoy composition grips; stainless finish. Marketed with plastic case, extra magazine, loading tool. Introduced 1991; dropped 1994.

New: $400   **Perf.:** $350   **Exc.:** $300

STURM RUGER P93 COMPACT

Semi-automatic; double action; 9mm Para.; 10-shot magazine; 3-15/16-inch barrel; 7 5/16-inch overall length; weighs 31 oz.; grooved black Xenoy composition grips; square post front sight, square notch windage-adjustable rear with white dot inserts; forward third of the slide tapered and polished to the muzzle; front of the slide crowned with a convex curve; seven finger grooves on slide; 400-series stainless steel slide; lightweight alloy frame. Available as decocker-only or double-action-only. Introduced 1993; still produced.

New: $425   **Perf.:** $375   **Exc.:** $325

STURM RUGER P94

Semi-automatic; double-action-only, decock only, or manual safety; 9mm Para., 40 S&W; 10-shot magazine; 4-1/4-inch barrel; 7-1/2-inch overall length; weighs 33 oz.; grooved Xenoy grips; square post front sight, windage-adjustable rear; three-dot system; slide gripping grooves roll over top of slide; ambidextrous safety-levers; ambidextrous decocking levers; matte finish stainless slide and barrel, alloy frame; frame size between full-size P-Series and compact P93. Introduced 1994; still produced.

New: $350   **Perf.:** $300   **Exc.:** $275

STURM RUGER P94L

Same specs as the KP94 except laser sight mounts in housing cast integrally with frame; Allen-head screws control windage and elevation adjustments. Made in U.S. by Sturm, Ruger. Introduced 1994; still produced for law enforcement only.

Sundance Model BOA

Sturm Ruger LCP

Sturm Ruger P95

Super Six Golden Bison

Sundance Laser 25

Sturm Ruger SR9

Sundance Point Blank

STURM RUGER KP94

Sized midway between the full-size P-Series and the compact P93. Has 4.25-inch barrel, 7.5-inch overall length and weighs about 33 oz. KP94 is manual safety model; KP94DAO is double-action-only (both 9mm Para., 10-shot magazine); KP94D is decocker-only in 40-caliber with 10-shot magazine. Slide gripping grooves roll over top of slide. KP94 has ambidextrous safety-levers; KP94DAO has no external safety, full-cock hammer position or decocking lever; KP94D has ambidextrous decocking levers. Matte finish stainless slide, barrel, alloy frame. Also available in blue. Introduced 1994.

New: $450   **Perf.:** $375   **Exc.:** $275

STURM RUGER P95 SEMI-AUTO PISTOL

Semi-automatic; double action; 9mm Para., 10-shot magazine. Barrel: 3.9-inch. Weight: 27 oz. Length: 7.3-inch overall. Stocks: Grooved; integral with frame. Sights: Blade front, rear drift adjustable for windage; three-dot system. Features: Molded polymer grip frame, stainless steel or chrome-moly slide. Suitable for +P+ ammunition. Decocker or DAO. Introduced 1996.

New: $325   **Perf.:** $300   **Exc.:** $250

Stainless finish

New: $350   **Perf.:** $325   **Exc.:** $275

STURM RUGER SR9

Introduced in 2008. Ruger's first striker-fired semi-auto pistol. Chambered in 9mm Parabellum. Double-action only with 4.14-inch barrel, 17+1 capacity. Available in three cofigurations: stainless steel slide with matte black frame; blackened stainless slide with matte black frame; and blackened slide with matte black frame. Note: Ruger re all early-production SR9 pistols with a "330" number prefix because of a potential safety issue.

New: $575   **Perf.:** $500   **Exc.:** $425

STURM RUGER LCP (LIGHTWEIGHT COMPACT PISTOL)

Introduced in 2008. Ruger's first true pocket pistol. Chambered in .380 (6+1 capacity) with a 2.75-inchc barrel. Double action only. Glass-filled nylon frame with steel barrel. Black matte finish.

New: $430   **Perf.:** $350   **Exc.:** $295

SUNDANCE MODEL A-25

Semi-automatic; 25 ACP; 7-shot; 2-1/2-inch barrel; 4-7/8-inch overall length; weighs 16 oz.; fixed sights; grooved black plastic or smooth simulated pearl stocks; rotary safety blocks rear; bright chrome or black Teflon finish. Introduced 1989.

New: $60   **Perf.:** $50   **Exc.:** $40

SUNDANCE MODEL BOA

Semi-automatic; 25 ACP; 7-shot; 2-1/2-inch barrel; 4-7/8-inch overall length; weighs 16 oz.; fixed sights; grooved ABS or simulated pearl grips; patented grip safety; manual rotary safety; button magazine release; bright chrome or black Teflon finish. Introduced 1991.

New: $75   **Perf.:** $60   **Exc.:** $50

SUNDANCE LASER 25

Semi-automatic; 25 ACP, 7-shot magazine. Barrel: 2-1/2-inch. Weight: 18 oz. Length: 4-7/8-inch overall. Stocks: Grooved black ABS. Sights: Class IIIa laser, 670 NM, 5mW, and fixed open. Features: Factory installed and sighted laser sight activated by squeezing the grip safety; manual rotary safety; button magazine release. Bright chrome or black finish. Introduced 1995.

New: $175   **Perf.:** $150   **Exc.:** $135

SUNDANCE POINT BLANK

Derringer; two-shot; 22 LR; 3-inch barrel; 4-5/8-inch overall length; weighs 8 oz.; grooved composition grips; blade front sight, fixed notch rear; double action trigger; push-bar safety; automatic chamber selection; fully enclosed hammer; matte black finish. Made in U.S. by Sundance Industries. Introduced 1994. Kind of a clone of the old High Standard derringer.

New: $75   **Perf.:** $60   **Exc.:** $50

SUPER SIX GOLDEN BISON

Revolver; single action; 45-70; 6-shot; 8-inch, 10-1/2-inch octagon barrel; 15-inch overall length (8-inch barrel); weighs 92 oz.; adjustable Millett rear sight, blaze orange blade on ramp front; walnut grips; manganese bronze used in cylinder frame, grip frame; coil springs; half-cock, cross-bolt traveling safeties; antique brown or blued finish. Marketed in fitted walnut presentation case. Discontinued 1992.

Perf.: $1500   **Exc.:** $1300   **VGood:** $1000

Tanarmi Model TA 76

Taurus Model 65

SUPER-SIX LTD. BISON BULL
Massive single-action .45-70 revolver with blued carbon steel (Bison Bull) or engraved molybdenum bronze (Golden Bison Bull) frame. Adjustable sights, 10.5" barrel, 17.5" overall length, weight 6 lbs. Value shown is for blued version. Add 350 percent for engraved version.

New: $995   **Exc.:** $800   **VGood:** $675

TANARMI MODEL BTA 90
Semi-automatic; double action; 9mm Para.; 12-shot; 3-1/2-inch barrel; weighs 30 oz.; blade front sight, white outline rear; checkered neoprene stocks; blued finish. Imported from Italy by Excam. Introduced 1987; discontinued 1990.

Perf.: $350   **Exc.:** $300   **VGood:** $250

Matte chrome finish

Perf.: $375   **Exc.:** $325   **VGood:** $275

TANARMI MODEL TA 22
Revolver; single action; 22 Short, 22 LR, 22 LR/22 WMR combo; 6-shot; 4-3/4-inch barrel; 10-inch overall length; blade front sight, drift-adjustable rear; checkered nylon grips, walnut optional; manual hammer-block safety frame; blued finish. Imported from Italy by Excam. Introduced 1978; discontinued 1991.

Perf.: $75   **Exc.:** $65   **VGood:** $50

TANARMI MODEL TA 38 OVER/UNDER DERRINGER
Single shot; tip-up action; 38 Spl.; 3-inch barrel; 4-3/4-inch overall length; weighs 14 oz.; fixed sights; checkered white nylon stocks; blued finish. Assembled in U.S. by Excam. Discontinued 1988.

Exc.: $75   **VGood:** $60   **Good:** $50

TANARMI MODEL TA 41
Semi-automatic; double action; 41 AE; 11-shot; 4-3/4-inch barrel; combat sights; black neoprene grips; matte blue finish. Imported from Italy by Excam; discontinued 1990.

Exc.: $400   **VGood:** $350   **Good:** $275

Matte chrome finish

Exc.: $425   **VGood:** $375   **Good:** $275

TANARMI MODEL TA 41 SS
Same general specs as Model TA 41 except 5-inch compensated barrel; competition sights; blue/chrome finish. Introduced 1989; discontinued 1990.

Exc.: $450   **VGood:** $400   **Good:** $350

TANARMI MODEL TA 76
Revolver; single action; 22 LR, 22 LR/22 WMR combo; 6-shot; 4-3/4-inch barrel; 10-inch overall length; weighs 32 oz.; adjustable rear sight, blade front; uncheckered walnut stocks; color case-hardened frame; brass backstrap, trigger guard; manual hammer-block safety; blued finish. Imported from Italy by Excam. Introduced 1987; discontinued 1991.

Exc.: $65   **VGood:** $50   **Good:** $40

TANARMI MODEL TA 90
Semi-automatic; double action; 9mm Para.; 15-shot; 4-3/4-inch barrel; 8-1/4-inch overall length; weighs 38 oz.; blade front sight, white-outline rear; checkered neoprene stocks; chromed barrel, trigger; extended slide release lever; blued finish. Imported from Italy by Excam. Introduced 1987; discontinued 1990.

Perf.: $350   **Exc.:** $295   **VGood:** $200

TANARMI MODEL TA 90 SS
Same specs as Model TA 90 except 5-inch compensated barrel; competition sights; blue/chrome finish. Imported from Italy by Excam. Introduced 1989; discontinued 1990.

Perf.: $425   **Exc.:** $375   **VGood:** $325

TARGA MODEL GT 22
Semi-automatic; single action; 22 LR; 10-shot; 3-7/8-inch barrel; weighs 26 oz.; blade ramp front sight, windage-adjustable rear; checkered walnut stocks; finger-rest magazine; steel frame; blued finish. Imported from Italy by Excam. Discontinued 1990.

Perf.: $150   **Exc.:** $125   **VGood:** $110

Chrome finish

Perf.: $165   **Exc.:** $135   **VGood:** $115

TARGA MODEL GT 22 TARGET
Same specs as Model GT 22 except 6-inch barrel; 12-shot; weighs 30 oz. Introduced 1988; discontinued 1990.

Perf.: $175   **Exc.:** $135   **VGood:** $125

TARGA MODEL GT 26
Semi-automatic; single action; 25 ACP; 6-shot; 2-1/2-inch barrel; weighs 13 oz.; fixed sights; wooden grips; blued finish. Imported from Italy by Excam. Discontinued 1990.

Exc.: $50   **VGood:** $40   **Good:** $30

(GT 26S) With steel frame

Exc.: $85   **VGood:** $65   **Good:** $50

TARGA MODEL GT 27
Semi-automatic; single action; 25 ACP; 6-shot; 2-1/2-inch barrel; 4-5/8-inch overall length; fixed sights; checkered nylon stocks; external hammer with half-cock feature; safety lever takedown; blued finish. Imported from Italy by Excam. Introduced 1977; discontinued 1990.

Exc.: $65   **VGood:** $50   **Good:** $40

TARGA MODEL GT 32
Semi-automatic; single action; 32 ACP; 7-shot; 3-7/8-inch barrel; 7-3/8-inch overall length; weighs 26 oz.; windage-adjustable rear sight, blade front; optional checkered nylon thumbrest or walnut stocks; external hammer; blued finish. Imported from Italy by Excam. Introduced 1977; discontinued 1990.

Exc.: $135   **VGood:** $110   **Good:** $100

TARGA MODEL GT 32 XE
Same general specs as Model GT 32 except 12-shot; blue finish. Introduced 1980; discontinued 1985.

Exc.: $175   **VGood:** $150   **Good:** $125

TARGA MODEL GT 380
Semi-automatic; single action; 380 ACP; 6-shot; 3-7/8-inch barrel; weighs 26 oz.; windage-adjustable rear sight, blade front; optional checkered nylon thumbrest or walnut stocks; blued finish. Introduced 1977; discontinued 1990.

Blue or chrome finish

Perf.: $150   **Exc.:** $135   **VGood:** $110

Light alloy frame

Perf.: $125   **Exc.:** $100   **VGood:** $85

TARGA MODEL GT 380 XE
Same specs as Model GT 380 except 12-shot; blue finish. Introduced 1980; discontinued 1990.

Perf.: $175   **Exc.:** $150   **VGood:** $125

TAURUS MODEL 44
Revolver; double action; 44 Mag.; 6-shot cylinder; 4-inch, 6-1/2-inch, 8-3/8-inch barrel; weighs 44-3/4-inch oz. (4-inch barrel); checkered Brazilian hardwood grips; serrated ramp front sight, micro-click fully-adjustable rear; heavy solid rib (4-inch), vent rib (6-1/2-inch, 8-3/8-inch barrel); compensated barrel; blued model with color case-hardened hammer and trigger. Imported by Taurus International. Introduced 1994; still in production.

Blue finish, 4-inch barrel

New: $375   **Perf.:** $325   **Exc.:** $275

Blue finish, 6-1/2-inch or 8-3/8-inch barrel

New: $400   **Perf.:** $350   **Exc.:** $325

Stainless steel, 4-inch barrel

New: $450   **Perf.:** $400   **Exc.:** $350

Stainless steel, 6-1/2-inch or 8-3/8-inch barrel

New: $475   **Perf.:** $425   **Exc.:** $375

TAURUS MODEL 65
Revolver; double action; 357 Mag.; 6-shot; 2-1/2-inch, 4-inch barrel; weighs 34 oz.; fixed sights; round butt grip; checkered wood grips; blue, satin nickel or stainless steel finish. Introduced 1978; still imported.

New: $225   **Perf.:** $185   **Exc.:** $150

Satin nickel finish

New: $250   **Perf.:** $200   **Exc.:** $175

Stainless steel

New: $275   **Perf.:** $235   **Exc.:** $200

TAURUS MODEL 66
Revolver; double action; 357 Mag.; 6-shot; 2-1/2-inch, 4-inch, 6-inch barrel; weighs 35 oz. (4-inch barrel); serrated ramp front sight, micro-click fully-adjustable rear; checkered wood grips; wide target hammer spur; floating firing pin; heavy barrel; shrouded ejector rod; blue, satin nickel or stainless steel finish. Introduced 1978; still imported.

New: $275   **Perf.:** $225   **Exc.:** $200

Stainless steel

New: $325   **Perf.:** $275   **Exc.:** $225

TAURUS MODEL 73 SPORT
Revolver; double action; 32 S&W Long; 6-shot; 3-inch heavy barrel; 8-1/4-inch overall length; weighs 20 oz.; target-type wood grips; ramp front sight,

Taurus Model 73 Sport

Taurus Model 74 Sport

Taurus Model 66

Taurus Model 80

Taurus Model 82

Taurus Model 85

Taurus Model 83

Taurus Model 85CH

notch rear; blue or satin nickel finish. Introduced 1979; discontinued 1992.

Perf.: $175   **Exc.:** $150   **VGood:** $125

Satin nickel finish

Perf.: $200   **Exc.:** $175   **VGood:** $150

TAURUS MODEL 74 SPORT
Revolver; double action; 32 S&W Long; 6-shot; 3-inch barrel; 8-1/4-inch overall length; adjustable rear sight, ramp front; hand-checkered walnut stocks; blued finish. Introduced 1971; discontinued 1978.

Exc.: $135   **VGood:** $110   **Good:** $100

Nickel finish

Exc.: $150   **VGood:** $125   **Good:** $110

TAURUS MODEL 76
Revolver; double action; 32 H&R Mag.; 6-shot; 6-inch heavy barrel with solid rib; weighs 34 oz.; Patridge-type front sight, fully-adjustable micro-click rear; checkered Brazilian hardwood grips; adjustable trigger; target hammer; blued finish. Introduced 1991; dropped 1994.

New: $225   **Perf.:** $185   **Exc.:** $135

TAURUS MODEL 80
Revolver; double action; 38 Spl.; 6-shot; 3-inch, 4-inch barrel; 9-1/4-inch overall length; weighs 30 oz.; fixed sights; hand-checkered Brazilian hardwood stocks; blue, satin nickel or stainless steel finish. Introduced 1971; still in production.

New: $200   **Perf.:** $150   **Exc.:** $125

Satin nickel finish

New: $225   **Perf.:** $175   **Exc.:** $135

Stainless steel

New: $250   **Perf.:** $200   **Exc.:** $175

TAURUS MODEL 82
Revolver; double action; 38 Spl.; 6-shot; 3-inch, 4-inch heavy barrel; 9-1/4-inch overall length; weighs 34 oz.; fixed sights; checkered Brazilian hardwood grips; blue, satin nickel or stainless steel finish. Introduced 1971; still in production.

New: $200   **Perf.:** $150   **Exc.:** $125

Satin nickel finish

New: $225   **Perf.:** $165   **Exc.:** $135

Stainless steel

New: $225   **Perf.:** $175   **Exc.:** $150

Price: Blue $296.00
Price: Stainless $344.00

TAURUS MODEL 83
Revolver; double action; 38 Spl.; 6-shot; 4-inch heavy barrel; 9-1/2-inch overall length; weighs 34 oz.; adjustable rear sight, ramp front; hand-checkered oversize Brazilian hardwood grips; blue or stainless steel finish. Introduced 1977; still in production.

New: $200   **Perf.:** $150   **Exc.:** $125

Stainless steel

New: $225   **Perf.:** $185   **Exc.:** $150

TAURUS MODEL 84
Revolver; double action; 38 Spl.; 6-shot; 4-inch barrel; 9-1/2-inch overall length; adjustable rear sight, ramp front; checkered wood grips; blued finish. Introduced 1971; discontinued 1978.

Exc.: $135   **VGood:** $115   **Good:** $100

TAURUS MODEL 85
Revolver; double action; 38 Spl.; 5-shot; 2-inch, 3-inch barrel; weighs 21 oz.; ramp front sight, square-notch rear; checkered Brazilian hardwood grips; blued, satin nickel or stainless finish. Introduced 1980; still imported.

New: $315   **Perf.:** $285   **Exc.:** $225

Satin nickel finish

New: $325   **Perf.:** $295   **Exc.:** $235

Stainless steel

New: $335   **Perf.:** $300   **Exc.:** $245

TAURUS MODEL 85CH
Same specs as Model 85 except 2-inch barrel; weighs 21 oz.; smooth Brazilian hardwood grips; concealed hammer. Introduced 1992; still in production.

Blue

New: $315   **Perf.:** $285   **Exc.:** $225

Stainless Steel

New: $325   **Perf.:** $295   **Exc.:** $235

TAURUS MODEL 85 HY-LITE MAGNESIUM
Similar to Model 85 but weighs only 13.8 oz. Gray alloy frame. Introduced 2007.

New: $450   **Perf.:** $350   **Exc.:** $295

MODEL 850 CIA
Similar to Model 85 but with lightweight alloy frame. Chamberd for .38 Special +P or .357. Concealed hammer. Introduced 2007.

New: $375   **Perf.:** $300   **Exc.:** $265

TAURUS MODEL 86 TARGET MASTER
Revolver; double action; 38 Spl.; 6-shot cylinder; 6-inch barrel; 11-1/4-inch overall length; weighs 34 oz.; oversize target-type grips of checkered Brazilian hardwood; Patridge front sight, micro-click fully-adjustable rear; blue finish with non-reflective finish on barrel. Imported from Brazil by Taurus International. Dropped 1994.

Perf.: $275   **Exc.:** $225   **VGood:** $200

Taurus Model 94

Taurus Model 94 UL

Taurus Model 96
Scout Master

Taurus Model 431

Taurus Model 441

Taurus Model
445, 445CH

Taurus Model 454
Raging Bull

Taurus Raging Bull
500 S&W

Taurus Model 605

TAURUS MODEL 94

Revolver; double action; 22 LR; 9-shot; 3-inch, 4-inch barrel; weighs 25 oz.; serrated ramp front sight, click-adjustable rear; checkered Brazilian hardwood stocks; color case-hardened hammer, trigger; floating firing pin; blued or stainless finish. Introduced 1988; still imported.

New: $265	**Perf.:** $245	**Exc.:** $175

Stainless steel		
New: $295	**Perf.:** $265	**Exc.:** $200

TAURUS MODEL 94 UL

Revolver, double action; 22 LR, 9-shot cylinder. Barrel: 2-inch, 4-inch, 5-inch. Weight: 25 oz. Stocks: Soft black rubber. Sights: Serrated ramp front, click-adjustable rear for windage and elevation. Floating firing pin, color case-hardened hammer and trigger. Introduced 1989. Imported by Taurus International.

New: $225	**Perf.:** $175	**Exc.:** $150

Stainless finish		
New: $275	**Perf.:** $200	**Exc.:** $175

TAURUS MODEL 96 SCOUT MASTER

Revolver; double action; 22 LR; 6-shot; 6-inch barrel; weighs 34 oz.; heavy solid barrel rib; adjustable target trigger; Patridge type front, micrometer click-adjustable rear; checkered Brazilian hardwood grips; blued finish. Introduced 1971; still in production.

New: $275	**Perf.:** $225	**Exc.:** $175

TAURUS MODEL 431

Revolver; double action; 44 Spl.; 5-shot; 3-inch, 4-inch, 6-inch barrel; weighs 40-1/2 oz. (6-inch barrel); checkered Brazilian hardwood grips; serrated ramp front sight, fixed rear; heavy barrel with solid rib and full-length ejector shroud; blue or stainless finish. Imported by Taurus International. Introduced 1992; still imported.

Blue finish		
New: $395	**Perf.:** $355	**Exc.:** $300

Stainless steel		
New: $425	**Perf.:** $395	**Exc.:** $345

TAURUS MODEL 441

Revolver; double action; 44 Spl.; 5-shot cylinder; 3-inch, 4-inch, 6-inch barrel; weighs 40-1/2 oz. (6-inch barrel); checkered Brazilian hardwood grips; serrated

ramp front sight, micrometer click fully-adjustable rear; heavy barrel with solid rib and full-length ejector shroud; blue or stainless finish. Imported by Taurus International. Introduced 1992; still imported.

Blue finish		
New: $395	**Perf.:** $355	**Exc.:** $300

Stainless steel		
New: $425	**Perf.:** $395	**Exc.:** $345

TAURUS MODEL 445, 445CH

Revolver; double action; 44 Special, 5-shot. Barrel: 2-inch. Weight: 28.25 oz. Length: 6-3/4-inch overall. Stocks: Soft black rubber. Sights: Serrated ramp front, notch rear. Features: Blue or stainless steel. Standard or concealed hammer. Introduced 1997. Imported by Taurus International.

Blue finish		
New: $395	**Perf.:** $355	**Exc.:** $300

Stainless steel		
New: $425	**Perf.:** $395	**Exc.:** $345

TAURUS MODEL RAGING BULL

Revolver; double action; 454 Casull or 480 Ruger, 5-shot. Barrel: 5-inch, 6-1/2-inch, 8-3/8-inch. Weight: 53 oz. (6-1/2-inch barrel). Length: 12-inch overall (6-1/2-inch barrel). Stocks: Soft black rubber. Sights: Patridge front, micrometer click adjustable rear. Features: Ventilated rib; integral compensating system. Introduced 1997. Imported by Taurus International.

Blue finish		
New: $650	**Perf.:** $550	**Exc.:** $450

Stainless steel		
New: $725	**Perf.:** $650	**Exc.:** $550

TAURUS RAGING BULL 500 S&W

Similar to Raging Bull 454 Casull stainless version but chambered in 500 S&W.

New: $725	**Perf.:** $650	**Exc.:** $550

TAURUS RAGING BULL .223

Similar to other Raging Bull models but chambered in .223 Remington with 7-shot cylinder. Ten-inch ventilated rib barrel. Announced in 2008 but apparently never actually produced.

New: $795	**Exc.:** $675	**VGood:** $495

TAURUS MODEL 96 SCOUT MASTER

Revolver; double action; 22 LR; 6-shot; 6-inch barrel; weighs 34 oz.; heavy solid barrel rib; adjustable target trigger; Patridge type front, micrometer click-adjustable rear; checkered Brazilian hardwood grips; blued finish. Introduced 1971; still in production.

New: $275	**Perf.:** $225	**Exc.:** $175

TAURUS MODEL 431

Revolver; double action; 44 Spl.; 5-shot; 3-inch, 4-inch, 6-inch barrel; weighs 40-1/2 oz. (6-inch barrel); checkered Brazilian hardwood grips; serrated ramp front sight, fixed rear; heavy barrel with solid rib and full-length ejector shroud; blue or stainless finish. Imported by Taurus International. Introduced 1992; still imported.

Blue finish		
New: $395	**Perf.:** $355	**Exc.:** $300

Stainless steel		
New: $425	**Perf.:** $395	**Exc.:** $345

TAURUS MODEL 441

Revolver; double action; 44 Spl.; 5-shot cylinder; 3-inch, 4-inch, 6-inch barrel; weighs 40-1/2 oz. (6-inch barrel); checkered Brazilian hardwood grips; serrated ramp front sight, micrometer click fully-adjustable rear; heavy barrel with solid rib and full-length ejector shroud; blue or stainless finish. Imported by Taurus International. Introduced 1992; still imported.

Blue finish		
New: $395	**Perf.:** $355	**Exc.:** $300

Stainless steel		
New: $425	**Perf.:** $395	**Exc.:** $345

Taurus Model 607

Taurus Model 617

Taurus Model 669

Taurus Model 689

Taurus
Model 741

Taurus Model 827

Taurus Tracker
10mm 10TSS4

Taurus
Model 941

TAURUS MODEL 605

Revolver; double action; 357 Mag.; 5-shot; 2-1/4-inch barrel; weighs 24-1/2 oz.; finger-groove Santoprene I grips; serrated ramp front sight, fixed notch rear; heavy, solid rib barrel; floating firing pin; blue or stainless finish. Imported by Taurus International. Introduced 1995; still imported.

Blue finish		
New: $250	**Perf.:** $200	**Exc.:** $175
Stainless steel		
New: $275	**Perf.:** $225	**Exc.:** $200

TAURUS MODEL 607

Revolver; double action; 357 Mag.; 7-shot, 4-inch, 6-1/2-inch barrel; weighs 44 oz.; Santoprene I grips with finger grooves; serrated ramp front sight, fully-adjustable rear; ventilated rib with built-in compensator (6-1/2-inch barrel). Imported by Taurus International. Introduced 1995; still imported.

Blue finish, 4-inch barrel		
New: $350	**Perf.:** $300	**Exc.:** $250
Blue finish, 6-1/2-inch barrel		
New: $350	**Perf.:** $300	**Exc.:** $250
Stainless steel, 4-inch barrel		
New: $400	**Perf.:** $350	**Exc.:** $300
Stainless steel, 6-1/2-inch barrel		
New: $425	**Perf.:** $375	**Exc.:** $325

TAURUS MODEL 608

Revolver; double action; 357 Mag., 8-shot. Barrel: 4-inch, 6-1/2-inch, 8-3/8. Weight: 44 oz. Length: NA. Stocks: Soft black rubber. Sights: Serrated ramp front, fully adjustable rear. Features: Ventilated rib with built-in compensator on 6-1/2-inch barrel. Available in blue or stainless. Introduced 1995. Imported by Taurus international.

Blue finish, 4-inch		
New: $375	**Perf.:** $300	**Exc.:** $250
Stainless steel, 4-inch		
New: $425	**Perf.:** $350	**Exc.:** $275
Blue finish, 6-1/2-inch, 8-3/8-inch		
New: $400	**Perf.:** $325	**Exc.:** $275
Stainless steel, 6-1/2-inch, 8-3/8-inch		
New: $450	**Perf.:** $375	**Exc.:** $300

TAURUS MODEL 617, 606CH

Revolver; double action; 357 Magnum, 7-shot. Barrel: 2-inch. Weight: 29 oz. Length: 6-3/4-inch overall. Stocks: Soft black rubber. Sights: Serrated ramp front, notch rear. Features: Heavy, solid barrel rib, ejector shroud. Available with porting, concealed hammer. Introduced 1998. Imported by Taurus International.

Blue finish		
New: $275	**Perf.:** $225	**Exc.:** $175
Stainless steel		
New: $325	**Perf.:** $275	**Exc.:** $225

TAURUS MODEL 669

Revolver; double action; 357 Mag.; 6-shot, 4-inch, 6-inch barrel; weighs 37 oz. (4-inch barrel); serrated ramp front sight, click-adjustable rear; checkered target-type Brazilian hardwood stocks; floating firing pin; full-length barrel shroud; target-type trigger; blued finish. Introduced 1988.

Blue		
New: $250	**Perf.:** $200	**Exc.:** $175
Stainless steel		
New: $350	**Perf.:** $300	**Exc.:** $250
With compensated barrel, blue		
New: $275	**Perf.:** $225	**Exc.:** $200
With compensated barrel, stainless		
New: $375	**Perf.:** $325	**Exc.:** $275

TAURUS MODEL 689

Revolver; double action; 357 Mag.; 6-shot cylinder; 4-inch, 6-inch barrel; weighs 37 oz. (4-inch barrel); checkered Brazilian walnut grips; serrated ramp front sight, fully-adjustable rear; wide target-type hammer; floating firing pin; full-length barrel shroud; full-length ventilated barrel rib. Imported by Taurus International. Introduced 1988.

Blue finish		
New: $275	**Perf.:** $225	**Exc.:** $175
Stainless steel		
New: $325	**Perf.:** $275	**Exc.:** $200

TAURUS MODEL 741

Revolver; double action; 32 H&R Mag.; 6-shot cylinder; 3-inch, 4-inch heavy barrel; weighs 32 oz. (4-inch barrel); checkered Brazilian hardwood grips; serrated ramp; target hammer; adjustable trigger. Imported by Taurus International. Introduced 1991; dropped 1995.

Blue finish		
Perf.: $295	**Exc.:** $275	**VGood:** $195
Stainless steel		
Perf.: $315	**Exc.:** $295	**VGood:** $245

TAURUS MODEL 761

Revolver; double action; 32 H&R Magnum; 6-shot cylinder; 6-inch heavy barrel with solid rib; weighs 34 oz.; checkered Brazilian hardwood grips; Patridge-type front sight, micro-click fully-adjustable rear; target hammer, adjustable target trigger; blue only. Imported by Taurus International. Introduced 1991; dropped 1995.

Perf.: $275	**Exc.:** $250	**VGood:** $185

TAURUS MODEL 827

Revolver; double action; 38 Special, 7-shot. Barrel: 4-inch. Weight: 36 oz. Length: NA. Stocks: Finger-groove Santoprene. Sights: Serrated ramp front, notch rear. Features: Solid rib; shrouded ejector rod. Introduced 1998. Imported by Taurus International.

Blue finish		
New: $250	**Perf.:** $200	**Exc.:** $175
Stainless steel		
New: $300	**Perf.:** $250	**Exc.:** $200

TAURUS MODEL 941

Revolver; double action; 22 WMR; 8-shot; 3-inch, 4-inch barrel; weighs 27-1/2 oz. (4-inch barrel); checkered Brazilian hardwood grips; serrated ramp front sight, fully-adjustable rear; solid rib heavy barrel with full-length ejector rod shroud. Imported by Taurus International. Introduced 1992; still imported.

Blue finish		
New: $250	**Perf.:** $225	**Exc.:** $175
Stainless steel		
New: $275	**Perf.:** $250	**Exc.:** $200

TAURUS TRACKER 10MM 10TSS4

Matte stainless 10mm single/double action revolver with 4-inch barrel and fixed sights. 5-shot, 34.8 oz, rubber grip.

New: $495	**Exc.:** $450	**VGood:** $395

TAURUS TRACKER 10SS8

10mm 6-shot matte stainless with either 6.5-inch (54.5 oz.) or 8.375-inch (59.5 oz.) barrel. Fixed sights and rubber grips.

New: $500	**Exc.:** $460	**VGood:** $400

Taurus Judge

Taurus Gaucho S/A-357-B

Taurus Gaucho S/A-45-B12

Taurus Model PT 22

Taurus Model PT 25

Taurus Model PT 58

Taurus Model PT 92AF

TAURUS TRACKER .45

Similar to other Tracker models but chambered in .45 ACP (via full-moon clips) with 5-shot cylinder. Four-inch ported barrel .

New: $500   **Exc.:** $460   **VGood:** $400

TAURUS MODEL 917

Lightweight, compact version of Model 92 chambered in 9mm Parabellum. Matte blue or stainless finish, 19+1 capacity.

New: $400   **Exc.:** $365   **VGood:** $295

TAURUS JUDGE

Stainless steel- or lightweight alloy-frame version of Tracker Model 4410. Chambered in 3" .410/.45 Colt (4510TKR-3MAG) or 2.5" .410/.45 Colt (4510TKR-3UL) with 3" (3" Magnum) or 2.5" barrel (2.5").

New: $475   **Exc.:** $415   **VGood:** $350

TAURUS TRACKER .45

Similar to other Tracker models but chambered in .45 ACP (via full-moon clips) with 5-shot cylinder. Four-inch barrel with Picatinny rail. Stainless steel frame and cylinder.

New: $495   **Exc.:** $450   **VGood:** $395

TAURUS TRACKER 4410 10TKR2SS

Shoots 2.5-inch .410 bore shells or .45 Colt. Holds 5 shots. Stainless or blued, 2.25-inch or 6.5-inch barrel, rubber grip. Single/double action, 32 oz., 9.1-inch LOA. Later version had 3-inch chamber.

New: $450   **Exc.:** $400   **VGood:** $315

TAURUS GAUCHO S/A-357-B, S/SM, S/S, CHSA

Single action 6-shot chambered for .357/.38 caliber. Barrel lengths 4.75-inch (36.2 oz.), 5.5-inch (36.7 oz.), 7.5-inch (37.7 oz.). Fixed sights. Blued, matte stainless, polished stainless or blued/case hardened receiver.

New: $415   **Exc.:** $325   **VGood:** $295

TAURUS GAUCHO S/A-44-40B, S/SM, S/S, CHSA

Single action 6-shot chambered for .44-40 caliber. Barrel lengths 4.75-inch (36.2 oz.), 5.5-inch (36.7 oz.), 7.5-inch (37.7 oz.). Fixed sights. Blued, matte stainless, polished stainless or blued/case hardened receiver.

New: $415   **Exc.:** $325   **VGood:** $295

TAURUS GAUCHO S/A-45-B12, S/SM12, S/S12, CHSA12

Single action Buntline-style 6-shot revolver chambered for .45 Colt. Barrel length 12-inch (41.5 oz.). Fixed sights. Blued, matte stainless, polished stainless or blued/case hardened receiver.

New: $415   **Exc.:** $325   **VGood:** $295

TAURUS MODEL PT 22

Semi-automatic; double action; 22 LR; 9-shot magazine; 2-3/4-inch barrel; 5-1/4-inch overall length; weighs 12-1/2 oz.; smooth Brazilian hardwood grips; blade front sight, fixed rear; tip-up barrel for loading, cleaning. Made in U.S. by Taurus International. Introduced 1992; still produced.

Blue finish		
New: $165	**Perf.:** $135	**Exc.:** $110
Stainless steel		
New: $175	**Perf.:** $150	**Exc.:** $135

TAURUS MODEL PT 25

Semi-automatic; double action; 25 ACP; 8-shot magazine; 2-3/4-inch barrel; 5-1/4-inch overall length; weighs 12-1/2 oz.; smooth Brazilian hardwood grips; blade front sight, fixed rear; tip-up barrel for loading, cleaning. Made in U.S. by Taurus International. Introduced 1992; still produced.

Blue finish		
New: $150	**Perf.:** $125	**Exc.:** $110
Stainless steel		
New: $175	**Perf.:** $150	**Exc.:** $135

TAURUS MODEL PT 58

Semi-automatic; double action; 380 ACP; 12-, 10-shot; 4-inch barrel; weighs 30 oz.; integral blade front sight, notch rear with three-dot system; Brazilian hardwood stocks; exposed hammer; inertia firing pin; blued finish. Introduced 1988; still imported.

New: $325	**Perf.:** $300	**Exc.:** $250
Stainless steel		
New: $400	**Perf.:** $350	**Exc.:** $300

TAURUS MODEL PT 91AF

Semi-automatic; double action; 41 AE; 10-shot; 5-inch barrel; weighs 34 oz.; fixed sights; smooth wood grips; exposed hammer; blued finish. Introduced 1990; discontinued 1991.

Perf.: $350	**Exc.:** $300	**VGood:** $250
Satin nickel finish		
Perf.: $375	**Exc.:** $325	**VGood:** $275

TAURUS MODEL PT 92AF AUTO PISTOL

Caliber: 9mm Para., 15-shot magazine. Barrel: 4.92-inch. Weight: 34 oz. Length: 8.54-inch overall. Stocks: Black rubber. Sights: Fixed notch rear. Three-dot sight system. Features: Double action, exposed hammer, chamber loaded indicator, ambidextrous safety, inertia firing pin. Imported by Taurus International.

Price: Blue $490.00
Price: Stainless steel $510.00

TAURUS MODEL PT 92AF

Semi-automatic; double action; 9mm Para.; 15-, 10-shot; 5-inch barrel; 8-1/2-inch overall length; weighs 34 oz.; fixed sights; black plastic stocks; exposed hammer; chamber loaded indicator; inertia firing pin; blued, nickel or stainless finish. Introduced 1983; still imported.

Blue, nickel finish		
New: $425	**Perf.:** $375	**Exc.:** $325
Stainless steel (PT 92SS)		
New: $450	**Perf.:** $425	**Exc.:** $375

TAURUS MODEL PT 92AFC

Same specs as PT 92AF except 4-inch barrel; 13-, 10-shot; 7-1/2-inch overall length; weighs 31 oz. Introduced 1991; still imported.

New: $350	**Perf.:** $325	**Exc.:** $275
Stainless steel		
New: $400	**Perf.:** $350	**Exc.:** $300

TAURUS MODEL PT 99AF

Semi-automatic; double action; 9mm Para.; 15-, 10-shot; 5-inch barrel; 8-1/2-inch overall length; adjustable sights; uncheckered Brazilian walnut stocks; exposed hammer; chamber-loaded indicator; inertia firing pin; blue, satin nickel or stainless steel finish. Introduced 1983; still in production.

Blue		
New: $450	**Perf.:** $375	**Exc.:** $300
Stainless steel		
New: $475	**Perf.:** $425	**Exc.:** $375

Taurus Model PT 101

Taurus Model PT-111
Millennium

Taurus Model PT 908

Taurus Model PT-911

Taurus Model PT-938

Taurus Model PT-940

Taurus Model PT 945

TAURUS MODEL PT 100

Semi-automatic; double action; 40 S&W; 11-, 10-shot; 5-inch barrel; weighs 34 oz.; fixed sights; three-dot combat system; uncheckered Brazilian hardwood grips; ambidextrous hammer-drop safety; exposed hammer; chamber-loaded indicator; inertia firing pin; blue or stainless steel finish. Introduced 1991; still imported.

Blue		
New: $450	**Perf.:** $400	**Exc.:** $325
Stainless steel		
New: $475	**Perf.:** $425	**Exc.:** $375

TAURUS MODEL PT 101

Semi-automatic; double action; 40 S&W; 11-, 10-shot; 5-inch barrel; 34 oz.; adjustable sights; uncheckered Brazilian hardwood grips; ambidextrous hammer-drop safety; exposed hammer; chamber-loaded indicator; inertia firing pin; blue or stainless steel finish. Introduced 1992; still imported.

Blue		
New: $450	**Perf.:** $375	**Exc.:** $300
Stainless steel		
New: $475	**Perf.:** $425	**Exc.:** $375

TAURUS MODEL PT-111 MILLENNIUM

Semi-automatic; double action only; 9mm Para., 10-shot magazine. Barrel: 3.30-inch. Weight: 19 oz. Length: 6 inches overall. Stocks: Polymer. Sights: Fixed. Low profile, three-dot combat. Features: Double action only. Firing pin lock; polymer frame; striker fired; push-button magazine release. Introduced 1998. Imported by Taurus International.

Blue finish		
New: $275	**Perf.:** $225	**Exc.:** $185
Stainless steel		
New: $300	**Perf.:** $250	**Exc.:** $200

TAURUS MODEL PT 908

Semi-automatic; double action; 9mm Para.; 8-shot magazine; 3-13/16-inch barrel; 7-inch overall length; weighs 30 oz.; checkered black composition grips; drift-adjustable front and rear sights, three-dot combat; exposed hammer; manual ambidextrous hammer-drop; inertia firing pin; chamber loaded indicator; blue or stainless steel finish. Imported by Taurus International. Introduced 1993; still imported.

Blue		
New: $325	**Perf.:** $300	**Exc.:** $250
Stainless steel		
New: $375	**Perf.:** $350	**Exc.:** $300

TAURUS MODEL PT-911

Semi-automatic; double action; 9mm Para., 10-shot magazine. Barrel: 3.85-inch. Weight: 28.2 oz. Length: 7.05-inch overall. Stocks: Black rubber. Sights: Fixed. Low profile, three-dot combat. Features: Double action, exposed hammer; ambidextrous hammer drop; chamber loaded indicator. Introduced 1997. Imported by Taurus International.

Blue finish		
New: $375	**Perf.:** $325	**Exc.:** $275
Stainless steel		
New: $400	**Perf.:** $350	**Exc.:** $325

TAURUS MODEL PT-938

Semi-automatic; double action only; 380 ACP, 10-shot magazine. Barrel: 3.72-inch. Weight: 27 oz. Length: 6.75-inch overall. Stocks: Black rubber. Sights: Fixed. Low profile, three-dot combat. Features: Double action only. Chamber loaded indicator; firing pin block; ambidextrous hammer drop. Introduced 1997. Imported by Taurus International.

Blue finish		
New: $350	**Perf.:** $300	**Exc.:** $225
Stainless steel		
New: $375	**Perf.:** $325	**Exc.:** $250

TAURUS 800 SERIES

Double-action semi-auto chambered in 9mm Parabellum (17+1), .40 S&W (15+1) and .45 ACP (12+1). Four-inch barrel; blued or stainless frame slide on polymer frame with integral grips. External hammer with "Strike Two" (trigger reset) feature. Model 809-B is a civilian version of the 24/7OSS. Introduced 2007.

New: $575	**Perf.:** $495	**Exc.:** $350

TAURUS MODEL PT-940

Semi-automatic; double action; 40 S&W, 10-shot magazine. Barrel: 3.35-inch. Weight: 28.2 oz. Length: 7.05-inch overall. Stocks: Black rubber. Sights: Drift-adjustable front and rear; three-dot combat. Features: Double action, exposed hammer; manual ambidextrous hammer-drop; inertia firing pin; chamber loaded indicator. Introduced 1996. Imported by Taurus International.

Blue finish		
New: $400	**Perf.:** $350	**Exc.:** $300
Stainless steel		
New: $425	**Perf.:** $375	**Exc.:** $325

TAURUS MODEL PT-945

Semi-automatic; double action; 45 ACP, 8-shot magazine. Barrel: 4.25. Weight: 29.5 oz. Length: 7.48 overall. Stocks: Black rubber. Sights: Drift-adjustable front and rear; three-dot system. Features: Double-action, manual ambidextrous hammer drop safety, intercept notch, firing pin block, chamber loaded indicator, last-shot hold-open. Introduced 1995. Imported by Taurus International.

Blue finish		
New: $400	**Perf.:** $350	**Exc.:** $300
Stainless steel		
New: $425	**Perf.:** $375	**Exc.:** $325
Blue finish, ported		
New: $450	**Perf.:** $375	**Exc.:** $325
Stainless steel		
New: $475	**Perf.:** $425	**Exc.:** $375

TAURUS PT24/7LS-9SS-17

Full-size stainless semi-auto chambered for 9mm. Long grip, long slide. Capacity 17+1. Single/double action. 5-inch barrel, 27.2 oz. Fixed, 2-dot rear sight. Also in short grip 10+1 capacity.

New: $455	**Exc.:** $395	**VGood:** $325

TAURUS PT24/79SSC-17

Compact stainless semi-auto chambered for 9mm, short grip, short slide. Capacity 15+1. Single/double action. 5-inch barrel, 27.2 oz. Fixed, 2-dot rear sight. Also in short grip 10+1 capacity.

New: $455	**Exc.:** $395	**VGood:** $325

TAURUS PT24/7PLS-9SSPTI-17

Full-size semi-auto chambered for 9mm. Capacity 17+1 or 10+1. Single/double action. Titanium slide, 4-inch barrel, 27.2 oz.

New: $515	**Exc.:** $465	**VGood:** $395

TAURUS PT24/7PLS-9SSCTI-17

Compact semi-auto chambered for 9mm. Capacity 17+1. Single/double action. Titanium slide, 3.3-inch barrel, 25.4 oz.

New: $515	**Exc.:** $465	**VGood:** $395

Taurus 24/7OSS

Taurus PT1911B

Taurus Model PT24/7PLS-9SSPTI-17

Texas Longhorn Texas Border Special

Texas Longhorn Grover's Improved No. 5

Texas Longhorn Jezebel

TAURUS PT1911B
Blued or stainless 1911-style single action in .45 ACP. 8+1 capacity. LOA 8.5-inch, 32 oz., 5-inch barrel, fixed Heinie two-dot straight-eight sight. Numerous options. Add 10 percent for stainless.

New: $515   **Exc.:** $465   **VGood 395:**

TAURUS PT-745GB
Blued semi-auto in .45 GAP with 7+1 capacity. 3.25-inch barrel, fixed sights, 22 oz., polymer grip plates.

New: $455   **Exc.:**400   **VGood** $335

TAURUS PT745B/SS-LS
Blued or stainless semi-auto in .45 ACP. 4.25-inch barrel, 23.3 oz. 7+1 capacity, polymer grip plates.

New: $455   **Exc.:** $400   **VGood** $335

TAURUS PT917 B20
9mm blued or stainless semi-auto with 20+1 capacity. Fixed sights, 4-inch barrel, 31.8 oz.

New: $510   **Exc.:** $465   **VGood** $355

TAURUS PT609TI-13
This 9mm semi-auto has a titanium finish plus 13+1 capacity, 3.25-inch barrel. Fixed sights, 19.2 oz.

New: $525   **Exc.:** $460   **VGood** $375

TAURUS PT59B/SS-15
Blued or stainless semi-auto in .380 ACP with 15+1 capacity. Fixed sights, 5-inch barrel, 32.8 oz.

New: $525   **Exc.:** $460   **VGood** $375

TAURUS 24/7OSS
Available in .45 ACP, .40 S&W and 9mm Parabellum. 12+ 1 capacity (.45), single-/double-action. Ambidextrous decock and safety, match grade barrel, polymer frame with steel upper. Claimed to exceed all requirements set by United States Special Operations Command and developed to compete in SOCOM pistol trials.

New: $595   **Exc.:** $515   **VGood** $395

TEXAS ARMORY DEFENDER
Derringer; 9mm Para., 357 Mag., 44 Mag., 45 ACP, 45 Colt/410; 2-shot; 3-inch barrel; 5-inch overall length; weighs 21 oz.; smooth wood grips; blade front sight, fixed rear; interchangeable barrels; retracting firing pins; rebounding hammer; cross-bolt safety; removable trigger guard; automatic extractor; blasted stainless steel finish. Made in U.S. by Texas Armory. Introduced 1993.

New: $250   **Perf.:** $200   **Exc.:** $175

TEXAS LONGHORN GROVER'S IMPROVED NO. 5
Revolver; single action; 44 Mag., 45 Colt; 6-shot; 5-1/2-inch barrel; weighs 44 oz.; square blade ramped front sight, fully-adjustable rear; fancy walnut stocks; double locking bolt; music wire coil springs; Elmer Keith design; polished blue finish. Introduced 1988; only 1200 made.

New: $1500   **Perf.:** $1150   **Exc.:** $850

TEXAS LONGHORN JEZEBEL
Single shot; top-break action; 22 LR, 22 WMR; 6-inch half-round, half-octagon; barrel; 8-inch overall length; weighs 15 oz.; automatic hammer-block safety; fixed rear sight, bead front; one-piece walnut grip; all stainless steel construction. Introduced 1986; discontinued 1992.

New: $500   **Perf.:** $175   **Exc.:** $135

TEXAS LONGHORN SOUTH TEXAS ARMY
Revolver; single action; 357 Mag., 44 Spl., 45 Colt; 4-3/4-inch barrel; blade front sight, grooved topstrap rear; one-piece fancy walnut grips; loading gate and ejector on left side of gun; cylinder rotates to left; all steel; color case-hardened frame; music wire coil springs; high-polish blue finish. Only 1000 made. Introduced 1984; no longer made.

New: $1250   **Perf.:** $1000   **Exc.:** $850

TEXAS LONGHORN TEXAS BORDER SPECIAL
Revolver; single action; 44 Spl., 45 Colt; 3-1/2-inch, 4-inch barrel; grooved topstrap rear sight, blade front; one-piece fancy walnut bird's-head-style stocks; loading gate, ejector housing on left side; cylinder rotates to left; color case-hardened frame; music wire coil springs; high-polish blue finish. Introduced 1984; 1000 made.

New: $1250   **Perf.:** $1000   **Exc.:** $850

TEXAS LONGHORN WEST TEXAS FLATTOP TARGET
Revolver; single action; 32-20, 357 Mag., 44 Spl./44 Mag., 45 Colt; 7-1/2-inch barrel; standard rear sight, contoured ramp front; one-piece walnut stock; flat-top style frame; polished blue finish. Introduced 1984; 1000 made.

New: $1250   **Perf.:** $1000   **Exc.:** $850

THOMAS 45
Semi-automatic; double action; 45 ACP; 6-shot magazine; 3-1/2-inch barrel; 6-1/2-inch overall length; checkered plastic stocks; windage-adjustable rear sight, blade front; blued finish; matte sighting surface; blowback action. Introduced 1977; dropped 1978. Only about 600 ever made. Collector value.

Exc.: $750   **VGood:** $450   **Good:** $375

THOMPSON/CENTER CONTENDER
Single shot; break-open action; chambered for 29 calibers; 8-3/4-inch, 10-inch, 14-inch round, heavy, octagon barrel; adjustable sights; checkered walnut grip, forearm; interchangeable barrels; detachable choke for shot cartridges; blued finish. Introduced 1967.

New: $550   **Perf.:** $395   **Exc.:** $325

Thompson/Center Encore

Thompson/Center Contender Super 16

Thompson/Center Contender Super 14

Thompson/Center Contender

Thompson/Center Super Contender 14 Stainless

THOMPSON/CENTER CONTENDER BULL BARREL ARMOUR ALLOY II
Same specs as Contender except chambered for 7 calibers; 10-inch round barrel; extra-hard satin finish. Introduced 1986; discontinued 1989.

Perf.: $500   **Exc.:** $350   **VGood:** $300

THOMPSON/CENTER CONTENDER STAINLESS
Same specs as Contender except stainless steel construction with blued sights; black Rynite forend; ambidextrous finger-groove grip with built-in rubber recoil cushion with sealed-in air pocket; receiver with different cougar etching; 10-inch bull barrel in 22 LR, 22 LR Match, 22 Hornet, 223 Rem., 30-30 Win., 357 Mag., 44 Mag., 45 Colt/410. Made in U.S. by Thompson/Center. Introduced 1993.

New: $500   **Perf.:** $350   **Exc.:** $300

THOMPSON/CENTER CONTENDER VENT RIB BARREL
Same specs as Contender except 357 Mag., 44 Mag., 45 Colt/410; 10-inch vent rib barrel.

Perf.: $465   **Exc.:** $350   **VGood:** $325

THOMPSON/CENTER CONTENDER VENT RIB BARREL ARMOUR ALLOY II
Same specs as Contender except 45 Colt/410 only; 10-inch vent rib barrel; extra hard satin finish. Introduced 1986; dropped 1997.

Perf.: $465   **Exc.:** $350   **VGood:** $325

THOMPSON/CENTER CONTENDER HUNTER
Single shot; break-open action; chambered for 8 calibers; 12-inch, 14-inch, barrel with muzzlebrake; 2-1/2x scope with illuminated reticle; walnut grips with rubber insert; interchangeable barrels; sling with studs and swivels; carrying case; blued finish. Introduced 1990; still in production.

New: $650   **Perf.:** $575   **Exc.:** $525

THOMPSON/CENTER ENCORE
Single shot, break-open action; 22-250, 223, 260 Rem., 7mmBR, 7mm-08, 243, 7.62x39, 308, 270, 30-06, 44 Mag., 444 Marlin single shot. Barrel: 10-inch, 15-inch, tapered round. Weight: NA. Length: 19-inch overall with 10-inch barrel. Stocks: American walnut with finger grooves, walnut forend. Sights: Blade on ramp front, adjustable rear, or none. Features: Interchangeable barrels; action opens by squeezing the trigger guard; drilled and tapped for scope mounting; blue finish. Announced 1996.

New: $575   **Perf.:** $400   **Exc.:** $325

THOMPSON/CENTER SUPER CONTENDER SUPER 14, SUPER 16
Single shot; break-open action; chambered for 13 calibers; 14-inch, 16-1/4-inch bull barrel; adjustable sights; walnut grips; beavertail forearm; interchangeable barrels; detachable choke for shot cartridges; blued finish. Introduced 1978;.

New: $550   **Perf.:** $400   **Exc.:** $335

45 Colt/410
New: $565   **Perf.:** $415   **Exc.:** $350

THOMPSON/CENTER SUPER CONTENDER ARMOUR ALLOY II
Same specs as Super Contender except chambered for only 5 calibers; extra-hard satin finish. Introduced 1986; discontinued 1989.

New: $565   **Perf.:** $415   **Exc.:** $350

THOMPSON/CENTER CONTENDER SUPER 14, SUPER 16 STAINLESS
Same specs as the standard Super Contender except stainless steel construction; blued sights; black Rynite forend and finger-groove; ambidextrous grip with built-in rubber recoil cushion with sealed-

in air pocket; different cougar etching on receiver. Introduced 1993.

With bull barrel
New: $565   **Perf.:** $415   **Exc.:** $350
45 Colt/410, 14-inch barrel
New: $565   **Perf.:** $415   **Exc.:** $350

THOMPSON/CENTER SUPER CONTENDER VENT RIB BARREL
Same specs as Super Contender except 45 Colt/410 only; 14-inch, 16-1/4-inch vent rib barrel.

New: $565   **Perf.:** $415   **Exc.:** $350

THUNDER FIVE
Revolver; double action; 45 Colt/410 shotshell, 2-inch, 3-inch; 5-shot cylinder; 2-inch barrel; 9-inch overall length; weighs 48 oz.; Pachmayr checkered rubber grips; fixed sights; ambidextrous hammer-block safety; squared triggerguard; internal draw bar safety; made of chrome moly steel; matte blue finish. Made in U.S. Marketed by Holston Ent., Dragun Ent. Introduced 1991.

Perf.: $400   **Exc.:** $350   **VGood:** $300

THUNDER FIVE T-70
Same specs as the Thunder Five except chambered for 45-70 cartridge. Marketed by Dragun Ent.

Perf.: $450   **Exc.:** $400   **VGood:** $350

TISAS FATIH 13
Beretta-style semi-auto clone chambered in .32 ACP.

New: $300   **Exc.:** $250   **VGood:** $195

TISAS KANUNI 16
Single-/double-action autopistol chambered in 9mm Parabellum with 15- or 17-shot capacity. Black, chrome or chrome/gold finish.

New: $325   **Exc.:** $275   **VGood:** $195

Tisas Kanuni 16

Tisas Kanuni S

Tisas Zigana M16

Tisas Fatih 13

Tisas Zigana Sport

Tisas Zigana C45

Tisas Zigana K

Tisas Zigana T

Tokarev TT-1930

Tisas Zigana F

TISAS KANUNI S

Lightweight version of Kanuni 16. Black, chrome or chrome/black finish.

New: $325   **Exc.:** $275   **VGood:** $195

TISAS ZIGANA M16

Single-/double-action autopistol chambered in 9mm Parabellum with 15- or 17-shot capacity and 5" barrel.

New: $375   **Exc.:** $325   **VGood:** $250

TISAS ZIGANA K

Compact version of Zigana M16 with 4" barrel.

New: $375   **Exc.:** $325   **VGood:** $250

TISAS ZIGANA T

Longer (5.5") barrel version of Zigana M16.

New: $375   **Exc.:** $325   **VGood:** $250

TISAS ZIGANA SPORT

Compensated version of Zigana K with 4.5" barrel.

New: $375   **Exc.:** $325   **VGood:** $250

TISAS ZIGANA C45

Similar to Zigana M16 but chambered in .45 ACP with 4.75" barrel.

New: $395   **Exc.:** $350   **VGood:** $275

TISAS ZIGANA F

"Meltdown" version of Zigana M16 with radiused edges and improved ergonomics.

New: $395   **Exc.:** $350   **VGood:** $275

TMI SINGLE SHOT

Single shot; 22 LR, 223, 7mm TCU, 7mm Int., 30 Herrett, 357 Maximum, 41 Mag., 44 Mag., 454 Casull, 375 Super Mag., others on special order; 10-1/2-inch, 14-inch barrel; smooth walnut grips with thumbrest; ramp front sight, open adjustable rear; interchangeable barrels of blue ordnance or bright stainless steel; ventilated barrel shroud; receiver has integral scope mount. From TMI Products. Introduced 1987; no longer produced.

Exc.: $450   **VGood:** $375   **Good:** $275

TOKAREV TT-1930

Semi-automatic; 7.62mm Tokarev (comparable to 7.63mm Mauser); 8-shot; 4-7/16-inch barrel; 7-3/4-inch overall length; grooved plastic grips. TT-30 is rare first model with separate block in rear of frame for hammer mechanism, dated 1933, 1934 or 1935.

Exc.: $750   **VGood:** $500   **Good:** $350

TOKAREV TT-33

Same as TT-30 except simplified mechanism, dates 1936-1945.

Exc.: $350   **VGood:** $250   **Good:** $175

TOKAREV POST-WAR

Same as TT-33, except made in various countries including China. Some countries and dates have some collector value, but recent China imports have sold new for under $100.

New: $125   **Perf.:** $100   **Exc.:** $85

TRADITIONS 1873

Revolver; single action; 22 LR, 357 Mag., 44-40, 45 Colt, 6-shot cylinder. Barrel: 4-3/4-inch, 5-1/2-inch, 7-1/2-inch. Weight: 44 oz. Length: 10-3/4-inch overall (5-1/2-inch barrel). Stocks: Walnut. Sights: Blade front, groove in topstrap rear. Features: Blued barrel, cylinder, color case-hardened frame, blue or brass trigger guard. Nickel-plated frame with polished brass trigger guard available in 357 Mag., 44-40, 45 Colt. Introduced 1998.

New: $300   **Perf.:** $250   **Exc.:** $185

TRADITIONS 1894 BISLEY

Similar to the 1873 except has special tight-curl grip frame, modified trigger guard, wide-spur hammer. Available in 45 Colt only with 4-3/4-inch barrel. Introduced 1998.

New: $325   **Perf.:** $275   **Exc.:** $200

TRADITIONS THUNDERER REVOLVER

Similar to the 1873 single-action revolver except has special birds-head grip with spur, and smooth or checkered walnut grips. Introduced 1998.

Smooth grips		
New: $300	**Perf.:** $250	**Exc.:** $185
Checkered grips		
New: $350	**Perf.:** $300	**Exc.:** $250

TRADITIONS 1875 SCHOFIELD

Revolver; single action; 44-40, 45 Schofield, 45 Colt, 6-shot cylinder. Barrel: 5-1/2-inch. Weight: 40 oz. Length: 11-1/4-inch overall. Stocks: Walnut. Sights: Blade front, notch rear. Features: Blue finish, case-hardened frame, hammer, trigger. Introduced 1998.

New: $750   **Perf.:** $650   **Exc.:** $525

TRADITIONS 1851 NAVY CONVERSION

Revolver; single action; 38 Spec. Barrel: 7-1/2-inch. Weight: 40 oz. Length: 14-1/2-inch overall. Stocks: Smooth walnut. Sights: Post front, hammer-notch rear. Features: Steel frame, brass trigger guard. Introduced 1998.

New: $425   **Perf.:** $395   **Exc.:** $335

UBERTI 1871 ROLLING BLOCK

Single shot; 22 LR, 22 WMR, 22 Hornet, 357 Mag., 45 Colt; 9-1/2-inch barrel; 14-inch overall length; weighs 44 oz.; fully-adjustable rear sight, blade front; walnut grip, forend; brass trigger guard; color case-hardened frame; blued barrel. Introduced 1987.

New: $350   **Perf.:** $300   **Exc.:** $250

UBERTI 1873 CATTLEMAN

Revolver; single action; 22 LR, 22 WMR, 38 Spl., 357 Mag., 38-40, 44 Spl., 44-40, 45 Colt; 6-shot; 4-3/4-inch, 5-1/2-inch, 7-1/2-inch barrel; 10-3/4-inch overall length (5-1/2-inch barrel); weighs 38 oz.; fixed or adjustable sights; wood grips; blued finish. Made in Italy, still imported.

Brass backstrap		
New: $325	**Perf.:** $275	**Exc.:** $200
Steel backstrap		
New: $350	**Perf.:** $275	**Exc.:** $225

Uberti 1871 Rolling Block

Uberti 1873 Cattleman

Uberti 1873 Cattleman

Uberti 1890 Army Outlaw

Uberti 1875 Remington Outlaw

Uberti Phantom

Uberti Inspector

Uberti Schofield

Ultra Light Arms Model 20 Hunter

UBERTI 1873 BUCKHORN

A slightly larger version of the Cattleman revolver. Available in 44 Magnum or 44 Magnum/44-40 convertible, otherwise has same specs.

New: $350 **Perf.:** $300 **Exc.:** $250

UBERTI 1873 CATTLEMAN, SHERIFF'S MODEL

Same specs as Cattleman except 44-40, 45 Colt only; 3-inch barrel; brass backstrap. Made in Italy, no longer imported.

Perf.: $300 **Exc.:** $250 **VGood:** $200

UBERTI 1873 CATTLEMAN, TARGET

Same specs as Cattleman except adjustable rear sight; brass backstrap. Discontinued 1990.

Perf.: $300 **Exc.:** $250 **VGood:** $200

Stainless steel

Perf.: $325 **Exc.:** $275 **VGood:** $225

UBERTI 1873 CATTLEMAN, BUNTLINE

Same specs as Cattleman except 357 Mag., 44-40, 45 Colt; 18-inch barrel; wood grips; steel backstrap cut for shoulder stock. Made in Italy. Importation discontinued 1989; reintroduced 1993; no longer imported.

Perf.: $375 **Exc.:** $325 **VGood:** $275

UBERTI 1873 COLT STALLION

Revolver; single action; 22 LR/22 WMR combo; 4-3/4-inch, 5-1/2-inch, 6-1/2-inch barrel; 10-3/4-inch overall length; weighs 36 oz.; grooved or adjustable rear sight, blade front; one-piece uncheckered European walnut stocks; brass triggerguard, backstrap; blued finish. Made in Italy. Introduced 1986; discontinued 1989.

Perf.: $275 **Exc.:** $200 **VGood:** $150

Stainless steel construction

Perf.: $325 **Exc.:** $250 **VGood:** $200

UBERTI 1875 REMINGTON OUTLAW

Revolver; single action; 357 Mag., 44-40, 45 Colt, 45 ACP; 6-shot; 7-1/2-inch barrel; 13 3/4-inch overall length; weighs 44 oz; notch rear sight, blade front; uncheckered European walnut stocks; brass triggerguard, color case-hardened frame; blued finish. Replica of 1875 Remington SAA. Made in Italy. Introduced 1987.

New: $350 **Perf.:** $275 **Exc.:** $225

UBERTI 1890 ARMY OUTLAW

Revolver; single action; 357 Mag., 44-40, 45 Colt, 45 Colt/45 ACP convertible, 6-shot. Barrel: 5-1/2-inch, 7-1/2-inch. Weight: 37 oz. Length: 12-1/2-inch overall. Stocks: American walnut. Sights: Blade front, groove rear. Features: Replica of the 1890 Remington single-action. Brass trigger guard, rest is blued. Imported by Uberti U.S.A.

New: $350 **Perf.:** $300 **Exc.:** $250

UBERTI BUCKHORN

Revolver; single action; 44-40, 44 Spl., 44 Mag.; 6-shot; 4-3/4-inch, 5-1/2-inch, 7-1/2-inch barrel; wood grips; brass or steel backstrap; blued finish. Made in Italy. Importation discontinued 1989; reintroduced 1992; still imported.

New: $350 **Perf.:** $275 **Exc.:** $200

UBERTI INSPECTOR

Revolver; double action; 32 S&W Long, 38 Spl.; 6-shot; 3-inch, 4-inch, 6-inch barrel; 8-inch overall length (3-inch barrel); weighs 24 oz.; fixed or adjustable rear sight, blade ramp front; checkered walnut stocks; blued finish. Made in Italy. Introduced 1986; discontinued 1990.

Perf.: $350 **Exc.:** $300 **VGood:** $275

Chrome finish

Perf.: $375 **Exc.:** $325 **VGood:** $300

UBERTI PHANTOM SILHOUETTE MODEL

Single shot; 357 Mag., 44 Mag.; 10-1/2-inch barrel; adjustable rear sight, blade ramp front; target-style walnut stocks; hooked trigger guard; blue finish. Made in Italy. Introduced 1986; discontinued 1989.

Perf.: $375 **Exc.:** $300 **VGood:** $250

UBERTI SCHOFIELD

Revolver; single action; 38 special, 44-40, 45 45 Colt, 6-shot cylinder. Barrel: 3-1/2, 5, and 7 inches. Weight: 40 oz. Stocks: Walnut. Sights: Blade front, notch rear. Features: Blue finish, case-hardened frame, hammer, trigger.

New: $850 **Perf.:** $750 **Exc.:** $625

ULTRA LIGHT ARMS MODEL 20 HUNTER

Bolt action; 22-250 through 308 Win., most silhouette calibers on request; 5-shot; 14-inch barrel; weighs 64 oz.; Kevlar/graphite reinforced stock in four colors; two-position safety; Timney adjustable trigger; matte or bright stock, metal finish; left- or right-hand action. Introduced 1987; discontinued 1989.

Perf.: $1250 **Exc.:** $1000 **VGood:** $850

Unique DES/69U Target

Unique Model L

Unique Model B/CF

Unique Model DES/69U Match

United Sporting Arms Seville

ULTRA LIGHT ARMS MODEL 20 REB

Same specs as Model 20 except includes hard case. Introduced 1994; still in production.

New: $1350 **Perf.:** $1250 **Exc.:** $1000

UNIQUE KRIEGSMODELL

Semi-automatic; 32 ACP; 9-shot; 3-7/16-inch barrel; 5-13/16-inch overall length; fixed sights; grooved plastic stocks; blued finish. Manufactured in France 1940 to 1945 during WWII German occupation.

Exc.: $300 **VGood:** $250 **Good:** $175

UNIQUE MODEL 2000-U MATCH

Semi-automatic; single action; 22 Short; 5-shot; 5-15/16-inch barrel; 11-3/8-inch overall length; weighs 43 oz.; anatomically shaped, adjustable, stippled French walnut grips; blade front sight, fully-adjustable rear; light alloy frame, steel slide and shock absorber; five barrel vents reduce recoil, three can be blocked; trigger adjustable for position and pull weight; comes with 340-gram weight housing, 160-gram available. Imported from France by Nygord Precision Products. Introduced 1984; dropped 1993.

Perf.: $1250 **Exc.:** $1000 **VGood:** $800

UNIQUE MODEL B/CF

Semi-automatic; 32 ACP, 380 ACP; 9-shot (32 ACP), 8-shot (380 ACP); 4-inch barrel; 6 5/8-inch overall length; fixed sights; thumbrest plastic stocks; blued finish. Manufactured in France. Introduced 1954; still in production, but not imported.

Exc.: $200 **VGood:** $175 **Good:** $150

UNIQUE MODEL D2

Semi-automatic; 22 LR; 10-shot; 4-1/2-inch barrel; 7-1/2-inch overall length; adjustable sights; thumbrest plastic stocks; blued finish. Introduced 1954; still in production, but not imported.

Perf.: $275 **Exc.:** $225 **VGood:** $185

UNIQUE MODEL D6

Semi-automatic; 22 LR; 10-shot; 6-inch barrel; 9-1/4-inch overall length; adjustable sights; thumbrest plastic stocks; blued finish. Introduced 1954; still in production, but not imported.

Perf.: $275 **Exc.:** $225 **VGood:** $185

UNIQUE DES/32U TARGET

Caliber: 32 S&W Long wadcutter. Barrel: 5.9. Weight: 40.2 oz. Stocks: Anatomically shaped, adjustable stippled French walnut. Sights: Blade front, micrometer click rear. Features: Trigger adjustable for weight and position; dry firing mechanism; slide stop catch. Optional sleeve weights. Introduced 1990. Imported from France by Nygord Precision Products. Price: Right-hand, about $1,350
Price: Left-hand, about $1,380

UNIQUE MODEL DES/32U

Semi-automatic; single action; 32 S&W Long wadcutter; 5-, 6-shot; 5-15/16-inch barrel; weighs 40 oz.; blade front sight, micrometer click rear; adjustable, stippled French walnut stocks; position-, weight-adjustable trigger; slide-stop catch; dry firing mechanism; optional sleeve weights of 120, 220, 320 grams. Made in France. Introduced 1990; still imported.

New: $1100 **Perf.:** $900 **Exc.:** $750

UNIQUE DES/69U TARGET

Semi-automatic; 22 LR, 5-shot magazine. Barrel: 5.91-inch. Weight: 35.3 oz. Length: 10.5-inch overall. Stocks: French walnut right- or left-hand target-style with thumbrest and adjustable shelf; hand-checkered panels. Sights: Ramp front, micro. adjustable rear mounted on frame; 8.66-inch sight radius. Features: Meets U.I.T. standards. Comes with 260-gram barrel weight; 100-, 150-, 350-gram weights available. Fully adjustable match trigger; dry-firing safety device. Imported from France by Nygord Precision Products.

New: $1100 **Perf.:** $900 **Exc.:** $750

UNIQUE MODEL DES/69U MATCH

Semi-automatic; 22 LR; 5-shot; 5-7/8-inch barrel; 10-1/2-inch overall length; click-adjustable rear sight mounted on frame, ramp front; checkered walnut thumbrest stocks; adjustable handrest; blued finish. Introduced 1969; still in production.

New: $1000 **Perf.:** $850 **Exc.:** $650

UNIQUE MODEL 96U TARGET

Semi-automatic; 22 LR, 5- or 6-shot magazine. Barrel: 5.9. Weight: 40.2 oz. Length: 11.2 overall. Stocks: French walnut. Target style with thumbrest and adjustable shelf. Sights: Blade front, micrometer rear mounted on frame. Features: Designed for Sport Pistol and Standard U.I.T. shooting. External hammer; fully adjustable and movable trigger; dry-firing device. Introduced 1997. Imported from France by Nygord Precision Products.

New: $1100 **Perf.:** $850 **Exc.:** $700

UNIQUE MODEL DES/823-U RAPID FIRE MATCH

Semi-automatic; 22 Short; 5-shot; 5-7/8-inch barrel; 10-7/16-inch overall length; adjustable rear sight, blade front; hand-checkered walnut thumbrest stocks; adjustable handrest; adjustable trigger; blued finish. Introduced 1974; importation dropped 1988.

Perf.: $1000 **Exc.:** $850 **VGood:** $700

UNIQUE MODEL L

Semi-automatic; 22 LR, 32 ACP, 380 ACP; 10-shot (22 LR), 7-shot (32 ACP), 6-shot (380 ACP); 3-5/16-inch barrel; 5-13/16-inch overall length; fixed sights; checkered plastic stocks; steel or alloy frame; blued finish. Introduced 1955; still in production but not imported.

Exc.: $175 **VGood:** $150 **Good:** $135

UNIQUE MODEL MIKROS POCKET

Semi-automatic; 22 Short, 22 LR; 6-shot; 2-1/4-inch barrel; 4-7/16-inch overall length; fixed sights; checkered plastic stocks; alloy or steel frame; blued finish. Introduced 1957; still in production, but not imported.

Exc.: $175 **VGood:** $150 **Good:** $125

UNIQUE MODEL RR

Semi-automatic; 32 ACP; 9-shot; 3-7/16-inch barrel; 5-13/16-inch overall length; fixed sights; grooved plastic stock; commercial version of Kriegsmodell with improved blued finish. No longer in production.

Exc.: $175 **VGood:** $150 **Good:** $125

UNITED SPORTING ARMS SEVILLE

Revolver; single action; 357 Mag., 41 Mag., 44 Mag., 45 Colt; 6-shot; 4-5/8-inch, 5-1/2-inch, 6-1/2-inch, 7-1/2-inch barrel; ramp front sight with red insert, fully-adjustable rear; smooth walnut, Pachmayr or thumbrest stocks; blued finish. Introduced 1981; discontinued 1986.

Exc.: $675 **VGood:** $475 **Good:** $300

UNITED SPORTING ARMS SEVILLE SHERIFF'S MODEL

Revolver; single action; 357 Mag., 38 Spl., 44 Spl., 44 Mag., 45 Colt; 6-shot; 3-1/2-inch barrel; ramp or blade front sight, adjustable or fixed rear; square-butt

USFA Custom Custer Battlefield Gun

USFA Ace

USFA Super .38

USFA Single Action Army

Voere VEC-RG Repeater

United States Firearms Rodeo II

or bird's-head smooth walnut grips; blued finish. Made in U.S. Introduced 1983; discontinued 1986.

Exc.: $525   **VGood:** $375   **Good:** $275

UNITED SPORTING ARMS SEVILLE SILHOUETTE

Revolver; single action; 357 Mag., 41 Mag., 44 Mag.; 6-shot; 10-1/2-inch barrel; weighs 55 oz.; undercut Patridge-style front sight, adjustable rear; smooth walnut thumbrest or Pachmayr stocks; stainless steel frame with blued barrel.

Exc.: $700   **VGood:** $500   **Good:** $325

UNITED STATES FIRE ARMS CUSTOM CUSTER BATTLEFIELD GUN

Replica of 1873 revolver used during height of Indian Wars, including Custer's Last Stand. Limited edition with cartouche of Ordnance Sub-inspector Orville W. Ainsworth; serial range 200-14,343. 7.5-inch barrel, six shot. Antique patina-aged blue. One-piece walnut stock.

New: $1395   **Exc.:** $1100   **VGood:** $875

UNITED STATES FIRE ARMS ACE .22 LR

Recreation of 1911-style Colt Ace. .22 LR with 10+1 capacity. Walnut grips.

New: $1875   **Exc.:** $1725   **VGood:** $1300

UNITED STATES FIRE ARMS SUPER .38

1911-style semi-auto. Blued finish; chambered for .38 Super Auto with 9+1 capacity. Walnut grips.

New: $1875   **Exc.:** $1725   **VGood:** $1300

UNITED STATES FIRE ARMS SINGLE ACTION ARMY

Revolver; single action; 22 LR, 22 WMR, 357 Mag., 44 Russian, 38-40, 44-40, 45 Colt, 6-shot cylinder. Barrel: 3-inch, 4-inch, 4-3/4-inch, 5-1/2-inch, 7-1/2-inch, 10-inch. Weight: 37 oz. Length: NA. Stocks: Smooth walnut. Sights: Blade front, notch rear. Features: Recreation of original guns; 3-inch and 4-inch have no ejector. Available with all-blue, blue with color case-hardening, or full nickel-plate finish. Made in USA; early production was assembled and finished in USA from components manufactured in

Italy. Available from United States Patent Fire-Arms Mfg. Co.

New: $1250   **Perf.:** $1050   **Exc.:** $900

UNITED STATES FIRE ARMS BISLEY

Revolver; single action; 45 Colt, 32WCF, 38S&W, 44S&W, 41 Colt, 38WCF, 44WCF. 6-shot cylinder. Barrel: 4-3/4-inch, 5-1/2-inch, 7-1/2-inch, 10-inch. Weight: 38 oz. (5-1/2-inch barrel). Length: NA. Stocks: Smooth walnut. Sights: Blade front, notch rear. Features: Available in all-blue, blue with color case-hardening, or full nickel plate finish.

New: $1100   **Perf.:** $850   **Exc.:** $500

UNITED STATES FIRE ARMS FLATTOP TARGET REVOLVER

Similar to the Single Action Army except 4-3/4-inch, 5-1/2-inch or 7-1/2-inch barrel, two-piece hard rubber stocks, flat top frame, adjustable rear sight.

New: $1100   **Perf.:** $1000   **Exc.:** $850

UNITED STATES FIRE ARMS NETTLETON CAVALRY REVOLVER

Similar to the single Action Army, except in 45 Colt only, with 7-1/2-inch barrel, color case-hardened/blue finish, and has old-style hand numbering, exact cartouche branding and correct inspector hand-stamp markings. Made in Italy, available from United States Patent Fire-Arms Mfg. Co.

New: $1395   **Exc.:** $1100   **VGood:** $875

UNITED STATES FIRE ARMS BIRD'S HEAD MODEL REVOLVER

Similar to the Single Action Army except has bird's-head grip and comes with 3-1/2-inch, 4-inch or 4-1/2-inch barrel.

New: $1250   **Perf.:** $1050   **Exc.:** $900

UNITED STATES FIRE ARMS RODEO/RODEO II

Entry-level but very high-quality 1873 clone. Rodeo has matte blue finish; Rodeo II has matte nickel finish. Add 10% for Rodeo II.

New: $600   **Exc.:** $525   **VGood:** $395

USELTON ARMS ULTRA COMPACT CLASSIC

1911-style semi-auto .45 with fixed sights. 4.25-inch barrel, 34 oz. 3-4 lb. trigger pull, 7+1 capacity. Rosewood or imitation ivory grips. Various finishes.

New: $2000   **Exc.:** $1750   **VGood:** $1300

UZI EAGLE AUTO PISTOL

Caliber: 9mm Para., 40 S&W, 45 ACP, 10-shot magazine. Barrel: 4.4. Weight: 35 oz. Length: 8.1 overall. Stocks: Textured, high-impact polymer. Sights: Three-dot tritium night sights. Features: Double-action mechanism with decocker; polygonal rifling; matte blue/black finish. Introduced 1997; dropped 1998. Imported from Israel by Uzi America, Inc.

New: $500   **Perf.:** $450   **Exc.:** $400

VEGA STAINLESS 45

Semi-automatic; 45 ACP; 7-shot; 5-inch barrel; 8-3/8-inch overall length; stainless steel construction; almost exact copy of 1911-A1 Colt; fixed sights or adjustable sights; polished slide, frame flats, balance sand-blasted. Introduced 1980 by Pacific International Merchandising; dropped about 1984.

Exc.: $525   **VGood:** $475   **Good:** $425

VOERE VEC-95CG

Bolt action; single shot; 5.56mm, 6mm UCC caseless; 12-inch, 14-inch barrel; weighs 3 lbs.; black synthetic, center-grip stock; no sights furnished; fires caseless ammunition via electronic ignition; two batteries in the grip last about 500 shots; two forward locking lugs; tang safety; drilled and tapped for scope mounting. Imported from Austria by JagerSport, Ltd. Introduced 1995; still imported.

New: $2000   **Perf.:** $1700   **Exc.:** $1350

VOERE VEC-RG REPEATER

Bolt action; 5.56mm, 6mm UCC caseless; 5-shot; 12-inch, 14-inch barrel; weighs 3 lbs.; black synthetic, rear-grip stock; no sights furnished; fires caseless ammunition via electronic ignition; two batteries in the grip last about 500 shots; two forward locking lugs; tang safety; drilled and tapped for scope mounting. Imported from Austria by JagerSport, Ltd. Introduced 1995; still imported.

New: $2000   **Perf.:** $1700   **Exc.:** $1350

WALTHER MODEL 1

Semi-automatic; 25 ACP; 6-shot magazine; 2-inch barrel; 4-7/16-inch overall length; checkered hard rubber stocks; fixed sights; blued finish. Manufactured in Germany 1908 to 1918; collector value.

Exc.: $550   **VGood:** $375   **Good:** $300

Walther Model 2

Walther Model 3

Walther Model 4

Walther Model 5

Walther Model 6

Walther Model 7

Walther Model 8

Walther Model 9

Walther Model HP

WALTHER MODEL 2

Semi-automatic; 25 ACP; 6-shot magazine; 2-inch barrel; 4-7/16-inch overall length; checkered hard rubber stocks; fixed sights; blued finish. Same general internal design as Model 1 but has a knurled takedown nut at the muzzle. Manufactured 1909 to 1918; collector value.

Exc.: $350   **VGood:** $300   **Good:** $250

WALTHER MODEL 3

Semi-automatic; 32 ACP; 8-shot magazine; 2-5/8-inch barrel; 5-inch overall length; checkered hard rubber stocks; fixed sights; blued finish. Manufactured 1909 to 1918. Rare; collector value.

Exc.: $950   **VGood:** $750   **Good:** $550

WALTHER MODEL 4

Semi-automatic; 32 ACP; 8-shot magazine; 3-1/2-inch barrel; 5-7/8-inch overall length; checkered hard rubber stocks; fixed sights; blued finish. Manufactured 1910 to 1920.

Exc.: $250   **VGood:** $150   **Good:** $100

WALTHER MODEL 5

Semi-automatic; 25 ACP; 6-shot magazine; 2-inch barrel; 4-7/16-inch overall length; checkered hard rubber stocks; fixed sights; blued finish. Same specs as Model 2 except better workmanship; improved finish. Manufactured 1913 to 1918; collector value.

Exc.: $350   **VGood:** $250   **Good:** $200

WALTHER MODEL 6

Semi-automatic; 9mm Para.; 8-shot magazine; 4-3/4-inch barrel; 8-1/4-inch overall length; checkered hard rubber stocks; fixed sights; blued finish. Manufactured 1915 to 1917. Rare.

Exc.: $4500   **VGood:** $3500   **Good:** $2750

WALTHER MODEL 7

Semi-automatic; 25 ACP; 8-shot magazine; 3-inch barrel; 5-5/16-inch overall length; checkered hard rubber stocks; fixed sights; blued finish. Manufactured 1917 to 1918.

Exc.: $500   **VGood:** $425   **Good:** $350

WALTHER MODEL 8

Semi-automatic; 25 ACP; 8-shot magazine; 2-7/8-inch barrel; 5-1/8-inch overall length; fixed sights; checkered plastic grips; blued. Manufactured by Waffenfabrik Walther, Zella-Mehlis, Germany. Introduced 1920; dropped 1945.

Exc.: $400   **VGood:** $325   **Good:** $275

WALTHER MODEL 8 LIGHTWEIGHT

Same specs as Model 8, except aluminum alloy. Introduced 1927; dropped about 1935.

Exc.: $1000   **VGood:** $750   **Good:** $600

WALTHER MODEL 9

Semi-automatic; 25 ACP; 6-shot magazine; 2-inch barrel; 3-15/16-inch overall length; checkered plastic grips; fixed sights; blued. Introduced 1921; dropped 1945.

Exc.: $450   **VGood:** $375   **Good:** $325

WALTHER MODEL HP

Semi-automatic; 9mm, 7.65mm Para. (very rare); 10-shot magazine; 5-inch barrel; 8-3/8-inch overall length; checkered (early) or grooved plastic or checkered wood (rare) grips; fixed sights; blued. Early examples have rectangular firing pin. Introduced 1939; dropped 1945.

Rectangular firing pin		
Exc.: $2250	**VGood:** $1850	**Good:** $1200
Round firing pin		
Exc.: $1500	**VGood:** $950	**Good:** $700

WALTHER MODEL PP

Semi-automatic; 22 LR, 25 ACP, 32 ACP, 380 ACP; 8-shot magazine; 3-7/8-inch barrel; 6-5/16-inch overall length; designed as law-enforcement model; fixed sights; checkered plastic grips; blued. WWII production has less value because of poorer workmanship. Introduced 1929; dropped 1945. RZM, PDM and other special markings bring a premium.

Wartime models		
Exc.: $350	**VGood:** $300	**Good:** $250
32 caliber		
Exc.: $400	**VGood:** $300	**Good:** $225
380 caliber		
Exc.: $1000	**VGood:** $750	**Good:** $500
22 caliber		
Exc.: $850	**VGood:** $650	**Good:** $450
25 caliber		
Exc.: $3000	**VGood:** $2500	**Good:** $2000

WALTHER MODEL PP LIGHTWEIGHT

Same specs as Model PP except aluminum alloy frame. Introduced 1929; dropped 1945.

32 caliber		
Exc.: $750	**VGood:** $450	**Good:** $375
380 caliber		
Exc.: $1200	**VGood:** $950	**Good:** $700

Walther Model PP

Walther Model PPK

Walther Model PPK/S

Walther Model TPH

Walther Model TP

Walther Sport Model 1926

Walther Olympia Sport Model

WALTHER MODEL PP MARK II
Same specs as pre-WWII model. Currently manufactured in France by Manufacture De Machines Du Haut-Rhin. Introduced 1953; still in production, but not imported.
Exc.: $250　**VGood:** $200　**Good:** $175

WALTHER MODEL PP POST-WWII
Same specs as pre-war except not made in 25-caliber. Currently manufactured by Carl Walther Waffenfabrik, Ulm/Donau, West Germany. Still in production. Imported by Interarms.
Exc.: $350　**VGood:** $275　**Good:** $200

WALTHER MODEL PPK
Semi-automatic; 22 LR, 25 ACP, 32 ACP, 380 ACP; 7-shot magazine; 3-1/4-inch barrel; 5-7/8-inch overall length; the Kurz (short) version of the PP; checkered plastic grips; fixed sights; blued finish. WWII production has less value due to poorer workmanship. Introduced 1931; dropped 1945. RZM, PDM and other special markings bring a premium.

Wartime models		
Exc.: $350	**VGood:** $300	**Good:** $250
32 caliber		
Exc.: $450	**VGood:** $375	**Good:** $325
380 caliber		
Exc.: $1250	**VGood:** $950	**Good:** $650
22 caliber		
Exc.: $900	**VGood:** $700	**Good:** $500
25 caliber		
Exc.: $4500	**VGood:** $4000	**Good:** $3500

WALTHER MODEL PPK AMERICAN
Same specs as PPK except 6-shot magazine; 3-7/8-inch barrel; 6-5/16-inch overall length; weighs 21 oz.; 380 ACP only; blued or stainless finish. Made in U.S. Introduced 1986; still marketed by Interarms.
New: $575　**Perf.:** $500　**Exc.:** $400

WALTHER MODEL PPK LIGHTWEIGHT
Same specs as standard model except for incorporation of aluminum alloys. Introduced 1933; dropped 1945.

32 caliber		
Exc.: $650	**VGood:** $550	**Good:** $450
380 caliber		
Exc.: $1600	**VGood:** $1350	**Good:** $1000
22 caliber		
Exc.: $1250	**VGood:** $950	**Good:** $800

WALTHER MODEL PPK MARK II
Same specs as pre-WWII PPK. Was manufactured in France by Manufacture De Machines Du Haut-Rhin. Introduced 1953; dropped 1960s.
Exc.: $300　**VGood:** $250　**Good:** $200

WALTHER MODEL PPK MARK II LIGHTWEIGHT
Same specs as standard model except receiver of Dural; 22 LR, 32 ACP only. Introduced 1953; still in production, but not imported.
Exc.: $350　**VGood:** $300　**Good:** $250

WALTHER MODEL PPK POST-WWII
Same specs as pre-war model except steel or aluminum alloy construction. Currently manufactured in Germany by Carl Walther Waffenfabrik. Still in production, although U.S. importation was dropped in 1968.

32 ACP		
Exc.: $350	**VGood:** $300	**Good:** $250
22 LR		
Exc.: $400	**VGood:** $350	**Good:** $275
380 ACP		
Exc.: $500	**VGood:** $400	**Good:** $300

WALTHER MODEL PPK/S (GERMAN)
Semi-automatic; 22 LR, 32 ACP, 380 ACP; 9-shot magazine; 3-1/4-inch barrel; 6-1/8-inch overall length; fixed sights; checkered plastic grips; blued. Same general specs as Walther PP except grip frame 1/2-inch longer and one shot larger magazine capacity to meet GCA '68 factoring system. Made in Germany. Introduced 1968; dropped 1982.

22 LR		
Exc.: $450	**VGood:** $400	**Good:** $325
32 ACP, 380 ACP		
Exc.: $350	**VGood:** $300	**Good:** $250

WALTHER MODEL PPK/S (AMERICAN)
Same specs as German-made PPK/S except made entirely in U.S. by Interarms. Made only in 380 ACP in blue ordnance steel or stainless. Introduced 1980; still in production.
New: $550　**Perf.:** $500　**Exc.:** $400

WALTHER MODEL TPH
Semi-automatic; 22 LR, 25 ACP; 6-shot magazine; 2-1/4-inch barrel; 5-3/8-inch overall length; weighs

14 oz.; drift-adjustable rear sight, blade front; constructed of stainless steel; scaled-down version of PP/PPK series. Made in U.S. by Interarms. Introduced 1987; still in production.
New: $600　**Perf.:** $525　**Exc.:** $450

WALTHER MODEL TP
Semi-automatic; 22 LR, 25 ACP; 6-shot magazine; 2-1/2-inch barrel; 5-1/8-inch overall length; checkered plastic grips; fixed front sight only; blued. Updated version of Model 9 with safety lever in center of slide. Introduced 1962; dropped 1968.
Exc.: $600　**VGood:** $400　**Good:** $300

WALTHER SPORT MODEL 1926
Semi-automatic; 22 LR; 6-inch, 9-inch barrels; 9-7/8-inch overall length (6-inch barrel); checkered one-piece walnut grip; adjustable target sights; blued. Introduced 1926; dropped 1936.
Exc.: $800　**VGood:** $650　**Good:** $500

WALTHER OLYMPIA SPORT MODEL
Semi-automatic; 22 LR; 7-3/8-inch barrel; 10-11/16-inch overall length; checkered wood grips; adjustable target sights; blued. Available with set of four detachable weights. Introduced 1936; dropped during WWII.
Exc.: $1000　**VGood:** $850　**Good:** $700

WALTHER OLYMPIA FUNKAMPF MODEL
Same specs as Sport model except 9-5/8-inch barrel; 13-inch overall length; set of four detachable weights. Introduced 1937; dropped during WWII.
Exc.: $1350　**VGood:** $1000　**Good:** $800

WALTHER OLYMPIA HUNTING MODEL
Same specs as Sport Model except 4-inch barrel. Introduced 1936; dropped during WWII.
Exc.: $950　**VGood:** $750　**Good:** $600

Walther OSP
Rapid-Fire

Walther Free Pistol

Walther
GSP Match

Walther P-38
Military Model

Walther P-38
(480 code marking)

Walther P-38
(banner, round firing pin)
Zero Series

Walther Model
P-88 Compact

Walther PP Super

Walther P99

WALTHER OLYMPIA RAPID FIRE MODEL

Same specs as Sport model except 22 Short; detachable muzzle weight. Introduced 1936; dropped during WWII.

Exc.: $1250   **VGood:** $950   **Good:** $700

WALTHER OSP RAPID-FIRE

Semi-automatic; single action; 22 Short; 5-shot; 5-3/4-inch barrel; 11-13/16-inch overall length; weighs 48 oz.; walnut, special adjustable free-style grip with hand rest; fixed front sight, fully-adjustable rear; available with either 2.2-lb. (1000 gm) or 3-lb. (1360 gm) trigger; spare mag., barrel weight, tools supplied in Match Pistol Kit. Imported from Germany by Interarms. Importation dropped 1992.

Perf.: $1350   **Exc.:** $1000   **VGood:** $800

WALTHER FREE PISTOL

Single shot; 22 LR; 11-11/16-inch barrel; 17-3/16-inch overall length; weighs 48 oz.; fully-adjustable match sights; hand-fitting walnut stocks; electronic trigger; matte blue finish. Made in Germany. Imported by Interarms; importation dropped 1991.

Perf.: $1400   **Exc.:** $1000   **VGood:** $850

WALTHER GSP MATCH

Semi-automatic; single action; 22 LR; 5-shot; 5-3/4-inch barrel; 11-13/16-inch overall length; weighs 45 oz.; walnut, special hand-fitting design grip; fixed front sight, fully-adjustable rear; available with either 2.2-lb. (1000 gm) or 3-lb. (1360 gm) trigger; spare mag., barrel weight, tools supplied in Match Pistol Kit. Imported from Germany by Interarms. Still imported.

New: $1250   **Perf.:** $1000   **Exc.:** $850

WALTHER GSP-C MATCH

Same specs as GSP except 32 S&W Long wadcutter cartridge; weighs 49-1/2 oz.; comes with case. Imported from Germany by Interarms. Still imported.

New: $1500   **Perf.:** $1350   **Exc.:** $1000

WALTHER P-5

Semi-automatic; 9mm Para.; 3-1/2-inch barrel; 7-inch overall length; same basic double-action mechanism

as P-38 but differs externally. Introduced 1978; still imported from Germany by Interarms.

New: $700   **Perf.:** $600   **Exc.:** $500

WALTHER MODEL P-38

Semi-automatic; 9mm Para.; 10-shot magazine; 5-inch barrel; 8-3/8-inch overall length; checkered (early) or grooved plastic grips; fixed sights; blued. Walther Model HP as adopted by German military in 1939 and produced by various makers (identified by code markings on slide) through 1945. Early Walther (-inchac code-inch) manufacture with high polish finish brings considerable premium from collectors; first few thousand had rectangular firing pin.

Walther banner, rectangular firing pin		
Exc.: $4500	**VGood:** $3500	**Good:** $2200
Walther banner marked, round firing pin		
Exc.: $1750	**VGood:** $1250	**Good:** $800
480 code marking		
Exc.: $3500	**VGood:** $1500	**Good:** $1000
ac Code, no date, with high polish finish		
Exc.: $3000	**VGood:** $2000	**Good:** $600
ac Code, dated 40, and 41, high polish finish		
Exc.: $1250	**VGood:** $750	**Good:** $400
Letter codes, dated 42 to 45		
Exc.: $450	**VGood:** $350	**Good:** $250

WALTHER P-38 POST-WAR

Same specs as WWII military model except improved workmanship; alloy frame.

New: $600   **Perf.:** $450   **Exc.:** $350

WALTHER P-1 POST-WAR

Same specs as WWII military model; manufactured for German police market until late 1960s. Alloy frame., blued finish. Deduct 20 percent for Manufrance manufacture. These pistols have been imported in great numbers and are not scarce. alloy frame.

New: $300   **Perf.:** $270   **Exc.:** $250

WALTHER P-38IV

Same specs as P-38 post-war except 4-1/2-inch barrel; 8-inch overall length. Introduced 1977; imported by Interarms.

Exc.: $475   **VGood:** $375   **Good:** $275

WALTHER P-38K

Same specs as P-38 except streamlined version of original with 2-1/4-inch barrel; 6-1/2-inch overall length; strengthened slide; no dust cover; windage-adjustable rear sight; hammer decocking lever; non-reflective matte finish. Imported from Germany by Interarms 1976; dropped 1980.

Exc.: $800   **VGood:** $650   **Good:** $450

WALTHER P-88 COMPACT

Semi-automatic; double action; 9mm Para., 14-shot; 4-inch barrel; 7-3/8-inch overall length; weighs 31-1/2 oz.; checkered black composition grips; blade front sight, fully-adjustable rear; ambidextrous decocking lever and magazine release; alloy frame; loaded chamber indicator; matte finish. Imported from Germany by Interarms. Introduced 1987; importation dropped 1994.

Perf.: $800   **Exc.:** $700   **VGood:** $550

WALTHER PP SUPER

Semi-automatic; 9mm Ultra, 380 ACP; 7-shot magazine; 3-5/8-inch barrel; 6-15/16-inch overall length; weighs 29 oz. loaded; utilizes P-38 mechanism; introduced for West German police in 1972 in 9mm Ultra. Several hundred 9mm Ultra models were imported in used condition, plus 1000 new guns in 380 ACP in 1984-85 by Interarms. Some collector value.

9mm Ultra		
Exc.: $500	**VGood:** $400	**Good:** $300
380 ACP		
Exc.: $600	**VGood:** $500	**Good:** $400

WALTHER P99

Semi-automatic; double action; 9mm Para., 10-shot magazine. Barrel: 4. Weight: 25 oz. Length: 7 overall. Stocks: Textured polymer. Sights: Blade front (comes with three interchangeable blades for elevation adjustment), micrometer rear adjustable for windage. Features: Double-action mechanism with trigger safety, decock safety, internal striker safety; chamber loaded indicator; ambidextrous magazine release levers; polymer frame with interchangeable backstrap inserts. Comes with two magazines. Introduced 1997. Imported from Germany by Interarms.

Exc.: $600   **VGood:** $500   **Good:** $40

Walther 75th Anniversary PPK

Warner Infallible

Webley Government Model

Weatherby Mark V CFP Pistol

Weatherby Mark V Silhouette

Walther SP22-M1

Webley-Fosbery Automatic Revolver

Walther SP22-M3

Walther SP22-M4a

Walther Model SP22-M2

Webley Mark III Police Model

WALTHER SEVENTY-FIFTH ANNIVERSARY PPK

Blued with wood grips, machine engraving and available in .380 ACP with 6+1 capacity. Special SN beginning with 0000PPK, shipped with glass-top display case. Single/double-action, 3.3-inch barrel, 20.8 oz. Windage-adjustable rear sight.

New: $700   **Exc.:** $595   **VGood:** $395

WALTHER MODEL SP22-M1

.22 LR autoloader with aluminum frame and 4-inch barrel.

Exc.: $400   **VGood:** $300   **Good:** $225

WALTHER MODEL SP22-M2

Similar to above but with a 6-inch barrel.

Exc.: $425   **VGood:** $325   **Good:** $250

WALTHER MODEL SP22-M3

Similar to above but with match-grade barrel and adjustable trigger.

Exc.: $475   **VGood:** $375   **Good:** $275

WALTHER MODEL SP22-M4

Similar to above but with wooden free-style grip assembly.

Exc.: $750   **VGood:** $600   **Good:** $425

WARNER INFALLIBLE

Semi-automatic; 32 ACP; 7-shot; 3-inch barrel; 6-1/2-inch overall length; checkered hard rubber stocks; fixed sights; blued finish. Manufactured 1917 to 1919.

Exc.: $300   **VGood:** $200   **Good:** $150

WEATHERBY MARK IV SILHOUETTE

Single shot; bolt action; 22, 250, 308; 15-inch barrel; globe front sight with inserts, target-type rear peep; thumbhole Claro walnut stock; rosewood forend tip with grip cap; modified Mark V Varmintmaster action; drilled and tapped for scope. Introduced 1980; dropped 1981.

Exc.: $3250   **VGood:** $2500   **Good:** $2000

WEATHERBY MARK V CFP PISTOL

Single shot; bolt action; 22-250, 243, 7mm-08, 308. Barrel: 15-inch fluted stainless. Weight: NA. Length: NA. Stock: Brown laminate with ambidextrous rear grip. Sights: None furnished; drilled and tapped for scope mounting. Features: Uses Mark V lightweight receiver of chrome moly steel, matte blue finish. Introduced 1998.

Exc.: $700   **VGood:** $500   **Good:** $350

WEBLEY-FOSBERY AUTOMATIC REVOLVER

Revolver; 455 Webley, 38 Colt Auto; 6-shot cylinder (455), 8-shot (38 Colt Auto); hinged frame; 6-inch barrel; 12-inch overall length; hand-checkered walnut stocks; fixed sights; blued finish. Recoil revolves cylinder, cocking hammer, leading to automatic terminology. Flat-top model was submitted for U.S. Army trials. Manufactured 1901 to 1924. Both calibers have collector value.

455 Webley		
Exc.: $5000	**VGood:** $4000	**Good:** $3200
38 Colt Auto		
Exc.: $7500	**VGood:** $5500	**Good:** $4500

GOVERNMENT MODEL

Revolver; 450 to 476; 6-shot; 4-inch to 7-1/2-inch barrels; hinged frame; Vulcanite or wood grips; bird's-head or square-butt grip configuration; fixed or target sights; bright blue or nickel finish. Standard Webley markings. Manufactured from 1886 to 1915.

Exc.: $800   **VGood:** $550   **Good:** $400

WEBLEY MARK I, II, III, IV, V REVOLVERS

Revolver; 455 Webley; 6-shot; 4-inch barrel; hinged frame; Vulcanite grips; brush blue finish. Standard proofs with Webley MKI through Webley MKV marks. Some models have commercial counterparts available in 450 through 476 calibers. Manufactured from 1887 to 1915. Deduct 25 percent if cylinder shortened for 45 Auto Rim cartridge.

Exc.: $850   **VGood:** $625   **Good:** $325

WEBLEY MARK III POLICE MODEL

Revolver; double action; 32 S&W, 320 S&W, 38 S&W; 6-shot cylinder; 3-inch, 4-inch barrel; 9-1/2-inch overall length; hinged frame; fixed sights; checkered Vulcanite or walnut grips; blued finish. Introduced 1897; dropped 1945. Beware of Indian/Pakistani copies.

Exc.: $575   **VGood:** $450   **Good:** $300

WEBLEY MARK III POLICE MODEL TARGET

Revolver; double action; 38 S&W; 6-shot cylinder; 3-inch, 4-inch, 6-inch, 10-inch barrel; 9-1/2-inch overall length; hinged frame; adjustable sights; checkered Vulcanite or walnut grips; blued finish. Introduced 1897; dropped 1945.

Exc.: $725   **VGood:** $550   **Good:** $400

Webley Mark IV Police Model

Webley Mark IV Revolver

Webley Mark VI

Webley Model 1912 Hammerless

Webley Mark IV Target Model

Webley Model 1907 Hammer Model

Webley Model 1911

Webley Model 1909 Target Pistol

Webley Model 1910

WEBLEY MARK IV POLICE MODEL

Revolver; double action; hinged frame; 38 S&W; 6-shot cylinder: 3-inch, 4-inch, 5-inch, 6-inch barrel; 9-1/8-inch overall length (5-inch barrel); fixed or target sights; checkered plastic grips; lanyard ring; blued finish. Introduced 1929; dropped 1968.

Exc.: $650   **VGood:** $450   **Good:** $400

WEBLEY MARK IV WAR MODEL

Same specs as the Police Model. Built during WWII, it usually has poor blueing over unpolished surfaces. To protect the corporate reputation, most were stamped "WAR FINISH." Deduct 15 percent for near-identical Enfield-manufactured model with bobbed hammer ("Tanker").

Exc.: $475   **VGood:** $315   **Good:** $225

WEBLEY MARK IV TARGET MODEL

Same specs as Police Model except 22 LR; adjustable rear sight. Built in small quantities; virtually a custom-produced handgun. Introduced 1931; dropped 1968.

Exc.: $550   **VGood:** $375   **Good:** $275

WEBLEY MARK IV 32 POLICE

Same specs as Police Model except 32 S&W. Introduced 1929; dropped 1968.

Exc.: $675   **VGood:** $450   **Good:** $300

WEBLEY MARK IV MILITARY REVOLVER

Revolver; 455 Webley; 6-shot; 4-inch, 6-inch barrel; hinged frame; Vulcanite grips; brush blue finish. Manufactured at Webley from 1915 to 1923 and at Enfield Arsenal from 1921 to 1926. Standard proofs: Webley Mark IV and date or Enfield MkVI and date. Manufactured from 1915 to 1926. Deduct 15 percent if cylinder shortend for 45 Auto Rim cartridge.

Webley 6-inch barrel		
Exc.: $725	**VGood:** $575	**Good:** $450
Webley 4-inch barrel		
Exc.: $725	**VGood:** $575	**Good:** $450
Enfield		
Exc.: $575	**VGood:** $425	**Good:** $375

WEBLEY MARK VI

Revolver; top-break; 6-shot double/single action. Caliber: 38/200 British WWII service cartridge, aka 38 S&W. Barrel: 4". Finish: Bright blue or matte "WAR FINISH. (see above). Very similar to the Enfield service revolver but generally commands a premium. Discontinued in the late 1960's. Commercial models in Excellent condition command as much as a 100 percent premium.

Exc.: $550   **VGood:** $350   **Good:** $275

WEBLEY 1905 POCKET 32

Semi-automatic; 32 ACP; 3-1/2-inch barrel; 6-1/4-inch overall length; 8-shot magazine; external hammer; checkered hard rubber grips; blue finish. Introduced 1905; extensively redesigned in 1908; dropped 1940.

Exc.: $550   **VGood:** $345   **Good:** $300

WEBLEY MODEL 1907 HAMMER MODEL

Semi-automatic; 25 ACP only; 2-1/8-inch barrel; 4-1/4-inch overall length; 6-shot magazine; checkered wood (early) or hard rubber grips. Introduced 1907; dropped 1940.

Exc.: $550   **VGood:** $345   **Good:** $300

WEBLEY MODEL 1909

Semi-automatic; 9mm Browning Long; 8-shot magazine; 5-inch barrel; 8-inch overall length; external hammer; checkered hard rubber or wood grips; blue finish; only 1694 made. Introduced 1909; dropped 1914.

Exc.: $1400   **VGood:** $950   **Good:** $700

WEBLEY MODEL 1909 TARGET PISTOL

Single shot; tip-up action; 22, 32 S&W, 38 S&W; 9-7/8-inch barrel; blade front sight; plastic thumbrest target grips; late versions had ballast chamber in butt to permit weight adjustment; rebounding hammer; matte-finish barrel; blued. Introduced 1909; dropped 1965.

Exc.: $650   **VGood:** $500   **Good:** $350

WEBLEY MODEL 1910

Semi-automatic; 380 ACP; 7-shot; 3-1/2-inch barrel; 6-1/4-inch overall length; exposed hammer; checkered hard rubber grips. Revised Model 1905 built for 380 cartridge. Introduced 1910; dropped 1932.

Exc.: $950   **VGood:** $625   **Good:** $475

WEBLEY MODEL 1910 HIGH VELOCITY

Semi-automatic; 38 ACP; 8-shot magazine; 5-inch barrel 8-1/2-inch overall length; internal hammer. Only about 1000 made. Introduced 1910; dropped 1911.

Exc.: $1950   **VGood:** $1350   **Good:** $850

WEBLEY MODEL 1911

Semi-automatic; single shot; 22 Long; 4-1/2-inch, 9-inch barrel; 6-1/2-inch overall length (4-1/2-inch barrel); external hammer; checkered hard rubber grips; blue finish. Built on revised 1905-32 ACP pistol frame for police practice; upon firing, action blows open to eject and be ready for reloading. Total production 1500. Introduced 1911; dropped 1932.

Exc.: $700   **VGood:** $500   **Good:** $250

Webley Model 1913

Webley R.I.C.
Royal Irish Constabulary

Webley No.2
British Bulldog

Wesson Firearms
45 Pin Gun

Wesson Firearms
FB744

WEBLEY MODEL 1913 (NAVY MODEL 455)

Semi-automatic; 455 Webley Self-Loading Pistol; 5-inch barrel; 8-1/2-inch overall length; external hammer; checkered hard rubber or wood grips; blue finish. About 1200 made for commercial sale; 7600 for the Royal Navy, and under 500 were "Royal Horse Artillery" models cut for shoulder stock and with adjustable rear sight. Introduced 1912; dropped 1933. Note: Serial numbers of all commercial Webley auto pistols were in a single series so do not reflect quantity actually produced of any model. Military 455 autos had their own series, from 1 through 8050.

Commercial production		
Exc.: $1700	**VGood:** $1200	**Good:** $1000
Navy production		
Exc.: $1750	**VGood:** $1000	**Good:** $850
Royal Horse Artillery		
Exc.: $3750	**VGood:** $3000	**Good:** $2575

WEBLEY MODEL 1912 HAMMERLESS

Semi-automatic; 25 ACP only; 6-shot; 2-1/8-inch barrel; 4-1/4-inch overall length; striker fired; hard rubber grips. Introduced 1912; dropped 1938.

Exc.: $550	**VGood:** $345	**Good:** $300

WEBLEY MODEL 1922

Semi-automatic; 9mm Browning Long; 8-shot; 5-inch barrel; 8-3/8-inch overall length; external hammer; checkered or plain wood grips; blued finish. Redesign of Model 1909 for possible military sale; of the 2000 made, 1000 were actually delivered to South African Defense Forces and 330 to Latvia. Introduced 1924; dropped 1932.

Exc.: $1800	**VGood:** $1150	**Good:** $900

WEBLEY NO. 2 BRITISH BULLDOG

Revolver; 320, 380, 450; 5-shot; 2-inch, 3-inch barrel; fluted or round cylinders; solid frame; wood grips; bright blue or nickel finish. Marked "Webley No. 2" and caliber; topstrap marked THE BRITISH BULLDOG or with name of British retailer. Many No. 2s are marked with name of California retailer since the Bulldog was very popular in the American West. Manufactured from 1878 to 1915.

Exc.: $600	**VGood:** $450	**Good:** $375
With American retailer or broad arrow marking		
Exc.: $650	**VGood:** $500	**Good:** $42

WEBLEY R.I.C. (ROYAL IRISH CONSTABULARY)

Revolver; 320 through 476; 5-, 6-shot cylinder; 2-inch, 6-inch barrels; solid frame; wood grips; bright blue or nickel finish. Early models had straighter grips and many had unfluted cylinders. Standard proofs with "Webley R.I.C." and caliber. Manufactured from 1868 to 1932.

Exc.: $650	**VGood:** $450	**Good:** $375

WEBLEY WP WEBLEY POCKET

Revolver; double action; hinged frame; 32 S&W only; 6-shot; 2-inch, 3-inch barrel; 6-inch overall length (2-inch); checkered plastic grips; fixed sights; blued finish. Introduced 1908; dropped 1940.

Exc.: $650	**VGood:** $395	**Good:** $300

WESSON FIREARMS 45 PIN GUN

Revolver; double action; 45 ACP; 6-shot; 5-inch barrel; 12-1/2-inch overall length; weighs 54 oz.; 1:14-inch twist; Taylor two-stage forcing cone; compensated shroud; finger-groove Hogue Monogrip grips; pin front sight, fully-adjustable rear; based on 44 Magnum frame; polished blue or brushed stainless steel; uses half-moon clips with 45 ACP, or 45 Auto Rim ammunition. Made in U.S. by Wesson Firearms Co., Inc. Introduced 1994; dropped 1995.

Blue finish, regular vent barrel shroud		
Perf.: $550	**Exc.:** $500	**VGood:** $400
Stainless steel, regular vent barrel shroud		
Perf.: $600	**Exc.:** $575	**VGood:** $500
Stainless steel vent heavy barrel shroud		
Perf.: $675	**Exc.:** $600	**VGood:** $550

WESSON FIREARMS ACTION CUP/PPC

Revolver; double action; 38 Spl., 357 Mag.; 6-shot; extra heavy 6-inch barrel with bull shroud, removable underweight; weighs 4-1/2 lbs.; Pachmayr Gripper grips; Tasco Pro Point II sight; competition tuned with narrow trigger; chamfered cylinder chambers;

stainless steel only. Made in U.S. by Wesson Firearms. Introduced 1989; dropped 1995.

Perf.: $700	**Exc.:** $625	**VGood:** $550

WESSON FIREARMS FB14-2

Revolver; double action; 357 Mag.; 2-1/2-inch, 4-inch fixed barrel; 8-1/4-inch overall length; weighs 36 oz. (2-1/2-inch barrel); service-style rubber grips; blade front sight, fixed rear; satin blue or stainless finish. Introduced 1993; dropped 1995.

New: $250	**Perf.:** $200	**Exc.:** $175

WESSON FIREARMS FB15, FB715

Revolver; double action; 357 Mag.; 6-shot; 3-inch, 4-inch, 5-inch, 6-inch fixed barrel; 8-3/4-inch overall length; weighs 37 oz. (3-inch barrel); Hogue rubber grips; blade front sight, adjustable rear; polished blue or stainless finish. FB715 is Service Model, with 2-1/2-inch or 4-inch barrel. Introduced 1993; dropped 1995.

New: $275	**Perf.:** $275	**Exc.:** $235

WESSON FIREARMS FB44

Revolver; double action; 44 Mag.; 6-shot; 4-inch, 5-inch, 6-inch, 8-inch barrel; 9-3/4-inch overall length (4-inch barrel); weighs 50 oz.; Hogue finger-groove rubber grips; interchangeable blade front sight, fully-adjustable rear; fixed, non-vented heavy barrel shrouds; polished blue finish. Introduced 1994; dropped 1995.

New: $350	**Perf.:** $300	**Exc.:** $275

WESSON FIREARMS FB744

Revolver; double action; 44 Mag.; 6-shot; 4-inch, 5-inch, 6-inch, 8-inch barrel; 9-3/4-inch overall length (4-inch barrel); weighs 50 oz.; Hogue finger-groove rubber grips; interchangeable blade front sight, fully-adjustable rear; fixed, non-vented heavy barrel shrouds; brushed stainless steel. Introduced 1994; dropped 1995.

New: $400	**Perf.:** $350	**Exc.:** $325

Wesson Firearms Model 14

Wesson Firearms Model 15

Wesson Firearms Model 22

Wesson Firearms Model 715VH

Wesson Firearms Model 22 Silhouette

Wesson Firearms Model 40 Silhouette

WESSON FIREARMS HUNTER SERIES

Revolver; double action; 357 Supermag, 41 Mag., 44 Mag., 445 Supermag; 6-shot cylinder; 6-inch, 7-1/2-inch fixed barrel; 14-inch overall length; weighs 64 oz.; Hogue finger-groove rubber or wood presentation grips; blade front sight, dovetailed Iron Sight Gunworks rear; 1:18-3/4-inch twist barrel; Alan Taylor two-stage forcing cone; non-fluted cylinder; bright blue or satin stainless. Introduced 1994; dropped 1995.

7-1/2-inch barrel, blue finish		
New: $700	**Perf.:** $650	**Exc.:** $600
7-1/2-inch barrel, stainless steel		
New: $750	**Perf.:** $700	**Exc.:** $650
6-inch compensated barrel, 7-inch shroud, blue finish		
New: $725	**Perf.:** $675	**Exc.:** $625
6-inch compensated barrel, 7-inch shroud), stainless steel		
New: $775	**Perf.:** $725	**Exc.:** $675
6-inch compensated barrel, 7-inch shroud, scope rings on shroud, blue finish		
New: $775	**Perf.:** $725	**Exc.:** $625
6-inch compensated barrel, 7-inch shroud, scope rings on shroud, stainless steel		
New: $800	**Perf.:** $750	**Exc.:** $700

WESSON FIREARMS MODEL 8-2

Revolver; double-action; 38 Spl.; 6-shot; 2-1/2-inch, 4-inch, 6-inch interchangeable barrels; 9 1/4-inch overall length (4-inch barrel); weighs 30 oz.; serrated front, fixed rear sight; checkered grips; stainless or bright blue finish. Introduced 1975; dropped 1995.

Perf.: $200   **Exc.:** $175   **VGood:** $150

WESSON FIREARMS MODEL 9-2H

Revolver; double action; 38 Spl.; 2-inch-15-inch barrel; ramp front, adjustable rear sight; heavy barrel options; blue or nickel finish. Introduced, 1975; dropped 1995, reintroduced 1997.

Perf.: $250   **Exc.:** $200   **VGood:** $175

WESSON FIREARMS MODEL 9-2V

Same specs as Model 9-2H except standard vent-rib barrel. Introduced 1975; discontinued 1995, reintroduced 1997.

Perf.: $275   **Exc.:** $225   **VGood:** $200

WESSON FIREARMS MODEL 9-2HV

Same specs as Model 9-2 except heavy vent-rib barrel; 38 Spl. only. Introduced 1975; discontinued 1995, reintroduced 1997.

Perf.: $325   **Exc.:** $275   **VGood:** $225

WESSON FIREARMS MODEL 11

Revolver; double action; 357 Mag.; 6-shot; 2-1/2-inch, 4-inch, 6-inch interchangeable barrel; 9-1/4-inch overall length (4-inch barrel); interchangeable grips; adjustable dovetail rear sight, serrated ramp front. Marketed with tools for changing barrels, grips; non-recessed barrel nut, blued. Introduced 1969; dropped 1974.

Perf.: $200   **Exc.:** $175   **VGood:** $150

WESSON FIREARMS MODEL 12

Revolver; 357 Mag.; 6-shot; 2-1/2-inch, 3-3/4-inch, 5-3/4-inch interchangeable barrels and grips; adjustable target-type rear sight, serrated ramp front. Marketed with tools for changing barrels, grips; blued. Introduced 1969; dropped 1974.

Perf.: $200   **Exc.:** $175   **VGood:** $150

WESSON FIREARMS MODEL 14

Revolver; double-action; 357 Mag.; 6-shot; 2-1/4-inch, 3-3/4-inch, 5-3/4-inch interchangeable barrel; 9-inch overall length (3-3/4-inch barrel); interchangeable walnut grips; fixed dovetail rear sight, serrated ramp front; wide trigger with adjustable over-travel stop; wide spur hammer; recessed barrel nut; blued, nickel, matte nickel finish. Introduced 1971; dropped 1975. Replaced by Model 14-2.

Perf.: $225   **Exc.:** $175   **VGood:** $150

WESSON FIREARMS MODEL 14-2

Same general specs as Model 14, except 2-1/2-inch, 4-inch Quickshift interchangeable barrels; Quickshift grips interchangeable with three other styles. Introduced 1976; dropped 1995.

New: $400   **Perf.:** $300   **Exc.:** $250

WESSON FIREARMS MODEL 15

Revolver; double action; 357 Mag.; 6-shot; 2-1/4-inch, 3-3/4-inch, 5-3/4-inch interchangeable barrel; fully-adjustable rear sight; wide trigger with adjustable over-travel stop; wide spur hammer; recessed barrel nut; blued, nickel, matte nickel finish. Introduced in 1971; dropped, 1975. Replaced by Model 15-2.

Perf.: $275   **Exc.:** $225   **VGood:** $175

WESSON FIREARMS MODEL 15-1

Same specs as Model 15 except reduced size of rear sight. Introduced, 1973; dropped, 1975.

Perf.: $250   **Exc.:** $200   **VGood:** $175

WESSON FIREARMS MODEL 15-2

Same specs as Model 15-1 except no barrel shroud. Introduced 1973; dropped, then reintroduced 1997.

Perf.: $300   **Exc.:** $200   **VGood:** $175

Wildey Hunter

Wichita Single-Shot

Wesson Firearms
Model 738P

Wesson Firearms
Model 44

WESSON FIREARMS MODEL 15-2H

Same specs as the Model 15-2, except heavy barrel options. Introduced 1975; dropped 1995.

Perf.: $300   **Exc.:** $200   **VGood:** $175

WESSON FIREARMS MODEL 15-2HV

Same specs as Model 15-2 except heavy vent-rib barrel, ranging from 2-inch to 15-inch. Introduced 1975; dropped 1995.

Perf.: $325   **Exc.:** $275   **VGood:** $225

WESSON FIREARMS MODEL 15 GOLD SERIES

Same specs as Model 15 except smoother tuned action; 6-inch or 8-inch vent heavy slotted barrel shroud; blued barrel; rosewood stocks; orange dot Patridge-type front sight, white triangle on rear blade; stamped "Gold Series" with gold-filled Dan Wesson signature. Introduced 1989; dropped 1994.

Perf.: $400   **Exc.:** $325   **VGood:** $275

WESSON FIREARMS MODEL 715VH

Same specs as Model 15-2 except stainless steel construction with compensated barrel. Discontinued 2005. (NOTE: In mid-2005, the assets of Wesson Firearms were acquired by CZ-USA. Future production of Dan Wesson revolvers is uncertain.)

Perf.: $700   **Exc.:** $550   **VGood:** $375

WESSON FIREARMS MODEL 22

Revolver; double action; 22 LR, 22 WMR; 6-shot cylinder; 2-1/2-inch, 4-inch, 6-inch, 8-inch, 10-inch interchangeable barrel; checkered, undercover, service or target stocks of American walnut; serrated, interchangeable front sight; adjustable white outline rear; blued or stainless steel; wide trigger; over-travel trigger adjustment; wide hammer spur. Introduced 1982; dropped, then reintroduced 1997.

Perf.: $300   **Exc.:** $200   **VGood:** $175

WESSON FIREARMS MODEL 22 SILHOUETTE

Revolver; single action; 22 LR; 6-shot; 10-inch regular vent or vent heavy barrel; weighs 53 oz.; combat-style grips; Patridge-style front sight, .080-inch rear. From Wesson Firearms Co., Inc. Introduced 1989; dropped 1995.

Blue finish, regular vent barrel		
New: $400	**Perf.:** $350	**Exc.:** $325
Blue finish, vent heavy barrel		
New: $425	**Perf.:** $375	**Exc.:** $350
Stainless steel, regular vent barrel		
New: $450	**Perf.:** $400	**Exc.:** $375
Stainless steel, vent heavy barrel		
New: $475	**Perf.:** $425	**Exc.:** $410

WESSON FIREARMS MODEL 32M

Revolver; 32 H&R Mag.; 6-shot; 2-1/2-inch, 3-3/4-inch, 5-3/4-inch barrel; adjustable rear sight, ramp front; blued or stainless steel. Introduced 1984.

Perf.: $300   **Exc.:** $200   **VGood:** $175

WESSON FIREARMS MODEL 40 SILHOUETTE

Revolver; 357 Maximum; 6-shot cylinder; 6-inch, 8-inch, 10-inch barrel; 14-5/16-inch overall length (8-inch barrel); weighs 64 oz.; adjustable rear sight, serrated front; blued or stainless steel; meets IHMSA competition criteria. Introduced 1986; dropped 1995.

Perf.: $600   **Exc.:** $525   **VGood:** $375

WESSON FIREARMS MODEL 41V

Revolver; double action; 41 Mag.; 6-shot cylinder; 4-inch, 6-inch, 8-inch, 10-inch interchangeable barrel; smooth walnut stocks; serrated front sight, adjustable white-outline rear; wide trigger; adjustable trigger over-travel feature; wide hammer spur; blued or stainless steel. Introduced 1982; dropped 1995.

Perf.: $350   **Exc.:** $300   **VGood:** $250

WESSON FIREARMS MODEL 44V

Revolver; double action; 44 Mag.; 6-shot; 4-inch, 6-inch, 8-inch, 10-inch interchangeable barrel; smooth walnut stocks; serrated front sight; adjustable white-outline rear; wide trigger with adjustable over-travel feature; wide hammer spur; blued or stainless finish. Introduced 1982; dropped 1995.

Perf.: $375   **Exc.:** $325   **VGood:** $275

WESSON FIREARMS MODEL 45V

Revolver; double action; 41 Mag., 44 Mag., 45 Colt; 6-shot cylinder; 4-inch, 6-inch, 8-inch, 10-inch interchangeable barrel; 12-inch overall length (6-inch barrel); weighs 48 oz. (4-inch barrel); smooth wood grips; 1/8-inch serrated front sight, fully-adjustable

white outline rear; smooth, wide trigger with adjustable over-travel; wide hammer spur. Made in U.S. by Wesson Firearms. Introduced 1993; dropped 1995.

Blue finish		
New: $400	**Perf.:** $350	**Exc.:** $300
Stainless steel		
New: $450	**Perf.:** $400	**Exc.:** $375

WESSON FIREARMS MODEL 322

Revolver; double action; 32-20; 6-shot cylinder; 2-1/2-inch, 4-inch, 6-inch, 8-inch barrel, standard, vent, vent heavy; 11-1/4-inch overall length; weighs 43 oz. (6-inch barrel); checkered walnut grips; red ramp interchangeable front sight, fully-adjustable rear; blue or stainless finish. Made in U.S. by Wesson Firearms Co., Inc. Introduced 1991; dropped 1995, reintroduced 1997. Longer barrels bring a premium.

New: $300   **Perf.:** $250   **Exc.:** $200

WESSON FIREARMS MODEL 738P

Revolver; double action; 38 Spl. +P; 5-shot cylinder; 2-inch barrel; 6-1/2-inch overall length; weighs 24-1/2 oz.; Pauferro wood or rubber grips; blade front sight, fixed notch rear; designed for +P ammunition; stainless steel construction. Made in U.S. by Wesson Firearms Co., Inc. Introduced 1992; dropped 1995. Reintroduced 1997.

New: $300   **Perf.:** $250   **Exc.:** $200

WESSON FIREARMS MODEL 7322

Revolver; double action; 32-20; 6-shot cylinder; 2-1/2-inch, 4-inch, 6-inch, 8-inch barrel, standard, vent, vent heavy; 11 1/4-inch overall length; weighs 43 oz. (6-inch barrel); checkered walnut grips; red ramp interchangeable front sight, fully-adjustable rear; stainless steel. Made in U.S. by Wesson Firearms Co., Inc. Introduced 1991; dropped 1995.

New: $375   **Perf.:** $325   **Exc.:** $300

WESSON FIREARMS .455 SUPERMAG

Revolver; has same general specs as Model 40 series; chambered for the .455 Supermag cartridge; blued or stainless steel; 4-inch, 6-inch, 8-inch, 10-inch barrel. Introduced, 1989; dropped, then reintroduced in 1997.

Perf.: $675   **Exc.:** $575   **VGood:** $500

WESSON FIREARMS PPC

Revolver; double action; 38 Spl., 357 Mag.; 6-shot cylinder; 6-inch extra heavy barrel with bull shroud, removable underweight; weighs 4 lbs., 7 oz.; Pachmayr Gripper grips; Aristocrat sights with three-postion rear; competition tuned with narrow trigger; chamfered cylinder chambers; bright blue finish or stainless steel. Made in U.S. by Wesson Firearms. Introduced 1989; dropped 1995.

Perf.: $550   **Exc.:** $500   **VGood:** $450

Wichita Silhouette

Wildey Automatic Pistol

Wildey Pin Gun

Wichita International

Whitney Wolverine

Wilkinson Diane

Wildey Jaws Viper

WHITNEY WOLVERINE

Semi-automatic; 22 LR; 4-1/2-inch barrel; 9-inch overall length; aluminum alloy frame; windage-adjustable rear; 1/8-inch Patridge-type front; top of slide serrated to reduce reflection; AAA American walnut stock with checkered pistol grip; checkered plastic grips; blued or nickel finish. Introduced 1956; dropped 1963. Reintroduced in polymer-frame version by Olympic Arms in 2005. Deduct 30 percent for Olympic production.

Exc.: $550   **VGood:** $395   **Good:** $300

Nickel finish

Exc.: $1000   **VGood:** $800   **Good:** $500

WICHITA CLASSIC SILHOUETTE

Bolt action; all standard calibers to 2.80-inch; 11-1/14-inch barrel; weighs 4 lbs.; hooded post front sight; open adjustable rear; AAA American walnut stock with checkered pistol grip; three locking lug bolts; three gas ports; adjustable trigger. From Wichita Arms. Introduced 1981; still in production.

Perf.: $3200   **Exc.:** $2400   **VGood:** $1900

WICHITA INTERNATIONAL

Single shot; 22 LR, 22 WMR, 32 H&R Mag., 357 Super Mag., 357 Mag., 7R, 7mm Super Mag., 7-30 Waters, 30-30 Win.; 10-inch, 10-1/2-inch, 14-inch barrel; weighs 3 lbs. 2 oz. (10-inch barrel); walnut grip and forend; Patridge front sight, adjustable rear; Wichita Multi-Range sight system optional; made of stainless steel; break-open action; grip dimensions same as Colt 45 Auto; drilled and tapped for furnished see-thru rings; extra barrels are factory fitted. Available from Wichita Arms. Introduced 1983; dropped 1994.

New: $750   **Perf.:** $650   **Exc.:** $550

WICHITA MASTER

Bolt action; 6mm BR, 7mm BR, 243, 7mm-08, 22-250, 308; 3-shot magazine; 13-inch, 14-7/8-inch barrel; weighs 4-1/2 lbs. (13-inch barrel); American walnut stock with oil finish; glass bedded; hooded post front sight, open adjustable rear; left-hand action with right-hand grip; round receiver and barrel; Wichita adjustable trigger. Made in U.S. by Wichita Arms. Introduced 1991; dropped 1994.

Perf.: $1275   **Exc.:** $850   **VGood:** $600

WICHITA SILHOUETTE PISTOL

Bolt action; 308 Win., 7mm IHSMA, 7mm-08; 14-15/16-inch barrel; 21-3/8-inch overall length; weighs 4-1/2 lbs.; Wichita Multi-Range sight system; American walnut glass-bedded stock; round barrel; fluted bolt with flat bolt handle; adjustable trigger. From Wichita Arms. Introduced 1979; still in production.

Perf.: $1500   **Exc.:** $1200   **VGood:** $950

WILDEY AUTOMATIC PISTOL

Semi-automatic; 10mm Wildey Mag., 11mm Wildey Mag., 357 Peterbuilt, 45 Win. Mag.; 7-shot; 5-inch, 6-inch, 7-inch, 8-inch, 10-inch, 12-inch, 14-inch (45 Win. Mag.); 8-inch, 10-inch, 12-inch, 15-inch (other calibers) interchangeable barrel; 11-inch overall length (7-inch barrel); weighs 64 oz. (5-inch barrel); ramp front sight, fully-adjustable rear; hardwood grips; stainless steel construction; three lug rotary belt; double or single action; polished and matte finish.

Perf.: $1400   **Exc.:** $1150   **VGood:** $900

WILDEY HUNTER

Semi-automatic; 44 Magnum, 45 Win. Mag.; 7-shot; 5-inch, 6-inch, 7-inch, 8-inch, 10-inch, 12-inch, 14-inch length; weighs 64 oz. (5-inch barrel); ramp front sight, fully-adjustable rear; hardwood grips; stainless steel construction; three lug rotary belt; double or single action; polished and matte finish.

Perf.: $1400   **Exc.:** $1150   **VGood:** $900

WILDEY PIN GUN

Gas-operated auto-loading pistol in polished or matte stainless for competition shooting. With muzzle brake; variety of calibers and barrel lengths (7-inch, 8-inch, 10-inch, 12-inch, 14-inch). 4.09 lb. (8-inch barrel).

New: $1550   **Exc.:** $1475   **VGood:** $1195

WILDEY JAWS VIPER

Jordanian Arms & Weapons System manufactured in Jordan. Semi-auto chambered for 9mm, .40 S&W, 45 ACP. Barrels: 4.4-inch and 5-inch. 10-round magazine. Stainless finish with rubberized grip.

New: $695   **Exc.:** $625   **VGood:** $495

WILKINSON DIANE

Semi-automatic; 22 LR, 25 ACP; 8-shot magazine; 2-1/8-inch barrel; 4-1/2-inch overall length; internal hammer; separate ejector; checkered styrene stocks; fixed sights integral with slide; matte blued finish. Introduced 1977; no longer in production.

Exc.: $200   **VGood:** $150   **Good:** $95

WILKINSON LINDA

Semi-automatic; 9mm Para.; 31-shot magazine; 8-5/16-inch barrel; 12-1/4-inch overall length; weighs 5 lbs.; protected blade front sight, Wiliams adjustable rear; maple forend; checkered black plastic stocks; blowback action; crossbolt safety. Introduced 1982.

New: $725   **Perf.:** $600   **Exc.:** $425

WILKINSON SHERRY

Semi-automatic; 22 LR; 8-shot magazine; 2-1/8-inch barrel; 4-3/4-inch overall length; weighs 9-1/4 oz.; no sights; checkered black plastic stocks; crossbolt safety; blue finish or gold-plated frame; blued slide, trigger. Introduced 1985.

New: $595   **Perf.:** $495   **Exc.:** $395

WILSON COMBAT KZ 9MM

Polymer-frame 1911 chambered for 9mm. Full size is 16+1 capacity with 5-inch barrel at 33 oz. Compact size is 14+1 capacity with 4.1-inch barrel at 31 oz.

New: $1300   **Exc.:** $1195   **VGood:** $895

WILSON COMBAT ADP 9MM

Wilson's first production pistol. 11-round capacity, polymer frame. 19.5 oz. 6.3-inch overall length, 3.75-inch barrel.

New: $579   **Exc.:** $515   **VGood:** $400

WYOMING ARMS PARKER AUTO

Semi-automatic; single action; 10mm Auto, 40 S&W, 45 ACP; 8-shot (10mm, 40 S&W), 7-shot (45 ACP); 3-3/8-inch, 5-inch, 7-inch barrel; 6-3/8-inch overall length; weighs 29 oz. to 44 oz.; grooved composition grips; fixed or Millett adjustable sights; made of stainless steel. Made in the U.S. by Wyoming Arms Mfg. Corp. Introduced 1990; dropped 1992.

3-3/8-inch, 5-inch barrel, fixed sights

Perf.: $425   **Exc.:** $375   **VGood:** $350

7-inch barrel, adjustable sights

Perf.: $450   **Exc.:** $350   **VGood:** $300

MODERN GUN VALUES
RIFLES
Directory of Manufacturers

A.A. ARMS AR9

Semi-automatic; 9mm Para.; 20-shot magazine; 16-1/4-inch barrel; 33-inch overall length; weighs 6-1/2 lbs.; folding buttstock, checkered plastic grip; adjustable post front sight in ring, fixed open rear; fires from closed bolt; lever safety blocks trigger and sear; vented barrel shroud; matte blue/black or nickel finish. Made in U.S. Marketed by Kimel Industries, later by A. A. Arms. Introduced 1991; no longer produced.

Exc.: $850   **VGood:** $600   **Good:** $450

AAO MODEL 2000 50 CALIBER

Bolt action; 50 BMG; 5-shot magazine; 30-inch barrel, 1:15-inch twist; weighs 24 lbs.; muzzlebrake; cast alloy stock with gray anodized finish; Kick-Ease recoil pad; no sights; drilled and tapped for scope base; controlled feeding via rotating enclosed claw extractor; 90-degree bolt rotation; cone bolt face and barrel; trigger-mounted safety blocks sear; fully-adjustable, detachable tripod. Made in U.S. by American Arms & Ordnance. Introduced 1994.

New: $3750   **Perf.:** $2995   **Exc.:** $1995

ACKLEY OLYMPUS GRADE

Bolt action; 22-250, 25-06, 257 Roberts, 270, 7x57, 30-06, 7mm Rem. Mag., 300 Win. Mag.; 4-shot magazine (standard calibers), 3-shot (magnums); 24-inch barrel; no sights; drilled, tapped for scope mounts; hand-checkered select American walnut stock; rubber buttpad; swivel studs; Ackley barrel; hinged floorplate; fully-adjustable trigger; Mark X Mauser action. Introduced 1971; discontinued 1975.

Perf.: $900   **Exc.:** $725   **VGood:** $550

ACKLEY OLYMPUS GRADE II

Same specs as Olympus Grade except finely hand-checkered select American walnut stock; rubber recoil pad. Custom offering only; precludes pricing.

ACKLEY STANDARD MODEL

Bolt action; 22-250, 25-06, 257 Roberts, 270, 7x57, 30-06, 7mm Rem. Mag., 300 Win. Mag.; 4-shot magazine (standard calibers), 3-shot (magnums); 24-inch barrel; engraved receiver; no sights, drilled, tapped for scope mounts; hand-checkered American walnut stock; rubber recoil pad, swivel studs; Ackley barrel; hinged floorplate; fully-adjustable trigger; Mark X Mauser action. Introduced 1971; discontinued 1975.

Perf.: $700   **Exc.:** $650   **VGood:** $450

ACKLEY VARMINT SPECIAL

Bolt action; 22-250, 220 Swift, 25-06, 257 Roberts, 270, 7x57, 30-06, 7mm Rem. Mag., 300 Win. Mag.; 4-shot magazine (standard calibers), 3-shot (magnums); 26-inch barrel; no sights; drilled tapped for scope mounts; hand-checkered American walnut stock; varmint forend; rubber recoil pad; swivel studs. Introduced 1971; discontinued 1975.

Perf.: $700   **Exc.:** $600   **VGood:** $450

ACTION ARMS TIMBERWOLF

Slide action; 38 Spl./357 Mag., 44 Mag.; 10-shot magazine; 18-1/2-inch barrel; 36-1/2-inch overall length; weighs 5-1/2 lbs.; blade front sight, adjustable rear; plain walnut stock; grooved slide handle; push-button safety on trigger guard; takedown; integral scope mount; blued or chrome finish. Was imported by Action Arms Ltd. (357 only) and Springfield Armory (357 Mag. and 44 Mag.). Made in Israel. Introduced 1989; no longer imported.

Exc.: $650   **VGood:** $495   **Good:** $290

Chrome finish

Exc.: $665   **VGood:** $510   **Good:** $305

ALPHA ALASKAN

Bolt action; 308 Win., 350 Rem. Mag., 358 Win., 458 Win. Mag.; 4-shot magazine; 20- to 24-inch barrel; weighs 6-3/4 to 7-1/2 lbs.; no sights; drilled tapped for scope mounts; Alphawood stock; Neidner-style grip cap; barrel band swivel stud; right- or left-hand models; stainless steel construction. Introduced 1985; discontinued 1987.

Exc.: $1400   **VGood:** $1100   **Good:** $825

Ackley Olympus Grade II

Action Arms Timberwolf

Alpha Alaskan

Alpha Custom Model

Alpha Jaguar Grade I

ALPHA BIG-FIVE

Bolt action; 300 H&H to 458 Win. Mag.; 4-shot magazine; 20-inch-24-inch Douglas barrel; no sights; drilled tapped for scope mounts; satin-finish American walnut reinforced stock; three-position safety; honed action and trigger; lightened action; swivel studs; decelerator recoil pad. Introduced 1987; discontinued 1987.

Exc.: $1500   **VGood:** $1200   **Good:** $875

ALPHA CUSTOM MODEL

Bolt action; 17 Rem., 222, 223, 22-250, 338-284, 25-06, 35 Whelen, 257 Weatherby, 338 Win. Mag.; other calibers available in short, medium, long actions; 20- to 24-inch barrel; 40- to 43-inch overall length; weighs 6 to 7 lbs.; no sights; drilled, tapped for scope mounts; hand-checkered classic-style California Claro walnut stock; hand-rubbed oil finish; ebony forend tip; custom steel grip cap; solid buttpad; inletted swivel studs; three-lug locking system; three-position safety; left- or right-hand models; satin blue finish. Introduced 1984; discontinued 1987.

Exc.: $1250   **VGood:** $1100   **Good:** $875

ALPHA GRAND SLAM

Bolt action; 17 Rem., 222, 223, 22-250, 338-284, 25-06, 35 Whelen, 257 Weatherby, 338 Win. Mag.; other calibers available in short, medium, long actions; 20- to 24-inch barrel; 40- to 43-inch overall length; weighs 6-1/2 lbs.; no sights; drilled, tapped for scope mounts; hand-checkered classic-style California Claro walnut stock; hand-rubbed oil finish; ebony forend tip; custom steel grip cap; solid buttpad; inletted swivel studs; three-lug locking system; three-position safety; fluted bolt; left- or right-hand models; matte blue finish. Introduced 1984; discontinued 1987.

Exc.: $1250   **VGood:** $975   **Good:** $750

ALPHA JAGUAR GRADE I

Bolt action; from 222 to 338 Win. Mag.; 4-shot magazine; 20- to 24-inch round tapered barrel; 39-1/2-inch overall length; weighs 6 lbs.; no sights; drilled, tapped for scope mounts; satin-finish American walnut Monte Carlo stock; rubber buttpad; swivel studs; medium-length Mauser-type action; slide safety; cocking indicator; aluminum bedding block; Teflon-coated trigger guard, floorplate assembly. Introduced 1987; discontinued 1987.

Exc.: $975   **VGood:** $875   **Good:** $700

ALPHA JAGUAR GRADE II

Same specs as Grade I except Douglas premium barrel.

Exc.: $970   **VGood:** $790   **Good:** $600

ALPHA JAGUAR GRADE III

Same specs as Grade I except Douglas barrel; three-position safety; honed action and trigger.

Exc.: $1225   **VGood:** $1100   **Good:** $875

ALPHA JAGUAR GRADE IV

Same specs as Grade I except Douglas barrel; three-position safety; honed action and trigger; lightened action; swivel studs.

Exc.: $1300   **VGood:** $1150   **Good:** $900

ALPINE SPORTER

Bolt action; 22-250, 243 Win., 264 Win., 270, 30-06, 308, 308 Norma Mag., 7mm Rem. Mag., 8mm, 300 Win. Mag.; 5-shot magazine (standard calibers), 3-shot (magnums); 23-inch barrel (standard calibers), 24-inch (magnums); ramp front sight, open adjustable rear; checkered pistol-grip Monte Carlo stock of European walnut; recoil pad; sling swivels. Imported from England by Mandall Shooting Supplies. Introduced 1978; no longer imported.

Perf.: $450   **Exc.:** $400   **VGood:** $270

AMAC TARGETMASTER

Slide-action; 22 Short, 22 Long, 22 LR; 19-shot magazine (22 Short), 15-shot (22 Long), 12-shot (22 LR); 18-1/2-inch barrel; 36-1/2-inch overall length; weighs 5-3/4 lbs.; hooded ramp front sight, open adjustable rear; receiver grooved for scope mounts; walnut-finished hardwood stock; polished blued finish. Made in standard and youth models. Introduced 1985 by Iver Johnson; dropped 1990.

Exc.: $245   **VGood:** $195   **Good:** $175

American Arms EXP-64

AMAC Wagonmaster

Alpine Sporter

American Arms SM-64

AMT Magnum Hunter

Anschutz Achiever

Anschutz BR-50

AMERICAN FIREARMS STAINLESS MODEL

Bolt action; 22-250, 243, 6mm Rem., 6mm Win. Mag., 25-06, 257 Win. Mag., 264 Win. Mag., 6.5mm Rem. Mag., 6.5x55, 270 Win. Mag., 284 Win., 7x57, 7mm Rem. Mag., 7.62x39, 308 Win., 30-06, 300 Win. Mag., 338 Win. Mag., 458 Mag.; 16-1/2-inch, 18-inch, 20-inch, 22-inch, 24-inch, 26-inch, 28-inch barrel; no sights; drilled, tapped for scope mounts; hand-checkered walnut or maple stock; side safety; hinged floorplate; adjustable trigger; made of blued or satin stainless steel. Manufactured in four grades. Introduced 1972; dropped 1974.

Grade I, Presentation		
Perf.: $1495	**Exc.:** $1095	**VGood:** $895
Grade II, Deluxe		
Perf.: $1095	**Exc.:** $895	**VGood:** $650
Grade III, Standard		
Perf.: $895	**Exc.:** $695	**VGood:** $495
Grade IV, 338 & 458 Standard		
Perf.: $995	**Exc.:** $795	**VGood:** $595

AMT LIGHTNING 25/22

Semi-automatic; 22 LR; 25 or 30-shot magazine; 17-1/2-inch tapered barrel; 26-1/2-inch overall length (folded), 37-inch (open); weighs 6 lbs.; folding stainless steel stock; ramp front sight, fixed rear; made of stainless steel with matte finish; receiver dovetailed for scope mounting; extended magazine release; adjustable rear sight optionally available; youth stock available. Made in U.S. by AMT. Introduced 1984; dropped 1994.

Perf.: $325   **Exc.:** $275   **VGood:** $195

AMT LIGHTNING SMALL-GAME HUNTING RIFLE (HUNTER) II

Same specs as Lightning 25/22 except conventional stock of black fiberglass-filled nylon, checkered at the grip and forend, and fitted with Uncle Mike's swivel studs; removable recoil pad for ammo storage, cleaning rod and survival knife; no sights, receiver grooved for scope mounting; 22-inch full-floating target weight barrel; 40-1/2-inch overall length; weighs 6 lbs.; 10-shot rotary magazine. Made in U.S. by AMT. Introduced 1987; 22 WMR introduced 1992; dropped 1994.

Perf.: $325   **Exc.:** $275   **VGood:** $195

AMT MAGNUM HUNTER

Semi-automatic; 22 WMR; 10-shot magazine; 22-inch barrel; 40-1/2-inch overall length; weighs 6 lbs.; black fiberglass-filled nylon stock with checkered grip and forend; no sights; drilled and tapped for Weaver mount; stainless steel construction; free-floating target-weight barrel. Made in U.S. by AMT. Introduced 1992; dropped 1994.

Exc.: $375   **VGood:** $295   **Good:** $195

ANSCHUTZ ACHIEVER

Bolt action; single shot; 22 LR; 5-shot magazine; 19-1/2-inch barrel; spacers allow 35-1/2-inch to 36-1/2-inch overall length; weighs 5 lbs.; fully-adjustable open rear sight, hooded front; walnut-finished European hardwood stock; Mark 2000-type action; adjustable two-stage trigger; grooved for scope mounts. Made in Germany. Introduced 1993.

Perf.: $440   **Exc.:** $365   **VGood:** $220

ANSCHUTZ ACHIEVER ST SUPER TARGET

Same specs as Achiever except single shot, 22-inch barrel with 3/4-inch diameter; accepts optional micrometer target sights; 38-3/4-inch to 39-3/4-inch overall length; weighs about 6-1/2 lbs.; 13-1/2-inch accessory rail on forend; designed for the advanced junior shooter with adjustable length of pull from 13-1/4-inch to 14-1/4-inch via removable butt spacers. Imported from Germany. Introduced 1994.

Perf.: $415   **Exc.:** $370   **VGood:** $280

ANSCHUTZ BR-50

Bolt action; 22 LR; single shot; 19-3/4-inch barrel (without 11-oz. muzzle weight); 37-3/4-inch to 42-1/2-inch overall length; weighs about 11 lbs.; benchrest-style stock of European hardwood with stippled grip; cheekpiece vertically adjustable to

AMAC WAGONMASTER

Lever action; 22 Short, 22 Long, 22 LR, 22 WMR; 21-shot magazine (22 Short), 17-shot (22 Long), 15-shot (22 LR), 12-shot (22 WMR); 18-inch barrel; 36-1/2-inch overall length; weighs 5-3/4 lbs.; hooded ramp front sight, open adjustable rear; receiver grooved for scope mount; walnut-finished stock, forend; polished blued finish. Add $20 for 22 WMR version. Introduced 1985 by Iver Johnson; dropped 1990.

Exc.: $225   **VGood:** $175   **Good:** $150

AMERICAN ARMS AKY 39

Semi-automatic; 7.62x39mm; 30-shot magazine; 19-1/2-inch barrel; 40-1/2-inch overall length; weighs 9 lbs.; hooded post front sight, open adjustable rear; flip-up tritium sights; teakwood stock. Manufactured in Yugoslavia. Introduced 1988; discontinued 1989.

Perf.: $950   **Exc.:** $800   **VGood:** $600

Folding stock model		
Perf.: $1000	**Exc.:** $850	**VGood:** $700

AMERICAN ARMS EXP-64 SURVIVAL RIFLE

Semi-automatic; 22 LR; 10-shot magazine; 21-inch barrel; 40-inch overall length; weighs 7 lbs.; blade front sight, adjustable rear; receiver grooved for scope mounts; synthetic stock with storage compartment; takedown feature; crossbolt safety. Made in Italy. Introduced 1989; discontinued 1990.

Exc.: $150   **VGood:** $1525   **Good:** $100

AMERICAN ARMS MINI-MAX

Semi-automatic; 22 LR; 10-shot magazine; 18-3/4-inch barrel; 36-1/2-inch overall length; weighs 4-1/2 lbs.; blade front sight, adjustable open rear; black synthetic or wood stock; trigger-block safety on trigger guard; receiver grooved for scope mounts. Introduced 1990; discontinued 1990.

Perf.: $80   **Exc.:** $70   **VGood:** $55

AMERICAN ARMS RS COMBO

Combination gun; over/under box lock; 222 or 308/12-ga. 3-inch; 24-inch barrel; weighs 7 lbs. 14 oz.; Full-choke tube; vent rib; blade front sight, folding rear; grooved for scope mounts; European walnut Monte Carlo stock; checkered pistol grip, forend; double triggers; extractors; silver finish, engraving; barrel connectors allow for windage/elevation adjustment of rifle barrel. Made in Italy. Introduced 1989; discontinued 1989.

Perf.: $795   **Exc.:** $695   **VGood:** $525

AMERICAN ARMS SM-64

Semi-automatic; 22 LR; 10-shot magazine; 21-inch barrel; 40-inch overall length; weighs 7 lbs.; hooded front sight, adjustable rear; checkered hardwood stock, forend; takedown feature. Made in Italy. Introduced 1989; discontinued 1990.

Exc.: $130   **VGood:** $110   **Good:** $90

1 inch; stock length adjustable via spacers and buttplate; glossy blue-black paint finish; no sights; receiver grooved for mounts; barrel drilled and tapped for target mounts; uses the Anschutz 2013 target action with #5018 two-stage adjustable target trigger. Imported from Germany. Introduced 1994.

Perf.: $2695　**Exc.:** $1995　**VGood:** $1125

ANSCHUTZ KADETT

Bolt action; 22 LR; 5-shot clip; 22-inch barrel; 40-inch overall length; weighs 5-1/2 lbs.; Lyman adjustable folding leaf rear sight, hooded bead on ramp front; checkered walnut-finish European hardwood stock; Mark 2000 target action; single-stage trigger; grooved for scope mount. Made in Germany. Introduced 1987; discontinued 1988.

Perf.: $335　**Exc.:** $300　**VGood:** $260

ANSCHUTZ MARK 525 DELUXE AUTO

Semi-automatic; 22 LR; 10-shot clip magazine; 24-inch barrel; 43-inch overall length; weighs 6-1/2 lbs.; European hardwood stock with checkered pistol grip, Monte Carlo comb, beavertail forend; hooded ramp front sight, folding leaf rear; rotary safety; empty shell deflector; single stage trigger; receiver grooved for scope mounting. Imported from Germany. Introduced 1984; no longer imported.

Perf.: $560　**Exc.:** $475　**VGood:** $390

ANSCHUTZ MARK 525 CARBINE

Same specs as Mark 525 except 20-inch barrel, handguard, adjustable peep sight. Discontinued 1985.

Perf.: $500　**Exc.:** $425　**VGood:** $295

ANSCHUTZ MARK 2000

Bolt action; single shot; 22 LR; heavy 26-inch barrel; 43-inch overall length; weighs 7-1/2 lbs.; globe insert front sight, micro-click peep rear; walnut-finish hardwood stock; thumb groove in stock; pistol grip swell. Made in Germany. Introduced 1980; importation discontinued 1988. Marketed in U. S. as Savage/Anschutz Mark 12.

Perf.: $440　**Exc.:** $390　**VGood:** $320

ANSCHUTZ MODEL 54.18MS

Bolt action; single shot; uses Super Match 54 action; for metallic silhouette shooting. 22 LR; 20, 22-1/2-inch barrel; 41-3/8-inch overall length; weighs 9 lbs. 4 oz.; no sights; stippled walnut stock, pistol grip, forearm; two-stage trigger. Introduced 1981.

Right-hand action		
Perf.: $1400	**Exc.:** $1075	**VGood:** $800
Left-hand action		
Perf.: $1450	**Exc.:** $1125	**VGood:** $825

ANSCHUTZ MODEL 54.18MS ED

Same specs as Model 54.18MS except 19-1/4-inch barrel; 14-1/4-inch extension tube; three removable muzzle weights. Introduced 1984; discontinued 1988.

Right-hand action		
Perf.: $1100	**Exc.:** $875	**VGood:** $625
Left-hand action		
Perf.: $1200	**Exc.:** $975	**VGood:** $700

ANSCHUTZ MODEL 54.18MS FORTNER SILHOUETTE RIFLE

Same specs as the 54.18MS except Anschutz/Fortner system straight-pull bolt action; 21-inch barrel, 3/4-inch-diameter; McMillan Fibergrain fiberglass silhouette stock; two-stage #5020 trigger adjustable from 3-1/2 oz. to 2 lbs.; extremely fast lock time. Imported from Germany. Introduced 1995.

Right-hand		
Perf.: $3250	**Exc.:** $2795	**VGood:** $1995
Left-hand		
Perf.: $3500	**Exc.:** $2995	**VGood:** $2125

ANSCHUTZ MODEL 54.18MS REP

Same specs as Model 54.18MS except repeater with 5-shot magazine; 22- to 30-inch barrel; weighs 7-3/4 lbs.; thumbhole wood or synthetic stock with vented forearm; Super Match 54 action. Introduced 1989.

Perf.: $1700　**Exc.:** $1300　**VGood:** $900

Anschutz Kadett

Anschutz Mark 525 Deluxe Auto

Anschutz Model 54.18MS

Anschutz 54.18MS Fortner Silhouette Rifle

Anschutz Model 64MS

ANSCHUTZ MODEL 54.18MS REP DELUXE

Same specs as Model 54.18 REP except Fibergrain McMillan thumbhole stock with stippling. Introduced 1990.

Perf.: $1700　**Exc.:** $1100　**VGood:** $900

ANSCHUTZ MODEL 64

Bolt action; single shot; 22 LR; 26-inch barrel, 11/16-inch diameter; 44-inch overall length; weighs 7-3/4 lbs.; no sights; scope blocks receiver grooved for Anschutz sights; walnut-finish hardwood stock; cheekpiece; hand-checkered pistol grip, beavertail forearm; adjustable buttplate; adjustable single-stage trigger; sliding side safety; forward sling swivel for competition sling. Marketed in U.S. as Savage/Anschutz Model 64. Introduced 1963; discontinued 1981.

Right-hand model		
Perf.: $500	**Exc.:** $400	**VGood:** $300
Left-hand model		
Perf.: $600	**Exc.:** $500	**VGood:** $400

ANSCHUTZ MODEL 64MS

Bolt action; single shot; 22 LR; 21-1/4-inch barrel; 39-1/2-inch overall length; weighs 8 lbs.; no sights; drilled, tapped for scope mounts; stippled thumbhole wood stock with pistol grip; adjustable two-stage trigger; Match 64 action. Introduced 1981; still imported.

Right-hand model		
Perf.: $800	**Exc.:** $700	**VGood:** $500
Left-hand model		
Perf.: $850	**Exc.:** $750	**VGood:** $550

ANSCHUTZ MODEL 64MS-FWT

Same specs as Model 64MS except weighs 6-1/4 lbs.; single-stage trigger. Introduced 1985; discontinued 1988.

Perf.: $595　**Exc.:** $525　**VGood:** $375

ANSCHUTZ MODEL 64MS LEFT-HAND SILHOUETTE

Same specs as Model 64MS except left-hand model. Imported from Germany. Introduced 1980; still imported.

Perf.: $895　**Exc.:** $775　**VGood:** $550

ANSCHUTZ 64-MSR SILHOUETTE RIFLE

Bolt action; 22 LR, 5-shot magazine. 21-1/2-inch barrel, medium heavy; 7/8-inch diameter; weighs 8 lbs. 39-1/2-inch overall. Walnut-finished hardwood stock, silhouette-type. Uses Match 64 action. Repeater designed for metallic silhouette competition. Stock has stippled checkering, contoured thumb groove with Wundhammer swell. Two-stage #5098 trigger. Slide safety locks sear and bolt. Imported from Germany by AcuSport Corp., Accuracy International, Gunsmithing, Inc.

Perf.: $800　**Exc.:** $700　**VGood:** $500

ANSCHUTZ MODEL 64S

Bolt action; single shot; 22 LR; 26-inch barrel; 44-inch overall length; target sights; walnut-finish hardwood stock; cheekpiece; hand-checkered pistol grip; beavertail forearm; adjustable buttplate; adjustable single-stage trigger; sliding side safety; forward sling swivel for competition sling. Marketed

Anschutz Model 54.18MS REP

Anschutz Model 1403B Biathlon

Anschutz Model 1407

Anschutz Model 1403D Match

Anschutz Model 1408ED

Anschutz Model 1411

Anschutz Model 1413

in U.S. as Savage/Anschutz Model 64S. Introduced 1963; discontinued 1981.

Right-hand model		
Perf.: $595	**Exc.:** $525	**VGood:** $350

Left-hand model		
Perf.: $625	**Exc.:** $550	**VGood:** $375

ANSCHUTZ MODEL 520/61

Semi-automatic; 22 LR; 10-shot clip magazine; 24-inch barrel; 43-inch overall length; weighs 6-1/2 lbs.; folding adjustable rear sight, hooded ramp front; receiver grooved for scope mounts; European Monte Carlo walnut stock, forend; hand checkering; rotary-style safety; single-stage trigger; swivel studs. Made in Germany. Introduced 1982; discontinued 1983.

Perf.: $375	**Exc.:** $300	**VGood:** $165

ANSCHUTZ MODEL 1403B BIATHLON

Bolt action; 22 LR; 5-shot magazine; 21-1/2-inch barrel; 42-1/2-inch overall length; weighs 8-1/2 lbs.; blonde-finish European hardwood stock; stippled pistol grip; globe front sight with snow cap and muzzle cover, optional micrometer peep rear with spring-hinged snow cap; uses Match 64 Target action with three-way adjustable two-stage trigger; slide safety; comes with five magazines; adjustable buttplate. Imported from Germany. Introduced 1991; no longer imported.

Perf.: $950	**Exc.:** $800	**VGood:** $525

ANSCHUTZ MODEL 1403D MATCH

Bolt action; single shot; 22 LR; 25-1/4-inch barrel; 43-1/4-inch overall length; weighs 8.6 lbs.; no sights;

receiver grooved for scope mounts; walnut-finished hardwood stock cheekpiece; checkered pistol grip, beavertail forend; adjustable buttplate; slide safety; #5053 adjustable single-stage trigger. Made in Germany. Introduced 1980; importation discontinued 1990.

Right-hand model		
Perf.: $750	**Exc.:** $650	**VGood:** $450

Left-hand model		
Perf.: $775	**Exc.:** $675	**VGood:** $475

ANSCHUTZ MODEL 1407

Bolt action; single shot; 22 LR; 26-inch barrel; 44-1/2-inch overall length; weighs 10 lbs.; weight conforms to ISU competition requirements, also suitable for NRA matches; no sights; receiver grooved for Anschutz sights; scope blocks; French walnut prone-style stock; Monte Carlo, cast-off cheekpiece; hand-stippled pistol grip, forearm; swivel rail, adjustable swivel; adjustable rubber buttplate; single-stage trigger; wing safety. Marketed in U.S. by Savage. Introduced in 1967; no longer in production.

Right-hand model		
Perf.: $475	**Exc.:** $425	**VGood:** $275

Left-hand model		
Perf.: $495	**Exc.:** $440	**VGood:** $290

ANSCHUTZ MODEL 1408

Bolt action; 22 LR; 5-, 10-shot magazine; 26-inch heavy barrel; weighs 10 lbs.; receiver grooved for micrometer sights; hooded ramp front sight; European walnut stock; checkered pistol grip, forearm; adjustable cheek-piece. Marketed in the U.S. by Savage. Introduced 1967; no longer in production.

Perf.: $375	**Exc.:** $325	**VGood:** $275

ANSCHUTZ MODEL 1408ED

Same specs as Model 1908 except 23-inch barrel; European walnut thumbhole stock; adjustable comb and buttplate; single-stage trigger; oversize bolt knob. Introduced in 1976; no longer in production.

Perf.: $550	**Exc.:** $500	**VGood:** $400

ANSCHUTZ MODEL 1411

Bolt action; single shot; 22 LR; 27-1/2-inch barrel; 46-inch overall length; weighs 11 lbs.; no sights; receiver grooved for Anschutz sights; scope blocks; French walnut prone-style stock; Monte Carlo, cast-off cheekpiece; hand-stippled pistol grip, forearm; swivel rail, adjustable swivel; adjustable rubber buttplate; single-stage trigger; wing safety. Marketed in U.S. by Savage. Introduced 1965; no longer in production.

Perf.: $450	**Exc.:** $400	**VGood:** $250

ANSCHUTZ MODEL 1413

Bolt action; single shot; heavy match rifle; 22 LR; 27-1/2-inch barrel; 50-inch overall length; weighs 15-1/2 lbs; no sights; receiver grooved for Anschutz sights; scope blocks; International-type French walnut stock; adjustable aluminum Schuetzen hook buttplate; adjustable cheekpiece; new yoke-type adjustable palm rest; single-stage trigger; wing safety. Marketed in the U.S. by Savage. Introduced 1967; no longer in production.

Perf.: $650	**Exc.:** $580	**VGood:** $400

ANSCHUTZ MODEL 1416D KL CLASSIC

Bolt action; 22 LR; 5-shot clip; 22-1/2-inch or 23-inch barrel; 41-inch overall length; weighs 5-1/2 to 6 lbs.; classic-style European walnut stock with straight comb, checkered pistol grip and forend; hooded ramp front sight, folding leaf rear; uses Match 64 action; adjustable single stage trigger; receiver grooved for scope mounting. Imported from Germany by Precision Sales International, later AcuSport.

Perf.: $700	**Exc.:** $600	**VGood:** $400

Left-hand		
Perf.: $725	**Exc.:** $620	**VGood:** $415

ANSCHUTZ MODEL 1416D CUSTOM

Same specs as Model 1416 Classic except European walnut stock with roll-over Monte Carlo cheekpiece; slim forend with schnabel tip; fine cut checkering on grip and forend. Imported from Germany by Precision Sales International, later AcuSport. Introduced 1988.

Perf.: $750   **Exc.:** $650   **VGood:** $450

ANSCHUTZ MODEL 1416D DELUXE

Same specs as Model 1416 except European walnut Monte Carlo stock with cheekpiece; schnabel forend; Model 1403 target rifle action. Imported from Germany by Precision Sales International. No longer imported.

Perf.: $750   **Exc.:** $675   **VGood:** $450

ANSCHUTZ MODEL 1416D FIBERGLASS

Same specs as Model 1416D except 40-1/4-inch overall length; weighs 5-1/4 lbs.; McMillan fiberglass Monte Carlo stock with roll-over cheekpiece; Wundhammer grip swell; adjustable trigger; slide safety; 10-shot magazine and single shot adaptor optional. Imported from Germany by Precision Sales International, Inc. Introduced 1991; no longer imported.

Perf.: $925   **Exc.:** $795   **VGood:** $495

ANSCHUTZ MODEL 1418D

Bolt action; 22 LR; 5-shot clip; 19-3/4-inch barrel; weighs 5-1/2 lbs.; European walnut Mannlicher-style stock with mahogany schnabel tip, checkered pistol grip and forend; hooded ramp front sight, folding leaf rear; uses Model 1403 target rifle action; adjustable single-stage trigger; receiver grooved for scope mounting. Imported from Germany by Precision Sales International, later AcuSport. Still imported.

Perf.: $975   **Exc.:** $800   **VGood:** $650

ANSCHUTZ MODEL 1422D CLASSIC

Bolt action; 22 LR; 5-shot clip; 24-inch barrel; 43-inch overall length; weighs 7-1/4 lbs.; hooded ramp front sight, folding leaf rear; drilled, tapped for scope mounting; select European walnut stock; checkered pistol grip, forend; adjustable single-stage trigger. Made in Germany. Introduced 1982; importation discontinued 1988.

Perf.: $995   **Exc.:** $850   **VGood:** $695

ANSCHUTZ MODEL 1422D CUSTOM

Same specs as Model 1422D Classic except weighs 6-1/2 lbs.; Monte Carlo stock with roll-over cheekpiece; slim forend; schnabel tip; palm swell on pistol grip; rosewood grip cap; diamond insert; skip-line checkering. Made in Germany. Introduced 1982; importation discontinued 1988.

Perf.: $1195   **Exc.:** $995   **VGood:** $695

ANSCHUTZ MODEL 1432 CLASSIC

Bolt action; 22 Hornet; 5-shot box magazine; 23-1/2-inch barrel; 42-1/2-inch overall length; weighs 7-3/4 lbs.; receiver grooved for scope mounting; folding leaf rear sight, hooded ramp front; European walnut Monte Carlo-type stock; hand-checkered pistol grip, forearm; cheekpiece. Introduced 1976; no longer in production.

Perf.: $1195   **Exc.:** $1095   **VGood:** $850

ANSCHUTZ MODEL 1432 CUSTOM

Same specs as Model 1432 except 24-inch barrel; 43-inch overall length; weighs 6-1/2 lbs.; Monte Carlo stock with roll-over cheekpiece; palm swell on pistol grip; rosewood grip cap; diamond insert. No longer in production.

Perf.: $1395   **Exc.:** $1125   **VGood:** $895

ANSCHUTZ MODEL 1433D

Bolt action; 22 Hornet; European walnut Mannlicher-type stock; 4-shot clip magazine; 19-3/4-inch barrel; 39-inch overall length; weighs 6-1/4 lbs.; receiver grooved for scope mounting; folding leaf rear sight, hooded ramp front; hand-checkered pistol grip, forearm; cheekpiece; Match 54 target action; single-stage or double-set trigger. Introduced 1976; discontinued 1986.

Perf.: $1000   **Exc.:** $800   **VGood:** $550

Anschutz Model 1416D/1516D Custom

Anschutz Model 1418D

Anschutz Model 1422D Classic

Anschutz Model 1432 Custom

Anschutz Model 1433D

Anschutz Model 1449 Youth

Anschutz Model 1451D KL Classic

ANSCHUTZ MODEL 1449 YOUTH

Bolt action; 22 LR; 5-shot clip; 16-1/4-inch barrel; 32-1/2-inch overall length; weighs 3-1/2 lbs.; hooded ramp front sight, open adjustable rear; grooved for scope mounts; walnut-finished European hardwood stock; built on Anschutz Mark 2000 action; single-shot clip adaptor and 10-shot magazine available. Made in Germany. Introduced 1990; discontinued 1991.

Perf.: $300   **Exc.:** $270   **VGood:** $130

ANSCHUTZ MODEL 1450B BIATHLON

Bolt action; single shot; 22 LR; 19-1/2-inch barrel; 36-inch overall length; weighs 5 lbs.; aperture sights; European hardwood stock with ventilated forend and adjustable buttplate; Mark 2000 action. Introduced 1993; discontinued 1993.

Perf.: $695   **Exc.:** $625   **VGood:** $460

ANSCHUTZ MODEL 1451D KL CLASSIC

Bolt action; 22LR; bbl. 22.5-inch; 5-shot magazine weighs 5.5 lbs.; overall length 41-inch folding leaf rear, ramp front sight, with hood; hardwood stock with checkered pistol grip and forearm; single-stage trigger. Introduced 1998. Imported from Germany.

Perf.: $400   **Exc.:** $350   **VGood:** $200

ANSCHUTZ MODEL 1451D KL MONTE CARLO CLASSIC

Same specs as 1451D KL Classic, but with walnut Monte Carlo stock with schnabel forearm, 1-inch sling swivels.

Perf.: $500   **Exc.:** $450   **VGood:** $300

Anschutz Model 1451R Sporter Target

Anschutz Model 1502 D HB Classic

Anschutz Model 1518D

Anschutz Model 1700D Bavarian

Anschutz Model 1700D Custom

ANSCHUTZ MODEL 1451R SPORTER TARGET

Same specs as 1451D KL, but designed as smallbore target and varmint rifle; stippled hardwood target stock, adjustable horizontally and vertically at butt, length can be extended with spacers; aluminum accessory rail; 22-inch heavy target barrel, grooved for target front sight; receiver grooved for target rear sight or scope mounting; weighs 6.3 lbs; 10-shot magazine; 2-stage trigger. Introduced 1998.

Perf.: $560   **Exc.:** $550   **VGood:** $400

ANSCHUTZ MODEL 1451ST R

Same specs as 1451D KL, but heavy-barrel repeater with multi-purpose beavertail hardwood stock; 22-inch bbl; grooved for sights or scope mounting; 5-shot magazine; 2-stage trigger; weighs 6.6 lbs.

Perf.: $600   **Exc.:** $550   **VGood:** $400

ANSCHUTZ MODEL 1502 D HB CLASSIC

Similar to Model 1702 D HB but with single-stage trigger, fewer refinements. Add 10 percent for beavertail forend.

NIB: $495   **Exc. $400   **VGood:** $300

ANSCHUTZ MODEL 1516D CLASSIC

Bolt action; 22 WMR; 4-shot clip; 22-1/2-inch barrel; 41-inch overall length; weighs 6 lbs.; classic-style European walnut stock with straight comb; checkered pistol grip and forend; hooded ramp front sight, folding leaf rear; uses Match 64 action; adjustable single-stage trigger; receiver grooved for scope mounting. Imported from Germany by Precision Sales International, later AcuSport.

Perf.: $695   **Exc.:** $525   **VGood:** $460

ANSCHUTZ MODEL 1516D CUSTOM

Same specs as Model 1516D Classic except European walnut stock with roll-over Monte Carlo cheekpiece; slim forend with schnabel tip; fine

cut checkering on grip and forend. Imported from Germany. Introduced 1988.

Perf.: $700   **Exc.:** $560   **VGood:** $340

ANSCHUTZ MODEL 1516D DELUXE

Same specs as Model 1516D Classic except European walnut Monte Carlo stock with cheekpiece; schnabel forend; Model 1403 target rifle action. Imported from Germany by Precision Sales International. No longer imported.

Perf.: $800   **Exc.:** $660   **VGood:** $450

ANSCHUTZ MODEL 1518D

Bolt action; 22 WMR; 4-shot clip; 19-3/4-inch barrel; 38-inch overall length; weighs 5-1/2 lbs.; European walnut Mannlicher-style stock with mahogany schnabel tip; checkered pistol grip and forend; hooded ramp front sight, folding leaf rear; set trigger. Introduced 1976; still in production.

Perf.: $850   **Exc.:** $740   **VGood:** $500

ANSCHUTZ MODEL 1518D DELUXE

Same specs as Model 1518D except Model 1403 target rifle action; adjustable single stage trigger; receiver grooved for scope mounting. Imported from Germany. No longer imported.

Perf.: $795   **Exc.:** $695   **VGood:** $470

ANSCHUTZ 1518D LUXUS BOLT-ACTION RIFLE

Bolt action, caliber: 22 WMR, 4-shot magazine. Barrel: 19-3/4-inch. Weight: 5-1/2 lbs. Length: 37-1/2-inch overall. Stock: European walnut. Sights: Blade on ramp front, folding leaf rear. Features: Receiver grooved for scope mounting; single stage trigger; skip-line checkering; rosewood forend tip; sling swivels. Imported from Germany by AcuSport Corp.

Perf.: $975   **Exc.:** $850   **VGood:** $700

ANSCHUTZ MODEL 1522D CLASSIC

Bolt action; 22 WMR; 5-shot clip; 24-inch barrel; 43-inch overall length; weighs 7-1/4 lbs.; hooded ramp front sight, folding leaf rear; drilled, tapped for scope mount; select European walnut stock; checkered pistol grip, forend; adjustable single-stage trigger. Made in Germany. Introduced 1982; importation discontinued 1988.

Perf.: $1050   **Exc.:** $950   **VGood:** $695

ANSCHUTZ MODEL 1522D CUSTOM

Same specs as Model 1522D except Monte Carlo cheekpiece; slim forend; schnabel tip; palm swell on pistol grip; rosewood grip cap, diamond insert; skip-line checkering. Introduced 1982; importation discontinued 1988.

Perf.: $1050   **Exc.:** $895   **VGood:** $595

ANSCHUTZ MODEL 1533D

Bolt action; 222 Rem.; 3-shot box magazine; 19-3/4-inch barrel; receiver grooved for scope mount; folding leaf rear sight, hooded ramp front; European walnut Mannlicher-style stock; hand-checkered pistol grip, forend; cheekpiece; single-stage or double-set trigger. Introduced 1976; no longer in production.

Perf.: $1050   **Exc.:** $950   **VGood:** $695

ANSCHUTZ MODEL 1700D BAVARIAN

Bolt action; 22 LR, 22 Hornet, 222 Rem.; 5-shot clip (22 Hornet); 24-inch barrel; 43-inch overall length; weighs 7-1/2 lbs.; European Monte Carlo walnut stock with Bavarian cheek rest; checkered pistol grip and forend; hooded ramp front sight, folding leaf rear; improved 1700 Match 54 action with adjustable #5096 trigger; drilled and tapped for scope mounting. Imported from Germany. Introduced 1988; still imported.

Rimfire		
Perf.: $995	**Exc.:** $895	**VGood:** $500
Centerfire		
Perf.: $1100	**Exc.:** $975	**VGood:** $700

ANSCHUTZ MODEL 1700D BAVARIAN MEISTERGRADE

Same specs as Model 1700D Bavarian except select European walnut stock; gold engraved trigger guard. Introduced 1988.

Rimfire		
Perf.: $1100	**Exc.:** $975	**VGood:** $720
Centerfire		
Perf.: $1250	**Exc.:** $1050	**VGood:** $725

ANSCHUTZ MODEL 1700D CLASSIC

Same specs as Model 1700D Bavarian except 22 LR; weighs 6-3/4 lbs.; #5095 trigger; select European walnut stock with checkered pistol grip and forend. Imported from Germany. Introduced 1988; importation dropped 1994.

Perf.: $1100   **Exc.:** $950   **VGood:** $600

ANSCHUTZ MODEL 1700D CLASSIC MEISTERGRADE

Same specs as 1700D Classic except better grade of wood; gold engraved trigger guard. Introduced 1988; importation dropped 1994.

Perf.: $1150   **Exc.:** $1000   **VGood:** $775

ANSCHUTZ MODEL 1700D CUSTOM

Same specs as Model 1700D Bavarian except European walnut stock with roll-over Monte Carlo cheekpiece; slim forend; schnabel tip; palm swell on pistol grip; skip-line checkering. Made in Germany. Introduced 1988; discontinued 1991.

Perf.: $1200   **Exc.:** $950   **VGood:** $675

ANSCHUTZ MODEL 1700D CUSTOM GRAPHITE

Same specs as Model 1700D Custom except 22 LR; 22-inch barrel; 41-inch overall length; weighs 7-1/2 lbs.; McMillan graphite-reinforced stock, roll-over cheekpiece; quick-detach sling swivels; embroidered sling. Introduced 1991; still imported.

Perf.: $1150   **Exc.:** $975   **VGood:** $695

ANSCHUTZ MODEL 1700D CUSTOM MEISTERGRADE

Same specs as Model 1700D Custom except select European walnut stock; gold, engraved trigger guard. Introduced 1988; discontinued 1991.

Perf.: $1100   **Exc.:** $900   **VGood:** $550

ANSCHUTZ MODEL 1700D FEATHERWEIGHT

Same specs as Model 1700D Bavarian except 22 LR; 22-inch barrel; 41-inch overall length; weighs 6-1/4 lbs.; matte black McMillan fiberglass stock; single-stage #5096 trigger. Introduced 1989; dropped about 1996.

Perf.: $1100   **Exc.:** $950   **VGood:** $715

ANSCHUTZ MODEL 1700D FEATHERWEIGHT DELUXE

Same specs as Model 1700D Featherweight except Fibergrain synthetic stock with simulated wood grain and skip-line checkering. Introduced 1990; no longer imported.

Perf.: $1150   **Exc.:** $1000   **VGood:** $750

ANSCHUTZ MODEL 1700D GRAPHITE HORNET

Same specs as Model 1700D Custom except 22 Hornet; 22-inch barrel; 41-inch overall length; weighs 7-1/2 lbs.; McMillan graphite-reinforced fiberglass stock with roll-over cheekpiece; built on Anschutz sporter action; fitted with Anschutz logo sling and quick-release swivels. Imported from Germany by Precision Sales International. Introduced 1995; still imported.

Perf.: $1150   **Exc.:** $975   **VGood:** $725

ANSCHUTZ MODEL 1702 D HB CLASSIC

Chambered in .17 Mach 2. Features include finely-tuned double-stage trigger, walnut stock, 23-inch blued heavy sightless barrel, 5-shot magazine.

NIB: $950   **Exc.:** $795   **VGood:** $600

ANSCHUTZ MODEL 1710D CUSTOM RIFLE

Bolt action; 22 LR, 5-shot clip. 24-1/4-inch barrel; weighs 7-3/8 lbs. 42-1/2-inch overall. Select European walnut stock. Sights: Hooded ramp front, folding leaf rear; drilled and tapped for scope mounting. Match 54 action with adjustable single-stage trigger; roll-over Monte Carlo cheekpiece, slim forend with schnabel tip, wundhammer palm swell on pistol grip, rosewood gripcap with white diamond insert; skip-line checkering on grip and forend. Imported from Germany by AcuSport Corp.

Perf.: $1100   **Exc.:** $8950   **VGood:** $700

ANSCHUTZ MODEL 1712 SILHOUETTE SPORTER

Chambered in .22 LR. Features include two-stage trigger, deluxe walnut stock with schnabel, 21.6-inch blued sightless barrel, 5-shot magazine.

NIB: $1375   **Exc.:** $1200   **VGood:** $900

ANSCHUTZ MODEL 1733D MANNLICHER

Bolt action; 22 Hornet; 5-shot clip; 19-3/4-inch barrel; 39-inch overall length; weighs 6-1/4 lbs.; full-length Mannlicher-style stock; hooded ramp front sight, Lyman folding rear; improved Match 54 action with #5096 single-stage trigger with 2-1/2-lb. adjustable pull weight; sling swivels. Imported from Germany. Introduced 1993.

Perf.: $1250   **Exc.:** $975   **VGood:** $600

ANSCHUTZ MODEL 1740 CUSTOM RIFLE

Bolt action; caliber: 22 Hornet, 5-shot clip; 222 Rem., 3-shot clip. Barrel: 24-inch. Weighs 6-1/2 lbs. 43-1/4-inch overall length. Select European walnut stock. Sights: Hooded ramp front, folding leaf rear; drilled and tapped for scope mounting. Uses match 54 action. Adjustable single stage trigger. Stock has roll-over Monte Carlo cheekpiece, slim forend with schnabel tip, Wundhammer palm swell on grip, rosewood gripcap with white diamond insert. Skip-

Anschutz Model 1700D Featherweight

Anschutz Model 1702 D HB Classic

Anschutz Model 1733D Mannlicher

Anschutz Model 1808ED Super

Anschutz Model 1907 Match

line checkering on grip and forend. Introduced 1997. Imported from Germany by AcuSport Corp.

Perf.: $1100   **Exc.:** $950   **VGood:** $700

ANSCHUTZ MODEL 1743D BOLT-ACTION RIFLE

Bolt action; caliber: 222 Rem., 3-shot magazine. 19.7-inch barrel. weighs 6.4 lbs; 39-inch overall length. Stock: European walnut, Mannlicher-style. Sights: Hooded blade front, folding leaf rear. Receiver grooved for scope mounting; single stage trigger; claw extractor; sling safety; sling swivels. Imported from Germany by AcuSport Corp.

Perf.: $1350   **Exc.:** $1050   **VGood:** $700

ANSCHUTZ MODEL 1803D

Bolt action; single shot; 22 LR; 25-1/2-inch heavy barrel; 43-3/4-inch overall length; weighs 8-3/8 lbs.; no sights; blonde or walnut-finished European hardwood target stock; adjustable cheekpiece; stippled grip, forend; built on Anschutz Match 64 action; #5091 two-stage trigger; right- or left-hand models. Made in Germany. Introduced 1987; discontinued 1993.

Perf.: $900   **Exc.:** $825   **VGood:** $585

ANSCHUTZ MODEL 1808D RT

Bolt action; single shot; 22 LR; 32-1/2-inch barrel; 50-1/2-inch overall length; weighs 9-3/8 lbs.; no sights furnished; grooved for scope mount; European walnut stock, heavy beavertail forend; adjustable cheekpiece, buttplate; stippled grip, forend; nine-way adjustable single-stage trigger; slide safety; right- or left-hand. Made in Germany. Introduced 1991.

Perf.: $1500   **Exc.:** $1400   **VGood:** $900

ANSCHUTZ MODEL 1808ED SUPER

Bolt action; single shot; designed for Running Target competition; 22 LR; 23-1/2-inch heavy barrel; 42-inch overall length; 9-1/4 lbs.; no sights; receiver grooved for scope mount; European hardwood stock; adjustable cheekpiece; beavertail forend; stippled pistol grip, forend; removable barrel weights; adjustable trigger; Special order only. Made in Germany. Introduced 1982; importation discontinued 1990.

Right-hand version		
Perf.: $1595	**Exc.:** $1395	**VGood:** $995
Left-hand version		
Perf.: $1600	**Exc.:** $1400	**VGood:** $1000

ANSCHUTZ MODEL 1827B BIATHLON

Bolt action; 22 LR; 5-shot magazine; 21-1/2-inch barrel; 42-1/2-inch overall length; weighs 8-1/2 lbs.; special Biathlon globe front sight, micrometer rear with snow cap; adjustable trigger; adjustable wooden buttplate; adjustable handstop rail; Biathlon butthook. Made in Germany. Introduced 1982.

Right-hand version		
Perf.: $1995	**Exc.:** $1595	**VGood:** $1100
Left-hand version		
Perf.: $2100	**Exc.:** $1675	**VGood:** $1150

ANSCHUTZ MODEL 1827BT FORTNER BIATHLON

Same specs as the Anschutz 1827B Biathlon rifle except Anschutz/Fortner system straight-pull bolt action. Imported from Germany. Introduced 1982.

Perf.: $2995	**Exc.:** $2195	**VGood:** $1600
Left-hand		
Perf.: $3050	**Exc.:** $2250	**VGood:** $1650

Anschutz Model 1913
Super Match

Anschutz Super Match 2013

Anschutz Model
1097 Club

Anschutz 1710 D HB Classic
150th Anniversary Model

Armalite AR-7 Explorer

ANSCHUTZ MODEL 1903 MATCH

Bolt action; single shot; 22 LR; 25-inch barrel, 3/4-inch diameter; 43-3/4-inch overall length; weighs 8-1/2 lbs.; walnut-finished hardwood stock with adjustable cheekpiece; stippled grip and forend; no sights; accepts #6825 sight set; Anschutz Match 64 action; #5098 two-stage trigger; designed for intermediate and advanced Junior Match competition. Imported from Germany. Introduced 1987.

Right-hand

| Perf.: $900 | Exc.: $800 | VGood: $525 |

Left-hand

| Perf.: $950 | Exc.: $850 | VGood: $575 |

ANSCHUTZ MODEL 1907 MATCH

Bolt action; single shot; 22 LR; 26-inch barrel with 7/8-inch diameter barrel; 44-1/2-inch overall length; weighs 10 lbs.; blonde-finished European hardwood target stock with vented forend; stippled pistol grip and forend; no sights; designed for ISU requirements; suitable for NRA matches. Imported from Germany.

| Perf.: $1695 | Exc.: $1350 | VGood: $895 |

ANSCHUTZ MODEL 1907-L MATCH

Same specs as Model 1907 Match except true left-hand action and stock. Imported from Germany.

| Perf.: $1750 | Exc.: $1400 | VGood: $950 |

ANSCHUTZ MODEL 1910 SUPER MATCH II

Bolt action; single shot; 22 LR; 27-1/4-inch barrel; 46-inch overall length; weighs about 14 lbs.; European walnut International-type stock with

adjustable cheekpiece; adjustable aluminum hook buttplate; adjustable hand stop; uses Match 54 action; sights not included. Imported from Germany. Introduced 1982; no longer imported.

Right-hand

| Perf.: $2400 | Exc.: $1995 | VGood: $1300 |

Left-hand

| Perf.: $2500 | Exc.: $2100 | VGood: $1400 |

ANSCHUTZ MODEL 1911 PRONE MATCH

Bolt action; 22 LR; single shot; 27-1/4-inch barrel; 46-inch overall length; weighs 12 lbs.; walnut-finished European hardwood stock of American prone style with Monte Carlo, cast-off cheekpiece; checkered pistol grip; beavertail forend with swivel rail and adjustable swivel; adjustable rubber buttplate; no sights; receiver grooved for Anschutz sights; scope blocks included; two-stage #5018 adjustable trigger. Imported from Germany.

| Perf.: $1850 | Exc.: $1350 | VGood: $950 |

ANSCHUTZ 1912 SPORT RIFLE

Bolt action; 22 LR, single shot. 25.9-inch barrel; weighs about 11.4 lbs. Length: 41.7 to 42.9-inch. European walnut or aluminum stock; no sights; Lightweight sport rifle version. Uses the 54 match action of the 1913 but weighs 1.5 pounds less. Stainless or blue barrel. Introduced 1997.

| Perf.:$1800 | Exc.: $1500 | VGood: $1100 |

ANSCHUTZ MODEL 1913 SUPER MATCH

Bolt action; single shot; 22 LR; 27-1/4-inch barrel; 46-inch overall length; weighs 15-1/2 lbs.; international diopter sights; match-grade European walnut International-type stock with adjustable cheekpiece, aluminum hook buttplate; fully-adjustable hand stop. Introduced 1988; still in production.

Right-hand action

| Perf.: $2700 | Exc.: $2000 | VGood: $1100 |

Left-hand action

| Perf.: $2800 | Exc.: $2100 | VGood: $1200 |

ANSCHUTZ SUPER MATCH 2007 ISU STANDARD

Bolt action; 22 LR; single shot; 19-3/4-inch barrel; 43-1/2-inch to 44-1/2-inch overall length; weighs about 11 lbs.; ISU Standard design stock of European walnut or blonde hardwood; no sights; uses improved Super Match 54 action, #5018 trigger; micro-honed barrel. Imported from Germany. Introduced 1992.

Right-hand

| Perf.: $2100 | Exc.: $1500 | VGood: $950 |

Left-hand

| Perf.: $2200 | Exc.: $1600 | VGood: $1050 |

ANSCHUTZ 2012 SPORT RIFLE

Bolt action; 22 LR. Barrel: 22.4-inch to 25.9-inch match; detachable muzzle tube; weighs 7.9 to 13 lbs. European walnut stock, thumbhole design. No sights; Uses Anschutz 54.18 barreled action with two-stage match trigger. Introduced 1997. Imported from Germany by AcuSport Corp.

| Perf.: $2100 | Exc.: $1600 | VGood: $1000 |

ANSCHUTZ SUPER MATCH 2013

Bolt action; single shot; 22 LR; 19-3/4-inch barrel (26-inch with tube installed); 43-1/2-inch to 45-1/2-inch overall length; weighs 15-1/2 lbs.; target adjustable European walnut stock; no sights; #7020/20 sight set optional; improved Super Match 54 action; #5018 trigger; micro-honed barrel; two-stage, nine-point adjustment trigger; slide safety. Imported from Germany. Introduced 1992.

Right-hand

| Perf.: $2995 | Exc.: $2495 | VGood: $1500 |

Left-hand

| Perf.: $3100 | Exc.: $2600 | VGood: $1600 |

ANSCHUTZ WOODCHUCKER

Bolt action; 22 LR; 5-shot clip; 16-1/4-inch barrel; 32-1/4-inch overall length; weighs 3-1/2 lbs.; bead front sight, U-notched rear; receiver grooved for scope mounting; walnut finished European hardwood stock; dual opposing extractors; built on Anschutz Mark 2000 action. Made in Germany. Introduced 1985; discontinued 1990.

| Perf.: $375 | Exc.: $275 | VGood: $150 |

ANSCHUTZ MODEL 1907 CLUB

Single-shot economy target rifle chambered in .22 LR. Features include target trigger, short lock time, 26-inch blued barrel, micrometer rear peep and hood front sights, ambidextrous removable cheekpiece and walnut buttstock with rubber buttplate and stock spacers. Weighs 9.7 lbs. Introduced 2006.

| NIB: $1300 | Exc.: N/A | VGood: N/A |

ANSCHUTZ MODEL 1710 D HB CLASSIC 150 YEARS ANNIVERSARY VERSION

Similar to Model 1710 D HB Classic but with heavy stainless barrel and stock laser-engraved with 150th anniversary and 1901 "Germania" logos. Introduced in 2007.

| NIB: $2150 | Exc.: N/A | VGood: N/A |

ARMALITE AR-7 CUSTOM

Semi-automatic; 22 LR; 8-shot box magazine; 16-inch cast aluminum barrel with steel liner; 33-1/2-inch overall length; peep rear sight, blade front; walnut stock; pistol grip; cheekpiece; variation of the AR-7 Explorer survival rifle, but not designed to float. Introduced 1964; discontinued 1970.

| Perf.: $200 | Exc.: $1355 | VGood: $100 |

ARMALITE AR-7 EXPLORER

Semi-automatic; 22 LR; takedown survival rifle with 8-shot box magazine; 16-inch aluminum barrel with steel liner; rear peep sight; weighs 2-3/4 lbs; length assembled 34-1/2-inch, stowed in stock, 16-1/2-inch; moulded Fiberglas, later Cycolac plastic stock, hollow for storing action, barrel, magazine; designed to float; snap-on rubber buttcap; modification of survival rifle designed for Air Force. Introduced in 1959 by Armalite; made by Charter Arms from 1973 to 1990; reintroduced 1992 by Survival Arms; discontinued 1995. Reintroduced 1997 by AR-7 Arms LLD.

Perf.: $175   **Exc.:** $135   **VGood:** $80

ARMALITE AR-10 (T) RIFLE

Semi-automatic, caliber: 308, 10-shot magazine; 24-inch target-weight custom barrel; weighs 10.4 lbs. Length: 43.5-inch overall. Green or black composition stock; N.M.fiberglass handguard tube. Detachable handle, front sight, or scope mount available. Comes with international-style flattop receiver with Picatinny rail. National Match two-stage trigger. Forged upper receiver. Receivers hard-coat anodized. Introduced 1995. Made in U.S.A. by ArmaLite, Inc.

Perf.: $1700   **Exc.:** $1400   **VGood:** $1000

AR-10 (T) Carbine; Lighter 16-inch barrel, single stage trigger, weighs 8.8 lbs.

Perf.: $1750   **Exc.:** $1500   **VGood:** $1000

ARMALITE AR-10A4 SPECIAL PURPOSE RIFLE

Semi-automatic; 308 Win., 243 Win., 10-shot magazine. 20-inch chrome-lined barrel, 1:12-inch twist; weighs 9.6 lbs. Length: 41-inch overall; Green or black composition stock; Detachable handle, front sight, or scope mount available; comes with international style flattop receiver with Picatinny rail. Proprietary recoil check. Forged upper receiver with case deflector. Receivers are hard-coat anodized. Introduced 1995. Made in U.S.A. by ArmaLite, Inc.

Perf.: $1200   **Exc.:** $1000   **VGood:** $800

AR-10A4 Carbine: Same specs except 16-inch barrel.

Perf.: $1200   **Exc.:** $1000   **VGood:** $800

ARMALITE M15A2 CARBINE

Semi-automatic; 223, 7-shot magazine; 16-inch heavy chrome lined barrel; 1:9 twist; weighs 7 lbs. 35-11/16-inch overall. Green or black composition stock. Standard A2 sights. Upper and lower receivers have push-type pivot pin; hard coat anodized; A2-style forward assist; M16A2- type raised fence around magazine release button. Made in U.S.A. by ArmaLite, Inc., still in production.

Perf.: $1000   **Exc.:** $750   **VGood:** $600

M15A2 Carbine; Same specs except 16-inch barrel.

Perf.: $1000   **Exc.:** $750   **VGood:** $600

ARMALITE M15A4

Semi-automatic; 223, 7-shot magazine. 20-inch heavy stainless barrel; 1:9-inch twist; weighs 9 lbs. 40-1/2-inch overall. Green or black plastic stock; N.M. fiberglass handguard tube. One-piece international-style flattop receiver with Weaver-type rail. Detachable carry handle, front sight and scope mount available. National Match two-stage trigger group; Picatinny rail; upper and lower receivers have push-type pivot pin; hard coat anodized finish. Made in U.S.A. by ArmaLite, Inc., still produced.

Perf.: $1300   **Exc.:** $1050   **VGood:** $700

ARMALITE M15A4(T)

Semi-automatic, 223, 7-shot magazine. 24-inch heavy stainless barrel; 1:8-inch twist. weighs 9.2 lbs. 42-3/8-inch overall. Green or black buttstock; N.M. fiberglass handguard tube. One-piece international-style flattop receiver with Weaver-type rail, including case deflector. Detachable carry handle, front sight and scope mount (30mm or 1-inch) available. Upper and lower receivers have push-type pivot pin, hard coat anodized. Made in U.S.A. by ArmaLite, Inc., still produced.

Perf.: $1200   **Exc.:** $900   **VGood:** $700

ARMSCOR MODEL 14D

Bolt action; 22 LR; 10-shot magazine; 23-inch barrel; 41-1/2-inch overall length; weighs 6-1/2 lbs.; fully-adjustable rear sight, bead ramp front; grooved for scope mounts; checkered walnut-finished mahogany

Armalite M15A2 Carbine

Armscor Model 14D

Armscor Model 20C

Armscor Model 50S

stock; blued finish. Made in Philippines. Introduced 1987.

Exc.: $100   **VGood:** $75   **Good:** $55

ARMSCOR MODEL 14P

Same specs as Model 14D except hooded bead ramp front sight; plain uncheckered stock. Made in the Philippines. Introduced 1987.

Exc.: $90   **VGood:** $70   **Good:** $50

ARMSCOR MODEL 20C

Semi-automatic; 22 LR; 10-shot or 15-shot magazine; 18-1/4-inch overall length; weighs 6-1/4 lbs.; fully-adjustable rear sight, bead ramp front; receiver grooved for scope mounts; walnut finished Philippine mahogany; carbine-style stock; steel barrel band, buttplate; blued finish. Introduced 1990.

Exc.: $110   **VGood:** $85   **Good:** $60

ARMSCOR MODEL 20P

Same specs as Model 20C except 20-3/4-inch barrel; 40-1/2-inch overall length; hooded bead ramp front sight; elevation-adjustable rear; no barrel band. Made in the Philippines. Introduced 1987.

Exc.: $90   **VGood:** $70   **Good:** $50

ARMSCOR MODEL 50S

Semi-automatic; 22 LR; 25-, 30-shot magazine; 18-1/4-inch ventilated barrel shroud; 38-inch overall length; weighs 6-1/2 lbs.; bead ramp front sight, open U-notch fully-adjustable rear; mahogany stock; blued finish. Introduced 1990. Reseembles Soviet PPSh.

Perf.: $300   **Exc.:** $275   **VGood:** $250

ARMSCOR MODEL 1400SC (SUPER CLASSIC)

Bolt action; 22 LR; 6-shot or 10-shot magazine; 22-1/2-inch barrel; 41-1/4-inch overall length; weighs 6-3/4 lbs.; hand-checkered American walnut Monte Carlo stock with cheekpiece; contrasting wood forend tip and grip cap; red recoil pad; engine-turned bolt; bead ramp front sight, fully-adjustable open

rear; grooved for scope mount; blue finish. Imported from the Philippines by Ruko Products. Introduced 1990; dropped 1994, reintroduced.

Perf.: $230   **Exc.:** $190   **VGood:** $130

ARMSCOR MODEL 1400LW

Same specs as 1400SC except weighs 6 lbs.; schnabel forend; hard rubber recoil pad; blued finish. Made in Philippines. Introduced 1990; discontinued 1992.

Perf.: $175   **Exc.:** $145   **VGood:** $105

ARMSCOR MODEL 1500S

Bolt action; 22 WMR; 5-shot magazine; 23-inch barrel; 41-inch overall length; weighs 6-1/2 lbs.; fixed sights; receiver grooved for scope mounts; double-lug bolt; plain mahogany stock; blued finish. Made in the Philippines. Introduced 1987.

Perf.: $160   **Exc.:** $135   **VGood:** $95

ARMSCOR MODEL 1500LW

Same specs as Model 1500S except lightweight European-style checkered walnut stock with recoil pad. Introduced 1990; discontinued 1992.

Perf.: $180   **Exc.:** $145   **VGood:** $105

ARMSCOR MODEL 1500SC (SUPER CLASSIC)

Same specs as Model 1500S except 41-1/4-inch overall length; hand-checkered Monte Carlo stock of American walnut; contrasting wood forend tip, grip cap; red rubber recoil pad; lathe-turned bolt. Introduced 1990; no longer in production.

Perf.: $225   **Exc.:** $175   **VGood:** $125

ARMSCOR MODEL 1600

Semi-automatic; 22 LR; military styling; 15-shot magazine; 19-1/2-inch barrel; 38-1/2-inch overall length; weighs 6 lbs.; peep rear sight, post front; black ebony wood stock; matte black finish; resembles Colt AR-15. Made in the Philippines. Introduced 1987.

Perf.: $165   **Exc.:** $135   **VGood:** $100

Armscor Model 1600

Armscor Model AK22

Armsport 1866 Sharps Carbine

Arnold Arms Alaskan Guide Rifle

Arnold Arms Grand Alaskan Rifle

Arnold Arms Alaskan Trophy Rifle

ARMSCOR MODEL 1600R

Same specs as Model 1600 except with stainless-steel retractable buttstock; weighs 7 lbs.; ventilated forend.

Perf.: $180 **Exc.:** $140 **VGood:** $100

ARMSCOR MODEL 2000SC (SUPER CLASSIC)

Semi-automatic; 22 LR; 15-shot magazine; 20-3/4-inch barrel; 40-1/2-inch overall length; weighs 6-1/4 lbs.; fully-adjustable open U-notch rear, bead ramp front sight; receiver grooved for scope mounts; checkered American walnut Monte Carlo sporter stock with cheekpiece; rubber recoil pad; blued finish. Made in Philippines. Introduced 1987.

Perf.: $110 **Exc.:** $75 **VGood:** $55

ARMSCOR MODEL AK22

Semi-automatic; 22 LR; military styling; 10-, 15-, 30-shot magazine; 18-1/4-inch barrel; 36-inch overall length; weighs 7 lbs.; plain mahogany stock; post front sight, open U-notch fully-adjustable rear; matte black finish; resembles the AK-47. Imported from the Philippines by Ruko Products. later KBI, Inc. Introduced 1987.

Perf.: $265 **Exc.:** $225 **VGood:** $110

With folding steel stock
Perf.: $295 **Exc.:** $250 **VGood:** $120

ARMSPORT 1866 SHARPS RIFLE

Single shot; 45-70; 28-inch round or octagonal barrel; 46-inch overall length; weighs 8 lbs.; walnut stock

and forend; blade front sight; folding adjustable rear; tang sight set optionally available; replica of the 1866 Sharps; color case-hardened frame, rest blued.

Perf.: $650 **Exc.:** $495 **VGood:** $395

With octagonal barrel
Perf.: $675 **Exc.:** $525 **VGood:** $425

ARMSPORT 1866 SHARPS CARBINE

Same specs as the 1866 Rifle except 22-inch round barrel.

Perf.: $650 **Exc.:** $495 **VGood:** $395

ARMSPORT 2800 SERIES

Bolt action; 30-06 (2801), 308 (2802), 270 Win. (2803), 243 Win. (2804), 7mm Rem. Mag. (2805), 300 Win. Mag. (2806); 24-inch barrel; weighs 8 lbs.; open adjustable rear, ramp front sight; checkered European walnut Monte Carlo stock; blued finish, Made in Italy. Introduced 1986; discontinued 1986.

Perf.: $595 **Exc.:** $495 **VGood:** $375

ARMSPORT 4000 SERIES

Double rifle; 243, 270, 284, 7.65mm, 308, 30-06, 7mm Rem. Mag., 9.3mm, 300 H&H, 375 H&H; interchangeable 16-, 20-ga. shotgun barrels; blade front sight with bead, windage-adjustable leaf rear; engraved receiver, sideplates; marketed in hand-fitted leather case. Introduced 1978; discontinued 1985.

Armsport 4010 (side-by-side version)
Perf.: $15,000 **Exc.:** $11,995 **VGood:** $8995

Armsport 401		
Perf.: $11,995	**Exc.:** $8995	**VGood:** $6995
Armsport 4012		
Perf.: $25,000	**Exc.:** $19,995	**VGood:** $15,000
Armsport 4013		
Perf.: $22,000	**Exc.:** $16,500	**VGood:** $12,000
Armsport 4020		
Perf.: $3600	**Exc.:** $2700	**VGood:** $2100
Armsport 4021		
Perf.: $3300	**Exc.:** $2400	**VGood:** $1800
Armsport 4022		
Perf.: $3350	**Exc.:** $2500	**VGood:** $1850
Armsport 4023		
Perf.: $2900	**Exc.:** $2200	**VGood:** $1750

ARMSPORT 4500 SERIES

Lever action; 20-inch barrel (carbine), 24-inch barrel (standard); adjustable rear, blade front sight; engraved sideplates; walnut stock; black chromed barrels; replica of Winchester 1873. Discontinued 1986.

Armsport 4500 Standard, 44-40		
Perf.: $1050	**Exc.:** $850	**VGood:** $650
Armsport 4501 Standard, 357 Mag.		
Perf.: $1000	**Exc.:** $800	**VGood:** $600
Armsport 4502 Carbine, 44-40		
Perf.: $1050	**Exc.:** $850	**VGood:** $650
Armsport 4503 Carbine, 357 Mag.		
Perf.: $1000	**Exc.:** $800	**VGood:** $600
Armsport 4504 Carbine, 357 Mag.		
Perf.: $500	**Exc.:** $410	**VGood:** $320

ARMSPORT TIKKA 4600 SERIES

Bolt action; 30-06 (4601), 308 Win. (4602), 270 Win. (4603), 243 Win. (4604), 7mm Rem. (4605), 300 Win. Mag. (4606), 222 Rem. (4607); adjustable rear, blade front sight; walnut stock; rubber recoil pad; blued finish. Discontinued 1984.

Perf.: $595 **Exc.:** $410 **VGood:** $380

ARNOLD ARMS ALASKAN RIFLE

Bolt action, calibers 300 Win. Magnum to 458 Arnold; 22-inch to 26-inch barrel. Synthetic stock; black, woodland or arctic camouflage; drilled and tapped for scope mounting. Uses Apollo, Remington or Winchester action with controlled round feed or push feed; chrome- moly steel or stainless; one-piece bolt, handle, knob; cone head bolt and breech; three-position safety; fully adjustable trigger. Introduced 1996. Made in U.S.A. by Arnold Arms Co.

Perf.: $2300 **Exc.:** $1700 **VGood:** $1300

ARNOLD ARMS ALASKAN GUIDE RIFLE

Similar to the Alaskan rifle except chambered for 257 to 338 Magnum; choice of A-grade English walnut or synthetic stock; three-position safety; scope mount only. Introduced 1996. Made in U.S.A. by Arnold Arms Co.

Perf.: $1800 **Exc.:** $1550 **VGood:** $1100

ARNOLD ARMS GRAND ALASKAN RIFLE

Similar to the Alaskan rifle except has AAA fancy select or exhibition-grade English walnut; barrel band swivel; comes with iron sights and scope mount; 24-inch to 26-inch barrel; 300 Magnum to 458 Win. Mag. Introduced 1996. Made in U.S.A. by Arnold Arms Co.

Perf.: $2800 **Exc.:** $2250 **VGood:** 1200

ARNOLD ARMS ALASKAN TROPHY RIFLE

Similar to the Alaskan rifle except chambered for 300 Magnum to 458 Win. Mag.; 24-inch to 26-inch barrel; black synthetic or laminated stock; comes with barrel band on 375 H&H and larger; scope mount; iron sights. Introduced 1996. Made in U.S.A. by Arnold Arms Co.

Perf.: $2400 **Exc.:** $1800 **VGood:** $1100

ARNOLD ARMS SAFARI RIFLE

Bolt action, calibers 300 Win. Mag. to 458 Win. Mag. 22-inch to 26-inch barrel; Grade A and AA Fancy English walnut stock; drilled and tapped for scope mounting. Uses Apollo, Remington or Winchester action with controlled or push round feed; one-piece bolt, handle, knob; cone head bolt and breech; three-position safety; fully adjustable trigger; chrome-moly steel in matte blue, polished, or bead blasted stainless. Introduced 1996. Made in U.S.A. by Arnold Arms Co.

Perf.: $2200　**Exc.:** $1600　**VGood:** $1100

ARNOLD ARMS AFRICAN TROPHY RIFLE

Similar to the Safari rifle except has AAA Extra Fancy English walnut stock with wrap-around checkering; matte blue chrome-moly or polished or bead blasted stainless steel; scope mount standard or optional Express sights. Introduced 1996. Made in U.S.A. by Arnold Arms Co.

Perf.: $6100　**Exc.:** $5000　**VGood:** $4000

ARNOLD ARMS GRAND AFRICAN RIFLE

Similar to the Safari rifle except has Exhibition Grade stock; polished blue chrome-moly steel or bead-blasted or Teflon-coated stainless; barrel band; scope mount, express sights; calibers 338 Magnum to 458 Win. Mag.; 24-inch to 26-inch barrel. Introduced 1996. Made in U.S.A. by Arnold Arms Co.

Perf.: $7500　**Exc.:** $6000　**VGood:** $5000

A-SQUARE CAESAR

Bolt action; numerous calibers; 20-inch to 26-inch barrel; weighs 8-1/2 to 11 lbs.; three-leaf express sights or scope; Claro walnut hand-rubbed oil-finish or synthetic stock; Coil-Chek recoil reducer; flush detachable swivels; double cross-bolts; claw extractor; right- or left-hand models; built on M700 receiver; matte blue finish. Introduced about 1985.

Perf.: $3500　**Exc.:** $2700　**VGood:** $1500

A-SQUARE GENGHIS KHAN

Similar to Hamilcar, but chambered for varmint calibers, 243 to 264 Win Mag.

Perf.: $3500　**Exc.:** $2700　**VGood:** $1500

A-SQUARE HAMILCAR "SMALL BORE" RIFLE

Bolt action; 25-06, 6.5x55, 270 Win., 7x57, 280 Rem., 30-06, 338-06, 9.3x62, 257 Wea. Mag., 264 Win. Mag., 270 Wea. Mag., 7mm Rem. Mag., 7mm Wea. Mag., 7mm STW, 300 Win. Mag., 300 Wea. Mag.; 4- or 6-shot magazine, depending upon caliber; custom barrel lengths to customer specifications; weighs 8-8-1/2 lbs.; oil-finished Claro walnut stock with A-Square Coil-Chek, recoil pad; choice of three-leaf express, forward or normal-mount scope; matte blue finish; Mauser-style claw extractor; two-position safety; three-way target trigger. From A-Square Co., Inc. Introduced 1994; still produced.

Perf.: $3200　**Exc.:** $2200　**VGood:** $1400

A-SQUARE HANNIBAL "BIG BORE" RIFLE

Bolt action; numerous calibers, up to and including 577 Tyrannosaur; 20-inch to 26-inch barrel; weighs 9 to 11-3/4 lbs.; three-leaf express sights or scope; Claro walnut hand-rubbed oil-finish or synthetic stock; Coil-Chek recoil reducer; double cross-bolts; claw extractor; two-position safety; three-way target trigger; built on P-17 Enfield receiver. Introduced about 1985.

Perf.: $4400　**Exc.:** $3200　**VGood:** $1400

AUTO-ORDNANCE 1927 A1 THOMPSON

Semi-automatic; 45 ACP; 30-shot magazine; 16-inch barrel; 42-inch overall length; weighs about 12 lbs.; walnut stock and vertical forend; blade front sight, open windage-adjustable rear; recreation of Thompson Model 1927; semi-auto only; finned barrel. Made in U.S. by Auto-Ordnance Corp. Add 20 percent for Auto-Ordnance (pre-Kahr) manufacture.

Perf.: $1200　**Exc.:** $900　**VGood:** $675

Arnold Arms Safari Rifle

A-Square Hannibal

Auto-Ordnance 1927A1 Commando

Auto-Ordnance Thompson M1

Auto-Ordnance M1 Carbine

AUTO-ORDNANCE 1927 A1C THOMPSON

Same specs as 1927 A1, except lightweight aluminum receiver, weighs 9-1/2 lbs. Add 20 percent for Auto-Ordnance (pre-Kahr) manufacture.

Perf.: $1200　**Exc.:** $900　**VGood:** $675

AUTO-ORDNANCE 1927A1 COMMANDO

Similar to the 1927A1 except has Parkerized finish, black-finish wood butt, pistol grip, horizontal forend. Comes with black nylon sling. Introduced 1998. Made in U.S.A. by Auto-Ordnance Corp. Add 20 percent for Auto-Ordnance (pre-Kahr) manufacture.

Perf.: $1100　**Exc.:** $750　**VGood:** $600

AUTO-ORDNANCE 1927A3

Semi-automatic; 22 LR; 10-, 30- or 50-shot magazine; 16-inch finned barrel; weighs about 7 lbs; walnut stock and forend; blade front sight, open fully-adjustable rear; recreation of the Thompson Model 1927; alloy receiver. Made in U.S. by Auto-Ordnance. No longer produced. Add 20% if drum magazine present.

Perf.: $1800　**Exc.:** $1600　**VGood:** $975

AUTO-ORDNANCE THOMPSON M1

Semi-automatic; 45 ACP; 30-shot magazine; 16-inch barrel; 42-inch overall length; weighs 11-1/2 lbs.; walnut stock and horizontal forend; blade front sight, fixed rear; side cocking knob; smooth unfinned barrel; sling swivels on butt and forend. Made in U.S by Auto-Ordnance Corp. Introduced 1985. Add 20 percent for Auto-Ordnance (pre-Kahr) manufacture.

Perf.: $1100　**Exc.:** $750　**VGood:** $600

AUTO-ORDNANCE M1 CARBINE

Newly-manufactured replica of military M1 carbine chambered in .30 Carbine. Introduced 2005. Birch stock, parkerized finish. (Add 5 percent for walnut stock.)

NIB: $675　**Exc.:** $625　**VGood:** $495

BALLARD NO. 1-3/4 FAR WEST RIFLE

Single shot, calibers 22 LR, 32-40, 38-55, 40-65, 40-70, 45-70, 45-110, 50-70, 50-90. 30-inch std. or heavyweight barrel; weighs 10-1/2 lbs. (std.) or 11-3/4 lbs. (heavyweight bbl.) Walnut stock. Blade front, Rocky Mountain rear sights. Single or double-set triggers, S-lever or ring-style lever; color case-hardened finish; hand polished and lapped Badger barrel. Made in U.S.A. by Ballard Rifle & Cartridge Co.

Perf.: $2600　**Exc.:** $2300　**VGood:** $1995

BALLARD NO. 4 PERFECTION RIFLE

Single shot, calibers 22 LR, 32-40, 38-55, 40-65, 40-70, 45-70, 45-90, 45-110, 50-70, 50-90. Barrel: 30-inch or 32-inch octagon, standard or heavyweight; weighs 10-1/2 lbs. (standard) or 11-3/4 lbs. (heavyweight bbl.) Smooth walnut stock. Blade front, Rocky Mountain rear sights. Rifle or shotgun-style buttstock, straight grip action, single or double-set trigger, "S" or right lever, hand polished and lapped Badger barrel. Made in U.S.A. by Ballard Rifle & Cartridge Co.

Perf.: $2700　**Exc.:** $2500　**VGood:** $2200

Ballard No. 5 Pacific

Ballard No. 7 Long Range

Ballard No. 8 Union Hill

Bayard Semi-Automatic Model

Beeman/HW 60J-ST

Beeman/HW 660 Match

50-caliber ammunition as the Browning machinegun. From Barrett Firearms. Introduced 1982; still produced.

Perf.: $7500   **Exc.:** $5300   **VGood:** $4300

BARRETT MODEL 90

Bolt action; 50 BMG; bullpup design; 5-shot magazine; 29-inch barrel; 45-inch overall length; weighs 22 lbs.; Sorbothane recoil pad on stock; no sights, scope optional; extendable bipod legs; match-grade barrel; high efficiency muzzlebrake. Made in U.S. by Barrett Firearms Mfg., Inc. Introduced 1990; dropped 1994.

Perf.: $4500   **Exc.:** $3500   **VGood:** $2000

BARRETT MODEL 95

Bolt action; 50 BMG; bullpup design; 5-shot magazine; 29-inch barrel; 45-inch overall length; weighs 22 lbs.; Sorbothane recoil pad on butt; no sights, scope optional; updated version of the Model 90; extendable bipod legs; match-grade barrel; high efficiency muzzlebrake. Made in U.S. by Barrett Firearms Mfg., Inc. Introduced 1995; still produced.

Perf.: $5700   **Exc.:** $4100   **VGood:** $2700

BARRETT MODEL 99 SINGLE SHOT RIFLE

Bolt action, 50 BMG. 33-inch barrel; weighs 25 lbs. 50.4-inch overall. Anodized aluminum stock with energy-absorbing recoil pad; no sights; integral M1913 scope rail; detachable bipod; match-grade barrel with high-efficiency muzzle brake. Introduced 1999. Made in U.S.A. by Barrett Firearms.

Perf.: $3800   **Exc.:** $2900   **VGood:** $2000

BAYARD SEMI-AUTOMATIC MODEL

Single shot; 22 Short, 22 Long; 19-inch barrel; 39-inch overall length; weighs 3-3/4 lbs.; fixed sights; loads cartridge when release stud is activated; American walnut stock. Originally priced at $4.50. Introduced 1908; discontinued 1914.

Perf.: $350   **Exc.:** $300   **VGood:** $190

BEEMAN/HW 60

Bolt action; single shot; 22 LR; 26-7/8-inch barrel; 45-3/4-inch overall length; weighs 11 lbs.; walnut target stock with adjustable buttplate; stippled pistol grip and forend; accessory rail with adjustable swivel; hooded ramp front sight, match-type aperture rear; adjustable match trigger with push-button safety. Imported from Germany by Beeman. Introduced 1981; no longer imported.

Right-hand		
Perf.: $595	**Exc.:** $450	**VGood:** $375
Left-hand		
Perf.: $795	**Exc.:** $595	**VGood:** $425

BEEMAN/HW 60J-ST

Bolt action; 22 LR; 22 7/8-inch barrel; 41-3/4-inch overall length; weighs 6-1/2 lbs.; walnut stock with cheekpiece; cut checkered pistol grip and forend; hooded blade front, open rear sight; polished blue finish; oil-finished walnut. Imported from Germany by Beeman. Introduced 1988; dropped 1992.

Perf.: $525	**Exc.:** $395	**VGood:** $295
222 Rem. caliber		
Perf.: $795	**Exc.:** $650	**VGood:** $495

BEEMAN/HW 660 MATCH

Bolt action; single shot; 22 LR; 26-inch barrel; weighs 10-3/4 lbs.; 45-5/16-inch overall length; match-type walnut stock with adjustable cheekpiece and buttplate; globe front sight, match aperture rear; adjustable match trigger; stippled pistol grip and forend; forend accessory rail. Imported from Germany by Beeman. Introduced 1988; no longer imported.

Perf.: $725   **Exc.:** $550   **VGood:** $400

BENELLI R1

Semi-auto rifle chambered in .270 WSM, .300 WSM, .308 Win., .30-06, or .300 WSM. Interchageable barrels. Blued finish with walnut, synthetic or ComforTech stock. Add 20 percent for ComforTech.

NIB: $925   **Exc.:** $875   **VGood:** $725

BALLARD NO. 5 PACIFIC SINGLE-SHOT RIFLE

Single shot; calibers 32-40, 38-55, 40-65, 40-90, 40-70 SS, 45-70 Govt., 45-110 SS, 50- 70 Govt., 50-90. 30-inch, or 32-inch octagonal barrel; weighs 10-1/2 lbs. High-grade walnut stock; rifle or shotgun style. Blade front, Rocky Mountain rear sights; Standard or heavy barrel; double-set triggers; under-barrel wiping rod; ring lever. Introduced 1999. Made in U.S.A. by Ballard Rifle & Cartridge Co.

Perf.: $2350   **Exc.:** $1950   **VGood:** $1650

BALLARD NO. 7 LONG RANGE RIFLE

Single shot; 32-40, 38-55, 40-65, 40-70 SS, 45-70 Govt., 45-90, 45-110. Barrel: 32-inch, 34-inch half-octagon; weighs 11-3/4 lbs. Walnut stock; checkered pistol grip shotgun butt, ebony forend cap. Globe front sight. Designed for shooting up to 1000 yards. Standard or heavy barrel; single or double-set trigger; hard rubber or steel buttplate. Introduced 1999. Made in U.S.A. by Ballard Rifle & Cartridge Co.

Perf.: $2350   **Exc.:** $1850   **VGood:** $1350

BALLARD NO. 8 UNION HILL RIFLE

Single shot; calibers 22 LR, 32-40, 38-55, 40-65 Win., 40-70. Barrel: 30-inch half-octagon; weighs about 10-1/2 lbs. Walnut stock; pistol grip butt with cheekpiece. Globe front sight; Designed for 200- yard offhand shooting. Standard or heavy barrel; double-set triggers; full loop lever; hook Schuetzen buttplate. Introduced 1999. Made in U.S.A. by Ballard Rifle & Cartridge Co.

Perf.: $2600   **Exc.:** $2100   **VGood:** $1600

BALLARD MODEL 1885 HIGH WALL SINGLE SHOT RIFLE

Single shot; calibers 17 Bee, 22 Hornet, 218 Bee, 219 Don Wasp, 219 Zipper, 22 Hi- Power, 225 Win., 25-20 WCF, 25-35 WCF, 25 Krag, 7mmx57R, 30-30, 30- 40 Krag, 303 British, 33 WCF, 348 WCF, 35 WCF, 35-30/30, 9.3x74R, 405 WCF, 50-110 WCF, 500 Express, 577 Express; barrel Lengths to 34-inch. Straight-grain American walnut stock; buckhorn or flat top rear sight, blade front. Faithful copy of original Model 1885 High Wall; parts interchange with original rifles; variety of options available. Introduced 2000. Made in U.S.A. by Ballard Rifle & Cartridge Co.

Perf.: $2000   **Exc.:** $1895   **VGood:** $1600

BARRETT MODEL 82A-1

Semi-automatic; 50 BMG; 10-shot detachable box magazine; 29-inch barrel; 57-inch overall length; weighs 28-1/2 lbs.; composition stock with Sorbothane recoil pad; no sights, scope optional; recoil operated with recoiling barrel; three-lug locking bolt; muzzlebrake; self-leveling bipod; fires same

BENTON & BROWN MODEL 93
Bolt action; 243, 6mm Rem., 25-06, 270, 280 Rem., 308, 30-06 (standard calibers); 257 Wea. Mag., 264 Win. Mag., 7mm Rem. Mag., 300 Wea. Mag., 300 Win. Mag., 338 Win. Mag., 340 Wea. Mag., 375 H&H (magnum calibers); 22-inch barrel (standard calibers), 24-inch (magnum calibers); 41-inch overall length (22-inch barrel); weighs about 8-1/2 lbs.; two-piece stock design of fancy walnut or fiberglass; oil finish; 20 lpi borderless checkering; sights optional; short-throw bolt action with 60° bolt throw; takedown design; interchangeable barrels and bolt assemblies; left-hand models available; safety locks firing pin and bolt. Made in U.S. by Benton & Brown Firearms, Inc. Introduced 1995.

Perf.: $1750   **Exc.:** $1300   **VGood:** $1000

Fiberglass stock model

Perf.: $1550   **Exc.:** $1100   **VGood:** $800

BERETTA AR-70
Semi-automatic; 223; 5-, 8-, 30-shot magazine; 17-3/4-inch barrel; weighs 8-1/4 lbs.; medium action; diopter adjustable sights; military-like epoxy resin finish. Offered with two magazines, cleaning kit and military-style carrying strap. Introduced 1984; discontinued 1989.

Perf.: $2200   **Exc.:** $1935   **VGood:** $170

BERETTA MATO
DELUXE BOLT-ACTION RIFLE
Bolt action; 270, 280 Rem., 30-06, 7mm Rem. Mag., 300 Win. Mag., 338 Win. Mag., 375 H&H. 23.6-inch barrel; weighs 7.9 lbs. 44-1/2-inch overall length. XXX claro walnut stock with ebony forend tip, hand-rubbed oil finish. Bead on ramp front, open fully adjustable rear sights; drilled and tapped for scope mounting. Mauser-style action with claw extractor; three-position safety; removable box magazine; 375 H&H has muzzle brake; premium for 375 caliber. Introduced 1997, dropped 2003. From Beretta U.S.A.

Perf.: $1000   **Exc.:** $800   **VGood:** $725

BERETTA MATO
SYNTHETIC BOLT-ACTION RIFLE
Similar to the Mato except has fiberglass/Kevlar/carbon-fiber stock in classic American style with shadow line cheekpiece, aluminum bedding block and checkering. Introduced 1998, dropped 2003. From Beretta U.S.A. Premium for 375 caliber.

Perf.: $1050   **Exc.:** $850   **VGood:** $675

BERETTA MODEL 455
Double rifle; side-by-side; sidelock action; 375 H&H, 416 Rigby, 458 Win. Mag., 470 NE, 500 NE 3-inch; 23-1/2-inch, 25-1/2-inch barrels; weighs 11 lbs.; blade front sight, folding leaf V-notch rear; hand-checkered European walnut stock; removable sideplates; double triggers; recoil pad; color case-hardened finish. Made in Italy. Introduced 1990; no longer imported.

Perf.: $46,000 **Exc.:** $38,000 **VGood:** $26,000

Model 455EELL with select walnut, engraving,

Perf.: $58,000 **Exc.:** $49,000 **VGood:** $39,000

BERETTA MODEL 500
Bolt action (short action); 222 Rem., 223 Rem.; 5-shot; 24-inch barrel; weighs 6-1/2-7/8 lbs.; short action; hood front sight, fully-adjustable rear; European walnut stock; oil-finished, hand-checkered; rubber buttpad. Made in Italy. Introduced 1984; importation discontinued 1990.

Perf.: $600   **Exc.:** $510   **VGood:** $420

BERETTA MODEL 500 S
Same specs as Model 500 except with iron sights.

Perf.: $625   **Exc.:** $550   **VGood:** $440

BERETTA MODEL 500 DL
Same specs as Model 500 except with select walnut, engraving, grip cap.

Perf.: $1300   **Exc.:** $1100   **VGood:** $900

BERETTA MODEL 500 DLS
Same specs as Model 500 except with iron sights, select walnut, engraving.

Perf.: $1400   **Exc.:** $1200   **VGood:** $1000

Benelli R1

Beretta Mato Deluxe

Beretta Model 455

Beretta Model 500

Beretta 455EELL

Beretta Model 501

BERETTA MODEL 500 EELL
Same specs as Model 500 except with fine walnut, more engraving.

Perf.: $1500   **Exc.:** $1300   **VGood:** $1100

BERETTA MODEL 500 EELLS
Same specs as Model 500 except with iron sights, fine walnut, more engraving.

Perf.: $1600   **Exc.:** $1400   **VGood:** $1200

BERETTA MODEL 501
(MEDIUM-LENGTH ACTION)
Bolt action; 243, 308; 5-shot magazine; 23-inch barrel; weighs 7 to 7-1/2 lbs.; hood front sight, fully-adjustable rear; checkered burled walnut stock; full pistol grip cap and palm swell; engraved receiver, trigger guard, magazine floorplate; rubber buttpad. Made in Italy. Introduced 1984; discontinued 1986.

Perf.: $595   **Exc.:** $510   **VGood:** $420

BERETTA MODEL 501 S
Same specs as Model 501 except with iron sights.

Perf.: $625   **Exc.:** $560   **VGood:** $475

BERETTA MODEL 501 DL
Same specs as Model 501 except with select walnut, engraving.

Perf.: $1285   **Exc.:** $1070   **VGood:** $900

BERETTA MODEL 501 DLS
Same specs as Model 501 except with iron sights, select walnut, engraving.

Perf.: $1400   **Exc.:** $1200   **VGood:** $1000

BERETTA MODEL 501 EELL
Same specs as Model 501 except with fine walnut, more engraving.

Perf.: $1550   **Exc.:** $1300   **VGood:** $1100

BERETTA MODEL 501 EELLS
Same specs as Model 501 except with iron sights, fine walnut, more engraving.

Perf.: $1575   **Exc.:** $1400   **VGood:** $1200

BERETTA MODEL 502
(LONG ACTION)
Bolt action; 6.5x55, 7mm Rem. Mag., 270, 7x64, 30-06, 300 Win. Mag., 375 H&H; 4-, 5-shot magazine; 24-1/2-inch barrel; weighs 8 to 8-1/2 lbs.; no sights; checkered walnut stock; schnabel forend; sling swivels; rubber buttpad. Made in Italy. Introduced, 1984; discontinued, 1986.

Perf.: $640   **Exc.:** $530   **VGood:** $480

BERETTA MODEL 502 DL
Same specs as Model 502 except with select walnut, engraving.

Perf.: $1450   **Exc.:** $1175   **VGood:** $950

BERETTA MODEL 502 DLS
Same specs as Model 502 except with iron sights, select walnut, engraving.

Perf.: $1425   **Exc.:** $1195   **VGood:** $975

BERETTA MODEL 502 EELL
Same specs as Model 502 except with fine walnut, more engraving.

Perf.: $1595   **Exc.:** $1295   **VGood:** $1050

BERETTA MODEL 502 EELLS
Same specs as Model 502 except with iron sights, fine walnut, more engraving

Perf.: $1595   **Exc.:** $1295   **VGood:** $1050

BERETTA MODEL 502 S
Same specs as Model 502 except with iron sights.

Perf.: $675   **Exc.:** $550   **VGood:** $495

Beretta Storm CX4 Carbine

Bernardelli Carbine

Bernardelli Express VB

Bernardelli Minerva

Big Horn Custom

BERETTA MODEL S689

Double rifle; over/under boxlock; 9.3x74R, 30-06; 23-inch barrel; weighs 7-3/4 lbs.; open V-notch rear sight, blade front on ramp; European walnut stock; checkered grip, forend; silvered, lightly engraved receiver; double triggers; ejectors; solid buttplate. Made in Italy. Introduced 1984; importation discontinued 1990.

Perf.: $3695   **Exc.:** $2995   **VGood:** $2200

BERETTA MODEL S689E

Same specs as Model S689 except auto ejectors.

Perf.: $3995   **Exc.:** $3250   **VGood:** $2250

BERETTA SPORTING CARBINE

Bolt action/semi-automatic; 22 LR; 4-, 8-, 20-shot magazine; 20-1/2-inch barrel; three-leaf folding rear sight, Patridge-type front; European walnut stock; sling swivels; hand-checkered pistol-grip. When bolt handle is dropped, acts as more-or-less conventional bolt-action; with bolt handle raised fires semi-auto. Produced in Italy following World War II.

Perf.: $370   **Exc.:** $300   **VGood:** $230

BERETTA SSO EXPRESS

Double rifle; over/under sidelock; 9.3x74R, 375 H&H, 458 Win. Mag.; 23-, 25-1/2-inch barrels; weighs 11 lbs.; blade front sight on ramp, open V-notch rear; hand-checkered European walnut stock; color case-hardened receiver, trigger, trigger guard; double triggers, ejectors; recoil pad. Made in Italy. Introduced 1984; discontinued 1990.

Perf.: $14,500   **Exc.:** $11,000   **VGood:** $8500

BERETTA SSO5 EXPRESS

Same specs as Model SSO except with select walnut, engraving

Perf.: $17,000   **Exc.:** $14,000   **VGood:** $12,000

BERETTA SSO6 EXPRESS CUSTOM

Double rifle; over/under sidelock; 9.3x74R, 375 H&H, 458 Win. Mag.; individually built to buyer's specifications; 25-1/2-inch barrel; weighs 11 lbs.; blade front sight on ramp; open V-notch rear; hand-checkered European walnut stock; color case-hardened receiver; double triggers, ejectors; recoil pad. Made in Italy. Introduced 1990.

Perf.: $34,500   **Exc.:** $28,500   **VGood:** $22,900

With gold engraving

Perf.: $39,500   **Exc.:** $33,500   **VGood:** $27,500

BERETTA STORM CX4 CARBINE

Semi-automatic; 9mm, 40 S&W, 45 ACP; 8 to 15-round magazines, 20 round 9mm magazines available as an option; 16.6-inch barrel; 29.7-inch overall length; weighs 5-3/4 lbs; black polymer stock with rubber recoil pad; aperture rear sight, adjustable post front sight. Introduced 2003, still produced.

Perf.: $685   **Exc.:** $550   **VGood:** $450

BERNARDELLI CARBINE

Semi-automatic; 22 LR; 5-, 10-shot magazine; 21-inch barrel; 40-inch overall length; weighs 5-3/8 lbs.; checkered Monte Carlo-style European walnut stock; steel receiver; hooded front sight, fully-adjustable rear; push-button safety; blued/black finish. Made in Italy. Introduced 1986; importation discontinued 1991.

Perf.: $550   **Exc.:** $500   **VGood:** $390

BERNARDELLI EXPRESS VB

Double rifle; 9.3x74R, 8x57 JRS, 7x65R, 30-06, 375 H&H; 25-1/2-inch barrels; weighs about 8 lbs.; select walnut stock with cheekpiece; long beavertail-schnabel forend; hand-checkered grip and forend; pistol grip or straight English; bead on ramp front sight, quarter-rib with leaf rear; coin-finished or color case-hardened boxlock action with automatic ejectors; double trigger; hand-cut rib. Imported from Italy by Magnum Research. Introduced 1990; no longer imported.

Perf.: $10,000   **Exc.:** $7400   **VGood:** $3000

With single trigger

Perf.: $12,000   **Exc.:** $8800   **VGood:** $3100

BERNARDELLI MINERVA

Double rifle, side-by-side, similar to Express, but with outside hammers; 9.3x74R only.

Perf.: $9000   **Exc.:** $7500   **VGood:** $6500

BERNARDELLI MODEL 120

Combination gun; over/under boxlock; 12-ga. over 22 Hornet, 222 Rem., 5.6x50R Mag., 243, 6.5x57R, 270, 7x57R, 308, 30-06, 6.5x55, 7x65R, 8x57JRS, 9.3x74R; iron sights; checkered walnut stock, forearm; double trigger; automatic ejectors or extractors; ventilated recoil pad; engraved action. Made in Italy. No longer in production.

Perf.: $3295   **Exc.:** $2275   **VGood:** $1400

BERNARDELLI MODEL 190

Combination gun; over/under boxlock; 12-, 16-, 20-ga. over 222, 243, 30-06, 308, 5.6x50R Mag. 5.6x57R, 6.5x55, 6.5x57R, 7x57R, 7x65R, 8x57JRS, 9.3x74R; iron sights; checkered walnut stock, forearm; double trigger; extractors. Made in Italy. Introduced 1989; discontinued 1989.

Perf.: $3295   **Exc.:** $2275   **VGood:** $1400

BERNARDELLI MODEL 2000

Combination gun; over/under boxlock action; 12-, 16-, 20-ga. over/under 22 Hornet, 222 Rem., 5.6x50R Mag., 243, 6.5x55, 6.5x57R, 270, 7x57R, 308, 30-06, 8x57JRS, 9.3x74R; 23-1/2-inch barrels; weighs 6-3/4 lbs.; blade front sight, open rear with quarter-rib for rail-type scope mount; hand-checkered, oil-finished select European walnut stock with Bavarian-type cheekpiece; double set triggers; auto ejectors; silvered, engraved action. Made in Italy. Introduced 1990; dropped 1991.

Perf.: $3295   **Exc.:** $2275   **VGood:** $1400

With extra set of barrels

Perf.: $4200   **Exc.:** $3300   **VGood:** $2000

BIG HORN CUSTOM

Bolt action; chambered to customer's specs; 22-250 through all magnums; furnished with two barrels to customer specs; weighs about 6-3/4 lbs.; no sights; drilled, tapped for scope mounts; Mauser action; classic-style Claro walnut stock; Pachmayr flush swivel sockets; adjustable trigger; recoil pad. Introduced 1983; discontinued 1984.

Perf.: $1900   **Exc.:** $1500   **VGood:** $1000

BLASER K77A

Single-shot, break-open; 22-250, 243, 6.5x55, 270, 280, 7x57R, 7x65R, 30-06, 7mm Rem. Mag., 300 Win. Mag., 300 Weatherby Mag.; 23-inch, 24-inch barrel; 39-1/2-inch overall length (23-inch barrel); weighs 5-1/2 lbs.; no sights; marketed with Blaser scope mount; checkered two-piece Turkish walnut stock; solid buttpad; three-piece take-down; tang-mounted sliding safety; interchangeable barrels. Made in Germany. Introduced 1988; dropped 1990.

Perf.: $2800   **Exc.:** $2700   **VGood:** $2300

Magnum calibers

Perf.: $2850   **Exc.:** $2750   **VGood:** $2400

With interchangeable barrels

Perf.: $3300   **Exc.:** $3200   **VGood:** $3100

BLASER K95

Single-shot, breakopen; 243, 270, 7x57, 30-06, 308, 7mm Rem Mag, 300 Win Mag, 300 Weatherby Mag; 20-, 24-, 26-inch barrels, 37-1/2 to 42-inch overall length, weighs about 5.8 lbs., Turkish walnut stock and forearm; locking block secures barrel into receiver.

Perf.: $4250   Exc.: $3850   VGood: $2600

BLASER R84

Bolt action; 22-250, 243, 6mm Rem., 25-06, 270, 280, 30-06 (standard calibers) 257 Wea., 264 Win. Mag., 7mm Rem. Mag., 300 Win. Mag., 300 Wea., 338 Win. Mag., 375 H&H; 23-inch barrel (standard calibers), 24-inch (magnum calibers); 41-inch overall length (23-inch barrel); weighs 7 to 7-1/4 lbs.; two-piece Turkish walnut stock and forend; solid black buttpad; no sights; comes with low-profile Blaser scope mounts; interchangeable barrels and magnum/standard caliber bolt assemblies; left-hand models available in all calibers. No longer imported.

Perf.: $2400   Exc.: $2000   VGood: $1400

Left-hand

Perf.: $2700   Exc.: $2200   VGood: $1500

BLASER R93

Bolt action, straight pull; 222, 243, 6.5x55, 270, 7x57, 308, 30-06, 7mm Rem. Mag., 300 Win. Mag., 300 Wea. Mag., 338 Win. Mag., 375 H&H, 416 Rem. Mag.; 3-shot magazine; 22-inch barrel (standard calibers), 24-inch (magnum calibers); 40-inch overall length (22-inch barrel); weighs 6-1/2 to 7-1/2 lbs.; two-piece European walnut stock; blade front sight on ramp, open rear, or no sights; thumb-activated safety slide/cocking mechanism; interchangeable barrels and bolt heads. Imported from Germany by Autumn Sales, later Sigarms. Introduced 1994. Add 10 percent-25 percent for premium grades, depending on degree of ornamentation.

Perf.: $4000   Exc.: $3850   VGood: $3300

BLASER R93 LONG RANGE RIFLE

Bolt action, straight pull; 308 Win., 10-shot detachable box magazine; 24-inch barrel; weighs 10.4 lbs. 44-inch overall; aluminum stock with synthetic lining, adjustable cheekpiece and butt, folding bipod; no sights furnished; accepts detachable scope mount; adjustable trigger; fully adjustable stock; quick takedown; corrosion resistant finish. Introduced 1998. Imported from Germany by Sigarms.

Perf.: $3700   Exc.: $2900   VGood: $2500

BLASER R93 SAFARI

Same specs as the R93 except 375 H&H, 416 Rem. Mag.; 24-inch barrel; weighs 9.5 lbs.; open sights; broad forend. Imported from Germany by Autumn Sales, Inc. Introduced 1994; no longer imported.

Perf.: $3900   Exc.: $3100   VGood: $2200

BLASER R93 SYNTHETIC

Same specs as R93 except one-piece black synthetic stock.

Perf.: $3050   Exc.: $2700   VGood: $2100

BLASER ULTIMATE BOLT ACTION

Bolt action; 60 degree bolt throw; bolt lugs lock into rear of barrel; 22-250, 243, 25-06, 270, 308, 30-06, 7x57, 7x64, 264 Win. Mag., 7mm Rem. Mag., 300 Win. Mag., 338 Win. Mag., 375 H&H; 22-inch, 24-inch barrel; interchangeable capability; weighs 6-3/4 lbs.; select checkered walnut stock, forearm; aluminum receiver with engraving;. Introduced 1985; discontinued 1989.

Perf.: $2900   Exc.: $2250   VGood: $1850

BORTMESS BIG HORN

Bolt action; calibers from 22-250 through 458 Win.; 24-inch, 25-inch barrel; no sights; drilled, tapped for scope mounts; Monte Carlo stock of American walnut; roll-over cheekpiece; half-curl pistol grip; rosewood cap; tapering forend; rosewood forend cap; high-gloss finish; steel buttplate or recoil pad; built on Ranger Arms action. Introduced 1974; discontinued 1977.

Perf.: $695   Exc.: $595   VGood: $435

BORTMESS CLASSIC MODEL

Bolt action; calibers from 22-250 through 458 Win.; 24-inch, 25-inch barrel; no sights; drilled, tapped for

scope mounts; hand-checkered American walnut stock; plastic pistol grip cap, forend tip; built on Ranger Arms action; Pachmayr solid rubber recoil pad. Introduced 1974; discontinued 1977.

Perf.: $695   Exc.: $595   VGood: $450

BORTMESS OMEGA

Bolt action; calibers from 22-250 through 358 Norma; 24-inch, 25-inch barrel; no sights; drilled, tapped for scope mounts; American walnut stock; high-gloss finish. Introduced 1974; discontinued 1977.

Perf.: $895   Exc.: $695   VGood: $550

Blaser K95

Blaser R84

Blaser R93 Long Range Rifle

Blaser R93 Synthetic

Bortmess Big Horn

Bortmess Omega

Bortmess Classic Model

Brno 500 Combination Gun

BRNO 500 COMBINATION GUN

Combination gun, breakopen; 12 gauge (2-3/4-inch chamber) over 5.6x52R, 5.6x50R, 222 Rem., 243, 6.x55, 308, 7x57R, 7x65R, 30-06. 23.6-inch barrel; weighs 7.6 lbs. 40-1/2-inch overall length. European walnut stock. Bead front, V-notch rear sights; grooved for scope mounting; hammerless boxlock action; double set trigger; blue finish with etched engraving; also available as double rifle. Announced 1998. Imported from the Czech Republic by Euro-Imports.

Perf.: $1700   Exc.: $1350   VGood: $850

Brno CZ 99 Precision 22

Brno CZ 537 Sporter

Brno ZH Series 300

Brno Model 21H

BRNO CZ 98 HUNTER CLASSIC

Bolt action, Mauser-type; 243, 6.5x55, 270, 7x57, 7x64, 308, 30-06, 7.92x57, 7mm Rem. Mag., 300 Win. Mag.; 24-inch barrel; 45-inch overall length; weighs 7-5/8 lbs.; walnut or synthetic stock; optional sights; integral Weaver-type base; controlled round feeding; fixed ejector; hinged floorplate; adjustable trigger; swivel studs. Imported from the Czech Republic by Springfield, Inc., later by Euro-Imports; Introduced 1995.

Perf.: $500   **Exc.:** $330   **VGood:** $280

With synthetic stock

Perf.: $415   **Exc.:** $300   **VGood:** $260

BRNO CZ 99 PRECISION 22

Bolt action; 22 LR; 5-shot magazine; 20-inch barrel; 41-inch overall length; weighs 6 lbs.; hooded bead on ramp front sight, fully-adjustable rear; receiver grooved for scope mount; checkered European hardwood stock; sliding safety; polished blue finish. Made in Yugoslavia. Introduced 1990; discontinued 1991.

Perf.: $300   **Exc.:** $270   **VGood:** $220

BRNO CZ 537 SPORTER

Bolt action; 270, 30-06 (internal 5-shot magazine), 243, 308 (detachable 5-shot magazine); 23 5/8-inch barrel; 44-3/4-inch overall length; weighs 7 lbs. 9 oz.; checkered walnut stock; hooded ramp front sight, adjustable folding leaf rear; improved standard-size Mauser-style action with non-rotating claw extractor; externally adjustable trigger; American-style safety; streamlined bolt shroud with cocking indicator. Imported from the Czech Republic by Magnum Research. Introduced 1992.

Perf.: $550   **Exc.:** $475   **VGood:** $375

With full stock, 308, 30-06

Perf.: $650   **Exc.:** $575   **VGood:** $475

BRNO CZ 550

Bolt action; 243, 308 (4-shot detachable magazine), 7x57, 270, 30-06, 7mm Rem. Mag., 300 Win. Mag. (5-shot internal magazine); 23-5/8-inch barrel; 44-3/4-inch overall length; weighs 7-1/4 lbs.; walnut stock with high comb; checkered grip and forend; no sights; drilled and tapped for Remington 700-style bases; polished blue finish. Imported from the Czech Republic by Magnum Research. Introduced 1995.

Perf.: $550   **Exc.:** $450   **VGood:** $375

BRNO ZH 300 COMBINATION GUN

Combination gun, breakopen; 22 Hornet, 5.6x50R Mag., 5.6x52R, 7x57R, 7x65R, 8x57JRS over 12, 16 (2-3/4-inch chamber); 23.6-inch barrel; weighs 7.9 lbs. 40-1/2-inch overall length. European walnut stock; Blade front, open adjustable rear sights. Boxlock action; double triggers; automatic safety; introduced 1986. Also available as double rifles. Imported from the Czech Republic by Pragotrade, later by Euro-Imports.

Perf.: $2995   **Exc.:** $2395   **VGood:** $1795

BRNO HORNET

Bolt action; 22 Hornet; 5-shot box magazine; 23-inch barrel; three-leaf rear sight, hooded ramp front; double-set trigger; sling swivels; hand-checkered pistol grip, forearm. Manufactured in Czechoslovakia from 1949 to 1973.

Exc.: $1000   **VGood:** $900   **Good:** $800

BRNO MODEL 1

Bolt action; 22 LR; 5-shot magazine; 23-inch barrel; weighs 6 lbs.; three-leaf rear sight, hooded ramp front; sporting stock; hand-checkered pistol grip; sling swivels. Introduced 1947; discontinued 1957.

Exc.: $450   **VGood:** $350   **Good:** $300

BRNO MODEL 2

Bolt action; 22 LR; 5-shot magazine; 23-inch barrel; weighs 6 lbs.; three-leaf rear sight, hooded ramp front; deluxe walnut sporting stock; hand-checkered pistol grip; sling swivels. Introduced 1946; discontinued 1957.

Exc.: $470   **VGood:** $380   **Good:** $310

BRNO MODEL 3

Bolt action; 22 LR; 5-shot magazine; 27-1/2-inch heavy barrel; weighs 9-1/2 lbs.; click-adjustable target sights; smooth target stock; sling swivels. Introduced 1949; discontinued 1956.

Exc.: $515   **VGood:** $430   **Good:** $325

BRNO MODEL 4

Bolt action; 22 LR; 5-shot magazine; 27-1/2-inch heavy barrel; weighs 9-1/2 lbs.; click-adjustable target sights; smooth target stock; sling swivels; improved safety, trigger. Introduced 1957; discontinued 1962.

Exc.: $635   **VGood:** $513   **Good:** $440

BRNO MODEL 5

Bolt action; 22 LR; 5-shot magazine; 23-inch barrel; weighs 6 lbs.; three-leaf rear sight, hooded ramp

front; sporting stock; hand-checkered pistol grip; sling swivels. Introduced 1957; discontinued 1973.

Exc.: $575   **VGood:** $495   **Good:** $400

BRNO MODEL 21H

Bolt action; 6.5x55, 7x57, 7x64, 8x57mm; 5-shot box magazine; 20-1/2-inch, 23-inch barrel; Mauser-type; two-leaf rear sight, ramp front; half-length sporting stock; hand-checkered pistol grip, forearm; sling swivels; double-set trigger. Introduced 1946; discontinued 1955.

Exc.: $900   **VGood:** $700   **Good:** $500

BRNO MODEL 22F

Bolt action; 6.5x55, 7x57, 7x64, 8x57mm; 5-shot box magazine; 20-1/2-inch, 23-inch barrel; Mauser-type; two-leaf rear sight, ramp front; Mannlicher-type stock; sling swivels; double-set trigger. Introduced 1946; discontinued 1955.

Perf.: $1100   **Exc.:** $850   **VGood:** $600

BRNO MODEL ZG-47

Bolt action; 270, 30-06, 7x57, 7x64, 8x64S, 8x57, 9.3x62, 10.75x68; 23-1/2-inch barrel; checkered walnut stock, pistol grip; schnabel forend; hinged floorplate; single trigger. Made in Czechoslovakia. Introduced 1956; discontinued 1962.

Perf.: $995   **Exc.:** $875   **VGood:** $700

BRNO MODEL ZKM-456

Bolt action; 22 LR; 5-, 10-shot magazine; 24-1/2-inch barrel; weighs 6-1/2 lbs.; folding rear sight, fixed front; Beechwood stock; pistol grip; blued finish. Introduced 1992; no longer imported.

Perf.: $330   **Exc.:** $270   **VGood:** $230

BRNO MODEL ZKM-456 L TARGET

Same specs as Model ZKM-456 except 27-1/2-inch barrel; adjustable front and rear sights; weighs 10 lbs. Introduced 1992; no longer imported.

Perf.: $330   **Exc.:** $270   **VGood:** $230

BRNO MODEL ZKM-456 MATCH

Same specs as Model ZKM-456 except single shot; 27-1/2-inch barrel; aperture sights; adjustable buttplate, cheekpiece; weighs 10 lbs. Introduced 1992; no longer imported.

Perf.: $375   **Exc.:** $300   **VGood:** $250

BRNO SUPER EXPRESS

Double rifle; over/under sidelock; 7x65R, 9.3x74R, 375 H&H, 458 Win. Mag.; 23-1/2-inch barrel; 40-inch overall length; weighs about 8-1/2 lbs.; quarter-rib with open rear sight, bead on ramp front; checkered European walnut stock; engraved sideplates; double-set triggers; selective auto ejectors; rubber recoil pad. Made in Czechoslovakia. Introduced 1986; discontinued 1992.

Perf.: $3450   **Exc.:** $2875   **VGood:** $1800

BRNO SUPER SAFARI

Double rifle; over/under sidelock; 7x64R, 375 H&H Mag., 9.3x74R; 23-1/2-inch barrel; weighs 9 lbs.; open sights; checkered walnut stock, forearm; double trigger with set trigger; ventilated recoil pad. Introduced 1992; no longer imported.

Perf.: $2295   **Exc.:** $1895   **VGood:** $1350

BRNO ZBK 110 SINGLE SHOT RIFLE

Single shot; 222 Rem., 5.6x52R, 22 Hornet, 5.6x50 Mag., 6.5x57R, 7x57R, 8x57JRS; 23.6-inch barrel; weighs 5.9 lbs. 40.1-inch overall. European walnut stock; no sights; drilled and tapped for scope mounting. Top tang opening lever; cross-bolt safety; polished blue finish. Announced 1998.

Perf.: $230   **Exc.:** $190   **VGood:** $150

BRNO ZKB 527 FOX

Bolt action; 22 Hornet, 222 Rem., 223 Rem.; 5-shot detachable magazine; 23-1/2-inch barrel, standard or heavy; 42-1/2-inch overall length; weighs 6 lbs. 1 oz.; European walnut Monte Carlo stock; hooded front sight, open adjustable rear; improved mini-Mauser action with non-rotating claw extractor; grooved receiver.

Perf.: $595   **Exc.:** $515   **VGood:** $415

BRNO ZKB 680 FOX
Bolt action; 22 Hornet, 222 Rem.; 5-shot detachable box magazine; 23-1/2-inch barrel; 42-1/2-inch overall length; weighs 5 lbs. 12 oz.; Turkish walnut Monte Carlo stock; hooded front sight, open adjustable rear; adjustable double-set triggers. Imported from Czechoslovakia by T.D. Arms. No longer imported.

Perf.: $445   **Exc.:** $380   **VGood:** $315

BRNO ZKK 600
Bolt action (medium-length action); 30-06, 270, 7x57, 7x64; 5-shot magazine; 23-1/2-inch barrel; 43-inch overall length; weighs 7-1/4 lbs.; open folding adjustable rear sight, hooded ramp front; synthetic or checkered walnut stock; improved Mauser action with controlled feed, claw extractor; adjustable set trigger; easy-release sling swivels. Made in Czechoslovakia. Introduced 1986.

Perf.: $500   **Exc.:** $425   **VGood:** $375

BRNO ZKK 601
Bolt action (short action); 223 Rem., 243 Win., 308 Win.; 5-shot magazine; 23-1/2-inch barrel; 43' overall length; 7-1/4 lbs.; open folding adjustable rear sight, hooded ramp front; synthetic or checkered walnut stock; improved Mauser action with controlled feed, claw extractor; adjustable set trigger; easy-release sling swivels. Made in Czechoslovakia. Introduced 1986.

Perf.:. $500   **Exc.:** $425   **VGood:** $370

BRNO ZKK 602
Bolt action (long action); 300 Win. Mag., 375 H&H, 8x68, 416 Rigby, 458 Win. Mag.; 5-shot magazine; 25-inch barrel; 9-5/8 lbs.; three-leaf express rear sight, hooded ramp front; synthetic or checkered walnut stock; adjustable set trigger; easy-release sling swivels. Made in Czechoslovakia. Introduced 1986.

Perf.: $650   **Exc.:** $575   **VGood:** $495

BRNO ZKM 452 STANDARD
Bolt action; 22 LR; 5-, 10-shot magazine; 25-inch barrel; 43-1/2-inch overall length; weighs 6 lbs. 9 oz.; beechwood stock; hooded bead front sight, open elevation-adjustable rear; blue finish; oiled stock; grooved receiver. Imported from Czechoslovakia by Action Arms, later Bauska. No longer imported.

Perf.: $285   **Exc.:** $225   **VGood:** $195

BRNO ZKM 452 DELUXE
Same specs as ZKM 452 except 23-5/8-inch barrel; 42-1/2-inch overall length; checkered walnut stock; sling swivels. Introduced 1992; no longer imported.

Perf.: $350   **Exc.:** $265   **VGood:** $210

BRNO ZKM 611
Semi-automatic; 22 WMR; 6-shot magazine; 20-inch barrel; 37-inch overall length; weighs 6 lbs. 2 oz.; European walnut stock with checkered grip and forend; blade front sight, open rear; removable box magazine; polished blue finish; grooved receiver for scope mounting; sling swivels; thumbscrew takedown.

Perf.: $460   **Exc.:** $400   **VGood:** $330

BRONCO
Single shot; 22 Short, 22 Long, 22 LR; 16-1/2-inch barrel; barrel pivots to side to load; weighs 3 lbs.; adjustable rear sight, blade front; early version solid construction, later, instant takedown; skeletonized crackle-finished alloy stock; cross-bolt safety. Introduced 1967; offered first by Firearms International, later by Garcia; discontinued 1978. Found in four versions: .22 LR single-shot, .22 Magnum single-shot, .410 single-shot, and .22/.410 O/U. Add 15% for .22/.410.

Perf.: $395   **Exc.:** $350   **VGood:** $190

ED BROWN SAVANNAH
Bolt-action medium-weight centerfire rifle. Chambered in a variety of short- and long-action standard and magnum chamberings. Fluted bolt, McMillan stock, optional muzzlebrake, blackened stainless barrel.

NIB: $3250   **Exc.:** $2995   **VGood:** $2100

Brno ZKB 527 Fox

Brno ZKB 680 Fox

Brno ZKK 600

Brno ZKK 602

Brno ZKM 452 Standard

Ed Brown Savannah

Ed Brown Damara

Ed Brown Compact Varmint

ED BROWN DAMARA
Similar to Savannah but in a lightweight configuration with natural-finish stainless barrel.

NIB: $3250   **Exc.:** $2995   **VGood:** $2100

ED BROWN COMPACT VARMINT
Similar to Damara but with shorter barrel, beavertail forend.

NIB: $3250   **Exc.:** $2995   **VGood:** $2100

BROWN MODEL ONE
Single shot; 22 LR, 357 Mag., 44 Mag., 7-30 Waters, 30-30 Win., 375 Win., 45-70; custom chamberings from 17 Rem. through 45-caliber available; 22-inch or custom length barrel, bull or tapered; weighs about 6 lbs.; smooth walnut stock; custom takedown design by Woodsmith; palm swell for right- or left-hand; rubber buttpad; sights optional; drilled and tapped for scope mounting; rigid barrel/receiver; falling-block action with short lock time, automatic case ejection; air-gauged barrels by Wilson and Douglas; muzzle has 11-degree target crown; matte black oxide finish standard, polished and electroless nickel optional. Made in U.S. by E.A. Brown Mfg. Introduced 1988.

Per.f: $1050   **Exc.:** $975   **VGood:** $550

BROWN MODEL 97D
Single shot, falling block; 17 Ackley through 45-70; barrels up to 26-inch; air-gauged match grade; weighs about 5 lbs., 11 oz.; sporter stock with pistol grip, cheekpiece and schnabel forearm; no sights furnished; drilled and tapped for scope mounting; polished blue-black finish; hand-fitted action; many options; Made in U. S. by E. Arthur Brown Co. Introduced about 1998.

Per.f: $1050   **Exc.:** $975   **VGood:** $550

BROWNING A-BOLT HUNTER
Bolt action; 25-06, 270, 30-06, 280, 7mm Rem. Mag., 300 Win. Mag., 338 Win. Mag., 375 H&H (long action); 22-250, 243 Win., 257 Roberts, 22-250, 7mm-08, 308 Win., also 223 WSSM, 243 WSSM, 270 WSM, 7mm WSM, 300 WSM (short action); 22-inch, 24-inch, 26-inch barrel; 44-3/4-inch overall length; weighs 6-1/2 to 7-1/2 lbs.; recessed muzzle; magnum and standard action; classic-style American walnut stock; recoil pad on magnum calibers; short throw fluted bolt; three locking lugs; plunger-type ejector; adjustable, grooved gold-plated trigger; hinged floorplate; detachable box magazine; slide tang safety; rosewood grip, forend caps. Made in

Browning A-Bolt Hunter

Browning A-Bolt Hunter, Left Hand

Browning A-Bolt Camo Stalker

Browning A-Bolt Micro Medallion

Browning A-Bolt Stainless Stalker

Browning A-Bolt 22

Browning A-Bolt II Hunter

Browning A-Bolt II Micro Hunter

Japan. Introduced 1985; redesigned in 1994 as A-Bolt II.

Perf.: $600   Exc.: $575   VGood: $395

BROWNING A-BOLT HUNTER, LEFT HAND
Similar to A-Bolt Hunter but in left-hand version.

Perf.: $650   Exc.: $625   VGood: $420

BROWNING A-BOLT CAMO STALKER
Same specs as A-Bolt Hunter except camo-stained laminated wood stock; cut checkering; non-glare finish on metal; 270, 30-06, 7mm Rem. Mag. Made in Japan. Introduced 1987; dropped 1989.

Perf.: $525   Exc.: $495   VGood: $375

BROWNING A-BOLT COMPOSITE STALKER
Same specs as the A-Bolt Hunter except checkered black composite stock. Imported from Japan by Browning. Introduced 1985.

Perf.: $595   Exc.: $560   VGood: $420

BROWNING A-BOLT EURO-BOLT
Same specs as the A-Bolt Hunter except satin-finished walnut stock with Continental-style cheekpiece; palm swell grip and schnabel forend; rounded bolt shroud and Mannlicher-style flattened bolt handle; 30-06, 270 (22-inch barrel), 7mm Rem.

Mag. (26-inch barrel); weighs about 6 lbs., 11 oz. Imported from Japan by Browning. Introduced 1993. Now known as Euro-Bolt II.

Perf.: $775   Exc.: $575   VGood: $450

BROWNING A-BOLT GOLD MEDALLION
Same specs as A-Bolt Hunter except select walnut stock; gold-filled inscription on barrel; engraved receiver; brass spacers between rubber recoil pad, rosewood grip cap, forend tip; palm swell pistol grip; Monte Carlo-style comb; double-border 22 lpi checkering; 270, 30-06, 300 Win. Mag., 7mm Rem. Mag. Made in Japan. Introduced 1988.

Perf.: $950   Exc.: $900   VGood: $700

BROWNING A-BOLT MEDALLION
Same specs as A-Bolt Hunter except 375 H&H Mag.; 1-inch deluxe sling swivels; rosewood pistol grip, forend cap; slide tang safety; with or without sights; glossy stock finish; high polish blue. Imported from Japan by Browning. Introduced 1985.

Perf.: $750	**Exc.: $700**	**VGood: $595**
375 H&H, with sights		
Perf.: $800	**Exc.: $750**	**VGood: $645**

BROWNING A-BOLT MEDALLION LEFT HAND
Same specs as the Medallion except left-hand action; 270, 30-06, 7mm Rem. Mag., 375 H&H. Imported from Japan by Browning. Introduced 1987.

Perf.: $800   Exc.: $750   VGood: $625

BROWNING A-BOLT MICRO MEDALLION
Same specs as A-Bolt Hunter except scaled-down version with 20-inch barrel; shortened, 13 5/16-inch length of pull; 3-shot magazine; weighs 6 lbs., 1 oz.; 243, 308, 7mm-08, 257 Roberts, 223, 22-250; no sights. Imported from Japan by Browning. Introduced 1988. Add 100% for .284.

Perf.: $695   Exc.: $650   VGood: $495

BROWNING A-BOLT STAINLESS STALKER
Same specs as A-Bolt Hunter except stainless steel receiver; matte silver-gray finish; graphite-fiberglass composite textured stock; no sights; 270, 30-06, 7mm Rem. Mag, 375 H&H. Made in Japan. Imported from Japan by Browning. Introduced 1987.

Perf.: $750	**Exc.: $700**	**VGood: $495**
Left-hand		
Perf.: $775	**Exc.: $725**	**VGood: $520**
375 H&H caliber		
Perf.: $950	**Exc.: $900**	**VGood: $695**

BROWNING A-BOLT 22
Bolt action; 22 LR, 22 WMR; 5-, 15-shot magazine; 22-inch barrel; 40-1/4-inch overall length; weighs 5 lbs. 9 oz.; walnut stock with cut checkering; rosewood grip cap and forend tip; with or without open sights; open sight model with ramp front and adjustable folding leaf rear; short 60°; bolt throw; top tang safety; grooved for 22 scope mount; drilled and tapped for full-size scope mounts; detachable magazine; gold-colored trigger. Imported from Japan by Browning. Introduced 1986; no longer imported.

22 LR		
Perf.: $750	**Exc.: $650**	**VGood: $525**
22 WMR		
Perf.: $775	**Exc.: $675**	**VGood: $550**

BROWNING A-BOLT 22 GOLD MEDALLION
Same specs as A-Bolt 22 except high-grade walnut stock with brass spacers between stock and rubber recoil pad, and rosewood grip cap and forend; Medallion-style engraving on receiver flats; "Gold Medallion" engraved and gold filled on right side of barrel; high-gloss stock finish; no sights. Imported from Japan by Browning. Introduced 1988; no longer imported.

Perf.: $800   Exc.: $750   VGood: $700

BROWNING A-BOLT II HUNTER
Bolt action; 223, 223 WSSM, 22-250, 243, 243 WSSM, 25-06, 270, 270 WSM, 280, 7mm-08, 7mm Rem. Mag., 308, 30-06, 300 Win. Mag., 300 WSM, 325 WSM, 338 Win. Mag., 375 H&H Mag.; 4-shot (standard calibers), 3-shot (magnum calibers) detachable box magazine; 22-inch medium sporter weight barrel with recessed muzzle; 26-inch on magnum calibers; 44-3/4-inch overall length, 41-3/4-inch (short action); weighs 6-1/2 to 7-1/2 lbs.; classic-style American walnut stock; recoil pad standard on magnum calibers; short-throw (60-degree) fluted bolt; three locking lugs; plunger-type ejector; grooved and gold-plated adjustable trigger; hinged floorplate; slide tang safety; glossy stock finish; rosewood grip and forend cap; high polish blue; BOSS barrel vibration modulator and muzzlebrake system not available in 375 H&H. Imported from Japan by Browning. Introduced 1994; still imported.

Perf.: $750	**Exc.: $550**	**VGood: $450**
With open sights		
Perf.: $700	**Exc.: $550**	**VGood: $480**
With BOSS		
Perf.: $740	**Exc.: $580**	**VGood: $500**

BROWNING A-BOLT II MICRO HUNTER

Similar to the A-Bolt II Hunter except has shorter barrel and stock, 13-5/16-inch length of pull, 20-inch barrel, and comes in 260 Rem., 243, 308, 7mm-08, 223, 22-250, 22 Hornet, also 270 WSM, 7mm WSM, 300 WSM. Weighs 6 lbs., 1 oz. Introduced 1999. Imported by Browning.

Perf.: $700   **Exc.:** $550   **VGood:** $500

BROWNING A-BOLT II COMPOSITE STALKER

Same specs as A-Bolt II Hunter except black graphite fiberglass stock with textured finish; matte blue finish on metal; .223 WSSM, .243 WSSM, .25 WSSM, .223, .243, .7mm-08, .270 WSM, 7mm WSM, .300 WSM, .325 WSM, .25-06, .270, .280, .30-06, 7mm RM, .300 WM, .338 WM. Add 10 percent for BOSS or left-hand version..; no sights; BOSS barrel vibration modulator and muzzlebrake system offered in all calibers. Imported from Japan by Browning. Introduced 1994; still imported.

Perf.: $650   **Exc.:** $500   **VGood:** $450

With BOSS

Perf.: $740   **Exc.:** $580   **VGood:** $500

BROWNING EURO-BOLT II

Same specs as A-Bolt II Hunter except satin-finished walnut stock with Continental-style cheekpiece; palm-swell grip and schnabel forend; rounded bolt shroud and Mannlicher-style flattened bolt handle; 30-06, 270 (22-inch barrel), 7mm Rem. Mag. (26-inch barrel); weighs about 6 lbs., 11 oz.; BOSS barrel vibration modulator and muzzlebrake system optional. Imported from Japan by Browning. Introduced 1993.

Perf.: $750   **Exc.:** $590   **VGood:** $450

With BOSS

Perf.: $825   **Exc.:** $700   **VGood:** $550

BROWNING A-BOLT II GOLD MEDALLION

Same specs as A-Bolt II Hunter except select walnut stock with brass spacers between rubber recoil pad, and rosewood grip cap and forend tip; gold-filled barrel inscription; palm swell pistol grip; Monte Carlo comb; 22 lpi checkering with double borders; engraved receiver flats; 270, 30-06, 7mm Rem. Mag. only. Imported from Japan by Browning. Introduced 1988.

Perf.: $700   **Exc.:** $590   **VGood:** $500

With BOSS

Perf.: $770   **Exc.:** $665   **VGood:** $550

BROWNING A-BOLT II HUNTER SHORT ACTION

Same specs as the standard A-Bolt II Hunter except short action for 223, 22-250, 243, 257 Roberts, 7mm-08, 284 Win., 308, new short magnum chamberings; weighs 6-1/2 lbs.; BOSS barrel vibration modulator and muzzlebrake system optional. Imported from Japan by Browning. Introduced 1994.

Perf.: $700   **Exc.:** $600   **VGood:** $500

With sights

Perf.: $750   **Exc.:** $650   **VGood:** $550

With BOSS

Perf.: $795   **Exc.:** $695   **VGood:** $595

BROWNING A-BOLT II MEDALLION

Same specs as A-Bolt II Hunter except .223 WSSM, .243 WSSM, .25 WSSM, .223, .243, .7mm-08, .270 WSM, 7mm WSM, .300 WSM, .325 WSM, .25-06, .270, .280, .30-06, 7mm RM, .300 WM, .338 WM. Add 10 percent for BOSS or left-hand version.istol grip, forend cap; slide tang safety; glossy stock finish; high polish blue. Imported from Japan by Browning. Introduced 1984; still imported.

Perf.: $725   **Exc.:** $650   **VGood:** $500

With BOSS

Perf.: $775   **Exc.:** $700   **VGood:** $575

375 H&H

Perf..: $900   **Exc.:** $825   **VGood:** $675

WSSM version, chambered for 223 WSSM and 243 WSSM, introduced 2003.

Perf.: $725   **Exc.:** $650   **VGood:** $500

Browning Euro-Bolt II

Browning A-Bolt II Varmint

Browning NRA A-Bolt

Browning A-Bolt Special Hunter RMEF

Browning A-Bolt White Gold RMEF

Browning Acera Straight Pull

223 WSSM, 243 WSSM, 25 WSSM chambering

Perf.: $725   **Exc.:** $650   **VGood:** $500

BROWNING A-BOLT II MEDALLION SHORT ACTION

Same specs as the standard A-Bolt II Medallion except short action for 223, 22-250, 243, 257 Roberts, 7mm-08, 284 Win., 308; weighs 6-1/2 lbs. BOSS barrel vibration modulator and muzzlebrake system optional. Imported from Japan by Browning. Introduced 1994.

Perf.: $725   **Exc.:** $650   **VGood:** $500

BROWNING A-BOLT II MICRO MEDALLION

Same specs as A-Bolt II Medallion except scaled-down version with 20-inch barrel; shortened length of pull (13-5/16-inch); 3-shot magazine; weighs 6 lbs. 1 oz.; 22 Hornet, 243, 308, 7mm-08, 257 Roberts, 223, 22-250; BOSS feature not available. Imported from Japan by Browning. Introduced 1994; no longer imported.

Perf.: $640   **Exc.:** $580   **VGood:** $500

BROWNING A-BOLT II STAINLESS STALKER

Bolt-action rifle. Calibers: .223 WSSM, .243 WSSM, .25 WSSM, .223, .243, .7mm-08, .270 WSM, 7mm WSM, .300 WSM, .325 WSM, .25-06, .270, .280, .30-06, 7mm RM, .300 WM, .338 WM, .375 H&H. Barrel: 22-inch, 23-inch, 24-inch, 26-inch stainless steel, sightless (except for .375 H&H). Magazine: Detachable box. Stock: Black composite. Add 10 percent for BOSS system and left-hand version.

Perf.: $745   **Exc.:** $695   **VGood:** $550

With BOSS

Perf.: $800   **Exc.:** $750   **VGood:** $600

375 H&H, with sights

Perf.: $715   **Exc.:** $670   **VGood:** $550

Left-hand, with BOSS

Perf.: $950   **Exc.:** $900   **VGood:** $750

BROWNING A-BOLT II VARMINT

Same specs as A-Bolt II Hunter except heavy varmint/target barrel; laminated wood stock with special dimensions; flat forend and palm swell grip; 223, 22-250, 243; comes with BOSS barrel vibration modulator and muzzlebrake system. Imported from Japan by Browning. Introduced 1994; no longer imported.

Perf.: $695   **Exc.:** $600   **VGood:** $500

BROWNING NRA A-BOLT WILDLIFE CONSERVATION COLLECTION

Commemorates NRA's Environment Conservation and Hunting Outreach Program. Caliber: .243 Win. Barrel: 22-inch blued sightless. Stock: Satin-finish walnut with NRA Heritage logo lasered on buttstock.

NIB: $750   **Exc.:** $695   **VGood:** $545

BROWNING A-BOLT SPECIAL HUNTER RMEF

Similar to A-Bolt Hunter but honors Rocky Mountain Elk Foundation. Chambered in .325 WSM. Satin finish. Introduced 2007.

NIB: $825   **Exc.:** $775   **VGood:** $650

BROWNING A-BOLT WHITE GOLD RMEF

Similar to A-Bolt Special Hunter RMEF but with stainless barrel and receiver and glossy finish. Introduced 2007.

NIB: $1200   **Exc.:** $1100   **VGood:** $895

Browning BBR

Browning Model 52

Browning (FN) High-Power Safari-Grade Medium-Action

Browning X-Bolt Composite Stalker

Browning X-Bolt Stainless Stalker

Browning X-Bolt Hunter

Browning (FN) High-Power Safari Olympian-Grade

Browning X-Bolt Medallion

BROWNING X-BOLT COMPOSITE STALKER

Features include steel receiver with matte blue finish, free-flaotinmg crowned barrel, matte black composite stock with palm swell, Inflex recoil pad. Various barrel lengths depending on chambering, which include both medium and long cartridges ranging from .243 Winchester to .338 Winchester Magnum. Introduced in 2008.

NIB: $800   **Exc.:** $700   **VGood:** $575

BROWNING X-BOLT STAINLESS STALKER

Similar to above but with stainless steel receiver and barrel. Various barrel lengths depending on chambering, which include both medium and long cartridges ranging from .243 Winchester to .375 H&H Magnum. Introduced in 2008.

NIB: $800   **Exc.:** $700   **VGood:** $575

BROWNING X-BOLT HUNTER

Similar to above but with sculpted, satin-finished walnut stock with cut checkering and low-luster blued barrel and receiver. Various barrel lengths depending on chambering, which include both medium and long cartridges ranging from .243 Winchester to .338 Winchester Magnum. Introduced in 2008.

NIB: $800   **Exc.:** $700   **VGood:** $575—

BROWNING X-BOLT MEDALLION

Similar to above but with high-gloss finish and engraved, blued barrel and receiver. Various barrel lengths depending on chambering, which include both medium and long cartridges ranging from .243 Winchester to .375 H&H Magnum. Introduced in 2008.

NIB: $1000   **Exc.:** $850   **VGood:** $675

BROWNING ACERA STRAIGHT-PULL RIFLE

Bolt action, straight pull; 30-06, 300 Win. Mag.; barrel length 22-inch; 24-inch for magnums; weighs 6 lbs., 9 oz. 41-1/4-inch overall. American walnut stock with high gloss finish. Optional blade on ramp front, open adjustable rear sights. Straight-pull action; detachable box magazine; Teflon coated breechblock; drilled and tapped for scope mounting. Introduced about 1999. No longer imported. Increasingly collectible.

Perf.: $900   **Exc.:** $850   **VGood:** $700

BROWNING BBR

Bolt action; 25-06, 270, 30-06, 7mm Rem. Mag., 300 Win. Mag., 338 Win. Mag. (long action), 22-250, 243 Win., 257 Roberts, 7mm-08 Rem., 308 Win. (short action); 4-shot (standard calibers), 3-shot (magnum calibers); 22-inch, 24-inch sporter barrel; recessed

muzzle; American walnut Monte Carlo stock; high cheek-piece; full/checkered pistol grip, forend; recoil pad on magnums; grooved, gold-plated adjustable trigger; detachable box magazine; tang slide safety; low-profile swing swivels. Made in Japan by Miroku. Introduced 1978; dropped 1984. Add $250 for 243 caliber.

Perf.:. $570   **Exc.:** $490   **VGood:** $375

BROWNING MODEL 52

Bolt action; 22 LR; 5-shot magazine; 24-inch barrel; weighs 7 lbs.; high-grade walnut stock with oil-like finish; cut-checkered grip and forend; metal grip cap, rosewood forend tip; no sights furnished; drilled and tapped for scope mounting or iron sights; recreation of the Winchester Model 52C Sporter with minor safety improvements; duplicates the adjustable Micro-Motion trigger system; button release magazine. Only 5000 made. Imported from Japan by Browning. Introduced 1991; dropped 1992.

Perf.: $750   **Exc.:** $595   **VGood:** $475

BROWNING (FN) HIGH-POWER SAFARI

Bolt action; 243, 257 Roberts, 264 Win Mag, 270, 284, 30-06, 7mm Rem Mag, 300 Win Mag, 308 Norma Mag., 300 H&H, 338 Win. Mag., 375 H&H Mag., 458 Win. Mag.; 4-shot magazine (magnum cartridges), 6-shot (standard calibers); 24-inch barrel (magnum calibers), 22-inch (standard calibers); European walnut stock; hand-checkered pistol grip, forearm; Monte Carlo cheekpiece; recoil pad on magnum models; folding leaf rear sight, hooded ramp front; quick-detachable sling swivels. Introduced 1960; dropped 1974. Premium for rare calibers.

Standard calibers
Exc.: $895   **VGood:** $675   **Good:** $550

Magnum calibers
Exc.: $995   **VGood:** $750   **Good:** $650

BROWNING (FN) HIGH-POWER SAFARI-GRADE MEDIUM-ACTION

Same specs as standard grade Safari except action length; 22-250, 243 Win., 284 Win., 308 Win.; 22-inch lightweight barrel standard, but available in 22-250, 243 with 24-inch heavy barrel. Dropped 1974.

Exc.: $895   **VGood:** $795   **Good:** $550

BROWNING (FN) HIGH-POWER SAFARI-GRADE SHORT-ACTION

Same specs as standard Safari except short action; 222 Rem., 222 Rem. Mag.; 22-inch lightweight, 24-inch heavy barrel. Dropped 1974.

Exc.: $895   **VGood:** $795   **Good:** $550

BROWNING (FN) HIGH-POWER SAFARI MEDALLION-GRADE

Same specs as standard Safari grade except scroll-engraved receiver, barrel; engraved ram's head on floorplate; select European walnut stock with rosewood grip cap, forearm tip. Dropped 1974.

Exc.: $1600   **VGood:** $1200   **Good:** $750

BROWNING (FN) HIGH-POWER SAFARI OLYMPIAN-GRADE

Same specs as Safari grade except engraving on barrel; chrome-plated floorplate, trigger guard, receiver, all engraved with game scenes; figured European walnut stock; 32 lpi checkering; rosewood forearm tip, grip cap; grip cap inlaid with 18-karat gold medallion. Discontinued 1974. Premium for rare cals.

Exc.: $3500   **VGood:** $2450   **Good:** $1595

BROWNING T-BOLT MODEL T-1

Bolt action; straight-pull; 22 LR; 5-shot clip magazine; 22-inch or 24-inch barrel; weighs 5-1/2 lbs.; uncheckered walnut pistol grip stock; peep rear sight, ramp blade front; left- or right-hand models available. Introduced 1965. Premium for left-hand model.

Perf.: $675   **Exc.:** $625   **VGood:** $585

BROWNING T-BOLT MODEL T-2
Same specs as Model T-1 except figured, hand-checkered walnut stock. 24-inch barrel. Not regularly imported. Last run T-2 was with plain stock.

Perf.: $650   **Exc.:** $600   **VGood:** $530

Late production model

Perf.: $600   **Exc.:** $550   **VGood:** $480

BROWNING T-BOLT (2006)
Reintroduction of classic and collectible T-bolt straight-pull .22 rifle but now with 10-shot rotary magazine. Introduced 2006. Add 5-10 percent for target/varmint version.

NIB: $525   **Exc.:** $475   **VGood:** $350

BROWNING T-BOLT TARGET/VARMINT STAINLESS
Similar to above but with stainless steel receiver and barrel. Introduced 2008.

Perf.: $850   **Exc.:** $725   **VGood:** $600

BROWNING T-BOLT COMPOSITE HUNTER
Sporter version of the new T-Bolt with black composite Monte Carlo stock and glossy blue barrel and receiver. Cham,bered in .17 HMR, .22 WMR or .22 LR. Scope not included. Introduced 2008.

Perf.: $675   **Exc.:** $575   **VGood:** $425

BROWNING T-BOLT COMPOSITE TARGET/VARMINT
Sporter version of the new T-Bolt Target/Varmint with black composite Monte Carlo stock and glossy blue barrel and receiver. Cham,bered in .17 HMR, .22 WMR or .22 LR. SCope not included. Introduced 2008.

Perf.: $700   **Exc.:** $550   **VGood:** $450

BROWNING T-BOLT SPORTER
Sporter version of the new T-Bolt with satin walnut stock and bright blue barrel and receiver. Scope not included. Introduced 2008.

Perf.: $700   **Exc.:** $550   **VGood:** $450

BROWNING AUTO 22 GRADE I
Semi-automatic; 22 LR, 22 Short; 11-shot (22 LR), 16-shot (22 Short); 19-1/4-inch barrel (22 LR), 22-1/4-inch barrel (22 Short); weighs 4-3/4 lbs.; buttstock tube magazine; select European walnut stock; hand-checkered pistol grip, semi-beaver tail forearm; open rear sight, bead front; engraved receiver, grooved for tip-off scope mount; cross-bolt safety. Introduced in 1958. Manufactured in Belgium until 1972; production transferred to Miroku in Japan; still in production.

Belgian manufacture

Perf.: $805   **Exc.:** $420   **VGood:** $360

Japanese manufacture

Perf.: $510   **Exc.:** $470   **VGood:** $310

BROWNING AUTO 22 GRADE II
Same specs as Grade I except gold-plated trigger; small game animal scenes engraved on receiver. No longer in production.

Belgian manufacture

Perf.: $1200   **Exc.:** $1000   **VGood:** $800

Japanese manufacture

Perf.: $500   **Exc.:** $400   **VGood:** $300

BROWNING AUTO 22 GRADE III
Same specs as Grade I except gold-plated trigger; extra-fancy walnut stock forearm; skip checkering on pistol grip, forearm; satin chrome-plated receiver; hand-carved, engraved scrolls, leaves, dog/game bird scenes; 22 LR only. No longer in production.

Belgian manufacture

Perf.: $3000   **Exc.:** $2600   **VGood:** $1900

Japanese manufacture

Perf.: $800   **Exc.:** $625   **VGood:** $495

BROWNING AUTO 22 GRADE VI
Same specs as Grade I except grayed or blued receiver; extensive engraving; gold-plated animals; stock forend of high-grade walnut with double-border cut checkering. Made in Japan. Introduced 1987.

Perf.: $715   **Exc.:** $645   **VGood:** $510

Browning T-Bolt Target/Varmint Stainless

Browning T-Bolt Composite Hunter

Browning T-Bolt Composite Target/Varmint

Browning T-Bolt Sporter

Browning T-Bolt 2006

Browning Auto 22 Grade I

Browning Auto 22 Grade III

Browning BAR Grade II

Browning BAR Grade IV

BROWNING BAR
Semi-automatic; 243 Win., 308 Win., 270 Win., 280 Rem., 30-06, 7mm Rem. Mag., 300 Win. Mag., 338 Win. Mag., also 270 WSM, 7mmWSM, 300 WSM; 22-inch barrel; 4-shot detachable box magazine (standard calibers), 3-shot (magnum calibers); adjustable folding leaf rear sight, gold bead hooded ramp front; receiver tapped for scope mounts; checkered walnut pistol-grip stock forearm. weighs 7-1/2 to 8-1/2 lbs. Not to be confused with the military Browning fully-automatic rifle. Grades I, II introduced in 1967; several grades still in production. Grades vary according to amount of checkering, carving, engraving, inlay work. Premium for Belgian marked.

Grade I

Perf.: $800   **Exc.:** $725   **VGood:** $400

Grade I Magnum

Perf.: $910   **Exc.:** $835   **VGood:** $550

Grade II

Perf.: $1000   **Exc.:** $920   **VGood:** $650

Grade II Magnum

Perf.: $1100   **Exc.:** $1050   **VGood:** $750

Grade III

Perf.: $1300   **Exc.:** $1250   **VGood:** $950

Grade III Magnum

Perf.: $1400   **Exc.:** $1350   **VGood:** $1050

Grade IV

Perf.: $1500   **Exc.:** $1450   **VGood:** $1150

Grade IV Magnum

Perf.: $1600   **Exc.:** $1550   **VGood:** $1250

Grade V

Perf.: $3000   **Exc.:** $2600   **VGood:** $2100

Grade V Magnum

Perf.: $3300   **Exc.:** $2900   **VGood:** $2300

BROWNING BAR-22
Semi-automatic; 22 LR; 15-shot, tubular magazine; 20-1/4-inch barrel; weighs 5 lbs. 2 oz.; receiver grooved for scope mount; folding leaf rear sight, gold bead ramp front; French walnut stock hand-checkered pistol grip, forearm. Introduced 1977; dropped 1986. Manufactured in Japan.

Grade I

Perf.: $495   **Exc.:** $425   **VGood:** $350

Grade II

Perf.: $595   **Exc.:** $525   **VGood:** $450

Browning BAR-22

Browning BAR Mark II Safari

Browning BAR Mark II Lightweight Semi-Auto

Browning BAR Stalker Auto Rifle

Browning BAR Shorttrac Left-Hand

Browning BAR Longtrac Left-Hand

Browning BAR Shorttrac Stalker

Browning Buck Mark Semi-Auto Rifle (Target)

Browning Buck Mark FLD Carbon

Browning B-92 Carbine

modulator and muzzlebrake system available only on models without sights. Imported from Belgium by Browning. Introduced 1993; still imported.

With sights		
Perf.: $775	**Exc.:** $660	**VGood:** $560
No sights		
Perf.: $725	**Exc.:** $645	**VGood:** $545
With BOSS, no sights		
Perf.: $825	**Exc.:** $725	**VGood:** $595

BROWNING BAR STALKER AUTO RIFLE

Semi-automatic; 243, 308, 270, 270 WSM, 7mm WSM, 30-06, 7mm Rem. Mag., 300 Win. Mag., 338 Win. Mag. Barrel: 20-inch, 22-inch and 24-inch; weighs 6 lbs., 12 oz. (243) to 8 lbs., 2 oz. (magnum cals.); 41-inch to 45-inch overall length. Black composite stock and forearm. Sights: Hooded front and adjustable rear or none. Optional BOSS (no sights); gas-operated action with seven-lug rotary bolt; dual action bars; 3- or 4-shot magazine (depending on caliber). Introduced 2001. Still imported by Browning. Premium for magnum calibers.

    Perf.: $775   **Exc.:** $650   **VGood:** $600

BROWNING BAR SHORTTRAC

A streamlined version of the BAR with walnut stock, blued barrel and receiver, and short-action design. Very similar to the Winchester SXR. Chambered for a variety of short-action calibers from .243 Winchester to 7mm WSM. Available in left-hand version and various synthetic and camo finishes.

    NIB: $925   **Exc.:** $865   **VGood:** $695

BROWNING BAR LONGTRAC

Similar to BAR ShortTrac but chambered in a variety of long-action calibers ranging from .270 Winchester to .300 Winchester Magnum. Available in left-hand version and various synthetic and camo finishes.

    NIB: $925   **Exc.:** $865   **VGood:** $695

BROWNING BAR SHORTTRAC STALKER

Similar to BAR ShortTrac but with matte blue barrel and composite stock. Introduced 2006.

    NIB: $900   **Exc.:** $840   **VGood:** $695

BROWNING BAR LONGTRAC STALKER

Long-action version of the BAR ShortTrac Stalker.

    NIB: $900   **Exc.:** $840   **VGood:** $695

BROWNING BUCK MARK SEMI-AUTO RIFLE

Semi-automatic; 22 LR, 10-shot magazine. 18-inch tapered barrel (Sporter) or heavy bull barrel (Target); weighs 4 lbs., 2 oz. (Sporter) or 5 lbs., 4 oz. (Target). 34-inch overall. Walnut stock and forearm with full pistol grip. Hi-Viz adjustable sights (Sporter); rifle version of the Buck Mark Pistol; straight blowback action; machined aluminum receiver with integral rail scope mount; recessed muzzle crown; manual thumb safety. Introduced 2001.

Sporter		
Perf.: $500	**Exc.:** $400	**VGood:** $350
Target, heavy bull barrel		
Perf.: $500	**Exc.:** $400	**VGood:** $350
FLD Target, bull barrel, gray laminated stock		
Perf.: $540	**Exc.:** $425	**VGood:** $375
FLD Carbon Rifle, light carbon composite barrel, introduced 2003		
Perf.: $610	**Exc.:** $475	**VGood:** $400

BROWNING B-92 CARBINE

Lever-action; 357 Mag., 44 Mag.; 11-shot magazine; 20-inch round barrel; post front sight, classic rear with notched elevation ramp; straight-grip European walnut stock; high-gloss finish; steel buttplate; tubular magazine. Designed from original Model 92 lever-action. Manufactured in Japan. Introduced 1978; dropped 1988. Premium for .357.

    Perf.: $750   **Exc.:** $650   **VGood:** $495

BROWNING BAR MARK II SAFARI

Semi-automatic; 243, 25-06, 270, 270 WSM, 7mm WSM, 300 WSM, 30-06, 308; 4-shot detachable magazine; 22-inch round tapered barrel; 43-inch overall length; weighs 7-3/8 lbs.; hand-checkered French walnut stock and forend; gold bead on hooded ramp front sight, click-adjustable rear, or no sights; updated version with new bolt release lever; removable trigger assembly with larger trigger guard; redesigned gas and buffer systems; scroll-engraved receiver tapped for scope mounting. BOSS barrel vibration modulator and muzzlebrake system available on models without sights. Imported from Belgium by Browning. Introduced 1993; still imported.

    Perf.: $730   **Exc.:** $610   **VGood:** $530

BROWNING BAR MARK II LIGHTWEIGHT SEMI-AUTO

Similar to the Mark II Safari except has lighter alloy receiver and 20-inch barrel. Available in 243, 308, 270, 30-06, 7mm Rem. Mag., 300 Win. Mag., 338 Win. Mag. Weighs 7 lbs., 2 oz.; overall length 41-inch. Has dovetailed, gold bead front sight on hooded ramp, open rear click adjustable for windage and elevation. Introduced 1997. Still imported by Browning. Premium for magnum calibers.

    Perf.: $750   **Exc.:** $650   **VGood:** $500

BROWNING BAR MARK II SAFARI MAGNUM

Same specs as the standard caliber model except weighs 8-3/8 lbs.; 45-inch overall length; 24-inch barrel; 3-round magazine; calibers 7mm Mag., 300 Win. Mag., 338 Win. Mag.; BOSS barrel vibration

BROWNING BL-22

Lever-action; 22 LR, 22 Long, 22 Short; 22-shot magazine (22 Short), 17-shot (22 Long), 15-shot (22 LR); 20-inch barrel; 36-3/4-inch overall length; weighs 5 lbs.; folding leaf rear sight, bead post front; two-piece uncheckered Western-style walnut stock, forearm; barrel band; half-cock safety; receiver grooved for tip-off mounts. Grade II with engraved receiver, checkered grip, forearm. Produced by Miroku Firearms. Introduced 1970; still in production.

Grade I

Perf.: $400	Exc.: $345	VGood: $290

Grade II

Perf.: $475	Exc.: $420	VGood: $320

BROWNING BL-22 NRA GRADE 1

Similar to BL-22 but with NRA logo lasered on buttstock.

NIB: $475	Exc.: $415	VGood: $365

BROWNING BL-22 GRAY LAMINATE STAINLESS

Similar to BL-22 but with gray laminated stock, nickeled receiver and stainless steel barrel.

NIB: $675	Exc.: $625	VGood: $500

BROWNING MODEL 53

Lever action; 32-20; 7-shot magazine; 22-inch round tapered barrel; 39-1/2-inch overall length; weighs 6 lbs. 8 oz.; full pistol grip stock of select walnut with semi-beavertail forend; high gloss finish; cut checkering on grip and forend; metal grip cap; post bead front sight, adjustable open rear; blue finish, including trigger. Based on the Model 92 Winchester with half-length magazine. Limited to 5000 guns. Imported from Japan by Browning. Made only in 1990.

Perf.: $900	Exc.: $750	VGood: $600

BROWNING MODEL 65 GRADE I

Lever action; 218 Bee; 7-shot magazine; 24-inch round tapered barrel; 41-3/4-inch overall length; weighs 6 lbs.; select walnut pistol-grip stock, semi-beavertail forend; hooded ramp front sight, adjustable buckhorn-type rear; blued finish. Limited edition reproduction of Winchester Model 65; half-length magazine. Made in Japan. Only 3500 manufactured. Introduced 1989; dropped 1990.

Perf.: 1000	Exc.: $900	VGood: $750

BROWNING MODEL 65 HIGH GRADE

Same specs as Grade I except better wood; cut checkering; high-gloss finish; receiver with grayed finish, scroll engraving, game scenes. Made in Japan. Only 1500 made. Introduced 1989; dropped 1990.

Perf.: $1300	Exc.: $1200	VGood: $1050

BROWNING MODEL 71 RIFLE AND CARBINE

Lever action; 348 Win.; 4-shot magazine; 20-inch, 24-inch barrel; 45-inch overall length; weighs 8 lb. 2 oz.; pistol-grip stock; classic-style forend; metal buttplate; reproduction of Winchester Model 71; half-length magazine; High Grade has blued barrel and magazine, grayed lever and receiver with scroll engraving, gold-plated game scene. Grade I production limited to 3000 rifles, 4000 carbines. Made in Japan. Introduced 1987; dropped 1989.

Grade I

Perf.: $1000	Exc.: $900	VGood: $795

High Grade

Perf.: $1300	Exc.: $1195	VGood: $950

BROWNING MODEL 81 BLR

Lever action; 223, 22-250, 243, 257 Roberts, 284 Win., 7mm-08, 308 Win., 358 Win.; 4-shot detachable box magazine; 20-inch round, tapered barrel; 39-3/4-inch overall length; weighs 7 lbs.; gold bead front sight, hooded ramp, square-notch adjustable rear; drilled, tapped for scope mounts; oil-finished, checkered, straight-grip walnut stock; recoil pad; half-cock hammer safety; wide, grooved trigger. Introduced 1971; made only in Japan after 1972; still imported by Browning.

Browning BL-22

Browning BL-22 Grade I

Browning BL-22 Gray Laminate Stainless

Browning Model 65 Grade I

Browning Model 65 High Grade

Browning Model 71 Rifle and Carbine

Browning Model 81 BLR Long Action

Browning BLR Lightweight Takedown

Browning BLR Light Weight 81 Stainless Takedown

Belgian manufacture

Perf.: $700	Exc.: $650	VGood: $500

Japanese manufacture

Perf.: $600	Exc.: $550	VGood: $400

BROWNING MODEL 81 BLR LONG ACTION

Same specs as Model 81 BLR except long action; 270, 30-06, 7mm Rem. Mag., 300 Win. Mag.; 22-inch, 24-inch barrel; weighs 8-1/2 lbs.; six-lug fluted, rotary bolt. Made in Japan. Introduced 1991.

Perf.: $700	Exc.: $650	VGood: $530

BROWNING BLR LIGHTWEIGHT TAKEDOWN

Similar to BLR Model 81 long- and short-action but with takedown feature.

NIB: $850	Exc.: $800	VGood: $695

BROWNING BLR LIGHT WEIGHT 81 STAINLESS TAKEDOWN

Similar to above but with stainless steel barrel and receiver. Introduced 2008.

NIB: $975	Exc.: $850	VGood: $695

BROWNING MODEL 1886 RIFLE AND CARBINE

Lever action; 45-70; 8-shot magazine; 22-inch barrel; 40-3/4-inch overall length; weighs 8 lbs. 3 oz.; satin-finished select walnut stock with metal crescent buttplate; blade front sight, open adjustable rear; full-length magazine; classic-style forend with barrel band, saddle ring; polished blue finish. Recreation of original John M. Browning-designed Winchester 1886. Limited to 7000 guns. Imported from Japan by Browning. Introduced 1992; dropped 1993.

Carbine

Perf.: $1000	Exc.: $900	VGood: $600

Rifle

Perf.: $1175	Exc.: $975	VGood: $695

Browning Model 1895

Browning Model 1885
High Wall

Browning Model 78

Browning BPR

Browning Continental

BROWNING MODEL 1886 RIFLE AND CARBINE, HIGH GRADE

Same specs as Model 1886 Rifle and Carbine except high grade walnut with cut-checkered grip and forend and gloss finish; grayed steel receiver and lever; scroll engraved receiver with game scenes highlighted by a special gold-plating and engraving process. Limited to 3000 guns. Introduced 1992; dropped 1993.

Rifle		
Perf.: $1500	**Exc.:** $1100	**VGood:** $900
Carbine		
Perf.: $1395	**Exc.:** $995	**VGood:** $795

BROWNING MODEL 1895

Lever action; 30-06, 30-40 Krag, 405 Winchester; 4-shot non-detachable box magazine; 24-inch round barrel; 42-inch overall length; weighs 8 lbs.; straight-grip walnut stock forend; matte finish; buckhorn rear sight with elevator, gold bead front on ramp; replica of John M. Browning's first box-magazine lever action; top loading magazine; half-cock hammer safety; High Grade Model with gold-plated moose, grizzly on gray engraved receiver. Made in Japan. Limited edition. Introduced 1985. 405 brings premium.

Grade I		
Perf.: $1000	**Exc.:** $750	**VGood:** $550
High Grade (2000 made)		
Perf.: $1400	**Exc.:** $1150	**VGood:** $895

BROWNING MODEL 1885 HIGH WALL

Single shot; falling block; 223, 22-250, 30-06, 270, 7mm Rem. Mag., 45-70; 28-inch octagon barrel with recessed muzzle; 43-1/2-inch overall length; weighs about 8-1/2 lbs.; walnut stock with straight grip; schnabel forend; no sights furnished; drilled and tapped for scope mounting; replica of John M. Browning's high-wall falling block rifle. Imported from Japan by Browning. Introduced 1985.

Perf.: $925	**Exc.:** $750	**VGood:** $595

BROWNING MODEL 1885 BPCR (BLACK POWDER CARTRIDGE RIFLE)

Similar to the 1885 High Wall rifle except the ejector system and shell deflector have been removed; chambered only for 40-65 and 45-70; color case-hardened full-tang receiver, lever, buttplate and gripcap; matte blue 30-inch part octagon, part round barrel. The Vernier tang sight has indexed elevation, is screw adjustable windage, and has three peep diameters. The hooded front sight has a built-in spirit level and comes with sight interchangeable inserts.

Adjustable trigger. Overall length 46-1/8-inch, weighs about 11 lbs. Introduced 1996. Imported from Japan.

Perf.: $1700	**Exc.:** $1400	**VGood:** $1100

BROWNING MODEL 1885 LOW WALL

Same specs as the Model 1885 High Wall except trimmer receiver; thinner 24-inch octagonal barrel; forend mounted to receiver; adjustable trigger; walnut pistol grip stock; trim schnabel forend with high-gloss finish; 22 Hornet, 223 Rem., 243 Win.; 39-1/2-inch overall length; weighs 6 lbs. 4 oz.; polished blue finish. Rifling twist rates: 1:16-inch (22 Hornet); 1:12-inch (223); 1:10-inch (243). Imported from Japan by Browning. Introduced 1995.

Perf.: $895	**Exc.:** $700	**VGood:** $575

BROWNING MODEL 1885 LOW WALL TRADITIONAL HUNTER

Similar to the Model 1885 Low Wall except chambered for 357 Mag., 44 Mag. and 45 Colt; steel crescent buttplate; 1/16-inch gold bead front sight, adjustable buckhorn rear, and tang-mounted peep sight with barrel-type elevation adjuster and knob-type windage adjustments. Barrel is drilled and tapped for a Browning scope base. Oil-finished select walnut stock with swivel studs. Introduced 1997.

Perf.: $900	**Exc.:** $800	**VGood:** $695

BROWNING MODEL 78

Single shot, falling block; 30-06, 25-06, 6mm Rem., 243, 22-250, 7mm Rem. Mag.; 26-inch tapered octagon or heavy round barrel; hand-rubbed, hand-checkered select walnut stock; rubber recoil pad; no sights; furnished with scope mounts and rings; falling-block action; exposed hammer; adjustable trigger; automatic ejector. Based on John M. Browning's first patent. Made in Japan. Introduced about 1974; dropped about 1983.

Perf.: $900	**Exc.:** $850	**VGood:** $695

BROWNING MODEL B-78

Same specs as Model 78 except 45-70; 24-inch heavy octagon barrel; blade front sight, step adjustable rear; drilled, tapped for scope mounts; straight-grip hand-checkered walnut stock; semi-schnabel forend; sling swivels; curved, blued steel buttplate. Introduced about 1978; dropped about 1983.

Perf.: $900	**Exc.:** $800	**VGood:** $725

BROWNING BPR PUMP RIFLE

Pump-action; 243, 308 (short action); 270, 30-06, 7mm Rem. Mag., 300 Win. Mag., 4-shot magazine (3 for magnums); 22-inch barrel; 24-inch for magnum calibers; weighs 7 lbs., 3 oz. 43-inch overall (22-inch

barrel). Select walnut stock with full pistol grip, high gloss finish. Gold bead on hooded ramp front sight, open click adjustable rear. Slide-action mechanism cams forend down away from the barrel on the rearward stroke. Seven-lug rotary bolt; cross-bolt safety behind trigger; removable magazine; alloy receiver. Introduced 1997. Imported from Belgium by Browning; no longer imported.

Perf.: $875	**Exc.:** $750	**VGood:** $600

BROWNING BPR-22

Pump-action; 22 LR, 22 WMR; 11-shot (22 WMR), 15-shot (22 LR) tube magazine; 20-1/2-inch barrel; hammerless. Grade II with engraved action; select walnut stocks. Made in Japan. Introduced in 1977; 22 LR dropped, 1982; 22 WMR dropped 1986.

22 LR		
Perf.: $525	**Exc.:** $450	**VGood:** $325
22 WMR		
Perf.: $600	**Exc.:** $495	**VGood:** $350
Grade II		
Perf.: $650	**Exc.:** $595	**VGood:** $500

BROWNING CONTINENTAL

Double rifle, superposed breakopen; 270 Win., 30-06, 9.3x74R; interchangeable 20-ga. barrels; 24-inch rifle barrels; 26-1/2-inch shotgun barrels; flat face gold bead front sight on matted ramp, folding leaf rear; straight-grip, oil-finished American walnut stock hand checkered; schnabel forend; action built on re-engineered Superposed 20-ga. frame; single selective inertia trigger; manual top tang safety barrel selector. Marketed in fitted case. Made in Belgium. Introduced 1979; dropped 1987.

Perf.: $11000	**Exc.:** $5700	**VGood:** $3750

BROWNING EXPRESS

Double rifle, superposed breakopen; 270, 30-06; 24-inch barrels; 41-inch overall length; weighs 7 lbs.; gold bead on ramp front sight, adjustable folding leaf rear; straight grip, oil-finished select European walnut stock; schnabel forend; hand checkered; reinforced breech face; single selective trigger; selective ejectors; manual safety; hand-engraved receiver; marketed in fitted case. Made in Belgium. Introduced 1981; dropped 1987.

Perf.: $8000	**Exc.:** $6500	**VGood:** $4650

BSA CENTURION

Single shot; Martini action; 22 LR; 24-inch match barrel; BSA No. 30 rear sight, No. 20 front; uncheckered walnut target stock; cheekpiece; pistol grip; long semi-beavertail forend. Discontinued 1932.

Exc.: $595	**VGood:** $485	**Good:** $300

BSA CF-2 CARBINE

Bolt action; 222 Rem., 22-250, 243, 6.5x55, 7mm Mauser, 7x64, 270, 308, 30-06, 7mm Rem. Mag., 300 Win. Mag.; 20-inch barrel; open adjustable rear sight, hooded ramp front; roll-over Monte Carlo stock of European walnut; high-gloss finish; pistol grip, skip-line checkering; adjustable single trigger or optional double-set trigger. Manufactured in England. Discontinued 1985.

Exc.: $450	**VGood:** $375	**Good:** $250

BSA CF-2 HEAVY BARREL

Same specs as CF-2 except 222 Rem., 22-250, 243; 23- to 26-inch heavy barrel; weighs 9 lbs.; no sights. No longer in production.

Exc.: $475	**VGood:** $400	**Good:** $270

BSA CF-2 SPORTER/CLASSIC

Same specs as CF-2 except 23- to 26-inch barrel; oil finished walnut stock. Manufactured in England. Introduced 1980; discontinued 1985.

Exc.: $420	**VGood:** $350	**Good:** $24

BSA CF-2 STUTZEN

Same specs as CF-2 except 222 Rem., 22-250, 243, 6.5x55, 7mm Mauser, 7x64, 270, 308, 30-06; 20-1/2-inch barrel; full-length Stutzen-style stock, contrasting schnabel forend tip, grip cap; improved bolt guide. Manufactured in England. Introduced 1982; discontinued 1985.

Exc.: $570	**VGood:** $470	**Good:** $270

BSA CF-2 VARMINTER
Same specs as CF-2 except 222 Rem., 22-250, 243; 23- to 26-inch heavy barrel; matte finish; sling swivels. Introduced 1986; discontinued 1986.

Exc.: $350 **VGood:** $280 **Good:** $255

BSA CFT TARGET
Bolt action; single shot; 308; 26-1/2-inch barrel; weighs 11 lbs.; globe front sight, aperture rear; European walnut stock. Introduced 1987. Discontinued 1987.

Exc.: $700 **VGood:** $595 **Good:** $475

BSA IMPERIAL
Bolt action; 270 Win., 308 Win., 30-06 (lightweight model), 22 Hornet, 222 Rem., 243 Win., 257 Roberts, 7x57mm, 300 Savage, 30-06 (standard weight); 22-inch barrel; recoil reducer cut into muzzle; European walnut cheekpiece stock; hand-checkered pistol grip, schnabel forend; black buttplate; pistol grip cap with white spacers; drilled, tapped for scope mounts; fully-adjustable trigger. Introduced 1959; discontinued 1964.

Exc.: $475 **VGood:** $380 **Good:** $300

BSA MAJESTIC DELUXE
Bolt action; 22 Hornet, 222 Rem., 243 Win., 308 Win., 30-06, 7x57mm; 4-shot magazine; 22-inch heavy barrel; weighs 6-1/4 lbs.; folding leaf rear, hooded ramp front sight; European walnut stock; checkered pistol grip, forend; cheekpiece; schnabel forend; sling swivels. Introduced 1959; discontinued 1965.

Exc.: $350 **VGood:** $300 **Good:** $250

BSA MAJESTIC DELUXE FEATHERWEIGHT
Same specs as Majestic Deluxe except recoil pad; lightweight 22-inch barrel; recoil reducer; 243, 270, 308, 30-06, 458. Premium for 458 chambering.

Exc.: $400 **VGood:** $300 **Good:** $230

BSA MARTINI INTERNATIONAL ISU MATCH
Single shot; 22 LR; 28-inch barrel; 43-inch-44-inch overall length; weighs 10-3/4 lbs.; Martini action; modified PH-1 Parker-Hale tunnel front sight, PH-25 aperture rear; match-type French butt and forend; flat cheekpiece; fully-adjustable trigger; designed for ISU specs. Introduced 1968; discontinued 1986.

Exc.: $700 **VGood:** $500 **Good:** $380

BSA MARTINI INTERNATIONAL MATCH
Single shot; 22 LR; 29-inch heavy barrel; Martini action; match sights; uncheckered two-piece target stock; full cheekpiece; pistol grip; broad beavertail forend; hand stop; swivels; right- or left-hand styles. Introduced 1950; discontinued 1953.

Exc.: $575 **VGood:** $375 **Good:** $300

BSA MARTINI INTERNATIONAL MATCH LIGHT
Same specs as Martini International Match except lightweight 26-inch barrel. Introduced 1950; discontinued 1953.

Exc.: $575 **VGood:** $375 **Good:** $300

BSA MARTINI INTERNATIONAL MATCH MARK II
Same specs as Martini International Match except choice of light (26-inch), heavy (29-inch) barrel; weighs 14 lbs. (29-inch barrel), 11 lbs. (26-inch barrel); redesigned stock forearm, trigger mechanism, ejection system; Introduced in 1953; discontinued 1959.

Exc.: $600 **VGood:** $400 **Good:** $320

BSA MARTINI INTERNATIONAL MATCH MARK III
Same specs as International Match Mark II heavy barrel model plus redesigned stock forend; free-floating barrel; longer frame with alloy strut to attach forend. Introduced 1959; discontinued 1967.

Exc.: $650 **VGood:** $450 **Good:** $375

BSA MARTINI INTERNATIONAL MATCH MARK V
Same specs as International Match except 28-inch heavy barrel; weighs 12-1/4 lbs. Introduced 1976; no longer produced.

Exc.: $650 **VGood:** $550 **Good:** $450

BSA MODEL 12/15 MATCH
Single shot; 22 LR; 29-inch barrel; Martini action; Parker-Hale PH-7A rear, PH-22 front sight; walnut target stock with high comb, cheekpiece, beavertail forend; forward sling swivel. Introduced 1938; production suspended during WWII; discontinued 1950.

Exc.: $450 **VGood:** $350 **Good:** $300

BSA MODEL 12/15
Same as 12/15 Match except heavy barrel. This was designation given rifle when reintroduced following WWII. Dropped 1950.

Exc.: $450 **VGood:** $350 **Good:** $300

BSA MODEL 13
Single shot; 22 LR; 25-inch barrel; Martini action; Parker-Hale No. 7 rear, hooded front sight; straight-grip walnut stock; hand-checkered forearm; lightweight version of BSA No. 12. Introduced 1913; discontinued 1929.

Exc.: $400 **VGood:** $350 **Good:** $300

BSA MODEL 13 SPORTER
Same specs as Model 13 except Parker-Hale Sportarget rear sight, bead front. Also available in 22 Hornet. discontinued 1932.

Exc.: $475 **VGood:** $325 **Good:** $275

22 Hornet
Exc.: $525 **VGood:** $375 **Good:** $325

BSA MODEL 15
Single shot; 22 LR; 29-inch barrel; Martini action; BSA No. 30 rear, No. 20 front sight; uncheckered walnut target stock; cheekpiece, pistol grip, long semi-beavertail forend. Introduced 1915; discontinued 1932.

Exc.: $395 **VGood:** $300 **Good:** $250

BSA MONARCH DELUXE
Bolt action; 22 Hornet, 222 Rem., 243 Win., 270 Win., 7mm Rem. Mag., 308 Win., 30-06; 22-inch barrel; weighs 6-1/4 lbs.; Mauser-type; fully-adjustable trigger; bolt head encloses cartridge and in turn enclosed by barrel extension; gas-proof cocking piece; hinged floorplate; silent safety with cocking indicator; folding leaf rear sight, hooded ramp front; checkered American-style stock; hardwood forend tip, grip cap; recoil pad. Introduced 1965; discontinued 1974.

Exc.: $395 **VGood:** $340 **Good:** $260

BSA CF-2 Varminter

BSA Majestic Deluxe Featherweight

BSA Model 12/15

BSA Model 13

BSA Model 15

BSA Monarch Deluxe

Bushmaster M17S Bullpup Rifle

Bushmaster Shorty XM15 E2S Carbine

Bushmaster XM15 E2S Dissipator Carbine

Bushmaster XM15 E2S Target Model Rifle

Bushmaster DCM Competition Rifle

Bushmaster XM15 E2S V-Match Rifle

BSA MONARCH DELUXE VARMINT
Same specs as Monarch Deluxe except 222 Rem., 243 Win; 24-inch heavy barrel. Introduced 1965; discontinued 1977.

Perf.: $395   **Exc.:** $350   **VGood:** $300

BSA NO. 12
Single shot; 22 LR; 29-inch barrel; Martini action; Parker-Hale No. 7 rear, hooded front sight; straight-grip walnut stock; hand-checkered forearm. Introduced 1912; discontinued 1929.

Exc.: $450   **VGood:** $300   **Good:** $200

BUSHMASTER M17S BULLPUP RIFLE
Semi-automatic; 223, 10-shot magazine. 21.5-inch barrel, chrome lined; 1:9-inch twist; weighs 8.2 lbs. 30-inch overall. Fiberglass-filled nylon stock. Designed for optics-carrying handle; incorporates scope mount rail for Weaver-type rings; also includes 25-meter open iron sights. Gas-operated, short-stroke piston system; ambidextrous magazine

release. Introduced 1993. Made in U.S.A. by Bushmaster Firearms, Inc./Quality Parts Co.

Perf.: $1000   **Exc.:** $900   **VGood:** $775

BUSHMASTER SHORTY XM15 E2S CARBINE
Semi-automatic, 223,10-shot magazine. 16-inch barrel, heavy; 1:9-inch twist; weighs 7.2 lbs. 34.75-inch overall. A2 type stock; fixed black composition. Fully adjustable M16A2 sight system; patterned after Colt M-16A2. Chrome-lined barrel with manganese phosphate finish. "Shorty"handguard. Has forged aluminum receivers with push-pin. Made in U.S.A. by Bushmaster Firearms Inc.

Perf.: $900   **Exc.:** $750   **VGood:** $600

BUSHMASTER XM15 E2S DISSIPATOR CARBINE
Similar to the XM15 E2S Shorty carbine except has full-length "Dissipator" handguard, longer sight radius; Weighs 7.6 lbs.; 34-3/4-inch overall length; forged aluminum receivers with push-pin style

takedown. Made in U.S.A. by Bushmaster Firearms, Inc.

Perf.: $900   **Exc.:** $750   **VGood:** $600

BUSHMASTER XM15 E25 AK SHORTY CARBINE
Similar to the XM15 E2S Shorty except has 14.5-inch barrel with an AK muzzle brake permanently attached giving 16-inch barrel length. Weighs 7.3 lbs. Introduced 1999. Made in U.S.A. by Bushmaster Firearms, Inc.

Perf.: $900   **Exc.:** $750   **VGood:** $600

BUSHMASTER XM15 E2S TARGET MODEL RIFLE
Semi-automatic; 223. 20-inch, 24-inch, 26-inch; 1:9-inch twist heavy barrel; weighs 8.3 lbs. 38.25-inch overall (20-inch barrel). Black composition stock; A2 type. Adjustable post front, adjustable aperture rear sights. Patterned after Colt M-16A2. Chrome-lined barrel with manganese phosphate exterior. Forged aluminum receivers with push-pin takedown. Made in U.S.A. by Bushmaster Firearms Co./Quality Parts Co.

Perf.: $900   **Exc.:** $750   **VGood:** $600

BUSHMASTER DCM COMPETITION RIFLE
Similar to the XM15 E2S Target Model except designed for DCM/CMP competition; has 20-inch extra-heavy (1-inch diameter) barrel with 1.8-inch twist for heavier competition bullets. Weighs about 12 lbs. with balance weights. Has special competition rear sight with interchangeable apertures, extra-fine 1/2- or 1/4-MOA windage and elevation adjustments; specially ground front sight post in choice of three widths. Full-length handguards over free-floating barrel tube. Introduced 1998. Comes in case with accessoriea. Made in U.S.A. by Bushmaster Firearms, Inc.

Perf.: $1300   **Exc.:** $1200   **VGood:** $1000

BUSHMASTER XM15 E2S V-MATCH RIFLE
Semi-automatic; 223. 20- or 24-inch, 1:9 twist heavy barrel; weighs 8.1 lbs. 38-1/4-inch overall (20-inch barrel). Black composition stock, A2 type; upper receiver has integral scope mount base. Chrome-lined .950-inch heavy barrel with counter-bored crown, manganese phosphate finish, free-floating aluminum handguard, forged aluminum receivers with push-pin takedown, hard anodized mil-spec finish. Competition trigger optional. Made in U.S.A. by Bushmaster Firearms, Inc.

Perf.: $950   **Exc.:** $800   **VGood $695**

BUSHMASTER VARMINTER RIFLE
Semi-automatic; 223 Rem., 5-shot. 24-inch barrel, 1:9-inch twist, fluted, heavy; weighs 8-3/4 lbs. 42-1/4-inch length. Stock has rubberized pistol grip. no sights; 1/2-inch scope risers. 2 stage trigger, slotted free floater forend, lockable hard case.

Perf.: $1000   **Exc.:** $900   **VGood:** $825

BUSHMASTER CARBON 15 9MM CARBINE
Semi-auto carbine chambered in 9mm Parabellum. Carbon fiber frame, 16-inch steel barrel, six-position telescoping stock, 30-rd. detachable magazine.

NIB: $850   **Exc.:** $800   **VGood:** $715

BUSHMASTER CARBON 15 TOP LOADING RIFLE
Semi-auto rifle chambered in .223. Carbon fiber frame, 16-inch steel barrel, retractable stock, Picatinny rail, 10-rd. fixed magazine. Based on AR-15.

NIB: $850   **Exc.:** $800   **VGood:** $715

BUSHMASTER PREDATOR
Semi-auto rifle chambered in .223. 20-inch DCM-type barrel, fixed composite buttstock, 2-stage competition trigger, Picatinny rail, 1/2-inch scope risers. Based on AR-15.

NIB: $1200   **Exc.:** $1100   **VGood:** $895

BUSHMASTER CARBON 15 .22 RIMFIRE RIFLE

Similar to Shorty but chambered in .22 LR. Blowback; 10-rd. magazine.

NIB: $675   **Exc.:** $615   **VGood:** $525

BUSHMASTER BA50 .50 BMG RIFLE

A bolt-action, 10-round repeater intended for long-range target shooting. 30-inch barrel, muzzle brake.

NIB: $5000   **Exc.:** $4250   **VGood:** $3300

BUSHMASTER BA50 .50 BMG CARBINE

Similar to above but with 22-inch barrel.

NIB: $5000   **Exc.:** $4250   **VGood:** $3300

CABANAS ESPRONCEDA

Bolt action, single shot; 177 pellet with 22 Blank cartridge; 18-3/4-inch barrel; 40-inch overall length; weighs 5-1/2 lbs.; open fully-adjustable rear sight, blade front; full sporter stock. Made in Mexico. Introduced 1986.

Perf.: $125   **Exc.:** $90   **VGood:** $65

CABANAS LASER RIFLE

Bolt action, single shot; 177 pellet with 22 Blank cartridge; 19-inch barrel; weighs 6 lbs., 12 oz. 42-inch overall. Target-type thumbhole stock; Blade front, open fully adjustable rear sights; Fires round ball or pellet with 22 blank cartridge. Imported from Mexico by Mandall Shooting Supplies.

Perf.: $145   **Exc.:** $110   **VGood:** $70

CABANAS LEYRE

Bolt action; single shot; 177 pellet with 22 Blank cartridge; 19-1/2-inch barrel; 44-inch overall length; weighs 8 lbs.; adjustable rear, blade front sight; sport/target walnut stock. Made in Mexico. Introduced 1984.

Perf.: $140   **Exc.:** $115   **VGood:** $100

CABANAS MASTER

Bolt action; single shot; 177 pellet with 22 Blank cartridge; 19-1/2-inch barrel; 45-1/2-inch overall length; weighs 8 lbs.; adjustable rear sight, blade front; Monte Carlo target-type walnut stock. Made in Mexico. Introduced 1984.

Perf.: $150   **Exc.:** $120   **VGood:** $90

CABANAS MINI-82 YOUTH PONY

Bolt action; single shot; 177 pellet with 22 Blank cartridge; 16-1/2-inch barrel; 34-inch overall length; weighs 3-1/8 lbs.; adjustable rear, blade front sight; youth-sized stock. Made in Mexico. Introduced 1984.

Perf.: $65   **Exc.:** $55   **VGood:** $50

CABANAS PHASER

Bolt action; single shot; 177 pellet with 22 Blank cartridge; 19-inch barrel; 42-inch overall length; weighs 6-3/4 lbs.; open fully-adjustable rear sight, blade front; target-type thumbhole stock. Made in Mexico. Introduced 1991; no longer imported.

Perf.: $150   **Exc.:** $120   **VGood:** $80

CABANAS R83

Bolt action; single shot; 177 pellet with 22 Blank cartridge; 17-inch barrel; 40-inch overall length; adjustable rear, blade front sight; large youth-sized hardwood stock. Made in Mexico. Introduced 1984.

Perf.: $75   **Exc.:** $70   **VGood:** $60

CABANAS TASER

Bolt action; single shot; 177 pellet with 22 Blank cartridge; 19-inch barrel; 42-inch overall length; weighs 6-3/4 lbs.; target-type thumbhole stock; blade front sight, open fully-adjustable rear; fires round ball or pellets with 22-caliber blank cartridge. Imported from Mexico by Mandall Shooting Supplies.

Perf.: $150   **Exc.:** $120   **VGood:** $80

CABANAS VARMINT

Bolt action; single shot; 177 pellet with 22 Blank cartridge; 21-1/2-inch barrel; 41-inch overall length;

Bushmaster BA50 .50 BMG Rifle

Cabanas Phaser

Cabanas Master

Bushmaster BA50 .50 BMG Carbine

weighs 4-1/2 lbs.; adjustable rear, blade front sight; varmint-type walnut stock. Made in Mexico. Introduced 1984.

Perf.: $110   **Exc.:** $90   **VGood:** $75

CABELA'S 1858 HENRY REPLICA

Lever action; 44-40; 13-shot magazine; 24-1/4-inch barrel; 43-inch overall length; weighs 9-1/2 lbs.; European walnut stock; bead front sight, open adjustable rear; brass receiver and buttplate; uses original Henry loading system; faithful to the original Henry rifle. Imported by Cabela's. Introduced 1994.

Perf.: $900   **Exc.:** $825   **VGood:** $695

CABELA'S 1866 WINCHESTER REPLICA

Lever action; 44-40; 13-shot magazine; 24-1/4-inch barrel; 43-inch overall length; weighs 9 lbs.; European walnut stock; bead front sight, open adjustable rear; solid brass receiver, buttplate; octagonal barrel. Faithful to the original Winchester '66 rifle. Imported by Cabela's. Introduced 1994.

Perf.: $750   **Exc.:** $650   **VGood:** $495

CABELA'S 1873 WINCHESTER REPLICA

Lever action; 44-40, 45 Colt; 13-shot magazine; 24-1/4-inch, 30-inch barrel; 43-1/4-inch overall length; weighs 8-1/2 lbs.; European walnut stock; bead front sight, open adjustable rear, or globe front, tang rear; color case-hardened steel receiver. Faithful to the original Model 1873 rifle. Imported by Cabela's. Introduced 1994.

Perf.: $825   **Exc.:** $695   **VGood:** $425

With tang sight, globe front

Perf.: $900   **Exc.:** $725   **VGood:** $495

CABELA'S 1873 WINCHESTER REPLICA SPORTING MODEL

Same specs as 1873 Winchester except 30-inch barrel. Imported by Cabela's. Introduced 1994.

Perf.: $740   **Exc.:** $595   **VGood:** $550

With half-round/half-octagon barrel, half magazine

Perf.: $750   **Exc.:** $650   **VGood:** $550

CABELA'S CATTLEMAN'S CARBINE

Revolver; 44-40; 6-shot cylinder; 18-inch barrel; 34-inch overall length; weighs 4 lbs.; European walnut

stock; blade front sight, notch rear; color case-hardened frame, rest blued. Imported by Cabela's. Introduced 1994.

Perf.: $460   **Exc.:** $395   **VGood:** $325

CABELA'S SHARPS SPORTING RIFLE

Single shot; 45-70; 32-inch tapered octagon barrel; 47-1/4-inch overall length; weighs 9 lbs.; checkered walnut stock; blade front sight, open adjustable rear; color case-hardened receiver and hammer, rest blued. Imported by Cabela's. Introduced 1995.

Perf.: $750   **Exc.:** $695   **VGood:** $550

CALICO LIBERTY 50 CARBINE

Semi-automatic; 9mm Para.; 50-shot magazine; 16-1/8-inch barrel; 34-1/2-inch overall length; weighs 7 lbs.; glass-filled, impact resistant polymer stock; adjustable post front sight, fixed notch and aperture flip rear; helical feed magazine; ambidextrous, rotating sear/striker block safety; static cocking handle; retarded blowback action; aluminum alloy receiver. Made in U.S. by Calico. Introduced 1995.

Perf.: $650   **Exc.:** $560   **VGood:** $470

CALICO LIBERTY 100 CARBINE

Semi-automatic; 9mm Para.; 100-shot magazine; 16-1/8-inch barrel; 34-1/2-inch overall length; weighs 7 lbs.; glass-filled, impact resistant polymer stock; adjustable post front sight, fixed notch and aperture flip rear; helical feed magazine; ambidextrous, rotating sear/striker block safety; static cocking handle; retarded blowback action; aluminum alloy receiver. Made in U.S. by Calico. Introduced 1995.

Perf.: $750   **Exc.:** $760   **VGood:** $590

CALICO MODEL M-100 CARBINE

Semi-automatic; 22 LR; 100-shot magazine; 16-inch barrel; 35 7/8-inch overall length with stock extended; weighs 5-3/4 lbs. (loaded); folding steel stock; post front sight elevation-adjustable, notch windage-adjustable rear; alloy frame and helical-feed magazine; ambidextrous safety; removable barrel assembly; pistol grip compartment; flash suppressor; bolt stop. Made in U.S. From Calico. Introduced 1986; dropped 1995.

Perf.: $625   **Exc.:** $535   **VGood:** $450

CALICO M-100FS CARBINE

Semi-automatic; 22 LR.; 16.25-inch barrel; weighs 5 lbs. 36-inch overall. Glass-filled, impact-resistant polymer stock. Adjustable post front, notch rear

Calico Liberty 50 Carbine

Carl Gustaf Grade II

Carl Gustaf "Swede" Deluxe

Carl Gustaf Varmint Target Model

Century Centurion P14 Sporter

Century Custom Sporting Rifle

sights. Has helical-feed magazine; aluminum receiver; ambidextrous safety. Made in U.S.A. by Calico. Introduced 1996, after federal magazine ban.

Perf.: $450   **Exc.:** $400   **VGood:** $190

CALICO MODEL M-105 SPORTER

Semi-automatic; 22 LR; 100-shot magazine; 16-inch barrel; 35 7/8-inch overall length; weighs 4-3/4 lbs. (empty); hand-rubbed wood buttstock and forend; post front sight elevation-adjustable, notch windage-adjustable rear; alloy frame and helical-feed magazine; ambidextrous safety; removable barrel assembly; pistol grip compartment; flash suppressor; bolt stop. Made in U.S. From Calico. Introduced 1987; dropped 1995.

Perf.: $310   **Exc.:** $230   **VGood:** $190

CALICO MODEL M-900 CARBINE

Semi-automatic; 9mm Para.; 50-, 100-shot magazine; 16-1/8-inch barrel; 28-1/2-inch overall length with stock collapsed; weighs 3-3/4 lbs (empty); sliding steel buttstock; post front sight fully-adjustable, fixed notch rear; helical feed magazine; ambidextrous safety; static cocking handle; retarded blowback action; glass-filled polymer grip. Made in U.S. by Calico. Introduced 1989; dropped 1995.

Perf.: $660   **Exc.:** $575   **VGood:** $480

CALICO MODEL M-951 TACTICAL CARBINE

Semi-automatic; 9mm Para.; 50-, 100-shot magazine; 16-1/8-inch barrel with long compensator; 28-3/4-inch overall length with stock collapsed; weighs 3-3/4 lbs. (empty); sliding steel buttstock, adjustable forward grip; fully-adjustable post front sight, fixed notch rear; helical feed magazine; ambidextrous safety; static cocking handle; retarded blowback action; glass-filled polymer grip. Made in U.S. by Calico. Introduced 1990; dropped 1995.

Perf.: $750   **Exc.:** $760   **VGood:** $590

CALICO MODEL M-951S TACTICAL CARBINE

Same specs as the M-951 except fixed stock. Made in U.S. by Calico. Introduced 1989; dropped 1995.

Perf.: $750   **Exc.:** $760   **VGood:** $590

CARL GUSTAF 2000

Bolt action; 243, 6.5x55, 7x64, 270, 308, 30-06, 7mm Rem. Mag., 300 Win. Mag., 9.3x62; 4-shot detachable magazine; 24-inch barrel; 44-inch overall length; weighs about 7-1/2 lbs.; sights optional; receiver drilled and tapped for scope mounting; select European walnut stock with hand-rubbed oil finish; Monte Carlo cheekpiece; Wundhammar swell pistol grip; 18 lpi checkering; three-way adjustable single-stage, roller bearing trigger; three-position safety; triple front locking lugs; 60-degree bolt rotation; free-floating barrel; swivel studs. Imported from Sweden by Precision Sales International. Introduced 1991; discontinued 1993.

Perf.: $900   **Exc.:** $750   **VGood:** $500

Magnum calibers
Perf.: $1000   **Exc.:** $850   **VGood:** $600

CARL GUSTAF GRADE II

Bolt action; 22-250, 243, 25-06, 6.5x55, 270, 308, 30-06; 5-shot magazine; 23-1/2-inch barrel; folding leaf rear, hooded ramp front sight; walnut Monte Carlo stock with cheekpiece; rosewood forearm tip, grip cap. Available as left-hand model in 25-06, 6.5x55, 270, 30-06. Made in Sweden. Introduced 1970; discontinued 1977.

Perf.: $795   **Exc.:** $595   **VGood:** $450

CARL GUSTAF GRADE II, MAGNUM MODEL

Same specs as Grade II except 7mm Rem. Mag., 300 Win. Mag.; 3-shot magazine; rubber recoil pad. Introduced 1970; discontinued 1977.

Perf.: $825   **Exc.:** $675   **VGood:** $475

CARL GUSTAF GRADE III

Bolt action; 22-250, 243, 25-06, 6.5x55, 270, 308, 30-06; 5-shot magazine; 23-1/2-inch barrel; 44-inch overall length; weighs 7-1/8 lbs.; no sights; deluxe high-gloss French walnut stock with additional checkering, rosewood forend tip; jeweled bolt; engraved floorplate; detachable swivels. Introduced 1970; discontinued 1977.

Perf.: $850   **Exc.:** $750   **VGood:** $595

CARL GUSTAF GRADE III, MAGNUM MODEL

Same specs as Grade III except 7mm Rem. Mag., 300 Win. Mag.; 3-shot magazine; recoil pad. Introduced 1970; discontinued 1977.

Perf.: $900   **Exc.:** $750   **VGood:** $625

CARL GUSTAF GRAND PRIX

Single shot; 22 LR; 26-3/4-inch barrel; adjustable weight; no sights; uncheckered French walnut target-style stock; adjustable cork buttplate; single-stage adjustable trigger. Introduced 1970; no longer in production.

Perf.: $700   **Exc.:** $600   **VGood:** $475

CARL GUSTAF "SWEDE" STANDARD

Bolt action; 22-250, 243, 25-06, 6.5x55, 270, 308, 30-06; 5-shot magazine; 23-1/2-inch barrel; folding leaf rear, hooded ramp front sight; Classic-style French walnut Monte Carlo or sloping comb with schnabel forend stock; hand-checkered pistol grip, forearm; sling swivels. Available as left-hand model. Made in Sweden. Introduced 1970; discontinued 1977.

Perf.: $600   **Exc.:** $500   **VGood:** $275

CARL GUSTAF "SWEDE" DELUXE

Same specs as "Swede" Standard except no sights; deluxe high-gloss walnut Monte Carlo stock; rosewood schnabel forend tip; jeweled bolt; engraved floorplate. Introduced 1970; discontinued 1977.

Perf.: $675   **Exc.:** $550   **VGood:** $325

CARL GUSTAF "SWEDE" STANDARD, MONTE CARLO MODEL

Same specs as "Swede" Standard except also 7mm Rem. Mag.; Monte Carlo-style stock with cheekpiece. Introduced 1970; discontinued 1977.

Perf.: $600   **Exc.:** $500   **VGood:** $300

CARL GUSTAF VARMINT TARGET MODEL

Bolt action; 222 Rem., 22-250, 243 Win., 6.5x55mm; 26-3/4-inch barrel; no sights; target-style stock, French walnut; adjustable trigger. Introduced 1970; no longer in production.

Perf.: $800   **Exc.:** $700   **VGood:** $500

CENTURY CENTURION P14 SPORTER

Bolt action; 303 British, 7mm Rem. Mag., 300 Win. Mag.; 5-shot magazine; 24-inch barrel; 43-5/8-inch overall length; no sights; drilled, tapped for scope mounts; checkered Monte Carlo European beechwood stock; uses modified Pattern 14 Enfield action; blued finish. Introduced 1987; no longer available.

Perf.: $2395   **Exc.:** $275   **VGood:** $160

CENTURY CUSTOM SPORTING RIFLE

Bolt action; 308, 7.62x39mm; 5-shot magazine; new 22-inch barrel; 43-3/4-inch overall length; weighs 6-3/4 lbs.; walnut-finished hardwood stock; no sights; two-piece Weaver-type base; uses small ring Model 98 action; low-swing safety; blue finish. From Century International Arms. Introduced 1994; no longer produced.

Perf.: $295   **Exc.:** $225   **VGood:** $120

CENTURY DELUXE CUSTOM SPORTER

Bolt action; 243, 270, 308, 30-06; 5-shot magazine; 24-inch barrel; 44-inch overall length; black synthetic stock; no sights, but scope base installed; Mauser 98 action; bent bolt handle for scope use; low-swing safety; matte black finish; blind magazine. From Century International Arms. Introduced 1992; no longer produced.

Perf.: $230   **Exc.:** $180   **VGood:** $140

CENTURY ENFIELD SPORTER NO.4

Bolt action; 303 British; 10-shot magazine; 25-1/4-inch barrel; 44-1/2-inch overall length; adjustable aperture rear sight, blade front; checkered beechwood Monte Carlo stock; built on Lee-Enfield No. 4 action; blued finish. Introduced 1987; no longer available.

Perf.: $225   **Exc.:** $190   **VGood:** $115

CENTURY INTERNATIONAL FAL SPORTER

Semi-automatic; 308 Win.; 20-3/4-inch barrel; 41-1/8-inch overall length; weighs 9 lbs., 13 oz.; Bell & Carlson thumbhole sporter stock; protected post front sight, adjustable aperture rear; matte blue finish; rubber buttpad. From Century International Arms. No longer produced.

Perf.: $700   **Exc.:** $575   **VGood:** $400

CENTURY INTERNATIONAL M-14

Semi-automatic; 308 Win.; 10-shot magazine; 22-inch barrel; 40-7/8-inch overall length; weighs 8-1/4 lbs.; walnut stock with rubber recoil pad; protected blade front sight, fully-adjustable aperture rear; gas-operated; forged receiver; Parkerized finish. Imported from China by Century International Arms. No longer imported.

Perf.: $950   **Exc.:** $850   **VGood:** $705

CENTURY MAUSER 98 SPORTER

Bolt action; 243, 270, 308, 30-06; 24-inch barrel; 44-inch overall length; black synthetic stock; no sights; scope base installed; Mauser 98 action; bent bolt handle for scope use; low-swing safety; matte black finish; blind magazine. From Century International Arms. Introduced 1992; no longer produced.

Perf.: $300   **Exc.:** $250   **VGood:** $140

CENTURY SWEDISH SPORTER #38

Bolt action; 6.5x55 Swede; 5-shot magazine; 24-inch barrel; 44-inch overall length; adjustable rear sight, blade front; checkered European hardwood Monte Carlo stock; marketed with Holden Ironsighter see-through scope mount; made on Model 38 Swedish Mauser action. Introduced 1987; no longer available.

Perf.: $255   **Exc.:** $180   **VGood:** $130

CENTURY TIGER DRAGUNOV

Semi-automatic; 7.62x54R; 5-shot magazine; 20-7/8-inch barrel; 42-15/16-inch overall length; weighs 8-1/2 lbs.; thumbhole stock of laminated European hardwood, black composition forend; blade front sight, open elevation-adjustable rear; 4x rangefinding scope with sunshade, lighted reticle; new manufacture of shortened version of Russian SVD sniper rifle; blued metal; quick-detachable scope mount; comes with sling, cleaning kit, gas regulator tool, case. Imported from Russia by Century International Arms. No longer imported. Deduct 25% for currently-imported Romanian model.

Perf.: $1100   **Exc.:** $1000   **VGood:** $850

CENTURY WEEKENDER

Bolt action; 22 LR; 5-shot magazine; 23-1/2-inch barrel; 42-inch overall length; open adjustable rear sight, hooded blade front; sling swivels; blued finish. Made in Europe. Introduced 1987; discontinued 1989.

Perf.: $175   **Exc.:** $140   **VGood:** $100

CHAPUIS AGEX EXPRESS SERIES

Double rifle; side-by-side boxlock; 375 H&H, 416 R Chapuis, 470 NE; 25-5/8-inch barrels; various grades of engraving; French walnut stock. Made in France. No longer imported.

Africa model		
Perf.: $17,995	**Exc.:** $15,995	**VGood:** $12,500
Brousse model		
Perf.: $9,995	**Exc.:** $7350	**VGood:** $5250

Century Enfield Sporter #4

Century International FAL Sporter

Century Swedish Sporter #38

Century Tiger Dragunov

Century Weekender

Chapuis Boxlock Double Rifle

Chipmunk Single Shot

Jungle model		
Perf.: $15,950	**Exc.:** $10,995	**VGood:** $5750
Safari model		
Perf.: $28,000	**Exc.:** $24,900	**VGood:** $17,995
Savanna model		
Perf.: $36,900	**Exc.:** $31,000	**VGood:** $18,995

CHAPUIS BOXLOCK DOUBLE RIFLE

Double rifle; side-by-side; 7x65R, 8x57 JRS, 9.3x74R, 375 H&H; 23 5/8-inch barrels; 40-5/16-inch overall length; weighs 8-3/8 lbs.; ramp bead front sight, adjustable express rear on quarter rib; oil-finished French walnut pistol-grip stock; engraved, coin-finished receiver; double-hook barrels, double triggers; automatic ejectors. Made in France. Introduced 1989; no longer imported.

Perf.: $6500   **Exc.:** $4850   **VGood:** $3650

CHAPUIS OURAL EXEL

Single shot; boxlock; 270, 300 Win. Mag., 7mm Rem. Mag.; 23-5/8-inch barrel; various grades of engraving; French walnut stocking. Made in France. No longer imported.

Perf.: $5995   **Exc.:** $4450   **VGood:** $3750

CHAPUIS RGEX EXPRESS

Double rifle; 30-06, 7x65R, 8x57 JRS, 9.3x74R; 23-5/8-inch barrel; weighs 8 to 9 lbs.; deluxe walnut stock with Monte Carlo comb, oil finish; bead on ramp front sight, adjustable express rear on quarter-rib; boxlock action with long trigger guard; automatic ejectors; double hook Blitz system action with coil springs; coin metal finish; trap grip cap for extra front sight. Imported from France by Armes de Chasse. No longer imported.

Perf.: $7100   **Exc.:** $5300   **VGood:** $4900

CHIPMUNK SINGLE SHOT

Bolt action; single-shot; 22 Short, 22 Long, 22 LR, also 22 WMR, 17 HMR, 17 Mach 2; 16-1/8-inch barrel; 30-inch overall length; weighs 2-1/2 lbs.; post on ramp front sight, adjustable peep rear; drilled, tapped for scope mounting; American walnut stock. Introduced 1982; offered by Chipmunk Manufacturing, Oregon Arms, then Rogue Rifle Co.; still in production. 17 and 22 WMR bring a premium.

Perf.: $170	**Exc.:** $135	**VGood:** $110
Deluxe model with hand checkering		
Perf.: $225	**Exc.:** $190	**VGood:** $140

Christensen Arms
Carbon One Hunter

Christensen Arms Carbon One
Bolt-Action Rifle

Churchill Highlander

Cimarron 1873 Winchester Replica
Sporting Rifle

Cimarron 1873 Winchester Replica
Long Range Model

CHIPMUNK TM (TARGET MODEL)

Bolt action, single shot; 22 LR.; heavier 18-inch barrel; weighs 5 lbs.; Length: 33-inch. Walnut stock with target accessory rail in forearm; 1/4-minute micrometer adjustable rear sight; Manually cocking single shot bolt action, blue receiver, adjustable butt plate and butt pad. Introduced 2002.

    Perf.: $300   **Exc.:** $245   **VGood:** $190

CHRISTENSEN ARMS CARBON ONE HUNTER

Semi-custom bolt action rifle built around choice of receivers; steel barrel encased in carbon alloy shroud; synthetic stock. All popular calibers. Weight: 6.5 – 7 lbs.

    NIB: $1550   **Exc.:** $1475   **VGood:** $1050

CHRISTENSEN ARMS CARBON RANGER REPEATER

Semi-custom bolt-action rifle chambered in .50 BMG. Five-shot magazine; steel Pac-Nor barrel encased in carbon alloy. Muzzle brake. Weight: 20 lbs.

    NIB: $5250   **Exc.:** $4900   **VGood:** $3500

CHRISTENSEN ARMS CARBON RANGER SINGLE SHOT

Similar to Christensen Carbon Ranger Repeater but single shot.

    NIB: $4675   **Exc.:** $1000   **VGood:** $3250

CHRISTENSEN ARMS CARBON ONE BOLT-ACTION RIFLE

Bolt action; 22-250 to 375 H&H calibers; barrel lengths up to 28-inch. Weight: 5-1/2 to 7-1/4 lbs. Synthetic or wood stock; No sights furnished. Choice of Remington, Browning or Winchester action with free-floated Christensen graphite/epoxy/steel barrel, trigger pull tuned to 3 to 3-1/2 lbs. Made in U.S.A.

by Christensen Arms. Prices will vary with custom features.

Carbon One Custom
    Perf.: $2500   **Exc.:** $2000   **VGood:** $1750

Carbon Lite, weighs about 5 lbs.
    Perf.: $2550   **Exc.:** $2100   **VGood:** $1800

Carbon Cannon (for belted magnum cartridges)
    Perf.: $2550   **Exc.:** $2100   **VGood:** $1800

CHURCHILL HIGHLANDER

Bolt action; 243, 25-06, 300 Win. Mag., 270, 308, 30-06, 7mm Rem. Mag.; 3-, 4-shot magazine, depending on caliber; 22-inch, 24-inch barrel; 42-1/2-inch overall length (22-inch barrel); weighs 7-1/2 to 8 lbs.; no sights or optional fully-adjustable rear sight, gold bead on ramp front; checkered classic-style European walnut stock; oil-finish wood; swivel posts; recoil pad; positive safety. Made in Europe. Introduced 1986; importation discontinued 1989.

    Perf.: $495   **Exc.:** $450   **VGood:** $350

With optional sights
    Perf.: $525   **Exc.:** $480   **VGood:** $390

CHURCHILL REGENT

Bolt action; 243, 25-06, 300 Win. Mag., 270, 308, 30-06, 7mm Rem. Mag.; 3-, 4-shot magazine, depending on caliber; 22-inch, 24-inch barrel; 42-1/2-inch overall length (22-inch barrel); weighs 7-1/2 to 8 lbs.; no sights or optional fully-adjustable rear sight, gold bead on ramp front; Monte Carlo stock with deluxe checkering; swivel posts; recoil pad; positive safety. Made in Europe. Introduced 1986; discontinued 1988.

    Perf.: $540   **Exc.:** $490   **VGood:** $420

With optional sights
    Perf.: $590   **Exc.:** $500   **VGood:** $430

CHURCHILL REGENT COMBO

Combination gun; over/under; 3-inch 12-ga. over 222, 223, 243, 270, 308, 30-06; 25-inch barrels; 42-inch

overall length; weighs 8 lbs.; open rear sight, blade on ramp front; hand-checkered, oil-finished European walnut Monte Carlo stock; dovetail scope mount; double triggers; silvered engraved receiver. Made in Europe. Introduced 1985; importation discontinued 1989.

    Perf.: $900   **Exc.:** $700   **VGood:** $600

CIMARRON 1860 HENRY REPLICA

Lever action; 44-40, 44 Spl., 45 Colt; 13-shot tubular magazine; 22-inch carbine, 24-1/2-inch rifle barrel; 43-inch overall length (24-1/2-inch barrel); weighs 9-1/2 lbs.; bead front sight, open adjustable rear; original Henry loading system; brass receiver, buttplate. Made in Italy. Introduced 1991; still imported.

    Perf.: $900   **Exc.:** $800   **VGood:** $700

Steel-frame version
    Perf.: $940   **Exc.:** $840   **VGood:** $740

CIMARRON 1866 WINCHESTER REPLICA

Lever action; 22 LR, 22 WMR, 44-40, 45 Colt; 24-1/4-inch octagonal barrel; 43-inch overall length; weighs 9 lbs.; bead front sight, open adjustable rear; European walnut stock; brass receiver, buttplate, forend cap. Made in Italy. Introduced 1991; still imported.

    Perf.: $800   **Exc.:** $650   **VGood:** $500

CIMARRON 1866 WINCHESTER REPLICA CARBINE

Lever action; 22 LR, 22 WMR, 38 Spl., 44-40, 45 Colt; 19-inch round barrel; bead front, open adjustable rear; smooth walnut stock, forearm; brass receiver, buttplate, forend cap. Made in Italy. Introduced 1991; still imported.

    Perf.: $800   **Exc.:** $650   **VGood:** $500

CIMARRON 1866 WINCHESTER REPLICA CARBINE, INDIAN MODEL

Same specs as 1866 Replica Carbine except engraved brass frame. Discontinued 1989.

    Perf.: $625   **Exc.:** $525   **VGood:** $405

CIMARRON 1866 WINCHESTER REPLICA CARBINE, TRAPPER MODEL

Same specs as 1866 Replica Carbine except 44-40 only; 16-inch round barrel. Discontinued 1990, reintroduced, still imported.

    Perf.: $725   **Exc.:** $585   **VGood:** $415

CIMARRON 1873 WINCHESTER REPLICA SPORTING RIFLE

Lever action; 44-40, 45 Colt; 24-inch octagon barrel; 43-inch overall length; 8 lbs.; adjustable semi-buckhorn rear sight, fixed front; walnut stock, forend; color case-hardened receiver. Introduced 1989.

    Perf.: $865   **Exc.:** $675   **VGood:** $625

CIMARRON 1873 WINCHESTER REPLICA, LONG RANGE MODEL

Same specs as 1873 Winchester except 22 LR, 22 WMR, 357 Mag., 38-40, 44-40, 45 Colt; 30-inch octagon barrel marked "Kings Improved"; 48-inch overall length; weighs 8-1/2 lbs. Introduced 1989.

    Perf.: $950   **Exc.:** $750   **VGood:** $650

CIMARRON 1873 WINCHESTER REPLICA, SADDLE RING CARBINE

Same specs as 1873 Winchester except 19-inch round barrel; blued receiver; saddle ring. Introduced 1989; still imported.

    Perf.: $950   **Exc.:** $675   **VGood:** $595

CIMARRON 1873 WINCHESTER REPLICA, SHORT MODEL

Same specs as 1873 Winchester except 22 LR, 22 WMR, 357 Mag., 44-40, 45 Colt; 20-inch octagon barrel; 39-inch overall length; weighs 7-1/2 lbs. Introduced 1989; still imported.

    Perf.: $865   **Exc.:** $675   **VGood:** $595

CIMARRON 1873 WINCHESTER REPLICA, TRAPPER CARBINE

Same specs as 1873 Winchester except 357 Mag., 44-40, 45 Colt; 16-inch barrel; blued finish. Introduced 1989; discontinued 1990; reintroduced, still imported.

Perf.: $800   **Exc.:** $595   **VGood:** $495

CIMARRON BILLY DIXON 1874 SHARPS SPORTING RIFLE

Single shot, falling block; 40-90, 45-70; 32-inch tapered octagonal barrel. European walnut stock; Blade front, Creedmoor rear sights; color case-hardened frame, blued barrel. Hand-checkered grip and forend; hand-rubbed oil finish. Introduced 1999. Made by Pedersoli, imported by Cimarron F.A. Co.

Perf.: $1400   **Exc.:** $1200   **VGood:** $1000

CIMARRON QUIGLEY MODEL 1874 SHARPS SPORTING RIFLE

Single shot, falling block; 45-70, 45-90, 45-120. Barrel: 34-inch octagonal. Checkered walnut stock; Blade front, adjustable rear sights; Blued finish; double set triggers. Replica of rifle used in movie, *Quigley Down Under*. Made by Pedersoli, imported by Cimarron F.A. Co. Introduced 1995, still available.

Perf.: $1550   **Exc.:** $1200   **VGood:** $$1000

CIMARRON SILHOUETTE MODEL 1874 SHARPS SPORTING RIFLE

Single shot, falling block; 45-70. 32-inch octagonal barrel; Blade front, adjustable rear sights; Pistol-grip walnut stock with shotgun-style butt plate; cut-rifled barrel; imported by Cimarron F.A. Co., still available.

Perf.: $1000   **Exc.:** $925   **VGood:** $840

CIMARRON MODEL 1885 HIGH WALL RIFLE

Single shot, falling block; 38-55, 40-65, 45-70, 45-90, 45-120. 30-inch octagonal barrel; European walnut stock; Bead front, semi-buckhorn rear sights; Replica of the Winchester 1885 High Wall rifle. Color case-hardened receiver and lever, blued barrel. Curved buttplate. Optional double set triggers. Introduced 1999. Imported by Cimarron F.A. Co., still available.

Perf.: $900   **Exc.:** $775   **VGood:** $650

CLARIDGE HI-TEC C CARBINE

Semi-automatic; 9mm Para., 40 S&W, 45 ACP; 18-shot magazine; 16-1/8-inch barrel; 31-3/4-inch overall length; weighs 4 lbs. 9 oz.; walnut stock; adjustable post in ring front sight, open windage-adjustable rear; aluminum or stainless frame; telescoping bolt, floating firing pin; safety locks the firing pin; sight radius of 20-1/8-inch; accepts same magazines as Claridge Hi-Tec pistols. Can be equipped with scope or Aimpoint sight. Made in U.S. From Claridge Hi-Tec, Inc. Introduced 1991; dropped 1993.

Perf.: $595   **Exc.:** $495   **VGood:** $395

CLARIDGE HI-TEC MODEL LEC-9 CARBINE

Semi-automatic; 9mm Para., 40 S&W, 45 ACP; 18-shot magazine; 16-1/8-inch barrel; 31-3/4-inch overall length; weighs 4 lbs. 9 oz.; graphite composite stock; adjustable post in ring front sight, open windage-adjustable rear; aluminum or stainless frame; telescoping bolt, floating firing pin; safety locks the firing pin; sight radius of 20-1/8-inch; accepts same magazines as Claridge Hi-Tec pistols. Can be equipped with scope or Aimpoint sight. Made in U.S. From Claridge Hi-Tec, Inc. Made only in 1992.

Perf.: $650   **Exc.:** $575   **VGood:** $485

CLARIDGE HI-TEC MODEL ZLEC-9 CARBINE

Same specs as the LEC-9 except laser sight system. Made in U.S. by Claridge Hi-Tec, Inc. Made only in 1992.

Perf.: $995   **Exc.:** $895   **VGood:** $795

Cimarron Billy Dixon 1874 Sharps Sporting Rifle

Cimarron Quigley Model 1874 Sharps Sporting Rifle

Cimarron Silhouette Model 1874 Sharps Sporting Rifle

Cimarron Model 1885 High Wall Rifle

Clayco Model 4

Clerke Hi-Wall

CLAYCO MODEL 4

Bolt action; 22 LR; 5-shot clip; 24-inch barrel; 42-inch overall length; weighs 5-3/4 lbs.; adjustable open rear sight, ramp front with bead; walnut-finished hardwood stock; wing-type safety; black composition buttplate; pistol-grip cap; receiver grooved for tip-off scope. Made in China. Introduced 1983 by Clayco Sports; discontinued 1985.

Perf.: $130   **Exc.:** $100   **VGood:** $80

CLERKE HI-WALL

Single shot; falling block; 223, 22-250, 243, 6mm Rem., 250 Savage, 257 Roberts, 25-06, 264 Win., 270, 7mm Rem. Mag., 30-30, 30-06, 300 Win., 375 H&H, 458 Win., 45-70; 26-inch barrel; no sights; drilled, tapped for scope mounts; walnut pistol-grip stock, forearm; no checkering; black buttplate; exposed hammer; schnabel forearm; curved finger lever. Introduced about 1970; discontinued about 1975.

Perf.: $800   **Exc.:** $650   **VGood:** $500

CLERKE HI-WALL DELUXE

Same specs as standard model except half-octagon barrel; adjustable trigger; checkered pistol grip, forearm, cheekpiece; plain or optional double-set trigger.

Perf.: $900   **Exc.:** $750   **VGood:** $600

With double-set trigger

Perf.: $950   **Exc.:** $800   **VGood:** $650

COLT 57

Bolt action; 243, 30-06; adjustable sights; checkered American walnut Monte Carlo stock; FN Mauser action; 5000 manufactured by Jefferson Manufacturing Co. Introduced 1957; discontinued 1957.

Exc.: $575   **VGood:** $485   **Good:** $350

Deluxe stock

Exc.: $600   **VGood:** $500   **Good:** $370

COLT AR-15A2 CARBINE

Semi-automatic; 223 Rem.; 5-shot magazine; 16-inch barrel; 5-13/16 lbs.; post front, adjustable rear sight; aluminum stock with collapsible butt; sling swivels. Introduced 1985; discontinued 1989.

Perf.: $1800   **Exc.:** $1500   **VGood:** $1000

COLT AR-15A2 RIFLE

Same specs as AR-15A2 Carbine except 20-inch barrel; 39-inch overall length; 7-1/2 lbs.; black composition stock, grip, forend; military matte black finish. Introduced 1985; discontinued 1989.

Perf.: $1700   **Exc.:** $1200   **VGood:** $850

COLT COLTEER

Semi-automatic; 22 LR; 19-3/8-inch barrel; 15-shot tube magazine; weighs 4-3/4 lbs.; open rear sight, hooded ramp front; uncheckered straight Western-style carbine stock; barrel band; alloy receiver. Introduced 1964; discontinued 1975.

Exc.: $375   **VGood:** $300   **Good:** $170

Colt Colteer

Colt Colteer 1-22

Colt Coltsman Sako Custom

Colt Courier

Colt Light Rifle Bolt Action

Colt Lightning

on hooded ramp, folding leaf rear; sliding safety; 243 Win., 308 Win. Introduced 1962; dropped 1965.

Exc.: $595   **VGood:** $495   **Good:** $395

COLT COLTSMAN SHORT-ACTION SAKO CUSTOM
Same specs as Coltsman Standard except Sako short action; 243, 308 Win. Introduced 1963; discontinued 1965.

Exc.: $595   **VGood:** $495   **Good:** $395

COLT COLTSMAN SHORT-ACTION SAKO DELUXE
Same specs as Coltsman Standard except Sako short action; 243, 308 Win.; action with integral scope blocks. Introduced 1963; discontinued 1965.

Exc.: $695   **VGood:** $595   **Good:** $495

COLT COURIER
Semi-automatic; 22 LR; 15-shot tubular magazine; 19-3/8-inch barrel; weighs 4-3/4 lbs.; receiver grooved for tip-off scope mount; American walnut stock forend; pistol grip. Introduced 1970; discontinued 1976.

Exc.: $375   **VGood:** $290   **Good:** $170

COLT LIGHT RIFLE BOLT ACTION
Bolt action; 243, 7x57, 7mm-08, 308 (short action); 25-06, 270, 280, 7mm Rem., Mag., 30-06, 300 Win. Mag. 24-inch barrel; weighs 5.4 to 6 lbs. Black synthetic stock; no sights furnished; low, medium, high scope mounts. Matte black finish; three-position safety. Introduced 1999, dropped 2002. Made in U.S.A. From Colt's Mfg., Inc.

Perf.: $500   **Exc.:** $450   **VGood:** 350

COLT LIGHTNING
Slide action; 22 LR, 32-20, 38-40, 44-40, 38-56, 50-96; 15-shot tubular magazine; 26-inch round or octagon barrel; open rear, blade front sight; American walnut stock, forend. Introduced 1884; discontinued 1902.

Small frame		
Exc.: $2250	**VGood:** $900	**Good:** $650
Medium frame		
Exc.: $2500	**VGood:** $1395	**Good:** $850
Large frame		
Exc.: $4750	**VGood:** $2795	**Good:** $1650

COLT LIGHTNING BABY CARBINE
Same specs as Colt Lightning except 10-shot tubular magazine; 15-inch, 16-inch barrel; weighs 5-1/4 lbs. Introduced 1884; discontinued 1902.

Medium frame		
Exc.: $5850	**VGood:** $3450	**Good:** $1950
Large frame		
Exc.: $10,000	**VGood:** $6950	**Good:** $5350

COLT LIGHTNING CARBINE
Same specs as Colt Lightning except 20-inch, 22-inch barrel; weighs 6-1/4 lbs. Introduced 1884; discontinued 1902.

Medium frame		
Exc.: $2700	**VGood:** $1000	**Good:** $600
Large frame		
Exc.: $8500	**VGood:** $6995	**Good:** $3950

COLT LIGHTNING SMALL FRAME
Same specs as Colt Lightning except 22 Short, 22 Long; 24-inch round or octagon barrel; 16-shot (22 Short), 15-shot (22 Long); bead front sight. Collector value. Manufactured 1887 to 1904.

Exc.: $1900   **VGood:** $900   **Good:** $650

COLT MATCH TARGET RIFLE
Semi-automatic; 223 Rem., 5-shot magazine. 16.1-inch or 20-inch barrel; weighs 7.1 to 8-1/2 lbs. 34-1/2-inch to 39-inch overall length; composition stock, grip, forend. Post front sight, rear sight adjustable for windage and elevation. 5-round detachable box magazine, flash suppressor, sling swivels. Forward bolt assist included. Introduced 1991. Made in U.S.A. by Colt's Manufacturing Co. Inc.

Perf.: $1100   **Exc.:** $900   **VGood:** $725

COLT COLTEER 1-22
Bolt action; single shot; 22 Short, 22 Long, 22 LR, 22 WMR; 20-inch, 22-inch barrel; open rear sight, ramp front; uncheckered walnut pistol grip; Monte Carlo stock. Introduced 1957; discontinued 1967.

Exc.: $320   **VGood:** $270   **Good:** $130

COLT COLTSMAN STANDARD
Bolt action; 223, 243, 264, 308, 30-06, 300 H&H Mag.; 5-, 6-shot box magazine; 22-inch, 24-inch barrel; weighs 6-1/2 to 7-1/2 lbs.; FN Mauser action; folding leaf rear sight, hooded post front; hand-checkered pistol-grip American walnut stock; Monte Carlo comb and cheekpiece; quick-detachable sling swivels. Introduced 1957; replaced in 1962 by Sako action model.

Exc.: $575   **VGood:** $500   **Good:** $440

COLT COLTSMAN CUSTOM
Same specs as Coltsman except 23-3/4-inch, 23-inch, 24-1/2-inch barrel; fancy select French walnut stock; rosewood forearm, pistol grip; Monte Carlo comb, cheekpiece, engraved floorplate; recoil pad; sling swivels. Introduced 1957; replaced in 1962 by Sako action.

Exc.: $695   **VGood:** $595   **Good:** $470

COLT COLTSMAN DELUXE
Same specs as Coltsman except better checkering, wood; adjustable rear sight, ramp front. Introduced 1957; discontinued 1962.

Exc.: $695   **VGood:** $595   **Good:** $495

COLT COLTSMAN LONG-ACTION SAKO CUSTOM
Same specs as Coltsman Standard except Sako action; fancy Monte Carlo stock; recoil pad; dark wood forend tip and pistol-grip cap; skip-line checkering. Introduced 1962; dropped 1965.

Exc.: $695   **VGood:** $595   **Good:** $495

300, 375 H&H calibers		
Exc.: $750	**VGood:** $650	**Good:** $525

COLT COLTSMAN LONG-ACTION SAKO STANDARD
Same specs as Coltsman Standard except Sako long action; 264 Win., 270 Win., 30-06, 300 H&H, 375 H&H; hinged floorplate; hand-checkered walnut stock; standard sling swivels; bead front sight on hooded ramp, folding leaf rear; sliding safety. Introduced 1962; dropped 1965.

Exc.: $695   **VGood:** $595   **Good:** $495

300, 375 magnum calibers		
Exc.: $850	**VGood:** $750	**Good:** $625

COLT COLTSMAN MEDIUM-ACTION SAKO CUSTOM
Same specs as Coltsman Standard except Sako medium action; fancy Monte Carlo stock; recoil pad; dark wood forend tip; pistol-grip cap; skip-line checkering. Introduced 1962; discontinued 1965.

Exc.: $695   **VGood:** $595   **Good:** $495

COLT COLTSMAN MEDIUM-ACTION SAKO STANDARD
Same specs as Coltsman Standard except Sako medium action; hinged floorplate; hand-checkered walnut stock; standard sling swivels; bead front sight

COLT ACCURIZED RIFLE

Similar to the Colt Match Target Model except has 24-inch stainless steel heavy barrel with 1:9-inch rifling, flattop receiver with scope mount and 1-inch rings, weighs 9.25 lbs. Introduced 1998, still in production. Made in U.S.A. by Colt's Mfg. Co., Inc.

Perf.: $1200 **Exc.:** 995 **VGood:** $750

COLT MATCH TARGET HBAR RIFLE

Similar to the Target Model except has heavy barrel, 800-meter rear sight adjustable for windage and elevation. Introduced 1991, still in production.

Perf.: $1100 **Exc.:** $900 **VGood:** $725

COLT SPORTER TARGET

Semi-automatic; 223 Rem.; 5-shot detachable box magazine; 20-inch barrel; 39-inch overall length; weighs 7-1/2 lbs.; composition stock, grip, forend; post front sight, aperture fully-adjustable rear; standard-weight barrel; flash suppressor; sling swivels; forward bolt assist; military matte black finish. Made in U.S. by Colt. Introduced 1991.

Perf.: $1100 **Exc.:** $800 **VGood:** $650

COLT SPORTER COMPETITION HBAR

Same specs as Sporter Target except flat-top receiver with integral Weaver-type base for scope mounting; counter-bored muzzle; 1:9-inch rifling twist. Made in U.S. by Colt. Introduced 1991.

Perf.: $1100 **Exc.:** $900 **VGood:** $725

COLT SPORTER COMPETITION HBAR RANGE SELECTED

Same specs as Sporter Competition HBAR except range selected for accuracy; 3-9x rubber armored scope, scope mount; carrying handle with iron sights; Cordura nylon carrying case. Made in U.S. by Colt. Introduced 1992; dropped 1994.

Perf.: $1450 **Exc.:** $1050 **VGood:** $850

COLT SPORTER LIGHTWEIGHT

Same specs as Sporter Target except 9mm Para., 223 Rem., 7.62x39mm; 16-inch barrel; 34-1/2-inch overall length; weighs 6-3/4 lbs. (223 Rem.), 7-1/8 lbs. (9mm Para.). Made in U.S. by Colt. Introduced 1991; no longer produced.

Perf.: $1000 **Exc.:** $800 **VGood:** $600

COLT SPORTER MATCH DELTA HBAR

Same specs as the Sporter Target except standard stock; heavy barrel; refined and inspected by the Colt Custom Shop; 3-9x rubber armored scope; removable cheekpiece; adjustable scope mount; black leather military-style sling; cleaning kit; hard carrying case; pistol grip with Delta medallion. Made in U.S. by Colt. Introduced 1987; dropped 1991.

Perf.: $1500 **Exc.:** $1150 **VGood:** $895

COLT SPORTER MATCH HBAR

Same specs as the Sporter Match Delta HBAR except with heavy barrel; 800-meter M-16A2 fully-adjustable rear sight. Made in U.S. by Colt. Introduced 1991; no longer produced.

Perf.: $1500 **Exc.:** $1000 **VGood:** $700

COLT SPORTER MATCH TARGET COMPETITION HBAR II

Same specs as the Sporter Match HBAR except 16-1/8-inch barrel; weighs 7-1/8 lbs.; 34-1/2-inch overall length; 1:9-inch twist barrel. Made in U.S. by Colt. Introduced 1995; still produced.

Perf.: $1275 **Exc.:** $1000 **VGood:** $800

COLT STAGECOACH

Semi automatic; 22 LR; 13-shot magazine; 16-1/2-inch barrel; 33-3/4-inch overall length; weighs 4-3/4 lbs.; deluxe American black walnut straight Western-style carbine stock with saddle ring; adjustable rear sight; engraved receiver. Introduced 1965; discontinued 1975.

Exc.: $400 **VGood:** $300 **Good:** $210

COLT-SAUER SPORTER

Bolt action; 22-250, 243, 308, 25-06, 270, 30-06, 7mm Rem. Mag., 300 Win. Mag., 300 Weatherby

Colt Lightning Small Frame

Colt Accurized Rifle

Colt Match Target HBAR Rifle

Colt Sporter Lightweight

Colt Sporter Match HBAR

Colt-Sauer Sporter

Mag.; 375 H&H Mag., 458 Win. Mag.; 3-, 4-shot detachable box magazine; 24-inch barrel; 43-3/4-inch overall length; weighs 8 lbs.; no sights; hand-checkered American walnut pistol-grip stock; rosewood pistol grip, forend caps; recoil pad; quick-detachable sling swivels. Introduced 1971; discontinued 1986.

Long action		
Exc.: $1050	**VGood:** $895	**Good:** $695
Short action		
Exc.: $1050	**VGood:** $895	**Good:** $695
Magnum action		
Exc.: $1150	**VGood:** $995	**Good:** $795
Grand Alaskan model		
Exc.: $1400	**VGood:** $1195	**Good:** $895
Grand African model		
Exc.: $1450	**VGood:** $1295	**Good:** $995

COLT-SHARPS FALLING BLOCK

Single shot; falling block; 17 Bee, 22-250, 243, 25-06, 7mm Rem. Mag., 30-06, 375 H&H Mag.; iron sights; checkered walnut stock, forearm; blued finish. Introduced 1970; discontinued 1977.

Perf.: $2900 **Exc.:** $2000 **VGood:** $1200

COMMANDO ARMS MARK 9

Semi-automatic; 9mm Para.; 5-, 15-, 30-, 90-shot magazine; 16-1/2-inch barrel; weighs 8 lbs.; peep-type rear sight, blade front; walnut stock, forearm; choice of vertical or horizontal foregrip; muzzlebrake; cooling sleeve. Introduced 1969 by Volunteer Enterprises.

Perf.: $495 **Exc.:** $425 **VGood:** $230

COMMANDO ARMS MARK 45

Semi-automatic; 45 ACP; 5-, 15-, 30-, 90-shot magazine; 16-1/2-inch barrel; weighs 8 lbs.; peep-type rear sight, blade front; walnut stock and forearm; available with choice of vertical or horizontal foregrip; muzzlebrake, cooling sleeve. Introduced 1969 by Volunteer Enterprises.

Perf.: $600 **Exc.:** $440 **VGood:** $350

COOPER ARMS MODEL 21 VARMINT EXTREME

Bolt action; single shot; 17 Rem., 17 Mach IV, 221 Fireball, 222, 222 Rem. Mag., 223, 22 PPC, 6x47;

Cooper Arms Model 22
Pro Varmint Extreme

Cooper Arms
Model BR-50

Cooper Arms Model
TRP-1 ISU Standard

Cumberland Mountain Plateau

23-3/4-inch stainless steel barrel with competition step crown; free-floated; AAA Claro walnut stock with flared oval forend, ambidextrous palm swell; 22 lpi checkering; oil finish; Pachmayr buttpad; weighs 8 lbs.; no sights; drilled and tapped for scope mounting; three mid-bolt locking lugs; adjustable trigger; glass bedded; swivel studs. Made in U.S. by Cooper Arms. Introduced 1994.

Perf.: $1500   **Exc.:** $1200   **VGood:** $900

COOPER ARMS MODEL 21 BENCHREST

Same specs as the Model 21 Varmint Extreme except 22 PPC, 223 Rem.; McMillan Benchrest composition stock; 24-inch, 1-inch straight taper stainless steel barrel with competition step crown, match chamber; Jewell two-stage, 1-oz. fully-adjustable trigger; weighs 7-1/4 lbs. Made in U.S. by Cooper Arms. Introduced 1994.

Perf.: $2000   **Exc.:** $1700   **VGood:** $1400

COOPER ARMS MODEL 22 PRO VARMINT EXTREME

Bolt action; single shot; 22-250, 220 Swift, 243, 25-06, 6mm PPC, 308; 26-inch stainless steel match-grade barrel with straight taper; free-floated; AAA Claro walnut stock with oil finish; 22 lpi wrap-around borderless ribbon checkering; beaded cheekpiece; steel grip cap; flared varminter forend; Pachmayr pad; no sights; drilled and tapped for scope mounting; three front locking lug system; available with sterling silver inlaid medallion, skeleton grip cap, and French walnut. Made in U.S. by Cooper Arms. Introduced 1995; still produced.

Perf.: $1650   **Exc.:** $1500   **VGood:** $1200

Black Jack model with McMillan synthetic stock

Perf.: $1750   **Exc.:** $1600   **VGood:** $1300

COOPER ARMS MODEL 22 BENCHREST

Same specs as the Model 22 Pro Varmint Extreme except 6mm PPC, 243, 308; McMillan Benchrest composition stock; 1-inch straight taper stainless steel barrel; competition step muzzle crown; match chamber. Made in U.S. by Cooper Arms. Introduced 1995; still produced.

Perf.: $2000   **Exc.:** $1700   **VGood:** $1300

COOPER ARMS MODEL 36 CENTERFIRE SPORTER

Bolt action; 17 CCM, 22 CCM, 22 Hornet; 5-shot magazine; 23-inch barrel; 42-1/2-inch overall length; weighs 7 lbs.; AA Claro walnut stock with 22 lpi checkering, oil finish (standard grade); AAA Claro

or AA French walnut (custom grade); no sights; three mid-bolt locking lugs, 45° bolt rotation; fully-adjustable trigger; swivel studs; Pachmayr buttpad. Made in U.S. by Cooper Arms. Introduced 1994; no longer made.

Perf.: $1395   **Exc.:** $995   **VGood:** $795

COOPER ARMS MODEL 36 RIMFIRE SPORTER

Bolt action; 22 LR; 5-shot magazine; 22-3/4-inch barrel; 42-1/2-inch overall length; weighs 7 lbs.; hand-checkered AAA Claro walnut stock (standard grade); AA fancy French walnut or AAA Claro walnut with beaded Monte Carlo cheekpiece (Custom grade); sights optional; three front locking lugs, 45-degree bolt rotation; fully-adjustable single stage trigger; Wiseman/McMillan competition barrel; swivel studs; Pachmayr buttpad; oil-finished wood. Made in U.S. by Cooper Arms. Introduced 1991.

Perf.: $1395   **Exc.:** $995   **VGood:** $795

Custom grade

Perf.: $1495   **Exc.:** $1100   **VGood:** $895

COOPER ARMS MODEL 36 RF CUSTOM CLASSIC

Same specs as the Model 36RF grade except ebony forend tip; steel grip cap; Brownell No. 1 checkering pattern. Made in U.S. by Cooper Arms. Introduced 1991; no longer made.

Perf.: $1500   **Exc.:** $1000   **VGood:** $700

COOPER ARMS MODEL 36 RF FEATHERWEIGHT

Same specs as the Model 36RF except custom stock shape with black textured finish. Made in U.S. by Cooper Arms. Introduced 1991; no longer made.

Perf.: $1400   **Exc.:** $950   **VGood:** $650

COOPER ARMS MODEL 38 CENTERFIRE SPORTER

Bolt action; 17 CCM, 22 CCM; 3-shot magazine; 23-3/4-inch Shilen match barrel; 42-1/2-inch overall length; weighs 8 lbs.; AA Claro walnut stock with 22 lpi checkering, oil finish (standard grade); AAA Claro or AA French walnut, beaded Monte Carlo cheekpiece (custom grade); no sights; three front locking lugs, 45-degree bolt rotation; fully-adjustable single stage match trigger; swivel studs. Pachmayr buttpad. Made in U.S. by Cooper Arms. Introduced 1991; no longer produced.

Perf.: $995   **Exc.:** $895   **VGood:** $795

Custom grade

Perf.: $1295   **Exc.:** $1095   **VGood:** $895

COOPER ARMS MODEL 40 CENTERFIRE SPORTER

Bolt action; 17 CCM, 17 Ackley Hornet, 22 CCM, 22 Hornet, 22 K-Hornet; 5-shot magazine; 23-inch barrel; 42-1/2-inch overall length; weighs 7 lbs.; AAA Claro walnut stock with 22 lpi borderless wrap-around ribbon checkering; oil finish; steel grip cap; Pachmayr pad; no sights; three mid-bolt locking lugs; 45-degree bolt rotation; fully-adjustable trigger; swivel studs. Made in U.S. by Cooper Arms. Introduced 1994.

Perf.: $1700   **Exc.:** $1400   **VGood:** $1100

COOPER ARMS MODEL 40 CUSTOM CLASSIC

Same specs as Model 40 except AAA Claro walnut; Monte Carlo beaded cheekpiece; oil finish. Made in U.S. by Cooper Arms. Introduced 1994.

Perf.: $1800   **Exc.:** $1500   **VGood:** $1200

COOPER ARMS MODEL 40 CLASSIC VARMINTER

Same specs as the Model 40 except AAA Claro walnut; wrap-around ribbon checkering; beaded cheekpiece; steel grip cap; flared varminter forend. Made in U.S. by Cooper Arms. Introduced 1994.

Perf.: $1490   **Exc.:** $1195   **VGood:** $995

COOPER ARMS MODEL 57-M BOLT-ACTION RIFLE

Bolt action; 22 LR, 22 WMR, 17 HMR. 23-3/4-inch stainless steel or 41-40 match grade barrel; weighs 6.6 lbs.; Claro walnut stock, 22 lpi hand checkering; no sights furnished. Three rear locking lug, repeating bolt-action with 5-shot mag. Fully adjustable trigger. Many options can affect price. Introduced 2002; Made in U.S.A. by Cooper Firearms of Montana, Inc.

Perf.: $1000   **Exc.:** $900   **VGood:** $800

COOPER ARMS MODEL BR-50

Bolt action; single shot; 22 LR; 22-inch barrel, .860-inch straight; 40-1/2-inch overall length; weighs 6-13/16 lbs.; McMillan Benchrest stock; no sights; three mid-bolt locking lugs; fully-adjustable match-grade trigger; stainless barrel. Made in U.S. by Cooper Arms. Introduced 1994.

Perf.: $1700   **Exc.:** $1400   **VGood:** $1100

COOPER ARMS MODEL TRP-1 ISU STANDARD

Bolt action; single shot; 22 LR; 22-inch barrel; 40-1/2-inch overall length; weighs 10 lbs.; walnut competition-style stock with adjustable cheekpiece and buttpad; no sights; accepts Anschutz sight packages; three front locking lugs, 45-degree bolt rotation; fully-adjustable single stage trigger; hand-lapped match-grade Shilen stainless barrel. Made in U.S. by Cooper Arms. Introduced 1991; no longer produced.

Perf.: $1450   **Exc.:** $1150   **VGood:** $895

With benchrest-style stock

Perf.: $1350   **Exc.:** $1050   **VGood:** $795

CUMBERLAND MOUNTAIN ARMS ELK RIVER

Single shot, falling block; 22 through 300 Win. Mag.; 32-40, 40-65, 45-70 single shot; 24-inch, 26-inch, 28-inch, round or octagon barrel; 44-inch overall length (28-inch barrel); weighs about 6-1/4 lbs.; American walnut stock; Marble's bead front sight, Marble's adjustable open rear; falling block action with underlever; blued barrel and receiver. Made in U.S. by Cumberland Mountain Arms, Inc. Introduced 1993; no longer produced.

Perf.: $895   **Exc.:** $795   **VGood:** $695

CUMBERLAND MOUNTAIN ARMS PLATEAU

Single shot, falling block; 40-65, 45-70, other calibers on special order; barrel length up to 32-inch, round; 48-inch overall length; weighs about 10-1/2 lbs. (32-inch barrel); American walnut stock; Marble's bead front sight, Marble's open rear; falling block action with underlever; blued barrel and receiver; lacquer finish stock; crescent buttplate. Made in U.S. by Cumberland Mountain Arms, Inc. Introduced 1995.

Perf.: $950   **Exc.:** $800   **VGood:** $675

CZ Model 3

CZ 452 American Classic
Bolt-Action Rifle

CZ 452 FS

CZ 452 Lux
Bolt-Action Rifle

CZ 452 Scout

CZ 452 Silhouette

CZ 452 Style

CZ 452 Varmint Rifle

CZ 511 Auto Rifle

CZ 513 Basic

CZ MODEL 3

Bolt action; 270 WSM, 7mm WSM, 300 WSM, 3-shot magazine; left or right hand action, blue or stainless steel, Mauser-style claw extractor; 3-position safety; adjustable trigger; introduced in 2004, still available.

Perf.: $800   **Exc.:** $750   **VGood:** $600

CZ 452 AMERICAN CLASSIC BOLT-ACTION RIFLE

Bolt action; 22 LR, 22 WMR, 17 HMR, 17 Mach 2; 5-shot or 10-shot detachable magazine, weighs 6.6 lbs.; has classic-style stock of Circassian walnut; 22-1/2-inch free-floating barrel with recessed target crown; receiver dovetail for scope mounting. No open sights furnished. Introduced 1999. Imported from the Czech Republic by CZ-USA, still available.

Perf.: $350   **Exc.:** $275   **VGood:** $225

CZ 452 FS

Bolt action; 22 LR, 22 WMR, 17 HMR; similar to 452 LUX, but with full-length Mannlicher-type stock; introduced 2004, still available.

Perf.: $420   **Exc.:** $320   **VGood:** $300

CZ 452 LUX BOLT-ACTION RIFLE

Bolt action; 22 LR, 22 WMR, 5-shot or 10-shot detachable magazine. 24.8-inch barrel; weighs 6.6 lbs. Length: 42.63-inch overall. Walnut stock with checkered pistol grip. Sights: Hooded front, fully adjustable tangent rear. All-steel construction, adjustable trigger, polished blue finish. Imported from the Czech Republic by CZ-USA, still available.

Perf.: $350   **Exc.:** $280   **VGood:** $220

CZ 452 SCOUT

Similar to 452 LUX, but has short stock with 12-inch pull for young shooters; 16.2-inch barrel; equipped with single-shot adapter; introduced 2000, still available.

Perf.: $210   **Exc.:** $160   **VGood:** $140

CZ 452 SILHOUETTE

Similar to 452 LUX, but with black synthetic stock; no sights furnished; 22 LR only.

Perf.: $375   **Exc.:** $275   **VGood:** $200

CZ 452 STYLE

Similar to 452 Silhouette, but with matte nickel finish on all metal surfaces; 22LR only.

Perf.: $375   **Exc.:** $275   **VGood:** $200

CZ 452 TRAINING RIFLE

Similar to 452 LUX, but with beechwood stock; comes with 5-round magazine; 22 LR only.

Perf.: $250   **Exc.:** $200   **VGood:** $180

CZ 452 VARMINT RIFLE

Similar to the 452 American Classic model except has heavy 20.8-inch barrel; stock has beavertail forend; weighs 7 lbs.; no sights furnished. Available in 22 LR, 22 WMR, 17 HMR, 17 Mach 2. Imported from the Czech Republic by CZ-USA, still available.

Perf.: $375   **Exc.:** $300   **VGood:** $250

CZ 511 AUTO RIFLE

Semi-automatic; 22 LR, 8-shot magazine. 22.2-inch barrel. weighs 5.39 lbs. 38.6-inch overall. Walnut stock with checkered pistol grip. Sights: Hooded front, adjustable rear. Features: Polished blue finish; detachable magazine; sling swivel studs. Imported from the Czech Republic by CZ-USA, still available.

Perf.: $325   **Exc.:** $275   **VGood:** $225

CZ 513 BASIC

Similar to CZ 452, but simplified; uncheckered beechwood stock and non-adjustable trigger; 22 LR only. Introduced 2004, still available.

Perf.: $210   **Exc.:** $165   **VGood:** $140

CZ 527 AMERICAN CLASSIC BOLT-ACTION RIFLE

Bolt action; 22 Hornet, 222 Rem., 223 Rem., 221 Fireball, 204 Ruger; detachable 5-shot magazine; 23-1/2-inch barrel; European walnut stock. Hooded front and open adjustable rear sights; Improved

CZ527 American Classic
Bolt-Action Rifle

CZ 527 Carbine

CZ 527 Lux
Bolt-Action Rifle

CZ 527 FS

CZ 527 Varmint
Kevlar

CZ 527 Varmint
Laminate

CZ 527 Varmint
Walnut

CZ 527 Prestige

CZ 550 American Classic
Bolt-Action Rifle

CZ 550 Lux
Bolt-Action Rifle

CZ 550 FS

mini-Mauser action with non-rotating claw extractor;
single set trigger; grooved receiver, imported from the
Czech Republic by CZ-USA. Still available.

    Perf.: $550   **Exc.:** $450   **VGood:** $350

CZ 527 CARBINE

Bolt action; 223, 7.62x39; detachable 5-shot
magazine; 18.5-inch bbl.; walnut stock; 5.8 lbs.;
introduced 2000, still made.

    Perf.: $525   **Exc.:** $450   **VGood:** $375

CZ 527 LUX
BOLT-ACTION RIFLE

Bolt action; 22 Hornet, 222 Rem., 223 Rem.,
detachable 5-shot magazine. 23-1/2-inch standard
or heavy barrel. weighs 6 lbs., 1 oz.; 42-1/2-inch
overall. Stock of European walnut with Monte Carlo.
Hooded front, open adjustable rear sights. Improved
mini-Mauser action with non-rotating claw extractor;
single set trigger; grooved receiver. Imported from the
Czech Republic by CZ-USA.

    Perf.: $550   **Exc.:** $550   **VGood:** $350

CZ 527 FS

Similar to 527 LUX, but with full-length Mannlicher-
type stock, steel muzzle cap; 20.5-inch bbl.; weighs
6.2 lbs.

    Perf.: $650   **Exc.:** $500   **VGood:** $400

CZ 527 VARMINT KEVLAR

Bolt action; 223; 527 action, 24-inch bbl.; Kevlar
varmint stock.

    Perf.: $740   **Exc.:** $600   **VGood:** $520

CZ 527 VARMINT LAMINATE

Bolt action; 223; similar to 527 Varmint Kevlar, but
with laminated wood stock.

    Perf.: $640   **Exc.:** $500   **VGood:** $420

CZ 527 VARMINT WALNUT

Bolt action; 17 Rem., 204 Ruger; 527 series Varmint
rifle with 24-inch bbl. and walnut stock.

    Perf.: $540   **Exc.:** $400   **VGood:** $320

CZ 527 PRESTIGE

Bolt action; 22 Hornet, 223; 21-inch barrel; prestige
version of 527 series.

    Perf.: $830   **Exc.:** $700   **VGood:** $600

CZ 550 AMERICAN CLASSIC
BOLT-ACTION RIFLE

Bolt action; 22-250, 243, 6.5x55, 270, 308, 30-06,
9.3x62; Similar to CZ 550 Lux except has American
classic-style stock with 18 lpi checkering; free-
floating barrel; recessed target crown. Has 25.6-
inch barrel; weighs 7.48 lbs. No sights furnished.
Introduced 1999. Imported from the Czech Republic
by CZ-USA. Still available.

    Perf.: $550   **Exc.:** $500   **VGood:** $450

CZ 550 LUX
BOLT-ACTION RIFLE

Bolt action; 22-250, 243, 6.5x55, 7x57, 7x64, 308
Win., 9.3x62, 270 Win., 30-06. 20.47 barrel-inch;
weighs 7.5 lbs. 44.68-inch overall length. Stock of
Turkish walnut in Bavarian style or FS (Mannlicher).
Hooded front sight, adjustable rear. Improved
Mauser-style action with claw extractor, fixed ejector,
square bridge dovetailed receiver; single set trigger.
Imported from the Czech Republic by CZ-USA.

    Perf.: $550   **Exc.:** $450   **VGood:** $400

CZ 550 FS

Similar to 550 LUX, but with full-length Mannlicher-
type stock, 20.5-inch bbl. Imported by CZ-USA; still
made.

    Perf.: $650   **Exc.:** $550   **VGood:** $500

CZ 550 MAGNUM
(AMERICAN SAFARI MAGNUM)

Bolt action, 375 H&H, 416 Rigby, 458 Win. Mag., 458
Lott; 25-inch bbl., weighs 9.9 lbs.; introduced 2004,
still made.

    Perf.: $875   **Exc.:** $640   **VGood:** $600

CZ 550 MAGNUM (MEDIUM MAGNUM)

Similar to the CZ 550 Lux except chambered for the 300 Win. Mag. and 7mm Rem. Mag.; 5-shot magazine. Adjustable iron sights, hammer-forged barrel, single-set trigger, Turkish walnut stock. Weighs 7.5 lbs. Introduced 2001. Still available. Imported from the Czech Republic by CZ USA.

Perf.: $600   **Exc.:** $500   **VGood:** $400

CZ 550 MAGNUM (SAFARI MAGNUM)

Similar to CZ 550 Lux and CZ 550 American Safari Magnum except has long action for 300 Win. Mag., 375 H&H, 416 Rigby, 458 Win. Mag. Overall length is 46.45 inches; barrel length 25 inches; weighs 9.24 lbs. Hooded front sight, express rear with one standing, two folding leaves. Imported from the Czech Republic by CZ-USA. Still available.

Perf.: $830   **Exc.:** $650   **VGood:** $600

CZ 550 VARMINT KEVLAR

Bolt action; 22-250, 308; 25.6-inch bbl.; heavy varmint rifle with Kevlar stock. Introduced 2004, still made.

Perf.: $700   **Exc.:** $600   **VGood:** $500

CZ 550 VARMINT LAMINATE

Bolt action; 22-250, 308; 25.6-inch bbl.; similar to Kevlar-stocked varmint rifle, but with laminated wood stock. Introduced 2002, still made.

Perf.: $620   **Exc.:** $500   **VGood:** $450

CZ 550 VARMINT WALNUT

Similar to Varmint Laminate rifle, but in 308 caliber only, with walnut stock.

Perf.: $600   **Exc.:** $500   **VGood:** $450

CZ 550 ULTIMATE HUNTING RIFLE

Similar to CZ550 American Safari Magnum but chambered for .300 WM only and with custom select wood. 23.6-inch barrel. Accuracy guaranteed at one MOA to 1000 yards. Introduced 2006.

NIB: $2300   **Exc.:** $1995   **VGood:** $1575

CZ 700 M1 SNIPER RIFLE

Bolt action; 308 Winchester, 10-shot magazine. 25.6-inch barrel; weighs 11.9 lbs. Length: 45 inches overall. Laminated wood thumbhole stock with adjustable buttplate and cheekpiece; permanently attached Weaver rail for scope mounting. 60-degree bolt throw; oversized trigger guard and bolt handle for use with gloves; full-length equipment rail on forend; fully adjustable trigger. Introduced 2001. Imported from the Czech Republic by CZ USA. No longer available.

Perf.: $1900   **Exc.:** $1700   **VGood:** $1500

CZ 750 SNIPER

Bolt-action rifle; .308 Win. 10-shot detachable magazine, 26-inch blued barrel, two scope mount systems, polymer stock, weighs 12 lbs. Replaces CZ 700 M1 sniper rifle. Introduced 2006.

NIB: $1925   **Exc.:** $1825   **VGood:** $1575

CZ 584 SOLO COMBINATION GUN

Combination gun; 7x57R; 12, 2-3/4-inch chamber. 24.4-inch barrels; weighs 7.37 lbs. 45-1/4 inches overall. Circassian walnut stock. Blade front sight, open rear adjustable for windage. Kersten-style double lump locking system; double-trigger Blitz-type mechanism with drop safety and adjustable set trigger for the rifle barrel; auto safety, dual extractors; receiver dovetailed for scope mounting. Imported from the Czech Republic by CZ-USA. Still available.

Per.f: $800   **Exc.:** $675   **VGood:** $590

CZ 589 STOPPER OVER/UNDER GUN

Double rifle, over/under; 458 Win. Magnum. 21.7-inch barrels. weighs 9.3 lbs. Length: 37-1/2 inches overall. Turkish walnut stock with sling swivels. Blade front, fixed rear sights. Kersten-style action; Blitz-type double trigger; hammer-forged, blued barrels; satin-nickel, engraved receiver. Introduced 2001, no longer available; Imported from the Czech Republic by CZ USA.

Perf.: $2700   **Exc.:** $2500   **VGood:** $2200

CZ 550 American Safari Magnum

CZ 550 Medium Magnum Bolt-Action Rifle

CZ 550 Safari Magnum

CZ550 Varmint Kevlar

CZ 550 Varmint Laminate

CZ 550 Varmint Walnut

CZ 700 M1 Sniper Rifle

CZ 584 Solo Combination Gun

CZ 589 Stopper Over/Under Gun

D-MAX AUTO CARBINE

Semi-automatic; 9mm Para., 10mm Auto, 40 S&W, 45 ACP; 30-shot magazine; 16-1/4-inch barrel; 38-1/2-inch overall length; weighs about 7-3/4 lbs.; walnut butt, grip, forend; post front sight, open fully-adjustable rear; aperture rear optional; blowback operation, fires from closed bolt; trigger-block safety; side-feed magazine; integral optical sight base; Max-Coat finish. Made in U.S. by D-Max Industries. No longer produced.

Perf.: $395   **Exc.:** $275   **VGood:** $200

Daewoo DR200 Varmint

Daisy Legacy Model 2201/2211

Daisy Legacy Model 2202/2212

Daisy Legacy Model 2203/2213

Daisy V/L Presentation

Dakota 10 Single Shot

Dakota 76 African

Dakota 76 Classic

dovetailed for scope mount; removable trigger assembly. Introduced 1988; discontinued 1991.

Model 2203		
Perf.: $145	**Exc.:** $120	**VGood:** $85
Model 2213		
Perf.: $150	**Exc.:** $125	**VGood:** $90

DAISY V/L

Single shot; underlever; 22 V/L caseless cartridge; 18-inch barrel; adjustable open rear sight, ramp blade front; stock of wood-grained Lustran plastic. Introduced 1968; discontinued 1969; only 19,000 manufactured. Values are for gun with ammo.

Perf.: $300　　**Exc.:** $225　　**VGood:** $175

DAISY V/L COLLECTOR KIT

Same specs as V/L except American walnut stock; gold-plate engraved with owner's name, gun's serial number; gun case; brass wall hangers; 300 rounds of V/L ammo. Introduced 1968; discontinued 1969; only 1000 produced.

Perf.: $375　　**Exc.:** $250　　**VGood:** $200

DAISY V/L PRESENTATION

Same specs as V/L except American walnut stock. Introduced 1968; discontinued 1969; only 4000 manufactured.

Perf.: $375　　**Exc.:** $250　　**VGood:** $200

DAKOTA 10 SINGLE SHOT

Lever action; chambered for most rimmed and rimless commercial cartridges; 23-inch barrel; 39-1/2-inch overall length; weighs 6 lbs.; falling block; no sights; drilled, tapped for scope mounts; medium-fancy classic-style walnut stock; checkered grip, forend; top tang safety; removable trigger plate. Made in U.S. Introduced 1993; still in production. Most Model 10 rifles have custom features, and prices vary widely.

Perf.: $3500　　**Exc.:** $2750　　**VGood:** $2000

DAKOTA 22 SPORTER

Bolt action; 22 LR, 22 Hornet; 5-shot magazine; 22-inch Premium barrel; 42-1/2-inch overall length; weighs about 6-1/2 lbs.; Claro or English walnut stock in classic design; 13-1/2-inch length of pull; point panel hand checkering; swivel studs; black buttpad; no sights; comes with mount bases; combines features of Winchester 52 and Dakota 76 rifles; full-sized receiver; rear locking lugs and bolt machined from bar stock; trigger and striker-blocking safety; adjustable trigger. Made in U.S. by Dakota Arms, Inc. Introduced 1992; out of production in 1998, reintroduced 2003. Premium for 22 Hornet chambering.

Perf.: $2000　　**Exc.:** $1500　　**VGood:** $1000

DAKOTA 76 AFRICAN

Bolt action; 338 Lapua Magnum, 404 Jeffery, 416 Rigby, 416 Dakota, 416 Remington, 450 Dakota; 4-shot magazine; 24-inch barrel; weighs 9 to 10 lbs.; select wood; two stock cross-bolts; ramp front sight, standing leaf rear. Made in U.S. by Dakota Arms, Inc. Introduced 1989; still produced.

Perf.: $4800　　**Exc.:** $3700　　**VGood:** $2900

DAKOTA 76 ALPINE

Bolt action; 22-250, 243, 6mm Rem., 250-3000, 7mm-08, 308, 358; 21-inch, 23-inch barrel; weighs 6-1/2 lbs.; slim checkered walnut stock; blind magazine. Introduced 1989; discontinued 1992.

Perf.: $1795　　**Exc.:** $1495　　**VGood:** $1200

DAKOTA 76 CLASSIC

Bolt action; 22-250, 243, 6mm Rem., 250-3000, 7mm-08, 308, 358, 257 Roberts, 270, 280, 30-06, 7mm Rem. Mag., 338 Win. Mag., 300 Win. Mag., 375 H&H, 458 Win. Mag.; 4-shot magazine; 21-inch, 23-inch barrel; weighs 7-1/2 lbs.; no sights; drilled, tapped for scope mounts; composite or classic-style medium-fancy walnut stock; one-piece rail trigger guard assembly; solid buttpad; steel grip cap; adjustable trigger. Based on original Winchester Model 70 design. Right- or left-handed. Introduced 1988; still in production.

Perf.: $3400　　**Exc.:** $2750　　**VGood:** $1400

DAEWOO DR200 VARMINT

Semi-automatic; 223 Rem.; 6-shot magazine; 18-3/8-inch barrel; 39-1/4-inch overall length; weighs 9 lbs.; synthetic thumbhole-style stock with rubber buttpad; post front sight in ring, aperture fully-adjustable rear; forged aluminum receiver; bolt, bolt carrier, firing pin, piston and recoil spring contained in one assembly; rotating bolt locking; uses AR-15 magazines. Imported from Korea by Kimber of America, Inc.; distributed by Nationwide Sports Dist. Introduced 1995; no longer imported.

Perf.: $650　　**Exc.:** $525　　**VGood:** $450

DAISY LEGACY MODEL 2201/2211

Bolt action; single shot; 22 LR; 19-inch barrel with octagonal shroud; weighs 6-1/2 lbs.; ramp blade front sight, fully-adjustable removable notch rear; moulded copolymer stock (Model 2201) or walnut stock (Model 2211); adjustable-length stock; removable bolt/trigger assembly; adjustable trigger; dovetailed for scope mounting; barrel interchanges with smoothbore. Introduced 1988; discontinued 1990.

Model 2201		
Perf.: $130	**Exc.:** $100	**VGood:** $70

Model 2211		
Perf.: $140	**Exc.:** $110	**VGood:** $80

DAISY LEGACY MODEL 2202/2212

Bolt action; 22 LR; 10-shot rotary magazine; 19-inch barrel with octagon shroud; weighs 6-1/2 lbs.; moulded copolymer stock (Model 2202) or walnut stock (Model 2212); ramp blade front sight, fully-adjustable removable rear; receiver dovetailed for scope mounting; adjustable butt length; removable bolt/trigger assembly; barrel interchanges with smoothbore. Introduced 1988; discontinued 1990.

Model 2202		
Perf.: $140	**Exc.:** $110	**VGood:** $80
Model 2212		
Perf.: $145	**Exc.:** $115	**VGood:** $85

DAISY LEGACY MODEL 2203/2213

Semi-automatic; 22 LR; 7-shot clip; 19-inch barrel; 34-3/4-inch overall length; weighs 6-1/2 lbs.; blade on ramp front sight, fully-adjustable, removable notch rear; moulded copolymer stock (Model 2203) or American hardwood stock (Model 2213); receiver

DAKOTA 76 CLASSIC SHORT ACTION

Same specs as Model 76 Classic except 22-250, 243, 6mm Rem., 250-3000, 7mm-08, 308; 21-inch barrel. Introduced 1989.

Perf.: $2095   **Exc.:** $1595   **VGood:** $1195

DAKOTA 76 SAFARI

Bolt action; 300 Win. Mag., 338 Win. Mag., 375 H&H, 458 Win. Mag.; 23-inch barrel; weighs 8-1/2 lbs.; ramp front sight, standing leaf rear; checkered plastic composite or English walnut stock; shadowline cheekpiece; barrel band front swivel, inletted rear. Introduced 1988; still in production.

Perf.: $4200   **Exc.:** $3200   **VGood:** $2200

With composite stock

Perf.: $2750   **Exc.:** $1995   **VGood:** $1495

DAKOTA 76 TRAVELER TAKEDOWN RIFLE

Bolt-action takedown rifle; 257 Roberts, 25-06, 7x57, 270, 280, 30-06, 338-06, 35 Whelen (standard length); 7mm Rem. Mag., 300 Win. Mag., 338 Win. Mag., 416 Taylor, 458 Win. Mag. (short magnums); 7mm, 300, 330, 375 Dakota Magnums. Other calibers available. 23-inch barrel; weighs 7-1/2 lbs. 43-1/2-inch overall. Medium fancy- grade walnut stock in classic style. Checkered grip and forend; solid butt pad; drilled and tapped for scope mounts. Threadless disassembly. Uses modified Model 76 design with many features of the Model 70 Winchester. Left-hand model also available. Introduced 1989, still available. Made in U.S.A. by Dakota Arms, Inc.

Classic,

Perf.: $4200   **Exc.:** $3200   **VGood:** $2700

Safari

Perf.: $5000   **Exc.:** $4000   **VGood:** $3200

DAKOTA 76 VARMINT

Bolt action; single shot; 17 Rem., 22 BR, 222 Rem., 22-250, 220 Swift, 223, 6mm BR, 6mm PPC; heavy barrel contour; special stock dimensions for varmint shooting. Made in U.S. by Dakota Arms, Inc. Introduced 1994; dropped 1998.

Perf.: $2200   **Exc.:** $1800   **VGood:** $1300

DAKOTA LIMITED EDITION .30-06 MODEL 76

Ultra-decked-out version of Model 76; commemorates 100th anniversary of .30-06 cartridge; production limited to 101 units.

NIB: $8500   **Exc.:** N/A   **VGood:** N/A

DAKOTA LIMITED EDITION .30-06 MODEL 10

Ultra-decked-out version of Model 76; commemorates 100th anniversary of .30-06 cartridge; production limited to 101 units.

NIB: $8000   **Exc.:** N/A   **VGood:** $775

DAKOTA 97 LIGHTWEIGHT HUNTER

Bolt action; 22-250 to 330 Dakota Magnum. 22-inch, 24-inch barrel; weighs 6.1 to 6.5 lbs. 43-inch overall length. Lightweight Fiberglass stock. Sights are optional. Matte blue finish, black stock. Right-hand action only. Introduced 1998. Made in U.S.A. by Dakota Arms, Inc.

Perf.: $1800   **Exc.:** $1400   **VGood:** $1000

DAKOTA 97 LONG RANGE HUNTER RIFLE

Bolt action; 25-06, 257 Roberts, 270 Win., 280 Rem., 7mm Rem. Mag., 7mm Dakota Mag., 30-06, 300 Win. Mag., 300 Dakota Mag., 338 Win. Mag., 330 Dakota Mag., 375 H&H Mag., 375 Dakota Mag. 24-inch, 26-inch match-quality; free-floating barrel; weighs 7.7 lbs. 45-inch to 47-inch overall length. H-S Precision black synthetic stock, with one-piece bedding block system. Drilled and tapped for scope mounting. Cylindrical machined receiver controlled round feed; Mauser-style extractor; three-position striker blocking safety; fully adjustable match trigger. Right-hand

Dakota 76 Safari

Dakota 76 Traveler Takedown Rifle

Dakota 76 Varmint

Dakota Limited Edition 76

Dakota 97 Long Range Hunter Rifle

Dakota Longbow Tactical E.R. Rifle

Charles Daly Bolt Action

action only. Introduced 1997, still available. Made in U.S.A. by Dakota Arms, Inc. \\

Perf.: $1800   **Exc.:** $1300   **VGood:** $1000

DAKOTA DOUBLE RIFLE

Double rifle, breakopen; 7x57R, 30-30, 9.3x74R, 375 H&H Flanged, 45-70, 470 Nitro Express, 500 Nitro Express. 25-inch barrel; Exhibition-grade walnut stock; Express sights; Round action; selective ejectors; engraving extra; recoil pad; Americase. From Dakota Arms Inc. Still available.

Perf.: $25,000   **Exc.:** $22,000   **VGood:** $20,000

DAKOTA LONGBOW TACTICAL E.R. RIFLE

Bolt action; 300 Dakota Magnum, 330 Dakota Magnum, 338 Lapua Magnum. 28-inch barrel, .950-inch at muzzle; weighs 13.7 lbs. 50-inch to 52-inch overall length. Ambidextrous McMillan A-2 fiberglass stock, black or olive green color; adjustable cheekpiece and buttplate. Comes with Picatinny one-piece optical rail. Uses the Dakota 76 action with controlled-round feed; three-position firing pin block safety; claw extractor; Model 70-style trigger. Comes with bipod, case, tool kit. Introduced 1997. Made in U.S.A. by Dakota Arms, Inc.

Perf.: $4200   **Exc.:** $3200   **VGood:** $2750

CHARLES DALY BOLT ACTION (EARLY)

Bolt action; 22 Hornet; 5-shot box magazine; 24-inch barrel; miniaturized Mauser; leaf rear, ramp front sight; walnut stock; hand-checkered pistol-grip forearm; hinged floorplate. Introduced 1931; discontinued 1939. Imported by Charles Daly; manufactured by Franz Jaeger Co. of Germany. Note: Same model was imported by A.F. Stoeger and sold as Herold Rifle.

Perf.: $850   **Exc.:** $600   **VGood:** $500

CHARLES DALY BOLT-ACTION CENTERFIRE RIFLE, FIELD GRADE

Bolt action; 22-250, 30-06, 22-inch bbl., 5-shot magazine, 43-inch OAL, walnut-finished hardwood stock, or black polymer stock, Mauser action.

Perf.: $380   **Exc.:** $320   **VGood:** $280

CHARLES DALY BOLT-ACTION CENTERFIRE RIFLE, FIELD GRADE, MAGNUM

Like the Field Grade, but chambered for 7mm Rem Mag, 300 Win Mag; 24-inch barrel, 44-5/8-inch OAL, weighs 7-1/4 lbs.

Perf.: $400   **Exc.:** $340   **VGood:** $300

Charles Daly Bolt-Action
22-Caliber Rifle, Field Grade

Charles Daly Bolt-Action
22-Caliber Rifle, Superior Grade

Dan Wesson Coyote Classic

Dan Wesson Coyote Target

Diana Model 820L

sling swivels; gold bead front sight. Introduced 1997.
Imported from Italy by K.B.I. Inc., still available.
Perf.: $1250 **Exc.:** $1100 **VGood:** $1000

CHARLES DALY EMPIRE COMBINATION GUN
Same as the Superior grade except has deluxe wood
with European-style comb and cheekpiece; slim
forend. Introduced 1997, still available. Imported from
Italy by K.B.I., Inc.
Perf.: $1650 **Exc.:** $1500 **VGood:** 1200

CHARLES DALY FIELD GRADE AUTO RIFLE
Semi-automatic; 22 LR, 10-shot magazine. 20-
3/4-inch barrel; weighs 6.5 lbs. 40-1/2-inch overall.
Walnut-finished hardwood stock with Monte Carlo;
hooded front sight, adjustable open rear. Receiver
grooved for scope mounting; blue finish; shell
deflector. Introduced 1998. Imported by K.B.I.
Perf.: $120 **Exc.:** $100 **VGood:** $80

CHARLES DALY EMPIRE GRADE AUTO RIFLE
Similar to the Field Grade except has select California
walnut stock with 24 lpi hand checkering, contrasting
forend and gripcaps, damascened bolt, high-polish
blue. Introduced 1998. Imported by K.B.I.; no longer
available.
Perf.: $170 **Exc.:** $130 **VGood:** $100

CHARLES DALY TRUE YOUTH BOLT-ACTION RIFLE
Bolt action; 22 LR, single shot. 16-1/4-inch barrel;
weighs about 3 lbs. 32-inch overall. Walnut-finished
hardwood stock; blade front, adjustable rear sights;
Scaled-down stock for small shooters. Blue finish.
Introduced 1998. Imported by K.B.I., Inc.
Perf.: $115 **Exc.:** $90 **VGood:** $65

DAN WESSON COYOTE CLASSIC BOLT-ACTION RIMFIRE RIFLE
Bolt action; 22 LR or 22 WMR. 5-shot magazine
(10-shot optional magazine). 22-3/4-inch barrel;
Laminated wood or exotic hardwood stock; fully
adjustable V-notch rear sight, brass bead ramp
front. Receiver drilled and tapped for scope mount;
checkered pistol grip and fore end with DW medallion
end cap; recessed target crown; sling swivel studs.
Introduced 2001, dropped 2003. From Dan Wesson
Firearms.
Perf.: $210 **Exc.:** $170 **VGood:** $120

DAN WESSON COYOTE TARGET BOLT-ACTION RIMFIRE RIFLE
Bolt action; 22 LR or 22 WMR, 5-shot magazine (10-
shot optional magazine). 18-3/8-inch heavy barrel;
laminated wood or exotic hardwood stock. Receiver
drilled and tapped for scope mount; target-crowned
muzzle; high comb, smooth pistol grip and rubber
butt plate. Introduced 2001, dropped 2003. From
Dan Wesson Firearms.
Perf.: $250 **Exc.:** $200 **VGood:** $150

DIANA MODEL 820F MATCH
Bolt action; single shot; 22 LR; 27-1/8-inch barrel;
44-1/2-inch overall length; weighs 15-1/2 lbs.; walnut
target stock; tunnel front sight, fully-adjustable match
rear; designed for free rifle events; adjustable hook
buttplate, adjustable cheekpiece, hand stop; stock
stabilizer and palm rest optional; trigger adjustable
from 1.4 to 8.8 oz. Imported from Germany by
Dynamit Nobel-RWS, Inc. Introduced 1990;
discontinued 1992.
Perf.: $1695 **Exc.:** $1395 **VGood:** $995

DIANA MODEL 820K
Same specs as Model 820F except 24-inch barrel;
41-inch overall length; weighs 9-1/2 lbs.; no sights;
detachable 3-piece barrel weight; designed for
running boar events; European walnut stock. Made in
Germany. Discontinued 1986.
Perf.: $895 **Exc.:** $750 **VGood:** $550

CHARLES DALY BOLT-ACTION CENTERFIRE RIFLE, SUPERIOR GRADE
Like the Field Grade, but highly-polished blued
barreled action with gold-plated trigger, hand-
checkered European walnut stock with Monte Carlo
comb, rollover cheekpiece.; open rear and ramp
front sights, or none, for scope mounting. Introduced
1996, imported by KBI.
Perf.: $420 **Exc.:** $375 **VGood:** 310

CHARLES DALY BOLT-ACTION CENTERFIRE RIFLE, SUPERIOR GRADE, MAGNUM
Like the Superior grade, but calibers 7mm Rem
Mag through 458 Win Mag; 24-inch, 26-inch barrels,
weighs about 8-1/4 lbs.
Perf.: $500 **Exc.:** $450 **VGood:** $400

CHARLES DALY BOLT-ACTION CENTERFIRE RIFLE, EMPIRE GRADE
Like the Superior Grade, but has oil-finished
American walnut stock with 18 lpi hand checkering;
black gripcap and forearm tip, highly-polished
barreled action, jeweled bolt, recoil pad, and swivel
studs. Imported by KBI, no longer available.
Perf.: $500 **Exc.:** $450 **VGood:** $400

CHARLES DALY BOLT-ACTION CENTERFIRE RIFLE, EMPIRE GRADE, MAGNUM
Like the Empire Grade, but for magnum calibers.
Imported by KBI; no longer available.
Perf.: $550 **Exc.:** $500 **VGood:** $450

CHARLES DALY BOLT-ACTION 22-CALIBER RIFLE, FIELD GRADE
Bolt action; 22 LR, 6- or 10-shot magazine; 22-5/8-
inch barrel, 6-1/8 lbs. walnut-finished hardwood
stock; bead front, adjustable rear sights; receiver
grooved for scope mounting. Introduced 1998 by
KBI.
Perf.: $110 **Exc.:** $90 **VGood:** $70

CHARLES DALY BOLT-ACTION 22-CALIBER RIFLE, SUPERIOR GRADE
Like the Field Grade, but high polished barreled
action, checkered Monte Carlo walnut stock; 22 LR,
22 WMR or 22 Hornet; premium for 22 Hornet.
Perf.: $160 **Exc.:** $130 **VGood:** $100

CHARLES DALY BOLT-ACTION 22-CALIBER RIFLE, EMPIRE GRADE
Like the Superior Grade, but Monte Carlo stock of
California walnut, 20 lpi hand checkering, black grip
cap and forearm cap, damascened bolt.
Perf.: $330 **Exc.:** $280 **VGood:** $210

CHARLES DALY SUPERIOR COMBINATION GUN
Combination gun; 12 ga. over 22 Hornet, 223 Rem.,
22-250, 243 Win., 270 Win., 308 Win., 30-06. 23.5-
inch barrels, shotgun choked Imp. Cyl.; weighs about
7.5 lbs. Checkered walnut pistol grip buttstock and
semi- beavertail forend. Silvered, engraved receiver;
chrome-moly steel barrels; double triggers; extractors;

DIANA MODEL 820L

Same specs as Model 820F except 24-inch, 26-inch barrel; weighs 10-1/2 lbs; designed for three-position match shooting. Made in Germany. Introduced 1990; discontinued 1992.

Perf.: $1195   **Exc.:** $895   **VGood:** $650

DIANA MODEL 820S

Same specs as Model 820L except 24-inch barrel; 41-inch overall length; weighs 10 5/16 lbs.; Model 82 or 75 aperture rear sight. Made in Germany. Introduced 1990; discontinued 1992.

Perf.: $995   **Exc.:** $795   **VGood:** $595

DIANA MODEL 820SF

Same specs as Model 820F except 41-inch overall length; weighs 11 lbs.; heavy barrel; Model 82 or 75 aperture rear sight. Made in Germany. Introduced 1990; discontinued 1992.

Perf.: $1095   **Exc.:** $895   **VGood:** $595

DIXIE MODEL 1873 RIFLE

Lever action; 44-40; 11-shot tubular magazine; 24-1/2-inch octagonal barrel; leaf rear sight, blade front; walnut stock forearm, receiver color case-hardened. Replica of Winchester '73. Introduced 1975.

Perf.: $795   **Exc.:** $695   **VGood:** $595

Engraved Model 1873 Rifle

Perf.: $1200   **Exc.:** $1000   **VGood:** $700

DIXIE MODEL 1873 CARBINE

Same specs as Model 1873 except 20-inch barrel, carbine bands.

Perf.: $695   **Exc.:** $595   **VGood:** $495

DIXIE 1874 SHARPS BLACKPOWDER SILHOUETTE

Single shot; falling block; 45-70; 30-inch tapered octagon barrel with 1:18-inch twist; 47-1/2-inch overall length; weighs 10-5/16 lbs.; oiled walnut shotgun-style butt with checkered metal buttplate; blade front sight, ladder-type hunting rear; replica of the Sharps #1 Sporter; color case-hardened receiver, hammer, lever and buttplate; blued barrel; tang drilled and tapped for tang sight; double-set triggers. Meets standards for NRA blackpowder cartridge matches. Imported from Italy by Dixie Gun Works. Introduced 1995; still imported.

Perf.: $1100   **Exc.:** $1000   **VGood:** $895

DIXIE 1874 SHARPS LIGHTWEIGHT HUNTER/TARGET

Same specs as Dixie 1874 Sharps Blackpowder Silhouette except straight-grip buttstock with military-style buttplate. Based on the 1874 military model. Imported from Italy by Dixie Gun Works. Introduced 1995.

Perf.: $1100   **Exc.:** $1000   **VGood:** $895

DIXIE REMINGTON CREEDMORE LONG RANGE

Rolling block; 45-70; 30-inch octagon barrel; weighs 13 lbs.; Creedmore sights; checkered wood stock; blued barrel; color case-hardening or exposed metal. No longer in production.

Perf.: $950   **Exc.:** $795   **VGood:** $695

DPMS PANTHER ARMS A-15 RIFLES

Semi-automatic; 223 Rem., 7.62x39. Barrel: 16-inch to 24-inch weighs 7-3/4 to 11-3/4 lbs. 34-1/2 to 42-1/4-inch overall. Black Zytel composite stock; Square front post, adjustable A2 rear sights; Steel or stainless steel heavy or bull barrel; hard-coat anodized receiver; aluminum free-float tube handguard; many options. From DPMS Panther Arms.

Panther Bull A-15 (20-inch stainless bull barrel)

Perf.: $875   **Exc.:** $700   **VGood:** $575

Panther Bull Twenty-Four (24-inch stainless bull barrel)

Perf.: $920   **Exc.:** $760   **VGood:** $610

Bulldog (20-inch stainless fluted barrel, flat top receiver)

Perf.: $1150   **Exc.:** $975   **VGood:** $850

Dixie Model 1873 Rifle

Dixie 1874 Sharps Blackpowder Silhouette

DPMS Panther Arms A-15 Rifles

DPMS Single Shot Rifle

DPMS Panther Race Gun

DPMS Panther Tuber

DPMS Panther Mark 12

Panther Bull Sweet Sixteen (16-inch stainless bull barrel)

Perf.: $840   **Exc.:** $710   **VGood:** $600

Panther DCM (20-inch stainless heavy bbl., national match sights).

Perf.: $1000   **Exc.:** $780   **VGood:** $630

Panther 7.62x39 (20-inch steel heavy barrel)

Perf.: $800   **Exc.:** $700   **VGood:** $575

DPMS PANTHER RACE GUN

Similar to Panther Bull but with 24-inch fluted bull barrel. Sights: JP Micro adjustable rear, JP front sight adjustable for height. Includes Lyman globe and Shaver inserts.

NIB: $1600   **Exc.:** $1475   **VGood:** $1150

DPMS PANTHER TUBER

Similar to Panther Bull 24 but with 16-inch barrel with cylindrical aluminum shroud.

NIB: $1600   **Exc.:** $1475   **VGood:** $1150

DPMS SINGLE SHOT RIFLE

AR-15-style single-shot rifle with manually-operated bolt, no magazine.

NIB: $775   **Exc.:** $725   **VGood:** $595

DPMS PANTHERA PARDUS

Similar to Panther Post-ban but with 16-inch bull barrel, telescoping buttstock and tan Teflon finish. Introduced 2006.

NIB: $1600   **Exc.:** $1475   **VGood:** $1150

DPMS Panther SDM-R

DSA SA58 Carbine

DSA SA58 Medium Contour

DSA SA58 Standard

DSA SA58 21" or 24" Bull Barrel

DuBiel Custom

Dumoulin Amazone

DPMS PANTHER 20TH ANNIVERSARY RIFLE
Similar to Panther Post-ban but with 20-inch bull barrel and engraved, chrome-plated lower receiver.
NIB: $2600   **Exc.:** $2475   **VGood:** $1950

DPMS PANTHER MARK 12
Similar to Panther but with flash hider and other refinements.
NIB: $1400   **Exc.:** $1325   **VGood:** $1075

DPMS PANTHER SDM-R
Similar to Panther but with stainless steel barrel and Harris bipod.
NIB: $1300   **Exc.:** $1225   **VGood:** $1000

DPMS LRT-SASS
Semi-automatic rifle based on AR-15 design. Chambered in .308 Win. With 18-inch stainless steel barrel with flash hider, collapsible Vitor Clubfoot carbine stock and 19-rd. detachable magazine.
NIB: $1800   **Exc.:** $1655   **VGood:** $1250

DPMS LR-260
Similar to LRT-SASS but with 24-inch stainless steel barrel and chambered in .260 Remington. Also available with 20-inch chrome-moly barrel as LR-260H. Introduced 2006.
NIB: $1200   **Exc.:** $1155   **VGood:** $975

DPMS LR-243
Similar to LR-260 but with 20-inch chrome-moly barrel and chambered in .243 Win. Introduced 2006.
NIB: $1200   **Exc.:** $1155   **VGood:** $975

DPMS LR-204
Similar to LRT-260 but chambered in .204 Ruger. Introduced 2006.
NIB: $1200   **Exc.:** $1155   **VGood:** $975

DSA SA58 CARBINE
Semi-automatic; 308 Win., limited 243 and 260; 16-1/4-inch barrel with integrally machined muzzle brake; weighs 8-3/4 lbs. Fiberglass stock with reinforced synthetic handguard. Adjustable post front, adjustable rear peep sights; Gas-operated semi-auto with fully adjustable gas system, high grade steel or 416 stainless upper receiver. In variety of camo finishes. Made in U.S.A. by DSA, Inc.
Perf.: $1250   **Exc.:** $1100   **VGood:** $900

DSA SA58 MEDIUM CONTOUR
Semi-automatic; 308 Win., limited 243 and 260; 21-inch barrel with integrally machined muzzle brake; weighs 9.75 lbs. 43-inch length; fiberglass reinforced stock with synthetic handguard. Adjustable post front sight with match rear peep. Gas-operated semi-auto with fully adjustable gas system, high grade steel or 416 stainless upper receiver. In variety of camo finishes. Made in U.S.A. by DSA, Inc.
Perf.: $1400   **Exc.:** $1250   **VGood:** $1000

DSA SA58 MEDIUM CONTOUR TACTICAL
Semi-automatic: 308 Win.; Fluted barrel, 16.25-inch; weighs 8 lbs.; 38-1/4-inch length. Fiberglass reinforced stock, short synthetic handguard. Adjustable post front sight, adjustable rear peep. Gas-operated semi-auto with fully adjustable gas system, high grade steel upper receiver. In variety of camo finishes. Made in U.S.A. by DSA, Inc.
Perf.: $1400   **Exc.:** $1250   **VGood:** $1000

DSA SA58 STANDARD
Semi-automatic; 308 Win.; 21-inch barrel with integrally machined muzzle brake; weighs 8-3/4 lbs.; 43-inch length; Fiberglass reinforced stock, synthetic handguard. Adjustable post front sight, adjustable rear peep. Gas-operated semi-auto with fully adjustable gas system, high grade steel upper receiver. In variety of camo finishes. Made in U.S.A. by DSA, Inc.
Perf.: $1250   **Exc.:** $1100   **VGood:** $900

DSA SA58 T48 TACTICAL
Semi-automatic; 308 Win.; 21-inch chrome-moly barrel with Browning flashhider; weighs 9.68 lbs.; 45-inch overall length; Field grade finish wood stock; Adjustable post front sight, adjustable rear peep. 10- or 20- round fixed magazine with stripper clip top cover. Gas operated semi-auto with fully adjustable gas system. Made in U.S.A. by DSA, Inc.
Perf.: $1650   **Exc.:** $1400   **VGood:** $1200

DSA SA58 BULL BARREL
Semi-automatic; 308 Win.; 21-inch or 24-inch bull barrel; weighs 11.1 or 11.5 lbs.; 41.5-inch and 44.5-inch lengths; Stock with free floating handguard. Elevation adjustable protected post front sight, match rear peep. Gas-operated semi-auto with fully adjustable gas system, high grade steel or stainless upper receiver. Extra for stainless barrel. Made in U.S.A. by DSA, Inc.
Perf.: $1700   **Exc.:** $1400   **VGood:** $1100

DUBIEL CUSTOM
Bolt action; 22-250 through 458 Win. Mag., selected wildcats; barrel weights, lengths depend upon caliber; Douglas Premium barrel; no sights; integral scope mount bases; walnut, maple or laminate stocks; hand-checkered; left- or right-hand models; 5-lug locking mechanism; 36-degree bolt rotation; adjustable Canjar trigger; oil or epoxy stock finish; slide-type safety; floorplate release; jeweled, chromed bolt; sling swivel studs; recoil pad. Introduced 1978; discontinued 1990.
Perf.: $2200   **Exc.:** $1900   **VGood:** $1500

DUMOULIN AMAZONE
Bolt action; various calibers from 270 to 458; 20-inch barrel; classic two-leaf rear sight, hooded blade on ramp front; full-length, hand-checkered, oil-finished European walnut stock; built on Mauser 98 action; adjustable trigger; Model 70-type safety. Made in Belgium. Introduced 1986; discontinued 1987.
Perf.: $1695   **Exc.:** $1495   **VGood:** $900

DUMOULIN BAVARIA DELUXE

Bolt action; various calibers from 222 to 458; 21-inch, 24-inch, 25-1/2-inch octagonal barrel; weighs about 7 lbs.; classic two-leaf rear sight, hooded blade on ramp front; hand-checkered, oil-finished select European walnut stock; built on Mauser or Sako action; adjustable trigger; Model 70-type safety; quick-detachable sling swivels; solid buttpad; deluxe engraving. Made in Belgium. Imported by Midwest Gun Sport. Introduced 1986; discontinued 1987.

Perf.: $1800   **Exc.:** $1400   **VGood:** $1000

DUMOULIN CENTURION

Bolt action; various calibers from 270 to 458; 21-1/2-inch, 24-inch, 25-inch barrel; no sights; hand-checkered, oil-finished select European walnut stock; built on Mauser or Sako action. Made in Belgium. Introduced 1986; discontinued 1987.

Perf.: $795   **Exc.:** $595   **VGood:** $495

DUMOULIN CENTURION CLASSIC

Same specs as Centurion except Mauser 98 action only; higher grade of wood stock. Introduced 1986; discontinued 1987.

Perf.: $950   **Exc.:** $795   **VGood:** $600

DUMOULIN DIANE

Bolt action; various calibers from 270 to 458; 22-inch barrel; classic two-leaf rear sight, hooded blade on ramp front; hand-checkered, oil-finished European walnut stock; built on Mauser 98 action; adjustable trigger; Model 70-type safety. Made in Belgium. Introduced 1986; discontinued 1987.

Perf.: $1450   **Exc.:** $1200   **VGood:** $800

DUMOULIN PIONEER EXPRESS

Double rifle; various calibers from 22 Hornet-600 Nitro Express; 24-inch, 26-inch barrel; 45-inch overall length (24-inch barrel); weighs 9-1/2 lbs.; two-leaf rear sight on quarter-rib, bead on ramp front; boxlock triple-lock system; Greener crossbolt; H&H type ejectors; articulated front trigger; various grades of engraving effect price. Made in Belgium. Introduced 1987; no longer imported. Prices range from $6500 to $12,000.

DUMOULIN SAFARI

Bolt action; magnum calibers up to 458; 24-inch to 26-inch barrel; 44-inch overall length (24-inch barrel); weighs 8-1/2 to 9 lbs.; two-leaf rear sight, hooded front on banded ramp; built on modified Sako or Mauser Oberndorf action; classic English-style deluxe European walnut stock; oil finish; buffalo horn grip cap; rubber buttpad; Model 70-type or side safety. Custom built in Belgium. Introduced 1986; discontinued 1987.

Perf.: $2400   **Exc.:** $1900   **VGood:** $1500

DUMOULIN SIDELOCK PRESTIGE

Double rifle; sidelock; traditional chopper lump or classic Ernest Dumoulin barrel system; 22-inch, 24-inch barrel, depending on caliber; deluxe European walnut stock; internal parts are gold-plated; Purdey lock system; ten grades, built to customer specs; differing engraving styles. Made in Belgium. Introduced 1986; no longer imported.

Perf.: $17,900 **Exc.:** $14,950 **VGood:** $9995

E.A.A./ANTONIO ZOLI EXPRESS RIFLE

Double rifle; boxlock; 7.65R, 30-06, 9.3x74R; 25-1/2-inch barrels; 40-1/2-inch overall length; weighs about 8 lbs.; fancy European walnut stock with raised cheekpiece, fine-line checkering; bead front sight, adjustable express rear on quarter-rib; engraved coin-finish frame; double-set triggers; selective automatic ejectors; rubber recoil pad; sling swivels. Imported from Italy by European American Armory. Importation dropped 1993.

Perf.: $3695   **Exc.:** $2995   **VGood:** $2195

Express Model E, better engraving, ejectors
Perf.: $4295   **Exc.:** $3495   **VGood:** $2495

Express Model EM, elaborate engraving, extra-fancy wood
Perf.: $4795   **Exc.:** $3995   **VGood:** $2995

E.A.A./HW 660 Match

EAA/Izhmash Biathlon Target Rifle

EAA/Izhmash Biathalon Basic Target Rifle

Eagle Arms EA-15 Golden Eagle

E.A.A./BAIKAL IZH-94 COMBINATION GUN

Combination gun; 12 gauge, 3-inch chamber; 222 Rem., 223, 5.6x50R, 5.6x55E, 7x57R, 7x65R, 7.62x39, 7.62x51, 308, 7.62x53R, 7.62x54R, 30-06; 24-inch or 26-inch barrels; imp., mod. and full choke tubes. weighs 7.28 lbs. Walnut stock; rubber butt pad. Express style sights. Hammer-forged barrels with chrome-lined bores; machined receiver; single-selective or double triggers. Imported by European American Armory.

Perf.: $600   **Exc.:** $545   **VGood:** $375

E.A.A./HW 660 MATCH

Bolt action; single shot; 22 LR; 26-inch barrel; 45-3/8-inch overall length; weighs 10-3/4 lbs.; match-type walnut stock with adjustable cheekpiece and buttplate; stippled pistol grip and forend; globe front sight, match aperture rear; adjustable match trigger; forend accessory rail. Imported from Germany by European American Armory. Introduced 1988; dropped 1994. Reintroduced, no longer available.

Perf.: $750   **Exc.:** $550   **VGood:** $425

E.A.A./IZHMASH BIATHLON TARGET RIFLE

Bolt Action; 22 LR; biathlon rifle with snow covers for barrel and sights, stock holding extra magazines, round trigger block. Unique bolt utilizes toggle action. Designed to compete in 40 meter biathlon event. 19.5-inch bbl.

Perf.: $900   **Exc.:** $800   **VGood:** $700

E.A.A./IZHMASH BIATHALON BASIC TARGET RIFLE

Same action as Biathlon but designed for plinking or fun. Beech stock, heavy barrel with Weaver rail for scope mount. 22 LR, 19.5-inch bbl.

Perf.: $300   **Exc.:** $200   **VGood:** $100

E.A.A./SABATTI MODEL 1822

Semi-automatic; 22 LR; 10-shot magazine; 18-1/2-inch round tapered barrel; 37-inch overall length; weighs 5-1/4 lbs.; stained hardwood stock; bead front sight, folding leaf elevation-adjustable rear; cross-bolt safety; blue finish. Imported from Italy by European American Armory. Introduced 1993; no longer imported.

Perf.: $180   **Exc.:** $150   **VGood:** $100

Heavy model, bull barrel, no sights
Perf.: $250   **Exc.:** $200   **VGood:** $150

Thumbhole model, heavy, bull barrel, no sights, one-piece stock
Perf.: $300   **Exc.:** $250   **VGood:** $200

E.A.A./SABATTI ROVER 870

Bolt action; 22-250, 243, 25-06, 270, 30-06, 308, 7mm Rem. Mag., 300 Win. Mag., 338 Win. Mag.; 23-inch barrel; 42-1/2-inch overall length; weighs about 7 lbs.; gold bead on ramp front sight, open adjustable rear; walnut stock with straight comb, cut checkering on grip and forend; positive safety locks trigger; blue finish. Imported by E.A.A. Introduced 1986; importation dropped 1987.

Perf.: $595   **Exc.:** $495   **VGood:** $395

E.A.A./SAIGA SEMI-AUTO RIFLE

Semi-automatic; 7.62x39, 308, 223. Barrel: 20.5-inch, 22-inch, 16.3-inch; weighs 7 to 8-1/2 lbs; 43-inch length; synthetic or wood stock; adjustable sights, sight base. Based on AK Combat rifle by Kalashnikov. Imported from Russia by EAA Corp.

Perf.: $250   **Exc.:** $210   **VGood:** $180

E.A.A./WEIHRAUCH HW 60

Bolt action; single shot; 22 LR; 26-7/8-inch barrel; 45-3/4-inch overall length; weighs 11 lbs.; walnut target stock with adjustable buttplate, stippled pistol grip and forend; forend rail with adjustable swivel; hooded ramp front sight, match-type aperture rear; adjustable match trigger with push-button safety. Imported from Germany by European American Armory. Introduced 1981; no longer imported.

Perf.: $595   **Exc.:** $450   **VGood:** $375

Left-hand model
Perf.: $795   **Exc.:** $595   **VGood:** $425

EAGLE ARMS EA-15

Semi-automatic; 223 Rem.; 30-shot magazine; 20-inch barrel; 39-inch overall length; weighs about 7 lbs.; black composition stock, trapdoor-style; post front sight, fully-adjustable rear; push-type receiver pivot pin for easy takedown; receivers hard coat anodized; E2-style forward assist mechanism; integral raised M-16A2-type fence around magazine release button. Made in U.S. by Eagle Arms, Inc. Introduced 1989; discontinued 1993.

Perf.: $750   **Exc.:** $650   **VGood:** $495

Eagle Arms M15A3
Post-Ban Predator

E.M.F. Sharps Carbine

E.M.F. Sharps Rifle

E.M.F. Remington-Style
Rolling-Block Carbine

E.M.F. 1866
Yellowboy Rifle

EAGLE ARMS EA-15 ACTION MASTER
Same specs as EA-15 except no sights, one-piece international-style upper receiver for scope mounting; solid aluminum handguard tube; free-floating 20-inch premium barrel; muzzle compensator; NM trigger group; weighs about 8-3/4 lbs. Renamed the 15A3 Action Master. Made in U.S. by Eagle Arms, Inc. Introduced 1991.

Perf.: $800   **Exc.:** $700   **VGood:** $500

EAGLE ARMS EA-15 EAGLE SPIRIT
Same specs as EA-15 rifle except 16-inch premium air-gauged barrel; weighs 8 lbs.; full-length tubular aluminum handguard; match accessories. Introduced 1993.

Perf.: $800   **Exc.:** $700   **VGood:** $500

EAGLE ARMS EA-15 GOLDEN EAGLE
Same specs as EA-15 except E2-style National Match rear sight with 1/2-MOA adjustments, elevation-adjustable NM front sight with set screw; 20-inch Douglas Premium extra-heavy match barrel with 1:9-inch twist; NM trigger group and bolt carrier group; weighs about 12-3/4 lbs. Made in U.S. by Eagle Arms, Inc. Introduced 1991.

Perf.: $800   **Exc.:** $700   **VGood:** $500

EAGLE ARMS EA-15A2 POST-BAN HEAVY BARREL
Same specs as EA-15 except 10-shot magazine; elevation-adjustable front sight; A2-style forward assist mechanism. Introduced 1995; no longer in production.

Perf.: $795   **Exc.:** $695   **VGood:** $595

EAGLE ARMS EA-15E2 CARBINE
Same specs as EA-15 except collapsible carbine-type buttstock; 16-inch heavy carbine barrel; M177-type flash supressor; weighs about 7-1/4 lbs. Made in U.S. by Eagle Arms, Inc. Introduced 1989; no longer in production.

Perf.: $795   **Exc.:** $695   **VGood:** $595

EAGLE ARMS EA-15E2 H-BAR
Same specs as EA-15 except 20-inch, slightly lighter and smaller heavy match barrel with 1:9-inch twist; weighs about 9 lbs. Made in U.S. by Eagle Arms, Inc. Introduced 1989; no longer in production.

Perf.: $895   **Exc.:** $795   **VGood:** $600

| With NM sights | | |
| **Perf.:** $1195 | **Exc.:** $995 | **VGood:** $725 |

EAGLE ARMS M15A3 POST-BAN PREDATOR
Semi-automatic; 223; 10-shot magazine; 18-inch, 1-1/4-inch diameter, stainless barrel with 1:8-inch twist; 34-3/8-inch overall length; weighs 9-1/4 lbs.; sights optional; one-piece international-style upper receiver; NM trigger; free-floating barrel; receiver hard-coat anodized; black composition stock; integral raised M16A2-type fence around magazine release button; A2-style forward assist. Made in U.S. by Eagle Arms, Inc. Introduced 1995.

Perf.: $800   **Exc.:** $700   **VGood:** $500

EAGLE ARMS EA-15A3 EAGLE EYE
Same specs as EA-15 except 24-inch, 1-1/4-inch diameter, stainless, air-gauged, free-floating heavy match barrel; weighted buttstock to counterbalance barrel; match-type hand-stop on handguard; 42-1/2-inch overall length; weighs about 13 lbs. Match sights

available on special order. Made in U.S. by Eagle Arms, Inc. Introduced 1994; no longer in production.

Perf.: $800   **Exc.:** $700   **VGood:** $500

EAGLE ARMS M15A3 S.P.R.
Same specs as M15A3 Predator except 18-inch barrel with 1:9-inch twist and front sight housing. Detachable carry handle. Made in U.S. by Eagle Arms, Inc. Introduced 1995; no longer produced.

Perf.: $1100   **Exc.:** $850   **VGood:** $595

E.M.F. 1860 HENRY
Lever action; 44-40, 44 rimfire; 24-1/4-inch barrel; 43-3/4-inch overall length; weighs about 9 lbs.; blade front sight, elevation-adjustable rear; oil-stained American walnut stock; reproduction of the original Henry rifle with brass frame and buttplate, rest blued. Imported by E.M.F.

Perf.: $895   **Exc.:** $695   **VGood:** $595

E.M.F. 1866 YELLOWBOY RIFLE
Lever action; 38 Spl., 44-40; 24-inch barrel; 43-inch overall length; weighs 9 lbs.; bead front sight, open adjustable rear; European walnut stock; solid brass frame; blued barrel, lever, hammer, buttplate. Imported from Italy by E.M.F.

Perf.: $795   **Exc.:** $695   **VGood:** $495

E.M.F. 1866 YELLOW BOY CARBINE
Same specs as 1866 Yellow Boy Rifle except 19-inch barrel; 38-inch overall length. Imported from Italy by E.M.F.

Perf.: $795   **Exc.:** $695   **VGood:** $495

E.M.F. MODEL 1873 RIFLE
Lever action; 357 Mag., 44-40, 45 Colt; 24-inch barrel; 43-1/4-inch overall length; weighs 8 lbs.; bead front sight, fully-adjustable rear; European walnut stock; color case-hardened frame. Imported by E.M.F.

Perf.: $950   **Exc.:** $850   **VGood:** $695

E.M.F. MODEL 1873 CARBINE
Same specs as Model 1873 Rifle except 19-inch barrel; blued frame. Imported by E.M.F.

Perf.: $950   **Exc.:** $850   **VGood:** $695

E.M.F. PREMIER MODEL 1873 CARBINE/RIFLE
Lever action; 45 Colt; 19-inch barrel (carbine), 24-1/2-inch barrel (rifle); 43-1/4-inch overall length; bead front, adjustable rear sight; uncheckered walnut stock, forearm; color case-hardened frame (rifle) or blued frame (carbine). Introduced 1988; discontinued 1989.

Rifle		
Perf.: $1000	**Exc.:** $950	**VGood:** $695
Carbine		
Perf.: $1000	**Exc.:** $950	**VGood:** $695

E.M.F. MODEL 1892 RIFLE
Lever action; 45 Colt, 44 Mag, 44-40, 357 Mag; 24-inch barrel, blued, round or octagon; case-colored frame. Introduced 1998.

Perf.: $500   **Exc.:** $425   **VGood:** $375

E.M.F MODEL 1892 CARBINE
Similar to Model 1892 rifle, except 20-inch barrel, carbine bands.

Perf.: $500   **Exc.:** $425   **VGood:** $375

E.M.F. REMINGTON-STYLE ROLLING-BLOCK RIFLE
Single shot; rolling block; 45-70; 30-inch octagon barrel; 46-1/2-inch OAL; weighs 11-3/4 lbs.; blade front, adjustable rear sights; walnut stock and forearm; color case-hardened receiver, brass trigger guard, buttplate and barrel band; blued barrel. Imported from Italy by E.M.F., still imported.

Perf.: $575   **Exc.:** $450   **VGood:** $350

E.M.F. REMINGTON-STYLE ROLLING-BLOCK CARBINE
Similar to Rolling-block rifle, except carbine with 26-inch barrel.

Perf.: $500   **Exc.:** $400   **VGood:** $300

E.M.F. SHARPS RIFLE

Single shot; falling block; 45-70; 28-inch octagonal barrel; weighs 10-3/4 lbs.; blade front sight, flip-up open rear; oiled walnut stock; color case-hardened lock; double-set trigger; blue finish. Replica of the 1874 Sharps Sporting rifle. Imported by E.M.F.

Perf.: $950   **Exc.:** $795   **VGood:** $695

With browned finish

Perf.: $975   **Exc.:** $825   **VGood:** $715

E.M.F. SHARPS CARBINE

Same specs as Sharps Rifle except has 22-inch round barrel; barrel band. Imported by E.M.F.

Perf.: $895   **Exc.:** $695   **VGood:** $595

E.M.F. TEXAS REMINGTON REVOLVING CARBINE

Single action; 22 LR; 6-shot cylinder; 21-inch barrel; 36-inch overall length; blade front sight, windage-adjustable rear; smooth walnut stock; brass frame, buttplate, trigger guard; blued cylinder, barrel. Made in Italy. Introduced 1991; no longer imported.

Perf.: $250   **Exc.:** $230   **VGood:** $190

ERMA EG72

Slide action; 22 LR; 15-shot magazine; 18-1/2-inch barrel; open rear sight, hooded ramp front; receiver grooved for scope mounts; straight hardwood stock; grooved slide handle; visible hammer. Made in Germany. Introduced 1970; discontinued 1976.

Perf.: $150   **Exc.:** $110   **VGood:** $90

ERMA EG73

Lever action; 22 WMR; 12-shot tube magazine; 18-1/2-inch barrel; open rear sight, hooded ramp front; receiver grooved for scope mount; European hardwood stock, forearm. Originally made in Germany. Introduced 1973; no longer in production.

Perf.: $200   **Exc.:** $160   **VGood:** $130

ERMA EG712

Lever action; 22 Short, 22 Long, 22 LR.; 21-shot (22 Short), 17-shot (22 Long), 15-shot (22 LR) tubular magazine; 18-1/2-inch barrel; open rear sight, hooded ramp front; carbine-style stock forearm of European hardwood, barrel band; receiver grooved for scope mount; near replica of Model 94 Winchester. Introduced 1976; no longer in production.

Perf.: $200   **Exc.:** $175   **VGood:** $150

ERMA MODEL EG712 L

Same specs as EG712 except European walnut stock; heavy octagon barrel; engraved, nickel silver finished receiver. Introduced 1978; no longer imported.

Perf.: $300   **Exc.:** $250   **VGood:** $200

ERMA EGM1

Semi-automatic; 22 LR; 5-shot magazine; 18-inch barrel; M-1-type sights with ramp front; receiver grooved for scope mounts; European walnut M-1 carbine-type stock; sling swivels; patterned after U.S. Cal. 30 M-1 Carbine. Introduced 1970; no longer imported.

Perf.: $190   **Exc.:** $160   **VGood:** $120

ERMA EM1

Semi-automatic; 22 LR; 10-, 15-shot magazine; 18-inch barrel; M1-type sights; receiver grooved for scope mounts; European walnut M1 Carbine-type stock; sling swivel in barrel band, oiler slot in stock; patterned after U.S. Cal. 30 M-1 Carbine. Introduced 1966; no longer imported.

Perf.: $265   **Exc.:** $245   **VGood:** $165

ERMA ESG22 CARBINE

Semi-automatic; 22 WMR; 5-, 12-shot magazine; 19-inch barrel; 38-inch overall length; military post front sight, adjustable peep rear; walnut stained beechwood stock; receiver grooved for scope mounts; gas-operated; styled after M-1 carbine. Made in Germany. Introduced 1978; no longer imported.

Perf.: $275   **Exc.:** $225   **VGood:** $175

Erma EG72

Erma EG712

Erma EM1

Fajen Acra S-24

Feather AT-9 Carbine

Feather AT-22 Carbine

FAJEN ACRA M-18

Bolt action; 270, 30-06, 243, 308, 284, 22-250, 6mm, 25-06, 7x57, 257 Roberts; 18-inch barrel; no sights; full-length Mannlicher-style stock; glass-bedded stock; rosewood pistol grip cap, forend tip; Santa Barbara Mauser action; recoil pad; blued finish. Introduced 1969; discontinued 1973.

Perf.: $595   **Exc.:** $495   **VGood:** $395

FAJEN ACRA RA

Bolt action; 270, 30-06, 243, 308, 284, 22-250, 6mm, 25-06, 7x57, 257 Roberts; 24-inch barrel; no sights; Monte Carlo stock of American walnut; glass-bedded stock; tenite buttplate, pistol-grip cap, forend tip; recoil pad; blued finish.

Perf.: $495   **Exc.:** $395   **VGood:** $325

FAJEN ACRA S-24

Bolt action; 270, 30-06, 243, 308, 284, 22-250, 6mm, 25-06, 7x57, 257 Roberts, 7mm Rem. Mag., 308 Norma Mag., 300 Win. Mag., 264 Win. Mag.; 24-inch barrel; no sights; checkered Monte Carlo stock of American walnut; recoil pad; glass-bedded stock; Santa Barbara Mauser action; blued finish; rosewood pistol-grip cap, forend tip. Introduced 1969; discontinued 1973.

Perf.: $495   **Exc.:** $420   **VGood:** $330

FAJEN ACRA VARMINT

Bolt action; 270, 30-06, 243, 308, 284, 22-250, 6mm, 25-06, 7x57, 257 Roberts, 7mm Rem. Mag., 308 Norma Mag., 300 Win. Mag., 264 Win. Mag.; 26-inch heavy barrel; no sights; checkered Monte Carlo stock of American walnut; glass-bedded stock; rosewood pistol grip cap, forend tip; recoil pad; blued finish. Introduced 1969; discontinued 1973.

Perf.: $495   **Exc.:** $395   **VGood:** $295

FEATHER AT-9 CARBINE

Semi-automatic; 9mm Para.; 17-inch barrel; 35-inch overall length (stock extended), 26-1/2-inch (stock closed); weighs 5 lbs.; hooded post front sight, adjustable aperture rear; telescoping wire stock, composition pistol grip; matte black finish. Made in U.S. by Feather Industries. Introduced 1988; no longer produced.

Perf.: $325   **Exc.:** $265   **VGood:** $200

FEATHER AT-22 CARBINE

Semi-automatic; 22 LR; 20-shot magazine; 17-inch barrel; 35-inch overall (stock extended), 26-inch (folded); weighs 3-1/4 lbs.; protected post front sight, adjustable aperture rear; telescoping wire stock, composition pistol grip; removable barrel; matte black finish. Made in U.S. by Feather Industries. Introduced 1986; still produced.

Perf.: $210   **Exc.:** $175   **VGood:** $130

Feather Model F9 Carbine

Federal Engineering XC222

Feinwerkbau Model 2000
Metallic Silhouette

Feinwerkbau Model 2000
Universal

FEATHER MODEL F2 CARBINE

Semi-automatic; 22 LR; 20-shot magazine; 17-inch barrel; 35-inch overall (stock extended); weighs 3-1/4 lbs.; protected post front sight, adjustable aperture rear; composition stock and pistol grip; removable barrel; matte black finish. Made in U.S. by Feather Industries. Introduced 1986; no longer produced.

Perf.: $240   **Exc.:** $200   **VGood:** $150

FEATHER MODEL F9 CARBINE

Semi-automatic; 9mm Para.; 17-inch barrel; 35-inch overall length; weighs 5 lbs.; hooded post front sight, adjustable aperture rear; composition stock and pistol grip; matte black finish. Made in U.S. by Feather Industries. Introduced 1988; no longer produced.

Perf.: $525   **Exc.:** $450   **VGood:** $325

FEDERAL ENGINEERING XC222

Semi-automatic; 22 LR; 30-shot magazine; 16-1/2-inch barrel with flash hider; 34-1/2-inch overall length; weighs 7-1/4 lbs.; hooded post front sight, Williams adjustable rear; sight bridge grooved for scope mounting; quick-detachable tube steel stock; quick takedown; all-steel Heli-arc welded construction; internal parts industrial hard chromed. Made in U.S. by Federal Engineering Corp. Introduced 1993; no longer produced.

Perf.: $380   **Exc.:** $320   **VGood:** $250

FEDERAL ENGINEERING XC450

Semi-automatic; 45 ACP; 16-shot magazine; 16-1/2-inch barrel with flash hider; 34-1/2-inch overall length; weighs 8 lbs.; hooded post front sight, Williams adjustable rear; sight bridge grooved for scope mounting; quick-detachable tube steel stock; quick takedown; all-steel Heli-arc welded construction; internal parts industrial hard chromed. Made in U.S.

by Federal Engineering Corp. Introduced 1984; dropped 1994.

Perf.: $650   **Exc.:** $535   **VGood:** $450

FEDERAL ENGINEERING XC900

Semi-automatic; 9mm Para.; 32-shot magazine; 16-1/2-inch barrel with flash hider; 34-1/2-inch overall length; weighs 8 lbs.; hooded post front sight, Williams adjustable rear; sight bridge grooved for scope mounting; quick-detachable tube steel stock; quick takedown; all-steel Heli-arc welded construction; internal parts industrial hard chromed. Made in U.S. by Federal Engineering Corp. Introduced 1984; dropped 1994.

Perf.: $550   **Exc.:** $435   **VGood:** $350

FEDERAL ORDNANCE M14SA TARGET

Semi-automatic; 7.62mm NATO; 20-shot magazine; 22-inch barrel; 48-inch overall length; weighs 9-1/2 lbs.; fully-adjustable G.I.-issue sights; fiberglass or wood stock; Parkerized metal finish. Civilian version of the M-14 service rifle. From Federal Ordnance. Introduced 1988; dropped 1992.

With fiberglass or black textured stock		
Perf.: $1050	**Exc.:** $825	**VGood:** $650
With walnut stock, forend		
Perf.: $1200	**Exc.:** $975	**VGood:** $795

FEDERAL ORDNANCE MODEL 713 MAUSER CARBINE, DELUXE GRADE

Semi-automatic; 7.63 Mauser, 9mm Para.; 10-, 20-shot detachable magazine; 16-inch barrel; weighs 5 lbs.; adjustable sights; deluxe walnut detachable stock. Introduced 1986; discontinued 1992.

Perf.: $1695   **Exc.:** $1250   **VGood:** $950

FEDERAL ORDNANCE MODEL 713 MAUSER CARBINE, FIELD GRADE

Same specs as Model 713 Mauser Carbine except 10-shot fixed magazine; walnut fixed stock. Introduced, 1987; discontinued 1992.

Perf.: $1050   **Exc.:** $795   **VGood:** $595

FEG SA-85M

Semi-automatic; AK STYLE; 7.62x39mm; 6-shot magazine; 16-3/8-inch barrel; 34-3/4-inch overall length; weighs 7-5/8 lbs.; hardwood handguard and thumbhole buttstock; cylindrical post front sight, fully-adjustable tangent rear; matte finish; chrome-lined barrel. Imported from Hungary by K.B.I., Inc. No longer imported.

Perf.: $695   **Exc.:** $545   **VGood:** $380

FEINWERKBAU MODEL 2000 MATCH

Bolt action; single shot; 22 LR; 26-1/4-inch barrel; 43-3/4-inch overall length; weighs 8-3/4 lbs.; micrometer match aperture rear sight, globe front with interchangeable inserts; standard walnut match stock; stippled pistol grip, forend; electronic or mechanical trigger. Made in Germany. Introduced 1979; discontinued 1988.

Perf.: $995   **Exc.:** $895   **VGood:** $695

With electronic trigger		
Perf.: $1250	**Exc.:** $1095	**VGood:** $895
Left-hand version		
Perf.: $1095	**Exc.:** $995	**VGood:** $795

FEINWERKBAU MODEL 2000 METALLIC SILHOUETTE

Bolt action; single-shot; 22 LR; 21-13/16-inch barrel; 39-inch overall length; weighs 6-1/2 lbs.; no sights; grooved for standard mounts; thumbhole walnut match stock; stippled pistol grip; fully-adjustable match trigger; heavy bull barrel. Made in Germany. Introduced 1985; no longer imported.

Perf.: $695   **Exc.:** $595   **VGood:** $450

| Left-hand version | | |
| **Perf.:** $725 | **Exc.:** $615 | **VGood:** $450 |

FEINWERKBAU MODEL 2000 MINI-MATCH

Bolt action; single shot; 22 LR; 22-inch barrel; walnut-stained birchwood match stock; stippled pistol grip; micrometer match aperture rear sight, globe front with interchangeable inserts; electronic or mechanical trigger. Made in Germany. Introduced 1979; discontinued 1988.

Perf.: $1000   **Exc.:** $750   **VGood:** $595

With electronic trigger		
Perf.: $1350	**Exc.:** $995	**VGood:** $695
Left-hand version		
Perf.: $1150	**Exc.:** $795	**VGood:** $595

FEINWERKBAU MODEL 2000 UNIVERSAL

Bolt action; single shot; 22 LR; 26-3/8-inch barrel; weighs 9-3/4 lbs.; standard walnut stock; stippled pistol grip, forend; micrometer match aperture rear sight, globe front with interchangeable inserts; electronic or mechanical trigger. Made in Germany. Introduced 1979; discontinued 1988.

Perf.: $1250   **Exc.:** $995   **VGood:** $795

With electronic trigger		
Perf.: $1400	**Exc.:** $1195	**VGood:** $1000
Left-hand version		
Perf.: $1300	**Exc.:** $1100	**VGood:** $900

FEINWERKBAU MODEL 2600 ULTRA FREE RIFLE

Bolt action; single-shot; 22 LR; 26-inch barrel; 40-7/16-inch overall length; weighs 14 lbs.; micrometer match aperture rear sight, globe front with interchangeable inserts; laminated wood thumbhole stock; electronic or mechanical trigger; accessory rails for movable weights; adjustable cheekpiece; hooked buttplate; right- or left-hand styles. Made in Germany. Introduced 1983; discontinued 1988.

Perf.: $1795   **Exc.:** $1295   **VGood:** $795

With electronic trigger
Perf.: $1995   **Exc.:** $1395   **VGood:** $1895

Left-hand version
Perf.: $1795   **Exc.:** $1395   **VGood:** $800

FEINWERKBAU MODEL 2600 UNIVERSAL

Single shot; 22 LR; 26-5/16-inch barrel; 43-3/4-inch overall length; weighs 10-1/2 lbs.; identical smallbore companion to the Model 600 air rifle; micrometer match aperture rear sight, globe front with interchangeable inserts; laminated European hardwood stock; free-floating barrel; match trigger with fingertip weight adjustment dial. Made in Germany. Introduced 1986; no longer imported.

Perf.: $1395   **Exc.:** $995   **VGood:** $750

Left-hand version
Perf.: $1495   **Exc.:** $995   **VGood:** $795

FERLACH CUSTOM DRILLING

Combination gun, drilling; Blitz action; various calibers/gauges; custom-built as to barrel length, sights, stock dimensions, wood; Greener crossbolt. Manufactured in Ferlach, Austria. Introduced 1976; no longer imported by Adler Arms of Pittsburgh. Because of the variety of grades and features, it is impossible to attribute used values. Have the rifle appraised by someone experienced and aware of quality in craftsmanship.

FERLACH DOUBLE RIFLE

Side-by-side or over/under; boxlock or sidelock; various calibers; any sighting combo desired; custom stocked; auto ejection. Introduced 1980; no longer imported by Adler Arms of Pittsburgh. Because of the variety of grades and features, it is impossible to attribute used values. Have the rifle appraised by someone experienced and aware of quality in craftsmanship.

F.I.E. GR-8 BLACK BEAUTY

Semi-automatic; 22 LR; 14-shot magazine; 19-1/2-inch barrel; 39-1/2-inch overall length; weighs 4 lbs.; adjustable open rear sight, band on ramp front; molded black nylon stock; checkered pistol grip, forend; top tang safety; receiver grooved for tip-off scope mounts. Similar to Remington Nylon 66 rifle. Made in Brazil. Introduced 1984; discontinued 1988.

Perf.: $190   **Exc.:** $170   **VGood:** $160

F.I.E. MODEL 122

Bolt action; 22 Short, 22 Long, 22 LR; 6- or 10-shot magazine; 21-inch barrel; 39-inch overall length; weighs 5-1/2 lbs.; fully-adjustable open rear sight, blade front; receiver grooved for scope mounts; Monte Carlo walnut stock; sliding wing safety lever; double extractors; red cocking indicator. Made in Brazil. Introduced 1986; discontinued 1988.

Perf.: $100   **Exc.:** $75   **VGood:** $65

F.I.E. MODEL 322

Bolt action; 22 Short, 22 Long, 22 LR; 6-, 10-shot magazine; 26-1/2-inch barrel; weighs 7 lbs.; adjustable sights; checkered wood stock; adjustable trigger. Introduced 1990; discontinued 1990.

Perf.: $475   **Exc.:** $350   **VGood:** $265

F.I.E. MODEL 422

Bolt action; 22 Short, 22 Long, 22 LR; 6-, 10-shot magazine; 26-1/2-inch heavy barrel; weighs 9 lbs.; adjustable sights; checkered wood stock; adjustable trigger. Introduced 1990; discontinued 1990.

Perf.: $475   **Exc.:** $375   **VGood:** $285

F.I.E./FRANCHI PARA CARBINE

Semi-automatic; 22 LR; 11-shot magazine; 19-inch barrel; 39-1/4-inch overall length; weighs 4-3/4 lbs.; open adjustable rear sight, hooded front; takedown; receiver grooved for scope mounts; magazine feeds through skeleton stock. Marketed in fitted carrying case. Made in Italy. Introduced 1986; discontinued 1988.

Perf.: $210   **Exc.:** $170   **VGood:** $120

Feinwerkbau Model 2600
Ultra Free Rifle

Feinwerkbau
Model 2600 Universal

Ferlach
Custom Drilling

Ferlach Double Rifle

F.I.E. GR-8
Black Beauty

F.I.E. Model 122

Finnish Lion
Champion Model

Finnish Lion
ISU Target Model

FINNISH LION CHAMPION MODEL

Bolt action; single shot; 22 LR; 28-3/4-inch barrel; free rifle design; extension-type rear peep sight, aperture front; European walnut stock; full pistol grip; beavertail forearm; thumbhole, palm rest, hand stop; hooked buttplate. Introduced 1965; discontinued 1972.

Perf.: $700   **Exc.:** $600   **VGood:** $500

FINNISH LION ISU TARGET MODEL

Bolt action; single shot; 22 LR; 27-1/2-inch barrel; extension-type rear peep sight, aperture front; European walnut target-design stock; hand-checkered beavertail forearm; full pistol grip; adjustable buttplate; swivel. Manufactured in Finland. Introduced 1966; discontinued 1977.

Perf.: $400   **Exc.:** $300   **VGood:** $250

Finnish Lion Match Model

Finnish Lion Standard Target Model

F.N. Deluxe Mauser

F.N. Supreme Mauser

Fox Model FB-1

FINNISH LION MATCH MODEL

Bolt action; single shot; 22 LR; 29-inch barrel; weight 14.3 lbs; extension-type rear peep sight, aperture front; European walnut free rifle-type stock; full pistol grip; beavertail forearm; thumbhole, palm rest, hand stop; hooked buttplate, swivel. Introduced 1937; discontinued 1972.

Perf.: $595   **Exc.:** $495   **VGood:** $395

FINNISH LION STANDARD TARGET MODEL

Bolt action; single shot; 22 LR; 27-5/8-inch barrel; 44-9/16-inch overall length; weighs 10-1/2 lbs.; aperture sights; French walnut target stock; adjustable trigger; many accessories available. Made in Finland. Introduced 1978; imported by Mandall Shooting Supplies.

Perf.: $675   **Exc.:** $575   **VGood:** $410

F.N. DELUXE MAUSER

Bolt action; 220 Swift, 243 Win., 244 Rem., 257 Roberts, 250-3000, 270 Win., 7mm, 300 Savage, 308 Win., 30-06, 8mm, 9.3x62, 9.5x57, 10.75x68; 5-shot box magazine; 24-inch barrel; Tri-range rear, hooded ramp front sight; hand-checkered European walnut stock; pistol-grip; cheekpiece; sling swivels. Manufactured in Belgium. Introduced 1947; discontinued 1963.

Exc.: $700   **VGood:** $500   **Good:** $400

F.N. DELUXE MAUSER, PRESENTATION GRADE

Same specs as Deluxe Mauser except engraved receiver, trigger guard, barrel breech, floorplate; select walnut stock. Introduced 1947; discontinued 1963.

Exc.: $995   **VGood:** $875   **Good:** $650

F.N. SUPREME MAUSER

Bolt action; 243 Win., 270 Win., 7mm, 308 Win., 30-06; 5-shot magazine, 4-shot (243 and 308); 22-inch barrel; Tri-range rear, hooded ramp front sight; hand-checkered European walnut stock; pistol grip; Monte Carlo cheekpiece, sling swivels. Introduced 1957; discontinued 1975.

Exc.: $750   **VGood:** $650   **Good:** $520

F.N. SUPREME MAUSER, MAGNUM MODEL

Same specs as Supreme Mauser except 264 Win. Mag., 7mm Rem. Mag., 300 Win. Mag.; 3-shot magazine. Introduced 1957; discontinued 1973.

Perf.: $800   **Exc.:** $695   **VGood:** $575

FOX MODEL FB-1

Bolt action; 22 LR; 5-shot clip; 24-inch barrel; 43-inch overall length; hooded ramp front, adjustable open rear sight; select walnut stock; palm swell grip, roll-over cheekpiece; rosewood pistol grip cap, forend tip; receiver grooved for tipoff scope mount; also drilled, tapped; double extractors. Marketed by Savage Arms. Introduced 1981; discontinued 1983.

Perf.: $250   **Exc.:** $175   **VGood:** $130

FRANCOTTE, AUGUSTE

Francotte rifles are custom made to the customer's specifications. Because of the individuality of rifles encountered used, values will fluctuate greatly within models. Options such as engraving, inlays, sights, wood and caliber will determine each rifle's worth. An individual expert appraisal is recommended. Priced new from $15,000 to $40,000. Used values range from 50 percent to 75 percent of new pricing.

FRANCOTTE BOXLOCK DOUBLE

Side-by-side; 243, 270, 30-06, 7x64, 7x65R, 8x57JRS, 9.3x74R, 375 H&H, 470 N.E.; 23-1/2-inch-26-inch barrel lengths; bead front sight on ramp, quarter-rib with fixed V rear; primarily custom-built gun; oil-finished European walnut stock; checkered butt; double triggers; manual safety; floating firing pins; gas-vent safety screws; coin finish or color case-hardening; English scroll engraving; numerous options. Made in Belgium. Still imported by Armes de Chasse.

FRANCOTTE CARPATHE MOUNTAIN

Single shot; 243, 270, 308, 30-06, 7x65R, 7x57R, 5.6x52R, 5.6x57R, 6.5x57R. 6.5x68R, 7mm Rem. Mag., 300 Win. Mag.; 23-1/2-inch-26-inch barrel; no sights furnished; scope mount extra; deluxe walnut

stock to customer specs; oil finish, fine checkering; boxlock or sidelock action with third fastener, extractor, manual safety; splinter forend. Many options available. Imported from Belgium by Armes de Chasse. No longer imported.

FRANCOTTE RIMAG

Bolt action; 358 Norma Mag., 375 H&H, 378 Wea. Mag., 404 Jeffery, 416 Rigby, 450 Watts, 460 Wea. Mag., 458 Win. Mag., 505 Gibbs, others on request; heavy round barrel, 23-5/8-inch to 26-inch; weighs 9 to 10 lbs.; ring-mounted front sight blade, fixed leaf rear; deluxe European walnut stock to customer specifications, oil finish, steel grip cap; A. Francotte Rimag action with three-position safety, round or square bridge. Imported from Belgium by Armes de Chasse. No longer imported.

FRANCOTTE SIDELOCK DOUBLE

Side-by-side; 243, 7x64, 7x65R, 8x57JRS, 270, 30-06, 9.3x74R, 375 H&H, 470 N.E.; 23-1/2-inch to 26-inch barrel lengths; weighs 7-5/8 lbs. (medium calibers), 11 lbs. (magnums); bead front sight on ramp, leaf rear on quarter-rib; hand-checkered, oil-finished European walnut stock; back-action sidelocks; double trigger, with hinged front trigger; auto or free safety; numerous options; largely a custom-built gun. Made in Belgium. Still imported by Armes de Chasse.

GALIL SPORTER

Semi-automatic; 223, 308; 5-shot magazine; 16-1/8-inch barrel (223), 18-1/2-inch (308); 40-1/2-inch overall length (223); weighs 8-3/4 lbs.; hardwood thumbhole stock; hooded post front, flip-type adjustable rear sight; black-finished wood and metal. Imported by Action Arms Ltd. Introduced 1991; discontinued 1993.

Perf.: $1000   **Exc.:** $850   **VGood:** $710

GAMBA BAYERN 88

Combo; boxlock over/under; 2-3/4-inch 12 ga. over 5.6x50R, 5.6x57R, 6.5x57R, 7x57R, 7x65R, 222 Rem. Mag., 243, 270, 30-06; 24-1/2-inch barrels; modified choke; weighs 7-1/2 lbs.; folding leaf rear sight, bead front on ramp; checkered European walnut stock; double-set trigger; case-hardened receiver; game, floral scene engraving; extractors; solid barrel rib. Made in Italy. Introduced 1987; no longer imported.

Perf.: $1395   **Exc.:** $995   **VGood:** $795

GAMBA MUSTANG

Single shot; sidelock; 5.6x50, 5.6x57R, 6.5x57R, 7x65R, 222 Rem. Mag., 243, 270, 30-06; 25-1/2-inch barrel; weighs 6-1/4 lbs.; leaf rear sight, bead on ramp front; hand-checkered, oil-finished figured European walnut stock; double-set trigger; silvered receiver; Renaissance engraving signed by engraver; claw-type scope mounts. Made in Italy. Introduced 1987; no longer in production.

Perf.: $10,500   **Exc.:** $8950   **VGood:** $6500

GAMBA RGZ 1000

Bolt action; 270, 7x64, 7mm Rem. Mag., 300 Win. Mag.; 20-1/2-inch barrel; weighs 7 lbs.; open notch ramp rear sight bead front; Monte Carlo-style European walnut stock; modified 98K Mauser action; single trigger. Introduced 1987; discontinued 1988.

Perf.: $1100   **Exc.:** $900   **VGood:** $720

GAMBA RGZ 1000 GAME

Same specs as RGZ 1000 except 23-3/4-inch barrel; 7-3/4 lbs.; double-set trigger.

Perf.: $1195   **Exc.:** $995   **VGood:** $795

GAMBA SAFARI EXPRESS

Double rifle; boxlock side-by-side; 7x65R, 9.3x74R, 375 H&H Mag.; 25-inch barrels; weighs about 10 lbs.; leaf rear sight, bead on ramp front; checkered select European walnut stock; cheekpiece; rubber recoil pad; triple Greener locking system; auto ejectors; double-set triggers; engraved floral, game scenes. Made in Italy. Introduced 1987; no longer imported.

Perf.: $5500   **Exc.:** $4250   **VGood:** $2595

GARBI EXPRESS DOUBLE RIFLE

Double rifle; 7x65R, 9.3x74R, 375 H&H. 24-3/4-inch barrel; weighs 7-3/4 to 8-1/2 lbs. 41-1/2-inch overall. Turkish walnut stock. Quarter-rib with express sight. Side-by-side double; H&H-pattern sidelock ejector with reinforced action, chopper lump barrels of Boehler steel; double triggers; fine scroll and rosette engraving, or full coverage ornamental; coin-finished action. Introduced 1997. Imported from Spain by Wm. Larkin Moore.

Perf.: $19,000   **Exc.:** $16,000   **VGood:** $12,000

GARCIA MUSKETEER

Bolt action; 243, 264, 270, 30-06, 308 Win., 308 Norma Mag., 7mm Rem. Mag., 300 Win. Mag.; 3-shot magazine (magnums), 5-shot (standard calibers); 44-1/2-inch overall length; Williams Guide open rear, hooded ramp front sight; checkered walnut Monte Carlo stock, pistol grip; FN Mauser Supreme action; adjustable trigger; sliding thumb safety; hinged floorplate. Introduced 1970; discontinued 1972.

Perf.: $595   **Exc.:** $495   **VGood:** $375

GARRETT ARMS ROLLING BLOCK

Single shot; 45-70; 30-inch octagon barrel; 48-inch overall length; weighs 9 lbs.; ladder-type tang sight, open folding rear on barrel, hooded globe front; European walnut stock; reproduction of Remington rolling block long-range sporter. Made in Italy. Introduced 1987; no longer imported.

Perf.: $595   **Exc.:** $475   **VGood:** $350

GEVARM E-1 AUTOLOADING

Semi-automatic; blowback; 22 LR; 10-shot magazine; 19-inch barrel; open sights; walnut stock, pistol grip; blued finish. No longer in production.

Exc.: $450   **VGood:** $340   **Good:** $275

GEVARM MODEL A2

Semi-automatic; blowback; 22 LR; 8-shot clip magazine; 21-1/2-inch barrel; takedown; tangent rear, hooded globe front sight; uncheckered walnut stock; schnabel forearm; no firing pin (as such) or extractor; fires from open bolt; ridge on bolt face offers twin ignition. Imported by Tradewinds, Inc. Introduced 1958; discontinued 1963.

Exc.: $550   **VGood:** $495   **Good:** $375

GOLDEN EAGLE MODEL 7000 GRADE I

Bolt action; 22-250, 243 Win., 25-06, 270 Win., 270 Weatherby Mag., 7mm Rem. Mag., 30-06, 300 Weatherby Mag., 300 Win. Mag., 338 Win. Mag.; 3-shot magazine, 4-shot (22-250); 24-inch, 26-inch barrel; no sights; checkered American walnut stock; contrasting grip cap; forend tip; golden eagle head inset in grip cap; recoil pad. Made in Japan. Introduced 1976; discontinued 1979.

Perf.: $610   **Exc.:** $495   **VGood:** $385

GOLDEN EAGLE MODEL 7000 GRADE I, AFRICAN

Same specs as Model 7000 Grade I except 375 H&H Mag., 458 Win. Mag.; open sights. Introduced 1976; discontinued 1979.

Perf.: $670   **Exc.:** $565   **VGood:** $450

GOLDEN EAGLE MODEL 7000 GRADE II

Bolt action; 22-250, 243 Win., 25-06, 270 Win., 270 Weatherby Mag., 300 Win. Mag., 338 Win. Mag.; 3-shot magazine, 4-shot (22-250); 24-inch, 26-inch barrel; no sights; best grade checkered American walnut stock, contrasting grip cap, forend tip, golden eagle head inset in grip cap; recoil pad; carrying case. Made in Japan. Introduced 1976; discontinued 1979.

Perf.: $695   **Exc.:** $595   **VGood:** $425

GREIFELT DRILLING

Combination gun; drilling; 12-, 16-, 20-, 28-ga., .410 over any standard rifle caliber; 24-inch, 26-inch

barrels; folding rear sight; matted rib; auto or non-auto ejectors. Manufactured prior to WWII.

Exc.: $3400   **VGood:** $2500   **Good:** $2000

Obsolete calibers

Exc.: $2500   **VGood:** $2200   **Good:** $1800

GREIFELT SPORT MODEL

Bolt action; 22 Hornet; 5-shot box magazine; 22-inch barrel; two-leaf rear, ramp front sight; hand-checkered European walnut stock; pistol grip. Made in Germany prior to World War II.

Perf.: $495   **Exc.:** $395   **VGood:** $295

GRENDEL R-31 CARBINE

Semi-automatic; 22 WMR; 30-shot magazine; 16-inch barrel; 23-1/2-inch overall length (stock collapsed); weighs 4 lbs.; fully-adjustable post front sight, aperture rear; telescoping tube stock, Zytel forend; blowback action with fluted chamber; ambidextrous safety; steel receiver; matte black finish; muzzlebrake. Scope mount optional. Made in U.S. by Grendel, Inc. Introduced 1991; discontinued 1994.

Perf.: $295   **Exc.:** $220   **VGood:** $180

GRENDEL SRT-20F COMPACT RIFLE

Bolt action; 243, 308 Win.; 9-shot magazine; 20-inch, fluted, unfluted barrel; weighs 6 5/8 lbs.; no sights; integral scope bases; muzzlebrake; folding fiberglass-reinforced Zytel stock; built on Sako A-2 action. Introduced 1987; discontinued 1990.

Perf.: $535   **Exc.:** $455   **VGood:** $350

With 24-inch barrel (SRT -24)

Perf.: $570   **Exc.:** $475   **VGood:** $375

HAENEL '88 MAUSER SPORTER

Bolt action; 7x57, 8x57, 9x57mm; 5-shot Mauser box magazine; 22-inch, 24-inch barrel, half or full octagon; leaf open rear, ramp front sight; hand-checkered European walnut sporting stock, cheekpiece, schnabel tip, pistol grip; raised matted rib; action based on Model '88 Mauser; double-set trigger; sling swivels. Manufactured in Germany prior to WWII.

Perf.: $800   **Exc.:** $675   **VGood:** $400

Garcia Musketeer

Golden Eagle Model 7000 Grade 1

Grendel R-31 Carbine

Hammerli Model 45 Match

HAENEL MAUSER MANNLICHER

Bolt action; 7x57, 8x57, 9x57mm; 5-shot Mannlicher-type box magazine; 22-inch, 24-inch barrel, half or full octagon; leaf open rear sight, ramp front; hand-checkered European walnut sporting stock, cheekpiece, schnabel tip, pistol grip; raised matted rib; action based on Model '88 Mauser; double-set trigger; sling swivels. Manufactured in Germany prior to WWII.

Perf.: $800   **Exc.:** $675   **VGood:** $400

HAENEL MODEL 900 MATCH

Bolt action; single shot; 22 LR; 25-15/16-inch barrel; 44-1/2-inch overall length; weighs 10-1/2 lbs.; match-type globe front sight, fully-adjustable aperture rear; sight radius adjustable from 31-inch to 32-1/2-inch; match-type beech stock with stippled grip and forend; adjustable comb and buttpad; adjustable trigger; polished blue finish. Imported from Germany by GSI, Inc. Introduced 1992; discontinued 1993.

Perf.: $695   **Exc.:** $550   **VGood:** $425

HAMMERLI MODEL 45 MATCH

Bolt action; single shot; 22 LR; 27-1/2-inch barrel; micrometer peep rear sight, blade front; free-rifle stock with full pistol grip, thumbhole, cheekpiece; palm rest, beavertail forearm; Swiss-type buttplate; sling swivels. Introduced 1945; discontinued 1957.

Exc.: $725   **VGood:** $610   **Good:** $500

HAMMERLI MODEL 54 MATCH

Bolt action; single shot; 22 LR; 27-1/2-inch barrel; micrometer peep rear, globe front sight; European walnut free-rifle stock; cheekpiece; adjustable hook buttplate; palm rest; thumbhole; swivel. Introduced 1954; discontinued 1957.

Exc.: $760   **VGood:** $640   **Good:** $550

HAMMERLI MODEL 503 FREE RIFLE

Bolt action; single shot; 22 LR; 27-1/2-inch barrel; micrometer rear, globe front sight; European walnut free-rifle stock; cheekpiece; adjustable hook buttplate; palm rest; thumbhole; swivel. Introduced 1957; discontinued 1962.

Exc.: $700   **VGood:** $580   **Good:** $510

Hammerli Model 503
Free Rifle

Hammerli Model 506
Match

Hammerli 1954 22
Match

Hammerli-Tanner 300 Meter

Harrington & Richardson
Model 60 Reising

Harrington & Richardson
Model 361

Harrington & Richardson
Model 700 Deluxe

HAMMERLI MODEL 505 MATCH

Bolt action; single shot; 22 LR; 27-1/2-inch barrel; aperture rear, globe front sight; European walnut free-rifle stock; cheekpiece; palm rest; thumbhole. Introduced 1957; discontinued 1962.

    Exc.: $695   **VGood:** $550   **Good:** $450

HAMMERLI MODEL 506 MATCH

Bolt action; single shot; 22 LR; 26-3/4-inch barrel; micrometer peep rear, globe front sight; European walnut free-rifle stock; cheekpiece; adjustable hook buttplate; palm rest; thumbhole; swivel. Introduced 1963; discontinued 1966.

    Exc.: $695   **VGood:** $600   **Good:** $550

HAMMERLI MODEL 1954 22 MATCH

Bolt action; single shot; 22 LR; 27-1/2-inch barrel; weighs 15 lbs.; double locking lugs; adjustable trigger, 5 to 16 oz.; hooded front sight, micrometer

peep rear; sling; palm rest; Swiss buttplate. Imported by H. Grieder.

    Exc.: $695   **VGood:** $575   **Good:** $480

HAMMERLI MODEL OLYMPIA

Bolt action; single shot; 6.5x55 and 7.5mm (Europe), 30-06 and 300 H&H Mag. (U.S.); other calibers on special order; 29-1/2-inch heavy barrel; designed for 300-meter event; micrometer peep rear, hooded front sight; double-pull or double-set trigger; free-type rifle stock with full pistol grip, thumbhole; cheekpiece; palm rest; beavertail forearm; swivels; Swiss-type buttplate. Imported by H. Grieder. Introduced 1949; discontinued 1962.

    Exc.: $895   **VGood:** $750   **Good:** $595

HAMMERLI-TANNER 300 METER

Bolt action; single shot; 7.5mm Swiss and other centerfires on request; 29-1/2-inch barrel; micrometer peep rear, globe front sight; uncheckered European walnut free-rifle stock; cheekpiece; adjustable hook buttplate; thumbhole; palm rest; swivel.

Manufactured in Switzerland. Introduced 1962; no longer in production.

    Exc.: $895   **VGood:** $795   **Good:** $630

HARRINGTON & RICHARDSON MODEL 60 REISING

Semi-automatic; 45 ACP; 12-, 20-shot detachable box magazine; 18-1/4-inch barrel; open rear, blade front sight; uncheckered hardwood pistol-grip stock. Introduced 1944; discontinued 1946. Some collector value.

    Exc.: $1900   **VGood:** $1600   **Good:** $1100

HARRINGTON & RICHARDSON MODEL 65

Semi-automatic; 22 LR; 10-shot detachable box magazine; 23-inch barrel; rear peep, blade front sight; uncheckered hardwood pistol-grip stock; used as training rifle by the Marine Corps in WWII; same general dimensions as M-1 Garand. Introduced 1944; discontinued 1946.

    Exc.: $295   **VGood:** $240   **Good:** $190

HARRINGTON & RICHARDSON MODEL 150

Semi-automatic; 22 LR; 5-shot detachable box magazine; 22-inch barrel; 42-inch overall length; weighs 7-1/4 lbs.; marble open rear, blade front sight on ramp; oil-finished uncheckered pistol-grip stock; cocking lever under forend; side safety; clip ejector. Introduced 1949; discontinued 1953.

    Exc.: $90   **VGood:** $70   **Good:** $55

HARRINGTON & RICHARDSON MODEL 151

Semi-automatic; 22 LR; 5-shot detachable box magazine; 22-inch barrel; 42-inch-inch overall length; weighs 7-1/4 lbs.; Redfield No. 70 peep rear sight. Introduced 1949; discontinued 1953.

    Exc.: $100   **VGood:** $80   **Good:** $60

HARRINGTON & RICHARDSON MODEL 165

Semi-automatic; 22 LR; 10-shot detachable box magazine; 23-inch barrel; Redfield No. 70 rear peep sight, blade front on ramp; uncheckered hardwood pistol-grip stock; sling swivels; web sling. Called the Leatherneck Model, it was a variation of Model 65 military autoloader used to train Marines in basic marksmanship during WWII. Introduced 1945; discontinued 1961.

    Exc.: $250   **VGood:** $200   **Good:** $150

HARRINGTON & RICHARDSON MODEL 360

Semi-automatic; gas operated; 243 Win., 308 Win.; 3-shot detachable box magazine; 22-inch barrel; 43-1/2-inch overall length; weighs 7-1/2 lbs.; open adjustable rear, gold bead front sight; one-piece American walnut hand-checkered stock; roll-over cheekpiece, full pistol grip; exotic wood pistol-grip cap, forearm tip; sling swivels. Introduced 1967; discontinued 1973.

    Exc.: $365   **VGood:** $310   **Good:** $240

HARRINGTON & RICHARDSON MODEL 361

Semi-automatic; gas operated; 243 Win., 308 Win.; 3-shot detachable box magazine; 22-inch barrel; open adjustable rear, gold bead front sight; hand-checkered walnut stock; full roll-over cheekpiece, full pistol grip; exotic wood pistol-grip cap, forearm tip; sling swivels. Introduced 1970; discontinued 1973.

    Exc.: $400   **VGood:** $340   **Good:** $280

HARRINGTON & RICHARDSON MODEL 700

Semi-automatic; 22 WMR; 5-, 10-shot magazine; 22-inch barrel; 43-1/4-inch overall length; weighs 6-1/2 lbs.; folding leaf rear, blade front sight on ramp; American walnut Monte Carlo stock with full pistol grip; composition buttplate. Introduced 1977; discontinued 1985.

    Exc.: $315   **VGood:** $265   **Good:** $180

HARRINGTON & RICHARDSON MODEL 700 DELUXE

Same specs as Model 700 except walnut stock with cheekpiece; checkered grip, forend; rubber recoil pad; no sights; marketed with H&R Model 432 4X scope, base and rings. Introduced 1979; discontinued 1985.

Exc.: $345   **VGood:** $300   **Good:** $190

HARRINGTON & RICHARDSON MODEL 755

"Semi-automatic"; single shot with automatic ejection; 22 LR, 22 Long, 22 Short; 22-inch barrel; open rear, military front sight; hardwood Mannlicher-type stock. Advertised as the Sahara Model. Introduced 1963; discontinued 1971. Some collector interest.

Exc.: $170   **VGood:** $140   **Good:** $100

HARRINGTON & RICHARDSON MODEL 760

"Semi-automatic"; Single shot with automatic ejection; 22 LR, 22 Long, 22 Short; 22-inch barrel; open rear, military front sight; hardwood sporter stock. Introduced 1965; discontinued 1970.

Exc.: $100   **VGood:** $90   **Good:** $70

HARRINGTON & RICHARDSON MODEL 800

Semi-automatic; 22 LR; 5-, 10-shot clip-type magazine; 22-inch barrel; open rear, bead ramp front sight; uncheckered walnut pistol-grip stock; solid frame; side thumb safety. Introduced 1958; discontinued 1960.

Exc.: $100   **VGood:** $80   **Good:** $60

HARRINGTON & RICHARDSON MODEL 058

Single shot; 30-30, 22 Hornet; 22-inch barrel; 37-1/2-inch overall length; weighs 6 lbs.; blade front sight; folding leaf rear; walnut finished hardwood stock; rubber buttplate.

Exc.: $195   **VGood:** $145   **Good:** $110

HARRINGTON & RICHARDSON MODEL 155 SHIKARI

Single shot; 44 Rem. Mag., 45-70; 24-inch (44, 45-70), 28-inch (45-70) barrel; 39-inch (24-inch barrel), 43-inch (28-inch barrel) overall length; weighs 7 lbs. (24-inch); adjustable folding leaf rear, blade front sight; uncheckered straight-grip walnut-finished hardwood stock forearm; blue-black finish with color case-hardened frame; barrel band; built on Model 158 action; brass cleaning rod. Introduced 1972; discontinued 1982.

Exc.: $325   **VGood:** $295   **Good:** $215

HARRINGTON & RICHARDSON MODEL 157

Single shot; 22 Hornet; 30-30; 22-inch barrel; 37-inch overall length; weighs 6-1/2 lbs.; adjustable folding leaf rear, ramp-mounted blade front sight; uncheckered walnut-finished hardwood pistol-grip buttstock; full-length forearm; drilled and tapped for scope mounts; sling swivels; built on Model 158 action. Introduced 1976; discontinued 1985.

Exc.: $195   **VGood:** $150   **Good:** $100

HARRINGTON & RICHARDSON MODEL 158 TOPPER

Single shot; 22 Jet, 22 Hornet, 30-30, 357 Mag., 44 Mag.; 22-inch interchangeable barrels; 37-1/2-inch overall length; weighs 5-1/4 lbs.; shotgun-type action; Lyman folding adjustable open rear sight; ramp front; visible hammer; side lever; automatic ejector; uncheckered walnut pistol-grip stock, forearm; recoil pad. Introduced 1963; no longer in production.

Exc.: $195   **VGood:** $150   **Good:** $100

HARRINGTON & RICHARDSON MODEL 158 MUSTANG

Same specs as Model 158 Topper except 30-30 only; fitted with 26-inch 20-ga. barrel as accessory. Introduced 1968; discontinued 1985.

Exc.: $210   **VGood:** $195   **Good:** $110

Harrington & Richardson Model 800

Harrington & Richardson Model 158 Topper Jet

Harrington & Richardson Model 171 Deluxe

Harrington & Richardson Model 258 Handy Gun II

HARRINGTON & RICHARDSON MODEL 158 TOPPER JET

Same specs as Model 158 Topper except 22 Rem. Jet; interchangeable with 20-ga., 410-bore, 30-30 barrels. Introduced 1963; discontinued 1967.

Exc.: $260   **VGood:** $240   **Good:** $200

30-30 barrel, combo
Exc.: $275   **VGood:** $255   **Good:** $215

20-ga. barrel, combo
Exc.: $275   **VGood:** $255   **Good:** $215

410 barrel, combo
Exc.: $275   **VGood:** $255   **Good:** $215

HARRINGTON & RICHARDSON MODEL 163

Single shot; break open action; 22 Hornet, 30-30, 357 Mag., 44 Mag.; 22-inch barrel; visible hammer; side lever; automatic ejector; straight-grip stock, contoured forearm; gold-plated hammer, trigger. Introduced 1964; discontinued 1967.

Exc.: $195   **VGood:** $150   **Good:** $100

HARRINGTON & RICHARDSON MODEL 164

Single shot; break open action; 22 Hornet, 30-30, 357 Mag., 44 Mag.; 22-inch barrel; visible hammer; side lever; automatic ejector; straight-grip uncheckered walnut stock; contoured forearm; gold-plated hammer, trigger. Introduced 1964; discontinued 1967.

Exc.: $195   **VGood:** $150   **Good:** $100

HARRINGTON & RICHARDSON MODEL 171

Single shot; trap door action; 45-70; 22-inch barrel; 41-inch overall length; weighs 7 lbs.; open fully-adjustable rear, blade front sight; uncheckered American walnut stock. Replica of Model 1873 Springfield cavalry carbine. Introduced 1972; discontinued 1985.

Exc.: $525   **VGood:** $475   **Good:** $395

HARRINGTON & RICHARDSON MODEL 171 DELUXE

Same specs as Model 171 except folding leaf rear sight; engraved breechblock, side lock, hammer. Introduced 1972; discontinued 1985.

Exc.: $675   **VGood:** $575   **Good:** $495

HARRINGTON & RICHARDSON MODEL 172

Single shot; trapdoor action; 45-70; 22-inch barrel; 41-inch overall length; weighs 7 lbs.; tang-mounted aperture sight; fancy checkered walnut stock; silver-plated hardware. Introduced 1972; discontinued 1977.

Exc.: $695   **VGood:** $595   **Good:** $475

HARRINGTON & RICHARDSON MODEL 173

Single shot; trapdoor action; 45-70; 26-inch barrel; 44-inch overall length; weighs 8 lbs.; Vernier tang rear, blade front sight; engraved breechblock receiver, hammer, barrel band, lock, buttplate; checkered walnut stock; ramrod. Replica of Model 1873 Springfield Officers Model. Introduced 1972; discontinued 1977.

Exc.: $695   **VGood:** $595   **Good:** $495

HARRINGTON & RICHARDSON MODEL 178

Single shot; trapdoor action; 45-70; 32-inch barrel; 52-inch overall length; weighs 8 5/8 lbs.; leaf rear, blade front sight; uncheckered full-length walnut stock; barrel bands, sling swivels, ramrod. Replica of Model 1873 Springfield Infantry Rifle. Introduced 1973; discontinued 1975.

Exc.: $350   **VGood:** $250   **Good:** $205

HARRINGTON & RICHARDSON MODEL 258 HANDY GUN II

Single shot; 22 Hornet, 30-30, 357 Mag., 357 Maximum, 44 Mag., 20-ga. 3-inch; 22-inch barrel; 37-inch overall length; weighs 6-1/2 lbs.; interchangeable rifle/shotgun barrels; ramp blade front, adjustable folding leaf rear sight; bead front sight on shotgun barrel; walnut-finished American hardwood stock; electroless matte nickel finish. Introduced 1982; discontinued 1985.

Exc.: $180   **VGood:** $150   **Good:** $120

HARRINGTON & RICHARDSON MODEL 422

Slide-action; 22 LR, 22 Long, 22 Short; 24-inch barrel; 15-shot (22 LR), 17-shot (22 Long), 21-shot (22 Short) tube magazine; open rear, ramp front sight; uncheckered walnut pistol-grip stock; grooved slide handle. Introduced 1952; discontinued 1958.

Exc.: $125   **VGood:** $100   **Good:** $70

HARRINGTON & RICHARDSON MODEL 424

Single shot; 22 Short, 22 Long, 22 LR; 24-inch barrel; open rear, blade front sight; manual cocking action; uncheckered American walnut stock. Introduced 1960; discontinued 1961. Some collector value.

Exc.: $100   **VGood:** $75   **Good:** $45

HARRINGTON & RICHARDSON MODEL 749

Pump action; 22 Short, 22 Long, 22 LR; 18-shot (22 Short), 15-shot (22 Long), 13-shot (22 LR) tube magazine; 19-inch barrel; 35-1/2-inch overall length; weighs 4 5/8 lbs.; dovetail blade front, adjustable rear sight; positive ejection; walnut-finished American hardwood stock, contoured forend. Introduced 1971; discontinued 1971.

Exc.: $150   **VGood:** $125   **Good:** $90

Harrington & Richardson Model 422

Harrington & Richardson Model 424

Harrington & Richardson Ultra Varmint

Harringtron & Richardson Ultra Comp Rifle

Harrington & Richardson Buffalo Classic

H&R Synthetic Handi-Rifle

H&R Synthetic Handi-Rifle with Iron Sights

H&R Superlite Synthetic Handi-Rifle/Slug Gun Combo

H&R Sportster

H&R HANDI SUPRLITE Compact Scope

HARRINGTON & RICHARDSON ULTRA HEAVY BARREL 22 MAG RIFLE

Single shot, breakopen; 22 WMR. 22-inch bull barrel. Cinnamon laminated wood stock with Monte Carlo cheekpiece; no sights furnished; scope mount rail included. Hand-checkered stock and forend; deep-crown rifling; tuned trigger; trigger locking system; hammer extension. Introduced 2001. From H&R 1871 LLC.

Perf.: $200   **Exc.:** $150   **VGood:** $120

HARRINGTON & RICHARDSON ULTRA HUNTER

Single shot; 223, 243, 25-06, 270, 308 Win., 450 Marlin; 26-inch (25-06), 24-inch (223 and 243), 22-inch (308 and 450 Marlin) barrel; weighs about 7-1/2 lbs.; no sights furnished; drilled, tapped for scope mounting; cinnamon-colored laminate stock and forend; hand-checkered grip and forend; break-open

action with side-lever release; positive ejection; comes with scope mount; swivel studs; blued receiver and barrel. From H&R 1871, Inc. Introduced 1995; still produced. Premium for 450 Marlin.

Perf.: $200   **Exc.:** $150   **VGood:** $110

HARRINGTON & RICHARDSON ULTRA VARMINT

Single shot; 204 Ruger, 223 Rem., 22-250; 22-inch heavy barrel; weighs about 7-1/2 lbs.; no sights; drilled, tapped for scope mounting; hand-checkered laminated birch stock with Monte Carlo comb; break-open action with side-lever release; positive ejection; comes with scope mount; swivel studs; blued receiver and barrel. From H&R 1971, Inc. Introduced 1993.

Perf.: $210   **Exc.:** $150   **VGood:** $110

HARRINGTON & RICHARDSON ULTRA COMP RIFLE

Similar to Ultra Varmint except chambered for 270 or

30-06; compensator to reduce recoil; camo-laminate stock and forend; blued, highly polished frame; scope mount. Made in U.S.A. by H&R 1871, LLC, no longer offered.

Perf.: $300   **Exc.:** $260   **VGood:** $210

HARRINGTON & RICHARDSON BUFFALO CLASSIC

This model, chambered in .38-55 Winchester or .45-70, employs a 28" heavy target barrel and original style rifling for consistent accuracy. It has a Williams receiver sight, and a Lyman target front sight with eight aperture inserts. Premium for special edition.

Perf.: $395   **Exc.:** $350   **VGood:** $310

HARRINGTON & RICHARDSON CR CARBINE

Single-shot rifle based on the Handi-Rifle design. Two-piece checkered walnut stock with schnabel forend. Marble's front and rear sights, crescent steel buttplate. Chambered in .45 Colt.

NIB: $400   **Exc.:** $365   **VGood:** $300

HARRINGTON & RICHARDSON SYNTHETIC HANDI-RIFLE

Basic Handi-Rifle design but with synthetic buttstock and forend (eather grooved or beavertail). Available with iron sights or picatinny rail for mounting optics.

NIB: $375   **Exc.:** $300   **VGood:** $215

HARRINGTON & RICHARDSON STAINLESS HANDI-RIFLE

Similar to above but with stainless barrel. Chambered in .223, .270 or .30-06.

NIB: $385   **Exc.:** $315   **VGood:** $225

HARRINGTON & RICHARDSON SYNTHETIC HANDI-RIFLE/SLUG GUN COMBO

Similar to above but with extra slug barrel. Available in .44 Mag/12 ga. and .357 Magnum/20 ga. Introduced in 2008.

NIB: $375   **Exc.:** $300   **VGood:** $215

HARRINGTON & RICHARDSON SUPERLITE HANDI-RIFLE COMPACT

Similar to Synthetic Handi-Rifle but weighs only 5.5 lbs. Chambered in .223 and .243. Alao available with optional scope. Values shown are for scoped model.

NIB: $395   **Exc.:** $325   **VGood:** $225

HARRINGTON & RICHARDSON SPORTSTER

A .22 LR or .22 WMR version of the Handi-Rifle with black polymer stock, flued forend and iron sights. Overall length 36-1/4 inches.

NIB: $175   **Exc.:** $145   **VGood:** $100

HARRINGTON & RICHARDSON MODEL 250

Bolt action; 22 LR; 5-, 10-shot detachable box magazine; 23-inch barrel; 40-inch overall length; weighs 6-1/2 lbs.; open rear sight, blade front on ramp; uncheckered oil-finished walnut pistol-grip stock. Advertised as the Sportster Model. Introduced 1948; discontinued 1961.

Exc.: $110   **VGood:** $90   **Good:** $70

HARRINGTON & RICHARDSON MODEL 251

Bolt action; 22 LR; 5-shot detachable box magazine; 22-inch barrel; Lyman No. 55H rear sight, blade front on ramp; uncheckered hardwood pistol-grip stock. Introduced 1948; discontinued 1961.

Exc.: $130   **VGood:** $100   **Good:** $80

HARRINGTON & RICHARDSON MODEL 265

Bolt action; 22 LR; 5-, 10-shot detachable box magazine; 22-inch barrel; 40-inch overall length; weighs 6-3/4 lbs.; Lyman No. 17A rear peep sight, blade front on ramp; uncheckered hardwood pistol-grip stock; spring-type bolt release; thumb-operated safety. Called the Reg'lar Model in advertising. Introduced 1946; discontinued 1949.

Exc.: $100   **VGood:** $75   **Good:** $50

HARRINGTON & RICHARDSON MODEL 265 TARGETEER JR.

Same specs as Model 265 except 20-inch barrel; 36-3/4-inch overall length; weighs 7 lbs.; Redfield No. 70 rear peep sight, Lyman No. 17A front; shorter youth uncheckered walnut pistol-grip stock; sling swivels; web sling. Introduced 1948; discontinued 1951.

Exc.: $165   **VGood:** $135   **Good:** $100

HARRINGTON & RICHARDSON MODEL 300 ULTRA

Bolt action; 22-250, 243 Win., 270 Win., 30-06, 308 Win., 300 Win. Mag., 7mm Rem. Mag.; 3-shot magazine (magnums), 5-shot (others); 22-inch, 24-inch barrel; FN Mauser action; with or without open rear sight, ramp front; hand-checkered American walnut stock; cheekpiece, full pistol grip; pistol-grip cap, forearm tip of contrasting exotic wood; rubber buttplate, sling swivels. Introduced 1965; discontinued 1978.

Exc.: $370   **VGood:** $295   **Good:** $250

HARRINGTON & RICHARDSON MODEL 301 ULTRA

Bolt action; 243 Win., 270 Win., 30-06, 308 Win., 300 Win. Mag., 7mm Rem. Mag.; 3-shot magazine (magnums), 5-shot (others); 18-inch barrel; FN Mauser action; with or without open rear sight, ramp front; Mannlicher-style stock; cheekpiece; full pistol grip; pistol-grip cap; metal forearm tip; rubber buttplate, sling swivels. Introduced 1978; discontinued 1978.

Exc.: $375   **VGood:** $300   **Good:** $250

HARRINGTON & RICHARDSON MODEL 317 ULTRA

Bolt action; 17 Rem., 222 Rem., 223 Rem., 17/223 handloads; 6-shot magazine; 20-inch tapered barrel; no sights; receiver dovetailed for scope mounts. Advertised as the Ultra Wildcat. Introduced 1966; discontinued 1976.

Exc.: $430   **VGood:** $350   **Good:** $290

HARRINGTON & RICHARDSON MODEL 317P ULTRA

Same specs as Ultra Model 317 except better grade of walnut; basketweave checkering. Discontinued 1976.

Exc.: $495   **VGood:** $395   **Good:** $320

HARRINGTON & RICHARDSON MODEL 330

Bolt action; 243, 270, 30-06, 308, 7mm Rem., 300 Win.; 22-inch tapered round barrel; 42-1/2-inch overall length; 7-1/8 lbs.; gold bead on ramp front sight, fully-adjustable rear; walnut hand-checkered stock with Monte Carlo; hinged floorplate; adjustable trigger; sliding side safety; receiver tapped for scope mounts. Introduced 1972; no longer in production.

Exc.: $395   **VGood:** $295   **Good:** $200

HARRINGTON & RICHARDSON MODEL 333

Bolt action; 30-06, 7mm Rem. Mag.; 22-inch barrel; 42-1/2-inch overall length; weighs 7-3/4 lbs.; no sights; walnut finished hardwood stock; adjustable trigger; Sako barrel and action; sliding thumb safety.

Exc.: $280   **VGood:** $210   **Good:** $180

HARRINGTON & RICHARDSON MODEL 340

Bolt action; 243, 7x57, 308, 270, 30-06; 5-shot; 22-inch barrel; 43-inch overall length; weighs 7-1/4 lbs.; no sights; drilled and tapped for scope mounts; American walnut stock; hand-checkered pistol grip, forend; carved, beaded cheekpiece; grip cap; recoil pad; Mauser-design action; hinged steel floorplate; adjustable trigger; high-luster blued finish. Introduced 1983; discontinued 1984.

Exc.: $395   **VGood:** $350   **Good:** $300

HARRINGTON & RICHARDSON MODEL 365

Bolt action; single shot; 22 LR; 22-inch barrel; Lyman No. 55 rear peep sight, blade front on ramp;

Harrington & Richardson Ultra Model 300

Harrington & Richardson Ultra Model 317

Harrington & Richardson Ultra Model 317P

Harrington & Richardson Model 330

Harrington & Richardson Model 340

Harrington & Richardson Ultra Model 370

Harrington & Richardson Model 465

uncheckered hardwood pistol-grip stock. Called the Ace in advertising. Introduced 1946; discontinued 1947.

Perf.: $110   **Exc.:** $90   **VGood:** $60

HARRINGTON & RICHARDSON MODEL 370 ULTRA

Bolt action; 22-250, 243 Win., 6mm Rem.; 24-inch heavy target/varmint barrel; built on Sako action; no sights; tapped for open sights and/or scope mounts; uncheckered, oil-finished walnut stock; roll-over comb; adjustable trigger; recoil pad; sling swivels. Advertised as Ultra Medalist. Introduced 1967; discontinued 1974.

Exc.: $375   **VGood:** $325   **Good:** $275

HARRINGTON & RICHARDSON MODEL 450

Bolt action; 22 LR; 5-, 10-shot detachable box magazine; 26-inch barrel; no sights; uncheckered American walnut target stock with full pistol grip, thick forend; scope bases; sling swivels, sling. Introduced 1948; discontinued 1961.

Exc.: $100   **VGood:** $80   **Good:** $65

HARRINGTON & RICHARDSON MODEL 451

Bolt action; 22 LR; 5-, 10-shot detachable box magazine; 26-inch barrel; Lyman 524F extension rear sight, Lyman No. 77 front sight; crowned muzzle; uncheckered American walnut stock with full pistol grip, thick forend; scope bases; sling swivels; sling. Introduced 1948; discontinued 1961.

Exc.: $175   **VGood:** $150   **Good:** $120

HARRINGTON & RICHARDSON MODEL 465

Bolt action; 22 LR; 10-shot detachable box magazine; 25-inch barrel; Lyman No. 57 rear peep sight, blade front on ramp; uncheckered walnut pistol-grip stock; sling swivels; web sling. Advertised as Targeteer Special. Introduced 1946; discontinued 1947.

Exc.: $160   **VGood:** $140   **Good:** $100

HARRINGTON & RICHARDSON MODEL 750

Bolt action; single shot; 22 LR, 22 Long, 22 Short; 22-inch (early), 24-inch barrel; 39-inch overall length; weighs 5 lbs.; open rear, blade front sight; double extractors; uncheckered walnut finished Monte

Harrington & Richardson
Model 750

Harrington & Richardson
Model 765

Harrington & Richardson
Model 865

Harrington & Richardson
Model 5200 Match

Harris-McMillan Antietam Sharps

Harris-McMillan Long Range Rifle

Harris-McMillan M-86 Sniper

mounts; oil-finish walnut (early), walnut-finished American hardwood stock with Monte Carlo pistol grip; sliding side safety; cocking indicator. Introduced 1949; discontinued 1985.

Exc.: $90   **VGood:** $80   **Good:** $65

HARRINGTON & RICHARDSON MODEL 866

Bolt action; 22 Short, 22 Long, 22 LR; 5-shot clip magazine; 22-inch round tapered barrel; 39-inch overall length; weighs 5 lbs.; blade front, step-adjustable open rear sight; receiver grooved for tip-off scope mounts; Mannlicher stock with Monte Carlo pistol grip; sliding side safety; cocking indicator. Introduced 1971; discontinued 1971.

Exc.: $120   **VGood:** $100   **Good:** $80

HARRINGTON & RICHARDSON MODEL 5200 SPORTER

Bolt action; single shot; 22 LR; 24-inch barrel; 42-inch overall length; weighs 6-1/2 lbs.; hooded ramp front sight; fully-adjustable Lyman peep rear; classic American walnut stock with hand cut checkering; rubber buttplate; adjustable trigger; drilled and tapped for scope mounts.

Exc.: $325   **VGood:** $270   **Good:** $210

HARRINGTON & RICHARDSON MODEL 5200 MATCH

Same specs as Model 5200 Sporter except 28-inch barrel; 46-inch overall length; weighs 11 lbs.; drilled, tapped for sights, scope; target-style American walnut stock; full-length accessory rail; rubber buttpad, palm stop; fully-adjustable trigger; dual extractors; polished blue-black metal finish. Introduced 1981; discontinued 1985.

Exc.: $420   **VGood:** $375   **Good:** $315

HARRIS-MCMILLAN ANTIETAM SHARPS

Falling block; single shot; 40-65, 45-75; 30-inch, 32-inch octagon or round barrel; 47-inch overall length; weighs 11-1/4 lbs.; hand-lapped stainless or chrome-moly barrel; Montana Vintage Arms #111 Low Profile Spirit Level front sight, #108 mid-range tang rear with windage adjustments; choice of straight grip, pistol grip or Creedmoor-style stock; schnabel forend; pewter tip optional; standard A Fancy wood, higher grades available; recreation of the 1874 Sharps sidehammer; action color case-hardened; barrel satin black; chrome-moly barrel optionally blued; optional sights include #112 Spirit Level Globe front with windage, #107 Long Range rear with windage. All parts and components made in U.S. by Harris Gunworks, Inc. Introduced 1994.

Perf.: $2300   **Exc.:** $2000   **VGood:** $1450

HARRIS-MCMILLAN LONG RANGE RIFLE

Bolt action; single shot; 300 Win. Mag., 7mm Rem. Mag., 300 Phoenix, 338 Lapua; 26-inch stainless steel match-grade barrel; 46-1/2-inch overall length; weighs 14 lbs.; barrel band and Tompkins front sight; no rear sight furnished; fiberglass stock with adjustable buttplate and cheekpiece; adjustable for length of pull, drop, cant and cast-off; solid bottom single shot action and Canjar trigger; barrel twist of 1:12-inch. All parts and components made in U.S. by Harris Gunworks, Inc. Introduced 1989.

Perf.: $3200   **Exc.:** $2750   **VGood:** $1600

HARRIS-MCMILLAN M-86 SNIPER

Bolt action; 308, 30-06, 300 Win. Mag.; 4-shot (308, 30-06), 3-shot (300 Win. Mag.) magazine; 24-inch McMillan match-grade barrel in heavy contour; 43-1/2-inch overall length; weighs 11-1/4 lbs. (308), 11-1/2 lbs. (30-06, 300); no sights; specially designed fiberglass stock with textured grip and forend, recoil pad; repeating action; comes with bipod; matte black finish; sling swivels. All parts and components made in U.S. by Harris Gunworks, Inc. Introduced 1989.

Perf.: $2500   **Exc.:** $2100   **VGood:** $1850

Takedown model

Perf.: $2200   **Exc.:** $1900   **VGood:** $1350

Carlo hardwood stock with pistol grip; feed ramp. Introduced 1954; no longer in production.

Exc.: $100   **VGood:** $80   **Good:** $55

HARRINGTON & RICHARDSON MODEL 751

Bolt action; single shot; 22 LR, 22 Long, 22 Short; 24-inch barrel; open rear, bead front sight; double extractors; Mannlicher stock; feed ramp. Introduced 1971; discontinued 1971.

Exc.: $125   **VGood:** $100   **Good:** $70

HARRINGTON & RICHARDSON MODEL 765

Bolt action; single shot; 22 LR, 22 Long, 22 Short; 24-inch barrel; 41-inch overall length; adjustable open rear sight, Red Devil hooded bead front;

uncheckered oil-finished walnut or hardwood pistol-grip stock. Introduced 1948; discontinued 1954.

Exc.: $95   **VGood:** $70   **Good:** $50

HARRINGTON & RICHARDSON MODEL 852

Bolt action; 22 LR, 22 Long, 22 Short; 24-inch barrel; 15-shot (22 LR), 17-shot (22 Long), 21-shot (22 Short) tube magazine; open rear, bead front sight; uncheckered pistol-grip hardwood stock. Introduced 1952; discontinued 1953.

Exc.: $100   **VGood:** $90   **Good:** $70

HARRINGTON & RICHARDSON MODEL 865

Bolt action; 22 Short, 22 Long, 22 LR; 5-shot clip magazine; 24-inch (early), 22-inch round tapered barrel; 40-1/2-inch overall length; weighs 5 lbs.; "Cottontail" bead (early), blade front, step-adjustable open rear sight; receiver grooved for tip-off scope

HARRIS-MCMILLAN M-87

Bolt action; single shot; 50 BMG; 29-inch barrel, with muzzlebrake; 53-inch overall length; weighs 21-1/2 lbs.; no sights; fiberglass stock; stainless steel receiver; chrome-moly barrel with 1:15-inch twist. All parts and components made in U.S. by Harris Gunworks, Inc. Introduced 1987; still in production.

Perf.: $3250   **Exc.:** $2800   **VGood:** $2000

HARRIS-MCMILLAN M-87R

Same specs as M-87 except 5-shot repeater. All parts and components made in U.S. by Harris Gunworks, Inc. Introduced 1990; still produced.

Perf.: $3795   **Exc.:** $3100   **VGood:** $2230

HARRIS-MCMILLAN M-89 SNIPER

Bolt action; 308 Win.; 5-shot magazine; 28-inch barrel with suppressor; weighs 15-1/4 lbs.; no sights; fiberglass stock adjustable for length; recoil pad; drilled and tapped for scope mounting; repeating action; comes with bipod. All parts and components made in U.S. by Harris Gunworks, Inc. Introduced 1990.

Perf.: $2700   **Exc.:** $2100   **VGood:** $1650

HARRIS-MCMILLAN M-92 BULLPUP

Bolt action; single shot; 50 BMG; bullpup barrel, with muzzlebrake; no sights; fiberglass bullpup stock; stainless steel receiver; chrome-moly barrel with 1:15-inch twist as on M87. All parts and components made in U.S. by Harris Gunworks, Inc. Introduced 1993.

Perf.: $4000   **Exc.:** $3200   **VGood:** $2100

HARRIS-MCMILLAN M-93

Bolt action; 50 BMG; 5-, 10-shot magazine; 29-inch barrel, with muzzlebrake; 53-inch overall length; weighs about 21-1/2 lbs.; no sights; folding fiberglass stock; right-handed stainless steel receiver; chrome-moly barrel with 1:15-inch twist. All parts and components made in U.S. by Harris Gunworks, Inc. Introduced 1987.

Perf.: $3995   **Exc.:** $3450   **VGood:** $2350

HARRIS-MCMILLAN NATIONAL MATCH

Bolt action; 7mm-08, 308; 5-shot magazine; 24-inch stainless steel barrel; 43-inch overall length; weighs about 11 lbs.; barrel band and Tompkins front sight, no rear sight; modified ISU fiberglass stock with adjustable buttplate; McMillan repeating action with clip slot, Canjar trigger; match-grade barrel. Fibergrain stock, sight installation, special machining and triggers optional. All parts and components made in U.S. by Harris Gunworks, Inc. Introduced 1989.

Perf.: $3200   **Exc.:** $2700   **VGood:** $2000

HARRIS-MCMILLAN SIGNATURE CLASSIC SPORTER

Bolt action; 22-250, 243, 6mm Rem., 7mm-08, 284, 308 (short action); 25-06, 270, 280 Rem., 30-06, 7mm Rem. Mag., 300 Win. Mag., 300 Wea. (long action); 338 Win. Mag., 340 Wea., 375 H&H (magnum); 4-shot magazine (standard calibers), 3-shot (magnums); 22-inch, 24-inch, 26-inch barrel; weighs about 7 lbs. (short action); no sights; fiberglass stock in green, beige, brown or black; recoil pad and 1-inch swivels installed; length of pull up to 14-1/4-inch; comes with 1-inch rings and bases; right- or left-hand action with matte black finish; aluminum floorplate. Fibergrain and wood stocks optional. All parts and components made in U.S. by Harris Gunworks, Inc. Introduced 1987; still produced.

Perf.: $2500   **Exc.:** $2150   **VGood:** $1500

HARRIS-MCMILLAN SIGNATURE ALASKAN

Same specs as Classic Sporter except 270, 280 Rem., 30-06, 7mm Rem. Mag., 300 Win. Mag., 300 Wea., 338 Win. Mag., 340 Wea., 375 H&H; match-grade barrel with single leaf rear sight, barrel band front; 1-inch detachable rings and mounts; steel floorplate;

electroless nickel finish; wood Monte Carlo stock with cheekpiece; palm swell grip; solid buttpad. All parts and components made in U.S. by Harris Gunworks, Inc. Introduced 1989.

Perf.: $3525   **Exc.:** $3000   **VGood:** $2100

HARRIS-MCMILLAN SIGNATURE CLASSIC STAINLESS SPORTER

Same specs as Classic Sporter except addition of 416 Rem. Mag.; barrel and action made of stainless steel; fiberglass stock; right- or left-hand action in natural stainless, glass bead or black chrome sulfide finishes. All parts and components made in U.S. by Harris Gunworks, Inc. Introduced 1990; still produced.

Perf.: $2700   **Exc.:** $2250   **VGood:** $1600

HARRIS-MCMILLAN SIGNATURE SUPER VARMINTER

Same specs as Classic Sporter except 223, 22-250, 220 Swift, 243, 6mm Rem., 25-06, 7mm-08, 7mm BR, 308, 350 Rem. Mag.; heavy-contour barrel; adjustable trigger; field bipod and special hand-bedded fiberglass stock; comes with 1-inch rings and bases. Fibergrain optional. All parts and components made in U.S. by Harris Gunworks, Inc. Introduced 1989.

Perf.: $2495   **Exc.:** $1995   **VGood:** $1395

HARRIS-MCMILLAN SIGNATURE TITANIUM MOUNTAIN RIFLE

Same specs as Classic Sporter except 270, 280 Rem., 30-06, 7mm Rem. Mag., 300 Win. Mag.; weighs 5-1/2 lbs.; action of titanium alloy; barrel of chrome-moly steel; graphite reinforced fiberglass stock. Fibergrain stock optional. All parts and components made in U.S. by Harris Gunworks, Inc. Introduced 1989; still produced. Premium for graphite-steel composite light weight barrel.

Perf.: $3000   **Exc.:** $2450   **VGood:** $1795

HARRIS GUNWORKS SIGNATURE VARMINTER

Similar to Signature Classic Sporter except has heavy contoured barrel, adjustable trigger, field bipod and special hand-bedded fiberglass stock. Chambered

for 223, 22-250, 220 Swift, 243, 6mm Rem., 25-06, 7mm-08, 7mm BR, 308, 350 Rem. Mag. Comes with 1-inch rings and bases. Introduced 1989.

Perf.: $2500   **Exc.:** $2000   **VGood:** $1400

HARRIS-MCMILLAN TALON SAFARI

Bolt action; 300 Win. Mag., 300 Wea. Mag., 300 Phoenix, 338 Win. Mag., 30-378, 338 Lapua, 300 H&H, 340 Wea. Mag., 375 H&H, 404 Jeffery, 416 Rem. Mag., 458 Win. Mag. (Safari Magnum); 378 Wea. Mag., 416 Rigby, 416 Wea. Mag., 460 Wea. Mag. (Safari Super Magnum); 24-inch match grade barrel; 43-inch overall length; weighs about 9-10 lbs.; barrel band front ramp sight, multi-leaf express rear; McMillan Safari action; fiberglass Safari stock; quick-detachable 1-inch scope mounts; positive locking steel floorplate; barrel band sling swivel; matte black finish standard. All parts and components made in U.S. by Harris Gunworks, Inc. Introduced 1989.

Perf.: $3200   **Exc.:** $2600   **VGood:** $2100

Talon Safari Super Magnum

Perf.: $3700   **Exc.:** $3200   **VGood:** $2600

HARRIS-MCMILLAN TALON SPORTER

Bolt action; 22-250, 243, 6mm Rem., 6mm BR, 7mm BR, 7mm-08, 25-06, 270, 280 Rem., 284, 308, 30-06, 350 Rem. Mag. (Long Action); 7mm Rem. Mag., 7mm STW, 300 Win. Mag., 300 Wea. Mag., 300 H&H, 338 Win. Mag., 340 Wea. Mag., 375 H&H, 416 Rem. Mag.; 24-inch barrel; no sights; weighs about 7-1/2 lbs.; choice of walnut or fiberglass stock; comes with rings and bases; uses pre-'64 Model 70-type action with cone breech, controlled feed, claw extractor and three-position safety; barrel and action of stainless steel; open sights optional and chrome-moly optional. All parts and components made in U.S. by Harris Gunworks, Inc. Introduced 1991.

Perf.: $2700   **Exc.:** $2295   **VGood:** $1710

HECKLER & KOCH HK91 A-2

Semi-automatic; 308 Win.; 5-, 20-shot detachable box magazine; 17-3/4-inch barrel; weighs 9-3/4 lbs.;

Harris-McMillan Signature Alaskan

Harris Gunworks Signature Titanium Mountain

Harris Gunworks Signature Varminter

Harris-McMillan Talon Safari

Heckler & Koch HK91 A-2

Heckler & Koch HK93 A-2

Heckler & Koch HK94 A-2

Heckler & Koch HK300

Heckler & Koch HK770

Heckler & Koch PSG-1 Marksman

Heckler & Koch SLB 2000 Rifle

V and aperture rear sight, post front; plastic buttstock forearm; delayed roller-lock blowback action. Introduced 1976; discontinued 1989. Imported for law enforcement sales only.

Perf.: $2700   **Exc.:** $2300   **VGood:** $1900

HECKLER & KOCH HK91 A-3
Same specs as HK91 A-2 except collapsible metal buttstock. Introduced 1976; discontinued 1989. Imported for law enforcement sales only.

Perf.: $3000   **Exc.:** $2600   **VGood:** $2100

HECKLER & KOCH HK93 A-2
Semi-automatic; 223 Rem.; 25-shot magazine; 16-1/8-inch barrel; weighs 8 lbs.; V and aperture rear sight, post front; plastic buttstock, forearm; delayed roller-lock blowback action. Introduced 1976; discontinued 1989. Imported for law enforcement sales only.

Perf.: $2950   **Exc.:** $2500   **VGood:** $2100

HECKLER & KOCH HK93 A-3
Same specs as HK93 A-2 except collapsible metal buttstock. Introduced 1976; discontinued 1989. Imported for law enforcement sales only.

Perf.: $3100   **Exc.:** $2650   **VGood:** $2250

HECKLER & KOCH HK94 A-2
Semi-automatic; 9mm Para.; 15-shot magazine; 16-inch barrel; 34-3/4-inch overall length; weighs 6-1/2 lbs. (fixed stock); hooded post front sight, fully-adjustable aperture rear; high-impact plastic butt and forend or retractable metal stock; delayed roller-locked action; accepts H&K quick-detachable scope mount. Imported from Germany by Heckler & Koch, Inc. Introduced 1983; discontinued 1994.

Perf.: $3800   **Exc.:** $3500   **VGood:** $3100

HECKLER & KOCH HK94 A-3
Same specs as HK94 A-2 except retractable metal stock. Imported from Germany by Heckler & Koch, Inc. Introduced 1983; discontinued 1994.

Perf.: $4100   **Exc.:** $3800   **VGood:** $3400

HECKLER & KOCH HK270
Semi-automatic; 22 LR; 5-, 20-shot magazine; 19-3/4-inch barrel; 38-1/4-inch overall length; weighs 5-3/4 lbs.; post front sight, fully-adjustable diopter rear; uncheckered European walnut cheekpiece stock; integral H&K scope mounts. Manufactured in Germany. Introduced 1977; discontinued 1985.

Perf.: $570   **Exc.:** $480   **VGood:** $410

HECKLER & KOCH HK300
Semi-automatic; 22 WMR; 5-, 15-shot detachable box magazine; 19-3/4-inch barrel; post windage-

adjustable front, adjustable V-notch rear; hand-checkered European walnut Monte Carlo stock with cheekpiece; checkered pistol grip and schnabel forend integral H&K scope mounts. Manufactured in Germany. Introduced 1977; discontinued 1989.

Perf.: $875   **Exc.:** $650   **VGood:** $525

HECKLER & KOCH HK630
Semi-automatic; 223; 4-, 10-shot magazine; 17-3/4-inch barrel; weighs 7 lbs.; V-notch rear, ramp front sight; European walnut stock with checkered forend, pistol grip; magazine catch at front of trigger guard; receiver dovetailed to accept clamp-type scope. Discontinued 1986.

Perf.: $1000   **Exc.:** $850   **VGood:** $650

HECKLER & KOCH HK770
Semi-automatic; 308 Win.; 3-, 10-shot magazine; 19-1/2-inch barrel; weighs 8 lbs.; vertically-adjustable blade front, open fold-down windage-adjustable rear sight; checkered European walnut pistol-grip stock; polygonal rifling; delayed roller-locked bolt system; receiver top dovetailed for clamp-type scope mount. Imported from Germany. Introduced 1976; discontinued 1986.

Perf.: $1450   **Exc.:** $1200   **VGood:** $800

HECKLER & KOCH HK940
Semi-automatic; 30-06; 3-, 10-shot magazine; 21-1/2-inch barrel; weighs 8-3/8 lbs.; vertically-adjustable blade front, open fold-down windage-adjustable rear sight; checkered European walnut pistol-grip stock; polygonal rifling; delayed roller-locked bolt system; receiver top dovetailed for clamp-type scope mount. Imported from Germany. Discontinued 1986.

Perf.: $1450   **Exc.:** $1200   **VGood:** $800

HECKLER & KOCH HK940K
Same specs as HK940 except 16-inch barrel; fuller cheekpiece. Introduced 1984; discontinued 1984.

Perf.: $1400   **Exc.:** $1100   **VGood:** $900

HECKLER & KOCH PSG-1 MARKSMAN
Semi-automatic; 308 Win.; 5-, 20-shot magazines; 25-1/2-inch heavy barrel; 47-1/2-inch overall length; weighs 17-1/2 lbs.; no iron sights; 6x42 Hensoldt scope; matte black high-impact plastic stock adjustable for length; pivoting buttcap; adjustable cheekpiece; target-type pistol grip, palm shelf; built on H&K 91 action; T-way rail for tripod, sling swivel. Made in Germany. Introduced 1986; no longer imported.

Perf.: $6250   **Exc.:** $5750   **VGood:** $4000

HECKLER & KOCH SLB 2000 RIFLE
Semi-automatic; 30-06; 2-, 5- and 10-shot magazines. 19.7-inch barrel; weighs 8 lb.; 41.3-inch long; Oil-finished, checkered walnut stock; Ramp front, Patridge notch rear sights; Short-stroke, piston-actuated gas operation; modular steel and polymer construction; free-floating barrel; pistol grip angled for natural feel. Introduced 2001. From H&K.

Perf.: $900   **Exc.:** $800   **VGood:** $650

HECKLER & KOCH SL6
Semi-automatic; 223 Rem.; 4-shot magazine; 17-1/2-inch barrel; weighs 8-3/8 lbs.; adjustable aperture rear, hooded post-front sight; oil-finished European walnut stock; polygonal rifling; delayed roller-locked action; dovetailed for quick-detachable scope mount. Made in Germany. Introduced 1983; discontinued 1986.

Perf.: $1300   **Exc.:** $1200   **VGood:** $950

HECKLER & KOCH SL7
Semi-automatic; 308 Win.; 3-shot magazine; 17-1/2-inch barrel; 39-3/4-inch overall length; weighs 8-3/8 lbs.; adjustable aperture rear, hooded post-front sight; oil-finished European walnut stock; polygon rifling; delayed roller-locked action; dovetailed for H&K quick-detachable scope mount. Made in Germany. Introduced 1983; no longer imported by H&K.

Perf.: $1300   **Exc.:** $1200   **VGood:** $950

HECKLER & KOCH SL8-1 RIFLE

Semi-automatic; 223; 10-shot magazine. 17.7-inch barrel; weighs 8.6 lbs.; 38.6-inch overall length; Polymer thumbhole stock; Blade front sight with integral hood; fully adjustable rear diopter. Picatinny rail. Based on German military G36 rifle. Uses short-stroke piston-actuated gas operation; almost entirely constructed of carbon fiber-reinforced polymer. Free-floating heavy target barrel. Introduced 2000, no longer available from H&K.

Perf.: $1800   **Exc.:** $1450   **VGood:** $1100

HECKLER & KOCH SR9

Semi-automatic; 308 Win.; 5-shot magazine; 19-3/4-inch bull barrel with polygonal rifling; 42-7/16-inch overall length; weighs 11 lbs.; post-front sight, fully-adjustable aperture rear; Kevlar reinforced fiberglass thumbhole stock with woodgrain finish; redesigned version of the HK91 rifle. Imported from Germany by Heckler & Koch, Inc. Introduced 1990; discontinued 1994.

Perf.: $3900   **Exc.:** $2600   **VGood:** $1900

HECKLER & KOCH SR9 (T) TARGET

Same specs as SR9 except MSG90 adjustable buttstock; trigger group from the PSG1 Marksman's Rifle; and the PSG1 contoured pistol grip with palm shelf. Imported from Germany by Heckler & Koch, Inc. Introduced 1992; discontinued 1994.

Perf.: $5000   **Exc.:** $4800   **VGood:** $3900

HECKLER & KOCH SR9 (TC) TARGET

Same specs as SR9 except PSG1 adjustable buttstock; target/competition version of the SR9 rifle; trigger group and contoured grip. Imported from Germany by Heckler & Koch, Inc. Introduced 1993; discontinued 1994.

Perf.: $4000   **Exc.:** $3700   **VGood:** $3200

HECKLER & KOCH USC CARBINE

Semi-automatic; 45 ACP, 10-shot magazine. 16-inch barrel; weighs 8.6 lb.; 35.4-inch overall length; Skeletonized polymer thumbhole. Blade front sight with integral hood, fully adjustable diopter rear. Based on German UMP submachine gun. Blowback operation; almost entirely constructed of carbon fiber-reinforced polymer. Free-floating heavy target barrel. Introduced 2000. Discontinued.

Perf.: $1600   **Exc.:** $1400   **VGood:** $1050

HENRY LEVER-ACTION 22

Lever action; 22 Long Rifle (15-shot); 18-1/4-inch round barrel; weighs 5-1/2 lbs.; 34-inch overall length. Walnut stock. Hooded blade front, open adjustable rear sights; Polished blue finish; full-length tubular magazine; side ejection; receiver grooved for scope mounting. Introduced 1997. Made in U.S.A. by Henry Repeating Arms Co.

Perf.: $245   **Exc.:** $180   **VGood:** $135

22 WMR; 11-shot, 19-1/4-inch bbl.

Perf.: $345   **Exc.:** $280   **VGood:** $235

17 HMR; 11-shot, 20-inch bbl.

Perf.: $345   **Exc.:** $280   **VGood:** $235

HENRY LEVER-ACTION FRONTIER MODEL

Similar to Henry Lever Action but with 20-inch octagon barrel. Chambered in .22 WMR and .17HMR.

NIB: $300   **Exc.:** $275   **VGood:** $225

HENRY BIG BOY LEVER-ACTION RIFLE

Lever action; 44 Mag., 45 Colt, .357 Magnum; 10-shot tubular magazine; 20-inch octogon bbl.; 38-1/2-inch long; weighs 8.6 pounds; solid-top brass receiver; straight-grip American walnut stock and forend; Marble semi-buckhorn rear sight and brass bead front sight.

Perf.: $650   **Exc.:** $595   **VGood:** 495

HENRY BIG BOY DELUXE ENGRAVED .44 MAGNUM

Similar to Henry Big Boy but with deluxe deep-cut German-style engraving on receiver. Introduced 2006.

NIB: $1350   **Exc.:** N/A   **VGood:** N/A

HENRY BIG BOY .44 MAGNUM "WILDLIFE EDITION"

Similar to Big Boy .44 Magnum but with forend and buttstock laser-engraved with whitetail deer scenes.

NIB: $1000   **Exc.:** $950   **VGood:** $775

Heckler & Koch SL7

Heckler & Koch SL8-1 Rifle

Heckler & Koch SR9

Heckler & Koch USC Carbine

Henry Lever-Action 22

Henry Lever-Action Frontier

Henry Big Boy Deluxe Engraved .44 Magnum

Henry Big Boy .44 Magnum "Wildlife Edition"

Henry Big Boy .44 Colt "Cowboy Edition"

Henry Pump-Action 22

Henry Pump Action .22 Octagon

Henry U.S. Survival Rifle .22

Heym Magnum Express

Heym Model 22S Safety Combo

Heym Model 33

HENRY BIG BOY .45 COLT "COWBOY EDITION"

Similar to Big Boy .45 Colt but with forend and buttstock laser-engraved with Old West scenes.

NIB: $1000   **Exc.:** $950   **VGood:** $775

HENRY GOLDEN BOY 22 LEVER-ACTION RIFLE

Lever action; 22 LR, 22 Magnum, 17 HRM; 16-shot. 20-inch octagonal barrel; weighs 6.25 lbs.; 38-inch overall length; American walnut stock; Blade front, open rear sights. Brasslite receiver, brass buttplate, blued barrel and lever. Introduced 1998. Made in U.S.A.; from Henry Repeating Arms Co.

Perf.: $375	**Exc.:** $300	**VGood:** $210
22 WMR		
Perf.: $425	**Exc.:** $350	**VGood:** $250
17 HMR		
Perf.: $430	**Exc.:** $360	**VGood:** N/A
Deluxe		
Perf.: $1000	**Exc.:** $900	**VGood:** N/A

HENRY DELUXE ENGRAVED GOLDEN BOY MAGNUM

Similar to Golden Boy Deluxe but chambered in .22 WMR. Features deluxe deep-cut German-style engraving on receiver. Discontinued.

NIB: $1100   **Exc.:** 950   **VGood:** N/A

HENRY "MINI" BOLT 22 RIFLE

Bolt action; single shot; 22 LR.; 16-inch stainless barrel, 8-groove rifling; 30-inch length; LOP 11-1/2-inch. Synthetic stock, pistol grip, wraparound checkering and beavertail forearm. Williams Fire sights. One piece bolt configuration, manually operated safety. Designed for beginners or ladies.

Perf.: $165   **Exc.:** $125   **VGood:** $100

HENRY PUMP-ACTION 22 PUMP RIFLE

Pump action; 22 LR, 15-shot; 18-1/4-inch barrel; weighs 5.5 lbs. American walnut stock. Bead on ramp front, open adjustable rear sights. Polished blue finish; receiver grooved for scope mount; grooved slide handle; two barrel bands. Introduced 1998. Made in U.S.A., from Henry Repeating Arms Co.

Perf.: $260   **Exc.:** $210   **VGood:** $170

HENRY PUMP ACTION .22 OCTAGON RIFLE

Similar to Henry Pump-Action Rifle but with 20-inch octagon barrel. Introduced 2006. Add 10 percent for .22 WMR.

NIB: $400   **Exc.:** $365   **VGood:** $300

HENRY U.S. SURVIVAL RIFLE .22

Semi-automatic; 22 LR, 8-shot magazine; 16-inch steel lined barrel; weighs 2.5 lbs. ABS plastic stock; Blade front sight on ramp, aperture rear. Takedown design stores barrel and action in hollow stock. Light enough to float. Silver, black or camo finish. Comes with two magazines. Introduced 1998. From Henry Repeating Arms Co.

Perf.: $175   **Exc.:** $145   **VGood:** $100

HEYM MODEL 55SS

Double rifle; over/under; 7x65R, 308, 30-06, 8x57JRS, 9.3x74R; 25-inch barrels; 42-inch overall length; weighs about 8 lbs.; silver bead ramp front, open V-type rear sight; dark European walnut stock with hand-checkered pistol grip and forend, oil finish; full sidelock action; Kersten double cross-bolt; cocking indicators; hand-engraved hunting scenes. Options include interchangeable barrels, Zeiss scopes in claw mounts, deluxe engravings and stock carving, etc. and increase values. Imported from Germany by Heckler & Koch, Inc. No longer imported.

Exc.: $8700   **VGood:** $8300   **Good:** $7200

HEYM MAGNUM EXPRESS

Bolt action; 338 Lapua Mag., 375 H&H, 378 Wea. Mag., 416 Rigby, 500 Nitro Express 3-inch 460 Wea. Mag., 500 A-Square, 450 Ackley, 600 N.E.; 5-shot magazine (416 Rigby); 24-inch barrel; 45-1/4-inch overall length; weighs about 10 lbs.; adjustable post front sight on ramp, three-leaf express rear; classic English stock of AAA-grade European walnut with cheekpiece; solid rubber buttpad; steel grip cap; modified magnum Mauser action with double square bridge; Timney single trigger; special hinged floorplate; barrel-mounted quick detachable swivel, quick detachable rear; vertical double recoil lug in rear of stock; three-position safety. Imported from Germany by JagerSport, Ltd. Introduced 1989; no longer imported.

Exc.: $5750   **VGood:** $4495   **Good:** $3250

600 Nitro Express caliber

Exc.: $9995   **VGood:** $7995   **Good:** $5150

HEYM MODEL 22S SAFETY COMBO

Combination gun; 16- or 20-ga. (2-3/4-inch, 3-inch), 12-ga. (2-3/4-inch) over 22 Hornet, 22 WMR, 222 Rem., 222 Rem Mag, 223, 22-250, 243 Win., 5.6x50R, 5.6x52R, 6.5x55, 6.5x57R, 7x57R, 8x57 JRS; 24-inch barrel with solid rib; weighs about 5-1/2 lbs.; silver bead ramp front, folding leaf rear sight; dark European walnut stock with hand-checkered pistol grip and forend; oil finish; tang-mounted cocking slide; floating rifle barrel; single-set trigger; base supplied for quick-detachable scope mounts; patented rocker-weight system automatically uncocks gun if accidentally dropped or bumped hard. Imported from Germany by Heckler & Koch, Inc. No longer imported.

Exc.: $3000   **VGood:** $2295   **Good:** $1895

HEYM MODEL 33

Drilling; side-by-side shotgun barrels with rifle barrel below; 5.6x50R Mag., 5.6x52R, 6.5x55, 6.5x57R, 7x57R, 7x65R, 8x57JRS, 9.3x74R, 222, 243, 270, 308, 30-06; 16x16 (2-3/4-inch), 20x20 (3-inch); 25-inch (Full & Mod.) barrels; 42-inch overall length; weighs about 6-1/2 lbs.; silver bead front, folding leaf rear sight; dark European walnut stock with checkered pistol grip and forend; oil finish; automatic sight positioner; boxlock action with Greener-type cross-bolt and safety, double under lugs; double-set triggers; plastic or steel trigger guard. Imported from Germany by Heckler and Koch, Inc. No longer imported.

Exc.: $6000   **VGood:** $5000   **Good:** $4350

HEYM MODEL 33 DELUXE

Same specs as Model 33 except extensive hunting scene engraving. Imported from Germany by Heckler & Koch, Inc. No longer imported.

Exc.: $7695 **VGood:** $6150 **Good:** $4595

HEYM MODEL 37B DOUBLE RIFLE DRILLING

Drilling; side-by-side rifle barrels with shotgun barrel below; 7x65R, 30-06, 8x57JRS, 9.3x74R; 20-ga. (3-inch); 25-inch barrels choked Full or Mod.; 42-inch overall length; weighs about 8-1/2 lbs.; silver bead front, folding leaf rear sight; dark European walnut stock with hand-checkered pistol grip and forend; oil finish; full sidelock construction; Greener-type cross-bolt; double under lugs; cocking indicators. Imported from Germany by Heckler & Koch, Inc. No longer imported.

Exc.: $12,995 **VGood:** $10,000 **Good:** $7995

HEYM MODEL 37B DELUXE

Same specs as Model 37B except extensive hunting scene engraving. Imported from Germany by Heckler & Koch, Inc. No longer imported.

Exc.: $15,500 **VGood:** $12,000 **Good:** $8995

HEYM MODEL 37 SIDELOCK DRILLING

Same specs as Model 37B except 12x12, 16x16 or 20x20 over 5.6x50R Mag., 5.6x52R, 6.5x55, 6.5x57R, 7x57R, 7x65R, 8x57JRS, 9.3x74R, 243, 308, 30-06; rifle barrel manually cocked and uncocked. Imported from Germany by Heckler & Koch, Inc. No longer imported.

Perf.: $11,995 **Exc.:** $8995 **VGood:** $6995

HEYM MODEL 55B

Double rifle; over/under; 7x65R, 308, 30-06, 8x57JRS, 8x75 RS, 9.3x74R, 375 H&H, 458 Win. Mag., 470 N.E.; 25-inch barrels; 42-inch overall length; weighs about 8 lbs., depending upon caliber; silver bead ramp front, open V-type rear sight; dark European walnut stock with hand-checkered pistol grip and forend; oil finish; boxlock or full sidelock action; Kersten double cross-bolt; cocking indicators; hand-engraved hunting scenes. Options include interchangeable barrels, Swarovski scopes in claw mounts, deluxe engravings and stock carving, etc. Imported from Germany by JagerSport, Ltd. No longer imported.

Exc.: $5000 **VGood:** $4500 **Good:** $4000

HEYM MODEL 55BF O/U COMBO GUN

Same specs as Model 55B O/U rifle except 12-, 16-, 20-ga. (2-3/4-inch or 3-inch) over 5.6x50R, 222 Rem., 223 Rem., 5.6x52R, 243, 6.5x57R, 270, 7x57R, 7x65R, 308, 30-06, 8x57JRS, 9.3x74R; solid rib barrel. Available with interchangeable shotgun and rifle barrels. No longer imported.

Exc.: $5000 **VGood:** $4500 **Good:** $4000

HEYM MODEL 55BW

Same specs as Model 55B except solid rib barrel. Available with interchangeable shotgun and rifle barrels. No longer imported.

Exc.: $9295 **VGood:** $7725 **Good:** $5495

HEYM MODEL 55FW O/U COMBO

Same specs as Model 55B O/U rifle except 12-, 16-, 20-ga. (2-3/4-inch or 3-inch) over 7x65R, 308, 30-06, 8x57JRS, 8x75 RS, 9.3x74R, 375 H&H, 458 Win. Mag., 470 N.E.; solid rib barrel. Available with interchangeable shotgun and rifle barrels. No longer imported.

Exc.: $10,995 **VGood:** $8995 **Good:** $6995

HEYM MODEL 77B

Double rifle; over/under boxlock; 9.3x74R, 375 H&H, 458 Win. Mag.; 25-inch, 28-inch barrels; weighs 8-1/2 lbs.; silver bead front, folding leaf rear sight; dark oil-finished European walnut stock; hand-checkered pistol grip, forend; fine engraving; Greener-type crossbolt; double under lugs. Introduced 1980; discontinued 1986.

Exc.: $5250 **VGood:** $4695 **Good:** $3395

Heym Model 33 Deluxe

Heym Model 55B

Heym Model 55BF O/U Combo

Heym Model 88B

Heym Model 88B Safari

Heym Model SR20 Trophy

HEYM MODEL 77BF

Same specs as Model 77B except over/under combo; boxlock or sidelock; 12-, 16-, 20-ga. over 5.6x50R, 222 Rem., 5.6x57R, 243, 6.5x57R, 270, 7x57R, 7x65R, 308, 30-06, 8x57 JRS, 9.3x74R, 375 H&H; solid rib barrel. Introduced 1986.

Boxlock (77BF)

Exc.: $5495 **VGood:** $4895 **Good:** $3695

Sidelock (77BFSS)

Exc.: $9500 **VGood:** $8250 **Good:** $5250

HEYM MODEL 88B

Side-by-side double rifle; 30-06, 300 Win Mag, 8x57JRS, 9.3x74R, 375 H&H; 25-inch Krupp steel barrels; 42-inch overall length; weighs 7-3/4 lbs. (standard calibers), 8-1/2 lbs. (magnums); silver bead post on ramp front sight, fixed or three-leaf express rear; fancy French walnut stock of classic North American design; Monte Carlo cheekpiece; hand-checkered forend; pistol grip; action with complete coverage hunting scene engraving; Anson-type boxlock action; Greener-type cross-bolt; double under-locking lugs; recoil pad. Imported from Germany by JagerSport, Ltd. No longer imported.

Exc.: $9600 **VGood:** $8795 **Good:** $7000

HEYM MODEL 88B SAFARI

Same specs as Model 88B except 375 H&H, 458 Win. Mag., 470 NE, 500 NE; weighs about 10 lbs.; large frame; ejectors. Imported from Germany by JagerSport, Ltd. No longer imported.

Exc.: $13,995 **VGood:** $10,995 **Good:** $8995

HEYM MODEL 88BSS

Same specs as Model 88B except quick detachable sidelocks. Imported from Germany by JagerSport, Ltd. No longer imported.

Perf.: $13,995 **Exc.:** $10,195 **VGood:** $8995

HEYM MODEL SR20 TROPHY

Bolt action; 243, 7x57, 270, 308, 30-06, 7mm Rem. Mag., 338 Win. Mag., 375 H&H, other calibers on request; 22-inch barrel (standard calibers), 24-inch (magnums); weighs about 7 lbs.; German silver bead ramp front sight, open rear on quarter-rib; drilled and tapped for scope mounting; AAA-grade European walnut stock with cheekpiece; solid rubber buttpad; checkered grip and forend; oil finish; rosewood grip cap; octagonal barrel; barrel-mounted quick detachable swivel, standard quick detachable rear swivel. Imported from Germany by Heckler & Koch, Inc. No longer imported.

Perf.: $2495 **Exc.:** $1995 **VGood:** $1195

HEYM MODEL SR20 ALPINE

Same specs as SR20 Trophy except 243, 270, 7x57, 308, 30-06, 6.5x55, 7x64, 8x57JS; 20-inch barrel; open sights; full-length "Mountain Rifle" stock with steel forend cap, steel grip cap. Imported from Germany by Heckler & Koch, Inc. Introduced 1989; no longer imported.

Perf.: $2400 **Exc.:** $2000 **VGood:** $1600

Heym Model SR20 Alpine

Heym Model SR20 Classic Safari

Heym Model SR20 Classic Sportsman

Hi-Point 9mm Carbine

Hi-Standard Flite King

Hi-Standard Hi-Power Field

Hi-Standard Hi-Power Field Deluxe

Hi-Standard Sport King Field

HEYM MODEL SR20 CLASSIC SAFARI

Same specs as SR20 Trophy except 404 Jeffery, 425 Express, 458 Win. Mag.; 24-inch barrel; large post front, three-leaf express rear sight; barrel-mounted ring-type front quick detachable swivel, quick detachable rear; double-lug recoil bolt in stock. Imported from Germany by Heckler & Koch, Inc. Introduced 1989; no longer imported.

Perf.: $3375   **Exc.:** $2895   **VGood:** $2495

HEYM MODEL SR20 CLASSIC SPORTSMAN

Same specs as SR20 Trophy except round barrel without sights. Imported from Germany by Heckler & Koch, Inc. Introduced 1989; no longer imported.

Perf.: $1695   **Exc.:** $1395   **VGood:** $995

Magnum calibers		
Perf.: $1795	**Exc.:** $1495	**VGood:** $1095

HEYM MODEL SR40

Bolt action, short action; 222, 222 Rem Mag, 223, 22-250, 5.6x50 Mag.; 24-inch barrel; 44-inch overall length; weighs 6-1/4 lbs.; silver bead ramp front, adjustable folding leaf rear sight; carbine-length Mannlicher-style stock; recoil pad; hinged floorplate; three-position safety. Made in Germany. Introduced 1984; discontinued 1988.

Perf.: $895   **Exc.:** $695   **VGood:** $495

Left-hand model		
Perf.: $995	**Exc.:** $795	**VGood:** $595

HEYM-RUGER MODEL HR30

Single shot; 243, 6.5x57R, 7x64, 7x65R, 270, 308, 30-06; 24-inch round barrel; weighs 6-3/8 lbs.; bead ramp front, leaf rear sight; hand-checkered European walnut Mannlicher or sporter stock; oil finish; recoil pad; Ruger No. 1 action. Custom-made gun, many options available. Introduced 1978; discontinued 1987.

Sporter stock		
Exc.: $3000	**VGood:** $2700	**Good:** $2100
Mannlicher stock		
Exc.: $3100	**VGood:** $2800	**Good:** $2200

HEYM-RUGER MODEL HR30G

Same specs as HR30 except 6.5x68R, 300 Win. Mag., 8x68S, 9.3x74R; 25-inch barrel.

Sporter stock		
Exc.: $3100	**VGood:** $2800	**Good:** $2200
Mannlicher stock		
Exc.: $3200	**VGood:** $2900	**Good:** $2300

HEYM-RUGER MODEL HR38

Single shot; 243, 6.5x57R, 7x64, 7x65R, 270, 308, 30-06; 24-inch octagon barrel; weighs 6-3/8 lbs.; bead ramp front, leaf rear sight; hand-checkered European walnut Mannlicher or sporter stock; oil finished; recoil pad; Ruger No. 1 action. Custom-made gun, many options available. Introduced 1978; discontinued 1987.

Sporter stock		
Exc.: $3200	**VGood:** $2900	**Good:** $2300
Mannlicher stock		
Exc.: $3300	**VGood:** $3000	**Good:** $2400

HEYM-RUGER MODEL HR38G

Same specs as HR38 except 6.5x68R, 300 Win. Mag., 8x68S.

Sporter stock		
Exc.: $3300	**VGood:** $3000	**Good:** $2400
Mannlicher stock		
Exc.: $3400	**VGood:** $3100	**Good:** $2500

HI-POINT 9MM CARBINE

Caliber: 9mm Para., 40 S&W, 10-shot magazine; 16-1/2 barrel-inch (17-1/2-inch for 40 S&W); weighs 4-1/2 lbs.; 31-1/2-inch overall; Black polymer stock; Protected post front, aperture rear sights. Scope mount, sling and swivels furnished. Grip-mounted magazine release. Black or chrome finish. Sling swivels. Introduced 1996, still available. Made in U.S.A. by MKS Supply, Inc.

Perf.: $255   **Exc.:** $225   **VGood:** $195

HI-POINT .40 S&W CARBINE

Similar to Hi-Point 9mm carbine but in .40 S&W. Features include all-weather, black, polymer stock, 10 shot maazine, 17.5-inch barrel, sling swivels, grip mounted clip release, quick on & off thumb safety, rear peep sight, 32.5-inch OAL and a scope mount.

NIB: $255   **Exc.:** $225   **VGood:** $195

HI-STANDARD FLITE KING

Pump-action; hammerless; 22 LR, 22 Long, 22 Short; 17-shot (22 LR), 19-shot (22 Long), 24-shot (22 Short) tubular magazine; 24-inch barrel; 41-3/4-inch overall length; weighs 5-1/2 lbs.; Patridge-type rear sight, bead front; checkered hardwood Monte Carlo pistol-grip stock; grooved slide handle. Introduced 1962; discontinued 1975.

Exc.: $195   **VGood:** $150   **Good:** $115

HI-STANDARD HI-POWER FIELD

Bolt action; 270, 30-06; 4-shot magazine; 22-inch barrel; 42-3/4-inch overall length; weighs 7 lbs.; built on Mauser-type action; folding leaf open rear sight, ramp front; uncheckered walnut field-style pistol-grip stock; sliding safety; quick-detachable sling swivels. Introduced 1962; discontinued 1966.

Exc.: $340   **VGood:** $290   **Good:** $240

HI-STANDARD HI-POWER FIELD DELUXE

Same specs as Hi-Power Field except impressed checkering on Monte Carlo stock; sling swivels. Introduced 1962; discontinued 1966.

Exc.: $375   **VGood:** $320   **Good:** $265

HI-STANDARD SPORT KING FIELD

Semi-automatic; 22 LR, 22 Long, 22 Short; 22-1/4-inch tapered barrel; 15-shot (22 LR), 17-shot (22 Long), 21-shot (22 Short) tubular magazine; open rear, bead post front sight; uncheckered pistol-grip stock. Introduced 1960; dropped 1966.

Exc.: $100   **VGood:** $90   **Good:** $75

HI-STANDARD SPORT KING CARBINE
Same specs as Sport King except 12-shot (22 LR), 14-shot (22 Long), 17-shot (22 Short) tubular magazine; 18-inch barrel; 38-1/2-inch overall length; weighs 5-1/2 lbs.; open rear, bead post front sight; receiver grooved for scope mounts; straight-grip stock; brass buttplate; sling swivels; golden trigger guard, trigger, safety. Introduced 1964; discontinued 1973.

Exc.: $140   **VGood:** $120   **Good:** $100

HI-STANDARD SPORT KING DELUXE
Same specs as Sport King Field except impressed checkering on stock. Introduced 1966; dropped 1975.

Exc.: $160   **VGood:** $140   **Good:** $110

HI-STANDARD SPORT KING SPECIAL
Same specs as Sport King Field except Monte Carlo stock; semi-beavertail forearm. Introduced 1960; discontinued 1966.

Exc.: $120   **VGood:** $100   **Good:** $90

HOENIG ROTARY ROUND ACTION DOUBLE RIFLE
Unique round action; Most popular calibers from 225 Win. to 9.3x74R.; 22-inch-26-inch barrel; English Walnut stock; to customer specs. Swivel hood front sight with button release (extra bead stored in trap door gripcap), express-style rear on quarter-rib adjustable for windage and elevation; scope mount. Round action opens by rotating barrels, pulling forward. Inertia extractor system; rotary safety blocks strikers. Single lever quick-detachable scope mount. Simple takedown without removing forend. Introduced 1997. Made in U.S.A. by George Hoenig.

Perf.: $24,000   **Exc.:** $22,000   **VGood:** $20,000

HOENIG ROTARY ROUND ACTION COMBINATION
Like double rifle, but with a 28-gauge shotgun barrel in combination with a rifle barrel; barrels 26-inch; weighs 7 lbs.; English Walnut stock to customer specs. Front ramp sight with button release blades. Foldable aperture tang sight windage and elevation adjustable. Quarter rib with scope mount. Round action opens by rotating barrels, pulling forward. Inertia extractor; rotary safety blocks strikers. Simple takedown without removing forend. Made in U.S.A. by George Hoenig.

Perf.: $24,000   **Exc.:** $22,000   **VGood:** $20,000

HOLLAND & HOLLAND BEST QUALITY
Bolt action; 240 Apex, 300 H&H Mag., 375 H&H Mag.; 4-shot box magazine; 24-inch barrel; built on Mauser or Enfield action; folding leaf rear, hooded ramp front; cheekpiece stock of European walnut; hand-checkered pistol grip, forearm; sling swivels, recoil pad; not imported to U.S. Prices can go higher than $30,000, depending on features.

HOLLAND & HOLLAND DELUXE
Bolt action; 240 Apex, 300 H&H Mag., 375 H&H Mag.; 4-shot box magazine; 24-inch barrel; built on Mauser or Enfield action; folding leaf rear, hooded ramp front sight; exhibition-grade European walnut cheekpiece stock; hand-checkered pistol grip, forearm; sling swivels; recoil pad. Introduced following World War II; not imported to U.S. Prices vary based on features.

HOLLAND & HOLLAND NO. 2 MODEL
Double rifle; sidelock; side-by-side; 240 Apex, 7mm H&H Mag., 300 H&H Mag., 375 H&H Mag., 458 Win. Mag., 465 H&H Mag., 577 H&H Mag.; 24-inch, 26-inch, 28-inch barrels; folding leaf rear, ramp front sight; two-piece European stock; hand-checkered pistol grip, forearm; swivels; not imported to U.S.

Exc.: $40,000   **VGood:** $28,500   **Good:** $12,000

Hoenig Rotary Round Action Double Rifle

Hoenig Rotary Round Action Combination

Holland & Holland Best Quality

Holland & Holland Royal

Howa Lightning

Howa M-1500 Ultralight

HOLLAND & HOLLAND ROYAL
Double rifle; hammerless sidelock; 240 Apex, 7mm H&H Mag., 300 H&H Mag., 375 H&H Mag., 458 Win., 465 H&H; 24-inch, 26-inch, 28-inch barrels; folding leaf rear, ramp front sight; two-piece choice European stock; hand-checkered pistol grip, forearm; swivels; custom-engraved receiver. Special-order rifle in the realm of semi-production, with original buyer's options available; not imported to U.S. Prices range from $20,000 to over $100,000 based on features.

HOLLAND & HOLLAND ROYAL DELUXE
Same specs as Royal Model except more ornate engraving; better grade European walnut stock; better fitting. Still in production; not imported to U.S. Prices vary based on features.

HOWA HEAVY BARREL VARMINT
Bolt action; 223, 22-250, 308; 24-inch heavy barrel; 42-inch overall length; weighs 7-1/2-7-3/4 lbs.; no sights; drilled and tapped for scope mounts; American walnut stock with Monte Carlo comb and cheekpiece; 18 lpi checkering on pistol grip and forend; single unit trigger guard and magazine box with hinged floorplate; Parkerized finish; quick detachable swivel studs; composition non-slip buttplate with white spacer. Imported from Japan by Interarms. Introduced 1989; discontinued 1992.

Perf.: $475   **Exc.:** $375   **VGood:** $300

HOWA LIGHTNING
Bolt action; 223, 22-250, 243, 270, 308, 30-06, 7mm Rem. Mag., 300 Win. Mag., 338 Win. Mag.; 22-inch barrel (standard calibers), 24-inch (magnums); 42-inch overall length (22-inch barrel); weighs 7-1/2 lbs.; no sights; drilled and tapped for scope mounting; black Bell & Carlson Carbelite composite stock with Monte Carlo comb; checkered grip and forend; sliding thumb safety; hinged floorplate; polished blue/black finish. From Interarms. Introduced 1993; still imported. Premium for magnum calibers.

Perf.: $425   **Exc.:** $335   **VGood:** $300

HOWA LIGHTNING WOODGRAIN
Same specs as Lightning except 243, 270, 30-06, 308, 7mm Rem. Mag.; 5-shot magazine; lightweight Carbelite synthetic stock with simulated woodgrain. Introduced 1994; no longer in production.

Perf.: $495   **Exc.:** $350   **VGood:** $320

HOWA M-1500 ULTRALIGHT
Similar to Howa M-1500 Lightning except receiver milled to reduce weight, tapered 22-inch barrel; 1-10-inch twist. Chambered for 243 Win. Stocks are black texture-finished hardwood. Weighs 6.4 lbs. Length 40-inch overall.

Perf.: $475   **Exc.:** $375   **VGood:** $300

HOWA M-1500 VARMINTER AND VARMINTER SUPREME RIFLES
Similar to M-1500 Lightning except has heavy 24-inch hammer-forged barrel. Chambered for 223, 22-250, 380. Weighs 9.3 lbs.; overall length 44-1/2-inch. Introduced 1999. Imported from Japan by Interarms/Howa. Varminter Supreme has heavy barrel, target crown muzzle. Heavy 24-inch barrel, laminated wood with raised comb stocks, rollover cheekpiece, vented beavertail forearm; available in 223 Rem., 22-250 Rem., 308 Win. Weighs 9.9 lbs. Introduced 2001. Imported from Japan by Legacy Sports International. Still available.

Perf.: $525   **Exc.:** $425   **VGood:** $300

Howa M-1500 Varminter and
Varminter Supreme Rifles

Howa Model 1500
Hunter

Husqvarna Hi-Power

Husqvarna Model 456

Husqvarna Series 1100

Husqvarna Series 3000

Husqvarna Series 3100

HUSQVARNA HI-POWER
Bolt action; 220 Swift, 270 Win., 30-06, 6.5x55, 8x57, 9.3x57; 23-3/4-inch barrel; 5-shot box magazine; Mauser-type action; open rear, hooded ramp front sight; hand-checkered pistol-grip beech stock; sling swivels. Introduced 1946; discontinued 1959.
   Exc.: $395   **VGood:** $340   **Good:** $310

HUSQVARNA MODEL 456
Bolt action; 243, 270, 30-06, 308, 7mm Rem. Mag.; 5-shot box magazine; 20-1/2-inch barrel; Husqvarna improved Mauser action; open adjustable rear, hooded ramp front sight; full-length European walnut stock; slope-away cheekpiece; metal forearm cap; sling swivels. Introduced 1959; discontinued 1970.
   Exc.: $425   **VGood:** $330   **Good:** $270

HUSQVARNA MODEL 1950
Bolt action; 220 Swift, 270 Win., 30-06; 5-shot box magazine; 23-3/4-inch barrel; Mauser-type action; open rear, hooded ramp front sight; hand-checkered pistol-grip beech stock; sling swivels. Introduced 1950; discontinued 1952.
   Exc.: $425   **VGood:** $350   **Good:** $280

HUSQVARNA MODEL 1951
Bolt action; 220 Swift, 30-06; 5-shot box magazine; 23-3/4-inch barrel; Mauser-type action; open rear, hooded ramp front sight; hand-checkered pistol-grip beech stock with high-comb, low safety. Introduced 1951; discontinued 1951.
   Exc.: $425   **VGood:** $365   **Good:** $300

HUSQVARNA MODEL 8000
Bolt action; 270 Win., 30-06, 300 Win. Mag., 7mm Rem. Mag.; 5-shot box magazine; 23-3/4-inch barrel; improved Husqvarna action; no sights; hand-checkered deluxe French walnut stock; Monte Carlo cheekpiece; rosewood forearm tip; pistol-grip cap; adjustable trigger; jeweled bolt; hinged engraved floorplate. Introduced 1971; discontinued 1972.
   Exc.: $695   **VGood:** $595   **Good:** $475

HUSQVARNA MODEL 9000
Bolt action; 270 Win., 30-06, 300 Win. Mag., 7mm Rem. Mag.; 5-shot box magazine; 23-3/4-inch barrel; improved Husqvarna action; folding leaf rear, hooded ramp front sight; Monte Carlo cheekpiece stock; adjustable trigger. Introduced 1971; discontinued 1972.
   Exc.: $495   **VGood:** $430   **Good:** $360

HUSQVARNA SERIES 1000
Bolt action; 220 Swift, 270, 30-06; 5-shot box magazine; 23-3/4-inch barrel; Mauser-type action; open rear, hooded ramp front sight; European walnut stock, with cheekpiece; Monte Carlo comb. Introduced 1952; discontinued 1956.
   Exc.: $450   **VGood:** $395   **Good:** $315

HUSQVARNA SERIES 1100
Bolt action; 220 Swift, 270, 30-06, 6.5x55, 8x57, 9.3x57; 5-shot box magazine; 23-1/2-inch barrel; Mauser-type action; open rear, hooded ramp front sight; European walnut Monte Carlo stock; jeweled bolt. Introduced 1952; discontinued 1956.
   Exc.: $475   **VGood:** $425   **Good:** $340

HUSQVARNA SERIES 3000
Bolt action; 243, 270, 30-06, 308, 7mm Rem. Mag.; 5-shot box magazine; 23-3/4-inch barrel; Husqvarna improved Mauser action; open rear, hooded ramp front sight; European walnut Monte Carlo-style stock; sling swivels. Introduced 1954; discontinued 1976.
   Exc.: $450   **VGood:** $395   **Good:** $320

HUSQVARNA SERIES 3100
Bolt action; 243 Win., 270 Win., 30-06, 308 Win.; 5-shot box magazine; 23-3/4-inch barrel; Husqvarna improved Mauser action; open rear, hooded ramp front sight; hand-checkered European walnut pistol-grip stock; cheekpiece; black forearm tip; pistol-grip cap; sling swivels. Introduced 1954; discontinued 1976.
   Exc.: $550   **VGood:** $430   **Good:** $360

HOWA MODEL 1500 HUNTER
Bolt action; 22-250, 223, 243, 270, 308, 30-06, 300 Win. Mag., 7mm Rem. Mag.; 3-, 5-shot magazine; 22-inch, 24-inch barrel; weighs 7-1/2 lbs.; ramped gold bead front, adjustable open rear sight; Monte-Carlo-type walnut stock; checkered pistol grip, forend; swivels; adjustable trigger. Made in Japan. Introduced 1988; discontinued 1988. Premium for magnum calibers.
   Perf.: $475   **Exc.:** $325   **VGood:** $29

HOWA MODEL 1500 TROPHY
Bolt action; 223, 22-250, 243, 270, 30-06, 308, 7mm Rem. Mag., 300 Win. Mag., 338 Win. Mag.; 22-inch barrel (standard calibers), 24-inch (magnums); 42-inch overall length; weighs 7-1/2 to 7-3/4 lbs.; hooded ramp gold bead front sight, open round-notch fully-adjustable rear; drilled and tapped for scope mounts; American walnut stock with Monte Carlo comb and cheekpiece; 18 lpi checkering on pistol grip and forend; single unit trigger guard and magazine box with hinged floorplate; quick detachable swivel studs; composition non-slip buttplate with white spacer; magnum models with rubber recoil pad. Imported from Japan by Interarms. Introduced 1979; discontinued 1992.
   Perf.: $495   **Exc.:** $395   **VGood:** $280

HOWA REALTREE CAMO
Bolt action; 270, 30-06; 5-shot magazine; 22-inch barrel; 42-1/4-inch overall length; weighs 8 lbs.; no sights; drilled and tapped for scope mounting; Bell & Carlson Carbelite composite stock with straight comb, checkered grip and forend; completely covered with Realtree camo finish, except bolt; sliding thumb safety; hinged floorplate; sling swivel studs; recoil pad. Imported from Japan by Interarms. Introduced 1993; discontinued 1994.
   Perf.: $495   **Exc.:** $395   **VGood:** $320

HUSQVARNA SERIES 4000

Bolt action; 243 Win., 270 Win., 30-06, 308 Win., 7mm Rem. Mag.; 5-shot box magazine; 20-1/2-inch barrel; Husqvarna improved Mauser action; no rear sight, hooded ramp front; drilled, tapped for scope mounts; European walnut Monte Carlo stock; hand-checkered pistol grip, forearm; sling swivels. Introduced 1954; discontinued 1976.

Exc.: $495   **VGood: $430**   **Good: $360**

HUSQVARNA SERIES 4100

Bolt action; 243 Win., 270 Win., 30-06, 308 Win., 7mm Rem. Mag.; 5-shot box magazine; 20-1/2-inch barrel; Husqvarna improved action; adjustable open rear, hooded ramp front sight; lightweight European walnut stock with cheekpiece; sling swivels. Introduced 1954; discontinued 1976.

Exc.: $575   **VGood: $460**   **Good: $350**

HUSQVARNA SERIES 6000

Bolt action; 243 Win., 270 Win., 30-06, 308 Win., 7mm Rem. Mag.; 5-shot box magazine; 23-3/4-inch barrel; three-leaf folding rear, hooded ramp front sight; fancy walnut stock; adjustable trigger; sling swivels. Introduced 1968; discontinued 1970.

Exc.: $595   **VGood: $495**   **Good: $385**

HUSQVARNA SERIES 7000

Bolt action; 243 Win., 270 Win., 30-06, 308 Win.; 5-shot box magazine; 20-1/2-inch barrel; three-leaf folding rear, hooded ramp front sight; lightweight fancy walnut stock; adjustable trigger; sling swivels. Introduced 1968; discontinued 1970.

Exc.: $595   **VGood: $495**   **Good: $395**

HUSQVARNA SERIES P-3000

Bolt action; 243 Win., 270 Win., 30-06, 7mm Rem. Mag.; 5-shot box magazine; 23-3/4-inch barrel; Husqvarna improved action; open rear, hooded ramp front sight; top-grade walnut stock; engraved action; adjustable trigger; sling swivels. Introduced 1968; discontinued 1970.

Perf.: $795   **Exc.: $650**   **VGood: $495**

IAI M-333 M1 GARAND

Semi-automatic; 30-06, 8-shot clip; 24-inch barrel; weighs 9-1/2 lbs.; 43.6-inch overall length; Hardwood stock; Blade front, aperture adjustable rear sights; Parkerized finish; gas-operated semi-automatic; remanufactured to military specifications. From IAI.

Perf.: $900   **Exc.: $810**   **VGood: $650**

IAI M-888 M1 CARBINE SEMI-AUTOMATIC RIFLE

Semi-automatic; 30 Carbine. 18-inch-20-inch barrel; weighs 5-1/2 lbs.; 35-inch- 37-inch overall length; Laminate, walnut or birch stock; Blade front, adjustable rear sights; gas-operated, air cooled, manufactured to military specifications. 10/15/30 round. magazines; scope available. From IAI.

Perf.: $450   **Exc.: $350**   **VGood: $300**

IAR MODEL 1873 REVOLVING CARBINE

Revolver, 357 Mag., 45 Colt. 18-inch barrel; weighs 4 lbs., 8 oz.; 34-inch overall length; One-piece walnut stock; Blade front, notch rear sights. Color case-hardened frame, blue barrel, backstrap and trigger guard. Introduced 1998. Imported from Italy by IAR, Inc.

Perf.: $500   **Exc.: $425**   **VGood: $350**

IBUS M17S 223 BULLPUP

Semi-automatic; 223 Remington; 10-shot magazine; 21-1/2" barrel; 30" overall length; no sights, but comes with scope mount for Weaver-type rings; Zytel glass-filled bullpup-style nylon stock; gas-operated; short-stroke piston action; ambidextrous magazine release. Made in USA by Bushmaster Firearms. Introduced 1993.

Perf.: $900   **Exc.: $800**   **VGood: $695**

INTERARMS MARK X ALASKAN

Bolt action; 375 H&H Mag., 458 Win. Mag.; 3-shot magazine; 24-inch barrel; 44-3/4-inch overall length; weighs 8-1/4 lbs.; adjustable folding leaf rear, ramp

Husqvarna Series 4000

Husqvarna Series 4100

Husqvarna Series 7000

Ibus M17S 223 Bullpup

Interarms Mark X Cavalier

Interarms Mark X Lightweight

front sight with removable hood; select walnut Monte Carlo-style stock with crossbolt; hand-checkered pistol grip, forend; sling swivels; heavy-duty recoil pad. Introduced 1976; discontinued 1985.

Exc.: $750   **VGood: $495**   **Good: $295**

INTERARMS MARK X AMERICAN FIELD

Bolt action; 22-250, 243, 25-06, 270, 7x57, 7mm Rem. Mag., 308 Win., 30-06, 300 Win. Mag.; 24-inch barrel; 45-inch overall length; weighs 7 lbs.; Mauser-system action; ramp front sight with removable hood, open fully-adjustable rear; drilled and tapped for scope mounts and receiver sight; hand-checkered walnut stock; 1-inch sling swivels; one-piece trigger guard with hinged floorplate; hammer-forged chrome vanadium steel barrel. Imported from Yugoslavia by Interarms. Discontinued 1994.

Exc.: $495   **VGood: $350**   **Good: $295**

INTERARMS MARK X CAVALIER

Bolt action; 22-250, 243, 25-06, 270, 7x57, 7mm Rem. Mag., 30-06, 300 Win. Mag., 308 Win.; 3-, 5-shot magazine; 24-inch barrel; 44-inch overall length; weighs 7-1/2 lbs.; adjustable folding leaf rear, ramp front sight with removable hood; drilled, tapped for receiver sights, scope mounts; checkered walnut stock with roll-over cheekpiece; rosewood grip cap and forend tip; recoil pad; adjustable trigger. Introduced 1974; discontinued 1983.

Exc.: $450   **VGood: $300**   **Good: $270**

INTERARMS MARK X CONTINENTAL CARBINE

Bolt action; 243, 270, 308, 30-06, 7x57; 3-, 5-shot magazine; 20-inch barrel; 40-inch overall length; weighs 7-1/2 lbs.; adjustable folding leaf rear, ramp front sight with removable hood; hand-checkered European walnut full-length stock with roll-over cheekpiece; recoil pad; double-set trigger; button-release hinged floorplate. Introduced 1976; discontinued 1983.

Exc.: $495   **VGood: $295**   **Good: $240**

INTERARMS MARK X LIGHTWEIGHT

Bolt action; 22-250, 270, 30-06, 7mm Rem. Mag.; 3-, 5-shot magazine; 20-inch barrel; adjustable folding leaf rear, ramp front sight with removable hood; lightweight Carbolite synthetic stock; adjustable trigger. Introduced 1988; discontinued 1990; reintroduced 1994; no longer in production.

Exc.: $450   **VGood: $290**   **Good: $245**

INTERARMS MARK X MARQUIS

Bolt action; 243, 270 Win., 308, 30-06, 7x57mm; 3-, 5-shot magazine; 20-inch barrel; 40-inch overall length; weighs 7-1/2 lbs.; adjustable folding leaf rear, ramp front sight with removable hood; hand-checkered European walnut full-length stock; adjustable trigger; quick-detachable sling swivels; blue steel forend cap; Mark X action; white line spacers buttplate, pistol grip cap. Discontinued 1984.

Exc.: $475   **VGood: $400**   **Good: $330**

Ithaca Model LSA-55

Ithaca Model 49 Saddlegun

Ithaca Model 49 Presentation

Ithaca Model 49 Saddlegun Repeater

INTERARMS MARK X MINI

Bolt action; 223 Rem., 7.62x39mm; 20-inch barrel; 39-3/4-inch overall length; weighs 6-3/8 lbs.; blade on ramp front sight, open adjustable rear; drilled and tapped for scope mounting; checkered European hardwood stock; adjustable trigger; miniature M98 Mauser action. Imported from Yugoslavia by Interarms. Introduced 1987; importation dropped 1994.

Exc.: $425   **VGood:** $375   **Good:** $350

INTERARMS MARK X REALTREE

Bolt action; 270, 30-06; 3-, 5-shot magazine; 22-inch barrel; 42-1/4-inch overall length; weighs 8 lbs.; adjustable folding leaf rear, ramp front sight with removable hood; Realtree camo stock; adjustable trigger; sliding thumb safety; hinged floorplate; mono-block receiver. Introduced 1994; no longer imported.

Exc.: $480   **VGood:** $320   **Good:** $290

INTERARMS MARK X VISCOUNT

Bolt action; 22-250, 243, 25-06, 270, 7x57, 308, 30-06, 7mm Rem. Mag., 300 Win. Mag.; 24-inch barrel; 44-inch overall length; weighs about 7 lbs.; blade on ramp front sight, open fully-adjustable rear; drilled and tapped for scope mounting; European hardwood stock with Monte Carlo comb; checkered grip and forend; polished blue finish; uses Mauser system action with sliding thumb safety, hinged floorplate, adjustable trigger. Imported from Yugoslavia by Interarms. Reintroduced 1987; discontinued 1994.

Exc.: $495   **VGood:** $330   **Good:** $290

INTERARMS MARK X WHITWORTH

Bolt action; 22-250, 243, 25-06, 270, 7x57, 308, 30-06, 7mm Rem. Mag., 300 Win. Mag.; 5-shot magazine, 3-shot (300 Win. Mag.); 24-inch barrel; 44-inch overall length; weighs 7 lbs.; hooded blade on ramp front sight, open fully-adjustable rear; select grade European walnut stock with checkered grip and forend, straight comb; Mauser system action with sliding thumb safety, hinged floorplate, adjustable trigger; polished blue finish; swivel studs.

Imported from Yugoslavia by Interarms. Introduced 1984; discontinued 1994.

Perf.: $475   **Exc.:** $395   **VGood:** $310

INTERARMS WHITWORTH EXPRESS

Bolt action; 375 H&H, 458 Win. Mag.; 24-inch barrel; 44-3/4-inch overall length; weighs about 8-1/4 to 8-1/2 lbs.; ramp front sight with removable hood, three-leaf open rear calibrated for 100, 200, 300 yards, on 1/4-rib; solid rubber recoil pad; classic English Express rifle design of hand-checkered, select European walnut; barrel-mounted sling swivel; adjustable trigger; hinged floorplate; solid steel recoil cross-bolt. From Interarms. Introduced 1974; no longer produced.

Perf.: $695   **Exc.:** $595   **VGood:** $475

INTERARMS WHITWORTH MANNLICHER-STYLE CARBINE

Bolt action; 243, 270, 308, 30-06, 7x57; 5-shot magazine; 20-inch barrel; 40-inch overall length; weighs 7 lbs.; hooded ramp front sight, fully-adjustable rear; full-length checkered European walnut stock with cheekpiece; sling swivels; rubber buttplate. Introduced 1984; discontinued 1987.

Perf.: $595   **Exc.:** $475   **VGood:** $350

ITHACA MODEL LSA-55

Bolt action; 22-250, 222 Rem., 6mm Rem., 243, 25-06, 270 Win., 30-06; 3-shot detachable box magazine; 23-inch free-floating barrel; 41-1/2-inch overall length; weighs 6-1/2 lbs.; adjustable rear, hooded ramp front sight; drilled, tapped for scope mounts; checkered European walnut pistol-grip Monte Carlo stock; adjustable trigger. Introduced 1972; discontinued 1976.

Exc.: $500   **VGood:** $450   **Good:** $350

ITHACA MODEL LSA-55 DELUXE

Same specs as LSA-55 except no sights; scope mounts; roll-over cheekpiece; rosewood forearm tip, grip cap; white spacers; sling swivel.

Exc.: $550   **VGood:** $475   **Good:** $395

ITHACA MODEL LSA-55 HEAVY BARREL

Same specs as LSA-55 except 22-250, 22 Rem.; 23-inch heavy barrel; no sights; redesigned stock;

beavertail forearm. Introduced 1974; discontinued 1976.

Exc.: $600   **VGood:** $525   **Good:** $495

ITHACA MODEL LSA-55 TURKEY GUN

Over/under rifle/shotgun combo; 12-ga./222 Rem.; 24-1/2-inch ribbed barrel; folding leaf rear sight, bead front; plain extractor; single trigger; exposed hammer. Imported from Finland. Introduced 1970; discontinued 1979.

Exc.: $900   **VGood:** $625   **Good:** $405

ITHACA MODEL LSA-65

Bolt action; 25-06, 270, 30-06; 4-shot magazine; 23-inch barrel; 41-1/2-inch overall length; weighs 6-1/2 lbs.; adjustable rear, hooded ramp front sight; drilled, tapped for scope mounts; checkered European walnut pistol-grip Monte Carlo stock; adjustable trigger. Introduced 1969; discontinued 1976.

Exc.: $550   **VGood:** $475   **Good:** $395

ITHACA MODEL LSA-65 DELUXE

Same specs as LSA-65 except no sights; scope mounts; roll-over cheekpiece; rosewood grip cap, forend tip. Introduced 1969; discontinued 1976.

Exc.: $600   **VGood:** $525   **Good:** $495

ITHACA MODEL 49 SADDLEGUN

Lever action; single shot; 22 Short, 22 Long, 22 LR, 22 WMR; 18-inch barrel; 34-1/2-inch overall length; weighs 5-1/2 lbs.; blank tube magazine for appearance only; open adjustable rear, bead post front sight; straight uncheckered two-piece Western-style carbine stock; barrel band on forearm; Martini-type action. Introduced 1961; discontinued 1976. Add 20 percent for 22 WMR.

Exc.: $165   **VGood:** $145   **Good:** $115

ITHACA MODEL 49 DELUXE

Same specs as Model 49 Saddlegun except figured walnut stock; gold-plated hammer, trigger, sling swivels. Introduced 1962; discontinued 1975.

Exc.: $295   **VGood:** $250   **Good:** $150

ITHACA MODEL 49 PRESENTATION

Same specs as Model 49 Saddlegun except fancy figured walnut stock; gold nameplate inlay; gold trigger, hammer; engraved receiver. Introduced 1962; discontinued 1974.

Exc.: $295   **VGood:** $250   **Good:** $150

ITHACA MODEL 49 SADDLEGUN REPEATER

Same specs as Model 49 Saddlegun except tubular magazine; 20-inch barrel; open rear, bead front sight; checkered grip. Introduced 1968; discontinued 1971.

Exc.: $210   **VGood:** $170   **Good:** $120

ITHACA MODEL 49 SADDLEGUN YOUTH

Same specs as Model 49 Saddlegun except shorter stock. Introduced 1961; discontinued 1976.

Exc.: $130   **VGood:** $100   **Good:** $80

ITHACA MODEL 72 SADDLEGUN

Lever action; 22 Short, 22 Long, 22 LR, 22 WMR; 11-, 15-shot tube magazine; 18-1/2-inch barrel; weighs 5 lbs.; step-adjustable open rear sight, hooded ramp front; grooved for scope mounts; uncheckered Western-style straight American walnut stock; barrel band on forearm; half-cock safety. Introduced 1972; discontinued 1977.

Exc.: $280   **VGood:** $210   **Good:** $160

ITHACA MODEL 72 SADDLEGUN DELUXE

Same specs as Model 72 Saddlegun except engraved, silver-finished receiver; octagon barrel; semi-fancy European walnut stock, forearm. Introduced 1974; discontinued 1976.

Exc.: $295   **VGood:** $230   **Good:** $180

ITHACA MODEL X5-C

Semi-automatic; 22 LR; 7-shot clip magazine; 22-inch barrel; 40-1/2-inch overall length; weighs 6 lbs.; open rear, Raybar front sight; uncheckered hardwood pistol-grip stock; grooved forearm. Introduced 1958; discontinued 1964.

Perf.: $350   **Exc.:** $220   **VGood:** $130

ITHACA MODEL X5-T

Same specs as Model X5-C except 16-shot tube magazine; smooth forearm. Introduced 1959; discontinued 1963.

Perf.: $360   **Exc.:** $210   **VGood:** $140

ITHACA MODEL X15

Semi-automatic; 22 LR; 7-shot clip magazine; 22-inch barrel; 40-1/2-inch overall length; weighs 6 lbs.; open rear, Raybar front sight; uncheckered walnut pistol-grip stock; beavertail forend. Introduced 1964; discontinued 1967.

Perf.: $380   **Exc.:** $220   **VGood:** $150

IVER JOHNSON 22 CARBINE MODEL EWHBA

Semi-automatic; 22 LR, 22 WMR; 15-shot; 18-1/2-inch barrel; 38-inch overall length; weighs 5-3/4 lbs.; 22 WMR gas-operated; military-style front sight protected by wings, fully-adjustable peep-style rear; sling swivels; walnut finished hardwood stock and front hand guard; blue finish. Imported from Germany. Introduced 1985; dropped 1988.

Exc.: $250   **VGood:** $225   **Good:** $195

IVER JOHNSON LI'L CHAMP

Bolt action; single shot; 22 Short, 22 Long, 22 LR; 16-1/4-inch barrel; 32-1/2-inch overall length; weighs 3-1/8 lbs.; front ramp sight, step-adjustable rear; black moulded stock; nickeled bolt; blue receiver and barrel; stock designed for young shooters. Introduced 1986; dropped 1988.

Exc.: $125   **VGood:** $100   **Good:** $75

IVER JOHNSON MODEL 2-X

Bolt action; single shot; 22 Short, 22 Long, 22 LR; 24-inch round tapered barrel; 41-inch overall length; weighs 4-1/2 lbs.; thumb-screw takedown; drop at comb 1-3/8-inch; drop at heel 2-3/8-inch; length of pull 14-inch; patented automatic safety; adjustable rear sight, blade front; steel buttplate; checkered full pistol grip; grooves in forend; chromium-plated bolt and trigger. Introduced 1930; dropped 1957.

Exc.: $200   **VGood:** $190   **Good:** $150

IVER JOHNSON MODEL 2-XA

Same specs as 2-X except Lyman #55 adjustable rear sight, Lyman #3 ivory 1/16-inch bead front; sling swivels; leather sling strap. Introduced 1930; dropped 1941.

Exc.: $220   **VGood:** $200   **Good:** $170

IVER JOHNSON MODEL 1003 UNIVERSAL CARBINE

Semi-automatic; 30 Carbine; 5-, 15-, 30-shot detachable magazine; 18-inch barrel; 35-3/4-inch overall length; weighs 5-1/2 lbs.; twin guide springs; drilled and tapped for scope mounting; hardwood stock with sling swivels; stainless or blue finish. Not made to military specifications. Manufactured 1986 only.

Exc.: $425   **VGood:** $345   **Good:** $215

IVER JOHNSON MODEL 1256 UNIVERSAL CARBINE

Semi-automatic; 256 Win. Mag.; 5-shot detachable magazine; 18-inch barrel; 35-3/4-inch overall length; weighs 5-1/2 lbs.; twin guide springs; drilled and tapped for scope mounting; hardwood stock with sling swivels; stainless or blue finish. Not made to military specifications. Manufactured 1986 only.

Perf.: $435   **Exc.:** $375   **VGood:** $315

IVER JOHNSON MODEL 5100 SPECIAL APPLICATION RIFLE

Bolt action; single shot; 338/416, 50 BMG; 29-inch free-floating fluted barrel; 51-1/2-inch overall length; weighs 36 lbs.; sniper rifle; marketed with Leupold

Ithaca Model X5-T

Iver Johnson 22 Carbine Model EWHBA

Iver Johnson Model 2-X

Iver Johnson Plainfield M1 Carbine

Iver Johnson Survival Carbine

Ultra M1 20x scope; adjustable composition stock; adjustable trigger; limited production in both calibers.

Exc.: $5000   **VGood:** $3950   **Good:** $2995

IVER JOHNSON MODEL X (EARLY MODEL)

Bolt action; single shot; 22 Short, 22 Long, 22 LR; 22-inch round tapered barrel; 39-1/4-inch overall length; weighs 4 lbs.; thumb-screw takedown; drop at comb 1-3/8-inch; drop at heel 2-5/8-inch; length of pull 13-1/4-inch; patented automatic safety; fixed open rear sight, blade front; steel buttplate; stock with large knob at front of forend; solid walnut stock. Introduced 1928; dropped 1932.

Exc.: $150   **VGood:** $95   **Good:** $50

IVER JOHNSON MODEL X (LATE MODEL)

Same specs as Early Model except 24-inch barrel; weighs 4-1/2 lbs.; larger, heavier stock; drop at heel 2-3/8-inch; length of pull 14-inch; overall length 41-inch; finger grooves in forend. Model X-A with adjustable sights. Introduced 1933; dropped 1941.

Exc.: $160   **VGood:** $100   **Good:** $60

IVER JOHNSON PLAINFIELD MODEL M1 CARBINE

Semi-automatic; 30 Carbine, 5.7mm MMJ, 9mm; 15-shot detachable magazine; 18-inch barrel; 35-1/2-inch overall length; weighs 6-1/2 lbs.; exact copy of WWII U.S. military carbine and manufactured to military specifications; American walnut or hardwood stock; blue or stainless finish; model names and numbers changed several times; M-2 full-automatic model available in early 1980s; Paratrooper Model with folding stock also available; 5.7mm MMJ caliber dropped early; 9mm caliber added in 1986. Introduced 1978; dropped 1992.

Exc.: $425   **VGood:** $345   **Good:** $215

IVER JOHNSON SURVIVAL CARBINE

Semi-automatic; 30 Carbine, 5.7mm MMJ; 15-shot detachable magazine; 18-1/2-inch barrel; 35-1/2-inch

overall length; weighs 6-1/2 lbs.; exact copy of U.S. WWII military carbine and manufactured to military specifications; Zytel plastic stock with pistol grip standard; folding stock available; stainless steel or blue finish. Introduced 1983; dropped 1985. Add 15 percent for 5.7.

Exc.: $425   **VGood:** $345   **Good:** $215

IVER JOHNSON TARGETMASTER EW22HBP

Pump action; 22 Short, 22 Long, 22 LR; 19-shot (22 Short), 15-shot (22 Long), 12-shot (22 LR); 18-1/2-inch barrel; 36-1/2-inch overall length; weighs 5-3/4 lbs.; tubular magazine under barrel; hooded front sight, step-adjustable rear; walnut finished hardwood buttstock and forearm; plastic buttplate; blue finish. Imported from Germany. Introduced 1985; dropped 1988.

Exc.: $190   **VGood:** $130   **Good:** $115

IVER JOHNSON TRAILBLAZER MODEL IJ22HBA

Semi-automatic; 22 LR; 10-shot magazine; 18-1/2-inch barrel; 38-inch overall length; weighs 5-3/4 lbs.; blade front sight, rear step-adjustable for elevation; Monte Carlo-styled checkered hardwood stock; plastic buttplate; blue finish. Imported from Canada. Introduced 1984; dropped 1986.

Exc.: $130   **VGood:** $95   **Good:** $70

IVER JOHNSON WAGONMASTER EW22HBL

Lever action; 22 LR, 22 Short, 22 Long, 22 WMR; 21-shot (22 Short), 17-shot (22 Long), 15-shot (22 LR), 12-shot (22 WMR); 18-1/2-inch barrel; 36-1/2-inch overall length; weighs 5-3/4 lbs.; tubular magazine under barrel; hooded front sight, step-adjustable rear; walnut finished hardwood buttstock and forearm; plastic buttplate; blue finish. Imported from Germany. Introduced 1985; dropped 1988.

Exc.: $190   **VGood:** $140   **Good:** $110

Jaeger Alaskan Model

Jaeger Hunter Model

KDF K15

KDF K15 Improved Model

KDF K22

Kel-Tec
SU-16B

IVER JOHNSON WAGONMASTER JUNIOR MODEL EW22HBLY

Same specs as Wagonmaster except 22 Short, 22 Long, 22 LR; 18-shot (22 Short), 15-shot (22 Long); 14-shot (22 LR); 16-1/4-inch barrel; 33-inch overall length; weighs 5-1/4 lbs. Imported from Germany. Introduced 1985; dropped 1988.

Exc.: $190   **VGood:** $140   **Good:** $110

IVER JOHNSON UNIVERSAL PARATROOPER

Semi-automatic; 30 Carbine; 5-, 15-, 30-shot detachable magazine; 18-inch barrel; 36-inch overall length (stock open), 27-inch overall length (stock folded); twin action guide springs; drilled and tapped for scope mounting; folding Schmeisser-type stock. Not manufactured to military specifications. Manufactured 1986 only.

Exc.: $400   **VGood:** $330   **Good:** $250

JAEGER AFRICAN MODEL

Bolt action; 375 H&H Mag., 416 Taylor, 458 Win. Mag.; 3-shot magazine; 22-inch, 24-inch barrel; weighs 9 lbs.; V-notch rear, hooded ramp front sight; deluxe black fiberglass stock with graphite-reinforcing; swivel studs; recoil pad; single-stage adjustable trigger; hinged floorplate; Mauser-type action; blue/black finish. Introduced 1989; discontinued 1990.

Perf.: $795   **Exc.:** $675   **VGood:** $495

JAEGER ALASKAN MODEL

Bolt action; 7mm Rem. Mag., 300 Win. Mag., 338 Win. Mag.; 4-shot magazine; 22-inch, 24-inch barrel; weighs 8 lbs.; Williams open rear, silver bead ramp front sight; black fiberglass stock; integral sling;

rubber recoil pad; checkered pistol-grip, forend; single-stage trigger; hinged floorplate; Mauser-type action; black wrinkle finish. Introduced 1989; discontinued 1990.

Perf.: $595   **Exc.:** $495   **VGood:** $395

JAEGER HUNTER MODEL

Bolt action; 243, 257 Roberts, 25-06, 7x57, 7mm-08, 280, 308, 30-06; 4-shot magazine; 22-inch, 24-inch barrel; weighs 7 lbs.; no sights; drilled, tapped for scope mounts; black fiberglass stock; integral sling; rubber recoil pad; checkered pistol grip, forend; single-stage adjustable trigger; hinged floorplate; Mauser-type action; black wrinkle finish. Introduced 1989; discontinued 1990.

Perf.: $595   **Exc.:** $495   **VGood:** $395

Laminated wood stock

Perf.: $550   **Exc.:** $495   **VGood:** $375

KBI SA-85M SEMI-AUTO RIFLE

Semi-automatic; 7.62x39mm; 6-shot magazine; 16-3/8-inch barrel; 34-3/4-inch overall length; weighs 7-1/2 lbs.; European hardwood thumbhole stock; post front sight, open adjustable rear; BATF-approved version of the gas-operated Kalashnikov rifle; black phosphate finish; comes with one magazine, cleaning

rod, cleaning/tool kit. Imported from Hungary by K.B.I., Inc. Introduced 1995; dropped 1995.

Perf.: $695   **Exc.:** $625   **VGood:** $475

KDF K15

Bolt action; 25-06, 257 Wea. Mag., 270, 270 Wea. Mag., 7mm Rem. Mag., 30-06, 300 Win. Mag., 300 Wea. Mag., 338 Win. Mag., 340 Wea. Mag., 375 H&H, 411 KDF Mag., 416 Rem. Mag., 458 Win. Mag.; 4-shot magazine (standard calibers), 3-shot (Magnums); 22-inch barrel (standard calibers), 24-inch optional; 44-inch overall (24-inch barrel); weighs about 8 lbs.; sights optional; drilled and tapped for scope mounting; laminated stock standard; Kevlar composite or AAA walnut in Monte Carlo, classic, schnabel or thumbhole styles optional; three-lug locking design with 60° bolt lift; ultra-fast lock time; fully-adjustable trigger. Imported from Germany by KDF, Inc. Introduced 1976; no longer imported.

Perf.: $1495   **Exc.:** $1000   **VGood:** $750

KDF K15 DANGEROUS GAME MODEL

Same specs as K15 except 411 KDF Mag.; choice of iron sights or scope mounts; oil-finished deluxe walnut stock; gloss blue, matte blue, Parkerized or electroless nickel finish; hinged floorplate. Introduced 1986; discontinued 1988.

Perf.: $1695   **Exc.:** $1395   **VGood:** $895

KDF K15 FIBERSTOCK PRO-HUNTER MODEL

Same specs as K15 except Brown Precision fiberglass stock in black, green, brown or camo with wrinkle finish; Parkerized, matte blue or electroless finish; recoil arrestor. Introduced 1986; discontinued 1988.

Perf.: $1650   **Exc.:** $1350   **VGood:** $875

KDF K15 IMPROVED MODEL

Same specs as K15 except 243, 25-06, 270, 7x57, 308, 30-06, 257 Weatherby, 270 Weatherby, 308 Norma Mag., 375 H&H Mag.; hand-checkered, oil-finished featherweight European walnut stock with schnabel or Monte Carlo style. Introduced 1987; discontinued 1988.

Perf.: $1695   **Exc.:** $1395   **VGood:** $895

KDF K15 SWAT MODEL

Same specs as K15 except 308; 24-inch, 26-inch barrel; weighs 10 lbs.; oil-finished walnut target stock; Parkerized metal. Introduced 1986; discontinued 1988.

Perf.: $1550   **Exc.:** $1495   **VGood:** $795

KDF K22

Bolt action; 22 LR, 22 WMR; 5-, 6-shot magazine; 21-1/2-inch barrel; 40-inch overall length; weighs 6-1/2 lbs.; no sights; receiver grooved for scope mounts; hand-checkered, oil-finished European walnut Monte Carlo stock; front-locking lugs on bolt; pillar bedding system. Made in Germany. Introduced 1984; discontinued 1988.

Perf.: $345   **Exc.:** $270   **VGood:** $220

KDF K22 DELUXE

Same specs as K22 except 22 LR only; quick-detachable swivels; rosewood forend tip; rubber recoil pad. Introduced 1984; discontinued 1988.

Perf.: $425   **Exc.:** $340   **VGood:** $280

KEL-TEC SU-16

Semi-automatic; 223; 18.5-inch bbl.; uses M-16 type locking and feeding system; polymer stock holds extra 5-round magazines, polymer forend opens to provide bipod; Picatinny rail on receiver; produced in black, NATO Green or Desert Beige colors. Variations: U-16A, 18.5-inch barrel; SU-16B, 16-inch lightweight barrel; SU-16C, 16-inch barrel, folding stock; SU-16CA, 16-inch standard barrel and standard stock.

Perf.: $500   **Exc.:** $400   **VGood:** $350

KEL-TEC SU-16B LIGHTWEIGHT

Similar to Kel-Tec SU-16, but lightweight version with 16-inch bbl.

Perf.: $500   **Exc.:** $400   **VGood:** $350

KEL-TEC SU-16C CARBINE

Similar to Kel-Tec SU-16, but 16-inch bbl.; polymer stock folds forward for carrying; length open 35.5-inch, length folded 25.5-inch; weighs 4.7 lbs.

Perf.: $500   **Exc.:** $400   **VGood:** $350

KEL-TEC SUB2000 CARBINE

Semi-automatic; 9mm, 40 S&W; 16.1-inch bbl., weighs 4 lbs.; different polymer housings accept S&W, Glock, Beretta, SIG or Kel-Tec magazines; folds to provide compact storage, overall length 30 inches, folded 16.1 inches. Blued, with black grip and forend; parkerized and chrome versions also made. Introduced 1996 by Kel-Tec CNC Industries, still in production.

Perf.: $375   **Exc.:** $ 350   **VGood:** $280

KEL-TEC RFB RIFLE

Bullpup semi-auto rifle with 32", 24" or 18" barrel, black laminated stock, third swivel for bipod. Forward ejection; takes FAL-type magazines. Chambered in .308 Winchester. Introduced in 2007. Price shown is for sporter.

NIB: $2300   **Exc.:** N/A   **VGood:** N/A

KIMBER 22 BOLT-ACTION RIFLE

Bolt action; 22 LR, 5-shot magazine. 18-inch, 22-inch, 24-inch match grade barrel; 11-degree target crown; weighs 5-8 lbs.; 35-inch to 43-inch length; Classic Claro walnut stock, hand-cut checkering, steel gripcap, swivel studs. Sights: None, drilled and tapped. All-new action with Mauser-style full-length claw extractor, two-position wing safety, match trigger, pillar-bedded action with recoil lug. Introduced 1999. Made in U.S.A. by Kimber Mfg., Inc.

Perf.: $950   **Exc.:** $850   **VGood:** $750

KIMBER 22 SUPERAMERICA BOLT-ACTION RIFLE

Similar to 22 Classic except has AAA Claro walnut stock with wrap- around 22 lpi hand-cut checkering, ebony forend tip, beaded cheekpiece. Introduced 1999. Made in U.S.A. by Kimber Mfg., Inc.

Perf.: $1550   **Exc.:** $1300   **VGood:** $1100

KIMBER 22 SVT BOLT-ACTION RIFLE (SHORT VARMINT/TARGET)

Similar to 22 Classic except has 18-inch stainless steel, fluted bull barrel, gray laminated, high-comb target-style stock with deep pistol grip, high comb, beavertail forend with bipod stud. Weighs 7.5 lbs., overall length 36-1/2 inches. Matte finish on action. Introduced 1999. Made in U.S.A. by Kimber Mfg., Inc.

Perf.: $900   **Exc.:** $800   **VGood:** $700

KIMBER 22 HS (HUNTER SILHOUETTE) BOLT-ACTION RIFLE

Similar to 22 Classic except 24-inch medium sporter match-grade barrel with half-fluting; high comb, walnut, Monte Carlo target stock with 18 lpi checkering; matte blue metal finish. Introduced 1999. Made in U.S.A. by Kimber Mfg., Inc.

Perf.: $775   **Exc.:** $675   **VGood:** $575

KIMBER MODEL 82

Bolt action; 22 Short, 22 Long, 22 LR, 22 WMR, 22 Hornet; 5-shot magazine (22 Short, 22 Long, 22 LR), 4-shot (22 WMR), 3-shot (22 Hornet); 22-inch, 24-inch barrel; weighs 6-1/2 lbs.; blade front sight on ramp, open adjustable rear; receiver grooved for special Kimber scope mounts; classic-style or Cascade-design select walnut stock; hand-checkered pistol grip, forend; rocker-type silent safety; checkered steel buttplate; steel grip cap; all-steel construction; blued finish. Classic model. Introduced 1980; discontinued 1988.

Perf.: $1100   **Exc.:** $1000   **VGood:** $795

KIMBER MODEL 82 ALL-AMERICAN MATCH

Same specs as Model 82 except 22 LR; 25-inch target barrel; weighs 9 lbs.; fully-adjustable stock; palm swell, thumb dent pistol grip; step-crowned .9-inch diameter free-floating barrel; forend inletted for weights;

adjustable trigger. Introduced 1990; discontinued 1991.

Perf.: $950   **Exc.:** $835   **VGood:** $695

KIMBER MODEL 82, CONTINENTAL

Same specs as Model 82 except deluxe full-length walnut stock. Introduced 1987; discontinued 1988.

Perf.: $1000   **Exc.:** $900   **VGood:** $695

KIMBER MODEL 82 GOVERNMENT TARGET

Same specs as Model 82 except 22 LR; 25-inch heavy target barrel; 43-1/2-inch overall length; weighs 10-3/4 lbs.; oversize target-type Claro walnut stock; single-stage adjustable trigger; designed as U.S. Army trainers. Introduced 1987; discontinued 1991.

Perf.: $900   **Exc.:** $800   **VGood:** $695

Kel-Tec SUB2000 Carbine

Kel-Tec RFB Rifle

Kimber 22 Bolt-Action Rifle

Kimber 22 SuperAmerica Bolt-Action Rifle

Kimber 22 SVT Bolt-Action Rifle

Kimber 22 HS Hunter Silhouette

Kimber Model 82

Kimber Model 82, Government Target Model

Kimber Model 82,
Varminter Model

Kimber Model 82C Classic

Kimber Model 82C
Custom Match

Kimber Model 82C SuperAmerica

Kimber Model 84, SuperAmerica

Kimber Model 84
Ultra Varminter

KIMBER MODEL 82, HUNTER
Same specs as Model 82 except 22 LR; 22-inch barrel; laminated stock; rubber recoil pad; matte finish. Introduced 1990; discontinued 1990.
Perf.: $750   **Exc.:** $635   **VGood:** $495

KIMBER MODEL 82, MINI CLASSIC
Same specs as Model 82 except 22 LR; 18-inch barrel; sling swivels. Introduced 1988; discontinued 1988.
Perf.: $795   **Exc.:** $695   **VGood:** $595

KIMBER MODEL 82, SPORTER
Same specs as Model 82 except 22 LR; 22-inch barrel; 4-shot magazine; round-top receiver. Introduced 1991; discontinued 1991.
Perf.: $895   **Exc.:** $795   **VGood:** $595

KIMBER MODEL 82, SUPERAMERICA
Same specs as Model 82 except checkered top quality California Claro walnut stock; beaded cheekpiece; ebony forend tip; detachable scope mounts. Introduced 1982; discontinued 1988; reintroduced 1990; discontinued 1991.
Perf.: $1500   **Exc.:** $1400   **VGood:** $1300

KIMBER MODEL 82, VARMINTER
Same specs as Model 82 except 22 LR; 5-, 10-shot magazine; 25-inch heavy barrel; weighs 8-1/4 lbs.; laminated stock; rubber recoil pad. Introduced 1990; discontinued 1991.
Perf.: $895   **Exc.:** $795   **VGood:** $695

KIMBER MODEL 82C CLASSIC
Bolt action; 22 LR; 4-shot magazine; 21-inch premium air-gauged barrel; 40-1/2-inch overall length; weighs 6-1/2 lbs.; no sights; drilled and tapped for Warne scope mounts optionally available from factory; classic-style stock of Claro walnut; 13-1/2-inch length of pull; hand-checkered; red rubber buttpad; polished steel grip cap; action with aluminum pillar bedding for consistent accuracy; single-set fully-adjustable trigger with 2-1/2-lb. pull. Made in U.S. by Kimber of America, Inc. Reintroduced 1994; no longer produced.
Perf.: $795   **Exc.:** $695   **VGood:** $595

KIMBER MODEL 82C CUSTOM MATCH
Same specs as Model 82C Classic except high-grade stock French walnut stock with black ebony forend tip; full coverage 22 lpi borderless checkering; steel Neidner (uncheckered) buttplate; satin rust blue finish. Made in U.S. by Kimber of America, Inc. Reintroduced 1995; no longer produced.
Perf.: $1650   **Exc.:** $1475   **VGood:** $995

KIMBER MODEL 82C SUPERAMERICA
Same specs as Model 82C except AAA fancy grade Claro walnut with beaded cheekpiece; ebony forend cap; hand-checkered 22 lpi patterns with wrap-around coverage; black rubber buttpad. Made in U.S. by Kimber of America, Inc. Reintroduced 1994; no longer produced.
Perf.: $1500   **Exc.:** $1400   **VGood:** $1050

KIMBER MODEL 82C SUPERAMERICA CUSTOM
Same specs as SuperAmerica except Neidner-style buttplate. Available options include: steel skeleton grip cap and buttplate; quarter-rib and open express sights; jewelled bolt; checkered bolt knob; special length of pull; rust blue finish. Made in U.S. by

Kimber of America, Inc. Reintroduced 1994; still produced.
Perf.: $1600   **Exc.:** $1500   **VGood:** $1150

KIMBER MODEL 82C SUPERCLASSIC
Same specs as Model 82C except AAA Claro walnut stock with black rubber buttpad, as used on the SuperAmerica. Made in U.S. by Kimber of America, Inc. Introduced 1995; no longer produced.
Perf.: $1500   **Exc.:** $1400   **VGood:** $1050

KIMBER MODEL 82C VARMINT
Same specs as Model 82C except slightly larger forend to accommodate the medium/heavy barrel profile; fluted, stainless steel match-grade barrel; weighs about 7-1/2 lbs. Made in U.S. by Kimber of America, Inc. Introduced 1995; no longer produced.
Perf.: $995   **Exc.:** $895   **VGood:** $795

KIMBER MODEL 84
Bolt action; 17 Rem., 17 Mach IV, 6x47, 5.6x50, 221 Rem. Fireball, 222 Rem. Mag., 222 Rem., 223 Rem.; 5-shot magazine; 22-inch barrel; 40-1/2-inch overall length; weighs 6-1/4 lbs.; hooded ramp front sight with bead, folding leaf rear are optional; grooved for scope mounts; Claro walnut plain straight comb stock with hand-cut borderless checkering; steel grip cap; checkered steel buttplate; new Mauser-type head locking action; steel trigger guard; three-position safety (new in '87); hinged floorplate; Mauser-type extractor; fully-adjustable trigger. Introduced 1984; discontinued 1989.
Perf.: $1050   **Exc.:** $995   **VGood:** $795

KIMBER MODEL 84, CONTINENTAL MODEL
Same specs as Model 84 except 221 Fireball, 222 Rem., 223 Rem.; 22-inch barrel; full-length deluxe checkered walnut stock. Introduced 1987; discontinued 1988.
Perf.: $1250   **Exc.:** $1095   **VGood:** $895

KIMBER MODEL 84, CUSTOM CLASSIC MODEL
Same specs as Model 84 except select-grade Claro walnut stock with ebony forend tip, Neidner-style buttplate. Introduced 1984; discontinued 1988.
Perf.: $995   **Exc.:** $895   **VGood:** $695

KIMBER MODEL 84, HUNTER MODEL
Same specs as Model 84 except 17 Rem., 222 Rem., 223 Rem.; 22-inch barrel; laminated stock; matte finish. Introduced 1990; discontinued 1990.
Perf.: $825   **Exc.:** $750   **VGood:** $595

KIMBER MODEL 84, SPORTER MODEL
Same specs as Model 84 except 17 Rem., 22 Hornet, 222 Rem., 22-250, 223 Rem., 250 Savage, 35 Rem.; 4-shot magazine; hand-checkered Claro walnut. Introduced 1991; discontinued 1991.
Perf.: $950   **Exc.:** $795   **VGood:** $695

KIMBER MODEL 84, SUPERAMERICA
Same specs as Model 84 except 17 Rem., 221 Rem., 22 Hornet, 22-250, 222 Rem., 223 Rem., 250 Savage, 35 Rem.; 4-shot magazine; 22-inch barrel; detachable scope mounts; top-quality stock; right- or left-hand versions. Introduced 1985; discontinued 1988; reintroduced 1990; discontinued 1991.
Perf.: $1525   **Exc.:** $1195   **VGood:** $995

KIMBER MODEL 84, SUPER GRADE
Same specs as Model 84 except 17 Rem., 222 Rem., 223 Rem.; Mauser bolt action; 22-inch barrel; grade AAA walnut stock. Introduced 1989; discontinued 1989.
Perf.: $1600   **Exc.:** $1250   **VGood:** $1050

KIMBER MODEL 84, ULTRA VARMINTER
Same specs as Model 84 except 17 Rem., 22 Hornet, 221 Rem., 222 Rem., 22-250, 223 Rem.; 24-inch barrel; weighs 7-3/4 lbs.; laminated birchwood stock. Introduced 1989; discontinued 1991.
Perf.: $1295   **Exc.:** $995   **VGood:** $795

KIMBER MODEL 84M BOLT-ACTION RIFLE

Bolt action; 22-250, 243, 260 Rem., 7mm-08, 308, 5-shot. Barrel: 22-inch, 24-inch, 26-inch; weighs 5 lbs., 10 oz. to 10 lbs.; 41-inch to 45-inch length; Claro walnut stock, checkered with steel grip cap or gray laminate; drilled and tapped for bases. Mauser claw extractor, two-position wing safety, action bedded on aluminum pillars, free-floated barrel, match-grade trigger set at 4 lbs., matte blue finish. Introduced 2001. Made in U.S.A. by Kimber Mfg. Inc.

Kimber Model 84M Classic; 22-250, 243, 260, 7mm-08, 308; 22-inch barrel.

Perf.: $900   **Exc.:** $800   **VGood:** $700

Kimber Model 84M Longmaster Classic; 223, 243, 308; 24-inch fluted stainless-steel bbl., introduced 2002.

Perf.: $950   **Exc.:** $850   **VGood:** $760

Kimber Model 84M LongMaster VT; 22-250, heavy varmint rifle, 24-inch or 26-inch stainless-steel bbl., laminated target stock.

Perf.: $1100   **Exc.:** $900   **VGood:** $800

Kimber Model 84M Montana; 243, 260, 7mm-08, 308; stainless steel, synthetic stock, introduced 2003.

Perf.: 1040   **Exc.:** $950   **VGood:** $890

Kimber Model 84M Varmint; 22-250; 26-inch bbl.

Perf.: $950   **Exc.:** $840   **VGood:** $750

Kimber Model 84M Pro Varmint; 204 Ruger, 22-250, 223, 308; introduced 2004.

Perf.: $1030   **Exc.:** $ 945   **VGood:** $850

Kimber Model 84M SuperAmerica; 223, 243, 260, 7mm-08, 308; has high-grade wood, checkering, ebony forend tip; introduced 2003.

Perf.: $1690   **Exc.:** $1430   **VGood:** $1250

KIMBER MODEL 84M LPT TACTICAL

Based on Model 84 action but with 24" mediumweight fluted match barrel, black laminated stock, third swivel for bipod. Chambered in .308 Winchester.

NIB: $1100   **Exc.:** $1000   **VGood:** $875

KIMBER MODEL 8400 SERIES

This series was introduced in 2003 and features the smallest action size compatible with the WSM family of cartridges.

KIMBER MODEL 8400 CLASSIC

This model is fitted with a select walnut stock with 20 lpi checkering. Chambered for the WSM calibers: .270, 7mm, .300, and .325. Barrel length is 24" with no sights. Magazine capacity is 3 rounds. Weight is about 6.6 lbs.

NIB: $1100   **Exc.:** $1000   **VGood:** $875

KIMBER MODEL 8400 MONTANA

This model features a 24" stainless steel barrel with no sights. Stock is black synthetic with no checkering. Same calibers as the Classic. Weight is about 6.25 lbs.

NIB: $1100   **Exc.:** $1000   **VGood:** $875

KIMBER MODEL 8400 SUPERAMERICA

This model is fitted with a AAA walnut stock with 24 lpi checkering. Cheekpiece and ebony forend tip are standard. Barrel length is 24" with no sights and chambered for the same calibers as the Classic. Weight is about 6.6 lbs.

NIB: $2100   **Exc.:** $1875   **VGood:** $1350

KIMBER 8400 CLASSIC SELECT GRADE

Similar to 8400 Classic but with hand-rubbed, oil-finished select stock of Claro or French walnut.

NIB: $1550   **Exc.:** $1350   **VGood:** $995

Kimber Model 84M Bolt-Action Rifle

Kimber 84M Longmaster Classic

Kimber 84M Longmaster VT

Kimber 84M Montana

Kimber 84M SuperAmerica

Kimber 8400 Classic

Kimber 8400 Montana

Kimber 8400 SuperAmerica

Kimber Model 89 African

KIMBER MODEL 8400 TACTICAL

Based on Model 8400 action (oversized bolt handle and knob, etc.) but with 24" heavyweight match barrel, stippled black McMillan stock, third swivel for bipod. Chambered in .308 Winchester.

NIB: $1550   **Exc.:** $1475   **VGood:** $1250

KIMBER MODEL 8400 ADVANCED TACTICAL

Similar to Model 8400 Tactical but with KimPro II Dark Earth finish, fully-adjustable stock and hard case. Introduced in 2007.

NIB: $2100   **Exc.:** $1950   **VGood:** $1695

KIMBER MODEL 89

Bolt action; 257 Roberts, 25-06, 7x57, 270, 280, 7mm Rem. Mag., 30-06, 300 Win. Mag., 300 H&H, 35 Whelen, 338 Win. Mag., 375 H&H Mag.; 3-, 5-shot magazine; 22-inch, 24-inch barrel; 42-inch overall length (22-inch barrel); weighs 7-3/4 lbs.; no sights; Claro or English walnut stock in Classic, Custom Classic design; Model 70-type trigger, ejector design; Mauser-type extractor; three-position safety. Introduced 1988; discontinued 1991.

Perf.: $900   **Exc.:** $800   **VGood:** $700

KIMBER MODEL 89 AFRICAN

Same specs as Model 89 except 375 H&H Mag., 404 Jeffery, 416 Rigby, 460 Weatherby Mag., 505 Gibbs; 5-shot magazine (375 H&H Mag.), 4-shot (404 Jeffery, 416 Rigby), 3-shot (460 Weatherby, 505 Gibbs); 26-inch heavy barrel; 47-inch overall length; weighs 10-1/2 lbs.; ramped blade front, express rear sight; English walnut stock with cheekpiece; rubber buttpad; double crossbolts. Introduced 1990; discontinued 1991.

Perf.: $4000   **Exc.:** $3595   **VGood:** $2495

Kimber Model 89, Medium Weight Deluxe

Kleinguenther K-15

Kleinguenther K-22

Kodiak Mk. IV Double Rifle

Krico Model 260

Krico Model 302

KIMBER MODEL 89, FEATHERWEIGHT DELUXE

Same specs as Model 89 except 257 Roberts, 25-06, 7x57, 270, 280, 30-06; 5-shot magazine; 22-inch light barrel; weighs 7-1/2 lbs.; deluxe walnut stock. Introduced 1989; discontinued 1990.

Perf.: $1295 **Exc.:** $1095 **VGood:** $895

KIMBER MODEL 89, HEAVYWEIGHT DELUXE

Same specs as Model 89 except 375 H&H Mag., 458 Win. Mag.; 3-shot magazine; 24-inch heavy barrel; weighs 9 lbs. Introduced 1989; discontinued 1990.

Perf.: $1500 **Exc.:** $1300 **VGood:** $1000

KIMBER MODEL 89, HUNTER

Same specs as Model 89 except 270, 30-06, 300 Win. Mag., 338 Win. Mag., 7mm Rem. Mag.; 22-inch barrel; laminated stock; matte finish. Introduced 1990; discontinued 1991.

Perf.: $1195 **Exc.:** $995 **VGood:** $750

KIMBER MODEL 89, MEDIUM WEIGHT DELUXE

Same specs as Model 89 except 300 Win. Mag., 300 H&H Mag., 300 Weatherby, 338 Win. Mag., 35 Whelen, 7mm Rem. Mag.; 3-shot magazine; 24-inch barrel; weighs 8 lbs. Introduced 1989; discontinued 1990.

Perf.: $1595 **Exc.:** $1095 **VGood:** $795

KIMBER MODEL 89, SUPER GRADE

Same specs as Model 89 except 22-inch barrel; grade AAA walnut stock; square receiver. Introduced 1989; discontinued 1989.

Perf.: $1595 **Exc.:** $1295 **VGood:** $995

KIMEL AR9

Semi-automatic; 9mm Para.; 20-shot magazine; 16-1/4-inch barrel; 33-inch overall length; weighs 6-1/2 lbs.; adjustable post front sight in ring, fixed open rear; folding buttstock, checkered plastic grip; fires from closed bolt; lever safety blocks trigger and sear; vented barrel shroud; matte blue/black or nickel finish. Made in U.S. Marketed by Kimel Industries. Introduced 1991; no longer produced.

Perf.: $510 **Exc.:** $450 **VGood:** $300

KINTREK MODEL KBP-1

Semi-automatic; 22 LR; 17-shot magazine; 25-inch barrel; 31-1/2-inch overall length; weighs 5-1/2 lbs.; post front sight, fully-adjustable aperture rear; drilled and tapped for scope mount; solid black synthetic bullpup stock with smooth pebble finish; grip safety and trigger-blocking safeties; ejects empties out through bottom of stock; bolt hold-open operated by grip safety; matte black finish. Made in U.S. by Kintrek, Inc. Introduced 1991; discontinued 1992.

Perf.: $175 **Exc.:** $150 **VGood:** $130

KLEINGUENTHER K-15

Bolt action; 243, 25-06, 270, 30-06, 308 Win., 7x57, 308 Norma Mag., 300 Weatherby Mag., 7mm Rem. Mag., 375 H&H, 257 Winchester, 270 Weatherby Mag., 300 Weatherby Mag.; 24-inch barrel (standard calibers) 26-inch (Magnums); no sights; drilled, tapped for scope mounts; hand-checkered Monte Carlo stock of European walnut; rosewood grip cap; high-luster or satin finish; recoil pad; many optional features available on special order. Manufactured in Germany. Imported and assembled by Kleinguenther; discontinued 1985.

Perf.: $1295 **Exc.:** $995 **VGood:** $750

KLEINGUENTHER K-22

Bolt action; 22 LR, 22 WMR; 5-shot magazine; 21-1/2-inch barrel; 40-inch overall length; weighs 6-1/2 lbs.; no sights; drilled, tapped for scope mounts; walnut-stained beechwood Monte Carlo stock; hand-cut checkering; sling swivels; no sights; two forward locking lugs; adjustable trigger; optional set trigger; silent safety. Made in Germany. Introduced 1984; discontinued 1985.

Perf.: $350 **Exc.:** $290 **VGood:** $200

With double-set trigger

Perf.: $395 **Exc.:** $320 **VGood:** $220

KODIAK MK. IV DOUBLE RIFLE

Double rifle; 45-70; 24-inch barrels; 42-1/2-inch overall length; weighs 10 lbs.; ramp front sight with bead, adjustable two-leaf rear; European walnut stock with semi-pistol grip; exposed hammers; color case-hardened locks; rubber recoil pad. Imported from Italy by Trail Guns Armory. Manufactured in Italy by Pedersoli. Introduced 1988; discontinued 1994.

Exc.: $2000 **VGood:** $1500 **Good:** $895

KRICO CARBINE

Bolt action; 22 Hornet, 222 Rem; 4-shot clip magazine; 20-inch, 22-inch barrel; open rear, hooded ramp front sight; hand-checkered European walnut full-length stock; miniature Mauser-type action; single- or double-set trigger; sling swivels. Made in Germany. Introduced 1956; discontinued 1962.

Exc.: $695 **VGood:** $575 **Good:** $450

KRICO MODEL 120M

Bolt action; 22 LR; 5-shot magazine; 19-1/2-inch barrel; 46-inch overall length; weighs 6 lbs.; military trainer; tangent elevation-adjustable rear, hooded blade front; receiver grooved for scope mounts; European hardwood stock; blued finish; adjustable trigger. Made in Germany. No longer imported.

Perf.: $350 **Exc.:** $290 **VGood:** $220

KRICO MODEL 260

Semi-automatic; 22 LR; 5-shot magazine; 19-1/2-inch barrel; 39-inch overall length; weighs 6-3/8 lbs.; ramp blade front sight, open adjustable rear; receiver grooved for scope mounting; beechwood stock; sliding safety. Made in Germany. Introduced 1989.

Perf.: $495 **Exc.:** $395 **VGood:** $285

KRICO MODEL 300

Bolt action; 22 LR, 22 WMR, 22 Hornet; 19-1/2-inch, 23-1/2-inch barrel; weighs 6 lbs.; ramp blade front sight, open adjustable rear; walnut-stained beech stock; double triggers; sliding safety; checkered grip, forend. Made in Germany. Introduced 1989.

Perf.: $600 **Exc.:** $485 **VGood:** $375

KRICO MODEL 300 DELUXE

Same specs as Model 300 except European walnut stock; better checkering. Introduced 1989.

Perf.: $625 **Exc.:** $495 **VGood:** $395

KRICO MODEL 300 SA

Same specs as Model 300 except Monte Carlo-style walnut stock. Introduced 1989.

Perf.: $575 **Exc.:** $450 **VGood:** $350

KRICO MODEL 300 STUTZEN

Same specs as Model 300 except full-length Stutzen-type walnut stock. Introduced 1989.

Perf.: $595 **Exc.:** $495 **VGood:** $395

KRICO MODEL 302

Bolt action; 22 LR; 5-, 10-shot magazine; 24-inch barrel; 43-inch overall length; weighs 6-1/2 lbs.; hooded post front, windage-adjustable rear sight; European walnut stock; checkered pistol grip, forend; single- or double-set trigger. Made in Germany. Introduced 1982; discontinued 1984.

Exc.: $575 **VGood:** $450 **Good:** $350

With double-set trigger

Exc.: $675 **VGood:** $495 **Good:** $395

KRICO MODEL 302DR C

Same specs as Model 302 except 22 LR, 22 WMR; classic-style European walnut stock. Introduced 1983; discontinued 1984.

Exc.: $595   **VGood:** $495   **Good:** $395

KRICO MODEL 302E

Same specs as Model 302 except straight forend; walnut-finished hardwood stock; single trigger. Introduced 1982; discontinued 1983.

Exc.: $625   **VGood:** $495   **Good:** $395

KRICO MODEL 304

Bolt action; 22 LR; 5-, 10-shot magazine; 20-inch barrel; weighs 6-1/4 lbs.; hooded ramp front, windage-adjustable rear sight; full-length Mannlicher-type stock; single- or double-set trigger. Made in Germany. Introduced 1982; discontinued 1984.

Exc.: $615   **VGood:** $525   **Good:** $395

KRICO MODEL 311

Bolt action; 22 LR; 5-, 10-shot clip magazine; 22-inch barrel; open rear sight, hooded ramp front; hand-checkered European walnut stock, pistol grip, cheekpiece; single- or double-set trigger; sling swivels. Also available with 2-1/2X scope. Introduced 1958; discontinued 1962.

Exc.: $340   **VGood:** $300   **Good:** $225

With scope

Exc.: $440   **VGood:** $380   **Good:** $290

KRICO MODEL 320

Bolt action; 22 LR; 5-shot magazine; 19-1/2-inch barrel; 38-1/2-inch overall length; weighs 6 lbs.; windage-adjustable open rear sight, blade front on ramp; Mannlicher-style select European walnut stock; cut-checkered grip, forend; blued steel forend cap; detachable box magazine; single- or double-set triggers. Made in Germany. Introduced 1986; discontinued 1988.

Exc.: $650   **VGood:** $570   **Good:** $480

KRICO MODEL 330S MATCH

Single shot; 22 LR; 25-1/2-inch heavy barrel; hooded front sight with interchangeable inserts, diopter match rear, rubber eye-cup; walnut-finished beechwood match stock; built-in hand stop; adjustable recoil pad; factory-set match trigger; stippled pistol grip. Introduced 1981; no longer imported.

Exc.: $705   **VGood:** $595   **Good:** $450

KRICO MODEL 340

Bolt action; 22 LR; 5-shot clip magazine; 21-inch match barrel; 39-1/2-inch overall length; weighs 7-1/2 lbs.; no sights; receiver grooved for tip-off mounts; European walnut match-style stock; stippled grip, forend; free-floating bull barrel; adjustable two-stage match trigger or double-set trigger; meets NRA MS rules. Made in Germany. Introduced 1983; discontinued 1988.

Exc.: $715   **VGood:** $605   **Good:** $480

KRICO MODEL 340 KRICOTRONIC

Same specs as Model 340 except electronic ignition system, replacing firing pin; fast lock time. Made in Germany. Introduced 1985; discontinued 1988.

Exc.: $1200   **VGood:** $900   **Good:** $750

KRICO MODEL 340 MINI-SNIPER

Same specs as Model 340 except weighs 8 lbs.; 40 overall length; high comb; palm swell, stippled ventilated forend; receiver grooved for scope mounts; free-floating bull barrel; muzzlebrake; large bolt knob; match-quality single trigger; sandblasted barrel, receiver. Made in Germany. Introduced 1984; discontinued 1986.

Exc.: $995   **VGood:** $795   **Good:** $575

KRICO MODEL 352E

Bolt action; 22 WMR; 24-inch barrel; 43-inch overall length; weighs 6-1/2 lbs.; hooded post front, windage-adjustable rear sight; walnut finished hard stock; wood straight forend; no white line spaces. Introduced 1982; discontinued 1984.

Exc.: $375   **VGood:** $325   **Good:** $235

Krico Model 304

Krico Model 320

Krico Model 340 Match

Krico Model 340 Mini-Sniper

Krico Model 360S Biathlon

Krico Model 400

KRICO MODEL 360S BIATHLON

Bolt action; 22 LR; 5-shot magazine; 21-1/4-inch barrel; 40-1/2-inch overall length; weighs 9-1/4 lbs.; globe front, fully-adjustable Diana 62 match peep rear sight; high-comb European walnut stock; adjustable buttplate; muzzle/sight snow cap; straight-pull action; match trigger. Marketed with five magazines, four stored in stock. Made in Germany. Introduced 1991.

Perf.: $1600   **Exc.:** $1300   **VGood:** $800

KRICO MODEL 360S2 BIATHLON

Same specs as Model 360S except weighs 9 lbs.; biathlon stock design of black epoxy-finished walnut with pistol grip; pistol-grip-activated action. Imported from Germany by Mandall Shooting Supplies. Introduced 1991; no longer imported.

Perf.: $1450   **Exc.:** $1150   **VGood:** $750

KRICO MODEL 400

Bolt action; 22 LR, 22 Hornet; 5-shot detachable magazine; 23-1/2-inch barrel; 41-inch overall length; weighs 8-1/2 lbs.; hooded post front, windage-adjustable open rear sight; hand-checkered deluxe European walnut stock; schnabel forend; solid rubber recoil pad; rear locking lugs; twin extractors; sling swivels; single- or double-set triggers. Introduced 1983; discontinued 1989.

Exc.: $765   **VGood:** $625   **Good:** $535

KRICO MODEL 400E

Same specs as Model 400 except straight forend; walnut-finished beech stock; no forend tip; hard rubber buttplate; single- or double-set trigger. Introduced 1982; discontinued 1983.

Perf.: $595   **Exc.:** $495   **VGood:** $375

KRICO MODEL 400L

Same specs as Model 400 except select French walnut stock; no schnabel. Introduced 1982; discontinued 1983.

Perf.: $795   **Exc.:** $695   **VGood:** $585

KRICO MODEL 400 MATCH

Same specs as Model 400 except single shot; 22 LR; 23-1/2-inch heavy barrel; no sights; match-type stock. Introduced Still in production.

Perf.: $850   **Exc.:** $705   **VGood:** $595

KRICO MODEL 420L

Bolt action; 22 Hornet; 5-shot magazine; 20-inch barrel; weighs 6-1/2 lbs.; hooded post front, windage-adjustable open rear sight; full-length walnut stock; solid rubber buttpad; rear locking lugs; twin extractors; sling swivels; single- or double-set trigger. Introduced 1982; discontinued 1983.

Exc.: $850   **VGood:** $725   **Good:** $575

KRICO MODEL 500 KRICOTRONIC MATCH

Bolt action; single shot; 22 LR; 23-1/2-inch barrel; 45-1/5-inch overall length; weighs 9-1/5 lbs.; globe front, match-type rear sight; match-type European walnut stock; adjustable butt; electronic ignition system; adjustable trigger. Made in Germany.

Perf.: $3700   **Exc.:** $2695   **VGood:** $1695

Krico Model 600 EAC

Krico Model 600 Match

Krico Model 620

Krico Model 640S

Krico Model 650S

Krico Model 700

KRICO MODEL 600

Bolt action; 17 Rem., 22-250, 222, 222 Rem. Mag., 223, 243, 308, 5.6x50 Mag.; 3-, 4-shot magazine; 23-1/2-inch barrel; 43-3/4-inch overall length; weighs 8 lbs.; hooded ramp front, fixed rear sight; tangent rear sight optional; hand-checkered European walnut Monte Carlo stock; schnabel forend; classic American-style stock also available; adjustable single- or double-set trigger, silent safety; double front locking lugs. Introduced 1983; no longer imported.
   Exc.: $995   **VGood:** $850   **Good:** $750

KRICO MODEL 600 EAC

Same specs as Model 600 except American-style classic stock; sling swivels. Introduced 1983; discontinued 1984.
   Exc.: $995   **VGood:** $795   **Good:** $595

KRICO MODEL 600 DELUXE

Same specs as Model 600 except traditional European-style select fancy walnut stock; rosewood schnabel forend tip; Bavarian cheekpiece; fine checkering; front sling swivel attaches to barrel; butterknife bolt handle; gold-plated single-set trigger. Introduced 1983; discontinued 1984.
   Exc.: $1095   **VGood:** $795   **Good:** $625

KRICO MODEL 600 MATCH

Same specs as Model 600 except no sights; drilled, tapped for scope mounts; cheekpiece match stock; vented forend; rubber recoil pad. Introduced 1983.
   Perf.: $1150   **Exc.:** $895   **VGood:** $750

KRICO MODEL 600 SINGLE SHOT

Same specs as Model 600 except match barrel; no sights; drilled, tapped for scope mounts; adjustable buttplate; match-type stock; flash hider; Parkerized

finish; large bolt knob; wide trigger shoe. Made in Germany. Introduced 1983.
   Perf.: $1150   **Exc.:** $895   **VGood:** $750

KRICO MODEL 600 SNIPER

Same specs as Model 600 except match barrel; no sights; drilled, tapped for scope mounts; adjustable buttplate; flash hider; Parkerized finish; large bolt knob; wide trigger shoe. Made in Germany. Introduced 1983.
   Perf.: $2550   **Exc.:** $2000   **VGood:** $1795

KRICO MODEL 620

Bolt action; 222 Rem., 223 Rem., 22-250, 243, 308, 5.6x50 Mag.; 3-shot magazine; 20-3/4-inch barrel; weighs 6-3/4 lbs.; hooded ramp front, fixed rear sight; tangent rear sight optional; drilled, tapped for scope mounts; full-length walnut stock; double-set trigger. Introduced 1988; discontinued 1988.
   Perf.: $1165   **Exc.:** $880   **VGood:** $790

KRICO MODEL 640S

Bolt action; 222, 223, 22-250, 308; 5-shot magazine; 20-inch semi-bull barrel; no sights; pistol-grip stock of French walnut; ventilated forend; single- or double-set triggers. Introduced 1981; discontinued 1988.
   Exc.: $1295   **VGood:** $995   **Good:** $750

KRICO MODEL 640 VARMINT

Bolt action; 22-250, 222 Rem., 223 Rem.; 4-shot magazine; 23-3/4-inch barrel; weighs 9-3/8 lbs.; no sights; drilled, tapped for scope mounts; cut-checkered select European walnut stock; high Monte Carlo comb; Wundhammer palm swell; rosewood forend tip. Made in Germany. Importation discontinued 1988.
   Exc.: $1125   **VGood:** $995   **Good:** $895

KRICO MODEL 650S

Bolt action; 222, 223, 308; 3-shot magazine; 23-inch bull barrel; muzzlebrake/flash hider; no sights; drilled, tapped for scope mounts; oil-finished select European walnut stock; adjustable cheekpiece, recoil pad; match trigger; single- or double-set trigger available; all metal; matte blue finish. Introduced 1981; discontinued 1988.
   Exc.: $1395   **VGood:** $995   **Good:** $795

KRICO MODEL 650S2

Same specs as Model 650 except special benchrest stock of French walnut. Introduced 1981; discontinued 1983.
   Exc.: $1395   **VGood:** $1095   **Good:** $825

KRICO MODEL 650 SUPER SNIPER

Same specs as Model 650 except 223, 308; 26-inch bull barrel. Made in Germany. Introduced 1981; discontinued 1988.
   Exc.: $1495   **VGood:** $1095   **Good:** $825

KRICO MODEL 700

Bolt action; 17 Rem., 222, 222 Rem. Mag., 223, 5.6x50 Mag., 243, 308, 5.6x57 RWS, 22-250, 6.5x55, 6.5x57, 7x57, 270, 7x64, 30-06, 9.3x62, 6.5x68, 7mm Rem. Mag., 300 Win. Mag., 8x68S, 7.5 Swiss, 9.3x64, 6x62 Freres; 23-1/2-inch barrel (standard calibers), 25-1/2-inch (magnums); 43-3/8-inch overall length (23-1/2-inch barrel); weighs about 7 lbs.; blade on ramp front sight, open adjustable rear; drilled, tapped for scope mounting; European walnut stock with Bavarian cheekpiece; removable box magazine; sliding safety. Imported from Germany by Mandall Shooting Supplies.
   Exc.: $1000   **VGood:** $795   **Good:** $680

KRICO MODEL 700 DELUXE

Same specs as Model 700 except better grade of wood, checkering. Imported from Germany by Mandall Shooting Supplies.
   Exc.: $1050   **VGood:** $875   **Good:** $725

KRICO MODEL 700 STUTZEN

Same specs as Model 700 except full-length stock. Imported from Germany by Mandall Shooting Supplies.
   Exc.: $1195   **VGood:** $895   **Good:** $695

KRICO MODEL 720

Bolt action; 17 Rem., 222, 222 Rem. Mag., 223, 5.6x50 Mag., 243, 308, 5.6x57 RWS, 22-250, 6.5x55, 6.5x57, 7x57, 270, 7x64, 30-06, 9.3x62, 6.5x68, 7mm Rem. Mag., 300 Win. Mag., 8x68S, 7.5 Swiss, 9.3x64, 6x62 Freres; 3-shot magazine; 20-3/4-inch barrel; weighs 6-3/4 lbs.; hooded ramp front, fixed rear sight; tangent rear sight optional; drilled, tapped for scope mounting; full-length walnut stock; double-set trigger. Introduced 1983; discontinued 1990.
   Exc.: $1095   **VGood:** $925   **Good:** $695

KRICO SPORTER

Bolt action; 22 Hornet, 222 Rem.; 4-shot clip magazine; 22-inch, 24-inch, 26-inch barrel; open rear, hooded ramp front sight; hand-checkered European walnut stock, cheekpiece, pistol grip, forend tip; miniature Mauser-type action; single- or double-set trigger; sling swivels. Made in Germany. Introduced 1956; discontinued 1962.
   Exc.: $645   **VGood:** $525   **Good:** $400

KRICO VARMINT MODEL

Bolt action; 222 Rem.; 4-shot magazine; 22-inch, 24-inch, 26-inch heavy barrel; no sights. Made in Germany. Introduced 1956; discontinued 1962.
   Exc.: $665   **VGood:** $575   **Good:** $435

KRIEGHOFF CLASSIC DOUBLE RIFLE

Double rifle; 7x65R, 308 Win., 30-06, 8x57 JRS, 8x75RS, 9.3x74R; 23.5-inch barrel; weighs 7.3 to 8 lbs. High grade European walnut stock. Standard has conventional rounded cheekpiece, Bavaria has Bavarian-style cheekpiece. Bead front sight with removable, adjustable wedge (375 H&H and below), standing leaf rear on quarter-rib. Boxlock action; double triggers; short opening angle for fast loading;

quiet extractors; sliding, self-adjusting wedge for secure bolting; Purdey-style barrel extension; horizontal firing pin placement. Many options available. Introduced 1997. Imported from Germany by Krieghoff International.

Perf.: $9700   **VGood:** $7500   **Good:** $5500

KRIEGHOFF CLASSIC BIG FIVE DOUBLE RIFLE

Similar to the standard Classic except available in 375 Flanged Mag. N.E., 500/416 N.E., 470 N.E., 500 N.E. 3-inch, 375 H&H, 416 Rigby, 458. Double trigger; has hinged front trigger, non-removable muzzle wedge (larger than 375-caliber), Universal Trigger System, Combi Cocking Device, steel trigger guard, specially weighted stock bolt for weight and balance. Many options available. Introduced 1997. Imported from Germany by Krieghoff International.

Perf.: $14500   **Exc.:** $11500   **VGood:** $7000

KRIEGHOFF HUBERTUS SINGLE-SHOT RIFLE

Single shot; 222, 243, 270, 308, 30-06, 5.6x50R Mag., 5.6x52R, 6x62R Freres, 6.5x57R, 6.5x65R, 7x57R, 7x65R, 8x57JRS, 8x75RS, 7mm Rem. Mag.; 300 Win. Mag.; 23-1/2-inch barrel; weighs 6-1/2 lbs. High-grade walnut stock; Blade front, open rear sights. Break-loading with manual cocking lever on top tang; take-down; extractor; schnabel forearm; many options. Imported from Germany by Krieghoff International Inc.

Perf.: $5700   **Exc.:** $4900   **VGood:** $3800

KRIEGHOFF NEPTUN

Drilling; 12-, 16-, 20-ga./22 Hornet, 222 Rem., 243, 270, 30-06, 308; standard European calibers also available up to 9.3x74R; 25-inch barrels; shot barrels choked Imp. Mod. & Full; optional free-floating rifle barrel available; weighs about 7-1/2 lbs.; bead front sight, automatic pop-up open rear; hand-checkered European walnut stock with German-style grip and cheekpiece, oil finish; full sidelock action with double or optional single trigger, top tang shotgun safety; fine, light scroll engraving. Imported from Germany by Krieghoff International, Inc. No longer imported.

Perf.: $17000   **Exc.:** $13000   **VGood:** $9100

KRIEGHOFF TECK COMBO

Combination gun; over/under; 12-, 16-, 20-ga./22 Hornet, 222, 243, 270, 30-06, 308 and standard European calibers; O/U rifle also available in 458 Win. on special order; 25-inch barrels on double rifle combo, 28-inch on O/U shotgun; optional free-floating rifle barrel; weighs about 7 to 7-1/2 lbs.; white bead front sight on shotgun, open or folding on rifle or combo; hand-checkered European walnut stock with German-style grip and cheekpiece; boxlock action with non-selective single trigger or optional single/double trigger; Greener cross-bolt; ejectors standard on all but O/U rifle; top tang safety; light scroll engraving. Imported from Germany by Krieghoff International, Inc. No longer imported. Premium for 458 Win Mag caliber.

Perf.: $9700   **Exc.:** $7000   **VGood:** $5000

KRIEGHOFF TECK DOUBLE RIFLE

Double rifle; boxlock; over/under; 7x57R, 7x64, 7x65R, 308 Win., 30-06, 300 Win. Mag., 8x57JRS, 9.3x74R, 375 H&H Mag., 458 Win. Mag.; 25-inch barrel; Express rear, ramp front sight; hand-checkered European walnut stock, forearm; double crossbolt; double underlugs. Introduced 1967; No longer imported. Premium for 458.

Perf.: $10,000   **Exc.:** $8000   **VGood:** $6000

KRIEGHOFF TRUMPF

Drilling; 12-, 16-, 20-ga./22 Hornet, 222 Rem., 243, 270, 30-06, 308; standard European calibers also available, up to 9.3x74R; 25-inch barrels; shot barrels choked Imp. Mod. & Full; optional free-floating rifle barrel; weighs about 7-1/2 lbs.; bead front sight, automatic pop-up open rear; hand-checkered European walnut stock with German-style grip and cheekpiece; oil finish; boxlock action with double or optional single trigger; top tang shotgun safety; fine,

Krieghoff Trumpf

Krieghoff Teck Double Rifle

Krieghoff Ulm

Krieghoff Ulm-Primus

Lakefield Arms Mark II Left Hand

Lakefield Arms Model 64B

light scroll engraving. Imported from Germany by Krieghoff International, Inc. No longer imported.

Perf.: $10,000   **Exc.:** $8000   **VGood:** $6000

KRIEGHOFF ULM COMBO

Combination gun; over/under; 12-, 16-, 20-ga./22 Hornet, 222, 243, 270, 30-06, 308 and standard European calibers; O/U rifle also available in 458 Win. on special order; 25-inch barrels (double rifle combo), 28-inch (O/U shotgun); optional free-floating rifle barrel; weighs about 7-7-1/2 lbs.; white bead front sight on shotgun, open or folding on rifle or combo; hand-checkered European walnut stock with German-style grip and cheekpiece; full sidelock action with non-selective single trigger or optional single/double trigger; Greener cross-bolt; ejectors standard on all but O/U rifle; top tang safety; light scroll engraving. Imported from Germany by Krieghoff International, Inc. No longer imported.

Perf.: $14,500   **Exc.:** $12,000   **VGood:** $8950

KRIEGHOFF ULM DOUBLE RIFLE

Double rifle; boxlock; over/under; 7x57R, 7x64, 7x65R, 308 Win., 30-06, 300 Win. Mag., 8x57JRS, 9.3x74R, 375 H&H Mag., 458 Win. Mag.; 25-inch barrel; express rear, ramp front sight; hand-checkered European walnut stock, forearm; double cross-bolt; double underlugs; leaf arabesque engraving. Introduced 1963; still imported.

Perf.: $16,800   **Exc.:** $14,500   **VGood:** $11,000

KRIEGHOFF ULM-PRIMUS

Same specs as Ulm except deluxe modifications including higher grade of engraving, wood;

detachable side locks. Introduced 1963; discontinued 1983.

Perf.: $24,500   **Exc.:** $20,500   **VGood:** $16,000

LAKEFIELD ARMS MARK I

Bolt action; single shot; 22 LR; 20-1/2-inch barrel; 39-1/2-inch overall length; weighs 5-1/2 lbs.; bead front, open adjustable rear sight; receiver grooved for scope mounts; checkered Monte Carlo-type stock of walnut-finished hardwood; thumb-activated rotating safety; right-, left-hand variations; youth model available with smaller dimensions; blued finish. Made in Canada. Introduced 1990.

Perf.: $100   **Exc.:** $75   **VGood:** $60

LAKEFIELD ARMS MARK II

Bolt action; 22 LR; 10-shot magazine; 20-1/2-inch barrel; 39-1/2-inch overall length; weighs 5-1/2 lbs.; bead front, open adjustable rear sight; receiver grooved for scope mounts; checkered Monte Carlo-type stock of walnut-finished hardwood; thumb-activated rotary safety; right-, left-hand variations; youth model available with smaller dimensions; blued finish. Made in Canada. Introduced 1990.

Perf.: $110   **Exc.:** $80   **VGood:** $65

LAKEFIELD ARMS MODEL 64B

Semi-automatic; 22 LR; 10-shot magazine; 20-inch barrel; 40-inch overall length; weighs 5-1/2 lbs.; bead front, open adjustable rear sight; checkered Monte Carlo-type walnut stained hardwood stock; side ejection; bolt hold-open device; thumb-activated rotary safety; blued finish. Made in Canada. Introduced 1990.

Perf.: $110   **Exc.:** $90   **VGood:** $80

Lakefield Arms Model 90 Biathlon

Lakefield Arms Model 91T

Lakefield Arms Model 92S Silhouette

Lakefield Arms Model 93M

L.A.R. Grizzly 50 Big Boar

Lebeau-Courally Sidelock

Legacy Sports International M-1500 Custom

stock with Monte Carlo-type comb; checkered grip and forend; thumb-operated rotary safety; blue finish. Made in Canada by Lakefield Arms Ltd. Introduced 1994.

Perf.: $130 **Exc.:** $100 **VGood:** $90

L.A.R. GRIZZLY 50 BIG BOAR

Bolt action; single shot; 50 BMG, 36-inch barrel; 45-1/2-inch overall length; weighs 28-1/2 lbs.; no sights; scope mount; integral stock; ventilated rubber recoil pad; bullpup design; thumb safety; all-steel construction. Made in U.S. by L.A.R. Mfg., Inc. Introduced 1994; still produced.

Perf.: $2150 **Exc.:** $2000 **VGood:** $1800

LEBEAU-COURALLY BOXLOCK

Double rifle; 8x57JRS, 9.3x74R; 23-1/2-inch to 26-inch chopper lump barrels; made to customer specs; weighs 8 lbs.; Express rear sight on quarter-rib, bead on ramp front; French walnut stock; pistol grip with cheekpiece, splinter or beavertail forend; steel grip cap; ejectors; several engraving patterns. Made in Belgium. Introduced 1987; no longer imported.

Perf.: $16,995 **Exc.:** $14,950 **VGood:** $9995

LEBEAU-COURALLY EXPRESS RIFLE SXS

Double rifle; 7x65R, 8x57JRS, 9.3x74R, 375 H&H, 470 N.E.; 24-inch to 26-inch barrels; weighs 7-3/4 to 10-1/2 lbs.; Fancy French walnut stock with cheekpiece; Bead on ramp front sight, standing express rear on quarter-rib. Holland & Holland-type sidelock with automatic ejectors; double triggers. Built to order only. Imported from Belgium by Wm. Larkin Moore.

Perf.: $38,000 **Exc.:** $30,000 **VGood:** $20,000

LEBEAU-COURALLY SIDELOCK

Double rifle; 8x57 JRS, 9.3x74R, 375 H&H, 458 Win. Mag., 470 NE, 577 NE; 23-1/2-inch to 26-inch chopper lump barrels; weighs 8 lbs.; made to customer specs; Express rear sight on quarter-rib, bead on ramp front; French walnut stock; pistol grip with cheekpiece, splinter or beavertail forend; steel grip cap; ejectors; reinforced action; several engraving patterns. Made in Belgium. Introduced 1987; no longer imported.

Perf.: $34,000 **Exc.:** $28,000 **VGood:** $19,000

LEGACY SPORTS INTERNATIONAL M-1500 CUSTOM RIFLES

Bolt action; 300 WSM, 300 Win. Mag.; 3 plus 1 in chamber; weighs 7.6 to 8.3 lbs.; 42-1/2-inch overall length. Black polymer or laminated wood stock; Built on Howa M-1500 stainless steel short-action, 3-position thumb safety, hinged floorplate, drilled and tapped for standard scope mounts. 300 WSM has stainless steel short action, 22-inch barrel. 300 Win. Mag. has blued long action, 24-inch bbl. with integral ported muzzle brake by Bill Wiseman. Introduced 2001 by Legacy Sports International.

Polymer stock		
Perf.: $850	**Exc.:** $750	**VGood:** $650
Laminated wood stock		
Perf.: $900	**Exc.:** $800	**VGood:** $700

LEGACY SPORTS INTERNATIONAL TEXAS SAFARI RIFLES

Bolt action; 270 Win., 300 Win. Mag. 270 Win.: 5 plus 1 in chamber; 300 Mag., 3 plus 1 in chamber; weighs 7.8 lbs; 42-1/2-inch overall length; 44-1/2 inches in 300 Win. Mag.; Brown/black laminated wood stock. Built on Howa M-1500 action customized by Bill Wiseman, College Station, TX; Wiseman-designed 3-position thumb safety and bolt-release, hinged floorplate, drilled and tapped for standard scope mounts. Action glass-bedded, Farrell free floated. 300 Win. Mag. has integral muzzle brake. Introduced 2001 by Legacy Sports International.

Perf.: $1495	**Exc.:** $1375	**VGood:** $1265
300 Win. Mag.		
Perf.: $1600	**Exc.:** $1550	**VGood:** $1450

LAKEFIELD ARMS MODEL 90 BIATHLON

Bolt action; 22 LR; 5-shot magazine; 21-inch barrel; 39-1/2-inch overall length; weighs 8-1/4 lbs.; target front sight with inserts, adjustable peep rear; natural-finish hardwood stock; clip holder; carrying, shooting rails; hand stop; butthook; snow-cap muzzle protector; right-, left-hand versions. Marketed with five magazines. Made in Canada. Introduced 1991; discontinued 1995.

Perf.: $400 **Exc.:** $360 **VGood:** $290

LAKEFIELD ARMS MODEL 91T

Bolt action; single shot; 22 LR; 25-inch barrel; 43-1/2-inch overall length; weighs 8 lbs.; target front sight with inserts; click-adjustable peep rear; target-type walnut-finished hardwood stock; shooting rail; hand stop. Made in Canada. Introduced 1991; discontinued 1995.

Perf.: $330 **Exc.:** $290 **VGood:** $220

LAKEFIELD ARMS MODEL 91TR

Same specs as Model 91T except repeater with 5-shot magazine. Made in Canada. Introduced 1991; discontinued 1995.

Perf.: $350 **Exc.:** $300 **VGood:** $230

LAKEFIELD ARMS MODEL 92S SILHOUETTE

Bolt action; 22 LR; 5-shot magazine; 21-inch barrel; 39-1/2-inch overall length; weighs 8 lbs.; no sights; receiver drilled, tapped for scope base; high-comb target-type stock of walnut-finished hardwood; right-, left-hand versions. Made in Canada by Lakefield Arms. Introduced 1992; discontinued 1995.

Perf.: $300	**Exc.:** $270	**VGood:** $200
Left-hand model		
Perf.: $320	**Exc.:** $280	**VGood:** $210

LAKEFIELD ARMS MODEL 93M

Bolt action; 22 WMR; 5-shot magazine; 20-3/4-inch barrel; 39-1/2-inch overall length; weighs 5-3/4 lbs.; bead front sight, adjustable open rear; receiver grooved for scope mount; walnut-finished hardwood

LEGACY SPORTS INTERNATIONAL MAUSER 98 RIFLE

Bolt action; 300 Win. Mag.; 24-inch barrel, 1-10-inch twist; weighs 8.4 lbs.; 45-inch overall length; Premium American walnut stock. Square-bridge Mauser 98 action dovetailed for ring mounts (scope and rings not included). 3-position thumb safety, hinged floorplate, adjustable trigger. Introduced 2001. Imported from Italy by Legacy Sports International.

Perf.: $875   **Exc.:** $775   **VGood:** $650

LES BAER CUSTOM ULTIMATE AR 223 RIFLE

Semi-automatic; 223. 18-inch barrel, 20-inch, 22-inch, 24-inch; weighs 7-3/4 to 9-3/4 lb.; Black synthetic stock; Picatinny-style flat top rail for scope mounting. Forged receiver; Ultra single-stage trigger (Jewell two-stage trigger optional); titanium firing pin; Versa-Pod bipod; chromed National Match carrier; stainless steel, hand-lapped and cryo-treated barrel; guaranteed to shoot 1/2 or 3/4 MOA, depending on model. Made in U.S.A. by Les Bear Custom Inc.

Super Varmint Model
Perf.: $2000   **Exc.:** $1700   **VGood:** $1400

M4 Flattop or IPSC Action Model
Perf.: $2200   **Exc.:** $1900   **VGood:** $1600

LJUTIC SPACE GUN

Single shot; 22-250, 30-30, 30-06, 308; 24-inch barrel; 44-inch overall length; iron sights or scope mounts; American walnut stock grip, forend; anti-recoil mechanism; twist-bolt action. Introduced 1981; discontinued 1988.

Perf.: $3000   **Exc.:** $2795   **VGood:** $2495

MAGNUM RESEARCH MAGNUM LITE TACTICAL RIFLE

Bolt action; 223 Rem., 22-250, 308 Win., 300 Win. Mag., 300 WSM; 26-inch Magnum Lite graphite barrel; weighs 8.3 lbs. H-S Precision tactical black synthetic stock; drilled and tapped for scope mount. Accurized Remington 700 action; adjustable trigger; adjustable comb height. Tuned to shoot 1/2-inch MOA or better. Introduced 2001. From Magnum Research Inc.

Perf.: $2250   **Exc.:** $2000   **VGood:** $1600

MAGNUM RESEARCH MAGNUMLITE GRAPHITE RIFLE

Bolt action rifle built on Remington or Sako action with H-S Precsion or Hogue stock. Chambered in .22-250, .223, 7mm Rem. Mag., .280, or .30-06.

NIB.: $2300   **Exc.:** $1900   **VGood:** $1200

MAGNUM RESEARCH MAGNUMLITE MLR-1722 RIFLE

Semi-auto rimfire rifle with graphite barrel and black Hogue overmolded stock. 10-shot rotary magazine.

NIB.: $600   **Exc.:** $500   **VGood:** $350

MAGNUM RESEARCH MAGNUMLITE MLR-1722 .17 MACH-2 RIFLE

Similar to above but chambered in .17 Mach-2.

NIB.: $600   **Exc.:** $500   **VGood:** $350

MAGNUM RESEARCH MAGNUMLITE MLR-1722 .22 WMR GRAPHITE RIFLE

Semi-auto rimfire rifle with graphite barrel and skeletonized laminated stock with thumbhole in a variety of laminate colors. Chambered in .22 WMR.

NIB.: $700   **Exc.:** $550   **VGood:** $395

MAGNUM RESEARCH MAGNUMLITE MLR-1722 .17 HMR GRAPHITE RIFLE

Similar to above but with conventional Hogue overmolded stock. Chamberd in 17 HMR.

NIB.: $700   **Exc.:** $550   **VGood:** $395

MAGNUM RESEARCH MAGNUMLITE MLR-1722 .17 HMR STAINLESS STEEL RIFLE

Similar to above but with stainless steel receiver and barrel.

NIB.: $700   **Exc.:** $550   **VGood:** $395

MAGTECH MODEL 122.2R

Bolt action; 22 Short, 22 Long, 22 LR; 6-, 10-shot magazines; 24-inch six-groove barrel; 43-inch overall length; weighs 6-1/2 lbs.; blade front sight, open fully-adjustable rear; receiver grooved for scope mount; Brazilian hardwood stock; sliding safety; double extractors. Imported from Brazil by Magtech Recreational Products, Inc. Introduced 1994; no longer imported.

Exc.: $100   **VGood:** $80   **Good:** $60

Legacy Sports International Mauser 98

Les Baer Ultimate AR 223 Super Varmint

Les Baer Ultimate AR 223 M4 Flattop

Les Baer Ultimate AR 223 IPSC

Ljutic Space Gun

Magnum Research Magnum-Lite Graphite Rifle

Magnum Research MagnumLite MLR-1722 .22 WMR Graphite Rifle

Magnum Research MagnumLite MLR-1722 Rifle

MAGTECH MODEL 122.2S

Same specs as Model 122.2R except no sights; receiver grooved for scope mounting. Imported from Brazil by Magtech Recreational Products, Inc. Introduced 1994; no longer imported.

Exc.: $90   **VGood:** $70   **Good:** $50

MAGTECH MODEL 122.2T

Same specs as Model 122.2R except ramp front sight, micrometer-adjustable open rear; receiver grooved for scope mounting. Imported from Brazil

Magnum Research Magnum Lite
Tactical Rifle

Magtech Model 122.2R

Magtech Model MT-52-T
Target

Magtech Model MT-66

Mannlicher-Schoenauer Model 1950
Carbine 6.5

by Magtech Recreational Products, Inc. Introduced 1994; no longer imported.

Exc.: $110   **VGood:** $100   **Good:** $80

MAGTECH MODEL MT-122C

Bolt action; 22 Short, 22 Long, 22 LR; 6-, 10-shot detachable magazines; 21-inch six-groove barrel; 39-inch overall length; weighs 5-3/4 lbs.; blade front sight, fully-adjustable open rear; receiver grooved for scope mount; Brazilian hardwood stock; sliding wing-type safety; double extractors; red cocking indicator. Imported from Brazil by Magtech Recreational Products, Inc. Introduced 1991; discontinued 1993.

Exc.: $90   **VGood:** $80   **Good:** $60

MAGTECH MODEL MT-122T

Same specs as MT-22C except 15-shot tubular magazine. Imported from Brazil by Magtech Recreational Products, Inc. Introduced 1991; discontinued 1993.

Exc.: $150   **VGood:** $120   **Good:** $90

MAGTECH MODEL MT-52-T TARGET

Bolt action; 22 LR; 6-, 10-shot magazine; 26-1/4-inch eight-groove barrel; 43-3/8-inch overall length; weighs about 9 lbs.; globe front sight with inserts, match-type aperture rear; receiver grooved for scope mounting; Brazilian hardwood stock with stippled grip; fully-adjustable rubber buttplate; aluminum forend rail with sling support; fully-adjustable trigger; free-floating barrel. Imported from Brazil by Magtech Recreational Products, Inc. Introduced 1991; discontinued 1993.

Exc.: $150   **VGood:** $120   **Good:** $90

MAGTECH MODEL MT-66

Semi-automatic; 22 LR; 14-shot tubular magazine; 19 5/8-inch six-groove barrel; 38-1/2-inch overall length; weighs 4-1/2 lbs.; blade front sight, open adjustable rear; receiver grooved for scope mounts; moulded black nylon stock with checkered pistol grip and forend; tube magazine loads through buttplate; top tang safety. Imported from Brazil by Magtech Recreational Products, Inc. Introduced 1991; discontinued 1993.

Exc.: $90   **VGood:** $80   **Good:** $70

MAGTECH MT 7022 AUTO RIFLE

Semi-automatic; 22 LR, 10-shot magazine. 18-inch barrel; weighs 4.8 lbs.; 37-inch overall length; Brazilian hardwood stock; Hooded blade front, fully adjustable open rear sights. Cross-bolt safety; last-shot bolt hold-open; alloy receiver is drilled and tapped for scope mounting. Introduced 1998. No longer offered. Imported from Brazil by Magtech Ammunition Co.

Perf.: $95   **Exc.:** $85   **VGood:** $75

With synthetic stock, as Model 7022 S

Perf.: $95   **Exc.:** $85   **VGood:** $75

MANNLICHER-SCHOENAUER HIGH VELOCITY

Bolt action; 30-06, 7x64 Brenneke, 8x60 Mag., 9.3x62, 10.75x57mm; 5-shot rotary magazine; 23-1/2-inch barrel; British-type three-leaf open rear sight, ramp front; hand-checkered traditional sporting stock of European walnut; cheekpiece, pistol grip; sling swivels. Introduced 1922; discontinued 1937.

Exc.: $2600   **VGood:** $2200   **Good:** $1725

MANNLICHER-SCHOENAUER MODEL 1903 CARBINE

Bolt action; 6.5x53mm; 5-shot rotary magazine; 17-1/2-inch barrel; two-leaf rear, ramp front sight; full-length uncheckered European walnut stock; metal forearm cap; pistol grip; cartridge trap in buttplate; double-set trigger; flat bolt handle; sling swivels. Introduced 1903; discontinued 1937.

Exc.: $1400   **VGood:** $1100   **Good:** $875

MANNLICHER-SCHOENAUER MODEL 1905 CARBINE

Bolt action; 9x56mm; 5-shot rotary magazine; 19-1/2-inch barrel; two-leaf rear, ramp front sight; full-length uncheckered European walnut stock; metal forearm cap; pistol grip; cartridge trap in buttplate; double-set trigger; flat bolt handle; sling swivels. Introduced 1905; discontinued 1937.

Exc.: $1600   **VGood:** $1300   **Good:** $975

MANNLICHER-SCHOENAUER MODEL 1908 CARBINE

Bolt action; 7x57mm, 8x56mm; 5-shot rotary magazine; 19-1/2-inch barrel; two-leaf rear, ramp front sight; full-length uncheckered European walnut stock; metal forearm cap; pistol grip; cartridge trap in buttplate; double-set trigger; flat bolt handle; sling swivels. Introduced 1908; discontinued 1947.

Exc.: $1600   **VGood:** $1300   **Good:** $975

MANNLICHER-SCHOENAUER MODEL 1910 CARBINE

Bolt action; 9x56, 9.5x57, 375 Express; 5-shot rotary magazine; 19-1/2-inch barrel; two-leaf rear, ramp front sight; full-length uncheckered European walnut stock; metal forearm cap; pistol grip; cartridge trap in buttplate; double-set trigger; flat bolt handle; sling swivels. Introduced 1910; discontinued 1937.

Exc.: $1500   **VGood:** $1200   **Good:** $875

MANNLICHER-SCHOENAUER MODEL 1924 CARBINE

Bolt action; 30-06; 5-shot rotary magazine; 19-1/2-inch barrel; two-leaf rear, ramp front sight; full-length uncheckered European walnut stock; metal forearm cap; pistol grip; cartridge trap in buttplate; double-set trigger; flat bolt handle; sling swivels. Introduced 1924; discontinued 1937.

Exc.: $2400   **VGood:** $1975   **Good:** $1425

MANNLICHER-SCHOENAUER MODEL 1950

Bolt action; 244, 257 Roberts, 270, 280, 30-06, 358 Win. Mag., 6.5x54, 7x57, 8x57, 9.3x62; 5-shot rotary magazine; 23-1/2-inch barrel; weighs 7-1/2 lbs.; folding leaf open rear sight, hooded ramp front; standard hand-checkered European walnut half-stock; pistol grip, cheekpiece; ebony forend tip; single- or double-set trigger; flat bolt handle; shotgun-type safety; sling swivels. Original price: $179. Introduced 1950; discontinued 1952.

Exc.: $1550   **VGood:** $1300   **Good:** $1000

MANNLICHER-SCHOENAUER MODEL 1950 CARBINE

Same specs as Model 1950 rifle except weighs 7 lbs.; full-length walnut stock; metal forend cap; 20-inch barrel. Introduced 1950; discontinued 1952.

Exc.: $1500   **VGood:** $1250   **Good:** $950

MANNLICHER-SCHOENAUER MODEL 1950 CARBINE 6.5

Same specs as Model 1950 except 6.5x54; 18-1/4-inch barrel; full-length walnut stock. Introduced 1950; discontinued 1952.

Exc.: $1400   **VGood:** $1100   **Good:** $950

MANNLICHER-SCHOENAUER MODEL 1952 IMPROVED

Bolt action; 244, 257 Roberts, 270, 280, 30-06, 358 Win. Mag., 6.5x54, 7x57, 8x57, 9.3x62; 5-shot rotary magazine; 24-inch barrel; weighs 7-1/4 lbs.; folding leaf open rear sight, hooded ramp front; improved hand-checkered European walnut half-stock; pistol grip; deluxe hand-carved cheekpiece; ebony forend tip; single- or double-set trigger; swept-back bolt handle; shotgun-type safety; sling swivels. Introduced 1952; discontinued 1956.

Exc.: $1500   **VGood:** $1200   **Good:** $1000

MANNLICHER-SCHOENAUER MODEL 1952 IMPROVED CARBINE

Same specs as Model 1952 Improved except 257 Roberts, 270, 30-06, 24-inch barrel; weighs 7 lbs.; improved full-length walnut stock design; swept back bolt handle. Introduced 1952; discontinued 1956.

Exc.: $1500   **VGood:** $1200   **Good:** $1000

MANNLICHER-SCHOENAUER MODEL 1952 IMPROVED CARBINE 6.5

Same specs Model 1952 Improved except 6.5x53; 18-1/4-inch barrel; weighs 6-3/4 lbs.; improved full-length walnut stock. Introduced 1952; discontinued 1956.

Exc.: $1450   **VGood:** $1150   **Good:** $950

MANNLICHER-SCHOENAUER MODEL 1956

Bolt action; 243 Win., 30-06; 5-shot rotary magazine; 22-inch barrel; folding leaf open rear sight, hooded ramp front; high-comb improved walnut half-stock; pistol grip; cheekpiece; ebony forend tip; single- or double-set trigger; swept-back bolt handle; shotgun-type safety; sling swivels. Introduced 1956; discontinued 1960.

Exc.: $1200   **VGood:** $1000   **Good:** $800

MANNLICHER-SCHOENAUER MODEL 1956 CARBINE

Same specs as Model 1956 except 243, 257 Roberts, 270, 30-06, 308, 6.5x53, 7mm; 20-inch barrel; redesigned high-comb walnut full-length stock. Introduced 1956; discontinued 1960.

Exc.: $1350   **VGood:** $1100   **Good:** $900

MANNLICHER-SCHOENAUER MODEL 1956 MAGNUM

Same specs as Model 1956 except 257 Weatherby Mag., 6.5x68, 8x68, 458 Win. Mag. Introduced 1956; discontinued 1960.

Exc.: $1400   **VGood:** $1200   **Good:** $975

MANNLICHER-SCHOENAUER MODEL 1961 MCA

Bolt action; 243 Win., 270 Win., 30-06; 5-shot rotary magazine; 22-inch barrel; folding leaf open rear sight, hooded ramp front; Monte Carlo walnut half-stock; pistol grip; cheekpiece; ebony forend tip; single- or double-set trigger; swept-back bolt handle; shotgun-type safety; sling swivels. Introduced 1961; discontinued 1971.

Exc.: $1300   **VGood:** $1135   **Good:** $950

MANNLICHER-SCHOENAUER 1961 MCA CARBINE

Same specs as Model 1956 except 243 Win., 270 Win., 30-06, 308 Win., 6.5x53; 20-inch barrel; Monte Carlo-style walnut full-length stock. Introduced 1961; discontinued 1971.

Exc.: $1350   **VGood:** $1180   **Good:** $995

MAPIZ ZANARDINI OXFORD

Double rifle; boxlock side-by-side; 444 Marlin, 7x65R, 6.5x57R, 9.3x74R, 375 H&H Mag., 458 Win. Mag., 465 N.E., 470 N.E., 577 N.E., 600 N.E., 375 Flanged N.E.; 24-inch, 25-inch, 25-1/2-inch barrel; oil-finished European walnut stock; rubber or hard buttplate; automatic ejectors; double triggers; heavy engraving. Made in Italy. Introduced 1989; discontinued 1990.

Perf.: $7900   **Exc.:** $6100   **VGood:** $4100

MARATHON CENTERFIRE

Bolt action; 243, 308, 7x57, 30-06, 270, 7mm Rem. Mag., 300 Win. Mag.; 5-shot magazine; 24-inch barrel; 45-inch overall length; weighs 8 lbs.; open adjustable rear sight, bead front on ramp; select walnut Monte Carlo stock; rubber recoil pad; Santa Barbara Mauser action; triple thumb locking safety; blued finish. Made in Spain. Introduced 1984; discontinued 1986.

Exc.: $310   **VGood:** $270   **Good:** $200

MARATHON SUPER SHOT 22

Bolt action; single shot; 22 LR; 24-inch barrel; 41-1/2-inch overall length; weighs 5 lbs.; step-adjustable open rear sight, bead front; receiver grooved for scope mounts; select hardwood stock; blued finish. Made in Spain. Introduced 1984; discontinued 1986.

Exc.: $65   **VGood:** $55   **Good:** $40

MARCEL THYS KING ROYAL

Double rifle; sidelock side-by-side; 22 LR, 22 Hornet, 30-06, 375 H&H Mag., 450 #2, 458 Win. Mag., 470 Nitro, 500-3-inch, 577, 600 Nitro; 24-inch to 27-inch chopper lump barrels; weighs 6 to 14 lbs. depending on caliber, accessories; bead on ramp front sight, one standing leaf, two folding leaves on quarter-rib; oil-finished European walnut stock; hand-detachable locks; reinforced top tang extension; reinforced Holland-type frame; full-coverage game scene engraving with gold inlay; coin finish or color case-

Mannlicher-Schoenauer 1961 MCA Carbine

Marathon Centerfire

Marathon Super Shot 22

Marlin Model 9 Camp Carbine

Marlin Model 45 Camp Carbine

Marlin Model 49

Marlin Model 49DL

Marlin Model 50

hardened action. Made in Belgium. Introduced 1990; discontinued 1992.

Exc.: $16,000   **VGood:** $13,900   **Good:** $11,500

MARCEL THYS LIEGE ROYAL LUX

Double rifle; sidelock side-by-side; 22 LR, 22 Hornet, 30-06, 375 H&H Mag., 450 #2, 458 Win. Mag., 470 Nitro, 500-3-inch, 577, 600 Nitro; 24-inch-27-inch chopper lump barrels; weighs 6-14 lbs. depending on caliber, accessories; bead on ramp front sight, one standing leaf, two folding leaves on quarter-rib; oil-finished dark European walnut stock; hand-detachable locks; reinforced top tang extension; reinforced Holland-type frame; full-coverage game scene engraving; coin finish or color case-hardened action. Made in Belgium. Introduced 1990; discontinued 1992.

Exc.: $14,500   **VGood:** $12,500   **Good:** $9950

MARLIN MODEL 9 CAMP CARBINE

Semi-automatic; 9mm Para.; 12-shot magazine; 16-1/2-inch barrel; 35-1/2-inch overall length; weighs 6-3/4 lbs.; adjustable open rear sight, ramp front with bead, hood; drilled, tapped for scope mount; wood stock; rubber buttpad; manual hold-open; Garand-type safety; magazine safety; loaded chamber indicator. Introduced 1985; discontinued 2000.

Perf.: $400   **Exc.:** $360   **VGood:** $275

MARLIN MODEL 9N

Same specs as Model 9 except nickel finish. Introduced 1991. No longer in production.

Perf.: $450   **Exc.:** $375   **VGood:** $300

MARLIN MODEL 45 CAMP CARBINE

Semi-automatic; 45 ACP; 7-shot magazine; 16-1/2-inch barrel; 35-1/2-inch overall length; weighs 6-3/4 lbs.; ramp front, open adjustable rear sight; walnut-finished hardwood stock; rubber buttpad; sling swivels. Introduced 1986, discontinued 2000.

Perf.: $600   **Exc.:** $500   **VGood:** $395

MARLIN MODEL 49

Semi-automatic; 22 LR; 19-shot tubular magazine; 22-inch barrel; 40-1/4-inch overall length; weighs 5-1/2 lbs.; open rear, hooded ramp front sight; two-piece checkered or uncheckered hardwood stock; same as Model 99C except solid top receiver; manual bolt hold-open. Introduced 1968; discontinued 1971.

Exc.: $100   **VGood:** $80   **Good:** $65

MARLIN MODEL 49DL

Same specs as Model 49 except capped pistol grip; checkered forearm and pistol grip; gold trigger; scroll-engraved receiver; grooved for tip-off scope mounts. Introduced 1970; no longer produced.

Exc.: $125   **VGood:** $100   **Good:** $70

Marlin Model 60

Scope.jpg
Model Model 60SN

Marlin Model 60'CF

Marlin Model 70HC

Marlin Model 70P Papoose

Marlin Model 70PSS

Marlin Model 75C

Marlin Model 88C

Marlin Model 98

MARLIN MODEL 50

Semi-automatic; 22 LR; 6-shot detachable box magazine; 22-inch barrel; take-down action; open adjustable rear sight, bead front; uncheckered pistol-grip walnut stock, grooved forearm. Introduced 1931; discontinued 1934.

Exc.: $125   **VGood:** $100   **Good:** $80

MARLIN MODEL 50E

Same specs as Model 50 except hooded front sight, peep rear.

Exc.: $135   **VGood:** $110   **Good:** $90

MARLIN MODEL 60

Semi-automatic; 22 LR; 14-shot tubular magazine; 22-inch round tapered barrel; 40-1/2-inch overall length; weighs 5-1/2 lbs.; ramp front sight, open adjustable rear; matted receiver; grooved for tip-off

mounts; walnut-finished Monte Carlo hardwood stock; auto last-shot bolt hold-open. Originally marketed as Marlin Glenfield Model 60. Introduced 1982; still in production, with variations in stock and finish options. Older, unremarkable examples frequently sell for less than $100.

Perf.: $175   **Exc.:** $150   **VGood:** $125

MARLIN MODEL 60SS

Same specs as Model 60 except breech bolt, barrel and outer magazine tube of stainless steel construction; most other parts either nickel-plated or coated to match the stainless finish; black/gray Maine birch laminate Monte Carlo stock; nickel-plated swivel studs; rubber buttpad. Made in U.S. by Marlin. Introduced 1993; still produced.

Perf.: $190   **Exc.:** $150   **VGood:** $130

Model 60SSK (black fiberglass-filled stock)
Perf.: $160   **Exc.:** $110   **VGood:** $80

Model 60SB (walnut-finished birch stock)
Perf.: $130   **Exc.:** $90   **VGood:** $70

MARLIN MODEL 60SN

Similar to Model 60SS but with black synthetic stock with molded checkering and swivel studs. Introduced in 2007. Available with factory-mounted 3x9 scope. Add 10 percent for scope package.

Perf.: $265   **Exc.:** $215   **VGood:** $150

MODEL 60S-CF

Similar to Model 60SN but with carbon fiber-dippedd black synthetic stock, giving it a – quote – "racy, high tech look."

Perf.: $265   **Exc.:** $215   **VGood:** $150

MARLIN MODEL 70HC

Semi-automatic; 22 LR; 7-, 15-shot clip magazine; 18-inch barrel; 36-3/4-inch overall length; weighs 5-1/2 lbs.; ramp front sight, adjustable open rear; receiver grooved for scope mount; Monte Carlo-type walnut-finished hardwood stock; cross-bolt safety; manual bolt hold-open. Introduced 1988; no longer in production.

Perf.: $160   **Exc.:** $140   **VGood:** $100

MARLIN MODEL 70P PAPOOSE

Same specs as Model 70HC except takedown model with easily removable barrel; 16-1/4-inch Micro-Groove barrel; walnut-finished hardwood stock; 35-1/4-inch overall length; weighs 3-1/4 lbs. Comes with zippered case. Made in U.S. by Marlin. Introduced 1986; discontinued 1995.

Perf.: $180   **Exc.:** $150   **VGood:** $120

MARLIN MODEL 70PSS

Same specs as Model 70P except stainless-steel barrel, other parts finished to match, fiberglass-filled synthetic stock; take-down model. Introduced 1986; still in production.

Perf.: $210   **Exc.:** $170   **VGood:** $140

MARLIN MODEL 75C

Semi-automatic; 22 LR; 13-shot tubular magazine; 18-inch barrel; 36-1/2-inch overall length; weighs 5 lbs.; ramp front, adjustable open rear sight; receiver grooved for scope mounts; walnut-finished Monte Carlo hardwood stock; cross-bolt safety; auto last-shot bolt hold-open. Introduced 1982; no longer in production.

Perf.: $150   **Exc.:** $125   **VGood:** $100

MARLIN MODEL 88C

Semi-automatic; 22 LR; 15-shot; 24-inch barrel; 45-inch overall length; weighs 6-3/4 lbs.; tube magazine in buttstock; open rear, hooded front sight; chrome-plated cocking handle; safety button; positive sear lock safety; black walnut uncheckered pistol-grip stock. Introduced 1948; discontinued 1956.

Exc.: $90   **VGood:** $80   **Good:** $70

MARLIN MODEL 88DL

Same specs as Model 88C except hand-checkered stock; sling swivels; receiver peep sight in rear. Introduced 1953; discontinued 1956.

Exc.: $100   **VGood:** $90   **Good:** $80

MARLIN MODEL 89C

Semi-automatic; 22 LR; 5-shot clip magazine (early model), 12-shot (late model); 24-inch barrel; 45-inch overall length; weighs 6-1/2 lbs.; hooded front, open rear sight; uncheckered pistol-grip stock. Introduced 1948; discontinued 1961.

Exc.: $90   **VGood:** $80   **Good:** $70

MARLIN MODEL 89DL

Same specs as Model 89C except sling swivels; receiver peep sight.

Exc.: $110   **VGood:** $90   **Good:** $70

MARLIN MODEL 98

Semi-automatic; 22 LR; 15-shot buttstock tube magazine; 22-inch barrel; 42-inch overall length; weighs 6-1/2 lbs.; fully-adjustable peep rear, hooded ramp front sight; solid frame; Bishop-style uncheckered Monte Carlo walnut stock, cheekpiece. Introduced 1957; discontinued 1959.

Exc.: $100   **VGood:** $90   **Good:** $70

MARLIN MODEL 99

Semi-automatic; 22 LR; 18-shot tube magazine; 22-inch barrel; 42-inch overall length; weighs 5-1/2 lbs.; open rear, hooded ramp front sight; uncheckered walnut pistol-grip stock. Introduced 1959; discontinued 1961.

Exc.: $100   **VGood:** $90   **Good:** $70

MARLIN MODEL 99C

Same specs as Model 99 except uncheckered walnut pistol-grip stock with fluted comb; grooved receiver for tip-off scope mounts; gold-plated trigger. Later production features checkering on pistol grip, forearm. Introduced 1962; discontinued 1978.

Exc.: $100   **VGood:** $90   **Good:** $80

MARLIN MODEL 99DL

Same specs as Model 99 except for uncheckered black walnut Monte Carlo stock; jeweled bolt; gold-plated trigger; sling, sling swivels. Introduced 1960; discontinued 1965.

Exc.: $110   **VGood:** $100   **Good:** $80

MARLIN MODEL 99G

Same specs as Model 99C except plainer stock; bead front sight. Introduced 1960; discontinued 1965.

Exc.: $100   **VGood:** $90   **Good:** $70

MARLIN MODEL 99M1 CARBINE

Same specs as Model 99C except designed after U.S. 30M1 carbine; 18-inch barrel; 37-inch overall length; weighs 4-3/4 lbs.; 10-shot tube magazine; uncheckered pistol grip carbine stock; hand guard with barrel band; open rear, military-type ramp front sight; drilled, tapped for receiver sights; grooved for tip-off mount; gold-plated trigger; sling swivels. Introduced 1964; discontinued 1978.

Exc.: $225   **VGood:** $200   **Good:** $150

MARLIN MODEL 922 MAGNUM

Semi-automatic; 22 WMR; 7-shot magazine; 20-1/2-inch barrel; 39-3/4-inch overall length; weighs 6-1/2 lbs.; ramp front sight with bead and removable Wide-Scan hood, adjustable folding semi-buckhorn rear; action based on the centerfire Model 9 Carbine; receiver drilled and tapped for scope mounting; checkered American black walnut stock with Monte Carlo comb; swivel studs; rubber buttpad; automatic last-shot bolt hold-open; magazine safety. Made in U.S. by Marlin Firearms Co. Introduced 1993; no longer in production.

Perf.: $400   **Exc.:** $355   **VGood:** $295

MARLIN MODEL 989M2 CARBINE

Semi-automatic; 22 LR; 7-shot detachable clip magazine; 18-inch barrel; 37-inch overall length; weighs 4-3/4 lbs.; open rear sight, military-type ramp front; uncheckered pistol-grip carbine walnut stock and handguard; barrel band; sling swivels; gold-plated trigger. Introduced 1965; discontinued 1978.

Exc.: $250   **VGood:** $225   **Good:** $195

MARLIN MODEL 990

Semi-automatic; 22 LR; 18-shot tubular magazine; 22-inch barrel; 40-3/4-inch overall length; weighs 5-1/2 lbs.; ramp bead hooded front, adjustable folding semi-buckhorn rear sight; American walnut Monte Carlo stock; checkered fluted comb; full pistol grip; cross-bolt safety; receiver grooved for tip-off mount. Introduced 1979; discontinued 1988.

Exc.: $135   **VGood:** $115   **Good:** $100

MARLIN MODEL 990L

Same specs as Model 990 except 14-shot magazine; 40-1/2-inch overall length; weighs about 5-3/4 lbs.; laminated hardwood stock with black rubber rifle buttpad and swivel studs; gold-plated trigger; manual bolt hold-open; automatic last-shot bolt hold-open. Made in U.S. by Marlin Firearms Co. Introduced 1992; dropped 1994.

Exc.: $110   **VGood:** $100   **Good:** $90

MARLIN MODEL 995

Semi-automatic; 22 LR; 7-shot clip magazine; 18-inch Micro-Groove barrel; 36-3/4-inch overall length;

Marlin Model 99M1 Carbine

Marlin Model 922 Magnum

Marlin Model 989M2 Carbine

Marlin Model 990L

Marlin Model 995

Marlin Model 995SS

Marlin Model 795 SS

weighs 5 lbs.; ramp bead front sight with Wide-Scan hood, adjustable folding semi-buckhorn rear; receiver grooved for scope mount; American black walnut stock with Monte Carlo; full pistol grip; checkered grip and forend; white buttplate spacer; Mar-Shield finish; bolt hold-open device; cross-bolt safety. Introduced 1979; dropped 1994.

Exc.: $125   **VGood:** $110   **Good:** $90

MARLIN MODEL 995SS

Same specs as Model 995 except stainless steel 18-inch barrel; ramp front sight with orange post and cut-away Wide-Scan hood, screw-adjustable open rear; black fiberglass-filled synthetic stock with nickel-plated swivel studs, moulded-in checkering; stainless steel breechbolt. Introduced 1979; no longer produced.

Perf.: $160   **Exc.:** $140   **VGood:** $110

MARLIN MODEL 7000 AUTO RIFLE

Semi-automatic; 22 LR, 10-shot box magazine; 18-inch heavy target barrel with 16-groove Micro-Groove rifling, recessed muzzle; weighs 5-1/2 lbs.; 37-inch overall length; Black fiberglass-filled synthetic stock with Monte Carlo comb, swivel studs, moulded-in checkering; comes with ring mounts. Automatic last-shot bolt hold-open, manual bolt hold-open; cross-bolt safety; steel charging handle; blue finish, nickel-plated magazine. Introduced 1997, still offered. Made in U.S.A. by Marlin Firearms Co.

Perf.: $200   **Exc.:** $150   **VGood:** $125

MARLIN MODEL 795 AUTO RIFLE

Similar to Model 7000 except standard-weight 18-inch barrel with 16-groove Micro-Groove rifling. Ramp front sight with brass bead, screw adjustable open rear. Receiver grooved for scope mount. Introduced 1997, still offered. Made in U.S.A. by Marlin Firearms Co.

Perf.: $175   **Exc.:** $125   **VGood:** $90

MARLIN MODEL 795SS AUTO RIFLE

Similar to Model 795 except stainless steel barrel. Most other parts nickel- plated. Adjustable folding semi-buckhorn rear sights, ramp front high-visibility post and removable cutaway wide scan hood. Still available.

Perf.: $200   **Exc.:** $175   **VGood:** $140

Marlin Model A-1

Marlin Model 15Y "Little Buckaroo"

Marlin Model 15YN "Little Buckaroo"

Marlin Model 17V Hornady Magnum

Marlin Model 17VS

Marlin Model 25

Marlin Model 25M

Marlin Model 25MNC

Marlin Model 25NC

sight, adjustable open rear; walnut finished hardwood Monte Carlo stock with full pistol grip; receiver grooved for tip-off scope mount; thumb safety; cocking indicator.

Exc.: $100   **VGood:** $80   **Good:** $65

MARLIN MODEL 15Y LITTLE BUCKAROO

Bolt action; single shot; 22 Short, 22 Long, 22 LR; 16-1/4-inch barrel; 33-1/4-inch overall length; weighs 4-1/4 lbs.; adjustable open rear sight, ramp front; marketed with 4x15 scope, mount; walnut-finished hardwood stock. Introduced 1984; discontinued 1986.

Perf.: $120   **Exc.:** $100   **VGood:** $80

MARLIN MODEL 15YN LITTLE BUCKAROO

Same specs as Model 15Y except without scope. Reintroduced 1989; still produced as Model 915Y.

Perf.: $165   **Exc.:** $125   **VGood:** $75

MARLIN MODEL 15YS

Stainless steel with fire sights.

Perf.: $175   **Exc.:** $135   **VGood:** $85

MARLIN MODEL 17V HORNADY MAGNUM

Bolt action; 17 HMR; 7-shot. 22-inch barrel; weighs 6 lbs., stainless; 41-inch overall length; Checkered walnut Monte Carlo stock, laminated black/grey. No sights but receiver grooved. Swivel studs, positive thumb safety, red cocking indicator, 1-inch scope rings, safety lock. Still offered as Model 917V.

Perf.: $240   **Exc.:** $200   **VGood:** $180

MARLIN MODEL 17VS

Same as Model 17V, but with stainless-steel barrel and action, laminated stock.

Perf.: $375   **Exc.:** $320   **VGood:** $ 290

MARLIN MODEL 25

Bolt action; 22 Short, 22 Long, 22 LR; 7-shot box magazine; 22-inch barrel; 41-inch overall length; weighs 5 lbs.; ramp front, open rear sight; walnut-finished hardwood pistol-grip stock. Introduced 1982; still produced as Model 925.

Perf.: $150   **Exc.:** $125   **VGood:** $90

MARLIN MODEL 25M

Same specs as Model 25 except 22 WMR.

Perf.: $165   **Exc.:** $140   **VGood:** $110

MARLIN MODEL 25MB MIDGET MAGNUM

Same specs as Model 25 except 22 WMR; 16-1/4-inch barrel; 35-1/4-inch overall length; weighs 4-3/4 lbs.; take-down; walnut-finished hardwood stock; grooved for tip-off scope; marketed with iron sights, 4x scope, zippered nylon case. Introduced 1987; discontinued 1988.

Perf.: $165   **Exc.:** $135   **VGood:** $115

MARLIN MODEL 25MN

Same specs as Model 25 except 22 WMR; weighs 6 lbs.; walnut-finished Maine birch pistol-grip Monte Carlo stock; ramp front sight, adjustable open rear. Introduced 1989; still in production as Model 915M.

Perf.: $150   **Exc.:** $125   **VGood:** $90

MARLIN MODEL 25MNC

Same specs as Model 25MN but with camo stock.

Perf.: $170   **Exc.:** $140   **VGood:** $120

MARLIN MODEL 25N

Same specs as Model 25 except 22 LR; adjustable open rear sight; receiver grooved for scope mounting. Introduced 1989; still in production as Model 925.

Perf.: $150   **Exc.:** $125   **VGood:** $95

MARLIN MODEL 25NC

Same specs as Model 25N but with camo stock.

Perf.: $155   **Exc.:** $130   **VGood:** $100

MARLIN MODEL A-1

Semi-automatic; 22 LR; 6-shot detachable box magazine; 24-inch barrel; open rear sight, bead front; uncheckered walnut pistol-grip stock. Introduced 1935; discontinued 1946.

Exc.: $175   **VGood:** $125   **Good:** $95

MARLIN MODEL A-1C

Same specs as Model A-1 except off/on safety; military-style one-piece buttstock with fluted comb and semi-beavertail forearm. Introduced 1940; discontinued 1946.

Exc.: $195   **VGood:** $150   **Good:** $125

MARLIN MODEL A-1DL

Same specs as Model A-1C except sling swivels; hooded front sight, peep rear.

Exc.: $195   **VGood:** $150   **Good:** $125

MARLIN MODEL A-1E

Same specs as Model A-1 except hooded front sight, peep rear.

Exc.: $195   **VGood:** $150   **Good:** $125

MARLIN MODEL 15

Bolt Action; 22 Short, 22 Long, 22 LR; 22-inch barrel; 41-inch overall length; weighs 5-1/2 lbs.; ramp front

MARLIN MODEL 65

Bolt action; single shot; 22 Short, 22 Long, 22 LR; 24-inch barrel; open rear, bead front sight; uncheckered walnut pistol-grip stock, grooved forearm. Introduced 1935; discontinued 1937.

Exc.: $100   **VGood:** $90   **Good:** $70

MARLIN MODEL 65E

Same specs as Model 65 except equipped with hooded front sight, peep rear.

Exc.: $125   **VGood:** $115   **Good:** $85

MARLIN MODEL 80

Bolt action; 22 Short, 22 Long, 22 LR; 8-shot detachable box magazine; 24-inch barrel; open rear, bead front sight; uncheckered walnut pistol-grip stock; black buttplate. Introduced 1934; discontinued 1939.

Exc.: $125   **VGood:** $115   **Good:** $85

MARLIN MODEL 80C

Same specs as Model 80 except one-piece military-style buttstock with fluted comb and semi-beavertail forearm; off/on safety. Model 80-C replaced standard Model 80 in 1940; discontinued 1970.

Exc.: $135   **VGood:** $125   **Good:** $95

MARLIN MODEL 80DL

Same specs as Model 80C except peep rear, hooded front sight; sling swivels. Introduced 1940; discontinued 1965.

Exc.: $145   **VGood:** $135   **Good:** $105

MARLIN MODEL 80E

Same specs as Model 80 except peep rear sight, hooded front.

Exc.: $155   **VGood:** $145   **Good:** $115

MARLIN MODEL 81

Bolt action; 22 Short, 22 Long, 22 LR; 18-shot tubular magazine (22 LR), 20-shot (22 Long), 25-shot (22 Short); 24-inch round tapered barrel; 42-1/2-inch overall length; weighs 6-1/2 lbs.; open rear, silver bead front sight; uncheckered pistol-grip stock. Introduced 1937; discontinued 1965.

Exc.: $125   **VGood:** $115   **Good:** $85

MARLIN MODEL 81C

Same specs as Model 81 except improved military-type one-piece buttstock with fluted comb and semi-beavertail forearm. Introduced 1940; discontinued 1971.

Exc.: $135   **VGood:** $125   **Good:** $95

MARLIN MODEL 81DL

Same specs as Model 81C except hooded front, peep rear sight; sling swivels. Introduced 1940; discontinued 1965.

Exc.: $155   **VGood:** $145   **Good:** $115

MARLIN MODEL 81E

Same specs as Model 81 except hooded front, peep rear sight.

Exc.: $155   **VGood:** $145   **Good:** $115

MARLIN MODEL 83TS BOLT-ACTION RIFLE

Bolt action; 22 LR, 12-shot tubular magazine, black Monte Carlo fiberglass-filled synthetic stock with sling swivel studs. Weighs 6 lbs.; length 41-inch overall. Introduced 2001, still offered. Made in U.S.A. by Marlin Firearms Co.

Perf.: $200   **Exc.:** $175   **VGood:** $100

MARLIN MODEL 100

Bolt action; take-down single shot; 22 Short, 22 Long, 22 LR; 24-inch barrel; weighs 4-1/2 lbs.; open adjustable rear sight, bead front; uncheckered walnut pistol-grip stock. Introduced 1936; discontinued 1941.

Exc.: $70   **VGood:** $60   **Good:** $50

MARLIN MODEL 100S

Same specs as Model 100 except sling; peep rear, hooded front sight. It is known as the Tom Mix Special, allegedly because Tom Mix used such a rifle in his vaudeville act in the '30s. Manufactured 1937 only. Value is based largely upon rarity.

Exc.: $300   **VGood:** $270   **Good:** $220

Marlin Model 80C

Marlin Model 83TS

Marlin Model 100

Marlin Model 101

Marlin Model 122

Marlin Model 322

Marlin Model 455

MARLIN MODEL 100SB

Same specs as Model 100 except smoothbore for use with 22 shot cartridge; shotgun sight. Actually, this may well have been the version used by Tom Mix in his act, as he used shot cartridges for breaking glass balls and other on-stage targets. Introduced 1936; discontinued 1941.

Exc.: $150   **VGood:** $110   **Good:** $80

MARLIN MODEL 101

Bolt action; single shot; 22 Short, 22 Long, 22 LR; 22-inch barrel; 40-inch overall length; weighs 4-1/2 lbs.; fully-adjustable semi-buckhorn rear sight, hooded Wide-Scan front; black plastic trigger guard; ring or T-shaped cocking piece; uncheckered walnut stock with beavertail forearm; receiver grooved for tip-off scope mount. Improved version of Model 100 with improved bolt, redesigned stock. Introduced 1941; discontinued 1976.

Exc.: $80   **VGood:** $60   **Good:** $50

MARLIN MODEL 101DL

Same specs as Model 101 except 24-inch barrel; 42-1/2-inch overall length; weighs 5 lbs.; peep rear, hooded front sight; sling swivels. Introduced 1941; discontinued 1945.

Exc.: $90   **VGood:** $75   **Good:** $55

MARLIN MODEL 122

Bolt action; single shot; 22 Short, 22 Long, 22 LR; 22-inch barrel; 40-inch overall length; weighs 5 lbs.; open rear, hooded ramp front sight; drilled, tapped for receiver sights, tip-off scope mount; junior target model with shortened uncheckered stock; walnut Monte Carlo pistol-grip stock. Introduced 1962; discontinued 1965.

Exc.: $80   **VGood:** $70   **Good:** $50

MARLIN MODEL 322

Bolt action; 222 Rem.; 3-shot clip-type magazine; 24-inch medium weight barrel; 42-inch overall length; weighs 7-1/2 lbs.; short Sako Mauser-type action; two-position peep sight rear, hooded ramp front with hunting bead; checkered walnut stock, forearm; sling swivels. Introduced 1954; discontinued 1958.

Exc.: $525   **VGood:** $485   **Good:** $350

MARLIN MODEL 455

Bolt action; 270, 308, 30-06; 5-shot box magazine; 24-inch medium-weight stainless steel barrel; 42-1/2-inch overall length; weighs 7-3/4 lbs.; Lyman No. 48 receiver sight, hooded ramp front; FN Mauser action; Sako trigger; checkered walnut Monte Carlo stock with cheekpiece; checkered forearm; receiver drilled, tapped for scope mounts. Introduced 1956; discontinued 1959.

Exc.: $525   **VGood:** $485   **Good:** $350

Marlin Model XL7

Marlin Model XL7C

Marlin Model XL7 RealTree

Marlin Model 780

Marlin Model 781

Marlin Model 783

Marlin Model 880

Marlin Model 880SQ Squirrel

Marlin Model 882

Marlin Model 882SS

MARLIN MODEL XL7 BOLT ACTION RIFLE

Introduced in 2008, this is a centerfire bolt-action rifle with adjustable Pro-Fire trigger system. 4+1 capacity. Chambered in .25-06, .270 and .30-06 with a crowned, precision-rifled 22-inch barrel that is joined to the receiver with a pressure nut. Black synthetic stock with raised cheekpiece and Soft-Tech recoil pad. No sights; drilled and tapped for mounts.

NIB.: $300   **Exc.:** $275   **VGood:** $225

MODEL XL7C BOLT ACTION RIFLE

Similar to above but with RealTree APG HD camo finish.

NIB.: $345   **Exc.:** $300   **VGood:** $350

MARLIN MODEL 780

Bolt action; 22 Short, 22 Long, 22 LR; 7-shot clip magazine; 22-inch barrel; 40-1/2-inch overall length; weighs 5-1/2 lbs.; open rear, ramp front sight; receiver grooved for scope mounts; Monte Carlo American walnut stock; checkered pistol grip, forearm; gold-plated trigger. Introduced 1971; discontinued 1988.

Exc.: $100   **VGood:** $80   **Good:** $65

MARLIN MODEL 781

Bolt action; 22 Short, 22 Long, 22 LR; 17-shot tubular magazine; 22-inch barrel; weighs 6 lbs.; open rear, ramp front sight; receiver grooved for scope mounts; American walnut Monte Carlo stock; checkered pistol-grip, forearm. Introduced 1971; discontinued 1988.

Exc.: $150   **VGood:** $130   **Good:** $100

MARLIN MODEL 782

Bolt action; 22 WMR; 7-shot clip magazine; 22-inch barrel; 41-inch overall length; weighs 6 lbs.; open rear, ramp front sight; receiver grooved for scope mounts; American walnut Monte Carlo stock; checkered pistol grip, forearm; sling swivels; leather sling. Introduced 1971; discontinued 1988.

Exc.: $175   **VGood:** $150   **Good:** $110

MARLIN MODEL 783

Bolt action; 22 WMR; 13-shot tubular magazine; 22-inch barrel; 41-inch overall length; weighs 6 lbs.; open rear, ramp front sight; receiver grooved for scope mounts; select American walnut Monte Carlo stock; checkered pistol grip, forearm; white line spacer; gold-plated trigger; sling swivels; leather sling. Introduced 1971; discontinued 1988.

Exc.: $175   **VGood:** $150   **Good:** $110

MARLIN MODEL 880

Bolt action; 22 LR; 7-shot clip magazine; 22-inch Micro Groove barrel; 41-inch overall length; weighs 5-1/2 lbs.; ramp front, adjustable semi-buckhorn rear sight; receiver grooved for tip-off scope mount; black walnut Monte Carlo stock; checkered pistol grip, forend; swivel studs; rubber buttpad. Mar-Shield finish. Replaces Model 780. Introduced 1989; no longer in production; replaced by Model 980.

Perf.: $170   **Exc.:** $140   **VGood:** $120

MARLIN MODEL 880SS

Same specs as Model 880 except barrel, receiver, front breech bolt, striker knob, trigger stud, cartridge lifter stud and outer magazine tube made of stainless steel; most other parts nickel-plated to match stainless finish; black fiberglass-filled AKZO synthetic stock with moulded-in checkering; stainless steel swivel studs. Made in U.S. by Marlin Firearms Co. Introduced 1994; no longer in production.

Perf.: $220   **Exc.:** $170   **VGood:** $120

MARLIN MODEL 880SQ SQUIRREL RIFLE

Similar to Model 880SS except uses heavy target barrel of Marlin's Model 2000L target rifle. Black synthetic stock with moulded-in checkering, double bedding screws, matte blue finish. Without sights, no dovetail or filler screws; receiver grooved for scope mount. Weighs 7 lbs. Introduced 1996, no longer offered. Made in U.S.A. by Marlin.

Perf.: $285   **Exc.:** $225   **VGood:** $210

MARLIN MODEL 881

Bolt action; 22 LR, 22 Short, 22 Long; 17-shot (22 LR), 19-shot (22 Long), 25-shot (22 Short) tubular magazine; 22-inch Micro Groove barrel; 41-inch overall length; weighs 6 lbs.; ramp front, adjustable semi-buckhorn rear sight; receiver grooved for tip-off scope mount; black walnut Monte Carlo stock; checkered pistol grip, forend; swivel studs; rubber buttpad. Mar-Shield finish. Replaced Model 781. Introduced 1989; no longer in production; replaced by Model 981.

Perf.: $180   **Exc.:** $150   **VGood:** $125

MARLIN MODEL 882

Bolt action; 22 WMR; 7-shot clip magazine; 22-inch Micro Groove barrel; 41-inch overall length; weighs 5-1/2 lbs.; ramp front, adjustable semi-buckhorn rear sight; receiver grooved for tip-off scope mount; black walnut Monte Carlo stock; checkered pistol grip, forend; swivel studs; rubber buttpad. Mar-Shield finish. Replaces Model 782. Introduced 1989; no longer in production; replaced by Model 982.

Perf.: $150   **Exc.:** $120   **VGood:** $100

MARLIN MODEL 882L

Same specs as Model 882 except laminated hardwood stock. No longer in production.

Perf.: $180   **Exc.:** $160   **VGood:** $120

MARLIN MODEL 882SS

Same specs as Model 882 except stainless steel front breech bolt, barrel, receiver and bolt knob; other parts either stainless steel or nickel-plated; black Monte Carlo stock of fiberglass-filled polycarbonate with moulded-in checkering; nickel-plated swivel studs. Made in U.S. by Marlin Firearms Co. Introduced 1995; no longer produced.

Perf.: $180   **Exc.:** $160   **VGood:** $130

MARLIN MODEL 882SSV
BOLT-ACTION RIFLE

Similar to the Model 882SS except chambered for 22 WMR, has selected heavy 22-inch stainless steel barrel with recessed muzzle, and comes without sights; receiver is grooved for scope mount and 1-inch ring mounts are included. Weighs 7 lbs. Introduced 1997, no longer in production. Made in U.S.A. by Marlin Firearms Co.

Perf.: $240   **Exc.:** $180   **VGood:** $120

MARLIN MODEL 883

Bolt action; 22 WMR; 12-shot tubular magazine; 22-inch Micro Groove barrel; 41-inch overall length; weighs 5-1/2 lbs.; ramp front, adjustable semi-buckhorn rear sight; receiver grooved for tip-off scope mount; black walnut Monte Carlo stock; checkered pistol grip, forend; swivel studs; rubber buttpad. Mar-Shield finish. Replaces Model 783. Introduced 1989; no longer in production; replaced by Model 983.

Perf.: $190   **Exc.:** $150   **VGood:** $100

MARLIN MODEL 883SS

Same specs as Model 883 except front breech bolt, striker knob, trigger stud, cartridge lifter stud, outer magazine tube of stainless steel; other parts nickel-plated; two-tone brown laminated Monte Carlo stock with swivel studs; rubber buttpad. Made in U.S. by Marlin Firearms Co. Introduced 1993; no longer in production; replaced by Model 983S.

Perf.: $200   **Exc.:** $150   **VGood:** $110

MARLIN MODEL 915Y
COMPACT

Single shot .22 rimfire rifle with 16-1/4-inch barrel, hardwood stock with impressed checkering and iron sights.

NIB.: $225   **Exc..:** $150   **VGood:** $110

MARLIN MODEL 915YS COMPACT

Similar to above but with stainless steel receiver and barrel, no checkering and fiber optic sights.

NIB.: $225   **Exc..:** $150   **VGood:** $110

MARLIN MODEL 917

Bolt-action rifle chambered in 17 Hornady Mag. Rimfire or .17 Mach 2; 7-shot clip magazine; fiberglass-filled synthetic stock with full pistol grip; swivel studs and molded-in checkering. Adjustable open rear sight, ramp front. 22-inch barrel. Introduced 2006.

NIB: $275   **Exc.:** $235   **VGood:** $195

MARLIN MODEL 917VT

Similar to above but with laminated brown thumbhole stock. Introduced 2008.

NIB: $410   **Exc.:** $350   **VGood:** $265

MARLIN MODEL 917VST

Similar to above but with laminated gray/black thumbhole stock. Introduced 2008.

NIB: $410   **Exc.:** $350   **VGood:** $265

MARLIN MODEL 925

This model is chambered for the .22 LR cartridge and fitted with a 22" standard weight barrel with adjustable sights. Monte Carlo hardwood stock with full pistol grip. Seven-round magazine. Weight is about 5.5 lbs.

NIB: $275   **Exc.:** $235   **VGood:** $190

MARLIN MODEL 925R

As above but with factory-mounted 3x9 scope.

NIB: $300   **Exc..:** $250   **VGood:** $190

MARLIN MODEL 925C

As above but with Monte Carlo hardwood stock with Mossy Oak Break-up camo pattern. Adjustable sights.

NIB.: $325   **Exc..:** $275   **VGood:** $215

MARLIN MODEL 980

Bolt action; 22 WMR; 8-shot clip-type magazine; 24-inch barrel; 43-inch overall length; weighs 6 lbs.; open adjustable rear sight, hooded ramp front; uncheckered walnut Monte Carlo-style stock with

Marlin Model 882SSV

Marlin Model 883

Marlin Model 915YS

Marlin Model 917VT

Marlin Model 925R

Marlin Model 925C

Marlin Model 980

Marlin Model 980 S

white spacers at pistol grip and buttplate; sling; sling swivels. Introduced 1966; discontinued 1971.

Exc.: $150   **VGood:** $130   **Good:** $100

MARLIN MODEL 980S

As above but with standard weight 22" barrel and 7-round nickel plated magazine and stainless steel barrel and receiver. Adjustable sights. Weight is about 6 lbs.

NIB: $250   **Exc.:** $200   **VGood:** $165

MARLIN MODEL 980S-CF

As above but with carbon fiber stock. Introduced in 2007.

NIB: $275   **Exc.:** $225   **VGood:** $195

MARLIN MODEL 981T

This model is chambered to handle interchangeably the .22 Short, Long, or LR cartridges in a tubular magazine. Black Monte Carlo fiberglass stock with full pistol grip. Adjustable sights. Fitted with a standard weight 22" barrel. Weight is about 6 lbs.

NIB: $275   **Exc.:** $225   **VGood:** $195

MARLIN MODEL 982VS

As above but with black fiberglass Monte Carlo stock. Heavy 22" stainless steel barrel. Nickel plated 7-round magazine. No sights. Weight is about 7 lbs.

NIB: $345   **Exc.:** $295   **VGood:** $200

MARLIN MODEL 982VS-CF

As above but with synthetic stock with dipped carbon-fiber textured finish.

NIB: $345   **Exc.:** $295   **VGood:** $200

MARLIN MODEL 983

This .22 WMR model features a Monte Carlo stock of American black walnut with full pistol grip and checkering.

NIB.: $345   **Exc.:** $300   **VGood:** $225

MARLIN MODEL 983T

Chambered for the .22 WMR cartridge and fitted with a 22" barrel. Monte Carlo black fiberglass stock with checkering. Adjustable sights. Tubular 12-round magazine. Weight is about 6 lbs.

NIB: $275   **Exc.:** $235   **VGood:** $195

MARLIN MODEL 983S

As above but with laminated two-tone stock.

NIB: $365   **Exc.:** $300   **VGood:** $200

MARLIN MODEL 2000 TARGET

Bolt action; single shot; 22 LR; 22-inch heavy barrel; 41-inch overall length; weighs 8 lbs.; hooded Lyman front sight, fully-adjustable Lyman target peep rear; high-comb, blue-enameled fiberglass/Kevlar stock; stippled grid forend; adjustable buttplate; aluminum forend rail; quick-detachable swivel; two-stage target trigger; red cocking indicator. Marketed with seven front sight inserts. Current models with Williams sights. Introduced 1991; no longer produced.

Perf.: $395   **Exc.:** $350   **VGood:** $295

MARLIN MODEL 2000A

Same specs as Model 2000 except adjustable comb; ambidextrous pistol grip; Marlin logo moulded into the blue Carbelite stock. Weighs 8-1/2 lbs. Made in U.S. by Marlin Firearms Co. Introduced 1994; discontinued 1995.

Perf.: $425   **Exc.:** $375   **VGood:** $310

Marlin Model 2000 Target

Marlin Model 2000A

Marlin Model 2000L Target

Marlin Model 18

Marlin Model 20

Marlin Model 27

Marlin Model 39A Mountie

MARLIN MODEL 2000L TARGET RIFLE

Bolt action; 22 LR, single shot. 22-inch heavy barrel, Micro-Groove rifling, match chamber, recessed muzzle; weighs 8 lbs; 41-inch overall length. Laminated black/gray stock with ambidextrous pistol grip. Hooded front sight with ten aperture inserts, fully adjustable target rear peep. Buttplate adjustable for length of pull, height and angle. Aluminum forend rail with stop and quick-detachable swivel. Two-stage target trigger; red cocking indicator. Introduced 1991, discontinued 2003.

Perf.: $425   **Exc.:** $375   **VGood:** $310

MARLIN MODEL 18

Slide action; 22 Short, 22 Long, 22 LR; tube magazine; 20-inch round or octagonal barrel; exposed hammer; open rear sight, bead front; solid frame; uncheckered straight stock, slide handle. Deluxe special-order models available. Introduced 1906; discontinued 1909. Some collector value.

Exc.: $400   **VGood:** $320   **Good:** $200

MARLIN MODEL 20

Slide action; 22 Short, 22 Long, 22 LR; 18-shot (22 LR) full-length tubular magazine, 10-shot (22 LR) half-length magazine; 24-inch octagonal barrel; open rear sight, bead front; uncheckered straight grip stock. Later versions designated as 20S and 20A. Introduced 1907; discontinued 1922. Some collector value.

Exc.: $400   **VGood:** $310   **Good:** $200

MARLIN MODEL 25

Slide action; 22 Short; 15-shot tubular magazine; 23-inch barrel; exposed hammer; open rear sight, bead front; uncheckered straight grip stock, slide handle. Introduced 1909; discontinued 1910. Some collector value.

Exc.: $400   **VGood:** $300   **Good:** $200

MARLIN MODEL 27

Slide action; 25-20, 32-20; 7-shot tubular magazine; 24-inch octagonal barrel; open rear, bead front sight; uncheckered straight-grip stock; grooved slide handle. Introduced 1910; discontinued 1916. Some collector value.

Exc.: $425   **VGood:** $400   **Good:** $365

MARLIN MODEL 27S

Same specs as Model 27 except available in caliber 25 Stevens RF; round barrel. Introduced 1920; discontinued 1932.

Exc.: $400   **VGood:** $350   **Good:** $280

MARLIN MODEL 30AS

Lever action; 30-30; 6-shot tube magazine; 20-inch barrel; 38-1/2-inch overall length; weighs 7 lbs.; adjustable rear sight, bead front; walnut-finished Maine birch pistol grip stock; hammer-block safety. Introduced 1985; later in production as Model 336AS.

Perf.: $300   **Exc.:** $275   **VGood:** $250

MARLIN MODEL 32

Slide action; 22 Short, 22 Long, 22 LR; 10-shot short tubular magazine, 18-shot full-length magazine; 24-inch octagonal barrel; open rear, bead front sight; uncheckered pistol-grip stock, grooved slide handle. Marlin's first hammerless slide action rifle, some collector value. Introduced 1914; discontinued 1915.

Exc.: $475   **VGood:** $420   **Good:** $300

MARLIN MODEL 36 RIFLE AND CARBINE

Lever action; 30-30, 32 Spl., 6-shot tube magazine, 20-inch (carbine), 24-inch (rifle) barrel. open rear sight, bead front; uncheckered walnut pistol grip stock, semibeavertail forearm. Introduced in 1936, designation changed to Model 36 in 1937. Discontinued 1948.

Exc.: $500   **VGood:** $400   **Good:** $350

MARLIN MODEL 36-DL DELUXE RIFLE

Lever action; 32 Spl., 30-30; 6-shot tubular magazine; 24-inch barrel; 42-inch overall length; weighs 6-3/4 lbs.; "Huntsmen" hooded ramp front sight with silver bead, flat-top rear; checkered American black walnut pistol-grip stock; semi-beavertail forearm; case-hardened receiver, lever; visible hammer; drilled, tapped for tang peep sight; detachable swivels; 1-inch leather sling. Introduced 1938; discontinued 1947.

Exc.: $600   **VGood:** $450   **Good:** $325

MARLIN MODEL 36-DL CARBINE

Same specs as Model 36A except 20-inch barrel; 38-inch overall length; no checkering, swivels, sling.

Exc.: $600   **VGood:** $450   **Good:** $325

MARLIN MODEL 36RC

Same specs as Model 36 Carbine except "Huntsman" ramp front sight with silver bead and hood. Introduced 1938; discontinued 1947.

Exc.: $600   **VGood:** $450   **VGood:** $325

MARLIN MODEL 38

Slide action; 22 Short, 22 Long, 22 LR; 10-shot tube magazine (22 LR), 12-shot (22 Long), 15-shot (22 Short); 24-inch octagon barrel; hammerless takedown; open rear, bead front sight; uncheckered pistol-grip walnut stock; grooved slide handle. Introduced 1920; discontinued 1930.

Exc.: $490   **VGood:** $360   **Good:** $290

MARLIN MODEL 39

Lever action; 22 Short, 22 Long, 22 LR; 18-shot (22 LR), 20-shot (22 Long), 25-shot (22 Short); 24-inch octagon barrel with tube magazine; open rear, bead front sight; uncheckered pistol-grip walnut stock, forearm. Introduced 1922; discontinued 1938.

Perf.: $1295   **Exc.:** $995   **VGood:** $450

MARLIN MODEL 39A

Same specs as Model 39 except heavier stock; semi-beavertail forearm; semi-heavy round barrel. Introduced 1939; a version still remains in production. Early variations, better condition bring a premium.

Exc.: $400   **VGood:** $300   **Good:** $200

MARLIN MODEL 39A GOLDEN

Same specs as Model 39 except gold-plated trigger, other refinements. Introduced 1960. No longer in production.

Perf.: $315   **Exc.:** $285   **VGood:** $255

MARLIN MODEL 39A MOUNTIE

Same specs as Model 39A except 15-shot tubular magazine (22 LR), 16-shot (22 Long), 21-shot (22 Short); American black walnut straight-grip stock; slim forearm; 20-inch barrel; 36-inch overall length; weighs 6 lbs. Designation changed in 1972 to Model 39M. Introduced 1953; discontinued 1969.

Exc.: $425   **VGood:** $355   **Good:** $295

MARLIN MODEL 39A MOUNTIE CARBINE

Same specs as Model 39A Mountie except weighs 5-1/4 lbs.; shorter tube magazine; 18-shot (22 Short, 14-shot (22 Long), 12-shot (22 LR).

Exc.: $425   **VGood:** $355   **Good:** $295

MARLIN MODEL 39D

Same specs as Model 39 except 20-1/2-inch barrel; 36-1/2-inch overall length; weighs 5-3/4 lbs.; 21-shot (22 Short), 16-shot (22 Long), 15-shot (22 LR); adjustable rear, target front sight; grip cap; white line spacers; offset hammer spur. Introduced 1971; discontinued 1973.

Exc.: $395   **VGood:** $295   **Good:** $250

MARLIN MODEL 39M

Same specs as Model 39 except 20-inch barrel; 36-inch overall length; weighs 6 lbs.; 21-shot (22 Short), 16-shot (22 Long), 15-shot (22 LR); straight-grip stock. Introduced 1963; discontinued 1987.

Exc.: $395   **VGood:** $295   **Good:** $250

MARLIN MODEL 39M OCTAGON
Same specs as Model 39M except octagon barrel; bead front sight; hard rubber buttplate; squared lever. Introduced 1973.

Exc.: $650   **VGood:** $500   **Good:** $400

MARLIN MODEL 39TDS CARBINE
Same specs as Model 39A except 16-shot magazine (22 Short), 12-shot (22 Long), 10-shot (22 LR); 16-1/2-inch Micro-Groove barrel; 32-5/8-inch overall length; weighs 5-1/4 lbs.; hooded ramp front sight, adjustable semi-buckhorn rear; straight-grip American black walnut stock; hammer-block safety; rebounding hammer; gold-plated trigger; take-down style; blued finish. Marketed with case. Introduced 1988; discontinued 1996.

Perf.: $340   **Exc.:** $250   **VGood:** $190

MARLIN MODEL 39AS GOLDEN
Lever action; 22 Short, 22 Long, 22 LR; 26-shot tubular magazine (22 Short), 21-shot (22 Long), 19-shot (22 LR); 24-inch Micro-Groove barrel; 40-inch overall length; weighs 6-1/2 lbs.; takedown action; bead on ramp front sight with detachable Wide-Scan hood, folding fully-adjustable semi-buckhorn rear; receiver tapped for scope mount (supplied); checkered American black walnut stock with white line spacers at pistol-grip cap and buttplate; Mar-Shield finish; swivel studs; rubber buttpad; hammer-block safety; rebounding hammer; offset hammer spur; gold-plated steel trigger. Made in U.S. by Marlin. Introduced 1988; no longer in production.

Exc.: $375   **VGood:** $325   **Good:** $275

MARLIN MODEL 56 LEVERMATIC
Lever action, short-throw lever; 22 Short, 22 Long, 22 LR; 7-shot clip magazine; 24-inch (early), 22-inch barrel; 41-inch overall length; weighs 6-1/4 lbs.; open rear, ramp front sight; one-piece Bishop-style uncheckered walnut Monte Carlo-type pistol-grip stock. Introduced 1955; discontinued 1964.

Exc.: $275   **VGood:** $250   **Good:** $175

MARLIN MODEL 56 CLIPPER KING LEVERMATIC
Special version of the Model 56. Came with mounted 4X scope, had special package and accessories, 10-shot magazine. Made in 1959 only, 152 specimens made, some collector value.

Exc.: $325   **VGood:** $290   **Good:** $250

MARLIN MODEL 57 LEVERMATIC
Lever action, short-throw lever; 22 Short, 22 Long, 22 LR; 25-shot tubular magazine (22 Short), 20-shot (22 Long), 18-shot (22 LR); 22-inch barrel; 41-inch overall length; weighs 6-1/4 lbs.; open rear sight, hooded ramp front; one-piece Bishop-style uncheckered walnut Monte Carlo-type pistol-grip stock. Introduced 1959; discontinued 1965.

Exc.: $275   **VGood:** $250   **Good:** $175

MARLIN MODEL 57M LEVERMATIC
Same specs as Model 57 except 22WMR, 24-inch barrel; 43-inch overall length; weighs 6-1/2 lbs.; 15-shot magazine; 25-degree lever throw. Introduced 1959; discontinued 1969.

Exc.: $295   **VGood:** $270   **Good:** $195

MARLIN MODEL 62 CENTERFIRE LEVERMATIC
Lever action, short-throw lever; 256 Mag., 22 Jet, 30 Carbine; 4-shot clip magazine; 24-inch barrel; 43-inch overall length; weighs 7 lbs.; open windage-adjustable rear sight, hooded ramp front; swivels; sling; uncheckered American black walnut Monte Carlo-type pistol-grip stock. The 256 Mag. was introduced in 1963; discontinued 1969. Premium for 22 Jet.

256 Magnum		
Exc.: $420	**VGood:** $365	**Good:** $325
30 Carbine		
Exc.: $425	**VGood:** $385	**Good:** $335

Marlin Model 39AS Golden

Marlin Model 56 Levermatic

Marlin Model 57 Levermatic

Marlin Model 62 Levermatic

Marlin Model 93

Marlin Model 94

MARLIN MODEL 92
Lever action; 22 Short, 22 Long, 22 LR, 32 Short, 32 LR, 32 Centerfire (with interchangeable firing pin); 16-inch, 24-inch, 26-inch, 28-inch barrel; tubular magazine; open rear, blade front sight; uncheckered straight-grip stock, forearm. Originally marketed as Model 1892. Introduced 1892; discontinued 1915. Collector value.

22 Caliber		
Exc.: $1350	**VGood:** $1095	**Good:** $600
32 Caliber		
Exc.: $1225	**VGood:** $995	**Good:** $500

MARLIN MODEL 93
Lever action; 25-36 Marlin, 30-30, 32 Spl., 32-40, 38-55; 10-shot tubular magazine; 26-inch, 28-inch, 30-inch, 32-inch round or octagonal barrel; solid frame or take-down; open rear, bead front sight; uncheckered straight-grip stock, forearm. Originally marketed as Model 1893. Introduced 1893; discontinued 1935. Collector value.

Exc.: $1500   **VGood:** $1025   **Good:** $795

MARLIN MODEL 93 CARBINE
Same specs as Model 93 except 20-inch barrel; 7-shot magazine; 30-30, 32 Spl.; carbine sights. Collector value.

Exc.: $1500   **VGood:** $1025   **Good:** $795

MARLIN MODEL 93SC
Same specs as Model 93 Carbine except shorter 5-shot magazine. Designated Sports Carbine. Collector value.

Exc.: $1500   **VGood:** $1025   **Good:** $795

MARLIN MODEL 94
Lever action; 25-20, 32-20, 38-40, 44-40; 10-shot magazine; 24-inch (standard), 15-inch, 20-inch, 26-inch, 28-inch, 30-inch, 32-inch round or octagonal barrel; solid frame or takedown; open rear, bead front sight; uncheckered pistol grip or straight stock, forearm. Originally marketed as Model 1894. Introduced 1894; discontinued 1933. Collector value.

Exc.: $1400   **VGood:** $895   **Good:** $695

MARLIN MODEL 95
Lever action; 33 WCF, 38-56, 40-65, 40-70, 40-82, 45-70; 9-shot tubular magazine; 24-inch round or octagonal barrel, other lengths on special order; open rear, bead front sight; uncheckered straight or pistol-grip stock, forearm. Originally marketed as Model 1895. Introduced 1895; discontinued 1915. Collector value.

Exc.: $2895   **VGood:** $2495   **Good:** $1700

MARLIN MODEL 97
Lever action; 22 Short, 22 Long, 22 LR; tubular magazine; 16-inch, 24-inch, 26-inch, 28-inch barrel; open rear, bead front sight; uncheckered straight or pistol grip stock, forearm. Originally marketed as Model 1897. Introduced 1897; discontinued 1916. Collector value.

Exc.: $1500   **VGood:** $1025   **Good:** $795

Marlin Model 336C

Marlin Model 336 Cowboy

Marlin Model 336A

Marlin Model 336CC

Marlin Model 336CS

Marlin Model 336T
Texan Carbine

MARLIN MODEL 336C

Lever-action; 30-30, 35 Rem., 32 Spl.; 6-shot tubular magazine; 20-inch barrel; 38-1/2-inch overall length; weighs 7 lbs.; updated version of Model 36 carbine; semi-buckhorn adjustable folding rear sight, ramp front with Wide-Scan hood; receiver tapped for scope mounts; round breech bolt; gold-plated trigger; offset hammer spur; top of receiver sandblasted to reduce glare. Introduced 1948; discontinued 1983; updated version still in production.

Exc.: $395　**VGood:** $350　**Good:** $295

MARLIN MODEL 336 COWBOY

Similar to the Model 336C except chambered for 30-30 and 38-55 Win., 24-inch tapered octagon barrel with deep-cut Ballard-type rifling; straight-grip walnut stock with hard rubber buttplate; blued steel forend cap; weighs 7-1/2 lbs.; 42-1/2-inch overall. Introduced 1999, no longer in production. Made in U.S.A. by Marlin.

Perf.: $650　**Exc.:** $525　**VGood:** $410

MARLIN MODEL 336A

Same specs as Model 336C except 24-inch round barrel; two-thirds magazine tube; 6-shot; blued forearm cap; sling swivels. Introduced 1950; temporarily discontinued 1962. Reintroduced 1973; discontinued 1980, no longer offered.

Exc.: $300　**VGood:** $250　**Good:** $200

MARLIN MODEL 336A LEVER-ACTION CARBINE

Same as the Marlin 336C except 20-inch barrel; has cut-checkered, walnut-finished hardwood pistol grip stock with swivel studs, 30-30 only, 6-shot. Hammer-block safety. Adjustable rear sight, brass bead front. Add 30 percent for 1/2 magazine tube version.

Exc.: $350　**VGood:** $325　**Good:** $300

MARLIN MODEL 336A-DL

Same specs as Model 336A except sling; swivels; hand-checkered stock, forearm. Discontinued 1962.

Exc.: $395　**VGood:** $350　**Good:** $295

MARLIN MODEL 336CC LEVER-ACTION CARBINE

Same as the Marlin 336A except has Mossy Oak Break-Up camouflage stock and forearm. 30-30 only, 6-shot; receiver tapped for scope mount or receiver sight. Introduced 2001, still in production. Made in U.S.A. by Marlin.

Perf.: $465　**Exc.:** $410　**VGood:** $375

MARLIN MODEL 336CS

Same specs as Model 336A except 30-30, 35 Rem.; 6-shot two-thirds tube magazine; 20-inch barrel; 38-1/2-inch overall length; weighs 7 lbs.; select black walnut stock; capped pistol grip; hammer-block safety; tapped for scope mounts; offset hammer spur. Introduced 1984; discontinued 2001.

Exc.: $395　**VGood:** $350　**Good:** $295

MARLIN MODEL 336 ER (EXTRA-RANGE) CARBINE

Same specs as Model 336A except 307 Win.(advertised), 356 Win.(produced); 4-shot tubular magazine; new hammer-block safety; rubber buttpad; marketed with detachable sling swivels, branded leather sling. Introduced 1983; discontinued 1986.

Exc.: $850　**VGood:** $700　**Good:** $450

MARLIN MODEL 336SS LEVER-ACTION CARBINE

Same as the 336C except receiver, barrel and other major parts are machined from stainless steel. 30-30 only, 6-shot; receiver tapped for scope. Still offered.

Perf.: $475　**Exc.:** $425　**VGood:** $170

MARLIN MODEL 336W LEVER-ACTION RIFLE

Similar to the Model 336CS except has walnut-finished, cut-checkered Maine birch stock; blued steel barrel band has integral sling swivel; no front sight hood; comes with padded nylon sling; hard rubber butt plate. Introduced 1998, still offered. Made in U.S.A. by Marlin.

Perf.: $310　**Exc.:** $230　**VGood:** $170

MARLIN MODEL 336 MARAUDER

Same specs as Model 336A except 30-30, 35 Rem.; 16-1/4-inch barrel. Introduced 1963; discontinued 1964.

Exc.: $410　**VGood:** $330　**Good:** $230

MARLIN MODEL 336 OCTAGON

Same specs as Model 336A except octagon barrel. Introduced 1973.

Exc.: $430　**VGood:** $390　**Good:** $310

MARLIN MODEL 336 SPORT CARBINE

Same specs as Model 336A rifle except 20-inch barrel; weighs 7 lbs.; two-thirds 6-shot magazine. Introduced 1948; discontinued 1963.

Exc.: $300　**VGood:** $250　**Good:** $180

MARLIN MODEL 336SC ZIPPER

Same specs as Model 336 Sport Carbine except chambered only for 219 Zipper; 20-inch heavy barrel; weighs 7-3/4 lbs. Introduced 1955; discontinued 1960.

Exc.: $800　**VGood:** $675　**Good:** $425

MARLIN MODEL 336SD

Same specs as Model 336A except 20-inch barrel; checkered pistol grip, forend; 38-1/2-inch overall length; weighs 7-1/2 lbs.; leather sling; deluxe sports carbine. Introduced 1954; discontinued 1962.

Exc.: $550　**VGood:** $325　**Good:** $220

MARLIN MODEL 336T TEXAN CARBINE

Same specs as Model 336A except 18-1/2-inch (1953), 20-inch barrel; straight-grip uncheckered walnut stock; squared lever. Called the Texan Model. Introduced in 1953; discontinued 1983. Originally chambered in 30-30, 35 Rem.; chambered in 44 Mag. from 1963 to 1967. Deluxe 336TDL version manufactured 1962-1963. No longer in production.

Exc.: $425　**VGood:** $375　**Good:** $325

Deluxe 336TDL

Exc.: $425　**VGood:** $325　**Good:** $300

MARLIN MODEL 336TS TEXAN

Same specs as Model 336CS except 30-30; 18-1/2-inch barrel; straight grip-stock; cross-bolt safety. Introduced 1984; discontinued 1987.

Exc.: $425　**VGood:** $325　**Good:** $275

MARLIN MODEL 336Y

Similar to Model 336C, but with 16-1/2-inch barrel, short stock with 12-1/2-inch length of pull; designed for young or smaller-stature hunters; 30-30 only.

Perf.: $500   **Exc.:** $400   **VGood:** N/A

MARLIN MODEL 336XLR

Lever-action chambered in .30/30, with 5-shot tubular magazine, 24-inch stainless steel barrel, along with stainless steel receiver, trigger, trigger guard plate, magazine tube, loading gate, and lever. Full pistol grip, swivel studs, and Ballard-type rifling precision fluted bolt. Features solid top receiver with side-ejection, adjustable folding semi-buckhorn rear sight, ramp front sight, tapped for scope mount. Designed for Hornady LEVERevolution cartridges.

NIB: $650   **Exc.:** $595   **VGood:** $475

MARLIN MODEL 375

Lever action; 375 Win.; 5-shot tube magazine; 20-inch barrel; 38-1/2-inch overall length; weighs 6-3/4 lbs.; hooded ramp front, adjustable semi-buckhorn folding rear sight; checkered American black walnut stocks; quick-detachable swivels; leather sling. Introduced 1980; discontinued 1983.

Exc.: $550   **VGood:** $475   **Good:** $350

MARLIN MODEL 444 RIFLE

Lever action; 444 Marlin; 5-shot tube magazine; 24-inch (early), 22-inch barrel; 42-1/2-inch overall length; weighs 7-1/2 lbs.; open elevation-adjustable rear sight, hooded ramp front; action is strengthened version of Model 336; straight-grip Monte Carlo stock of uncheckered American walnut; recoil pad; carbine forearm; barrel band; sling; sling swivels. Introduced 1965; discontinued 1972.

Exc.: $425   **VGood:** $390   **Good:** $345

MARLIN MODEL 444 SPORTER

Same specs as Model 444 Rifle except 22-inch barrel, 40-1/2-inch overall length; folding rear, brass bead front sight; Model 336A-type pistol-grip stock, forearm; recoil pad; detachable swivels; sling. Introduced 1972; discontinued 1983; updated version still offered.

Exc.: $445   **VGood:** $390   **Good:** $345

MARLIN MODEL 444P OUTFITTER LEVER-ACTION

Similar to the 444 with 18-1/2-inch ported barrel; weighs 6-3/4 lbs.; overall length 37-inch. Available only in 444 Marlin. Introduced 1999, dropped 2003.

Perf.: $475   **Exc.:** $425   **VGood:** $400

MARLIN MODEL 444SS

Same specs as Model 444 Sporter except 22-inch barrel with deep-cut Ballard-type rifling; fully-adjustable folding semi-buckhorn rear sight; hammer-block safety; offset hammer spur; Mar-Shield finish. Introduced 1984; dropped 2001.

Perf.: $450   **Exc.:** $425   **VGood:** $395

MARLIN MODEL 1894

Lever action; 41 Mag., 44 Mag., 45 Colt; 10-shot tube magazine; 20-inch carbine barrel; 37-1/2-inch overall length; weighs 6 lbs.; hooded ramp front sight, semi-buckhorn adjustable rear; uncheckered straight grip black walnut stock, forearm; gold-plated trigger; receiver tapped for scope mount; offset hammer spur; solid top receiver sand blasted to reduce glare. 41 Mag. produced 1985-1988; 45 Colt produced 1989-1990. Introduced 1969; later production as Model 1894S.

Perf.: $400   **Exc.:** $370   **VGood:** $320

MARLIN MODEL 1894C

Same specs as Model 1894 except 357 Mag.; 9-shot tube magazine; 18-1/2-inch barrel; 35-1/2-inch overall length; weighs 6 lbs. Introduced 1979; discontinued 1985. Improved version still offered.

Perf.: $400   **Exc.:** $370   **VGood:** $320

MARLIN MODEL 1894CL CLASSIC

Same specs as 1894CL except 218 Bee, 25-20, 32-20; brass bead front sight, adjustable semi-buckhorn folding rear; hammer-block safety; rubber rifle buttpad; swivel studs. Introduced 1988; discontinued

1994. Later reintroduced in .32-20; add 15% for earlier .25-20/.218 production.

Perf.: $600   **Exc.:** $500   **VGood:** $395

MARLIN MODEL 1894CS CARBINE

Same specs Model 1894 except 38 Spl., 357 Mag.; 18-1/2-inch barrel; 9-shot magazine; brass bead front sight; hammer-block safety. Introduced 1985; dropped 2001.

Perf.: $495   **Exc.:** $395   **VGood:** $320

MARLIN MODEL 1894FG

Similar to Model 1894, but current production chambered for 41 Magnum cartridge only; 20-inch barrel.

Perf.: $515   **Exc.:** $475   **VGood:** 400

MARLIN MODEL 1894M

Same specs as Model 1894 except 22 WMR; 11-shot magazine; no gold-plated trigger; receiver tapped for scope mount or receiver sight. Introduced 1982; discontinued 1986.

Exc.: $400   **VGood:** $365   **Good:** $290

MARLIN MODEL 1894P/1894CP CARBINE

Similar to the Model 1894 except has ported 16-1/4-inch barrel with 8-shot magazine. Overall length 33-1/4-inch, weighs 5-3/4 lbs. Discontinued 2003.

Model 1894P (44 Spec./44 Mag.)
Perf.: $530   **Exc.:** $450   **VGood:** $370

Model 1894CP (38 Spec./357 Mag.)
Perf.: $530   **Exc.:** $450   **VGood:** $350

Marlin Model 336XLR

Marlin Model 375

Marlin Model 444 Sporter

Marlin Model 444P Outfitter Lever-Action

Marlin Model 1894C

Marlin Model 1894CL Classic

Marlin Model 1894CS Carbine

Marlin Model 1894P/1894CP Carbine

Marlin Model 1894 Cowboy

Marlin Model 1894 Cowboy Competition Rifle

Marlin Model 1894SS

Marlin Model 1895

Marlin Model 1895 Cowboy

Marlin Model 1895G Guide Gun

Marlin Model 1895GS Guide Gun

Marlin Model 1895XLR

MARLIN MODEL 1894 COWBOY

Lever action; 357 Mag., 44 Mag., 45 Colt, 10-shot magazine. 24-inch tapered octagon barrel, deep cut rifling; weighs 7-1/2 lbs.; 41-1/2-inch overall length; straight grip American black walnut stock, hard rubber buttplate, Marble carbine front, adjustable Marble semi- buckhorn rear sights. Squared finger lever; straight grip stock; blued steel forend tip. Designed for Cowboy Action shooting events. Introduced 1996.

Perf.: $600   **Exc.:** $480   **VGood:** $370

MARLIN MODEL 1894 COWBOY COMPETITION RIFLE

Similar to Model 1894 except 38 Spl. or 45 Colt only; 20-inch barrel, 37-1/2-inch long, weighs only 6 lbs.,

antique finish on receiver, lever and bolt. Factory-tuned for competitive cowboy action shooting.

Perf.: $790   **Exc.:** $680   **VGood:** $575

MARLIN MODEL 1894 OCTAGON

Same specs as Model 1894CS Carbine except octagon barrel; bead front sight. Introduced 1973. No longer produced.

Exc.: $450   **VGood:** $400   **Good:** $315

MARLIN MODEL 1894 SPORTER

Same specs as Model 1894CS Carbine except 22-inch barrel, 6-shot magazine. Introduced 1973.

Exc.: $390   **VGood:** $275   **Good:** $190

MARLIN MODEL 1894S

Same specs as Model 1894 except 41 Mag., 44 Spl., 44 Mag.; buttpad; swivel studs; hammer-block safety; offset hammer spur. Discontinued 2001, reintroduced as updated Model 1894 (without letter suffix).

Perf.: $550   **Exc.:** $475   **VGood:** $375

MARLIN MODEL 1894SS

Similar to Model 1894 except has stainless steel barrel, receiver, lever, guard plate, magazine tube and loading plate. Nickel-plated swivel studs.

Perf.: $615   **Exc.:** $580   **VGood:** $500

MARLIN MODEL 1895

Lever action; 45-70; 4-shot tube magazine; 22-inch round barrel; 40-1/2-inch overall length; weighs 7 lbs.; offset hammer spur; adjustable semi-buckhorn folding rear sight, bead front; solid receiver tapped for scope mounts, receiver sights; two-piece uncheckered straight grip American walnut stock, forearm of black walnut; rubber buttplate; blued steel forend cap. Meant to be a recreation of the original Model 1895 discontinued in 1915. Actually built on action of Marlin Model 444. Introduced 1972; discontinued 1979. Updated version still in production.

Exc.: $495   **VGood:** $400   **Good:** $395

MARLIN MODEL 1895 COWBOY LEVER-ACTION RIFLE

Similar to Model 1895 except has 26-inch tapered octagon barrel with Ballard- type rifling, Marble carbine front sight and Marble adjustable semi-buckhorn rear sight. Receiver tapped for scope or receiver sight. Overall length is 44-1/2-inch, weighs about 8 lbs. Introduced 2001. Made in U.S.A. by Marlin.

Perf.: $600   **Exc.:** $550   **VGood:** $400

MARLIN MODEL 1895G GUIDE GUN LEVER-ACTION RIFLE

Similar to Model 1895 with deep-cut Ballard-type rifling; 18-1/2-inch ported barrel; straight-grip walnut stock. Overall length is 37 inches, weight 7 lbs. Introduced 1998. Discontinued.

Perf.: $450   **Exc.:** $350   **VGood:** $275

MARLIN MODEL 1895GS GUIDE GUN

Similar to Model 1895G except receiver, barrel and most metal parts are machined from stainless steel. Chambered for 45-70, 4-shot, 18-1/2-inch barrel. Overall length is 37 inches, weight 7 lbs. Introduced 2001. Current production features non-ported barrel.

Perf.: $700   **Exc.:** $575   **VGood:** $500

MARLIN MODEL 1895M LEVER-ACTION RIFLE

Similar to Model 1895 except has an 18-1/2-inch ported barrel with Ballard-type cut rifling. Chambered for 450 Marlin. Introduced 2000, still offered without ported barrel.

Perf.: $550   **Exc.:** $500   **VGood:** $425

MARLIN MODEL 1895S

Same specs as Model 1895 except full pistol-grip stock; straight buttpad. Introduced 1980; discontinued 1983.

Exc.: $425   **VGood:** $365   **Good:** $315

MARLIN MODEL 1895SS

Same specs as Model 1895 except full pistol-grip stock; hammer-block safety. Introduced 1984; discontinued 2001.

Exc.: $450   **VGood:** $365   **Good:** $315

MARLIN MODEL 1895XLR

Lever-action chambered in .45-70 Government or .450 Marlin with a 4-shot tubular magazine, 24-inch stainless steel barrel, along with stainless steel receiver, trigger, trigger guard plate, magazine tube, loading gate, and lever. Full pistol grip, swivel studs, and Ballard-type rifling precision fluted bolt. Features solid top receiver with side-ejection, adjustable folding semi-buckhorn rear sight, ramp front sight, tapped for scope mount. Designed for Hornady LEVERevolution cartridges.

NIB: $650   **Exc.:** $595   **VGood:** $475

MARLIN MODEL 444XLR
Similar to Model 1895XLR but chambered in .444 Marlin.

NIB: $650   **Exc.:** $595   **VGood:** $475

MARLIN MODEL 1897 COWBOY RIFLE
Lever Action; 22 S,L,LR; 24-inch octagon barrel; 40-inch OAL; American walnut stock and forearm with cut checkering; Marble semibuckhorn rear, gold bead front sights; introduced 1999, discontinued 2002.

Perf.: $575   **Exc.:** $500   **VGood:** 425

MARLIN MODEL 1897T RIFLE
Lever action 22, S (21), L (16), LR (14), tubular mag. 20-inch tapered octagon barrel. Marble semi-buckhorn rear, Marble front brass bead sights. Hammer block safety, solid top receiver tapped, base for scope rings. Introduced 2002, no longer offered.

Perf.: $525   **Exc.:** $450   **VGood:** $375

MARLIN-GLENFIELD MODEL 15
Bolt action; single shot; 22 Short, 22 Long, 22 LR; 22-inch barrel; 41-inch overall length; weighs 5-1/2 lbs.; ramp front, adjustable open rear sight; receiver grooved for tip-off scope mount; Monte Carlo walnut-finished hardwood stock; checkered full pistol grip; red cocking indicator; thumb safety. Introduced 1979; discontinued 1983.

Exc.: $75   **VGood:** $60   **Good:** $50

MARLIN-GLENFIELD MODEL 20
Bolt action; 22 Short, 22 Long, 22 LR; 8-shot clip magazine; 22-inch barrel; bead front sight; walnut finished stock.

Exc.: $75   **VGood:** $65   **Good:** $55

MARLIN-GLENFIELD MODEL 30
Lever action; 30-30, some made in 35 Rem.; 4-shot tubular magazine; 20-inch barrel; 38-1/2-inch overall length; weighs 7 lbs.; adjustable rear sight, bead front; receiver tapped for scope mounts; walnut finished hardwood stock with semi-beavertail forend; round breech bolt; offset hammer spur; top of receiver sandblasted to reduce glare; blued forearm cap. Introduced 1966; discontinued 1972.

Exc.: $225   **VGood:** $195   **Good:** $150

MARLIN-GLENFIELD MODEL 30A
Same specs as Model 30 except impressed checkering on stock, forearm. Introduced 1969; still in production as Marlin Model 30AS.

Exc.: $225   **VGood:** $195   **Good:** $150

MARLIN-GLENFIELD MODEL 30GT
Same specs as Marlin-Glenfield Model 30 except 18-1/2-inch barrel; brass bead front, adjustable rear sight; straight grip walnut-finished hardwood stock; receiver sandblasted. Introduced 1979; discontinued 1981.

Exc.: $210   **VGood:** $180   **Good:** $135

MARLIN-GLENFIELD MODEL 60
Semi-automatic; 22 LR; 14-, 18-shot tubular magazine; 22-inch tapered, round barrel; 40-1/2-inch overall length; weighs 5-1/2 lbs.; ramp front, fully-adjustable rear sight; press-checkered, walnut-finished Maine birch stock with Monte Carlo full pistol grip; manual bolt hold-open; Mar-Shield finish. Introduced 1966; still in production as Marlin Model 60.

Exc.: $125   **VGood:** $95   **Good:** $75

MARLIN-GLENFIELD MODEL 70
Semi-automatic; 22 LR; 7-shot detachable clip magazine; 18-inch barrel; 36-1/2-inch overall length; weighs 4-1/2 lbs.; open adjustable rear, ramp front sight; chrome-plated trigger; cross-bolt safety; bolt hold-open; chrome-plated magazine; sling swivels; walnut-finished hardwood stock. Introduced 1967; discontinued 1994.

Exc.: $125   **VGood:** $95   **Good:** $75

MARLIN-GLENFIELD MODEL 75C
Semi-automatic; 22 LR; 14-shot magazine; 18-inch barrel; 36-3/4-inch overall length; weighs 5 lbs.; ramp front, open adjustable rear sight; walnut finished hardwood Monte Carlo stock with full pistol grip; bolt hold-open; cross-bolt safety; receiver grooved for scope mounts. Introduced 1980. No longer in production.

Exc.: $125   **VGood:** $95   **Good:** $75

MARLIN-GLENFIELD MODEL 81G
Bolt action; 22 Short, 22 Long, 22 LR; 18-shot (22 LR), 20-shot (22 Long), 24-shot (22 Short) tube magazine; open rear, bead front sight; standard uncheckered pistol-grip stock; chrome-plated trigger. Introduced 1937; discontinued 1971.

Exc.: $110   **VGood:** $95   **Good:** $70

MARLIN-GLENFIELD MODEL 101G
Bolt action; single shot; 22 Short, 22 Long, 22 LR; 22-inch barrel; semi-buckhorn fully-adjustable rear sight, hooded wide-scan front; black plastic trigger guard; T-shaped cocking piece; uncheckered hardwood stock with beavertail forearm; receiver grooved for tip-off scope mount. Introduced 1960; discontinued 1965.

Exc.: $110   **VGood:** $95   **Good:** $70

MARLIN-GLENFIELD MODEL 989G
Semi-automatic; 22 LR; 7-shot clip detachable magazine; 18-inch barrel; bead front, open rear sight; plain stock. Same as Marlin Model 989M2. Introduced 1962; discontinued 1964.

Exc.: $175   **VGood:** $150   **Good:** $115

MAUSER MODEL 10 VARMINTER
Bolt action; 22-250; 5-shot box magazine; 24-inch heavy barrel; no sights; drilled, tapped for scope mounts; hand-checkered European walnut Monte

Marlin Model 1897 Cowboy Rifle

Marlin Model 1897T Rifle

Mauser Model 10 Varminter

Mauser Model 66 Magnum

Mauser Model 66SP Match

Carlo pistol-grip stock; externally adjustable trigger; hammer-forged Krupp Special Ordnance steel barrel. Introduced 1973; discontinued 1975.

Exc.: $595   **VGood:** $540   **Good:** $400

MAUSER MODEL 66
Bolt action; 243, 270, 308, 30-06, 5.6x57, 6.5x57, 7x64, 9.3x62, 7mm Rem. Mag., 300 Wea. Mag., 300 Win. Mag., 6.5x68, 8x68S, 9.3x64; 3-shot magazine; 24-inch barrel (standard calibers), 26-inch (magnum caliber); 39-inch overall length (standard calibers); weighs 7-1/2 to 9-3/8 lbs.; blade front sight on ramp, fully-adjustable open rear; hand-checkered European walnut stock with Monte Carlo comb; hand-rubbed oil finish; rosewood forend and grip caps; telescoping short-stroke action; interchangeable, free-floated, medium-heavy barrels; mini-claw extractor; adjustable single-stage trigger; internal magazine. Imported from Germany by Precision Imports, Inc. Introduced 1989; discontinued 1994.

Perf.: $1400   **Exc.:** $1200   **VGood:** $795

Magnum calibers

Perf.: $1500   **Exc.:** $1300   **VGood:** $900

MAUSER MODEL 66 SAFARI
Same specs as Model 66 except 375 H&H, 458 Win. Mag.; weighs 9-3/8 lbs. Imported from Germany by Precision Imports, Inc. Introduced 1989; discontinued 1994.

Perf.: $2000   **Exc.:** $1600   **VGood:** $1200

MAUSER MODEL 66 STUTZEN
Same specs as Model 66 except 21-inch barrel; full-length Stutzen stock. Imported from Germany by Precision Imports, Inc. Introduced 1989; discontinued 1994.

Perf.: $1500   **Exc.:** $1250   **VGood:** $1000

MAUSER MODEL 66SP MATCH
Bolt action; 308 Win.; 3-shot magazine; 27-1/2-inch barrel, muzzle brake; no sights; scope supplied; match-design European walnut stock; thumbhole pistol grip; spring-loaded cheekpiece; Morgan adjustable recoil pad; adjustable match trigger. Introduced 1976; discontinued 1990.

Perf.: $2200   **Exc.:** $1800   **VGood:** $1600

Mauser Model 77 Big Game

Mauser Model 77 Sportsman

Mauser Model 98 Standard

Mauser Model 99 Monte Carlo Stock

Mauser Model 99 Classic Stock

Mauser Model 107

Mauser Model 201

MAUSER MODEL 77

Bolt action; 243, 270, 6.5x57, 7x64, 308, 30-06; 3-shot detachable magazine; 24-inch barrel; weighs 7-1/4 lbs.; ramp front sight, open adjustable rear; oil-finished European walnut stock; rosewood grip cap; forend tip; palm-swell pistol grip; Bavarian cheekpiece; recoil pad; interchangeable double-set or single trigger. Introduced 1981; no longer imported.

Perf.: $1150   **Exc.:** $910   **VGood:** $750

MAUSER MODEL 77 BIG GAME

Same specs as Model 77 except 375 H&H, 458 Win. Mag.; 26-inch barrel; weighs 8-1/2 lbs. Introduced 1981; no longer imported.

Perf.: $1295   **Exc.:** $995   **VGood:** $810

MAUSER MODEL 77 MAGNUM

Same specs as Model 77 except 7mm Rem. Mag., 6.5x68, 300 Win. Mag., 300 Weatherby Mag., 9.3x62, 9.3x64, 8x68S; 26-inch barrel; weighs 8-1/8 lbs. Introduced 1981; no longer imported.

Perf.: $1365   **Exc.:** $1100   **VGood:** $895

MAUSER MODEL 77 MANNLICHER

Same specs as Model 77 except 20-inch barrel; 7-3/4 lbs.; European walnut full-stock; set trigger. Introduced 1981; no longer imported.

Perf.: $1195   **Exc.:** $995   **VGood:** $750

MAUSER MODEL 77 SPORTSMAN

Same specs as Model 77 except 243, 308; weighs 9 lbs.; no sights; set trigger. No longer imported.

Perf.: $1395   **Exc.:** $995   **VGood:** $750

MAUSER MODEL 77 ULTRA

Same specs as Model 77 except 6.5x57, 7x64, 30-06; 20-inch barrel; weighs 7-3/4 lbs. Introduced 1981; no longer imported.

Perf.: $1250   **Exc.:** $995   **VGood:** $725

MAUSER MODEL 83

Bolt action; 308; 10-shot magazine; 26-inch barrel; European walnut match stock; adjustable buttplate comb; match trigger. No longer imported.

Perf.: $2195   **Exc.:** $1695   **VGood:** $1345

MAUSER MODEL 83 SINGLE SHOT

Same specs as Model 83 except single shot action. No longer imported.

Perf.: $1995   **Exc.:** $1495   **VGood:** $995

MAUSER MODEL 83 MATCH UIT

Same specs as Model 83 except single shot action; free rifle designed for UIT competition. No longer imported.

Perf.: $2250   **Exc.:** $1795   **VGood:** $1375

MAUSER MODEL 86-SR SPECIALTY RIFLE

Bolt action; 308 Win.; 9-shot detachable magazine; 25-5/8-inch fluted barrel with 1:12-inch twist; 47-3/4-inch overall length; weighs about 11 lbs.; no sights; competition metallic sights or scope mount optional; laminated wood, fiberglass, or special match thumbhole wood stock with rail in forend and adjustable recoil pad; match barrel with muzzle brake; action with two front bolt locking lugs and bedded in stock with free-floated barrel; match trigger adjustable as single or two-stage, fully-adjustable for weight, slack, and position; silent safety locks bolt, firing pin. Imported from Germany by Precision Imports, Inc. Introduced 1989; discontinued 1994.

With fiberglass stock
Perf.: $3395   **Exc.:** $2500   **VGood:** $2150

With match thumbhole stock
Perf.: $3595   **Exc.:** $3295   **VGood:** $2500

MAUSER MODEL 98 STANDARD

Bolt action; 7mm Mauser, 7.9mm (8mm) Mauser; 5-shot box magazine; 23-1/2-inch barrel; adjustable rear, blade front sight; military-style uncheckered European walnut stock; straight military-type bolt handle; Mauser trademark on receiver ring; commercial version of German military rifle. Introduced post-WWI; discontinued 1938.

Exc.: $795   **VGood:** $525   **Good:** $375

MAUSER MODEL 99

Bolt action; 243, 25-06, 270, 308, 30-06, 5.6x57, 6.5x57, 7x57, 7x64 (standard calibers); 7mm Rem. Mag., 257 Wea. Mag., 270 Wea. Mag., 300 Wea. Mag., 300 Win. Mag., 338 Win. Mag., 375 H&H, 8x68S, 9.3x64 (magnum calibers); removable 4-shot magazine (standard calibers), 3-shot (magnums); 24-inch barrel (standard calibers), 26-inch (magnums); 44-inch overall length (standard calibers); weighs about 8 lbs.; no sights; drilled and tapped for scope mounting; hand-checkered European walnut stock with rosewood grip cap; accuracy bedding with free-floated barrel, three front-locking bolt lugs, 60-degree bolt lift; adjustable single-stage trigger; silent safety locks bolt, sear, trigger. Imported from Germany by Precision Imports, Inc. Introduced 1989; discontinued 1994.

Classic stock, oil finish
Perf.: $900   **Exc.:** $700   **VGood:** $600

Classic stock, high luster finish
Perf.: $900   **Exc.:** $725   **VGood:** $600

Monte Carlo stock, oil finish
Perf.: $925   **Exc.:** $710   **VGood:** $610

Monte Carlo stock, high luster finish
Perf.: $915   **Exc.:** $700   **VGood:** $600

MAUSER MODEL 107

Bolt action; 22 LR; 5-shot magazine; 21-1/2-inch barrel; 40-inch overall length; weighs about 5 lbs.; hooded blade front sight, adjustable open rear; grooved receiver for scope mounting; walnut-stained beechwood stock with Monte Carlo comb; checkered grip and forend; sling swivels; dual extractors; 60-degree bolt throw; steel trigger guard and floorplate; satin blue finish. Imported from Germany by Precision Imports, Inc. Introduced 1992; discontinued 1994.

Perf.: $250   **Exc.:** $215   **VGood:** $190

MAUSER MODEL 201

Bolt action; 22 LR, 22 WMR; 5-shot magazine; 21-inch barrel; 40-inch overall length; weighs about 6-1/2 lbs.; sold with or without sights; receiver accepts rail mounts and drilled, tapped for scope mounting; walnut-stained beechwood stock with Monte Carlo comb and cheekpiece; checkered grip and forend; hammer forged medium-heavy, free-floated barrel; bolt with two front locking lugs, dual extractors; adjustable trigger; safety locks bolt, sear and trigger. Imported from Germany by Precision Imports, Inc. Introduced 1989; discontinued 1994.

22 LR
Perf.: $400   **Exc.:** $325   **VGood:** $250

22 WMR
Perf.: $425   **Exc.:** $350   **VGood:** $300

MAUSER MODEL 201 LUXUS

Same specs as Model 201 except walnut stock with rosewood forend tip. Imported from Germany by Precision Imports, Inc. Introduced 1989; discontinued 1994.

22 LR		
Perf.: $550	**Exc.:** $475	**VGood:** $400
22 WMR		
Perf.: $600	**Exc.:** $500	**VGood:** $425

MAUSER MODEL 225

Bolt action; 243, 25-06, 270, 7x57, 308, 30-06, 257 Weatherby, 270 Weatherby, 7mm Rem. Mag., 300 Win. Mag., 300 Weatherby, 308 Norma Mag., 375 H&H Mag.; 3-shot magazine (magnums), 4-shot (standard); 24-inch barrel (standard), 26-inch (magnums); 44-1/2-inch overall length with longer barrel; weighs 8 lbs.; no sights; drilled, tapped for scope mounts; hand-checkered, oil-finished European Monte Carlo stock; recoil pad; swivel studs. Made in Germany. Introduced 1988; discontinued 1989.

Standard calibers		
Perf.: $1350	**Exc.:** $1200	**VGood:** $950
Magnum calibers		
Perf.: $1450	**Exc.:** $1300	**VGood:** $1000

MAUSER MODEL 660

Bolt action; 243 Win., 25-06, 270 Win., 308 Win., 30-06, 7x57, 7mm Rem. Mag.; 24-inch barrel; no sights; drilled, tapped for scope mounts; checkered European Monte Carlo walnut stock; white line pistol-grip cap, recoil pad; adjustable single-stage trigger; push-button safety. Introduced 1973; discontinued 1975.

Exc.: $895	**VGood:** $795	**Good:** $595

MAUSER MODEL 660 SAFARI

Same specs as Model 660 except only 458 Win. Mag., 375 H&H Mag., 338 Win. Mag., 7mm Rem. Mag.; 28-inch barrel; express rear sight, fixed ramp front. Introduced 1973; discontinued 1975.

Exc.: $995	**VGood:** $795	**Good:** $595

MAUSER MODEL 660 ULTRA

Same specs Model 660 except 21-inch barrel. Introduced 1965; discontinued 1975.

Exc.: $795	**VGood:** $695	**Good:** $495

MAUSER MODEL 660P TARGET

Same specs as Model 660 except 308 Win., other calibers on special order; 3-shot magazine; 26-1/2-inch heavy barrel, muzzle brake; dovetail rib for scope mounting; European walnut target stock with full pistol-grip, thumbhole, adjustable cheekpiece, adjustable rubber buttplate. Not imported.

Exc.: $1295	**VGood:** $895	**Good:** $695

MAUSER MODEL 660S DELUXE

Same specs as Model 660 except 21-inch barrel; carbine version; engraving; gold/silver inlay work; heavy carving on select walnut stock. Special order only; no longer imported. Prices vary depending on special order features. $2500+

MAUSER MODEL 660SH

Same specs as Model 660 except 6.5x68, 7mm Rem. Mag., 7mm SE v. Hoff, 300 Win. Mag., 8x68S, 9.3x64. Introduced 1965; discontinued 1975.

Exc.: $995	**VGood:** $795	**Good:** $595

MAUSER MODEL 660T CARBINE

Same specs as Model 660 except 21-inch barrel; full-length stock. Introduced 1965; discontinued 1975.

Exc.: $1050	**VGood:** $875	**Good:** $695

MAUSER MODEL 2000

Bolt action; 270 Win., 308 Win., 30-06; 5-shot magazine; 24-inch barrel; folding leaf rear sight, hooded ramp front; hand-checkered European walnut stock; Monte Carlo comb; cheekpiece; forend tip; sling swivels. Introduced 1969; discontinued 1971.

Exc.: $350	**VGood:** $300	**Good:** $270

Mauser Model 225

Mauser Model 660

Mauser Model 660 Safari

Mauser Model 3000

Mauser Model 4000 Varmint

Mauser Model KKW

MAUSER MODEL 3000

Bolt action; 243 Win., 270 Win., 308 Win., 30-06, 375 H&H Mag., 7mm Rem. Mag.; 3-shot magazine (magnum), 4-shot (standard); 22-inch barrel (standard calibers), 26-inch (magnums); no sights; drilled, tapped for scope mounts; hand-checkered European walnut Monte Carlo stock; white line spacer on pistol-grip cap; recoil pad; sliding safety; fully-adjustable trigger; detachable sling swivels. Left-hand action available. Introduced 1971; discontinued 1975.

Exc.: $495	**VGood:** $450	**Good:** $400
Left-hand model		
Exc.: $550	**VGood:** $500	**Good:** $460
Magnum calibers		
Exc.: $535	**VGood:** $480	**Good:** $440
Left-hand model		
Exc.: $625	**VGood:** $575	**Good:** $500

MAUSER MODEL 4000 VARMINT

Bolt action; 222 Rem., 223 Rem.; 4-shot magazine; 22-inch barrel; folding leaf rear sight, hooded ramp front; hand-checkered European walnut Monte Carlo stock; rubber buttplate. Introduced 1971; discontinued 1975.

Exc.: $425	**VGood:** $365	**Good:** $310

MAUSER MODEL DSM34

Bolt action; single shot; 22 LR; 26-inch barrel; tangent curve open rear sight, barleycorn front; Model 98 Mauser military-type stock; no checkering; sling swivels. Introduced 1934; discontinued 1939.

Exc.: $325	**VGood:** $270	**Good:** $230

MAUSER MODEL EL320

Bolt action; single shot; 22 LR; 23-1/2-inch barrel; adjustable open rear sight, bead front; sporting-style European walnut stock; hand-checkered pistol grip, forearm; grip cap; sling swivels. Introduced 1927; discontinued 1935.

Exc.: $275	**VGood:** $240	**Good:** $200

MAUSER MODEL EN310

Bolt action; single shot; 22 LR; 19-3/4-inch barrel; fixed open rear sight, blade front; uncheckered European walnut pistol-grip stock. Introduced post-WWI; discontinued 1935.

Exc.: $250	**VGood:** $230	**Good:** $200

MAUSER MODEL ES340

Bolt action; single shot; 22 LR; 25-1/2-inch barrel; tangent curve rear sight, ramp front; European walnut sporting stock; hand-checkered pistol grip; grooved forearm; sling swivels. Introduced 1923; discontinued 1935.

Exc.: $290	**VGood:** $250	**Good:** $220

MAUSER MODEL ES340B

Same specs as Model ES340 except 26-3/4-inch barrel; uncheckered pistol-grip stock. Introduced 1935; discontinued 1939.

Exc.: $290	**VGood:** $260	**Good:** $240

MAUSER MODEL ES350

Bolt action; repeater; 22 LR; 27-1/2-inch barrel; open micrometer rear sight, ramp front; target-style walnut stock; hand-checkered pistol grip, forend; grip cap. Introduced 1925; discontinued 1935.

Exc.: $450	**VGood:** $400	**Good:** $350

MAUSER MODEL ES350B

Same specs as Model ES350 except single shot; 26-3/4-inch barrel; receiver grooved for scope mount. Introduced 1935; discontinued 1938.

Exc.: $375	**VGood:** $315	**Good:** $260

MAUSER MODEL KKW

Bolt action; single shot; 22 LR; 26-inch barrel; tangent curve open rear sight, barleycorn front; Model 98 Mauser military-type walnut stock; no checkering; sling swivels; used in training German troops in WWII. Introduced 1935; discontinued 1939.

Exc.: $395	**VGood:** $325	**Good:** $275

Mauser Model MS420B

Mauser Sporter

Mauser Special British Model Type A

Mauser Special British Model Type A Magnum

Mauser Type B

McMillan 300 Phoenix Long Range Rifle

McMillan M-86 Sniper

MAUSER SPORTER, MILITARY MODEL

Same specs as Sporter except 7x57, 8x57, 9x57; military front sight; Model 98-type barrel; two-stage trigger. Manufactured prior to WWI.

Exc.: $600   **VGood:** $500   **Good:** $450

MAUSER SPORTER, SHORT MODEL

Same specs as Sporter except only 6.5x54, 8x58; 19-3/4-inch barrel. Manufactured prior to WWI.

Exc.: $3295   **VGood:** $2995   **Good:** $2195

MAUSER SPECIAL BRITISH MODEL TYPE A

Bolt action; 7x57, 8x60, 9x57, 9.3x62mm, 30-06; 5-shot box magazine; 23-1/2-inch barrel; express rear sight, hooded ramp front; hand-checkered pistol grip; Circassian walnut sporting stock; buffalo horn grip cap, forearm tip; military-type trigger; detachable sling swivels. Introduced before WWI; discontinued 1938.

Exc.: $2995   **VGood:** $2395   **Good:** $1695

MAUSER SPECIAL BRITISH MODEL TYPE A MAGNUM

Same specs as Type A except magnum action; 10.75x68mm, 280 Ross, 318 Westley Richards Express, 404 Jeffery. Introduced before WWI; discontinued 1939.

Exc.: $3995   **VGood:** $3750   **Good:** $3225

MAUSER SPECIAL BRITISH MODEL TYPE A SHORT

Same specs as Type A except short action; 6.5x54, 8x51mm, 250-3000; 21-1/2-inch barrel. Introduced before WWI; discontinued 1938.

Exc.: $3900   **VGood:** $3395   **Good:** $2995

MAUSER TYPE B

Bolt action; 7x57, 8x57, 8x60, 9x57, 9.3x62, 10.75x68mm, 30-06; 5-shot box magazine; 23-1/2-inch barrel; three-leaf rear sight, ramp front; hand-checkered walnut pistol-grip stock; schnabel forearm tip; grip cap; double-set triggers; sling swivels. Introduced before WWI; discontinued 1938.

Exc.: $4000   **VGood:** $3600   **Good:** $3000

MCMILLAN 300 PHOENIX LONG RANGE RIFLE

Bolt action; 300 Phoenix; 28-inch barrel; weighs 12-1/2 lbs.; no sights furnished; fiberglass stock with adjustable cheekpiece, adjustable buttplate; comes with rings and bases; matte black finish; textured stock. All parts and components made in U.S. by Harris Gunworks. Introduced 1992; no longer produced.

Perf.: $2600   **Exc.:** $2100   **VGood:** $1300

MCMILLAN M-40 SNIPER MODEL

Bolt action; 308 Win.; 4-shot magazine; 24-inch, 26-inch match-grade heavy contour barrel; weighs 9 lbs.; no sights; fiberglass stock; recoil pad. Introduced 1990; no longer in production.

Perf.: $1800   **Exc.:** $1450   **VGood:** $995

MCMILLAN M-86 SNIPER

Bolt action; 308, 30-06, 300 Win. Mag.; 4-shot (308, 30-06), 3-shot (300 Win. Mag.); 24-inch heavy match-grade barrel; 43-1/2-inch overall length; weighs 11-1/4 lbs. (308), 11-1/2 lbs. (30-06, 300); McHale fiberglass stock with textured grip and forend; recoil pad; no sights; bipod; sling swivels; matte black finish. Introduced 1989; no longer in production.

Perf.: $1800   **Exc.:** $1100   **VGood:** $850

MCMILLAN M-87

Bolt action; 50 BMG; single shot; 29-inch barrel, with muzzle brake; 53-inch overall length; weighs about 21-1/2 lbs.; no sights furnished; McMillan fiberglass stock; right-handed McMillan stainless steel receiver, chrome-moly barrel with 1:15-inch twist. All parts and components made in U.S. by Harris Gunworks. Introduced 1987; still produced.

Perf.: $2950   **Exc.:** $2400   **VGood:** $1900

MAUSER MODEL MM410

Bolt action; 22 LR; 5-shot detachable box magazine; 23-1/2-inch barrel; tangent curve open rear sight, ramp front; European walnut sporting stock; hand-checkered pistol grip; sling swivels. Introduced 1926; discontinued 1935.

Exc.: $395   **VGood:** $325   **Good:** $310

MAUSER MODEL MM410B

Same specs as MM410 except lightweight sporting stock. Introduced 1935; discontinued 1939.

Exc.: $390   **VGood:** $320   **Good:** $300

MAUSER MODEL MS350B

Bolt action; 22 LR; 5-shot detachable box magazine; 26-3/4-inch barrel; micrometer open rear sight, ramp front; barrel grooved for detachable rear sight/scope; target stock of European walnut; hand-checkered pistol grip, forearm; sling swivels. Replaced Model ES350. Introduced 1935; discontinued 1939.

Exc.: $495   **VGood:** $420   **Good:** $305

MAUSER MODEL MS420

Bolt action; 22 LR; 5-shot detachable box magazine; 25-1/2-inch barrel; tangent curve open rear sight,

ramp front; European walnut sporting stock; hand-checkered pistol grip; grooved forearm; sling swivels. Introduced 1925; discontinued 1935.

Exc.: $400   **VGood:** $320   **Good:** $290

MAUSER MODEL MS420B

Same specs as Model MS420 except 25-3/4-inch barrel; better stock wood. Introduced 1935; discontinued 1939.

Exc.: $425   **VGood:** $340   **Good:** $300

MAUSER SPORTER (EARLY)

Bolt action; 6.5x55, 6.5x58, 7x57, 9x57, 9.3x62, 10.75x68; 5-shot box magazine; 23-1/2-inch barrel; tangent-curve rear sight, ramp front; uncheckered European walnut stock, pistol grip; schnabel-tipped forearm; sling swivels; double-set trigger. Made in Germany prior to World War I.

Exc.: $1250   **VGood:** $995   **Good:** $700

MAUSER SPORTER CARBINE

Same specs Sporter except only 6.5x54, 6.5x58, 7x57, 8x57, 9x57; 19-3/4-inch barrel. Manufactured prior to WWI.

Perf.: $1395   **Exc.:** $1095   **VGood:** $750

RIFLES

MCMILLAN M-87R
Same specs as M-87 except 5-shot repeater. All parts and components made in U.S. by Harris Gunworks. Introduced 1987; still produced.
> **Perf.:** $3795   **Exc.:** $3100   **VGood:** $2230

MCMILLAN M-89 SNIPER
Bolt action; 308 Win.; 5-shot magazine; 28-inch barrel with optional suppressor; weighs 15-1/4 lbs.; drilled, tapped for scope mounts; length-adjustable McMillan fiberglass stock; bipod. Introduced 1990.
> **Perf.:** $2700   **Exc.:** $2100   **VGood:** $1650

MCMILLAN M-92 BULLPUP
Bolt action; single shot; 50 BMG; 24-inch, 26-inch barrel; no sights; fiberglass bullpup-style stock; recoil pad. Introduced 1995; still in production.
> **Perf.:** $4000   **Exc.:** $3200   **VGood:** $2100

MCMILLAN M-93
Bolt action; 50 BMG; 5-, 10-shot detachable magazine; 29-inch chrome-moly with muzzle brake; 53-inch overall length; 21-1/2 lbs.; no sights; folding fiberglass stock. Introduced 1995.
> **Perf.:** $3975   **Exc.:** $3550   **VGood:** $2595

MCMILLAN NATIONAL MATCH
Bolt action; 308; 5-shot magazine; 24-inch stainless steel barrel; 43-inch overall length; weighs 11 lbs.; barrel band-type Tomkins front sight, no rear sight; modified ISU fiberglass stock; adjustable buttplate; Canjar trigger; right-hand only. Options include Fibergrain stock, sights. Introduced 1989; still in production.
> **Perf.:** $3200   **Exc.:** $2700   **VGood:** $2000

MCMILLAN SIGNATURE ALASKAN
Bolt action; 270, 280 Rem., 30-06, 7mm Rem. Mag., 300 Win. Mag., 300 Weatherby, 358 Win. Mag., 340 Weatherby, 375 H&H Mag.; 3-shot magazine (magnums), 4-shot (standard calibers); 22-inch, 24-inch, 26-inch match-grade barrel; single-leaf rear sight, barrel band front; Monte Carlo walnut stock, cheekpiece, palm-swell grip; steel floorplate; Teflon or electroless nickel finish. Introduced 1989; still in production.
> **Perf.:** $3125   **Exc.:** $2800   **VGood:** $2100

MCMILLAN SIGNATURE CLASSIC SPORTER
Bolt action; 22-250, 243, 6mm Rem., 7mm-08, 284, 308, 25-06, 270, 280 Rem., 30-06, 7mm Rem. Mag., 300 Win. Mag., 300 Weatherby, 338 Win. Mag., 340 Weatherby Mag., 375 H&H Mag.; 3-shot magazine (magnum), 4-shot (standard); 22-inch, 24-inch, 26-inch barrel; weighs 7 lbs. (magnums); no sights; 1-inch rings, bases furnished; McMillan fiberglass stock; recoil pad; sling swivels; matte-black McMillan right- or left-hand action; aluminum floorplate; Fibergrain, wood stocks optional. Introduced 1987.
> **Perf.:** $2100   **Exc.:** $1695   **VGood:** $1095

MCMILLAN SIGNATURE CLASSIC SPORTER STAINLESS
Same specs as Classic Sporter except barrel and action made of stainless steel; same calibers in addition to 416 Rem. Mag.; fiberglass stock; right- or left-hand action; natural stainless, glass bead or black chrome sulfide finishes. All parts and components made in U.S. by Harris Gunworks. Introduced 1990; still produced.
> **Perf.:** $2300   **Exc.:** $2150   **VGood:** $1300

MCMILLAN SIGNATURE TITANIUM MOUNTAIN
Bolt action; 270, 280, 30-06, 300 Win. Mag., 338 Win. Mag., 7mm Rem. Mag; 3-shot magazine (magnum), 4-shot (standard); 22-inch, 24-inch, 26-inch barrel; chrome-moly steel or titanium match-grade barrel; weighs 6-1/2 lbs.; graphite-reinforced fiberglass stock; titanium-alloy action. Introduced 1989; still in production.

> Steel barrel
> **Perf.:** $2695   **Exc.:** $2250   **VGood:** $1795
> Titatium barrel
> **Perf.:** $2995   **Exc.:** $2395   **VGood:** $1895

McMillan M-89 Sniper

McMillan Signature Alaskan

McMillan Signature Classic Sporter

McMillan Signature Classic Sporter Stainless

McMillan Signature Titanium Mountain

McMillan Signature Varminter

McMillan Talon Safari

McMillan Talon Sporter

MCMILLAN SIGNATURE VARMINTER
Bolt action; 223, 22-250, 220 Swift, 243, 6mm Rem., 25-06, 7mm-08, 308; 4-shot magazine; 22-inch, 24-inch, 26-inch barrel; weighs 7 lbs.; heavy contoured barrel; hand-bedded fiberglass or Fibergrain stock; adjustable trigger; field bipod; marketed with rings, bases. Introduced 1989.
> **Perf.:** $2495   **Exc.:** $1995   **VGood:** $1395

MCMILLAN STANDARD SPORTER
Bolt action; 6.5x55, 7mm-08, 308, 270, 280 Rem., 30-06, 7mm Rem. Mag., 300 Win. Mag., 338 Win. Mag.; 24-inch barrel; weighs 7-1/2 lbs.; no sights; drilled, tapped for scope mounts; American walnut or painted fiberglass stock; chrome-moly action; button rifled barrel; Shilen trigger; hinged floorplate. Introduced 1991; discontinued 1992.
> **Perf.:** $995   **Exc.:** $795   **VGood:** $695

MCMILLAN TALON SAFARI
Bolt action; 300 Win. Mag., 300 Weatherby, 338 Win. Mag., 340 Weatherby, 375 Weatherby, 375 H&H Mag., 378 Weatherby, 416 Taylor, 416 Rigby, 458 Win. Mag.; 4-shot magazine; 24-inch stainless barrel; 43-inch overall length; weighs 10 lbs.; barrel-band ramp front sight, multi-leaf express rear; fiberglass stock; barrel-band sling swivels; 1-inch scope mounts; steel floorplate; matte black finish. Introduced 1989; still in production.
> **Perf.:** $3300   **Exc.:** $2800   **VGood:** $2100

MCMILLAN TALON SAFARI SUPER MAG
Same specs as Talon Safari except 338 Lapua, 378 Wea. Mag., 416 Rigby, 460 Weatherby, 416 Weatherby, 300 Phoenix, 30-378. Still in production.
> **Perf.:** $3700   **Exc.:** $3200   **VGood:** $2600

Merkel Model 96K Drilling

Merkel Model 140-1

Merkel Model 140-1.1

Merkel Model 210E
Combination Gun

MCMILLAN TALON SPORTER

Bolt action; 25-06, 270, 280 Rem., 30-06, 7mm Rem. Mag., 300 Win. Mag., 300 Weatherby Mag., 300 H&H, 338 Win. Mag., 340 Weatherby Mag., 375 H&H Mag., 416 Rem. Mag.; 24-inch barrel; weighs 7-1/2 lbs.; no sights; drilled, tapped for scope mounts; American walnut or McMillan fiberglass stock; built on pre-'64 Model 70-type action; cone breech; controlled feed; claw extractor; three-position safety; stainless steel barrel, action; chrome-moly optional. Introduced 1991.

Perf.: $2600   **Exc.:** $2200   **VGood:** $1710

MERKEL MODEL 90S DRILLING

Drilling; 12-, 20-ga., 3-inch chambers, 16-ga., 2-3/4-inch chambers; 22 Hornet, 5.6x50R Mag., 5.6x52R, 222 Rem., 243 Win., 6.5x55, 6.5x57R, 7x57R, 7x65R, 308, 30-06, 8x57JRS, 9.3x74R, 375 H&H; 25-5/8-inch barrels; weighs 8 to 8-1/2 lbs. depending upon caliber; blade front sight, fixed rear; oil-finished walnut stock with pistol-grip; cheekpiece on 12-, 16-gauge; selective sear safety; double barrel locking lug with Greener cross-bolt; scroll-engraved, case-hardened receiver; automatic trigger safety; Blitz action; double triggers. Imported from Germany by GSI. No longer imported.

Perf.: $5500   **Exc.:** $4995   **VGood:** $3495

MERKEL MODEL 90K DRILLING

Same specs as Model 90S Drilling except manually cocked rifle system. Imported from Germany by GSI. No longer imported.

Perf.: $5995   **Exc.:** $5250   **VGood:** $3995

MERKEL MODEL 95S DRILLING

Drilling; 12, 20, 3-inch chambers, 16, 2-3/4-inch chambers; 22 Hornet, 5.6x50R Mag., 5.6x52R, 222 Rem., 243 Win., 6.5x55, 6.5x57R, 7x57R, 7x65R, 308, 30-06, 8x57JRS, 9.3x74R, 375 H&H; 25-5/8-inch barrels; weighs 8 to 8-1/2 lbs. depending upon caliber; blade front sight, fixed rear; oil-finished walnut stock with pistol grip; cheekpiece on 12-, 16-gauge; double barrel locking lug with Greener cross-bolt; scroll-engraved, case-hardened receiver; selective sear safety; Blitz action; double triggers. Imported from Germany by GSI; no longer imported.

Perf.: $6995   **Exc.:** $5995   **VGood:** $4995

MERKEL MODEL 95K DRILLING

Same specs as Model 95S Drilling except manually cocked rifle system. Still imported.

Perf.: $7950   **Exc.:** $6650   **VGood:** $4995

MERKEL MODEL 96K DRILLING

Drilling; 23.6-inch barrels; 12 or 20 gauge over 22 Hornet, 243, 308, 30-06. Greener cross bolt; case-hardened receiver with scroll engraving; automatic safety; Rifle system manually cocked from tang slide; double triggers; fitted baggage case furnished with gun. Imported by GSI.

Perf.: $6700   **Exc.:** $5000   **VGood:** $4150

MERKEL MODEL 140-1 DOUBLE RIFLE

Double rifle; side-by-side; 22 Hornet, 5.6x50R Mag., 5.6x52R, 222 Rem., 243 Win., 6.5x55, 6.5x57R, 7x57R, 7x65R, 308, 30-06, 8x57JRS, 9.3x74R, 375 H&H; 25-5/8-inch barrels; weighs about 7-3/4 lbs., depending upon caliber; blade front sight on ramp, fixed rear; oil-finished walnut stock with pistol grip, cheekpiece; Anson & Deeley boxlock action with cocking indicators, double triggers; engraved color case-hardened receiver. Imported from Germany by GSI. Still imported.

Perf.: $5900   **Exc.:** $4770   **VGood:** $3795

MERKEL MODEL 140-1.1 DOUBLE RIFLE

Same as Model 140-1 Double Rifle except engraved; silver-gray receiver. Imported from Germany by GSI. Still imported.

Perf.: $6800   **Exc.:** $5795   **VGood:** $3995

MERKEL MODEL 150-1 DOUBLE RIFLE

Double rifle; side-by-side; 22 Hornet, 5.6x50R Mag., 5.6x52R, 222 Rem., 243 Win., 6.5x55, 6.5x57R, 7x57R, 7x65R, 308, 30-06, 8x57JRS, 9.3x74R, 375 H&H; 25-5/8-inch barrels; weighs about 7-3/4 lbs., depending upon caliber; blade front sight on ramp, fixed rear; oil-finished walnut stock with pistol grip, cheekpiece; Anson & Deeley boxlock action with cocking indicators, double triggers, false sideplates; silver-gray receiver with Arabesque engraving. Imported from Germany by GSI. No longer imported.

Perf.: $7500   **Exc.:** $5695   **VGood:** $4495

MERKEL MODEL 150-1.1 DOUBLE RIFLE

Same specs as Model 150-1 Double Rifle except English Arabesque engraving. Imported from Germany by GSI. No longer imported.

Perf.: $8500   **Exc.:** $7250   **VGood:** $5295

MERKEL MODEL 160 DOUBLE RIFLE

Double rifle; side-by-side; 22 Hornet, 5.6x50R Mag., 5.6x52R, 222 Rem., 243 Win., 6.5x55, 6.5x57R, 7x57R, 7x65R, 308, 30-06, 8x57JRS, 9.3x74R, 375 H&H; 25-5/8-inch barrels; weighs about 7-3/4 lbs., depending upon caliber; blade front sight on ramp, fixed rear; oil-finished walnut stock with pistol grip, cheekpiece; sidelock action; double barrel locking lug with Greener cross-bolt; fine engraved hunting scenes on sideplates; Holland & Holland ejectors; double triggers. Imported from Germany by GSI. No longer imported.

Perf.: $12,875   **Exc.:** $10,875   **VGood:** $7995

MERKEL MODEL 210E COMBINATION GUN

Combination gun; over/under; 12-, 16-, 20-ga. (2-3/4-inch chamber) over 22 Hornet, 5.6x50R, 5.6x52R, 222 Rem., 243 Win., 6.5x55, 6.5x57R, 7x57R, 7x65R, 308 Win., 30-06, 8x57JRS, 9.3x74R, 375 H&H; 25-5/8-inch barrels; weighs about 7-1/2 lbs.; bead front sight, fixed rear; oil-finished walnut stock with pistol grip, cheekpiece; Kersten double cross-bolt lock; scroll-engraved, color case-hardened receiver; Blitz action; double triggers. Imported from Germany by GSI. No longer imported.

Perf.: $5780   **Exc.:** $4395   **VGood:** $3550

MERKEL MODEL 211E COMBINATION GUN

Combination gun; over/under; 12-, 16-, 20-ga. (2-3/4-inch chamber) over 22 Hornet, 5.6x50R, 5.6x52R, 222 Rem., 243 Win., 6.5x55, 6.5x57R, 7x57R, 7x65R, 308 Win., 30-06, 8x57JRS, 9.3x74R, 375 H&H; 25-5/8-inch barrels; weighs about 7-1/2 lbs.; bead front sight, fixed rear; oil-finished walnut stock with pistol grip, cheekpiece; Kersten double cross-bolt lock; silver-grayed receiver with fine hunting scene engraving; Blitz action; double triggers. Imported from Germany by GSI. No longer imported.

Perf.: $6700   **Exc.:** $4995   **VGood:** $3995

MERKEL MODEL 213E COMBINATION GUN

Combination gun; over/under; 12-, 16-, 20-ga. (2-3/4-inch chamber) over 22 Hornet, 5.6x50R, 5.6x52R, 222 Rem., 243 Win., 6.5x55, 6.5x57R, 7x57R, 7x65R, 308 Win., 30-06, 8x57JRS, 9.3x74R, 375 H&H; 25-5/8-inch barrels; weighs about 7-1/2 lbs.; bead front sight, fixed rear; oil-finished walnut stock with pistol grip, cheekpiece; Kersten double cross-bolt lock; English-style, large scroll Arabesque engraving; sidelock action; double triggers. Imported from Germany by GSI. No longer imported.

Perf.: $11,995   **Exc.:** $9995   **VGood:** $6995

MERKEL MODEL 220E DOUBLE RIFLE

Double rifle; over/under; boxlock; 22 Hornet, 5.6x50R Mag., 5.6x52R, 222 Rem., 243 Win., 6.5x55, 6.5x57R, 7x57R, 7x65R, 308, 30-06, 8x57JRS, 9.3x74R; 25-5/8-inch barrels; weighs about 7-3/4 lbs., depending upon caliber; blade front sight, fixed rear; oil-finished walnut stock with pistol grip, cheekpiece; Kersten double cross-bolt lock; scroll-engraved, case-hardened receiver; Blitz action with double triggers. Imported from Germany by GSI. No longer imported.

Perf.: $9295   **Exc.:** $7195   **VGood:** $5495

MERKEL MODEL 221E DOUBLE RIFLE

Double rifle; over/under; boxlock; 22 Hornet, 5.6x50R Mag., 5.6x52R, 222 Rem., 243 Win., 6.5x55, 6.5x57R, 7x57R, 7x65R, 308, 30-06, 8x57JRS, 9.3x74R; 25-5/8-inch barrels; weighs about 7-3/4 lbs., depending upon caliber; blade front sight, fixed rear; oil-finished walnut stock with pistol grip, cheekpiece; Kersten double cross-bolt lock; silver-grayed receiver with hunting scene engraving; Blitz action with double triggers. Imported from Germany by GSI. No longer imported.

Perf.: $9900   **Exc.:** $7995   **VGood:** $5995

MERKEL MODEL 223E DOUBLE RIFLE

Double rifle; over/under; sidelock; 22 Hornet, 5.6x50R Mag., 5.6x52R, 222 Rem., 243 Win., 6.5x55, 6.5x57R, 7x57R, 7x65R, 308, 30-06, 8x57JRS, 9.3x74R; 25-5/8-inch barrels; weighs about 7-3/4 lbs, depending upon caliber; blade front sight, fixed rear; oil-finished walnut stock with pistol grip, cheekpiece; sidelock action; English-style large-scroll Arabesque engraving; Blitz action with double triggers. Imported from Germany by GSI. No longer imported.

Perf.: $14,995 **Exc.:** $12,500 **VGood:** $9500

MERKEL MODEL 313E COMBINATION GUN

Combination gun; over/under; 12-, 16-, 20-ga. (2-3/4-inch chamber) over 22 Hornet, 5.6x50R, 5.6x52R, 222 Rem., 243 Win., 6.5x55, 6.5x57R, 7x57R, 7x65R, 308 Win., 30-06, 8x57JRS, 9.3x74R, 375 H&H; 25-5/8-inch barrels; weighs about 7-1/2 lbs.; bead front sight, fixed rear; oil-finished walnut stock with pistol grip, cheekpiece; Kersten double cross-bolt lock; medium-scroll engraving on receiver; sidelock action; double triggers. Imported from Germany by GSI. No longer imported.

Perf.: $13,950 **Exc.:** $10,995 **VGood:** $9250

MERKEL MODEL 323E DOUBLE RIFLE

Double rifle; over/under; sidelock; 22 Hornet, 5.6x50R Mag., 5.6x52R, 222 Rem., 243 Win., 6.5x55, 6.5x57R, 7x57R, 7x65R, 308, 30-06, 8x57JRS, 9.3x74R; 25-5/8-inch barrels; weighs about 7-3/4 lbs., depending upon caliber; blade front sight, fixed rear; oil-finished walnut stock with pistol grip, cheekpiece; medium-scroll engraving on action; Blitz action with double triggers. Imported from Germany by GSI. No longer imported.

Perf.: $20,000 **Exc.:** $17,500 **VGood:** $13,500

MERKEL MODEL K-1 LIGHTWEIGHT STALKING RIFLE

Single shot, breakopen; 243 Win., 270 Win., 7x57R, 308 Win., 30-06, 7mm Rem. Mag., 300 Win. Mag., 9.3x74R; 23.6-inch barrels; weighs 5.6 lbs. unscoped; Satin-finished walnut stock, fluted and checkered; sling-swivel studs; scope base furnished. Franz Jager single-shot break-open action, cocking/uncocking slide-type safety, matte silver receiver, selectable trigger pull weights, integrated, quick detach 1-inch or 30mm optic mounts. Imported from Germany by GSI. Still imported.

Standard, simple border engraving
Perf.: $3800 **Exc.:** $3200 **VGood:** $2600
Premium, light arabesque scroll
Perf.: $4300 **Exc.:** $3500 **VGood:** $2900
Jagd, fine engraved hunting scenes
Perf.: $4700 **Exc.:** $3900 **VGood:** $3200

MIDLAND 1500S SURVIVOR

Bolt action; 308 Win.; 5-shot magazine; 22-inch barrel; 43-inch overall length; weighs 7 lbs.; hooded ramp front sight, open adjustable rear; black composite stock with recoil pad; Monte Carlo cheekpiece; stainless steel barreled action with satin chromed bolt. Made by Gibbs Rifle Co. Introduced 1993; discontinued 1994.

Perf.: $650 **Exc.:** $550 **VGood:** $450

MIDLAND MODEL 1500C SURVIVOR

Same specs as Model 1500S Survivor except detachable clip magazine. Made by Gibbs Rifle Co. Introduced 1993; discontinued 1994.

Perf.: $600 **Exc.:** $500 **VGood:** $400

MITCHELL 1858 HENRY REPLICA

Lever action; 44-40; 13-shot magazine; 24-1/4-inch barrel; 43-inch overall length; weighs 9-1/2 lbs.; bead front sight, open adjustable rear; European walnut stock; brass receiver and buttplate; uses original Henry loading system; faithful to the original rifle. Imported by Mitchell Arms, Inc. Introduced 1990; discontinued 1993.

Perf.: $800 **Exc.:** $630 **VGood:** $500

Mitchell 1858 Henry Replica

Mitchell 1873 Winchester Replica

Mitchell AK-22

Mitchell CAR-15/22

Mitchell Galil/22

MITCHELL 1866 WINCHESTER REPLICA

Lever action; 44-40; 13-shot magazine; 24-1/4-inch barrel; 43-inch overall length; weighs 9 lbs.; bead front sight, open adjustable rear; European walnut stock; solid brass receiver, buttplate, forend cap; octagonal barrel; faithful to the original Winchester '66 rifle. Imported by Mitchell Arms, Inc. Introduced 1990; discontinued 1993.

Perf.: $700 **Exc.:** $530 **VGood:** $430

MITCHELL 1873 WINCHESTER REPLICA

Lever action; 45 Colt; 13-shot magazine; 24-1/4-inch barrel; 43-inch overall length; weighs 9-1/2 lbs.; bead front sight, open adjustable rear; European walnut stock; color case-hardened steel receiver; faithful to the original Model 1873 rifle. Imported by Mitchell Arms, Inc. Introduced 1990; discontinued 1993.

Perf.: $750 **Exc.:** $625 **VGood:** $495

MITCHELL AK-22

Semi-automatic; 22 LR, 22 WMR; 20-shot magazine (22 LR), 10-shot (22 WMR); 18-inch barrel; 36-inch overall length; weighs 6-1/2 lbs.; post front sight, open adjustable rear; European walnut stock; 22-caliber rimfire replica of the AK-47 rifle; wide magazine to maintain appearance. Imported from Italy by Mitchell Arms, Inc. Introduced 1985; discontinued 1993.

Perf.: $295 **Exc.:** $250 **VGood:** $175

MITCHELL CAR-15/22

Semi-automatic; 22 LR; 15-shot magazine; 16-3/4-inch barrel; telescoping butt; 32-inch overall length when collapsed; adjustable post front sight, adjustable aperture rear. Scope mount available. Replica of the CAR-15 rifle. Imported by Mitchell Arms, Inc. Introduced 1990; discontinued 1993.

Perf.: $230 **Exc.:** $200 **VGood:** $150

MITCHELL GALIL/22

Semi-automatic; 22 LR, 22 WMR; 20-shot magazine (22 LR), 10-shot (22 WMR); 18-inch barrel; 36-inch overall length; weighs 6-1/2 lbs.; elevation-adjustable post front sight, windage-adjustable rear; European walnut grip and forend with metal folding or wood fixed stock; replica of the Israeli Galil rifle. Imported by Mitchell Arms, Inc. Introduced 1987; discontinued 1993.

Perf.: $270 **Exc.:** $230 **VGood:** $190

MITCHELL HIGH STANDARD 15/22

Semi-automatic; 22 LR; 15-shot magazine, 30-shot available; 21-1/2-inch barrel; 37-1/2-inch overall length; weighs 6-1/4 lbs.; blade on ramp front sight, open adjustable rear; American walnut stock; polished blue finish; barrel band on forend. Imported from Philippines by Mitchell Arms, Inc. Introduced 1994; discontinued 1995.

Perf.: $130 **Exc.:** $110 **VGood:** $80

MITCHELL HIGH STANDARD 15/22D

Same specs as Mitchell High Standard 15/22 except fancy walnut stock with checkering; rosewood grip and forend caps. Imported from the Philippines by Mitchell Arms, Inc. Introduced 1994; discontinued 1995.

Perf.: $140 **Exc.:** $120 **VGood:** $90

Mitchell High Standard 20/22

Mitchell High Standard 9302

Mitchell High Standard 16/22

Mitchell MAS/22

Mitchell PPS/5

Mossberg Model 26B

MITCHELL
HIGH STANDARD 20/22

Semi-automatic; 22 LR; 10-shot magazine; 20-1/2-inch barrel; 37-1/2-inch overall length; weighs 6-1/4 lbs.; blade on ramp front sight, open adjustable rear; American walnut stock; polished blue finish; barrel band on forend. Imported from Philippines by Mitchell Arms, Inc. Introduced 1994; discontinued 1995.

Perf.: $100   **Exc.: $80**   **VGood: $70**

MITCHELL HIGH STANDARD 20/22D

Same specs as Mitchell High Standard 20/22 except fancy walnut stock with checkering; rosewood grip and forend caps. Imported from the Philippines by Mitchell Arms, Inc. Introduced 1994; discontinued 1995.

Perf.: $110   **Exc.: $90**   **VGood: $80**

MITCHELL HIGH STANDARD 20/22 SPECIAL

Same specs as Mitchell High Standard 20/22 except heavy barrel. Imported from the Philippines by Mitchell Arms, Inc. Introduced 1994; discontinued 1995.

Perf.: $110   **Exc.: $90**   **VGood: $70**

MITCHELL
HIGH STANDARD 9301

Bolt action; 22 LR; 10-shot magazine; 22-1/2-inch barrel; 40-3/4-inch overall length; weighs about 6-1/2 lbs.; bead on ramp front sight, open adjustable rear; American walnut with rosewood grip and forend caps; checkering; polished blue finish. Imported from the Philippines by Mitchell Arms, Inc. Introduced 1994; discontinued 1995.

Perf.: $200   **Exc.: $160**   **VGood: $110**

MITCHELL
HIGH STANDARD 9302

Bolt action; 22 WMR; 5-shot magazine; 22-1/2-inch barrel; 40-3/4-inch overall length; weighs about 6-1/2 lbs.; bead on ramp front sight, open adjustable rear; American walnut stock with rosewood grip and forend caps; checkering; polished blue finish. Imported from the Philippines by Mitchell Arms, Inc. Introduced 1994; discontinued 1995.

Perf.: $250   **Exc.: $200**   **VGood: $150**

MITCHELL
HIGH STANDARD 9303

Bolt action; 22 LR; 10-shot magazine; 22-1/2-inch barrel; 40-3/4-inch overall length; weighs about 6-1/2 lbs.; bead on ramp front sight, open adjustable rear; American walnut stock; polished blue finish. Imported

from the Philippines by Mitchell Arms, Inc. Introduced 1994; discontinued 1995.

Perf.: $200   **Exc.: $150**   **VGood: $110**

MITCHELL
HIGH STANDARD 9304

Bolt action; 22 WMR; 5-shot magazine; 22-1/2-inch barrel; 40-3/4-inch overall length; weighs about 6-1/2 lbs.; bead on ramp front sight, open adjustable rear; American walnut stock; rosewood grip and forend caps; checkering; polished blue finish. Imported from the Philippines by Mitchell Arms, Inc. Introduced 1994; discontinued 1995.

Perf.: $220   **Exc.: $165**   **VGood: $120**

MITCHELL
HIGH STANDARD 9305

Bolt action; 22 LR; 10-shot magazine; 22-1/2-inch heavy barrel; 40-3/4-inch overall length; weighs about 7 lbs.; bead on ramp front sight, open adjustable rear; American walnut stock; polished blue finish. Imported from the Philippines by Mitchell Arms, Inc. Introduced 1994; discontinued 1995.

Perf.: $250   **Exc.: $175**   **VGood: $130**

MITCHELL M-16A1

Semi-automatic; 22 LR; 15-shot magazine; 20-1/2-inch barrel; 38-1/2-inch overall length; weighs 7 lbs.; adjustable post front sight, adjustable aperture rear; full width magazine; black composition stock; comes with military-type sling. 22 rimfire replica of the AR-15 rifle. Imported by Mitchell Arms, Inc. Introduced 1990; discontinued 1994.

Perf.: $240   **Exc.: $190**   **VGood: $150**

MITCHELL MAS/22

Semi-automatic; 22 LR; 20-shot magazine; 18-inch barrel; 28-1/2-inch overall length; weighs 7-1/2 lbs.; adjustable post front sight, flip-type aperture rear; walnut butt, grip and forend; top cocking lever; flash hider; bullpup design resembles French armed forces rifle. Imported by Mitchell Arms, Inc. Introduced 1987; discontinued 1993.

Perf.: $300   **Exc.: $250**   **VGood: $210**

MITCHELL PPS/50

Semi-automatic; 22 LR; 20- or 50-shot magazine; styled after Russian PPSh submachinegun; 16-1/2-inch barrel; 33-1/2-inch overall length; weighs 5-1/2 lbs.; blade front sight, adjustable rear; walnut stock; full-length perforated barrel shroud; matte finish. Imported by Mitchell Arms, Inc. Introduced 1989; discontinued 1993.

20-shot		
Perf.: $325	**Exc.: $295**	**VGood: $250**
50-shot		
Perf.: $350	**Exc.: $320**	**VGood: $275**

MONTANA ARMORY
MODEL 1885 HIGH WALL

Single shot, falling block; 30-40, 32-40, 38-55, 40-65, 45-70; 26-inch barrel (30-40), 28-inch other calibers; Douglas premium tapered octagon barrel; American black walnut stock. Marble's ivory bead front, number 66 rear sights; recreation of early High Wall, with coil-spring action. Tang drilled and tapped for tang sight; color case hardened receiver, lever, hammer and breechblock. Introduced 1991, no longer in production.

Perf.: $1200   **Exc.: $1050**   **VGood: $925**

MOSSBERG MODEL 10

Bolt action; single shot; 22 Short, 22 Long, 22 LR; 22-inch barrel; take-down; open rear sight, bead front; uncheckered walnut pistol-grip stock; swivels, sling. Introduced 1933; discontinued 1935.

Exc.: $125   **VGood: $95**   **Good: $60**

MOSSBERG MODEL 14

Bolt action; single shot; 22 Short, 22 Long, 22 LR; 24-inch barrel; take down; rear peep sight, hooded ramp front; uncheckered pistol-grip stock; semi-beavertail forearm; sling swivels. Introduced 1934; discontinued 1935.

Exc.: $125   **VGood: $95**   **Good: $60**

MOSSBERG MODEL 20

Bolt action; single shot; 22 Short, 22 Long, 22 LR; 24-inch barrel; take down; open rear sight, bead front; uncheckered pistol-grip stock; forearm with finger grooves. Introduced 1933; discontinued 1935.

Exc.: $125   **VGood:** $95   **Good:** $60

MOSSBERG MODEL 21

Bolt action; single shot; 22 Short, 22 Long, 22 LR; 24-inch barrel; take down. Similar to Model 20. Introduced 1934; discontinued 1935.

Exc.: $125   **VGood:** $95   **Good:** $60

MOSSBERG MODEL 25

Bolt action; single shot; 22 Short, 22 Long, 22 LR; 24-inch barrel; take down; rear peep sight, hooded ramp front; uncheckered pistol-grip stock; semi-beavertail forearm; sling swivels. Introduced 1935; discontinued 1936.

Exc.: $145   **VGood:** $110   **Good:** $70

MOSSBERG MODEL 25A

Same specs as Model 25 except with master action; better wood and finish. Introduced 1937; discontinued 1938.

Exc.: $175   **VGood:** $130   **Good:** $90

MOSSBERG MODEL 26B

Bolt action; single shot; 22 Short, 22 Long, 22 LR; 26-inch tapered barrel; 41-3/4-inch overall length; weighs 5-1/2 lbs.; No.2A open sporting or No.4 micrometer peep rear sight, hooded ramp front; uncheckered pistol-grip stock; sling swivels. Manufactured 1938 to 1941.

Exc.: $155   **VGood:** $115   **Good:** $80

MOSSBERG MODEL 26C

Same specs as Model 26B except open sights; no sling swivels.

Exc.: $155   **VGood:** $115   **Good:** $80

MOSSBERG MODEL 26T TARGO RIFLE/SHOTGUN

Bolt action; single shot; Targo 22 smoothbore with smoothbore and rifled screw-on adapters. Fewer than 1000 manufactured. Introduced 1940; discontinued 1942. Add 15 percent premium for target thrower and clay birds.

Exc.: $450   **VGood:** $350   **Good:** $240

MOSSBERG MODEL 30

Bolt action; single shot; 22 Short, 22 Long, 22 LR; 24-inch barrel; takedown; rear peep sight, hooded ramp bead front; uncheckered pistol-grip stock; grooved forearm. Introduced 1933; discontinued 1935.

Exc.: $125   **VGood:** $105   **Good:** $80

MOSSBERG MODEL 34

Bolt action; single shot; 22 Short, 22 Long, 22 LR; 24-inch barrel; takedown; rear peep sight, hooded ramp bead front; uncheckered pistol-grip stock with semi-beavertail forearm. Introduced 1934; discontinued 1935.

Exc.: $125   **VGood:** $105   **Good:** $80

MOSSBERG MODEL 35

Bolt action; single shot; 22 LR; 26-inch barrel, target grade; micrometer rear peep sight; hooded ramp front; target stock with full pistol grip, beavertail forearm; sling swivels. Introduced 1935; discontinued 1937.

Exc.: $295   **VGood:** $250   **Good:** $135

MOSSBERG MODEL 35A

Same specs as Model 35 except heavy barrel; new Master action; uncheckered target stock with cheekpiece, full pistol grip. Introduced 1937; discontinued 1938.

Exc.: $295   **VGood:** $250   **Good:** $135

MOSSBERG MODEL 35A-LS

Same specs as Model 35A except Lyman 17A front, Lyman No. 57 rear sight.

Exc.: $310   **VGood:** $260   **Good:** $150

Mossberg Model 35

Mossberg Model L42A

Mossberg Model 42B

Mossberg Model 42C

Mossberg Model 42TR Targo Rifle/Shotgun

Mossberg Model 43B

MOSSBERG MODEL 40

Bolt action; 22 Short, 22 Long, 22 LR; 16-shot tube magazine (22 LR), 18-shot (22 Long), 22-shot (22 Short); takedown repeater. Introduced 1933; discontinued 1935.

Exc.: $165   **VGood:** $130   **Good:** $90

MOSSBERG MODEL 42

Bolt action; 22 Short, 22 Long, 22 LR; 7-shot detachable box magazine; 24-inch barrel; takedown; receiver peep sight, open rear sight, hooded ramp front; uncheckered walnut pistol-grip stock; sling swivels. Introduced 1935; discontinued 1937.

Exc.: $200   **VGood:** $165   **Good:** $125

MOSSBERG MODEL 42A

Same specs as Model 42 with Master action, minor upgrading. Introduced 1937 to replace dropped Model 42; discontinued 1938.

Exc.: $245   **VGood:** $175   **Good:** $125

MOSSBERG MODEL L42A

Same specs as Model 42A except left-handed action. Introduced 1938; discontinued 1941.

Exc.: $255   **VGood:** $185   **Good:** $135

MOSSBERG MODEL 42B

Same specs as Model 42A except design improvements; replaced the Model 42A; micrometer peep sight in addition to open rear; 5-shot detachable box magazine. Introduced 1938; discontinued 1941.

Exc.: $245   **VGood:** $175   **Good:** $125

MOSSBERG MODEL 42C

Same specs as Model 42B except no rear peep sight.

Exc.: $235   **VGood:** $165   **Good:** $115

MOSSBERG MODEL 42M

Same specs as Model 42 except 23-inch tapered barrel; 40-inch overall length; weighs 6-3/4 lbs.; two-piece Mannlicher-type long stock with pistol grip, cheekpiece; micrometer receiver peep sight, open rear sight, hooded ramp front. Introduced 1940; discontinued 1950.

Exc.: $245   **VGood:** $175   **Good:** $125

MOSSBERG MODEL 42M (A), 42M (B), 42M (C)

Same specs as Model 42M except minor changes in extractors and sights. No military markings. Introduced 1944; discontinued 1950.

Exc.: $245   **VGood:** $175   **Good:** $125

MOSSBERG MODEL 42MB

Same same specs as Model 42M except no cheekpiece; approximately 50,000 made for U.S. and Great Britain; U.S. Property and British proofmarks. Produced only during World War II. Some collector value.

U.S. Property marked
Exc.: $475   **VGood:** $425   **Good:** $395

British proof marks
Exc.: $390   **VGood:** $335   **Good:** $265

MOSSBERG MODEL 42TR TARGO RIFLE/SHOTGUN

Bolt action; 22 Short; Long, Long Rifle, 22 Long Rifle Shot, 7-shot box magazine; smoothbore and rifled screw-on adapters; no sling swivels. Introduced commercially 1940; discontinued 1942.

Exc.: $350   **VGood:** $295   **Good:** $200

MOSSBERG MODEL 42T TARGO RIFLE/SHOTGUN

Same specs as Model 42TR except not provided with rifled adapter; front sight hood or rear sight, which

Mossberg Model 44B

Mossberg Model 44US

Mossberg Model 45

Mossberg Model 46

Mossberg Model 46B

Mossberg Model 140B

were available separately. Introduced commercially 1940; discontinued 1942.

Exc.: $350   **VGood:** $295   **Good:** $200

MOSSBERG MODEL 43

Bolt action; 22 LR; 7-shot detachable box magazine; 26-inch barrel; Lyman No. 57 rear sight, selective aperture front; adjustable trigger, speed lock; target stock with cheekpiece, full pistol grip; beavertail forend; adjustable front swivel. Introduced 1937; discontinued 1938.

Exc.: $200   **VGood:** $165   **Good:** $125

MOSSBERG MODEL L43

Same specs as Model 43 except left-hand action.

Exc.: $265   **VGood:** $225   **Good:** $200

MOSSBERG MODEL 43B

Bolt action; 22 LR; 7-shot detachable magazine; 26-inch barrel; Lyman No. 57 receiver sight, Lyman No. 17A front sight; walnut target stock with cheekpiece, full pistol-grip; beavertail forearm; not styled after standard Model 43. Introduced 1938; discontinued 1939.

Exc.: $310   **VGood:** $260   **Good:** $150

MOSSBERG MODEL 44B

Bolt action; target configuration; 22 LR; 7-shot clip magazine; 26-inch heavy barrel; 43-inch overall length; weighs 8-1/2 lbs.; micrometer receiver peep sight, hooded front; speed lock; thumb safety; grooved adjustable trigger; walnut target stock with cheekpiece, full pistol grip; beavertail forearm; adjustable sling swivels. Introduced 1938; discontinued 1943.

Exc.: $310   **VGood:** $260   **Good:** $150

MOSSBERG MODEL 44US

Bolt action; 22 LR; 7-shot detachable box magazine; 26-inch heavy barrel; 43-inch overall length; weighs 8-1/2 lbs.; same specs as Model 44B except designed primarily for teaching marksmanship to Armed Forces during World War II; uncheckered walnut target stock; sling swivels. Introduced 1943; discontinued 1948. Collector value.

Exc.: $310   **VGood:** $260   **Good:** $150

U.S. Property marked

Exc.: $475   **VGood:** $425   **Good:** $395

MOSSBERG MODEL 44US(A), 44US(B), 44US(C), 44US(D)

Same specs as Model 44US except minor changes in sights and extractors.

Exc.: $310   **VGood:** $260   **Good:** $150

U.S. Property marked

Exc.: $475   **VGood:** $425   **Good:** $395

MOSSBERG MODEL 45

Bolt action; 22 Short, 22 Long, 22 LR; 15-shot tube magazine (22 LR), 18-shot (22 Long), 22-shot (22 Short); 24-inch heavy barrel; 42-1/2-inch overall length; weighs 6-3/4 lbs.; take-down, repeater; receiver peep sight, open rear, hooded ramp front; uncheckered pistol-grip stock; sling swivels. Introduced 1935; discontinued 1937.

Exc.: $200   **VGood:** $165   **Good:** $125

MOSSBERG MODEL 45A

Same specs as Model 45 except improved version of discontinued Model 45 with Master action, minor design variations. Introduced 1937; discontinued 1938.

Exc.: $200   **VGood:** $165   **Good:** $125

MOSSBERG MODEL 45AC

Same specs as Model 45A except without receiver peep sight.

Exc.: $175   **VGood:** $155   **Good:** $125

MOSSBERG MODEL 45B

Same specs as Model 45A except open rear sight. Introduced 1938; discontinued 1940.

Exc.: $175   **VGood:** $155   **Good:** $125

MOSSBERG MODEL 45C

Same specs as Model 45 except no sights; designed for use only with scope sight.

Exc.: $175   **VGood:** $155   **Good:** $125

MOSSBERG MODEL L45A

Same specs as Model 45A except left-hand action. Introduced 1937; discontinued 1938.

Exc.: $195   **VGood:** $140   **Good:** $130

MOSSBERG MODEL 46

Bolt action; 22 Short, 22 Long, 22 LR; 15-shot (22 LR), 18-shot (22 Long), 22-shot (22 Short) tube magazine; 26-inch barrel; 44-1/2-inch overall length; weighs 7-1/2 lbs.; takedown repeater; micrometer rear peep sight; hooded ramp front; uncheckered walnut pistol-grip stock with cheekpiece; beavertail forearm; sling swivels. Introduced 1935; discontinued 1937.

Exc.: $175   **VGood:** $155   **Good:** $125

MOSSBERG MODEL 46A

Same specs as discontinued Model 46 with Master action and minor design improvements; detachable sling swivels. Introduced 1937; discontinued 1938.

Exc.: $175   **VGood:** $155   **Good:** $125

MOSSBERG MODEL 46AC

Same specs as Model 46A except open rear sight instead of micrometer peep sight.

Exc.: $175   **VGood:** $155   **Good:** $125

MOSSBERG MODEL 46A-LS

Same specs as Model 46A except equipped with factory-supplied Lyman No. 57 receiver sight.

Exc.: $235   **VGood:** $165   **Good:** $115

MOSSBERG MODEL 46B

Same specs as Model 46A except receiver peep and open rear sights. Introduced 1938; discontinued 1940.

Exc.: $175   **VGood:** $155   **Good:** $125

MOSSBERG MODEL 46BT

Same specs as Model 46B except heavier barrel; target-styled stock. Introduced 1938; discontinued 1939.

Exc.: $150   **VGood:** $110   **Good:** $90

MOSSBERG MODEL 46C

Same specs as Model 46 except heavier barrel.

Exc.: $175   **VGood:** $150   **Good:** $100

MOSSBERG MODEL 46M

Same specs as Model 46 except 23-inch barrel; 40-inch overall length; weighs 7 lbs.; micrometer receiver peep sight, open rear, hooded ramp front; two-piece Mannlicher-type stock with pistol grip, cheekpiece; sling swivels. Introduced 1940; discontinued 1952.

Exc.: $150   **VGood:** $110   **Good:** $90

MOSSBERG MODEL 46M(A), 46M(B)

Same specs as Model 46M except minor sight changes.

Exc.: $150   **VGood:** $110   **Good:** $90

MOSSBERG MODEL 46T

Same specs as Model 46 except heavier barrel and stock; target version. Introduced 1936; discontinued 1937.

Exc.: $175   **VGood:** $155   **Good:** $125

MOSSBERG MODEL L46A-LS

Same specs as Model 46A-LS except left-hand action.

Exc.: $260   **VGood:** $220   **Good:** $170

MOSSBERG MODEL 140B

Bolt action; 22 Short, 22 Long, 22 LR; 7-shot clip magazine; 24-1/2-inch barrel; 42-inch overall length; weighs 5-3/4 lbs.; target/sporter version of Model 140K; peep rear sight, ramp front. Introduced 1957; discontinued 1958

Exc.: $120   VGood: $95   Good: $65

MOSSBERG MODEL 140K

Same specs as Model 140B except uncheckered walnut pistol-grip stock; Monte Carlo with cheekpiece; open rear sight, bead front; sling swivels. Introduced 1955; discontinued 1958.

Exc.: $110   VGood: $80   Good: $65

MOSSBERG MODEL 142

Bolt action; 22 Short, 22 Long, 22 LR; 7-shot removable box magazine; 18-inch tapered barrel; 36-inch overall length; weighs 5 lbs.; rear fully-adjustable peep sight, military-style ramp front; walnut Monte Carlo pistol-grip stock; as with Model 152, sling swivels, sling mount on left side of stock; forearm hinges down to act as handgrip. Some barrels marked 142A. Introduced 1949; discontinued 1957.

Exc.: $245   VGood: $175   Good: $125

MOSSBERG MODEL 142K

Same specs as Model 142 except peep sight is replaced by open rear sight. Introduced 1953; discontinued 1957.

Exc.: $225   VGood: $165   Good: $95

MOSSBERG MODEL 144

Bolt action; 22 LR; 26-inch heavy barrel; 7-shot detachable clip magazine; 43-inch overall length; weighs 8 lbs.; target model; micrometer receiver peep sight, hooded front; pistol-grip target stock; grooved trigger; grooved receiver for Mossberg No. 4M4 scope; thumb safety; T-shaped bolt handle; adjustable hand stop; beavertail forearm; sling swivels. Introduced 1949; discontinued 1954.

Exc.: $170   VGood: $140   Good: $110

MOSSBERG MODEL 144LS

Same specs as Model 144 except Lyman No. 57MS receiver peep sight, Lyman No. 17A front. Introduced 1954; discontinued 1960.

Exc.: $230   VGood: $195   Good: $155

MOSSBERG MODEL 144LS-A

Same specs as Model 144LS except Mossberg 330 rear peep sight. Introduced 1960; discontinued 1978.

Exc.: $220   VGood: $160   Good: $120

MOSSBERG MODEL 144LS-B (TARGET)

Same specs as Model 144 except 27-inch round barrel; Lyman 17A hooded front sight with inserts, Mossberg 5331 receiver peep sight; target-style American walnut stock; adjustable forend hand stop. Introduced 1978; discontinued 1985.

Exc.: $235   VGood: $190   Good: $165

MOSSBERG MODEL 146B

Bolt action; 22 Short, 22 Long, 22 LR; 20-shot (22 LR), 23-shot (22 Long), 30-shot (22 Short) tube magazine; 26-inch barrel; 43-1/4-inch overall length; weighs 7 lbs.; takedown repeater; micrometer fully-adjustable peep rear sight on receiver, hooded front sight, open fully-adjustable rear; uncheckered walnut pistol-grip Monte Carlo-type stock with cheekpiece; adjustable trigger; moulded finger-groove trigger guard; schnabel forearm; sling swivels. Introduced 1949; discontinued 1954.

Exc.: $135   VGood: $100   Good: $65

MOSSBERG MODEL 146B-A

Same specs as Model 146B except different sights. Introduced 1954; discontinued 1958.

Exc.: $135   VGood: $100   Good: $65

MOSSBERG MODEL 320B

Bolt action; single shot; 22 LR, 22 Short, 22 Long; 24-inch tapered barrel; 43-1/2-inch overall length; weighs 5-3/4 lbs.; hooded ramp front, rear target precision peep sight; automatic safety; hammerless; walnut pistol-grip Monte Carlo stock; sling swivels.

Mossberg Model 140K

Mossberg Model 144

Mossberg Model 144LS

Mossberg Model 146B

Mossberg Model 320K

Mossberg Model 340B

Mossberg Model 340TR Targo Rifle/Shotgun

Designated by manufacturer as a Boy Scout target model. Introduced 1960; discontinued 1971.

Exc.: $125   VGood: $90   Good: $70

MOSSBERG MODEL 320K

Same specs as Model 320B except open sights; no sling swivels; drop-in loading platform; automatic safety. Introduced 1958; discontinued 1960.

Exc.: $85   VGood: $75   Good: $60

MOSSBERG MODEL 320K-A

Same specs as Model 320K.

Exc.: $85   VGood: $75   Good: $60

MOSSBERG MODEL 320TR TARGO RIFLE/SHOTGUN

Bolt action; single shot; 22 Short, 22 Long, 22 LR; smoothbore with interchangeable rifled and smoothbore barrel adapters; adjustable open sight, blade front; sold with Model 1A hand trap thrower. Introduced 1961; discontinued 1962.

Exc.: $230   VGood: $160   Good: $120

MOSSBERG MODEL 321B

Bolt action; single shot; 22 Short, 22 Long, 22 LR; 24-inch barrel; 43-1/2-inch overall length; weighs 6-1/2 lbs.; S330 peep sight with 1/4-minute click adjustments; hardwood stock with walnut finish; cheekpiece; checkered pistol grip, forearm; hammerless bolt-action with drop-in loading platform; automatic safety. Discontinued 1976.

Exc.: $80   VGood: $60   VGood: $50

MOSSBERG MODEL 321K

Same specs as Model 321B except adjustable open rear sight, ramp front. Introduced 1972; no longer in production.

Exc.: $70   VGood: $55   VGood: $45

MOSSBERG MODEL 340B, 340B-A

Bolt action; 22 Short, 22 Long, 22 LR; 7-shot box magazine; 24-inch barrel; 43-1/2-inch overall length; weighs 6-1/2 lbs.; hammerless; rear precision target peep sight, hooded ramp front; walnut Monte Carlo stock with cheekpiece, pistol-grip; buttplate white line spacer. Introduced 1958; no longer in production.

Exc.: $125   VGood: $90   VGood: $60

MOSSBERG MODEL 340K, 340K-A

Same specs as Model 340B except for open rear sight, bead front. Introduced 1958; discontinued 1971.

Exc.: $100   VGood: $80   Good: $50

MOSSBERG MODEL 340M

Same specs as Model 340K except for 18-1/2-inch barrel; 38-1/2-inch overall length; weighs 5-1/4 lbs.; one-piece Mannlicher-style Monte Carlo pistol-grip stock; sling; sling swivels. Introduced 1970; discontinued 1971.

Exc.: $230   VGood: $180   Good: $130

MOSSBERG MODEL 340TR TARGO RIFLE/SHOTGUN

Bolt action; 22 Short, 22 Long, 22 LR; 22LR-shot; smoothbore; rifled and choke adapters screw into muzzle for shooting bullets or shot. Smoothbore was

Mossberg Model 342

Mossberg Model 640KS

Mossberg Model 800

Mossberg Model 800M

Mossberg Model 800VT

Mossberg Model 810

designed for short-range trap shooting; the special Mossberg trap could be fastened to the barrel to allow the shooter to throw his own miniature targets. Introduced 1961; discontinued 1962.

Exc.: $240   **VGood:** $185   **Good:** $150

MOSSBERG MODEL 341

Bolt action; 22 Short, 22 Long, 22 LR; 7-shot clip magazine; 24-inch barrel; 43-1/2-inch overall length; weighs 6-1/2 lbs.; fully-adjustable open rear sight, bead post ramp front; walnut Monte Carlo stock with cheekpiece; checkered pistol grip, forearm; plastic buttplate with white line spacer; sliding side safety; sling swivels. Introduced 1972; discontinued 1976.

Exc.: $90   **VGood:** $70   **Good:** $65

MOSSBERG MODEL 342

Bolt action; 22 Short, 22 Long, 22 LR; 7-shot clip magazine; 18-inch tapered barrel; hammerless action; peep rear sight, bead front; receiver grooved for scope mounts; uncheckered walnut Monte Carlo pistol-grip stock; two-position forearm that folds down for rest or handgrip; thumb safety; sling swivels; web sling. Introduced 1957; discontinued 1959.

Exc.: $150   **VGood:** $95   **VGood:** $60

MOSSBERG MODEL 342K, 342K-A

Same specs as Model 342 except with open rear sight. Introduced 1958; discontinued 1971.

Exc.: $120   **VGood:** $90   **Good:** $55

MOSSBERG MODEL 344

Bolt action; 22 LR; 7-shot clip magazine; walnut finished, checkered stock. Introduced 1985.

Exc.: $125   **VGood:** $105   **Good:** $85

MOSSBERG MODEL 344K

Same specs as Model 344 except carbine length.

Exc.: $125   **VGood:** $105   **Good:** $85

MOSSBERG MODEL 346B

Bolt action; 22 Short, 22 Long, 22 LR; 18-shot tube magazine (22 LR), 20-shot (22 Long), 25-shot (22 Short); 24-inch barrel; hammerless action; triple

sight combination; hooded ramp front, receiver peep with open rear sight; uncheckered walnut stock with pistol grip; Monte Carlo comb; cheekpiece; quick-detachable sling swivels. Introduced 1958; discontinued 1967.

Exc.: $125   **VGood:** $95   **Good:** $60

MOSSBERG MODEL 346K, 346K-A

Same specs as Model 346B except open rear sight, bead front. Introduced 1958; discontinued 1971.

Exc.: $110   **VGood:** $80   **Good:** $55

MOSSBERG MODEL 620K, 620K-A

Bolt action; single shot; 22 WMR; 24-inch barrel; 44-3/4-inch overall length; weighs 6 lbs.; fully-adjustable open rear sight, bead front; extra heavy duty receiver and bolt; grooved trigger; thumb safety; receiver grooved for scope mounts; hammerless action; walnut Monte Carlo pistol-grip stock with cheekpiece; sling swivels; impressed checkering on pistol-grip, forearm. Introduced 1958; discontinued 1974.

Exc.: $120   **VGood:** $100   **Good:** $70

MOSSBERG MODEL 640K

Bolt action; 22 WMR; 5-shot detachable box magazine; 24-inch barrel; 44-3/4-inch overall length; weighs 6 lbs.; hammerless action; fully-adjustable open rear sight, bead front; receiver grooved for scope mounts; extra heavy duty receiver and bolt; grooved trigger; thumb safety; walnut Monte Carlo pistol-grip stock with cheekpiece; open rear sight, bead front; sling swivels; impressed checkering on pistol grip, forearm. Called the "Chuckster". Introduced 1959; no longer in production.

Exc.: $140   **VGood:** $110   **Good:** $80

MOSSBERG MODEL 640KS

Same specs as Model 640K except select walnut stock, checkered pistol grip, forearm; gold-plated front sight, rear sight elevator and trigger. Discontinued 1974.

Exc.: $180   **VGood:** $140   **VGood:** $110

MOSSBERG MODEL 640M

Same specs as Model 640K except full-length checkered Monte Carlo Mannlicher stock; 20-inch barrel; heavy receiver; jeweled bolt. Manufactured 1971.

Exc.: $200   **VGood:** $170   **Good:** $140

MOSSBERG MODEL 642K

Bolt action; 22 WMR; 5-shot box magazine; 18-inch barrel; 38-1/4-inch overall length; weighs 5 lbs.; bead front sight, fully-adjustable open rear; fold-down forend; walnut Monte Carlo pistol-grip stock; grip cap and buttplate white line spacers; web sling. Introduced 1960; discontinued 1968.

Exc.: $190   **VGood:** $140   **Good:** $110

MOSSBERG MODEL 800

Bolt action; 222 Rem., 22-250, 243 Win., 308 Win.; 4-shot magazine, 3-shot (22-250); 22-inch barrel; 42-inch overall length; weighs 6-1/2 lbs.; folding-leaf rear sight, ramp front; checkered pistol-grip Monte Carlo stock, forearm; recessed bolt head with six locking lugs; top tang safety; hinged floorplate with button release; cheekpiece; sling swivels. Manufactured 1967; discontinued 1980.

Exc.: $350   **VGood:** $300   **Good:** $215

MOSSBERG MODEL 800D SUPER GRADE

Same specs as Model 800 except 22-250, 243 Win., 308 Win.; Monte Carlo stock with roll-over comb, cheekpiece; rosewood forend tip, pistol-grip cap; hand-Damascened bolt. Manufactured 1970 to 1973.

Exc.: $375   **VGood:** $325   **Good:** $230

MOSSBERG MODEL 800M

Same specs as Model 800 except 20-inch barrel; 40-inch overall length; 22-250, 243 Win., 308 Win.; full-length Mannlicher-type stock; flat bolt handle. Manufactured 1969 to 1972.

Exc.: $350   **VGood:** $300   **Good:** $215

MOSSBERG MODEL 800SM

Same specs as Model 800 except weighs 7-1/2 lbs.; equipped with Mossberg Model 84 4x scope.

Exc.: $350   **VGood:** $300   **Good:** $215

MOSSBERG MODEL 800VT

Same specs as Model 800 except varmint/target model; 222 Rem., 22-250, 243 Win.; 24-inch heavy barrel; weighs 9-1/2 lbs.; 44-inch overall length; no sights; Marksman-style stock; scope mount blocks. Manufactured 1968 to 1980.

Exc.: $350   **VGood:** $300   **Good:** $215

MOSSBERG MODEL 810, 810A

Bolt action; 270 Win., 30-06, 7mm Rem. Mag., 338 Win. Mag.; 4-shot (standard calibers), 3-shot (magnum calibers) detachable or internal magazine; 22-inch barrel (standard calibers), 24-inch (magnum calibers); 42-inch overall length; weighs 7-1/2-8 lbs.; folding leaf rear sight, ramp front with gold bead, fully-adjustable folding leaf middle sight; receiver drilled, tapped for peep or scope; hinged floorplate; checkered pistol-grip walnut stock, forearm; Monte Carlo comb, cheekpiece; pistol-grip cap; recoil pad with white liners; sling swivels. Manufactured 1970 to 1980.

Standard calibers		
Exc.: $300	**VGood:** $265	**Good:** $215

Magnum calibers		
Exc.: $350	**VGood:** $300	**Good:** $215

MOSSBERG MODEL 810ASM

Same Specs as Model 810 except 30-06; no sights; comes fitted with Mossberg Model 84 4x scope. Introduced 1972.

Exc.: $350   **VGood:** $300   **Good:** $215

MOSSBERG MODEL 810B

Same specs as Model 810 except 24-inch barrel; 44-inch overall length. Introduced 1972.

Exc.: $350   **VGood:** $300   **Good:** $215

MOSSBERG MODEL 810BSM
Same specs as Model 810B except 7mm Rem. Mag.; no sights; comes fitted with Mossberg Model 84 4x scope. Introduced 1972.

Exc.: $350 **VGood:** $300 **Good:** $215

MOSSBERG MODEL 810C
Same specs as Model 810 except 270 Win. Introduced 1973.

Exc.: $350 **VGood:** $300 **Good:** $215

MOSSBERG MODEL 810D
Same specs as Model 810 except 338 Win. Mag. Introduced 1973.

Exc.: $350 **VGood:** $300 **Good:** $215

MOSSBERG MODEL 1500 MOUNTAINEER
Bolt action; 222, 223, 22-250, 243, 25-06, 270, 30-06, 308, 7mm Rem. Mag., 300 Win. Mag., 338 Win. Mag., 22-inch, 24-inch barrel; weighs 7-1/2 lbs.; open round-notch adjustable rear sight, hooded ramp gold bead front; American walnut stock; Monte Carlo comb, cheekpiece; cut checkering; single-unit triggerguard/magazine box; hinged floorplate; swivel studs; composition buttplate; magnums with rubber recoil pad. Made in Japan by Howa. Originally marketed by S&W. Introduced 1979; discontinued 1987.

Standard calibers
Exc.: $300 **VGood:** $250 **Good:** $220

Magnum calibers
Exc.: $350 **VGood:** $310 **Good:** $270

MOSSBERG MODEL 1500 MOUNTAINEER DELUXE
Same specs as Model 1500 except sans sights; engine-turned bolt; decorated floorplate with scrollwork; skip-line checkering; sling, swivels, swivel posts included; magnum models with vent, recoil pad.

Standard calibers
Exc.: $350 **VGood:** $300 **Good:** $250

Magnum calibers
Exc.: $370 **VGood:** $320 **Good:** $270

MOSSBERG MODEL 1500 MOUNTAINEER VARMINT DELUXE
Same specs as Model 1500 except 222, 22-250, 223, 308; 24-inch heavy barrel; no sights; fully-adjustable trigger; skip-line checkering; quick-detachable swivels. Originally marketed by S&W. Introduced 1986; discontinued by Mossberg, 1987.

Exc.: $370 **VGood:** $310 **Good:** $280

MOSSBERG MODEL 1550
Bolt action; 243, 270, 30-06; box magazine; 22-inch, 24-inch barrel; weighs 7-1/2 lbs.; with or without sights; American walnut stock; Monte Carlo comb, cheekpiece; cut checkering; swivel studs; composition buttplate; magnums with rubber recoil pad. Made in Japan by Howa. Introduced 1986; discontinued 1987.

Exc.: $330 **VGood:** $280 **Good:** $250

MOSSBERG MODEL 1700LS
Bolt action; 243, 270, 30-06; 22-inch barrel; 4-shot removable box magazine; classic-style stock; tapered forend; schnabel tip; hand-checkering; black rubber buttpad; flush-mounted sling swivels; jeweled bolt body. Marketed as Classic Hunter. Made in Japan. Originally marketed by S&W. Introduced 1986; discontinued 1987.

Exc.: $400 **VGood:** $350 **Good:** $275

MOSSBERG MODEL B
Bolt action; single shot; 22 Short, 22 Long, 22 LR; 22-inch barrel; take-down; uncheckered pistol-grip walnut stock. Introduced 1930; discontinued 1932.

Exc.: $105 **VGood:** $70 **Good:** $55

MOSSBERG MODEL C
Bolt action; single shot; 22 Short, 22 Long, 22 LR; 24-inch barrel; ivory bead front sight, open sporting rear. Introduced 1931; discontinued 1932.

Exc.: $100 **VGood:** $70 **Good:** $55

MOSSBERG MODEL C-1
Same specs as Model C except Lyman front and rear sights; leather sling, swivels.

Exc.: $125 **VGood:** $100 **Good:** $85

MOSSBERG MODEL R
Bolt action; 22 Short, 22 Long, 22 LR; 24-inch barrel; tube magazine; take-down; open rear sight, bead front; uncheckered pistol-grip stock. Introduced 1930; discontinued 1932.

Exc.: $165 **VGood:** $125 **Good:** $90

MOSSBERG MODEL RM-7A
Bolt action; 30-06; 22-inch barrel; 5-shot magazine; gold bead front sight on ramp, adjustable folding leaf rear; drilled, tapped for scope mounts; classic-style checkered pistol-grip stock of American walnut; rotary magazine; three-position bolt safety; sling swivel studs. Introduced 1978; discontinued 1981. Few made.

Perf.: $500 **Exc.:** $400 **VGood:** $300

MOSSBERG MODEL RM-7B
Same specs as Model RM-7A except 7mm Rem. Mag.; 4-shot magazine; 24-inch barrel; 45-1/4-inch overall length. Introduced 1978; discontinued 1981. Very rare.

Perf.: $550 **Exc.:** $450 **VGood:** $350

MOSSBERG MODEL 50
Semi-automatic; 22 LR; 24-inch barrel; 15-shot tube magazine in buttstock; 43-3/4-inch overall length; weighs 6-3/4 lbs.; takedown; open rear sight, hooded ramp front; uncheckered walnut pistol-grip stock; finger grooves in grip; no sling swivels. Introduced 1939; discontinued 1942.

Exc.: $130 **VGood:** $110 **VGood:** $100

MOSSBERG MODEL 51
Semi-automatic; 22 LR; 15-shot tube magazine; 24-inch barrel; 43-3/4-inch overall length; weighs 7-1/4 lbs.; receiver peep sight; sling swivels; cheekpiece stock; heavy beavertail forearm. Made only in 1939.

Exc.: $175 **VGood:** $130 **Good:** $110

MOSSBERG MODEL 51M
Same specs as Model 51 except 20-inch round tapered barrel; 40-inch overall length; weighs 7 lbs.; two-piece Mannlicher-style stock. Introduced 1939; discontinued 1946.

Exc.: $185 **VGood:** $150 **Good:** $100

MOSSBERG MODEL 151K
Semi-automatic; 22LR; 24-inch tapered barrel; 44-inch overall length; weighs 6 lbs.; no peep sight; sling swivels; uncheckered sporting stock; Monte Carlo comb; cheekpiece; schnabel forearm. Introduced 1950; discontinued 1951.

Exc.: $210 **VGood:** $165 **VGood:** $100

MOSSBERG MODEL 151M
Semi-automatic; 22 LR; 15-shot tube magazine; 20-inch barrel; 40-inch overall length; weighs 7 lbs.; No. S101 hooded ramp front, No. S107 open sporting rear or No. S130 micro-click adjustable rear; two-piece Mannlicher stock; sling swivels; steel buttplate. Introduced 1946; discontinued 1958.

Exc.: $210 **VGood:** $165 **VGood:** $100

MOSSBERG MODEL 151M(A), 151M(B), 151M(C)
Same specs as Model 151M except minor changes in sights and buttplate. Introduced 1947; discontinued 1958.

Exc.: $210 **VGood:** $165 **VGood:** $100

Mossberg Model 1500 Mountaineer Deluxe

Mossberg Model RM-7A

Mossberg Model Model 50

Mossberg Model 51

Mossberg Model 51M

Mossberg Model 151M

Mossberg Model 152

Mossberg Model 350K

Mossberg Model 351K

Mossberg Model 352K

Mossberg Model 353

Mossberg Model 377

Mossberg Model 380

Mossberg Model 430

Mossberg Model 432

MOSSBERG MODEL 351K, 351K-A

Semi-automatic; 22 LR; 15-shot tube magazine in buttstock; 24-inch barrel; 43-inch overall length; weighs 6 lbs.; fully-adjustable open rear sight with U-notch, bead front; receiver grooved for scope mount; walnut Monte Carlo pistol-grip stock. Introduced 1960; discontinued 1971.

Exc.: $100   VGood: $90   Good: $80

MOSSBERG MODEL 351C

Same specs as Model 351K except 18-1/2-inch barrel; 38-1/2-inch overall length; weighs 5-1/2 lbs.; straight Western-type carbine stock with barrel band; sling swivels. Called the "Jack Rabbit Special." Introduced 1965; discontinued 1971.

Exc.: $120   VGood: $100   Good: $90

MOSSBERG MODEL 352

Semi-automatic; 22 Short, 22 Long, 22 LR; 7-shot detachable box magazine; 18-inch barrel; 38-inch overall length; weighs 5 lbs.; peep rear sight, bead front; unchecked walnut Monte Carlo pistol-grip stock; two-position Tenite forearm extension folds down for rest or hand grip; sling swivels; web sling. Introduced 1958; discontinued 1971.

Exc.: $125   VGood: $110   Good: $90

MOSSBERG MODEL 352K, 352K-A, 352K-B

Same specs as Model 352 except with fully-adjustable open rear sight. Introduced 1960; discontinued 1971.

Perf.: $115   Exc.: $110   VGood: $80

MOSSBERG MODEL 353

Semi-automatic; 22 LR; 7-shot detachable box magazine; 18-inch barrel; 38-inch overall length; weighs 5 lbs.; fully-adjustable open rear sight, ramp front with bead; American walnut Monte Carlo Pistol-grip stock; black Tenite fold down forend extension; checkered pistol grip, forend; receiver grooved for scope mount; sling swivels, web strap on left side of stock. Introduced 1972.

Exc.: $125   VGood: $110   Good: $90

MOSSBERG MODEL 377

Semi-automatic; 22 LR; 15-shot tubular magazine; 20-inch barrel; 40-inch overall length; weighs 6-1/4 lbs.; no open sights; 4x scope mounted; moulded polystyrene straight-line thumbhole stock; roll-over cheekpiece; Monte Carlo comb; checkered forearm. Advertised as the Plinkster. Introduced 1977; discontinued 1985.

Exc.: $135   VGood: $110   Good: $80

MOSSBERG MODEL 380, 380S

Semi-automatic; 22 LR; 15-shot tubular magazine in stock; 20-inch tapered barrel; weighs about 5-1/2 lbs.; bead front sight, adjustable open rear; receiver grooved for scope mounting; walnut-finished hardwood stock; black plastic buttplate. Introduced 1981; discontinued 1985.

Exc.: $100   VGood: $85   Good: $70

MOSSBERG MODEL 430

Semi-automatic; 22 LR; 18-shot tube magazine; 24-inch barrel; 43-inch overall length; weighs 6-1/4 lbs.; open rear sight, gold bead front; two-piece walnut Monte Carlo stock; checkered pistol grip, forearm; gold-plated, grooved trigger; Damascened bolt; buttplate, pistol grip cap white line spacers; top tang safety; hammerless action. Introduced 1970; discontinued 1971.

Exc.: $110   VGood: $100   Good: $80

MOSSBERG MODEL 432

Semi-automatic; 22 LR; 15-shot magazine; 20-inch barrel; 39-1/2-inch overall length; weighs 6 lbs.; gold-plated, grooved trigger; Damascened bolt; buttplate, pistol grip white line spacers; top tang safety; hammerless action; carbine; unchecked straight-grip carbine stock, forearm; barrel band; sling swivels. Introduced 1970; discontinued 1971.

Exc.: $110   VGood: $100   Good: $80

MOSSBERG MODEL 152

Semi-automatic; 22 LR; 7-shot detachable box magazine; 18-inch barrel; 38-inch overall length; weighs 5 lbs.; rear peep sight, military-type ramp front; walnut Monte Carlo pistol-grip stock; hinged forearm swings down to act as forward handgrip; sling swivels and adjustable sling mounted on left side. Introduced 1948; discontinued 1957.

Exc.: $210   VGood: $165   VGood: $100

MOSSBERG MODEL 152K

Same specs as Model 152 except open rear sight. Introduced 1950; discontinued 1957.

Exc.: $210   VGood: $165   VGood: $100

MOSSBERG MODEL 333

Semi-automatic; 22 LR; 15-shot tubular magazine; 20-inch barrel; 39-1/2-inch overall length; weighs 6-1/4 lbs.; fully-adjustable open rear sight, beaded ramp front; checkered pistol-grip Monte Carlo American walnut stock, forearm; buttplate, pistol grip white line spacers; automatic bolt hold-open; tang safety; gold-plated, grooved trigger; Damascened bolt; receiver grooved for scope mounts; barrel band; sling swivels. Manufactured 1972 to 1973.

Exc.: $130   VGood: $100   Good: $70

MOSSBERG MODEL 350K, 350K-A

Semi-automatic; 22 high-speed Short, 22 Long, 22 LR; 7-shot clip magazine; 23-1/2-inch barrel; 43-1/2-inch overall length; weighs 6 lbs.; fully-adjustable open rear sight with U-notch, bead front; receiver grooved for scope mount; walnut Monte Carlo pistol-grip stock. Introduced 1958; discontinued 1971.

Exc.: $100   VGood: $100   Good: $80

MOSSBERG MODEL 400 PALOMINO

Lever action; 22 Short, 22 Long, 22 LR; 15-shot (22 LR), 17-shot (22 Long), 20-shot (22 Short) tube magazine; 24-inch barrel; 41-inch overall length; weighs 5-1/2 lbs.; fully-adjustable open notch rear sight, bead front; walnut Monte Carlo stock; moulded pistol-grip cap and buttplate; beavertail forearm; hammerless action; lightweight high-tensile alloy receiver; removable sideplate; grooved trigger; cross-bolt safety; blued finish; receiver grooved for scope. Introduced 1959; discontinued 1963.

Exc.: $180   **VGood:** $130   **Good:** $100

MOSSBERG MODEL 402 PALOMINO

Same specs as Model 400 except 18-1/2-inch, 20-inch barrel; 36-1/2-inch overall length; weighs 4-3/4 lbs.; barrel band on forearm, sling swivels; magazine holds two fewer rounds in 22 Long, 22 LR lengths. Manufactured 1961 to 1971.

Exc.: $190   **VGood:** $135   **VGood:** $105

MOSSBERG MODEL 472 CARBINE

Lever action; 30-30, 35 Rem.; 6-shot tubular magazine; 20-inch barrel; adjustable buckhorn rear sight, ramp front; with gold bead; barrel tapped for scope mounting; off-set hammer spur; side-ejecting; pistol-grip or straight stock; barrel band on forearm; sling swivels on pistol-grip style, removable saddle ring on straight-stock model. Manufactured 1972 to 1980.

Exc.: $350   **VGood:** $300   **Good:** $230

MOSSBERG MODEL 472 BRUSH GUN

Same specs as Model 472 Carbine except 18-inch barrel; 30-30; 5-shot magazine; straight stock. Manufactured 1974 to 1976.

Exc.: $375   **VGood:** $325   **Good:** $295

MOSSBERG MODEL 472 RIFLE

Same specs as Model 472 Carbine except 24-inch barrel; 5-shot magazine; pistol-grip stock only. Manufactured 1974 to 1976.

Exc.: $350   **VGood:** $300   **Good:** $230

MOSSBERG MODEL 472 "1 OF 5000"

Same specs as Model 472 Brush Gun except etched Native American frontier scenes on receiver; gold-plated trigger; brass saddle ring, buttplate, barrel bands; select walnut stock forearm; limited edition, numbered 1 through 5000. Manufactured 1974.

Exc.: $430   **VGood:** $255   **Good:** $200

MOSSBERG MODEL 479PC

Lever action; 30-30, 35 Rem.; 6-shot tube magazine; 20-inch barrel; 38-1/2-inch overall length; weighs 6-3/4-7 lbs.; ramp front sight, elevation-adjustable rear; American walnut stock with pistol grip and fluted comb; composition buttplate; pistol-grip cap; hammer-block safety; side ejection. Introduced 1978; discontinued 1981.

Exc.: $325   **VGood:** $300   **Good:** $250

MOSSBERG MODEL 479PCA

Same specs as Model 479PC except 30-30 only; bead on ramp front sight, adjustable open rear; walnut-finished hardwood stock; rebounding hammer; trigger built into cocking lever; blued finish. Reintroduced 1983; no longer in production.

Exc.: $325   **VGood:** $300   **Good:** $250

MOSSBERG MODEL 479RR ROY ROGERS

Same specs as Model 479PCA except 5-shot magazine; 18-inch barrel; 36-1/2-inch overall length; gold bead on ramp front sight, adjustable semi-buckhorn rear; American walnut stock; gold-finished trigger; barrel bands; Rogers' signature, American eagle, stars and stripes etched in receiver. 5000 guns produced only in 1983.

Perf.: $375   **Exc.:** $275   **VGood:** $225

MOSSBERG MODEL 479SC

Same specs as Model 479PC except straight grip stock. Introduced 1978; discontinued 1981.

Exc.: $325   **VGood:** $300   **Good:** $250

MOSSBERG MODEL 464 LEVER ACTION CENTERFIRE RIFLE

Side-loading, top-ejecting lever rifle with button-rifled 20-inch barrel, blued finish and hardwood stock. Tang-mounted thumb safety. Chambered in .30-30.

NIB.: $375   **Exc.:** $275   **VGood:** $225

MOSSBERG MODEL 464 LEVER ACTION RIMFIRE RIFLE

A .22 LR version of the above with 18-inch barrel. Not in production as of 10/08.

NIB: $295   **Exc.:** N/A   **VGood:** N/A

MOSSBERG MODEL K

Slide action; 22 Short, 22 Long, 22 LR; 14-shot (22 LR), 16-shot (22 Long), 20-shot (22 Short) tube magazine; 22-inch barrel; take-down; hammerless; open rear sight, bead front; uncheckered straight-grip walnut stock; grooved slide handle. Introduced 1922; discontinued 1931.

Exc.: $200   **VGood:** $175   **Good:** $150

MOSSBERG MODEL L

Lever action, single shot, falling block; 22 Short, 22 Long, 22 LR; 24-inch barrel; take-down; Martini-design falling-block lever-action; open rear sight, bead front; uncheckered walnut pistol-grip stock, forearm. Introduced 1929; discontinued 1932. This is a very scarce Mossberg and would be the foundation or the finishing touch to any Mossberg collection.

Exc.: $550   **VGood:** $450   **Good:** $325

MOSSBERG MODEL L-1

Same specs as Model L except target version with Lyman 2A tang sight; factory sling. Introduced about 1930; discontinued about 1931.

Exc.: $575   **VGood:** $475   **Good:** $350

MOSSBERG MODEL M

Slide action; 22 Short, 22 Long, 22 LR; 14-shot (22 LR), 16-shot (22 Long), 20-shot (22 Short) tube magazine; 24-inch octagonal barrel; take-down; hammerless; open rear sight, bead front; uncheckered pistol-grip stock; grooved slide handle. Introduced 1928; discontinued 1931.

Exc.: $200   **VGood:** $180   **Good:** $150

MOSSBERG MODEL S

Slide action; 22 Short, 22 Long, 22 LR; 19-3/4-inch barrel; similar to Model K except shorter magazine tube. Introduced 1927; dropped 1931.

Exc.: $210   **VGood:** $185   **Good:** $145

MOSSBERG/NEW HAVEN MODEL 220K

Bolt action; single shot; 22 Short, 22 Long, 22 LR; 24-inch barrel with crowned muzzle; weighs 5-3/4 lbs.; open adjustable rear sight, bead front; walnut finished Monte Carlo pistol-grip stock; hand-rubbed oil finish; automatic safety. Introduced 1961.

Exc.: $80   **VGood:** $65   **Good:** $55

MOSSBERG/NEW HAVEN MODEL 240K

Bolt action; 22 Short, 22 Long, 22 LR; 24-inch barrel with crowned muzzle; fully-adjustable open rear sight, bead front; walnut finished Monte Carlo pistol-grip stock; hammerless; takedown; grooved trigger; thumb safety. Lower-priced version of the Mossberg Model 340K. Introduced 1961.

Exc.: $90   **VGood:** $70   **Good:** $50

MOSSBERG/NEW HAVEN MODEL 246K

Bolt action; 22 Short, 22 Long, 22 LR; 25-shot (22 Short), 20-shot (22 Long), 18-shot (22 LR); 24-inch round tapered barrel with crowned muzzle; 43-1/4 overall length; weighs 6-1/4 lbs.; fully-adjustable open rear sight, sporting front; receiver grooved for scope mounts; tapped and drilled for Mossberg No. S-330 peep; hammerless; takedown; grooved trigger; thumb safety. A lower-priced version of the Mossberg Model 346K. Introduced 1961.

Exc.: $90   **VGood:** $70   **Good:** $50

MOSSBERG/NEW HAVEN MODEL 250K

Semi-automatic; 22 LR; 7-shot detachable box magazine; 24-inch round tapered barrel; 44-inch overall length; weighs 5-1/2 lbs.; open adjustable rear sight, bead front; American walnut Monte Carlo stock with tapered forend; hand-rubbed oil finish; receiver

Mossberg Model 400 Palomino

Mossberg Model 464

Mossberg Model 472 Carbine

Mossberg Model 479PC

Mossberg Model K

Mossberg Model L

Mossberg Model 702 Plinkster

Mossberg Model 817 Plinkster

Mossberg SSi-One

Mossberg Model 100 ATR

M-S Safari Arms 1000-Yard Match Model

M-S Safari Arms Silhouette Model

M-S Safari Arms Varmint Model

---

grooved for scope mounting. A lower-priced version of the Mossberg Model 350K. Introduced 1960.

Exc.: $90   **VGood:** $80   **Good:** $60

MOSSBERG/NEW HAVEN MODEL 250KB

Same specs as Model 250K except 22 Long, 22 LR; weighs 6 lbs.; Ac-Kro-Gruv rifling; fully-adjustable rear peep sight. Introduced 1961.

Exc.: $95   **VGood:** $85   **Good:** $65

MOSSBERG MODEL 702 PLINKSTER

Semi-auto chambered for .22 LR. Black synthetic stock with schnabel forend; silver-finished barrel and receiver. Ten-shot magazine. Also available as scope package (add 10 percent) and with tiger maple or carbon fiber stock and chromed barrel and receiver.

NIB: $130   **Exc.:** $110   **VGood:** $90

MOSSBERG MODEL 802 PLINKSTER BOLT ACTION

Bolt-action rifle chambered in .22 LR with 18-inch steel barrel and black synthetic stock with schnabel. Also available with 4X scope package (add 10 percent).

NIB: $130   **Exc.:** $110   **VGood:** $90

MOSSBERG 817 PLINKSTER RIFLE

Similar to Model 802 Plinkster but chambered in .17 HMR.

NIB: $130   **Exc.:** $110   **VGood:** $90

MODEL 817 VARMINT

Introduced in 2008, this offering by Mossberg International features a 21-inch free-floating blued or brushed chrome barrel, hardwood or black synthetic stock, factory Weaver mounts, detachable box magazine and .17 HMR chambering.

NIB: $235   **Exc.:** $175   **VGood:** $115

MOSSBERG SSI-ONE SINGLE SHOT RIFLE

Lever action, single shot, breakopen; 223 Rem., 22-250 Rem., 243 Win., 270 Win., 308 Rem., 30-06; 24-inch barrel; weighs 8 lbs.; 40-inch long; Satin-finished walnut stock, fluted and checkered; sling-swivel studs. no sights (scope base furnished); Frame accepts interchangeable barrels, including 12- gauge, fully rifled slug barrel and 12 ga., 3-1/2-inch chambered barrel with Ulti- Full Turkey choke tube. Lever-opening, break-action design; single-stage trigger; ambidextrous, top-tang safety; internal eject/extract selector. Introduced 2000, no longer in production.

SSi-One Sporter (standard barrel)
Perf.: $450   **Exc.:** $350   **VGood:** $250
SSi-One Varmint (bull barrel, 22-250 Rem. only.
Perf.: $475   **Exc.:** $375   **VGood:** $270

MOSSBERG MODEL 100 ATR (ALL TERRAIN RIFLE)

Bolt-action rifle chambered in .243 Win, .270 Win, .30-06, or .308 Win. 22" free-floated barrel, matte blue or Marinecote, wood, black synth, Durawood synthetic or 100 percent Mossy Oak Break Up camo coverage stock with recoil pad, three-shot

top loading magazine. Weight around 7 lbs. Also available as 3X9 scope package (add 10 percent).

NIB: $300   **Exc.:** $260   **VGood:** $190

MOSSBERG 100 ATR SUPER BANTAM

Similar to Model 100 ATR but chambered only in .243 and .308. No sights. Synthetic black stock adjustable for length of pull.

NIB: $275   **Exc.:** $230   **VGood:** $175

MOSSBERG 4X4 RIFLE

Bolt-action centerfire rifle chambered in .25-06, .270, .30-06, 7mm Rem Mag, .300 Win Mag, .338 Win Mag. Barrel length 22" (iron sight) or 24" (sightless). Detachable box magazine, two-position safety. Walnut, laminated or black synthetic stock with lightening cutouts in butt and forend. Scope package also available.

NIB: $450   **Exc.:** $395   **VGood:** $275

MOUNTAIN EAGLE MAGNUM LITE RIFLE

Bolt action; 22-250, 223 Rem. (Varmint); 280, 30-06 (long action); 7mm Rem. Mag., 300 Win. Mag., (magnum action); 24-inch, 26-inch, free floating barrel; weighs 7 lbs., 13 oz.; 44-inch overall length (24-inch barrel); Kevlar-graphite stock with aluminum bedding block, high comb, recoil pad, swivel studs; made by H-S Precision; no sights; accepts any Remington 700-type base. Special Sako action with one-piece forged bolt, hinged steel floorplate, lengthened receiver ring; adjustable trigger. Krieger cut-rifled benchrest barrel. Introduced 1996. From Magnum Research, Inc.

Perf.: $2000   **Exc.:** $1500   **VGood:** $900
Later rifles with Remington actions
Perf.: $1650   **Exc.:** $1200   **VGood:** $650

M-S SAFARI ARMS 1000-YARD MATCH MODEL

Bolt action; single shot; 28-inch heavy barrel; no sights; drilled/tapped for scope mount; sleeved stainless steel action; electronic trigger; custom-painted fully-adjustable fiberglass stock; custom-built to buyer's specs. Introduced 1982; discontinued 1985.

Exc.: $1385   **VGood:** $995   **Good:** $750

M-S SAFARI ARMS SILHOUETTE MODEL

Bolt action; single shot; 22 LR, all standard centerfires; 23-inch barrel (22 LR), 24-inch (centerfires); no sights; drilled/tapped for scope mounts; custom-painted fiberglass silhouette stock; stainless steel action; electronic trigger; custom built to buyer's specs. Introduced 1982; discontinued 1985.

Exc.: $700   **VGood:** $600   **Good:** $450

M-S SAFARI ARMS VARMINT MODEL

Bolt action; single shot; any standard centerfire chambering; 24-inch stainless steel barrel; no sights; drilled, tapped for scope mounts; custom-painted thumbhole or pistol-grip fiberglass stock; stainless steel action; electronic trigger; custom built to buyer's specs. Introduced 1983; discontinued 1985.

Exc.: $925   **VGood:** $700   **Good:** $525

MUSGRAVE PREMIER NR5

Bolt action; 243 Win., 270 Win., 30-06, 308 Win., 7mm Rem. Mag.; 5-shot magazine; 25-1/2-inch barrel; no sights; European walnut Monte Carlo stock; cheekpiece; hand-checkered pistol-grip, forearm; pistol-grip cap, forend tip; recoil pad; sling swivel studs. Introduced 1972; discontinued 1973.

Exc.: $400   **VGood:** $300   **Good:** $220

MUSGRAVE RSA SINGLE SHOT NR1

Bolt action; 308 Win.; 26-inch barrel; target aperture rear sight, tunnel front; European walnut target stock with handguard; barrel band; rubber buttplate; sling swivels. Introduced 1972; discontinued 1973.

Exc.: $450   **VGood:** $325   **Good:** $240

MUSGRAVE VALIANT NR6

Bolt action; 243 Win., 270 Win., 30-06, 308 Win., 7mm Rem. Mag; 5-shot magazine; 24-inch barrel; removable leaf rear sight, hooded ramp front; straight-comb stock; skip-line checkering; sans grip cap, forend tip. Introduced 1972; discontinued.

Exc.: $365   **VGood:** $250   **Good:** $200

NAVY ARMS 45-70 MAUSER RIFLE

Bolt action; 45-70 Government; 3-shot magazine; 24-inch, 26-inch barrel; open rear sight, ramp front; hand-checkered Monte Carlo stock; built on Siamese Mauser action. Introduced 1973; no longer in production.

Exc.: $395   **VGood:** $350   **Good:** $295

NAVY ARMS 45-70 MAUSER CARBINE

Same specs as 45-70 Mauser except 18-inch barrel; straight walnut stock.

Exc.: $375   **VGood:** $330   **Good:** $275

NAVY ARMS 1860 HENRY RIFLE

Lever action; 44-40, 45 Colt. 24-1/4-inch octagonal barrel, 1:16-inch twist; weighs 9.26 lbs.; 43-3/4-inch overall length; Walnut stock; Blade front, adjustable folding rear sights; Steel color-case hardened or brass receiver; 13- shot magazine. Introduced 2001. Imported from Uberti by Navy Arms.

Steel color-case hardened receiver

Perf.: $900   **Exc.:** $700   **VGood:** $620

Brass receiver

Perf.: $925   **Exc.:** $725   **VGood:** $655

NAVY ARMS 1860 HENRY MILITARY RIFLE

Lever action; 44-40, 44 Rem.; 13-shot magazine; 24-1/4-inch barrel; weighs 9-1/4 lbs.; blade front sight, elevation-adjustable rear; oil-stained American walnut stock; brass frame, buttplate; sling swivels; no forend; blued barrel; optional engraving. Recreation of the model used by cavalry units in the Civil War. Introduced 1985; still in production.

Perf.: $895   **Exc.:** $725   **VGood:** $600

NAVY ARMS 1860 HENRY CARBINE

Same specs as Henry except 22-inch barrel; 41-inch overall length; weighs 8-3/4 lbs.; no sling swivels. Imported from Italy by Navy Arms. Introduced 1992; no longer imported.

Perf.: $795   **Exc.:** $695   **VGood:** $595

NAVY ARMS 1860 HENRY IRON FRAME

Same specs as Henry except receiver of blued or color case-hardened steel. Made in Italy. Introduced 1991.

Perf.: $925   **Exc.:** $750   **VGood:** $650

NAVY ARMS 1860 HENRY TRAPPER MODEL

Same specs as Henry except 8-shot magazine; 16-1/2-inch barrel; weighs 7-1/2 lbs.; brass frame, buttplate; blued barrel. Made in Italy. Introduced, 1991.

Perf.: $795   **Exc.:** $675   **VGood:** $575

NAVY ARMS MODEL 1866 WINCHESTER-STYLE RIFLE

Lever action; 38 Spl., 357 Mag., 44-40, 45 Colt; full-length tube magazine; 24-inch octagon barrel; 39-1/2-inch overall length; weighs 9-1/4 lbs.; open leaf rear sight, fixed blade front; walnut straight grip stock, forearm; barrel band; polished brass frame, buttplate; other parts blued. Introduced in 1966; similar model still imported.

Perf.: $695   **Exc.:** $595   **VGood:** $495

NAVY ARMS MODEL 1866 CARBINE

Same specs as Model 1866 except 10-shot magazine; 19-inch barrel; carbine forearm, barrel band. Introduced 1967; no longer in production.

Perf.: $695   **Exc.:** $595   **VGood:** $495

NAVY ARMS MODEL 1866 TRAPPER

Same specs as Model 1866 except 22 LR; 8-shot magazine; 16-1/2-inch barrel.

Perf.: $695   **Exc.:** $595   **VGood:** $495

NAVY ARMS MODEL 1866 YELLOWBOY

Same specs as Model 1866 except 44-40; 12-shot tubular magazine; 24-inch full-octagon barrel; 42-1/2-inch overall length; weighs 8-1/2 lbs.; ladder-type adjustable rear sight; European walnut stock; brass forend tip; blued barrel, hammer, lever. Made in Italy. Introduced 1991; still imported.

Perf.: $675   **Exc.:** $525   **VGood:** $385

NAVY ARMS MODEL 1866 YELLOWBOY CARBINE

Same specs as Model 1866 Yellowboy except 10-shot magazine; 19-inch barrel. Made in Italy. Introduced 1991.

Perf.: $770   **Exc.:** $620   **VGood:** $565

NAVY ARMS 1873 SPRINGFIELD INFANTRY RIFLE

Single shot, trapdoor; 45-70; 32.5-inch barrel; weighs about 8 lbs.; walnut stock; blade front, long-range military ladder-type rear sights; blued lockplate and barrel; case-hardened breechblock; cleaning rod

Musgrave RSA Single Shot NR1

Musgrave Premier NR5

Navy Arms 45-70 Mauser Rifle

Navy Arms Henry Military Rifle

Navy Arms 1860 Henry Military Rifle

Navy Arms 1860 Henry Iron Frame

Navy Arms 1860 Henry Trapper Model

Navy Arms Model 1866

Navy Arms Model 1866 Yellowboy

Navy Arms 1873 Springfield Cavalry Carbine

Navy Arms 1873 Winchester

Navy Arms 1874 Sharps Buffalo Rifle

Navy Arms 1874 Sharps Sporting Rifle

Navy Arms 1874 Sharps Infantry Rifle

Navy Arms 1874 Sharps Sniper Rifle

Navy Arms 1885 High Wall Rifle

Navy Arms 1892 Rifle

under barrel; replica of standard military rifle used by U.S. after 1873. Imported by Navy Arms.

Perf.: $975   **Exc.:** $800   **VGood:** $600

NAVY ARMS 1873 SPRINGFIELD CAVALRY CARBINE

Single shot, trapdoor; 45-70. 22-inch barrel; weighs 7 lbs.; 40-1/2-inch overall length; Walnut stock; Blade front, military ladder rear sights; Blued lockplate and barrel; color case-hardened breechblock; saddle ring with bar. Replica of 7th Cavalry gun. Imported by Navy Arms.

Perf.: $875   **Exc.:** $700   **VGood:** $550

NAVY ARMS 1873 WINCHESTER-STYLE RIFLE

Lever action; 44-40, 45 Colt; 12-shot magazine; 24-inch barrel; 43-inch overall length; weighs 8-1/4 lbs.; blade front sight, buckhorn rear; European walnut stock and forend; color case-hardened frame, rest blued; full-octagon barrel. Imported by Navy Arms. Introduced 1991; still imported.

Perf.: $795   **Exc.:** $695   **VGood:** $550

NAVY ARMS 1873 WINCHESTER-STYLE SPORTING RIFLE

Same specs as 1873 Winchester-Style rifle except checkered pistol-grip stock; 30-inch octagonal barrel (24-inch available). Imported by Navy Arms. Introduced 1992; still imported.

Perf.: $870   **Exc.:** $775   **VGood:** $695

NAVY ARMS 1873 WINCHESTER-STYLE CARBINE

Same specs as 1873 Winchester-Style Rifle except 19-inch barrel. Imported by Navy Arms. Introduced 1991; still imported.

Perf.: $795   **Exc.:** $650   **VGood:** $500

NAVY ARMS 1874 SHARPS CAVALRY CARBINE

Falling block; single shot; 45-70; 22-inch barrel; 39-inch overall length; weighs 7-3/4 lbs.; blade front sight, military ladder-type rear; walnut stock; color case-hardened receiver and furniture. Replica of the 1874 Sharps miltary carbine. Imported by Navy Arms. Introduced 1991.

Perf.: $995   **Exc.:** $795   **VGood:** $595

NAVY ARMS 1874 SHARPS BUFFALO RIFLE

Caliber: 45-70, 45-90. 28-inch heavy octagon barrel; weighs 10 lbs., 10 oz.; 46-inch overall length; Walnut stock; checkered grip and forend; Blade front, ladder rear sights; tang sight optional. Color case-hardened receiver, blued barrel; double-set triggers.

Perf.: $1100   **Exc.:** $950   **VGood:** $765

NAVY ARMS SHARPS PLAINS RIFLE

Similar to Sharps Buffalo rifle except 45-70 only, 32-inch medium-weight barrel, weighs 9 lbs., 8 oz., and is 49-inch overall. Imported by Navy Arms.

Perf.: $1100   **Exc.:** $950   **VGood:** $765

NAVY ARMS SHARPS SPORTING RIFLE

Same as the Navy Arms Sharps Plains Rifle except has pistol grip stock. Introduced 1997. Imported by Navy Arms.

Perf.: $1050   **Exc.:** $925   **VGood:** $745

NAVY ARMS 1874 SHARPS INFANTRY RIFLE

Same specs as 1874 Sharps Calvary Carbine except 30-inch barrel; double-set triggers; weighs 8-1/2 lbs.; 46-3/4-inch overall length; three-band model. Imported by Navy Arms. Introduced 1984; still imported.

Perf.: $1100   **Exc.:** $950   **VGood:** $765

NAVY ARMS 1874 SHARPS SNIPER RIFLE

Same specs as Navy Arms 1874 Sharps Carbine except 30-inch barrel; double-set triggers; weighs 8-1/2 lbs.; 46-3/4-inch overall length. Imported by Navy Arms. Introduced 1984; still imported.

Perf.: $1200   **Exc.:** $1050   **VGood:** $865

NAVY ARMS 1885 HIGH WALL RIFLE

Single shot, falling block; 45-70; others available on special order; 28-inch round, 30-inch octagonal barrel; weighs 9.5 lbs.; 45-1/2-inch overall length (30-inch barrel)); walnut stock; blade front sight, vernier tang-mounted peep rear. Replica of Winchester's High Wall designed by Browning. Color case-hardened receiver, blued barrel. Introduced 1998. Imported by Navy Arms.

Perf.: $900   **Exc.:** $700   **VGood:** $600

NAVY ARMS 1892 RIFLE

Lever action; 357 Mag., 44-40, 45 Colt. 24-1/4-inch octagonal barrel; weighs 7 lbs.; 42-inch overall length; American walnut stock; Blade front sight, semi- buckhorn rear. Replica of Winchester's early Model 1892 with octagonal barrel, forend cap and crescent buttplate. Blued or color case- hardened receiver. Introduced 1998. Imported by Navy Arms.

Perf.: $520   **Exc.:** $425   **VGood:** $350

NAVY ARMS 1892 STAINLESS CARBINE

Similar to the 1892 Rifle except stainless steel, has 20-inch round barrel, weighs 5-3/4 lbs., and is 37-1/2-inch overall. Introduced 1998. Imported by Navy Arms.

Perf.: $530   **Exc.:** $445   **VGood:** $360

NAVY ARMS 1892 SHORT RIFLE

Similar to the 1892 Rifle except has 20-inch octagonal barrel, weighs 6-1/4 lbs., and is 37-3/4-inch overall. Replica of the rare, special order 1892 Winchester nicknamed the "Texas Special." Blued or color case-hardened receiver and furniture. Introduced 1998.

Perf.: $520   **Exc.:** $420   **VGood:** $355

NAVY ARMS 1892 STAINLESS RIFLE

Lever action; 357 Mag., 44-40, 45 Colt; 24-1/4-inch octagonal barrel; weighs 7 lbs.; 42-inch length; American walnut stock; brass bead front sight, semi-buckhorn rear; designed for the Cowboy Action shooter. Stainless steel barrel, receiver and furniture. Introduced 2000.

Perf.: $530   **Exc.:** $445   **VGood:** $360

NAVY ARMS EM-331

Bolt action; 7.62x39mm; 5-shot detachable magazine; 21-inch barrel; 42-inch overall length; weighs 7-1/2 lbs.; hooded ramp front sight, open adjustable rear; receiver dovetailed for scope rings; Monte Carlo style stock with sling swivels, rubber recoil pad, contrasting forend tip; polished blue finish. Imported by Navy Arms. Introduced 1994; discontinued 1994.

Perf.: $300   **Exc.:** $265   **VGood:** $225

NAVY ARMS MARTINI

Single shot; 444 Marlin, 45-70; 26-inch, 30-inch half or full octagon barrel; Creedmore tang peep sight, open middle sight, blade front; checkered pistol-grip stock; schnabel forend; cheekpiece. Introduced 1972; discontinued 1984.

Perf.: $495   **Exc.:** $420   **VGood:** $350

NAVY ARMS REVOLVING CARBINE

Carbine; 357 Mag., 44-40, 45 Colt; 6-shot cylinder; 20-inch barrel; 38-inch overall length; weighs 5 lbs.; open rear sight, blade front; straight-grip stock; brass buttplate, triggerguard. Action based on Remington Model 1874 revolver. Manufactured in Italy. Introduced, 1968; discontinued 1984.

Perf.: $575   **Exc.:** $450   **VGood:** $360

NAVY ARMS ROLLING BLOCK BABY CARBINE

Single shot; 22 LR, 22 Hornet, 357 Mag., 44-40; 20-inch octagon barrel, 22-inch round barrel; open rear sight; blade front; uncheckered straight-grip stock forearm; case-hardened frame; brass triggerguard; brass buttplate. Introduced, 1968; discontinued 1984.

Perf.: $375   **Exc.:** $350   **VGood:** $295

NAVY ARMS ROLLING BLOCK BUFFALO RIFLE

Single shot, rolling block; 45-70; 26-inch, 30-inch half or full octagonal barrel; brass barrel band; open rear sight, blade front. Introduced 1971; still in production.

Perf.: $670   **Exc.:** $595   **VGood:** $425

NAVY ARMS ROLLING BLOCK BUFFALO CARBINE

Same specs as Rolling Block Buffalo except 18-inch barrel. Introduced 1971; discontinued 1985.

Perf.: $650   **Exc.:** $395   **VGood:** $420

NAVY ARMS ROLLING BLOCK RIFLE

Single shot, rolling block; 45-70. 26-inch, 30-inch barrel; Walnut stock; Blade front sight, adjustable rear. Reproduction of classic rolling block action. Available with full-octagon or half-octagon-half-round barrel. Color case-hardened action, steel fittings.

Perf.: $700   **Exc.:** $600   **VGood:** $500

Navy Arms 1892 Short Rifle

Navy Arms Martini

Navy Arms Revolving Carbine

Navy Arms Rolling Block Buffalo

Navy Arms "John Bodine" Rolling Block

Navy Arms Rolling Block #2 Creedmore

Navy Arms TU--33/40 Carbine

NAVY ARMS "JOHN BODINE" ROLLING BLOCK RIFLE

Single shot, rolling block; 45-70; 30-inch heavy octagonal barrel; Walnut stock; Globe front sight, Soule tang rear. Double set triggers.

Perf.: $1300   **Exc.:** $1100   **VGood:** $900

NAVY ARMS ROLLING BLOCK #2 CREEDMORE

Single shot; 45-70, 45-90; 26-inch, 28-inch, 30-inch heavy half or full octagon barrel; Creedmore tang peep sight; checkered walnut stock; color case-hardened receiver. Still in production.

Perf.: $875   **Exc.:** $695   **VGood:** $600

NAVY ARMS SHARPS NO. 3 LONG RANGE RIFLE

Single shot, falling block; 45-70, 45-90; 34-inch octagon barrel; weighs 10 lbs., 12 oz.; 51-1/2-inch length; Deluxe walnut stock; Globe target front and match grade rear tang sights; Shotgun buttplate, German silver forend cap, color case hardenend receiver.

Perf.: $1700   **Exc.:** $1300   **VGood:** $950

NAVY ARMS SHARPS PLAINS RIFLE

Single shot; falling block; 45-70; 28-1/2-inch barrel; 45-3/4-inch overall length; weighs 8 lbs., 10 oz.; blade front sight, open windage-adjustable rear; checkered walnut butt and forend; color case-hardened action, rest blued. Imported by Navy Arms. Introduced 1991; no longer imported.

Perf.: $795   **Exc.:** $625   **VGood:** $520

NAVY ARMS TU-33/40 CARBINE

Bolt action; 7.62x39mm; 4-shot magazine; 20-3/4-inch barrel; 38-inch overall length; weighs 6-1/2 lbs.; hooded barleycorn front sight, military V-notch adjustable rear; miniature Mauser-style action; hardwood stock; comes with leather sling. Based on Mauser G.33/40 carbine. Imported by Navy Arms. Introduced 1992; discontinued 1994.

Exc.: $250   **VGood:** $225   **Good:** $175

Navy Arms TU-KKW
Sniper Trainer

New England Firearms
Handi-Rifle

New England Firearms
Super Light

New England Firearms
Sportster Single-Shot Rifle

New England Firearms
Survivor Rifle

Noble Model 10

Noble Model 20

lightweight synthetic stock and forend. No sights furnished on 223 and 243 versions, but have factory-mounted scope base and offset hammer spur; Monte Carlo stock; 22 Hornet has ramp front, fully adjustable open rear. Overall length 36-inch, weighs about 5.5 lbs. Introduced 1997. Made in U.S.A. by New England Firearms.

    Perf.: $175   **Exc.:** $125   **VGood:** $100

NEW ENGLAND FIREARMS SPORTSTER SINGLE-SHOT RIFLE

Single shot, breakopen; 22 LR, 22 WMR, 17 HMR, 17 Mach 2; 20-inch barrel; weighs 5-1/2 lbs.; 36-1/4-inch overall length; Black polymer stock; no sights; scope mount included; Break open, side-lever release; automatic ejection; recoil pad; sling swivel studs; trigger locking system. Introduced 2001.

    Perf.: $105   **Exc.:** $95   **VGood:** $80

Youth model. 20-inch bbl., shorter stock, 33-inch overall

    Perf.: $105   **Exc.:** $95   **VGood:** $85

17-caliber

    Perf.: $140   **Exc.:** $115   **VGood:** N/A

NEW ENGLAND FIREARMS SURVIVOR RIFLE

Single shot, breakopen; 223, 357 Mag., 308 Win., 45 Colt/410; 22-inch barrel; weighs 6 lbs.; 36-inch overall length; Black polymer stock, thumbhole design; no sights; scope mount provided. Receiver drilled and tapped for scope mounting. Stock and forend have storage compartments for ammo, etc.; comes with integral swivels and black nylon sling. Introduced 1996. Made in U.S.A. by New England Firearms.

    Perf.: $200   **Exc.:** $180   **VGood:** $150

NEWTON BUFFALO SPORTER

Bolt action; 256, 30, 35 Newton, 30-06; 5-shot box magazine; 24-inch barrel; open rear sight, ramp front; hand-checkered pistol-grip stock; reversed set-trigger; Enfield-designed bolt handle. Introduced 1922; discontinued 1924. Collector value.

    Exc.: $1700   **VGood:** $950   **Good:** $650

NEWTON-MAUSER SPORTER

Bolt action; 256 Newton; 5-shot box magazine; 24-inch barrel; open rear sight, ramp front; checkered American walnut pistol-grip stock; double-set triggers; hinged floorplate. Introduced 1914; discontinued 1915.

    Exc.: $1975   **VGood:** $1350   **VGood:** $825

NEWTON STANDARD SPORTER (TYPE I)

Bolt action; 22, 256, 280, 30, 33, 35 Newton, 30-06; 24-inch barrel; open rear sight, ramp front; hand-checkered pistol-grip stock; double-set triggers. Introduced 1916; discontinued 1918. Collector value.

    Exc.: $1680   **VGood:** $950   **Good:** $750

NEWTON STANDARD SPORTER (TYPE II)

Same specs as Sporter Type I except improved bolt-action design; 256, 30, 35 Newton, 30-06; 5-shot box magazine; reversed set-trigger; Enfield-design bolt handle. Collector value. Introduced 1921; discontinued 1922.

    Exc.: $1650   **VGood:** $950   **Good:** $670

NOBLE MODEL 10

Bolt action; single shot; 22 Short, 22 Long, 22 LR; 24-inch barrel; open rear sight, bead front; uncheckered hardwood pistol-grip stock. Introduced 1955; discontinued 1958.

    Exc.: $95   **VGood:** $80   **Good:** $50

NOBLE MODEL 20

Bolt action; single shot; 22 Short, 22 Long, 22 LR; 22-inch barrel; weighs 5 lbs.; open rear sight, bead front; uncheckered walnut pistol-grip stock. Introduced 1958; discontinued 1963.

    Exc.: $95   **VGood:** $80   **Good:** $50

NAVY ARMS TU-KKW SNIPER TRAINER

Bolt action; 7.62x39mm; 4-shot magazine; 20-3/4-inch barrel; 38-inch overall length; weighs 7-3/8 lbs.; hooded barleycorn front sight, military V-notch adjustable rear; Type 89 2-3/4x scope with quick detachable mount system; hardwood stock; miniature Mauser-style action; comes with leather sling; cleaning rod. Based on Mauser G.33/40 carbine. Imported by Navy Arms. Introduced 1992; discontinued 1994.

    Exc.: $250   **VGood:** $225   **Good:** $175

NEW ENGLAND FIREARMS HANDI-RIFLE

Break-open; single shot; 204 Ruger, 22 Hornet, 223, 22-250, 243, 25-06, 270, 280, 30-30, 44 Mag., 45-70; 22-inch barrel; weighs 7 lbs.; ramp front sight, folding rear; drilled, tapped for scope mounts; walnut-finished hardwood stock; break-open action; side-lever release; blued finish or stainless steel. Introduced 1989; still in production.

    Perf.: $200   **Exc.:** $170   **VGood:** $140

NEW ENGLAND FIREARMS SUPER LIGHT RIFLE

Similar to Handi-Rifle except different barrel taper, shorter 20-inch barrel with recessed muzzle, special

NOBLE MODEL 33
Slide action; 22 Short, 22 Long, 22 LR; 21-shot (22 Short), 17-shot (22 Long), 15-shot (22 LR) tube magazine; 24-inch barrel; 41-3/4-inch overall length; weighs 6 lbs.; hammerless; open rear sight, bead front; Tenite stock; grooved wood slide handle. Introduced 1949; discontinued 1953.

Exc.: $185   VGood: $145   Good: $95

NOBLE MODEL 33A
Same specs as Model 33 except hardwood stock and slide handle. Introduced 1953, as replacement for Model 33; discontinued 1955.

Exc.: $175   VGood: $135   Good: $85

NOBLE MODEL 222
Bolt action; single shot; 22 Short, 22 Long, 22 LR; 22-inch barrel; 38-inch overall length; weighs 5 lbs.; barrel, receiver milled as integral unit; interchangeable peep and V-notch rear sight, ramp front; scope mounting base; uncheckered hardwood pistol-grip stock. Introduced 1958; discontinued 1971.

Exc.: $95   VGood: $80   Good: $50

NOBLE MODEL 235
Slide-action; 22 Short, 22 Long, 22 LR; 21-shot (22 Short), 17-shot (22 Long), 15-shot (22 LR) tube magazine; 24-inch barrel; hammerless; open rear sight, ramp front; hardwood pistol-grip stock; grooved wood slide handle. Introduced 1951; discontinued 1973.

Exc.: $185   VGood: $150   Good: $135

NOBLE MODEL 275
Lever action; 22 Short, 22 Long, 22 LR; 21-shot (22 Short), 17-shot (22 Long), 15-shot (22 LR) tube magazine; 24-inch barrel; 42-inch overall length; weighs 5-1/2 lbs.; hammerless; open rear sight, ramp front; receiver grooved for tip-off scope mount; uncheckered one-piece hardwood full pistol-grip stock. Introduced 1958; discontinued 1971. Funny, dopey little rifle.

Exc.: $165   VGood: $135   Good: $95

NOBLE MODEL 285
Semi-automatic; 22 LR; 15-shot tube magazine; 22-inch barrel; 40-inch overall length; weighs 5-1/2 lbs.; ramp front sight, adjustable open rear; top thumb safety; receiver grooved for tip-off mount; walnut finished pistol-grip stock.

Exc.: $150   VGood: $125   Good: $95

NORINCO MAK 90
Semi-automatic, AK-47 type action; 7.62x39, 223; 5-shot magazine; 16-1/4-inch barrel; 35-1/2-inch overall length; weighs 8 lbs.; adjustable post front sight, open adjustable rear; walnut-finished thumbhole stock with recoil pad; chrome-lined barrel; forged receiver; black oxide finish. Comes with extra magazine, oil bottle, cleaning kit, sling. Imported from China by Century International Arms. No longer imported. Add 25 percent for milled receiver side panels. NOTE: Add 10% for MAK-91 heavy-barrel National Match.

Perf.: $650   Exc.: $550   VGood: $450

NORINCO MODEL ATD
Semi-automatic; 22 LR; modeled after Browning 22 rifle; 11-shot magazine; 19-3/8-inch barrel; 36 5/8-inch overall length; weighs 4-3/8 lbs.; blade front sight, open adjustable rear; checkered hardwood stock; Browning-type take-down action; tube magazine loads through buttplate; cross-bolt safety; blued finish; engraved receiver. Made in China. Introduced 1987; no longer imported.

Perf.: $170   Exc.: $140   VGood: $120

NORINCO MODEL EM-321
Slide action; 22 LR; 9-shot tubular magazine; 19-1/2-inch barrel; 37-inch overall length; weighs 6 lbs.; blade front sight, open folding rear; hardwood stock; blue finish; grooved slide handle. Imported from China by China Sports, Inc. No longer imported.

Perf.: $135   Exc.: $100   VGood: $80

NORINCO MODEL JW-14
Semi-automatic; 22 LR; 10-shot magazine, 20-inch barrel, 40-inch OAL, post front sight with ears, Mauser-style military rear sight to 200M; walnut-finished hardwood stock. Imported from China by Interstate Arms Corp. No longer imported.

Perf.: $100   Exc.: $80   VGood: $70

NORINCO MODEL JW-15
Bolt action; 22 LR; 5-shot detachable magazine; 24-inch barrel; 41-3/4-inch overall length; weighs 5-3/4 lbs.; hooded blade front sight, windage-adjustable open rear; walnut-stained hardwood stock; sling swivels; wing-type safety. Made in China. No longer imported.

Perf.: $90   Exc.: $80   VGood: $70

NORINCO MODEL JW-27
Bolt action; 22 LR; 5-shot magazine; 22-3/4-inch barrel; 41-3/4-inch overall length; weighs 5-3/4 lbs.; dovetailed bead on blade front sight, fully-adjustable rear; receiver grooved for scope mounting; walnut-finished hardwood stock with checkered grip and forend; blued finish. Imported from China by Century International Arms. Introduced 1992; no longer imported.

Perf.: $85   Exc.: $75   VGood: $65

NORINCO TYPE EM-332
Bolt action; 22 LR; 5-shot magazine; 18-1/2-inch barrel; 41-1/2-inch overall length; weighs 4-1/2 lbs.; blade front sight on ramp, open adjustable rear; hardwood stock; magazine holder on right side of butt for two extra magazines; blue finish. Imported from China by China Sports, Inc. Introduced 1990; no longer imported.

Perf.: $140   Exc.: $100   VGood: $80

NORRAHAMMAR MODEL N-900
Bolt action; 243 Win., 270 Win., 308 Win., 30-06; 20-1/4-inch barrel; hooded front sight, adjustable rear; hand-checkered European walnut pistol-grip stock, forearm; single-stage trigger; ebony grip cap; buttplate; side safety; hinged floorplate; sling swivels. Made in Sweden. Introduced 1957; discontinued 1967.

Exc.: $325   VGood: $270   Good: $210

NOSLER CUSTOM MODEL 48 SPORTER
Bolt-action centerfire rifle chambered in .270 Winchester Short Magnum. 24" barrel, round top

Noble Model 222

Noble Model 235

Norinco Model ATD

Norinco Model EM-321

Norinco Model JW-27

Norrahammar Model N-900

Nosler Custom Model 48 Sporter

Modern Collectible Firearms: What's Hot (and What Might Be)

Chances are, when most people think of collectible firearms, they think of guns that most of us can only dream about: First Generation Colt Single Action Armys, Winchester Model 1886s, Smith & Wesson Triple Locks, and other top-tier collectibles.

Yet part of the fun of gun collecting is trying to identify those modern makes and models that will someday become top-tier collectibles themselves. On the following pages you'll find guns that are obtainable on today's market and show signs of becoming tomorrow's hot collectibles. All have demonstrated sustained demand; some have been discontinued in the recent past; others are still in production and have attracted a nearly cult-like following. Still others might well be rendered collectible by future legislation.

The bottom line: If you find any of these guns at a reasonable price, considering giving them a new home. Chances are you won't be sorry!

Above: The semi-auto M72 RPK by Century International Arms is a close copy of the Soviet RPK light machinegun.

Above: Century International Arms' version of the Soviet Dragunov sniper rifle garnered good reviews and is already becoming a bit scarce.

Right: In 2006, Auto Ordnance (now owned by Kahr Arms) introduced its TA5 pistol, a modified reintroduction of its original Model 1927 A5 pistol, which was discontinued in 1994 after only around 3,300 had been produced. The TA5 accepts stick mags and 10-, 50- and 100-round drums.

Left: A Yugoslavian-licensed copy of the German MG 42, Century International Arms' belt-fed M53 semi-auto in 8mm Mauser is a big hit with WWII buffs.

Above: *Nylon 76 (MB) "Trailrider," the only lever action repeater Remington ever produced. Note the extremely short lever throw.*

Top: *Nylon 76 (MB) "Trailrider": Lever action, .22 LR only, 14-rd. tubular magazine. Blued metal parts, Mohawk brown stock with white trim. Approximately 25,300 produced from 1962-1964.*

Bottom: *Nylon 76 (not catalogued): Lever action, .22 LR only, 14-rd. tubular magazine. Blued metal parts, black stock with white trim. Production numbers for this model do not exist.*

Remington's "Nylon 66" line of .22 rifles (1959-1989) have become very hot collectibles among "older kids" who remember when they were the latest and greatest. In fact, some models – especially the black-and-chrome Apache Black models – frequently sell in the $1000+ price range! We hope you enjoy these samples from the Jim Stark collection.

Nylon 66 (BD) "Black Diamond." Semi-auto, .22 LR only, 14-rd. tubular magazine. Blued metal parts with a black stock having black diamonds on the balance of trim in white. Approximately 56,000 produced from 1962-1983.

Above: BC GR-8 "Black Beauty" receiver cover stamped with manufacturer's and importer's identification as required by BATF.

— — — — — — MADE IN BRAZIL BY CBC — — — — — —
IMPORTED BY CENTURY ARMS—ST. ALBANS, V.T.

Left: Brazilian import, manufactured by CBC (Cia Brazileire Cartouchos, Santo Andre, Brazil, SA). This "nylon" rifle is an almost identical copy of the Remington Nylon 66. It was sometimes marketed as the model GR-8 "Black Beauty." Internal parts are not interchangeable. It was imported by several different companies.

REMINGTON

NYLON

Top: Nylon "Apache 77": Manufactured exclusively for K-Mart from 1987-1989. Metal parts are coated with a matte black sprayed-on finish; the stock is a swirled green, orange and black. It is fed through a 10-rd. box magazine made of plastic; magazines are marked "77." Not to be confused with the 66 (SG) Seneca green or the 77 (MB) Mohawk.

Bottom: Nylon 66 (AB) "Apache Black": Semi-auto, .22 LR only, 14-rd. tubular magazine. Chrome plated metal parts, black stock with white trim. Approximately 220,000 produced from 1962-1983.

Below: Nylon 66 (AB) "Apache Black" lifetime warranty sticker. The conventional wisdom is that all factory replacement stickers were lost or destroyed.

THIS TOUGH RIFLE STOCK has a full **LIFETIME WARRANTY** Made of tough DuPont structural nylon, this stock is so much stronger and more durable than one made of wood that we guarantee it will not warp, crack, chip, fade or peel for the life of the rifle or we will replace it free. The gun should be sent Collect to ARMS SERVICE DIVISION, REMINGTON ARMS COMPANY, INC., ILION, NEW YORK 13357. This Warranty gives you specific legal rights and you may also have other rights which may vary from state to state. This warranty does not cover stock damage caused intentionally or by unreasonable use. **Remington** ® DUPONT Remington Arms Company, Inc. and Remington Arms of Canada, Ltd. and Remington GmbH

Above: Nylon 12s in 19-5/8" and 24" barrel lengths. Note tubular magazine feed ports.

Right: Nylon 12: Bolt action, 22 S, L, or LR ammunition fed through a tube under the barrel, silver spoon-shaped bolt handle. Blued metal parts, Mohawk brown stock with white trim. Shown with 24" barrel. Production numbers for this barrel length are not available.

Left: Nylon 12: Bolt action, 22 S,L, or LR ammunition fed through a tube under the barrel, silver spoon-shaped bolt handle. Blued metal parts, Mohawk brown stock with white trim. Shown with 19-5/8" barrel. Also available in 24" barrel configuration. Approximately 27,600 produced from 1962-1964.

REMINGTON
NYLON

Above: Gold-filled, embossed receiver cover of Nylon 66 (AN) "150th Anniversary."

Left: Nylon 66 (AN): "150th Anniversary" commemorative edition. Blued metal parts, Mohawk brown stock with white trim, 22 LR only. Distinguished by the 150th Anniversary stamping on the left side of the receiver cover. Approximately 4000 produced in 1966 only.

Right: Nylon 66 (BI): "Bicentennial" commemorative edition. Blued metal parts, Mohawk brown stock with white trim, .22 LR ONLY. Distinguished by the Eagle and "1776/1976" stamping on the left side of the receiver cover. Approximately 10,000 produced in 1976 only.

Below: Gold-filled, embossed receiver cover of Nylon 66 (BI) "Bicentennial."

Packaging and box label for the Nylon Mohawk 10 C.

Packaging and box label for the Nylon 11.

When it was discontinued in 1998, the Browning Auto-5 was without a doubt the most beloved semi-auto shotgun of all time. Today, virtually all A-5s have become collectible, with certain models – the Belgian Magnums and Sweet Sixteens among them – being particularly hot. Even the Japanese A-5s, long considered the red-haired stepchildren of the A-5 family, have achieved respectability (as they should). Here we see the grandest Auto-5 of all, the 1998 limited-edition Final Tribute.

The Winchester Model 1894 is said to be the best-selling American rifle of all time, with well over 7,000,000 units sold between 1893 and 2006, when it was discontinued. Of course, pre-1964 Model 94s (the name changed from "Model "1894" to "Model 94" around 1927) have been collectible since 1964. However, when the Model 94 was finally discontinued, values for all Model 94s rose tremendously. The following pages illustrate some of the later Model 94s that are still encountered fairly often – and some not so often. The .410 shotgun model and limited-edition rifles are particularly coveted.

Model 94 Ranger.

Model 94 Trail's End.

Model 94 Trapper.

Model 94 Legacy.

Below: *M94 Heritage 1 of 1000 receiver detail.*

Model 94 Heritage 1 of 100 Custom Edition.

Model 94 Heritage 1 of 1000 Custom Edition.

Model 9410 2-1/2" .410 shotgun.

Model 9422 Traditional .22 rifle.

Model 9422 Legacy .22 rifle.

Model 9410 Packer 2-1/2" .410 shotgun.

Right: M94 Heritage 1 of 100 receiver detail.

GRIP CAPS

Each of the Remington Nylon rifles is simple to identify. The model number is on the grip cap. The Brazilian "Black Beauty" grip cap is unmarked.

Nylon 76

Nylon 66

Brazilian "Black Beauty"

Nylon 77

Nylon Apache 77

Nylon Mohawk 10 C

Shooters who had only dreamed about owning Teddy Roosevelt's "Lion Medicine" were thrilled in 2002 when Winchester reintroduced its Model 1895 rifle chambered in the mighty .405 Winchester cartridge, which for most of the 20th century was the most powerful lever-action cartridge available. The modern Model 1895 was offered in two grades, and as of this writing is still available as a Limited Edition Theodore Roosevelt commemorative. Oddly, the Grade I .405, rather than the High Grade, seems to be preferred by many collectors.

Left: *Winchester Model 1895 High Grade in .405 Winchester.*

Right: *Winchester Model 1895 Grade I in .405 Winchester.*

In 2006, Smith & Wesson introduced its blued, nickeled or casehardened "Classic" series of revolvers, modeled after many of the post-war Hand Ejectors that enjoy such popularity among collectors. The modern "Classics" vary from the originals in some ways (e.g., keyed safeties and different manufacturing techniques) but they certainly capture their spirit. Among the most collectible of the modern "Classics" are the N-frames, a few of which are shown below. (Other modern S&W "Classics" include various J- and K-frames.)

Right: *S&W Classic Model 25 in .45 Colt.*

Right: *S&W Classic Model 24 in .44 Special.*

Right: *S&W Classic Model 29 in .44 Magnum.*

Right: *S&W Classic Model 27 in .357 Magnum.*

STI International of Georgetown, Texas, began in the 1980s when gunsmith Virgil Tripp began building competition 1911-style pistols. In the years since, STI has expanded its line and, in the process, has built a reputation second to none, with its "carry" models being regarded as absolutely top-shelf. It's safe to say that STI pistols will continued to be well-regarded by 1911 collectors and enthusiasts for the foreseeable future.

Above Right: *STI Escort, a chopped and channeled 1911 chambered in .45 ACP and 9mm Parabellum.*

Left: *STI's LS 1911 is one of the "skinniest" 1911 pistols ever made, measuring only .765" across the slide and 1.065" across the grip panels. It's chambered in 9mm Parabellum.*

Above Left: *STI's Rogue is built on the company's LS frame, but the frame is made of aluminum alloy for an overall weight of only 21 oz.*

Right: *With its 3" barrel and "Officer"-sized frame, STI's OffDuty is a compact handful chambered in .45 ACP and 9mm Parabellum.*

One of Hollywood's favorite movie guns, the Desert Eagle chambered in .50 AE has appeared in more than 30 films, including Harley Davidson and the Marlboro Man, RoboCop, RoboCop2, RoboCop3, Escape from LA, Alien vs. Predator and Get Smart. Available in a variety of eye-catching finishes, the Desert Eagle .50 is collectible if for no other reason than it's the most powerful production semi-auto pistol ever built.

NS Firearms Model 522

Olympic Arms CAR-97

Olympic Arms International Match

receiver, onyx gray composite stock. Introduced 2007. Price includes scope.

NIB: $2200   **Exc.:** $N/A   **VGood:** $N/A

NS FIREARMS MODEL 522

Bolt action; 22 LR; 5-shot magazine; 21-inch barrel; 39-1/2-inch overall length; weighs 7-3/4 lbs.; no sights; receiver grooved for scope mount; walnut stock with cut-checkered grip and forend; satin finish; free-floated hammer-forged heavy barrel; forged receiver and bolt with two locking lugs, dual extractors; safety locks bolt and trigger. Imported by Keng's Firearms Specialty. Introduced 1993; discontinued 1994.

Exc.: $170   **VGood:** $220   **VGood:** $95

OLYMPIC ARMS AR-15 MATCH

Semi-automatic; 223; 20- or 30-shot magazine; 20-inch stainless steel barrel; 39-1/2-inch overall length; weighs 8-3/4 lbs.; post front sight, fully-adjustable aperture rear; cut-off carrying handle with scope rail attached; button-rifled 4140 ordnance steel or stainless barrel with 1:9-inch twist standard, 1:7, 1:12, 1:14 twists optional; weighs 8-1/2 lbs. Made in U.S. by Olympic Arms, Inc. Introduced 1993; discontinued 1994.

Perf.: $695   **Exc.:** $595   **VGood:** $495

OLYMPIC ARMS CAR-97 RIFLES

Semi-automatic; 223, 7-shot; 9mm Para., 45 ACP, 40 S&W, 10mm, 10-shot; 16-inch barrel; weighs 7 lbs.; 34.75-inch overall length; A2 stowaway grip stock, telescoping-look butt; post front sight, fully adjustable aperature rear. Based on AR-15 rifle. Post-ban version of the CAR-15. Made in U.S.A. by Olympic Arms, Inc.

Perf.: $800   **Exc.:** $650   **VGood:** $550

OLYMPIC ARMS INTERCONTINENTAL MATCH

Semi-automatic; 223; 5-shot magazine; 20-inch stainless steel barrel; 39-1/2-inch overall length; weighs about 10 lbs.; no sights; cut-off carrying handle with scope rail attached; synthetic woodgrain thumbhole buttstock; broach-cut, free-floated barrel with 1:10 or 1:8.5 twist; magazine well floorplate; fluting optional. Made in U.S. by Olympic Arms, Inc. Introduced 1992; discontinued 1994.

Perf.: $1595   **Exc.:** $1195   **VGood:** $950

OLYMPIC ARMS INTERNATIONAL MATCH

Semi-automatic; 223; 20- or 30-shot magazine; 20-inch or 24-inch stainless steel barrel; 39-1/2-inch overall length (20-inch barrel); weighs 10 lbs.;

standard AR-15-type post front sight, adjustable target peep rear; cut-off carrying handle with scope rail attached; black composition A2 stow-away butt and grip; broach-cut, free-floating barrel with 1:10 or 1:8.5 twist; fluting optional. Based on the AR-15 rifle. Made in U.S. by Olympic Arms, Inc. Introduced 1985; no longer made.

Perf.: $1395   **Exc.:** $995   **VGood:** $825

OLYMPIC ARMS UM-1P

Premium-grade gas-operated .223 semi-auto target rifle based on AR-15 chassis. Features include 24-inch stainless steel bull barrel, anodized finish, pistol grip with bottom swell, Picatinny rail, Harris bipod, and competition trigger.

NIB: $1600   **Exc.:** N/A   **VGood:** N/A

OLYMPIC ARMS UM-1

Plain-jane variant of UM-1P but with 20-inch stainless steel bull barrel, standard pistol grip, no bipod.

NIB: $1100   **Exc.:** N/A   **VGood:** N/A

OLYMPIC ARMS SM-1P

Tricked-out AR-15 in .223 with 20-inch stainless steel barrel, free-floating sleeve handguard, carry handle upper or Picatinny rail flattop, pneumatic recoil buffer, Bob Jones interchangeable sight system, competition trigger, and Maxhard receivers.

NIB: $1600   **Exc.:** N/A   **VGood:** N/A

OLYMPIC ARMS SM-1

Plain-jane variant of SM-1P but with standard receivers, trigger and sights. No pneumatic recoil buffer.

NIB: $1100   **Exc.:** N/A   **VGood:** N/A

OLYMPIC ARMS ML-1

Similar to SM-1 but with 16-inch barrel with flash hider, 6-position collapsible buttstock and free-floating aluminum tube handguard.

NIB: $950   **Exc.:** N/A   **VGood:** N/A

OLYMPIC ARMS ML-2

Similar to ML-1 but with flat-top upper receiver with Picatinny rails, standard buttstock and bull barrel.

NIB: $950   **Exc.:** N/A   **VGood:** N/A

OLYMPIC ARMS MODEL K8

Similar to ML-2 but with 20-inch barrel and extended aluminum tube handguard.

NIB: $850   **Exc.:** N/A   **VGood:** N/A

OLYMPIC ARMS MODEL K8-MAG

Similar to K8 but with 24-inch bull barrel and chambered in .223 WSM, .243 WSM or .25 WSM.

NIB: $1100   **Exc.:** N/A   **VGood:** N/A

OLYMPIC ARMS K3B

Features include 16-inch chrome-moly barrel with flash-hidefully adjustable rear sight, 6-position collapsible buttstock and carbine-length handguard.

NIB: $775   **Exc.:** N/A   **VGood:** N/A

OLYMPIC ARMS K3B-M4

Similar to K3B but with M4S fiberite handguard with heatshield and 32.25-inch overall length.

NIB: $835   **Exc.:** N/A   **VGood:** N/A

OLYMPIC ARMS K3B-CAR

Similar to K3B but with 30.5-inch overall length.

NIB: $810   **Exc.:** N/A   **VGood:** N/A

OLYMPIC ARMS K3B-FAR

Similar to K3B but with featherweight barrel and weight of 5.84 lbs.

NIB: $825   **Exc.:** N/A   **VGood:** N/A

OLYMPIC ARMS K4B

Similar to K3B but with 20-inch barrel and rifle-length fiberite handguard.

NIB: $800   **Exc.:** N/A   **VGood:** N/A

OLYMPIC ARMS K4B-A4

Similar to K4B but with ventilated FIRSH rifle-length handguard.

NIB: $905   **Exc.:** N/A   **VGood:** N/A

OLYMPIC ARMS LTF

Features include 16-inch chrome-molybdenum barrel, free-floating FIRSH handguard with Picatinny rails, ACE FX skeleton stock, ERGO pistol grip and multiple-aperture flipup sight system.

NIB: $1225   **Exc.:** N/A   **VGood:** N/A

OLYMPIC ARMS LT-M4

Similar to LTF but with 16-inch stainless steel barrel.
NIB: $1150 Exc.: N/A   VGood: N/A

OLYMPIC ARMS K16

Similar to K8 but with 16-inch bull chrome-moly barrel.

NIB: $725   **Exc.:** N/A   **VGood:** N/A

OLYMPIC ARMS GI-16

Basic military AR-15-inspired semi-auto rifle chambered in .223. 16-inch chrome-moly barrel with flash-hider, 6-position collapsible buttstock, carbine-length handguard and rear sight adjustable for windage only.

NIB: $650   **Exc.:** N/A   **VGood:** N/A

OLYMPIC ARMS K30

Similar to GI-16 but chambered in .30 Carbine. Includes mag well insert to accept military-spec magazines.

NIB: $900   **Exc.:** N/A   **VGood:** N/A

OLYMPIC ARMS K9/K10/K40/K45

Similar to K30 but chambered, respectively, for 9mm Parabellum, 10mm, .40 S&W and .45ACP. Models use converted surplus military magazines.

NIB: $800   **Exc.:** N/A   **VGood:** N/A

OLYMPIC ARMS K9-GL/K40-GL

Similar to K9 and K40 but accept standard Glock pistol magazines.

NIB: $925   **Exc.:** N/A   **VGood:** N/A

OLYMPIC ARMS PLINKER PLUS

Similar to GI-16 but with standard buttstock.

NIB: $650   **Exc.:** N/A   **VGood:** N/A

OLYMPIC ARMS PLINKER PLUS 20

Similar to Plinker Plus but with 20-inch barrel and rifle-length handguard.

NIB: $575   **Exc.:** N/A   **VGood:** N/A

OLYMPIC ARMS K7 ELIMINATOR

Similar to K4 but with 16-inch barrel with extended handguard and sight radius of 20-inch-barreled models.

NIB: $845   **Exc.:** N/A   **VGood:** N/A

OLYMPIC ARMS K-4 AR-15

Semi-automatic; 223; 30-shot magazine; 20-inch barrel; 39-inch overall length; weighs about 8 lbs.; post elevation-adjustable front sight, peep-style windage-adjustable rear; E-2-style sight system optionally available; full-length M-16-style black composition stock; heavy match-grade barrel; trapdoor in buttstock; A-2 stow-away pistol grip. Made in U.S. by Olympic Arms, Inc. Introduced 1975; no longer produced.

Perf.: $795   **Exc.:** $695   **VGood:** $595

OLYMPIC ARMS MULTIMATCH

Semi-automatic; 223; 30-shot magazine; 16-inch free-floating, broach-cut, stainless steel barrel with 1:10-inch or 1:8-1/2-inch twist; 36-inch overall length; weighs 7-1/2 lbs.; E2 fully adjustable or International Match upper receiver for scope mounting; telescoping stock or collapsible aluminum buttstock; cut-off carrying handle with scope rail attached (ML2); based on the AR-15 rifle. Made in U.S. by Olympic Arms, Inc. Introduced 1991; still produced.

Perf.: $715   **Exc.:** $650   **VGood:** $600

OLYMPIC ARMS PCR-1

Semi-automatic; 223; 10-shot magazine; 20-inch barrel of 416 stainless steel; 38-1/4-inch overall length; weighs about 10 lbs.; no sights; flat-top upper receiver, cut-down front sight base; black composition A2 stowaway grip and trapdoor butt; broach-cut, free-floating barrel with 1:8.5 or 1:10 twist; no bayonet lug; crowned barrel; fluting available. Based on the AR-15 rifle. Made in U.S. by Olympic Arms, Inc. Introduced 1994; discontinued 1995. Reintroduced.

Perf.: $1095   **Exc.:** $950   **VGood:** $800

OLYMPIC ARMS PCR-2

Same specs as PCR-1 except 16-inch barrel; weighs about 8 lbs.; post front sight, fully-adjustable aperture rear. Made in U.S. by Olympic Arms, Inc. Introduced 1994; discontinued 1995. Reintroduced.

Perf.: $925   **Exc.:** $825   **VGood:** $650

OLYMPIC ARMS PCR-3

Same specs as PCR-1 except 16-inch barrel; flat-top upper receiver, cut-down front sight base. Made in U.S. by Olympic Arms, Inc. Introduced 1994; dropped 1995. Reintroduced.

Perf.: $975   **Exc.:** $825   **VGood:** $650

OLYMPIC ARMS PCR-4

Same specs as PCR-1 except 16-inch barrel, weighs 8-1/2 lbs.; post front sight, A1 windage-adjustable rear; button-rifled 1:7, 1:9, 1:12 or 1:14 twist barrel. Made in U.S. by Olympic Arms, Inc. Introduced 1994; discontinued 1995. Reintroduced.

Perf.: $750   **Exc.:** $575   **VGood:** $470

OLYMPIC ARMS PCR-5

Same specs as PCR-1 except 9mm Para., 40 S&W, 45 ACP, 223; 16-inch barrel; 34-3/4-inch overall length; weighs 7 lbs.; post front sight, A1 windage-adjustable rear. Based on the CAR-15. Made in U.S. by Olympic Arms, Inc. Introduced 1994; discontinued 1995, reintroduced; still produced as K-series pistol-caliber carbines.

Perf.: $700   **Exc.:** $550   **VGood:** $425

OLYMPIC ARMS PCR-6

Same specs as PCR-1 except 7.62x39mm; 16-inch barrel; 34-3/4-inch overall length; weighs 7 lbs.; post front sight, A1 windage-adjustable rear. Based on the CAR-15. Made in U.S. by Olympic Arms, Inc. Introduced 1994; discontinued 1995. Reintroduced, then discontinued again.

Perf.: $865   **Exc.:** $700   **VGood:** $565

OLYMPIC ARMS PCR-9

Same specs as PCR-5 except 9mm Para; 16-inch barrel; 34-inch overall length (stock extended); weighs 7 lbs.; post elevation-adjustable front sight, windage-adjustable rear; telescoping buttstock. Made in U.S. by Olympic Arms, Inc. Introduced 1982; still produced as K3B-9.

Perf.: $795   **Exc.:** $695   **VGood:** $550

OLYMPIC ARMS PCR-10

Same specs as PCR-5 except 16-inch barrel; 34-inch overall length (stock extended); weighs 7 lbs.; post elevation-adjustable front sight, windage-adjustable rear; telescoping buttstock. Based on the AR-15 rifle. Made in U.S. by Olympic Arms, Inc. Introduced 1982.

Perf.: $1095   **Exc.:** $995   **VGood:** $895

OLYMPIC ARMS PCR-40

Same specs as PCR-1 except 40 S&W; 16-inch barrel; 34-inch overall length (stock extended); weighs 7 lbs.; post elevation-adjustable front sight, windage-adjustable rear; telescoping buttstock. Made in U.S. by Olympic Arms, Inc. Introduced 1982; still made as K3B-40.

Perf.: $995   **Exc.:** $895   **VGood:** $795

OLYMPIC ARMS PCR-45

Same specs as PCR-1 except 45 ACP; 16-inch barrel; 34-inch overall length (stock extended); weighs 7 lbs.; post elevation-adjustable front sight, windage-adjustable rear; telescoping buttstock. Made in U.S. by Olympic Arms, Inc. Introduced 1982; still made as K3B-45.

Perf.: $995   **Exc.:** $895   **VGood:** $795

OLYMPIC ARMS SERVICE MATCH

Semi-automatic; 223; 20-, 30-shot magazine; 20-inch stainless steel barrel; 39-1/2-inch overall length; weighs 8-3/4 lbs.; post front sight, fully-adjustable aperture rear; black composition A2 standard stock; barrel broach-cut and free-floating with 1:10 or 1:8.5 twist; fluting optional. Based on the AR-15 rifle. Conforms to all DCM standards. Made in U.S. by Olympic Arms, Inc. Introduced 1989; reintroduced as PCR-SM.

Perf.: $900   **Exc.:** $800   **VGood:** $700

OLYMPIC ARMS ULTRAMATCH

Semi-automatic; 223; 20-, 30-shot magazine; 20-inch or 24-inch stainless steel barrel; 39-1/2-inch overall length (20-inch barrel); weighs about 10 lbs.; no sights; cut-off carrying handle with scope rail attached; black composition A2 stowaway butt and grip; broach-cut, free-floating barrel with 1:10 or 1:8.5 twist; fluting optional. Based on the AR-15 rifle. Made in U.S. by Olympic Arms, Inc. Introduced 1985; discontinued 2002.

Perf.: $1550   **Exc.:** $1250   **VGood:** $925

Olympic Arms Multimatch

Olympic Arms PCR-1

Olympic Arms PCR-2

Olympic Arms PCR-5

Olympic Arms Service Match

Olympic Arms Ultramatch

Omega III

Parker-Hale Model 81 Classic

Parker-Hale Model 81 Classic African

Parker-Hale Model 85 Sniper

Parker-Hale Model 87 Target

Parker-Hale Model 1000

Parker-Hale Model 1100 Lightweight

Parker-Hale Model 1100M African Magnum

PARKER-HALE MODEL 81 CLASSIC AFRICAN

Same specs as Model 81 Classic except 375 H&H, 9.3x62; African express rear sight; adjustable trigger; barrel band front swivel; engraved receiver; classic-style stock with solid buttpad; checkered pistol grip and forend. Introduced 1986; no longer produced.

Exc.: $1200   **VGood:** $970   **Good:** $625

PARKER-HALE MODEL 85 SNIPER RIFLE

Bolt action; 308 Win.; 10-shot magazine; 24-1/4-inch barrel; 45-inch overall length; weighs 12-1/2 lbs. (with scope); post front windage-adjustable sight, fold-down elevation-adjustable rear; McMillan fiberglass stock with several color patterns available; quick-detachable bipod; palm stop with rail; sling swivels; matte finish. No longer made.

Exc.: $2695   **VGood:** $2350   **Good:** $1200

PARKER-HALE MODEL 87 TARGET

Bolt action; 308 Win., 243, 6.5x55, 308, 30-06, 300 Win. Mag. (other calibers on request); 5-shot detachable box magazine; 26-inch heavy barrel; 45-inch overall length; weighs about 10 lbs.; no sights; walnut target-style stock adjustable for length of pull; solid buttpad; accessory rail with hand-stop; deeply stippled grip and forend; receiver dovetailed for Parker-Hale "Roll-Off" scope mounts; Mauser-style action with large bolt knob; Parkerized finish. Made by Gibbs Rifle Co. Introduced 1987; no longer made.

Exc.: $1200   **VGood:** $950   **Good:** $750

PARKER-HALE MODEL 1000

Bolt action; 22-250, 243, 6mm, 270, 6.5x55, 7x57, 7x64, 308, 30-06, 7mm Rem. Mag.; 4-shot magazine; 22-inch barrel, 24-inch (22-250); 42-1/2-inch overall length; weighs 7-1/4 lbs.; no sights; drilled and tapped for scope mounting; walnut Monte Carlo stock with checkered palm swell pistol grip and forend; rosewood grip cap; Mauser-style action; one-piece steel Oberndorf-style trigger guard with hinged floorplate. Introduced 1992; no longer made.

Exc.: $395   **VGood:** $340   **Good:** $300

PARKER-HALE MODEL 1000 CLIP

Same specs as Model 1000 except detachable box magazine. Introduced 1992; no longer made.

Exc.: $395   **VGood:** $340   **Good:** $300

PARKER-HALE MODEL 1100 LIGHTWEIGHT

Bolt action; 22-250, 243, 6mm Rem., 270, 6.5x55, 7x57, 7x64, 308, 30-06, 7mm Rem. Mag.; 4-shot magazine; 24-inch barrel; 44-1/2-inch overall length; weighs 7-3/4 lbs.; no sights; drilled, tapped for open sights or scope mounting; classic-style European walnut stock with hand-cut checkering; palm swell; rosewood grip cap; Mauser-style action; Oberndort-style triggerguard; buttpad; sling swivels. Imported from England by Precision Sports. Introduced 1984; no longer imported.

Exc.: $450   **VGood:** $350   **Good:** $300

PARKER-HALE MODEL 1100M AFRICAN

Same specs as Model 1100 except 375 H&H Mag., 458 Win. Mag; 46-inch overall length; weighs 9-1/2 lbs.; hooded post front sight; V-notch rear; heavily reinforced, glass-beaded, weighted stock; vent recoil pad. Introduced 1984; no longer imported.

Exc.: $625   **VGood:** $490   **Good:** $400

PARKER-HALE MODEL 1200 SUPER

Bolt action; 22-250, 243, 6mm, 270, 6.5x55, 7x57, 7x64, 308, 30-06, 300 Win. Mag., 7mm Rem. Mag.; 22-inch barrel; 43-inch overall length; weighs about 7 lbs.; Mauser-type action with twin locking lugs; hinged floorplate; adjustable single stage trigger; silent side safety; hooded post front, flip-up rear sight; European walnut stock; cut-checkered pistol grip and forend; sling swivels. Introduced 1984; no longer produced.

Exc.: $525   **VGood:** $450   **Good:** $375

OMEGA III

Bolt action; 25-06, 270, 30-06, 7mm Rem. Mag., 300 Win. Mag., 338 Win. Mag., 358 Norma Mag.; 4-shot (belted), 5-shot (standard) rotary magazine; 22-inch, 24-inch barrel; no sights; choice of Monte Carlo, Classic or thumbhole varminter; Claro walnut English laminated or laminated walnut/maple; right- or left-hand action; octagonal bolt; square locking system, enclosed bolt face; fully-adjustable trigger. Introduced 1973; discontinued 1976.

Exc.: $695   **VGood:** $550   **Good:** $425

PARKER-HALE MODEL 81 CLASSIC

Bolt action; 22-250, 243, 6mm Rem., 270, 6.5x55, 7x57, 7x64, 308, 30-06, 300 Win. Mag., 7mm Rem. Mag.; 4-shot magazine; 24-inch barrel; 44-1/2-inch overall length; weighs 7-3/4 lbs.; Mauser-style action; one-piece steel Oberndorf-style triggerguard with hinged floorplate; drilled and tapped for open sights and scope mounting; scope bases included; rubber buttpad; quick-detachable sling swivels. Introduced 1985; no longer produced.

Exc.: $750   **VGood:** $600   **Good:** $485

PARKER-HALE MODEL 1200P PRESENTATION

Same specs as Model 1200 Super except 243, 30-06; no sights; engraved action, floorplate, triggerguard; detachable sling swivels. Introduced 1969; discontinued 1975.

Exc.: $495   **VGood:** $450   **Good:** $395

PARKER-HALE MODEL 1200V VARMINTER

Same specs as Model 1200 Super except 22-250, 6mm Rem., 25-06, 243; 24-inch barrel; no sights. Introduced 1969; discontinued 1983.

Exc.: $510   **VGood:** $450   **Good:** $380

PARKER-HALE MODEL 1300C SCOUT

Bolt action; 243, 308; 10-shot magazine; 20-inch barrel; 41-inch overall length; weighs 8-1/2 lbs.; no sights; drilled and tapped for scope mounting; checkered laminated birch stock; detachable magazine; muzzle brake; polished blue finish. Introduced 1992; no longer made.

Exc.: $650   **VGood:** $540   **Good:** $400

PARKER-HALE MODEL 2100 MIDLAND

Bolt action; 22-250, 243, 6mm, 270, 6.5x55, 7x57, 7x64, 308, 30-06; 22-inch barrel; 43-inch overall length; weighs about 7 lbs.; hooded post front, flip-up open rear; Mauser-type action has twin front locking lugs; rear safety lug, claw extractor; hinged floorplate; adjustable single stage trigger; silent slide safety. Imported from England by Precision Sports, Inc. Introduced 1984; discontinued 1989.

Exc.: $300   **VGood:** $250   **Good:** $200

PARKER-HALE MODEL 2600 MIDLAND

Bolt action; 22-250, 243, 6mm, 270, 6.5x55, 7x57, 7x64, 308, 30-06, 300 Win. Mag., 7mm Rem. Mag.; 22-inch barrel; 43-inch overall length; weighs about 7 lbs.; hooded post front sight, flip-up open rear; European hardwood stock with cut-checkered pistol grip and forend; sling swivels; Mauser-type action with twin front locking lugs, rear safety lug, and claw extractor; hinged floorplate; adjustable single-stage trigger; silent side safety. Introduced 1984; no longer produced.

Exc.: $295   **VGood:** $250   **Good:** $220

PARKER-HALE MODEL 2700 LIGHTWEIGHT MIDLAND

Bolt action; 22-250, 243, 6mm, 270, 6.5x55, 7x57, 7x64, 308, 30-06, 7mm Rem. Mag.; 22-inch light barrel; 43-inch overall length; weighs about 6-1/2 lbs.; hooded post front sight, flip-up open rear; receiver drilled and tapped for scope mounting; lightweight European walnut stock with checkered pistol grip and forend; sling swivels. Introduced 1992; no longer made.

Exc.: $350   **VGood:** $300   **Good:** $240

PARKER-HALE MODEL 2800 MIDLAND

Bolt action; 22-250, 243, 6mm, 270, 6.5x55, 7x57, 7x64, 308, 30-06, 300 Win. Mag., 7mm Rem. Mag.; 22-inch barrel; 43-inch overall length; weighs about 7 lbs.; hooded post front sight, flip-up open rear; laminated birch Monte Carlo stock with cut-checkered pistol grip and forend; sling swivels; Mauser-type action with twin front locking lugs, rear safety lug, and claw extractor; hinged floorplate; adjustable single-stage trigger; silent side safety. No longer produced.

Exc.: $325   **VGood:** $275   **Good:** $230

PEDERSEN MODEL 3000

Bolt action; 270, 30-06, 7mm Rem. Mag., 338 Win. Mag.; 3-shot magazine; 22-inch barrel (270, 30-06); 24-inch (magnums); no sights; drilled, tapped for scope mount; American walnut stock, roll-over cheekpiece; hand-checkered pistol-grip, forearm; Mossberg Model 800 action; adjustable trigger; sling swivels. Grades differ in amount of engraving and quality of stock wood. Introduced 1972; discontinued

Parker-Hale Model 1200 Super

Parker-Hale Model 2100 Midland

Pedersen Model 3000

Perugini-Visini Boxlock Express

Perugini-Visini Sidelock Express

1975. Pedersen was a upper-shelf Mossberg name brand.

Grade I		
Exc.: $950	**VGood:** $750	**Good:** $550
Grade II		
Exc.: $650	**VGood:** $550	**Good:** $450
Grade III		
Exc.: $550	**VGood:** $450	**Good:** $385

PEDERSEN MODEL 3500

Bolt action; 270 Win., 30-06, 7mm Rem. Mag.; 22-inch barrel (standard calibers), 24-inch (7mm Mag.); 3-shot magazine; drilled, tapped for scope mounts; hand-checkered black walnut stock, forearm; rosewood pistol-grip cap, forearm tip; hinged steel floorplate; Damascened bolt; adjustable trigger. Introduced 1973; discontinued 1975.

Exc.: $550   **VGood:** $480   **Good:** $420

PEDERSEN MODEL 4700

Lever action; 30-30, 35 Rem.; 5-shot tubular magazine; 24-inch barrel; open rear sight, hooded ramp front; black walnut stock beavertail forearm; Mossberg Model 472 action; barrel band swivels. Introduced 1975; discontinued 1975.

Exc.: $360   **VGood:** $330   **Good:** $290

PERUGINI-VISINI BOXLOCK EXPRESS

Double rifle; side-by-side; 9.3x74R, 444 Marlin; 25-inch barrel; 41-1/2-inch overall length; bead on ramp front sight, express rear on rib; oil-finished European walnut stock; hand-checkered pistol grip, forend; cheekpiece; non-ejector action; double triggers; color case-hardened receiver; rubber recoil pad; marketed in trunk-type case. Made in Italy. Introduced 1983; discontinued 1989.

Perf.: $2995   **Exc.:** $2675   **VGood:** $1900

PERUGINI-VISINI BOXLOCK MAGNUM

Double rifle; over/under; 7mm Rem. Mag., 7x65R, 9.3x74R, 270 Win., 338 Win. Mag., 375 H&H Mag., 458 Win. Mag.; 24-inch barrels; 40-1/2-inch overall length; bead on ramp front sight, express rear on rib; oil-finished European walnut stock; cheekpiece; hand-checkered pistol grip, forend; ejectors; silvered receiver, other metal parts blued; marketed in trunk-type case. Made in Italy. Introduced 1983; discontinued 1989.

Perf.: $5495   **Exc.:** $4895   **VGood:** $3695

PERUGINI-VISINI EAGLE

Single shot; boxlock; 17 Rem., 222, 22-250, 243, 270, 30-06, 7mm Rem. Mag., 300 Win. Mag., 5.6x50R, 5.6x57R, 6.5x68R, 7x57R, 9.3x74R, 10.3x60R; 24-inch, 26-inch barrel; no sights; claw-type scope mounts; oil-finished European walnut stock; adjustable set trigger ejector; engraved, case-hardened receiver. Made in Italy. Introduced 1986; discontinued 1989.

Perf.: $4995   **Exc.:** $4250   **VGood:** $2995

PERUGINI-VISINI MODEL SELOUS

Double rifle; 30-06, 7mm Rem. Mag., 7x65R, 9.3x74R, 270 Win., 338 Win., 375 H&H, 458 Win. Mag., 470 Nitro; 22-inch-26-inch barrels; 41-inch overall length (24-inch barrels); weighs 7-1/4 to 10-1/2 lbs.; bead on ramp front sight, express rear on quarter-rib; oil-finished walnut stock with checkered grip and forend, cheekpiece; true sidelock action with ejectors; sideplates hand detachable; comes with leather trunk case. Imported from Italy by Wm. Larkin Moore. Introduced 1983; discontinued 1992.

Perf.: $21,995   **Exc.:** $17,995   **VGood:** $10,975

Phillips & Rodgers
Wilderness Explorer

Plainfield M-1 Carbine

Plainfield M-1 Carbine
Deluxe Sporter

Plainfield M-1 Carbine,
Commando Model

Professional Ordnance
Carbon 15 (Type 97S)

Quality Parts/Bushmaster
V Match

PERUGINI-VISINI PROFESSIONAL

Bolt action; 222 Rem. through 458 Win. Mag.; 24-inch, 26-inch barrel; no sights; oil-finished European walnut stock; modified Mauser 98k bolt action; single or double-set triggers. Made in Italy. Introduced 1986; discontinued 1987.

Perf.: $3495   **Exc.:** $2995   **VGood:** $1995

PERUGINI-VISINI PROFESSIONAL DELUXE

Same specs as Professional except open sights; checkered oil-finished European walnut stock; knurled bolt handle. Made in Italy. Introduced 1986; discontinued 1987.

Perf.: $3495   **Exc.:** $2995   **VGood:** $1995

PERUGINI-VISINI SIDELOCK EXPRESS

Double rifle; side-by-side; various up to 470 Nitro Express; 22-inch, 26-inch barrels; bead on ramp front sight, express rear on rib; oil-finished walnut stock;

hand-checkered grip, forend; cheekpiece; ejectors; hand-detachable side plates; marketed in trunk-type case. Made in Italy. Introduced 1983; discontinued 1989.

Perf.: $10,000   **Exc.:** $7995   **VGood:** $6495

PERUGINI-VISINI VICTORIA

Double rifle; 30-06, 7x65R, 9.3x74R, 375 H&H, 458 Win. Mag., 470 Nitro; 22-inch-26-inch barrels; 41-inch overall length (24-inch barrels); weighs 7-1/4 to 10-1/2 lbs.; bead on ramp front sight, express rear on quarter-rib; oil-finished walnut stock with checkered grip and forend, cheekpiece; true sidelock action with automatic ejectors; sideplates hand detachable; double triggers; comes with leather trunk case. Imported from Italy by Wm. Larkin Moore. Introduced 1983; discontinued 1992.

Perf.: $10500   **Exc.:** $5490   **VGood:** $3700

PHILLIPS & RODGERS WILDERNESS EXPLORER

Bolt action; 22 Hornet, 218 Bee, 44 Mag, 50 AE (interchangeable barrels). 18-inch barrel; weighs

5.5 lbs.; 38-1/2-inch OAL; quick-change bolt faces and barrels allow using four different cartridges. Introduced 1997, discontinued 1997. Few made.

Perf.: $900   **Exc.:** $700   **VGood:** N/A

PLAINFIELD M-1 CARBINE

Semi-automatic; 5.7mm, 30 Carbine, 256 Ferret; 15-shot magazine; 18-inch barrel; weighs 5-1/2 lbs.; open sights; military-style wood stock; early models with standard military fittings, some from surplus parts; later models with ventilated metal hand guard, no bayonet lug. Introduced 1960; discontinued 1976.

30 Carbine		
Exc.: $325	**VGood:** $275	**Good:** $200
256 Ferret		
Perf.: $400	**Exc.:** $375	**VGood:** $315

PLAINFIELD M-1 CARBINE, COMMANDO OR PARATROOPER MODEL

Same specs as M-1 Carbine except telescoping wire stock; pistol-grips front and rear.

Exc.: $400   **VGood:** $365   **Good:** $250

PLAINFIELD M-1 CARBINE, DELUXE SPORTER

Same specs as M-1 Carbine except Monte Carlo sporting stock. Introduced 1960; discontinued 1973.

Exc.: $325   **VGood:** $275   **Good:** $200

PLAINFIELD M-1 CARBINE, MILITARY SPORTER

Same specs as M-1 Carbine except unslotted buttstock; wood handguard.

Exc.: $325   **VGood:** $275   **Good:** $200

PROFESSIONAL ORDNANCE CARBON 15 (TYPE 97)

Semi-automatic; 223; 16-inch barrel, weighs 3.9 lbs., 35-inch OAL; carbon fiber buttstock and forearm, with rubberized pistol grip; no sights, base for optics. Carbon fiber upper and lower carriers; QD compensator. Made in US by Professional Ordnance.

Perf.: $1000   **Exc.:** $800   **VGood:** $600

PROFESSIONAL ORDNANCE CARBON 15 TYPE 97S (INSULATED FOREND, OTHER IMPROVEMENTS)

Perf.: $1200   **Exc.:** $900   **VGood:** $700

PURDEY BIG GAME SPORTER

Bolt action; 7x57, 300 H&H Mag., 375 H&H Mag., 404 Jeffery, 10.75x73; 3-shot magazine; 24-inch barrel; Mauser-design; folding leaf rear sight, hooded ramp front; hand-checkered European walnut pistol-grip stock. Introduced post World War I; not imported.

Exc.: $6995   **VGood:** $5695   **Good:** $4295

PURDEY DOUBLE RIFLE

Double rifle; sidelock; 300 H&H Mag., 375 H&H Mag., 375 Flanged Nitro Express, 500-465 Nitro Express, 470 Nitro Express, 577 Nitro Express, 600 Nitro Express; 25-1/2-inch barrel; hammerless; folding leaf rear sight, hooded ramp front; hand-checkered European cheekpiece stock; ejectors; sling swivels; recoil pad. Introduced prior to World War I; not imported. Prices range from $25,000 to $85,000.

QUALITY PARTS/ BUSHMASTER V MATCH

Semi-automatic; 223; 10-shot magazine; 20-inch, 24-inch, 26-inch barrel with 1:9-inch twist; 38-1/4-inch overall length (20-inch barrel); weighs 8-1/4 lbs.; .950-inch barrel diameter with counter-bored crown, integral flash suppressor; no sights; comes with scope mount base installed; black composition stock; hand-built match gun with E2 lower receiver, push-pin-style takedown; upper receiver with brass deflector; free-floating steel handguard accepts laser sight, flashlight, bipod. Made in U.S. by Quality Parts Co./Bushmaster Firearms Co.

Perf.: $920   **Exc.:** $800   **VGood:** $695

QUALITY PARTS/ BUSHMASTER XM-15 E-2 SHORTY CARBINE

Semi-automatic; 223; 10-shot magazine; 16-inch barrel; 34-1/2-inch overall length; weighs 7-1/4 lbs.; adjustable post front sight, adjustable aperture rear; fixed black composition stock; chrome-lined barrel with manganese phosphate finish; "Shorty" handguards; E-2 lower receiver with push-pin takedown. Patterned after Colt M-16A2.

Perf.: $900 **Exc.: $750** **VGood: $600**

QUALITY PARTS/BUSHMASTER XM-15 E-2 DISSIPATOR

Same specs as Shorty XM-15 E-2 Carbine except "Dissipator" handguard and fixed stock, longer sight radius.

Perf.: $900 **Exc.: $750** **VGood: $600**

QUALITY PARTS/BUSHMASTER XM-15 E2 TARGET

Same specs as XM-15 Carbine except 20-inch, 24-inch, 26-inch heavy barrel with 1:7-inch or 1:9-inch twist; 38-inch overall length (20-inch barrel); weighs 8-3/8 lbs.

Perf.: $900 **Exc.: $750** **VGood: $600**

RAHN DEER SERIES

Bolt action; 25-06, 308, 270; 24-inch barrel; open adjustable rear sight, bead front; drilled, tapped for scope mounts; Circassian walnut stock with rosewood forend, grip caps or Monte Carlo-style with semi-schnabel forend; hand-checkered; one-piece triggerguard; hinged, engraved floorplate; rubber recoil pad; 22 rimfire conversion insert available. Introduced 1986; discontinued 1993.

Perf.: $695 **Exc.: $595** **VGood: $495**

RAHN ELK SERIES

Same specs as Rahn Deer Series except 6x56, 30-06, 7mm Rem. Mag.; elk head engraved on floorplate. Introduced 1986; discontinued 1993.

Perf.: $695 **Exc.: $595** **VGood: $495**

RAHN HIMALAYAN SERIES

Same specs as Deer Series except 5.6x57, 6.5x68S; short stock of walnut or fiberglass; yak engraved on floorplate with scroll border. Introduced 1986; discontinued 1993.

Perf.: $725 **Exc.: $625** **VGood: $525**

RAHN SAFARI SERIES

Same specs as Deer Series except 308 Norma Mag., 300 Win. Mag., 8x68S, 9x64; choice of Cape buffalo, rhino, elephant engraving; gold oval nameplate with three initials. Introduced 1986; discontinued 1993.

Perf.: $795 **Exc.: $695** **VGood: $595**

RANGER ARMS STANDARD MODEL

Bolt action; various from 22-250 through 458 Win. Mag.; various barrel lengths, contour to order; no sights; drilled, tapped for scope mounting; hand-checkered roll-over cheekpiece, thumbhole, Mannlicher stock in variety of woods; rosewood pistol-grip cap, forend tip; recoil pad; push-button safety; adjustable trigger; left- or right-hand models. Introduced 1969; discontinued 1974.

Exc.: $600 **VGood: $550** **Good: $350**

RANGER ARMS TEXAS MAGNUM

Bolt action; 270 Win., 30-06, 7mm Rem. Mag., 300 Win. Mag., 338 Win. Mag., 358 Norma Mag.; 24-inch, 25-inch barrel; no sights; drilled, tapped for scope mounts; hand-checkered American walnut or Claro stock; hand-rubbed to high polish, epoxy finish; recoil pad; swivel studs; jeweled, chromed bolt body; rosewood pistol-grip cap; forend tip. Introduced 1969; discontinued 1974.

Exc.: $650 **VGood: $575** **Good: $375**

RANGER ARMS TEXAS MAVERICK

Bolt action; 22-250, 243, 6mm Rem., 308 Win., 6.5mm, 350 Rem. Mag.; 22-inch, 24-inch round

Quality Parts/Bushmaster
XM-15 E-2 Shorty Carbine

Quality Parts/Bushmaster
XM-15 E-2 Dissipator

Quality Parts/Bushmaster
XM-15 E-2 Target

Rahn Elk Series

Raptor Bolt-Action Rifle

tapered barrels; no sights; drilled, tapped for scope mounts; Monte Carlo stock of English or Claro walnut; skip-line checkering; cheekpiece; rosewood pistol-grip cap, forend tip; recoil pad; adjustable trigger; push-button safety; right- and left-hand models. Introduced 1969; discontinued 1974.

Exc.: $700 **VGood: $625** **Good: $400**

With thumbhole stock

Exc.: $550 **VGood: $470** **Good: $400**

With full-length stock

Exc.: $575 **VGood: $475** **Good: $410**

RAPTOR BOLT-ACTION RIFLE

Bolt action; 270, 30-06, 243, 25-06, 308; 4-shot magazine; 22-inch barrel; weighs 7 lbs., 6 oz.; 42.5-inch overall length; Black synthetic stock, fiberglass reinforced; checkered grip and forend; vented recoil pad; Monte Carlo cheekpiece; drilled and tapped for scope mounts. Rust-resistant "Taloncote" treated barreled action; pillar bedded; stainless bolt with three locking lugs; adjustable trigger. Introduced 1997. Made in U.S.A. by Raptor Arms Co.

Perf.: $450 **Exc.: $395** **VGood: $275**

RED WILLOW ARMORY BALLARD NO. 1-1/2 HUNTING RIFLE

Single shot; dropping block; 32-40 Win., 38-55, 40-65 Win., 40-70 Ballard, 40-85 Ballard, 45-70; other calibers on special order; 30-inch medium-heavy tapered round barrel; weighs 9 lbs.; blade front sight, buckhorn rear; oil-finished American walnut stock with crescent butt, schnabel forend; exact recreation of the Ballard No. 1-1/2; single trigger; under-barrel wiping rod; drilled and tapped for tang sight; ring lever; mid- and long-range tang sights; Swiss tube

with bead or Lyman globe front sight; fancy wood, double-set triggers optionally available. Made in U.S. by Red Willow Tool & Armory, Inc. Introduced 1992; discontinued 1993.

Perf.: $1400 **Exc.: $1200** **VGood: $1000**

RED WILLOW ARMORY BALLARD NO. 4-1/2 TARGET RIFLE

Single shot; dropping block; 32-40 Win., 38-55, 40-65 Win., 40-85, 45-70; 30-inch part-round, part-octagon medium-heavy barrel; weighs 10 to 11-1/2 lbs.; Swiss bead front sight, buckhorn rear; oil-finished American walnut stock with pistol grip; checkered steel shotgun-style buttplate; double-set triggers; under-barrel wiping rod; drilled and tapped for tang sight; full loop lever. Made in U.S. by Red Willow Tool & Armory, Inc. Introduced 1992; discontinued 1993.

Perf.: $2400 **Exc.: $2200** **VGood: $2000**

RED WILLOW ARMORY BALLARD NO. 5 PACIFIC

Single shot; dropping block; 32-40 Win., 38-55, 40-65 Win., 40-70 Ballard, 40-85 Ballard, 45-70; other calibers on special order; 30-inch tapered octagon barrel; weighs 10 to 11-1/2 lbs.; blade front sight, buckhorn rear; oil-finished American walnut stock with crescent butt, schnabel forend; exact recreation of the Ballard No. 5 Pacific; double-set triggers; under-barrel wiping rod; drilled and tapped for tang sight; ring lever; mid- and long-range sights, fancy wood, single trigger optionally available. Made in U.S. by Red Willow Tool & Armory, Inc. Introduced 1992; discontinued 1993.

Perf.: $1950 **Exc.: $1700** **VGood: $1400**

Remington Model Four

Remington Model 8A

Remington Model 74 Sportsman

Remington Model 81A Woodsmaster

Remington Model 16

Remington Model 550A

Remington Model 552A Speedmaster

RED WILLOW ARMORY BALLARD NO. 8 UNION HILL

Single shot; dropping block; 32-40 Win., 38-55, 40-65 Win., 40-70 Ballard, 40-85 Ballard, 45-70; other calibers on special order; 30-inch part round-part octagon barrel; weighs 10 lbs.; Swiss tube sight with bead front, drilled and tapped for tang sight; oil-finished American walnut stock with cheek rest, pistol grip, nickeled off-hand-style buttplate; exact recreation of the original model, with double-set triggers; mid- and long range tang sights, Lyman globe front fancy wood, single trigger, buckhorn rear sight optionally available. Made in U.S. by Red Willow Tool & Armory, Inc. Introduced 1992; discontinued 1993.

Perf.: $2600   Exc.: $2400   VGood: $2000

RED WILLOW ARMORY BALLARD NO. 8 UNION HILL DELUXE RIFLE

Same specs as Ballard No. 8 Union Hill except mid-range tang sight; fancy wood and checkering. Made in U.S. by Red Willow Tool & Armory, Inc. Introduced 1992; discontinued 1993.

Perf.: $3200   Exc.: $2800   VGood: $2500

REMINGTON MODEL FOUR

Semi-automatic; 243 Win., 6mm Rem., 270, 7mm Express Rem., 280 Rem., 308 Win., 30-06; 4-shot clip magazine; 22-inch round tapered barrel; 42-inch overall length; weighs 7-1/2 lbs.; gold bead ramp front sight, windage-adjustable sliding ramp rear; checkered American walnut Monte Carlo pistol-grip stock; cartridge head inset on receiver bottom denotes caliber; positive cross-bolt safety; tapped for scope

mount. Redesign of Model 742. Introduced 1981; discontinued 1988.

	Exc.: $350	VGood: $325	Good: $295
D Peerless Grade			
	Perf.: $1995	Exc.: $1695	VGood: $995
F Premier Grade			
	Perf.: $4195	Exc.: $3795	VGood: $2695
F Premier Gold Grade			
	Perf.: $6495	Exc.: $4995	VGood: $3995

REMINGTON MODEL FOUR COLLECTORS EDITION

Same specs as Model Four except 30-06; etched receiver; 24K gold inlays; all metal parts with high-luster finish. Only 1500 made in 1982.

Perf.: $1000   Exc.: $795   VGood: $595

REMINGTON MODEL 8, 8A

Semi-automatic; 25, 30, 32, 35 Rem.; 5-shot fixed box magazine; 22-inch barrel; bead front sight, open rear; plain walnut straight stock forearm. Introduced 1906; discontinued 1936.

Exc.: $525   VGood: $370   Good: $250

REMINGTON MODEL 81, 81A WOODSMASTER

Semi-automatic; 30, 32, 35 Rem., 300 Savage; 5-shot non-detachable box magazine; 22-inch barrel; 41-1/2-inch overall length; weighs 8 lbs.; white metal bead front sight, step-adjustable rear; takedown; hammerless; solid breech; uncheckered American walnut pistol-grip stock, forearm; shotgun-style buttplate. Introduced 1936 to replace Model 8; discontinued 1950.

Exc.: $625   VGood: $450   Good: $275

REMINGTON MODEL 74 SPORTSMAN

Semi-automatic; 30-06; 4-shot magazine; 22-inch barrel; weighs 7-1/2 lbs.; open adjustable sights; walnut-finished hardwood stock, forend; cartridge head inset on receiver bottom denotes caliber; positive cross-bolt safety; tapped for scope mounts. Introduced 1984; discontinued 1987.

Exc.: $300   VGood: $260   Good: $210

REMINGTON MODEL 16, 16A

Semi-automatic; 22 LR; tube magazine in buttstock; 22-inch barrel; takedown; bead front sight, open rear; uncheckered straight walnut stock. Introduced 1914; discontinued 1928.

Exc.: $385   VGood: $340   Good: $225

REMINGTON MODEL 24, 24A

Semi-automatic; 22 Short, 22 LR; 15-shot (22 Short), 10-shot (22 LR) tube magazine in buttstock; 21-inch barrel; takedown; bead front sight, open rear; uncheckered walnut stock, forearm. Introduced 1922; discontinued 1935.

Exc.: $380   VGood: $295   Good: $250

REMINGTON MODEL 241A SPEEDMASTER

Semi-automatic; 22 Short, 22 LR; 15-shot (22 Short), 10-shot (22 LR) tube magazine; 24-inch barrel; 41-1/2-inch overall length; weighs 6 lbs.; takedown; white metal bead front sight, step-adjustable sporting rear; uncheckered walnut stock, semi-beavertail forearm, shotgun-style checkered buttplate. Introduced 1935; discontinued 1951.

Exc.: $475   VGood: $375   Good: $260

REMINGTON MODEL 522 VIPER

Semi-automatic; 22 LR; 10-shot magazine; 20-inch barrel; 40-inch overall length; weighs 4-5/8 lbs.; bead on ramp front sight, fully-adjustable open rear; integral grooved rail on receiver for scope mounting; black synthetic stock with positive checkering; beavertail forend; synthetic receiver; magazine safety; cocking indicator; manual and last-shot hold-open; trigger mechanism with primary and secondary sears; integral ejection port shield. Made in U.S. by Remington. Introduced 1993; discontinued 1997.

Perf.: $150   Exc.: $125   VGood: $100

REMINGTON MODEL 550A

Semi-automatic; 22 Short, 22 Long, 22 LR; 22-shot (22 Short), 17-shot (22 Long), 15-shot (22 LR) tube magazine; 24-inch barrel; 43-1/2-inch overall length; weighs 6-1/4 lbs.; white metal bead front sight, step-adjustable rear; uncheckered American walnut one-piece pistol-grip stock; semi-beavertail forend; thumb safety; shotgun-style Bakelite checkered buttplate. Introduced 1941; discontinued 1971.

Exc.: $250   VGood: $160   Good: $140

REMINGTON MODEL 550GS

Same specs as Model 550A except 22-inch barrel; fired shell deflector; screw eye for counter chain; originally listed as Gallery Special.

Exc.: $295   VGood: $195   Good: $150

REMINGTON MODEL 550P

Same specs as Model 550A except Patridge-type ramp blade front sight on ramp, peep-type rear.

Exc.: $200   VGood: $180   Good: $155

REMINGTON MODEL 552A SPEEDMASTER

Semi-automatic; 22 Short, 22 Long, 22 LR; 20-shot (22 Short), 17-shot (22 Long), 15-shot (22 LR); 23-inch, 25-inch barrel; 42-inch overall length; weighs 5-1/2 lbs.; white metal bead front sight, step-adjustable rear; uncheckered walnut-finished hardwood half-pistol-grip stock; semi-beavertail forearm; composition checkered buttplate; cross-bolt safety. Introduced 1958, still in production.

Exc.: $295   VGood: $250   Good: $175

REMINGTON MODEL 552BDL DELUXE
Same specs as Model 552A except 21-inch barrel; 41-inch overall length; weighs 5-3/4 lbs.; Du Pont RKW-finished walnut stock; checkered forend; capped pistol-grip stock; semi-beavertail forearm. Introduced 1958; still in production.

Perf.: $325   **Exc.:** $295   **VGood:** $250

REMINGTON MODEL 552C
Same specs as Model 552A except 21-inch barrel; 41-inch overall length. Introduced 1961; discontinued 1977.

Perf.: $325   **Exc.:** $295   **VGood:** $250

REMINGTON MODEL 552GS GALLERY SPECIAL
Same specs as Model 552A except 22 Short. No longer produced.

Perf.: $355   **Exc.:** $310   **VGood:** $250

REMINGTON MODEL 552 NRA EDITION SPEEDMASTER
Similar to Model 552 BDL but with NRA logo lasered on receiver.

NIB: $455   **Exc.:** $425   **VGood:** $325

REMINGTON 597 AUTO RIFLE
Caliber: 22 LR, 10-shot box magazine; 20-inch barrel; weighs 5-1/2 lbs.; 40-inch overall length; Black synthetic stock; Matte black finish, nickel-plated bolt. Receiver is grooved and drilled and tapped for scope mounts. Introduced 1997, still offered. Made in U.S.A. by Remington.

Perf.: $150   **Exc.:** $125   **VGood:** $100

Model 597 Magnum, 22 WMR, 8-shot clip (add 35 percent for 17 HMR)

Perf.: $275   **Exc.:** $225   **VGood:** $175

Model 597 Magnum LS, laminated stock

Perf.: $350   **Exc.:** $275   **VGood:** $220

Model 597 SS, 22 LR, stainless steel, black synthetic

Perf.: $195   **Exc.:** $150   **VGood:** $110

REMINGTON MODEL 597 LSS
Similar to Model 597 but with laminated stock, stainless barrel and 3-9X scope. Dealer exclusive for 2007.

NIB: $300   **Exc.:** $275   **VGood:** $200

REMINGTON MODEL 597 SYNTHETIC SCOPE COMBO
"Package rifle" similar to Model 597 but with 3-9X scope included.

NIB: $200   **Exc.:** $175   **VGood:** $125

REMINGTON MODEL 740, 740A
Semi-automatic; 244, 280, 308 Win., 30-06; 4-shot detachable box magazine; 22-inch barrel; 42-1/2-inch overall length; weighs 7-1/2 lbs.; white metal bead ramp front sight, step-adjustable, semi-buckhorn rear; hammerless; solid frame; side ejection; uncheckered American walnut pistol-grip stock; grooved semi-beavertail forearm. Introduced 1955; discontinued 1960.

Exc.: $345   **VGood:** $285   **Good:** $235

REMINGTON MODEL 740ADL
Same specs as Model 740A except deluxe checkered walnut stock, forend; grip cap; sling swivels; standard or high comb.

Exc.: $350   **VGood:** $295   **Good:** $255

REMINGTON MODEL 740BDL
Same specs as Model 740A except select checkered highly-figured walnut stock, forend; grip cap; sling swivels; standard or high comb.

Exc.: $365   **VGood:** $320   **Good:** $270

REMINGTON MODEL 742, 742A
Semi-automatic; 6mm Rem., 243 Win., 280 Rem., 308 Win., 30-06; 4-shot box magazine; 22-inch barrel; 42-inch overall length; weighs 7-1/2 lbs.; gold bead front sight on ramp, step-adjustable rear; versions in 1960s with impressed checkering on stock, forearm; later versions, cut checkering. Introduced 1960; discontinued 1980.

Exc.: $300   **VGood:** $275   **Good:** $250

Remington Model 597 SS

Remington Model 597 Magnum LS

Remington Model 740A

Remington Model 742

Remington Model 742BDL

Remington Model 7400

Remington Model 750 Woodsmaster

Remington Model R15 VTR

Remington Model R15 VTR Carbine

REMINGTON MODEL 742ADL
Same specs as Model 742A except deluxe checkered walnut stock; engraved receiver; sling swivels; grip cap. Introduced 1960.

Exc.: $350   **VGood:** $300   **Good:** $260

REMINGTON MODEL 742BDL
Same specs as Model 742A except 308 Win., 30-06; Monte Carlo cheekpiece; black tip on forearm; basketweave checkering.

Exc.: $370   **VGood:** $320   **Good:** $280

Left-hand model

Exc.: $370   **VGood:** $320   **Good:** $290

REMINGTON MODEL 742C CARBINE
Same specs as Model 742A except 280, 308 Win., 30-06; 18-1/2-inch barrel; 38-1/2-inch overall length; weighs 6-1/2 lbs.

Exc.: $350   **VGood:** $300   **Good:** $260

REMINGTON MODEL 742CDL CARBINE
Same specs as Model 742C except checkered stock, forend; decorated receiver.

Exc.: $390   **VGood:** $325   **Good:** $290

REMINGTON MODEL 742D PEERLESS
Same specs as Model 742A except fancy wood; scroll engraving.

Exc.: $2000   **VGood:** $1600   **Good:** $1100

REMINGTON MODEL 742F PREMIER
Same specs as Model 742A except figured American walnut best-grade stock, cheekpiece; extensive engraved receiver, barrel.

Exc.: $3995   **VGood:** $3495   **Good:** $2750

REMINGTON MODEL 742F PREMIER GOLD
Same specs as Model 742A except best-grade wood; extensive engraving; gold inlays.

Exc.: $5995   **VGood:** $4995   **Good:** $3985

REMINGTON MODEL 7400
Semi-automatic; 6mm Rem., 243, 270, 280, 30-06, 308, 35 Whelen; 4-shot detachable magazine; 22-inch barrel; 42-inch overall length; weighs 7-1/2 lbs.; gold bead ramp front sight, windage-adjustable sliding ramp rear; tapped for scope mounts; impressed checkered American walnut pistol-grip stock; positive cross-bolt safety. Introduced 1981; still in production.

Perf.: $485   **Exc.:** $370   **VGood:** $310

With black synthetic stock, matte black metal, rifle or carbine

Perf.: $450   **Exc.:** $350   **VGood:** $275

REMINGTON MODEL 7400 CARBINE
Same specs as Model 7400 except 30-06 only; 18-1/2-inch barrel; weighs 7-1/4 lbs. Introduced 1988; no longer in production.

Perf.: $485   **Exc.:** $370   **VGood:** $310

Remington Model R15CS VTR Predator Carbine

Remington Model 597 TVP

Remington Model 597 Blaze Camo

Remington Model 597 Pink Camo

REMINGTON MODEL 7400D PEERLESS

Same specs as Model 7400 except fine checkered fancy walnut stock; engraving.

Perf.: $2495   **Exc.:** $1995   **VGood:** $1395

REMINGTON MODEL 7400F PREMIER

Same specs as Model 7400 except best-grade fine checkered walnut stock; extensive engraving.

Perf.: $5295   **Exc.:** $4495   **VGood:** $2695

REMINGTON MODEL 7400F PREMIER GOLD

Same specs as Model 7400 except best-grade fine checkered walnut stock; extensive engraving with gold inlays.

Perf.: $7995   **Exc.:** $6450   **VGood:** $2995

REMINGTON MODEL 7400 SPECIAL PURPOSE

Same specs as Model 7400 except 270, 30-06; non-glare finish on the American walnut stock; all exposed metal with non-reflective matte black finish; quick-detachable sling swivels; camo-pattern Cordura carrying sling. Made in U.S. by Remington. Introduced 1993; discontinued 1994.

Perf.: $430   **Exc.:** $350   **VGood:** $290

REMINGTON MODEL 750 WOODSMASTER

Wood-stocked, traditionally-styled, updated version of Model 7400 semi-auto. Reminiscent of the old M740 semi-auto. Rifle version has 22-inch barrel; carbine has 18.5-inch barrel. Introduced 2006.

NIB: $625   **Exc.:** $565   **VGood:** $400

REMINGTON MODEL 750 SYNTHETIC

Similar to Model 750 Woodsmaster but with black synthetic stock and forend. Introduced in 2007.

NIB: $675   **Exc.:** $625   **VGood:** $475

REMINGTON MODEL R15 VTR PREDATOR RIFLE

AR-style rifle chambered for .223 Remington or .204 Ruger. Supplied with one 5-shot magazine but accepts AR-style higher-cap magazines. 22-inch fluted barrel; fixed stock. Finish: Advantage MAX-12 HD overall.

Perf.: $1145   **Exc.:** $950   **VGood:** $795

REMINGTON MODEL R15 VTR PREDATOR CARBINE

Similar to above but with 18-inch barrel.

Perf.: $1145   **Exc.:** $950   **VGood:** $795

REMINGTON MODEL R15CS VTR PREDATOR CARBINE

Similar to above but with collapsible buttstock.

Perf.: $1145   **Exc.:** $950   **VGood:** $795

REMINGTON "NYLON" SERIES .22 RIFLES

These rifles are becoming increasingly collectible. Buyers should note that the Hohawk Brown rifles are the most common, followed in order by the "Apache Black" and "Seneca Green". Values shown are for Mohawk Brown. Increase given values by 100 percent for Apache Black and 175 percent for Seneca Green.

REMINGTON NYLON 10

Single-shot bolt action. Add 40% for rare 24" barrel version.,

Exc.: $600   **VGood:** $475   **Good:** $350

REMINGTON NYLON 10-C

Semi-automatic, 22 LR; succeeded and virtually identical to Nylon 77. Introduced 1971; discontinued 1978.

Exc.: $200   **VGood:** $175   **Good:** $150

REMINGTON NYLON 11

Bolt action; 22 Short, 22 Long, 22 LR; 6-, 10-shot detachable box magazines; 19 5/8-inch barrel; 38-1/2-inch overall length; weighs 4-1/2 lbs.; blade front sight, thumb-screw adjustable rear; Mohawk brown nylon stock with diamond inlay; checkered pistol grip, forearm grip cap, buttplate with white line spacers. Introduced 1962; discontinued 1964.

Exc.: $250   **VGood:** $225   **Good:** $175

REMINGTON NYLON 12

Bolt action; 22 Short, 22 Long, 22 LR; 22-shot (22 Short), 17-shot (22 Long), 15-shot (22 LR) tube magazine; 19-5/8-inch barrel; 38-1/2-inch overall length; weighs 4-1/2 lbs.; blade front sight, thumb-screw adjustable rear; Mohawk brown nylon stock with diamond inlay; checkered pistol grip, forearm grip cap, buttplate with white line spacers. Introduced 1962; discontinued 1964.

Exc.: $275   **VGood:** $250   **Good:** $195

REMINGTON NYLON 66

Semi-automatic; 22 LR; 14-shot tube magazine in buttstock; 19-1/2-inch barrel; 38-1/2-inch overall length; weighs 4 lbs.; blade front sight, fully-adjustable open rear; receiver grooved for tip-off mounts; moulded nylon stock with checkered pistol grip; white diamond forend inlay; black pistol-grip cap.Introduced 1959; discontinued 1988.

Exc.: $285   **VGood:** $225   **Good:** $175

REMINGTON NYLON 76

Lever-action; 22 LR; 14-shot tube magazine in buttstock; 19-1/2-inch barrel; weighs 4-1/2 lbs.; blade front sight, open rear; receiver grooved for tip-off mounts; moulded nylon stock with checkered pistol grip, forearm; available in two stock colors: Mohawk brown and Apache black; latter has chrome-plated receiver. Introduced 1962; discontinued 1964. Values shown are for Mohawk Brown. Add as much as 300% for Apache Black.

Exc.: $700   **VGood:** $525   **Good:** $350

REMINGTON NYLON 77

Semi-automatic; 22 LR; 5-shot detachable box magazine; 19-1/2-inch barrel; 38-1/2-inch overall length; weighs 4 lbs.; blade front sight, open rear; receiver grooved for tip-off mounts; moulded nylon stock with checkered pistol grip, forearm. Available in same colors as Nylon 66. Introduced 1970; discontinued 1971.

Exc.: $300   **VGood:** $250   **Good:** $200

REMINGTON NYLON 77 APACHE

Same specs as Nylon 77 except red-green speckled nylon stock; 10-shot detachable box magazine; made for K-Mart. Introduced 1987; discontinued 1987.

Exc.: $300   **VGood:** $250   **Good:** $200

MODEL 597 TVP (TARGET/VARMINT/PLINKER)

Ultra-funky .22 LR autoloader built on the Model 597 chassis. Features include bolt-guidance system with twin, tool-steel guide rails; laminated, skeletonized wood stock; non-glare matte finish; 10-shot metal detachable magazine; and last-shot hold-open bolt for added safety. Scope rail. Introduced in 2008.

Exc.: $530   **VGood:** $425   **Good:** $250

REMINGTON MODEL 597 YELLOW JACKET

Similar to above but with yellow and black laminated stock.

Exc.: $505   **VGood:** $415   **Good:** $235

REMINGTON MODEL 597 BLAZE CAMO

A Model 597 with synthetic stock molded in screamin' blaze orange and black.

Exc.: $250   **VGood:** $225   **Good:** $150

REMINGTON MODEL 597 PINK CAMO

Similar to above but with a pink – yes, pink – and black camo-pattern stock.

Exc.: $250   **VGood:** $225   **Good:** $150

REMINGTON BOLT-ACTION RIFLES REMINGTON MODEL 30A

Bolt action; 25, 30, 32, 35 Rem., 7mm Mauser, 30-06; 5-shot box magazine; early models with 24-inch barrel; military-type double-stage trigger; schnabel forearm tip; later versions with 22-inch barrel, checkered walnut stock forearm; uncheckered on earlier version with finger groove in forearm; pistol grip; bead front sight, open rear; modified commercial version of 1917 Enfield action. Introduced 1921; discontinued 1940.

Exc.: $695   **VGood:** $575   **Good:** $390

REMINGTON MODEL 30R CARBINE

Same specs as Model 30A except 20-inch barrel; plain stock.

Exc.: $695   **VGood:** $575   **Good:** $390

REMINGTON MODEL 30S SPORTING

Same specs as Model 30A except 25 Rem., 257 Roberts, 7mm Mauser, 30-06; 5-shot box magazine, 24-inch barrel; bead front sight, No. 48 Lyman receiver sight; long full forearm, high-comb checkered stock. Introduced 1930; discontinued 1940. Add 25 percent for 25 Remington.

Exc.: $695   **VGood:** $575   **Good:** $390

REMINGTON MODEL 33

Bolt action; single shot; 22 Short, 22 Long, 22 LR; 24-inch barrel; takedown; bead front sight, open rear; uncheckered pistol-grip stock; grooved forearm. Introduced 1931; discontinued 1936.

Exc.: $200   **VGood:** $150   **Good:** $75

REMINGTON MODEL 33 NRA JUNIOR

Same specs as Model 33 except Patridge front sight, Lyman peep-style rear; 7/8-inch sling; swivels.

Exc.: $250   **VGood:** $195   **Good:** $125

REMINGTON MODEL 34

Bolt action; 22 Short, 22 Long, 22 LR; 22-shot (22 Short), 17-shot (22 Long), 15-shot (22 LR) tube magazine; 24-inch barrel; takedown; bead front sight, open rear; uncheckered hardwood pistol-grip stock; grooved forearm. Introduced 1932; discontinued 1936.

Exc.: $200   **VGood:** $150   **Good:** $75

REMINGTON MODEL 34 NRA

Same specs as Model 34 except Patridge front sight, Lyman peep rear; swivels; 7/8-inch sling.

Exc.: $250   **VGood:** $195   **Good:** $125

REMINGTON MODEL 37 RANGEMASTER

Bolt action; 22 LR; 5-shot box magazine; single shot adapter supplied as standard; 28-inch heavy barrel; 46-1/2-inch overall length; weighs 12 lbs.; Remington peep rear sight, hooded front; models available with Wittek Vaver or Marble-Goss receiver sight; scope bases; uncheckered target stock with or without sling; swivels. When introduced, barrel band held forward section of stock to barrel; with modification of forearm, barrel band eliminated in 1938. Introduced 1937; original version discontinued 1940.

Exc.: $550   **VGood:** $470   **Good:** $400

REMINGTON MODEL 37 OF 1940

Same specs as Model 37 except Miracle trigger mechanism; high-comb stock; beavertail forearm. Introduced 1940; discontinued 1954.

Exc.: $650   **VGood:** $550   **Good:** $440

REMINGTON MODEL 40X

Bolt action; single shot; 22 LR; 28-inch standard or heavy barrel; 46-3/4-inch overall length; weighs 12-3/4 lbs. (heavy barrel); Redfield Olympic sights optional; scope bases; American walnut, high comb target stock; built-in adjustable bedding device; adjustable swivel; rubber buttplate; action similar to Model 722; adjustable trigger. Introduced 1955; discontinued 1964.

Exc.: $1050   **VGood:** $895   **Good:** $595

With sights

Exc.: $1250   **VGood:** $995   **Good:** $650

REMINGTON MODEL 40X CENTERFIRE

Same specs as Model 40X except only 222 Rem., 222 Rem. Mag., 30-06, 308, other calibers on special request at additional cost. Introduced 1961; discontinued 1964.

Exc.: $1400   **VGood:** $950   **Good:** $650

With sights

Exc.: $1500   **VGood:** $1050   **Good:** $730

REMINGTON MODEL 40X STANDARD

Same specs as Model 40X except lighter standard-weight 28-inch barrel; weighs 10-3/4 lbs.

Exc.: $1000   **VGood:** $900   **Good:** $750

With sights

Exc.: $1100   **VGood:** $1000   **Good:** $850

REMINGTON MODEL 40-XB RANGEMASTER RIMFIRE

Bolt action; single shot; 22 LR; 28-inch barrel, standard or heavyweight; 47-inch overall length; weighs 10-3/4 lbs. (standard barrel); no sights; American walnut target stock, with palm rest; adjustable swivel block on guide rail; adjustable trigger; rubber buttplate. Replaced Model 40X. Introduced 1964; discontinued 1974.

Exc.: $500   **VGood:** $400   **Good:** $350

REMINGTON MODEL 40-XB RANGEMASTER CENTERFIRE

Same specs as Model 40-XB Rangemaster except 222 Rem., 222 Rem. Mag., 223 Rem., 6mm, 7.62mm, 220 Swift, 243, 25-06, 7mm BR, 7mm Rem. Mag., 30-338, 300 Win. Mag., 30-06, 6mmx47, 6.5x55, 22-250, 244, 30-06, 308; stainless steel 27-1/4-inch barrel, standard or heavyweight; 47-inch overall length; weighs 11-1/4 lbs.; no sights; target stock; adjustable swivel block on guide rail; rubber buttplate. Introduced 1964; still in production.

Exc.: $1400   **VGood:** $1125   **Good:** $950

REMINGTON MODEL 40-XB RANGEMASTER REPEATER

Same specs as Model 40-XB Rangemaster except repeater with 5-shot magazine. No longer in production.

Exc.: $1300   **VGood:** $1025   **Good:** $850

REMINGTON MODEL 40-XB RANGEMASTER VARMINT SPECIAL KS

Same specs as Model 40-XB except single shot or repeater; 220 Swift; 27-1/4-inch stainless steel barrel; 45-3/4-inch overall length; weighs 9-3/4 lbs.; no sights; Kevlar aramid fiber stock; straight comb; cheekpiece; palm swell grip; black recoil pad; removable swivel studs; custom-built to order. Introduced 1987; discontinued 1990.

Perf.: $1395   **Exc.:** $1095   **VGood:** $930

Remington Model 34

Remington Model 37 Rangemaster

Remington Model 40X Centerfire

Remington Model 40-XB

Remington Model 40-XB Rangemaster Rimfire

Remington Model 40-XB Rangemaster Centerfire

Remington Model 40-XB Varmint Special

Remington Model 40XB-BR

Remington Model 40-XC National Match

REMINGTON MODEL 40-XB-BR

Bolt action; single shot; 22 BR Rem., 222, 222 Rem. Mag., 223, 6mmx47, 6mm BR Rem., 7.62 NATO; stainless steel 20-inch light varmint, 26-inch heavy varmint barrel; 38-inch overall length (20-inch barrel); weighs 9-1/4 lbs.; no sights; supplied with scope blocks; select walnut stock; wide squared-off forend; adjustable trigger. Introduced 1978; discontinued 1989.

Perf.: $995   **Exc.:** $795   **VGood:** $650

REMINGTON MODEL 40-XB-BR KS

Same specs as Model 40XB-BR except Kevlar stock. Introduced 1989; still in production.

Perf.: $1195   **Exc.:** $895   **VGood:** $730

REMINGTON MODEL 40-XC NATIONAL MATCH

Bolt action; 7.62 NATO (308 Win); 5-shot magazine; receiver has clip-slot for top-loading; 24-inch stainless steel barrel; 43-1/2-inch overall length; weighs 11 lbs.; no sights; position-style American walnut stock; palm swell; adjustable buttplate; adjustable trigger to meet all ISU Army Rifle specs. Introduced 1978; later production made with Kevlar stock as 40-XC KS.

Perf.: $1195   **Exc.:** $895   **VGood:** $730

Remington Model 40-XR

Remington Model 40-XR KS

Remington Model 41P

Remington Model 78 Sportsman

Remington Model 341A

Remington Model 510A

Remington Model 512X

REMINGTON MODEL 40-XC KS NATIONAL MATCH

Same specs as Model 40-XC except Kevlar stock. Introduced 1992.

Perf.: $1250 **Exc.:** $995 **VGood:** $795

REMINGTON MODEL 40-XR

Bolt-action; single-shot; 22 LR; 24-inch heavy target barrel; 42-1/2-inch overall length; weighs 9-1/4 lbs.; no sights; drilled, tapped, furnished with scope blocks; American walnut position-style stock, with front swivel block, forend guide rail; adjustable buttplate; adjustable trigger. Meets ISU specs. Introduced 1975; discontinued 1991.

Exc.: $995 **VGood:** $850 **Good:** $695

REMINGTON MODEL 40-XR CUSTOM SPORTER

Same specs as Model 40-XR except Custom Shop model; available in four grades. Duplicates Model 700 Centerfire rifle. Introduced 1986; discontinued 1991. Premium for higher grades.

Perf.: $1100 **Exc.:** $925 **VGood:** $795

REMINGTON MODEL 40-XR KS

Same specs as Model 40-XR except 43-1/2-inch overall length; weighs 10-1/2 lbs.; Kevlar stock. Introduced 1989.

Exc.: $1150 **VGood:** $895 **Good:** $695

REMINGTON MODEL 40-XR KS SPORTER

Same specs as Model 40-XR except match chamber; Kevlar stock; special order only. Introduced 1994.

Exc.: $925 **VGood:** $680 **Good:** $535

REMINGTON MODEL 41A TARGETMASTER

Bolt action; single shot; 22 Short, 22 Long, 22 LR; 27-inch barrel; takedown; bead front sight, open rear; unchecked pistol-grip stock. Introduced 1936; discontinued 1940.

Exc.: $150 **VGood:** $130 **Good:** $110

REMINGTON MODEL 41AS

Same specs as Model 41A Targetmaster except 22 Remington Special (22WRF) cartridge.

Exc.: $175 **Vgood:** $150 **Good:** $120

REMINGTON MODEL 41P

Same specs as Model 41A Targetmaster except hooded front sight, peep-type rear.

Exc.: $140 **VGood:** $120 **Good:** $100

REMINGTON MODEL 41SB

Same specs as Model 41A Targetmaster except smoothbore barrel for 22 shot cartridges.

Exc.: $230 **VGood:** $160 **Good:** $130

REMINGTON MODEL 78 SPORTSMAN

Bolt action; 223, 243, 308, 270, 30-06; 4-shot magazine; 22-inch barrel; 42-1/2-inch overall length; weighs 7-1/2 lbs.; open adjustable sights; straight-comb walnut-finished hardwood stock; cartridge head inset on receiver bottom denotes caliber; positive cross-bolt safety; tapped for scope mount. Introduced 1984; discontinued 1989.

Exc.: $305 **VGood:** $275 **Good:** $250

REMINGTON MODEL 341A

Bolt action; 22 Short, 22 Long, 22 LR; 22-shot (22 Short), 17-shot (22 Long), 15-shot (22 LR) tube magazine; 27-inch barrel; takedown; bead front sight, open rear; unchecked hardwood pistol-grip stock. Introduced 1936; discontinued 1940.

Exc.: $175 **VGood:** $140 **Good:** $105

REMINGTON MODEL 341P

Same specs as Model 341A except hooded front sight, peep rear.

Exc.: $190 **VGood:** $140 **Good:** $110

REMINGTON MODEL 341SB

Same specs as Model 341A except smoothbore barrel for 22 shot cartridges.

Exc.: $250 **VGood:** $200 **Good:** $150

REMINGTON MODEL 510A

Bolt action; single shot; 22 Short, 22 Long, 22 LR; 25-inch barrel; 43-inch overall length; 5-3/4 lbs.; takedown; bead front sight, open rear; unchecked American walnut pistol-grip stock; shotgun-style checkered buttplate; semi-beavertail forend; grooved trigger; double locking lugs, extractors; thumb safety; auto ejector. Introduced 1939; discontinued 1963.

Exc.: $120 **VGood:** $90 **Good:** $70

REMINGTON MODEL 510P

Same specs as Model 510A except Patridge-design front sight on ramp,"Point-crometer" peep rear.

Exc.: $140 **VGood:** $120 **Good:** $80

REMINGTON MODEL 510SB

Same specs as Model 510A except smoothbore barrel for 22 shot cartridge; shotgun bead front sight, no rear sight.

Exc.: $175 **VGood:** $140 **Good:** $100

REMINGTON MODEL 510X

Same specs as Model 510A except redesigned fully-adjustable rear sight, ramped front sight. Introduced 1964; discontinued 1966.

Exc.: $120 **VGood:** $90 **Good:** $70

REMINGTON 510X-SB

Same specs as Model 510X except smoothbore barrel for use with 22-shot cartridge.

Exc.: $175 **VGood:** $140 **Good:** $110

REMINGTON MODEL 511A

Bolt action; 22 Short, 22 Long, 22 LR; 6-shot detachable box magazine; 25-inch barrel; 43-inch overall length; weighs 5-3/4 lbs.; takedown; white metal bead front sight, step-adjustable rear; unchecked pistol-grip stock; grooved trigger; thumb safety. Introduced 1939; discontinued 1962.

Exc.: $130 **VGood:** $100 **Good:** $85

REMINGTON MODEL 511P

Same specs as Model 511A except "Point-crometer" peep sight on rear of receiver; Patridge-type ramp blade front.

Exc.: $140 **VGood:** $110 **Good:** $95

REMINGTON MODEL 511SB

Same specs as Model 511A except smoothbore for use with 22 shot cartridge; open sights.

Exc.: $175 **VGood:** $140 **Good:** $110

REMINGTON MODEL 511X

Same specs as Model 511A except box or clip-type magazine; improved sights. Introduced 1965; discontinued 1966.

Exc.: $130 **VGood:** $100 **Good:** $85

REMINGTON MODEL 512A

Bolt action; 22 Short, 22 Long, 22 LR; 22-shot (22 Short), 17-shot (22 Long), 15-shot (22 LR) tube magazine; 25-inch barrel; 43-inch overall length; weighs 6 lbs.; takedown; double extractors, locking lugs; automatic ejector; thumb safety; white metal bead front sight, open rear; unchecked pistol-grip stock; semi-beavertail forearm. Introduced 1940; discontinued 1963.

Exc.: $140 **VGood:** $110 **Good:** $90

REMINGTON MODEL 512P

Same specs as Model 512A except Patridge-type blade front sight on ramp, "Point-crometer" peep rear.

Exc.: $150 **VGood:** $120 **Good:** $100

REMINGTON MODEL 512SB

Same specs as Model 512 except smoothbore for use with 22-shot cartridge; open sights.

Exc.: $170 **VGood:** $135 **Good:** $110

REMINGTON MODEL 512X

Same specs as Model 512A except one cartridge shorter magazine; improved sights. Introduced 1964; discontinued 1966.

Exc.: $130 **VGood:** $100 **Good:** $80

REMINGTON MODEL 513S SPORTER

Bolt action; 22 LR; 6-shot detachable box magazine; 27-inch barrel; 45-inch overall length; weighs 6-3/4 lbs.; Patridge-type ramp front sight, Marble open rear; receiver drilled, tapped for Redfield No. 75 micrometer sight; adjustable trigger stop; double extractors, locking lugs; side-lever safety; checkered American walnut sporter-style stock; checkered steel buttplate; sling swivels. Introduced 1940; discontinued 1956.

Exc.: $550   **VGood:** $450   **Good:** $360

REMINGTON MODEL 513TR MATCHMASTER

Same specs as Model 513TR except weighs 9 lbs.; Redfield globe front sight, Redfield No. 75 peep-type rear; uncheckered target-style stock; 1-1/4-inch government-style leather sling; adjustable trigger stop; double extractors, locking lugs; side-lever safety. Introduced 1940; discontinued 1969.

Exc.: $370   **VGood:** $310   **Good:** $210

REMINGTON MODEL 514

Bolt action; single shot; 22 Short, 22 Long, 22 LR; 24-3/4-inch barrel; 42-inch overall length; weighs 5-1/4 lbs.; flat integral bead front sight, step-adjustable rear; uncheckered pistol-grip stock; black plastic buttplate. Introduced 1948; discontinued 1971. Add 5 percent for short-stocked, short-barrelled youth model (514 Boy's Rifle).

Exc.: $175   **VGood:** $150   **Good:** $125

REMINGTON MODEL 514P

Same specs as Model 514 except for ramp front sight, peep-type rear.

Exc.: $195   **VGood:** $170   **Good:** $145

REMINGTON MODEL 514SB

Same specs as Model 514 except smoothbore barrel for 22 shot cartridge.

Perf.: $225   **Exc.:** $200   **VGood:** $100

REMINGTON MODEL 521T

Bolt action; 22 LR; 6-shot detachable box magazine; 25-inch barrel; 43-inch overall length; weighs 7 lbs.; takedown; Patridge-type blade front sight, Lyman 57RS peep-type rear; double locking lugs, extractors; firing indicator; side-lever safety; uncheckered American walnut target stock; black Bakelite buttplate; sling; swivels. Named "The Junior Special." Introduced 1947; discontinued 1969.

Exc.: $295   **VGood:** $230   **Good:** $180

REMINGTON MODEL 540X

Bolt action; single shot; 22 LR; 26-inch heavy barrel; 43-1/2-inch-47-inch overall length; weighs 8 lbs.; no sights; drilled, tapped for scope blocks; fitted with front sight base; target-style stock with Monte Carlo comb and thumb rest groove; full-length guide rail; adjustable buttplate. Introduced 1969; discontinued 1974.

Exc.: $400   **VGood:** $350   **Good:** $275

REMINGTON MODEL 540XR

Bolt action; single shot; 22 LR; 26-inch medium-weight barrel; 43-1/2-inch to 46-3/4-inch overall length; weighs 8-7/8 lbs.; no sights; drilled, tapped for scope blocks; fitted with front sight base; Monte Carlo position-style stock; thumb groove, cheekpiece; adjustable buttplate; full-length guide rail; adjustable match trigger. Introduced 1974; discontinued 1983.

Exc.: $425   **VGood:** $365   **Good:** $280

REMINGTON MODEL 540XR JR

Same specs as Model 540XR except 1-3/4-inch shorter stock to fit junior shooter; adjustable length of pull. Introduced 1974; discontinued 1983.

Exc.: $350   **VGood:** $300   **Good:** $275

REMINGTON MODEL 541S

Bolt action; 22 Short, 22 Long, 22 LR; 5-shot clip magazine; 24-inch barrel; 42-5/8-inch overall length; weighs 5-1/2 lbs.; no sights; drilled, tapped for scope mounts, receiver sights; American walnut Monte Carlo stock; checkered pistol grip,

Remington Model 513TR Matchmaster

Remington Model 514

Remington Model 521T

Remington Model 541S

Remington Model 541T

Remington Model XR-100 Rangemaster

Remington Model 580

Remington Model 581

forearm; rosewood colored forend tip, pistol grip cap; checkered buttplate; thumb safety; engraved receiver, trigger guard. Introduced 1972; discontinued 1983.

Exc.: $395   **VGood:** $350   **Good:** $275

REMINGTON MODEL 541T

Same specs as Model 541S except drilled, tapped for scope mounts only; satin finish; no engraving. Introduced 1986.

Perf.: $350   **Exc.:** $275   **VGood:** $240

REMINGTON MODEL 541T HB

Same specs as Model 541T except weighs about 6-1/2 lbs; heavy target-type barrel without sights; receiver drilled and tapped for scope mounting; American walnut stock with straight comb, satin finish, cut checkering, black checkered buttplate, black grip cap and forend tip. Made in U.S. by Remington. Introduced 1993.

Perf.: $375   **Exc.:** $320   **VGood:** $280

REMINGTON MODEL XR-100 RANGEMASTER

Single-shot target rifle built on Model Seven/XP-100 action and chambered in .204 Ruger, .223 Remington, and .22-250. Laminated thumbhole stock with cutouts in forend and 26" heavy varmint barrel.

NIB: $850   **Exc.:** $700   **VGood:** $575

REMINGTON MODEL 580

Bolt action; single shot; 22 Short, 22 Long, 22 LR; 24-inch tapered barrel; 42-3/8-inch overall length; weighs 5 lbs.; screw-lock adjustable rear sight, bead post front; hardwood stock with Monte Carlo comb, pistol grip; black composition buttplate; side safety; integral loading platform; receiver grooved for tipoff mounts. Introduced 1957; discontinued 1976.

Exc.: $175   **VGood:** $150   **Good:** $125

REMINGTON MODEL 580BR "BOYS' RIFLE"

Same specs as Model 580 except youth model with stock 1-inch shorter. Introduced 1971; discontinued 1978.

Exc.: $150   **VGood:** $125   **Good:** $100

REMINGTON MODEL 580SB

Same specs as Model 580 except smoothbore barrel for 22 shot cartridges.

Exc.: $200   **VGood:** $175   **Good:** $150

REMINGTON MODEL 581

Bolt action; 22 Short, 22 Long, 22 LR; 5-shot box magazine; 24-inch round barrel; 42-3/8-inch overall length; weighs 5-1/4 lbs.; screw-adjustable open rear sight, bead on post front; hardwood Monte Carlo pistol-grip stock; side safety; wide trigger;

Remington Model 581
Sportsman

Remington Model 582

Remington Model 591

Remington Model 592

Remington Model 504

Remington Model 547

Remington Model Five

Remington Model 600

Remington Model 660

REMINGTON MODEL 504

.22 rimfire bolt-action sporter. Calibers: .22 LR, .22 WMR, .17 Mach 2, .17 HMR; five-shot detachable magazine. Barrel: 22-inch blued with iron sights; receiver blued for scope mounts. Stock: laminated walnut with QD swivels. Add 20 percent for target version.

NIB: $550   **Exc.:** $495   **VGood:** $375

REMINGTON MODEL 547

High-quality magazine-fed bolt-action .17 or .22 rimfire sporter with walnut stock, crowned muzzle, tuned trigger and other goodies. A dealer exclusive for 2007.

NIB: $975   **Exc.:** $225   **VGood:** $175

REMINGTON MODEL FIVE

A more economical, Serbian-made version of the discontinued Model 504. Chambered for .22 LR.

NIB: $350   **Exc.:** $300   **VGood:** $265

REMINGTON MODEL 600

Bolt action; 222 Rem., 6mm Rem., 243, 308, 35 Rem.; 5-, 6-shot (222 Rem. only) magazine; 18-1/2-inch round barrel with ventilated nylon rib; 37-1/4-inch overall length; weighs 5-1/2 lbs.; blade ramp front sight, fully-adjustable open rear; drilled, tapped for scope mounts; checkered walnut Monte Carlo pistol-grip stock. Introduced 1964; discontinued 1967.

Exc.: $650   **VGood:** $525   **Good:** $425

223 Rem. (Rare)

Exc.: $750   **VGood:** $600   **Good:** $500

REMINGTON MODEL 600 MAGNUM

Same specs as Model 600 except 6.5mm Rem. Mag., 350 Rem. Mag.; 4-shot box magazine; heavy Magnum-type barrel; weighs 6-1/2 lbs.; laminated walnut/beech stock; recoil pad; swivels; sling. Introduced 1965; discontinued 1967.

Exc.: $900   **VGood:** $700   **Good:** $500

REMINGTON MODEL 600 MOHAWK

Same specs as Model 600 except 222 Rem., 6mm Rem., 243, 308; 18-1/2-inch barrel with no rib; promotional model. Introduced 1971; discontinued 1980.

Exc.: $500   **VGood:** 425   **Good:** $350

REMINGTON MODEL 660

Bolt action; 222 Rem., 6mm Rem., 243, 308; 5-, 6-shot (222 Rem. only) magazine; 20-inch barrel; 38-3/4-inch overall length; weighs 6-1/2 lbs.; brass bead front sight on ramp, open adjustable rear; checkered Monte Carlo stock; black pistol-grip cap, forearm tip. Introduced 1968; discontinued 1971.

Exc.: $525   **VGood:** $450   **Good:** $350

REMINGTON MODEL 660 MAGNUM

Same specs as Model 660 except 6.5mm Rem. Mag., 350 Rem. Mag.; 4-shot magazine; laminated walnut/beech stock for added strength; quick-detachable sling swivels; sling; recoil pad. Introduced 1968; discontinued 1971.

Exc.: $850   **VGood:** $670   **Good:** $550

REMINGTON MODEL 673

Bolt action, 6.5 Rem. Mag., 308, 300 Rem. SAUM, 350 Rem. Mag.; 3-shot magazine; 22-inch bbl., 41-3/16-inch long; weighs 7-1/2 lbs.; laminated stock; ventilated rib on blued barrel; adjustable open sights. Introduced 2003, considered a modern replacement for the discontinued Model 600 and 660 Magnum rifles.

Perf.: $600   **Exc.:** $525   **VGood:** $395

REMINGTON MODEL 700ADL

Bolt action; 222, 222 Rem. Mag., 22-250, 243, 25-06, 264 Win. Mag., 6mm Rem., 270, 280, 7mm Rem. Mag., 308, 30-06; 4-shot (264, 7mm), 6-shot (222, 222 Rem. Mag.), 5-shot (others); 20-inch, 22-inch, 24-inch round tapered barrel; 39-1/2-inch overall length (222, 222 Rem. Mag., 243 Win.); removable, adjustable rear sight with windage screw; gold bead ramp front; tapped for scope mounts; walnut Monte Carlo stock, with pistol grip; originally introduced

receiver grooved for tip-off mounts. Introduced 1967; discontinued 1984.

Exc.: $195   **VGood:** $175   **Good:** $125

REMINGTON MODEL 581 SPORTSMAN

Same specs as Model 581 except with single-shot adapter. Reintroduced 1986.

Exc.: $195   **VGood:** $175   **Good:** $125

REMINGTON MODEL 582

Bolt action; 22 Short, 22 Long, 22 LR; 20-shot (22 Short), 15-shot (22 Long), 14-shot (22 LR) tube magazine; 24-inch round barrel; 42-3/8-inch overall length; weighs 5-1/4 lbs.; screw-adjustable open rear sight, bead on post front; hardwood Monte Carlo pistol-grip stock; side safety; wide trigger; receiver grooved for tip-off mounts. Introduced 1967; discontinued 1983.

Exc.: $195   **VGood:** $175   **Good:** $125

REMINGTON MODEL 591

Bolt action; 5mm Rem. Mag. caliber; 4-shot box magazine; 24-inch barrel; 42-3/8-inch overall length; weighs 5 lbs.; screw-adjustable open rear sight, bead post front; uncheckered hardwood stock, with Monte Carlo comb; black composition pistol-grip cap, buttplate; side safety; wide trigger; receiver grooved for tip-off scope mounts. Introduced 1970; discontinued 1974.

Perf.: $225   **Exc.:** $200   **VGood:** $165

REMINGTON MODEL 592

Bolt action; 5mm Rem. rimfire; 10-shot tube magazine; 24-inch barrel; 42-3/8-inch overall length; weighs 5-1/2 lbs.; screw-adjustable open rear sight, bead post front; uncheckered hardwood stock, with Monte Carlo comb; black composition pistol-grip cap, buttplate; side safety; wide trigger; receiver grooved for tip-off scope mounts. Introduced 1970; discontinued 1974.

Perf.: $225   **Exc.:** $200   **VGood:** $165

with hand-checkered pistol grip, forearm; made for several years with RKW finish, impressed checkering; more recent models with computerized cut checkering. Introduced 1962; still in production.

Perf.: $400   **Exc.:** $320   **VGood:** $285

With optional laminated stock

Perf.: $420   **Exc.:** $350   **VGood:** $300

REMINGTON MODEL 700 ADL SYNTHETIC

Similar to the 700 ADL except has a fiberglass-reinforced synthetic stock with straight comb, raised cheekpiece, positive checkering, and black rubber butt pad. Metal has matte finish. Available in 22-250, 223, 243, 270, 308, 30-06 with 22-inch barrel, 300 Win. Mag., 7mm Rem. Mag. with 24-inch barrel. Introduced 1996. Still offered.

Perf.: $350   **Exc.:** $300   **VGood:** $260

REMINGTON MODEL 700 ADL SYNTHETIC YOUTH

Similar to the Model 700 ADL Synthetic except has 1-inch shorter stock, 20-inch barrel. Chambered for 243, 308. Introduced 1998.

Perf.: $375   **Exc.:** $315   **VGood:** $265

REMINGTON MODEL 700APR AFRICAN PLAINS RIFLE

Bolt action; 7mm Rem. Mag., 300 Win. Mag., 300 Wea. Mag., 338 Win. Mag., 375 H&H, 375 Rem Ultra Mag; 26-inch Custom Shop barrel with satin finish; Magnum receiver; laminated wood stock with raised cheekpiece; satin finish; black buttpad; 20 lpi cut checkering. Made in U.S. by Remington. Introduced 1994; still produced as a custom shop item.

Perf.: $1450   **Exc.:** $1350   **VGood:** $950

REMINGTON MODEL 700AS

Bolt action; 22-250, 243, 270, 280, 30-06, 308, 7mm Rem. Mag., 300 Weatherby Mag.; 4-shot magazine, 3-shot (7mm, 300 Wea. Mag.); 22-inch, 24-inch (22-250, 7mm Rem. Mag., 300 Wea. Mag.) barrel; weighs 6-1/2 to 7 lbs.; no sights; Arylon thermoplastic resin stock; black, lightly textured finish; hinged floorplate; solid buttpad; right-hand only. Introduced 1989; discontinued 1991.

Perf.: $450   **Exc.:** $400   **VGood:** $330

REMINGTON MODEL 700AWR ALASKAN WILDERNESS RIFLE

Bolt action; 7mm Rem. Mag., 300 Win. Mag., 300 Weatherby Mag., 338 Win. Mag., 375 H&H; 24-inch Custom Shop barrel profile; stainless barreled action with satin blue finish; matte gray stock of fiberglass and graphite, reinforced with DuPont Kevlar; straight comb with raised cheekpiece; Magnum-grade black rubber recoil pad. Made in U.S. by Remington. Introduced 1994; still produced as a custom shop rifle.

Perf.: $1200   **Exc.:** $950   **VGood:** $750

REMINGTON MODEL 700BDL

Bolt action; 17 Rem., 22-250, 222 Rem., 222 Rem. Mag., 243, 25-06, 264 Win. Mag., 270, 280, 300 Savage, 30-06, 308, 35 Whelen, 6mm Rem., 7mm Rem. Mag., 7mm-08, 300 Win. Mag., 338 Win. Mag., 8mm Rem. Mag.; 4-shot magazine; 20-inch, 22-inch, 24-inch barrel; stainless barrel (7mm Rem. Mag., 264, 300 Win. Mag.); with or without sights; select walnut, hand-checkered Monte Carlo stock; black forearm tip, pistol-grip cap, skip-line fleur-de-lis checkering; matted receiver top; quick-release floorplate; quick-detachable swivels, sling.

Perf.: $465   **Exc.:** $400   **VGood:** $325

Left-hand model

Perf.: $545   **Exc.:** $470   **VGood:** $370

REMINGTON MODEL 700 LSS RIFLE

Similar to 700 BDL except stainless steel barreled action, gray laminated wood stock with Monte Carlo comb and cheekpiece. No sights furnished. Available in 7mm Rem. Mag., 7mm Rem. Ultra Mag., 375 Rem. Ultra Mag., LH 7mm Rem. Ultra Mag., 300 Rem. Ultra Mag., 300 Win. Mag., and 338 Rem. Ultra Mag. in right-hand, and 30-06, 300 Rem. Ultra Mag., 338 Rem. Ultra Mag. in left-hand model; premium for left-hand. Introduced 1996.

Perf.: $600   **Exc.:** $485   **VGood:** $410

Remington Model 700ADL Synthetic Youth

Remington Model 700APR African Plains Rifle

Remington Model 700AS

Remington Model 700AWR Alaskan Wilderness Rifle

Remington Model 700BDL

Remington Model 700BDL SS DM

Remington Model 700BDL DM

REMINGTON MODEL 700BDL DM

Same specs as Model 700BDL except right-hand action calibers: 6mm, 243, 25-06, 270, 280, 7mm-08, 30-06, 308, 7mm Rem. Mag., 300 Win. Mag., 338 Win. Mag.; left-hand calibers: 243, 270, 7mm-08, 30-06, 7mm Rem. Mag., 300 Win. Mag.; 3-shot (Magnums), 4-shot (standard) detachable box magazine; glossy stock finish; open sights; recoil pad; sling swivels. Made in U.S. by Remington. Introduced 1995.

Right-hand, standard calibers		
Perf.: $500	**Exc.:** $450	**VGood:** $380

Left-hand, standard calibers, right-hand Magnums		
Perf.: $525	**Exc.:** $475	**VGood:** $400

Left-hand, Magnum calibers		
Perf.: $550	**Exc.:** $485	**VGood:** $425

REMINGTON MODEL 700BDL EUROPEAN

Same specs as Model 700BDL except 243, 270, 7mm-08, 280 Rem., 30-06 (22-inch barrel), 7mm Rem. Mag. (24-inch barrel); oil-finished walnut stock. Made in U.S. by Remington. Introduced 1993.

Standard calibers		
Perf.: $440	**Exc.:** $385	**VGood:** $325

7mm Rem. Mag.		
Perf.: $465	**Exc.:** $425	**VGood:** $375

REMINGTON MODEL 700BDL LIMITED CLASSIC

Same specs as Model 700BDL except made in classic style, with a different single chambering for each year; In sequence, from 1981 through 2005, the calibers were: 1981: 7x57, 1982: 257 Roberts.,

1983: 300 H&H, 1984: 250-3000, 1985: 350 Rem Mag, 1986: 264 Win Mag, 1987: 338 Win Mag, 1988: 35 Whelen, 1989: 300 Wby Mag, 1990: 25-06, 1991: 7mm Wby Mag, 1992: 220 Swift, 1993: 222, 1994: 6.5x55, 1995: 300 Win Mag, 1996: 375 H&H, 1997: 280, 1998: 8mm Rem Mag, 1999: 17 Rem, 2000: 223, 2001: 7mm-08, 2002: 221 Fireball, 2003: 300 Savage, 2004: 8x57, 2005: 308; classic-style, hand-checkered walnut straight stock; black forearm tip, pistol-grip cap; high gloss blued finish. New caliber announced annually and produced for that year only. Introduced 1981; still in production.

Perf.: $635   **Exc.:** $480   **VGood:** $385

REMINGTON MODEL 700BDL MOUNTAIN RIFLE

Same specs as Model 700BDL except 243, 25-06, 257 Roberts, 270, 7mm-08, 280, 30-06, 308, 7x57; 22-inch tapered barrel; checkered American walnut stock with cheekpiece; ebony forend tip. Introduced 1986; no longer in production.

Perf.: $435   **Exc.:** $375   **VGood:** $325

REMINGTON MODEL 700BDL MOUNTAIN CUSTOM KS WOOD GRAINED

Same specs as Model 700BDL Mountain except 375 H&H Mag., 416 Rem. Mag., 458 Win. Mag.; wood-grained Kevlar stock. Introduced 1992; discontinued 1993.

Perf.: $900   **Exc.:** $795   **VGood:** $625

REMINGTON MODEL 700BDL MOUNTAIN STAINLESS

Same specs as Model 700BDL Mountain except 25-06, 270, 280, 30-06; 22-inch stainless barrel; weighs

Remington Model 700BDL
SS DM Magnum

Remington Model 700BDL
Varmint Special

Remington Model 700 Classic

Remington Model 700
Custom Mountain KS

Remington Model 700
LSS Mountain

Remington Model 700FS

7-1/4 lbs.; black synthetic stock with checkering. Introduced 1993; discontinued 1993.

Perf.: $460   **Exc.:** $400   **VGood:** $375

REMINGTON MODEL 700BDL SAFARI

Same specs as Model 700BDL except 375 H&H Mag., 8mm Rem. Mag., 416 Rem. Mag., 458 Win. Mag.; 3-shot magazine; 24-inch, 26-inch barrel; 46-3/8-inch overall length; weighs 9 lbs.; no sights; Classic or Monte Carlo hand-checkered walnut stock; recoil pad. Introduced 1962; still in production.

Perf.: $875   **Exc.:** $695   **VGood:** $530

Left-hand model

Perf.: $925   **Exc.:** $750   **VGood:** $565

REMINGTON MODEL 700BDL SAFARI CUSTOM KS

Same specs as Model 700BDL Safari except 8mm Rem. Mag., 375 H&H Mag., 416 Rem. Mag., 458 Win. Mag.; lightweight Kevlar straight-line classic stock; comb; no cheekpiece. Introduced 1989; still in production.

Perf.: $1100   **Exc.:** $925   **VGood:** $700

Left-hand model

Perf.: $1150   **Exc.:** $950   **VGood:** $725

REMINGTON MODEL 700BDL SAFARI CUSTOM KS STAINLESS

Same specs as Model 700BDL Safari except 375 H&H Mag., 416 Rem. Mag., 458 Win. Mag.; Kevlar stock; stainless barrel and action. Introduced 1993; still in production.

Perf.: $1200   **Exc.:** $950   **VGood:** $750

REMINGTON MODEL 700BDL SS

Same specs as Model 700BDL Safari Custom KS Stainless rifle except 223, 243, 6mm Rem., 7mm-08 Rem., 308 (short action), 25-06, 270, 280 Rem., 30-06, 7mm Rem. Mag., 7mm Weatherby Mag., 300 Win. Mag., 300 Weatherby Mag., 338 Win. Mag. (standard long action); 24-inch barrel; Magnum-contour barrel (Magnums); weighs 6-3/4 to 7 lbs;

corrosion-resistant follower and fire control; stainless #416 BDL-style barreled action with fine matte finish; synthetic stock with straight comb and cheekpiece, textured finish, positive checkering, plated swivel studs. Made in U.S. by Remington. Introduced 1993; still produced.

Standard calibers		
Perf.: $500	**Exc.:** $450	**VGood:** $400
Magnum calibers		
Perf.: $535	**Exc.:** $465	**VGood:** $410

REMINGTON MODEL 700BDL SS DM

Same specs as Model 700BDL SS except 6mm, 243, 25-06, 270, 280, 7mm-08, 7mm Rem. Mag., 300 Win. Mag., 300 Weatherby Mag.; detachable box magazine; black synthetic stock. Made in U.S. by Remington. Introduced 1995; still produced.

Standard calibers		
Perf.: $520	**Exc.:** $450	**VGood:** $400
Magnum calibers		
Perf.: $545	**Exc.:** $475	**VGood:** $425

REMINGTON MODEL 700BDL VARMINT SPECIAL

Same specs as Model 700BDL except 24-inch heavy barrel; 43-1/2-inch overall length; weighs 9 lbs.; no sights; 222, 223, 22-250, 25-06, 6mm Rem., 243, 7mm-08 Rem., 308; 5-, 6-shot magazine. Introduced 1967.

Perf.: $470   **Exc.:** $400   **VGood:** $325

REMINGTON MODEL 700BDL VARMINT SYNTHETIC

Same specs as Model 700BDL Varmint except 220 Swift, 22-250, 223 Rem., 308; black/gray synthetic stock; aluminum bedding block; matte metal finish. Introduced 1992; still in production.

Perf.: $540   **Exc.:** $420   **VGood:** $350

REMINGTON MODEL 700C

Bolt action; 17 Rem., 22-250, 222 Rem., 222 Rem. Mag., 223 Rem., 243, 25-06, 264 Mag., 270, 280,

300 Savage, 30-06, 308, 35 Whelen, 6mm Rem., 6.5mm Rem. Mag., 7mm Rem. Mag., 7mm-08, 300 Win. Mag., 338 Win. Mag., 350 Rem. Mag., 8mm Mag.; 4-shot magazine; 20-inch, 22-inch, 24-inch barrel; with or without sights; select walnut, hand-checkered stock; rosewood forearm tip, grip cap; hand-lapped barrel; hinged floorplate; Custom Shop rifle. Introduced 1964; discontinued 1983.

Perf.: $895   **Exc.:** $795   **VGood:** $650

REMINGTON MODEL 700D PEERLESS

Same specs as Model 700C except best-grade wood; scroll engraving.

Perf.: $1695   **Exc.:** $1295   **VGood:** $995

REMINGTON MODEL 700F PREMIER

Same specs as Model C except best-grade wood; extensive engraving.

Perf.: $3125   **Exc.:** $2625   **VGood:** $2100

REMINGTON MODEL 700 CAMO SYNTHETIC RIFLE

Bolt action; 22-250, 243, 7mm-08, 270, 280, 30-06, 308, 7mm Rem. Mag., 300 Weatherby Mag.; 4-shot, 3-shot (7mm, 300 Wea. Mag.) magazine; open adjustable sights; synthetic stock, stock and metal (except bolt and sights) fully camouflaged in Mossy Oak Bottomland camo; swivel studs. Made in U.S. by Remington. Introduced 1992; discontinued 1994.

Perf.: $450   **Exc.:** $375   **VGood:** $330

REMINGTON MODEL 700 CLASSIC

Bolt action; 22-250, 6mm Rem., 243, 270, 7mm Mauser, 30-06, 7mm Rem. Mag., 350 Rem. Mag., 375 H&H, 300 Win. Mag.; 24-inch barrel; 44-1/2-inch overall length; weighs 7-3/4 lbs.; no sights; drilled and tapped for scope mounting; American walnut straight-comb stock with 20 lpi checkered pistol grip, forend; rubber recoil pad; sling swivel studs; hinged floorplate. Introduced 1978. Considreable premium for scarce chamberings such as .264 WM.

Perf.: $500   **Exc.:** $450   **VGood:** $400

REMINGTON MODEL 700 CUSTOM MOUNTAIN KS

Bolt action; 270, 280, 300 Win. Mag., 300 Weatherby Mag., 30-06, 338 Win. Mag., 35 Whelen, 7mm Rem. Mag., 8mm Rem. Mag., 375 H&H Mag. 375 Rem Ultra Mag.; 4-shot magazine; 22-inch barrel; 42-1/2-inch overall length; weighs 6-3/8 lbs.; no sights; Kevlar reinforced resin stock; left- and right-hand versions; Custom Shop rifle. Introduced 1986; still in production.

Perf.: $995   **Exc.:** $895   **VGood:** $650

Left-hand model

Perf.: $1025   **Exc.:** $925   **VGood:** $675

REMINGTON MODEL 700 MOUNTAIN

Same specs as Model 700 Custom Mountain KS except walnut stock with satin finish, fine-line checkering. Introduced 1986; no longer in production.

Perf.: $450   **Exc.:** $375   **VGood:** $300

REMINGTON MODEL 700 LSS MOUNTAIN RIFLE

Similar to Model 700 Custom KS Mountain Rifle except stainless steel 22-inch barrel and two-tone laminated stock. Chambered in 260 Rem., 7mm-08, 270 Winchester and 30-06. Overall length 42-1/2-inch, weighs 6-5/8 oz. Introduced 1999.

Perf.: $675   **Exc.:** $550   **VGood:** $450

REMINGTON MODEL 700FS

Bolt action; 243, 270, 30-06, 308, 7mm Rem. Mag.; 4-shot magazine; 22-inch, 24-inch (7mm) barrel; weighs 6-1/4 to 6-3/4 lbs.; open sights; classic-style gray or gray camo fiberglass stock reinforced with Kevlar; black Old English-type rubber recoil pad; right- or left-hand actions. Introduced 1987; discontinued 1988.

Perf.: $635   **Exc.:** $565   **VGood:** $400

REMINGTON MODEL 700LS

Bolt action; 243, 270, 30-06, 7mm Rem. Mag.; 5-shot, 4-shot (7mm); 22-inch, 24-inch barrel (7mm); weighs 7-1/4 lbs.; open sights; laminated light/dark wood Monte Carlo pistol-grip stock with cut checkering; sling swivels. Introduced 1990; no longer in production.

Perf.: $450　　**Exc.:** $385　　**VGood:** $310

REMINGTON MODEL 700MTN DM

Bolt action; 243, 260 Rem., 270 Win., 7mm-08, 25-06, 280 Rem., 30-06; 4-shot detachable box magazine; 22-inch barrel; 42-1/2-inch overall length; weighs 6-3/4 lbs.; no sights; drilled, tapped for scope mounting; redesigned pistol grip; straight comb; contoured cheekpiece; hand-rubbed oil satin finish; two position thumb safety. Introduced 1986; still in production.

Perf.: $450　　**Exc.:** $400　　**VGood:** $335

REMINGTON MODEL 700MTRSS

Bolt action; 25-06, 270, 280 Rem., 30-06; weighs 6-3/4 lbs.; 22-inch barrel; stainless steel barreled action; textured black Rynite synthetic stock with positive checkering; straight comb and cheekpiece. Made in U.S. by Remington. Introduced 1993; discontinued 1994.

Perf.: $510　　**Exc.:** $420　　**VGood:** $360

REMINGTON MODEL 700RS

Bolt action; 270, 280, 30-06; 4-shot magazine; 22-inch barrel; weighs 7-1/4 lbs.; open sights; glass-reinforced Rynite synthetic thermoplastic resin stock; textured gray or camouflage finish; solid buttpad; hinged floorplate. Introduced 1987; discontinued 1989.

Perf.: $500　　**Exc.:** $425　　**VGood:** $380

REMINGTON MODEL 700 SENDERO

Bolt action; 25-06, 270, 7mm Rem. Mag., 300 Win. Mag.; 26-inch heavy barrel with spherical concave crown; long action for Magnum calibers; composite stock. Made in U.S. by Remington. Introduced 1994; still produced.

Perf.: $585　　**Exc.:** $475　　**VGood:** $400

REMINGTON MODEL 700 SENDERO SF RIFLE

Similar to 700 Sendero except stainless-steel action and 26-inch stainless-steel fluted barrel. Weighs 8-1/2 lbs. Chambered for 25-06, 7mm Rem. Mag., 7mm Rem. Ultra Mag., 7mm STW, 300 Win. Mag., 300 Rem. Ultra Mag., 338 Rem. Ultra Mag., Introduced 1996. Still offered.

Perf.: $850　　**Exc.:** $715　　**VGood:** $600

REMINGTON MODEL 700 TITANIUM

Similar to 700 BDL except has titanium receiver, spiral-cut fluted bolt, skeletonized bolt handle and carbon-fiber and aramid fiber reinforced stock with sling swivel studs. Barrel 22-inch; weighs 5-1/4 lbs. (short action) or 5-1/2 lbs. (long action). Satin stainless finish. 260 Rem., 270 Win., 7mm-08, 30-06, 308 Win. Introduced 2001.

Perf.: $1000　　**Exc.:** $800　　**VGood:** $700

REMINGTON MODEL 700VLS VARMINT LAMINATED STOCK

Bolt action; 222 Rem., 223 Rem., 22-250, 243, 308; 26-inch heavy barrel; no sights; brown laminated stock with forend tip, grip cap, rubber buttpad; polished blue finish. Made in U.S. by Remington. Introduced 1995; still produced.

Perf.: $580　　**Exc.:** $475　　**VGood:** $380

REMINGTON MODEL 700 VS VARMINT SYNTHETIC RIFLES

Similar to 700 BDL Varmint Laminated except composite stock reinforced with aramid fiber reinforced, fiberglass and graphite. Aluminum bedding block that runs full length of receiver. Free-floating 26-inch barrel. Metal has black matte finish; stock has textured black and gray finish and swivel studs. Available in 223, 22-250, 308. Right- and left-hand. Introduced 1992, still offered.

Perf.: $580　　**Exc.:** $445　　**VGood:** $410

REMINGTON MODEL 700VS SF

Bolt action; 223, 220 Swift, 22-250, 243, 308; 26-inch fluted barrel; satin-finish stainless barreled action; spherical concave muzzle crown. Made in U.S. by Remington. Introduced 1994; still produced.

Perf.: $750　　**Exc.:** $565　　**VGood:** $465

REMINGTON MODEL 700 ETRONX ELECTRONIC IGNITION RIFLE

Similar to Model 700 VS SF except features battery-powered ignition system for near-zero lock time and electronic trigger mechanism. Requires ammunition with EtronX electrically fired primers. Aluminum-bedded 26-inch heavy, stainless steel, fluted barrel; overall length 45-7/8-inch; weight 8 lbs., 14 oz. Black, Kevlar-reinforced composite stock. Light-emitting diode display on grip top indicates fire or safe mode, loaded or unloaded chamber, battery condition. Available in 220 Swift, 22-250 or 243 Win. Introduced 2000.

Perf.: $1700　　**Exc.:** $1500　　**VGood:** $1200

REMINGTON MODEL 700 RMEF

Bolt action; 7mm Rem. Ultra Mag., 300 Rem. Ultra Mag.; 26-inch barrel; weighs 7-5/8 lbs.; 46.5-inch overall length; Synthetic stock, Realtree hardwood finish; no sights, drilled and tapped. Special Edition (sold one year only), Rocky Mountain Elk Foundation rifle, 416 stainless bolt, varrel, receiver. Portion of proceeds to RMEF.

Perf.: $780　　**Exc.:** $585　　**VGood:** $470

REMINGTON MODEL 700 SENDERO SF-II

Similar to Sendero SF but with HS Precision synthetic stock. Chambered in .264 WM, 7mm RM, 7mm RUM, .300 WM, and .300 RUM.

NIB: $925　　**Exc.:** $865　　**VGood:** $695

REMINGTON MODEL 700 CDL

Similar to Model 700 Classic with straight-comb, oil-finished walnut stock with ebony tip, satin blue receiver and barrel (24" standard calibers, 26" magnum) and fine-cut checkering. Available in a variety of standard, magnum, and short magnum chamberings. Add 25 percent for .30-06 commemorative version.

NIB: $525　　**Exc.:** $485　　**VGood:** $395

REMINGTON MODEL 700 CDL SF LTD.

Similar to Model 700 CDL but with engraved floorplate and stainless, fluted barrel. Chambered in .30-06 and .17 Remington Fireball. 2006 "Centennial" model commemorates the centennial of the .30-06 cartridge and was introduced in 2006 for one year only. Reintroduced in .260 Remington in 2008.

NIB: $995　　**Exc.:** $895　　**VGood:** $695

Remington Model 700 MTN DM

Remington Model 700 Sendero

Remington Model 700 Sendero SF

Remington Model 700 Titanium

Remington Model 700VLS Varmint Laminated Stock

Remington Model 700VS SF

Remington Model 700 EtronX Electronic Ignition Rifle

Remington Model 700 Sendero SF-!!

Remington Model 710

Remington Model 700 CDL SF Ltd.

Remington Model 700 VTR

Remington Model 770

Remington Model 715 Sportsman

Remington Model 721A Magnum

Remington Model 725ADL

Remington Model 788

REMINGTON MODEL 700 VTR (VARMINT TACTICAL)

Similar to Model 700 but with green stock with black overmold grips (similar to XCR models); tactical-style 1 in 9" twist (223 caliber) or tactical-style 1 in 12" twist (308 caliber):22" barrel with integrated muzzle brake design and triangular barrel contour to enhance accuracy. Chambered in .204, .223, .22-250 and .308. Introduced in 2008.

NIB: $900   **Exc.:** $800   **VGood:** $675

REMINGTON MODEL 710 BOLT-ACTION RIFLE

Bolt action; 270 Win., 30-06, 7mm Rem. Mag., 300 Win. Mag.; 22-inch barrel; weighs 7-1/8 lbs.; 42-1/2-inch overall length; Gray synthetic stock; Bushnell Sharpshooter 3-9x scope mounted and bore-sighted. Unique action locks bolt directly into barrel; 60-degree bolt throw; 4-shot dual-stack magazine; key-operated Integrated Security System locks bolt open. Introduced 2001. Discontinued.

Perf.: $ 295   **Exc.:** $250   **VGood:** $175

REMINGTON MODEL 770 YOUTH

Similar to Model 770 but with shorter barrel and stock.

NIB: $375   **Exc.:** $325   **VGood:** $265

REMINGTON MODEL 715 SPORTSMAN

Similar to Model 770. A dealer exclusive for 2007.

NIB: $325   **Exc.:** $295   **VGood:** $250

REMINGTON MODEL 720A

Bolt action; 257 Roberts, 270, 30-06; 5-shot detachable box magazine; 22-inch barrel; 42-1/2-inch overall length; weighs 8 lbs.; bead front sight on ramp, open rear; models available with Redfield No. 70RST micrometer or Lyman No. 48 receiver sights; checkered American walnut pistol-grip stock; modified Model 1917 Enfield action. Made only in

1941 as factory facilities were afterwards converted to wartime production. Note: Most 720s were made in 30-06; few in 270; and only a handful in 257 Roberts. Add premium for rarer calibers.

Exc.: $1250   **VGood:** $1000   **Good:** $700

REMINGTON MODEL 720R

Same specs as Model 720A except 20-inch barrel; models available with Redfield No. 70RST micrometer or Lyman No. 48 receiver sights.

Exc.: $1250   **VGood:** $1000   **Good:** $700

REMINGTON MODEL 720S

Same specs as Model 720A except 24-inch barrel; models available with Redfield No. 70RST micrometer or Lyman No. 48 receiver sights.

Exc.: $1250   **VGood:** $1000   **Good:** $700

REMINGTON MODEL 721A

Bolt action; 270, 280, 30-06; 4-shot box magazine; 24-inch barrel; 44-1/4-inch overall length; weighs 7-1/4 lbs.; white metal bead front sight on ramp, step-adjustable sporting rear; uncheckered American walnut sporter stock with pistol grip; semi-beavertail forend; checkered shotgun-style buttplate; thumb safety; receiver drilled, tapped for scope mounts, micrometer sights. Introduced 1948; discontinued 1962.

Exc.: $400   **VGood:** $335   **Good:** $275

REMINGTON MODEL 721A MAGNUM

Same specs as Model 721A except only 264 Win. Mag., 300 H&H Mag.; 3-shot magazine; heavy 26-inch barrel; 46-1/4-inch overall length; weighs 8-1/4 lbs.; recoil pad. Values shown are for .264; deduct 15% for .300.

Exc.: $675   **VGood:** $550   **Good:** $340

REMINGTON MODEL 721ADL

Same specs as Model 721A except deluxe checkered walnut sporter stock, forearm. Introduced 1948; discontinued 1962.

Exc.: $425   **VGood:** $375   **Good:** $295

REMINGTON MODEL 721ADL MAGNUM

Same specs as Model 721ADL except 264 Win. Mag., 300 H&H Mag.; 3-shot magazine; 26-inch barrel; recoil pad. Values shown are for .264; deduct 15% for .300.

Exc.: $625   **VGood:** $500   **Good:** $300

REMINGTON MODEL 721BDL

Bolt action; 270, 280, 30-06; 4-shot magazine; 24-inch barrel; bead front sight on ramp, open rear; select checkered walnut sporter stock, forearm. Introduced 1948; discontinued 1962.

Exc.: $415   **VGood:** $365   **Good:** $310

REMINGTON MODEL 721BDL MAGNUM

Same specs as Model 721BDL except 264 Win. Mag., 300 H&H Mag.; 3-shot magazine; 26-inch barrel; recoil pad.

Exc.: $625   **VGood:** $500   **Good:** $300

REMINGTON MODEL 722A

Bolt action, short action version of Model 721; 222 Rem., 222 Rem. Mag., 243 Win., 244 Rem., 257 Roberts, 300 Savage, 308; 4-, 5-shot (222 Rem.) magazine; 24-inch, 26-inch (222 Rem., 244 Rem.) barrel; 43-1/4-inch overall length; weighs 7 lbs.; shorter action than Model 721A; white metal bead front sight on ramp, step-adjustable sporting rear; receiver drilled, tapped for scope mounts or micrometer sights; uncheckered walnut sporter stock. Introduced 1948; discontinued 1962.

Exc.: $415   **VGood:** $365   **Good:** $310

REMINGTON MODEL 722ADL

Same specs as Model 722A except deluxe checkered walnut sporter stock.

Exc.: $425   **VGood:** $375   **Good:** $325

REMINGTON MODEL 722BDL

Same specs as Model 722A except select checkered walnut sporter stock.

Exc.: $450   **VGood:** $350   **Good:** $250

REMINGTON MODEL 725ADL

Bolt action; 222 Rem., 243, 244, 270, 280, 30-06; 4-, 5-shot (222 Rem.) box magazine; 22-inch, 24-inch (222 Rem.) barrel; 42-1/2-inch, 43-1/2-inch (222) overall length; weighs 7 lbs.; removable hood ramp front sight, adjustable open rear; Monte Carlo comb, walnut stock; hand-checkered pistol grip, forearm; hinged floorplate; swivels. Some calibers bring premium. Introduced 1958; discontinued 1961.

Exc.: $385   **VGood:** $290   **Good:** $210

REMINGTON MODEL 725ADL KODIAK MAGNUM

Same specs as Model 725ADL except 375 H&H Mag., 458 Win. Mag.; 3-shot box magazine; 26-inch barrel; reinforced deluxe Monte Carlo stock; recoil pad; special recoil reduction device built into barrel; black forearm tip; sling, swivels. Made only in 1962.

Exc.: $950   **VGood:** $850   **Good:** $700

REMINGTON MODEL 788

Bolt action; 222, 22-250, 223, 6mm Rem., 243, 7mm-08, 308, 30-30, 44 Mag.; 3-, 4-shot (222) detachable box magazine; 22-inch, 24-inch (222, 22-250) barrel; 41-inch to 43-5/8-inch overall length; weighs 7-7-1/2 lbs.; open fully-adjustable rear sight, blade ramp front; receiver tapped for scope mounts; American walnut or walnut-finished hardwood pistol-grip stock, uncheckered with Monte Carlo comb; thumb safety; artillery-type bolt. Introduced 1967; discontinued 1983.

Exc.: $360   **VGood:** $305   **Good:** $270

44 Mag., 7mm-08

Exc.: $600   **VGood:** $500   **Good:** $395

REMINGTON MODEL 788 CARBINE
Same specs as Model 788 except 18-1/2-inch barrel.
Exc.: $370 **VGood:** $315 **Good:** $280

REMINGTON MODEL 788 LEFT-HAND
Same specs as Model 788 except 6mm, 308; left-hand version. Introduced 1969.
Exc.: $375 **VGood:** $310 **Good:** $260

REMINGTON MODEL INTERNATIONAL FREE RIFLE
Bolt action; single shot; used 40XB action; 22 LR; 222 Rem., 222 Rem. Mag., 223 Rem., 7.62 NATO, 30-06; 27-1/4-inch barrel; 47-inch overall length; weighs 15 lbs.; no sights; hand-finished stock; adjustable buttplate and hook; movable front sling swivel; adjustable palm rest; 2-oz. adjustable trigger. Introduced 1964; discontinued 1974.
Perf.: $1900 **Exc.:** $1600 **VGood:** $1300

REMINGTON MODEL INTERNATIONAL MATCH FREE RIFLE
Bolt action; single shot; 22 LR, 222 Rem., 222 Rem. Mag., 30-06, 7.62mm NATO, others on special order; 28-inch barrel; no sights; freestyle hand-finished stock with thumbhole; interchangeable, adjustable rubber buttplate and hook-type buttplate; adjustable palm rest; adjustable sling swivel; 2-oz. adjustable trigger. Introduced 1961; discontinued 1964.
Perf.: $2000 **Exc.:** $1700 **VGood:** $1400

REMINGTON MODEL SEVEN
Bolt action; 17 Rem., 222 Rem., 223 Rem., 243, 7mm-08, 6mm, 308; 4-shot magazine, 5-shot (222 only); 18-1/2-inch barrel; 37-1/2-inch overall length; weighs 6-1/4 lbs.; ramp front sight, adjustable open rear; American walnut stock; modified schnabel forend; machine-cut checkering; short action; silent side safety; free-floated barrel. Introduced 1983.
Perf.: $450 **Exc.:** $370 **VGood:** $320

REMINGTON MODEL SEVEN CUSTOM KS
Same specs as Model Seven except 223 Rem., 7mm BR, 7mm-08, 308, 35 Rem., 350 Rem. Mag.; 20-inch barrel; weighs 5-3/4 lbs.; Kevlar aramid fiber stock; iron sights; drilled, tapped for scope mounts. Special order through Remington Custom Shop. Introduced 1987.
Perf.: $950 **Exc.:** $750 **VGood:** $600

REMINGTON MODEL SEVEN CUSTOM MS
Same specs as Model Seven except 222 Rem., 223, 22-250, 243, 6mm Rem., 7mm-08 Rem., 308, 350 Rem. Mag.; 20-inch barrel; weighs 6-3/4 lbs.; full-length Mannlicher-style stock of laminated wood with straight comb, solid black recoil pad, black steel forend tip, cut checkering, gloss finish; polished blue finish; calibers 250 Savage, 257 Roberts, 35 Rem. available on special order. From Remington Custom Shop. Introduced 1993; no longer produced.
Perf.: $910 **Exc.:** $710 **VGood:** $650

REMINGTON MODEL SEVEN FS
Same specs as Model Seven except 243, 7mm-08, 308; weighs 5-1/4 lbs.; fiberglass/Kevlar classic-style stock gray or camo; rubber buttpad. Introduced 1987; discontinued 1989.
Perf.: $550 **Exc.:** $475 **VGood:** $400

REMINGTON MODEL SEVEN LS
Similar to Model Seven except has satin-finished, brown laminated stock with 20-inch carbon steel barrel. 223, 243 Win., 7mm-08, 300 Win. Introduced 2000, still produced.
Perf.: $600 **Exc.:** $500 **VGood:** $400

REMINGTON MODEL SEVEN SS
Same specs as Model Seven except 243, 260, 7mm-08, 308, also 7mm Rem SA Ultra Mag, 300 Rem SA Ultra Mag; 20-inch or 22-inch barrel; stainless steel barreled action; black synthetic stock. Made in U.S. by Remington. Introduced 1994; still produced.

Remington International Match Free Rifle

Remington Model Seven

Remington Model Seven Custom KS

Remington Model Seven FS

Remington Model Seven LS

Remington Model Seven LSS

Remington Model Seven XCR Camo

Remington Model Seven 25th Anniversary

Remington Model Seven Predator

Perf.: $475 **Exc.:** $430 **VGood:** $390
7mm Rem.SAUM, 300 Rem. SAUM, 22-inch bbl.
Perf.: $500 **Exc.:** $450 **VGood:** $400

REMINGTON MODEL SEVEN LSS
Bolt action; 22-250, 7mm-08; 20-inch barrel; weighs 6-1/2 lbs.; 39-1/4-inch overall length; Brown laminated stock; Cut checkering. Short-action design; silent side safety; free-floated barrel except for single pressure point at forend tip. Stainless barreled action. Introduced 1983.
Perf.: $690 **Exc.:** $580 **VGood:** $450

REMINGTON MODEL SEVEN YOUTH
Same specs as Model Seven except 6mm Rem., 243, 7mm-08; hardwood stock with 12-3/16-inch length of pull. Made in U.S. by Remington. Introduced 1993; still produced.
Perf.: $450 **Exc.:** $400 **VGood:** $325

Model Seven Youth Synthetic, short gray synthetic stock
Perf.: $425 **Exc.:** $375 **VGood:** $300

REMINGTON MODEL SEVEN CDL
Similar to Model Seven but with satin walnut.satin blue finish, sightless barrel, and Limbsaver recoil pad.
NIB: $650 **Exc.:** $595 **VGood:** $450

REMINGTON MODEL SEVEN XCR CAMO
Similar to Model Seven LSS but with camo stock, fluted barrel and weather-resistant coating. Chambered in .243, 7mm-08, .308, .270 WSM and .300 WSM. Introduced in 2007.
NIB: $850 **Exc.:** $700 **VGood:** $575

REMINGTON MODEL SEVEN 25TH ANNIVERSARY VERSION
Similar to Model Seven but in 7mm-08 only with 25th anniversary medallion inset at the pistol grip cap

Remington Model 770

Remington Model 798 Stainless Laminate

Remington Model 798 SPS

Remington Model 798 Safari

Remington-Lee Sporter

Remington Model Six

Remington Model 14-½

Remington Model 25A

REMINGTON MODEL SIX

Slide action; 6mm Rem., 243, 270, 308 Win., 308 Accelerator, 30-06, 30-06 Accelerator; 4-shot detachable clip magazine; 22-inch round tapered barrel; 42-inch overall length; weighs 7-1/2 lbs.; gold bead front sight on matted ramp, open adjustable sliding ramp rear; cut-checkered Monte Carlo walnut stock with full cheekpiece; cross-bolt safety; tapped for scope mount; cartridge head medallion on receiver bottom to denote caliber. Special version of Model 760. Introduced 1981; discontinued 1988.

Perf.: $395   Exc.: $350   VGood: $300

D Peerless Grade
Perf.: $1995   Exc.: $1795   VGood: $1095

F Premier Grade
Perf.: $4195   Exc.: $3795   VGood: $2695

F Premier Gold Grade
Perf.: $6495   Exc.: $5195   VGood: $3995

REMINGTON MODEL 12, 12A

Slide action; 22 Short, 22 Long, 22 LR; 15-shot (22 Short), 12-shot (22 Long), 10-shot (22 LR) tube magazine; 22-inch barrel; hammerless takedown; bead front sight, open rear; uncheckered straight stock; grooved slide handle. Introduced 1909; discontinued 1936.

Exc.: $450   VGood: $350   Good: $300

REMINGTON MODEL 12B

Same specs as Model 12A except 22 Short only; octagonal barrel.

Exc.: $475   VGood: $350   Good: $300

REMINGTON MODEL 12C

Same specs as Model 12A except 24-inch octagonal barrel; pistol-grip stock.

Exc.: $460   VGood: $385   Good: $315

REMINGTON MODEL 12CS

Same specs as Model 12A except 22 Rem. Spl. (22 WRF); 12-shot magazine; 14-inch octagonal barrel; pistol-grip stock.

Exc.: $460   VGood: $360   Good: $310

REMINGTON MODEL 14, 14A

Slide action; 25, 30, 32, 35 Rem.; 5-shot tube magazine; 22-inch barrel; hammerless; takedown; bead front sight, open rear; uncheckered walnut straight stock; grooved slide handle. Introduced 1912; discontinued 1935. Add 25 percent for 25 Remington.

Exc.: $550   VGood: $450   Good: $320

REMINGTON MODEL 14R CARBINE

Same specs as Model 14 except 18-inch barrel.

Exc.: $625   VGood: $495   Good: $345

REMINGTON MODEL 14-1/2

Slide action; 38-40, 44-40; 11-shot tube magazine; 22-1/2-inch barrel; hammerless; takedown; bead front sight, open rear; uncheckered walnut straight stock; grooved slide handle. Introduced 1912; discontinued 1925.

Exc.: $830   VGood: $560   Good: $470

REMINGTON MODEL 14-1/2 CARBINE

Same specs as Model 14-1/2 except 9-shot full-length tube magazine; 18-1/2-inch barrel. Introduced 1912; discontinued 1925.

Exc.: $860   VGood: $580   Good: $490

REMINGTON MODEL 25, 25A

Slide action; 25-20, 32-20; 10-shot tube magazine; 24-inch barrel; hammerless; takedown; blade front sight, open rear; uncheckered walnut pistol-grip stock; grooved slide handle. Introduced 1923; discontinued 1936.

Exc.: $650   VGood: $495   Good: $365

REMINGTON MODEL 25R CARBINE

Same specs as Model 25A except 6-shot magazine; 18-inch barrel; straight stock.

Exc.: $675   VGood: $525   Good: $390

---

area, high-sheen blued finish on the receiver, bolt and 22" standard-contour barrel, X-Mark Pro Trigger and SuperCell recoil pad. Introduced 2008.

NIB: $950   Exc.: $825   VGood: $675

MODEL SEVEN PREDATOR

Similar to Model Seven but with full coverage in Mossy Oak® Brush® camo; fluted, magnum contour 22" barrel, synthetic stock as on Model Seven XCR; X-Mark Pro Trigger. Chambered in .17 Remington Fireball, .204, .223, .22-250 and .243.

NIB: $800   Exc.: $650   VGood: $525

MODEL 770

Package rifle similar to Model 710 but with redesigned bolt assembly and magazine catch. Chambered in .243, .270, 7mm-08, .308, .30-06, and .300 WM. Also available in Youth model chambered in .243 only. Introduced in 2007. In 2008 a version with stainless steel barrel and receiver and full camo finish was introduced.

NIB: $400   Exc.: $350   VGood: $250

REMINGTON MODEL 798

Long-action sporting rifle built on reworked 98 Mauser action. Calibers: .243, .308, .30-06, .270, .300 WM, .375 H&H, .458 WM. Barrel: 22-inch or 24-inch blued sightless. Stock: Brown laminated with recoil pad. Claw extractor, 2-position safety, hinged floorplate. Add 10 percent for Magnum chamberings; add 40 percent for .375 and .458.

NIB: $550   Exc.: $495   VGood: $365

REMINGTON MODEL 798 STAINLESS LAMINATE

Similar to Model 798 but with laminated stock and stainless barrel. Chambered in .243, .25-06, .270,

---

.30-06, 7mm Mag, .300 WM, .375 H&H Mag and .458 Win Mag. Add 30 percent for .458.

NIB: $695   Exc.: $625   VGood: $495

MODEL 798 SPS

Similar to Model 798 but with blued barrel and black synthetic stock. Introduced 2008.

NIB: $525   Exc.: $425   VGood: $300

MODEL 798 SAFARI

Similar to Model 798 but chambered in .375 H&H or .458 Winchester Magnum. Introduced 2008.

NIB: $1150   Exc.: $900   VGood: $675

REMINGTON MODEL 799

Similar to Model 798 but short-action without recoil pad. Calibers: .22 Hornet, .222 Remington, .22-250, .223, 762X39.

NIB: $525   Exc.: $470   VGood: $340

REMINGTON-LEE SPORTER

Bolt action; 6mm USN, 30-30, 30-40, 303 British, 7mm Mauser, 7.65 Mauser, 32 Spl., 32-40, 35 Spl., 38-55, 38-72, 405 Win., 43 Spanish, 45-70, 45-90; 5-shot detachable box magazine; 24-inch, 26-inch barrel; open rear sight, bead front; hand-checkered American walnut pistol-grip stock. Collector value. Introduced 1886; discontinued 1906.

Exc.: $1550   VGood: $965   Good: $595

REMINGTON-LEE SPORTER DELUXE

Same specs as Remington-Lee Sporter except half-octagon barrel; Lyman sights; deluxe walnut stock. Collector value. Introduced 1886; discontinued 1906.

Exc.: $1795   VGood: $995   Good: $695

REMINGTON MODEL 76 SPORTSMAN

Slide action; 30-06; 4-shot magazine; 22-inch barrel; 42-inch overall length; weighs 7-1/2 lbs.; open adjustable sights; walnut-finished hardwood stock, forend; cartridge head inset on receiver bottom denotes caliber; cross-bolt safety; tapped for scope mounts. Introduced 1984; discontinued 1987.

Perf.: $300   **Exc.:** $270   **VGood:** $225

REMINGTON MODEL 121A FIELDMASTER

Slide action; 22 Short, 22 Long, 22 LR; 20-shot (22 Short), 15-shot (22 Long), 14-shot (22 LR); 24-inch round barrel; weighs 6 lbs.; hammerless; takedown; white metal bead ramp front sights, step-adjustable rear; uncheckered pistol-grip stock; grooved semi-beavertail slide handle. Introduced 1936; discontinued 1954.

Exc.: $375   **VGood:** $325   **Good:** $250

REMINGTON MODEL 121S

Same specs as Model 121A except 22 Rem. Spl.; 12-shot magazine.

Exc.: $520   **VGood:** $430   **Good:** $335

REMINGTON MODEL 121SB

Same specs as Model 121A except smoothbore barrel for 22 shot cartridge.

Exc.: $600   **VGood:** $500   **Good:** $400

REMINGTON MODEL 141, 141A GAMEMASTER

Slide action; 30, 32, 35 Rem.; 5-shot tube magazine; 24-inch barrel; 42-3/4-inch overall length; weighs 7-3/4 lbs.; hammerless; takedown; white metal bead ramp front sight, step-adjustable rear; uncheckered American walnut half-pistol-grip stock; grooved slide handle. Introduced 1936; discontinued 1950.

Exc.: $470   **VGood:** $325   **Good:** $270

REMINGTON MODEL 141R CARBINE

Same specs as Model 141 except 30, 32 Rem., 18-1/2-inch barrel.

Exc.: $490   **VGood:** $350   **Good:** $285

REMINGTON MODEL 572A FIELDMASTER

Slide action; 22 Short, 22 Long, 22 LR; 20-shot (22 Short), 17-shot (22 Long), 15-shot (22 LR) tube magazine; 25-inch barrel; weighs 5-1/2 lbs.; hammerless; ramp front sight, open rear; uncheckered hardwood pistol-grip stock, grooved forearm. Introduced 1955; discontinued 1988.

Perf.: $250   **Exc.:** $225   **VGood:** $190

REMINGTON MODEL 572 FIELDMASTER

Same specs as Model 572A except 23-inch barrel; weighs 4 lbs.; "Sun-Grain" stock, forend in Buckskin tan or Crow-Wing black colors; chrome-plated magazine tube, trigger, floorplate. Add 20 percent for Crow Wing black.

Perf.: $450   **Exc.:** $425   **VGood:** $325

REMINGTON MODEL 572BDL DELUXE

Same specs as Model 572A except pistol-grip cap; RKW wood finish; checkered grip, slide handle; adjustable rear sight, ramp front. Still in production.

Perf.: $365   **Exc.:** $335   **VGood:** $275

REMINGTON MODEL 572SB

Same specs as Model 572A except smoothbore barrel for 22 shot cartridge. No longer produced.

Perf.: $395   **Exc.:** $230   **VGood:** $160

REMINGTON MODEL 572BDL SMOOTHBORE (2007)

Similar to Model 572 but with unrifled barrel for use with shot cartridges. Introduced in 2007.

NIB: $550   **Exc.:** $475   **VGood:** $315

REMINGTON MODEL 760

Slide action; 222 Rem., 223 Rem., 6mm Rem., 243 Win., 244 Rem., 257 Roberts, 270 Win., 280 Rem.,

Remington Model 121A
Fieldmaster

Remington Model 141A
Gamemaster

Remington Model 572A
Fieldmaster

Remington Model 572BDL Deluxe

Remington Model 572BDL
Smoothbore

Remington Model 760BDL

Remington Model 7600

30-06, 300 Savage, 308 Win., 35 Rem.; 4-shot magazine; 22-inch barrel; 42-1/4-inch overall length; weighs 7-1/2 lbs.; hammerless; white metal bead front sight on ramp, step-adjustable, semi-buckhorn rear. Models from mid-'60s to early '70s with impressed checkering; others hand-checkered on pistol grip, slide handle; early versions with grooved slide handle, no checkering on stock. Introduced 1952; discontinued 1980.

Perf.: $325   **Exc.:** $220   **VGood:** $180

222 Rem., 223 Rem.

Perf.: $1195   **Exc.:** $895   **VGood:** $695

257 Roberts

Perf.: $710   **Exc.:** $570   **VGood:** $375

REMINGTON MODEL 760ADL

Same specs as Model 760 except deluxe checkered stock, forend; grip cap; sling swivels; standard or high comb. Introduced 1953; discontinued 1963.

Perf.: $335   **Exc.:** $240   **VGood:** $200

REMINGTON MODEL 760BDL

Same specs as Model 760 except 270, 30-06, 308; basketweave checkering on pistol grip, forearm; black forearm tip; early versions in right- or left-hand styles.

Perf.: $350   **Exc.:** $250   **VGood:** $220

REMINGTON MODEL 760 CARBINE

Same specs as Model 760 except 270, 280, 30-06, 308, 35 Rem.; 18-1/2-inch barrel; 38-1/2-inch overall length; weighs 6-1/2 lbs.

Perf.: $410   **Exc.:** $300   **VGood:** $260

REMINGTON MODEL 760CDL

Same specs as Model 760 Carbine except checkered stock, forend; decorated receiver.

Perf.: $435   **Exc.:** $375   **VGood:** $310

REMINGTON MODEL 760D PEERLESS

Same specs as Model 760 except fine checkered fancy stock; engraving.

Perf.: $1000   **Exc.:** $850   **VGood:** $650

REMINGTON MODEL 760F PREMIER

Same specs as Model 760 except figured American walnut best-grade stock; fine checkered stock, forend; extensive engraved game scenes.

Perf.: $2420   **Exc.:** $1910   **VGood:** $1500

REMINGTON MODEL 760F PREMIER GOLD

Same specs as Model 760 except best-grade fine checkered fancy stock; extensive engraving with gold inlay.

Perf.: $5000   **Exc.:** $4000   **VGood:** $3000

REMINGTON MODEL 7600

Slide action; 6mm Rem., 243, 270, 280, 30-06, 308, 35 Whelen; 4-shot detachable magazine; 22-inch barrel; 42-inch overall length; weighs 7-1/2 lbs.; removable gold bead ramp front, windage-adjustable sliding ramp rear sight; tapped for scope mount; impressed checkered American walnut pistol-grip stock; positive cross-bolt safety. Introduced 1981; still in production in a number of variations.

Perf.: $425   **Exc.:** $350   **VGood:** $275

Remington 7600P Patrol Rifle

Remington Baby Carbine

Remington No. 1
Rolling Block Mid-Range Sporter

Remington No. 2

Remington No. 3

Remington No. 4

Remington No. 4-S Military

Remington No. 5

REMINGTON MODEL 7600 CARBINE
Same specs as Model 7600 except 30-06 only; 18-1/2-inch barrel; weighs 7-1/4 lbs.
   Perf.: $425   **Exc.:** $350   **VGood:** $275

REMINGTON 7600 SPECIAL PURPOSE
Same specs as Model 7600 except 270, 30-06; non-glare finished American walnut stock; all exposed metal with non-reflective matte black finish; quick-detachable sling swivels; camo-pattern Cordura carrying sling. Made in U.S. by Remington. Introduced 1993; discontinued 1994.
   Perf.: $400   **Exc.:** $360   **VGood:** $280

REMINGTON 7600D PEERLESS
Same specs as Model 7600 except fine checkered fancy walnut stock; engraving.
   Perf.: $2100   **Exc.:** $1600   **VGood:** $1200

REMINGTON 7600F PREMIER
Same specs as Model 7600 except best-grade fine checkered walnut stock; extensive engraving.
   Perf.: $4600   **Exc.:** $4000   **VGood:** $2600

REMINGTON 7600F PREMIER GOLD
Same specs as Model 7600 except best-grade fine checkered walnut stock; extensive engraving with gold inlays.
   Perf.: $7000   **Exc.:** $5100   **VGood:** $3400

REMINGTON 7600P PATROL RIFLE
Same specs as Model 7600, except 308 only, 16.5-inch barrel, 4-shot magazine; parkerized metal, black synthetic stock and forend, with sling swivel studs; weighs 7 lbs. Wilson Combat ghost-ring rear sight. Introduced 2002.
   Perf.: $460   **Exc.:** $375   **VGood:** $285

REMINGTON MODEL 7615 TACTICAL PUMP CARBINE
Pump-action rifle based on Model 7600 action and chambered in .223 Remington with 16-1/2" barrel. Folding synthetic stock. Introduced in 2007.
   Perf.: $700   **Exc.:** $575   **VGood:** N/A

REMINGTON MODEL 7615 SPECIAL PURPOSE SYNTHETIC
Similar to Model 7615 but with fixed stock and picatinny rail. A dealer exclusive for 2007.
   Perf.: $535   **Exc.:** N/A   **VGood:** N/A

REMINGTON MODEL 7615 CAMO HUNTER
Similar to Model 7615 Tactical but with fixed buttstock and entirely camo-finished except for action parts and trigger guard assembly. Introduced in 2007.
   Perf.: $535   **Exc.:** N/A   **VGood:** N/A

REMINGTON MODEL 7615 RANCH CARBINE
Similar to Model 7615 Tactical but with fixed buttstock, walnut buttstock and forend, and 18-1/2" barrel. No iron sights but drilled and tapped for scope mounts. Introduced in 2007.
   Perf.: $535   **Exc.:** N/A   **VGood:** N/A

REMINGTON BABY CARBINE
Single shot; rolling block; 44 Win.; 20-inch barrel; open rear sight, blade front; uncheckered American walnut carbine-style straight stock, forearm; barrel band. Introduced 1902; discontinued 1902.
   Exc.: $3000   **VGood:** $2500   **Good:** $1500

REMINGTON NO. 1 ROLLING BLOCK MID-RANGE SPORTER
Single shot, modern-production rolling block; 45-70, later 30-30, 444 Marlin; 30-inch round barrel; weighs 8-3/4 lbs.; 46-1/2-inch overall length; American walnut stock with checkered pistol grip and forend; Beaded blade front sight, adjustable center-notch buckhorn rear. Recreation of the original Remington rolling block, made new in U.S.A. by Remington. Reintroduced in 1998. Discontinued.
   Perf.: $1200   **Exc.:** $900   **VGood:** $700

REMINGTON NO. 2
Single shot; rolling block; 22, 25, 32, 38, 44 rimfire or centerfire; 24-inch, 26-inch, 28-inch, 30-inch barrel; open rear sight, bead front; American walnut straight-grip stock, schnabel forearm. Collector value. Introduced 1873; discontinued 1910.
   Exc.: N/A   **VGood:** $950   **Good:** $500

REMINGTON NO. 3
Single shot; falling block side-lever; 22 WCF, 22 Extra Long, 25-20 Stevens, 25-21 Stevens, 25-25 Stevens, 32 WCF, 32 Ballard & Marlin, 32-40 Rem., 38 WCF, 38-40 Rem., 38-50 Rem., 38-55 Ballard & Marlin, 40-60 Ballard & Marlin, 40-60 WCF, 45-60 Rem., 40-82 WCF, 45-70 Govt., 45-90 WCF; 28-inch, 30-inch half- or full-octagon barrel; open rear sight, blade front; hand-checkered pistol-grip stock. Collector value. Introduced 1880; discontinued 1911.
   VGood: $1100   **Good:** $800

REMINGTON NO. 3 HIGH POWER
Same specs as Model No. 3 except 30-30, 30-40, 32 Spl., 32-40, 38-55, 38-72; open rear sight, bead front; hand-checkered pistol-grip stock, forearm. Introduced 1893; discontinued 1907. Collector value.
   VGood: $1150   **Good:** $850

REMINGTON NO. 4
Single shot; rolling block; 22 Short, 22 Long, 22 LR, 25 Stevens rimfire; 32 Short, 32 Long, 32 Rimfire; 22-1/2-inch, 24-inch (32 Rimfire) octagonal barrel; blade front sight, open rear; plain walnut stock, forearm; solid-frame and takedown models. 1890 to 1901, solid frame; 1901 to 1926 first takedown with lever on right side; 1926 to 1933, second takedown with large screw head. Some collector value. Introduced 1890; discontinued 1933.
   VGood: $625   **Good:** $300

REMINGTON NO. 4-S MILITARY
Same specs as No. 4 except 22 Short, 22 Long, 22 LR; 26-inch barrel; military style, including stacking swivel, sling; bayonet stud on barrel; bayonet, scabbard originally included. Early production was marked "American Boy Scout"; later production was marked "Military Model." This rifle was never the officially adopted arm of the Boy Scouts of America; the reasons behind the early production markings are still unknown. Collector value. Introduced 1913; discontinued 1923.
   VGood: $1895   **Good:** $875

REMINGTON NO. 5
Single shot; rolling block; 7mm Mauser, 30-30, 30-40 Krag, 303 British, 32-40, 32 Spl., 38-55; 24-inch, 26-inch, 28-inch barrel; open sporting rear sight, blade front; uncheckered straight-grip stock. Some collector value. Introduced 1897; discontinued 1905.
   VGood: $1595   **Good:** $695

REMINGTON NO. 5 MILITARY
Same specs as No. 5 except only 8mm Lebel, 7mm Mauser, 7.62 Russian, 30 U.S.; 30-inch barrel. Also known as Model 1902.
VGood: $1595 **Good:** $695

REMINGTON NO. 6
Single shot; rolling block; 22 Short, 22 Long, 22 LR, 32 Rimfire Short, 32 Rimfire Long; 20-inch barrel; takedown; open front, rear sights; tang peep sight optional; plain straight stock, forearm. Introduced 1901; discontinued 1933.
VGood: $425 **Good:** $350

REMINGTON NO. 7
Single shot; 22 Short, 22 Long, 22 LR, 22 Stevens RF; other calibers on special order; 24-inch, 26-inch, 28-inch half-octagon barrel; Lyman combination rear sight, Beach combination front; rear tang sight on projection from curved pistol-grip tang; hand-checkered American walnut stock, forearm. About 1000 made, collector value. Introduced 1903; discontinued 1911.
VGood: $4195 **Good:** $1995

REMINGTON MODEL SPR18 SINGLE-SHOT RIFLE
An imported (Baikal) break-action rifle with silvertone receiver and fluted barrel. Formerly branded as "Remington Spartan." Calibers: .223, .243, .270, .30-06, .308. Weight: 6-3/4 lbs. Introduced 2005.
NIB: $350 **Exc.:** $300 **VGood:** $225

REMINGTON MODEL SPR94 COMBO GUN
Over/under rifle shotgun. Combinations: .410/.22 rimfire, .410/.17HMR, .41o/.22WMR, 12-ga./.223, 12-ga./.30-06, 12-ga./.308. Double triggers, tang safety. Imported; formerly branded as "Remington Spartan."
NIB: $575 **Exc.:** $500 **VGood:** $395

REMINGTON MODEL 412 SINGLE-SHOT RIFLE
Compact single-shot chambered for .22 LR. 19.5-inch blued barrel, hardwood stock.
NIB: $135 **Exc.:** $110 **VGood:** $75

RIGBY NOTE: RIFLES SHOULD BE INDIVIDUALLY APPRAISED AS CALIBER AND OPTIONS CAN AFFECT VALUES.

RIGBY 350 MAGNUM
Bolt action; 350 Mag.; 24-inch barrel; 5-shot box magazine; high-quality walnut stock with checkered full pistol grip, forearm; folding leaf rear sight, bead front. No longer in production.
Perf.: $3995 **Exc.:** $3400 **VGood:** $2600

RIGBY 416 MAGNUM
Bolt action; 375 H&H, 404, 416 Rigby, 416 Rem. Mag., 458 Win. Mag., 505; 24-inch barrel; 4-shot box magazine; walnut sporting stock with checkered pistol grip, forearm; folding leaf rear sight, bead front.
Perf.: $9250 **Exc.:** $7995 **VGood:** $5495

RIGBY BEST QUALITY
Double rifle; sidelock; 22 LR, 275 Mag., 350 Mag., 416 Rigby, 458 Win. Mag., 465, 470 NE, 577 NE, 600 NE; 24-inch-28-inch barrel; hammerless ejector; folding leaf rear sight, bead front; hand-checkered walnut stock; pistol-grip forearm; engraved receiver.
Perf.: $40,000 **Exc.:** $32,500 **VGood:** $25,000

RIGBY BIG GAME BOLT ACTION
Bolt action; 350 Mag., 375 H&H Mag., 404, 416 Rigby, 416 Rem. Mag., 458 Win. Mag., 505; 4-, 5-shot magazine; 21-inch-24-inch barrel; folding leaf rear sight, bead front; high-quality walnut sporting stock with checkered pistol grip, forearm.
Perf.: $8500 **Exc.:** $7600 **VGood:** $4900

Remington No. 6

Remington No. 7

Remington Model SPR18

Remington Model 412

Rigby 350 Magnum

Rigby Best Quality

Rigby Second Quality

Rigby Standard Bolt Action

RIGBY SECOND QUALITY
Double rifle; boxlock; 22 LR, 275 Mag., 350 Mag., 416 Rigby, 458 Win. Mag., 465, 470 NE, 577 NE, 600 NE; 22-inch-26-inch barrel; hammerless ejector; folding leaf rear sight, bead front; hand-checkered walnut stock; pistol grip, forearm; engraved receiver.
Perf.: $16,500 **Exc.:** $12,995 **VGood:** $9995

RIGBY STANDARD BOLT ACTION
Bolt action; 243, 270, 275 Rigby, 7x57, 30-06, 300 H&H Mag., 300 Win. Mag., 308, 7mm Rem. Mag., 375 H&H Mag., 404 Rigby, 458 Win. Mag.; 3-, 4-, 5-shot magazine; 20- to 25-inch barrel; folding leaf rear sight, bead front; walnut sporting stock with hand-checkered half pistol grip, forearm.
Perf.: $7995 **Exc.:** $5500 **VGood:** $3250
Magnum calibers
Perf.: $8500 **Exc.:** $5995 **VGood:** $3650

RIGBY STANDARD LIGHTWEIGHT
Same specs as Standard Bolt Action except 24-inch barrel; lighter weight.
Perf.: $7995 **Exc.:** $5500 **VGood:** $3250
Magnum calibers
Perf.: $8500 **Exc.:** $5995 **VGood:** $3650

RIGBY THIRD QUALITY
Double rifle; boxlock; 22 LR, 275 Mag., 350 Mag., 416 Rigby, 458 Win. Mag., 465, 470 NE, 577 NE, 600 NE; 22-inch-26-inch barrel; hammerless ejector; folding leaf rear sight, bead front; checkered walnut stock; engraved receiver. No longer in production.
Perf.: $12,000 **Exc.:** $10,000 **VGood:** $7500

RIZZINI EXPRESS 90L DOUBLE RIFLE
Double rifle, over/under; 30-06, 7x65R, 9.3x74R; 24-inch barrel; weighs 7-1/2 lbs; 40-inch overall length; Select European walnut stock with satin oil finish; English- style cheekpiece. Ramp front sight, quarter-rib with express sight. Color case-hardened boxlock action; automatic ejectors; single selective trigger; polished blue barrels. Extra 20-gauge shotshell barrels available. Comes with case. Imported for Italy by Wm. Larkin Moore.
Perf.: $4100 **Exc.:** $3200 **VGood:** $2500

ROCK RIVER ARMS STANDARD A2 RIFLE
Semi-automatic; 45 ACP; weighs 8.2 lbs.; Thermoplastic stock; Standard AR-15 style sights. Two-stage, national match trigger; optional muzzle brake. Made in U.S.A. From River Rock Arms.
Perf.: $8750 **Exc.:** $800 **VGood:** $660

Rock River Arms Standard A2

Rossi Model 62 SA

Rossi Model 62 SAC Carbine

Rossi Model 92 SRC

Rossi Model 92 SRS Puma Short Carbine

Sako Classic

Sako Fiberglass

Sako Finnbear Sporter

ROSS MODEL 1905 MARK II

Bolt action; 303 British; 4-shot magazine; 28-inch barrel; two-leaf open rear sight, bead front; hand-checkered American walnut sporting stock; straight-pull action. Introduced prior to WWI; no longer in production.

Exc.: $600   **VGood:** $495   **Good:** $395

ROSS MODEL 1910 MARK III

Bolt action; 280 Ross, 303 British; 4- or 5-shot magazine; 22-inch, 24-inch, 26-inch barrel; two-leaf open rear sight, bead front; hand-checkered American walnut sporting stock. Made in Canada. Some collector value. Some may be unsafe to fire. Introduced 1910; discontinued 1918.

Exc.: $600   **VGood:** $495   **Good:** $395

ROSSI MATCHED PAIR CENTERFIRE RIFLE/ SHOTGUN

Single shot, breakopen, 12 or 20 ga. shotgun barrel with interchangeable rifle barrel in 243, 270, 308, 30-06; weighs 5 to 7 lbs, depending on variant. Adjustable rifle sights, bead front on shotgun; internal transfer-bar mechanism, manual safety, trigger-block system.

Perf.: $190   **Exc.:** $160   **VGood:** $120

ROSSI MATCHED PAIR RIMFIRE RIFLE/SHOTGUN

Single shot, breakopen; 22 LR or 22 Mag. or 17 HMR; 18-1/2-inch or 23-inch barrel; weighs 6 lbs.; Hardwood stock (brown or black finish); Fully adjustable front and rear sights; Break-open action, transfer-bar manual safety, includes matched 410-, 20- or 12-gauge shotgun barrel with bead front sight. Introduced 2001. Imported by BrazTech/Taurus.

Perf.: $110   **Exc.:** $90   **VGood:** $80

ROSSI MODEL 59 SA

Slide action; 22 WMR; 23-inch round or octagonal barrel; 39-1/4-inch overall length; weighs 5-3/4 lbs.; takedown; blade front sight, adjustable rear; walnut stock with straight grip, grooved forend; blue finish. Imported from Brazil by Interarms. Introduced by Interarms 1978; no longer imported.

Exc.: $190   **VGood:** $145   **Good:** $130

ROSSI MODEL 62 SA

Slide action; 22 Short, 22 Long, 22 LR; 20-shot (22 Short), 16-shot (22 Long), 14-shot (22 LR) tube magazine; 23-inch round or octagon barrel; 39-1/4-inch overall length; weighs 5-3/4 lbs.; takedown; blade front sight, adjustable rear; walnut stock with straight grip, grooved forend; blued or nickel finish. Imported from Brazil. Introduced by Interarms 1978.

Exc.: $275   **VGood:** $235   **Good:** $150
Nickel finish
Exc.: $295   **VGood:** $250   **Good:** $155
Blue, with octagonal barrel
Exc.: $295   **VGood:** $250   **Good:** $155

ROSSI MODEL 62 SAC CARBINE

Same specs as Model 62 SA except 16-1/4-inch barrel. Introduced 1975.

Exc.: $160   **VGood:** $125   **Good:** $115

ROSSI MODEL 62 SA STAINLESS

Same specs as Model 62 SA except stainless steel barrel and action. Introduced 1986; discontinued 1986.

Exc.: $295   **VGood:** $250   **Good:** $155

ROSSI MODEL 65 SRC

Lever action; 44 Spl./44 Mag., 44-40; 10-shot tube magazine; 20-inch barrel; weighs 5-3/4 lbs.; blade front sight, buckhorn rear; uncheckered walnut stock; saddle ring. Introduced 1989.

Exc.: $260   **VGood:** $220   **Good:** $190

ROSSI MODEL 92 SRC

Lever action; 38 Spl., 357 Mag., 44-40, 44 Mag.; 9-shot (38 Spl.), 8-shot (other calibers); 20-inch barrel; blade front sight, buckhorn rear; uncheckered walnut stock. Made in Brazil. Introduced 1978.

Exc.: $300   **VGood:** $245   **Good:** $190
Engraved model
Exc.: $350   **VGood:** $300   **Good:** $250

ROSSI MODEL 92 SRS PUMA SHORT CARBINE

Same specs as Model 92 except 38-357; 16-inch barrel; 33-inch overall length. Early production with Puma medallion on side of receiver. Imported from Brazil by Interarms. Introduced 1986.

Exc.: $375   **VGood:** $295   **Good:** $225

ROSSI SINGLE SHOT CENTERFIRE RIFLE

Single shot, breakopen; 308 Win., 270 Win., 30-06 Spfld., 223 Rem., 243 Win.; 23-inch barrel; weighs 6-6.5 lbs.; Monte carlo stock, exotic woods, walnut finish & swivels with white line space and recoil pad. Scope rails and hammer extension included. Break Open, positive ejection, internal transfer bar mechanism and manual external safety. Trigger block system included.

Perf.: $200   **Exc.:** $175   **VGood:** $150

SAKO CLASSIC

Bolt action; 243, 270, 30-06, 7mm Rem. Mag.; 21-3/4-inch barrel; weighs 6 lbs.; classic-style stock with straight comb; matte finish wood. Imported from Finland by Stoeger. Introduced 1993.

Exc.: $700   **VGood:** $560   **Good:** $440

SAKO FIBERGLASS

Bolt action; 22-250, 243, 308, 7mm-08, 25-06, 270, 30-06, 7mm Rem. Mag., 300 Win. Mag., 338 Win. Mag., 375 H&H Mag.; 4-shot (Magnums), 5-shot magazine (standard calibers); 23-inch barrel; no sights; marketed with scope mounts; black fiberglass stock; wrinkle finish; rubber buttpad. Made in Finland. Introduced 1985.

Perf.: $1050   **Exc.:** $800   **VGood:** $600
Left-hand model
Perf.: $1100   **Exc.:** $1000   **VGood:** $800

SAKO FIBERGLASS CARBINE

Same specs as Fiberglass except 18-1/2-inch barrel; 243, 25-06, 270, 30-06, 7mm Rem. Mag., 300 Win. Mag., 375 H&H Mag. Introduced 1986; discontinued 1991.

Perf.: $1050   **Exc.:** $800   **VGood:** $600

SAKO FINNBEAR SPORTER

Bolt action; 25-06, 264 Win. Mag., 270, 30-06, 300 Win. Mag., 338 Mag., 7mm Rem. Mag., 375 H&H Mag.; 4-shot (Magnums), 5-shot magazine (standard calibers); 24-inch barrel; no rear sight, hooded ramp front; drilled, tapped for scope mounts; hand-checkered European walnut, Monte Carlo, pistol-grip stock; recoil pad; sling swivels. Introduced 1961; discontinued 1971.

Exc.: $795   **VGood:** $650   **Good:** $550

SAKO FINNFIRE

Bolt action; 22 LR; 5-shot magazine; 22-inch barrel; 40-inch overall length; weighs 5-1/4 lbs.; hooded blade front sight, open adjustable rear; European walnut stock with checkered grip and forend; adjustable single-stage trigger; 50-degree bolt lift. Imported from Finland by Stoeger Industries. Introduced 1994.

Exc.: $670   **VGood:** $490   **Good:** $410

SAKO FINNFIRE HUNTER BOLT-ACTION RIFLE

Bolt action; 22 LR, 5-shot magazine; 22-inch barrel; weighs 5.75 lbs.; 39-1/2-inch overall length; European walnut stock with checkered grip and forend; Hooded blade front sight, open adjustable rear; Adjustable single-stage trigger; has 50-degree bolt lift. Introduced 1994. Imported from Finland by Beretta USA.

Perf.: $820   **Exc.:** $700   **VGood:** $600

SAKO FINNFIRE SPORTER RIFLE

Bolt action; 22 LR. 22-inch barrel; heavy, free-floating; Match style stock of European walnut; adjustable cheekpiece and buttplate; stippled pistol grip and forend; no sights; has 11mm integral dovetail scope mount. Based on the Sako P94S action with two bolt locking lugs, 50-degree bolt lift and 30mm throw; adjustable trigger. Introduced 1999. Imported from Finland by Beretta USA.

Perf.: $890   **Exc.:** $770   **VGood:** $660

SAKO FINNSPORT MODEL 2700

Bolt action; 270, 300 Win. Mag.; 4-shot magazine; 21-inch, 22-inch barrel; no sights; scope mounts; Monte Carlo stock design. Introduced 1983; no longer in production.

Perf.: $795   **Exc.:** $675   **VGood:** $550

SAKO FINNWOLF

Lever action; 243 Win., 308 Win.; 3-, 4-shot magazine (early models); 23-inch barrel; hammerless; no rear sight, hooded ramp front; drilled, tapped for scope mounts; hand-checkered European walnut Monte Carlo stock in left- or right-hand styling; sling swivels. Introduced 1964; discontinued 1972.

Exc.: $1700   **VGood:** $1300   **Good:** $995

SAKO FORESTER SPORTER

Bolt action; 22-250, 243 Win., 308 Win.; 5-shot magazine; 23-inch barrel; no rear sight, hooded ramp front; drilled, tapped for scope mounts; hand-checkered walnut Monte Carlo pistol-grip stock; sling swivel studs. Introduced 1957; discontinued 1971.

Exc.: $775   **VGood:** $600   **Good:** $500

SAKO FORESTER SPORTER CARBINE

Same specs as Forester Sporter except 20-inch barrel; Mannlicher-type stock.

Exc.: $925   **VGood:** $695   **Good:** $600

SAKO FORESTER SPORTER HEAVY BARREL

Same specs as Forester Sporter except 24-inch heavy barrel.

Exc.: $800   **VGood:** $625   **Good:** $525

SAKO HUNTER

Bolt action; 17 Rem., 222 Rem., 223 Rem., 22-250, 243, 308, 7mm-08, 25-06, 270, 280, 30-06, 7mm Rem. Mag., 300 Win. Mag., 300 Weatherby Mag., 338 Win. Mag., 375 H&H Mag., 416 Rem. Mag.; 4-shot (Magnums), 5-shot magazine (standard calibers); 21-1/4-inch, 21-3/4-inch, 22-inch barrel; no sights; scope mounts; checkered classic-style French walnut stock; sling swivels. Made in Finland. Introduced 1986.

Exc.: $675   **VGood:** $495   **Good:** $410

Left-hand model

Exc.: $750   **VGood:** $575   **Good:** $440

SAKO HUNTER CARBINE

Same specs as Hunter except 22-250, 243, 7mm-08, 308, 300 Win. Mag., 25-06, 6.5x55, 270, 7x64, 30-06,

Sako Finnfire

Sako Finnfire Hunter

Sako Finnfire Sporter

Sako Finnsport Model 2700

Sako Finnwolf

Sako Forester Sporter

Sako Hunter Carbine

Sako Hunter LS

Sako Lightweight Deluxe

7mm Rem. Mag., 375 H&H Mag.; 18-1/2-inch barrel; oil-finished stock. Introduced 1986; discontinued 1991.

Exc.: $650   **VGood:** $450   **Good:** $400

SAKO HUNTER LS

Same specs as Hunter except laminated stock with dull finish. Introduced 1987.

Perf.: $975   **Exc.:** $795   **VGood:** $595

Left-hand model

Perf.: $995   **Exc.:** $825   **VGood:** $595

SAKO LIGHTWEIGHT DELUXE

Bolt action; 17 Rem., 222, 223, 22-250, 243, 308, 7mm-08, 25-06, 270, 280 Rem., 30-06, 7mm Rem. Mag., 300 Win. Mag., 338 Win. Mag., 300 Wea., 375 H&H, 416 Rem. Mag.; 21-inch, 22-inch barrel; select wood with skip-line checkering; rosewood grip cap and forend tip; ventilated recoil pad; fine checkering

on top surfaces of integral dovetail bases, bolt sleeve, bolt handle root and bolt knob; mirror finish bluing. Imported from Finland by Stoeger Industries.

Standard calibers

Perf.: $1125   **Exc.:** $925   **VGood:** $675

Magnum calibers

Perf.: $1175   **Exc.:** $950   **VGood:** $695

SAKO MANNLICHER CARBINE

Bolt action; 17 Rem., 222, 223, 243, 25-06, 270, 308, 30-06, 7mm Rem. Mag., 300 Win. Mag., 375 H&H Mag.; 4-shot (Magnums), 5-shot magazine (standard calibers); 18-1/2-inch barrel; open sights; full Mannlicher-style stock. Made in Finland. Introduced 1977.

Perf.: $895   **Exc.:** $695   **VGood:** $495

Magnum calibers

Perf.: $950   **Exc.:** $750   **VGood:** $550

Sako Mauser

Sako Model 74

Sako 75 Hunter

Sako 75 Stainless Synthetic Rifle

Sako 75 Deluxe Rifle

Sako 75 Finnlight

Sako 75 Single Shot Custom

Sako 75 Varmint

STW, 7mm Wea. Mag., 300 Win. Mag., 300 Wea. Mag., 338 Win. Mag., 340 Wea. Mag., 375 H&H, 416 Rem. Mag.; 22-inch barrel, standard calibers; 24-inch, 26-inch magnum calibers. weighs about 6 lbs.; European walnut stock with matte lacquer finish; no sights; dovetail scope mount rails. New design with three locking lugs and a mechanical ejector, key locks firing pin and bolt, cold hammer-forged barrel is free-floating, 2- position safety, hinged floorplate or detachable magazine that can be loaded from the top, short 70 degree bolt lift. Five action lengths. Introduced 1997. Imported from Finland by Beretta USA.

    Perf.: $1010   **VGood:** $800   **Good:** $660

SAKO 75 HUNTER LEFT-HAND
Similar to Sako 75 Hunter, but true left-hand action, 25-06, 270, 30-06.
    Perf.: $1200   **Exc.:** $1000   **VGood:** N/A

SAKO 75 HUNTER STAINLESS RIFLE
Similar to Sako 75 Hunter except all metal is stainless steel. Walnut stock with matte lacquer finish, rubber butt pad. Introduced 1999. Imported from Finland by Beretta USA. Still available.
    Perf.: $1100   **Exc.:** $880   **VGood:** $700

SAKO 75 DELUXE RIFLE
Similar to 75 Hunter except select wood rosewood gripcap and forend tip. Available in 17 Rem., 222, 223, 243, 260, 7mm-08, 7mm WSM, 308, 25-06, 270, 280, 30-06; 270 Wea. Mag., 7mm Rem. Mag., 7mm STW, 7mm Wea. Mag., 300 Win. Mag., 300 Wea. Mag., 338 Win. Mag., 340 Wea. Mag., 375 H&H, 416 Rem. Mag. Introduced 1997. Imported from Finland by Beretta USA.
    Perf.: $1550   **Exc.:** $1200   **VGood:** $900

SAKO 75 FINNLIGHT
Similar to Sako 75 Hunter, but stainless-steel metal parts and synthetic stock; calibers 243 Win., 7mm-08 Rem., 308 Win., 25-06 Rem., 270 Win., 280 Rem, 30-06 Spfld, 6.5x55, 7mm Rem. Mag., 300 Win. Mag.; 20-inch, 22-inch barrel, weighs 6-1/2 lbs.; no sights; introduced 2001, still imported from Finland by Beretta USA.
    Perf.: $1300   **Exc.:** $1000   **VGood:** 800

SAKO 75 SINGLE SHOT CUSTOM
Similar to Sako 75 Hunter, but single-shot only, 308, heavy 23.6-inch fluted stainless-steel barrel; laminated stock with beavertail forend; single set trigger; weighs 9 lbs.; introduced 2004.
    Perf.: $2800   **Exc.:** $2100   **VGood:** N/A

SAKO 75 STAINLESS SYNTHETIC RIFLE
Similar to 75 Hunter except all metal is stainless steel, synthetic stock has soft composite panels moulded into forend and pistol grip. Available in 22-250, 243, 308 Win., 25-06, 270, 30-06 with 22-inch barrel, 7mm Rem. Mag., 7mm STW, 300 Win. Mag., 338 Win. Mag. and 375 H&H Mag. with 24-inch barrel and 300 Wea. Mag., 300 Rem.Ultra Mag. with 26-inch barrel. Introduced 1997. Imported from Finland by Beretta USA.
    Perf.: $1100   **VGood:** $900   **Good:** $700

SAKO 75 VARMINT RIFLE
Similar to Model 75 Hunter except chambered only for 17 Rem., 204 Ruger, 222 Rem., 223 Rem., 22-250 Rem., 22 PPC, 243, 260, 6mm PPC, 308, 24-inch heavy barrel with recessed crown, beavertail forend. Introduced 1998. Imported from Finland by Beretta USA.
    Perf.: $1200   **Exc.:** $980   **VGood:** $770

SAKO 75 VARMINT STAINLESS LAMINATED RIFLE
Similar to Sako 75 Hunter except chambered only for 204 Ruger, 222, 223, 22-250, 22 PPC USA, 6mm PPC, 243, 260, 308, heavy 24-inch barrel with recessed crown, all metal is stainless steel, laminated wood stock with beavertail forend. Introduced 1999. Imported from Finland by Beretta USA.
    Perf.: $1350   **Exc.:** $1100   **VGood:** $900

SAKO MAUSER
Bolt action; 270, 30-06; 5-shot magazine; 24-inch barrel; open leaf rear sight, Patridge front; hand-checkered European walnut, Monte Carlo cheekpiece stock; sling swivel studs. Introduced 1946; discontinued 1961.
    Exc.: $550   **VGood:** $500   **Good:** $420

SAKO MAUSER MAGNUM
Same specs as Mauser except 8x60S, 8,2x57, 300 H&H Mag., 375 H&H Mag.; recoil pad. Discontinued 1961.
    Exc.: $650   **VGood:** $560   **Good:** $450

SAKO MODEL 72
Bolt action; 222 Rem., 223 Rem., 22-250, 243 Win., 25-06, 270 Win., 30-06, 308, 7mm Rem. Mag., 300 Win. Mag., 338 Win. Mag., 375 H&H Mag.; 23-inch, 24-inch barrel; adjustable rear sight, hooded front; hand-checkered European walnut stock; adjustable trigger; hinged floorplate. Introduced 1973; discontinued 1976.
    Exc.: $530   **VGood:** $470   **Good:** $400

SAKO MODEL 73
Lever action; 243 Win., 308 Win.; 3-shot clip magazine; 23-inch barrel; no rear sight, hooded ramp front; drilled, tapped for scope mounts; hand-checkered European walnut Monte Carlo stock; sling swivels; flush floorplate. Introduced 1973; discontinued 1975.
    Exc.: $495   **VGood:** $420   **Good:** $330

SAKO MODEL 74
Bolt action; 222 Rem., 223 Rem., 220 Swift, 22-250, 243, 25-06, 270, 7mm Rem. Mag., 30-06, 300 Win. Mag., 338 Win. Mag., 375 H&H Mag.; 4-shot (Magnums), 5-shot (standard calibers) magazine; 23-1/2-inch, 24-inch standard or heavy barrel; no sights; hand-checkered European walnut Monte Carlo stock; Mauser-type action; detachable sling swivels. Introduced 1974; no longer in production.
    Exc.: $575   **VGood:** $450   **Good:** $380

SAKO MODEL 74 CARBINE
Same specs as Model 74 except only 30-06; 20-inch barrel; Mannlicher-design full-length stock. Introduced 1974; no longer in production.
    Exc.: $595   **VGood:** $495   **Good:** $400

SAKO 75 HUNTER BOLT-ACTION RIFLE
Bolt action; 17 Rem., 222, 223, 22-250, 243, 260, 7mm-08, 308 Win., 25-06, 270, 6.5x55, 280, 30-06; 270 Wea. Mag., 7mm WSM, 7mm Rem. Mag., 7mm

SAKO MODEL 78

Bolt action; 22 WMR, 22 LR, 22 Hornet; 4-shot (22 Hornet), 5-shot magazine; 22-1/2-inch barrel; no sights; hand-checkered European walnut Monte Carlo stock. Introduced 1977; discontinued 1986.

Rimfire:
Exc.: $420   **VGood:** $400   **Good:** $350
22 Hornet:
Exc.: $480   **VGood:** $420   **Good:** $400

SAKO 85 HUNTER

Bolt-action centerfire rifle chambered in short and long calibers ranging from .223 Remington to .375 H&H Mag. Controlled round feeding, checkered walnut stock, satin blued sightless 22-7/16", 22-7/8", or 24-3/8" barrel.

NIB: $1250   **Exc.:** $1150   **VGood:** $875

SAKO 85 STAINLESS SYNTHETIC

Similar to Sako 85 Hunter but with stainless steel receiver and barrel.

NIB: $1300   **Exc.:** $1200   **VGood:** $900

SAKO 85 FINNLIGHT

Similar to Sako 85 Stainless Synthetic but with recoil pad and ultra-lightweight synthetic stock. Chambered in long and short cartridges ranging from .243 to .300 Win Mag.

NIB: $1200   **Exc.:** $1100   **VGood:** $850

SAKO 85 VARMINT

Similar to Sako 85 Hunter but with recoil pad and 7.5-oz. set trigger. Chambered in .204 Ruger, .243, .22-250 or .308.

NIB: $1350   **Exc.:** $1250   **VGood:** $950

SAKO 85 LAMINATED SS VARMINT

Similar to Sako 85 Varmint but with laminated stock and stainless steel barrel. Introduced 2007.

NIB: $1500   **Exc.:** $1400   **VGood:** $1100

SAKO QUAD

Bolt-action rimfire rifle with four interchangeable barrels for .22 LR, .22 Magnum, .17 Mach 2 and .17 HMR. Available with satin walnut or grey synthetic stock. Four- and two-barrel combos available. Pricing is for four-barrel Hunter version (walnut stock).

NIB: $1500   **Exc.:** $1400   **VGood:** $1050

SAKO PPC MODEL

Bolt action; single shot; 22 PPC, 6mm PPC; 5-shot magazine; 21-3/4-inch, 23-3/4-inch (Benchrest) barrel; weighs 8-1/2 lbs. (heavy barrel); checkered walnut stock; beavertail forend; rosewood pistol grip, forearm (Deluxe). Introduced 1989; no longer in production.

Hunter model
Perf.: $1100   **Exc.:** $900   **VGood:** $650
Deluxe model
Perf.: $1350   **Exc.:** $1050   **VGood:** $900
Benchrest model
Perf.: $995   **Exc.:** $895   **VGood:** $695

SAKO SAFARI GRADE

Bolt action; 338 Win. Mag., 375 H&H Mag., 416 Rem. Mag.; 4-shot magazine; 22-inch barrel; quarter-rib "express" rear sight, hooded ramp front; French walnut stock; checkered 20 lpi, solid rubber buttpad; grip cap and forend tip; front sling swivel band-mounted on barrel. Imported from Finland by Stoeger Industries.

Exc.: $1750   **VGood:** $1100   **Good:** $700

SAKO STANDARD SPORTER

Bolt action; 17 Rem., 222, 223 (short action); 22-250, 220 Swift, 243, 308 (medium action); 25-06, 270, 30-06, 7mm Rem. Mag., 300 Win. Mag., 338 Win. Mag., 375 Mag., 375 H&H Mag. (long action); 23-inch, 24-inch barrel; no sights; hand-checkered European walnut pistol-grip stock, with hinged floorplate; adjustable trigger. Imported from Finland. Introduced 1978; no longer imported.

Short action
Exc.: $670   **VGood:** $550   **Good:** $450

Sako 75 Varmint Stainless Laminated Rifle

Sako Model 78

Sako Standard Sporter

Sako Standard Sporter Deluxe

Sako Standard Sporter Safari

Sako TRG-21

Medium action
Exc.: $670   **VGood:** $550   **Good:** $450
Long action
Exc.: $670   **VGood:** $550   **Good:** $450

SAKO STANDARD SPORTER CARBINE

Same specs as Standard Sporter except 222, 243, 270, 30-06; 20-inch barrel; full Mannlicher-type stock. Introduced 1977; no longer imported.

Exc.: $675   **VGood:** $565   **Good:** $460

SAKO STANDARD SPORTER CLASSIC

Same specs as Standard Sporter except 243, 270, 30-06, 7mm Rem. Mag.; receiver drilled, tapped for scope mounts; straight-comb stock with oil finish; solid rubber recoil pad; recoil lug. Introduced 1980; no longer imported.

Exc.: $675   **VGood:** $545   **Good:** $450

SAKO STANDARD SPORTER DELUXE

Same specs as Standard Sporter except select wood; rosewood pistol-grip cap, forend tip; metal checkering on dovetail bases, bolt sleeve, bolt handle; ventilated recoil pad; skip-line checkering. No longer imported.

Exc.: $865   **VGood:** $725   **Good:** $600

SAKO STANDARD SPORTER HEAVY BARREL

Same specs as Standard Sporter except beavertail forend; made with short, medium actions only.

Exc.: $695   **VGood:** $595   **Good:** $450

SAKO STANDARD SPORTER SAFARI

Same specs as Standard Sporter except long action; 7mm Rem. Mag., 300 Win. Mag., 338 Win Mag., 375 H&H Mag.; quarter-rib express rear sights, hooded ramp front; hand-checkered European walnut stock, solid rubber recoil pad; pistol-grip cap, forend tip; front sling swivel mounted on barrel. No longer imported.

Exc.: $1900   **VGood:** $1125   **Good:** $800

SAKO STANDARD SPORTER SUPER DELUXE

Same specs as Standard Sporter Deluxe except select European walnut stock with deep-cut oak leaf carving; rosewood pistol-grip cap, forend tip; high-gloss finish; metal checkering on dovetail bases, bolt sleeve, bolt handle; metal has super-high polish. No longer imported.

Perf.: $2500   **Exc.:** $1800   **VGood:** $1000

SAKO STANDARD SPORTER VARMINT HEAVY BARREL

Same specs as Standard Sporter Super Deluxe except 17 Rem., 222, 223 (short action), 22-250, 243, 308, 7mm-08 (medium action); 5-shot magazine; weighs from 8-1/4 to 8-1/2 lbs.; beavertail forend. Imported from Finland by Stoeger Industries.

Perf.: $900   **Exc.:** $750   **VGood:** $600

SAKO TRG-21

Bolt action; 308 Win.; 10-shot magazine; free-floating 25-3/4-inch heavy stainless barrel; 46-1/2-inch overall length; weighs 10-1/2 lbs.; no sights; optional quick-detachable, one-piece scope mount base, 1-inch or 30mm rings; reinforced polyurethane stock with fully-adjustable cheekpiece and buttplate; resistance-free bolt; 60-degree bolt lift; two-stage trigger adjustable for length, pull, horizontal or vertical pitch. Imported from Finland by Stoeger. Introduced 1993.

Perf.: $3200   **Exc.:** $2600   **VGood:** $1800

Sako TRG-22

Sako TRG-S

Sako Vixen Sporter Carbine

Sako Vixen Sporter Heavy Barrel

Sauer Model 90

Sauer Model 90 Safari

Sauer Model 90 Supreme

SAKO TRG-22 BOLT-ACTION RIFLE
Bolt action; 308 Win., 10-shot magazine; 26-inch barrel; weighs 10-1/4 lbs.; 45-1/4-inch overall length; Reinforced polyurethane stock with fully adjustable cheekpiece and buttplate; no sights; Optional quick-detachable, one-piece scope mount base, 1-inch or 30mm rings. Resistance-free bolt, free-floating heavy stainless barrel, 60-degree bolt lift. Two-stage trigger adjustable for length, pull, horizontal or vertical pitch. Introduced 2000.

Perf.: $2500   Exc.: $2000   VGood: $1700

SAKO TRG-S
Bolt action; 243, 7mm-08, 270, 30-06, 7mm Rem. Mag., 300 Win. Mag., 338 Win. Mag., 375 H&H, 416 Rem. Mag.; 5-shot magazine (4-shot for 375 H&H); 22-inch, 24-inch (Magnum calibers) barrel; 45-1/2-inch overall length; weighs 7-3/4 lbs.; no sights; reinforced polyurethane stock with Monte Carlo comb; resistance-free bolt with 60-degree lift; recoil pad adjustable for length; free-floating barrel; detachable magazine; fully-adjustable trigger; matte blue metal. Imported from Finland by Stoeger. Introduced 1993.

Perf.: $720   Exc.: $650   VGood: $475

SAKO TRG-42 BOLT-ACTION RIFLE
Similar to TRG-S except 5-shot magazine, fully adjustable stock and competition trigger. Offered in 338 Lapua Mag. and 300 Win. Mag. Still imported from Finland by Beretta USA.

Perf.: $2950   Exc.: $2100   VGood: $1700

SAKO VIXEN SPORTER
Bolt action (short action); 218 Bee, 22 Hornet, 222 Rem., 222 Rem. Mag., 223; 5-shot magazine; 23-1/2-inch barrel; no rear sight, hooded ramp front; drilled, tapped for scope mounts; checkered European walnut, Monte Carlo, pistol-grip stock; cheekpiece; sling swivels. Introduced 1946; discontinued 1976.

Exc.: $795   VGood: $650   Good: $500

SAKO VIXEN SPORTER CARBINE
Same specs as Vixen Sporter except 20-inch barrel; Mannlicher-type stock.

Exc.: $895   VGood: $695   Good: $550

SAKO VIXEN SPORTER HEAVY BARREL
Same specs as Vixen Sporter except only 222 Rem., 222 Rem. Mag., 223; heavy barrel; target-style stock; beavertail forearm.

Exc.: $1050   VGood: $795   Good: $550

SAUER DRILLING
Drilling; side-by-side; 12-gauge, 2-3/4-inch chambers/243, 6.5x57R, 7x57R, 7x65R, 30-06, 9.3x74R; 16-gauge, 2-3/4-inch chambers/6.5x57R, 7x57R, 7x65R, 30-06; 25-inch barrel; 46-inch overall length; weighs 7-1/2 lbs.; bead front sight, automatic pop-up rifle rear; fancy French walnut stock with checkered grip and forend, hog-back comb, sculptured cheekpiece, hand-rubbed oil finish; Greener boxlock cross-bolt action with double underlugs; Greener side safety; separate rifle cartridge extractor; nitride-coated, hand-engraved receiver available with English Arabesque or relief game animal scene engraving; Lux Model with profuse relief-engraved game scenes, extra-fancy stump wood. Was imported from Germany by Paul Co.

Standard		
Perf.: $3795	**Exc.: $3050**	**VGood: $2495**
Lux		
Perf.: $5295	**Exc.: $4495**	**VGood: $3750**

SAUER MAUSER SPORTER
Bolt action; 7x57, 8x57, 30-06; other calibers on special order; 5-shot box magazine; 22-inch, 24-inch half-octagon barrels, matted raised rib; three-leaf open rear sight, ramp front; hand-checkered pistol-grip European walnut stock; raised side panels; schnabel tip; double-set triggers; sling swivels; also manufactured with full-length Mannlicher-style stock, 20-inch barrel. Manufactured prior to WWII.

Exc.: $695   VGood: $595   Good: $495

Full-length stock		
Exc.: $795	**VGood: $695**	**Good: $550**

SAUER MODEL 90
Bolt action; 222, 22-250, 243, 308, 25-06, 270, 30-06, 7mm Rem. Mag., 300 Win. Mag., 300 Weatherby Mag., 338 Win. Mag., 375 H&H Mag., 458 Win. Mag.; 3-shot (Magnums), 4-shot detachable box magazine (standard calibers); 22-1/2-inch, 26-inch barrel; windage-adjustable open rear sight, post front on ramp; oil-finished European walnut stock; recoil pad; rear bolt-locking lugs; front sling swivel on barrel band. Made in Germany. Introduced 1986; discontinued 1989.

Exc.: $895   VGood: $650   Good: $600

SAUER MODEL 90 LUX
Same specs as Model 90 except only 300 Win. Mag., 300 Weatherby Mag., 338 Win. Mag., 375 H&H Mag.; deluxe oil-finished European walnut stock; rosewood forearm tip, pistol-grip cap; gold trigger.

Exc.: $1395   VGood: $995   Good: $660

SAUER MODEL 90 SAFARI
Same specs as Model 90 except 458 Win. Mag.; 23-2/3-inch barrel. Introduced 1986; discontinued 1988.

Perf.: $1295   Exc.: $995   VGood: $795

SAUER MODEL 90 SAFARI LUX
Same specs as Model 90 except 458 Win. Mag.; 23-2/3-inch barrel; Williams sights; rosewood forearm, pistol-grip cap; gold trigger.

Exc.: $1400   VGood: $1100   Good: $900

SAUER MODEL 90 STUTZEN
Same specs as Model 90 except 222, 22-250, 243, 308, 25-06, 270, 30-06; Mannlicher-style full stock. Introduced 1986; discontinued 1989.

Exc.: $800   VGood: $700   Good: $600

SAUER MODEL 90 STUTZEN LUX
Same specs as Model 90 Lux except Mannlicher-style stock.

Exc.: $1195   VGood: $895   Good: $795

SAUER MODEL 90 SUPREME
Same specs as Model 90 except 25-06, 270, 30-06, 300 Win. Mag., 300 Weatherby Mag., 7mm Rem. Mag., 338 Win. Mag., 375 H&H Mag.; high-gloss European walnut stock; jeweled bolt; gold trigger. Introduced 1987; still in production.

Grade I engraving		
Perf.: $1295	**Exc.: $995**	**VGood: $875**
Grade II engraving		
Perf.: $2595	**Exc.: $1995**	**VGood: $1195**
Grade III engraving		
Perf.: $2895	**Exc.: $2295**	**VGood: $1395**
Grade IV engraving		
Perf.: $3495	**Exc.: $2995**	**VGood: $1995**

SAUER MODEL 200

Bolt action; various calibers from 243 to 375 H&H Mag.; 3-shot (Magnums), 4-shot detachable box magazine (standard calibers); 24-inch interchangeable barrels; 44-inch overall length; no sights; drilled, tapped for iron sights or scope mounts; checkered European walnut pistol-grip stock; left-hand model available; steel or alloy versions. Made in Germany. Introduced 1986; discontinued 1993.

Exc.: $795   **VGood:** $595   **Good:** $500

Left-hand model

Exc.: $850   **VGood:** $650   **Good:** $550

SAUER MODEL 200 CARBON FIBER

Same specs as Model 200 except carbon fiber stock. Introduced 1986; discontinued 1988.

Exc.: $800   **VGood:** $725   **Good:** $660

SAUER MODEL 200 LUX

Same specs as Model 200 except deluxe walnut stock; rosewood forearm tip, pistol-grip cap; gold trigger. Introduced 1986; discontinued 1988.

Exc.: $765   **VGood:** $645   **Good:** $550

Left-hand model

Exc.: $860   **VGood:** $750   **Good:** $600

SAUER MODEL 202

Bolt action; 22 LR, 243, 6.5x55, 6.5x57, 25-06, 270, 280, 7x64, 308, 30-06, 9,3x62 (standard calibers); 6.5x68, 8x68S, 7mm Rem. Mag., 300 Win. Mag., 300 Wea. Mag., 338 Win. Mag., 375 H&H (Magnum calibers); interchangeable 24-inch barrel (standard calibers), 26-inch (Magnum calibers); weighs 7-1/2 lbs. (steel), 6-1/2 lbs. (alloy); sights optional; drilled, tapped for scope mounting; modular receiver accepts interchangeable barrels; steel or alloy receiver; standard stock of fancy Claro walnut, two-piece, with Monte Carlo comb, palm swell grip, semi-schnabel forend tip; Super Grade with extra-fancy Claro walnut with rosewood grip cap, forend tip, high-gloss epoxy finish; French walnut Eurostock with oil finish available; right- or left-hand bolt; tang safety; fully-adjustable trigger; cocking indicator; detachable magazine. Was imported from Germany by Paul Co., now by Sigarms. Introduced 1994.

Exc.: $855   **VGood:** $755   **Good:** $625

Super Grade

Exc.: $895   **VGood:** $795   **Good:** $675

375 H&H Magnum

Exc.: $950   **VGood:** $795   **Good:** $695

375 H&H Magnum Super Grade

Exc.: $1050   **VGood:** $895   **Good:** $750

SAUER MODEL 202 ALASKA

Same specs as Model 202 except 300 Wea. Mag. or 300 Win. Mag.; 26-inch barrel; weighs 8-1/4 lbs.; laminated brown stock; metal coated with "Ilaflon" for protection. Accepts any Model 202 Magnum barrel. Was imported from Germany by Paul Co. Introduced 1994.

Perf.: $1095   **Exc.:** $925   **VGood:** $750

SAUER MODEL 202 HUNTER MATCH

Same specs as Model 202 except 6.5x55, 308; 28-inch match barrel; French walnut sporter stock; matte black finish. Introduced 1994.

Perf.: $1295   **Exc.:** $995   **VGood:** $795

SAUER 202 TR TARGET

Bolt action; 6.5x55mm, 308 Win.; 5-shot magazine; 26-inch, 28-1/2-inch heavy match target barrel; 44-1/2-inch overall length; weighs 12 lbs.; globe front sight, Sauer-Busk 200-600m diopter rear; drilled, tapped for scope mounting; one-piece true target-type stock of laminated beechwood/ epoxy; adjustable buttplate and cheekpiece; interchangeable free-floating, hammer-forged barrel; two-stage adjustable trigger; vertical slide safety; 3 millisecond lock time; rail for swivel, bipod; right- or left-hand; converts to 22 rimfire. Was imported from Germany by Paul Co. Introduced 1994.

Exc.: $1500   **VGood:** $1100   **Good:** $800

SAUER MODEL SSG 2000

Bolt action; 223, 308, 7.5 Swiss, 300 Weatherby Mag.; 4-shot detachable box magazine; 24-inch, 26-inch barrel; weighs 13-1/5 lbs.; no sights; scope

Sauer Model 200

Savage Mark I

Savage Mark II

Savage Mark II-LV Heavy Barrel

Savage Model 3

Savage Model 4

mounts; thumbhole walnut stock; adjustable comb, buttplate, forend rail; stippled grip, forend; right- or left-hand models; flash hider/muzzlebrake; double-set triggers; sliding safety. Made in Germany. Introduced 1985; discontinued 1986.

Exc.: $4495   **VGood:** $2595   **Good:** $1750

SAVAGE CUB

Bolt action, single shot; 22LR, 17 Mach 2; 16-1/8-inch barrel; weighs 3.3 lbs; rear peep, post front sights; uses Mark I bolt action in scaled-down junior-size rifle; blued barrel and action; walnut-finished hardwood stock. Made in Canada, from Savage Arms; Introduced 2003, still in production.

Perf.: $135   **Exc.:** 100   **VGood:** $75

SAVAGE MODEL CUB-T

Similar to Model CUB but with laminated thumbhole stock.

NIB: $235   **Exc.:** $200   **VGood:** $175

SAVAGE MARK I BOLT-ACTION RIFLE

Bolt action; 22 LR, single shot, 22 LR Shot version also available; 20-3/4-inch barrel; weighs 5-1/2 lbs.; 39-1/2-inch overall length; Walnut-finished hardwood stock with Monte Carlo-type comb, checkered grip and forend, synthetic stock also available; Bead front sight, open adjustable rear. Receiver grooved for scope mounting. Thumb-operated rotating safety. Blue finish. Youth models with camo or color-laminate stocks also produced. Introduced 1990. Made in Canada, from Savage Arms Inc.

Perf.: $115   **Exc.:** $95   **VGood:** $70

SAVAGE MARK II BOLT-ACTION RIFLE

Bolt action; 22 LR, 17 Mach 2; repeater with 10-shot detachable box magazine; 20-1/2-inch barrel; weighs 5-1/2 lbs.; 39-1/2-inch overall length; Walnut-finished hardwood stock with Monte Carlo-type comb, checkered grip and forend, synthetic stock also available; Bead front sight, open adjustable rear. Receiver grooved for scope mounting. Thumb-operated rotating safety; left-hand version also available. Blue finish. Introduced 1990. Made in Canada, from Savage Arms, Inc.

Mark II standard model

Perf.: $125   **Exc.:** $100   **VGood:** $80

Mark II (youth), 19-inch barrel, 37-inch overall, 5 lbs.

Perf.: $125   **Exc.:** $100   **VGood:** $80

SAVAGE MARK II-LV HEAVY BARREL RIFLE

Similar to Mark II-G except heavy 21-inch barrel with recessed target-style crown, laminated hardwood stock with cut checkering. No sights furnished, has dovetailed receiver for scope mounting. Overall length is 39-3/4-inch, weighs 6-1/2 lbs. Comes with 10-shot detachable box magazine. Introduced 1997. Imported from Canada by Savage Arms, Inc.

Perf.: $170   **Exc.:** $150   **VGood:** $120

With black synthetic stock

Perf.: $160   **Exc.:** $140   **VGood:** $110

SAVAGE MODEL MARK II CLASSIC

Similar to Mark II but with sporter-weight barrel and oil-finished premium walnut stock. AccuTrigger.

NIB: $415   **Exc.:** $375   **VGood:** $300

SAVAGE MODEL 3

Bolt action; single shot; 22 Short, 22 Long, 22 LR; 26-inch barrel (pre-WWII), 24-inch (post-WWII); 43-inch overall length; weighs 5 lbs.; takedown; chromium-plated bolt, trigger; adjustable flat-top rear sight, gold bead front; receiver drilled, tapped for scope mounting; uncheckered American walnut one-piece pistol-grip stock; early forearm with finger grooves; checkered hard rubber or steel buttplate. Introduced 1933; discontinued 1952.

Exc.: $90   **VGood:** $80   **Good:** $60

SAVAGE MODEL 3S

Same specs as Model 3 except rear peep sight, hooded front sight with three inserts. Introduced 1933; discontinued 1942.

Exc.: $100   **VGood:** $90   **Good:** $70

SAVAGE MODEL 3ST

Same specs as Model 3S except rear peep sight, hooded front sight; swivels, sling. Introduced 1933; discontinued 1942.

Exc.: $110   **VGood:** $90   **Good:** $80

Savage Model 5

Savage Model 19

Savage Model 10FM
Sierrra

Savage Model 10FCM
Scout

Savage Model 19 NRA

Savage Model 23AA

quick-detachable swivels. Introduced 1998, still
offered. Made in U.S.A. by Savage Arms, Inc.

Perf.: $390   **Exc.:** $290   **VGood:** $220

SAVAGE MODEL 10FCM SCOUT ULTRA LIGHT RIFLE

Bolt action; 7mm-08 Rem., 308 Win. 20-inch barrel;
weighs 6.25 lbs.; 39.75-inch overall length; Synthetic
stock with checkering, dual pillar bed. Ghost ring rear
sight, gold bead front. Blued, detachable 4-shot box
magazine, Savage shooting sling/carry strap. Quick
detachable swivels. Introduced 1999, discontinued
after two years; reintroduced 2007.

Perf.: $525   **Exc.:** $460   **VGood:** $310

SAVAGE MODEL 19

Bolt action; 22 LR; 5-shot detachable box magazine;
25-inch barrel; weighs 8 lbs.; early model with
adjustable rear peep sight, blade front; later model
with hooded front sight, Savage No. 15 fully-
adjustable aperture extension rear; target-type
uncheckered one-piece walnut stock; full pistol grip,
2-inch wide beavertail forearm; checkered buttplate;
receiver drilled for scope blocks; 1-1/4-inch sling;
sling swivels. Introduced 1933; discontinued 1946.

Exc.: $230   **VGood:** $190   **Good:** $150

SAVAGE MODEL 19H

Same specs as Model 19 except chambered for 22
Hornet. Introduced 1933; discontinued 1942.

Exc.: $495   **VGood:** $440   **Good:** $300

SAVAGE MODEL 19L

Same specs as Model 19 except Lyman 48Y
receiver sight, No. 17A front sight. Introduced 1933;
discontinued 1942.

Exc.: $325   **VGood:** $265   **Good:** $200

SAVAGE MODEL 19M

Same specs as Model 19 except heavy 28-inch
barrel; scope bases. Introduced 1933; discontinued
1942.

Exc.: $350   **VGood:** $290   **Good:** $220

SAVAGE MODEL 19 NRA

Same specs as Model 19 except adjustable rear
sight, blade front; American walnut military-type full
stock, pistol grip; uncheckered. Introduced 1919;
discontinued 1933.

Exc.: $230   **VGood:** $190   **Good:** $150

SAVAGE MODEL 23A

Bolt action; 22 LR; 5-shot detachable box magazine;
23-inch barrel; open rear sight, blade or bead front;
uncheckered American walnut pistol-grip stock, thin
forearm, schnabel tip. Introduced 1923; discontinued
1933.

Exc.: $220   **VGood:** $180   **Good:** $130

SAVAGE MODEL 23AA

Same specs as Model 23A except 22 Short, 22 Long,
22 LR; checkered stock; swivel studs; speed lock;
receiver tapped for No. 10 Savage aperture rear
sight. Introduced 1933; discontinued 1942.

Exc.: $270   **VGood:** $220   **Good:** $170

SAVAGE MODEL 23B

Same specs as Model 23A except 25-20; 25-inch
barrel; weighs 6-1/2 lbs.; swivel studs; no schnabel
tip. Introduced 1923; discontinued 1942.

Exc.: $250   **VGood:** $200   **Good:** $150

SAVAGE MODEL 23C

Same specs as Model 23B except 32-20; 25-inch
barrel; swivel studs; no schnabel tip. Introduced
1923; discontinued 1942.

Exc.: $250   **VGood:** $200   **Good:** $150

SAVAGE MODEL 23D

Same specs as Model 23B except 22 Hornet;
25-inch barrel; weighs 6-1/2 lbs.; swivel studs; no
schnabel tip; flat-top adjustable rear sight, gold bead
front. Introduced 1923; discontinued 1947.

Exc.: $310   **VGood:** $270   **Good:** $220

SAVAGE MODEL 4

Bolt action; 22 Short, 22 Long, 22 LR; 5-shot
detachable box magazine; 24-inch barrel; weighs
5-1/2 lbs.; takedown; chromium-plated bolt,
trigger; pre-WWII version with open rear sight,
bead front; checkered pistol grip; American walnut
stock, grooved forearm; post-WWII model with
uncheckered stock; rubber buttplate. Introduced
1933; discontinued 1965.

Pre-WWII model
Exc.: $110   **VGood:** $95   **Good:** $80
Post-WWII model
Exc.: $115   **VGood:** $100   **Good:** $90

SAVAGE MODEL 4M

Same specs as post-war Model 4 except 22 WMR;
gold-plated trigger. Introduced 1961; discontinued
1965.

Exc.: $120   **VGood:** $95   **Good:** $80

SAVAGE MODEL 4S

Same specs as Model 4 except fully-adjustable
rear peep sight, hooded front with three inserts.
Introduced 1933; discontinued 1942.

Exc.: $120   **VGood:** $100   **Good:** $90

SAVAGE MODEL 5

Bolt action; 22 Short, 22 Long, 22 LR; 21-shot (22
Short), 17-shot (22 Long), 15-shot (22 LR) tubular
magazine; 24-inch tapered barrel with crowned
muzzle; weighs 6 lbs.; takedown; chromium-plated
bolt, trigger; fully-adjustable sporting rear sight,
gold bead front; redesigned American walnut stock,
bolt handle, trigger guard; hard rubber buttplate.
Introduced 1936; discontinued 1961.

Exc.: $120   **VGood:** $105   **Good:** $90

SAVAGE MODEL 5S

Same specs as Model 5 except No. 15 Micro peep
rear sight, hooded No. 150 front. Introduced 1936;
discontinued 1942.

Exc.: $125   **VGood:** $110   **Good:** $90

SAVAGE MODEL 10FM SIERRA ULTRA LIGHT RIFLE

Bolt action; 223, 243, 308. 20-inch barrel; weighs 6
lbs.; 41-1/2-inch overall length; "Dual Pillar" bedding
in black synthetic stock with silver medallion in
gripcap; no sights; drilled and tapped for scope
mounting. True short action. Comes with sling and

SAVAGE MODEL 30 STEVENS FAVORITE

Single shot, falling block; 22 LR, 22WMR, 17 HMR; 20-1/2-inch barrel; weighs 4.25 lbs.; 36.75-inch overall length; Walnut stock, straight grip, schnabel forend; Adjustable rear sight, bead post front. Lever action falling block, inertia firing pin system, half octagonal or full octagonal bbl. Add $20 for camo finish.

Perf.: $200   **Exc.:** $170   **VGood:** $140

SAVAGE MODEL 34

Bolt action; 22 Short, 22 Long, 22 LR; 5-shot magazine; 20-inch barrel; open rear sight, blade front; uncheckered hardwood pistol grip or checkered Monte Carlo stock. Introduced 1969; discontinued 1973.

Exc.: $90   **VGood:** $80   **Good:** $50

SAVAGE MODEL 34M

Same specs as Model 34 except 22 WMR. Introduced 1969; discontinued 1973.

Exc.: $100   **VGood:** $90   **Good:** $70

SAVAGE MODEL 35

Bolt action; 22 LR; 5-shot magazine; 22-inch barrel; 41-inch overall length; ramp front sight, step-adjustable open rear; walnut-finished hardwood Monte Carlo stock; checkered pistol grip, forend; receiver grooved for scope mount. Introduced 1982; discontinued 1985.

Exc.: $90   **VGood:** $80   **Good:** $50

SAVAGE MODEL 35M

Same specs as Model 35 except 22 WMR. Introduced 1982; discontinued 1985.

Exc.: $100   **VGood:** $90   **Good:** $60

SAVAGE MODEL 36

Bolt action; single shot; 22 LR; 22-inch barrel; 41-inch overall length; ramp front sight, step-adjustable rear; walnut-finished hardwood Monte Carlo stock; checkered pistol grip, forend; receiver grooved for scope mount. Introduced 1982; discontinued 1985.

Exc.: $80   **VGood:** $65   **Good:** $40

SAVAGE MODEL 40

Bolt action; 250-3000, 30-30, 300 Savage, 30-06; 4-shot detachable box magazine; 22-inch, 24-inch barrel (300 Savage, 30-06); weighs 7-1/2 lbs.; semi-buckhorn rear sight, white metal bead front on ramp; uncheckered American walnut pistol-grip stock; tapered forearm; schnabel tip; steel buttplate. Introduced 1928; discontinued 1940.

Exc.: $350   **VGood:** $300   **Good:** $250

SAVAGE MODEL 40 VARMINT HUNTER

Bolt action, single shot; 22 Hornet, 223; 24-inch heavy barrel; new Model 40 action with AccuTrigger; heavy laminated stock with beavertail forend; no sights. 223 chambering was dropped shortly after introduction, will bring a premium. Introduced 2004, still produced.

Perf.: $375   **Exc.:** $300   **VGood:** N/A

SAVAGE MODEL 45

Bolt action; 250-3000, 30-30, 300 Savage, 30-06; 4-shot detachable box magazine; 22-inch (250-3000, 30-30), 24-inch barrel; Deluxe version of Model 40 rifle. Lyman receiver sight, bead front on ramp; hand-checkered pistol-grip stock, forearm, schnabel tip. Introduced 1928; discontinued 1940.

Exc.: $400   **VGood:** $350   **Good:** $300

SAVAGE MODEL 46

Bolt action; 22 Short, 22 Long, 22 LR; 20-shot (22 Short), 17-shot (22 Long), 15-shot (22 LR) tubular magazine; open rear sight, blade front; uncheckered hardwood pistol grip or checkered Monte Carlo stock. Introduced 1969; discontinued 1973.

Exc.: $90   **VGood:** $75   **Good:** $60

SAVAGE MODEL 63

Bolt action; single shot; 22 Short, 22 Long, 22 LR; 18-inch barrel; 36-inch overall length; weighs 4 lbs.;

Savage Model 23D

Savage Model 30 Stevens "Favorite"

Savage Model 40

Savage Model 40 Varmint Hunter

Savage Model 63

Savage Model 65

Savage Model 93 Magnum

Savage Model 93 Classic Thumbhole

Savage Model 93XP

open rear sight, hooded ramp front; one-piece full-length walnut-finished hardwood pistol-grip stock; sling swivels; furnished with key to lock trigger. Introduced 1970; discontinued 1972.

Exc.: $85   **VGood:** $70   **Good:** $40

SAVAGE MODEL 63M

Same specs as Model 63K except only 22 WMR. Introduced 1970; discontinued 1972.

Exc.: $90   **VGood:** $80   **Good:** $60

SAVAGE MODEL 65

Bolt action; 22 LR; 5-shot detachable clip magazine; 20-inch lightweight tapered barrel; 39-inch overall length; weighs 4-3/4 lbs.; gold bead ramp front sight, open rear with elevator; receiver grooved for scope mounting; select walnut Monte Carlo pistol-grip stock; buttplate with white line spacer; raised fluted comb; thumb safety; double extractors. Introduced 1965; discontinued 1974.

Exc.: $100   **VGood:** $80   **Good:** $60

SAVAGE MODEL 65M

Same specs as Model 65 except 22 WMR. Introduced 1966; discontinued 1981.

Exc.: $130   **VGood:** $110   **Good:** $80

SAVAGE MODEL 93 MAGNUM BOLT-ACTION RIFLE

Bolt action; 22 WMR, 17 HMR; 5-shot magazine. 20-

3/4-inch barrel; weighs 5-3/4 lbs.; 39-1/2-inch overall length; Walnut-finished hardwood stock with Monte Carlo-type comb, checkered grip and forend. Bead front sight, adjustable open rear. Receiver grooved for scope mount. Thumb-operated rotary safety. Blue finish. Introduced 1994. Made in Canada, from Savage Arms.

Perf.: $140   **Exc.:** $120   **VGood:** $100

With black synthetic stock

Perf.: $130   **Exc.:** $110   **VGood:** $90

SAVAGE MODEL 93 CLASSIC THUMBHOLE

Similar to above but with thumbhole stock.

NIB: $350   **Exc.:** $295   **VGood:** $350

SAVAGE MODEL 93XP

.22 WMR package gun with 22-inch barrel and factory-mounted 3x9 scope. Finished overall with Mossy Oak Brush stock.

NIB: $375   **Exc.:** $295   **VGood:** $250

SAVAGE MODEL 93FSS MAGNUM RIFLE

Similar to Model 93G except stainless steel barreled action and black synthetic stock with positive checkering. Weighs 5-1/2 lbs. Introduced 1997. Imported from Canada by Savage Arms, Inc.

Perf.: $190   **Exc.:** $150   **VGood:** $100

Savage Model 93FVSS
Magnum

Savage Model 10FP
Tactical

Savage Model 110B

Savage Model 110C

Savage Model 110C
Left-Hand

Savage Model 110CY
Ladies/Youth

Savage Model 110D

Savage Model 110D
Left-Hand

Savage Model 110E

SAVAGE MODEL 93FVSS MAGNUM RIFLE

Similar to Model 93FSS Magnum except 21-inch heavy barrel with recessed target-style crown, satin-finished stainless barreled action, black graphite/fiberglass stock. Drilled and tapped for scope mounting; comes with Weaver-style bases. Introduced 1998. Made in Canada by Savage Arms, Inc.

Perf.: $200   **Exc.:** $160   **VGood:** $120

SAVAGE MODEL 93BTVS

Similar to Model 93FVSS but with laminated thumbhole stock.

NIB: $390   **Exc.:** $335   **VGood:** $290

SAVAGE MODEL 93R17 CLASSIC

Similar to Model 93 but in .17HMR only with sporter-weight barrel and oil-finished premium walnut stock. AccuTrigger. Introduced in 2007.

NIB: $450   **Exc.:** $395   **VGood:** $295

SAVAGE MODEL 10 PREDATOR HUNTER

Similar to Model 110FC but with overall camo

finish, 22" medium-contour barrel, and AccuTrigger. Chambered in .204 Ruger, .22-250 and .223.

NIB: $575   **Exc.:** $525   **VGood:** $400

SAVAGE MODEL 10FP TACTICAL RIFLE

Similar to the Model 110FP except has true short action, chambered for 223, 308; black synthetic stock with Pillar bedding. Introduced 1998. Made in U.S.A. by Savage Arms, Inc.

Perf.: $500   **Exc.:** $400   **VGood:** $320

SAVAGE MODEL 10FCP-HS PRECISION

Similar to Model 110FP but with one-piece HS Precision synthetic target stock and detachable box magazine. Introduced in 2007.

NIB: $795   **Exc.:** $725   **VGood:** $595

SAVAGE MODEL 10FCP CHOATE

Similar to Model 10FP but with Choate synthetic stock.

NIB: $650   **Exc.:** $600   **VGood:** $495

SAVAGE MODEL 10FCP MCMILLAN

Similar to Model 10FP but with synthetic McMillan precision stock.

NIB: $725   **Exc.:** $685   **VGood:** $595

SAVAGE MODEL 110

Bolt action; 243, 270, 308, 30-06; 4-shot box magazine; 22-inch medium-weight barrel; 43-inch overall length; weighs 6-3/4 lbs.; step-adjustable rear sight, gold bead ramp front; hand-checkered American walnut pistol-grip stock; aluminum buttplate; pistol-grip cap. Introduced 1958; discontinued 1963.

Exc.: $200   **VGood:** $175   **Good:** $140

SAVAGE MODEL 110B

Same specs as Model 110 except 243, 270, 30-06; 4-shot internal magazine; checkered American walnut Monte Carlo pistol-grip stock, forearm. Introduced 1977; discontinued 1979.

Perf.: $300   **Exc.:** $275   **VGood:** $200

Left-hand model

Exc.: $300   **VGood:** $270   **Good:** $190

SAVAGE MODEL 110B LAMINATE

Same specs as Model 110 except 300 Win. Mag., 338 Win. Mag.; 3-shot internal magazine; 24-inch barrel; brown laminated hardwood Monte Carlo pistol-grip stock, forearm. Introduced 1989; discontinued 1991.

Exc.: $270   **VGood:** $240   **Good:** $180

SAVAGE MODEL 110C

Same specs as Model 110 except 22-250, 243 Win., 25-06, 270 Win., 30-06, 308 Win., 7mm Rem. Mag., 300 Win. Mag.; 3-shot (Magnums), 4-shot detachable box magazine; 22-inch, 24-inch (22-250, Magnums) barrel; open folding leaf rear sight, gold bead ramp front; hand-checkered Monte Carlo American walnut pistol-grip stock; recoil pad (Magnums). Introduced 1966.

Exc.: $265   **VGood:** $230   **Good:** $200

Left-hand model

Exc.: $270   **VGood:** $240   **Good:** $210

SAVAGE MODEL 110CY LADIES/ YOUTH

Same specs as Model 110 except 223, 243, 270, 300 Sav., 308; 5-shot magazine; ramp front sight, fully-adjustable rear; drilled and tapped for scope mounting; walnut-stained hardwood stock with high comb, cut checkering; 12-1/2-inch length of pull; red rubber buttpad. Made in U.S. by Savage. Introduced 1991.

Perf.: $325   **Exc.:** $275   **VGood:** $225

SAVAGE MODEL 110D

Same specs as Model 110 except 22-250, 223 Rem., 243, 25-06, 270, 308, 30-06, 7mm Rem. Mag., 264, 300 Win. Mag., 338 Win. Mag.; 3-shot (Magnums), 4-shot magazine; 22-inch, 24-inch (22-250) barrel; 42-1/2 to 45-inch overall length; weighs 6-3/4 to 8 lbs. (22-250); semi-buckhorn step-adjustable folding rear sight; hinged floorplate; aluminum buttplate or hard rubber (22-250) recoil pad. Introduced 1966; discontinued 1988.

Exc.: $340   **VGood:** $290   **Good:** $260

Left-hand model

Exc.: $350   **VGood:** $300   **Good:** $270

SAVAGE MODEL 110E

Same specs as Model 110 except 22-250, 223, 243 Win., 30-06, 270, 7mm Rem. Mag., 308; 3-shot (Magnum), 4-shot box magazine; 20-inch, 24-inch (7mm, stainless) barrel; 40-1/2-inch overall length (20-inch barrel), 45-1/2-inch (24-inch); weighs 6-3/4 lbs.; uncheckered Monte Carlo stock (early versions); checkered pistol grip, forearm (later models); recoil pad (Magnum). Introduced 1963; discontinued 1989.

Exc.: $300   **VGood:** $250   **Good:** $200

Left-hand model

Exc.: $310   **VGood:** $260   **Good:** $210

SAVAGE MODEL 110ES

Same specs as Model 110E except 30-06, 243, 308 Win.; comes with 4x scope and mount. Introduced 1983.

Exc.: $340   **VGood:** $300   **Good:** $250

SAVAGE 110F

Same as Model 110 except 22-250, 223 Rem., 243 Win., 250 Savage, 25-06, 308 Win., 30-06, 270 Win., 7mm Rem Mag., 300 Savage, 300 Win. Mag., 7mm-08, 338 Win. Mag.; removable open sights; black Du Pont Rynite stock with black buttpad, swivel studs; right-hand only. Made in U.S. by Savage. Introduced 1988; discontinued 1994.

Exc.: $380   **VGood:** $300   **Good:** $270

SAVAGE 110FNS

Same specs as Model 110F except no sights; black composite stock. Made in U.S. by Savage. No longer made.

Exc.: $320   **VGood:** $240   **Good:** $190

SAVAGE MODEL 110FP POLICE

Same specs as Model 110F except 223, 308, 30-06, 300 Win. Mag., 7mm Rem. Mag., 25-06; 4-shot internal magazine; 24-inch heavy barrel; 45-1/2-inch overall length; weighs 8-1/2 lbs.; no sights; drilled, tapped for scope mounts; black graphite/fiberglass composition stock; double swivel studs on forend for swivels or bipod; matte finish on all metal parts. Introduced 1990; still in production.

Exc.: $400   **VGood:** $330   **Good:** $280

SAVAGE MODEL 110FP

Composite stock and 24" heavy barrel. In 2003 the Savage AccuTrigger was added to this model. Discontinued.

Exc.: $285   **VGood:** $250   **Good:** $175

SAVAGE MODEL 110FP TACTICAL RIFLE

Bolt action, long action; 223, 25-06, 308, 30-06, 300 Win. Mag., 7mm Rem. Mag.; 4-shot magazine; 24-inch heavy barrel; recessed target muzzle crown; weighs 8-1/2 lbs.; 45-1/2-inch overall length; Black graphite/fiberglass composition stock; positive checkering; no sights; receiver drilled and tapped for scope mounting; pillar-bedded stock; black matte finish on all metal parts. Double swivel studs on the forend for sling and/or bipod mount. Right or left-hand. Introduced 1990. From Savage Arms, Inc.

Perf.: $500   **Exc.:** $400   **VGood:** $320

SAVAGE MODEL 110G

Same specs as Model 110 except 22-250, 223 Rem., 250 Savage, 25-06, 270 Win., 300 Savage, 308 Win., 30-06, 243 Win., 7mm-08, 7mm Rem. Mag., 300 Win. Mag.; 5-shot (standard calibers), 4-shot (Magnums); 22-inch 24-inch round tapered barrels; 42-inch overall length (22-inch barrel); checkered walnut-finished Monte Carlo hardwood stock; hard rubber buttplate; ramp front sight, step-adjustable rear; top tang safety; tapped for scope mounts; floating barrel; adjustable trigger. Introduced, 1989.

Exc.: $335   **VGood:** $285   **Good:** $250

Left-hand model (110GL)
Exc.: $345   **VGood:** $300   **Good:** $260

SAVAGE 110GC

Same specs as Model 110G except 30-06, 270, 7mm Rem. Mag., 300 Win. Mag.; detachable box magazine. Made in U.S. by Savage. No longer made.

Perf.: $340   **Exc.:** $300   **VGood:** $250

SAVAGE MODEL 110GCXP3 PACKAGE

Same specs as Model 110G except 270, 30-06, 7mm Rem. Mag., 300 Win. Mag.; detachable box magazine; factory-mounted and bore-sighted 3-9x32 scope, rings and bases; quick-detachable swivels; sling; Monte Carlo-style hardwood stock with walnut finish; left-hand models available in all calibers. Made in U.S. by Savage Arms, Inc. Introduced 1994

Exc.: $410   **VGood:** $370   **Good:** $320

SAVAGE 110GLNS

Same specs as Model 110G except 30-06, 270, 7mm Rem. Mag.; true left-hand action; no sights. Made in U.S. by Savage. No longer made.

Exc.: $320   **VGood:** $260   **Good:** $220

SAVAGE 110GNS

Same specs as Model 110G except no sights. Made in U.S. by Savage. No longer made.

Exc.: $300   **VGood:** $270   **Good:** $230

Savage Model 110FP
Police

Savage Model 10FP
Tactical

Savage Model 110S

Savage Model 110
50th Anniversary

SAVAGE 110GV VARMINT

Same as Model 110G except 22-250, 223; no sights; receiver drilled and tapped for scope mounting; medium-weight varmint barrel. Made in U.S. by Savage. Introduced 1989; discontinued 1993.

Exc.: $330   **VGood:** $290   **Good:** $240

SAVAGE MODEL 110GXP3 PACKAGE

Same specs as Model 110G except package with scope and sling; 223, 22-250, 243, 250 Savage, 25-06, 270, 300 Sav., 30-06, 308, 7mm Rem. Mag., 7mm-08, 300 Win. Mag.; factory mounted bore-sighted 3-9x32 scope, rings and bases; quick-detachable swivels; sling; Monte Carlo-style hardwood stock with walnut finish; left-hand models available in all calibers. Made in U.S. by Savage Arms, Inc. Introduced 1991; still produced.

Exc.: $385   **VGood:** $330   **Good:** $280

SAVAGE MODEL 110K

Same specs as Model 110 except laminated camouflage stock; 243, 270, 30-06, 7mm Rem. Mag., 338 Win. Mag.; Introduced 1986; discontinued 1988.

Exc.: $330   **VGood:** $290   **Good:** $240

SAVAGE MODEL 110M

Same specs as Model 110 except 264 Win. Mag., 300 Win. Mag., 7mm Rem. Mag., 338 Win. Mag.; 3-shot magazine; 24-inch stainless steel barrel; 45-inch overall length; weighs 8 lbs. (338); hand-checkered American walnut pistol-grip Monte Carlo stock; recoil pad. Introduced 1963; discontinued 1969.

Exc.: $320   **VGood:** $270   **Good:** $220

Left-hand model (110ML)
Exc.: $340   **VGood:** $300   **Good:** $240

SAVAGE MODEL 110MC

Same specs as Model 110 except 22-250; 24-inch barrel; hand-checkered American walnut pistol-grip Monte Carlo stock. Introduced 1959; discontinued 1969.

Exc.: $370   **VGood:** $330   **Good:** $270

Left-hand model (110MC-L)
Exc.: $390   **VGood:** $340   **Good:** $300

SAVAGE MODEL 110P PREMIER GRADE

Same specs as Model 110 except 243 Win., 30-06, 7mm Rem. Mag.; 3-shot (Magnum), 4-shot magazine; 22-inch, 24-inch (7mm, stainless) barrel; 43-inch-45-inch overall length; weighs 7-7-3/4 lbs.; recessed bolt head; double front locking lugs; top tang safety; aluminum buttplate; skip-checkered Monte Carlo select French walnut stock; hand-carved roll-over cheekpiece; rosewood pistol-grip cap, forearm tip with white inlay; recoil pad (Magnum); left- or right-hand action. Introduced 1964; discontinued 1970.

Exc.: $440   **VGood:** $330   **Good:** $310

7mm Rem. Mag. model
Exc.: $460   **VGood:** $350   **Good:** $330

SAVAGE MODEL 110PE PRESENTATION GRADE

Same specs as Model 110 except 243 Win., 30-06, 7mm Rem. Mag.; 3-shot (Magnum), 4-shot magazine; 22-inch, 24-inch (Magnum) barrel; skip-checkered Monte Carlo fancy French walnut stock; rosewood pistol-grip cap, forearm tip; recoil pad (Magnum); right-, or left-hand action; engraved receiver, trigger guard, floorplate. Introduced 1958; discontinued 1970.

Exc.: $695   **VGood:** $595   **Good:** $495

7mm Rem. Mag. model
Exc.: $725   **VGood:** $625   **Good:** $525

SAVAGE MODEL 110S

Same specs as Model 110 except 308, 7mm-08; 5-shot magazine; 22-inch heavy tapered barrel; weighs 8-1/2 lbs.; no sights; drilled, tapped for scope mounts; special silhouette stock with Wundhammer swell stippled pistol grip, forend; rubber recoil pad. Introduced 1978; discontinued 1985.

Exc.: $350   **VGood:** $300   **Good:** $275

SAVAGE MODEL 110V

Same specs as Model 110 except 22-250, 223; 5-shot magazine; 26-inch heavy barrel; no sights; checkered American walnut varmint stock. Introduced 1983; discontinued 1989.

Exc.: $350   **VGood:** $300   **Good:** $250

SAVAGE 110WLE LIMITED EDITION ONE OF ONE THOUSAND

Same specs as Model 110 except 7x57mm Mauser, 250-3000 Savage, 300 Savage; high-luster #2 fancy-grade American walnut stock with cut checkering; swivel studs, and recoil pad; highly polished blue; the bolt with laser-etched Savage logo. Sold with gun lock, ear plugs, sight-in target and shooting glasses. Made in U.S. by Savage. Introduced 1992; no longer made.

Exc.: $460   **VGood:** $400   **Good:** $360

SAVAGE MODEL 110 - FIFTIETH ANNIVERSARY

Short-action rifle commemorating the 50th anniversary of the Model 10. Chambered in .300 Savage with 22-inch barrel. 1000 numbered rifles, high-luster blued barrel and action, unique checkering pattern on select walnut stock, high-grade hinged floorplate, Scroll pattern on receiver, 24-inch double barrel bands, 24-karat gold plated double barrel bands, 24-karat gold plated AccuTrigger, embossed recoil pad.

NIB.: $700   **Exc.:** $525   **VGood:** $375

SAVAGE MODEL 111 CHIEFTAIN

Bolt action; 243 Win., 270 Win., 7x57, 7mm Rem. Mag., 30-06; 3-shot (Magnum), 3-shot detachable clip magazine; 22-inch, 24-inch (Magnum, stainless) barrel; 43- to 45-inch overall length; 7-1/2 to 8-1/4 lbs.; leaf rear sight, hooded ramp front; select checkered American walnut pistol-grip stock;

Savage Model 111G Classic Hunter

Savage Model 11BTH

Savage Model 12BTCSS

Savage Model 112V

Monte Carlo comb; cheekpiece; pistol-grip cap; hard rubber or recoil pad (Magnum) with white line spacer; detachable swivels; sling. Introduced 1974; discontinued 1978.

Exc.: $370   **VGood:** $330   **Good:** $280

SAVAGE MODEL 111 HUNTER
Bolt action; 25-06, 270, 30-06, 7mm Rem. Mag., 300 Win. Mag., 338 Win. Mag., 300 Rem. Ultra Mag., 7mm WSM, 300 Rem. Ultra Mag., 7mm Rem. Ultra Mag., 270 WSM, 300 Win. Short Mag., 7mm Rem. Short Ultra Mag. Barrel: 22-inch, 24-inch (magnum calibers). Stock: Walnut-finished hardwood or synthetic. Sights: Ramp front, open fully adjustable rear; drilled and tapped for scope mounting. Three-position top tang safety, double front locking lugs, free-floated button-rifled barrel. Introduced 1994, still produced. Made in U.S.A. by Savage Arms, Inc.

Perf.: $340   **Exc.:** $320   **VGood:** $270

SAVAGE MODEL 11 HUNTER RIFLE
Similar to the Model 111 except has true short action, chambered for 223, 22-250, 243, 308; black synthetic or walnut-finished hardwood stock. Introduced 1998, still produced. Made in U.S.A. by Savage Arms, Inc.

Perf.: $320   **Exc.:** $300   **VGood:** $250

SAVAGE MODEL 11FYCAK
Short-action youth model chambered in .243, 7mm-08, and .308. Barrel: 22-inch blued with muzzlebrake, no sights. Stock: Black composite. Weight 6.5 lbs.; 41.5-inch overall length.

NIB: $495   **Exc.:** $460   **VGood:** $355

SAVAGE MODEL 111FYCAK
Similar to Model 11FYCAK but long-action chambered for .25-06, .270 and .30-06.

NIB: $495   **Exc.:** $460   **VGood:** $355

SAVAGE MODEL 11BTH
Laminated, thumbhole-stock version of the Model 11 chambered in .204, .223, .22-250 and .22 Hornet. 22-inch blued barrel.

Exc.: $460   **VGood:** $400   **Good:** $360

SAVAGE MODEL 111F CLASSIC HUNTER
Same specs as Model 111 except calibers from 25-06 to 338 Win. Mag.; top-loading magazine; graphite/fiberglass filled classic-style stock with non-glare finish; positive checkering; black recoil pad; swivel studs. Right- or left-hand action. Made in U.S. by Savage Arms, Inc. Model number reintroduced 1994; still produced.

With sights		
Exc.: $350	**VGood:** $300	**Good:** $250
Without sights as Model 111FNS		
Exc.: $290	**VGood:** $250	**Good:** $210
With detachable magazine as Model 111FC		
Exc.: $300	**VGood:** $270	**Good:** $230

SAVAGE MODEL 111G CLASSIC HUNTER
Same specs as Model 111 except 223, 22-250, 243, 250 Sav., 25-06, 270, 300 Sav., 30-06, 308, 7mm Rem. Mag., 7mm-08, 300 Win. Mag.; weighs about 6-1/2 lbs.; ramp front sight, open fully-adjustable rear (or no sights); receiver drilled, tapped for scope mounting; classic-style, walnut-finished hardwood stock with straight comb, ventilated red rubber recoil pad; three-position top tang safety; double front locking lugs; free-floated button-rifled barrel; trigger lock, target, ear puffs. Right- or left-hand action. Made in U.S. by Savage Arms, Inc. Model number reintroduced 1994; still produced.

With sights		
Perf.: $325	**Exc.:** $300	**VGood:** $250
Without sights as Model 111GNS		
Perf.: $300	**Exc.:** $275	**VGood:** $225
With detachable magazine as Model 111GC		
Perf.: $300	**Exc.:** $270	**VGood:** $230

SAVAGE MODEL 112 LONG RANGE RIFLE
Bolt action; 25-06, 30-06, 7mm Rem Mag, 300 Win Mag; 5-shot magazine; 26-inch heavy barrel; weighs 8.8 lbs.; 47-1/2-inch overall length; Black graphite/fiberglass filled composite stock with positive checkering. no sights; drilled and tapped for scope mounting; pillar-bedded stock; Blued barrel with recessed target-style muzzle crown; double front swivel studs for attaching bipod. Introduced 1991. Made in U.S.A. by Savage Arms, Inc.

Perf.: $450   **Exc.:** $400   **VGood:** $350

SAVAGE MODEL 12 LONG RANGE RIFLE
Similar to the Model 112 Long Range except with true short action, chambered for 223, 22-250, 308; black synthetic stock or brown laminated stock; fluted stainless barrel. Introduced 1998. Made in U.S.A. by Savage Arms, Inc.

Perf.: $440   **Exc.:** $390   **VGood:** $340

SAVAGE MODEL 12 LONG RANGE PRECISION VARMINTER (LRPV)
Single-shot bolt action chambered in .204 Ruger, .223 or .22-250. Features include AccuTrigger and oversized bolt handle. Composite stock, sightless stainless steel fluted barrel. Weight: 11.25 lbs.

NIB: $875   **Exc.:** $825   **VGood:** $675

SAVAGE MODEL 12VSS VARMINTER RIFLE
Similar to other Model 12s except blue/stainless steel action, fluted stainless barrel, Choate full pistol-grip, adjustable synthetic stock, Sharp Shooter trigger. Overall length 47-1/2 inches, weighs appx. 15 lbs. No sights; drilled and tapped for scope mounts. Chambered in 223, 22-250, 308 Win. Made in U.S.A. by Savage Arms Inc.

Perf.: $640   **Exc.:** $500   **VGood:** $400

SAVAGE MODEL 12BTCSS
Similar to Model 12VSS but with laminated thumbhole MonteCarlo stock with short action and detachable box magazine.

NIB: $725   **Exc.:** $595   **VGood:** $350

SAVAGE MODEL 12 F/TR F-CLASS TARGET RIFLE
International-class target rifle chambered in .6.5x284 Norma. Ventilated forend, laminated "underhold" target stock, oversize bolt knob, AccuTrigger, 30" stainless barrel. Also available in Model 12F/TR version with conventional buttstock and elevated cheekpiece.

NIB: $1100   **Exc.:** $995   **VGood:** $850

SAVAGE MODEL 112BV
Bolt action; 22-250, 223 Rem.; 4-shot magazine; 26-inch barrel; no sights; drilled, tapped for scope mounts; brown laminate stock, Wundhammer pistol grip; alloy steel construction. Introduced 1993; discontinued 1993.

Exc.: $475   **VGood:** $430   **Good:** $365

SAVAGE MODEL 112BT COMPETITION GRADE
Same specs as Model 112BV except 223, 300 Win. Mag., 308 Win.; 5-shot (223, 308 Win.) magazine; single shot (300 Win.); stainless barrel with black finish; laminated wood stock with straight comb, adjustable cheek rest, Wundhammer palm swell, ventilated forend; recoil pad adjustable for length of pull; matte black alloy receiver; bolt with black titanium nitride coating, large handle ball; alloy accessory rail on forend. Sold with safety gun lock, target and ear puffs. Made in U.S. by Savage Arms, Inc. Introduced 1994.

Perf.: $910   **Exc.:** $800   **VGood:** $675

SAVAGE MODEL 112FV VARMINT RIFLE
Same specs as Model 112BV except 220 Swift (single shot), 22-250, 223 (4-shot magazine); weighs 8-1/2 lbs.; blued, heavy 26-inch barrel with recessed target-style muzzle; black graphite/fiberglass composite stock with positive checkering; double front swivel studs for attaching bipod. Made in U.S. by Savage Arms, Inc. Introduced 1991; no longer produced.

Exc.: $360   **VGood:** $300   **Good:** $240

SAVAGE MODEL 112FVSS
Same specs as Model 112BV except 223, 22-250, 25-06, 7mm Rem. Mag., 300 Win. Mag.; heavy 26-inch barrel with recessed target-style muzzle; stainless fluted steel barrel, bolt handle, trigger guard; black graphite/fiberglass filled composite stock with positive checkering; double front swivel studs for attaching bipod. Made in U.S.A. by Savage Arms, Inc. Introduced 1991; no longer produced.

Perf.: $470   **Exc.:** $400   **VGood:** $345

SAVAGE MODEL 112FVSS-S
Same specs as Model 112BV except solid bottom single shot action; 223, 22-250, 220 Swift; ; heavy 26-inch barrel with recessed target-style muzzle; fluted stainless steel barrel, bolt handle, trigger guard; black graphite/fiberglass filled composite stock with positive checkering; double front swivel studs for attaching bipod. Made in U.S.A. by Savage Arms, Inc. Introduced 1991; no longer produced.

Perf.: $450   **Exc.:** $380   **VGood:** $320

SAVAGE MODEL 112R
Same specs as Model 112BV except 22-250, 243, 25-06; 5-shot magazine; 26-inch tapered free-floating barrel; no sights; drilled, tapped for scope mounts; American walnut stock; fluted comb, Wundhammer swell at pistol grip; top tang safety. Introduced 1979; discontinued 1980.

Exc.: $330   **VGood:** $280   **Good:** $240

SAVAGE MODEL 112V
Same specs as Model 112BV except 220 Swift, 222 Rem., 223 Rem., 225 Win., 22-250 Rem., 243 Win., 25-06 Rem; 26-inch heavy barrel; 47-inch overall length; weighs 9-1/4 lbs.; scope bases; select American walnut varminter stock; high comb;

checkered pistol grip; detachable sling swivels; recoil pad with white line spacer. Introduced 1975; discontinued 1979.

Exc.: $340   **VGood:** $290   **Good:** $250

SAVAGE MODEL 112 VARMINT, LOW PROFILE

Long-action bolt rifle chambered for .25-06 (4) and .300 WM (3). Stock: Brown laminated with recoil pad. Barrel: 26-inch sightless stainless steel bull. Weight: 11.25 lbs.

NIB: $675   **Exc.:** $625   **VGood:** $495

SAVAGE MODEL 14 CLASSIC

Short-action bolt-action rifle chambered for .22-250, .243, .270 WSM, 7mm-08, .300 WSM and .308. Barrel: 22-inch or 24-inch polished blue without sights. Stock: Select lacquered walnut with contrasting forend.

NIB: $540   **Exc.:** $495   **VGood:** $375

SAVAGE MODEL 14 EURO CLASSIC

Similar to Model 14 Classic but with iron sights.

NIB: $540   **Exc.:** $495   **VGood:** $375

SAVAGE MODEL 114 CLASSIC

Similar to Model 14 Classic but long-action chambered for .270, 7mm RM and .300 WM.

NIB: $540   **Exc.:** $495   **VGood:** $375

SAVAGE MODEL 114U ULTRA RIFLE

Similar to the Model 114C except has high-luster blued finish, high-gloss walnut stock with custom cut checkering, ebony tip. No sights; drilled and tapped for scope. Chambered for 270, 30-06, 7mm Rem. Mag., 7mm STW and 300 Win. Mag.

Exc.: $400   **VGood:** $300   **Good:** $250

SAVAGE MODEL 114CU CLASSIC ULTRA

Bolt action; 270, 30-06, 7mm Rem. Mag., 300 Win. Mag.; 4-shot (Magnums), 5-shot removable box magazine; 22-inch, 24-inch (Magnums) barrel; weighs 7-1/8 lbs.; ramp front sight, step-adjustable rear; tapped for scope mounts; checkered, high-gloss straight American walnut stock; grip cap; recoil pad; cut checkering; tang safety. Introduced 1991.

Exc.: $460   **VGood:** $410   **Good:** $350

SAVAGE MODEL 114 EURO CLASSIC

Similar to Model 114 Classic but with iron sights.

NIB: $540   **Exc.:** $495   **VGood:** $375

SAVAGE MODEL 116FSS WEATHER WARRIOR

Bolt action; 223, 243, 270, 30-06, 308, 7mm Rem. Mag., 300 Win. Mag., 338 Win. Mag.; free-floated 22-inch barrel (standard calibers), 24-inch (Magnums); weighs 6-3/4 lbs.; no sights; drilled, tapped for scope mounting; graphite/ fiberglass filled black composite stock; stainless steel barreled action; right- or left-hand action. Made in U.S. by Savage Arms, Inc. Introduced 1991; still produced as a long action rifle only.

Perf.: $420   **Exc.:** $380   **VGood:** $320

With detachable magazine as Model 116FCS

Perf.: $430   **Exc.:** $385   **VGood:** $340

SAVAGE MODEL 116FHSS

Similar to Model 116FSS but with hinged floorplate.

NIB: $550   **Exc.:** $500   **VGood:** $395

SAVAGE MODEL 16FSS RIFLE

Similar to Model 116FSS except true short action, chambered for 204, 223, 22-250, 243, 270 WSM, 7-08, 7mm WSR, 300 WSM; 22-inch free-floated barrel; black graphite/fiberglass stock with "Dual Pillar" bedding. Also left-hand. Introduced 1998, still available. Made in U.S.A. by Savage Arms, Inc.

Perf.: $420   **Exc.:** $380   **VGood:** $320

SAVAGE MODEL 16FHSS

Similar to Model 16FSS but with hinged floorplate. Introduced 2006.

NIB: $550   **Exc.:** $500   **VGood:** $395

Savage Model 114CU Classic Ultra

Savage Model 116FSS Weather Warrior

Savage Model 116FSAK

Savage Model 116SE Safari Express

Savage Model 340C

Savage Model 25 Lightweight Varminter

Savage Model 25 Classic Sporter

SAVAGE MODEL 16 FLHSS WEATHER WARRIOR

Similar to Model 16 FSS but in left-hand version.

NIB: $475   **Exc.:** $425   **VGood:** $325

SAVAGE MODEL 116FSAK

Same specs as Model 116FSS except 270, 30-06, 7mm Rem. Mag., 338 Win. Mag.; Savage "Adjustable Muzzle Brake" with fluted barrel. Made in U.S. by Savage Arms, Inc. Introduced 1994.

Perf.: $510   **Exc.:** $445   **VGood:** $380

With detachable magazine as Model 116FCSAK

Perf.: $500   **Exc.:** $440   **VGood:** $370

SAVAGE MODEL 116FSK

Same specs as Model 116FSS except 270, 30-06, 7mm-Rem. Mag., 338 Win. Mag.; 22-inch "Shock-Suppressor" barrel; fixed muzzle brake. Made in U.S. by Savage Arms, Inc. Introduced 1993; no longer produced.

Exc.: $500   **VGood:** $430   **Good:** $370

SAVAGE MODEL 116FHSAK

Similar to 116FSAK but with hinged floorplate.

NIB: $550   **Exc.:** $500   **VGood:** $395

SAVAGE MODEL 16FHSAK

Similar to Model 116FHSAK but short-action only.

NIB: $550   **Exc.:** $500   **VGood:** $395

SAVAGE MODEL 116SE SAFARI EXPRESS

Bolt action; 300 Win. Mag., 338 Win. Mag., 425 Express, 458 Win. Mag.; 3-shot magazine; 24-inch barrel; 45-1/2-inch overall length; weighs 8-1/2 lbs.; bead on ramp front sight, three-leaf rear; select grade classic-style American walnut stock with ebony forend tip; cut-checkered grip and forend; two stainless steel cross-bolts; internally vented recoil pad; 400 series stainless steel barreled action; controlled round feeding; adjustable muzzlebrake; barrel band-mounted front swivel stud. Made in U.S. by Savage Arms, Inc. Introduced 1994.

Exc.: $795   **VGood:** $675   **Good:** $580

SAVAGE MODEL 116US ULTRA STAINLESS RIFLE

Same specs as Model 116SE except 270, 30-06, 7mm Rem. Mag., 300 Win. Mag.; stock has high-gloss finish; no open sights; stainless steel action with satin finish. Made in U.S. by Savage Arms, Inc. Introduced 1995; no longer produced.

Perf.: $600   **Exc.:** $500   **VGood:** $400

SAVAGE MODEL 25 LIGHTWEIGHT VARMINTER

Short-action rifle chambered in .204 and .223. Medium-contour fluted barrel with recessed target crown, free-floating sleved barrel, dual pillar bedding, three locking lugs, 60-degree bolt lift, AccuTrigger adjustable from 2.5 to 3.25 lbs., detachable box magazine. Weight 8.25 lbs.

NIB: $700   **Exc.:** $550   **VGood:** $395

SAVAGE MODEL 25 LIGHTWEIGHT VARMINTER THUMBHOLE

Similar to above but with thumbhole stock.

NIB: $725   **Exc.:** $575   **VGood:** $415

SAVAGE MODEL 25 CLASSIC SPORTER

Short-action rifle chambered in .204 and .223. Free-floating sleeved barrel, Dual pillar bedding, three locking lugs, 60-degree bolt lift, AccuTrigger adjustable from 2.5 to 3.25 lbs., Detachable box magazine. Satin lacquer American walnut stock with contrasting forend tip and wraparound checkering.

NIB: $700   **Exc.:** $550   **VGood:** $395

SAVAGE MODEL 340

Bolt action; 22 Hornet, 222 Rem., 30-30; 3-, 4-shot detachable box magazine; 20-inch, 22-inch, 24-inch medium-weight barrel; 40-inch overall length (20-inch barrel); weighs 6-3/4 lbs.; click-adjustable middle sight, ramp front; unchecked one-piece American walnut pistol-grip stock; thumb safety at right rear of receiver. Introduced 1950; discontinued 1986.

Exc.: $300   **VGood:** $275   **Good:** $250

Savage Model 29

Savage Model 99A

Savage Model 99E

SAVAGE MODEL 340C

Same specs as Model 340 except 30-30; 3-shot detachable box magazine; 18-1/2-inch medium-weight barrel; 36-1/2-inch overall length; weighs 6-1/4 lbs.; checkered American walnut pistol-grip stock; pistol grip, buttplate white line spacer; sling swivels. Introduced 1962; discontinued 1965.

Exc.: $275   **VGood:** $250   **Good:** $225

SAVAGE MODEL 340S DELUXE

Same specs as Model 340 Savage No. 175 except peep rear sight, hooded gold bead front; 3-shot magazine (30-30) hand-checkered American walnut pistol-grip stock; swivel studs. Introduced 1952; discontinued 1960.

Exc.: $300   **VGood:** $275   **Good:** $250

SAVAGE MODEL 340V

Same specs as Model 340 except 225 Win.; 24-inch barrel; American walnut varmint-style stock. Introduced 1967; no longer in production.

Exc.: $425   **VGood:** $400   **Good:** $375

SAVAGE MODEL 342

Bolt action; 22 Hornet; 4-shot detachable box magazine; 22-inch, 24-inch barrel; 40-inch overall length; weighs 6-3/4 lbs.; click-adjustable middle sight, ramp front; tapped for Weaver scope side mounts; uncheckered one-piece American walnut pistol-grip stock; after 1953 was incorporated into Model 340 line. Introduced 1950; discontinued 1953.

Exc.: $300   **VGood:** $275   **Good:** $250

SAVAGE MODEL 342S DELUXE

Same specs as Model 340 Savage No. 175 peep rear sight, hooded ramp front with gold bead; hand-checkered American walnut pistol-grip stock; swivel studs; after 1953 was incorporated into Model 340 line.

Exc.: $325   **VGood:** $295   **Good:** $275

SAVAGE MODEL 1904

Bolt action; single shot; 22 Short, 22 Long, 22 LR; 18-inch barrel; takedown; open rear sight, bead front; uncheckered one-piece straight stock. Introduced 1904; discontinued 1917.

Exc.: $150   **VGood:** $100   **Good:** $75

SAVAGE MODEL 1905

Bolt action; single shot; 22 Short, 22 Long, 22 LR; 22-inch barrel; takedown; open rear sight, bead front; uncheckered one-piece straight stock. Introduced 1905; discontinued 1918.

Exc.: $150   **VGood:** $100   **Good:** $75

SAVAGE MODEL 1920

Bolt action; 250-3000, 300 Savage; 5-shot box magazine; 22-inch (250-3000), 24-inch (300 Savage) barrel; Mauser-type action; open rear sight, bead front; hand-checkered American walnut pistol-grip stock; slender schnabel forearm. Introduced 1920; discontinued 1926.

Exc.: $400   **VGood:** $360   **Good:** $300

SAVAGE MODEL 1920 (1926 VERSION)

Bolt action; 250-3000, 300 Savage; 5-shot box magazine; 24-inch barrel; Mauser-type action; Lyman

No. 54 rear peep sight; redesigned stock. Introduced 1926; discontinued 1929.

Exc.: $410   **VGood:** $375   **Good:** $310

SAVAGE MODEL 25

Slide action; 22 Short, 22 Long, 22 LR; 20-shot (22 Short), 17-shot (22 Long), 15-shot (22 LR) tube magazine; 24-inch octagon barrel; hammerless; takedown; open rear sight, blade front; uncheckered American walnut pistol-grip stock; grooved slide handle. Introduced 1925; discontinued 1929.

Exc.: $290   **VGood:** $250   **Good:** $210

SAVAGE MODEL 29

Slide action; 22 Short, 22 Long, 22 LR; 20-shot (22 Short), 17-shot (22 Long), 15-shot (22 LR) tube magazine; hammerless; takedown; 21-inch overall length; weighs 5-3/4 lbs.; push-button safety rear of trigger guard; flat-top sporting rear sight, gold beat front; open rear sight, blade front; pre-WWII model with 24-inch octagon barrel, hand-checkered walnut pistol-grip stock, slide handle; post-WWII model with 24-inch round barrel, uncheckered stock. Introduced 1929; discontinued 1967.

Pre-WWII model		
Exc.: $295	**VGood:** $250	**Good:** $200
Post-WWII model		
Exc.: $235	**VGood:** $200	**Good:** $160

SAVAGE MODEL 29-G

Same specs as Model 29 post-WWII except shorter magazine, 16-shot (22 Long), 14-shot (22 LR); short 1-1/4-inch slide action. Introduced 1955.

Exc.: $235   **VGood:** $200   **Good:** $160

SAVAGE MODEL 99 (MODEL 1899, ORIGINAL VERSION)

Lever action; 25-35, 30-30, 303 Savage, 32-40, 38-55,; 5-shot rotary magazine; 22-inch (round), 26-inch (half, full octagon) barrel; hammerless; open rear sight, bead front; uncheckered walnut straight-grip stock, tapered forearm. Introduced, 1899; discontinued 1922.

Exc.: $1200   **VGood:** $900   **Good:** $695

SAVAGE MODEL 99-358

Same specs as Model 99 except only 358 Win. caliber; grooved forend; recoil pad. Introduced 1977; discontinued 1980.

Exc.: $695   **VGood:** $550   **Good:** $400

SAVAGE MODEL 99-375

Same specs as Model 99 except only 375 Win. caliber; recoil pad. Introduced 1980; discontinued 1980.

Exc.: $650   **VGood:** $505   **Good:** $355

SAVAGE MODEL 99A (EARLY MODEL)

Same specs as Model 99 except 30-30, 300 Savage, 303 Savage; 24-inch or 26-inch barrel. Introduced 1920; discontinued 1936.

Exc.: $950   **VGood:** $700   **Good:** $500

SAVAGE MODEL 99A (LATE MODEL)

Same specs as Model 99 except 243, 250 Savage, 300 Savage, 308, 375 Win.; 20-inch, 22-inch barrel; 39-3/4-inch (20-inch barrel) overall length; weighs 7 lbs.; grooved trigger; straight walnut stock with schnabel forend. Introduced 1971; discontinued 1981.

Exc.: $475   **VGood:** $375   **Good:** $300

SAVAGE MODEL 99B

Same specs as original Model 99 except takedown design. Introduced 1922; discontinued 1936.

Exc.: $925   **VGood:** $595   **Good:** $475

SAVAGE MODEL 99C

Same specs as late-production Model 99 except detachable clip magazine replaces rotary type; 22-250, 243 Win., 284 Win., 308 Win. (284 dropped in 1974); 4-shot detachable magazine, 3-shot (284); 22-inch barrel; 41-3/4-inch overall length; weighs 6-3/4 lbs.; hammerless; solid breech; Damascened bolt; case-hardened lever; blue receiver; gold-plated trigger; top tang safety; hooded gold bead ramp front, adjustable folding ramp rear sight; receiver tapped for scope mounts; walnut stock with checkered pistol grip, forend; Monte Carlo comb; swivel studs. Introduced in 1965; last variation of the Model 99; production discontinued 1998.

Exc.: $520   **VGood:** $430   **Good:** $370

SAVAGE MODEL 99CD

Same specs as Model 99C except 22-250, 243, 284 Win., 7mm-08, 308; white line recoil pad, pistol-grip cap; quick-detachable swivels, sling. Introduced 1976; discontinued 1980.

Exc.: $530   **VGood:** $430   **Good:** $370

SAVAGE MODEL 99DE CITATION

Same specs as Model 99 except 243, 284 Win., 308; 22-inch barrel; checkered American walnut Monte Carlo pistol-grip stock, forearm; engraved, receiver, tang, lever; quick detachable swivels. Introduced 1968; discontinued 1970.

Exc.: $1050   **VGood:** $795   **Good:** $650

SAVAGE MODEL 99DL

Same specs as Model 99 except 243, 250-3000, 284, 300 Savage, 308, 358 Win.; 24-inch, 22-inch barrel; 43-3/4-inch overall length; 6-3/4 lbs.; hammerless; solid breach; Damascened bolt; case-hardened laver; blued receiver; gold-plated trigger; top tang safety; high comb, checkered; walnut Monte Carlo pistol-grip stock; step adjustable, rear sight, gold bead front; semi-buckhorn; sling swivels; deluxe model. Introduced 1960; discontinued 1974.

Exc.: $450   **VGood:** $385   **Good:** $345

SAVAGE MODEL 99E (EARLY MODEL)

Same specs as Model 99 except 22 Hi-Power, 250-3000, 30-30, 300 Savage, 303 Savage; 22-inch 24-inch (300 Savage) barrel; solid frame. Introduced 1920; discontinued 1936. Add 20 percent for 22 Hi-Power.

Exc.: $800   **VGood:** $550   **Good:** $480

SAVAGE MODEL 99E (LATE MODEL)

Same specs as Model 99 except 243, 250 Savage, 300 Savage, 308; 20-inch, 22-inch, 24-inch medium-weight barrel; weighs 7-1/4 lbs.; hardwood pistol-grip stock; trigger guard safety. Introduced 1960 as "economy" version; discontinued 1982.

Exc.: $425   **VGood:** $395   **Good:** $300

SAVAGE MODEL 99EG (EARLY MODEL)

Same specs as Model 99 except 22 Hi-Power, 250-3000, 30-30, 300 Savage, 303 Savage; 22-inch, 24-inch (300 Savage) barrel; solid frame model; no checkering. Introduced 1936; discontinued 1941.

Exc.: $695   **VGood:** $395   **Good:** $260

SAVAGE MODEL 99EG (LATE MODEL)

Same specs as Model 99 except 243, 250-3000, 250 Savage, 300 Savage, 308, 358 Win.; 24-inch barrel; 43-1/4 overall length; weighs 7-1/4 lbs.; checkered pistol-grip stock. Introduced 1946; discontinued 1960. 20 percent premium for .358.

Exc.: $425   **VGood:** $395   **Good:** $300

SAVAGE MODEL 99F CARBINE
Lever action, early-production carbine; 303, 30-30, 25-35, 32-40, 38-55; produced before 1919 and below serial number 200,000; some made with barrel bands or saddle rings.

Exc.: $890   **VGood:** $680   **Good:** $410

SAVAGE MODEL 99F FEATHERWEIGHT (EARLY MODEL)
Same specs as Model 99 except 22 Hi-Power, 250-3000, 30-30, 300 Savage, 303 Savage; 22-inch, 24-inch (300 Savage) barrel; lightweight takedown model. Introduced 1920; discontinued 1942. Add 20 percent for 22 Hi-Power.

Exc.: $695   **VGood:** $475   **Good:** $210

SAVAGE MODEL 99F FEATHERWEIGHT (LATE MODEL)
Same specs as Model 99 except 243, 250-3000, 284 Win., 300 Savage, 308, 358 Win.; 22-inch lightweight barrel; 41-1/4-inch overall length; weighs 6-1/2 lbs.; solid breech; polished Damascened finish bolt; case-hardened lever; blued receiver; grooved trigger; checkered walnut pistol-grip stock; featherweight solid frame model. Introduced 1955; discontinued 1972. 20 percent premium for .358; 10 percent premium for 284 Win.

Exc.: $595   **VGood:** $420   **Good:** $310

SAVAGE MODEL 99G
Same specs as Model 99 except 22 Hi-Power, 250-3000, 30-30, 300 Savage, 308, 303 Savage; 5-shot rotary box-type magazine; 22-inch, 24-inch (300 Savage) medium-weight barrel; weighs 7-3/4 lbs.; takedown; hand-checkered full pistol grip, tapered forearm; shotgun butt. Introduced 1920; discontinued 1942.

Exc.: $595   **VGood:** $475   **Good:** $270

SAVAGE MODEL 99H
Same specs as Model 99 except 250-3000, 30-30, 303 Savage; 20-inch barrel; solid frame; carbine stock with barrel band. Introduced 1931; discontinued 1942.

Exc.: $795   **VGood:** $575   **Good:** $280

SAVAGE MODEL 99K
Same specs as Model 99 except 22 Hi-Power, 250-3000, 30-30, 300 Savage, 303 Savage; 22-inch 24-inch (300 Savage) barrel; takedown; Lyman peep rear sight, folding middle sight; fancy grade checkered walnut pistol-grip stock, forearm; engraved receiver, barrel. Introduced 1931; discontinued 1942. Add 15 percent for 22 Hi-Power.

Exc.: $1995   **VGood:** $1495   **Good:** $860

SAVAGE MODEL 99PE
Same specs as Model 99 except 243, 284 Win., 308; 22-inch barrel; 41-3/4-inch overall length; weighs 6-3/4 lbs.; Damascened bolt; gold-plated trigger; case-hardened lever; hand-checkered fancy American walnut Monte Carlo pistol-grip stock, forearm; game scene engraved on receiver sides; engraved tang, lever; quick-detachable swivels. Introduced 1966; discontinued 1970. Add 10 percent for 284 Win.

Exc.: $1175   **VGood:** $925   **Good:** $570

SAVAGE MODEL 99R (EARLY MODEL)
Same specs as Model 99 except 250-3000, 300 Savage; 22-inch (250-3000), 24-inch (300 Savage) tapered medium-weight barrel; weighs 7-1/4 lbs.; hand-checkered American walnut oversize pistol-grip stock, forearm; solid frame model; semi-buckhorn rear sight, raised ramp gold bead front. Introduced 1936; discontinued 1942.

Exc.: $695   **VGood:** $450   **Good:** $230

SAVAGE MODEL 99R (LATE MODEL)
Same specs as Model 99 except 243, 250-3000, 300 Savage, 308, 358 Win.; 24-inch barrel; 43-3/4-inch overall length; weighs 7-1/2 lbs.; tapped for Weaver scope mount; hand-checkered American walnut oversize pistol-grip stock, semi-beavertail forearm; sling swivel studs. Introduced 1946; discontinued 1960.

Exc.: $640   **VGood:** $390   **Good:** $220

Savage Model 99EG
Late Model

Savage Model 99K

Savage Model 99PE

Savage Model 99T Featherweight

Savage Model 170

Savage Model 170C
Carbine

Savage Model 1903

SAVAGE MODEL 99RS (EARLY MODEL)
Same specs as Model 99 except 250-3000, 300 Savage; 22-inch, 24-inch (300 Savage) tapered medium-weight barrel; weighs 7-1/2 lbs.; Lyman rear peep sight, gold bead front; hand-checkered American walnut oversize pistol-grip stock, forearm; sling, swivels; solid frame model. Introduced 1936; discontinued 1942.

Exc.: $795   **VGood:** $495   **Good:** $240

SAVAGE MODEL 99RS (LATE MODEL)
Same specs as Model 99 except 243, 250 Savage, 300 Savage, 308, 358 Win.; 24-inch barrel; weighs 7-1/2 lbs.; Redfield 70LH adjustable receiver sight; milled slot for a middle sight; No. 34 Lyman gold bead front; hand-checkered American walnut oversize pistol-grip stock, forearm; quick-release sling swivel; leather sling. Introduced 1946; discontinued 1958. Add 20 percent for 358.

Exc.: $550   **VGood:** $450   **Good:** $350

SAVAGE MODEL 99T FEATHERWEIGHT
Same specs as Model 99 except 22 Hi-Power, 30-30, 300 Savage, 303 Savage; 20-inch 22-inch (300 Savage) barrel; hand-checkered walnut pistol-grip stock; beavertail forend; solid frame model. Introduced 1936; discontinued 1942. Add 15 percent for 22 Hi-Power.

Exc.: $575   **VGood:** $475   **Good:** $310

SAVAGE MODEL 170
Slide action; 30-30, 35 Rem.; 3-shot tubular magazine; 22-inch barrel; 41-1/2-inch overall length; weighs 6-3/4 lbs.; folding leaf rear sight, gold bead ramp front; receiver drilled, tapped for scope mount; select checkered American walnut pistol-grip stock; Monte Carlo comb, grooved slide handle; hard rubber buttplate. Introduced 1970; discontinued 1981. Deduct 10 percent for 30-30.

Exc.: $375   **VGood:** $325   **Good:** $295

SAVAGE MODEL 170C CARBINE
Same specs as Model 170 except 30-30; 18-1/2-inch barrel; weighs 6 lbs.; straight-comb stock. Introduced 1974; discontinued 1981.

Exc.: $350   **VGood:** $325   **Good:** $275

SAVAGE MODEL 1903
Slide action; 22 Short, 22 Long, 22 LR; hammerless; takedown; detachable box magazine; 24-inch octagonal barrel; open rear sight, bead front; checkered one-piece pistol grip or straight stock. Introduced 1903; discontinued 1921.

Exc.: $270   **VGood:** $220   **Good:** $160

SAVAGE MODEL 1909
Slide action; 22 Short, 22 Long, 22 LR; detachable box magazine; 20-inch round barrel; open rear sight, bead front; uncheckered one-piece pistol grip or straight stock. Introduced 1909; discontinued 1915.

Exc.: $200   **VGood:** $165   **Good:** $130

Savage Model 1914

Savage Model 6

Savage Model 6S

Savage Model 7

Savage Model 7S

Savage Model 24

Savage Model 24F

walnut stock; storage in buttstock for ten 22 LR cartridges and one 20-ga. shell; some with nickel finish. Introduced 1972; discontinued 1988.

Exc.: $500   **VGood:** $400   **Good:** $250

SAVAGE MODEL 24D

Same specs as Model 24 except 22 LR, 22 WMR/20-ga., 410; black or color case-hardened frame with engraving; checkered walnut pistol-grip stock. Introduced 1981; no longer in production.

Exc.: $400   **VGood:** $300   **Good:** $225

SAVAGE MODEL 24DL

Same specs as Model 24 except 22/20-ga., 410; checkered walnut Monte Carlo pistol-grip stock; checkered forend; top lever; scope dovetails; satin chrome frame with game scenes; pistol grip cap; pistol grip, buttplate white line spacer. Introduced 1962; discontinued 1969.

Exc.: $425   **VGood:** $325   **Good:** $250

SAVAGE MODEL 24F

Same specs as Model 24 except 22 LR, 22 Hornet, 223, 30-30/12-, 20-ga.; black Rynite composition or walnut stock; removable buttcap for storage; removable grip cap with integral compass, screwdriver. Introduced 1989; still in production.

Exc.: $540   **VGood:** $475   **Good:** $320

SAVAGE MODEL 24F-12T TURKEY GUN

Same specs as Model 24F except 22 Hornet, 223 over 12-gauge with 3-inch chamber; camouflage Rynite stock and Full, Imp. Cyl., Mod. choke tubes. Made in U.S. by Savage. Introduced 1989.

Exc.: $560   **VGood:** $475   **Good:** $350

SAVAGE MODEL 24FG

Same specs as Model 24 except 22 LR/20-ga., 410; top lever; scope dovetails; color case-hardened frame; walnut finish hardwood straight stock; no checkering. Introduced 1972; no longer in production.

Exc.: $400   **VGood:** $350   **Good:** $265

SAVAGE MODEL 24 FIELD

Same specs as Model 24 except 22 LR, 22 WMR/20-ga., 410; weighs 6-3/4 lbs.; lightweight field model. Discontinued 1989.

Exc.: $400   **VGood:** $310   **Good:** $260

SAVAGE MODEL 24MDL

Same specs as Model 24 except 22 WMR/20-ga., 410; checkered walnut pistol-grip stock; top lever; scope dovetails; satin chrome frame. Introduced 1965; discontinued 1969.

Exc.: $425   **VGood:** $395   **Good:** $350

SAVAGE MODEL 24MS

Same specs as Model 24 except 22 WMR/20-ga., 410; sidelever; scope dovetails. Introduced 1962; discontinued 1971.

Exc.: $425   **VGood:** $395   **Good:** $350

SAVAGE MODEL 24S

Same specs as Model 24 except 22 LR/20-ga., 410; sidelever; scope dovetails. Introduced 1965; discontinued 1971.

Exc.: $400   **VGood:** $375   **Good:** $325

SAVAGE MODEL 24V

Same specs as Model 24 except 22 Hornet, 222, 223, 30-30, 357 Mag., 357 Max./20-ga. 3-inch; stronger receiver; color case-hardened frame; scope dovetails; walnut finished hardwood stock. Introduced 1971; discontinued 1989. Add 20 percent for 357 Mag or Max.

Exc.: $550   **VGood:** $495   **Good:** $425

SAVAGE MODEL 24VS

Same specs as Model 24 except 357 Mag./20-ga.; 20-inch barrel; cylinder bore; pistol-grip walnut stock; nickel finish. No longer in production.

Exc.: $625   **VGood:** $595   **Good:** $475

SAVAGE MODEL 1914

Slide action; 22 Short, 22 Long, 22 LR; 17-shot (22 LR) tubular magazine; 24-inch octagonal barrel; hammerless; takedown; open rear sight, bead front; uncheckered pistol-grip stock, grooved slide handle. Introduced 1914; discontinued 1924.

Exc.: $190   **VGood:** $150   **Good:** $100

SAVAGE MODEL 6

Semi-automatic; 22 Short, 22 Long, 22 LR; 21-shot (22 Short), 17-shot (22 Long), 15-shot (22 LR) tube magazine; 24-inch tapered barrel with crowned muzzle; weighs 6 lbs.; takedown; open fully-adjustable sporting rear sight, gold bead front; receiver tapped for Weaver scope; pre-WWII version has checkered pistol-grip walnut stock; post-WWII model has uncheckered stock; receiver, triggerguard with silver-gray finish. Introduced 1938; discontinued 1968.

Pre-WWII model
Exc.: $150   **VGood:** $130   **Good:** $110

Post-WWII model
Exc.: $140   **VGood:** $120   **Good:** $100

SAVAGE MODEL 6P

Same specs as Model 6 except checkered pistol grip, forend; rosewood forend tip come with 0420 scope and mount. Introduced 1965.

Exc.: $175   **VGood:** $150   **Good:** $110

SAVAGE MODEL 6S

Same specs as Model 6 except fully-adjustable peep rear sight with two discs, hooded front with three inserts. Introduced 1938; discontinued 1942.

Exc.: $160   **VGood:** $140   **Good:** $100

SAVAGE MODEL 7

Semi-automatic; 22 Short, 22 Long, 22 LR; 5-shot detachable clip magazine; 24-inch tapered barrel with crowned muzzle; weighs 6 lbs.; takedown; fully-adjustable sporting rear sight, gold bead front; takedown; pre-WWII model with checkered pistol-grip walnut stock; post-WWII model with uncheckered stock; hard rubber buttplate. Introduced 1939; discontinued 1951.

Pre-WWII model
Exc.: $140   **VGood:** $120   **Good:** $100

Post-WWII model
Exc.: $150   **VGood:** $130   **Good:** $100

SAVAGE MODEL 7S

Same specs as Model 7 except fully-adjustable peep rear sight with two discs, hooded front with three inserts. Introduced 1938; discontinued 1942.

Exc.: $150   **VGood:** $130   **Good:** $100

SAVAGE MODEL 24

Over/under combo; 22 LR, 22 Short, 22 Long/410-3-inch or 2-1/2-inch; 24-inch barrels; 40-1/2-inch overall length; weighs 7 lbs.; takedown; barrel selection slide button on right side of receiver; full choke shotgun barrel; top-lever break-open; ramp front sight, elevation-adjustable rear; uncheckered walnut pistol-grip stock; visible hammer; single trigger; barrel selector on frame, later on hammer. Introduced 1950; discontinued 1965.

Exc.: $300   **VGood:** $275   **Good:** $200

SAVAGE MODEL 24C CAMPER'S COMPANION

Same specs as Model 24 except 22 LR/20-ga.; 20-inch barrel; Cylinder bore; weighs 5-3/4 lbs.; straight

SAVAGE MODEL 60

Semi-automatic; 22 LR; 15-shot tubular magazine; 20-inch barrel; 40-1/2-inch overall length; weighs 6 lbs.; open rear sight, gold bead ramp front; tang slide safety; American walnut Monte Carlo stock; checkered pistol-grip, forearm; Wundhammer swell pistol grip; beavertail forend; buttplate white line spacer. Introduced 1969; discontinued 1972.

Exc.: $100   **VGood:** $75   **Good:** $70

SAVAGE MODEL 64 AUTO RIFLE

Semi-automatic; 22 LR; 10-shot magazine; 20-inch, 21-inch barrel; weighs 5-1/2 lbs.; 40-inch, 41-inch overall length; Walnut-finished hardwood stock with Monte Carlo-type comb, checkered grip and forend. Bead front, open adjustable rear sights. Receiver grooved for scope mounting. Thumb-operated rotating safety. Blue finish. Side ejection, bolt hold-open device. Introduced 1990. Made in Canada, from Savage Arms.

Perf.: $120   **Exc.:** $90   **VGood:** $70

Model 64FSS, stainless

Perf.: $160   **Exc.:** $140   **VGood:** $110

Model 64F, black synthetic stock

Perf.: $130   **Exc.:** $110   **VGood:** $100

SAVAGE MODEL 64FV AUTO RIFLE

Similar to the Model 64F except has heavy 21-inch barrel with recessed crown; no sights provided-comes with Weaver-style bases. Introduced 1998. Imported from Canada by Savage Arms, Inc.

Perf.: $150   **Exc.:** $130   **VGood:** $100

SAVAGE MODEL 64FVSS

Like Model 64, but with stainless-steel action and barrel; Introduced 2002, still offered.

Perf.: $200   **Exc.:** $170   **VGood:** $130

SAVAGE MODEL 64 BTV

Similar to Model 64 but with laminated thumbhole stock.

Perf.: $175   **Exc.:** $145   **VGood:** $100

SAVAGE MODEL 88

Semi-automatic; 22 LR; 15-shot tubular magazine; 20-inch barrel; open rear sight, bead front; checkered American walnut pistol-grip stock; side safety. Introduced 1969; discontinued 1972.

Exc.: $100   **VGood:** $90   **Good:** $75

SAVAGE MODEL 90 CARBINE

Semi-automatic; 22 LR; 10-shot tubular magazine; 16-1/2-inch barrel; 37-1/2-inch overall length; weighs 5-3/4 lbs.; satin blued receiver; tang slide safety; folding leaf rear sight, gold bead front; uncheckered walnut carbine stock; barrel band; sling swivels. Introduced 1969; discontinued 1972.

Exc.: $100   **VGood:** $90   **Good:** $75

SAVAGE MODEL 219

Single shot; 22 Hornet, 25-20, 30-30, 32-20; 26-inch tapered medium-weight barrel; weighs 6 lbs.; hammerless; takedown; break-open; top tang safety; adjustable flat-top rear sight, bead front on ramp; uncheckered walnut pistol-grip stock, forearm; top lever. Introduced 1938; discontinued 1965. Add 20 percent for 22 Hornet, 25-20 or 32-20. Barrels alone $150-$200.

Exc.: $425   **VGood:** $395   **Good:** $325

SAVAGE MODEL 219L

Same specs as Model 219 except sidelever action. Introduced 1965; discontinued 1967.

Exc.: $400   **VGood:** $370   **Good:** $300

SAVAGE MODEL 221

Single shot; 30-30; 26-inch barrel; takedown; hammerless; break-open; open rear sight, bead front on ramp; uncheckered walnut pistol-grip stock, forearm; top lever; interchangeable 30-inch 12-ga. shotgun barrel. Introduced 1939; discontinued 1960.

Exc.: $325   **VGood:** $295   **Good:** $245

Savage Model 60

Savage Model 64

Savage Model 64FV

Savage Model 64FVSS

Savage Model 64 BTV

Savage Model 88

Savage Model 90 Carbine

Savage Model 219

Savage Model 219L

SAVAGE MODEL 222

Single shot; 30-30; 26-inch barrel; takedown; hammerless; break-open; open rear sight, bead front on ramp; uncheckered walnut pistol-grip stock, forearm; top lever; interchangeable 28-inch 16-ga. shotgun barrel.

Exc.: $295   **VGood:** $265   **Good:** $225

SAVAGE MODEL 223

Single shot; 30-30; 26-inch barrel; takedown; hammerless; break-open; open rear sight, bead front on ramp; uncheckered walnut pistol-grip stock, forearm; top lever; interchangeable 28-inch 20-ga. shotgun barrel.

Exc.: $325   **VGood:** $295   **Good:** $245

SAVAGE MODEL 227

Single shot; 22 Hornet; 26-inch barrel; takedown; hammerless; break-open; open rear sight, bead front on ramp; uncheckered walnut pistol-grip stock, forearm; top lever; interchangeable 30-inch 12-ga. shotgun barrel.

Exc.: $325   **VGood:** $295   **Good:** $245

SAVAGE MODEL 228

Single shot; 22 Hornet; 26-inch barrel; takedown; hammerless; break-open; open rear sight, bead

front on ramp; uncheckered walnut pistol-grip stock, forearm; top lever; interchangeable 28-inch 16-ga. shotgun barrel.

Exc.: $325   **VGood:** $295   **Good:** $245

SAVAGE MODEL 229

Single shot; 22 Hornet; 26-inch barrel; takedown; hammerless; break-open; open rear sight, bead front on ramp; uncheckered walnut pistol-grip stock, forearm; top lever; interchangeable 28-inch 20-ga. shotgun barrel.

Exc.: $325   **VGood:** $295   **Good:** $245

SAVAGE MODEL 389

Over/under combo; 12-ga./222, 308; 25-3/4-inch barrels; hammerless; floating front mount for windage, elevation adjustment; blade front sight, folding leaf rear; oil-finished walnut stock; recoil pad; checkered grip, forend; matte finish; double triggers; swivel studs. Introduced 1988; discontinued 1990. Manufactured in Finland by Valmet.

Exc.: $650   **VGood:** $550   **Good:** $400

SAVAGE MODEL 980DL

Semi-automatic; 22 LR; 15-shot tube magazine; 20-inch barrel; 40-1/2-inch overall length; weighs 6 lbs.; solid steel receiver; receiver grooved for scope

Savage Model 221

Savage Model 1912

Savage/Anschutz Mark 10D

Savage/Anschutz Mark 12

Savage/Anschutz Model 54

Savage/Anschutz Model 164M

Savage/Anschutz Model 184

adjustable single-stage trigger; folding leaf open rear sight, hooded ramp front; skip-checkered high grade French walnut stock; hand-carved roll-over cheekpiece; rosewood grip cap, forearm tip with white inlay; sling swivels. Introduced 1964; discontinued 1967.

    Exc.: $540   **VGood:** $430   **Good:** $240

SAVAGE-ANSCHUTZ MODEL 164

Bolt action; 22 LR; 5-shot detachable clip magazine; 24-inch barrel; 40-3/4-inch overall length; weighs 6 lbs.; receiver grooved for tip-off mount; hooded ramp gold bead front, folding leaf rear; European walnut stock; hand-checkered pistol grip, forearm; Monte Carlo comb, cheekpiece; sliding side safety; schnabel forearm; fully-adjustable single-stage trigger. Introduced 1966; discontinued 1981.

    Exc.: $350   **VGood:** $300   **Good:** $180

SAVAGE-ANSCHUTZ MODEL 164M
Same specs as Model 164 except 22 WMR; 4-shot magazine.

    Exc.: $380   **VGood:** $330   **Good:** $190

SAVAGE-ANSCHUTZ MODEL 184

Bolt action; 22 LR; 5-shot detachable clip magazine; 21-1/2-inch barrel; folding leaf rear sight, hooded ramp front; receiver grooved for scope mounts; European walnut stock with Monte Carlo comb, schnabel forearm; hand-checkered pistol grip, forearm. Introduced 1966; discontinued 1974.

    Exc.: $350   **VGood:** $300   **Good:** $160

SAVAGE-ANSCHUTZ MODEL 1410

Bolt action; single shot; 22 LR; 27-1/2-inch barrel; 50-inch overall length; weighs 15-1/2 lbs.; no sights; receiver grooved for Anschutz sights; scope blocks; International-type stock with thumb hole, aluminum hook buttplate; vertically adjustable buttplate. Introduced 1968.

    Exc.: $350   **VGood:** $300   **Good:** $140

SAVAGE-ANSCHUTZ MODEL 1418 SPORTER

Bolt action; 22 LR; 5-shot detachable clip magazine; 24-inch barrel; receiver grooved for tip-off mount; European Mannlicher stock, inlays, skip-line hand-checkering; double-set or single-stage trigger. Made in Germany. Introduced 1981; discontinued 1981.

    Exc.: $595   **VGood:** $495   **Good:** $260

SAVAGE-ANSCHUTZ MODEL 1518 SPORTER

Bolt action; 22 WMR; 5-shot detachable clip magazine; 24-inch barrel; receiver grooved for tip-off mount; European Mannlicher stock, inlays, skip-line hand-checkering; double-set or single-stage trigger. Made in Germany. Introduced 1981; discontinued 1981.

    Exc.: $645   **VGood:** $535   **Good:** $280

SAVAGE-STEVENS MODEL 35

Bolt action; 22 LR; 5-shot clip magazine; 22-inch barrel; 41-inch overall length; weighs 4-3/4 lbs.; ramp front sight, step-adjustable rear; walnut finished hardwood stock; checkered pistol grip, forend; receiver grooved for scope mounts. Introduced 1982; discontinued 1985.

    Exc.: $80   **VGood:** $55   **Good:** $40

SAVAGE-STEVENS MODEL 35M
Same specs as Model 35 except 22 WMR.

    Exc.: $90   **VGood:** $70   **Good:** $50

SAVAGE-STEVENS MODEL 36

Bolt action; single shot; 22 LR; 22-inch barrel; 41-inch overall length; weighs 4-3/4 lbs.; ramp front sight, step-adjustable open rear; walnut-finished hardwood stock; checkered pistol grip, forend; receiver grooved for scope mounts. Introduced 1983.

    Exc.: $80   **VGood:** $60   **Good:** $40

mounting; hooded ramp front sight, folding leaf adjustable rear; checkered walnut Monte Carlo stock, pistol grip, forend. Introduced 1981.

    Exc.: $120   **VGood:** $90   **Good:** $60

SAVAGE MODEL 1912

Semi-automatic; 22 LR; 7-shot detachable box magazine; takedown; open rear sight, bead front; uncheckered straight stock. Introduced 1912; discontinued 1916.

    Exc.: $310   **VGood:** $225   **Good:** $185

SAVAGE-ANSCHUTZ MARK 10

Bolt action; single shot; 22 LR; 26-inch barrel; 44-inch overall length; weighs 8-1/2 lbs.; micrometer click-adjustable rear sight, globe front; European walnut pistol-grip target stock; cheekpiece; adjustable hand stop; adjustable single-stage trigger; sling swivels. Imported from Germany. Introduced 1967; discontinued 1972.

    Exc.: $320   **VGood:** $270   **Good:** $150

SAVAGE-ANSCHUTZ MARK 10D
Same specs as Mark 10 except different rear sight; Monte Carlo stock. Imported 1972 only.

    Exc.: $330   **VGood:** $280   **Good:** $150

SAVAGE-ANSCHUTZ MARK 12

Bolt action; single shot; 22 LR; 26-inch heavy barrel; 43-inch overall length; weighs 8 lbs.; globe front sight, micro-click peep rear; walnut-finished hardwood target stock; thumb groove, Wundhammer pistol-grip swell, adjustable hand stop; sling swivels. Imported from Germany. Introduced 1978; discontinued 1981.

    Exc.: $350   **VGood:** $300   **Good:** $150

SAVAGE-ANSCHUTZ MODEL 54

Bolt action; 22 LR; 5-shot clip magazine; 22-1/2-inch barrel; 42-inch overall length; weighs 6-3/4 lbs.; folding leaf sight, hooded ramp gold bead front; receiver grooved for tip-off mount, tapped for scope blocks; French walnut stock with Monte Carlo roll-over comb; schnabel forearm tip; hand-checkered pistol grip, forearm; adjustable single-stage trigger; wing safety. Introduced 1966; discontinued 1981.

    Exc.: $595   **VGood:** $495   **Good:** $270

SAVAGE-ANSCHUTZ MODEL 54M
Same specs as Model 54 except 22 WMR. Introduced 1973; discontinued 1981.

    Exc.: $625   **VGood:** $525   **Good:** $300

SAVAGE-ANSCHUTZ MODEL 141

Bolt action; 22 LR; 5-shot clip magazine; 22-inch barrel; 40-3/4-inch overall length; weighs 5-1/2 lbs.; right side slide safety; adjustable single-stage trigger; gold bead hooded ramp front sight, folding leaf rear; receiver grooved for scope mount, tapped for aperture sight; French walnut Monte Carlo stock with cheekpiece; skip-line hand-checkered pistol grip, forend; rosewood forend tip with white inlay; buttplate with white-line spacer; sling swivel studs. Introduced 1966.

    Exc.: $125   **VGood:** $100   **Good:** $90

SAVAGE-ANSCHUTZ MODEL 153

Bolt action; 222 Rem.; 24-inch barrel; 43-inch overall length; weighs 6-3/4 lbs.; recessed bolt head with double locking lugs; wing-type safety;

SAVAGE-STEVENS MODEL 72 CRACKSHOT

Lever action; single shot; 22 Short, 22 Long, 22 LR; 22-inch octagonal barrel; falling block; open rear sight, bead front; uncheckered American walnut straight-grip stock, forearm; color case-hardened frame. Introduced 1972; discontinued 1987.

Exc.: $140   **VGood:** $110   **Good:** $90

SAVAGE-STEVENS MODEL 73

Bolt action; single shot; 22 Short, 22 Long, 22 LR; 20-inch barrel; 38-inch overall length; weighs 4-1/2 lbs.; plated trigger; takedown screw; cocking knob; open rear sight, blade front; receiver grooved for scope mounting; one-piece uncheckered hardwood pistol grip stock. Introduced 1965; discontinued 1980.

Exc.: $70   **VGood:** $60   **Good:** $45

SAVAGE-STEVENS MODEL 73Y

Same specs as Model 73 except 18-inch barrel; 35-inch overall length; weighs 4 lbs.; shorter buttstock. Introduced 1965; discontinued 1980.

Exc.: $70   **VGood:** $60   **Good:** $40

SAVAGE-STEVENS MODEL 74

Lever action; single shot; 22 Short, 22 Long, 22 LR; 22-inch round barrel; hardwood stock; black-finished frame. Introduced 1972; discontinued 1974.

Exc.: $135   **VGood:** $110   **Good:** $85

SAVAGE-STEVENS MODEL 80

Semi-automatic; 22 LR; 15-shot tube magazine; 20-inch barrel; 40-inch overall length; weighs 6 lbs.; blade front sight, fully-adjustable open rear; select walnut Monte Carlo stock with checkered forens, pistol grip; buttplate, pistol grip white line spacers; receiver grooved for scope mounting. Introduced 1977; no longer in production.

Exc.: $90   **VGood:** $80   **Good:** $65

SAVAGE-STEVENS MODEL 88

Semi-automatic; 22 LR; 15-shot tube magazine; 20-inch barrel; 40-1/2-inch overall length; weighs 5-3/4 lbs.; open rear sight, ramp gold bead front; checkered hardwood straight stock with pistol grip; slide safety on tang. Introduced 1969; discontinued 1972.

Exc.: $100   **VGood:** $80   **Good:** $60

SAVAGE-STEVENS MODEL 89 CRACKSHOT

Lever action; single shot; 22 LR; 18-1/2-inch barrel; 35-inch overall length; weighs 5 lbs.; sporting front sight, open rear; walnut finished hardwood straight stock; hammer cocked by hand; automatic ejection; hard rubber buttplate black satin finish. Introduced 1977; discontinued 1985.

Exc.: $140   **VGood:** $105   **Good:** $70

SAVAGE-STEVENS MODEL 120

Bolt action; single shot; 22 Short, 22 Long, 22 LR; tubular magazine; 20-inch round, tapered barrel; action cocks on opening of bolt; sporting front/rear sights; grooved for scope mounts; walnut-finished hardwood stock; pistol-grip; thumb safety; double extractors; recessed bolt face. Introduced 1979; discontinued 1983.

Exc.: $60   **VGood:** $50   **Good:** $40

SAVAGE-STEVENS MODEL 125

Bolt action; single shot; 22-inch barrel; 39-inch overall length; sporting front sight, open rear with elevator; walnut-finished stock; manual cocking; blued finish. Introduced 1981; no longer made.

Exc.: $70   **VGood:** $60   **Good:** $40

SCHULTZ & LARSEN MODEL 47

Bolt action; single shot; 22 LR; 28-1/2-inch barrel; micrometer receiver sight, globe front; free-rifle style European walnut stock; cheekpiece; thumbhole; buttplate; palm rest; sling swivels; set trigger. Made in Germany. No longer in production.

Exc.: $695   **VGood:** $610   **Good:** $495

Savage-Stevens Model 80

Savage-Stevens Model 88

Savage-Stevens Model 125

Sedgely Springfield Sporter

SCHULTZ & LARSEN MODEL 54

Bolt action; single shot; 6.5x55mm, American calibers available on special order; 27-1/2-inch barrel; micrometer receiver sight, globe front; free-rifle style European walnut stock; adjustable buttplate; cheekpiece; palm rest; sling swivels. No longer in production.

Exc.: $895   **VGood:** $795   **Good:** $625

SCHULTZ & LARSEN MODEL 54J

Bolt action; 270 Win., 30-06, 7x61 Sharpe & Hart; 3-shot magazine; 24-inch, 26-inch barrels; no sights; hand-checkered European walnut sporter stock; Monte Carlo comb, cheekpiece.

Exc.: $725   **VGood:** $615   **Good:** $535

SCHULTZ & LARSEN MODEL 61

Bolt action; single shot; 22 LR; 28-1/2-inch barrel; micrometer receiver sight, globe front; free-rifle style European walnut stock; cheekpiece; buttplate; palm rest; sling swivels; set trigger. No longer in production.

Exc.: $895   **VGood:** $795   **Good:** $685

SCHULTZ & LARSEN MODEL 62

Bolt action; single shot; various calibers; 28-1/2-inch barrel; micrometer receiver sight, globe front; free-rifle style European walnut stock; cheekpiece; buttplate; palm rest; sling swivels; set trigger. No longer in production.

Exc.: $1025   **VGood:** $895   **Good:** $710

SCHULTZ & LARSEN MODEL 68

Bolt action; 22-250, 243, 6mm Rem., 264 Win. Mag., 270, 30-06, 308, 7x61 Sharpe & Hart, 7mm Rem. Mag., 8x57JS, 300 Win. Mag., 308 Norma Mag., 338 Win. Mag., 358 Norma Mag., 458 Win. Mag.; 24-inch barrel; no sights; select French walnut sporting stock; adjustable trigger. No longer in production.

Exc.: $795   **VGood:** $695   **Good:** $595

SEDGELY SPRINGFIELD SPORTER

Bolt action; 218 Bee, 22-3000, 220 Swift, 22-4000, 22 Hornet, 25-35, 250-3000, 257 Roberts, 270 Win., 30-06, 7mm; 24-inch barrel; Lyman No. 48 rear sight, bead front on matted ramp; hand-checkered

walnut stock; sling swivels, grip cap; many variations. Introduced 1928; discontinued 1941.

Perf.: $1295   **Exc.:** $1125   **VGood:** $895

Left-hand model
Perf.: $1495   **Exc.:** $1295   **VGood:** $995

SEDGELY SPRINGFIELD SPORTER CARBINE

Same specs as Springfield Sporter except 20-inch barrel; full-length walnut stock.

Perf.: $1495   **Exc.:** $1295   **VGood:** $995

SERRIFLE SCHUETZEN MODEL

Single shot, falling block; 22, 32, 38, 41, 44, 45; octagon, half-octagon or round barrel to 32-inch at customer's preference; no sights; furnished with scope blocks; fancy Helm-pattern walnut stock; Niedner-type firing pin; coil spring striker based on Winchester Hi-Wall action. Introduced 1984; discontinued 1986.

Perf.: $1295   **Exc.:** $1050   **VGood:** $895

C. SHARPS ARMS MODEL 1874 SPORTING

Single shot; 40, 45, 50; 30-inch octagon barrel; weighs 9-1/2 lbs.; Lawrence-type open rear sight, blade front; American walnut stock; color case-hardened receiver, buttplate, barrel bands; blued barrel; recreation of original Sharps models in several variations. Introduced 1985; discontinued 1987.

Sporting Rifle No. 1
Exc.: $1400   **VGood:** $1200   **Good:** $895

Sporting Rifle No. 3
Exc.: $1400   **VGood:** $1200   **Good:** $895

Long Range Express Rifle
Exc.: $1500   **VGood:** $1300   **Good:** $995

Military Rifle
Exc.: $1200   **VGood:** $1100   **Good:** $795

Carbine
Exc.: $1100   **VGood:** $1000   **Good:** $695

Business Rifle
Exc.: $1400   **VGood:** $1200   **Good:** $995

C. SHARPS ARMS NEW MODEL 1874 OLD RELIABLE

Single shot; 40-50, 40-70, 40-90, 45-70, 45-90, 45-100, 45-110, 45-120, 50-70, 50-90, 50-140; 26-inch, 28-inch, 30-inch tapered, octagon barrel; weighs 10 lbs.; blade front sight, buckhorn rear; drilled, tapped for tang sight installation; straight-grip American black walnut stock; shotgun butt; heavy forend with schnabel tip; recreation of original C. Sharps

Serrifle Schuetzen Model

C. Sharps Arms New Model 1875 Rifle

C. Sharps Arms New Model 1875 Rifle

C. Sharps Arms New Model 1875 Classic

Shilen DGA Silhouette

Shiloh Sharps Model 1874 Jaeger

Shiloh Sharps Model 1874 Long Range Express

Shiloh Sharps 1874 No. 1 Sporting

design; double-set triggers. Manufactured by Shiloh Products. Reintroduced 1991.

Exc.: $2000   **VGood:** $1895   **Good:** $1695

C. SHARPS ARMS NEW MODEL 1875 RIFLE

Single shot, falling block; 22 LR, 32-40 Ballard, 38-55 Ballard, 38-56 WCF, 40-65 WCF, 40-90-3-1/4-inch, 40-90-2-5/8-inch, 40-70-2-1/10-inch, 40-70-2-1/4-inch, 40-7- 2-1/2-inch, 40-50-1-11/16-inch, 40-50-1-7/8-inch, 45-90, 40-70, 45-100, 45-110, 45-120, 50-70, 50-90, 50-140; 24-inch, 26-inch, 28-inch, 30-inch, 32-inch, 34-inch barrel; weighs 8 to 12 lbs; buckhorn rear sight, blade front; straight-grip walnut stock; case-colored receiver; reproduction of 1875 Sharps rifle. Manufactured by Shiloh Rifle Mfg. Co. Introduced 1986.

Carbine model
Exc.: $2000   **VGood:** $1800   **Good:** $1495
Saddle Rifle
Exc.: $2100   **VGood:** $1900   **Good:** $1610
Sporting model
Exc.: $2000   **VGood:** $1800   **Good:** $1595
Business model
Exc.: $2200   **VGood:** $1975   **Good:** $1495

C. SHARPS ARMS NEW MODEL 1875 CLASSIC

Same specs as New Model 1875 except 30-inch full octagon barrel; weighs 10 lbs.; Rocky Mountain buckhorn rear sight; crescent buttplate with toe plate; Hartford-style forend with German silver nose cap. Introduced 1987.

Exc.: $1895   **VGood:** $1795   **Good:** $1150

C. SHARPS ARMS NEW MODEL 1875 TARGET & LONG RANGE

Same specs as New Model 1875 except available in all listed calibers except 22 LR; 34-inch tapered octagon barrel; globe with post front sight, Long Range Vernier tang sight with windage adjustments; pistol-grip stock with cheek rest; checkered steel buttplate. Made in U.S. by C. Sharps Arms Co., distributed by Montana Armory, Inc. Introduced 1991.

Exc.: $1995   **VGood:** $1895   **Good:** $1250

C. SHARPS ARMS NEW MODEL 1885 HIGH WALL

Single shot; 22 LR, 22 Hornet, 219 Zipper, 30-40 Krag, 32-40, 38-55, 40-65 WCF, 45-70; 26-inch, 28-inch, 30-inch Douglas Premium tapered octagon barrels; Marble's ivory bead front sight, #66 long-blade, flat-top rear with reversible notch, elevator; American black walnut stock; recreation of original octagon-top High Wall; coil-spring action; tang drilled for tang sight; color case-hardened finish on most external parts. Introduced 1991; no longer in production.

Exc.: $1400   **VGood:** $1150   **Good:** $975

SHILEN DGA SPORTER

Bolt action; 17 Rem., 222, 223, 22-250, 220 Swift, 6mm Rem., 243 Win., 250 Savage, 257 Roberts, 284 Win., 308 Win., 358 Win.; 3-shot magazine; 24-inch barrel; no sights; uncheckered Monte Carlo walnut or fiberglass stock; cheekpiece; pistol-grip; sling swivels. Introduced 1976; discontinued 1987.

Exc.: $650   **VGood:** $550   **Good:** $450

SHILEN DGA BENCHREST MODEL

Same specs as DGA Model except single shot; 26-inch medium or heavy barrel; classic or thumbhole

walnut or fiberglass stock. Introduced 1977; no longer in production.

Exc.: $700   **VGood:** $600   **Good:** $500

SHILEN DGA SILHOUETTE

Same specs as DGA Model except 308 Win.; 25-inch heavy barrel. No longer in production.

Exc.: $700   **VGood:** $600   **Good:** $500

SHILEN DGA VARMINTER

Same specs as DGA Model except 25-inch heavy barrel. Introduced 1976; discontinued 1987.

Exc.: $650   **VGood:** $550   **Good:** $500

SHILOH SHARPS MODEL 1874 BUSINESS RIFLE

Single shot; 40-50 BN, 40-70 BN, 40-90 BN, 45-70 ST, 45-90 ST, 50-70 ST, 50-100 ST, 32-40, 38-55; 28-inch heavy round barrel; blade front sight, buckhorn rear; straight-grip steel buttplate; double-set trigger. Introduced 1986; still in production.

Exc.: $2200   **VGood:** $1975   **Good:** $1495

SHILOH SHARPS MODEL 1874 CARBINE

Same specs as other Model 1874 series rifles except 24-inch round barrel; single trigger. Introduced 1986; no longer in production.

Exc.: $1900   **VGood:** $1675   **Good:** $1195

SHILOH SHARPS MODEL 1874 JAEGER

Same specs as other Model 1874 series rifles except 30-40, 30-30, 307 Win., 45-70; 26-inch half-octagon lightweight barrel; standard supreme black walnut stock; shotgun, pistol grip or military-style butt. Introduced 1986; no longer in production.

Exc.: $2200   **VGood:** $1975   **Good:** $1495

SHILOH SHARPS MODEL 1874 LONG RANGE EXPRESS

Same specs as other Model 1874 series rifles except 34-inch tapered octagon barrel; sporting tang rear sight, globe front; semi-fancy, oil-finished pistol-grip walnut stock; shotgun-type buttplate; schnabel forend. Introduced 1985; still in production.

Exc.: $2200   **VGood:** $1975   **Good:** $1495

SHILOH SHARPS MODEL 1874 MILITARY

Same specs as other Model 1874 series rifles except 30-inch round barrel; Lawrence-style rear ladder sight, iron block front; military buttstock with steel buttplate and patchbox; long forend with three barrel bands; sling swivels; single trigger. Introduced 1985; no longer in production.

PExc.: $2000   **VGood:** $1775   **Good:** $1295

SHILOH SHARPS MODEL 1874 MILITARY CARBINE

Same specs as other Model 1874 series rifles except 40-70 BN, 45-70, 50-70; 22-inch round barrel; blade-type front sight, ladder-type rear; oil-finished military-type buttstock with steel buttplate; carbine forend with barrel band; saddle bar and ring; single trigger. Introduced 1989; no longer in production.

Perf.: $1300   **Exc.:** $1100   **VGood:** $975

SHILOH SHARPS MODEL 1874 MONTANA ROUGHRIDER

Same specs as other Model 1874 series rifles except 30-40, 30-30, 40-50x1-11/16 BN, 40-70x2-1/10, 45-70x2-1/10 ST; 24-inch, 26-inch, 28-inch, 30-inch, 34-inch half-octagon or full-octagon barrel; globe front and tang sight optional; standard supreme or semi-fancy oil-finished pistol-grip walnut stock; shotgun, pistol grip or military-style butt; schnabel forend. Introduced 1985; still in production.

Exc.: $2200   **VGood:** $1975   **Good:** $1495

SHILOH SHARPS MODEL 1874 NO. 1 SPORTING

Same specs as other Model 1874 rifles except 40-50 BN, 40-90 BN, 45-70 ST, 45-110 ST, 50-70 ST, 50-90 ST, 50-110 ST, 32-40, 38-55, 40-70 ST, 40-90 ST; 30-inch octagon barrel; semi-fancy, oil-finished pistol-grip walnut stock; shotgun-type buttplate; schnabel forend. Introduced 1985; still in production.

Exc.: $2200   VGood: $1975   Good: $1495

SHILOH SHARPS MODEL 1874 NO. 2 SPORTING

Same specs as other Model 1874 rifles except 45-70, 45-90, 45-120, 50-90, 50-140; 30-inch octagon barrel; semi-fancy, oil-finished pistol-grip walnut stock; shotgun-type buttplate; schnabel forend. No longer in production.

Exc.: $2200   VGood: $1975   Good: $1495

SHILOH SHARPS MODEL 1874 NO. 3 SPORTING

Same specs as other Model 1874 rifles except 40-50 BN, 40-90 BN, 45-70 ST, 45-110 ST, 50-70 ST, 50-90 ST, 50-110 ST, 32-40, 38-55, 40-70 ST, 40-90 ST; 30-inch octagon barrel; oil-finished straight-grip stock standard wood; shotgun-type buttplate. Introduced 1985; still in production.

Exc.: $2200   VGood: $1975   Good: $1495

SHILOH SHARPS MODEL 1874 SADDLE RIFLE

Same specs as other Model 1874 rifles except 26-inch octagon barrel; semi-fancy shotgun-type butt. Introduced 1986; still in production.

Perf.: $1400   Exc.: $1100   VGood: $900

SHILOH SHARPS 1874 QUIGLEY

Single shot, falling block; 45-70, 45-110. 34-inch heavy octagon barrel; Military-style stock with patch box, standard grade American walnut; Semi buckhorn rear sight, interchangeable front and midrange vernier tang sight with windage; replica of rifle used in the motion picture, "Quigley Down Under." Gold inlay initials, pewter tip, hartford collar, case color or antique finish. Double set triggers.

Perf.: $2800   Exc.: $2500   VGood: $2000

SHILOH SHARPS 1874 CREEDMOOR TARGET

Single shot, falling block; 38-55, 40-50 BN, 40-65 Win., 40-70 BN, 40-70 ST, 40-90 BN, 40- 90 ST, 44-77 BN, 44-90 BN, 45-70 ST, 45-90 ST, 45-100 ST, 45-110 ST, 45-120 ST, 50-70 ST, 50-90 ST; 32-inch barrel, half round-half octagon. Extra fancy American walnut shotgun style stock with pistol grip. Single trigger. AA finish on stock, polished barrel and screws, pewter tip.

Exc.: $2200   VGood: $1975   Good: $1495

SIGARMS SHR 970 SYNTHETIC RIFLE

Bolt action; 25-06, 270, 280, 308, 30-06. 22-inch barrel; weighs 7.2 lbs.; 41.9-inch overall length; black fiberglass or walnut stock; drilled and tapped for scope mounting. Quick takedown; interchangeable barrels; removable box magazine; cocking indicator; three-position safety. Introduced 1998. Imported by Sigarms, Inc.

Perf.: $720   Exc.: $660   VGood: $500

SIGARMS SIG 556

Generally similar to the Swiss-made SIG 556 tactical rifle but made in the USA. Chambered in 5.56 NATO. Collapsible stock, 16" mil-spec barrel, picatinny rail and all the trendy tactical goodies.

NIB: $1275   Exc.: $1175   VGood: $1050

SIGARMS SIG 556 HOLO

Similar to above but with holographic sight.

NIB: $1575   Exc.: $1375   VGood: $11250

SIGARMS SIG 556 DMR

A sniper version of the SIG 556 SWAT with bipod and other accurizing features.

NIB	Exc	V.G.	Good	Fair	Poor
NIB: $2100	**Exc.: $1775**	**VGood: $1250**			

SIGARMS SAUER SSG 3000

Imported by SIGARMS. A 5-round bolt action sniper rifle chambered in .308 Winchester. The heavy-contoured, hammer forged barrel is fitted with a flash

Shiloh Sharps 1874 Montana Roughrider

Shiloh Sharps 1874 Quigley

Shiloh Sharps 1874 Creedmoor Target

Sigarms SHR 970

Sigarms SIG 556

SIGARMS Sauer SSG 3000

Smith & Wesson Model 125

Smith & Wesson Model 1500

Smith & Wesson Model 1500 Deluxe

suppressor/muzzle brake to provide greater accuracy with reduced muzzle signature. Both the barrel and the receiver feature a black oxide finish to eliminate glare. The short, smooth 60 degree bolt throw allows for rapid operation and, like the safety release, the bolt action is quiet. A massive six-lug lockup system is used to give the SSG 3000 greater strength and accuracy. Pistol grip and fully adjustable stock to give the shooter a custom fit. The trigger is adjustable for trigger position, trigger take up, let-off point, and trigger pull weight. The receiver on the SSG 3000 features a dovetail that will accept a wide range of sighting systems, including a factory available M1913 rail.

NIB: $3750   Exc.: $3000   VGood: $2250

SMITH & WESSON MODEL 125

Bolt action; 270 Win., 30-06; 5-shot magazine; 24-inch barrel; step-adjustable rear sight, hooded ramp front; action drilled, tapped for scope mounts; thumb safety; standard grade with hand-checkered stock of European walnut; deluxe grade adds rosewood forearm tip, pistol-grip cap. Introduced 1973; discontinued 1973.

Standard grade		
Exc.: $450	**VGood: $400**	**Good: $280**
Deluxe grade		
Exc.: $500	**VGood: $450**	**Good: $290**

SMITH & WESSON MODEL 1500

Bolt action; 22-250, 222, 223, 25-06, 243, 270, 30-06, 308, 7mm Rem. Mag., 300 Win. Mag., 338 Win. Mag.; 5-shot box magazine; 22-inch, 24-inch (magnum) barrel; hooded gold bead front sight, open round-notch fully-adjustable rear; checkered American walnut stock; single-set trigger; one-piece trigger guard; hinged floorplate; quick-detachable swivel studs; composition non-slip buttplate; rubber recoil pad (magnums). Introduced 1979; discontinued 1984.

Exc.: $425   VGood: $400   Good: $300

SMITH & WESSON MODEL 1500 DELUXE

Same specs as Model 1500 except no sights; decorative scrollwork on floorplate; skip-line checkering; pistol-grip cap with S&W seal; sling, swivels. Introduced 1980; discontinued 1984.

Exc.: $450   VGood: $425   Good: $325

SMITH & WESSON MODEL 1500 MOUNTAINEER

Same specs as Model 1500 except 22-inch, 24-inch barrel; no sights; drilled, tapped for scope mounts; satin-finished, checkered American walnut stock;

Smith & Wesson Model 1500 Mountaineer

Smith & Wesson Model 1700LS Classic Hunter

Smith & Wesson Model B

Smith & Wesson Model C

Smith & Wesson Model D

Smith & Wesson M&P15 PC

Springfield, Inc. M-1 Garand

Springfield, Inc. M1A

recoil pad (magnum). Introduced 1983; discontinued 1984.

Exc.: $450   **VGood:** $425   **Good:** $325

SMITH & WESSON MODEL 1500 VARMINT DELUXE

Same specs as Model 1500 except 222, 22-250, 223; 22-inch heavy barrel; oil-finished stock; quick-detachable swivels; fully-adjustable trigger; blued or Parkerized finish. Introduced 1982; discontinued 1984.

Exc.: $450   **VGood:** $425   **Good:** $325

SMITH & WESSON MODEL 1700LS CLASSIC HUNTER

Bolt action; 243, 270, 30-06; 5-shot removable magazine; hooded globe bead front sight, open round-notch fully-adjustable rear; checkered American classic walnut stock, tapered forend, schnabel tip; ribbon checkering pattern; black rubber buttpad; flush-mounted sling swivels; jeweled bolt body; knurled bolt knob. Introduced 1983; discontinued 1984.

Exc.: $550   **VGood:** $425   **Good:** $325

SMITH & WESSON MODEL A

Bolt action; 22-250, 243 Win., 270 Win., 308 Win., 30-06, 7mm Rem. Mag., 300 Win. Mag.; 3-shot (magnum), 5-shot magazine; 23-3/4-inch barrel; folding leaf rear sight, hooded ramp front; hand-checkered European walnut stock; Monte Carlo,

rosewood pistol-grip cap, forend tip; sling swivels. Manufactured in Sweden by Husqvarna. Introduced 1969; discontinued 1972.

Exc.: $475   **VGood:** $450   **Good:** $350

SMITH & WESSON MODEL B

Same specs as Model A except 243 Win., 270 Win., 30-06, 308; 23-3/4-inch light barrel; three-leaf folding rear sight, hooded German silver bead front; Monte Carlo stock; schnabel forend tip. Introduced 1969; discontinued 1972.

Exc.: $475   **VGood:** $450   **Good:** $350

SMITH & WESSON MODEL C

Same specs as Model A except 243 Win., 270 Win., 30-06, 308; 23-3/4-inch light barrel; open sporting rear sight, hooded German silver bead front; straight-comb stock; cheekpiece, schnabel forend tip. Introduced 1969; discontinued 1972.

Exc.: $475   **VGood:** $450   **Good:** $350

SMITH & WESSON MODEL D

Same specs as Model A except 243 Win., 270 Win., 30-06, 308; 20-3/4-inch light barrel; straight comb full-length Mannlicher-type stock; cheekpiece; open sporting rear sight, hooded German silver bead front. Introduced 1969; discontinued 1972.

Exc.: $475   **VGood:** $450   **Good:** $350

SMITH & WESSON MODEL E

Same specs as Model A except 243 Win., 270 Win., 30-06, 308; 20-3/4-inch light barrel; full-length

Mannlicher-type Monte Carlo stock; schnabel forend tip; open sporting rear sight, hooded German silver bead front. Introduced 1969; discontinued 1972.

Exc.: $475   **VGood:** $450   **Good:** $350

SMITH & WESSON M&P15 MILITARY AND POLICE TACTICAL RIFLE

Gas-operated semi-auto built along lines of AR-15. Caliber: 5.56mm NATO. Magazine capacity: 30. Barrel: 16-inch 1:9. Stock: Six-position telescoping composite. Weight: 6.74 lbs. unloaded. Sights: Adjustable front and rear. Variants: M&P15A & M&P15T (no carry handle; folding battle sight).

NIB: $1150   **Exc.:** $1075   **VGood:** $950

SMITH & WESSON M&P 15 PC

Generally similar to the M&P rifle but with accurized tubular floated barrel, 2-stage match trigger, 20" matte stainless barrel. No sights.

NIB: $1375   **Exc.:** $1295   **VGood:** $1100

SOVEREIGN TD 22

Semi-automatic; 22 LR; 10-shot clip; 21-inch barrel; 41-inch overall length; weighs 6-1/2 lbs.; takedown; fully-adjustable open rear sight, hooded ramp front; walnut-finished hardwood stock; blued finish. Introduced 1986; no longer in production.

Exc.: $80   **VGood:** $60   **Good:** $45

SPRINGFIELD INC. BM-59 (ITALIAN MODEL)

Semi-automatic; 7.62mm NATO (308 Win.); 20-shot box magazine; 19-3/8-inch barrel; 43-3/4-inch overall length; weighs 9-1/4 lbs.; military square-blade front sight, click-adjustable peep rear; walnut stock with trapped rubber buttpad; full military-dress Italian service rifle with winter trigger, grenade launcher and sights, tri-compensator, bipod. Refined version of the M-1 Garand. Made in Italy, assembled by Springfield Armory, Inc. Introduced 1981; no longer available.

Exc.: $1495   **VGood:** $1195   **Good:** $880

SPRINGFIELD INC. BM-59 ALPINE PARATROOPER

Same specs as BM-59 Italian Model except Beretta-made folding metal buttstock with pistol grip. Made in Italy, assembled in U.S. by Springfield Armory, Inc. Introduced 1981; no longer available.

Exc.: $1695   **VGood:** $1295   **Good:** $900

SPRINGFIELD INC. BM-59 NIGERIAN MODEL

Same specs as BM-59 Italian Model except Beretta-made vertical pistol grip stock. Made in Italy, assembled in U.S. by Springfield Armory, Inc. Introduced 1981; no longer available.

Exc.: $1695   **VGood:** $1350   **Good:** $900

SPRINGFIELD INC. M-1 GARAND

Semi-automatic; 30-06, 308 Win., 270 Win., 8-shot. 24-inch barrel; weighs 9.5 lbs.; 43.6-inch overall length; American walnut stock. Military square post front, military aperture, MOA adjustable rear sights. Limited production, certificate of authenticity, all new receiver, barrel and stock with remaining parts USGI mil-spec. 2-stage military trigger; discontinued 1990; reintroduced in 2002 in 30-06 and 308 only, still in production; premium for 270 caliber.

Exc.: $1200   **VGood:** $995   **Good:** $695

SPRINGFIELD INC. M1A

Semi-automatic; gas-operated; 308 Win. (7.62 NATO), 243 Win., 7mm-08; 5-, 10-, 20-shot box magazine; 22-inch barrel, flash suppressor; adjustable aperture rear sight, blade front; walnut, birch or fiberglass stock; fiberglass hand guard; sling swivels, sling. Same general specs as military M14 but without full-auto capability. Maker is private Illinois firm, not a U.S. government facility. Introduced 1974; still in production.

Exc.: $1200   **VGood:** $995   **Good:** $695

Fiberglass stock

Perf.: $1050   **Exc.:** $950   **VGood:** $750

SPRINGFIELD INC. M1A MATCH
Same specs as M1A except National Match grade barrel, sights; glass-bedded American walnut or fiberglass stock; better trigger pull; modified gas system, mainspring guide. Still in production.

Perf.: $1550   **Exc.:** $1200   **VGood:** $955

SPRINGFIELD INC. M1A SCOUT SQUAD RIFLE
Same specs as M1A except 18-inch barrel with muzzle brake, 308, weighs 9.3 pounds, 10 or 20 round magazine.

Perf.: $1525   **Exc.:** $1100   **VGood:** $800

SPRINGFIELD INC. M1A SOCOM RIFLE
Same specs as M1A except 16.25-inch barrel with muzzle brake, forward-positioned scope mount, fiberglass stock; 308, weighs 8.9 pounds, 10 or 20 round magazine. Introduced 2004, still in production.

Perf.: $1675   **Exc.:** $1250   **VGood:** N/A

SPRINGFIELD ARMORY M1A SOCOM 16
Similar to SOCOM but with walnut stock and 16-inch barrel.

NIB: $1550   **Exc.:** $1450   **VGood:** $1195

SPRINGFIELD INC. M1A SUPER MATCH
Same specs as M1A except heavier, premium-grade barrel; National Match sights; glass-bedded oversize American walnut or fiberglass stock; better trigger pull; modified gas system, mainspring guide. Still in production.

Perf.: $2100   **Exc.:** $1695   **VGood:** $1100

SPRINGFIELD INC. M1A/M21 TACTICAL
Same specs as M1A Super Match except Douglas Premium match barrel and special sniper stock with adjustable cheekpiece; weighs 11-1/4 lbs. From Springfield, Inc.

Perf.: $2000   **Exc.:** $1400   **VGood:** $1100

SPRINGFIELD INC. M1A/M21 LAW ENFORCEMENT
Semi-automatic; 243, 7mm-08, 308 Win.; 20-shot magazine; air-gauged 22-inch Douglas heavy barrel; 44-1/4-inch overall length; weighs 11-7/8 lbs.; National Match front and rear sights; glass-bedded heavy walnut stock with adjustable comb, ventilated recoil pad. Refinement of the standard M1A rifle with specially knurled shoulder for figure-eight operating rod guide. From Springfield Armory, Inc. Introduced 1987; no longer made.

Perf.: $2000   **Exc.:** $1400   **VGood:** $1100

SPRINGFIELD INC. M1A/M21 SNIPER
Semi-automatic; 308 Win.; 20-shot box magazine; 22-inch heavy barrel; 44-1/4-inch overall length; weighs 15-1/4 lbs. with bipod, scope mount; National Match sights; heavy American walnut stock with adjustable comb, ventilated recoil pad; based on M1A rifle; folding, removable bipod; leather military sling. Introduced 1987; discontinued 1992.

Perf.: $2100   **Exc.:** $1500   **VGood:** $1200

SPRINGFIELD INC. M1A/M25 CARLOS HATHCOCK MODEL
Same specs as M1A/M21 except synthetic stock with adjustable comb, 308, 22-inch barrel, 12.75 pounds; Picatinny rail for optical sights only, no provision for iron sights; Harris bipod. Special model in honor of U.S. Marine Gunnery Sergeant Carlos N. Hathcock; rifle bears a facsimile of his signature. Introduced in 2001, still in production. Top dollar for unfired, absolutely mint specimens.

Perf.: $3700   **Exc.:** $2700   **VGood:** $1700

SPRINGFIELD INC. M-6 SCOUT RIFLE/SHOTGUN
Combination gun; 22 LR, 22 WMR, 22 Hornet over 410-bore; 18-1/4-inch barrel; 32-inch overall length; weighs 4-1/2 lbs.; blade front sight, military aperture for 22, V-notch for 410; folding steel stock with storage for fifteen 22 LR, four 410 shells; all-metal construction; designed for quick disassembly and minimum maintenance; folds for compact storage. Early examples made in U.S. by Springfield, Inc., later guns imported from the Czech Republic. Introduced 1982; reintroduced 1995, no longer in production.

Springfield, Inc. M1A Super Match

Springfield, Inc. M-6 Scout Rifle/Shotgun

Squires Bingham Model 14D

Stevens Buckhorn Model 056

Pricing shown is for later CZ production; 100 percent premium for marked USA production.

Perf.: $250   **Exc.:** $225   **VGood:** $185

Stainless steel version

Perf.: $275   **Exc.:** $250   **VGood:** $210

SPRINGFIELD INC. MODEL 700 BASR
Bolt action; 308 Win.; 5-shot magazine; 26-inch heavy Douglas Premium barrel; 46-1/4-inch overall length; weighs 13-1/2 lbs.; no sights; synthetic fiber stock; rubber recoil pad; marketed with military leather sling; adjustable, folding Parker-Hale bipod. Introduced 1987; discontinued 1988.

Exc.: $695   **VGood:** $595   **Good:** $440

SPRINGFIELD INC. SAR-8 SPORTER
Semi-automatic; 308 Win.; 20-shot magazine; 18-inch barrel; 40-3/8-inch overall length; weighs 8-3/4 lbs.; protected front sight, rotary-style adjustble rear; black or green composition forend; wood thumbhole butt; delayed roller-lock action; fluted chamber; matte black finish. From Springfield Inc. Introduced 1990; discontinued; reintroduced 1995, no longer in production.

Perf.: $2200   **Exc.:** $1900   **VGood:** $1500

SPRINGFIELD INC. SAR-4800
Semi-automatic; 5.56, 7.62 NATO (308 Win.); 10-shot magazine; 21-inch barrel; 43-3/8-inch overall length; weighs 9-1/2 lbs.; protected post front sight, adjustable peep rear; fiberglass forend; wood thumbhole butt. New production. From Springfield Inc. Reintroduced 1995, no longer in production.

Perf.: $2100   **Exc.:** $1800   **VGood:** $1400

SPRINGFIELD INC. SAR-4800 22
Same specs as SAR-4800 except 22 LR. No longer in production.

Perf.: $1100   **Exc.:** $950   **VGood:** $695

SPRINGFIELD INC. SAR-4800 BUSH
Same specs as SAR-4800 except 18-inch barrel. No longer in production.

Perf.: $2100   **Exc.:** $1800   **VGood:** $1400

SQUIRES BINGHAM MODEL 14D
Bolt action; 22 LR; 5-shot box magazine; 24-inch barrel; V-notch rear sight, hooded ramp front; grooved receiver for scope mounts; exotic hand-checkered wood stock, contrasting forend tip, pistol-grip cap. Made in the Philippines. No longer in production.

Exc.: $70   **VGood:** $50   **Good:** $45

SQUIRES BINGHAM MODEL 15
Bolt action; 22 WMR; 5-shot box magazine; 24-inch barrel; V-notch rear sight, hooded ramp front; grooved receiver for scope mounts; exotic hand-checkered wood stock, contrasting forend tip; pistol-grip cap. Made in the Philippines. No longer in production.

Exc.: $80   **VGood:** $60   **Good:** $50

SQUIRES BINGHAM MODEL M16
Semi-automatic; 22 LR; 15-shot detachable box magazine; 19-1/2-inch barrel; muzzlebrake/flash hider; integral rear sight, ramped post front; black painted mahogany buttstock, forearm; similar to military M16. No longer imported.

Exc.: $200   **VGood:** $165   **Good:** $115

SQUIRES BINGHAM MODEL M20D
Semi-automatic; 22 LR; 15-shot detachable box magazine; 19-1/2-inch barrel; muzzlebrake/flash hider; V-notch rear sight, blade front; grooved receiver for scope mount; hand-checkered exotic wood stock; contrasting pistol-grip cap, forend tip. No longer imported.

Exc.: $90   **VGood:** $70   **Good:** $60

SPRINGFIELD ARMORY MODEL P9 SUBCOMPACT
Same specs as Model P9 except 9mm Para., 40 S&W; 12-shot (9mm), 9-shot (40 S&W); 3-1/2-inch barrel; weighs 32 oz.; compact slide frame; squared triggerguard; extended magazine floorplate. Introduced 1990; discontinued 1992.

Perf.: $350   **Exc.:** $300   **VGood:** $250

SPRINGFIELD ARMORY MODEL P9 ULTRA LSP
Same specs as Model P9 except 5-inch barrel; 8-3/8-inch overall length; weighs 34-1/4 oz.; long slide ported; rubber or walnut stocks; blued, Parkerized or blue/stainless finish. Introduced 1991; discontinued 1993.

Perf.: $550   **Exc.:** $450   **VGood:** $350

Phosphated finish

Perf.: $575   **Exc.:** $475   **VGood:** $375

Stainless steel

Perf.: $600   **Exc.:** $500   **VGood:** $450

Stainless frame/matte black slide

Perf.: $600   **Exc.:** $525   **VGood:** $450

SPRINGFIELD ARMORY OMEGA
Semi-automatic; single action; 38 Super, 10mm, 40 S&W, 45 ACP; 5-shot (10mm, 40 S&W), 7-shot (45 ACP), 9-shot (38 Super) magazine; 5-inch, 6-inch barrel; weighs 46 oz.; polygonal rifling; rubberized wrap-around grips; removable ramp front sight, fully-adjustable rear. Convertible between calibers; double serrated slide; built on 1911-A1 frame. Made in U.S. by Springfield Armory; now Springfield, Inc. Introduced 1987; discontinued 1990.

Exc.: $650   **VGood:** $500   **Good:** $350

Stag Arms Stag-15 Model 2
Pre-Ban

Stag Arms Stag-15 Model 3
Pre-Ban

Stag Arms Stag 6.8 Model 5
Pre-Ban

Stag Arms Stag-15 Model 6
Pre-Ban Super Varminter

SPRINGFIELD ARMORY OMEGA MATCH

Same specs as Omega except adjustable breech face; new extractor system; low profile combat sights; double serrated slide. Introduced 1991; discontinued 1992.

Perf.: $750   **Exc.:** $650   **VGood:** $500

SPRINGFIELD ARMORY PANTHER

Semi-automatic; double action; 9mm Para., 40 S&W, 45 ACP; 15-shot (9mm Para.), 11-shot (40 S&W), 9-shot (45 ACP); 40 S&W, 11-shot; 45 ACP, 9-shot magazine; 3-3/4-inch barrel; 7-inch overall length; weighs 29 oz.; narrow profile checkered walnut grips; low profile blade front sight, windage-adjustable rear; three-dot system; hammer drop and firing pin safeties; serrated front and rear straps; serrated slide top; Commander hammer; frame-mounted slide stop; button magazine release; matte blue finish. From Springfield Armory; now Springfield, Inc. Introduced 1991; dropped 1992.

Perf.: $500   **Exc.:** $400   **VGood:** $350

SPRINGFIELD ARMORY XD 45ACP

Polymer semi-auto in black, green or bi-tone holds 13+1 .45 ACP. Imported from Croatia. Fixed sights. Service model: 4-inch barrel, 30 oz. Tactical model: 5-inch barrel, 32 oz. Picatinny rail. Introduced 2006.

New: $600   **Exc.:** $495   **VGood:** $395

SPRINGFIELD ARMORY LIGHTWEIGHT OPERATOR

Blued, semi-auto .45 ACP with 5-inch bull barrel. Fixed sights, 5-6-lb. trigger pull, Cocobolo grips, 31 oz. Picatinny rail.

New: $995   **Exc.:** $875   **VGood:** $550

SPRINGFIELD ARMORY LIGHTWEIGHT CHAMPION OPERATOR

Similar to above but with 4-inch bull barrel.

New: $995   **Exc.:** $875   **VGood:** $550

SPRINGFIELD ARMORY ENHANCED MICRO PISTOL (EMP)

Tiny little 1911-style semi-auto chambered in 9mm Parabellum or .40 S&W. Short-action single-action design, 7-shot capacity, 3" bull barrel, fixed sights, stainless frame that is 1/8" shorter than the company's Compact models.

New: $1050   **Exc.:** $950   **VGood:** $675

SPRINGFIELD ARMORY XD(M)

Polymer-framed 16+1 autoloader chambered in .40 S&W. Features include easy-access magazine release, "minimal error disassembly" design, interchangeable backstraps. Introduced 2008.

New: $650   **Exc.:** $495   **VGood:** $395

STAG ARMS STAG-15 MODEL 1 PRE-BAN

Basic M-4 Carbine pattern. Cal. 5.56mm/.223. 16-inch M-4 barrel with flash hider and bayonet lug. A2 upper receiver with adjustable rear sight. Six-position collapsible buttstock.

New: $950   **Exc.:** $825   **VGood:** $695

STAG ARMS STAG-15 MODEL 2 PRE-BAN

As above but with a flat top upper receiver. Includes MI ERS flip type rear sight assembly.

New: $975   **Exc.:** $850   **VGood:** $715

STAG ARMS STAG-15 MODEL 2 T

As above but with a A.R.M.S. sight system and Samson MRFS-C four sided hand guard.

New: $1125   **Exc.:** $995   **VGood:** $750

STAG ARMS STAG-15 MODEL 3 PRE-BAN

M-4 type carbine featuring a flat top receiver and gas block with picatinny rails. Six position collapsible buttstock.

New: $900   **Exc.:** $800   **VGood:** $675

STAG ARMS STAG-15 MODEL 4 PRE-BAN

An A-2 type rifle featuring a 20-inch barrel. Flash hider and bayonet lug.

New: $1000   **Exc.:** $900   **VGood:** $700

STAG ARMS STAG 6.8 MODEL 5 PRE-BAN

Cal. 6.8 SPC. 16-inch barrel. Flat top receiver with picitinny rail. Six position collapsible buttstock. 25-round magazine.

New: $1050   **Exc.:** $950   **VGood:** $750

STAG ARMS STAG-15 MODEL 6 PRE-BAN SUPER VARMINTER

24-inch heavy barrel. No flash hider. Flat top receiver with picitinny rail. Two stage trigger. Free float round hand guard. A2 type fixed stock.

New: $1075   **Exc.:** $975   **VGood:** $775

STANDARD ARMS MODEL G

Semi-automatic; 25 Rem., 30 Rem., 35 Rem.; 4-shot (35 Rem.), 5-shot magazine; 22-3/8-inch barrel; gas operated; hammerless; takedown; open rear sight, ivory bead front; American walnut buttstock; slide handle-type forearm; gas port, when closed, could be used as a manual slide action. Introduced 1912. Notorious for malfunctioning!

VGood: $650   **Good:** $395   **Fair:** $250

STANDARD ARMS MODEL M

Slide action; 25 Rem., 30 Rem., 35 Rem.; 4-shot (35 Rem.), 5-shot magazine; 22-3/8-inch barrel; hammerless; takedown; open rear sight, ivory bead front; American walnut buttstock, slide handle-type forearm. Introduced 1912. Some collector value.

VGood: $675   **Good:** $420   **Fair:** $275

STEVENS BUCKHORN MODEL 053

Bolt action; single shot; 25 Stevens, 22 Short, 22 Long, 22 LR, 22 WMR; 24-inch barrel; 41-1/4-inch overall length; weighs 5-1/2 lbs.; takedown; receiver peep sight, open folding middle sight, hooded ramp front with three inserts, removable hood; uncheckered walnut stock; pistol grip; black forearm tip. Introduced 1935; discontinued 1948.

Exc.: $150   **VGood:** $130   **Good:** $95

STEVENS BUCKHORN MODEL 53

Same specs as Buckhorn Model 053 except open rear sight, gold bead front.

Exc.: $150   **VGood:** $130   **Good:** $95

STEVENS BUCKHORN MODEL 056

Bolt action; 22 Short, 22 Long, 22 LR; 5-shot detachable box magazine; 24-inch barrel; 43-1/2-inch overall length; weighs 6 lbs.; takedown; receiver peep sight, open middle sight, hooded front; uncheckered walnut sporter-type stock; pistol grip, black forearm tip; rubber buttplate. Introduced 1935; discontinued 1948.

Exc.: $175   **VGood:** $155   **Good:** $120

STEVENS BUCKHORN MODEL 56

Same specs as Buckhorn Model 056 except open rear sight, gold bead front.

Exc.: $175   **VGood:** $155   **Good:** $120

STEVENS BUCKHORN MODEL 066

Bolt action; 22 Short, 22 Long, 22 LR; 21-shot (22 Short), 17-shot (22 Long), 15-shot (22 LR) tube magazine; 24-inch barrel; 43-1/2-inch overall length; weighs 6 lbs.; receiver peep sight, folding sporting middle sight, hooded front; uncheckered walnut sporting stock; pistol grip, black forearm tip; rubber buttplate. Introduced 1935; discontinued 1948.

Exc.: $150   **VGood:** $130   **Good:** $95

STEVENS BUCKHORN MODEL 66
Same specs as Model 066 except fully-adjustable sporting rear sight, gold bead front.

Exc.: $150   **VGood:** $130   **Good:** $95

STEVENS BUCKHORN NO. 057
Semi-automatic; 22 LR; 5-shot detachable box magazine; 24-inch barrel; takedown; peep receiver sight, hooded front; uncheckered sporter-style stock; black forearm tip. Introduced 1939; discontinued 1948.

Exc.: $125   **VGood:** $100   **Good:** $75

STEVENS BUCKHORN NO. 57
Same specs as Buckhorn No. 057 except open rear sight, plain bead front.

Exc.: $125   **VGood:** $100   **Good:** $75

STEVENS BUCKHORN NO. 076
Semi-automatic; 22 LR; 15-shot tube magazine; 24-inch barrel; weighs 6 lbs.; takedown; cross-bolt locks for use as single shot with 22 Short, 22 Long, 22 LR; peep rear receiver sight, folding flat-top middle sight, hooded front; uncheckered sporter-style stock; black forearm tip; rubber buttplate. Introduced 1938; discontinued 1948.

Exc.: $150   **VGood:** $130   **Good:** $115

STEVENS BUCKHORN NO. 76
Same specs as Buckhorn No. 076 except open rear sight; gold bead front.

Exc.: $150   **VGood:** $130   **Good:** $115

STEVENS MODEL 15
Bolt action; single shot; 22 Short, 22 Long, 22 LR; 22-inch, 24-inch barrel; 43-inch overall length; weighs 4 lbs.; elevation-adjustable open rear sight, gold bead front; uncheckered walnut pistol-grip stock. Introduced 1948; discontinued 1965.

Exc.: $100   **VGood:** $75   **Good:** $55

STEVENS MODEL 15Y
Same specs as Model 15 except 21-inch barrel; 35-1/4-inch overall length; shorter youth-size buttstock. Introduced 1958; discontinued 1965.

Exc.: $100   **VGood:** $75   **Good:** $55

STEVENS MODEL 66
Bolt action; 22 Short, 22 Long, 22 LR; 19-shot (22 Short), 15-shot (22 Long), 13-shot (22 LR) tube magazine; 24-inch barrel; takedown; open rear sight, bead front; uncheckered walnut pistol-grip stock; grooved forearm. Introduced 1931; discontinued 1935.

Exc.: $100   **VGood:** $75   **Good:** $55

STEVENS MODEL 76
Semi-automatic; usable as repeater or single shot; 22 LR (semi-auto), 22 Short, 22 Long, 22 LR (repeater or single shot); 15-shot tubular magazine; 24-inch tapered barrel with crowned muzzle; weighs 6 lbs.; hammer release mechanism for single shot operation; open rear sight, gold bead front; American walnut full pistol-grip stock; hard rubber buttplate. Introduced 1947.

Exc.: $150   **VGood:** $130   **Good:** $115

STEVENS MODEL 84
Bolt action; 22 Short, 22 Long, 22 LR; 15-shot (22 LR), 17-shot (22 Long), 21-shot (22 Short) tube magazine; 24-inch barrel; 43-inch overall length; weighs 6 lbs.; cross-bolt locks for single shot operation; takedown; elevation-adjustable micro peep rear sight, gold bead front; uncheckered walnut military-style full pistol-grip stock; plated bolt, trigger. Introduced 1949; discontinued 1965.

Exc.: $100   **VGood:** $75   **Good:** $55

STEVENS MODEL 84S
Same specs as Model 84 except No. 150 micro peep rear sight, No. 150 hooded front. Introduced 1948; discontinued 1952.

Exc.: $100   **VGood:** $75   **Good:** $55

STEVENS MODEL 85
Semi-automatic; 22 LR; 5-shot detachable box magazine; 24-inch barrel; 44-inch overall length;

Stevens Buckhorn Model 066

Stevens Buckhorn Model 66

Stevens Buckhorn No. 076

Stevens Model 15Y

Stevens Model 84

Stevens Model 84S

Stevens Model 86S

Stevens Model 87

weighs 6 lbs.; takedown; cross-bolt locks for repeater or single shot operation; open rear sight, bead front; uncheckered American walnut full pistol-grip stock; black forearm tip; hard rubber buttplate. Introduced 1948; discontinued 1976.

Exc.: $125   **VGood:** $100   **Good:** $75

STEVENS MODEL 85K
Same specs as Model 85 except 20-inch barrel; 40-inch overall length; weighs 5 3/4 lbs. Introduced 1959.

Exc.: $125   **VGood:** $100   **Good:** $75

STEVENS MODEL 85S
Same specs as Model 85 except peep rear sight, hooded front. Introduced 1948; discontinued 1976.

Exc.: $125   **VGood:** $100   **Good:** $75

STEVENS MODEL 86
Bolt action; 22 Short, 22 Long, 22 LR; 21-shot (22 Short), 17-shot (22 Long), 15-shot (22 LR) tube magazine; 24-inch barrel; 43-1/2-inch overall length; weighs 6 lbs.; takedown; sporting elevation-adjustable rear sight, gold bead front; uncheckered walnut military-style full pistol-grip stock; plated bolt, trigger. Introduced 1935; discontinued 1948.

Exc.: $100   **VGood:** $75   **Good:** $55

STEVENS MODEL 86S
Same specs as Model 86 except No. 150 peep rear sight, hooded front. Introduced 1948; discontinued 1952.

Exc.: $100   **VGood:** $75   **Good:** $55

STEVENS MODEL 87, 87A
Semi-automatic; 22 LR; can also be used as repeater or single shot; 15-shot tube magazine; 24-inch barrel (until late '60s), 20-inch barrel (later version); weighs 6 lbs.; takedown; cross-bolt locks for single shot operation; open rear sight, bead front; uncheckered American walnut full pistol-grip stock; black forearm tip; hard rubber buttplate. Marketed as Springfield Model 87 from 1938 to 1948, when trade name dropped. Introduced as the Stevens Model 87 in 1948; discontinued 1976.

Exc.: $100   **VGood:** $75   **Good:** $55

STEVENS MODEL 87K
Same specs as Model 87 except 20-inch barrel; 40-inch overall length; weighs 5-3/4 lbs. Introduced 1959.

Exc.: $100   **VGood:** $75   **Good:** $55

STEVENS MODEL 87S
Same specs as Model 87 except peep rear sight, hooded front. Introduced with Stevens name in 1948; discontinued 1953.

Exc.: $105   **VGood:** $80   **Good:** $60

STEVENS MODEL 110E
Bolt action; 243, 308, 30-06; 4-shot magazine; 22-inch round tapered barrel; removable bead ramp front sight, step-adjustable rear; drilled, tapped for peep sight or scope mounts; walnut-finished hardwood Monte Carlo stock; checkered pistol grip, forend; hard rubber buttplate; top tang safety. Introduced 1978; discontinued 1984.

Exc.: $275   **VGood:** $2225   **Good:** $145

Stevens Model 110ES

Stevens Model 325

Stevens No. 419
Junior Target

Stevens Favorite No. 17

Stevens Ideal No. 44

STEVENS MODEL 110ES
Same specs as Model 110E except 5-shot magazine; free-floating barrel; marketed with 4x scope, mounts. Introduced 1981; discontinued 1985.

Exc.: $295 **VGood:** $250 **Good:** $155

STEVENS MODEL 120
Bolt action; single shot; 22 Short, 22 Long, 22 LR; 20-inch round tapered barrel; sporting front/rear sights; grooved for scope mounts; walnut-finished hardwood stock; pistol grip; action cocks on opening of bolt; thumb safety; double extractors; recessed bolt face. Introduced 1979; discontinued 1983.

Exc.: $80 **VGood:** $70 **Good:** $50

STEVENS MODEL 125
Bolt action; single shot; 22 Short, 22 Long, 22 LR; 22-inch barrel; 39-inch overall length; sporting front sight, open rear with elevator; walnut-finished stock; manual cocking; blued finish. Introduced 1981; no longer made.

Exc.: $100 **VGood:** $75 **Good:** $55

STEVENS MODEL 322
Bolt action; 22 Hornet; 4-shot detachable box magazine; 21-inch barrel; open rear sight, ramp front; uncheckered walnut pistol grip stock. Introduced 1947; discontinued 1950.

Exc.: $260 **VGood:** $240 **Good:** $150

STEVENS MODEL 322S
Same specs as Model 322 except peep rear sight. Introduced 1947; discontinued 1950.

Exc.: $270 **VGood:** $250 **Good:** $160

STEVENS MODEL 325
Bolt action; 30-30; 4-shot detachable box magazine; 21-inch barrel; open rear sight, bead front; uncheckered pistol-grip stock; flat bolt handle. Introduced 1947; discontinued 1950.

Exc.: $240 **VGood:** $200 **Good:** $170

STEVENS MODEL 325S
Same specs as Model 325 except peep rear sight. Introduced 1947; discontinued 1950.

Exc.: $250 **VGood:** $210 **Good:** $190

STEVENS MODEL 416-2
Bolt action; 22 LR; 5-shot detachable box magazine; 26-inch heavy barrel; weighs 9-1/2 lbs.; No. 106 receiver peep sight, No. 25 hooded front; uncheckered American walnut target-type stock; checkered steel buttplate; sling swivels, 1-1/4-inch sling. Introduced 1937; discontinued 1949.

Exc.: $325 **VGood:** $230 **Good:** $150

With U.S. Property markings

Exc.: $395 **VGood:** $300 **Good:** $200

STEVENS NO. 419 JUNIOR TARGET
Bolt action; single shot; 22 LR; 26-inch barrel; takedown; Lyman No. 55 peep rear sight, blade front; uncheckered walnut junior target stock; pistol grip; sling; swivels. Introduced 1932; discontinued 1936.

Exc.: $170 **VGood:** $140 **Good:** $100

STEVENS FAVORITE NO. 17
Lever action; single shot; 22 LR, 25 rimfire, 32 rimfire; 24-inch barrel, other lengths available on special order; takedown; open rear sight, Rocky Mountain front; uncheckered walnut straight-grip stock; tapered forearm. Introduced 1894; discontinued 1935. Collector value.

Exc.: $270 **VGood:** $200 **Good:** $165

STEVENS FAVORITE NO. 18
Lever action; single shot; 22 LR, 25 rimfire, 32 rimfire; 24-inch barrel, other lengths available on special order; takedown; Vernier peep rear sight, Beach combination front, leaf middle sight; uncheckered walnut straight-grip stock, tapered forearm. Introduced 1894; discontinued 1917. Collector value.

Exc.: $290 **VGood:** $230 **Good:** $180

STEVENS FAVORITE NO. 19
Lever action; single shot; 22 LR, 25 rimfire, 32 rimfire; 24-inch barrel, other lengths available on special order; takedown; Lyman combination rear sight, Lyman front, leaf middle sight; uncheckered walnut straight-grip stock, tapered forearm. Introduced 1895; discontinued 1917. Collector value.

Exc.: $290 **VGood:** $230 **Good:** $170

STEVENS FAVORITE NO. 20
Lever action; single shot; 22 rimfire, 32 rimfire only; smoothbore barrel; takedown; open rear sight, Rocky Mountain front; uncheckered walnut straight-grip stock; tapered forearm. Introduced 1895; discontinued 1935. Collector value.

Exc.: $290 **VGood:** $240 **Good:** $170

STEVENS FAVORITE NO. 26 CRACKSHOT
Lever action; single shot; 22 LR, 32 rimfire; 18-inch, 22-inch barrel; takedown; open rear sight, blade front; uncheckered straight-grip walnut stock, tapered forearm. Introduced 1913; discontinued 1939. Collector value.

Exc.: $220 **VGood:** $180 **Good:** $145

STEVENS FAVORITE NO. 26-1/2 CRACKSHOT
Same specs as No. 26 Crackshot except smoothbore barrel for 22, 32 rimfire shot cartridges. Introduced 1914; discontinued 1939. Collector value.

Exc.: $240 **VGood:** $175 **Good:** $135

STEVENS FAVORITE NO. 27
Lever action; single shot; 22 LR, 25 rimfire, 32 rimfire; 24-inch octagon barrel, other lengths available on special order; takedown; open rear sight, Rocky Mountain front; uncheckered walnut straight-grip stock; tapered forearm. Introduced 1912; discontinued 1939. Collector value.

Exc.: $210 **VGood:** $170 **Good:** $140

STEVENS FAVORITE NO. 28
Lever action; single shot; 22 LR, 25 rimfire, 32 rimfire; 24-inch octagon barrel, other lengths available on special order; takedown; Vernier peep sight, Beach combination front, leaf middle sight; uncheckered walnut straight-grip stock, tapered forearm. Introduced 1896; discontinued 1935. Collector value.

Exc.: $280 **VGood:** $190 **Good:** $160

STEVENS FAVORITE NO. 29
Lever action; single shot; 22 LR, 25 rimfire, 32 rimfire; 24-inch octagon barrel, other lengths available on special order; takedown; Lyman combination rear sight, Lyman front, leaf middle sight; uncheckered walnut straight-grip stock, tapered forearm. Introduced 1896; discontinued 1935. Collector value.

Exc.: $290 **VGood:** $190 **Good:** $165

STEVENS FAVORITE MODEL 30
Lever action, single shot; modern recreation of older Stevens Favorite series of rifles, still in production; 22 LR, 22 WMR, 17 HMR; 21-inch half-octagon barrel; weighs 4 ¼ pounds; open sights.

Perf.: $190 **Exc.:** $170 **VGood:** $140

Takedown version

Perf.: $210 **Exc.:** $190 **VGood:** $160

STEVENS IDEAL NO. 44
Lever action; single shot; 22 LR, 25 rimfire, 32 rimfire, 25-20, 32-20, 32-40, 38-40, 38-55, 44-40; 24-inch, 26-inch round, full- or half-octagon barrel; rolling block; takedown; open rear sight, Rocky Mountain front; uncheckered straight-grip walnut stock, forearm. Introduced 1894; discontinued 1932. Primarily of collector interest.

Exc.: $685 **VGood:** $550 **Good:** $465

STEVENS IDEAL NO. 44-1/2
Same specs as Ideal No. 44 except improved falling block, lever action. Introduced 1903; discontinued 1916. Collector interest.

Exc.: $980 **VGood:** $790 **Good:** $585

STEVENS IDEAL NOS. 45 THROUGH 56
Lever actions; rolling and falling block; 22 LR, 25 rimfire, 32 rimfire, 25-20, 32-20, 32-40, 38-40, 38-55, 44-40; 24-inch, 26-inch round, full-, half-octagon barrel; other lengths available on special order; various sights available; various walnut stock options; similar to Ideal No. 44 with numerous updated improvements. Introduced 1896; discontinued 1916. Because of special order features, triggers, barrel makers, stocks and engraving, these models require

separate evaluation. Higher grades and Schuetzens are very collectible and desirable.

STEVENS NO. 70 VISIBLE LOADER

Slide action; 22 Short, 22 Long, 22 LR; 15-shot (22 Short), 13-shot (22 Long), 11-shot (22 LR) tube magazine; 22-inch barrel; open rear sight, bead front; uncheckered straight-grip stock; grooved slide handle. Introduced 1907; discontinued 1934. Collector value.

Exc.: $360   **VGood:** $280   **Good:** $210

STEVENS NO. 414 ARMORY MODEL

Lever action; single shot; 22 Short, 22 LR; 26-inch barrel; rolling block; Lyman receiver peep sight, blade front; checkered straight-grip walnut stock; military-style forearm; sling swivels. Introduced 1912; discontinued 1932.

Exc.: $700   **VGood:** $500   **Good:** $400

STEVENS NO. 417 WALNUT HILL

Lever action; single shot; 22 Short, 22 LR, 22 Hornet; 28-inch heavy, 29-inch extra heavy barrel; Lyman No. 52L extension rear sight, No. 17A front; uncheckered walnut target stock; full pistol grip, beavertail forearm; sling swivels; barrel band; sling. Introduced 1932; discontinued 1947.

Exc.: $1200   **VGood:** $1000   **Good:** $750

STEVENS NO. 417-1 WALNUT HILL

Same specs as No. 417 Walnut Hill except Lyman No. 48L receiver sight. Introduced 1932; discontinued 1947.

Exc.: $1200   **VGood:** $900   **Good:** $700

STEVENS NO. 417-2 WALNUT HILL

Same specs as No. 417 Walnut Hill except Lyman No. 1441 tang sight. Introduced 1932; discontinued 1947.

Exc.: $1200   **VGood:** $900   **Good:** $700

STEVENS NO. 417-3 WALNUT HILL

Same specs as No. 417 Walnut Hill except no sights. Introduced 1932; discontinued 1947.

Exc.: $1150   **VGood:** $800   **Good:** $650

STEVENS NO. 417-1/2 WALNUT HILL

Same specs as No. 417 Walnut Hill except 22 Hornet, 25 rimfire, 22 WRF, 22 LR; 28-inch barrel; Lyman No. 144 tang peep sight, folding middle sight, bead front; uncheckered walnut sporting-style stock; pistol grip; semi-beavertail forearm. Introduced 1932; discontinued 1940.

Exc.: $1200   **VGood:** $1000   **Good:** $800

STEVENS NO. 418 WALNUT HILL

Lever action; single shot; 22 Short, 22 LR; 26-inch barrel; takedown; Lyman No. 144 tang peep sight, blade front; uncheckered walnut stock; pistol grip, semi-beavertail forearm; sling swivels, sling. Introduced 1932; discontinued 1940.

Exc.: $775   **VGood:** $595   **Good:** $300

STEVENS NO. 418-1/2 WALNUT HILL

Same specs as No. 418 Walnut Hill except 22 Short, 22 LR, 22 WRF, 25 Stevens; Lyman No. 2A tang peep sight, bead front. Introduced 1932; discontinued 1940.

Exc.: $795   **VGood:** $595   **Good:** $300

STEVENS SPRINGFIELD MODEL 15

Bolt action; single shot; 22 Short, 22 Long, 22 LR; 22-inch barrel; 37-inch overall length; weighs 4 lbs.; takedown; elevation-adjustable sporting rear sight, gold bead front; uncheckered walnut-finished pistol-grip stock. Introduced 1937; discontinued 1948.

Exc.: $60   **VGood:** $50   **Good:** $40

NOTE: Springfield was used as a brand name from 1935 until 1948, with the designation being dropped at that time. It should not be confused with Springfield Armory, although the name may have been registered with such mistaken identity in mind. After the Springfield brand name was dropped, rifles were known strictly by the Stevens name.

Stevens No. 70
"Visible Loader"

Stevens No. 414
Armory

Stevens No. 417-0
Walnut Hill

Stevens No. 417½
Walnut Hill

Stevens No. 418
Walnut Hill

Stevens No. 418½ Walnut Hill

Stevens Springfield Model 82

Stevens Springfield Model 83

STEVENS SPRINGFIELD MODEL 82

Bolt action; single shot; 22 Short, 22 Long, 22 LR; 22-inch barrel; takedown; open rear sight, bead front; uncheckered walnut pistol-grip stock; grooved forearm. Introduced 1935; discontinued 1939.

Exc.: $65   **VGood:** $50   **Good:** $40

STEVENS SPRINGFIELD MODEL 83

Bolt action; single shot; 25 Stevens, 22 WRF, 22 Short, 22 Long, 22 LR; 24-inch barrel; takedown; open rear sight, bead front; uncheckered walnut pistol-grip stock; grooved forearm. Introduced 1935; discontinued 1939.

Exc.: $70   **VGood:** $55   **Good:** $50

STEVENS SPRINGFIELD MODEL 084

Bolt action; 22 Short, 22 Long, 22 LR; 5-shot detachable clip magazine; 24-inch barrel; 43-1/2-inch overall length; weighs 6 lbs.; takedown; rear peep sight, hooded front; uncheckered walnut pistol-grip stock; black forearm tip; plated bolt, trigger. Introduced 1935; discontinued 1948.

Exc.: $80   **VGood:** $70   **Good:** $50

STEVENS SPRINGFIELD MODEL 84

Same specs Model 084 except open sights. Introduced 1935; discontinued 1948.

Exc.: $70   **VGood:** $65   **Good:** $45

Steyr Classic Mannlicher SBS Rifle

Steyr Model 90 Carbine

Steyr-Mannlicher Model L Luxus

Steyr-Mannlicher Model L Varmint

STEVENS SPRINGFIELD MODEL 085

Semi-automatic; 22 LR; 5-shot detachable box magazine; 24-inch barrel; takedown; peep rear sight, hooded front; uncheckered pistol-grip stock; black forend tip. Introduced 1939; discontinued 1948.

Exc.: $80   **VGood:** $70   **Good:** $50

STEVENS SPRINGFIELD MODEL 85

Same specs as Model 085 except open sights. Introduced 1939; discontinued 1948.

Exc.: $75   **VGood:** $65   **Good:** $45

STEVENS SPRINGFIELD MODEL 086

Bolt action; 22 Short, 22 Long, 22 LR; 21-shot (22 Short), 17-shot (22 Long), 15-shot (22 LR) tube magazine; 24-inch barrel; 41-1/2-inch overall length; weighs 5-1/2 lbs.; chromium-plated bolt, trigger; takedown; peep rear sight, folding sporting middle, hooded front; uncheckered walnut pistol-grip stock; black forearm tip; plated bolt, trigger. Introduced 1935; discontinued 1948.

Exc.: $85   **VGood:** $70   **Good:** $50

STEVENS SPRINGFIELD MODEL 86

Same specs as Model 086 except open sights. Introduced 1935; discontinued 1948.

Exc.: $80   **VGood:** $65   **Good:** $45

STEVENS SPRINGFIELD MODEL 087

Semi-automatic; 22 LR; 24-inch barrel; takedown; peep rear sight, hooded front; uncheckered pistol-grip stock; black forearm tip. Introduced 1938; discontinued 1948.

Exc.: $90   **VGood:** $70   **Good:** $50

STEVENS SPRINGFIELD MODEL 87

Same specs as Model 087 except open rear sight, bead front. Introduced 1938; discontinued 1948.

Exc.: $85   **VGood:** $65   **Good:** $50

NOTE: In 2005 Savage reintroduced the Stevens brand to designate a new series of entry-level rimfire and centerfire rifles.

STEVENS MODEL 200

Long- or short-action bolt rifle chambered in .223, .22-250, .243, 7MM-08, .308, .25-06, .270, .30-06, 7mm RM, or .300 WM. Gray checkered synthetic stock and 22-inch (short-action) or 24-inch (long-action) blued sightless barrel.

NIB: $300   **Exc.:** $265   **VGood:** $195

STEVENS CADET MINI-YOUTH

Single-shot bolt-action .22 with hardwood stock. Similar to Savage Cub .22 rimfire. Introduced 2006.

NIB: $150   **Exc.:** $120   **VGood:** $75

STEVENS MODEL 315 YOUTH

Similar to Cadet Mini-Youth but with sightless barrel.

NIB: $155   **Exc.:** $130   **VGood:** $95

STEVENS MODEL 310

Five-shot bolt-action repeater chambered for .17 HMR. Detachable box magazine, synthetic stock, blued 20.75-inch sightless barrel.

NIB: $199   **Exc.:** $165   **VGood:** $100

STEVENS MODEL 310 HEAVY BARREL

Similar to Stevens Model 310 but with 21-inch bull barrel.

NIB: $225   **Exc.:** $200   **VGood:** $155

STEVENS MODEL 300

Clip-fed bolt-action repeater chambered for .22 rimfire. Gray synthetic stock and 20.75-inch blued barrel. Also available with scope package (add 10 percent).

NIB: $155   **Exc.:** $125   **VGood:** $85

STEVENS MODEL 305

Similar to Stevens Model 310 but chambered in .22 WMR.

NIB: $189   **Exc.:** $165   **VGood:** $115

STEYR A.U.G.-SA

Semi-automatic; 223 Rem.; 30- or 42-shot magazine; 20-inch barrel; 31-inch overall length; weighs 8-1/2 lbs.; synthetic green stock; one-piece molding houses receiver group, hammer mechanism and magazine; integral 1.5x scope; scope and mount form the carrying handle; gas-operated action; conversion to suit right- or left-handed shooters, including ejection port; folding vertical front grip. Imported from Austria by Gun South, Inc. Introduced 1983; no longer imported. Values were greatly affected by 1994 import ban, can still fluctuate widely.

Perf.: $3500   **Exc.:** $2700   **VGood:** $2400

STEYR CLASSIC MANNLICHER SBS RIFLE

Bolt action; 243, 25-06, 308, 6.5x55, 6.5x57, 270, 7x64 Brenneke, 7mm-08, 7.5x55, 30-06, 9.3x62, 6.5x68, 7mm Rem. Mag., 300 Win. Mag., 8x685, 4-shot magazine. Barrel: 23.6-inch standard; 26-inch magnum; 20-inch full stock standard calibers. Weighs 7 lbs.; 40.1-inch overall length. Stock: Hand-checkered fancy European oiled walnut with standard forend. Sights: Ramp front adjustable for elevation, V-notch rear adjustable for windage. Single adjustable trigger; 3-position roller safety with "safe-bolt" setting; drilled and tapped for Steyr factory scope mounts. Introduced 1997. Imported from Austria by GSI, Inc.

Perf.: $1200   **Exc.:** $1000   **VGood:** $800

STEYR MODEL 90 CARBINE

Bolt action; 22 LR; 5-shot detachable box magazine; 19-inch barrel; leaf rear sight, hooded bead front; hand-checkered European walnut Mannlicher-type stock; sling swivels. Manufactured in Austria. Introduced 1953; discontinued 1967.

Perf.: $1195   **Exc.:** $995   **VGood:** $725

STEYR MODEL 95

Bolt action; 8x50R Mannlicher; 30-inch barrel; straight pull; adjustable leaf rear sight, hooded bead front; military walnut Mannlicher-style stock; sling swivels. No longer produced.

Perf.: $165   **Exc.:** $115   **VGood:** $85

STEYR-MANNLICHER JAGD MATCH

Bolt action; 222 Rem., 243 Win., 308 Win.; 23-1/2-inch heavy rear; Mannlicher sights; checkered laminate half-stock. Still in production.

Perf.: $1595   **Exc.:** $1295   **VGood:** $895

STEYR-MANNLICHER MATCH SPG-UIT

Bolt action; 308 Win.; 25-1/2-inch barrel; 44-inch overall length; weighs 10 lbs.; Steyr globe front sight, Steyr peep rear; laminated and ventilated stock of special UIT Match design; double-pull trigger adjustable for let-off point, slack, weight of first-stage pull, release force and length; buttplate adjustable for height and length. Meets UIT specifications. Imported from Austria by GSI, Inc. Introduced 1992.

Perf.: $3495   **Exc.:** $2995   **VGood:** $2395

STEYR-MANNLICHER MODEL L

Bolt action; 22-250, 5.6x57mm, 243 Win., 6mm Rem., 308 Win.; 5-shot detachable rotary magazine; 23-5/8-inch barrel; 42-1/2-inch overall length; open rear sight, hooded ramp front; European walnut half-stock; Monte Carlo comb, cheekpiece; skip-checkered pistol grip, forearm; double-set triggers; detachable sling-swivels; buttpad. Introduced 1968.

Perf.: $1750   **Exc.:** $1380   **VGood:** $850

STEYR-MANNLICHER MODEL L CARBINE

Same specs as Model L except 20-inch barrel; 39-inch overall length; full-length checkered European walnut stock. Introduced 1968.

Perf.: $1790   **Exc.:** $1410   **VGood:** $900

STEYR-MANNLICHER MODEL L LUXUS

Same specs as Model L except only 5.6x57, 6mm Rem., 22-250, 243, 308; 3-shot detachable steel magazine; single set trigger; rear tang slide safety; European walnut full- or half-stock.

Perf.: $2100   **Exc.:** $1495   **VGood:** $1190

With full stock

Perf.: $2400   **Exc.:** $1595   **VGood:** $1290

STEYR-MANNLICHER MODEL L LUXUS CARBINE

Same specs as Model L except 5.6x57, 6mm Rem., 22-250, 243, 308; 3-shot magazine; 20-inch barrel; European walnut full-stock.

Perf.: $2450   **Exc.:** $1595   **VGood:** $1295

STEYR-MANNLICHER MODEL L VARMINT

Same specs as Model L except 22-250, 243 Win.; 26-inch heavy barrel; no sights; ventilated square forearm. Introduced 1969.

Perf.: $1775   **Exc.:** $1100   **VGood:** $890

STEYR-MANNLICHER MODEL M

Bolt action; 6.5x57mm, 7x57mm, 7x64mm, 25-06, 270 Win., 30-06, 8x57JS, 9.3x62; 5-shot detachable rotary magazine; 23-1/2-inch barrel; open rear sight, hooded ramp front; European walnut full- or half-stock; forend tip, recoil pad; detachable sling swivels. Also left-hand model, with 6.5x55, 7.5mm Swiss as additional calibers. Standard version introduced, 1969; left-hand version, 1977.

Perf.: $1900   **Exc.:** $1295   **VGood:** $895

Left-hand model
Perf.: $2100   **Exc.:** $1495   **VGood:** $995

STEYR-MANNLICHER MODEL M CARBINE

Same specs as Model M except 20-inch barrel; full-length stock. Introduced 1977.

Perf.: $1950   **Exc.:** $1350   **VGood:** $995

Left-hand model
Perf.: $2200   **Exc.:** $1550   **VGood:** $1050

STEYR-MANNLICHER MODEL M LUXUS

Same specs as Model M except 6.5x57, 270, 7x64, 30-06, 9.3x62, 7.5 Swiss; 3-shot detachable, in-line steel magazine; single set trigger; rear tang slide safety; full or half-stock. Imported from Austria by GSI, Inc.

Perf.: $2000   **Exc.:** $1295   **VGood:** $895

With full stock
Perf.: $2300   **Exc.:** $1595   **VGood:** $1095

STEYR-MANNLICHER MODEL M LUXUS CARBINE

Same specs as Model M except only 6.5x55, 6.5x57, 7x64, 7.5 Swiss, 270, 30-06; 3-shot magazine; 20-inch barrel; European walnut full-stock.

Perf.: $2300   **Exc.:** $1595   **VGood:** $1095

STEYR-MANNLICHER MODEL M PROFESSIONAL

Same specs as Model M except 270, 7x57, 7x64, 30-06, 9.3x62; 20-inch , 23-2/3-inch barrel; Cycolac synthetic stock; Parkerized finish. Introduced 1977; discontinued 1993.

Perf.: $1475   **Exc.:** $995   **VGood:** $795

STEYR-MANNLICHER MODEL MIII PROFESSIONAL

Same specs as the Model M except 6.5x57, 270, 30-06, 7x64, 9.3x62; 23-1/2-inch barrel; weighs about 7-1/2 lbs.; no sights; black ABS Cycolac or stippled, checkered European wood half-stock; single or optional double-set trigger. Imported from Austria by GSI, Inc. Reintroduced 1994.

Perf.: $895   **Exc.:** $695   **VGood:** $595

STEYR-MANNLICHER MODEL M72 L/M

Bolt action; 22-250, 5.6x57mm, 6mm Rem., 243 Win., 6.5x57mm, 270 Win., 7x57mm, 7x64mm, 308 Win., 30-06; 23-2/3-inch barrel; 5-shot rotary magazine; open rear sight, hooded ramp front; European walnut half-stock; hand-checkered pistol-grip forearm, rosewood forend tip; recoil pad; interchangeable single- or double-set trigger; detachable sling swivels; front locking bolt. Introduced 1972; no longer in production.

Exc.: $995   **VGood:** $795   **Good:** $595

STEYR-MANNLICHER MODEL M72 MODEL L/M CARBINE

Same specs as Model M72 L/M except 20-inch barrel; full-length stock. Introduced 1972; no longer in production.

Exc.: $1100   **VGood:** $850   **Good:** $650

STEYR-MANNLICHER MODEL S

Bolt action; 6.5x68mm, 257 Weatherby Mag., 264 Win. Mag., 7mm Rem. Mag., 300 Win. Mag., 300 H&H Mag., 308 Norma Mag., 8x68S, 338 Win. Mag., 9.3x64mm, 375 H&H Mag., 458 Win. Mag.; 5-shot detachable rotary magazine; 26-inch barrel; open

Steyr-Mannlicher Model M

Steyr-Mannlicher Model M Luxus

Steyr-Mannlicher Model MIII Professional

Steyr-Mannlicher Model S

Steyr SBS Forester Rifle

Steyr SBS Prohunter Rifle with camo stock

Steyr Scout Bolt-Action Rifle

rear sight, hooded ramp front; European walnut half-stock; Monte Carlo comb, cheekpiece; skip-checkered pistol grip, forearm; forend tip; recoil pad. Introduced 1969.

Perf.: $1725   **Exc.:** $1195   **VGood:** $950

STEYR SBS FORESTER RIFLE

Caliber: 243, 25-06, 270, 7mm-08, 308 Win., 30-06, 7mm Rem. Mag., 300 Win. Mag. Detachable 4-shot magazine. 23.6-inch barrel, standard calibers; 25.6-inch, magnum calibers; weighs 7-1/2 lbs.; 44-1/2-inch overall length (23.6-inch barrel); oil-finished American walnut stock with Monte Carlo cheekpiece. Pachmayr 1-inch swivels; no sights; drilled and tapped for Browning A-Bolt mounts; Steyr Safe Bolt system, three-position ambidextrous roller tang safety, for Safe, Loading, Fire. Matte finish on barrel and receiver; adjustable trigger. Rotary cold-hammer forged barrel. Introduced 1997. Imported by GSI, Inc.

Standard calibers
Perf.: $650   **Exc.:** $600   **VGood:** $500

Magnum calibers
Perf.: $700   **Exc.:** $650   **VGood:** $550

STEYR SBS PROHUNTER RIFLE

Similar to the SBS Forester except has ABS synthetic stock with adjustable butt spacers, straight comb without cheekpiece, palm swell, Pachmayr 1-inch

swivels. Special 10-round magazine conversion kit available. Introduced 1997. Imported by GSI.

Standard calibers
Perf.: $650   **Exc.:** $580   **VGood:** $475

Magnum calibers
Perf.: $700   **Exc.:** $625   **VGood:** $500

STEYR SCOUT BOLT-ACTION RIFLE

Bolt action; 308 Win., 376 Steyr; 5-shot magazine. 19-inch barrel, fluted; Gray Zytel stock; Pop-up front & rear sights; Leupold M8 2.5x28 IER scope on Picatinny optic rail with Steyr mounts. offered with luggage case, scout sling, two stock spacers, two magazines. Introduced 1998. Imported by GSI. Add 10 percent for Jeff Cooper memorial version.

Perf.: $1750   **Exc.:** $1500   **VGood:** $1200

STEYR-MANNLICHER MODEL SL

Bolt action; 5.6x50, 22-250, 222 Rem., 222 Rem. Mag., 223 Rem.; 5-shot detachable rotary Makrolon magazine; 23-5/8-inch barrel; 42-1/2-inch overall length; open rear sight, hooded ramp front with .080 gold bead; European walnut half-stock; Monte Carlo comb, cheekpiece; skip-checkered pistol-grip, forearm; interchangeable single- or double-

Steyr-Mannlicher Model SL

Steyr-Mannlicher Model SSG Match

Steyr-Mannlicher SSG Match UIT

Steyr-Mannlicher SSG P-IV

Stoner SR-15 M-5

Stoner SR-15 Match

STEYR-MANNLICHER MODEL SSG MATCH

Same specs as Model SSG except 26-inch heavy barrel; weighs 11 lbs.; Walther target peep sights; brown synthetic or walnut stock; adjustable rail in forend; match bolt. Introduced 1981; discontinued 1991.

Synthetic stock

Perf.: $2500   **Exc.:** $2000   **VGood:** $1400

Walnut stock

Perf.: $2600   **Exc.:** $2100   **VGood:** $1500

STEYR-MANNLICHER MODEL SSG MATCH UIT

Same specs as Model SSG except 243, 308; weighs 11 lbs.; 10-shot magazine; Walther rear peep sight, globe front; UIT Match walnut stock; stippled grip, forend; adjustable double-pull trigger; adjustable buttplate. Introduced 1984; still in production.

Perf.: $3375   **Exc.:** $3000   **VGood:** $2000

STEYR-MANNLICHER SSG P-II

Same specs as Model SSG except 243, 308; large modified bolt handle; no sights; forend rail. Still in production.

Perf.: $1650   **Exc.:** $1350   **VGood:** $995

STEYR-MANNLICHER SSG P-IIK

Same specs as Model SSG P-II except 20-inch heavy barrel.

Perf.: $1650   **Exc.:** $1350   **VGood:** $995

STEYR-MANNLICHER SSG P-III

Same specs as Model SSG except 26-inch heavy barrel; diopter match sight bases; H-S Precision Pro-Series stock (black only). Imported from Austria by GSI, Inc. Introduced 1992; discontinued 1993.

Perf.: $2025   **Exc.:** $1695   **VGood:** $995

STEYR-MANNLICHER SSG P-IV

Same specs as Model SSG except 16-3/4-inch heavy barrel with flash hider; ABS Cycolac synthetic stock in green or black. Imported from Austria by GSI, Inc. Introduced 1992.

Perf.: $2300   **Exc.:** $1800   **VGood:** $1200

STEYR-MANNLICHER MODEL S/T

Bolt action; 9.3x64, 375 H&H Mag., 458 Win. Mag.; 5-shot detachable rotary magazine; 26-inch heavy barrel; open rear sight, hooded ramp front; European walnut half-stock; Monte Carlo comb, cheekpiece; skip-checkered pistol grip, forearm; forend tip; recoil pad. Introduced 1975.

Perf.: $2050   **Exc.:** $1695   **VGood:** $1200

STEYR-MANNLICHER MODEL S LUXUS

Same specs as the Model S/T except 6.5x68, 7mm Rem. Mag., 300 Win. Mag., 8x68S; 3-shot detachable steel, in-line magazine; single set trigger; rear tang slide safety; half-stock only. Imported from Austria by GSI, Inc.

Perf.: $2300   **Exc.:** $1900   **VGood:** $995

STONER SR-15 M-5 RIFLE

Semi-automatic; 223; 20-inch barrel; weighs 7.6 lbs.; 38-inch overall length; Black synthetic stock; Post front sight, fully adjustable rear (300-meter sight); Modular weapon system; two-stage trigger. Black finish. Introduced 1998. Made in U.S.A. by Knight's Mfg. Add 100 percent for "1 of 100" edition.

Perf.: $2200   **Exc.:** $1900   **VGood:** $1500

STONER SR-15 MATCH RIFLE

Semi-automatic; 223; 20-inch barrel; weighs 7.9 lbs.; 38-inch overall length; Black synthetic stock; no sights furnished; flat-top upper receiver for scope mounting; Short Picatinny rail, two-stage match trigger. Introduced 1998. Made in U.S.A. by Knight's Mfg.Co.

Perf.: $2300   **Exc.:** $2000   **VGood:** $1600

set triggers; detachable sling swivels; buttpad. Introduced 1968.

Perf.: $1700   **Exc.:** $1495   **VGood:** $895

STEYR-MANNLICHER MODEL SL CARBINE

Same specs as Model SL except 20-inch barrel; 39-inch overall length; full-length stock. Introduced 1968.

Perf.: $1800   **Exc.:** $1595   **VGood:** $995

STEYR-MANNLICHER MODEL SL VARMINT

Same specs as Model SL except only 22-250, 222 Rem., 222 Rem. Mag., 223; 26-inch barrel; no sights; vent. square forearm. Introduced 1969.

Perf.: $1900   **Exc.:** $1695   **VGood:** $1100

STEYR-MANNLICHER MODEL SSG

Bolt action; 308 Win.; 5- or 10-shot magazine; 25-1/2-inch heavy barrel; 44-1/2-inch overall length; weighs 8-3/8 lbs.; micrometer peep rear sight, globe front; European walnut or synthetic target stock; full pistol grip; wide forearm; swivel rail; adjustable buttplate; single trigger; single shot plug; also made with high-impact ABS Cycolac plastic stock. Introduced 1969.

Perf.: $1550   **Exc.:** $1200   **VGood:** $1000

With plastic stock

Perf.: $1500   **Exc.:** $1150   **VGood:** $950

STONER SR-25 MATCH

Semi-automatic; 7.62 NATO; (308); 10-shot steel magazine, 5-shot optional; 24-inch heavy match barrel with 1:11.25-inch twist; 44-inch overall length; weighs 10-3/4 lbs.; no sights; black synthetic stock of AR-15A2 design; full floating forend of Mil-spec synthetic attaches to upper receiver at a single point; integral Weaver-style rail; rings and iron sights optional; improved AR-15 trigger; AR-15-style seven-lug rotating bolt; gas block rail mounts detachable front sight. Made in U.S. by Knight's Mfg. Co. Introduced 1993.

Perf.: $3100 **Exc.:** $2200 **VGood:** $1500

STONER SR-25 MATCH LIGHTWEIGHT

Same specs as SR-25 Match except 20-inch medium match target contour barrel; 40-inch overall length; weighs 9-1/2 lbs.

Perf.: $2995 **Exc.:** $2100 **VGood:** $1500

STONER SR-25 SPORTER

Same specs as SR-25 Match except 20-inch barrel; 40-inch overall length; weighs 83/4 lbs.; AR-15A2-style elevation-adjustable front sight, detachable windage-adjustable rear; upper and lower receivers made of lightweight aircraft aluminum alloy; quick-detachable carrying handle/rear sight assembly; two-stage target trigger, shell deflector, bore guide, scope rings optional. Made in U.S. by Knight's Mfg. Co. Introduced 1993.

Perf.: $2695 **Exc.:** $1995 **VGood:** $1200

STONER SR-25 CARBINE

Same as the SR-25 Sporter except 16-inch light/hunting contour barrel; 36-inch overall length; weighs 7-3/4 lbs.; no sights; integral Weaver-style rail; scope rings; iron sights optional. Made in U.S. by Knight's Mfg. Co. Introduced 1995.

Perf.: $2995 **Exc.:** $2100 **VGood:** $1400

STURM RUGER DEERFIELD 99/44 CARBINE

Semi-automatic; 44 Mag., 4-shot rotary magazine; 18-1/2-inch barrel; weighs 6-1/4 lbs.; 36-7/8-inch overall length; Hardwood stock; Gold bead front, folding adjustable aperture rear sights; Semi-automatic action; dual front-locking lugs lock directly into receiver; integral scope mount; push-button safety; marketed with 1-inch rings and gun lock. Introduced 2000. Made in U.S.A. by Sturm, Ruger & Co.

Perf.: $475 **Exc.:** $450 **VGood:** $375

STURM RUGER MINI-14

Semi-automatic; 223 Rem., 222 Rem.; 5-shot detachable box magazine; 18-1/2-inch barrel; weighs 6-1/2 lbs.; gas-operated, fixed-piston carbine; unchecked, reinforced American hardwood carbine-type stock (early versions with walnut); positive primary extraction; fully-adjustable rear sight, gold bead front. Introduced 1973.

Perf.: $450 **Exc.:** $370 **VGood:** $330

STURM RUGER MINI-14 RANCH RIFLE

Same specs as Mini-14 except 222 (1984 only), 223; steel-reinforced hardwood stock; ramp-type front sight; marketed with Sturm Ruger S100R scope rings; 20-shot magazine available; blued or stainless steel.

Perf.: $460 **Exc.:** $390 **VGood:** $340

STURM RUGER MINI-14 STAINLESS

Same specs as Mini-14 except barrel, action built of stainless steel. Introduced 1978.

Perf.: $480 **Exc.:** $400 **VGood:** $355

STURM RUGER MINI-14 WITH FOLDING STOCK

Same specs as Mini-14 Ranch Rifle except metal folding stock; checkered plastic vertical pistol grip; 47-3/4-inch overall length with stock extended, 27-1/2-inch with stock closed; weighs 7-3/4 lbs.; blued or stainless steel; no longer in production.

Perf.: $550 **Exc.:** $480 **VGood:** $435

Stoner SR-25 Match

Stoner SR-25 Match Lightweight

Stoner SR-25 Sporter

Stoner SR-25 Carbine

Sturm Ruger Deerfield 99/44 Carbine

Sturm Ruger Mini-14

Sturm Ruger Mini-14 Ranch

Sturm Ruger Mini-14 Folding Stock

Sturm Ruger Mini-14/5

Sturm Ruger NRA Mini-14

Sturm Ruger Model 10/22
Carbine Stainless Steel

Sturm Ruger Model 10/22
Deluxe Sporter

Sturm Ruger Model 10/22
International

Sturm Ruger 10-22

Sturm Ruger 10-22
All-Weather

Sturm Ruger 10-22
CRR Compact

Sturm Ruger K10/22T
10/22 Target

STURM RUGER MODEL 10/22 CARBINE

Semi-automatic; 22 LR; 10-shot detachable rotary magazine; 18-1/2-inch barrel; uncheckered walnut carbine stock on early versions; as of 1980, standard models with birch stocks; barrel band; receiver tapped for scope blocks or tip-off mount; adjustable folding leaf rear sight, gold bead front; blue or stainless finish. Introduced 1964; still in production.

Perf.: $150	Exc.: $120	VGood: $100
Uncheckered walnut stock		
Perf.: $185	Exc.: $145	VGood: $130
Stainless steel finish		
Perf.: $220	Exc.: $185	VGood: $150

STURM RUGER MODEL 10/22 DELUXE SPORTER

Same specs as Model 10/22 except checkered walnut stock; flat buttplate; sling swivels; no barrel band. Introduced 1971, still in production.

| Perf.: $215 | Exc.: $185 | VGood: $140 |

STURM RUGER MODEL 10/22 INTERNATIONAL

Same specs as Model 10/22 except full-length Mannlicher-type walnut stock (early manufacture); birch full-length Mannlicher stock (1994); sling swivels. Introduced 1964; discontinued 1971. Reintroduced 1994. Premium for early production.

Perf.: $220	Exc.: $170	VGood: $140
Checkered stock		
Perf.: $300	Exc.: $250	VGood: $200

STURM RUGER 10/22 RIFLE

Same specs as 10/22 Carbine except 20-inch barrel, rifle stock with flat butt, no barrel band.

| Perf.: $240 | Exc.: $ 180 | VGood: $120 |

STURM RUGER MODEL 10/22 SPORTER

Same specs as Model 10/22 except Monte Carlo stock with grooved forearm; grip cap; sling swivels. Dropped in 1971, but reintroduced in 1973, with hand-checkered walnut pistol-grip stock. Dropped 1975. Reintroduced, still in production. Premium for early model.

| Exc.: $300 | VGood: $270 | Good: $190 |

STURM RUGER 10/22T TARGET RIFLE

Similar to the 10/22 except has 20-inch heavy, hammer-forged barrel with tight chamber dimensions, improved trigger pull, laminated hardwood stock dimensioned for optical sights; no iron sights supplied; weighs 7-1/4 lbs. Introduced 1996; still offered.

| Perf.: $420 | Exc.: $350 | VGood: $280 |

STURM RUGER 10/22 ALL-WEATHER RIFLE

Similar to the stainless 10/22 except has black composite stock of thermoplastic polyester resin reinforced with fiberglass; checkered grip and forend. Brushed satin, natural metal finish with clear hardcoat finish. Weighs 5 lbs., measures 36-3/4-inch overall. Introduced 1997, still in production.

| Perf.: $230 | Exc.: $200 | VGood: $150 |

STURM RUGER 10/22 CRR COMPACT RIFLE

Similar to 10/22 standard rifle but with 16.25-inch blued barrel, shorter hardwood stock, fiber optic sights and 34.5-inch overall length.

| NIB: $250 | Exc.: $205 | VGood: $175 |

STURM RUGER K10/22T RUGER 10/22 TARGET STAINLESS

Similar to 10/22 Target but with stainless steel barrel and laminated stock.

| NIB: $375 | Exc.: $335 | VGood: $295 |

STURM RUGER 10/22-T

Similar to 100/22 Target Stainless but with blued steel barrel and blued receiver.

| NIB: $295 | Exc.: $245 | VGood: $180 |

STURM RUGER MINI 14/5

Same as Mini 14 but with five-round magazine; hardwood stock, 18-1/2-inch barrel, blued or stainless metal.

| Perf.: $480 | Exc.: $420 | VGood: $375 |

STURM RUGER MINI-14 TARGET RIFLE

Accurized version of the Mini-14 but with matte stainless barrel and receiver, black laminated thumbhole stock, adjustable harmonic dampener. No sights.

| NIB: $825 | Exc.: $765 | VGood: $595 |

STURM RUGER NRA MINI-14

Ruger NRA Mini-14 Rifle with two 20-round magazines, gold-tone medallion in grip cap, and special serial number sequence (NRA8XXXXX).

Produced in 2008 only. Also available with 5-round magazines.

| Perf.: $900 | Exc.: $695 | VGood: $450 |

STURM RUGER MINI THIRTY RIFLE

Semi-automatic; 7.62x39mm Russian or 6.8 Remington; 5-shot detachable staggered box magazine; 18-1/2-inch barrel; weighs 7-1/4 lbs.; six-groove barrel; Sturm Ruger integral scope mount bases; folding peep sight; blued or stainless finish. Introduced 1987; still in production.

Perf.: $560	Exc.: $490	VGood: $390
Stainless finish		
Perf.: $580	Exc.: $4750	VGood: $340

STURM RUGER 10/22 MAGNUM AUTOLOADING CARBINE

Semi-automatic; 22 WMR, 9-shot rotary magazine; 18-1/2-inch barrel; weighs 6 lbs.; 37-1/4-inch overall length; Birch stock; Gold bead front, folding rear sights. All-steel receiver has integral Ruger scope bases for the included 1-inch rings. Introduced 1999. Discontinued.

Perf.: $700   **Exc.:** $595   **VGood:** $400

STURM RUGER MODEL 44 CARBINE

Semi-automatic; 44 Mag.; 4-shot tubular magazine; 18-1/2-inch barrel; magazine release button incorporated in 1967; uncheckered walnut pistol-grip carbine stock; barrel band; receiver tapped for scope mount; folding leaf rear sight, gold bead front. Introduced 1961; dropped 1985. Premium for 1961-1962 specimens marked "Deerstalker."

Exc.: $495   **VGood:** $380   **Good:** $300

STURM RUGER MODEL 44 INTERNATIONAL

Same specs as Model 44 except full-length Mannlicher-type walnut stock; sling swivels. Dropped 1971.

Exc.: $795   **VGood:** $625   **Good:** $395

STURM RUGER MODEL 44RS

Same specs as Model 44 except sling swivels; built-in peep sight.

Exc.: $480   **VGood:** $390   **Good:** $330

STURM RUGER MODEL 44 SPORTER

Same specs as Model 44 except sling swivels; Monte Carlo sporter stock; grooved forearm; grip cap; flat buttplate. Dropped 1971.

Exc.: $545   **VGood:** $450   **Good:** $380

STURM RUGER MODEL 77R

Bolt-action; 22-250, 220 Swift, 243 Win., 7mm-08, 6.5 Rem. Mag., 280 Rem., 284 Win., 308 Win., 300 Win. Mag., 338 Win. Mag., 350 Rem. Mag., 25-06, 257 Roberts, 250-3000, 6mm Rem., 270 Win., 7x57mm, 7mm Rem. Mag., 30-06; 3-, 5-shot magazine, depending upon caliber; 22-inch tapered barrel; hinged floorplate; adjustable trigger; hand-checkered American walnut stock; pistol-grip cap; sling swivel studs; recoil pad; integral scope mount base; optional folding leaf adjustable rear sight, gold bead ramp front. Introduced in 1968; no longer in production. Replaced by the Model M77 Mark II.

Perf.: $420   **Exc.:** $350   **VGood:** $320

350 Rem. Mag. caliber

Perf.: $470   **Exc.:** $390   **VGood:** $360

STURM RUGER MODEL 77RL ULTRA LIGHT

Same specs as Model 77R except 243, 308, 270, 30-06, 257, 22-250, 250-3000; 20-inch light barrel; Sturm Ruger 1-inch scope rings. Introduced 1983.

Perf.: $420   **Exc.:** $350   **VGood:** $300

STURM RUGER MODEL 77RS

Same specs as Model 77R except magnum-size action; 257 Roberts, 25-06, 270 Win., 7mm Rem. Mag., 300 Win. Mag., 338 Win. Mag.; 3-, 5-shot, depending upon caliber; 22-inch barrel (270, 30-06, 7x57, 280 Rem.); 24-inch barrel (all others).

Perf.: $510   **Exc.:** $450   **VGood:** $400

STURM RUGER MODEL 77RS TROPICAL

Same specs as Model 77RS except 458 Win. Mag.; 24-inch barrel; steel triggerguard, floorplate; weighs 8-3/4 lbs.; open sights; 1-inch scope rings. Introduced 1990; dropped 1991.

Perf.: $550   **Exc.:** $480   **VGood:** $400

STURM RUGER MODEL 77 ROUND TOP MAGNUM

Same specs as Model 77R except round top action; drilled, tapped for standard scope mounts, open sights; 25-06, 270 Win., 7mm Rem. Mag., 30-06, 300

Sturm Ruger 10/22-T

Sturm Ruger 10/22 Magnum Autoloading Carbine

Sturm Ruger Model 44

Sturm Ruger Model 77R

Sturm Ruger Model 77RL Ultra Light

Sturm Ruger Model 77RS Tropical

Sturm Ruger Model 77 Round Top Magnum

Sturm Ruger Model 77V Varmint

Sturm Ruger Model 77R Mark II

Win. Mag., 338 Win. Mag. Introduced 1971; dropped 1985.

Perf.: $390   **Exc.:** $350   **VGood:** $300

STURM RUGER MODEL 77V VARMINT

Same specs as Model 77R except 22-250, 220 Swift, 243 Win., 25-06, 308; 24-inch heavy straight tapered barrel, 26-inch (220 Swift); drilled, tapped for target scope mounts or integral scope mount bases on receiver; checkered American walnut stock. Introduced 1970; dropped 1992. Replaced by Model 77V Mark II in 1992.

Perf.: $430   **Exc.:** $380   **VGood:** $340

STURM RUGER MODEL 77 RSI INTERNATIONAL

Same specs as Model 77R except 18-1/2-inch barrel; full-length Mannlicher-style stock; steel forend cap; loop-type sling swivels; open sights; Sturm Ruger steel scope rings; improved front sight; 22-250, 250-3000, 243, 308, 270, 30-06; weighs 7 lbs; 38-3/8-inch overall length. Introduced 1986.

Perf.: $495   **Exc.:** $410   **VGood:** $350

STURM RUGER MODEL 77 RLS ULTRA LIGHT CARBINE

Same specs as Model 77R except 18-1/2-inch barrel; Sturm Ruger scope mounting system; iron sights; hinged floorplate; 270, 30-06, 243, 308; 38-7/8-inch overall length; weighs 6 lbs. Introduced 1987; no longer in production.

Perf.: $430   **Exc.:** $370   **VGood:** $310

STURM RUGER MODEL 77R MARK II

Bolt-action; 223, 22-250, 243 Win., 25-06, 257 Roberts, 270 Roberts, 270 Win., 280 Rem., 6mm Rem., 6.5x55, 7x57, 30-06, 308 Win. Mag., 7mm Rem. Mag., 300 Win. Mag., 338 Win. Mag.; 4-shot magazine; 20-inch barrel; 39-1/2-inch overall length; weighs 6-1/2 lbs.; American walnut stock; no sights; Ruger integral scope mount base; marketed with 1-inch scope rings; new three-position wing safety; redesigned trigger; short action. Introduced 1989; still in production.

Perf.: $590   **Exc.:** $450   **VGood:** $340

Sturm Ruger Model 77R
Mark II Express

Sturm Ruger Model 77R Mark II
Magnum

Sturm Ruger HK77RFP
Hawkeye

Sturm Ruger Hawkeye African

Sturm Ruger Model 77/22

Sturm Ruger Model 77/22RMP
Stainless

Sturm Ruger Model 77/22RSH Hornet

STURM RUGER MODEL 77R MARK II EXPRESS

Same specs as Model 77R Mark II except 270, 30-06, 7mm Rem. Mag., 300 Win. Mag., 338 Win. Mag., 375 H&H, 416 Rigby, 458 Lott; 4-shot magazine (3-shot for magnums); 22-inch barrel with integral sight rib; checkered French walnut stock; live-rubber recoil pad; steel grip cap; rear swivel stud, barrel-mounted front swivel stud; blade front sight, adjustable V-notch folding-leaf express rear sight with one standing leaf, one folding; three-position safety; Mauser-type extractor; controlled feeding. Introduced 1991.

Perf.: $1250   **Exc.:** $900   **VGood:** $650

STURM RUGER MODEL 77R MARK II MAGNUM

Same specs as Model 77R Mark II except 7/16-inch longer receiver with increased locking area and lengthened front; 375 H&H, 404 Jeffery, 416 Rigby, 458 Lott; 4-shot magazine (375, 404, 458), 3-shot (416) magazine; 22-inch barrel with integral sight rib; ramp front, three-leaf express sight; high-grade Circassian walnut stock with checkered grip and forend; black live-rubber recoil pad; steel floorplate and triggerguard. Introduced 1989, still in production.

Perf.: $1495   **Exc.:** $1100   **VGood:** $795

STURM RUGER MODEL 77 MARK II ALL-WEATHER STAINLESS

Same specs as Model 77R Mark II except all metal parts of stainless steel; fiberglass-reinforced Zytel stock; 223, 243, 270, 308, 30-06, 7mm Rem. Mag, 300 Win Mag, 338 Win Mag; fixed blade-type ejector; new triggerguard; patented floorplate latch; three-position safety; integral scope base, 1-inch Sturm

Ruger scope rings; built-in swivel loops. Introduced 1990, still in production.

Perf.: $595   **Exc.:** $480   **VGood:** $400

STURM RUGER M77VT MARK II TARGET RIFLE

Bolt action; 22-250, 220 Swift, 223, 243, 25-06, 308; 26-inch heavy stainless steel barrel with target gray finish; weighs 9-3/4 lbs.; Approx. 44-inch overall length; Laminated American hardwood stock with beavertail forend, steel swivel studs; no checkering or gripcap; Integral scope mount bases in receiver. Ruger diagonal bedding system. Ruger steel 1-inch scope rings supplied. Fully adjustable trigger. Steel floorplate and trigger guard. New version introduced 1992.

Perf.: $650   **Exc.:** $500   **VGood:** $370

STURM RUGER M77 MKII FRONTIER RIFLE

Bolt-action rifle based on M77 MkII chassis but configured for scout-style scope mount system. Chambered in .243, .308, 7mm-08, .300 WSM, .325 WSM. Gray laminated stock, 16.5-inch blued or stainless barrel (add 15 percent for stainless). Introduced 2005; stainless model introduced 2006 (add 10 percent).

NIB: $585   **Exc.:** $510   **VGood:** $25

STURM RUGER HM77R HAWKEYE

Slimmed-down version of the M77. American walnut stock, blued barrel, Mauser-style controlled feed

extractor, soft red rubber recoil pad, stainless steel bolt, new LC6 trigger, engraved solid steel floorplate. Chambered in 7mm-08, 7mm Magnum, .308, .30-06, .300 Win Mag, .338 Win Mag. Left-hand version available.

NIB: $550   **Exc.:** $765   **VGood:** $595

STURM RUGER HK77RFP HAWKEYE

All-weather version of the HM77R Hawkeye but with synthetic stock and stainless barrel. Same chamberings as HM77R but with .338 Federal and .358 Winchester as well.

NIB: $1000   **Exc.:** $790   **VGood:** $620

STURM RUGER HM77RSPHAB HAWKEYE ALASKAN

Similar to HK77RFP but with iron sights, Diamondblack finish and Hogue stock. Chambered in .375 Ruger. Add 5% for left-hand model.

NIB: $1075   **Exc.:** $995   **VGood:** $850

STURM RUGER HKM77PRCM HAWKEYE COMPACT MAGNUM

Similar to Hawkeye but with 1/2-inch shorter synthetic stock and stainless steel barrel and receiver. Chambered for .300 and .338 RCM (Ruger Compact Magnum). Introduced 2008.

NIB: $1000   **Exc.:** $790   **VGood:** $620

STURM RUGER HKM77RCM HAWKEYE COMPACT MAGNUM

Similar to above but with blued barrel and walnut stock. Introduced 2008.

NIB: $1000   **Exc.:** $790   **VGood:** $620

STURM RUGER HM77RSPHAB HAWKEYE AFRICAN

Similar to HK77RFP but with checkered walnut stock and express-style sights. Chambered in .375 Ruger. Chambered in .375 Ruger. Introduced in 2007. A left-hand version was introduced in 2008.

NIB: $1175   **Exc.:** $825   **VGood:** $695

STURM RUGER MODEL 77/17

Bolt action; 17 HMR, 17 Mach 2; 9-shot detachable rotary magazine (17 HMR) or 10-shot (17 Mach 2); similar to earlier Model 77/22 rifles chambered for 22 WMR and 22 LR, but for the new 17 HMR and 17 Mach 2 cartridges; several variations; introduced 2002, still in production.

For 17 HMR versions, 22-inch barrel		
Perf.: $520	**Exc.:** $410	**VGood:** $350
For 17 Mach 2 versions, 20-inch barrel		
Perf.: $620	**Exc.:** N/A	**VGood:** N/A

STURM RUGER MODEL 77/22

Bolt action; 22 LR; 10-shot rotary magazine; 20-inch barrel; 39-3/4-inch overall length; weighs 5-3/4 lb.; checkered American walnut or nylon-reinforced Zytel stock; gold bead front sight, adjustable folding leaf rear; 1-inch Sturm Ruger rings optional; Mauser-type action; three-position safety simplified bolt stop; 10/22 dual screw barrel attachment system. Blued model introduced 1983; stainless steel and blued models with synthetic stock introduced 1989; still in production.

Perf.: $480   **Exc.:** $390   **VGood:** $290

With synthetic stock		
Perf.: $480	**Exc.:** $390	**VGood:** $290

STURM RUGER MODEL 77/22 HORNET

Same specs as Model 77/22 except 22 Hornet; 6-shot rotary magazine; weighs about 6 lbs.; checkered American walnut stock; black rubber buttpad; brass bead front sight, open adjustable rear; slightly lengthened receiver; comes with 1-inch Sturm Ruger scope rings. Made in U.S. by Sturm Ruger & Co. Introduced 1994; still produced.

Perf.: $490   **Exc.:** $400   **VGood:** $370

STURM RUGER MODEL 77/22MP
Same specs as Model 77/22 except 22 WMR; stainless steel; synthetic stock. Introduced 1989.
Perf.: $450   **Exc.:** $390   **VGood:** $290

STURM RUGER MODEL 77/22RM
Same specs as Model 77/22 except 22 WMR.; blued metal; walnut stock. Introduced 1989; still produced.
Perf.: $460   **Exc.:** $400   **VGood:** $300

STURM RUGER MODEL 77/22 RMP
Same specs as Ruger Model 77/22 RM except stainless finish; synthetic stock. Still in production.
Perf.: $460   **Exc.:** $400   **VGood:** $300

STURM RUGER MODEL 77/22RP
Same specs as Model 77/22 except synthetic stock; no iron sights; comes with scope rings. Made in U.S. by Sturm, Ruger & Co. Introduced 1989; still in production.
Perf.: $445   **Exc.:** $390   **VGood:** $260

STURM RUGER MODEL 77/22RS
Same specs as the Model 77/22 except blade front sight, fully-adjustable open rear; comes with scope rings. Made in U.S. by Sturm, Ruger & Co. Still produced.
Perf.: $370   **Exc.:** $250   **VGood:** $230

STURM RUGER MODEL 77/22RSH HORNET
Same as the 77/22 except 22 Hornet; blade front sight, fully-adjustable open rear adjustable. Made in U.S. by Sturm, Ruger & Co. Introduced 1994.
Perf.: $420   **Exc.:** $320   **VGood:** $290

STURM RUGER MODEL 77/22RSM
Same specs as the Model 77/22R except 22 WMR; blade front sight, fully-adjustable open rear; blue finish; checkered walnut stock. Made in U.S. by Sturm Ruger & Co. Still produced.
Perf.: $400   **Exc.:** $260   **VGood:** $230

STURM RUGER MODEL 77/22 RSMP
Same specs as Model 77/22 RSM except stainless finish; synthetic stock.
Perf.: $390   **Exc.:** $260   **VGood:** $230

STURM RUGER MODEL 77/22 RSP
Same specs as Model 77/22 except stainless finish; synthetic stock.
Perf.: $390   **Exc.:** $260   **VGood:** $230

STURM RUGER MODEL 77/22 VH
Same specs as Model 77/22 except 22 Hornet; laminated stock. Still in production.
Perf.: $500   **Exc.:** $425   **VGood:** $290

STURM RUGER MODEL 77/44 BOLT-ACTION RIFLE
Bolt action; 44 Magnum, 4-shot magazine; 18-1/2-inch barrel; seighs 6 lbs.; 38-1/4-inch overall length; American walnut stock with rubber butt pad and swivel studs, or black polymer (stainless only). Gold bead front, folding leaf rear sights; Comes with Ruger 1-inch scope rings. Uses same action as the Ruger 77/22. Short bolt stroke; rotary magazine; three-position safety. Introduced 1997.
Perf.: $520   **Exc.:** $440   **VGood:** $360

STURM RUGER MODEL 96/22
Lever action, short-throw lever; 22LR; 10-round rotary magazine; 18-1/2-inch barrel; weighs 5-1/4 lbs. 37-1/4-inch OAL; hardwood stock; gold bead front,folding leaf rear sights; cross-button safety; visible cocking indicator. Introduced 1996, still in production.
Perf.: $320   **Exc.:** $265   **VGood:** $210

STURM RUGER MODEL 96/17
Like Model 96/22, but chambered for 17 HRM cartridge, 9-round magazine. Introduced 2003, still in production.
Perf.: $350   **Exc.:** $275   **VGood:** $230

STURM RUGER MODEL 96/22M
Like Model 96/22, but chambered for 22 WMR cartridge, 9-round magazine.
Perf.: $350   **Exc.:** $275   **VGood:** $230

Sturm Ruger Model 77/22RSM

Sturm Ruger Model 77/22RSP

Sturm Ruger Model 96-22

Sturm Ruger Model 96-44

Sturm Ruger No. 1B

Sturm Ruger No. 1A Light Sporter

Sturm Ruger No. 1S Medium Sporter

Sturm Ruger No. 1H Tropical

STURM RUGER MODEL 96/44M
Like Model 96/22, but chambered for 44 Mag. cartridge; 4-round magazine.
Perf.: $500   **Exc.:** $400   **VGood:** $315

STURM RUGER NO. 1B STANDARD SINGLE SHOT
Single-shot; 204 Ruger, 218 Bee, 22 Hornet, 22-250, 220 Swift, 243 Win., 223, 257 Roberts, 280, 6mm Rem., 25-06, 270 Win., 308, 30-06, 7mm Rem. Mag., 300 Win. Mag., 338 Mag., 270 Weatherby, 300 Weatherby; 26-inch barrel with quarter rib; American walnut, two-piece stock; hand-checkered pistol grip, forearm; open sights or integral scope mounts; hammerless falling-block design; automatic ejector; top-tang safety. Introduced 1967; still in production.
Perf.: $670   **Exc.:** $580   **VGood:** $385

STURM RUGER NO. 1A LIGHT SPORTER
Same specs as No. 1B except 22-inch barrel; Alex Henry-style forearm; iron sights; 204 Ruger, 243 Win., 270 Win., 30-06, 7x57mm. Introduced 1968; still in production.
Perf.: $665   **Exc.:** $580   **VGood:** $385

STURM RUGER NO. 1S MEDIUM SPORTER
Same specs as No. 1A Light Sporter except 7mm Rem. Mag., 300 Win. Mag., 338 Win. Mag., 45-70; 26-inch barrel, 22-inch (45-70) barrel. Introduced 1968; still in production.
Perf.: $770   **Exc.:** $530   **VGood:** $420

STURM RUGER NO. 1H TROPICAL MODEL
Same specs as No. 1S Medium Sporter except 375 H&H Mag., 405 Win., 416 Rigby, 458 Win. Mag., 458 Lott; 24-inch heavy barrel; open sights. Introduced 1968; still in production.
Perf.: $790   **Exc.:** $630   **VGood:** $470

Sturm Ruger No. 1 RSI International

Sturm Ruger No. 1 Light Standard 1-AB

Sturm Ruger No. 3

Sturm Ruger PC9 Carbine

Swiss K-31 Target Model

Tanner 300-Meter Free Rifle

Tanner 300-Meter UIT Standard Free Rifle

Taurus Model 62

STURM RUGER PC9 CARBINE
Like PC4 Carbine, but chambered for 9mm cartridge, 10- or 15-shot magazine. Introduced 1997; still produced.

    Perf.: $450   **Exc.: $400**   **VGood: $350**

SURVIVAL ARMS AR-7 EXPLORER
Semi-automatic; 22 LR; 8-shot magazine; 16-inch barrel; 34-1/2-inch overall length with barrel mounted, 16-1/2-inch stowed; weighs 2-1/2 lbs.; square blade front sight, aperture elevation-adjustable rear; moulded Cycolac stock with snap-on buttcap; takedown design stores barrel and action in hollow stock; black, silvertone or camouflage finish. Light enough to float. Survival Arms took over manufacture of the AR-7 from Charter Arms. Reintroduced 1992; discontinued 1995.

    Perf.: $130   **Exc.: $115**   **VGood: $90**

SURVIVAL ARMS AR-7 SPORTER
Same specs as AR-7 Explorer except 25-shot magazine; black finish with telescoping stock. Made in U.S. by Survival Arms, Inc. Introduced 1992; discontinued 1995.

    Perf.: $180   **Exc.: $150**   **VGood: $125**

SURVIVAL ARMS AR-7 WILDCAT
Same specs as AR-7 Explorer except black finish and wood stock. Made in U.S. by Survival Arms, Inc. Introduced 1992; discontinued 1995.

    Perf.: $165   **Exc.: $130**   **VGood: $110**

SWISS K-31 TARGET MODEL
Bolt action; 308; 6-shot magazine; 26-inch barrel; 44-inch overall length; straight pull; protected blade front sight, ladder-type adjustable rear; European walnut stock; sling, muzzle cap; based on straight-pull Schmidt-Rubin design. Made in Switzerland. Introduced 1982; no longer in production.

    Perf.: $395   **Exc.: $350**   **VGood: $300**

TANNER 50-METER FREE RIFLE
Bolt action; single shot; 22 LR; 27-2/3-inch barrel; 43-2/5-inch overall length; weighs 14 lbs.; micrometer-diopter rear sight, globe front with interchangeable inserts; nutwood stock with palm rest; accessory rail; adjustable hook buttplate; adjustable set trigger. Made in Switzerland. Introduced 1984; dropped 1988.

    Perf.: $2995   **Exc.: $2495**   **VGood: $1895**

TANNER 300-METER FREE RIFLE
Bolt action; single shot; 308, 7.5 Swiss; 28-5/8-inch barrel; 45-5/16-inch overall length; weighs 15 lbs.; Tanner micrometer-diopter rear sight, globe front with interchangeable inserts; thumbhole walnut stock; accessory rail; palm rest; adjustable hook buttplate; three-lug revolving bolt design; adjustable set trigger. Made in Switzerland. Introduced 1984; discontinued 1988.

    Perf.: $4750   **Exc.: $3700**   **VGood: $2800**

TANNER 300-METER UIT STANDARD FREE RIFLE
Same specs as 300-Meter Free Rifle except repeater with 10-shot magazine; 24-13/16-inch barrel; 40-5/8-inch overall length; weighs 10-1/2 lbs.; no palm rest; no adjustable buttplate. Made in Switzerland. Introduced 1984; discontinued 1988.

    Perf.: $4800   **Exc.: $3900**   **VGood: $3000**

TAURUS MODEL 62 PUMP RIFLE
Slide action; 22 LR, 17 Mach 2; 12- or 13-shot magazine; 16-1/2-inch or 23-inch round barrel; weighs 5.9 lbs.; 39-inch overall length; premium hardwood stock; adjustable rear sight, bead blade front, optional tang sight; blue, case-hardened or stainless finishes; bolt-mounted safety, pump action, manual firing pin block, integral security lock system. Imported from Brazil by Taurus International, still available.

    Perf.: $250   **Exc.: $200**   **VGood: $150**

STURM RUGER NO. 1 RSI INTERNATIONAL
Same specs as No. 1B, except full-length Mannlicher-style stock of American walnut, 20-inch barrel; 243, 30-06, 7x57, 270. Introduced 1983; still in production.

    Perf.: $780   **Exc.: $580**   **VGood: $410**

STURM RUGER NO. 1V SPECIAL VARMINTER
Same specs as No. 1B except 24-inch heavy barrel; 22-250, 220 Swift, 223, 25-06, 6mm; supplied with target scope bases. Introduced 1970; still in production.

    Perf.: $760   **Exc.: $620**   **VGood: $475**

RUGER NO. 1 LIGHT STANDARD 1-AB
Similar to Light Sporter 1-A but with 22-inch sightless blued barrel. Chambered in .204 Ruger only; introduced 2006.

    NIB: $725   **Exc.: $665**   **VGood: $525**

STURM RUGER NO. 3
Single-shot; 22 Hornet, 223, 30-40 Krag, 375 Win., 44 Mag., 45-70; 22-inch barrel; same action as Sturm Ruger No. 1, except for different lever; uncheckered American walnut, two-piece carbine-type stock; folding leaf rear sight, gold bead front; adjustable trigger; barrel band on forearm; automatic ejector. Introduced 1969; 30-40 chambering dropped 1978; model discontinued 1986. Premium for 30-40.

    Perf.: $650   **Exc.: $595**   **VGood: $475**

223, 44 Mag. calibers

    Perf.: $615   **Exc.: $560**   **VGood: $440**

STURM RUGER PC4 CARBINE
Semi-automatic; 40 S&W cal., 10-shot magazine; 16.25-inch barrel; weighs 6 lbs., 4 oz.; 34.75-inch overall length; Black high impact synthetic stock with checkered grip and forend; blade front, open adjustable rear sights or ghost ring peep sights; integral Ruger scope mounts; delayed blowback action; manual push-button cross bolt safety and internal firing pin block safety automatic slide lock. Introduced 1997. Still produced.

    Perf.: $450   **Exc.: $400**   **VGood: $350**

RIFLES

TAURUS MODEL 62LAR LEVER RIFLE
Lever-action rifle based on Model 62 pump action and chambered in .22 LR. 23-inch blued barrel, walnut-finish hardwood stock. Introduced 2006. Add 10 percent for stainless steel.

NIB: $265   **Exc.:** $225   **VGood:** $175

TAURUS MODEL 72 PUMP RIFLE
Same as Model 62 except chambered in 22 WMR, 17 HMR; 16-1/2-inch bbl. holds 10 shots, 23-inch bbl. holds 11 shots. Weighs 108.8 oz. Introduced 2001, still in production. Imported from Brazil by Taurus International, still available.

Perf.: $260   **Exc.:** $210   **VGood:** $160

TAURUS THUNDERBOLT
Clone of old Colt Lightning Magazine Rifle. Chambered in .45 Colt and .38/.357 with 14-round tubular magazine. Blued finish with hardwood buttstock and forend. Add 15 percent for stainless steel.

NIB: $550   **Exc.:** $450   **VGood:** $365

TAURUS MODEL 63 SEMI-AUTOMATIC RIFLE
Semi-automatic; 22 LR; 10-shot tube magazine in buttstock; 23-inch round barrel; blued metal; walnut-finished hardwood stock and forearm; Based on the Winshester Model 63 rifle. Introduced 2002, still in production.

Perf.: $270   **Exc.:** $220   **VGood:** $170

THOMPSON/CENTER CONTENDER CARBINE
Single shot, breakopen; 17 HMR, 17 Mach 2, 204 Ruger, 22 LR, 22 Hornet, 223 Rem., 6.8 Rem., 7mm TCU, 7-30 Waters, 30-30, 357 Rem. Max., 35 Rem., 375 JDJ, 44 Mag., 410; 21-inch barrel; 35-inch overall length; weighs 5-1/8 lbs.; open adjustable rear sight, blade front; drilled, tapped for scope mounts; checkered American walnut stock; rubber buttpad; built on T/C Contender action; interchangeable barrels. Introduced 1985; still in production with new G2 frame.

Perf.: $400   **Exc.:** $325   **VGood:** $270

THOMPSON/CENTER CONTENDER CARBINE RYNITE
Same specs as Contender Carbine except Rynite stock, forend. Introduced 1990; discontinued 1993.

Perf.: $390   **Exc.:** $280   **VGood:** $230

THOMPSON/CENTER CONTENDER CARBINE STAINLESS
Same specs as Contender Carbine except stainless steel with blued sights; walnut or Rynite stock, forend. Made in U.S. by Thompson/Center. Introduced 1993; no longer produced.

Perf.: $420   **Exc.:** $330   **VGood:** $280

THOMPSON/CENTER CONTENDER CARBINE SURVIVAL SYSTEM
Same specs as Contender Carbine except Rynite stock; two 16-1/4-inch barrels, 223 Rem., 45 Colt/410. Marketed in Cordura nylon case. Introduced 1991; no longer in production.

Perf.: $470   **Exc.:** $410   **VGood:** $340

THOMPSON/CENTER CONTENDER CARBINE YOUTH MODEL
Same specs as Contender Carbine except 22 LR, 22 WMR, 223, 7-30 Waters, 30-30, 35 Rem., 44 Mag.; 16-1/4-inch barrel; 29-inch overall length; fully-adjustable open sights; shorter buttstock; also available with rifled vent rib barrel chambered for 45/410. Introduced 1987.

Perf.: $350   **Exc.:** $300   **VGood:** $250

THOMPSON/CENTER CUSTOM SHOP TCR '87
Single shot, breakopen; 22 Hornet, 222 Rem., 22-250, 243 Win., 270, 308, 7mm-08, 30-06, 32-40 Win., 12-ga. slug, 10-ga. and 12-ga. field barrels; 23-inch (standard), 25-7/8-inch (heavy) barrel; 39-1/2-inch overall length; weighs about 6-3/4 lbs.; break-open; no sights; checkered American black walnut stock,

Taurus Thunderbolt

Taurus Model 63

Thompson/Center Contender Carbine Stainless

Thompson/Center Stainless Encore Rifle

Thompson/Center TCR '83 Hunter

Thompson/Center 22 LR Classic

forend; interchangeable barrels; single-stage trigger; cross-bolt safety. Made in U.S. by T/C. Available only through the T/C custom shop. Introduced 1987; no longer offered. Values shown are for complete rifle.

Perf.: $800   **Exc.:** $600   **VGood:** $375

THOMPSON/CENTER ENCORE RIFLE
Single shot, breakopen; 204 Ruger, 22 Hornet, 22-250, 223, 243, 260, 25-06, 270, 7mm-08, 280, 308, 30-06, 7mm Rem. Mag., 300 Win. Mag., 405 Win., 45-70; 24-inch, 26-inch barrel; weighs 6 lbs., 12 oz. (24-inch barrel); 38-1/2-inch overall length (24-inch barrel); American walnut stock, Monte Carlo style, with schnabel forend, or black composite stock; Ramp-style white bead front, fully adjustable leaf-type rear sights; Interchangeable barrels; action opens by squeezing trigger guard; drilled and tapped for T/C scope mounts; polished blue finish. Introduced 1996, still in production.

Perf.: $570   **Exc.:** $450   **VGood:** $410

With black composite stock and forend
Perf.: $530   **Exc.:** $400   **VGood:** $350

THOMPSON/CENTER STAINLESS ENCORE RIFLE
Similar to blued Encore except stainless steel with blued sights, black composite stock and forend or camp composite stock and forend. Available in 22-250, 223, 7mm-08, 30-06, 308. Introduced 1999, still available. Made in U.S.A. by Thompson/Center Arms.

Perf.: $590   **Exc.:** $470   **VGood:** $420

THOMPSON/CENTER TCR '83 HUNTER
Single shot, breakopen, hammerless; 223, 22-250, 243 Win., 7mm Rem. Mag., 30-06; 23-inch barrel; 39-1/2-inch overall length; weighs 6-7/8 lbs.; blade on ramp front sight, windage-adjustable open rear; American black walnut stock; cut-checkering on pistol-grip, forend; interchangeable barrels; cross-bolt safety; single-stage or double-set trigger. Introduced 1983; discontinued 1986.

Perf.: $580   **Exc.:** $525   **VGood:** $450

THOMPSON/CENTER TCR '87 HUNTER
Single shot, breakopen, hammerless; 22 Hornet, 222 Rem., 223 Rem., 22-250, 243 Win., 270, 308, 7mm-08, 30-06, 32-40 Win., 375 H&H, 416 Rem. Mag.; 12-gauge slug; 23-inch (standard), 25 7/8-inch heavy barrel; no sights; checkered American black walnut stock; interchangeable barrels; single-stage trigger; cross-bolt safety. Introduced 1987; discontinued 1992.

Perf.: $600   **Exc.:** $550   **VGood:** $475

THOMPSON/CENTER 22 CLASSIC RIFLE
Semi-automatic; 22 LR, 8-shot magazine; 22-inch match-grade barrel; weighs 5-1/2 pounds; 39-1/2-inch overall length; Satin-finished American walnut stock with Monte Carlo-type comb and pistol grip cap, swivel studs; Ramp-style front sight and fully adjustable rear, both with fiber optics; All-steel receiver drilled and tapped for scope mounting; barrel threaded to receiver; thumb-operated safety. Introduced 2000, still offered.

Perf.: $290   **Exc.:** $220   **VGood:** $180

THOMPSON/CENTER 22 BENCHMARK
Similar to 22 Classic, but has 18-inch heavy target barrel, laminated stock; no sights, drilled and tapped for scope base; weighs 6.8 pounds; 10-round detachable magazine. Introduced in 2003, still produced.

Perf.: $430   **Exc.:** $360   **VGood:** N/A

THOMPSON/CENTER SILVER LYNX
Similar to 22 Classic, but stainless steel, with 20-inch match-grade barrel, black composite stock; adjustable open sights; trap in buttplate holds extra 5- or 10-shot magazine. Introduced in 2004, still produced.

Perf.: $ 385   **Exc.:** $260   **VGood:** N/A

Thompson/Center SilverLynx

Thompson/Center Icon

Thompson/Center Icon Classic Long Action

Thompson/Center Icon Classic Weather-shield

Thompson/Center Icon Weathershield Camo

Thompson/Center Triumph

Thompson/Center Pro Hunter

Tikka Model 55

Tikka Model 65

THOMPSON/CENTER ICON

Bolt-action centerfire rifle chambered in .22-250, .243, .308 and .30 Thompson-Center. Premium checkered walnut stock. Barrel length 22" (iron sight) or 24" (sightless). Detachable box magazine.

NIB: $695   **Exc.:** 550   **VGood:** 400

THOMPSON/CENTER ICON CLASSIC LONG ACTION RIFLE

Similar to Icon but with long-action design and chambered for .270, .30-06, .300 Winchester Magnum and 7mm Remington Magnum.

NIB: $750   **Exc.:** 650   **VGood:** 475

THOMPSON/CENTER ICON WEATHERSHIELD MEDIUM ACTION RIFLE

Similar to Icon but with stainless steel barrel and receiver and black synthetic or RealTree AP Camo stock. Add 5% for camo.

NIB: $750   **Exc.:** 650   **VGood:** 475

THOMPSON/CENTER TRIUMPH

Fifty-caliber toggle-breech inline muzzleloader with only four moving parts. Blued/synthetic, Weathershield/synthetic, or Weathershield/stainless finish.

NIB: $395   **Exc.:** $335   **VGood:** $250

THOMPSON/CENTER PRO HUNTER

Similar to Encore rifle but with plain or fluted barrel and various finish and stock options. Barrels interchange with standard Encore barrels. Muzzleloading and pistol versions available. Introduced 2007.

NIB: $775   **Exc.:** $695   **VGood:** $550

TIKKA MODEL 07

Over/under combination gun; 222, 5.6x52R, 5.6x50R Mag., beneath 12-ga. barrel; 22-3/4-inch barrels; bead front sight, open windage-adjustable rear; Monte Carlo stock of European walnut; palm swell with pistol grip; exposed hammer, sling swivels;

vent rib, rosewood pistol-grip cap. Introduced 1979; discontinued 1982.

Exc.: $595   **VGood:** $495   **Good:** $395

TIKKA MODEL 55

Bolt action; 17 Rem., 222, 22-250, 6mm Rem., 243, 308; 3-shot detachable magazine; 23-inch barrel; bead ramped front sight, fully-adjustable rear; drilled, tapped for scope mounts; hand-checkered Monte Carlo stock of European walnut; palm swell on pistol grip. Introduced 1979; discontinued 1981.

Exc.: $370   **VGood:** $300   **Good:** $250

TIKKA MODEL 55 DELUXE

Same specs as Model 55 except roll-over cheekpiece; forend tip; grip cap of rosewood. Introduced 1979; discontinued 1981.

Exc.: $430   **VGood:** $370   **Good:** $300

TIKKA MODEL 55 SPORTER

Same specs as Model 55 except 222, 22-250, 243, 308; 5-, 10-shot magazine; 23-inch heavy barrel; no sights; varmint-type stock; oil-finish. Introduced 1979; discontinued 1981.

Exc.: $390   **VGood:** $330   **Good:** $260

TIKKA MODEL 65

Bolt action; 25-06, 6.5x55, 7x57, 7x64, 270, 308, 30-06, 7mm Rem. Mag., 300 Win. Mag.; 5-shot magazine; 22-inch barrel; bead ramped front sight, fully-adjustable rear; drilled, tapped for scope mounts; hand-checkered Monte Carlo stock of European walnut; palm swell on pistol grip; adjustable trigger. Introduced 1979; discontinued 1981.

Exc.: $420   **VGood:** $370   **Good:** $300

TIKKA MODEL 65 DELUXE

Same specs as Model 65 except roll-over cheekpiece; forend tip; rosewood grip cap. Introduced 1979; discontinued 1981.

Exc.: $430   **VGood:** $370   **Good:** $300

TIKKA MODEL 65 TARGET

Same specs as Model 65 except 25-06, 6.5x55, 270, 308, 30-06; 22-inch heavy barrel; no sights; target-type walnut stock; stock designed to meet ISU requirements, with stippled forend, palm swell. Introduced 1969; discontinued 1981.

Exc.: $500   **VGood:** $430   **Good:** $360

TIKKA MODEL 77K

Combo; over/under; 222, 5.6x52R, 6.5x55, 7x57R, 7x65R, 308 beneath 12-ga. barrel; 22-3/4-inch barrel; hammerless; bead front sight, open windage-adjustable rear; Monte Carlo stock of European walnut; palm swell with pistol-grip; sling swivels; ventilated rib; rosewood pistol-grip cap. Introduced 1979; discontinued 1982.

Exc.: $795   **VGood:** $625   **Good:** $475

TIKKA MODEL 412S DOUBLE RIFLE

Double rifle; 9.3x74R; 24-inch barrel; weighs 8-5/8 lbs.; ramp front sight, adjustable open rear; American walnut stock with Monte Carlo-style comb; barrel selector mounted in trigger; cocking indicators in tang; recoil pad; ejectors. Imported from Italy by Stoeger. Introduced 1980; no longer imported.

Perf.: $1700   **Exc.:** $1400   **VGood:** $1050

TIKKA MODEL 512S COMBINATION GUN

Combination gun, over/under; replaced Model 412S; 12 gauge over 222, 308; 24-inch barrels, shotgun barrel choked Imp. Mod.; weighs 7-5/8 lbs.; blade front sight, flip-up-type open rear; American walnut stock with recoil pad, Monte Carlo comb; barrel selector on trigger; hand-checkered stock and forend; barrels are screw-adjustable to change point of bullet impact; interchangeable barrels. Imported from Italy by Stoeger. Introduced 1980, no longer imported.

Perf.: $1100   **Exc.:** $920   **VGood:** $710

TIKKA MODEL 512S DOUBLE RIFLE

Double rifle; 9.3x74R; 24-inch barrel; weighs 8-5/8 lbs.; ramp front sight, adjustable open rear; American walnut stock with Monte Carlo-style comb; barrel selector mounted in trigger; cocking indicators in tang; recoil pad; ejectors. Imported from Italy by Stoeger. Introduced 1980; no longer imported.

Perf.: $1700   **Exc.:** $1400   **VGood:** $1050

TIKKA PREMIUM GRADE

Bolt action; 22-250, 223, 243, 270, 30-06, 7mm Rem. Mag., 300 Win. Mag., 338 Win. Mag.; 3-, 5-shot magazine; 22-inch (standard), 24-inch (magnum) barrel; 43-inch overall length; weighs 7-1/4 lbs.; no sights; Monte Carlo select walnut stock with roll-over cheekpiece; rosewood grip, forend caps; hand-checkered grip, forend; polished, blued barrel. Made in Finland. Introduced 1990; no longer in production.

Exc.: $680   **VGood:** $520   **Good:** $400

TIKKA SPORTER RIFLE

Bolt action; 223, 22-250, 308, detachable 5-shot magazine; 23-1/2-inch heavy barrel; weighs 9 lbs.; 43-5/8-inch overall length; European walnut stock with adjustable comb, adjustable buttplate; stippled grip and forend; no sights; drilled and tapped for scope mounting. Buttplate adjustable for length, angle, height and pitch, adjustable trigger, free-floating barrel. Introduced 1998. Imported from Finland by Beretta USA.

Perf.: $900   **Exc.:** $750   **Good:** $650

TIKKA STANDARD

Bolt action; 22-250, 223, 243, 270, 30-06, 7mm Rem. Mag., 300 Win. Mag., 338 Win. Mag.; 3-, 5-shot magazine; 22-inch barrel (standard), 24-inch (magnums); 43-inch overall length; weighs 7-1/4 lbs.; no sights; Monte Carlo European walnut stock; checkered grip, forend; rubber buttplate; receiver dovetailed for scope mounts. Made in Finland. Introduced 1988; no longer in production.

Exc.: $595   **VGood:** $475   **Good:** $350

TIKKA T3 HUNTER

Bolt action; 223, 22-250, 243, 308, 25-06, 270, 6.5x55, 270 WSM, 7mm Rem Mag, 30-06, 300 WSM, 300 Win Mag, 338 Win Mag; 22-7/16-inch barrel (24-3/8-inch magnum calibers) 6-3/4 lbs.; no sights; walnut stock with rubber butt pad; introduced 2003, still imported by Beretta USA.

Perf.: $600   **Exc.:** $500   **VGood:** $400

TIKKA T3 LAMINATED STAINLESS

Similar to T3 Hunter, but with laminated stock and barrel and action of stainless steel.

Perf.: $800   **Exc.:** $750   **VGood:** N/A

TIKKA T3 LITE

Similar to T3 Hunter, but with synthetic stock; weighs 6 lbs, 3 oz; introduced 2003, still imported by Beretta USA.

Perf.: $550   **Exc.:** $450   **VGood:** $400

TIKKA T3 LITE STAINLESS

Similar to T3 Lite, but barrel and action of stainless steel.

Perf.: $600   **Exc.:** $475   **VGood:** $400

TIKKA T3 TACTICAL

Similar to T3 Hunter, but tactical rifle for law enforcement; 223, 308; 20-inch barrel; black phosphate finish, synthetic stock with adjustable comb; 5-shot detachable magazine; Picatinny rail on action; fitted for muzzle brake and bipod. Imported by Beretta USA.

Perf.: $1300   **Exc.:** $1100   **VGood:** $900

TIKKA T3 VARMINT

Similar to T3 Hunter, but with bull barrel, synthetic stock, adjustable trigger; 223, 22-250, 308, 5-shot detachable magazine. Imported by Beretta USA.

Perf.: $750   **Exc.:** $690   **VGood:** N/A

Tikka Model 512S Double Rifle

Tikka Premium Grade

Tikka Sporter Rifle

Tikka Standard Model

Tikka T3 Hunter

Tikka T3 Lite

Tikka T3 Lite Stainless

Tikka Whitetail/Battue

Tikka Whitetail Hunter

TIKKA T3 VARMINT STAINLESS

Similar to T3 Varmint, but barrel and action of stainless steel. Imported by Beretta USA.

Perf.: $800   **Exc.:** $750   **VGood:** N/A

TIKKA WHITETAIL/BATTUE

Bolt action; 270, 308, 30-06, 7mm Rem. Mag., 300 Win. Mag., 338 Win. Mag.; 3-, 5-shot magazine; 20-1/2-inch barrel; raised quarter-rib; V-shaped rear sight, blade front; Monte Carlo European walnut stock; checkered pistol grip, forend; rubber buttplate; receiver dovetailed for scope mounts. Made in Finland. Introduced 1991; no longer in production.

Perf.: $530   **Exc.:** $440   **VGood:** $370

TIKKA WHITETAIL HUNTER BOLT-ACTION RIFLE

Bolt action; 22-250, 223, 243, 7mm-08, 25-06, 270, 308, 30-06, 7mm Rem. Mag., 300 Win. Mag., 338 Win. Mag; 22-1/2-inch barrel (std. cals.), 24-1/2-inch (magnum cals.); weighs 7-1/8 lbs.; 43-inch overall length (std. cals.); European walnut stock with Monte Carlo comb, rubber butt pad, checkered grip and forend; Detachable four-shot magazine (standard calibers), three-shot in magnums. Receiver dovetailed for scope mounting. Reintroduced 1996. Imported from Finland by Beretta USA.

Standard calibers
Perf.: $620   **Exc.:** $500   **VGood:** $400

Tikka Continental Varmint

Tikka Whitetail Hunter Deluxe

Tikka Continental Long Range Hunting Rifle

Tradewinds Husky Model 5000

Tradewinds Model 260-A

Traditions 1874 Sharps

Traditions Rolling Block

Magnum calibers		
Perf.: $650	**Exc.:** $520	**VGood:** $430
Left-hand		
Perf.: $660	**Exc.:** $540	**VGood:** $440

TIKKA CONTINENTAL VARMINT RIFLE

Similar to the standard Tikka rifle except has 26-inch heavy barrel, extra-wide forend. Chambered for 17 Rem., 22-250, 223, 308. Made in Finland by Sako. Imported by Beretta USA.

Perf.: $690   **Exc.:** $550   **VGood:** $490

TIKKA WHITETAIL HUNTER DELUXE RIFLE

Similar to the Whitetail Hunter except has select walnut stock with rollover Monte Carlo comb, rosewood grip cap and forend tip. Has adjustable trigger, detachable magazine, free-floating barrel. Same calibers as the Hunter. Introduced 1999. Imported from Finland by Beretta USA.

Standard calibers		
Perf.: $720	**Exc.:** $600	**VGood:** $500
Magnum calibers		
Perf.: $775	**Exc.:** $625	**VGood:** $525

TIKKA WHITETAIL HUNTER SYNTHETIC RIFLE

Similar to the Whitetail Hunter except has black synthetic stock; calibers 223, 22-250, 243, 7mm-08, 25-06, 270 Win., 30-06, 7mm Rem. Mag., 300 Win.

Mag., 338 Win. Mag. Introduced 1996. Imported from Finland by Beretta USA.

Perf.: $600   **Exc.:** $500   **VGood:** $400

TIKKA CONTINENTAL LONG RANGE HUNTING RIFLE

Similar to the Whitetail Hunter except has 26-inch heavy barrel. Available in 25-06, 270 Win., 7mm Rem. Mag., 300 Win. Mag. Introduced 1996. Imported from Finland by Beretta USA.

Perf.: 680   **Exc.:** $550   **VGood:** 480

TIKKA WHITETAIL HUNTER STAINLESS SYNTHETIC

Similar to the Whitetail Hunter except all metal is of stainless steel, and it has a black synthetic stock. Available in 22-250, 223, 243, 7mm-08, 25- 06, 270, 308, 30-06, 7mm Rem. Mag., 300 Win. Mag., 338 Win. Mag. Introduced 1997. Imported from Finland by Beretta USA.

Perf.: $600   **Exc.:** $500   **VGood:** $410

TRADEWINDS HUSKY MODEL 5000

Bolt action; 22-250, 243, 270, 30-06, 308; removable 4-shot magazine; 23-3/4-inch barrel; fixed hooded front sight, adjustable rear; hand-checkered Monte Carlo stock of European walnut; white-line spacers on pistol-grip cap, forend tip, buttplate; recessed bolt head; adjustable trigger. Imported from Europe. Introduced 1973; discontinued 1983.

Exc.: $350   **VGood:** $320   **Good:** $290

TRADEWINDS MODEL 260-A

Semi-automatic; 22 LR; 5-shot magazine; 22-1/2-inch barrel; 41-1/2-inch overall length; hooded ramp front sight, three-leaf folding rear; walnut stock; hand-checkered pistol grip, forend; double extractors; sliding safety; sling swivels; receiver grooved for scope mount. Made in Japan. Introduced 1975; discontinued 1989.

Exc.: $200   **VGood:** $170   **Good:** $130

TRADEWINDS MODEL 311-A

Bolt action; 22 LR; 5-shot magazine; 22-1/2-inch barrel; 41-1/4-inch overall length; hooded ramp front sight, folding leaf rear; receiver grooved for scope mount; Monte Carlo walnut stock; hand-checkered pistol grip, forend; sliding safety. Made in Europe. Introduced 1976; no longer in production.

Exc.: $180   **VGood:** $150   **Good:** $110

TRADITIONS 1874 SHARPS DELUXE RIFLE

Single shot; falling block; 45-70; 32-inch octagonal barrel with 1:18-inch twist; weighs 11.67 lbs.; 48.8-inch overall length; Checkered walnut stock with German silver nose cap and steel butt plate. Globe front sight, adjustable creedmore rear with 12 inserts. Color-case hardened receiver; double-set triggers. Introduced 2001. Imported from Pedersoli by Traditions.

Perf.: $900   **Exc.:** $700   **VGood:** $550

TRADITIONS 1874 SHARPS SPORTING DELUXE RIFLE

Similar to Sharps Deluxe but custom silver engraved receiver, European walnut stock and forend, satin finish, set trigger, fully adjustable.

Perf.: $1600   **Exc.:** $1200   **VGood:** $1000

TRADITIONS 1874 SHARPS STANDARD RIFLE

Similar to 1874 Sharps Deluxe Rifle, except has blade front and adjustable buckhorn-style rear sight. Weighs 10.67 pounds. Introduced 2001. Imported from Pedersoli by Traditions.

Perf.: $1100   **Exc.:** $975   **VGood:** $800

TRADITIONS ROLLING BLOCK SPORTING RIFLE

Single shot, rolling block; 45-70; 30-inch octagonal barrel with 1:18-inch twist; 46.7-inch overall length; weighs 11.67 lbs.; walnut stock, blade front, adjustable rear sights; Antique silver, color-case hardened receiver, drilled and tapped for tang/globe sights; brass butt plate and trigger guard. Introduced 2001. Imported from Pedersoli by Traditions.

Perf.: $900   **Exc.:** $775   **VGood:** $650

TRISTAR 1860 HENRY RIFLE

Lever action; 44-40, 45 Colt; 24-1/4-inch barrel; half-octagon; weighs 9.2 lbs.; 43-3/4-inch overall length; American walnut stock; blade front sight, rear adjustable for elevation. Frame, elevator, magazine follower, buttplate are brass, balance blue. Made by Uberti. Imported by Tristar Sporting Arms Ltd. Arms, Inc.

Perf.: $890   **Exc.:** $700   **VGood:** $540

TRISTAR 1860 HENRY TRAPPER CARBINE

Similar to the 1860 Henry Rifle except has 18-1/2-inch barrel, measures 37- 3/4-inch overall, and weighs 8 lbs. Introduced 1999. Imported from Uberti of Italy by Tristar Sporting Arms Ltd.

Perf.: $860   **Exc.:** $700   **VGood:** $540

TRISTAR 1874 SHARPS SPORTING RIFLE

Single shot, falling block; 45-70; 28-inch, 32-inch, 34-inch octagonal barrel; 44.5-inch overall length; weighs 9.75 lbs.; Walnut stock; Dovetail front, adjustable rear sights. Cut checkering, case colored frame finish.

Perf.: $1150   **Exc.:** $1000   **VGood:** $850

TRISTAR 1885 SINGLE SHOT

Single shot, falling block; 45-70; 28-inch barrel; 44.5-inch overall length; weighs 8.75 lbs.; European walnut stock; bead on blade front sight, open step-adjustable rear; Recreation of the 1885 Winchester by Uberti. Color case-hardened receiver and lever, blued barrel. Introduced 1998. Imported from Italy by Tristar Sporting Arms Ltd.

Perf.: $680   **Exc.:** $560   **VGood:** $400

TYROL CUSTOM CRAFTED MODEL

Bolt action; 243, 25-06, 30-06, 308, 7mm, 300 Win.; 23-3/4-inch barrel; hooded ramp front sight, adjustable rear; drilled, tapped for scope mounts; hand-checkered Monte Carlo stock of European walnut; adjustable trigger; shotgun-type tang safety. Manufactured in Austria. Introduced 1973; discontinued 1975.

Exc.: $400   **VGood:** $320   **Good:** $210

UBERTI HENRY RIFLE

Lever action; 44-40; 24-1/2-inch half-octagon barrel; 43-3/4-inch overall length; weighs 9 lbs.; elevation-adjustable rear sight, blade front; unchecked walnut stock; brass buttplate, frame, elevator, magazine follower; rest charcoal blued or of polished steel. Made in Italy. Introduced 1987.

Perf.: $850   **Exc.:** $720   **VGood:** $510

UBERTI HENRY CARBINE

Same specs as Henry Rifle except 22-1/4-inch barrel. Improted by Uberti USA; still in production.

Perf.: $850   **Exc.:** $720   **VGood:** $510

UBERTI HENRY TRAPPER

Same specs as Henry Rifle except 16-inch or 18-inch barrel. Imported by Uberti USA; still in production.

Perf.: $850   **Exc.:** $720   **VGood:** $510

UBERTI MODEL 1866 SPORTING RIFLE

Lever action; 22 LR, 22 WMR, 38 Spl., 44-40; 24-1/2-inch octagonal barrel; 43-1/4-inch overall length; weighs 8 lbs.; elevation-adjustable rear sight, windage-adjustable blade front; polished brass frame, buttplate, forend cap; rest charcoal blued. Made in Italy. Introduced 1987.

Perf.: $710   **Exc.:** $570   **VGood:** $440

UBERTI MODEL 1866 YELLOWBOY CARBINE

Same specs as Model 1866 except 19-inch round barrel, carbine bands; 38-1/4-inch overall length; weighs 7 7/16 lbs. Introduced 1987; still in production.

Perf.: $710   **Exc.:** $570   **VGood:** $440

UBERTI MODEL 1866 TRAPPER CARBINE

Same specs as Model 1866 except 22 LR, 38 Spl., 44-40; 16-1/8-inch barrel. Introduced 1987; discontinued 1989.

Perf.: $710   **Exc.:** $570   **VGood:** $440

UBERTI MODEL 1873 BUCKHORN

Revolving carbine; 44 Mag., 44 Spl., 44-40; 6-shot cylinder; 18-inch barrel; 34-inch overall length; weighs 4-1/2 lbs.; grooved or target rear sight, blade front; carbine version of single-action revolver; color case-hardened frame; blued cylinder, barrel; brass buttplate. Introduced 1987; discontinued 1989.

Perf.: $410   **Exc.:** $350   **VGood:** $290

With target sights

Perf.: $440   **Exc.:** $380   **VGood:** $320

UBERTI MODEL 1873 CATTLEMAN

Revolving carbine; 22 LR/22 WMR, 38 Spl., 357 Mag., 44-40, 45 Colt; 6-shot cylinder; 18-inch barrel; 34-inch overall length; weighs 4-1/2 lbs.; grooved or target rear sight, blade front; carbine version of single-action revolver; case hardened frame;

Tyrol Custom Crafted Model

Uberti Henry

Uberti Model 1873
Sporting Rifle

Uberti 1886 Yellowboy Carbine

Uberti Rolling Block
Baby Carbine

Ultra-Hi Model 2200

blued cylinder, barrel; brass buttplate. Made in Italy. Introduced 1987; discontinued 1989, reintroduced.

Perf.: $400   **Exc.:** $330   **VGood:** $270

With target sights

Perf.: $425   **Exc.:** $350   **VGood:** $280

UBERTI MODEL 1873 SPORTING RIFLE

Lever action; 22 LR, 22 WMR, 38 Spl., 357 Mag., 44-40, 45 Colt; 24-1/4-inch, 30-inch octagonal barrel; 43-1/4-inch overall length; weighs 8 lbs.; elevation-adjustable rear sight, windage-adjustable blade front; unchecked walnut stock; brass elevator; color case-hardened frame; blued barrel, hammer, lever, buttplate. Reproduction of 1873 Winchester, made in Italy. Introduced 1987; still in production.

Perf.: $820   **Exc.:** $675   **VGood:** $540

UBERTI MODEL 1873 SPORTING CARBINE

Same specs as Model 1873 Sporting except 19-inch round barrel; 38-1/4-inch overall length; weighs 7-1/4 lbs.; available with nickel plating. Introduced 1987; still in production.

Perf.: $790   **Exc.:** $625   **VGood:** $500

Nickel finish

Perf.: $820   **Exc.:** $645   **VGood:** $525

UBERTI MODEL 1873 SPORTING CARBINE, TRAPPER MODEL

Same specs as Model 1873 Sporting except 357 Mag., 44-40, 45 Colt; 16-inch barrel. Discontinued 1990.

Perf.: $800   **Exc.:** $630   **VGood:** $500

UBERTI MODEL 1875 ARMY TARGET

Revolving carbine; 357 Mag., 44-40, 45 Colt; 6-shot cylinder; 18-inch barrel; 37-inch overall length; weighs 4-1/2 lbs.; carbine version of 1875 single-

action revolver; elevation-adjustable rear sight, ramp front; unchecked walnut stock; polished brass buttplate, triggerguard; case-hardened frame; blued or nickel-plated cylinder, barrel. Made in Italy. Introduced 1987; discontinued 1989.

Blued finish

Perf.: $400   **Exc.:** $325   **VGood:** $260

Nickel finish

Perf.: $430   **Exc.:** $350   **VGood:** $285

UBERTI ROLLING BLOCK BABY CARBINE

Single shot; 22 LR, 22 WMR, 22 Hornet, 357 Mag.; 22-inch barrel; 35-1/2-inch overall length; weighs 4-13/16 lbs.; copy of Remington New Model No. 4 carbine; brass buttplate, triggerguard; blued barrel; color case-hardened frame. Introduced 1986, still available.

Perf.: $375   **Exc.:** $300   **VGood:** $270

Rifle version, 26-inch bbl.

Perf.: $500   **Exc.:** $400   **VGood:** $375

ULTIMATE ACCURACY MODEL 5100A1 LONG-RANGE RIFLE

Bolt action; 50 BMG; 5-shot magazine; 29-inch fully fluted, free-floating barrel; 51-1/2-inch overall length; weighs 36 lbs.; no sights; optional Leupold Ultra M1-16x scope; composition buttstock with comb adjustment for drop; adjustable trigger; breaks down for transport, storage. Made in U.S. by Ultimate Accuracy. Introduced 1994; no longer in production.

Perf.: $2995   **Exc.:** $2495   **VGood:** $1995

ULTIMATE ACCURACY MODEL 5100A1 IMPROVED MODEL

Same specs as Model 5100A1 except receiver is drilled and tapped for scope mount; manual safety; one-piece muzzle brake. Made in U.S. by Ultimate Accuracy. No longer in production.

Perf.: $2995   **Exc.:** $2495   **VGood:** $1995

Ultra Light Arms Model 20

Ultra Light Arms Model 20 Rimfire

Ultra Light Arms Model 28

Unique Model T.66 Match

Universal Model 1000

ULTRA-HI MODEL 2200
Bolt action; single shot; 22 Short, 22 Long, 22 LR; 23-inch barrel; weighs 5 lbs.; blade front sight, open rear; pistol-grip Monte Carlo hardwood stock. Made in Japan. Introduced 1977; no longer in production.
Perf.: $60   **Exc.:** $50   **VGood:** $40

ULTRA LIGHT ARMS MODEL 20
Bolt action (short action); 17 Rem., 222, 223, 22 Hornet, 22-250, 243, 6mm Rem., 250 Savage, 257 Roberts, 260 Rem., 7x57, 7x57 Ackley, 7mm-08, 284, 300 Savage, 308, 358 Win.; other calibers on request; 22-inch barrel; 41-1/2-inch overall length; weighs only 4-1/2 lbs.; no sights; marketed with scope mount; Kevlar/graphite stock in green, black brown or camo; two-position, three-function safety; Timney trigger; bright or matte finish; marketed in hard case; left- or right-hand action. Introduced 1986. Company name changed to New Ultra Light Arms LLC in 2002.
Perf.: $2400   **Exc.:** $1950   **VGood:** $1250
Left-hand model
Perf.: $2550   **Exc.:** $2000   **VGood:** $1300

ULTRA LIGHT ARMS MODEL 20 RIMFIRE
Bolt action; 22 LR; single shot or 5-shot repeater with removable magazine; 22-inch Douglas Premium, #1 contour barrel; 41-1/2-inch overall length; weighs 5-1/4 lbs.; no sights; drilled, tapped for scope mount; scope mounts; composite Kevlar, graphite reinforced stock with Du Pont Imron paint; 13-1/2-inch length of pull. Made in U.S. by New Ultra Light Arms. Introduced 1993.
Perf.: $800   **Exc.:** $670   **VGood:** $600

ULTRA LIGHT ARMS MODEL 24
Bolt action (long action); 25-06, 270, 280, 30-06, 7mm Express; 22-inch barrel; weighs 5-1/4 lbs.; no sights; marketed with scope mount; Kevlar/graphite stock; two-position, three-function safety; Timney trigger; bright or matte finish; left- or right-hand action. Introduced 1986, still in production.
Perf.: $2600   **Exc.:** $1900   **VGood:** $1600

Left-hand model
Perf.: $2650   **Exc.:** $1950   **VGood:** $1650

ULTRA LIGHT ARMS MODEL 28
Bolt action (magnum action); 264, 7mm Rem. Mag., 300 Win. Mag., 338 Win. Mag.; 24-inch Douglas Premium No. 2 contour barrel; 45-inch overall length; weighs 5-1/2 lbs.; Timney adjustable trigger; two-position, three-function safety; benchrest-quality action; matte or gloss metal and stock finish; KDF or ULA recoil arrestor built in. Right- or left-hand action. Made in U.S. by New Ultra Light Arms. Introduced 1993.
Perf.: $2900   **Exc.:** $2200   **VGood:** $1700
Left-hand model
Perf.: $2925   **Exc.:** $2225   **VGood:** $1725

ULTRA LIGHT ARMS MODEL 40 MAGNUM
Bolt action; 300 Wea. Mag., 416 Rigby; 24-inch or 26-inch Douglas Premium No. 2 contour barrel; 45-inch overall length; weighs 5-1/2 lbs.; Timney adjustable trigger; two-position, three-function safety; benchrest-quality action; matte or gloss metal and stock finish; KDF or ULA recoil arrestor built in; right- or left-hand action. Made in U.S. by New Ultra Light Arms. Introduced 1993.
Perf.: $2950   **Exc.:** $2300   **VGood:** $1800
Left-hand model
Perf.: $3000   **Exc.:** $2350   **VGood:** $1850

UNIQUE MODEL G.21
Semi-automatic; 22 LR; 5-, 10-shot magazine; 18-inch barrel; 33-1/2-inch overall length; weighs 6 lbs.; adjustable rear peep sight; French walnut stock; magazine and manual safeties. Was imported by Nygord Precision Products; no longer imported.
Perf.: $300   **Exc.:** $280   **VGood:** $250

UNIQUE MODEL T AUDAX
Bolt action; 22 LR, 22 Short; 5-shot (22 Short), 10-shot magazine; 21-1/2-inch barrel; 39-1/4-inch overall length; weighs 6-1/2 lbs.; adjustable rear sight; dovetailed grooves on receiver for scope or

target sight; lateral safety; French walnut stock. Was imported by Nygord Precision Products; no longer imported.
Perf.: $545   **Exc.:** $500   **VGood:** $400

UNIQUE MODEL T DIOPTRA
Bolt action; 22 LR, 22 WMR; 5-shot (22 WMR), 10-shot (22 LR) magazine; 23-1/2-inch barrel; 41-inch overall length; weighs 6-1/2 lbs.; adjustable rear sight; dovetailed grooves on receiver for scope or target sight; lateral safety; French Monte Carlo walnut stock. Was imported by Nygord Precision Products; no longer imported.
Perf.: $750   **Exc.:** $620   **VGood:** $510

UNIQUE MODEL T/SM
Bolt action; 22 LR, 22 WMR; 5-shot (22 WMR), 10-shot (22 LR) magazine; 20-1/2-inch barrel; 38-1/2-inch overall length; weighs 6-1/2 lbs.; adjustable rear sight; adjustable trigger; dovetailed grooves on receiver for scope or target sight; French Monte Carlo walnut stock; left-handed stock available. Was imported by Nygord Precision Products; no longer imported.
Perf.: $770   **Exc.:** $630   **VGood:** $525

UNIQUE MODEL T/SM BIATHALON JUNIOR
Same specs as Model T/SM except metallic grooves on stock for sling and harness mounting. Was imported by Nygord Precision Products; no longer imported.
Perf.: $725   **Exc.:** $595   **VGood:** $495

UNIQUE MODEL T/SM MATCH JUNIOR
Same specs as Model T/SM except adjustable buttplate; metallic grooves on stock for sling and harness mounting. Was imported by Nygord Precision Products; no longer imported.
Perf.: $725   **Exc.:** $595   **VGood:** $495

UNIQUE MODEL T.66 MATCH
Bolt action; single shot; 22 LR; 25-1/2-inch barrel; 44-1/8-inch overall length; weighs 10 7/8 lbs.; interchangeable globe front sight, Micro-Match rear; French walnut stock; stippled forend, pistol-grip; left-hand model available; meets NRA, UIT standards. Imported from France. Introduced 1980; no longer in production.
Perf.: $450   **Exc.:** $410   **VGood:** $360

UNIQUE MODEL T.791 BIATHLON
Bolt action; 22 LR; 5-shot magazine; 22-1/2-inch barrel; 40-1/4-inch overall length; weighs 10 lbs.; interchangeable globe front sight, MIcro-Match rear; French walnut stock; stippled forend, pistol grip; left-hand model available; meets NRA, UIT standards. Imported from France. Introduced 1980; no longer in production.
Perf.: $750   **Exc.:** $695   **VGood:** $475

UNIQUE MODEL X51 BIS
Semi-automatic; 22 LR; 5-, 10-shot magazine; 23-1/2-inch barrel; 40-1/2-inch overall length; weighs 6 lbs.; adjustable rear sight; French walnut stock; magazine and manual safeties. Was imported by Nygord Precision Products; no longer imported.
Perf.: $350   **Exc.:** $290   **VGood:** $240

UNIVERSAL MODEL 1000
Semi-automatic; 30 Carbine; 5-shot magazine; 18-inch barrel; 35-1/4-inch overall length; weighs 6 lbs.; military iron sights; receiver tapped for scope mount; birchwood stock; copy of G.I. version of M1 Carbine with bayonet lug. Introduced about 1965. No longer in production.
Exc.: $475   **VGood:** $450   **Good:** $275

UNIVERSAL MODEL 1002
Same specs as Model 1003 except military type, but with metal handguard.
Exc.: $325   **VGood:** $295   **Good:** $200

UNIVERSAL MODEL 1003
Semi-automatic; 30 carbine; 5-shot magazine; 18-inch barrel (other lengths have been reported); 35-1/2-inch overall length; weighs 5-1/2 lbs.; military iron sights; receiver tapped for scope mount; birchwood stock; similar to 30 M1 Carbine without bayonet lug. No longer in production.

   Exc.: $475   **VGood:** $450   **Good:** $275

UNIVERSAL MODEL 1005 DELUXE
Same specs as Model 1003 except polished super-mirror blue finish; Monte Carlo walnut stock; weighs 6-1/2 lbs. No longer in production.

   Exc.: $500   **VGood:** $475   **Good:** $450

UNIVERSAL MODEL 1010
Same specs as Model 1003 except nickel-plated.

   Exc.: $500   **VGood:** $475   **Good:** $450

UNIVERSAL MODEL 1015
Same specs as Model 1003 except gold-plated finish.

   Exc.: $575   **VGood:** $495   **Good:** $295

UNIVERSAL MODEL 1020
Same specs as Model 1003 except black DuPont teflon coated.

   Exc.: $500   **VGood:** $475   **Good:** $450

UNIVERSAL MODEL 1025
Same specs as Model 1003 except camouflage olive DuPont teflon coated.

   Exc.: $500   **VGood:** $475   **Good:** $450

UNIVERSAL MODEL 1256 FERRET
Semi-automatic; 256 Win. Mag.; 5-shot magazine; 18-inch barrel; no sights; 4x Universal scope; birchwood stock; M1 Carbine action; satin blue finish. No longer in production.

   Exc.: $500   **VGood:** $475   **Good:** $450

VALMET HUNTER MODEL
Semi-automatic; 223, 243, 308; 5-, 9-, 20-shot magazine; 20-1/2-inch barrel; 42-inch overall length; weighs 8 lbs.; open rear sight, blade front; American walnut stock, butt, forend; checkered palm swell pistol grip, forend; Kalashnikov-type action. Made in Finland. Introduced 1986; discontinued 1989.

   Perf.: $1400   **Exc.:** $1195   **VGood:** $795

VALMET MODEL 412 DOUBLE RIFLE
Double rifle; 243, 308, 30-06, 375 Win, 9.3x74R; 24-inch barrels; weighs 8-5/8 lbs.; ramp front sight, adjustable open rear; barrel selector mounted on trigger; hand-checkered Monte Carlo stock of American walnut; recoil pad. Importation began 1980; no longer imported from Finland by Valmet.

   Perf.: $1300   **Exc.:** $1200   **VGood:** $1000

VALMET MODEL 412S COMBO GUN
Combination gun; 12 ga. over 222, 223, 243, 308, 30-06; 24-inch barrel (Imp. & Mod.); weighs 7-5/8 lbs.; blade front, flip-up-type open rear; hand-checkered American walnut stock, forend; recoil pad. Importation began 1980; no longer imported from Finland by Valmet.

   Perf.: $1150   **Exc.:** $910   **VGood:** $705

VARNER FAVORITE HUNTER
Single shot; 22 LR; 21-1/2-inch half-round/half-octagon barrel; weighs 5 lbs.; takedown; blade front sight, open step-adjustable rear and peep; checkered American walnut stock; recreation of Stevens Favorite rifle with takedown barrel. Introduced 1988; discontinued 1990.

   Perf.: $375   **Exc.:** $300   **VGood:** $230

VARNER FAVORITE SCHEUTZEN
Same specs as Favorite Hunter except 24-inch half-round/half-octagon target-grade barrel; ladder-type tang-mounted peep sight, globe-type front with six inserts; checkered AAA fancy walnut pistol-grip perch-belly stock, extended forend; scroll-engraved color case-hardened frame, lever; recreation of

Valmet Hunter Model

Valmet 412 Double Rifle

Varner Favorite Hunter

Vektor Model 98

Vickers Empire Model

Vickers Jubilee Model

Voere Model 1007

the Stevens Ladies Favorite Scheutzen, originally produced 1910 to 1916. Reintroduced 1989; discontinued 1990.

   Perf.: $995   **Exc.:** $825   **VGood:** $685

VEKTOR H5 SLIDE-ACTION RIFLE
Slide action; 223 Rem., 5-shot magazine; 18-inch, 22-inch barrel; 42-1/2-inch overall length (22-inch barrel); weighs 9 lbs., 15 oz.; walnut thumbhole stock; comes with 1-inch 4x32 scope with low-light reticle. AR-15 type rotating bolt mechanism. Matte black finish. Introduced 1999. Imported from South Africa by Vektor USA; no longer imported.

   Perf.: $800   **Exc.:** $700   **VGood:** $560

VEKTOR BUSHVELD BOLT-ACTION RIFLE
Bolt action; 243, 308, 7x57, 7x64 Brenneke, 270 Win., 30-06, 300 Win. Mag., 300 H&H, 9.3x62. 22- to 26-inch barrel; Turkish walnut stock with wrap-around hand checkering; blade on ramp front, fixed standing leaf rear sights. Controlled-round feed; Mauser-type extractor; no cut-away through the bolt locking lug; M70-type three-position safety; Timney-type adjustable trigger. Introduced 1999. Imported from South Africa by Vektor USA; no longer imported.

   Perf.: $1400   **Exc.:** $1100   **VGood:** $900

VEKTOR MODEL 98 BOLT-ACTION RIFLE
Bolt action; 243, 308, 7x57, 7x64 Brenneke, 270 Win., 30-06, 300 Win. Mag., 300 H&H, 375 H&H, 9.3x62; 22- to 26-inch barrel; Turkish walnut stock with hand-checkered grip and forend; no sights furnished; drilled and tapped for scope mounting. Bolt has guide rib; non- rotating, long extractor enhances positive feeding; polished blue finish. Updated Mauser 98 action. Introduced 1999. Imported from South Africa by Vektor USA; no longer imported.

   Perf.: $980   **Exc.:** $840   **VGood:** $670

VICKERS EMPIRE MODEL
Single shot; 22 LR; 27-inch, 30-inch barrel; Martini-type action; perfection rear peep sight, Parker-Hale No. 2 front; straight-grip walnut stock. Manufactured prior to WWII.

   Exc.: $475   **VGood:** $350   **Good:** $275

VICKERS JUBILEE MODEL
Single-shot; 22 LR; 28-inch heavy barrel; Martini-type action; Perfection rear peep sight, Parker-Hale No. 2 front; single-piece European walnut target stock; full pistol grip; forearm. Manufactured prior to World War II.

   Exc.: $470   **VGood:** $380   **Good:** $310

Voere Model 2107

Voere Model 2115

Voere Model 2155

Voere Titan

Voere Titan Menor

Voere VEC-91 Lightning

VOERE MODEL 2155

Bolt action; 270, 243, 30-06 (standard), 308, 22-250, 7x64, 5.6x57, 6.5x55, 8x57 JRS, 7mm Rem. Mag., 300 Win. Mag., 8x68S, 9.3x62, 9.3x64, 6.5x68; 5-shot non-detachable box magazine; 22-inch (standard), 24-inch barrel; Mauser-type action; no sights; drilled, tapped for scope mount; European walnut stock; checkered pistol grip, forend; single- or double-set trigger. Made in Austria. Introduced 1984; importation dropped 1995.

Perf.: $800   **Exc.:** $650   **VGood:** $530

VOERE MODEL 2165

Bolt action; 22-250, 243, 270, 7x57, 7x64, 308, 30-06 (standard), 7mm Rem. Mag., 300 Win. Mag., 9.3x64 (magnum); 5-shot magazine (standard calibers), 3-shot (magnums); 22-inch barrel (standard calibers), 24-inch (magnums); 44-1/2-inch overall length (22-inch barrel); weighs 7 to 7-1/2 lbs.; ramp front sight, open adjustable rear; European walnut stock with Bavarian cheekpiece, schnabel forend tip, rosewood grip cap; built on Mauser 98-type action; tang safety; detachable box magazine; comes with extra magazine. No longer imported.

Perf.: $850   **Exc.:** $690   **VGood:** $550

VOERE MODEL 2185

Semi-automatic; 7x64, 308, 30-06; 2-shot detachable magazine; 20-inch barrel; 43-1/2-inch overall length; weighs 7-3/4 lbs.; blade on ramp front sight, open adjustable rear; receiver drilled, tapped for scope mounts; European walnut stock with checkered grip and forend; ventilated rubber recoil pad; oil finish; gas-operated action with three forward locking lugs; hammer-forged free-floating barrel; two-stage trigger; cocking indicator inside trigger guard. Importation dropped 1994.

Perf.: $1700   **Exc.:** $1350   **VGood:** $900

With Mannlicher-style full stock
Perf.: $1750   **Exc.:** $1400   **VGood:** $975

VOERE MODEL 2185 MATCH

Same specs as Model 2185 except 5-shot magazine; hooded post front sight, aperture rear; laminated match-type stock with glass bedding; adjustable cheekpiece and buttplate. Introduced 1992; discontinued 1994.

Perf.: $2900   **Exc.:** $2300   **VGood:** $1600

VOERE TITAN

Bolt action; 243, 25-06, 270, 7x57, 308, 30-06, 257 Weatherby, 270 Weatherby, 7mm Rem. Mag., 300 Win. Mag., 300 Weatherby, 308 Norma Mag., 375 H&H; 3-, 4-shot magazine, depending on caliber; 24-inch, 26-inch barrel; 44-1/2-inch overall length (24-inch barrel); weighs 8 lbs.; no sights; drilled, tapped for scope mounts; hand-checkered, oil-finished European walnut Monte Carlo stock; recoil pad; swivel studs; three-lug, front-locking action. Made in Austria. Introduced 1986; discontinued 1988.

Perf.: $800   **Exc.:** $675   **VGood:** $535

VOERE TITAN MENOR

Bolt action; 222 Rem., 223 Rem.; 3-shot magazine; 23-1/2-inch barrel; 42-inch overall length; weighs 6 lbs.; no sights; drilled, tapped for scope mounts; hand-checkered, oil-finished European walnut Monte Carlo stock; rosewood grip cap, forend tip. Made in Austria. Introduced 1986; discontinued 1988.

Perf.: $600   **Exc.:** $500   **VGood:** $400

VOERE VEC-91 LIGHTNING

Bolt action, electronic ignition; 5.56 UCC (223-cal.), 6mm UCC caseless ammunition; 5-shot magazine; 20-inch barrel; 39-inch overall length; weighs 6 lbs.; blade on ramp front sight, open adjustable rear; drilled, tapped for scope mounts; European walnut stock with cheekpiece; checkered grip and schnabel forend; top tang safety; fires caseless ammunition via electric ignition; two batteries housed in pistol grip last about 5000 shots; trigger adjustable from 5 oz. to 7 lbs.; twin forward locking lugs. Imported from Austria. Introduced 1991. Without ammunition, this gun is a paperweight – buyer beware!

Perf.: $850   **Exc.:** $700   **VGood:** $575

VOERE MODEL 1007

Bolt action; 22 LR; 18-inch barrel; weighs 5-1/2 lbs.; open adjustable rear sight, hooded front; military-type oil-finished beech stock; single-stage trigger; sling swivels; convertible to single-shot; Biathlon model. Made in Austria. Introduced 1984; discontinued 1991.

Perf.: $230   **Exc.:** $180   **VGood:** $150

VOERE MODEL 1013

Bolt action; 22 WMR; 5-, 8-shot magazine; 18-inch barrel; weighs 5-1/2 lbs.; open adjustable rear sight, hooded front; military-type oil-finished stock; double-set trigger; sling swivels. Made in Austria. Introduced 1984; discontinued 1991.

Perf.: $280   **Exc.:** $230   **VGood:** $190

VOERE MODEL 2107

Bolt action; 22 LR; 5-, 8-shot magazine; 19-1/2-inch barrel; 41-inch overall length; weighs 6 lbs.; fully adjustable open rear sight, hooded front; European hardwood Monte Carlo stock; swivel studs; buttpad. Made in Germany. Introduced 1986; discontinued 1988.

Perf.: $325   **Exc.:** $290   **VGood:** $230

VOERE MODEL 2107 DELUXE

Same specs as Model 2107 except checkered stock; raised cheekpiece. Introduced 1986; discontinued 1988.

Perf.: $350   **Exc.:** $280   **VGood:** $230

VOERE MODEL 2114S

Semi-automatic; 22 LR; 8-, 15-shot clip magazine; 18-inch barrel; 37-2/3-inch overall length; weighs 5-3/4 lbs.; leaf rear sight, hooded ramp front; walnut-finished beechwood stock, pistol grip, forend; single-stage trigger; wing-type safety. Made in Austria. Introduced 1984; no longer in production.

Perf.: $265   **Exc.:** $210   **VGood:** $170

VOERE MODEL 2115

Semi-automatic; 22 LR; 8-, 10-, 15-shot clip magazine; 18-inch barrel; 37-3/4-inch overall length; weighs 5-3/4 lbs.; leaf rear sight, hooded ramp front; walnut-finished beechwood stock; checkered pistol grip, forend; cheekpiece; single-stage trigger wing type safety. Made in Austria. Introduced 1984; discontinued 1995.

Perf.: $300   **Exc.:** $260   **VGood:** $230

VOERE MODEL 2150

Bolt action; 22-250, 243, 270, 7x57, 7x64, 308, 30-06 (standard), 7mm Rem. Mag., 300 Win. Mag., 9.3x64, 338 Win. Mag. (375 H&H, 458 Win. Mag. on special order); 22-inch barrel, 24-inch (magnums); weighs about 8 lbs.; ramp front sight, adjustable open rear; walnut stock with hand-rubbed oil finish, hand-checkered grip and forend; barrel-mounted front sling swivel; K-98 Mauser action with hinged floorplate; Was imported from Austria; importation dropped 1995.

Perf.: $800   **Exc.:** $675   **VGood:** $520

VOERE VEC-91BR
Same specs as VEC-91 except single shot; heavy 20-inch barrel; synthetic benchrest stock. Imported from Austria. Introduced 1995. Deduct 50 percent if no ammunition.
Perf.: $1700 **Exc.:** $1400 **VGood:** $900

VOERE VEC-91HB VARMINT SPECIAL
Same specs as VEC-91 except 22-inch heavy sporter barrel; black synthetic or laminated wood stock. Imported from Austria. Introduced 1995. Deduct 50 percent if no ammunition.
Perf.: $1350 **Exc.:** $1000 **VGood:** $720

VOERE VEC-91SS
Same specs as VEC-91 except no sights; synthetic stock with straight comb, matte-finished metal. Imported from Austria. Introduced 1995. Deduct 50 percent if no ammunition.
Perf.: $1200 **Exc.:** $930 **VGood:** $700

WALTHER MODEL 1
Semi-automatic; 22 LR; 5-, 9-shot detachable box magazine; 20-inch barrel; tangent curve rear sight, ramp front; hand-checkered European walnut sporting stock; pistol grip; grooved forend; sling swivels; with bolt-action feature makes it possible to fire as semi-automatic, single-shot or as bolt-operated repeater. Manufactured prior to WWII.
Exc.: $600 **VGood:** $525 **Good:** $350

WALTHER MODEL 2
Semi-automatic; 22 LR; 5-, 9-shot detachable box magazine; 24-1/2-inch barrel; tangent curve rear sight, ramp front; hand-checkered European walnut sporting stock; pistol grip; grooved forend; sling swivels; bolt-action feature makes it possible to fire as semi-automatic, single-shot or as bolt-operated repeater. Manufactured prior to WWII.
Exc.: $590 **VGood:** $490 **Good:** $365

WALTHER MODEL 2 LIGHTWEIGHT
Same specs as Model 2 except 20-inch barrel; lightweight stock.
Exc.: $590 **VGood:** $490 **Good:** $365

WALTHER MODEL G22
Semi-automatic, bullpup design, 22 LR; polymer frame and stock; 10-shot detachable box magazine, stock holds spare magazine; 20-inch barrel; 29-1/2-inch overall length; weighs 5.9 pounds; adjustable sights, rails will mount optical or laser sights, combination packages offered; introduced 2004, still available from Walther USA.
Perf.: $390 **Exc.:** $300 **VGood:** $275

WALTHER MODEL GX-1 MATCH
Bolt action; single shot; 22 LR; 25-1/2-inch heavy barrel; micrometer aperture rear sight, globe front; European walnut thumbhole stock; adjustable cheekpiece, buttplate; removable butthook; accessory rail; hand stop; palm rest; counterweight; sling swivels; free rifle design. No longer in production.
Perf.: $1875 **Exc.:** $1375 **VGood:** $1100

WALTHER MODEL KK/MS METALLIC SILHOUETTE
Bolt action; single shot; 22 LR; 25-1/2-inch barrel; 44-3/4-inch overall length; weighs 8-3/4 lbs.; no sights; receiver grooved for scope mounts; thumbhole European walnut stock; stippled grip, forend; adjustable trigger; oversize bolt knob; rubber buttpad. Made in Germany. Introduced 1989; discontinued 1991.
Exc.: $1230 **VGood:** $1000 **Good:** $800

WALTHER MODEL KKJ
Bolt action; 22 LR; 5-shot box magazine; 22-1/2-inch medium-heavy target barrel; open rear sight, ramp front; checkered European walnut pistol-grip stock forearm; high tapered comb; sling swivels. Introduced in 1957; no longer imported.
Exc.: $700 **VGood:** $575 **Good:** $420

Voere VEC-91HB Varmint Special

Voere VEC-91SS

Walther Model 2

Walther G22

Walther Model KKJ

Walther Model KKM Match

Walther Model Prone 400

WALTHER MODEL KKJ-HO
Same specs as Model KKJ except chambered for 22 Hornet.
Exc.: $800 **VGood:** $680 **Good:** $550

WALTHER MODEL KKJ-MA
Same specs as Model KKJ except 22 WMR.
Exc.: $760 **VGood:** $600 **Good:** $420

WALTHER MODEL KKM MATCH
Bolt action; single shot; 22 LR; 26-inch barrel; micrometer rear sight, Olympic front with post, aperture inserts; European walnut stock with adjustable hook buttplate, hand shelf, ball-type offset yoke palm rest; fully-adjustable match trigger. Imported from Germany. Introduced 1957; no longer in production.
Exc.: $1400 **VGood:** $1100 **Good:** $800

WALTHER MODEL KKM-S
Same specs as Model KKM except adjustable cheekpiece.
Exc.: $1500 **VGood:** $1175 **Good:** $900

WALTHER MODEL KKW
Bolt action; single shot; 22 LR; tangent curve rear sight, ramp front; walnut military-style stock. Manufactured prior to WWII.
Exc.: $695 **VGood:** $575 **Good:** $390

WALTHER MODEL PRONE 400
Bolt action; single shot; 22 LR; 25-1/2-inch barrel; micrometer rear sight, interchangeable post or aperture front; European walnut stock with adjustable length, drop; cheekpiece; forearm guide rail for sling or palm rest; fully-adjustable trigger; especially designed for prone shooting. Introduced 1972; no longer in production.
Exc.: $750 **VGood:** $630 **Good:** $510

Walther Model SSV

Walther MovingTarget Model

Walther Running Boar Model 500

Walther U.I.T. BV Universal

Walther U.I.T. Match Model

Weatherby Deluxe Magnum

Weatherby Mark V Accumark

globe-type front sight, fully-adjustable aperture rear; European walnut stock, adjustable for length, drop; forend rail; meets NRA, UIT requirements; fully-adjustable trigger. Made in Germany. Introduced 1988; discontinued 1990.

Exc.: $1450 **VGood:** $1300 **Good:** $1050

WALTHER U.I.T. MATCH MODEL
Same specs as U.I.T. BV except new tapered forend profile; scope mount bases; fully stippled forend. Imported from Germany by Interarms. Introduced 1966; no longer imported.

Exc.: $1300 **VGood:** $1000 **Good:** $775

WALTHER U.I.T.-E MATCH MODEL
Same specs as U.I.T. BV except state-of-the-art electronic trigger. Introduced 1984; no longer imported.

Exc.: $1350 **VGood:** $1050 **Good:** $875

WEATHERBY CLASSICMARK I
Bolt action; 240 through 460 Wea. Mag.; 22-inch, 26-inch barrel; straight comb stock of hand-selected American Claro walnut with oil finish; 18 lpi panel point checkering; 1-inch Presentation recoil pad; all metal satin finished; Mark V action. Available in right- or left-hand versions. Imported from Japan by Weatherby. Introduced 1992; discontinued 1993.

Perf.: $1050 **Exc.:** $825 **VGood:** $700

Calibers 300, 340 Wea. Mag., 378 Wea. Mag., 416 Wea. Mag., 460 Wea. Mag.

Perf.: $1125 **Exc.:** $895 **VGood:** $695

WEATHERBY CLASSICMARK II
Same as the Classicmark I except stock of deluxe hand-selected American walnut with shadow-line cheekpiece, rounded forend; 22 lpi wrap-around point checkering, oil finish; steel grip cap; Old English recoil pad; satin-finished metal; uses Mark V action. Available in right-hand version only. Imported from Japan by Weatherby. Made only in 1992.

Perf.: $1400 **Exc.:** $1175 **VGood:** $985

Calibers 300, 340 Wea. Mag., 378 Wea. Mag.

Perf.: $1500 **Exc.:** $1275 **VGood:** $1075

Calibers 416 Wea. Mag., 460 Wea. Mag.

Perf.: $1800 **Exc.:** $1475 **VGood:** $1275

WEATHERBY CLASSICMARK II SAFARI CLASSIC
Same specs as Classicmark II except 375 H&H; 24-inch barrel; engraved floorplate; ramp front sight, quarter-rib express rear; barrel band front sling swivel. Made in 1992 only.

Perf.: $2200 **Exc.:** $1850 **VGood:** $1450

WEATHERBY DELUXE (EARLY)
Bolt action; 270, 30-06; 24-inch barrel; no sights; Monte Carlo stock with cheekpiece; hand-checkered pistol-grip, forearm; black grip cap, forearm tip; quick-detachable sling swivels; Mauser action built to Weatherby specs by FN; some Springfield actions were used. Introduced 1948; discontinued 1955.

Exc.: $1695 **VGood:** $1495 **Good:** $975

WEATHERBY DELUXE MAGNUM (EARLY)
Same specs as Deluxe except 220 Rocket, 257 Weatherby Mag., 7mm Weatherby Mag., 300 Weatherby Mag., 375 Weatherby Mag., 378 Weatherby Mag.; 24-inch, 26-inch barrel. Introduced 1948; discontinued 1955.

Exc.: $1895 **VGood:** $1695 **Good:** $1175

WEATHERBY MARK V ACCUMARK RIFLE
Bolt action; 223, 22-250, 243, 25-06, 240 Wea Mag, 257, 270, 7mm, 300, 340 Wea. Mags., 338-378 Wea. Mag., 30-378 Wea. Mag., 7mm STW, 7mm Rem. Mag., 300 Win. Mag.; 26-inch, 28-inch barrel; weighs 8-1/2 lbs.; 46-5/8-inch overall length; Bell & Carlson stock with full length aluminum bedding block. Drilled and tapped for scope mounting. Uses Mark V action with heavy-contour fluted stainless barrel with black oxidized flutes, muzzle diameter of .705-inch. Introduced 1996; still offered. Made in U.S.A. From Weatherby.

Perf.: $1200 **Exc.:** $1000 **VGood:** $850

WALTHER MODEL SSV VARMINT RIFLE
Bolt action; single shot; 22 LR, 22 Hornet; 25-1/2-inch barrel; no sights; European walnut Monte Carlo stock; high cheekpiece; full pistol grip, forend. No longer in production.

Exc.: $600 **VGood:** $520 **Good:** $420

22 Hornet model

Exc.: $700 **VGood:** $620 **Good:** $510

WALTHER MODEL V
Bolt action; single shot; 22 LR; 26-inch barrel; open rear sight, ramp front; uncheckered European walnut pistol-grip sporting stock, grooved forend; sling swivels. Manufactured prior to World War II.

Exc.: $400 **VGood:** $375 **Good:** $300

WALTHER MODEL V MEISTERBUSCHE
Same specs as Model V except micrometer open rear sight; checkered pistol grip.

Exc.: $480 **VGood:** $440 **Good:** $340

WALTHER MOVING TARGET MODEL
Bolt action; single shot; 22 LR; 23-1/2-inch barrel; micrometer rear sight, globe front; receiver grooved for dovetail scope mounts; European walnut

thumbhole stock; stippled forearm, pistol grip; adjustable cheekpiece, buttplate; especially designed for running boar competition. Imported from Germany. Introduced 1972; no longer in production.

Exc.: $1295 **VGood:** $1095 **Good:** $850

WALTHER OLYMPIC MODEL
Bolt action; single shot; 22 LR; 26-inch heavy barrel; extension micrometer rear sight, interchangeable front; hand-checkered pistol-grip target stock of European walnut; full rubber-covered beavertail forend; thumbhole; palm rest; adjustable buttplate; sling swivels. Manufactured in Germany prior to WWII.

Exc.: $950 **VGood:** $850 **Good:** $695

WALTHER RUNNING BOAR MODEL 500
Bolt action; single shot; 22 LR; 23-1/2-inch barrel; no sights; receiver grooved for dovetail scope mounts; European walnut thumbhole stock; stippled pistol grip; forend; adjustable cheekpiece, buttplate; left-hand stock available. Introduced 1975; discontinued 1990.

Exc.: $1200 **VGood:** $1000 **Good:** $800

WALTHER U.I.T. BV UNIVERSAL
Bolt action; single shot; 22 LR; 25-1/2-inch barrel; 44-3/4-inch overall length; weighs about 10 lbs.;

WEATHERBY MARK V ACCUMARK ULTRA LIGHTWEIGHT RIFLES

Similar to the Mark V Accumark except weighs 5-3/4 lbs.; 24-inch, 26-inch fluted barrel with recessed target crown; hand-laminated stock with CNC-machined aluminum bedding plate and faint gray "spider web" finish. Available in 257, 270, 7mm, 300 Wea. Mags., (26-inch); 243, 240 Wea. Mag., 25-06, 270 Win., 280 Rem., 7mm-08, 7mm Rem. Mag., 30-06, 338-06 A-Square, 308, 300 Win. Mag. (24-inch). Introduced 1998. Made in U.S.A. by Weatherby.

Perf.: $1100   **Exc.:** 900   **VGood:** $800

WEATHERBY MARK V SVM SUPER VARMINT MASTER RIFLE

Similar to the Mark V Accumark except has 26-inch fluted Krieger barrel, spiderweb-pattern tan laminated synthetic stock; fully adjustable trigger. Chambered for 223, 22-250, 220 Swift, 243; 220 Swift made as a single-shot rifle. Made in U.S.A. by Weatherby, introduced in 2000, still in production.

Perf.: $1380   **Exc.:** $1100   **VGood:** $900

WEATHERBY MARK V FIBERMARK RIFLES

Similar to other Mark V models except has black Kevlar and fiberglass composite stock and bead-blast blue or stainless finish. Chambered for 19 standard and magnum calibers. Introduced 1983; reintroduced 2001; still offered. Made in U.S.A. by Weatherby.

Perf.: $980   **Exc.:** $810   **VGood:** $620

WEATHERBY MARK V FIBERMARK ALASKAN

Same specs as Fibermark except 270 Weatherby Mag., 7mm Weatherby Mag., 300 Weatherby Mag., 340 Weatherby Mag.; all metal parts plated with electroless nickel for corrosion protection. Introduced 1991; discontinued 1994.

Perf.: $1150   **Exc.:** $995   **VGood:** $895

WEATHERBY MARK V CROWN CUSTOM MODEL

Bolt action; 240 Weatherby Mag., 257 Weatherby Mag., 7mm Weatherby Mag., 300 Weatherby Mag., 30-06, 340 Weatherby Mag.; 3-, 5-shot magazine; 24-inch, 26-inch barrel; optional sights; super-fancy walnut stock with carving, inlays; utilizes hand-honed, engraved Mark V barreled action; fully checkered bolt knob; engraved floorplate; damascened bolt, follower; gold monogramed name or initials; right-hand only. Introduced 1989; still offered by Weatherby Custom Shop.

Perf.: $5695   **Exc.:** $4995   **VGood:** $2900

WEATHERBY MARK V CUSTOM MODEL

Bolt action; 22-250, 30-06, 224 Weatherby Varmintmaster (standard action), 240, 257, 270, 7mm, 300, 340, 378, 460 (magnum action); 2-, 5-shot box magazine, depending on caliber; 24-inch, 26-inch barrel; available in right- or left-hand model; scope mounts; super deluxe stock with buttstock inlay, two forend inlays; gold monogram inlay; engraved with name or initials; stock carving with stained background; fully checkered bolt knob; damascened bolt and follower; hand-honed action; engraved floorplate.

Perf.: $2995   **Exc.:** $2485   **VGood:** $1775

WEATHERBY MARK V DANGEROUS GAME RIFLE

Bolt action; 375 H&H, 375 Wea. Mag., 378 Wea. Mag., 416 Rem. Mag., 416 Wea. Mag., 458 Win. Mag., 458 Lott, 460 Wea. Mag. 300 Win. Mag., 300 Wby. Mag., 338 Win. Mag., 340 Wby. Mag.; 24-inch or 26-inch barrel; weighs 8-3/4 to 9-1/2 lbs.; 44-5/8-inch to 46-5/8-inch overall length; Kevlar and fiberglass composite stock; Barrel-band hooded front sight with large gold bead, adjustable ramp/shallow V rear. Designed for dangerous-game hunting. Black oxide matte finish on all metalwork; Pachmayr Decelerator recoil pad, short-throw Mark V action. Introduced 2001, still produced. Made in U.S.A. by Weatherby.

Perf.: $2400   **Exc.:** $1795   **VGood:** $1150

Weatherby Mark V Accumark Ultra Lightweight

Weatherby Mark V SVM Super Varmint Master

Weatherby Mark V Fibermark Rifles

Weatherby Mark V Crown Custom Model

Weatherby Mark V Dangerous Game

Weatherby Mark V Deluxe

Weatherby Mark V Euromark

WEATHERBY MARK V DELUXE

Bolt action; 22-250, 30-06, 224 Weatherby Varmintmaster (standard action), 240, 257, 270, 7mm, 300, 340, 378, 416, 460 Weatherby Magnums (magnum action); 2-, 5-shot box magazine, depending on caliber; 24-inch, 26-inch barrel; available in right- or left-hand model; some actions made by Sauer in Germany to Weatherby specs; no sights; drilled, tapped for scope mounts; Monte Carlo stock with cheekpiece; skip checkering on pistol grip, forearm; forearm tip, pistol grip cap, recoil pad; quick-detachable sling swivels. Introduced in 1958; made in U.S. from 1958 to 1960, then production transferred to Germany, later to Japan; still in production.

Standard calibers, German-made		
Exc.: $1295	**VGood:** $1085	**Good:** $820
Standard calibers, Japan-made		
Exc.: $995	**VGood:** $890	**Good:** $750
Magnum calibers, German-made		
Exc.: $1595	**VGood:** $1285	**Good:** $1090
Magnum calibers, Japanese-made		
Exc.: $1195	**VGood:** $1090	**Good:** $950

WEATHERBY MARK V EUROMARK

Bolt action; chambered for all Weatherby calibers except 224, 22-250; 24-inch, 26-inch round tapered barrel; 44-1/4-inch overall length (24-inch barrel); weighs 6-1/2 to 10-1/2 lbs.; open sights optional; walnut Monte Carlo stock with extended tail, fine-line hand checkering; satin oil finish; ebony forend tip and grip cap with maple diamond; solid buttpad; cocking indicator; adjustable trigger; hinged floorplate; thumb safety; quick-detachable sling swivels. Uses Mark V action. Introduced 1986.

Perf.: $1050	**Exc.:** $900	**VGood:** $750
Calibers 378 Wea. Mag., 416 Wea. Mag., 460 Wea. Mag.		
Perf.: $1400	**Exc.:** $1050	**VGood:** $925

WEATHERBY MARK V EUROSPORT

Bolt action; 22-250, 30-06, 224 Weatherby Varmintmaster (standard action), 240, 257, 270, 7mm, 300, 340, 378, 460 Wby. Mag. (magnum action); 2-, 5-shot box magazine, depending on caliber; 24-inch barrel; Mark V action; available in right-hand only; no sights; drilled, tapped for scope mounts; raised-comb Monte Carlo stock with hand-rubbed satin oil finish; no grip cap, forend tip; recoil pad; quick-detachable sling swivels. Introduced 1995.

Perf.: $775	**Exc.:** $660	**VGood:** $580
375 caliber		
Perf.: $825	**Exc.:** $690	**VGood:** $610

Weatherby Mark V
Lazermark

Weatherby Mark V
Royal Custom

Weatherby Mark V
Safari Grade Custom

Weatherby Mark V
Sporter

Weatherby Mark V SLS
Stainless Laminate Sporter

Weatherby Mark V
Super Big Game
Master Deer Rifle

Weatherby Mark V
Synthetic

Weatherby Mark V
Deluxe

Weatherby Mark XXII Clip

WEATHERBY MARK V LAZERMARK

Bolt action; 240, 257, 270, 7mm Wea. Mag., 300, 340, 378 WM, 416 WM, 460 WM, 300 WM; 3-, 5-shot magazine; 24-inch, 26-inch round tapered barrel; checkered pistol-grip American walnut stock; rosewood forearm, pistol grip; lazer-carved stock, forend. Introduced 1981; still in production. (Add $250 for 416 WM & 460 WM calibers.)

Perf.: $1200   **Exc.:** $1100   **VGood:** $835

WEATHERBY MARK V ROYAL CUSTOM RIFLE

Bolt action; 257, 270, 7mm, 300, 340 all Wby. Mags. Other calibers available upon request. Barrel: 26-

inch. Stock: Monte Carlo hand-checkered claro walnut with high gloss finish. Bolt and follower are damascened with checkered knob. Engraved receiver, bolt sleeve and floorplate sport scroll pattern. Animal images on floorplate optional. High gloss blue, 24-karat gold and nickel-plating. Made in U.S.A., still offered by Weatherby Custom Shop.

Perf.: $5200   **Exc.:** $4300   **VGood:** $3100

WEATHERBY MARK V SAFARI GRADE CUSTOM

Bolt action; 300 WM, 340 WM, 378 WM, 416 WM, 460 WM; 24-inch barrel; satin oil-finished European walnut stock; ebony forend tip, pistol grip cap; black recoil pad; fine-line checkering; matte blue finish; barrel band front sling swivel; quarter-rib rear

sight, hooded ramp front with brass bead; engraved floorplate; custom-built rifle; Introduced, 1989; still offered by Weatherby Custom Shop. (Add $200 for 378 WM and larger calibers.)

Perf.: $5100   **Exc.:** $3965   **VGood:** $2800

WEATHERBY MARK V SPORTER

Bolt action; 257, 270, 7mm, 300, 340 Wea. Mag., 7mm Rem Mag., 300 Win Mag., 338 Win. Mag., 375 H&H; 24-inch, 26-inch barrel; Mark V action; low-luster blue metal; Monte Claro walnut stock with high-gloss epoxy finish; Monte Carlo comb, recoil pad. Introduced 1993; still produced.

Perf.: $850   **Exc.:** $695   **VGood:** $580

WEATHERBY MARK V STAINLESS

Bolt action; 22-250, 30-06, 224 Weatherby Varmintmaster (standard action); 240, 257, 270, 7mm, 300, 340, 378, 460 (magnum action); 2-, 5-shot box magazine, depending on caliber; 24-inch, 26-inch barrel; available in right-hand only; 400 series stainless steel construction; lightweight injection-moulded synthetic stock with raised Monte Carlo comb; checkered grip and forend; custom floorplate release. Made in U.S. From Weatherby. Introduced 1995.

Perf.: $885   **Exc.:** $695   **VGood:** $585

375 H&H

Perf.: $995   **Exc.:** $795   **VGood:** $700

WEATHERBY MARK V SLS STAINLESS LAMINATE SPORTER

Similar to the Mark V Stainless except all metalwork is 400 series stainless with a corrosion-resistant black oxide bead-blast matte finish. Action is hand-bedded in a laminated stock with a 1-inch recoil pad. Weighs 8-1/2 lbs. Introduced 1997, no longer offered. Made in U.S.A. From Weatherby.

Perf.: $1100   **Exc.:** $970   **VGood:** $800

WEATHERBY MARK V SUPER BIG GAME MASTER DEER RIFLE

Bolt action; 240 Wby. Mag., 25-06 Rem., 270 Win., 280 Rem., 30-06 Spfld., 257 Wby. Mag., 270 Wby. Mag., 7mm Rem., Mag., 7mm Wby. Mag., 338- 06 A- Square, 300 Win. Mag., 300 Wby. Mag.; 26-inch barrel with target crown; weighs 5-3/4 lbs., (6-3/4 lbs. Magnum); raised comb Monte Carlo composite stock; fluted barrel, aluminum bedding block, Pachmayr decelerator, 54-degree bolt lift, adj. trigger.

Perf.: $1100   **Exc.:** $970   **VGood:** $850

WEATHERBY MARK V SYNTHETIC

Bolt action; 7mm Rem Mag, 300 Win Mag, 338 Win Mag, 375 H&H Mag.; 24-inch barrel; weighs 7-1/2 lbs.; synthetic stock with raised Monte Carlo comb, dual-taper checkered forend; low-luster blued metal; uses Mark V action. Right-hand only. Made in U.S. From Weatherby. Introduced 1995; still produced.

Perf.: $750   **Exc.:** $540   **VGood:** $475

WEATHERBY MARK V DELUXE

Step-up version of classic Mark V. Features include deluxe Claro walnut Monte Carlo stock with rosewood forend, 26-inch or 28-inch high-polish blued sightless barrel. Chambered in .257, .270, 7mm, .300, .340, .378, .416, and .460 Weatherby Magnum. Add 40 percent for .460.

NIB: $1750   **Exc.:** $1595   **VGood:** $1375

WEATHERBY MARK XXII CLIP

Semi-automatic; 22 LR; 5-, 10-shot clip magazine; 24-inch barrel; folding leaf open rear sight; ramp front; Monte Carlo stock cheekpiece; skip checkering on pistol grip, forearm; forearm tip, grip cap, quick-detachable sling swivels. Introduced 1963; discontinued 1989. Made in Italy. Deduct 5 percent for Japanese manufacture.

Perf.: $700   **Exc.:** $600   **VGood:** $375

WEATHERBY MARK XXII TUBULAR
Same specs as Mark XXII Clip except 15-shot tube magazine. Introduced 1973; discontinued 1989.
  Perf.: $700   **Exc.:** $600   **VGood:** $375

WEATHERBY MARK XXII BOLT ACTION RIFLE (2007)
Bolt action rifle chambered in 22 LR and 17 HMR. Checkered walnut Monte Carlo stock, 23-inch barrel, rubber rifle buttpad, blued receiver and barrel, magazine capacity 4+1 (17) or 5+1 (22). Introduced 2007.
  Perf.: $775   **Exc.:** 550   **VGood:** 395

WEATHERBY THREAT RESPONSE RIFLES (TRR) SERIES
Bolt action; 223 Rem., 308 Win., 300 Win. Mag., 300 Wby. Mag., 30-378 Wby. Mag., 338-378 Wby. Mag. 22-inch or 26-inch barrel, target crown. Laminated composite stock. Adjustable trigger, aluminum bedding block, beavertail forearms dual tapered, flat-bottomed. "Rocker Arm" lockdown scope mounting. 54-degree bolt lift. Pachmayr decelerator pad. Made in U.S.A., still in production.

Standard calibers		
Perf.: $1400	**Exc.:** $1200	**VGood:** $950
Magnum calibers		
Perf.: $1500	**Exc.:** $1300	**VGood:** $1000

WEATHERBY ULTRAMARK
Bolt action; 240 Wea. Mag., 257 Wea. Mag., 270 Wea. Mag., 30-06, 7mm Wea. Mag., 300 Wea. Mag., 378 Wea. Mag., 416 Wea. Mag.; 3-, 5-shot magazine; 24-inch, 26-inch barrel; fancy American walnut stock, basketweave checkering; hand-honed jeweled action; engraved floorplate; right- or left-hand models. Introduced 1989; discontinued 1990.

Perf.: $995	**Exc.:** $895	**VGood:** $795
378 Wea. Mag.		
Perf.: $1250	**Exc.:** $1100	**VGood:** $950
416 Wea. Mag.		
Perf.: $1350	**Exc.:** $1200	**VGood:** $1050

WEATHERBY VANGUARD
Bolt action; 25-06, 243, 270, 30-06, 308, 264, 7mm Rem. Mag., 300 Win. Mag.; 3-, 5-shot magazine, depending on caliber; 24-inch hammer-forged barrel; 44-1/2-inch overall length; weighs 7-7/8 lbs.; no sights; receiver drilled, tapped for scope mounts; American walnut stock; pistol-grip cap; forearm tip; hand checkered forearm, pistol grip; adjustable trigger; hinged floorplate. Introduced 1970; discontinued 1983; reintroduced as Vanguard Sporter, still in production.
  Perf.: $480   **Exc.:** $385   **VGood:** $325

WEATHERBY VANGUARD ALASKAN
Same as the Vanguard except 223, 243, 7mm-08, 270 Win., 7mm Rem. Mag., 308, 30-06; forest green or black wrinkle-finished synthetic stock; all metal finished with electroless nickel; right-hand only. Introduced 1992; discontinued 1993.
  Perf.: $650   **Exc.:** $550   **VGood:** $475

WEATHERBY VANGUARD CLASSIC I
Same specs as Vanguard except 223, 243, 270, 7mm-08, 7mm Rem. Mag., 30-06, 308; 24-inch barrel; classic-style stock without Monte Carlo comb, no forend tip; distinctive Weatherby grip cap; satin finish on stock. Introduced 1989; discontinued 1993.
  Perf.: $475   **Exc.:** $400   **VGood:** $335

WEATHERBY VANGUARD CLASSIC II
Same specs as Vanguard except 22-250, 243, 270, 7mm Rem. Mag., 30-06, 300 Win. Mag., 338 Win. Mag., 270 Wea. Mag., 300 Wea. Mag.; rounded forearm with black tip, black grip cap with walnut diamond inlay, 20 lpi checkering; solid black recoil pad; oil-finished stock. Introduced 1989; discontinued 1993.
  Perf.: $625   **Exc.:** $510   **VGood:** $410

WEATHERBY VANGUARD FIBERGUARD
Same specs as Vanguard except 223, 243, 308, 270, 7mm Rem. Mag., 30-06; 20-inch barrel; weighs 6-1/2

lbs.; forest green wrinkle-finished fiberglass stock; matte blued metal. Made in Japan. Introduced 1985; discontinued 1988.
  Perf.: $475   **Exc.:** $395   **VGood:** $350

WEATHERBY VANGUARD STAINLESS
Similar to Vanguard, but matte-finish stainless-steel parts, synthetic stock; 223, 22-250, 243, 257 Wby. Mag., 270, 270 WSM, 270, 7mm Rem. Mag., 308, 300 Win. Mag., 300 WSM, 300 Win. Mag., 300 Wby. Mag., 338 Win. Mag.
  Perf.: $500   **Exc.:** $400   **VGood:** $300

WEATHERBY VANGUARD SYNTHETIC
Similar to Vanguard, but black synthetic stock, metal parts have matte black finish; same cartridge chamberings as Vanguard Stainless.
  Perf.: $475   **Exc.:** $375   **VGood:** $245

WEATHERBY VANGUARD VGL LIGHTWEIGHT RIFLE
Same specs as Vanguard except 223, 243, 270, 30-06, 7mm Rem. Mag., 308; 5-, 6-shot magazine; 20-inch barrel; non-glare blued finish; satin-finished stock; hand checkering; black buttpad, spacer. Made in Japan. Introduced 1984; discontinued 1988.
  Perf.: $415   **Exc.:** $360   **VGood:** $300

WEATHERBY VANGUARD VGS
Same specs as Vanguard except 222-250, 25-06, 243, 270, 30-06, 7 mm Rem. Mag., 300 Win. Mag.; side safety. Made in Japan. Introduced 1984; discontinued 1988.
  Perf.: $415   **Exc.:** $360   **VGood:** $300

WEATHERBY VANGUARD VGX
Same specs as Vanguard except 22-250, 243, 270, 270 Wea. Mag., 7mm Rem. Mag., 30-06, 300 Win.

Mag., 300 Wea. Mag., 338 Win. Mag.; 24-inch No. 2 contour barrel; walnut stock with high luster finish; rosewood grip cap and forend tip. Imported from Japan by Weatherby. Introduced 1984; discontinued 1993.
  Perf.: $500   **Exc.:** $415   **VGood:** $360

WEATHERBY VANGUARD WEATHERGUARD
Same specs as Vanguard except 223, 243, 308, 270, 7mm Rem. Mag., 30-06; 24-inch barrel; 44-1/2-inch overall length; weighs 7-1/2 lbs.; accepts same scope mount bases as Mark V action; forest green or black wrinkle-finished synthetic stock; all metal is matte blue. Right-hand only. Introduced 1989; discontinued 1993.
  Perf.: $400   **Exc.:** $350   **VGood:** $300

WEATHERBY VANGUARD SPORTER STAINLESS
Similar to Vanguard but with sporter-style stock, stainless steel barrel and receiver.
  NIB: $750   **Exc.:** $695   **VGood:** $600

WEATHERBY VANGUARD VARMINT SPECIAL
Chambered in .223, .22-250, or .308. 22-inch blued #3 contour heavy crowned barrel, adjustable trigger, synthetic tan composite stock with black spiderweb pattern. Introduced 2006.
  NIB: $575   **Exc.:** $525   **VGood:** $450

WEATHERBY VANGUARD SUB-MOA VARMINT SPECIAL
Similar to Vanguard Varmint Special but with ventilated beavertail forend and other accuracy refinements.
  NIB: $825   **Exc.:** $750   **VGood:** $625

Weatherby Mark XXII Tubular

Weatherby Threat Response

Weatherby Ultramark

Weatherby Vanguard Classic I

Weatherby Vanguard Fiberguard

Weatherby Vanguard Stainless

Weatherby Vanguard Weatherguard

Weatherby Vanguard Sporter Stainless

Weatherby Vanguard Varmint Special

Weatherby Vanguard Sub-MOA Varmint Special

Weatherby Vanguard Sub-MOA Stainless

Weatherby Vanguard Youth Compact

Weatherby Vanguard Sage Country Custom

Weatherby Vanguard Back Country Custom

Weihrauch Model HW 60

WEATHERBY VANGUARD SUB-MOA MATTE OR STAINLESS

Introduced in 2005 this model features a guarantee to shoot .99" at 100 yards. Calibers from .223 Rem. to .338 Win. Mag. Barrel length is 24" with Monte Carlo Fiberguard stock. Adjustable trigger. Weight is about 7.75 lbs. Also available in stainless steel. Add 15% for stainless steel.

NIB: $825   **Exc.:** $750   **VGood:** $625

WEATHERBY VANGUARD DELUXE

Similar to Vanguard but features 24-inch polished blued barrel, glossy select Monte Carlo walnut stock with rosewood forend, adjustable trigger. Chambered in .270, .30-06, .257 Weatherby Mag., and .300 Weatherby Mag. Introduced 2006.

NIB: $725   **Exc.:** $655   **VGood:** $525\

WEATHERBY VANGUARD COMPACT

This model, chambered for the ..223, 22-250, .243, or .308, is fitted with a 20" barrel and scaled-down hardwood stock with shorter length of pull. Also included is a full size composite stock. Weight is about 6.75 lbs. Introduced in 2005.

Perf.: $550   **Exc.:** $500   **VGood:** $425

WEATHERBY VANGUARD YOUTH COMPACT

Similar to above but with synthetic stock. Introduced 2008.

Perf.: $550   **Exc.:** $500   **VGood:** $425

WEATHERBY VANGUARD SAGE COUNTRY CUSTOM

Introduced in 2008, this is similar to the Vanguard Synthetic but with injection-molded Desert Camo stock. Available in a variety of chamberings from ..223 to .338 Winchester Magnum.

Perf.: $950   **Exc.:** $795   **VGood:** $525

WEATHERBY VANGUARD BACK COUNTRY CUSTOM

Introduced in 2008, this is a lightweight version of the Vanguard Synthetic with a fluted barrel, textured stock and overall weight of 6-3/4 lbs. Available in a variety of chamberings from ..257 Weatherby Magnum to .300 Weatherby Magnum.

Perf.: $950   **Exc.:** $795   **VGood:** $525

WEATHERBY WEATHERMARK

Bolt action; 240, 257, 270, 7mm, 300, 340 Wea. Mags, 7mm Rem. Mag., 270 Win., 30-06; 22-inch, 24-inch barrel; weighs 7-1/2 lbs.; impregnated-color black composite stock with raised point checkering; Mark V action; right-hand only. Introduced 1992; no longer made.

Perf.: $800   **Exc.:** $675   **VGood:** $425

375 H&H		

Perf.: $900   **Exc.:** $775   **VGood:** $500

WEATHERBY WEATHERMARK ALASKAN

Same specs as Weathermark except all metal plated with electroless nickel. Available in right-hand only. Introduced 1992; no longer produced.

Perf.: $750   **Exc.:** $615   **VGood:** $515

375 H&H		

Perf.: $800   **Exc.:** $720   **VGood:** $545

WEIHRAUCH MODEL HW 60

Single shot; 22 LR; 26-3/4-inch barrel; hooded ramp front sight, match-type aperture rear; European walnut stock with stippled pistol-grip, forend; adjustable buttplate; rail with adjustable swivel; adjustable trigger; push-button safety. Introduced 1981; no longer imported from Germany.

Perf.: $670   **Exc.:** $550   **VGood:** $430

WEIHRAUCH MODEL HW 60J

Same specs as Model HW 60 except 22 LR, 222; checkered walnut sporter-style stock. Discontinued 1992.

Perf.: $535   **Exc.:** $420   **VGood:** $375

222 caliber		

Perf.: $725   **Exc.:** $625   **VGood:** $595

WEIHRAUCH MODEL HW 66

Bolt action; 22 Hornet, 222; 22-3/4-inch barrel; 41-3/4-inch overall length; weighs 6-1/2 lbs.; hooded blade ramp front sight, open rear; oil-finished walnut stock with cheekpiece; checkered pistol grip, forend. Introduced 1988; discontinued 1990.

Perf.: $625   **Exc.:** $515   **VGood:** $400

Double-set trigger		

Perf.: $665   **Exc.:** $560   **VGood:** $460

WEIHRAUCH MODEL HW 660 MATCH

Bolt action; 22 LR; 26-inch barrel; 45-1/3-inch overall length; weighs 10-3/4 lbs.; globe front sight, match aperture rear; match-type walnut stock with adjustable cheekpiece, buttplate; checkered pistol grip, forend; forend accessory rail; adjustable match trigger. Introduced 1990; no longer in production.

Perf.: $735   **Exc.:** $660   **VGood:** $560

WESSON & HARRINGTON BUFFALO CLASSIC

Single shot; 45-70; 32-inch heavy barrel; 52-inch overall length; weighs 9 lbs.; no sights; drilled and tapped for peep sight; American black walnut stock and forend; barrel dovetailed for front sight; color case-hardened Handi-Rifle action with exposed hammer; color case-hardened crescent buttplate; 19th century checkering pattern. Made in U.S. by H&R 1871, Inc. Introduced 1995; still produced.

Perf.: $400   **Exc.:** $335   **VGood:** $250

WESSON & HARRINGTON 38-55 TARGET CLASSIC RIFLE

Similar to the Buffalo Classic rifle except chambered for 38-55 Win., has 28-inch barrel; barrel and steel furniture, including steel trigger guard and forend spacer, are highly polished and blued. Color case-hardened receiver and buttplate. Barrel is dovetailed for a front sight, and drilled and tapped for receiver sight or scope mount. Introduced 1998. Made in U.S.A. by H&R 1871, Inc.

Perf.: $400   **Exc.:** $335   **VGood:** $250

WESTLEY RICHARDS DOUBLE

Double rifle; boxlock; 30-06, 318 Accelerated Express, 375 Mag., 425 Mag. Express, 465 Nitro Express, 470 Nitro Express; 25-inch barrels; hammerless; leaf rear sight, hooded front; French walnut stock; hand-checkered pistol-grip, forearm; cheekpiece; horn forearm tip; sling swivels; ejectors. Favored for African big game. Values vary according to caliber and engraving; range $16,000 to $45,000.

WESTLEY RICHARDS MAGAZINE MODEL

Bolt action; 30-06, 7mm high velocity, 318 Accelerated Express, 375 Mag., 404 Nitro Express, 425 Mag.; 22-inch barrel (7mm High Velocity), 25-inch (425 Mag.)

24-inch other calibers; leaf rear sight, hooded front; sporting stock of French walnut; hand-checkered pistol grip, forearm; cheekpiece; horn forearm tip; sling swivels.

Perf.: $7700   **Exc.:** $6800   **VGood:** $5600

WHITWORTH EXPRESS

Bolt action; 22-250, 243, 25-06, 270, 7x57, 308, 30-06, 300 Win. Mag., 7mm Rem. Mag., 375 H&H, 458 Win. Mag.; 24-inch barrel; 44-inch overall length; 3-leaf open sight (magnums); open sights (others); classic European walnut English Express stock; hand checkering; adjustable trigger; hinged floorplate; steel recoil crossbolt; solid recoil pad; barrel-mounted sling swivel. Made originally in England; barreled actions later produced in Yugoslavia. Introduced 1974; no longer imported. Add 20 percent for African chamberings.

Exc.: $650   **VGood:** $425   **Good:** $300

WHITWORTH EXPRESS CARBINE

Same specs as Safari Express except 243, 270, 308, 7x57, 30-06; 20-inch barrel; Mannlicher-style stock. Introduced 1986; discontinued 1988.

Exc.: $500   **VGood:** $430   **Good:** $340

WHITWORTH SAFARI EXPRESS

Bolt action; 375 H&H, 458 Win. Mag.; 24-inch barrel; 44-inch overall length; weighs 7-1/2 to 8 lbs.; ramp front sight with removable hood, three-leaf open rear calibrated for 100, 200, 300 yards on 1/4-rib; classic English Express rifle stock design of hand checkered, select European walnut; solid rubber recoil pad; barrel-mounted sling swivel; adjustable trigger; hinged floorplate; solid steel recoil crossbolt. From Interarms. No longer imported.

Exc.: $700   **VGood:** $500   **Good:** $375

WICHITA CLASSIC MODEL

Bolt action; single shot; calibers 17 through 308 Win.; 21-1/8-inch octagon barrel; no sights; drilled, tapped for scope mounts; hand-checkered American walnut pistol-grip stock; steel grip cap; Pachmayr rubber recoil pad; right-, left-hand action; Canjar trigger; checkered bolt handle; jeweled bolt; non-glare blue finish. Introduced 1978.

Perf.: $1700   **Exc.:** $1200   **VGood:** $900

Left-hand model

Perf.: $1800   **Exc.:** $1300   **VGood:** $925

WICHITA SILHOUETTE MODEL

Bolt action; single shot; all standard calibers; 24-inch free-floated barrel; no sights; drilled/tapped for scope mounts; metallic gray fiberthane stock; vent rubber recoil pad; 2-oz. Canjar trigger; fluted bolt; left- or right-hand; marketed in hard case. Introduced 1983; no longer in production.

Perf.: $1900   **Exc.:** $1600   **VGood:** $1200

Left-hand model

Perf.: $2000   **Exc.:** $1700   **VGood:** $1300

WICHITA STAINLESS MAGNUM

Bolt action; calibers 270 Win. through 458 Win. Mag.; single shot or with blind magazine; 22-inch, 24-inch target-grade barrel; no sights; drilled, tapped for Burris scope mounts; hand-inletted, glass-bedded fancy American walnut stock; hand-checkered; steel pistol-grip cap; Pachmayr rubber recoil pad; fully-adjustable trigger; stainless steel barrel, action. Introduced 1980; no longer in production.

Perf.: $1725   **Exc.:** $1350   **VGood:** $1000

WICHITA VARMINT MODEL

Bolt action; calibers 17 Rem. through 308 Win.; 3-shot magazine; 21-1/8-inch Atkinson chrome-moly barrel; no sights; drilled, tapped for scope mounts; hand inletted, hand-rubbed, hand-checkered American walnut pistol-grip stock; steel grip cap; Pachmayr rubber recoil pad; right- or left-hand action; checkered bolt handle; jeweled bolt; non-glare blued finish. Introduced 1978.

Perf.: $1725   **Exc.:** $1350   **VGood:** $1000

Westley Richards Magazine Model

Whitworth Express

Wichita Classic Model

Wichita Silhouette Model

Wichita Stainless Magnum

Wickliffe Stinger

Wickliffe Traditionalist

WICKLIFFE MODEL 76

Single shot; 22 Hornet, 223 Rem., 22-250, 243 Win., 25-06, 308 Win., 30-06, 45-70; 22-inch lightweight, 26-inch heavy sporter barrel; falling block; no sights; American walnut Monte Carlo stock; cheekpiece, pistol grip, semi-beavertail forend. Introduced 1976; discontinued 1979.

Exc.: $900   **VGood:** $650   **Good:** $500

WICKLIFFE MODEL 76 DELUXE

Same specs as Model 76 except 30-06; 22-inch barrel; high-luster blue finish; nickel-silver grip cap; better wood. Introduced 1976; discontinued 1979.

Exc.: $975   **VGood:** $725   **Good:** $575

WICKLIFFE STINGER

Single shot; 22 Hornet, 223 Rem.; 22-inch barrel; falling block; no sights; American walnut Monte Carlo stock, Continental-type forend; etched receiver logo; quick-detachable sling swivels. Introduced 1979; discontinued 1980.

Exc.: $900   **VGood:** $650   **Good:** $500

WICKLIFFE STINGER DELUXE

Same specs as Stinger except 22-inch lightweight barrel; high-luster blue finish; nickel-silver grip cap; better wood. Introduced 1979; discontinued 1980.

Exc.: $975   **VGood:** $725   **Good:** $575

WICKLIFFE TRADITIONALIST

Single shot; 30-06, 45-70; 24-inch chrome-moly barrel; falling block; open sights; American walnut classic-style buttstock; hand-cut checkering; sling; sling swivels. Introduced 1979; discontinued 1980.

Exc.: $975   **VGood:** $725   **Good:** $575

WILKINSON LINDA CARBINE

Semi-automatic; 9mm Para.; 16-3/16-inch barrel; weighs 7 lbs.; fixed tubular stock with wood pad. Aperture rear sight. Aluminum receiver, pre-ban configuration, vent. barrel shroud, small wooden forearm, 18 or 31 shot mag. Pre-ban receivers made into carbines by Northwest Arms.

Perf.: $1000   **Exc.:** $770   **VGood:** $560

WILDEY CARBINE

Semi-automatic; 44 AutoMag, 45 Win. Mag., 45 Wildey Mag., 475 Wildey Mag.; based on Wildey pistol with 18-inch barrel; walnut stock and forend; available with polished or matte stainless-steel finish. Made by Wildey Fire Arms.

Perf.: $2850   **Exc.:** $2100   **VGood:** N/A

WILKINSON TERRY CARBINE

Semi-automatic; 9mm Para.; 30-shot magazine; 16-3/16-inch barrel; 30-inch overall length; weighs about 6 lbs.; protected post front sight, aperture rear;

Wilkinson Terry Carbine

Winchester Lee Sporter

Winchester Model 43

Winchester Model 43
Special Grade

Winchester Model 47

Winchester Model 52A

Winchester Model 52A
Heavy Barrel

Winchester Model 52B
Heavy Barrel

dovetailed receiver for scope mounting; uncheckered maple or black synthetic stock forend; bolt-type safety; ejection port has automatic trap door; blowback action; fires from closed bolt. Introduced 1975.

Exc.: $425   **VGood:** $325   **Good:** $275

WINCHESTER LEE MUSKET

Bolt action; 6mm (236 USN); 5-shot box magazine; 28-inch barrel; folding leaf rear sight, post front; military semi-pistol-grip stock; blued finish. Commercial version of Lee Navy Model 1895 rifle. Introduced 1897; discontinued 1905. Collector value.

Exc.: $2300   **VGood:** $2000   **Good:** $1770

WINCHESTER LEE SPORTER

Same specs as Lee Musket except 24-inch barrel; open rear sight, bead front; sporter-style walnut stock. Introduced 1897; discontinued 1905. Collector value.

Exc.: $2350   **VGood:** $2050   **Good:** $1820

WINCHESTER MODEL 43

Bolt action; 218 Bee, 22 Hornet, 25-20, 32-20; 3-shot box magazine, 2-shot (32-20); 24-inch barrel; 42-1/2-inch overall length; weighs 6 lbs.; open rear sight, No. 103 bead front on hooded ramp; uncheckered

American walnut pistol-grip stock; swivels. Introduced 1950; discontinued 1957.

Exc.: $600   **VGood:** $500   **Good:** $400

WINCHESTER MODEL 43 SPECIAL GRADE

Same specs as Model 43 except for grip cap; checkered pistol grip, forearm; Lyman 59A micrometer rear sight.

Exc.: $680   **VGood:** $570   **Good:** $485

WINCHESTER MODEL 47

Bolt action; single shot; 22 Short, 22 Long, 22 LR; 25-inch barrel; peep or open rear sight, No. 97 bead front on ramp with detachable sight-cover or No. 95 bead; uncheckered American walnut pistol grip stock. Introduced 1949; discontinued 1954.

Exc.: $380   **VGood:** $310   **Good:** $240

WINCHESTER MODEL 52 (EARLY PRODUCTION)

Bolt action; 22 Short, 22 LR; 5-shot box magazine; 28-inch barrel; folding leaf peep rear sight, blade front; scope bases; semi-military stock; pistol grip; grooves on forearm. Later versions had higher comb, semi-beavertail forearm; slow lock model was replaced in 1929 by speed lock. Last arms of this model bore serial numbers followed by the letter "A." Introduced 1919; discontinued 1937.

Exc.: $1050   **VGood:** $815   **Good:** $625

WINCHESTER MODEL 52 SPORTER

Same specs as Model 52 except for 24-inch lightweight barrel; weighs 7-1/4 lbs.; Lyman No. 48F receiver sight, Redfield gold bead on hooded ramp at front; deluxe walnut sporting stock with cheekpiece; checkered forend, pistol grip; black forend tip; leather sling. Beware of fakes. Introduced 1934; discontinued 1958.

Exc.: $3500   **VGood:** $3000   **Good:** $1900

WINCHESTER MODEL 52A

Bolt action; 22 Short, 22 LR; 5-shot box magazine; 28-inch barrel; folding leaf peep rear sight, blade front; scope bases; semi-military stock; pistol grip; grooves on forearm; speedlock action. Introduced 1929; discontinued 1939.

Exc.: $975   **VGood:** $825   **Good:** $675

WINCHESTER MODEL 52A HEAVY BARREL

Same specs as Model 52A except 28-inch heavy barrel; Lyman 17G front sight. Discontinued 1939.

Exc.: 1100   **VGood:** $900   **Good:** $700

WINCHESTER MODEL 52A SPORTER

Same specs as Model 52A except 24-inch lightweight barrel; Lyman No. 48 receiver sight, gold bead on hooded ramp front; deluxe walnut sporting stock, checkered; black forend tip; cheekpiece. Introduced 1937; discontinued 1939.

Exc.: $4500   **VGood:** $4000   **Good:** $2500

WINCHESTER MODEL 52B

Bolt action; 22 Short, 22 LR; 5-shot box magazine; 28-inch barrel; various sighting options; target or Marksman pistol-grip stock with high comb, beavertail forearm; round-top receiver; redesigned Model 52A action. Introduced 1940; discontinued 1947.

Exc.: $900   **VGood:** $720   **Good:** $585

WINCHESTER MODEL 52B BULL GUN

Same specs as Model 52B except 28-inch extra-heavy barrel; Marksman pistol-grip stock; Vaver No. 35 Mielt extension receiver sight, Vaver WIIAT front.

Exc.: $1000   **VGood:** $820   **Good:** $695

WINCHESTER MODEL 52B HEAVY BARREL

Same specs as Model 52B except 28-inch heavy barrel; Lyman No. 48FH rear sight, Lyman No. 77 front.

Exc.: $1195   **VGood:** $900   **Good:** $600

WINCHESTER MODEL 52B SPORTER

Same specs as Model 52 except 5-shot detachable box magazine; 24-inch lightweight barrel; Lyman No. 48 receiver sight, gold bead on hooded ramp front; deluxe walnut sporting stock, checkered; black forend tip; cheekpiece; sling swivels; single shot adapter.

Exc.: $3500 **VGood:** $2900 **Good:** $2000

WINCHESTER MODEL 52B SPORTER (1993)

Same specs as Model 52B except no sights; drilled, tapped for scope mounting; Remake of early Model 52 Sporter; Model 52C mechanism with stock configuration of the Model 52B; Micro-Motion trigger. Production limited to 6000 rifles. Introduced 1993; discontinued 1993.

Perf.: $700 **Exc.:** $575 **VGood:** $390

WINCHESTER MODEL 52C

Bolt action; 22 Short, 22 LR; 5-, 10-shot box magazine; 28-inch barrel; various sighting systems; Marksman pistol-grip stock with high comb, beavertail forearm; Micro-Motion trigger; single shot adapter. Introduced 1947; discontinued 1961.

Exc.: $1125 **VGood:** $920 **Good:** $680

WINCHESTER MODEL 52C BULL GUN

Same specs as Model 52C except 28-inch extra-heavy bull barrel; weighs 12 lbs.

Exc.: $1200 **VGood:** $1000 **Good:** $795

WINCHESTER MODEL 52C HEAVY BARREL

Same specs as Model 52C except 28-inch heavy barrel.

Exc.: $1120 **VGood:** $940 **Good:** $670

WINCHESTER MODEL 52C SPORTER

Same specs as Model 52C except 24-inch lightweight barrel; Lyman No. 48 receiver sight, gold bead on hooded ramp front; deluxe walnut sporting stock, checkered; black forend tip; cheekpiece; sling swivels; single shot adapter; Micro-Motion trigger.

Exc.: $3400 **VGood:** $2900 **Good:** $2000

WINCHESTER MODEL 52D

Bolt action; single shot; 22 LR; 28-inch free-floating standard or heavy barrel; 46-inch overall length; weighs 9-3/4 lbs. (standard barrel), 11 lbs. (heavy barrel); no sights; scope blocks for standard target scopes; redesigned Marksman stock; rubber buttplate; accessory channel in stock with forend stop. Introduced 1961; discontinued 1980.

Exc.: $1100 **VGood:** $920 **Good:** $750

WINCHESTER MODEL 52D INTERNATIONAL MATCH

Same specs as Model 52D except laminated international-style stock with aluminum forend assembly; hook butt plate; adjustable palm rest; ISU or Kenyon trigger. Introduced 1969; discontinued 1980.

ISU trigger		
Exc.: $1960	**Vgood:** $1850	**Good:** $1740
Kenyon trigger		
Exc.: $2000	**VGood:** $1900	**Good:** $1800

WINCHESTER MODEL 52D INTERNATIONAL PRONE

Same specs as Model 52D International Match except stock designed for prone shooting only; no hook butt plate or palm rest; oil-finished stock with removable roll-over cheekpiece for easy bore cleaning. Introduced 1975; discontinued 1980.

Exc.: $1000 **VGood:** $900 **Good:** $700

WINCHESTER MODEL 54

Bolt action; 270, 7x57mm, 30-30, 30-06, 7.65x53mm, 9x57mm; 5-shot box magazine; 24-inch barrel; open rear sight, bead front; checkered pistol-grip stock; two-piece firing pin; steel buttplate (checkered from 1930 on). Introduced 1925; discontinued 1930.

Exc.: $775 **VGood:** $675 **Good:** $525

Winchester Model 52B Sporter

Winchester Model 52C Bull Gun

Winchester Model 52D

Winchester Model 52D International Match

Winchester Model 54 Improved

Winchester Model 54 Super Grade

Winchester Model 56

WINCHESTER MODEL 54 CARBINE

Same specs as Model 54 except 20-inch barrel; plain pistol-grip stock; grooves on forearm. Introduced 1927; discontinued 1930.

Exc.: $850 **VGood:** $775 **Good:** $550

WINCHESTER MODEL 54 IMPROVED

Same specs as Model 54 except with mechanical improvements; 22 Hornet, 220 Swift, 250-3000, 257 Roberts, 270, 7x57mm, 30-06; 24-inch, 26-inch (220 Swift) barrel; NRA-type stock; checkered pistol-grip, forearm; one-piece firing pin; speed lock. Introduced 1930; discontinued 1936.

Exc.: $775 **VGood:** $700 **Good:** $545

WINCHESTER MODEL 54 IMPROVED CARBINE

Same specs as Model 54 except 22 Hornet, 220 Swift, 250-3000, 257 Roberts, 270, 7x57mm, 30-06; 20-inch barrel; lightweight or NRA-type stock; checkered pistol-grip, forearm; one-piece firing pin; speed lock. Introduced 1930; discontinued 1936.

Exc.: $800 **VGood:** $750 **Good:** $575

WINCHESTER MODEL 54 NATIONAL MATCH

Same specs as Model 54 except Lyman sights; Marksman target stock; scope bases. Introduced 1935; no longer in production.

Exc.: $995 **VGood:** $890 **Good:** $695

WINCHESTER MODEL 54 SNIPER'S RIFLE

Same specs as Model 54 except 30-06; heavy 26-inch barrel; Lyman No. 48 rear peep sight, blade front sight; semi-military type stock.

Exc.: $1095 **VGood:** $995 **Good:** $795

WINCHESTER MODEL 54 SUPER GRADE

Same specs as Model 54 except deluxe stock with pistol grip cap, cheekpiece, black forend tip; quick-detachable sling swivels; 1-inch leather sling. Introduced 1934; discontinued 1935.

Exc.: $1100 **VGood:** $950 **Good:** $800

WINCHESTER MODEL 56

Bolt action; 22 Short, 22 LR; 5-, 10-shot magazine; 22-inch barrel; open rear sight, bead front; uncheckered pistol-grip stock; schnabel-type forearm. Introduced 1926; discontinued 1929. Premium for 22 Short chambering.

Exc.: $1145 **VGood:** $795 **Good:** $550

Deluxe model with checkering		
Exc.: $1595	**VGood:** $995	**Good:** $795

WINCHESTER MODEL 57

Bolt action; 22 Short, 22 LR; 5-, 10-shot magazine; 22-inch barrel; Lyman peep sight, blade front; drilled, tapped receiver; semi-military-type pistol-grip target

Winchester Model 57

Winchester Model 58

Winchester Model 59

Winchester Model 60

Winchester Model 60A

Winchester Model 67 Junior

Winchester Model 68

Winchester Model 69

Winchester Model 70
(1936-1963)

WINCHESTER MODEL 67

Bolt action; single shot; 22 Short, 22 Long, 22 LR, 22 WMR, 22-shot cartridge; 24-inch rifled, 27-inch rifled or smoothbore barrel; takedown; open rear sight, bead front; uncheckered pistol-grip stock; grooved forearm (early models); manual cocking. Introduced 1934; discontinued 1963.

Exc.: $190   VGood: $150   Good: $125

WINCHESTER MODEL 67 JUNIOR (BOY'S RIFLE)

Same specs as Model 67 except 20-inch barrel; shorter stock.

Exc.: $240   VGood: $200   Good: $130

WINCHESTER MODEL 68

Bolt action; single shot; 22 Short, 22 Long, 22 LR, 22 WMR; 24-inch, 27-inch; takedown; adjustable rear peep sight, ramp front; uncheckered walnut pistol-grip stock; grooved forearm (early models); manual cocking. Introduced 1934; discontinued 1946.

Exc.: $285   VGood: $205   Good: $145

WINCHESTER MODEL 69, 69A

Bolt action; 22 Short, 22 Long, 22 LR; 5-, 10-shot detachable box magazine; 25-inch barrel; takedown; open rear sight, bead ramp front; uncheckered pistol-grip stock. Introduced 1935; discontinued 1963.

Exc.: $315   VGood: $230   Good: $190

WINCHESTER MODEL 69 MATCH

Same specs as Model 69 except Lyman No. 57EW receiver sight, Winchester No. 101 front; Army-type leather sling.

Exc.: $335   VGood: $245   Good: $210

WINCHESTER MODEL 69 TARGET

Same specs as Model 69 except rear peep sight, Winchester No. 93 blade front sight; sling swivels; Army-type leather sling.

Exc.: $325   VGood: $240   Good: $200

WINCHESTER MODEL 70

This bolt action, centerfire repeating rifle is a versatile longarm, having been produced in more variations and configurations than any other of the manufacturer's firearms. The rifle is divided into roughly three historical categories, the original variations having been made from 1936 to 1963; at that time, the rifle was redesigned to a large degree, actually downgraded in an effort to meet rising costs, but to hold the retail price. This series of variations was produced from 1964 until 1972, at which time the rifle was upgraded and the retail price increased. Additional changes have been made in years since. The venerable Winchester Model 70 was discontinued in 2006.

WINCHESTER MODEL 70 (1936-1963)

Bolt action; 22 Hornet, 220 Swift, 243, 250-3000, 7mm, 257 Roberts, 264 Win. Mag., 270, 7x57mm, 300 Savage, 300 H&H Mag., 300 Win. Mag., 30-06, 308, 338 Win. Mag., 35 Rem., 358 Win., 375 H&H Mag., (other calibers on special order such as 9x57mm and 7.65mm); 4-shot box magazine (magnums); 5-shot (other calibers); 20-inch, 24-inch, 25-inch, 26-inch barrel; claw extractor; hooded ramp front sight, open rear; hand-checkered walnut pistol-grip stock; Monte Carlo comb on later productions. Introduced 1936; discontinued 1963. In many cases, the value depends largely on the caliber of the rifle. Note: 300 Savage, 35 Rem., 7.65mm, 9x57mm very rare; see appraiser.

PRE-WWII (1936-1945)

Standard calibers
Exc.: $1100   VGood: $850   Good: $650
220 Swift, 257 Roberts, 300 H&H Mag.
Exc.: $1400   VGood: $900   Good: $700
375 H&H Mag., 7x57mm, 250-3000
Exc.: $1800   VGood: $1100   Good: $900

POST-WWII (1946-1963)

Standard calibers
Exc.: $1000   VGood: $800   Good: $600

---

stock; swivels; web sling; barrel band. Introduced 1927; discontinued 1936. Premium for 22 Short chambering.

Exc.: $650   VGood: $495   Good: $385

WINCHESTER MODEL 58

Bolt action; single shot; 22 Short, 22 Long, 22 LR; 18-inch barrel; open rear sight, blade front sight; uncheckered straight-grip hardwood stock; takedown; manual cocking. Introduced 1928; discontinued 1931.

Exc.: $420   VGood: $320   Good: $270

WINCHESTER MODEL 59

Bolt action; single shot; 22 Short, 22 Long, 22 LR; 23-inch barrel; open rear sight, blade front; pistol grip, uncheckered one-piece hardwood stock;

buttplate; takedown; manual cocking. Introduced 1930; discontinued 1931.

Exc.: $600   VGood: $500   Good: $370

WINCHESTER MODEL 60

Bolt action; single shot; 22 Short, 22 Long, 22 LR; 23-inch barrel (until 1933), 27-inch thereafter; open rear sight, blade front; uncheckered pistol-grip hardwood stock; buttplate; takedown; manual cocking. Introduced 1931; discontinued 1934.

Exc.: $325   VGood: $200   Good: $160

WINCHESTER MODEL 60A

Same specs as Model 60 except 27-inch barrel; Lyman rear peep sight, square-top front; heavy semi-military target stock; web sling. Introduced 1933; discontinued 1939.

Exc.: $495   VGood: $295   Good: $200

220 Swift, 243, 257 Roberts
Exc.: $1300   **VGood:** $900   **Good:** $650

22 Hornet, 300 H&H Mag.,
Exc.: $1700   **VGood:** $1300   **Good:** $1100

300 Win. Mag., 338 Win. Mag., 375 H&H Mag.
Exc.: $1700   **VGood:** $1200   **Good:** $1000
Note: 250-3000, 300 Savage, 358, 35 Rem., 7x57mm
Very rare; see appraiser.

WINCHESTER MODEL 70 ALASKAN
Same specs as Model 70 (1936-1963) except 300 Win. Mag., 338 Win. Mag., 375 H&H Mag.; 3-, 4-shot (375 H&H Mag.) magazine; 24-inch barrel (300 Win. Mag.), 25-inch barrel; 45-5/8-inch overall length; weighs 8 to 8-3/4 lbs.; bead front, sight, folding leaf rear; tapped for scope mounts, receiver sights; Monte Carlo stock; recoil pad. Introduced 1960; discontinued 1963.
Exc.: $1900   **VGood:** $1400   **Good:** $995

WINCHESTER MODEL 70 BULL GUN
Same specs as Model 70 (1936-1963) except 30-06, 300 H&H Mag.; 28-inch extra heavy barrel; scope bases; walnut target Marksman stock; Lyman No. 77 front sight, Lyman No. 48WH rear; Army-type leather sling strap. Discontinued 1963.
Exc.: $2300   **VGood:** $1700   **Good:** $1295

WINCHESTER MODEL 70 CARBINE
Same specs as Model 70 (1936-1963) except 22 Hornet, 250-3000, 257 Roberts, 270, 7x57mm, 30-06; 20-inch barrel. The 250-3000, 7x57mm are rare; see appraiser. Introduced 1936; discontinued 1946.

Calibers 270, 30-06
Exc.: $1695   **VGood:** $1195   **Good:** $895

22 Hornet, 257 Roberts
Exc.: $2695   **VGood:** $1995   **Good:** $1295

WINCHESTER MODEL 70 FEATHERWEIGHT
Same specs as Model 70 (1936-1963) except 243, 264 Win. Mag., 270, 308, 30-06, 358 Win.; 22-inch lightweight barrel, 24-inch (special order); weighs 6-1/2 lbs.; lightweight American walnut Monte Carlo or straight comb stock; checkered pistol grip, forend; aluminum triggerguard, checkered buttplate, floorplate; 1-inch swivels. Introduced 1952; discontinued 1963.

Calibers 243, 270, 30-06, 308
Exc.: $1050   **VGood:** $800   **Good:** $650

264 Win. Mag., 358 Win.
Exc.: $1600   **VGood:** $1300   **Good:** $1000

WINCHESTER MODEL 70 NATIONAL MATCH
Same specs as Model 70 (1936-1963) except 30-06; 24-inch barrel; Lyman No. 77 front ramp sight, Lyman No. 48WH rear; Army-type leather sling strap; scope bases; checkered walnut Marksman target stock. Discontinued 1960.
Exc.: $1775   **VGood:** $1200   **Good:** $850

WINCHESTER MODEL 70 SUPER GRADE
Same specs as Model 70 (1936-1963) except 24-inch, 25-inch, 26-inch barrel; Winchester 22G open sporting rear sight; deluxe stock, cheekpiece; black forearm tip; sling; quick-detachable sling swivels; grip cap. Introduced 1936; discontinued 1960.
Exc.: $1950   **VGood:** $1300   **Good:** $1000

375 H&H Mag.
Exc.: $3000   **VGood:** $2300   **Good:** $1600

WINCHESTER MODEL 70 SUPER GRADE AFRICAN
Same specs as Model 70 (1936-1963) except 458 Win. Mag.; 3-shot magazine; 25-inch barrel; weighs 9-1/2 lbs.; Monte Carlo checkered walnut pistol-grip stock; cheekpiece; recoil pad; stock crossbolts; front sling swivel stud mounted on barrel. Introduced 1956; discontinued 1963.
Exc.: $3700   **VGood:** $3000   **Good:** $2300

Winchester Model 70 Alaskan

Winchester Model 70 Bull Gun

Winchester Model 70 Featherweight

Winchester Model 70 Featherweight Monte Carlo

Winchester Model 70 National Match

Winchester Model 70 Super Grade

Winchester Model 70 Super Grade African

Winchester Model 70 Target

Winchester Model 70 Varmint

WINCHESTER MODEL 70 SUPER GRADE FEATHERWEIGHT
Same specs as Model 70 (1936-1963) except 243, 270, 30-06, 308; 22-inch barrel; lightweight deluxe Monte Carlo stock, cheekpiece; black pistol-grip cap, forearm tip; aluminum buttplate, triggerguard, floorplate; sling; quick-detachable swivels. Discontinued 1960.
Exc.: $3050   **VGood:** $1995   **Good:** $1095

WINCHESTER MODEL 70 TARGET
Same specs as Model 70 (1936-1963) except 24-inch, 26-inch medium-weight barrel; scope bases; walnut target Marksman stock; Lyman No. 77 front sight, Lyman No. 48WH rear, Army-type leather sling strap.
Exc.: $1995   **VGood:** $1100   **Good:** $795

WINCHESTER MODEL 70 VARMINT
Same specs as Model 70 (1936-1963) except 220 Swift, 243 Win.; 26-inch stainless heavy barrel; weighs 9-3/4 lbs. scope bases; checkered walnut varminter stock. Introduced 1956; discontinued 1963.
Exc.: $1195   **VGood:** $895   **Good:** $750

Winchester Model 70 Standard
(1964-1971)

Winchester Model 70 African

Winchester Model 70 Deluxe

Winchester Model 70
International Army Match

Winchester Model 70 Magnum

Winchester Model 70 Mannlicher

Winchester Model 70 Target

Winchester Model 70 Black Shadow

Winchester Model 70
Classic Custom Grade

Winchester Model 70
Featherweight Classic

WINCHESTER MODEL 70 DELUXE

Same specs as Model 70 (1964-1971) except 243, 270 Win., 30-06, 300 Win. Mag.; 3-shot magazine (magnum), 5-shot (other calibers); 22-inch, 24-inch barrel (magnum); hand-checkered walnut Monte Carlo stock, forearm; ebony forearm tip; recoil pad (magnum). Introduced 1964; discontinued 1971.

Perf.: $550   **Exc.:** $300   **VGood:** $250

WINCHESTER MODEL 70 INTERNATIONAL ARMY MATCH

Same specs as Model 70 (1964-1971) except 308; 5-shot box magazine; 24-inch heavy barrel; optional sights; International Shooting Union stock; forearm rail for accessories; adjustable buttplate; externally adjustable trigger. Introduced 1971; discontinued 1971.

Perf.: $850   **Exc.:** $650   **VGood:** $500

WINCHESTER MODEL 70 MAGNUM

Same specs as Model 70 (1964-1971) except 264 Win. Mag., 7mm Rem. Mag., 300 H&H Mag., 300 Win. Mag., 338 Win. Mag., 375 H&H Mag.; 3-shot magazine; 24-inch barrel; 4-41/2-inch overall length; weighs 7-1/4 lbs.

Perf.: $550   **Exc.:** $395   **VGood:** $260

WINCHESTER MODEL 70 MANNLICHER

Same specs as Model 70 (1964-1971) except 243, 220, 30-06, 308; 19-inch barrel; checkered Mannlicher stock with Monte Carlo comb, cheekpiece; steel forearm cap. Introduced 1969; discontinued 1972.

Perf.: $815   **Exc.:** $595   **VGood:** $495

WINCHESTER MODEL 70 TARGET

Same specs as Model 70 (1964-1971) except 30-06, 308; 5-shot box magazine; 24-inch heavy barrel; 44-1/2-inch overall length; weighs 10-1/4 lbs.; no sights; target scope blocks; checkered heavy high-comb Marksman stock; aluminum hand stop. Introduced 1964; discontinued 1971.

Perf.: $750   **Exc.:** $500   **VGood:** $400

WINCHESTER MODEL 70 (1972 TO PRESENT)

Bolt action; 22-250, 222, 25-06, 243, 270, 308, 30-06; 5-shot box magazine; 22-inch swaged, floating barrel; removable hooded ramp bead front sight, open rear; tapped for scope mounts; walnut Monte Carlo stock; cut checkering on pistol grip, forearm; forend tip; hinged floorplate; steel grip cap; sling swivels. Introduced 1972; discontinued 1980.

Perf.: $460   **Exc.:** $300   **VGood:** $220

WINCHESTER MODEL 70 BLACK SHADOW

Bolt action; 270, 30-06, 7mm Rem Mag, 300 Win Mag; 22-inch or 24-inch barrel; black composite stock, matte blue barrel and action. Push-feed bolt design; hinged floorplate. Made in U.S.A. by U.S. Repeating Arms Co. Introduced in 2000.

Perf.: $475   **Exc.:** $350   **VGood:** $300

WINCHESTER MODEL 70 CLASSIC CUSTOM GRADE

Same specs as Model 70 (1972 to present) except 270, 30-06, 7mm Rem. Mag., 300 Win. Mag., 338 Win. Mag.; 3-shot (magnum), 5-shot magazine; 24-inch, 26-inch barrel; fancy satin-finished walnut stock; hand-honed and fitted parts; Introduced 1990; discontinued 1994.

Perf.: $1350   **Exc.:** $995   **VGood:** $695

WINCHESTER MODEL 70 CLASSIC CUSTOM GRADE FEATHERWEIGHT

Same specs as Model 70 (1972 to present) except 22-250, 223, 243, 270, 280, 30-06, 308, 7mm-08 Rem.; no sights; checkered, satin-finished, high-grade American walnut stock, schnabel forend; rubber buttpad; high polish blued finish; controlled round feeding. Introduced 1992; no longer in production.

Perf.: $950   **Exc.:** $650   **VGood:** $500

WINCHESTER MODEL 70 (1964-1971)

Bolt action; 22-250, 222, 225, 243, 270, 308, 30-06, (standard calibers); 5-shot box magazine; 22-inch heavy barrel; 42-1/2-inch overall length; weighs 7 lbs.; plunger-type extractor; hooded ramp front sight, adjustable open rear; checkered walnut Monte Carlo stock, cheekpiece; sling swivels. Introduced 1964; discontinued 1971.

Exc.: $395   **VGood:** $325   **Good:** $300

WINCHESTER MODEL 70 AFRICAN

Same specs as Model 70 (1964-1971) except 375 H&H Mag., 458 Win. Mag.; 22-inch barrel (375 H&H Mag.), 24-inch (458 Win. Mag.); 42-1/2-inch overall length; weighs 8-1/2 lbs.; special sights; hand-checkered walnut Monte Carlo stock; ebony forearm tip; recoil pad; quick-detachable swivels; sling; twin crossbolts. Introduced 1964; discontinued 1971.

Perf.: $795   **Exc.:** $525   **VGood:** $450

WINCHESTER MODEL 70 CLASSIC CUSTOM GRADE SHARPSHOOTER

Same specs as Model 70 (1972 to present) except 223, 22-250, 308 Win., 300 Win. Mag.; 24-inch (308), 26-inch (223, 22-250, 300 Win. Mag.) barrel; 44-1/2-inch overall length (24-inch barrel); weighs 11 lbs.; no sights; scope bases and rings; glass-bedded McMillan A-2 target style stock with recoil pad, swivel studs; controlled round feeding; hand-honed and fitted action; Schneider barrel; matte blue finish. Introduced 1992; discontinued 1994.

Perf.: $1795   **Exc.:** $1395   **VGood:** $795

WINCHESTER MODEL 70 CLASSIC CUSTOM GRADE SPORTING SHARPSHOOTER

Same specs as Model 70 (1972 to present) except 220 Swift, 270, 7mm STW, 300 Win. Mag.; 24-inch (270), 26-inch stainless steel Schneider barrel, glass-bedded with natural finish; 44-1/2-inch overall length (24-inch barrel); no sights; scope bases and rings; McMillan sporter-style, gray-finished composite stock; blued receiver; pre-'64-style action with controlled round feeding. Introduced 1994; discontinued 1994.

Perf.: $1650   **Exc.:** $1195   **VGood:** $895

WINCHESTER MODEL 70 CLASSIC DBM (DETACHABLE BOX MAGAZINE)

Same specs as Model 70 (1972 to present) except 22-250, 243, 308, 284 Win., 270, 30-06, 7mm Rem. Mag., 300 Win. Mag.; 3-shot detachable box magazine; 24-inch, 26-inch barrel; with or without sights; scope bases and rings; pre-'64-type action with controlled round feeding. Introduced 1994; discontinued 1995.

Perf.: $485   **Exc.:** $395   **VGood:** $330

WINCHESTER MODEL 70 CLASSIC DBM-S

Same specs as Model 70 (1972 to present) except 270, 30-06, 7mm Rem. Mag., 300 Win. Mag.; 3-shot detachable box magazine; 24-inch barrel; with or without sights; scope bases and rings; black fiberglass/graphite composite stock; pre-'64-type controlled round feeding. Introduced 1994; discontinued 1994.

Perf.: $560   **Exc.:** $390   **VGood:** $330

WINCHESTER MODEL 70 CLASSIC FEATHERWEIGHT

Same specs as Model 70 (1972 to present) except 22-250, 223, 243, 270, 280, 30-06, 308, 7mm-08; no sights; scope bases and rings; standard-grade walnut stock; claw extractor; controlled-round feeding system. Introduced 1992.

Perf.: $590   **Exc.:** $510   **VGood:** $330

WINCHESTER MODEL 70 CLASSIC FEATHERWEIGHT COMPACT

Similar to Classic Featherweight except scaled down for smaller shooters. 20-inch barrel, 12-1/2-inch length of pull. Pre-'64-type action. Available in 243, 308 or 7mm-08. Introduced 1998. Made in U.S.A. by U. S. Repeating Arms Co.

Perf.: $650   **Exc.:** $560   **VGood:** $385

WINCHESTER MODEL 70 CLASSIC SAFARI EXPRESS

Bolt action; 375 H&H Mag., 416 Rem. Mag., 458 Win. Mag., 3-shot magazine; 24-inch barrel; weighs 8-1/4 to 8-1/2 lbs. American walnut stock with Monte Carlo cheekpiece. Wrap-around checkering and finish. Sights: Hooded ramp front, open rear. Controlled round feeding. Two steel cross bolts in stock for added strength. Front sling swivel stud mounted on barrel. Contoured rubber butt pad. From U.S. Repeating Arms Co. Introduced 1999.

Perf.: $925   **Exc.:** $750   **VGood:** $670

WINCHESTER MODEL 70 CLASSIC SM

Same specs as Model 70 (1972 to present) except black composite, graphite-impregnated stock; black matte-finished metal; pre-'64-type action with controlled feeding; 264 Win. Mag., 270, 30-06, 7mm Rem. Mag., 300 Win. Mag., 300 Weatherby Mag.,

Winchester Model 70 Classic Safari Express

Winchester Model 70 Classic Sporter LT

Winchester Model 70 Classic Stainless

Winchester Model 70 Classic Super Grade

Winchester Model 70 Coyote

338 Win. Mag., 375 H&H Mag.; 3-shot magazine (magnum), 5-shot (others); 24-inch, 26-inch barrel; weighs 7-3/4 lbs.; with or without sights; scope bases and rings; BOSS barrel vibration modulator and muzzle brake system optional. Introduced 1994.

Perf.: $495   **Exc.:** $410   **VGood:** $360

375 H&H
Perf.: $560   **Exc.:** $460   **VGood:** $390

With BOSS (270, 30-06, 7mm Rem. Mag., 300 Win. Mag., 338 Win. Mag.)
Perf.: $600   **Exc.:** $510   **VGood:** $440

WINCHESTER MODEL 70 CLASSIC SPORTER

Same specs as Model 70 (1972 to present) except 25-06, 264 Win. Mag., 270, 270 Win. Mag., 300 Win. Mag., 300 Weatherby Mag., 338 Win. Mag., 7mm Rem. Mag.; 3-shot magazine (magnum), 5-shot (others); 24-inch, 26-inch barrel; controlled round feeding. Introduced 1994.

Perf.: $705   **Exc.:** $610   **VGood:** $560

WINCHESTER MODEL 70 CLASSIC SPORTER LT

Bolt action; 25-06, 270 Win., 30-06, 7mm STW, 7mm Rem. Mag., 300 Win. Mag., 338 Win. Mag., 3-shot magazine; 5-shot for 25-06, 270 Win., 30-06; 24-inch barrel, 26-inch for magnums; weighs 7-3/4 to 8 lbs.; 46-3/4-inch overall length (26-inch bbl.); American walnut stock with cut checkering and satin finish, classic style with straight comb. Drilled and tapped for scope mounting. Uses pre-64-type action with controlled round feeding. Three-position safety, stainless steel magazine follower; rubber butt pad; epoxy bedded receiver recoil lug. From U.S. Repeating Arms Co. Introduced 1999; premium for left-hand action.

Perf.: $610   **Exc.:** $510   **VGood:** $400

WINCHESTER MODEL 70 CLASSIC STAINLESS

Same specs as Model 70 (1972 to present) except 22-250, 243, 308, 270, 30-06, 7mm Rem. Mag., 300 Win. Mag., 300 WSM, 300 Weatherby Mag., 338 Win. Mag., 375 H&H Mag.; 3-shot magazine (magnum), 5-shot (others); 22-inch, 24-inch, 26-inch stainless steel barrel; weighs 6-3/4 lbs.; no sights; drilled, tapped for scope mounts; black fiberglass/graphite composite stock; matte gray finish; stainless steel

pre-'64-type action with controlled feeding; BOSS barrel vibration modulator and muzzlebrake system optional. Introduced 1994.

Perf.: $625   **Exc.:** $420   **VGood:** $360

375 H&H Mag., with sights
Perf.: $875   **Exc.:** $670   **VGood:** $610

With BOSS (all except 300 Wea. Mag., 375 H&H Mag.)
Perf.: $700   **Exc.:** $535   **VGood:** $430

WINCHESTER MODEL 70 CLASSIC SUPER GRADE

Same specs as Model 70 (1972 to present) except 270, 30-06, 7mm Rem. Mag., 300 Win. Mag., 338 Win. Mag.; 3-shot magazine (magnum), 5-shot (others); 24-inch barrel; no sights; scope bases and rings; straight-comb walnut stock with sculptured cheekpiece, tapered forend; wraparound cut checkering; solid buttpad; stainless steel claw extractor, magazine follower, bolt guide rail; three-position safety; hinged floorplate; pre-'64-type action with controlled round feeding; BOSS barrel vibration modulator and muzzlebrake system optional. Introduced 1994.

Perf.: $1050   **Exc.:** $975   **VGood:** $795

With BOSS system
Perf.: $1100   **Exc.:** $1025   **VGood:** $975

WINCHESTER MODEL 70 CLASSIC SUPER EXPRESS MAGNUM

Same specs as Model 70 (1972 to present) except 375 H&H, 375 JRS, 7mm STW, 416 Rem. Mag., 458 Win. Mag., 470 Capstick; 3-shot magazine; 22-inch barrel (458 Win. Mag.), 24-inch (others); weighs 8-1/2 lbs.; three-leaf express rear sight; deluxe checkered, satin-finished walnut stock; controlled round feed action; two steel crossbolts; barrel mounted front swivel stud. Introduced 1990.

Perf.: $1500   **Exc.:** $1200   **VGood:** $975

WINCHESTER MODEL 70 COYOTE

Similar to Model 70 Black Shadow except laminated wood stock, 24-inch medium-heavy stainless steel barrel. 223, 223 WSSM, 22-250, 243, 243 WSSM, 25 WSSM, 270, 270 WSM, 7mm WSM, 300 WSM, 325 WSM. Introduced 2000. Add 15 percent for short magnum chamberings.

Perf.: $680   **Exc.:** $500   **VGood:** $430

Winchester Model 70 Heavy Varmint

Winchester Model 70 Lightweight

Winchester Model 70 Lightweight Carbine

Winchester Model 70 Ranger

Winchester Model 70 Ranger Youth/Ladies

Winchester Model 70 Stealth

Winchester Model 70 Target

WINCHESTER MODEL 70 CUSTOM SHARPSHOOTER

Same specs as Model 70 (1972 to present) except 223, 22-250, 308 Win., 300 Win. Mag.; 24-inch barrel (308), 26-inch (others); weighs 11 lbs.; no sights; scope bases and rings; McMillan A-2 target-style stock, glass bedded; hand-honed and fitted action; Schneider barrel; matte blue finish. Introduced 1992; discontinued 1994.

Perf.: $1300   **Exc.:** $950   **VGood:** $750

WINCHESTER MODEL 70 DBM

Same specs as Model 70 (1972 to present) except 22-250, 223, 243, 270, 30-06, 308, 7mm Rem. Mag., 300 Win. Mag.; 3-shot detachable box magazine; 24-inch, 26-inch barrel; with or without sights; scope bases and rings. Introduced 1992; discontinued 1994.

Perf.: $780   **Exc.:** $695   **VGood:** $525

WINCHESTER MODEL 70 FEATHERWEIGHT WINTUFF

Same specs as Model 70 (1972 to present) except 22-250, 223, 243, 270, 30-06, 308; no sights; scope bases and rings; brown laminated checkered pistol-grip stock; schnabel forend. Introduced 1988; discontinued 1990.

Perf.: $750   **Exc.:** $675   **VGood:** $510

WINCHESTER MODEL 70 HEAVY BARREL VARMINT

Same specs as Model 70 (1972 to present) except 22-250, 223, 243, 308; heavy 26-inch barrel with counter-bored muzzle; 46-inch overall length; weighs 9 lbs.; no sights; drilled, tapped for scope mounts; sporter-style stock; rubber buttpad. Introduced 1989; discontinued 1994.

Perf.: $650   **Exc.:** $500   **VGood:** $420

WINCHESTER MODEL 70 HEAVY VARMINT

Same specs as Model 70 (1972 to present) except 220 Swift, 22-250, 223, 243, 308; weighs 10-3/4 lbs.; heavy 26-inch stainless barrel with counter-bored muzzle; no sights; black synthetic stock with full-length Pillar Plus AccuBlock, beavertail forend; rubber buttpad. Introduced 1989; discontinued 1994.

Perf.: $685   **Exc.:** $610   **VGood:** $530

WINCHESTER MODEL 70 LIGHTWEIGHT

Same specs as Model 70 (1972 to present) except 22-250, 223 Rem., 243 Win., 270 Win., 280, 308 Win., 30-06; 5-shot magazine, 6-shot (223 Rem.); 22-inch barrel; no sights; drilled, tapped for scope mounts; satin-finished American walnut stock; machine-cut checkering; three-position safety; stainless steel magazine follower; hinged floorplate. Introduced 1984.

Perf.: $520   **Exc.:** $430   **VGood:** $400

WINCHESTER MODEL 70 LIGHTWEIGHT CARBINE

Same specs as Model 70 (1972 to present) except 22-250, 222, 223, 243, 250 Savage, 270, 308, 30-06; 5-shot magazine, 6-shot (223); 20-inch barrel;

drilled, tapped for scope mounts; satin-finished American walnut stock; cut checkering; stainless steel magazine follower; three-position safety; hinged floorplate. Introduced 1984; discontinued 1986.

Perf.: $520   **Exc.:** $410   **VGood:** $380

WINCHESTER MODEL 70 RANGER

Bolt action; 223, 243, 270, 30-06, 7mm Rem. Mag.; 3-shot magazine (7mm Rem. Mag.), 4-shot (others); 22-inch, 24-inch barrel; weighs 7-1/8 lbs.; economy version of Winchester Model 70; American hardwood stock; no checkering; composition buttplate; matte blue finish. Introduced 1985.

Perf.: $370   **Exc.:** $320   **VGood:** $235

WINCHESTER MODEL 70 RANGER YOUTH/LADIES RIFLE

Same specs as Ranger; 223, 243, 308; 7mm-08; 4-shot magazine; 20-inch, 22-inch barrel; weighs 5-3/4 lbs.; scaled-down American hardwood stock with 1-inch shorter length of pull; no checkering; composition buttplate; matte blue finish. Introduced 1985.

Perf.: $370   **Exc.:** $320   **VGood:** $220

WINCHESTER MODEL 70 SHB (SYNTHETIC HEAVY BARREL)

Same specs as Model 70 (1972 to present) except 308; heavy 26-inch barrel with counter-bored muzzle; weighs 9 lbs.; black synthetic stock with checkering; matte blue finish. Introduced 1992; discontinued 1992.

Perf.: $460   **Exc.:** $400   **VGood:** $340

WINCHESTER MODEL 70 SPORTER SSM

Same specs as Model 70 (1972 to present) except 223, 22-250, 243, 270, 308, 30-06, 7mm Rem. Mag., 300 Win. Mag., 338 Win. Mag., 375 H&H Mag.; 3-shot magazine (magnum), 5-shot (others); 24-inch, 26-inch barrel; weighs 7-3/4 lbs.; no sights; scope bases and rings; black composite, graphite-impregnated stock; matte finish metal. Introduced 1992; discontinued 1993.

Perf.: $450   **Exc.:** $360   **VGood:** $310

WINCHESTER MODEL 70 SPORTER WINTUFF

Same specs as Model 70 (1972 to present) except 270, 30-06, 7mm Rem. Mag., 300 Win. Mag., 300 Weatherby Mag., 338 Win. Mag.; 3-shot magazine (magnum), 5-shot (others); 24-inch barrel; bases and rings for scope mounts; checkered brown laminated stock; rubber recoil pad. Introduced 1992; discontinued 1992.

Perf.: $560   **Exc.:** $470   **VGood:** $420

WINCHESTER MODEL 70 STEALTH RIFLE

Bolt action; 223, 223 WSSM, 22-250, 243 WSSM, 25 WSSM, 308 Win.; 26-inch barrel; weighs 10-3/4 lbs.; 46-inch overall length; Kevlar/fiberglass/graphite stock, Pillar Plus Accu-Block with full-length aluminum bedding block. Push-feed bolt design; matte finish. Introduced 1999. Made in U.S.A. by U.S. Repeating Arms Co

Perf.: $820   **Exc.:** $650   **VGood:** $560

WINCHESTER MODEL 70 SYNTHETIC HEAVY VARMINT

Same specs as Model 70 (1972 to present) except 223, 22-250, 243, 308; 26-inch heavy stainless steel barrel; weighs 10-3/4 lbs.; fiberglass/graphite stock; full-length Pillar Plus AccuBlock stock bedding system. Introduced 1993.

Perf.: $625   **Exc.:** $495   **VGood:** $410

WINCHESTER MODEL 70 TARGET

Same specs as Model 70 (1972 to present) except 30-06, 308; 26-inch heavy barrel; contoured aluminum hand stop for either left- or right-handed shooter; high-comb target stock; tapped for micrometer sights. No longer in production.

Perf.: $710   **Exc.:** $520   **VGood:** $480

WINCHESTER MODEL 70 VARMINT

Same specs as Model 70 (1972 to present) except 22-250, 223, 225, 243, 308; 24-inch heavy barrel; no sights; black serrated buttplate; black forend tip; high-luster finish on walnut stock. Introduced 1972; designated XTR 1978; designation dropped 1989; discontinued 1993.

Perf.: $560   **Exc.:** $500   **VGood:** $440

WINCHESTER MODEL 70 WINLITE

Same specs as Model 70 (1972 to present) except 25-06, 270, 280, 30-06, 7mm Rem. Mag., 300 Win. Mag., 300 Weatherby Mag., 338 Win. Mag.; 3-, 4-shot magazine; 22-inch, 24-inch (magnum) barrel; McMillan brown fiberglass stock. Introduced 1986; discontinued 1990.

Perf.: $470   **Exc.:** $400   **VGood:** $350

WINCHESTER MODEL 70 XTR

Same specs as Model 70 (1972 to present) except 222, 22-250, 25-06, 243, 270, 308, 30-06, 264 Win. Mag., 7mm Rem. Mag., 300 Win. Mag., 338 Win. Mag.; 3-shot magazine (magnum), 5-shot (others); 22-inch, 24-inch (magnum) barrel; satin-finished stock. Introduced 1978; discontinued 1989.

Perf.: $495   **Exc.:** $440   **VGood:** $400

WINCHESTER MODEL 70 XTR FEATHERWEIGHT

Same specs as Model 70 (1972 to present) except 22-250, 223, 243, 25-06, 257 Roberts, 270, 280, 7x57, 6.5x55 Swedish, 30-06, 308, 7mm-08, 7mm Rem. Mag., 300 Win. Mag.; 22-inch, 24-inch (300 Win. Mag.) tapered barrel; no sights; checkered satin-finished American walnut stock, schnabel forend; red rubber buttpad; high-polish blued finish on metal; optional blade front sight, adjustable folding rear. Introduced 1981; XTR designation dropped 1989; no longer in production. Add 10 percent for 257, 6.5 chamberings.

Perf.: $510   **Exc.:** $450   **VGood:** $400

With sights
Perf.: $530   **Exc.:** $460   **VGood:** $400

WINCHESTER MODEL 70 XTR FEATHERWEIGHT EUROPEAN

Same specs as Model 70 (1972 to present) except 6.5x55 Swedish chambering; weighs 6-3/4 lbs. Introduced 1986; discontinued 1986.

Perf.: $570   **Exc.:** $530   **VGood:** $490

WINCHESTER MODEL 70 XTR SPORTER

Same specs as Model 70 (1972 to present) except 22-250, 223, 243, 25-06, 264 Win. Mag., 270, 270 Weatherby Mag., 30-06, 300 Win. Mag., 300 Weatherby Mag., 300 H&H, 308, 7mm Rem. Mag., 338 Win. Mag.; 3-shot magazine (magnum), 5-shot (others); 24-inch barrel; three-position safety; stainless steel magazine follower; rubber buttpad. Introduced 1980; XTR designation dropped 1989; no longer in production.

Perf.: $395   **Exc.:** $330   **VGood:** $300

WINCHESTER MODEL 70 XTR SUPER EXPRESS MAGNUM

Same specs as Model 70 (1972 to present) except 375 H&H Mag., 458 Win Mag.; 3-shot magazine; 22-inch, 24-inch barrel; steel crossbolts; contoured rubber buttpad. Introduced 1981; discontinued 1989.

Perf.: $1100   **Exc.:** $1000   **VGood:** $850

WINCHESTER MODEL 70 SHADOW ELITE STAINLESS

Bolt-action rifle. Calibers: .22-250, .243, .308, .270, .30-06, .300 WM, .338 WM, .375 H&H, .270 WSM, 7mm WSM, .300 WSM, .325 WSM. Barrel: Stainless steel, 24-inch or 26-inch (.300, .338 WM). Stock: Overmolded composite. Weight: 6-1/2 – 7-3/4 lbs. Magazine capacity: 3 or 5 (.22-250, .243, .308, .270, .30-06).

NIB: $700   **Exc.:** $620   **VGood:** $495

WINCHESTER MODEL 70 SHADOW ELITE CAMO STAINLESS

Similar to Shadow Elite Stainless but with Mossy Oak New Break Up camo synthetic stock.

NIB: $775   **Exc.:** $675   **VGood:** $495

Winchester Model 70 Varmint

Winchester Model 70 Winlite

Winchester Model 70 XTR Featherweight

Winchester Model 70 Varmint

Winchester Model 70 Featherweight Deluxe (2008 Production)

Winchester Model 70 Sporter Deluxe (2008 Production)

Winchester Model 70 Extreme Weather SS (2008 Production)

Winchester Model 70A

WINCHESTER MODEL 70 PRO SHADOW BLUED

Bolt-action rifle. Calibers: .22-250, .243, .308, .270, .30-06, 7mm RM, .300 WM, .270 WSM, 7mm WSM, .300 WSM, .325 WSM. Barrel: Blued steel, 22-inch (standard) or 24-inch (magnum). Stock: Overmolded composite. Weight: 6-1/2 – 7 lbs. Magazine capacity: 3 (magnum) or 5 (standard).

NIB: $550   **Exc.:** $495   **VGood:** $375

WINCHESTER MODEL 70 PRO SHADOW STAINLESS

Similar to Pro Shadow blued but with stainless steel barrel and .338 WM and .375 H&H chamberings.

NIB: $650   **Exc.:** $595   **VGood:** $495

WINCHESTER MODEL 70 LAMINATED COYOTE OUTBACK STAINLESS

Similar to Model 70 Coyote Lite but with skeletonized laminated stock and stainless steel only. Calibers: .22-250, .243, .308, .270, .30-06, 7mm RM, .300 WM, .270 WSM, 7mm WSM, .300 WSM, .325 WSM. Weight: 7-3/4 lbs.

NIB: $975   **Exc.:** $895   **VGood:** $625

WINCHESTER MODEL 70 LAMINATED COYOTE GRAY OR BROWN STAINLESS

Similar to Model 70 Laminated Coyote Outback but with non-fluted barrel and choice of brown or gray laminated stock.

NIB: $675   **Exc.:** $600   **VGood:** $475

WINCHESTER MODEL 70 FEATHERWEIGHT DELUXE (2008 PRODUCTION)

Pre-64 action, three-position safety, jewelled bolt, knurled bolt handle, walnut stock with slight schnabel, cut checkering, Pachmayr Decelerator recoil pad., 22- or 24-inch barrel depending on caliber. Chambered for a variety of cartridges from .243 to .325 Winchester Short Magnum. Weight 6.5 to 7 lbs.

New: $1100   **Exc.:** $890   **VGood:** $650

WINCHESTER MODEL 70 SPORTER DELUXE (2008 PRODUCTION)

Similar to above but with non-schnabel forend and cheekpiece.

New: $1000   **Exc.:** $790   **VGood:** $550

WINCHESTER NEW MODEL 70 SUPER GRADE SPECIAL LIMITED EDITION

Very fancy version of the Model 70 featuring post-'64 action, ultra-premium walnut, gold-filled engraving, black forend cap, steel grip cap, and shadowline cheekpiece. Only 250 produced in 2008. Chambered in .300 Winchester Magnum only.

New: $2400   **Exc.:** $1775   **VGood:** $1200

WINCHESTER MODEL 70 EXTREME WEATHER SS (2008 PRODUCTION)

Post-'64 style action with 22-, 24- or 26-inch barrel depending on chambering. Three-position safety, fluted stainless barrel and Bell and Carlson composite stock. Chambered for a variety of cartridges from .308 to .325 Winchester Short Magnum.

New: $1100   **Exc.:** $890   **VGood:** $650

WINCHESTER MODEL 70A

Bolt action; 222 Rem., 22-250, 243 Win., 25-06, 264 Win. Mag., 270 Win., 30-06, 308 Win., 7mm Rem. Mag., 300 Win. Mag.; 22-inch, 24-inch barrel;

Winchester Model 75 Sporter

Winchester Model 75 Target

Winchester Model 121

Winchester Model 131

Winchester Model 141

Winchester Model 310

Winchester Model 320

Winchester Wildcat

Winchester Model 670

serves as trigger. Introduced 1904; discontinued 1923. Some collector interest.

Exc.: $1995   **VGood:** $995   **Good:** $695

WINCHESTER MODEL 121

Bolt action; single shot; 22 Short, 22 Long, 22 LR; 20-3/4-inch barrel; weighs 5 lbs.; standard post bead front sight, adjustable V rear; one-piece American hardwood pistol-grip stock with modified Monte Carlo profile; grooved for tip-off scope mounts. Introduced 1967; discontinued 1973.

Exc.: $200   **VGood:** $175   **Good:** $150

Winchester Model 121Y Youth with shortened stock

Exc.: $185   **VGood:** $160   **Good:** $135

Winchester Model 121 Deluxe with ramp front sight, swivels

Exc.: $225   **VGood:** $200   **Good:** $175

WINCHESTER MODEL 131

Bolt action; 22 Short, 22 Long, 22 LR; 7-shot clip magazine; 20-inch barrel; weighs 5 lbs.; ramped bead post front sight, adjustable rear; receiver grooved for telescopic sight mounts; one-piece American hardwood stock with fluted comb, modified Monte Carlo profile; red safety; red cocking indicator. Introduced 1967; discontinued 1973.

Exc.: $200   **VGood:** $175   **Good:** $150

WINCHESTER MODEL 141

Bolt action; 22 Short, 22 Long, 22 LR; 19-shot tube magazine (22 Short), 15-shot (22 Long), 13-shot (22 LR); 20-3/4-inch barrel; weighs 5 lbs.; ramped bead post front, adjustable rear sight; American hardwood stock with fluted comb, modified Monte Carlo; red cocking indicator; red-marked safety. Introduced 1967; discontinued 1973.

Exc.: $200   **VGood:** $175   **Good:** $150

WINCHESTER MODEL 310

Bolt action; single shot; 22 Short, 22 Long, 22 LR; 22-inch barrel; 39-inch overall length; weighs 5-5/8 lbs.; ramped bead post front sight, adjustable rear; grooved for scope sight; drilled, tapped for micrometer rear sight; checkered American walnut Monte Carlo pistol-grip stock, forearm; serrated trigger; positive safety lever; swivels. Introduced 1971; discontinued 1974.

Exc.: $180   **VGood:** $150   **Good:** $115

WINCHESTER MODEL 320

Bolt action; 22 Short, 22 Long, 22 LR; 5-shot magazine; 22-inch barrel; 30-1/2-inch overall length; weighs 5-5/8 lbs.; ramped bead post front sight, adjustable rear; grooved for scope mounts; drilled, tapped for micrometer rear sight; American walnut Monte Carlo pistol-grip stock, forearm; sling swivels; serrated trigger; positive safety. Introduced 1971; discontinued 1974.

Exc.: $310   **VGood:** $250   **Good:** $1390

WINCHESTER WILDCAT

Bolt-action repeater styled after Mosin-Nagant military sporter. Caliber: .22 LR. Magazine: 5- and 10-round detachable. Stock: checkered walnut with Schnabel. Barrel: 21-inch blued. Weight:4.5 lbs. Imported.

NIB: $275   **Exc.:** $225   **VGood:** $175

WINCHESTER MODEL 670

Bolt action; Introduced in 1967 as economy version of Model 70; 225, 243, 270, 308, 30-06; 4-shot magazine; 19-inch, 24-inch barrel; ramp bead front sight, adjustable rear; sights easily detached for scope mounting; hardwood Monte Carlo pistol-grip stock; 2-position safety; discontinued 1973.

Exc.: $375   **VGood:** $265   **Good:** $200

WINCHESTER MODEL 670 MAGNUM

Same specs as Model 670 except 264 Win. Mag., 7mm Rem. Mag., 300 Win. Mag.; 3-shot magazine. Introduced 1967; discontinued 1970.

Exc.: $400   **VGood:** $300   **Good:** $275

adjustable leaf rear sight with white diamond for quick sighting, hooded ramp front; dark American walnut with high-comb Monte Carlo, undercut cheekpiece; three-position safety. Introduced 1972 as replacement for Model 770, more closely following style of Model 70; discontinued 1978.

Perf.: $320   **Exc.:** $290   **VGood:** $240

WINCHESTER MODEL 72

Bolt action; 22 Short, 22 Long, 22 LR; 22-shot tubular magazine (22 Short), 16-shot (22 Long), 15-shot (22 LR); 25-inch barrel; takedown; peep or open rear sight, bead front; uncheckered pistol-grip stock. Introduced 1938; discontinued 1959.

Exc.: $390   **VGood:** $280   **Good:** $245

WINCHESTER MODEL 72 GALLERY

Same specs as Model 72 except 22 Short only. Introduced 1939; discontinued 1942.

Perf.: $465   **Exc.:** $295   **VGood:** $260

WINCHESTER MODEL 72 TARGET

Same specs as Model 72 except rear peep sight, blade front; sling swivels.

Exc.: $415   **VGood:** $290   **Good:** $250

WINCHESTER MODEL 75 SPORTER

Bolt action; 22 LR; 5-, 10-shot clip magazine; 24-inch barrel; weighs 5-1/2 lbs.; open rear sight, hooded ramp blade front; checkered select walnut stock, pistol grip; hard rubber grip cap; swivels; checkered steel buttplate; cocked with opening movement of bolt. Introduced 1939; discontinued 1958.

Exc.: $750   **VGood:** $625   **Good:** $525

WINCHESTER MODEL 75 TARGET

Same specs as Model 75 except 28-inch barrel; 44-3/4-inch overall length; weighs 8-5/8 lbs.; target scope or variety of sights; uncheckered walnut stock, semi-beavertail forearm, pistol grip; 1-inch Army-type leather sling. Introduced 1938; discontinued 1958.

Exc.: $570   **VGood:** $440   **Good:** $300

WINCHESTER MODEL 99 THUMB TRIGGER

Bolt action; single shot; 22 Short, 22 Long, 22 Extra Long; 18-inch round barrel; takedown; open rear sight, blade front; straight-grip one-piece American walnut stock; thumb button at rear of cocking piece

RIFLES

WINCHESTER MODEL 677

Bolt action; single shot; scoped version of Model 67; 22 Short, 22 Long, 22 LR, 22 WRF; 24-inch barrel; takedown; no sights; scope mounts mounted on barrel, Winchester 5A scope provided; uncheckered pistol-grip stock, grooved forearm. Enjoyed little success due to poor scope-mounting system. Introduced 1937; discontinued 1939. Only 2239 produced. Some collector value with original scope. Premium for 22 WMRFchambering.

Exc.: $895   **VGood:** $595   **Good:** $395

WINCHESTER MODEL 697

Bolt action; repeater; scoped version of Model 69; 22 Short, 22 Long, 22 LR; 5-, 10-shot detachable box magazine; 25-inch barrel; no sights; scope bases attached to barrel; choice of 2-3/4x or 5x Winchester scope. Introduced 1937; discontinued 1941. Collector interest with original scope.

Exc.: $995   **VGood:** $695   **Good:** $425

WINCHESTER MODEL 770

Bolt action; 222 Rem., 22-250, 243 Win., 270 Win., 308 Win., 30-06; 22-inch barrel; weighs 7-1/2 lbs.; hooded ramp front sight, adjustable rear; checkered walnut Monte Carlo pistol-grip stock, cheekpiece, forearm; composition buttplate; red cocking indicator. This rifle was designed as a lower-echelon Model 70 but failed to meet acceptance, and was dropped after only four years and replaced by Model 70A. Introduced 1969; discontinued 1972.

Exc.: $330   **VGood:** $300   **Good:** $250

WINCHESTER MODEL 770 MAGNUM

Same specs as Model 770 except 264 Win. Mag., 7mm Rem. Mag., 300 Win. Mag.; 3-shot magazine; 24-inch barrel; rubber recoil pad. Introduced 1969; discontinued 1972. Replaced by Model 70A.

Exc.: $350   **VGood:** $320   **Good:** $270

WINCHESTER MODEL 1900

Bolt action; single shot; 22 Short, 22 Long; 18-inch round barrel; takedown; open rear sight, blade front; straight-grip one-piece American walnut stock. Introduced 1899; discontinued 1902. Some collector interest.

VGood: $450   **Good:** $325   **Fair:** $220

WINCHESTER MODEL 1902

Bolt action; single shot; 22 Short, 22 Long, 22 Extra Long; 18-inch round barrel; takedown; open rear sight, blade front; straight-grip one-piece American walnut stock; enlarged trigger guard forms pistol grip. Introduced 1902; discontinued 1931.

VGood: $275   **Good:** $175   **Fair:** $125

WINCHESTER MODEL 1904

Bolt action; single shot; 22 Short, 22 Long, 22 Extra Long, 22 LR; 21-inch round barrel; takedown; open rear sight, blade front; straight-grip one-piece American walnut stock; enlarged trigger guard forms pistol grip. Introduced 1904; discontinued 1931. Some collector interest.

VGood: $300   **Good:** $200   **Fair:** $160

WINCHESTER MODEL 1904/1899 THUMB TRIGGER

Similar to basic Model 1904 but has no traditional trigger. Trigger is loctaed on upper tang and is operated with thumb. A John Browning design (who else)?

VGood: $550   **Good:** $2450   **Fair:** $275

WINCHESTER MODEL 1904-A

Same specs as Model 1904 except 22 LR. Introduced 1927; discontinued 1931.

VGood: $300   **Good:** $200   **Fair:** $160

WINCHESTER MODEL 53

Lever action; 25-20, 32-20, 44-40; 6-shot half-magazine; 22-inch barrel; open rear sight, bead front; walnut pistol-grip or straight-grip stock; blued finish; based on the Model 92 design. Introduced 1924; discontinued 1932.

Exc.: $2295   **VGood:** $1295   **Good:** $795

Winchester Model 770

Winchester Model 1900

Winchester Model 1902

Winchester Model 1904

Winchester Model 55 Centerfire

Winchester Model 64 (Early Production)

Winchester Model 64 Deer Rifle

Takedown model
Exc.: $2495   **VGood:** $1495   **Good:** $995
(Premium for .44-40 Cal)

WINCHESTER MODEL 55 CENTERFIRE

Lever action; 25-35, 30-30, 32 Spl.; 3-shot tubular magazine; 24-inch round barrel; open rear sight, bead front; uncheckered American walnut straight grip stock, forend. Based on Model 94 design. Collector value. Introduced 1924; discontinued 1932.

Exc.: $1495   **VGood:** $895   **Good:** $595

Takedown model
Exc.: $1595   **VGood:** $995   **Good:** $650

WINCHESTER MODEL 64 (EARLY PRODUCTION)

Lever action; 219 Zipper, 25-35, 30-30, 32 Spl.; 20-inch, 24-inch barrel; weighs 7 lbs.; Winchester No. 22H open sporting or Lyman No. 56 (20-inch barrel) open rear sight, hooded ramp bead front;

uncheckered American walnut pistol-grip stock, forend. Originally manufactured 1933 to 1957. Collector value on original production. Premium for .219 Zipp[er.

Exc.: $1295   **VGood:** $895   **Good:** $540

WINCHESTER MODEL 64 (LATE PRODUCTION)

Lever action; 30-30; 5-shot tube magazine; 24-inch barrel; open rear sight, ramped bead front; uncheckered American walnut pistol-grip stock, forend. Introduced 1972; discontinued 1973.

Exc.: $395   **VGood:** $300   **Good:** $250

WINCHESTER MODEL 64 DEER RIFLE

Same specs as Model 64 except 30-30, 32 Spl.; weighs 7-3/4 lbs.; hand-checkered pistol-grip stock, forend; 1-inch sling swivels; sling; checkered steel buttplate; discontinued 1957.

Exc.: $1320   **VGood:** $950   **Good:** $650

Winchester Model 65
Winchester Model 71 Deluxe
Winchester Model 88
Winchester Model 88 Carbine
Winchester Model 94 Antique
Winchester Model 94 Classic
Winchester Model 94 Legacy
Winchester Model 94 Limited Edition Centennial Grade 1

barrel; 39-1/2-inch overall length; weighs 6-1/2 lbs.; hammerless; hooded white metal bead front sight, Lyman folding leaf middle sight; one-piece checkered walnut stock with steel-capped pistol grip, fluted comb, sling swivels; three-lug bolt; crossbolt safety; side ejection. Introduced 1955; discontinued 1974. Add 10 percent for 358.

308 Win.
Exc.: $695   VGood: $650   Good: $390
243 Win. (pre-1964)
Exc.: $715   VGood: $600   Good: $410
243 Win. (post-1964)
Exc.: $595   VGood: $450   Good: $390
284 Win. (pre-1964)
Exc.: $1575   VGood: $1150   Good: $650
284 Win. (post-1964)
Exc.: $995   VGood: $695   Good: $430
358 Win.
Exc.: $1350   VGood: $920   Good: $740

WINCHESTER MODEL 88 CARBINE
Same specs as Model 88 except 243, 284, 308; 19-inch barrel; barrel band. Introduced 1968; discontinued 1973.
Perf.: $1200   Exc.: $1090   VGood: $710

Note: The Winchester Model 94 was discontinued in 2006. Values fluctuate wildly.

WINCHESTER MODEL 94 (POST-1964 PRODUCTION)
Lever action; 30-30, 32 Spl., 7-30 Waters, 44 Mag.; 6-tube magazine; 20-inch, 24-inch barrel; weighs 6-1/4 lbs.; open rear sight, ramp front; plain American walnut straight-grip stock; barrel band on forearm; saddle ring; side or angle ejection (post-1982); blued finish. Introduced 1964; modified variations still in production. Premium for 7-30.
Exc.: $540   VGood: $480   Good: $350
Side or Angle Eject Model
Exc.: $550   VGood: $495   Good: $360

WINCHESTER MODEL 94 ANTIQUE
Same specs as Model 94 except 20-inch barrel; case-hardened receiver with scrollwork; gold-colored saddle ring. Introduced 1964; discontinued 1983.
Exc.: $530   VGood: $500   Good: $380

WINCHESTER MODEL 94 CLASSIC
Same specs as Model 94 except 30-30; 20-inch, 26-inch octagonal barrel; semi-fancy American walnut stock, forearm; steel buttplate; scrollwork on receiver. Introduced 1967; discontinued 1970.
Exc.: $610   VGood: $550   Good: $400

WINCHESTER MODEL 94 DELUXE
Same specs as Model 94 except 30-30; checkered walnut stock, forearm. Introduced 1988; later in production as Model 94 Traditional.
Exc.: $650   VGood: $605   Good: $480

WINCHESTER MODEL 94 LEGACY
Same specs as Model 94 except half-pistol-grip walnut stock; checkered grip and forend. 30-30, 357 Mag., 38-55, 44 Mag., 45 Colt. Introduced 1995.
Perf.: $575   Exc.: $425   VGood: $560

WINCHESTER MODEL 94 LIMITED EDITION CENTENNIAL GRADE I
Same specs as Model 94 except made to commemorate the 100th anniversary of the Model 94; 30-30; 26-inch half-octagon barrel; tube half-magazine; drilled, tapped for tang sight; close reproduction of the turn-of-the-century #9 factory engraving; diamond-style "H" checkering pattern on the pistol-grip stock, forend; engraving on receiver sides shows whitetail deer profiles. Introduced 1994; discontinued 1994.
Perf.: $1000   Exc.: $950   VGood: $795

WINCHESTER MODEL 64 ZIPPER
Same specs as Model 64 except chambered for 219 Zipper; 26-inch barrel; weighs 7 lbs.; Winchester No. 98A peep rear sight. Introduced 1938; discontinued 1941. Collector value.
Exc.: $1695   VGood: $1295   Good: $995

WINCHESTER MODEL 65
Lever action; 218 Bee, 25-20, 32-20; 7-shot tube half-magazine; 22-inch, 24-inch (218 Bee) barrel; based on the Model 92 design; weighs 6-1/2 lbs.; open or peep rear sight, Lyman gold bead front on ramp base; plain pistol-grip stock, forearm; shotgun-type butt with checkered steel buttplate. Introduced 1933; discontinued 1947.
Exc.: $2795   VGood: $1995   Good: $1050

WINCHESTER MODEL 71
Lever action; 348 Win.; 4-shot tube magazine; 24-inch barrel; weighs 8 lbs.; open rear sight, bead front on ramp with hood; plain walnut pistol-grip stock, beavertail forend; blued finish; action is improved version of Model 1886. Introduced 1936; discontinued 1957. Premium for pre-war/long-tang models.
Exc.: $2100   VGood: $1395   Good: $825

WINCHESTER MODEL 71 CARBINE
Same specs as Model 71 except 20-inch barrel. Introduced 1936; discontinued 1938.
Exc.: $2500   VGood: $1750   Good: $1350

WINCHESTER MODEL 71 DELUXE
Same specs as Model 71 except No. 98A rear peep sight; checkered stock, forearm, grip cap; quick-detachable sling swivels; leather sling.
Exc.: $1795   VGood: $995   Good: $750

WINCHESTER MODEL 88
Lever action; 243 Win., 284 Win., 308 Win., 358 Win.; 5-shot detachable box magazine; 22-inch

WINCHESTER MODEL 94 LIMITED EDITION CENTENNIAL HIGH GRADE RIFLE

Same specs as Model 94 except high-grade rifle made to commemorate the 100th anniversary of the Model 94; 30-30; 26-inch half-octagon barrel; tube half-magazine; Lyman No. 2 tang sight; spade-pattern checkering on pistol-grip stock; blued receiver with gold inlays and #6-style engraving pattern showing a gold deer on the right, gold mountain sheep on the left. Only 3,000 produced. Introduced 1994; discontinued 1994.

Perf.: $1350   **Exc.:** $1050   **VGood:** $795

WINCHESTER MODEL 94 LIMITED EDITION CENTENNIAL HIGH GRADE CUSTOM

Same specs as Model 94 except highest grade rifle made to commemorate the 100th anniversary of the Model 94; 30-30; 26-inch half-octagon barrel; tube half-magazine; Lyman No. 2 tang sight; spade-pattern checkering on pistol-grip stock; top ejection; hand-engraved, grayed action with inking in #5 style with gold inlaid ovals containing a pair of pronghorns on the right, caribou on the left; crescent buttplate. Only 94 produced. Introduced 1994; discontinued 1994.

Perf.: $6995   **Exc.:** $5995   **VGood:** $3550

WINCHESTER MODEL 94 RANGER

Same specs as Model 94 except economy version; 30-30 only; 5-shot or 6-shot magazine; 20-inch barrel; uncheckered hardwood stock, forearm. Introduced 1985.

Perf.: $475   **Exc.:** $400   **VGood:** $365

WINCHESTER MODEL 94 RANGER COMPACT

Similar to the Model 94 Ranger except has shorter 16-inch barrel and 12-1/2-inch length of pull, rubber recoil pad, post front sight. 30-30, 357 Mag; Introduced 1998. Made in U.S.A. by U.S. Repeating Arms Co., Inc.

Perf.: $475   **Exc.:** $400   **VGood:** $365

WINCHESTER MODEL 94 SADDLE RING CARBINE

Same specs as Model 94 except saddle ring; 44 Mag.; 20-inch barrel; top ejection. Introduced 1967; discontinued 1972.

Perf.: $775   **Exc.:** $625   **VGood:** $560

WINCHESTER MODEL 94 TIMBER CARBINE

Similar to the Model 94 Big Bore and XTR Big Bore rifles. Chambered for 444 Marlin, later 450 Marlin; 18-inch ported barrel; half-pistol grip stock with butt pad; checkered walnut grip and forend. Introduced 1999; still offered. Made in U.S.A. by U.S. Repeating Arms Co., Inc.

Perf.: $750   **Exc.:** $625   **VGood:** $560

WINCHESTER MODEL 94 TRADITIONAL

Lever action; 30-30 Win., 6-shot; 44 Mag., 11-shot tubular magazine; 20-inch barrel; weighs 6-1/2 lbs.; 37-3/4-inch overall length; Straight grip checkered walnut stock and forend; Hooded blade front, semi-buckhorn rear. Drilled and tapped for scope mount; forged steel receiver; side ejection, exposed rebounding hammer with automatic trigger-activated transfer bar. Introduced 1984.

Perf.: $600   **Exc.:** $550   **VGood:** $490

WINCHESTER MODEL 94 TRAILS END

Similar to the Model 94 except chambered only for 357 Mag., 44-40, 44 Mag., 45 Colt, 25-35, 30-30; 11-shot magazine. Walnut stock and forearm; saddle ring. Introduced 1997. From U.S. Repeating Arms Co., Inc.. Add 20 percent for 25-35.

Perf.: $950   **Exc.:** $825   **VGood:** $650

WINCHESTER MODEL 94 TRAPPER

Same specs as Model 94 except short 16-inch barrel; 30-30 (standard), 357 Mag., 44 Mag./44 Spl., 45 Colt; 5-shot tube magazine in 30-30, 9 shots in other calibers; side ejection. Introduced 1985.

Perf.: $650   **Exc.:** $540   **VGood:** $500

WINCHESTER MODEL 94 WIN-TUFF

Same specs as Model 94 except 30-30; drilled, tapped for scope mounts; checkered hardwood stock, forearm. Introduced 1987.

Perf.: $650   **Exc.:** $540   **VGood:** $500

WINCHESTER MODEL 94 WRANGLER

Same specs as Model 94 except 32 Spl.; 16-inch barrel; top ejection; roll-engraved Western scene on receiver. Introduced 1983; no longer in production.

Exc.: $610   **VGood:** $475   **Good:** $190

WINCHESTER MODEL 94 WRANGLER II

Same specs as Model 94 except 32 Spl., 38-55; 16-inch barrel; angle ejection; loop-type finger lever; roll-engraved Western scenes on receiver. Introduced 1983; discontinued 1986.

Exc.: $740   **VGood:** $650   **Good:** $510

WINCHESTER MODEL 94 WRANGLER LARGE LOOP

Same specs as Model 94 except 30-30, 44 Mag.; 16-inch barrel; extra-large loop lever. Introduced 1992.

Exc.: $640   **VGood:** $550   **Good:** $390

Side or Angle Eject Model
Exc.: $650   **VGood:** $560   **Good:** $400

WINCHESTER MODEL 94 XTR

Same specs as Model 94 except higher-grade version; 30-30, 7-30 Waters; 20-inch, 24-inch barrel (7-30 Waters); hooded front sight; select checkered walnut straight-grip stock. Introduced 1978; discontinued 1988.

Exc.: $650   **VGood:** $575   **Good:** $350

7-30 Waters
Exc.: $800   **VGood:** $750   **Good:** $575

WINCHESTER MODEL 94 XTR BIG BORE

Same specs as Model 94 XTR except 307 Win., 356 Win., 375 Win.; 6-shot tube magazine; 20-inch barrel; cut-checkered satin-finish American walnut stock, rubber recoil pad. XTR designation dropped 1989. Introduced 1978. Deduct 10 percent for 375.

Exc.: $800   **VGood:** $650   **Good:** $575

Side or Angle Eject model
Exc.: $825   **VGood:** $675   **Good:** $600

Winchester Model 94 Ranger

Winchester Model 94 Ranger Compact

Winchester Model 94 Traditional

Winchester Model 94 Trails End

Winchester Model 94 Trapper

Winchester Model 94 Wrangler II

Winchester Model 94 Side Eject

Winchester Model 94 XTR
Big Bore

Winchester Model 150

Winchester Model 250

Winchester Model 250
Deluxe

Winchester Model 255

Winchester Model 1873

Winchester Model 1873
Carbine

uncheckered American walnut straight-grip stock, forend; blued finish. Introduced 1873; discontinued 1924. 1 of 1000, and 1 of 100 are extremely rare. Appraisal recommended. Beware of fakes. Collector value.

> **Exc.:** $4000 to $11000
> **VGood:** $2500 to $6000
> **Good:** $900 to $4000

WINCHESTER MODEL 1873 CARBINE
Same specs as Model 1873 except 20-inch barrel; 12-shot magazine; two barrel bands. Collector value.

> **Exc.:** $5000 to $14000
> **VGood:** $2900 to $10000
> **Good:** $1000 to $5000

WINCHESTER MODEL 1873 MUSKET
Same specs as Model 1873 except 30-inch barrel; extra capacity tube magazine; three barrel bands. Values from $1000 to $7000.

WINCHESTER MODEL 1873 RIMFIRE
Same specs as Model 1873 except 22 Short, 22 Long, 22 Extra Long. Introduced 1884; discontinued 1904. Collector value.

> **Exc.:** $10,000   **VGood:** $6750   **Good:** $2500

WINCHESTER MODEL 1873 SPECIAL
Same specs as Model 1873 except octagon barrel only; color case-hardened receiver; select American walnut pistol-grip stock. Case-hardened receivers brings substantial premium. Need appraisal. Collector value.

WINCHESTER MODEL 1876
Lever action; 40-60, 45-60, 45-75, 50-95; tube magazine; 26-inch, 28-inch barrel; open rear sight, bead or blade front; uncheckered American walnut straight-grip stock, forend; blued finish. Model 1876 values to over $6000. 1 of 1000 and 1 of 100 Model values to $75,000, an appraiser is needed. Introduced 1876; discontinued 1897.

WINCHESTER MODEL 1876 CARBINE
Same specs as Model 1876 except 22-inch barrel; full-length forearm; one barrel band. Values to $7500.

WINCHESTER MODEL 1876 MUSKET
Same specs as Model 1876 except 32-inch barrel; carbine-like forend tip; one barrel band. Values to $8000.

Model 1885 Note: All Model 1885 Single Shot rifles were available in many calibers and barrel contours. Each example merits expert appraisal.

WINCHESTER MODEL 1885 HIGH WALL
Lever action; single shot; 22 RF through 50; 30-inch barrel of various weights; open rear sight, blade front; uncheckered American walnut straight-grip stock, forend; solid frame. Introduced 1885; discontinued 1920. Collector value.

> Color case-hardened (pre-1901)
> **Exc.:** $3495   **VGood:** $2995   **Good:** $1995
> Blued finish (post-1901)
> **Exc.:** $2695   **VGood:** $2195   **Good:** $1650

WINCHESTER MODEL 1885 HIGH WALL DELUXE GRADE
Same specs as Model 1885 High Wall except better wood; hand-checkered stock, forend. Collector value.

> **Exc.:** $4995   **VGood:** $4250   **Good:** $3295

WINCHESTER MODEL 1885 HIGH WALL SCHUETZEN
Same specs as Model 1885 High Wall except 30-inch octagonal barrel; Vernier rear tang peep sight, wind-gauge front; European walnut Schuetzen-type stock; hand-checkered forend, pistol grip; Schuetzen buttplate, adjustable palm rest; spur finger lever; double-set trigger. Collector value.

> **Exc.:** $8995   **VGood:** $6995   **Good:** $4250
> Takedown model
> **Exc.:** $9995   **VGood:** $7995   **Good:** $5250

WINCHESTER MODEL 94 XTR DELUXE
Same specs as Model 94 XTR except 30-30; 20-inch barrel; deluxe checkered walnut straight-grip stock, long forearm; rubber buttplate. Introduced 1987; discontinued 1988.

> **Exc.:** $670   **VGood:** $610   **Good:** $550

WINCHESTER MODEL 150
Lever action; 22 Short, 22 Long, 22 LR; 21-shot tube magazine (22 Short), 17-shot (22 Long), 15-shot (22 LR); 20-1/2-inch barrel; weighs 5 lbs.; aluminum alloy receiver grooved for scope sight; walnut-finished American hardwood stock; forearm has frontier-style barrel band; straight grip; no checkering. Introduced 1967; discontinued 1974.

> **Exc.:** $150   **VGood:** $100   **Good:** $85

WINCHESTER MODEL 250
Lever action; 22 Short, 22 Long, 22 LR; 21-shot tube magazine (22 Short), 17-shot (22 Long), 15-shot (22 LR); 20-1/2-inch barrel; 39-inch overall length; weighs 5 lbs.; hammerless; ramped square post front sight, adjustable square notch rear; aluminum alloy receiver grooved for tip-off scope mounts; walnut-finished hardwood stock; crossbolt safety on front of trigger guard. Introduced 1963; discontinued 1973.

> **Exc.:** $175   **VGood:** $110   **Good:** $90

WINCHESTER MODEL 250 DELUXE
Same specs as Model 250 except select walnut stock, fluted comb, cheekpiece; basketweave checkering; white spacer between buttplate and stock; sling swivels. Introduced 1965; discontinued 1971.

> **Exc.:** $215   **VGood:** $150   **Good:** $100

WINCHESTER MODEL 255
Lever action; 22 WMR; 11-shot tube magazine; 20-1/2-inch barrel; 39-inch overall length; weighs 5 lbs.; hammerless; ramped square post front sight, adjustable square notch rear; aluminum alloy receiver grooved for scope mounts; walnut-finish hardwood pistol-grip stock; crossbolt safety. Introduced 1964; discontinued 1970.

> **Exc.:** $215   **VGood:** $150   **Good:** $100

WINCHESTER MODEL 255 DELUXE
Same specs as Model 255 except high-gloss Monte Carlo select walnut stock, fluted comb, cheekpiece; basketweave checkering; white spacer between butt-plate and stock; sling swivels. Introduced 1965; discontinued 1971.

> **Exc.:** $250   **VGood:** $230   **Good:** $175

WINCHESTER MODEL 1873
Lever action; 32-20, 38-40, 44-40; 6-, 12-, 15- or 17-shot tubular magazine; 24-inch barrel standard, other lengths made; open rear sight, bead or blade front;

WINCHESTER MODEL 1885 LOW WALL SPORTER

Lever action; single shot; 22 RF; 28-inch round, octagonal barrel; solid frame; open rear sight, blade front; unchecked American walnut straight stock, forend. Introduced 1885; discontinued 1920. Collector value. Premium for optional features and for rifles made before 1898.

Exc.: $1295   **VGood:** $995   **Good:** $795

WINCHESTER MODEL 1885 LOW WALL RIMFIRE (RECENT MANUFACTURE)

Single shot, falling block; 22 LR, later 17 HMR, with 17 Mach 2 introduced in 2005; 24-1/2-inch barrel, half-octagon; 41-inch overall length; weighs 8 lbs; Walnut stock; Blade front, semi-buckhorn rear sights; Drilled and tapped for scope mount or tang sight; target chamber. Introduced 1999; Limited production. From U.S. Repeating Arms Co.

Grade I (2,400 made)
Perf.: $750   **Exc.:** $600   **VGood:** $515

High Grade (1,100 made; engraved/gold inlaid)
Perf.: $1100   **Exc.:** $900   **VGood:** $700

WINCHESTER MODEL 1885 LOW WALL WINDER MUSKET

Same specs as Model 1885 Low Wall except 22 Short, 22 LR; 28-inch round barrel; solid frame or takedown; musket-type rear sight, blade front; straight-grip military-type stock, forend. Collector value.

Exc.: $2100   **VGood:** $1450   **Good:** $695

WINCHESTER MODEL 1885 HIGH WALL HUNTER

Single shot; patterned after original Model 1885 designed by John Browning. Calibers: .223, .22-250, .270 WSM, 7mm WSM, .300 WSM, .325 WSM. Stock: Checkered walnut. Barrel: 28-inch blued, sightless octagon with Pachmayr pad. Weight: 8-1/2 lbs.

NIB: $800   **Exc.:** $725   **VGood:** $625

WINCHESTER MODEL 1885 .30-06 CENTENNIAL HIGH WALL HUNTER

Similar to Model 1885 High Wall Hunter but with premium wood and gold inlay on receiver. Commemorates centennial of .30-06 cartridge.

NIB: $1500   **Exc.:** $1375   **VGood:** $1095

WINCHESTER MODEL 1885 LOW WALL 17 MACH 2

Similar to Model 1885 High Wall but with low-profile receiver, crescent buttplate, and 24-inch barrel. Chambered for 17 Mach 2 rimfire cartridge. Introduced 2006.

NIB: $995   **Exc.:** $820   **VGood:** $695

WINCHESTER MODEL 1886

Lever action; 33 WCF, 45-70, 45-90, 40-82, 40-65, 38-56, 40-70, 38-70, 50-100-450, 50-110 Express; 8-shot tube magazine or 4-shot half-magazine; 26-inch round, half-octagonal, octagonal barrel; open rear sight, bead or blade front; plain straight stock, forearm; color case-hardened (pre-1901) or blued (post-1901) finish. Premiums for many features and calibers. Appraisal necessary. Introduced 1886; discontinued 1935. Collector value.

Exc.: $9000   **VGood:** $6000   **Good:** $4500

With deluxe checkered stock
Exc.: $15000   **VGood:** $9995   **Good:** $5250

WINCHESTER MODEL 1886 CARBINE

Same specs as Model 1886 except 22-inch round barrel. Rare.

Exc.: $13950   **VGood:** $9450   **Good:** $5995

WINCHESTER MODEL 1886 LIGHTWEIGHT

Same specs as Model 1886 except lightened; 33 WCF, 45-70; 22-inch, 24-inch round barrel; rubber buttplate; blued finish.

Exc.: $3995   **VGood:** $2850   **Good:** $1495

WINCHESTER MODEL 1886 MUSKET

Same specs as Model 1886 except 30-inch round barrel; one barrel band.

Exc.: $18995   **VGood:** $9995   **Good:** $6700

WINCHESTER MODEL 1886 TAKEDOWN

Same specs as Model 1886 except 24-inch round barrel; takedown feature.

Exc.: $7495   **VGood:** $4500   **Good:** $2450

WINCHESTER MODEL 1886 LEVER-ACTION RIFLE (RECENT MANUFACTURE)

Lever action; 45-70, 4-shot magazine; 22-inch round tapered barrel; 40-1/2-inch overall length; weighs 7-1/4 lbs.; Smooth walnut stock; Bead front sight, ramp-adjustable buckhorn-style rear. Recreation of the Model 1886 lightweight rifle. Polished blue finish; crescent metal butt plate; metal forend cap; pistol grip stock. Reintroduced 1998. From U.S. Repeating Arms Co., Inc. Add 10% for takedown version.

Grade I
Perf.: $1200   **Exc.:** $900   **VGood:** $650

High Grade
Perf.: $1450   **Exc.:** $1200   **VGood:** $900

WINCHESTER MODEL 1892

Lever action; 218 Bee (rare), 25-20, 32-20, 38-40, 44-40; 13-shot tube magazine, 7-shot half-magazine, 10-shot two-thirds magazine; 24-inch round or octagonal barrel; open rear sight, bead front; plain, straight stock, forearm; blued finish. Introduced 1892; discontinued 1941.

Exc.: $2745   **VGood:** $1495   **Good:** $875

With takedown feature
Exc.: $3105   **VGood:** $1995   **Good:** $1250

WINCHESTER MODEL 1892 CARBINE

Same specs as Model 1892 except 5-, 11-shot magazine; 20-inch barrel; two barrel bands.

Exc.: $2995   **VGood:** $1995   **Good:** $1250

WINCHESTER MODEL 1892 MUSKET

Same specs as Model 1892 except 30-inch barrel; three barrel bands; buttplate.

Exc.: $8995   **VGood:** $5350   **Good:** $3450

Winchester Model 1885 Low Wall Rimfire

Winchester Model 1886

Winchester Model 1892

Winchester Model 1895

Winchester Model 1895 Limited Edition Grade I

Winchester Model 1895 High Wall Hunter

Winchester Model 1895 Centennial High Wall Hunter

Winchester Model 1895
Saddle Ring Carbine

Winchester Model 9417

Winchester Model 9422

Winchester Model 9422
High Grade

Winchester Model 9422
Legacy

Winchester Model 9422 XTR
Classic

WINCHESTER MODEL 1892 TRAPPER'S CARBINE

Same specs as Model 1892 except 12-inch, 14-inch, 15-inch, 16-inch, 18-inch barrel; shortened tube magazine; two barrel bands; browned finish.

Exc.: $9995   **VGood:** $5995   **Good:** $2550

WINCHESTER MODEL 1894

Lever action; 25-35, 30-30, 32-40, 32 Spl., 38-55; 4-, 6-shot tube magazine; 22-inch, 26-inch barrel; open rear sight, blade or ramp (post-1931) front; plain American walnut straight-grip stock; blued finish. Introduced 1894; discontinued 1936. Premium for those made before 1898.

Exc.: $2495   **VGood:** $1295   **Good:** $695

Takedown model

Exc.: $2995   **VGood:** $1895   **Good:** $895

WINCHESTER MODEL 1894 CARBINE

Same specs as Model 1894 except 20-inch barrel. Premium for original saddle ring.

Exc.: $2495   **VGood:** $1370   **Good:** $700

WINCHESTER MODEL 1894 TRAPPER CARBINE

Same specs as Model 1894 except 14-inch, 15-inch, 16-inch, 17-inch, 18-inch barrel. No longer in production.

Exc.: $5550   **VGood:** $3500   **Good:** $1570

WINCHESTER MODEL 1895

Lever action; 30-40 Krag, 30 Govt.'03 (30-03), 30 Govt.'06 (30-06), 303 British, 7.62mm Russian, 35 Win., 38-72, 405 Win., 40-72; 4-, 5-shot (30-40, 303 British) box magazine; 24-inch, 28-inch barrel; open rear sight, bead or blade front; uncheckered American walnut straight-grip stock, forend; blued finish. Introduced 1895; discontinued 1931. Collector value. Premium for .405.

Exc.: $4000   **VGood:** $2500   **Good:** $1400

Takedown model

Exc.: $4400   **VGood:** $2800   **Good:** $1600

WINCHESTER MODEL 1895 CARBINE

Same specs as Model 1895 except 30-40 Krag, 30-03, 30-06, 303 British; 22-inch barrel; one barrel band; carbine stock; solid frame. Collector value.

Exc.: $2900   **VGood:** $2000   **Good:** $1000

With U.S. Government markings

Exc.: $4000   **VGood:** $3300   **Good:** $1800

WINCHESTER MODEL 1895 LIMITED EDITION (RECENT PRODUCTION)

Lever action; 30-06, 270, 405 Win, 4-shot non-datachable box magazine; 24-inch round barrel; 42-inch overall length; weighs 8 lbs.; American walnut stock; Gold bead front sight, buckhorn rear adjustable for elevation. Recreation of the original Model 1895 for its 100th anniversary. Polished blue finish with Nimschke-style scroll engraving on receiver. Scalloped receiver, two-piece cocking lever, schnabel forend, straight-grip stock. Introduced 1995; standard version no longer in production.

Grade

Perf.: $900   **Exc.:** $800   **VGood:** $695

High Grade, extensive engraving, 4000 rifles made.

Perf.: $1600   **Exc.:** $1400   **VGood:** $995

405 caliber, Grade I, Introduced 2000, discontinued 2003.

Perf.: $1425   **Exc.:** $1125   **VGood:** $900

405 High Grade

Perf.: $1700   **Exc.:** $1300   **VGood:** $950

WINCHESTER MODEL 1895 MUSKET

Same specs as Model 1895 except 30-40 Krag, 30 Govt'03, 30 Govt'06; 28-inch, 30-inch barrel; two-barrel bands; handguard over barrel.

Exc.: $2000   **VGood:** $1495   **Good:** $1095

With U.S. Government markings

Exc.: $2995   **VGood:** $1650   **Good:** $1295

WINCHESTER MODEL 1895 NRA MUSKET

Same specs as Model 1895 except 24-inch barrel; meets NRA specs for competition.

Exc.: $4500   **VGood:** $1900   **Good:** $1400

WINCHESTER MODEL 1895 SADDLE RING CARBINE (RECENT MFR.)

Patterned after original Model 1895 carbine. Features include blued 22-inch barrel, ladder style rear sight; D&T for Lyman side mount; saddle ring on left side of receiver; .30-'06. Chambered in .30-06 only; commemorates centennial of .30-06 cartridge.

NIB: $1275   **Exc.:** $1050   **VGood:** $875

WINCHESTER MODEL 9417

Lever action; 17 HMR; 11-shot tube magazine; 20-1/2-inch or 22-1/2-inch barrel; weighs 6 lbs; adjustable rear, ramp front sights; grooved for scope mounting; introduced 2003 as 17-caliber variant of Model 9422.

Perf.: $1000   **Exc.:** $800   **VGood:** $570

WINCHESTER MODEL 9422

Lever action; 22 Short, 22 Long, 22 LR; 21-shot tube magazine (22 Short), 17-shot (22 Long), 15-shot (22 LR); 20-1/2-inch barrel; weighs 6-1/2 lbs.; hooded ramp bead front sight, adjustable semi-buckhorn rear; grooved for scope mounts; checkered American walnut straight-grip stock, forearm. Introduced 1972; designated XTR 1978; XTR designation dropped 1989; still in production.

Perf.: $740   **Exc.:** $670   **VGood:** $515

WINCHESTER MODEL 9422 HIGH GRADE

Same specs as Model 9422 except 22 LR; high grade walnut with gloss finish; blued and engraved receiver with coonhound on right side, racoon profile on left, both framed with detailed Nimschke-style scrollwork. Introduced 1995.

Perf.: $900   **Exc.:** $795   **VGood:** $495

WINCHESTER MODEL 9422 LEGACY

Like Model 9422, but checkered pistol-grip walnut stock and forearm; longer 22-1/2-inch barrel; adjustable rear, ramp front sights; receiver grooved for scope mounting; hammer extension; 22 LR or 22WMR; still in production.

Perf.: $1000   **Exc.:** $900   **VGood:** $780

WINCHESTER MODEL 9422 MAGNUM

Same specs as Model 9422 except 22 WMR; 11-shot tube magazine. Introduced 1972.

Perf.: $950   **Exc.:** $825   **VGood:** $525

WINCHESTER MODEL 9422 WIN-CAM

Same specs as Model 9422 except 22 WMR only; 11-shot tube magazine; checkered green laminated hardwood stock, forearm. Introduced 1987.

Perf.: $1050   **Exc.:** $950   **VGood:** $830

WINCHESTER MODEL 9422 WIN-TUFF

Same specs as Model 9422 except 22 LR, 22 WMR; checkered brown laminated hardwood stock, forearm. Introduced 1988.

Perf.: $1050   **Exc.:** $950   **VGood:** $830

WINCHESTER MODEL 9422 XTR CLASSIC

Same specs as Model 9422 except 22-1/2-inch barrel; 39-1/8-inch overall length; satin-finished walnut stock fluted comb; no checkering; crescent steel buttplate; curved finger lever; capped pistol grip. Introduced 1985; discontinued 1988.

Perf.: $1050   **Exc.:** $950   **VGood:** $830

WINCHESTER MODEL 55 RIMFIRE

Single shot, "semi-automatic;" 22 Short, 22 Long, 22 LR; 22-inch barrel; weighs 5-1/2 lbs.; action automatically ejects the fired case, recocks, and remains open for loading after each shot; top loading; open rear sight, bead front; one-piece unchecked walnut stock. Introduced 1958; discontinued 1961.

Exc.: $210   **VGood:** $170   **Good:** $100

WINCHESTER MODEL 63 (1933-1958)

Semi-automatic; 22 LR Super Speed or Super-X; 10-shot tube magazine in buttstock; 20-inch barrel (early series), 23-inch (later series); takedown; open rear sight, bead front; unchecked walnut pistol-grip stock and forearm. Introduced 1933; discontinued 1958.

20-inch barrel		
Exc.: $800	**VGood:** $700	**Good:** $575
23-inch barrel		
Exc.: $900	**VGood:** $775	**Good:** $595

WINCHESTER MODEL 63 (1997-1998)

Semi-automatic; 22 LR; 10-shot tube magazine; 23-inch barrel; 39-inch overall length; weighs 6-1/4 lbs.; Recreation of the original Model 63. Magazine tube loads through a port in the buttstock. Reintroduced 1997. From U. S. Repeating Arms Co.

Grade I		
Perf.: $700	**Exc.:** $650	**VGood:** $570
High grade, select walnut, cut checkering, engraved scenes,		
Perf.: $950	**Exc.:** $825	**VGood:** $700

WINCHESTER MODEL 74

Semi-automatic; 22 Short or 22 LR; 20-shot tube magazine in buttstock (22 Short), 14-shot (22 LR); 24-inch barrel; takedown; open rear sight, bead front; unchecked one-piece pistol-grip stock; safety on top of receiver. Introduced 1939; discontinued 1955. Premium for 22 Short (Gallery) model.

Exc.: $295   **VGood:** $195   **Good:** $180

WINCHESTER MODEL 77 CLIP

Semi-automatic; 22 LR; 8-shot clip magazine; 22-inch barrel; weighs 5-1/2 lbs.; #75C bead front sight, #32B open rear; plain, American walnut one-piece stock; pistol grip; beavertail forend; rotary thumb safety; black composition buttplate. Introduced 1955; discontinued 1963.

Exc.: $230   **VGood:** $190   **Good:** $150

WINCHESTER MODEL 77 TUBE

Same specs as Model 77 Clip except for 15-shot tube magazine.

Exc.: $280   **VGood:** $240   **Good:** $180

WINCHESTER MODEL 100

Semi-automatic; gas-operated; 243 Win., 284 Win., 308 Win.; 3-shot magazine (284 Win.), 4-shot (others); 22-inch barrel; 42-1/2-inch overall length; weighs 7-1/2 lbs.; hooded bead front sight, folding leaf rear; tapped for receiver sights, scope mounts; one-piece walnut with checkered pistol-grip stock, forearm; sling swivels. Introduced 1960; discontinued 1974. 284 chambering brings a premium.

Pre-1964 Model		
Exc.: $725	**VGood:** $650	**Good:** $560
Post-1964 Model		
Exc.: $675	**VGood:** $500	**Good:** $415

WINCHESTER MODEL 100 CARBINE

Same specs as Model 100 except 19-inch barrel; no checkering; barrel band. Introduced 1967; discontinued 1973.

Exc.: $750   **VGood:** $675   **Good:** $500

WINCHESTER MODEL 190

Semi-automatic; 22 Short, 22 Long, 22 LR; 21-shot tube magazine (22 Short), 17-shot (22 Long), 15-shot (22 LR); 20-1/2-inch, 24-inch barrel with 1:16-inch twist; 39-inch overall length; weighs 5 lbs; bead post front sight, adjustable V rear; aluminum alloy receiver grooved for scope mounts; American hardwood stock with plain, unchecked pistol-grip, forearm; Introduced 1967; discontinued 1980.

Exc.: $175   **VGood:** $140   **Good:** $70

WINCHESTER MODEL 290

Semi-automatic; 22 Short, 22 Long, 22 LR; 21-shot tube magazine (22 Short), 17-shot (22 Long), 15-shot (22 LR); 39-inch overall length; weighs 5 lbs.; open rear sight, ramp front; unchecked or impress-checkered hardwood pistol-grip stock, forend. Introduced 1963; discontinued 1977.

Exc.: $185   **VGood:** $150   **Good:** $90

WINCHESTER MODEL 290 DELUXE

Same specs as Model 290 except fancy American walnut Monte Carlo stock, forend. Introduced 1965; discontinued 1977.

Exc.: $190   **VGood:** $155   **Good:** $95

Winchester Model 63

Winchester Model 74

Winchester Model 77 Tube

Winchester Model 100

Winchester Model 190

Winchester Model 290

Winchester Model 1903

WINCHESTER MODEL 490

Semi-automatic; 22 LR; 5-shot detachable box magazine; 22-inch barrel; folding leaf rear sight, hooded ramp front; one-piece checkered American walnut pistol-grip stock, resembles Model 100 centerfire rifle. Introduced 1975; discontinued 1978.

Exc.: $185   **VGood:** $150   **Good:** $90

NOTE: FOR THE FOLLOWING WINCHESTER SELF-LOADING RIFLES (MODELS 1903, 1905, 1907 AND 1910), A CONSIDERABLE PREMIUM CAN BE EXPECTED FOR 98% OR BETTER AND FOR SPECIAL-ORDER EXAMPLES.

WINCHESTER MODEL 1903

Semi-automatic; 22 Winchester Automatic RF cartridge; 10-shot tube magazine in butt; 20-inch barrel; takedown; open rear sight, bead front; unchecked straight-grip stock, forend; special

Winchester Model 1905

Winchester Model 1907

Winchester Model 1910

Winchester Model SXR Super X

Winchester Super Grade Combo

Winchester Double Express

Winchester Model 61

Winchester Model 62

Winchester Model 270

WINCHESTER MODEL SXR SUPER X RIFLE

Gas-operated semi-automatic patterned after Browning BAR ShortTrac and LongTrac. Calibers: .30-06, .300WM, .270 WSM, .300 WSM. Barrel: 22-inch (.30-06), 24-inch. Weight: 7-1/4 lbs. Stock: Two-piece checkered walnut.

NIB: $850   **Exc.:** $775   **VGood:** $625

WINCHESTER COMBINATION GUN SUPER GRADE

Over/under; 30-06/12-ga.; 25-inch Winchoke shot barrel; 41-1/4-inch overall length; bead front sight, folding leaf rear; fancy American walnut stock; hand-checkered pistol grip, forend; full-length top barrel rib; silvered, engraved receiver; blued barrels; integral scope bases; single selective mechanical trigger. Made in Japan. Introduced 1982; discontinued 1985.

Exc.: $2400   **VGood:** $1700   **Good:** $1400

WINCHESTER DOUBLE EXPRESS RIFLE

Double rifle; over/under; 30-06, 9.3x74R, 6.5mm, 270, 7.65R, 257 Roberts; 23-1/2-inch barrel; 39-5/8-inch overall length; bead on ramp front sight, folding leaf rear on quarter-rib; integral scope bases; fancy American walnut stock; hand-checkered pistol grip, forend; uses Model 101 shotgun action; silvered, engraved receiver; blued barrels; quick-detachable sling swivels; marketed in hard case. Made in Japan. Introduced 1982; discontinued 1985.

Exc.: $3100   **VGood:** $2495   **Good:** $2195

WINCHESTER MODEL 61

Slide action; 22 Short, 22 Long, 22 LR; 20-shot tube magazine (22 Short), 16-shot (22 Long), 14-shot (22 LR); 24-inch round or octagon barrel; hammerless; takedown; open rear sight, bead front; uncheckered pistol-grip stock; grooved semi-beavertail slide handle. Introduced 1932; discontinued 1963. Premium for early examples.

Exc.: $850   **VGood:** $650   **Good:** $465

Octagon barrel model
Exc.: $1095   **VGood:** $795   **Good:** $495

WINCHESTER MODEL 61 MAGNUM

Same specs as Model 61 except 22 WMR; 12-shot tube magazine. Introduced 1960; discontinued 1963.

Exc.: $1000   **VGood:** $750   **Good:** $575

WINCHESTER MODEL 62

Slide action; 22 Short, 22 Long, 22 LR; 20-shot tube magazine (20 Short), 16-shot (22 Long), 14-shot (22 LR); 23-inch barrel; visible hammer; bead front sight, open rear; plain, straight-grip stock; grooved semi-beavertail slide handle; also available in gallery model in 22 Short only. Introduced 1932; discontinued 1959.

Exc.: $645   **VGood:** $465   **Good:** $350

WINCHESTER MODEL 270

Slide action; 22 Short, 22 Long, 22 LR; 21-shot tube magazine (22 Short), 17-shot (22 Long), 15-shot (22 LR); 20-1/2-inch barrel; 39-inch overall length; weighs 5 lbs.; ramped square post front sight, adjustable square notch rear; aluminum alloy receiver grooved for tip-off scope mounts; walnut-finished hardwood, or black or brown cycolac plastic pistol-grip stock; crossbolt safety. Introduced 1963; discontinued 1973.

Walnut stock
Exc.: $185   **VGood:** $140   **Good:** $90

Plastic stock
Exc.: $165   **Vgood:** $125   **Good:** $70

WINCHESTER MODEL 270 DELUXE

Same specs as Model 270 except high-gloss Monte Carlo select walnut stock, fluted comb, cheekpiece; basketweave checkering; white buttspacer. Introduced 1965; discontinued 1973.

Exc.: $190   **VGood:** $145   **Good:** $95

wood and factory checkering bring a premium. Introduced 1903; discontinued 1932. Collector value.

Exc.: $985   **VGood:** $815   **Good:** $645

Deluxe rifle with checkered pistol-grip stock and forearm
Exc.: $1200   **VGood:** $730   **Good:** $560

WINCHESTER MODEL 1905

Semi-automatic; 32 Win. Self-Loading, 35 Win. Self-loading; 5-, 10-shot box magazine; 22-inch barrel; takedown; open rear sight, bead front; uncheckered American walnut pistol-grip stock, forend. Introduced 1905; discontinued 1920. Collector value.

Exc.: $645   **VGood:** $525   **Good:** $445

WINCHESTER MODEL 1907

Semi-automatic; 351 Win. Self-Loading; 5-, 10-shot box magazine; 20-inch barrel; takedown; open rear sight, bead front; uncheckered walnut pistol-grip stock, forend. Introduced 1907; discontinued 1957. Collector value.

Exc.: $700   **VGood:** $585   **Good:** $375

WINCHESTER MODEL 1910

Semi-automatic; 401 Win. Self-Loading; 4-shot box magazine; 20-inch barrel; takedown; open rear sight, bead front; uncheckered walnut pistol-grip stock, forend. Introduced 1910; discontinued 1936. Collector value. Add 15 percent for high grade.

Exc.: $700   **VGood:** $585   **Good:** $375

WINCHESTER MODEL 275

Slide action; similar to Model 270, but chambered for 22 WMR; 11-shot tube magazine; 20-1/2-inch barrel; 39-inch overall length; weighs 5 lbs.; ramped square post front sight, adjustable square notch rear; aluminum alloy receiver grooved for tip-off scope mounts; walnut-finished hardwood pistol-grip stock; crossbolt safety. Introduced 1964; discontinued 1971.

Exc.: $290   **VGood:** $215   **Good:** $145

WINCHESTER MODEL 275 DELUXE

Same specs as Model 275 except Monte Carlo select American walnut stock, fluted comb, cheekpiece; basketweave checkering; white buttspacer. Introduced 1965; discontinued 1971.

Exc.: $300   **VGood:** $225   **Good:** $155

WINCHESTER MODEL 1890

Slide action; 22 Short, 22 Long, (not interchangeable), 22 WRF, (22 LR was added after 1919); 15-shot tube magazine (22 Short), 12-shot (22 Long), 11-shot (22 LR), 10-shot (22 WRF); 24-inch octagonal barrel; open rear, bead front sight; plain, straight stock, grooved slide handle; visible hammer; originally solid-frame design; after serial No. 15,552, all were takedowns; color case-hardened (pre-1901) or blued (post-1901) finish. Collector value. Because of production variations, expert appraisal is recommended. Introduced 1890; discontinued 1934.

Color case-hardened model		
Exc.: $4500	**VGood:** $3600	**Good:** $2100
Blued finish		
Exc.: $1295	**VGood:** $795	**Good:** $565

WINCHESTER MODEL 1906

Slide action; 22 Short, 22 Long, 22 LR; 15-shot tube magazine (22 Short), 12-shot (22 Long), 11-shot (22 LR); takedown; open rear sight, bead front; straight-grip uncheckered gumwood or walnut stock, grooved forend; visible hammer; shotgun buttplate. Originally offered as low-cost variant of the Model 1890; first rifles for 22 Short only; in 1908 a new version handled Short, Long and Long Rifle cartridges interchangeably; Introduced 1906; discontinued 1932. Collector value. Because of production variations, expert appraisal is recommended.

Exc.: $995   **VGood:** $695   **Good:** $465

WINCHESTER MODEL 1906 EXPERT

Same specs as Model 1906 except pistol-grip stock, redesigned forend; blue/nickel or nickel finish. Introduced 1918; discontinued 1924.

Exc.: $1695   **VGood:** $950   **Good:** $620

WINCHESTER CUSTOM SHOP MODEL 70 CUSTOM 100TH ANNIVERSARY .30-06

Semi-fancy walnut Featherweight stock with single steel crossbolt, one-piece engraved floorplate, high-lustre blued and engraved 22-inch barrel. Commemorates centennial of .30-06 cartridge. Only 100 manufactured.

NIB: $2600   **Exc.:** $2000   **VGood:** $1450

WINCHESTER CUSTOM SHOP MODEL 70 CUSTOM SPECIAL "70 YEARS OF THE MODEL 70"

Calibers: .270, .30-06 Springfield, .300 WM. Barrel: 24-inch or 26-inch (.300 WM) blued sightless. Engraved floorplate and barrel. Stock: semi-fancy checkered walnut. Introduced 2006, only 70 manufactured per caliber.

NIB: 3000   **Exc.:** N/A   **VGood:** N/A

WINCHESTER CUSTOM SHOP MODEL 70 CUSTOM MAPLE

Calibers: .284, .270, .308, .30-06. Barrel: 24-inch blued. Weight: 7-3/4 lbs. Stocked in fiddleback maple with pre-'64 pattern checkering. Quantities "very limited." Introduced 2006.

NIB: 4300   **Exc.:** N/A   **VGood:** N/A

Winchester Model 275

Winchester Model 1890

Winchester Model 1906

Winslow Bolt-Action Sporter

A. Zoli AZ-1900 Classic

WINCHESTER CUSTOM SHOP MODEL 70 CUSTOM CONTINENTAL HUNTER

Calibers: .284, .270, .308, .30-06. Barrel: 22-inch blued or stainless Krieger. Stock: glossy claro walnut, round knob pistol grip, schnabel forend.

NIB: $5200   **Exc.:** N/A   **VGood:** N/A

WINCHESTER CUSTOM SHOP MODEL 70 CUSTOM STAINLESS LAMINATE

Calibers: .270 WSM, 7mm WSM, .300 WSM, .325 WSM. Barrel: 24-inch stainless sporter. Stock: black/gray or brown Featherweight laminated with Schnabel and Pachmayr pad.

NIB: $2300   **Exc.:** N/A   **VGood:** N/A

WINSLOW BOLT-ACTION SPORTER

Bolt action; all popular standard and magnum centerfire calibers; 3-, 4-shot magazine; 24-inch barrel, 26-inch (magnums); two stock styles: slim pistol grip with beavertail forearm or hooked pistol grip with wide flat forearm; Monte Carlo stock with cheekpiece in walnut, maple or myrtle; rosewood pistol grip, forend tip; custom rifle in eight grades. Introduced 1963; discontinued 1978.

Commander Grade		
Exc.: $495	**VGood:** $430	**Good:** $350
Regal Grade		
Exc.: $595	**VGood:** $530	**Good:** $450
Regent Grade		
Exc.: $750	**VGood:** $650	**Good:** $550
Regimental Grade		
Exc.: $950	**VGood:** $825	**Good:** $635
Crown Grade		
Exc.: $1395	**VGood:** $1195	**Good:** $930
Royal Grade		
Exc.: $1595	**VGood:** $1295	**Good:** $1100

Imperial Grade		
Exc.: $3495	**VGood:** $2895	**Good:** $2000
Emperor Grade		
Exc.: $6100	**VGood:** $4695	**Good:** $4000

ZOLI COMBINATO

Combination gun; over/under; boxlock; 222, 243/12. ga.; 24-inch barrels; blade front sight, flip-up rear; checkered European walnut stock; double triggers. From Antonio Zoli in Italy. Introduced 1980; discontinued 1993.

Perf.: $1695   **Exc.:** $1295   **VGood:** $935

ZOLI MODEL AZ-1900 CLASSIC

Bolt action; 243, 6.5x55, 270, 308, 30-06, 7mm Rem. Mag., 300 Win. Mag.; 21-inch barrel (24-inch on 7mm Rem. Mag., 300 Win. Mag.); 41-3/4-inch overall length with 21-inch barrel; weighs 7-1/4 lbs.; open sights were supplied with gun but not mounted; drilled, tapped for scope mounts; checkered Turkish circassian walnut stock; polished blue finish; oil-finished stock; engine-turned bolt. Made by Angelo Zoli; Imported from Italy by European American Armory. Introduced 1989; discontinued 1993.

Perf.: $800   **Exc.:** $670   **VGood:** $500

ZOLI MODEL AZ-1900M

Same specs as Model AZ-1900 except Bell & Carlson composite stock. Made by Angelo Zoli. Imported from Italy by European American Armory. Imported only in 1991.

Perf.: $695   **Exc.:** $495   **VGood:** $425

ZOLI SAVANA DOUBLE RIFLE

Double rifle; 7x65R, 30-06, 9.3x74R; 25-1/2-inch barrels; gold bead front sight, fixed V-notch rear in quarter-rib; premium grade French walnut stock with full pistol grip, cheekpiece; Anson & Deeley boxlock action with choice of single or double triggers; bushed firing pins; cocking indicators; silvered, engraved frame. Made by Angelo Zoli. Imported from Italy by European American Armory. Introduced 1989; discontinued 1991.

Perf.: $6095   **Exc.:** $5000   **VGood:** $3895

MODERN GUN VALUES
SHOTGUNS
Directory of Manufacturers

AMERICAN ARMS BRISTOL

Over/under; boxlock; 12-, 20-ga.; 3-inch chambers; 24-inch, 26-inch, 28-inch barrels; standard choke combos or choke tubes; front bead sight; glossy hand-checkered walnut stock; ejectors; single set trigger; engraved dummy sideplates; silver-finished frame; gold trigger. Made in Spain. Introduced 1987; discontinued 1988.

Fixed chokes		
Perf.: $625	**Exc.:** $500	**VGood:** $425
Choke tubes		
Perf.: $685	**Exc.:** $550	**VGood:** $470

AMERICAN ARMS BRITTANY

Side-by-side; boxlock ejectors; 12-, 20-ga; 3-inch chambers; 27-inch barrel (12-ga.), 25-inch barrel (20-ga.); weighs 6-1/2 lbs.; Imp. Cyl., Mod., Full choke tubes; straight English-style hand-checkered European walnut stock; semi-beavertail forend; engraving; single selective trigger; automatic safety; rubber recoil pad; case-color finish. Made in Spain. Introduced 1989; dropped 2000.

Perf.: $725	**Exc.:** $575	**VGood:** $485

AMERICAN ARMS DERBY

Side-by-side; sidelock; 12-, 20-, 28-ga., .410; 3-inch chambers, 2-3/4-inch (28-ga.); 26-inch, 28-inch barrel; weighs 6-1/2 to 6-3/4 lbs.; standard chokes; chromed bores; metal bead front sight; hand-checkered European walnut straight-grip stock, splinter forend; single selective trigger; hand rubbed oil finish; chromed receiver. Made in Spain. Introduced 1987; dropped 1994.

Perf.: $1150	**Exc.:** $975	**VGood:** $850

Add 10 percent to above prices for 28 gauge or .410 bore

AMERICAN ARMS EXCELSIOR

Over/under; sidelock; 12-, 20-ga.; 3-inch chambers; 26-inch, 28-inch barrels; standard choke combos or choke tubes; metal middle bead sight, glow worm front; hand-checkered European walnut stock, forend; auto selective ejectors; single non-selective trigger; manual safety; raised relief hand-engraved, gold-plated hunting scenes on sideplates. Made in Spain. Introduced 1987; discontinued 1987.

Fixed chokes		
Perf.: $1725	**Exc.:** $1510	**VGood:** $1250
Choke tubes		
Perf.: $1795	**Exc.:** $1580	**VGood:** $1320

AMERICAN ARMS FS200 COMPETITION

Over/under; boxlock; 12-ga.; 2-3/4-inch chambers; 26-inch, 32-inch barrels; Skeet/Skeet, Improved/Full; weighs 7-3/4 lbs.; hand-checkered, oil-finished European walnut stock; palm swell; ventilated recoil pad; selective auto ejectors; single selective trigger; black or satin chrome-finished frame. Made in Spain. Introduced 1987; discontinued 1987.

Perf.: $685	**Exc.:** $550	**VGood:** $470

AMERICAN ARMS FS300 COMPETITION

Same specs as FS200 Competition except 26-inch, 30-inch, 32-inch barrels; engraved false sideplates; satin chrome-finished receiver. Introduced 1986; discontinued 1986.

Perf.: $785	**Exc.:** $625	**VGood:** $530

AMERICAN ARMS FS400 COMPETITION

Same specs as FS200 Competition except sidelock; 26-inch, 30-inch, 32-inch barrels; single trigger; engraved chrome-finished receiver. Introduced 1986; discontinued 1986.

Perf.: $1125	**Exc.:** $900	**VGood:** $765

AMERICAN ARMS FS500 COMPETITION

Same specs as FS200 Competition except sidelock; 26-inch, 30-inch, 32-inch barrels; single trigger; engraved chrome-finished receiver. Introduced 1985; discontinued 1985.

Perf.: $1125	**Exc.:** $895	**VGood:** $775

American Arms Bristol

American Arms Brittany

American Arms Derby

American Arms Gentry

American Arms Grulla #2

American Arms Silver I

American Arms Silver II

AMERICAN ARMS GENTRY

Side-by-side; boxlock; 12-, 20-, 28-ga., .410; 3-inch chambers, 2-3/4-inch (28-ga.); 26-inch, 28-inch barrel; weighs about 6-1/4 to 6-3/4 lbs.; standard chokes; chromed bores; metal bead front sight; hand-checkered European walnut stock with semi-gloss finish; English-type scroll engraving; extractors; floating firing pin; silver finish on receiver. Introduced 1987; dropped 2000.

Perf.: $675	**Exc.:** $475	**VGood:** $375

Add $50 to above prices for 28 gauge or .410 bore

AMERICAN ARMS GRULLA #2

Side-by-side; sidelock; 12-, 20-, 28-ga., .410; 26-inch, 28-inch barrel; weighs about 6 lbs.; standard choke combos; select European walnut straight English stock; splinter forend; hand-rubbed oil finish; checkered grip, forend, butt; double triggers; detachable locks; automatic selective ejectors; cocking indicators; gas escape valves; English-style concave rib; color case-hardened receiver; scroll engraving. Made in Spain. Introduced 1989.

Perf.: $2575	**Exc.:** $2050	**VGood:** $1750

AMERICAN ARMS LINCE

Over/under; boxlock ejector; 12-, 20-ga., .410; 3-inch chambers; weighs 6-3/4 lbs.; metal bead front sight; standard choke combinations; checkered European walnut stock; single selective trigger; manual safety; rubber recoil pad; chrome-lined barrels; scroll engraving; blue or silver finish. Introduced 1986; discontinued 1986.

Perf.: $510	**Exc.:** $400	**VGood:** $380
.410		
Perf.: $555	**Exc.:** $450	**VGood:** $420

Add $75 to above prices for choke tubes

AMERICAN ARMS ROYAL

Over/under; sidelock; 12-, 20-ga.; 3-inch chambers; 26-inch, 28-inch barrels; weighs 7-1/4 lbs.; standard

choke combos or choke tubes; metal middle bead sight, glow worm front; hand-checkered European walnut stock, forend; auto selective ejectors; single non-selective trigger; manual safety; silvered sideplates; English-style hand-engraved scrollwork. Made in Spain. Introduced 1987; discontinued 1987.

Fixed chokes		
Perf.: $1595	**Exc.:** $1310	**VGood:** $1080
Choke tubes		
Perf.: $1660	**Exc.:** $1385	**VGood:** $1140

AMERICAN ARMS SHOTGUN

Side-by-side; boxlock ejector; 10-ga.; 3-1/2-inch chambers; double triggers; English-style hand-engraved scrollwork; chrome-finished receiver. Introduced 1986; discontinued 1986.

Perf.: $450	**Exc.:** $335	**VGood:** $295

AMERICAN ARMS SILVER I

Over/under; boxlock; 12-, 20-, 28-ga., .410; 2-3/4-inch chamber (28-ga.), 3-inch chamber (others); 26-inch, 28-inch barrels; standard choke combinations; weighs 6-3/4 lbs.; checkered European walnut stock with cast-off; single selective trigger; extractors; manual safety; rubber recoil pad; chrome-lined barrels; scroll engraving; metal bead front sight; silver finish. Made in Europe. Introduced 1987; dropped 2000.

Perf.: $535	**Exc.:** $430	**VGood:** $350

Add $40 to above prices for 28 gauge or .410 bore

AMERICAN ARMS SILVER II

Same specs as Silver I except 26-inch, 28-inch barrels in 12-ga., 26-inch (others); choke tubes. Also available in two-barrel set in 28/.410. Introduced 1987; still in production.

Perf.: $660	**Exc.:** $560	**VGood:** $475

Add $50 to above prices for 28 gauge or .410 bore (fixed chokes only)

American Arms Silver Sporting

American Arms Silver WS/OU 12

American Arms WS/SS 10

American Arms York

Apollo TR 30 Field

Arizaga Model 31

Armalite AR-17 Golden Gun

AMERICAN ARMS TS/OU 12

Over/under; boxlock ejector; 12-ga.; 3-1/2-inch chambers; 24-inch barrels; 46-inch overall length; weighs 6 lbs., 14 oz.; cut-checkered European walnut stock; black vented recoil pad; single selective trigger; chromed bores; matte metal finish. Made in Italy. Introduced 1988; no longer in production.

Perf.: $685   **Exc.:** $545   **VGood:** $475

AMERICAN ARMS TS/SS 12 DOUBLE

Side-by-side; boxlock; 12-ga.; 3-1/2-inch chambers; 26-inch barrels; choke tubes; extractors; single selective trigger; camouflage sling, sling swivels; recoil pad; chromed bores; raised matted rib; wood and metal matte finish. Made in Spain. Introduced 1988; dropped 2000.

Perf.: $665   **Exc.:** $550   **VGood:** $450

AMERICAN ARMS TS/SS 10 DOUBLE

Same specs as TS/SS 12 except 10-ga.; weighs about 11 lbs.; double triggers; AAI choke tubes Full/Full. Made in Spain. Introduced 1988; DISC. 2000.

Perf.: $665   **Exc.:** $550   **VGood:** $450

AMERICAN ARMS WS/SS 10

Side-by-side; boxlock; 10-ga.; 3-1/2-inch chambers; 32-inch barrels choked Full & Full; weighs 11-1/4 lbs.; flat rib; hand-checkered European walnut stock with beavertail forend; full pistol grip; dull finish; rubber recoil pad; double triggers; extractors; camouflaged sling; sling swivels. All metal with Parkerized finish. Introduced 1987; no longer produced.

Perf.: $775   **Exc.:** $650   **VGood:** $550

AMERICAN ARMS YORK

Side-by-side; boxlock; 12-, 20-, 28-ga., .410; 3-inch chambers; 25-inch, 28-inch barrels; standard choke combos; weighs 7-1/4 lbs.; gold bead front sight; gloss-finished, hand-checkered European walnut stock; beavertail forend; pistol grip; double triggers; extractors; manual safety; independent floating firing pins. Made in Spain. Introduced 1987; discontinued 1988.

Perf.: $625   **Exc.:** $475   **VGood:** $375

Optional single selective trigger

Perf.: $650   **Exc.:** $500   **VGood:** $400

Add $50 to above prices for 28 gauge or .410 bore

APOLLO TR AND TT SHOTGUNS

Gauge: 12, 20 and .410, 3" chambers; 28 ga. 2-3/4" chambers. Barrels: 26", 28", 20" or 32". Weight: 6 to 7-1/4 lbs. Stock: Oil-finished European walnut. Features include bioxlock action, chromed bores, automatic ejectors, single selective trigger, choke tubes (12and 20 ga. only). Introduced 2000 by SIGarms. TR30 Field (color case-hardened sideplates).

Perf.: $1800   **Exc.:** $1550   **VGood:** $1100

TR40 Gold (with gold inlay over engraving)

Perf.: $2200   **Exc.:** $1750   **VGood:** $1300

TT25 Competition (wide vent rib with mid-bead)

Perf.: $1750   **Exc.:** $1400   **VGood:** $1100

ARIZAGA MODEL 31

Side-by-side; boxlock; 12-, 16-. 20-, 28-ga., .410; 26-inch, 28-inch barrels; standard choke combos; 45-inch overall length; weighs 6-5/8 lbs; European walnut; English-style straight or pistol-grip stock; double triggers; engraved receiver; blued finish. Made in Spain. Introduced 1986; still in production.

Perf.: $475   **Exc.:** $395   **VGood:** $340

ARMALITE AR-17 GOLDEN GUN

Semi-auto; 12-ga.; 2-shot; 28-inch barrel; recoil operated; interchangeable choke tubes for Improved, Modified, Full chokes; polycarbonate stock, forearm; barrel, receiver housing of aluminum alloy; recoil pad; gold-anodized finish; also with black anodized finish. Introduced 1964; discontinued 1965. Only 2000 made.

Exc.: $750   **VGood:** $575   **Good:** $475

AMERICAN ARMS SILVER II UPLAND LIGHT

Same specs as Silver II except 12-, 20-ga.; 26-inch barrels; Franchoke tubes; weighs 6-1/4 lbs. (12-ga.), 5-3/4 lbs. (20-ga.); ejectors; ventilated rib; engraved frame with antique silver finish. Made in Spain. Introduced 1994; dropped 1998.

Perf.: $800   **Exc.:** $625   **VGood:** $550

AMERICAN ARMS SILVER SPORTING

Over/under; boxlock; 12-, 20-ga.; 2-3/4-inch (12-ga.), 3-inch (20-ga.) chambers; 28-inch (20-ga.), 30-inch barrels; weighs 7-3/8 lbs.; wide vent rib; Franchoke choke tubes; figured walnut stock with cut checkering; elongated forcing cones; ported barrels; pistol-grip stock with palm swell; radiused recoil pad; tapered target rib; target bead sights; mechanical single selective trigger; nickel finish. Introduced 1990; dropped 2000.

Perf.: $835   **Exc.:** $680   **VGood:** $550

AMERICAN ARMS SILVER SPORTING SKEET

Same specs as Silver Sporting except 26-inch ported barrels with elongated forcing cones; weighs 7-3/8 lbs.; stock dimensions of 14-3/8-inch by 1-3/8-inch by 2-3/8-inch; target-type ventilated rib with two bead sights; Skeet, Skeet, Imp. Cyl., Mod. choke tubes. Introduced 1992; no longer in production.

Perf.: $790   **Exc.:** $685   **VGood:** $575

AMERICAN ARMS SILVER SPORTING TRAP

Same specs as Silver Sporting except 30-inch ported barrels with elongated forcing cones; weighs 7-3/4 lbs.; stock dimensions of 14 3/8-inchx 1-1/2-inch by 1-5/8-inch; Mod., Imp. Mod., Full, Full choke tubes; target-type ventilated rib with two sight beads. Introduced 1992; dropped 1993.

Perf.: $790   **Exc.:** $685   **VGood:** $575

AMERICAN ARMS SILVER WS/OU 12

Over/under; boxlock ejector; 12-ga.; 3-1/2-inch chambers; 28-inch barrels; 46-inch overall length; weighs 7 lbs., 2 oz.; cut-checkered European walnut stock; black vented recoil pad; single selective trigger; chromed bores; matte metal finish. Made in Italy. Introduced 1988; dropped 2000.

Perf.: $675   **Exc.:** $365   **VGood:** $300

AMERICAN ARMS SILVER WT/OU 10

Over/under; boxlock; 10-ga.; 3-1/2-inch chambers; 26-inch barrels; Full/Full choke tubes; weighs 9-3/8 lbs.; extractors; chromed bores; non-reflective wood stock; dull metal finish; recoil pad; single trigger; ventilated rib; top tang safety. Introduced 1988; discontinued 2000.

Perf.: $775   **Exc.:** $750   **VGood:** $650

ARMSCOR MODEL 30D

Slide-action; 12-ga.; 5-shot magazine; 26-inch Modified, 30-inch Full barrel; 47-inch overall length; weighs 7-1/4 lbs.; metal bead front sight; Philippine plain mahogany stock; checkered double slidebars; blued finish. Made in the Philippines. Introduced 1990; discontinued 1991.

Perf.: $195   **Exc.:** $160   **VGood:** $135

ARMSCOR MODEL 30D/IC

Same specs as Model 30D except interchangeable choke tubes; checkered stock. No longer imported.

Perf.: $220   **Exc.:** $185   **VGood:** $160

ARMSCOR MODEL 30DG

Same specs as Model 30D except 20-inch plain barrel; rifle sights; 6-, 8-shot; plain pistol grip and grooved forend. Introduced 1987; discontinued 1991; reintroduced 2001.

Perf.: $185   **Exc.:** $150   **VGood:** $130

ARMSCOR MODEL 30FS

Same specs as Model 30D except black folding stock, pistol grip. Introduced 1990; discontinued 1991.

Perf.: $240   **Exc.:** $215   **VGood:** $190

ARMSCOR MODEL 30K

Same specs as Model 30D except 7-shot magazine; 21-inch barrel; olive green butt, forend. Introduced 1990; discontinued 1991.

Perf.: $215   **Exc.:** $190   **VGood:** $165

ARMSCOR MODEL 30P

Same specs as Model 30D except 11-1/2-inch barrel; 3-, 5-shot; bolo-type short stock; 22-1/2-inch overall length; weighs 5-1/2 lbs. For law enforcement. No longer imported.

Perf.: $250   **Exc.:** $225   **VGood:** $200

ARMSCOR MODEL 30R

Same specs as Model 30D except 6-, 8-shot; 20-inch Cylinder-bore barrel; 39-inch overall length; weighs 6-3/4 lbs.; bead front sight; smooth pistol-grip stock and grooved forend. No longer imported.

Perf.: $175   **Exc.:** $150   **VGood:** $125

ARMSCOR MODEL 30RP

Same specs as Model 30D except 18-inch barrel; 27-inch overall length; weighs 6-1/8 lbs.; black wood butt, forend. For law enforcement. Introduced 1987; discontinued 1991; reintroduced 2001.

Perf.: $210   **Exc.:** $175   **VGood:** $145

ARMSCOR M-30F FIELD PUMP SHOTGUN

Gauge: 12, 3-inch chamber. Barrel: 28-inch fixed Mod., or with Mod. and Full choke tubes; weighs: 7.6 lbs.; walnut-finished hardwood; double action slide bars; blued steel receiver; damascened bolt. Introduced 1996. Imported from the Philippines by K.B.I., Inc.

Perf.: $175   **Exc.:** $170   **VGood:** $160

ARMSPORT MODEL 1032 GOOSE GUN

Side-by-side; 10-ga.; 3-1/2-inch chambers: 32-inch barrels; weighs 11 lbs.; solid matted rib; engraved; checkered pistol-grip European walnut stock, forend; double triggers; vent rubber recoil pad with white spacer. Made in Spain. Introduced 1979; no longer imported.

Perf.: $365   **Exc.:** $310   **VGood:** $275

ARMSPORT MODEL 1040

Side-by-side; 12-ga.; 26-inch barrel; Imp./Mod.; oil-finished walnut stock and forend; hand-engraved receiver. No longer imported.

Perf.: $375   **Exc.:** $335   **VGood:** $295

ARMSPORT MODEL 1041

Side-by-side; 12-ga.; 28-inch barrel; Mod./Full; oil-finished walnut stock and forend; hand-engraved receiver. No longer imported.

Perf.: $375   **Exc.:** $335   **VGood:** $295

Armscor Model 30D

Armscor Model 30DG

Armscor Model 30R

Armsport Model 1050 Series

Armsport Model 2500 Series

ARMSPORT MODEL 1042

Side-by-side; 20-ga.; 26-inch barrel; Imp./Mod.; oil-finished walnut stock and forend; hand-engraved receiver. No longer imported.

Perf.: $380   **Exc.:** $345   **VGood:** $295

ARMSPORT MODEL 1043

Side-by-side; 20-ga.; 28-inch barrel; Mod./Full; oil-finished walnut stock and forend; hand-engraved receiver. No longer imported.

Perf.: $375   **Exc.:** $335   **VGood:** $295

ARMSPORT MODEL 1050 SERIES

Side-by-side; boxlock; 12-, 20-, 28-ga., .410; 3-inch chambers; 26-inch, 28-inch barrels; weighs 6-3/4 lbs.; chrome-lined barrels; European walnut stock; double triggers; extractors; silvered, engraved receiver. Made in Italy. Introduced 1986; no longer imported.

Model 1050 (12-ga.)			
Perf.: $595	**Exc.:** $475		**VGood:** $395
Model 1053 (20-ga.)			
Perf.: $610	**Exc.:** $485		**VGood:** $400
Model 1054 (.410)			
Perf.: $635	**Exc.:** $520		**VGood:** $425
Model 1055 (28-ga.)			
Perf.: $635	**Exc.:** $520		**VGood:** $425

ARMSPORT MODEL 1212 WESTERN

Side-by-side; 12-ga.; 3-inch chambers; 20-inch barrels; weighs 6-1/2 lbs.; checkered pistol-grip stock of European walnut, beavertail forend; metal front bead on matted solid rib; exposed hammers. Made in Spain. Introduced 1979; no longer imported.

Perf.: $350   **Exc.:** $275   **VGood:** $240

ARMSPORT MODEL 1626

Over/under; boxlock; 12-ga.; 3-inch chambers; 26-inch barrels; Improved/Modified; non-ejector; single selective trigger; vent rib; hand-checkered European walnut stock, forend; recoil pad; engraved. Made in Italy. No longer imported.

Perf.: $565   **Exc.:** $365   **VGood:** $300

ARMSPORT MODEL 1628

Over/under; boxlock; 12-ga.; 3-inch chambers; 28-inch barrels; Modified/Full; non-ejector; single selective trigger; vent rib; hand-checkered European walnut stock, forend; recoil pad; engraved. Made in Italy. No longer imported.

Perf.: $565   **Exc.:** $365   **VGood:** $300

ARMSPORT MODEL 1726

Over/under; boxlock; 20-ga.; 3-inch chambers; 26-inch barrels; Improved/Modified; non-ejector; single selective trigger; vent rib; hand-checkered European walnut stock, forend; recoil pad; engraved. Made in Italy. No longer imported.

Perf.: $565   **Exc.:** $365   **VGood:** $300

ARMSPORT MODEL 1728

Over/under; boxlock; 20-ga.; 3-inch chambers; 28-inch barrels; Modified/Full; non-ejector; single selective trigger; vent rib; hand-checkered European walnut stock, forend; recoil pad; engraved. Made in Italy. No longer imported.

Perf.: $575   **Exc.:** $375   **VGood:** $300

ARMSPORT MODEL 1810

Over/under; .410-bore; 3-inch chambers; 26-inch barrels; Full/Full chokes; blued receiver and barrels. No longer imported.

Perf.: $575   **Exc.:** $375   **VGood:** $300

ARMSPORT MODEL 2526

Over/under; 12-ga.; 26-inch barrels; Imp./Mod.; vent rib; hand-checkered European walnut pistol-grip stock; single selective trigger; auto ejectors; engraved receiver. Manufactured in Europe. Introduced 1979; no longer imported.

Perf.: $585   **Exc.:** $375   **VGood:** $300

ARMSPORT MODEL 2528

Over/under; 12-ga.; 28-inch barrels; Modified/Full; vent rib; hand-checkered European walnut pistol-grip stock; single selective trigger; auto ejectors; engraved receiver. Manufactured in Europe. Introduced 1979; no longer imported.

Perf.: $585   **Exc.:** $375   **VGood:** $300

Armsport Model 2700 Series

Amsport Model 2700 Goose Gun

Armsport Models 2720, 2725

Armsport Models 2730, 2731

Armsport Models 2734, 2736, 2742, 2744

Armsport Models 2741

ARMSPORT MODEL 2626

Over/under; boxlock; 20-ga.; 26-inch barrels; Imp./Mod.; automatic ejectors; vent rib; single selective trigger; walnut stock and forend; recoil pad; engraved. No longer imported.

Perf.: $595 **Exc.:** $395 **VGood:** $330

ARMSPORT MODEL 2628

Over/under; boxlock; 20-ga.; 28-inch barrels; Mod./Full; automatic ejectors; vent rib; single selective trigger; walnut stock and forend; recoil pad; engraved. No longer imported.

Perf.: $585 **Exc.:** $375 **VGood:** $330

ARMSPORT MODEL 2697

Over/under; boxlock; 10-ga. Magnum; 3-1/2-inch chambers; 28-inch chrome-lined barrels; choke tubes; engraved silver finished receiver; wide vent rib; hand-checkered walnut forend and stock. No longer imported.

Perf.: $925 **Exc.:** $700 **VGood:** $600

ARMSPORT MODEL 2698

Over/under; boxlock; 10-ga. Magnum; 3-1/2-inch chambers; 32-inch chrome-lined barrels; choke tubes; engraved silver finished receiver; wide vent rib; hand-checkered walnut forend and stock. No longer imported.

Perf.: $925 **Exc.:** $700 **VGood:** $600

ARMSPORT MODEL 2699

Over/under; boxlock; 10-ga. Magnum; 3-1/2-inch chambers; 28-inch chrome-lined barrels; Full/Improved-Modified chokes; engraved silver finished receiver; wide vent rib; hand-checkered walnut forend and stock. No longer imported.

Perf.: $995 **Exc.:** $605 **VGood:** $565

ARMSPORT MODEL 2700 GOOSE GUN

Over/under; 10-ga.; 3-1/2-inch chambers; 28-inch Full/Imp. Mod., 32-inch Full/Full barrels; weighs 9-1/2 lbs.; Boss-type action; European walnut stock; double triggers; extractors. Made in Italy. Introduced 1986; still in production.

Perf.: $875 **Exc.:** $605 **VGood:** $565

ARMSPORT MODEL 2700 SERIES

Over/under; boxlock; 10-ga. Mag.; 3-1/2-inch chambers; 32-inch chrome-lined barrels; Full/Full chokes; engraved silver finished receiver; extractors; wide vent rib; hand-checkered walnut forend and stock. No longer imported.

Perf.: $875 **Exc.:** $615 **VGood:** $565

ARMSPORT MODEL 2701, 2702

Same specs as 2700 except 12-ga.; 3-inch Mag. chambers; 28-inch barrels; Modified/Full. No longer imported by Armsport.

Perf.: $450 **Exc.:** $355 **VGood:** $290

ARMSPORT MODEL 2703, 2704

Same specs as 2700 except 20-ga.; 3-inch Mag. chambers; Improved/Modified chokes. No longer imported by Armsport.

Perf.: $475 **Exc.:** $355 **VGood:** $290

ARMSPORT MODEL 2705

Same specs as 2700 except .410; 26-inch barrels; Modified/Full chokes. Made in Italy. No longer imported.

Perf.: $625 **Exc.:** $425 **VGood:** $355

ARMSPORT MODEL 2706 COMMANDER

Same specs as 2700 except 12-ga.; 20-inch barrels; double triggers; extractors. No longer imported by Armsport.

Perf.: $300 **Exc.:** $250 **VGood:** $225

ARMSPORT MODEL 2707

Same specs as 2700 except 28-ga.; Improved/Modified; double trigger. No longer imported by Armsport.

Perf.: $625 **Exc.:** $425 **VGood:** $355

ARMSPORT MODEL 2708 SLUG GUN

Same specs as 2700 except 12-ga.; 20-inch or 23-inch barrels; double or single trigger. No longer imported by Armsport.

Perf.: $575 **Exc.:** $450 **VGood:** $390

ARMSPORT MODEL 27 16, 2717

Same specs as 2700 except 12-ga.; 3-inch Mag. chambers; 28-inch barrels; Modified/Full chokes; single selective trigger; extractors. No longer imported.

Perf.: $600 **Exc.:** $475 **VGood:** $390

ARMSPORT MODEL 2718, 2719

Same specs as 2700 except 20-ga.; 3-inch Mag. chambers; 26-inch barrels; Improved/Modified chokes; single selective trigger; extractors. No longer imported.

Perf.: $600 **Exc.:** $475 **VGood:** $390

ARMSPORT MODEL 2720

Same specs as 2700 except .410; 26-inch barrels; Modified/Full chokes; single selective trigger; extractors. No longer imported.

Perf.: $640 **Exc.:** $515 **VGood:** $430

ARMSPORT MODEL 2725

Same specs as 2700 except 28-ga.; 26-inch barrels; Improved/Modified choke tubes. No longer imported.

Perf.: $640 **Exc.:** $515 **VGood:** $430

ARMSPORT MODEL 2730

Same specs as 2700 except 12-ga.; 28-inch barrels; Skeet set with choke tubes; single trigger; ejectors. No longer imported.

Perf.: $740 **Exc.:** $525 **VGood:** $475

ARMSPORT MODEL 2731

Same specs as 2700 except 20-ga.; 26-inch barrels; Skeet set with choke tubes; single trigger; ejectors. No longer imported.

Perf.: $740 **Exc.:** $525 **VGood:** $475

ARMSPORT MODEL 2733

Same specs as 2700 except 12-ga.; 28-inch barrels; Modified/Full; Boss-type action; extractors; single selective trigger. No longer imported.

Perf.: $685 **Exc.:** $460 **VGood:** $370

ARMSPORT MODEL 2734

Same specs as 2700 except 12-ga.; 28-inch barrels; choke tubes; extractors; single selective trigger. No longer imported.

Perf.: $720 **Exc.:** $505 **VGood:** $455

ARMSPORT MODEL 2735

Same specs as 2700 except 20-ga.; 26-inch barrels; Improved/Modified; Boss-type action; extractors; single selective trigger. No longer imported.

Perf.: $685 **Exc.:** $460 **VGood:** $370

ARMSPORT MODEL 2736

Same specs as 2700 except 20-ga.; 26-inch barrels; choke tubes; Boss-type action; extractors; single selective trigger. No longer imported.

Perf.: $600 **Exc.:** $475 **VGood:** $425

ARMSPORT MODEL 2741

Same specs as 2700 except 12-ga.; 28-inch barrels; Modified/Full; Boss-type action; ejectors; single selective trigger. No longer imported.

Perf.: $640 **Exc.:** $440 **VGood:** $375

ARMSPORT MODEL 2742 SPORTING CLAYS
Same specs as 2700 except 12-ga.; 28-inch barrels; choke tubes; single selective trigger. No longer imported.

Perf.: $600   **Exc.:** $450   **VGood:** $390

ARMSPORT MODEL 2744 SPORTING CLAYS
Same specs as 2700 except 20-ga.; 26-inch barrels; choke tubes; ejectors; single selective trigger. No longer imported.

Perf.: $625   **Exc.:** $450   **VGood:** $390

ARMSPORT MODEL 2746
Same specs as 2700 except 12-ga. Mag.; 3-1/2-inch chambers; 28-inch barrels; choke tubes. No longer imported.

Perf.: $695   **Exc.:** $425   **VGood:** $390

ARMSPORT MODEL 2747
Same specs as 2700 except 12-ga. Mag.; 3-1/2-inch chambers; 32-inch barrels; choke tubes. No longer imported.

Perf.: $695   **Exc.:** $425   **VGood:** $390

ARMSPORT MODEL 2750 SPORTING CLAYS
Same specs as 2700 except 12-ga.; 28-inch barrels; choke tubes; single selective trigger; ejectors; equipped with decorative sideplates. No longer imported.

Perf.: $725   **Exc.:** $575   **VGood:** $525

ARMSPORT MODEL 2751 SPORTING CLAY
Same specs as 2700 except 20-ga.; 26-inch barrels; choke tubes; single selective trigger; ejectors; equipped with decorative sideplates. No longer imported.

Perf.: $925   **Exc.:** $575   **VGood:** $525

ARMSPORT MODEL 2751
Semi-automatic; 12-ga.; 3-inch chamber; 28-inch Modified, 30-inch Full (2751A) choke barrels; weighs 7 lbs.; choke tube version available; European walnut stock; rubber recoil pad; blued or silvered receiver with engraving. Made in Italy. Introduced 1986; no longer imported.

Perf.: $400   **Exc.:** $320   **VGood:** $275

With choke tubes

Perf.: $420   **Exc.:** $340   **VGood:** $285

Silvered receiver

Perf.: $420   **Exc.:** $340   **VGood:** $285

ARMSPORT MODEL 2755
Pump-action; 12-ga.; 3-inch chamber; 28-inch Modified, 30-inch Full (2755A) barrel; weighs 7 lbs.; choke tubes available; vent rib; European walnut stock; rubber recoil pad; blued finish. Made in Italy. Introduced 1986; no longer imported.

Perf.: $320   **Exc.:** $225   **VGood:** $165

With choke tubes

Perf.: $335   **Exc.:** $245   **VGood:** $195

ARMSPORT MODEL 2900 TRI-BARREL
Over/under; 12-ga.; 3-inch chambers; 28-inch barrels; weighs 7-3/4 lbs.; choked Improved/Modified/Full; standard choke combos; European walnut stock; double triggers; top-tang barrel selector; silvered, engraved frame. Made in Italy. Introduced 1986; no longer imported.

Perf.: $2675   **Exc.:** $2150   **VGood:** $1700

ARMSPORT MODEL 2901 TRI-BARREL
Same specs as 2900 Tri-Barrel except 12-ga.; 3-inch Mag. chambers; choked Modified/Full/Full. No longer imported.

Perf.: $2675   **Exc.:** $2150   **VGood:** $1700

ARMSPORT MODEL 3030 DELUXE GRADE TRAP
Over/under; 12-ga.; 32-inch barrels; wide ventilated rib; ventilated lateral rib; single selective trigger;

Armsport Models 2746, 2747

Armsport Models 2750, 2751 Sporting Clays

Armsport Model 2900 Tri-Barrel

automatic ejectors; fluorescent bead front sight; checkered walnut stock; beavertail forend; Greener-type cross-bolt; engraved sideplates. No longer imported.

Perf.: $625   **Exc.:** $475   **VGood:** $375

ARMSPORT MODEL 3032 DELUXE GRADE TRAP
Over/under; 12-ga.; 30-inch barrels; wide ventilated rib; ventilated lateral rib; single selective trigger; automatic ejectors; fluorescent bead front sight; checkered walnut stock; beavertail forend; Greener-type cross-bolt; engraved sideplates. No longer imported.

Perf.: $645   **Exc.:** $495   **VGood:** $385

ARMSPORT MODEL 3101 DELUXE MONO TRAP
Single or over/under; 12-ga.; 30-inch (O/U), 32-inch (single) barrels; single selective trigger; automatic ejectors; highly grained walnut stock, forend with high-lustre finish; choice of mono trap or as a combo set should be 30 percent higher with over/under barrels. No longer imported.

Perf.: $650   **Exc.:** $500   **VGood:** $400

ARMSPORT MODEL 3102 DELUXE MONO TRAP SET
Single or over/under; 12-ga.; 32-inch (O/U), 34-inch (single) barrels; single selective trigger; automatic ejectors; highly grained walnut stock, forend with high lustre finish; choice of mono trap or as a set; combo set should be 30 percent higher with over/under barrels. No longer imported.

Perf.: $1100   **Exc.:** $895   **VGood:** $700

ARMSPORT MODEL 3103 DELUXE MONO TRAP
Single shot; 12-ga.; 32-inch barrels; single selective trigger; automatic ejectors; highly grained walnut stock, forend with high lustre finish; choice of mono trap or as a set; combo set should be 30 percent higher with over/under barrels. No longer imported.

Perf.: $700   **Exc.:** $575   **VGood:** $400

ARMSPORT MODEL 3104 DELUXE MONO TRAP
Single shot; 12-ga.; 34-inch barrels; single selective trigger; automatic ejectors; highly grained walnut stock, forend with high lustre finish; choice of mono trap or as a set; combo set should be 30 percent higher with over/under barrels. No longer imported.

Perf.: $700   **Exc.:** $575   **VGood:** $400

ARMSPORT MODEL 4000 EMPEROR OVER/UNDER
Over/under; 12-, 16-, 20-ga.; any barrel length; any choke; handcrafted barrels, action, root walnut stock, forend; hand engraved receiver, sideplate; custom made to order; luggage-type case. No longer imported.

Perf.: $1200   **Exc.:** $975   **VGood:** $725

ARMSPORT MODEL 4010 EMPEROR SIDE-BY-SIDE
Side-by-side; sidelock; 12- 16-, 20-ga.; any barrel length; any choke; handcrafted barrels, action, root walnut stock, forend; engraved receiver, sideplate; luggage-type case; custom made. No longer imported.

Perf.: $1750   **Exc.:** $1425   **VGood:** $1200

ARMSPORT MODEL 4031
Side-by-side; sidelock; 12-, 20-ga. 26-inch, 28-inch barrels; Improved/Modified or Modified/Full chokes; English-style straight walnut stock; hand detachable locks; silver finish hand-engraved receiver; highly polished steel barrels. Made in Italy. No longer imported.

Perf.: $3800   **Exc.:** $2500   **VGood:** $1950

ARMSPORT MODEL 4032 MONO TRAP
Single shot; 12-ga.; 32-inch barrel; vent rib; single trigger; walnut stock with pistol grip; recoil pad; automatic ejector; premier grade; hand engraved. No longer imported.

Perf.: $1750   **Exc.:** $1300   **VGood:** $1100

ARMSPORT MODEL 4033 MONO TRAP
Single shot; 12-ga.; 34-inch barrel; vent rib; single trigger; walnut stock with pistol grip; recoil pad; automatic ejector; premier grade; hand engraved. No longer imported.

Perf.: $1750   **Exc.:** $1300   **VGood:** $1100

ARMSPORT MODEL 4034 MONO TRAP SET
Single shot; 12-ga.; 32-inch barrel; vent rib; single trigger; walnut stock with pistol grip; recoil pad; automatic ejector; premier grade; hand engraved. Additional set of 30-inch O/U barrels. No longer imported.

Perf.: $2500   **Exc.:** $1900   **VGood:** $1000

ARMSPORT MODEL 4034 O/U TRAP SET
Single shot; 12-ga.; 30-inch barrels; vent rib; single trigger; walnut stock with pistol grip; recoil pad; automatic ejector; premier grade; hand engraved. Additional set of 30-inch O/U barrels. No longer imported.

Perf.: $2500   **Exc.:** $1900   **VGood:** $1650

ARMSPORT MODEL 4035 MONO TRAP SET
Single shot; 12-ga.; 34-inch barrel; vent rib; single trigger; walnut stock with pistol grip; recoil pad; ejector; premier grade; hand engraved. Additional set of 32-inch O/U barrels. No longer imported.

Perf.: $2500   **Exc.:** $1900   **VGood:** $1650

Arrieta Model 557

Arrieta Model 570

Arrieta Model 578

Arrieta Model 600
Imperial

Arrieta Model 600
Imperial Tiro

Arrieta Model 800

Arrieta Model 802

Arrieta Model 803

Arrieta Model 871

Arrieta Model 872

Arrieta Model 873

Arrieta Model 874

Arrieta Model 875

ARMSPORT MODEL 4035 O/U TRAP SET

Single shot; 12-ga.; 32-inch barrels; vent rib; single trigger; walnut stock with pistol grip; recoil pad; automatic ejectors; premier grade; hand engraved. Additional set of 32-inch O/U barrels. No longer imported.

Perf.: $2500   **Exc.:** $1900   **VGood:** $1650

ARMSPORT MODEL 4040 PREMIER SLUG

Side-by-side; 12-ga.; 23-inch barrels; Cyl./Imp. Cyl.; rib with leaf rear sight; blade front; hand-checkered walnut stock with half pistol grip and beavertail forend; hand relief engraved receiver. No longer imported.

Perf.: $1250   **Exc.:** $800   **VGood:** $700

ARMSPORT MODEL 4041 PREMIER SLUG

Side-by-side; 12-ga.; 23-inch, 28-inch barrels; Cyl./Imp. Cyl. (23-inch), Mod./Full (28-inch); rib with leaf rear sight, blade front; hand-checkered walnut stock with half pistol grip and beavertail forend; hand relief-engraved receiver. No longer imported.

Perf.: $1250   **Exc.:** $800   **VGood:** $700

ARMSPORT MODEL 4046 MONO TRAP

Single shot; 12-ga.; 34-inch barrel; specially reinforced receiver carved from a solid block of gun steel; unique coil spring trigger assembly; handcrafted Italian leather fitted case. No longer imported.

Perf.: $2750   **Exc.:** $2150   **VGood:** $1800

ARMSPORT MODEL 4047 MONO TRAP

Single shot; 12-ga.; 32-inch barrel; specially reinforced receiver carved from a solid block of gun steel; unique coil spring trigger assembly;

handcrafted Italian leather fitted case. No longer imported.

Perf.: $2750   **Exc.:** $2150   **VGood:** $1800

ARMSPORT MODEL 4048 MONO TRAP SET

Single shot; 12-ga.; 32-inch (over/under), 34-inch (mono) barrel; specially reinforced receiver carved from a solid block of gun steel; unique coil spring trigger assembly; comes with extra trigger assembly; handcrafted Italian leather fitted case. No longer imported.

Perf.: $1100   **Exc.:** $875   **VGood:** $700

ARMSPORT MODEL 4049 MONO TRAP SET

Single shot; 12-ga.; 30-inch (over/under), 32-inch (mono) barrel; specially reinforced receiver carved from a solid block of gun steel; unique coil spring trigger assembly; comes with extra trigger assembly; handcrafted Italian leather fitted case. No longer imported.

Perf.: $1100   **Exc.:** $875   **VGood:** $700

ARMSPORT SINGLE

Single-shot; 12-, 20-ga.; 3-inch chamber; 26-inch, 28-inch barrel; weighs 6-1/2 lbs.; oil-finished hardwood stock; chrome-lined barrel; cocking indicator opening lever behind trigger guard; manual safety. Made in Europe. Introduced 1987; no longer imported.

Perf.: $85   **Exc.:** $55   **VGood:** $45

Model 1125 (12-ga., Modified)

Perf.: $85   **Exc.:** $55   **VGood:** $45

Model 1126 (12-ga., Full)

Perf.: $85   **Exc.:** $55   **VGood:** $45

Model 1127 (20-ga., Modified)

Perf.: $85   **Exc.:** $55   **VGood:** $45

ARRIETA SIDELOCK DOUBLE SHOTGUNS

Side-by-side; sidelock; 12-, 16-, 20-, 28-ga., .410; barrel length and chokes to customer specs.; select European walnut stock with oil finish, straight English grip, checkered butt (standard), or pistol-grip; essentially a custom gun with myriad options; Holland & Holland-pattern hand-detachable sidelocks, selective automatic ejectors, double triggers (hinged front) standard. Some have self-opening action. Finish and engraving to customer specs. Imported from Spain by importers including Wingshooting Adventures, Orvis, Griffin & Howe, New England Arms Corp. and Quality Arms.

Model 557, detachable engraved sidelocks, auto ejectors

Perf.: $3000   **Exc.:** $2100   **VGood:** $1600

Model 570, non-detachable sidelocks, auto ejectors

Perf.: $3475   **Exc.:** $2450   **VGood:** $1825

Model 578, scrollwork engraved, auto ejectors

Perf.: $4050   **Exc.:** $2800   **VGood:** $1975

Model 600 Imperial, lightly engraved, self-opening

Perf.: $5275   **Exc.:** $4150   **VGood:** $3300

Model 601 Imperial Tiro, nickel-plated action, self-opening

Perf.: $6600   **Exc.:** $4250   **VGood:** $3500

Model 801, detachable sidelocks, fine engraving, self-opening

Perf.: $8175   **Exc.:** $7200   **VGood:** $6325

Model 802, non-detachable sidelocks, finely engraved
Perf.: $8135   **Exc.:** $7200   **VGood:** $6300

Model 803, detachable sidelocks, finely engraved, self-opening
Perf.: $6175   **Exc.:** $5300   **VGood:** $4175

Model 871, auto ejectors, scroll engraved, rounded frame action
Perf.: $4400   **Exc.:** $3425   **VGood:** $2750

Model 872, self-opening, rounded frame action, finely engraved
Perf.: $11,000   **Exc.:** $9500   **VGood:** $8200

Model 873, self-opening, automatic ejectors, engraved with game scene
Perf.: $7525   **Exc.:** $5500   **VGood:** $4325

Model 874, self-opening, gold engraved
Perf.: $8225   **Exc.:** $7200   **VGood:** $6200

Model 875, self-opening, custom-made only
Perf.: $13,000   **Exc .:** $10,650   **VGood:** $9450

Model 931, self-opening, all gauges, elaborate engraving, H&H selective ejectors
Perf.: 250   **Exc.:** $11,000   **VGood:** $9500

ASTRA MODEL 650

Over/under; 12-ga; 28-inch, 30-inch barrels; standard chokes; vent rib; hand-checkered European walnut stock; double triggers; ejectors or extractors; scroll-engraved receiver. Was imported from Spain. Introduced 1980; discontinued 1987.

Perf.: $450   **Exc.:** $375   **VGood:** $300

Extractors
Perf.: $410   **Exc.:** $335   **VGood:** $260

Trap and Skeet models
Perf.: $460   **Exc.:** $375   **VGood:** $300

ASTRA MODEL 750

Over/under; 12-ga.; 28-inch, 30-inch barrels; vent rib; hand-checkered European walnut stock; single selective trigger; ejectors or extractors; scroll-engraved receiver. Introduced 1980; discontinued 1987.

Perf.: $440   **Exc.:** $365   **VGood:** $290

Extractors only
Perf.: $410   **Exc.:** $335   **VGood:** $275

AyA AUGUSTA

Over/under; sidelock; 12-ga.; vent rib; single or double trigger; high-grade scroll engraving; fancy walnut; Kersten cross bolts. A deluxe gun modeled after the Merkel.

Perf.: $20,000   **Exc.:** $5600   **VGood:** $4500

AyA BOLERO

Side-by-side; boxlock; extractors; 12-, 16-, 20-, 28-ga., .410; single non-selective trigger. Imported as Model 400 by Firearms International. Introduced 1955; discontinued 1963.

Perf.: $350   **Exc.:** $275   **VGood:** $225

AyA CORAL

Over/under; 12-, 16-ga.; 26-inch, 28-inch, 30-inch barrels; 2-3/4-inch chambers; any choke desired; Kersten crossbolt; ejectors; pistol-grip stock; single or double trigger; two grades of engraving. No longer imported; discontinued 1985.

Perf.: $1300   **Exc.:** $1000   **VGood:** $800

AyA COSMOS

Single barrel; single shot; 12 Mag., 12-, 16-, 20-, 24-, 28-ga., .410; ejector; hammer; top lever; pistol-grip walnut stock; buttpad; sling swivels; interchangeable barrels. No longer imported.

Perf.: $345   **Exc.:** $295   **VGood:** $250

AyA IBERIA

Side-by-side; boxlock; 12-ga.; 2-3/4-inch chambers; 28-inch barrels; straight, half or full pistol-grip stock; hand checkered walnut; minimal engraving; extractors; double trigger. No longer imported; discontinued 1984.

Perf.: $545   **Exc.:** $395   **VGood:** $359

AyA Cosmos

AyA Coral Grade A

AyA Iberia II

AyA Matador II

AyA Model 37 Super Grade A

AyA Model 37 Super Grade B

AyA Model 53-E

AyA Model 53-E

AyA IBERIA/E

Same specs as Iberia except ejectors. No longer imported.

Perf.: $575   **Exc.:** $425   **VGood:** $395

AyA IBERIA II

Same specs as Iberia except 12-, 16-ga.; no engraving; earlier version had straight receiver-to-wood joint; newer Iberia has a single scallop. No longer imported.

Perf.: $520   **Exc.:** $360   **VGood:** $310

AyA MATADOR

Side-by-side; boxlock; ejectors; 10-, 12-, 16-, 20-, 28-ga., .410; 2-3/4-inch, 3-inch (20-ga.), 3-1/2-inch (10-ga.) chambers; 26-inch, 28-inch, 30-inch barrels; any standard choke combo; European walnut stock; checkered pistol grip; beavertail forearm; single-selective trigger. Imported as Model 400E by Firearms International. Introduced 1955; discontinued 1963.

Exc.: $350   **VGood:** $300   **Good:** $220

AyA MATADOR II

Same specs as Matador except 12-, 20-ga.; better wood. Manufactured 1964 to 1969.

Exc.: $350   **VGood:** $315   **Good:** $265

AyA MODEL 4 DELUXE

Side-by-side; boxlock; 12-, 16-, 20-, 28-ga., .410; 26-inch, 27-inch, 28-inch barrels, depending upon gauge; weighs 5 to 7 lbs.; select European walnut stock and forend; Anson & Deeley system with double locking lugs; chopper lump barrels; bushed firing pins; automatic safety and ejectors; articulated front trigger. Still imported.

Perf.:: $2750   **Exc.:** $2575   **VGood:** $1095

AyA MODEL 37 SUPER

Over/under; sidelock; 12-, 16-, 20-ga.; 26-inch, 30-inch barrels; any standard choke combo; vent rib; single selective or double trigger(s); automatic ejectors; hand-checkered stock, forearm; heavily engraved pistol-grip or straight stock. Introduced 1963; no longer in production.

Perf.: $2000   **Exc.:** $1600   **VGood:** $1350

AyA MODEL 53-E

Side-by-side; sidelock ejector; 12-, 16-, 20-ga.; 2-3/4-inch chambers, 3-inch Mag. (available in 20-ga.); 26-inch, 28-inch, 30-inch barrels; any choke; finely hand-engraved with full coverage; hand-detachable locks; side clips; third locking bite; gas vents; single or double trigger; straight grip; half or full pistol grip on request; stock made to measure on request; plain or vent rib. Still imported.

Perf.: $3750   **Exc.:** $1850   **VGood:** $1250

AyA Model 56

AyA Model 106

AyA Model 107

AyA Model 107LI

AyA Model 110

AyA Model 112

AyA Model 116

AyA Model 117

AyA Model XXV/SL

AyA Model XXV/BL

AyA Model XXV (BL) Boxlock

AyA MODEL 56

Side-by-side; sidelock ejectors; triple-bolting; 12-, 16-, 20-ga.; barrel length, chokes to customers specs; European walnut stock to customer's specs; semi-custom manufacture; matted rib, vent rib available; automatic safety; cocking indicators; gas escape valves; folding front trigger; highly engraved receiver. Introduced 1972. 12-, 20-ga. still imported by Armes de Chasse.

Perf.: $6500   **Exc.:** $2900   **VGood:** $2350

AyA MODEL 106

Side-by-side; boxlock; 12-, 16-, 20-ga.; 2-3/4-inch chambers; 28-inch barrels; half or full pistol-grip with or without cheekpiece; almost no engraving; Greener-type cross bolt. No longer imported; discontinued 1985.

Perf.: $570   **Exc.:** $460   **VGood:** $420

AyA MODEL 107

Side-by-side; boxlock; 12-, 16-, 20-ga.; 2-3/4-inch chambers; 26-inch, 28-inch, 30-inch barrels; Modified/Full; cross bolt; brightly-finished receiver or color case-hardened; extractors; double trigger; checkered wood. No longer imported.

Perf.: $570   **Exc.:** $450   **VGood:** $390

AyA MODEL 107LI

Same specs as Model 107 except 12-, 16-ga.; Half/Full choke; side clips; scalloped receiver; modest engraving. No longer imported.

Perf.: $695   **Exc.:** $565   **VGood:** $525

AyA MODEL 110

Side-by-side; hammer gun; sidelock; 12-, 16-ga.; 2-3/4-inch chambers; 28-inch, 30-inch barrels; cross bolt and double underlugs; hand-checkered walnut; extractors. No longer imported.

Perf.: $750   **Exc.:** $550   **VGood:** $450

AyA MODEL 112

Side-by-side; sidelock; 12-, 16-, 20-ga.; 2-3/4-inch chambers; 28-inch, 30-inch barrels; hand-checkered walnut stock and forend; sideclips; cross bolt; extractors; modest engraving; double triggers; straight, semi- or full pistol grip. No longer imported.

Perf.: $695   **Exc.:** $525   **VGood:** $450

AyA MODEL 116

Side-by-side; sidelock; 12-, 16-, 20-ga.; 2-3/4-inch chambers; 27-inch, 28-inch, 30-inch barrels; hand-detachable locks; double trigger; third bite; hand-checkered walnut stock, forend; extractors. No longer imported.

Perf.: $1000   **Exc.:** $845   **VGood:** $795

AyA MODEL 117

Side-by-side; sidelock ejector; 12-, 16-, 20-ga.; 2-3/4-inch chambers; 26-inch, 27-inch, 28-inch, 30-inch barrels; standard choke combos; hand-checkered European walnut stock; beavertail forend; straight, half or full pistol grip; Holland & Holland design hand-detachable locks; double or selective single trigger. Was imported by Precision Sports. No longer in production.

Perf.: $850   **Exc.:** $715   **VGood:** $660

AyA MODEL 931

Over/under; boxlock; 12-, 16-, 20-, 28-ga., .410; 26-inch, 27-inch, 28-inch barrels; weighs 5 to 7 lbs; self-opening; Anson & Deeley system with double locking lugs; chopper lump barrels; bushed firing pins; automatic safety, ejectors; articulated front trigger. Imported by Armes de Chasse. Still in production.

Perf.: $1000   **Exc.:** $750   **VGood:** $555

AyA MODEL XXV/SL

Side-by-side; boxlock; 12-, 20-ga.; 26-inch, 27-inch, 28-inch, 29-inch barrels, depending upon gauge; weighs 5 to 7 lbs.; European walnut stock and forend; Holland & Holland system with double locking lugs; chopper lump barrels; bushed firing pins; automatic safety and ejectors; articulated front trigger. Still imported.

Perf.: $2850   **Exc.:** $1850   **VGood:** $1550

AyA MODEL XXV/BL

Side-by-side; boxlock ejector; 12- or 20-ga.; 2-1/2-inch chambers; 2-3/4-inch chambers on request; 25-inch barrels; standard chokes; straight-grip European walnut stock; half or full pistol grip on request; checkered butt; fine hand engraving; double triggers; Churchill-type narrow rib; color case-hardened or coin-finished receiver. Made in Spain. Introduced 1981; still imported by Armes de Chasse.

Perf.: $2000   **Exc.:** $1225   **VGood:** $995

AyA NO. 1

Side-by-side; sidelock; 12-, 20-ga.; 26-inch, 27-inch, 28-inch, 29-inch barrels; weighs 5-7 lbs.; double triggers; articulated front trigger; automatic safety; selective automatic ejectors; cocking indicators; bushed firing pins; replaceable hinge pins and chopper lump barrels; hand-cut checkered walnut stocks with oil finish; metal oval on buttstock for engraved initials; concave rib; straight hand; double triggers; engraved. Still imported by Armes de Chasse.

Perf.: $6325   **Exc.:** $2350   **VGood:** $1850

AyA NO. 2

Side-by-side; sidelock; 12-, 16-, 20-, 28-ga., .410; 3-inch chambers; 28-inch barrels; standard choke combos; weighs 7 lbs.; silver bead front sight; English-style oil-finished walnut stock, splinter forend; checkered butt; single selective or double triggers; engraved sideplates; auto safety; gas escape valves. Made in Spain. Introduced 1987; discontinued 1988. Now imported by Armes de Chasse.

12-, 20-ga., double triggers		
Perf.: $2775	**Exc.:** $1150	**VGood:** $900
12-, 20-ga., single trigger		
Perf.: $2825	**Exc.:** $1200	**VGood:** $950
28-ga., .410, double triggers		
Perf.: $2850	**Exc.:** $1350	**VGood:** $1000
28-ga., .410, single trigger		
Perf.: $2875	**Exc.:** $1275	**VGood:** $1000

AyA MODEL 3-A

Side-by-side; boxlock; 12-, 16-, 20-, 28-ga., .410; 26-inch, 28-inch, 30-inch barrels; 3-inch chambers (12-ga.); standard chokes; straight, half or full pistol grip; double triggers; border-engraved only; Spanish walnut stock; hand-checkered; chopper lump barrels; double underlug lock only. Discontinued 1985.

Perf.: $645   **Exc.:** $545   **VGood:** $495

AyA NO. 4

Side-by-side; boxlock; 12-, 16-, 20-, 28-ga., .410; 26-inch, 28-inch, 30-inch barrels; standard chokes; hand-checkered straight-grip European walnut stock; other stock types made to order; checkered butt; classic forend; automatic ejectors, safety; double or single triggers; color case-hardened receiver. Made in Spain. Introduced 1981; still imported by Armes de Chasse.

12-, 16-ga.		
Perf.: $1400	**Exc.:** $625	**VGood:** $525
20-ga.		
Perf.: $1400	**Exc.:** $625	**VGood:** $525
28-ga., .410		
Perf.: $1450	**Exc.:** $675	**VGood:** $575

AyA YEOMAN

Side-by-side; boxlock; 12-ga.; ejectors; very plain gun with no engraving; color-hardened receiver; hand-checkered walnut stock. No longer imported.

Perf.: $495   **Exc.:** $395   **VGood:** $355

BAIKAL 66 COACH GUN

Side-by-side; exposed hammers; 12-ga.; 2-3/4-inch chambers; 20-inch Improved/Modified, 28-inch Modified/ Full barrels; weighs 6-1/4 lbs. (20-inch), 7-1/4 lbs. (28-inch); hand-checkered European hardwood pistol-grip stock, beavertail forearm; chromed bores, chambers; hand engraved receiver; extractors. Also known as the TOZ-66/54. Made in Russia. No longer imported.

Perf.: $175   **Exc.:** $140   **VGood:** $125

AyA No. 1

AyA No. 1

AyA No. 2

AyA No. 2

AyA No. 3-A

AyA No. 4

Baikal IJ-18M

Baikal IJ-27

BAIKAL IJ-18

Single shot; single barrel; exposed hammer; 12-, 16-, 20-ga., .410; 2-3/4-inch chamber; 26-inch Modified, 28-inch Modified, 30-inch Full choke barrel; 44-1/2-inch overall length; weighs 6 lbs.; hand-checkered European walnut pistol-grip stock, forearm; white spacers at pistol grip, plastic buttplate; chrome-lined bore, chamber; extractor; cocking indicator; crossbolt safety. Made in Russia. Introduced 1973; still in production.

Perf.: $75   **Exc.:** $65   **VGood:** $55

BAIKAL IJ-18EM

Same specs as IJ-18 except automatic ejector. Imported from Russia by Century International Arms. Still imported.

Perf.: $80   **Exc.:** $65   **VGood:** $55

BAIKAL IJ-18M

Same specs as IJ-18 except 12-, 16-, 20-ga., .410; 2-3/4-inch chamber (12, 16), 3-inch chamber (20, .410); 26-inch, 28-inch barrel; choked Improved Cylinder, Full, Modified; trigger block safety; engraved, blued receiver. Imported from Russia by K.B.I., Inc. Reintroduced 1994; still imported.

Perf.: $65   **Exc.:** $55   **VGood:** $45

BAIKAL IJ-25

Over/under; 12-ga; 2-3/4-inch chambers; 26-inch Skeet/ Skeet, 28-inch Modified/Full, 30-inch Improved/Full barrels; vent rib; hand-checkered European walnut pistol-grip stock, ventilated forearm; white spacers at pistol-grip cap, recoil pad; single non-selective trigger; chrome-lined barrels, chambers, internal parts; hand-engraved, silver inlaid receiver, forearm latch, triggerguard. Made in Russia. Introduced 1973; discontinued 1978.

Perf.: $305   **Exc.:** $225   **VGood:** $175

BAIKAL IJ-27

Over/under; 12- (2-3/4-inch), 20-ga. (3-inch); 26-inch Skeet/Skeet, 28-inch Modified/Full barrels; hand-fitted ventilated rib; hand-checkered European walnut pistol-grip stock, ventilated forend; white spacers at pistol-grip cap, rubber recoil pad; double triggers; automatic safety; extractors; chrome-lined barrels, chambers, internal parts; hand-engraved, silver inlaid receiver, forearm latch, triggerguard. Made in Russia. Introduced 1973; dropped 1996.

Perf.: $330   **Exc.:** $275   **VGood:** $250

Baikal IJ-27EIC

Baikal IJ-43

Baikal MC-110

Baikal TOZ-34P

BAIKAL IJ-27EIC
Same specs as IJ-27 except automatic ejectors; single trigger; dropped 1996. M

Perf.: $370   **Exc.:** $315   **VGood:** $290

BAIKAL IJ-27EM
Same specs as IJ-27 except 12-ga.; 2-3/4-inch chambers; 28-1/2-inch chrome-lined barrels; weighs 7-1/2 lbs.; European hardwood stock; double triggers; selective automatic ejectors. Imported from Russia by Century International Arms. Still imported.

Perf.: $330   **Exc.:** $260   **VGood:** $215

BAIKAL IJ-27M
Same specs as IJ-27 except 12-ga.; 2-3/4-inch chambers; 28-1/2-inch chrome-lined barrels; European hardwood stock; double triggers; extractors; sling swivels. Imported from Russia by Century International Arms; still imported.

Perf.: $350   **Exc.:** $325   **VGood:** $295

BAIKAL IJ-43
Side-by-side; boxlock; 12-ga.; 2-3/4-inch chambers; 20-inch Cylinder/Cylinder, 28-inch Modified/Full barrels; weighs 6-3/4 lbs.; checkered walnut stock, forend; double triggers; extractors; blued, engraved receiver. Imported from Russia by K.B.I., Inc. Reintroduced 1994; dropped 1996.

Perf.: $235   **Exc.:** $200   **VGood:** $130

BAIKAL IJ-43EM
Same specs as IJ-43 except 28-1/2-inch chrome-lined barrels; European hardwood stock; automatic ejectors. Imported from Russia by Century International Arms. Still imported.

Perf.: $250   **Exc.:** $190   **VGood:** $150

BAIKAL IJ-43M
Same specs as IJ-43 except 28-1/2-inch chrome-lined barrels; European hardwood stock; automatic safety. Imported from Russia by Century International Arms. Still imported.

Perf.: $250   **Exc.:** $200   **VGood:** $165

BAIKAL IJ-58M
Side-by-side; hammerless; 12-ga.; 2-3/4-inch chambers; 26-inch Improved/Modified, 28-inch Modified/Full barrels; hand-checkered European walnut pistol-grip stock, beavertail forend; hinged front double trigger; chrome-lined barrels, chambers; hand-engraved receiver; hammer interceptors; recoil pad; extractors. Made in Russia. Introduced 1973; discontinued 1982.

Perf.: $235   **Exc.:** $185   **VGood:** $145

BAIKAL MC-5
Over/under; 12-, 20-ga.; 2-3/4-inch chambers; 26-inch Improved/Modified, Skeet/Skeet barrels;

weighs 5-3/4 lbs.; hand-fitted solid rib; fancy hand-checkered walnut stock; straight or pistol grip, with or without cheekpiece; non-removable forend; double triggers; extractors; hammer interceptors; silver-finished, fully engraved receiver; chrome-lined barrels, chambers, internal parts; marketed with case. Made in Russia. Introduced 1973; discontinued 1982.

Perf.: $325   **Exc.:** $350   **VGood:** $295

BAIKAL MC-6
Over/under; 12-ga.; 2-3/4-inch chambers; 26-inch Skeet/ Skeet, Improved Cylinder/Modified barrels; hand-fitted solid raised rib; fancy hand-checkered walnut stock; pistol grip or straight stock, with or without cheekpiece; non-removable forend; single non-selective or double triggers; extractors; hammer interceptors; silver-finished, fully engraved receiver; chrome-lined barrels, chambers, internal parts; marketed with case. Made in Russia. Introduced 1973; discontinued 1982.

Perf.: $495   **Exc.:** $395   **VGood:** $300

BAIKAL MC-7
Over/under; 12-, 20-ga.; 2-3/4-inch chambers; 26-inch Improved/Modified, 28-inch Modified/Full barrels; solid raised rib; hand-checkered fancy walnut straight or pistol-grip stock, beavertail forend; ejectors; double triggers; optional single selective trigger; hand-chiseled, engraved receiver; chrome-lined barrels, chambers, internal parts; marketed with case. Made in Russia. Introduced 1973; discontinued 1982.

Perf.: $900   **Exc.:** $750   **VGood:** $625

BAIKAL MC-8
Over/under; 12-ga.; 2-3/4-inch chambers; 2-barrel set of 26-inch Skeet/Skeet, 28-inch Modified/Full; hand-fitted vent rib; weighs 7-3/4 lbs.; hand-checkered fancy European walnut Monte Carlo pistol-grip stock, non-removable beavertail forend; double triggers; extractors; optional single selective trigger, selective ejectors; hand-engraved, blued receiver; chrome-lined barrels, chambers, internal parts; marketed with case. Made in Russia. Introduced 1973; discontinued 1982.

Perf.: $875   **Exc.:** $700   **VGood:** $595

With single selective trigger, selective ejectors

Perf.: $925   **Exc.:** $750   **VGood:** $625

BAIKAL MC-10
Side-by-side; hammerless; 12-, 20-ga.; 2-3/4-inch chambers; 26-inch Improved/Modified, 28-inch Modified/Full barrels; raised solid rib; hand-checkered fancy European walnut stock, semi-beavertail forearm; straight or pistol grip; chrome-lined barrels, chambers, internal parts; double triggers; auto safety; extractors or selective ejectors;

receiver engraved with animal, bird scenes; engraved trigger guard, tang. Made in Russia. Introduced 1973; discontinued 1978.

Perf.: $375   **Exc.:** $310   **VGood:** $275

BAIKAL MC-21
Autoloader; takedown; 12-ga.; 5-shot magazine; 26-inch Improved, 28-inch Modified, 30-inch Full choke barrel; vent rib; hand-rubbed, hand-checkered European walnut cheekpiece stock, grooved forearm; white spacers at pistol grip, buttplate; chrome-lined barrel, chamber; reversible safety; target-grade trigger. Made in Russia. Introduced 1973; discontinued 1978.

Perf.: $275   **Exc.:** $200   **VGood:** $175

BAIKAL MC-109
Over/under; hand-detachable sidelock; 12-ga.; 2-3/4-inch chambers; 28-inch barrels; raised rib; weighs 7-1/4 lbs.; hand-carved, checkered fancy walnut stock, beavertail forend; straight or pistol grip with or without cheekpiece; single selective trigger; chromed barrels, chambers, internal parts; hand-chiseled scenes on receiver to customer specs; marketed with case. Made in Russia. Introduced 1975; discontinued 1982.

Perf.: $925   **Exc.:** $700   **VGood:** $595

BAIKAL MC-110
Side-by-side; 12-, 20-ga.; 2-3/4-inch chambers; 26-inch Improved Cylinder/Modified (20-ga.), 28-inch Modified/Full (12-ga.) barrels; raised solid rib; weighs 6 lbs. (20-ga.), 6-3/4 lbs. (12-ga.); hand-checkered fancy walnut straight or pistol-grip stock, semi-beavertail forend; double triggers; chromed barrels, chambers, internal parts; hammer interceptors; extractors; auto safety; fully engraved receiver, triggerguard, tang; marketed in case. Made in Russia. Introduced 1975; discontinued 1982.

Perf.: $500   **Exc.:** $400   **VGood:** $300

BAIKAL MC-111
Side-by-side; hand-detachable sidelock; 12-ga.; 2-3/4-inch chambers; barrel lengths, chokes to customer's specifications; hand-checkered European walnut straight or pistol-grip stock, semi-beavertail forend; single selective trigger; hammer interceptors; cocking indicators; gold, silver inlays in butt; hand-chiseled bird, animal scenes on receiver; chromed barrels, chambers, internal parts; marketed with case. Made in Russia. Introduced 1975; discontinued 1982.

Perf.: $975   **Exc.:** $750   **VGood:** $625

BAIKAL TOZ-34P
Over/under; boxlock; 12-ga.; 2-3/4-inch chambers; 28-inch Full/ Improved Cylinder barrels; vent rib; 44-inch overall length; weighs 7-1/2 lbs.; European walnut stock, forend; extractors; optional ejectors; cocking indicator; double triggers; engraved, blued receiver; ventilated rubber buttpad. Imported from Russia by Century International Arms. Still imported.

Perf.: $350   **Exc.:** $280   **VGood:** $210

With ejectors

Perf.: $375   **Exc.:** $300   **VGood:** $235

BAIKAL TOZ-66
Side-by-side; exposed hammers; 12-ga.; 2-3/4-inch chambers; 20-inch Improved/Modified, 28-inch Modified/Full barrels; hand-checkered European hardwood pistol-grip stock, beavertail forearm; chrome-lined barrels, chambers; hand-engraved receiver; extractors. Made in Russia. Introduced 1973; discontinued 1978.

Perf.: $225   **Exc.:** $150   **VGood:** $100

BAKER BATAVIA EJECTOR
Side-by-side; sidelock; hammerless; 12-, 16-, 20-ga.; 26-inch to 32-inch Damascus or forged steel barrels; any standard choke combo; best-grade hand-checkered American walnut pistol-grip stock, forearm; auto ejectors. Introduced 1921; discontinued 1930.

Exc.: $880   **VGood:** $770   **Good:** $745

Damascus

Exc.: $500   **VGood:** $400   **Good:** $305

BAKER BATAVIA LEADER

Same specs as Batavia Ejector except forged steel barrels; extractors or auto ejectors; less expensive finish. Discontinued around 1930.

Extractors		
Exc.: $500	**VGood:** $425	**Good:** $375

Auto ejectors		
Exc.: $595	**VGood:** $510	**Good:** $470

BAKER BATAVIA SPECIAL

Same specs as Batavia Ejector except forged steel barrels; extractors; less expensive finish. Discontinued around 1930.

Exc.: $495   **VGood:** $405   **Good:** $375

BAKER BLACK BEAUTY SPECIAL

Side-by-side; sidelock; hammerless; 12-, 16-, 20-ga.; 26-inch to 32-inch barrels; any standard choke combination; ejectors or extractors; hand-checkered American walnut pistol-grip stock, forearm; engraved. Introduced 1921; discontinued 1930.

Extractors		
Exc.: $745	**VGood:** $650	**Good:** $615

Auto ejectors		
Exc.: $855	**VGood:** $760	**Good:** $725

BAKER GRADE R

Side-by-side; sidelock; hammerless; 12-, 16-, 20-ga.; 26-inch, 28-inch, 30-inch, 32-inch Damascus or Krupp steel barrels; select hand-checkered European walnut pistol-grip stock, forend; extractors or auto ejectors; extensive engraving with game scenes. Introduced 1915; discontinued 1933.

Extractors		
Exc.: $1000	**VGood:** $925	**Good:** $800

Auto ejectors		
Exc.: $1200	**VGood:** $1125	**Good:** $1000

Paragon Grade, extractors		
Exc.: $1300	**VGood:** $1125	**Good:** $1000

Paragon Grade, auto ejectors		
Exc.: $1500	**VGood:** $1275	**Good:** $1000

Expert Grade, ejectors, select finish		
Exc.: $1975	**VGood:** $1350	**Good:** $1100

Deluxe Grade, best-grade finish		
Exc.: $3250	**VGood:** $2650	**Good:** $2000

BAKER GRADE S

Side-by-side; sidelock; hammerless; 12-, 16-, 20-ga.; 26-inch, 28-inch, 30-inch, 32-inch fluid-tempered steel barrels; select hand-checkered European walnut pistol-grip stock, forend; scroll, line engraving; extractors or auto ejectors. Introduced 1915; discontinued 1933.

Extractors		
Exc.: $880	**VGood:** $775	**Good:** $745

Auto ejectors		
Exc.: $1100	**VGood:** $990	**Good:** $965

BEEMAN FABARM

Over/under; boxlock; 12-ga.; 2-3/4-inch chambers; 26-1/2-inch Skeet/Skeet, 29-inch Full/Modified barrels; weighs about 7-1/2 lbs.; red bead front sight, white bead middle; select cut-checkered walnut stock, schnabel forend; single selective trigger; auto ejectors; chrome-lined bores, chambers; silvered, engraved receiver; Skeet/Trap combo with interchangeable barrels cased. Made in Italy. Introduced 1984; discontinued 1984.

Field Grade		
Perf.: $650	**Exc.:** $525	**VGood:** $410

Trap/Skeet		
Perf.: $750	**Exc.:** $625	**VGood:** $500

Combo		
Perf.: $1100	**Exc.:** $860	**VGood:** $750

BENELLI CORDOBA

Autoloader; black synthetic stock; 12- or 20-ga., 2-3/4- and 3-inch chamber; 28- and 30-inch barrels with 4 extended choke tubes; red bar sights; 7.2 to 7.3 lbs. overall weight.

Perf.: $1510   **Exc.:** $1210   **VGood:** $975

Baker Batavia Leader

Baker Batavia Special

Baker Grade R

Baker Paragon Grade

Baker Grade S

Beeman Fabarm

Benelli Cordoba

Benelli Black Eagle

Benelli Black Eagle Competition

BENELLI BLACK EAGLE

Autoloader; Montefeltro recoil action; 12-ga.; 3-inch chambers; 5-shot magazine; 21-inch, 24-inch, 26-inch, 28-inch vent-rib barrels; choke tubes; weighs 7-3/8 lbs.; high-gloss European walnut stock; marketed with drop adjustment kit; two-piece steel/aluminum receiver; silver finish on lower receiver, blued upper. Made in Italy. Introduced 1989; discontinued 1991.

Perf.: $825   **Exc.:** $675   **VGood:** $550

BENELLI BLACK EAGLE COMPETITION

Same specs as Black Eagle except 26-inch, 28-inch barrel; mid-bead sight; competition stock; two-piece etched aluminum receiver. Made in Italy. Introduced 1989; dropped 1997.

Perf.: $1025   **Exc.:** $795   **VGood:** $675

BENELLI BLACK EAGLE COMPETITION "LIMITED EDITION"

Same specs as Black Eagle except gold inlays; fancy wood; special serial numbers.

Perf.: $1850   **Exc.:** $1500   **VGood:** $1225

BENELLI BLACK EAGLE SLUG GUN

Same specs as Black Eagle except 24-inch rifled barrel; no rib; weighs 7-1/8 lbs.; two-piece steel/alloy receiver; drilled, tapped for scope mount; marketed with scope mount. Made in Italy. Introduced 1989; discontinued 1991; reintroduced 1992; dropped 2003.

Perf.: $1110   **Exc.:** $910   **VGood:** $775

BENELLI BLACK EAGLE SUPER

Same specs as Black Eagle except 3-1/2-inch chamber; 24-inch, 26-inch, 28-inch barrels; 49-3/8-

Benelli Black Eagle Super

Benelli Black Eagle Super Slug

Benelli Executive Series Type III

Benelli Executive Series Type I

Benelli Executive Series Type II

Benelli Executive Series Type III

Benelli Legacy

Benelli Sport

inch overall length (28-inch barrel); weighs 7-1/2 lbs.; bead front sight; European walnut stock adjustable for drop; satin or gloss finish. Introduced 1991; still imported.

Perf.: $1075	Exc.: $895	VGood: $775
Timber HD Camo 24-inch, 26-inch, 28-inch barrel		
With 24-inch, 26-inch and 28-inch barrel, polymer stock		
Left-hand, 24-inch, 26-inch, 28-inch, polymer stock		
Perf.: $1200	Exc.: $995	VGood: $875
Left-hand, 24-inch, 26-inch, 28-inch, camo stock		
Perf.: $1275	Exc.: $1025	VGood: $925

BENELLI BLACK EAGLE SUPER SLUG

Same specs as Benelli Black Eagle except 3-1/2-inch chamber; 24-inch E.R. Shaw Custom rifled barrel; 45-1/2-inch overall length; weighs 7-1/2 lbs.; scope mount base; matte-finish receiver; wood or polymer stocks available. Imported from Italy by Heckler & Koch, Inc. Introduced 1992.

With wood stock		
Perf.: $1120	Exc.: $920	VGood: $785
With polymer stock		
Perf.: $1110	Exc.: $910	VGood: $775
24-inch barrel, Timber HD Camo		
Perf.: $1235	Exc.: $1035	VGood: $900

BENELLI EXECUTIVE SERIES

Autoloader; Montefeltro recoil action; 12-ga.; 3-inch chamber; 5-shot magazine; 21-inch, 24-inch, 26-inch, 28-inch barrel; choke tubes; weighs 7-3/8 lbs.; highest grade of walnut stock with drop adjustment kit; two-piece steel/aluminum receiver; grayed steel lower receiver; hand-engraved and gold inlaid (Type III). Special order only. Made in Italy. Introduced 1995.

Type I (about two-thirds engraving coverage)		
Perf.: $4825	Exc.: $3775	VGood: $2550
Type II (full coverage engraving)		
Perf.: $5375	Exc.: $4175	VGood: $3075
Type III (full coverage, gold inlays)		
Perf.: $6200	Exc.: $4600	VGood: $3500

BENELLI EXTRALUXE

Autoloader; inertial action; 12-ga.; 2-3/4-inch chamber; 5-shot magazine; 26-inch, 28-inch barrel; vent rib; weighs 6-3/4 lbs.; hand-checkered walnut stock; crossbolt safety; interchangeable barrels; similar to SL-121 but with extra-fancy wood; fine hand engraving; gold trigger; carrying case. No longer imported.

Perf.: $295	Exc.: $250	VGood: $220

BENELLI LEGACY SHOTGUN

Gauge: 12, 20; 2-3/4-inch and 3-inch chamber; 24-inch, 26-inch, 28-inch barrel (Full, Mod., Imp. Cyl., Imp. Mod., cylinder choke tubes); mid-bead sight; weighs 5.8 to 7.6 lbs.; 49-5/8-inch overall (28-inch barrel); select European walnut with satin finish. Uses the rotating bolt inertia recoil operating system with a two-piece steel/aluminum etched receiver (bright on lower, blue upper). Drop adjustment kit allows the stock to be custom fitted without modifying the stock. Introduced 1998. Imported from Italy by Benelli USA, Corp.

Perf.: $1175	Exc.: $935	VGood: $785

BENELLI SPORT SHOTGUN

Similar to the Legacy model except has matte blue receiver, two carbon fiber interchangeable ventilated ribs, adjustable butt pad, adjustable buttstock, and functions with ultra-light target loads. Walnut stock with satin finish. Introduced 1997. Imported from Italy.

Perf.: $1125	Exc.: $895	VGood: $750

BENELLI M1 FIELD SHOTGUN

Gauge: 20-ga., 2-3/4- and 3-inch chamber; 24- and 26-inch barrel; weighs 5.7 to 5.8 lbs.; black or camo synthetic stock; stepped ventilated rib with red bar sights. Comes with set of five choke tubes. Imported from Italy.

Black synthetic stock version
Perf.: $800   **Exc.:** $675   **VGood:** $575
Camo stock version
Perf.: $815   **Exc.:** $690   **VGood:** $590

BENELLI M2 FIELD SHOTGUN

Autoloader; 12-ga., 2-3/4- and 3-inch chamber; 21-inch, 24-inch, 26-inch, 28-inch barrel; weighs 6.9 to 7.2 lbs.; high impact polymer stock; wood on 26-inch, 28-inch; red bar sights; ventilated rib; blue finish. Available with or without ComforTech stock. Uses the rotating Montefeltro bolt system. Comes with set of five choke tubes. Imported from Italy. Add 5% for SteadyGrip.

Black synthetic stock version
Perf.: $1000   **Exc.:** $875   **VGood:** $575
Walnut stock version
Perf.: $1075   **Exc.:** $925   **VGood:** $590
Camo stock
Perf.: $1100   **Exc.:** $950   **VGood:** $610

BENELLI M2 PRACTICAL

Similar to M2 Tactical but with 26-inch barrel, 9-shot capacity, and oversized controls.
Exc.: $1000   **VGood:** $925   **Good:** $800

BENELLI M1 SUPER 90

Autoloader; rotating Montefeltro bolt system; 12-ga; 3-inch chamber; 3-shot magazine; extended magazine available with 26-inch, 28-inch barrels; 21-inch, 24-inch, 26-inch, 28-inch barrels; choke tubes; vent rib; weighs 7-1/2 lbs.; metal bead front sight; wood or polymer stock, forearm; blued finish. Made in Italy. Introduced 1987; still imported.
Perf.: $865   **Exc.:** $685   **VGood:** $600

BENELLI M1 SUPER 90 DEFENSE

Same specs as M1 Super 90 except 5-shot magazine; 18-1/2-inch Cylinder barrel; open or aperture (ghost ring) rifle-type sights; polymer pistol-grip stock; matte black finish. Introduced 1993; dropped 1998.
Perf.: $685   **Exc.:** $525   **VGood:** $395
Add $45 to above prices for ghost ring sighting system

BENELLI M1 SUPER 90 ENTRY

Same specs as M1 Super 90 except 5-shot magazine; 14-inch Cylinder barrel; open or aperture (ghost ring) rifle-type sights; polymer straight or pistol-grip stock; matte black finish. Introduced 1992; still imported.
Perf.: $810   **Exc.:** $675   **VGood:** $585
Add $15 to above prices for synthetic pistol grip stock
Add $65 for ghost ring sights
Note: Ownership of this model requires special registration under the National Firearms Act due to its short barrel.

BENELLI M1 SUPER 90 MONTEFELTRO

Same specs as M1 Super 90 except 12- or 20-ga.; 4-shot magazine; checkered European walnut drop-adjustable stock with satin finish; matte blue metal finish. Made in Italy. Introduced 1987; still imported.
Perf.: $865   **Exc.:** $725   **VGood:** $600
Left-hand, 26-inch, 28-inch bbl.
Perf.: $880   **Exc.:** $740   **VGood:** $615
Timber HD Camo, 21-inch, 24-inch barrel
Perf.: $920   **Exc.:** $780   **VGood:** $685
20 ga., 24-inch, 26-inch bbl. syn.

BENELLI M1 SUPER 90 MONTEFELTRO 20-GAUGE LIMITED EDITION

Same specs as M1 Super 90 except 20-ga.; 3-inch chamber; 4-shot magazine; 26-inch barrel; weighs 5-3/4 lbs.; checkered European walnut drop-adjustable stock with satin finish; special nickel-plated and engraved receiver inlaid with gold. Made in Italy. Introduced 1993; still imported.
Perf.: $1700   **Exc.:** $1250   **VGood:** $900

Benelli M1 Field

Benelli M2 Walnutstock

Benelli M2 Practical

Benelli M2 Tactical

Benelli M1 Super 90

Benelli M1 Super 90 Defense

Benelli M1 Super 90 Montefeltro

BENELLI M1 SUPER 90 MONTEFELTRO, LEFT-HAND

Same specs as M1 Super 90 except left-hand action; 12- or 20-ga.; 4-shot magazine; checkered European walnut drop-adjustable stock with satin finish; matte blue metal finish. Made in Italy. Introduced 1987; still imported.
Perf.: $750   **Exc.:** $470   **VGood:** $.410

BENELLI M1 SUPER 90 MONTEFELTRO UPLANDER

Same specs as M1 Super 90 except 12-, 20-ga.; 4-shot magazine; 21-inch, 24-inch barrels; checkered European walnut drop-adjustable stock with satin finish. Made in Italy. Introduced 1987; discontinued 1992.
Perf.: $600   **Exc.:** $350   **VGood:** $300

BENELLI M1 SUPER 90 MONTEFELTRO SLUG

Same specs as M1 Super 90 except 12-ga.; 3-inch chamber; 4-shot magazine; 24-inch barrel; Cylinder choke; 45-1/2-inch overall length; weighs 7 lbs.; checkered European walnut drop-adjustable stock with satin finish; matte blue metal finish. Made in Italy. Introduced, 1988; discontinued, 1992.
Perf.: $590   **Exc.:** $340   **VGood:** $290

BENELLI M1 SUPER 90 SLUG

Same specs as M1 Super 90 except 5-shot magazine; 18-1/2-inch Cylinder barrel; open or aperture (ghost ring) rifle-type sights; polymer straight stock; matte black finish. Introduced 1986; still imported.
Perf.: $615   **Exc.:** $310   **VGood:** $280

BENELLI M1 SUPER 90 SPORTING SPECIAL

Same specs as M1 Super 90 except 18-1/2-inch barrel; Improved Cylinder, Modified, Full choke tubes; 39-3/4-inch overall length; weighs 6-1/2 lbs.; ghost ring sight; sporting-style polymer stock with drop adjustment; matte black finish receiver. Made in Italy. Introduced 1993; still imported.
Perf.: $680   **Exc.:** $410   **VGood:** $375

BENELLI M1 SUPER 90 TACTICAL

Same specs as M1 Super 90 except 5-shot magazine; 18-1/2-inch Improved Cylinder, Modified, Full barrel; open or aperture (ghost ring) rifle-type sights; polymer straight or pistol-grip stock; matte black finish. Numerous law enforcement and military options. Introduced 1993; still imported.
Perf.: $810   **Exc.:** $675   **VGood:** $575

Benelli M1 Super 90 Tactical

Benelli M1 Practical

Benelli M2 Field with ComforTech

Benelli M2 Field w/o ComforTech

Benelli M3 Convertible Standard Stock

Benelli M3 Convertible with folding stock

Benelli M3 Pistolgrip Ghostring

Benelli M4

BENELLI M1 PRACTICAL

Similar to M1 Field Shotgun, Picatinny receiver rail for scope mounting, nine-round magazine, 26-inch compensated barrel and ghost ring sights. Designed for IPSC competition.

Perf.: $1055	**Exc.:** $875	**VGood:** $750

BENELLI MONTEFELTRO SHOTGUN

Gauge: 12-, 20-ga., 2-3/4-inch and 3-inch chamber. Barrel: 24-inch, 26-inch, 28-inch with 5 choke tubes. Stock: Satin walnut. Sights: Red bar. Features: Lightweight, one-piece receiver.

12-, 20-ga.		
Perf.: $865	**Exc.:** $725	**VGood:** $600
Left-hand 26-inch, 28-inch, 12 ga.		
Perf.: $855	**Exc.:** $720	**VGood:** $600
20 ga. short stock		
Perf.: $860	**Exc.:** $715	**VGood:** $615

BENELLI M2 TACTICAL

Inertia-operated semi-auto; 12 ga., 2-3/4" and 3"; 5+1 capacity. 18-1/2" barrel, pistol grip synthetic ComforTech stock, ghost ring aperture rear sight and bead front sight with tritium inserts. Standard stock model available. Introduced 2005 by Benelli USA.

New: $1065	**Exc.:** $800	**VGood:** $650

BENELLI M2 FIELD WITH COMFORTECH

In 12 gauge, this model is offered with a 21", 24", 26" or 28" barrel with a black matte synthetic finish or Max-4, Timber or APG camo. The 20 gauge has a 24" or 26" barrel in black, Timber or APG. Average 12 gauge weight is 7 lbs.; average 20 gauge weight is 5.8 lbs. Add $120 for camo.

NIB: $995	**Exc.:** $820	**VGood:** $695

BENELLI M2 FIELD WITHOUT COMFORTECH

Same features as above without ComforTech features. Available only in satin walnut with 26" or 28" barrel.

NIB: $900	**Exc.:** $725	**VGood:** $600

BENELLI M3 CONVERTIBLE SHOTGUN

Combination pump/auto action; 12-ga., 2-3/4-inch, 3-inch chambers; 5-shot magazine; 19-3/4-inch barrel (Cyl.); weighs 7 lbs., 4oz.; 41-inch overall; high-impact polymer stock with sling loop in side of butt; rubberized pistol grip on stock; open rifle sights, fully adjustable; ghost ring and rifle type; alloy receiver with inertia recoil rotating locking lug bolt; matte finish; automatic shell release lever. Introduced 1989. Imported from Italy.

With standard stock, open rifle sights		
Perf.: $955	**Exc.:** $745	**VGood:** $630
With ghost ring sight system, standard stock		
Perf.: $1010	**Exc.:** $795	**VGood:** $685
With ghost ring sights, pistol-grip stock		
Perf.: $1010	**Exc.:** $805	**VGood:** $695

BENELLI M4

Proprietary ARGO system semi-auto; 12-ga., 2-3/4" and 3", 5+1 capacity. 18-1/2" barrel, pistol grip synthetic ComforTech stock or optional standard or folding stock. Ghost ring aperture rear sight and bead front sight with tritium inserts. Picatinny rail for optics mounting. Civilian version of military M1014. Introduced 2005 by Benelli USA.

New: $1529	**Perf.:** $1100	**VGood:** $900

BENELLI NOVA PUMP SHOTGUN

Gauge: 12-, 20-ga., 2-3/4-inch, 3-inch chamber (3-1/2-inch 12-ga. only) 24-inch, 26-inch, 28-inch barrel; synthetic stock, X-tra Brown 12 ga., Timber HD 20-ga.; red bar sights. Montefeltro rotating bolt design with dual action bars, magazine cut-off, synthetic trigger assembly, 4-shot magazine. Introduced 1999. Imported from Italy.

Black stock, 12-ga.		
Perf.: $295	**Exc.:** $265	**VGood:** $235

BENELLI M1 TACTICAL SHOTGUN

Gauge: 12; 2-3/4-inch, 3-inch chambers; 5-shot magazine; 18.5-inch barrel, IC, M, F choke tubes; weighs 6.7 lbs.; 39.75-inch overall; black polymer stock; rifle type sights with ghost ring system, tritium night sights optional; semi-auto inertia recoil action; cross-bolt safety; bolt release button; matte-finish metal. Introduced 1993. Imported from Italy.

With rifle sights, standard stock		
Perf.: $900	**Exc.:** $700	**VGood:** $600
With ghost ring rifle sights, standard stock		
Perf.: $795	**Exc.:** $595	**VGood:** $435
With ghost ring sights, pistol grip stock		
Perf.: $810	**Exc.:** $610	**VGood:** $450
With rifle sights, pistol grip stock		
Perf.: $810	**Exc.:** $610	**VGood:** $450

X-tra Brown, 12-ga.
Perf.: $360   **Exc.:** $330   **VGood:** $300

Black stock, 20-ga.
Perf.: $295   **Exc.:** $265   **VGood:** $235

Timber HD, 20-ga.
Perf.: $360   **Exc.:** $330   **VGood:** $300

Add $15 to above prices for Youth Model with 13-inch length of pull
Add $55 for 2- or 4-shot magazine extension
Add $70 for 24-inch barrel with full Timber HD camo coverage (Turkey Model)
Add $42 for recoil reducer (10 oz.) or mercury (14 oz.) installed in stock

BENELLI NOVA PUMP SLUG GUN
Similar to the Nova except has 18.5-inch barrel with adjustable rifle-type or ghost ring sights; weighs 7.2 lbs.; black synthetic stock. Introduced 1999. Imported from Italy.

With rifle sights

With ghost-ring sight
Perf.: $425   **Exc.:** $385   **VGood:** $350

Add $75 to above prices for Advantage Timber HD camo

BENELLI NOVA PUMP RIFLED SLUG GUN
Similar to Nova Pump Slug Gun except has 24-inch barrel and rifled bore; open rifle sights; synthetic stock; weighs 8.1 pounds.
Perf.: $425   **Exc.:** $385   **VGood:** $350

BENELLI SUPERNOVA
Introduced in 2006, the Supernova incorporates Benelli's ComforTech stock system into the Nova pump shotgun. Available in 24-inch, 26-inch and 28-inch barrel lengths in matte black synthetic, 24-inch and 26-inch barrel lengths in Advantage Timber camo, and 26-inch and 28-inch barrel lengths in Max-4 camo. Weight is about 8 lbs. with 28-inch barrel. All versions are chambered for 3.5-inch shells. Three choke tubes. Add 15 percent for camo versions.
NIB: $395   **Exc.:** $350   **VGood:** $295

BENELLI SUPERNOVA STEADYGRIP
As above but with extended pistol grip in 24-inch barrel only. Matte black synthetic or Advantage Timber stock. Add 15 percent for camo model.
NIB: $405   **Exc.:** $360   **VGood:** $300

BENELLI SUPERNOVA TACTICAL
Matte black synthetic stock with 18-inch barrel. Available with ComforTech or pistol grip stock. Fixed cylinder bore. Open rifle sights. Ghost ring sights optional.
NIB: $400   **Exc.:** $355   **VGood:** $295

BENELLI SL-121
Autoloader; 12-ga.; 2-3/4-inch chamber; 5-shot magazine; 26-inch, 28-inch barrel; plain or vent rib (SL-121V); 6-3/4 lbs.; metal bead front sight; hand-checkered European walnut pistol-grip stock; crossbolt safety; quick-interchangeable barrels; optional engraving; slug model available. Made in Italy. Introduced 1977; dropped 1985.
Perf.: $385   **Exc.:** $360   **VGood:** $325

Engraved model
Perf.: $420   **Exc.:** $375   **VGood:** $295

Slug model
Perf.: $400   **Exc.:** $360   **VGood:** $325

BENELLI SL-123
Autoloader; 12-ga; 2-3/4-inch chamber; 5-shot magazine; 26-inch, 28-inch barrels; plain or vent rib (SL-123V); weighs 6-3/4 lbs.; metal bead front sight; fancy hand-checkered European walnut pistol-grip stock; crossbolt safety; quick-interchangeable barrels; optional engraving; slug model available. Made in Italy. Introduced 1977; dropped 1985.
Perf.: $420   **Exc.:** $365   **VGood:** $350

Engraved model
Perf.: $495   **Exc.:** $395   **VGood:** $315

Benelli Nova Pump Shotgun

Benelli Nova Turkey HD

Benelli Nova Pump Slug Gun

Benelli Nova Pump Rifled Slug Gun

Benelli Supernova

Benelli Supernova Steadygrip

Benelli Supernova Tactical

Benelli SL-121

Benelli SL-121 Slug

Benelli SL-123

Slug model
Perf.: $400   **Exc.:** $320   **VGood:** $365

BENELLI SL-201
Autoloader; 20-ga.; 4-shot magazine; 26-inch barrel; vent rib; weighs 5-3/4 lbs.; hand-checkered walnut stock; crossbolt safety; quick-interchangeable barrels; similar to SL-121. No longer imported.
Perf.: $350   **Exc.:** $250   **VGood:** $200

BENELLI ULTRA LIGHT
Inertia-driven 12 gauge semi-auto features an alloy receiver, carbon fiber rib and small proportions to

Benelli Ultra Light

Beretta A-301 Field

Beretta A-301 Slug

Beretta A-301 Trap

Beretta A-302

Beretta A-302 Slug

Beretta A-303

Beretta A-303 Youth

Beretta A391 Xtrema 3.5

BERETTA A-301 TRAP
Same specs as A-310 Field except 30-inch Full choke barrel; checkered European walnut Monte Carlo stock; recoil pad; gold-plated trigger. Introduced 1977; discontinued 1982.

Perf.: $390 **Exc.:** $350 **VGood:** $295

BERETTA A-302
Gas-operated autoloader; 12-, 20-ga.; 2-3/4-inch, 3-inch chamber; 3-shot magazine; 22-inch Slug, 26-inch Improved or Skeet, 28-inch Modified or Full, 30-inch (12-ga. only) Full or Full Trap barrel; optional Mobilchokes; cut-checkered European walnut pistol-grip stock, forend; scroll-engraved alloy receiver; push-button safety. Made in Italy. Introduced 1983; discontinued 1987.

Standard chokes		
Perf.: $400	**Exc.:** $350	**VGood:** $340
Mobilchokes		
Perf.: $430	**Exc.:** $380	**VGood:** $370

BERETTA A-303
Gas-operated autoloader; 12-, 20-ga.; 2-3/4-inch, 3-inch chamber; 3-shot magazine; 22-inch, 24-inch, 26-inch, 28-inch, 30-inch, 32-inch barrel; optional Mobilchokes; weighs 6 lbs. (20-ga.), 7 lbs. (12-ga.); hand-checkered American walnut stock; alloy receiver; magazine cut-off; push-button safety. Made in Italy. Introduced 1983; 20-ga. still imported.

Standard chokes		
Perf.: $600	**Exc.:** $340	**VGood:** $300
Mobilchokes		
Perf.: $650	**Exc.:** $390	**VGood:** $340

BERETTA A-303 MATTE FINISH
Same specs as A-303 except 3-inch chamber; 24-inch, 26-inch, 28-inch, 30-inch barrel; Mobilchoke tubes; non-reflective finish on all wood, metal surfaces; studs, sling swivels. Introduced 1991; discontinued 1992.

Perf.: $650 **Exc.:** $390 **VGood:** $340

BERETTA A-303 SPORTING CLAYS
Same specs as A-303 except 12-, 20-ga.; 2-3/4-inch chamber; 28-inch barrel; Mobilchoke tubes; wide competition-style vent rib; slightly different stock dimensions; special rubber buttpad. Made in Italy. Introduced 1989; still imported.

Perf.: $670 **Exc.:** $450 **VGood:** $380

BERETTA A-303 UPLAND MODEL
Same specs as A-303 except 12-, 20-ga.; 2-3/4-inch, 3-inch chamber; 24-inch vent rib barrel; Mobilchoke tubes; straight English-style stock. Made in Italy. Introduced 1989; still imported.

Perf.: $600 **Exc.:** $360 **VGood:** $330

BERETTA A-303 YOUTH
Same specs as A-303 except shorter length of pull; weighs 6 lbs. Introduced 1991; dropped 1996.

Perf.: $500 **Exc.:** $360 **VGood:** $300

BERETTA A391 XTREMA 3.5 AUTO SHOTGUNS
Gauge: 12-ga. 3-1/2-inch chamber. Barrel: 24-inch, 26-inch, 28-inch. Weight: 7.8 lbs. Stock: Synthetic. Features: Semi-auto goes with two-lug rotating bolt and self-compensating gas valve, extended tang, cross bolt safety, self-cleaning, with case.

Synthetic; MSR		
Perf.: $950	**Exc.:** $825	**VGood:** $750
Realtree Hardwood HD Camo		
Perf.: $1075	**Exc.:** $900	**VGood:** $825

Add $135 to above prices for 24-inch barrel in Hardwoods Camo

BERETTA A391 XTREMA2
An upgraded version of the Xtrema with additional recoil-reducing features was introduced in 2005. Available with 24-inch, 26-inch or 28-inch barrels with black, Max-4 HD or Hardwoods HD synthetic stock. Optima-Bore five choke system. Optional Kick Off recoil reduction feature available. Add 10 percent for camo finish. Add 30 percent for Kick Off option.

NIB: 1100 **Exc.:** 950 **VGood:** 800

bring weight down to about 6 lbs. Walnut stock with Weathercoat finish. Chambered for 3-inch shells. Offered in 24-inch barrel only with 5 Crio chokes. Introduced 2006.

NIB: $1175 **Exc.:** $1050 **VGood:** $900

BERETTA (DR. FRANCO) ARIETE STANDARD
Autoloader, gas-operated; 12 gauge; 2-3/4-inch, 3-inch chamber; various barrel lengths with or without choke tubes; aluminum receiver; checkered stock and forearm; weighs 6.9 lbs. Imported during 1993 only.

Perf.: $995 **Exc.:** $795 **VGood:** $525

BERETTA (DR. FRANCO) ARIETE
Slide-action; 12-ga.; 3-inch chamber; various barrel lengths without ventilated rib; twice action bars; matte finish; recoil pad. Imported during 1993 only.

Perf.: $780 **Exc.:** $695 **VGood:** $550

BERETTA AUTOLOADING SHOTGUNS

BERETTA A-301 FIELD
Gas-operated autoloader; 12- (2-3/4-inch), 20-ga. (3-inch); 3-shot magazine; 26-inch Improved, 28-inch Full, Modified barrels; vent rib; checkered European walnut pistol-grip stock, forend. Introduced 1977; discontinued 1982.

Perf.: $395 **Exc.:** $360 **VGood:** $330

BERETTA A-301 MAGNUM
Same specs as A-301 Field except 12-ga.; 3-inch chamber; 30-inch Full choke barrel; recoil pad. Introduced 1977; discontinued 1982.

Perf.: $425 **Exc.:** $385 **VGood:** $330

BERETTA A-301 SKEET
Same specs as A-301 Field except 26-inch Skeet barrel; checkered European walnut Skeet-style stock; gold-plated trigger. Introduced 1977; discontinued 1982.

Perf.: $400 **Exc.:** $360 **VGood:** $330

BERETTA A-301 SLUG
Same specs as A-301 Field except 22-inch barrel; Slug choke; no rib; rifle sights. Introduced 1977; discontinued 1982.

Perf.: $395 **Exc.:** $360 **VGood:** $330

BERETTA A391 XTREMA2 SLUG GUN

24-inch rifled barrel version of Xtrema2. Black synthetic only. Add 10 percent for Kick Off option.

NIB: 1000 **Exc.:** 900 **VGood:** 800

BERETTA AL-2

Gas-operated autoloader; 12-, 20-ga.; 3-shot magazine; 2-3/4-inch, 3-inch chamber; 26-inch, 28-inch, 30-inch interchangeable barrel; Full, Modified, Improved Cylinder, Skeet chokes; vent rib; medium front bead sight; diamond-point hand-checkered European walnut pistol-grip stock, forend. Introduced 1969; discontinued 1975.

Standard grade
Perf.: $330 **Exc.:** $305 **VGood:** $275
Trap/Skeet model
Perf.: $380 **Exc.:** $320 **VGood:** $290
Magnum model
Perf.: $415 **Exc.:** $385 **VGood:** $330

BERETTA AL-3

Gas-operated autoloader; 12-, 20-ga.; 3-shot magazine; 2-3/4-inch, 3-inch chamber; 26-inch, 28-inch, 30-inch interchangeable barrel; Full, Modified, Improved Cylinder, Skeet chokes; vent rib; medium front bead sight; diamond-point hand-checkered select European walnut pistol-grip stock, forend; hand-engraved receiver. Introduced 1969; discontinued 1975.

Standard grade
Perf.: $380 **Exc.:** $350 **VGood:** $295
Trap/Skeet model
Perf.: $390 **Exc.:** $350 **VGood:** $295
Magnum model
Perf.: $.425 **Exc.:** $385 **VGood:** $330

BERETTA GOLD LARK

Gas-operated autoloader; takedown; 12-ga.; 26-inch, 28-inch, 30-inch, 32-inch vent-rib barrels; Improved Cylinder, Modified, Full choke; hand-checkered European walnut pistol-grip stock, beavertail forearm; push-button safety in triggerguard; all parts hand polished; fine engraving. Introduced 1960; discontinued 1967.

Exc.: $480 **VGood:** $400 **Good:** $325

BERETTA MODEL 390 FIELD GRADE

Gas-operated autoloader; 12-ga.; 3-inch chamber; 3-shot magazine; 22-inch, 24-inch, 26-inch, 30-inch barrel; Mobilchoke tubes; floating vent rib; weighs 7 lbs.; select walnut stock adjustable for drop and cast; self-compensating valve allows action to shoot all loads without adjustment; alloy receiver; reversible safety; chrome-plated bore. Made in Italy. Introduced 1992; still imported.

Perf.: $680 **Exc.:** $420 **VGood:** $360

BERETTA MODEL 390 FIELD GRADE GOLD MALLARD

Same specs as Model 390 Field Grade except highly select walnut stock; receiver with gold engraved animals. Introduced 1992; still imported.

Perf.: $850 **Exc.:** $575 **VGood:** $460

BERETTA MODEL 390 FIELD GRADE SILVER MALLARD

Same specs as Model 390 Field Grade except select walnut stock with gloss or matte finish; medium or thin rubber buttpad. Introduced 1992; dropped 1997.

Perf.: $680 **Exc.:** $520 **VGood:** $415

BERETTA MODEL 390 FIELD GRADE SILVER SLUG

Same specs as Model 390 Field Grade except 22-inch slug barrel; no rib; weighs 7 1/4 lbs.; grooved receiver for scope mount; blade front sight, adjustable rear; swivels. Introduced 1992; dropped 1997.

Perf.: $680 **Exc.:** $420 **VGood:** $360

Beretta A391 Xtrema 2

Beretta AL-2

Beretta Model 390 Field Grade

Beretta Model 390 Competition Skeet Sport

Beretta Model 390 Competition Trap Sport

Beretta AL391 Urika

BERETTA MODEL 390 COMPETITION SKEET SPORT

Gas-operated autoloader; 12-ga.; 3-inch chamber; 3-shot magazine; 26-inch, 28-inch Skeet-choke barrel; vent rib; select walnut Skeet-style stock, forearm; self-compensating valve allows action to shoot all loads without adjustment; reversible safety; chrome-plated bore; lower-contour, rounded alloy receiver; recoil pad; ported barrel available. Made in Italy. Introduced 1995; still imported.

Perf.: $680 **Exc.:** $420 **VGood:** $360
With ported barrel
Perf.: $750 **Exc.:** $520 **VGood:** $460

BERETTA MODEL 390 COMPETITION SKEET SPORT SUPER

Same specs as Model 390 Competition Skeet Sport except 28-inch Skeet-choke ported barrel; wide ventilated rib with orange front sight; select walnut Skeet-style stock; adjustable comb and length of pull. Made in Italy. Introduced 1993; still imported.

Perf.: $900 **Exc.:** $600 **VGood:** $500

BERETTA MODEL 390 COMPETITION SPORTING

Same specs as Model 390 Competition Skeet Sport except 28-inch, 30-inch vent-rib barrel; Full, Modified, Improved Cylinder, Skeet choke tubes; select walnut Monte Carlo stock. Made in Italy. Introduced 1995; still imported.

Perf.: $650 **Exc.:** $380 **VGood:** $300
With ported barrel
Perf.: $680 **Exc.:** $.410 **VGood:** $330

BERETTA MODEL 390 COMPETITION TRAP SPORT

Same specs as Model 390 Competition Skeet Sport except 30-inch, 32-inch step-tapered vent-rib barrel; Full, Improved Modified, Modified choke tubes; white

front bead; select walnut trap-style stock. Made in Italy. Introduced 1995; still imported.

Perf.: $680 **Exc.:** $375 **VGood:** $340
With ported barrel
Perf.: $750 **Exc.:** $475 **VGood:** $440

BERETTA MODEL 390 COMPETITION TRAP SUPER

Same specs as 390 Competition Skeet Sport except 30-inch, 32-inch ported barrel; Mobilchoke tubes; wide ventilated rib with orange front sight; select walnut trap-style stock; adjustable comb and length of pull. Made in Italy. Introduced 1993; still imported.

Perf.: $1000 **Exc.:** $620 **VGood:** $580

BERETTA AL391 URIKA AUTO SHOTGUNS

Gauge: 12-, 20-gauge; 3" chamber. Barrel: 22", 24", 26", 28", 30"; five Mobilchoke choke tubes. Weight: 5.95 to 7.28 lbs. Length: Varies by model. Stock: Walnut, black or camo synthetic; shims, spacers and interchangeable recoil pads allow custom fit. Features: self-compensating gas operation handles full range of loads; recoil reducer in receiver; enlarged trigger guard; reduced-weight receiver, barrel and forend; hard-chromed bore. Introduced 2000. Imported from Italy by Beretta USA.

Urika (12-ga., 26", 28", 30" barrels)
Perf.: $835 **Exc.:** $700 **VGood:** $600
Urika (20-ga., 24", 26", 28" barrels)
Perf.: $835 **Exc.:** $700 **VGood:** $600
Urika Synthetic (12-ga., 24", 26", 28", 30" barrels)
Perf.: $835 **Exc.:** $700 **VGood:** $600
Urika Camo. (12-ga., Realtree Hardwoods or Advantage Wetlands)
Perf.: $925 **Exc.:** $795 **VGood:** $675

BERETTA AL391 URIKA GOLD AND GOLD SPORTING AUTO SHOTGUNS

Similar to AL391 Urika except features deluxe wood, jeweled bolt and carrier, gold-inlaid receiver with

Beretta AL391 Urika Trap

Beretta AL391 Urika Gold Sporting

Beretta AL391 Urika Parallel Target RL

Beretta AL391 Teknys Gold

Beretta AL391 Teknys

Beretta 3901 Target RL

Beretta Model 1200F

Beretta Model 1201FP3

black or silver finish. Introduced 2000. Imported from Italy.

Urika Gold (12- or 20-ga., black receiver)
Perf.: $995   **Exc.:** $700   **VGood:** $540

Urika Gold (silver, lightweight receiver)
Perf.: $1035   **Exc.:** $741   **VGood:** $581

Urika Gold Sporting (12 or 20, black receiver, engraving)
Perf.: $995   **Exc.:** $700   **VGood:** $540

Urika Gold Sporting (12-ga., silver receiver, engraving)
Perf.: $1035   **Exc.:** $741   **VGood:** $581

BERETTA AL391 URIKA SPORTING AUTO SHOTGUNS

Similar to AL391 Urika except has competition sporting stock with rounded rubber recoil pad, wide ventilated rib with white front and mid-rib beads, satin-black receiver with silver markings. Available in 12- and 20-gauge. Introduced 2000. Imported from Italy by Beretta USA.

Perf.: $880   **Exc.:** $650   **VGood:** $525

BERETTA AL391 URIKA TRAP AND GOLD TRAP AUTO SHOTGUNS

Similar to AL391 Urika except in 12-ga. only, has wide ventilated rib with white front and mid-rib beads, Monte Carlo stock and special trap recoil pad. Gold Trap features highly figured walnut stock and forend, gold-filled Beretta logo and signature on receiver. Introduced 2000. Imported from Italy.

Urika Trap
Perf.: $995   **Exc.:** $700   **VGood:** $540

Urika Gold Trap
Perf.: $995   **Exc.:** $700   **VGood:** $540

BERETTA AL391 URIKA PARALLEL TARGET RL AND SL AUTO SHOTGUNS

Similar to AL391 Urika except has parallel-comb, Monte Carlo stock with tighter grip radius to reduce trigger reach and stepped ventilated rib. SL model has same features but with 13.5-inch length of pull stock. Introduced 2000. Imported from Italy by Beretta USA.

Urika Parallel Target RL; $1027
Perf.: $880   **Exc.:** $650   **VGood:** $525

Urika Parallel Target SL
Perf.: $880   **Exc.:** $650   **VGood:** $525

BERETTA AL391 URIKA YOUTH SHOTGUN

Similar to AL391 except has a 24-inch or 26-inch barrel with 13.5-inch stock for youth and smaller shooters. Introduced 2000. From Beretta USA.

Perf.: $835   **Exc.:** $700   **VGood:** $600

BERETTA AL391 TEKNYS

This model features a nickel receiver with polished sides and anti-glare top. Offered in 12 or 20 gauge with 26" or 28" vent rib barrel. X-wood stock with Gel-Tek recoil. Weight is about 7.2 lbs. for 12 gauge and 5.9 lbs. for the 20 gauge. Introduced in 2003.

Perf.: $935   **Exc.:** $800   **VGood:** $675

BERETTA AL391 TEKNYS GOLD

As above, but with engraved hunting scene on the receiver, gold plated trigger, jeweled breech bolt and carrier. Select walnut checkered stock with oil finish. Introduced in 2003.

Perf.: $1035   **Exc.:** $900   **VGood:** $775

BERETTA AL391 TEKNYS GOLD TARGET

Similar to AL391 Teknys Gold but with adjustable comb, 8.5 oz. recoil reducer and additional stepped rib for trap shooting. 30-inch barrel.

NIB: $1700   **Exc.:** $1595   **VGood:** $11

BERETTA 3901 TARGET RL

Gas-operated semi-auto chambered in 3-inch 12-gauge. Specifically designed for smaller-stature shooters with adjustable length of pull from 12 to 13 inches. Stock is adjustable for cast on or cast off. Adjustable comb and Sporting style flat rib. Available in 12 gauge only with 26-inch or 28-inch barrel.

NIB: $800   **Exc.:** $750   **VGood:** $625

BERETTA MODEL 1200F

Recoil-operated autoloader; 12-ga.; 2-3/4-inch chamber; 4-shot magazine; 26-inch, 28-inch vent-rib barrel; Mobilchokes; weighs 7-1/8 lbs.; checkered European walnut or matte-black finished polymer stock, forend; recoil pad. Left-handed model available. Made in Italy. Introduced 1984; discontinued 1990.

Perf.: $500   **Exc.:** $415   **VGood:** $350

BERETTA MODEL 1200FP

Same specs as Model 1200F except 6-shot magazine; 20-inch Cylinder barrel; no vent rib; adjustable rifle-type sights; designed for law enforcement. Made in Italy. Introduced 1988; discontinued 1990.

Perf.: $725   **Exc.:** $595   **VGood:** $500

BERETTA MODEL 1201F

Recoil-operated autoloader; 12-ga.; 3-inch chamber; 4-shot magazine; 24-inch, 26-inch, 28-inch vent-rib barrel; Mobilchokes; weighs 7-1/4 lbs.; matte-black finished polymer stock, forend; adjustable butt, recoil pad. Made in Italy. Introduced 1988; discontinued 1994.

Perf.: $725   **Exc.:** $595   **VGood:** $500

BERETTA MODEL 1201FP

Same specs as Model 1201F except 6-shot magazine; 20-inch Cylinder barrel; no vent rib; adjustable rifle-type sights; designed for law enforcement. Made in Italy. Introduced 1991; still imported.

Perf.: $725   **Exc.:** $595   **VGood:** $500

BERETTA MODEL 1201FP3

Same specs as Model 1201F except 20-inch Cylinder barrel; fixed rifle type sight; 6-shot magazine. Introduced 1988; still in production.

Perf.: $475   **Exc.:** $300   **VGood:** $225

BERETTA MODEL 1201FP GHOST RING AUTO SHOTGUN

Gauge: 12, 3-inch chamber; 18-inch barel (Cyl.); weighs 6.3 lbs.; special strengthened technopolymer stock; matte black finish; 5-shot magazine. Adjustable Ghost Ring rear sight, tritium front. Introduced 1988. Imported from Italy.

Perf.: $695   **Exc.:** $515   **VGood:** $385

BERETTA PINTAIL

Recoil-operated autoloader; 12-ga.; 3-inch chamber; 24-inch rifled Slug choke, 24-inch, 26-inch Mobilchoke barrels; weighs 7 lbs.; metal bead front sight; select checkered hardwood stock, forend with matte finish; recoil pad; crossbolt safety; matte-black receiver. Slug version has rifle sights, sling swivels. Imported from Italy. Introduced 1993; dropped 2001; reintroduced 2003.

Perf.: $575   **Exc.:** $475   **VGood:** $425

BERETTA RUBY LARK

Gas-operated autoloader; takedown; 12-ga.; 26-inch, 28-inch, 30-inch, 32-inch vent-rib stainless barrels; Improved Cylinder, Modified, Full choke; hand-checkered European walnut pistol-grip stock, beavertail forearm; push-button safety in triggerguard; all parts hand-polished; extensive engraving. Introduced 1960; discontinued 1967.

Exc.: $675   **VGood:** $550   **Good:** $475

BERETTA SILVER LARK

Gas-operated autoloader; takedown; 12-ga.; 26-inch, 28-inch, 30-inch, 32-inch barrels; Improved Cylinder, Modified, Full choke; hand-checkered European walnut pistol-grip stock, beavertail forearm; push-button safety in trigger guard; all parts hand polished. Introduced 1960; discontinued 1967.

Exc.: $295   **VGood:** $260   **Good:** $240

BERETTA AL391 URIKA 2

Introduced in 2007, the Urika 2 is an enhanced version of the original AL391 Urika semi-auto. Improvements include the addition of a spinning, self-cleaning action for faster cycling and longer functioning periods between cleanings.

NIB: $975   **Exc.:** $895   **VGood:** $775

BERETTA AL391 URIKA 2 X-TRA GRAIN

This series features Beretta's wood-enhancement treatment to highlight the color contrast of the wood. Offered in 3" 12 and 20 gauge with 26" and 28" barrels. A 20 gauge youth model with shorter stock and 24" barrel is also offered.

NIB: $1125   **Exc.:** $1075   **VGood:** $895

BERETTA AL391 URIKA 2 GOLD

Select oil-finished wood stock and forend with gold-filled game bird inlays on the receiver. The 12 gauge has a 28" barrel and the 20 gauge has a 26" barrel.

NIB: $1225   **Exc.:** $1175   **VGood:** $995

BERETTA AL391 URIKA 2 KICK-OFF

These waterfowl models feature Beretta's Kick-Off recoil reduction system. Matte black synthetic, Max-4 or Realtree AP finish with 26" or 28" barrel. Deduct 30 percent for models without Kick-Off. Add 10 percent for camo finish.

NIB: $1125   **Exc.:** $1075   **VGood:** $895

BERETTA AL391 URIKA 2 GOLD SPORTING

Enhanced wood with gold inlays and floral motif engraving on receiver in 12 gauge with 28" or 30" barrel.

NIB: $1375   **Exc.:** $1200   **VGood:** $900

BERETTA AL391 URIKA 2 PARALLEL TARGET X-TRA GRAIN

Target model in 12 gauge with 28", 30" or 32" barrel.

NIB: $1150   **Exc.:** $1100   **VGood:** $925

Beretta Silver Lark

Beretta AL391 Urika 2 X-tra Grain

Beretta AL391 Urika 2 Gold

Beretta ASE 90 Gold Trap

Beretta BL-1

Beretta BL-2/S

BERETTA AL391 URIKA 2 GOLD PARALLEL TARGET

Enhanced wood with gold inlays and floral motif engraving on receiver in 12 gauge with 30" or 32" barrel.

NIB: $1225   **Exc.:** $1175   **VGood:** $1050

BERETTA OVER/UNDER SHOTGUNS

BERETTA ASE 90 PIGEON

Over/Under; 12-ga.; 2-3/4-inch chambers; 3-shot magazine; 28-inch Improved Modified/Full barrels; vent rib; weighs about 8 lbs.; high-grade checkered walnut stock, forend; drop-out trigger assembly; recoil pad; silver-finished or blued receiver; gold etching; hard-chrome bores; comes with hard case. Made in Italy. Introduced 1992; discontinued 1994.

Perf.: $7100   **Exc.:** $5000   **VGood:** $4000

BERETTA ASE 90 GOLD SKEET

Same specs as ASE 90 Gold Pigeon except 28-inch Skeet/Skeet barrels; high-grade checkered walnut Skeet-style stock, forend. Made in Italy. Introduced 1992; still imported.

Perf.: $7500   **Exc.:** $5000   **VGood:** $4000

BERETTA ASE 90 GOLD SPORTING CLAYS

Same specs as ASE 90 Gold Pigeon except 28-inch, 30-inch vent-rib barrel; Mobilchoke tubes; high-grade checkered walnut Monte Carlo stock, forend. Introduced 1992; still imported.

Perf.: $7550   **Exc.:** $5000   **VGood:** $4000

BERETTA ASE 90 GOLD TRAP

Same specs as ASE 90 Gold Pigeon except 30-inch vent-rib barrel; fixed chokes or Mobilchokes; high-grade checkered walnut trap-style stock, forend; extra trigger group. Introduced 1992; still imported.

Perf.: $7550   **Exc.:** $5000   **VGood:** $4000

BERETTA ASE 90 GOLD TRAP COMBO

Same specs as ASE 90 Gold Pigeon except two-barrel set with 30-inch vent-rib over/under and 32-inch or 34-inch single over barrel; fixed chokes or Mobilchokes; high-grade checkered walnut trap-style stock, forend; extra trigger group. Introduced 1992; still imported.

Perf.: $9500   **Exc.:** $7000   **VGood:** $5000

BERETTA ASEL

Over/under; boxlock; 12-, 20-ga.; 26-inch, 28-inch, 30-inch barrels; Improved/Modified, Modified/Full chokes; hand-checkered pistol-grip stock, forend; single nonselective trigger; selective automatic ejectors. Introduced 1947; discontinued 1964.

12-ga.		
Exc.: $2750	**VGood:** $2375	**Good:** $1975
20-ga.		
Exc.: $4650	**VGood:** $3950	**Good:** $3500

BERETTA BL-1

Over/under; boxlock; 12-ga.; 2-3/4-inch chambers; 26-inch, 28-inch, 30-inch chrome-moly steel barrels; Improved/Modified, Modified/Full chokes; ramp front sight with fluorescent inserts; hand-checkered European walnut pistol-grip stock, forearm; double triggers; extractors; automatic safety; Monoblock design. Introduced 1969; discontinued 1972.

Exc.: $395   **VGood:** $350   **Good:** $285

BERETTA BL-2

Over/under; boxlock; 12-ga.; 2-3/4-inch chambers; 26-inch, 28-inch, 30-inch chrome-moly steel barrels; Improved/Modified, Modified/Full chokes; ramp front sight with fluorescent inserts; hand-checkered European walnut pistol-grip stock, forearm; single selective triggers; extractors; automatic safety; Monoblock design; engraving. Introduced 1969; discontinued 1972.

Exc.: $450   **VGood:** $395   **Good:** $350

BERETTA BL-2/S

Same specs as BL-2 except 2-3/4-inch, 3-inch chambers; vent rib. Introduced 1974; discontinued 1976.

Perf.: $475   **Exc.:** $425   **VGood:** $365

Beretta BL-3

Beretta BL-4

Beretta BL-5

Beretta DT10 Trident Trap

Beretta DT10 Trident Trap Combo

Beretta DT10 Trident Trap Bottom Single Combo

Beretta DT10 Trident Skeet

BERETTA BL-3

Over/under; boxlock; 12-, 20-ga; 2-3/4-inch, 3-inch chambers; 26-inch, 28-inch, 30-inch chrome-moly steel barrels; vent rib; Improved/Modified, Modified/Full chokes; ramp front sight with fluorescent inserts; hand-checkered European walnut pistol-grip stock, forearm; single selective triggers; ejectors; automatic safety; Monoblock design; engraved receiver. Introduced 1968; discontinued 1976.

Perf.: $600   **Exc.:** $550   **VGood:** $525

BERETTA BL-2

Over/under; boxlock; 12-ga.; 2-3/4-inch chambers; 26-inch, 28-inch, 30-inch chrome-moly steel barrels; Improved/Modified, Modified/Full chokes; ramp front sight with fluorescent inserts; hand-checkered European walnut pistol-grip stock, forearm; single selective triggers; extractors; automatic safety; Monoblock design; engraving. Introduced 1969; discontinued 1972.

Exc.: $450   **VGood:** $395   **Good:** $350

BERETTA BL-2/S

Same specs as BL-2 except 2-3/4-inch, 3-inch chambers; vent rib. Introduced 1974; discontinued 1976.

Perf.: $475   **Exc.:** $425   **VGood:** $365

BERETTA BL-3

Over/under; boxlock; 12-, 20-ga; 2-3/4-inch, 3-inch chambers; 26-inch, 28-inch, 30-inch chrome-moly steel barrels; vent rib; Improved/Modified, Modified/Full chokes; ramp front sight with fluorescent inserts; hand-checkered European walnut pistol-grip stock, forearm; single selective triggers; ejectors; automatic

safety; Monoblock design; engraved receiver. Introduced 1968; discontinued 1976.

Perf.: $600   **Exc.:** $550   **VGood:** $525
Add 50 percent to above prices for 20 gauge in at least 90 percent condition.

BERETTA BL-4

Over/under; boxlock; 12-, 20-, 28-ga; 2-3/4-inch, 3-inch chambers; 26-inch, 28-inch, 30-inch chrome-moly steel barrels; vent rib; Improved/Modified, Modified/Full chokes; ramp front sight with fluorescent inserts; hand-checkered select European walnut pistol-grip stock, forearm; single selective triggers; ejectors; automatic safety; Monoblock design; heavily engraved receiver. Introduced 1968; discontinued 1976.

Perf.: $900   **Exc.:** $800   **VGood:** $725
Add 20 percent to above price for 20 gauge
Add 50 percent for 28 gauge

BERETTA BL-5

Over/under; boxlock; 12-, 20-ga; 2-3/4-inch, 3-inch chambers; 26-inch, 28-inch, 30-inch chrome-moly steel barrels; vent rib; Improved/Modified, Modified/Full chokes; ramp front sight with fluorescent inserts; hand-checkered fancy European walnut pistol-grip stock, forearm; single selective triggers; ejectors; automatic safety; Monoblock design; heavily engraved receiver. Introduced 1968; discontinued 1976.

Perf.: $1050   **Exc.:** $900   **VGood:** $825

BERETTA BL-6

Over/under; boxlock; 12-, 20-ga; 2-3/4-inch, 3-inch chambers; 26-inch, 28-inch, 30-inch chrome-moly

steel barrels; vent rib; Improved/Modified, Modified/Full chokes; ramp front sight with fluorescent inserts; best-grade hand-checkered fancy European walnut pistol-grip stock, forearm; single selective triggers; ejectors; automatic safety; Monoblock design; false sideplates; extensive engraving. Introduced 1973; discontinued 1976.

Perf.: $1400   **Exc.:** $1100   **VGood:** $1000
Add 20 percent to above prices for 20 gauge.

BERETTA DT10 TRIDENT SHOTGUNS

Gauge: 12, 2-3/4-inch, 3-inch chambers; 28-inch, 30-inch, 32-inch, 34-inch barrel; competition-style vent rib; fixed or Optima Choke tubes; weighs 7.9 to 9 lbs.; High-grade walnut stock with oil finish; hand-checkered grip and forend, adjustable stocks available; detachable, adjustable trigger group; raised and thickened receiver; forend iron has replaceable nut to guarantee wood-to-metal fit; Optima Bore to improve shot pattern and reduce felt recoil. Introduced 2000. Imported from Italy.

Trident Trap (selective, lockable single trigger, adjustable stock)
Perf.: $6850   **Exc.:** $5650   **VGood:** $4950
Trident Trap Combo (single and O/U barrels)
Perf.: $9250   **Exc.:** $7750   **VGood:** $6500
Trident Trap Bottom Single Combo (adj. point of impact rib on single bbl.)
Perf.: $9500   **Exc.:** $7875   **VGood:** $6600
Trident Skeet (skeet stock with rounded recoil pad, tapered rib)
Perf.: $7200   **Exc.:** $6500   **VGood:** $5200
Trident Sporting (sporting clays stock with rounded recoil pad)
Perf.: $6850   **Exc.:** $5650   **VGood:** $4950

BERETTA GOLDEN SNIPE

Over/under; boxlock; 12-, 20-ga.; 2-3/4-inch, 3-inch chambers; 26-inch, 28-inch, 30-inch barrels; Improved/Modified, Modified/Full, Full/Full chokes; vent rib; hand-checkered European walnut pistol-grip stock, forearm; non-selective, selective trigger; auto ejectors; nickel steel receiver. Introduced 1955; discontinued 1975.

Nonselective trigger
Exc.: $995   **VGood:** $875   **Good:** $775
Selective trigger
Exc.: $995   **VGood:** $875   **Good:** $775

BERETTA GOLDEN SNIPE DELUXE

Same specs as Golden Snipe except finer engraving; better walnut. Available in Skeet, Trap models. Introduced 1955; discontinued 1975.
Exc.: $1140   **VGood:** $1000   **Good:** $890

BERETTA GRADE 100

Over/under; sidelock; 12-ga.; 26-inch, 28-inch, 30-inch barrel; any standard choke combination; hand-checkered straight or pistol-grip European walnut stock, forend; double triggers; automatic ejectors. Introduced post-World War II; discontinued 1960s.
Exc.: $1500   **VGood:** $1000   **Good:** $775

BERETTA GRADE 200

Over/under; sidelock; 12-ga.; 26-inch, 28-inch, 30-inch barrel; any standard choke combination; hand-checkered select European walnut straight or pistol-grip stock, forend; double triggers; automatic ejectors; chrome-plated bores, action; engraving. Introduced post-World War II; discontinued 1960s.
Exc.: $1750   **VGood:** $1400   **Good:** $1000

BERETTA MODEL 57E

Over/under; boxlock; 12-, 20-ga.; 2-3/4-inch, 3-inch chambers; 26-inch, 28-inch, 30-inch vent-rib barrel; hand-checkered European walnut pistol-grip stock, beavertail forend; automatic ejectors; single non-selective trigger; optional single selective trigger; similar to Golden Snipe model but overall quality is higher. Introduced 1955; discontinued 1967.
Exc.: $825   **VGood:** $770   **Good:** $660
Single selective trigger
Exc.: $850   **VGood:** $800   **Good:** $690

BERETTA SERIES 682 GOLD E SKEET, TRAP, SPORTING OVER/UNDERS

Gauge: 12, 2-3/4-inch chambers; Skeet-28-inch barrel, trap-30-inch and 32-inch; Imp., Mod. & Full and Mobilchoke; trap mono shotguns-32-inch and 34-inch Mobilchoke; trap top single guns-32-inch and 34-inch full and Mobilchoke; trap combo sets from 30-inch barrel O/U, to 32-inch O/U, 34-inch top single; close-grained walnut, hand checkered; white Bradley bead front sight and center bead; Greystone gunmetal gray finish receiver with gold accents. Trap Monte Carlo stock has deluxe trap recoil pad. Various grades available. Imported from Italy.

S682 Gold E Skeet, adjustable stock
Perf.: $2575   **Exc.:** $2250   **VGood:** $2125

S682 Gold E Trap Top Combo
Perf.: $2950   **Exc.:** $2350   **VGood:** $1900

S682 Gold E Trap with adjustable stock
Perf.: $2700   **Exc.:** $2200   **VGood:** $1800

S692 Gold E Sporting
Perf.: $2950   **Exc.:** $2400   **VGood:** $1975

S687 EELL Diamond Pigeon Skeet; discontinued 2002
Perf.: $4155   **Exc.:** $3075   **VGood:** $2550

S687 EELL Diamond Pigeon Skeet, adjustable stock
Perf.: $5295   **Exc.:** $4675   **VGood:** $4125

S687 EELL Diamond Pigeon Sporting
Perf.: $3850   **Exc.:** $3175   **VGood:** $2475

BERETTA MODEL 682 COMPETITION GOLD SKEET

Over/under; low-profile, improved boxlock; 12-, 20-, 28-ga., .410; 26-inch, 28-inch Skeet/Skeet barrels; weighs 7-1/2 lbs.; white bead front sight; highly select hand-checkered European walnut Skeet-type stock, beavertail forearm with matte finish; manual safety; single selective trigger with adjustable length of pull; recoil pad; gray-finished receiver. Introduced 1991; still in production.
Perf.: $2200   **Exc.:** $1350   **VGood:** $1000

Four-barrel set in all four gauges
Perf.: $4895   **Exc.:** $3000   **VGood:** $2700

BERETTA MODEL 682 COMPETITION GOLD SKEET SUPER

Same specs as Model 682 Competition Gold Skeet except adjustable comb and buttpads; ported barrel. Introduced 1991; still imported.
Perf.: $2650   **Exc.:** $1720   **VGood:** $1500

BERETTA MODEL 682 COMPETITION GOLD SPORTING

Same specs as Model 682 Competition Gold Skeet except 12-ga.; 2-3/4-inch chamber; 28-inch, 30-inch, 32-inch barrels; Mobilchokes; 1/2-inch wide ventilated rib; weighs 7-3/8 lbs.; highly select hand-checkered European walnut Sporting stock, schnabel forend with matte finish. Made in Italy. Still imported.
Perf.: $2750   **Exc.:** $2500   **VGood:** $2300

BERETTA MODEL 682 COMPETITION GOLD SPORTING PORTED

Same specs as Model 682 Competition Gold Skeet except 12-ga.; 2-3/4-inch chamber; 28-inch, 30-inch ported barrels; Mobilchokes; 1/2-inch wide ventilated rib; weighs 7-3/8 lbs.; highly select hand-checkered European walnut Sporting stock, schnabel forend with matte finish. Made in Italy. Still imported.
Perf.: $2300   **Exc.:** $1350   **VGood:** $1000

BERETTA MODEL 682 COMPETITION GOLD SPORTING SUPER

Same specs as Model 682 Competition Gold Skeet except 12-ga.; 2-3/4-inch chamber; 28-inch, 30-inch ported barrels; Mobilchokes; 1/2-inch wide ventilated tapered rib; weighs 7-3/8 lbs.; adjustable highly select hand-checkered European walnut Sporting stock, schnabel forend with matte finish. Made in Italy. Still imported.
Perf.: $2600   **Exc.:** $1750   **VGood:** $1000

BERETTA MODEL 682 COMPETITION GOLD TRAP

Same specs as Model 682 Competition Gold Skeet except 12-ga.; 2-3/4-inch chamber; 30-inch, 32-inch barrel; Mobilchokes; stepped, tapered rib; highly select hand-checkered European walnut Monte Carlo stock. Made in Italy. Introduced 1987; still imported.
Perf.: $2500   **Exc.:** $1700   **VGood:** $1200

Combo with extra single 32-inch, 34-inch over barrel
Perf.: $3000   **Exc.:** $2100   **VGood:** $1500

BERETTA MODEL 682 COMPETITION GOLD TRAP LIVE BIRD

Same specs as Model 682 Competition Gold Skeet except 12-ga.; 2-3/4-inch chamber; 30-inch barrel; Mobilchokes; Strada or flat tapered rib; highly select hand-checkered European walnut trap-style stock, beavertail forend with matte finish. Still in production.
Perf.: $2200   **Exc.:** $1500   **VGood:** $1000

BERETTA MODEL 682 COMPETITION GOLD TRAP MONO

Same specs as Model 682 Competition Gold Skeet except 12-ga.; 2-3/4-inch chambers; single 32-inch, 34-inch over barrel; Multichokes; vent rib; highly select hand-checkered European walnut Monte Carlo stock. Made in Italy. Introduced 1987; still imported.
Perf.: $2300   **Exc.:** $1500   **VGood:** $1000

BERETTA MODEL 682 COMPETITION GOLD TRAP MONO SUPER

Same specs as Model 682 Competition Skeet except 12-ga.; 2-3/4-inch chambers; single 32-inch, 34-inch over barrel; fixed or Mobilchokes; vent rib; highly select hand-checkered European walnut Monte Carlo stock. Made in Italy. Introduced 1991; still imported.
Perf.: $2500   **Exc.:** $1650   **VGood:** $1000

Beretta S682 Gold E Skeet

Beretta S682 Gold E Trap Combo

Beretta S682 Gold E Trap

Beretta S682 Gold E Sporting

Beretta S687 EELL Diamond Pigeon Skeet

Beretta S687 EELL Diamond Pigeon Skeet w/adjustable stock

Beretta S687 EELL Diamond Pigeon Sporting

Beretta Model 682 Competition Gold Skeet

Beretta Model 682 Competition Gold Trap Super

Beretta Model 685

Beretta Model 686 Competition Sporting Onyx

Beretta Model 686 Competetion Sporting Silver Perdiz

Beretta Model 686 Field

Beretta Model 686 Field EL Gold Perdiz

Beretta Model 686 Field Essential

BERETTA MODEL 682 COMPETITION GOLD TRAP SUPER

Same specs as Model 682 Competition Gold Skeet except 12-ga.; 2-3/4-inch chamber; 30-inch, 32-inch ported barrels; Mobilchokes; stepped, tapered rib; adjustable highly select hand-checkered European walnut Monte Carlo stock with matte finish; silver sideplates with hand engraved game scenes. Introduced 1991; still imported.

Perf.: $2500   **Exc.:** $1650   **VGood:** $1000

Combo with extra single 32-inch, 34-inch over barrel

Perf.: $3000   **Exc.:** $2000   **VGood:** $1400

BERETTA MODEL 682 COMPETITION SPORTING CONTINENTAL COURSE

Same specs as Model 682 Competition Gold Skeet except 12-ga.; 2-3/4-inch chambers; 28-inch, 30-inch Mobilchoke barrel; reverse tapered rib; Highly select hand-checkered European walnut stock, schnabel forend with matte finish; palm swell; black receiver; made for English Sporting Clays competition. Introduced 1994; still in production.

Perf.: $2400   **Exc.:** $1500   **VGood:** $1000

BERETTA MODEL 685

Over/under; boxlock; 12-, 20-ga.; 2-3/4-inch or 3-inch chambers; 26-inch, 28-inch, 30-inch barrels; standard chokes; hand-checkered walnut stock; steel receiver; single trigger; extractors; light engraving. Discontinued 1986.

Perf.: $620   **Exc.:** $490   **VGood:** $400

BERETTA MODEL 686 COMPETITION SKEET SILVER PERDIZ

Over/under; low-profile, improved boxlock; 12-ga.; 2-3/4-inch chambers; 28-inch Skeet/Skeet barrels; tapered rib; weighs 7-5/8 lbs.; white front bead sight; select checkered walnut stock, beavertail forend with matte finish; manual safety; single trigger; recoil pad;

silver receiver with scroll engraving. Made in Italy. Introduced 1994; still imported.

Perf.: $1150   **Exc.:** $890   **VGood:** $690

BERETTA MODEL 686 COMPETITION SPORTING COLLECTION SPORT

Same specs as Model 686 Competition Skeet Silver Perdiz except 12-ga.; 3-inch chambers; 28-inch Strada-rib barrel; Mobilchokes; select checkered multi-colored walnut stock, beavertail forend with matte finish; single selective trigger; multi-colored receiver. Made in Italy. Introduced 1996; still imported.

Perf.: $1200   **Exc.:** $850   **VGood:** $700

BERETTA MODEL 686 COMPETITION SPORTING ONYX

Same specs as Model 686 Competition Skeet Silver Perdiz except 12-ga.; 3-inch chambers; 28-inch, 30-inch Strada-rib barrels; Mobilchokes; single selective trigger; semi-matte black receiver with gold lettering. Made in Italy. Introduced 1994; still imported.

Perf.: $1150   **Exc.:** $950   **VGood:** $850

BERETTA MODEL 686 COMPETITION SPORTING ONYX ENGLISH COURSE

Same specs as Model 686 Competition Skeet Silver Perdiz except 12-ga.; 3-inch chamber; 28-inch vent-rib barrels; Mobilchokes; semi-matte black receiver; designed for English Sporting Clays competition. Made in Italy. Introduced 1991; discontinued 1992.

Perf.: $1700   **Exc.:** $1100   **VGood:** $950

BERETTA MODEL 686 COMPETITION SPORTING SILVER PERDIZ

Same specs as Model 686 Competition Skeet Silver Perdiz except 12-, 20-ga.; 3-inch chamber; 28-inch, 30-inch barrels; Mobilchokes; Strada rib (12-ga.), flat rib (20-ga.); weighs 7-3/4 lbs.; checkered select walnut, semi-beavertail forend with matte

finish. Made in Italy. Introduced 1994; discontinued 1996.

Perf.: $1200   **Exc.:** $775   **VGood:** $500

Combo with two-barrel set

Perf.: $1800   **Exc.:** $1300   **VGood:** $1100

BERETTA MODEL 686 COMPETITION SPORTING SILVER PIGEON

Same specs as Model 686 Competition Skeet Silver Perdiz except 12-, 20-ga.; 3-inch chamber; 28-inch, 30-inch barrels; Mobilchokes; Strada rib (12-ga.), flat rib (20-ga.); weighs 7-3/4 lbs.; checkered select walnut stock, schnabel forend with matte finish; single selective trigger. Made in Italy. Introduced 1996; still imported.

Perf.: $1250   **Exc.:** $900   **VGood:** $600

BERETTA MODEL 686 COMPETITION TRAP INTERNATIONAL

Same specs as Model 686 Competition Skeet Silver Perdiz except 30-inch Improved Modified/Full barrels; vent rib; select checkered walnut trap-style stock, forearm. Made in Italy. Introduced, 1994; discontinued 1995.

Perf.: $1000   **Exc.:** $600   **VGood:** $525

BERETTA MODEL 686 FIELD EL GOLD PERDIZ

Over/under; low-profile, improved boxlock; 12-, 20-ga.; 3-inch chamber; 26-inch, 28-inch vent-rib barrels; Mobilchokes; weighs 6-7/8 lbs.; highly select checkered walnut stock, beavertail forend with gloss finish; auto safety; single selective trigger; rubber recoil pad; silver receiver with full sideplates and floral scroll engraving. Made in Italy. Introduced 1994; still imported.

Perf.: $1800   **Exc.:** $1120   **VGood:** $910

BERETTA MODEL 686 FIELD ESSENTIAL

Same specs as Model 686 Field EL Gold Perdiz except 12-ga.; 3-inch chamber; weighs 6-3/4 lbs.; matte black plain receiver. Made in Italy. Introduced 1994; still imported.

Perf.: $910   **Exc.:** $590   **VGood:** $510

BERETTA MODEL 686 FIELD ONYX

Same specs as Model 686 Field EL Gold Perdiz except 12-, 20-ga.; 3-inch, 3-1/2-inch chambers; weighs 6-7/8 lbs.; checkered select walnut straight English-style or pistol-grip stock, semi-beavertail forend (schnabel forend for English stock) with matte finish; semi-matte black receiver; ventilated rib. Imported from Italy by Beretta U.S.A. Introduced 1988; still imported.

Perf.: $1100   **Exc.:** $650   **VGood:** $540

BERETTA MODEL 686 FIELD ONYX MAGNUM

Same specs as Model 686 Field EL Gold Perdiz except 12-ga.; 3-1/2-inch chambers; checkered select walnut straight English-style or pistol-grip stock, semi-beavertail forend (schnabel forend for English stock) with matte finish; matte black plain receiver. Made in Italy. Introduced 1990; discontinued 1993.

Perf.: $1175   **Exc.:** $700   **VGood:** $600

BERETTA MODEL 686 FIELD SILVER PERDIZ

Same specs as Model 686 Field EL Gold Perdiz except 12-, 20-, 28-ga.; 2-3/4-inch, 3-inch chambers; checkered select walnut straight English-style or pistol-grip stock, semi-beavertail forend (schnabel forend for English stock) with gloss finish; silver receiver with floral scroll engraving. Made in Italy. Introduced 1994; discontinued 1996.

Perf.: $1100   **Exc.:** $750   **VGood:** $650

Combo with two-barrel set for 20-, 28-ga.

Perf.: $1475   **Exc.:** $1250   **VGood:** $1100

BERETTA MODEL 686 FIELD SILVER PIGEON

Same specs as Model 686 Field EL Gold Perdiz except 12-, 20-, 28-ga.; 2-3/4-inch, 3-inch chambers; highly select checkered walnut stock, schnabel forend with gloss finish; silver receiver with floral scroll engraving. Made in Italy. Introduced 1996; still imported.

Perf.: $1225   **Exc.:** $825   **VGood:** $575

BERETTA MODEL 686 FIELD ULTRALIGHT

Same specs as Model 686 Field EL Gold Perdiz except 12-ga.; 2-3/4-inch chamber; weighs 5-3/4 lbs.; checkered select walnut stock, schnabel forend with matte finish; aluminum alloy receiver with titanium plate; game scene engraving. Made in Italy. Introduced 1994; still imported.

Perf.: $1450   **Exc.:** $1000   **VGood:** $750

BERETTA MODEL S686 WHITEWING AND BLACKWING O/U

Gauge: 12, 3-inch chambers; 26-inch, 28-inch barrel; Mobilchoke tubes (Imp. Cyl., Mod., Full); weighs 6.7 lbs.; 45.7-inch overall (28-inch barrels). 14.5-inch by 2.2-inch by 1.4-inch dimensioned American walnut stock with radiused black buttplate; matte chrome finish on receiver; matte blue barrels; hard-chrome bores; low- profile receiver with dual conical locking lugs; single selective trigger; ejectors. Imported from Italy.

Whitewing
Perf.: $1155   **Exc.:** $995   **VGood:** $875

Blackwing (Rugged Blue, schnabel forend)
Perf.: $1155   **Exc.:** $995   **VGood:** $875

BERETTA S686 ONYX O/U SHOTGUN

Gauge: 12, 3-inch chambers; 28-inch, 30-inch barrel (Mobilchoke tubes); weighs 7.7 lbs.; checkered American walnut; wide, vented 12.5mm target rib; radiused recoil pad; polished black finish on receiver and barrels. Intended for the beginning Sporting Clays shooter. Introduced 1993. Imported from Italy.

Perf.: $1375   **Exc.:** $1100   **VGood:** $900

With X-Tra Wood (highly figured)
Perf.: $1439   **Exc.:** $1109   **VGood:** $919

BERETTA S686 SILVER PIGEON O/U SHOTGUN

Gauge: 12, 20, 28; 3-inch chambers (2-3/4-inch 28-ga.); 26-inch, 28-inch barrel; weighs 6.8 lbs.; checkered walnut; interchangeable barrels (20- and 28-ga.); single selective gold-plated trigger; boxlock action; auto safety; schnabel forend.

Perf.: $1565   **Exc.:** $1150   **VGood:** $950

20 ga. and 28 ga.
Perf.: $1877   **Exc.:** $1462   **VGood:** $1262

BERETTA MODEL 687 COMPETITION SKEET EELL DIAMOND PIGEON

Over/under; low-profile, improved boxlock; 12-ga.; 2-3/4-inch chambers; 28-inch Skeet/Skeet barrels; tapered rib; weighs 7-1/2 lbs.; white front bead sight; highly select checkered walnut forend with matte finish; rubber recoil pad; manual safety; single selective trigger; silver receiver with full sideplates; hand-engraved game scenes; comes with a case. Made in Italy. Introduced 1994; still imported.

Perf.: $4775   **Exc.:** $4000   **VGood:** $3550

Four-barrel set in 12-, 20-, 28-ga., .410
Perf.: $6750   **Exc.:** $4900   **VGood:** $4000

BERETTA MODEL 687 COMPETITION SPORTING EELL DIAMOND PIGEON

Same specs as Model 687 Competition Skeet EELL Diamond Pigeon except 12-ga.; 2-3/4-inch, 3-inch chambers; 28-inch, 30-inch Strada-rib barrels; Mobilchokes; highly select checkered walnut stock, schnabel forend with matte finish; stock oval plate. Made in Italy. Introduced 1994; still imported.

Perf.: $4350   **Exc.:** $2700   **VGood:** $2000

Beretta Model S686 Whitewing

Beretta S686 Onyx

Beretta Model 687 Field EL Onyx

Beretta Model 687 Field Golden Onyx

BERETTA MODEL 687 COMPETITION SPORTING EL GOLD PIGEON

Same specs as Model 687 Competition Skeet Diamond Pigeon except 12-ga.; 3-inch chambers; 28-inch, 30-inch Strada-rib barrels; Mobilchokes; weighs 7-1/4 lbs.; highly select checkered walnut stock, schnabel forend with matte finish; stock oval plate; silver receiver with full sideplates; gold engraved animals. Made in Italy. Introduced 1994; still imported.

Perf.: $2800   **Exc.:** $1500   **VGood:** $1100

BERETTA MODEL 687 COMPETITION SPORTING L SILVER PIGEON

Same specs as Model 687 Competition Skeet EELL Diamond Pigeon except 12-, 20-ga.; 3-inch chambers; 28-inch, 30-inch barrel; Mobilchokes; Strada rib (12-ga.), flat rib (20-ga.); weighs 7-1/4 lbs.; select checkered walnut stock, schnabel forend with matte finish; stock oval plate. Made in Italy. Introduced 1994; still imported.

Perf.: $2150   **Exc.:** $1600   **VGood:** $1200

BERETTA MODEL 687 COMPETITION SPORTING SILVER PERDIZ ENGLISH COURSE

Same specs as Model 687 Competition Skeet EELL Diamond Pigeon except 28-inch vent-rib barrels; Mobilchokes; designed for English Sporting Clays competition. Made in Italy. Introduced 1991; discontinued 1992.

Perf.: $2350   **Exc.:** $1400   **VGood:** $1125

BERETTA MODEL 687 COMPETITION TRAP EELL DIAMOND PIGEON

Same specs as Model 687 Competition Skeet EELL Diamond Pigeon except 30-inch barrel; Mobilchokes; stepped, tapered rib; weighs 8-7/8 lbs.; highly select checkered walnut Monte Carlo stock, beavertail forend with matte finish; single adjustable trigger. Made in Italy. Introduced 1994; still imported.

Perf.: $4250   **Exc.:** $2700   **VGood:** $2200

BERETTA MODEL 687 COMPETITION TRAP EELL DIAMOND PIGEON COMBO

Same specs as Model 687 Competition Skeet EELL Diamond Pigeon except two-barrel set with 32-inch over/under and single 34-inch over; Mobilchokes; stepped, tapered rib; weighs 8-7/8 lbs.; highly select checkered walnut Monte Carlo stock, beavertail

forend with matte finish; single adjustable trigger. Made in Italy. Introduced 1994; still imported.

Perf.: $5000   **Exc.:** $3500   **VGood:** $3000

BERETTA MODEL 687 COMPETITION TRAP EELL DIAMOND PIGEON MONO

Same specs as Model 687 Competition Skeet EELL Diamond Pigeon except 32-inch, 34-inch barrel; Full or Mobilchokes; stepped, tapered rib; weighs 8-1/8 lbs.; highly select checkered walnut Monte Carlo stock, beavertail forend with gloss finish; single adjustable trigger. Made in Italy. Introduced 1994; still imported.

Perf.: $3250   **Exc.:** $2600   **VGood:** $2300

BERETTA MODEL 687 FIELD EELL DIAMOND PIGEON

Over/under; low-profile, improved boxlock; 12-, 20-, 28-ga.; 2-3/4-inch, 3-inch chambers; 26-inch, 28-inch vent-rib barrels; Mobilchokes; weighs 6-7/8 lbs.; metal front bead sight; highly select checkered walnut stock, schnabel forend with gloss finish; rubber recoil pad; stock oval plate; auto safety; single selective trigger; silver receiver with full sideplates; hand-engraved game scenes; comes with case. Made in Italy. Introduced 1994; still imported.

Perf.: $4775   **Exc.:** $4000   **VGood:** $3550

BERETTA MODEL 687 FIELD EL GOLD PIGEON

Same specs as Model 687 Field EELL Diamond Pigeon except 12-, 20-, 28-ga., .410; 2-3/4-inch, 3-inch chambers; silver receiver with full sideplates; gold engraved animals. Made in Italy. Introduced 1994; still imported.

Perf.: $2925   **Exc.:** $1975   **VGood:** $1700

Combo (28 and .410)
Perf.: $4775   **Exc.:** $4075   **VGood:** $3425

BERETTA MODEL 687 FIELD EL ONYX

Same specs as Model 687 Field EELL Diamond Pigeon except 12-, 20-ga.; 3-inch chambers; black receiver with dummy sideplates; engraving. Made in Italy. Introduced 1990; discontinued 1991.

Perf.: $2350   **Exc.:** $1775   **VGood:** $1520

BERETTA MODEL 687 FIELD GOLDEN ONYX

Same specs as Model 687 Field EELL Diamond Pigeon except 12-, 20-ga.; 3-inch chambers; black receiver; gold engraving. Made in Italy. Introduced 1988; discontinued 1989.

Perf.: $1400   **Exc.:** $900   **VGood:** $795

Beretta Silver Pigeon S Combo

Beretta Silver Pigeon V

Beretta Silver Snipe

Beretta Sporting Clays

Beretta SO-2 Presentation

Beretta SO-3

Beretta SO-4

BERETTA S-58 SKEET

Over/under; boxlock; 12-, 20-ga.; 2-3/4-inch, 3-inch chambers; 26-inch Skeet/Skeet barrels; vent rib; checkered European walnut Skeet-style stock, forend; recoil pad; selective single trigger; ejectors; scroll engraved. Introduced 1977; no longer in production.

    Perf.: $750   **Exc.:** $620   **VGood:** $500

BERETTA S-58 TRAP

Same specs as S-58 Skeet except 30-inch Improved Modified/Full; checkered European walnut Monte Carlo stock, forend. Introduced 1977; no longer in production.

    Perf.: $680   **Exc.:** $520   **VGood:** $450

BERETTA SILVER SNIPE

Over/under; boxlock; 12-, 20-ga.; 2-3/4-inch, 3-inch chambers; 26-inch, 28-inch, 30-inch barrels; Improved/Modified, Modified/Full, Full/Full chokes; plain or vent rib; hand-checkered European walnut pistol-grip stock, forearm; nonselective, selective trigger; extractors; nickel steel receiver. Introduced 1955; discontinued 1967.

Nonselective trigger		
Exc.: $725	**VGood:** $650	**Good:** $595

Selective trigger		
Exc.: $775	**VGood:** $695	**Good:** $650

BERETTA SPORTING CLAYS SHOTGUNS

Over/under; 12-, 20-ga.; 2-3/4-inch, 3-inch chambers; 28-inch, 30-inch, 32-inch barrel Mobilchoke; close-grained walnut; Beretta Mobilchoke flush-mounted screw-in choke tube system; wide 12.5mm top rib with 2.5mm center groove; 686 Silver Pigeon has silver receiver with scroll engraving; 687 Silver Pigeon Sporting has silver receiver, highly figured walnut; 687 EL Pigeon Sporting has game scene engraving with gold inlaid animals on full sideplate. Introduced 1994. Imported from Italy by Beretta USA.

    Perf.: $1795   **Exc.:** $1550   **VGood:** $1325

BERETTA SO-2 PRESENTATION

Over/under; sidelock; 12-ga.; 26-inch Improved/Modified, 28-inch Modified/Full Boehler anti-rust barrels; vent rib; hand-checkered European walnut straight or pistol-grip stock; chrome-nickel receiver; all interior parts chromed; checkered trigger, safety, top lever; scroll engraving; silver pigeon inlaid in top lever. Made in Field, Skeet, Trap models. Made in Italy. Introduced 1965; no longer in production.

    Perf.: $3995   **Exc.:** $2950   **VGood:** $2350

BERETTA SO-3

Over/under; sidelock; 12-ga.; 26-inch Improved/Modified, 28-inch Modified/Full Boehler anti-rust barrels; vent rib; fancy hand-checkered European walnut straight or pistol-grip stock; chrome-nickel receiver; all interior parts chromed; checkered trigger, safety, top lever; profuse scroll and relief engraving; silver pigeon inlaid in top lever. Made in Field, Skeet, Trap models. Made in Italy. Introduced 1965; no longer in production.

    Perf.: $6500   **Exc.:** $4800   **VGood:** $4300

BERETTA SO-4

Over/under; hand-detachable sidelock; 12-ga.; 26-inch Improved/Modified, 28-inch Modified/Full Boehler anti-rust barrels; vent rib; fancy hand-checkered European full-grain walnut straight or pistol-grip stock; chrome-nickel receiver; all interior parts chromed; checkered trigger, safety, top lever; elaborate scroll and relief engraving; silver pigeon inlaid in top lever. Made in Field, Skeet, Trap models. Made in Italy. Introduced 1965; no longer in production.

    Perf.: $7500   **Exc.:** $6000   **VGood:** $5500

BERETTA SO-5

Over/under; hand-detachable sidelock; 12-ga.; handmade gun built to customer specs; fancy hand-checkered European full-grain walnut straight or pistol-grip stock; chrome-nickel receiver; all interior parts chromed; checkered trigger, safety, top lever;

BERETTA MODEL 687 FIELD L ONYX

Same specs as Model 687 Field EELL Diamond Pigeon except 12-, 20-ga.; 3-inch chambers; black receiver; engraved game scenes. Made in Italy. Introduced 1990; discontinued 1991.

    Perf.: $1300   **Exc.:** $860   **VGood:** $720

BERETTA MODEL 687 FIELD L SILVER PIGEON

Same specs as Model 687 Field EELL Diamond Pigeon except 12-, 20-ga.; 3-inch chambers; silver receiver with game scenes. Made in Italy. Introduced 1994; still imported.

    Perf.: $1625   **Exc.:** $950   **VGood:** $800

BERETTA SILVER PIGEON S

New in 2007, the Silver Pigeon S Series features scroll and floral engraving on a satin nickel-alloy finished receiver. It is available in 12, 20 and 28 gauge with 26" or 28" barrels, and .410 bore with 28" barrels. All come with five chokes. Weight is about 6.8 lbs.

    NIB: $1875   **Exc.:** $1725   **VGood:** $1500

BERETTA SILVER PIGEON S COMBO

Combo model comes with 26" 20 gauge barrels and 28" 28 gauge barrels.

    NIB: $2250   **Exc.:** $2050   **VGood:** $1700

BERETTA 687 SILVER PIGEON V

This is the top-of-the-line model in the Silver Pigeon Series. Available in 12, 20 and 28 gauges with 26-inch and 28-inch barrels and .410-bore (added in 2006). Pistol-grip stock of richly figured walnut with oil finish. Color case-hardened receiver with gold-filled game bird inlays. English stocked versions of the 20 and 28 gauges and .410 bore were added in 2006.

    NIB: $3150   **Exc.:** $2900   **VGood:** $2375

BERETTA S-55B

Over/under; boxlock; 12-, 20-ga.; 2-3/4-inch, 3-inch chambers; 26-inch, 28-inch, 30-inch vent-rib barrels; standard choke combos; checkered European walnut pistol-grip stock, forend; selective single trigger; extractors. Introduced 1977; no longer in production.

    Perf.: $565   **Exc.:** $455   **VGood:** $390

BERETTA S-56E

Over/under; boxlock; 12-, 20-ga.; 2-3/4-inch, 3-inch chambers; 26-inch, 28-inch, 30-inch vent-rib barrels; standard choke combos; checkered European walnut pistol-grip stock, forend; selective single trigger; ejectors; scroll engraved. Introduced 1977; no longer in production.

    Perf.: $620   **Exc.:** $525   **VGood:** $480

elaborate scroll and relief engraving; Crown Grade symbol inlaid in top lever. Made in Field, Skeet, Trap models. Made in Italy. Still in production on special-order basis.

Perf.: $15,500   **Exc.:** $9500   **VGood:** $7750

BERETTA SO-6

Over/under; hand-detachable sidelock; 12-ga.; handmade gun built to customer specs; fancy hand-checkered European full-grain walnut straight or pistol-grip stock; chrome-nickel receiver; all interior parts chromed; checkered trigger, safety, top lever; elaborate scroll and relief engraving; Crown Grade symbol inlaid in top lever. Made in Skeet, Trap, Sporting models. Made in Italy. Still in production on special-order basis.

Perf.: $16,650   **Exc.:** $13,500   **VGood:** $10,750

BERETTA SO-6 EELL

Same specs as SO-6 except produced on custom order to buyer's specs; special engraving and inlays. Made in Italy. Introduced 1989; still imported.

Perf.: $27,500   **Exc.:** $21,500   **VGood:** $16,750

BERETTA SO-7

Over/under; sidelock; 12-ga.; 26-inch Improved/ Modified, 28-inch Modified/Full Boehler anti-rust barrels; vent rib; fancy hand-checkered European full-grain walnut straight or pistol-grip stock; chrome-nickel receiver; all interior parts chromed; checkered trigger, safety, top lever; elaborate scroll and relief engraving; silver pigeon inlaid in top lever. Made in Field model. Made in Italy. Introduced 1948; no longer in production.

Perf.: $9000   **Exc.:** $8300   **VGood:** $7500

BERETTA SO-9

Over/under; hand-detachable sidelock; 12-, 20-, 28-ga., .410; handmade gun built to customer specs; Boehler anti-rust steel barrels; fixed or screw-in Mobilchoke system; fancy hand-checkered European full-grain walnut straight or pistol-grip stock; chrome-nickel receiver; all interior parts chromed; checkered trigger, safety, top lever; highly decorated, engraved. Made in Skeet, Trap, Sporting models. Made in Italy. Introduced 1989; still imported.

Perf.: $35,000   **Exc.:** $27,500   **VGood:** $20,500

BERETTA ULTRALIGHT OVER/UNDER

Gauge: 12, 2-3/4-inch chambers; 26-inch, 28-inch barrel, Mobilchoke choke tubes; weighs about 5 lbs., 13 oz.; select American walnut with checkered grip and forend; low-profile aluminum alloy receiver with titanium breech face insert; game scene engraving; single selective trigger; automatic safety. Introduced 1992. Imported from Italy.

Perf.: $1600   **Exc.:** $1195   **VGood:** $895

BERETTA ULTRALIGHT DELUXE OVER/UNDER SHOTGUN

Similar to the Ultralight except has matte electroless nickel finish receiver with gold game scene engraving; matte oil-finished, select walnut stock and forend. Imported from Italy.

Perf.: $1875   **Exc.:** $1550   **VGood:** $1250

BERETTA OVER/UNDER FIELD SHOTGUNS

Gauge: 12-, 20-, 28-ga., .410, 2-3/4-inch, 3-inch and 3-1/2-inch chambers; 26-inch and 28-inch barrel (Mobilchoke tubes); close-grained, highly-figured, American walnut stocks and forends; unique, weather-resistant finish on barrels. Silver designates standard 686, 687 models with silver receivers; 686 Silver Pigeon has enhanced engraving pattern, schnabel forend; 686 Silver Essential has matte chrome finish; Gold indicates higher grade 686EL, 687EL models with full sideplates; Diamond is for 687EELL models with highest grade wood, engraving. Case provided with Gold and Diamond grades. Imported from Italy by Beretta U.S.A.

S686 Silver Pigeon two-bbl. set
Perf.: $2125   **Exc.:** $1575   **VGood:** $1300
S686 Silver Pigeon
Perf.: $1565   **Exc.:** $1150   **VGood:** $950

Beretta SO-5

Beretta SO-6 EELL

Beretta SO-6 EELL close-up

Beretta SO-7

Beretta SO-9

Beretta SO-9 engraving patterns

Beretta SO-9 engraving patterns

Beretta Ultralight

Beretta Ultralight Deluxe

Beretta GR-2

Beretta GR-3

Beretta GR-4

Beretta Model 409PB

Beretta Model 410E

Beretta Model 424

Beretta Model 452 EELL

S687 Silver Pigeon II Sporting
Perf.: $1825   **Exc.:** $1600   **VGood:** $1450
Combo 29-inch and 30-inch
Perf.: $2500   **Exc.;** **$2200**   **VGood:** $1900
S687EL Gold Pigeon (gold inlays, sideplates)
Perf.: $3335   **Exc.:** $2475   **VGood:** $1950
S687EL Gold Pigeon, .410, 26-inch; 28 ga., 28-inch
Perf.: $4395   **Exc.:** $3475   **VGood:** $2950
S687 EL Gold Pigeon II (deep relief engraving)
Perf.: $3700   **Exc.:** $3300   **VGood:** $2900
S687 EL Gold Pigeon II Sporting (d.r. engraving)
Perf.: $3950   **Exc.:** $3500   **VGood:** $3100

BERETTA GR-2

Side-by-side; boxlock; 12-(2-3/4-inch), 20-ga. (3-inch); 26-inch, 28-inch 30-inch barrels; standard choke combos; checkered European walnut pistol-grip stock, forend; plain extractors; double triggers. Introduced 1968; discontinued 1976.

Perf.: $670   **Exc.:** $560   **VGood:** $520

BERETTA GR-3

Side-by-side; boxlock; 12-, 20-ga.; 3-inch chambers; 26-inch, 28-inch 30-inch barrels; standard choke combos; checkered European walnut pistol-grip stock, forend; plain extractors; single selective trigger; recoil pad. Introduced 1968; discontinued 1976.

Perf.: $780   **Exc.:** $660   **VGood:** $575

BERETTA GR-4

Side-by-side; boxlock; 12-ga.; 2-3/4-inch chambers; 26-inch, 28-inch 30-inch barrel; standard choke combos; checkered select European walnut pistol-grip stock, forend; auto ejectors; single selective trigger; engraving. Introduced 1968; discontinued 1976.

Perf.: $1500   **Exc.:** $1215   **VGood:** $1075

BERETTA MODEL 409PB

Side-by-side; boxlock; hammerless; 12-, 16-, 20-, 28-ga.; 27-1/2-inch, 28-1/2-inch, 30-inch barrels; Improved/Modified, Modified/Full chokes; hand-checkered European walnut straight or pistol-grip stock, beavertail forearm; double triggers; plain

extractors; engraved action. Introduced 1934; discontinued 1964.

Exc.: $775   **VGood:** $675   **Good:** $600
Add 25 percent to above prices for 20 gauge
Add 50 percent for 28 gauge

BERETTA MODEL 410

Side-by-side; boxlock; hammerless; 10-ga.; 3-1/2-inch chambers; 27-1/2-inch, 28-1/2-inch, 30-inch barrels; Improved/Modified, Modified/Full chokes; hand-checkered European walnut straight stock; recoil pad; plain extractors; double triggers. Introduced 1934; discontinued 1963.

Exc.: $1200   **VGood:** $995   **Good:** $880

BERETTA MODEL 410E

Same specs as Model .410 except 12-, 16-, 20-, 28-ga.; hand-checkered European walnut straight or pistol-grip stock, beavertail forend; double triggers; automatic ejectors; engraved action. Introduced 1934; discontinued 1964.

12 Gauge		
Exc.: $1275	**VGood:** $1000	**Good:** $895
20 Gauge		
Exc.: $1750	**VGood:** $1550	**Good:** $1275
28 Gauge		
Exc.: $3775	**VGood:** $3300	**Good:** $2800

BERETTA MODEL 411E

Side-by-side; boxlock; hammerless; 12-, 16-, 20-, 28-ga.; 27-1/2-inch, 28-1/2-inch, 30-inch barrels; Improved/Modified, Modified/Full chokes; hand-checkered European walnut straight or pistol-grip stock; beavertail forend; sideplates; engraved action; automatic ejectors; double triggers. Introduced 1934; discontinued 1964.

12 Gauge		
Exc.: $2000	**VGood:** $1750	**Good:** $1350
20 Gauge		
Exc.: $2750	**VGood:** $2325	**Good:** $1750
28 Gauge		
Exc.: $4250	**VGood:** $3775	**Good:** $3300

BERETTA MODEL 424

Side-by-side; boxlock; hammerless; 12-, 20-ga.; 26-inch Improved/Modified, 28-inch Modified/Full barrels; checkered European walnut straight-grip stock, forend; plain extractors; border engraving on action. Introduced 1977; discontinued 1984. Redesignated as Model 625.

Perf.: $1475   **Exc.:** $1175   **VGood:** $975
Add 50 percent to above prices for 20 gauge

BERETTA MODEL 426

Side-by-side; boxlock; hammerless; 12-, 20-ga.; 26-inch Improved/Modified, 28-inch Modified/Full barrels; high-grade checkered European walnut straight-grip stock, forend; ejectors; finely engraved action; silver pigeon inlaid on top lever. Introduced 1977; discontinued 1984. Redesignated as Model 626.

Perf.: $1575   **Exc.:** $1275   **VGood:** $1075

BERETTA MODEL 452 CUSTOM

Side-by-side; detachable sidelock; 12-ga; 26-inch, 28-inch, 30-inch barrels; choked to customer specs; weighs 6-3/4 lbs.; highly figured European walnut stock; double bolting; ejectors; double triggers; optional single non-selective trigger; manual safety; coin-finished frame. Essentially custom built. Made in Italy. Introduced 1990; still in production.

Perf.: $28,750 **Exc.:** $20,500 **VGood:** $15,750

BERETTA MODEL 452 EELL

Same specs as Model 452 except walnut briar stock; full engraving. Introduced 1992; still imported.

Perf.: $38,950 **Exc.:** $27,750 **VGood:** $21,000

BERETTA MODEL 626

Side-by-side; boxlock; 12-, 20-ga.; 2-3/4-inch chambers; 26-inch, 28-inch barrels; standard choke combos; concave matted rib; hand-checkered European walnut straight or pistol-grip stock, forearm; coil springs; double underlugs, bolts;

double triggers; auto safety; ejectors. Made in Italy. Introduced 1985; discontinued 1988. Formerly designated as Beretta 426.

Perf.: $1450   **Exc.:** $1050   **VGood:** $875

BERETTA MODEL 626 ONYX

Same specs as Model 626 except 12-, 20-ga.; 3-1/2-inch, 3-inch chambers; choke tubes; select hand-checkered European walnut stock, forearm. Introduced 1988; discontinued 1993.

Perf.: $1650   **Exc.:** $1250   **VGood:** $1000

BERETTA MODEL 627 EL

Side-by-side; boxlock; 12-, 20-ga.; 2-3/4-inch, 3-inch chambers; 26-inch, 28-inch barrels; fixed or Mobilchokes; front , center bead sights; concave matted barrel rib; fine-quality hand-checkered European walnut straight or pistol-grip stock, forend; coil springs; double underlugs, bolts; single trigger; auto safety ejectors; fine engraving; gold inlays on dummy sideplates; comes with case. Made in Italy. Introduced 1985; discontinued 1993.

Perf.: $2700   **Exc.:** $1600   **VGood:** $1400
Add 25 percent to above prices for 20 gauge
Subtract 5 percent from above prices for fixed choke and 2 ¾-inch chambers

BERETTA MODEL 627 EELL

Same specs as 627 EL except profuse engraving on dummy sideplates. Made in Italy. Introduced 1985; discontinued 1993.

Perf.: $4500   **Exc.:** $3000   **VGood:** $2700

BERETTA MODEL 470 SILVER HAWK SHOTGUN

Side-by-side; boxlock; 12-, 20-ga.; 3-inch chambers; 26-inch (Imp. Cyl. & Imp. Mod.), 28-inch (Mod. & Full) barrel; weighs 5.9 lbs. (20-gauge); select European walnut stock; straight English grip; single selective trigger; selector provides automatic ejection or extraction; silver-chrome action and forend iron with fine engraving; top lever highlighted with gold inlaid hawk's head. ABS case. Imported from Italy.

Perf.: $1950   **Exc.:** $1700   **VGood:** $1475
Add 15 percent to above prices for 20 gauge
Add $130 for multi-chokes

BERETTA SILVER HAWK FEATHERWEIGHT

Side-by-side; boxlock; 12-, 16-, 20-, 28-ga.; 26-inch to 32-inch barrels; all standard choke combos; matted rib; hand-checkered European walnut stock, beavertail forearm; plain extractors; double or nonselective single trigger. Introduced 1954; discontinued 1967.

Single trigger		
Exc.: $495	**VGood:** $440	**Good:** $413
Double triggers		
Exc.: $550	**VGood:** $495	**Good:** $440

BERETTA SILVER HAWK MAGNUM

Same specs as Silver Hawk Featherweight except 10- (3-1/2-inch), 12-ga. (3-inch); 30-inch, 32-inch barrels; chrome-plated bores; raised rib; recoil pad. Introduced 1954; discontinued 1967.

Single trigger		
Exc.: $495	**VGood:** $.450	**Good:** $395
Double triggers		
Exc.: $530	**VGood:** $500	**Good:** $450

BERETTA SO-6 SXS

Side-by-side; sidelock; 12-ga.; 26-inch, 30-inch barrels; any choke; walnut stock; ejectors; single selective trigger; entire gun made-to-order. No longer in production.

Perf.: $7200   **Exc.:** $6500   **VGood:** $5925

BERETTA SO-7 SXS

Side-by-side; sidelock; 12-ga.; 26-inch, 30-inch barrels; any choke; select walnut stock; ejectors; single selective trigger; entire gun made-to-order. No longer in production.

Exc.: $7950   **VGood:** $6875

Beretta Model 626

Beretta Model 470 Silver Hawk

Beretta Model SO-7 SXS

Beretta FS-1

Beretta Mark II

Beretta Silver Pigeon

BERETTA DT 10 TRIDENT TRAP TOP SINGLE SHOTGUN

Gauge: 12, 3-inch chamber; 34-inch barrel; five Optima Choke tubes (Full, Full Imp., Modified, Mod. and Imp. Cyl.); weighs 8.8 lbs.; high-grade walnut; adjustable stock;.detachable, adjustable trigger group; Optima Bore for improved shot pattern and reduced recoil; slim Optima Choke tubes; raised and thickened receiver for long life. Introduced 2000. Imported from Italy.

Perf.: $7550   **Exc.:** $6500   **VGood:** $5750

BERETTA FS-1

Single barrel; single shot; hammerless under-lever; 12-, 16-, 20-, 28-ga., .410; 26-inch (28-ga., .410), 28-inch (16-, 20-ga.), 30-inch barrel (12-ga.); Full choke; hand-checkered pistol-grip stock, forearm; folds to length of barrel; barrel release ahead of trigger guard. Advertised as the Companion. Introduced 1959; no longer in production.

Exc.: $175   **VGood:** $150   **Good:** $125

BERETTA GOLD PIGEON

Slide action; 12-ga.; 5-shot magazine; 26-inch, 30-inch, 32-inch vent-rib barrels; standard chokes; hand-checkered walnut pistol-grip stock, beavertail forearm; hand-polished, engine-turned bolt; gold trigger; moderate engraving; inlaid gold pigeon. Introduced 1959; discontinued 1966.

Exc.: $475   **VGood:** $375   **Good:** $310

BERETTA MARK II

Single shot; boxlock; 12-ga.; 32-inch, 34-inch barrel; wide vent rib; weighs about 8-3/8 lbs.; checkered European walnut Monte Carlo pistol-grip stock, beavertail forend; ejector; recoil pad. Introduced 1972; discontinued 1976.

Perf.: $550   **Exc.:** $450   **VGood:** $400

BERETTA MODEL 680 COMPETITION MONO TRAP

Single shot; boxlock; 12-ga.; 2-3/4-inch chamber; 32-inch, 34-inch barrel; ventilated rib; weighs about 8 lbs.; luminous front sight, center bead; hand-checkered European walnut Monte Carlo stock, forearm; automatic ejector; single trigger; deluxe trap recoil pad; silver finish. Introduced 1979; no longer in production.

Perf.: $1050   **Exc.:** $700   **VGood:** $650

BERETTA MODEL 680 COMPETITION TRAP

Same specs as Model 680 Competition Mono Trap except over/under; 29-1/2-inch Improved Modified/Full barrels. No longer imported.

Perf.: $1150   **Exc.:** $800   **VGood:** $710

BERETTA MODEL 680 COMPETITION TRAP COMBO

Same specs as Model 680 Competition Mono Trap except over/under; two-barrel set with 29-1/2-inch Improved Modified/Full over/under and 32-inch or 34-inch single over barrels. No longer in production.

Perf.: $1150   **Exc.:** $800   **VGood:** $700

BERETTA MODEL 680 COMPETITION SKEET

Same specs as Model 680 Competition Mono Trap except over/under; 28-inch Skeet/Skeet barrels; smooth recoil pad. No longer in production.

Perf.: $1150   **Exc.:** $800   **VGood:** $700

BERETTA RUBY PIGEON

Slide action; 12-ga.; 5-shot magazine; 26-inch, 30-inch, 32-inch vent-rib barrels; standard chokes; hand-checkered walnut pistol-grip stock, beavertail forearm; hand-polished, engine-turned bolt; gold trigger; elaborate engraving; inlaid gold pigeon with ruby eye. Introduced 1959; discontinued 1966.

Exc.: $600   **VGood:** $475   **Good:** $395

BERETTA SILVER PIGEON

Slide action; 12-ga.; 5-shot magazine; 26-inch, 30-inch, 32-inch barrels; standard chokes; hand-checkered walnut pistol-grip stock, beavertail forearm; hand-polished, engine-turned bolt; chromed trigger; light engraving; inlaid silver pigeon. Introduced 1959; discontinued 1966.

Exc.: $250   **VGood:** $200   **Good:** $175

Beretta SL-2

Bernardelli Model 115S Target

Bernardelli Model 190

Bernardelli Model 192

Bernardelli Model 220MS

Bernardelli Brescia

BERETTA SL-2

Slide action; 12-ga.; 3-shot magazine; 26-inch Improved, 28-inch Full or Modified, 30-inch Full barrels; vent rib; checkered European walnut stock, forend. Introduced 1968; discontinued 1971.

Exc.: $225 **VGood:** $175 **Good:** $150

BERETTA TR-1

Single shot; underlever; 12-ga.; 32-inch vent-rib barrel; checkered European walnut Monte Carlo pistol-grip stock, beavertail forend; engraved frame; recoil pad. Introduced 1968; discontinued 1971.

Exc.: $250 **VGood:** $165 **Good:** $110

BERETTA TR-2

Single shot; underlever; 12-ga.; 32-inch extended vent-rib barrel; checkered European walnut Monte Carlo pistol-grip stock, beavertail forend; engraved frame; recoil pad. Introduced 1968; discontinued 1972.

Exc.: $250 **VGood:** $165 **Good:** $110

BERNARDELLI OVER/UNDER SHOTGUNS

BERNARDELLI MODEL 115

Over/under; boxlock; 12-ga.; 2-3/4-inch chambers; 25-1/2-inch, 26-3/4-inch, 29-1/2-inch barrels; Multichokes or standard chokes; concave top rib, vented middle rib; specially designed anatomical grip stock for competition; schnabel forend; leather-faced recoil pad; inclined-plane locking; ejectors; selective or non-selective trigger. Made in Italy. Introduced 1989; discontinued 1991.

Perf.: $1770 **Exc.:** $1175 **VGood:** $950

BERNARDELLI MODEL 115E

Same specs as Model 115 except sideplates; engraving; silver finish.

Perf.: $4500 **Exc.:** $3525 **VGood:** $3000

BERNARDELLI MODEL 115L

Same specs as Model 115 except engraving; silver finish.

Perf.: $2600 **Exc.:** $2375 **VGood:** $2050

BERNARDELLI MODEL 115S

Same specs as Model 115 except engraving.

Perf.: $2150 **Exc.:** $1925 **VGood:** $1745

BERNARDELLI MODEL 115 TARGET

Same specs as Model 115 except configured for trap shooting. Introduced 1989; discontinued 1991.

Perf.: $1800 **Exc.:** $1595 **VGood:** $1375

BERNARDELLI MODEL 115E TARGET

Same specs as Model 115 Target except sideplates; engraving; silver finish.

Perf.: $5950 **Exc.:** $4800 **VGood:** $4125

BERNARDELLI MODEL 115L TARGET

Same specs as Model 115 Target except engraving; silver finish.

Perf.: $3700 **Exc.:** $2995 **VGood:** $2600

BERNARDELLI MODEL 115S TARGET

Same specs as Model 115 Target except engraving.

Perf.: $3275 **Exc.:** $2425 **VGood:** $1825

BERNARDELLI MODEL 115S TARGET MONOTRAP

Same specs as Model 115 Target except single barrel.

Perf.: $1550 **Exc.:** $1100 **VGood:** $900

BERNARDELLI MODEL 190

Over/under; 12-ga.; various barrel lengths; checkered walnut English straight or pistol-grip stock, forearm; ejectors; single selective trigger; silver finished receiver; engraving. Introduced 1986; discontinued 1989.

Perf.: $1400 **Exc.:** $900 **VGood:** $750

BERNARDELLI MODEL 190MC

Same specs as Model 190 except Monte Carlo stock.

Perf.: $1000 **Exc.:** $825 **VGood:** $700

BERNARDELLI MODEL 190 SPECIAL

Same specs as Model 190 except select walnut; elaborate engraving.

Perf.: $1335 **Exc.:** $1000 **VGood:** $895

BERNARDELLI MODEL 190 SPECIAL MS

Same specs as Model 190 except select walnut stock; single trigger; elaborate engraving.

Perf.: $1300 **Exc.:** $850 **VGood:** $750

BERNARDELLI MODEL 192

Over/under; boxlock; 12-ga.; 2-3/4-inch chambers; 25-1/2-inch, 26-3/4-inch, 28-inch, 29-1/2-inch barrels; standard choke combos or multichoke tubes; weighs 7 lbs.; hand-checkered European walnut English straight or pistol-grip stock; ejectors; single selective trigger silvered, engraved action. Made in Italy. Introduced 1989; still imported.

Perf.: $1175 **Exc.:** $895 **VGood:** $750

Add $65 to above prices for single trigger
Add $200 for choke tubes
Add $350 for Model 192 Special (includes double triggers and ejectors)

BERNARDELLI MODEL 192MS MC

Same specs as Model 192 except 3-inch chambers; five choke tubes. Introduced 1989; still imported.

Perf.: $1750 **Exc.:** $1200 **VGood:** $900

BERNARDELLI MODEL 192MS MC WF

Same specs as Model 192 except 3-1/2-inch chambers; three choke tubes. Introduced 1989; still imported.

Perf.: $1275 **Exc.:** $950 **VGood:** $875

BERNARDELLI MODEL 220MS

Over/under; boxlock; 12-, 20-ga.; 25-1/2-inch, 26-3/4-inch, 28-inch, 29-1/2-inch barrels; standard choke combos or multichoke tubes; hand-checkered walnut English straight or pistol-grip stock; ejectors; double triggers; silver-gray receiver with engraving. Made in Italy. Introduced 1989; still in production.

Perf.: $1350 **Exc.:** $995 **VGood:** $850

With selective trigger

Perf.: $1410 **Exc.:** $1050 **VGood:** $920

BERNARDELLI 9MM GARDEN GUN

Autoloader; rimfire 9mm Flobert shot cartridge; 3-shot magazine; 24-2/5-inch barrel; uncheckered walnut stock, forearm. Introduced 1987.

Perf.: $500 **Exc.:** $465 **VGood:** $325

BERNARDELLI BRESCIA

Side-by-side; sidelock; exposed hammer; 12-, 16-, 20-ga.; 2-3/4-inch, 3-inch chambers; 25-1/2-inch Cylinder/Modified or Improved Cylinder/Improved Modified, 26-3/4-inch Improved Cylinder/Improved Modified or Modified/Full, 29-1/2-inch Improved Modified/Full barrels; weighs about 7 lbs.; checkered European walnut English straight-grip stock; extractors; double triggers; color case-hardened action. Made in Italy. Introduced 1960; no longer imported.

Perf.: $2050 **Exc.:** $795 **VGood:** $600

BERNARDELLI ELIO

Side-by-side; boxlock; hammerless; 12-ga.; 25-inch Improved/Modified, 28-inch Modified/Full barrels; hand-checkered European walnut straight stock; double triggers; extractors; silver-finished receiver;

English-style scroll engraving; lightweight game model. Introduced 1970; no longer imported.

Perf.: $1200   **Exc.:** $900   **VGood:** $750

Elio E with ejectors
Perf.: $1250   **Exc.:** $950   **VGood:** $800

Elio M with single trigger
Perf.: $1250   **Exc.:** $950   **VGood:** $800

Elio EM
Perf.: $1300   **Exc.:** $1000   **VGood:** $850

BERNARDELLI GAMECOCK

Side-by-side; boxlock; hammerless; 12-, 16-, 20-, 28-ga.; 25-inch Improved/Modified, 28-inch Modified/Full barrels; hand-checkered European walnut straight stock; extractors; double triggers. Introduced 1970; no longer imported.

Perf.: $900   **Exc.:** $620   **VGood:** $580

With ejectors
Perf.: $1050   **Exc.:** $770   **VGood:** $620

With Deluxe engraving
Perf.: $1250   **Exc.:** $950   **VGood:** $800

BERNARDELLI HEMINGWAY

Side-by-side; boxlock; 12-, 16-, 20-, 28-ga; 2-3/4-inch, 3-inch chambers; 23-1/2-inch to 28-inch barrels; weighs 6-1/4 lbs.; European walnut stock; ejectors; front trigger folds on double-trigger; silvered, engraved action. Introduced 1990; dropped 1997.

Perf.: $2050   **Exc.:** $1500   **VGood:** $1050

With single trigger
Perf.: $2120   **Exc.:** $1570   **VGood:** $1120

With single selective trigger
Perf.: $2170   **Exc.:** $1620   **VGood:** $1170

BERNARDELLI HEMINGWAY DELUXE

Same specs as Hemingway except sideplates; select wood; elaborate engraving.

Perf.: $2350   **Exc.:** $1750   **VGood:** $1150

With single trigger
Perf.: $2475   **Exc.:** $1875   **VGood:** $1275

BERNARDELLI HOLLAND VB

Side-by-side; Holland & Holland-design sidelock; 12-ga.; 26-inch to 32-inch barrels; all standard choke combos; hand-checkered European walnut straight or pistol-grip stock, forearm; double triggers; automatic ejectors. Introduced 1946; discontinued 1992.

Liscio Model
Perf.: $10,350   **Exc.:** $5300   **VGood:** $4450

Inciso Model with engraving
Perf.: $10,700   **Exc.:** $7000   **VGood:** $5500

Lusso Model with engraving, select walnut
Perf.: $9000   **Exc.:** $7900   **VGood:** $6500

Extra Model with deluxe engraving, select wood
Perf.: $13,250   **Exc.:** $9700   **VGood:** $7450
Add $625 to above prices for single trigger
Add $1035 for engraving pattern No. 4
Add $4550 for engraving pattern No. 12
Add $9000 for engraving pattern No. 20

Gold Model
Perf.: $47,500   **Exc.:** $32,500   **VGood:** $24,000

BERNARDELLI ITALIA

Side-by-side; sidelock; exposed hammer; 12-, 16-, 20-ga.; 2-3/4-inch, 3-inch chambers; 25-1/2-inch Cylinder/Modified or Improved Cylinder/Improved Modified, 26-3/4-inch Improved Cylinder/Improved Modified or Modified/Full, 29-1/2-inch Improved Modified/Full barrels; weighs about 7 lbs.; checkered high-grade European walnut English straight-grip stock; profuse engraving. Made in Italy. Introduced 1990; no longer imported.

Perf.: $2275   **Exc.:** $1200   **VGood:** $900

BERNARDELLI ITALIA EXTRA

Same specs as Italia except highest grade of engraving and wood. Made in Italy. Introduced 1990; no longer imported.

Perf.: $6400   **Exc.:** $3150   **VGood:** $2200

Bernardelli Game Cock

Bernardelli Hemingway Deluxe

Bernardelli Holland VB Liscio

Bernardelli Holland VB Lusso

Bernardelli Holland VB Deluxe

Bernardelli Italia

walnut stock; extractors; double triggers. Made in Italy. Introduced 1989; discontinued 1989.

Perf.: $850   **Exc.:** $750   **VGood:** $675

Model 112E with engraving
Perf.: $995   **Exc.:** $850   **VGood:** $775

Model 112M with single trigger
Perf.: $925   **Exc.:** $825   **VGood:** $750

BERNARDELLI MODEL 112EM
Same specs as Model 112 except engraving; single trigger. Introduced 1989; dropped 1997.

Perf.: $1200   **Exc.:** $800   **VGood:** $650

BERNARDELLI MODEL 112EM MC
Same specs as Model 112EM except 3-inch chamber; 5 choke tubes; engraving; single trigger. Introduced 1990; discontinued 1992.

Perf.: $1600   **Exc.:** $1000   **VGood:** $850

BERNARDELLI MODEL 112EM MC WF
Same specs as Model 112EM except 3-1/2-inch chamber; 3 choke tubes; engraving; single trigger. Introduced 1990; discontinued 1991.

Perf.: $1275   **Exc.:** $975   **VGood:** $850

BERNARDELLI ROMA 3
Side-by-side; Anson & Deeley boxlock; false sideplates; hammerless; 12-, 16-, 20-, 28-ga.; 27-1/2-inch, 29-1/2-inch barrels; Modified/Full chokes; hand-checkered European walnut straight or pistol-grip stock, forearm; extractors; double triggers; color case-hardened receiver. Introduced 1946; dropped 1997.

Perf.: $1425   **Exc.:** $1200   **VGood:** $895

BERNARDELLI ROMA 3E
Same specs as Roma 3 except ejectors; dropped 1997.

Perf.: $1600   **Exc.:** $1325   **VGood:** $1050

BERNARDELLI ROMA 3EM
Same specs as Roma 3 except ejectors; single trigger. No longer in production.

Perf.: $1700   **Exc.:** $1400   **VGood:** $1125

BERNARDELLI ROMA 3M
Same specs as Roma 3 except single trigger. No longer in production.

Perf.: $1450   **Exc.:** $900   **VGood:** $775

BERNARDELLI ROMA 4
Side-by-side; Anson & Deeley boxlock; false sideplates; hammerless; 12-, 16-, 20-, 28-ga.; 27-1/2-inch, 29-1/2-inch barrels; Modified/Full chokes; hand-checkered European walnut straight or pistol-grip stock, forearm; extractors; double triggers; scroll engraving; silver finish; dropped 1989.

Perf.: $1550   **Exc.:** $900   **VGood:** $695

BERNARDELLI ROMA 4E
Same specs as Roma 4 except ejectors. Still in production.

Perf.: $1775   **Exc.:** $1475   **VGood:** $1150

BERNARDELLI ROMA 4EM
Same specs as Roma 4 except ejectors; single trigger. No longer in production.

Perf.: $1850   **Exc.:** $1550   **VGood:** $1250

BERNARDELLI ROMA 4M
Same specs as Roma 4 except single trigger; dropped 1989.

Perf.: $1650   **Exc.:** $1100   **VGood:** $975

BERNARDELLI ROMA 6
Side-by-side; Anson & Deeley boxlock; hammerless; 12-, 16-, 20-, 28-ga.; 27-1/2-inch, 29-1/2-inch barrels; Modified/Full chokes; hand-checkered European walnut straight or pistol-grip stock, forearm; extractors; double triggers; elaborate engraved sideplates; silver finish. Importation dropped 1989.

Perf.: $1700   **Exc.:** $1100   **VGood:** $900

Bernardelli Las Palomas

Bernardelli Model 112EM

Bernardelli Roma 3

Bernardelli Roma 4

Bernardelli Roma 6

BERNARDELLI LAS PALOMAS
Side-by-side; Anson & Deeley boxlock; 12-ga.; 2-3/4-inch chambers; 28-inch barrels bored for pigeon shooting; select European walnut stock; Australian pistol grip with shaped heel, palm swell; double trigger; special trigger guard; manual safety; auto safety optional; vent recoil pad; optional features. Made in Italy. Introduced 1984; dropped 1997.

Perf.: $3000   **Exc.:** $1850   **VGood:** $1600

Las Palomas M with single trigger
Perf.: $3600   **Exc.:** $2400   **VGood:** $2150

BERNARDELLI MODEL 112
Side-by-side; 12-ga.; Anson & Deeley boxlock; 12-ga.; 2-3/4-inch chambers; 25-5/8-inch, 26-3/4-inch, 28-inch, 29-1/8-inch barrels; Modified/Full; European

BERNARDELLI ROMA 6E
Same specs as Roma 6 except ejectors. Importation discontinued 1997.
Perf.: $2400   **Exc.:** $1825   **VGood:** $1475

BERNARDELLI ROMA 6EM
Same specs as Roma 6 except ejectors; single trigger. No longer in production.
Perf.: $2475   **Exc.:** $2000   **VGood:** $1550

BERNARDELLI ROMA 6M
Same specs as Roma 6 except single trigger. Importation discontinued 1989.
Perf.: $1850   **Exc.:** $1295   **VGood:** $1150

BERNARDELLI ROMA 7
Side-by-side; Anson & Deeley boxlock; hammerless; 12-ga.; 27-1/2-inch, 29-1/2-inch barrels; Modified/Full chokes; fancy hand-checkered European walnut straight or pistol-grip stock, forearm; ejectors; double triggers; elaborately engraved, silver-finished sideplates. Introduced 1994; dropped 1997.
Perf.: $3200   **Exc.:** $2200   **VGood:** $1675

BERNARDELLI ROMA 8
Side-by-side; Anson & Deeley boxlock; hammerless; 12-ga.; 27-1/2-inch, 29-1/2-inch barrels; Modified/Full chokes; fancy select hand-checkered European walnut straight or pistol-grip stock, forearm; ejectors; double triggers; elaborately engraved, silver-finished sideplates. Introduced 1994; dropped 1997.
Perf.: $3700   **Exc.:** $2700   **VGood:** $1950

BERNARDELLI ROMA 9
Side-by-side; Anson & Deeley boxlock; hammerless; 12-ga.; 27-1/2-inch, 29 1/2-inch barrels; Modified/Full chokes; best-grade hand-checkered European walnut straight or pistol-grip stock, forearm; ejectors; double triggers; very elaborately engraved, silver-finished sideplates. Introduced 1994; dropped 1997.
Perf.: $4550   **Exc.:** $3200   **VGood:** $2500

BERNARDELLI S. UBERTO 1
Side-by-side; Anson & Deeley-style boxlock; Purdey locks; 12-, 16-, 20-, 28-ga.; 2-3/4-inch, 3-inch chambers; 25-5/8-inch, 26-3/4-inch, 28-inch, 29-1/8-inch barrels; Modified/Full; select hand-checkered European walnut stock; extractors; double triggers; color case-hardened receiver. Made in Italy. Introduced 1946; discontinued 1990.
Perf.: $1050   **Exc.:** $950   **VGood:** $800

BERNARDELLI S UBERTO 1E
Same specs as S. Uberto 1 except ejectors. No longer in production.
Perf.: $1175   **Exc.:** $950   **VGood:** $850

BERNARDELLI S. UBERTO 1EM
Same specs as S. Uberto 1 except ejectors; single trigger. No longer in production.
Perf.: $1225   **Exc.:** $1020   **VGood:** $920

BERNARDELLI S. UBERTO 1M
Same specs as S. Uberto 1 except single trigger. No longer in production.
Perf.: $1050   **Exc.:** $800   **VGood:** $650

BERNARDELLI S. UBERTO 2
Side-by-side; Anson & Deeley-style boxlock; Purdey locks; 12-, 16-, 20-, 28-ga.; 2-3/4-inch, 3-inch chambers; 25-5/8-inch, 26-3/4-inch, 28-inch, 29-1/8-inch barrels; Modified/Full; select hand-checkered European walnut stock; extractors; double triggers; engraved, silver-finished receiver. Made in Italy. Introduced 1946; dropped 1997.
Perf.: $1375   **Exc.:** $1150   **VGood:** $875

BERNARDELLI S UBERTO 2E
Same specs as S. Uberto 2 except ejectors. No longer in production.
Perf.: $1525   **Exc.:** $1300   **VGood:** $1050

BERNARDELLI S. UBERTO 2EM
Same specs as S. Uberto 2 except ejectors; single trigger. No longer in production.
Perf.: $1600   **Exc.:** $1375   **VGood:** $1125

Bernardelli S. Uberto

Bernardelli S. Uberto 1

Bernardelli S. Uberto 2

Bernardelli S. Uberto FS

BERNARDELLI S. UBERTO 2M
Same specs as S. Uberto 2 except single trigger. No longer in production.
Perf.: $1410   **Exc.:** $1110   **VGood:** $910

BERNARDELLI S. UBERTO FS
Side-by-side; Anson & Deeley-style boxlock; Purdey locks; 12-, 16-, 20-, 28-ga.; 2-3/4-inch, 3-inch chambers; 25-5/8-inch, 26-3/4-inch, 28-inch, 29-1/8-inch barrels; Modified/Full; select hand-checkered European walnut stock; extractors; double triggers; elaborately engraved, silver-finished receiver. Made in Italy. Introduced 1987; no longer in production.
Perf.: $1695   **Exc.:** $1450   **VGood:** $1125

BERNARDELLI S UBERTO FSE
Same specs as S. Uberto FS except ejectors. Still in production.
Perf.: $1400   **Exc.:** $1100   **VGood:** $975

BERNARDELLI S. UBERTO FSEM
Same specs as S. Uberto FS except ejectors; single trigger. No longer in production.
Perf.: $1500   **Exc.:** $1165   **VGood:** $1025

BERNARDELLI S. UBERTO FSM
Same specs as S. Uberto FS except single trigger. No longer in production.
Perf.: $1760   **Exc.:** $1510   **VGood:** $1185

BERNARDELLI SLUG GUN
Side-by-side; Anson & Deeley boxlock; 12-ga.; 23-3/4-inch barrels; slug bores; walnut English straight or pistol-grip stock, forearm; extractors; double trigger; silver finished receiver; engraving. Discontinued 1990.
Perf.: $1325   **Exc.:** $1000   **VGood:** $895

BERNARDELLI SLUG LUSSO
Same specs as Slug Gun except ejectors; sideplates; elaborate engraving. Discontinued 1992.
Perf.: $2325   **Exc.:** $1550   **VGood:** $1200

BERNARDELLI SLUG LUSSO M
Same specs as Slug Gun single trigger; ejectors; sideplates; elaborate engraving. No longer in production.
Perf.: $2400   **Exc.:** $1625   **VGood:** $1265

BERNARDELLI SLUG M GUN
Same specs as Slug Gun except single trigger. No longer in production.
Perf.: $1495   **Exc.:** $1065   **VGood:** $970

BERNARDELLI XXVSL
Side-by-side; Holland & Holland-type sidelock; 12-ga.; 25-inch demi-block barrels; standard chokes; custom-fitted European walnut stock, classic or beavertail forend; selective ejectors; manual or auto safety; double sears; fitted luggage case. Made in Italy. Introduced 1982; discontinued 1984.
Perf.: $1700   **Exc.:** $1200   **VGood:** $800

Boss Over/Under

Breda Pegaso Hunter

Bretton Baby

Brno CZ-581

Brno Model 500

Brno Super

BOSS SIDE-BY-SIDE

Side-by-side; sidelock; 12-, 16-, 20-, 28-ga.; .410; 26-inch, 28-inch, 30-inch barrels; any desired choke combo; hand-checkered European walnut stock, forearm; straight or pistol-grip stock; automatic ejectors; double or non-selective single trigger; selective single trigger extra; round or flat action sides. Made to order. Introduced 1880; still in production.

> 12-ga.
> **Perf.:** $40,000 **Exc.:** $30,000 **VGood:** $20,000
> Smaller gauges
> **Perf.:** $45,000 **Exc.:** $35,000 **VGood:** $25,000

BOSS OVER/UNDER

Over/under; sidelock; 12-, 16-, 20-, 28-ga.; .410; 26-inch, 28-inch, 30-inch, 34-inch barrels; any desired choke combo; matted or vent rib; hand-checkered European walnut stock, forearm; recoil pad; automatic ejectors; double or non-selective single trigger; selective single trigger. Made to order. Introduced 1909; still in production.

> 12-ga.
> **Perf.:** $60,000 **Exc.:** $40,000 **VGood:** $30,000
> Smaller gauges
> **Perf.:** $65,000 **Exc.:** $45,000 **VGood:** $35,000

BREDA AUTOLOADER

Autoloader; takedown; 12-, 20-ga.; 4-shot tube magazine; 25-1/2-inch, 27-1/2-inch barrels; chrome bore; plain or with matted rib; hand-checkered European walnut straight or pistol-grip stock, forearm; available in 3 grades with chromed receivers, engraving. Grade, value depends upon amount of engraving, quality of wood. Made in Italy. Introduced 1946; no longer imported.

> Standard
> **Exc.:** $300 **VGood:** $275 **Good:** $255
> Grade I
> **Exc.:** $575 **VGood:** $530 **Good:** $485
> Grade II
> **Exc.:** $685 **VGood:** $620 **Good:** $560

> Grade III
> **Exc.:** $850 **VGood:** $790 **Good:** $700

BREDA AUTOLOADER MAGNUM 12

Same specs as Autoloader except 12-ga.; 3-inch chamber. Introduced 1950; no longer imported.

> Plain barrel
> **Exc.:** $470 **VGood:** $375 **Good:** $380
> Matte rib
> **Exc.:** $495 **VGood:** $355 **Good:** $395

BREDA VEGA SPECIAL

Over/under; box lock action; 12-, 20-ga.; 26-inch, 28-inch barrels; single trigger; ejectors; blue finish.
> **Exc.:** $575 **VGood:** $495 **Good:** $460

BREDA VEGA SPECIAL TRAP

Over/under; boxlock action; 12 ga.; trigger and lock designed for competition shooting; 30-inch, 32-inch barrels; single trigger; ejectors; blue finish. Still imported.
> **Exc.:** $885 **VGood:** $820 **Good:** $760

BREDA VEGA LUSSO

Over/under; scalloped boxlock action; 12 ga.; 3-inch chambers; SST; ejectors; 26-inch, 28-inch barrels; vent rib; coin finished receiver with light perimeter engraving; checkered Circassian walnut stock and forearm. Introduced 2001; dropped 2002.
> **Exc.:** $1695 **VGood:** $820 **Good:** $760

BREDA SIRIO STANDARD

Over/under; box lock action; 12-, 20-ga.; 26-inch, 28-inch barrels; single trigger; ejectors; action extensively engraved; blue finish. Also available in skeet configuration (28-inch barrels).
> **Exc.:** $2000 **VGood:** $1850 **Good:** $1630

BREDA PEGASO HUNTER

Over/under; boxlock action; 12-, 20-ga.; 3-inch chambers; 26-inch, 28-inch (12 ga. Only), 30-inch (Sporting Clays only); vent rib barrels with 7mm (Hunter) or 11mm (sporting Clays) rib; 5

interchangable chokes; removable trigger group; engraved silver steel (Hunter Model) or blue finished (Sporting Clays), inertia SST; oil finished deluxe walnut stock and forearm; weighs 7 – 7-1/2 lbs.. Importation began 2004.
> **Exc.:** $2739 **VGood:** $2400 **Good:** $2050

BREDA PEGASO SPORTING CLAYS

Similar to Pegaso Hunter, except 12 ga. Only; upgraded wood; Breda logos in 24 Kt. Gold; supplied with ABS fitted case. Importation began 2004.
> **Exc.:** $3300 **VGood:** $2875 **Good:** $2400

BREDA ANDROMEDA SPECIAL

Side-by-side; 12 ga. Only; single trigger; ejectors; select checkered walnut; satin finished receiver with elaborate engraving.
> **Exc.:** $640 **VGood:** $550 **Good:** $480

BRETTON BABY

Over/under; 12-, 20-ga.; 2-3/4-inch chambers; 27-1/2-inch barrels; standard choke tubes; weighs 5 lbs.; oil-finished checkered European walnut stock; receiver slides open on guide rods, locks with thumblever; extractors. Made in France. Introduced 1986; still in production.
> **Perf.:** $995 **Exc.:** $885 **VGood:** $700

BRETTON BABY DELUXE

Same specs as Bretton Baby except 12-, 16-, 20-ga.; double triggers; silvered engraved receiver. Discontinued 1994.
> **Perf.:** $1050 **Exc.:** $925 **VGood:** $800

BRETTON SPRINT DELUXE

Over/under; sliding breech; 12-, 16 (disc.), 20-ga.; engraved coin finished receiver; 27-1/2-inch separated barrels; deluxe checkered walnut stock and forearm; weighs 4.8 lbs.; Importation discontinued 1994.
> **Perf.:** $895 **Exc.:** $725 **VGood:** $625

BRETTON FAIR PLAY

Similar to Sprint deluxe, except that action pivots like a normal O/U; 12-, 20 ga.; 27-1/2-inch separated barrels; weighs 4.8 lbs.; No longer imported.
> **Perf.:** $966 **Exc.:** $850 **VGood:** $675

BRI SPECIAL MODEL

Slide action; 12-ga.; 3-inch chamber; 24-inch rifled Cylinder barrel; 44-inch overall length; weighs 7-1/2 lbs.; no sights; scope mount on barrel; high, straight comb walnut stock; rubber recoil pad; built on Mossberg Model 500 Trophy Slugster action. Made by Ballistic Research Industries. Introduced, 1988; discontinued, 1990.
> **Perf.:** $300 **Exc.:** $225 **VGood:** $180

BRNO CZ-581

Over/under; boxlock; 12-ga.; 2-3/4-inch chambers; 28-inch barrels; vent rib; 45-1/2-inch overall length; weighs 7-1/3 lbs.; Turkish walnut stock; raised cheekpiece; auto safety; sling swivels; selective ejectors; double triggers. Made in Czechoslovakia. Introduced 1986; discontinued 1991.
> **Perf.:** $550 **Exc.:** $425 **VGood:** $350

BRNO MODEL 500

Over/under; boxlock; 2-3/4-inch chambers; 27-inch Full/Modified barrels; weighs 7 lbs.; European walnut raised cheekpiece stock; ejectors; double triggers; acid-etched engraving. Made in Czechoslovakia. Introduced 1987; discontinued 1991.
> **Perf.:** $845 **Exc.:** $725 **VGood:** $625
> Add $50 to above prices for single trigger (disc. 1999)

BRNO SUPER

Over/under; sidelock; 12-ga.; 2-3/4-inch chambers; 27-1/2-inch Full/Modified barrels; weighs 7-1/4 lbs.; European walnut raised cheekpiece stock; double safety interceptor sears; selective ejectors; double or single triggers; engraved sideplates. Made in Czechoslovakia. Introduced 1987; discontinued 1991.
> **Perf.:** $800 **Exc.:** $700 **VGood:** $640

BRNO ZBK 100 SINGLE BARREL SHOTGUN

Gauge: 12 or 20. Barrel: 27.5-inch. Weight: 5.5 lbs. Length: 44-inch overall. Stock: Beech. Features: Polished blue finish; sling swivels. Announced 1998. Imported from The Czech Republic by Euro-Imports.

Perf.: $180   **Exc.:** $160   **VGood:** $140

BRNO ZH-301 SERIES

Over/under; boxlock; 12-ga.; 2-3/4-inch chambers; 27-1/2-inch barrels; Modified/Full; weighs 7 lbs.; European walnut stock; double triggers; acid-etched engraving. Made in Czechoslovakia. Introduced 1987; discontinued 1991.

Brno ZH-301 Field
Perf.: $600   **Exc.:** $475   **VGood:** $375

Brno ZH-302 Skeet with 26-inch Skeet/Skeet barrels
Perf.: $650   **Exc.:** $515   **VGood:** $375

Brno ZH-303 Trap with 30-inch barrels
Perf.: $600   **Exc.:** $450   **VGood:** $350

BRNO ZH 300 OVER/UNDER SHOTGUN

Gauge: 12, 2-3/4-inch chambers. Barrel: 26-inch, 27-1/2-inch, 29-inch (Skeet, Imp. Cyl., Mod., Full). Weight: 7 lbs. Length: 44.4-inch overall. Stock: European walnut. Features: Double triggers; automatic safety; polished blue finish engraved receiver. Announced 1998. Imported from the Czech Republic by Euro-Imports.

ZH 301, Field
Perf.: $600   **Exc.:** $475   **VGood:** $395

ZH 302, Skeet
Perf.: $650   **Exc.:** $515   **VGood:** $375

ZH 303, 12 ga. Trap
Perf.: $650   **Exc.:** $515   **VGood:** $375

ZH 321, 16 ga.
Perf.: $600   **Exc.:** $475   **VGood:** $375
Add $20 to above prices for Monte Carlo stock

BRNO ZP-49

Side-by-side; sidelock; 12-ga.; 2-3/4-inch chambers; 28-1/2-inch Full/Modified barrels; Turkish or Yugoslavian walnut straight or pistol-grip stock; barrel indicators; ejectors; double triggers; auto safety; sling swivels. Introduced 1986; discontinued 1994.

Perf.: $535   **Exc.:** $.460   **VGood:** $420

BRNO ZP-149

Side-by-side; sidelock; 12-ga.; 2-3/4-inch chambers; 28-1/2-inch Full/Modified barrels; weighs 7-1/4 lbs.; Turkish or Yugoslavian walnut straight or pistol-grip stock; raised cheekpiece; barrel indicators; ejectors; double triggers; auto safety; engraving available. Made in Czechoslovakia. Introduced 1986; discontinued 1991.

Perf.: $575   **Exc.:** $495   **VGood:** $425

With engraving
Perf.: $550   **Exc.:** $450   **VGood:** $350
Add $25 to above prices for pistol grip stock

BRNO ZP-349

Side-by-side; sidelock; 12-ga.; 2-3/4-inch chambers; 28-1/2-inch Full/Modified barrels; weighs 7-1/4 lbs.; Turkish or Yugoslavian walnut straight or pistol-grip stock, beavertail forearm; raised cheekpiece; barrel indicators; extractors; double triggers; auto safety; engraving available. Made in Czechoslovakia. Introduced 1986; discontinued 1991.

Perf.: $450   **Exc.:** $390   **VGood:** $360

With engraving
Perf.: $470   **Exc.:** $410   **VGood:** $380

BRNO 501.2 OVER/UNDER SHOTGUN

Gauge: 12, 2-3/4-inch chambers. Barrel: 27.5-inch (Full & Mod.). Weight: 7 lbs. Length: 44-inch overall. Stock: European walnut. Features: Boxlock action with double triggers, ejectors; automatic safety; hand-cut checkering. Announced 1998. Imported from The Czech Republic by Euro-Imports.

Perf.: $845   **Exc.:** $725   **VGood:** $625

Brno ZH-301 Series

Brno ZP-149

Browning A-500

Browning A-500G

Browning Auto-5 American Grade I (1940-1949)

BROWNING A-500G

Gas-operated autoloader; 12-ga.; 3-inch chamber; 26-inch, 28-inch, 30-inch interchangeable barrel with Invector choke tubes; ventilated rib; weighs 7-3/4 lbs.; 47-1/2-inch overall length; select walnut rounded pistol-grip stock with gloss finish; recoil pad; four-lug rotary bolt; crossbolt safety; patented gas metering system to handle all loads; built-in buffering system to absorb recoil, reduce stress on internal parts; high-polish blue finish with light engraving on receiver and "A-500G" in gold color. Made in Japan. Introduced 1990; discontinued 1993.

Perf.: $555   **Exc.:** $425   **VGood:** $375

BROWNING A-500G BUCK SPECIAL

Same specs as A-500G except 24-inch barrel; 45-1/2-inch overall length; weighs 7-3/4 lbs.; screw adjustable rear sight, countoured ramp front with gold bead. Made in Japan. Introduced 1990; discontinued 1992.

Perf.: $540   **Exc.:** $395   **VGood:** $350

BROWNING A-500G SPORTING CLAYS

Same specs as A-500G except 28-inch, 30-inch Invector choke barrel; receiver has semi-gloss finish with "Sporting Clays" in gold lettering. Made in Japan. Introduced 1992; discontinued 1993.

Perf.: $555   **Exc.:** $425   **VGood:** $375

BROWNING A-500R

Short-recoil autoloader; 12-ga.; 3-inch chamber; 26-inch, 28-inch, 30-inch barrel; Invector choke tubes; weighs about 7-1/2 lbs.; select walnut pistol-grip stock, forend with gloss finish; black ventilated recoil pad; four-lug rotary bolt; composite and coil spring buffering system; shoots all loads without adjustment; magazine cut-off. Made in Belgium. Introduced 1987; discontinued 1993.

Perf.: $475   **Exc.:** $425   **VGood:** $375

BROWNING A-500R BUCK SPECIAL

Same specs as A-500R except 24-inch barrel; ramp front sight, open adjustable rear. Made in Belgium. Introduced 1987; discontinued 1993.

Perf.: $510   **Exc.:** $460   **VGood:** $410

BROWNING AUTO-5 (1900-1940)

Recoil-operated autoloader; takedown; 12-, 16-ga.; 3- (pre-WWII), 4-shot magazine; 26-inch to 32-inch barrels; various chokes; plain barrel, vent or raised matted rib; hand-checkered European walnut pistol-grip stock, forearm. Made by FN. Introduced 1900; has been made in a wide variety of configurations grades and gauges; redesignated as Grade I in 1940. Deduct 25 percent for "suicide safety" inset into the front end of the trigger guard.

With plain barrel
Exc.: $675   **VGood:** $575   **Good:** $475

With raised rib
Exc.: $750   **VGood:** $675   **Good:** $575

With ventilated rib
Exc.: $825   **VGood:** $725   **Good:** $650

BROWNING AUTO-5 (1900-1940) GRADE III

Same specs as Auto-5 (1900-1940) except better wood, checkering and more engraving. Discontinued 1940.

Exc.: $2350   **VGood:** $2100   **Good:** $1900

With raised matted rib
Exc.: $2500   **VGood:** $2250   **Good:** $2050

With ventilated rib
Exc.: $2795   **VGood:** $2475   **Good:** $2225

BROWNING AUTO-5 (1900-1940) GRADE IV

Same specs as Auto-5 (1900-1940) except better wood, checkering and engraving; profuse inlays of green, yellow gold. Sometimes called Midas Grade. Discontinued 1940.

Exc.: $3655   **VGood:** $3300   **Good:** $2995

With raised matted rib
Exc.: $3995   **VGood:** $3655   **Good:** $3300

BROWNING AUTO-5 AMERICAN GRADE I (1940-1949)

Autoloader; 12-, 16-, 20-ga.; 2-3/4-inch chamber; 3-, 5-shot tube magazine; 26-inch, 28-inch, 30-inch, 32-inch barrel; standard chokes; no rib; weighs 6-7/8

Browning Auto-5 American Utility Field Model (1940-1949)

Browning Auto-5 Belgium Standard (1947-1953)

Browning Auto-5 Classic

Browning Auto-5 Classic Gold

Browning Auto-5 Light Buck Special (Miroku)

Browning Auto-5 Light Sweet 16 (FN)

lbs. (20-ga.), 7-1/4 lbs. (16-ga.), 8 lbs. (12-ga.); hand-checkered American walnut pistol-grip stock, forend; identical to the Remington Model 11A; manufactured by Remington for Browning. Introduced 1940; discontinued 1949.

Exc.: $495   **VGood:** $395   **Good:** $350
Add 10 percent to above prices for vent. Rib or 20 ga.

BROWNING AUTO-5 AMERICAN SPECIAL (1940-1949)
Same specs as Auto-5 American Grade I (1940-1949) except either ventilated rib or matted raised rib. Introduced 1940; discontinued 1949.

With ventilated rib		
Exc.: $375	**VGood:** $320	**Good:** $290
With raised rib		
Exc.: $360	**VGood:** $300	**Good:** $280

BROWNING AUTO-5 AMERICAN SPECIAL SKEET (1940-1949)
Same specs as Auto-5 American Grade I (1940-1949) except 26-inch barrel; ventilated rib; Cutts Compensator. Introduced 1940; discontinued 1949.

Exc.: $375   **VGood:** $325   **Good:** $295

BROWNING AUTO-5 AMERICAN UTILITY FIELD MODEL (1940-1949)
Same specs as Auto-5 American Grade I (1940-1949) except 28-inch barrel; PolyChoke. Introduced 1940; discontinued 1949.

Exc.: $395   **VGood:** $255   **Good:** $220

BROWNING AUTO-5 BELGIUM STANDARD (1947-1953)
Autoloader; 12-, 16-ga.; 3-, 5-shot magazine; 2-3/4-inch chambers; 26-inch, 28-inch, 30-inch, 32-inch barrel; standard choke tubes; plain, matted or ventilated rib; weighs 8 lbs.; hand-checkered French

walnut stock with high-gloss finish; hand-engraved receiver. Introduced 1947; discontinued 1953.

With plain barrel		
Exc.: $595	**VGood:** $425	**Good:** $375
With hollow matted rib		
Exc.: $680	**VGood:** $335	**Good:** $315
With ventilated rib		
Exc.: $695	**VGood:** $550	**Good:** $500

BROWNING AUTO-5 CLASSIC
Autoloader; 12-ga.; 2-3/4-inch chamber; 5-shot magazine with 3-shot plug furnished; 28-inch Modified barrel; select figured walnut stock; special checkering; hunting, wildlife scenes engraved in satin gray receiver; engraved portrait of John M. Browning; engraved legend, "Browning Classic. One of Five Thousand." Only 5000 manufactured. Introduced 1984; discontinued 1984.

Exc.: $1195   **VGood:** $945   **Good:** $725

BROWNING AUTO-5 CLASSIC GOLD
Same specs as Auto-5 Classic except engraved scenes are inlaid with gold animals portrait; engraved with "Browning Gold Classic One of Five Hundred." Only 500 made. Introduced 1984; discontinued 1984.

Perf.: $4195   **Exc.:** $3495   **VGood:** $2495

BROWNING AUTO-5 LIGHT (FN)
Autoloader; 12-, 20-ga.; 2-3/4-inch chamber; 5-shot magazine with 3-shot plug furnished; 26-inch, 28-inch, 30-inch barrel; standard chokes; checkered walnut pistol-grip stock, forend; hand-engraved receiver; gold-plated trigger; double extractors; interchangeable barrels; with or without ventilated rib. Made by FN Belgium. Introduced 1952; discontinued 1976.

Without rib		
Perf.: $650	**Exc.:** $550	**VGood:** $450
With ventilated rib		
Perf.: $950	**Exc.:** $795	**VGood:** $645

BROWNING AUTO-5 LIGHT (MIROKU)
Same specs as Auto-5 Light (FN) except ventilated rib; Invector choke tubes. Made by Miroku of Japan. Introduced 1976.

Perf.: $775   **Exc.:** $595   **VGood:** $525

BROWNING AUTO-5 LIGHT BUCK SPECIAL (MIROKU)
Same specs as Auto-5 Light (FN) except 24-inch barrel; choked for slugs; vent rib; adjustable rear sight, gold bead front on contoured ramp; detachable swivels, sling optional on current model. Made by Miroku of Japan. Introduced 1976; discontinued 1985; reintroduced 1989.

Perf.: $700   **Exc.:** $400   **VGood:** $350

BROWNING AUTO-5 LIGHT SKEET (FN)
Same specs as the Auto-5 Light (FN) except for 26-inch, 28-inch Skeet/Skeet barrel; plain barrel or vent rib (late models). Made by FN Belgium. Introduced 1952; discontinued 1976.

Perf.: $675   **Exc.:** $575   **VGood:** $400

BROWNING AUTO-5 LIGHT SKEET (MIROKU)
Same specs as the Auto-5 Light (FN) except for 26-inch, 28-inch Skeet/Skeet barrel; vent rib. Made by Miroku of Japan. Introduced 1976; discontinued 1983.

Perf.: $650   **Exc.:** $585   **VGood:** $400

BROWNING AUTO-5 LIGHT STALKER
Same specs as Auto-5 Light (FN) except 12-ga.; 2-3/4-inch chamber; 26-inch, 28-inch vent-rib barrel; Invector choke tubes; weighs 8 lbs. (26-inch); black graphite-fiberglass stock, forend with checkered panels; matte blue metal finish. Made by Miroku of Japan. Introduced 1992.

Perf.: $650   **Exc.:** $595   **VGood:** $425

BROWNING AUTO-5 SWEET 16 (FN)
Same specs as Auto-5 (FN) except 16-ga.; 2-9/16-inch, 2-3/4-inch chamber; weighs 6-3/4 lbs. (without rib); gold-plated trigger, safety, safety latch. Introduced 1937; discontinued 1976. Deduct 10 percent for suicide safety.

Without rib		
Exc.: $860	**VGood:** $660	**Good:** $600
With hollow matted rib		
Exc.: $1295	**VGood:** $995	**Good:** $825
With ventilated rib		
Exc.: $1595	**VGood:** $1295	**Good:** $950

BROWNING AUTO-5 SWEET 16 (MIROKU)
Same specs as Auto-5 (FN) except 16-ga.; 2-3/4-inch chamber; Invector chokes; vent rib; weighs 7-1/4 lbs. Made by Miroku of Japan. Introduced 1987; discontinued 1992.

Perf.: $1295   **Exc.:** $925   **VGood:** $850

BROWNING AUTO-5 TRAP (FN)
Same specs as Auto-5 Light (FN) except 12-ga.; 30-inch Full barrel; vent rib; weighs 8-1/4 lbs.; trap stock. Made by FN Belgium. Discontinued 1971.

Exc.: $850   **VGood:** $665   **Good:** $625

BROWNING AUTO-5 MAGNUM (FN)
Autoloader; 12-, 20-ga.; 3-inch chamber; 26-inch, 28-inch, 30-inch, 32-inch barrels; Full, Modified, Improved Cylinder chokes; plain or vent-rib; checkered walnut pistol-grip stock, forend; recoil pad. Made by FN Belgium. Introduced 1958; discontinued 1976.

With plain barrel		
Perf.: $725	**Exc.:** $650	**VGood:** $550
With ventilated rib		
Perf.: $825	**Exc.:** $795	**VGood:** $695

BROWNING AUTO-5 MAGNUM (MIROKU)

Same specs as Auto-5 Magnum (FN) except 26-inch, 28-inch barrel; Invector choke tubes. Made by Miroku of Japan. Introduced 1976.

Perf.: $825   **Exc.:** $650   **VGood:** $595

BROWNING AUTO-5 MAGNUM STALKER

Same specs as the Auto-5 Magnum (FN) except 26-inch, 28-inch back-bored vent-rib barrel; Invector choke tubes; weighs 8-3/4 lbs. (28-inch); black graphite-fiberglass stock, forend with checkered panels; matte blue metal finish. Made by Miroku of Japan. Introduced 1992.

Perf.: $750   **Exc.:** $650   **VGood:** $400

BROWNING B-80

Autoloader; 12-, 20-ga.; 2-3/4-inch, 3-inch chamber; 5-shot magazine; 22-inch slug barrel, 26-inch Improved Cylinder, Cylinder, Cylinder Skeet, Full, Modified, 28-inch Full, Modified, 30-inch Full, 32-inch Full choke barrels; ventilated rib; hand-checkered French walnut stock; solid black recoil pad; steel receiver; interchangeable barrels. Made in Belgium. Introduced 1981; discontinued 1989.

Perf.: $425   **Exc.:** $300   **VGood:** $275

BROWNING B-80 UPLAND SPECIAL

Same specs as B-80 except 2-3/4-inch chamber; 22-inch barrel; hand-checkered French walnut straight-grip stock. Made in Belgium. Introduced 1986; discontinued 1989.

Perf.: $450   **Exc.:** $320   **VGood:** $290

BROWNING B-2000

Autoloader; 12-, 20-ga.; 2-3/4-inch chamber; 4-shot magazine; 26-inch, 28-inch, 30-inch barrel; choice of standard chokes; vent rib or plain matted barrel; checkered pistol-grip stock of European walnut. Manufactured in Belgium, assembled in Portugal. Introduced 1974; discontinued 1982.

Perf.: $345   **Exc.:** $280   **VGood:** $240

BROWNING B-2000 BUCK SPECIAL

Same specs as B-2000 except 12- (2-3/4-inch), 20-ga. (3-inch); 24-inch slug barrel; no rib; open rear sight, front ramp. Introduced 1974; discontinued 1982.

Perf.: $350   **Exc.:** $280   **VGood:** $250

BROWNING B-2000 MAGNUM

Same specs as B-2000 except 3-inch chamber; 3-shot magazine; 26-inch, 28-inch, 30-inch, 32-inch barrel; vent rib. Introduced 1974; discontinued 1982.

Perf.: $350   **Exc.:** $300   **VGood:** $275

BROWNING B-2000 SKEET

Same specs as B-2000 except 26-inch Skeet-choke barrel; Skeet stock; recoil pad. Introduced 1974; discontinued 1982.

Perf.: $350   **Exc.:** $290   **VGood:** $260

BROWNING B-2000 TRAP

Same specs as B-2000 except 12-ga.; 2-3/4-inch chamber; 30-inch, 32-inch barrel; high post vent rib; Modified, Improved, Full chokes; Monte Carlo-style stock; recoil pad. Introduced 1974; discontinued 1982.

Perf.: $350   **Exc.:** $290   **VGood:** $260

BROWNING DOUBLE AUTO

Short-recoil autoloader; takedown; 12-ga.; 2-shot magazine; 26-inch, 28-inch, 30-inch barrel; any standard choke; plain or recessed rib barrel; weighs about 7-3/4 lbs; hand-checkered European walnut pistol-grip stock, forearm; steel receiver; conservative engraving. Introduced 1955; discontinued 1961.

Exc.: $650   **VGood:** $525   **Good:** $450

With ventilated rib

Exc.: $750   **VGood:** $550   **Good:** $475

BROWNING DOUBLE AUTO TWELVETTE

Same specs as Double Auto except aluminum receiver; barrel with plain matted top or vent rib; black anodized receiver with gold-wiped engraving; some receivers anodized in brown, gray or green with silver-wiped engraving; weighs about a pound less than standard model. Introduced 1955; discontinued 1971.

Exc.: $650   **VGood:** $525   **Good:** $450

With ventilated rib

Exc.: $750   **VGood:** $650   **Good:** $575

BROWNING DOUBLE AUTO TWENTYWEIGHT

Same specs as Double Auto except 26-1/2-inch barrel; weighs almost 2 lbs. less, largely due to thinner stock. Introduced 1956; discontinued 1971.

Exc.: $650   **VGood:** $525   **Good:** $450

With ventilated rib

Exc.: $825   **VGood:** $735   **Good:** $625

BROWNING GOLD

Gas-operated autoloader; 12-, 20-ga; 3-inch chamber; 4-shot magazine; 26-inch, 28-inch, 30-inch back-bored (12-ga.) or 26-inch, 30-inch (20-ga.) barrel; Invector choke tubes; weighs about 7-5/8 lbs. (12-ga.); cut-checkered select walnut stock,

Browning Auto-5 Magnum (FN)

Browning Auto-5 Magnum Stalker

Browning B-80

Browning B-80 Upland Special

Browning B-2000

Browning B-2000 Skeet

Browning B-2000 Trap

Browning Double Auto

Browning Double Auto Twelvette

Browning Double Auto Twentyweight

Browning Gold

Browning Gold Deer Stalker

Browning Gold Sporting Clays

Browning Gold Ladies/Youth Sporting Clays

Browning Gold Micro

Browning Gold Stalker

Browning Gold Mossy Oak Break-Up

Browning Gold Classic Hunter

Browning Gold Classic Stalker

palm swell grip with gloss finish; self-regulating, self-cleaning gas system shoots all loads; lightweight receiver with special non-glare deep black finish; large reversible safety button; large rounded trigger guard, gold trigger; crossbolt safety; recoil pad. Made in Japan. Introduced 1994; still imported.

Perf.: $660   Exc.: $340   VGood: $300

Price: 12 ga., 3-1/2-inch chamber		
Perf.: $895	**Exc.: $725**	**VGood: $625**

BROWNING GOLD RIFLED DEER HUNTER AUTO SHOTGUN
Similar to the Gold Hunter except 12- or 20-gauge, 22-inch rifled barrel with cantilever scope mount, walnut stock with extra-thick recoil pad. Weighs 7 lbs., 12 oz., overall length 42-1/2-inch. Sling swivel studs fitted on the magazine cap and butt. Introduced 1997. Imported by Browning.

12-gauge		
Perf.: $860	**Exc.: $625**	**VGood: $525**
With Mossy Oak Break-up camouflage		
Perf.: $945	**Exc.: $745**	**VGood: $610**

20-gauge (satin-finish walnut stock, 3-inch chamber)		
Perf.: $875	**Exc.: $695**	**VGood: $600**

BROWNING GOLD DEER STALKER
Similar to the Gold Deer Hunter except has black composite stock and forend, fully rifled 12-gauge barrel, cantilever scope mount. Introduced 1999. Imported by Browning.

Perf.: $755   Exc.: $550   VGood: $450

BROWNING GOLD SPORTING CLAYS AUTO
Similar to the Gold Hunter except 12-gauge only with 28-inch or 30-inch barrel; front Hi-Viz Pro-Comp and center bead on tapered ventilated rib; ported and back-bored Invector Plus barrel; 2-3/4-inch chamber; satin-finished stock with solid, radiused recoil pad with hard heel insert; non-glare black alloy receiver has "Sporting Clays" inscribed in gold. Introduced 1996. Imported from Japan.

Perf.: $825   Exc.: $570   VGood: $460

BROWNING GOLD SPORTING GOLDEN CLAYS
Similar to the Sporting Clays except has silvered receiver with gold engraving, high-grade wood. Introduced 1999. Imported by Browning.

Perf.: $1275   Exc.: $1025   VGood: $840

BROWNING GOLD LADIES/YOUTH SPORTING CLAYS AUTO
Similar to the Gold Sporting Clays except has stock dimensions of 14-1/4-inch by 1-3/4-inch by 2-inch for women and younger shooters. Introduced 1999. Imported by Browning.

Perf.: $780   Exc.: $550   VGood: $455

BROWNING GOLD MICRO AUTO SHOTGUN
Similar to the Gold Hunter except has a 26-inch barrel, 13-7/8-inch pull length and smaller pistol grip for youths and other small shooters. Weighs 6 lbs., 10 oz. Introduced 2001.

Perf.: $780   Exc.: $550   VGood: $435

BROWNING GOLD STALKER AUTO SHOTGUNS
Similar to the Gold Hunter except has black composite stock and forend. Choice of 3-inch or 3-1/2-inch chamber.

12 ga. with 3-inch chamber		
Perf.: $755	**Exc.: $550**	**VGood: $430**
With 3-1/2-inch chamber		
Perf.: $765	**Exc.: $565**	**VGood: $950**

BROWNING GOLD MOSSY OAK® SHADOW GRASS SHOTGUNS
Similar to the Gold Hunter except 12-gauge only, completely covered with Mossy Oak Shadow Grass camouflage. Choice of 3-inch or 3-1/2-inch chamber and 26-inch or 28-inch barrel. Introduced 1999. Imported by Browning.

12 ga. 3-inch chamber		
Perf.: $1035	**Exc.: $800**	**VGood: $675**
12 ga., 3-1/2-inch chamber		
Perf.: $1075	**Exc.: $870**	**VGood: $750**

BROWNING GOLD MOSSY OAK® BREAK-UP SHOTGUNS
Similar to the Gold Hunter except 12-gauge only, completely covered with Mossy Oak Break-Up camouflage. Imported by Browning.

3-inch chamber		
Perf.: $855	**Exc.: $585**	**VGood: $475**
3-1/2-inch chamber		
Perf.: $875	**Exc.: $635**	**VGood: $500**
NWTF model, 3-inch chamber, 24-inch bbl. with Hi-Viz sight		
Perf.: $885	**Exc.: $610**	**VGood: $495**
NWTF model, 3-1/2-inch chamber, 24-inch bbl. with Hi-Viz sight.		
Perf.: $950	**Exc.: $700**	**VGood: $600**
Gold Rifled Deer (22-inch rifled bbl., cantilever scope mount)		
Perf.: $795	**Exc.: $565**	**VGood: $455**

BROWNING GOLD CLASSIC HUNTER AUTO SHOTGUN
Similar to the Gold Hunter 3-inch except has semi-hump back receiver, magazine cut-off, adjustable comb, and satin-finish wood. Introduced 1999. Imported by Browning.

12 or 20 gauge		
Perf.: $780	**Exc.: $550**	**VGood: $435**
Classic High Grade (silvered, gold engraved receiver, high-grade wood)		
Perf.: $1575	**Exc.: $1250**	**VGood: $1050**

BROWNING GOLD CLASSIC STALKER
Similar to the Gold Classic Hunter except has adjustable composite stock and forend. Introduced 1999. Imported by Browning.

Perf.: $725   Exc.: $530   VGood: $430

BROWNING GOLD FUSION AUTO SHOTGUN

Similar to the Gold Hunter except is 1/2 lb. lighter, has a new-style vent rib, adjustable comb system, Hi-Viz Pro-Comp front sight and five choke tubes. Offered with 26-inch, 28-inch or 30-inch barrel, 12-gauge, 3-inch chamber only. Includes hard case. Introduced 2001. Imported by Browning.

Perf.: $865   **Exc.:** $600   **VGood:** $475

BROWNING NWTF GOLD TURKEY STALKER

Similar to the Gold Hunter except 12-ga., 3-inch chamber only, has 24-inch barrel with Hi-Viz front sight and National Wild Turkey Federation logo on stock. Imported by Browning.

Perf.: $710   **Exc.:** $525   **VGood:** $425

BROWNING GOLD TURKEY/ WATERFOWL CAMO SHOTGUN

Similar to the Gold Turkey/Waterfowl Hunter except 12-gauge only, 3-inch or 3-1/2-inch chamber, 24-inch barrel with extra-full turkey choke tube, Hi-Viz front sight. Completely covered with Mossy Oak Break-Up camouflage. Introduced 1999. Imported by Browning.

Perf.: $715   **Exc.:** $500   **VGood:** $400

Turkey/Waterfowl Stalker (black stock and metal)
Perf.: $875   **Exc.:** $695   **VGood:** $600

BROWNING GOLD NWTF TURKEY SERIES CAMO SHOTGUN

Similar to the Gold Turkey/Waterfowl model except 10- or 12-gauge (3-inch or 3-1/2-inch chamber), 24-inch barrel with extra-full choke tube, Hi-Viz fiber-optic sights and complete gun coverage in Mossy Oak Break-Up camouflage with National Wild Turkey Federation logo on stock. Introduced 2001.

10 gauge
Perf.: $1075   **Exc.:** $875   **VGood:** $775

12 gauge, 3-1/2-inch chamber
Perf.: $1075   **Exc.:** $875   **VGood:** $775

12 gauge, 3-inch chamber
Perf.: $635   **Exc.:** $475   **VGood:** $415

BROWNING GOLD UPLAND SPECIAL AUTO SHOTGUN

Similar to the Gold Classic Hunter except has straight-grip walnut stock, 12- or 20-gauge, 3-inch chamber. Introduced 2001.

12-gauge (24-inch bbl., weighs 7 lbs.)
Perf.: $750   **Exc.:** $535   **VGood:** $425

20-gauge (26-inch bbl., weighs 6 lbs., 12 oz.)
Perf.: $750   **Exc.:** $535   **VGood:** $425

BROWNING GOLD SUPERLITE HUNTER

Introduced in 2006, this gun uses an aluminum alloy receiver and alloy magazine tube to reduce weight to about 7 lbs. in 12 gauge. Gloss finish walnut stock. Available with 3-inch or 3.5-inch chamber and 26-inch or 28-inch barrel. Magazine cut-off feature on 3.5-inch model. A 6.5 lb. 20 gauge with 3-inch chamber and 26-inch or 28-inch barrel is also offered. Three choke tubes. Add 15 percent for 3.5-inch chamber.

NIB: $950   **Exc.:** $875   **VGood:** $725

BROWNING GOLD SUPERLITE FIELD HUNTER

Similar to Gold Superlite Hunter but with semi-humpback style receiver and satin finish walnut stock and 3-inch chamber only. Magazine cut-off on 12 gauge models. Adjustable shim system and three choke tubes.

NIB: $950   **Exc.:** $875   **VGood:** $725

BROWNING GOLD SUPERLITE MICRO

Similar to Gold Superlite Hunter but with compact dimensions for smaller shooters. Only in 20 gauge with 26-inch barrel. Weighs about 6.25 pounds. Three choke tubes.

NIB: $945   **Exc.:** $870   **VGood:** $720

BROWNING GOLD 10

Same specs as Gold except 10-ga.; 3-1/2-inch chamber; 26-inch, 28-inch, 30-inch barrel; Invector tubes choked Improved Cylinder, Modified, Full; weighs about 10-1/2 lbs.; forged steel receiver with polished blue finish. Made in Japan. Introduced 1993; still imported.

Perf.: $820   **Exc.:** $550   **VGood:** $480

BROWNING GOLD 10-GAUGE AUTO COMBO

Similar to the Gold 10 except comes with 24-inch and 26-inch barrels with Imp. Cyl., Mod., Full Invector choke tubes. Introduced 1999. Imported by Browning.

Perf.: $880   **Exc.:** $764   **VGood:** $633

BROWNING GOLD LIGHT 10-GAUGE AUTO SHOTGUN

Similar to the Browning Gold 10, except has an alloy receiver that is 1 lb. lighter than standard model. Offered in 26-inch or 28-inch bbls. With Mossy Oak Break-Up or Shadow Grass coverage; 5-shot magazine. Weighs 9 lbs., 10 oz. (28-inch bbl.). Introduced 2001. Imported by Browning.

Perf.: $1025   **Exc.:** $800   **VGood:** $695

Stalker (black composite stock and forearm)
Perf.: $1127   **Exc.:** $880   **VGood:** $764

BROWNING GOLD 10 STALKER

Same specs as Gold except 10-ga.; 3-1/2-inch chamber; 26-inch, 28-inch, 30-inch barrel; Invector tubes choked Improved Cylinder, Modified, Full; weighs about 10-1/2 lbs.; checkered black graphite-fiberglass composite stock with dull finish; non-glare metal finish. Made in Japan. Introduced 1993; still imported.

Perf.: $820   **Exc.:** $550   **VGood:** $480

BROWNING SILVER HUNTER

This semi-auto features a satin finish walnut stock and forend. It is available with a 3-inch chamber in 26-inch, 28-inch and 30-inch barrel lengths or with a 3.5-inch chamber in 26-inch or 28-inch barrel length. Add 15 percent for 3.5-inch chamber.

NIB: $800   **Exc.:** $725   **VGood:** $600

BROWNING SILVER STALKER

Similar to Silver Hunter but with matte black composite stock and forend. Sling swivel studs. 3.5-inch chamber only.

NIB: $775   **Exc.:** $710   **VGood:** $575

BROWNING SILVER–MOSSY OAK

Similar to Silver Stalker but in choice of Mossy Oak New Break-Up with 26-inch barrel or Mossy Oak New Shadow Grass with 26-inch or 28-inch barrel.

NIB: $975   **Exc.:** $895   **VGood:** $675

Browning Gold Fusion

Browning Gold Turkey/Waterfowl Camo

Browning Gold Upland Special

Browning Gold Superlite Field Hunter

Browning Gold 10-Gauge Auto Combo

Browning Gold Light 10-Gauge

Browning Silver Hunter

Browning Silver Stalker

Browning Silver Mossy Oak

Browning BSS Sporter

Browning Silver Sporting Micro

Browning Silver NWTF

Browning Silver Rifled Deer

Browning Satin Hunter

Browning Citori Gran Lightning Hunting

Browning Citori Hunting Lightning Micro

BROWNING SILVER MICRO
This is a 20 gauge with a 26" barrel and shorter stock dimensions for smaller shooters.
NIB: $825   **Exc.:** $750   **VGood:** $625

BROWNING SILVER SPORTING MICRO
This 2.75" 12 gauge includes adjustment spacers for changing stock length. Barrel is 28". Three choke tubes included. Weight is about 7 lbs.
NIB: $825   **Exc.:** $750   **VGood:** $625

BROWNING SILVER NWTF
New in 2008, this 3" 12 gauge turkey gun is fully camouflaged with Mossy Oak's New Break-Up pattern. The 24" barrel is outfitted with fiber-optic rifle sights. Weight is about 7 lbs. Add 10% for 3.5" chamber.
NIB: $1100   **Exc.:** $900   **VGood:** $725

BROWNING SILVER RIFLED DEER
New in 2008, this 3" 12 gauge slug gun features a rifled barrel with cantilever scope mount. Finishes include satin walnut, black composite and Mossy Oak New Break-Up camo. Add 10% for camo finish.
NIB: $1100   **Exc.:** $900   **VGood:** $725

BROWNING BSS
Side-by-side; boxlock; hammerless; 12-, 20-ga.; 3-inch chambers; 26-inch, 28-inch, 30-inch barrel; standard choke combos; checkered walnut pistol grip stock, beavertail forend; non-selective single trigger. Made in Japan. Introduced 1972; discontinued 1987.
Perf.: $925   **Exc.:** $750   **VGood:** $550

Add 50 percent to above prices for 20 gauge in 95+ percent condition
Subtract 20 percent from above prices for early guns with single, non-selective trigger

BROWNING BSS SPORTER
Same specs as BSS except 20-ga.; 26-inch, 28-inch barrel; walnut straight stock, forend; selective trigger. Made in Japan. Introduced 1977; discontinued 1987.
Perf.: $1150   **Exc.:** $950   **VGood:** $800

BROWNING B-SS SPORTER GRADE II
Similar to Sporter, except has satin grey finished receiver with an engraved pheasant, duck, quail and dogs. Discontinued 1983.
Perf.: $1750   **Exc.:** $1475   **VGood:** $1100
Add 50 percent to above prices for 20 ga. In 95 percent + condition

BROWNING BSS SIDELOCK
Side-by-side; sidelock; 12-, 20-ga.; 26-inch, 28-inch, barrel; straight-grip French walnut stock; checkered butt; double triggers; auto safety; cocking indicator; receiver, forend iron, trigger guard, top lever, tang are satin gray with rosettes, scrollwork. Made in Japan. Introduced 1984; discontinued 1987.

12-Gauge		
Perf.: $3500	**Exc.:** $3100	**VGood:** $2600
20-Gauge		
Perf.: $4750	**Exc.:** $4100	**VGood:** $3500

BROWNING CITORI (HUNTING) MODELS
Over/under; boxlock; 12-, 16-, 20-, 28-ga., .410; 3-inch, 3-1/2-inch chambers; 26-inch, 28-inch, 30-inch barrel; Improved/Modified, Modified/Full, Full/Full chokes or Invector choke tubes; checkered pistol-grip stock, semi-beavertail forearm; automatic ejectors; selective single trigger; recoil pad. Various grades available with price dependent on type of engraving. Made in Japan. Introduced 1973; dropped 2001.

Grade I		
Perf.: $750	**Exc.:** $675	**VGood:** $575
Grade I, 12-ga., 3-1/2-inch		
Perf.: $950	**Exc.:** $720	**VGood:** $600
Grade I, Hunter (discontinued 2001); Invector, 12 and 20		
Grade I, Lightning; Invector Plus; 12, 20		
Grade I, Lightning; 28 and .410; Invector		
Grade II		
Perf.: $995	**Exc.:** $810	**VGood:** $740
Grade III, grayed steel receiver, light engraving. Lightning; Invector Plus; 12, 20		
Lightning; 28 and .410; Invector Plus		
Perf.: $1350	**Exc.:** $800	**VGood:** $700
Grade V, extensive engraving		
Perf.: $1450	**Exc.:** $1000	**VGood:** $950
Grade VI, blue or grayed receiver, extensive engraving and inlays. Grade VI, Lightning, Invector Plus; 12, 20		
Grade VI, Lightning; 28-ga. and .410; Invector		
Perf.: $2000	**Exc.:** $1200	**VGood:** $1000
Gran Lightning; 26-inch, 28-inch, Invector Plus; 12, 20		
Perf.: $1825	**Exc.:** $1300	**VGood:** $1050
Gran Lightning; 28-ga., .410		
Perf.: $1948	**Exc.:** $1423	**VGood:** $1173
Micro Lightning, 20-ga., 24-inch bbl.; discontinued 2001		
Perf.: $1250	**Exc.:** $945	**VGood:** $785
White Lightning (silver nitride receiver w/engraving, 12- or 20-ga., 26-inch, 28-inch)		
Perf.: $1265	**Exc.:** $960	**VGood:** $800
White Lightning, 28-ga. or .410-bore		
Perf.: $1337	**Exc.:** $1032	**VGood:** $872

BROWNING CITORI SATIN HUNTER
12-ga., satin-finished wood, matte-finished bbls and receiver, 3-1/2-inch chambers. Discontinued 2001.
Perf.: $1150   **Exc.:** $825   **VGood:** $650

BROWNING CITORI LIGHTNING (HUNTING)
Same specs as Citori Hunting except Invector choke tubes; hand-checkered French walnut pistol-grip stock, slim forearm; ivory bead sights. Introduced 1988; still in production.

Grade I		
Perf.: $950	**Exc.:** $520	**VGood:** $480
Grade III, grayed steel receiver, light engraving		
Perf.: $1850	**Exc.:** $1350	**VGood:** $1035
Grade VI, blue or grayed receiver, extensive engraving and inlays		
Perf.: $2825	**Exc.:** $2100	**VGood:** $1475

BROWNING CITORI GRAN LIGHTNING (HUNTING)
Same specs as Citori Hunting except 3-inch chambers; 26-inch, 28-inch barrels; Invector choke tubes; high-grade walnut stock; satin-oil finish. Introduced 1990; still in production.
Perf.: $1400   **Exc.:** $800   **VGood:** $650

BROWNING CITORI LIGHTNING MICRO (HUNTING)
Same specs as Citori Hunting except scaled down for smaller shooters; 24-inch barrels; Invector choke system; weighs 6-1/8 lbs. Introduced 1991; discontinued 2001.

Grade I		
Perf.: $1250	**Exc.:** $945	**VGood:** $785

BROWNING CITORI HUNTING SPORTER

Same specs as Citori Hunting except 3-inch chamber; 26-inch barrel; walnut straight-grip stock, schnabel forend with satin oil finish. Introduced 1978; no longer in production.

Grade I		
Perf.: $800	**Exc.:** $550	**VGood:** $500
Grade II		
Perf.: $1150	**Exc.:** $980	**VGood:** $850
Grade V		
Perf.: $1450	**Exc.:** $1150	**VGood:** $1000

BROWNING CITORI SPORTING HUNTER

Similar to the Citori Hunting I except has Sporting Clays stock dimensions, a Superposed-style forend, and Sporting Clays butt pad. Available in 12-gauge with 3-inch chambers, back-bored 26-inch, 28-inch and 30-inch, all with Invector Plus choke tube system. Introduced 1998; discontinued 2001. Imported from Japan by Browning.

12-gauge, 3-1/2-inch		
Perf.: $1352	**Exc.:** $997	**VGood:** $827
12-, 20-gauge, 3-inch		
Perf.: $1250	**Exc.:** $895	**VGood:** $725

BROWNING CITORI HUNTING SUPERLIGHT

Same specs as Citori Hunting except 12-, 20-, 28-ga., .410; 2-3/4-inch chambers; 24-inch, 26-inch, 28-inch barrels; straight-grip stock; schnabel forend. Made in Japan. Introduced 1982; all but Superlight Feather discontinued 2001.

Grade I		
Perf.: $950	**Exc.:** $575	**VGood:** $480
Grade III, grayed steel receiver, light engraving		
Perf.: $1750	**Exc.:** $1275	**VGood:** $975

Subtract 10 percent from above prices if without Invector choke tubes
Add $275 to above prices for 28 ga. Or .410 bore

Grade VI, blue or grayed receiver, extensive engraving and inlays		
Perf.: $1950	**Exc.:** $1175	**VGood:** $1000
Grade I, 28 or .410, Invector		
Perf.: $1325	**Exc.:** $925	**VGood:** $775
Grade III, Invector, 12-ga.		
Perf.: $1750	**Exc.:** $1275	**VGood:** $975
Grade VI, Invector, 12 or 20, gray or blue		
Perf.: $2625	**Exc.:** $1875	**VGood:** $1425
Grade VI, 28 or .410, Invector, gray or blue		
Perf.: $2895	**Exc.:** $2145	**VGood:** $1695
Grade I Invector, 12 or 20		
Perf.: $1175	**Exc.:** $875	**VGood:** $675
Grade I Invector, White Upland Special (24-inch bbls.); 12 or 20		
Perf.: $1175	**Exc.:** $875	**VGood:** $675
Citori Superlight Feather (12 ga., alloy receiver)		
Perf.: $1415	**Exc.:** $1025	**VGood:** $800

BROWNING CITORI LIGHTNING FEATHER O/U

Similar to the 12 gauge Citori Grade I except has 2-3/4-inch chambers, rounded pistol grip, Lightning-style forend, and lighweight alloy receiver. Weighs 6 lbs. 15 oz. with 26-inch barrels (12-ga.); 6 lbs., 2 oz. (20-ga., 26-inch bbl.). Silvered, engraved receiver. Introduced 1999. Imported by Browning.

12- or 20-ga., 26-inch or 28-inch barrels		
Perf.: $1385	**Exc.:** $1000	**VGood:** $785
Lightning Feather Combo (20- and 28-ga. bbls., 27-inch each)		
Perf.: $2475	**Exc.:** $2025	**VGood:** $1850

BROWNING CITORI SKEET, SPECIAL SKEET, ULTRA XS SKEET, XS SKEET

Over/under; boxlock; 12-, 20-, 28-ga., .410; 26-inch, 28-inch barrels; Skeet/Skeet fixed choke of Invector choke tubes; ventilated rib or target high-post wide rib; checkered walnut pistol-grip Skeet-style stock, forearm; single selective trigger; ejectors; recoil pad.

Browning Citori Sporting Hunter

Browning Citori Superlight

Browning Citori Superlight Feather

Browning Citori Lightning Feather

Browning Citori Ultra XS Skeet

Browning Citori Ultra XT Trap

Browning Citori Feather XS

Various grades available with price dependent on type of engraving. Made in Japan. Introduced 1974; still in production as XS Skeet.

Grade I		
Perf.: $1150	**Exc.:** $700	**VGood:** $550
Grade I with 3-barrel set		
Perf.: $2400	**Exc.:** $1750	**VGood:** $1350
Grade III		
Perf.: $1500	**Exc.:** $820	**VGood:** $700
Grade III with 4-barrel set		
Perf.: $4500	**Exc.:** $2650	**VGood:** $2100
Grade III with 3-barrel set		
Perf.: $3000	**Exc.:** $2000	**VGood:** $1400
Grade VI		
Perf.: $1950	**Exc.:** $1500	**VGood:** $1100
Grade VI with 3-barrel set		
Perf.: $3100	**Exc.:** $1850	**VGood:** $1650
Grade VI with 4-barrel set		
Perf.: $4450	**Exc.:** $2650	**VGood:** $2100
Golden Clays		
Perf.: $2300	**Exc.:** $1500	**VGood:** $1100
Golden Clays with 3-barrel set		
Perf.: $4000	**Exc.:** $2750	**VGood:** $2000
Golden Clays with 4-barrel set		
Perf.: $5400	**Exc.:** $3250	**VGood:** $2500

BROWNING CITORI ULTRA XS SKEET

Similar to other Citori Ultra models except features a semi-beavertail forearm with deep finger grooves, ported barrels and triple system. Adjustable comb is optional. Introduced 2000.
Price: 12- and 20-ga.; 28-inch or 30-inch barrel

Perf.: $1825	**Exc.:** $1350	**VGood:** $1025
Adjustable comb model; 12- or 20-ga.		
Perf.: $2056	**Exc.:** $1581	**VGood:** $1256

BROWNING CITORI ULTRA XT TRAP

Similar to other Citori Ultra models except offered in 12-ga. only with 30-inch or 32-inch ported barrel, high-post rib, ventilated side ribs, Triple Trigger System and silver nitride receiver. Includes Full, Modified and Imp. Cyl. choke tubes. From Browning.
Price: 30-inch or 32-inch barrel

Perf.: $1700	**Exc.:** $1250	**VGood:** $950
Adjustable-comb model		
Perf.: $1978	**Exc.:** $1528	**VGood:** $1228

BROWNING CITORI ULTRA XS SPORTING

Similar to other Citori Ultra XS models except offered in 12-, 20-, 28-ga., and .410-bore. Silver nitride receiver, schnabel forearm, ventilated side rib. Imported by Browning.

.410 or 28-ga.		
Perf.: $1901	**Exc.:** $1426	**VGood:** $1226
12- or 20-ga.		
Perf.: $1825	**Exc.:** $1350	**VGood:** $1150

BROWNING CITORI FEATHER XS SHOTGUNS

Similar to the standard Citori except has lightweight alloy receiver, silver nitrade Nitex receiver, 28-inch or 30-inch barrel, schnabel forearm, ventilated side rib and Hi-Viz Comp fiber optics sight. Available in 12-, 20-, 28-ga., and .410-bore. Introduced 2000; discontinued 2001. Add 10 percent for .410 and 28.

Perf.: $1800	**Exc.:** $1375	**VGood:** $1150

BROWNING CITORI HIGH GRADE SHOTGUNS

Similar to standard Citori except has full sideplates with engraved hunting scenes and gold inlays, high-grade, hand-oiled walnut stock and forearm. Introduced 2000. From Browning.

Citori Privilege (fully embellished sideplates), 12- or 20-ga.		
Perf.: $4775	**Exc.:** $4075	**VGood:** $3450
Citori BG VI Lightning (gold inlays of ducks and pheasants); 28-inch or 30-inch barrel		
Perf.: $2775	**Exc.:** $1975	**VGood:** $1475

Browning Citori 525 Feather

Browning Citori 625 Sporting

Browning Citori Ultra XS Prestige

Browning Citori XS Sporting Clay

Browning Citori Sporting Clays 325

Browning Citori Sporting Clays 425

Browning Citori Sporting Clays GTI

Citori BG III Superlight (scroll engraving on grayed receiver, gold inlays)
Perf.: $1415   **Exc.:** $1025   **VGood:** $800

Citori 425 Golden Clays (engraving of game bird-clay bird transition, gold accents); 12- or 20-ga.
Perf.: $3150   **Exc.:** $2275   **VGood:** $1675

BROWNING CITORI XS SPORTING CLAYS

Similar to the Citori Grade I except has silver nitride receiver with gold accents, stock dimensions of 14-3/4-inch by 1-1/2-inch by 2-1/4-inch with satin finish, right- hand palm swell, schnabel forend. Comes with Modified, Imp. Cyl. and Skeet Invector-Plus choke tubes. Back-bored barrels; vented side ribs. Introduced 1999. Imported by Browning.

12-, 20-ga.
Perf.: $1825   **Exc.:** $1350   **VGood:** $1025

28-ga., .410-bore
Perf.: $1825   **Exc.:** $1350   **VGood:** $1025

CITORI 525 FEATHER

This lightweight Citori features an alloy receiver with a steel breech face and high-relief engraving. The stock and Schnabel forend are Grade II/III oil finished walnut. Available in 12, 20 and 28 gauges and .410 bore with 26" or 28" barrels. All but 28 gauge have 3" chambers. Weight is about 6.9 lbs. in12 gauge and 5.5 to 5.7 lbs. in others. Three choke tubes.

Perf.: $2275   **Exc.:** $1875   **VGood:** $1500

CITORI 625 SPORTING

Introduced in 2008, this 2.75" 12 gauge has 28", 30" or 32" ported barrels with Browning's Vector Pro lengthened forcing cones system. The stock and Schnabel forend are Grade III/IV walnut. The steel receiver has a silver nitride finish with high-relief engraving and gold embellishment. Five choke tubes included. Weight is 7.9 to 8.2 lbs. Add 5% for adjustable comb stock.

Perf.: $3300   **Exc.:** $2875   **VGood:** $2250

CITORI 625 FIELD

This 3" 12 gauge has 26" or 28" barrels and a gloss oil finish Grade II/III walnut stock and schnabel forend. Steel receiver with silver nitride finish and high-relief engraving. Three choke tubes. Weight is about 7.8 lbs.

Perf.: $2275   **Exc.:** $1875   **VGood:** $1500

CITORI ULTRA XS PRESTIGE

New in 2008, this 12 gauge sporting clays model features an adjustable comb and Grade III/IV walnut stock with right hand palm swell. Ported barrels are 28", 30" or 32". Gold accented, high relief Ultra XS Special engraving on the steel/silver nitride finish receiver. Weight is about 8 lbs.

Perf.: $4500   **Exc.:** $3875   **VGood:** $3250

BROWNING SPECIAL SPORTING CLAYS

Similar to the Citori Ultra Sporter except has full pistol grip stock with palm swell, gloss finish, 28-inch, 30-inch or 32-inch barrels with back-bored Invector Plus chokes (ported or non-ported); high post tapered rib. Also available as 28-inch and 30-inch two-barrel set. Introduced 1989; discontinued 2001.

With ported barrels
Perf.: $1300   **Exc.:** $925   **VGood:** $775

As above, adjustable comb
Perf.: $1520   **Exc.:** $1145   **VGood:** $995

BROWNING LIGHTNING SPORTING CLAYS

Similar to the Citori Lightning with rounded pistol grip and classic forend. Has high post tapered rib or lower hunting-style rib with 30-inch back-bored Invector Plus barrels, ported or non-ported, 3-inch chambers. Gloss stock finish, radiused recoil pad. Has "Lightning Sporting Clays Edition" engraved and gold filled on receiver. Introduced 1989.

Low-rib, ported
Perf.: $1425   **Exc.:** $1025   **VGood:** $875

High-rib, ported
Perf.: $1506   **Exc.:** $1106   **VGood:** $956

BROWNING LIGHT SPORTING 802 ES O/U

Gauge: 12, 2-3/4-inch chambers. Barrel: 28-inch, back-bored Invector Plus. Comes with flush-mounted Imp. Cyl. and Skeet; 2-inch extended Imp. Cyl. and Mod.; and 4-inch extended Imp. Cyl. and Mod. tubes. Weight: 7 lbs., 5 oz. Length: 45-inch overall. Stock: 14-3/8-inch by 1/8-inch by 1-9/16-inch by 1-3/4-inch. Select walnut with radiused solid recoil pad, schnabel-type forend. Features: Trigger adjustable for length of pull; narrow 6.2mm ventilated rib; ventilated barrel side rib; blued receiver. Introduced 1996; discontinued 2001. Imported from Japan.

Perf.: $1700   **Exc.:** $1175   **VGood:** $975

BROWNING CITORI SPORTING CLAYS 325

Over/under; boxlock; 12-, 20-ga.; 2-3/4-inch chambers; back-bored 28-inch, 30-inch, 32-inch vent-rib barrels; barrels are ported on 12-gauge guns; Invector Plus choke tubes; weighs about 7-3/4 lbs.; select cut-checkered walnut stock, schnabel forend with gloss finish; three interchangeable trigger shoes to adjust length of pull; grayed receiver with engraving; blued barrels. Made in Japan. Introduced 1993; discontinued 1994.

Perf.: $1250   **Exc.:** $800   **VGood:** $700

BROWNING CITORI SPORTING CLAYS 325 GOLDEN CLAYS

Same specs as Citori Sporting Clays 325 except high-grade walnut; grayed receiver highlighted with 24-karat gold. Made in Japan. Introduced 1993; discontinued 1994.

Perf.: $2250   **Exc.:** $1350   **VGood:** $1050

BROWNING CITORI SPORTING CLAYS 425

Over/under; 12-, 20-ga.; 2-3/4-inch chambers; back-bored 28-inch, 30-inch, 32-inch vent-rib barrels; barrels are ported on 12-ga. guns; Invector Plus choke tubes; weighs about 7-3/4 lbs.; select cut-checkered walnut stock, schnabel forend with gloss finish; three interchangeable trigger shoes to adjust length of pull; grayed receiver with engraving, blued barrels. Made in Japan. Introduced 1993; still imported.

Perf.: $1380   **Exc.:** $800   **VGood:** $700

Price: Grade I, 12-, 20-ga., Invector Plus
Perf.: $1665 **Exc.:** $1150 **VGood:** $935

Price: Golden Clays, 12-, 20-ga., Invector Plus
Perf.: $3150   **Exc.:** $2275   **VGood:** $1675

BROWNING CITORI SPORTING CLAYS 425 GOLDEN CLAYS

Same specs as Sporting Clays 425 except high-grade walnut; grayed receiver highlighted with 24-karat gold. Made in Japan. Introduced 1995; discontinued 2001.

Perf.: $2500   **Exc.:** $1350   **VGood:** $1000

BROWNING CITORI SPORTING CLAYS 425 WSSF

Same specs as Sporting Clays 425 except 12-ga.; stock dimensions specifically tailored to women shooters; top lever and takedown lever are easier to operate; stock and forend have teal-colored finish with WSSF logo. Made in Japan. Introduced 1995; discontinued.

Perf.: $1400   **Exc.:** $800   **VGood:** $700

BROWNING CITORI SPORTING CLAYS GTI

Over/under; boxlock; 12-ga.; 28-inch, 30-inch vent-rib barrels (ported or non-ported); Invector Plus choke tubes; ventilated side ribs; checkered walnut semi-pistol grip stock, grooved semi-beavertail forend with satin finish; radiused rubber buttpad; three interchangeable trigger shoes for three length of pull adjustments. Made in Japan. Introduced 1989; discontinued 1994.

Grade I, non-ported barrels
Perf.: $1100   **Exc.:** $550   **VGood:** $450

Grade I, ported barrels
Perf.: $1200   **Exc.:** $650   **VGood:** $550

Golden Clays, ported barrels
Perf.: $2200   **Exc.:** $1350   **VGood:** $1000

BROWNING CITORI SPORTING CLAYS LIGHTNING

Over/under; boxlock; 12-ga.; back-bored 30-inch Invector Plus barrels (ported or non-ported); high-post tapered rib or hunting-type rib; checkered walnut pistol-grip stock, forend with gloss stock finish; adjustable comb, recoil pad; engraved, gold-filled receiver. Made in Japan. Introduced, 1989; still imported.

Grade I, non-ported
Perf.: $1100   **Exc.:** $625   **VGood:** $490

Grade I, ported
Perf.: $1150   **Exc.:** $700   **VGood:** $550

Pigeon Grade, ported
Perf.: $1250   **Exc.:** $800   **VGood:** $650

Golden Clays, ported
Perf.: $2200   **Exc.:** $1350   **VGood:** $1000

BROWNING CITORI SPECIAL SPORTING CLAYS

Over/under; boxlock; 12-ga.; back-bored 28-inch, 30-inch, 32-inch barrels (ported or non-ported); Invector Plus choke tubes; high-post tapered rib; checkered walnut pistol-grip stock, forend with gloss finish; palm swell. Also available as 28-inch, 30-inch two-barrel set. Made in Japan. Introduced 1989; discontinued.

Grade I, non-ported
Perf.: $1050   **Exc.:** $900   **VGood:** $700

Grade I, ported
Perf.: $1100   **Exc.:** $950   **VGood:** $750

Grade I, two-barrel set
Perf.: $1900   **Exc.:** $1700   **VGood:** $1500

Golden Clays, ported
Perf.: $3100   **Exc.:** $2800   **VGood:** $2200

BROWNING CITORI SPORTING CLAYS ULTRA SPORTER

Over/under; boxlock; 12-ga.; back-bored 28-inch or 30-inch barrels (ported or non-ported); Invector Plus choke tubes; ventilated side ribs; checkered walnut pistol-grip stock, grooved semi-beavertail forend with satin finish; radiused rubber buttpad; three interchangeable trigger shoes for three length of pull adjustments. Made in Japan. Introduced 1995; discontinued 1999.

Grade I, non-ported
Perf.: $1500   **Exc.:** $1250   **VGood:** $1000

Grade I, ported
Perf.: $1595   **Exc.:** $1300   **VGood:** $1100

Golden Clays
Perf.: $3300   **Exc.:** $2850   **VGood:** $2200

BROWNING CITORI TRAP, SPECIAL TRAP, ULTRA XT AND XT

Over/under; boxlock; 12-ga.; 30-inch, 32-inch ported or non-ported barrels; Full/Full, Improved Modified/Full, Modified/Full, or Invector Plus choke tubes; vent rib and high-post target wide vent rib; fitted with trap-style recoil pad; checkered walnut Monte Carlo cheekpiece stock, beavertail forearm. Introduced 1974; still in production.

Grade I, Invector Plus, ported
Perf.: $1500   **Exc.:** $1250   **VGood:** $1000

Grade I Combo, with extra 34-inch single barrel, Invector Plus, ported
Perf.: $1800   **Exc.:** $1500   **VGood:** $1300

Grade III, Invector Plus, ported
Perf.: $1500   **Exc.:** $1250   **VGood:** $1000

Grade V, Invector Plus, ported
Perf.: $2650   **Exc.:** $2200   **VGood:** $1950

Grade VI, Invector Plus, ported
Perf.: $2100   **Exc.:** $1800   **VGood:** $1650

Golden Clays, satin-gray receiver with engraving, inlays
Perf.: $3000   **Exc.:** $2750   **VGood:** $2400

Pigeon Grade, deluxe wood, inlays
Perf.: $3200   **Exc.:** $2950   **VGood:** $2650

Browning Citori Sporting Clays Ultra Sporter

Browning Citori Trap

Browning Citori Trap Plus

Browning Liege

Browning ST-100

Browning Superposed Broadway Trap

Singature Painted, red and black painted stock
Perf.: $1475   **Exc.:** $1175   **VGood:** $950

BROWNING CITORI TRAP PLUS

Same specs as Citori Trap except back-bored 30-inch, 32-inch barrels; .745-inch over-bore; Invector Plus choke tubes with Full, Improved Modified and Modified; high post, ventilated, tapered, target rib adjustable for impact from 3-inch to 12-inch above point of aim; with or without ported barrels; select walnut Monte Carlo stock, modified beavertail forend with high-gloss finish; fully adjustable for length of pull, drop at comb, drop at Monte Carlo; Browning Recoil Reduction System. Made in Japan. Introduced 1989; no longer imported.

Grade I, Invector Plus, ported
Perf.: $1500   **Exc.:** $900   **VGood:** $750

Grade I Combo with extra 34-inch single barrel, Invector Plus, ported
Perf.: $2600   **Exc.:** $1900   **VGood:** $1700

Golden Clays, satin-gray receiver with engraving, inlays
Perf.: $4300   **Exc.:** $2650   **VGood:** $2100

Pigeon Grade, deluxe wood, inlays
Perf.: $1650   **Exc.:** $850   **VGood:** $700

BROWNING CITORI XT TRAP OVER/UNDER

Similar to the Citori Special Trap except has engraved silver nitride receiver with gold highlights, vented side barrel rib. Available in 12-gauge with 30-inch or 32-inch barrels, Invector-Plus choke tubes. Introduced 1999. Imported by Browning.

Perf.: $1715   **Exc.:** $1250   **VGood:** $950

With adjustable-comb stock
Perf.: $1935   **Exc.:** $1470   **VGood:** $1170

BROWNING LIEGE

Over/under; boxlock; 12-ga.; 2-3/4-inch, 3-inch chamber; 26-1/2-inch, 28-inch, 30-inch barrels; standard choke combos; vent rib; checkered walnut pistol-grip stock, forearm; automatic ejectors; non-selective single trigger. Introduced 1973; discontinued 1975.

Perf.: $720   **Exc.:** $550   **VGood:** $490

BROWNING ST-100

Over/under; 12-ga.; 30-inch barrels; floating Broadway rib; five-position impact adjustment; hand-checkered select walnut stock, semi-beavertail forend with high-gloss finish; selective auto ejectors; single selective mechanical trigger; manual top tang safety. Introduced 1979; discontinued 1982.

Perf.: $2200   **Exc.:** $1650   **VGood:** $1400

BROWNING SUPERPOSED

Over/under; 12-, 20-, 28-ga.; .410; 26-1/2-inch, 28-inch, 30-inch, 32-inch (discontinued WWII) barrels; gun is made in a wide spectrum of variations, grades, choke combinations; early models and pre-WWII had double triggers, twin single triggers or non-selective single trigger (pre-WWII production ended when Belgium was invaded); hand-checkered French walnut pistol-grip or straight stock, forearm. Standard Grade is listed as Grade I, with raised matted rib or vent rib. Introduced 1928; no longer in production.

Exc.: $950   **VGood:** $800   **Good:** $575

BROWNING SUPERPOSED BROADWAY TRAP

Same specs as Superposed except 30-inch, 32-inch barrel; 5/8-inch-wide Broadway vent rib. No longer in production.

Exc.: $850   **VGood:** $720   **Good:** $500

Browning Superposed
Diana Grade

Browning Superposed
Midas Grade

Browning Superposed
Presentation 1

Browning Superposed
Presentation 2 Magnum

Browning Superposed Presentation 2
Magnum

Browning Superposed Presentation 2
Magnum

Browning Superposed Presentation 2 Magnum Bottom View

Browning Superposed
Presentation 3

Browning Superposed
Presentation 4

Browning Superposed
Super-Light Field Grade

BROWNING SUPERPOSED MAGNUM

Same specs as Superposed except 12-ga.; 3-inch chamber; 30-inch vent-rib barrel; choked Full/Full or Full/Mod.; recoil pad. No longer in production.

Perf.: $1350 **Exc.:** $875 **VGood:** $800

BROWNING SUPERPOSED MIDAS GRADE

Same specs as Superposed except heavily engraved, gold inlaid; pre-war versions with raised matted rib or vent rib; later versions have only wide vent rib. No longer in production.

Perf.: $6950 **Exc.:** $6000 **VGood:** $4950

BROWNING SUPERPOSED PIGEON GRADE

Same specs as Superposed except better wood, finer checkering, more engraving than Standard Superposed model; raised matted rib or vent rib. Was redesignated as Grade II after WWII. No longer in production.

Perf.: $4000 **Exc.:** $3400 **VGood:** $2150

BROWNING SUPERPOSED SKEET

Same specs as Superposed except 12-, 20-, 28-ga., .410; 26-1/2-inch, 28-inch barrel; choked Skeet/Skeet. No longer in production.

Exc.: $900 **VGood:** $750 **Good:** $560

BROWNING SUPERPOSED PRESENTATION SUPERLIGHT

Over/under; boxlock; 12-, 20-ga. 26-1/2-inch barrel; solid or vent rib; hand-checkered straight-grip stock of select walnut; top lever single selective trigger barrel selector combined with manual tang safety. Options too numerous to mention; available in 4 grades. Introduced 1977; no longer imported.

Grade I		
Perf.: $2800	**Exc.:** $1900	**VGood:** $1680
Grade II		
Perf.: $3300	**Exc.:** $2200	**VGood:** $2000
Grade III		
Perf.: $5500	**Exc.:** $4000	**VGood:** $3500
Grade IV		
Perf.: $6500	**Exc.:** $4500	**VGood:** $3900

BROWNING SUPERPOSED PRESENTATION SUPERLIGHT BROADWAY TRAP

Same specs as Superposed Presentation Superlight except 30-inch, 32-inch barrel; wide vent rib; different stock measurements. Discontinued 1984.

Grade I		
Perf.: $2500	**Exc.:** $1650	**VGood:** $1500
Grade II		
Perf.: $3000	**Exc.:** $1900	**VGood:** $1750
Grade III		
Perf.: $5000	**Exc.:** $3600	**VGood:** $3200
Grade IV		
Perf.: $6000	**Exc.:** $4000	**VGood:** $3500

BROWNING SUPERPOSED PRESENTATION SUPERLIGHT LIGHTNING SKEET

Same specs as Superposed Presentation Superlight except 12-, 20-, 28-ga., .410; center and front ivory bead sights; special Skeet stock, forend. Introduced 1977; discontinued 1982.

Grade I		
Perf.: $2500	**Exc.:** $1650	**VGood:** $1500
Grade II		
Perf.: $3000	**Exc.:** $1900	**VGood:** $1750
Grade III		
Perf.: $5000	**Exc.:** $3600	**VGood:** $3200
Grade IV		
Perf.: $6000	**Exc.:** $4000	**VGood:** $3500

BROWNING SUPERPOSED DIANA GRADE

Same specs as Superposed except raised matted rib or vent rib before WWII; post-war models have only vent rib; better wood, more extensive engraving; redesignated as Grade V after WWII; improved general quality. No longer in production.

Perf.: $4700 **Exc.:** $2700 **VGood:** $2100

BROWNING SUPERPOSED GRADE I LIGHTNING MODEL

Same specs as Superposed except matted barrel; no rib before WWII; post-war models have vent rib. Other specs generally the same as Standard Superposed model. No longer in production.

Perf.: $1550 **Exc.:** $1275 **VGood:** $995

BROWNING SUPERPOSED PRESENTATION SUPERLIGHT LIGHTNING TRAP

Same specs as Superposed Presentation Superlight except 30-inch barrels; trap stock, semi-beavertail forend. Discontinued 1984.

Grade I
Perf.: $2500   **Exc.:** $1650   **VGood:** $1500

Grade II
Perf.: $3000   **Exc.:** $1900   **VGood:** $1750

Grade III
Perf.: $5000   **Exc.:** $3600   **VGood:** $3200

Grade IV
Perf.: $6000   **Exc.:** $4000   **VGood:** $3500

BROWNING SUPERPOSED PRESENTATION SUPERLIGHT MAGNUM

Same specs as Superposed Presentation Superlight except 3-inch chambers; 30-inch barrels; factory fitted recoil pad. Discontinued 1984.

Grade I
Perf.: $2500   **Exc.:** $1650   **VGood:** $1500

Grade II
Perf.: $3000   **Exc.:** $1900   **VGood:** $1750

Grade III
Perf.: $5000   **Exc.:** $3600   **VGood:** $3200

Grade IV
Perf.: $6000   **Exc.:** $4000   **VGood:** $3500

BROWNING SUPERPOSED SUPERLIGHT

Over/under; boxlock; 12-, 20-ga.; 2-3/4-inch chambers; 26-1/2-inch vent-rib barrels; choked Modified/Full or Improved/Modified; hand-checkered select walnut straight-grip stock, forearm; top lever; barrel selector combined with manual tang safety; single selective trigger; engraved receiver. Introduced 1967; discontinued 1976.

12-ga.
Perf.: $1650   **Exc.:** $1150   **VGood:** $1000

20-ga.
Perf.: $2300   **Exc.:** $1400   **VGood:** $1200

BROWNING CYNERGY CLASSIC FIELD

This more traditionally styled 12 gauge was added to the Cynergy line in 2006. It features a steel receiver with silver nitride finish and game bird scenes on each side. Satin finish walnut stock and schnabel style forend. Three choke tubes. Available in barrel lengths of 26-inch and 28-inch with an average weight of 7.75 lbs.

NIB: $1875   **Exc.:** $1775   **VGood:** $1500

BROWNING CYNERGY CLASSIC SPORTING

New for 2006, this traditionally styled version of the Cynergy Sporting is available in 12 gauge with 28-inch, 30-inch or 32-inch ported barrels. Oil finish walnut stock with Schnabel forend and Browning logo on steel receiver with silver nitride finish. Three Invector-Plus Midas Grade choke tubes. Average weight 7.75 lbs.

NIB: $2825   **Exc.:** $2695   **VGood:** $2000

BROWNING CYNERGY SPORTING, ADJUSTABLE COMB

Similar to Cynergy Sporting but with a comb adjustable for cast and drop. Average weight 8.2 lbs.

NIB: $2900   **Exc.:** $2725   **VGood:** $2375

BROWNING CYNERGY FEATHER

This lightweight Cynergy 12 gauge was introduced in 2006, followed by 20 and 28 gauge and .410 bore versions in 2008. Satin finish walnut stock. Weight is about 6.5 lbs. in 12 gauge and about 5 lbs. in others.

NIB: $2400   **Exc.:** $2195   **VGood:** $1700

CYNERGY FEATHER COMPOSITE

As above but with synthetic stock and forend in 12 gauge only.

NIB: $2400   **Exc.:** $2195   **VGood:** $1700

Browning Superposed Presentation Superlight Lightning Trap

Browning Cynergy Classic Field

Browning Cynergy Classic Sporting

Browning Cynergy Feather

Browning Cynergy Euro Sporting

Browning Cynergy Trap Unsingle

Browning A-Bolt Stalker Shotgun

Browning BPS

BROWNING CYNERGY EURO SPORTING

Sporting clays and skeet version comes in 2.75" 12 and 20 gauge with 28", 30" or 32" barrels. Stock is oil finish Grade III/IV walnut. Three choke tubes. Weight is about 8 lbs. in 12 gauge and 6.5 lbs. in 20 gauge.

NIB: $3500   **Exc.:** $3000   **VGood:** $2700

BROWNING CYNERGY CLASSIC TRAP UNSINGLE COMBO

Trap shotgun in 12 gauge comes with a double barrel set in 32/34", 32/32", 30/34" or 30/32". Gloss finish Monte Carlo Grade III/IV walnut stock with right hand palm swell and adjustable comb. Weight is about 8.9 lbs. Four choke tubes. Aluminum fitted carrying case.

NIB: $5000   **Exc.:** $4195   **VGood:** $3500

BROWNING A-BOLT HUNTER SHOTGUN

Bolt action; 12-ga.; 3-inch chamber; 2-shot detachable magazine; 22-inch fully rifled barrel or 23-inch barrel with 5-inch Invector choke tube; weighs 7-1/8 lbs.; 44-3/4-inch overall length; blade front sight with red insert, open adjustable rear, or no sights; drilled and tapped for scope mount; walnut stock with satin finish; A-Bolt rifle action with 60° bolt throw; front-locking bolt with claw extractor; hinged floorplate; swivel studs; matte finish on barrel, receiver. Imported by Browning. Introduced 1995.

Rifled barrel
Perf.: $1000   **Exc.:** $875   **VGood:** $700

Invector barrel
Perf.: $1100   **Exc.:** $925   **VGood:** $750

BROWNING A-BOLT STALKER SHOTGUN

Same specs as A-Bolt Hunter except black, non-glare composite pistol-grip stock, forend. Imported by Browning. Introduced 1995.

Rifled barrel
Perf.: $900   **Exc.:** $800   **VGood:** $650

Invector barrel
Perf.: $950   **Exc.:** $850   **VGood:** $750

BROWNING BPS

Slide action; 10-, 12-, 20-, 28-ga.; 3-inch, 3-1/2-inch chamber; 4-, 5-shot magazine; 24-inch, 26-inch, 28-inch, 30-inch barrel; Invector chokes; high-post vent rib; 48-3/4-inch overall length; weighs 7-1/2 lbs.; select walnut pistol-grip stock, semi-beavertail forend; bottom feeding, ejection; receiver top safety. Made in Japan. Introduced 1977; still imported by Browning.

Perf.: $400   **Exc.:** $325   **VGood:** $290

10-ga., Hunter, Invector
Perf.: $445   **Exc.:** $380   **VGood:** $335

12-ga., 3-1/2-inch Magnum Hunter, Invector Plus
Perf.: $540   **Exc.:** $495   **VGood:** $.410

12-ga., 3-1/2-inch Magnum Stalker (black syn. stock)
Perf.: $465   **Exc.:** $400   **VGood:** $355

12-, 20-ga., Hunter, Invector Plus
Perf.: $445   **Exc.:** $380   **VGood:** $335

12-ga. Deer Hunter (22-inch rifled bbl., cantilever mount)
Perf.: $460   **Exc.:** $385   **VGood:** $310

28-ga., Hunter, Invector
Perf.: $423   **Exc.:** $343   **VGood:** $298

.410 bore, Hunter, Invector
Perf.: $423   **Exc.:** $343   **VGood:** $298

BROWNING BPS BUCK SPECIAL

Same specs as BPS except 24-inch Cylinder barrel; no Invector choke tubes. Introduced 1977; reintroduced 1989; still in production.

Perf.: $375   **Exc.:** $240   **VGood:** $200

10-ga.
Perf.: $525   **Exc.:** $375   **VGood:** $340

Browning BPS Game
Gun Deer Special

Browning BPS NWTF
Turkey Series

Browning BPS Waterfowl
10-Gauge

BROWNING BPS GAME GUN DEER SPECIAL

Same specs as BPS except 12-ga.; 3-inch chamber; heavy 20-1/2-inch barrel with rifled choke tube; rifle-type sights with adjustable rear; solid receiver scope mount; "rifle" stock dimensions for scope or open sights; gloss or matte finished wood with checkering; newly designed receiver/magazine tube/ barrel mounting system to eliminate play; sling swivel studs; polished blue metal. Made by Miroku in Japan. Introduced 1992.

Perf.: $430   **Exc.:** $240   **VGood:** $200

BROWNING BPS GAME GUN TURKEY SPECIAL

Same specs as BPS except 12-ga.; 3-inch chamber; light 20-1/2-inch barrel; Extra-Full Invector choke tube; drilled and tapped for scope mounting; rifle-style satin-finished walnut stock; swivel studs; dull-finished barrel, receiver. Made in Japan by Miroku. Introduced 1992.

Perf.: $400   **Exc.:** $275   **VGood:** $240

BROWNING BPS LADIES & YOUTH MODEL

Same specs as BPS except 20-ga.; 22-inch barrel; shortened walnut pistol-grip stock; recoil pad. Made in Japan. Introduced 1986.

Perf.: $380   **Exc.:** $220   **VGood:** $195

BROWNING BPS PIGEON GRADE

Same specs as BPS except 12-ga.; 3-inch chamber; 26-inch, 28-inch vent-rib barrel; select high grade walnut stock, forend; gold-trimmed receiver. Made in Japan. Introduced 1992; still imported.

Perf.: $500   **Exc.:** $420   **VGood:** $345

BROWNING BPS STALKER

Same specs as BPS except 10-, 12-ga.; 3-inch, 3-1/2-inch chamber; 24-inch, 26-inch, 28-inch, 30-inch barrel; black-finished synthetic stock, forearm; matte blued finish on metal; black recoil pad. Made in Japan. Introduced 1987; still imported.

Perf.: $445   **Exc.:** $380   **VGood:** $335

BROWNING BPS NWTF TURKEY SERIES PUMP SHOTGUN

Similar to the BPS Stalker except has full coverage Mossy Oak Break- Up camo finish on synthetic stock, forearm and exposed metal parts. Offered in 10 and 12 gauge, 3-inch or 3-1/2-inch chamber; 24-inch bbl. has extra-full choke tube and Hi-Viz fiber optic sights. Introduced 2001.

10-ga., 3-1/2-inch chamber		
Perf.: $400	**Exc.:** $340	**VGood:** $275
12-ga., 3-1/2-inch chamber		
Perf.: $400	**Exc.:** $340	**VGood:** $275
12-ga., 3-inch chamber		
Perf.: $400	**Exc.:** $340	**VGood:** $275

BROWNING BPS UPLAND SPECIAL

Same specs as BPS except 12-, 20-ga.; 22-inch barrel; walnut straight-grip stock, forearm. Made in Japan. Introduced 1989.

Perf.: $575   **Exc.:** $440   **VGood:** $300

BROWNING BPS MICRO PUMP SHOTGUN

Same as BPS Upland Special except 20-ga. only, 22-inch Invector barrel, stock has pistol grip with recoil pad. Length of pull is 13-1/4-inch; weighs 6 lbs., 12 oz. Introduced 1986.

Perf.: $395   **Exc.:** $310   **VGood:** $265

BROWNING BPS WATERFOWL 10-GAUGE

Same specs as BPS except 10-ga.; 3 1/2-inch chamber; 28-inch, 30-inch vent-rib barrel; high grade stock; gold-trimmed receiver. Made in Japan. Introduced 1993.

Perf.: $625   **Exc.:** $430   **VGood:** $375

BROWNING BPS WATERFOWL CAMO PUMP SHOTGUN

Similar to the BPS Hunter except completely covered with Mossy Oak Shadow Grass camouflage. Available in 12-gauge, with 24-inch, 26-inch or 28-inch barrel, 3-inch chamber. Introduced 1999.

Perf.: $460   **Exc.:** $385   **VGood:** $340

BROWNING BPS 10 GAUGE SHOTGUNS

Chambered for the 10-gauge, 3-1/2-inch load. Offered in 24-inch, 26-inch and 28-inch barrels. Offered with walnut, black composite (Stalker models) or camouflage stock and forend. Introduced 1999. Imported.

Hunter (walnut)		
Perf.: $460	**Exc.:** $395	**VGood:** $350
Stalker (composite)		
Perf.: $465	**Exc.:** $400	**VGood:** $355
Mossy Oak Shadow Grass or Break-Up Camo		
Perf.: $540	**Exc.:** $495	**VGood:** $.410

BROWNING BPS 10-GAUGE CAMO PUMP

Similar to the BPS 10-gauge Hunter except completely covered with Mossy Oak Shadow Grass camouflage. Available with 24-inch, 26-inch, 28-inch barrel. Introduced 1999. Imported.

Perf.: $540   **Exc.:** $495   **VGood:** $.410

BROWNING MODEL 12

Slide action; 20-, 28-ga.; 2-3/4-inch chamber; 26-inch Modified barrel; high post floating rib with grooved sighting plane; weighs about 7 lbs.; cut-checkered select walnut stock, forearm with semi-gloss finish; Grade V has high-grade walnut; crossbolt safety in trigger guard; polished blue finish. Made in Japan. Reproduction of the Winchester Model 12. The 20-ga. was limited to 8000 guns; introduced 1988, discontinued 1990. The 28-ga. was limited to 8500 Grade I and 4000 Grade V guns; introduced 1991, discontinued 1992.

Grade I		
Perf.: $450	**Exc.:** $320	**VGood:** $280
Grade V		
Perf.: $795	**Exc.:** $600	**VGood:** $450

BROWNING MODEL 42

Slide action; .410; 3-inch chamber; 26-inch Full barrel; high post floating rib with grooved sighting plane; weighs about 6-3/4 lbs.; cut-checkered select walnut stock, forearm with semi-gloss finish; Grade V has high-grade walnut; crossbolt safety in trigger guard; polished blue finish. Made in Japan. Reproduction of the Winchester Model 42. Limited to 6000 Grade I and 6000 Grade V guns. Introduced 1991; discontinued 1993.

Grade I		
Perf.: $500	**Exc.:** $370	**VGood:** $300
Grade V		
Perf.: $795	**Exc.:** $625	**VGood:** $500

BROWNING RECOILLESS TRAP

Bolt action; single shot; 12-ga.; 2-3/4-inch chamber; back-bored 30-inch barrel; Invector Plus tubes; ventilated rib adjusts to move point of impact; weighs about 9 lbs.; cut-checkered select walnut stock, forearm with high gloss finish; adjustable for drop at comb and length of pull; bolt action eliminates up to 72 percent of recoil; forend is used to cock action when the action is forward. Made in Japan. Introduced 1993.

Perf.: $825   **Exc.:** $790   **VGood:** $680

BROWNING RECOILLESS TRAP MICRO

Same specs as Recoilless Trap except 27-inch barrel; weighs 8-5/8 lbs.; stock length of pull is adjustable from 13-inch to 13-3/4-inch. Made in Japan. Introduced 1995; still imported.

Perf.: $825   **Exc.:** $790   **VGood:** $680

BROWNING SINGLE SHOT SHOTGUNS BROWNING BT-99 MAX

Single shot; boxlock; 12-ga.; 2-3/4-inch chamber; 32-inch, 34-inch vent-rib barrel; Invector Plus choke tubes; weighs 8-5/8 lbs.; ivory front sight, middle bead; hand-checkered walnut pistol-grip Monte Carlo or standard stock, forend; gold-plated trigger; automatic ejector; recoil pad. Made in Japan. Introduced 1995; still in production.

Perf.: $1200	**Exc.:** $710	**VGood:** $580
Stainless model with black ported barrel		
Perf.: $1450	**Exc.:** $825	**VGood:** $650

BROWNING BT-99 TRAP

Same specs as BT-99 Max except Improved, Full fixed choke or Invector Plus chokes (standard 1992); no gold plating; also available in stainless version with black barrel. Made in Japan. Introduced 1969; discontinued 1994. Reintroduced 2001.

Perf.: $800	**Exc.:** $500	**VGood:** $420
Stainless model with black barrel		
Perf.: $1275	**Exc.:** $850	**VGood:** $650
Pigeon Grade high-grade stock		
Perf.: $1150	**Exc.:** $700	**VGood:** $600
Signature Painted with red, black stock		
Perf.: $950	**Exc.:** $500	**VGood:** $450
Golden Clays with gold inlays		
Perf.: $1950	**Exc.:** $1400	**VGood:** $1150
Conventional stock, 32-inch or 34-inch barrel		
Perf.: $895	**Exc.:** $700	**VGood:** $550
Adj.-comb stock, 32-inch or 34-inch barrel		
Perf.: $1298	**Exc.:** $1063	**VGood:** $938

BROWNING BT-99 PLUS

Same specs as BT-99 Max except high, wide rib, Monte Carlo-style stock. Introduced 1976; Competition name dropped 1978; discontinued 1994.

Perf.: $1200	**Exc.:** $900	**VGood:** $750
Stainless model with black barrel		
Perf.: $1475	**Exc.:** $900	**VGood:** $750
Pigeon Grade high grade stock		
Perf.: $1425	**Exc.:** $900	**VGood:** $750
Signature Painted with red, black stock		
Perf.: $1400	**Exc.:** $900	**VGood:** $780
Golden Clays with gold inlays		
Perf.: $2475	**Exc.:** $2000	**VGood:** $1775

BROWNING BT-99 PLUS MICRO

Same specs as BT-99 Max except 28-inch, 30-inch ported barrel with adjustable rib system; Invector Plus choke system and back-bored barrel; buttstock with adjustable length of pull range of 13-1/2-inch to 14-inch; Browning's recoil reducer system; scaled down for smaller shooters; marketed in Travel Vault case. Made in Japan. Introduced 1991; discontinued 1994.

Perf.: $1325	**Exc.:** $900	**VGood:** $750

Stainless model with black barrel

Perf.: $1625	**Exc.:** $1400	**VGood:** $1200

Pigeon Grade high grade stock

Perf.: $1475	**Exc.:** $1250	**VGood:** $1000

Signature Painted with red, black stock

Perf.: $1475	**Exc.:** $1250	**VGood:** $1000

Golden Clays with gold inlays

Perf.: $2625	**Exc.:** $2000	**VGood:** $1600

BROWNING BT-100 TRAP

Single shot; 12-ga.; 2-3/4-inch chamber; back-bored 32-inch, 34-inch barrel with Invector Plus, or fixed Full choke; weighs 8-5/8 lbs.; 48-1/2-inch overall length (32-inch barrel); cut-checkered walnut Monte Carlo stock, wedge-shaped forend with finger groove; high gloss finish; drop-out trigger adjustable for weight of pull from 3-1/2 to 5-1/2 lbs., and for three length positions; Ejector-Selector allows ejection or extraction of shells; stainless steel or blue finish; optional adjustable comb stock with thumbhole. Made in Japan. Introduced 1995; still imported. Blue finish.

Grade I, blue, Monte Carlo, Invector Plus

Perf.: $1835	**Exc.:** $1225	**VGood:** $985

Grade I, blue, adj. comb, Invector Plus

Perf.: $2073	**Exc.:** $1463	**VGood:** $1223

Stainless steel, Monte Carlo, Invector Plus

Perf.: $2310	**Exc.:** $1475	**VGood:** $1125

Stainless steel, adj. comb, Invector Plus

Perf.: $2549	**Exc.:** $1714	**VGood:** $1364

CAPRINUS SWEDEN

Over/under; 12-ga.; 2-3/4-inch chamber; 28-inch, 30-inch barrel; interchangeable choke tubes; high-grade European walnut, optional Monte Carlo stock; oil finish; checkered butt; single selective trigger ejectors; double safety system; stainless steel construction. Made in Sweden. Introduced 1982; discontinued 1985.

Skeet Special

Perf.: $3600	**Exc.:** $2700	**VGood:** $2350

Skeet Game

Perf.: $3650	**Exc.:** $2750	**VGood:** $2400

Game

Perf.: $3700	**Exc.:** $2800	**VGood:** $2400

Trap

Perf.: $3600	**Exc.:** $2700	**VGood:** $2350

CARLO CASARTELLI

Side-by-side; sidelock; various gauges; elaborate game scene and/or scroll engraving was available. Essentially a custom order gun. No longer imported.

Perf.: $13,000	**Exc.:** $9700	**VGood:** $7900

CENTURION ORDNANCE POSEIDON

Slide action; 12 ga.; 1-3/4-inch chamber (shoots mini-shells and slugs); 18-1/4-inch smoothbore barrel; 13-inch LOP; black synthetic stock and forearm; 6-shot magazine; adjustable rear sight; weighs 5 lbs., 5 oz.. Imported in prototype form only 2001.

Perf.: $295	**Exc.:** $250	**VGood:** $225

CENTURY KHAN ARTHEMIS (SUPER ARTHEMIS)

Over/under; 12-, 20, 28 ga., .410 bore; 3-inch chambers, 28-inch barrels; vent. Rib; SST; extractors; checkered walnut stock and forearm; weighs 5.3 to 7.4 lbs. Imported from Turkey by Century International Arms, Inc. until late 2004. Importation resumed by Legacy Sports International, early 2005.

Perf.: $450	**Exc.:** $395	**VGood:** $350

Browning BT-99 Plus Micro

Browning BT-100 Trap

Century Kahn Super Arthemis

Century Centurion

Century Centurion New Model

Chapuis Progress RBV

Add $25 to above prices for 20 ga or 28 ga.
Add $50 for .410 bore.

CENTURY PHANTOM

Semi-auto.; 12 ga.; 3-inch chamber; 24-inch, 26-inch 28-inch barrel; vent. Rib; 3 choke tubes; black synthetic stock and forearm. Imported from Turkey by Century International Arms, Inc.

Perf.: $265	**Exc.:** $225	**VGood:** $200

CENTURY SAS-12

Semi-auto.; 12 ga.; 2-3/4-inch chamber; 22-inch, 23-1/2-inch barrel; detachable 3- or 5-shot magazine; black synthetic stock and forearm. Manufactured by PRC in China. Imported by Century International Arms, Inc.

Perf.: $225	**Exc.:** $185	**VGood:** $165

CENTURY COACH GUN

Side-by-side; 12-, 20-ga., .410 bore; exposed hammers; 20-inch barrels; steel construction; checkered walnut stock and forearm; sling swivels. Imported from China by Century International Arms, Inc.

Perf.: $240	**Exc.:** $195	**VGood:** $175

CENTURY MODEL YL12

Slide action; 12 ga.; 2-3/4-inch, 3-inch chamber; 19-inch barrel; bead or rifle sights; fixed choke; weighs 7.2 lbs. Imported from China by Century International Arms, Inc.

Perf.: $140	**Exc.:** $115	**VGood:** $100

CENTURY CENTURION (OLD MODEL)

Over/under; boxlock; 12-ga.; 2-3/4-inch chamber; 28-inch Modofied/Full barrel; weighs 7-1/4 lbs.; European Walnut stock; double triggers; extractors; polished blue finish. Introduced 1993; formerly imported by Century International Arms, Inc.

Perf.: $320	**Exc.:** $220	**VGood:** $200

CENTURY CENTURION (NEW MODEL)

Over/under; 12-, 20-, 28-ga., .410 bore; bead sight; SST; 3-inch chambers (2-3/4-inch 28 ga.); 5 choke tubes (12 and 20 ga.); gloss finish Turkish walnut stock; automatic safety; hand checkering, extractors; 4140 drilled steel barrel; ventilated recoil pad; weighs 5.3 to 7.35 lbs.; 8mm top rib (12 & 20 ga.), 7mm top rib (28 ga. & .410 bore). Imported from Turkey beginning 2005 by Century International Arms, Inc.

Perf.: $390	**Exc.:** $295	**VGood:** $235

CENTURY BLACK DIAMOND

Semi-auto.; 12 ga.; 22-inch barrel. Imported from Turkey by Century International Arms, Inc.

Perf.: $180	**Exc.:** $140	**VGood:** $120

CENTURY TOZ MODEL 34

Over/under; 12-, 20, 28-ga.; full choke over modified; ejectors (20 ga. only); 28-inch barrel (26-inch 28 ga.); overall length 45-inches (28 ga. 43-inches); blued receiver; 1-inch recoil pad; weighs 6.7 to 7.5 lbs. Imported from Russia by Century International Arms, Inc.

Perf.: $190	**Exc.:** $150	**VGood:** $130

CHAPUIS PROGRESS RBV

Side-by-side; boxlock, sideplates; 12-, 20-ga.; 26-1/2-inch, 27-1/2-inch barrels; ventilated rib; weighs about 6-1/4 lbs.; fine-checkered oil-finished French or American walnut straight or pistol-grip stock; auto ejectors; double triggers; chromed bores; scroll engraving. Made in France. Introduced 1979; discontinued 1982.

Perf.: $1800	**Exc.:** $1400	**VGood:** $1200

CHAPUIS PROGRESS RG

Same specs as Progress RBV except boxlock. Introduced 1979; discontinued 1982; reintroduced 1989; no longer imported.

Perf.: $1200	**Exc.:** $900	**VGood:** $750

Chapuis Progress RG

Charles Daly Diamond Grade Trap (1971)

Charles Daly Diamond Grade (1984)

CHAPUIS PROGRESS SLUG
Same specs as Progress RBV except boxlock; right barrel is rifled for slugs. No longer imported.
Perf.: $1200   **Exc.:** $900   **VGood:** $750

CHAPUIS ST. BONETT
Side-by-side; 12-, 16-, 20-ga.; boxlock with case colored or coin finished sideplates with fine English scroll or game scene engraving; 27 ½-inch monobloc barrels; ejectors; DTs; checkered straight grip walnut stock and forearm; hardshell case. Limited importation began 1997.
Perf.: $2675   **Exc.:** $2300   **VGood:** $2000

CHAPUIS O/U
Over/under; sidelock; 12-, 16-, 20-ga.; 22-inch, 23-1/2-inch, 26-2/3-inch, 27-1/2-inch, 31-1/2-inch barrel; choked to customer specs; choice of rib styles; French walnut straight English or pistol-grip stock; auto ejectors or extractors; long trigger guard. Made in France. Introduced 1989; no longer imported.
Perf.: $3450   **Exc.:** $2250   **VGood:** $1900
NOTE: 20-, 28-gauges bring 25 percent to 35 percent more than prices shown. The .410 is as much as 50 percent higher.

CHARLES DALY AUTO
Recoil-operated autoloader; 12-ga.; 5-shot magazine; 3-shot plug furnished; 26-inch Improved, 28-inch Modified or Full, 30-inch Full barrels; vent rib; hand-checkered walnut pistol-grip stock, forearm; button safety; copy of early Browning patents. Made in Japan. Introduced 1973; discontinued 1975.
Perf.: $300   **Exc.:** $250   **VGood:** $210

CHARLES DALY DIAMOND GRADE
Over/under; boxlock; 12-, 20-, 28-ga.; .410; 26-inch, 28-inch, 30-inch barrels; choked Skeet/Skeet, Improved/Modified, Modified/Full, Full/Full; vent rib; extensive hand-checkered French walnut pistol-grip stock, beavertail forearm; selective single trigger; selective ejection system; safety/barrel selector; engraved receiver, trigger guard. Made in Japan. Introduced 1967; discontinued 1973.

Field model		
Perf.: $1000	**Exc.:** $900	**VGood:** $800
Skeet model		
Perf.: $1050	**Exc.:** $900	**VGood:** $800
Trap model		
Perf.: $900	**Exc.:** $780	**VGood:** $700

CHARLES DALY DIAMOND-REGENT GRADE
Same specs as Diamond Grade except highly figured French walnut stock; profuse engraving; hunting scenes inlaid in gold, silver; firing pins removable through breech face. Made in Japan. Introduced 1967; discontinued 1973.
Perf.: $1900   **Exc.:** $1350   **VGood:** $1150

CHARLES DALY DIAMOND DL DOUBLE SHOTGUN
Side-by-side; 12-, 20-ga., .410 bore; 3-inch chambers; 28, 2-3/4-inch chambers; 28-inch barrel (Mod. & Full), 26-inch (Imp. Cyl. & Mod.), 26-inch (Full & Full, .410); weighs about 5-7 lbs.; select fancy European walnut; English-style butt; beavertail forend; hand-checkered, hand-rubbed oil finish; drop-forged action with gas escape valves; demiblock barrels with concave rib; selective automatic ejectors; hand-detachable double safety sidelocks with hand-engraved rose and scrollwork; hinged front trigger; color case-hardened receiver. Introduced 1997. Imported from Spain by K.B.I., Inc.

12- or 20-gauge		
Perf.: $6060	**Exc.:** $4950	**VGood:** $4375
28 gauge		
Perf.: $6160	**Exc.:** $4995	**VGood:** $4575
.410		
Perf.: $6160	**Exc.:** $4995	**VGood:** $4575

CHARLES DALY DIAMOND REGENT DL DOUBLE SHOTGUN
Side-by-side; 12-, 20-ga.;.410, bore; 3-inch chambers; 28, 2-3/4-inch chambers; 28-inch barrel (Mod. & Full), 26-inch (Imp. Cyl. & Mod.), 26-inch (Full & Full, .410); weighs about 5-7 lbs.; special select fancy European walnut, English-style butt, splinter forend; hand-checkered; hand-rubbed oil finish; drop-forged action with gas escape valves; demiblock barrels of chrome- nickel steel with concave rib; selective automatic-ejectors; hand-detachable, double-safety H&H sidelocks with demi-relief hand engraving; H&H pattern easy-opening feature; hinged trigger; coin-finished action. Introduced 1997. Imported from Spain by K.B.I., Inc.

12- or 20-gauge		
Perf.: $18,950	**Exc.:** $15,750	**VGood:** $13,250
28-gauge		
Perf.: $18,950	**Exc.:** $15,750	**VGood:** $13,250
.410		
Perf.: $18,950	**Exc.:** $15,750	**VGood:** $13,250

CHARLES DALY DIAMOND REGENT GTX DL HUNTER O/U
Over/under; 12-, 20-ga.; .410 bore; 3-inch chambers; 28, 2-3/4-inch chambers; 26-inch, 28-inch, 30-inch barrel (choke tubes), 26-inch (Imp. Cyl. & Mod. in 28, 26-inch (Full & Full) in .410; weighs about 7 lbs.; extra select fancy European walnut with 24-inch hand checkering; hand rubbed oil finish; Boss-type action with internal side lumps; deep cut hand-engraved scrollwork and game scene set in full sideplates; GTX detachable single selective trigger system with coil springs; chrome-moly steel barrels; automatic safety; automatic ejectors; white bead front sight; metal bead center sight. Introduced 1997; dropped 1997. Imported from Italy by K.B.I., Inc.

12 or 20		
Perf.: $19,750	**Exc.:** $16,250	**VGood:** $13,750
28; MSR		
Perf.: $19,750	**Exc.:** $16,2500	**VGood:** $13,750
.410		
Perf.: $19,7500	**Exc.:** $16,250	**VGood:** $13,750
Diamond Regent GTX EDL Hunter (as above with engraved scroll and birds, 10 gold inlays), 12 or 20		
As above, 28		
Perf.: $23,000	**Exc.:** $19,500	**VGood:** $16,000
As above, .410		
Perf.: $23,000	**Exc.:** $19,500	**VGood:** $16,000

CHARLES DALY DIAMOND GTX SPORTING O/U SHOTGUN
Over/under: 12-, 20-ga.; 3-inch chambers; 28-inch, 30-inch barrel with choke tubes; weighs about 8.5 lbs.; checkered deluxe walnut stock; Sporting Clays dimensions; pistol grip; semi-beavertail forend; hand-rubbed oil finish; chromed, hand-engraved receiver; chrome-moly steel barrels; GTX detachable single selective trigger system with coil springs; automatic safety; automatic ejectors; red bead front sight; ported barrels. Introduced 1997. Imported from Italy by K.B.I., Inc.
Perf.: $5260   **Exc.:** $4750   **VGood:** $4275

CHARLES DALY DIAMOND GTX TRAP AE-MC O/U SHOTGUN
Over/under; 12-ga.; 2-3/4-inch chambers; 30-inch barrel (Full & Full); weighs about 8.5 lbs.; checkered deluxe walnut stock; pistol grip; trap dimensions; semi- beavertail forend; hand-rubbed oil finish; silvered, hand-engraved receiver; chrome-moly steel barrels; GTX detachable single selective trigger system with coil springs; automatic safety; automatic-ejectors; red bead front sight; metal bead middle; recoil pad. Introduced 1997. Imported from Italy by K.B.I., Inc.
Perf.: $5865   **Exc.:** $4900   **VGood:** $4400

CHARLES DALY DIAMOND GTX DL HUNTER O/U
Over/under; 12-, 20-ga.; .410 bore; 3-inch chambers; 28, 2-3/4-inch chambers; 26, 28-inch barrels; choke tubes in 12- and 20-ga.; 26-inch (Imp. Cyl. & Mod.), 26-inch (Full & Full) in .410- bore; weighs about 8.5 lbs.; select fancy European walnut stock; 24 lpi hand checkering; hand-rubbed oil finish; Boss-type action with internal side lugs; hand-engraved scrollwork and game scene; GTX detachable single selective trigger system with coil springs; chrome-moly steel barrels; automatic safety; automatic ejectors; red bead front sight; recoil pad. Introduced 1997. Imported from Italy by K.B.I., Inc.

12 or 20		
Perf.: $11,250.00	**Exc.:** $9000	**VGood:** $7000
28		
Perf.: $11,250	**Exc.:** $9000	**VGood:** $7000
.410		
Perf.: $11,250	**Exc.:** $9000	**VGood:** $7000
GTX EDL Hunter (with gold inlays), 12, 20		
Perf.: $13,750	**Exc.:** $11,250	**VGood:** $9000
As above, 28		
Perf.: $13,750	**Exc.:** $11,250	**VGood:** $9000
As above, .410		
Perf.: $13,750	**Exc.:** $11,250	**VGood:** $9000

CHARLES DALY DIAMOND GRADE (1984)
Over/under; boxlock; 12-, 20-ga.; 27-inch barrels; three choke tubes; hand-checkered oil-finished European walnut stock; single selective competition trigger; selective auto ejectors; silvered, engraved receiver. Made in Italy. Introduced 1984; discontinued 1987.
Perf.: $650   **Exc.:** $500   **VGood:** $480

CHARLES DALY DIAMOND SKEET (1984)
Same specs as Diamond Grade (1984) except 12-ga.; 26-inch Skeet/Skeet barrels; competition vent rib; Skeet stock; target trigger. Introduced 1984; discontinued 1988.
Perf.: $750   **Exc.:** $450   **VGood:** $400

CHARLES DALY DIAMOND TRAP (1984)

Same specs as Diamond Grade (1984) except 12-ga.; 30-inch barrels; competition vent top and middle ribs; Monte Carlo stock; target trigger. Introduced 1984; discontinued 1988.

Perf.: $800   **Exc.:** $500   **VGood:** $450

CHARLES DALY EMPIRE DOUBLE

Side-by-side; boxlock; hammerless; 12-, 16-, 20-ga; 2-3/4-inch (16-ga.), 3-inch (12-, 20-ga.) chamber; 26-inch, 28-inch, 30-inch barrels; standard choke combos; checkered walnut pistol-grip stock, beavertail forearm; plain extractors; non-selective single trigger. Made in Japan. Introduced 1968; discontinued 1971.

Exc.: $500   **VGood:** $380   **Good:** $300

CHARLES DALY EMPIRE EDL HUNTER O/U

Over/under; 12-, 20-ga.; .410 bore; 3-inch chambers; 28 ga., 2-3/4-inch; 26-inch, 28-inch barrels (12, 20, choke tubes), 26-inch (Imp. Cyl. & Mod., 28 ga.), 26-inch (Full & Full, .410); weighs about 7 lbs.; checkered walnut pistol grip buttstock; semi-beavertail forend; recoil pad; silvered, engraved receiver; chrome-moly barrels; gold single selective trigger; automatic safety; automatic ejectors; red bead front sight, metal bead middle sight. Introduced 1997. Imported from Italy by K.B.I., Inc.

Empire EDL (dummy sideplates) 12 or 20		
Perf.: $1365	**Exc.:** $1070	**VGood:** $875
Empire EDL		
Perf.: $1351	**Exc.:** $1056	**VGood:** $864
Empire EDL, .410		
Perf.: $1351	**Exc.:** $1056	**VGood: $864**

CHARLES DALY EMPIRE SPORTING O/U

Similar to the Empire EDL Hunter except 12- or 20-gauge only, 28-inch, 30-inch barrels with choke tubes; ported barrels; special stock dimensions. Introduced 1997. Imported from Italy by K.B.I., Inc.

Perf.: $1375   **Exc.:** $1075   **VGood:** $900

CHARLES DALY EMPIRE QUALITY TRAP

Single barrel; Anson & Deeley-type boxlock; 12-ga.; 30-inch, 32-inch, 34-inch vent-rib barrel; hand-checkered European walnut pistol-grip stock, forearm; automatic ejector. Made in Suhl, Germany. Introduced 1920; discontinued 1933.

Exc.: $1200   **VGood:** $900   **Good:** $700

CHARLES DALY EMPIRE TRAP AE MC

Single barrel; 12-ga.; 2-3/4-inch chambers; 30-inch barrel choke tubes; weighs about 7 lbs.; checkered walnut; pistol grip, semi-beavertail forend; silvered, engraved, reinforced receiver; chrome-moly steel barrels; gold single selective trigger; automatic safety; automatic ejector; red bead front sight; metal bead center; recoil pad. Introduced 1997. Imported from Italy by K.B.I., Inc.

Perf.: $1415   **Exc.:** $1075   **VGood:** $900

CHARLES DALY FIELD AUTO

Autoloader; 12-ga.; 2-3/4-inch, 3-inch chamber; 27-inch barrel; standard chokes or Invector choke tubes; weighs 7 1/4 lbs.; checkered walnut pistol-grip stock, forend; crossbolt safety; alloy receiver; chromed bolt; stainless steel gas piston. Made in Japan. Introduced 1984; discontinued 1987.

Perf.: $300   **Exc.:** $250   **VGood:** $210

CHARLES DALY FIELD GRADE

Over/under; boxlock; 12-, 20-, 28-ga., .410; 2-3/4-inch, 3-inch chambers (12-, 20-ga.); 26-inch, 28-inch, 30-inch barrels; choked Skeet/Skeet, Improved/Modified, Modified/Full, Full/Full; vent rib; hand-checkered walnut pistol-grip stock, fluted forearm; recoil pad (12-ga. Magnum); selective single trigger; automatic selective ejectors; safety/barrel selector; engraved receiver. Made in Japan. Introduced

Charles Daly Empire Double

Charles Daly Empire Quality Trap

Charles Daly Field Grade

Charles Daly Field III

1963 (12-, 20-ga.); introduced 1965 (28-ga., .410); discontinued 1976.

Perf.: $600   **Exc.:** $500   **VGood:** $450

CHARLES DALY FIELD GRADE (1989)

Over/under; boxlock; 12-, 20-ga.; 3-inch chambers; 26-inch, 28-inch barrels; standard fixed choke combos; cut-checkered walnut pistol-grip stock, forend with semi-gloss finish; black vent rubber recoil pad; manual safety extractors; single-stage selective trigger; color case-hardened, engraved receiver. Made in Europe. Introduced 1989; still in production.

Perf.: $450   **Exc.:** $350   **VGood:** $280

CHARLES DALY FIELD GRADE DELUXE (1989)

Same specs as Field Grade (1989) except 12-, 20-ga.; Improved Cylinder, Modified and Full choke tubes; automatic selective ejectors; antique silver finish on frame. Introduced 1989; still imported.

Perf.: $670   **Exc.:** $450   **VGood:** $400

CHARLES DALY FIELD III

Over/under; boxlock; 12-, 20-ga.; 26-inch, 28-inch, 30-inch chrome-lined barrels; standard choke combos; vent rib; checkered European walnut stock, forend; single selective trigger extractors; blued, engraved frame. Made in Italy. Introduced 1984; discontinued 1988.

Perf.: $375   **Exc.:** $320   **VGood:** $295

CHARLES DALY FIELD HUNTER DOUBLE SHOTGUN

Side-by-side; 10-, 12-, 20, 28-ga., .410 bore (3-inch chambers; 28 has 2-3/4-inch); 32-inch barrel (Mod. & Mod.), 28, 30-inch (Mod. & Full), 26-inch (Imp. Cyl. & Mod.), .410 (Full & Full); weighs 6 lbs. to 11.4 lbs.; checkered walnut pistol grip and forend; silvered, engraved receiver; gold single selective trigger in 10-, 12-, and 20 ga.; double triggers in 28 and .410; automatic safety; extractors; gold bead front sight. Introduced 1997. Imported from Spain by K.B.I., Inc.

10-ga.		
Perf.: $665	**Exc.:** $465	**VGood:** $400
12- or 20-ga.		
Perf.: $665	**Exc.:** $465	**VGood:** $400
28-ga.		
Perf.: $595	**Exc.:** $395	**VGood:** $330
.410-bore		
Perf.: $595	**Exc.:** $395	**VGood:** $330
As above, 12 or 20 AE. MC		
Perf.: $665	**Exc.:** $465	**VGood:** $400

CHARLES DALY FIELD HUNTER OVER/UNDER SHOTGUN

Over/under; 12-, 20-, 28-ga. and .410 bore (3-inch chambers, 28 ga. has 2-3/4-inch); 28-inch barrel Mod & Full, 26-inch Imp. Cyl. & Mod (.410 is Full & Full); weighs about 7 lbs.; checkered walnut pistol grip and forend; blued engraved receiver; chrome-moly steel barrels; gold single selective trigger; automatic safety; extractors; gold bead front sight. Introduced 1997. Imported from Italy by K.B.I., Inc.

12- or 20-ga.		
Perf.: $670	**Exc.:** $475	**VGood:** $395
28-ga.		
Perf.: $750	**Exc.:** $555	**VGood:** $475
.410 bore		
Perf.: $750	**Exc.:** $555	**VGood:** $475

CHARLES DALY FIELD HUNTER AE SHOTGUN

Similar to the Field Hunter except 28-gauge and .410-bore only; 26-inch (Imp. Cyl. & Mod., 28-gauge), 26-inch (Full & Full, .410); automatic; ejectors. Introduced 1997. Imported from Italy by K.B.I., Inc.

28		
Perf.: $865	**Exc.:** $745	**VGood:** $640
.410		
Perf.: $865	**Exc.:** $745	**VGood:** $640

CHARLES DALY SUPERIOR HUNTER AE SHOTGUN

Similar to the Field Hunter AE except has silvered, engraved receiver. Introduced 1997. Imported from Italy by F.B.I., Inc.

Charles Daly Superior Sporting

Charles Daly Lux Over/Under

28-ga.
Perf.: $1025   **Exc.:** $895   **VGood:** $720
.410 bore
Perf.: $1025   **Exc.:** $895   **VGood:** $720

CHARLES DALY FIELD HUNTER AE-MC

Similar to the Field Hunter except in 12 or 20 only, 26-inch or 28-inch barrels with five multichoke tubes; automatic ejectors. Introduced 1997. Imported from Italy by K.B.I., Inc.

12 or 20
Perf.: $865   **Exc.:** $745   **VGood:** $640

CHARLES DALY SUPERIOR SPORTING O/U

Similar to the Field Hunter AE-MC except 28-inch or 30-inch barrels; silvered, engraved receiver; five choke tubes; ported barrels; red bead front sight. Introduced 1997. Imported from Italy by K.B.I., Inc.
Perf.: $1130   **Exc.:** $955   **VGood:** $790

CHARLES DALY HAMMERLESS DRILLING

Anson & Deeley-type boxlock; 12-, 16-, 20-ga.; rifle barrel chambered for 25-20, 25-35, 30-30; automatic rear sight; hand-checkered European walnut pistol-grip stock, forearm; plain extractors. Made in three grades that differ only in checkering, amount of engraving, wood, overall quality. Made in Suhl, Germany. H.A. Linder models exhibit extensive higher grade engraving, and inlays which affect value. Introduced 1921; discontinued 1933.

Superior Quality
Exc.: $2200   **VGood:** $1650   **Good:** $1300
Diamond Quality
Exc.: $4000   **VGood:** $3000   **Good:** $2500
Regent Diamond Quality (Linder)
Exc.: $7500   **VGood:** $6850   **Good:** $6000
Regent Diamond Quality (Sauer)
Exc.: $6500   **VGood:** $4500   **Good:** $3800

CHARLES DALY HAMMERLESS OVER/UNDER

Over/under; Anson & Deeley-type boxlock; 12-, 16-, 20-ga.; 26-inch to 30-inch barrels; any standard choke combo; European walnut stock hand-checkered pistol grip, forearm; double triggers; automatic ejectors. Made in two grades that differ in grade of wood, checkering, amount of engraving, general overall quality. Made in Suhl, Germany. Introduced 1920; discontinued 1933.

Empire Quality
Exc.: $2500   **VGood:** $2150   **Good:** $1750
Diamond Quality
Exc.: $3600   **VGood:** $2800   **Good:** $2200

CHARLES DALY HAMMERLESS SIDE-BY-SIDE

Side-by-side; Anson & Deeley-type boxlock; 10-, 12-, 16-, 20-, 28-ga., .410; 26-inch to 28-inch barrels; any choke combo; checkered walnut pistol-grip stock, forearm; made in four grades; all have automatic ejectors, except Superior Quality; grades differ in grade of wood, checkering, amount of engraving, general overall quality. Made in Suhl, Germany. Shotguns made by H.A. Linder exhibit extensive higher-grade engraving, inlays and other custom features which affect value. Introduced 1920; discontinued 1933.

Superior Quality
Exc.: $700   **VGood:** $500   **Good:** $400
Empire Quality (Linder)
Exc.: $4000   **VGood:** $3000   **Good:** $2000
Diamond Quality (Linder)
Exc.: $9500   **VGood:** $7000   **Good:** $5000
Regent Diamond Quality (Linder)
Exc.: $13,000   **VGood:** $9000   **Good:** $7000
Empire Quality (Sauer)
Exc.: $3000   **VGood:** $2000   **Good:** $1500
Diamond Quality (Sauer)
Exc.: $5000   **VGood:** $3500   **Good:** $2200
Regent Diamond Quality (Sauer)
Exc.: $6500   **VGood:** $4800   **Good:** $3600

CHARLES DALY LUX OVER/UNDER

Over/under; boxlock; 12-, 20-, 28-ga., .410; 26-inch, 28-inch vent rib, chrome-lined barrels; three internal choke tubes; cut-checkered walnut pistol-grip stock, forend with semi-gloss finish; single selective trigger; auto selective ejectors; antique silver-finished frame. Made in Europe. Introduced 1989; no longer in production.
Perf.: $600   **Exc.:** $440   **VGood:** $390

CHARLES DALY LUX SIDE-BY-SIDE

Side-by-side; boxlock; 12-, 20-ga.; 26-inch barrel; choke tubes; cut-checkered walnut pistol-grip stock, semi-beavertail forend; single selective trigger; ejectors; recoil pad. Introduced 1990; discontinued 1994.
Perf.: $520   **Exc.:** $370   **VGood:** $300

CHARLES DALY MODEL 100 COMMANDER

Over/under; Anson & Deeley-type boxlock; 12-, 16-, 20-, 28-ga., .410; 26-inch, 28-inch, 30-inch barrels; Improved/Modified, Modified/Full chokes; hand-checkered European walnut straight or pistol-grip stock, forearm; automatic ejectors; double triggers or Miller single selective trigger; engraved receiver. Made in Liege, Belgium. Introduced 1933; discontinued at beginning of WWII.
Exc.: $425   **VGood:** $350   **Good:** $275
With single selective trigger
Exc.: $450   **VGood:** $370   **Good:** $300

CHARLES DALY MODEL 200 COMMANDER

Over/under; Anson & Deeley-type boxlock; 12-, 16-, 20-, 28-ga., .410; 26-inch, 28-inch, 30-inch barrels; Improved/Modified, Modified/Full chokes; hand-checkered select European walnut straight or pistol-grip stock, forearm; automatic ejectors; double triggers or Miller single selective trigger; elaborate engraved receiver. Made in Liege, Belgium. Introduced 1933; discontinued at beginning of WWII.
Exc.: $495   **VGood:** $350   **Good:** $290
With single selective trigger
Exc.: $525   **VGood:** $425   **Good:** $360

CHARLES DALY MODEL DSS

Side-by-side; boxlock; 12-, 20-ga.; 3-inch chambers; 26-inch barrels; choke tubes; weighs about 6-3/4 lbs.; cut-checkered figured walnut pistol-grip stock, semi-beavertail forend; black rubber recoil pad; automatic selective ejectors; automatic safety; gold single trigger; engraved, silvered frame. Introduced 1990; no longer imported.
Exc.: $550   **VGood:** $400   **Good:** $325

CHARLES DALY MODEL DSS

Side-by-side; boxlock; 12-, 20-ga.; 3-inch chambers; 26-inch barrels; choke tubes; weighs about 6-3/4 lbs.; cut-checkered figured walnut pistol-grip stock, semi-beavertail forend; black rubber recoil pad; automatic selective ejectors; automatic safety; gold single trigger; engraved, silvered frame. Introduced 1990; no longer imported.
Exc.: $550   **VGood:** $400   **Good:** $325

CHARLES DALY MULTI-XII

Gas-operated autoloader; 12-ga.; 3-inch chamber; 27-inch vent-rib barrel; Invector choke system; checkered walnut pistol-grip stock, forend; rosewood grip cap; brown vent recoil pad; shoots all loads without adjustment; scroll engraved receiver. Made in Japan. Introduced 1986; discontinued 1987.
Perf.: $400   **Exc.:** $300   **VGood:** $220

CHARLES DALY NOVAMATIC LIGHTWEIGHT

Autoloader; 12-ga.; 2-3/4-inch chamber; 4-shot tubular magazine; 26-inch, 28-inch barrel; Improved Cylinder or three-tube Quick-Choke system; plain or vent-rib barrel; checkered walnut pistol-grip stock, forearm. Made in Italy by Breda. Introduced 1968; discontinued 1968.

With plain barrel
Exc.: $265   **VGood:** $200   **Good:** $150
With vent rib
Exc.: $295   **VGood:** $230   **Good:** $180

CHARLES DALY NOVAMATIC LIGHTWEIGHT MAGNUM

Same specs as Novamatic Lightweight except 12-, 20-ga.; 3-inch chambers; 3-shot magazine; 28-inch vent-rib barrel; Full choke. Introduced 1968; discontinued 1968.
Exc.: $285   **VGood:** $250   **Good:** $190

CHARLES DALY NOVAMATIC LIGHTWEIGHT TRAP

Same specs as Novamatic Lightweight except 30-inch vent-rib barrel; Full choke; Monte Carlo trap stock; recoil pad. Introduced 1968; discontinued 1968.
Exc.: $300   **VGood:** $240   **Good:** $190

CHARLES DALY NOVAMATIC LIGHTWEIGHT SUPER

Same specs as Novamatic Lightweight except 12-, 20-ga.; 26-inch, 28-inch (only 12-ga.) barrel; Skeet choke available; standard vent rib (only 12-ga.); lighter weight. Introduced 1968; discontinued 1968.
Exc.: $280   **VGood:** $240   **Good:** $180

CHARLES DALY PRESENTATION GRADE

Over/under; boxlock; 12-, 20-ga.; 27-inch barrel; three choke tubes; hand-checkered, oil-finished European walnut stock; single selective competition trigger; selective auto ejectors; silvered, engraved receiver, sideplates. Made in Italy. Introduced 1984; discontinued 1986.
Perf.: $1000   **Exc.:** $800   **VGood:** $695

CHARLES DALY SEXTUPLE TRAP

Single barrel; Anson & Deeley-type boxlock; 12-ga.; 30-inch, 32-inch, 34-inch vent-rib barrel; hand-checkered European walnut pistol-grip stock, forearm; six locking bolts; automatic ejector. Made in two grades that differ only in checkering, amount of engraving, grade of wood, improved overall quality. Made in Suhl, Germany. Introduced 1920; discontinued 1933.

Empire Quality
Exc.: $1850   **VGood:** $1300   **Good:** $1050
Regent Diamond Quality
Exc.: $2500   **VGood:** $1750   **Good:** $1100

CHARLES DALY SUPERIOR GRADE OVER/UNDER

Over/under; boxlock; 12-, 20-, 28-ga., .410; 26-inch, 28-inch, 30-inch barrels; choked Skeet/Skeet, Improved/Modified, Modified/Full, Full/Full; vent-rib; hand-checkered walnut pistol-grip stock, beavertail forearm; selective single trigger; selective ejection system; safety/barrel selector; engraved receiver. Made in Japan. Introduced 1963; discontinued 1976.

Standard model		
Perf.: $700	**Exc.:** $550	**VGood:** $425
Trap model		
Perf.: $750	**Exc.:** $600	**VGood:** $460

CHARLES DALY SUPERIOR GRADE SIDE-BY-SIDE

Side-by-side; boxlock; 12-, 20-ga.; 26-inch, 28-inch, 30-inch chrome-lined barrels; standard choke combos; vent-rib; checkered European walnut stock, forend; single selective trigger. Introduced 1984; discontinued 1985.

Perf.: $510	**Exc.:** $395	**VGood:** $320

CHARLES DALY SUPERIOR HUNTER DOUBLE SHOTGUN

Side-by-side; 12-, 20-ga.; 3-inch chambers; 28-ga. 2-3/4-inch chambers; 28-inch barrel (Mod. & Full) 26-inch (Imp. Cyl. & Mod.); weighs about 7 lbs.; checkered walnut; pistol grip; splinter forend; silvered, engraved receiver; chrome-lined barrels; gold single trigger; automatic safety; extractors; gold bead front sight. Introduced 1997. Imported from Italy by K.B.I., Inc.

Exc. $890	**VGood:** $775	**Good:** $650
28-ga., 26-inch		
Exc.: $860	**VGood:** $745	**Good:** $620
470 EL		

CHARLES DALY EMPIRE HUNTER DOUBLE SHOTGUN

Similar to Superior Hunter except deluxe wood, game scene engraving, automatic ejectors. Introduced 1997. Imported from Italy by K.B.I., Inc.

12 or 20		
Perf.: $1165	**Exc.:** $975	**VGood:** $790

CHARLES DALY MODEL 306

This 3" side-by-side is offered in 12 and 20 gauge with 26" or 28" barrels. Turkish walnut stock, gold-plated single selective trigger and extractors. Three choke tubes.

NIB: $575	**Exc.:** $530	**VGood:** $475

CHARLES DALY SUPERIOR II

Over/under; boxlock; 12-, 20-ga.; 2-3/4-inch, 3-inch chambers (12-ga.); 26-inch, 28-inch, 30-inch chrome-lined barrels; vent-rib; standard choke combos; checkered European walnut stock, forend; single selective trigger; automatic ejectors; silvered receiver; engraving. Introduced 1984; discontinued 1988.

Perf.: $650	**Exc.:** $440	**VGood:** $390

CHARLES DALY SUPERIOR SINGLE TRAP

Single shot; boxlock; hammerless; 12-ga.; 32-inch, 34-inch barrels; Full choke; vent-rib; checkered walnut Monte Carlo pistol-grip stock, forearm; recoil pad; auto ejector. Made in Japan. Introduced 1968; discontinued 1976.

Perf.: $575	**Exc.:** $500	**VGood:** $400

CHARLES DALY SUPERIOR TRAP AE MC

Single barrel; 12-ga.; 2-3/4-inch chamber; 30-inch barrel choke tubes; weighs 7 lbs.; checkered walnut stock; pistol grip, semi-beavertail forend; silver engraved receiver; chrome-moly steel barrels; gold single selective trigger; automatic safety; automatic ejectors; red bead front sight; metal bead center; recoil pad. Introduced 1997. Imported from Italy by K.B.I., Inc.

Perf.: $1160	**Exc.:** $990	**VGood:** $815

Charles Daly Sextuple Trap

Charles Daly Superior Grade Over/Under

Charles Daly Superior Single Trap (postwar)

Charles Daly Superior Grade Over/Under Trap

Charles Daly Model 306

Charles Daly Superior Grade Engraving

Charles Daly Venture Grade

Charles Daly Venture Grade Trap

Charles Daly Model 105

CHARLES DALY VENTURE GRADE

Over/under; boxlock; 12-, 20-ga; 26-inch Skeet/Skeet or Improved/Modified, 28-inch Modified/Full, 30-inch Improved/Full barrels; vent rib; checkered walnut pistol-grip stock, forearm; manual safety; automatic ejectors; single selective trigger. Made in three variations. Made in Japan. Introduced 1973; discontinued 1976.

Standard model		
Perf.: $575	**Exc.:** $500	**VGood:** $400
Trap model, Monte Carlo stock, 30-inch barrel		
Perf.: $550	**Exc.:** $480	**VGood:** $390
Skeet model, 26-inch barrel		
Perf.: $600	**Exc.:** $520	**VGood:** $490

CHARLES DALY MODEL 105

This 3" 12 gauge over-and-under features an engraved nickel-plated steel receiver, double triggers

Charles Daly Model 106

Charles Daly VR-MC Semi-Auto

Charles Daly VR-MC Semi-Auto Youth

Charles Daly VR-MC Pump Youth

Charles Daly Maxi-Mag Pump

E.J. Churchill Field

and extractors. Chokes are fixed Modified and Full with 28" barrels or Modified and Improved Cylinder with 26" barrels.

NIB: $375   **Exc.:** $335   **VGood:** $295

CHARLES DALY MODEL 106

Available in 12, 20 and 28 gauge and .410 bore, the Model 106 O/U has a blued receiver with raised gold ducks and a rounded pistol grip. All but the .410 include three screw-in chokes. Barrels are 26" or 28" in 12 and 20 gauge and 26" in 28 gauge and .410. Frames are scaled to gauge.

NIB: $400   **Exc.:** $365   **VGood:** $300

CHARLES DALY FIELD HUNTER SEMI-AUTO LEFT HAND
Same as above but left hand only.

Perf.: $350   **Exc.:** $300   **VGood:** $275

CHARLES DALY FIELD HUNTER SEMI-AUTO BLACK CHROME TACTICAL
Same as above but with 22-inch Cylinder-bore smoothbore barrel, rifle sights.

Perf.: $350   **Exc.:** $300   **VGood:** $275

CHARLES DALY FIELD HUNTER VR-MC
This series of 3" semi-automatic 12 gauges is finished in one of four Realtree/Advantage camo patterns or matte black. Barrels are 24", 26" or 28". Advantage Timber model is available in 20 gauge and black matte is available in 20 and 28 gauge. Add 15 percent for camo.

NIB: $200   **Exc.:** $165   **VGood:** $130

CHARLES DALY HUNTER VR-MC YOUTH
As above but with a 1.6-inch shorter stock and 22" barrel. In 20 gauge only.

NIB: $190   **Exc.:** $150   **VGood:** $120

CHARLES DALY SUPERIOR II HUNTER
Semi-auto featuring oil-finished Turkish walnut stocks and three chokes. Available in 12 and 20 gauge with 26" or 28" barrel and 28 gauge with 26" barrel.

NIB: $500   **Exc.:** $435   **VGood:** $375

CHARLES DALY SUPERIOR II SPORT
Semi-auto in 12 gauge only with 28" or 30" ported barrel and wide rib.

NIB: $525   **Exc.:** $460   **VGood:** $400

CHARLES DALY SUPERIOR II TRAP
Semi-auto in 12 gauge, 30" ported barrel only with Monte Carlo comb and wide rib.

NIB: $535   **Exc.:** $470   **VGood:** $410

CHARLES DALY FIELD HUNTER MAXI-MAG VR-MC SEMI-AUTO
This 3.5" 12 gauge comes in one of three Realtree/Advantage camos and matte black with 24", 26" or 28" ported barrel. Add 15 percent for camo.

NIB: $550   **Exc.:** $500   **VGood:** $395

CHARLES DALY FIELD HUNTER PUMP
Slide-action; 12- and 20-ga.; 24-, 26-, 28- or 30-inch barrels; ventilated rib; black synthetic stock; 3 choke tubes. Still in production.

Perf.: $200   **Exc.:** $175   **VGood:** $150

Camo

Perf.: $250   **Exc.:** $200   **VGood:** $175

CHARLES DALY FIELD BLACK CHROME TACTICAL PUMP
Same as above but with 18-1/2-inch Cylinder-bore barrel, rifle sights.

Perf.: $175   **Exc.:** $150   **VGood:** $125

CHARLES DALY FIELD NICKEL TACTICAL PUMP
Same as above but with nickel finish.

Perf.: $185   **Exc.:** $160   **VGood:** $135

CHARLES DALY FIELD HUNTER 20-GA. YOUTH PUMP
Same as Field Hunter but in 20-ga. only and 22-inch barrel.

Perf.: $200   **Exc.:** $175   **VGood:** $150

Camo

Perf.: $250   **Exc.:** $200   **VGood:** $175

CHARLES DALY FIELD HUNTER MAXI-MAG VR-MC PUMP
Newer versions of the Maxi-Mag are recognized by an updated forend and availability in Timber or Hardwoods camo or matte black. All are 3.5" 12 gauges with a 24", 26" or 28" ported barrel. Add 15 percent for camo.

NIB: $200   **Exc.:** $175   **VGood:** $135

CHIPMUNK .410 YOUTH SHOTGUN
Gauge: .410 bore; 18-1/4-inch tapered, barrel; blue finish; weighs 3.25 lbs.; length: 33-inch; walnut stock; manually cocking single shot bolt; blued receiver.

Perf.: $185   **Exc.:** $160   **VGood:** $145

CHURCHILL, E.J., CROWN
Side-by-side; boxlock; hammerless; 12-, 16-, 20-, 28-ga., .410; 25-inch, 28-inch, 30-inch, 32-inch barrel; any desired choke combo; third-grade, hand-checkered European walnut stock, forearm; pistol grip or straight English-style; double triggers or single selective trigger; ejectors; Introduced 1900; discontinued 1982. Made in England.

Perf.: $4750   **Exc.:** $3200   **VGood:** $2600

With single selective trigger

Perf.: $5200   **Exc.:** $3700   **VGood:** $3000

20-ga.

Perf.: $5500   **Exc.:** $3800   **VGood:** $3000

28-ga.

Perf.: $6500   **Exc.:** $4500   **VGood:** $3500

.410-bore

Perf.: $7500   **Exc.:** $5000   **VGood:** $4200

CHURCHILL, E.J., FIELD
Side-by-side; sidelock; hammerless; 12-, 16-, 20-, 28-ga.; 25-inch, 28-inch, 30-inch, 32-inch barrel; any desired choke combo; third grade, hand-checkered European walnut stock, forearm; pistol grip or straight English-style; ejectors; double triggers or single selective trigger; engraving. Introduced 1900; discontinued 1982. Made in England.

Perf.: $9500   **Exc.:** $7500   **VGood:** $6500

With single selective trigger

Perf.: $10,500   **Exc.:** $8500   **VGood:** $7500

20-ga.

Perf.: $12,500   **Exc.:** $9000   **VGood:** $8000

28-ga.

Perf.: $14,500   **Exc.:** $10,500   **VGood:** $9000

CHURCHILL, E.J., HERCULES

Side-by-side; boxlock; hammerless; 12-, 16-, 20-, 28-ga.; 25-inch, 28-inch, 30-inch, 32-inch barrel; any desired choke combo; top-grade, hand-checkered European walnut stock, forearm; pistol grip or straight English-style; ejectors; double triggers or single selective trigger; engraving. Introduced 1900; discontinued 1982. Made in England.

   Perf.: $9000   **Exc.:** $7000   **VGood:** $6000

With single selective trigger

   Perf.: $10,000   **Exc.:** $8000   **VGood:** $7000

20-ga.

   Perf.: $12,000   **Exc.:** $8500   **VGood:** $7500

28-ga.

   Perf.: $14,000   **Exc.:** $9500   **VGood:** $8000

CHURCHILL, E.J., IMPERIAL

Side-by-side; boxlock; hammerless; 12-, 16-, 20-, 28-ga.; 25-inch, 28-inch, 30-inch, 32-inch barrel; any desired choke combo; second-grade, hand-checkered European walnut stock, forearm; pistol grip or straight English-style; ejectors; double triggers or single selective trigger; engraving. Introduced 1900; discontinued 1982. Made in England.

   Perf.: $19,500   **Exc.:** $13,500   **VGood:** $11,500

With single selective trigger

   Perf.: $20,000   **Exc.:** $14,000   **VGood:** $12,000

20-ga.

   Perf.: $24,000   **Exc.:** $16,000   **VGood:** $13,500

28-ga.

   Perf.: $28,000   **Exc.:** $19,000   **VGood:** $16,000

CHURCHILL, E.J., PREMIER

Over/under; sidelock; hammerless; 12-, 16-, 20-, 28-ga.; 25-inch, 28-inch, 30-inch, 32-inch barrel; hand-checkered European walnut stock, forearm; pistol grip or straight English-style; ejectors; double triggers or single selective trigger; English engraving. Introduced 1925; discontinued 1955. Made in England.

   Perf.: $18,000   **Exc.:** $12,000   **VGood:** $9000

With single selective trigger

   Perf.: $19,000   **Exc.:** $13,000   **VGood:** $10,000

20-ga.

   Perf.: $22,000   **Exc.:** $14,500   **VGood:** $11,000

28-ga.

   Perf.: $25,000   **Exc.:** $16,500   **VGood:** $13,000

CHURCHILL, E.J., PREMIER QUALITY

Side-by-side; sidelock; hammerless; 12-, 16-, 20-, 28-ga.; 25-inch, 28-inch, 30-inch, 32-inch barrel; any desired choke combo; top-grade, hand-checkered European walnut stock, forearm; pistol grip or straight English-style; ejectors; double triggers or single selective trigger; English engraving. Introduced 1900; discontinued 1982. Made in England.

   Perf.: $17,000   **Exc.:** $11,000   **VGood:** $8000

With single selective trigger

   Perf.: $18,000   **Exc.:** $12,000   **VGood:** $9000

20-ga.

   Perf.: $21,000   **Exc.:** $13,500   **VGood:** $10,000

28-ga.

   Perf.: $24,000   **Exc.:** $15,500   **VGood:** $12,000

CHURCHILL, E.J., REGAL

Side-by-side; boxlock; hammerless; 12-, 16-, 20-, 28-ga., .410; 25-inch, 28-inch, 30-inch, 32-inch barrel; any desired choke combo; second-grade, hand-checkered European walnut stock, forearm; pistol grip or single selective trigger. Introduced during WWII; discontinued 1982. Made in England.

   Perf.: $5500   **Exc.:** $3800   **VGood:** $3200

With single selective trigger

   Perf.: $6000   **Exc.:** $4300   **VGood:** $3700

20-ga.

   Perf.: $6700   **Exc.:** $4500   **VGood:** $3850

28-ga.

   Perf.: $7500   **Exc.:** $4500   **VGood:** $3800

E.J. Churchill Hercules

E.J. Churchill Premier

Churchill Utility

Churchill Regent IV S/S

.410-bore

   Perf.: $8500   **Exc.:** $6000   **VGood:** $5000

CHURCHILL, E.J., UTILITY

Side-by-side; boxlock; hammerless; 12-, 16-, 20-, 28-ga., .410; 25-inch, 28-inch, 30-inch, 32-inch barrel; any desired choke combo; second-grade, hand-checkered European walnut stock, forearm; pistol grip or straight English-style; ejectors; double triggers or single selective trigger. Introduced 1900; discontinued WWII. Made in England.

   Exc.: $5600   **VGood:** $4600   **Good:** $3000

With single selective trigger

   Exc.: $6000   **VGood:** $5100   **Good:** $3400

20-ga.

   Exc.: $6300   **VGood:** $5500   **Good:** $3800

28-ga.

   Exc.: $6500   **VGood:** $6000   **Good:** $5000

.410-bore

   Exc.: $6700   **VGood:** $6300   **Good:** $5400

Subtract 10 percent for 16 ga.

CHURCHILL DEERFIELD SEMI-AUTO

Autoloader; 12-ga.; 2-3/4-inch, 3-inch chamber; 20-inch slug barrel; standard chokes or ICT choke tubes; weighs 7-1/2 lbs.; checkered select Claro walnut pistol -grip stock, forend; high gloss or matte finish wood; rosewood grip cap; stainless steel gas piston; crossbolt safety; aluminum alloy receiver.

Made in Japan. Introduced 1984; discontinued 1986. Previously imported by Ellett Brothers.

   Perf.: $450   **Exc.:** $350   **VGood:** $300

CHURCHILL REGENT IV S/S BOXLOCK

Side-by-side; boxlock; 12-, 20-ga.; 2-3/4-inch chamber; 25-inch, 28-inch barrel; tapered Churchill rib; hand-checkered European walnut straight stock; double triggers. Made in Spain. Introduced 1984; discontinued 1987. Previously imported by Ellett Brothers.

   Perf.: $525   **Exc.:** $400   **VGood:** $325

Left-hand version

   Perf.: $575   **Exc.:** $450   **VGood:** $375

CHURCHILL REGENT VI S/S SIDELOCK

Same specs as Regent IV S/S except sidelock. No longer in production. Previously imported by Ellett Brothers.

   Perf.: $800   **Exc.:** $600   **VGood:** $500

CHURCHILL REGENT V O/U

Over/under; boxlock; 12-, 20-ga.; 27-inch barrel; interchangeable choke tubes; ventilated rib; ejectors; SST; pewter finish. Made in Italy. Introduced 1984; discontinued 1991.Previously imported by Ellett Brothers.

   Perf.: $850   **Exc.:** $690   **VGood:** $600

Churchill Regent O/U Flyweight

Churchill Regent O/U Trap

Churchill Regent O/U Skeet

Churchill Regent VII O/U

Churchill Regent Semi-Auto

Churchill Windsor O/U III

Churchill Windsor S/S

Churchill Windsor Semi-Auto

CHURCHILL REGENT O/U COMPETITION

Same specs as Regent V except available with trap and Skeet models. 12-ga.; 2-3/4-inch chamber; 26-inch Skeet/Skeet, 30-inch Improved Modified/Full (trap) barrel; checkered European walnut stock, schnabel forend; oil finish; single selective trigger; automatic ejectors; silvered, engraved receiver. Introduced 1991; discontinued 1992. Previously imported by Ellett Brothers.

Trap version		
Perf.: $800	**Exc.:** $575	**VGood:** $550
Skeet version		
Perf.: $750	**Exc.:** $525	**VGood:** $500

CHURCHILL REGENT O/U FLYWEIGHT

Same specs as Regent V except 23-inch barrel; choke tubes. Made in Japan. Introduced 1984; discontinued 1986. Previously imported by Ellett Brothers.

Perf.: $850   **Exc.:** $790   **VGood:** $700

CHURCHILL REGENT O/U TRAP/SKEET

Same specs as Regent V except sideplates; 26-inch, 30-inch barrel; checkered Monte Carlo stock (trap model); oil-finished wood; vent recoil pad; chrome bores; silvered, engraved receivers. Introduced 1984;

discontinued 1991. Previously imported by Ellett Brothers.

Perf.: $800   **Exc.:** $600   **VGood:** $500

CHURCHILL REGENT VII O/U

Same specs as Regent V except sideplates. No longer imported.

Perf.: $850   **Exc.:** $690   **VGood:** $600

CHURCHILL REGENT SEMI-AUTO

Autoloader; 12-ga.; 2-3/4-inch, 3-inch chamber; 26-inch, 28-inch, 30-inch barrel; standard chokes or ICT choke tubes; weighs 7-1/2 lbs.; checkered select Monte Claro walnut pistol-grip stock, forend; high gloss or matte finish wood; rosewood grip cap; stainless steel gas piston; crossbolt safety; etched, polished aluminum receiver. Made in Japan. Introduced 1984; discontinued 1986. Previously imported by Ellett Brothers.

Perf.: $400   **Exc.:** $300   **VGood:** $280

CHURCHILL ROYAL

Side-by-side; boxlock; 10-, 12-, 20-, 28-ga., .410; 3-inch, 3-1/2-inch chamber; 26-inch, 28-inch barrel; standard choke combos; concave rib; checkered European walnut straight-grip stock; double triggers; extractors; chromed bores; color case-hardened finish. Made in Spain. Introduced 1988; discontinued 1991. Previously imported by Ellett Brothers.

10-ga.		
Perf.: $450	**Exc.:** $350	**VGood:** $300

12-, 20-ga.		
Perf.: $450	**Exc.:** $350	**VGood:** $300
28-ga.		
Perf.: $480	**Exc.:** $380	**VGood:** $330
.410		
Perf.: $525	**Exc.:** $425	**VGood:** $375

CHURCHILL TURKEY AUTOMATIC SHOTGUN

Gas-operated autoloader; 12-ga.; 3-inch chamber; 5-shot magazine; 25-inch barrel; Modified, Full, Extra Full choke tubes; weighs 7 lbs.; hand-checkered walnut stock with satin finish; magazine cut-off; non-glare metal finish; gold-colored trigger. Introduced 1990;. Previously imported by Ellett Brothers.

Perf.: $480   **Exc.:** $360   **VGood:** $300

CHURCHILL WINDSOR III O/U

Over/under; boxlock; 12-, 20-ga., .410; 3-inch chamber; 26-inch, 28-inch, 30-inch barrel; standard choke combos or interchangeable choke tubes; checkered European walnut pistol-grip stock, forend; extractors; single selective trigger; silvered, engraved finish. Made in Italy. Introduced 1984; no longer in production. Previously imported by Ellett Brothers.

Perf.: $500   **Exc.:** $400   **VGood:** $340

CHURCHILL WINDSOR IV O/U

Same specs as Windsor O/U III except 12-, 20-ga.; ejectors. Introduced 1984; no longer imported.

Perf.: $750   **Exc.:** $525   **VGood:** $440

CHURCHILL WINDSOR O/U FLYWEIGHT

Same specs as Windsor O/U except 23-inch barrel; ICT choke tubes; checkered walnut straight-grip stock. No longer imported.

Perf.: $600   **Exc.:** $500   **VGood:** $450

CHURCHILL WINDSOR O/U SPORTING CLAYS

Same specs as Windsor IV except 12-ga.; 28-inch, 30-inch ported, back-bored barrels; choke tubes; tapered ventilated rib, ventilated side rib; select walnut stock, sporting-style forend with finger grooves; palm swell grip; lengthened forcing cones. Introduced 1995; no longer imported.

Perf.: $900   **Exc.:** $750   **VGood:** $600

CHURCHILL WINDSOR S/S

Side-by-side; boxlock; 10-, 12-, 16-, 20-, 28-ga., .410; 2-3/4-inch (16-ga.), 3-inch chamber; 24-inch, 26-inch, 28-inch, 30-inch, 32-inch barrel; hand-checkered European walnut stock, beavertail forend; rubber butt pad; auto safety; double triggers; extractors; silvered, engraved finish. Made in Spain. Introduced 1984; discontinued 1991.

Perf.: $500	**Exc.:** $410	**VGood:** $320
10-ga.		
Perf.: $495	**Exc.:** $380	**VGood:** $300

CHURCHILL WINDSOR S/S II

Same specs as Windsor S/S except ejectors. No longer in production.

Perf.: $550   **Exc.:** $460   **VGood:** $370

CHURCHILL WINDSOR SEMI-AUTO

Autoloader; 12-ga.; 2-3/4-inch, 3-inch chamber; 26-inch to 30-inch barrel; standard chokes or ICT choke tubes; weighs 7-1/2 lbs.; checkered select Monte Claro walnut pistol-grip stock, forend; high gloss or matte finish wood; rosewood grip cap; stainless steel gas piston; crossbolt safety; anodized alloy receiver. Made in Japan. Introduced 1984; discontinued 1991.

Perf.: $350   **Exc.:** $275   **VGood:** $210

CLAYCO MODEL 6

Over/under; 12-ga.; 2-3/4-inch chamber; 26-inch, 28-inch, barrel; vent top rib; checkered walnut-finished hardwood pistol-grip stock, forend; single non-selective trigger; auto safety; vent rubber recoil pad; blued scroll-engraved receiver. Made in China. Introduced 1983; discontinued 1985.

Perf.: $200   **Exc.:** $150   **VGood:** $100

COGSWELL & HARRISON AMBASSADOR

Side-by-side; boxlock; 12-, 16-, 20-ga.; 26-inch, 28-inch, 30-inch barrel; any choke combo; hand-checkered European walnut straight-grip stock, forearm; ejectors; double triggers; sideplates feature game engraving or rose and scroll engraving. Introduced 1970; no longer in production. Made in England.

Perf.: $5500   **Exc.:** $4950   **VGood:** $4450

COGSWELL & HARRISON AVANT TOUT KONOR

Side-by-side; boxlock; hammerless; 12-, 16-, 20-ga.; 25-inch, 27-1/2-inch, 30-inch barrels; any desired choke combo; hand-checkered European walnut straight-grip stock, forearm; pistol-grip stock available on special order; sideplates; double, single or single selective triggers; engraving. Introduced 1920s; no longer in production. Made in England.

Exc.: $2500   **VGood:** $2200   **Good:** $1800
Add $400 to above prices for SST
Add 20 percent for 20 ga.
Subtract 10 percent for 16 ga.

COGSWELL & HARRISON AVANT TOUT REX

Same specs as Avant Tout Konor except no sideplates; lower grade wood, checkering, engraving, overall finish. No longer in production. Made in England.

Exc.: $2150   **VGood:** $1800   **Good:** $1650

COGSWELL & HARRISON AVANT TOUT SANDHURST

Same specs as Avant Tout Konor except less intricate engraving, checkering; lower grade of wood, overall workmanship. No longer in production. Made in England.

Exc.: $2500   **VGood:** $2300   **Good:** $2150

COGSWELL & HARRISON HUNTIC MODEL

Side-by-side; sidelock; 12-, 16-, 20-ga.; 25-inch, 27-1/2-inch, 30-inch barrel; any desired choke combo; hand-checkered European walnut straight-grip stock, forearm; pistol-grip stock on special order; ejectors; double, single or single selective triggers. Introduced in late 1920s; no longer in production. Made in England.

Exc.: $3500   **VGood:** $3200   **Good:** $3000
Add $400 to above prices for SST

COGSWELL & HARRISON MARKOR MODEL

Side-by-side; boxlock; 12-, 16-, 20-ga.; 27-1/2-inch, 30-inch barrels; any standard choke combo; hand-checkered European walnut straight-grip stock, forearm; double triggers; ejectors or extractors. Introduced in late 1920s; no longer in production. Made in England.

Extractors
Exc.: $1475   **VGood:** $1300   **Good:** $1050
Ejectors
Exc.: $1750   **VGood:** $1650   **Good:** $1350

COGSWELL & HARRISON PRIMAC MODEL

Side-by-side; hand-detachable sidelock; 12-, 16-, 20-ga.; 25-inch, 26-inch, 27-1/2-inch, 30-inch barrels; any choke combo; hand-checkered European walnut straight-grip stock, forearm; ejectors; double triggers, single or single selective triggers; English-style engraving. Introduced in 1920s; no longer in production. Made in England.

Exc.: $4950   **VGood:** $3750   **Good:** $2400

COGSWELL & HARRISON VICTOR MODEL

Side-by-side; hand-detachable sidelock; 12-, 16-, 20-ga.; 25-inch, 26-inch, 27-1/2-inch, 30-inch barrels; any choke combo; hand-checkered European walnut straight-grip stock, forearm; ejectors; double triggers, single or single selective triggers; high quality English-style engraving. Introduced in 1920s; no longer in production. Made in England.

Exc.: $6000   **VGood:** $4000   **Good:** $3000

Cogswell & Harrison
Avant Tout Konor

Colt Coltsman Pump

Colt Custom Double Barrel

Colt Magnum Auto Custom

Colt Sauer Drilling

Colt Ultra Light Auto

Connecticut Valley Classics
Classic Sporter

COLT COLTSMAN PUMP

Slide action; takedown; 12-, 16-, 20-ga.; 4-shot magazine; 26-inch Improved, 28-inch Modified, 30-inch Full choke barrel; weighs about 6 lbs.; uncheckered European walnut stock. Introduced 1961; discontinued 1965.

Exc.: $350   **VGood:** $260   **Good:** $230

COLT COLTSMAN PUMP CUSTOM

Same specs as Coltsman Pump except vent rib; hand-checkered pistol grip, forearm. Introduced 1961; discontinued 1963.

Exc.: $375   **VGood:** $275   **Good:** $255

COLT CUSTOM DOUBLE BARREL

Boxlock; 12-, 16-ga.; 2-3/4-inch, 3-inch chamber (12-ga.); 26-inch Improved/Modified, 28-inch Modified/Full, 30-inch Full/Full choke barrels; hand-checkered European walnut pistol-grip stock, beavertail forearm. Introduced 1961; discontinued 1961.

Exc.: $600   **VGood:** $450   **Good:** $225

COLT MAGNUM AUTO

Autoloader; takedown; 12-, 20-ga.; 3-inch chamber; 28-inch (20-ga.), 32-inch (12-ga.) interchangeable chrome-lined barrels; Full choke; plain, solid or vent rib; weighs 8-1/4 lbs. (12-ga.) or 6 lbs. (20-ga.); walnut stock; steel receiver. Introduced 1964; discontinued 1966.

Exc.: $350   **VGood:** $290   **Good:** $230

COLT MAGNUM AUTO CUSTOM

Same specs as Magnum Auto except solid or vent rib; select walnut stock, forearm; engraved receiver. Introduced 1964; discontinued 1966.

Exc.: $395   **VGood:** $330   **Good:** $270

COLT SAUER DRILLING

Side-by-side; boxlock; top lever; 30-06 or 243 Winchester under 12-ga.; 25-inch barrels; shotgun barrels choked Modified/Full; folding leaf rear sight, blade front with brass bead; hand-checkered oil-finished American walnut pistol-grip stock, forearm; black pistol-grip cap; recoil pad; cocking indicators; tang barrel selector; automatic sight positioner; set rifle trigger; side safety; crossbolt safety. Made for Colt by Sauer in Germany. No longer imported by Colt.

Perf.: $3200   **Exc.:** $2300   **VGood:** $1900

COLT ULTRA LIGHT AUTO

Autoloader; takedown; 12-, 20-ga.; 2-3/4-inch chamber; 4-shot magazine; 26-inch Improved or Modified, 28-inch Modified or Full, 30-inch Full chrome-lined interchangeable barrels; plain, solid or vent rib; weighs 6-1/4 lbs. (12-ga.), 5 lbs. (20-ga.); walnut stock; crossbolt safety; aluminum alloy receiver. Introduced 1964; discontinued 1966.

Perf.: $280   **Exc.:** $250   **VGood:** $195

COLT ULTRA LIGHT AUTO CUSTOM

Same specs as Ultra Light Auto except solid or vent rib; select walnut stock, forearm; engraved with bird scenes. Introduced 1964; discontinued 1966.

Perf.: $225   **Exc.:** $175   **VGood:** $140

CONNECTICUT SHOTGUN MANUFACTURING CO. MODEL 21

Side-by-side; 12-, 16-, 20-, 28-ga., .410 bore; 4 frame sizes (12, 16, 20 and 28 ga./.410 bore); barrels lengths up to 32-inch; matte, solid or vent. Rib; fixed chokes; best quality checkered wood; Limited manufacture beginning 2002. Each is built on a custom order basis.

Cosmi Semi-Auto

CZ Grouse

CZ Sporting

CONNECTICUT SHOTGUN MANUFACTURING MODEL 21-1

Similar to Model 21, except features light scroll engraving patterned after the Winchester no. 1; A fancy wood. Introduced 2002.

Perf.: $8750 **Exc.:** $7250 **VGood:** $6500
Add $1000 to above prices for 28 ga.
Add $3500 for .410 bore

CONNECTICUT SHOTGUN MANUFACTURING MODEL 21-5

Similar to Model 21, except has both scroll and three hunting scenes engraved patterned after Winchester's No. 5 style on barrels and frame; AA fancy wood. Introduced 2002.

Perf.: $12,900 **Exc.:** $9950 **VGood:** $8750
Add $2100 to above prices for 28 ga.
Add $2600 for .410 bore

CONNECTICUT SHOTGUN MANUFACTURING MODEL 21-6

Similar to Model 21, except has tight scroll and dog and game bird engraving patterned after Winchester's No. 6 style on frame and barrels; AAA fancy wood. Introduced 2002.

Perf.: $13,800 **Exc.:** $11,250 **VGood:** $9250
Add $2100 to above prices for 28 ga.
Add $2600 for .410 bore

CONNECTICUT SHOTGUN MANUFACTURING MODEL 21 GRAND AMERICAN

Similar to Model 21, except is top of the line model; 2 sets of barrels; elaborate scroll engraving on barrels and frame; 5 gold inlays; B carved stock and forearm; AAA full fancy feather crotch American walnut. Introduced 2002.

Perf.: $16,995 **Exc.:** $14,250 **VGood:** $11,650

CONNECTICUT VALLEY CLASSICS CLASSIC SPORTER

Over/under; boxlock; 12-ga.; 3-inch chambers; 28-inch, 30-inch, 32-inch barrels; Skeet, Improved Cylinder, Modified, Full CV choke tubes; weighs 7-3/4 lbs.; hand-checkered American black walnut pistol-grip stock, forend; elongated forcing cones; stainless receiver with fine engraving; chrome-lined bores and chambers suitable for steel shot; receiver duplicates Classic Doubles M101 specifications. Introduced 1993; no longer in production.

Perf.: $2450 **Exc.:** $2000 **VGood:** $1500

CONNECTICUT VALLEY CLASSICS CLASSIC FIELD WATERFOWLER

Over/under; boxlock; 12-ga.; 3-inch chambers; 30-inch barrels; Skeet, Improved Cylinder, Modified, Full CV choke tubes; weighs 7-3/4 lbs.; hand-checkered American black walnut pistol-grip stock, forend; elongated forcing cones; blued, non-reflective receiver with fine engraving; chrome-lined bores and chambers suitable for steel shot; receiver duplicates Classic Doubles M101 specifications. Introduced 1995; no longer in production.

Perf.: $2200 **Exc.:** $1300 **VGood:** $1000

COSMI SEMI-AUTOMATIC

Recoil-operated autoloader; break-open; 12-, 20-ga.; 2-3/4-inch, 3-inch chamber; 3-, 8-shot magazine in buttstock; 22-inch to 34-inch barrel to customers specs; choke tubes; weighs 6-1/4 lbs.; hand-checkered exhibition-grade Circassian walnut stock; double ejectors; double safety system; stainless steel construction; various grades of engraving can double price; marketed in fitted leather case; essentially a hand-made custom gun. Made in Italy. Introduced 1985; still imported.

Perf.: $12,000 **Exc.:** $5000 **VGood:** $4500

COSMI ALUMINUM MODEL

Similar to standard Cosmi, except 12-, 20-ga.; receiver made of machined aluminum; weighs 7 lbs. (12-ga.), 5.9 lbs. (20 ga.).

Perf.: $14,000 **Exc.:** $5000 **VGood:** $4595

COSMI TITANIUM MODEL

Similar to standard Cosmi, except 12-, 20-ga.; receiver made of machined titanium; weighs 6.8 lbs. (12-ga.), 5.7 lbs. (20-ga.). Introduced in 1990.

Perf.: $16,500 **Exc.:** $5750 **VGood:** $4950

CROSSFIRE SHOTGUN/RIFLE

Gauge/Caliber: 12, 2-3/4-inch; Chamber: 4-shot/223 Rem. (5-shot). Barrel: 20-inch (shotgun), 18-inch (rifle). Weight: About 8.6 lbs. Length: 40-inch overall. Stock: Composite. Sights: Meprolight night sights. Integral Weaver-style scope rail. Features: Combination pump-action shotgun, rifle; single selector, single trigger; dual action bars for both upper and lower actions; ambidextrous selector and safety. Introduced 1997. Made in U.S. From Hesco.

Perf.: $1750 **Exc.:** $1550 **VGood:** $1350
With camo finish
Perf.: $1850 **Exc.:** $1650 **VGood:** $1450

CRUCELEGUI HERMANOS MODEL 150

Side-by-side; Greener triple crossbolt action; exposed hammers; 12-, 20-ga.; 20-inch, 26-inch, 28-inch, 30-inch, 32-inch barrels; hand-checkered European walnut stock, beavertail forend; double triggers; color case-hardened receiver; chromed bores; sling swivels. Made in Spain. Introduced 1979; still in production.

Perf.: $350 **Exc.:** $290 **VGood:** $240
NOTE: On this model, .410 is worth 50 percent more than prices shown, 28-gauge worth 40 percent more, 20-gauge, 25 percent more.

CZ 581 SOLO OVER/UNDER SHOTGUN

Over/under; 12-ga.; 2-3/4-inch chambers; 27.6-inch barrel (Mod. & Full); weighs 7.37 lbs.; 44.5-inch overall; circassian walnut stock; automatic ejectors; double triggers; Kersten-style double lump locking system. Imported from the Czech Republic by CZ-USA.

Exc.: $740 **VGood:** $625 **Good:** $570

CZ GROUSE

New in 2008, the Grouse is a single trigger side-by-side in 12, 20 and 28 gauge and .410 bore with 3" chambers (2.75" in 28 gauge). White chrome-plated receiver with scroll engraving. Prince of Wales grip and semi-beavertail Schnabel forend. Barrels are 28" in 12 and 20 gauge and 26" in 28 and .410. Includes five choke tubes (.410 is choked IC/MOD). Add 20% for 28 gauge and .410 bore.

Exc.: $900 **VGood:** $725 **Good:** $600

CZ SPORTING

This dedicated sporting clays over/under is a 12 gauge with an adjustable comb stock and forend of #3 Circassian walnut. It features chrome-lined barrels back-bored to .736 and automatic ejectors. Barrels are 30" or 32". Five choke tubes included. Weight is about 9 lbs.

Exc.: $2200 **VGood:** $1125 **Good:** $850

DAKOTA PREMIER GRADE SHOTGUNS

Side-by-side; 12-, 16-, 20-, 28-ga.; .410 bore. 27-inch barrel; exhibition-grade English walnut, hand-rubbed oil finish with straight grip and splinter forend; French grey finish; 50 percent coverage engraving; double triggers; selective ejectors. Finished to customer specifications. Made in U.S. by Dakota Arms.

12-, 16-, 20-gauge		
Exc.: $8300	**VGood:** $6950	**Good:** $5650

28 gauge and .4105		
Perf.: $13,950	**Exc.:** $10,250	**VGood:** $8300

DAKOTA LEGEND

Similar to Premier Grade except has special selection English walnut, full- coverage scroll engraving, oak and leather case. Made in U.S. by Dakota Arms.

12-, 16-, 20-gauge		
Perf.: $16,000	**Exc.:** $13,000	**VGood:** $11,000

28-gauge and .410		
Perf.: $17,600	**Exc.:** $14,300	**VGood:** $12,100

DARNE MODEL R11 BIRD HUNTER

Side-by-side; sliding breech action; 12-, 20-ga.; 25-1/2-inch Improved Cylinder/Modified barrels; raised rib; deluxe hand-checkered walnut stock, forearm; double triggers; automatic selective ejection; case-hardened receiver. Made in France. Discontinued 1979.

Perf.: $1700 **Exc.:** $1550 **VGood:** $1300

DARNE MODEL R15 PHEASANT HUNTER

Side-by-side; sliding breech action; 12-ga.; 27-1/2-inch Modified/Full barrels; raised rib; fancy hand-checkered walnut stock, forearm; double triggers; automatic selective ejection system; case-hardened engraved receiver. Discontinued 1979.

Perf.: $2250 **Exc.:** $2000 **VGood:** $1850

DARNE MODEL V19 QUAIL HUNTER SUPREME

Side-by-side; sliding breech action; 20-, 28-ga.; 25-1/2-inch Improved/Modified barrels; raised rib; extra-fancy hand-checkered walnut stock, forearm; double triggers; automatic selective ejection; case-hardened receiver; elaborate engraving. Discontinued 1979.

Perf.: $4500 **Exc.:** $4150 **VGood:** $3700

DARNE MODEL MAGNUM R16

Similar to other Darne models in the R series, but higher grade of wood and greater amount of engraving. Discontinued 1979.

Perf.: $3500 **Exc.:** $3150 **VGood:** $2650

DARNE MODEL V22

Similar to other Darne models in the V series, except higher grade of wood and greater amount of engraving. Discontinued 1979.

Perf.: $5750 **Exc.:** $5300 **VGood:** $4600

DAVIDSON MODEL 63B

Double barrel; Anson & Deeley boxlock; 12-, 16-, 20-, 28-ga., .410; 25-inch (.410), 26-inch, 28-inch 30-inch (12-ga.) barrels; Improved Cylinder/Modified, Modified/Full, Full/Full chokes; hand-checkered walnut pistol-grip stock; plain extractors; automatic safety; engraved, nickel-plated frame. Made in Spain. Introduced 1963; no longer in production.

Exc.: $275 **VGood:** $260 **Good:** $220

DAVIDSON MODEL 63B MAGNUM

Same specs as Model 63B except 10-, 12-, 20-ga.; 3-inch (12-, 20-ga.), 3-1/2-inch (10-ga.) chambers; 32-inch Full/Full barrels (10-ga. only). Made in Spain. No longer in production.

12-, 20-ga. Magnum		
Exc.: $360	**VGood:** $340	**Good:** $310

10-ga. Magnum		
Exc.: $385	**VGood:** $370	**Good:** $340

DAVIDSON MODEL 69SL

Double barrel; sidelock; 12-, 20-ga.; 26-inch, 28-inch barrels; Modified/Improved (26-inch), Modified/Full (28-inch) choke; hand-checkered European walnut stock; detachable locks; nickel-plated, engraved action. Introduced 1963; discontinued 1976.

Perf.: $415	**Exc.:** $395	**VGood:** $375

DAVIDSON MODEL 73

Side-by-side; sidelock; exposed hammer; 12-, 20-ga.; 3-inch chambers; 20-inch barrels; checkered European walnut pistol-grip stock, forearm; detachable sideplates; plain extractors; double triggers. Made in Spain. Introduced 1976; no longer in production.

Perf.: $275	**Exc.:** $260	**VGood:** $220

DESERT INDUSTRIES BIG TWENTY

Single shot; 20-ga.; 19-inch Cylinder bore barrel; 31-3/4-inch overall length; weighs 4-3/4 lbs.; bead front sight; fixed formed-wire stock with buttplate; walnut forend, grip; all-steel construction; blued finish. Introduced 1990; no longer in production.

Perf.: $180	**Exc.:** $155	**VGood:** $125

DIAMOND 12-GA. PUMP SHOTGUN

Pump-action; 12-ga.; 2-3/4-inch and 3-inch chambers; 18-inch-30-inch barrel; weighs 7 lbs.; walnut or synthetic stock; aluminum one-piece receiver sculpted for lighter weight; double locking on fixed bolt; Gold, Elite and Panther series with vented barrels and 3 chokes. Imported from Turkey by ADCO Sales.

Gold, 28-inch, walnut		
Perf.: $450	**Exc.:** $375	**VGood:** $325

Gold, 28-inch, synthetic		
Perf.: $400	**Exc.:** $325	**VGood:** $275

Gold Slug, 24-inch, same as above		
Perf.: $400	**Exc.:** $325	**VGood:** $275

Silver Mariner 20-inch Slug, synthetic		
Perf.: $425	**Exc.:** $350	**VGood:** $300

Elite, 20-inch-28-inch, walnut		
Perf.: $285	**Exc.:** $240	**VGood:** $200

Elite, 20-inch Slug, walnut		
Perf.: $245	**Exc.:** $200	**VGood** $165

Panther, 20-inch, 28-inch, synthetic		
Perf.: $225	**Exc.** $200	**VGood:** $165

Panther,18.5-inch Slug, synthetic		
Perf.: $211	**VGood:** $186	**VGood:** $151

DUMOULIN EUROPA

Side-by-side; 12-, 20-, 28-ga., .410 bore; Anson & Deeley boxlock action; single or double trigger; moderately engraved; oil finished stock and forearm; choice of 6 engraving options. Discontinued 1989. Formerly imported from Belgium.

Perf.: $3300	**VGood:** $2750	**VGood:** $2350

DUMOULIN LIEGE

Side-by-side; Anson & Deeley boxlock or sidelock; 12-, 16-, 20-, 28-ga.; 2-3/4-inch, 3-inch chambers; 26-inch to 32-inch barrels choked to customers specs; weighs 6-1/4 lbs. Custom-built in Belgium. Introduced 1986; discontinued 1988.

Luxe Model		
Perf.: $5500	**Exc.:** $.4100	**VGood:** $3450

Grand Luxe		
Perf.: $7200	**Exc.:** $5200	**VGood:** $4400

Add 15 percent to above prices for 28 ga.
Add 15 percent for sideplates

Davidson Model 63B

E.A.A./Baikal Bounty Hunter IZH-43K

E.A.A./Baikal IZH-18 Single Barrel

E.A.A./Baikal IZH-18 Max Single Barrel

E.A.A./Baikal IZH-43 Bounty Hunter

E.A.A./Baikal MP-133 Pump

EAA/BAIKAL BOUNTY HUNTER IZH-43K SHOTGUN

Gauge: 12 (2-3/4-inch, 3-inch chambers), 20 (3-inch chambers), 28 (2-3/4-inch chambers), .410 (3-inch chambers); 18-1/2-inch, 20-inch, 24-inch, 26-inch, 28-inch barrel, three choke tubes; weighs 7.28 lbs.; walnut, checkered forearm and grip; machined receiver; hammer-forged barrels with chrome-line bores; external hammers; double triggers (single, selective trigger available); rifle barrel inserts optional. Imported by European American Armory.

Perf.: $365	**Exc.:** $300	**VGood:** $260

EAA/BAIKAL IZH-18 SINGLE BARREL SHOTGUN

Single barrel; 12-ga. (2-3/4-inch and 3-inch chambers), 20-ga. (2-3/4-inch and 3-inch), 16-ga. (2-3/4-inch), .410 bore (3-inch); 26-1/2-inch, 28-1/2-inch barrel; modified or full choke (12 and 20 gauge); full only (16-gauge); improved cylinder (20-gauge); full or improved modified (.410); walnut-stained hardwood; rubber recoil pad; hammer-forged steel barrel; machined receiver; cross-block safety; cocking lever with external cocking indicator; optional automatic ejector; screw-in chokes and rifle barrel. Imported by European American Armory.

IZH-18 (12, 16, 20 or .410)		
Perf.: $80	**Exc.:** $65	**VGood:** $55

IZH-18 (20-gauge with Imp. Cyl. or .410 with Imp. Mod.)		
Perf.: $94	**Exc.:** $79	**VGood:** $69

EAA/BAIKAL IZH-18MAX SINGLE BARREL SHOTGUN

Single barrel; 12-ga. 3-inch chamber; 20-ga. 3-inch; .410, 3-inch; 24-inch barrel (.410), 26-inch (.410 or 20-ga.) or 28-inch (12-ga.); weighs 6.4 to 6.6 lbs.; walnut stock; polished nickel receiver; ventilated rib; I.C., Mod. and Full choke tubes; titanium-coated

trigger; internal hammer; selectable ejector/extractor; rubber butt pad; decocking system. Imported by European American Armory.

12- or 20-ga., choke tubes		
Perf.: $154	**Exc.:** $135	**VGood:** $129

.410 bore, full choke only		
Perf.: $94	**Exc.:** $79	**VGood:** $69

Sporting, 12-ga., ported, Monte Carlo stock		
Perf.: $185	**Exc.:** $160	**VGood:** $135

EAA/BAIKAL IZH-43 BOUNTY HUNTER SHOTGUNS

Gauge: 12 (2-3/4-inch, 3-inch chambers), 16 (2-3/4-inch chambers), 20 (2-3/4-inch and 3-inch chambers); 20-inch, 24-inch, 26-inch, 28-inch barrel; Imp., Mod. and Full choke tubes; hardwood or walnut; checkered forend and grip; hammer forged barrel; internal hammers; extractors; engraved receiver; automatic tang safety; non-glare rib. Imported by European American Armory.

12-gauge, 2-3/4-inch chambers, 20-inch bbls., dbl. triggers, hardwood stock		
Perf.: $260	**Exc.:** $225	**VGood:** $200

12- or 20-gauge, 2-3/4-inch chambers, 20-inch bbls., dbl. triggers, walnut stock		
Perf.: $320	**Exc.:** $285	**VGood:** $260

EAA/BAIKAL MP-133 PUMP SHOTGUN

Pump action; 12-ga., 3-1/2-inch chamber; 18-1/2-inch, 20-inch, 24-inch, 26-inch, 28-inch barrel; Imp., Mod. and Full choke tubes; walnut, checkered grip and grooved forearm; hammer-forged, chrome-lined barrel with ventilated rib; machined steel parts; dual action bars; trigger-block safety; 4-shot magazine tube; handles 2-3/4-inch through 3-1/2-inch shells. Introduced 2000. Imported by European American Armory.

Perf.: $275	**Exc.:** $215	**VGood:** $185

E.A.A./Baikal Bounty Hunter MP-213 Coach Gun

E.A.A./Baikal MP-233 Over/Under

E.A.A./Baikal IZH-27 Over/Under

ERA Bird Hunter

ERA Full Limit

Erbi Model 76ST

EAA/BAIKAL MP-153 AUTO SHOTGUN

Semi-auto; 12-ga., 3-1/2-inch chamber; 18-1/2-inch, 20-inch, 24-inch, 26-inch, 28-inch barrel; Imp., Mod. and Full choke tubes; weighs 7.8 lbs.; walnut stock; gas-operated action with automatic gas-adjustment valve allows use of light and heavy loads interchangeably; 4-round magazine; rubber recoil pad. Introduced 2000. Imported by European American Armory.

Blued finish, walnut stock and forend
Perf.: $445   **Exc. $375**   **VGood:** $320

Field grade, synthetic stock
Perf.: $355   **Exc.:** $285   **VGood:** $230

EAA/BAIKAL MP-213 SHOTGUN

Gauge: 12, 3-inch chambers; 24-inch, 26-inch, 28-inch barrel; Imp., Mod. and Full choke tubes; weighs 7.28 lbs.; walnut, checkered forearm and grip; rubber butt pad; hammer-forged barrels; chrome-lined bores; machined receiver; double trigger (each trigger fires both barrels independently); ejectors. Introduced 2000. Imported by European American Armory.
Perf.: $795   **Exc.:** $675   **VGood:** $595

EAA/BAIKAL BOUNTY HUNTER MP-213 COACH GUN

Side-by-side; 12-ga.; 2-3/4-inch chambers; 20-inch barrel; Imp., Mod. and Full choke tubes; weighs 7 lbs.; walnut, checkered forend and grip; selective double trigger with removable assembly (single trigger and varied pull weights available); ejectors; engraved receiver. Imported by European American Armory.
Perf.: $954   **Exc.:** $834   **VGood:** $754

EAA/BAIKAL MP-233 OVER/UNDER SHOTGUN

Over/under; 12-ga., 3-inch chambers; 26-inch, 28-inch, 30-inch barrel; Imp., Mod. and Full choke tubes; weighs 7.28 lbs.; walnut; checkered forearm and grip; hammer-forged barrels; chrome-lined bores; removable trigger assembly (optional single selective trigger or double trigger); ejectors. Introduced 2000. Imported by European American Armory.
Perf.: $795   **Exc.:** $650   **VGood:** $575

EAA/BAIKAL IZH-27 OVER/UNDER SHOTGUN

Over/under; 12-ga. (3-inch chambers), 16-ga. (2-3/4-inch chambers), 20-ga. (3-inch chambers), 28-ga. (2-3/4-inch chambers), .410 bore (3-inch); 26-1/2-inch barrel, 28-1/2-inch (Imp., Mod. and Full choke tubes for 12 and 20 gauges; Improved Cylinder and Modified for 16 and 28 gauges; Improved Modified and Full for .410; 16 also offered in Mod. and Full); walnut, checkered forearm and grip. Imported by European American Armory.

12-, 16- and 20-gauge
Perf.: $420   **Exc.:** $350   **VGood:** $295

28-gauge and .410
Perf.: $479   **Exc.:** $409   **VGood:** $354

EAA IZH-27 SPORTING O/U

Basic IZH-27 with barrel porting, wide vent rib with double sight beads, engraved nickel receiver, checkered walnut stock and forend with palm swell and semi-beavertail, 3 screw chokes, SS trigger, selectable ejectors, auto tang safety
Perf.: $500   **Exc.:** $430   **VGood:** $375

E.A.A./SABATTI FALCON-MON

Over/under; boxlock; 12-, 20-, 28-ga., .410; 3-inch chambers; 26-inch, 28-inch barrels; standard chokes; ventilated rib; weighs about 7 lbs.; cut-checkered select walnut pistol-grip stock, beavertail forend with gloss finish; gold-plated single selective trigger; extractors; engraved, blued receiver. Made in Italy. Introduced 1993; discontinued 1994.

12- or 20-ga.
Perf.: $600   **Exc.:** $420   **VGood:** $350

28-ga. or .410
Perf.: $650   **Exc.:** $470   **VGood:** $400

E.A.A./SABATTI SABA-MON DOUBLE

Side-by-side; boxlock; 12-, 20-, 28-ga., .410; 3-inch chambers; 26-inch, 28-inch barrels; standard chokes; European walnut straight English or pistol-grip stock; single selective trigger; automatic selective

ejectors; blue finish. Made in Italy. Introduced 1993; discontinued 1994.
Perf.: $920   **Exc.:** $680   **VGood:** $500

E.A.A./SABATTI SPORTING CLAYS PRO-GOLD

Over/under; boxlock; 12-ga.; 3-inch chambers; 28-inch, 30-inch barrels; six choke tubes; weighs 7-3/4 lbs.; target-style fluorescent bar front sight; European walnut pistol-grip stock, forend with gloss finish; special Sporting Clays recoil pad; automatic ejectors; gold-plated single selective trigger; engraved, blued receiver with gold inlays. Comes with lockable hard shell plastic case. Made in Italy. Introduced 1993; no longer imported.
Perf.: $800   **Exc.:** $600   **VGood:** $500

EAA/SAIGA AUTO SHOTGUN

Semi-automatic; 12-ga, 20-ga., .410 bore; 3-inch chamber; 19-inch, 21-inch, 22-inch barrel; weighs 6.6-7.6 lbs.; length: 40-inch-45-inch; synthetic stock; retains best features of the AK rifle by Kalashnikov as a semi-auto shotgun; magazine fed. Imported from Russia by EAA Corp.

.410 bore
Perf.: $210   **Exc.:** $160   **VGood:** $145

20-ga.
Perf.: $340   **Exc.:** $300   **VGood:** $275

12-ga.
Perf.: $380   **Exc.:** $340   **VGood:** $315

E.M.F. HARTFORD MODEL COWBOY SHOTGUN

Gauge: 12; 20-inch barrel; checkered walnut; center bead sight; exposed hammers; color-case hardened receiver; blued barrel. Introduced 2001. Formerly imported from Spain (during 2001 and 2002) by E.M.F. Co. Inc.
Perf.: $550   **Exc.:** $495   **VGood:** $450

E.M.F. STAGECOACH MODEL

Side-by-side; exposed hammers, 12 ga. only; 20-inch brown barrels; made by S.I.A.C.E. Imported 2000-2002.
Perf.: $300   **Exc.:** $275   **VGood:** $215

E.M.F. MARK V CONQUEST

Side-by-side; 12 ga.; 28-inch barrels; choke tubes. Importation began 2003.
Perf.: $385   **Exc.:** $325   **VGood:** $275

ERA BIRD HUNTER

Side-by-side; boxlock; 12-, 16-, 20-ga., .410; 26-inch, 28-inch, 30-inch barrels; raised matted rib; hand-checkered walnut stock, beavertail forend; extractors; auto disconnector; double triggers; engraved receiver. Made in Brazil. Introduced 1979; no longer in production.
Perf.: $150   **Exc.:** $125   **VGood:** $100

ERA FULL LIMIT

Over/under; 12-, 20-ga.; 28-inch barrels; vent, top and middle ribs; hand-checkered walnut-finished hardwood stock; Monte Carlo or straight styles; auto safety, extractors; double triggers; engraved receiver. Made in Brazil. Introduced 1980; no longer in production.
Perf.: $250   **Exc.:** $200   **VGood:** $180

ERA WINNER

Single barrel; exposed hammer; 12-, 16-, 20-ga.,.410; 28-inch barrel; metal bead front sight; walnut-stained hardwood stock, beavertail forend; triggerguard button opens action; auto ejectors. Made in Brazil. Introduced 1980; no longer in production.
Perf.: $125   **Exc.:** $100   **VGood:** $75

ERBI MODEL 76AJ

Side-by-side; 10-, 12-, 20-, 28-ga.; 26-inch, 28-inch Modified/Full barrels; medium bead front sight; hand-checkered European walnut straight-grip stock; double triggers; automatic ejectors; engraved, silvered receiver. Made in Spain. Introduced 1982 by Toledo Armas; discontinued 1984.
Perf.: $550   **Exc.:** $460   **VGood:** $400

ERBI MODEL 76ST
Same specs as Model 76AJ except automatic extractors. Introduced 1982 by Toledo Armas; discontinued 1984.

Perf.: $500   **Exc.:** $400   **VGood:** $350

ERBI MODEL 80
Side-by-side; sidelock; 10-, 12-, 20-, 28-ga.; 26-inch, 28-inch Modified/Full barrels; medium bead front sight; hand-checkered European walnut straight-grip stock; double triggers; extractors; engraved silvered receiver. Introduced 1982 by Toledo Armas; discontinued 1984.

Perf.: $850   **Exc.:** $675   **VGood:** $550

ESCORT MODEL AS
Semi-auto.; 12-ga.; 28-inch barrel (choke tubes, M, IM, F); 3-inch chambers; weighs 7 lbs.; Turkish walnut; checkered pistol grip and forend; aluminum-alloy receiver; blued finish; chrome-plated bolt; adjustment for normal and magnum loads; gold-plated trigger; trigger-guard safety; magazine cut-off; choke tube wrench; two stock-adjustment shims; waterfowl plug; 7-shot magazine extender. Introduced 2002. Imported from Turkey by Legacy Sports International.

Perf.: $332   **Exc.:** $297   **VGood:** $272

Model PS, black polymer stock

Perf.: $320   **Exc.:** $285   **VGood:** $260

ESCORT SERIES
Slide action; 12-ga.; 3-inch chamber; matte blue or camo finish with polymer stock and forearm; 20-inch, 24-inch, 28-inch barrel; alloy receiver with 3/8-inch milled dovetail for sight mounting; trigger guard safety; 5-shot magazine with cut-off button; two stock adjustment shims; weighs 6.4 to 7 lbs. Importation began 2003.

Aimguard Model; 20-inch barrel; black synthetic stock; fixed cyl. Bore choke; 6.4 lbs.

Perf.: $160   **Exc.:** $135   **VGood:** $120

Field Hunter; 24-inch, 28-inch barrel; 100 percent camo coverage or matte blue finish; includes 3 choke tubes.

Perf.: $175   **Exc.:** $155   **VGood:** $135

Add $50 to above prices for camo stock
Add $105 for FH TriViz sight combo

EXEL MODEL 101
Over/under; boxlock; 12-ga.; 2-3/4-inch, 3-inch chambers; 26-inch Improved Cylinder/Modified barrels; vent-rib; checkered European walnut stock; single selective trigger; extractors. Made in Spain. Introduced 1984; discontinued 1987.

Perf.: $350   **Exc.:** $300   **VGood:** $260

EXEL MODEL 102
Over/under; boxlock; 12-ga.; 2-3/4-inch, 3-inch chambers; 27-5/8-inch Improved Cylinder/Modified barrels; vent-rib; checkered European walnut stock; single selective trigger; extractors. Made in Spain. Introduced 1984; discontinued 1987.

Perf.: $360   **Exc.:** $300   **VGood:** $260

EXEL MODEL 103
Over/under; boxlock; 12-ga.; 2-3/4-inch, 3-inch chambers; 29 1/2-inch Modified/Full barrels; vent-rib; checkered European walnut stock; single selective trigger; extractors. Made in Spain. Introduced 1984; discontinued 1987.

Perf.: $360   **Exc.:** $300   **VGood:** $260

EXEL MODEL 104
Over/under; boxlock; 12-ga.; 2-3/4-inch, 3-inch chambers; 27-5/8-inch Improved Cylinder/Improved Modified barrels; vent-rib; checkered European walnut stock; single selective trigger; selective auto ejectors. Made in Spain. Introduced 1984; discontinued 1987.

Perf.: $360   **Exc.:** $300   **VGood:** $260

EXEL MODEL 105
Over/under; boxlock; 12-ga.; 2-3/4-inch, 3-inch chambers; 27-5/8-inch barrel with screw-in choke tubes; vent-rib; deluxe checkered European walnut stock; single selective trigger; selective auto ejectors;

Escort Aimguard

Escort Field Hunter

Exel Series 100

Exel Model 201

engraved satin finish. Made in Spain. Introduced 1984; discontinued 1987.

Perf.: $525   **Exc.:** $410   **VGood:** $380

EXEL MODEL 106
Over/under; boxlock; 12-ga.; 2-3/4-inch, 3-inch chambers; 27-5/8-inch barrel with screw-in choke tubes; vent-rib; deluxe checkered European walnut stock; single selective trigger; selective auto ejectors; engraved blue finish. Made in Spain. Introduced 1984; discontinued 1987.

Perf.: $700   **Exc.:** $500   **VGood:** $430

EXEL MODEL 107
Over/under; boxlock; 12-ga.; 2-3/4-inch, 3-inch chambers; 29-1/2-inch barrel with Full/interchangeable tubes; vent-rib; deluxe checkered European walnut stock; single selective trigger; selective auto ejectors; engraved blue finish. Made in Spain. Introduced 1984; discontinued 1987.

Perf.: $700   **Exc.:** $500   **VGood:** $430

EXEL MODEL 201
Side-by-side; boxlock; 12-, 20-ga.; 2-3/4-inch chambers; 28-inch barrels; high matted rib; metal bead front sight; hand-checkered European walnut straight or pistol-grip stock; double triggers; extractors; color case-hardened finish. Made in Spain. Introduced 1984; discontinued 1987.

Perf.: $350   **Exc.:** $220   **VGood:** $190

EXEL MODEL 202
Side-by-side; boxlock; 12-, 20-ga.; 2-3/4-inch chambers; 26-inch barrels; high matted rib; metal bead front sight; hand-checkered European walnut straight or pistol-grip stock; double triggers; extractors; color case-hardened finish. Made in Spain. Introduced 1984; discontinued 1987.

Perf.: $350   **Exc.:** $220   **VGood:** $190

EXEL MODEL 203
Side-by-side; boxlock; 12-, 20-ga.; 3-inch chambers; 27-inch barrels; high matted rib; metal bead front sight; hand-checkered European walnut straight or pistol-grip stock; double triggers; extractors; color case-hardened finish. Made in Spain. Introduced 1984; discontinued 1987.

Perf.: $350   **Exc.:** $220   **VGood:** $190

EXEL MODEL 204
Side-by-side; boxlock; 12-, 20-ga.; 2-3/4-inch chambers; 28-inch barrels; high matted rib; metal

bead front sight; hand-checkered European walnut straight or pistol-grip stock; single or double triggers; automatic selective ejectors; silvered, engraved receiver. Made in Spain. Introduced 1984; discontinued 1987.

Perf.: $525   **Exc.:** $400   **VGood:** $340

EXEL MODEL 205
Side-by-side; boxlock; 12-, 20-ga.; 2-3/4-inch chambers; 26-inch barrels; high matted rib; metal bead front sight; hand-checkered European walnut straight or pistol-grip stock; single or double triggers; automatic selective ejectors; silvered, engraved receiver. Made in Spain. Introduced 1984; discontinued 1987.

Perf.: $525   **Exc.:** $400   **VGood:** $340

EXEL MODEL 206
Side-by-side; boxlock; 12-, 20-ga.; 2-3/4-inch chambers; 27-inch barrels; high matted rib; metal bead front sight; hand-checkered European walnut stock; straight or full pistol-grip; single or double triggers; automatic selective ejectors; silvered, engraved receiver. Made in Spain. Introduced 1984; discontinued 1987.

Perf.: $525   **Exc.:** $400   **VGood:** $340

EXEL MODEL 207
Side-by-side; sidelock; 12-ga.; 2-3/4-inch chambers; 28-inch barrels; high matted rib; metal bead front sight; hand-checkered European walnut straight or pistol-grip stock; double triggers; extractors or ejectors; color case-hardened finish. Made in Spain. Introduced 1984; discontinued 1987.

Perf.: $600   **Exc.:** $490   **VGood:** $400

EXEL MODEL 208
Side-by-side; sidelock; 12-ga.; 2-3/4-inch chambers; 28-inch barrels; high matted rib; metal bead front sight; deluxe hand-checkered European walnut straight or pistol-grip stock; double triggers; extractors or ejectors; color case-hardened finish; engraved receiver. Made in Spain. Introduced 1984; discontinued 1987.

Perf.: $675   **Exc.:** $525   **VGood:** $500

EXEL MODEL 209
Side-by-side; sidelock; 20-ga.; 2-3/4-inch chambers; 26-inch barrel; high matted rib; metal bead front sight; deluxe hand-checkered European walnut straight or pistol-grip stock; double triggers; extractors or ejectors; color case-hardened finish;

Exel Model 251

Exel Series 300

Fabarm Camo Turkey Mag

Fabarm Ultra Camo

Fabarm Classic Lion
Grade I

Fabarm Classic Lion
Grade II

Fabarm Classic Lion Elite

Fabarm FP6 Pump

EXEL SERIES 300

Over/under; boxlock; 12-ga.; 2-3/4-inch chambers;
28-inch, 29-inch barrels, vent-rib; checkered European
walnut pistol-grip field or Monte Carlo stock, forend;
auto selective ejectors; silvered, engraved finish.
Offered in ten variations with differing degrees of
ornamentation. Made in Spain. Introduced 1984;
discontinued 1987.

Models 301 & 302		
Perf.: $450	**Exc.:** $360	**VGood:** $300
Models 303 & 304		
Perf.: $520	**Exc.:** $430	**VGood:** $390
Models 305 & 306		
Perf.: $600	**Exc.:** $500	**VGood:** $450
Models 307 & 308		
Perf.: $550	**Exc.:** $450	**VGood:** $400
Models 309 & 310		
Perf.: $600	**Exc.:** $500	**VGood:** $450

FABARM CAMO TURKEY MAG SHOTGUN

Over/under; 12-ga.; 3-1/2-inch chambers; 20-inch
barrel TriBore (Ultra-Full ported tubes); weighs 7.5 lbs.;
length: 46-inch overall; stock dimensions 14.5 inches
by 1.5 inches by 2.29 inches; front bar sight; Picatinny
rail scope base; completely covered with Xtra Brown
camouflage finish; unported barrels. Introduced 1999.
Imported from Italy by Heckler & Koch, Inc.

    Perf.: $995   **Exc.:** $875   **VGood:** $775

FABARM ULTRA CAMO

Similar to Camo Turkey but without front bar sight
and Picatinny base.

FABARM CLASSIC LION DOUBLE SHOTGUN

Side-by-side; 12-ga.; 3-inch chambers; 26-inch, 28-
inch, 30-inch barrel (Cyl., Imp. Cyl., Mod., Imp. Mod.,
Full choke tubes); weighs 7.2 lbs.; length: 44.5-inch-
48.5; English-style or pistol grip oil-finished European
walnut; boxlock action with double triggers;
automatic ejectors; automatic safety. Introduced
1998. Imported from Italy by Heckler & Koch, Inc.

Grade I		
Perf.: $1375	**Exc.:** $1125	**VGood:** $850
Grade II		
Perf.: $1875	**Exc.:** $1525	**VGood:** $1200
Grade II Bill Hanus Birdgun Model		
Similar to Grade II, except has best quality wood. Importation discontinued 2000.		
Perf.: $2275	**Exc.:** $1925	**VGood:** $1550
Elite (color-case hardened finish, 44.5-inch)		
Perf.: $1395	**Exc.:** $1150	**VGood:** $875

FABARM FIELD PUMP SHOTGUN

Pump action; 12-ga.; 3-inch chamber; 28-inch barrel
(24-inch rifled slug barrel available); weighs 76.6 lbs.;
length 48.25-inch overall; polymer stock; similar to
Fabarm FP6 pump shotgun; alloy receiver; twin action
bars; available in black or Mossy Oak Break-Up camo
finish; includes Cyl., Mod. and Full choke tubes.
Introduced 2001. Imported from Italy by Heckler &
Koch Inc.

Matte black finish		
Perf.: $325	**Exc.:** $285	**VGood:** $260
Mossy Oak Break-Up finish		
Perf.: $400	**Exc.:** $355	**VGood:** $320

FABARM FP6 PUMP SHOTGUN

Pump action; 12-ga.; 3-inch chamber; 20-inch barrel;
(Cyl.); accepts choke tubes; weighs 6.6 lbs.; 41.25-
inch overall; black polymer stock with textured grip;
grooved slide handle; blade front sight; twin action
bars; anodized finish; free carrier for smooth reloading.
Introduced 1998. Imported from Italy by Heckler &
Koch, Inc.

Carbon fiber finish		
Perf.: $460	**Exc.:** $400	**VGood:** $365
With flip-up front sight, Picatinny rail with rear sight, oversize safety button		
Perf.: $480	**Exc.:** $440	**VGood:** $400

---

engraved receiver. Made in Spain. Introduced 1984;
discontinued 1987.

    Perf.: $550   **Exc.:** $465   **VGood:** $400

EXEL MODEL 210

Side-by-side; sidelock; 20-ga.; 2-3/4-inch chambers;
27-inch barrel; high matted rib; metal bead front
sight; deluxe hand-checkered European walnut
straight or pistol-grip stock; double triggers;
extractors or ejectors; color case-hardened finish;
engraved receiver. Made in Spain. Introduced 1984;
discontinued 1987.

    Perf.: $550   **Exc.:** $465   **VGood:** $400

EXEL MODEL 240

Side-by-side; boxlock; .410; 2-3/4-inch chambers;
28-inch barrel; high matted rib; metal bead front
sight; hand-checkered European walnut straight or
pistol-grip stock; double triggers; extractors; color

---

case-hardened finish. Made in Spain. Introduced
1984; discontinued 1987.

    Perf.: $425   **Exc.:** $280   **VGood:** $210

EXEL MODEL 251

Single shot; exposed hammer; .410; 3-inch chamber;
folding stock; splinter forend; non-ejector; case-
hardened frame. Made in Spain. Introduced 1985;
discontinued 1987.

    Perf.: $160   **Exc.:** $125   **VGood:** $100

EXEL MODEL 281

Side-by-side; boxlock; 28-ga.; 2-3/4-inch chambers;
28-inch barrel; high matted rib; metal bead front sight;
hand-checkered European walnut straight or pistol-
grip stock; double triggers; extractors; color case-
hardened finish. Made in Spain. Introduced 1984;
discontinued 1987.

    Perf.: $400   **Exc.:** $295   **VGood:** $250

FABARM GOLD LION MARK II AUTO SHOTGUN

Semi-auto.; 12-ga.; 3-inch chamber; 24-inch, 26-inch, 28-inch barrel; choke tubes; weighs 7 lbs.; length: 45.5-inch overall; European walnut stock with gloss finish; olive wood grip cap; TriBore barrel; reversible safety; gold-plated trigger and carrier release button; leather-covered rubber recoil pad. Introduced 1998. Imported from Italy by Heckler & Koch, Inc.

Perf.: $750   **Exc.:** $675   **VGood:** $595

FABARM CAMO LION AUTO SHOTGUN

Similar to Gold Lion except 24-inch, 26-inch or 28-inch ported TriBore barrel system with five choke tubes, completely covered with Wetlands camouflage pattern. Red front sight bead and mid-rib bead. Introduced 1999. Imported from Italy by Heckler & Koch, Inc.

Perf.: $850   **Exc.:** $725   **VGood:** $650

FABARM SPORTING CLAYS EXTRA AUTO SHOTGUN

Similar to Gold Lion except 28-inch TriBore ported barrel with interchangeable colored front-sight beads, mid-rib bead, 10mm channeled vent rib, carbon-fiber finish, oil-finished walnut stock and forend with olive wood grip cap. Distinctive gold-colored receiver logo. Available in 12-gauge only, 3-inch chamber. Introduced 1999. Imported from Italy by Heckler & Koch, Inc.

Perf.: $1025   **Exc.:** $895   **VGood:** $775

FABARM MAX LION OVER/UNDER SHOTGUNS

Over/under: 12-ga.; 3-inch chambers; 20, 3-inch chambers; 26-inch, 28-inch, 30-inch barrel (12 ga.); 26-inch, 28-inch barrel (20-ga.); choke tubes; weighs 7.4 lbs.; 47-1/2-inch overall (26-inch barrel); European walnut; leather-covered recoil pad; TriBore barrel; boxlock action with single selective trigger; manual safety; automatic ejectors; chrome-lined barrels; adjustable trigger; silvered, engraved receiver; locking, fitted luggage case. Introduced 1998. Imported from Italy by Heckler & Koch, Inc.

Perf.: $1625   **Exc.:** $1350   **VGood:** $1150

FABARM MAX LION PARADOX

Over/under; 12-ga.; 3-inch chambers; 24-inch barrel; weighs 7.6 lbs.; 44.5-inch overall; walnut with special enhancing finish; TriBore upper barrel and lower barrel with paradox rifling; both wood and receiver are enhanced with special finishes; color case-hardened type finish.

Perf.: $975   **Exc.:** $875   **VGood:** $775

FABARM MONOTRAP SHOTGUN

Single barrel; 12-ga.; 2-3/4-inch chamber; 30-inch, 34-inch barrel; weighs 6.7 to 6.9 lbs.; 48-1/2-inch overall length (30-inch bbl.); walnut; adjustable comb competition-style stock; red front sight bar, mid-rib bead; built on 20-gauge receiver for quick handling; silver receiver with blued barrel; special trap rib (micrometer adjustable); includes three choke tubes (M, IM, F). Introduced 2000.

Perf.: $1625   **Exc.:** $1375   **VGood: $1150**

FABARM RED LION

Semi-auto.; 12-ga.; 3-inch chamber; 26-inch, 28-inch barrel; five screw-in chokes; weighs 7 to 7.2 lbs.; premium walnut; olive grip cap; red bar sights; TriBore barrel system. Limited edition Gold Lion, black and silver finish receiver with English-style gold inlaid engraving, Fabarm semi-automatic operating system. Blue finish.

Perf.: $710   **Exc.:** $635   **VGood:** $550

FABARM SILVER LION OVER/ UNDER SHOTGUNS

Over/under; 12-ga.; 3-inch chambers; 20, 3-inch chambers; 26-inch, 28-inch, 30-inch barrel (12-ga.); 26-inch, 28-inch barrel (20-ga.); choke tubes; weighs: 7.2 lbs.; 47-1/2-inch overall length(26-inch barrels); walnut; leather-covered recoil pad; TriBore barrel; boxlock action with single selective trigger; silvered receiver with engraving; automatic ejectors; locking

Fabarm Camo Lion
Auto Shotgun

Fabarm Sporting Clays
Extra Auto

Fabarm Max Lion
Over/Under

Fabarm Max Lion Paradox

Fabarm Monotrap

Fabarm Red Lion

Fabarm Silver Lion
Over/Under

Fabarm Silver Lion Cub
Model O/U

Fabarm Ultra Cam
Mag Lion

Fabarm Sporting Clays
Competition Extra O/U

hard plastic case. Introduced 1998. Imported from Italy by Heckler & Koch, Inc.

Perf.: $1075   **Exc.:** $925   **VGood:** $825

FABARM SILVER LION CUB MODEL O/U

Similar to the Silver Lion except has 12.5-inch length of pull, is in 20-gauge only (3-1/2-inch chambers), and comes with 24-inch TriBore barrel system.

Weight is 6 lbs. Introduced 1999. Imported from Italy by Heckler & Koch, Inc.

Perf.: $1075   **Exc.:** $925   **VGood:** $825

FABARM ULTRA CAMO MAG LION

Similar to Silver Lion but with all-camo finish. Introduced 1998. Imported from Italy by Heckler & Koch, Inc. 12- or 20-gauge.

Perf.: $1075   **Exc.:** $925   **VGood:** $825

Fabarm Tactical Shotgun

Ferlib Model F VII

F.I.E. Brute

F.I.E. CBC

F.I.E. Hamilton & Hunter

F.I.E. S.O.B.

FABARM SPORTING CLAYS COMPETITION EXTRA O/U

Over/under; 12-, 20-ga.; 3-inch chambers; 12-ga. has 30-inch barrel; 20 ga. has 28-inch; ported TriBore barrel system with five tubes; weighs 7 to 7.8 lbs.; deluxe walnut; leather-covered recoil pad; single selective trigger; auto ejectors; 10mm channeled rib; carbon fiber finish. Introduced 1999. Imported from Italy by Heckler & Koch, Inc.

Perf.: $1575　　**Exc.:** $1325　　**VGood:** $1100

FABARM TACTICAL SEMI-AUTOMATIC SHOTGUN

Semi-auto.; 12-ga.; 3-inch chamber; 20-inch barrel; weighs 6.6 lbs.; length: 41.2-inch overall; polymer or folding stock; ghost ring sights (tritium night sights optional); gas-operated; matte receiver; twin forged action bars; oversized bolt handle and safety button; Picatinny rail; includes cylinder bore choke tube. Introduced 2001. Imported from Italy by Heckler & Koch Inc.

Perf.: $865　　**Exc.:** $750　　**VGood:** $650

FERLACH CONSTANT COMPANION

Side-by-side; Anson & Deeley-type action; 12-, 16-, 20-ga.; 28-inch, 30-inch barrels; tapered boring; hand-checkered black walnut pistol-grip stock, cheekpiece; quadruple Greener bolt; auto safety; ejectors; double triggers; engraved receiver. Made in Austria. Introduced 1956; discontinued 1958.

Perf.: $875　　**Exc.:** $775　　**VGood:** $700

FERLIB MODEL F VII

Side-by-side; boxlock; 12-, 16-, 20-, 28-ga., .410; 25-inch, 26-inch, 27-inch, 28-inch barrels; standard chokes; oil-finished checkered European walnut straight-grip stock, forend; beavertail forend optional; single or double triggers; silvered, scroll-engraved receiver. Made in Italy. Introduced 1983; still in production.

12-, 16-, 20-ga.		
Perf.: $9950	**Exc.:** $8750	**VGood:** $7600
28-ga., .410		
Perf.: $10,200	**Exc.:** $9100	**VGood:** $7900

FERLIB MODEL F VII/SC

Same specs as Model F VII except elaborate engraving with gold inlays. Made in Italy. Introduced 1983; still in production.

12-, 16-, 20-ga.		
Perf.: $7500	**Exc.:** $6000	**VGood:** $5000
28-ga., .410		
Perf.: $8100	**Exc.:** $6500	**VGood:** $5400

FERLIB MODEL F VII SIDEPLATE

Same specs as Model F VII except sideplates; single trigger; elaborate engraving. Made in Italy. Introduced 1983; still in production.

12-, 16-, 20-ga.		
Perf.: $12,950	**Exc.:** $10,500	**VGood:** $9000
28-ga., .410		
Perf.: $13,200	**Exc.:** $10,750	**VGood:** $9220

FERLIB MODEL F VII SIDEPLATE SC

Same specs as Model F VII except sideplates; single trigger; elaborate engraving with gold inlays. Made in Italy. Introduced 1983; still in production.

12-, 16-, 20-ga.		
Perf.: $10,000	**Exc.:** $8500	**VGood:** $7000
28-ga., .410		
Perf.: $11,000	**Exc.:** $9000	**VGood:** $7500

FIAS MODEL SK-1

Over/under; boxlock; 12-, 20-ga.; 3-inch chambers; 26-inch Improved Cylinder/Modified, 28-inch Modified/Full, 30-inch Modified/Full or Full/Full, 32-inch Full/Full barrels; vent-rib; hand-checkered select European walnut pistol-grip stock, forearm; top lever break; Greener crossbolt; double triggers; extractors. Made in Europe. Introduced 1974; discontinued 1984.

Perf.: $275　　**Exc.:** $230　　**VGood:** $190

FIAS MODEL SK-3

Over/under; boxlock; 12-, 20-ga.; 3-inch chambers; 26-inch Improved Cylinder/Modified, 28-inch Modified/ Full, 30-inch Modified/Full or Full/Full, 32-inch Full/Full barrels; vent-rib; hand-checkered select European walnut pistol-grip stock, forearm; top lever break; Greener crossbolt; selective single trigger; extractors. Made in Europe. Introduced 1974; discontinued 1984.

Perf.: $290　　**Exc.:** $240　　**VGood:** $200

FIAS MODEL SK-4

Over/under; boxlock; 12-, 20-ga.; 3-inch chambers; 26-inch Improved Cylinder/Modified, 28-inch Modified/Full, 30-inch Modified/Full or Full/Full, 32-inch Full/Full barrels; vent-rib; hand-checkered select European walnut pistol-grip stock; beavertail forearm; top lever break; Greener crossbolt; selective single trigger; selective auto ejectors. Made in Europe. Introduced 1974; discontinued 1984.

Perf.: $350　　**Exc.:** $280　　**VGood:** $210

FIAS MODEL SK-4D

Same specs as SK-4 except sideplates; better grade wood; deluxe engraving. Introduced 1974; discontinued 1984.

Perf.: $480　　**Exc.:** $320　　**VGood:** $270

FIAS MODEL SK-4S

Same specs as SK-4 except 26-inch Skeet 1/Skeet 2 barrels. Introduced 1974; discontinued 1984.

Perf.: $320　　**Exc.:** $280　　**VGood:** $210

FIAS MODEL SK-4T

Same specs as Model SK-4 except 12-ga.; 2-3/4-inch chambers; 30-inch Improved Modified/Full, 32-inch Improved Modified/Full barrels; middle sight; select European walnut Monte Carlo pistol-grip stock, beavertail forearm. Introduced 1974; discontinued 1984.

Perf.: $350　　**Exc.:** $280　　**VGood:** $210

F.I.E. BRUTE

Side-by-side; boxlock; 12-, 20-ga., .410; 19-inch barrels; 30-inch overall length; short hand-checkered walnut stock. Made in Brazil. Introduced 1979; no longer in production.

Perf.: $195　　**Exc.:** $150　　**VGood:** $130

F.I.E. CBC

Single shot; takedown; exposed hammer; 12-, 16-, 20-ga., .410; 28-inch Full-choke barrel; metal bead front sight; walnut-stained hardwood stock, beavertail forend; trigger guard button breaks action; auto ejector. Made in Brazil. Introduced 1982; discontinued 1984.

Perf.: $90　　**Exc.:** $75　　**VGood:** $50

F.I.E. HAMILTON & HUNTER

Single shot; takedown; exposed hammer; 12-, 20-ga., .410; 3-inch chamber; 28-inch barrel; weighs 6-1/2 lbs.; metal bead front sight; walnut-stained hardwood stock, beavertail forend; break-button on trigger guard; auto ejector. Made in Brazil. Introduced 1986; discontinued 1990.

Perf.: $100　　**Exc.:** $80　　**VGood:** $60

F.I.E. S.O.B.

Single barrel; exposed hammer; 12-, 20-ga., .410; 18-1/2-inch barrel; metal bead front sight; short walnut-finished hardwood stock, beavertail forend; auto ejector. Made in Brazil. Introduced 1980; discontinued 1984.

Perf.: $110　　**Exc.:** $80　　**VGood:** $60

F.I.E. S.S.S. MODEL
Single barrel; exposed hammer; 12-, 20-ga., .410; 3-inch chamber; 18 1/2-inch Cylinder barrel; weighs 6-1/2 lbs.; walnut-finished hardwood stock, full beavertail forend; auto ejectors; break-button on trigger guard. Made in Brazil. Introduced 1986; discontinued 1990.

Perf.: $90   **Exc.:** $75   **VGood:** $50

F.I.E. STURDY
Over/under; 12-, 20-ga.; 3-inch chamber; 28-inch vent-rib barrel; walnut stock; double triggers; extractors; engraved silver finished receiver. Introduced 1985; discontinued 1988.

Perf.: $300   **Exc.:** $275   **VGood:** $250

F.I.E. STURDY DELUXE PRITI
Same specs as Sturdy except deluxe walnut stock. Introduced 1985; discontinued 1988.

Perf.: $325   **Exc.:** $290   **VGood:** $260

With optional single selective trigger; ejectors; choke tubes

Perf.: $395   **Exc.:** $360   **VGood:** $330

F.I.E. STURDY MODEL 12 DELUXE
Same specs as Sturdy except only 12-ga.; choke tubes; select walnut stock; single selective trigger; ejectors. Introduced 1988; discontinued 1988.

Perf.: $320   **Exc.:** $290   **VGood:** $260

FOX FA-1
Autoloader; 12-ga.; 28-inch Modified, 30-inch Full choke barrels; metal bead front sight; walnut pistol-grip stock; rosewood grip cap with inlay; self-compensating gas system; crossbolt safety; chrome-moly barrel, polished receiver. Made in Japan. Introduced 1981 by Savage Arms; discontinued 1982.

Perf.: $300   **Exc.:** $260   **VGood:** $225

FOX FP-1
Slide action; 12-ga.; 28-inch, 30-inch barrels; vent. rib; metal bead front sight; checkered pistol-grip walnut stock; rosewood pistol-grip cap; crossbolt safety; dual action bars. Made in Japan. Introduced 1981 by Savage Arms; discontinued 1982.

Perf.: $290   **Exc.:** $250   **VGood:** $210

STEVENS/FOX MODEL B
Side-by-side; boxlock; hammerless; 12-, 16-, 20-ga.,.410; 26-inch, 28-inch, 30-inch barrels; Modified/Full, Improved/ Modified, Full/Full chokes; hand-checkered American walnut pistol-grip stock, forearm; double triggers; plain extractors; case-hardened frame. Introduced 1940; no longer in production.

Exc.: $320   **VGood:** $270   **Good:** $225

STEVENS/FOX MODEL B-DE
Same specs as Model B except for checkered select walnut pistol-grip stock, beavertail forearm; non-selective single trigger; satin chrome-finished frame; replaced Model B-DL. Introduced 1965; discontinued 1966.

Exc.: $340   **VGood:** $290   **Good:** $215

STEVENS/FOX MODEL B-DL
Same specs as Model B except for checkered select walnut pistol-grip stock, beavertail forearm; non-selective single trigger; satin chrome-finished frame; sideplates. Introduced 1962; discontinued 1965.

Exc.: $360   **VGood:** $310   **Good:** $225

STEVENS/FOX MODEL B-SE
Same specs as Model B except single trigger; selective ejectors. Introduced 1966; discontinued 1987.

Perf.: $450   **Exc.:** $425   **VGood:** $290

STEVENS/FOX MODEL B-ST
Same specs as Model B except non-selective single trigger. Introduced 1955; discontinued 1966.

Exc.: $475   **VGood:** $400   **Good:** $320

Fox FA-1

Fox FP-1

Stevens/Fox Model B-DE

Stevens/Fox Model B

Stevens/Fox Model B-DL

Stevens/Fox Model B-SE

Stevens/Fox Model B-ST

A.H. FOX MODEL B LIGHTWEIGHT
Side-by-side; boxlock; hammerless; 12-, 20-ga., .410; 24-inch Improved/Modified (12-, 20-ga. only), 26-inch Full/Full (.410 only), 26-inch Improved/Modified, 28-inch Modified/Full, 30-inch Modified/Full (12-ga. only) barrels; vent rib; checkered select walnut pistol-grip stock, beavertail forearm; double triggers; color case-hardened frame. Introduced 1973; no longer in production.

Perf.: $350   **Exc.:** $320   **VGood:** $200

A.H. FOX HAMMERLESS DOUBLE BARREL (1902-1905)
Side-by-side; boxlock; 12-ga.; 28-inch, 30-inch, 32-inch Krupp fluid steel barrels; Damascus barrels optional in grades C and higher; Whitworth fluid steel barrels optional in Grade H; English walnut stocks; pistol grip in Grade A, straight or pistol grip in others; made by Philadelphia Gun Company, Philadelphia. Introduced 1902; discontinued 1905.

Grade A		
Perf.: $1250	**Exc.:** $875	**VGood:** $700
Grade B		
Perf.: $2000	**Exc.:** $1400	**VGood:** $1100
Grade C		
Perf.: $2900	**Exc.:** $2000	**VGood:** $1600

Grade D		
Perf.: $6500	**Exc.:** $4900	**VGood:** $3600
Grade E		
Perf.: $10,000	**Exc.:** $7500	**VGood:** $5500
Grade F		
Perf.: $13,500	**Exc.:** $10,000	**VGood:** $7400
Grade H		
Perf.: $15,500	**Exc.:** $12,000	**VGood:** $8600

A.H. FOX HAMMERLESS DOUBLE BARREL (1905-1946)
Side-by-side; boxlock; 12-, 16-, 20-ga.; 2-9/16-inch (until mid-1930s), 2-3/4-inch, 3-inch chambers; Krupp fluid steel (until about 1910), Chromox steel barrels (used exclusively after the early 1920s); walnut half-pistol-grip stock standard, straight or pistol grip optional; earliest graded smallbores have snap-on forend latch; standard engraving patterns for all grades except CE were changed 1913-1914; all graded 12-ga. and graded smallbores built after 1913 have Deeley finger-lever forend latch; Fox-Kautzky single trigger available in all grades after 1914; other options included beavertail forend, vent rib, skeleton steel butt, recoil pad, extra sets of barrels, custom stocks. 12-ga. introduced 1905; 16-, 20-ga. introduced 1912 and built on the same, scaled-down frame. Made by A.H. Fox Gun Company,

A.H. Fox Hammerless
Double Barrel B Grade

A.H. Fox Hammerless
Double Barrel DE Grade

A.H. Fox Hammerless
Double Barrel CE Grade

A.H. Fox Hammerless
Double Barrel XE Grade

Philadelphia, 1905-1929; taken over by Savage Arms Company in late 1929 and production moved to Utica, New York in 1930; production of the original A.H. Fox gun discontinued in 1946. Approximate production totals: graded 12-ga., 35,000; graded 16-ga., 3521; graded 20-ga., 3434.

A.H. FOX HAMMERLESS DOUBLE BARREL A GRADE

Same specs as Hammerless Double Barrel (1905-1946) except 26-inch to 32-inch barrels; American walnut stocks; double or single trigger; extractors. Introduced 1905; discontinued 1942.

Exc.: $1400   **VGood:** $950   **Good:** $800

A.H. FOX HAMMERLESS DOUBLE BARREL AE GRADE

Same specs as Hammerless Double Barrel (1905-1946) except 26-inch to 32-inch barrels; American walnut stocks; double or single trigger; ejectors. Introduced 1905; discontinued 1946.

Exc.: $1600   **VGood:** $1150   **Good:** $950

A.H. FOX HAMMERLESS DOUBLE BARREL B GRADE

Same specs as Hammerless Double Barrel (1905-1946) except 26-inch to 32-inch barrels; English walnut stocks; double or single trigger; extractors. Introduced 1905; discontinued 1918.

Exc.: $2300   **VGood:** $1700   **Good:** $1450

A.H. FOX HAMMERLESS DOUBLE BARREL BE GRADE

Same specs as Hammerless Double Barrel (1905-1946) except 26-inch to 32-inch barrels; English walnut stocks; double or single trigger; ejectors. Introduced 1905; discontinued 1918.

Exc.: $2500   **VGood:** $1900   **Good:** $1650

A.H. FOX HAMMERLESS DOUBLE BARREL C GRADE

Same specs as Hammerless Double Barrel (1905-1946) except 26-inch to 32-inch barrels; English walnut stocks; double or single trigger; extractors. Introduced 1905; discontinued 1913.

Exc.: $3400   **VGood:** $2900   **Good:** $2400

A.H. FOX HAMMERLESS DOUBLE BARREL CE GRADE

Same specs as Hammerless Double Barrel (1905-1946) except 26-inch to 32-inch barrels; English walnut stocks; double or single trigger; ejectors. Introduced 1905; discontinued 1946.

Exc.: $3800   **VGood:** $3100   **Good:** $2600

A.H. FOX HAMMERLESS DOUBLE BARREL D GRADE

Same specs as Hammerless Double Barrel (1905-1946) except 26-inch to 32-inch barrels; Circassian

walnut stocks; double or single trigger; extractors. Introduced 1905; discontinued 1913.

Exc.: $7700   **VGood:** $5700   **Good:** $4300

A.H. FOX HAMMERLESS DOUBLE BARREL DE GRADE

Same specs as Hammerless Double Barrel (1905-1946) except 26-inch to 32-inch barrels; Circassian walnut stocks; double or single trigger; ejectors. Introduced 1905; discontinued 1945.

Exc.: $8000   **VGood:** $6000   **Good:** $4500

A.H. FOX HAMMERLESS DOUBLE BARREL F GRADE

Same specs as Hammerless Double Barrel (1905-1946) except 26-inch to 32-inch barrels; Circassian walnut stocks; extractors; made to order with any available option at no extra charge. Introduced 1906; discontinued 1913.

Exc.: $16,000   **VGood:** $11,000   **Good:** $9500

A.H. FOX HAMMERLESS DOUBLE BARREL FE GRADE

Same specs as Hammerless Double Barrel (1905-1946) except 26-inch to 32-inch barrels; Circassian walnut stocks; ejectors; made to order with any available option at no extra charge. Introduced 1906; discontinued 1940.

Exc.: $16,500   **VGood:** $12,000   **Good:** $10,000

A.H. FOX HAMMERLESS DOUBLE BARREL GE GRADE

Same specs as Hammerless Double Barrel (1905-1946) except reputedly the highest-grade A.H. Fox gun; included in price lists from 1922 through 1930, but never shown in catalogs.

A.H. FOX HAMMERLESS DOUBLE BARREL SKEETER

Same specs as Hammerless Double Barrel (1905-1946) except 12-, 20-ga.; 28-inch barrels; vent rib; ivory beads; walnut pistol-grip stock, beavertail forend; recoil pad; ejectors; double triggers; single trigger optional. Introduced 1931; discontinued 1931.

Exc.: $2500   **VGood:** $1800   **Good:** $1400

A.H. FOX HAMMERLESS DOUBLE BARREL TRAP GRADE

Same specs as Hammerless Double Barrel (1905-1946) except 26-inch to 32-inch barrels; vent rib; ivory beads; walnut pistol-grip stock, beavertail forend; recoil pad; double triggers; single trigger optional. Introduced 1932; discontinued 1936.

Exc.: $2500   **VGood:** $1800   **Good:** $1400

A.H. FOX HAMMERLESS DOUBLE BARREL XE GRADE

Same specs as Hammerless Double Barrel (1905-1946) except 26-inch to 32-inch barrels; Circassian

walnut stocks; Monte Carlo comb optional; double or single trigger; ejectors. Introduced 1914; discontinued 1945.

Exc.: $5750   **VGood:** $4800   **Good:** $3800

A.H. FOX HAMMERLESS DOUBLE BARREL (CURRENT PRODUCTION)

Side-by-side; boxlock; 20-ga.; 26-inch, 28-inch, 30-inch barrels; American walnut stock, splinter forend; stocks made to order; double triggers; optional beavertail forend, skeleton steel butt, recoil pad, checkered butt, single trigger; grades CE, DE, FE, Exhibition. Introduced 1993 by Connecticut Shotgun Manufacturing Company, New Britain, Connecticut; still in production.

CE Grade		
Perf.: $10,950	**Exc.:** $8500	**VGood:** $.6250
DE Grade		
Perf.: $14,800	**Exc.:** $11,500	**VGood:** $9500
FE Grade		
Perf.: $19,700	**Exc.:** $16,500	**VGood:** $12,750
Exhibition Grade		
Perf.: $22,500	**Exc.:** $17,500	**VGood:** $12,500

A.H. FOX SIDE-BY-SIDE SHOTGUNS

Gauge: 16, 20, 28, .410. Barrel: Length and chokes to customer specifications. Rust-blued Chromox or Krupp steel. Weight: 5-1/2 to 6-3/4 lbs. Stock: Dimensions to customer specifications. Hand-checkered Turkish Circassian walnut with hand-rubbed oil finish. Straight, semi or full pistol grip; splinter, schnabel or beavertail forend; traditional pad, hard rubber buttplate or skeleton butt. Features: Boxlock action with automatic ejectors; double or Fox single selective trigger. Scalloped, rebated and color case-hardened receiver; hand finished and hand-engraved. Grades differ in engraving, inlays, grade of wood, amount of hand finishing. Add $1,500 for 28 or .410-bore. Introduced 1993. Made in U.S. by Connecticut Shotgun Mfg.

Price: CE Grade $11,000		
Perf.: $11,000	**Exc.:** $8,500	**VGood:** $6,250
Price: XE Grade $12,500.00		
Perf.: $12,500	**Exc.:** 9,250	**VGood:** $6,500
Price: DE Grade $15,000.00		
Perf.: $15,000	**Exc.:** $11,500	**VGood:** $9,500
Price: FE Grade $20,000.00		
Perf.: $20,000	**Exc.:** $16,500	**VGood:** $12,750
Price: Exhibition Grade $30,000.00		
Price: 28/.410 CE Grade $12,500.00		
Perf.: $12,500	**Exc.** $10,000	**VGood:** $7,750
Price: 28/.410 XE Grade $14,000		
Perf.: $14,000	**Exc.:** $10,750	**VGood:** $8,000
Price: 28/.410 DE Grade $16,500		
Perf.: $16,500	**Exc.:** $13,000	**VGood:** $11,000
Price: 28/.410 FE Grade $21,500		
Perf.: $21,500	**Exc.:** $18,000	**VGood:** $14,250
Price: 28/.410 Exhibition Grade $30,000		

A.H. FOX SINGLE-BARREL TRAP

Single shot; boxlock; 12-ga.; 30-inch, 32-inch barrel; vent rib; American walnut straight, half- or pistol-grip stock; Monte Carlo comb optional for early guns, standard after 1931; ejector; available in four grades. Introduced 1919; discontinued 1939. Approximate production totals: J Grade, 460; K Grade, 77; L Grade, 25; M Grade, 9.

J Grade		
Exc.: $3860	**VGood:** $3550	**Good:** $3200
K Grade		
Exc.: $5200	**VGood:** $4650	**Good:** $4000
L Grade		
Exc.: $6500	**VGood:** $5750	**Good:** $5000
M Grade		
Exc.: $8000	**VGood:** $7250	**Good:** $6000

A.H. FOX SP GRADE

Side-by-side; boxlock; 12-, 16-, 20-ga.; 26-inch, 28-inch, 30-inch, 32-inch barrels; American walnut pistol-grip stock; double triggers; extractors; optional single trigger, beavertail forend, recoil pad, ivory beads; a distinct model mechanically identical to standard Fox guns but with a squarer, smooth-sided frame and no cheek panels on the stock; originally called Fox Special Grade, changed to SP Grade. Introduced 1932; discontinued 1946.

Perf.: $2000   **Exc.:** $1400   **VGood:** $1100

A.H. FOX SPE GRADE

Same specs as SP Grade except ejectors. Introduced 1932; discontinued 1946.

Perf.: $2100   **Exc.:** $1500   **VGood:** $1200

A.H. FOX SPE SKEET GRADE

Same specs as SP Grade except ejectors; double or single trigger. Introduced 1934; discontinued 1934.

Perf.: $2100   **Exc.:** $1500   **VGood:** $1200

A.H. FOX SPE SKEET AND UPLAND GAME GUN

Same specs as SP Grade except 26-inch, 28-inch Cylinder/Quarter barrels; American walnut straight or pistol-grip stock, beavertail forend; single trigger; ejectors; optional double triggers, vent rib, recoil pad. Introduced 1935; discontinued 1939.

Perf.: $2100   **Exc.:** $1500   **VGood:** $1200

A.H. FOX SPR GRADE

Same specs as SP Grade except vent rib; ejectors. Introduced 1936; discontinued 1936.

Perf.: $2300   **Exc.:** $1700   **VGood:** $1400

A.H. FOX STERLINGWORTH

Side-by-side; boxlock; 12-, 16-, 20-ga.; 2-9/16-inch (until mid-1930s), 2-3/4-inch, 3-inch chambers; 26-inch to 32-inch Krupp fluid steel (until about 1910), Chromox steel barrels (used exclusively after the early 1920s); checkered American walnut half-pistol-grip stock, snap-on forend standard; straight or pistol grip optional; snap-on forend latch; double triggers; optional Fox-Kautzky single trigger available in all grades after 1914; extractors; standard engraving patterns for all grades except CE were changed 1913-1914; other options include beavertail forend, vent rib, skeleton steel butt, recoil pad, extra sets of barrels, custom stocks; mechanically same as other A.H. Fox doubles, but purely production-line guns without much handwork. Introduced 1911; discontinued 1946. Made by A.H. Fox Gun Company, Philadelphia, 1905-1929; taken over by Savage Arms Company in late 1929 and production moved to Utica, New York in 1930; production of the original A.H. Fox gun discontinued in 1946. Approximate production totals: 12-ga. Sterlingworth, 110,000; Sterlingworth 16-ga., 28,000; 20-ga. Sterlingworth, 21,000.

Exc.: $1000   **VGood:** $700   **Good:** $450

A.H. FOX STERLINGWORTH BRUSH

Same specs as Fox Sterlingworth except 26-inch Cylinder/Modified barrels. Introduced 1911; discontinued 1930.

Exc.: $1000   **VGood:** $700   **Good:** $450

A.H. FOX STERLINGWORTH DELUXE

Same specs as Fox Sterlingworth except Lyman ivory beads; recoil pad. Introduced 1930; discontinued 1945.

Exc.: $1250   **VGood:** $1000   **Good:** $800

A.H. FOX STERLINGWORTH DELUXE EJECTOR

Same specs as Fox Sterlingworth except Lyman ivory beads; ejectors; recoil pad. Introduced 1931; discontinued 1945.

Exc.: $1400   **VGood:** $1150   **Good:** $950

A.H. FOX STERLINGWORTH EJECTOR

Same specs as Fox Sterlingworth except ejectors. Introduced 1911; discontinued 1946.

Exc.: $1200   **VGood:** $900   **Good:** $650

A.H. Fox Sterlingworth

A.H. Fox Sterlingworth Standard

Franchi Black Magic 48/AL

Franchi Black Magic Game

A.H. FOX STERLINGWORTH FIELD

Same specs as Fox Sterlingworth except 28-inch Modified/Full barrels. Introduced 1911; discontinued 1930.

Exc.: $1000   **VGood:** $700   **Good:** $450

A.H. FOX STERLINGWORTH SKEET

Same specs as Fox Sterlingworth except 26-inch, 28-inch barrels; checkered American walnut straight-grip stock; extractors; double triggers; optional single trigger, beavertail forend, recoil pad. Introduced 1935; discontinued 1945.

Perf.: $2200   **Exc.:** $1600   **VGood:** $1200

A.H. FOX STERLINGWORTH SKEET EJECTOR

Same specs as Fox Sterlingworth except 26-inch, 28-inch barrels; checkered American walnut straight-grip stock; ejectors; double triggers; optional single trigger, beavertail forend, recoil pad. Introduced 1935; discontinued 1945.

Perf.: $2250   **Exc.:** $1650   **VGood:** $1250

A.H. FOX STERLINGWORTH STANDARD

Same specs as Fox Sterlingworth except 30-inch Full/Full barrels. Introduced 1911; discontinued 1930.

Exc.: $1000   **VGood:** $700   **Good:** $450

A.H. FOX STERLINGWORTH TRAP

Same specs as Fox Sterlingworth except 32-inch Full/Full barrels. Introduced 1911; discontinued 1930.

Exc.: $1100   **VGood:** $750   **Good:** $500

A.H. FOX STERLINGWORTH WILDFOWL

Same specs as Fox Sterlingworth except 12-ga.; 30-inch, 32-inch barrels; ejectors; not a true Sterlingworth but rather a Super-Fox engraved and stamped "Fox Sterlingworth." Introduced 1934; discontinued 1940.

Exc.: $1300   **VGood:** $850   **Good:** $700

A.H. FOX SUPER-FOX

Over/Under; boxlock; 12-, 20-ga.; over-bored 30-inch, 32-inch Chromox steel barrels; checkered American walnut half-pistol-grip stock, snap-on forend standard; straight or pistol grip optional; snap-on forend latch; double triggers; optional Fox-Kautzky single trigger available; ejectors; standard engraving patterns; built on special, oversized frames; other options include beavertail forend, vent rib, ivory beads; skeleton steel butt, recoil pad, extra sets of barrels, custom stocks; special Fox model designed for long-range shooting; although designated HE Grade, it was also available in any standard Fox grade on special order; high grades rare. A few very early Super-Foxes are stamped "Barrels Guaranteed - See Tag"; most later ones are stamped "Barrels Not Guaranteed - See Tag"; both stamps refer to pattern density, not quality of barrels. 12-ga. introduced 1923; 20-ga. introduced 1925; 20-ga. discontinued 1931; 12-ga. discontinued 1942. Produced in very small numbers, about 300 guns in 12-ga. and only about 60 in 20-ga.

Exc.: $2000   **VGood:** $1400   **Good:** $1100

FRANCHI BLACK MAGIC 48/AL

Recoil-operated autoloader; 12-, 20-ga.; 2-3/4-inch chamber; 5-shot magazine; 24-inch rifled, 24-inch, 26-inch, 28-inch barrel; Improved Cylinder, Modified, Full Franchoke tubes; vent rib; weighs 5-1/4 lbs.; checkered walnut pistol-grip stock, forend; chrome-lined bore; crossbolt safety. Made in Italy. Introduced 1950; still in production.

Perf.: $585   **Exc.:** $530   **VGood:** $430

FRANCHI BLACK MAGIC GAME

Autoloader; 12-, 20-ga.; 3-inch chamber; 24-inch, 26-inch, 28-inch barrel; vent rib; choke tubes; bead front sight; checkered walnut stock, forearm; crossbolt safety; magazine cut-off; recoil pad. Made in Italy. Introduced 1989; discontinued 1991.

Perf.: $550   **Exc.:** $450   **VGood:** $395

Franchi Black Magic Skeet

Franchi Crown Grade

Franchi Diamond Grade

Franchi Eldorado

Franchi Hunter Semi-Automatic

Franchi Imperial Grade

Franchi Imperial Extra

Franchi LAW-12

FRANCHI CROWN GRADE

Recoil-operated autoloader; 12-, 20-ga.; 5-shot magazine; 24-inch, 26-inch, 28-inch, 30-inch interchangeable vent-rib barrel; Improved, Modified, Full chokes; hand-checkered European walnut pistol-grip stock, forearm; alloy receiver; chrome-lined barrels; simplified takedown; engraved hunting scene. Introduced 1954; discontinued 1975.

Perf.: $1540   **Exc.:** $1320   **VGood:** $1210

FRANCHI DIAMOND GRADE

Recoil-operated autoloader; 12-, 20-ga.; 5-shot magazine; 24-inch, 26-inch, 28-inch, 30-inch interchangeable vent-rib barrel; Improved, Modified, Full chokes; hand-checkered European walnut pistol-grip stock, forearm; alloy receiver; chrome-lined barrels; simplified takedown; scroll engraved with silver inlay. Introduced 1954; discontinued 1975.

Perf.: $1980   **Exc.:** $1735   **VGood:** $1540

FRANCHI ELDORADO

Recoil-operated autoloader; 12-, 20-ga.; 5-shot magazine; 24-inch, 26-inch, 28-inch, 30-inch interchangeable vent-rib barrel; Improved, Modified, Full chokes; select hand-checkered European walnut pistol-grip stock, forearm; alloy receiver; chrome-lined barrels; simplified takedown; scroll engraving covering 75 percent of receiver surfaces; gold-plated trigger; chrome-plated breech bolt. Introduced 1955; discontinued 1975.

Perf.: $450   **Exc.:** $420   **VGood:** $395

FRANCHI ELITE

Gas-operated autoloader; 12-ga.; 2-3/4-inch, 3-inch chamber; 24-inch, 26-inch, 28-inch, 30-inch, 32-inch barrel; 7mm vent rib; all standard chokes; weighs 7-3/8 lbs.; oil-finished, checkered European walnut stock; blued receiver; stainless steel gas piston; engraved receiver. Made in Italy. Introduced 1985; discontinued 1989.

Perf.: $595   **Exc.:** $500   **VGood:** $425

FRANCHI HUNTER SEMI-AUTOMATIC

Recoil-operated autoloader; 12-, 20-ga.; 5-shot magazine; 24-inch, 26-inch, 28-inch, 30-inch interchangeable vent-rib barrel; Improved, Modified, Full chokes; hand-checkered select European walnut pistol-grip stock, forearm; alloy receiver; chrome-lined barrels; simplified takedown; etched receiver. Introduced 1950; discontinued 1990.

Perf.: $415   **Exc.:** $360   **VGood:** $300

FRANCHI HUNTER MAGNUM

Same specs as Hunter Semi-Automatic except 12-, 20-ga.; 3-inch chamber; 32-inch (12-ga.), 28-inch (20-ga.) vent-rib, Full-choke barrel; recoil pad. Introduced 1955; discontinued 1973.

Perf.: $430   **Exc.:** $380   **VGood:** $370

FRANCHI IMPERIAL GRADE

Recoil-operated autoloader; 12-, 20-ga.; 5-shot magazine; 24-inch, 26-inch, 28-inch, 30-inch interchangeable vent-rib barrels; Improved, Modified, Full chokes; hand-checkered European walnut pistol-grip stock, forearm; alloy receiver; chrome-lined barrels; simplified takedown; elaborate engraving with gold inlay. Introduced 1954; discontinued 1975.

Perf.: $2420   **Exc.:** $2090   **VGood:** $1925

FRANCHI LAW-12

Autoloader; 12-ga.; 2-3/4-inch chamber; 5-, 8-shot tube magazine; 21-1/2-inch barrel; synthetic pistol-grip stock; alloy receiver. Introduced 1988; discontinued 1994.

Perf.: $575   **Exc.:** $485   **VGood:** $400

FRANCHI MODEL 500

Gas-operated autoloader; 12-ga.; 4-shot magazine; 26-inch, 28-inch barrel; vent rib; any standard choke; checkered European walnut pistol-grip stock. Introduced 1976; no longer in production.

Perf.: $330   **Exc.:** $310   **VGood:** $305

FRANCHI BLACK MAGIC SKEET

Autoloader; 12-, 20-ga.; 2-3/4-inch chamber; 28-inch barrel; vent rib; choke tubes; bead front sight; checkered walnut stock, forearm; crossbolt safety; magazine cut-off; recoil pad. Made in Italy. Introduced 1989; discontinued 1991.

Perf.: $580   **Exc.:** $475   **VGood:** $425

FRANCHI BLACK MAGIC TRAP

Autoloader; 12-ga.; 2-3/4-inch chamber; 30-inch barrel; vent rib; choke tubes; bead front sight; checkered European walnut trap-style stock, forearm; crossbolt safety; magazine cut-off; recoil pad. Made in Italy. Introduced 1989; discontinued 1991.

Perf.: $615   **Exc.:** $.495   **VGood:** $430

FRANCHI MODEL 520 DELUXE

Gas-operated autoloader; 12-ga.; 4-shot magazine; 26-inch, 28-inch barrel; vent rib; any standard choke; checkered select European walnut pistol-grip stock; engraved receiver. Introduced 1976; no longer in production.

Perf.: $385   **Exc.:** $365   **VGood:** $330

FRANCHI MODEL 520 ELDORADO GOLD

Same specs as Model 520 Deluxe except high quality of wood; better engraving; gold inlays in receiver. Introduced 1977; no longer in production.

Perf.: $990   **Exc.:** $770   **VGood:** $715

FRANCHI MODEL 530

Autoloader; 12-, 20-, 28-ga.; 2-3/4-inch, 3-inch chamber; 5-shot magazine; 30-inch barrel; interchangeable choke tubes; vent rib; oil finished, hand-checkered French walnut straight or Monte Carlo stock; interchangeable stock drilled, tapped for recoil reducer; specially tuned gas system; target-grade trigger; chrome-lined bore, chamber; matte blue finish. Introduced 1978; discontinued 1982.

Perf.: $660   **Exc.:** $550   **VGood:** $525

FRANCHI 612 AND 620

Autoloader; 12-, 20-ga.; 3-inch chamber; 24-inch, 26-inch, 28-inch barrel; IC, M, F tubes; weighs 7 lbs.; European walnut, synthetic and Timber HD stocks; alloy frame with matte black finish; gas-operated with Vario System; four-lug rotating bolt. Introduced 1996. Imported from Italy by Benelli U.S.A.

Walnut
Perf.: $565   **Exc.:** $490   **VGood:** $430
Camo, Timber HD
Perf.: $655   **Exc.:** $580   **VGood:** $520
Synthetic (black synthetic stock, forend)
Perf.: $550   **Exc.:** $475   **VGood:** $415
20-ga., 24-inch, 26-inch, 28-inch, walnut
Perf.: $565   **Exc.:** $490   **VGood:** $430
Variopress 620 (Timber HD Camo)
Perf.: $655   **Exc.:** $485   **VGood:** $520

FRANCHI 612 DEFENSE SHOTGUN

Similar to 612 except has 18-1/2-inch, Cylinder-bore barrel with black, synthetic stock. Available in 12-gauge, 3-inch chamber only. Weighs 6-1/2 lbs. 2-shot magazine extension available. Introduced 2000.

Perf.: $525   **Exc.:** $450   **VGood:** $375

FRANCHI 612 SPORTING SHOTGUN

Similar to 612 except has 30-inch ported barrel to reduce muzzle jump. Available in 12-gauge, 3-inch chamber only. Introduced 2000.

Perf.: $825   **Exc.:** $750   **VGood:** $625

FRANCHI 620 SHORT STOCK SHOTGUN

Similar to 620 but with stock shortened to 12-1/2-inch length of pull for smaller shooters. Introduced 2000.

Perf.: $565   **Exc.:** $490   **VGood:** $430

FRANCHI 720

Autoloader; 20-ga.; 3-inch chamber; 24-inch, 26-inch, 28-inch barrel; IC, M, F tubes; weighs 6 lbs.; European walnut, Max-4, and Timber HD stocks; four-lug rotating bolt. Imported from Italy by Benelli U.S.A.

Walnut
Perf.: $565   **Exc.:** $490   **VGood:** $430
Camo, Timber HD/Max-4
Perf.: $655   **Exc.:** $580   **VGood:** $520
Youth version (12-1/2-inch LOP)
Perf.: $550   **Exc.:** $475   **VGood:** $415

FRANCHI 712 RAPTOR

Autoloader; 12-ga.; 2-3/4 and 3-inch chamber; 30-inch barrel; IC, M, F tubes; weighs 7.1 lbs.; WeatherCoat stock; four-lug rotating bolt. Imported from Italy by Benelli U.S.A.

Perf.: $565   **Exc.:** $490   **VGood:** $430

Franchi Model 530

Franchi 612 Defense Shotgun

Franchi 612 Sporting Shotgun

Franchi 620 Short Stock Shotgun

Franchi Model 720

Franchi 712 Raptor

Franchi Model 912 Timber HD Max4 Camo

Franchi Model 912 Timber HD Camo

Franchi Prestige

FRANCHI MODEL 720 RAPTOR

Similar to above but in 20-ga., 2-3/4- and 3-inch barrel.

Perf.: $565   **Exc.:** $490   **VGood:** $430

FRANCHI 912

Autoloader; 12-ga.; 3-1/2-inch chamber; 24-inch, 26-inch, 28-, 30-inch barrel; IC, M, F tubes; weighs 7-1/2 lbs.; European walnut, synthetic, Timber HD and Max-4 HD stocks; gas-operated with Vario System; four-lug rotating bolt. Imported from Italy by Benelli U.S.A.

Walnut
Perf.: $665   **Exc.:** $590   **VGood:** $530
Camo, Timber HD
Perf.: $755   **Exc.:** $680   **VGood:** $620
Synthetic (black synthetic stock, forend)
Perf.: $650   **Exc.:** $575   **VGood:** $515
SteadyGrip (full pistol grip) stock

FRANCHI PRESTIGE

Gas-operated autoloader; 12-ga.; 2-3/4-inch, 3-inch chamber; 24-inch, 26-inch, 28-inch, 30-inch, 32-inch barrel; 7mm vent-rib; all standard chokes; weighs 7-3/8 lbs.; oil-finished, checkered European walnut stock; blued receiver; stainless steel gas piston. Made in Italy. Introduced 1985; discontinued 1989.

Perf.: $600   **Exc.:** $390   **VGood:** $290

FRANCHI SKEET GUN

Recoil-operated autoloader; 12-, 20-ga.; 5-shot magazine; 26-inch vent-rib barrel; Skeet choke; hand-checkered fancy European walnut pistol-grip stock, forearm; alloy receiver; chrome-lined barrels; simplified takedown. Introduced 1972; discontinued 1974.

Perf.: $385   **Exc.:** $370   **VGood:** $350

FRANCHI SLUG GUN

Recoil-operated autoloader; 12-, 20-ga.; 5-shot magazine; 22-inch Cylinder-bore barrel; raised gold bead front sight, Lyman folding leaf open rear; hand-checkered European walnut pistol-grip stock, forearm; sling swivels. Introduced 1955; no longer in production.

Exc.: $360   **VGood:** $330   **Good:** $350

FRANCHI 48AL SHOTGUN

Autoloader; 20 or 28 ga.; 2-3/4-inch chamber; 24-inch, 26-inch, 28-inch barrel (Full, Cyl., Mod., choke tubes); weighs 5.5 lbs. (20-gauge); length: 44-inch-48-inch; 14- 1/4-inchx1-5/ 8-inchx2-1/2-inch stock dimensions; walnut with checkered grip and forend; long recoil-operated action; chrome-lined bore; cross-bolt safety. Imported from Italy by Benelli U.S.A.

20 ga.
Perf.: $585   **Exc.:** $530   **VGood:** $430
28 ga.
Perf.: $695   **Exc.:** $640   **VGood:** $540

Franchi Slug Gun

Franchi 48AL Deluxe Shotgun

Franchi 48AL English

Franchi SPAS-12

Franchi Standard Semi-Automatic (48/AL)

Franchi Standard Magnum (48/AL)

Franchi I-12 Walnut

Franchi I-12 Camo

FRANCHI 48AL DELUXE SHOTGUN
Similar to 48AL but with select walnut stock and forend and high-polish blue finish with gold trigger. Introduced 2000.

20-gauge, 26-inch barrel
Perf.: $775 **Exc.:** $625 **VGood:** $525

28-gauge, 26-inch barrel
Perf.: $825 **Exc.:** $675 **VGood:** $575

FRANCHI 48AL ENGLISH
Similar to 48AL Deluxe but with straight grip "English style" stock. 20-ga., 28-ga., 26-inch bbl.; IC, M, F tubes.

20-gauge
Perf.: $775 **Exc.:** $625 **VGood:** $525

28-gauge
Perf.: $825 **Exc.:** $675 **VGood:** $575

FRANCHI 48AL SHORT STOCK SHOTGUN
Similar to 48AL but with stock shortened to 12-1/2-inch length of pull. 20-gauge, 26-inch barrel.
Perf.: $585 **Exc.:** $530 **VGood:** $430

FRANCHI VARIOMAX 912
Introduced in 2001 this model is chambered for the 12 gauge 3.5" shell. It is offered with a choice of 24", 26", 28", or 30" barrels with vent-rib. Black synthetic

stock. Weight is about 7.6 lbs. Choke tubes. In 2002 a walnut stock was added as an option.
Perf.: $625 **Exc.:** $550 **VGood:** $450

FRANCHI VARIOMAX 912 CAMO
Same as above but with Advantage Timber camo finish.
Perf.: $650 **Exc.:** $575 **VGood:** $475

FRANCHI VARIOMAX 912 STEADYGRIP
Introduced in 2005 this model features a extended pistol grip and Advantage H-D camo stock with 24" vent rib barrel and choke tubes. Weight is about 8 lbs.
Perf.: $700 **Exc.:** $575 **VGood:** $495

FRANCHI VARIOPRESS 612 SPORTING
This is a 12 gauge semi-automatic gas-operated shotgun with 30" ported barrel. Extended choke tubes. Select walnut stock with stock drop kit. Magazine capacity is 5 rounds. Weight is about 7 lbs. First imported in 2000.
Perf.: $675 **Exc.:** $595 **VGood:** $450

FRANCHI VARIOPRESS 612 FIELD
This 12 gauge model is offered with barrel lengths from 24" to 28". Stock configurations are walnut,

synthetic, or camo. Magazine capacity is 5 rounds. Weight is about 7 lbs. depending on barrel length.
Perf.: $500 **Exc.:** $425 **VGood:** $350

FRANCHI VARIOPRESS 612 DEFENSE
This 12 gauge gun is fitted with an 18.5" barrel and black synthetic stock. Matte black finish. Choke is cylinder. Weight is about 6.5 lbs. Magazine capacity is 5 rounds. First imported in 2000.
Perf.: $425 **Exc.:** $350 **VGood:** $275

FRANCHI VARIOPRESS 620 FIELD
This model is offered in 20 gauge with a choice of walnut or camo stock. Barrel lengths from 24" to 28". Magazine capacity is 5 rounds. Weight is about 6 lbs.
Perf.: $675 **Exc.:** $595 **VGood:** $465

FRANCHI VARIOPRESS 620 SHORT STOCK
Same as above but with 12.5" length of pull and walnut stock. First imported in 2000.
Perf.: $675 **Exc.:** $595 **VGood:** $465

FRANCHI SPAS-12
Autoloader/slide action; 12-ga.; 2-3/4-inch chamber; 5-, 8-shot tube magazine; 21-1/2-inch barrel; synthetic pistol-grip stock; alloy receiver; button-activated switch to change action type. Introduced 1988; discontinued 1994.
Perf.: $675 **Exc.:** $575 **VGood:** $475

FRANCHI STANDARD SEMI-AUTOMATIC (48/AL)
Recoil-operated autoloader; 12-, 20-ga.; 5-shot magazine; 24-inch, 26-inch, 28-inch, 30-inch interchangeable vent-rib barrel; Improved, Modified, Full chokes; hand-checkered European walnut pistol-grip stock, forearm; alloy receiver; chrome-lined barrels; simplified takedown. Introduced 1950; still in production.
Perf.: $480 **Exc.:** $290 **VGood:** $240

FRANCHI STANDARD MAGNUM (48/AL)
Same specs as Standard Semi-automatic (48/AL) except 12-, 20-ga.; 3-inch chamber; 28-inch (20-ga.), 32-inch (12-ga.) plain or vent-rib barrel; recoil pad. Introduced 1952; discontinued 1990.
Perf.: $400 **Exc.:** $300 **VGood:** $225

FRANCHI TURKEY GUN
Recoil-operated autoloader; 12-ga.; 3-inch chamber; 5-shot magazine; 32-inch vent-rib barrel; Extra Full choke; hand-checkered European walnut pistol-grip stock, forearm; alloy receiver; chrome-lined barrels; simplified takedown; engraved turkey scene on receiver. Introduced 1963; discontinued 1965.
Perf.: $415 **Exc.:** $385 **VGood:** $370

FRANCHI I-12
Introduced in 2005 this 12 gauge model is offered with 3" chambers and choice of 24", 26", or 28" vent rib barrels. Available with synthetic, walnut, Max-4, or Timber H-D stock. Choke tubes. Weight is about 7.5 lbs. depending on barrel length.
Perf.: $900 **Exc.:** $750 **VGood:** $575

FRANCHI I-12 WHITE GOLD
Similar to Inertia I-12 but with highly figured walnut stock and white gold game bird scene on a satin nickel receiver. Introduced in 2006. Available only with 28-inch barrel. Weight is about 7.7 lbs.
NIB: $1150 **Exc.:** $1025 **VGood:** $850

FRANCHI ALCIONE
Over/under; 12-ga.; 2-3/4-inch chamber; 28-inch Modified/Full barrel; cut-checkered French walnut pistol-grip stock, forend; top tang safety; single selective trigger; auto ejectors; chrome-plated bores; silvered receiver; decorative scroll engraving. Made in Italy. Introduced 1982; discontinued 1989.
Perf.: $675 **Exc.:** $550 **VGood:** $495

FRANCHI ALCIONE SL
Same specs as Alcione except 27-inch Improved/Modified, 28-inch Modified/Full barrels; ivory bead front sight; better engraving; silvered receiver; gold-plated trigger; gold-inlaid receiver; marketed in fitted case. Made in Italy. Introduced 1982; discontinued 1986.

Perf.: $1150　**Exc.:** $995　**VGood:** $875

FRANCHI ALCIONE FIELD OVER/UNDER SHOTGUN
Over/under; 12-, 20-ga.; 3-inch chambers; 26-inch, 28-inch barrel; IC, M, F tubes; weighs 7-1/2 lbs.; length: 43-inch overall with 26-inch barrels; European walnut; boxlock action with ejectors; barrel selector mounted on trigger; silvered, engraved receiver; vent center rib; automatic safety; interchangeable 20-ga. barrels.; left-hand available. Imported from Italy by Benelli USA.

Perf.: $1100　**Exc.:** $950　**VGood:** $800
Price: (20-gauge barrel set) $460

FRANCHI SX O/U SHOTGUN
Similar to Alcione Field model with high-grade walnut stock and forend. Gold engraved removable sideplates, interchangeable barrels.

Perf.: $1675　**Exc.:** $1495　**VGood:** $1275

FRANCHI ALCIONE SPORT SL O/U SHOTGUN
Similar to Alcione except 2-3/4-inch chambers, elongated forcing cones and porting for Sporting Clays shooting. 10mm vent rib, tightly curved pistol grip, manual safety, removable sideplates. Imported from Italy by Benelli USA.

Perf.: $1400　**Exc.:** $1200　**VGood:** $950

FRANCHI ALCIONE TITANIUM OVER/UNDER SHOTGUN
Over/under; 12-, 20-ga.;3-inch chambers; 26-inch, 28-inch barrels; IC, M, F tubes; weighs 6.8 lbs.; 43-inch, 45-inch overall; select walnut; front/mid bead sight; receiver (titanium inserts) made of aluminum alloy; 7mm vent rib; fast locking triggers. Left-hand available.

Perf.: $1225　**Exc.:** $1050　**VGood:** $950
Add $450 to above prices for 2 barrel set (includes extra 20 ga. barrels)

FRANCHI ARISTOCRAT
Over/under; 12-ga.; 24-inch Cylinder/Improved Cylinder, 26-inch Improved/Modified, 28-inch Modified/Full, 30-inch Modified/Full vent-rib barrel; hand-checkered Italian walnut pistol-grip stock, forearm; selective automatic ejectors; automatic safety; selective single trigger; English scroll engraving on receiver; blue-black finish. Introduced 1960; discontinued 1968.

Exc.: $660　**VGood:** $470　**Good:** $440

FRANCHI ARISTOCRAT DELUXE
Same specs as Aristocrat except select walnut stock forearm; heavy relief engraving on receiver, tang and trigger guard. Introduced 1960; discontinued 1965.

Exc.: $800　**VGood:** $700　**Good:** $640

FRANCHI ARISTOCRAT IMPERIAL
Same specs as Aristocrat except top-quality European walnut stock; exquisite engraving. Introduced 1967 on customer-order basis; discontinued 1969.

Exc.: $2200　**VGood:** $2090　**Good:** $1925

FRANCHI ARISTOCRAT MAGNUM
Same specs as Aristocrat except 3-inch chamber; 32-inch Full choke barrels; recoil pad. Introduced 1962; discontinued 1965.

Exc.: $470　**VGood:** $440　**Good:** $395

FRANCHI ARISTOCRAT MONTE CARLO
Same specs as Aristocrat except top-of-the-line European walnut stock; top-of-the-line engraving. Introduced 1967 on customer-order basis; discontinued 1969.

Exc.: $3080　**VGood:** $2915　**Good:** $2640

Franchi Alcione Field

Franchi SX O/U

Franchi Alcione Sport SL

Franchi Alcione Titanium

Franchi Aristocrat Deluxe

Franchi Aristocrat Silver-King

Franchi Aristocrat Skeet

FRANCHI ARISTOCRAT SILVER-KING
Same specs as Aristocrat except selected ultra-deluxe walnut stock forearm, cut from the same blank for match of grain, color, finish; hand-checkered pistol grip, forearm; engraved, bright-finish receiver. Introduced 1965; discontinued 1968.

Exc.: $750　**VGood:** $560　**Good:** $535

FRANCHI ARISTOCRAT SKEET
Same specs as Aristocrat except 26-inch Skeet/Skeet vent-rib barrel; grooved beavertail forearm. Introduced 1962; discontinued 1968.

Exc.: $425　**VGood:** $390　**Good:** $350

FRANCHI ARISTOCRAT SUPREME
Same specs as Aristocrat except select walnut stock, forearm; heavy relief engraving on receiver, tang and trigger guard; gold-inlaid game bird figures on receiver. Introduced 1960; discontinued 1965.

Exc.: $1265　**VGood:** $1155　**Good:** $1075

FRANCHI ARISTOCRAT TRAP
Same specs as Aristocrat except 30-inch Modified/Full vent-rib barrels; hand-checkered select deluxe-grade European walnut pistol-grip stock, beavertail forend; Monte Carlo comb; color case-hardened receiver. Introduced 1962; discontinued 1968.

Exc.: $550　**VGood:** $525　**Good:** $480

FRANCHI BLACK MAGIC LIGHTWEIGHT HUNTER
Over/under; boxlock; 12-, 20-ga.; 2-3/4-inch chambers; 25-inch barrel; choke tubes; weighs 6 lbs.; cut-checkered figured walnut stock, schnabel forend with semi-gloss finish; solid black recoil pad; single selective trigger auto safety; auto selective ejectors; polished blue finish; gold accents. Made in Italy. Introduced 1989; discontinued 1991.

Perf.: $975　**Exc.:** $850　**VGood:** $775

FRANCHI BLACK MAGIC SPORTING HUNTER
Over/under; boxlock; 12-ga.; 3-inch chambers; 28-inch barrel; choke tubes; weighs 7 lbs.; cut-checkered figured walnut stock, schnabel forend with semi-gloss finish; solid black recoil pad; single selective trigger auto safety; auto selective ejectors; polished blue finish; gold accents. Made in Italy. Introduced 1989; discontinued 1991.

Perf.: $995　**Exc.:** $875　**VGood:** $800

FRANCHI FALCONET
Over/under; 12-, 16-, 20-, 28-ga., .410; 24-inch, 26-inch, 28-inch, 30-inch (12-ga. only) barrels; standard choke combos; checkered walnut pistol-grip stock, forearm; epoxy finish; selective single trigger; barrel selector; automatic safety; selective automatic

Franchi Aristocrat Supreme

Franchi Aristocrat Trap

Franchi Black Magic Lightweight Hunter

Franchi Falconet

Franchi Flaconet International Skeet

Franchi Falconet International Trap

Franchi Falconet 2000

Franchi Model 2000 Sporting

FRANCHI FALCONET 2000

Over/under; boxlock; 12-ga.; 2-3/4-inch chambers; 26-inch barrels; Improved Cylinder, Modified, Full Franchoke tubes; weighs 6 lbs.; white fluorescent bead front sight; checkered walnut stock; silvered action with gold-plated game scene; single selective trigger; automatic selective ejectors. Made in Italy. Reintroduced 1992; no longer imported.

Perf.: $1245   **Exc.:** $975   **VGood:** $850

FRANCHI MODEL 2000 SPORTING

Over/under; boxlock; 12-ga.; 2-3/4-inch chambers; 28-inch ported barrels; Skeet, Improved Cylinder, Modified, Full Franchoke tubes; weighs 7 3/4 lbs.; white fluorescent bead front sight; checkered walnut stock; single selective mechanical trigger; automatic selective ejectors; blued action. Made in Italy. Introduced 1992; no longer imported.

Perf.: $1275   **Exc.:** $1025   **VGood:** $875

FRANCHI MODEL 2003 TRAP

Over/under; boxlock; 12-ga.; 30-inch, 32-inch, Improved Modified/Full, Full/Full barrels; high vent rib; checkered European walnut straight or Monte Carlo stock, beavertail forearm; single selective trigger; auto ejectors; recoil pad; marketed with carrying case. Introduced 1976; discontinued 1982.

Perf.: $1150   **Exc.:** $1000   **VGood:** $900

FRANCHI MODEL 2004 TRAP

Single barrel; boxlock; 12-ga.; 32-inch, 34-inch, Full choke barrel; high vent rib; checkered European walnut straight or Monte Carlo stock, beavertail forearm; single selective trigger; auto ejectors; recoil pad; marketed with carrying case. Introduced 1976; discontinued 1982.

Perf.: $1205   **Exc.:** $1090   **VGood:** $1045

FRANCHI MODEL 2005 COMBINATION TRAP

Over/under; boxlock; 12-ga.; incorporates barrels of Model 2003, single barrel of Model 2004 as interchangeable set; high vent rib; checkered European walnut straight or Monte Carlo stock, beavertail forearm; single selective trigger; auto ejectors; recoil pad. Introduced 1976; discontinued 1982.

Perf.: $1815   **Exc.:** $1595   **VGood:** $1515

FRANCHI MODEL 2005/3 COMBINATION TRAP

Same specs as Model 2005 Combination Trap except three-barrel set incorporating over/under barrels of Model 2003, single barrel of Model 2004. Introduced 1976; discontinued 1982.

Perf.: $2420   **Exc.:** $2090   **VGood:** $1980

FRANCHI MODEL 3000/2

Over/under; 12-ga.; 30-inch, 32-inch over and 32-inch, 34-inch under barrel; 3 interchangeable choke tubes; high vent rib; checkered European walnut straight or Monte Carlo stock, beavertail forearm; single selective trigger; auto ejectors; recoil pad. Marketed with fitted case. No longer in production.

Perf.: $2600   **Exc.:** $2200   **VGood:** $1950

FRANCHI PEREGRIN MODEL 400

Over/under; 12-ga.; 26-1/2-inch, 28-inch vent-rib barrels; standard choke combos; checkered European walnut pistol-grip stock, forearm; steel receiver; auto ejectors; selective single trigger. Introduced 1975; no longer in production.

Perf.: $660   **Exc.:** $605   **VGood:** $570

FRANCHI PEREGRIN MODEL 451

Over/under; 12-ga.; 26 1/2-inch, 28-inch vent-rib barrels; standard choke combos; checkered European walnut pistol-grip stock, forearm; alloy receiver; auto ejectors; selective single trigger. Introduced 1975; no longer in production.

Perf.: $605   **Exc.:** $550   **VGood:** $525

---

ejectors; alloy receiver, fully engraved. Introduced 1969 as Falcon; discontinued 1985.

Perf.: $530   **Exc.:** $450   **VGood:** $.410

FRANCHI FALCONET INTERNATIONAL SKEET

Same specs as Falconet except 26-inch Skeet-choked barrels; wide vent rib; select Skeet-style stock, forearm; engraved color case-hardened receiver. Introduced 1970; discontinued 1974.

Perf.: $935   **Exc.:** $865   **VGood:** $825

FRANCHI FALCONET INTERNATIONAL TRAP

Same specs as Falconet except 12-ga.; 30-inch Modified/Full choke barrels; wide vent rib; select checkered trap-style Monte Carlo stock, forearm; engraved color case-hardened receiver; recoil pad. Introduced 1970; discontinued 1974.

Perf.: $935   **Exc.:** $855   **VGood:** $825

FRANCHI FALCONET SKEET

Same specs as Falconet except 26-inch Skeet-choked barrels; wide vent rib; Skeet-style stock, forearm; color case-hardened receiver. Introduced 1970; discontinued 1974.

Perf.: $935   **Exc.:** $855   **VGood:** $825

FRANCHI FALCONET SUPER

Same specs as Falconet except 12-ga.; 27-inch, 28-inch barrels; translucent front sight; engraved silver finish lightweight alloy receiver; rubber buttplate. Made in Italy. Introduced 1982; discontinued 1986.

Perf.: $825   **Exc.:** $610   **VGood:** $525

FRANCHI FALCONET TRAP

Same specs as Falconet except 12-ga.; 30-inch Modified/Full choke barrel; wide vent rib; checkered trap-style Monte Carlo stock, forearm; color case-hardened receiver; recoil pad. Introduced 1970; discontinued 1974.

Perf.: $935   **Exc.:** $855   **VGood:** $825

FRANCHI VELOCE OVER/UNDER SHOTGUN

Over/under; 20-, 28-ga.; 26-inch, 28-inch barrel; IC, M, F tubes; weighs 5.5 to 5.8 lbs.; 43-inch to 45-inch length; high-grade walnut stock; aluminum receiver with steel reinforcement scaled to 20-gauge for light weight; pistol grip stock with slip recoil pad. Imported by Benelli USA.

Perf.: $1250   **Exc.:** $1050   **VGood:** $925
28-ga.
Perf.: $1325   **Exc.:** $1125   **VGood:** $1000

FRANCHI VELOCE ENGLISH OVER/UNDER SHOTGUN

Similar to Veloce standard model with straight grip English style stock. Available with 26-inch barrels in 20- and 28-gauge.

Perf.: $1250   **Exc.:** $1050   **VGood:** $925
28-ga.
Perf.: $1325   **Exc.:** $1125   **VGood:** $1000

FRANCHI RENAISSANCE FIELD

The Renaissance Series was introduced in 2006. These over-and-unders feature ultra-light alloy receivers, oil-finished walnut stocks, Prince of Wales pistol grips, cut checkering and Twin Shock Absorber recoil pads with gel insert. The 3" 12 and 20 gauges have 26" or 28" barrels; the 28 gauge has a 26" barrel. Weights average 6.2 lbs. in 12 gauge, 5.8 lbs. in 20 gauge and 5.5 lbs. in 28 gauge. Add 5 percent to values shown for 28 gauge.

NIB: $1175   **Exc.:** $995   **VGood:** $800

FRANCHI RENAISSANCE CLASSIC

A-Grade walnut with gold inlaid receiver.

NIB: $1250   **Exc.:** $1150   **VGood:** $895

FRANCHI RENAISSANCE ELITE

AA-Grade Walnut with gold inlaid receiver.

NIB: $2000   **Exc.:** $1700   **VGood:** $1400

FRANCHI RENAISSANCE SPORTING

This 3" 12 gauge model was introduced in 2007. It features a 30" barrel, A-Grade walnut stock, engraved receiver with gold inlay and adjustable comb. Weight is about 7.9 lbs.

NIB: $1750   **Exc.:** $1500   **VGood:** $1195

FRANCHI SIDE-BY-SIDE SHOTGUNS FRANCHI AIRONE

Side-by-side; boxlock; 12-ga.; all standard barrel lengths, choke combinations; hand-checkered European walnut straight-grip stock, forearm; automatic ejectors; double triggers. Introduced 1956; special order only; discontinued 1968.

Exc.: $1320   **VGood:** $1100   **Good:** $900

FRANCHI ASTORE

Side-by-side; boxlock; 12-ga.; all standard barrel lengths, choke combinations; hand-checkered European walnut straight-grip stock, forearm; plain extractors; double triggers. Introduced 1956; special order only; discontinued 1968.

Exc.: $910   **VGood:** $770   **Good:** $715

FRANCHI ASTORE S

Same specs as Astore except high-grade hand-checkered European walnut straight-grip stock, forearm; auto ejectors; fine engraving on frame. No longer in production.

Exc.: $1700   **VGood:** $1540   **Good:** $1450

FRANCHI ASTORE II

Same specs as Astore except 27-inch, 28-inch barrels; standard chokes; European walnut pistol-grip stock; plain extractors or auto ejectors; engraving. No longer in production.

Exc.: $935   **VGood:** $880   **Good:** $800

Franchi Veloce Over/Under

Franchi Veloce Over/Under close up

Franchi Veloce English Over/Under

Franchi Renaissance Field

Franchi Renaissance Classic

Franchi Renaissance Elite

Franchi Astore S

FRANCHI CUSTOM SIDELOCK

Side-by-side; 12-, 16-, 20-, 28-ga.; barrel lengths, chokes custom-ordered; hand-checkered European walnut straight or pistol-grip stock, forearm; automatic ejectors; hand-detachable locks; self-opening action; single trigger optional. Made in six grades; variations depending upon quality of wood, amount of engraving, checkering, overall workmanship. For self-opening action, add $75; for single trigger, add $200. Introduced 1956, special order only; discontinued 1968.

Condor
Exc.: $6500   **VGood:** $5700   **Good:** $4000
Imperial
Exc.: $9000   **VGood:** $7500   **Good:** $6000

Imperial
Exc.: $9200   **VGood:** $7900   **Good:** $6500
No. 5 Imperial Monte Carlo
Exc.: $12,000   **VGood:** $9500   **Good:** $7500
No. 11 Imperial Monte Carlo
Exc.: $12,500   **VGood:** $10,000   **Good:** $9000
Imperial Monte Carlo Extra
Exc.: $15,000   **VGood:** $13,000   **Good:** $10,000

FRANCHI SAS-12

Slide action; 12-ga.; 3-inch chamber; 8-shot tube magazine; 21-1/2-inch barrel; synthetic pistol-grip stock; alloy receiver. Introduced 1988; discontinued 1990.

Perf.: $415   **Exc.:** $360   **VGood:** $300

Francotte Boxlock

Francotte Jubilee No. 14

Francotte Jubilee No. 18

Francotte Jubilee No. 20

Francotte Jubilee No. 25

Francotte Jubilee No. 30

Francotte Jubilee No. 45

Francotte
Model 9/40SE

Francotte
Model 6886

FRANCOTTE BOXLOCK

Side-by-side; boxlock; 12-, 16-, 20-, 28-ga., .410; 2-3/4-inch, 3-inch chambers; 26-inch to 29-inch barrels; bead front sight; custom deluxe oil-finished European walnut straight or pistol-grip stock, splinter or beavertail forend; checkered butt; double locks, triggers; manual or auto safety; ejectors; English scroll engraving, coin finish or color case-hardening; many custom options. Made in Belgium. Introduced 1989. Considerable premium for small guages.

Perf.: $2,650   **Exc.:** $1950   **VGood:** $900

FRANCOTTE JUBILEE

Side-by-side; boxlock with sideplates; 12-, 16-, 20-, 28-ga., .410; 2-3/4-inch, 3-inch chambers; customer-specified chokes, triggers and stock style; ejectors; imported in numbered grades 14, 18, 20, 25, 30 and No. 45 Eagle Grade.

No. 14		
Exc.: $1325	**VGood:** $1100	**Good:** $975
No. 18		
Exc.: $1925	**VGood:** $1700	**Good:** $1550
No. 20		
Exc.: $2900	**VGood:** $2525	**Good:** $1950

No. 25		
Exc.: $3550	**VGood:** $3000	**Good:** $2500
No. 30		
Exc.: $4975	**VGood:** $4500	**Good:** $4000
No. 45 Eagle Grade		
Exc.: $5850	**VGood:** $4950	**Good:** $4250

FRANCOTTE KNOCKABOUT

Side-by-side; boxlock; 12-, 16-, 20-, 28-ga., .410; 26-inch to 32-inch (12-ga.), 26-inch to 28-inch barrels in other gauges; any desired choke combo; crossbolt safety; double triggers; ejectors; series was made in several grades for distribution exclusively in this country by Abercrombie & Fitch; grades varied only in overall quality, grade of wood, checkering and engraving. Introduced prior to WWII; discontinued in 1960s. A&F applied the Knockabout name to a different gun imported from Italy.

Exc.: $1265   **VGood:** $1100   **Good:** $935

FRANCOTTE MODEL 9/40E/38321

Side-by-side; Anson & Deeley boxlock; sideplates; 12-, 16-, 20-, 28-ga., .410; all standard barrel lengths, choke combos; hand-checkered European walnut stock, straight or pistol-grip design; reinforced frame, side clips; Purdey-type bolt; automatic ejectors; fine English engraving. Introduced about 1950; no longer in production.

Perf.: $4200   **Exc.:** $3000   **VGood:** $2200

FRANCOTTE MODEL 9/40SE

Over/under; Anson & Deeley boxlock; 12-, 16-, 20-, 28-ga., .410; all standard barrel lengths choke combos; hand-checkered European walnut straight or pistol-grip stock, forearm; automatic ejectors; double triggers; elaborate engraving. Introduced about 1950; no longer in production.

Perf.: $8700   **Exc.:** $6000   **VGood:** $4800

FRANCOTTE MODEL 10/18E/628

Side-by-side; Anson & Deeley boxlock; 12-, 16-, 20-, 28-ga., .410; all standard barrel lengths, choke combos; hand-checkered European walnut straight or pistol-grip stock, forearm; Purdey-type bolt; Greener crossbolt; side clips; automatic ejectors; double triggers. Manufactured before World War II.

Perf.: $3000   **Exc.:** $2100   **VGood:** $1650

FRANCOTTE MODEL 11/18E

Side-by-side; Anson & Deeley boxlock; 12-, 16-, 20-, 28-ga., .410; all standard barrel lengths, choke combos; hand-checkered European walnut straight or pistol-grip stock, forearm; Purdey-type bolt; Greener crossbolt; side clips; automatic ejectors; double triggers. Manufactured before World War II.

Perf.: $3000   **Exc.:** $2100   **VGood:** $1650

FRANCOTTE MODEL 120.HE/328

Side-by-side; sidelock; made in all standard gauges; chokes, barrel lengths to customer's order; hand-checkered European walnut straight or pistol-grip stock, forearm; automatic ejectors; double triggers. Introduced about 1950; no longer in production.

Perf.: $8100   **Exc.:** $5700   **VGood:** $4450

FRANCOTTE MODEL 4996

Side-by-side; Anson & Deeley boxlock; 12-, 16-, 20-, 28-ga., .410; all standard barrel lengths, choke combinations available; hand-checkered European walnut straight or pistol-grip stock, forearm; Greener crossbolt; side clips; automatic ejectors; double triggers. Manufactured before World War II.

Perf.: $2750   **Exc.:** $1900   **VGood:** $1500

FRANCOTTE MODEL 6886

Side-by-side; boxlock; 12-, 16-, 20-, 28-ga., .410; all standard barrel lengths, choke combinations available; hand-checkered European walnut straight or pistol-grip stock, forearm; automatic ejectors; double triggers. Manufactured before World War II.

Perf.: $2250   **Exc.:** $1600   **VGood:** $1250

FRANCOTTE MODEL 6930

Side-by-side; boxlock; 12-, 16-, 20-, 28-ga., .410; all standard barrel lengths, choke combos; hand-checkered European walnut straight or pistol-grip stock, forearm; square crossbolt; automatic ejectors; double triggers. Manufactured before World War II.

Perf.: $2350   **Exc.:** $1850   **VGood:** $1300

FRANCOTTE MODEL 6982

Side-by-side; Anson & Deeley boxlock; sideplates; 12-, 16-, 20-, 28-ga., .410; all standard barrel lengths, choke combos; hand-checkered European walnut stock, straight or pistol-grip design; reinforced frame, side clips; Purdey-type bolt; automatic ejectors. Introduced about 1950; no longer in production.

Perf.: $3125   **Exc.:** $2200   **VGood:** $1700

FRANCOTTE MODEL 8446

Side-by-side; boxlock; 12-, 16-, 20-, 28-ga., .410; all standard barrel lengths, choke combinations available; hand-checkered European walnut straight or pistol-grip stock, forearm; Greener crossbolt; side clips; automatic ejectors; double triggers. Manufactured before World War II.

Perf.: $2700   **Exc.:** $1900   **VGood:** $1500

FRANCOTTE MODEL 8455

Side-by-side; Anson & Deeley boxlock; sideplates; 12-, 16-, 20-, 28-ga., .410; all standard barrel lengths, choke combos; hand-checkered European walnut stock, straight or pistol-grip design; reinforced frame, side clips; Greener crossbolt; Purdey-type bolt; automatic ejectors; engraving. Introduced about 1950; no longer in production.

Perf.: $3100   **Exc.:** $2200   **VGood:** $1700

FRANCOTTE MODEL 8457

Side-by-side; Anson & Deeley boxlock; 12-, 16-, 20-, 28-ga., .410; all standard barrel lengths, choke combos; hand-checkered European walnut straight or pistol-grip stock, forearm; Greener-Scott crossbolt; side clips; automatic ejectors; double triggers. Manufactured before World War II.

Perf.: $3000   **Exc.:** $2100   **VGood:** $1700

FRANCOTTE MODEL 9261

Side-by-side; Anson & Deeley boxlock; 12-, 16-, 20-, 28-ga., .410; all standard barrel lengths, choke combos; hand-checkered European walnut straight or pistol-grip stock, forearm; Greener crossbolt; side clips; automatic ejectors; double triggers. Manufactured before World War II.

Perf.: $2350   **Exc.:** $1650   **VGood:** $1300

FRANCOTTE MODEL 10594

Side-by-side; Anson & Deeley boxlock; sideplates; 12-, 16-, 20-, 28-ga., .410; all standard barrel lengths, choke combos; hand-checkered European walnut stock, straight or pistol-grip design; reinforced frame, side clips; Purdey-type bolt; automatic ejectors. Introduced about 1950; no longer in production.

Perf.: $3000   **Exc.:** $2100   **VGood:** $1650

FRANCOTTE MODEL SOB. E/11082

Over/under; Anson & Deeley boxlock; 12-, 16-, 20-, 28-ga., .410; all standard barrel lengths, choke combos; hand-checkered European walnut straight or pistol-grip stock, forearm; automatic ejectors; double triggers; engraving. Introduced about 1950; no longer in production.

Perf.: $6300   **Exc.:** $4400   **VGood:** $3500

FRANCOTTE SIDELOCK

Side-by-side; sidelock; 12-, 16-, 20-, 28-ga., .410; 2-3/4-inch, 3-inch chamber; 26-inch, 29-inch barrel; custom chokes; bead front sight; deluxe oil-finished European walnut straight or pistol-grip stock, splinter or beavertail forend; checkered butt; double intercepting sears; double triggers; ejectors; English scroll engraving, coin finish or color case-hardening; numerous custom options. Made in Belgium. Introduced 1989; imported by Armes de Chasse.

Perf.: $24,000   **Exc.:** $20,000   **VGood:** $17,500

Francotte
Model 6982

Francotte
Model 8446

Francotte
Model 9261

Francotte Sidelock

Galef Companion

GALEF COMPANION

Single shot; 12-, 16-, 20-, 28-ga., .410; 26-inch, 28-inch, 30-inch barrel; plain or vent rib; European walnut pistol-grip stock, forearm; special folding feature. Made in Italy. Introduced 1968; no longer imported.

Exc.: $125   **VGood:** $100   **Good:** $85

GALEF MONTE CARLO TRAP

Single shot; underlever; 12-ga.; 32-inch barrel; Full choke; vent rib; checkered European walnut pistol-grip stock, beavertail forearm; extractor; recoil pad. Made in Italy. Introduced 1968; no longer imported.

Exc.: $185   **VGood:** $175   **Good:** $150

GALEF/ZABALA

Side-by side; boxlock; 10-, 12-, 16-, 20-, 28-ga., .410; 22-inch (12-ga.) Improved/Modified, 26-inch (12-, 20-, 28-ga.) Improved/Modified or (.410) Modified/Full, 28-inch (10-, 12-, 16-, 20-, 28-ga.) Modified/Full, 30-inch (12-ga.) Modified/Full, 32-inch (10-, 12-ga.) Full/Full barrels; hand-checkered European walnut stock, beavertail forearm; recoil pad; automatic safety; extractors. Made in Spain; no longer in production.

Standard gauges		
Exc.: $175	**VGood:** $150	**Good:** $130
.410-bore		
Exc.: $190	**VGood:** $170	**Good:** $140

Galef/Zabala

Galef/Zoli Silver Hawk

Galef/Zoli Silver Snipe

Gamba Daytona

Gamba Daytona Grade 4 Engraving

Gamba Daytona Grade 5 Engraving

Gamba Daytona Grade 6 Engraving

GALEF/ZOLI SILVER SNIPE
Over/under; boxlock; 12-, 20-ga.; 3-inch chambers; 26-inch Improved/Modified, 28-inch Modified/Full, 30-inch Modified/Full (12-ga. only) barrels; vent rib; hand-checkered European walnut pistol-grip stock, forearm; crossbolt safety; automatic safety; single trigger; chrome-lined barrels. Made in Italy. No longer imported.

Exc.: $500   **VGood:** $475   **Good:** $400

GALEF/ZOLI SILVER SNIPE TRAP
Same specs as Silver Snipe except 30-inch Full/Full barrel; non-automatic safety. No longer imported.

Exc.: $395   **VGood:** $295   **Good:** $220

GALEF/ZOLI SILVER SNIPE SKEET
Same specs as Silver Snipe except 26-inch Skeet/Skeet barrels; non-automatic safety. No longer imported.

Exc.: $385   **VGood:** $295   **Good:** $220

GAMBA 2100
Slide action; 12-ga.; 7-shot magazine; 20-inch barrel; weighs 7 lbs.; European walnut stock; flat black finish; designed for law enforcement. No longer imported.

Perf.: $590   **Exc.:** $375   **VGood:** $300

GAMBA AMBASSADOR
Side-by-side; sidelock; 12-, 20-ga.; 2-3/4-inch chamber; 27-1/2-inch barrels; choked to customer's specs; checkered straight English-style root walnut stock; double or single trigger; ejectors; inlaid gold shield in forend; engraved, gold-inlaid blued barrels. Made in Italy. Introduced 1987; discontinued 1987.

Perf.: $35,500 **Exc.:** $22,500 **VGood:** $15,000
Add $950 to above prices for English scroll engraving

GAMBA AMBASSADOR EXECUTIVE
Same specs as Ambassador except custom built to customer's specs; has better wood; extensive signed engraving. Made in Italy. Introduced 1987; discontinued 1987.

Perf.: $47,750 **Exc.:** $28,750 **VGood:** $21,250

GAMBA DAYTONA
Over/under; boxlock; 12-, 20-ga.; 2-3/4-inch chambers; 26-3/4-inch, 28-inch, 29-inch, 32-inch barrel; weighs 5-1/2 to 8-1/2 lbs.; European walnut stock in Monte Carlo, traditional, Skeet/Sporting Clays or hunting configuration; interchangeable schnabel, half or full beavertail forend; ejectors; single selective, adjustable or release trigger available. Made in Italy. Introduced 1990. New Daytona series introduced 2000.

Perf.: $8500   **Exc.:** $6000   **VGood:** $4300
Add $2000 to above prices for Daytona combo package
Add $3700 - $4300 for extra set of barrels

GAMBA DAYTONA SL
Same specs as Daytona except sidelock; cased. Limited importation 1990-1994; reintroduced 2000.

Perf.: $26,000 **Exc.:** $18000 **VGood:** $11050

GAMBA DAYTONA GRADE 4
Same specs as Daytona, except is the most elaborately engraved number Daytona Model; buyer's choice of fine scroll engraving or eagle panel scene.

Perf.: $26,000 **Exc.:** $18000 **VGood:** $11050

GAMBA DAYTONA GRADE 5/5E
One grade below Grade 4 in ornamentation.

Perf.: $18,000 **Exc.:** $15,000 **VGood:** $11,750

GAMBA DAYTONA GRADE 6/6SCE
One grade below Daytona Grade 5 with choice of tight scroll engraving or duck game scene.

Perf.: $17,000 **Exc.:** $14,000 **VGood:** $10,450

GAMBA DAYTONA GRADE 7
One grade below Grade 6; oval game scene engraving with English scroll around perimeter.

Perf.: $16,000 **Exc.:** $12,750 **VGood:** $9,750

GALEF/ZOLI GOLDEN SNIPE
Over/under; boxlock; 12-, 20-ga.; 3-inch chambers; 26-inch Improved/Modified, 28-inch Modified/Full, 30-inch Modified/Full (12-ga. only) barrels; vent rib; hand-checkered European walnut pistol-grip stock, forearm; crossbolt safety; automatic safety; automatic selective ejectors; single trigger; chrome-lined barrels. Made in Italy. No longer imported.

Field model
Exc.: $400   **VGood:** $300   **Good:** $225
Trap/Skeet models
Exc.: $480   **VGood:** $380   **Good:** $310

GALEF/ZOLI SILVER HAWK
Side-by-side; boxlock; 12-, 20-ga.; 3-inch chambers; 26-inch, 28-inch, 30-inch barrels; Improved/Modified, Modified/Full chokes; hand-checkered European walnut pistol-grip stock. Made in Italy. Introduced 1967; discontinued 1972.

Exc.: $500   **VGood:** $475   **Good:** $400

GAMBA DAYTONA GRADE 8
One grade below Grade 7 with English scroll engraving.
Perf.: $14,000 **Exc.:** $11,250 **VGood:** $8,950

GAMBA DAYTONA SL HH
Same specs as Daytona except hand-detachable sidelocks; cased.
Perf.: $45,500 **Exc.:** $30,000 **VGood:** $20,500

GAMBA DAYTONA SL
Over/under; boxlock; 12-ga.; deluxe variation of the Daytona Model; sideplates have extensive engraving; newer manufactured examples have detachable trigger group; includes case. Limited importation 199 to 1994; reintroduced 2000.
Perf.: $26,000 **Exc.:** $18,000 **VGood:** $11,500

GAMBA DAYTONA GRADE ROYALE
Same features as Daytona SL, except is the top-of-the-line Daytona Model.
Perf.: $27,000 **Exc.:** $19,750 **VGood:** $12,500

GAMBA DAYTONA GRADE PURDEY
Same features as Daytona SL, except has Purdey locking system.
Perf.: $26,000 **Exc.:** $19,000 **VGood:** $12,000

GAMBA DAYTONA SLE TIGER
Same features as Daytona SL, except has sideplates engraved with African game scenes.
Perf.: $40,500 **Exc.:** $27,500 **VGood:** $17,950

GAMBA DAYTONA SLE BEST
Same features as Daytona SL, except has elaborate scroll and 24 Kt. Gold game scene inlays.
Perf.: $45,000 **Exc.:** $30,000 **VGood:** $20,000

GAMBA DAYTONA SLE VENUS
Same features as Dayton SL, except has elaborate scroll and game scene engraving.
Perf.: $41,750 **Exc.:** $28,500 **VGood:** $18,750

GAMBA DAYTONA GRADE 1 SL
Same features as Daytona SL, except has elaborate engraving with 24 Kt. Gold game scene engraving.
Perf.: $40,000 **Exc.:** $26,750 **VGood:** $17,500

GAMBA DAYTONA GRADE 2 SL
Same features as Daytona SL, except has elaborate game scene and scroll engraving without gold inlays.
Perf.: $28,250 **Exc.:** $21,000 **VGood:** $13,500

GAMBA DAYTONA GRADE 3 SL
Same features as Daytona SL, except has hand engraved sideplates with English scroll and game scenes.
Perf.: $26,000 **Exc.:** $18,750 **VGood:** $11,750

GAMBA DAYTONA COMPETITION
Over/under; boxlock; 12-, 20-ga.; 2-3/4-inch, 3-inch chambers; 26-3/4-inch Skeet/Skeet, 28-inch Skeet/Skeet, 28-inch Modified/Full (SC model), 30-inch Improved Modified/Full (SC model), 30-inch Improved Modified/Full (trap), 32-inch Modified/Full (trap), 32-inch Full (monotrap) barrels; hand-checkered select walnut stock with oil finish; detachable trigger mechanism; Boss-type locking system; automatic ejectors; anatomical single trigger; optional single selective, release or adjustable trigger; black or chrome frame. Made in Italy. Introduced 1990; still imported.

Trap, 12- or 20-ga.
Perf.: $5200 **Exc.:** $3200 **VGood:** $2750
Skeet, 12-ga.
Perf.: $5250 **Exc.:** $3750 **VGood:** $3300
Pigeon, 12-ga.
Perf.: $5500 **Exc.:** $3500 **VGood:** $3250
Sporting, 12-ga.
Perf.: $5800 **Exc.:** $3700 **VGood:** $3200
American Trap, 12-ga.
Perf.: $5950 **Exc.:** $4400 **VGood:** $3850

Gamba Edinburgh Trap

Gamba London

Gamba Oxford 90

Gamba Principessa

GAMBA EDINBURGH SKEET
Over/under; 12-ga.; 2-3/4-inch chambers; 26-1/2-inch Skeet/Skeet barrels; European walnut stock with high-gloss lacquer finish; recoil pad; chrome-lined barrels; double vent ribs; single trigger; auto ejectors; scroll border engraving; silver-finished receiver. Made in Italy. Introduced 1980; no longer imported.
Perf.: $1450 **Exc.:** $1050 **VGood:** $950

GAMBA EDINBURGH TRAP
Same specs as Edinburgh except 30-inch, 32-inch, 34-inch barrels; oil-finished walnut Monte Carlo stock. No longer imported.
Perf.: $1450 **Exc.:** $1050 **VGood:** $950

GAMBA EUROPA 2000
Over/under; boxlock; 12-ga.; 2-3/4-inch chamber; 27-inch Improved/Modified or Modified/Full barrels; oil-finished, select walnut stock; dummy sideplates; ejectors; anti-recoil buttplate; floral, English engraving patterns. Made in Italy. Introduced 1987; discontinued 1987.
Perf.: $1250 **Exc.:** $995 **VGood:** $895

GAMBA GRIFONE
Over/under; boxlock; 12-, 20-ga.; 2-3/4-inch chambers; 27-inch Improved/Modified, Modified/Full barrels; weighs 7 lbs.; checkered European walnut stock; ejectors; double or single triggers; silvered receiver engraved game, floral scenes. Made in Italy. Introduced 1987; discontinued 1987.
Perf.: $750 **Exc.:** $600 **VGood:** $500

GAMBA GRINTA SKEET
Over/under; boxlock; 12-ga.; 2-3/4-inch chambers; 27-inch Skeet/Skeet barrels; weighs 8 lbs.; checkered European walnut Skeet-style stock; ejectors; single selective trigger. No longer imported.
Perf.: $1400 **Exc.:** $900 **VGood:** $750

GAMBA GRINTA TRAP
Same specs as Grinta Skeet except 29-inch Modified/Full barrels; checkered European walnut trap-style stock. No longer imported.
Perf.: $1400 **Exc.:** $900 **VGood:** $750

GAMBA HUNTER SUPER
Side-by-side; boxlock; 12-ga.; 2-3/4-inch chambers; 26-3/4-inch Modified/Full, 28-inch Improved/Modified barrels; weighs 6-3/4 lbs.; checkered European walnut stock; double triggers; extractors; silvered, engraved receiver. Made in Italy. Introduced 1987; importation by Armes de Chasse discontinued 1987.
Perf.: $1750 **Exc.:** $1275 **VGood:** $895

GAMBA LONDON
Side-by-side; sidelock; 12-, 20-ga.; 2-3/4-inch chambers; 26-3/4-inch, 27-1/2-inch barrels; weighs 6-3/4 lbs.; checkered straight English-style root walnut stock; double sear safety; ejectors; double triggers; silvered receiver; fine English-type scroll, rosette engraving. Made in Italy. Originally marketed by Renato Gamba. Introduced 1981; discontinued 1987.
Perf.: $8800 **Exc.:** $8500 **VGood:** $7000

GAMBA LS2000
Over/under; boxlock; 12-, 20-, 28-ga., .410; 27-1/2-inch Modified/Full barrels; weighs 6-1/4 lbs.; European walnut stock; single trigger extractors; game scene engraving; folding design. Made in Italy. Introduced 1987; discontinued 1987.
Perf.: $500 **Exc.:** $300 **VGood:** $250

GAMBA MILANO
Single shot; 12-, 16-, 20-, 28-, 32-ga., .410; 27-1/2-inch Full choke barrel; vent rib; weighs 5-3/4 lbs.; checkered European hardwood stock; chromed, photo-engraved receiver; folding design. Made in Italy. Introduced 1987; discontinued 1987.
Perf.: $300 **Exc.:** $210 **VGood:** $175

GAMBA OXFORD 90
Side-by-side; boxlock with sideplates; 12-, 20-ga.; 26-3/4-inch, 27-1/2-inch barrels; straight English or pistol-grip root walnut stock; double or single trigger auto ejectors; better grade of engraving. Made in Italy. Introduced 1981; discontinued 1987; reintroduced by Heckler & Koch 1990; discontinued 1991.
Perf.: $3650 **Exc.:** $2700 **VGood:** $2300

GAMBA PRINCIPESSA
Side-by-side; 12-, 20-ga.; 2-3/4-inch chambers; straight English-style walnut stock; double or single trigger; ejectors; fine English-style scroll engraving; silvered receiver. Made in Italy. Introduced 1981; discontinued 1987; reintroduced by Heckler & Koch 1990; discontinued 1991.
Perf.: $2750 **Exc.:** $1900 **VGood:** $1525

GAMBA VICTORY SKEET
Over/under; boxlock; 12-ga.; 2-3/4-inch chambers; 27-inch Skeet/Skeet barrels; recessed chokes; weighs 7-3/4 lbs.; stippled European walnut Skeet-style stock; removable rubber recoil pad; ejectors; single trigger; blued receiver; light engraving; gold nameplate. Made in Italy. Introduced 1987; discontinued 1987.
Perf.: $1450 **Exc.:** $1050 **VGood:** $950

Garbi Model 51B

Garbi Model 60A

Garbi Model 71

Garbi Model 100

Garbi Model 102

Garbi Model 101 Engraving

Garbi Model 103A Engraving

Garbi Model 103A

Garbi Model 200

GARBI MODEL 71

Side-by-side; hand-detachable sidelock; 12-, 16-, 20-ga.; 26-inch, 28-inch barrels; oil-finished checkered European walnut straight-grip stock, classic forend; ejectors; double triggers; color case-hardened action. Made in Spain. Introduced 1980; discontinued 1988.

Perf.: $2100   **Exc.:** $1450   **VGood:** $1300

GARBI MODEL 100

Side-by-side; hand-detachable sidelock; 12-, 16-, 20-ga.; 26-inch, 28-inch custom-choked barrels; checkered European walnut straight-grip stock, classic forend; ejectors; double triggers; forged barrel lumps; color case-hardened action; numerous options. Made in Spain. Introduced 1986; still imported.

Perf.: $4750   **Exc.:** $3800   **VGood:** $3250

GARBI MODEL 100 DOUBLE

Side-by-side; sidelock; 12-, 16-, 20-, 28-ga.; 26-inch, 28-inch barrel choked to customer specs.; weighs 5-1/2 to 7-1/2 lbs.; European walnut stock, straight grip, checkered butt, classic forend; automatic ejectors; double triggers standard; color case-hardened action; coin finish optional; single trigger; beavertail forend, etc. optional. Five other models are available. Imported from Spain by Wm. Larkin Moore.

Perf.: $4800   **Exc.:** $3850   **VGood:** $3250

GARBI MODEL 101

Side-by-side; hand-detachable sidelock; 12-, 16-, 20-ga.; file-cut Churchill or vent top rib; select European walnut stock; ejectors; Continental-style floral, scroll engraving; 12-ga. pigeon or wildfowl designs available; better quality than Model 71.

Perf.: $6200   **Exc.:** $4900   **VGood:** $4100

GARBI MODEL 102

Side-by-side; 12-, 16-, 20-, 28-ga.; 25-inch to 30-inch barrels; standard chokes; select European walnut stock; Holland sidelock ejector; chopper lump barrels; scroll engraving; hinged double triggers; non-selective single trigger optional; other options. Made in Spain. Introduced 1982; dropped 1988. Was imported by Wm. Larkin Moore, L. Joseph Rahn.

Perf.: $4500   **Exc.:** $4000   **VGood:** $3000

GARBI MODEL 103A

Side-by-side; 12-, 16-, 20-ga.; 25-inch to 30-inch barrels; chopper lump barrels; select European walnut stock; ejectors; hinged double triggers; non-selective single trigger optional; Purdey-type scroll, rosette engraving. Made in Spain. Introduced 1982.

Perf.: $8000   **Exc.:** $6300   **VGood:** $4890

GARBI MODEL 103B

Same specs as 103 except Holland & Holland-type assisted-opening mechanism; nickel-chrome steel barrels. Introduced 1982.

Perf.: $11,800 **Exc.:** $8850 **VGood:** $7100

GARBI MODEL 103B ROYAL

Same specs. as the 103B, except is a deluxe variation with engraving similar to the H&H Royal style; extra fancy walnut stock; gold oval stock plate; matted concave rib.

Perf.: $15,800 **Exc.:** $12,300 **VGood:** $10,000

GARBI MODEL 110

Side-by-side; sidelock; 12-, 20-, 28-ga.; barrel lengths, chokes, stocks to custom order. Made in Spain. Introduced 1982 by Toledo Armas; discontinued 1984.

Perf.: $7300   **Exc.:** $4500   **VGood:** $4000

GARBI MODEL 200

Side-by-side; sidelock; 12-, 16-, 20-, 28-ga.; 26-inch, 28-inch chopper-lump, nickel-chrome steel barrels; finely figured European walnut stock; ejectors; double triggers; heavy-duty locks; Continental-style floral, scroll engraving. Made in Spain. Introduced 1982; still imported.

Perf.: $11,200 **Exc.:** $8300 **VGood:** $6350

GAMBA VICTORY TRAP

Same specs as Victory Skeet except 29-inch Modified/Full barrels; stippled European walnut trap-style stock. Made in Italy. Introduced 1987; discontinued 1987.

Perf.: $1450   **Exc.:** $1050   **VGood:** $950

GARBI MODEL 51A

Side-by-side; boxlock; 12-ga.; 2-3/4-inch chambers; 28-inch Modified/Full barrels; hand-checkered European walnut pistol-grip stock, forend; double triggers; extractors; hand-engraved receiver. Made in Spain. Introduced 1980; no longer imported.

Perf.: $475   **Exc.:** $340   **VGood:** $310

GARBI MODEL 51B

Same specs as Model 51A except 12-, 16-, 20-ga.; automatic ejectors. Introduced 1980; discontinued 1988.

Perf.: $800   **Exc.:** $540   **VGood:** $500

GARBI MODEL 60A

Side-by-side; sidelock; 12-ga.; 2-3/4-inch chambers; 26-inch, 28-inch, 30-inch barrel; custom chokes; hand-checkered select European walnut custom pistol-grip stock, forend; double triggers; extractors; scroll-engraved receiver. Made in Spain. Introduced 1981; discontinued 1988.

Perf.: $735   **Exc.:** $550   **VGood:** $495

GARBI MODEL 60B

Same specs as 60A except 12-, 16-, 20-ga.; ejectors; demi-block barrels. Introduced 1981; no longer imported.

Perf.: $1150   **Exc.:** $800   **VGood:** $700

GARBI MODEL 62A

Side-by-side; sidelock; 12-ga.; 2-3/4-inch chamber; 26-inch-30-inch barrels; Modified/Full chokes; demi-block barrels; gas exhaust valves; extractors; jointed double triggers; plain receiver with engraved border. Made in Spain. Introduced 1981; discontinued 1988.

Perf.: $695   **Exc.:** $550   **VGood:** $490

GARBI MODEL 62B

Same specs as 62A except 12-, 16-, 20-ga.; ejectors. Introduced 1982; discontinued 1988.

Perf.: $1100   **Exc.:** $740   **VGood:** $700

GARBI MODEL 300

Side-by-side; sidelock; 12-, 20-, 28-ga.; barrel lengths, chokes, stocks to custom order; engraving. Made in Spain. No longer imported.

Perf.: $8900   **Exc.:** $6500   **VGood:** $5000

GARBI SPECIAL MODEL

Side-by-side; sidelock; 12-, 16-, 20-, 28-ga.; 26-inch, 28-inch barrels; fancy European walnut stock; ejectors; game scene engraved in receiver some with gold inlays; top quality metalwork, wood. Made in Spain. Introduced 1982; discontinued 1988.

Perf.: $7600   **Exc.:** $5000   **VGood:** $4100

GARCIA BRONCO

Single shot; swing-out action; takedown; .410; 18-1/2-inch barrel; weighs 3-1/2 lbs.; one-piece metal frame skeletonized stock, receiver; crinkle finish. Made in USA by Firearms International; later bought by Garcia. Introduced 1968; discontinued 1978.

Perf.: $350   **Exc.:** $325   **VGood:** $295

GARCIA BRONCO .22/.410

Over/under combo; swing-out action; takedown; 22 LR over, .410 under, 18 1/2-inch barrel; one-piece metal frame stock, receiver; crinkle finish. Introduced 1976; discontinued 1978.

Perf.: $325   **Exc.:** $300   **VGood:** $285

GOLDEN EAGLE MODEL 5000 GRADE I FIELD

Over/under; boxlock; 12-, 20-ga.; 2-3/4-inch, 3-inch chambers; 26-inch, 28-inch, 30-inch barrels; Improved/Modified, Modified/Full chokes; vent rib; checkered walnut pistol-grip stock, semi-beavertail forearm; selective single trigger; auto ejectors; engraved receiver; gold eagle head inlaid in frame. Made in Japan. Introduced 1975; discontinued 1980.

Perf.: $850   **Exc.:** $775   **VGood:** $700

GOLDEN EAGLE MODEL 5000 GRADE II FIELD

Same specs as Model 5000 Grade I Field except more elaborate engraving; spread-wing eagle inlaid in gold; fancier wood. Introduced 1975; discontinued 1980.

Perf.: $950   **Exc.:** $875   **VGood:** $790

GOLDEN EAGLE MODEL 5000 GRADE I TRAP

Same specs as Model 5000 Grade I Field except 30-inch, 32-inch barrels; Modified/Full, Improved Modified/Full, Full/Full choke; wide vent rib; trap-style stock; recoil pad. Introduced 1975; discontinued 1980.

Perf.: $875   **Exc.:** $800   **VGood:** $725

GOLDEN EAGLE MODEL 5000 GRADE II TRAP

Same specs as Model 5000 Grade I Field except 30-inch, 32-inch barrels; Modified/Full, Improved Modified/Full, Full/Full choke; wide vent rib; vent side ribs; trap-style stock; recoil pad; more elaborate engraving; spread-wing eagle gold inlay; inertia trigger; fancier wood. Introduced 1975; discontinued 1980.

Perf.: $975   **Exc.:** $895   **VGood:** $810

GOLDEN EAGLE MODEL 5000 GRADE I SKEET

Same specs as Model 5000 Grade I Field except 26-inch, 28-inch Skeet/Skeet barrels; vent rib. Introduced 1975; discontinued 1980.

Perf.: $875   **Exc.:** $800   **VGood:** $725

GOLDEN EAGLE MODEL 5000 GRADE II SKEET

Same specs as Model 5000 Grade I Field except 26-inch, 28-inch Skeet/Skeet barrels; vent rib; vent side ribs; more elaborate engraving; spread-wing eagle gold inlay; inertia trigger; fancier wood. Introduced 1975; discontinued 1980.

Perf.: $975   **Exc.:** $895   **VGood:** $810

Garcia Bronco

Garcia Bronco 22/410

Golden Eagle Model 5000 Grade II Field

Golden Eagle Model 5000 Grade III Trap

Greener Crown Grade DH75

Greener Empire

GOLDEN EAGLE MODEL 5000 GRADE III

Same specs as Grade I Field except game scene engraving; scroll-engraved frame, barrels, sideplates; fancy wood; available in Field, Trap and Skeet versions; Trap model has Monte Carlo comb, full pistol grip, recoil pad. Introduced 1976; discontinued 1980.

Field version		
Perf.: $2250	**Exc.:** $1900	**VGood:** $1600
Trap/Skeet versions		
Perf.: $2200	**Exc.:** $1800	**VGood:** $1500

GOROSABEL 501

Side-by-side; boxlock; 12-, 16-, 20-, 28-ga., .410; 26-inch, 27-inch, 28-inch barrels; standard choke combos; hand-checkered select walnut English or pistol-grip stock, splinter or beavertail forend; ejectors. Introduced 1986; discontinued 1988.

Perf.: $700   **Exc.:** $590   **VGood:** $500

GOROSABEL 502

Side-by-side; boxlock; 12-, 16-, 20-, 28-ga.,.410; 26-inch, 27-inch, 28-inch barrels; standard choke combos; hand-checkered English or pistol-grip select walnut stock, splinter or beavertail forend; ejectors; engraving. Introduced 1986; discontinued 1988.

Perf.: $890   **Exc.:** $790   **VGood:** $700

GOROSABEL 503

Side-by-side; boxlock; 12-, 16-, 20-, 28-ga., .410; 26-inch, 27-inch, 28-inch barrels; standard choke combos; hand-checkered fancy walnut English or pistol-grip stock; splinter or beavertail forend; ejectors; scalloped frame; scroll engraving. Introduced 1986; discontinued 1988.

Perf.: $1000   **Exc.:** $850   **VGood:** $750

GOROSABEL BLACKPOINT

Side-by-side; sidelock; 12-, 20-ga.; 2-3/4-inch, 3-inch chambers; 26-inch, 27-inch, 28-inch barrels; standard choke combos; hand-checkered select European walnut stock, splinter or beavertail forend; Purdey-style scroll, rose engraving; numerous options. Made in Italy. Introduced 1986, discontinued 1988.

Perf.: $1550   **Exc.:** $1200   **VGood:** $1000

GOROSABEL SILVERPOINT

Side-by-side; sidelock; 12-, 20-ga.; 2-3/4-inch, 3-inch chambers; 26-inch, 27-inch, 28-inch barrels; standard choke combos; hand-checkered European walnut straight or pistol-grip stock, splinter or beavertail forend; large scroll engraving. Made in Italy. Introduced 1986, discontinued 1988.

Perf.: $1000   **Exc.:** $800   **VGood:** $700
Note: On all variations, add $175 for non-selective single trigger; $350 for selective trigger.

GREENER CROWN GRADE DH75

Side-by-side; boxlock; 12-, 16-, 20-ga.; 26-inch, 28-inch, 30-inch barrels; any choke combo; top-quality hand-checkered European walnut straight or pistol-grip stock, forearm; Greener crossbolt; ejectors; double triggers; non-selective or selective single trigger at added cost; best-grade engraved action. Introduced 1875; discontinued 1965.

Exc.: $8200   **VGood:** $6975   **Good:** $5350

GREENER EMPIRE

Side-by-side; boxlock; 12-ga.; 28-inch, 30-inch, 32-inch barrels; any choke combo; hand-checkered European walnut straight or half-pistol-grip stock, forearm; non-ejector; ejectors at additional cost. Introduced about 1893; discontinued 1962.

Exc.: $1760   **VGood:** $1540   **Good:** $1300
Add approximately $200 to above prices for auto. ejectors.

Greener
Far-Killer

Greener Jubilee
Grade DH35

Greener Sovereign
Grade DH40

Greifelt Grade No. 1

Bill Hanus Birdgun

Harrington & Richardson
Folding Model

Harrington & Richardson
Model 088

Add approximately $400 to above prices for SST. Subtract about 10 percent from above prices for 16 ga.

GREIFELT GRADE NO. 3

Over/under; boxlock; 12-, 16-, 20-, 28-ga., .410; 26-, 28-inch, 30-inch, 32-inch barrels; any desired choke combo; solid matted rib standard; vent rib at added cost; hand-checkered European walnut straight or pistol-grip stock; ejectors; double triggers; single trigger at added cost; engraving. Made in Germany prior to World War II.

Solid rib
Exc.: $2250   **VGood:** $1650   **Good:** $1250
Vent rib
Exc.: $2400   **VGood:** $1850   **Good:** $1450
.410-bore or 28 ga.
Exc.: $2500   **VGood:** $1900   **Good:** $1500
Add about $400 to above prices for SST. Subtract about 10 percent from above prices for 16 ga.

GREIFELT MODEL 22

Side-by-side; boxlock; 12-, 20-ga.; 28-inch, 30-inch barrels; Modified/Full choke; hand-checkered straight English or pistol-grip stock, forend; cheekpiece; plain extractors; double triggers; sideplates. Introduced about 1950; no longer in production.
Exc.: $1760   **VGood:** $1595   **Good:** $1320

GREIFELT MODEL 22E

Same specs as Model 22 except ejectors. Introduced about 1950; no longer in production.
Exc.: $2200   **VGood:** $1950   **Good:** $1700

GREIFELT MODEL 103

Side-by-side; boxlock; 12-, 16-ga.; 28-inch, 30-inch barrels; Modified/Full chokes; hand-checkered European walnut straight English or pistol-grip stock, forearm; extractors; double triggers. Introduced about 1950; no longer in production.
Exc.: $1650   **VGood:** $1485   **Good:** $1210

GREIFELT MODEL 103E

Same specs as Model 103 except ejectors. Introduced about 1950; no longer in production.
Exc.: $1760   **VGood:** $1595   **Good:** $1320

GREIFELT MODEL 143E

Over/under; boxlock; 12-, 16-, 20-ga.; 26-inch, 28-inch, 30-inch barrels; any desired choke; solid or vent rib; hand-checkered European walnut straight or pistol-grip stock; single or double trigger; engraved; post-WWII version of the Grade I but of lower quality. Introduced about 1950. No longer imported.
Exc.: $2150   **VGood:** $1850   **Good:** $1550

BILL HANUS BIRDGUN

Side-by-side; boxlock; 16-, 20-, 28-ga.; 26-inch Skeet/Skeet barrels; weighs 6-1/4 lbs. (12-ga.); hand-checkered straight-grip walnut stock, semi-beavertail forend; single non-selective trigger; raised Churchill rib; auto safety; ejectors; color case-hardened action. Made in Spain. Introduced 1991; still imported.
Perf.: $1800   **Exc.:** $1450   **VGood:** $950

HARRINGTON & RICHARDSON FOLDING MODEL

Single barrel; 12-, 16-, 20-, 28-ga. or .410 with 26-inch barrel (Heavy Frame model); 28-ga., .410 with 22-inch barrel (Light Frame model); Full choke; bead front sight; checkered pistol-grip stock, forearm; gun is hinged at front of frame so barrel folds against stock for storage, transport. Introduced about 1910; discontinued 1942.
Exc.: $175   **VGood:** $150   **Good:** $125
Add about 75 percent to above prices for 28 ga. or .410 bore

HARRINGTON & RICHARDSON MODEL 088

Single shot; sidelever; external hammer; takedown; 12-, 16-, 20-, 28-ga., .410; 26-inch, 28-inch, 30-inch, 32-inch, 36-inch barrels; walnut-finished hardwood semi-pistol-grip stock; auto ejector; case-hardened frame. No longer in production.
Exc.: $85   **VGood:** $75   **Good:** $55

GREENER EMPIRE DELUXE

Same specs as Empire except deluxe finish and better craftsmanship.
Exc.: $1850   **VGood:** $1660   **Good:** $1500

GREENER FAR-KILLER

Side-by-side; boxlock; 12-, 10-, 8-ga.; 28-inch, 30-inch, 32-inch barrels; any desired choke combination; hand-checkered European walnut straight or half-pistol-grip stock; non-ejectors; automatic ejectors at added cost. Introduced about 1895; discontinued 1962.

12-ga.
Exc.: $2300   **VGood:** $1900   **Good:** $1650
10-, 8-ga.
Exc.: $2500   **VGood:** $2100   **Good:** $1790
Add approximately $800 to above prices for auto. ejectors.

GREENER GENERAL PURPOSE

Single shot; Martini-type action; takedown; 12-ga.; 26-inch, 30-inch, 32-inch barrel; Modified, Full choke; hand-checkered European walnut straight-grip stock, forearm; ejector. Introduced 1910; discontinued 1964. Subtract 25 percent for 14-ga. police model (shells very rare).
Exc.: $400   **VGood:** $325   **Good:** $250

GREENER JUBILEE GRADE DH35

Side-by-side; boxlock; 12-, 16-, 20-ga.; 26-inch, 28-inch, 30-inch barrels; any choke combo; hand-checkered European walnut straight or pistol-grip stock, forearm; Greener crossbolt; ejectors; double triggers; non-selective or selective single trigger at added cost; engraved action. Introduced 1875; discontinued 1965.
Exc.: $2400   **VGood:** $1700   **Good:** $1550

GREENER SOVEREIGN GRADE DH40

Side-by-side; boxlock; 12-, 16-, 20-ga.; 26-inch, 28-inch, 30-inch barrels; any choke combo; hand-checkered select European walnut straight or pistol-grip stock, forearm; Greener crossbolt; ejectors; double triggers; non-selective or selective single trigger at added cost; engraved action. Introduced 1875; discontinued 1965.
Exc.: $2500   **VGood:** $2000   **Good:** $1895

GREIFELT GRADE NO. 1

Over/under; boxlock; 12-, 16-, 20-, 28-ga., .410; 26-inch, 28-inch, 30-inch, 32-inch barrels; any desired choke combo; solid matted rib standard; vent rib at added cost; hand-checkered European walnut straight or pistol-grip stock; ejectors; double triggers; single trigger at added cost; elaborate engraving. Made in Germany prior to World War II.

Solid rib
Exc.: $2850   **VGood:** $2100   **Good:** $1750
Vent rib
Exc.: $3100   **VGood:** $2350   **Good:** $2000
.410-bore or 28 ga.
Exc.: $3650   **VGood:** $2650   **Good:** $2400

HARRINGTON & RICHARDSON
MODEL 088 JUNIOR
Same specs as Model 088 except 20-ga., .410; 25-inch Modified (20-ga.) or Full (.410) choke barrel; stock dimensions for smaller shooters.

Exc.: $75   **VGood:** $60   **Good:** $50

HARRINGTON & RICHARDSON
MODEL 099 DELUXE
Single shot; 12-, 16-, 20-ga., .410; 2-3/4-inch, 3-inch chamber; 25-inch, 26-inch, 28-inch barrel; bead front sight; walnut-finished hardwood semi-pistol-grip stock, semi-beavertail forend; electroless matte nickel finish. Introduced 1982; discontinued 1985.

Perf.: $85   **Exc.:** $60   **VGood:** $50

HARRINGTON & RICHARDSON
MODEL 159 GOLDEN SQUIRE
Single barrel; exposed hammer; 12-, 20-ga.; 28-inch (20-ga.), 30-inch (12-ga.) barrel; Full choke; bead front sight; uncheckered hardwood straight-grip stock, schnabel forearm. Introduced 1964; discontinued 1966.

Exc.: $75   **VGood:** $65   **Good:** $55

HARRINGTON & RICHARDSON
MODEL 162 SLUG GUN
Single barrel; sidelever break-open; exposed hammer; takedown; 12-, 20-ga.; 3-inch chamber; 24-inch Cylinder choke barrel; rifle sights; uncheckered hardwood pistol-grip stock, forend; recoil pad. Introduced 1968; discontinued 1985.

Perf.: $105   **Exc.:** $85   **VGood:** $75

HARRINGTON & RICHARDSON
MODEL 176
Single shot; sidelever break-open; exposed hammer; takedown; 10-, 12-ga.; 3-inch, 3-1/2-inch chamber; 32-inch, 36-inch heavy barrel; Full choke; weighs 9-1/4 lbs.; bead front sight; uncheckered hardwood pistol-grip stock, special long forend; recoil pad. Introduced 1978; discontinued 1985.

Perf.: $110   **Exc.:** $85   **VGood:** $65

HARRINGTON & RICHARDSON
MODEL 176 SLUG GUN
Same specs as Model 176 except 10-ga. rifled slugs; 3-1/2-inch chamber; 28-inch Cylinder barrel; weighs 9-1/4 lbs.; ramp front sight, folding leaf rear; uncheckered hardwood pistol-grip stock, magnum-type forend; recoil pad; sling swivels. Introduced 1982; discontinued 1985.

Perf.: $125   **Exc.:** $95   **VGood:** $80

HARRINGTON & RICHARDSON
MODEL 348 GAMESTER
Bolt action; takedown; 12-, 16-ga.; 2-shot tube magazine; 28-inch barrel; Full choke; uncheckered hardwood pistol-grip stock, forearm. Introduced 1949; discontinued 1954.

Exc.: $95   **VGood:** $75   **Good:** $50

HARRINGTON & RICHARDSON
MODEL 349 GAMESTER DELUXE
Bolt action; takedown; 12-, 16-ga.; 2-shot tube magazine; 26-inch barrel; adjustable choke device; uncheckered hardwood pistol-grip stock, forearm; recoil pad. Introduced 1953; discontinued 1955.

Exc.: $100   **VGood:** $85   **Good:** $60

HARRINGTON & RICHARDSON
MODEL 351 HUNTSMAN
Bolt action; takedown; 12-, 16-ga.; 2-shot tube magazine; 26-inch barrel; adjustable choke device; uncheckered American hardwood Monte Carlo stock; recoil pad; push-button safety. Introduced 1956; discontinued 1958.

Exc.: $95   **VGood:** $75   **Good:** $55

HARRINGTON & RICHARDSON
MODEL 400
Slide action; hammerless; 12-, 16-, 20-ga.; 5-shot tube magazine; 28-inch Full choke barrel;

Harrington & Richardson
Model 099 Deluxe

Harrington & Richardson
Model 162 Slug Gun

Harrington & Richardson
Model 176

Harrington & Richardson
Model 176 Slug Gun

Harrington & Richardson
Model 400

Harrington & Richardson
Model 402

Harrington & Richardson
Model 403

uncheckered pistol-grip stock, grooved slide handle; recoil pad (12-, 16-ga. only). Introduced 1955; discontinued 1967.

Exc.: $145   **VGood:** $125   **Good:** $110

HARRINGTON & RICHARDSON
MODEL 401
Slide action; hammerless; 12-, 16-, 20-ga.; 5-shot tube magazine; 28-inch barrel; adjustable choke device; uncheckered pistol-grip stock, grooved slide handle; recoil pad (12-, 16-ga. only). Introduced 1956; discontinued 1963.

Exc.: $155   **VGood:** $140   **Good:** $120

HARRINGTON & RICHARDSON
MODEL 402
Slide action; hammerless; .410; 5-shot tube magazine; 28-inch Full choke barrel; uncheckered pistol-grip stock, grooved slide handle; recoil pad

(12-, 16-ga. only). Introduced 1959; discontinued 1963. Premium for .410.

Exc.: $175   **VGood:** $125   **Good:** $95

HARRINGTON & RICHARDSON
MODEL 403
Autoloader; takedown; .410; 4-shot tube magazine; 26-inch barrel; Full choke; uncheckered walnut pistol-grip stock, forearm. Introduced 1964; discontinued 1964.

Exc.: $375   **VGood:** $325   **Good:** $260

HARRINGTON & RICHARDSON
MODEL 404
Side-by-side; boxlock; 12-, 20-ga., .410; 25-inch Full/Full (.410), 26-inch Modified/Improved (20-ga.), 28-inch Modified/Full (12-ga.) barrels; checkered hardwood pistol-grip stock, forearm; double triggers; plain extractors. Made to H&R specifications in Brazil. Introduced 1968; discontinued 1972.

Exc.: $315   **VGood:** $265   **Good:** $245

Harrington & Richardson Model 404C

Harrington & Richardson Model 440

Harrington & Richardson Model 442

Harrington & Richardson Model 1212

Harrington & Richardson Model 1212 Waterfowler

Harrington & Richardson No. 1 Harrich

Harrington & Richardson No. 3

Harrington & Richardson No. 5

Harrington & Richardson No. 6

Harrington & Richardson No. 7 Bay State

Harrington & Richardson No. 8

HARRINGTON & RICHARDSON MODEL 404C

Same specs as Model 404 except Monte Carlo stock. No longer in production.

Exc.: $325   **VGood:** $275   **Good:** $255

HARRINGTON & RICHARDSON MODEL 440

Slide action; hammerless; 12-, 16-, 20-ga.; 4-shot magazine; 24-inch, 26-inch, 28-inch barrel; standard chokes; uncheckered American walnut pistol-grip

stock, forend; recoil pad; slide ejection. Introduced 1972; discontinued 1975.

Exc.: $250   **VGood:** $230   **Good:** $180

HARRINGTON & RICHARDSON MODEL 442

Slide action; hammerless; 12-, 16-, 20-ga.; 4-shot magazine; 24-inch, 26-inch, 28-inch barrel; standard chokes; vent rib; checkered American walnut pistol-

grip stock, forend; recoil pad; slide ejection. No longer in production.

Exc.: $165   **VGood:** $155   **Good:** $140

HARRINGTON & RICHARDSON MODEL 459 GOLDEN SQUIRE JUNIOR

Single barrel; exposed hammer; 20-ga., .410; 26-inch barrel; Full choke; bead front sight; youth-sized uncheckered hardwood straight-grip stock, schnabel forearm. Introduced 1964; discontinued 1964.

Exc.: $75   **VGood:** $65   **Good:** $55

HARRINGTON & RICHARDSON MODEL 1212

Over/under; boxlock; 12-ga.; 2-3/4-inch chambers; 28-inch barrels; Improved Cylinder/Improved Modified chokes; vent rib; checkered European walnut pistol-grip stock, fluted forearm; selective single trigger; plain extractors. Made in Spain by Lanber. Introduced 1976; discontinued 1981.

Perf.: $300   **Exc.:** $270   **VGood:** $240

HARRINGTON & RICHARDSON MODEL 1212 WATERFOWLER

Same specs as Model 1212 except 3-inch chamber; 30-inch barrels; Modified/Full choke; recoil pad. Introduced 1976; discontinued 1981.

Perf.: $310   **Exc.:** $280   **VGood:** $250

HARRINGTON & RICHARDSON NO. 1 HARRICH

Single shot; 12-ga.; 32-inch, 34-inch barrel; Full choke; high vent rib; hand-checkered European walnut Monte Carlo pistol-grip stock, beavertail forearm; Kersten top locks, double under lugs; recoil pad; trap model. Made in Austria. Introduced 1971; discontinued 1974.

Perf.: $1700   **Exc.:** $1550   **VGood:** $1400

HARRINGTON & RICHARDSON NO. 3

Single barrel; top-lever break-open; hammerless; takedown; 12-, 16-, 20-, 24-, 28-ga., .410; 26-inch, 28-inch, 30-inch, 32-inch barrels; Full choke; bead front sight; uncheckered American walnut pistol-grip stock, forearm; automatic ejector. Introduced 1908; discontinued 1942.

Exc.: $75   **VGood:** $50   **Good:** $40

HARRINGTON & RICHARDSON NO. 5

Single barrel; toplever break-open; exposed hammer; takedown; 28-ga., .410; 26-inch, 28-inch barrel; Full choke; bead front sight; uncheckered American walnut pistol-grip stock, forearm; automatic ejector; lightweight configuration. Introduced 1908; discontinued 1942.

Exc.: $90   **VGood:** $65   **Good:** $45

HARRINGTON & RICHARDSON NO. 6

Single barrel; top-lever break-open; exposed hammer; takedown; 10-, 12-, 16-, 20-ga.; 28-inch, 30-inch, 32-inch, 34-inch, 36-inch barrels; bead front sight; uncheckered American walnut pistol-grip stock, forearm; heavy breech; automatic ejector. Introduced 1908; discontinued 1942.

Exc.: $85   **VGood:** $65   **Good:** $55

HARRINGTON & RICHARDSON NO. 7 BAY STATE

Single barrel; exposed hammer; takedown; 12-, 16-, 20-ga., .410; 26-inch, 28-inch, 30-inch, 32-inch barrels; Full choke; bead front sight; uncheckered American walnut pistol-grip stock, slim forearm. Also known as Model No. 9. Introduced 1908; discontinued 1942.

Exc.: $85   **VGood:** $65   **Good:** $55

HARRINGTON & RICHARDSON NO. 8

Single barrel; exposed hammer; takedown; 12-, 16-, 20-, 28-ga., .410; 26-inch, 28-inch, 30-inch, 32-inch barrel; Full choke; bead front sight; uncheckered

American walnut pistol-grip stock, forearm; different forearm design than No. 5; automatic ejector. Introduced 1908; discontinued 1942.

Exc.: $125　**VGood:** $95　**Good:** $75
Add 100 percent to above prices for 28 ga. or .410 bore.

HARRINGTON & RICHARDSON NO. 48 TOPPER

Single barrel; top-lever break-open; exposed hammer; takedown; 12-, 16-, 20-ga., .410; 26-inch, 28-inch, 30-inch, 32-inch barrel; Modified, Full choke; bead front sight; unchecked American walnut pistol-grip stock, forearm; automatic ejector. Introduced 1946; discontinued 1957.

Exc.: $110　**VGood:** $75　**Good:** $65
Add about 15 percent to above prices for Topper Deluxe.

HARRINGTON & RICHARDSON N.W.T.F. SHOTGUNS

Single shot; 12-ga., 3-1/2-inch chamber, fixed full choke; 20-ga., 3-inch chamber, fixed modified choke; 24-inch barrel (12-ga.) or 22-inch (20-ga.); weighs 5 to 6 lbs.; straight-grip camo laminate with recoil pad and sling swivel studs; bead front sight; break-open action with side lever release; hand-checkered stock and forearm; includes trigger lock. National Wild Turkey Federation logo on receiver.

Perf.: $145　**Exc.:** $120　**VGood:** $100
20-ga. youth gun (12-1/2-inch length of pull, weighs 5 lbs.)
Perf.: $140　**Exc.:** $110　**VGood; $95

HARRINGTON & RICHARDSON N.W.T.F TURKEY

Single shot; break-open; sidelever; 12-ga.; 3-1/2-inch chamber; 24-inch barrel; Turkey Full choke tube; weighs 6 lbs.; 40-inch overall length; gold bead front sight; Mossy Oak camouflage hardwood pistol-grip stock, semi-beavertail forend; auto ejector; Mossy Oak sling; swivels; studs; satin-nickel frame; blued barrel. Introduced, 1992; still in production.

Perf.: $140　**Exc.:** $105　**VGood:** $80

HARRINGTON & RICHARDSON N.W.T.F. TURKEY YOUTH

Same specs as N.W.T.F. Turkey except 20-ga.; 3-inch chamber; 22-inch Full choke barrel; recoil pad. Introduced 1992; still in production.

Perf.: $135　**Exc.:** $100　**VGood:** $75

HARRINGTON & RICHARDSON SB2-980 ULTRA SLUG

Single shot; 12-ga.; 3-inch chamber; 24-inch fully rifled barrel; weighs 9 lbs.; scope mount; walnut-stained hardwood Monte Carlo stock; sling swivels; black nylon sling; H&R 10-gauge action with heavy-wall barrel. Introduced 1995; still in production.

Perf.: $180　**Exc.:** $140　**VGood:** $110

HARRINGTON & RICHARDSON MODEL 928 ULTRA SLUG HUNTER DELUXE

Similar to the SB2-980 Ultra Slug except uses 12 gauge action and 12 gauge barrel blank bored to 20 gauge, then fully rifled with 1:35-inch twist. Has hand-checkered camo laminate Monte Carlo stock and forend. Comes with Weaver-style scope base, offset hammer extension, ventilated recoil pad, sling swivels and nylon sling. Introduced 1997. Made in U.S. by H&R 1871 LLC.

Perf.: $260　**Exc.:** $205　**VGood:** $165

HARRINGTON & RICHARDSON TAMER

Single shot; .410; 3-inch chamber; 19-1/2-inch barrel; Full choke; weighs 5-6 lbs.; 33-inch overall length; high-density black-polymer thumbhole stock holds four spare shotshells; H&R Topper action with matte electroless nickel finish. Introduced 1994.

Perf.: $110　**Exc.:** $90　**VGood:** $75

Harrington & Richardson No. 48 Topper

Harrington & Richardson No. 48 Topper Engraving

Harrington & Richardson Tamer

Harrington & Richardson Topper Model 098

Harrington & Richardson Topper Model 098 Deluxe

Harrington & Richardson Topper Model 098 Junior

HARRINGTON & RICHARDSON TOPPER MODEL 058

Single shot; sidelever; exposed hammer; takedown; 12-, 16-, 20-, 28-ga., .410; 26-inch, 28-inch, 30-inch barrel; walnut-finished hardwood pistol-grip stock; auto ejector; case-hardened frame. Introduced 1978; discontinued 1981.

Perf.: $80　**Exc.:** $65　**VGood:** $50

HARRINGTON & RICHARDSON TOPPER MODEL 098

Single shot; break-open; sidelever; 12-, 16- (2-3/4-inch), 20-, 28-ga., .410; 3-inch chamber; 26-inch, 28-inch barrel; Modified, Full choke; gold bead front sight; black-finish hardwood pistol-grip stock, semi-beavertail forend; auto ejector; satin nickel frame; blued barrel. Introduced 1992.

Perf.: $90　**Exc.:** $75　**VGood:** $60

HARRINGTON & RICHARDSON TOPPER JUNIOR 098

As above except 22-inch barrel, 20 ga. (Mod.), .410-bore (Full), 12-1/2-inch length of pull)

HARRINGTON & RICHARDSON TOPPER MODEL 098 CLASSIC YOUTH

Same specs as Topper Model 098 except 20-, 28-ga. (2-3/4-inch), .410; 3-inch chamber; Modified, Full choke; 22-inch barrel; cut-checkered American black

walnut pistol-grip stock, forend; ventilated rubber recoil pad with white line spacers; blued barrel, blued frame. Introduced 1992; still produced.

Perf.: $115　**Exc.:** $90　**VGood:** $65

HARRINGTON & RICHARDSON TOPPER MODEL 098 DELUXE

Same specs as Topper Model 098 except 12-ga.; 3-1/2-inch chamber; 28-inch barrel; Modified choke tube. Introduced 1992; still in production.

Perf.: $105　**Exc.:** $85　**VGood:** $60

HARRINGTON & RICHARDSON TOPPER MODEL 098 DELUXE RIFLED SLUG GUN

Same specs as Topper Model 098 except 12-ga.; 3-inch chamber; 28-inch fully rifled and ported barrel; ramp front sight, fully adjustable rear; black-finish hardwood pistol-grip stock, semi-beavertail forend; barrel twist is 1:35-inch; nickel-plated frame; blued barrel. Introduced 1995; still produced.

Perf.: $150　**Exc.:** $125　**VGood:** $100

HARRINGTON & RICHARDSON TOPPER MODEL 098 JUNIOR

Same specs as Topper Model 098 except 20-ga., .410; 22-inch barrel; Modified, Full choke; stock dimensions for smaller shooters. Introduced 1992; still in production.

Perf.: $90　**Exc.:** $75　**VGood:** $60

Harrington & Richardson Topper Model 158

Harrington & Richardson Topper Model 198 Deluxe

Harrington & Richardson Topper Model 490 Greenwing

Harrington & Richardson Topper Model 590 Junior

Hatfield Uplander

Heym Model 55F

HARRINGTON & RICHARDSON TOPPER MODEL 148
Single barrel; sidelever; exposed hammer; takedown; 12-, 16-, 20-ga., .410; 28-inch, 30-inch, 32-inch, 36-inch barrel; Full choke; uncheckered American walnut pistol-grip stock, forearm; recoil pad. Introduced 1958; discontinued 1961.
Exc.: $100　**VGood:** $75　**Good:** $60

HARRINGTON & RICHARDSON TOPPER MODEL 158
Single barrel; sidelever; exposed hammer; takedown; 12-, 16-, 20-ga., .410; 28-inch, 30-inch, 32-inch, 36-inch barrel; Full, Modified choke; bead front sight; uncheckered hardwood pistol-grip stock, forearm; recoil pad; improved version of Topper Model 148. Introduced 1962; discontinued 1985.
Perf.: $90　**Exc.:** $75　**VGood:** $60

HARRINGTON & RICHARDSON TOPPER MODEL 188 DELUXE
Single barrel; sidelever; exposed hammer; takedown; .410; 28-inch, 30-inch, 32-inch, 36-inch barrels; Full choke; uncheckered American walnut pistol-grip stock, forearm finished with black, red, yellow, blue, green, pink or purple lacquer; recoil pad; chrome-plated frame. Introduced 1958; discontinued 1961.
Exc.: $125　**VGood:** $100　**Good:** $75

HARRINGTON & RICHARDSON TOPPER MODEL 198 DELUXE
Single barrel; sidelever; exposed hammer; takedown; 20-ga., .410; 28-inch barrel; Full, Modified choke; uncheckered American walnut pistol-grip stock, forearm finished with black lacquer; chrome-plated frame. Introduced 1962; discontinued 1985.
Perf.: $90　**Exc.:** $75　**VGood:** $60

HARRINGTON & RICHARDSON TOPPER MODEL 480 JUNIOR
Single barrel; top-lever break-open; exposed hammer; .410; 26-inch barrel; Modified, Full choke; bead front sight; youth-sized uncheckered American walnut pistol-grip stock, forearm; automatic ejector. Introduced 1958; discontinued 1960.
Exc.: $70　**VGood:** $60　**Good:** $50

HARRINGTON & RICHARDSON TOPPER MODEL 488 DELUXE
Single barrel; top-lever break-open; exposed hammer; 12-, 16-, 20-ga., .410; 26-inch, 28-inch, 30-inch, 32-inch barrel; Modified, Full choke; bead front sight; uncheckered American walnut pistol-grip stock, forearm with black-lacquer finish; recoil pad; automatic ejector; chrome-plated frame. Introduced 1946; discontinued 1957.
Exc.: $75　**VGood:** $65　**Good:** $55

HARRINGTON & RICHARDSON TOPPER MODEL 490 JUNIOR
Single shot; sidelever break-open; takedown; 20-, 28-ga., .410; 26-inch barrel; Modified (20-, 28-ga.), Full (.410) choke; weighs 5 lbs.; bead front sight; youth-sized uncheckered hardwood pistol-grip stock, forend; recoil pad. Introduced 1962; discontinued 1985.
Perf.: $90　**Exc.:** $75　**VGood:** $60

HARRINGTON & RICHARDSON TOPPER MODEL 490 GREENWING
Same specs as Topper Model 490 Junior except gold-finished trigger; inscription on frame; polished blued finish. Discontinued 1984.
Perf.: $100　**Exc.:** $85　**VGood:** $75

HARRINGTON & RICHARDSON TOPPER MODEL 580 JUNIOR
Single barrel; top-lever break-open; exposed hammer; takedown; 12-, 16-, 20-ga., .410; 26-inch, 28-inch, 30-inch, 32-inch barrel; Modified, Full choke; bead front sight; uncheckered American walnut pistol-grip stock, forearm with black, red, yellow, blue, green, pink or purple lacquer finish; automatic ejector. Introduced 1958; discontinued 1961.
Exc.: $120　**VGood:** $90　**Good:** $70

HARRINGTON & RICHARDSON TOPPER MODEL 590 JUNIOR
Single shot; sidelever break-open; exposed hammer; takedown; 20-, 28-ga., .410; 26-inch barrel; Modified (20-, 28-ga.), Full (.410) choke; weighs 5 lbs.; bead front sight; youth-sized uncheckered hardwood pistol-grip stock, forearm with black lacquer finish; chrome-plated frame; recoil pad. Introduced 1962; discontinued 1963.
Exc.: $75　**VGood:** $60　**Good:** $50

HATFIELD UPLANDER
Side-by-side; boxlock; 20-ga.; 3-inch chambers; 26-inch Improved Cylinder/Modified barrel; weighs 5-3/4 lbs.; fancy maple straight English-style stock, splinter forend; double locking underlug; single non-selective trigger; color case-hardened frame; half-coverage hand-engraved action with French gray finish; comes with English-style oxblood leather luggage case with billiard felt interior. Made in eight grades with various levels of engraving, inlays and fancy wood. Introduced 1988; dropped 1996. Production resumed of some models in 2003.

Grade I		
Perf.: $1700	**Exc.:** $1500	**VGood:** $1325
Grade II		
Perf.: $2650	**Exc.:** $2250	**VGood:** $1825
Grade III		
Perf.: $2350	**Exc.:** $1900	**VGood:** $1575
Grade IV		
Perf.: $3995	**Exc.:** $3575	**VGood:** $2900
Grade V		
Perf.: $4700	**Exc.:** $4400	**VGood:** $3350
Grade VI		
Perf.: $5200	**Exc.:** $4850	**VGood:** $3700
Grade VII		
Perf.: $5250	**Exc.:** $4895	**VGood:** $3750
Grade VIII		
Perf.: $12,000	**Exc.:** $9750	**VGood:** $8750

HATFIELD'S UPLANDER 28
Side-by-side; boxlock; 28 ga.; 26-inch monobloc barrels; matte rib; small scalloped frame; extractors; SST or DT; checkered Circassian walnut straight grip stock; splinter forend; case colored frame; weighs 4 lbs. Introduced 2004.
Perf.: $1350　**Exc.:** $1200　**VGood:** $1000

HEYM MODEL 55 F
Over/under; boxlock; 12-, 16-, 20-ga.; 28-inch barrel; hand-checkered European walnut stock; Kersten double crossbolt; double underlugs; Arabesque or hunting engraving; numerous options at added cost. Introduced 1979; discontinued 1992.
Perf.: $5100　**Exc.:** $4525　**VGood:** $3950

HEYM MODEL 55 SS
Same specs as Model 55 F except sidelock action; large engraving scenes. No longer in production.
Perf.: $4800　**Exc.:** $3825　**VGood:** $3300

HEYM MODEL 200
Over/under; boxlock; 20-ga.; 3-inch chambers; 28-inch vent rib barrels; light engraving; no longer imported.
Perf.: $895　**Exc.:** $795　**VGood:** $700

HHF (HUGLU) MODEL 101 B 12 AT-DT

Over/under; boxlock; 12-ga.; 3-inch chambers; combo set with 30-inch and 32-inch barrels; fixed chokes or choke tubes; 16mm rib; weighs about 8 lbs.; Circassian walnut Monte Carlo stock to trap dimensions; palm swell grip; recoil pad; single selective trigger; manual safety; automatic ejectors or extractors; silvered frame with 50 percent engraving coverage. Many custom features available. Made in Turkey. Introduced 1995; still imported.

With extractors
| Perf.: $2000 | Exc.: $1750 | VGood: $1500 |

With ejectors
| Perf.: $2100 | Exc.: $1850 | VGood: $1600 |

HHF MODEL 101 B 12 ST TRAP

Same specs as Model 101 B 12 AT-DT except 30-inch over/under barrels. Made in Turkey. Introduced 1995; still imported.

With extractors
| Perf.: $950 | Exc.: $750 | VGood: $600 |

With ejectors
| Perf.: $1025 | Exc.: $825 | VGood: $675 |

HHF (HUGLU) MODEL 103 B 12 ST

Over/under boxlock; 12-, 20-, 28-ga., .410; 3-inch chambers; 28-inch barrels; choke tubes or fixed chokes; weighs about 7-1/2 lbs.; Circassian walnut stock; dummy sideplates; double triggers; manual safety; extractors; 80- percent engraving coverage, inlaid animals on blackened sideplates. Made in Turkey. Introduced 1995; still imported.

12-, 20-ga., fixed chokes
| Perf.: $900 | Exc.: $725 | VGood: $550 |

12-, 20-ga., choke tubes
| Perf.: $950 | Exc.: $775 | VGood: $600 |

28-ga., .410, fixed chokes
| Perf.: $950 | Exc.: $775 | VGood: $600 |

HHF (HUGLU) MODEL 103 C 12 ST

Same specs as Model 103 B 12 ST except 12-, 20-ga.; 3-inch chambers; extractors or ejectors; black receiver with 50- percent engraving coverage. Made in Turkey. Introduced 1995; still imported.

With extractors
| Perf.: $950 | Exc.: $750 | VGood: $600 |

With ejectors
| Perf.: $1025 | Exc.: $825 | VGood: $675 |

HHF (HUGLU) MODEL 103 D 12 ST

Same specs as Model 103 B 12 ST except standard boxlock; 12-, 20-ga.; 3-inch chambers; extractors or ejectors; 80 percent engraving coverage. Made in Turkey. Introduced 1995; still imported.

With extractors
| Perf.: $950 | Exc.: $750 | VGood: $600 |

With ejectors
| Perf.: $1025 | Exc.: $825 | VGood: $675 |

HHF MODEL 103 F 12 ST

Same specs as Model 103 B 12 ST except 12-, 20-ga.; 3-inch chambers; extractors or ejectors; 100- percent engraving coverage. Made in Turkey. Introduced 1995; still imported.

With extractors
| Perf.: $1000 | Exc.: $800 | VGood: $650 |

With ejectors
| Perf.: $1075 | Exc.: $875 | VGood: $725 |

HHF (HUGLU) MODEL 104 A 12 ST

Over/under; boxlock; 12-, 20-, 28-ga., .410; 3-inch chambers; 28-inch barrels; fixed chokes or choke tubes; weighs about 7-1/2 lbs.; Circassian walnut stock with field dimensions; manual safety; extractors or ejectors; double triggers; silvered, engraved receiver with 15- percent engraving coverage. Made in Turkey. Introduced 1995; still imported.

12-, 20-ga., fixed chokes, extractors

HHF Model 103 C 12 ST

Hi-Standard Flite-King Brush

Hi-Standard Flite-King Brush Deluxe

Hi-Standard Flite-King Brush Deluxe (1966)

Hi-Standard Flite-King Deluxe Rib (1966)

| Perf.: $850 | Exc.: $675 | VGood: $500 |

12-, 20-ga., choke tubes, ejectors
| Perf.: $900 | Exc.: $725 | VGood: $550 |

28-ga., .410, fixed chokes, extractors
| Perf.: $900 | Exc.: $725 | VGood: $550 |

HHF (HUGLU) MODEL 200 A 12 ST DOUBLE

Side-by-side; boxlock; 12-, 20-, 28-ga., .410; 3-inch chambers; 28-inch barrels; fixed chokes or choke tubes; weighs about 7-1/2 lbs.; Circassian walnut stock; single selective trigger; extractors; manual safety; silvered receiver with 15 percent engraving coverage. Made in Turkey. Introduced 1995; still imported.

12-, 20-ga.
| Perf.: $950 | Exc.: $750 | VGood: $600 |

28-ga., .410
| Perf.: $1025 | Exc.: $825 | VGood: $675 |

HHF (HUGLU) MODEL 202 A 12 ST

Side-by-side; boxlock; 12-, 20-, 28-ga., .410; 3-inch chambers; 28-inch barrels; fixed chokes or choke tubes; weighs about 7-1/2 lbs.; Circassian walnut stock; double triggers; extractors; manual safety; silvered receiver with 30 percent engraving coverage. Made in Turkey. Introduced 1995; still imported.

12-, 20-ga.
| Perf.: $925 | Exc.: $725 | VGood: $575 |

28-ga., .410
| Perf.: $1000 | Exc.: $800 | VGood: $700 |

HI-STANDARD FLITE-KING BRUSH

Slide action; 12-ga.; 2-3/4-inch chamber; 4-shot magazine; 18-inch, 20-inch Cylinder-bore barrel; rifle sights; unchecked walnut pistol-grip stock, slide handle. Introduced 1962; discontinued 1964.

| Exc.: $160 | VGood: $150 | Good: $140 |

HI-STANDARD FLITE-KING BRUSH DELUXE

Same specs as Flite-King Brush except 20-inch Cylinder barrel; adjustable peep rear sight; checkered pistol grip, fluted slide handle; recoil pad; sling swivels; sling. Introduced 1964; discontinued 1966.

| Exc.: $190 | VGood: $160 | Good: $150 |

HI-STANDARD FLITE-KING BRUSH (1966)

Slide action; 12-ga.; 2-3/4-inch chamber; 5-shot magazine; 20-inch Cylinder barrel; rifle sights; checkered American walnut pistol-grip stock, slide handle; recoil pad. General specs follow Flite-King series dropped in 1966, except for damascened bolt, new checkering design. Introduced 1966; discontinued 1975.

| Perf.: $195 | Exc.: $170 | VGood: $150 |

HI-STANDARD FLITE-KING BRUSH DELUXE (1966)

Same specs as Flite-King Brush (1966) except adjustable peep rear sight; sling swivels; sling. Introduced 1966; discontinued 1975.

| Perf.: $270 | Exc.: $200 | VGood: $180 |

HI-STANDARD FLITE-KING DELUXE RIB

Slide action; 12-, 16-, 20-, 28-ga., .410; 2-3/4-inch (12-ga.), 3-inch chamber; 3- (20-ga.), 4-shot magazine; 28-inch Full or Modified, 30-inch Full barrel; vent rib; checkered walnut pistol-grip stock, slide handle. Introduced 1961; discontinued 1966. 50% premium for small gauges.

| Exc.: $215 | VGood: $195 | Good: $160 |

HI-STANDARD FLITE-KING DELUXE (1966)

Slide action; 12-, 20-, 28-ga., .410; 2-3/4-inch (12-ga.), 3-inch chamber; 5-shot magazine; 26-inch Improved Cylinder, 27-inch adjustable choke, 28-inch

Hi-Standard Flite-King
Deluxe (1966)

Hi-Standard Flite-King Deluxe 28 (1966)

Hi-Standard Flite-King Deluxe Rib 12

Hi-Standard Flite-King Field

Hi-Standard Flite-King 410 Field
Deluxe (1966)

Hi-Standard Flite-King Special

Hi-Standard Flite-King Trophy

Hi-Standard Shadow Auto

Hi-Standard Shadow Indy

Modified or Full, 30-inch Full choke barrel; checkered
American walnut pistol-grip stock, slide handle; recoil
pad. General specs follow Flite-King series dropped in
1966, except for damascened bolt, new checkering
design. Introduced 1966; discontinued
1975. 50% premium for small gauges.

Fixed choke		
Perf.: $195	**Exc.:** $175	**VGood:** $150
Adjustable choke		
Perf.: $200	**Exc.:** $180	**VGood:** $160

HI-STANDARD FLITE-KING DELUXE RIB (1966)

Same specs as Flite-King Deluxe (1966) except
27-inch adjustable choke, 28-inch Modified or Full,
30-inch Full choke barrel; vent rib. General specs
follow Flite-King series dropped in 1966, except for
damascened bolt, new checkering design.
Introduced 1966; discontinued 1975. 50% premium
for small gauges.

Fixed choke		
Perf.: $210	**Exc.:** $180	**VGood:** $150
Adjustable choke		
Perf.: $220	**Exc.:** $190	**VGood:** $160

HI-STANDARD FLITE-KING DELUXE SKEET (1966)

Same specs as Flite-King Deluxe (1966) except 26-
inch vent-rib barrel; Skeet choke; optional recoil pad.
General specs follow Flite-King series dropped 1966,
except for damascened bolt, new checkering design.
Introduced 1966; discontinued 1975. 50% premium
for small gauges.

Perf.: $270	**Exc.:** $200	**VGood:** $175

HI-STANDARD FLITE-KING DELUXE TRAP (1966)

Same specs as Flite-King Deluxe (1966) except 12-
ga.; 2-3/4-inch chamber; 30-inch Full choke barrel;
vent rib; trap-style checkered walnut pistol-grip
stock, slide handle. General specs follow Flite-King
series dropped in 1966, except for damascened
bolt, new checkering design. Introduced 1966;
discontinued 1975.

Perf.: $270	**Exc.:** $200	**VGood:** $175

HI-STANDARD FLITE-KING FIELD

Slide action; 12-, 16-, 20-, 28-ga., .410; 2-3/4-inch
(12-ga.), 3-inch chamber; 3- (20-ga.), 4-shot magazine;
26-inch Improved Cylinder, 28-inch Modified or
Full, 30-inch Full barrel; uncheckered walnut pistol-
grip stock, grooved slide handle. Introduced 1960;
discontinued 1966. 50% premium for small gauges.

Exc.: $165	**VGood:** $150	**Good:** $140

HI-STANDARD FLITE-KING SKEET

Same specs as Flite-King Field except 12-, 20-, 28-
ga., .410; 2-3/4-inch (12-ga.), 3-inch chamber; 26-inch
Skeet-choked barrel; vent rib; checkered walnut
pistol-grip stock, slide handle. Introduced 1962;
discontinued 1966. 50% premium for small gauges.

Exc.: $250	**VGood:** $225	**Good:** $200

Add 35 percent to above prices for 28 ga. or .410
bore.

HI-STANDARD FLITE-KING SPECIAL

Same specs as Flite-King Field except 12-, 16-,
20-, 28-ga.; 2-3/4-inch (12-ga.), 3-inch chamber;
27-inch adjustable choke barrel. Introduced 1960;
discontinued 1966. 50% premium for 28 ga.

Exc.: $165	**VGood:** $150	**Good:** $140

HI-STANDARD FLITE-KING TRAP

Same specs as Flite-King Field except 12-ga.; 2-3/4-
inch chamber; 4-shot magazine; 30-inch barrel; Full
choke; vent rib; trap-style checkered walnut pistol-
grip stock, slide handle; recoil pad. Introduced 1962;
discontinued 1966.

Exc.: $190	**VGood:** $150	**Good:** $135

HI-STANDARD FLITE-KING TROPHY

Same specs as Flite-King Field except Slide-action;
12-, 16-, 20-, 28-ga.; 2-3/4-inch (12-ga.), 3-inch
chamber; 3- (20-ga.), 4-shot magazine; 27-inch
adjustable choke, 28-inch Modified or Full barrel
(20-ga.); vent rib; checkered walnut pistol-grip stock,
slide handle. Introduced 1960; discontinued 1966.
50% premium for 28 ga.

Exc.: $190	**VGood:** $180	**Good:** $170

HI-STANDARD SHADOW AUTO

Gas-operated autoloader; 12-, 20-ga.; 2-3/4-inch,
3-inch chamber; 3- (3-inch), 4-shot magazine; 26-
inch Improved Cylinder or Skeet, 28-inch Modified,
Improved Modified or Full, 30-inch Trap or Full
barrel; magnum available only with 30-inch barrel;
checkered walnut pistol-grip stock, forearm. Made in
Japan. Introduced 1974; discontinued 1975.

Perf.: $375	**Exc.:** $345	**VGood:** $330

HI-STANDARD SHADOW INDY

Over/under; boxlock; 12-ga.; 2-3/4-inch chamber;
27-1/2-inch Skeet, 29-3/4-inch Improved Modified/
Full or Full/Full barrels; Airflow vent rib; skip-
checkered walnut pistol-grip stock, ventilated
forearm; selective auto ejectors; selective single
trigger; engraved receiver; recoil pad. Made in Japan.
Introduced 1974; discontinued 1975.

Perf.: $850	**Exc.:** $800	**VGood:** $760

HI-STANDARD SHADOW SEVEN

Same specs as Shadow Indy except 27-1/2-inch Improved Cylinder/Modified or Modified/Full barrels; vent rib; skip-checkered walnut pistol-grip stock, forearm; no recoil pad. Made in Japan. Introduced 1974; discontinued 1975.

Perf.: $700   **Exc.:** $640   **VGood:** $550

HI-STANDARD SUPERMATIC DEER

Autoloader; 12-ga.; 4-shot magazine; 22-inch Cylinder barrel; rifle sights; checkered American walnut stock, forearm; recoil pad. Introduced 1965; discontinued 1965.

Exc.: $225   **VGood:** $205   **Good:** $185

HI-STANDARD SUPERMATIC DELUXE

Autoloader; 12-, 20-ga.; 2-3/4-inch (12-ga.), 3-inch chamber; 3- (20-ga.), 4-shot magazine; 27-inch adjustable-choke barrel (discontinued 1970), 26-inch Improved, 28-inch Modified or Full, 30-inch Full choke barrels; checkered American walnut pistol-grip stock, forearm; recoil pad. Differs from original Supermatic; has new checkering, damascened bolt. Introduced 1966; discontinued 1975. This gun has never received the credit it deserves; although heavy, it was America's first successful gas-operated sporting arm.

Fixed choke		
Perf.: $240	**Exc.:** $225	**VGood:** $195

Adjustable choke		
Perf.: $255	**Exc.:** $240	**VGood:** $215

HI-STANDARD SUPERMATIC DELUXE RIB

Same specs as Supermatic Deluxe except 28-inch Modified or Full, 30-inch Full choke barrels; vent rib. Introduced 1966; discontinued 1975.

Fixed choke		
Perf.: $260	**Exc.:** $245	**VGood:** $215

Adjustable choke		
Perf.: $275	**Exc.:** $260	**VGood:** $230

HI-STANDARD SUPERMATIC DUCK

Autoloader; 12-ga.; 3-inch chamber; 3-shot magazine; 30-inch Full-choke barrel; uncheckered American walnut pistol-grip stock, forearm; recoil pad. Introduced 1961; discontinued 1966.

Exc.: $265   **VGood:** $235   **Good:** $190

HI-STANDARD SUPERMATIC DUCK DELUXE

Same specs as Supermatic Duck except checkered American walnut pistol-grip stock, forearm. Introduced 1966; discontinued 1975.

Perf.: $280   **Exc.:** $250   **VGood:** $205

HI-STANDARD SUPERMATIC DUCK RIB

Same specs as Supermatic Duck except vent rib. Introduced 1961; discontinued 1966.

Exc.: $285   **VGood:** $255   **Good:** $210

HI-STANDARD SUPERMATIC DUCK RIB DELUXE

Same specs as Supermatic Duck Rib except vent rib; checkered American walnut pistol-grip stock, forearm. Introduced 1966; discontinued 1975.

Perf.: $295   **Exc.:** $275   **VGood:** $225

HI-STANDARD SUPERMATIC FIELD

Gas-operated autoloader; 12-, 20-ga.; 2-3/4-inch (12-ga.), 3-inch chamber; 3- (20-ga.), 4-shot magazine; 26-inch Improved, 28-inch Modified or Full, 30-inch Full barrel; uncheckered American walnut pistol-grip stock, forearm. Introduced 1960; discontinued 1966.

Exc.: $200   **VGood:** $190   **Good:** $180
Add 5 percent to above prices for 20 gauge.

Hi-Standard Shadow Seven

Hi-Standard Supermatic Deer

Hi-Standard Supermatic Deluxe

Hi-Standard Supermatic Duck

Hi-Standard Supermatic Duck Rib

Hi-Standard Supermatic Field

Hi-Standard Supermatic Skeet

Hi-Standard Supermatic Special

Hi-Standard Supermatic Trap

HI-STANDARD SUPERMATIC SKEET

Autoloader; 12-, 20-ga.; 2-3/4-inch (12-ga.), 3-inch chamber; 3- (20-ga.), 4-shot magazine; 26-inch vent-rib barrel; Skeet choke; uncheckered Skeet-style American walnut pistol-grip stock, forearm; recoil pad. Introduced 1962; discontinued 1966.

Exc.: $260   **VGood:** $230   **Good:** $240

HI-STANDARD SUPERMATIC SKEET DELUXE

Same specs as Supermatic Skeet except checkered Skeet-style American walnut pistol-grip stock, forearm. Introduced 1966; discontinued 1975.

Perf.: $310   **Exc.:** $240   **VGood:** $250

HI-STANDARD SUPERMATIC SPECIAL

Autoloader; 12-, 20-ga.; 2-3/4-inch (12-ga.), 3-inch chamber; 3- (20-ga.), 4-shot magazine; 27-inch barrel; adjustable choke; uncheckered American walnut pistol-grip stock, forearm. Introduced 1960; discontinued 1966.

Exc.: $180   **VGood:** $145   **Good:** $125

HI-STANDARD SUPERMATIC TRAP

Autoloader; 12-ga.; 4-shot magazine; 30-inch Full barrel; vent rib; trap-style uncheckered American walnut pistol-grip stock, forearm; recoil pad. Introduced 1962; discontinued 1966.

Exc.: $240   **VGood:** $200   **Good:** $150

Hi-Standard Supermatic Trap Deluxe

Hi-Standard Supermatic Trophy

Hoenig Rotary Round Action Game Gun

Holland & Holland Badminton

Holland & Holland Dominion Game Gun

Holland & Holland Royal Game Gun

HI-STANDARD SUPERMATIC TRAP DELUXE

Same specs as Supermatic Trap except trap-style checkered American walnut pistol-grip stock, forearm. Introduced 1966; discontinued 1975.

Perf.: $250   **Exc.:** $235   **VGood:** $215

HI-STANDARD SUPERMATIC TROPHY

Autoloader; 12-, 20-ga.; 2-3/4-inch (12-ga.), 3-inch chamber; 3- (20-ga.), 4-shot magazine; 27-inch adjustable choke barrel; vent rib; checkered American walnut pistol-grip stock, forearm; recoil pad. Introduced 1961; discontinued 1966.

Exc.: $235   **VGood:** $210   **Good:** $195

HOENIG ROTARY ROUND ACTION GAME GUN

Gauge: 28. Barrel: 26-inch, 28-inch, solid tapered rib. Weight: 6 lbs. Stock: English walnut. Features: Round action opens by rotating barrels, pulling forward. Inertia extractor, rotary safety blocks strikers. Simple takedown without removing forend. Elegance and class of guns of yesteryear. Made in U.S.A. by George Hoenig. Price: $19,995

HOLLAND & HOLLAND

NOTE: 20-gauge versions are valued at 20 percent more than indicated prices; 28-gauge, 40 percent additional; .410 at 60 percent higher.

HOLLAND & HOLLAND BADMINTON

Side-by-side; sidelock; hammerless; 12-, 16-, 20-, 28-ga.; barrel lengths, chokes to customer specs; hand-checkered straight-grip or pistol-grip stock, forearm; non-self-opening action; auto ejectors; double triggers or single trigger; engraving. Introduced 1902; no longer in production.

Double triggers		
Perf.: $10,000	**Exc.:** $8000	**VGood:** $7000
Single trigger		
Perf.: $11,000	**Exc.:** $9000	**VGood:** $8000

HOLLAND & HOLLAND BADMINTON GAME GUN

Same specs as Badminton except only 12-, 20-ga. Discontinued 1988.

Double trigger		
Perf.: $20,000	**Exc.:** $15,000	**VGood:** $12,000
Single trigger		
Perf.: $22,000	**Exc.:** $17,000	**VGood:** $14,000

HOLLAND & HOLLAND CAVALIER

Side-by-side; boxlock; 12-, 20-, 28-ga.; 28-inch, 30-inch barrels; any standard choke combo; hand-checkered European walnut pistol-grip or straight-grip stock, forearm; double trigger; auto ejectors; engraving; color case-hardened receiver. Discontinued 1993.

Perf.: $9500   **Exc.:** $7750   **VGood:** $6350
Add about 10 percent to above prices for 20 ga.
Add approximately 10 percent to above prices for 28 ga.

HOLLAND & HOLLAND CAVALIER DELUXE

Same specs as Cavalier except better engraving and select wood. Discontinued 1993.

Perf.: $10,000   **Exc.:** $8000   **VGood:** $7000

HOLLAND & HOLLAND DOMINION GAME GUN

Side-by-side; sidelock; hammerless; 12-, 16-, 20-ga.; 25-inch, 28-inch, 30-inch barrels; choked to customer's specs; hand-checkered European walnut straight-grip stock, forearm; double triggers; automatic ejectors. Introduced 1935; discontinued 1989.

Perf.: $6750   **Exc.:** $6150   **VGood:** $5650
Add approximately 20 percent to above prices for 20 ga.

HOLLAND & HOLLAND NORTHWOOD

Side-by-side; boxlock; 12-, 16-, 20-, 28-ga.; 28-inch, 30-inch barrels; any standard choke combo; hand-checkered European walnut pistol-grip stock or straight-grip stock, forearm; double triggers; auto ejectors; engraving; color case-hardened receiver. Discontinued 1993.

Perf.: $6000   **Exc.:** $4800   **VGood:** $4400
Add approximately 10 percent to above prices for 20 ga.
Add approximately 20 percent for 28 ga.

HOLLAND & HOLLAND NORTHWOOD DELUXE

Same specs as Northwood except better engraving and select wood. Discontinued 1993.

Perf.: $7000   **Exc.:** $5500   **VGood:** $4500
Add approximately 10 percent to above prices for 20 ga.
Add approximately 20 percent for 28 ga.

HOLLAND & HOLLAND NORTHWOOD GAME MODEL

Side-by-side; Anson & Deeley boxlock; 12-, 16-, 20-, 28-ga.; 28-inch barrels; any standard choke combo; hand-checkered European walnut straight-grip or pistol-grip stock, forearm; double triggers, automatic ejectors. Introduced prior to World War II; discontinued late 1960s.

Perf.: $7000   **Exc.:** $5500   **VGood:** $4500

HOLLAND & HOLLAND NORTHWOOD PIGEON MODEL

Same specs as Northwood Game Model except 12-, 16-, 20-ga.; more engraving. No longer in production.

Perf.: $8000   **Exc.:** $6500   **VGood:** $5000

HOLLAND & HOLLAND NORTHWOOD WILDFOWL MODEL

Same specs as Northwood Game Model except 12-ga.; 3-inch chamber; 30-inch barrels. No longer in production.

Perf.: $8000   **Exc.:** $6500   **VGood:** $5000

HOLLAND & HOLLAND RIVIERA

Side-by-side; sidelock; hammerless; 12-, 16-, 20-, 28-ga.; barrel lengths, chokes to customer specs; hand-checkered straight-grip or pistol-grip stock, forearm; non-self-opening action; auto ejectors; double triggers; two interchangeable barrels; engraving. Introduced 1945; discontinued 1967.

12 Gauge		
Exc.: $11,000	**VGood:** $9300	**Good:** $7500
20 Gauge		
Exc.: $13,000	**VGood:** $11,500	**Good:** $9500

HOLLAND & HOLLAND ROYAL

Side-by-side; sidelock; hammerless; 12-, 16-, 20-, 28-ga.; barrel lengths, chokes to customer's specs; hand-checkered straight-grip or pistol-grip stock, forearm; non-self-opening action; automatic ejectors; double triggers or single non-selective trigger; English engraving. Introduced 1885; no longer in production.

Double triggers		
Exc.: $20,000	**VGood:** $17,500	**Good:** $7000
Single trigger		
Exc.: $21,500	**VGood:** $18,500	**Good:** $8000

HOLLAND & HOLLAND ROYAL GAME GUN

Side-by-side; sidelock; hammerless; 12-, 16-, 20-, 28-ga.; .410; barrel lengths, chokes to customer's specs; hand-checkered straight-grip or pistol-grip stock, forearm; self-opening action; double triggers or single non-selective trigger; ornate engraving. Introduced 1922; still in production.

Double triggers		
Perf.: $48,000	**Exc.:** $27,000	**VGood:** $19,000
Single trigger		
Perf.: $48,000	**Exc.:** $30,000	**VGood:** $22,000
Add approximately 10 percent for 28 ga. or .410 bore
Add about $3000 for vent. rib.

HOLLAND & HOLLAND ROYAL GAME GUN DELUXE

Same specs as Royal Game Gun except top-of-the-line model with better engraving and wood. Still in production.

Double triggers		
Perf.: $56,900	**Exc.:** $35,000	**VGood:** $20,000
Single trigger		
Perf.: $56,900	**Exc.:** $39,000	**VGood:** $24,000

HOLLAND & HOLLAND ROYAL OVER/UNDER

Over/under; hand-detachable sidelocks; hammerless; 12-ga.; barrel lengths, chokes to customer's specs; hand-checkered European walnut straight-grip stock, forearm; automatic ejectors; double triggers or single trigger. Introduced 1925; discontinued 1950.

HOLLAND & HOLLAND ROYAL OVER/UNDER (NEW MODEL)

Same specs as Royal Over/Under except narrower, improved action. Introduced 1951; discontinued 1965.

HOLLAND & HOLLAND ROYAL OVER/UNDER GAME GUN

Over/under; hand-detachable sidelocks; hammerless; 12-, 20-ga.; 2-3/4-inch chambers; 25-inch to 30-inch barrels; any standard choke combo; select hand-checkered walnut straight-grip or pistol-grip stock, forearm; automatic ejectors; single or double triggers; engraved color case-hardened receiver. Introduced 1992; still in production.

Double triggers		
Perf.: $60,375	**Exc.:** $35,000	**VGood:** $24,000
Single trigger		
Perf.: $60,375	**Exc.:** $39,000	**VGood:** $28,000

HOLLAND & HOLLAND SINGLE BARREL TRAP

Single barrel; boxlock; 12-ga.; 30-inch, 32-inch barrel; Full choke; vent rib; European walnut Monte Carlo pistol-grip stock, forearm; auto ejector; recoil pad. Discontinued 1992.

Perf.: $14,500 **Exc.:** $12,000 **VGood:** $10,000

HOLLAND & HOLLAND SPORTING OVER/UNDER

Blitz action; 12-, 20-ga.; 2-3/4-inch chambers; 28-inch to 32-inch barrels; screw-in choke tubes; hand-checkered European walnut straight-grip or pistol-grip stock, forearm; single selective trigger; auto ejectors. Introduced 1993; still in production.

Perf.: $25,000 **Exc.:** $22,000 **VGood:** $16,000

HOLLAND & HOLLAND SPORTING OVER/UNDER DELUXE

Same specs as Sporting Over/Under except better engraving and select wood. Introduced 1993; still in production.

Perf.: $34,775 **Exc.:** $23,000 **VGood:** $18,000

HOLLAND & HOLLAND SUPER TRAP

Single barrel; Anson & Deeley boxlock; 12-ga.; 30-inch, 32-inch barrel; Extra-Full choke; European walnut Monte Carlo stock, full beavertail forearm; automatic ejector; no safety; recoil pad. Made in three grades with varying types of engraving and wood. Introduced prior to World War II; discontinued late 1960s.

Standard Grade		
Perf.: $4500	**Exc.:** $4000	**VGood:** $3500
Deluxe Grade		
Perf.: $7500	**Exc.:** $6000	**VGood:** $4500
Exhibition Grade		
Perf.: $10,250	**Exc.:** $8500	**VGood:** $7000

HUNTER FULTON

Side-by-side; boxlock; hammerless; 12-, 16-, 20-ga., .410; 26-inch to 32-inch barrels; standard choke combos; walnut stock; hand-checkered pistol grip, forearm; double triggers or non-selective

Holland & Holland Royal Over/Under

Hunter Fulton

Hunter Special

IGA Condor O/U

IGA Reuna Single Barrel

single trigger. Introduced 1920; discontinued 1948. Made by Hunter Arms Company, Fulton, New York. Considerable premium for .410.

Double triggers		
Exc.: $500	**VGood:** $390	**Good:** $295
Single trigger		
Exc.: $600	**VGood:** $425	**Good:** $325

HUNTER SPECIAL

Side-by-side; boxlock; hammerless; 12-, 16-, 20-ga.; 26-inch to 30-inch barrels; standard choke combos; hand-checkered walnut pistol-grip stock, forearm; extractors. Introduced 1920; discontinued 1948.

Double triggers		
Exc.: $525	**VGood:** $425	**Good:** $325
Single trigger		
Exc.: $625	**VGood:** $525	**Good:** $425

IGA COACH MODEL

Side-by-side; 12-, 20-ga., .410; 2-3/4-inch (12-, 20-ga.), 3-inch (.410) chambers; 20-inch barrels; Improved Cylinder/ Modified chokes; solid matted rib; oil-finished hand-checkered Brazilian hardwood pistol grip stock, forend; extractors; auto safety; double triggers. Made in Brazil. Introduced 1983; still imported by Stoeger.

Perf.: $240 **Exc.:** $170 **VGood:** $135

IGA CONDOR O/U

Over/under; boxlock; 12-, 20-ga.; 3-inch chambers; 26-inch. 28-inch barrels; Improved Cylinder/Modified, Modified/Full choke tubes; vent top rib; weighs 7 lbs.; oil-finished checkered Brazilian hardwood pistol-grip stock, forend; manual safety; single trigger; extractors. Made in Brazil. Introduced 1983.

Perf.: $280 **Exc.:** $225 **VGood:** $150

IGA CONDOR I

Same specs as the Condor except single trigger, deluxe checkered walnut stock; vent. rib; separated barrels; choke tubes.

Perf.: $295 **Exc.:** $250 **VGood:** $175

IGA CONDOR II

Same specs as the Condor except double triggers, molded buttplate. Made in Brazil. Introduced 1983; still imported by Stoeger.

Perf.: $295 **Exc.:** $250 **VGood:** $175

IGA CONDOR I SPECIAL

Similar to Condor I, except has matte nickel finish, oil finished hardwood stock and forearm. Importation began 2002.

Perf.: $355 **Exc.:** $300 **VGood:** $240

IGA CONDOR SUPREME

Same specs as the Condor except automatic ejectors. Made in Brazil. Introduced 1983; still imported by Stoeger.

Perf.: $395 **Exc.:** $250 **VGood:** $195

IGA CONDOR SUPREME DELUXE

Same specs. as the Condor Supreme, except high polish blue; gold SST. Importation began 2000.

Perf.: $355 **Exc.:** $430 **VGood:** $260

IGA HUNTER CLAYS MODEL

Over/under; 12-ga.; single trigger; ejectors; 28-inch barrels; choke tubes; deluxe checkered stock and forearm; gold trigger. Mfg. 1997-99.

Perf.: $495 **Exc.:** $415 **VGood:** $335

IGA TURKEY SERIES

Over/under; 12-ga.; 3-inch chambers; 26-inch barrels; vent. rib; choke tubes; single trigger; ejectors; Advantage camo on wood and metal (except receiver. Produced 1997 to 2000.

Perf.: $415 **Exc.:** $325 **VGood:** $250

IGA WATERFOWL SERIES

Similar to Turkey Series, except has 30-inch barrels; 12-ga.; 3-inch chamber. Produced 1998-2000.

Perf.: $415 **Exc.:** $325 **VGood:** $250

IGA ERA 2000

Over/under; boxlock; 12-ga.; 3-inch chambers; 26-inch, 28-inch barrels; Full, Modified, Improved Cylinder choke tubes; oil-finished hand-checkered Brazilian hardwood pistol grip stock, forend; single trigger; blue finish. Made in Brazil. Introduced 1992; still imported by Stoeger.

Perf.: $385 **Exc.:** $275 **VGood:** $195

IGA REUNA SINGLE BARREL

Single shot; exposed hammer; 12-, 20-ga., .410; 2-3/4-inch (12-ga), 3-inch (20-ga., .410) chamber; 26-inch, 28-inch barrel; Full choke tube; weighs 5-1/4 lbs.; metal bead front sight; Brazilian hardwood

IGA Uplander

Ithaca Mag-10

Ithaca Mag-10 Supreme

Ithaca Model 51

Ithaca Model 51 Deerslayer

Ithaca Model 300

stock; half-cock safety; extractor; blued finish. Made in Brazil. Introduced 1987; still imported by Stoeger.

Perf.: $95   **Exc.:** $70   **VGood:** $60

IGA UPLANDER

Side-by-side; boxlock; 12-, 20-, 28-ga., .410; 2-3/4-inch (12, 20-, 28-ga.), 3-inch (.410) chambers; 26-inch. 28-inch barrels; Improved Cylinder/Modified, Modified/Full, Full/Full (.410) chokes; solid matted rib; oil-finished hand-checkered hardwood pistol-grip stock, forend; extractors; auto safety; double triggers. Made in Brazil. Introduced 1983; still imported by Stoeger.

Perf.: $300   **Exc.:** $235   **VGood:** $185

INDUSTRIAS DANOK RED PRINCE

Side-by-side; 12-ga.; 2-3/4-inch chambers; Modified/Full barrels; medium bead front sight; checkered European walnut straight-grip stock, forend; double triggers; auto ejectors; hand-engraved action. Made in Spain. Introduced 1982 by Toledo Armas; discontinued 1984.

Perf.: $900   **Exc.:** $700   **VGood:** $550

ITHACA MAG-10

Gas-operated autoloader; 10-ga.; 3-1/2-inch chamber; various barrel lengths, chokes; plain or vent rib; walnut stock, forearm; recoil pad. Introduced 1977; discontinued 1986.

With plain barrel		
Perf.: $650	**Exc.:** $520	**VGood:** $440
With vent rib		
Perf.: $700	**Exc.:** $570	**VGood:** $490

ITHACA MAG-10 DELUXE

Same specs as Mag-10 except vent rib; checkered semi-fancy walnut stock, forearm; sling swivels. Introduced 1977; discontinued 1986.

Perf.: $800   **Exc.:** $5725   **VGood:** $575

ITHACA MAG-10 SUPREME

Same specs as Mag-10 except vent rib; checkered fancy walnut stock, forearm; sling swivels. Introduced 1974; discontinued 1986. M

Perf.: $850   **Exc.:** $740   **VGood:** $625

ITHACA MAG-10 ROADBLOCKER

Similar to the standard Mag-10, except 22-inch cylinder bore ribless barrel; parkerized finish. Was marketed to police departments as a tactical shotgun for stopping moving cars.

Perf.: $750   **Exc.:** $625   **VGood:** $575

ITHACA MODEL 51

Gas-operated autoloader; takedown; 12-, 20-ga.; 2-3/4-inch chamber; 3-shot tube magazine; 26-inch Improved or Skeet, 28-inch Full or Modified or Skeet, 30-inch Full barrel; optional vent rib; Raybar front sight; hand-checkered American walnut pistol-grip stock, forend; white spacer on pistol grip; reversible safety; engraved receiver. Introduced 1970; discontinued 1982.

Plain barrel		
Perf.: $260	**Exc.:** $210	**VGood:** $180
Vent rib		
Perf.: $290	**Exc.:** $240	**VGood:** $210

ITHACA MODEL 51A

Same specs as Model 51 except cosmetic improvements. Introduced 1982; discontinued 1986.

Perf.: $260   **Exc.:** $210   **VGood:** $180

ITHACA MODEL 51A DEERSLAYER

Same specs as Model 51 except special 24-inch slug barrel; Raybar front sight, open adjustable rear; sight base grooved for scope mounts. Introduced 1983; discontinued 1984.

Perf.: $355   **Exc.:** $300   **VGood:** $260

ITHACA MODEL 51A MAGNUM

Same specs as Model 51 except 12-ga.; 3-inch chamber. Introduced 1984; discontinued 1985.

Perf.: $375   **Exc.:** $320   **VGood:** $225
Add approximately 10 percent to above prices for vent rib.

ITHACA MODEL 51A MAGNUM WATERFOWLER

Same specs as Model 51 except 12-ga.; 3-inch chamber; vent rib; matte-finished metal; sling; swivels. Introduced 1985; discontinued 1986.

Perf.: $325   **Exc.:** $290   **VGood:** $210
Add approximately $50 for camouflage exterior finish.

ITHACA MODEL 51A PRESENTATION

Same specs as Model 51 except 12-ga.; deluxe checkered walnut pistol-grip stock, forearm; elaborate engraving. Introduced 1984; discontinued 1986.

Perf.: $850   **Exc.:** $775   **VGood:** $675

ITHACA MODEL 51A SUPREME SKEET

Same specs as Model 51 except 12-, 20-ga.; 26-inch Skeet barrel; fancy American walnut Skeet stock. Introduced 1983; discontinued 1986.

Perf.: $465   **Exc.:** $395   **VGood:** $340

ITHACA MODEL 51A SUPREME TRAP

Same specs as Model 51 except 30-inch Full-choke barrel; fancy American walnut trap stock; Monte Carlo stock optional; recoil pad. Introduced 1983; discontinued 1986.

Perf.: $450   **Exc.:** $375   **VGood:** $320

ITHACA MODEL 51 DEERSLAYER

Same specs as Model 51 except 12-, 20-ga.; special 24-inch slug barrel; Raybar front sight, open adjustable rear; sight base grooved for scope. Introduced 1972; discontinued 1983.

Perf.: $335   **Exc.:** $275   **VGood:** $225

ITHACA MODEL 51 FEATHERLIGHT

Same specs as Model 51 except hand-fitted; engraved receiver; weighs 7-1/2 lbs. Introduced 1978; discontinued 1982.

Perf.: $375   **Exc.:** $300   **VGood:** $275

ITHACA MODEL 51 FEATHERLIGHT DELUXE TRAP

Same specs as Model 51 except 28-inch Full or Improved Modified, 30-inch Full or Improved Cylinder barrel; weighs 7-1/2 lbs.; fancy walnut trap-style stock; hand-fitted, engraved receiver. No longer produced.

Perf.: $400   **Exc.:** $315   **VGood:** $270

ITHACA MODEL 51 MAGNUM

Same specs as Model 51 except 12-ga.; 3-inch chamber. Introduced 1970; discontinued 1985.

Plain barrel		
Perf.: $255	**Exc.:** $200	**VGood:** $175
Vent rib		
Perf.: $285	**Exc.:** $235	**VGood:** $200

ITHACA MODEL 51 SKEET

Same specs as Model 51 except 12-, 20-ga.; 26-inch Skeet barrel; vent rib; select Skeet-style stock; recoil pad. Introduced 1970; discontinued 1986.

Perf.: $360   **Exc.:** $310   **VGood:** $260

ITHACA MODEL 51 TRAP

Same specs as Model 51 except 30-inch. 32-inch barrel; Full choke; vent rib; select trap-style stock; recoil pad. Introduced 1970; discontinued 1986.

Perf.: $360   **Exc.:** $310   **VGood:** $260

ITHACA MODEL 51 TURKEY

Same specs as Model 51 except 12-ga.; 3-inch chamber; 26-inch barrel; sling; swivels; matte finish. Introduced 1984; discontinued 1986.

Perf.: $350   **Exc.:** $270   **VGood:** $240

ITHACA MODEL 300

Recoil-operated autoloader; takedown; 12-ga.; 26-inch Improved Cylinder, 28-inch Full or Modified, 30-inch Full-choke barrel; optional vent rib; checkered American walnut pistol-grip stock, fluted forearm; crossbolt safety; automatic magazine cutoff allows changing loads without unloading magazine. Introduced 1969; discontinued 1973.

Plain barrel		
Perf.: $275	**Exc.:** $200	**VGood:** $150
Vent rib		
Perf.: $295	**Exc.:** $220	**VGood:** $170

ITHACA MODEL 900 DELUXE

Recoil-operated autoloader; takedown; 12-, 20-ga.; 25-inch Improved Cylinder; 28-inch Full or Modified, 30-inch Full-choke (12-ga.) vent-rib barrel; hand-checkered American walnut pistol-grip stock, forearm; white spacers on grip cap, buttplate; interchangeable barrels; crossbolt safety; gold-filled engraving on receiver; gold-plated trigger; nameplate inlaid in stock. Introduced 1969; discontinued 1973.

Perf.: $420   **Exc.:** $340   **VGood:** $270

ITHACA MODEL 900 DELUXE SLUG

Same specs as Model 900 Deluxe except 24-inch barrel; rifle sights. Introduced 1969; discontinued 1973.

Perf.: $420   **Exc.:** $340   **VGood:** $270

ITHACA MODEL XL 300

Gas-operated autoloader; 12-, 20-ga.; 26-inch Improved Cylinder or Skeet, 28-inch Full or Modified, 30-inch Full or Modified barrel; optional vent rib; checkered American walnut pistol-grip stock, fluted forearm; self-compensating gas system; reversible safety. Introduced 1973; discontinued 1976.

Perf.: $325   **Exc.:** $250   **VGood:** $200
Add approximately 10 percent to above prices for vent. rib.

ITHACA MODEL XL 900

Gas-operated autoloader; 12-, 20-ga.; 5-shot tube magazine; 26-inch Improved Cylinder or Skeet, 28-inch Full or Modified, 30-inch Full or Improved Cylinder barrels; Bradley-type front sight on target-grade guns; Raybar front sight on vent-rib field guns; checkered walnut-finished stock; self-compensating gas system; reversible safety; action release button. Introduced 1973; discontinued 1978.

Perf.: $350   **Exc.:** $270   **VGood:** $200

Vent rib
Perf.: $370   **Exc.:** $290   **VGood:** $220

Skeet grade
Perf.: $385   **Exc.:** $300   **VGood:** $250

Trap grade
Perf.: $385   **Exc.:** $300   **VGood:** $250

ITHACA MODEL XL 900 SLUG GUN

Same specs as Model XL 900 except 24-inch slug barrel; rifle sights. Introduced 1973; discontinued 1978.

Perf.: $335   **Exc.:** $270   **VGood:** $240

ITHACA MODEL 37

Slide action; hammerless; takedown; 12-, 16-, 20-ga.; 4-shot tube magazine; 26-inch, 28-inch, 30-inch barrel; hand-checkered American walnut pistol-grip stock, slide handle, or uncheckered stock, grooved slide handle. Introduced 1937; discontinued 1986.

Checkered stock
Perf.: $250   **Exc.:** $200   **VGood:** $160

Uncheckered stock
Perf.: $240   **Exc.:** $190   **VGood:** $150

ITHACA MODEL 37 $3000 GRADE

Same specs as Model 37 except custom-built; hand-finished parts; hand-checkered pistol-grip stock, slide handle of select figured walnut; gold-inlaid engraving; recoil pad. Was listed as $1000 Grade prior to World War II. Introduced 1937; discontinued 1967.

Exc.: $4000   **VGood:** $3500   **Good:** $2800

ITHACA MODEL 37 BASIC FEATHERLIGHT

Same specs as Model 37 except plain or vent rib; tung-oil-finished walnut stock, traditional ringtail forend; matte finish on all metal. Introduced 1980; discontinued 1983.

Perf.: $295   **Exc.:** $190   **VGood:** $150

ITHACA MODEL 37D FEATHERLIGHT

Same specs as Model 37 except 12-, 20-ga.; 5-shot magazine; Ithaca Raybar front sight; checkered American walnut pistol-grip stock, beavertail forend;

Ithaca Model XL 900

Ithaca Model 37

Ithaca Model 37 (1983)

Ithaca Model 37 $3000 Grade

Ithaca Model 37 Basic Featherlight

Ithaca Model 37 Deerslayer

Ithaca Model 37DV Featherweight

Ithaca Model 37 English Ultralight

decorated receiver; crossbolt safety; recoil pad. Introduced 1954; discontinued 1981.

Perf.: $300   **Exc.:** $225   **VGood:** $190

ITHACA MODEL 37 DEERSLAYER

Same specs as Model 37 except 20-inch, 26-inch barrel bored for rifled slugs; open rifle-type rear sight, ramp front. Introduced 1969; discontinued 1986.

Perf.: $300   **Exc.:** $240   **VGood:** $195

ITHACA MODEL 37 DELUXE FEATHERLIGHT

Same specs as Model 37 except vent rib; deluxe oil-finished cut-checkered straight-grip stock, slide handle. Introduced 1981; discontinued 1986.

Perf.: $350   **Exc.:** $325   **VGood:** $295

ITHACA MODEL 37DV FEATHERWEIGHT

Same specs as Model 37 except 12-, 20-ga.; 5-shot magazine; Ithaca Raybar front sight; vent rib; checkered American walnut pistol-grip stock, beavertail forend; decorated receiver; crossbolt safety; recoil pad. Introduced 1962; discontinued 1981.

Perf.: $300   **Exc.:** $240   **VGood:** $195

ITHACA MODEL 37 ENGLISH ULTRALIGHT

Same specs as Model 37 except 12-, 20-ga.; 25-inch vent-rib barrel; oil-finished cut-checkered straight-grip stock, slide handle. Introduced 1981; discontinued 1986.

Perf.: $475   **Exc.:** $400   **VGood:** $350

Ithaca Model 37R Deluxe

Ithaca Model 37 Super Deerslayer

Ithaca Model 37T Target Grade

Ithaca Model 37 Deluxe

Ithaca Model 37 Deerslayer II

ITHACA MODEL 37 FEATHERLIGHT
Same specs as Model 37 except 12-, 20-ga.; 5-shot magazine; Ithaca Raybar front sight; checkered American walnut pistol-grip stock; decorated receiver; crossbolt safety. Introduced 1980; discontinued 1986.
Perf.: $300 **Exc.:** $240 **VGood:** $195

ITHACA MODEL 37 FEATHERLIGHT PRESENTATION
Same specs as Model 37 except 12-ga.; 5-shot magazine; Ithaca Raybar front sight; fancy checkered American walnut pistol-grip stock; gold decorated receiver; engraving; crossbolt safety. Introduced 1981; discontinued 1986.
Perf.: $1175 **Exc.:** $1000 **VGood:** $890

ITHACA MODEL 37 FIELD GRADE
Same specs as Model 37 except 12-, 20-ga.; 2-3/4-inch chamber; standard or vent rib barrel; Raybar front sight; American hardwood stock, ring-tail forend. Introduced 1983; discontinued 1986.
Perf.: $300 **Exc.:** $240 **VGood:** $195

ITHACA MODEL 37 FIELD GRADE MAGNUM
Same specs as Model 37 except 12-, 20-ga.; 3-inch chamber; 28-inch, 30-inch vent-rib barrel; Raybar front sight; American hardwood stock, ringtail forend; elongated receiver; grip cap has flying mallard; recoil pad. Introduced 1978; discontinued 1986.
Perf.: $370 **Exc.:** $340 **VGood:** $310

ITHACA MODEL 37R
Same general specs as Model 37 except raised solid rib. Introduced 1937; discontinued 1967.

Checkered stock
Exc.: $275 **VGood:** $250 **Good:** $185
Uncheckered stock
Exc.: $265 **VGood:** $240 **Good:** $175

ITHACA MODEL 37R DELUXE
Same specs as Model 37 except raised solid rib; hand-checkered fancy walnut stock, slide handle. Introduced 1955; discontinued 1961.
Exc.: $350 **VGood:** $275 **Good:** $250

ITHACA MODEL 37S SKEET GRADE
Same specs as Model 37 except vent rib; checkered stock, extension slide handle. Introduced 1937; discontinued 1955.
Exc.: $445 **VGood:** $375 **Good:** $335

ITHACA MODEL 37 SUPER DEERSLAYER
Same specs as Model 37 except 20-inch, 26-inch barrel bored for rifled slugs; open rifle-type rear sight; ramp front; improved wood in stock, slide handle. Introduced 1962; discontinued 1979.
Exc.: $330 **VGood:** $250 **Good:** $185

ITHACA MODEL 37 SUPREME GRADE
Same specs as Model 37 except hand-checkered fancy walnut stock, slide handle; available in Skeet or trap configurations. Introduced 1967; discontinued 1979.
Perf.: $500 **Exc.:** $400 **VGood:** $350

ITHACA MODEL 37T TARGET GRADE
Same specs as Model 37 except vent rib; hand-checkered fancy walnut stock, slide handle; choice of Skeet or Trap stock. Replaced Model 37S Skeet Grade and Model 37T Trap Grade. Introduced 1955; discontinued 1961.
Perf.: $425 **Exc.:** $375 **VGood:** $325

ITHACA MODEL 37T TRAP GRADE
Same specs as Model 37 except vent rib; checkered select walnut straight trap-style stock, extension slide-handle; recoil pad. Introduced 1937; discontinued 1955.
Perf.: $425 **Exc.:** $375 **VGood:** $325

ITHACA MODEL 37 ULTRA-LIGHT
Same specs as Model 37 except 12-, 20-ga.; 5-shot magazine; 25-inch vent-rib barrel; checkered American walnut pistol-grip stock; recoil pad; gold-plated trigger; Sid Bell-designed grip cap. No longer in production.
Perf.: $390 **Exc.:** $275 **VGood:** $220

ITHACA MODEL 37V FEATHERWEIGHT
Same specs as Model 37 except 12-, 20-ga.; 5-shot magazine; vent rib; Ithaca Raybar front sight; checkered American walnut pistol-grip stock; decorated receiver; crossbolt safety. No longer in production.
Perf.: $260 **Exc.:** $240 **VGood:** $195

ITHACA MODEL 37 DELUXE PUMP SHOTGUN
Gauge: 12, 16, 20, 3-inch chamber. Barrel: 26-inch, 28-inch, 30-inch (12 gauge), 26-inch, 28-inch (16 and 20 gauge), choke tubes. Weight: 7 lbs. Stock: Walnut with cut-checkered grip and forend. Features: Steel receiver; bottom ejection; brushed blue finish, vent rib barrels. Reintroduced 1996. Made in U.S. by Ithaca Gun Co.
Perf.: $485 **Exc.:** $365 **VGood:** $275
With straight English-style stock
Perf.: $675 **Exc.:** $580 **VGood:** 5340

ITHACA MODEL 37 NEW CLASSIC
Ringtail forend, sunburst recoil pad, hand-finished walnut stock, 26-inch or 28-inch barrel)
Perf.: $665 **Exc.:** $525 **VGood:** $400

ITHACA MODEL 37 WATERFOWLER
Similar to Model 37 Deluxe except in 12-gauge only with 28-inch barrel, special extended steel shot choke tube system. Complete coverage of Advantage Wetlands or Hardwoods camouflage. Introduced 1999. Made in U.S. by Ithaca Gun Co.
Perf.: $540 **Exc.:** $400 **VGood:** $315

ITHACA MODEL 37 DEERSLAYER II PUMP SHOTGUN
Gauge: 12, 20, 3-inch chamber. Barrel: 20-inch, 25-inch, fully rifled. Weight: 7 lbs. Stock: Cut-checkered American walnut with Monte Carlo comb. Sights: Rifle-type. Features: Integral barrel and receiver. Bottom ejection. Brushed blue finish. Reintroduced 1997. Made in U.S. by Ithaca Gun Co.
Perf.: $500 **Exc.:** $375 **VGood:** $295
Smooth Bore Deluxe
Perf.: $475 **Exc.:** $395 **VGood:** $325
Rifled Deluxe
Perf.: $475 **Exc.:** $395 **VGood:** $325

ITHACA MODEL 37 DEERSLAYER III PUMP SHOTGUN
Gauge: 12, 20, 2-3/4-inch and 3-inch chambers; 26-inch rifled barrel free floated; weighs 9 lbs.; Monte Carlo laminate stock; barrel length gives increased velocity; trigger and sear set hand filed and stoned for creep free operation; Weaver-style scope base; swivel studs; matte blue.
Perf.: $550 **Exc.:** $475 **VGood:** $300

ITHACA MODEL 37 RUFFED GROUSE SPECIAL EDITION
Gauge: 20. Barrel: 22-inch, 24-inch, interchangeable choke tubes. Weight: 5.25 lbs. Stock: American black walnut. Features: Laser engraved stock wtih line art drawing. Bottom eject. Vent rib and English style. Right- or left-hand via simple safety change. Aluminum receiver. Made in U.S.A. by Ithaca Gun Co.
Perf.: $715 **Exc.:** $565 **VGood:** $435

ITHACA ELLETT SPECIAL MODEL 37 TURKEYSLAYER
Gauge: 12, 3-inch chamber. Barrel: 22-inch ported. Stock: Composite. Sights: Fully adjustable, TruGlo front and rear. Features: Recreated from "Golden Age." Complete camo covering. Drilled and tapped. Extended turkey chokes. Matte metal, Realtree Hardwoods 20/200 or Advantage Timber patterns.
Perf.: $500 **Exc.:** $375 **VGood:** $295

ITHACA QUAD BORE MODEL 37 TURKEYSLAYER

Gauge: 20. Barrel: 22-inch ported. Weight: 6.25 lbs. Stock: Black walnut stock and forend. Sights: Fully adjustable, TruGlo. Features: Sling swivel studs, matte blue, turkey Full choke tube, 100 percent American made.

Perf.: $520   **Exc.:** $395   **VGood:** $315

ITHACA MODEL 37 ULTRALIGHT DELUXE

Gauge: 16, 2-3/4-inch chamber. Barrel: 24-inch, 26-inch, 28-inch. Weight: 5.25 lbs. Stock: Standard deluxe. Sights: Raybar. Features: Vent rib, drilled and tapped, interchangeable barrel. F, M, IC choke tubes.

Deluxe
Perf.: $475   **Exc.:** $380   **VGood:** $340
Classic/English
Perf.: $475   **Exc.:** $380   **VGood:** $340
Classic/Pistol
Perf.: $475   **Exc.:** $380   **VGood:** $340

ITHACA MODEL 66

Lever action; single shot; manually cocked hammer; 12-, 20-ga., .410; 26-inch Full (.410), 28-inch Full or Modified (12-, 20-ga.), 30-inch Full (12-ga.) barrel; vent. rib (special order); checkered straight stock, uncheckered forearm. Introduced 1963; discontinued 1979.

Exc.: $225   **VGood:** $195   **Good:** $115
Add about 35 percent to above prices for .410 bore. Add 10 percent for vent. rib.

ITHACA MODEL 66 LONG TOM

Same specs as Model 66 except 12-ga.; 36-inch Full-choke barrel; recoil pad. Introduced 1969; discontinued 1974.

Exc.: $265   **VGood:** $235   **Good:** $195

ITHACA MODEL 66RS BUCK BUSTER

Same specs as Model 66 except 12-, 20-ga.; 22-inch Cylinder barrel; rifle sights. Introduced 1967; 12-ga. discontinued 1970; 20-ga. discontinued 1979.

Perf.: $265   **Exc.:** $250   **VGood:** $175

ITHACA MODEL 66 VENT RIB

Same specs as Model 66 except vent-rib barrel. Introduced 1969; discontinued 1974.

Perf.: $250   **Exc.:** $210   **VGood:** $125

ITHACA MODEL 66 YOUTH MODEL

Same specs as Model 66 except 20-ga., .410; 25-inch barrel; shorter stock; recoil pad. Introduced 1965; discontinued 1979.

Exc.: $150   **VGood:** $125   **Good:** $100

ITHACA MODEL 87

Slide action; 12-, 20-ga.; 3-inch chamber; 5-shot magazine; 26-inch, 28-inch, 30-inch barrel; choke tubes; Raybar front sight; checkered walnut pistol-grip stock, forend; bottom ejection; crossbolt safety. Introduced 1988.

Perf.: $350   **Exc.:** $220   **VGood:** $180

ITHACA MODEL 87 CAMO

Same specs as Model 87 except 12-ga.; 24-inch, 26-inch, 28-inch vent-rib barrel; Modified choke tube; camouflage finish. Introduced 1988; still in production.

Perf.: $.410   **Exc.:** $240   **VGood:** $180

ITHACA MODEL 87 COMBO

Same specs as Model 87 except 28-inch barrel with choke tubes, 20-inch, 25-inch rifled barrel; no checkering. No longer in production.

Perf.: $400   **Exc.:** $315   **VGood:** $275

ITHACA MODEL 87 DEERSLAYER

Same specs as Model 87 except 20-inch, 25-inch slug or rifled barrel; Raybar blade front sight on ramp, rear adjustable for windage, elevation; grooved for scope mounting. Introduced 1988; discontinued 1993.

Perf.: $325   **Exc.:** $210   **VGood:** $180

ITHACA MODEL 87 DEERSLAYER II

Same specs as Model 87 except rifled barrel; Raybar blade front sight on ramp, rear adjustable for windage and elevation; grooved for scope mounting; high-gloss checkered American walnut Monte Carlo stock, forend; solid-frame construction. Introduced 1988.

Perf.: $425   **Exc.:** $275   **VGood:** $210

ITHACA MODEL 87 DEERSLAYER II FAST TWIST

Same specs as Model 87 except 12-ga.; 25-inch non-removable rifled barrel; Raybar blade front sight on ramp, rear adjustable for windage and elevation; grooved for scope mounting; high-gloss checkered American walnut Monte Carlo stock, forend; solid-frame construction. Introduced 1992; discontinued 1993.

Perf.: $420   **Exc.:** $300   **VGood:** $250

ITHACA MODEL 87 DEERSLAYER DELUXE

Same specs as Model 87 except 20-inch, 25-inch slug or rifled barrel; Raybar blade front sight on ramp, rear adjustable for windage and elevation; grooved for scope mounting; high-gloss checkered walnut pistol-grip stock, forend; gold trigger. Introduced 1989.

Perf.: $375   **Exc.:** $240   **VGood:** $195

ITHACA MODEL 87 DEERSLAYER DELUXE COMBO

Same specs as Model 87 except 20, 25-inch slug or rifled barrel; extra 28-inch barrel; Raybar front sight on ramp, rear adjustable for windage and elevation; grooved for scope mounting; high-gloss checkered walnut pistol-grip stock, forend; gold trigger. Introduced 1989; still in production.

Perf.: $475   **Exc.:** $340   **VGood:** $295

ITHACA MODEL 87 DELUXE

Same specs as Model 87 except vent-rib barrel; choke tubes; high-gloss walnut stock, forend; gold trigger. Introduced 1988; still in production.

Perf.: $400   **Exc.:** $300   **VGood:** $240

ITHACA MODEL 87 DELUXE COMBO

Same specs as Model 87 except extra 28-inch barrel; vent rib; choke tubes; high-gloss walnut stock, forend; gold trigger. No longer in production.

Perf.: $450   **Exc.:** $350   **VGood:** $290

ITHACA MODEL 87 DELUXE MAGNUM

Same specs as Model 87 except vent-rib barrel; choke tubes; high-gloss walnut stock, forend; gold trigger. Introduced 1981; discontinued 1988.

Perf.: $320   **Exc.:** $270   **VGood:** $230

Ithaca Model 66

Ithaca Model 66 Long Tom

Ithaca Model 66RS Buck Buster

Ithaca Model 66 Youth Model

Ithaca Model 87 Deerslayer

Ithaca Model 87 Deerslayer II

Ithaca Model 87 Deluxe

Ithaca Model 87 Supreme

Ithaca Model 87 Turkey

Ithaca Model 87 Ultralight

New Ithaca Double (NID) Field Grade

ITHACA MODEL 87 ENGLISH
Same specs as Model 87 except 20-ga.; 3-inch chamber; 24-inch, 26-inch vent-rib barrel; choke tubes; recoil pad. Introduced 1991.
Perf.: $.410   **Exc.:** $275   **VGood:** $225

ITHACA MODEL 87 M&P
Same specs as Model 87 except 5-, 8-shot magazine; 18-1/2-inch, 20-inch Cylinder bore barrel; weighs 7 lbs.; black polymer pistol-grip stock, forearm; Parkerized finish. Introduced 1988; discontinued 1993.
Perf.: $250   **Exc.:** $200   **VGood:** $170

ITHACA MODEL 87 SUPREME
Same specs as Model 87 except vent-rib; fancy-grade walnut stock, forend; engraving. Introduced 1988; still in production.
Perf.: $650   **Exc.:** $400   **VGood:** $300

ITHACA MODEL 87 TURKEY GUN
Same specs as Model 87 except 12-ga.; 24-inch barrel; fixed Full choke or Full choke tube; matte blue or Camoseal finish. Introduced 1988; still in production.
Perf.: $375   **Exc.:** $280   **VGood:** $200

ITHACA MODEL 87 ULTRA DEERSLAYER
Same specs as Model 87 except 20-inch, 25-inch slug or rifled barrel; Raybar blade front sight on ramp, rear adjustable for windage and elevation; grooved for scope mounting; high-gloss checkered walnut pistol-grip stock, forend; gold trigger; aluminum construction. Introduced 1989; discontinued 1990.
Perf.: $325   **Exc.:** $225   **VGood:** $180

ITHACA MODEL 87 ULTRALIGHT
Same specs as Model 87 except 12-, 20-ga.; 3-inch chamber; 20-inch, 24-inch, 25-inch, 26-inch barrel; fixed or choke tubes; aluminum construction. Introduced 1988; discontinued 1990.
Perf.: $375   **Exc.:** $295   **VGood:** $240

ITHACA MODEL 87 ULTRALIGHT DELUXE
Same specs as Model 87 except 12-, 20-ga.; 3-inch chamber; 20-inch, 24-inch, 25-inch, 26-inch barrel; fixed or choke tubes; high-gloss select-grade checkered walnut stock, forend; gold trigger; aluminum construction. Introduced 1989; discontinued 1991.
Perf.: $.410   **Exc.:** $300   **VGood:** $235

ITHACA HOMELAND SECURITY GUNS
Gauge: 12 ga., 2-3/4-inch and 3-inch chambers. Barrel: 18-1/2-inch interchangeable. Weight: 6.5 lbs. Stock: Synthetic deluxe and oil finish. Sights: Bead. Discontinued 2002.

Synthetic/Standard		
Perf.: $450	**Exc.:** $400	**VGood:** $300
Synthetic/Ported		
Perf.: $465	**Exc.:** $415	**VGood:** $315

ITHACA CLASSIC DOUBLES SPECIAL FIELD GRADE SXS
Gauge: 20, 28, 2-3/4-inch chambers, .410, 3-inch. Barrel: 26-inch, 28-inch, 30-inch, fixed chokes. Weight: 5 lbs., 14 oz. (20-gauge). Stock: 14-1/2-inchx2-1/4-inchx1-3/8-inch. High-grade American black walnut, hand-rubbed oil finish; splinter or beavertail forend; straight or pistol grip. Features: Double triggers, ejectors; color case-hardened, engraved action body with matted top surfaces. Introduced 1999. Made in U.S. by Ithaca Classic Doubles. Discontinued.
Perf.: $5999   **Exc.:** $5200   **VGood:** $4650

ITHACA CLASSIC DOUBLES GRADE 4E CLASSIC SXS SHOTGUN
Similar to Special Field Grade except gold-plated triggers, jeweled barrel flats and hand-turned locks. Feather crotch and flame-grained black walnut hand-checkered 28 lpi with fleur-de-lis pattern. Action body engraved with three game scenes and bank note scroll, color case-hardened. Introduced 1999. Made in U.S. by Ithaca Classic Doubles. Discontinued.
Perf.: $7500   **Exc.:** $6750   **VGood:** $5750

ITHACA CLASSIC DOUBLES GRADE 7E CLASSIC SXS SHOTGUN
Similar to Special Field Grade except engraved with bank note scroll and flat 24k gold game scenes: gold setter and gold pointer on opposite action sides, American bald eagle inlaid on bottom plate. Hand-timed, polished, jeweled ejectors and locks. Exhibition grade American black walnut stock and forend with eight-panel fleur-de-lis borders.

Introduced 1999. Made in U.S. by Ithaca Classic Doubles. Discontinued.
Perf.: $11,000   **Exc.:** $9900   **VGood:** $8950

ITHACA CLASSIC DOUBLES SOUSA SPECIAL GRADE SXS SHOTGUN
Similar to the Special Field Grade except presentation grade American black walnut, hand-carved and checkered; hand-engraving with 24-karat gold inlays; tuned action and hand-applied finishes. Made in U.S. by Ithaca Classic Doubles.
Perf.: $18,000   **Exc.:** $16,200   **VGood:** $15,125

ITHACA CRASS MODEL NO. 1
Side-by-side; boxlock; hammerless; (also available with exposed hammers); 10-, 12-, 16-ga. (introduced about 1898); twist barrels; American walnut pistol-grip stock; double triggers; extractors (ejectors optional after 1897). Ithaca's first hammerless model; original grades, No. 1 through No. 7; No. 1 Special and No. 1-1/2 added about 1898. Introduced, about 1888; discontinued, 1901; serial number range: 6981 to 49104.
Exc.: $350   **VGood:** $300   **Good:** $240

ITHACA CRASS MODEL NO. 1 SPECIAL
Same specs as Crass Model No. 1 except steel barrels.
Exc.: $400   **VGood:** $350   **Good:** $295

ITHACA CRASS MODEL NO. 1-1/2
Same specs as Crass Model No. 1.
Exc.: $450   **VGood:** $400   **Good:** $325

ITHACA CRASS MODEL NO. 2
Same specs as Crass Model No. 1 except English walnut pistol-grip stock.
Exc.: $570   **VGood:** $425   **Good:** $350

ITHACA CRASS MODEL NO. 3
Same specs as Crass Model No. 1 except twist or steel barrels; English walnut pistol-grip stock.
Exc.: $660   **VGood:** $500   **Good:** $400

ITHACA CRASS MODEL NO. 4
Same specs as Crass Model No. 1 except twist or steel barrels; French walnut pistol-grip stock.
Exc.: $1350   **VGood:** $1000   **Good:** $800

ITHACA CRASS MODEL NO. 5
Same specs as Crass Model No. 1 except twist or Krupp steel barrels; French walnut pistol-grip stock.
Exc.: $1800   **VGood:** $1450   **Good:** $1100

ITHACA CRASS MODEL NO. 6
Same specs as Crass Model No. 1 except twist or Krupp steel barrels; French walnut pistol-grip stock.
Exc.: $2200   **VGood:** $1850   **Good:** $1500

ITHACA CRASS MODEL NO. 7
Same specs as Crass Model No. 1 except twist or Whitworth steel barrels; French walnut pistol-grip stock.
Exc.: $2500   **VGood:** $2150   **Good:** $1800

NEW ITHACA DOUBLE (NID) FIELD GRADE
Side-by-side; boxlock; hammerless; 10- (3-inch, 3-1/2-inch chambers), 12- (2-3/4-inch, 3-inch chambers), 16-, 20-ga., .410; 26-inch (12-, 16-, 20-ga., .410), 28-inch (12-, 16-, 20-ga., .410), 30-inch (12-, 16-, 20-ga.), 32-inch (10-ga.), 34-inch (10-ga.) fluid-steel barrels; American walnut pistol-grip stock; extractors (ejectors optional); double triggers (single trigger optional); optional recoil pad, ivory sight. Produced in nine grades. Magnum 10-ga. available in any grade, on special-order only, 1932-1942; total production about 887. Magnum 12-ga. available on special-order only, after 1937; total production about 87. Early NIDs (1926-1936) have snail-ear cocking indicators at the top of the frame. Introduced 1926; discontinued 1948; serial number range: 425000 to 470099. Minimum 150% premium for .410.
Exc.: $590   **VGood:** $480   **Good:** $400

NEW ITHACA DOUBLE (NID) SKEET MODEL FIELD GRADE

Same specs as New Ithaca Double (NID) Field Grade except ivory sight; American walnut pistol-grip stock, beavertail forend; ejectors; recoil pad. Introduced 1935; discontinued 1948.

Exc.: $750   **VGood:** $600   **Good:** $475

NEW ITHACA DOUBLE (NID) NO. 2

Same specs as New Ithaca Double (NID) Field Grade.

Exc.: $950   **VGood:** $550   **Good:** $525

NEW ITHACA DOUBLE (NID) NO. 3

Same specs as New Ithaca Double (NID) Field Grade; ejectors standard after 1935.

Exc.: $1100   **VGood:** $700   **Good:** $600

NEW ITHACA DOUBLE (NID) NO. 4

Same specs as New Ithaca Double (NID) Field Grade except extractors (ejectors optional until 1935, then standard); double triggers (single trigger optional); optional beavertail forend, vent rib, recoil pad, ivory sight.

Exc.: $2250   **VGood:** $1600   **Good:** $1200

NEW ITHACA DOUBLE (NID) NO. 5

Same specs as New Ithaca Double (NID) Field Grade except extractors (ejectors optional until 1926, then standard); double triggers (single trigger optional); optional beavertail forend, vent rib, recoil pad, ivory sight.

Exc.: $3000   **VGood:** $2650   **Good:** $1900

NEW ITHACA DOUBLE (NID) NO. 7

Same specs as New Ithaca Double (NID) Field Grade except extractors (ejectors optional until 1926, then standard); double triggers (single trigger optional); optional beavertail forend, vent rib, recoil pad, ivory sight.

Exc.: $6000   **VGood:** $5000   **Good:** $4500

NEW ITHACA DOUBLE (NID) SOUSA SPECIAL

Same specs as New Ithaca Double (NID) Field Grade except extractors (ejectors optional until 1926, then standard); double triggers (single trigger optional); optional beavertail forend, vent rib, recoil pad, ivory sight. Extreme rarity precludes pricing.

ITHACA FLUES MODEL FIELD GRADE

Side-by-side; boxlock; hammerless (also available with exposed hammers until about 1915); 10-, 12-, 16-, 20-ga.; 24-inch (20-ga.), 26-inch (12-, 16-, 20-ga.), 28-inch (12-, 16-, 20-ga.), 30-inch (10-, 12-, 16-ga.), 32-inch (10-, 12-ga.) fluid-steel barrels; American walnut half-pistol-grip stock; extractors (ejectors optional); double triggers (Infallible single trigger optional, 1915-1916); produced in eleven grades. Introduced 1908; discontinued 1926; serial number range: 175000 to 398365.

Exc.: $750   **VGood:** $500   **Good:** $350

ITHACA FLUES MODEL NO. 1

Same specs as Flues Model Field Grade except also 28-ga. with 24-inch, 26-inch barrels; twist barrels; American walnut pistol-grip stock.

Exc.: $800   **VGood:** $650   **Good:** $400

ITHACA FLUES MODEL NO. 1 SPECIAL

Same specs as Flues Model Field Grade except also 28-ga. with 24-inch, 26-inch barrels; American walnut pistol-grip stock.

Exc.: $850   **VGood:** $700   **Good:** $500

ITHACA FLUES MODEL NO. 1-1/2

Same specs as Flues Model Field Grade except also 28-ga. with 24-inch, 26-inch barrels; twist barrels; American walnut pistol-grip stock.

Perf.: $750   **Exc.:** $500   **VGood:** $350

ITHACA FLUES MODEL NO. 2

Same specs as Flues Model Field Grade except also 28-ga. with 24-inch, 26-inch barrels; twist barrels; American walnut pistol-grip stock.

Exc.: $750   **VGood:** $500   **Good:** $350

New Ithaca Double (NID) Skeet Model Field Grade

New Ithaca Double (NID) No. 2

New Ithaca Double (NID) No. 4

ITHACA FLUES MODEL NO. 2 KRUPP PIGEON GUN

Same specs as Flues Model Field Grade except also 28-ga. with 24-inch, 26-inch barrels; Krupp steel barrels; European walnut stock; pistol, half-pistol or straight grip.

Exc.: $800   **VGood:** $550   **Good:** $400

ITHACA FLUES MODEL NO. 3

Same specs as Flues Model Field Grade except also 28-ga. with 24-inch, 26-inch barrels; twist or Krupp steel barrels; European walnut stock; pistol, half-pistol or straight grip.

Krupp steel		
Exc.: $825	**VGood:** $550	**Good:** $400

ITHACA FLUES MODEL NO. 4

Same specs as Flues Model Field Grade except also 28-ga. with 24-inch, 26-inch barrels; twist or Krupp steel barrels; European walnut stock; pistol, half-pistol or straight grip.

Krupp steel		
Exc.: $1350	**VGood:** $1000	**Good:** $800

ITHACA FLUES MODEL NO. 5

Same specs as Flues Model Field Grade except also 28-ga. with 24-inch, 26-inch barrels; twist or Krupp steel barrels; European walnut stock; pistol, half-pistol or straight grip.

Krupp steel		
Exc.: $1800	**VGood:** $1450	**Good:** $1100

ITHACA FLUES MODEL NO. 6

Same specs as Flues Model Field Grade, except also 28-ga. with 24-inch, 26-inch barrels; twist or Krupp steel barrels; English walnut stock; pistol, half-pistol or straight grip. Extreme rarity precludes pricing.

ITHACA FLUES MODEL NO. 7

Same specs as Flues Model Field Grade, except also 28-ga. with 24-inch, 26-inch barrels; Whitworth steel barrels; English walnut stock; pistol, half-pistol or straight grip. Extreme rarity precludes pricing.

ITHACA FLUES ONE-BARREL TRAP GUN NO. 4

Side-by-side; boxlock; hammerless; 12-ga.; 30-inch, 32-inch, 34-inch Krupp steel barrels; vent rib;

American walnut stock; pistol, half-pistol or straight grip; ejector; decoration similar to equivalent grades of Flues Model double guns. Introduced 1914; discontinued 1922; serial number range same as Flues Model doubles; total production about 4700.

Exc.: $1050   **VGood:** $800   **Good:** $650

ITHACA FLUES ONE-BARREL TRAP GUN NO. 5

Same specs as Flues One-Barrel Trap Gun No. 4.

Exc.: $1350   **VGood:** $1000   **Good:** $800

ITHACA FLUES ONE-BARREL TRAP GUN NO. 6

Same specs as Flues One-Barrel Trap Gun No. 4. Extreme rarity precludes pricing.

ITHACA FLUES ONE-BARREL TRAP GUN NO. 7

Same specs as Flues One-Barrel Trap Gun No. 4.

Exc.: $2500   **VGood:** $2200   **Good:** $1900

ITHACA FLUES ONE-BARREL TRAP GUN SOUSA SPECIAL

Same specs as Flues One-Barrel Trap Gun No. 4. Introduced 1918; discontinued 1922. Extreme rarity precludes pricing.

ITHACA FLUES ONE-BARREL TRAP GUN VICTORY GRADE

Same specs as Flues One-Barrel Trap Gun No. 4 except extractor; straight-grip stock. Introduced 1919; discontinued 1922.

Exc.: $800   **VGood:** $600   **Good:** $450

ITHACA KNICKERBOCKER ONE-BARREL TRAP GUN NO. 4

Boxlock; hammerless; 12-ga.; 30-inch, 32-inch, 34-inch fluid-steel barrel; vent rib; American walnut straight or pistol-grip stock; recoil pad; ejector; decoration similar to equivalent grades of New Ithaca Double guns; named for its designer, Frank Knickerbocker, it was widely known among shooters as the Knick. Introduced 1922; discontinued 1977, except on special order; serial number range: 400000 to 405739.

Exc.: $1495   **VGood:** $995   **Good:** $750

Ithaca Knickerbocker
One-Barrel Trap Victory Grade

Ithaca Minier
Model 3

Ithaca Minier
Model 4

Ithaca Lewis
Model No 1 Special

ITHACA KNICKERBOCKER ONE-BARREL TRAP NO. 5
Same specs as Ithaca Knickerbocker One-Barrel Trap Gun No. 4. Introduced 1922; discontinued 1982.
Exc.: $3500   **VGood:** $3000   **Good:** $2500

ITHACA KNICKERBOCKER ONE-BARREL TRAP NO. 6
Same specs as Ithaca Knickerbocker One-Barrel Trap Gun No. 4. Though never a catalogue item, a few Knicks in grade No. 6 were built in 1922-1923.
Exc.: $3800   **VGood:** $2900   **Good:** $2200

ITHACA KNICKERBOCKER ONE-BARREL TRAP NO. 7
Same specs as Ithaca Knickerbocker One-Barrel Trap Gun No. 4. Introduced 1922; discontinued early 1960s.
Exc.: $4200   **VGood:** $3200   **Good:** $2500

ITHACA KNICKERBOCKER ONE-BARREL TRAP SOUSA SPECIAL
Same specs as Ithaca Knickerbocker One-Barrel Trap Gun No. 4. Introduced 1922; discontinued 1937. Extreme rarity precludes pricing.

ITHACA KNICKERBOCKER ONE-BARREL TRAP VICTORY GRADE
Same specs as Ithaca Knickerbocker One-Barrel Trap Gun No. 4 except 32-inch barrel; straight-grip stock. Introduced 1922; discontinued 1937.
Exc.: $795   **VGood:** $600   **Good:** $455

ITHACA KNICKERBOCKER ONE-BARREL TRAP $1000 GRADE
Same specs as Ithaca Knickerbocker One-Barrel Trap Gun No. 4. Introduced in 1937 to replace Sousa Special Grade; the name was changed periodically to reflect price increases: $1500 Grade, $2000 Grade, $6500 Grade; after 1980, it was simply Dollar Grade; discontinued 1981.
Perf.: $6000   **Exc.:** $4800   **VGood:** $4000

ITHACA MINIER MODEL FIELD GRADE
Side-by-side; boxlock; hammerless (also available with exposed hammers); 10-, 12-, 16-ga.; 26-inch. 28-inch. 30-inch. 32-inch fluid-steel barrels; American walnut half-pistol-grip stock, forearm; extractors (ejectors optional except as noted); double triggers; mechanically quite different from the Lewis Model; produced in eleven grades. Introduced 1906;

discontinued 1908; serial number range: 130000 to 151770.
Exc.: $400   **VGood:** $350   **Good:** $290

ITHACA MINIER MODEL NO. 1
Same specs as Minier Model Field Grade except 10-, 12-, 16-, 20-ga.; twist barrels; American walnut pistol-grip stock.
Exc.: $400   **VGood:** $350   **Good:** $290

ITHACA MINIER MODEL NO. 1 SPECIAL
Same specs as Minier Model Field Grade except American walnut pistol-grip stock.
Exc.: $425   **VGood:** $375   **Good:** $300

ITHACA MINIER MODEL NO. 1-1/2
Same specs as Minier Model Field Grade except 10-, 12-, 16-, 20-ga.; twist barrels; American walnut pistol-grip stock.
Perf.: $400   **Exc.:** $350   **VGood:** $290

ITHACA MINIER MODEL NO. 2
Same specs as Minier Model Field Grade except 10-, 12-, 16-, 20-ga.; twist barrels; American walnut pistol-grip stock.
Exc.: $470   **VGood:** $400   **Good:** $350

ITHACA MINIER MODEL NO. 2 KRUPP PIGEON GUN
Same specs as Minier Model Field Grade except 10-, 12-, 16-, 20-ga.; Krupp steel barrels; American walnut pistol-grip stock.
Exc.: $750   **VGood:** $550   **Good:** $400

ITHACA MINIER MODEL NO. 3
Same specs as Minier Model Field Grade except 10-, 12-, 16-, 20-ga.; twist or Krupp steel barrels; American walnut pistol-grip stock.
Exc.: $850   **VGood:** $625   **Good:** $450

ITHACA MINIER MODEL NO. 4
Same specs as Minier Model Field Grade except 10-, 12-, 16-, 20-ga.; twist or Krupp steel barrels; American walnut straight or pistol-grip stock.
Exc.: $1400   **VGood:** $1100   **Good:** $900

ITHACA MINIER MODEL NO. 5
Same specs as Minier Model Field Grade except 10-, 12-, 16-, 20-ga.; twist or Krupp steel barrels; American walnut straight or pistol-grip stock.
Exc.: $2000   **VGood:** $1650   **Good:** $1400

ITHACA MINIER MODEL NO. 6
Same specs as Minier Model Field Grade except 10-, 12-, 16-, 20-ga.; twist or Krupp steel barrels; American walnut straight or pistol-grip stock.
Exc.: $3500   **VGood:** $3000   **Good:** $1500

ITHACA MINIER MODEL NO. 7
Same specs as Minier Model Field Grade, except 10-, 12-, 16-, 20-ga.; twist or Whitworth steel barrels; American walnut straight or pistol-grip stock.
Exc.: $3600   **VGood:** $3200   **Good:** $1700

ITHACA LEWIS MODEL NO. 1
Side-by-side; boxlock; hammerless; 10-, 12-, 16-, 20-ga. (intro. 1904); twist barrels; American walnut pistol-grip stock; extractors (ejectors optional); same grades as and slightly redesigned version of Crass Model. Introduced 1901; discontinued 1906; serial number range: 9.4109 to 123677.
Exc.: $500   **VGood:** $300   **Good:** $240

ITHACA LEWIS MODEL NO. 1 SPECIAL
Same specs as Lewis Model No. 1 except steel barrels.
Exc.: $800   **VGood:** $525   **Good:** $240

ITHACA LEWIS MODEL NO. 1-1/2
Same specs as Lewis Model No. 1.
Exc.: $800   **VGood:** $550   **Good:** $240

ITHACA LEWIS MODEL NO. 2
Same specs as Lewis Model No. 1 except English walnut pistol-grip stock.

Exc.: $825   **VGood:** $600   **Good:** $350

ITHACA LEWIS MODEL NO. 3
Same specs as Lewis Model No. 1 except twist or steel barrels; English walnut pistol-grip stock.

Exc.: $1400   **VGood:** $750   **Good:** $400

ITHACA LEWIS MODEL NO. 4
Same specs as Lewis Model No. 1 except twist or steel barrels; French walnut pistol-grip stock.

Exc.: $1900   **VGood:** $1700   **Good:** $800

ITHACA LEWIS MODEL NO. 5
Same specs as Lewis Model No. 1 except twist or Krupp steel barrels; French walnut pistol-grip stock.

Exc.: $1800   **VGood:** $1450   **Good:** $1100

ITHACA LEWIS MODEL NO. 6
Same specs as Lewis Model No. 1 except twist or Krupp steel barrels; French walnut pistol-grip stock.

Exc.: $4250   **VGood:** $3000   **Good:** $2400

ITHACA LEWIS MODEL NO. 7
Same specs as Lewis Model No. 1 except twist or Whitworth steel barrels; French walnut pistol-grip stock.

Exc.: $4250   **VGood:** $3200   **Good:** $2400

ITHACA LSA-55 TURKEY GUN
Over/under combo; exposed hammers; 12-ga./222 Rem.; 24-1/2-inch vent-rib barrels; folding leaf rear sight, bead front; checkered walnut Monte Carlo stock, forearm; plain extractor; single trigger. Made in Finland. Introduced 1970; discontinued 1979.

Perf.: $800   **Exc.:** $680   **VGood:** $575

ITHACA SINGLE BARREL 5E CUSTOM TRAP
Single barrel; boxlock; 12-ga.; 2-3/4-inch chamber; 32-inch, 34-inch Full choke barrel; weighs about 8-1/2 lbs.; white front bead, brass middle bead sights; checkered fancy American walnut stock, forend; extensively engraved and gold inlaid frame, top lever, trigger guard. Reintroduced 1988; discontinued 1991.

Perf.: $3000   **Exc.:** $2400   **VGood:** $2000

IVER JOHNSON CHAMPION MATTED RIB MODEL
Single shot; top-lever breaking; 12-, 16-, 20-ga., .410 (intro. 1928); 28-inch, 30-inch, 32-inch barrel; Full choke; solid raised full-length rib finely matted; 45-inch overall length (30-inch barrel); weighs 7-1/4 lbs. (12-ga.), 7 lbs. (16-, 20-ga.); full-checkered pistol-grip stock; automatic extractor; optional automatic ejector; hard rubber pistol-grip cap, buttplate; large knob on forend. Introduced 1913; discontinued 1941.

Exc.: $125   **VGood:** $95   **Good:** $65

IVER JOHNSON CHAMPION MODEL 36
Single shot; top lever breaking; 12-, 16-, 20-, 24-, 28-ga., .410; 28-inch, 30-inch, 32-inch barrel; Full choke; 45-inch overall length (30-inch barrel); weighs 6-3/4 lbs.; American black walnut stock, forend; rebounding hammer; barrel and lug forged in one; extractor; optional automatic ejector; case-hardened frame, nickel optional; browned barrel; Introduced 1909; name changed to Champion Single Barrel Shotgun in 1913; .410, 24-, 28-ga. introduced 1913; 24-ga. discontinued 1928; 16-, 20-, 28-ga., .410 discontinued 1941; 12-ga. discontinued 1957.

Exc.: $125   **VGood:** $100   **Good:** $85

IVER JOHNSON CHAMPION MODEL 36 JUNIOR
Same specs as Champion Model 36 except 26-inch barrel; shortened stock. Introduced 1909; dropped 1941.

Exc.: $115   **VGood:** $100   **Good:** $75

Ithaca LSA-55 Turkey Gun

Ithaca Single Barrel 5E Custom Trap

Iver Johnson Matted Rib Grade

Iver Johnson Champion Grade

Iver Johnson Champion Top Snap

Iver Johnson Ejector Single

IVER JOHNSON CHAMPION MODEL 39
Single shot; top-lever breaking; 24-, 28-ga.; 28-inch. 30-inch plain barrel; Full choke; 45-inch overall length (30-inch barrel); weighs 5-3/4 lbs.; American black walnut stock, forend; hard rubber pistol-grip cap, buttplate; barrel and lug forged as one; rebounding hammer; extractor; optional automatic ejector; case-hardened frame, nickel optional; brown barrel. Introduced 1909; discontinued 1913.

Exc.: $135   **VGood:** $120   **Good:** $100

IVER JOHNSON CHAMPION MODEL 39 JUNIOR
Same specs as Champion Model 39 except 26-inch. 28-inch barrel; shortened stock. Introduced 1909; dropped 1913.

Exc.: $135   **VGood:** $120   **Good:** $100

IVER JOHNSON CHAMPION TOP SNAP
Single shot; top lever breaking; 12-ga.; 30-inch plain twist steel barrel; 45-3/4-inch overall length; weighs 6-1/2 lbs.; American black walnut stock, forend; rebounding hammer; double locking bolt; extractor; nickeled frame; browned barrel imported from Belgium. Introduced 1880; discontinued 1905.

Exc.: $85   **VGood:** $70   **Good:** $50

IVER JOHNSON CHAMPION TOP SNAP NEW MODEL
Single shot; top lever breaking; 12-, 16-ga.; 28-inch, 30-inch, 32-inch steel barrel; Full choke; 45-inch overall length (30-inch barrel); weighs 6-3/4 lbs.; American black walnut stock, forend; hard rubber pistol grip, buttplate cap; rebounding hammer; automatic extractor; case-hardened frame; browned barrel. Introduced 1900; discontinued 1908.

Exc.: $90   **VGood:** $65   **Good:** $55

IVER JOHNSON CHAMPION TOP SNAP NEW MODEL JUNIOR
Same specs as Champion Top Snap New Model except shortened stock. Introduced 1900; dropped 1908.

Exc.: $90   **VGood:** $65   **Good:** $55

IVER JOHNSON EJECTOR SINGLE
Single shot; ring trigger break-open; semi-hammerless; 12-, 16-ga.; 28-inch, 30-inch, 32-inch plain twist steel barrel; 43-3/4-inch overall length (28-inch barrel); weighs 7 lbs.; American black walnut stock, forend; bobbed rebounding hammer; automatic ejector; case-hardened frame; browned barrel; after 1900 ring trigger model available with full hammer. Introduced 1885; 16-ga. introduced 1900; discontinued 1905.

Exc.: $85   **VGood:** $60   **Good:** $45

Iver Johnson Silver Shadow

Iver Johnson SKEET-ER

Iver Johnson Special Trap Model

Iver Johnson Hercules Grade Hammerless Double Barrel

Iver Johnson Hercules Grade Hammerless Supertrap

Iver Johnson Hercules Grade Hammerless

Ga.	Barrel (ins.)	Optional Barrels	Choke Lt./Rt.	Wgt./lbs. Extractor	Wgt./lbs. Ejector
12	30	28, 32	Full/Mod.	7	7¼
16	28	30, 32	Full/Mod.	6¾	7
20	28	None	Full/Mod.	6¾	6¾
410	26	None	Full/Full	5¾	6
	32		Full/Full		

IVER JOHNSON EJECTOR SINGLE JUNIOR

Same specs as Ejector Single except shortened stock. Introduced 1900; dropped 1905.

Exc.: $90   **VGood:** $65   **Good:** $55

IVER JOHNSON HAMMERLESS DOUBLE BARREL

Side-by-side; boxlock; 12-ga.; 28-inch, 30-inch, 32-inch barrel; 28-inch, 30-inch Full (left barrel) and Modified (right), 32-inch Full choke; 46-3/8-inch overall length; weighs 7-1/2 lbs.; American black walnut stock, forend; hard rubber buttplate, pistol-grip cap; breech sleeve area is solid drop-forged piece; hammer can be lowered without snapping on empty chambers; automatic safety; automatic ejectors; double triggers. Introduced 1913; discontinued 1923.

Exc.: $400   **VGood:** $365   **Good:** $250

IVER JOHNSON HERCULES GRADE HAMMERLESS DOUBLE BARREL

Side-by-side; boxlock; 12-, 16-, 20-ga., .410; 26-inch, 28-inch, 30-inch barrels; 46-3/8-inch overall length (30-inch barrels); hand-checkered American black walnut stock with 14-inch pull; .410 has straight stock with 13-1/2-inch pull; stock drop at comb, 1-3/4-inch; drop at heel, 2-3/4-inch; plain extractor model with slim forend; automatic ejector model with beavertail forend with D&E fastener; hard rubber buttplate and pistol grip cap; barrels, lugs forged as

one then joined together; automatic safety; double triggers. Introduced 1924; discontinued 1941.

Exc.: $850   **VGood:** $650   **Good:** $400

Add 10 percent to above prices for 16 ga.
Add 20 percent for 20 ga.
Add 100 percent for .410 bore
Add 200 percent for 28 ga.

IVER JOHNSON HERCULES GRADE HAMMERLESS SUPERTRAP

Side-by-side; boxlock; 12-ga.; 32-inch barrel; raised full-length ventilated rib; 48-3/8-inch overall length; 8-1/2 lbs.; two Lyman ivory bead sights; hand-checkered American black walnut stock, wide beavertail forend with Deeley & Edge fastener; 14 1/2-inch length of stock; 1-1/2-inch drop at comb; 2-inch drop at heel; hard rubber buttplate and pistol-grip cap; each barrel and lug forged in one, proof-tested, then joined together; automatic selective ejectors; double triggers; anti-flinch recoil pad; automatic safety. Introduced 1924; discontinued 1941.

Exc.: $1100   **VGood:** $800   **Good:** $700

IVER JOHNSON SEMI-OCTAGON BARREL

Single shot; 12-, 16-ga.; 28-inch, 30-inch, 32-inch barrel; top half of barrel 5-inch from breech semi-octagon; top surface of barrel matted; Full choke; 45-inch overall length; weighs 6-3/4 lbs. (12-ga.), 6-1/2 lbs. (16-ga.); American black walnut, plain-finished forend with large knob; hard rubber buttplate and pistol-grip cap; extractor; optional

automatic ejector; case-hardened frame; browned barrel. Introduced 1913; discontinued 1927.

Exc.: $95   **VGood:** $85   **Good:** $75

IVER JOHNSON SILVER SHADOW

Over/under; boxlock; 12-ga.; 3-inch chambers; 26-inch Improved Cylinder/Modified, 28-inch Modified/Full, 30-inch Full/Full barrels; full-length ventilated rib; checkered European walnut pistol-grip stock, forend; plastic pistol-grip cap; plain extractors; double triggers; optional non-selective single trigger. Made in Italy. Introduced 1973; discontinued 1978.

Perf.: $400   **Exc.:** $350   **VGood:** $300

IVER JOHNSON SKEET-ER

Side-by-side; boxlock; 12-, 16- 20-, 28-ga., .410; 2-3/4-inch, 3-inch (.410) chamber; optional 2-1/2-inch chamber; 26-inch, 28-inch barrel; 8-1/2 lbs. (12-, 16-, 20-, 28-ga.), 7-1/2 lbs. (.410); Skeet choke, 75 percent at 30 yds. (right barrel), 75 percent at 20 yds. (left); hand-checkered, lacquer-finished select fancy figured American black walnut straight (.410) or pistol-grip stock, large beavertail forend with Deeley & Edge fastener; 14-1/2-inch length; drop at heel 2 -5/8-inch; hard rubber grip cap; each barrel, lug forged in one, proofed then joined together; automatic extractors or automatic ejectors; automatic or manual safety. Introduced 1927; discontinued 1941.

Exc.: $1800   **VGood:** $1350   **Good:** $1000

Add 20 percent to above prices for automatic ejectors.
Add 50 percent for factory vent. rib.
Add 20 percent for 20 ga.
Add 40 percent for SST.
Add 100 percent for 16 ga., 28 ga. or .410 bore.
Add 200 percent for factory engraving (rare).

IVER JOHNSON SPECIAL TRAP MODEL

Single shot; top-lever breaking; 12-ga.; 32-inch barrel; Full choke; raised full-length ventilated rib, finely matted; 47-inch overall length; weighs 7 lbs.; two Lyman ivory sight beads; hand-checkered American black walnut stock, large trap-style forend; hard rubber buttplate, pistol-grip cap; length of stock, 14-1/2-inch; drop at comb, 1-1/2-inch; drop at heel, 2-inch; automatic ejectors; optional rubber recoil pad. Introduced 1927; discontinued 1941.

Exc.: $250   **VGood:** $225   **Good:** $200

IVER JOHNSON TRIGGER ACTION EJECTOR SINGLE

Single shot; 12-, 16-ga.; 28-inch, 30-inch, 32-inch barrel; Full choke; 45-inch overall length (30-inch barrel); weighs 6 lbs.; American black walnut stock, forend; hard rubber pistol-grip cap, buttplate; automatic ejectors; trigger operates locking bolt; fires by small trigger inset in main trigger; case-hardened frame; browned barrel. Introduced 1900; discontinued 1908.

Exc.: $100   **VGood:** $80   **Good:** $60

IVER JOHNSON TRIGGER ACTION EJECTOR SINGLE JUNIOR

Same specs as Trigger Action Ejector Single except shortened stock; weighs 5-1/2 lbs.; 42-inch overall length. Introduced 1900; dropped 1908.

Exc.: $110   **VGood:** $90   **Good:** $70

KASSNAR FOX

Autoloader; 12-ga.; 26-inch, 28-inch, 30-inch barrels; standard choke combos; vent rib; metal bead front sight; American walnut stock; crossbolt safety; interchangeable barrel. Imported by Kassnar. Introduced 1979; discontinued 1983.

Perf.: $275   **Exc.:** $240   **VGood:** $200

KASSNAR GRADE I

Over/under; boxlock; 12-, 20-, 28-ga., .410; 3-inch chambers; 26-inch, 28-inch barrels; fixed or choke tubes; vent rib; checkered European walnut stock, forend; extractors; gold-plated single selective trigger; blued, engraved receiver. Introduced 1990; still imported by K.B.I. Inc.

With fixed chokes, extractors		
Perf.: $500	**Exc.:** $400	**VGood:** $350
With choke tubes, extractors		
Perf.: $550	**Exc.:** $450	**VGood:** $400
With choke tubes; automatic ejectors		
Perf.: $600	**Exc.:** $500	**VGood:** $450

KASSNAR GRADE II

Side-by-side; boxlock; 10-, 12-, 16-, 20-, 28-ga., .410; 3-inch, 3-1/2-inch chambers; 26-inch, 28-inch, 32-inch barrels; concave rib; checkered European walnut stock; double triggers; auto top tang safety; extractors; color case-hardened action. Made in Europe. Introduced 1989; discontinued 1990.

Perf.: $500   **Exc.:** $395   **VGood:** $300

KASSNAR OMEGA O/U

Over/under; .410; 3-inch chambers; 24-inch Full/Full barrels; vent rib; checkered European walnut stock; auto safety; single trigger; folds for storage, transport. Made in Italy. Introduced 1984; discontinued 1985.

Perf.: $380   **Exc.:** $320   **VGood:** $290

KASSNAR OMEGA PUMP

Slide action; 12-ga.; 2-3/4-inch chambers; 5-, 8-shot magazine; 20-inch, 26-inch, 28-inch, 30-inch barrels; bead front sight; rifle-type on slug gun; stained hardwood or Philippine mahogany stock; damascened bolt; crossbolt safety. Made in the Philippines. Introduced 1984; discontinued 1986.

Perf.: $240   **Exc.:** $190   **VGood:** $150

KASSNAR OMEGA SXS

Side-by-side; .410; 3-inch chambers; 24-inch barrels; checkered beech (standard) or walnut (deluxe) semi-pistol-grip stock; top tang safety; blued barrels, receiver; folds for storage, transport. Made in Spain. Introduced 1984; discontinued 1985.

Standard		
Perf.: $210	**Exc.:** $185	**VGood:** $150
Deluxe		
Perf.: $230	**Exc.:** $205	**VGood:** $170

KASSNAR OMEGA SINGLE BARREL

Single barrel; 12-, 16-, 20-, 28-ga., .410; 2-3/4-inch, 3-inch chambers; 26-inch, 28-inch, 30-inch Full choke barrel; checkered hardwood (standard) or walnut (deluxe) stock, forearm; chromed (standard) or blued (deluxe) receiver; bottom lever (standard) or top lever (deluxe) break; folds for storage, transport. Introduced 1984; discontinued 1985.

Standard		
Perf.: $100	**Exc.:** $80	**VGood:** $70
Deluxe		
Perf.: $120	**Exc.:** $100	**VGood:** $80

KASSNAR OMEGA STANDARD FOLDING SINGLE BARREL

Single barrel; 12-, 16-, 20-, 28-ga., .410 bore; 28-inch, 30-inch barrel; checkered hardwood stock; matte chrome receiver; weighs 5-1/2 lbs. Importation discontinued 1987.

Perf.: $160   **Exc.:** $135   **VGood:** $115

KASSNAR DELUXE FOLDING SINGLE BARREL

Similar to the standard, except has checkered walnut stock and forearm; blue receiver. Importation discontinued 1987.

Perf.: $195   **Exc.:** $160   **VGood:** $135

Kassnar Grade I

Kassnar Grade II

Kassnar Omega O/U

Kassnar Omega SxS

Kemen KM-4 Over/Under

KAWAGUCHIYA FG

Over/under; boxlock; 12-ga.; 2-3/4-inch chambers; 26-inch, 28-inch barrels; vent rib; sterling silver front bead sight; high-grade French walnut stock; selective single trigger; selective auto ejectors; chrome-lined bore; chromed trigger. Made in Japan. Introduced 1981 by La Paloma Marketing; discontinued 1985.

Perf.: $625   **Exc.:** $500   **VGood:** $450

KAWAGUCHIYA M-250

Gas-operated autoloader; 12-ga.; 2-3/4-inch chamber; 26-inch, 28-inch, 30-inch barrel; standard fixed chokes or Tru-Choke System; vent rib; checkered French walnut pistol-grip stock; reversible crossbolt safety. Made in Japan. Introduced 1980 by La Paloma Marketing; discontinued 1986.

With fixed chokes		
Perf.: $325	**Exc.:** $245	**VGood:** $200
With Tru-Choke System		
Perf.: $375	**Exc.:** $300	**VGood:** $250

KAWAGUCHIYA M-250 DELUXE

Same specs as M-250 except silvered, etched receiver. Introduced 1980; discontinued 1986.

With fixed chokes		
Perf.: $410	**Exc.:** $300	**VGood:** $260
With Tru-Choke System		
Perf.: $460	**Exc.:** $350	**VGood:** $310

KAWAGUCHIYA OT-SKEET E1

Over/under; boxlock; 12-ga.; 2-3/4-inch chambers; 26-inch, 28-inch Skeet/Skeet barrels; 13mm vent rib; middle and front bead sights; high-grade French walnut stock; gold-colored wide trigger; plastic buttplate; push-button forend release. Introduced 1981 by La Paloma Marketing; discontinued 1985.

Perf.: $900   **Exc.:** $750   **VGood:** $690

KAWAGUCHIYA OT-SKEET E2

Same specs as OT-Skeet E1 except super-deluxe French Walnut stock, forend; chromed receiver; better scroll engraving. Introduced 1981 by La Paloma Marketing; discontinued 1985.

Perf.: $1350   **Exc.:** $1000   **VGood:** $900

KAWAGUCHIYA OT-TRAP E1

Over/under; boxlock; 12-ga.; 2-3/4-inch chamber; 30-inch barrels; 13mm vent rib; bone white middle, front bead sights; high-grade oil-finished French walnut stock; rubber recoil pad; blued scroll-engraved receiver. Introduced 1981 by LaPaloma Marketing; discontinued 1985.

Perf.: $910   **Exc.:** $725   **VGood:** $650

KAWAGUCHIYA OT-TRAP E2

Same specs as OT-Trap E1 except super-deluxe French walnut stock, forend; chromed receiver; better scroll engraving. Introduced 1981 by LaPaloma Marketing; discontinued 1985.

Perf.: $1295   **Exc.:** $1000   **VGood:** $900

KDF BRESCIA

Side-by-side; 12-, 20-ga.; Anson & Deeley-type action; 28-inch Full/Modified or Improved/Modified chrome-lined barrels; hand-checkered European walnut pistol-grip stock, forearm; recoil pad; double triggers; engraved action. Made in Italy. No longer imported.

Perf.: $330   **Exc.:** $290   **VGood:** $250

KDF CONDOR

Over/under; boxlock; 26-inch Improved/Modified or Skeet/Skeet; 28-inch Full/Modified or Modified/Modified, 30-inch (12-ga.) Full/Modified or Full/Full barrels; vent rib; Skeet model has extra-wide rib; hand-checkered European walnut pistol-grip stock, forearm; single selective trigger; automatic ejectors. Made in Italy. No longer imported.

Field Grade		
Perf.: $600	**Exc.:** $570	**VGood:** $525
Skeet Grade		
Perf.: $625	**Exc.:** $595	**VGood:** $550

KDF CONDOR TRAP

Same specs as Condor except 12-ga.; 28-inch Full/Modified, 30-inch, 32-inch Modified/Full or Full/Full barrels; wide vent rib; Monte Carlo stock. No longer imported.

Perf.: $625   **Exc.:** $595   **VGood:** $550

Kessler Model 28
Three-Shot Repeater

Kessler Model 50
Lever-Matic

Kimber Valier Grade I

Kimber Valier Grade II

Kolar Sporting Clays

KEMEN KM-4 OVER/UNDER

Over/under; boxlock; 12-ga.; 2-3/4-inch, 3-inch chambers; 27-5/8-inch barrels choked Hunting, Pigeon, Sporting Clays, Skeet; 30-inch, 32-inch barrels choked Sporting Clays, Trap; ventilated flat or step top rib; ventilated, solid or no side ribs; weighs 7-1/4 to 8-1/2 lbs.; high-grade walnut stock made to customer dimensions; drop-out trigger assembly; low-profile receiver with black finish on Standard model, antique silver on sideplate models and all engraved, gold inlaid models; barrels, forend, trigger parts interchangeable with Perazzi. Comes with hard case, accessory tools, spares. Imported from Spain by USA Sporting Clays. Introduced 1989.

KM-4 Standard		
Perf.: $7450	**Exc.:** $5900	**VGood:** $5000
KM-4 Luxe-A (engraved scroll), Luxe-B (game scenes)		
Perf.: $9000	**Exc.:** $7000	**VGood:** $5000
KM-4 Super Luxe (engraved game scene)		
Perf.: $13,500	**Exc.:** $9950	**VGood:** $8250
KM-4 Extra Luxe-A (scroll engraved sideplates)		
Perf.: $14,000	**Exc.:** $10,500	**VGood:** $9000
KM-4 Extra Luxe-B (game scene sideplates)		
Perf.: $16,000	**Exc.:** $15,500	**VGood:** $15,000
KM-4 Extra Gold (inlays, game scene)		
Perf.: $22,500	**Exc.:** $18,000	**VGood:** $15,500

KESSLER MODEL 28 THREE-SHOT REPEATER

Bolt action; takedown; 12-, 16-, 20-ga.; 3-shot detachable box magazine; 26-inch (20-ga.), 28-inch (12-,16-ga.) barrel; Full choke; uncheckered one-piece pistol-grip stock; recoil pad. Introduced 1951; discontinued 1953.

Exc.: $95	**VGood:** $75	**Good:** $50

KESSLER MODEL 50 LEVER-MATIC

Lever action; takedown; 12-, 16-, 20-ga.; 3-shot magazine; 26-inch, 28-inch, 30-inch barrels; Full choke; uncheckered pistol-grip stock; recoil pad. Introduced 1951; discontinued 1953.

Exc.: $190	**VGood:** $150	**Good:** $125

KIMBER AUGUSTA SHOTGUN

Premium over/under, Boss type action. 12-ga. only. Tri-alloy barrel with choke tubes. Backbored 736. Long forcing cones. HiViz sight with center bead on vent rib. Available with many features. Custom dimensions available. Imported from Italy by Kimber Mfg., Inc.

Perf.: $995	**Exc.:** $3500	**VGood:** $3150

KIMBER VALIER GRADE I

A lightweight, properly-scaled side-by-side in 16- and 20-gauge. Double triggers and extractors. Choked IC and Mod. Color case-hardened receiver, straight stock and splinter forend. Hand checkered wood at 24 lpi. Chambered for 2.75-inch shells in 16 gauge and 3-inch shells in 20 gauge.

NIB: 3300	**Exc.:** 2900	**VGood:** 2300

KIMBER VALIER GRADE II

Similar to Valier Grade I but with higher grade wood and choice of color case, blued or bone charcoal receiver in 20 gauge; bone charcoal only in 16 gauge. Automatic ejectors.

NIB: 4000	**Exc.:** 3350	**VGood:** 2400

KIMBER MARIAS GRADE I

This single-trigger sidelock over-and-under features scroll hand engraving and bone charcoal case colors with 24 lpi checkered wood. Grade I is available with 28-inch barrels and Prince of Wales stock in 12 and 20 gauge. Chambered for 3-inch shells. Automatic ejectors. Comes with 5 choke tubes.

NIB: 4500	**Exc.:** 3795	**VGood:** 2600

KIMBER MARIAS GRADE II

Similar to Marias Grade I but with higher grade wood. Available in 12 gauge with PW stock or 20 gauge with PW or straight stock in 26-inch, 28-inch or 30-inch barrels.

NIB: 4995	**Exc.:** 4100	**VGood:** 3200

KOLAR SPORTING CLAYS O/U SHOTGUN

Gauge: 12, 2-3/4-inch chambers. Barrel: 30-inch, 32-inch; extended choke tubes. Stock: French walnut. Features: Single selective trigger, detachable, adjustable for length; overbored barrels with long forcing cones; flat tramline rib; matte blue finish. Made in U.S. by Kolar.

Standard		
Perf.: $6100	**Exc.:** $5500	**VGood:** $4800
Elite Gold		
Perf.: $11,100	**Exc.:** $9500	**VGood:** $8800
Legend		
Perf.: $13,100	**Exc.:** $12,500	**VGood:** $10,800
Custom Gold		
Perf.: $23,190	**Exc.:** $22,500	**VGood:** $19,900

KOLAR AAA COMPETITION TRAP OVER/UNDER SHOTGUN

Similar to the Sporting Clays gun except has 32-inch O/U; 34-inch Unsingle or 30-inch barrels. Stock: American or French walnut; step parallel rib standard. Contact maker for full listings. Made in U.S. by Kolar.

Over/under, choke tubes, Standard		
Perf.: $6900	**Exc.:** $6200	**VGood:** $5900
Unsingle, choke tubes, Standard		
Perf.: $7650	**Exc.:** $7500	**VGood:** $7200
Combo (30-inch/34-inch, 32-inch/34-inch), Standard		
Perf.: $9995	**Exc.:** $9700	**VGood:** $8900

KOLAR AAA COMPETITION SKEET OVER/UNDER SHOTGUN

Similar to the Sporting Clays gun except has 28-inch or 30-inch barrels with Kolarite AAA sub-gauge tubes; stock of American or French walnut with matte finish; flat tramline rib; under barrel adjustable for point of impact. Many options available. Contact maker for complete listing. Made in U.S. by Kolar.

Standard, choke tubes		
Perf.: $8500	**Exc.:** $7900	**VGood:** $7450
Standard, choke tubes, two-barrel set		
Perf.: $10,690	**Exc.:** $9990	**VGood:** $8900

NOTE: The following values for Krieghoff shotguns are suggested. With Krieghoffs, values are whatever the local market will bear.

KRIEGHOFF K-80 LIVE BIRD

Over/under; 12-ga.; 2-3/4-inch chambers; 28-inch, 29-inch, 30-inch barrels; Improved Modified/Extra-Full chokes; weighs 8 lbs.; checkered European walnut stock; free-floating barrels; steel receiver satin gray finish; engraving; marketed in aluminum case made in four grades with differing wood and engraving options. Introduced 1980; still in production.

Perf.: $5100	**Exc.:** $3500	**VGood:** $2800
Bavaria Model		
Perf.: $9200	**Exc.:** $6000	**VGood:** $4800
Danube Model		
Perf.: $15,000	**Exc.:** $10,000	**VGood:** $8000
Gold Target Model		
Perf.: $18,500	**Exc.:** $12,000	**VGood:** $9000

KRIEGHOFF K-80 LIVE BIRD LIGHTWEIGHT

Same specs as K-80 Live Bird except lightweight barrels and action. Introduced 1980; still in production.

Perf.: $5100	**Exc.:** $3500	**VGood:** $2800
Bavaria Model		
Perf.: $9200	**Exc.:** $6000	**VGood:** $4800
Danube Model		
Perf.: $15,000	**Exc.:** $10,000	**VGood:** $8000
Gold Medal Target		
Perf.: $18,500	**Exc.:** $12,000	**VGood:** $9000

KRIEGHOFF K-80 SKEET

Over/under; 12-ga.; 2-1/2-inch chambers; 28-inch Skeet/Skeet barrels; optional Tula or choke tubes; vent rib; Skeet-style checkered European walnut stock; selective adjustable trigger; satin-gray finish receiver; made in four grades with differing wood and engraving options. Made in Germany. Introduced 1980; still in production.

Perf.: $5700 **Exc.:** $3500 **VGood:** $2900
Bavaria Model
Perf.: $14,975 **Exc.:** $11,250 **VGood:** $8575
Danube Model
Perf.: $22,945 **Exc.:** $19,250 **VGood:** $17,750
Gold Medal Target
Perf.: $25,975 **Exc.:** $20,500 **VGood:** $15,950
Standard, Skeet chokes
Perf.: $5700 **Exc.:** $3500 **VGood:** $3150
Skeet Special (28-inch or 30-inch, tapered flat rib, Skeet & Skeet choke tubes)
Perf.: $6000 **Exc.:** $4600 **VGood:** $3500

KRIEGHOFF K-80 SKEET FOUR-BARREL SET
Same specs as K-80 Skeet except comes with four 28-inch barrels for 12-, 20-, 28-ga., .410; marketed in aluminum case; made in four grades with differing wood and engraving options. Introduced 1980; still in production.
Perf.: $13,000 **Exc.:** $7600 **VGood:** $6200
Bavaria Model
Perf.: $18,200 **Exc.:** $12,500 **VGood:** $9750
Danube Model
Perf.: $26,100 **Exc.:** $17,000 **VGood:** $13,000
Gold Medal Target
Perf.: $29,650 **Exc.:** $17,300 **VGood:** $13,000

KRIEGHOFF K-80 SKEET INTERNATIONAL
Same specs as K-80 Skeet except Tula chokes with gas release ports; 1/2-inch vent Broadway-type rib; International Skeet stock; marketed in fitted aluminum case. Introduced 1980; still in production.
Perf.: $6200 **Exc.:** $4000 **VGood:** $3400

KRIEGHOFF K-80 SKEET LIGHTWEIGHT
Same specs as K-80 Skeet except weighs 7 lbs.; made in three grades with differing wood and engraving options. Made in Germany. Introduced 1980; still in production.
Perf.: $6000 **Exc.:** $3800 **VGood:** $3200
Bavaria Model
Perf.: $9700 **Exc.:** $5500 **VGood:** $5000
Danube Model
Perf.: $16,000 **Exc.:** $10,500 **VGood:** $9000

KRIEGHOFF K-80 SKEET LIGHTWEIGHT TWO-BARREL SET
Same specs as K-80 Skeet except set of two 28-inch, 30-inch barrels; weighs 7 lbs.; made in four grades with differing wood and engraving options. Made in Germany. Introduced 1988; still in production.
Perf.: $9400 **Exc.:** $7000 **VGood:** $5150
Bavaria Model
Perf.: $14,975 **Exc.:** $11,250 **VGood:** $8575
Danube Model
Perf.: $22,945 **Exc.:** $15,250 **VGood:** $17,750
Gold Medal Target
Perf.: $25,975 **Exc.:** $20,500 **VGood:** $15,500

KRIEGHOFF K-80 SKEET SPECIAL
Same specs as K-80 Skeet except Skeet/Skeet choke tubes; tapered flat rib. Introduced 1980; still in production.
Perf.: $6100 **Exc.:** $3900 **VGood:** $3300
Bavaria Model
Perf.: $10,000 **Exc.:** $7000 **VGood:** $5900
Danube Model
Perf.: $16,000 **Exc.:** $11,500 **VGood:** $9000
Gold Medal Target
Perf.: $19,000 **Exc.:** $12,500 **VGood:** $10,000

KRIEGHOFF K-80 SPORTING CLAYS
Over/under; 12-ga.; 2-3/4-inch chambers; 28-inch, 30-inch, 32-inch barrels; choke tubes; tapered flat or step rib styles; checkered European walnut sporting stock for gun-down shooting style; free-

Krieghoff K-80 Skeet

Krieghoff K-80 Skeet International

Krieghoff K-80 Sporting Clays

Krieghoff K-80 Trap

Krieghoff K-80 Trap Combo

Krieghoff K-80 Trap Topsingle

floating barrels; standard or lightweight receiver; satin nickel finish; scroll engraving; marketed in aluminum case; made in four grades with differing wood and engraving options. Made in Germany. Introduced 1988; still in production.
Standard grade with five choke tubes
Perf.: $6750 **Exc.:** $6000 **VGood:** $5500
Bavaria Model
Perf.: $10,000 **Exc.:** $6400 **VGood:** $5000
Danube Model
Perf.: $15,500 **Exc.:** $10,000 **VGood:** $8000
Gold Medal Target
Perf.: $20,000 **Exc.:** $11,500 **VGood:** $9200

KRIEGHOFF K-80 SINGLE BARREL TRAP GUN
Gauge: 12, 2-3/4-inch chamber; 32-inch or 34-inch barrel unsingle; fixed full or choke tubes; weighs about 8-3/4 lbs.; four stock dimensions or adjustable stock available; all hand-checkered European walnut; satin nickel finish; selective mechanical trigger adjustable for finger position; tapered step vent. rib; adjustable point of impact.
Standard grade full Unsingle
Perf.: $6600 **Exc.:** $5300 **VGood:** $4350

KRIEGHOFF K-80 TRAP
Over/under; 12-ga.; 2-3/4-inch chambers; 30-inch, 32-inch barrels; standard choke combos or choke tubes; vent step rib; weighs 8-1/2 lbs.; checkered European walnut stock; palm swell grip; four stock dimensions or adjustable stock; selective adjustable trigger; satin nickel receiver; made in four grades with differing wood and engraving options. Made in Germany. Introduced 1980; still in production.
Standard
Perf.: $7750 **Exc.:** $6750 **VGood:** $5300
Bavaria Model
Perf.: $10,000 **Exc.:** $6200 **VGood:** $5000
Danube Model
Perf.: $15,500 **Exc.:** $9500 **VGood:** $8500

Gold Medal Target
Perf.: $19,500 **Exc.:** $12,000 **VGood:** $9000

KRIEGHOFF K-20 O/U SHOTGUNS
Similar to the K-80 except built on a 20-gauge frame. Designed for skeet, sporting clays and field use. Offered in 20-, 28-gauge and .410-bore, 28-inch and 30-inch barrels. Imported from Germany by Krieghoff International Inc.
K-20, 20-gauge
Perf.: $8000 **Exc.:** $7500 **VGood:** $6500
K-20, 28-gauge
Perf.: $8775 **Exc.:** $7775 **VGood:** $6775
K-20, .410-bore
Perf.: $8775 **Exc.:** $7775 **VGood:** $6775

KRIEGHOFF K-80 TRAP COMBO
Same specs as K-80 Trap except two-barrel set cased with standard frame; made in four grades with differing wood and engraving options. Introduced 1980; still in production.
Perf.: $9000 **Exc.:** $6000 **VGood:** $4000
Bavaria Model
Perf.: $12,000 **Exc.:** $8200 **VGood:** $7000
Danube Model
Perf.: $20,500 **Exc.:** $15,000 **VGood:** $11,000
Gold Medal Target
Perf.: $24,000 **Exc.:** $17,500 **VGood:** $14,000

KRIEGHOFF K-80 TRAP TOPSINGLE
Same specs as K-80 Trap except single top 34-inch barrel; Full choke; made in four grades with differing wood and engraving options. Introduced 1980; still in production.
Perf.: $6600 **Exc.:** $4500 **VGood:** $3500
Bavaria Model
Perf.: $11,000 **Exc.:** $6900 **VGood:** $6000
Danube Model
Perf.: $19,000 **Exc.:** $12,500 **VGood:** $10,000
Gold Medal Target
Perf.: $21,000 **Exc.:** $14,000 **VGood:** $11,000

Krieghoff K-80 Trap Unsingle

Krieghoff KS-5 Trap

S-1807
Krieghoff Model 32

Krieghoff Teck

Krieghoff Ulm

KRIEGHOFF K-80 TRAP UNSINGLE

Same specs as K-80 Trap except single lower 32-inch, 34-inch barrel; Full choke; made in four grades with differing wood and engraving options. Introduced 1980; still in production.

Perf.: $8400	Exc.: $6200	VGood: $5500
Bavaria Model		
Perf.: $10,000	Exc.: $6400	VGood: $5000
Danube Model		
Perf.: $15,500	Exc.: $10,000	VGood: $8000
Gold Medal Target		
Perf.: $20,000	Exc.: $11,500	VGood: $9200

KRIEGHOFF KS-5 TRAP

Single shot; 12-ga.; 2-3/4-inch chamber; 32-inch, 34-inch barrels; Full choke or choke tubes; vent tapered step rib; weighs 8-1/2 lbs.; high Monte Carlo, low Monte Carlo or factory-adjustable stock of European walnut; adjustable trigger; blued or nickel receiver; marketed in fitted aluminum case. Made in Germany. Introduced 1988; still in production.

With fixed chokes		
Perf.: $3000	Exc.: $2000	VGood: $1600
With choke tubes		
Perf.: $3300	Exc.: $2300	VGood: $1900

KRIEGHOFF KS-5 SPECIAL

Same specs as KS-5 Trap except fully adjustable rib; adjustable stock. Made in Germany. Introduced 1990; still in production.

With fixed chokes		
Perf.: $3300	Exc.: $2200	VGood: $1750
With choke tubes		
Perf.: $3600	Exc.: $2500	VGood: $2000

KRIEGHOFF KX-5 TRAP GUN

Gauge: 12, 2-3/4-inch chamber. Barrel: 34-inch; choke tubes. Weight: About 8-1/2 lbs. Stock: Factory adjustable stock. European walnut. Features: Ventilated tapered step rib. Adjustable position trigger, optional release trigger. Fully adjustable rib; shooter to adjust point of impact from 50 percent/50 percent to nearly 90 percent/10 percent. Satin gray electroless nickel receiver. Fitted aluminum case.

Imported from Germany by Krieghoff International, Inc.

Perf.: $3700   Exc.: $3200   VGood: $2650

KRIEGHOFF MODEL 32

Over/under; boxlock; 12-, 20-, 28-ga., .410; 26-1/2-inch, 28-inch, 30-inch, 32-inch barrels; any choke combo; checkered European walnut pistol-grip stock, forend; single trigger; auto ejectors; manufactured in Field, Skeet, Trap configurations; patterned after Remington Model 32. Introduced 1958; discontinued 1980.

Perf.: $2500	Exc.: $2250	VGood: $2000
Low-rib two-barrel trap		
Perf.: $3200	Exc.: $2500	VGood: $2000
High-rib Vandalia two-barrel trap		
Perf.: $3200	Exc.: $2500	VGood: $2000

Add approximately 20 percent to above prices for two-barrel set.

KRIEGHOFF MODEL 32 FOUR-BARREL SKEET SET

Same specs as Model 32 except four sets of matched barrels (12-, 20-, 28-ga., .410); Skeet chokes, stock design; marketed in fitted case; made in seven grades depending upon quality of wood, amount and quality of engraving. No longer in production.

Standard Grade		
Perf.: $11,000	Exc.: $8400	VGood: $7300
Munchen Grade		
Perf.: $12,500	Exc.: $9200	VGood: $8000
San Remo Grade		
Perf.: $15,800	Exc.: $10,000	VGood: $8500
Monte Carlo Grade		
Perf.: $18,800	Exc.: $13,500	VGood: $10,500
Crown Grade		
Perf.: $23,000	Exc.: $16,500	VGood: $13,500
Super Crown Grade		
Perf.: $28,000	Exc.: $19,500	VGood: $16,000
Exhibition Grade		
Perf.: $32,000	Exc.: $23,000	VGood: $18,500

KRIEGHOFF MODEL 32 SINGLE-BARREL TRAP

Same specs as Model 32 except single shot; 12-ga.; 32-inch, 34-inch barrel; Modified, Improved Modified, Full choke; high vent rib; checkered Monte Carlo stock, beavertail forend; recoil pad. Introduced 1959; no longer in production.

Perf.: $1700   Exc.: $1100   VGood: $900

KRIEGHOFF NEPTUN

Drilling; sidelock; 12-, 20-ga. (2-3/4-inch, 3-inch chamber); 22 Hornet, 222 Remington, 243 Winchester, 270 Winchester, 6.5x57R, 7x57R, 7x65R, 30-06, other calibers available on special order; 25-inch barrels; solid rib; folding leaf rear sight, post or bead front; checkered European walnut pistol-grip stock, forend; cheekpiece; steel or dural receiver; slit extractor or ejector for shotgun barrels; double triggers; sling swivels; engraving. Introduced 1960; still in production.

Perf.: $13,500   Exc.: $9500   VGood: $7500

KRIEGHOFF NEPTUN PRIMUS

Same specs as Neptun except detachable sidelocks; fancier figured walnut; higher grade of engraving. Introduced 1962; still in production.

Perf.: $18,000   Exc.: $12,500   VGood: $9000

KRIEGHOFF PLUS

Drilling; boxlock; 12-, 20-ga. (2-3/4-inch, 3-inch chamber); 222 Remington, 243 Winchester, 270 Winchester, 6.5x57R, 7x65R, 30-06, other calibers on special order; 25-inch barrels; solid rib; folding leaf rear sight, post or bead front; checkered European walnut pistol-grip stock, forend; cheekpiece; slit extractor or ejector for shotgun barrels; double triggers. Introduced 1988; still in production.

Perf.: $4600   Exc.: $2800   VGood: $2000

KRIEGHOFF TECK

Over/under; boxlock; 12-, 16-, 20-ga.; 28-inch vent-rib barrel; Modified/Full choke; checkered European walnut pistol-grip stock, forend; Kersten double crossbolt; auto ejectors; double or single triggers; steel or Dural receiver. Made in Germany. Introduced 1967; still in production.

Perf.: $6500   Exc.: $4400   VGood: $3750

KRIEGHOFF TECK COMBINATION

Same specs as Teck except rifle barrel in 22 Hornet, 222 Remington, 222 Remington Magnum, 7x57R, 7x64, 7x65R, 30-30, 300 Winchester Magnum, 30-06, 308, 9.3x-74R; solid rib; folding leaf rear sight, post or bead front; cheekpiece; semi-beavertail forend; sling swivels. Introduced 1967; still in production.

Perf.: $6500   Exc.: $4400   VGood: $3750

KRIEGHOFF TRUMPF

Drilling; boxlock; 12-, 16-, 20-ga. (2-3/4-inch, 3-inch chamber); 22 Hornet, 222 Remington, 243 Winchester, 270 Winchester, 6.5x57R, 7x57R, 7x65R, 30-06, other calibers available on special order; 25-inch barrels; solid rib; folding leaf rear sight, post or bead front; checkered European walnut pistol-grip stock, forend; cheekpiece; steel or Dural receiver; slit extractor or ejector for shotgun barrels; double triggers; sling swivels. Introduced 1953; still in production.

Perf.: $8000   Exc.: $5200   VGood: $4400

KRIEGHOFF ULM

Over/under; sidelock; 12-, 16-, 20-ga.; 28-inch vent-rib barrel; Modified/Full choke; checkered European walnut pistol-grip stock, forend; Kersten double crossbolt; auto ejectors; double or single triggers; steel or Dural receiver; Arabesque engraving. Introduced 1958; still in production.

Perf.: $10,500   Exc.: $8200   VGood: $7000

KRIEGHOFF ULM COMBINATION

Same specs as Ulm except rifle barrel in 22 Hornet, 222 Remington, 222 Remington Magnum, 7x57R, 7x64, 7x65R, 30-30, 300 Winchester Magnum, 30-06, 308, 9.3x74R; solid rib; folding leaf rear sight, post or bead front; cheekpiece; semi-beavertail forend; sling swivels. Introduced 1963; still in production.

Perf.: $10,500   Exc.: $7200   VGood: $6000

KRIEGHOFF ULM-PRIMUS

Over/under; detachable sidelock; 28-inch vent-rib barrel; Modified/Full choke; fancy checkered European walnut pistol-grip stock, forend; Kersten double crossbolt; auto ejectors; double or single triggers; steel or dural receiver; high-grade engraving. Introduced 1958; still in production.

Perf.: $18,100 **Exc.:** $12,850 **VGood:** $9000

KRIEGHOFF ULM-PRIMUS COMBINATION

Same specs as Ulm-Primus except rifle barrel in 22 Hornet, 222 Remington, 222 Remington Magnum, 7x57R, 7x64, 7x65R, 30-30, 300 Winchester Magnum, 30-06, 308, 9.3x74R; solid rib; folding leaf rear sight, post or bead front; cheekpiece; semi-beavertail forend; sling swivels. Introduced 1963; still in production.

Perf.: $15,500 **Exc.:** $8500 **VGood:** $7000

KRIEGHOFF ULTRA COMBINATION

Over/under; boxlock; 12-ga. over 7x57R, 7x64, 7x65R, 30-06, 308; 25-inch vent-rib barrel; folding leaf rear sight, post or bead front; checkered European walnut pistol-grip stock, forend; Kersten double crossbolt; auto ejectors; double triggers; thumb-cocking mechanism; satin finish receiver. Introduced 1985; still in production.

Perf.: $3500 **Exc.:** $1750 **VGood:** $1400

KRIEGHOFF ULTRA-B COMBINATION

Same specs as Ultra Combo except barrel selector for front set trigger. Introduced 1985; still in production.

Perf.: $4200 **Exc.:** $1900 **VGood:** $1500

KRIEGHOFF VANDALIA TRAP

Single barrel or over/under; boxlock; 12-ga.; 30-inch, 32-inch, 34-inch barrels; vent rib; hand-checkered European walnut pistol-grip stock, beavertail forearm; three-way safety; selective single trigger; ejectors; optional silver, gold inlays, relief engraving, fancier wood. Made in Germany. Introduced 1973; discontinued 1976.

Perf.: $2200 **Exc.:** $1850 **VGood:** $1500

LANBER 82

Over/under; boxlock; 12-, 20-ga.; 3-inch chambers; 26-inch Improved Cylinder/Modified, 28-inch Modified/Full barrels; European walnut stock, forend; double triggers; silvered, engraved receiver. Imported from Spain by Eagle Imports, Inc. Introduced 1994; still imported.

Perf.: $480 **Exc.:** $375 **VGood:** $325

LANBER 87 DELUXE

Over/under; boxlock; 12-, 20-ga.; 3-inch chambers; 26-inch, 28-inch barrels; choke tubes; single selective trigger; silvered, engraved receiver. Imported from Spain by Eagle Imports, Inc. Introduced 1994; still imported.

Perf.: $820 **Exc.:** $550 **VGood:** $480

LANBER 97 SPORTING CLAYS

Over/under; boxlock; 12-ga.; 2-3/4-inch chambers; 28-inch barrels; choke tubes; European walnut stock, forend; single selective trigger; silvered, engraved receiver. Imported from Spain by Eagle Imports, Inc. Introduced 1994; still imported.

Perf.: $870 **Exc.:** $575 **VGood:** $500

LANBER MODEL 844

Over/under; boxlock; 12-ga.; 2-3/4-inch chambers; 28-inch Improved Cylinder/Improved Modified barrels; checkered European walnut pistol-grip stock, forend; single trigger; extractors. Made in Spain. Introduced 1981; discontinued 1986.

Exc.: $375 **VGood:** $300 **Good:** $275

LANBER MODEL 844 EST

Same specs as Model 844, except ejectors. Introduced 1981; discontinued 1986.

Exc.: $395 **VGood:** $320 **Good:** $295

Krieghoff Ulm-Primus

Krieghoff Vandalia Trap

Lanber Model 844

Lanber Model 2004 LCH

Lanber Model 2008 LCH

Lanber Model 2009 LCH

LANBER MODEL 844 MST

Same specs as Model 844, except 12-ga.; 3-inch chambers; 30-inch Modified/Full barrels. Introduced 1981; discontinued 1986.

Exc.: $375 **VGood:** $300 **Good:** $275

LANBER MODEL 2004 LCH

Over/under; boxlock; 12-ga.; 2-3/4-inch chambers; 28-inch barrels; interchangeable LanberChoke system; middle rib between barrels; checkered European walnut pistol-grip stock, forend; single selective trigger; ejectors; satin finish. Made in Spain. Introduced 1981; discontinued 1986.

Perf.: $650 **Exc.:** $500 **VGood:** $390

LANBER MODEL 2004 LCH SKEET

Same specs as Model 2004 LCH, except select walnut stock; engraving; blued finish. Made in Spain. Introduced 1981; discontinued 1986

Perf.: $710 **Exc.:** $550 **VGood:** $500

LANBER MODEL 2004 LCH TRAP

Same specs as Model 2004 LCH, except 30-inch barrels; trap-style walnut stock; blued finish. Introduced 1981; discontinued 1986.

Perf.: $650 **Exc.:** $540 **VGood:** $500

LANBER MODEL 2008 LCH

Over/under; boxlock; 12-ga.; 2-3/4-inch chambers; 28-inch barrels; interchangeable LanberChoke system; checkered European walnut pistol-grip

stock, forend; single selective trigger; ejectors; blued finish. Introduced 1981; discontinued 1986.

Perf.: $750 **Exc.:** $625 **VGood:** $410

LANBER MODEL 2009 LCH

Over/under; boxlock; 12-ga.; 2-3/4-inch chambers; 30-inch barrels; interchangeable LanberChoke system; checkered European walnut pistol-grip stock, forend; single selective trigger; ejectors; blued finish. Introduced 1981; discontinued 1986.

Perf.: $570 **Exc.:** $460 **VGood:** $410

MIGUEL LARRANAGA TRADITIONAL

Side-by-side; exposed hammers; 12-, 20-ga.; 2-3/4-inch chambers; 28-inch Modified/Full barrels; medium bead front sight; hand-checkered European walnut straight-grip stock, checkered butt; hand-engraved locks. Made in Spain. Introduced 1982 by Toledo Armas; discontinued 1984.

Perf.: $395 **Exc.:** $325 **VGood:** $295

LAURONA 82 SUPER GAME

Over/under; boxlock; 12-, 20-ga.; 2-3/4-inch chambers; 28-inch Full/Modified, Improved Cylinder/Improved Modified barrels; vent rib; checkered European walnut stock, forend; twin single triggers; auto selective ejectors; silvered, engraved frame; black chrome barrels. Made in Spain. Inroduced 1986; discontinued 1989

Perf.: $925 **Exc.:** $750 **VGood:** $650

Laurona 83 Super Game

Laurona 85 Super Game

Laurona Silhouette 300 Trap

Laurona Silhouette 300 Sporting Clays

LAURONA 82 TRAP COMPETITION
Same specs as 82 Super Game except 29-inch barrels; checkered European walnut Monte Carlo stock, forend; single trigger; rubber recoil pad. Introduced 1986; discontinued 1986.

Perf.: $600   **Exc.:** $475   **VGood:** $375

LAURONA 83 SUPER GAME
Over/under; boxlock; 12-, 20-ga.; 2-3/4-inch, 3-inch chambers; 28-inch vent-rib barrels; Multichokes; checkered European walnut stock, forend; twin single triggers; auto selective ejectors; silvered, engraved frame; black chrome barrels. Made in Spain. Introduced 1986; no longer in production.

Perf.: $1150   **Exc.:** $850   **VGood:** $750

LAURONA 84 SUPER GAME
Over/under; boxlock; 12-, 20-ga.; 2-3/4-inch, 3-inch chambers; 28-inch Full/Modified, Improved Cylinder/Improved Modified barrels; vent rib; checkered European walnut stock, forend; single selective trigger; auto selective ejectors; silvered, engraved frame; black chrome barrels. Made in Spain. Introduce 1986; discontinued 1989.

Perf.: $900   **Exc.:** $740   **VGood:** $650

LAURONA 84 SUPER TRAP
Same specs as 84 Super Game, except 29-inch Improved Modified/Full, Modified/Full barrels; checkered European walnut pistol-grip stock, beavertail forend; rubber recoil pad. Made in Spain. Introduced 1986; no longer in production.

Perf.: $1250   **Exc.:** $925   **VGood:** $830

LAURONA 85 SUPER GAME
Over/under; boxlock; 12-, 20-ga.; 2-3/4-inch, 3-inch chambers; 28-inch vent-rib barrels; Multichokes; checkered European walnut stock, forend; single selective trigger; auto selective ejectors; silvered, engraved frame; black chrome barrels. Made in Spain. Introduced 1986; no longer in production.

Perf.: $1150   **Exc.:** $825   **VGood:** $750

LAURONA 85 SUPER SKEET
Same specs as 85 Super Game, except only 12-ga.; 2-3/4-inch chambers; mechanical triggers. Made in Spain. Introduced 1986; no longer in production.

Perf.: $1450   **Exc.:** $925   **VGood:** $825

LAURONA 85 SUPER TRAP
Same specs as 85 Super Game, except 29-inch vent-rib barrels; Full/Multichokes; checkered European walnut pistol-grip stock, beavertail forend;

rubber recoil pad. Made in Spain. Introduced 1986; no longer in production.

Perf.: $1575   **Exc.:** $950   **VGood:** $850

LAURONA GRAND TRAP GTO COMBO
Single shot or over/under; 12-ga.; 3-inch chambers; 34-inch single top barrel; 29-inch over/under barrels; Multichokes; 10mm steel rib; European walnut Monte Carlo stock, full beavertail, finger-grooved forend; curved trap recoil pad; elongated forcing cone; bottom chamber area fitted with buffered recoil system. Made in Spain. Introduced 1990; discontinued 1991.

Perf.: $2000   **Exc.:** $1250   **VGood:** $1000

LAURONA GRAND TRAP GTU COMBO
Same specs as Grand Trap GTO Combo, except single barrel is on bottom; floating steel rib; teardrop forend. Introduced 1990; discontinued 1991.

Perf.: $2100   **Exc.:** $1350   **VGood:** $1100

LAURONA SILHOUETTE 300 SPORTING CLAYS
Over/under; 12-ga.; 3-inch chambers; 28-inch vent-rib barrels; Multichokes; weighs 7-1/4 lbs.; European walnut pistol-grip stock, beavertail forend; selective single trigger; auto selective ejectors; rubber buttpad; blued finish. Made in Spain. Introduced 1988; no longer in production.

Perf.: $1350   **Exc.:** $900   **VGood:** $800

LAURONA SILHOUETTE 300 TRAP
Same specs as Silhouette 300 Sporting Clays, except 29-inch barrels; weighs about 8 lbs.; trap-style European walnut pistol-grip stock, forend. Introduced 1988; no longer in production.

Perf.: $1500   **Exc.:** $950   **VGood:** $850

LAURONA SILHOUETTE SINGLE BARREL TRAP
Single shot; 12-ga.; 2-3/4-inch chamber; top single or bottom single 34-inch vent-rib barrel; Multichokes; European walnut pistol-grip stock, beavertail forend; rubber buttpad. Made in Spain. Introduced 1991; no longer in production.

Perf.: $1000   **Exc.:** $850   **VGood:** $700

LAURONA SILHOUETTE ULTRA-MAGNUM
Over/under; boxlock; 12-ga.; 3-1/2-inch chamber; 28-inch barrels; Multichokes; checkered European walnut pistol-grip stock, beavertail forend; single selective trigger; auto selective ejectors; rubber buttpad. Made in Spain. Introduced 1990; no longer in production.

Perf.: $1350   **Exc.:** $925   **VGood:** $825

LEBEAU-COURALLY BOSS-VEREES O/U
Gauge: 12, 20; 2-3/4-inch chambers. Barrel: 25-inch to 32-inch. Weight: To customer specifications. Stock: Exhibition-quality French walnut. Features: Boss- type sidelock with automatic ejectors; single or double triggers; chopper lump barrels. A custom gun built to customer specifications. Imported from Belgium by Wm. Larkin Moore.

Exc.: $59,000 **VGood:** $47,000 **Good:** $41,000

LEBEAU-COURALLY BOXLOCK
Side-by-side; Anson & Deeley boxlock; 12-, 16-, 20-, 28-ga.; 26-inch to 30-inch barrels; choked to custom specs; hand-rubbed, oil-finished French walnut stock, forend; double triggers; ejectors; optional sideplates; Purdey-type fastener; choice of rib style, engraving. Made in Belgium to custom order. Introduced 1987; still in production.

Perf.: $13,000   **Exc.:** $9000   **VGood:** $7500

LEBEAU-COURALLY BOXLOCK SXS SHOTGUN
Gauge: 12-, 16-, 20-, 28-ga., .410-bore. 25-inch to 32-inch barrel; weight to customer specifications; French walnut; Anson & Deely-type action with automatic ejectors; single or double triggers. Essentially a custom gun built to customer specifications. Imported from Belgium by Wm. Larkin Moore.

Exc.: $16,750 **VGood:** $14,000 **Good:** $11,500

LEBEAU-COURALLY MODEL 1225
Side-by-side; Holland & Holland sidelock; 12-, 20-, 28-ga.; 2-3/4-inch, 3-inch chambers; 26-inch to 28-inch custom-choked barrels; weighs 6-3/8 lbs.; custom Grand Luxe walnut stock; double triggers; auto ejectors; color case-hardened frame; English engraving. Made to order in Belgium. Introduced 1987; discontinued 1988.

Perf.: $25,000 **Exc.:** $17,500 **VGood:** $12,000

LEBEAU-COURALLY SIDELOCK
Side-by-side; Holland & Holland sidelock; 12-, 16-, 20-, 28-ga., .410; 26-inch to 30-inch custom-choked barrels; best-quality checkered French walnut custom pistol-grip stock, splinter forend; ejectors; chopper lump barrels; choice of rib type, engraving pattern; some have H&H-type self-opening mechanism. Made to custom order in Belgium. Introduced 1987; no longer in production.

Perf.: $32,000 **Exc.:** $22,500 **VGood:** $19,000

LEBEAU-COURALLY SIDELOCK SXS SHOTGUN
Gauge: 12-, 16-, 20-, 28-ga., .410-bore; 25-inch to 32-inch barrel; weight to customer specifications; fancy French walnut; Holland & Holland-type action with automatic ejectors; single or double triggers. Essentially a custom gun built to customer specifications. Imported from Belgium by Wm. Larkin Moore.

Exc.: $33,000 **VGood:** $26,250 **Good:** $22,500

LEFEVER ARMS AUTOMATIC HAMMERLESS DOUBLES
Side-by-side; sidelock; hammerless; 8-, 10-, 12-, 16-, 20-ga.; 26-inch (only 12-, 16-, 20-ga.), 28-inch (only 10-, 12-, 16-, 20-ga.), 30-inch, 32-inch, 34-inch (only 8-ga.) twist and fluid-steel barrels; ejectors optional in some grades, standard in others; double triggers standard; single trigger catalogue option after 1913; earliest guns semi-boxlock, later ones fully boxlock,

both with decorative sideplates. Originally called the Automatic Hammerless, the Lefever Arms gun has an unusual ball-and-socket hinge joint and numerous adjustable features in the action, fastening system, triggers, safety and ejectors. Originally offered in eight grades; several more were added after 1890; grades differ in quality of finish, amount and quality of engraving and checkering, quality of wood, and in some cases simply the addition of ejectors. Introduced 1885; discontinued 1915. Lefever Arms was purchased by Ithaca Gun Company in 1915; all subsequent guns bearing the Lefever name – Nitro Special, Long Range, Grade A, and Single Barrel Trap – were manufactured by Ithaca. None of these was built on the same mechanical system as either the Lefever Arms or D.M. Lefever guns.

LeFever Grade A

LEFEVER ARMS AUTOMATIC HAMMERLESS DOUBLE GRADE I

Same specs as Automatic Hammerless Double except 12-, 16-, 20-ga.; steel barrels; walnut half-pistol-grip stock; double triggers; extractors. The Grade I never appeared in Lefever Arms catalogues and may have been made on contract for Schoverling, Daly & Gales sporting-goods company of New York. It is the only grade Lefever Arms ever discontinued. Introduced 1899; discontinued 1907.

Exc.: $1000 **VGood:** $830 **Good:** $700

LEFEVER ARMS AUTOMATIC HAMMERLESS DOUBLE GRADE A

Same specs as Automatic Hammerless Double except 8-, 10-, 12-, 16-, 20-ga.; twist or Krupp steel barrels; Circassian or French walnut stock; pistol, half-pistol or straight grip; horn or skeleton-steel buttplate; ejectors. 8-gauge extremely rare, precludes pricing.

Other gauges
Exc.: $14,500 **VGood:** $10,000 **Good:** $9000

LEFEVER ARMS AUTOMATIC HAMMERLESS DOUBLE GRADE AA

Same specs as Automatic Hammerless Double except 8-, 10-, 12-, 16-, 20-ga.; twist or Krupp steel barrels; Circassian or French walnut stock; pistol, half-pistol or straight grip; horn or skeleton-steel buttplate; ejectors. 8-gauge extremely rare, precludes pricing.

Other gauges
Exc.: $20,000 **VGood:** $15,000 **Good:** $11,000

LEFEVER ARMS AUTOMATIC HAMMERLESS DOUBLE GRADE B

Same specs as Automatic Hammerless Double except 8-, 10-, 12-, 16-, 20-ga.; twist or Krupp steel barrels; English walnut stock; pistol, half-pistol or straight grip; extractors. 8-gauge extremely rare, precludes pricing.

Other gauges
Exc.: $4700 **VGood:** $4000 **Good:** $3000

LEFEVER ARMS AUTOMATIC HAMMERLESS DOUBLE GRADE BE

Same specs as Automatic Hammerless Double except 8-, 10-, 12-, 16-, 20-ga.; twist or Krupp steel barrels; English walnut stock; pistol, half-pistol or straight grip; ejectors. 8-gauge extremely rare, precludes pricing.

Other gauges
Exc.: $8000 **VGood:** $6500 **Good:** $5500

LEFEVER ARMS AUTOMATIC HAMMERLESS DOUBLE GRADE C

Same specs as Automatic Hammerless Double except 8-, 10-, 12-, 16-, 20-ga.; twist or Krupp steel barrels; English walnut stock; pistol, half-pistol or straight grip; extractors. 8-gauge extremely rare, precludes pricing.

Other gauges
Exc.: $3850 **VGood:** $2650 **Good:** $2400

LEFEVER ARMS AUTOMATIC HAMMERLESS DOUBLE GRADE CE

Same specs as Automatic Hammerless Double except 8-, 10-, 12-, 16-, 20-ga.; twist or Krupp steel barrels; English walnut stock; pistol, half-pistol

or straight grip; ejectors. 8-gauge extremely rare, precludes pricing.

Other gauges
Exc.: $6500 **VGood:** $4300 **Good:** $3900

LEFEVER ARMS AUTOMATIC HAMMERLESS DOUBLE GRADE D

Same specs as Automatic Hammerless Double except 8-, 10-, 12-, 16-, 20-ga.; twist or Krupp steel barrels; English walnut stock; pistol, half-pistol or straight grip; extractors. 8-gauge extremely rare, precludes pricing.

Other gauges
Exc.: $2400 **VGood:** $1900 **Good:** $1750

LEFEVER ARMS AUTOMATIC HAMMERLESS DOUBLE GRADE DE

Same specs as Automatic Hammerless Double except 8-, 10-, 12-, 16-, 20-ga.; twist or Krupp steel barrels; English walnut stock; pistol, half-pistol or straight grip; ejectors. 8-gauge extremely rare, precludes pricing.

Other gauges
Exc.: $3900 **VGood:** $3000 **Good:** $2500

LEFEVER ARMS AUTOMATIC HAMMERLESS DOUBLE GRADE DS

Same specs as Automatic Hammerless Double except 12-, 16-, 20-ga.; steel barrels; walnut half-pistol-grip stock; double triggers; extractors; grade stamp on water table.

Exc.: $1000 **VGood:** $800 **Good:** $700

LEFEVER ARMS AUTOMATIC HAMMERLESS DOUBLE GRADE DSE

Same specs as Automatic Hammerless Double except 12-, 16-, 20-ga.; steel barrels; walnut half-pistol-grip stock; double triggers; ejectors; grade stamp on water table.

Exc.: $1150 **VGood:** $900 **Good:** $790

LEFEVER ARMS AUTOMATIC HAMMERLESS DOUBLE GRADE E

Same specs as Automatic Hammerless Double except 8-, 10-, 12-, 16-, 20-ga.; twist or Krupp steel barrels; English walnut stock; pistol, half-pistol or straight grip; extractors. 8-gauge extremely rare, precludes pricing.

Other gauges
Exc.: $2200 **VGood:** $1800 **Good:** $1700

LEFEVER ARMS AUTOMATIC HAMMERLESS DOUBLE GRADE EE

Same specs as Automatic Hammerless Double except 8-, 10-, 12-, 16-, 20-ga.; twist or Krupp steel barrels; English walnut stock; pistol, half-pistol or straight grip; ejectors. 8-gauge extremely rare, precludes pricing.

Other gauges
Exc.: $3000 **VGood:** $2500 **Good:** $2200

LEFEVER ARMS AUTOMATIC HAMMERLESS DOUBLE GRADE F

Same specs as Automatic Hammerless Double except 10-, 12-, 16-, 20-ga.; twist or steel barrels; English walnut stock; pistol, half-pistol or straight grip; double triggers; extractors.

Exc.: $1650 **VGood:** $1450 **Good:** $1300

LEFEVER ARMS AUTOMATIC HAMMERLESS DOUBLE GRADE FE

Same specs as Automatic Hammerless Double except 10-, 12-, 16-, 20-ga.; twist or steel barrels;

English walnut stock; pistol, half-pistol or straight grip; double triggers; ejectors.

Exc.: $2200 **VGood:** $1650 **Good:** $1400

LEFEVER ARMS AUTOMATIC HAMMERLESS DOUBLE GRADE G

Same specs as Automatic Hammerless Double except 10-, 12-, 16-, 20-ga.; twist or steel barrels; English walnut stock; pistol, half-pistol or straight grip; double triggers; extractors.

Exc.: $1500 **VGood:** $1350 **Good:** $1200

LEFEVER ARMS AUTOMATIC HAMMERLESS DOUBLE GRADE GE

Same specs as Automatic Hammerless Double except 10-, 12-, 16-, 20-ga.; twist or steel barrels; English walnut stock; pistol, half-pistol or straight grip; double triggers; ejectors.

Exc.: $2100 **VGood:** $1600 **Good:** $1350

LEFEVER ARMS AUTOMATIC HAMMERLESS DOUBLE GRADE H

Same specs as Automatic Hammerless Double except 12-, 16-, 20-ga.; twist (12-, 16-ga.) or steel (12-, 16-, 20-ga.) barrels; English walnut stock; pistol, half-pistol or straight grip; double triggers; extractors.

Exc.: $1250 **VGood:** $1000 **Good:** $900

LEFEVER ARMS AUTOMATIC HAMMERLESS DOUBLE GRADE HE

Same specs as Automatic Hammerless Double except 12-, 16-, 20-ga.; twist (12-, 16-ga.) or steel (12-, 16-, 20-ga.) barrels; English walnut stock; pistol, half-pistol or straight grip; double triggers; ejectors.

Exc.: $1700 **VGood:** $1300 **Good:** $1000

LEFEVER ARMS AUTOMATIC HAMMERLESS DOUBLE OPTIMUS

Same specs as Automatic Hammerless Double except 8-, 10-, 12-, 16-, 20-ga.; twist or Whitworth steel barrels; Circassian or French walnut stock; pistol, half-pistol or straight grip; horn or skeleton-steel buttplate.

8-ga.
Exc.: $5000 **VGood:** $3700 **Good:** $3000
Other gauges
Exc.: $4000 **VGood:** $3000 **Good:** $2000

LEFEVER ARMS AUTOMATIC HAMMERLESS DOUBLE THOUSAND DOLLAR GRADE

Same specs as Automatic Hammerless Double except built to order.

8-ga.
Exc.: $10,000 **VGood:** $8000 **Good:** $6500
Other gauges
Exc.: $9000 **VGood:** $7000 **Good:** $5500

LEFEVER GRADE A

Side-by-side; boxlock; hammerless; 12-, 16-, 20-ga., .410; 26-inch, 28-inch, 30-inch, 32-inch barrels; standard choke combos; hand-checkered American walnut pistol-grip stock, forend; plain extractors or auto ejectors; double, single triggers. Made by Ithaca. Introduced 1934; discontinued 1942.

With extractors, double triggers
Exc.: $700 **VGood:** $500 **Good:** $390
With ejectors, double triggers
Exc.: $900 **VGood:** $700 **Good:** $550
With extractors, single trigger
Exc.: $760 **VGood:** $560 **Good:** $450

LeFever Grade A Skeet

LeFever Long Range

LeFever Nitro Special

Ljutic Bi-Gun

With ejectors, single trigger
Exc.: $900   **VGood:** $700   **Good:** $600
NOTE: 16-gauge 20 percent higher; 20-gauge 50 percent higher; .410 200 percent higher.

LEFEVER GRADE A SKEET
Same specs as Grade A, except 26-inch barrels, Skeet chokes; beavertail forend; integral auto ejector; single trigger. Introduced 1934; discontinued 1942.
Exc.: $950   **VGood:** $800   **Good:** $700
NOTE: 16-gauge 50 percent higher; 20-gauge 100 percent higher; .410 200 percent higher.

LEFEVER LONG RANGE
Single shot; boxlock; hammerless; 12-, 16-, 20-ga., .410; 26-inch, 28-inch, 30-inch, 32-inch barrels; standard chokes; vent-rib; bead front sight; hand-checkered American walnut pistol-grip stock, forearm; ejector. Introduced 1923; discontinued 1942.
Exc.: $225   **VGood:** $150   **Good:** $100

LEFEVER NITRO SPECIAL
Side-by-side; boxlock; 12-, 16-, 20-ga., .410; 26-inch, 28-inch, 30-inch, 32-inch barrels; standard choke combos; hand-checkered American walnut pistol-grip stock, forearm; single nonselective trigger; optional double triggers; plain extractors. Introduced 1921; discontinued 1948.

With double triggers
Exc.: $440   **VGood:** $310   **Good:** $195
With single trigger
Exc.: $470   **VGood:** $350   **Good:** $250
NOTE: 16-gauge 20 percent higher; 20-gauge 50 percent higher than prices shown; .410, 200 percent higher.

LEFEVER SINGLE BARREL TRAP
Single shot; boxlock; hammerless; 12-ga.; 30-inch, 32-inch barrels; Full choke; vent rib; bead front sight; hand-checkered American walnut pistol-grip stock, forearm; ejector; recoil pad. Introduced 1923; discontinued 1942.
Exc.: $350   **VGood:** $240   **Good:** $200
NOTE: 16-gauge 20 percent higher; 20-gauge 50 percent higher; .410 200 percent higher.

D.M. LEFEVER HAMMERLESS DOUBLE
Side-by-side; boxlock; hammerless; 12-, 16-, 20-ga.; 26-inch, 28-inch, 30-inch 32-inch twist or fluid-steel barrels; double triggers; optional single trigger; ejectors standard in most grades; same ball-and-socket hinge joint as Lefever Arms and most of the same adjustable features; quite rare, only about 1000 were built. Introduced 1901; discontinued 1906. Extreme rarity precludes pricing.

D.M. LEFEVER HAMMERLESS DOUBLE GRADE NO. 4, AA
Same specs as Hammerless Double except twist, Krupp steel or Whitworth steel barrels; French walnut stock; pistol, half-pistol or straight grip; ejectors; double triggers; optional single trigger; skeleton-steel or Lefever buttplate.

With double triggers
Exc.: $9000   **VGood:** $8000   **Good:** $6000
With single trigger
Exc.: $10,500   **VGood:** $9000   **Good:** $7000

D.M. LEFEVER HAMMERLESS DOUBLE GRADE NO. 5, B
Same specs as Hammerless Double except twist or Krupp steel barrels; English walnut stock; pistol, half-pistol or straight grip; skeleton-steel or Lefever buttplate; ejectors; double triggers; optional single trigger.

With double triggers
Exc.: $7500   **VGood:** $6000   **Good:** $5000
With single trigger
Exc.: $8000   **VGood:** $7000   **Good:** $6000

D.M. LEFEVER HAMMERLESS DOUBLE GRADE NO. 6, C
Same specs as Hammerless Double except twist or Krupp steel barrels; English walnut stock; pistol, half-pistol or straight grip; skeleton-steel or Lefever buttplate; ejectors; double triggers; optional single trigger.

With double triggers
Exc.: $5000   **VGood:** $4000   **Good:** $3000
With single trigger
Exc.: $6000   **VGood:** $5000   **Good:** $4000

D.M. LEFEVER HAMMERLESS DOUBLE GRADE NO. 8, E
Same specs as Hammerless Double except twist, steel, or Krupp steel barrels; English walnut stock; pistol, half-pistol or straight grip; ejectors; double triggers; optional single trigger.

With double triggers
Exc.: $4000   **VGood:** $3500   **Good:** $2500
With single trigger
Exc.: $5200   **VGood:** $4500   **Good:** $3500

D.M. LEFEVER HAMMERLESS DOUBLE GRADE NO. 9, F
Same specs as Hammerless Double except twist, steel or Krupp steel barrels; American walnut stock; pistol, half-pistol or straight grip; ejectors; double triggers; optional single trigger.

With double triggers
Exc.: $3000   **VGood:** $2750   **Good:** $2000
With single trigger
Exc.: $3750   **VGood:** $3400   **Good:** $3000

D.M. LEFEVER HAMMERLESS DOUBLE GRADE O EXCELSIOR
Same specs as Hammerless Double except twist or steel barrels; American walnut stock; pistol, half-pistol or straight grip; extractors; optional ejectors; double triggers only.

With extractors
Exc.: $2500   **VGood:** $2000   **Good:** $1500
With ejectors
Exc.: $3100   **VGood:** $2800   **Good:** $2300

D.M. LEFEVER HAMMERLESS DOUBLE UNCLE DAN GRADE
Same specs as Hammerless Double except made to order.
Exc.: $7000   **VGood:** $6200   **Good:** $5000

D.M. LEFEVER SINGLE BARREL TRAP
Single shot; boxlock; 12-ga.; 26-inch, 28-inch, 30-inch, 32-inch steel barrel; Full choke; checkered American walnut pistol-grip stock, forend; ejector; presumably available in same grades as double guns; extremely rare, total production fewer than 50; have the gun appraised by an expert. Introduced 1904; discontinued 1906.
Exc.: $1000   **VGood:** $850   **Good:** $700

LJUTIC BI-GUN
Over/under; 12-ga.; 28-inch, 33-inch barrels; choked to customer specs; hollow-milled rib; oil-finished, hand-checkered American walnut stock; choice of pull or release trigger; push-button opener in front of trigger guard; custom-made gun. Introduced 1978; no longer in production.
Perf.: $9000   **Exc.:** $8400   **VGood:** $7000

LJUTIC BI-GUN COMBO
Same specs as Bi-Gun except interchangeable single barrel; two trigger assemblies (one for single trigger, one for double). No longer in production.
Perf.: $15,000 **Exc.:** $12,500 **VGood:** $8500

LJUTIC BI-GUN FOUR-BARREL SKEET
Same specs as Bi-Gun except comes with matched 28-inch barrels in 12-, 20-, 28-ga., .410; custom checkered fancy American or French walnut stock; Ljutic Paternator chokes integral to barrels. No longer in production.
Perf.: $19,000 **Exc.:** $17,500 **VGood:** $15,500

LJUTIC BI-MATIC
Autoloader; 12-ga.; 2-3/4-inch chamber; 2-shot magazine; 26-inch, 28-inch, 30-inch, 32-inch barrel; choked to customer's specs; oil-finished, hand-checkered American walnut stock; designed for trap, Skeet; left- or right-hand ejection; many options. Introduced 1983.
Perf.: $3500 **Exc.:** $2900 **VGood:** $1990

LJUTIC DYNA TRAP
Single barrel; 12-ga.; 33-inch Full barrel; trap-style walnut stock; extractor; push-button opening. Introduced 1981; discontinued 1984.
Perf.: $2500 **Exc.:** $2150 **VGood:** $1650
Add approximately $300 to above prices for release trigger.
Add $400 for extra release trigger.
Add $250 for extra pull trigger.

LJUTIC LM-6
Over/under; 12-ga.; 2-3/4-inch chambers; 28-inch to 32-inch barrels; choked to customer's specs; hollow-milled rib; custom oil-finished, hand-checkered walnut stock; pull or release trigger push-button opener. Introduced 1988; still in production.
Perf.: $19,990 **Exc.:** $15,750 **VGood:** $11,800

LJUTIC LM-6 COMBO
Same specs as LM-6 except interchangeable single barrel; two trigger guards (one for single trigger, one for double triggers). Introduced 1988.
Perf.: $20,000 **Exc.:** $16,000 **VGood:** $12,000

LJUTIC LM-6 FOUR-BARREL SKEET SET
Same specs as LM-6, except matched set of 28-inch barrels in 12-, 20-, 28-ga. and .410; integral Ljutic Paternator chokes; custom-checkered American or French walnut stock. Introduced 1988; still in production to order.
Perf.: $28,500 **Exc.:** $20,000 **VGood:** $18,000

LJUTIC LM-6 SUPER DELUXE O/U SHOTGUN
Gauge: 12. Barrel: 28-inch to 34-inch, choked to customer specs for live birds, trap, International Trap. Weight: To customer specs. Stock: To customer specs. Oil finish, hand checkered. Features: Custom-made gun. Hollow-milled rib, pull or release trigger, pushbutton opener in front of trigger guard. From Ljutic Industries.

Super Deluxe LM-6 O/U
Perf.: $19,995 **Exc.:** $15,750 **VGood:** $11,000

LJUTIC OVER/UNDER COMBO
Interchangeable single barrel, two trigger guards, one for single trigger, one for doubles.
Perf.: $25,995 **Exc.:** $21,750 **VGood:** $17,000

Extra over/under barrel sets, 29-inch to 32-inch

LJUTIC MODEL X-73
Single barrel; 12-ga.; 33-inch Full barrel; Monte Carlo walnut stock; extractor; push-button opening. Introduced 1981; no longer in production.
Perf.: $2400 **Exc.:** $1900 **VGood:** $1800

LJUTIC MONO GUN
Single barrel; 12-ga.; 34-inch barrel; fixed or choke tubes; choice of Olympic, step-style or standard rib; hand-checkered, oil-finished fancy walnut stock; pull

Ljutic Dyna Trap

Ljutic LM-6 Deluxe

Ljutic Mono Gun

Ljutic Mono Gun LTX

Ljutic LTX Pro 3 Deluxe Mono Gun

Ljutic Space Gun

Ljutic Space Gun Vent Rib

or release trigger; removable trigger guard; push-button opening. Introduced 1962; still in production.

With fixed choke
Perf.: $5950 **Exc.:** $4000 **VGood:** $3500
With choke tubes
Perf.: $6300 **Exc.:** $4400 **VGood:** $3900
Stainless steel mono gun
Perf.: $6995 **Exc.:** $5500 **VGood:** $4450

LJUTIC MONO GUN ADJUSTABLE BARREL
Same specs as Mono Gun, except adjustable choke to adjust pattern. Introduced 1978; discontinued 1983.
Perf.: $4600 **Exc.:** $3200 **VGood:** $2700

LJUTIC MONO GUN LTX
Same specs as Mono Gun, except 33-inch extra-light barrel; double recessed choking; Olympic rib; exhibition-quality wood; extra-fancy checkering. Introduced 1985.

With fixed choke
Perf.: $7400 **Exc.:** $5600 **VGood:** $4000
With choke tubes
Perf.: $7750 **Exc.:** $5950 **VGood:** $4300

LJUTIC MONO GUN LTX SUPER DELUXE
Same specs as Mono Gun, except 33-inch extra-light barrel; double recessed choking; medium rib; exhibition-quality wood; extra-fancy checkering; release trigger. Introduced 1984; still in production.
Perf.: $6000 **Exc.:** $5000 **VGood:** $3900
With choke tubes
Exc.: $5200 **VGood:** $4100
Perf.: $6200

LJUTIC LTX PRO 3 DELUXE MONO GUN
Deluxe lightweight version of the Mono Gun with high quality wood, upgrade checkering, special rib height, screw in chokes, ported and cased.
Perf.: $8995 **Exc.:** $7750 **VGood:** $6500
Stainless steel model
Perf.: $9995 **Exc.:** $8750 **VGood:** $7500

LJUTIC SPACE GUN
Single barrel; 12-ga.; 30-inch barrel; front sight on vent rib; fancy American walnut stock with medium or large pistol grip; universal comb; pull or release button trigger; anti-recoil device. Introduced 1981; still in production.
Perf.: $5500 **Exc.:** $4500 **VGood:** $3500

LUGER CLASSIC O/U SHOTGUNS
Gauge: 12, 3-inch and 3-1/2-inch chambers; 26-inch, 28-inch, 30-inch barrel; Imp. Cyl. Mod. and Full choke tubes; weighs 7-1/2 lbs.; 45-inch overall (28-inch barrel); select-grade European walnut, hand-checkered grip and forend; gold, single selective trigger; automatic ejectors. Introduced 2000.

Classic (26-inch, 28-inch or 30-inch barrel; 3-1/2-inch chambers)

Classic Sporting (30-inch barrel; 3-inch chambers): limited importation precludes pricing.

LUGER SEMI-AUTO SHOTGUN
Gas-operated 12-ga semi-auto manufactured by Khan in Turkey. Resembles Benelli semi-auto; no longer imported.
Perf.: $400 **Exc.:** $300 **VGood:** $195

Magtech Model MT-586.2

Magtech Model MT-586P

Manufrance Falcor Pheasant Gun

Manufrance Falcor Trap

Marlin Model 17

Marlin Model 19

MAGTECH MT-151

Single shot; exposed hammer; three-piece takedown; 12-, 16-, 20-ga., .410; 2-3/4-inch (16-ga.), 3-inch chamber; 25-inch (.410 only), 26-inch, 28-inch, 30-inch barrel; weighs about 5 3/4 lbs.; Brazilian hardwood stock, beavertail forend; trigger guard opener button. Made in Brazil. Introduced 1991; dropped 1992.

Perf.: $100   Exc.: $80   VGood: $60

MAGTECH MODEL MT-586.2

Slide action; 12-ga.; 2-3/4-inch, 3-inch chamber; 28-inch Full, Modified or Improved Modified barrel; Brazilian Embuia hardwood stock, grooved slide handle; crossbolt safety; dual-action slide bars; blued finish. Made in Brazil. Introduced 1991; discontinued 1995.

Perf.: $190   Exc.: $175   VGood: $160

MAGTECH MODEL MT-586.2-VR

Same specs as Model MT-586.2 except 12-ga.; 3-inch chamber; 26-inch, 28-inch barrel; choke tubes; weighs 7-1/4 lbs.; 46-1/2-inch overall length (26-inch barrel); ventilated rib with bead front sight. Made in Brazil. Introduced 1995; no longer imported.

Perf.: $230   Exc.: $180   VGood: $150

MAGTECH MODEL MT-586 SLUG

Same specs as Model MT-586.2 except 24-inch Cylinder barrel; rifle sights; Brazilian Embuia hardwood Monte Carlo stock, slide handle; matte finish. Made in Brazil. Introduced 1991; discontinued 1995.

Perf.: $180   Exc.: $150   VGood: $130

MAGTECH MODEL MT-586P

Slide action; 12-ga.; 3-inch chamber; 7-shot magazine; 19-inch Cylinder bore barrel; weighs 7-1/4 lbs.; bead front sight; Brazilian hardwood stock,

pump handle; crossbolt safety dual-action slide bars; blued finish. Made in Brazil. Introduced 1991; still in production.

Perf.: $180   Exc.: $150   VGood: $130

MANUFRANCE AUTO

Gas-operated autoloader; 12-ga.; 2-3/4-inch, 3-inch chamber; 3-shot magazine; 26-inch Improved Cylinder, 28-inch Modified, 30-inch Full choke barrels; vent rib; hand-checkered French walnut pistol-grip stock; black matte finish; quick takedown; interchangeable barrels. Made in France. Introduced 1978; no longer in production.

Perf.: $325   Exc.: $260   VGood: $230

MANUFRANCE FALCOR COMPETITION TRAP

Over/under; boxlock; 12-ga.; 2-3/4-inch chambers; 30-inch chrome-lined barrels; alloy high-post rib; 48-inch overall length; ivory bead front sight on metal sleeve, middle ivory bead; hand-checkered French walnut stock, smooth beavertail forend; hand-rubbed oil finish; inertia-type trigger; top tang safety/barrel selector; auto ejectors. Made in France. Introduced 1984; discontinued 1985.

Perf.: $700   Exc.: $600   VGood: $540

MANUFRANCE FALCOR PHEASANT GUN

Same specs as Falcor Competition Trap, except 27-1/2-inch chrome-lined barrels; metal bead front sight; checkered forend; single trigger; silver-gray finish; scroll engraving on receiver top lever, trigger guard. Made in France. Introduced 1984; discontinued 1985.

Perf.: $800   Exc.: $700   VGood: $640

MANUFRANCE FALCOR SKEET

Same specs as Falcor Competition Trap except 27-1/2-inch Skeet barrels; vent top and middle rib; luminous yellow front bead in metal sleeve;

checkered forend; smooth Skeet buttpad. Introduced 1984; discontinued 1985.

Perf.: $700   Exc.: $600   VGood: $540

MANUFRANCE FALCOR TRAP

Same specs as Falcor Competition Trap, except vent top and middle rib; luminous yellow front bead in metal sleeve; checkered forend. Made in France. Introduced 1984; discontinued 1985.

Perf.: $700   Exc.: $600   VGood: $540

MANUFRANCE ROBUST

Side-by-side; boxlock; 12-ga.; 2-3/4-inch chambers; 20-1/2-inch, 27-1/2-inch barrels; hand-checkered French walnut stock, beavertail forend; double triggers; extractors; top tang safety; color case-hardened receiver. Introduced 1984; discontinued 1985.

Perf.: $500   Exc.: $400   VGood: $340

MANUFRANCE ROBUST DELUXE

Same specs as Robust except 27-1/2-inch chrome-lined barrels; auto ejectors; silver-gray finish; scroll engraving on receiver, top lever, trigger guard; optional retractable sling in butt. Made in France. Introduced 1984; discontinued 1985.

Perf.: $550   Exc.: $450   VGood: $390

MARLIN MODEL 16

Slide action; visible hammer; takedown; 16-ga.; 5-shot tubular magazine; 26-inch, 28-inch barrel; standard chokes; American walnut pistol-grip stock, grooved slide handle; made in four grades, differing in quality of wood, engraving and checkering on Grades C, D. Introduced 1903; discontinued 1910.

Grade A		
Exc.: $275	**VGood: $225**	**Good: $200**
Grade B		
Exc.: $485	**VGood: $400**	**Good: $375**
Grade C		
Exc.: $715	**VGood: $635**	**Good: $580**
Grade D		
Exc.: $120	**VGood: $1050**	**Good: $900**

MARLIN MODEL 17

Slide action; visible hammer; solid frame; 12-ga.; 5-shot tubular magazine; 30-inch, 32-inch barrel; Full choke; uncheckered American walnut straight-grip stock, grooved slide handle. Introduced 1906; discontinued 1908.

Exc.: $300   VGood: $210   Good: $150

MARLIN MODEL 17 BRUSH

Same specs as Model 17, except for 26-inch Cylinder barrel. Introduced 1906; discontinued 1908.

Exc.: $275   VGood: $150   Good: $130

MARLIN MODEL 17 RIOT

Same specs as Model 17, except for 20-inch Cylinder barrel. Introduced 1906; discontinued 1908.

Exc.: $260   VGood: $150   Good: $140

MARLIN MODEL 19

Slide action; visible hammer; 12-ga.; 5-shot tubular magazine; 26-inch, 28-inch, 30-inch, 32-inch barrel; standard chokes; American walnut pistol-grip stock, grooved slide handle; checkering on higher grades; two extractors; matted sighting groove on top of lightweight receiver; made in four grades, differing in quality of workmanship, wood and amount of engraving. Introduced 1906; discontinued 1907.

Grade A		
Exc.: $325	**VGood: $240**	**Good: $150**
Grade B		
Exc.: $425	**VGood: $325**	**Good: $240**
Grade C		
Exc.: $550	**VGood: $475**	**Good: $325**
Grade D		
Exc.: $1000	**VGood: $750**	**Good: $650**

MARLIN MODEL 21 TRAP

Slide action; visible hammer; 12-ga.; 5-shot tubular magazine; 26-inch, 28-inch, 30-inch, 32-inch barrel; standard chokes; American walnut straight-grip stock, grooved slide handle; checkering on higher grades; two extractors; matted sighting groove on top of lightweight receiver; made in four grades, differing in workmanship, quality of wood and engraving. Introduced 1907; discontinued 1908.

Grade A		
Exc.: $375	**VGood:** $225	**Good:** $120
Grade B		
Exc.: $425	**VGood:** $325	**Good:** $225
Grade C		
Exc.: $550	**VGood:** $450	**Good:** $300
Grade D		
Exc.: $1175	**VGood:** $1050	**Good:** $600

MARLIN MODEL 24

Slide action; visible hammer; improved takedown; 12-ga.; 5-shot tubular magazine; 26-inch, 28-inch, 30-inch, 32-inch barrel; standard chokes; solid matted rib attached to frame; American walnut pistol-grip stock, grooved slide handle; checkering or higher grades; two extractors; matted sighting groove on top of lightweight receiver; automatic recoil safety lock; made in four grades. Introduced 1908; discontinued 1917.

Grade A		
Exc.: $325	**VGood:** $275	**Good:** $150
Grade B		
Exc.: $450	**VGood:** $400	**Good:** $280
Grade C		
Exc.: $575	**VGood:** $500	**Good:** $350
Grade D		
Exc.: $1100	**VGood:** $800	**Good:** $600

MARLIN MODEL 25MG GARDEN GUN SHOTGUN

Gauge: 22 WMR shotshell; 7-shot magazine; 22-inch smoothbore barrel; weighs 6 lbs.; 41-inch overall; press-checkered hardwood; high-visibility bead front sight; bolt action; thumb safety; red cocking indicator. Introduced 1999. Discontinued 2002. Made in U.S. by Marlin.

   Perf.: $190   **Exc.:** $155   **VGood:** $130

MARLIN MODEL 26

Slide action; visible hammer; solid frame; 12-ga.; 5-shot tubular magazine; 30-inch, 32-inch Full-choke barrel; solid matted rib attached to frame; American walnut straight-grip stock, grooved slide handle; two extractors; matted sighting groove on top of lightweight receiver; automatic recoil safety lock. Introduced 1909; discontinued 1916.

   Exc.: $250   **VGood:** $200   **Good:** $120

MARLIN MODEL 26 BRUSH

Same specs as Model 26, except 26-inch Cylinder barrel. Introduced 1909; discontinued 1916.

   Exc.: $250   **VGood:** $180   **Good:** $120

MARLIN MODEL 26 RIOT

Same specs as Model 26, except 20-inch Cylinder barrel. Introduced 1909; discontinued 1915.

   Exc.: $250   **VGood:** $175   **Good:** $120

MARLIN MODEL 28

Slide action; hammerless; takedown; 12-ga.; 5-shot tubular magazine; 26-inch, 28-inch, 30-inch, 32-inch barrel; standard chokes; American walnut pistol-grip stock, grooved slide handle; matted barrel top or solid matted rib (28D); made in four grades, differing in quality of wood, amount of engraving on 28C, 28D. Introduced 1913; 28B, 28C, 28D discontinued 1915; 28A discontinued 1922.

Grade A		
Exc.: $275	**VGood:** $225	**Good:** $175
Grade B		
Exc.: $475	**VGood:** $325	**Good:** $250
Grade C		
Exc.: $600	**VGood:** $500	**Good:** $395
Grade D		
Exc.: $1200	**VGood:** $875	**Good:** $625

MARLIN MODEL 28T

Same specs as Model 28, except 30-inch Full-choke barrel; matted rib; hand-checkered American walnut

straight-grip stock; high fluted comb; fancier wood. Introduced 1915; discontinued 1915.

   Exc.: $500   **VGood:** $420   **Good:** $355

MARLIN MODEL 28TS

Same specs as Model 28, except 30-inch Full-choke barrel; American walnut straight-grip stock; matted barrel top. Introduced 1915; discontinued 1915.

   Exc.: $400   **VGood:** $350   **Good:** $250

MARLIN MODEL 30

Slide action; visible hammer; improved takedown; 16-ga.; 5-shot tubular magazine; 26-inch, 28-inch barrel; standard chokes; solid matted rib on frame; American walnut pistol-grip stock, grooved slide handle; auto recoil safety lock; made in four grades depending upon quality of wood, amount and quality of engraving. Introduced 1911; discontinued 1917.

Grade A		
Exc.: $325	**VGood:** $275	**Good:** $225
Grade B		
Exc.: $475	**VGood:** $375	**Good:** $300
Grade C		
Exc.: $575	**VGood:** $495	**Good:** $375
Grade D		
Exc.: $1200	**VGood:** $975	**Good:** $695

MARLIN MODEL 30 FIELD

Same specs as Model 30, except 25-inch barrel; Modified choke; American walnut straight-grip stock. Introduced 1911; discontinued 1917.

   Exc.: $300   **VGood:** $200   **Good:** $100

MARLIN MODEL 31

Slide action; hammerless; 16-, 20-ga.; 5-shot tubular magazine; 25-inch, 26-inch, 28-inch barrel; standard chokes; American walnut pistol-grip stock, grooved slide handle; matted barrel top; scaled-down version of Model 28; made in four grades, differing in quality

Marlin Model 24
Grade A

Marlin Model 28
Grade B

Marlin Model
30 Grade D

Marlin Model 31
Grade A

Marlin Model 42A

Marlin Model 43A

wood, checkering and engraving. Introduced 1914; discontinued 1917.

Grade A		
Exc.: $350	**VGood:** $250	**Good:** $140
Grade B		
Exc.: $400	**VGood:** $300	**Good:** $260
Grade C		
Exc.: $550	**VGood:** $475	**Good:** $350
Grade D		
Exc.: $1100	**VGood:** $800	**Good:** $500

MARLIN MODEL 31 FIELD

Same specs as Model 31, except 25-inch barrel; Modified choke; American walnut straight- or pistol-grip stock. Introduced 1914; discontinued 1917.

   Exc.: $350   **VGood:** $325   **Good:** $290

MARLIN MODEL 42A

Slide action; visible hammer; takedown; 12-ga.; 5-shot tubular magazine; 26-inch Cylinder, 28-inch Modified, 30-inch or 32-inch Full barrel; bead front sight; unchecked American walnut pistol-grip stock, grooved slide handle. Introduced 1922; discontinued 1933.

   Exc.: $260   **VGood:** $225   **Good:** $175

MARLIN MODEL 43A

Slide action; hammerless; takedown; 12-ga.; 5-shot tubular magazine; 26-inch 28-inch, 30-inch, 32-inch barrel; standard chokes; American walnut pistol-grip stock, grooved slide handle; matted barrel top. Introduced 1922; discontinued 1930.

   Exc.: $275   **VGood:** $250   **Good:** $200

MARLIN MODEL 43T

Same specs as Model 43A, except 30-inch Full-choke barrel; matted rib; American walnut straight-grip stock. Introduced 1922; discontinued 1930.

   Exc.: $350   **VGood:** $300   **Good:** $250

Marlin Model 43T

Marlin Model 44A

Marlin Model 50

Marlin Model 53

Marlin Model 55

Marlin Model 55
Fixed Choke

Marlin Model 55
Adjustable Choke

Marlin Model 55
Goose Gun

Marlin Model 55 Swamp Gun

Marlin Model 59 Olympic

MARLIN MODEL 50

Bolt action; 12-, 20-ga.; 2-shot clip magazine; 28-inch (12-ga.), 26-inch (20-ga.) barrel; Full or adjustable choke; uncheckered American walnut one-piece pistol-grip stock; thumb safety; sling swivels; leather sling; double extractors; tapped for receiver sights. Introduced 1967; discontinued 1975.

With fixed choke
Perf.: $125   **Exc.:** $80   **VGood:** $60

With adjustable choke
Perf.: $140   **Exc.:** $90   **VGood:** $70

MARLIN MODEL 53

Slide action; hammerless; takedown; 12-ga.; 5-shot tubular magazine; 26-inch, 28-inch, 30-inch, 32-inch barrel; standard chokes; American walnut pistol-grip stock, grooved slide handle; matted barrel top. Introduced 1929; discontinued 1931.

Exc.: $300   **VGood:** $250   **Good:** $200

MARLIN MODEL 55

Bolt action; takedown; 12-, 16-, 20-ga.; 28-inch (12-, 16-ga.); 26-inch (20-ga.) barrel; Full or adjustable choke; uncheckered American walnut one-piece pistol-grip stock; recoil pad (12-ga.). Introduced 1954; discontinued 1965.

With fixed choke
Exc.: $200   **VGood:** $160   **Good:** $140

With adjustable choke
Exc.: $250   **VGood:** $190   **Good:** $150

MARLIN MODEL 55 GOOSE GUN

Same general specs as Model 55 except 3" 12-ga.; 2-shot clip magazine; 36-inch barrel; Full choke; thumb safety; sling swivels; leather carrying strap; double extractors; tapped for receiver sights. Introduced 1962.

Perf.: $300   **Exc.:** $260   **VGood:** $175

MARLIN MODEL 55 SWAMP GUN

Same specs as Model 55, except 12-ga., 3-inch chamber; 20-1/2-inch barrel; adjustable choke; sling swivels. Introduced 1963; discontinued 1965.

Exc.: $300   **VGood:** $200   **Good:** $100

MARLIN MODEL 55S SLUG

Same specs as Model 55, except 12-ga.; 2-shot clip magazine; 24-inch Cylinder barrel; rifle sights; tapped for receiver sights; thumb safety; sling swivels; leather carrying strap; double extractors. Introduced 1973; discontinued 1979.

Perf.: $275   **Exc.:** $250   **VGood:** $185

MARLIN MODEL 59 OLYMPIC

Single shot; bolt action; .410; 2-1/2-inch, 3-inch chamber; 24-inch Full barrel; bead front sight; uncheckered one-piece walnut pistol-grip stock, also available with Junior stock with 12-inch length of pull; self-cocking bolt; automatic thumb safety. Introduced 1959; discontinued 1965.

Exc.: $150   **VGood:** $125   **Good:** $100

MARLIN MODEL 59 OLYMPIC JUNIOR

Same specs as Model 59 Olympic except smaller sized stock with 12-inch length of pull. No longer in production.

Exc.: $165   **VGood:** $140   **Good:** $115

MARLIN MODEL 60

Single shot; boxlock; visible hammer; takedown; 12-ga.; 30-inch, 32-inch Full barrel; walnut pistol-grip stock, beavertail forend; automatic ejector. Limited production of 600 to 3000. Introduced 1923; discontinued 1923.

Exc.: $300   **VGood:** $225   **Good:** $175

MARLIN MODEL 63A

Slide action; hammerless; takedown; 12-ga.; 5-shot magazine; 26-inch, 28-inch, 30-inch, 32-inch barrel; standard chokes; American walnut pistol-grip stock, grooved slide handle; matted barrel top. Replaced model 43A. Introduced 1931; discontinued 1933.

Exc.: $300   **VGood:** $225   **Good:** $125

MARLIN MODEL 43TS

Same specs as Model 43, except 30-inch Full-choke barrel; American walnut straight-grip stock. Introduced 1922; discontinued 1930.

Exc.: $400   **VGood:** $340   **Good:** $290

MARLIN MODEL 44A

Slide action; hammerless; 20-ga.; 5-shot tubular magazine; 25-inch, 26-inch, 28-inch barrel; standard chokes; American walnut pistol-grip stock, grooved slide handle; matted barrel top. Introduced 1922; discontinued 1933.

Exc.: $325   **VGood:** $275   **Good:** $225

MARLIN MODEL 44S

Same specs as Model 44A, except select hand-checkered American walnut stock, slide handle. Introduced 1922; discontinued 1933.

Exc.: $350   **VGood:** $300   **Good:** $250

MARLIN MODEL 49

Slide action; visible hammer; takedown; 12-ga.; 5-shot tubular magazine; 26-inch Cylinder, 28-inch Modified, 30-inch or 32-inch Full barrel; bead front sight; uncheckered American walnut pistol-grip stock, grooved slide handle. Used by Marlin as a premium, with purchase of four shares of corporate stock; fewer than 3000 made. Introduced 1928; discontinued 1930.

Exc.: $400   **VGood:** $350   **Good:** $275

MARLIN MODEL 63T

Same specs as Model 63A, except 30-inch Full-choke barrel; matted rib; American walnut straight-grip stock. Introduced 1931; discontinued 1933.

Exc.: $325   **VGood:** $275   **Good:** $225

MARLIN MODEL 63TS TRAP SPECIAL

Same specs as Model 63A, except 30-inch Full-choke barrel; matted rib; American walnut trap-style stock with dimensions to special order. Introduced 1931; discontinued 1933.

Exc.: $375   **VGood:** $325   **Good:** $275

MARLIN MODEL 90

Over/under; boxlock; 12-, 16-, 20-ga.; .410; 26-inch, 28-inch, 30-inch barrels; Improved/Modified, Modified/Full chokes; full-length rib between barrels; bead front sight; hand-checkered American walnut pistol-grip stock, forearm; double triggers; optional single non-selective trigger; recoil pad. Introduced 1937; discontinued during WWII.

With double triggers		
Exc.: $440	**VGood:** $280	**Good:** $200
With single trigger		
Exc.: $550	**VGood:** $380	**Good:** $300
.410 model, double triggers		
Exc.: $900	**VGood:** $520	**Good:** $350
.410 model, single trigger		
Exc.: $950	**VGood:** $575	**Good:** $400

MARLIN MODEL 90-DT

Same specs as Model 90 except post-WWII version with double triggers; no rib between barrels; no recoil pad. Introduced 1949; discontinued 1958. Deduct 15 percent for 16-ga.

Exc.: $400	**VGood:** $350	**Good:** $295
.410 model		
Exc.: $1000	**VGood:** $875	**Good:** $550

MARLIN MODEL 90-ST

Same specs as Model 90, except post-WWII version with single non-selective trigger; no rib between barrels; no recoil pad. Introduced 1949; discontinued 1958.

Exc.: $500	**VGood:** $380	**Good:** $300
.410 model		
Exc.: $1050	**VGood:** $925	**Good:** $600

MARLIN MODEL 120 MAGNUM

Slide action; hammerless; 12-ga.; 2-3/4-inch, 3-inch chamber; 26-inch Improved Cylinder, 28-inch Modified, 30-inch Full barrel; vent rib; checkered walnut pistol-grip stock, semi-beavertail forearm; slide release button; crossbolt safety; interchangeable barrels; side ejection. Introduced 1971; discontinued 1984. Add 20 percent for 40-inch "Long Tom" barrel.

Exc.: $325   **VGood:** $275   **Good:** $200

MARLIN MODEL 120 TRAP

Same specs as Model 120 Magnum, except 30-inch Full or Modified barrel; hand-checkered Monte Carlo stock, full forearm. Introduced 1973; discontinued 1975.

Exc.: $345   **VGood:** $295   **Good:** $220

MARLIN MODEL .410

Lever action; visible hammer; solid frame; .410, 2-1/2-inch shell; 4-shot tubular magazine; 22-inch, 26-inch barrel; Full choke; uncheckered American walnut pistol-grip stock, grooved beavertail forend. Used by Marlin as a promotional firearm for shareholders. Introduced 1929; discontinued 1932.

Exc.: $1000   **VGood:** $850   **Good:** $675

MARLIN LEVER ACTION .410 (RECENT)

Lever action shotgun based on 1895 lever action rifle action, chambered for 2-1/2-inch shells. Cylinder bore, rubber buttplate, fold-down rear sight. Discontinued.

Exc.: $1100   **VGood:** $850   **Good:** $675

Marlin Model 90-DT

Marlin Model 120 Magnum

Marlin Model 410

Marlin Model 512 Slugmaster

Marlin Model 1898 Grade A

Marlin Model 5510

Marlin Premier Mark I

Marlin Premier Mark II

MARLIN MODEL 512 SLUGMASTER

Bolt action; 12-ga.; 3-inch chamber; 2-shot detachable box magazine; 21-inch rifled barrel with 1:28-inch twist; weighs 8 lbs.; 44-3/4-inch overall length; ramp front sight with brass bead and removable hood, adjustable folding semi-buckhorn rear; drilled and tapped for scope mounting; press-checkered, walnut-finished Maine birch stock; ventilated recoil pad. Uses Model 55 action with thumb safety. Designed for shooting saboted slugs. Introduced 1994; dropped 1999.

Perf.: $295   **Exc.:** $220   **VGood:** $195

MARLIN MODEL 1898

Slide action; visible hammer; takedown; 12-ga.; 5-shot tubular magazine; 26-inch, 28-inch, 30-inch, 32-inch barrel; standard chokes; American walnut pistol-grip stock, grooved slide handle; checkering on higher grades; grades differ in quality of woods, amount of engraving; Marlin's first shotgun. Introduced 1898; discontinued 1905.

Grade A		
Exc.: $325	**VGood:** $250	**Good:** $190
Grade B		
Exc.: $420	**VGood:** $320	**Good:** $275

Grade C		
Exc.: $600	**VGood:** $500	**Good:** $420
Grade D		
Exc.: $1250	**VGood:** $1000	**Good:** $850

MARLIN MODEL 5510 GOOSE GUN

Bolt action; takedown; 10-ga.; 3-1/2-inch chamber; 2-shot clip magazine; 34-inch heavy barrel; Full choke; uncheckered American walnut one-piece pistol-grip stock; recoil pad; sling swivels; leather sling. Introduced 1976; discontinued 1985.

Perf.: $395   **Exc.:** $350   **VGood:** $290

MARLIN PREMIER MARK I

Slide-action; hammerless; takedown; 12-ga.; 3-shot magazine; 26-inch Improved or Skeet, 28-inch Modified, 30-inch Full barrel; bead front sight; French walnut pistol-grip stock, forearm; bead front sight; side ejection; crossbolt safety. Made in France by Manufrance. Introduced 1961; discontinued 1963.

Exc.: $200   **VGood:** $175   **Good:** $100

MARLIN PREMIER MARK II

Same specs as Premier Mark I, except checkered pistol grip, forearm; scroll-engraved receiver. Made in France. Introduced 1961; discontinued 1963.

Exc.: $210   **VGood:** $190   **Good:** $110

Marlin Premier Mark IV

Marlin-Glenfield Model 778

Marocchi America

Marocchi Avanza

Marocchi Conquista
Sporting Clays

Marocchi Contrast

MARLIN PREMIER MARK IV
Same specs as Premier Mark I except optional vent rib; fine checkering; better wood; pistol-grip cap; full-coverage engraved receiver; engraved trigger guard. Made in France. Introduced 1961; discontinued 1963.

Exc.: $275   **VGood:** $225   **Good:** $175

With vent rib

Exc.: $305   **VGood:** $250   **Good:** $190

MARLIN-GLENFIELD MODEL 55G
Bolt action; takedown; 12-, 16-, 20-ga.; 28-inch (12-, 16-ga.); 26-inch (20-ga.) barrel; Full or adjustable choke; uncheckered walnut-finished hardwood one-piece pistol-grip stock; recoil pad (12-ga.). Introduced 1954; discontinued 1965.

With fixed choke

Exc.: $185   **VGood:** $160   **Good:** $140

With adjustable choke

Exc.: $195   **VGood:** $170   **Good:** $150

MARLIN-GLENFIELD MODEL 60G
Single shot; bolt action; .410; 2-1/2-inch, 3-inch chamber; 24-inch Full barrel; bead front sight; uncheckered walnut-finished hardwood one-piece pistol-grip stock; also available with junior stock with 12-inch length of pull; self-cocking bolt; automatic thumb safety. Introduced 1960; discontinued 1964.

Exc.: $75   **VGood:** $60   **Good:** $40

MARLIN-GLENFIELD MODEL 60G JUNIOR
Same specs as Model 60G except smaller-sized stock with 12-inch length of pull. No longer in production.

Exc.: $75   **VGood:** $60   **Good:** $40

MARLIN-GLENFIELD MODEL 778
Slide action; 12-ga.; 2-3/4-inch, 3-inch chambers; 5-shot magazine; 20-inch slug barrel with sights, 26-inch Improved, 28-inch Modified, 30-inch Full barrel; plain or vent rib; walnut-finished hardwood stock, semi-beavertail forend; steel receiver; engine-turned bolt; double action bars; vent recoil pad. Introduced 1979; discontinued 1984. Glenfield-labaled version of Marlin Model 120.

With plain barrel

Perf.: $230   **Exc.:** $180   **VGood:** $125

With vent rib

Perf.: $250   **Exc.:** $200   **VGood:** $150

MAROCCHI AMERICA
Over/under; 12-, 20-ga.; 2-3/4-inch chambers; 26-inch to 29-inch Skeet, 27-inch to 32-inch trap, barrels, 30-inch, 32-inch single barrel; hand-checkered select European walnut stock, schnabel or beavertail forend; left- or right-hand palm swell; medium engraving coverage on frame; custom engraving, inlays offered. Marketed in fitted hard case. Made in Italy. Introduced 1983; discontinued 1986.

Perf.: $1800   **Exc.:** $1550   **VGood:** $1200

With deluxe engraving

Perf.: $1950   **Exc.:** $1700   **VGood:** $1350

MAROCCHI AVANZA
Over/under; 12-, 20-ga.; 2-3/4-inch chambers; 26-inch, 28-inch barrels; fixed or Interchokes; vent top, middle ribs; weighs 6-3/4 lbs.; cut-checkered select walnut stock; recoil pad; auto mechanical barrel cycling; auto selective ejectors; auto safety; single selective trigger. Made in Italy. Introduced 1990; discontinued 1993.

Perf.: $700   **Exc.:** $575   **VGood:** $480

MAROCCHI AVANZA SPORTING CLAYS
Same specs as Avanza except 12-ga.; 28-inch vent-rib barrels; Interchokes; trigger adjustable for length. Made in Italy. Introduced 1990; still in production.

Perf.: $800   **Exc.:** $550   **VGood:** $490

MAROCCHI CONQUISTA SKEET
Over/under; boxlock; 12-ga.; 2-3/4-inch chambers; 28-inch Skeet/Skeet barrels; 10mm concave vent rib; checkered American walnut pistol-grip stock, forend; buttpad. Weighs about 7-3/4 lbs. Introduced 1994. Ergonomically shaped trigger adjustable for pull length and weight; automatic selective ejectors; coin-finished receiver, blued barrels; hard case; stock wrench. Also available as true left-hand model-opening lever operates from left to right; stock has left-hand cast. Made in Italy. Introduced 1994; still imported.

Grade I, right-hand

Perf.: $1725   **Exc.:** $1475   **VGood:** $1225

Grade II, right-hand

Perf.: $1995   **Exc.:** $1675   **VGood:** $1450

Grade III, right-hand; MSR

Perf.: $3225   **Exc.:** $2650   **VGood:** $2250

MAROCCHI CONQUISTA SPORTING CLAYS
Same specs as Conquista Skeet except 28-inch, 30-inch, 32-inch barrels; Contrechoke tubes; Sporting Clays buttpad; no left-hand model. Made in Italy. Introduced 1994; still imported.

Grade I

Perf.: $1725   **Exc.:** $1450   **VGood:** $1200

Add approximately $125 to above prices for left-hand version.

Grade II

Perf.: $1995   **Exc.:** $1675   **VGood:** $1425

Add approximately $355 to above prices for left-hand version.

Grade III

Perf.: $3225   **Exc.:** $2650   **VGood:** $2250

Add approximately $396 to above prices for left-hand version.

MAROCCHI CONQUISTA TRAP
Same specs as the Conquista Skeet except 30-inch, 32-inch barrels; Full/Full; weighs about 8-1/4 lbs.; trap stock dimensions; no left-hand model. Made in Italy. Introduced 1994; still imported.

Grade I (RH)

Perf.: $1700   **Exc.:** $1450   **VGood:** $1250

Grade II (RH)

Perf.: $1890   **Exc.:** $1600   **VGood:** $1400

Grade III

Perf.: $3225   **Exc.:** $2650   **VGood:** $2200

MAROCCHI LADY SPORT
Over/under; boxlock; 12-ga.; 2-3/4-inch chambers; 28-inch, 30-inch barrels; five Contrechoke tubes; 10mm concave vent rib; weighs about 7-1/2 lbs.; checkered American walnut pistol-grip stock, forend; buttpad; ergonomically shaped trigger adjustable for pull length and weight; automatic selective ejectors; coin-finished receiver, blued barrels; hard case; stock wrench; ergonomically designed specifically for women shooters; available with colored graphics finish on frame and opening lever. Also available as true left-hand model-opening lever operates from left to right; stock has left-hand cast. Made in Italy. Introduced 1995.

Grade I

Perf.: $1750   **Exc.:** $1200   **VGood:** $1100

Grade II

Perf.: $1850   **Exc.:** $1450   **VGood:** $1250

Grade III

Perf.: $2850   **Exc.:** $2050   **VGood:** $1850

MAROCCHI CONTRAST
Over/under; 12-, 20-ga.; 2-3/4-inch chambers; 26-inch to 29-inch Skeet, 27-inch to 32-inch trap barrels; select European walnut stock; hand-checkered pistol grip, schnabel or beavertail forend; hand-rubbed wax finish; left or right-hand palm swell; light engraving on standard grade; custom engraving, inlays at added cost. Marketed in fitted hard case. Made in Italy. Introduced 1983; discontinued 1986.

Perf.: $1800   **Exc.:** $1450   **VGood:** $1100

With deluxe engraving

Perf.: $1950   **Exc.:** $1600   **VGood:** $1250

MAROCCHI CONQUISTA USA MODEL 92 SPORTING CLAYS O/U SHOTGUN

Gauge: 12, 3-inch chambers; 30-inch barrel; back-bored, ported (ContreChoke Plus tubes); 10mm concave ventilated top rib, ventilated middle rib; weighs 8 lbs. 2 oz.; stock dimensions 14-1/4-inch-14-5/8-inchx 2-1/8-inchx1-3/8-inch; American walnut with checkered grip and forend; Sporting Clays butt pad; low profile frame; fast lock time; automatic selective ejectors; blued receiver and barrels; three choke tubes; ergonomically shaped trigger adjustable for pull length without tools; barrels are back-bored and ported. Introduced 1996. Imported from Italy by Precision Sales International.

Perf.: $1450   **Exc.:** $1175   **VGood:** $950

MAROCCHI MODEL 99 SPORTING TRAP AND SKEET

Gauge: 12, 2-3/4-inch, 3-inch chambers; 28-inch, 30-inch, 32-inch barrel; French walnut; Boss Locking system; screw-in chokes; low recoil, lightweight monoblock barrels and ribs. Imported from Italy by Precision Sales International.

Grade I
Perf.: $1995   **Exc.:** $1750   **VGood:** $1500
Grade II
Perf.: $2475   **Exc.:** $2125   **VGood:** $1725
Grade II Gold
Perf.: $2630   **Exc.:** $2280   **VGood:** $1880
Grade III
Perf.: $2925   **Exc.:** $2400   **VGood:** $2000
Grade III Gold
Perf.: $3110   **Exc.:** $2585   **VGood:** $2185
Blackgold
Perf.: $3650   **Exc.:** $3200   **VGood:** $2600
Lodestar
Perf.: $4625   **Exc.:** $4175   **VGood:** $3575
Brittania
Perf.: $4625   **Exc.:** $4175   **VGood:** $3575
Diana
Perf.: $5850   **Exc.:** $5400   **VGood:** $4800

MAROCCHI SM-28 SXS

Side-by-side; 12-, 20-ga.; 2-3/4-inch chamber; totally handmade to customers specs and dimensions. Supplied with fitted leather luggage case. Introduced 1983; discontinued 1986.

Perf.: $10,000   **Exc.:** $8500   **VGood:** $7500

MAROCCHI PRITI

Over/under; 12-, 20-ga.; 3-inch chambers; 28-inch barrels; vent top and middle ribs; hand-checkered walnut stock; auto safety; extractors; double triggers; engraved antique silver receiver. Made in Italy. Introduced 1984; discontinued 1988.

Perf.: $324   **Exc.:** $285   **VGood:** $250

MAUSER MODEL CONTEST

Over/under; 12-ga.; 27-1/2-inch chrome-lined barrels; select European walnut stock; receiver engraved with hunting scenes; dummy sideplates; auto ejectors; single selective trigger. Made in Germany. Introduced 1981; no longer in production.

Trap Model
Perf.: $1100   **Exc.:** $950   **VGood:** $800
Skeet Model
Perf.: $1500   **Exc.:** $1200   **VGood:** $900

MAUSER-BAUER MODEL 71E

Over/under; Greener crossbolt boxlock; 12-ga.; 28-inch Modified/Full, Improved/Modified barrels; vent rib; hand-checkered European walnut pistol-grip stock, beavertail forearm; double triggers; automatic ejectors. Made in Italy. Introduced 1972; discontinued 1973.

Perf.: $375   **Exc.:** $250   **VGood:** $200

MAUSER-BAUER MODEL 72E

Over/under; boxlock; 12-ga.; 28-inch Full/Modified, 30-inch Full/Full barrels; wide vent rib; hand-checkered European walnut pistol-grip stock,

Marocchi Conquista USA Model 92 Sporting Clays

Maroccini Priti

Mauser-Bauer Model 71E

Mauser-Bauer Model 72E

Mauser-Bauer Model 496

Mauser-Bauer Model 496 Competition Grade

Mauser-Bauer Model 610 Phantom

Mauser-Bauer Model 620

beavertail forearm; Greener crossbolt; single trigger; automatic ejectors; engraved receiver. Made in Italy. Introduced 1972; discontinued 1973.

Perf.: $300   **Exc.:** $260   **VGood:** $225

MAUSER-BAUER MODEL 496

Single barrel; single shot; boxlock; 12-ga.; 32-inch Modified, 34-inch Full-choke barrel; matted vent rib; hand-checkered European walnut Monte Carlo stock, forearm; recoil pad; automatic ejector; auto safety; Greener crossbolt; double underlocking blocks; color case-hardened action; scroll engraving. Introduced 1972; discontinued 1974.

Perf.: $495   **Exc.:** $385   **VGood:** $295

MAUSER-BAUER MODEL 496 COMPETITION GRADE

Same specs as Model 496 except high ramp rib; front, middle sight bead; hand finishing on wood and metal parts. Introduced 1973; discontinued 1974.

Perf.: $600   **Exc.:** $435   **VGood:** $325

MAUSER-BAUER MODEL 580 ST. VINCENT

Side-by-side; Holland & Holland sidelock; 12-ga.; 28-inch, 30-inch, 32-inch barrels; standard choke combos; hand-checkered European walnut straight

stock, forearm; split sear levers; coil hammer springs; single or double triggers; scroll-engraved receiver. Introduced 1973; discontinued 1974.

Perf.: $900   **Exc.:** $795   **VGood:** $695

MAUSER-BAUER MODEL 610 PHANTOM

Over/under; 12-ga.; 30-inch, 32-inch barrels; standard choke combos; raised rib; vent rib between barrels for heat reduction; hand-checkered European walnut stock, forearm; recoil pad; coil springs throughout working parts; color case-hardened action. Introduced 1973; discontinued 1974.

Perf.: $695   **Exc.:** $580   **VGood:** $500

MAUSER-BAUER MODEL 610 SKEET

Same specs as Model 610 except three Purbaugh tubes to convert gun for all-gauge competition (20-, 28-ga., .410). Introduced 1973; discontinued 1974.

Perf.: $1100   **Exc.:** $850   **VGood:** $700

MAUSER-BAUER MODEL 620

Over/under; boxlock; 12-ga.; 28-inch Modified/Full, Improved/Modified, Skeet/Skeet, 30-inch Full/Modified barrels; vent rib; hand-checkered European walnut pistol-grip stock, beavertail forearm; Greener crossbolt; single nonselective adjustable trigger;

Maverick Model 88

Maverick Model 88
Security

Maverick Model 91
Accu-Mag

Maverick Model 95

Merkel Model 47S

optional selective or double triggers; automatic ejectors; recoil pad. Made in Italy. Introduced 1972; discontinued 1974.

With double triggers		
Perf.: $750	**Exc.:** $650	**VGood:** $575
With single selective trigger		
Perf.: $795	**Exc.:** $680	**VGood:** $600

MAVERICK MODEL 60

Autoloader; 12-ga.; 2-3/4-inch, 3-inch chamber; 5-shot magazine; 18-1/2-inch (2-3/4-inch chamber only) Cylinder, 24-inch Full and rifled choke tubes, 28-inch vent-rib Modified Accu-Choke barrel; weighs 7-1/4 lbs.; black synthetic stock and forend; designated barrels for magnum and non-magnum loads; action release button; blued receiver. Introduced 1993; limited production; no longer in production.

Perf.: $175   **Exc.:** $150   **VGood:** $125

MAVERICK MODEL 88

Slide action; 12-ga.; 3-inch chamber; 6-shot magazine; 24-inch with rifle sights, 28-inch, 32-inch barrels; fixed or Accu-chokes; plain or vent rib; 48-inch overall length with 28-inch barrel; weighs 7-1/4 lb.; bead front sight; black synthetic stock, ribbed forend; alloy receiver; interchangeable barrels; crossbolt safety; rubber recoil pad; blue finish. Marketed with Mossberg Cablelock. Introduced 1988.

With plain barrel		
Perf.: $195	**Exc.:** $150	**VGood:** $125
With vent rib		
Perf.: $200	**Exc.:** $160	**VGood:** $140
With 24-inch barrel with rifle sights		
Perf.: $205	**Exc.:** $145	**VGood:** $115

MAVERICK MODEL 88 COMBAT

Same specs as Model 88 except 18-1/2-inch Cylinder barrel with vented shroud; black synthetic pistol-grip stock; built-in carrying handle. Introduced 1990; discontinued 1992.

Perf.: $280   **Exc.:** $250   **VGood:** $195

MAVERICK MODEL 88 SECURITY

Same specs as Model 88 except 6-, 8-shot magazine; 18-1/2-inch Cylinder barrel; synthetic

straight- or pistol-grip stock, unribbed forend. Introduced 1993; still in production.

Perf.: $195   **Exc.:** $130   **VGood:** $100

Add $10 to above prices for 8-shot model with 20-inch barrel.
Add up to $65 for combo package.
Add $100 for Bullpup configuration (6- to 9-shot); discontinued 1994.

MAVERICK MODEL 91 ACCU-MAG

Slide action; 12-ga.; 3-1/2-inch chamber; 28-inch vent-rib barrel; ACCU-MAG Modified tube; weighs about 7-3/4 lbs.; black synthetic stock, slide handle; dual slide bars; crossbolt safety; rubber recoil pad. Accessories interchangeable with Mossberg Model 835. Introduced 1993; still in production.

Perf.: $250   **Exc.:** $205   **VGood:** $180

MAVERICK MODEL 95

Bolt action; 12-ga.; 3-inch chamber; 2-shot magazine; 25-inch Modified barrel; weighs 6-1/2 lbs.; full-length textured black synthetic stock with integral magazine; ambidextrous rotating safety; twin extractors; rubber recoil pad; blue finish. Introduced 1995; still in production.

Perf.: $160   **Exc.:** $120   **VGood:** $100

MERCURY MAGNUM

Side-by-side; boxlock; 10-, 12-, 20-ga.; 3-inch, 3-1/2-inch chambers; 28-inch, 32-inch barrels; checkered European walnut pistol-grip stock; double triggers; auto safety; extractors; safety gas ports; engraved frame. Made in Spain and imported by Tradewinds, Inc. Also called Model G1032. Introduced 1970; discontinued 1989.

10-ga.		
Perf.: $500	**Exc.:** $410	**VGood:** $380
12-, 20-ga.		
Perf.: $300	**Exc.:** $260	**VGood:** $210

MERKEL MODEL 8

Side-by-side; boxlock; 12-, 16-, 20-ga.; 2-3/4-inch chambers; 26-inch, 26 3/4-inch, 28-inch barrels; weighs 6+ lbs.; checkered European walnut English straight-grip or pistol-grip stock, forend; double triggers or single selective trigger; double

lugs; Greener crossbolt locking system; automatic ejectors; sling swivels; built to handle steel shot; engraved, color case-hardened receiver. Made in Germany. Discontinued 1994.

Perf.: $1250   **Exc.:** $900   **VGood:** $750

MERKEL MODEL 47E

Side-by-side; boxlock; hammerless; 12-, 20-ga.; 2-3/4-inch chambers; standard barrel lengths, choke combos; hand-checkered European walnut stock, forearm; pistol grip and cheekpiece or straight English style; double hook bolting; Greener crossbolt; double triggers or single selective trigger; automatic ejectors; cocking indicators; engraving; sling swivels; built to handle steel shot. Still in production.

Perf.: $3025   **Exc.:** $2150   **VGood:** $1500

MERKEL MODEL 47LSC SPORTING CLAYS

Same specs as Model 47E except 12-ga.; 3-inch chambers; 28-inch barrel; Briley choke tubes; weighs about 7-1/4 lbs.; fancy figured walnut pistol-grip stock, beavertail forend; recoil pad; single selective trigger adjustable for length of pull; H&H-type ejectors; manual safety; cocking indicators; lengthened forcing cones; color case-hardened receiver with Arabesque engraving. Comes with fitted leather luggage case. Made in Germany. Introduced 1993; no longer imported.

Perf.: $2600   **Exc.:** $1950   **VGood:** $1700

MERKEL MODEL 47S

Same specs as Model 47E except sidelock; 12-, 16-, 20-, 28-ga., .410; 2-3/4-inch, 3-inch chambers; double triggers or single trigger. Introduced prior to WWII; still in production.

Perf.: $3950   **Exc.:** $2800   **VGood:** $2400

MERKEL MODEL 47SL, 147SL SIDE-BY-SIDES

Similar to Model 122 except H&H style sidelock action with cocking indicators, ejectors. Silver-grayed receiver and sideplates have Arabesque engraving, engraved border and screws (Model 47S), or fine hunting scene engraving (Model 147S). Imported from Germany by GSI.

Model 47SL		
Perf.: $5650	**Exc.:** $4650	**VGood:** $3800
Model 147SL		
Perf.: $7650	**Exc.:** $5350	**VGood:** $4300
Model 247SL (English-style engraving, large scrolls)		
Perf.: $7700	**Exc.:** $5300	**VGood:** $4250
Model 447SL (English-style engraving, small scrolls)		
Perf.: $9250	**Exc.:** $8350	**VGood:** $7500

MERKEL MODEL 280EL AND 360EL SHOTGUNS

Similar to Model 47E except smaller frame. Greener cross bolt with double under-barrel locking lugs, fine engraved hunting scenes on silver-grayed receiver, luxury-grade wood, Anson and Deely box-lock action. H&H ejectors, single-selective or double triggers. Introduced 2000. From Merkel.

Model 280EL (28-gauge, 28-inch barrel, Imp. Cyl. and Mod. chokes)		
Perf.: $5500	**Exc.:** $4400	**VGood:** $3700
Model 360EL (.410-bore, 28-inch barrel, Mod. and Full chokes)		
Perf.: $5625	**Exc.:** $4400	**VGood:** $3700
Model 280/360EL two-barrel set (28-ga. and .410-bore)		
Perf.: $8050	**Exc.:** $6950	**VGood:** $6250

MERKEL MODEL 280SL AND 360SL SHOTGUNS

Similar to Model 280EL and 360EL except has sidelock action, double triggers, English-style Arabesque engraving. Introduced 2000. From Merkel.

Model 280SL (28-gauge, 28-inch barrel, Imp. Cyl. and Mod. chokes)		
Perf.: $8050	**Exc.:** $6850	**VGood:** $6150

Model 360SL (.410-bore, 28-inch barrel, Mod. and Full chokes)

Perf.: $8100   **Exc.:** $7000   **VGood:** $6150

Model 280/360SL two-barrel set

Perf.: $11,650   **Exc.:** $10,250   **VGood:** $9250

MERKEL MODEL 100

Over/under; boxlock; hammerless; 12-, 16-, 20-ga.; standard barrel lengths, choke combos; plain or optional ribbed barrel; hand-checkered European walnut stock, forearm; pistol grip and cheekpiece or straight English style; Greener crossbolt safety; double triggers; plain extractors. Made in Germany prior to World War II.

With plain barrel

Exc.: $1250   **VGood:** $900   **Good:** $700

With ribbed barrel

Exc.: $1350   **VGood:** $1000   **Good:** $900

MERKEL MODEL 101

Over/under; boxlock; hammerless; 12-, 16-, 20-ga.; standard barrel lengths, choke combos; ribbed barrel; hand-checkered European walnut stock, forearm; pistol grip and cheekpiece or straight English style; Greener crossbolt safety; double triggers; separate extractors; engraving. Made in Germany prior to World War II.

Exc.: $1850   **VGood:** $1600   **Good:** $1325

MERKEL MODEL 101E

Same specs as Model 101 except ejectors. Made in Germany prior to World War II.

Exc.: $2000   **VGood:** $1750   **Good:** $1425

MERKEL MODEL 122

Side-by-side; Anson & Deely boxlock; 12-, 16-, 20-ga.; 3-inch chambers; 26-3/4-inch, 28-inch barrels; any standard choke combo; hand-checkered straight-grip or pistol-grip stock, forend; automatic ejectors; double triggers or single selective trigger; dummy sideplates; Greener crossbolt. Made in Germany. Introduced 1993; still in production.

Perf.: $3200   **Exc.:** $2000   **VGood:** $1650

MERKEL MODEL 127

Side-by-side; Holland & Holland-type hand-detachable sidelocks; hammerless; 12-, 16-, 20-, 28-ga., .410; standard barrel lengths, choke combos; hand-checkered European walnut stock, forearm; pistol-grip and cheekpiece or straight English style; double triggers; automatic ejectors; elaborately engraved with Arabesque or hunting scene. Manufactured in Germany prior to WWII.

Perf.: $13,500   **Exc.:** $9000   **VGood:** $7000

MERKEL MODEL 130

Side-by-side; Anson & Deeley-type boxlock; hammerless; 12-, 16-, 20-, 28-ga., .410; standard barrel lengths, choke combos; hand-checkered European walnut stock, forearm; pistol-grip and cheekpiece or straight English style; dummy sideplates; double triggers; automatic ejectors; elaborate Arabesque or hunting-scene engraving. Made in Germany prior to World War II.

Perf.: $9,999   **Exc.:** $8500   **VGood:** $6000

MERKEL MODEL 147

Side-by-side; Anson & Deeley boxlock; 12-, 16-, 20-ga.; 26-3/4-inch, 28-inch barrels; other lengths on special order; any standard choke combo; hand-checkered straight-grip or pistol-grip stock, forend; extractors; double triggers or single selective trigger. Made in Germany since World War II; still in production.

Perf.: $1600   **Exc.:** $1100   **VGood:** $900

MERKEL MODEL 147E

Same specs as Model 147 except 12-, 16-, 20-, 28-ga.; automatic ejectors. Made in Germany since World War II; still in production.

Perf.: $2150   **Exc.:** $1850   **VGood:** $1600

MERKEL MODEL 147S

Same specs as Model 147 except sidelock; 12-, 16-, 20-, 28-ga., .410; 25-1/2-inch, 26-inch, 26-3/4-inch, 28-inch barrels; automatic ejectors; engraved hunting

Merkel Model 101

Merkel Model 130

Merkel Model 147E

Merkel Model 201

Merkel Model 201E

scene on action. Made in Germany since World War II; still in production.

Perf.: $5300   **Exc.:** $3600   **VGood:** $3100

28-ga.

Perf.: $2250   **Exc.:** $1950   **VGood:** $1700

MERKEL MODEL 200

Over/under; boxlock; hammerless; 12-, 16-, 20-, 24-, 28-, 32-ga.; standard barrel lengths, choke combos; ribbed barrels; hand-checkered European walnut stock, forearm; pistol grip and cheekpiece or straight English style; Kersten double crossbolt; separate extractors; double triggers; scalloped frame; Arabesque engraving. Made in Germany prior to World War II.

Exc.: $1000   **VGood:** $800   **Good:** $700

MERKEL MODEL 200E

Same specs as the Model 200 except ejectors; double, single or single selective trigger. Introduced prior to WWII; 24-, 28-, 32-ga. dropped during WWII; still in production.

Perf.: $3300   **Exc.:** $2450   **VGood:** $1995

MERKEL MODEL 200E SKEET

Same specs as the Model 200 except 12-ga.; 2-3/4-inch chambers; 26-inch Skeet/Skeet barrels; tapered ventilated rib; competition pistol-grip stock; single selective trigger; half-coverage Arabesque engraving on silver-grayed receiver. Made in Germany. Introduced 1993; still imported.

Perf.: $4650   **Exc.:** $3700   **VGood:** $3500

MERKEL MODEL 200ET TRAP

Same specs as the Model 200 except 12-ga.; 2-3/4-inch chambers; 30-inch Full/Full barrels; tapered ventilated rib; competition pistol-grip stock; single selective trigger; half-coverage Arabesque engraving

on silver-grayed receiver. Made in Germany. Introduced 1993; still imported.

Perf.: $4650   **Exc.:** $3700   **VGood:** $3300

MERKEL MODEL 200SC SPORTING CLAYS

Same specs as the Model 200 except Blitz action; 30-inch barrels with lengthened forcing cones; fixed or five Briley choke tubes; tapered vent rib select-grade stock; single selective trigger adjustable for length of pull; Kersten double crossbolt lock; competition recoil pad; color case-hardened receiver; fitted luggage case. Made in Germany. Introduced 1995; still imported.

With fixed chokes

Perf.: $6700   **Exc.:** $3900   **VGood:** $3200

With choke tubes

Perf.: $7100   **Exc.:** $4300   **VGood:** $3600

MERKEL MODEL 201

Over/under; boxlock; hammerless; 12-, 16-, 20-ga.; standard barrel lengths, choke combos; ribbed barrels; hand-checkered European walnut stock, forearm; pistol grip and cheekpiece or straight English style; separate extractors; double triggers; Greener crossbolt; scalloped frame; engraving. Made in Germany prior to World War II. No longer in production.

Exc.: $1600   **VGood:** $1200   **Good:** $990

MERKEL MODEL 201E

Same specs as Model 201 except ejectors. Made in Germany prior to World War II.

Exc.: $2550   **VGood:** $2150   **Good:** $1950

Merkel Model 202E

Merkel
Model 247S

Merkel Model 303E

Merkel
Model 347S

MERKEL MODEL 201E (RECENT)
Same specs as Model 201 except 12-, 16-, 20-, 28-ga.; ejectors; double, single or single selective trigger. Made in Germany. Still in production.

Perf.: $4200   **Exc.:** $2750   **VGood:** $2200

28-ga. model

Perf.: $5000   **Exc.:** $3250   **VGood:** $2700

MERKEL MODEL 201ES
Same specs as Model 201 except 12-ga.; 2-3/4-inch chamber; 26-3/4-inch Skeet/Skeet barrels; full-coverage engraving. Made in Germany. Still in production.

Perf.: $6800   **Exc.:** $4350   **VGood:** $3200

MERKEL MODEL 201ET
Same specs as Model 201 except 12-ga.; 2-3/4-inch chamber; 30-inch Full/Full barrels; full-coverage engraving. Made in Germany. Still in production.

Perf.: $3000   **Exc.:** $2800   **VGood:** $2600

MERKEL MODEL 202
Over/under; boxlock; hammerless; 12-, 16-, 20-ga.; standard barrel lengths, choke combos; ribbed barrels; selective hand-checkered European walnut stock, forearm; pistol grip and cheekpiece or straight English style; Greener separate extractors; double triggers; dummy sideplates. Made in Germany prior to World War II.

Exc.: $2950   **VGood:** $2500   **Good:** $2300

MERKEL MODEL 202E
Same specs as Model 202 except ejectors. Made in Germany prior to World War II.

Exc.: $3200   **VGood:** $2750   **Good:** $2400

MERKEL MODEL 202E (RECENT)
Same specs as Model 202, except automatic ejectors; full-coverage engraving. Made in Germany. Introduced 1993; still in production.

Perf.: $8200   **Exc.:** $5500   **VGood:** $4000

MERKEL MODEL 203
Over/under; hand-detachable sidelocks; hammerless; 12-, 16-, 20-ga.; ribbed barrels in standard lengths, choke combos; hand-checkered European walnut stock, forearm; pistol grip and cheekpiece or straight English style; Kersten double crossbolt; automatic ejectors; double triggers; optional single selective or non-selective trigger; Arabesque or hunting scene engraving. Made in Germany prior to World War II.

With double triggers

Perf.: $5000   **Exc.:** $3500   **VGood:** $2800

With single trigger

Perf.: $5500   **Exc.:** $4000   **VGood:** $3000

With single selective trigger

Perf.: $6000   **Exc.:** $4500   **VGood:** $3500

MERKEL MODEL 203E
Same specs as Model 203 except standard sidelocks. Made in Germany. Still in production.

Perf.: $9500   **Exc.:** $4900   **VGood:** $3800

MERKEL MODEL 203ES
Same specs as Model 203 except standard sidelocks; 12-ga.; 2-3/4-inch chamber; 26 3/4-inch Skeet/Skeet barrels; full coverage engraving. Made in Germany. No longer imported.

Perf.: $13,500   **Exc.:** $9500   **VGood:** $7500

MERKEL MODEL 203ET
Same specs as Model 203 except standard sidelocks; 12-ga.; 2-3/4-inch chamber; 30-inch Full/Full barrels; full coverage engraving. Made in Germany. Still in production.

Perf.: $12,500   **Exc.:** $9500   **VGood:** $7500

MERKEL MODEL 204E
Over/under; Merkel sidelocks; hammerless; 12-, 16-, 20-ga.; ribbed barrels in standard lengths, choke combos; hand-checkered European walnut stock, forearm; pistol grip and cheekpiece or straight English style; Kersten double crossbolt; automatic ejectors; double triggers; fine English-style engraving. Made in Germany prior to World War II.

Exc.: $6000   **VGood:** $4200   **Good:** $3400

MERKEL MODEL 210
Over/under; boxlock; hammerless; 12-, 16-, 20-, 24-, 28-, 32-ga.; ribbed barrels in standard lengths, choke combos; select hand-checkered European walnut stock, forearm; pistol grip and cheekpiece or straight English style; Kersten double crossbolt; scalloped frame; elaborate engraving; separate extractors; double triggers. Made in Germany prior to World War II.

Exc.: $2150   **VGood:** $1900   **Good:** $1500

MERKEL MODEL 247S
Side-by-side; sidelock; 12-, 16-, 20-ga.; 25 1/2-inch, 26-inch, 26-3/4-inch barrels; standard choke combos; hand-checkered straight-grip or pistol-grip stock, forend; automatic ejectors; double triggers or single selective trigger; engraving. Made in Germany. Still in production.

Perf.: $6500   **Exc.:** $3800   **VGood:** $3200

MERKEL MODEL 300
Over/under; Merkel-Anson boxlock; hammerless; 12-, 16-, 20-, 24-, 28-, 32-ga.; ribbed barrels in standard lengths, choke combos; hand-checkered European walnut stock; pistol grip and cheekpiece or straight English style; Kersten double crossbolt; two underlugs; scalloped frame; Arabesque or hunting scene engraving; separate extractors. Made in Germany prior to World War II.

Exc.: $1950   **VGood:** $1700   **Good:** $1500

MERKEL MODEL 300E
Same general specs as Model 300 except automatic ejectors. Made in Germany prior to World War II.

Exc.: $2650   **VGood:** $1950   **Good:** $1650

MERKEL MODEL 301
Over/under; Merkel-Anson boxlock; hammerless; 12-, 16-, 20-, 24-, 28-, 32-ga.; ribbed barrels in standard lengths, choke combos; select hand-checkered European walnut stock; pistol grip and cheekpiece or straight English style; Kersten double crossbolt; two underlugs; scalloped frame; elaborate engraving; separate extractors. Made in Germany prior to World War II.

Exc.: $6000   **VGood:** $4500   **Good:** $3400

MERKEL MODEL 301E
Same specs as Model 301 except automatic ejectors. Made in Germany prior to World War II.

Exc.: $4200   **VGood:** $3200   **Good:** $2600

MERKEL MODEL 302
Over/under; hammerless; 12-, 16-, 20-, 24-, 38-, 32-ga.; ribbed barrels in standard lengths, choke combos; select hand-checkered European walnut stock; pistol grip and cheekpiece or straight English style; Kersten double crossbolt; two underlugs; scalloped frame; elaborate engraving; automatic ejectors; dummy sideplates. Made in Germany prior to World War II.

Exc.: $9000   **VGood:** $7500   **Good:** $6000

MERKEL MODEL 303E
Over/under; Holland & Holland-type hand-detachable sidelocks; hammerless; ribbed barrels in standard lengths, choke combos; select hand-checkered European walnut stock, forearm; pistol grip and cheekpiece or straight English style; Kersten crossbolt; double underlugs; automatic ejectors. Introduced prior to World War II; still in production.

Perf.: $18,000 **Exc.:** $13,000 **VGood:** $10,000

MERKEL MODEL 304E
Over/under; Holland & Holland-type hand-detachable sidelocks; hammerless; 12-, 16-, 20-, 24-, 28-, 32-ga.; ribbed barrels in standard lengths, choke combos; fancy hand-checkered European walnut stock; pistol grip and cheekpiece or straight English style; Kersten double crossbolt; two underlugs; automatic ejectors; scalloped frame; elaborate engraving. Made in Germany prior to World War II. Optional extras can greatly affect price.

Perf.: $20,000 **Exc.:** $15,000 **VGood:** $10,000

MERKEL MODEL 310E
Over/under; Merkel-Anson boxlock; hammerless; 12-, 16-, 20-, 24-, 28-, 32-ga.; ribbed barrels in standard lengths, choke combos; hand-checkered European walnut stock; pistol grip and cheekpiece or straight English style; Kersten double crossbolt; two underlugs; automatic ejectors; scalloped frame; Arabesque or hunting scene engraving. Made in Germany prior to World War II.

Exc.: $6500   **VGood:** $4900   **Good:** $3500

MERKEL MODEL 347S
Side-by-side; sidelock; 12-,16-, 20-ga.; 25 1/2-inch, 26-inch, 26 3/4-inch barrels; any standard choke combo; select hand-checkered straight-grip or pistol-grip stock, forend; automatic ejectors; double triggers or single selective trigger; elaborate engraving. Made in Germany. Still in production.

Perf.: $7300   **Exc.:** $4200   **VGood:** $3500

MERKEL MODEL 400

Over/under; boxlock; hammerless; 12-, 16-, 20-ga.; ribbed barrels in standard lengths, choke combos; hand-checkered European walnut stock, forearm; pistol grip and cheekpiece or straight English style; Kersten double crossbolt; double triggers; separate extractors; Arabesque engraving on receiver. Made in Germany prior to World War II.

Exc.: $1850   **VGood:** $1450   **Good:** $1100

MERKEL MODEL 400E

Same specs as Model 400 except for ejectors. Made in Germany prior to World War II.

Exc.: $1900   **VGood:** $1500   **Good:** $1250

MERKEL MODEL 410

Over/under; boxlock; hammerless; 12-, 16-, 20-ga.; ribbed barrels in standard lengths, choke combos; select hand-checkered European walnut stock, forearm; pistol grip and cheekpiece or straight English style; Kersten double crossbolt; double triggers; separate extractors; elaborate engraving. Made in Germany prior to World War II.

Exc.: $1900   **VGood:** $1600   **Good:** $1250

MERKEL MODEL 410E

Same specs as Model 410 except ejectors. Made in Germany prior to World War II.

Exc.: $2175   **VGood:** $1900   **Good:** $1600

MERKEL MODEL 447S

Side-by-side; sidelock; 12-, 16-, 20-ga.; 25-1/2-inch, 26-inch, 26-3/4-inch barrels; standard choke combos; select hand-checkered straight-grip or pistol-grip stock, forend; automatic ejectors; double triggers or single selective trigger; fancy engraving. Made in Germany. Still in production.

Perf.: $8500   **Exc.:** $4400   **VGood:** $3200

MERKEL MODEL 2001EL O/U SHOTGUN

Gauge: 12, 20, 3-inch chambers, 28, 2-3/4-inch chambers. Barrel: 12-28-inch; 20, 28 ga.-26-3/4-inch. Weight: About 7 lbs. (12 ga.). Stock: Oil-finished walnut; English or pistol grip. Features: Self-cocking Blitz boxlock action with cocking indicators; Kersten double cross-bolt lock; silver-grayed receiver with engraved hunting scenes; coil spring ejectors; single selective or double triggers. Imported from Germany by GSI, Inc.

Perf.: $7100   **Exc.:** $5600   **VGood:** $4250

MERKEL MODEL 303EL O/U SHOTGUN

Similar to Model 2001 EL except Holland & Holland-style sidelock action with cocking indicators; English-style Arabesque engraving. Available in 12-, 20-, 28-gauge. Imported from Germany by GSI, Inc.

Perf.: $19,750   **Exc.:** $16,250   **VGood:** $13,000

MERKEL MODEL 2002 EL O/U SHOTGUN

Similar to Model 2001 EL except dummy sideplates, Arabesque engraving with hunting scenes; 12-, 20-, 28-gauge. Imported from Germany by GSI, Inc.

Perf.: $10,625   **Exc.:** $8000   **VGood:** $6000

MERKEL 1622

Introduced in 2006, this 16-gauge boxlock side-by-side features full sideplates, case hardened receiver with cocking indicators, ejectors, single selective or double triggers and pistol grip or English style stock. Fixed IC and Mod. chokes. Add 50 percent for 2-barrel set (second set is 28-inch 20 gauge).

NIB: 5200   **Exc.:** 4600   **VGood:** 3250

MERKEL 1622E

Similar to 1622 but with fine engraved hunting scenes on silver-grayed receiver.

NIB: 6200   **Exc.:** 5600   **VGood:** 2250

MERKEL 1622EL

Similar to Model 1622E but with luxury grade wood. Add 30 percent for 2-barrel set (second set is 28-inch 20 gauge).

NIB: 8895   **Exc.:** 8175   **VGood:** 7675

Merkel Model 400

Merkel Model 2001EL

Merkel Model 447S

Merkel Model 303EL

Merkel Model 2002EL

Miida Model 612

Miida Model 2100 Skeet

MERKEL 2000CL

Introduced in 2006, this model is similar to the 2000EL but has a scroll engraved case hardened receiver and luxury grade wood. Semi-pistol grip or English style stock and three-piece forearm. Available in 12, 20 and 28 gauge, all with 28-inch barrel and fixed IC and Mod. chokes.

NIB: 6995   **Exc.:** 6250   **VGood:** 5200

MERKEL 2000CL SPORTER

Similar to 2000CL but in following configurations: 12-gauge with 30-inch vent rib barrels; 20-gauge with 28-inch solid rib barrels; and 28-gauge with 28-inch solid rib barrels. All are fixed choke Skeet and IC.

NIB: 6995   **Exc.:** 6250   **VGood:** 5200

MIIDA MODEL 612

Over/under; boxlock; 12-ga.; 26-inch Improved Cylinder/Modified; 28-inch Modified/Full barrels; vent rib; checkered walnut pistol-grip stock, forearm; auto ejectors; single selective trigger; engraving. Made in Japan; imported by Marubeni America Corp. Introduced 1972; discontinued 1974.

Perf.: $825   **Exc.:** $700   **VGood:** $600

MIIDA MODEL 2100 SKEET

Over/under; boxlock; 12-ga.; 27-inch vent-rib barrels; 12-ga.; 27-inch Skeet/Skeet barrels; vent rib; select checkered walnut pistol-grip stock, forearm; selective single trigger; auto ejectors; 50 percent engraving coverage. Made in Japan; imported by Marubeni America Corp. Introduced 1972; discontinued 1974.

Perf.: $875   **Exc.:** $780   **VGood:** $700

MIIDA MODEL 2200S SKEET

Over/under; boxlock; 12-ga.; 27-inch Skeet/Skeet barrels; vent rib; checkered fancy walnut Skeet stock, semi-beavertail forearm; 60 percent engraving coverage. Made in Japan; imported by Marubeni America Corp. Introduced 1972; discontinued 1974.

Perf.: $950   **Exc.:** $800   **VGood:** $700

MIIDA MODEL 2200T TRAP

Same specs as 2200S, except 29-3/4-inch Improved Modified/Full barrels; trap stock; recoil pad. Made in Japan; imported by Marubeni America Corp. Introduced 1972; discontinued 1974.

Perf.: $950   **Exc.:** $800   **VGood:** $700

MIIDA MODEL 2300S SKEET

Over/under; boxlock; 12-ga.; 27-inch Skeet/Skeet barrels; vent rib; checkered fancy walnut Skeet stock, semi-beavertail forearm; 70 percent engraving coverage. Made in Japan; imported by Marubeni America Corp. Introduced 1972; discontinued 1974.

Perf.: $900   **Exc.:** $750   **VGood:** $650

MIIDA MODEL 2300T TRAP

Same specs as Model 2300S Skeet, except 29-3/4-inch Improved Modified/Full barrels; trap stock; recoil pad. Made in Japan; imported by Marubeni America Corp. Introduced 1972; discontinued 1974.

Perf.: $900   **Exc.:** $750   **VGood:** $650

Miida Model Grandee GRT Trap

Mitchell High Standard Model 9104

Mitchell High Standard Model 9105

Mitchell High Standard
Model 9108-B

Mitchell High Standard Model 9109

Mitchell High Standard Model 9114-PG

brown-finished hardwood stock, slide handle; fixed
barrel with steel receiver; polished blue finish. Made
in the Philippines. Introduced 1994; discontinued
1996.

 Perf.: $230 **Exc.:** $180 **VGood:** $140

MITCHELL HIGH STANDARD MODEL 9108-BL
Same specs as Model 9108-B except black-finished
hardwood stock, slide handle. Introduced 1994;
discontinued 1996.

 Perf.: $230 **Exc.:** $180 **VGood:** $140

MITCHELL HIGH STANDARD MODEL 9108-CT
Same specs as Model 9108-B except Improved
Cylinder, Modified, Full choke tubes. Introduced
1994; discontinued 1996.

 Perf.: $250 **Exc.:** $200 **VGood:** $160

MITCHELL HIGH STANDARD MODEL 9108-HG-B
Same specs as Model 9108-B except brown-finished
hardwood stock, slide handle. Introduced 1994;
discontinued 1996.

 Perf.: $250 **Exc.:** $200 **VGood:** $160

MITCHELL HIGH STANDARD MODEL 9108-HG-BL
Same specs as Model 9108-B except black-finished
hardwood stock, slide handle. Introduced 1994;
discontinued 1996.

 Perf.: $250 **Exc.:** $200 **VGood:** $150

MITCHELL HIGH STANDARD MODEL 9109
Slide action; 12-ga.; 2-3/4-inch chamber; 8-shot
magazine; 20-inch Cylinder barrel; rifle sights; walnut-
finished hardwood stock, slide handle; fixed barrel
with steel receiver; polished blue finish. Made in the
Philippines. Introduced 1994; discontinued 1996.

 Perf.: $250 **Exc.:** $200 **VGood:** $150

MITCHELL HIGH STANDARD MODEL 9111-B
Slide action; 12-ga.; 2-3/4-inch chamber; 7-shot
magazine; 18-1/2-inch Cylinder barrel; bead sight;
brown-finished hardwood hand-grip stock, slide
handle; fixed barrel with steel receiver; polished blue
finish. Made in the Philippines. Introduced 1994;
discontinued 1996.

 Perf.: $250 **Exc.:** $200 **VGood:** $150

MITCHELL HIGH STANDARD MODEL 9111-BL
Same specs as Model 9108-B except black-finished
hardwood stock, slide handle. Introduced 1994;
discontinued 1996.

 Perf.: $250 **Exc.:** $200 **VGood:** $150

MITCHELL HIGH STANDARD MODEL 9111-CT
Same specs as Model 9108-B except Improved
Cylinder, Modified, Full choke tubes. Introduced
1994; discontinued 1996.

 Perf.: $250 **Exc.:** $200 **VGood:** $150

MITCHELL HIGH STANDARD MODEL 9113-B
Slide action; 12-ga.; 2-3/4-inch chamber; 7-shot
magazine; 18-1/2-inch Cylinder barrel; rifle sights;
brown-finished hardwood hand-grip stock, slide
handle; fixed barrel with steel receiver; polished blue
finish. Made in the Philippines. Introduced 1994;
discontinued 1996.

 Perf.: $250 **Exc.:** $200 **VGood:** $150

MITCHELL HIGH STANDARD MODEL 9114-PG
Slide action; 12-ga.; 2-3/4-inch chamber; 7-shot
magazine; 18-1/2-inch Cylinder barrel; rifle sights;
pistol-grip stock; slide handle; fixed barrel with steel
receiver; polished blue finish. Introduced 1994;
discontinued 1996.

 Perf.: $290 **Exc.:** $220 **VGood:** $180

MIIDA MODEL GRANDEE GRS SKEET
Over/under; boxlock; 12-ga.; 27-inch Skeet/Skeet
barrels; wide vent rib; extra fancy walnut Skeet stock,
semi-beavertail forearm; single selective trigger; auto
ejectors; sideplates; gold-inlaid, fully engraved frame,
breech ends of barrels, locking lever, trigger guard.
Made in Japan; imported by Marubeni America Corp.
Introduced 1972; discontinued 1974.

 Perf.: $2250 **Exc.:** $1800 **VGood:** $1600

MIIDA MODEL GRANDEE GRT TRAP
Same specs as Model Grandee GRS Skeet, except
29-3/4-inch Full/Full barrels; trap stock; recoil pad.
Made in Japan; imported by Marubeni America Corp.
Introduced 1972; discontinued 1974.

 Perf.: $2250 **Exc.:** $1800 **VGood:** $1800

MITCHELL HIGH STANDARD MODEL 9104
Slide action; 12-ga.; 2-3/4-inch chamber; 6-shot
magazine; 20-inch Cylinder barrel; bead sight;
walnut-finished hardwood stock, slide handle; fixed
barrel with steel receiver; polished blue finish. Made

in the Philippines. Introduced 1994; discontinued
1996.

 Perf.: $230 **Exc.:** $180 **VGood:** $160

MITCHELL HIGH STANDARD MODEL 9104-CT
Same specs as Model 9104 except Improved
Cylinder, Modified, Full choke tubes. Introduced
1994; discontinued 1996.

 Perf.: $250 **Exc.:** $200 **VGood:** $160

MITCHELL HIGH STANDARD MODEL 9105
Slide action; 12-ga.; 2-3/4-inch chamber; 6-shot
magazine; 20-inch Cylinder barrel; rifle sights; walnut-
finished hardwood stock, slide handle; fixed barrel
with steel receiver; polished blue finish. Made in the
Philippines. Introduced 1994; discontinued 1996.

 Perf.: $250 **Exc.:** $200 **VGood:** $160

MITCHELL HIGH STANDARD MODEL 9108-B
Slide action; 12-ga.; 2-3/4-inch chamber; 8-shot
magazine; 20-inch Cylinder barrel; bead sight;

MITCHELL HIGH STANDARD MODEL 9115

Slide action; 12-ga.; 2-3/4-inch chamber; 7-shot magazine; 18-1/2-inch Cylinder barrel with ventilated heat shield; bead sight; walnut-finished hardwood SAS-style stock, slide handle; stock stores four shells; fixed barrel with steel receiver; Parkerized finish. Made in the Philippines. Introduced 1994; discontinued 1996.

Perf.: $290   **Exc.:** $220   **VGood:** $180

MITCHELL HIGH STANDARD MODEL 9115-CT

Same specs as Model 9115 except Improved Cylinder, Modified, Full choke tubes. Introduced 1994; discontinued 1996.

Perf.: $310   **Exc.:** $230   **VGood:** $190

MITCHELL HIGH STANDARD MODEL 9115-HG

Same specs as Model 9115 except walnut finished hardwood SAS-style hand-grip stock, slide handle. Introduced 1994; discontinued 1996.

Perf.: $290   **Exc.:** $220   **VGood:** $180

MONTE CARLO SINGLE

Single barrel; 12-ga.; 32-inch trap barrel; hand-checkered European walnut pistol-grip stock, beavertail forend; recoil pad; auto ejector; slide safety; gold-plated trigger. Made in Italy. Introduced 1968; no longer in production.

Exc.: $275   **VGood:** $240   **Good:** $180

MOSSBERG SEMI-AUTOMATIC SHOTGUNS MOSSBERG MODEL 1000

Gas-operated autoloader; 12-, 20-ga.; 2-3/4-inch chamber; 4-shot tube magazine; 26-inch, 28-inch vent-rib barrel; standard chokes; optional screw-in choke tubes; front, middle bead sights; checkered American walnut stock; interchangeable crossbolt safety; pressure compensator, floating piston for recoil control; engraved alloy receiver. Made in Japan. Formerly marketed by Smith & Wesson; discontinued 1987.

Perf.: $390   **Exc.:** $320   **VGood:** $280
Add $30 to above prices for Multi-Choke II.

MOSSBERG MODEL 1000 JUNIOR

Same specs as Model 1000 except 20-ga.; 22-inch Multi-Choke barrel; vent rib; junior-sized stock. Introduced 1986; discontinued 1987.

Perf.: $410   **Exc.:** $330   **VGood:** $290

MOSSBERG MODEL 1000 SKEET

Same specs as Model 1000 except 26-inch Skeet barrel; vent rib; Skeet-style stock; steel receiver. Introduced 1986; discontinued 1986.

Perf.: $375   **Exc.:** $300   **VGood:** $250

MOSSBERG MODEL 1000 SLUG

Same specs as Model 1000 except 22-inch barrel; rifle sights; recoil pad. Introduced 1986; discontinued 1987.

Perf.: $400   **Exc.:** $320   **VGood:** $260

MOSSBERG MODEL 1000 SUPER

Same specs as Model 1000 except gas-metering system for 2-3/4-inch, 3-inch shells; 26-inch, 28-inch, 30-inch Multi-Choke barrel; recoil pad. Introduced 1986; discontinued 1987.

Perf.: $480   **Exc.:** $375   **VGood:** $315

MOSSBERG MODEL 1000 SUPER SKEET

Same specs as Model 1000 except gas-metering system for 2-3/4-inch, 3-inch shells; 25-inch; recessed-type Skeet choke; oil-finished, select-grade walnut stock, forend; palm swell; recoil-reduction compensator; contoured trigger; forend cap weights for changing balance. Introduced 1986; discontinued 1987.

Perf.: $550   **Exc.:** $450   **VGood:** $400

Mitchell High Standard Model 9115

Mossberg Model 1000 Junior

Mossberg Model 5500

Mossberg Model 5500 MkII

Mossberg Model 9200 Crown Grade

Mossberg Model 9200 Crown Grade Camo

Mossberg Home Security 410

MOSSBERG MODEL 1000 SUPER TRAP

Same specs as Model 1000 except 12-ga.; gas-metering system for 2-3/4-inch, 3-inch shells; 30-inch Multi-choke barrel; vent rib; walnut-finished hardwood Monte Carlo stock; recoil pad. Introduced 1986; discontinued 1987.

Perf.: $465   **Exc.:** $370   **VGood:** $300

MOSSBERG MODEL 1000 SUPER WATERFOWLER

Same specs as Model 1000 except 12-ga.; gas-metering system for 2-3/4-inch, 3-inch shells; 28-inch Multi-choke barrel; sling swivels; camo sling; Parkerized finish. Introduced 1986; discontinued 1987.

Perf.: $500   **Exc.:** $400   **VGood:** $360

MOSSBERG MODEL 5500

Autoloader; 12-ga.; 2-3/4-inch, 3-inch chamber; interchangeable 18-1/2-inch Cylinder, 24-inch Slugster, 26-inch Improved, 28-inch Modified, 30-inch Full barrel; Accu-Choke tubes; bead front sight; walnut-finished hardwood stock. Introduced 1983; discontinued 1985.

Perf.: $235   **Exc.:** $200   **VGood:** $170

Slugster model
Perf.: $260   **Exc.:** $215   **VGood:** $190

MOSSBERG MODEL 5500 MKII

Same specs as Model 5500 except 24-inch rifled, 24-inch, 26-inch, 28-inch vent-rib barrel; Accu-II choke tubes. Also marketed as two-barrel set with both 26-inch (2-3/4-inch) and 28-inch (3-inch) barrels. Introduced 1988; discontinued 1992.

Perf.: $250   **Exc.:** $200   **VGood:** $175

Combo set
Perf.: $300   **Exc.:** $250   **VGood:** $225

MOSSBERG MODEL 5500 MARK II CAMO

Same specs as Model 5500 except 28-inch barrel; Accu-II choke tubes; synthetic stock; camouflage finish. Introduced 1988; discontinued 1992.

Perf.: $280   **Exc.:** $230   **VGood:** $200

MOSSBERG MODEL 6000

Autoloader; 12-ga.; 3-inch chamber; 28-inch barrel; Modified Accu-Choke tube; weighs about 7-1/2 lbs.; walnut-finished stock with high-gloss finish; alloy receiver; shoots all 2-3/4-inch or 3-inch loads without adjustment. Introduced 1993; discontinued 1993.

Perf.: $275   **Exc.:** $200   **VGood:** $180

MOSSBERG MODEL 9200 CROWN GRADE

Autoloader; 12-ga.; 3-inch chamber; 24-inch rifled, 24-inch, 28-inch vent-rib barrel; Accu-Choke tubes; weighs about 7 1/2 lbs.; cut-checkered walnut stock with high-gloss finish; ambidextrous safety; alloy receiver; shoots all 2-3/4-inch or 3-inch loads without adjustment. Introduced 1992; dropped 2001.

With standard barrel
Perf.: $425   **Exc.:** $350   **VGood:** $290

With 24-inch rifled barrel; scope base; Dual-Comb stock
Perf.: $445   **Exc.:** $370   **VGood:** $310

MOSSBERG MODEL 9200 CROWN GRADE CAMO

Same specs as Model 9200 Crown Grade except 24-inch vent-rib barrel; Accu-Choke tubes; synthetic stock, forend; completely covered with Mossy Oak Tree Stand or OFM camouflage finish. Introduced 1993; dropped 1999.

With Mossy Oak finish
Perf.: $400   **Exc.:** $325   **VGood:** $265

With OFM camo finish
Perf.: $400   **Exc.:** $325   **VGood:** $265

Mossberg Model 500

Mossberg Model 500AHT
(Hi-Rib Trap)

Mossberg Model 500ASG
Slugster

Mossberg Model 500 Bullpup

Mossberg Model 500
Camo

MOSSBERG MODEL 9200 NWTF EDITION

Same specs as Model 9200 Crown Grade except black matte receiver with turkey scenes etched on both sides; Realtree camo finish on rest of gun. Introduced 1994; still in production.

Perf.: $490   **Exc.:** $395   **VGood:** $350

MOSSBERG MODEL 9200 REGAL

Same specs as Model 9200 Crown Grade except 24-inch rifled, 28-inch vent-rib barrel; Accu-Choke tubes; less fancy wood. Introduced 1992; discontinued 1993.

Perf.: $425   **Exc.:** $350   **VGood:** $290

MOSSBERG MODEL 9200 USST

Same specs as Model 9200 Crown Grade except 26-inch vent-rib barrel; Accu-Choke tubes (including Skeet); cut-checkered walnut-finished stock, forend; "United States Shooting Team" custom engraved receiver. Introduced 1993; still in production.

Perf.: $415   **Exc.:** $330   **VGood:** $280

MOSSBERG SLIDE-ACTION SHOTGUNS MOSSBERG HOME SECURITY 410

Slide action; .410; 3-inch chamber; 18-1/2-inch barrel; spreader choke; 37-1/2-inch overall length; weighs 6-1/4 lbs; synthetic pistol-grip stock, forend; recoil pad; blued finish; also available with laser installed in forend. Marketed with Mossberg Cablelock. Introduced 1990; still in production.

Perf.: $260   **Exc.:** $195   **VGood:** $165

With laser
Perf.: $375   **Exc.:** $300   **VGood:** $275

MOSSBERG MODEL HS410 SHOTGUN

Similar to the Model 500 Security pump except chambered for 20 gauge or 410 with 3-inch chamber; has pistol grip forend, thick recoil pad, muzzle brake and has special spreader choke on the 18.5-inch barrel. Overall length is 37-1/2-inch; weight is 6-1/4 lbs. Blue finish; synthetic field stock. Mossberg Cablelock and video included. Introduced 1990.

Perf.: $280   **Exc.:** $230   **VGood:** $200

MOSSBERG MODEL 200D

Slide action; 12-ga.; 3-shot detachable box magazine; 28-inch barrel; interchangeable choke tubes; uncheckered, walnut-finished hardwood pistol-grip stock, grooved black nylon slide handle; recoil pad. Introduced 1955; discontinued 1959.

Exc.: $135   **VGood:** $95   **Good:** $50

MOSSBERG MODEL 200K

Same specs as Model 200D except variable C-Lect-Choke instead of interchangeable choke tubes. Introduced 1955; discontinued 1959.

Exc.: $140   **VGood:** $100   **Good:** $50

MOSSBERG MODEL 500

Slide action; hammerless; takedown; 12-, 20-ga., .410; 6-shot tube magazine; 3-shot plug furnished; 24-inch Slugster Cylinder with rifle sights (12-ga. only), 26-inch Improved, 28-inch Modified or Full, 30-inch Full (12-ga. only) barrel; adjustable C-Lect-Choke, Accu-Choke, Accu-II, Accu-Steel tubes; white bead front sight, brass mid-bead; checkered or uncheckered American walnut pistol-grip stock, grooved slide handle; recoil pad; twin extractors; ambidextrous safety; disconnecting safety dual action bars. Marketed with Cablelock. Introduced 1961; still in production.

With fixed-choke barrel
Perf.: $220   **Exc.:** $150   **VGood:** $130

With adjustable-choke barrel
Perf.: $240   **Exc.:** $170   **VGood:** $140

Combo with extra barrel
Perf.: $280   **Exc.:** $210   **VGood:** $180

MOSSBERG MODEL 500AGVD

Same specs as Model 500 except 12-, 20-ga.; 3-inch chamber; 28-inch vent-rib barrel with Accu-Choke system for Improved, Modified, Full. No longer in production.

Perf.: $240   **Exc.:** $170   **VGood:** $140

MOSSBERG MODEL 500AHT (HI-RIB TRAP)

Same specs as Model 500 except 12-ga.; 28-inch, 30-inch Full-choke barrel; Simmons Olympic-style

free-floating rib; built-up Monte Carlo trap stock. Introduced 1978; discontinued 1986.

Perf.: $275   **Exc.:** $240   **VGood:** $200

MOSSBERG MODEL 500AHTD (HI-RIB TRAP)

Same specs as Model 500 except 12-ga.; 28-inch, 30-inch barrel; three choke tubes; Simmons Olympic-style free-floating rib; built-up Monte Carlo trap stock. Introduced 1978; discontinued 1986.

Perf.: $305   **Exc.:** $255   **VGood:** $215

MOSSBERG MODEL 500ALD

Same specs as Model 500 except 12-ga.; 2-3/4-inch, 3-inch chamber; 28-inch vent-rib barrel; Accu-Choke or three interchangeable choke tubes; game scene etched in receiver. Introduced 1977; no longer in production.

Perf.: $245   **Exc.:** $180   **VGood:** $150

MOSSBERG MODEL 500 ALMR (HEAVY DUCK)

Same specs as Model 500 except 12-ga.; 3-inch chamber; 30-inch, 32-inch Full-choke barrel; vent rib. Introduced 1977; no longer in production.

Perf.: $250   **Exc.:** $185   **VGood:** $155

MOSSBERG MODEL 500ALS SLUGSTER

Same specs as Model 500 except 12-ga.; 2-3/4-inch, 3-inch chamber; 18-1/2-inch, 24-inch Cylinder-bore barrel; rifle sights; game scene etched in receiver. Introduced 1977; no longer in production.

Perf.: $230   **Exc.:** $160   **VGood:** $130

MOSSBERG MODEL 500ASG SLUGSTER

Same specs as Model 500 except 12-, 20-ga.; 2-3/4-inch, 3-inch chamber; 18-1/2-inch, 24-inch slug barrel; ramp front sight, open adjustable folding leaf rear; running deer etched on receiver. No longer in production.

Perf.: $225   **Exc.:** $180   **VGood:** $150

MOSSBERG MODEL 500APR PIGEON GRADE TRAP

Same specs as Model 500 except for 30-inch Full-choke barrel; vent rib; checkered walnut Monte Carlo trap-style stock, beavertail slide handle. Introduced 1968; discontinued 1975.

Perf.: $425   **Exc.:** $310   **VGood:** $240

MOSSBERG MODEL 500 BANTAM

Same specs as Model 500 except 20-ga.; 22-inch vent rib barrel; Modified Accu-Choke tube; 1-inch shorter stock with reduced length from pistol grip to trigger, reduced forend reach. Introduced 1992; still in production.

Perf.: $245   **Exc.:** $200   **VGood:** $160

MOSSBERG MODEL 500 BULLPUP

Same specs as Model 500 except 12-ga.; 3-inch chamber; 6-, 9-shot magazine; 18-1/2-inch, 20-inch Cylinder-bore barrel; weighs 9-1/2 lbs.; fixed sights mounted in carrying handle; plastic bullpup-design stock; crossbolt, grip safeties; marketed with Cablelock. Designed for law enforcement; may be illegal in some jurisdictions. Introduced 1986; discontinued 1990.

6-shot model
Perf.: $480   **Exc.:** $390   **VGood:** $350

8-shot model
Perf.: $500   **Exc.:** $410   **VGood:** $370

MOSSBERG MODEL 500 CAMO

Same specs as Model 500 except 12-ga.; receiver drilled, tapped for scope mount; synthetic field or Speedfeed stock; sling swivels; camo sling; entire surface covered with camo finish; marketed with Mossberg Cablelock. Introduced 1986; still in production.

Perf.: $250   **Exc.:** $150   **VGood:** $100

Camo Combo with extra barrel
Perf.: $340   **Exc.:** $220   **VGood:** $170

MOSSBERG MODEL 500 CAMPER
Same specs as Model 500 except .410 bore only; 18-1/2-inch Cylinder-bore barrel; synthetic pistol-grip stock; carry case. Introduced 1988; dropped 1988.
Perf.: $325   **Exc.:** $280   **VGood:** $250

MOSSBERG MODEL 500CLD
Same specs as Model 500 except 20-ga.; 2-3/4-inch chamber; 28-inch barrel; Accu-Choke or three interchangeable choke tubes; game scene etched on receiver. Introduced 1977; no longer in production.
Perf.: $250   **Exc.:** $175   **VGood:** $130

MOSSBERG MODEL 500CLDR
Same specs as Model 500 except 20-ga.; 2-3/4-inch chamber; 28-inch vent-rib barrel; Accu-Choke or three interchangeable choke tubes; game scene etched on receiver. Introduced 1977; no longer in production.
Perf.: $270   **Exc.:** $195   **VGood:** $150

MOSSBERG MODEL 500CLS SLUGSTER
Same specs as Model 500 except 20-ga.; 2-3/4-inch, 3-inch chamber; 24-inch Cylinder-bore barrel; rifle sights; game scene etched in receiver. Introduced 1977; no longer in production.
Perf.: $235   **Exc.:** $170   **VGood:** $130

MOSSBERG MODEL 500E
Same specs as Model 500 except .410; 26-inch barrel; Full, Modified, Improved chokes; fluted comb. No longer in production.
Perf.: $245   **Exc.:** $175   **VGood:** $145

Skeet barrel with vent rib, checkering
Perf.: $275   **Exc.:** $195   **VGood:** $175

MOSSBERG MODEL 500EGV
Same specs as Model 500 except .410; 26-inch Full-choke barrel; vent rib; checkered pistol grip, forend; fluted comb; recoil pad. No longer in production.
Perf.: $275   **Exc.:** $195   **VGood:** $175

MOSSBERG MODEL 500EL
Same specs as Model 500 except .410; 2 1/2-inch, 3-inch chamber; 26-inch Full-choke barrel; game scene etched in receiver. Introduced 1977; no longer in production.
Perf.: $275   **Exc.:** $195   **VGood:** $175

MOSSBERG MODEL 500ELR
Same specs as Model 500 except .410; 2-1/2-inch, 3-inch chamber; 26-inch Full-choke barrel; vent rib; game scene etched in receiver. Introduced 1977; no longer in production.
Perf.: $275   **Exc.:** $195   **VGood:** $175

MOSSBERG MODEL 500 GHOST RING
Same specs as Model 500 except 12-ga., 3-inch chamber; 6-, 9-shot magazine; 18-1/2-inch Cylinder or Accu-Choke barrel; adjustable blade front sight, adjustable Ghost Ring rear with protective ears; synthetic or Speedfeed stock; blue or Parkerized finish. Introduced 1990; dropped 1997.

Blue finish
Perf.: $270   **Exc.:** $190   **VGood:** $150

Parkerized finish
Perf.: $300   **Exc.:** $210   **VGood:** $180

Parkerized finish, Accu-Choke barrel
Perf.: $350   **Exc.:** $260   **VGood:** $225
Add $50 to above prices for 9-shot magazine.
Add $125 for Accu-Choke barrel.
Add $135 for Speedfeed stock.

MOSSBERG MODEL 500 INTIMIDATOR
Same specs as Model 500 except 12-ga.; 3-inch chamber; 6-, 9-shot magazine; 18-1/2-inch Cylinder-bore barrel; integral laser sight incorporated in synthetic forend; blued or Parkerized finish; marketed with Mossberg Cablelock. Introduced 1990; discontinued 1993.

With blue finish
Perf.: $450   **Exc.:** $360   **VGood:** $300

Mossberg Model 500 Camper

Mossberg Model 500 Mariner

Mossberg Model 500 Persuader

Mossberg Model 590

Mossberg Model 500 Rolling Thunder

With Parkerized finish
Perf.: $460   **Exc.:** $370   **VGood:** $310

MOSSBERG MODEL 500 MARINER
Same specs as Model 500 except 12-ga.; 3-inch chamber; 6-, 9-shot magazine; 18-1/2-inch, 20-inch Cylinder-bore barrel; weighs 7 lbs.; ghost ring or metal bead front sight; walnut-finished hardwood, synthetic or Speedfeed stock; all metal parts are finished with Marinecoat to resist rust, corrosion; marketed with Cablelock. Still in production.
Perf.: $350   **Exc.:** $220   **VGood:** $180

Mini Combo with extra barrel, handguard, pistol grip
Perf.: $450   **Exc.:** $320   **VGood:** $280
Add $20 to above prices for 9-shot variation.
Add $70 for ghost ring sights.
Add $25 for Speedfeed stock.

MOSSBERG MODEL 500 MEDALLION
Same specs as Model 500 except 12-, 20-ga.; 28-inch vent-rib barrel; Accu-Choke tubes; game bird medallion inset in receiver: pheasant or duck (12-ga.), grouse or quail (20-ga.); only 5000 made in each category. Introduced 1983; discontinued 1984.
Perf.: $260   **Exc.:** $190   **VGood:** $175

MOSSBERG MODEL 500 MUZZLELOADER COMBO
Same specs as Model 500 except two-barrel set with 24-inch rifled Slugster barrel with rifle sights and 24-inch fully rifled 50-caliber muzzle-loading barrel with ramrod; Uses #209 standard primer. Introduced 1992; still in production.
Perf.: $390   **Exc.:** $280   **VGood:** $220

MOSSBERG MODEL 500 PERSUADER
Same specs as Model 500 except 12-, 20-ga.; 6-, 8-shot magazine; 18-1/2-inch, 20-inch barrel; Cylinder bore or Accu-Choke tubes; shotgun or rifle sights; uncheckered wood or synthetic pistol-grip stock, grooved slide handle; blue or Parkerized finish; optional bayonet lug. Designed specifically for law enforcement. Introduced 1977; still in production.
Perf.: $245   **Exc.:** $175   **VGood:** $150

With bayonet lug
Perf.: $260   **Exc.:** $190   **VGood:** $165

12 gauge, Parkerized finish, 6-shot, 18-1/2-inch barrel, ghost ring sights.
Perf.: $377   **Exc.:** $317   **VGood:** $287

Home Security 410 (.410-bore, 18-1/2-inch barrel with spreader choke)
Perf.: $280   **Exc.:** $230   **VGood:** $200

12- or 20-ga., 18-1/2-inch, blue, wood or synthetic stock, 6-shot.
Perf.: $265   **Exc.:** $205   **VGood:** $175

Cruiser, 12- or 20-ga., 18-1/2-inch, blue, pistol grip, heat shield.
Perf.: $282   **Exc.:** $217   **VGood:** $192

As above, .410-bore.
Perf.: $270   **Exc.:** $205   **VGood:** $180

MOSSBERG MODEL 500 SECURITY SERIES
Same specs as Model 500 except 12-ga.; 3-inch chamber; 6-, 8-shot magazine; 18-1/2-inch, 20-inch Cylinder bore barrel; weighs 7 lbs.; metal bead front sight; walnut-finished hardwood, synthetic or Speedfeed stock; blue, Parkerized or nickel finish.

With blue or nickel finish
Perf.: $240   **Exc.:** $170   **VGood:** $150

With Parkerized finish
Perf.: $260   **Exc.:** $190   **VGood:** $170

Mini Combo with extra barrel
Perf.: $290   **Exc.:** $220   **VGood:** $190

MOSSBERG MODEL 500 SUPER GRADE
Same specs as Model 500 except vent-rib barrel; checkered pistol grip, slide handle. Introduced 1961; discontinued 1976.

With fixed-choke barrel
Perf.: $245   **Exc.:** $190   **VGood:** $150

With adjustable-choke barrel
Perf.: $265   **Exc.:** $210   **VGood:** $170

MOSSBERG MODEL 500 TROPHY SLUGSTER
Same specs as Model 500 except 12-ga.; 3-inch chamber; 24-inch smooth or rifled bore; 44-inch overall length; weighs 7-1/4 lbs.; scope mount; walnut-stained hardwood stock; swivel studs; recoil pad; Introduced 1988; still in production.
Perf.: $285   **Exc.:** $200   **VGood:** $180

Mossberg JIC Mariner

Mosberg JIC Cruiser

Mossberg JIC Sandstorm Tube

Mossberg Model 930 Tactical

MOSSBERG MODEL 500 TURKEY

Same specs as Model 500 except 24-inch Accu-Choke barrel with Improved Cylinder, Modified, Full, Extra-Full lead shot choke tubes; Ghost-Ring sights; swivel studs; camo sling; overall OFM camo finish. Introduced 1992. Still in production.

Perf.: $300   **Exc.:** $240   **VGood:** $200

MOSSBERG MODEL 500 ROLLING THUNDER

This home defense/tactical model is a 3" 12 gauge featuring a pistol grip, 23" barrel with heat shield and recoil-reducing stabilizer and six-round capacity.

Perf.: $375   **Exc.:** $315   **VGood:** $250

MOSSBERG MODEL 500 JIC (JUST IN CASE)

This survival model is a 3" 12 gauge featuring a pistol grip, 18.5" barrel and a weatherproof pack tube. Three different models available with different finishes and accessory packages.

Perf.: $375   **Exc.:** $325   **VGood:** $250

MOSSBERG MODEL 590 SPECIAL PURPOSE SHOTGUNS

Similar to Model 500 except has Parkerized or Marinecote finish, 9-shot magazine and black synthetic stock (some models feature Speed Feed.

Available in 12-gauge only with 20-inch, cylinder bore barrel. Weighs 7-1/4 lbs. Still in production.

Bead sight, heat shield over barrel.
Perf.: $335   **Exc.:** $275   **VGood:** $225
Ghost ring sight, Speedfeed stock.
Perf.: $456   **Exc.:** $396   **VGood:** $346
Add $60 to above prices for parkerized finish. Add $90 for heavy barrel variation with metal triggerguard and safety.

MOSSBERG MODEL 590

Slide action; 12-ga.; 3-inch chamber; 9-shot magazine; 20-inch Cylinder-bore barrel; synthetic field or Speedfeed stock with heat shield; bayonet lug; swivel studs; rubber recoil pad; blued or Parkerized finish; marketed with Cablelock. Introduced 1990; still in production.

With blued finish, field stock
Perf.: $290   **Exc.:** $220   **VGood:** $190
With blued finish, Speedfeed stock
Perf.: $310   **Exc.:** $240   **VGood:** $210
With Parkerized finish, field stock
Perf.: $340   **Exc.:** $270   **VGood:** $240
With Parkerized finish, Speedfeed stock
Perf.: $360   **Exc.:** $290   **VGood:** $260

MOSSBERG 590DA DOUBLE-ACTION PUMP SHOTGUN

Similar to Model 590 except trigger requires a long stroke for each shot, duplicating the trigger pull of double-action-only pistols and revolvers. Available in 12-gauge only with black synthetic stock and Parkerized finish with 14-inch (law enforcement only), 18-1/2-inch and 20-inch barrels. Six-shot magazine tube (9-shot for 20-inch barrel). Front bead or ghost ring sights. Weighs 7 pounds (18 1/2-inch barrel). Introduced 2000; dropped 2003. From Mossberg. Bead sight, 6-shot magazine.
Perf.: $450   **Exc.:** $415   **VGood:** $360
Ghost ring sights, 6-shot magazine. Still in production.
Perf.: $498   **Exc.:** $463   **VGood:** $408
Bead sight, 9-shot magazine. Still in production.
Perf.: $450   **Exc.:** $415   **VGood:** $360
Ghost ring sights, 9-shot magazine. Still in production.
Perf.: $498   **Exc.:** $463   **VGood:** $408

MOSSBERG MODEL 590 BULLPUP

Same specs as Model 590 except shrouded 20-inch Cylinder-bore barrel; fixed sights mounted in carrying handle; bullpup-configuration plastic stock; crossbolt, grip safties. Designed for law enforcement. Introduced 1989; discontinued 1990.
Perf.: $410   **Exc.:** $310   **VGood:** $260

MOSSBERG MODEL 590 GHOST RING

Same specs as Model 590 except ghost-ring sights. Introduced 1990; still in production.

With blued finish, field stock
Perf.: $310   **Exc.:** $240   **VGood:** $210
With blued finish, Speedfeed stock
Perf.: $330   **Exc.:** $260   **VGood:** $230
With Parkerized finish, field stock
Perf.: $360   **Exc.:** $290   **VGood:** $260
With Parkerized finish, Speedfeed stock
Perf.: $380   **Exc.:** $310   **VGood:** $280

MOSSBERG MODEL 590 INTIMIDATOR

Same specs as Model 590 except has integral laser sight built into synthetic field stock, forend; marketed with Mossberg Cablelock. Introduced 1990; discontinued 1993.

With blued finish
Perf.: $425   **Exc.:** $330   **VGood:** $280
With Parkerized finish
Perf.: $450   **Exc.:** $365   **VGood:** $300

MOSSBERG MODEL 590 MARINER

Same specs as Model 590 except all parts coated with Marinecoat. Introduced 1989; discontinued 1993.

With field stock
Perf.: $300   **Exc.:** $210   **VGood:** $170
With Speedfeed stock
Perf.: $320   **Exc.:** $230   **VGood:** $190

MOSSBERG MODEL 930 TACTICAL

This 3" 12 gauge has an 18.5" barrel and cylinder bore. Synthetic stock with matte black finish.
Perf.: $495   **Exc.:** $495   **VGood:** $275

MOSSBERG MODEL 835 AMERICAN FIELD

Slide action; 12-ga.; 3-1/2-inch chamber handles all size shells; backbored 28-inch Accu-Mag Modified choke tube for steel or lead shot; weighs 7-3/4 lbs.; cut-checkered, walnut-stained hardwood stock; ambidextrous thumb safety; twin extractors; dual slide bars. Introduced 1988; still in production.
Perf.: $225   **Exc.:** $180   **VGood:** $150

MOSSBERG MODEL 835 ULTI-MAG

Same specs as Model 835 American Field except 24-inch rifled bore with rifle sights, 24-inch, 28-inch backbored vent-rib barrel; four Accu-Mag choke tubes for steel or lead shot; cut-checkered,

walnut-stained hardwood or camo synthetic stock.
Introduced 1988; discontinued 1991.

Perf.: $380   **Exc.:** $275   **VGood:** $200

MOSSBERG MODEL 835 ULTI-MAG CROWN GRADE

Same specs as Model 835 American Field except 24-inch rifled bore with rifle sights, 24-inch, 28-inch backbored vent-rib barrel; four Accu-Mag choke tubes for steel or lead shot; cut-checkered walnut standard or Dual-Comb, or camo synthetic stock. Introduced 1988; still in production.

With standard barrel; standard walnut stock

Perf.: $380   **Exc.:** $310   **VGood:** $270

With standard barrel; Dual-Comb walnut stock

Perf.: $385   **Exc.:** $315   **VGood:** $275

With rifled barrel; scope base; Dual-Comb walnut stock

Perf.: $400   **Exc.:** $320   **VGood:** $290

Combo with 24-inch rifled, 28-inch barrels; Dual-Comb walnut stock

Perf.: $420   **Exc.:** $340   **VGood:** $300

Realtree or Mossy Oak Camo with standard barrel; synthetic stock

Perf.: $430   **Exc.:** $350   **VGood:** $310

Realtree Camo Combo with 24-inch rifled, 24-inch smoothbore barrels; synthetic stock, hard case

Perf.: $525   **Exc.:** $450   **VGood:** $400

OFM Camo with standard barrel; synthetic stock

Perf.: $410   **Exc.:** $330   **VGood:** $300

OFM Camo Combo with 24-inch rifled, 28-inch barrels; synthetic stock

Perf.: $460   **Exc.:** $400   **VGood:** $360

MOSSBERG MODEL 835 ULTI-MAG PUMP

Gauge: 12, 3-1/2-inch chamber; ported 24-inch rifled bore, 24-inch, 28-inch barrel; Accu-Mag choke tubes for steel or lead shot; weighs 7-3/4 lbs. ; 48-1/2-inch overall; dual comb; cut-checkered hardwood or camo synthetic; both have recoil pad; white bead front, brass mid-bead sights, fiber optic; shoots 2-3/4-inch, 3-inch or 3-1/2-inch shells; back-bored and ported barrel to reduce recoil, improve patterns; ambidextrous thumb safety; twin extractors; dual slide bars. Mossberg Cablelock included. Introduced 1988.

28-inch vent. rib, hardwood stock

Perf.: $375   **Exc.:** $310   **VGood:** $265

Combo, 24-inch rifled bore, rifle sights, 24-inch vent. rib, Accu-Mag Ulti-Full choke tube, Woodlands camo finish

Perf.: $425   **Exc.:** $350   **VGood:** $305

RealTree Camo Turkey, 24-inch vent. rib, Accu-Mag, Extra-Full tube, synthetic stock

Perf.: $450   **Exc.:** $380   **VGood:** $345

Mossy Oak Camo, 28-inch vent. rib, Accu-Mag tubes, synthetic stock

Perf.: $460   **Exc.:** $385   **VGood:** $350

OFM Camo, 28-inch vent. rib, Accu-Mag Mod. tube, synthetic stock

Perf.: $460   **Exc.:** $385   **VGood:** $350

MOSSBERG MODEL 835 SYNTHETIC STOCK

Similar to the Model 835, except with 28-inch ported barrel with Accu-Mag Mod. choke tube, Parkerized finish, black synthetic stock and forend. Introduced 1998. Still in production.

Perf.: $260   **Exc.:** $225   **VGood:** $200

MOSSBERG 835 ULTI-MAG THUMBHOLE TURKEY

New in 2006, this dedicated pump-action 12 gauge turkey gun features a thumbhole stock and overbored barrel. Chambered for 3.5 inch shells. X-Factor ported choke tube. Barrel is 20 inches and has adjustable fiber-optic front and rear sights. Weight is about 7.75 lbs. Available in Mossy Oak New Break-Up camo or Realtree Hardwoods Green camo.

NIB: $400   **Exc.:** $350   **VGood:** $295

Mossberg Model 835 Ulti-Mag

Mossberg Model 835 Ulti-Mag Crown Grade

Mossberg Model 835 Ulti-Mag Thumbhole Turkey

Mossberg Model 835 Ulti-Mag Tactical Turkey

Mossberg Model SA-20

Mossberg Model 190D

Mossberg Model 195D

MOSSBERG 835 ULTI-MAG TACTICAL TURKEY

Same as above but with extended pistol grip stock that is adjustable for length of pull from 10.75-inch to 14.5-inch.

NIB: $425   **Exc.:** $375   **VGood:** $320

MOSSBERG MODEL SA-20

This synthetic-stocked, matte black 20 gauge autoloader is chambered for 3-inch shells. It has a 28" or 26" vent-rib barrel and comes with five choke tubes. Weight is about 6 lbs. The Bantam model has a 1-inch shorter length of pull and 24" barrel and weighs about 5.6 lbs. Introduced in 2008.

NIB: $350   **Exc.:** $295   **VGood:** $195

MOSSBERG MODEL 70

Bolt action; single shot; takedown; .410; 24-inch barrel; interchangeable Modified, Full choke tubes; uncheckered one-piece, finger-grooved, pistol-grip stock. Introduced 1933; discontinued 1935.

Exc.: $100   **VGood:** $75   **Good:** $50

MOSSBERG MODEL 73

Bolt action; single shot; takedown; .410; 24-inch barrel; interchangeable Modified, Full choke tubes; uncheckered one-piece, finger-grooved, pistol-grip stock. Introduced 1936; discontinued 1939.

Exc.: $125   **VGood:** $95   **Good:** $75

MOSSBERG MODEL 75

Bolt action; single shot; takedown; 20-ga.; 26-inch barrel; interchangeable Modified, Full choke tubes; uncheckered one-piece, finger-grooved, pistol-grip stock. Introduced 1934; discontinued 1937.

Exc.: $125   **VGood:** $95   **Good:** $75

MOSSBERG MODEL 80

Bolt action; takedown; .410; 2-shot fixed top-loading magazine; 24-inch barrel; interchangeable Modified, Full choke tubes; uncheckered one-piece, finger-grooved, pistol-grip stock. Introduced 1934; discontinued 1935.

Exc.: $100   **VGood:** $80   **Good:** $60

MOSSBERG MODEL 83D

Bolt action; takedown; .410; 2-shot fixed top-loading magazine; 23-inch barrel; interchangeable Modified, Full choke tubes; uncheckered one-piece, finger-grooved, pistol grip stock. Introduced 1940; discontinued 1947 replaced by Model 183D.

Exc.: $100   **VGood:** $80   **Good:** $60

MOSSBERG MODEL 85

Bolt action; takedown; 20-ga.; 2-shot fixed top-loading magazine; 26-inch barrel; interchangeable Modified, Full choke tubes; uncheckered one-piece, finger-grooved, pistol-grip stock. Introduced 1934; discontinued 1939.

Exc.: $90   **VGood:** $60   **Good:** $45

MOSSBERG MODEL 85D

Same specs as Model 85 except 2-shot detachable box magazine; 25-inch barrel; interchangeable Full, Modified, Improved Cylinder choke tubes; black plastic buttplate. Introduced 1940; discontinued 1947 & replaced by Model 185D.

Exc.: $80   **VGood:** $60   **Good:** $45

MOSSBERG MODEL 173

Bolt action; single shot; takedown; .410; 2-1/2-inch, 3-inch chamber; 24-inch Full-choke barrel; 43-1/2-inch overall length; weighs 5-1/2 lbs.; uncheckered one-piece, finger-grooved, pistol-grip stock; plastic buttplate. Introduced 1957; discontinued 1973.

Exc.: $80   **VGood:** $60   **Good:** $45

Mossberg SSi-One Slug

Mossberg Onyx Reserve Sporting

Mossberg Silver Reserve SXS

Mossberg Onyx Reserve Sporting Clays

Navy Arms Model 83
Bird Hunter

MOSSBERG MODEL 173Y
Same specs as Model 173 except 22-inch Full-choke barrel; youth-size uncheckered one-piece, finger-grooved, pistol-grip stock. Introduced 1957; discontinued 1973.

Exc.: $80   VGood: $60   Good: $45

MOSSBERG MODEL 183D
Bolt action; takedown; .410; 2-shot fixed top-loading magazine; 24-inch barrel; interchangeable Modified, Full choke tubes; 43-1/2-inch overall length; weighs 5-1/2 lbs.; uncheckered one-piece, finger-grooved, pistol-grip stock. Introduced 1947; discontinued 1971.

Exc.: $90   VGood: $60   Good: $45

MOSSBERG MODEL 183K
Same specs as Model 183D, except variable C-Lect-Choke instead of interchangeable tubes; 44-1/2-inch overall length. Introduced 1953; discontinued 1985.

Exc.: $95   VGood: $60   Good: $45

MOSSBERG MODEL 185D
Bolt action; takedown; 20-ga.; 2-3/4-inch chamber; 2-shot detachable box magazine; 26-inch barrel; Full, Improved Cylinder choke tubes; 44-1/2-inch overall length; weighs 6-1/4 lbs.; uncheckered one-piece, finger-grooved, pistol-grip stock; black plastic buttplate. Introduced 1947; discontinued 1971.

Exc.: $95   VGood: $60   Good: $45

MOSSBERG MODEL 185K
Same specs as Model 185D except variable C-Lect-Choke instead of interchangeable tubes; 45 1/2-inch overall length. Introduced 1951; discontinued 1963.

Exc.: $95   VGood: $60   Good: $45

MOSSBERG MODEL 190D
Bolt action; takedown; 16-ga.; 2-3/4-inch chamber; 2-shot detachable box magazine; 26-inch barrel; Full, Improved Cylinder choke tubes; 44-1/2-inch overall length; weighs 6-3/4 lbs.; uncheckered one-piece, finger-grooved, pistol-grip stock; black plastic buttplate. Introduced 1955; discontinued 1971.

Exc.: $100   VGood: $65   Good: $50

MOSSBERG MODEL 190K
Same specs as Model 190D except variable C-Lect-Choke instead of interchangeable choke tubes; 45 1/2-inch overall length. Introduced 1956; discontinued 1963.

Exc.: $90   VGood: $60   Good: $45

MOSSBERG MODEL 195D
Bolt action; takedown; 12-ga.; 2-3/4-inch chamber; 2-shot detachable box magazine; 26-inch barrel;

interchangeable Full, Improved Cylinder choke tubes; 45-1/2-inch overall length; weighs 7-1/2 lbs.; uncheckered one-piece, finger-grooved, pistol-grip stock; black plastic buttplate. Introduced 1955; discontinued 1971.

Exc.: $90   VGood: $60   Good: $45

MOSSBERG MODEL 195K
Same specs as the Model 195D except variable C-Lect-Choke instead of interchangeable choke tubes; 46-1/2-inch overall length. Introduced 1956; discontinued 1963.

Exc.: $95   VGood: $65   Good: $50

MOSSBERG MODEL 385K
Bolt action; takedown; 20-ga.; 3-inch chamber; 2-shot detachable clip magazine; 26-inch barrel; C-Lect-Choke; walnut-finished hardwood Monte Carlo stock; recoil pad. Introduced 1963; no longer in production.

Exc.: $95   VGood: $70   Good: $50

MOSSBERG MODEL 390K
Bolt action; takedown; 16-ga.; 3-inch chamber; 2-shot detachable clip magazine; 28-inch barrel; C-Lect-Choke; walnut-finished hardwood Monte Carlo stock; recoil pad. Introduced 1963; no longer in production.

Exc.: $95   VGood: $70   Good: $50

MOSSBERG MODEL 395K
Bolt action; takedown; 12-ga.; 3-inch chamber; 2-shot detachable clip magazine; 28-inch barrel; C-Lect-Choke; walnut-finished hardwood Monte Carlo stock; recoil pad. Introduced 1963; no longer in production.

Exc.: $95   VGood: $70   Good: $50

MOSSBERG MODEL 695 SLUGSTER
Gauge: 12, 3-inch chamber; 22-inch barrel, fully rifled, ported; weighs 7-1/2 lbs.; black synthetic, with swivel studs and rubber recoil pad; blade front, folding rifle-style leaf rear sights; fiber optic; Weaver-style scope bases; matte metal finish; rotating thumb safety; detachable 2-shot magazine; Mossberg cablelock. Made in U.S. by Mossberg. Introduced 1996.

Perf.: $275   Exc.: $220   VGood: $185

With Fiber Optic rifle sights

Perf.: $297   Exc.: $242   VGood: $207

With woodlands camo stock, Fiber Optic sights

Perf.: $327   Exc.: $272   VGood: $237

MOSSBERG SSI-ONE 12-GAUGE SLUG SHOTGUN
Gauge: 12, 3-inch chamber; 24-inch, fully rifled barrel; weighs 8 lbs.; 40-inch overall length; walnut, fluted and cut checkered stock; sling-swivel studs; drilled and tapped for scope base; no sights (scope base supplied); frame accepts interchangeable rifle barrels (see Mossberg SSi- One rifle listing); lever-opening, break-action design; ambidextrous, top-tang safety; internal eject/extract selector. Introduced 2000.

Perf.: $390   Exc.: $310   VGood: $250

MOSSBERG SSI-ONE TURKEY SHOTGUN
Similar to SSi-One 12-gauge Slug Shotgun, but chambered for 12-ga., 3-1/2-inch loads. Includes Accu-Mag Turkey Tube. Introduced 2001.

Perf.: $390   Exc.: $310   VGood: $250

MOSSBERG ONYX RESERVE SPORTING
12-ga. O/U with 26- or 28-inch barrels. Similar to Silver Reserve Sporting but with blued receiver.

NIB: $575   Exc.: $475   VGood: $325

MOSSBERG SILVER RESERVE SIDE-BY-SIDE
New in 2008, the side-by-side version of the Silver Reserve comes in 12 gauge with 28" or 26" barrels and 20 and 28 gauge with 26" barrels. The stock and forend is select black walnut with satin finish. The receiver is satin-finished silver with scroll engraving and barrels are blued. Bores are chrome-plated. All models come with five choke tubes. Weight is 6.4 to 6.5 lbs. for 20 and 28 gauges; 7.2 lbs. for 12 gauge.

NIB: $700   Exc.: 475   VGood: 325

MOSSBERG ONYX RESERVE SPORTING SXS
Similar to Silver Reserve Sporting but with blued receiver.

NIB: $700   Exc.: 475   VGood: 325

ONYX RESERVE SIDE-BY-SIDE
This model is similar to the Silver Reserve but with a blued receiver.

NIB: $700   Exc.: 475   VGood: 325

NAVY ARMS MODEL 83 BIRD HUNTER
Over/under; boxlock; 12-, 20-ga.; 3-inch chambers; 28-inch barrels; standard choke combos; vent top, middle ribs; weighs 7-1/2 lbs.; metal bead front sight; checkered European walnut stock; double triggers; extractors; silvered, engraved receiver. Made in Italy. Introduced 1984; discontinued 1990.

Perf.: $260   Exc.: $200   VGood: $180

NAVY ARMS MODEL 93
Over/under; boxlock; 12-, 20-ga.; 3-inch chambers; 28-inch barrels; standard choke tubes; vent top, middle ribs; metal bead front sight; checkered European walnut stock, forend; double triggers; ejectors; silvered engraved receiver. Made in Italy. Introduced 1985; discontinued 1990.

Perf.: $315   Exc.: $240   VGood: $200

NAVY ARMS MODEL 95
Over/under; boxlock; 12-, 20-ga.; 3-inch chambers; 28-inch barrels; five choke tubes; vent top, middle ribs; weighs 7-1/2 lbs.; metal bead front sight; checkered European walnut stock; single trigger; extractors; silvered, engraved receiver. Made in Italy. Introduced 1985; discontinued 1990.

Perf.: $365   Exc.: $300   VGood: $270

NAVY ARMS MODEL 96
Over/under; boxlock; 12-, 20-ga.; 3-inch chambers; 28-inch barrels; five choke tubes; vent top, middle ribs; weighs 7-1/2 lbs.; metal bead front sight; checkered European walnut stock; single trigger; ejectors; gold-plated, engraved receiver. Made in Italy. Introduced 1986; discontinued 1990.

Perf.: $450   Exc.: $360   VGood: $300

NAVY ARMS MODEL 100 SXS
Side-by-side; 12-, 20-ga.; 3-inch chambers; 28-inch Improved Cylinder/Modified, Modified/Full chrome-lined barrels; weighs 7 lbs.; checkered European walnut stock; extractors; gold-plated double triggers; engraved, hard-chromed receiver. Made in Italy. Introduced 1985; discontinued 1987.
Perf.: $300   **Exc.:** $290   **VGood:** $225

NAVY ARMS MODEL 100 O/U
Over/under; 12-, 20-, 28-ga., .410; 3-inch chambers; 26-inch vent-rib, chrome-lined barrels; checkered walnut stock; single trigger; extractors; engraved, hard-chrome finished receiver. Introduced 1985; discontinued 1988.
Perf.: $375   **Exc.:** $290   **VGood:** $260

NAVY ARMS MODEL 105
Single shot; top lever; hammerless; 12-, 20-ga., .410; 3-inch chamber; 26-inch, 28-inch Full-choke barrel; metal bead front sight; checkered walnut-stained hardwood stock; folds for storage, transport; engraved chrome receiver. Made in Italy. Introduced 1987; discontinued 1990.
Perf.: $80   **Exc.:** $60   **VGood:** $40

NAVY ARMS MODEL 105 DELUXE
Similar to the standard Model 105, except has European walnut stock and vent. rib.
Perf.: $95   **Exc.:** $85   **VGood:** $75

NAVY ARMS MODEL 150
Side-by-side; 12-, 20-ga.; 3-inch chambers; 28-inch Improved Cylinder/Modified, Modified/Full chrome-lined barrels; weighs 7 lbs.; checkered European walnut stock; ejectors; gold-plated double triggers; engraved, hard-chromed receiver. Introduced 1985; discontinued 1987.
Perf.: $465   **Exc.:** $375   **VGood:** $315

NAVY ARMS MODEL 600
Single shot; top lever; hammerless; 12-, 20-ga., .410; 26-inch, 28-inch chrome-lined barrel; checkered beech stock; engraved hard-chromed receiver; folds for storage, transport. Made in Italy. Introduced 1986; discontinued 1987.
Perf.: $80   **Exc.:** $60   **VGood:** $40

NEW ENGLAND FIREARMS CAMO TURKEY SHOTGUNS
Gauge: 10, 3-1/2-inch; 12, 20, 3-inch chamber; 24-inch barrel; Extra-Full, screw-in choke tube (10 ga.); fixed Full choke (12, 20); American hardwood, green and black camouflage finish with sling swivels and ventilated recoil pad; bead front sight; matte metal finish; stock counterweight to reduce recoil; patented transfer bar system for hammer-down safety; includes camo sling and trigger lock. Accepts other factory-fitted barrels. Introduced 2000.

10-, 12-ga.
Perf.: $145   **Exc.:** $120   **VGood:** $100
20-ga. youth model (22-inch bbl.)
Perf.: $150   **Exc.:** $115   **VGood:** $95

NEW ENGLAND FIREARMS HANDI-RIFLE
Single shot; break-open; interchangeable rifle, shotgun barrels; 22 Hornet, 223, 243, 30-30, 30-06, 45-70; 12-, 20-ga. with 3-inch chamber; 22-inch barrel; 37-inch overall length; weighs 6-1/2 lbs.; American hardwood stock; rifle barrels have ramp front sight, open rear; drilled, tapped for scope mounts; matte electroless nickel or blued finish. Introduced 1987; still produced.
Perf.: $200   **Exc.:** $160   **VGood:** $130

NEW ENGLAND FIREARMS PARDNER
Single shot; sidelever; 12-, 16-, 20-, 28-ga., .410; 2-3/4-inch, 3-inch chambers; 24-inch, 26-inch, 28-inch, 32-inch barrel; standard chokes; weighs 5-1/2 lbs.; walnut-finished hardwood stock; transfer-bar ignition; blued finish. Introduced 1987; still in production.
Perf.: $90   **Exc.:** $65   **VGood:** $50
Youth model (12-, 20-, 28-ga., .410, 22-inch barrel, recoil pad)
Perf.: $115   **Exc.:** $95   **VGood:** $80

Navy Arms Model 100 SxS

New England Firearms Excell Synthetic

New England Firearms Excell Waterfowl

12-ga., 32-inch (Full)
Perf.: $110   **Exc.:** $90   **VGood:** $75

NEW ENGLAND FIREARMS PARDNER DELUXE
Same specs as Pardner except Double Back-up buttstock holding two extra shotshells. Introduced 1987; discontinued 1991.
Perf.: $100   **Exc.:** $75   **VGood:** $60

NEW ENGLAND FIREARMS PARDNER SPECIAL PURPOSE
Same specs as Pardner except 10-ga.; 3 1/2-inch chamber; 28-inch barrel; weighs 9-1/2 lbs.; recoil pad; blued or camo finish. Introduced 1988; still in production.
Perf.: $135   **Exc.:** $115   **VGood:** $95

NEW ENGLAND FIREARMS PARDNER YOUTH
Same specs as Pardner except 20-, 28-ga., .410; 22-inch barrel; shorter stock. Introduced 1989; still in production.
Perf.: $95   **Exc.:** $65   **VGood:** $55

NEW ENGLAND FIREARMS SPECIAL PURPOSE SHOTGUNS
Gauge: 10, 3-1/2-inch chamber; 28-inch barrel (Full), 32-inch barrel (Mod.); weighs 9-1/2 lbs.; 44-inch overall (28-inch barrel); American hardwood with walnut or matte camo finish; ventilated rubber recoil pad; bead front sight; break-open action with side-lever release; ejector; matte finish on metal. Introduced 1992.

Walnut-finish wood sling and swivels
Perf.: $135   **Exc.:** $115   **VGood:** $95
Camo finish, sling and swivels
Camo finish, 32-inch, sling and swivels
Perf.: $238   **Exc.:** $218   **VGood:** $198
Black matte finish, 24-inch, Turkey Full choke tube, sling and swivels
Perf.: $190   **Exc.:** $160   **VGood:** $135

NEW ENGLAND FIREARMS SURVIVOR
Single shot; 12-, 20-ga., .410/45 Colt; 3-inch chamber; 20-inch rifled (.410/45 Colt), 22-inch smoothbore with Modified choke tube; weighs 6 lbs.; 36-inch overall length; black polymer thumbhole/pistol-grip stock, beavertail forend; sling swivels; buttplate removes for extra ammunition storage; forend also holds extra ammunition; black or nickel finish. Introduced 1993.

With black finish
Perf.: $100   **Exc.:** $75   **VGood:** $50
With nickel finish
Perf.: $110   **Exc.:** $85   **VGood:** $60
With black finish, .410/45 Colt
Perf.: $135   **Exc.:** $95   **VGood:** $75
With nickel finish, .410/45 Colt
Perf.: $140   **Exc.:** $100   **VGood:** $80

NEW ENGLAND FIREARMS TRACKER SLUG GUN
Single shot; break-open; sidelever; 12-, 20-ga.; 3-inch chamber; 24-inch barrel; Cylinder choke; weighs

6 lbs.; 40-inch overall length; blade front sight, fully adjustable rifle-type rear; walnut-finished hardwood pistol-grip stock, recoil pad; blued barrel, color case-hardened frame. Introduced 1992; dropped 2001.
Perf.: $100   **Exc.:** $60   **VGood:** $55

NEW ENGLAND FIREARMS TRACKER II SLUG GUN
Same specs as the Tracker Slug Gun except fully rifled bore. Introduced 1992; still in production.
Perf.: $125   **Exc.:** $95   **VGood:** $55

NEW ENGLAND FIREARMS TURKEY/GOOSE GUN
Single shot; break-open; sidelever; 10-ga.; 3-1/2-inch chamber; 28-inch barrel; Full choke; weighs 9 1/2 lbs.; 44-inch overall length; walnut- or camo-finished American hardwood stock; ventilated rubber recoil pad; ejector; matte finish on metal. Introduced 1992; still in production.
Perf.: $140   **Exc.:** $90   **VGood:** $70

NEW ENGLAND FIREARMS TURKEY/GOOSE N.W.T.F.
Same specs as Turkey/Goose Gun except 10-, 20-ga.; 24-inch barrel; interchangeable choke tubes (comes with Turkey Full, others optional); drilled, tapped for long-eye relief scope mount; completely covered with Mossy Oak camouflage finish; Mossy Oak sling included. Introduced 1992; still in production.

10-ga. model
Perf.: $200   **Exc.:** $145   **VGood:** $100
20-ga. model
Perf.: $125   **Exc.:** $70   **VGood:** $50

NEW ENGLAND FIREARMS TURKEY/GOOSE SPECIAL
Same specs as the Turkey/Goose Gun except 12-ga.; 3-inch chamber; 24-inch (fixed Full Turkey choke); weighs 5 to 6 lbs; 40-inch overall length; modified pistol-grip stock; recoil pad; swivel studs; full coverage Realtree camouflage. Introduced 1994; still in production.
Perf.: $95   **Exc.:** $75   **VGood:** $55

NEW ENGLAND FIREARMS/ H&R 1871 TOPPER
Single-shot, break-open; 12 gauge (SB1-198), 16 gauge (SB1-698), 20 gauge (SB1-298), 28 gauge (SB1-898), .410 bore (SB1-498); American hardwood stock, black finish, pistol grip; barrel lengths: 26- (20 ga., 28 ga., .410 Bore) and 28-inch (12 ga., 16 ga.); chamber: Up to 3-inch (12 ga., 20 ga., .410 bore), 2-3/4-inch (16 ga., 28 ga.); bead front sight; weighs 5-6 lbs.
Perf.: $95   **Exc.:** $75   **VGood:** $55

NEW ENGLAND FIREARMS TOPPER DELUXE CLASSIC
Similar to the Topper; available in 20 as well as 12 gauge with a ventilated rib and choke tube system (modified tube provided); 28-inch (26-inch in 20 gauge) barrel with bead front sight; nickel-plated receiver; genuine American Walnut stock with ventilated recoil pad.
Perf.: $175   **Exc.:** $135   **VGood:** $95

NEW ENGLAND FIREARMS TOPPER DELUXE

New England Firearms
Excell Turkey

New England
Firearms Excell Combo

New England Firearms Pardner
Pump Synthetic

New England Firearms Pardner
Pump Field Shotgun

New England Firearms Pardner
Pump Compact Walnut Shotgun

New England Firearms Pardner
Pump Compact Synthetic Shotgun

Similar to Topper; available in 12 gauge with a 3-1/2-inch chamber and a screw-in choke that can handle both lead and steel shot.

Perf.: $125   **Exc.:** $70   **VGood:** $50

NEW ENGLAND FIREARMS TOPPER JUNIOR

Similar to Topper; 22-inch barrel is scaled ideally for smaller-framed shooters.

Perf.: $125   **Exc.:** $70   **VGood:** $50

NEW ENGLAND FIREARMS TOPPER JUNIOR CLASSIC

Similar to Topper Jr. but with blued frame, and cut-checkered American black walnut stock and fore-end.

Perf.: $125   **Exc.:** $70   **VGood:** $50

NEW ENGLAND FIREARMS EXCELL

Introduced in 2005 this model is chambered for the 12 gauge 3" shell and fitted with a 28" vent rib barrel with choke tubes. Checkered black synthetic stock. Magazine capacity is 5 rounds. Weight is about 7 lbs.

Exc.: $300   **VGood:** $200   **Good:** $135

NEW ENGLAND FIREARMS EXCELL WATERFOWL

As above but with Real Tree Advantage Wetlands camo finish. Introduced in 2005.

Exc.: $350   **VGood:** $250   **Good:** $165

NEW ENGLAND FIREARMS EXCELL TURKEY

This model is fitted with a 22" barrel with choke tubes and fiber optic front sight. Real Tree Advantage Hardwoods camo finish. Weight is 7 lbs. Introduced in 2005.

Exc.: $350   **VGood:** $250   **Good:** $165

NEW ENGLAND FIREARMS EXCELL COMBO

This model has a black synthetic stock and two barrels: 28" vent rib with choke tubes, and 24" rifled barrel. Weight is about 7 lbs. depending on barrel length. Introduced in 2005.

Exc.: $350   **VGood:** $250   **Good:** $165

NEW ENGLAND FIREARMS PARDNER PUMP WALNUT SHOTGUN

12- or 20-gauge pump-actio shotgun with American walnut furniture, 28- or 26-inch vent rib barrel, 3-inch chamber and screw-in choke tube. Weight 7-1/2 lbs.

Perf.: $180   **Exc.:** $115   **VGood:** $85

NEW ENGLAND FIREARMS PARDNER PUMP SYNTHETIC SHOTGUN

Similar to above but with black synthetic buttstock and forend.

Perf.: $150   **Exc.:** $100   **VGood:** $75

NEW ENGLAND FIREARMS PARDNER PUMP FIELD SHOTGUN

Similar to above but with Realtree APG HD camo finish.

Perf.: $180   **Exc.:** $115   **VGood:** $85

NEW ENGLAND FIREARMS PARDNER PUMP COMPACT FIELD SHOTGUN

Similar to above but with 1-1/4-inch shorter length of pull and 21 inch barrel.

Perf.: $180   **Exc.:** $115   **VGood:** $85

NEW ENGLAND FIREARMS PARDNER PUMP COMPACT WALNUT SHOTGUN

Similar to Pardner Pump Walnut model but with 1-1/4 inch shorter length of pull and 21 inch barrel. Weight 6-1/4 lbs.

Perf.: $180   **Exc.:** $115   **VGood:** $85

NEW ENGLAND FIREARMS PARDNER PUMP COMPACT SYNTHETIC SHOTGUN

Similar to above but with black synthetic buttstock and forend.

Perf.: $180   **Exc.:** $115   **VGood:** $85

NEW ENGLAND FIREARMS PARDNER PUMP COMBO

Introduced in 2005 this model features two 12 gauge 3" barrels. One 28" with vent rib and choke tubes,

and the other 22" rifled slug barrel. Walnut stock. Weight is about 7.5 lbs. depending on barrel length.

Perf.: $180   **Exc.:** $115   **VGood:** $85

NEW ENGLAND FIREARMS SPECIAL PURPOSE

This is a similar model but it is offered only in 10 gauge. It is available in several different configurations: A 10 gauge model with hardwood stock with 28" barrel, a camo model with 28" barrel, a camo model with 32" barrel choked Modified, and a black matte finish model with 24" barrel with screw-in turkey Full choke. Weight is about 9.5 lbs.

Perf.: $180   **Exc.:** $115   **VGood:** $85

NEW ENGLAND FIREARMS PARDNER PUMP PROTECTOR

Similar to Pardner Pump but with matte black finish throughout and synthetic buttstock and forend. Also available with carbon fiber dipped stock.

Perf.: $180   **Exc.:** $115   **VGood:** $85

NEW ENGLAND FIREARMS PARDNER PUMP COMBO

Similar to Pardner Pump but with two barrels: 28-inch smoothbore with vent rib and 22-inch rifled slug barrel with iron sights and drilled and tapped for scope base.

Perf.: $150   **Exc.:** $100   **VGood:** $75

NEW ENGLAND FIREARMS PARDNER PUMP TURKEY

Similar to Pardner Pump but with Realtree APG HD full-camo dip or Realtree Hardwoods camo finish. Fiber optics front and rear sights. Comes with screw-in XF Turkey choke tube.

Perf.: $180   **Exc.:** $115   **VGood:** $85

NEW HAVEN MODEL 273

Bolt action; single shot; top-loading; .410; 24-inch tapered barrel; Full choke; oil-finished American walnut Monte Carlo-style, pistol-grip stock; thumb safety. Made by Mossberg. Introduced 1960; discontinued 1965.

Exc.: $75   **VGood:** $50   **Good:** $45

NEW HAVEN MODEL 283

Bolt action; takedown; .410; 3-inch chamber; 2-shot clip detachable clip magazine; 25-inch barrel; detachable Full-choke tube; other chokes available at added cost; oil-finished American walnut Monte Carlo-style, pistol-grip stock; thumb safety. Made by Mossberg. Introduced 1960; discontinued 1965.

Exc.: $80   **VGood:** $55   **Good:** $45

NEW HAVEN MODEL 285

Bolt action; takedown; 20-ga.; 3-inch chamber; 2-shot clip detachable clip magazine; 25-inch barrel; detachable Full-choke tube; other chokes available at added cost; oil-finished American walnut Monte Carlo-style, pistol-grip stock; thumb safety. Made by Mossberg. Introduced 1960; discontinued 1965.

Exc.: $80   **VGood:** $55   **Good:** $45

NEW HAVEN MODEL 290

Bolt action; takedown; 16-ga.; 2-shot detachable clip magazine; 28-inch barrel; detachable Full-choke tube; other choke tubes available at added cost; oil-finished American walnut Monte Carlo-style, pistol-grip stock; thumb safety. Made by Mossberg. Introduced 1960; discontinued 1965.

Exc.: $80   **VGood:** $55   **Good:** $45

NEW HAVEN MODEL 295

Bolt action; takedown; 12-ga.; 2-shot detachable clip magazine; 28-inch barrel; detachable Full-choke tube; other choke tubes available at added cost; oil-finished American walnut Monte Carlo-style pistol-grip stock; thumb safety. Made by Mossberg. Introduced 1960; discontinued 1965.

Exc.: $80   **VGood:** $55   **Good:** $45

NEW HAVEN MODEL 495

Bolt action; takedown; 12-ga.; 2-shot detachable clip magazine; 28-inch Full-choke barrel; unchecked walnut-finished hardwood Monte Carlo-style, pistol-grip stock; thumb safety. Introduced 1964; discontinued 1965.

Exc.: $80   **VGood:** $55   **Good:** $45

NEW HAVEN MODEL 600

Slide action; takedown; 12-ga.; 2-3/4-inch, 3-inch chamber; 6-shot magazine; 26-inch Improved Cylinder, 28-inch Full or Modified, 30-inch Full-choke barrel; choice of standard or magnum barrel; uncheckered walnut pistol-grip stock, extension slide handle; safety on top of receiver. Same general design as Mossberg Model 500. Introduced 1962; discontinued 1965.

Exc.: $140   **VGood:** $110   **Good:** $90

NEW HAVEN MODEL 600AST SLUGSTER

Same specs as Model 600 except 12-, 20-ga.; 18-1/2-inch, 24-inch Slugster barrel; ramp front sight, open adjustable folding leaf rear; running deer scene etched on receiver. Introduced 1978; no longer in production.

Exc.: $140   **VGood:** $110   **Good:** $90

NEW HAVEN MODEL 600ETV

Same specs as Model 600 except .410; 26-inch vent-rib barrels; checkered walnut-finished, pistol-grip stock, forend; fluted comb; recoil pad. No longer in production.

Exc.: $150   **VGood:** $120   **Good:** $100

NEW HAVEN MODEL 600K

Same specs as Model 600 except C-Lect-Choke feature. No longer in production.

Exc.: $150   **VGood:** $120   **Good:** $100

NOBLE MODEL 40

Slide action; solid frame; 12-, 16-ga.; 6-shot magazine; 28-inch barrel; Multi-choke; uncheckered American walnut pistol-grip stock, grooved forearm; recoil pad; push-button safety. Introduced 1952; discontinued 1956.

Exc.: $150   **VGood:** $110   **Good:** $75

NOBLE MODEL 50

Slide action; solid frame; 12-, 16-ga.; 6-shot magazine; 28-inch barrel; uncheckered American walnut pistol-grip stock, grooved forearm; push-button safety. Introduced 1954; discontinued 1956.

Exc.: $150   **VGood:** $110   **Good:** $75

NOBLE MODEL 60

Slide action; solid frame; 12-, 16-ga.; 6-shot magazine; 28-inch barrel; Master choke; uncheckered American walnut pistol-grip stock, grooved slide handle; crossbolt safety; recoil pad. Introduced 1957; discontinued 1969.

Exc.: $150   **VGood:** $110   **Good:** $75

NOBLE MODEL 60ACP

Same specs as Model 60 except receiver is machined from single block of steel, all lock surfaces are hardened. Replaced Model 60 and Model 60AF. Introduced 1967; discontinued 1971.

Exc.: $160   **VGood:** $120   **Good:** $85

NOBLE MODEL 60AF

Same specs as Model 60 except selected steel barrel; damascened bolt; select walnut stock with fluted comb. Introduced 1965; discontinued 1966.

Exc.: $150   **VGood:** $110   **Good:** $75

NOBLE MODEL 65

Slide action; solid frame; 12-, 16-ga.; 6-shot magazine; 28-inch barrel; Full or Modified choke; uncheckered American walnut pistol-grip stock, grooved slide handle; crossbolt safety. Introduced 1967; discontinued 1969.

Exc.: $150   **VGood:** $110   **Good:** $75

NOBLE MODEL 66CLP

Slide action; solid frame; 12-, 16-ga.; 3-inch (12-ga.) chamber; 6-shot tubular magazine; 28-inch barrel; adjustable choke; checkered American walnut pistol-grip stock, slide handle; keylock safety mechanism; recoil pad. Introduced 1967; discontinued 1979.

Exc.: $155   **VGood:** $115   **Good:** $85

New Haven Model 600AST Slugster

Noble Model 60

Noble Model 60ACP

Noble Model 65

Noble Model 66CLP

Noble Model 66RLP

Noble Model 66XL

Noble Model 70

NOBLE MODEL 66RCLP

Same specs as Model 66CLP except vent-rib barrel. Introduced 1967; discontinued 1970.

Exc.: $160   **VGood:** $120   **Good:** $85

NOBLE MODEL 66RLP

Same specs as Model 66CLP except Modified or Full choke. Introduced 1967; discontinued 1970.

Exc.: $160   **VGood:** $120   **Good:** $85

NOBLE MODEL 66XL

Same specs as Model 66CLP except Modified or Full choke; checkered slide handle; no recoil pad. Introduced 1967; discontinued 1970.

Exc.: $155   **VGood:** $115   **Good:** $85

NOBLE MODEL 70

Slide action; solid frame; .410; 3-inch chamber; 6-shot magazine; 26-inch barrel; Full choke; uncheckered walnut pistol-grip stock, grooved forearm; top safety. Introduced 1959; discontinued 1967.

Exc.: $150   **VGood:** $110   **Good:** $75

NOBLE MODEL 70CLP

Same specs as Model 70 except adjustable choke. Introduced 1958; discontinued 1970.

Exc.: $150   **VGood:** $110   **Good:** $75

NOBLE MODEL 70RCLP

Same specs as Model 70 except adjustable choke; vent rib. Introduced 1967; discontinued 1970.

Exc.: $155   **VGood:** $115   **Good:** $89

NOBLE MODEL 70RLP

Same specs as Model 70 except vent rib. Introduced 1967; discontinued 1970.

Exc.: $155   **VGood:** $115   **Good:** $80

Noble Model 70X

Noble Model 80

Noble Model 166L Deergun

Noble Model 602

Noble Model 662

Noble Model 450E

NOBLE MODEL 70X
Same specs as Model 70 except side ejection; damascened bolt. Replaced Model 70. Introduced 1967; discontinued 1971.

    Exc.: $160   **VGood:** $120   **Good:** $85

NOBLE MODEL 70XL
Same specs as Model 70 except checkered buttstock. Introduced 1958; discontinued 1970.

    Exc.: $160   **VGood:** $120   **Good:** $85

NOBLE MODEL 80
Recoil-operated autoloader; .410; 2-1/2-inch, 3-inch chamber; 6-shot magazine; 26-inch barrel; Full choke; uncheckered American walnut pistol-grip stock, grooved forearm; fluted comb; action release button; push-button safety. Introduced 1965; discontinued 1967.

    Exc.: $225   **VGood:** $200   **Good:** $140

NOBLE MODEL 160 DEERGUN
Slide action; 12-, 16-ga.; 6-shot magazine; 24-inch barrel; Lyman adjustable peep rear sight, ramp post front; tapped for scope; uncheckered American walnut pistol-grip stock, grooved slide handle; hard rubber buttplate; sling swivels; detachable carrying strap. Introduced 1965; discontinued 1966.

    Exc.: $140   **VGood:** $90   **Good:** $75

NOBLE MODEL 166L DEERGUN
Slide action; 12-, 16-ga.; 6-shot magazine; 24-inch barrel; Lyman adjustable peep rear sight, ramp post

front; tapped for scope; uncheckered American walnut pistol-grip stock, grooved slide handle; hard rubber buttplate; sling swivels; detachable carrying strap. Replaced Model 160 Deergun. Introduced 1967; discontinued 1971.

    Exc.: $185   **VGood:** $150   **Good:** $120

NOBLE MODEL 390 DEERGUN
Slide action; solid frame; 12-ga.; 3-inch chamber; 6-shot magazine; 24-inch rifled slug barrel; Lyman adjustable peep rear sight, ramp post front; impressed-checkered American walnut stock, slide handle; tang safety; sling swivels; detachable carrying strap. Introduced 1972; discontinued 1972.

    Exc.: $185   **VGood:** $150   **Good:** $125

NOBLE MODEL 420
Double barrel; hammerless; top lever; 12-, 16-, 20-ga.; 28-inch barrels; Full/Modified chokes; matted rib; checkered pistol-grip stock, forearm; double triggers; automatic safety. Introduced 1959; discontinued 1971. Made in Spain.

    Exc.: $275   **VGood:** $225   **Good:** $95

NOBLE MODEL 420EK
Same specs as Model 420 except demi-block with triple lock; front, middle bead sights; hand-checkered Circassian walnut pistol-grip stock, beavertail forearm; recoil pad; automatic selective ejectors; hand-engraved action; gold inlay on top lever. Introduced 1968; discontinued 1968. Made in Spain.

    Exc.: $290   **VGood:** $240   **Good:** $125

NOBLE MODEL 450E
Double barrel; demi-block with triple lock; 12-, 16-, 20-ga.; 28-inch barrel; Modified/Full chokes; front, middle bead sights; hand-checkered Circassian walnut pistol-grip stock, beavertail forend; double triggers; engraving; gold inlay; recoil pad. Replaced Model 420EK. Introduced 1969; discontinued 1971. Made in Spain.

    Exc.: $290   **VGood:** $240   **Good:** $125

NOBLE MODEL 520
Side-by-side; hammerless; 12-, 20-, 16-, 28-ga. .410; 2-3/4-inch chamber; 26-inch, 28-inch barrels; standard choke combos; matted top rib; hand-

checkered Circassian walnut stock, forend; double triggers; Holland-design extractors; hand-engraved frame. Introduced 1970; discontinued 1972. Made in Spain.

    Exc.: $250   **VGood:** $150   **Good:** $125

NOBLE MODEL 550
Side-by-side; hammerless; 12-, 20-ga.; 2-3/4-inch chambers; 28-inch barrels; Modified/Full chokes; front, middle bead sights; hand-checkered Circassian walnut pistol-grip stock, beavertail forend; grip cap; double triggers; double auto selective ejectors; tang safety; rubber recoil pad; custom hand-engraved frame; knight's head medallion inlaid on top snap. Introduced 1970; discontinued 1972. Made in Spain.

    Exc.: $270   **VGood:** $160   **Good:** $130

NOBLE MODEL 602
Slide action; solid frame; 20-ga.; 3-inch chamber; 6-shot magazine; 28-inch barrel; adjustable choke; uncheckered American walnut pistol-grip stock, grooved slide handle; top safety; side ejection; recoil pad. Introduced 1963; discontinued 1971.

    Exc.: $175   **VGood:** $140   **Good:** $80

NOBLE MODEL 602CLP
Same specs as Model 602 except keylock safety mechanism; checkered pistol-grip stock, slide handle. Introduced 1958; discontinued 1970.

    Exc.: $175   **VGood:** $140   **Good:** $85

NOBLE MODEL 602RCLP
Same specs as Model 602 except keylock safety mechanism; vent rib; checkered pistol-grip stock, slide handle. Introduced 1967; discontinued 1970.

    Exc.: $175   **VGood:** $140   **Good:** $85

NOBLE MODEL 602RLP
Same specs as Model 602 except keylock safety mechanism; vent rib; Full or Modified choke; checkered pistol-grip stock, slide handle. Introduced 1967; discontinued 1970.

    Exc.: $175   **VGood:** $140   **Good:** $85

NOBLE MODEL 602XL
Same specs as Model 602 except keylock safety mechanism; Full or Modified choke; checkered slide handle; no recoil pad. Introduced 1958; discontinued 1970.

    Exc.: $165   **VGood:** $125   **Good:** $80

NOBLE MODEL 662
Slide action; solid frame; 20-ga.; 6-shot magazine; 26-inch barrel; Full choke; uncheckered walnut pistol-grip stock, grooved slide forearm; top safety; aluminum alloy barrel, receiver. Introduced 1966; discontinued 1970.

    Exc.: $170   **VGood:** $140   **Good:** $100

NOBLE MODEL 757
Slide action; solid frame; 20-ga.; 2-3/4-inch chamber; 5-shot magazine; 28-inch aircraft alloy barrel; adjustable choke; impressed-checkered American walnut pistol-grip stock, slide handle; tang safety; barrel, receiver black anodized; decorated receiver. Introduced 1972; discontinued 1972.

    Exc.: $170   **VGood:** $120   **Good:** $100

NOBLE SERIES 200
Slide action; solid frame; 20-ga.; 3-inch chamber; 6-shot magazine; 28-inch barrel; optional vent rib; adjustable choke or Modified, Full choke; impressed-checkered American walnut stock, slide handle; tang safety; side ejection; keylock safety mechanism; recoil pad. Introduced 1972; discontinued 1972.

With fixed choke
    Exc.: $150   **VGood:** $100   **Good:** $80

With fixed choke, vent rib
    Exc.: $155   **VGood:** $105   **Good:** $85

With adjustable choke
    Exc.: $155   **VGood:** $105   **Good:** $85

With adjustable choke, vent rib
    Exc.: $160   **VGood:** $110   **Good:** $90

NOBLE SERIES 300

Slide action; solid frame; 12-, 16-ga.; 3-inch (12-ga.) chamber; 6-shot magazine, 3-shot plug furnished; 28-inch barrel; adjustable choke or Modified, Full choke; optional vent rib; impressed-checkered American walnut stock, slide handle; tang safety; side ejection; keylock safety mechanism; damascened bolt. Introduced 1972; discontinued 1972.

With fixed choke		
Exc.: $150	**VGood:** $100	**Good:** $80
With fixed choke, vent rib		
Exc.: $155	**VGood:** $105	**Good:** $85
With adjustable choke		
Exc.: $155	**VGood:** $105	**Good:** $85
With adjustable choke, vent rib		
Exc.: $160	**VGood:** $110	**Good:** $90

NOBLE SERIES 400

Slide action; solid frame; .410; 3-inch chamber; 6-shot magazine; 25-inch barrel; adjustable choke or Modified, Full choke; optional vent rib; impressed-checkered American walnut pistol-grip stock, slide handle; tang safety; side ejection; keylock safety mechanism; damascened bolt. Introduced 1972; discontinued 1972.

With fixed choke		
Exc.: $155	**VGood:** $105	**Good:** $85
With fixed choke, vent rib		
Exc.: $160	**VGood:** $110	**Good:** $90
With adjustable choke		
Exc.: $160	**VGood:** $110	**Good:** $90
With adjustable choke, vent rib		
Exc.: $165	**VGood:** $115	**Good:** $95

NORINCO TYPE HL12-203

Over/under; boxlock action; 12-ga. only; 2-3/4-inch chambers; ejectors; 30-inch barrels; vent. rib; single trigger; multi-chokes; checkered stock and forearm; 7-1/2 lbs. Importation began 1989; dropped 1993.

Exc.: $350   **VGood:** $300   **Good:** $265

NORINCO MODEL 99 COACH GUN

Side-by-side; 12-ga. only; 2-3/4-inch chambers; exposed hammers; 20-inch barrels; Fjull/Modified choke tubes; blue finish; checkered stock and forearm; weighs 7-1/5 lbs.

Exc.: $215   **VGood:** $190   **Good:** $175

NORINCO MODEL 87L

Lever action; 12-ga. only; 2-3/4-inch chamber; styled after Winchester Model 1887; 20-inch barrel; walnut stock and forearm. Importation began 2003.

Exc.: $335   **VGood:** $275   **Good:** $235

NORINCO MODEL 2000 FIELD

Autoloader; 12-ga. only; 2-3/4-inch chamber; steel receiver; aluminum alloy triggerguard; 26-inch, 28-inch barrel; vent. rib; Modified choke tube; choice of black synthetic or checkered hardwood stock and forearm; weighs 7-1/2 lbs. Limited importation during 1999 only.

Exc.: $230   **VGood:** $200   **Good:** $185
Add $10 to above prices for wood stock and forearm.

NORINCO MODEL 2000 DEFENSE

Similar to Model 2000 Field, except 18-1/2-inch barrel; cyl. Choke tube; choice of bead, rifle or ghost ring sights; matte black metal finish; black synthetic stock and forearm with recoil pad. Limited importation during 1999 only.

Exc.: $230   **VGood:** $200   **Good:** $185
Add $10 to above prices for rifle sights.
Add $20 for ghost ring sights.

NORINCO TYPE HL12-102

Slide-action; 12-ga. only; 2-3/4-inch chamber; 28.4-inch barrel; 3-shot mag.; crossbolt safety; fixed chokes; weighs 9.3 lbs. Importation began 1989; dropped 1993.

Perf.: $230   **Exc.:** $200   **VGood:** $175

Omega Folding Over/Under

Omega Folding Single Barrel

Parker Hammerless Grade A-1 Special

NORINCO MODEL 984/985/987

Slide-action; 12-ga. only; 3-inch chamber; 26-inch, 28-inch-barrel, vent. rib; Modified choke tube; black synthetic or uncheckered hardwood stock and forearm; matte black metal finish. Importation began 2001; dropped 2002.

Perf.: $200   **Exc.:** $170   **VGood:** $155
Add $10 to above prices for hardwood stock (models 985 & 987).

NORINCO MODEL 97W HAMMER

Slide-action; 12-ga. only; styled similar to the Winchester Model 97; outside hammer; 20-inch plain barrel; cylinder bore fixed choke; solid frame; hardwood stock with grooved "corn cob" forearm. Importation began 2001.

Perf.: $400   **Exc.:** $350   **VGood:** $250

NORINCO MODEL 97T TRENCH GUN

Slide-action; 12-ga. only; reproduction of the original Winchester WWI Trench Gun; shrouded barrel; proper markings same as original.

Perf.: $500   **Exc.:** $400   **VGood:** $300

NORINCO MODEL 981/982T

Slide-action; 12 ga. only; 3-inch chamber; 18-1/2-inch cylinder bore barrel; fixed choke; black synthetic stock and forearm; matte black metal fin ish. Importation began 2001.

Perf.: $200   **Exc.:** $170   **VGood:** $150
Add $20 to above prices for ghost ring sights (Model 982T).

NORINCO MODEL 983

Slide-action; 12-ga. only; 22-inch barrel; external rifled choke tube; adjustable rifle sights; synthetic black stock. Imported during 2002 only.

Perf.: $215   **Exc.:** $170   **VGood:** $155

OMEGA FOLDING OVER/UNDER

Over/under; boxlock; 12-, 20-, 28-ga., .410; 3-inch chambers; 26-inch, 28-inch barrels; standard choke combos; vent rib; weighs 5-1/2 lbs.; checkered European walnut stock; auto safety; single trigger; extractors; folding takedown design. Made in Italy. Introduced 1986; discontinued 1994.

Perf.: $330   **Exc.:** $250   **VGood:** $200

OMEGA FOLDING OVER/UNDER DELUXE

Same specs as Folding Over/Under except select walnut stock. Introduced 1986; discontinued 1990.

Perf.: $400   **Exc.:** $310   **VGood:** $265

OMEGA FOLDING SIDE-BY-SIDE

Side-by-side; boxlock; 10-, 28-ga., .410; 26-inch barrels; standard choke combos; vent rib; weighs 5 1/2 lbs.; checkered beechwood stock, forearm; auto safety; double triggers; extractors; folding takedown design. Introduced 1986; discontinued 1989.

Perf.: $180   **Exc.:** $130   **VGood:** $100

OMEGA FOLDING SIDE-BY-SIDE DELUXE

Same specs as Folding Side-By-Side except select walnut stock. Introduced 1986; discontinued 1990.

Perf.: $210   **Exc.:** $180   **VGood:** $130

OMEGA FOLDING SINGLE BARREL

Single shot; 12-, 16-, 20-, 28-ga., .410; 2-3/4-inch, 3-inch chambers; 26-inch, 28-inch, 30-inch barrel; Full choke; metal bead front sight; checkered beech stock; top opening lever; matte chromed receiver; folds for storage, transport. Made in Italy. Introduced 1984; discontinued 1988.

Perf.: $145   **Exc.:** $100   **VGood:** $80

OMEGA FOLDING SINGLE BARREL DELUXE

Same specs as Folding Single Barrel except vent rib; checkered walnut stock; blued receiver. Introduced 1984; discontinued 1988.

Perf.: $190   **Exc.:** $165   **VGood:** $130

PARKER HAMMERLESS DOUBLE

Side-by-side; boxlock; 10-, 12-, 16-, 20-, 28-ga., .410; 26-inch to 32-inch barrels; any standard choke combo; hand-checkered select walnut stock, forearm; choice of straight, half- or pistol-grip stock; automatic ejectors; double or selective single trigger. After Parker Brothers was absorbed by Remington Arms in 1934, shotgun was designated as Remington Parker Model 920. Because of the wide variations in styles and extras, as well as the number of grades-differing in engraving, checkering and general workmanship-there is a wide range of values. The selective trigger was introduced in 1922, with the raised vent rib; the beavertail forend was introduced in 1923; all add to used value. Some guns were put together from available parts and stocks by Remington until 1942. Grades are in descending values, with the A-designated model being worth several times that of the V model. Non-ejector models (pre-1934) are worth about 30 percent less than value shown for ejector models; if gun has interchangeable barrels, it is worth 30 to 35 percent more than shown. Those in 20-ga. are 35

Parker Hammerless Double Grade AAHE

Parker Hammerless Double Grade AHE

Parker Hammerless Double Grade BHE

Parker Hammerless Double Grade CHE

Parker Hammerless Double Grade GHE

Parker Hammerless Double Grade DHE

Parker Trojan

Parker Single-Barrel Trap

Parker Reproductions Grade DHE

PARKER SINGLE-BARREL TRAP

Single barrel; boxlock; hammerless; 12-ga.; 30-inch, 32-inch, 34-inch barrel; any designated choke; vent rib; hand-checkered select walnut pistol grip stock, forearm; choice of straight, half- or pistol grip; ejector. Various grades differ with amount of workmanship, checkering, engraving, etc. General specs are the same for all variations. After absorption of Parker by Remington, model was listed as Remington Parker Model 930. Introduced 1917; discontinued 1942.

Grade SA-1 Special		
Exc.: $12,500	VGood: $9500	Good: $8000
Grade SAA		
Exc.: $5200	VGood: $4000	Good: $3000
Grade SA		
Exc.: $4000	VGood: $3500	Good: $2500
Grade SB		
Exc.: $3500	VGood: $3000	Good: $2600
Grade SC		
Exc.: $3000	VGood: $2100	Good: $1700

PARKER TROJAN

Double barrel; boxlock; hammerless; 12-, 16-, 20-ga.; 26-inch, 28-inch Modified/Full, 30-inch Full barrels; hand-checkered American walnut pistol grip stock, forearm; plain extractors; double or single triggers. Introduced 1915; discontinued 1939.

12-, 16-ga. model with double triggers		
Exc.: $1600	VGood: $1000	Good: $800
12-, 16-ga. model with single trigger		
Exc.: $1900	VGood: $1200	Good: $950
20-ga. model with double triggers		
Exc.: $2400	VGood: $1650	Good: $1400
20-ga. model with single trigger		
Exc.: $2900	VGood: $2000	Good: $1700

PARKER REPRODUCTIONS GRADE A-1 SPECIAL

Side-by-side; boxlock; 12-, 20-, 28-ga.; 2-3/4-inch, 3-inch chambers; 26-inch, 28-inch barrels; metal bead front sight; checkered select American walnut straight or pistol-grip stock, forend; double or single trigger; skeleton or hard rubber buttplate; two-barrel set; engraving; reproduction of original; all parts interchange with original. Introduced 1988; no longer in production.

Perf.: $10,000   Exc.: $7500   VGood: $7250

PARKER REPRODUCTIONS GRADE BHE

Side-by-side; 12-, 20-, 28-ga.; 2-3/4-inch, 3-inch chambers; checkered fancy American walnut straight or pistol-grip stock, splinter or beavertail forend; checkered butt; double or single selective triggers; selective ejectors; hand engraving; case-hardened frame; marketed in fitted leather trunk-type case; reproduction of original; all parts interchange with original. Made in Japan. Introduced 1984; discontinued 1989. Premium for 28 ga.

Perf.: $4500   Exc.: $3800   VGood: $2900

PARKER REPRODUCTIONS GRADE DHE

Side-by-side; boxlock; 12-, 20-, 28-ga.; 2-3/4-inch, 3-inch chambers; 26-inch, 28-inch barrels; metal bead front sight; checkered American walnut straight or pistol-grip stock, forend; double or single trigger; skeleton or hard rubber buttplate; reproduction of original; all parts interchange with original. Made in Japan. Introduced 1984; no longer in production. Premium for 28 ga.

Perf.: $3700   Exc.: $2800   VGood: $2500

PARKER-HALE MODEL 630

Side-by-side; boxlock; 12-ga.; 3-inch chambers; 26-inch, 28-inch barrels; standard choke combos; checkered straight-grip English-style stock, forend; auto safety; extractors; double triggers; color case-hardened action. Made in Spain. Introduced 1993; discontinued 1993.

Perf.: $600   Exc.: $425   VGood: $380

percent higher, 28-ga. are 75 percent higher and .410 are 100 percent higher than values shown. Prices shown are for 12-, 16-ga. configurations. For single trigger, add $250; vent rib, add $300; single selective trigger, add $200 to $300; raised vent rib, add $325 to $350; beavertail forearm addition in grades VHE, GHE, DHE, CHE, add $200 to $250 to base price; for grades BHE, AHE, AAHE, add $450 to $500 to base; for A1 Special, add $500 to $750.

Grade A-1 Special		
Exc.: $65,000	VGood: $50,000	Good: $42,000
Grade AAHE		
Exc.: $30,000	VGood: $22,500	Good: $18,500

Grade AHE		
Exc.: $17,500	VGood: $10,000	Good: $8000
Grade BHE		
Exc.: $7500	VGood: $5000	Good: $4000
Grade CHE		
Exc.: $5000	VGood: $3500	Good: $2500
Grade DHE		
Exc.: $4000	VGood: $2500	Good: $2000
Grade GHE		
Exc.: $3000	VGood: $2000	Good: $1500
Grade VHE		
Exc.: $2100	VGood: $1250	Good: $1000

PARKER-HALE MODEL 640A

Side-by-side; boxlock; 12-, 16-, 20-, 28-ga., .410; 2-3/4-inch, 3-inch chambers; 25-inch, 26-inch, 27-inch, 28-inch barrels; raised rib; hand-checkered, oil-finished walnut pistol-grip stock, beavertail forend; auto safety; extractors; single trigger; buttplate; silvered, engraved action. Made in Spain. Introduced 1986; discontinued 1993.

Perf.: $800   **Exc.:** $600   **VGood:** $540

PARKER-HALE MODEL 640E

Same specs as Model 640A except concave rib; hand-checkered, oil-finished straight-grip English-style walnut stock, splinter forend; checkered butt; double triggers. Available in a wide variety of styles. Made in Spain. Introduced 1986; discontinued 1993. Name changed to Precision Sports Model 800 Series in 1990.

Perf.: $760   **Exc.:** $520   **VGood:** $450

PARKER-HALE MODEL 640M

Same specs as Model 640A except 10-ga.; 3-1/2-inch chambers; 26-inch, 30-inch, 32-inch Full/Full barrels; checkered straight-grip English-style stock, forend; auto safety; extractors; double triggers; recoil pad. Made in Spain. Introduced 1989; discontinued 1993.

Perf.: $825   **Exc.:** $625   **VGood:** $550

PARKER-HALE MODEL 640 SLUG

Same specs as Model 640A except 12-ga.; 25-inch Improved Cylinder/Improved Cylinder barrels. Made in Spain. Introduced 1991; discontinued 1993.

Perf.: $900   **Exc.:** $700   **VGood:** $600

PARKER-HALE MODEL 645A

Side-by-side; boxlock; 12-, 16-, 20-, 28-ga., .410; 2-3/4-inch, 3-inch chambers; 26-inch, 28-inch barrels; raised rib; hand-checkered, oil-finished walnut pistol-grip stock, beavertail forend; auto safety; ejectors; single trigger; buttplate; silvered, engraved action. Made in Spain. Introduced 1986; discontinued 1993.

Perf.: $1000   **Exc.:** $725   **VGood:** $600

PARKER-HALE MODEL 645E

Same specs as Model 645A except concave rib; hand-checkered, oil-finished straight-grip English-style walnut stock, splinter forend; checkered butt; double triggers. Made in Spain. Introduced 1986; discontinued 1993.

Perf.: $910   **Exc.:** $600   **VGood:** $550

PARKER-HALE MODEL 645E-XXV

Same specs as Model 645E except 25-inch barrels; Churchill rib; hand-checkered, oil-finished straight-grip English-style walnut stock, splinter forend; checkered butt; double triggers. Made in Spain. Introduced 1986; discontinued 1993.

Perf.: $900   **Exc.:** $600   **VGood:** $550

PARKER-HALE MODEL 650A

Side-by-side; boxlock; 12-ga.; 28-inch barrels; choke tubes; raised rib; checkered pistol-grip walnut stock, beavertail forend; auto safety; extractors; single trigger; buttplate; silvered action. Made in Spain. Introduced 1992; discontinued 1993.

Perf.: $850   **Exc.:** $650   **VGood:** $600

PARKER-HALE MODEL 650E

Same specs as Model 650A except concave rib; straight-grip English-style stock, splinter forend; checkered butt; double triggers. Made in Spain. Introduced 1992; discontinued 1993.

Perf.: $800   **Exc.:** $600   **VGood:** $550

PARKER-HALE MODEL 655A

Side-by-side; boxlock; 12-ga.; 28-inch barrels; choke tubes; raised rib; checkered pistol-grip walnut stock, beavertail forend; auto safety; ejectors; single trigger; buttplate; silvered action. Made in Spain. Introduced 1992; discontinued 1993.

Perf.: $975   **Exc.:** $775   **VGood:** $700

PARKER-HALE MODEL 655E

Same specs as Model 655A except concave rib; straight-gip English-style walnut stock, splinter

Parker-Hale Model 645A

Parker-Hale Model 645E

Pedersen Model 1000 Grade I

Pedersen Model 1000 Grade II

Pedersen Model 1500 Trap

forend; checkered butt; double triggers. Made in Spain. Introduced 1992; discontinued 1993.

Perf.: $900   **Exc.:** $700   **VGood:** $625

PARKER-HALE MODEL 670E

Side-by-side; sidelock; 12-, 16-, 20-ga.; 2-3/4-inch, 3-inch chambers; 26-inch, 27-inch, 28-inch barrels; concave rib; hand-checkered, oil-finished straight-grip English-style walnut stock, splinter forend; auto safety; ejectors; double triggers; checkered butt; silvered, engraved action. Made in Spain. Introduced 1986; discontinued 1993.

Perf.: $3500   **Exc.:** $2500   **VGood:** $1900

PARKER-HALE MODEL 680E-XXV

Side-by-side; sidelock; 12-, 16-, 20-ga.; 2-3/4-inch, 3-inch chambers; 25-inch barrels; Churchill rib; hand-checkered, oil-finished straight-grip English-style walnut stock, splinter forend; auto safety; ejectors; double triggers; checkered butt; color case-hardened action. Made in Spain. Introduced 1986; discontinued 1993.

Perf.: $3300   **Exc.:** $2300   **VGood:** $1700

PARQUEMY MODEL 48

Side-by-side; .410; 3-inch chambers; Modified/Full barrels; medium bead front sight; hand-checkered straight-grip European walnut stock; double triggers; checkered butt; extractors; hand-engraved locks. Made in Spain. Introduced 1983 by Toledo Armas; discontinued 1984.

Perf.: $525   **Exc.:** $400   **VGood:** $350

PARQUEMY MODEL 48E

Same specs as Model 48 except 12-, 20-, 28-ga.; 2-3/4-inch chambers; ejectors. Introduced 1982 by Toledo Armas; discontinued 1984.

Perf.: $650   **Exc.:** $525   **VGood:** $450

PEDERSEN MODEL 1000

Over/under; boxlock; 12-, 20-ga.; 2-3/4-inch chambers; 26-inch, 28-inch, 30-inch barrels; vent rib; hand-checkered American walnut pistol-grip stock, forearm; rubber recoil pad; automatic ejectors; single

selective trigger; hand-engraved, gold-filled receiver; silver inlays. Introduced 1973; discontinued 1975.

Grade I		
Perf.: $2000	**Exc.:** $1700	**VGood:** $1600
Grade II		
Perf.: $1700	**Exc.:** $1400	**VGood:** $1200

PEDERSEN 1000 MAGNUM

Same specs as Model 1000 except 12-ga.; 3-inch chamber; 30-inch barrels; Improved Modified/Full chokes. Introduced 1973; discontinued 1975.

Grade I		
Perf.: $2000	**Exc.:** $1700	**VGood:** $1600
Grade II		
Perf.: $1700	**Exc.:** $1400	**VGood:** $1300

PEDERSEN MODEL 1000 SKEET

Same specs as Model 1000 except 12-ga.; 2-3/4-inch chambers; 26-inch, 28-inch barrels; Skeet chokes; Skeet-style walnut stock. Introduced 1973; discontinued 1975.

Grade I		
Perf.: $2100	**Exc.:** $1950	**VGood:** $1700
Grade II		
Perf.: $1900	**Exc.:** $1450	**VGood:** $1300

PEDERSEN MODEL 1000 TRAP

Same specs as Model 1000 except made in 12-ga.; 2-3/4-inch chambers; 30-inch, 32-inch barrels; Modified/Full or Improved Modified/Full chokes; Monte Carlo trap-style walnut stock. Introduced 1973; discontinued 1975.

Grade I		
Perf.: $2000	**Exc.:** $1600	**VGood:** $1400
Grade II		
Perf.: $1550	**Exc.:** $1300	**VGood:** $1100

PEDERSEN MODEL 1500

Over/under; boxlock; 12-ga.; 2-3/4-inch, 3-inch chambers; 26-inch, 28-inch, 30-inch, 32-inch barrels; standard choke combos; vent rib; hand-checkered European walnut pistol-grip stock, forearm; rubber recoil pad; automatic selective ejectors; choice of sights. Introduced 1973; discontinued 1975.

Perf.: $650   **Exc.:** $450   **VGood:** $350

Pedersen Model 2500

Perazzi Competition I Single Barrel Trap

Perazzi Competition I Trap

Perazzi Competition IV Trap

Perazzi DB81 Special American Trap Combo

Perazzi DB81 Special American Trap Single Barrel

PEDERSEN MODEL 1500 SKEET
Same specs as Model 1500 except 27-inch barrels; Skeet choke; Skeet-style walnut stock. Introduced 1973; discontinued 1975.

Perf.: $700 **Exc.:** $530 **VGood:** $450

PEDERSEN MODEL 1500 TRAP
Same specs as Model 1500 except 30-inch, 32-inch barrels; Modified/Full or Improved Modified/Full chokes; Monte Carlo trap-style walnut stock. Introduced 1973; discontinued 1975.

Perf.: $750 **Exc.:** $500 **VGood:** $400

PEDERSEN MODEL 2000
Side-by-side; boxlock; 12-, 20-ga.; 26-inch, 28-inch, 30-inch barrels; hand-checkered American walnut pistol-grip stock forearm; automatic selective ejectors; barrel selector/safety; single selective trigger; automatic safety; gold-filled, hand-engraved receiver. Introduced 1973; discontinued 1975.

Grade I		
Perf.: $2500	**Exc.:** $2100	**VGood:** $1800
Grade II		
Perf.: $2250	**Exc.:** $1900	**VGood:** $1650

PEDERSEN MODEL 2500
Side-by-side; boxlock; 12-, 20-ga.; hand-checkered European walnut pistol-grip stock, beavertail forearm; automatic selective ejectors; barrel selector/safety; single selective trigger; automatic safety; no receiver engraving. Introduced 1973; discontinued 1975.

Perf.: $450 **Exc.:** $375 **VGood:** $300

PEDERSEN MODEL 4000
Slide action; 12-, 20-ga., .410; 3-inch chambers; 26-inch, 28-inch, 30-inch vent-rib barrel; standard chokes; checkered select American walnut stock,

slide handle; full-coverage engraving on receiver. Based upon Mossberg Model 500. Introduced 1973; discontinued 1973.

Perf.: $450 **Exc.:** $375 **VGood:** $300

PEDERSEN MODEL 4000 TRAP
Same specs as Model 4000 except 12-ga.; 30-inch Full-choke barrel; Monte Carlo trap-style walnut stock; recoil pad. Introduced 1975; discontinued 1975.

Perf.: $475 **Exc.:** $365 **VGood:** $325

PEDERSEN MODEL 4500
Slide action; 12-, 20-ga., .410; 3-inch chamber; 26-inch, 28-inch, 30-inch vent-rib barrel; standard chokes; checkered select American walnut stock, slide handle; some engraving on receiver. Introduced 1975; discontinued 1975.

Perf.: $400 **Exc.:** $320 **VGood:** $280

PEDERSEN MODEL 4500 TRAP
Same specs as Model 4500 except 12-ga.; 30-inch Full-choke barrel; Monte Carlo trap-style walnut stock; recoil pad. Introduced 1975; discontinued 1975.

Perf.: $420 **Exc.:** $330 **VGood:** $290

PERAZZI COMPETITION I SINGLE BARREL TRAP
Single shot; boxlock; 12-ga.; 32-inch, 34-inch vent-rib barrel; Full choke; checkered Monte Carlo stock, beavertail forend; auto ejectors; single trigger; recoil pad. Introduced by Ithaca 1973; discontinued 1978.

Perf.: $2650 **Exc.:** $1950 **VGood:** $1700

PERAZZI COMPETITION I SKEET
Same specs as Competition I Single Barrel Trap except over/under; 26 3/4-inch barrels; integral

muzzlebrakes; Skeet chokes; Skeet-style checkered European walnut pistol-grip stock, forend. Introduced by Ithaca 1969; discontinued 1974.

Perf.: $4400 **Exc.:** $3300 **VGood:** $2800

PERAZZI COMPETITION I TRAP
Same specs as Competition I Single Barrel Trap except over/under; 30-inch, 32-inch barrels; Improved Modified/Full chokes; checkered European walnut pistol-grip stock, forend. Introduced by Ithaca 1969; discontinued 1974.

Perf.: $4000 **Exc.:** $3200 **VGood:** $2700

PERAZZI COMPETITION IV TRAP
Single barrel; boxlock; 12-ga.; 32-inch, 34-inch barrel; four interchangeable choke tubes; high, wide vent rib; checkered European walnut stock, beavertail forend; auto ejectors; single selective trigger; recoil pad; marketed in fitted case. Introduced by Ithaca 1977; discontinued 1978.

Perf.: $2000 **Exc.:** $1400 **VGood:** $1100

PERAZZI DB81 SPECIAL AMERICAN TRAP COMBO
Over/under; boxlock; 12-ga.; two-barrel set of 29-1/2-inch or 31-1/2-inch O/U and 32-inch or 34-inch single; fixed or choke tubes; high vent rib; checkered European walnut Monte Carlo stock, beavertail forend; removable trigger group; external selector. Made in Italy. Introduced 1988; still in production.

Standard Grade		
Perf.: $10,000	**Exc.:** $7000	**VGood:** $5000
SC3 Grade		
Perf.: $16,000	**Exc.:** $11,200	**VGood:** $8000
SC0 Grade		
Perf.: $27,500	**Exc.:** $19,250	**VGood:** $13,750
SC0 Gold Grade		
Perf.: $30,000	**Exc.:** $20,000	**VGood:** $15,000
SC0 Sideplates Grade		
Perf.: $40,000	**Exc.:** $28,000	**VGood:** $20,000
SC0 Gold Sideplates Grade		
Perf.: $45,000	**Exc.:** $31,500	**VGood:** $22,500

PERAZZI DB81 SPECIAL AMERICAN TRAP SINGLE BARREL
Same specs as DB81 Special American Trap Combo except only single shot; 32-inch, 34-inch barrel. Made in Italy. Introduced 1988; discontinued 1994.

Standard Grade		
Perf.: $5800	**Exc.:** $3650	**VGood:** $3100
SC3 Grade		
Perf.: $9500	**Exc.:** $6100	**VGood:** $5000
SC0 Grade		
Perf.: $16,000	**Exc.:** $10,000	**VGood:** $8500
SC0 Gold Grade		
Perf.: $17,500	**Exc.:** $11,000	**VGood:** $9000
SC0 Sideplates Grade		
Perf.: $23,000	**Exc.:** $15,500	**VGood:** $12,500
SC0 Gold Sideplates Grade		
Perf.: $26,500	**Exc.:** $20,000	**VGood:** $16,000

PERAZZI DB81 SPECIAL TRAP O/U
Same specs as DB81 Special American Trap Combo except over/under; 29-1/2-inch, 31-1/2-inch O/U barrels. Made in Italy. Introduced 1988; still in production.

Standard Grade		
Perf.: $8000	**Exc.:** $5600	**VGood:** $4100
SC3 Grade		
Perf.: $12,500	**Exc.:** $8500	**VGood:** $6500
SC0 Grade		
Perf.: $22,000	**Exc.:** $14,500	**VGood:** $11,500
SC0 Gold Grade		
Perf.: $25,500	**Exc.:** $17,500	**VGood:** $13,250
SC0 Sideplates Grade		
Perf.: $34,000	**Exc.:** $23,500	**VGood:** $17,500
SC0 Gold Sideplates Grade		
Perf.: $40,000	**Exc.:** $28,000	**VGood:** $21,000

PERAZZI GRAND AMERICAN 88 SPECIAL AMERICAN TRAP COMBO

Over/under; boxlock; 12-ga.; two-barrel set with 29-1/2-inch or 31-1/2-inch O/U and 32-inch or 34-inch single; fixed or choke tubes; vent rib; checkered European walnut Monte Carlo stock, beavertail forend; removable, adjustable trigger group; single selective trigger; external selector. Made in Italy. Discontinued 1992.

Standard Grade
Perf.: $9500   **Exc.:** $6150   **VGood:** $4950
SC3 Grade
Perf.: $15,000   **Exc.:** $9750   **VGood:** $7800
SC0 Grade
Perf.: $23,000   **Exc.:** $15,000   **VGood:** $11,950
SC0 Gold Grade
Perf.: $26,000   **Exc.:** $16,900   **VGood:** $13,500
SC0 Sideplates Grade
Perf.: $33,500   **Exc.:** $21,950   **VGood:** $17,500
SC0 Gold Sideplates Grade
Perf.: $38,500   **Exc.:** $25,000   **VGood:** $20,000

PERAZZI GRAND AMERICAN 88 SPECIAL AMERICAN TRAP SINGLE BARREL

Same specs as Grand American 88 Special American Trap Combo except 32-inch, 34-inch single barrel only. Made in Italy. Discontinued 1992.

Standard Grade
Perf.: $6500   **Exc.:** $3800   **VGood:** $3000
SC3 Grade
Perf.: $12,000   **Exc.:** $7000   **VGood:** $5500
SC0 Grade
Perf.: $20,000   **Exc.:** $11,500   **VGood:** $9000
SC0 Gold Grade
Perf.: $22,000   **Exc.:** $13,500   **VGood:** $10,000
SC0 Sideplates Grade
Perf.: $29,500   **Exc.:** $18,000   **VGood:** $13,000
SC0 Gold Sideplates Grade
Perf.: $34,500   **Exc.:** $21,000   **VGood:** $17,000

PERAZZI GRAND AMERICAN 88 SPECIAL TRAP O/U

Same specs as Grand American 88 Special American Trap Combo except 29-1/2-inch, 30-3/4-inch, 31-1/2-inch O/U barrels; checkered European walnut pistol-grip stock, beavertail forend. Made in Italy. Discontinued 1992.

Standard Grade
Perf.: $6900   **Exc.:** $4500   **VGood:** $3600
SC3 Grade
Perf.: $12,500   **Exc.:** $8150   **VGood:** $6500
SC0 Grade
Perf.: $20,500   **Exc.:** $13,300   **VGood:** $10,500
SC0 Gold Grade
Perf.: $23,000   **Exc.:** $14,500   **VGood:** $12,000
SC0 Sideplates Grade
Perf.: $31,000   **Exc.:** $20,000   **VGood:** $16,100
SC0 Gold Sideplates Grade
Perf.: $35,500   **Exc.:** $23,000   **VGood:** $18,500

PERAZZI LIGHT GAME MODEL

Over/under; boxlock; 12-ga.; 27-1/2-inch barrels; Modified/Full, Improved Cylinder/Modified chokes; checkered European walnut field stock, forend; single trigger; auto ejectors. Introduced by Ithaca 1972; discontinued 1974.

Perf.: $4300   **Exc.:** $3100   **VGood:** $2750

PERAZZI MIRAGE CLASSIC SPORTING O/U

Over/under; boxlock; 12-ga.; 28-3/8-inch, 29 1/2-inch, 31-1/2-inch barrels; fixed or choke tubes; vent rib; checkered European walnut pistol-grip stock, beavertail forend; single selective trigger; removable trigger group; external selector; engraving. Made in Italy. Still in production.

Perf.: $9000   **Exc.:** $6300   **VGood:** $4900

Perazzi DB81 Special Trap O/U

Perazzi Light Game Model

Perazzi Mirage Classic Sporting O/U

PERAZZI MIRAGE LIVE BIRD (EARLY MFG.)

Over/under; boxlock; 12-ga.; 28-inch Modified/Extra-Full barrels; vent rib; checkered European walnut pistol-grip stock, forend; selective ejectors; non-selective single trigger; recoil pad. Introduced by Ithaca 1973; discontinued 1978.

Perf.: $2500   **Exc.:** $1700   **VGood:** $1300

PERAZZI MIRAGE SKEET (EARLY MFG.)

Same specs as Mirage Live Bird (Early Mfg.) except 28-inch barrels; integral muzzle brakes; Skeet chokes; Skeet-style checkered European walnut pistol-grip stock, forend. Introduced by Ithaca 1973; discontinued 1978.

Perf.: $2500   **Exc.:** $1700   **VGood:** $1300

PERAZZI MIRAGE TRAP (EARLY MFG.)

Same specs as Mirage Live Bird (Early Mfg.) except 30-inch, 32-inch barrels; Improved Modified/Full chokes; tapered vent rib; checkered European Monte Carlo stock, forend. Introduced by Ithaca 1973; discontinued 1978.

Perf.: $2500   **Exc.:** $1700   **VGood:** $1300

PERAZZI MIRAGE PIGEON-ELECTROCIBLES O/U

Over/under; boxlock; 12-ga.; 27-1/2-inch, 28-3/8-inch, 29-1/2-inch, 31-1/2-inch barrels; fixed or choke tubes; vent rib; checkered European walnut pistol-grip stock, schnabel beavertail forend; removable trigger group. Made in Italy. Introduced 1995; still in production.

Standard Grade
Perf.: $7000   **Exc.:** $4500   **VGood:** $3600
SC3 Grade
Perf.: $12,500   **Exc.:** $8000   **VGood:** $6500
SC0 Grade
Perf.: $21,500   **Exc.:** $14,000   **VGood:** $11,000
SC0 Gold Grade
Perf.: $24,000   **Exc.:** $15,500   **VGood:** $12,500
SC0 Sideplates Grade
Perf.: $32,500   **Exc.:** $21,000   **VGood:** $17,000
SC0 Gold Sideplates Grade
Perf.: $38,500   **Exc.:** $25,000   **VGood:** $20,000

PERAZZI MIRAGE SKEET O/U

Same specs as Mirage Pigeon-Electrocibles O/U except 26-3/4-inch, 27-1/2-inch barrels; beavertail forend. Made in Italy. Introduced 1993; still in production.

Standard Grade
Perf.: $7000   **Exc.:** $4500   **VGood:** $3600
SC3 Grade
Perf.: $12,500   **Exc.:** $8000   **VGood:** $6500
SC0 Grade
Perf.: $21,500   **Exc.:** $14,000   **VGood:** $11,000
SC0 Gold Grade
Perf.: $24,000   **Exc.:** $15,500   **VGood:** $12,500
SC0 Sideplates Grade
Perf.: $32,500   **Exc.:** $21,000   **VGood:** $17,000
SC0 Gold Sideplates Grade
Perf.: $38,500   **Exc.:** $25,000   **VGood:** $20,000

PERAZZI MIRAGE TRAP O/U

Same specs as Mirage Pigeon-Electrocibles O/U except 29 1/2-inch, 30 3/4-inch, 31-1/2-inch barrels; beavertail forend. Made in Italy. Still in production.

Standard Grade
Perf.: $7000   **Exc.:** $4500   **VGood:** $3600
SC3 Grade
Perf.: $12,500   **Exc.:** $8000   **VGood:** $6500
SC0 Grade
Perf.: $21,500   **Exc.:** $14,000   **VGood:** $11,000
SC0 Gold Grade
Perf.: $24,000   **Exc.:** $15,500   **VGood:** $12,500
SC0 Sideplates Grade
Perf.: $32,500   **Exc.:** $21,000   **VGood:** $17,000
SC0 Gold Sideplates Grade
Perf.: $38,500   **Exc.:** $25,000   **VGood:** $20,000

PERAZZI MIRAGE SPECIAL PIGEON-ELECTROCIBLES O/U

Over/under; boxlock; 12-ga.; 28-3/8-inch, 29 1/2-inch, 31-1/2-inch barrels; fixed or choke tubes; vent rib; checkered European walnut pistol-grip stock; schnabel beavertail forend; removable, adjustable trigger. Made in Italy. Introduced 1995; still in production.

Standard Grade
Perf.: $7500   **Exc.:** $5000   **VGood:** $3900
SC3 Grade
Perf.: $12,500   **Exc.:** $8000   **VGood:** $6500

Perazzi Mirage Special Sporting O/U Standard Grade

Perazzi Mirage Special Sporting O/U SC3 Grade

Perazzi MT-6 Trap

Perazzi MX3 SC0 Grade Engraving

SC0 Grade
Perf.: $22,000 **Exc.:** $14,000 **VGood:** $11,500
SC0 Gold Grade
Perf.: $25,000 **Exc.:** $16,250 **VGood:** $13,000
SC0 Sideplates Grade
Perf.: $33,000 **Exc.:** $21,500 **VGood:** $17,000
SC0 Gold Sideplates Grade
Perf.: $38,000 **Exc.:** $25,000 **VGood:** $19,750

PERAZZI MIRAGE SPECIAL SKEET O/U
Same specs as Mirage Special Pigeon-Electrocibles O/U except 26-3/4-inch, 27-1/2-inch barrels; beavertail forend. Made in Italy. Still in production.
Standard Grade
Perf.: $7500 **Exc.:** $5000 **VGood:** $3900
SC3 Grade
Perf.: $12,500 **Exc.:** $8000 **VGood:** $6500
SC0 Grade
Perf.: $22,000 **Exc.:** $14,000 **VGood:** $11,500
SC0 Gold Grade
Perf.: $25,000 **Exc.:** $16,250 **VGood:** $13,000
SC0 Sideplates Grade
Perf.: $33,000 **Exc.:** $21,500 **VGood:** $17,000
SC0 Gold Sideplates Grade
Perf.: $38,000 **Exc.:** $25,000 **VGood:** $19,750

PERAZZI MIRAGE SPECIAL SPORTING O/U
Same specs as Mirage Special Pigeon-Electrocibles O/U except 28-3/8-inch, 29-1/2-inch, 31-1/2-inch barrels; beavertail forend; single selective trigger; external selector. Made in Italy. Still in production.
Standard Grade
Perf.: $7500 **Exc.:** $5000 **VGood:** $3900
SC3 Grade
Perf.: $12,500 **Exc.:** $8000 **VGood:** $6500
SC0 Grade
Perf.: $22,000 **Exc.:** $14,000 **VGood:** $11,500
SC0 Gold Grade
Perf.: $25,000 **Exc.:** $16,250 **VGood:** $13,000
SC0 Sideplates Grade
Perf.: $33,000 **Exc.:** $21,500 **VGood:** $17,000
SC0 Gold Sideplates Grade
Perf.: $38,000 **Exc.:** $25,000 **VGood:** $19,750

PERAZZI MIRAGE SPECIAL TRAP O/U
Same specs as Mirage Special Pigeon-Electrocibles O/U except 29-1/2-inch, 30-3/4-inch, 31-1/2-inch barrels; beavertail forend. Made in Italy. Still in production.
Standard Grade
Perf.: $7500 **Exc.:** $5000 **VGood:** $3900
SC3 Grade
Perf.: $12,500 **Exc.:** $8000 **VGood:** $6500
SC0 Grade
Perf.: $22,000 **Exc.:** $14,000 **VGood:** $11,500
SC0 Gold Grade
Perf.: $25,000 **Exc.:** $16,250 **VGood:** $13,000
SC0 Sideplates Grade
Perf.: $33,000 **Exc.:** $21,500 **VGood:** $17,000
SC0 Gold Sideplates Grade
Perf.: $38,000 **Exc.:** $25,000 **VGood:** $19,750

PERAZZI MT-6 SKEET
Over/under; boxlock; 12-ga.; 28-inch separated barrels; five interchangeable choke tubes; wide vent rib; Skeet-style checkered European walnut pistol-grip stock, forend; non-selective single trigger; auto selective ejectors; recoil pad; marketed in fitted case. Introduced by Ithaca 1976; discontinued 1978.
Perf.: $4000 **Exc.:** $3100 **VGood:** $2750

PERAZZI MT-6 TRAP
Same specs as MT-6 Skeet except 30-inch, 32-inch barrels; trap-style checkered European walnut pistol-grip stock, forend. Introduced by Ithaca 1976; discontinued 1978.
Perf.: $2500 **Exc.:** $1700 **VGood:** $1300

PERAZZI MT-6 TRAP COMBO
Same specs as MT-6 Skeet except two-barrel set with 30-inch or 32-inch O/U and 32-inch or 34-inch single under barrel; seven interchangeable choke tubes; high aluminum vent rib; trap-style checkered European walnut pistol-grip stock, forend; marketed in fitted case. Introduced by Ithaca 1977; discontinued 1978.
Perf.: $4200 **Exc.:** $3000 **VGood:** $2200

PERAZZI MX1B PIGEON-ELECTROCIBLES O/U
Over/Under; boxlock; 12-ga.; 27-1/2-inch barrels; fixed or choke tubes; vent rib; checkered European pistol-grip walnut stock, schnabel forend; removable

trigger group. Made in Italy. Introduced 1995; still in production.
Standard Grade
Perf.: $7000 **Exc.:** $4500 **VGood:** $3600
SC3 Grade
Perf.: $12,500 **Exc.:** $8000 **VGood:** $6500
SC0 Grade
Perf.: $21,500 **Exc.:** $14,000 **VGood:** $11,000
SC0 Gold Grade
Perf.: $24,000 **Exc.:** $15,000 **VGood:** $12,500
SC0 Sideplates Grade
Perf.: $32,500 **Exc.:** $21,000 **VGood:** $17,000
SC0 Gold Sideplates Grade
Perf.: $38,500 **Exc.:** $25,000 **VGood:** $20,000

PERAZZI MX1B SPORTING O/U
Same specs as MX1B Pigeon-Electrocibles O/U except 28-3/8-inch, 29-1/2-inch, 31-1/2-inch barrels; choke tubes; single selective trigger; external selector. Made in Italy. No longer in production.
Standard Grade
Perf.: $7000 **Exc.:** $4500 **VGood:** $3600
SC3 Grade
Perf.: $12,500 **Exc.:** $8000 **VGood:** $6500
SC0 Grade
Perf.: $21,500 **Exc.:** $14,000 **VGood:** $11,000
SC0 Gold Grade
Perf.: $24,000 **Exc.:** $15,000 **VGood:** $12,500
SC0 Sideplates Grade
Perf.: $32,500 **Exc.:** $21,000 **VGood:** $17,000
SC0 Gold Sideplates Grade
Perf.: $38,500 **Exc.:** $25,000 **VGood:** $20,000

PERAZZI MX3 SPECIAL AMERICAN TRAP COMBO
Over/under; boxlock; 12-ga.; two-barrel set with 29-1/2-inch or 31-1/2-inch and 32-inch O/U or 34-inch single; fixed or choke tubes; vent rib; checkered European walnut Monte Carlo stock, beavertail forend; removable, adjustable trigger group; single selective trigger; external selector. Made in Italy. Discontinued 1992.
Perf.: $7500 **Exc.:** $4900 **VGood:** $3900
SC3 Grade
Perf.: $13,000 **Exc.:** $8500 **VGood:** $6750
SC0 Grade
Perf.: $21,500 **Exc.:** $14,000 **VGood:** $11,000
SC0 Gold Grade
Perf.: $24,000 **Exc.:** $15,500 **VGood:** $12,500

PERAZZI MX3 SPECIAL AMERICAN TRAP SINGLE BARREL
Same specs as MX3 Special American Trap Combo except 32-inch, 34-inch single barrel. Made in Italy. Discontinued 1992.
Standard Grade
Perf.: $5500 **Exc.:** $3500 **VGood:** $2850
SC3 Grade
Perf.: $9500 **Exc.:** $6200 **VGood:** $5000
SC0 Grade
Perf.: $17,500 **Exc.:** $11,500 **VGood:** $9100
SC0 Gold Grade
Perf.: $18,000 **Exc.:** $11,750 **VGood:** $9500

PERAZZI MX3 SPECIAL SKEET O/U
Same specs as MX3 Special American Trap Combo except 26-3/4-inch, 27-1/2-inch barrels; checkered European walnut pistol-grip stock, beavertail forend. Made in Italy. Discontinued 1992.
Standard Grade
Perf.: $6000 **Exc.:** $3900 **VGood:** $3100
SC3 Grade
Perf.: $10,000 **Exc.:** $6500 **VGood:** $5200
SC0 Grade
Perf.: $17,500 **Exc.:** $11,500 **VGood:** $9100
SC0 Gold Grade
Perf.: $20,000 **Exc.:** $13,000 **VGood:** $10,500

PERAZZI MX3 SPECIAL SPORTING O/U

Same specs as MX3 Special American Trap Combo except 28-3/8-inch, 29-1/2-inch, 31-1/2-inch barrels; checkered European walnut pistol-grip stock, beavertail forend. Made in Italy. Discontinued 1992.

Standard Grade
Perf.: $6200   **Exc.:** $4000   **VGood:** $3200
SC3 Grade
Perf.: $10,500   **Exc.:** $6800   **VGood:** $5500
SC0 Grade
Perf.: $18,000   **Exc.:** $11,700   **VGood:** $9400
SC0 Gold Grade
Perf.: $20,500   **Exc.:** $13,500   **VGood:** $10,500

PERAZZI MX3 SPECIAL TRAP O/U

Same specs as MX3 Special American Trap Combo except 29-1/2-inch, 30-3/4-inch, 31-1/2-inch barrels; checkered European walnut pistol-grip stock, beavertail forend. Made in Italy. Discontinued 1992.

Standard Grade
Perf.: $6000   **Exc.:** $3900   **VGood:** $3100
SC3 Grade
Perf.: $10,000   **Exc.:** $6500   **VGood:** $5200
SC0 Grade
Perf.: $17,500   **Exc.:** $11,500   **VGood:** $9100
SC0 Gold Grade
Perf.: $20,000   **Exc.:** $13,000   **VGood:** $10,500

PERAZZI MX6 AMERICAN TRAP SINGLE BARREL

Single shot; 12-ga.; 32-inch, 34-inch barrel; fixed or choke tubes; raised vent rib; checkered European walnut Monte Carlo stock, beavertail forend; removable trigger group. Made in Italy. Introduced 1995; still in production.

Perf.: $4200   **Exc.:** $2900   **VGood:** $2200
Combo model with extra O/U barrels
Perf.: $6800   **Exc.:** $4500   **VGood:** $3600

PERAZZI MX6 SKEET O/U

Same specs as MX6 American Trap Single Barrel except over/under; boxlock; 26-3/4-inch, 27-1/2-inch barrels. Made in Italy. Introduced 1995.

Exc.: $3500   **VGood:** $2650

PERAZZI MX6 SPORTING O/U

Same specs as MX6 American Trap Single Barrel except over/under; boxlock; 28-3/8-inch, 29-1/2-inch, 31-1/2-inch barrels; single selective trigger; external selector. Made in Italy. Introduced 1995; still in production.

Perf.: $6000   **Exc.:** $4000   **VGood:** $3100

PERAZZI MX6 TRAP O/U

Same specs as MX6 American Trap Single Barrel except over/under; boxlock; 29-1/2-inch, 30-3/4-inch, 31-1/2-inch barrels. Made in Italy. Introduced 1995.

Perf.: $5000   **Exc.:** $3500   **VGood:** $2650

PERAZZI MX7 AMERICAN TRAP SINGLE BARREL

Single shot; 12-ga.; 32-inch, 34-inch barrel; fixed or choke tubes; raised vent rib; checkered European walnut Monte Carlo stock, beavertail forend; fixed trigger group. Made in Italy. Introduced 1995.

Perf.: $4900   **Exc.:** $3500   **VGood:** $2600
Combo model with extra O/U barrels
Perf.: $7000   **Exc.:** $4900   **VGood:** $3700

PERAZZI MX7 SKEET O/U

Same specs as MX7 American Trap Single Barrel except over/under; boxlock; 27-1/2-inch barrels; checkered European walnut pistol-grip stock, beavertail forend; single selective trigger; external selector. Made in Italy. Introduced 1993.

Perf.: $5200   **Exc.:** $3700   **VGood:** $2800

PERAZZI MX7 SPORTING O/U

Same specs as MX7 American Trap Single Barrel except over/under; boxlock; 28-3/8-inch, 29-1/2-inch, 31-1/2-inch barrels; checkered European walnut pistol-grip stock, beavertail forend; single selective

Perazzi MX3
American Trap Combo

Perazzi MX3 Special
American Trap Single Barrel

Perazzi MX3 Special Skeet O/U

Perazzi MX3 Special Trap O/U

Perazzi MX7
Sporting O/U

trigger; external selector. Made in Italy. Introduced 1992.

Perf.: $5800   **Exc.:** $4000   **VGood:** $3000

PERAZZI MX7 TRAP O/U

Same specs as MX7 American Trap Single Barrel except over/under; boxlock; 29-1/2-inch, 30-3/4-inch, 31-1/2-inch barrels; checkered European walnut pistol-grip stock, beavertail forend; single selective trigger; external selector. Made in Italy. Introduced 1993.

Perf.: $5200   **Exc.:** $3700   **VGood:** $2800

PERAZZI MX8 OVER/UNDER SHOTGUNS

Gauge: 12, 2-3/4-inch chambers; 28-3/8-inch barrel (Imp. Mod. & Extra Full), 29-1/2-inch barrel (choke tubes); weighs 7 lbs., 12 oz.; special stock specifications; single selective trigger. Many options available. Imported from Italy by Perazzi U.S.A., Inc.

Sporting
N/A
Trap Double Trap (removable trigger group)
Exc.: $3800   **VGood:** $3750   **Good:** $3100
Skeet
Exc.: $5900   **VGood:** $4400   **Good:** $3600
SC3 grade (variety of engraving patterns)
SCO grade (more intricate engraving, gold inlays).

PERAZZI MX8 GAME O/U

Over/under; boxlock; 12-, 20-ga.; 26-3/4-inch, 27-1/2-inch barrels; fixed or choke tubes; vent rib; checkered European walnut pistol-grip (12-ga.) or straight-grip (20-ga.) stock; schnabel or tapered forend; removable trigger group; single selective trigger; external selector. Made in Italy. Introduced 1993.

Standard Grade
Perf.: $7000   **Exc.:** $4500   **VGood:** $3600
SC3 Grade
Perf.: $12,500   **Exc.:** $8000   **VGood:** $6500
SC0 Grade
Perf.: $21,500   **Exc.:** $14,000   **VGood:** $11,000
SC0 Gold Grade
Perf.: $24,000   **Exc.:** $15,500   **VGood:** $12,500

SC0 Sideplates Grade
Perf.: $32,500   **Exc.:** $21,000   **VGood:** $17,000
SC0 Gold Sideplates Grade
Perf.: $38,500   **Exc.:** $25,000   **VGood:** $20,000

PERAZZI MX8 SKEET O/U

Same specs as MX8 Game O/U except 26-3/4-inch, 27-1/2-inch barrels; checkered European walnut pistol-grip stock, beavertail forend. Made in Italy. Introduced 1993.

Standard Grade
Perf.: $7000   **Exc.:** $4500   **VGood:** $3600
SC3 Grade
Perf.: $12,500   **Exc.:** $8000   **VGood:** $6500
SC0 Grade
Perf.: $21,500   **Exc.:** $14,000   **VGood:** $11,000
SC0 Gold Grade
Perf.: $24,000   **Exc.:** $15,500   **VGood:** $12,500
SC0 Sideplates Grade
Perf.: $32,500   **Exc.:** $21,000   **VGood:** $17,000
SC0 Gold Sideplates Grade
Perf.: $38,500   **Exc.:** $25,000   **VGood:** $20,000

PERAZZI MX8 TRAP O/U

Same specs as MX8 Game O/U except 29-1/2-inch, 30-3/4-inch, 31-1/2-inch barrels; checkered European walnut pistol-grip stock, beavertail forend. Made in Italy. Introduced by Ithaca 1969; still in production by Perazzi.

Standard Grade
Perf.: $7000   **Exc.:** $4500   **VGood:** $3600
SC3 Grade
Perf.: $12,500   **Exc.:** $8000   **VGood:** $6500
SC0 Grade
Perf.: $21,500   **Exc.:** $14,000   **VGood:** $11,000
SC0 Gold Grade
Perf.: $24,000   **Exc.:** $15,500   **VGood:** $12,500
SC0 Sideplates Grade
Perf.: $32,500   **Exc.:** $21,000   **VGood:** $17,000
SC0 Gold Sideplates Grade
Perf.: $38,500   **Exc.:** $25,000   **VGood:** $20,000

PERAZZI MX8 TRAP COMBO

Same specs as MX8 Game O/U except two-barrel set with 29-1/2-inch or 31-1/2-inch O/U and 32-inch or 34-inch single; checkered European walnut pistol-

Perazzi MX8 Trap O/U

Perazzi MX8 Trap Combo

Perazzi MX8 Special Skeet O/U

Perazzi MX9 American Trap Combo

grip stock, forend; two trigger groups. Introduced by Ithaca 1973; discontinued 1978.

Perf.: $3500   **Exc.:** $2300   **VGood:** $1800

PERAZZI MX8/MX8 SPECIAL TRAP, SKEET

Gauge: 12, 2-3/4-inch chambers; Trap 29-1/2-inch barrel (Imp. Mod. & Extra Full), 31-1/2-inch barrel (Full & Extra Full); choke tubes optional; Skeet 27-5/8-inch barrel (Skeet & Skeet); weighs about 8-1/2 lbs. (Trap); 7 lbs., 15 oz. (Skeet); interchangeable and custom made stock to customer specs; detachable and interchangeable trigger group with flat V springs; flat 7/16-inch ventilated rib. Many options available. Imported from Italy by Perazzi U.S.A., Inc.: **$3900** **VGood:** $3525 **Good:** $3100

MX8 Special (adj. four-position trigger)
Exc.: $3900   **VGood:** $3525   **Good:** $3100

MX8 Special Combo (O/U and single barrel sets)
Exc.: $9450   **VGood:** $8000   **Good:** $7150

PERAZZI MX8 SPECIAL SKEET OVER/UNDER

Similar to the MX8 Skeet except has adjustable four-position trigger, Skeet stock dimensions.

Exc.: $3900   **VGood:** $3525   **Good:** $3100

PERAZZI MX8/20 OVER/UNDER SHOTGUN

Similar to the MX8 except has smaller frame and has a removable trigger mechanism. Available in trap, Skeet, sporting or game models with fixed chokes or choke tubes. Stock is made to customer specifications. Introduced 1993.

Exc.: $4350   **VGood:** $4000   **Good:** $3650

PERAZZI MX8 SPECIAL AMERICAN TRAP COMBO

Over/under; boxlock; 12-ga.; two-barrel set of 29-1/2-inch or 31-1/2-inch O/U and 32-inch or 34-inch single; fixed or choke tubes; raised vent rib; checkered European walnut Monte Carlo stock, beavertail forend; adjustable, removable trigger group; external selector. Made in Italy. Introduced 1988.

Standard Grade
Perf.: $9200   **Exc.:** $6000   **VGood:** $4800

PERAZZI MX8 SPECIAL AMERICAN TRAP SINGLE BARREL

Same specs as MX8 Special American Trap Combo except 32-inch, 34-inch single barrel. Made in Italy. Introduced 1988; discontinued 1994.

Standard Grade
Perf.: $6000   **Exc.:** $3900   **VGood:** $3100

SC3 Grade
Perf.: $11,000   **Exc.:** $7100   **VGood:** $5700

SC0 Grade
Perf.: $19,000   **Exc.:** $12,300   **VGood:** $9900

SC0 Gold Grade
Perf.: $21,000   **Exc.:** $13,500   **VGood:** $11,000

SC0 Sideplates Grade
Perf.: $30,000   **Exc.:** $17,500   **VGood:** $15,500

SC0 Gold Sideplates Grade
Perf.: $35,000   **Exc.:** $22,750   **VGood:** $18,000

PERAZZI MX8 SPECIAL SKEET O/U

Same specs as MX8 Special American Trap Combo except 26-3/4-inch, 27-1/2-inch O/U barrels; checkered European walnut pistol-grip stock, beavertail forend. Made in Italy.

Standard Grade
Perf.: $7500   **Exc.:** $5000   **VGood:** $3900

SC3 Grade
Perf.: $12,500   **Exc.:** $8000   **VGood:** $6500

SC0 Grade
Perf.: $22,000   **Exc.:** $14,000   **VGood:** $11,500

SC0 Gold Grade
Perf.: $25,000   **Exc.:** $16,250   **VGood:** $13,000

SC0 Sideplates Grade
Perf.: $33,000   **Exc.:** $21,500   **VGood:** $17,000

SC0 Gold Sideplates Grade
Perf.: $38,000   **Exc.:** $25,000   **VGood:** $19,750

PERAZZI MX8 SPECIAL SPORTING O/U

Same specs as MX8 Special American Trap Combo except 12-, 20-ga.; 28-3/8-inch, 29-1/2-inch, 31-1/2-inch O/U barrels; checkered European walnut pistol-grip stock, beavertail forend. Made in Italy. Still in production.

Standard Grade
Perf.: $7800   **Exc.:** $5000   **VGood:** $4000

SC3 Grade
Perf.: $13,000   **Exc.:** $8500   **VGood:** $6750

SC0 Grade
Perf.: $22,500   **Exc.:** $14,600   **VGood:** $11,700

SC0 Gold Grade
Perf.: $25,500   **Exc.:** $16,500   **VGood:** $13,250

PERAZZI MX8 SPECIAL TRAP O/U

Same specs as MX8 Special American Trap Combo except 29-1/2-inch, 30-3/4-inch, 31-1/2-inch O/U barrels; checkered European walnut pistol-grip stock, beavertail forend. Made in Italy.

Standard Grade
Perf.: $7500   **Exc.:** $5000   **VGood:** $3900

SC3 Grade
Perf.: $12,500   **Exc.:** $8000   **VGood:** $6500

SC0 Grade
Perf.: $22,000   **Exc.:** $14,000   **VGood:** $11,500

SC0 Gold Grade
Perf.: $25,000   **Exc.:** $16,250   **VGood:** $13,000

SC0 Sideplates Grade
Perf.: $33,000   **Exc.:** $21,500   **VGood:** $17,000

SC0 Gold Sideplates Grade
Perf.: $38,000   **Exc.:** $25,000   **VGood:** $19,750

PERAZZI MX9 AMERICAN TRAP COMBO

Over/under; boxlock; 12-ga.; two-barrel set of 29-1/2-inch or 31-1/2-inch O/U and 32-inch or 34-inch single; fixed or choke tubes; adjustable rib to change point of impact; checkered European walnut Monte Carlo adjustable stock, beavertail forend; removable trigger. Made in Italy. Introduced 1993; discontinued 1994.

Standard Grade
Perf.: $11,500   **Exc.:** $7500   **VGood:** $6000

SC3 Grade
Perf.: $17,000   **Exc.:** $11,000   **VGood:** $8800

SC0 Grade
Perf.: $26,500   **Exc.:** $17,000   **VGood:** $13,800

SC0 Gold Grade
Perf.: $29,000   **Exc.:** $19,000   **VGood:** $15,000

SC0 Sideplates Grade
Perf.: $37,500   **Exc.:** $24,000   **VGood:** $19,500

SC0 Gold Sideplates Grade
Perf.: $42,000   **Exc.:** $27,000   **VGood:** $21,800

PERAZZI MX9 AMERICAN TRAP SINGLE BARREL

Same specs as MX9 American Trap Combo except 32-inch, 34-inch single barrel. Made in Italy. Introduced 1993; discontinued 1994.

Standard Grade
Perf.: $8500   **Exc.:** $5500   **VGood:** $4400

SC3 Grade
Perf.: $13,000   **Exc.:** $8500   **VGood:** $6700

SC0 Grade
Perf.: $21,500   **Exc.:** $14,000   **VGood:** $11,000

SC0 Gold Grade
Perf.: $23,500   **Exc.:** $15,000   **VGood:** $12,000

SC0 Sideplates Grade
Perf.: $32,500   **Exc.:** $21,000   **VGood:** $17,000

SC0 Gold Sideplates Grade
Perf.: $37,500   **Exc.:** $24,000   **VGood:** $19,500

PERAZZI MX9 TRAP O/U

Same specs as MX9 American Trap Combo except 29-1/2-inch, 30-3/4-inch, 31-1/2-inch O/U barrels; checkered European walnut pistol-grip adjustable stock, beavertail forend. Made in Italy. Introduced 1993; discontinued 1994.

Standard Grade
Perf.: $8800   **Exc.:** $5700   **VGood:** $4500

SC3 Grade
Perf.: $13,400   **Exc.:** $8700   **VGood:** $7000

SC0 Grade
Perf.: $22,000   **Exc.:** $14,000   **VGood:** $11,500

SC0 Gold Grade
Perf.: $24,100   **Exc.:** $15,600   **VGood:** $12,500

SC0 Sideplates Grade
Perf.: $33,200   **Exc.:** $21,600   **VGood:** $17,000

SC0 Gold Sideplates Grade
Perf.: $38,300   **Exc.:** $25,000   **VGood:** $20,000

PERAZZI MX10 OVER/UNDER SHOTGUN

Gauge: 12, 2-3/4-inch chambers; 29-1/2-inch barrel, 31.5-inch barrel (fixed chokes); walnut, cheekpiece adjustable for elevation and cast; adjustable rib; vent. side rib; externally selective trigger; available in single barrel, combo, over/under trap, Skeet, pigeon and sporting models. Introduced 1993. Imported from Italy by Perazzi U.S.A., Inc.

    Perf.: $9000   **Exc.:** $4550   **VGood:** $4400

PERAZZI MX10 AMERICAN TRAP COMBO

Over/under; boxlock; 12-ga.; two-barrel set of 29-1/2-inch or 31-1/2-inch O/U and 32-inch or 34-inch single; fixed or choke tubes; checkered European walnut adjustable stock, beavertail forend; removable trigger group; external selector. Made in Italy. Introduced 1993.

    Standard Grade
    Perf.: $12,000   **Exc.:** $7800   **VGood:** $6200
    SC3 Grade
    Perf.: $18,000   **Exc.:** $11,700   **VGood:** $9400
    SC0 Grade
    Perf.: $28,000   **Exc.:** $18,200   **VGood:** $14,500
    SC0 Gold Grade
    Perf.: $31,000   **Exc.:** $20,000   **VGood:** $16,000

PERAZZI MX10 AMERICAN TRAP SINGLE BARREL

Same specs as MX10 American Trap Combo except 32-inch, 34-inch single barrel. Made in Italy. Introduced 1993; discontinued 1993.

    Standard Grade
    Perf.: $8500   **Exc.:** $5500   **VGood:** $4400
    SC3 Grade
    Perf.: $13,000   **Exc.:** $8500   **VGood:** $6700
    SC0 Grade
    Perf.: $21,000   **Exc.:** $13,600   **VGood:** $11,000
    SC0 Gold Grade
    Perf.: $24,000   **Exc.:** $15,600   **VGood:** $12,500
    SC0 Sideplates Grade
    Perf.: $32,000   **Exc.:** $20,800   **VGood:** $16,500
    SC0 Gold Sideplates Grade
    Perf.: $38,000   **Exc.:** $25,000   **VGood:** $20,000

PERAZZI MX10 PIGEON-ELECTROCIBLES O/U

Same specs as MX10 American Trap Combo except 27-1/2-inch, 29-1/2-inch O/U barrels. Made in Italy. Introduced 1995; still in production.

    Standard Grade
    Perf.: $9000   **Exc.:** $5800   **VGood:** $4700
    SC3 Grade
    Perf.: $14,000   **Exc.:** $9100   **VGood:** $7300
    SC0 Grade
    Perf.: $23,500   **Exc.:** $15,000   **VGood:** $12,000
    SC0 Gold Grade
    Perf.: $26,000   **Exc.:** $17,000   **VGood:** $13,500

PERAZZI MX10 SKEET O/U

Same specs as MX10 American Trap Combo except 27-1/2-inch, 29-1/2-inch O/U barrels. Made in Italy. Introduced 1995; still in production.

    Standard Grade
    Perf.: $9000   **Exc.:** $5800   **VGood:** $4700
    SC3 Grade
    Perf.: $14,000   **Exc.:** $9100   **VGood:** $7300
    SC0 Grade
    Perf.: $23,500   **Exc.:** $15,000   **VGood:** $12,000
    SC0 Gold Grade
    Perf.: $26,000   **Exc.:** $17,000   **VGood:** $13,500

PERAZZI MX10 SPORTING O/U

Same specs as MX10 American Trap Combo except 28-3/8-inch, 29-1/2-inch, 31-1/2-inch O/U barrel. Made in Italy. Introduced 1993; still in production.

    Standard Grade
    Perf.: $10,000   **Exc.:** $6500   **VGood:** $5200

Perazzi MX10
American Trap Combo

Perazzi MX20 Game O/U

    SC3 Grade
    Perf.: $15,000   **Exc.:** $9750   **VGood:** $7800
    SC0 Grade
    Perf.: $24,500   **Exc.:** $16,000   **VGood:** $13,000
    SC0 Gold Grade
    Perf.: $27,500   **Exc.:** $18,000   **VGood:** $14,300

PERAZZI MX10 TRAP O/U

Same specs as MX10 American Trap Combo except 12-, 20-ga.; 29-1/2-inch, 30-3/4-inch, 31-1/2-inch O/U barrels. Made in Germany. Introduced 1993; still in production.

    Standard Grade
    Perf.: $9000   **Exc.:** $5800   **VGood:** $4700
    SC3 Grade
    Perf.: $14,000   **Exc.:** $9100   **VGood:** $7300
    SC0 Grade
    Perf.: $23,500   **Exc.:** $15,000   **VGood:** $12,000
    SC0 Gold Grade
    Perf.: $26,000   **Exc.:** $17,000   **VGood:** $13,500

PERAZZI MX11 AMERICAN TRAP COMBO

Over/under; boxlock; 12-ga.; two-barrel set of 29-1/2-inch or 31-1/2-inch O/U and 32-inch or 34-inch single; fixed or choke tubes; vent rib; checkered European walnut Monte Carlo adjustable stock, beavertail forend; removable trigger group; single selective trigger; external selector. Made in Italy. Introduced 1995.

    Perf.: $8200   **Exc.:** $5800   **VGood:** $4300

PERAZZI MX11 AMERICAN TRAP SINGLE BARREL

Same specs as MX11 American Trap Combo except 32-inch, 34-inch single barrel. Made in Italy. Introduced 1995.

    Perf.: $6200   **Exc.:** $4300   **VGood:** $3300

PERAZZI MX11 PIGEON-ELECTROCIBLES O/U

Same specs as MX11 American Trap Combo except 27-1/2-inch O/U barrels; checkered European walnut pistol grip adjustable stock, beavertail forend. Made in Italy. Introduced 1995.

    Perf.: $6500   **Exc.:** $4500   **VGood:** $3400

PERAZZI MX11 SKEET O/U

Same specs as MX11 American Trap Combo except 26-3/4-inch, 27-1/2-inch O/U barrels; checkered European walnut pistol-grip adjustable stock, beavertail forend. Made in Italy. Introduced 1995; still in production.

    Perf.: $6500   **Exc.:** $4500   **VGood:** $3400

PERAZZI MX11 SPORTING O/U

Same specs as MX11 American Trap Combo except 28-3/8-inch, 29-1/2-inch, 31-1/2-inch O/U barrels; checkered European walnut pistol-grip adjustable stock, beavertail forend. Made in Italy. Introduced 1995; still in production.

    Perf.: $7500   **Exc.:** $5000   **VGood:** $4000

PERAZZI MX11 TRAP O/U

Same specs as MX11 American Trap Combo except 29-1/2-inch, 30-3/4-inch, 31-1/2-inch O/U barrels; checkered European walnut pistol-grip adjustable

stock, beavertail forend. Made in Italy. Introduced 1995; still in production.

    Perf.: $6500   **Exc.:** $4500   **VGood:** $3400

PERAZZI MX12 HUNTING OVER/UNDER

Gauge: 12, 2-3/4-inch chambers; 26-3/4-inch, 27-1/2-inch, 28-3/8-inch, 29-1/2-inch barrel (Mod. & Full); choke tubes available in 27-5/8-inch, 29-1/2-inch only (MX12C); weighs 7 lbs., 4 oz.; stock to customer specs; interchangeable; single selective trigger; coil springs used in action; schnabel forend tip. Imported from Italy by Perazzi U.S.A., Inc.

    Exc.: $4650   **VGood:** $4350   **Good:** $3950
    MX12C (with choke tubes)

PERAZZI MX20 HUNTING OVER/UNDER

Similar to the MX12 except 20 ga. frame size. Non-removable trigger group. Available in 20, 28, 410 with 2-3/4-inch or 3-inch chambers. 26-inch standard, and choked Mod. & Full. Weight is 6 lbs., 6 oz.

    Exc.: $4500   **VGood:** $4300   **Good:** $3650
    MX20C (as above, 20-ga. only, choke tubes)

PERAZZI MX12 GAME O/U

Over/under; boxlock; 12-ga.; 26-3/4-inch, 27-1/2-inch barrels; fixed or choke tubes; vent rib; checkered European walnut straight-grip stock, schnabel or tapered forend; single selective trigger; non-removable trigger group; engraving. Made in Italy.

    Standard Grade
    Perf.: $6200   **Exc.:** $4400   **VGood:** $3500
    SC3 Grade
    Perf.: $12,500   **Exc.:** $8000   **VGood:** $6500
    SC0 Grade
    Perf.: $21,000   **Exc.:** $13,500   **VGood:** $11,000
    SC0 Gold Grade
    Perf.: $24,000   **Exc.:** $15,500   **VGood:** $12,500
    SC0 Sideplates Grade
    Perf.: $33,000   **Exc.:** $21,500   **VGood:** $17,000
    SC0 Gold Sideplates Grade
    Perf.: $38,500   **Exc.:** $25,000   **VGood:** $20,000

PERAZZI MX14 AMERICAN TRAP SINGLE BARREL

Single shot; 12-ga.; 34-inch barrel; fixed or choke tubes; vent rib; checkered European walnut Monte Carlo adjustable stock, beavertail forend; removable trigger group; unsingle configuration. Made in Italy. Introduced 1995.

    Perf.: $6200   **Exc.:** $4300   **VGood:** $3300
    Combo model with extra O/U barrels
    Perf.: $8500   **Exc.:** $5500   **VGood:** $4400

PERAZZI MX20 GAME O/U

Over/under; boxlock; 20-ga.; 26-inch, 26-3/4-inch, 27-1/2-inch barrels; fixed or choke tubes; vent rib; checkered European walnut straight-grip stock, schnabel or tapered forend; single selective trigger; non-removable trigger group; engraving. Made in Italy.

    Standard Grade
    Perf.: $6700   **Exc.:** $4400   **VGood:** $3500
    SC3 Grade
    Perf.: $12,500   **Exc.:** $8000   **VGood:** $6500

Perazzi TMX Special
American Trap Single Barrel

Perazzi TM1 Special
American Trap Single Barrel

Piotti King No. 1

Piotti King No. 1
Engraving

Piotti King No. 1
EELL Engraving

SC0 Grade
Perf.: $21,000 **Exc.:** $13,500 **VGood:** $11,000
SC0 Gold Grade
Perf.: $24,000 **Exc.:** $15,500 **VGood:** $12,500
SC0 Sideplates Grade
Perf.: $33,000 **Exc.:** $21,500 **VGood:** $17,000
SC0 Gold Sideplates Grade
Perf.: $38,500 **Exc.:** $25,000 **VGood:** $20,000

PERAZZI MX28, MX410 GAME O/U SHOTGUNS

Gauge: 28, 2-3/4-inch chambers, 410, 3-inch chambers; 26-inch barrel (Imp. Cyl. & Full); stock to customer specifications; made on scaled-down frames proportioned to the gauge. Introduced 1993. Imported from Italy by Perazzi U.S.A., Inc.
Exc.: $8100 **VGood:** $7750 **Good:** $7250

PERAZZI MX28 GAME O/U

Over/under; boxlock; 28-ga.; 26-inch, 26-3/4-inch, 27-1/2-inch barrels; fixed or choke tubes; vent rib; checkered European walnut straight-grip stock, tapered forend; non-removable trigger group; engraving. Made in Italy. Introduced 1993.
Standard Grade
Perf.: $11,500 **Exc.:** $9700 **VGood:** $7300
SC3 Grade
Perf.: $20,000 **Exc.:** $13,000 **VGood:** $10,500
SC0 Grade
Perf.: $29,000 **Exc.:** $19,000 **VGood:** $15,000
SC0 Gold Grade
Perf.: $31,500 **Exc.:** $20,500 **VGood:** $16,000
SC0 Sideplates Grade
Perf.: $40,000 **Exc.:** $26,000 **VGood:** $21,000
SC0 Gold Sideplates Grade
Perf.: $46,000 **Exc.:** $30,000 **VGood:** $24,000

PERAZZI MX410 GAME O/U

Over/under; boxlock; .410; 26-inch, 26-3/4-inch, 27-1/2-inch barrels; fixed chokes; vent rib; checkered European walnut straight-grip stock, tapered forend; non-removable trigger group; engraving. Made in Italy. Introduced 1993; still in production.
Standard Grade
Perf.: $11,500 **Exc.:** $9700 **VGood:** $7300
SC3 Grade
Perf.: $20,000 **Exc.:** $13,000 **VGood:** $10,500
SC0 Grade
Perf.: $29,000 **Exc.:** $19,000 **VGood:** $15,000

SC0 Gold Grade
Perf.: $31,500 **Exc.:** $20,500 **VGood:** $16,000
SC0 Sideplates Grade
Perf.: $40,000 **Exc.:** $26,000 **VGood:** $21,000
SC0 Gold Sideplates Grade
Perf.: $46,000 **Exc.:** $30,000 **VGood:** $24,000

PERAZZI SINGLE BARREL TRAP

Single shot; boxlock; 12-ga.; 34-inch barrel; Full choke; vent rib; checkered European walnut pistol-grip stock, forend; auto ejector; recoil pad. Introduced by Ithaca 1971; discontinued 1972.
Perf.: $2200 **Exc.:** $1700 **VGood:** $1500

PERAZZI TM1 SPECIAL AMERICAN TRAP SINGLE BARREL

Single shot; 12-ga.; 32-inch, 34-inch barrel; fixed or choke tubes; raised vent rib; checkered European walnut Monte Carlo stock, beavertail forend; removable, adjustable four-position trigger. Made in Italy. Introduced 1988; still in production.
Standard Grade
Perf.: $5200 **Exc.:** $3400 **VGood:** $2700
SC0 Grade
Perf.: $16,000 **Exc.:** $10,500 **VGood:** $8300
SC0 Gold Grade
Perf.: $18,500 **Exc.:** $12,000 **VGood:** $9600

PERAZZI TMX SPECIAL AMERICAN TRAP SINGLE BARREL

Single shot; 12-ga.; 32-inch, 34-inch barrel; fixed or choke tubes; high vent rib; checkered European walnut Monte Carlo stock, beavertail forend; removable, adjustable four-position trigger. Made in Italy. Introduced 1988.
Standard Grade
Perf.: $5500 **Exc.:** $3600 **VGood:** $2900
SC0 Grade
Perf.: $17,000 **Exc.:** $11,000 **VGood:** $8900
SC0 Gold Grade
Perf.: $19,500 **Exc.:** $12,500 **VGood:** $10,000

PERUGINI-VISINI CLASSIC DOUBLE

Side-by-side; sidelock; 12-, 20-ga.; 2-3/4-inch, 3-inch chambers; various barrel lengths, chokes; high-grade oil-finished straight English briar walnut stock; H&H-type hand-detachable sidelocks; internal parts

gold-plated; single or double triggers; auto ejectors; numerous options. Made in Italy. Introduced, 1986; discontinued 1989.
Perf.: $20,000 **Exc.:** $17,000 **VGood:** $15,000

PERUGINI-VISINI LIBERTY DOUBLE

Side-by-side; boxlock; 12-, 20-, 28-ga.; 410; 2-3/4-inch, 3-inch chambers; various barrel lengths, chokes; high-grade oil-finished straight English briar walnut stock; internal parts gold-plated; single or double trigger; auto ejectors; numerous options. Made in Italy. Introduced 1986; discontinued 1989.
Perf.: $10,750 **Exc.:** $9000 **VGood:** $7750

PERUGINI-VISINI AUSONIA

Side-by-side; sidelock; 12-, 20-ga.; exposed hammers; double Purdey type sidelock action; demibloc barrels; variety of engraving options. No longer produced.
Perf.: $7140 **Exc.:** $6500 **VGood:** $5750

PERUGINI-VISINI REGINA

Side-by-side; 12-ga.; heavy frame construction intended for hunting and competition; removable trigger group; chopper lump barrels; many options.
Exc.: $11,500 **VGood:** $9950 **Good:** $8700

PERUGINI-VISINI ROMAGNA HAMMER GUN

Best quality Zanotti-stylke bar action hammer gun; 12-, 16-, 20-, 28-ga., .410 bore; heavy frame configuration for competition use. Engraved by master engraver.
Exc.: $19,500 **VGood:** $16,950 **Good:** $13,000

PERUGINI-VISINI NOVA

Over/under; best quality Boss-style sidelock with back action locks; Boss-style forend iron and side ribs; best quality English rose and scroll engraving is standard.
Exc.: $38,500 **VGood:** $32,950 **Good:** $26,000

PIOTTI BOSS OVER/UNDER

Over/under; sidelock; 12-, 16-, 20-, 28-ga.; 26-inch to 32-inch barrels; standard chokes; stock dimensions to customer specs; best quality figured walnut. Essentially a custom-made gun with many options. Made in Italy. Introduced 1993; still imported by William Larkin Moore & Co.
Perf.: $48,000 **Exc.:** $34,000 **VGood:** $28,750
Add $8,900 to above prices for 28 ga.
Add $3,200 for 16- or 20-ga.
Add $3,100 for single trigger.

PIOTTI KING NO. 1

Side-by-side; H&H sidelock; 12-, 16-, 20-, 28-ga., .410; 25-inch to 30-inch (12-ga.), 25-inch to 28-inch (other gauges) barrels; file-cut or concave vent rib; fine-figured straight-grip European walnut stock, split or beavertail forend; oil or satin luster finish; double triggers; optional single non-selective trigger; coin finish or color case-hardening; full-coverage engraving; gold crown on top lever; name in gold; gold crest on forend. Made in Italy to customer's requirements. Introduced 1983; still in production.
Perf.: $29,600 **Exc.:** $20,900 **VGood:** $17,750
With single trigger
Perf.: $32,000 **Exc.:** $22,300 **VGood:** $20,000

PIOTTI KING NO. 1 EELL

Same specs as King No. 1 except highest quality wood, metal work; engraved scenes, gold inlays; signed by master engraver. Made in Italy. Introduced 1983; no longer imported. Extremely rare, precludes pricing.

PIOTTI KING NO. 1 EXTRA

Same specs as King No. 1 except exhibition grade wood; better metal work; Bulino game scene engraving or game scene engraving with gold inlay work signed by master engraver. Made in Italy.
Perf.: $35,000 **Exc.:** $32,000 **VGood:** $28,250
With single trigger
Perf.: $37,000 **Exc.:** $34,000 **VGood:** $30,250

PIOTTI LUNIK

Side-by-side; H&H sidelock; 12-, 16-, 20-, 28-ga., .410; 25-inch to 30-inch (12-ga.), 25-inch to 28-inch (other gauges) barrels; fine-figured straight-grip European walnut stock, split or beavertail forend; oil or satin luster finish; double triggers; optional single non-selective trigger; Renaissance-style scroll engraving, gold crown on top lever, gold name and gold crest in forend; demi-block barrels. Made in Italy. Introduced 1983.

Perf.: $30,900 **Exc.:** $21,900 **VGood:** $18,750

With single trigger

Perf.: $32,900 **Exc.:** $23,900 **VGood:** $20,750

PIOTTI MONTE CARLO

Side-by-side; H&H sidelock; 12-, 16-, 20-, 28-ga., .410; 25-inch to 30-inch (12-ga.), 25-inch to 28-inch (other gauges) barrels; fine-figured straight-grip European walnut stock, split or beavertail forend; oil or satin luster finish; double triggers; optional single non-selective trigger; ejectors; Purdey-type engraving. Made in Italy. Introduced 1983; discontinued 1989.

Perf.: $10,500 **Exc.:** $9250 **VGood:** $8200

With single trigger

Perf.: $11,500 **Exc.:** $10,250 **VGood:** $9200

PIOTTI PIUMA

Side-by-side; Anson & Deeley boxlock; 12-, 16-, 20-, 28-ga., .410; 25-inch to 30-inch (12-ga.), 25-inch to 28-inch (other gauges) barrels; file-cut rib; oil-finished, straight-grip European walnut stock, splinter type or beavertail forend; satin luster finish optional; ejectors; chopper lump barrels; double triggers, hinged front; optional single non-selective trigger; coin finish or color case-hardening; scroll, rosette, scallop engraving. Made in Italy. Introduced 1983.

Perf.: $14,800 **Exc.:** $10,900 **VGood:** $9,500

With single trigger

Perf.: $16,000 **Exc.:** $12,100 **VGood:** $10,700

PIOTTI WESTLAKE

Side-by-side; H & H sidelock action; 12-, 16-, 20, 28-ga., .410 bore; scroll engraving. Discontinued 1989.

Perf.: $8500 **Exc.:** $7500 **VGood:** $6000

PIOTTI HAMMER GUN

Side-by-side; 12-ga.; self-cocking; ejector; double triggers; exposed hammers; back action with fine scroll engraving. Importation began 2001.

Perf.: $29,800 **Exc.:** $23,200 **VGood:** $18,750

PIOTTI KING EXTRA

Side-by-side; sidelock; 12-, 16-, 20-, 28-ga., .410 bore; best quality H&H pattern; ejectors; chopper lump barrels; level-file cut rib; choice of Burlino game scene or standard cameo game scene engraving with gold inlays; signed by a master engraver; exhibition grade wood.

Perf.: $35,000 **Exc.:** $25,900 **VGood:** $22,000

PRECISION SPORTS MODEL 640A

Side-by-side; boxlock; 12-, 16-, 20-, 28-ga., .410; 2-3/4-inch chambers; 26-inch, 28-inch barrels; Improved Cylinder/Modified or Modified/Full chokes; raised matte rib; hand-checkered walnut pistol-grip stock, beavertail forend with oil finish; checkered butt; buttplate; automatic safety; ejectors or extractors; single non-selective trigger; silvered, engraved action. Made in Spain by Ugartechea. Originally imported as Parker-Hale brand. Introduced 1986; discontinued 1993.

Exc.: $800 **VGood:** $650 **Good:** $500

28-ga., .410, ejectors

Perf.: $900 **Exc.:** $750 **VGood:** $600

PRECISION SPORTS MODEL 640E

Same specs as Model 640A except concave rib; hand-checkered walnut straight-grip stock, splinter forend with oil finish; double triggers. Made in Spain by Ugartechea. Originally imported as Parker-Hale brand. Introduced 1986; discontinued 1993.

Perf.: $700 **Exc.:** $500 **VGood:** $400

28-ga., .410, ejectors

Perf.: $800 **Exc.:** $600 **VGood:** $500

Piotti Lunik

Piotti Lunik Engraving

Piotti Monte Carlo Engraving

Piotti Piuma

Precision Sports Model 600 English Series

PRECISION SPORTS MODEL 600 ENGLISH SERIES

Similar to the Model 640E but with oil finished English-style straight stock.

Perf.: $900 **Exc.:** $800 **VGood:** $650

PRECISION SPORTS MODEL 640M BIG TEN

Same specs as Model 640A except chambered for 10-ga.; 26-inch, 30-inch, 32-inch barrels; Full/Full. Originally imported as Parker-Hale brand. Introduced 1986; discontinued 1993.

Perf.: $800 **Exc.:** $650 **VGood:** $550

PRECISION SPORTS MODEL 640 SLUG GUN

Same specs as Model 640A except 12-ga. only; 25-inch barrels; Improved Cylinder/Improved Cylinder. Originally imported as Parker-Hale brand. Introduced 1986; discontinued 1993.

Perf.: $950 **Exc.:** $700 **VGood:** $600

PRECISION SPORTS MODEL 645A

Side-by-side; boxlock; 12-, 16-, 20-, 28-ga., .410; 2-3/4-inch chambers; 26-inch, 28-inch barrels; Improved Cylinder/Modified or Modified/Full; raised matte rib; hand-checkered walnut pistol-grip stock, beavertail forend with oil finish; checkered butt; buttplate; automatic safety; ejectors; single non-selective trigger; silvered, engraved action. Made in Spain by Ugartechea. Originally imported as Parker-Hale brand. Introduced 1986; discontinued 1993.

Perf.: $1100 **Exc.:** $750 **VGood:** 600

28-ga., .410, ejectors

Perf.: $1200 **Exc.:** $850 **VGood:** $700

PRECISION SPORTS MODEL 645E

Same specs as Model 645A except concave rib; hand-checkered walnut straight-grip stock, splinter forend with oil finish; double triggers. Made in Spain by Ugartechea. Originally imported as Parker-Hale brand. Introduced 1986; discontinued 1993.

Perf.: $900 **Exc.:** $650 **VGood:** $550

28-ga., .410, ejectors

Perf.: $980 **Exc.:** $730 **VGood:** $630

PRECISION SPORTS MODEL 645E-XXV

Same specs as Model 645A except 25-inch barrels; Churchill-type rib. Originally imported as Parker-Hale brand. Introduced 1986; discontinued 1993.

Perf.: $900 **Exc.:** $650 **VGood:** $550

28-ga., .410, ejectors

Perf.: $980 **Exc.:** $730 **VGood:** $630

PRECISION SPORTS MODEL 650A

Side-by-side; boxlock; 12-ga.; 2-3/4-inch chambers; 26-inch, 28-inch barrels; Improved Cylinder/Modified choke tubes; raised matte rib; hand-checkered walnut pistol-grip stock, beavertail forend with oil finish; checkered butt; buttplate; automatic safety; extractors; single non-selective trigger; silvered, engraved action. Made in Spain by Ugartechea. Originally imported as Parker-Hale brand. Introduced 1986; discontinued 1993.

Perf.: $800 **Exc.:** $650 **VGood:** $550

PRECISION SPORTS MODEL 650E

Same specs as Model 650A except concave rib; hand-checkered walnut straight-grip stock, splinter forend with oil finish; double triggers. Made in Spain by Ugartechea. Originally imported as Parker-Hale brand. Introduced 1986; discontinued 1993.

Perf.: $800 **Exc.:** $650 **VGood:** $550

Premier Ambassador

Premier Brush King

Premier Continental

Premier Monarch Supreme

Premier Regent

Premier Regent Magnum

Purdey Over/Under

Purdey Single Barrel Trap

automatic safety. Made in Europe. No longer in production.
Perf.: $225 **Exc.:** $190 **VGood:** $170

PREMIER MONARCH SUPREME
Side-by-side; boxlock; 12-, 20-ga.; 2-3/4-inch (12-ga.), 3-inch (20-ga.) chambers; 26-inch Improved Cylinder/Modified, 28-inch Modified/Full barrels; checkered fancy European walnut pistol-grip stock, beavertail forearm; double triggers; auto ejectors. Introduced 1959; discontinued 1981.
Perf.: $440 **Exc.:** $385 **VGood:** $360

PREMIER PRESENTATION CUSTOM GRADE
Side-by-side; boxlock; 12-, 20-ga.; 2-3/4-inch (12-ga.), 3-inch (20-ga.) chambers; 26-inch Improved Cylinder/Modified, 28-inch Modified/Full barrels; hand-checkered high-grade European walnut pistol-grip stock, beavertail forearm; engraved hunting scene; gold and silver inlays; custom-order gun. Introduced 1959; discontinued 1981.
Perf.: $1150 **Exc.:** $950 **VGood:** $825

PREMIER REGENT
Side-by-side; 12-, 16-, 20-, 28-ga., .410; 26-inch Improved/Modified, Modified/Full, 28-inch Modified/Full barrels; matted tapered rib; hand-checkered European walnut pistol-grip stock, forearm; double triggers; automatic safety. Introduced 1955; discontinued 1981.
Perf.: $280 **Exc.:** $250 **VGood:** $210

PREMIER REGENT MAGNUM
Same specs as Regent except 10-, 12-ga.; 3-inch, 3-1/2-inch chambers; 30-inch, 32-inch Full/Full barrels; hand-checkered European walnut pistol-grip stock, beavertail forearm; recoil pad. Discontinued 1981.

10-ga.
Perf.: $330 **Exc.:** $285 **VGood:** $265
12-ga.
Perf.: $305 **Exc.:** $275 **VGood:** $250

PURDEY SIDE-BY-SIDE
Side-by-side; sidelock; 12-, 16-, 20-, 28-ga., .410-ga.; 26-inch, 27-inch, 28-inch, 30-inch barrels; 2-1/2, 2-3/4, or 3-inch; any choke combo; choice of rib style; hand-checkered European walnut straight-grip stock, forearm; pistol-grip stock on special order; double triggers or single trigger; automatic ejectors; made in several variations including Game Model, Featherweight Game, Pigeon Gun, with side clips. Prices are identical for all. Introduced 1880.
With double triggers
Perf.: $44,000 **Exc.:** $35,000 **VGood:** $30,000
With single trigger
Perf.: $45,000 **Exc.:** $36,000 **VGood:** $31,000

PURDEY OVER/UNDER
Over/under; sidelock; pre-WWII guns are built on Purdey action, post-war versions on Woodward action; 12-, 16-, 20-, 28-ga., .410-bore; 26-inch, 27-inch, 28-inch barrels; any choke combo; any rib style to customer's preference; hand-checkered European walnut straight or pistol-grip stock, forearm; double or single trigger; engraved receiver. Introduced 1925.
With Purdey action, double triggers
Perf.: $50,000 **Exc.:** $36,000 **VGood:** $33,000
With Purdey action, single trigger
Perf.: $52,000 **Exc.:** $38,000 **VGood:** $35,000
With Woodward action, double trigger
Perf.: $56,000 **Exc.:** $40,000 **VGood:** $37,000
With Woodward action, single trigger
Perf.: $60,000 **Exc.:** $44,000 **VGood:** $40,000

PURDEY SINGLE BARREL TRAP
Single shot; Purdey action; 12-ga.; barrel length, choke to customer's specs; vent rib; hand-checkered European walnut straight or pistol-grip stock, forearm; engraved receiver. Introduced 1917; discontinued prior to WWII.
Perf.: $12,500 **Exc.:** $9000 **VGood:** $8200

PRECISION SPORTS MODEL 655A
Side-by-side; boxlock; 12-ga.; 2-3/4-inch chambers; 28-inch barrels; Improved Cylinder/Modified choke tubes; concave rib; hand-checkered walnut pistol-grip stock, beavertail forend with oil finish; automatic safety; ejectors; checkered butt; buttplate; single non-selective trigger; silvered, engraved action. Made in Spain by Ugartechea. Originally imported as Parker-Hale brand. Introduced 1986; discontinued 1993.
Perf.: $900 **Exc.:** $700 **VGood:** $600

PRECISION SPORTS MODEL 655E
Same specs as Model 655A except concave rib; hand-checkered walnut straight-grip stock, splinter forend with oil finish; double triggers. Made in Spain by Ugartechea. Originally imported as Parker-Hale brand. Introduced 1986; discontinued 1993.
Perf.: $900 **Exc.:** $700 **VGood:** $600

PRECISION SPORTS MODEL 800 AMERICAN SERIES
Side-by side; boxlock; 10-, 12-, 16-, 20-, 28-ga., .410; 2-3/4-inch, 3-inch, 3-1/2-inch chambers depending upon gauge; 25-inch, 26-inch, 27-inch, 28-inch barrels; raised matte rib; hand-checkered

European walnut pistol-grip stock, beavertail forend; buttplate; auto safety; ejectors or extractors; single non-selective trigger; engraved, silvered frame. Made in Spain. Introduced 1986; discontinued 1993.
Perf.: $1000 **Exc.:** $750 **VGood:** $650

PREMIER AMBASSADOR
Side-by-side; 12-, 16-, 20-ga., .410; 22-inch (except .410), 26-inch barrels; Modified/Full chokes; European walnut stock, hand-checkered pistol-grip stock, forearm; double triggers; cocking indicators; automatic safety. Made in Europe. Introduced 1957; discontinued 1981.
Perf.: $385 **Exc.:** $360 **VGood:** $295

PREMIER BRUSH KING
Side-by-side; 12-, 20-ga.; 22-inch Improved/Modified barrels; matted tapered rib; hand-checkered European walnut pistol-grip stock, forearm; double triggers; automatic safety. Introduced 1959; discontinued 1981.
Perf.: $275 **Exc.:** $250 **VGood:** $220

PREMIER CONTINENTAL
Side-by-side; exposed hammers; 12-, 16-, 20-ga.; 22-inch, 26-inch barrels; Modified/Full chokes; hand-checkered European walnut pistol-grip stock, forearm; double triggers; cocking indicators;

REMINGTON MODEL 11A

Autoloader; hammerless; takedown; 12-, 16-, 20-ga.; 5-shot tube magazine; 26-inch, 28-inch, 30-inch, 32-inch barrel; Full, Modified, Improved Cylinder, Skeet chokes; plain, solid or vent rib; checkered pistol-grip stock, forearm. Introduced 1905; discontinued 1949. Deduct 10 percent for 16-ga.

Plain barrel

Exc.: $300	VGood: $225	Good: $185

Solid rib

Exc.: $315	VGood: $235	Good: $200

Vent rib

Exc.: $360	VGood: $335	Good: $305

NOTE: THE FOLLOWING GRADES OF THE REMINGTON MODEL 11 (11B - 11F) FEATURE PROGRESSIVELY HIGHER-QUALITY WOOD AND ORNAMENTATION. PRICES FLUCTUATE BUT MAY APPROACH $10,000 FOR THE 11F PREMIERE.

REMINGTON MODEL 11B SPECIAL

Same specs as Model 11A except higher grade of walnut, checkering and engraving. Discontinued 1948.

REMINGTON MODEL 11D TOURNAMENT

Same specs as Model 11A except select grade of walnut, checkering and engraving. Discontinued 1948.

REMINGTON MODEL 11E EXPERT

Same specs as Model 11A except fine grade of walnut, checkering and engraving. Discontinued 1948.

REMINGTON MODEL 11F PREMIER

Same specs as Model 11A except best grade of walnut, checkering and engraving. Discontinued 1948.

REMINGTON MODEL 11R RIOT GUN

Same specs as Model 11A except 12-ga.; special 20-inch barrel; sling swivels. Introduced 1921; discontinued 1948. 100% premium for US Ordnance/Army markings.

Exc.: $360	VGood: $295	Good: $210

REMINGTON MODEL 11-48A

Recoiling-barrel autoloader; hammerless; takedown; 12-, 16-, 20-, 28-ga., .410; 4-, 5-shot tube magazine; 26-inch Cylinder, 28-inch Modified or Full, 30-inch Full barrels; plain matted or vent-rib barrel; hand-checkered half-pistol-grip stock, forend; redesigned version of Model 11. Introduced 1949; discontinued 1969. Designated the 11-48 to draw on the popularity of the previous Model 11; i.e., "the new Model 11 of 1948." Premium for small gauge.

Plain barrel

Exc.: $300	VGood: $240	Good: $195

Vent-rib barrel

Exc.: $450	VGood: $350	Good: $300

REMINGTON MODEL 11-48A RIOT

Same specs as Model 11-48A except 12-ga.; 20-inch plain barrel. Introduced 1949; discontinued 1969.

Exc.: $300	VGood: $240	Good: $195

Note: Values for the following higher grades of the Remington 11-48 fluctuate and may approach $10,000 for the 11-48F Premiere grade.

REMINGTON MODEL 11-48B SPECIAL

Same specs as Model 11-48A except higher grade of wood, checkering and engraving. Introduced 1949; discontinued 1969. Premium for small gauge.

REMINGTON MODEL 11-48D TOURNAMENT

Same specs as Model 11-48A except select grade of wood, checkering and engraving. Introduced 1949; discontinued 1969.

REMINGTON MODEL 11-48F PREMIER

Same specs as Model 11-48A except best grade of wood, checkering and engraving. Introduced 1949;

Remington Model 11A

Remington Model 11-48A

Remington Model 11-48RSS Slug

Remington Model 11-48SA Skeet

Remington Model 11-87 Premier

Remingtom Model 11-87 Premier Special Purpose Deer Gun

discontinued 1969.

REMINGTON MODEL 11-48 RSS SLUG GUN

Same specs as Model 11-48 except 12-ga. slug; 26-inch plain barrel; adjustable rifle-type gold bead front sight, step-adjustable rear. Introduced 1959; no longer in production.

Exc.: $350	VGood: $265	Good: $200

REMINGTON MODEL 11-48SA SKEET

Same specs as Model 11-48A except 25-inch vent-rib barrel; Skeet choke; Skeet-style walnut stock, forend. Introduced 1952; discontinued 1969.

Exc.: $550	VGood: $480	Good: $400

REMINGTON MODEL 11-87 PREMIER

Gas-operated autoloader; 12-ga.; 3-inch chamber; 26-inch, 28-inch, 30-inch vent-rib barrel; Rem-Choke tubes; weighs 8-1/4 lb.; metal bead middle sight, Bradley-type white-faced front; high-gloss or satin-finished, cut-checkered walnut stock, pinned forend; brown buttpad; pressure compensating system handles 2-3/4-inch or 3-inch shells; stainless steel magazine tube; barrel support ring on operating bars; left- or right-hand versions. Introduced, 1987; still in production. Add $150 for nickel plated version.

Right-hand model

Perf.: $630	Exc.: $495	VGood: $410

Left-hand model

Perf.: $670	Exc.: $555	VGood: $475

REMINGTON MODEL 11-87 PREMIER 175TH ANNIVERSARY

Same specs as Model 11-87 Premier except 28-inch vent-rib barrel; walnut wood with high-gloss finish; receiver engraved with Remington's 175th anniversary scroll design with an American eagle. Introduced 1991; discontinued 1991.

Perf.: $6505	Exc.: $505	VGood: $335

REMINGTON MODEL 11-87 PREMIER N.W.T.F.

Same specs as Model 11-87 Premier except 21-inch vent-rib barrel; Rem-Choke Improved Cylinder and Turkey Extra-Full tubes; synthetic brown Trebark camouflage-finished stock; camo sling; swivels. Introduced 1992; discontinued 1993.

Perf.: $525	Exc.: $375	VGood: $285

REMINGTON MODEL 11-87 PREMIER SKEET

Same specs as Model 11-87 Premier except 12-ga.; 2-3/4-inch chamber; 26-inch vent-rib barrel; cut-checkered, deluxe walnut Skeet-style stock with satin finish; two-piece buttplate, Introduced 1987; still in production.

Perf.: $650	Exc.: $550	VGood: $475

REMINGTON MODEL 11-87 PREMIER SPECIAL PURPOSE DEER GUN

Same specs as Model 11-87 Premier except 21-inch barrel; rifled and Improved Cylinder choke tubes; rifle sights; cantilever scope mount, rings; gas system handles all 2-3/4-inch and 3-inch slug, buckshot, high-velocity field and magnum loads; not designed to function with light 2-3/4-inch field loads; dull stock finish, Parkerized exposed metal surfaces; bolt and carrier have blackened color. Introduced 1987; discontinued 1995.

Perf.: $690	Exc.: $495	VGood: $425

REMINGTON MODEL 11-87 PREMIER SPECIAL PURPOSE MAGNUM

Same specs as Model 11-87 Premier except black synthetic or satin wood stock; Parkerized metal finish; blackened bolt, carrier; quick-detachable sling swivels; camo padded nylon sling. Introduced 1987; still in production.

Perf.: $500	Exc.: $350	VGood: $260

With synthetic stock and forend (SPS).

Perf.: $610	Exc.: $475	VGood: $400

Remington Model 11-87
Premier Special Purpose
Magnum

Remingtom Model 11-87
Premier Sporting Clays

Remingtom Model 11-87
SP Super Magnum

Remingtom Model 11-87
SPS Super Magnum

Remington Model 11-87
Premier SPS-BG-Camo
Deer/Turkey

Remington Model 11-87
Premier SPS-Deer

Remington Model 11-87
Premier SPS-T Camo

Remington Model 11-87 SPS-T
Turkey Camo

Remington Model 11-87
Premier Trap

REMINGTON MODEL 11-87 PREMIER SPECIAL PURPOSE SYNTHETIC CAMO

Same specs as Model 11-87 Premier except 26-inch vent-rib barrel; synthetic stock; camo sling; swivels; all surfaces (except bolt and trigger guard) covered with Mossy Oak Bottomland camo finish. Introduced 1992; still in production.

Perf.: $710   **Exc.:** $520   **VGood:** $435

REMINGTON MODEL 11-87 PREMIER SPORTING CLAYS

Same specs as Model 11-87 Premier except 12-ga.; 2-3/4-inch chamber; 26-inch, 28-inch medium-height vent-rib Light Contour barrel; Skeet, Improved Cylinder, Modified, Full long Rem-Choke tubes; ivory bead front sight; special stock dimensions; shortened magazine tube and forend; Sporting Clays buttpad; lengthened forcing cone; competition trigger; top

of receiver, barrel and rib matte finished; comes in two-barrel fitted hard case. Introduced 1992; still in production.

Perf.: $675   **Exc.:** $570   **VGood:** $450

REMINGTON MODEL 11-87 SP AND SPS SUPER MAGNUM SHOTGUNS

Similar to Model 11-87 Special Purpose Magnum except has 3-1/2-inch chamber. Available in flat-finish American walnut or black synthetic stock, 26-inch or 28-inch black-matte finished barrel and receiver; Imp. Cyl., Modified and Full Rem-Choke tubes. Overall length 45-3/4-inch, weighs 8 lbs., 2 oz. Introduced 2000.

SP Super Magnum (walnut stock)
Perf.: $695   **Exc.:** $495   **VGood:** $435
SPS Super Magnum (synthetic stock)
Perf.: $610   **Exc.:** $475   **VGood:** $400

SPS Super Magnum (camo)
Perf.: $710   **Exc.:** $510   **VGood:** $435

REMINGTON MODEL 11-87 PREMIER SPS-BG-CAMO DEER/TURKEY

Same specs as Model 11-87 Premier except 21-inch barrel; Improved Cylinder, Super-Full Turkey (.665-inch diameter with knurled extension) Rem-Choke tubes and rifled choke tube insert; rifle sights; synthetic stock, forend; quick-detachable swivels; camo Cordura carrying sling; all surfaces Mossy Oak Bottomland camouflage-finished. Introduced 1993; discontinued 1995.

Perf.: $525   **Exc.:** $365   **VGood:** $300

REMINGTON MODEL 11-87 PREMIER SPS CANTILEVER

Same specs as Model 11-87 Premier except 20-inch barrel; Improved Cylinder, 3 1/2-inch rifled Rem-Choke tubes; cantilever scope mount; synthetic Monte Carlo stock; sling; swivels. Introduced 1994; still in production.

Perf.: $600   **Exc.:** $420   **VGood:** $320

REMINGTON MODEL 11-87 PREMIER SPS-DEER

Same specs as Model 11-87 Premier except fully-rifled 21-inch barrel; rifle sights; black non-reflective synthetic stock, forend; black carrying sling. Introduced 1993; still in production.

Perf.: $525   **Exc.:** $375   **VGood:** $290

With wood stock (Model 11-87 SP Deer Gun) Rem-Choke, 21-inch barrel w/rifle sights

REMINGTON MODEL 11-87 SPS CANTILEVER SHOTGUN

Similar to the 11-87 SPS except has fully rifled barrel; synthetic stock with Monte Carlo comb; cantilever scope mount deer barrel. Comes with sling and swivels. Introduced 1994.

Perf.: $650   **Exc.:** $525   **VGood:** $453

REMINGTON MODEL 11-87 PREMIER SPS-T CAMO

Same specs as Model 11-87 Premier except 21-inch vent-rib barrel; Improved Cylinder, Super-Full Turkey (.665-inch diameter with knurled extension) Rem-Choke tubes; synthetic stock; all surfaces Mossy Oak Green Leaf camouflage-finished; non-reflective black bolt body, trigger guard and recoil pad. Introduced 1993; still in production.

Perf.: $620   **Exc.:** $440   **VGood:** $340

REMINGTON MODEL 11-87 SPS-T TURKEY CAMO

Similar to the 11-87 Special Purpose Magnum except with synthetic stock, 21-inch vent. rib barrel with Rem-Choke tube. Completely covered with Mossy Oak Break-Up Brown camouflage. Bolt body, trigger guard and recoil pad are non-reflective black.

Exc.: $700   **VGood:** $500   **Good:** $420
Model 11-87 SPS-T RS/TG (TruGlo fiber optics sights)
Exc.: $720   **VGood:** $520   **Good:** $440
Model 11-87 SPS-T Camo CL cantilever
Exc.: $702   **VGood:** $502   **Good:** $422

REMINGTON MODEL 11-87 SPS-T SUPER MAGNUM SYNTHETIC CAMO

Similar to the 11-87 SPS-T Turkey Camo except has 23-inch vent rib barrel with Turkey Super full choke tube, chambered for 12 ga., 3-1/2-inch, TruGlo rifle sights. Introduced 2001.

Exc.: $720   **VGood:** $520   **Good:** $440

REMINGTON MODEL 11-87 PREMIER TRAP

Same specs as Model 11-87 Premier except 12-ga.; 2-3/4-inch chamber; 30-inch vent-rib barrel; checkered deluxe walnut Trap-style stock with satin-finish; straight or Monte Carlo comb; right- or left-hand models. Introduced 1987; dropped 1999.

Right-hand model
Perf.: $625   **Exc.:** $450   **VGood:** $345
Left-hand model
Perf.: $675   **Exc.:** $500   **VGood:** $395

REMINGTON MODEL 11-87 UPLAND SPECIAL SHOTGUN

Similar to 11-87 Premier except has 23-inch ventilated rib barrel with straight- grip, English-style walnut stock. Available in 12- or 20-gauge. Overall length 43-1/2-inch, weighs 7-1/4 lbs. (6-1/2 lbs. in 20-ga.). Comes with Imp. Cyl., Modified and Full choke tubes. Introduced 2000.

12- or 20-gauge		
Perf.: $600	**Exc.:** $475	**VGood:** $400

REMINGTON MODEL 11-87 SPORTSMAN

No-frills 11-87 with matte black synthetic stock. Available in 12 and 20 gauge with 3-inch chamber and 26-inch or 28-inch barrel. One choke tube included. Youth model 20 gauge with smaller dimensions also available.

NIB: $415   **Exc.:** $375   **VGood:** $315

REMINGTON MODEL 11-87 SPORTSMAN NRA EDITION

Similar to 11-87 Sportsman but in 12 gauge only with NRA logo on receiver and Mossy Oak New Break-Up stock and forend.

NIB: $460   **Exc.:** $420   **VGood:** $360

REMINGTON MODEL 11-87 SPORTSMAN CAMO

New in 2007, the camo version of the Sportsman comes in 12 and 20 gauge with 26" or 28" barrel. Finished in Mossy Oak Break-Up camo.

NIB: $795   **Exc.:** $695   **VGood:** $525

REMINGTON MODEL 11-87 SPORTSMAN CAMO RIFLED

Camo 12 gauge slug gun with 21" barrel and cantilever scope mount.

NIB: $525   **Exc.:** $485   **VGood:** $425

REMINGTON MODEL 11-87 SPORTSMAN CAMO YOUTH

Youth model in 20 gauge with shorter length of pull was introduced in 2007. Weight is about 6.5 lbs.

NIB: $725   **Exc.:** $665   **VGood:** $575

REMINGTON MODEL 11-87 SPS SUPER MAGNUM WATERFOWL

This 3.5" 12 gauge is finished in Mossy Oak Duck Blind camo. It has a 30" barrel and includes three chokes. Weight is 8.25 lbs.

NIB: $1050   **Exc.:** $975   **VGood:** $850

REMINGTON MODEL 11-87 SP-T THUMBHOLE

This 12 gauge with 3.5-inch chamber is made specifically for turkey hunting. Camouflaged in Mossy Oak Obsession with an R3 recoil pad and thumbhole stock. The 23-inch barrel has fiber-optic adjustable rifle sights and is drilled and tapped for scope mounting. Includes a turkey super full choke tube and sling/swivels.

NIB: $725   **Exc.:** $675   **VGood:** $575

REMINGTON MODEL 11-87 SP THUMBHOLE

Laminated, thumbhole-stock 12 gauge slug gun with 3-inch chamber and 21-inch fully rifled cantilever barrel.

NIB: $700   **Exc.:** $650   **VGood:** $550

REMINGTON MODEL 11-87 SPS-T SUPER MAGNUM

Similar to Model 11-87 SP Thumbhole but with pistol-grip stock and vent rib barrel.

NIB: $650   **Exc.:** $550   **VGood:** $450

REMINGTON MODEL 11-87 SPORTSMAN SUPER MAG SHURSHOT TURKEY

New in 2008, this specialized turkey shotgun with ShurShot stock is a 3.5-inch-chamber 12 gauge

with a 23-inch non-vent-rib barrel. It comes with fiber-optic rifle-type sights, and a synthetic stock and forend. The gun is fully covered in Realtree APG HD camo. Weight is about 7.6 lbs.

NIB: $800   **Exc.:** $675   **VGood:** $550

REMINGTON MODEL 11-87 SPORTSMAN SUPER MAGNUM WATERFOWL

As above, but with full coverage in Mossy Oak Duck Blind camo and shell-holding Speedfeed stock and three choke tubes.

NIB: $750   **Exc.:** $675   **VGood:** $550

REMINGTON MODEL 11-87 SPORTSMAN SHURSHOT CANTILEVER

This dedicated slug gun in 3-inch 12-gauge features a 23-inch, fully rifled barrel with cantilever scope mount. It is matte black with synthetic stock and forend finished in Realtree Hardwoods HD camo. Weight is about 8 lbs.

NIB: $750   **Exc.:** $675   **VGood:** $550

Remington Model 11-87 Upland Special

Remington Model 11-87 Sportsman Youth

Remington Model 11-87 Sportsman NRA Edition

Remington Model 11-87 Sportsman Camo

Remington Model 11-87 SPS Super Magnum Waterfowl

Remington Model 11-87 Sportsman Super Mag ShurShot Turkey

Remington Model 11-87 Sportsman Super Magnum Waterfowl

Remington Model 11-87 Sportsman ShurShot Cantilever

Remington Model 878A Automaster

REMINGTON MODEL 878A AUTOMASTER

Gas-operated autoloader; 12-ga.; 3-shot tube magazine; plain or vent rib; 26-inch Improved Cylinder; 28-inch Modified, 30-inch Full choke barrels; uncheckered pistol-grip stock, forend. Introduced 1959; discontinued 1962.

Plain barrel		
Exc.: $190	**VGood:** $160	**Good:** $130
Vent-rib barrel		
Exc.: $215	**VGood:** $185	**Good:** $155

REMINGTON MODEL 1100D TOURNAMENT

Gas-operated autoloader; hammerless; takedown; 12-, 16-, 20-, 28-ga., .410; 5-shot magazine; 26-inch, 28-inch, 30-inch vent-rib barrel; fixed or choke tubes; high-grade checkered walnut pistol-grip stock, forend; buttplate; engraving; custom-order gun. Introduced 1963.

Perf.: $2900   **Exc.:** $2050   **VGood:** $1425

Remington Model 1100D
Tournament

Remington Model 1100
Deer

Remington Model 1100F Premier

Remington Model 1100 Field

Remington Model 1100 Special Field

Remington Model 1100 LT-20

Remington Model 110
Synthetic LT-20

Remington Model 1100 LT-20
Deer Gun

Remington Model 110
Synthetic

REMINGTON MODEL 1100 DEER

Gas-operated autoloader; hammerless; takedown; 12-, 20-ga.; 5-shot magazine; 20-inch, 21-inch, 22-inch Improved Cylinder barrel; rifle sights; checkered walnut pistol-grip stock, forend; recoil pad. No longer in production.

Perf.: $430   **Exc.:** $350   **VGood:** $275

Left-hand model

Perf.: $450   **Exc.:** $370   **VGood:** $295

REMINGTON MODEL 1100 DEER SPECIAL PURPOSE

Same specs as Model 1100 Deer except matte finish on checkered walnut pistol-grip stock, forend; matte metal finish. Introduced 1986; discontinued 1986.

Perf.: $335   **Exc.:** $295   **VGood:** $275

REMINGTON MODEL 1100 DEER CANTILEVER 20-GAUGE

Same specs as Model 1100 Deer except 20-ga.; fully rifled 21-inch slug barrel; cantilever scope mount; sling; swivels. Introduced 1994; still in production.

Perf.: $500   **Exc.:** $350   **VGood:** $260

REMINGTON MODEL 1100F PREMIER

Gas-operated autoloader; hammerless; takedown; 12-, 16-, 20-, 28-ga., .410; 5-shot magazine; 26-inch, 28-inch, 30-inch vent-rib barrel; fixed or choke tubes; best-grade checkered walnut pistol-grip stock, forend; buttplate; engraving; custom-order gun. Introduced 1963; still in production.

Perf.: $6000   **Exc.:** $4400   **VGood:** $2850

REMINGTON MODEL 1100F PREMIER GOLD

Same specs as Model 110F Premier except gold inlays. Introduced 1963.

Perf.: $9030   **Exc.:** $5150   **VGood:** $3425

REMINGTON MODEL 1100 FIELD

Gas-operated autoloader; hammerless; takedown; 12-, 16-, 20-ga.; 5-shot magazine; 26-inch, 28-inch, 30-inch barrel; fixed or choke tubes; plain or vent rib; checkered walnut pistol-grip stock, forend; buttplate. Introduced 1963; discontinued 1988.

Plain barrel

Perf.: $350   **Exc.:** $290   **VGood:** $250

Vent-rib barrel

Perf.: $395   **Exc.:** $340   **VGood:** $295

REMINGTON MODEL 1100 FIELD COLLECTORS EDITION

Same specs as Model 1100 Field except positive cut-checkered, richly figured walnut stock; deep-relief etching; gold highlights; marketed with certificate showing serial number. Only 3000 made. Introduced 1981; discontinued 1981.

Perf.: $1000   **Exc.:** $650   **VGood:** $550

REMINGTON MODEL 1100 SPECIAL FIELD

Same specs as Model 1100 Field except 12-, 20-ga., .410; 23-inch vent-rib barrel; fixed or choke tubes; checkered walnut straight-grip stock, shortened forend; matte-finished receiver; no engraving. Introduced 1983.

Perf.: $510   **Exc.:** $410   **VGood:** $360

REMINGTON MODEL 1100 LIGHTWEIGHT MAGNUM

Same specs as Model 1100 Field except 20-ga.; 3-inch chamber; lightweight frame. Introduced 1977; no longer in production.

Plain barrel

Perf.: $395   **Exc.:** $320   **VGood:** $270

Vent rib

Perf.: $425   **Exc.:** $360   **VGood:** $310

REMINGTON MODEL 1100 LT-20

Same specs as Model 1100 Field except 20-ga.; 2-3/4-inch chamber; 26-inch, 28-inch plain barrel; 6-1/2 lbs.; satin or high-gloss mahogany pistol-grip stock, forend; lightweight receiver. Still in production.

Perf.: $500   **Exc.:** $415   **VGood:** $325

REMINGTON MODEL 1100 SYNTHETIC LT-20

Gauge: 20. Barrel: 26-inch Rem-Chokes. Weight: 6-3/4 lbs. Stock: black synthetic, checkered pistol grip and forend. Features: Matted receiver top with scroll work on both sides of receiver.

Perf.: $510   **Exc.:** $410   **VGood:** $360

REMINGTON MODEL 1100 YOUTH GUN LT-20

Shortened synthetic stock with 21-inch barrel with Rem-Chokes.

Perf.: $500   **Exc.:** $400   **VGood:** $350

REMINGTON MODEL 1100 YOUTH SYNTHETIC TURKEY CAMO

Similar to the Model 1100 LT-20 except has 1-inch shorter stock, 21-inch vent rib barrel with Full Rem-Choke tube; 3-inch chamber; synthetic stock and forend are covered with RealTree Advantage camo, and barrel and receiver have non-reflective, black matte finish. Introduced 1999.

Perf.: $500   **VGood:** $415   **Good:** $325

REMINGTON MODEL 1100 LT-20 SYNTHETIC DEER SHOTGUN

Similar to the Model 1100 LT-20 except has 21-inch fully rifled barrel with rifle sights, 2-3/4-inch chamber, and fiberglass-reinforced synthetic stock. Introduced 1997.

Perf.: $495   **Exc.:** $375   **VGood:** $300

REMINGTON MODEL 1100 SYNTHETIC

12 gauge, and has black synthetic stock; vent. rib 28-inch barrel on 12 gauge, both with Mod. Rem-Choke tube. Weighs about 7-1/2 lbs. Introduced 1996.

Perf.: $430   **Exc.:** $340   **VGood:** $275

REMINGTON MODEL 1100 LT-20 TOURNAMENT SKEET

Same specs as Model 1100 except 20-, 28-ga., .410; 26-inch plain barrel; special Skeet choke; vent rib; ivory bead front, metal bead middle sights. No longer in production.

Perf.: $500   **Exc.:** $380   **VGood:** $300

REMINGTON MODEL 1100 MAGNUM DUCK GUN

Same specs as Model 1100 Field except 12-, 20-ga.; 3-inch chamber; 28-inch (20-ga.), 30-inch (12-ga.) barrel; recoil pad. Introduced 1963; discontinued 1988.

Plain barrel
Perf.: $400   **Exc.:** $300   **VGood:** $200
Vent-rib barrel
Perf.: $425   **Exc.:** $270   **VGood:** $225

REMINGTON MODEL 1100 MAGNUM SPECIAL PURPOSE

Same specs as Model 1100 Field except 12-ga.; 3-inch chamber; 26-inch, 30-inch vent-rib barrel; oil-finished wood; dark recoil pad; quick-detachable swivels; padded sling; chrome-lined bore; all exposed metal finished in nonreflective black. Introduced 1985; discontinued 1986.
Perf.: $400   **Exc.:** $300   **VGood:** $225

REMINGTON MODEL 1100 SPORTING 28

Similar to the 1100 LT-20 except in 28-gauge with 25-inch barrel; comes with Skeet, Imp. Cyl., Light Mod., Mod. Rem-Choke tube. Semi-Fancy walnut with gloss finish, Sporting rubber butt pad. Introduced 1996.
Perf.: $750   **Exc.:** $600   **VGood:** $525

REMINGTON MODEL 1100 SPORTING 20 SHOTGUN

Similar to Model 1100 LT-20 except tournament-grade American walnut stock with gloss finish and sporting-style recoil pad, 28-inch Rem-Choke barrel for Skeet, Imp. Cyl., Light Modified and Modified. Introduced 1998.\
Perf.: $720   **Exc.:** $550   **VGood:** $475

REMINGTON MODEL 1100 CLASSIC TRAP SHOTGUN

Similar to Standard Model 1100 except 12 gauge with 30-inch, low-profile barrel, semi-fancy American walnut stock, high-polish blued receiver with engraving and gold eagle inlay. Singles, mid handicap and long handicap choke tubes. Overall length 50-1/2-inch, weighs 8 lbs., 4 oz. Introduced 2000.
Perf.: $735   **Exc.:** $570   **VGood:** $485

REMINGTON MODEL 1100 SPORTING 12 SHOTGUN

Similar to Model 1100 Sporting 20 Shotgun except in 12-gauge, 28-inch ventilated barrel with semi-fancy American walnut stock, gold-plated trigger. Overall length 49-inch, weighs 8 lbs. Introduced 2000.
Perf.: $720   **Exc.:** $550   **VGood:** $475

REMINGTON MODEL 1100 SYNTHETIC DEER SHOTGUN

Similar to Model 1100 LT-20 except 12-gauge, 21-inch fully rifled barrel with cantilever scope mount and fiberglass-reinforced synthetic stock with Monte Carlo comb. Introduced 1997.
Exc.: $495   **VGood:** $375   **Good:** $310

REMINGTON MODEL 1100SA SKEET

Same specs as Model 1100 Field except Skeet boring; vent rib; ivory bead front sight, metal bead middle; cut checkering; new receiver scroll pattern. Introduced 1963; no longer made. Premium for small gauge.
Perf.: $460   **Exc.:** $375   **VGood:** $300

REMINGTON MODEL 1100SC SKEET

Same specs as Model 1100 Field except Skeet boring; vent rib; ivory bead front sight, metal bead middle; new receiver scroll pattern; selected wood. No longer made. Premium for small gauge.
Perf.: $460   **Exc.:** $375   **VGood:** $300

REMINGTON MODEL 1100TA TRAP

Same specs as Model 1100 Field except 12-ga.; 30-inch Full-choke barrel; recoil pad; right- or left-hand models. Introduced 1979; discontinued 1986.
Perf.: $410   **Exc.:** $330   **VGood:** $295

Remington Model 1100 Magnum Duck Gun

Remington Model 1100 Magnum Special Purpose

Remington Model 1100 Sporting 20 Shotgun

Remington Model 1100 Classic Trap Shotgun

Remington Model 1100 Sporting 12 Shotgun

Remington Model 1100SA Skeet

Remington Model 1100TB Trap

Remington Model 1100 Youth Synthetic

Remington Model 1100 Youth Synthetic Camo

REMINGTON MODEL 1100TB TRAP

Same specs as Model 1100 Field except 12-ga.; 30-inch Full-choke barrel; vent rib; trap-style stock; Monte Carlo or straight comb; recoil pad. Introduced 1963; discontinued 1981.

Straight-comb stock
Perf.: $475   **Exc.:** $400   **VGood:** $325
Monte Carlo stock
Perf.: $495   **Exc.:** $415   **VGood:** $340

REMINGTON MODEL 1100TD TRAP TOURNAMENT

Same specs as Model 1100 Field except 12-ga.; 30-inch Full-choke barrel; vent rib; select-grade trap-style stock; Monte Carlo or straight comb; recoil pad. Introduced 1979; discontinued 1986.

Straight-comb stock
Perf.: $550   **Exc.:** $400   **VGood:** $350
Monte Carlo stock
Perf.: $570   **Exc.:** $420   **VGood:** $370

REMINGTON MODEL 1100 YOUTH

Same specs as Model 1100 Field except 20-ga.; 2-3/4-inch chamber; 21-inch barrel; youth-sized

mahogany stock, forend; lightweight receiver. Still in production.
Perf.: $475   **Exc.:** $340   **VGood:** $260

REMINGTON MODEL 1100 TACTICAL SPEEDFEED IV

All-black 2.75" 12 gauge has an 18" barrel with fixed Improved Cylinder choke and Speedfeed IV stock. Extended 6-round magazine. Weight is 7.5 lbs.
NIB: $725   **Exc.:** $650   **VGood:** $535

REMINGTON MODEL 1100 TACTICAL STANDARD STOCK

Tactical 2.75" 12 gauge has 22" barrel threaded for Remchokes. Extended 8-round magazine.
NIB: $650   **Exc.:** $595   **VGood:** $460

REMINGTON MODEL 1100 G3

Introduced in 2006, this updated 1100 features a Realwood high gloss semi-fancy stock and forend. Available in 12 and 20 gauges with 26-inch or 28-inch barrel and chambered for 3-inch shells. Includes five Pro Bore chokes for 12 gauge and five Rem chokes for 20 gauge, R3 recoil pad and high-grade travel case.
NIB: $695   **Exc.:** $610   **VGood:** $500

Remington Model 1100 G3

Remington Model 1100 Competition

Remington Model 1100 Premier Sporting

Remington Model 105 CTI

Remington SP-10 Magnum

Remington Model SP10 Magnum Camo

Remington SP-10 Magnum Waterfowl

Remington SP-10 Magnum Thumbhole Camo

Remington Sportsman Auto

Remington Sportsman Model 48A

REMINGTON MODEL 1100 COMPETITION

This 12 gauge with 2.75-inch chamber is optimized for target shooting with a 30-inch overbored barrel and R3 recoil pad. Nickel-teflon receiver and semi-fancy walnut stock and forend. Includes five ProBore chokes. Weight is about 8 lbs. Add 10 percent for adjustable-comb model.

NIB: $915   **Exc.:** $865   **VGood:** $695

REMINGTON MODEL 1100 PREMIER SPORTING

Introduced in 2008 as a dedicated sporting clays gun, the Premier Sporting comes in 12, 20 and 28 gauge and .410 bore with 2.75" chamber (3" in .410). Polished nickel receiver with fine-line embellishments and gold accents. Stock and forend are semi-fancy American walnut with high-gloss finish. A full line of Briley choke tubes and Premier Sporting hard case

are included. Weights are about 8 lbs. in 12 gauge; 7 lbs. in 20 gauge; and 6.5 lbs. in 28 gauge and .410. Add 5 percent for 28 and .410.

BIN.: $1250   **Exc.:** $1050   **VGood:** $895

REMINGTON MODEL 105CTI

New in 2006, this ultralight gas-operated 12 gauge autoloader features advanced recoil reduction and bottom feed and ejection. Available with 26-inch or 28-inch barrel. Satin finish walnut stock. Chambered for 3-inch shells. Includes three Pro Bore chokes. Weighs about 7 lbs.

NIB: $825   **Exc.:** $750   **VGood:** N/A

REMINGTON SP-10 MAGNUM

Autoloader; 10-ga.; 3-1/2-inch chamber; 3-shot magazine; 26-inch, 30-1/2-inch barrel; Full, Modified Rem-Choke tubes; 47-1/2-inch overall length with shorter barrel; weighs about 11 lbs.; metal bead front sight; checkered satin-finished American

walnut stock; brown recoil pad; padded Cordura sling; stainless steel gas system that lessens recoil; matte-finished receiver, barrel. Introduced 1989; still in production.

Perf.: $995   **Exc.:** $875   **VGood:** $785

Turkey Camo (26-inch vent rib barrel, Rem-Choke tube, Mossy Oak Break-up)

Exc.: $1075   **VGood:** $885   **Good:** $785

REMINGTON SP-10 MAGNUM CAMO

Same specs as Model SP-10 Magnum except 23-inch vent-rib barrel; Extra-Full Turkey Rem-Choke tube; mid-rib bead, Bradley-style front sight; swivel studs; quick-detachable swivels; non-slip camo Cordura carrying sling; Mossy Oak Bottomland camo-finished buttstock, forend, receiver, barrel and magazine cap; matte black bolt body and trigger guard. Introduced 1993.

Perf.: $1000   **Exc.:** $900   **VGood:** $800

REMINGTON SP-10 MAGNUM TURKEY COMBO

Same specs as Model SP-10 except two-barrel set with 26-inch or 30-inch vent-rib barrel and extra 22-inch rifle-sighted barrel; Modified, Full, Extra-Full Turkey Rem-Choke tubes; camo sling; swivels. Introduced 1991; discontinued 1995.

Perf.: $1295   **Exc.:** $1125   **VGood:** $925

REMINGTON MODEL SP-10 MAGNUM WATERFOWL

New in 2007, this waterfowl-specific model is a synthetic-stock 3.5" 10 gauge with Mossy Oak Duck Blind camo finish and 26" barrel. Includes three Briley ported choke tubes. Weight is about 10.9 lbs

NIB: $1475   **Exc.:** $1325   **VGood:** $1095

REMINGTON MODEL SP-10 MAGNUM THUMBHOLE CAMO

Special turkey model features a synthetic thumbhole stock and complete Mossy Oak Obsession camo finish. Barrel is 23". Briley ported turkey choke included. Weight is 10.9 lbs.

NIB: $1675   **Exc.:** $1595   **VGood:** $1295

REMINGTON SPORTSMAN AUTO

Autoloader; 12-ga.; 2-3/4-inch chamber; 5-shot tube magazine; 28-inch, 30-inch vent-rib barrel; fixed or choke tubes; 7 3/4-inch lbs.; walnut-stained hardwood pistol-grip stock, forend; buttplate. Introduced 1985; discontinued 1986.

Perf.: $300   **Exc.:** $260   **VGood:** $220

REMINGTON SPORTSMAN MODEL 48A

Autoloader; hammerless; takedown; 12-, 16-, 20-ga.; 3-shot tube magazine; 26-inch Improved Cylinder, 28-inch Modified or Full, 30-inch Full-choke barrel; plain matted or vent-rib barrel available; hand-checkered American walnut pistol-grip stock, grooved forend; streamlined receiver. Introduced 1949; discontinued 1959. The last of Remington's recoil-operated autoloaders.

Plain barrel

Exc.: $210   **VGood:** $165   **Good:** $130

Vent-rib barrel

Exc.: $240   **VGood:** $195   **Good:** $160

Note: Values for the following higher grades of the Remington 48 fluctuate and may approach $10,000 for the 48F Premiere grade.

REMINGTON SPORTSMAN MODEL 48B SPECIAL

Same specs as Model 48A except high-quality wood, checkering; engraved receiver. Introduced 1949; discontinued 1959.

REMINGTON SPORTSMAN MODEL 48D TOURNAMENT

Same specs as 48A except improved wood; finer checkering; more engraving. Introduced 1949; discontinued 1959.

REMINGTON SPORTSMAN MODEL 48F PREMIER

Same specs as 48A except top-quality wood; fully engraved receiver. Introduced 1949; discontinued 1959.

REMINGTON SPORTSMAN MODEL 48SA SKEET

Autoloader; hammerless; takedown; 12-, 16-, 20-ga.; 3-shot magazine; 26-inch Skeet-choke barrel; plain matted surface or vent rib; ivory bead front sight, metal bead rear; checkered American walnut pistol-grip stock, forend. Introduced 1949; discontinued 1960.

Plain barrel
Exc.: $305   **VGood:** $275   **Good:** $255

Vent-rib barrel
Exc.: $395   **VGood:** $350   **Good:** $300

REMINGTON SPORTSMAN MODEL 48SC SKEET TARGET

Same specs as Model 48SA Skeet except higher grade of wood, checkering and engraving. Introduced 1949; discontinued 1960.

Exc.: $360   **VGood:** $330   **Good:** $290

REMINGTON MODEL 48SF SKEET PREMIER

Same specs as Model 48SA Skeet except best grade of wood, checkering and engraving. Introduced 1949; discontinued 1960.

Exc.: $2035   **VGood:** $1500   **Good:** $1200

REMINGTON SPORTSMAN MODEL 58ADL

Gas-operated autoloader; 12-ga.; 3-shot tube magazine; 26-inch, 28-inch, 30-inch barrels; plain or vent rib; Improved Cylinder, Modified, Full choke, Remington Skeet boring; checkered pistol-grip stock, forend. Introduced 1956; discontinued 1964.

Plain barrel
Exc.: $250   **VGood:** $220   **Good:** $190

Vent-rib barrel
Exc.: $300   **VGood:** $275   **Good:** $250

REMINGTON SPORTSMAN MODEL 58BDL DELUXE SPECIAL

Same specs as Sportsman Model 58ADL except higher grade of walnut wood. Introduced 1956; discontinued 1964.

Exc.: $260   **VGood:** $220   **Good:** $190

REMINGTON SPORTSMAN MODEL 58D TOURNAMENT

Same specs as Sportsman Model 58ADL except vent rib; select grade of wood, checkering and engraving. Introduced 1956; discontinued 1964.

Exc.: $700   **VGood:** $600   **Good:** $530

REMINGTON SPORTSMAN MODEL 58F PREMIER

Same specs as Sportsman Model 58ADL except vent rib; best grade of wood, checkering and engraving. Introduced 1956; discontinued 1964.

Exc.: $1375   **VGood:** $1210   **Good:** $1000

REMINGTON SPORTSMAN MODEL 58SA SKEET

Gas-operated autoloader; 12-ga.; 3-shot tube magazine; 26-inch vent-rib barrel; Skeet choke; special Skeet-style stock, forend. Introduced 1956; discontinued 1964.

Exc.: $330   **VGood:** $300   **Good:** $270

REMINGTON SPORTSMAN MODEL 58SC SKEET TARGET

Same specs as Sportsman Model 58SA Skeet except higher grade of wood, checkering and engraving. Introduced 1956; discontinued 1964.

Exc.: $400   **VGood:** $325   **Good:** $260

Remington Sportsman Model 58ADL

Remington Sportsman Model 58SA Skeet

Remington Model 10A

Remington Model 17A

Remington Model 31A

REMINGTON SPORTSMAN MODEL 58SD SKEET TOURNAMENT

Same specs as Model 58SA Skeet except select grade of wood, checkering and engraving. Introduced 1956; discontinued 1964.

Exc.: $605   **VGood:** $500   **Good:** $430

REMINGTON SPORTSMAN MODEL 58SF SKEET PREMIER

Same specs as Sportsman Model 58SA Skeet except best grade of wood, checkering and engraving. Introduced 1956; discontinued 1964.

Exc.: $1125   **VGood:** $1025   **Good:** $950

REMINGTON MODEL 10A

Slide action; hammerless; takedown; 12-ga.; 6-shot tube magazine; 26-inch, 28-inch, 30-inch, 32-inch barrel; Full, Modified, Cylinder choke; uncheckered pistol-grip stock, grooved slide handle. Introduced 1907; discontinued 1929.

Exc.: $270   **VGood:** $195   **Good:** $170

REMINGTON MODEL 17A

Slide action; hammerless; takedown; 26-inch, 28-inch, 30-inch, 32-inch barrel; plain barrel or solid rib; Modified, Full, Cylinder choke; uncheckered stock with pistol grip, grooved slide handle; Browning design. Introduced 1921; discontinued 1933.

Plain barrel
Exc.: $275   **VGood:** $220   **Good:** $195

Solid rib
Exc.: $375   **VGood:** $325   **Good:** $290

REMINGTON MODEL 29A

Slide action; hammerless; takedown; 12-ga.; 5-shot tubular magazine; 26-inch, 28-inch, 30-inch, 32-inch barrel; plain barrel, solid or vent rib; Full, Modified, Cylinder choke; hand-checkered pistol-grip stock, slide handle. Introduced 1929; discontinued 1933.

Plain barrel
Exc.: $250   **VGood:** $230   **Good:** $200

Solid rib
Exc.: $290   **VGood:** $265   **Good:** $230

Vent rib
Exc.: $310   **VGood:** $275   **Good:** $240

REMINGTON MODEL 29S TRAP SPECIAL

Same specs as Model 29A except ventilated rib; on trap-style straight-grip stock, longer slide handle. No longer in production.

Exc.: $450   **VGood:** $425   **Good:** $370

REMINGTON MODEL 31A

Slide action; hammerless; takedown 12-, 16-, 20-ga.; 3-, 5-shot magazine; 26-inch, 28-inch, 30-inch, 32-inch barrel; plain barrel, solid or vent rib; Full, Modified, Improved Cylinder, Skeet choke; early models had checkered pistol-grip stock, slide handle; later styles had plain stock, grooved slide handle. Introduced 1931; discontinued 1949.

Plain barrel
Exc.: $345   **VGood:** $300   **Good:** $265

Solid rib
Exc.: $385   **VGood:** $345   **Good:** $300

Vent rib
Exc.: $415   **VGood:** $375   **Good:** $325
Note: Values for the following higher grades of the Remington 31 fluctuate and may approach $10,000 for the 31F Premiere grade.

REMINGTON MODEL 31B SPECIAL

Same specs as Model 31A except higher grade of wood, checkering and engraving. Introduced 1931; discontinued 1949.

REMINGTON MODEL 31D TOURNAMENT

Same specs as Model 31A except select grade of wood, checkering and engraving. Introduced 1931; discontinued 1949.

REMINGTON MODEL 31E EXPERT

Same specs as Model 31A except fine grade of wood, checkering and engraving. Introduced 1931; discontinued 1949.

REMINGTON MODEL 31F PREMIER

Same specs as Model 31A except best grade of wood, checkering and engraving. Introduced 1931; discontinued 1949.

Remington Model 31S
Trap Special

Remington Model 870
Competition Trap

Remington Model 870
Express

Remington Model 870 SPS
Super Slug Deer Gun

Remington Model 870 Express Youth

REMINGTON MODEL 31H HUNTER'S SPECIAL
Same specs as Model 31A except 12-ga.; 30-inch, 32-inch solid-rib barrel; Full choke; sporting uncheckered walnut pistol-grip stock, forend. Introduced 1931; discontinued 1949.

Exc.: $350   **VGood:** $300   **Good:** $250

REMINGTON MODEL 31R RIOT GUN
Same specs as Model 31A except 12-ga.; 20-inch barrel. Introduced 1931; discontinued 1949.

Exc.: $365   **VGood:** $325   **Good:** $295

REMINGTON MODEL 31S TRAP SPECIAL
Same specs as Model 31A except 12-ga.; 30-inch, 32-inch solid-rib barrel; Full choke; trap-style uncheckered walnut half-pistol-grip stock, forend. Introduced 1931; discontinued 1949.

Exc.: $500   **VGood:** $450   **Good:** $400

REMINGTON MODEL 31 SKEET
Same specs as Model 31A except 26-inch barrel; solid or vent rib; Skeet choke; beavertail forend. Introduced 1931; discontinued 1949.

Solid rib		
Exc.: $450	**VGood:** $395	**Good:** $365
Vent rib		
Exc.: $550	**VGood:** $495	**Good:** $425

REMINGTON MODEL 31TC TRAP
Same as Model 31A except 12-ga.; 30-inch, 32-inch vent-rib barrel; Full choke; trap-style checkered walnut pistol-grip stock, beavertail forend; recoil pad. Introduced 1931; discontinued 1948.

Exc.: $750   **VGood:** $600   **Good:** $520

REMINGTON MODEL 870ADL WINGMASTER
Slide action; hammerless; takedown; 12-, 16-, 20-ga.; 5-shot tube magazine; 3-shot plug furnished with gun; 26-inch Improved Cylinder, 28-inch Modified or Full, 30-inch Full barrel; choice of plain, matted top surface or vent rib; fine-checkered pistol-grip stock, beavertail forend. Introduced 1950; discontinued 1963.

Plain barrel		
Exc.: $220	**VGood:** $200	**Good:** $180
Vent rib		
Exc.: $275	**VGood:** $250	**Good:** $225

REMINGTON MODEL 870 ALL-AMERICAN TRAP
Slide action; hammerless; takedown; 12-ga.; 5-shot tube magazine; 30-inch Full-choke barrel; fancy American walnut straight-comb or Monte Carlo stock, forend; custom-grade engraved receiver, trigger guard, barrel. Introduced 1972; discontinued 1976.

Exc.: $600   **VGood:** $500   **Good:** $425

REMINGTON MODEL 870AP WINGMASTER
Slide action; hammerless; takedown; 12-, 16-, 20-ga.; 5-shot tube magazine; 3-shot plug furnished with gun; 26-inch Improved Cylinder, 28-inch Modified or Full, 30-inch Full barrel; choice of plain, matted top surface or vent rib; walnut stock, grooved slide handle. Introduced 1950; discontinued 1963.

Plain barrel		
Exc.: $190	**VGood:** $170	**Good:** $150
Vent rib		
Exc.: $220	**VGood:** $200	**Good:** $190

REMINGTON MODEL 870AP WINGMASTER MAGNUM
Same specs as Model 870AP Wingmaster except 12-ga.; 3-inch chamber; 30-inch Full-choke barrel; recoil pad. Introduced 1955; discontinued 1963.

Plain barrel		
Exc.: $170	**VGood:** $140	**Good:** $110
Vent rib		
Exc.: $200	**VGood:** $170	**Good:** $140

REMINGTON MODEL 870AP WINGMASTER MAGNUM DELUXE
Same specs as Model 870AP Wingmaster except 12-ga.; 3-inch chamber; 30-inch Full-choke barrel; checkered stock, extension beavertail slide handle; matte top surface barrel.

Exc.: $180   **VGood:** $150   **Good:** $120

REMINGTON MODEL 870BDL WINGMASTER
Same specs as Model 870AP Wingmaster except select American walnut pistol-grip stock, forend. Introduced 1950; discontinued 1963.

Plain barrel		
Exc.: $190	**VGood:** $155	**Good:** $125
Vent rib		
Exc.: $240	**VGood:** $190	**Good:** $165

REMINGTON MODEL 870 BRUSHMASTER DELUXE
Same specs as Model 870AP Wingmaster except 12-, 20-ga.; 2-3/4-inch, 3-inch chamber; 20-inch barrel; Improved Cylinder or choke tube; adjustable rear sight, ramp front; satin-finished checkered wood stock, forearm; recoil pad; right- or left-hand model. Discontinued 1994.

Right-hand model		
Perf.: $340	**Exc.:** $240	**VGood:** $190
Left-hand model		
Perf.: $380	**Exc.:** $270	**VGood:** $220

REMINGTON MODEL 870 COMPETITION TRAP
Same specs as Model 870AP Wingmaster except single shot; 12-ga.; 30-inch vent-rib barrel; Full choke; select walnut Trap-style stock, forend; gas reduction system to lessen recoil. Introduced 1980; discontinued 1986.

Perf.: $480   **Exc.:** $390   **VGood:** $300

REMINGTON MODEL 870 EXPRESS
Slide action; hammerless; takedown; 12-, 20-, 28-ga., .410; 5-shot tube magazine; 3-shot plug furnished with gun; 20-inch, 25-inch, 26-inch, 28-inch vent. rib barrel; Modified Rem-Choke tube; press-checkered, walnut-finished hardwood stock, forearm; solid black recoil pad; Parkerized metal surfaces. Introduced 1987.

12-ga., 20-ga.		
Perf.: $265	**Exc.:** $215	**VGood:** $180
Express Combo, 12-ga., 26-inch vent rib with mod. Rem-Choke and 20-inch fully rifled barrel with rifle sights, or Rem. Choke		
Perf.: $412	**Exc.:** $362	**VGood:** $327
Express L-H (left-hand), 12-ga., 28-inch vent rib with Mod. Rem-Choke tube		
Perf.: $562	**Exc.:** $472	**VGood:** $412
Synthetic, 12-ga, 26-inch or 28-inch		
Perf.: $265	**Exc.:** $215	**VGood:** $180
Express Combo (20-ga.) with extra Deer rifled barrel, fully rifled or Rem. Choke		
Perf.: $412	**Exc.:** $362	**VGood:** $327

REMINGTON MODEL 870 EXPRESS SYNTHETIC 18-INCH
Similar to 870 Express with 18-inch barrel except synthetic stock and forend. Introduced 1994.

Perf.: $250   **Exc.:** $205   **VGood:** $170

REMINGTON MODEL 870 SPS SUPER SLUG DEER GUN
Similar to the Model 870 Express Synthetic except has 23-inch fully rifled, modified contour barrel with cantilever scope mount. Comes with black synthetic stock and forend with swivel studs, black Cordura nylon sling. Introduced 1999.

Perf.: $470   **Exc.:** $375   **VGood:** $310

REMINGTON MODEL 870 EXPRESS YOUTH GUN
Same as Model 870 Express except 13-inch length of pull, 20-gauge, 23-inch barrel with Mod. Rem-Choke tube. Weighs 6.25 lbs. Hardwood stock with low-luster finish. Introduced 1991.

Youth (1-inch shorter stock)		
Perf.: $265	**Exc.:** $215	**VGood:** $180
Youth Deer 20-inch FR/RS		
Perf.: $298	**Exc.:** $248	**VGood:** $213

REMINGTON MODEL 870 EXPRESS RIFLE-SIGHTED DEER GUN

Same as Model 870 Express except 20-inch barrel with fixed Imp. Cyl. choke, open iron sights, Monte Carlo stock. Introduced 1991.

Perf.: $265   **Exc.:** $215   **VGood:** $180

W/fully rifled barrel

Perf.: $298   **Exc.:** $248   **VGood:** $213

Synthetic Deer (black synthetic stock, black matte metal)

Perf.: $295   **Exc.:** $225   **VGood:** $185

REMINGTON MODEL 870 EXPRESS DEER CANTILEVER

Same specs as Model 870 Express except 12-ga.; 20-inch smooth bore or rifled barrel; fixed Improved Cylinder Rem-Chokes for slugs or buckshot; barrel-mounted cantilever scope mount; scope rings; Monte Carlo stock; sling; swivels; Introduced 1991; discontinued 1992.

Smooth bore barrel

Perf.: $300   **Exc.:** $235   **VGood:** $200

Rifled barrel

Perf.: $330   **Exc.:** $265   **VGood:** $230

REMINGTON MODEL 870 EXPRESS HD

Same specs as Model 870 Express except 12-ga.; 18-inch Cylinder barrel; bead front sight; positive-checkered synthetic stock, forend with non-reflective black finish. Introduced 1995; still in production.

Perf.: $250   **Exc.:** $180   **VGood:** $160

REMINGTON MODEL 870 EXPRESS SYNTHETIC

Same specs as Model 870 Express except 12-, 20-ga.; 26-inch, 28-inch barrel; synthetic stock, forend. Made in U.S. by Remington. Introduced 1994; still in production.

Perf.: $265   **Exc.:** $215   **VGood:** $180

REMINGTON MODEL 870 EXPRESS TURKEY

Same specs as Model 870 Express except 12-ga.; 3-chamber; 21-inch vent-rib barrel; Extra-Full Rem-Choke turkey tube. Introduced 1991; still in production.

Perf.: $275   **Exc.:** $215   **VGood:** $185

REMINGTON MODEL 870 EXPRESS YOUTH

Same specs as Model 870 Express except 20-ga.; 21-inch vent-rib barrel; Modified Rem-Choke; low-luster hardwood stock; 12-inch length of pull. Introduced 1991; still in production.

Perf.: $265   **Exc.:** $215   **VGood:** $180

REMINGTON MODEL 870 EXPRESS TURKEY

Same as Model 870 Express except 3-inch chamber, 21-inch vent rib turkey barrel and Extra-Full Rem. choke turkey tube; 12-ga. only. Introduced 1991.

Perf.: $270   **Exc.:** $215   **VGood:** $185

Camo stock w/RealTree Advantage camo, matte black metal

Perf.: $324   **Exc.:** $269   **VGood:** $239

Youth Turkey camo (as above with 1-inch shorter length of pull)

Perf.: $332   **Exc.:** $282   **VGood:** $247

REMINGTON MODEL 870 EXPRESS SUPER MAGNUM

Introduced in 1998, this 870 is similar to the 870 Express but is chambered for 3.5" 12 gauge. Offered in walnut stock with blued 28" barrel, matte black synthetic with 26" or 28" barrel or various camo finishes. Also available as a combo with extra 20" rifled deer barrel. Add $100 for camo. Add 20 percent for combo with deer barrel.

Perf.: $295   **Exc.:** $230   **VGood:** $190

Price: Super Magnum Synthetic

Perf.: $308   **Exc.:** $243   **VGood:** $203

Remington Model 870 Express Deer

Remington Model 870 Express HD

Remington Model 870 Express Turkey

Remington Model 870 Express Super Magnum

Remington Model 870 Express Deer/Turkey Combo

Remington Model 870 50th Anniversary Classic Trap Shotgun

Turkey Camo (Turkey Extra Full Rem-Choke, full-coverage RealTree Advantage camo)

Perf.: $395   **Exc.:** $315   **VGood:** $250

Combo (26-inch with Mod. Rem-Choke and 20-inch fully rifled deer barrel with 3-inch chamber and rifle sights; wood stock)

Perf.: $442   **Exc.:** $377   **VGood:** $337

Synthetic Turkey (black)

Perf.: $308   **Exc.:** $243   **VGood:** $203

REMINGTON MODEL 870 EXPRESS DEER/TURKEY COMBO

This 3" 12 gauge has a 21-inch barrel threaded for Remchokes for turkey hunting and a 23" rifled slug barrel with cantilever scope mount for deer hunting. Receiver and barrel are matte black; synthetic stock is Mossy Oak Break-Up camo.

NIB: $545   **Exc.:** $485   **VGood:** $375

REMINGTON MODEL 870 WINGMASTER

Gauge: 12-, 16-ga., 3-inch chamber; 26-inch, 28-inch, 30-inch barrel (Rem-Chokes); weighs 7-1/4 lbs.; 46-inch, 48-inch overall; walnut, hardwood, synthetic; single bead sight (Twin bead Wingmaster); ballistically balanced performance, milder recoil; light contour barrel; double action bars; cross-bolt safety; blue finish.

Walnut; blued; 26-inch, 28-inch

Exc.: $275   **VGood:** $250   **Good:** $220

Super Magnum, 3-1/2-inch chamber

Exc.: $295   **VGood:** $230   **Good:** $190

Express, 28-inch, vent rib

Exc.: $250   **VGood:** $220   **Good:** $200

Synthetic

Exc.: $265   **VGood:** $215   **Good:** $180

REMINGTON MODEL 870 50TH ANNIVERSARY CLASSIC TRAP SHOTGUN

Similar to Model 870 Wingmaster except has 30-inch ventilated rib, light contour barrel, singles, mid and long handicap choke tubes, semi-fancy American walnut stock, high-polish blued receiver with engraving.

Perf.: $695   **Exc.:** $565   **VGood:** $470

REMINGTON MODEL 870 MARINE MAGNUM

Similar to Model 870 Wingmaster except all metal plated with electroless nickel, black synthetic stock and forend. Has 18-inch plain barrel (Cyl.), bead front sight, 7-shot magazine. Introduced 1992.

Perf.: $430   **Exc.:** $355   **VGood:** $275

REMINGTON MODEL 870 WINGMASTER LW SMALL BORE

Similar to Model 870 Wingmaster except in 28-gauge and .410-bore only, 25-inch vent rib barrel with Rem-Choke tubes, high-gloss wood finish. 26-inch & 28-inch barrels/20-ga.

20-gauge

Perf.: $535   **Exc.:** $445   **VGood:** $385

Remington Model 870 Special Purpose Synthetic Camo

Remington Model 870 Lightweight

Remington Model 870 Police

Remington Model 870SA Skeet

Remington Model 870 Special Field

Remington Model 870 Special Purpose Deer Gun

.410-bore
Perf.: $535   **Exc.:** $445   **VGood:** $385
28-gauge
Perf.: $588   **Exc.:** $498   **VGood:** $438

REMINGTON MODEL 870 WINGMASTER SUPER MAGNUM SHOTGUN
Similar to Model 870 Express Super Magnum except high-polish blued finish, 28-inch vent-rib barrel with Imp. Cyl., Modified and Full choke tubes, 3-1/2-inch chamber, checkered high-gloss walnut stock. Overall length 48-inch, weighs 7 1/2 lbs. Introduced 2000.
Perf.: $560   **Exc.:** $475   **VGood:** $395

REMINGTON MODEL 870 SPS-T SYNTHETIC CAMO SHOTGUN
Chambered for 12-ga., 3-inch shells, has Mossy Oak Break-Up synthetic stock and metal treatment, TruGlo fiber optic sights. Introduced 2001.

20-inch RS, Rem. Choke
Perf.: $445   **Exc.:** $350   **VGood:** $280

REMINGTON MODEL 870 SPS SUPER MAGNUM CAMO
Has synthetic stock and all metal (except bolt and trigger guard) and stock covered with Mossy Oak Break-Up camo finish. In 12 gauge 3-1/2-inch, 26-inch, 28-inch vent rib, Rem-Choke. Comes with camo sling, swivels.
Perf.: $385   **Exc.:** $320   **VGood:** $265

REMINGTON MODEL 870 FIELD WINGMASTER
Slide action; hammerless; takedown; 12-, 16-, 20-, 28-ga., .410; 5-shot tube magazine; 25-inch Full or Modified, 26-inch Improved Cylinder, 28-inch Modified or Full, 30-inch Full barrel; fixed or Rem-Choke tubes; choice of plain, matted top surface or vent rib;

checkered walnut stock, slide handle with high-gloss or satin finish. Introduced 1965; still in production.

Plain barrel
Perf.: $300   **Exc.:** $200   **VGood:** $140
Vent rib
Perf.: $425   **Exc.:** $350   **VGood:** $295

REMINGTON MODEL 870 LIGHTWEIGHT
Slide action; hammerless; takedown; 20-ga.; 5-shot magazine; 23-inch barrel; plain or vent rib; 5 lbs.; lightweight mahogany stock, forearm. Introduced 1972; discontinued 1983.

Plain barrel
Perf.: $265   **Exc.:** $200   **VGood:** $175
Vent rib
Perf.: $300   **Exc.:** $235   **VGood:** $210

REMINGTON MODEL 870 LIGHTWEIGHT MAGNUM
Same specs as Model 870 Lightweight except 3-inch chamber; 26-inch, 28-inch barrel; fixed or choke tubes; plain or vent rib; 6 lbs.; lightweight mahogany stock, forearm. Introduced 1972; discontinued 1994.

Plain barrel
Perf.: $300   **Exc.:** $210   **VGood:** $175
Vent rib
Perf.: $350   **Exc.:** $250   **VGood:** $200

REMINGTON MODEL 870 MAGNUM DUCK GUN
Slide action; hammerless; takedown; 12-, 20-ga.; 3-inch chamber; 26-inch, 28-inch, 30-inch vent-rib barrel; Full or Modified choke; checkered walnut stock, slide handle; recoil pad. Introduced 1964; still in production.
Perf.: $385   **Exc.:** $265   **VGood:** $210

REMINGTON MODEL 870 MARINE MAGNUM
Slide action; hammerless; takedown; 12-ga.; 3-inch chamber; 7-shot magazine; 18-inch plain barrel; Cylinder choke; bead front sight; black synthetic stock, forend; electroless nickel-plated metal surfaces. Introduced 1992; still in production.
Perf.: $400   **Exc.:** $280   **VGood:** $210

REMINGTON MODEL 870 POLICE
Slide action; hammerless; takedown; 12-ga.; 3-inch chamber; 18-inch, 20-inch Police Cylinder or 20-inch Improved Cylinder; weighs 7 lbs.; metal bead front or rifle sights; lacquered hardwood stock; steel receiver; double slide bars; blued or Parkerized finish. Introduced 1994; still in production.
Perf.: $350   **Exc.:** $295   **VGood:** $230

REMINGTON MODEL 870SA SKEET
Slide action; hammerless; takedown; 12-, 20-, 28-ga., .410; 5-shot tube magazine; 26-inch vent-rib barrel; Skeet choke; ivory bead front sight, metal bead in rear; checkered pistol-grip stock, extension beavertail slide handle. Introduced 1950; discontinued 1982.
Perf.: $300   **Exc.:** $250   **VGood:** $200

REMINGTON MODEL 870SC SKEET TARGET
Same specs as Model 870SA Skeet except higher grade of wood, checkering and engraving. Introduced 1950; discontinued 1982.
Perf.: $350   **Exc.:** $300   **VGood:** $250

REMINGTON MODEL 870SD SKEET TOURNAMENT
Same specs as Model 870SA Skeet except select grade of wood, checkering and engraving. Introduced 1950; discontinued 1982.
Perf.: $450   **Exc.:** $375   **VGood:** $275

REMINGTON MODEL 870SF SKEET PREMIER
Same specs as Model 870SA Skeet except best grade of wood, checkering and engraving. Introduced 1950; discontinued 1982.
Perf.: $500   **Exc.:** $450   **VGood:** $300

REMINGTON MODEL 870 SPECIAL FIELD
Slide action; hammerless; takedown; 12-, 20-ga.; 3-inch chamber; 5-shot tube magazine; 21-inch, 23-inch vent-rib barrel; fixed or choke tubes; checkered straight-grip stock, short forend. Introduced 1984.
Perf.: $500   **Exc.:** $465   **VGood:** $410

REMINGTON MODEL 870 SPECIAL PURPOSE
Slide action; hammerless; takedown; 12-ga.; 3-inch chamber; 26-inch, 28-inch vent-rib barrel; Rem-Choke tubes; oil-finished wood or black synthetic stock, forend; quick detachable sling swivels; padded sling; black metal finish; chrome-lined bore. Introduced 1985.

Synthetic stock
Perf.: $325   **Exc.:** $250   **VGood:** $200
Wood stock
Perf.: $385   **Exc.:** $310   **VGood:** $260

REMINGTON MODEL 870 SPECIAL PURPOSE DEER GUN
Same specs as Model 870 Special Purpose except 20-inch barrel; rifled and Improved Cylinder choke tubes; rifle sights or cantilever scope mount with rings; walnut Monte Carlo stock with satin finish; recoil pad; detachable camo Cordura nylon sling; black, non-glare metal finish. Introduced 1989.

With rifle sights
Perf.: $350   **Exc.:** $250   **VGood:** $200
With scope mount and rings
Perf.: $400   **Exc.:** $300   **VGood:** $250

REMINGTON MODEL 870 SPECIAL PURPOSE SYNTHETIC CAMO

Same specs as Model 870 Special Purpose except 26-inch vent-rib barrel; Rem-Choke tubes; synthetic stock; all surfaces (except bolt and trigger guard) Mossy Oak Bottomland camo-finished; camo sling; swivels. Introduced 1992.

Perf.: $380 **Exc.:** $260 **VGood:** $205

REMINGTON MODEL 870 SPS-BG-CAMO DEER/TURKEY

Same specs as Model 870 Special Purpose except 20-inch barrel; Improved Cylinder, Super-Full Turkey (.665-inch diameter with knurled extension) Rem-Choke tubes and rifled choke tube insert; rifle sights, synthetic stock, forend; quick-detachable swivels; camo Cordura carrying sling; all surfaces Mossy Oak Bottomland camouflage-finished. Introduced 1993; discontinued 1995.

Perf.: $340 **Exc.:** $240 **VGood:** $200

REMINGTON MODEL 870 SPS CANTILEVER

Same specs as Model 870 Special Purpose except 20-inch smooth bore barrel; optional rifled barrel; Improved Cylinder and 3-1/2-inch rifled Rem-Choke tubes; cantilever scope mount; synthetic Monte Carlo stock; sling; swivels. Introduced 1994.

Perf.: $350 **Exc.:** $250 **VGood:** $200

With fully rifled barrel

Perf.: $400 **Exc.:** $300 **VGood:** $250

REMINGTON MODEL 870 SPS DEER

Same specs as Model 870 Special Purpose except fully-rifled 20-inch barrel; rifle sights; black non-reflective synthetic stock, forend; black carrying sling. Introduced 1993.

Perf.: $340 **Exc.:** $240 **VGood:** $190

REMINGTON MODEL 870 SPS SPECIAL PURPOSE MAGNUM

Same specs as Model 870 Special Purpose except 26-inch, 28-inch barrel; Rem-Choke tubes; black synthetic stock, forend; dark recoil pad; padded Cordura 2-inch wide sling; quick-detachable swivels; dull, non-reflective black metal finish. Introduced 1985; still in production as SPS-T Special Purpose Magnum.

Perf.: $310 **Exc.:** $230 **VGood:** $190

REMINGTON MODEL 870 SPS-T CAMO

Same specs as Model 870 Special Purpose except 21-inch vent-rib barrel; Improved Cylinder and Super-Full Turkey (.665-inch diameter with knurled extension) Rem-Choke tubes; synthetic stock; Mossy Oak Green Leaf camouflage-finished; non-reflective black bolt body, trigger guard and recoil pad. Introduced 1993; still in production.

Perf.: $390 **Exc.:** $270 **VGood:** $215

REMINGTON MODEL 870TA TRAP

Slide action; hammerless; takedown; 12-ga. 5-shot tube magazine; 30-inch Modified, Full barrel; ivory front bead, white metal middle; deluxe checkered walnut trap-style stock, forend; hand-fitted action, parts; recoil pad; special hammer, sear, trigger assembly. Discontinued 1986.

Perf.: $350 **Exc.:** $260 **VGood:** $210

REMINGTON MODEL 870TB TRAP

Same specs as Model 870TA Trap except 28-inch, 30-inch vent-rib barrel; Full choke; metal bead front; no rear sight. Introduced 1950; discontinued 1981.

Perf.: $425 **Exc.:** $300 **VGood:** $225

REMINGTON MODEL 870TC TRAP

Same specs as Model 870TA Trap except 30-inch vent-rib barrel; Rem-Choke; vent rib; optional Monte Carlo stock.

Perf.: $550 **Exc.:** $355 **VGood:** $295

With Monte Carlo stock

Perf.: $570 **Exc.:** $375 **VGood:** $310

Remington Model 870 SPS-T Camo

Remington Model 870TB Trap

Remington Model 870TC Trap

Remington Model 870 XCS Marine Magnum

Remington Model 870 SPS Max Gobbler

Remington Model 870 Tac-2 SpecOps

Remington Model 870 Tac-3 Folding Stock

REMINGTON MODEL 870 XCS MARINE MAGNUM

New in 2007, this weather-resistant 870 is a 3" 12 gauge with full black TriNyte coverage, 18" fixed Cylinder barrel and 7 round capacity. Weight is 7.5 lbs.

NIB: $750 **Exc.:** $695 **VGood:** $575

REMINGTON MODEL 870 SPS MAX GOBBLER

This dedicated turkey gun is a 3.5" 12 gauge featuring a length-adjustable Knoxx SpecOps stock, 23" barrel, fiber-optic rifle sights, Super Full turkey choke tube and full coverage in Realtree APG camo. Drilled and tapped for Weaver style mount. Weight is 8 lbs.

NIB: $700 **Exc.:** $635 **VGood:** $525

REMINGTON MODEL 870 TAC-2 SPECOPS STOCK

Tactical 3" 12 gauge is available with a Knoxx pistol-grip or folding stock. Barrel is 18" with fixed Cylinder choke. Magazine capacity is 6 shells. Weight is 7 lbs.

NIB: $575 **Exc.:** $525 **VGood:** $425

REMINGTON MODEL 870 TAC-3 SPEEDFEED IV

Tactical 3" 12 gauge with pistol-grip stock and 20" barrel. Extended 7-round magazine. Weight is 7.5 lbs.

NIB: $535 **Exc.:** $485 **VGood:** $395

REMINGTON MODEL 870 TAC-3 FOLDER

As above but with Knoxx Spec-Ops folding stock. Weight is 7 lbs.

NIB: $595 **Exc.:** $545 **VGood:** $475

REMINGTON MODEL 870 SP-T THUMBHOLE

Introduced in 2005, this 3.5-inch 12 gauge is designed specifically for turkey hunting with full coverage in Mossy Oak Obsession camo and thumbhole stock. The 23-inch barrel features fiber-optic adjustable rifle sights and is drilled and tapped for scope mounting. Includes R3 recoil pad, sling, swivels and turkey super full choke tube.

NIB: $435 **Exc.:** $395 **VGood:** $300

REMINGTON MODEL 870 SPS-T SUPER MAG

Similar to Model 870 SP-T Thumbhole but with pistol-grip stock and vent-rib barrel.

NIB: $435 **Exc.:** $395 **VGood:** $300

REMINGTON MODEL 870 SPS-T/20

This 20-gauge turkey gun features a 3-inch chamber, 23-inch vent rib barrel, R3 recoil pad and full coverage in Mossy Oak New Break-Up camo. Drilled and tapped for scope mount.

NIB: $350 **Exc.:** $315 **VGood:** $265

REMINGTON MODEL 870 WINGMASTER NRA EDITION

Special edition with NRA logo on receiver. Available in 12 gauge with 3-inch chamber, 12 gauge Super Mag with 3.5-inch chamber, and 16, 20 and 28 gauges and .410 bore.

NIB: $500 **Exc.:** $375 **VGood:** $295

REMINGTON MODEL 870 SPECIAL PURPOSE THUMBHOLE

Laminated stock 12 gauge slug gun with 3-inch chamber and 23-inch fully rifled cantilever barrel.

NIB: $445 **Exc.:** $395 **VGood:** $315

Remington Model 870 SPS-T Super Mag

Remington Model 870 Special Purpose Thumbhole

Remington Model 870 Wingmaster 100th Anniversary

Remington Model 870 Express Magnum ShurShot Turkey

Remington Model 870 Express Magnum ShurShot Cantilever

Remington Model 870 Express Super Magnum Waterfowl

Remington Model 870 SPS ShurShot Turke

Remington Model 870 Tactical Desert Recon

Remington 90-T Super Single

Remington Model 32A

Realtree's APG HD camo. It has a 23-inch non-vent-rib barrel outfitted with fiber-optic rifle-type sights and includes an extended Turkey Rem Choke. Weight is about 7.5 lbs.

NIB: $650   **Exc.:** $525   **VGood:** $315

REMINGTON MODEL 870 TACTICAL DESERT RECON

This tactical version 870 features Digital Tiger desert camo on the synthetic stock and forend and an olive-drab powder-coated barrel and receiver. It is available with an 18" (six round mag. capacity) or 20" (seven round mag. capacity) barrel. Speedfeed I (shell holding) or Speedfeed IV (pistol grip) stock. Add 10 percent for Speedfeed IV stock.

NIB: $650   **Exc.:** $525   **VGood:** $315

REMINGTON SPORTSMAN

Slide action; 12-, 16-, 20-ga; 5-shot tube magazine; 20-inch, 26-inch barrel; various choke options; walnut pistol-grip stock, forearm; made in Field, Riot and Skeet models. Introduced 1931; discontinued 1948.

Plain barrel		
Exc.: $295	**VGood:** $180	**Good:** $140
Solid rib		
Exc.: $310	**VGood:** $225	**Good:** $170
Vent rib		
Exc.: $375	**VGood:** $290	**Good:** $235

REMINGTON SPORTSMAN PUMP

Slide action; 12-ga.; 3-inch chamber; 28-inch, 30-inch vent-rib barrel; 7 1/2 lbs.; checkered walnut-stained hardwood stock, forend; recoil pad; similar to Model 870. Introduced 1984; discontinued 1986.

Perf.: $285   **Exc.:** $195   **VGood:** $150

REMINGTON 90-T SUPER SINGLE

Single shot; 12-ga.; 2-3/4-inch chamber; 30-inch, 32-inch, 34-inch barrel; fixed choke or Rem-Chokes; ported or non-ported barrel; weighs 8-3/4 lb.; figured, checkered American walnut stock; cavities in forend, buttstock for added weights; black vented rubber recoil pad; elongated forcing cones; drop-out trigger unit. Introduced 1990; discontinued 1998.

Perf.: $2000   **Exc.:** $1800   **VGood:** $1600

With adjustable rib		
Perf.: $2300	**Exc.:** $2100	**VGood:** $1850

REMINGTON RIDER NO. 3

Single shot; break-open; hammerless; 10-, 12-, 16-, 20-, 24-, 28-ga.; 30-inch, 32-inch barrel; uncheckered American walnut pistol-grip stock, forearm. Introduced 1893; discontinued 1903.

Exc.: $425   **VGood:** $360   **Good:** $220

REMINGTON RIDER NO. 9

Single shot; break-open; hammerless; 10-, 12-, 16-, 20-, 24-, 28-ga.; 30-inch, 32-inch barrel; uncheckered American walnut pistol-grip stock, forearm; automatic ejector. Introduced 1902; discontinued 1910.

Exc.: $325   **VGood:** $295   **Good:** $260

REMINGTON MODEL 32A

Over/under; double lock; hammerless; takedown; 12-ga.; 26-inch, 28-inch, 30-inch barrels; various fixed chokes; plain barrels, solid or vent rib; walnut checkered pistol-grip stock, forend; double or single trigger; auto ejectors. Introduced 1931; discontinued 1947.

Single trigger, plain barrels		
Exc.: $1500	**VGood:** $1100	**Good:** $900
Single trigger, solid or vent rib		
Exc.: $1600	**VGood:** $1200	**Good:** $1000
Double triggers, plain barrels		
Exc.: $1450	**VGood:** $1050	**Good:** $800
Double triggers, solid or vent rib		
Exc.: $1500	**VGood:** $1100	**Good:** $900

REMINGTON MODEL 870 WINGMASTER 100TH ANNIVERSARY

This Commemorative Edition 12 gauge celebrating 100 years of Remington pump shotguns (dating from the introduction of the Model 10 in 1908) was introduced in 2008 and offered only for one year. Gold-inlaid logos on both sides of receiver and "B" Grade American Walnut stock with high-gloss finish. Includes three choke tubes. MSRP: $1035.

NIB: $875   **Exc.:** $700   **VGood:** $550

REMINGTON MODEL 870 EXPRESS MAGNUM SHURSHOT TURKEY

This turkey-dedicated model has a matte black finish with a ShurShot pistol grip/thumbhole stock and forend finished in Mossy Oak Obsession camo. The 3-inch 12 gauge has a 21-inch barrel. Includes a Turkey Extra Full choke tube. Weight is about 7.5 lbs.

NIB: $500   **Exc.:** $375   **VGood:** $295

REMINGTON MODEL 870 EXPRESS MAGNUM SHURSHOT CANTILEVER

This 3 inch 12 gauge has a 23", fully rifled barrel with cantilever scope mount. Matte black finish. Weight is about 7.75 lbs.

NIB: $550   **Exc.:** $425   **VGood:** $315

REMINGTON MODEL 870 EXPRESS SUPER MAGNUM WATERFOWL

Introduced in 2008, his dedicated waterfowl gun is completely finished in Mossy Oak Duck Blind camo. The 3.5" 12 gauge has a 28" barrel, HiViz single bead sight and weighs about 7.5 lbs. Includes one choke tube.

NIB: $575   **Exc.:** $475   **VGood:** $250

REMINGTON MODEL 870 SPS SHURSHOT TURKEY

New in 2008, this 12 gauge 870 is chambered for shells up to 3.5". It features Remington's ShurShot pistol grip/thumbhole stock and is fully covered in

REMINGTON MODEL 32D TOURNAMENT

Same specs as Model 32A except higher grade of wood, checkering and engraving. Introduced 1931; discontinued 1947.

Single trigger, plain barrels
Exc.: $2700 **VGood:** $2350 **Good:** $1400
Single trigger, solid or vent rib
Exc.: $3000 **VGood:** $2475 **Good:** $1700
Double triggers, plain barrels
Exc.: $2500 **VGood:** $2000 **Good:** $1200
Double triggers, solid or vent rib
Exc.: $2700 **VGood:** $2200 **Good:** $1400

REMINGTON MODEL 32 EXPERT

Same specs as Model 32A except select grade of wood, checkering and engraving. Introduced 1931; discontinued 1947.

Single trigger, plain barrels
Exc.: $4300 **VGood:** $3200 **Good:** $2600
Single trigger, solid or vent rib
Exc.: $4700 **VGood:** $3600 **Good:** $3000
Double triggers, plain barrels
Exc.: $3900 **VGood:** $2800 **Good:** $2200
Double triggers, solid or vent rib
Exc.: $4300 **VGood:** $3200 **Good:** $2600

REMINGTON MODEL 32F PREMIER

Same specs as Model 32A except best grade of wood, checkering and engraving. Introduced 1931; discontinued 1947.

Single trigger, plain barrels
Exc.: $5300 **VGood:** $3900 **Good:** $3000
Single trigger, solid or vent rib
Exc.: $5800 **VGood:** $4400 **Good:** $3500
Double triggers, plain barrels
Exc.: $4800 **VGood:** $3400 **Good:** $2500
Double triggers, solid or vent rib
Exc.: $5300 **VGood:** $3900 **Good:** $3000

REMINGTON MODEL 32 SKEET GRADE

Same specs as Model 32A except 26-inch, 28-inch barrels; Skeet boring; single selective trigger, beavertail forend. Introduced 1932; discontinued 1942.

Plain barrels
Exc.: $1400 **VGood:** $1000 **Good:** $750
Solid or vent rib
Exc.: $1500 **VGood:** $1100 **Good:** $850

REMINGTON MODEL 32TC TRAP

Same specs as Model 32A except 30-inch, 32-inch vent-rib barrel; Full choke; checkered trap-style pistol-grip stock, beavertail forend.

Double triggers
Exc.: $2200 **VGood:** $1500 **Good:** $1100
Single trigger
Exc.: $2400 **VGood:** $1700 **Good:** $1200

REMINGTON MODEL 332 O/U SHOTGUN

Gauge: 12, 3-inch chambers; 26-inch, 28-inch, 30-inch barrel; weighs 7-3/4 lbs.; 42 inches to 47 inches overall; satin-finished American walnut; twin bead sights; light-contour, vent rib; Rem chock barrel; blued; traditional M-32 experience with M-300 Ideal performance; standard auto ejectors; set trigger. Boxlock action.

Perf.: $1325 **Exc.:** $1025 **VGood:** $895

REMINGTON MODEL 3200

Over/under; boxlock; 12-ga.; 2-3/4-inch chamber; 26-inch Improved Cylinder/Modified, 28-inch Modified/Full, 30-inch Modified/Full barrels; vent rib; checkered American walnut pistol-grip stock, forearm; auto ejectors; selective single trigger. Similar to earlier Model 32. Introduced 1973; discontinued 1984.

Perf.: $1100 **Exc.:** $995 **VGood:** $900

Remington Model 32 Expert

Remington Model 332 O/U

Remington Model 3200 Competition Skeet

Remington Model 3200 Competition Trap

Remington Model 3200 Skeet

Remington Model 3200 Trap

Remington Premier STS Competition

Remington Premier STS Competition Adjustable

REMINGTON MODEL 3200 COMPETITION SKEET

Same specs as Model 3200 except 26-inch, 28-inch Skeet-choke barrels; select walnut Skeet-style stock, full beavertail forearm; engraved forend latch plate, trigger guard; gilt scrollwork on frame. Introduced 1973; discontinued 1984.

Perf.: $1750 **Exc.:** $1400 **VGood:** $1200

REMINGTON MODEL 3200 COMPETITION TRAP

Same specs as Model 3200 except 30-inch, 32-inch Improved Modified/Full or Full/Full barrels; select fancy walnut straight comb or Monte Carlo stock, beavertail forend; engraved forend latch plate, trigger guard; gilt scrollwork on frame. Introduced 1973; discontinued 1984.

Perf.: $2000 **Exc.:** $1300 **VGood:** $1100

REMINGTON MODEL 3200 MAGNUM

Same specs as Model 3200 except 12-ga.; 3-inch chamber; 30-inch Modified/Full or Full/Full barrels. Introduced 1973; discontinued 1984.

Perf.: $1950 **Exc.:** $1800 **VGood:** $1670

REMINGTON MODEL 3200 SKEET

Same specs as Model 3200 except for 26-inch, 28-inch Skeet-choke barrels; Skeet-style stock, full beavertail forearm. Introduced 1973; discontinued 1984.

Perf.: $1250 **Exc.:** $1000 **VGood:** $950

REMINGTON MODEL 3200 SPECIAL TRAP

Same specs as Model 3200 except 30-inch, 32-inch Improved Modified/Full or Full/Full barrels; higher grade select walnut straight comb or Monte Carlo trap-style stock, beavertail forearm. Introduced 1973; discontinued 1984.

Perf.: $1400 **Exc.:** $1350 **VGood:** $1200

REMINGTON MODEL 3200 TRAP

Same specs as Model 3200 except 30-inch, 32-inch Improved Modified/Full or Full/Full barrels; straight comb or Monte Carlo trap-style stock, beavertail forearm. Introduced 1973; discontinued 1984.

Perf.: $1375 **Exc.:** $1100 **VGood:** $950

REMINGTON PREMIER STS COMPETITION

This 12 gauge O/U with 28-inch or 30-inch barrels has a titanium receiver, overbored barrel, gloss finish stock and 5 extended chokes. Weight is about 7.5 lbs.

Perf.: $1975 **Exc.:** $1830 **VGood:** $1600

REMINGTON PREMIER FIELD GRADE

O/U available in 12, 20 and 28 gauges with satin finish and nickel receiver. Available with 26-inch or 28-inch barrels. Includes three flush chokes. Weight is about 6.5 lbs. for 20 and 28 gauges and 7.5 lbs. for 12 gauge.

NIB: $1600 **Exc.:** $1450 **VGood:** $1175

Remington Premier Field Grade

Remington Premier Upland Grade

Remington Model 1882

Remington Model 1894

Remington Model 1900

Remington Parker (2008)

Remington Peerless

Richland Model 200

Richland Model 707 Deluxe

REMINGTON MODEL 1900

Side-by-side; boxlock; hammerless; 10-, 12-, 16-ga.; 28-inch, 30-inch barrels; hand-checkered American walnut straight-grip stock, heavy forearm; double triggers; auto ejectors. Introduced 1900; discontinued 1910.

Exc.: $1200   **VGood:** $1100   **Good:** $1000

REMINGTON PARKER AAHE 28 GAUGE OVER/UNDER SHOTGUN

A reintroduction of the Charles Parker O/U shotgun. Built to customer specs with a variety of options. Pricing starts at $49,000 (as of 2008).

NIB: $49,000   **VGood:** N/A   **Good:** $N/A

REMINGTON MODEL 1900 TRAP

Same specs as Model 1900 except 32-inch Full-Choke barrels; select trap-style walnut stock. Introduced 1900; discontinued 1910.

Exc.: $700   **VGood:** $425   **Good:** $390

REMINGTON PEERLESS

Over/under; boxlock; 12-ga.; 3-inch chamber; 26-inch, 28-inch, 30-inch barrels; Improved, Modified, Full Rem-Choke tubes; weighs 7-1/4 lbs.; cut-checkered American walnut pistol-grip stock, forend with Imron gloss finish; black ventilated recoil pad; gold-plated, single selective trigger; automatic safety; automatic ejectors; polished blue finish with light scrollwork on removable sideplates; Remington logo on bottom of receiver. Introduced 1993;.

Perf.: $925   **Exc.:** $700   **VGood:** $600

RHODE ISLAND ARMS MORONNE MODEL 46

Over/under; boxlock; 12-, 20-ga.; 26-inch Improved Cylinder/Modified, 28-inch Modified/Full barrels; plain barrel or vent rib; checkered straight or pistol-grip stock; non-selective single trigger; plain extractors. Fewer than 500 made. Introduced 1949; discontinued 1953.

12-ga., plain barrel		
Exc.: $875	**VGood:** $675	**Good:** $600
12-ga., vent rib		
Exc.: $1000	**VGood:** $825	**Good:** $750
20-ga., plain barrel		
Exc.: $1000	**VGood:** $825	**Good:** $750
20-ga., vent rib		
Exc.: $1150	**VGood:** $975	**Good:** $900

RICHLAND MODEL 200

Side-by-side; Anson & Deeley-type boxlock; hammerless; 12-, 16-, 20-, 28-ga., .410; 26-inch Improved/Modified or Modified/Full, 28-inch Modified/Full barrels; hand-checkered European walnut pistol-grip stock, beavertail forearm; cheekpiece; double triggers; plain extractors; recoil pad. Made in Spain. Introduced 1963; discontinued 1985.

Perf.: $330   **Exc.:** $300   **VGood:** $275

RICHLAND MODEL 202

Side-by-side; Anson & Deeley boxlock; hammerless; 12-, 20-ga.; comes in two-barrel set for a single gauge; 26-inch Improved/Modified and 30-inch Full/Full (12-ga.) or 22-inch Improved/Modified and 26-inch Modified/Full (20-ga.) barrels; hand-checkered European walnut pistol-grip stock, beavertail forearm; cheekpiece; double triggers; plain extractors; recoil pad. Made in Spain. Introduced 1963; discontinued 1971.

Exc.: $450   **VGood:** $390   **Good:** $275

RICHLAND MODEL 707 DELUXE

Side-by-side; boxlock; hammerless; 12-, 20-ga.; 26-inch Improved/Modified, 28-inch Modified/Full, 30-inch Full/Full barrels; hand-checkered European walnut stock, forearm; triple bolting system; double triggers; plain extractors; recoil pad. Made in Spain. Introduced 1963; discontinued 1972.

Exc.: $300   **VGood:** $275   **Good:** $250

REMINGTON PREMIER UPLAND GRADE

As above but with oil finish stock and case colored receiver with gold game bird scene.

NIB: $1150   **Exc.:** $995   **VGood:** $735

REMINGTON MODEL 1882

Side-by-side; visible hammers; 10-, 12-, 16-ga.; 28-inch, 30-inch, 32-inch steel or Damascus barrels; hand-checkered American walnut pistol-grip stock, forearm; double triggers. Introduced 1882; discontinued 1910.

Damascus barrels		
Exc.: $1500	**VGood:** $1400	**Good:** $1200
Steel barrels		
Exc.: $1000	**VGood:** $900	**Good:** $800

REMINGTON MODEL 1889

Side-by-side; visible hammers; 10-, 12-, 16-ga.; 28-inch, 30-inch, 32-inch steel or Damascus barrels; double triggers; hand-checkered American walnut stock, slim forend. Introduced 1889; discontinued 1908. Prices shown are for lowest grade.

Damascus barrels		
Exc.: $2100	**VGood:** $1800	**Good:** $1700
Steel barrels		
Exc.: $1350	**VGood:** $1250	**Good:** $900

REMINGTON MODEL 1894

Side-by-side; boxlock; hammerless; 10-, 12-, 16-ga.; 26-inch, 28-inch, 30-inch, 32-inch barrels; hand-checkered American walnut straight-grip stock, forearm; double triggers; auto ejectors. Introduced 1894; discontinued 1910.

Exc.: $1350   **VGood:** $1225   **Good:** $1025

REMINGTON MODEL 1894 TRAP

Same specs as Model 1894 except 32-inch Full-choke barrels; trap-style walnut stock. Introduced 1894; discontinued 1910.

Exc.: $2750   **VGood:** $2625   **Good:** $2525

RICHLAND MODEL 711 MAGNUM

Side-by-side; hammerless; Anson & Deeley-type boxlock; Purdey-type triple lock; 10- (3 1/2-inch), 12- (3-inch), 20-ga.; 30-inch, 32-inch Full/Full barrels; hand-checkered European walnut pistol-grip stock, forearm; double triggers; plain extractors; automatic safety; recoil pad. Advertised as Long Range Waterfowl Magnum. Made in Spain. Introduced 1963; discontinued 1985.

10-ga.		
Perf.: $400	Exc.: $325	VGood: $275
12-ga.		
Perf.: $340	Exc.: $295	VGood: $265
20-ga.		
Perf.: $450	Exc.: $340	VGood: $295

RICHLAND MODEL 808

Over/under; boxlock; 12-ga.; 26-inch Improved/Modified, 28-inch Modified/Full, 30-inch Full/Full barrels; vent rib; hand-checkered European walnut stock, forearm; plain extractors; non-selective single trigger. Made in Italy. Introduced 1963; discontinued 1968.

Exc.: $425	VGood: $375	Good: $330

RICHLAND MODEL 828

Over/under; boxlock; 28-ga.; 26-inch Improved/Modified, 28-inch Full/Modified barrels; vent rib; hand-checkered European walnut stock, quick-detachable forearm; sliding crossbolt lock; non-automatic safety; plain extractors; single selective trigger; color case-hardened receiver; rosette engraving. Made in Italy. Introduced 1971; no longer in production. Available on special order only.

Perf.: $650	Exc.: $550	VGood: $500

RICHLAND MODEL 844

Over/under; boxlock; 12-ga.; 2-3/4-inch, 3-inch chambers; 26-inch Improved/Modified, 28-inch Modified/Full, 30-inch Full/Full barrels; hand-checkered European walnut pistol-grip stock, forearm; plain extractors; non-selective single trigger. Made in Italy. Introduced 1971; no longer in production.

Perf.: $325	Exc.: $280	VGood: $250

RIGBY BEST QUALITY SIDELOCK

Side-by-side; 12-, 20-ga.; various barrel lengths, chokes to customer's specs; hand-checkered European walnut straight-grip stock, forearm; automatic ejectors; double triggers; English engraving. Still in production.

Perf.: $36,000	Exc.: $32,000	VGood: $26,000

RIGBY SIDELOCK DOUBLE

Side-by-side; all gauges; various barrel lengths, chokes to customer's specs; hand-checkered European walnut straight-grip stock, forearm; automatic ejectors; double triggers; English engraving; made in two grades, differing in overall quality, amount of engraving. Introduced 1885; discontinued 1955.

Sandringham Grade		
Exc.: $8500	VGood: $6000	Good: $5000
Regal Grade		
Exc.: $12,000	VGood: $9000	Good: $7500

RIGBY BOXLOCK DOUBLE

Side-by-side; all gauges; various barrel lengths, chokes to customer's specs; hand-checkered European walnut straight-grip stock, forearm; automatic ejectors; double triggers; English engraving; made in two grades, differing in amount and nature of engraving, overall quality. Introduced 1900; discontinued 1955.

Chatsworth Grade		
Exc.: $4000	VGood: $3000	Good: $2500
Sackville Grade		
Exc.: $5500	VGood: $4500	Good: $4000

RIZZINI S790 EMEL OVER/UNDER SHOTGUN

Gauge: 20-, 28-ga., .410; 26-inch, 27.5-inch barrel (Imp. Cyl. & Imp. Mod.); weighs about 6 lbs.; extra-fancy select walnut stock; boxlock action with profuse engraving; automatic ejectors; single selective trigger; silvered receiver. Comes with Nizzoli leather case. Introduced 1996. Imported from Italy by Wm. Larkin Moore & Co.

Perf.: $7800	Exc.: $6800	VGood: $5900

RIZZINI S792 EMEL OVER/UNDER SHOTGUN

Similar to S790 EMEL except dummy sideplates with extensive engraving coverage. Nizzoli leather case. Introduced 1996. Imported from Italy by Wm. Larkin Moore & Co.0

Perf.: $7500	Exc.: $6600	VGood: $5650

RIZZINI UPLAND EL OVER/UNDER SHOTGUN

Gauge: 12, 16, 20, 28, .410. Barrel: 26-inch, 27-1/2-inch, Mod. & Full, Imp. Cyl. & Imp. Mod. choke tubes. Weight: About 6.6 lbs. Features: Boxlock action; single selective trigger; ejectors; profuse engraving on silvered receiver. Comes with fitted case. Introduced 1996. Imported from Italy by Wm. Larkin Moore & Co.

Perf.: $2800	Exc.: $2400	VGood: $2100

Richland Model 711 Magnum

Richland Model 808

Richland Model 828

Richland Model 844

Rizzini S790 Emel Over/Under

Rizzini S792 Emel Over/Under

Rizzini Artemis Over/Under

Rizzini S782 Emel Over/Under

RIZZINI ARTEMIS OVER/UNDER SHOTGUN

Same as Upland EL model except dummy sideplates with extensive game scene engraving. Fancy European walnut stock. Fitted case. Introduced 1996. Imported from Italy by Wm. Larkin Moore & Co.

Perf.: $1850	Exc.: $1575	VGood: $1300

RIZZINI S782 EMEL OVER/UNDER SHOTGUN

Gauge: 12, 2-3/4-inch chambers; 26-inch, 27-1/2-inch barrel (Imp. Cyl. & Imp. Mod.); weighs about 6.75 lbs.; extra fancy select walnut; boxlock action with dummy sideplates; extensive engraving with gold inlaid game birds; silvered receiver; automatic ejectors; single selective trigger; Nizzoli leather case. Introduced 1996. Imported from Italy by Wm. Larkin Moore & Co.

Perf.: $9500	Exc.: $8525	VGood: $7200

RIZZINI BOXLOCK

Side-by-side; Anson & Deeley boxlock: 12-, 16-, 20-, 28-ga., .410; 25-inch to 30-inch barrels; file-cut rib; weighs 5-1/2 to 6-1/4 lbs., depending upon gauge; hand-rubbed oil finish stock; ejectors; chopper lump barrels; double triggers, single non-selective optional; scroll, rosette engraving on scalloped

Rossi Matched Pair

Rossi Overland

Rossi Turkey Gun

Rossi Squire

Rottweil Model 72
American Trap Single

Rottweil Model 72
Field Supreme

Rottweil Model 72
International Skeet

ROSSI SINGLE-SHOT SHOTGUN

Gauge: 12-, 20-ga., 2-3/4-inch chamber; .410, 3-inch chamber; 28-inch barrel full, 22-inch barrel Youth; weighs 5 lbs.; stained hardwood; bead sight; break-open, positive ejection; internal transfer bar; trigger block.

Perf.: $90   **Exc.:** $80   **VGood:** $70

ROSSI TURKEY GUN

Introduced in 2008. A specialized version of Roosi's 12-ga. single-shot shotgun. Features a 3-1/2 inch chamber, fiber optic sights, drilled and tapped barrel, included scope mount base and a removable Briley® Extended Turkey Choke.

Perf.: $175   **Exc.:** $140   **VGood:** $95

ROSSI SQUIRE

Side-by-side; hammerless; 12-, 20-ga., .410; 20-inch, 28-inch barrels; raised matted rib; walnut-finished hardwood pistol-grip stock, beavertail forearm; double triggers; twin underlugs; synchronized sliding bolts. Made in Brazil. Introduced 1978; discontinued 1990.

Perf.: $300   **Exc.:** $245   **VGood:** $195

ROTTWEIL MODEL 72 AMERICAN SKEET

Over/under; boxlock; 12-ga.; 26-3/4-inch barrels; vent rib; metal bead front sight; hand-checkered French walnut pistol-grip stock, forend; ejectors; single trigger; engraved. Introduced 1977; discontinued 1986.

Perf.: $1800   **Exc.:** $1650   **VGood:** $1450

ROTTWEIL MODEL 72 AMERICAN TRAP SINGLE

Same specs as Model 72 American Skeet except 34-inch single barrel; hand-honed chokes; high vent rib; center bead sight, plastic front in metal sleeve; hand-checkered, oil-finished French walnut Monte Carlo stock; muzzle collar changes point of impact; double vent recoil pad; single selective or double triggers. Introduced 1977; discontinued 1986.

Perf.: $950   **Exc.:** $850   **VGood:** $700

ROTTWEIL MODEL 72 AMERICAN TRAP COMBO

Same specs as Model 72 American Skeet except two-barrel set with 32-inch separated over/under barrels, 34-inch single-barrel; hand-honed chokes; high vent rib; center bead sight, plastic front in metal sleeve; hand-checkered, rubbed European walnut Monte Carlo stock; muzzle collar changes point of impact; double vent recoil pad; single selective or double triggers. Introduced 1977; discontinued 1986.

Perf.: $1850   **Exc.:** $1700   **VGood:** $1600

ROTTWEIL MODEL 72 AMERICAN TRAP DOUBLE

Same specs as Model 72 American Skeet except 32-inch barrels; hand-honed chokes; high vent rib; center bead sight, plastic front in metal sleeve; hand-checkered, oil-finished Monte Carlo French walnut stock; muzzle collar changes point of impact; double vent recoil pad; single selective or double triggers. Introduced 1977; discontinued 1986.

Perf.: $1750   **Exc.:** $1400   **VGood:** $1200

ROTTWEIL MODEL 72 FIELD SUPREME

Same specs as Model 72 American Skeet except 28-inch barrels; plastic buttplate; removable interchangeable single trigger assembly; engraved action. Made in Germany. Introduced 1976; discontinued 1986.

Perf.: $1750   **Exc.:** $1300   **VGood:** $1100

ROTTWEIL MODEL 72 INTERNATIONAL SKEET

Same specs as Model 72 American Skeet except 26-3/4-inch chrome-lined barrels; flared chokes; hand-checkered, oil-finished French walnut stock, modified beavertail forend; retracting spring-mounted firing pins; selective single inertia-type trigger. Introduced 1976; discontinued 1986.

Perf.: $1850   **Exc.:** $1600   **VGood:** $1400

---

frame; coin finish; optional color case-hardening; primarily a custom gun with stock, choke tubes to customer specs. Made in Italy. Introduced 1989; still in production.

12-, 16-, 20-ga.			
Perf.: $22,000	**Exc.:** $11,000	**VGood:** $9000	
28-ga., .410			
Perf.: $25,000	**Exc.:** $12,000	**VGood:** $10,000	

RIZZINI SIDELOCK

Side-by-side; Holland & Holland sidelock; 12-, 16-, 20-, 28-ga., .410; 25-inch to 30-inch barrels; optional rib styles; weighs 6-1/2 to 8 lbs., depending upon gauge; rubbed oil finish or optional satin luster finish stock; auto ejectors; double triggers; single selective trigger optional; coin finish or optional color case-hardening; full coverage scroll engraving, with floral bouquets, gold crown on top lever; customer's name in gold; gold crest inset in forend. Primarily a custom gun with stock, choke tubes to customer specs. Made in Italy. Introduced 1989; still in production.

12-, 16-, 20-ga.			
Perf.: $35,000	**Exc.:** $17,500	**VGood:** $15,000	
28-ga., .410			
Perf.: $40,000	**Exc.:** $21,000	**VGood:** $16,500	

ROSSI MATCHED PAIR SINGLE-SHOT SHOTGUN/RIFLE

Gauge: 12,- 20-ga., .410 22-inch barrel (18-1/2-inch Youth), 28-inch barrel (23-inch full); weighs 4 to 6 lbs.; hardwood (brown or black finish); bead front sight; break-open internal transfer bar manual external safety; blued or stainless steel finish; sling-swivel studs; includes matched 22 LR or 22 Mag. barrel with fully adjustable front and rear sight; trigger block system. Introduced 2001. Imported by BrazTech/Taurus.

Blue			
Perf.: $125	**Exc.:** $100	**VGood:** $90	
Stainless steel			
Perf.: $120	**Exc.:** $100	**VGood:** $90	

ROSSI OVERLAND

Side-by-side; sidelock; 12-, 20-ga., .410; 20-inch, 26-inch, 28-inch barrels; solid raised matted rib; European walnut pistol-grip stock, beavertail forend; double triggers; external hammers; Greener crossbolt. Made in Brazil. Introduced 1978; discontinued 1988.

Perf.: $275   **Exc.:** $230   **VGood:** $185

ROTTWEIL MODEL 72 INTERNATIONAL TRAP
Same specs as Model 72 American Skeet except 30-inch barrels; raised vent rib. Introduced 1976; discontinued 1986.

Perf.: $1850   **Exc.:** $1600   **VGood:** $1400

ROTTWEIL PARAGON OVER/UNDER
Gauge: 12, 2-3/4-inch chambers; 28-inch, 30-inch barrel; five choke tubes; weighs 7 lbs.; European walnut; boxlock action; detachable trigger assembly; ejectors can be deactivated; convertible top lever for right- or left-hand use; trigger adjustable for position. Imported from Germany by Dynamit Nobel-RWS, Inc..

Perf.: $6950   **Exc.:** $6500   **VGood:** $5750

ROYAL ARMS MODEL 87SC
Over/under; boxlock; 12-ga.; 2-3/4-inch chambers; 27-5/8-inch barrels; choke tubes; tapered raised rib; weighs 7 3/8 lb.; select walnut stock; auto ejectors; auto safety; single selective trigger; coin-finish receiver; arabesque scroll engraving. Made in Italy. Introduced 1987; discontinued 1987.

Perf.: $575   **Exc.:** $475   **VGood:** $400

ROYAL ARMS MODEL 87T TRAP
Same specs as Model 87SC except Trap-style stock; other Trap configurations. Introduced 1987; discontinued 1987.

Perf.: $600   **Exc.:** $440   **VGood:** $340

SAE MODEL 66C
Over/under; 12-ga.; 26-inch Skeet/Skeet, 28-inch Modified/Full barrels; oil-finished Monte Carlo walnut stock, beavertail forearm; selective auto ejectors; auto safety; single mechanical trigger; dummy sideplates; gold inlays; extensive engraving. Made in Spain. Introduced 1987; discontinued 1988.

Perf.: $950   **Exc.:** $725   **VGood:** $650

SAE MODEL 70
Over/under; boxlock; 12-, 20-ga.; 3-inch chambers; 26-inch Modified/Full, 28-inch Improved/Modified barrels; weighs 6 3/4 lbs.; European walnut stock; selective auto ejectors; auto safety; single mechanical trigger; engraved receiver; blued finish. Made in Spain. Introduced 1987; discontinued 1988.

Perf.: $400   **Exc.:** $275   **VGood:** $260

SAE MODEL 70 MULTICHOKE
Same specs as Model 70 except 12-ga.; 27-inch barrels; choke tubes; silvered receiver. Made in Spain. Introduced 1987; discontinued 1988.

Perf.: $425   **Exc.:** $350   **VGood:** $300

SAE MODEL 209E
Side-by-side; sidelock; 12-, 20-ga., .410; 2-3/4-inch chambers; 26-inch Modified/Full, 28-inch Modified/Improved Cylinder barrels; fancy oil-finished checkered select walnut stock, forend; double triggers; selective ejectors; engraved, coin-finished receiver. Made in Spain. Introduced 1987; discontinued 1988.

Perf.: $925   **Exc.:** $700   **VGood:** $650

SAE MODEL 210S
Side-by-side; boxlock; 12-, 20-ga., .410; 3-inch chambers; 25-inch Modified/Full, 28-inch Modified Improved barrels; weighs 7 lbs.; checkered pistol-grip European walnut stock, splinter forend; auto safety; extractors; double triggers; silver-finished, engraved action. Made in Spain. Introduced 1987; discontinued 1988.

Perf.: $420   **Exc.:** $300   **VGood:** $210

SAE MODEL 340X
Side-by-side; sidelock; 12-, 20-ga.; 2-3/4-inch chambers; 26-inch Modified/Full, 28-inch Modified/Improved Cylinder barrels; weighs about 7 lbs.; high-gloss straight-grip select walnut stock, forearm; double triggers; selective ejectors; color case-hardened receiver, engraving. Made in Spain. Introduced 1987; discontinued 1988.

Perf.: $700   **Exc.:** $550   **VGood:** $495

Royal Arms Model 87SC

SAE Model 210S

Sarasqueta Model 119E

Sarasqueta Model 119

Sarasqueta Sidelock Double No. 4

Sarasqueta Sidelock Double No. 6E

Sarasqueta Sidelock Double No. 7E

SAN MARCO 10-GAUGE
Over/under; boxlock; 10-ga.; 3-1/2-inch chambers; 28-inch Modified/Modified, 32-inch Modified/Full barrels; chrome-lined bores; solid 3/8-inch barrel rib; weighs 9 to 9-1/2 lbs.; walnut stock with waterproof finish; long forcing cones; double triggers; extractors; Deluxe grade has automatic ejectors; engraved receiver with game scenes, matte finish. Made in Italy. Introduced 1990; discontinued 1994.

Perf.: $700   **Exc.:** $500   **VGood:** $370

Deluxe grade

Perf.: $800   **Exc.:** $600   **VGood:** $470

SAN MARCO FIELD SPECIAL
Over/under; boxlock; 12-, 20-, 28-ga.; 3-inch chambers; 26-inch Improved Cylinder/Modified, 28-inch Full/Modified barrels; vented top and middle ribs; weighs 5-1/2 to 6 lbs.; engraved, silvered receiver; single trigger. Made in Italy. Introduced 1990; discontinued 1994.

Perf.: $600   **Exc.:** $430   **VGood:** $330

SAN MARCO WILDFOWLER
Over/under; boxlock; 12-ga.; 3-1/2-inch chambers; 28-inch Modified/Modified, Full/Modified barrels; chrome-lined bores; vented top and middle ribs; weighs 7-3/4 lbs.; checkered waterproof walnut pistol-grip stock, forend; long forcing cones; single non-selective trigger; extractors on Standard, automatic ejectors on Deluxe; silvered, engraved action. Made in Italy. Introduced 1990; discontinued 1994.

Perf.: $525   **Exc.:** $380   **VGood:** $300

Deluxe grade

Perf.: $600   **Exc.:** $430   **VGood:** $330

SARASQUETA BOXLOCK DOUBLE
Side-by-side; boxlock; hammerless; 12-, 16-, 20-, 28-ga.; various standard barrel lengths, choke combinations; hand-checkered European walnut straight-grip stock, forearm; plain extractors; double triggers; Greener crossbolt (No.2); optional ejectors; engraved. Introduced mid-1930s; no longer in production.

No. 2		
Perf.: $325	**Exc.:** $250	**VGood:** $180
No. 2E		
Perf.: $375	**Exc.:** $280	**VGood:** $230
No. 3		
Perf.: $375	**Exc.:** $280	**VGood:** $230
No. 3E		
Perf.: $425	**Exc.:** $330	**VGood:** $280

SARASQUETA MODEL 119E
Side-by-side; 12-ga.; 2-3/4-inch chambers; 28-inch Modified/Full, Improved/Modified barrels; medium bead front sight; European walnut straight-grip stock; auto ejectors; double triggers; hand-engraved locks. Made in Spain. Introduced 1982 by Toledo Armas; discontinued 1984.

Perf.: $450   **Exc.:** $350   **VGood:** $300

SARASQUETA SIDELOCK DOUBLE
Side-by-side; hammerless; 12-, 16-, 20-, 28-ga., .410; barrel lengths, choke combinations to customer's order; hand-checkered European walnut straight-grip stock, forearm; double triggers; optional automatic ejectors; made in 18 grades, differing in

Sarasqueta Sidelock Double Model 11E

Sarasqueta Sidelock Double Model 12E

Sarasqueta Super Deluxe

Sarriugarte Model 101E

Sarriugarte Model 501E Special

Sarriugarte Model 200 Trap

Sauer Artemis Model Grade I

Sauer Model BBF

quality of wood, checkering and engraving. Made in Spain.

No. 4		
Perf.: $600	**Exc.:** $500	**VGood:** $450
No. 4E		
Perf.: $650	**Exc.:** $550	**VGood:** $500
No. 6E		
Perf.: $780	**Exc.:** $680	**VGood:** $600
No. 7E		
Perf.: $850	**Exc.:** $750	**VGood:** $700
No. 10E		
Perf.: $1650	**Exc.:** $1400	**VGood:** $1300
No. 11E		
Perf.: $1700	**Exc.:** $1500	**VGood:** $1400
No. 12E		
Perf.: $2000	**Exc.:** $1800	**VGood:** $1650

SARASQUETA SUPER DELUXE
Side-by-side; sidelock; hammerless; 12-ga.; barrel lengths, choke combos to customer's order; hand-checkered European walnut pistol-grip stock, forearm; automatic ejectors; double triggers; engraved action. Introduced 1930s; no longer in production.

    Perf.: $1800   **Exc.:** $1600   **VGood:** $1200

SARRIUGARTE MODEL 101DS
Over/under; 12-ga.; 2-3/4-inch chambers; 26-inch Improved/Modified, 28-inch Modified/Full barrels; medium bead front sight; hand-checkered European walnut pistol-grip stock; extractors; selective trigger; border engraving on receiver. Made in Spain. Introduced 1982 by Toledo Armas; discontinued 1984.

    Perf.: $425   **Exc.:** $340   **VGood:** $295

SARRIUGARTE MODEL 101E
Same specs as Model 101DS except single trigger; auto ejectors. Introduced 1982; discontinued 1984.

    Perf.: $500   **Exc.:** $375   **VGood:** $320

SARRIUGARTE MODEL 101E DS
Same specs as Model 101DS except ejectors. Introduced 1982; discontinued 1984.

    Perf.: $550   **Exc.:** $425   **VGood:** $350

SARRIUGARTE MODEL 200 TRAP
Over/under; 12-ga.; 2-3/4-inch chambers; 30-inch Full/Full barrels; vent middle rib; European walnut Monte Carlo stock; single trigger; auto ejectors. Made in Spain. Introduced 1982 by Toledo Armas; discontinued 1984.

    Perf.: $700   **Exc.:** $570   **VGood:** $500

SARRIUGARTE MODEL 501E SPECIAL
Over/under; 12-ga.; 2-3/4-inch chambers; 30-inch Full/Full barrels; vent middle rib; select European walnut Monte Carlo stock; single trigger; auto ejectors; elaborate engraving. Introduced 1982; discontinued 1984.

    Perf.: $1500   **Exc.:** $1150   **VGood:** $900

SARRIUGARTE MODEL 501E SPECIAL EXCELSIOR
Same specs as Model 501E Special except top of the line with best wood available; best grade of engraving. Introduced 1982; discontinued 1984.

    Perf.: $2000   **Exc.:** $1550   **VGood:** $1300

SARRIUGARTE MODEL 501E SPECIAL NIGER
Same specs as Model 501E Special except higher-grade wood; better engraving. Introduced 1982; discontinued 1984.

    Perf.: $1900   **Exc.:** $1400   **VGood:** $1100

SARSILMAZ SEMI-AUTOMATIC SHOTGUN
Gauge: 12, 3-inch chamber; 26-inch or 28-inch barrel; fixed chokes; Walnut or synthetic; handles 2-3/4-inch or 3-inch Magnum loads. Introduced 2000. Imported from Turkey by PMC.

    Perf.: $325   **Exc.:** $250   **VGood:** $180

SARSILMAZ PUMP SHOTGUN
Gauge: 12, 3-inch chamber. Barrel: 26-inch or 28-inch. Stocks: Oil-finished hardwood. Features: Includes extra pistol-grip stock. Introduced 2000. Imported from Turkey by PMC.

    Perf.: $300   **Exc.:** $250   **VGood:** $180

SARSILMAZ OVER/UNDER SHOTGUN
Over/under; 12-ga.; 3-inch chambers; 26-inch, 28-inch barrel; fixed chokes or choke tubes; oil-finished hardwood stock; double or single selective trigger; wide ventilated rib; chrome-plated parts; blued finish. Introduced 2000. Imported from Turkey by PMC.

    Perf.: $425   **Exc.:** $375   **VGood:** $315

SAUER ARTEMIS MODEL
Side-by-side; Holland & Holland-type sidelock; 12-ga.; 28-inch Modified/Full barrels; hand-checkered European walnut pistol-grip stock, beavertail forearm; Greener-type crossbolt; double underlugs; double sear safeties; automatic ejectors; single selective trigger; recoil pad; Grade I has fine-line engraving; Grade II has English arabesque motif. Introduced 1960s; discontinued 1977.

Grade I		
Perf.: $5500	**Exc.:** $4600	**VGood:** $3800
Grade II		
Perf.: $6600	**Exc.:** $5500	**VGood:** $4800

SAUER MODEL BBF
Over/under combo; blitz action; Kersten lock; 16-ga. top barrel; choice of 30-30, 30-06, 7x65R rifle barrel; 25-inch barrels; shotgun barrel Full choke; folding leaf rear sight; hand-checkered European walnut pistol-grip stock, forearm; modified Monte Carlo comb; cheekpiece; front set trigger activates rifle

barrel; sling swivels; arabesque engraving pattern. Introduced 1950s; discontinued 1985.

Standard Grade		
Perf.: $2150	**Exc.:** $1600	**VGood:** $1250
Deluxe Grade		
Perf.: $2350	**Exc.:** $1800	**VGood:** $1450

SAUER MODEL 66 FIELD

Over/under; Holland & Holland sideplates; 12-ga.; 28-inch Modified/Full barrels; hand-checkered European walnut stock, forearm; automatic safety; selective automatic ejectors; single selective trigger; recoil pad; three grades of engraving. Introduced 1960s; discontinued 1975.

Grade I		
Perf.: $2200	**Exc.:** $1750	**VGood:** $1500
Grade II		
Perf.: $2995	**Exc.:** $2400	**VGood:** $1900
Grade III		
Perf.: $3850	**Exc.:** $3300	**VGood:** $2800

SAUER MODEL 66 TRAP

Same specs as Model 66 Field except 30-inch Full/Full or Modified/Full barrels; wide vent rib; trap-style checkered European walnut stock, ventilated beavertail forearm; non-automatic safety. Introduced 1960s; discontinued 1975.

Grade I		
Perf.: $2090	**Exc.:** $1760	**VGood:** $1540
Grade II		
Perf.: $3080	**Exc.:** $2420	**VGood:** $1980
Grade III		
Perf.: $3800	**Exc.:** $3300	**VGood:** $2800

SAUER MODEL 66 SKEET

Same specs as Model 66 Field except 26-inch Skeet/Skeet barrels; vent rib; Skeet-style checkered European walnut stock, ventilated beavertail forearm. Introduced 1966; discontinued 1975.

Grade I		
Perf.: $2000	**Exc.:** $1650	**VGood:** $1300
Grade II		
Perf.: $2900	**Exc.:** $2000	**VGood:** $1700
Grade III		
Perf.: $3750	**Exc.:** $3000	**VGood:** $2600

SAUER ROYAL MODEL

Side-by-side; Anson & Deeley-type boxlock; 12-, 16-, 20-ga.; 26-inch Improved/Modified, 28-inch Modified/Full, 30-inch Full/Full barrels; hand-checkered European walnut pistol-grip stock, beavertail forearm; Greener crossbolt; single selective trigger; automatic ejectors; automatic safety; double underlugs; scalloped frame; recoil pad; arabesque engraving. Introduced 1955; discontinued 1977.

Perf.: $1500	**Exc.:** $1100	**VGood:** $900

SAUER/FRANCHI STANDARD GRADE

Over/under; 12-ga.; 28-inch, 29-inch barrels; vent rib; standard choke combos; weighs 7 lbs.; checkered European walnut stock; single selective trigger; selective auto ejectors; blued finish; made in four grades with differing wood, finish and engraving. Made in Germany. Introduced 1986; discontinued 1988.

Standard Grade		
Perf.: $350	**Exc.:** $300	**VGood:** $280
Regent Grade		
Perf.: $475	**Exc.:** $390	**VGood:** $350
Favorite Grade		
Perf.: $550	**Exc.:** $495	**VGood:** $450
Diplomat Grade		
Perf.: $875	**Exc.:** $750	**VGood:** $625

SAUER/FRANCHI SKEET

Over/under; 12-ga.; 28-inch Skeet/Skeet barrels; vent rib; checkered select European walnut stock, forearm; ejectors; single selective trigger; silvered receiver. Introduced 1986; discontinued 1988.

Perf.: $900	**Exc.:** $690	**VGood:** $600

Sauer Model 66 Field

Sauer Royal Model

Sauer/Franchi Sporting S

Savage Model 24

Savage Model 30

Savage Model 30AC

SAUER/FRANCHI SPORTING S

Over/under; 12-ga.; 28-inch barrels; standard choke combos; vent rib; checkered select European walnut stock, forearm; ejectors; single selective trigger; silvered receiver. Introduced 1986; discontinued 1988.

Perf.: $800	**Exc.:** $700	**VGood:** $600

SAUER/FRANCHI TRAP

Over/under; 12-ga.; 29-inch barrels; standard choke combos; vent rib; checkered select European walnut trap-style stock, forearm; ejectors; single selective trigger; silvered receiver. Introduced 1986; discontinued 1988.

Perf.: $850	**Exc.:** $700	**VGood:** $600

SAVAGE MODEL 24

Over/under combo; break-open; 22 Short, Long, LR upper barrel; .410; 3-inch, Full-choke lower barrel; 24-inch barrels; open rear sight; ramp front rifle sight; uncheckered walnut pistol-grip stock; sliding button selector; single trigger. Introduced 1950; discontinued 1965.

Exc.: $435	**VGood:** $380	**Good:** $260

SAVAGE MODEL 24DL

Same specs as Model 24 except top lever; 20-ga., .410 lower barrel; checkered Monte Carlo stock, beavertail forearm; satin chrome-finished receiver, trigger guard. No longer in production.

Exc.: $425	**VGood:** $325	**Good:** $260

SAVAGE MODEL 24M

Same specs as Model 24 except 22 WMR upper barrel. Introduced 1965; discontinued 1971.

Exc.: $525	**VGood:** $450	**Good:** $400

SAVAGE MODEL 24MDL

Same specs as Model 24L except top lever; 20-ga., .410 lower barrel; 22 WMR upper barrel; checkered Monte Carlo stock, beavertail forearm; satin chrome-finished receiver, trigger guard. Introduced 1965; discontinued 1969.

Exc.: $500	**VGood:** $405	**Good:** $315

SAVAGE MODEL 28A

Slide action; hammerless; takedown; 12-, 16-, 20-ga.; 5-shot tube magazine; 26-inch, 28-inch, 30-inch, 32-inch plain barrel; Modified, Cylinder, Full choke; uncheckered American walnut pistol-grip stock, grooved slide handle; black plastic buttplate. Introduced 1920s; discontinued 1940.

Exc.: $225	**VGood:** $175	**Good:** $150

SAVAGE MODEL 28B

Same specs as Model 28A except raised matted rib. No longer in production.

Exc.: $235	**VGood:** $185	**Good:** $160

SAVAGE MODEL 28D

Same specs as Model 28A except Full-choke barrel; matted rib; hand-checkered pistol-grip trap-style stock, slide handle. No longer in production.

Exc.: $235	**VGood:** $185	**Good:** $160

SAVAGE MODEL 30

Slide action; hammerless; solid frame; 12-, 16-, 20-ga., .410; 4-shot (.410), 5-shot magazine; 26-inch, 28-inch, 30-inch barrel; Improved Modified, Full chokes; vent rib; uncheckered American walnut stock, grooved slide handle; hard rubber buttplate. Introduced 1958; discontinued 1979.

Exc.: $170	**VGood:** $150	**Good:** $130

Savage Model 30D

Savage Model 30 Slug Gun

Savage Model 220

Savage Model 311

Savage Model 312 Field

Savage Model 333

Savage Model 333T Trap

SAVAGE MODEL 30AC
Same specs as Model 30 except 12-ga.; 26-inch barrel; adjustable choke; checkered stock. Introduced 1959; discontinued 1975.

    Exc.: $200   **VGood:** $175   **Good:** $160

SAVAGE MODEL 30ACL
Same specs as Model 30 except 12-ga.; 26-inch barrel; adjustable choke; checkered stock; ejection port, safety on left side. Introduced 1960; discontinued 1964.

    Exc.: $180   **VGood:** $150   **Good:** $120

SAVAGE MODEL 30D
Same specs as Model 30 except takedown; 12-, 20-ga., .410; 3-inch chamber; vent rib; checkered pistol-grip stock, fluted extension slide handle; recoil pad; alloy receiver; etched pattern on receiver. Introduced 1972; discontinued 1979.

    Exc.: $180   **VGood:** $165   **Good:** $150

SAVAGE MODEL 30FG
Same specs as Model 30 except takedown; 12-, 20-ga., .410; 3-inch chamber; checkered pistol-grip stock, fluted extension slide handle; recoil pad; alloy receiver. Introduced 1970; discontinued 1975.

    Perf.: $180   **Exc.:** $130   **VGood:** $100

SAVAGE MODEL 30 SLUG GUN
Same specs as Model 30 except 12-, 20-ga.; 22-inch slug barrel; rifle sights. Introduced 1964; discontinued 1982.

    Perf.: $180   **Exc.:** $150   **VGood:** $130

SAVAGE MODEL 30T
Same specs as Model 30 except 12-ga.; 30-inch Full-choke barrel; Monte Carlo trap-style stock; recoil pad. Introduced 1964; discontinued 1975.

    Perf.: $180   **Exc.:** $150   **VGood:** $130

SAVAGE MODEL 210F MASTER SHOT SLUG GUN
Gauge: 12, 3-inch chamber; 2-shot magazine; 24-inch barrel 1:35-inch rifling twist; weighs 7-1/2 lbs.; 43-1/2-inch overall; glass-filled polymer with positive checkering; based on the Savage Model 110 action; 60-degree bolt lift; controlled round feed; comes with scope mount. Introduced 1996. Made in U.S. by Savage Arms.

    Perf.: $495   **Exc.:** $325   **VGood:** $280

SAVAGE MODEL 220
Single barrel; single shot; hammerless; takedown; 12-, 16-, 20-ga., .410; 28-inch to 32-inch barrels; Full choke; uncheckered American walnut pistol-grip stock, forearm; automatic ejector. Introduced 1947; discontinued 1965. Separate barrels $100 in Excellent condition.

    Exc.: $300   **VGood:** $240   **Good:** $150

SAVAGE MODEL 220AC
Same specs as Model 220 except Savage adjustable choke. No longer in production.

    Exc.: $285   **VGood:** $25   **Good:** $135

SAVAGE MODEL 220L
Same specs as Model 220 except side lever. Introduced 1965; discontinued 1972.

    Exc.: $285   **VGood:** $220   **Good:** $150

SAVAGE MODEL 220P
Same specs as Model 220 except 12-, 16-, 20-, 28-ga.; Poly Choke; recoil pad. No longer in production.

    Exc.: $285   **VGood:** $25   **Good:** $135

SAVAGE MODEL 242
Over/under; .410; 24-inch barrels; Full choke; open rear, ramp front sight; single exposed hammer; uncheckered walnut pistol-grip stock; lever barrel selector; single trigger. Introduced 1977; discontinued 1979.

    Perf.: $425   **Exc.:** $375   **VGood:** $255

SAVAGE MODEL 312 FIELD
Over/under; boxlock; 12-ga.; 3-inch chambers; 26-inch, 28-inch barrels; Improved Cylinder, Modified, Full choke tubes; ventilated top, middle ribs; weighs 7 lbs.; checkered walnut stock; ventilated recoil pad; single trigger; satin chrome-finished frame. Introduced 1990; discontinued 1993.

    Perf.: $475   **Exc.:** $365   **VGood:** $300

SAVAGE MODEL 312SC SPORTING CLAYS
Same as the Model 312 Field except 28-inch barrels; Skeet 1, Skeet 2, Improved Cylinder, Modified, Full choke tubes; curved target-type recoil pad; receiver marked "Sporting Clays" on each side. Introduced 1990; discontinued 1993.

    Perf.: $575   **Exc.:** $460   **VGood:** $400

SAVAGE MODEL 312T TRAP
Same as the Model 312 Field except 30-inch barrels; Full, Modified choke tubes; weighs 7-1/4 lbs.; checkered walnut Monte Carlo stock; rubber recoil pad. Introduced 1990; discontinued 1993.

    Perf.: $500   **Exc.:** $425   **VGood:** $430

SAVAGE MODEL 320
Over/under; 20-ga.; 3-inch chambers; 26-inch barrels; choke tubes; vent top, middle ribs; weighs 6-3/4 lbs.; high-gloss, uncheckered stock, forend; recoil pad; single trigger; marketed with gun lock, shooting glasses, ear protection. Introduced 1991; discontinued 1992.

    Perf.: $500   **Exc.:** $425   **VGood:** $325

SAVAGE MODEL 330
Over/under; boxlock; 12- (2-3/4-inch), 20-ga. (3-inch); 26-inch Improved Cylinder/Modified, 28-inch Modified/Full, 30-inch Modified/Full barrels; checkered European walnut pistol-grip stock, forearm; selective single trigger; plain extractors. Made in Finland by Valmet. Introduced 1969; discontinued 1979.

    Perf.: $500   **Exc.:** $400   **VGood:** $325

SAVAGE MODEL 333
Over/under; boxlock; 12- (2-3/4-inch), 20-ga. (3-inch); 26-inch Improved Cylinder/Modified or Skeet/Skeet, 28-inch Modified/Full, 30-inch Modified/Full barrels; vent rib; checkered European walnut pistol-grip stock, broad forearm; single selective triggers; auto ejectors. Made in Finland by Valmet.

    Perf.: $575   **Exc.:** $475   **VGood:** $425
Add 30 percent to above prices for 20-ga.
Add 25 percent for extra set of barrels.

SAVAGE MODEL 333T TRAP
Same specs as Model 333 except 12-ga.; 30-inch Improved Cylinder/Modified or Skeet/Skeet, 28-inch Modified/Full, checkered European walnut Monte Carlo pistol-grip trap stock; extractors; recoil pad. Introduced 1972; discontinued 1979.

    Perf.: $550   **Exc.:** $425   **VGood:** $375

SAVAGE MODEL 420

Over/under; boxlock; hammerless; takedown; 12-, 16-, 20-ga.; 26-inch, 28-inch, 30-inch barrels; Modified/Full or Cylinder/Improved; uncheckered American walnut pistol-grip stock, forearm; double triggers; optional single non-selective trigger; extractors; automatic safety. Introduced 1930s; discontinued 1942.

Double triggers		
Exc.: $300	**VGood:** $200	**Good:** $175

Single trigger		
Exc.: $340	**VGood:** $235	**Good:** $200

SAVAGE MODEL 430

Over/under; boxlock; hammerless; takedown; 12-, 16-, 20-ga.; 26-inch, 28-inch, 30-inch barrels; Modified/Full, Cylinder/Improved chokes; matted top barrel; hand-checkered American walnut stock, forearm; double triggers; optional single non-selective trigger; automatic safety; recoil pad. Introduced 1930s; discontinued 1942.

Double triggers		
Exc.: $350	**VGood:** $250	**Good:** $200

Single trigger		
Exc.: $395	**VGood:** $300	**Good:** $250

SAVAGE MODEL 440

Over/under; boxlock; 12- (2-3/4-inch), 20-ga. (3-inch); 26-inch Improved Cylinder/Modified or Skeet/Skeet, 28-inch Modified/Full, 30-inch Modified/Full barrels; checkered American walnut pistol-grip stock, forearm; single selective trigger; plain extractors. Introduced 1968; discontinued 1972.

Perf.: $480	**Exc.:** $400	**VGood:** $375

SAVAGE MODEL 440T TRAP

Same specs as Model 440, except 12-ga.; 30-inch Improved Modified/Full barrels; wide vent rib; checkered select American walnut Monte Carlo trap stock, semi-beavertail forearm; recoil pad. Introduced 1969; discontinued 1972.

Perf.: $550	**Exc.:** $450	**VGood:** $400

SAVAGE MODEL 444 DELUXE

Over/under; boxlock; 12- (2-3/4-inch), 20-ga. (3-inch); 26-inch Improved Cylinder/Modified or Skeet/Skeet, 28-inch Modified/Full, 30-inch Modified/Full barrels; select checkered American walnut pistol-grip stock, semi-beavertail forearm; single selective trigger; auto ejectors. Introduced 1969; discontinued 1972.

Perf.: $550	**Exc.:** $450	**VGood:** $400

SAVAGE MODEL 550

Side-by-side; boxlock; hammerless; 12- (2-3/4-inch), 20-ga. (3-inch); 26-inch Improved Cylinder/Modified, 28-inch Modified/Full, 30-inch Modified/Full barrels; checkered American walnut pistol-grip stock, semi-beavertail forearm; non-selective single trigger; auto ejectors. Introduced 1971; discontinued 1973.

Perf.: $325	**Exc.:** $275	**VGood:** $175

SAVAGE MODEL 720

Autoloader; Browning humpback design; takedown; 12-, 16-ga.; 4-shot tube magazine; 26-inch, 28-inch, 30-inch, 32-inch barrels; Cylinder, Modified, Full chokes; hand-checkered American walnut pistol-grip stock forearm; black plastic buttplate. Introduced 1930; discontinued 1949.

Exc.: $345	**VGood:** $275	**Good:** $250

SAVAGE MODEL 726

Autoloader; takedown; 12-, 16-ga.; 2-shot tube magazine; 26-inch, 28-inch, 30-inch, 32-inch barrels; Cylinder, Modified, Full chokes; hand-checkered American walnut pistol-grip stock, forearm; black plastic buttplate; engraved receiver. Introduced 1930; discontinued 1949.

Exc.: $345	**VGood:** $275	**Good:** $250

SAVAGE MODEL 740C

Autoloader; takedown; 12-, 16-ga.; 2-shot tube magazine; 24-1/2-inch barrel; Skeet choke; hand-checkered American walnut pistol-grip Skeet-style stock, beavertail forearm; Cutts Compensator; black

Savage Model 420

Savage Model 430

Savage Model 440

Savage Model 440T Trap

Savage Model 550

Savage Model 720

Savage Model 726

Savage Model 755

plastic buttplate. Introduced 1939; discontinued 1949.

Exc.: $350	**VGood:** $230	**Good:** $195

SAVAGE MODEL 745 LIGHTWEIGHT

Autoloader; takedown; 12-ga.; 3-, 5-shot tube magazine; 28-inch barrel; Cylinder, Modified, Full chokes; hand-checkered American walnut pistol-grip stock, forearm; black plastic buttplate; alloy receiver. Introduced 1946; discontinued 1949.

Exc.: $345	**VGood:** $275	**Good:** $250

SAVAGE MODEL 750

Autoloader; Browning design; takedown; 12-ga. 4-shot tube magazine; 26-inch Improved, 28-inch Full or Modified barrel; checkered American walnut pistol-grip stock, grooved forearm. Introduced 1960; discontinued 1963.

Exc.: $345	**VGood:** $275	**Good:** $250

SAVAGE MODEL 750AC

Same specs as Model 750 except 26-inch barrel; adjustable choke. Introduced 1964; discontinued 1967.

Exc.: $345	**VGood:** $275	**Good:** $250

SAVAGE MODEL 750SC

Same specs as Model 750 except 26-inch barrel; Savage Super Choke. Introduced 1962; discontinued 1963.

Exc.: $225	**VGood:** $150	**Good:** $120

SAVAGE MODEL 755

Autoloader; takedown; 12-, 16-ga.; 2-, 4-shot tube magazine; 26-inch Improved Cylinder, 28-inch Full or Modified, 30-inch Full barrel; hand-checkered American walnut pistol-grip stock, forearm; rounded receiver. Introduced 1949; discontinued 1958.

Exc.: $210	**VGood:** $160	**Good:** $120

SAVAGE MODEL 755SC

Same specs as Model 755 except 25-inch barrel; Savage Super Choke. No longer in production.

Exc.: $210	**VGood:** $160	**Good:** $120

Savage Model 775
Lightweight

Savage Model 775SC
Lightweight

Savage Model 2400 Combo

Savage Milano

Scattergun Technologies
Tactical Response TR-870

Scattergun Technologies
SWAT

SAVAGE MODEL 775 LIGHTWEIGHT

Autoloader; takedown; 12-, 16-ga.; 2-, 4-shot magazine; 26-inch Improved Cylinder, 28-inch Full or Modified, 30-inch Full barrel; hand-checkered American walnut pistol-grip stock, forearm; alloy receiver. Introduced 1953; discontinued 1960.

Exc.: $210   **VGood:** $150   **Good:** $125

SAVAGE MODEL 775SC LIGHTWEIGHT

Same specs as Model 775 Lightweight, except 26-inch barrel; Savage Super Choke. No longer in production.

Exc.: $225   **VGood:** $165   **Good:** $120

SAVAGE MODEL 2400 COMBO

Over/under; boxlock; 12-ga.; Full-choke upper barrel, 308 Win. or 222 Rem. lower barrel; 23-1/2-inch barrels; solid matted rib; blade front sight; folding leaf rear; dovetail for scope mounting; checkered European walnut Monte Carlo pistol-grip stock, semi-beavertail forearm; recoil pad. Made by Valmet in Finland. Introduced 1975; discontinued 1979.

Perf.: $775   **Exc.:** $600   **VGood:** $450

SAVAGE MILANO

This Italian-made over-and-under is available in 12, 20 and 28 gauges and .410-bore on frames scaled to match, all with 28-inch barrels and 3-inch chambers.

Single selective trigger. Three choke tubes (fixed IC and Mod. on .410-bore). Automatic ejectors.

NIB: $1225   **Exc.:** $1100   **VGood:** $875

SCATTERGUN TECHNOLOGIES TACTICAL RESPONSE TR-870

Slide action; 12-ga.; 3-inch chamber; 7-shot magazine; 18-inch Cylinder-choked barrel; ramp front sight with tritium insert, adjustable Ghost Ring rear; Davis Speed Feed II synthetic stock; adjustable nylon sling; Jumbo Head safety; 6-shot ammo holder on left side of receiver; modified Remington 870P; additions include recoil-absorbing buttplate; nylon forend with flashlight. Made in variety of law enforcement versions. Introduced 1991; still in production.

Perf.: $650   **Exc.:** $400   **VGood:** $300

FBI model (Discontinued 1999)
Perf.: $715   **Exc.:** $625   **VGood:** $490

Patrol model (Discontinued 1999)
Perf.: $545   **Exc.:** $500   **VGood:** $465

Border Patrol model
Perf.: $650   **Exc.:** $550   **VGood:** $475

Louis Awerbuck model
Perf.: $625   **Exc.:** $490   **VGood:** $385

Practical Turkey model
Perf.: $545   **Exc.:** $500   **VGood:** $465

Expert model
Perf.: $1200   **Exc.:** $995   **VGood:** $775

Professional model
Perf.: $895   **Exc.:** $735   **VGood:** $580

Entry model
Perf.: $995   **Exc.:** $800   **VGood:** $600

Compact model
Perf.: $575   **Exc.:** $510   **VGood:** $420

SCATTERGUN TECHNOLOGIES K-9

Autoloader; 12-ga.; 18-inch barrel; adj. ghost ring sight; 7-shot mag.; side saddle; synthetic buttstock and forearm. Discontinued 2003.

Perf.: $1100   **Exc.:** $875   **VGood:** $775

SCATTERGUN TECHNOLOGIES SWAT

Similar to K-9 Model, except has 14-inch barrel and forearm with 11,000CP flashlight. Discontinued 2003. This model was available for police and military sales only.

Perf.: $1400   **Exc.:** $1150   **VGood:** $895

SCATTERGUN TECHNOLOGIES URBAN SNIPER

Autoloader; 12-ga.; 18-inch rifled barrel; scout optics; 7-shot mag.; side saddle; synthetic butt stock and forearm; bipod. Descontinued 1999.

Perf.: $1225   **Exc.:** $1075   **VGood:** $950

W&C SCOTT (GUNMAKERS) LTD. BLENHEIM

Side-by-side; bar-action sidelock; 12-ga.; 25-inch to 30-inch barrels; choking to order; concave, Churchill or flat rib; figured walnut with 28 lpi checkering; gold oval on belly at stock; fine scroll and floral engraving; optional full or half pistol grip stock, semi-beavertail forend. Introduced 1983; discontinued 1991. A best quality gun. Made in England.

Perf.: $25,000 **Exc.:** $18,500 **VGood:** $15,000

Deluxe, upgraded wood and metal work
Perf.: $30,000 **Exc.:** $23,000 **VGood:** $19,000

W&C SCOTT (GUNMAKERS) LTD. BOWOOD DELUXE

Side-by-side; boxlock; 12-, 16-, 20-, 28-ga.; 25-inch to 30-inch barrels; Improved/Modified choking or to order; concave, Churchill or flat rib; hand-checkered custom French walnut stock; scroll engraving. Made in England. Introduced 1980; discontinued 1991.

12-, 16-ga.
Perf.: $7500   **Exc.:** $6000   **VGood:** $5000

20-, 28-ga.
Perf.: $8500   **Exc.:** $7000   **VGood:** $6000

W&C SCOTT (GUNMAKERS) LTD. CHATSWORTH GRANDELUXE

Side-by-side; boxlock; 12-, 16-, 20-, 28-ga.; 25-inch to 30-inch barrels; Improved/Modified choking or to order; concave, Churchill or flat rib; fine hand-checkered custom French walnut stock; hand-fitted; extensive scroll engraving. Made in England. Introduced 1980; discontinued 1991.

12-, 16-ga.
Perf.: $9500   **Exc.:** $7000   **VGood:** $6000

20-, 28-ga.
Perf.: $10,500   **Exc.:** $8000   **VGood:** $7000

W&C SCOTT (GUNMAKERS) LTD. CROWN

Side-by-side; hammerless boxlock; 12-, 16-, 20-, 28-ga.; 25-inch to 30-inch barrels; Improved/Modified choking or to order; concave, Churchill or flat rib; checkered French walnut stock with side panels and drop points; engraved case-colored action. Introduced 1982; discontinued 1991. Made in England.

Perf.: N/A   **Exc.:** N/A   **VGood:** N/A   **Good:** N/A

W&C SCOTT (GUNMAKERS) LTD. KINMOUNT

Side-by-side; boxlock; 12-, 16-, 20-, 28-ga.; 25-inch to 30-inch barrels; Improved/Modified choking or to order; concave, Churchill or flat rib; checkered French walnut stock; engraving. Introduced 1981; discontinued 1991. Made in England.

12-, 16-ga.
Perf.: $7000   **Exc.:** $5500   **VGood:** $4500
20-, 28-ga.
Perf.: $8000   **Exc.:** $6500   **VGood:** $5500

W&C SCOTT (GUNMAKERS) LTD. TEXAN

Side-by-side; hammerless boxlock with false sideplates; 12-, 16-, 20-, 28-ga.; 25-inch to 30-inch barrels; standard chokes; flat rib; single trigger; ejectors; fancy walnut; pistol grip stock, beavertail forend. Made for the American market. Introduced 1981; discontinued 1991. Made in England.

Perf.: $7000   **Exc.:** $5500   **VGood:** $4500

W&C SCOTT & SON MONTE CARLO B

Side-by-side; hammerless; bar-action sidelock; 10-, 12-, 16-, 20-ga.; 28-inch to 32-inch Damascus or fluid steel barrels; choking to order; solid flat rib; figured walnut stock and forend; extractors or ejectors; double or single trigger; early examples have crystal (cocking) indicators on sideplate; two grades of engraving; case-colored action. This was the company's most popular sidelock. Introduced 1898; discontinued 1935. Made in England.

Perf.: $5000   **Exc.:** $3500   **VGood:** $2500

W&C SCOTT & SON PIGEON CLUB GUN

Side-by-side; bar-action sidelock; exposed hammers; 10-, 12-ga.; 27-inch to 32-inch Damascus or fluid steel barrel; choking to order; solid flat rib; figured walnut stock and forend; fully engraved case-colored action; made in grades A, B, C, but not marked. Made in England. Introduced 1879; discontinued 1924.

Perf.: $4500   **Exc.:** $3500   **VGood:** $2850

W&C SCOTT & SON PREMIER HAMMERLESS

Side-by-side; bar-action sidelock; hammerless; 10-, 12-, 16-, 20-ga.; 28-inch to 32-inch Damascus or fluid steel barrel; choking to order; solid flat rib; figured walnut stock and forend; ejectors; square cross bolt third lock; sideclips; fully engraved case-colored action. Made in England. This was the company's best gun. Introduced 1897; discontinued 1927.

Perf.: $9000   **Exc.:** $7500   **VGood:** $6000

W&C SCOTT & SON IMPERIAL PREMIER HAMMERLESS

Same specs as the Premier Hammerless except with extensive high-quality engraving; finest Italian walnut with fleur-de-lis checkering. Introduced 1897; discontinued 1932.

Perf.: $11,500   **Exc.:** $9000   **VGood:** $7000

W&C SCOTT & SON PREMIER QUALITY HAMMER

Side-by-side; bar-action sidelock; exposed hammers; 4-, 8-, 10-, 12-, 16-ga.; 27-inch to 32-inch Damascus or fluid steel barrels; choking to order; solid flat rib; figured walnut stock and forend; fully engraved case-colored action. Made in England. Introduced 1873; discontinued 1921.

Perf.: $2800   **Exc.:** $2000   **VGood:** $1750

W&C SCOTT & SON RELIANCE/CONTINENTAL

Side-by-side; hammerless boxlock; 10-, 12-, 16-, 20-ga.; 28-inch to 32-inch Damascus or fluid steel barrels; standard choking; solid flat rib; figured walnut; ejectors; double trigger; Greener cross bolt; sideclips fully engraved, case-colored scalloped

W&C Scott (Gunmakers) Ltd. Kinmount

W&C Scott (Gunmakers) Ltd. Crown

W&C Scott & Son Premier Hammerless

W&C Scott (Gunmakers) Ltd. Texan

Secolo Model 250

Senator Folding Model

action. This was the company's best boxlock shotgun. Made in England. Discontinued 1933.

Perf.: $3000   **Exc.:** $2400   **VGood:** $1900

W&C SCOTT & SON SINGLE BARREL TRAP

Single shot; bar-action sidelock; 12-ga.; 27-inch to 36-inch fluid steel barrel; vent-rib with twin ivory sight beads; pistol grip Monte Carlo stock, beavertail forend; recoil pad; engraved action; Italian walnut. Sold for $400 in 1928; 70 guns made. Made in England. Introduced 1914; discontinued 1929. Extreme rarity precludes pricing.

SECOLO MODEL 250

Over/under; 12-ga.; 2-3/4-inch chambers; 28-inch Modified/Full barrels; vent rib; hand-checkered European walnut pistol-grip stock, forend; extractors; single or double triggers; sling swivels; silvered frame; light engraving. Made in Spain. Introduced 1983; discontinued 1984.

Perf.: $375   **Exc.:** $295   **VGood:** $225

SECOLO MODEL 530

Single barrel; 12-ga.; 2-3/4-inch chamber; 30-inch, 32-inch lower barrel; 5 interchangeable choke tubes; vent rib; European walnut Monte Carlo stock; silvered or case-hardened receiver. Made in Spain. Introduced 1983; discontinued 1984.

Perf.: $900   **Exc.:** $775   **VGood:** $675

SECOLO MODEL 540 MONO TRAP

Single barrel; 12-ga.; 2-3/4-inch chamber; 30-inch, 32-inch upper barrel; 5 interchangeable choke tubes; vent rib; European walnut Monte Carlo stock; silvered or case-hardened receiver. Made in Spain. Introduced 1983; discontinued 1984.

Perf.: $900   **Exc.:** $775   **VGood:** $675

SECOLO MODEL 550 TRAP

Over/under; 12-ga.; 2-3/4-inch chambers, 30-inch, 32-inch barrels; 5 interchangeable choke tubes; vent rib; European walnut Monte Carlo stock; silvered or case-hardened receiver. Made in Spain. Introduced 1983; discontinued 1984.

Perf.: $800   **Exc.:** $625   **VGood:** $540

SECOLO MODEL 560 SKEET

Over/under; 12-ga.; 2-3/4-inch chambers; 30-inch, 32-inch Skeet/Skeet barrels; vent rib; Skeet-style European walnut stock; silvered or case-hardened receiver. Made in Spain. Introduced 1983; discontinued 1984.

Perf.: $825   **Exc.:** $650   **VGood:** $575

SENATOR FOLDING MODEL

Over/under; boxlock; 12-, 20-ga., .410; 3-inch chambers; 26-inch, 28-inch barrels; vent top, middle ribs; weighs 7 lbs.; European walnut stock; engraved; underlever cocking/opening system. Made in Italy. Introduced 1986; discontinued 1988.

Perf.: $210   **Exc.:** $160   **VGood:** $110

SIGARMS APOLLO TR AND TT SHOTGUNS

Over/under; boxlock action; 12-, 20-gauge, .410, 3-inch chambers; 28-gauge 2-3/4-inch chambers; 26-inch, 28-inch, 30-inch, 32-inch barrels; weighs 6 to 7-1/4 lbs.; oil-finished European walnut stock; hard-chromed bores; automatic ejectors; single selective trigger; choke tubes (12 and 20 ga. only). Introduced 2000. From Sigarms.

TR 30 Field (color casehardened side plates)
Perf.: $2275   **Exc.:** $1900   **VGood:** $1675
TR 40 Gold (gold overlays on game scenes)
Perf.: $2575   **Exc.:** $2125   **VGood:** $1850
TT 25 Competition (wide vent. rib with mid-bead)
Perf.: $2475   **Exc.:** $2000   **VGood:** $1750

Sigarms SA 3

Sile Sky Stalker

Silma Model 70

Silma Model 70 EJ Deluxe

Silma Model 70 EJ Superlight

Silma Model 70 EJ Standard

SKB Model 1300 Upland Mag

SKB Model 1900 Field

checkered select European walnut, pistol grip, solid rubber recoil pad; monobloc construction; chrome-moly blued steel barrels; raised vent rib; automatic safety and ejectors; single mechanical gold-plated trigger; bead front sight; brushed, engraved receiver. Introduced 2002. Imported from Italy by Legacy sports International.

12-, 20-ga. w/multichokes (IC, M, F)		
Perf.: $815	**Exc.:** $750	**VGood:** $675
28-ga., .410 w/multichokes (IC, M, F), fixed (M&F)		
Perf.: $868	**Exc.:** $813	**VGood:** $733

SILMA MODEL 70 EJ SUPERLIGHT
Similar to Silma 70EJ Deluxe except 12-gauge, 3-inch chambers, alloy receiver, weighs 5.6 lbs.

12-, 20-ga. w/multichokes (IC, M, F)		
Perf.: $1001	**Exc.:** $896	**VGood:** $806
12-, 20-ga. w/fixed chokes (M&F)		
Perf.: $890	**Exc.:** $785	**VGood:** $695

SILMA MODEL 70 EJ STANDARD
Similar to Silma 70EJ Deluxe except 12- and 20-gauge only, standard walnut stock, light engraving, silver-plated trigger.

12-ga. w/multichokes (IC, M, F)		
Perf.: $686	**Exc.:** $611	**VGood:** $576

SKB MODEL 300
Recoil-operated autoloader; takedown; 12-, 20-ga.; 5-shot magazine; 26-inch Improved Cylinder, 28-inch Full or Modified, 30-inch Full barrel; optional vent rib; checkered American walnut pistol-grip stock, fluted forearm; crossbolt safety; automatic magazine cutoff allows changing loads without unloading magazine. Introduced 1969; discontinued 1973.

With plain barrel		
Perf.: $300	**Exc.:** $200	**VGood:** $150
With vent rib		
Perf.: $325	**Exc.:** $225	**VGood:** $175

SKB MODEL 900 DELUXE
Recoil-operated autoloader; takedown; 12-, 20-ga; 5-shot magazine; 25-inch Improved Cylinder, 28-inch Full or Modified, 30-inch Full barrel; vent rib; hand-checkered American walnut pistol-grip stock, forearm; white spacers on grip cap, buttplate; interchangeable barrels; crossbolt safety; gold-filled engraving on receiver; gold-plated trigger; nameplate inlaid in stock. Introduced 1969; discontinued 1973.

Perf.: $300   **Exc.:** $250   **VGood:** $200

SKB MODEL 900 DELUXE SLUG
Same specs as Model 900 Deluxe except 24-inch slug barrel; rifle sights. Introduced 1969; discontinued 1973.

Perf.: $275   **Exc.:** $220   **VGood:** $200

SKB MODEL 1300 UPLAND MAG
Gas-operated autoloader; 12-, 20-ga.; 2-3/4-inch, 3-inch chamber; 22-inch Slug barrel, 26-inch, 28-inch vent-rib barrel; Inter-Choke tubes; hand-checkered walnut pistol-grip stock, forend; magazine cut-off system; blued receiver. Made in Japan. Introduced 1988; discontinued 1992.

Perf.: $400   **Exc.:** $325   **VGood:** $290

SKB MODEL 1900 FIELD
Gas-operated autoloader; 12-, 20-ga.; 2-3/4-inch, 3-inch chamber; 22-inch Slug barrel, 26-inch, 28-inch vent-rib barrel; Inter-Choke tubes; hand-checkered walnut pistol-grip stock, forend; magazine cut-off system; gold-plated trigger; engraved bright-finish receiver. Made in Japan. Introduced 1988; discontinued 1992.

Perf.: $450   **Exc.:** $375   **VGood:** $300

SKB MODEL 1900 TRAP
Same specs as Model 1900 Field except 12-ga.; 2-3/4-inch chamber; 30-inch barrel; Inter-Choke tubes; 9.5mm wide raised rib. Made in Japan. Introduced 1988; discontinued 1992.

Perf.: $450   **Exc.:** $375   **VGood:** $300

SIGARMS SA 3
Over-under; boxlock action; 12-, 20-gauge; 3-inch chambers; 26-inch, 28-inch, 30-inch separated barrels; weighs 7 lbs.; scalloped coin finished monoblock with game scene engraving; field or Sporting Clays (introduced 1998) configuration; vent rib; choke tubes; ejectors; SST; checkered walnut stock and forearm. Introduced 1997; dropped 1998.

Perf.: $1175   **Exc.:** $925   **VGood:** $775

SIGARMS SA 5
Over-under; boxlock action; 12-, 20-gauge; 3-inch chambers; coin finished monoblock action; hand engraved detachable side plates; ejectors; SST; select checkered walnut stock and forearm; field or Sporting Clays (introduced 1998) configuration; 26-1/2-inch, 28-inch, 30-inch (Sporting Clays only) barrels; vent rib; choke tubes; lockable case; weighs 6 to 7 lbs. Introduced 1997; dropped 1999.

Perf.: $2175   **Exc.:** $1775   **VGood:** $1450

SILE SKY STALKER
Over/under; .410; 3-inch chambers; 26-inch barrels; checkered walnut stock, schnabel forend; folds for storage, carrying; chrome-lined bores; matted hard chrome finish on receiver. Made in Italy. Introduced 1984; discontinued 1990.

Perf.: $275   **Exc.:** $230   **VGood:** $185

SILMA MODEL 70
Over/under; boxlock; 12-ga.; 3-inch chambers; 27-1/2-inch barrels; Modified/Improved Cylinder; weighs 7 lbs.; European walnut pistol-grip stock; single trigger; sling swivels; engraved, blued action. Made in Italy. Introduced 1995; still in production.

Perf.: $725   **Exc.:** $600   **VGood:** $515

SILMA MODEL 70EJ DELUXE
Gauge: 12 (3-1/2-inch chambers), 20, .410 (3-inch chambers), 28 (2-3/4-inch chambers); 28-inch barrel (12- and 20-gauge, fixed and tubed, 28-ga. and .410 fixed), 26-inch barrel (12- and 20-ga. fixed); weighs 7.6 lbs 12-gauge; 6.9 lbs. 20-, 28-ga. and .410;

SKB MODEL XL 100

Gas-operated autoloader; slug gun; 12-ga.; 2-3/4-inch chamber; 4-shot magazine; 20-inch Cylinder barrel; 40-3/8-inch overall length; red ramp front sight with Raybar-type blade, adjustable rifle rear sight; French walnut stock forend; reversible crossbolt safety; marketed with sling swivels; aluminum alloy receiver black anodized finish. Made in Japan. Introduced 1978; discontinued 1980.

Perf.: $225   **Exc.:** $175   **VGood:** $150

SKB MODEL XL 300

Gas-operated autoloader; 12-, 20-ga.; 5-shot magazine; 26-inch Improved Cylinder or Skeet, 28-inch Full or Modified, 30-inch Full barrel; optional vent rib; checkered American walnut pistol-grip stock, fluted forearm; self-compensating gas system; reversible safety. Introduced 1973; discontinued 1976.

With plain barrel

Perf.: $275   **Exc.:** $225   **VGood:** $190

With vent rib

Perf.: $300   **Exc.:** $250   **VGood:** $210

SKB MODEL XL 900

Gas-operated autoloader; 12-, 20-ga; 5-shot tube magazine; 26-inch Improved Cylinder; 28-inch Full or Modified, 30-inch Full barrel; vent rib; Raybar front sight; checkered walnut-finished stock; self-compensating gas system; reversible safety; action release button. Introduced 1973; discontinued 1978.

Perf.: $300   **Exc.:** $250   **VGood:** $220

SKB MODEL XL 900 SKEET

Same specs as Model XL 900 except 26-inch Skeet barrel; Bradley front sight. Introduced 1973; discontinued 1978.

Perf.: $400   **Exc.:** $350   **VGood:** $265

SKB MODEL XL 900 SLUG GUN

Same specs as Model XL 900 except 24-inch slug barrel; rifle sights. Introduced 1973; discontinued 1978.

Perf.: $350   **Exc.:** $295   **VGood:** $260

SKB MODEL XL 900 TRAP

Same specs as Model XL 900 except 12-ga.; 30-inch Full or Improved Cylinder barrel; Bradley front sight. Introduced 1973; discontinued 1978.

Perf.: $395   **Exc.:** $350   **VGood:** $320

SKB MODEL 500

Over/under; boxlock; hammerless; 12-, 20-, 28-ga., .410; 26-inch Improved/Modified, 28-inch Improved/Modified or Modified/Full, 30-inch Modified/Full barrels; Raybar front sight; hand-checkered walnut pistol-grip stock, forearm; pistol-grip cap; fluted comb; gold-plated single selective trigger; automatic ejectors; non-automatic safety; chrome-lined barrels, action; scroll-engraved border on receiver. Introduced 1967; discontinued 1979.

Perf.: $500   **Exc.:** $400   **VGood:** $350

SKB MODEL 500 MAGNUM

Same specs as Model 500 except 12-ga.; 3-inch chambers. Introduced 1967; discontinued 1979.

Perf.: $550   **Exc.:** $450   **VGood:** $400

SKB MODEL 500 SKEET

Same specs as Model 500 except 12-, 20-ga.; fixed Skeet/Skeet chokes; recoil pad with white line spacer; white front sight with middle bead. Introduced 1979; no longer in production.

Perf.: $500   **Exc.:** $400   **VGood:** $350

SKB MODEL 505 DELUXE

Over/under; boxlock; 12-, 20-, 28-ga. (2-3/4-inch), 410; 3-inch chambers; 26-inch, 28-inch, 30-inch, 32-inch, 34-inch barrels; all 12-ga. barrels are back-bored, have lengthened forcing cones and longer choke tube system; Inter-Choke tubes or fixed (.410 only) Improved Cylinder/Modified, Modified/Full chokes; ventilated side ribs; weighs 6-1/2 to 8-1/2 lbs.; hand-checkered walnut stock with high-gloss finish; manual safety; automatic ejectors; single selective trigger; silver nitride-finish receiver with

SKB Model 500

SKB Model 500 Skeet

SKB Model 505 Deluxe

SKB Model 505 Field

SKB Model 585 Field

Field or Target pattern engraving, gold inlay. Made in Japan. Introduced 1987; discontinued 1993.

Field

Perf.: $850   **Exc.:** $700   **VGood:** $600

Two-barrel Field Set (12- & 20-ga., 20- & 28-ga. or 28-ga. & .410)

Perf.: $1150   **Exc.:** $1000   **VGood:** $900

SKB MODEL 505 SKEET

Same specs as the Model 505 Deluxe except 12-, 20-, 28-ga., .410; 26-inch 28-inch barrels; Skeet/Skeet chokes; Skeet stock dimensions. Made in Japan. Introduced 1987; discontinued 1993.

Perf.: $750   **Exc.:** $600   **VGood:** $500

SKB MODEL 505 SKEET SET

Same specs as the Model 505 Deluxe except 12-ga. gun comes with 20-, 28-ga. and .410 barrel sets in 26-inch or 28-inch lengths; fixed Skeet/Skeet chokes; Skeet stock dimensions. Made in Japan. Introduced 1987; discontinued 1993.

Perf.: $1750   **Exc.:** $1400   **VGood:** $1050

SKB MODEL 505 TRAP

Same specs as the Model 505 Deluxe except 12-ga.; 2-3/4-inch chambers; 30-inch barrels; fixed Improved Modified/Full chokes; Trap stock dimensions. Made in Japan. Introduced 1987; discontinued 1993.

Perf.: $850   **Exc.:** $600   **VGood:** $500

SKB MODEL 505 TRAP COMBO

Same specs as the Model 505 Deluxe except comes with 30-inch or 32-inch over/under barrels and 32-inch or 34-inch top single barrel; standard or Monte Carlo stock. Made in Japan. Introduced 1987; discontinued 1993.

Perf.: $1150   **Exc.:** $900   **VGood:** $800

SKB MODEL 585 FIELD

Over/under; boxlock; 12-, 20-, 28-ga. (2-3/4-inch), .410; 3-inch chambers; 26-inch, 28-inch, 30-inch, 32-inch, 34-inch barrels; all 12-gauge barrels are back-bored, have lengthened forcing cones and longer choke tube system; Inter-Choke tubes or fixed (.410 only) Improved Cylinder/Modified or Modified/Full chokes; ventilated side ribs; hand checkered walnut stock with high-gloss finish; target stocks available in

standard and Monte Carlo; manual safety, automatic ejectors, single selective trigger; silver nitride-finished receiver with Field or Target pattern engraving. Made in Japan. Introduced 1992; still in production.

Perf.: $1255   **Exc.:** $945   **VGood:** $760

Two-barrel Field Set (12- & 20-ga., 20- & 28-ga. or 28-ga. & .410)

Perf.: $2115   **Exc.:** $1775   **VGood:** $1475

Price: Trap, Skeet

Perf.: $1310   **Exc.:** $975   **VGood:** $800

Two-barrel trap combo

Perf.: $2110   **Exc.:** $1775   **VGood:** $1600

Sporting Clays

Perf.: $1410   **Exc.:** $1050   **VGood:** $850

Price: Skeet Set (20-, 28-, .410)

Perf.: $3175   **Exc.:** $2550   **VGood:** $2000

SKB MODEL 585 GOLD PACKAGE

Similar to Model 585 Field except gold-plated trigger, two gold-plated game inlays, schnabel forend. Silver or blue receiver. Introduced 1998. Imported from Japan by G.U. Inc.

12-, 20-ga.

Perf.: $1375   **Exc.:** $1065   **VGood:** $880

28-ga., .410

Perf.: $1445   **Exc.:** $1135   **VGood:** $950

SKB MODEL 585 SKEET

Same specs as Model 585 Field except Competition series choke tubes; Skeet-dimensioned stock, radiused recoil pad; oversize bores and lengthened forcing cones (12-ga. models); chrome-plated bores, chambers, ejectors. Made in Japan. Introduced 1992; still in production.

Perf.: $1050   **Exc.:** $800   **VGood:** $750

Four-barrel Skeet set

Perf.: $2400   **Exc.:** $1725   **VGood:** $1200

SKB MODEL 585 SPORTING CLAYS

Same specs as Model 585 Field except 12-, 20-, 28-ga.; 28-inch, 30-inch, 32-inch barrels; Competition series choke tubes (12-ga.), standard Inter-Choke tubes (20-, 28-ga.); traditional 3/8-inch narrow stepped rib or semi-wide channeled 15/16-inch stepped rib; nickel center bead, white front; special

SKB Model 600

SKB Model 600 Field

SKB Model 600 Magnum

SKB Model 600 Trap Grade

SKB Model 605 Trap

SKB Model 680 English

stock dimensions. Made in Japan. Introduced 1992; still in production.

> **Perf.:** $1100 **Exc.:** $850 **VGood:** $750

SKB MODEL 585 TRAP

Same specs as Model 585 Field except 12-ga.; 30-inch, 32-inch barrels; Competition series choke tubes; wide step rib; nickel center bead; white front; standard trap stock or Monte Carlo; oversize bores; lengthened forcing cones. Made in Japan. Introduced 1992; still in production.

> **Perf.:** $1050 **Exc.:** $800 **VGood:** $750

SKB TWO-BARREL COMBO

> **Perf.:** $1550 **Exc.:** $1300 **VGood:** $1150

SKB MODEL 585 WATERFOWLER

Same specs as Model 585 Field except 12-ga.; 28-inch, 30-inch barrels; Improved Cylinder, Skeet 1, Modified Inter-Choke tubes; oil-finished stock, forend; bead-blasted receiver with silver nitride finish; bead-blasted, blued barrels. Made in Japan. Introduced 1995; still in production.

> **Perf.:** $1100 **Exc.:** $850 **VGood:** $750

SKB MODEL 585 YOUTH

Same specs as Model 585 Field except 12-, 20-ga.; 26-inch, 28-inch barrels; 13-1/2-inch length of pull; .755-inch bores, lengthened forcing cones and Competition series choke tubes. Made in Japan. Introduced 1994; still in production.

> **Perf.:** $950 **Exc.:** $750 **VGood:** $650

SKB MODEL 600

Over/under; boxlock; hammerless; 12-, 20-, 28-ga.; .410; 26-inch Improved/Modified, 28-inch Improved/ Modified or Modified/Full, 30-inch Modified/Full barrel; Raybar front sight; select hand-checkered walnut pistol-grip stock, forearm; pistol-grip cap; fluted comb; gold-plated single selective trigger;

automatic ejectors; non-automatic safety; chrome-lined barrels; silver-finished, scroll-engraved receiver. Introduced 1967; discontinued 1979.

> **Perf.:** $950 **Exc.:** $875 **VGood:** $700

SKB MODEL 600 MAGNUM

Same specs as Model 600 except 12-ga.; 3-inch chamber. Introduced 1969; discontinued 1972.

> **Perf.:** $1050 **Exc.:** $875 **VGood:** $730

SKB MODEL 600 SKEET GRADE

Same specs as Model 600 except 26-inch, 28-inch Skeet/Skeet barrels; recoil pad. Introduced 1967; discontinued 1979.

> **Perf.:** $995 **Exc.:** $850 **VGood:** $725

SKB MODEL 600 SMALL BORE

Same specs as Model 600 except 20-, 28-ga., .410; 28-inch Skeet/Skeet three-barrel set; recoil pad. Introduced 1979; discontinued 1979.

> **Perf.:** $1400 **Exc.:** $1100 **VGood:** $925

SKB MODEL 600 TRAP GRADE

Same specs as Model 600, except 12-ga; 30-inch, 32-inch barrels; Full/Full or Full/Improved; walnut straight or Monte Carlo pistol-grip stock; recoil pad. Introduced 1967; discontinued 1979.

> **Perf.:** $990 **Exc.:** $850 **VGood:** $700

SKB MODEL 605 FIELD

Over/under; boxlock; 12-, 20-, 28-ga. (2-3/4-inch), .410; 3-inch chambers; 26-inch, 28-inch, 30-inch, 32-inch, 34-inch barrels; all 12-gauge barrels are back-bored, have lengthened forcing cones and longer choke tube system; Inter-Choke tubes or fixed Improved Cylinder/Modified, Modified/Full chokes; ventilated side ribs; weighs 6-1/2 to 8-1/2 lbs.; hand-checkered semi-fancy American walnut stock with high-gloss finish; manual safety; automatic ejectors; single selective trigger; silver nitride-finished receiver

with Field or Target pattern engraving, gold inlay. Made in Japan. Introduced 1987; discontinued 1992.

Field
> **Perf.:** $1075 **Exc.:** $850 **VGood:** $750

Two-barrel Field Set (12- & 20-ga. or 28-ga. & .410)
> **Perf.:** $1575 **Exc.:** $1300 **VGood:** $1250

SKB MODEL 605 SKEET

Same specs as Model 605 Field except 12-, 20-, 28-ga., .410; 28-inch barrels; Skeet/Skeet chokes; Skeet stock dimensions. Made in Japan. Introduced 1987; discontinued 1992.

> **Perf.:** $1100 **Exc.:** $850 **VGood:** $750

Four-barrel Skeet set
> **Perf.:** $1850 **Exc.:** $1500 **VGood:** $1100

SKB MODEL 605 SPORTING CLAYS

Same specs as Model 605 Field except 12-ga.; 2-3/4-inch chambers; 28-inch, 30-inch barrels; Inter-Choke tubes; Sporting Clays stock dimensions. Made in Japan. Introduced 1987; discontinued 1993.

> **Perf.:** $1050 **Exc.:** $800 **VGood:** $700

SKB MODEL 605 TRAP

Same specs as Model 605 Field except 12-ga.; 2-3/4-inch chambers; 30-inch, 32-inch barrels; Improved Modified/Full choke tubes; trap stock dimensions. Made in Japan. Introduced 1987; discontinued 1992.

> **Perf.:** $1000 **Exc.:** $750 **VGood:** $650

Two-barrel trap combo
> **Perf.:** $1300 **Exc.:** $1050 **VGood:** $950

SKB MODEL 680 ENGLISH

Over/under; boxlock; hammerless; 12-, 20-, 28-ga., .410; 26-inch, 28-inch chrome-lined barrels; Full/Modified or Modified/Improved chokes; vent rib; Bradley sights; checkered select walnut English-style straight-grip stock; single selective trigger; automatic selective ejectors; black chromed exterior surfaces. Introduced 1973; discontinued 1979.

> **Perf.:** $1300 **Exc.:** $1150 **VGood:** $975

SKB MODEL 685 FIELD

Over/under; boxlock; 12- 20-, 28-ga. (2-3/4-inch), .410; 3-inch chambers; 26-inch, 28-inch, 30-inch, 32-inch, 34-inch barrels; all 12-gauge barrels are back-bored, have lengthened forcing cones and longer choke tube system; Inter-Choke tubes or fixed (.410 only) Improved Cylinder/Modified or Modified/Full chokes; hand-checkered walnut stock with high-gloss finish; target stocks available in standard and Monte Carlo; manual safety; automatic ejectors; single selective trigger; jeweled barrel block; silver-finished receiver with fine engraving, gold inlay. Made in Japan. No longer imported.

> **Perf.:** $1250 **Exc.:** $925 **VGood:** $750

Two-barrel Field set (12- & 20-ga. or 28-ga. & .410)
> **Perf.:** $1650 **Exc.:** $1350 **VGood:** $1200

SKB MODEL 685 SPORTING CLAYS

Same specs as Model 685 Field except 12-, 20-, 28-ga.; 28-inch, 30-inch, 32-inch barrels; choke tubes; 3/8-inch stepped target-style rib optional; nickel center bead, white front; special stock dimensions; matte finish receiver. Made in Japan. No longer imported.

> **Perf.:** $1250 **Exc.:** $850 **VGood:** $750

Two-barrel Sporting Clays set (12-, 20-ga.)
> **Perf.:** $1650 **Exc.:** $1250 **VGood:** $1150

SKB MODEL 685 TRAP

Same specs as Model 685 Field except 12-ga.; 30-inch, 32-inch barrels; wide step rib; nickel center bead, white front; Competition series choke tubes; standard trap or Monte Carlo stock; oversize bores and lengthened forcing cones. Made in Japan. No longer imported.

> **Perf.:** $1350 **Exc.:** $950 **VGood:** $850

Two-barrel combo
> **Perf.:** $1650 **Exc.:** $1250 **VGood:** $1150

SKB MODEL 685 SKEET
Same specs as Model 685 Field except Competition series choke tubes; Skeet-dimensioned stock, radiused recoil pad; all 12-ga. models have oversize bores and lengthened forcing cones; chrome-plated bores, chambers, ejectors. Made in Japan. No longer imported.

Perf.: $1250   **Exc.:** $850   **VGood:** $750

Four-barrel Skeet set

Perf.: $1750   **Exc.:** $1350   **VGood:** $1200

SKB MODEL 700 SKEET
Over/under; boxlock; hammerless; 12-, 20-, 28-ga., .410; 26-inch, 28-inch Skeet/Skeet chrome-lined barrels; Raybar front sight; select hand-checkered oil-finished walnut pistol-grip stock, forearm; pistol-grip cap; fluted comb; gold-plated single selective trigger; automatic ejectors; non-automatic safety; recoil pad; silver-finished engraved receiver. Introduced 1967; discontinued 1979.

Perf.: $800   **Exc.:** $700   **VGood:** $625

SKB MODEL 700 TRAP
Same specs as Model 700 Skeet except 12-, 20-ga.; 30-inch, 32-inch barrels; Full/Full or Full/Improved chokes; straight or Monte Carlo walnut pistol-grip stock. Introduced 1967; discontinued 1979.

Perf.: $850   **Exc.:** $705   **VGood:** $625

SKB MODEL 785 FIELD
Over/under; boxlock; 12-, 20-, 28-ga. (2-3/4-inch), .410; 3-inch chambers; 26-inch, 28-inch, 30-inch, 32-inch barrels; chrome-plated, oversize, back-bored barrels with lengthened forcing cones; Inter-Choke tubes; hand-checkered American black walnut stock, semi-beavertail forend with high-gloss finish; single selective chrome-plated trigger; chrome-plated selective ejectors; manual safety. Made in Japan. Introduced 1995.

Perf.: $1750   **Exc.:** $1400   **VGood:** $1200

Field set (12- and 20-ga.)

Perf.: $2200   **Exc.:** $1800   **VGood:** $1500

Field, 12- or 20-ga.

Perf.: $1900   **Exc.:** $1650   **VGood:** $1400

Field, 28-ga. or .410

Perf.: $1980   **Exc.:** $1730   **VGood:** $1480

Field set, 20- & 28-ga., 28-ga. & .410

Perf.: $2780   **Exc.:** $2400   **VGood:** $2025

Sporting Clays, 12- or 20-ga.

Perf.: $2000   **Exc.:** $1675   **VGood:** $1375

Sporting Clays, 28-ga.

Perf.: $2080   **Exc.:** $1755   **VGood:** $1455

Sporting Clays set, 12- and 20-ga.

Perf.: $2775   **Exc.:** $2450   **VGood:** $2125

Skeet, 12- or 20-ga.

Perf.: $1940   **Exc.:** $1625   **VGood:** $1365

Skeet, 28-ga. or .410

Perf.: $1980   **Exc.:** $1665   **VGood:** $1405

Skeet, three-barrel set, 20-, 28-ga.,.410

Perf.: $3835   **Exc.:** $2975   **VGood:** $2350

Trap, standard or Monte Carlo

Perf.: $1940   **Exc.:** $1625   **VGood:** $1365

Trap combo, standard or Monte Carlo

Perf.: $2820   **Exc.:** $2505   **VGood:** $2245

SKB MODEL 785 SKEET
Same specs as Model 785 Field except Competition series choke tubes; Skeet-dimensioned stock, radiused recoil pad; all 12-ga. barrels back-bored with lengthened forcing cones. Made in Japan. Introduced 1995; still in production.

Perf.: $1750   **Exc.:** $1400   **VGood:** $1200

Three-barrel Skeet set (20-, 28-ga., .410)

Perf.: $2350   **Exc.:** $1800   **VGood:** $1500

SKB MODEL 785 SPORTING CLAYS
Same specs as Model 785 Field except 12-, 20-, 28-ga.; 28-inch, 30-inch, 32-inch barrels; target-style ventilated rib; Sporting Clays stock dimensions; radiused recoil pad. Made in Japan. Introduced 1995; still in production.

Perf.: $1800   **Exc.:** $1400   **VGood:** $1150

SKB Model 700 Trap

SKB Model 785 Field

SKB Model 885 Field

Sporting Clays set (12- and 20-ga.)

Perf.: $2400   **Exc.:** $2000   **VGood:** $1550

SKB MODEL 785 TRAP
Same specs as Model 785 Field except 12-ga.; 30-inch, 32-inch barrels; back-bored barrels with lengthened forcing cones, chrome-plated chambers; Competition series choke tubes; standard trap or Monte Carlo stock. Made in Japan. Introduced 1995; dropped 2002.

Perf.: $1750   **Exc.:** $1400   **VGood:** $1200

Two-barrel combo

Perf.: $2200   **Exc.:** $1800   **VGood:** $1500

SKB MODEL 800 FIELD
Over/under; boxlock; hammerless; 12-, 20-, 28-ga., .410; 26-inch Improved/Modified, 28-inch Improved/Modified or Modified/Full, 30-inch Modified/Full barrels; Raybar front sight; select hand-checkered walnut pistol-grip stock, forearm; pistol-grip cap; fluted comb; gold-plated single selective trigger; automatic ejectors; non-automatic safety; chrome-lined barrels, action; fine scroll-engraved border on receiver. Introduced 1979; discontinued 1980.

Perf.: $1100   **Exc.:** $800   **VGood:** $700

SKB MODEL 800 SKEET
Same specs as Model 800 Field except 12-, 20-ga.; 26-inch, 28-inch Skeet/Skeet chrome-lined barrels; recoil pad. Introduced 1969; discontinued 1979.

Perf.: $1250   **Exc.:** $900   **VGood:** $800

SKB MODEL 800 TRAP
Same specs as Model 800 Field except 12-ga.; 30-inch, 32-inch barrels; Full/Full or Full/Improved; straight or Monte Carlo walnut pistol-grip stock. Introduced 1967; discontinued 1979.

Perf.: $1250   **Exc.:** $900   **VGood:** $800

SKB MODEL 880 CROWN GRADE
Over/under; boxlock; sideplates; 12-, 20-, 28-ga., .410; 26-inch Skeet/Skeet, 28-inch Skeet/Skeet, 30-inch Full/Improved, 32-inch Full/Improved barrels; Bradley-type front sight; trap or Skeet hand-checkered fancy French walnut pistol-grip stock, forearm; hand-honed action; engraved receiver; gold-inlaid crown on bottom of frame. Introduced 1973; discontinued 1976.

Perf.: $1900   **Exc.:** $1800   **VGood:** $1600

SKB MODEL 885 FIELD
Over/under; boxlock; dummy sideplates; 12-, 20-, 28-ga. (2-3/4-inch), .410; 3-inch chambers; 26-inch, 28-inch, 30-inch, 32-inch, 34-inch barrels; all 12-gauge barrels are back-bored, have lengthened forcing cones and longer choke tube system; Inter-Choke tubes or fixed (.410 only) Improved Cylinder/Modified or Modified/Full chokes; hand-checkered select-grade walnut stock with high-gloss finish; target stocks available in standard and Monte Carlo; manual safety; automatic ejectors; single selective trigger; jeweled barrel block; silver-finished receiver with fine engraving, gold inlay. Made in Japan. No longer imported.

Perf.: $1650   **Exc.:** $1200   **VGood:** $900

Two-barrel Field set (12- & 20-ga. or 28-ga. & .410)

Perf.: $2100   **Exc.:** $1500   **VGood:** $1300

SKB MODEL 885 SPORTING CLAYS
Same specs as Model 885 Field except 12-, 20-, 28-ga.; 28-inch, 30-inch 32-inch barrels; choke tubes; 3/8-inch stepped target-style rib optional; nickel center bead, white front; special stock dimensions; matte finish receiver. Made in Japan. No longer imported.

Perf.: $1450   **Exc.:** $800   **VGood:** $700

SKB MODEL 885 SKEET
Same specs as Model 885 Field except Competition series choke tubes; Skeet-dimensioned stock, radiused recoil pad; all 12-ga. barrels oversize with lengthened forcing cones; chrome-plated bores, chambers, ejectors. Made in Japan. No longer imported.

Perf.: $1450   **Exc.:** $800   **VGood:** $700

Four-barrel Skeet set

Perf.: $2800   **Exc.:** $2000   **VGood:** $1800

SKB MODEL 885 TRAP
Same specs as Model 885 Field except 12-ga.; 30-inch, 32-inch barrels; Competition series choke tubes; wide step rib; nickel center bead, white front; standard trap stock or Monte Carlo; oversize bores and lengthened forcing cones. Made in Japan. No longer imported.

Perf.: $1650   **Exc.:** $900   **VGood:** $800

Two-barrel combo

Perf.: $2100   **Exc.:** $1500   **VGood:** $1300

SKB MODEL 5600
Over/under; 12-ga.; 26-inch, 28-inch, 30-inch barrels; vent rib; checkered walnut pistol-grip stock; auto selective ejectors; mechanical single trigger; hand-polished, blued frame, barrels; made in trap and Skeet configurations. Made in Japan. Introduced 1979; discontinued 1980.

Perf.: $575   **Exc.:** $495   **VGood:** $430

SKB MODEL 5700
Over/under; 12-ga.; 26-inch, 28-inch, 30-inch barrels; vent rib; high-grade checkered walnut pistol-grip stock; auto selective ejectors; mechanical single trigger; hand-polished, blued frame, barrels; engraving; made in trap and Skeet configurations. Introduced 1979; discontinued 1980.

Perf.: $695   **Exc.:** $530   **VGood:** $455

SKB MODEL 5800
Over/under; 12-ga.; 26-inch, 28-inch, 30-inch barrels; vent rib; best-grade checkered walnut pistol-grip stock; auto selective ejectors; mechanical single trigger; hand-polished, blued frame, barrels; elaborate engraving; made in trap and Skeet configurations. Introduced 1979; discontinued 1980.

Perf.: $950   **Exc.:** $850   **VGood:** $775

SKB 85TSS Unsingle Combo

SKB Model 100

SKB Model 200E

SKB Model 200 Magnum

SKB Model 280

SKB Model 385

SKB MODEL 85 TSS TRAP

Over/under; 12-ga.; 3-inch chamber; 32-inch barrel (Mag-na-ported barrel optional); weighs 8-3/4 lbs.; fixed or adjustable comb; 12 mm step-up rib.

SKB 85TSS UNSINGLE COMBO

Same as 85TSS above but with extra "unsingle" single-shot barrel set.

SKB SIDE-BY-SIDE SHOTGUNS SKB MODEL 100

Side-by side; boxlock; 12-, 20-ga.; 26-inch Improved/ Modified, 28-inch Full/Modified, 30-inch Full/Full barrels; hand-checkered pistol grip stock, forearm; single selective trigger; plain extractors; automatic safety. Made in Japan. Introduced 1967; discontinued 1979.

   Perf.: $795   **Exc.:** $575   **VGood:** $400
Add 20 percent to above prices for 20-ga. Add 10-15 percent for fully engraved receiver with hunting scene.

SKB MODEL 150

Side-by-side; boxlock; 12-, 20-ga.; 26-inch Improved/Modified, 28-inch Full/Modified, 30-inch Full/Full barrels; hand-checkered pistol-grip stock, beavertail forearm; single selective trigger; plain extractors; automatic safety. Introduced 1972; discontinued 1974.

   Perf.: $895   **Exc.:** $46455   **VGood:** $425
Add 20 percent to above prices for 20-ga.

SKB MODEL 200E

Side-by-side; boxlock; 12-, 20-ga.; 2-3/4-inch chambers; 26-inch Improved/Modified, 28-inch Full/ Modified, 30-inch Full/Full barrels; hand-checkered pistol-grip stock, beavertail forearm; recoil pad; automatic selective ejectors; engraved, silver-plated frame; gold-plated nameplate, trigger. Introduced 1967; discontinued 1979.

   Perf.: $1100   **Exc.:** $995   **VGood:** $875

SKB MODEL 200E SKEET GRADE

Same specs as Model 200E except 25-inch Skeet/ Skeet barrels; straight-grip English-style stock; non-automatic safety; recoil pad. Introduced 1967; discontinued 1979.

   Perf.: $1150   **Exc.:** $1025   **VGood:** $900

SKB MODEL 200 MAGNUM

Same specs as Model 200E except 3-inch chambers; 26-inch, 28-inch, 30-inch barrels; white line spacer recoil pad. Introduced 1979; no longer in production.

   Perf.: $1150   **Exc.:** $1025   **VGood:** $900

SKB MODEL 280

Side-by-side; boxlock; 12-, 20-ga.; 2-3/4-inch chambers; 25-inch, 26-inch, 28-inch barrels; standard choke combos; hand-checkered straight-grip stock, forearm; automatic selective ejectors; single selective trigger; gold-plated nameplate, trigger; game scene engraving. Introduced 1971; discontinued 1979.

   Perf.: $1400   **Exc.:** $900   **VGood:** $650

SKB MODEL 385 SIDE-BY-SIDE

Gauge: 12, 20, 3-inch chambers; 28, 2-3/4-inch chambers. Barrel: 26-inch (Imp. Cyl., Mod., Skeet choke tubes). Weight: 6-3/4 lbs. Length: 42 1/2-inch overall; American walnut with straight or pistol grip stock, semi-beavertail forend. Features: Boxlock action. Silver nitrided receiver with engraving; solid barrel rib; single selective trigger, selective automatic ejectors, automatic safety. Introduced 1996. Imported from Japan by G.U. Inc.

   Perf.: $1750   **Exc.:** $1425   **VGood:** $1050
   Field Set, 20-, 28-ga., 26-inch or 28-inch, English or pistol grip
   Perf.: $2475   **Exc.:** $2100   **VGood:** $1750

SKB MODEL 385 SPORTING CLAYS

Similar to the Field Model 385 except 12-gauge only; 28-inch barrel with choke tubes; raised ventilated rib with metal middle bead and white front. Introduced 1998. Imported from Japan by G.U. Inc.

   Perf.: $1850   **Exc.:** $1425   **VGood:** $1050
   Sporting Clays set, 20-, 28-ga.
   Perf.: $2575   **Exc.:** $2100   **VGood:** $1750

SKB MODEL 485 SIDE-BY-SIDE

Similar to the Model 385 except has dummy sideplates, raised ventilated rib with metal middle bead and white front, extensive upland game scene engraving, semi-fancy American walnut English or pistol grip stock. Imported from Japan by G.U. Inc.

   Perf.: $2400   **Exc.:** $2050   **VGood:** $1725
   Field set, 20-, 28-ga., 26-inch
   Perf.: $3400   **Exc.:** $2825   **VGood:** $2300

SKB MODEL 400E

Side-by-side; boxlock; 12-, 20-ga.; 3-inch chambers; 26-inch Improved/Modified, 28-inch Full/Modified, 30-inch Full/Full barrels; hand-checkered pistol-grip stock, beavertail forearm; recoil pad; automatic selective ejectors; engraved, silver-plated frame, sideplates, gold-plated nameplate, trigger. No longer in production.

   Perf.: $1595   **Exc.:** $1495   **VGood:** $1395

SKB MODEL 400E SKEET GRADE

Same specs as Model 400E except 25-inch Skeet/ Skeet barrel; straight-grip English-style stock; non-automatic safety; recoil pad. Introduced 1967; discontinued 1979.

   Perf.: $650   **Exc.:** $500   **VGood:** $450

SKB MODEL 480

Side-by-side; boxlock; 12-, 20-ga.; 3-inch chambers; 25-inch, 26-inch, 28-inch barrels; standard choke combos; hand-checkered straight-grip stock, forearm; automatic selective ejectors; single selective trigger; gold-plated nameplate, trigger; game scene engraving. Introduced 1971; discontinued 1979.

   Perf.: $1000   **Exc.:** $750   **VGood:** $600

SKB SINGLE BARREL & SLIDE-ACTION SHOTGUNS

SKB CENTURY

Single-barrel trap; boxlock; 12-ga.; 30-inch, 32-inch barrel; vent rib; full choke; checkered pistol-grip walnut stock, beavertail forearm; straight or Monte Carlo comb; recoil pad; auto ejector. Introduced 1973; discontinued 1974.

   Perf.: $550   **Exc.:** $475   **VGood:** $430

SKB CENTURY II

Same specs as Century except redesigned locking iron; Monte Carlo stock, reverse-taper forearm. Introduced 1975; discontinued 1979.

   Perf.: $575   **Exc.:** $495   **VGood:** $455

SKB MODEL 7300

Slide action; 12-, 20-ga.; 2-3/4-inch, 3-inch chambers; 24-inch, 26-inch, 28-inch, 30-inch barrels; vent rib; Ray-type front sights; hand-checkered French walnut stock, beavertail forend; recoil pad; white line spacer; double action bars. Made in Japan. Introduced 1979; discontinued 1980.

   Perf.: $275   **Exc.:** $200   **VGood:** $180

SKB Model 7300

SKB MODEL 7900 TARGET GRADE

Slide action; 12-, 20-ga.; 2-3/4-inch, 3-inch chambers; 26-inch Skeet/Skeet, 30-inch trap-choked barrels; white front sight, middle bead; hand-checkered French walnut stock, beavertail forend; recoil pad (Trap) or composition buttplate (Skeet); blued scroll-etched receiver; made in Trap and Skeet configurations. Introduced 1979; discontinued 1980.

Perf.: $325 **Exc.:** $275 **VGood:** $225

S&M 10-GAUGE

Over/under; boxlock; 10-ga.; 3-1/2-inch chambers; 28-inch, 32-1/2-inch Full/Full barrels; weighs 9 lbs.; checkered walnut stock; double triggers; extractors; matte-finished metal. Made in Europe. Introduced by Ballistic Products 1986; discontinued 1988.

Perf.: $475 **Exc.:** $375 **VGood:** $300

L.C. SMITH HAMMERLESS DOUBLE BARRELS (1890-1912)

Side-by-side; sidelock; hammerless; 8-, 10-, 12-, 16-, 20-ga.; 26-inch, 28-inch, 30-inch, 32-inch twist or fluid steel barrels; lowest grades stocked in American walnut, high grades in European walnut; splinter or beavertail forend; straight, half-, or pistol grip; double triggers; selective single trigger optional after 1904; ejectors optional in lower grades, standard in high grades; Featherweight frame was available in certain grades after 1909; only 30 made in 8-ga., 1895 to 1897; made in 12 grades until revised in 1913. Manufactured by Hunter Arms Co., Fulton, New York. Introduced 1890; discontinued 1912.

L.C. SMITH HAMMERLESS DOUBLE BARREL NO. 00 (1890-1912)

Same specs as Hammerless Double Barrel (1890-1912), except 12-, 16-, 20-ga.; fluid steel barrels; double trigger, extractors standard; single trigger, ejectors optional; total production, 57,795; with ejectors, 5,874. Introduced 1889; discontinued 1912.

Exc.: $1250 **VGood:** $800 **Good:** $650

L.C. SMITH HAMMERLESS DOUBLE BARREL NO. 0 (1890-1912)

Same specs as Hammerless Double Barrel (1890 to 1912), except twist (10-, 12-, 16-ga.) or fluid steel (10-, 12-, 16-, 20-ga.) barrels; double triggers, extractors standard; ejectors optional after 1898; Featherweight frame available after 1907; total production, 29,360; with ejectors, 6607. Introduced 1895; discontinued 1912.

Exc.: $1450 **VGood:** $950 **Good:** $750

L.C. SMITH HAMMERLESS DOUBLE BARREL NO. 1 (1890-1912)

Same specs as Hammerless Double Barrel (1890 to 1912), except twist (10-, 12-, 16-ga.) or fluid steel (10-, 12-, 16-, 20-ga.) barrels; fluid steel barrels available after 1907; double triggers, extractors standard; single trigger, ejectors optional; Featherweight frame available after 1907; in decoration, corresponds to the earlier Quality 2; total production, 10,221; with ejectors, 1640. Introduced 1890; discontinued 1912.

Exc.: $1800 **VGood:** $1100 **Good:** $900

L.C. SMITH HAMMERLESS DOUBLE BARREL PIGEON GUN (1890-1912)

Same specs as Hammerless Double Barrel (1890 to 1912), except twist (10-, 12-, 16-ga.) or fluid steel (12-, 16-, 20-ga.) barrels; French walnut straight or pistol grip stock; Monte Carlo comb optional; double triggers, ejectors standard; single trigger optional; lightweight version available in 12- and 16-ga.; total production, 1214. Introduced 1895; discontinued 1912.

Exc.: $1950 **VGood:** $1500 **Good:** $1300

L.C. SMITH HAMMERLESS DOUBLE BARREL NO. 2 (1890-1912)

Same specs as Hammerless Double Barrel (1890 to 1912), except 28-inch to 32-inch fluid steel barrels standard; twist barrels optional; European walnut pistol-grip stock; double triggers, extractors standard; ejectors optional; Featherweight frame

SKB Model 7900
Target Grade, Trap

SKB Model 7900
Target Grade, Skeet

L.C. Smith
Hammerless Double Barrel
Crown Grade (1913-1945)

L.C. Smith
Hammerless Double Barrel
Ideal Grade (1913-1945)

L.C. Smith
Hammerless Double Barrel
Trap Grade (1913-1945)

L.C. Smith Hammerless
Double Barrel
Skeet Special (1913-1945)

L.C. Smith Hammerless
Double Barrel
Specialty Grade (1913-1945)

follow the same basic specifications in gauges, barrel lengths, and other features as those made earlier. Their appearance is somewhat different, however, in that the frames and lockplates lack many of the complex, graceful curves and planes that characterize the older guns; this simpler, more straightforward shaping was an attempt by Hunter Arms to reduce the amount of milling and handwork that went into the guns, and thereby reduce the cost of manufacture. Beavertail forends became available in 1920; .410-bore guns in 1926; 10-ga. phased out in early 1920s; Featherweight frame available in some grades up to 1927, in all grades after 1927; special, extra-high solid rib available in all grades after 1939; manufactured by Hunter Arms Co., Fulton, New York. Introduced 1913; discontinued 1945.

L.C. SMITH HAMMERLESS DOUBLE BARREL FIELD GRADE (1913-1945)

Same specs as Hammerless Double Barrel (1913 to 1945), except 12-, 16-, 20-ga., .410; fluid steel barrels; American walnut pistol-grip stock; double triggers, extractors standard; single trigger, ejectors optional; a version featuring ivory sights and recoil pad was introduced in 1939 as the Field Special; total production, 141,844. Introduced 1913; discontinued 1945.

Exc.: $995   **VGood:** $700   **Good:** $600

L.C. SMITH HAMMERLESS DOUBLE BARREL IDEAL GRADE (1913-1945)

Same specs as Hammerless Double Barrel (1913 to 1945), except twist or fluid steel barrels; fluid steel barrels only, after 1917; 26-inch, 28-inch barrels only in .410; American walnut pistol-grip stock; straight or half-pistol grip optional; double triggers, extractors standard; single trigger, ejectors optional; total production, 21,862. Introduced 1913; discontinued 1945.

Exc.: $1300   **VGood:** $900   **Good:** $800

L.C. SMITH HAMMERLESS DOUBLE BARREL TRAP GRADE (1913-1945)

Same specs as Hammerless Double Barrel (1913 to 1945), except fluid steel barrels standard; twist barrels optional until 1917; American walnut pistol-grip stock standard; straight or half-pistol grip optional; ejectors and single trigger standard; double triggers optional; total production 3335. Introduced 1913; discontinued 1939.

Exc.: $1500   **VGood:** $1300   **Good:** $900

L.C. SMITH HAMMERLESS DOUBLE BARREL SKEET SPECIAL (1913-1945)

Same specs as Hammerless Double Barrel (1913 to 1945), except 12-, 16-, 20-ga., .410; 26-inch, 27-inch, 28-inch fluid steel barrels; American walnut straight-grip stock, beavertail forend standard; half- and pistol grip optional; single trigger; ejectors; checkered butt standard; Featherweight frame standard; total production 771. Introduced 1929; discontinued 1944.

Exc.: $1950   **VGood:** $1400   **Good:** $1100

L.C. SMITH HAMMERLESS DOUBLE BARREL OLYMPIC GRADE (1913-1945)

Same specs as Hammerless Double Barrel (1913 to 1945), except 12-, 16-, 20-ga.; 28-inch to 32-inch fluid steel barrels; vent rib; ivory bead sight; American walnut pistol-grip stock, beavertail forend standard; straight or half-pistol grip optional; single trigger; recoil pad; total production, 26. Introduced 1932; discontinued 1938. Extremely rare; precludes pricing.

L.C. SMITH HAMMERLESS DOUBLE BARREL SPECIALTY GRADE (1913-1945)

Same specs as Hammerless Double Barrel (1913 to 1945), except fluid steel barrels standard; twist barrels optional until 1917; vent rib optional; American walnut straight-, half- or pistol-grip stock; double triggers, extractors standard; single trigger, ejectors optional; total production, 6,565. Introduced 1913; discontinued 1945.

Exc.: $2000   **VGood:** $1400   **Good:** $1100

available; total production, 12,887; with ejectors, 5044. Introduced 1892; discontinued 1912.

Exc.: $2600   **VGood:** $1800   **Good:** $1400

L.C. SMITH HAMMERLESS DOUBLE BARREL NO. 3 (1890-1912)

Same specs as Hammerless Double Barrel (1890 to 1912), except fluid steel (12-, 16-, 20-ga.) or twist (10-, 12-, 16-, 20-ga.) barrels; English walnut straight or pistol-grip stock; double triggers, extractors standard; single trigger, ejectors optional; total production, 3790; with ejectors, 2093. Introduced 1892; discontinued 1912.

Exc.: $2800   **VGood:** $2000   **Good:** $1500

L.C. SMITH HAMMERLESS DOUBLE BARREL NO. 4 (1890-1912)

Same specs as Hammerless Double Barrel (1890 to 1912), except twist (10-, 12-, 16-, 20-ga.) or fluid steel (12-, 16-, 20-ga.) barrels; French or English walnut straight or pistol-grip stock; Monte Carlo comb optional; double triggers, extractors standard; ejectors optional; total production, 455; with ejectors, 321. Introduced 1892; discontinued 1913.

Exc.: $7500   **VGood:** $5900   **Good:** $3500

L.C. SMITH HAMMERLESS DOUBLE BARREL A1 GRADE (1890-1912)

Same specs as Hammerless Double Barrel (1890 to 1912), except 10-, 12-, 16-ga.; 28-inch to 32-inch twist barrels; English walnut half-, three-quarter- or pistol-grip stock; double triggers, ejectors standard; total production, 739. Introduced 1890; discontinued 1898.

Exc.: $4500   **VGood:** $3100   **Good:** $2500

L.C. SMITH HAMMERLESS DOUBLE BARREL NO. 5 (1890-1912)

Same specs as Hammerless Double Barrel (1890 to 1912), except twist (10-, 12-, 16-ga.) or fluid steel (12-, 16-, 20-ga.) barrels; English or French walnut stocks; double triggers, ejectors standard; extractors, single trigger optional; in 1913, No. 5 was renamed Crown Grade; total production before 1913, 484; with ejectors, 373. Introduced 1892; discontinued 1912.

Exc.: $7000   **VGood:** $4200   **Good:** $3300

L.C. SMITH HAMMERLESS DOUBLE BARREL MONOGRAM (1890-1912)

Same specs as Hammerless Double Barrel (1890 to 1912), except twist barrels; Whitworth fluid steel barrels available after 1896; English, French or Circassian walnut straight or pistol-grip stock; Monte Carlo comb optional; ejectors standard after 1896; double triggers standard; single trigger optional; Featherweight frame, with Whitworth steel barrels, available after 1907; Monogram was the only grade not changed in 1913; total production (1895-1912), 102. Introduced 1895; discontinued 1945.

Exc.: $9000   **VGood:** $6300   **Good:** $5000

L.C. SMITH HAMMERLESS DOUBLE BARREL A2 GRADE (1890-1912)

Same specs as Hammerless Double Barrel (1890 to 1912), except twist or Whitworth fluid steel barrels; French, English or Circassian walnut straight or pistol-grip stock; Monte Carlo comb optional; ejectors, double triggers standard; single trigger optional; lightweight version with Krupp steel barrels available; total production, 100. Introduced 1892; discontinued 1912.

Exc.: $12,000   **VGood:** $8500   **Good:** $6600

L.C. SMITH HAMMERLESS DOUBLE BARREL A3 GRADE (1890-1912)

Same specs as Hammerless Double Barrel (1890 to 1912), except Whitworth steel barrels; Krupp steel barrels optional; ejectors, double triggers standard; single trigger optional; Circassian walnut straight or pistol-grip stock; Monte Carlo comb optional; lightweight version available; total production, 17. Introduced 1896; discontinued 1915. Extremely rare, precludes pricing.

L.C. SMITH HAMMERLESS DOUBLE BARRELS (1913-1945)

Side-by-side; sidelock; hammerless; 10-, 12-, 16-, 20-ga., .410; 26-inch, 28-inch, 30-inch, 32-inch twist or fluid steel barrels; lowest grades stocked in American walnut, high grades in European walnut; straight-, half- or pistol-grip; splinter or beavertail forend. L.C. Smith guns built after 1912

L.C. SMITH HAMMERLESS DOUBLE BARREL EAGLE GRADE (1913-1945)
Same specs as Hammerless Double Barrel (1913 to 1945), except 10-, 12-, 16-, 20-ga.; fluid steel barrels standard; twist barrels optional until 1917; European walnut straight-, half- or pistol-grip stock; double triggers, extractors standard; single trigger, ejectors optional; total production, 580. Introduced 1913; discontinued 1932.

Exc.: $4000   **VGood:** $2800   **Good:** $2200

L.C. SMITH HAMMERLESS DOUBLE BARREL CROWN GRADE (1913-1945)
Same specs as Hammerless Double Barrel (1913 to 1945), except fluid steel barrels standard; twist barrels optional until 1917; made largely to order, with all options: vent rib; European walnut straight-, half- or pistol-grip stock, beavertail forend; single trigger; ejectors; total production, 842. Introduced 1913; discontinued 1945.

Exc.: $5000   **VGood:** $3500   **Good:** $2750

L.C. SMITH HAMMERLESS DOUBLE BARREL MONOGRAM GRADE (1913-1945)
Same specs as Hammerless Double Barrel (1913 to 1945), except twist or Whitworth fluid steel barrels; English, French or Circassian walnut straight or pistol-grip stock; Monte Carlo comb optional; ejectors; double triggers standard; single trigger optional; Featherweight frame, with Whitworth steel barrels, available; same specifications as pre-1913 Monogram Grade; total production (1913-1945), 164. Introduced 1895; discontinued 1945.

Exc.: $9000   **VGood:** $6300   **Good:** $5000

L.C. SMITH HAMMERLESS DOUBLE BARREL PREMIER GRADE (1913-1945)
Same specs as Hammerless Double Barrel (1913 to 1945), except 12-, 16-, 20-ga.; Whitworth fluid steel barrels; made to order; all options available; total production, 28. Introduced 1913; discontinued 1941. Extremely rare; precludes pricing.

L.C. SMITH HAMMERLESS DOUBLE BARREL DELUXE GRADE (1913-1945)
Same specs as Hammerless Double Barrel (1913 to 1945), except 12-, 16-, 20-ga.; Whitworth fluid steel barrels; made to order; all options available; total production, 30. Introduced 1913; discontinued 1945. Extreme rarity precludes pricing.

L.C. SMITH HAMMERLESS DOUBLE BARREL LONG RANGE WILD FOWL GUN (1913-1945)
Same specs as Hammerless Double Barrel (1913 to 1945), except 12-ga.; 3-inch chambers; 30-inch or 32-inch barrels; European walnut pistol-grip stock; straight- or -pistol-grip optional; extractors or ejectors; double or single trigger; available in any standard grade. Introduced 1924; discontinued 1945.

Exc.: $900   **VGood:** $600   **Good:** $500

L.C. SMITH HAMMERLESS DOUBLE BARRELS (1945-1950)
Side-by-side; sidelock; hammerless; 10-, 12-, 16-, 20-ga., .410; 26-inch, 28-inch, 30-inch, 32-inch twist or fluid steel barrels; lowest grades stocked in American walnut, high grades in European walnut; straight-, half- or pistol-grip; splinter or beavertail forend. Marlin Firearms Company purchased Hunter Arms Company in 1945; guns built after 1945 were stamped L.C. SMITH GUN COMPANY; all grades of double gun except Field, Ideal, Specialty and Crown were discontinued; specifications for these grades remained same as before; manufactured by Marlin Firearms, Co. Introduced 1945; discontinued 1950.

L.C. SMITH HAMMERLESS DOUBLE BARREL FIELD GRADE (1945-1950)
Same specs as Hammerless Double Barrel (1945 to 1950), except 12-, 16-, 20-ga., .410; fluid steel barrels; American walnut pistol-grip stock; double triggers, extractors standard; single trigger, ejectors

L.C. Smith
Hammerless Double Barrel
Premier Grade (1913-1945)

L.C. Smith
Hammerless Double Barrel
Eagle Grade (1913-1945)

L.C. Smith
Hammerless Double Barrel
Olympic Grade (1913-1945)

optional; total production, 43,312. Introduced 1945; discontinued 1950.

Exc.: $900   **VGood:** $600   **Good:** $500

L.C. SMITH HAMMERLESS DOUBLE BARREL IDEAL GRADE (1945-1950)
Same specs as Hammerless Double Barrel (1945 to 1950), except fluid steel barrels; 26-inch, 28-inch barrels only in .410; American walnut pistol-grip stock; straight or half-pistol optional; double triggers, extractors standard; single trigger, ejectors optional; total production, 3950. Introduced 1945; discontinued 1950.

Exc.: $1300   **VGood:** $900   **Good:** $700

L.C. SMITH HAMMERLESS DOUBLE BARREL SPECIALTY GRADE (1945-1950)
Same specs as Hammerless Double Barrel (1945 to 1950), except fluid steel barrels standard; vent rib optional; American walnut straight-, half- or pistol-grip stock; double triggers, extractors standard; single trigger, ejectors optional; total production, 109. Introduced 1945; discontinued 1950.

Exc.: $2100   **VGood:** $1500   **Good:** $1200

L.C. SMITH HAMMERLESS DOUBLE BARREL CROWN GRADE (1945-1950)
Same specs as Hammerless Double Barrel (1945 to 1950), except fluid steel barrels standard; made largely to order, with all options: vent rib; European walnut straight-, half- or pistol-grip stock, beavertail forend; single trigger; ejectors; total production, 48. Introduced 1945; discontinued 1950.

Exc.: $5000   **VGood:** $3500   **Good:** $2750

L.C. SMITH HAMMERLESS DOUBLE BARREL PREMIER SKEET GRADE (1945-1950)
Same specs as Hammerless Double Barrel (1945 to 1950), except 12-, 20-ga.; 26-inch or 28-inch barrels; high solid rib; European walnut straight-grip stock, beavertail forend; ejectors; single trigger; checkered butt; manufactured 1949 to 1950; total production, 507. Introduced 1949; discontinued 1950.

Exc.: $1850   **VGood:** $1300   **Good:** $1000

L.C. Smith
Hammerless Double Barrel
Monogram Grade (1913-1945)

L.C. Smith Hammerless
Double Barrel Premier
Skeet Grade (1945-1950)

L.C. SMITH HAMMERLESS DOUBLE BARREL FIELD GRADE (1967-1971)
Side-by-side; sidelock; hammerless; 12-ga.; 28-inch barrels; vent rib; American walnut pistol-grip stock, splinter forend; double triggers; extractors. Marlin Firearms Co. briefly reintroduced to L.C. Smith double gun; total production, 2351. Introduced 1967; discontinued 1971.

Exc.: $700   **VGood:** $550   **Good:** $450

L.C. SMITH HAMMERLESS DOUBLE BARREL FIELD GRADE DELUXE
Same specs as Hammerless Double Barrel Field Grade (1967 to 1971), except Simmons vent rib; select American walnut pistol-grip stock, beavertail forend; total production, 188. Introduced 1971; discontinued 1971.

Exc.: $950   **VGood:** $725   **Good:** $550

L.C. SMITH SINGLE-BARREL TRAP GUN
Single shot; boxlock; hammerless; 12-ga.; 30-inch to 34-inch barrels (Olympic Grade 32-inch only); vent rib; hand-checkered American walnut pistol-grip stock, beavertail forend; ejectors; recoil pad; made in 10 grades with differing quality of workmanship, engraving and wood. Specialty, Eagle, Crown and Monogram grades introduced 1917; other grades introduced later (Olympic in 1928); Eagle Grade discontinued 1932; all others (except Olympic and Specialty) discontinued 1945; Olympic and Specialty grades discontinued 1950. Production totals as follows: Field Grade, 1; Ideal Grade, 5; Olympic Grade, 622; Specialty Grade, 1861; Trap Grade, 1; Eagle Grade, 56; Crown Grade, 88; Monogram Grade, 15; Premier Grade, 2; DeLuxe Grade, 3. The rarity of some grades precludes pricing.

Olympic Grade		
Exc.: $1900	**VGood:** $1400	**Good:** $1000
Specialty Grade		
Exc.: $2500	**VGood:** $1800	**Good:** $1400
Crown Grade		
Exc.: $4500	**VGood:** $3000	**Good:** $2500
Monogram Grade		
Exc.: $9000	**VGood:** $6000	**Good:** $5000

Smith & Wesson Model 916

Smith & Wesson Model 1000 Trap

Smith & Wesson Model 1000 Waterfowler

Smith & Wesson Model 3000

Smith & Wesson Model 3000 Waterfowler

Sporting Arms Snake Charmer

Stevens Model 22-410

Stevens Model 58

SMITH & WESSON MODEL 916

Slide action; 12-, 16-, 20-ga.; 6-shot magazine; 20-inch Cylinder, 26-inch Improved Cylinder, 28-inch Modified, Full or adjustable choke, 30-inch Full barrel; vent rib (26-inch, 28-inch barrel); uncheckered walnut stock, fluted comb, grooved slide handle; optional recoil pad; satin-finished steel receiver, no-glare top. Introduced 1973; discontinued 1980.

With plain barrel

Perf.: $230   **Exc.:** $200   **VGood:** $180

With plain barrel, recoil pad

Perf.: $235   **Exc.:** $205   **VGood:** $185

With vent rib

Perf.: $250   **Exc.:** $220   **VGood:** $200

With vent rib, recoil pad

Perf.: $260   **Exc.:** $230   **VGood:** $210

SMITH & WESSON MODEL 916T

Same specs as Model 916 except takedown; 12-ga.; no 20-inch barrel. Introduced 1976; discontinued 1980.

With plain barrel

Perf.: $235   **Exc.:** $205   **VGood:** $185

With plain barrel, recoil pad

Perf.: $240   **Exc.:** $210   **VGood:** $185

With vent rib

Perf.: $255   **Exc.:** $225   **VGood:** $205

With vent rib, recoil pad

Perf.: $265   **Exc.:** $235   **VGood:** $215

SMITH & WESSON MODEL 1000

Gas-operated autoloader; 12-, 20-ga.; 2-3/4-inch chamber; 4-shot magazine; 26-inch Skeet or Improved Cylinder, 28-inch Improved, Modified or Full barrel; vent rib; front, middle beads; walnut checkered pistol-grip stock, forearm; crossbolt safety; pressure compensator; engraved alloy receiver. Made in Japan. Introduced 1973; discontinued 1984.

Perf.: $325   **Exc.:** $280   **VGood:** $250

SMITH & WESSON MODEL 1000 MAGNUM

Same specs as Model 1000 except 12-, 20-ga.; 3-inch chamber; 28-inch, 30-inch Modified or Full choke barrel; recoil pad. Introduced 1977; discontinued 1984.

Perf.: $330   **Exc.:** $285   **VGood:** $255

SMITH & WESSON MODEL 1000S

Same specs as Model 1000 except recessed-type Skeet choke with compensator to soften recoil, reduce muzzle jump; fluorescent red front bead; oil-finished select walnut stock with palm swell. Introduced 1979; discontinued 1984.

Perf.: $375   **Exc.:** $325   **VGood:** $280

SMITH & WESSON MODEL 1000 TRAP

Same specs as Model 1000 except 30-inch Multi-Choke barrel; stepped rib; white middle bead, Bradley front; Monte Carlo trap-style stock; shell catcher; steel receiver. Introduced 1983; discontinued 1984.

Perf.: $550   **Exc.:** $400   **VGood:** $350

SMITH & WESSON MODEL 1000 WATERFOWLER

Same specs as Model 1000 except 3-inch chamber; 30-inch Full-choke barrel; dull oil stock finish; quick-detachable swivels; padded camouflage sling; Parkerized finish; black oxidized bolt. Introduced 1982; discontinued 1984.

Perf.: $375   **Exc.:** $325   **VGood:** $285

SMITH & WESSON MODEL 3000

Slide action; 12-, 20-ga.; 3-inch chamber; 22-inch slug with rifle sights, 26-inch Improved, 28-inch Modified, 30-inch Full plain or vent-rib barrel; Multi-Choke available; American walnut stock; cross-bolt reversible safety for left-handers; dual action bars; chrome-plated bolt; steel receiver; rubber recoil pad. Introduced 1980; discontinued 1984.

Perf.: $345   **Exc.:** $275   **VGood:** $215

With slug barrel

Perf.: $375   **Exc.:** $305   **VGood:** $245

SMITH & WESSON MODEL 3000 WATERFOWLER

Same specs as Model 3000 except 3-inch chamber; 30-inch Full-choke barrel; dull oil-finished stock; quick-detachable sling swivels; padded camo sling; Parkerized finish; black oxidized bolt. Introduced 1982; discontinued 1984.

Perf.: $355   **Exc.:** $285   **VGood:** $225

SPORTING ARMS SNAKE CHARMER

Single barrel; break-open; .410; 3-inch chamber; 18 1/8-inch barrel; no sights; plastic thumbhole stock; storage compartment in buttstock for spare ammo; all stainless steel construction. Introduced 1978; discontinued 1988.

Perf.: $110   **Exc.:** $85   **VGood:** $70

SPORTING ARMS SNAKE CHARMER II

Same specs as Snake Charmer. Reintroduced 1989; still in production.

Perf.: $120   **Exc.:** $95   **VGood:** $80

SPORTING ARMS SNAKE CHARMER II NEW GENERATION

Same specs as Snake Charmer I except black carbon steel barrel. Introduced 1989; still in production.

Perf.: $130   **Exc.:** $90   **VGood:** $75

STEVENS MODEL 22-410

Over/under combo; exposed hammer; takedown; 22 Short, 22 Long, 22 LR barrel over .410 shotgun barrel; 24-inch barrels; Full choke; open rear sight, rifle-type ramp front; original models had uncheckered American walnut pistol-grip stock, forearm; later production had Tenite plastic stock, forearm; single trigger. Introduced 1938; discontinued 1950. Still in production by Savage Arms as Model 24, with variations.

With walnut stock

Exc.: $410   **VGood:** $320   **Good:** $170

With Tenite stock

Exc.: $1405   **VGood:** $315   **Good:** $165

STEVENS MODEL 58

Bolt action; takedown; .410; 3-shot detachable box magazine; 24-inch barrel; Full choke; uncheckered, one-piece, walnut-finished hardwood pistol-grip stock; late models had checkering; plastic buttplate. Introduced 1937; discontinued 1945.

Exc.: $125   **VGood:** $100   **Good:** $65

STEVENS MODEL 59

Bolt action; takedown; .410; 5-shot tube magazine; 24-inch barrel; Full choke; uncheckered one-piece walnut-finished hardwood pistol-grip stock; plastic buttplate. Introduced 1934; discontinued 1973.

Exc.: $135 **VGood:** $110 **Good:** $75

STEVENS MODEL 67

Slide action; 12-, 20-ga., .410; 3-inch chamber; 5-shot tube magazine; 26-inch, 28-inch, 30-inch barrel; optional vent rib; fixed or choke tubes; metal bead front sight; checkered walnut-finished hardwood pistol-grip stock, tapered slide handle; top tang safety; steel receiver. Introduced 1981; discontinued 1988. Add 25 percent for 410.

Perf.: $175 **Exc.:** $150 **VGood:** $125

With vent rib

Perf.: $185 **Exc.:** $160 **VGood:** $135

STEVENS MODEL 67 SLUG

Same specs as Model 67 except 12-ga.; 21-inch slug barrel; rifle sights. Introduced 1986; discontinued 1989.

Perf.: $175 **Exc.:** $150 **VGood:** $125

STEVENS MODEL 67 VRT-K CAMO

Same specs as Model 67 except 12-, 20-ga.; 28-inch vent-rib barrel; choke tubes; laminated hardwood camouflage stock, slide handle. Introduced 1986; discontinued 1988.

Perf.: $225 **Exc.:** $180 **VGood:** $160

STEVENS MODEL 67 VRT-Y

Same specs as Model 67 except 20-ga.; 22-inch vent-rib barrel; choke tubes; youth-sized checkered walnut-finish hardwood stock, forearm. Introduced 1987; discontinued 1988.

Perf.: $200 **Exc.:** $150 **VGood:** $125

STEVENS MODEL 69 RXL

Slide action; 12-ga.; 5-shot tube magazine; 18-1/4-inch Cylinder barrel; checkered walnut-finished hardwood stock, slide handle; recoil pad. Introduced 1981; discontinued 1989.

Perf.: $200 **Exc.:** $150 **VGood:** $125

STEVENS MODEL 77

Slide action; hammerless; solid frame; 12, 16-, 20-ga.; 5-shot tube magazine; 26-inch Improved; 28-inch Modified or Full barrel; uncheckered walnut-finished hardwood stock, grooved slide handle. Introduced 1954; discontinued 1971.

Exc.: $130 **VGood:** $90 **Good:** $70

STEVENS MODEL 77SC

Same specs as Model 77 except Savage Super Choke. No longer in production.

Exc.: $130 **VGood:** $90 **Good:** $70

STEVENS MODEL 79-VR

Slide action; 12-, 20-ga.; 26-inch, 28-inch, 30-inch vent-rib barrel; metal bead front sight; checkered walnut-finished hardwood pistol-grip stock, tapered slide handle; top tang safety; interchangeable barrels. Introduced 1981; discontinued 1983.

Perf.: $200 **Exc.:** $150 **VGood:** $125

STEVENS MODEL 94C

Single barrel; single shot; exposed hammer; break-open; early models side lever breaking; 12-, 16-, 20-ga., .410; 28-inch, 30-inch, 32-inch, 36-inch barrel; Full choke; checkered walnut finished hardwood pistol-grip stock, forearm; automatic ejector; color case-hardened frame. Introduced 1937; discontinued 1984.

Perf.: $100 **Exc.:** $80 **VGood:** $60

STEVENS MODEL 94Y

Same specs as Model 94C except top lever breaking; 20-ga., .410; 26-inch barrel; youth stock; recoil pad. Discontinued 1984.

Perf.: $100 **Exc.:** $80 **VGood:** $60

STEVENS MODEL 107

Single barrel; exposed hammer; takedown; 12-, 16-, 20-ga., .410; 26-inch, 28-inch, 30-inch barrel;

Stevens Model 59

Stevens Model 67

Stevens Model 79-VR

Stevens Model 94C

Stevens Model 94Y

Stevens Model 107

Stevens Model 124

Stevens Model 240

Stevens Model 258

Full choke; uncheckered walnut-finished hardwood pistol-grip stock, forearm automatic ejector. Introduced 1937; discontinued 1953.

Exc.: $75 **VGood:** $50 **Good:** $40

STEVENS MODEL 124

Straight-pull bolt action; solid frame, hammerless; 12-ga.; 2-shot tube magazine; 28-inch barrel; Improved, Modified, Full chokes; checkered Tenite plastic stock, forearm. Introduced 1947; discontinued 1952.

Exc.: $175 **VGood:** $140 **Good:** $125

STEVENS MODEL 240

Over/under; takedown; .410; 26-inch barrels; Full choke; early models had uncheckered American walnut pistol-grip stock, forearm; later versions had Tenite plastic stock forearm; double triggers. Introduced 1939; discontinued 1942.

With walnut stock

Exc.: $475 **VGood:** $340 **Good:** $240

With Tenite stock

Exc.: $470 **VGood:** $335 **Good:** $225

STEVENS MODEL 258

Bolt action; takedown; 20-ga.; 3-shot detachable box magazine; 25-inch barrel; Full choke; uncheckered hardwood, one-piece, pistol-grip stock; black plastic forearm cap, buttplate. Introduced 1937; discontinued 1965.

Exc.: $100 **VGood:** $75 **Good:** $50

Stevens Model 311

Stevens Model 520

Stevens Model 530

Stevens Model 620

Stoeger P-350

Stoeger P-350 Camo

Stoeger P-350 Defense

STEVENS MODEL 530ST
Same specs as Model 530 except single selective trigger. Introduced 1947; discontinued 1954.

Exc.: $375   **VGood:** $325   **Good:** $235

STEVENS MODEL 620
Slide action; hammerless; takedown; 12-, 16-, 20-ga.; 5-shot tube magazine; 26-inch, 28-inch, 30-inch, 32-inch barrel; Cylinder, Improved, Modified, Full choke; hand-checkered American walnut pistol-grip stock, slide handle; black plastic buttplate. Introduced 1927; discontinued 1953.

Exc.: $250   **VGood:** $185   **Good:** $125

STEVENS MODEL 621
Slide action; hammerless; takedown; 12-, 16-, 20-ga.; 5-shot tube magazine; 26-inch, 28-inch, 30-inch, 32-inch barrel; Cylinder, Improved, Modified Full choke; raised solid matted rib; hand-checkered American walnut pistol-grip stock, slide handle; black plastic buttplate. Introduced 1927; discontinued 1953.

Exc.: $250   **VGood:** $185   **Good:** $125

STEVENS MODEL 675
Slide action; 12-ga.; 5-shot tube magazine; 24-inch vent-rib barrel; choke tubes; rifle iron sights; checkered walnut-finished hardwood pistol-grip stock, forearm; recoil pad. Introduced 1987; discontinued 1988.

Perf.: $240   **Exc.:** $185   **VGood:** $160

STEVENS MODEL 5151
Side-by-side; boxlock; hammerless; 12-, 16-, 20-ga., .410; 3-inch chambers; 26-inch, 28-inch, 30-inch, 32-inch barrels; Ivoroid sights; hand-checkered American walnut pistol-grip stock, forearm; recoil pad. Introduced 1936; discontinued 1942.

Exc.: $200   **VGood:** $140   **Good:** $110

STEVENS MODEL 5151-ST
Same specs as Model 5151 except non-selective single trigger. No longer in production.

Exc.: $220   **VGood:** $160   **Good:** $120

STEVENS MODEL 9478 SUPER VALUE
Single barrel; exposed hammer; 10-, 12-, 20-ga., .410; 26-inch, 28-inch, 30-inch, 36-inch barrel; walnut-finished hardwood stock; bottom action opening button; auto ejection; color case-hardened frame. Introduced 1979; discontinued 1986.

Perf.: $110   **Exc.:** $90   **VGood:** $70

STOEGER P-350
This pump-action 12 gauge is chambered for 3.5" shells. It has a 24", 26" or 28" barrel and a matte black, Max-4, Timber or APG finish. There are also some pistol-grip stock offerings with 24" barrels. Includes five choke tubes. Weight is about 6.8 lbs. Add $20 for pistol-grip stock. Add $75 for camo finish.

NIB: $275   **Exc.:** $230   **VGood:** $175

STOEGER P-350 DEFENSE
Same as above in a matte black finish with 18.5", fixed cylinder choke barrel. Add $20 for pistol-grip stock.

NIB: $275   **Exc.:** $230   **VGood:** $175

STOEGER/IGA UPLANDER SIDE-BY SIDE SHOTGUN
Gauge: 16-, 28-ga., 2-3/4-inch chambers. 12, 20, .410, 3-inch chambers. Barrel: 26-inch, 28-inch. Weight: 7.3 lbs. Sights: Brass bead. Features: Double trigger, IC, Mod. choke tubes with gun.

Perf.: $300   **Exc.:** $235   **VGood:** $185

With screw-in chokes

Perf.: $315   **Exc.:** $250   **VGood:** $200

Upland Special

Perf.: $340   **Exc.:** $300   **VGood:** $260

Upland Supreme with SST, red bar sights

Perf.: $395   **Exc.:** $355   **VGood:** $300

STEVENS MODEL 311
Side-by-side; boxlock; hammerless; 12-, 16-, 20-ga., .410; 3-inch chambers; 26-inch, 28-inch, 30-inch, 32-inch barrels; standard choke combos; early models had uncheckered American walnut pistol-grip stock, forearm; later models had walnut-finished hardwood pistol-grip stock, fluted comb; double triggers, auto top tang safety; plastic buttplate; case-hardened finish on frame. Originally introduced 1931 as Model 311, but stamped Model 5000; in 1941 stamp was changed to Model 5100, but still listed in catalog as Model 311A; in 1950 gun marked Model 311; discontinued 1988.

Perf.: $375   **Exc.:** $325   **VGood:** $250

STEVENS MODEL 520
Slide action; 12-, 16-, 20-ga.; 5-shot magazine; 30-inch barrel; weighs 7-1/2 lbs.; checkered American walnut stock, forend; safety inside trigger guard; made exclusively for Sears, Roebuck; marketed as Sears Ranger. Discontinued about 1930.

Exc.: $160   **VGood:** $120   **Good:** $95

STEVENS MODEL 530
Side-by-side; boxlock; hammerless; 12-, 16-, 20-ga., .410; 26-inch, 28-inch, 30-inch, 32-inch barrels; Modified/Full, Cylinder/Modified, Full/Full chokes; hand-checkered American walnut pistol-grip stock, forearm; double triggers; early models have recoil pads. Introduced 1936; discontinued 1954.

Exc.: $350   **VGood:** $300   **Good:** $225

STEVENS MODEL 530M
Same specs as Model 530 except Tenite plastic stock, forearm. Introduced before WWII; discontinued 1947.

Exc.: $345   **VGood:** $295   **Good:** $220

STOEGER/IGA ENGLISH STOCK SIDE-BY-SIDE
Similar to Uplander except in .410 or 20-ga. only with 24-inch barrels, straight English stock and beavertail forend. Automatic safety, extractors, double triggers. Introduced 1996. Imported from Brazil by Stoeger.

.410 (Mod. chokes)
Perf.: $300   **Exc.:** $235   **VGood:** $185

20-ga. (IC and Mod. choke tubes)
Perf.: $300   **Exc.:** $235   **VGood:** $185

STOEGER UPLAND SHORT STOCK SIDE-BY-SIDE
Similar to English stock, only 13-inch length of pull. Excellent for ladies and youth. 20-ga., IC, Mod. fixed, .410 Mod.& Full. Rubber recoil.

Perf.: $300   **Exc.:** $235   **VGood:** $185

STOEGER MODEL 2000
Gauge: 12, 3-inch chamber, set of 5 choke tubes; 24-inch, 26-inch, 28-inch, 30-inch barrel; walnut, deluxe, synthetic, and Timber HD/Max-4 camo stock; white bar sight; inertia-recoil for light target to turkey leads; single trigger combo 26-inch/24-inch pack wtih optional 24-inch slug barrel.

Walnut, 26-inch, 28-inch, 30-inch bbl.
Perf.: $355   **Exc.:** $315   **VGood:** $285

Deluxe Camo, 26-inch, 28-inch bbl.
Perf.: $476   **Exc.:** $436   **VGood:** $406

Synthetic, 24-inch, 26-inch, 28-inch bbl.
Perf.: $355   **Exc.:** $315   **VGood:** $285

Price: Synthetic combo, 26-inch/24-inch bbl.
Perf.: $430   **Exc.:** $390   **VGood:** $360

Optional slug bbl., 26-inch

Timber HD, 24-inch, 26-inch, 28-inch bbl.
Perf.: $430   **Exc.:** $390   **VGood:** $360

STOEGER SILVERADO COACH SIDE-BY-SIDE
Gauge: 12, 20, .410, 2-3/4-inch, 3-inch chambers; 20-inch barrel; weighs 6-1/2 lbs.; brown hardwood, classic beavertail forend; brass bead sight; IC & Mod. fixed chokes; tang auto safety; auto extractors; silvered finish; black plastic butt plate; 12-ga. and 20-ga. also with English style stock.

Perf.: $320   **Exc.:** $270   **VGood:** $215

STOEGER COACH GUN SUPREME
Similar to Coach Gun but with walnut stock, blued, stainless, or nickeled finish.

STOEGER UPLANDER SHOTGUN
Gauge: 12, 20, .410 (3-inch chambers); 28 (2-3/4-inch chambers). Barrel: 24-inch, 26-inch, 28-inch. Weight: 6-3/4 lbs. Length: 40-inch to 44-inch overall. Stock: Brazilian hardwood; checkered grip and forearm. Features: Automatic safety; extractors; handles steel shot. Introduced 1997. Imported from Brazil by Stoeger. With chokes tubes.

Perf.: $315   **Exc.:** $250   **VGood:** $185

STOEGER UPLANDER SUPREME SHOTGUN
Similar to Uplander except American walnut soft black rubber recoil pad, gloss finish. Choke tubes and 3-inch chambers standard 12-, 20-ga.; 28-ga. has 26-inch, 3-inch chambers; chokes, fixed IC and Mod. Single selective gold plated triggers; extractors. Introduced 1997. Imported from Brazil by Stoeger.

Perf.: $395   **Exc.:** $355   **VGood:** $300

STOEGER 2002 SINGLE-SHOT SHOTGUN
Gauge: 12, 20, .410, 2-3/4-inch, 3-inch chambers. Blued. Barrel: 26-inch, 28-inch. Weight: 5.4 lbs. Sights: Brass bead. Features: .410/Full fixed choke tubes, rest Mod. screw-in. .410 24-inch bbl. available (l.o.p. 13-inch). 12-ga. hardwood pistol-grip stock and forend. 20-ga. 26-inch bbl., hardwood forend.

Perf.: $90   **Exc.:** $75   **VGood:** $65

Stoeger Model 2000
Deluxe Camo

Stoeger Model 2000
Deluxe

Stoeger Model 2000
Synthetic

Stoeger Model 2000 Synthetic Combo

Stoeger Silverado Coach

Stoeger Coach Gun Supreme

Stoeger Uplander

Stoeger Uplander Supreme

Stoeger Condor

STOEGER CONDOR O/U
Over/under; boxlock; 12-, 20-ga.; 3-inch chambers; 26-inch. 28-inch barrels; Improved Cylinder/Modified, Modified/Full choke tubes; vent top rib; weighs 7 lbs.; oil-finished checkered Brazilian hardwood pistol-grip stock, forend; manual safety; single trigger; extractors. Introduced 1983; still imported by Stoeger.

Perf.: $320   **Exc.:** $300   **VGood:** $275

Stoeger Condor Special

Stoeger Condor Combo

Stoeger Condor Youth

Sturm, Ruger Red Label

Sturm, Ruger Woodside

Tar-Hunt RSG-12

CONDOR SPECIAL

Same specs as the Condor except 12- and 20-ga.; deluxe checkered walnut stock; vent. rib; stainless steel receiver; choke tubes.

Perf.: $350   **Exc.:** $325   **VGood:** $300

CONDOR COMBO

Same specs as the Condor except with matched 12- and 20-ga., 26- and 28-inch barrel set; deluxe checkered walnut stock; vent. rib; separated barrels; choke tubes.

Perf.: $400   **Exc.:** $380   **VGood:** $355

CONDOR SUPREME

Same specs as the Condor except with single selective trigger.

Perf.: $395   **Exc.:** $365   **VGood:** $320

CONDOR YOUTH

Similar to Condor but in .410 and 20-ga. only with 13-inch LOP.

Perf.: $320   **Exc.:** $300   **VGood:** $275

STOEGER CONDOR COMPETITION

These 3" 12 and 20 gauge over-and-unders feature 30" barrels, AA Grade wood and adjustable combs. Three choke tubes. Weight is about 7.3 lbs. in 20 gauge and 7.8 lbs. in 12 gauge.

NIB: $525   **Exc.:** $495   **VGood:** $375

STOEGER CONDOR COMPETITION COMBO

As above with 12- and 20-gauge barrels.

NIB: $635   **Exc.:** $595   **VGood:** $475

STOEGER CONDOR OUTBACK

New in 2007, the Outback O/U comes in 12 and 20 gauge chambered for 3" shells. The finish is either A Grade satin walnut stock with blued barrels and receiver or matte black walnut stock with polished barrels and receiver. Barrels are 20" with rifle sights. Includes two choke tubes. Add $40 for black/nickel.

NIB: $425   **Exc.:** $375   **VGood:** $275

STURM RUGER GOLD LABEL SIDE-BY-SIDE SHOTGUN

Gauge: 12, 3-inch chambers; 28-inch barrel with skeet tubes; weighs 6-1/2 lbs.; 45-inch overall; American walnut straight or pistol grip; gold bead front; full-length rib, serrated top; spring-assisted break-open; SS trigger; auto eject; five interchangeable screw-in choke tubes; combination safety/barrel selector with auto safety reset.

Perf.: $2775   **Exc.:** $2075   **VGood:** $1450

STURM RUGER KTS-1234-BRE RED LABEL TRAP MODEL SINGLE-BARREL SHOTGUN

Gauge: 12; 2-3/4-inch chamber; 34-inch barrel; weighs 9 lbs.; 50-1/2-inch overall; select walnut checkered; adjustable pull length 13-1/2 to 15-inch; fully adjustable rib for pattern position; adjustable stock comb cast for right- or left-handed shooters; straight grooves the length of barrel to keep wad from rotating for pattern improvement; Full and Modified choke tubes; gold-inlaid eagle and Ruger name on receiver. Introduced 2000. Only 300 produced.

Perf.: $3000   **Exc.:** $2575   **VGood:** $1725

STURM RUGER RED LABEL

Over/under; boxlock; 12-, 20-ga.; 3-inch chambers; 26-inch, 28-inch vent-rib barrels; Full/Modified,

Improved Cylinder/Modified, Skeet choke tubes; checkered American walnut pistol-grip stock, forearm; optional straight-grip stock; single selective trigger; auto ejectors. Introduced (20-ga.) 1977; (12-ga.) 1982; still in production.

Perf.: $1050   **Exc.:** $860   **VGood:** $725

English Field with straight-grip stock

Perf.: $965   **Exc.:** $775   **VGood:** $685

All-Weather Red Label with black synthetic stock

Perf.: $1125   **Exc.:** $860   **VGood:** $715

Factory engraved All-Weather models

Perf.: $1225   **Exc.:** $1050   **VGood:** $815

RUGER ENGRAVED RED LABEL O/U SHOTGUNS

Similar to Red Label except scroll-engraved receiver with 24-carat gold game bird (pheasant in 12-ga., grouse in 20-ga., woodcock in 28-ga., duck on All-Weather 12-ga.). Introduced 2000.

Engraved, 12 gauge, 30-inch bbls.

Perf.: $1225   **Exc.:** $1050   **VGood:** $815

Engraved,(12-, 20- and 28-gauge; 26-inch and 28-inch bbls.)

Perf.: $1225   **Exc.:** $1050   **VGood:** $815

Engraved, All-Weather (synthetic stock, 12-gauge only; 26-inch and 28-inch bbls.)

Perf.: $1225   **Exc.:** $1050   **VGood:** $815

Engraved, All-Weather (synthetic stock, 12-ga. only, 30-inch bbls.)

Perf.: $1300   **Exc.:** $1125   **VGood:** $890

STURM RUGER RED LABEL SPORTING CLAYS

Same specs as Red Label except 12-ga.; 3-inch chambers; 30-inch barrels backbored to .744-inch diameter; two Skeet, one Improved Cylinder, one Modified stainless steel choke tubes; optional Full and Extra-Full tubes available; free-floating serrated vent rib; brass front, mid-rib beads; weighs 7-3/4 lbs.; overall length 47-inch; no barrel side ribs. Introduced 1992; still in production.

Perf.: $1100   **Exc.:** $800   **VGood:** $700

STURM RUGER RED LABEL SPORTING CLAYS 20-GAUGE

Same specs as the Red Label except 20-ga.; 3-inch chambers; 30-inch barrels backbored to .631-inch-.635-inch diameter; four special 2-inch long interchangeable, screw-in choke tubes: two Skeet, one Modified, one Improved Cylinder; optional Full and Extra-Full tubes available; no barrel side spacers. Introduced 1994; still in production.

Perf.: $1100   **Exc.:** $800   **VGood:** $700

STURM RUGER RED LABEL WOODSIDE

Over/under; boxlock; 12-, 20-ga.; 3-inch chambers; 26-inch, 28-inch, 30-inch backbored barrels; Full, Modified, Improved Cylinder and two Skeet stainless steel choke tubes; serrated free-floating rib; weighs 7-1/2 to 8 lbs.; select Circassian walnut pistol-grip or straight-grip stock; buttstock extends forward into action as two side panels; newly patented Ruger cocking mechanism for easier, smoother opening; single selective mechanical trigger; selective automatic ejectors; blued barrels; stainless steel receiver; optional engraved action. Introduced 1995.

Perf.: $1500   **Exc.:** $1100   **VGood:** $850

Woodside Sporting Clays (30-inch bbls.)

Perf.: $1525   **Exc.:** $1250   **VGood:** $1000

TAR-HUNT RSG-12 PROFESSIONAL

Bolt action; 12-, 20-ga.; 2-3/4-inch chamber; 21-1/2-inch fully rifled barrel with muzzlebrake; weighs 7-3/4 lbs.; Weaver-style scope mounting bases and Burris steel rings; matte black McMillan fiberglass stock; Pachmayr Decelerator pad; rifle-style action with two locking lugs; two-position safety; single-stage, adjustable rifle trigger; right- and left-hand models at same prices. Introduced 1991; still in production.

Perf.: $1200   **Exc.:** $850   **VGood:** $750

Professional 16-ga. Elite model, right- or left-hand

Perf.: $1750 **Exc.:** $1475 **VGood:** $1150

Millennium/10th Anniversary models (limited to 25 guns): NP-3 nickel/Teflon metal finish, black McMillan Fibergrain stock, Jewell adj. Trigger.

Perf.: $2075 **Exc.:** $1825 **VGood:** $1500

TAR-HUNT RSG-12 PROFESSIONAL MATCHLESS MODEL
Same specs as RSG-12 Professional except McMillan Fibergrain or camouflage stock; 400-grit gloss metal finish. Introduced 1991.

Perf.: $1500 **Exc.:** $1100 **VGood:** $950

TAR-HUNT RSG-12 PROFESSIONAL PEERLESS MODEL
Same specs as RSG-12 Professional except McMillan Fibergrain fiberglass stock; NP-3 nickel/teflon metal finish. Introduced 1991.

Perf.: $1750 **Exc.:** $1200 **VGood:** $1000

TAR-HUNT RSG-12 TURKEY MODEL
Same specs as RSG-12 Professional except smoothbore barrel; Remington Rem-Choke thread system. Introduced 1991.

Perf.: $1200 **Exc.:** $850 **VGood:** $750

TAR-HUNT RSG-20 MOUNTAINEER SLUG GUN
Similar to the RSG-12 Professional except chambered for 20-ga. (2-3/4-inch) shells; 21-inch Shaw rifled barrel, with muzzle brake; two-lug bolt; one- shot blind magazine; matte black finish; McMillan fiberglass stock with Pachmayr Decelerator pad; receiver drilled and tapped for Rem. 700 bases. Weighs 6 -1/2 lbs. Introduced 1997. Made in U.S. by Tar-Hunt Custom Rifles, Inc.

Perf.: $1750 **Exc.:** $1475 **VGood:** $1150

TECHNI-MEC MODEL 610
Over/under; boxlock; 10-ga.; 3-1/2-inch chambers; 32-inch barrels; Improved Modified/Full chokes; hand-checkered walnut stock, forend; rubber recoil pad; single selective trigger; silvered and engraved frame, blued barrels. Made in Italy. Introduced 1991; no longer imported.

Perf.: $875 **Exc.:** $700 **VGood:** $625

TECHNI-MEC MODEL SPL 640
Over/under; boxlock; 12-, 16-, 20-, 28-ga.; 2-3/4-inch chambers; 26-inch chrome-lined barrel; Modified/Full chokes; ventilated rib; weighs 5-1/2 lbs.; European walnut stock; single or double triggers; folds in half for storage, transportation; photo-engraved silvered receiver. Made in Italy. Introduced 1984; no longer imported.

Perf.: $440 **Exc.:** $300 **VGood:** $250

TECHNI-MEC MODEL SPL 642
Folding over/under; 12-, 16-, 20-, 28-ga., .410; 26-inch Modified/Full barrels; vent rib; checkered European walnut stock, forearm; single or double triggers; chrome-lined barrels; photo-engraved, silvered receiver. No longer in production.

With single trigger

Perf.: $440 **Exc.:** $300 **VGood:** $250

With double triggers

Perf.: $420 **Exc.:** $280 **VGood:** $230

TECHNI-MEC MODEL SR 690 SKEET
Over/under; boxlock; 12-ga.; 2-3/4-inch chambers; 25-inch, 28-inch barrels; Skeet/Skeet chokes; Ray-type sights; select European walnut Monte Carlo stock with Skeet dimensions; single selective trigger; automatic ejectors; antique silver finish on receiver. Made in Italy. Introduced 1984; no longer imported.

Perf.: $525 **Exc.:** $375 **VGood:** $300

TECHNI-MEC MODEL SR 690 TRAP
Same specs as Model SR 690 Skeet except 30-inch barrels; Full/Full chokes; select European walnut

Monte Carlo stock with trap dimensions. Made in Italy. Introduced 1984; no longer imported.

Perf.: $525 **Exc.:** $375 **VGood:** $300

TECHNI-MEC MODEL SR 692 EM
Over/under; boxlock; 12-, 16-, 20-ga.; 2-3/4-inch, 3-inch chambers; 26-inch, 28-inch, 30-inch barrels; Modified, Full, Improved Cylinder, Cylinder chokes; checkered European walnut pistol-grip stock, forend; single selective trigger; automatic ejectors; dummy sideplates with fine game scene engraving. Made in Italy. Introduced 1984; no longer imported.

Perf.: $440 **Exc.:** $350 **VGood:** $290

THOMPSON/CENTER CUSTOM SHOP TCR '87 HUNTER
Single shot; boxlock; 10-, 12-ga.; 3, 3-1/2-inch chamber; 25-inch barrel; Full choke designed for steel shot; weighs 8 lbs.; uncheckered walnut stock; stock has extra 7/16-inch drop at heel; same receiver as TCR '87 rifle models. Introduced through T/C custom shop 1989; discontinued 1994.

Perf.: $725 **Exc.:** $495 **VGood:** $325

THOMPSON/CENTER ENCORE RIFLED SLUG GUN
Gauge: 20, 3-inch chamber; 26-inch barrel, fully rifled; weighs about 7 lbs. ; 40-1/2-inch overall;

Tar-Hunt RSG-20 Mountaineer Slug Gun

Techni-Mec Model 610

Techni-Mec Model SPL 640

Thompson/Center Custom Shop TCR '87 Hunter

Thompson/Center Encore Rifled Slug Gun

Tikka Model 77

Tikka Model 412S Field Grade

walnut with walnut forearm; steel, click-adjustable rear and ramp-style front, both with fiber optics; break-open design uses interchangeable barrels; composite stock and forearm available. Introduced 2000.

Perf.: $620 **Exc.:** $465 **VGood:** $395

THOMPSON/CENTER ENCORE TURKEY GUN
Gauge: 12-ga. Barrel: 24-inch. Features: Blued, high definition Adv. Timber camo.

Perf.: $575 **Exc.:** $500 **VGood:** $430

TIKKA MODEL 77
Over/under; 12-ga.; 27-inch, 30-inch vent-rib barrels; skip-line-checkered European walnut Monte Carlo pistol-grip stock with roll-over cheekpiece, forend; ejectors; barrel selector; single trigger. Made in Finland. Introduced 1979; no longer imported.

Perf.: $675 **Exc.:** $525 **VGood:** $475

TIKKA MODEL 412S FIELD GRADE
Over/under; boxlock; 12-, 20-ga.; 3-inch chambers; 24-inch, 26-inch, 28-inch, 30-inch barrels; Improved Cylinder, Modified, Improved Modified, Full stainless steel screw-in chokes; weighs about 7-1/4 lbs.; checkered American walnut pistol-grip stock, forend; barrel selector in trigger; automatic top tang safety; barrel cocking indicators; system allows free interchangeability of barrels, stocks and forends

Tikka Model 412S
Sporting Clays

Tradewinds H-170

Traditions ALS 2100 Turkey

Traditions ALS 2100 Waterfowl

Traditions Elite Series
Side-by-Side

into double rifle model, combination gun, etc. Name changed to Model 512S in 1993. Made in Finland and Italy. Introduced 1980; still imported as Tikka Model 512S.

Perf.: $1000   **Exc.:** $700   **VGood:** $525

TIKKA MODEL 412S SPORTING CLAYS

Same as the Model 412S except 12-ga.; 28-inch, 30-inch barrels; five choke tubes; manual safety. Made in Finland and Italy. Introduced 1992; still imported as Model 512S.

Perf.: $1050   **Exc.:** $750   **VGood:** $600

TIKKA MODEL 412ST SKEET

Over/under; 12-, 20-ga.; 28-inch stepped-rib barrels; choke tubes; European walnut Skeet-style stock; mechanical single trigger; auto ejectors; elongated forcing cone; cocking indicators; hand-honed action. Made in Finland. Introduced 1980; discontinued 1990.

Perf.: $1000   **Exc.:** $750   **VGood:** $650

TIKKA MODEL 412ST SKEET GRADE II

Same specs as Model 412ST Skeet except checkered semi-fancy European walnut Skeet-style stock; drilled for recoil-reducing unit; matte nickel receiver; matte blue locking bolt, lever; gold trigger. Made in Finland. Introduced 1989; discontinued 1990.

Perf.: $1200   **Exc.:** $850   **VGood:** $775

TIKKA MODEL 412ST TRAP

Same specs as Model 412ST Skeet except 12-ga.; 30-inch, 32-inch barrels; European walnut stock; palm swell. Made in Finland. Introduced 1980; discontinued 1990.

Perf.: $1000   **Exc.:** $750   **VGood:** $650

TIKKA MODEL 412ST TRAP GRADE II

Same specs as Model 412ST Skeet except 12-ga.; 30-inch, 32-inch barrels; checkered semi-fancy European walnut stock, palm swell; drilled for recoil-reducing unit; matte nickel receiver; matte blue locking bolt, lever; gold trigger. Made in Finland. Introduced 1989; discontinued 1990.

Perf.: $1200   **Exc.:** $850   **VGood:** $775

TOLEDO ARMAS VALEZQUEZ

Side-by-side; 12-ga. 2-3/4-inch chambers; custom barrel lengths, chokes; custom exhibition-grade European walnut stock; auto ejectors; hand-engraved action; many options. Made in Spain. Introduced 1982; discontinued 1984.

Perf.: $2600   **Exc.:** $2000   **VGood:** $1700

TRADEWINDS H-170

Recoil-operated autoloader; 12-ga.; 2-3/4-inch chambers; 5-shot tube magazine; 26-inch Modified, 28-inch Full barrel; vent rib; hand-checkered select European walnut pistol-grip stock; light alloy receiver. Made in Japan. Introduced 1970; no longer in production.

Perf.: $275   **Exc.:** $250   **VGood:** $195

TRADITIONS ALS 2100 SERIES SEMI-AUTOMATIC SHOTGUNS

Gauge: 12, 3-inch chamber; 20, 3-inch chamber; 24-inch, 26-inch, 28-inch barrel (imp. cyl., mod. and full choke tubes); weighs 5 lbs., 10 oz. to 6 lbs., 5 oz.; 44-inch to 48-inch overall; walnut or black composite; gas-operated; vent-rib barrel with Beretta-style threaded muzzle. Introduced 2001 by Traditions.

12- or 20-ga., 26-inch or 28-inch barrel, walnut stock		
Perf.: $430	**Exc.:** $390	**VGood:** $355
12- or 20-ga., 24-inch barrel Youth Model, walnut stock		
Perf.: $430	**Exc.:** $390	**VGood:** $355
12- or 20-ga., 26-inch or 28-inch barrel, composite stock		
Perf.: $410	**Exc.:** $375	**VGood:** $335

TRADITIONS ALS 2100 TURKEY SEMI-AUTOMATIC SHOTGUN

Similar to ALS 2100 Field Model except chambered in 12-gauge, 3-inch only with 21-inch barrel and Mossy Oak Break Up camo finish. Weighs 6 lbs., 1 oz.; 41-inch overall.

Perf.: $465	**Exc.:** $410	**VGood:** $365
26-inch vent rib bbl.		
Perf.: $455	**Exc.:** $400	**VGood:** $360

TRADITIONS ALS 2100 WATERFOWL SEMI-AUTOMATIC SHOTGUN

Similar to ALS 2100 Field Model except chambered in 12-ga., 3-inch only with 28-inch barrel (w/steel chokes for 2002) and Advantage Wetlands camo finish. Weighs 6 lbs., 5 oz.; 48-inch overall.

Perf.: $465   **Exc.:** $410   **VGood:** $365

TRADITIONS ALS 2100 HUNTER COMBO

Similar to ALS 2100 Field Model except 2 barrels, 28-inch vent rib and 24-inch fully rifled deer. Choice TruGlo adj. sights or fixed cantilever mount on rifled barrel. Multi chokes.

Perf.: $590   **Exc.:** $535   **VGood:** $500

TRADITIONS CLASSIC SERIES O/U SHOTGUNS

Gauge: 12, 3-inch; 20, 3-inch; 16, 2-3/4-inch; 28, 2-3/4-inch; 410, 3-inch; 26-inch barrel, 28-inch; weighs 6 lbs., 5 oz. to 7 lbs., 6 oz.; 43-inch to 45-inch overall; walnut stock; single-selective trigger; chrome-lined barrels with screw-in choke tubes; extractors (Field Hunter and Field I models) or automatic ejectors (Field II and Field III models); rubber butt pad; top tang safety. Imported from Fausti of Italy by Traditions.

Field Hunter - blued receiver; 12- or 20-ga.; 26-inch bbl. has I.C. and mod. tubes, 28-inch has mod. and full tubes)		
Perf.: $710	**Exc.:** $655	**VGood:** $580
Field I - blued receiver; 12-, 20-, 28-ga. or .410; fixed chokes (26-inch IC/Mod., 28-inch Mod./Full)		
Perf.: $675	**Exc.:** $555	**VGood:** $485
Field II - coin-finish receiver; 12-, 16-, 20-, 28-ga. or .410; gold trigger; choke tubes)		
Perf.: $710	**Exc.:** $635	**VGood:** $575
Field III - coin-finish receiver; gold engraving and trigger; 12 ga.; 26-inch or 28-inch bbl.; choke tubes		
Perf.: $1000	**Exc.:** $850	**VGood:** $775
Upland I - blued receiver; 12- or 20-ga.; English-style straight walnut stock; choke tubes		
Perf.: $975	**Exc.:** $875	**VGood:** $715
Upland III - blued receiver, gold engraving; 20-ga.; high-grade pistol grip walnut stock; choke tubes		
Perf.: $1320	**Exc.:** $1095	**VGood:** $925
Upland III - blued, gold engraved receiver, 12-ga. Round pistol grip stock, choke tubes		
Perf.: $1320	**Exc.:** $1095	**VGood:** $925
Sporting Clay II - silver receiver; 12-ga.; ported barrels with skeet, I.C., mod. and full extended tubes		
Perf.: $915	**Exc.:** $810	**VGood:** $700
Sporting Clay III - engraved receivers, 12- and 20-ga., walnut stock, vent rib, extended choke tubes		
Perf.: $1175	**Exc.:** $975	**VGood:** $850

TRADITIONS ELITE SERIES SIDE-BY-SIDE SHOTGUNS

Gauge: 12, 3-inch; 20, 3-inch; 28, 2-3/4-inch; .410, 3-inch; 26-inch barrel; weighs 5-3/4 to 6-1/2 lbs.; 43-inch overall; walnut stock; chrome-lined barrels; fixed chokes (Elite Field III ST, Field I DT and Field I ST) or choke tubes (Elite Hunter ST); extractors (Hunter ST and Field I models) or automatic ejectors (Field III ST); top tang safety. Imported from Fausti of Italy by Traditions.

Elite Field I DT – 12-, 20-, 28-ga. or .410; I.C. and Mod. fixed chokes (F/F on .410); double triggers		
Perf.: $780	**Exc.:** $720	**VGood:** $595
Elite Field I ST - 12-, 20-, 28-ga. or .410; same as DT but with single trigger		
Perf.: $860	**Exc.:** $750	**VGood:** $625
Elite Field III ST – 28-ga. or .410; gold-engraved receiver; high-grade walnut stock		
Perf.: $1825	**Exc.:** $1550	**VGood:** $1275
Elite Hunter ST – 12- or 20-ga.; blued receiver; IC and Mod. choke tubes		
Perf.: $995	**Exc.:** $850	**VGood:** $775

TRADITIONS MAG 350 SERIES O/U SHOTGUNS

Gauge: 12, 3-1/2-inch; 24-inch, 26-inch and 28-inch barrel; weighs 7 lbs. to 7 lbs., 4 oz.; 41-inch to 45-inch overall; walnut or composite with Mossy Oak Break-Up or Advantage Wetlands camouflage; black matte, engraved receiver; vent rib; automatic ejectors; single-selective trigger; three screw-in choke tubes; rubber recoil pad; top tang safety. Imported from Fausti of Italy by Traditions.

Mag Hunter II - 28-inch black matte barrels, walnut stock, includes IC, Mod. and Full tubes

Perf.: $700	**Exc.:** $630	**VGood:** $575

Turkey II - 24-inch or 26-inch camo barrels, Break-Up camo stock, includes Mod., Full and X-Full tubes

Perf.: $825	**Exc.:** $715	**VGood:** $625

Waterfowl II - 28-inch camo barrels, Advantage Wetlands camo stock, includes IC, Mod. and Full tubes

Perf.: $835	**Exc.:** $715	**VGood:** $635

TRIDENT SUPERTRAP II

Single shot; 12-ga.; 32-inch, 34-inch ported barrel; Multi-Choke tubes; weighs 8-1/2 lbs.; white front bead, brass middle bead; checkered American walnut stock, forend; vent rubber recoil pad; pull/release-convertible trigger; long forcing cone. Introduced 1990; discontinued 1992.

Perf.: $1800	**Exc.:** $1400	**VGood:** $1200

TRISTAR BRITTANY

This SxS features a boxlock action with case-colored frame with scroll engraving. Straight grip walnut stock with semi-beavertail forend. Offered in 12, 16, 20 and 28 gauge and .410 bore with 3-inch chambers and choke tubes. Weight is 6.2 - 7.4 lbs. depending on gauge.

NIB: $900	**Exc.:** $840	**VGood:** $725

TRISTAR BRITTANY CLASSIC

Enhanced Brittany model features fancy walnut wood and rounded pistol grip, cut checkering, engraved case colored frame and auto selective ejectors. Available in 12, 16, 20 and 28 gauges and .410 bore, all with 3" chambers and 27" barrels. Weight is about 6.7 lbs. in 12 gauge and slightly less in sub-gauges. Deduct 15 percent for standard Brittany model.

NIB: $925	**Exc.:** $865	**VGood:** $750

TRISTAR TSA FIELD

Semi-auto with walnut forend and pistol grip stock, 3-inch chamber, 3 choke tubes and magazine cut-off feature. Weight is around 5.7 lbs. in 20 gauge and 6.5 lbs. in 12 gauge depending on barrel length. 20 gauge available in youth model.

NIB: $350	**Exc.:** $300	**VGood:** $250

TRISTAR TSA SYNTHETIC AND SYNTHETIC MAG

Same features as TSA Field Model but with non-glare black synthetic stock and forend. Also available with complete Realtree Max-4 coverage. Mag model has 3.5-inch chamber. Add 15 percent for camo.

NIB: $325	**Exc.:** $275	**VGood:** $225

TRISTAR DERBY CLASSIC SIDE-BY-SIDE

Gauge: 12. Barrel: 28-inch Mod. & Full fixed chokes. Features: Sidelock action, engraved, double trigger, auto ejectors, English straight stock. Made in Europe for Tristar Sporting Arms Ltd.

Perf.: $1075	**Exc.:** $925	**VGood:** $825

TRISTAR MODEL 1887

Lever-action; 12-ga.; 22-inch barrel; weighs 8-3/4 lbs.; 40-1/2-inch overall; walnut w/pistol grip; improved cylinder choke; oil finish. Introduced 2002. Made in Australia. Available through AcuSport Corp.

Perf.: $995	**Exc.:** $850	**VGood:** $750

TRISTAR PHANTOM AUTO SHOTGUNS

Gauge: 12, shoots 2-3/4-inch or 3-inch interchangeably; 24-inch, 26-inch, 28-inch barrel (Imp. Cyl., Mod., Full choke tubes); European walnut or black synthetic; gas-operated action; blued barrel; checkered pistol grip and forend; vent rib barrel. Introduced 1999. Imported by Tristar Sporting Arms Ltd.

Perf.: $385	**Exc.:** $350	**VGood:** $315

TRISTAR PHANTOM HP AUTO SHOTGUN

Gauge: 12, 3-inch chamber. Barrel: 19-inch; threaded for external choke tubes. Stock: Black synthetic. Sights: Bead front. Features: Gas-operated action; blue/ black finish; five-shot extended magazine tube. Imported by Tristar Sporting Arms Ltd.

Perf.: $341	**Exc.:** $306	**VGood:** $271

TRISTAR YORK

This side-by-side with blued engraved receiver and 3-inch chambers comes in 12 and 20 gauge with 26- inch or 28-inch barrels. Walnut, pistol grip stock and rubber recoil pad.

NIB: $825	**Exc.:** $765	**VGood:** $600

TRISTAR ROTA MODEL 411 SIDE-BY-SIDE

Gauge: 12, 16, 20, .410, 3-inch chambers; 28, 2-3/4-inch; 12-ga., 26-inch barrel; 28-inch; 16-, 20-, 28-ga., 410-bore, 26-inch; 12- and 20-ga. have three choke tubes, 16, 28 (Imp. Cyl. & Mod.), .410 (Mod. & Full) fixed chokes; weighs 6-1/2 to 7-1/4 lbs.; 14-3/8-inch l.o.p.; standard walnut with pistol grip, splinter-style forend; hand checkered; engraved, color case-hardened boxlock action; double triggers, extractors; solid barrel rib. Introduced 1998. Imported from Italy by Tristar Sporting Arms, Ltd.

Perf.: $710	**Exc.:** $650	**VGood:** $575

TRISTAR ROTA MODEL 411D SIDE-BY-SIDE

Similar to Model 411 except automatic ejectors, straight English-style stock, single trigger. Solid barrel rib with matted surface; chrome bores; color case-hardened frame; splinter forend. Introduced 1999. Imported from Italy by Tristar Sporting Arms, Ltd.

Perf.: $915	**Exc.:** $800	**VGood:** $700

Traditions Mag 350 Series O/U Turkey II

Traditions Mag 350 Series O/U Waterfowl II

Tristar Brittany

Tristar Brittany Classic

Tristar Derby Classic

Tristar Phantom

Tristar Phantom HP Auto

Tristar Rota Model 411D
Side-by-Side

Tristar Rota Model 411R
Coach Gun Side-by-Side

Tristar Rota Model 411F
Side-by-Side

Tristar Silver Sporting O/U

Tristar Silver II

Tristar TR-SC "Emilio Rizzini"
Over/Under

Tristar TR-L "Emilio Rizzini"
Over/Under

Tristar TR-I "Emilio Rizzini"
Over/Under

Tristar TR-Mag "Emilio Rizzini"
Over/Under

TRISTAR ROTA MODEL 411R COACH GUN SIDE-BY-SIDE

Similar to Model 411 except in 12- or 20-gauge only with 20-inch barrels and fixed chokes (Cyl. & Cyl.). Double triggers, extractors, choke tubes. Introduced 1999. Imported from Italy by Tristar Sporting Arms, Ltd.

Perf.: $650   **Exc.:** $575   **VGood:** $525

TRISTAR ROTA MODEL 411F SIDE-BY-SIDE

Similar to Model 411 except silver, engraved receiver, ejectors, IC, Mod. and Full choke tubes, English-style stock, single gold trigger, cut checkering. Imported from Italy by Tristar Sporting Arms, Ltd.

Perf.: $1425   **Exc.:** $1200   **VGood:** $995

TRISTAR SILVER SPORTING O/U

Gauge: 12, 2-3/4-inch chambers, 20 3-inch chambers; 28-inch barrel, 30-inch (Skeet, Imp. Cyl., Mod., Full choke tubes); weighs 7-3/8 lbs.; 45-1/2-inch overall; figured walnut, cut checkering; Sporting Clays quick-mount buttpad; target bead front sight; boxlock action with single selective trigger, automatic selective ejectors; special broadway channeled rib; vented barrel rib; chrome bores; chrome-nickel finish on frame, with engraving. Introduced 1990. Imported from Italy by Tristar Sporting Arms Ltd.

Perf.: $675   **Exc.:** $575   **VGood:** $495

TRISTAR SILVER II SHOTGUN

Similar to the Silver I except 26-inch barrel (Imp. Cyl., Mod., Full choke tubes, 12- and 20-ga.), 28-inch (Imp. Cyl., Mod., Full choke tubes, 12-ga. only), 26-inch (Imp. Cyl. & Mod. fixed chokes, 28-ga. and .410), automatic selective ejectors. Weight about 6 lbs., 15 oz. (12-ga., 26-inch).

Perf.: $565   **Exc.:** $475   **VGood:** $425

TRISTAR TR-SC "EMILIO RIZZINI" OVER/UNDER

Gauge: 12, 20, 3-inch chambers; 28-inch barrel, 30-inch (Imp. Cyl., Mod., Full choke tubes); weighs 7-1/2 lbs.; 46-inch overall (28-inch barrel); semi-fancy walnut; pistol grip with palm swell; semi-beavertail forend; black Sporting Clays recoil pad; silvered boxlock action with Four Locks locking system; auto ejectors; single selective (inertia) trigger; auto safety; hard chrome bores; vent. 10mm rib with target-style front and mid-rib beads. Introduced 1998. Imported from Italy by Tristar Sporting Arms, Ltd.

Sporting Clays model		
Perf.: $885	**Exc.:** $775	**VGood:** $675
20 ga.		
Perf.: $965	**Exc.:** $855	**VGood:** $755

TRISTAR TR-ROYAL "EMILIO RIZZINI" OVER/UNDER

Similar to the TR-SC except has special parallel stock dimensions to give low felt recoil; Rhino-ported, extended 12-, 20-, 28-ga. or .410 choke tubes; solid barrel spacer; has "TR-Royal" gold engraved on the silvered receiver. Available in 12- (28-inch, 30-inch), 20- and 28-gauge (28-inch only). Introduced 1999. Imported from Italy by Tristar Sporting Arms, Ltd.

12-ga.		
Perf.: $1075	**Exc.:** $935	**VGood:** $825
20-, 28-ga.		
Perf.: $1075	**Exc.:** $935	**VGood:** $825

TRISTAR TR-L "EMILIO RIZZINI" OVER/UNDER

Similar to the TR-SC except has stock dimensions designed for female shooters. Standard grade walnut. Introduced 1998. Imported from Italy by Tristar Sporting Arms, Ltd.

Perf.: $890   **Exc.:** $780   **VGood:** $680

TRISTAR TR-I, II "EMILIO RIZZINI" OVER/UNDERS

Gauge: 12, 20, 3-inch chambers (TR-I); 12-, 16-, 20-, 28-ga., .410/3-inch chambers; 12-ga., 26-inch barrel (Imp. Cyl. & Mod.), 28-inch (Mod. & Full); 20-ga., 26-inch barrel (Imp. Cyl. & Mod.); fixed chokes; weighs 7-1/2 lbs.; walnut with palm swell pistol grip, hand checkering, semi-beavertail forend, black recoil pad; boxlock action with blued finish; Four Locks locking system; gold single selective (inertia) trigger system; automatic safety; extractors. Introduced 1998. Imported from Italy by Tristar Sporting Arms, Ltd.

TR-I		
Perf.: $585	**Exc.:** $485	**VGood:** $430
TR-II (automatic ejectors, choke tubes) 12-, 16-ga.		
Perf.: $795	**Exc.:** $675	**VGood:** $575
20-, 28-ga., .410		
Perf.: $845	**Exc.:** $725	**VGood:** $625

TRISTAR TR-MAG "EMILIO RIZZINI" OVER/UNDER

Similar to TR-I, 3-1/2-inch chambers; choke tubes; 24-inch or 28-inch barrels with three choke tubes; extractors; auto safety. Matte blue finish on all metal, non-reflective wood finish. Introduced 1998. Imported from Italy by Tristar Sporting Arms, Ltd.

Perf.: $650	**Exc.:** $575	**VGood:** $475
Mossy Oak Break-Up camo		
Perf.: $820	**Exc.:** $745	**VGood:** $645
Mossy Oak Shadow Grass camo		
Perf.: $820	**Exc.:** $745	**VGood:** $645
10 ga., Mossy Oak camo patterns		
Perf.: $1018	**Exc.:** $943	**VGood:** $843

TRISTAR TR-CLASS SL "EMILIO RIZZINI" O/U

Gauge: 12, 2-3/4-inch chambers; 28-inch, 30-inch barrel; weighs 7-3/4 lbs.; fancy walnut, hand checkering, semi-beavertail forend, black recoil pad, gloss finish; boxlock action with silvered, engraved sideplates; Four Lock locking system; automatic ejectors; hard chrome bores; vent tapered 7mm rib with target-style front bead; hand-fitted gun. Introduced 1999. Imported from Italy by Tristar Sporting Arms, Ltd.

Perf.: $1625   **Exc.:** $1400   **VGood:** $1125

TRISTAR WS/OU 12 SHOTGUN

Gauge: 12, 3 1/2-inch chambers; 28-inch or 30-inch barrel (Imp. Cyl., Mod., Full choke tubes); weighs 6 lbs., 15 oz.; 46-inch overall; European walnut with cut checkering, black vented recoil pad, matte finish; boxlock action with single selective trigger; automatic selective ejectors; chrome bores; matte metal finish. Imported by Tristar Sporting Arms Ltd.

Perf.: $550   **Exc.:** $475   **VGood:** $425

TRISTAR HUNTER LITE

Over-and-under with silver alloy engraved frame, 3-inch chambers, extractors, choke tubes and walnut pistol grip stock and forearm. 20-gauge with 26-inch barrels weighs 5.4 lbs.; 12 gauge with 28-inch barrels weighs 6 lbs.

NIB: $400   **Exc.:** $350   **VGood:** $295

TRISTAR HUNTER

Similar to Hunter Lite But with blued steel frame.

NIB: $390   **Exc.:** $340   **VGood:** $275

TRISTAR FIELD HUNTER

Over/under 12-ga with 28-inch barrels, walnut stocks and three interchangeable chokes; this model includes selective auto ejectors and five choke tubes.

NIB: $500   **Exc.:** $450   **VGood:** $395

UGARTECHEA 10-GAUGE MAGNUM

Side-by-side; boxlock; 10-ga.; 3-1/2-inch chambers; 32-inch barrels; matted rib; weighs 11 lbs.; front, center metal beads; checkered European walnut stock; vent rubber recoil pad; Purdey-type forend release; double triggers; color case-hardened action; rest is blued. Made in Spain. Introduced 1990; still in production.

Perf.: $725   **Exc.:** $645   **VGood:** $545

UNION ARMERA LUXE

Side-by-side; 12-, 20-ga.; 2-3/4-inch chambers; custom built to customer's specs; top-grade European walnut stock; auto ejectors; hand-engraved action; numerous options. Made in Spain. Introduced 1982; discontinued 1984.

Perf.: $5200   **Exc.:** $3750   **VGood:** $3200

UNION ARMERA WINNER

Side-by-side; 12-, 20-ga.; 2-3/4-inch chambers; custom built to customer's specs; top-grade European walnut stock; auto ejectors; hand-engraved action; numerous options. Made in Spain. Introduced 1982; discontinued 1984.

Perf.: $2700   **Exc.:** $2250   **VGood:** $1900

UNIVERSAL FIREARMS AUTO WING

Recoil-operated autoloader; takedown; 12-ga.; 2-3/4-inch chamber; 5-shot magazine, 3-shot plug furnished; 25-inch, 28-inch, 30-inch barrel; Improved, Modified, Full chokes; vent rib; ivory bead front, middle sights; checkered European walnut pistol-grip stock, grooved forearm; crossbolt safety; interchangeable barrels. Introduced 1970; discontinued 1974.

Perf.: $150   **Exc.:** $125   **VGood:** $100

UNIVERSAL FIREARMS DOUBLE WING

Side-by-side; boxlock; 10-, 12-, 20-ga.; 26-inch Improved/Modified, 28-inch or 30-inch Modified/Full barrels; checkered European walnut pistol-grip stock, beavertail forearm; double triggers; recoil pad. Introduced 1970; discontinued 1974.

Perf.: $350   **Exc.:** $295   **VGood:** $250

UNIVERSAL FIREARMS DUCK WING

Recoil-operated autoloader; takedown; 12-ga.; 2-3/4-inch chamber; 5-shot magazine, 3-shot plug furnished; 28-inch, 30-inch barrel; Full choke; ivory bead front, middle sights; checkered European walnut pistol-grip stock, grooved forearm; crossbolt safety; interchangeable barrels; exposed metal parts coated with olive green Teflon-S. Introduced 1970; discontinued 1972.

Perf.: $200   **Exc.:** $125   **VGood:** $95

UNIVERSAL FIREARMS MODEL 101

Single shot; top break; external hammer; takedown; 12-ga.; 3-inch chamber; 28-inch, 30-inch Full-choke barrel; uncheckered pistol-grip stock, beavertail forearm. Introduced 1967; discontinued 1969. Replaced by Single Wing model.

Perf.: $75   **Exc.:** $45   **VGood:** $30

UNIVERSAL FIREARMS MODEL 202

Side-by-side; boxlock; 12-, 20-ga.; 3-inch chambers; 26-inch Improved/Modified, 28-inch Modified/Full barrels; hand-checkered European walnut pistol-grip stock, European-style forearm; double triggers. Introduced 1967; discontinued 1969. Replaced by Double Wing model.

Perf.: $275   **Exc.:** $195   **VGood:** $8145

UNIVERSAL FIREARMS MODEL 203

Side-by-side; boxlock; 10-ga.; 3 1/2-inch chambers; 32-inch Full/Full barrels; hand-checkered European walnut pistol-grip stock, European-style forearm; double triggers. Introduced 1967; discontinued 1969.

Perf.: $440   **Exc.:** $420   **VGood:** $295

UNIVERSAL FIREARMS MODEL 2030

Side-by-side; boxlock; 10-ga.; 3-1/2-inch chambers; 32-inch Full/Full barrels; checkered European walnut pistol-grip stock, beavertail forearm; double triggers; recoil pad. Introduced 1970; discontinued 1974.

Perf.: $440   **Exc.:** $420   **VGood:** $295

UNIVERSAL FIREARMS OVER WING

Over/under; boxlock; hammerless; 12-, 20-ga.; 3-inch chambers; 26-inch Improved/Modified, 28-inch or 30-inch Modified/Full barrels; vent rib; front, middle sights; checkered European walnut pistol-grip stock, forearm; double triggers; single-trigger model

Tristar TR-Class SL "Emilio Rizzini" Over/Under

Tristar Field Hunter

Ugartechea 10-Gauge Magnum

Union Armera Winner

Universal Firearms Auto Wing

Universal Firearms Double Wing

Universal Firearms Duck Wing

Universal Firearms Over Wing

Universal Firearms Single Wing

Urbiola Model 160E

Valmet Lion

Valmet Model 412K

Valmet Model 412S American

Ventura Model 51

Ventura Model 53

with engraved receiver at added cost. Introduced 1970; discontinued 1974.

With double triggers
Perf.: $295   **Exc.:** $195   **VGood:** $150

With single trigger, engraved receiver
Perf.: $325   **Exc.:** $220   **VGood:** $175

UNIVERSAL FIREARMS SINGLE WING

Single-shot; top break; external hammer; takedown; 12-ga.; 3-inch chamber; 28-inch Full or Modified barrel; uncheckered European walnut pistol-grip stock, beavertail forearm; automatic ejector. Introduced 1970; discontinued 1974.
Perf.: $75   **Exc.:** $45   **VGood:** $30

URBIOLA MODEL 160E

Side-by-side; 12-, 20-ga.; 2-3/4-inch chambers; 26-inch Improved/Full, 28-inch Modified/Full barrels; hand-checkered European walnut straight-grip stock; checkered butt; automatic ejectors; double triggers; hand-engraved locks. Made in Spain. Introduced 1982 by Toledo Armas; discontinued 1984.
Perf.: $625   **Exc.:** $500   **VGood:** $425

VALMET LION

Over/under; boxlock; 12-ga.; 26-inch Improved/Modified, 28-inch Modified/Full, 30-inch Modified/Full or Full/Full barrels; hand-checkered walnut stock; single selective trigger; plain extractors. Made in Finland. Introduced 1951; discontinued 1967.
Exc.: $360   **VGood:** $300   **Good:** $275

VALMET MODEL 412K

Over/under; 12-, 20-ga.; 26-inch, 28-inch, 30-inch barrels; vent rib; checkered American walnut stock; extractors; interchangeable barrels, stocks, forends; barrel selector on trigger; auto top tang safety; barrel cocking indicators; optional double triggers. Made in Finland. Introduced 1980; discontinued 1990.
Perf.: $700   **Exc.:** $500   **VGood:** $400

VALMET MODEL 412KE

Same specs as Model 412K except auto ejectors; non-auto safety. Introduced 1980; discontinued 1983.
Perf.: $775   **Exc.:** $575   **VGood:** $475

VALMET MODEL 412S AMERICAN

Same specs as Model 412K except luminous sights; better wood; checkering; palm swell on pistol grip; new forend latch spring mechanism; improved firing pin; made in Trap, Skeet, Field versions. Made in Finland. Introduced 1980; discontinued 1984.
Perf.: $1000   **Exc.:** $750   **VGood:** $600

VALMET MODEL 412ST SKEET

Over/under; 12-, 20-ga.; 28-inch stepped-rib barrels; choke tubes; European walnut Skeet-style stock; mechanical single trigger; auto ejectors; elongated forcing cone; cocking indicators; hand-honed action. Made in Finland. Introduced 1980; discontinued 1990.
Perf.: $995   **Exc.:** $750   **VGood:** $650

VALMET MODEL 412ST SKEET GRADE II

Same specs as Model 412ST Skeet except checkered semi-fancy European walnut Skeet-style stock drilled for recoil-reducing unit; matte nickel receiver; matte blue locking bolt, lever; gold trigger. Made in Finland. Introduced 1989; discontinued 1990.
Perf.: $1200   **Exc.:** $800   **VGood:** $700

VALMET MODEL 412ST TRAP

Same specs as Model 412ST Skeet except 12-ga.; 30-inch, 32-inch barrels; European walnut stock, palm swell. Made in Finland. Introduced 1980; discontinued 1990.
Perf.: $1200   **Exc.:** $800   **VGood:** $700

VALMET MODEL 412ST TRAP GRADE II

Same specs as Model 412ST Skeet except 12-ga.; 30-inch, 32-inch barrels; checkered semi-fancy European walnut stock, palm swell; stock drilled for recoil-reducing unit; matte nickel receiver; matte blue locking bolt, lever; gold trigger. Made in Finland. Introduced 1989; discontinued 1990.
Perf.: $1200   **Exc.:** $800   **VGood:** $700

VENTURA AVANTI SMALL GAUGE

Over/under; boxlock; 28-ga. (2-3/4-inch), .410 (3-inch); 26-inch barrels; vent top, side ribs; weighs 5 3/4 lbs.; straight English-type French walnut stock; single selective trigger; auto ejectors; fully engraved. Made in Italy. Introduced 1987; discontinued 1988.
Perf.: $750   **Exc.:** $600   **VGood:** $525

VENTURA AVANTI SMALL GAUGE EXTRA LUSSO

Same specs as Avanti Small Gauge except highly figured French walnut stock; more ornate engraving. Introduced 1987; discontinued 1988.
Perf.: $1050   **Exc.:** $850   **VGood:** $750

VENTURA CONTENTO

Over/under; boxlock; 12-ga.; 26-inch, 28-inch, 29-1/2-inch, 32-inch barrels; high post rib, vent side ribs; hand-checkered European walnut Monte Carlo stock; Woodward side lugs, double internal bolts; selective single trigger; auto ejectors. Introduced 1975, discontinued 1982.
Perf.: $1800   **Exc.:** $1250   **VGood:** $1000

VENTURA CONTENTO EXTRA LUSSO

Same specs as Contento except best-grade fancy walnut stock; extensive Florentine engraving. No longer in production.
Perf.: $2000   **Exc.:** $1475   **VGood:** $1200

VENTURA CONTENTO LUSSO GRADE

Same specs as Contento except better wood; engraved action. No longer in production.
Perf.: $1900   **Exc.:** $1350   **VGood:** $1100

VENTURA MODEL 51

Side-by-side; 12-, 20-ga.; 27-1/2-inch, 30-inch barrels; hand-checkered select European walnut straight or pistol-grip stock, slender beavertail forend; single selective trigger; auto ejectors; hand-engraved action. Made in Spain. Introduced 1980; discontinued 1985.
Perf.: $600   **Exc.:** $450   **VGood:** $375

VENTURA MODEL 53

Side-by-side; 12-, 20-, 28-ga., .410; 25-inch, 27-1/2-inch, 30-inch barrels; hand-checkered select European walnut straight or pistol-grip stock, slender beavertail forend; single selective or double triggers; auto ejectors; hand-engraved frame. Made in Spain. Introduced 1980; discontinued 1985.
Perf.: $640   **Exc.:** $490   **VGood:** $410

VENTURA MODEL 62

Side-by-side; H&H sidelock; 12-, 20-, 28-ga.; 25-inch, 27-1/2-inch, 30-inch barrels; select figured

English walnut straight or pistol-grip stock, slender beavertail forend; single selective or double triggers; auto ejectors; cocking indicator; gas escape valve; intercepting safety; double underbolts; Purdey-style engraving. Made in Spain. Introduced 1980; discontinued 1982.

Perf.: $1125   **Exc.:** $850   **VGood:** $750

VENTURA MODEL 64

Side-by-side; H&H sidelock; 12-, 20-, 28-ga.; 25-inch, 27-1/2-inch, 30-inch barrels; select figured English walnut straight or pistol-grip stock, slender beavertail forend; single selective or double triggers; auto ejectors; cocking indicator; gas escape valve; intercepting safety; Florentine engraving. Introduced 1978; no longer in production.

Perf.: $1125   **Exc.:** $850   **VGood:** $750

VENTURA MODEL 66

Side-by-side; H&H sidelock; 12-, 20-, 28-ga.; 25-inch, 27-1/2-inch, 30-inch barrels; select figured English walnut straight or pistol-grip stock, slender beavertail forend; single selective or double triggers; auto ejectors; cocking indicator; gas escape valve; intercepting safety; treble bolting; side clips; Florentine engraving. Introduced 1980; no longer in production.

Perf.: $1125   **Exc.:** $850   **VGood:** $750

VENTURA MODEL XXV

Side-by-side; 12-, 20-, 28-ga., .410; 25-inch barrels; Churchill rib; hand-checkered select European walnut straight or pistol grip stock, slender beavertail forend; single selective or double triggers; auto ejectors; hand-engraved frame. Made in Spain. Introduced 1980; no longer in production.

Perf.: $850   **Exc.:** $625   **VGood:** $550

VENTURA REGIS MODEL

Side-by-side; H&H sidelock; 12-, 20-, 28-ga., .410; 2-3/4-inch, 3-inch chambers; 26-inch, 28-inch barrels; weighs 6-1/2 lbs.; hand-checkered select figured French walnut stock, sliver beavertail forend; intercepting safeties; triple locks; auto ejectors; single selective, double triggers; floral engraving; several options. Made in Italy. Introduced 1986; discontinued 1988.

Perf.: $1500   **Exc.:** $1350   **VGood:** $1100

VENTURA VICTRIX

Side-by-side; Anson & Deeley boxlock; 12-, 20-, 28-ga., .410; 2-3/4-inch, 3-inch chambers; 26-inch, 28-inch barrels; fixed chokes; optional screw-in chokes; weighs 6-1/2 lbs.; hand-checkered French walnut stock, beavertail forend; triple locks; auto ejectors; double or single selective trigger; marketed in leather trunk-type case. Made in Italy. Introduced 1986; discontinued 1988.

With fixed chokes		
Perf.: $800	**Exc.:** $600	**VGood:** $500
With choke tubes		
Perf.: $850	**Exc.:** $650	**VGood:** $550

VENTURA VICTRIX EXTRA LUSSO

Same specs as Victrix except better quality wood; full floral engraving. Made in Italy. Introduced 1986; discontinued 1988.

With fixed chokes		
Perf.: $1125	**Exc.:** $850	**VGood:** $750
With choke tubes		
Perf.: $1175	**Exc.:** $900	**VGood:** $800

VERONA LX501 HUNTING O/U SHOTGUNS

Gauge: 12, 20, 28, 410 (2-3/4-inch, 3-inch chambers); 28-inch barrel; 12-, 20-ga. have Interchoke tubes, 28-ga. and .410 have fixed Full & Mod.; weighs 6 to 7 lbs.; matte-finished walnut with machine-cut checkering; gold-plated single-selective trigger; ejectors; engraved, blued receiver; non-automatic safety; coil spring-operated firing pins. Introduced 1999. Imported from Italy by B.C. Outdoors.

12- and 20-ga.		
Perf.: $650	**Exc.:** $550	**VGood:** $495

28-ga. and .410		
Perf.: $675	**Exc.:** $595	**VGood:** $525
Combos 20/28, 28/410		
Perf.: $1300	**Exc.:** $1200	**VGood:** $1150

VERONA LX692 GOLD HUNTING OVER/UNDER SHOTGUNS

Similar to Verona LX501 except engraved, silvered receiver with false sideplates showing gold-inlaid bird hunting scenes on three sides; schnabel forend tip; hand-cut checkering; black rubber butt pad. Available in 12- and 20-gauge only, five InterChoke tubes. Introduced 1999. Imported from Italy by B.C. Outdoors.

Perf.: $1195	**Exc.:** $995	**VGood:** $875
Combo 28/410		
Perf.: $2100	**Exc.:** $1900	**VGood:** $1750

VERONA LX680 SPORTING OVER/UNDER SHOTGUNS

Similar to Verona LX501 except engraved, silvered receiver; ventilated middle rib; beavertail forend; hand-cut checkering; available in 12- or 20-gauge only with 2-3/4-inch chambers. Introduced 1999. Imported from Italy by B.C. Outdoors.

Perf.: $975   **Exc.:** $800   **VGood:** $700

VERONA LX680 SKEET/SPORTING, TRAP OVER/UNDER SHOTGUNS

Similar to Verona LX501 except Skeet or trap stock dimensions; beavertail forend, palm swell on pistol grip; ventilated center barrel rib. Introduced 1999. Imported from Italy by B.C. Outdoors.

Perf.: $1100	**Exc.:** $900	**VGood:** $800
Gold Competition (false sideplates with gold-inlaid hunting scenes)		
Perf.: $1475	**Exc.:** $1300	**VGood:** $1100

VERONA LX692 GOLD SPORTING OVER/UNDER SHOTGUNS

Similar to Verona LX680 except false sideplates have gold-inlaid bird hunting scenes on three sides; red high-visibility front sight. Introduced 1999. Imported from Italy by B.C. Outdoors.

Perf.: $1275   **Exc.:** $1100   **VGood:** $100

VERONA LX680 COMPETITION TRAP

Gauge: 12; 30-inch barrel O/U, 32-inch single bbl.; weighs 8-3/8 lbs. combo, 7 lbs. single; walnut stock; white front, mid-rib bead sights; interchangeable barrels switch from O/U to single configurations; 5

Briley chokes in combo, 4 in single bbl.; extended forcing cones, parted barrels 32-inch with raised rib.

Trap Single		
Perf.: $1499	**Exc.:** $1395	**VGood:** $1200
Trap Combo		
Perf.: $2300	**Exc.:** $2200	**VGood:** $2000

VERONA LX702 GOLD TRAP COMBO

Gauge: 20 & 28, 2-3/4-inch chamber; 30-inch barrel; weighs 7 lbs.; Turkish walnut with beavertail forearm; white front bead sight; 2-barrel competition gun; color case-hardened sideplates and receiver with gold inlaid pheasant; ventilated rib between barrels; 5 interchokes. Imported from Italy by B.C. Outdoors.

Combo		
Perf.: $1475	**Exc.:** $1300	**VGood:** $1100
20-gauge		
Perf.: $1475	**Exc.:** $1300	**VGood:** $1100

VERONA MODEL SX400 SEMI-AUTO SHOTGUN

Gauge: 12; 26-inch, 30-inch barrel; weighs 6-1/2 lbs.; walnut, black composite stock; red dot sights; aluminum receivers; gas-operated; 2-3/4-inch or 3-inch Magnum shells (without adj.); 4 screw-in chokes and wrench included; sling swivels; gold trigger; blued barrel. Imported from Italy by B.C. Outdoors.

401S, 12-gauge		
Perf.: $375	**Exc.:** $325	**VGood:** $290
405SDS, 12-gauge		
Perf.: $570	**Exc.:** $495	**VGood:** $395
405L, 12-gauge		
Perf.: $295	**Exc.:** $250	**VGood:** $210

WEATHERBY ATHENA SIDE-BY-SIDE

Side-by-side; 12-, 20-ga.; 26-inch, 28-inch barrel; Turkish walnut, straight grip stock; brass bead front sight; barrel selector independent of crossbolt safety; integral multi-choke system; interchangeable screw-in Briley choke tubes (excepting .410 bored IC & Mod.); receiver engraved with rose and scroll.

Perf.: $1285   **Exc.:** $1025   **VGood:** $865

WEATHERBY ATHENA GRADE IV

Over/under; boxlock; dummy sideplates; 12-, 20-ga.; 3-inch chambers; 26-inch, 28-inch barrels; three

Ventura Model 64

Verona LX501
Skeet/Sporting, Trap O/U

Verona LX680
Skeet/Sporting, Trap O/U

Verona LX692
Gold Sporting Over/Under

Weatherby Athena Grade IV

Weatherby Athena Grade V Classic Field

Weatherby Athena III Classic Field

Weatherby Athena Single Barrel Trap

Weatherby Centurion

Weatherby Model Eighty-Two

Weatherby Model Ninety-Two

Weatherby Olympian

Weatherby Orion I

IMC Multi-Choke tubes; checkered American walnut pistol-grip stock, forend; mechanically operated single selective trigger (selector inside trigger guard); selective auto ejectors; top tang safety, Greener crossbolt; fully engraved receiver. Made in Japan. Introduced 1982; still in production.

Perf.: $2000 **Exc.:** $1495 **VGood:** $1150

WEATHERBY ATHENA GRADE V CLASSIC FIELD

Same specs as the Athena Grade IV except 26-inch, 28-inch, 30-inch barrels; oil-finished, fine-line-checkered Claro walnut, rounded pistol-grip stock w/slender forend; Old English recoil pad; sideplate receiver rose and scroll engraved. Made in Japan. Introduced 1993; still imported.

Perf.: $2500 **Exc.:** $2000 **VGood:** $1500

WEATHERBY ATHENA III CLASSIC FIELD O/U

Has Grade III Claro walnut with oil finish, rounded pistol grip, slender forend; silver nitride/gray receiver has rose and scroll engraving with gold- overlay upland game scenes. Introduced 1999. Imported from Japan by Weatherby.

12-, 20-, 28-gauge		
Perf.: $1900	**Exc.:** $1550	**VGood:** $1275

WEATHERBY ATHENA SINGLE BARREL TRAP

Same specs as the Athena Grade IV except 12-ga.; 2-3/4-inch chambers; 32-inch, 34-inch single top

barrel; Full, Modified, Improved Modified Multi-Choke tubes; white front sight, brass middle bead; trap stock dimensions. Made in Japan. Introduced 1988; discontinued 1992.

Perf.: $1550	**Exc.:** $950	**VGood:** $850
Combo with extra O/U barrel set		
Perf.: $2000	**Exc.:** $1500	**VGood:** $1200

WEATHERBY CENTURION

Autoloader; 12-ga.; 2-3/4-inch chamber; 26-inch Skeet or Improved Cylinder, 28-inch Improved or Modified or Full, 30-inch Full barrel; vent rib; front, middle bead sights; hand-checkered American walnut pistol-grip stock, forearm; pressure compensator; engraved alloy receiver. Made in Japan. Introduced 1970; discontinued 1982; replaced by Model Eighty-Two.

Perf.: $325 **Exc.:** $275 **VGood:** $225

WEATHERBY CENTURION DELUXE

Same specs as Centurion except fancy-grade wood; etched receiver. Introduced 1972; discontinued 1982.

Perf.: $395 **Exc.:** $325 **VGood:** $250

WEATHERBY CENTURION TRAP

Same specs as Centurion except 30-inch Full-choke barrel; trap-style walnut stock. Introduced 1972; discontinued 1982.

Perf.: $370 **Exc.:** $350 **VGood:** $310

WEATHERBY MODEL EIGHTY-TWO

Gas-operated autoloader; 12-ga.; 2-3/4-inch, 3-inch chamber; 26-inch, 28-inch, 30-inch barrels; 22-inch slug barrel with rifle sights available; fixed or interchangeable choke tubes; hand-checkered pistol-grip stock, forend; rubber recoil pad; floating piston; fluted bolt; crossbolt safety; gold-plated trigger. Made in Japan. Introduced 1982; discontinued 1988.

With fixed choke		
Perf.: $395	**Exc.:** $295	**VGood:** $255
With choke tubes		
Perf.: $425	**Exc.:** $320	**VGood:** $285

WEATHERBY MODEL EIGHTY-TWO BUCKMASTER

Same specs as Model Eighty-Two except 22-inch Skeet barrel; rifle sights. Introduced 1982; discontinued 1987.

Perf.: $375 **Exc.:** $350 **VGood:** $295

WEATHERBY MODEL EIGHTY-TWO TRAP

Same specs as Model Eighty-Two except 30-inch Full-choke barrel; trap-style walnut stock. Introduced 1982; discontinued 1984.

With fixed choke		
Perf.: $350	**Exc.:** $275	**VGood:** $250
With choke tubes		
Perf.: $375	**Exc.:** $300	**VGood:** $275

WEATHERBY MODEL NINETY-TWO

Slide action; 12-ga.; 2-3/4-inch, 3-inch chamber; 26-inch Modified or Improved or Skeet, 28-inch Full or Modified, 30-inch Full barrel; vent rib; hand-checkered American walnut pistol-grip stock, forend; grip cap; recoil pad; crossbolt safety; engraved black alloy receiver. Made in Japan. Introduced 1982; discontinued 1988.

With fixed choke		
Perf.: $325	**Exc.:** $275	**VGood:** $240
With Multi-chokes		
Perf.: $350	**Exc.:** $325	**VGood:** $270

WEATHERBY MODEL NINETY-TWO BUCKMASTER

Same specs as Model Ninety-two except 22-inch Skeet barrel; rifle sights. Introduced 1982; discontinued 1987.

Perf.: $345 **Exc.:** $285 **VGood:** $250

WEATHERBY MODEL NINETY-TWO TRAP

Same specs as Model Ninety-two except 30-inch Full-choke barrel; trap-style walnut stock. Introduced 1982; discontinued 1984.

With fixed choke		
Perf.: $300	**Exc.:** $220	**VGood:** $190
With Multi-chokes		
Perf.: $325	**Exc.:** $240	**VGood:** $200

WEATHERBY OLYMPIAN

Over/under; boxlock; 12-, 20-ga.; 26-inch, 28-inch, 30-inch barrels; checkered American walnut pistol-grip stock; selective auto ejectors; single selective trigger; top tang safety; Greener crossbolt. Made in Italy. Introduced 1978; discontinued 1982; replaced by Athena.

Perf.: $875 **Exc.:** $750 **VGood:** $650

WEATHERBY OLYMPIAN TRAP

Same specs as Olympian except 12-ga.; 30-inch, 32-inch barrels; vent rib; trap-style walnut stock. Introduced 1978; discontinued 1982.

Perf.: $875 **Exc.:** $750 **VGood:** $650

WEATHERBY ORION I

Over/under; boxlock; 12-, 20-ga.; 3-inch chambers; 26-inch, 28-inch Full/Modified or Modified/Improved or Skeet/Skeet, 30-inch Full/Modified barrels; Multi-chokes; checkered American walnut pistol-grip stock, forend; rubber recoil pad; selective auto ejectors;

single selective trigger; top tang safety; Greener-type crossbolt. Made in Japan. Introduced 1982.

Perf.: $1000   Exc.: $750   VGood: $600

WEATHERBY ORION I SPORTING CLAYS

Same specs as Orion I except 12-ga.; 28-inch barrels; IMC choke tubes; raised rib; center and front beads; special Sporting Clays stock dimensions; rounded buttpad; elongated forcing cones; blued receiver with two 24-Karat gold clay targets on the bottom. Made in Japan. Introduced 1991; discontinued 1992.

Perf.: $1200   Exc.: $950   VGood: $800

WEATHERBY ORION UPLAND O/U

Similar to Orion Grade I. Plain blued receiver, gold W on trigger guard; rounded pistol grip, slender forend of Claro walnut with high-gloss finish; black butt pad. Available in 12- and 20-gauge with 26-inch and 28-inch barrels. Introduced 1999. Imported from Japan by Weatherby.

Perf.: $1095   Exc.: $965   VGood: $800

WEATHERBY ORION II

Over/under; boxlock; 12-, 20-, 28-ga., .410; 3-inch chambers; 26-inch, 28-inch, 30-inch barrels; fixed or choke tubes; high-gloss checkered American walnut pistol-grip stock, forend; rubber recoil pad; selective auto ejectors; single selective trigger; top tang safety; Greener crossbolt; engraving. Discontinued 1993.

Perf.: $1100   Exc.: $800   VGood: $675

WEATHERBY ORION II CLASSIC

Same specs as Orion II except 12-, 20-, 28-ga.; 3-inch chambers; fine-line-checkered Claro walnut rounded-pistol-grip, slender forend with high-gloss finish; Old English recoil pad; silver-gray nitride receiver with engraved waterfowl and upland scenes. Made in Japan. Introduced 1993; still in production.

Perf.: $1300   Exc.: $1095   VGood: $875

WEATHERBY ORION II CLASSIC SPORTING CLAYS

Same specs as Orion II except 12-ga.; 28-inch, 30-inch barrels; IMC choke tubes; stepped Broadway-style competition vent top, side rib; Sporting Clays rounded-pistol-grip stock, slender forend with high-gloss finish; rounded buttpad; elongated forcing cones; silver-gray nitride receiver; scroll engraving with clay pigeon monogram in gold-plate overlay. Made in Japan. Introduced 1993; still in production.

Perf.: $1450   Exc.: $1100   VGood: $950

WEATHERBY ORION II SPORTING CLAYS

Same specs as Orion II except 12-ga.; 2-3/4-inch chambers; 28-inch, 30-inch barrels; Improved Cylinder, Modified, Full chokes; competition center vent rib; mid-barrel and enlarged front beads; Sporting Clays rounded-pistol-grip stock, slender forend with high-gloss finish; rounded recoil pad; lengthened forcing cones; silver nitride receiver with acid-etched, gold-plate clay pigeon monogram. Made in Japan. Introduced 1992.

Perf.: $1550   Exc.: $1400   VGood: $1250

WEATHERBY ORION III

Over/under; boxlock; 12-, 20-ga.; 3-inch chambers; 26-inch, 28-inch, 30-inch barrels; Multi-chokes; high-gloss checkered American walnut pistol-grip stock, forend; rubber recoil pad; selective auto ejectors; single selective trigger; top tang safety; Greener crossbolt; silvered, engraved receiver. Introduced 1989; still in production.

Perf.: $1250   Exc.: $850   VGood: $700

WEATHERBY ORION III CLASSIC

Same specs as Orion III except fine-line-checkered Claro walnut rounded-pistol-grip stock, slender forend with oil finish; Old English recoil pad; silver-gray nitride receiver with engraved waterfowl and upland scenes and gold-plate overlay. Made in Japan. Introduced 1993; still in production.

Perf.: $1400   Exc.: $1200   VGood: $950

Weatherby Orion Upland

Weatherby Orion II Classic Sporting Clays

Weatherby Orion III

Weatherby Orion III English Field

Weatherby Orion D'Italia

Weatherby Orion Side-by-Side

WEATHERBY ORION GRADE III FIELD O/U SHOTGUNS

Over/under; 12-, 20-ga.; 3-inch chambers; 26-inch, 28-inch barrel; IMC Multi-Choke tubes; weighs 6-1/2 to 9 lbs.; American walnut, checkered grip and forend; rubber recoil pad; selective automatic ejectors; single selective inertia trigger; top tang safety; Greener cross bolt; silver-gray receiver with engraving and gold duck/pheasant. Imported from Japan by Weatherby.

Perf.: $1545   Exc.: $1225   VGood: $965

WEATHERBY ORION GRADE III CLASSIC FIELD O/U

Similar to Orion III Field except stock has rounded pistol grip, satin oil finish, slender forend, Old English recoil pad. Introduced 1993. Imported from Japan by Weatherby.

Perf.: $1565   Exc.: $1250   VGood: $1075

WEATHERBY ORION III ENGLISH FIELD O/U

Similar to Orion III Classic Field except straight grip English-style stock. Available in 12-gauge (28-inch), 20-gauge (26-inch, 28-inch) with IMC Multi-Choke tubes. Silver/gray nitride receiver engraved and gold-plate overlay. Introduced 1997. Imported from Japan by Weatherby.

Perf.: $1695   Exc.: $1300   VGood: $1175

WEATHERBY ORION GRADE II CLASSIC FIELD O/U

Similar to Orion III Classic Field except stock has high-gloss finish, and bird on receiver is not gold. Available in 12-gauge, 26-inch, 28-inch, 30-inch barrels; 20-gauge, 26-inch 28-inch, both with 3-inch chambers; 28-gauge, 26-inch, 2-3/4-inch chambers.

All have IMC choke tubes. Imported from Japan by Weatherby.

Perf.: $1300 E   Exc.: $1095   VGood: $875

WEATHERBY ORION GRADE I FIELD O/U

Similar to Orion Grade III Field except blued receiver with engraving, and the bird is not gold. Available in 12-gauge, 26-inch, 28-inch, 30-inch; 20-gauge, 20-inch, 28-inch, both with 3-inch chambers and IMC choke tubes. Imported from Japan by Weatherby.

Perf.: $1240   Exc.: $1040   VGood: $860

WEATHERBY ORION D'ITALIA

Engraved silver-finish metalwork and fineline, 20 lpi checkering. Turkish walnut stock with high-gloss finish. Available in 12 gauge with 28" barrel and 20 gauge with 26" barrel.

Perf.: $1695   Exc.: $1300   VGood: $1175

WEATHERBY ORION SIDE-BY-SIDE

Gauge: 12, 20, 28, .410. Barrel: 26-inch, 28-inch. Stock: Turkish walnut, half round pistol grip. Sights: Brass bead front. Features: Barrel selector independent of crossbolt safety. Integral multi-choke system, interchangeable screw-in Briley choke tubes (excepting .410 bored IC & Mod.). Receivers engraved with rose and scroll.

Perf.: $960   Exc.: $845   VGood: $735

WEATHERBY ORION SSC OVER/UNDER SHOTGUN

Gauge: 12, 3-inch chambers; 28-inch, 30-inch, 32-inch barrel (Skeet, SC1, Imp. Cyl., SC2, Mod. IMC choke tubes); weighs about 8 lbs.; Claro walnut with satin oil finish; schnabel forend tip; sporter-

Weatherby Orion SSC

Weatherby Athena D'Italia

Weatherby Athena D'Italia PG

Weatherby Athena D'Italia Deluxe

Weatherby Patrician

Weatherby Patrician Deluxe

Weatherby Regency

Weatherby Regency Trap

Weatherby SAS Sporting Clays

Weatherby SASSlug Gun

Weatherby SA-08 Upland

style pistol grip; Pachmayr Decelerator recoil pad; lengthened forcing cones and back-boring; ported barrels with 12mm grooved rib with mid-bead sight; mechanical trigger is adjustable for length of pull. Introduced 1998. Imported from Japan by Weatherby.

SSC (Super Sporting Clays)
Perf.: $1645   **Exc.:** $1350   **VGood:** $1125

WEATHERBY ATHENA D'ITALIA

This model features a boxlock action with intricately engraved sideplates, straight grip stock and double triggers. Available in 12, 20 and 28 gauges. Three chokes in 12 and 20 gauges; fixed IC and Mod. in 28 gauge. 3-inch chambers in 12 and 20 gauges; 2.75-inch chambers in 28 gauge. Automatic ejectors. Weight 6.75 to 7.25 lbs.

NIB: $2500   **Exc.:** $2250   **VGood:** $1695

WEATHERBY ATHENA D'ITALIA PG

Introduced in 2006, this model is offered in the same configurations as the D'Italia. It is identical in action and frame to the D'Italia but with a rounded pistol grip stock and single gold trigger. Laser-cut checkering at 20 lpi.

NIB: $2750   **Exc.:** $2500   **VGood:** $1825

WEATHERBY ATHENA D'ITALIA DELUXE

Renaissance floral engraving with Bolino style game scene and AAA Fancy Turkish walnut with 24 lpi hand checkering adorn this straight grip stocked model. Available in 12, 20 and 28 gauges with 26-inch or 28-inch barrels with fixed IC and Mod. chokes. Single trigger.

NIB: $6700   **Exc.:** $5750   **VGood:** $3995

WEATHERBY PATRICIAN

Slide action; 12-ga.; 2-3/4-inch chamber; 26-inch Modified or Improved or Skeet, 28-inch Full or Modified, 30-inch Full barrels; vent rib; hand-checkered stock, pistol-grip & forearm; recoil pad; hidden magazine cap; crossbolt safety. Made in Japan. Introduced 1970; discontinued 1982; replaced by Model Ninety-Two.

Perf.: $280   **Exc.:** $200   **VGood:** $170

WEATHERBY PATRICIAN DELUXE

Same specs as Patrician except fancy-grade wood; etched receiver. Introduced 1972; discontinued 1982.

Perf.: $310   **Exc.:** $275   **VGood:** $240

WEATHERBY PATRICIAN TRAP

Same specs as Patrician except 30-inch Full-choke barrel; Trap-style walnut stock. Introduced 1972; discontinued 1982.

Perf.: $280   **Exc.:** $230   **VGood:** $195

WEATHERBY REGENCY

Over/under; 12-, 20-ga.; boxlock; 28-inch Full/Modified, Modified/Improved, Skeet/Skeet barrels; vent rib; bead front sight; hand-checkered American walnut pistol-grip stock, forearm; recoil pad; selective automatic ejectors; single selective trigger; simulated sidelocks; fully engraved receiver. Made first in Italy; then Japan. Introduced 1972; discontinued 1982; replaced by Orion.

Perf.: $950   **Exc.:** $800   **VGood:** $725

WEATHERBY REGENCY TRAP

Same specs as Regency except 30-inch, 32-inch barrels; Modified/Full, Improved Modified/Full, Full/Full chokes; vent side, top ribs; walnut Monte Carlo or straight Trap-style stock. Introduced 1965; discontinued 1982.

Perf.: $895   **Exc.:** $800   **VGood:** $725

WEATHERBY SAS (SEMI-AUTOMATIC SHOTGUNS)

6 Models: SAS Field, SAS Sporting Clays, SAS Shadow Grass, SAS Break-Up, SAS Synthetic, SAS Slug Gun Gauge: 12. Barrel: Vent ribbed, 24-inch-30-inch. Stock: SAS Field and Sporting Clays, walnut. SAS Shadow Grass, Break-Up, Synthetic, composite. Sights: SAS Sporting Clays, brass front and mid-point back. SAS Shadow Grass and Break-Up, HiViz front and brass mid. Synthetic has brass front. Features: IMC system includes 3 Briley screw-in choke tubes. Case included.

Sporting Clays
Perf.: $695   **Exc.:** $595   **VGood:** $495

Slug Gun
Perf.: $675   **Exc.:** $625   **VGood:** $525

WEATHERBY SA-08 UPLAND

This semi-automatic was new in 2008. It features a walnut stock with oil finish. Available in 12 and 20 gauge with 3" chambers and 28" or 26" barrels. Three choke tubes included.

Perf.: $525   **Exc.:** $475   **VGood:** $375

WEATHERBY SA-08 YOUTH
As above but in 20 gauge with 26" barrel only and shorter 12.5" length of pull.

Perf.: $525 **Exc.:** $475 **VGood:** $375

WEATHERBY PA-08 SERIES
Weatherby introduced this line of pump-action shotguns in 2008. All models come in 12 gauge with 3" chambers and have chrome-lined barrels. Knoxx stock models reduced recoil and are adjustable in length.

WEATHERBY PA-08 UPLAND
This model has a walnut stock and forend with low-lustre finish and matte black metal work. Available with 28" or 26" barrel. Includes three choke tubes.

Perf.: $325 **Exc.:** $295 **VGood:** $250

WEATHERBY PA-08 KNOXX STRUTTER X
Strutter models feature a synthetic stock and 24" vent rib barrel. Three choke tubes included. Add 15 percent for Apparition Excel camo pattern.

Perf.: $435 **Exc.:** $325 **VGood:** $295

WEATHERBY PA-08 KNOXX HD
Home defense model features an 18" non-vent-rib barrel and cylinder choke.

Perf.: $435 **Exc.:** $325 **VGood:** $295

WESSON & HARRINGTON LONG TOM CLASSIC SHOTGUN
Gauge: 12, 3-inch chamber; 32-inch barrel (Full); weighs 7-1/2 lbs.; length 46-inch overall; American black walnut with hand- checkered grip and forend; color case-hardened receiver and crescent steel buttplate, blued barrel; receiver engraved with the National Wild Turkey Federation logo. Introduced 1998; dropped 2001.

Perf.: $275 **Exc.:** $240 **VGood:** $195

WESTERN ARMS LONG RANGE HAMMERLESS
Side-by-side; boxlock; 12-, 16-, 20-ga., .410; 26-inch to 32-inch Modified/Full barrels; uncheckered walnut stock, forearm; double or single trigger; plain extractors. Introduced 1924; discontinued 1942. Made by Western Arms Corp., later absorbed by Ithaca Gun Co.

With double triggers		
Exc.: $250	**VGood:** $175	**Good:** $150
With single trigger		
Exc.: $275	**VGood:** $200	**Good:** $175

WESTLEY RICHARDS BEST QUALITY BOXLOCK
Side-by-side; hand-detachable boxlock; hammerless; 12-, 16-, 20-, 28-ga., .410; barrel lengths, chokes to order; hand-checkered walnut straight or half-pistol-grip stock, forearm; hinged lockplate; selective ejectors; double or single selective trigger. Still in production.

With double triggers		
Perf.: $15,500	**Exc.:** $9000	**VGood:** $7000
With single trigger		
Perf.: $16,500	**Exc.:** $10,000	**VGood:** $8000

WESTLEY RICHARDS BEST QUALITY SIDELOCK
Side-by-side; hand-detachable sidelocks; hammerless; 12-, 16-, 20-, 28-ga., .410; barrel lengths, chokes to order; hand-checkered walnut straight or half-pistol-grip stock, forearm; selective ejectors; double or single selective trigger. Introduced 1910; still in production.

With double triggers		
Perf.: $25,000	**Exc.:** $18,000	**VGood:** $12,000
With single trigger		
Perf.: $26,000	**Exc.:** $19,000	**VGood:** $13,000

Weatherby SA-08 Youth

Weatherby PA-08 Upland

Weatherby PA-08 Knoxx Strutter X

Weatherby PA-08 Knoxx HD

Westley Richards Best Quality Boxlock

Westley Richards Best Quality Sidelock

Westley Richards

Westley Richards Boxlock Model Deluxe Quality

WESTLEY RICHARDS BOXLOCK MODEL DELUXE QUALITY
Side-by-side; hand-detachable boxlock; hammerless; 12-, 16-, 20-, 28-, .410-ga.; barrel lengths, chokes to order; hand-checkered European stock, forearm; straight or half-pistol grip available in Pigeon or Wildfowl Model at same price; triple-bite leverwork; selective ejectors; double triggers or single selective trigger. Introduced 1890; still in production.

With double triggers		
Perf.: $11,500	**Exc.:** $8500	**VGood:** $7000
With single trigger		
Perf.: $12,500	**Exc.:** $9500	**VGood:** $8000

WESTLEY RICHARDS MODEL B
Side-by-side; Anson & Deeley boxlock; hammerless; 12-, 16-, 20-ga.; barrel lengths, choking to order; hand-checkered European walnut straight or half-pistol-grip stock, forearm; Pigeon or Wildfowl Model available at same price; selective ejectors or extractors; double triggers. Introduced late 1920s; still in production.

With ejectors		
Perf.: $5500	**Exc.:** $4000	**VGood:** $3000
With extractors		
Perf.: $5000	**Exc.:** $3500	**VGood:** $2500

WESTLEY RICHARDS OVUNDO
Over/under; hand-detachable boxlock; hammerless; 12-ga.; barrel lengths, chokes to order; hand-checkered European walnut straight or half-pistol-grip stock, forearm; dummy sideplates; single selective trigger. Introduced 1920.

Perf.: $17,500 **Exc.:** $15,500 **VGood:** $12,000

WINCHESTER MODEL 40
Recoil-operated autoloader; 12-ga.; 4-shot tube magazine; 28-inch, 30-inch barrel; Modified, Full choke; ramp bead front sight; uncheckered pistol-grip stock, semi-beavertail forend; streamlined receiver. Introduced 1940; discontinued 1941.

Exc.: $590 **VGood:** $475 **Good:** $350

WINCHESTER MODEL 40 SKEET
Same specs as Model 40 except 24-inch barrel; Cutts Compensator; checkered pistol-grip stock, forearm; grip cap. No longer in production.

Exc.: $560 **VGood:** $450 **Good:** $280

WINCHESTER MODEL 50
Autoloader; 12-, 20-ga.; 2-shot magazine; 28-inch, 30-inch barrel; Improved, Modified, Full chokes; optional vent rib; 7-1/4 lbs.; bead-front sight; hand-checkered American walnut stock; fluted comb; composition buttplate; side ejection; short recoil action; interchangeable barrels. Introduced 1954; discontinued 1961.

Exc.: $500	**VGood:** $450	**Good:** $390
With vent rib		
Exc.: $540	**VGood:** $475	**Good:** $420

Winchester Model 50

Winchester Model 59

Winchester Model 1400

Winchester Model 1400
(Left-Hand)

Winchester Model 1400 Mark II

Winchester Model 1500 XTR

Winchester Model 1911

WINCHESTER MODEL 50 FEATHERWEIGHT
Same specs as Model 50 except 12-ga. weighs 7 lbs.; 20-ga. weighs 5-3/4 lbs.; alloy construction. Introduced 1958; discontinued 1961.

Exc.: $425   **VGood:** $365   **Good:** $310

WINCHESTER MODEL 50 PIGEON
Same specs as Model 50 except best-grade wood, carving and engraving. Introduced 1954; discontinued 1961.

Standard model
Exc.: $1000   **VGood:** $825   **Good:** $650
Featherweight model
Exc.: $1100   **VGood:** $800   **Good:** $600
Skeet model
Exc.: $1100   **VGood:** $900   **Good:** $750
Trap model
Exc.: $1100   **VGood:** $900   **Good:** $750

WINCHESTER MODEL 50 SKEET
Same specs as Model 50 except 12-ga.; 26-inch vent-rib barrel; Skeet choke; hand-checkered American walnut Skeet-style stock. Introduced 1954; discontinued 1961.

Exc.: $600   **VGood:** $525   **Good:** $420

WINCHESTER MODEL 50 TRAP
Same specs as Model 50 except 12-ga.; 30-inch vent-rib barrel; Full choke; hand-checkered American walnut Monte Carlo stock. Introduced 1954; discontinued 1961.

Exc.: $600   **VGood:** $525   **Good:** $420

WINCHESTER MODEL 59
Autoloader; 12-ga.; 3-shot magazine; 26-inch Improved Cylinder, 28-inch Modified or Full, 30-inch Full choke barrel; special-order 26-inch fiberglass-wrapped steel barrel (Winlite) with Versalite choke system of cylinder tubes (introduced in 1961) to allow any choke variation; checkered walnut stock, forearm. (Winchester also made a Model 59 rimfire rifle in 1930-don't be confused by the model numbers.) Introduced 1959; discontinued 1965.

Perf.: $600   **Exc.:** $500   **VGood:** $400

WINCHESTER MODEL 1400
Gas-operated autoloader; takedown; 12-, 16-, 20-ga.; 2-3/4-inch chamber; 2-shot magazine; 26-inch, 28-inch, 30-inch barrel; fixed Improved Cylinder, Modified, Full chokes or Winchoke tubes; plain or vent rib; checkered walnut stock, forearm; optional Cycolac stock and recoil pad with recoil-reduction system. Introduced 1964; discontinued 1968; replaced by Model 1400 Mark II.

With plain barrel, walnut stock
Exc.: $300   **VGood:** $225   **Good:** $190
With vent rib, walnut stock
Exc.: $310   **VGood:** $235   **Good:** $195
With plain barrel, Cycolac stock
Exc.: $275   **VGood:** $210   **Good:** $180
With vent rib, Cycolac stock
Exc.: $325   **VGood:** $245   **Good:** $200

WINCHESTER MODEL 1400 DEER GUN
Same specs as Model 1400 except 12-ga.; 22-inch barrel for slugs or buckshot; rifle sight; walnut stock, forearm. Introduced 1965; discontinued 1974.

Perf.: $265   **Exc.:** $240   **VGood:** $195

WINCHESTER MODEL 1400 MARK II
Same specs as Model 1400 except restyled walnut stock, forearm; push-button carrier release; front-locking, rotating bolt locking into barrel extension; self-compensating gas system for standard and magnum 2-3/4-inch loads; aluminum receiver; engine turned bolt; push-button action release; crossbolt safety. Made in right- or left-hand versions. Introduced 1968; replaced Model 1400; discontinued 1980.

With plain barrel
Perf.: $305   **Exc.:** $230   **VGood:** $200
With vent rib
Perf.: $315   **Exc.:** $255   **VGood:** $230

WINCHESTER MODEL 1400 SKEET
Same specs as Model 1400 except 12-, 20-ga.; 26-inch vent-rib barrel; Skeet choke; semi-fancy walnut Skeet-style stock, forearm; optional Cycolac

stock with recoil reduction system. Introduced 1965; discontinued 1968.

With walnut stock
Exc.: $350   **VGood:** $260   **Good:** $210
With Cycolac stock with recoil reduction
Exc.: $375   **VGood:** $310   **Good:** $245

WINCHESTER MODEL 1400 TRAP
Same specs as Model 1400 except 12-ga.; 30-inch vent-rib barrel; Full choke; semi-fancy walnut Monte Carlo stock, forearm; optional Cycolac stock with recoil reduction system. Introduced 1965; discontinued 1973.

With walnut stock
Exc.: $300   **VGood:** $230   **Good:** $190
With Cycolac stock with recoil reduction
Exc.: $350   **VGood:** $280   **Good:** $240

WINCHESTER MODEL 1400 (RECENT)
Gas-operated autoloader; 12-, 20-ga.; 2-3/4-inch chamber; 3-shot magazine; 22-inch, 26-inch, 28-inch vent-rib barrel; WinChoke tubes; cut-checkered American walnut stock, forearm. Introduced 1989; discontinued 1994.

Perf.: $340   **Exc.:** $270   **VGood:** $230

WINCHESTER MODEL 1400 CUSTOM (RECENT)
Same specs as Model 1400 (Recent) except 12-ga.; 28-inch vent-rib barrel; semi-fancy walnut stock, forend; hand-engraved receiver; made in Winchester custom shop. Introduced 1991; discontinued 1992.

Perf.: $750   **Exc.:** $600   **VGood:** $500

WINCHESTER MODEL 1400 SLUG HUNTER (RECENT)
Same specs as Model 1400 (Recent) except 12-ga.; 22-inch smoothbore barrel; Improved Cylinder, Sabot Winchoke tubes; adjustable open sights; drill, tapped for scope mounts. Introduced 1990; no longer in production.

Perf.: $300   **Exc.:** $275   **VGood:** $235

WINCHESTER MODEL 1500 XTR
Gas-operated autoloader; 12-, 20-ga.; 26-inch, 28-inch, 30-inch barrel; plain or vent rib; WinChoke tubes; metal bead front sight; cut-checkered American walnut pistol-grip stock; front locking, rotating bolt; nickel-plated carrier, crossbolt safety. Introduced 1978; discontinued 1983.

Perf.: $300   **Exc.:** $250   **VGood:** $210

WINCHESTER MODEL 1911
Autoloading; hammerless; takedown; 12-ga.; 26-inch, 28-inch barrel standard chokes; uncheckered laminated birch stock, forend. Introduced 1911; discontinued 1925. Popularly called "The Widowmaker" because of its quirky cocking system (i.e., pulling the barrel rearward).

Exc.: $425   **VGood:** $325   **Good:** $210

WINCHESTER MODEL 1911 FANCY FINISHED
Same specs as Model 1911 except checkered walnut stock, forend. Introduced 1911; discontinued 1918.

Exc.: $525   **VGood:** $425   **Good:** $310

WINCHESTER MODEL 1911 PIGEON
Same specs as Model 1911 except matted barrel; checkered fancy walnut straight-grip stock, forend; pistol grip optional; elaborate engraving. Introduced 1913; discontinued 1926.

Exc.: $750   **VGood:** $500   **Good:** $350

WINCHESTER MODEL 1911 TRAP
Same specs as Model 1911 except matted barrel; checkered fancy walnut straight-grip stock, forend; pistol grip optional. Introduced 1913; discontinued 1926.

Exc.: $525   **VGood:** $3425   **Good:** $310

WINCHESTER SUPER-X MODEL 1

Gas-operated autoloader; takedown; 12-ga.; 2-3/4-inch chamber; 4-shot magazine; 26-inch Improved Cylinder, 28-inch Modified or Full, 30-inch Full-choke barrel; vent rib; checkered American walnut pistol-grip stock, forearm. Introduced 1974; discontinued 1981.

Perf.: $500   **Exc.:** $450   **VGood:** $400

WINCHESTER SUPER-X MODEL 1 SKEET

Same specs as Super-X Model 1 except 26-inch Skeet-choke barrel; select American walnut Skeet-style stock. Introduced 1974; discontinued 1981.

Exc.: $695   **VGood:** $550   **Good:** $450

WINCHESTER SUPER-X MODEL 1 TRAP

Same specs as Super-X Model 1 except 30-inch barrel; Improved Modified or Full choke; select American walnut straight or Monte Carlo trap-style stock, forearm; recoil pad. Introduced 1974; discontinued 1981.

Exc.: $525   **VGood:** $400   **Good:** $375

WINCHESTER SUPER X2 AUTO SHOTGUN

Gauge: 12, 3-inch, 3-1/2-inch chamber; 24-inch, 26-inch, 28-inch barrel; Invector Plus choke tubes; weighs 7-1/4 to 7-1/2 lbs.; walnut or black synthetic; gas-operated action shoots all loads without adjustment; vent. rib barrels; 4-shot magazine. Introduced 1999. Made in U.S.A. by U.S. Repeating Arms Co.

Field, 3-inch, walnut or synthetic stock		
Perf.: $720	**Exc.:** $645	**VGood:** $565
Magnum, 3-1/2-inch, synthetic stock, 26-inch or 28-inch bbl.		
Perf.: $850	**Exc.:** $710	**VGood:** $610
Camo Waterfowl, 3-1/2-inch, Mossy Oak Shadow Grass		
Perf.: $960	**Exc.:** $815	**VGood:** $675
NWTF Turkey, 3-1/2-inch, black synthetic stock, 24-inch bbl.		
Perf.: $970	**Exc.:** $815	**VGood:** $685
NWTF Turkey, 3-1/2-inch, Mossy Oak Break-Up camo		
Perf.: $970	**Exc.:** $815	**VGood:** $685

WINCHESTER SUPER X2 SPORTING CLAYS AUTO SHOTGUN

Similar to the Super X2 except has two gas pistons (one for target loads, one for heavy 3-inch loads), adjustable comb system and high-post rib. Back-bored barrel with Invector Plus choke tubes. Offered in 28-inch and 30-inch barrels. Introduced 2001. From U.S. Repeating Arms Co.

Perf.: $830   **Exc.:** $710   **VGood:** $600

WINCHESTER SUPER X2 FIELD 3-INCH AUTO SHOTGUN

Similar to the Super X2 except has a 3-inch chamber, walnut stock and forearm and high-profile rib. Back-bored barrel (26-inch or 28-inch) and Invector Plus choke tubes. Introduced 2001. From U.S. Repeating Arms Co.

Perf.: $720   **Exc.:** $645   **VGood:** $565

WINCHESTER SUPER X3

Introduced in 2006, The Super X3 12 gauge features weight and recoil reducing features and a .742-inch back-bored barrel. It is available in a variety of configurations weighing under 7 lbs. in the 3-inch Field model and about 7.5 lbs. in composite, camo and 3.5-inch models. All models except Cantilever Deer include three choke tubes.

NIB: $900   **Exc.:** $825   **VGood:** $650

WINCHESTER SUPER X3 "FLANIGUN" EXHIBITION/SPORTING

With a red receiver and forend cap, this is a duplicate of the gun used by exhibition shooter Patrick Flanigan but with a shorter magazine tube. It has a 3" chamber and 28" barrel.

NIB: $1250   **Exc.:** $1025   **VGood:** $750

Winchester Super-X Model 1

Winchester Super X2 Magnum

Winchester Super X2 Sporting Clays

Winchester Super X3 Camo

Winchester Super X3 "Flanigun"

Winchester Super X3 Classic Field

Winchester Super X3 Turkey

WINCHESTER SUPER X3 CLASSIC FIELD

Introduced in 2008, the Classic Field is similar to the Super X3 Field but with traditional sharp checkering on pistol grip and forend. Barrel length is 26" or 28".

NIB: $975   **Exc.:** $850   **VGood:** $650

WINCHESTER SUPER X3 TURKEY

New in 2008, this dedicated turkey model has a 3.5" chamber, 24" barrel, extra-full choke tube and complete coverage in Mossy Oak New Breakup camo. Price includes a TruGlo red-dot scope. Weight is 7.5 lbs.

NIB: $1200   **Exc.:** $1000   **VGood:** $750

WINCHESTER MODEL 12

Slide action; hammerless; 12-, 16-, 20-, 28-ga.; 2-3/4-inch, 3-inch chamber; 5-shot magazine; 26-inch, 28-inch, 30-inch, 32-inch barrel; Improved Cylinder, Modified, Full choke; optional matted or vent rib; unchecked walnut pistol-grip stock, forearm; blued. Introduced 1912; discontinued 1963.

With plain barrel		
Exc.: $575	**VGood:** $480	**Good:** $325
With matted rib		
Exc.: $600	**VGood:** $550	**Good:** $375
With vent rib		
Exc.: $700	**VGood:** $600	**Good:** $475

WINCHESTER MODEL 12 FEATHERWEIGHT

Same specs as Model 12 except 12-ga.; 26-inch Improved Cylinder, 28-inch Modified or Full, 30-inch Full barrel; alloy guard. Introduced 1959; discontinued 1962.

Exc.: $695   **VGood:** $625   **Good:** $490

WINCHESTER MODEL 12 HEAVY DUCK

Same specs as Model 12 except 12-ga.; 3-inch chamber; 3-shot magazine; 30-inch, 32-inch Full barrel; plain, matted or vent rib; recoil pad. Introduced 1937; discontinued 1963.

With plain barrel		
Exc.: $850	**VGood:** $750	**Good:** $600
With matted rib		
Exc.: $875	**VGood:** $775	**Good:** $625
With vent rib		
Exc.: $1000	**VGood:** $800	**Good:** $650

WINCHESTER MODEL 12 PIGEON

Same specs as Model 12 except hand-checkered fancy walnut stock, forearm; engine-turned bolt, carrier; hand-worked action; optional carving and engraving. Introduced 1912; discontinued 1963.

Standard model with plain barrel		
Exc.: $1250	**VGood:** $800	**Good:** $700
Standard model with vent rib		
Exc.: $1375	**VGood:** $950	**Good:** $800
Skeet model with plain barrel		
Exc.: $1250	**VGood:** $800	**Good:** $700
Skeet model with plain barrel, Cutts Compensator		
Exc.: $1000	**VGood:** $600	**Good:** $500
Skeet model with vent rib		
Exc.: $1250	**VGood:** $950	**Good:** $800
Trap model with matted rib		
Exc.: $1200	**VGood:** $900	**Good:** $800
Trap model with vent rib		
Exc.: $1250	**VGood:** $950	**Good:** $850

WINCHESTER MODEL 12 RIOT

Same specs as Model 12 except 12-ga.; 20-inch Cylinder barrel; vent handguard. Introduced 1918; discontinued 1963.

Military Version		
Exc.: $1150	**VGood:** $850	**Good:** $600
Civilian Version		
Exc.: $850	**VGood:** $775	**Good:** $575

WINCHESTER MODEL 12 SKEET

Same specs as Model 12 except 26-inch Skeet barrel; plain barrel or vent rib; red or ivory bead front sight; 94B middle; checkered walnut pistol-grip stock, extension slide handle; recoil pad. Introduced 1937; discontinued 1963.

With plain barrel		
Exc.: $625	**VGood:** $575	**Good:** $500
With plain barrel, Cutts Compensator		
Exc.: $475	**VGood:** $375	**Good:** $300
With vent rib		
Exc.: $825	**VGood:** $775	**Good:** $700

Winchester Model 12

Winchester Model 12 Trap (1972)

Winchester Model 12 (1993)

Winchester Model 25

Winchester Model 42 Skeet

Winchester Model 1200

WINCHESTER MODEL 12 SUPER PIGEON

Same specs as Model 12 except 12-ga.; 26-inch, 28-inch, 30-inch vent-rib barrel; hand-checkered fancy walnut stock, forearm; hand-honed and fitted action; engine-turned bolt, carrier, carving; engraving; top-of-the-line custom gun. Introduced 1965; discontinued 1975.

Standard model with plain barrel		
Exc.: $1750	**VGood:** $1300	**Good:** $1200
Standard model with vent rib		
Exc.: $1950	**VGood:** $1600	**Good:** $1350
Skeet model with plain barrel		
Exc.: $1750	**VGood:** $1500	**Good:** $1200
Skeet model with plain barrel, Cutts Compensator		
Exc.: $1500	**VGood:** $1000	**Good:** $850
Skeet model with vent rib		
Exc.: $1950	**VGood:** $1600	**Good:** $1350
Trap model with matted rib		
Exc.: $1800	**VGood:** $1500	**Good:** $1350
Trap model with vent rib		
Exc.: $1950	**VGood:** $1600	**Good:** $1450

WINCHESTER MODEL 12 TRAP

Same specs as Model 12 except 12-ga.; 30-inch Full-choke barrel; vent or matted rib; checkered walnut pistol-grip stock, extension slide handle; optional Monte Carlo stock; recoil pad. Introduced 1937; discontinued 1963.

With matted rib		
Exc.: $700	**VGood:** $500	**Good:** $425
With vent rib		
Exc.: $850	**VGood:** $650	**Good:** $575
With vent rib, Monte Carlo stock		
Exc.: $975	**VGood:** $775	**Good:** $725

WINCHESTER MODEL 12 (1972)

Same specs as Model 12 except 12-ga.; 26-inch, 28-inch, 30-inch barrels; standard chokes; vent rib; hand-checkered American walnut stock, slide handle; engine-turned bolt, carrier. Introduced 1972; discontinued 1975.

Perf.: $575   **Exc.:** $525   **VGood:** $425

WINCHESTER MODEL 12 (1993)

Same specs as Model 12 except limited production. Introduced 1993, still in production.

Perf.: $950   **Exc.:** $800   **VGood:** $650

WINCHESTER MODEL 12 SKEET (1972)

Same specs as Model 12 except 26-inch Skeet-choke barrel; hand-checkered American walnut Skeet-style stock, slide handle; engine-turned bolt, carrier; recoil pad. Introduced 1972; discontinued 1975.

Perf.: $900   **Exc.:** $650   **VGood:** $525

WINCHESTER MODEL 12 TRAP (1972)

Same specs as Model 12 except 30-inch Full-choke barrel; vent rib; checkered American walnut straight or Monte Carlo trap-style stock; engine-turned bolt, carrier; recoil pad. Introduced 1972; discontinued 1975.

Perf.: $700   **Exc.:** $575   **VGood:** $475

WINCHESTER MODEL 25

Slide action; hammerless; solid frame; 12-ga.; 4-shot tubular magazine; 26-inch, 28-inch plain barrel; Improved Cylinder, Modified or Full choke; metal bead front sight; uncheckered walnut pistol grip stock, grooved slide handle. Introduced 1950; discontinued 1954.

Exc.: $325   **VGood:** $275   **Good:** $225

WINCHESTER MODEL 25 RIOT

Same specs as Model 25 except 20-inch Cylinder barrel. Introduced 1949; discontinued 1955.

Exc.: $250   **VGood:** $190   **Good:** $230

WINCHESTER MODEL 42

Slide action; hammerless; .410; 2-1/2-inch, 3-inch chamber; 5- (3-inch), 6-shot (2-1/2-inch) magazine; 26-inch; 28-inch barrel; Full, Modified, Cylinder choke; plain, matted or vent rib; uncheckered walnut stock, grooved slide handle. Introduced 1933; discontinued 1963.

With plain barrel		
Exc.: $850	**VGood:** $700	**Good:** $600
With matted rib		
Exc.: $1250	**VGood:** $1100	**Good:** $950
With vent rib		
Exc.: $1450	**VGood:** $1300	**Good:** $1050

WINCHESTER MODEL 42 DELUXE

Same specs as Model 42 except top-of-the-line model with best-grade wood and finish. Introduced 1933; discontinued 1963.

Exc.: $2200   **VGood:** $1750   **Good:** $1300

WINCHESTER MODEL 42 SKEET

Same specs as Model 42 except Skeet choke; matted rib; checkered fancy walnut Skeet-style stock, forearm. Introduced 1933; discontinued 1963.

Exc.: $1850   **VGood:** $1350   **Good:** $1200

WINCHESTER MODEL 42 TRAP

Same specs as Model 42 except matted rib; checkered fancy walnut trap-style stock, forearm. Introduced 1933; discontinued 1940.

Exc.: $1850   **VGood:** $1350   **Good:** $1200

WINCHESTER MODEL 42 HIGH GRADE (1993)

Slide action; hammerless; .410; 2-3/4-inch chamber; 26-inch vent-rib barrel; Full choke; weighs 7 lbs.; checkered high-grade walnut pistol-grip stock, forend; engraved receiver with gold inlays. Only 850 guns made. Made in Japan. Introduced 1993; discontinued 1993.

Perf.: $1350   **Exc.:** $1000   **VGood:** $850

WINCHESTER MODEL 1200

Slide action; takedown; 12-, 16-, 20-ga.; 2-3/4-inch chambers; 4-shot magazine; 26-inch, 28-inch, 30-inch barrel; Improved Cylinder, Modified, Full fixed choke or interchangeable WinChoke tubes for Cylinder, Modified, Full; plain or vent rib; press-checkered walnut stock, slide handle; optional Cycolac stock with recoil-reduction system; front-lock rotary bolt; recoil pad. Introduced 1964; discontinued 1981.

With plain barrel, walnut stock		
Perf.: $200	**Exc.:** $170	**VGood:** $150
With vent-rib barrel, walnut stock		
Perf.: $240	**Exc.:** $210	**VGood:** $190
With plain barrel, Cycolac stock		
Perf.: $260	**Exc.:** $230	**VGood:** $200
With vent-rib barrel, Cycolac stock		
Perf.: $300	**Exc.:** $270	**VGood:** $240

WINCHESTER MODEL 1200 DEER

Same specs as Model 1200 except 12-ga.; 22-inch barrel for rifled slugs or buckshot; rifle-type sights; walnut stock only; sling swivels. Introduced 1965; discontinued 1974.

Perf.: $210   **Exc.:** $150   **VGood:** $140

WINCHESTER MODEL 1200 MAGNUM

Same specs as Model 1200 except 12-, 20-, 28-ga.; 3-inch chamber; 28-inch, 30-inch Full-choke barrel; plain or vent rib. Introduced 1964; discontinued 1981.

With plain barrel, walnut stock		
Perf.: $290	**Exc.:** $265	**VGood:** $250
With vent-rib barrel, walnut stock		
Perf.: $300	**Exc.:** $275	**VGood:** $260
With plain barrel, Cycolac stock		
Perf.: $280	**Exc.:** $240	**VGood:** $200
With vent-rib barrel, Cycolac stock		
Perf.: $325	**Exc.:** $260	**VGood:** $230

WINCHESTER MODEL 1200 SKEET

Same specs as Model 1200 except 12-, 20- ga.; 2-shot magazine; 26-inch vent-rib barrel; Skeet choke; semi-fancy walnut stock, forend; optional Cycolac stock with recoil-reduction system; tuned trigger. Introduced 1965; discontinued 1974.

With walnut stock		
Perf.: $295	**Exc.:** $240	**VGood:** $200
With Cycolac stock		
Perf.: $350	**Exc.:** $300	**VGood:** $250

WINCHESTER MODEL 1200 TRAP

Same specs as Model 1200 except 12-ga.; 2-shot magazine; 28-inch WinChoke, 30-inch Full-choke barrel; vent rib; semi-fancy walnut standard or Monte Carlo trap-style stock, forearm; optional Cycolac stock with recoil-reduction system. Introduced 1965; discontinued 1974.

With standard stock		
Perf.: $325	**Exc.:** $275	**VGood:** $200

With Monte Carlo stock
Perf.: $345   **Exc.:** $300   **VGood:** $220

With Cycolac stock
Perf.: $360   **Exc.:** $325   **VGood:** $250

WINCHESTER MODEL 1300 DEFENDER PUMP GUNS

Gauge: 12, 20, 3-inch chamber, 5- or 8-shot capacity; 18-inch barrel (Cyl.); weighs 6-3/4 lbs.; 38-5/8-inch overall; walnut-finished hardwood stock and ribbed forend, synthetic or pistol grip; metal bead front sight or TRUGLO fiber-optic; front-locking rotary bolt; twin action slide bars; black rubber butt pad.

8-Shot (black synthetic stock, TRUGLO sight)
Perf.: $265   **Exc.:** $205   **VGood:** $160

8-Shot Pistol Grip (pistol grip synthetic stock)
Perf.: $278   **Exc.:** $218   **VGood:** $173

WINCHESTER MODEL 1300 STAINLESS MARINE PUMP GUN

Same as the Defender 8-Shot except has bright chrome finish, stainless steel barrel, bead front sight. Phosphate coated receiver for corrosion resistance.
Perf.: $435   **Exc.:** $360   **VGood:** $265

WINCHESTER MODEL 1300 CAMP DEFENDER

Same as the Defender 8-Shot except has hardwood stock and forearm, fully adjustable open sights and 22-inch barrel with WinChoke choke tube system (cylinder choke tube included). Weighs 6-7/8 lbs. Introduced 2001.
Perf.: $295   **Exc.:** $225   **VGood:** $175

WINCHESTER MODEL 1300 WALNUT FIELD PUMP

Gauge: 12, 20, 3-inch chamber; 5-shot capacity; 26-inch, 28-inch barrel; vent. rib, with Full, Mod. & Imp. Cyl. Winchoke tubes; weighs 6-3/8 lbs.; 42-5/8-inch overall; American walnut, with deep cut checkering on pistol grip, traditional ribbed forend; high luster finish; metal bead front sight; twin action slide bars; front-locking rotary bolt; roll-engraved receiver; blued, highly polished metal; cross-bolt safety with red indicator. Introduced 1984.
Perf.: $345   **Exc.:** $250   **VGood:** $200

WINCHESTER MODEL 1300 UPLAND PUMP GUN

Similar to Model 1300 Walnut except straight-grip stock, 24-inch barrel. Introduced 1999. Made in U.S.A. by U.S. Repeating Arms Co.
Perf.: $325   **Exc.:** $240   **VGood:** $195

WINCHESTER MODEL 1300 BLACK SHADOW

Slide action; hammerless; 12-, 20-ga.; 3-inch chamber; 5-shot magazine; 26-inch, 28-inch vent-rib barrel; Modified WinChoke tubes; metal bead front sight; black composite pistol-grip stock, forend; black rubber recoil pad; crossbolt safety; twin action slide bars; front-locking rotating bolt; matte black finish. Introduced 1995.
Perf.: $270   **Exc.:** $210   **VGood:** $180

WINCHESTER MODEL 1300 BLACK SHADOW DEER

Same specs as Model 1300 Black Shadow except 12-ga.; 3-inch chamber; 22-inch vent-rib barrel; Improved Cylinder WinChoke tube; ramp-type front sight, fully adjustable rear; receiver drilled and tapped for scope mounts. Introduced 1994.
Perf.: $270   **Exc.:** $210   **VGood:** $180

With rifled barrel
Perf.: $301   **Exc.:** $231   **VGood:** $186

With cantilever scope mount
Perf.: $344   **Exc.:** $274   **VGood:** $229

Combo (22-inch rifled and 28-inch smoothbore bbls.)
Perf.: $395   **Exc.:** $325   **VGood:** $280

Compact (20-ga., 22-inch rifled barrel, shorter stock)
Perf.: $295   **Exc.:** $225   **VGood:** $165

Winchester Model 1300 Defender 8-shot

Winchester Model 1300 Camp Defender

Winchester Model 1300 Walnut Field

Winchester Model 1300 Black Shadow

Winchester Model 1300 Ranger

Winchester Model 1300 Ranger Combo

WINCHESTER MODEL 1300 BLACK SHADOW TURKEY

Same specs as Model 1300 Black Shadow except 12-ga.; 3-inch chamber; 22-inch vent-rib barrel; Full WinChoke tube; receiver drilled and tapped for scope mounts. Introduced 1994; discontinued 2000.
Perf.: $270   **Exc.:** $210   **VGood:** $180

WINCHESTER MODEL 1300 N.W.T.F. SERIES I

Slide action; hammerless; 12-ga.; 3-inch chamber; 5-shot magazine; 22-inch vent-rib barrel; Extra Full, Full, Modified WinChoke tubes; checkered green WinCam laminated stock, forend; black rubber recoil pad; crossbolt safety; twin action slide bars; front-locking rotating bolt; camo sling and swivels; receiver roll-engraved with turkey scenes; right side has National Wild Turkey Federation name in script; matte finish metal. Introduced 1989; no longer in production.
Perf.: $420   **Exc.:** $365   **VGood:** $260
Add approximately $45 to above prices for Buck & Tom Superflauge configuration.

WINCHESTER MODEL 1300 N.W.T.F. SERIES II

Same specs as the Model 1300 N.W.T.F. Series I except 12-, 20-ga.; WinCam green laminated stock, ribbed forend; ladies/youth-sized stock available. Introduced 1990; discontinued 1991.
Perf.: $350   **Exc.:** $265   **VGood:** $210

WINCHESTER MODEL 1300 N.W.T.F. SERIES III

Same specs as the Model 1300 N.W.T.F. Series I except rifle-type adjustable sights; WinCam green

laminated stock, ribbed forend. Introduced 1992; discontinued 1993.
Perf.: $350   **Exc.:** $265   **VGood:** $210

WINCHESTER MODEL 1300 N.W.T.F. SERIES IV

Same specs as the Model 1300 N.W.T.F. Series I except WinTuff black laminated stock, ribbed forend. Introduced 1993; discontinued 1994.
Perf.: $350   **Exc.:** $265   **VGood:** $210

WINCHESTER MODEL 1300 RANGER

Slide action; hammerless; 12-, 20-ga.; 3-inch chamber; 5-shot magazine; 26-inch, 28-inch vent-rib barrel; Full, Modified, Improved Cylinder WinChoke tubes; checkered walnut-finished hardwood pistol-grip stock, forend; black rubber recoil pad; crossbolt safety; twin action slide bars; front-locking rotating bolt. Introduced 1983.
Perf.: $280   **Exc.:** $220   **VGood:** $185

Model 1300 Compact, 24-inch vent. rib
Perf.: $280   **Exc.:** $210   **VGood:** $165

WINCHESTER MODEL 1300 RANGER COMBO

Same specs as Model 1300 Ranger except two-barrel set with 22-inch Cylinder smoothbore or rifled deer barrel with rifle-type sights and an interchangeable 28-inch vent-rib barrel with Full, Modified, Improved Cylinder WinChoke tubes; drilled and tapped for scope mounts; rings and bases. Introduced 1983.
Perf.: $330   **Exc.:** $270   **VGood:** $230

Winchester Model 1300 Ranger
Deer Gun

Winchester Model 1300 Ranger
Ladies/Youth

Winchester Model 1300
Slug Hunter

Winchester Model 1300 Turkey

Winchester Model 1300 Turkey
Buck and Tom

Winchester Model 1300 Turkey
Short Turkey

Winchester Model 1300 XTR

Winchester Model 1300 XTR Defender

WINCHESTER MODEL 1300 RANGER DEER

Same specs as Model 1300 Ranger except 22-inch Cylinder smoothbore or rifled deer barrel with rifle-type sights; drilled and tapped for scope mounts; rings and bases. Introduced 1983.

Perf.: $300   **Exc.:** $245   **VGood:** $200

WINCHESTER MODEL 1300 RANGER LADIES/YOUTH

Same specs as Model 1300 Ranger except 20-ga.; 3-inch chamber; 22-inch vent-rib barrel; Full, Modified, Improved Cylinder WinChoke tubes; weighs 6-1/2 lbs.; overall length 41-5/8-inch; hardwood stock (walnut available) with 13-inch pull length. Introduced 1983.

With hardwood stock		
Perf.: $280	**Exc.:** $220	**VGood:** $185
With walnut stock		
Perf.: $300	**Exc.:** $240	**VGood:** $200

WINCHESTER MODEL 1300 REALTREE TURKEY GUN

Same specs as Model 1300 Ranger except 12-ga.; 3-inch chamber; 22-inch barrel; Extra Full, Full, Modified WinChoke tubes; drilled and tapped for

scope mounts; synthetic Realtree(r) camo stock, forend; padded, adjustable sling; matte finished barrel, receiver. Introduced 1994.

Perf.: $325   **Exc.:** $285   **VGood:** $225

WINCHESTER MODEL 1300 SLUG HUNTER

Same specs as Model 1300 Ranger except 12-ga.; 22-inch smoothbore or rifled barrel; Improved Cylinder, Sabot choke tubes (smoothbore only); adjustable open sights; receiver drilled and tapped for scope mounts; scope bases; cut-checkered walnut stock, forend. Introduced 1990; smoothbore dropped 1992; still in production as Model 1300 Slug Hunter Deer.

Perf.: $350   **Exc.:** $265   **VGood:** $200

WINCHESTER MODEL 1300 STAINLESS MARINE

Same specs as Model 1300 Ranger except 5-, 8-shot magazine; 18-inch Cylinder stainless barrel; rifle-type sights; bright chrome finish; phosphate-coated receiver for corrosion resistance. Introduced 1989.

Perf.: $395   **Exc.:** $275   **VGood:** $210

WINCHESTER MODEL 1300 TURKEY

Same specs as Model 1300 Ranger except 12-ga.; 22-inch barrel; Modified, Full, Extra Full WinChoke

tubes; WinCam green camo laminated stock; recoil pad, Cordura sling; swivels; matte finish wood and metal. Introduced 1985; discontinued 1988.

Perf.: $300   **Exc.:** $240   **VGood:** $185

WINCHESTER MODEL 1300 TURKEY AND UNIVERSAL HUNTER MODELS

12-gauge w/3-inch chamber. Rotary bolt action. Mossy oak break-up finish on 26-inch VR barrel Extra Full turkey, Improved Cylinder, Modified and Full WinChoke tubes included.

Universal Hunter		
Perf.: $365	**Exc.:** $315	**VGood:** $280
Buck and Tom		
Perf.: $401	**Exc.:** $351	**VGood:** $316
Short Turkey		
Perf.: $405	**Exc.:** $355	**VGood:** $320

WINCHESTER MODEL 1300 XTR

Slide action; 12-, 20-ga.; 3-inch chamber; 4-shot magazine; 26, 28-inch plain or vent-rib barrel; WinChoke tubes; metal bead front sight; cut-checkered American walnut stock, grooved forearm; twin action bars; crossbolt safety; engine-turned bolt; alloy receiver, trigger guard. Introduced 1978; XTR designation dropped 1989; discontinued 1993.

With plain barrel		
Perf.: $260	**Exc.:** $200	**VGood:** $160
With vent-rib barrel		
Perf.: $295	**Exc.:** $240	**VGood:** $185

WINCHESTER MODEL 1300 XTR DEER GUN

Same specs as Model 1300 XTR except 12-ga.; 24-1/8-inch barrel; rifle-type sights. No longer in production.

Perf.: $295   **Exc.:** $240   **VGood:** $185

WINCHESTER MODEL 1300 XTR DEFENDER

Same specs as Model 1300 XTR except 5-, 8-shot magazine; 18-inch, 24-inch Cylinder barrel; 38-3/5-inch overall length; weighs 6-3/4 lb.; metal bead front sight; walnut-finished hardwood or synthetic pistol-grip stock, ribbed forend; crossbolt safety; front-locking rotary bolt; twin slide bars; black rubber buttpad. Introduced 1984; XTR designation dropped 1989.

Perf.: $240	**Exc.:** $165	**VGood:** $120
Defender Combo with extra 28-inch vent-rib barrel		
Perf.: $320	**Exc.:** $240	**VGood:** $180

WINCHESTER MODEL 1300 XTR FEATHERWEIGHT

Same specs as Model 1300 XTR except 22-inch vent-rib barrel; crossbolt safety with red indicator; roll-engraved alloy receiver. Introduced 1984; XTR designation dropped 1989; discontinued 1993.

Perf.: $320   **Exc.:** $240   **VGood:** $200

WINCHESTER MODEL 1300 XTR LADIES/YOUTH

Same specs as Model 1300 XTR except 22-inch vent-rib barrel; youth-sized walnut stock with high luster finish; crossbolt safety with red safety indicator; highly polished blue finish. Introduced 1983; XTR designation dropped 1989.

Perf.: $250   **Exc.:** $220   **VGood:** $185

WINCHESTER MODEL 1300 XTR WALNUT

Same specs as Model 1300 XTR 26-inch, 28-inch vent-rib barrel; walnut stock with high luster finish; crossbolt safety with red safety indicator; highly polished blued finish. Introduced, 1984; XTR designation dropped 1989.

Perf.: $300   **Exc.:** $245   **VGood:** $200

WINCHESTER MODEL 1300 XTR WATERFOWL

Same specs as Model 1300 XTR except 12-ga.; 28-inch, 30-inch vent-rib barrel; matte walnut or brown WinTuff stock, forearm; recoil pad; camo sling; swivels. Introduced 1984; XTR designation dropped 1989; discontinued 1991.

Perf.: $280   **Exc.:** $230   **VGood:** $200

WINCHESTER SPEED PUMP SERIES

This family of inertia-assisted slide-action shotguns was introduced in 2008 to take the place of the discontinued Model 1300. The 3" 12 gauge is available with a 26" or 28" barrel. Three choke tubes included. Weight is 7 to 7.25 lbs.

WINCHESTER SPEED PUMP WALNUT FIELD

High-gloss walnut with traditional checkering.

Perf.: $375   **Exc.:** $315   **VGood:** $295

WINCHESTER SPEED PUMP BLACK SHADOW FIELD

Synthetic stock and forend with matte black metal. MSRP:

Perf.: $375   **Exc.:** $315   **VGood:** $295

WINCHESTER SPEED PUMP DEFENDER

This home-security 12 gauge has an 18", cylinder choke barrel and 5-round magazine tube. Weight is about 6.5 lbs.

Perf.: $295   **Exc.:** $265   **VGood:** $215

WINCHESTER MODEL 1893

Slide action; exposed hammer; solid frame; 12-ga.; 2-5/8-inch chamber; 5-shot tubular magazine; 30-inch, 32-inch steel barrel; Damascus barrel optional; Full choke standard; Modified or Cylinder bore optional; uncheckered American walnut half-pistol-grip stock; fancy wood, checkering optional. Introduced 1893; discontinued 1897.

Exc.: $800   **VGood:** $600   **Good:** $500

With fancy wood, checkering

Exc.: $900   **VGood:** $675   **Good:** $550

WINCHESTER MODEL 1897

Slide action; visible hammer; takedown or solid frame; 12-, 16-ga.; 2-3/4-inch chamber; 5-shot tube magazine; 26-inch, 28-inch, 30-inch, 32-inch (12-ga. only) barrel; Full, Modified, Cylinder bore; intermediate chokes added 1931; uncheckered walnut half-pistol-grip stock, grooved forend. Introduced 1897; discontinued 1957.

Exc.: $900   **VGood:** $600   **Good:** $435

WINCHESTER MODEL 1897 BRUSH

Same specs as Model 1897 except 26-inch Cylinder bore barrel. Introduced 1897; discontinued 1931.

Exc.: $825   **VGood:** $600   **Good:** $335

WINCHESTER MODEL 1897 PIGEON

Same specs as Model 1897 except checkered fancy walnut stock, standard or beavertail forearm; engraving. Introduced 1897; discontinued 1939.

Exc.: $3500   **VGood:** $2250   **Good:** $1800

WINCHESTER MODEL 1897 SPECIAL TRAP

Same specs as Model 1897 except checkered fancy walnut trap-style stock, standard or beavertail forearm; engraving. Introduced 1931; discontinued 1939.

Exc.: $3500   **VGood:** $2250   **Good:** $1800

WINCHESTER MODEL 1897 STANDARD TRAP

Same specs as Model 1897 except Trap-style stock; replaced Model 1897 Trap. Introduced 1931; discontinued 1939.

Exc.: $1100   **VGood:** $700   **Good:** $500

WINCHESTER MODEL 1897 TOURNAMENT

Same specs as Model 1897 except checkered fancy walnut stock, standard or beavertail forearm; engraving. Introduced 1910; discontinued 1931.

Exc.: $1200   **VGood:** $750   **Good:** $600

WINCHESTER MODEL 1897 TRAP

Same specs as Model 1897 except Trap-style stock. Introduced 1897; discontinued 1931.

Exc.: $1100   **VGood:** $700   **Good:** $500

WINCHESTER MODEL 1897 TRENCH

Same specs as Model 1897 except ventilated steel handguard; bayonet stud; built for U.S. Army during WWI. Introduced 1920; discontinued 1935.

Exc.: $2500   **VGood:** $1500   **Good:** $1300

WINCHESTER MODEL 101

Over/under; boxlock; 12- (2-3/4-inch), 20- (3-inch), 28-ga. (2-3/4-inch), .410 (3-inch); 26-1/2-inch Improved/Modified, 28-inch Modified/Full, 30-inch Modified/Full (12-ga. only) barrels; vent rib; checkered french walnut stock, forearm; auto ejectors; single selective trigger; combo barrel selector, safety; engraving. Made in Japan by Olin Kodensha. Introduced 1963; discontinued 1978.

12-, 20-ga. model

Perf.: $1200   **Exc.:** $800   **VGood:** $700

28-ga., .410 model

Exc.: $1600   **VGood:** $1275   **VGood:** $850

WINCHESTER MODEL 101 MAGNUM

Same specs as Model 101 except 12-, 20-ga.; 3-inch chambers; 30-inch Full/Full, Modified/Full barrels; recoil pad. Introduced 1966; discontinued 1981.

Perf.: $1150   **Exc.:** $850   **VGood:** $700

Add approximately 20 percent 9o above prices for 20-ga.

WINCHESTER MODEL 101 PIGEON GRADE

Same specs as Model 101 except best-grade wood, checkering and engraving. Introduced 1963; discontinued 1984.

Field model

Perf.: $1500   **Exc.:** $1200   **VGood:** $1000

Skeet model

Perf.: $1300   **Exc.:** $900   **VGood:** $800

Trap model

Perf.: $1400   **Exc.:** $1000   **VGood:** $900

WINCHESTER MODEL 101 SKEET

Same specs as Model 101 except 26-inch (12-ga.), 26-1/2-inch (20-ga.), 28-inch (28-ga., .410) barrels; Skeet chokes; Skeet-style stock, forearm. Introduced 1966; discontinued 1984. Considerable premium for small gauges.

Perf.: $1000   **Exc.:** $850   **VGood:** $695

WINCHESTER MODEL 101 TRAP

Same specs as Model 101 except 12-ga.; 30-inch, 32-inch Improved Modified/Full, Full/Full barrels; Trap-style stock; Monte Carlo or straight comb. Introduced 1966; discontinued 1984.

With Monte Carlo stock

Perf.: $1250   **Exc.:** $900   **VGood:** $800

With straight stock

Perf.: $1250   **Exc.:** $900   **VGood:** $800

WINCHESTER MODEL 101 TRAP SINGLE BARREL

Same specs as Model 101 except 12-ga.; 32-inch, 34-inch single over barrel; Full choke; Trap-style Monte Carlo stock. Introduced 1967; discontinued 1971.

Perf.: $900   **Exc.:** $600   **VGood:** $500

WINCHESTER MODEL 101 WATERFOWL

Same specs as Model 101 except 12-ga.; 3-inch chambers; 32-inch barrels; WinChokes. Introduced 1981; discontinued 1982.

Perf.: $1350   **Exc.:** $1000   **VGood:** $900

WINCHESTER MODEL 101 DIAMOND GRADE SKEET

Over/under; boxlock; 12-, 20-, 28-ga., .410; 27-1/2-inch barrels; WinChokes; tapered, elevated vent rib; hand-checkered select walnut Skeet-style stock, beavertail forearm; auto ejectors; contoured single selective trigger; combo barrel selector, safety;

Winchester Model 1300 XTR Waterfowl

Winchester Speed Pump Walnut Field

Winchester Speed Pump Black Shadow

Winchester Speed Pump Defender

Winchester Model 1897

Winchester Model 101 Pigeon Grade

WINCHESTER MODEL 101 XTR

Winchester Model 101 XTR American Flyer Live Bird

Winchester Model 101 XTR Waterfowl

Winchester Model 501 Grand European

Winchester Select Model 101 Field (2007)

Winchester Supreme Field

WINCHESTER MODEL 101 XTR PIGEON GRADE LIGHTWEIGHT

Same specs as Model 101 XTR except 12-, 20-, 28-ga., .410; 26-inch to 32-inch barrels; hand-checkered French walnut stock; knurled non-slip trigger; alloy construction; hand-engraved satin-finished receiver; marketed in hard case. Made in Japan. Introduced, 1983; discontinued 1987.

Perf.: $1800   **Exc.:** $1350   **VGood:** $1200

WINCHESTER MODEL 101 XTR PIGEON GRADE SKEET

Same specs as Model 101 XTR except 12-, 20-, 28-ga., .410; select checkered Skeet-style stock. Introduced 1980; discontinued 1987.

Perf.: $1200   **Exc.:** $950   **VGood:** $850

WINCHESTER MODEL 101 XTR PIGEON GRADE TRAP

Same specs as Model 101 XTR except 12-ga.; select checkered trap-style stock. Introduced 1980; discontinued 1987.

Perf.: $1200   **Exc.:** $950   **VGood:** $850

WINCHESTER MODEL 101 XTR QUAIL SPECIAL

Same specs as Model 101 XTR except 12-, 20-, 28-ga., .410; 25 1/2-inch vent-rib barrels; Winchokes; checkered American walnut straight-grip stock; silvered engraved receiver. Made in Japan. Introduced 1987; discontinued 1988.

12-ga., .410 models		
Perf.: $1850	**Exc.:** $1400	**VGood:** $1200
20-ga. model		
Perf.: $2300	**Exc.:** $1700	**VGood:** $1450
28-ga. model		
Perf.: $3000	**Exc.:** $2000	**VGood:** $1800

WINCHESTER MODEL XTR WATERFOWL

Same specs as Model 101 XTR except 25-1/2-inch, 27-inch, 28-inch barrels; weighs 8-1/4 lbs.; vent-rib; bead front and middle sights; hand-checkered French walnut stock, forend. Made in Japan. Introduced 1981; discontinued 1982.

Perf.: $1900   **Exc.:** $1475   **VGood:** $975

WINCHESTER MODEL 501 GRAND EUROPEAN

Over/under; 12-, 20-ga.; 27-inch, 30-inch, 32-inch barrels; tapered vent rib; hand-rubbed oil-finish American walnut stock; Trap model has Monte Carlo or regular stock; Skeevt version has rosewood buttplate; engine-turned breech interior; selective auto ejectors; chromed bores; engraved silvered receiver. Made in Japan. Introduced 1981; discontinued 1986.

Perf.: $2195   **Exc.:** $1995   **VGood:** $1895

WINCHESTER MODEL 1001 O/U

Over/under; 12-ga.; 3-inch chamber; 28-inch barrel; Imp. Cyl., Mod., Imp. Mod., Skeet WinPlus; 45-inch overall length; weighs 7 lbs.; select walnut stock; checkered grip, forend; single selective trigger; automatic ejectors; wide vent rib; matte finished receiver top; blued receiver with scroll engraving. Although carried in the 1993 catalog and advertised for a year, the Model 1001 never reached full production status because of technical and quality control difficulties in Italy. Both Field and Sporting Clays versions were planned. Some guns reached consumers, but in late 1994 all were recalled and the project was cancelled.
Note: Since none are in the marketplace, no sales performance can be established and no values are given.

WINCHESTER SELECT MODEL 101 FIELD (2007)

This Belgian-made version of Winchester's popular Model 101 was introduced in 2007. It features Grade II/III walnut, 26" or 28" barrels and deep-relief engraving on the blued receiver that mimics the original 101. Classic white line spacer and vented recoil pad. Three choke tubes. Weight is about 7.2 lbs.

NIB: $1700   **Exc.:** $1495   **VGood:** 1050

---

diamond-pattern engraved satin-finished receiver. Made in Japan. Introduced 1982; discontinued 1987.

Perf.: $1750   **Exc.:** $1300   **VGood:** $1100

WINCHESTER MODEL 101 DIAMOND GRADE TRAP

Same specs as Model 101 Diamond Grade Skeet except 12-ga.; 30-inch, 32-inch barrels; hand-checkered select walnut trap-style stock, beavertail forearm. Introduced 1982; discontinued 1987.

Perf.: $1750   **Exc.:** $1300   **VGood:** $1100

WINCHESTER MODEL 101 DIAMOND GRADE TRAP COMBO

Same specs as Model 101 Diamond Grade Skeet except 12-ga.; two-barrel set with 30-inch or 32-inch over/under barrels and 32-inch or 34-inch single barrel; hand-checkered select walnut trap-style stock, beavertail forearm. Introduced 1982; discontinued 1987.

Perf.: $2600   **Exc.:** $2100   **VGood:** $1900

WINCHESTER MODEL 101 DIAMOND GRADE TRAP SINGLE

Same specs as Model 101 Diamond Grade Skeet except 12-ga.; 32-inch, 34-inch single barrel; hand-checkered select walnut Trap-style stock, beavertail forearm. Introduced 1982; discontinued 1987.

Perf.: $2000   **Exc.:** $1650   **VGood:** $1450

WINCHESTER MODEL 101 XTR

Over/under; boxlock; 12-, 20-ga.; 26-inch, 28-inch, 30-inch barrels; WinChokes; vent rib; metal bead front sight; cut-checkered American walnut pistol-grip stock, beavertail forearm; chrome-plated chambers, bores; manual safety; barrel selector; single selective trigger; auto ejectors; hand

engraving; replaced Model 101. Introduced 1978; discontinued 1987.

Perf.: $1850   **Exc.:** $1400   **VGood:** $1200

WINCHESTER MODEL 101 XTR AMERICAN FLYER LIVE BIRD

Same specs as Model 101 XTR except 12-ga.; 2-3/4-inch chambers; 28-inch, 29-1/2-inch barrels; under barrel fitted for internal WinChokes, over barrel has Extra-Full choke; competition vent-rib; full fancy American walnut stock; blued receiver, gold wire border inlays; matte finish on top of receiver; marketed in luggage-type case. Made in Japan. Introduced 1987; discontinued 1987.

Perf.: $2450   **Exc.:** $1900   **VGood:** $1700

WINCHESTER MODEL 101 XTR AMERICAN FLYER LIVE BIRD COMBO SET

Same specs as Model 101 XTR except 12-ga.; 2-3/4-inch chambers; two-barrel set with 28-inch, 29-1/2-inch barrels; under barrel fitted for internal WinChokes, over barrel has Extra-Full choke; competition vent rib; full fancy American walnut stock; blued receiver, gold wire border inlays; matte finish on top of receiver. Made in Japan. Introduced 1987; discontinued 1987.

Perf.: $3500   **Exc.:** $2900   **VGood:** $2600

WINCHESTER MODEL 101 XTR PIGEON GRADE FEATHERWEIGHT

Same specs as Model 101 XTR except 12-, 20-ga.; 25 1/2-inch Improved Cylinder/Improved Modified barrels; checkered walnut straight-grip stock. Introduced 1983; discontinued 1987.

Perf.: $1400   **Exc.:** $950   **VGood:** $850

MODEL 101 PIGEON GRADE TRAP

This deluxe dedicated trap gun was introduced in 2008. It features a Grade III/IV walnut stock with a high-gloss finish and a raised comb. Barrels are 30" or 32". Three choke tubes included. Weight is 7.5 to 7.75 lbs. Add 5% for adjustable comb stock.

NIB: $1700   **Exc.:** $1495   **VGood:** 1050

WINCHESTER SUPREME O/U SHOTGUNS

Gauge: 12, 2-3/4-inch, 3-inch chambers; 28-inch, 30-inch barrel, Invector Plus choke tubes; weighs 7 lbs. 6 oz. to 7 lbs. 12. oz.; 45-inch overall (28-inch barrel); checkered walnut stock; chrome-plated chambers; back-bored barrels; tang barrel selector/safety; deep-blued finish. Introduced 2000.

Supreme Field (26-inch or 28-inch barrel, 6mm ventilated rib)

Perf.: $1075   **Exc.:** $895   **VGood:** $825

Supreme Sporting (28-inch or 30-inch barrel, 10mm rib, adj. trigger)

Perf.: $1200   **Exc.:** $995   **VGood:** $900

WINCHESTER XPERT MODEL 96

Over/under; boxlock; 12-, 20-ga.; 3-inch chambers; 26-inch, 28-inch, 30-inch barrels; vent rib; depending on gauge, barrel length, weighs 6-1/4 to 8-1/4 lbs.; checkered walnut pistol-grip stock, forend; similar to Model 101. Made in Japan. Introduced 1976; discontinued 1981.

Exc.: $800   **VGood:** $600   **Good:** $500

WINCHESTER XPERT MODEL 96 SKEET

Same specs as Xpert Model 96 except 2-3/4-inch chambers; 27-inch barrels; Skeet choke; checkered walnut Skeet-style stock. Made in Japan. Introduced 1976; discontinued 1981.

Exc.: $825   **VGood:** $625   **Good:** $500

WINCHESTER XPERT MODEL 96 TRAP

Same specs as Xpert Model 96 except 12-ga.; 2-3/4-inch chambers; 30-inch barrels; checkered walnut straight or Monte Carlo trap-style stock; recoil pad. Made in Japan. Introduced 1976; discontinued 1981.

Exc.: $775   **VGood:** $595   **Good:** $495

WINCHESTER SELECT DELUXE FIELD

New in 2007, this Belgian-made 3" 12 gauge O/U features an engraved steel receiver with silver nitride finish and Grade II walnut. Barrels are 26", 28" or 30". Three chokes included. Weight is about 7.25 lbs.

NIB: $1325   **Exc.:** $1250   **VGood:** $1050

WINCHESTER SELECT PLATINUM FIELD

This 3" 12 gauge O/U was introduced in 2007. It is Belgian-made and comes with 28" or 30" barrels, Grade II/III walnut and deep relief engraving. Includes three Signature extended choke tubes and hard case.

NIB: $1950   **Exc.:** $1795   **VGood:** $1395

WINCHESTER SELECT PLATINUM SPORTING

Similar to the Platinum Field with 28", 30" or 32" ported barrels, wide rib, adjustable trigger shoe and five Signature extended choke tubes and hard case.

NIB: $2195   **Exc.:** $1995   **VGood:** $1700

WINCHESTER SELECT MIDNIGHT

High-gloss bluing on receiver and barrels with gold accent game bird pattern on both sides and bottom of the receiver. Satin finished Grade II/III walnut. Oval checkering pattern. Choke tubes. Introduced 2006. Available in 26-inch and 28-inch barrels.

NIB: 2000   **Exc.:** 1695   **VGood:** 1050

Winchester 101 Pigeon Grade Trap

Winchester Supreme Sporting

Winchester Xpert Model 96

Winchester Xpert Model 96 Skeet

Winchester Select Deluxe Field

Winchester Select Platinum Field

Winchester Select Platinum Sporting

WINCHESTER SELECT WHITE FIELD

An engraved silver nitride receiver is featured on both versions of the White Field. The Traditional model has traditional checkering and the Extreme model features the Select Series' unique oval checkering pattern. Both versions have choke tubes and are available in 26-inch and 28-inch barrels. Introduced 2006.

NIB: 1400   **Exc.:** 1050   **VGood:** 795

WINCHESTER MODEL 21

Side-by-side; boxlock; hammerless; 12-, 16-, 20-, 28-ga., .410; 20-inch, 28-inch, 30-inch, 32-inch (12-ga. only) barrels; raised matted or vent rib; Full, Improved Modified, Modified, Improved Cylinder, Skeet chokes; checkered walnut straight or pistol-grip stock, regular or beavertail forend; automatic safety; early models (1931-1944) have double triggers and extractors, single trigger and ejectors optional; later models (1945-1959) have selective single trigger and selective ejectors. Introduced 1931; discontinued 1959.

With double triggers, extractors

Exc.: $3500   **VGood:** $2900   **Good:** $2000

With double triggers, selective ejectors

Exc.: $4200   **VGood:** $3700   **Good:** $2850

With single selective trigger, extractors

Exc.: $5900   **VGood:** $4400   **Good:** $3100

With single selective trigger, selective ejectors

Exc.: $6500   **VGood:** $5500   **Good:** $4750

.410 model

Exc.: $30,000   **VGood:** $20,000   **Good:** $14,000

28-ga. model

Exc.: $20,000   **VGood:** $14,000   **Good:** $9000

WINCHESTER MODEL 21 CUSTOM

Same specs as Model 21 except hand-checkered fancy American walnut stock, forearm; hand-honed internal parts; optional carving, engraving and gold inlays. Introduced 1960; discontinued 1982.

Perf.: $7500   **Exc.:** $5500   **VGood:** $4500

WINCHESTER MODEL 21 DUCK

Same specs as Model 21 except 12-ga.; 3-inch chamber; 30-inch, 32-inch barrels; Full choke; checkered walnut pistol-grip stock, beavertail forearm; selective ejection; selective single trigger; recoil pad. Introduced 1940; discontinued 1954.

With matted rib

Exc.: $6000   **VGood:** $5000   **Good:** $3750

With vent rib

Exc.: $6300   **VGood:** $5300   **Good:** $4050

WINCHESTER MODEL 21 GRAND AMERICAN

Same specs as Model 21 except two barrel sets; hand-checkered fancy American walnut stock, forearm; hand-honed internal parts; optional

Winchester Select Midnight

Winchester Select White Field

Winchester Model 21
Grand American

Winchester Model 23 XTR
Golden Quail

Winchester Model 23 XTR
Pigeon Grade

Winchester Model 23 XTR
Pigeon Grade Lightweight

Winchester Model 24

mechanical single trigger; selective ejectors; silver-gray satin finish on receiver, top lever, trigger guard; fine-line scroll engraving. Made in Japan. Introduced 1978; discontinued 1986.

Perf.: $1000   **Exc.:** $700   **VGood:** $600

WINCHESTER MODEL 23 XTR GOLDEN QUAIL

Same specs as Model 23 XTR except different chamberings produced each year; 12- (1986), 20- (1984), 28-ga. (1985), .410 (1987); 25-1/2-inch solid-rib barrel; fixed chokes; English-style straight-grip stock, beavertail forearm; engraving; gold inlays. Only 500 made each year. Introduced 1984; discontinued 1987.

12 Gauge		
Perf.: $2500	**Exc.:** $2300	**VGood:** $2000
20 Gauge		
Perf.: $2850	**Exc.:** $2500	**VGood:** $2150
28 Gauge		
Perf.: $3950	**Exc.:** $3750	**VGood:** $3450
.410 Bore		
Perf.: $3950	**Exc.:** $3750	**VGood:** $3450

WINCHESTER MODEL 23 XTR HEAVY DUCK

Same specs as Model 23 XTR except 12-ga.; 3-inch chambers; 30-inch Full/Extra-Full barrels; select American walnut stock, beavertail forend; blued receivers, barrels; marketed in hard case. Only 500 made. Made in Japan. Introduced 1983; discontinued 1984.

Perf.: $2150   **Exc.:** $1750   **VGood:** $1450

WINCHESTER MODEL 23 XTR LIGHT DUCK

Same specs as Model 23 XTR except 20-ga.; 3-inch chambers, 28-inch Full/Full barrels; select American walnut stock, beavertail forend; blued receiver, barrels; marketed in hard case. Only 500 made. Made in Japan. Introduced 1984; discontinued 1985.

Perf.: $2495   **Exc.:** $2150   **VGood:** $1850

WINCHESTER MODEL 23 XTR PIGEON GRADE

Same specs as Model 23 XTR except higher grade of wood, checkering and engraving; marketed in hard case. Made in Japan. Introduced, 1983; discontinued 1986.

Perf.: $2220   **Exc.:** $2000   **VGood:** $1750

WINCHESTER MODEL 23 XTR PIGEON GRADE LIGHTWEIGHT

Same specs as Model 23 XTR except 25-1/2-inch barrels; fixed or choke tubes; English-style straight-grip stock, thin semi-beavertail forend; engraved bird scene. Marketed in hard case. Made in Japan. Introduced 1982; discontinued 1988.

Perf.: $2250   **Exc.:** $2000   **VGood:** $1800

WINCHESTER MODEL 23 XTR TWO-BARREL SET

Same specs as Model 23 XTR except 20-, 28-ga.; two-barrel set in each gauge of 25-1/2-inch barrel, each fitted with its own full fancy American walnut semi-beavertail forend; marketed in handmade leather luggage-style carrying case. Only 500 made. Introduced 1986; discontinued 1986

Perf.: $4900   **Exc.:** $4100   **VGood:** $3100

WINCHESTER MODEL 24

Side-by-side; hammerless; takedown; 12-, 16-, 20-ga.; 26-inch Improved/Modified, 28-inch Modified/Full or Improved/ Modified, 30-inch Modified/Full (12-ga. only) barrels; uncheckered walnut straight or pistol-grip stock, semi-beavertail forearm; composition buttplate; double triggers; automatic ejectors. Introduced 1940; discontinued 1957.

12-, 16-ga. model.		
Exc.: $575	**VGood:** $395	**Good:** $275
20-ga. model		
Exc.: $600	**VGood:** $425	**Good:** $300

carving, engraving and gold inlays. Introduced 1960; discontinued 1982.

Perf.: $49,750 **Exc.:** $37,500 **VGood:** $25,000

WINCHESTER MODEL 21 PIGEON
Same specs as Model 21 except hand-checkered fancy American walnut stock, forearm; hand-honed internal parts; optional carving, engraving and gold inlays. Introduced 1960; discontinued 1982.

Perf.: $15,500 **Exc.:** $14,500 **VGood:** $13,000

WINCHESTER MODEL 21 SKEET
Same specs as Model 21 except 26-inch, 28-inch barrels; Skeet chokes; red bead front sight; checkered French walnut stock, beavertail forearm; selective single trigger, selective ejection; non-auto safety. Introduced 1933; discontinued 1958.

With matted rib		
Exc.: $1900	**VGood:** $1600	**Good:** $1300
With vent rib		
Exc.: $2100	**VGood:** $1800	**Good:** $1500

WINCHESTER MODEL 21 TRAP
Same specs as Model 21 except 30-inch, 32-inch barrels; Full choke; checkered walnut pistol-grip or straight stock, beavertail forearm; selective trigger; non-auto safety; selective ejection. Introduced 1932; discontinued 1940.

With matted rib		
Exc.: $6000	**VGood:** $4995	**Good:** $3000

With vent rib		
Exc.: $6300	**VGood:** $5295	**Good:** $3150

WINCHESTER MODEL 23 CLASSIC
Side-by-side; 12-, 20-, 28-ga., .410; 26-inch vent-rib barrels; deluxe hand-checkered walnut stock, beavertail forend; auto safety; auto ejectors; single selective trigger; solid recoil pad; gold inlay on bottom of receiver; gold initial plate in stock; ebony inlay in forend; blued, engraved receiver. Made in Japan. Introduced 1986; discontinued 1988.

12-, 20-ga.		
Perf.: $1600	**Exc.:** $1200	**VGood:** $1000
28-ga., .410		
Perf.: $2100	**Exc.:** $1500	**VGood:** $1250

WINCHESTER MODEL 23 CUSTOM
Same specs as Model 23 Classic except 12-ga.; 27-inch WinChoke barrels; chrome-lined bores, chambers for steel shot; high-luster blued receiver, no engraving; marketed in luggage-style case. Made in Japan. Introduced 1986; discontinued 1988.

Perf.: $2000   **Exc.:** $1200   **VGood:** $1000

WINCHESTER MODEL 23 XTR
Side-by-side; 12-, 20-ga.; 3-inch chambers; 25-1/2-inch, 26-inch, 28-inch, 30-inch barrels; tapered vent rib; WinChokes; tapered vent rib; cut-checkered high-luster American walnut stock, beavertail forend;

WINCHESTER MODEL 20

Single shot; exposed hammer; takedown; .410; 2-1/2-inch chamber; 26-inch Full-choke barrel; checkered pistol-grip stock, forearm. Introduced 1919; discontinued 1924.

Exc.: $475   **VGood:** $350   **Good:** $290

WINCHESTER MODEL 36

Single shot; bolt action; takedown; 9mm short shot, 9mm long shot, 9mm ball cartridges interchangeably; 18-inch round barrel; one-piece plain wood stock, forearm; special trigger guard forms pistol grip; composition buttplate; cocks by pulling rearward on knurled firing pin head, same mechanism used in some Winchester single-shot rifles; guns were not serialized. Introduced 1920; discontinued 1927.

Exc.: $600   **VGood:** $475   **Good:** $300

WINCHESTER MODEL 37

Single shot; break-open; semi-hammerless; 12-, 16-, 20-, 28-ga., .410; 26-inch, 28-inch, 30-inch, 32-inch barrel; Full, Modified, Cylinder choke; metal bead front sight; uncheckered American walnut pistol-grip stock, semi-beavertail forearm; automatic ejector; checkered composition buttplate. Introduced 1936; discontinued 1968. Some buyers pay a slight premium for "red lettering" on Winchester logo.

12-ga. model
Exc.: $350   **VGood:** $275   **Good:** $125
16-ga. model
Exc.: $295   **VGood:** $275   **Good:** $115
20-ga. model
Exc.: $295   **VGood:** $225   **Good:** $145
28-ga. model
Exc.: $950   **VGood:** $650   **Good:** $500
.410 model
Exc.: $425   **VGood:** $295   **Good:** $250

WINCHESTER MODEL 37A

Single barrel; break-open; 12- (3-inch), 16- (2-3/4-inch), 20- (3-inch), 28-ga. (2-3/4-inch), .410 (3-inch); 25-inch, 28-inch, 30-inch, 32-inch, 36-inch barrel; Full choke; checkered walnut-stained hardwood pistol-grip stock; concave hammer spur; white spacer between grip cap and buttplate; gold trigger; engraving. Introduced 1973; discontinued 1980.

12-, 16-, 20-ga. model
Perf.: $140   **Exc.:** $100   **VGood:** $80
28-ga., .410 model
Perf.: $190   **Exc.:** $140   **VGood:** $120

WINCHESTER MODEL 37A YOUTH

Same specs as Model 37A except 20-ga., .410; 26-inch barrel; Improved Modified, Full chokes; youth-sized hardwood stock. Introduced 1973; discontinued 1980.

Perf.: $180   **Exc.:** $110   **VGood:** $90

WINCHESTER MODEL 41

Single shot; bolt action; takedown; .410; 2-1/2-inch (pre-1933), 3-inch (post-1933) chamber; 24-inch full-choke barrel; uncheckered one-piece walnut pistol-grip or straight-grip stock; checkering on special order; guns were not numbered serially. Introduced 1920; discontinued 1934.

Exc.: $400   **VGood:** $300   **Good:** $250

WINCHESTER MODEL 370

Single barrel; break-open; 12- (3-inch), 16- (2-3/4-inch), 20- (3-inch), 28-ga. (2-3/4-inch), .410 (3-inch); 26-inch, 28-inch, 30-inch, 32-inch, 36-inch barrel; Full choke; weight varies with gauges and barrel lengths, from 5-1/2 to 6-1/4 lbs.; bead front sight; plain American hardwood pistol-grip stock, forearm; hard-rubber buttplate; auto ejectors. Introduced 1968; discontinued 1973, replaced by Model 37A.

12-, 16-, 20-ga. model
Perf.: $125   **Exc.:** $100   **VGood:** $80
28-ga., .410 model
Perf.: $175   **Exc.:** $140   **VGood:** $120

WINCHESTER MODEL 370 YOUTH

Same specs as Model 370 except 20-ga., .410; 26-inch Improved Modified barrel; youth-sized

Winchester Model 20

Winchester Model 37A

Winchester Model 37A Youth

Winchester Model 41

Winchester Model 370

Winchester Model 1887

Winchester Model 1901

hardwood stock; rubber recoil pad. Introduced 1969; discontinued 1973.

Perf.: $160   **Exc.:** $110   **VGood:** $90

WINCHESTER MODEL 1885 SINGLE SHOT

Falling block; takedown or solid frame; 20-ga.; 3-inch chamber; 26-inch nickel-steel barrel; extra barrels or matted top barrels optional; Full choke standard; Modified or Cylinder bore optional; uncheckered walnut pistol-grip stock; shotgun version of Model 1885 Hi-Wall rifle. Introduced 1913; discontinued 1918.

Exc.: $3000   **VGood:** $2300   **Good:** $1800

WINCHESTER MODEL 1887

Lever action; solid frame; 10-, 12-ga.; 4-shot tubular magazine; 30-inch, 32-inch barrel; Full choke; uncheckered American walnut half-pistol-grip stock, forend. Introduced 1887; discontinued 1901.

Exc.: $1950   **VGood:** $1400   **Good:** $1100

WINCHESTER MODEL 1887 DELUXE

Same specs as Model 1887 except Damascus barrel; hand-checkered stock, forend. Introduced 1887; discontinued 1901.

Exc.: $2400   **VGood:** $1850   **Good:** $1400

WINCHESTER MODEL 1901

Lever action; solid frame; 10-ga.; 4-shot tube magazine; 30-inch, 32-inch barrel; Full choke; uncheckered American walnut half-pistol-grip stock,

forend; replaced Model 1887 in line with internal redesign features. Introduced 1901; discontinued 1920.

Exc.: $1900   **VGood:** $1500   **Good:** $1300

WINCHESTER MODEL 9410 LEVER-ACTION SHOTGUN

Gauge: .410, 2-1/2-inch chamber; 24-inch barrel (Cyl. bore); weighs 6-3/4 lbs.; 42-1/8-inch overall; checkered walnut straight-grip, checkered walnut forearm; V rear sight, TruGlo front; Model 94 rifle action (smoothbore) chambered for .410 shotshell. 9-shot tubular magazine; 13-1/2-inch length of pull. Introduced 2001. From U.S. Repeating Arms Co.

Price: 9410 Lever-Action Shotgun
Perf.: $1100   **Exc.:** $875   **VGood:** $600
Price: 9410 Packer Shotgun
Perf.: $1100   **Exc.:** $875   **VGood:** $600

WOODWARD BEST QUALITY DOUBLE

Side-by-side; sidelock; built to customer order in any standard gauge, barrel length, choke; double or single trigger; automatic ejectors; produced in field, wildfowl, Skeet or Trap configurations. Made in England. Manufactured prior to WWII.

With single trigger
Perf.: $28,500   **Exc.:** $21,000   **VGood:** $19,500
With double trigger
Perf.: $27,500   **Exc.:** $20,000   **VGood:** $18,500

Zoli Delfino

Zoli Silver Falcon

Zoli Silver Fox

Zoli Uplander

Zoli Woodsman

Zoli Z90 Mono-Trap Model

WOODWARD BEST QUALITY OVER/UNDER

Over/under; sidelock; built to customer order in any standard gauge, barrel length, choke; plain barrel or vent rib; double or single trigger; auto ejectors. Made in England. Introduced 1909; discontinued WWII.

With single triggers
Perf.: $34,000 **Exc.:** $25,000 **VGood:** $20,500

With double triggers
Perf.: $33,000 **Exc.:** $24,000 **VGood:** $19,000

WOODWARD SINGLE BARREL TRAP

Single shot; sidelock; 12-ga.; built to customer order in any standard barrel length, choke; plain barrel or vent rib; single trigger; auto ejectors. Made in England. Manufactured prior to WWII.

Perf.: $13,000 **Exc.:** $9000 **VGood:** $8000

ZABALA DOUBLE

Side-by-side; 10-, 12-, 20-ga., .410; 26-inch, 28-inch, 30-inch, 32-inch barrels; raised matted solid rib; metal bead front sight; hand-checkered French walnut pistol-grip stock, plastic-finished beavertail forend; double triggers; front trigger hinged; hand-engraved action, blued finish. Made in Spain. Introduced 1980; discontinued 1982. Add 25 percent for 10-ga.

Perf.: $475 **Exc.:** $395 **VGood:** $325

PIETRO ZANOLETTI MODEL 2000 FIELD

Over/under; boxlock; 12-ga.; 28-inch barrels; gold bead front sight; checkered European walnut pistol-grip stock, forend; auto ejectors; double triggers;

engraved receiver. Made in Italy. Introduced 1984; no longer in production.

Perf.: $500 **Exc.:** $385 **VGood:** $325

ZOLI DELFINO

Over/under; 12-, 20-ga.; 3-inch chambers; 28-inch barrels; vent rib; hand-checkered European walnut pistol-grip stock, cheekpiece; chromed bores; double triggers; auto sliding safety; color case-hardened receiver; light engraving. Made in Italy. Introduced 1980; discontinued 1989.

Perf.: $650 **Exc.:** $560 **VGood:** $490

ZOLI GOLDEN SNIPE

Over/under; boxlock; 12-, 20-ga.; 26-inch, 28-inch, 30-inch vent-rib barrels; standard choke combos; hand-checkered European walnut pistol-grip stock, forend; single trigger; auto ejectors; engraving. No longer in production.

Perf.: $700 **Exc.:** $560 **VGood:** $490

ZOLI SILVER FALCON

Over/under; boxlock; 12-, 20-ga.; 3-inch chambers; 26-inch, 28-inch barrels; standard choke combos or Full choke tubes; Turkish Circassian walnut stock; single selective trigger, auto ejectors; silvered finish, floral engraving on frame. Made in Italy. Introduced 1989; discontinued 1990.

Perf.: $950 **Exc.:** $700 **VGood:** $550

ZOLI SILVER FOX

Side-by-side; boxlock; 12-, 20-ga.; 3-inch chambers; 26-inch, 28-inch barrels; standard choke combos; select Turkish Circassian walnut straight-grip stock, splinter forend; solid recoil pad; single trigger;

selective ejectors; engraved, silvered receiver. Made in Italy. Introduced 1989; discontinued 1990.

Perf.: $1750 **Exc.:** $1425 **VGood:** $1250

ZOLI UPLANDER

Side-by-side; boxlock; 12-, 20-ga.; 3-inch chambers; 25-inch Improved Cylinder/Modified barrels; hand-checkered Turkish Circassian walnut straight English-style stock, splinter forend; single trigger; auto ejectors; color case-hardened frame. Introduced 1989; discontinued 1990.

Perf.: $975 **Exc.:** $875 **VGood:** $775

ZOLI WOODSMAN

Over/under; boxlock; 12-ga.; 3-inch chambers; 23-inch vent-rib barrels for rifled slugs; five choke tubes; rifle sights on raised rib; skip-line-checkered, oil-finished Turkish Circassian walnut stock; rubber buttpad; single selective trigger; auto selective ejectors; with or without sling swivels; blued, engraved frame. Made in Italy. Introduced 1989; discontinued 1990.

Perf.: $1600 **Exc.:** $1150 **VGood:** $900

ZOLI Z90 MONO-TRAP MODEL

Single barrel; break-open; 12-ga.; 2-3/4-inch chamber; 32-inch, 34-inch single barrel; choke tubes; raised vent rib; two sight beads; checkered Turkish Circassian walnut Monte Carlo pistol-grip stock, forearm; single selective trigger; selective auto ejectors; recoil pad; matte blue finish on receiver. Made in Italy. Introduced 1989; discontinued 1990.

Perf.: $2150 **Exc.:** $1450 **VGood:** $1200

ZOLI Z90 SKEET MODEL

Same specs as Z90 Mono-Trap except over/under; boxlock; 28-inch barrels; checkered Turkish Circassian walnut Skeet-style stock, forearm. Made in Italy. Introduced 1989; discontinued 1990.

Perf.: $2150 **Exc.:** $1450 **VGood:** $1200

ZOLI Z90 SPORTING CLAYS

Same specs as Z90 Mono-Trap except over/under; sidelock; 28-inch barrels; weighs 7-1/4 lbs.; checkered Turkish Circassian walnut pistol-grip stock, forend; schnabel forend tip; single selective trigger; selective auto ejectors; solid rubber buttpad; silvered, engraved frame. Made in Italy. Introduced 1989; discontinued 1990.

Perf.: $2150 **Exc.:** $1450 **VGood:** $1200

ZOLI Z90 TRAP

Same specs as Z90 Mono-Trap except over/under; boxlock; 29-1/2-inch, 32-inch barrels; step-type vent rib; vent center rib; weighs 8-1/2 lbs.; adjustable single selective trigger. Made in Italy. Introduced 1989; discontinued 1990.

Perf.: $2150 **Exc.:** $1450 **VGood:** $1200

MODERN GUN VALUES
COMMEMORATIVES
Directory of Dates

Commemoratives & Limited Editions, 1960 - 1995 Introduction

I will be frank: as far as I know, no one has ever compiled an exhaustive list of all the commemorative, special-issue, and special-order firearms offered during the twentieth and twenty-first centuries. The mere thought of compiling such a list makes my head hurt.

Here's why: back in the sixties and seventies, the only major manufacturers of commemorative guns were Colt and Winchester. Colt's platform was the Single Action Army; Winchester's, the Model 94. The speculation at the time was that these two companies made these guns to spur sales of their two aging flagship models. This explanation is still valid, to some extent at least, four decades later.

Today, however, it's a different story. During the last two decades, most American gunmakers invested in computer-aided manufacturing, which meant that making special-run guns presented no particular problems in terms of tooling and scrap. If, say, the Upper Sandusky Conservation and Hog Roast Club wanted to commemorate their fiftieth anniversary with a special rifle, pistol or shotgun, gunmakers will usually be happy to comply as long as a minimum buy is guaranteed.

Then major gun distributors got into the act. Sales and marketing firms such as TALO began offering exclusives, which they sold to their dealers as non-catalogued specialty items. Most of these special-run guns were, and are, very attractive, but their uncatalogued status makes them very difficult to classify. I get probably two calls a month inquiring about these guns, which don't usually appear in any price guides.

In general, there are four different types of commemorative firearms: those released directly from the manufacturer into their normal distribution channel; those exclusively made for a specific distributor; those made as fund-raisers for non-profit organizations; and those commissioned from a specialty retailer for direct sales to the public. Let's take a look at them.

The Factory Commemorative

The first type is exemplified by the Winchester 94 and Colt SAA commemoratives that we all love – or hate. These firearms have lately acquired a legitimacy among collectors that they didn't always enjoy – in fact, most serious Winchester collectors would have spit in your face 20 years ago if you had asked them if they had a Crazy Horse commemorative among their holdings. Until recently, the NRA commemorative Colt SAA was a pariah among collectors. This situation is changing; the discontinuance of the Model 94 in 2006 has made all 94s collectible, and the value of second-generation SAAs is appreciating rapidly.

The Distributor Special

The second type includes the TALO and Davidson's special-run guns that are released to key retailers who buy from such distributors. As discussed above, these guns are usually uncatalogued, and most of the general gun-owning public is usually unaware of their existence.

The Fund-Raiser

The third type is exemplified by the various not-for-profit guns that we have all seen, often unfired, in the used-gun racks of our local retailers. The Ithaca Model 37 shotgun was a big favorite of Ducks Unlimited some years back, for example, but I know of no comprehensive source that lists all of the variations of these fund-raiser guns or how many were produced.

The Distributor Special

The fourth type of commemorative or special-issue gun includes the various historical and personality-cult commemoratives that are built on the chassis of both domestic and offshore firearms. American Historical Foundation, for example, offers at least 60 commemorative firearms at this writing, ranging from fancy .25 Colt semi-autos to Thompsons. And right now, at this very moment, you can buy an Elvis Presley commemorative Smith & Wesson revolver from a collectibles company doing business as America Remembers. The revolver itself is called the Elvis Presley Taking Care of Business, and it can be yours for a mere $2195. If you're you're the kind of person whose living room motif features imitation velvet Elvis tapestries and Presley collector plates, you might also consider America Remembers' Elvis Presley Western Tribute, which is based on an Italian-made Uberti Single Action Army clone. America Remembers offers dozens of other special-run commemorative or tribute guns should your tastes run in that direction.

Often the definitions of these four types becomes blurred or disappears altogether. Was the Charter Arms "Bonnie & Clyde" matched set of revolvers that was produced 30 years ago a true commemorative, or just a marketing gimmick? Is the Remington Model Seven 25th Anniversary Edition bolt action rifle a true commemorative? The mind boggles.

In this book, we pretty much limit ourselves to factory-built commemoratives that hit the market between 1960 and 1995. We apologize in advance who are searching for, say, a Colt El Capitan or El Presidente in these pages. We might also go ahead and apologize to those who find commemorative firearms listed herein for sale at figures substantially above or below the values shown in this section. These things happen. By the way, values shown are for examples in mint, unfired condition.

One thing is for sure: like all guns, commemorative or special-run firearms are worth precis ely what someone is willing to pay for them, no more or less. The fact that a gun might be a "distributor special," for example, does not inherently add to or detract from its value. If someone is willing to pay a certain amount for the privilege of being the only kid on the block with a [fill in the blank], then that figure is what that gun is worth to that buyer in those circumstances. To generalize beyond that is misleading.

I have always thought that the most fascinating collectors are those who are just slightly mad on the subject of their interest. I once knew a man, for example, who would energetically expound on the RCA/Victor recordings of Spike Jones until he was literally frothing at the mouth. Was he a nut? Yes. Was he MY kind of nut? Absolutely! Passionate people are always the most interesting.

So let us not turn up our noses at someone who's saving his pennies for a Gene Autry, Smiley Burnette and Pat Buttram Tribute Rifle from America Remembers. You may not find such a rifle listed in the following section, but that doesn't mean it's inherently less valuable than some of the guns that are listed.

Besides, I'm kind of a Gene Autry fan myself.

Cheers,

Dan Shideler

1960 Marlin 90th Anniversary Model

1962 Colt New Mexico Golden Anniversary

1961 Colt Sheriff's Model

1960

MARLIN 90TH ANNIVERSARY MODEL

Model 39A rifle commemorating firm's ninth decade. Has same general specs as Golden 39A, except for chrome-plated barrel, action; stock forearm of hand-checkered select American walnut; squirrel figure carved on right side of butt stock. Manufactured 1960; only 500 made.
Market Value: $995

1961

COLT 125TH ANNIVERSARY MODEL

Single Action Army revolver; "125th Anniversary—SAA Model .45 Cal." on left side of 7-1/2-inch barrel; 45 Colt only; varnished walnut grips; gold-plated Colt medallions; gold-plated hammer, trigger, trigger guard; balance blued. Originally cased in red velvet-lined box; 7390 made in 1961 only.
Issue Price: $150
Market Value: $1495

COLT CIVIL WAR CENTENNIAL

Single shot replica of Colt Model 1860 Army revolver; "Civil War Centennial Model—.22 Caliber Short" on left side of 6-inch barrel; 22 Short only; varnished walnut grips; gold-plated Colt medallions; gold-plated frame, backstrap, trigger guard assembly, balance blued; originally in leatherette case; 24,114 made in 1961 only.
Issue Price: $32.50
Market Value: $175

COLT GENESEO ANNIVERSARY

No. 4 derringer replica; "1836—Geneseo Anniversary Model—1961" on left side of 2-1/2-inch barrel; 22 Short only; walnut grips; gold plated in entirety; originally cased in velvet/satin-lined box; made especially for Cherry's Sporting Goods, Geneseo, Illinois; 104 made in 1961 only.
Issue Price: $27.50
Market Value: $650

COLT KANSAS STATEHOOD CENTENNIAL

Frontier Scout revolver; "1861—Kansas Centennial—1961" on left side of 4-3/4-inch barrel; 22 LR only; walnut grips; no medallions; gold-plated in entirety; originally cased in velvet-lined box with Kansas state seal inlaid in lid; made in 1961 only.
Issue Price: $75
Market Value: $450

COLT PONY EXPRESS CENTENNIAL

Frontier Scout revolver; "1860-61—Russell, Majors and Waddell/Pony Express Centennial Model—1960-61" on left side of 4-3/4-inch barrel; 22 LR only; varnished walnut grips; gold-plated Colt medallions; gold plated in entirety; originally cased in rosewood box with gold-plated centennial medallion in lid; 1007 made in 1961 only.
Issue Price: $80
Market Value: $450

COLT SHERIFF'S MODEL

Single Action Army revolver; made exclusively for Centennial Arms Corp.; "Colt Sheriff's Model .45" on left side of 3-inch barrel; 45 Colt only; walnut grips without medallions; 25 made with nickel finish; 478 blued; made only in 1961.
Issue Price: Nickel, $139.50; Blued, $150
Nickel
Market Value: $5500
Blued
Market Value: $1995

1962

COLT COLUMBUS, OHIO, SESQUICENTENNIAL

Frontier Scout revolver; "1812—Columbus Sesquicentennial—1962" on left side of 4-3/4-inch barrel; 22 LR only; varnished walnut grips with gold-plated medallions; gold-plated in entirety; originally cased in velvet/satin-lined walnut case; 200 made in 1962 only.
Issue Price: $100
Market Value: $550

COLT FORT FINDLAY, OHIO, SESQUICENTENNIAL

Frontier Scout revolver; "1812—Fort Findlay Sesquicentennial—1962" on left side of 4-3/4-inch, barrel; 22 LR, 22 WMR; varnished walnut grips; gold-

plated in entirety; originally cased in red velvet/satin-lined walnut box; 110 made in 1962 only.
Issue Price: $89.50
Market Value: $650
Cased Pair, 22 LR, 22 WMR (20 made in 1962)
Market Value: $2500

COLT NEW MEXICO GOLDEN ANNIVERSARY

Frontier Scout revolver; "1912—New Mexico Golden Anniversary—1962" wiped in gold on left side of 4-3/4-inch barrel; 22 LR only; varnished walnut grips; gold-plated medallions; barrel, frame, base pin screw, ejector rod, rod tube, tube plug and screw, bolt and trigger, hammer screws blued; balance gold-plated; originally cased in redwood box with yellow satin/velvet lining; 1000 made in 1962 only.
Issue Price: $79.95
Market Value: $450

COLT ROCK ISLAND ARSENAL CENTENNIAL

Single shot version of Colt Model 1860 Army revolver; "1862—Rock Island Arsenal Centennial Model—1962" on left side of 6-inch barrel; 22 Short only; varnished walnut grips; blued finish; originally in blue and gray leatherette case; 550 made in 1962 only.
Issue Price: $38.50
Market Value: $250

COLT WEST VIRGINIA STATEHOOD CENTENNIAL

Frontier Scout revolver; "1863—West Virginia Centennial—1963" wiped in gold on left side of 4-3/4-inch barrel; 22 LR only; pearlite grips, gold-plated medallions; blued, with gold-plated backstrap, trigger guard assembly and screws, stock screw; originally cased in blonde wood box with gold velvet/satin lining; 3452 made in 1962 only.
Issue Price: $75
Market Value: $450

COLT WEST VIRGINIA STATEHOOD CENTENNIAL SINGLE ACTION ARMY

Same legend on barrel as 22 version; 5-1/2-inch barrel; 45 Colt only; same blue/gold finish as Scout version; same type of casing; 600 made in 1963 only.
Issue Price: $150
Market Value: $1495

1963 Colt
Idaho Territorial
Centennial

1963 Colt
Arizona Territorial Centennial

C-2246
1963 Colt
General John Hunt
Morgan Indian Raid

1964 Colt
Nevada Battle Born Commemorative
Frontier Scout/Single-Action Army Set

1963

COLT ARIZONA TERRITORIAL CENTENNIAL
Frontier Scout revolver "1863—Arizona Territorial Centennial—1963" wiped in gold on left side of 4-3/4-inch barrel; 22 LR only; pearlite grips, gold-plated medallions; gold plated, with blue barrel, frame, base pin screw, ejector rod, rod tube, tube plug and screw, bolt and trigger screws, hammer and hammer screw; originally cased in blonde-finished box with yellow velvet/satin lining; 5355 made in 1963 only.
Issue Price: $75
Market Value: $500

COLT ARIZONA TERRITORIAL CENTENNIAL SINGLE ACTION ARMY
Same as Colt Arizona Territorial Centennial Frontier Scout with same legend on barrel; 5 1/2-inch barrel; 45 Colt only; same blue/gold-plated finish; same type case; 1280 made in 1963 only.
Issue Price: $150
Market Value: $1495

COLT BATTLE OF GETTYSBURG CENTENNIAL
Frontier Scout revolver "1863—Battle of Gettysburg Centennial—1963" wiped in gold on left side of 4-3/4-inch barrel; 22 LR only; walnut grips; gold-plated medallions; gold plated with blued barrel, frame, base pin screw, ejector rod tube, tube plug and screw, and bolt, trigger and hammer screws; originally cased in blonde-finished wood with yellow velvet in bottom, blue satin in lid; 1019 made in 1963 only.
Issue Price: $89.95
Market Value: $800

COLT CAROLINA CHARTER TERCENTENARY
Frontier Scout revolver "1663—Carolina Charter Tercentenary—1963" wiped in gold on left side of 4-3/4-inch barrel; 22 LR only; walnut grips; gold-plated medallions; gold-plated, with barrel, frame, cylinder, base pin screw, ejector rod, rod tube, tube plug, tube screw, bolt, trigger and hammer screws blued; originally cased in blonde-finished box with yellow velvet/satin lining; 300 made in 1963 only.
Issue Price: $75
Market Value: $460

COLT CAROLINA CHARTER TERCENTENARY 22/45 COMBO SET
Includes Frontier Scout described above and Single Action Army revolver, with same legend on 5-1/2-inch barrel, 45 Colt only; same finish on grips as Frontier version; larger case to fit both guns; 251 sets made in 1963 only.
Issue Price: $240
Market Value: $1995

COLT FORT McPHERSON, NEBRASKA, CENTENNIAL
No. 4 Derringer replica; "Fort McPherson/1863—Centennial—1963" wiped in gold on left side of 2-1/2-inch barrel; 22 Short only; ivorylite grips, no medallions; gold-plated with blued barrel, bolt, trigger screw, hammer and screw, trigger and stock screw; originally cased in walnut-finished box, with gold velvet/satin lining; 300 made in 1963 only.
Issue Price: $28.95
Market Value: $600

COLT FORT STEPHENSON, OHIO, SESQUICENTENNIAL
Frontier Scout revolver "1813—Fort Stephenson Sesquicentennial—1963" wiped in silver on left side of 4-3/4-inch barrel; 22 LR only; laminated rosewood grips, nickel-plated medallions; nickel-plated finish, with blued barrel, frame, base pin screw, ejector rod, rod tube, tube plug and screw, bolt and trigger and hammer screws; originally cased in blonde-finished wood, with yellow velvet/satin lining; 200 made only in 1963.
Issue Price: $75
Market Value: $750

COLT GENERAL JOHN HUNT MORGAN INDIAN RAID
Frontier Scout revolver; "1863—Gen. John Hunt Morgan Indian Raid—1963" wiped in gold on left side of 4-3/4-inch barrel; 22 LR; pearlite grips, gold-plated medallions; gold-plated with blued frame, barrel, cylinder, base pin screw, ejector rod, rod tube, tube plug and tube screw and bolt and trigger screw; originally cased in blonde-finished wood, with gold velvet/satin lining; 100 made in 1963 only.
Issue Price: $74.50
Market Value: $850

COLT H. COOK 1 OF 100
Frontier Scout/Single Action Army revolvers; sold as set; "H. Cook 1 of 100" on left side of barrels; Scout has 4-3/4-inch barrel, 22 LR only; SA Army has 7-1/2-inch barrel, 45 Colt only; pearlite grips; nickel-plated medallions; both nickel-plated with blued frame, base pin, trigger and hammer screws; originally cased in silver-colored box with blue satin/velvet lining; 100 sets made in 1963 only for H. Cook Sporting Goods, Albuquerque, N.M.
Issue Price: $275
Market Value: $1995

COLT IDAHO TERRITORIAL CENTENNIAL
Frontier Scout revolver; "1863—Idaho Territorial Centennial—1963" wiped in silver on left side of 4-3/4-inch barrel; 22 LR only; pearlite grips; nickel-plated medallions; nickel-plated with blue frame, barrel, base pin screw, ejector rod tube, tube plug and screw, and bolt, trigger and hammer screws; originally cased in blonde-finished wood, with gold velvet/satin lining; 902 made in 1963 only.
Issue Price: $75
Market Value: $650

1964

COLT CALIFORNIA GOLD RUSH COMMEMORATIVE
Frontier Scout revolver; "California Gold Rush Model" on left side of 4-3/4-inch barrel; 22 LR only; ivorylite grips; gold-plated medallions; gold-plated in entirety; originally cased in blonde wood box; blue velvet lining in bottom, gold in lid; 500 made in 1964 only.
Issue Price: $79.50
Market Value: $675

COLT CALIFORNIA GOLD RUSH SINGLE ACTION ARMY
Same barrel legend as Frontier Scout version; 5-1/2-inch barrel; 45 Colt only; same finish, grips, casing; 130 made in 1966 only.
Issue Price: $175
Market Value: $1250 to $1500

COLT CHERRY'S SPORTING GOODS 35TH ANNIVERSARY
Frontier Scout/Single Action Army revolvers, sold as set; "1929—Cherry's Sporting Goods 1964" on left side of barrel; Scout has 4-3/4-inch barrel, 22 LR only; SA Army has 4-3/4-inch barrel, 45 Colt only; both have laminated rosewood grips; gold-plated medallions; gold-plated in entirety; originally cased in embossed black leatherette, with black velvet/satin lining; 100 sets made in 1964 only.
Issue Price: $275
Market Value: $1995

1964 Colt
General Hood Centennial

1964 Colt
California Gold Rush
Commemorative

1964 Colt
New Jersey Tercentenary

COLT CHAMIZAL TREATY COMMEMORATIVE

Frontier Scout revolver; "1867 Chamizal Treaty—1964" wiped in gold on left side of 4-3/4-inch barrel; 22 LR only; pearlite grips; gold-plated medallions; gold-plated finish; blued frame, barrel, ejector rod, ejector tube, rod plug and screw, base pin and base pin screw and hammer, trigger and bolt screws; originally cased in blonde-finished wood; yellow velvet/satin lining; 450 made in 1964.
Issue Price: $85
Market Value: $650

COLT CHAMIZAL TREATY SINGLE ACTION ARMY

Same legend on 5-1/2-inch barrel; 45 Colt only; same grips, finish as Frontier Scout version; same type of case; 50 made in 1964.
Issue Price: $170
Market Value: $1595

COLT CHAMIZAL TREATY FRONTIER SCOUT/SINGLE ACTION ARMY COMBO

Includes the two revolvers described above in one oversize case; 50 pairs made in 1965.
Issue Price: $280
Market Value: $1995

COLT COL. SAM COLT SESQUICENTENNIAL PRESENTATION

Single Action Army revolver; "1815—Col. Sam Colt Sesquicentennial Model—1964" on left side of 7-1/2-inch barrel; 45 Colt only; rosewood grips; roll-engraved scene on cylinder; nickel-plated medallions; silver-plated finish, with blued frame, barrel, ejector rod tube and screw, hammer and trigger; originally cased in varnished walnut box with 12 dummy nickel-plated cartridges in cartridge block; burgundy velvet lining; 4750 made in 1964 only.
Issue Price: $225
Market Value: $1595

COLT COL. SAM COLT SESQUICENTENNIAL DELUXE

Same specs as Col. Sam Colt Sesquicentennial Presentation model except hand-fitted rosewood grips with escutcheons rather than medallions; hand-engraved cylinder; case has plate marked "1 of 200"; 200 made in 1964 only.
Issue Price: $500
Market Value: $2600

COLT COL. SAM COLT SESQUICENTENNIAL CUSTOM DELUXE

Same specs as Col. Sam Colt Sesquicentennial Deluxe except facsimile of Samuel Colt's signature engraved on backstrap; lid of case engraved with "1 of 50"; name of purchaser engraved when requested; 50 made in 1965.
Issue Price: $1000
Market Value: $4200

COLT GENERAL HOOD CENTENNIAL

Frontier Scout revolver; "1864—General Hood's Tennessee Campaign—1964" on left side of 4-3/4-inch barrel; 22 LR only; laminated rosewood grips, gold-plated medallions; gold-plated finish, except for blued trigger, hammer, base pin, ejector rod, rod head and screw and screws for base pin, hammer, trigger, backstrap and trigger guard; originally cased in blonde-finished wood box with green velvet/satin lining; 1503 made in 1964 only.
Issue Price: $75
Market Value: $650

COLT MONTANA TERRITORY CENTENNIAL

Frontier Scout revolver; "1864—Montana Territory Centennial—1964" on left side of barrel; "1889—Diamond Jubilee Statehood—1964" on right side; both markings wiped in gold; 4-3/4-inch barrel; 22 LR only; rosewood or pearlite grips; gold-plated medallions; gold-plated finish, except for blued barrel, frame, base pin screw, cylinder, ejector rod, rod tube, tube plug and tube screw, bolt, and trigger and hammer screws; originally cased in walnut-finished box with red velvet/satin lining; 2300 made in 1964 only.
Issue Price: $75
Market Value: $650

COLT MONTANA TERRITORY CENTENNIAL SINGLE ACTION ARMY

Same barrel markings as Frontier Scout version; 7-1/2-inch barrel, 45 Colt only; same grips, finish, except frame is color case-hardened; same casing as Frontier Scout; 851 made in 1964 only.
Issue Price: $150
Market Value: $1595

COLT NEVADA STATEHOOD CENTENNIAL

Frontier Scout revolver "1864—Nevada Centennial—1964" wiped in silver on left side of 4-3/4-inch barrel; 22 LR only; pearlite grips; nickel-plated medallions; nickel-plated finish, with blued barrel, frame, base pin screw, cylinder ejector rod, rod tube, tube plug and tube screw, hammer, bolt, trigger screws; originally cased in gray-finished wood with blue velvet-lined bottom, silver satin-lined lid; 3984 made in 1964 only.
Issue Price: $75
Market Value: $650

COLT NEVADA STATEHOOD CENTENNIAL SINGLE ACTION ARMY

Same legend on barrel as Frontier Scout; 5-1/2-inch barrel; 45 Colt only; grips, medallions, finish identical to Scout; same casing motif; 1688 made in 1964 only.
Issue Price: $150
Market Value: $1595

COLT NEVADA STATE CENTENNIAL FRONTIER SCOUT SINGLE ACTION ARMY SET

Includes the two handguns described above in oversized case; 189 standard sets were made, plus

577 sets featuring extra engraved cylinders; made in 1964 only.
Issue Price: $240
        ($350 with extra engraved cylinders).

Standard Set
Market Value: $1895

With extra engraved cylinders
Market Value: $1995

COLT NEVADA BATTLE BORN COMMEMORATIVE

Frontier Scout revolver; "1864—Nevada 'Battle Born'—1964" wiped in silver on left side of 4-3/4-inch barrel; 22 LR only; pearlite grips; nickel-plated medallions; nickel-plated, with blued frame, barrel, base pin screw, ejector rod, tube, tube plug and screw, bolt, trigger and hammer screws; cased in blue-finished wood box, with blue velvet/satin lining; 981 made in 1964 only.
Issue Price: $85
Market Value: $650

COLT NEVADA BATTLE BORN COMMEMORATIVE SINGLE ACTION ARMY

Same legend on barrel as Frontier Scout version; 5-1/2-inch barrel; 45 Colt only; same grips, finish, casing as Frontier Scout; 80 made in 1964 only.
Issue Price: $175
Market Value: $1595

COLT NEVADA BATTLE BORN COMMEMORATIVE FRONTIER SCOUT/SINGLE ACTION ARMY SET

Includes the two handguns previously described in oversize case; 20 sets were made in 1964 only.
Issue Price: $265
Market Value: $2695

COLT NEW JERSEY TERCENTENARY

Frontier Scout revolver; "1664—New Jersey Tercentenary—1964" on left side of barrel; 4-3/4-inch barrel; 22 LR only; laminated rosewood grips; nickel-plated medallions; blued finish, with nickel-plated barrel, frame, ejector rod tube, tube plug and screw; originally cased in blonde-finished box with blue velvet lining in bottom, silver satin in lid; 1001 made in 1964 only.
Issue Price: $75
Market Value: $650

COLT NEW JERSEY TERCENTENARY SINGLE ACTION ARMY

Same legend on barrel as Frontier Scout; 5-1/2-inch barrel; 45 Colt only; grips, medallions, finish the same as on Frontier Scout version; same casing; 250 made in 1964 only.
Issue Price: $150
Market Value: $1595

1965 Colt Dodge City
Commemorative

1966 Colt Abilene
Commemorative

COLT PONY EXPRESS PRESENTATION

Single Action Army revolver; "Russell, Majors and Waddell—Pony Express Presentation Model" on left side of barrel. Various Pony Express stop markings on backstrap; 7-1/2-inch barrel; 45 Colt; walnut grips; nickel-plated medallions; nickel-plated in entirety; originally cased in walnut-finished wood with transparent Lucite lid; lined with burgundy velvet; 1004 made in 1964 only.
Issue Price: $250
Market Value: $1595

COLT ST. LOUIS BICENTENNIAL

Frontier Scout revolver; "1764—St. Louis Bicentennial—1964" wiped in gold on left side of 4-3/4-inch barrel; 22 LR only; laminated rosewood grips; gold-plated medallions; gold-plated, except for blued frame, barrel, cylinder, ejector rod, rod tube, tube plug and screw; non-fluted cylinder: originally cased in blonde-finished wood box; yellow velvet/satin lining; 802 made in 1964 only.
Issue Price: $75
Market Value: $650

COLT ST. LOUIS BICENTENNIAL SINGLE ACTION ARMY

Same legend on barrel as Frontier Scout version; 5-1/2-inch barrel; 45 Colt only; same grips, medallions, finish, casing as Scout version; 200 made in 1964 only.
Issue Price: $150
Market Value: $1595

COLT ST. LOUIS BICENTENNIAL FRONTIER SCOUT/SINGLE ACTION ARMY SET

Includes the two handguns described above in oversize case; 200 sets made in 1964 only.
Issue Price: $240
Market Value: $1995

COLT WICHITA COMMEMORATIVE

Frontier Scout revolver; "1864—Kansas Series-Wichita—1964" wiped in silver on left side of 4-3/4-inch barrel; 22 LR only; pearlite grips; gold-plated medallions; gold-plated in entirety; originally cased in blonde-finished wood; lined with red velvet/satin; 500 made in 1964 only.
Issue Price: $85
Market Value: $650

COLT WYATT EARP BUNTLINE

Single Action Army revolver; "Wyatt Earp Buntline Special" on left side of 12-inch barrel; 45 Colt only; laminated black rosewood grips; gold-plated medallions; gold-plated in entirety; originally cased in black-finished wood, lined with green velvet/satin; 150 made only in 1964.
Issue Price: $250
Market Value: $2850

COLT WYOMING DIAMOND JUBILEE

Frontier Scout revolver "1890—Wyoming Diamond Jubilee—1965" on left side of barrel; 4-3/4-inch barrel; 22 LR only; rosewood grips, nickel-plated medallions; nickel-plated finish, except for blued barrel, frame, ejector rod, rod tube, tube plug and plug screw; cased in blond-finished box, with blue velvet bottom lining, silver satin-lined lid; 2357 made in 1964 only.
Issue Price: $75
Market Value: $650

ITHACA MODEL 48 ST. LOUIS BICENTENNIAL

Lever-action; single shot; hand-operated rebounding hammer; 22 LR, 22 Long, 22 Short; 18-inch barrel; Western carbine-style straight stock; open rear sight, ramp front. Only 200 manufactured in 1964.
Issue Price: $34.95
Market Value: $295

REMINGTON MONTANA CENTENNIAL

Model 600 carbine; bolt action; 6mm Rem. only; deviates from standard Model 600 specs only in better walnut; commemorative medallion inlaid into the stock; barrel inscription reads, "1889-1964/75th Anniversary"; 1000 made in 1964 only.
Issue Price: $124.95
Market Value: $595

WINCHESTER WYOMING DIAMOND JUBILEE COMMEMORATIVE

Model 94 carbine; 30-30 only; 1500 made, distributed exclusively by Billings Hardware Co.; same as standard M94, except for color case-hardened, engraved receiver, commemorative inscription on barrel; brass saddle ring, loading gate; state medallion embedded in stock; made only in 1964.
Issue Price: $100
Market Value: $1495

1965

COLT APPOMATTOX CENTENNIAL

Frontier Scout revolver; "1865—Appomattox Commemorative Model—1965" wiped in silver on left side of 4-3/4-inch barrel; 22 LR only; laminated rosewood grips; nickel-plated medallions; nickel-plated finish, with blued barrel, frame, backstrap and trigger guard screws, ejector rod tube, tube plug and tube screw; originally cased in blonde-finished wood lined with blue velvet on bottom, gray satin in lid; 1001 made in 1965 only.
Issue Price: $75
Market Value: $650

COLT APPOMATTOX CENTENNIAL FRONTIER SINGLE ACTION ARMY

Same legend on 5-1/2-inch barrel; 45 Colt only; grips, finish, casing the same as for Frontier Scout version; 250 made in 1965.
Issue Price: $150
Market Value: $1595

COLT APPOMATTOX CENTENNIAL FRONTIER SCOUT/SINGLE ACTION ARMY COMBO

Same specs as the two revolvers described above in one oversize case; 250 sets made in 1965 only.
Issue Price: $240
Market Value: $1995

COLT COLORADO GOLD RUSH COMMEMORATIVE

Frontier Scout revolver; "1858—Colorado Gold Rush—1878" wiped in silver on left side of 4-3/4-inch barrel; 22 LR only; laminated rosewood grips; nickel-plated medallions; gold-plated finish, with nickel-plated hammer, base pin and screw, ejector rod head, hammer and trigger screws, trigger, grip screw; originally cased in blonde-finished wood; black velvet/satin lining; 1350 made in 1965 only.
Issue Price: $85
Market Value: $675

COLT DODGE CITY COMMEMORATIVE

Frontier Scout revolver; "1864—Kansas Series-Dodge City—1964" wiped in silver on left side of 4-3/4-inch barrel; 22 LR only; ivorylite grips; gold-plated medallions; gold-plated finish, with blued base pin and screw, ejector rod, ejector rod head, bolt and trigger screw, hammer and hammer screw, trigger; originally cased in blonde-finished wood; lined with kelly green velvet/satin; 500 made in 1965 only.
Issue Price: $85
Market Value: $650

COLT FORTY-NINER MINER

Frontier Scout revolver: "The '49er Miner" wiped in gold on left side of 4-3/4-inch barrel; 22 LR only; laminated rosewood grips; gold-plated medallions; gold-plated finish with blued barrel, frame, backstrap and trigger guard assembly, ejector rod, tube and tube plug, ejector tube screw; originally cased in walnut-finished wood; lined with velvet in bottom, blue satin in lid; 500 made only in 1965.
Issue Price: $85
Market Value: $650

COLT GENERAL MEADE CAMPAIGN COMMEMORATIVE

Frontier Scout revolver: "Gen. Meade Pennsylvania Campaign Model" wiped in gold on left side of 4-3/4-inch barrel; 22 LR only; ivorylite grips, gold-plated medallions; gold-plated finish; blued frame, barrel, cylinder, ejector rod tube, tube plug and screw, hammer and trigger screws; originally cased in walnut-finished wood; blue velvet lining in bottom, gold satin in lid; 1197 made in 1965 only.
Issue Price: $75
Market Value: $650

COLT GENERAL MEADE CAMPAIGN SINGLE ACTION ARMY REVOLVER

Same legend on the 5-1/2-inch barrel; 45 Colt only; same finish, casing as Frontier Scout version; 200 made in 1965 only.
Issue Price: $165
Market Value: $1695

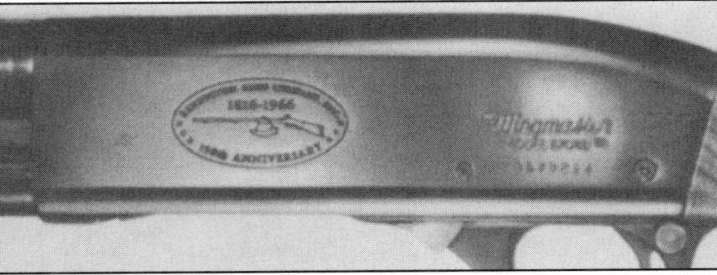

1966 Remington 150th Anniversary Model 1100SA   1966 Remington 150th Anniversary Model 870SA

COLT OLD FORT DES MOINES RECONSTRUCTION COMMEMORATIVE

Frontier Scout revolver; "Reconstruction of Old Fort Des Moines" wiped in silver on left side of 4-3/4-inch barrel; 22 LR only; pearlite grips; gold-plated medallions; gold-plated in entirety; originally cased in white-finished wood; royal purple velvet lining in bottom; white satin in lid; 700 made in 1965 only.
Issue Price: $89.95
Market Value: $675

COLT OLD FORT DES MOINES RECONSTRUCTION SINGLE ACTION ARMY

Same legend on 5-1/2-inch barrel; 45 Colt only; grips, finish the same as on Frontier Scout version; same casing; 100 made in 1965 only.
Issue Price: $169.95
Market Value: $1695

COLT OLD FORT DES MOINES FRONTIER SCOUT/SINGLE ACTION ARMY COMBO

Same specs as the two revolvers described above, in one oversize case; 100 sets made in 1965 only.
Issue Price: $289.95
Market Value: $2195

COLT OREGON TRAIL COMMEMORATIVE

Frontier Scout revolver; "Oregon Trail Model," wiped in gold, on left side of 4-3/4-inch barrel; 22 LR only; pearlite grips; gold-plated medallions; blued finish with gold-plated backstrap and trigger guard assembly and screws, hammer, trigger and screws, base pin, base pin screw and ejector rod head; originally cased in blonde-finished wood; lined with blue velvet in bottom, gold satin in lid; 1995 made only in 1965.
Issue Price: $75
Market Value: $650

COLT JOAQUIN MURRIETTA 1 OF 100

Frontier Scout/Single Action Army combo; both have "Joaquin Murrietta 1 of 100" on left side of barrels; Scout has 4-3/4-inch barrel, 22 LR only; SAA has 5-1/2-inch barrel, 45 Colt only; grips on both are pearlite, with gold-plated medallions; finish for both is gold-plated with blued barrels, frames, ejector rod tubes; originally in one oversize case of walnut-finished wood; blue velvet/satin lining; 100 sets made in 1965 only.
Issue Price: $350
Market Value: $1995

COLT ST. AUGUSTINE QUADRICENTENNIAL

Frontier Scout revolver; "1565—St. Augustine Quadricentennial—1965" wiped in gold on left side of 4-3/4-inch barrel; 22 LR only; pearlite grips; gold-plated medallions; blued finish, with blued barrel, base pin, ejector rod, tube, tube plug and screw, frame, hammer and trigger screws, backstrap and trigger guard assembly and screws; cased in blonde-finished wood; gold velvet/satin lining; 500 made in 1965 only.
Issue Price: $85
Market Value: $675

1966

COLT ABERCROMBIE & FITCH TRAILBLAZER

New Frontier Single Action Army revolver: "Abercrombie & Fitch Co." wiped in gold on left side of 7-1/2-inch barrel; 45 Colt only; rosewood grips; gold-plated medallions; gold-plated finish, blued barrel, cylinder, hammer, sights, ejector rod tube, ejector rod screw, case-hardened frame; roll-engraved, nonfluted cylinder; originally cased in varnished American walnut with brass-framed glass cover; bottom lined with crushed blue velvet; 200 made in 1966 with "New York" marked on butt, 100 with "Chicago" butt marking; 200 with "San Francisco" butt marking.
Issue Price: $275
Market Value: $1495

COLT ABILENE COMMEMORATIVE

Frontier Scout revolver; "1866—Kansas Series Abilene—1966" wiped in silver on left side of 4-3/4-inch barrel; 22 LR only; laminated rosewood grips; gold-plated medallions; gold-plated in entirety; originally cased in blonde-finished wood; blue velvet/satin lining; 500 made in 1966 only.
Issue Price: $95
Market Value: $650

COLT DAKOTA TERRITORY COMMEMORATIVE

Frontier Scout revolver; "1861—Dakota Territory—1889" wiped in gold on left side of 4-3/4-inch barrel; 22 LR only; laminated rosewood grips; gold-plated medallions; blued finish with gold-plated backstrap and trigger guard assembly and screws, ejector rod and head, base pin, trigger, hammer, stock screw; originally cased in blonde-finished wood; red velvet/satin lining; 1000 made in 1966 only.
Issue Price: $85
Market Value: $650

COLT INDIANA SESQUICENTENNIAL

Frontier Scout revolver; "1816—Indiana Sesquicentennial—1966" wiped in gold on left side of 4-3/4-inch barrel; 22 LR only; pearlite grips; gold-plated medallions; blued finish, with gold-plated backstrap and trigger guard assembly, base pin and screw, ejector rod head, cylinder, bolt and trigger screw, hammer and hammer screw, trigger, stock screw; originally cased in blonde-finished wood; bottom lined with gold velvet, lid with blue satin; 1500 made in 1966 only.
Issue Price: $85
Market Value: $650

COLT OKLAHOMA TERRITORY COMMEMORATIVE

Frontier Scout revolver; "1890—Oklahoma Diamond Jubilee—1965" wiped in gold on left side of 4-3/4-inch barrel; 22 LR only; laminated rosewood grips; gold-plated medallions; blued finish with gold-plated backstrap and trigger guard assembly and screws, cylinder, ejector rod head, base pin and screw, bolt and trigger; cased in blonde-finished wood; red velvet/satin lining; 1343 made only in 1966.
Issue Price: $85
Market Value: $650

REMINGTON 150TH ANNIVERSARY MODEL 552A

Semi-automatic rifle; 22 LR, 22 Long, 22 Short; same specs as standard Model 552 except stamp-engraved legend on left side of receiver: "Remington Arms Company Inc., 1816-1966, 150th Anniversary," with corporate logo; 1000 made in 1966 only.
Issue Price: $58
Market Value: $475

REMINGTON 150TH ANNIVERSARY MODEL 572A

Slide-action rifle; 22 Short, 22 Long, 22 LR; same specs as standard model 572 except stamp-engraved legend on left side of receiver: "Remington Arms Company, Inc., 1816-1966, 150th Anniversary," with corporate logo; 1000 made in 1966 only.
Issue Price: $60
Market Value: $475

REMINGTON 150TH ANNIVERSARY MODEL 742 ADL

Semi-automatic rifle; 30-06 only; impressed basketweave checkering; has same specs as standard 742 ADL, except for stamp-engraved legend on left side of receiver; "Remington Arms Company Inc., 1816-1966, 150th Anniversary" with corporate logo; 1000 made in 1966 only.
Issue Price: $150
Market Value: $500

REMINGTON 150TH ANNIVERSARY MODEL 760 ADL

Pump-action rifle; 30-06 only; same specs as standard 760 BDL Deluxe model except stamp-engraved legend on left side of receiver: "Remington Arms Company Inc., 1816-1966, 150th Anniversary," with corporate logo; 1000 made in 1966 only.
Issue Price: $135
Market Value: $595

REMINGTON 150TH ANNIVERSARY MODEL 870 SA

Slide-action Skeet gun; 12-ga. only; 26-inch barrel; vent rib; specs the same as standard Model 870, except for stamp-engraved legend on left side of receiver: "Remington Arms Company, Inc., 1816-1966, 150th Anniversary" with corporate logo; 1000 made in 1966 only.
Issue Price: $130
Market Value: $550

REMINGTON 150TH ANNIVERSARY MODEL 870 TB

Same specs as Remington 150th Anniversary Model 870 SA except recoil pad; 30-inch barrel; trap stock; same stamp-engraved legend on receiver; 1000 made in 1966 only.
Issue Price: $165
Market Value: $700

REMINGTON 150TH ANNIVERSARY MODEL 1100 SA

Semi-automatic Skeet shotgun; 12-ga. only; 26-inch barrel; vent rib; specs the same as standard Model 1100, except for stamp-engraved legend on left side of receiver: "Remington Arms Company, Inc., 1816-1966, 150th Anniversary" with corporate logo; 1000 made in 1966 only.
Issue Price: $185
Market Value: $700

1966 Winchester Centennial '66 Commemorative 20″ Barrel

1966 Winchester Centennial '66 Commemorative 26″ Barrel

REMINGTON 150TH ANNIVERSARY MODEL 1100 TB

Same specs as Remington 150th Anniversary Model 1100 SA except recoil pad; 30-inch barrel; trap stock; same stamp-engraved legend on receiver; 1000 made in 1966 only.
Issue Price: $220
Market Value: $750

REMINGTON 150TH ANNIVERSARY NYLON 66

Semi-automatic; 22 LR; same specs as standard Nylon 66 Apache Black model except stamp-engraved legend on left side of receiver "Remington Arms Company Inc., 1816-1966, 150th Anniversary," with corporate logo; 1000 made in 1966 only.
Issue Price: $50
Market Value: $495

WINCHESTER NEBRASKA CENTENNIAL COMMEMORATIVE

Model 94 carbine; 30-30 only; same as standard M94 except gold-plated loading gate, buttplate, rear barrel band, hammer; commemorative inscription on barrel, medallion in stock; only 2500 made and distributed only in Nebraska; made only in 1966.
Issue Price: $100
Market Value: $1395

WINCHESTER CENTENNIAL '66 COMMEMORATIVE

Model 94; rifle and carbine versions commemorate Winchester's 100th anniversary; produced in 1966 only; 100,478 were made; 30-30 only; rifle version with 26-inch half-octagon barrel; full-length 8-shot magazine; gold-plated forearm cap, receiver; post front sight, open rear; walnut stock forearm with epoxy finish; saddle ring; brass buttplate; commemorative inscription on barrel and top tang. Carbine differs only in shorter forearm; 20-inch barrel; 6-shot magazine.
Issue Price: $125

RIFLE, CARBINE

Market Value: $1206

MATCHED SET WITH CONSECUTIVE SERIAL NUMBERS

Market Value: $2400

1967

COLT ALAMO COMMEMORATIVE

Frontier Scout revolver; "Alamo Model," flanked by stars, wiped in gold on left side of 4-3/4-inch barrel; 22 LR only; ivorylite grips, with inlaid gold-plated Texas star below screw on left grip. Gold-plated finish; blued barrel, frame, ejector rod tube, tube plug and screw; originally cased in blonde-finished wood box; blue velvet/satin lining; 4250 made in 1967 only.
Issue Price: $85
Market Value: $650

COLT ALAMO COMMEMORATIVE SINGLE ACTION ARMY

Same legend on barrel; same grips, finish, but with blued barrel, frame and ejector rod tube and tube screw; same casing; 750 made in 1967 only.
Issue Price: $165
Market Value: $1595

COLT ALAMO COMMEMORATIVE FRONTIER SCOUT/SINGLE ACTION ARMY COMBO

Includes two revolvers described above in one oversize case; 250 sets made in 1967 only.
Issue Price: $265
Market Value: $1995

COLT BAT MASTERSON

Frontier Scout revolver; "Lawman Series—Bat Masterson" on left side of 4-3/4-inch barrel; 22 LR only; checkered rubber eagle grips; nickel-plated finish; cased originally in black leatherette; red velvet/satin lining; 3000 made in 1967 only.
Issue Price: $90
Market Value: $675

COLT BAT MASTERSON SINGLE ACTION ARMY

Same legend on 4-3/4-inch barrel; 45 Colt only; grips, finish, casing are the same as for Frontier Scout version; 500 made in 1967 only.
Issue Price: $180
Market Value: $1600

COLT CHATEAU THIERRY COMMEMORATIVE

Semi-automatic; Model 1911 A1; "1917 World War I Commemorative 1967" on right side of slide; roll-engraved scene on left depicting WWI battle; 5-inch barrel; 45 auto; checkered walnut grips; inlaid commemorative medallions; left grip inlaid with Chateau Thierry battle bar; blued finish with slide scene, serial number, banner, Colt markings wiped in gold; several features including no trigger finger relief cuts, non-grooved trigger, safety lever, adapted from original M1911 design; Standard model cased in olive drab box; Deluxe and Custom models have oiled, waxed teak cases; Deluxe model case inscribed "One of Seventy-Five/Deluxe Engraved/Chateau Thierry Commemoratives"; Custom model case inscribed "One of Twenty-Five/Custom Engraved/ Chateau Thierry Commemoratives"; gun bears gold-filled signature of A.A White, engraver; 7400 Standard versions made in 1967-68, 75 Deluxe, 25 Custom.
Issue Price: Standard, $200; Deluxe, $500; Custom, $1000

Standard
Market Value: $995

Deluxe
Market Value: $1450

Custom
Market Value: $2850

COLT CHISHOLM TRAIL COMMEMORATIVE

Frontier Scout revolver; "1867—Kansas Series— Chisholm Trail—1967" wiped with silver on left side of 4-3/4-inch barrel; 22 LR; pearlite grips; nickel-plated medallions; blued finish, with nickel-plated backstrap and trigger guard assembly and screws, trigger, hammer base pin, ejector rod head, stock screw; originally cased in blonde-finished wood, gold velvet/ satin lining; 500 made in 1967 only.
Issue Price: $100
Market Value: $650

COLT COFFEYVILLE COMMEMORATIVE

Frontier Scout revolver; "1866—Kansas Series— Coffeyville—1966" wiped in silver on left side of 4-3/4-inch barrel; 22 LR only; walnut grips; gold-plated medallions; gold-plated finish; blued backstrap and trigger guard assembly screws, base pin and screw, ejector rod, ejector rod head, hammer and hammer screw, trigger; originally cased in blonde-finished wood; black velvet/satin lining; 500 made in 1967 only.
Issue Price: $95
Market Value: $650

REMINGTON CANADIAN CENTENNIAL

Model 742 rifle; semi-automatic; 30-06 only; same as standard model except impressed checkering on pistol grip; left side of receiver is engraved with maple leaves, special insignia, "1867-1967—Canadian Centennial Gun," wiped in white; serial number is preceded by letter C; 1000 made in 1967 only.
Issue Price: $119.95
Market Value: $495

RUGER CANADIAN CENTENNIAL 10/22

Standard model of 22 rimfire rifle with silver commemorative medal set in the stock; top of the receiver is engraved with a design composed of the Canadian Exposition symbol, branches of the Canadian maple leaf and the words, "Canadian Centennial Guns." Issued in 1967; 4430 made.
Issue Price: $99.50
Market Value: $550

WINCHESTER ALASKAN PURCHASE CENTENNIAL

Model 94 rifle; sold only in Alaska; receiver engraved in 19th Century filigree for "antique" appeal; centered in stock is the official Alaskan Purchase centennial medallion with totem pole symbol of the state; barrel is 26-inch, with magazine capacity of 8 shots; other facets are standard of Model 94. Introduced, 1967.
Issue Price: $125
Market Value: $1695

WINCHESTER CANADIAN CENTENNIAL

Model 64; action obviously is the Model 94; not to be confused with Winchester's Model 64 boy's rifle discontinued in 1963. Canadian commemorative is in 30-30 caliber; octagonal 26-inch rifle or 20-inch carbine barrel; black-chromed receiver engraved with maple leaf motif; forearm tip black-chromed; straight stock finished with "antique gloss." Both versions have a dovetail bead post front sight, buckhorn rear. Carbine comes with saddle ring; 6-shot magazine; the rifle comes with 8-shot magazine. Gold-filled inscription on barrel reads, "Canadian Centennial 1867-1967." Introduced in 1967.
Issue Price: Rifle or Carbine, $125; Matching Set with consecutive serial numbers, $275

Rifle
Market Value: $1095

Carbine
Market Value: $1075

Matched Set
Market Value: $1950

1968 Colt Nebraska Centennial

1967 Colt Bat Masterson

1968 Colt Pat Garrett
Commemorative

1967 Winchester Canadian Centennial

1968 Colt Belleau Wood Commemorative

1968

COLT BELLEAU WOOD COMMEMORATIVE
Semi-automatic; Model 1911 A1; "1917 World War I Commemorative 1967" on right side of slide; roll engraved scene on left side of machine gun battle; 5-inch barrel; 45 Auto only; rosewood grips inlaid with commemorative medallions; left grip inlaid with Belleau Wood battle bar; blued finish; slide scene, serial number, banner, Colt markings wiped in gold on Standard model; Deluxe version has slide, frame hand engraved, serial numbers gold-inlaid; Custom has more elaborate engraving; the same features of 1911 model adapted to Chateau Thierry model are incorporated; cases are same as Chateau Thierry model, with brass plate for Deluxe engraved "One of Seventy Five/Deluxe Engraved/Belleau Wood Commemorative"; plate on Custom model reads "One of Twenty-Five/Custom Engraved/Belleau Wood Commemoratives"; production began in 1968, with 7400 Standard types, 75 Deluxe, 25 Custom.
Issue Price: Standard, $200; Deluxe, $500; Custom, $1000.

Standard
Market Value: $895

Deluxe
Market Value: $1450

Custom
Market Value: $2850

COLT GEN. NATHAN BEDFORD FORREST
Frontier Scout revolver; "General Nathan Bedford Forrest" on left side of 4-3/4-inch barrel; 22 LR only; laminated rosewood grips; gold-plated medallions; gold-plated finish; blued cylinder, backstrap and trigger guard assembly; originally cased in dark brown leatherette; red velvet/satin lining; 3000 made in 1968-69.
Issue Price: $110
Market Value: $650

COLT NEBRASKA CENTENNIAL
Frontier Scout revolver; "1867—Nebraska Centennial—1967" on left side of 4-3/4-inch barrel; 22 LR; pearlite grips; gold-plated barrel, frame, hammer, trigger, ejector rod head, stock screw; originally cased in blonde-finished wood; lined with

blue velvet in bottom, gold satin in lid; 7001 made in 1968 only.
Issue Price: $100
Market Value: $625

COLT PAT GARRETT COMMEMORATIVE
Frontier Scout revolver; "Lawman Series Pat Garrett" on right side of 4-3/4-inch barrel; 22 LR only; pearlite grips; gold-plated medallions; gold-plated finish; nickel-plated barrel, frame, backstrap and trigger guard assembly, ejector rod; loading gate is gold-plated; originally cased in black leatherette with gold velvet/satin lining; 3000 made in 1968 only.
Issue Price: $110
Market Value: $475

COLT PAT GARRETT SINGLE ACTION ARMY REVOLVER
Same barrel legend; 5-1/2-inch barrel; 45 Colt only; same grips, finish, casing as Frontier Scout version; 500 made in 1968.
Issue Price: $200
Market Value: $1595

COLT PAWNEE TRAIL COMMEMORATIVE
Frontier Scout revolver; "1868-Kansas Series—Pawnee Trail—1968" wiped in silver on left side of 4-3/4-inch barrel; 22 LR; laminated rosewood grips; nickel-plated medallions; blued finish; nickel-plated backstrap and trigger guard assembly and screws, cylinder, base pin, ejector rod head, trigger hammer, stock screw; originally cased in blonde-finished wood; lined with blue velvet in bottom, silver satin in lid; 501 made in 1968.
Issue Price: $110
Market Value: $650

COLT SANTA FE TRAIL COMMEMORATIVE
Frontier Scout revolver; "Kansas Series—Santa Fe Trail—1968" wiped in silver on left side of 4-3/4-inch barrel; 22 LR; ivorylite grips; nickel-plated medallions; blued finish with nickel-plated backstrap and trigger guard assembly and screws, hammer, trigger, stock screw, base pin, ejector rod head; originally cased in blonde-finished wood; green velvet/satin lining; 501 made in 1968-69.
Issue Price: $120
Market Value: $650

FRANCHI CENTENNIAL
Semi-automatic take-down rifle; 22 LR only; commemorates 1868-1968 centennial of S.A. Luigi Franchi; centennial seal engraved on receiver; 21-inch barrel; 11-shot buttstock magazine; hand-checkered European walnut stock forearm; open rear sight, gold bead front on ramp. Deluxe model has better grade wood, fully engraved receiver. Made only in 1968.
Issue Price: Standard, $86.95; Deluxe, $124.95.

Standard
Market Value: $425 to $450

Deluxe
Market Value: $550 to $575

WINCHESTER BUFFALO BILL COMMEMORATIVE
Model 94; available with either 20-inch or 26-inch barrel, both with bead post front sights, semi-buckhorn rear sights. Hammer, trigger, loading gate, forearm tip, saddle ring, crescent buttplate nickel-plated. Barrel, tang inscribed respectively, "Buffalo Bill Commemorative" and "W.F. Cody—Chief of Scouts." Receiver embellished with scrollwork. American walnut stock with embedded Buffalo Bill Memorial Assn. medallion; rifle with 8-shot tubular magazine, carbine with 6-shot magazine. Introduced, 1968.
Issue Price: Rifle, Carbine, $129.95 Rifle marked "1 of 300", $1000

Rifle
Market Value: $1200

Rifle marked "1 of 300"
Market Value: $2750

Carbine
Market Value: $1200

WINCHESTER ILLINOIS SESQUICENTENNIAL
Model 94; "Land of Lincoln," and a profile of Lincoln engraved on the receiver, with gold-filled inscription on barrel, "Illinois Sesquicentennial, 1818-1968"; gold-plated metal buttplate, trigger, loading gate and saddle ring. Official souvenir medallion embedded in walnut stock. First state commemorative to be sold outside the celebrating state by Winchester. Introduced in 1968.
Issue Price: $110
Market Value: $1495

1969 Colt Alabama Sesquicentennial

1969 Colt Second Battle of the Marne Commemorative

1969 Colt Meuse Argonne Commemorative

1969

COLT ALABAMA SESQUICENTENNIAL

Frontier Scout revolver; "1819—Alabama Sesquicentennial—1969" on left side of 4-3/4-inch barrel; 22 LR only; ivorylite grips; gold-plated medallions; gold-plated finish; nickel-plated loading gate, cylinder, ejector rod, rod head, and tube, base pin and screw, bolt and trigger guard assembly screws, hammer and screw, trigger; originally cased in red leatherette covered wood box; white velvet lining in bottom, red satin in lid; 3001 made in 1969.
Issue Price: $110
Market Value: $650

COLT ARKANSAS TERRITORIAL SESQUICENTENNIAL

Frontier Scout revolver; "1819—Arkansas Territory Sesquicentennial—1969" on left side of 4-3/4-inch barrel; 22 LR only; laminated rosewood grips; gold-plated medallions; blued frame, backstrap and trigger guard assembly, ejector rod head; gold-plated stock screw nut; originally cased in blonde-finished basswood; red velvet/satin lining; 3500 made; production began in 1969.
Issue Price: $110
Market Value: $650

COLT CALIFORNIA BICENTENNIAL

Frontier Scout revolver; "1769—California Bicentennial—1969" on left side of 6-inch barrel; 22 LR only; laminated rosewood grips; gold-plated medallions; gold-plated finish; all screws nickel-plated, except base pin, grip screws; hammer, trigger also nickel-plated; originally cased in California redwood; black velvet/satin lining; 5000 made in 1969-70.
Issue Price: $135
Market Value: $650

COLT FORT LARNED COMMEMORATIVE

Frontier Scout revolver; "1869—Kansas Series-Fort Larned—1969" on left side of 4-3/4-inch barrel; 22 LR; pearlite grips; nickel-plated medallions; nickel-plated finish; blued backstrap and trigger guard assembly, base pin and screw, cylinder, ejector rod head and tube screw, hammer and stock screw, bolt and trigger screw; originally cased in blonde finished wood; blue velvet lining in bottom; silver satin in lid; 500 made in 1969-70.
Issue Price: $120
Market Value: $650

COLT GOLDEN SPIKE

Frontier Scout revolver; "1869—Golden Spike—1969" on right side of 6-inch barrel; standard barrel markings on left; both wiped in gold; 22 LR only; sand-blasted walnut-stained fir grips; gold-plated medallions; gold-plated finish; blued barrel, frame, backstrap and trigger guard assembly and ejector tube plug and screw; originally cased in hand-stained, embossed simulated mahogany; 11,000 made in 1969.
Issue Price: $135
Market Value: $650

COLT WILD BILL HICKOK COMMEMORATIVE

Frontier Scout revolver; "Lawman Series—Wild Bill Hickok" wiped in silver on right side of 6-inch barrel; 22 LR only; nonfluted cylinder; pearlite grips; nickel-plated medallions; nickel-plated finish; blued barrel, frame, ejector tube screw; originally cased in black leatherette covered box; bottom lined in blue velvet, lid in silver satin; 3000 made, production began in 1969.
Issue Price: $116.60
Market Value: $675

COLT WILD BILL HICKOK COMMEMORATIVE SINGLE ACTION ARMY

Same legend on 7-1/2-inch barrel; 45 Colt only; same finish as Frontier Scout version, except for nickel-plated loading gate; same casing; 500 made, production beginning in 1969.
Issue Price: $220
Market Value: $1695

COLT MEUSE ARGONNE COMMEMORATIVE

Semi-automatic; Model 1911A1; "1917 World War I Commemorative 1967" on right side of slide; left has roll-engraved charge on pillbox on Standard; slides, frames on Deluxe, Custom models are hand engraved, serial numbers inlaid in gold; Custom model is more elaborately engraved, inlaid; 5-inch barrel, 45 Auto only; varnished crotch walnut grips; inlaid commemorative medallions left grip inlaid with Meuse Argonne battle bar; blued finish; engraving, numbers et. al., gold wiped on Standard model; same case as earlier WWI Commemoratives; brass plate for Deluxe reads "One of Seventy-Five/ Deluxe Engraved/Meuse Argonne Commemoratives"; plate on Custom case is inscribed "One of Seventy Five/Custom Engraved/Meuse Argonne Commemoratives"; production began in 1969; 7400 Standard, 75 Deluxe, 25 Custom.
Issue Price: Standard, $220; Deluxe, $500; Custom, $1000

Standard		
Market Value: $495		
Deluxe		
Market Value: $1550		
Custom		
Market Value: $2950		

COLT SECOND BATTLE OF THE MARNE COMMEMORATIVE

Semi-automatic; Model 1911A1; "1917 World War I Commemorative 1967" on right side of slide; roll-engraved combat scene on left side of slide; 5-inch barrel; 45 Auto; white French holly grips; inlaid commemorative medallions; left grip inlaid with 2nd Battle of the Marne battle bar; blue finish, with slide engraving, serial number on Standard, banner, other markings wiped in gold; Deluxe and Custom models are hand engraved, with serial numbers gold inlaid; work on Custom model is in greater detail; cases are same as others in series, except Deluxe case has brass plate inscribed "One of Seventy-Five/Deluxe Engraved/2nd Battle of the Marne Commemorative"; Custom case has same type of plate inscribed "One of Twenty-Five/Custom Engraved/2nd Battle of the Marne Commemorative"; 7400 Standard guns made in 1969; 75 Deluxe; 25 Custom.
Issue Price: Standard, $220; Deluxe, $500; Custom, $1000

Standard		
Market Value: $995		
Deluxe		
Market Value: $1550		
Custom		
Market Value: $2950		

COLT SHAWNEE TRAIL COMMEMORATIVE

Frontier Scout revolver; "1869—Kansas Series—Shawnee Trail 1969" wiped in silver on left side of 4-3/4-inch barrel; 22 LR only; laminated rosewood grips; nickel-plated medallions; blued finish; nickel-plated backstrap and trigger guard assembly and screws, cylinder, base pin, ejector rod head, hammer, trigger and stock screw; originally cased in blonde-finished wood; red velvet/satin lining; 501 made in 1969 only.
Issue Price: $120
Market Value: $650

COLT TEXAS RANGER COMMEMORATIVE

Single Action Army revolver; "Texas Ranger Commemoratives/One Riot-One Ranger" wiped in silver on left side of barrel; "Texas Rangers" roll engraved on backstrap; sterling silver star, wreath on top of backstrap behind hammer; YO Ranch brand stamped on bottom of backstrap; 7-1/2-inch barrel; 45 Colt only; Standard model has rosewood grips, silver miniature Ranger badge inlaid in left grip; blued finish; case-hardened frame; nickel-plated trigger guard, base pin and screw, ejector rod and head, ejector tube screw; gold-plated stock screw, stock escutcheons, medallions. First 200 are custom models, with finish decoration to customer's desires at increasing prices; custom finished guns had deluxe engraved serial numbers, ivory grips with star inlay; originally cased in special hand-rubbed box with drawers, glass top; red velvet lining; 200 Custom, 800 Standard guns made; production began in 1969.
Issue Price: Custom, varying with customers desires; Standard, $650

Standard		
Market Value: $2450		
Grade III		
Market Value: $5200		
Grade II		
Market Value: $5700		
Grade I		
Market Value: $6200		

1969 Winchester
Golden Spike

1970 Colt World War II
Pacific Theater

1969 Winchester
Cowboy Commemorative

1970 Colt World War II
European Theater

1970 Colt Missouri Territorial
Sesquicentennial

WINCHESTER COWBOY COMMEMORATIVE

Model 94; receiver, upper and lower tang, lever, barrel bands are nickel-plated; butt plate is stainless steel, with tang that extends over top of stock for square comb look; stock is straight grip with extended forearm of American walnut; embedded in right side of stock is medallion of cowboy roping a steer; etched on left side of receiver, "Brave Land—Bold Men." Opposite side is engraved with coiled lariat, spurs; barrel is 20-inch, carrying "Cowboy Commemorative"; upper tang has inscription, "Winchester Model 1894." Has adjustable semi-buckhorn rear sight, blued saddle ring; in 30-30 only. Introduced in 1969.
Issue Price: $125; Marked "1 of 300", $1000
Market Value: $1300

Marked "1 of 300"
Market Value: $2950

WINCHESTER GOLDEN SPIKE

Model 94; features 20-inch barrel with twin barrel bands plated in yellow gold; yellow gold receiver, engraved with decorative scrolled border on right side, inscribed on other side with railroad spike flanked by dates, 1869 and 1969. Barrel carries "Golden Spike Commemorative" inscription; upper tang bears words "Oceans United By Rail." Buttstock, forearm are straight-line design of satin-finished American walnut, with fluted comb. Inset in stock is centennial medallion of engines of Central Pacific, Union Pacific meeting on May 10, 1869. It has straight brass buttplate, blued saddle ring; chambered for 30-30; weight is 7 lbs. Introduced in 1969.
Issue Price: $119.95
Market Value: $1295

WINCHESTER THEODORE ROOSEVELT COMMEMORATIVE

Model 94 rifle and carbine; made in 1969 only; 49,505 manufactured; 30-30 only; rifle has 26-inch octagonal barrel; 6-shot half-magazine; forearm cap, upper tang, receiver plated with white gold; receiver engraved with American eagle, "26th President 1901-1909," Roosevelt's facsimile signature; contoured lever, half pistol grip; medallion in stock. Carbine differs from rifle in shorter forearm, full-length 6-shot tubular magazine; 20-inch barrel.
Issue Price: $125

Rifle
Market Value: $1500

Carbine
Market Value: $1400

Matched set with consecutive serial numbers
Market Value: $2600

1970

COLT FORT HAYS COMMEMORATIVE

Frontier Scout revolver; "1870—Fort Hays—1970" wiped in silver on left side of 4-3/4-inch barrel; 22 LR only; hard rubber grips; nickel-plated finish; blued barrel, backstrap and trigger guard assembly screws, cylinder, base pin screw, ejector tube screw, bolt and trigger screw, hammer screw, trigger; originally cased in blonde finished wood; bottom lined with blue velvet, gold satin in lid; 500 made in 1970.
Issue Price: $130
Market Value: $650

COLT FORT RILEY COMMEMORATIVE

Frontier Scout revolver; "1870—Kansas Series—Fort Riley—1970" wiped in black on left side of 4-3/4-inch barrel; 22 LR only; ivorylite grips; nickel-plated medallions; nickel-plated finish; blued backstrap and trigger guard assembly, cylinder, base pin and screw, ejector rod head and tube screw, bolt and trigger screw, hammer and screw, trigger, stock screw; originally cased in blonde-finished wood; black velvet/satin lining; 500 made in 1970.
Issue Price: $130
Market Value: $650

COLT MAINE SESQUICENTENNIAL

Frontier Scout revolver; "1820—Maine Sesquicentennial—1970" on left side of 4-3/4-inch barrel; 22 LR only nonfluted cylinder; pearlite grips; gold-plated medallions; gold-plated finish; nickel-plated backstrap and trigger guard assembly, cylinder, base pin screw, hammer and hammer screw, ejector rod head, ejector tube screw, bolt and trigger screw; originally cased in natural knotty white pine; lined with royal blue velvet in bottom; light blue satin in lid; 3000 made in 1970.
Issue Price: $120
Market Value: $650

COLT MISSOURI TERRITORIAL SESQUICENTENNIAL

Frontier Scout revolver; "1820-Missouri Sesquicentennial—1970" wiped in gold on left side of 4-3/4-inch barrel; 22 LR only; walnut grips; gold-plated medallions; blued finish; gold-plated cylinder, loading gate, base pin, ejector rod head, ejector tube, tube screw, bolt and trigger screw, hammer, trigger, stock screw, top backstrap screws; originally cased in natural finish willow, lined in red velvet; 3000 made in 1970.
Issue Price: $125
Market Value: $650

COLT MISSOURI TERRITORIAL SESQUICENTENNIAL SINGLE ACTION ARMY

Same legend on the 5-1/2-inch barrel; 45 Colt only; grips, medallions, finish and plating are same as Frontier Scout version, except for case-hardened frame, loading gate; same casing; 900 made; production started in 1970.
Issue Price: $220
Market Value: $1695

COLT WORLD WAR II/EUROPEAN THEATER

Semi-automatic; Model 1911A1; slide is marked "World War II Commemorative/European Theater of Operations" on left side; right side is roll-engraved with major sites of activity; 5-inch barrel; 45 Auto only; bird's-eye maple grips; gold-plated medallions; nickel-plated finish in entirety; originally cased in oak box with oak cartridge block; lid removable; seven dummy cartridges included; infantry blue velvet lining; 11,500 made; production began in 1970.
Issue Price: $250
Market Value: $995

COLT WORLD WAR II/PACIFIC THEATER

Semi-automatic; Model 1911A1; slide is marked "World War II Commemorative/Pacific Theater of Operations" on right side; left side roll-engraved with names of ten major battle areas; both sides of slide bordered in roll-marked palm leaf design; 5-inch barrel; 45 Auto only; Brazilian rosewood grips; gold-plated medallions; nickel-plated in entirety; originally cased in Obichee wood; light green velvet lining; seven nickel-plated dummy cartridges in cartridge block; 11,500 made; production began in 1970.
Issue Price: $250
Market Value: $995

1970 Savage Anniversary Model 1895

1971 Harrington & Richardson Anniversary Model 1873

1971 Marlin 39A Article II

1971 Colt NRA Centennial
Commemorative Autoloader

1971 Colt NRA Centennial
Commemorative Single Action

COLT WYATT EARP COMMEMORATIVE

Frontier Scout revolver; "Lawman Series—Wyatt Earp" on right side of barrel; standard model markings on left side; 12-inch Buntline barrel; 22 LR only; walnut grips; nickel-plated medallions blued finish; nickel-plated barrel, cylinder, ejector tube plug, ejector tube screw, rod head, base pin and base pin screw, hammer, trigger and backstrap and trigger guard assembly; originally cased in black leatherette-covered box; bottom lined with burgundy velvet; lid with red satin; 3000 made; production started in 1970.
Issue Price: $125
Market Value: $695

COLT WYATT EARP SINGLE ACTION ARMY

Same legend on barrel, but wiped in silver; 16-1/8-inch barrel; 45 Colt only; same grips, medallions as Frontier Scout version; blued finish; case-hardened frame; nickel-plated hammer, trigger, base pin, base pin cross latch assembly; same casing as Frontier Scout; 500 made; production began in 1970.
Issue Price: $395
Market Value: $2950

MARLIN MODEL 39 CENTURY LTD.

Marking the Marlin Centennial, 1870 to 1970; same specs as standard Model 39A except for square lever; fancy walnut straight-grip uncheckered stock; forearm; 20-inch octagonal barrel; brass forearm cap; nameplate inset in stock buttplate. Produced only in 1970.
Issue Price: $125
Market Value: $850

MARLIN CENTENNIAL MATCHED PAIR

Combines presentation-grade Model 336 centerfire, rimfire Model 39, in luggage-type case; matching serial numbers, for additional collector value. Both rifles have fancy walnut straight-grip stocks, forearms; brass forearm caps, brass buttplates, engraved receivers with inlaid medallions. Model 336 is chambered for 30-30 only; Model 39 for 22 LR, 22

Long, 22 Short. Only 1000 sets were manufactured in 1970.
Issue Price: $750
Market Value: $1550

SAVAGE ANNIVERSARY MODEL 1895

Replica of Savage Model 1895; hammerless lever-action; marks 75th anniversary of Savage Arms Corp. (1895-1970); 308 Win. only; 24-inch octagon barrel; 5-shot rotary magazine; engraved receiver, brass-plated lever; brass buttplate; brass medallion inlaid in stock; uncheckered walnut straight grip stock, Schnabel-type forearm. Made only in 1970; 9999 produced.
Issue Price: $195
Market Value: $895

WINCHESTER LONE STAR COMMEMORATIVE

Model 94; produced in rifle version with 26-inch barrel and carbine with 20-inch length. Receiver, upper and lower tang, lever, forearm cap, magazine tube cap all are gold-plated; buttplate is crescent shaped, solid brass. Stocks are American walnut with half pistol grip, fluted comb; commemorative medal with faces of Sam Houston, Stephen F. Austin, William Travis, Jim Bowie and Davy Crockett is inset in right side of stock. Left side of receiver is engraved with star and dates, 1845, 1970; both sides are bordered with series of stars; barrel carries inscription, "Lone Star Commemorative." Upper tang has "Under Six Flags," referring to banners of Spain, France, Mexico, Texas Republic, Confederacy and United States, which have flown over territory. It has bead post front sight, semi-buckhorn rear, plus saddle ring. Introduced in 1970.
Issue Price: Rifle, Carbine, $140; Matched Set with consecutive serial numbers $305

Carbine
Market Value: $1500

Rifle
Market Value: $1600

Matched set
Market Value: $2500

1971

COLT FORT SCOTT COMMEMORATIVE

Frontier Scout revolver; "1871 Kansas Series—Fort Scott—1971" on left side of 4-3/4-inch barrel; 22 LR only; checkered rubber, eagle-style grips; nickel-plated finish; blued barrel, cylinder, base pin screw, ejector tube screw, bolt and trigger screw, hammer, hammer screw, trigger; originally cased in blonde-finished wood; gold velvet/satin lining; 500 made in 1971.
Issue Price: $130
Market Value: $450

COLT NRA CENTENNIAL COMMEMORATIVE

Single Action Army; "1871 NRA Centennial 1971" wiped in gold on left side of 4-3/4-inch, 5-1/2-inch, or 7-1/2-inch barrels; 357 Magnum, 45 Colt; Goncalo Alves grips; gold-plated NRA medallion inlays; blued finish; case-hardened frame; nickel-silver grip screw escutcheons; originally cased in walnut, with inlaid NRA plate; gold velvet/satin lining; 2412 357 Magnums, 4131 45 Colts made; production began in 1971.
Issue Price: $250

357 Magnum
Market Value: $1495

45 Colt
Market Value: $1695

COLT NRA CENTENNIAL COMMEMORATIVE

Semi-automatic; Gold Cup National Match model; "1871 NRA Centennial 1971/The First 100 Years of Service/.45 Automatic Caliber" wiped in gold on left side of slide; MK IV barrel; Eliason rear sight; 5-inch barrel; 45 Auto only; checkered walnut grips; gold-plated NRA medallion inlays; blued; same type of case as NRA commemorative SAA; 2500 made; production began in 1971.
Issue Price: $250
Market Value: $1495

1971 Savage Model 71

1971 Winchester National Rifle
Association Centennial Model

1972 High Standard
Benner Commemorative

1972 Colt Florida Territorial Sesquicentennial

HARRINGTON & RICHARDSON ANNIVERSARY MODEL 1873
Replica of Officer's Model 1873 Trapdoor Springfield commemorating 100th anniversary of H&R (1871-1971); single shot action; 45-70 only; 26-inch barrel; engraved receiver, breech block, hammer, lock plate, buttplate; hand-checkered walnut stock with inlaid brass commemorative plate; peep rear sight, blade front; ramrod. Made only in 1971. Production limited to 10,000.
Market Value: $895

MARLIN 39A ARTICLE II
Same general specs as Model 39A; commemorates National Rifle Association Centennial, 1871-1971. Medallion with legend "The Right to Bear Arms" set on blued receiver; 24-inch octagonal barrel; tube magazine holds 19 LR, 21 Long, 25 Short; fancy uncheckered walnut pistol-grip stock forearm; brass buttplate, forearm cap. Produced only in 1971.
Issue Price: $135
Market Value: $575

MARLIN ARTICLE II CARBINE
Same specs as Marlin 39A Article II rifle except straight grip stock; square lever; shorter magazine; reduced capacity; 20-inch octagonal barrel. Produced only in 1971.
Issue Price: $135; Cased Set, $750

Carbine
Market Value: $175
Cased Set
Market Value: $1100

SAVAGE MODEL 71
Single shot lever-action; replica of Stevens Favorite, issued as commemorative to Joshua Stevens, founder of Stevens Arms Co.; 22 LR only; 22-inch octagonal barrel; brass-plated hammer, lever; uncheckered straight-grip stock, Schnabel forearm; brass commemorative medallion inlaid in stock; brass butt plate; open rear sight, brass blade front. Made in 1971; only 10,000 produced.
Issue Price: $75
Market Value: $395

WINCHESTER NATIONAL RIFLE ASSOCIATION CENTENNIAL MODEL
Introduced in two versions: musket and rifle, both on Model 94 actions; musket resembles Model 1895 NRA musket with military lever to meet requirements for NRA match competition at turn of century; has

26-inch tapered round barrel; full-length American walnut forearm; black-chromed steel buttplate; rear sight has calibrated folding rear leaf, blade front sight; 7-shot magazine. Rifle model resembles Model 64, also made on 94 action with 5-shot half-magazine; 24-inch tapered, round barrel; hooded ramp and bead post front sight; adjustable semi-buckhorn rear sight; contoured lever, blued steel forearm cap. Both models are 30-30; have quick-detachable sling swivels; receivers are black-chromed steel; NRA seal in silver-colored metal is set in right side of stocks; left side of receivers inscribed appropriately with "NRA Centennial Musket" or "NRA Centennial Rifle." Both were introduced in 1971.
Issue Price: $149.95; Matched set with consecutive serial numbers, $325

Musket
Market Value: $1200
Rifle
Market Value: $1300
Cased set
Market Value: $2400

1972

COLT FLORIDA TERRITORIAL SESQUICENTENNIAL
Frontier Scout revolver; "1822—Florida Territory—1972" on left side of 4-3/4-inch barrel; 22 LR only; cypress wood grips; gold-plated medallions, blued finish; case-hardened frame, loading gate; gold-plated base pin, base pin screw, ejector rod head and screws, hammer, trigger and trigger screws; originally cased in cypress wood box; gold velvet/satin lining; 2001 made; production began in 1972.
Issue Price: $125
Market Value: $650

HIGH STANDARD BENNER COMMEMORATIVE
Super Military Trophy auto; 22 Long only; 5-1/2-inch bull barrel; checkered American walnut thumbrest grip; micro rear sight; grip angle is that of the 1911 Government model; engraved with the five-ring Olympic insignia to denote the twentieth anniversary of Huelet O. "Joe" Benner's Olympic Gold Medal win; 1000 guns made; serial numbers, 1 to 1000. Made in 1972.
Issue Price: $550
Market Value: $1650

MARLIN MODEL 336 ZANE GREY
Same specs as Model 336A except 30-30 only; 22-inch octagonal barrel. Commemorates centennial of Zane Grey's birth, 1872 to 1972; commemorative medallion attached to receiver; selected uncheckered walnut pistol grip stock forearm; brass forearm cap, buttplate; 10,000 produced with special serial numbers, ZG1 through ZG10,000. Produced only in 1972.
Issue Price: $150
Market Value: $495

1973

CHURCHILL ONE OF ONE THOUSAND
Bolt-action; 270 Win., 7mm Rem. Magnum, 308, 30-06, 300 Win. Magnum, 375 H&H Magnum, 458 Win. Magnum; 5-shot magazine in standard calibers, 3-shot in magnum; made on Mauser-type action; classic French walnut stock; hand-checkered pistol-grip, forearm; recoil pad, cartridge trap in butt; sling swivels. Manufactured in England in 1973 to commemorate Interarms' 20th anniversary. Only 1000 made.
Market Value: $2500

COLT ARIZONA RANGER COMMEMORATIVE
Frontier Scout revolver; "Arizona Ranger Commemorative" on left side of 4-3/4-inch barrel; 22 LR only; laminated rosewood grips; nickel-plated medallions; blued finish; case-hardened frame; nickel-plated backstrap and trigger guard assembly, hammer trigger, base pin, base pin assembly, screw for backstrap/trigger guard assembly, grips; originally cased in walnut with glass window lid; replica Arizona Ranger badge included in case; lined with maroon velvet; 3001 made; production began in 1973.
Issue Price: $135
Market Value: $650

COLT PEACEMAKER CENTENNIAL
Single Action Army revolver, Frontier Six Shooter configuration; "The Frontier Six-Shooter" etched on left side of barrel, "1873 Peacemaker Centennial 1973" roll-marked on right side; 7-1/2-inch barrel; 44-40 only; checkered rubber eagle-style grips; nickel-plated in entirety; originally cased in leather-covered wood box; brown velvet lining; 1500 made; production began in 1973.
Issue Price: $300
Market Value: $1695

1973 Sako Golden Anniversary Model

1974 Charles Daly Wildlife Commemorative

1973 Winchester Texas Ranger
Commemorative

1974 Remington 1974 Ducks
Unlimited Commemorative

1973 Remington 1973 Ducks Unlimited
Commemorative

1973 Colt Peacemaker
Centennial in 45 Colt
Peacemaker

COLT PEACEMAKER CENTENNIAL 45 COLT
Configuration has "1873 Peacemaker Centennial 1973" roll marked on left side of 7-1/2-inch barrel; 45 Colt only; one-piece varnished walnut grip; blued finish; case-hardened frame, hammer; originally cased in oiled walnut with brass-framed glass cover; maroon velvet lining; 1500 made; production began in 1973.
Issue Price: $300
Market Value: $1695

COLT PEACEMAKER CENTENNIAL 45 COLT/44-40 COMBO
Includes the two revolvers described above in oversize case of walnut-stained willow; lined with dark maroon velvet; matching serial numbers on guns; 500 sets made in 1973.
Issue Price: $625
Market Value: $3195

HARRINGTON & RICHARDSON CUSTER MEMORIAL EDITION
Replica of blackpowder 1873 Springfield carbine; 54-caliber; inlaid with gold; heavy engraving; fancy-grade walnut stock; marketed in mahogany case. Each rifle bears the name of a cavalryman who died in the Battle of the Little Big Horn. Manufactured, 1973, in two versions; 25 Officers' Model, 243 Enlisted Men's Model.
Issue Price: Officer's Model, $3000; Enlisted Men's Model, $2000

Officer's Model
Market Value: $3995

Enlisted Men's Model
Market Value: $1995

REMINGTON 1973 DUCKS UNLIMITED COMMEMORATIVES
Model 1100 autoloading shotgun; 12-ga. only; 30-inch barrel; Full choke; vent rib. Other specs the same as standard Model 1100, except that serial number is preceded by DU; Ducks Unlimited medallion,

surrounded by gilded scrollwork is attached to left side of receiver; 500 made in 1973 only.
Issue Price: $230
Market Value: $595

SAKO GOLDEN ANNIVERSARY MODEL
Same specs as Sako long-action Deluxe sporter; 7mm Rem. Magnum only; floorplate, trigger guard, receiver feature gold oak leaf, acorn decoration; hand-checkered select European walnut stock hand-carved oak leaf pattern. Commemorates firm's 50th anniversary only; 1000 made in 1973.
Market Value: $1095

SMITH & WESSON TEXAS RANGER COMMEMORATIVE
Model 19 357 Combat Magnum; 4-inch barrel; sideplate stamped with Texas Ranger commemorative seal; uncheckered Goncalo Alves stocks; marketed with specially designed Bowie-type knife in presentation case. Commemorated the 150th anniversary of the Texas Rangers. Reported 8000 sets made in 1973.
Market Value: $895

STOEGER LIMITED EDITION LUGER CARBINE
Semi-automatic; 22 LR; 11-inch barrel; forged aluminum frame; walnut pistol grips and forearm. Marketed in a black leatherette, red velvet-lined case. Due to lack of buttstock was classified as a handgun and was legal. Reported 300 made in 1973. Original price unknown.
Market Value: $1000

WINCHESTER TEXAS RANGER COMMEMORATIVE
Model 94; features stock forearm of semi-fancy walnut, with the buttstock having square comb, metal butt plate. Chambered in 30-30; 6-shot tube magazine; a facsimile of Texas Ranger star badge is embedded in the stock; saddle ring is included. Of standard grade, only 4850 were released in April

1973, all of them in the state of Texas. Another 150 Special Edition guns, at $1000 each, were released, in presentation cases, only to the Texas Ranger Association. These were hand-checkered, with full fancy walnut stocks, barrel and receiver highly polished; 4-shot magazine; 16-inch barrel; weighs 6 lbs.; standard model weighs 7 lbs.; 20-inch barrel. With Special Edition guns, commemorative star is mounted inside the presentation case instead of in the stock. Also introduced April 1973. Standard model, Issue Price: $134.95; Special Edition, $1000.

Standard model
Market Value: $1395

Special Edition
Market Value: $2950

1974

CHARLES DALY WILDLIFE COMMEMORATIVE
Over/under; 12-ga.; trap and Skeet models only; same general specs as Diamond Grade over/under; fine scrollwork on left side of receiver, duck scene engraved on right side. Manufactured in Japan 1974. Reported 500 guns made.
Market Value: $795

MOSSBERG MODEL 472 ONE IN 5000
Same specs as Model 472 Brush Gun except brass buttplate; barrel bands and saddle ring; gold-plated trigger; bright blued finish; Indian scenes etched on receiver; select walnut stock and forearm. Limited edition manufactured, 1974 only; numbered 1 through 5,000.
Market Value: $395

REMINGTON 1974 DUCKS UNLIMITED COMMEMORATIVE
Model 870 pump-action, with gilded scroll-engraved receiver; special serial numbers; DU color medallion set in receiver. Made only in 1974 for auction by DU.
Market Value: $495

1976 Mag-Na-Port Mark V Limited Edition

1976 Remington Bicentennial Nylon 66

1976 Remington Bicentennial Model 742

1976 Remington Bicentennial Model 760

1976 Winchester Bicentennial '76 Carbine

1975

MOSSBERG DUCK STAMP COMMEMORATIVE

Same specs as the Model 500DSPR Pigeon Grade 12-ga. magnum heavy duck gun; features a heavy 30-inch vent-rib barrel; Full choke only; receiver carries an etching of a wood duck. Gun was marketed with a special wall plaque commemorating, with the shotgun, the Migratory Bird Hunting Stamp Program. Only 1000 made in 1975.
Market Value: $375

RUGER COLORADO CENTENNIAL

Single-Six revolver; 22 LR; stainless steel grip frame; rosewood grip panels; historic scene roll engraved on cylinder; 6-1/2-inch barrel; inscribed to signify its purpose as a centennial commemorative; marketed in walnut presentation case; 15,000 made in 1975.
Issue Price: $250
Market Value: $595

1976

BROWNING BICENTENNIAL 78

Single shot Model 78; 45-70; same specs as standard model, except for bison and eagle engraved on receiver; scroll engraving on lever, both ends of barrel, buttplate, top of receiver; high-grade walnut stock forearm. Manufactured in Japan. Marketed with engraved hunting knife, commemorative medallion, alder presentation case. Gun and knife serial numbers match, beginning with 1776. Only 1000 sets made. Manufactured only in 1976.
Issue Price: $150
Market Value: $1950

BROWNING BICENTENNIAL SUPERPOSED

Over/under; 12-ga.; same basic specs as standard Superposed shotgun, but sideplates engraved, gold-inlaid turkey-hunting scene on right side, U.S. flag, bald eagle on left. State markings are in gold on blue background; hand-checkered American walnut straight-grip stock, Schnabel forearm; marketed in velvet-lined walnut presentation case. Only 51 made; one for each state and District of Columbia. Manufactured in Belgium, 1976.
Market Value: $10,000

COLT BICENTENNIAL SET

Includes Colt SAA revolver, Python revolver and 3rd Model Dragoon revolver, with accessories; all have rosewood stocks, matching roll-engraved unfluted cylinders, blued finish, silver medallion bearing the Seal of the United States; Dragoon has silver grip frame; all revolvers in set have matching serial numbers, 0001 through 1776. Marketed with deluxe three-drawer walnut presentation case, reproduction volume of Armsmear. Made only in 1976.
Market Value: $3195

ITHACA BICENTENNIAL MODEL 37

Slide-action; 12-ga.; basic specs of Model 37 Supreme, except for Bicentennial design etched into receiver; serialized USA 0001 to USA 1976; full fancy walnut stock slide handle. Only 1976 made in 1976. Marketed in presentation case.
Market Value: $795

MAG-NA-PORT MARK V LIMITED EDITION

Revolver; built on Ruger Super Blackhawk; 44 Magnum; 5-inch barrel; jeweled, plated hammer and trigger; smoothed trigger pull; front sight altered with red insert; satin nickel backstrap, trigger guard, ejector rod housing, center pin; deluxe blue finish; Mag-na-ported barrel. Marketed in presentation case; made in 1976.
Issue Price: $395
Market Value: $3500 to $3700

REMINGTON BICENTENNIAL NYLON 66

Rifle; semi-automatic; 22 LR; same specs as standard Nylon 66 except specially marked with eagle, shield flanked with scrollwork and underlined with "1776-1976"; dates are gilded; Mohawk brown stock only; 12,000 made.
Issue Price: $84.95
Market Value: $575

REMINGTON BICENTENNIAL MODEL 742

Same specs as standard Model 742 Woodsmaster except Bicentennial commemorative inscription etched on receiver; different checkering pattern. Manufactured 1976 only.
Market Value: $495

1975 Ruger Colorado Centennial

REMINGTON BICENTENNIAL MODEL 760

Same specs as standard Model 760 Gamemaster except Bicentennial commemorative inscription etched on receiver; different checkering pattern. Manufactured 1976 only.
Market Value: $475

WICKLIFFE '76 COMMEMORATIVE

Single shot; same specs as '76 Deluxe model except filled etching on sidewalls of receiver; 26-inch barrel only; U.S. silver dollar inlaid in stock; marketed in presentation case. Manufactured 1976 only. Only 100 made.
Market Value: $850

WINCHESTER BICENTENNIAL '76 CARBINE

Model 94; same specs as standard model except 30-30 only; engraved antique silver finish; American eagle on left side of receiver, "76" encircled with thirteen stars on right side; engraved on right side of barrel is legend "Bicentennial 1776-1976." Originally marketed with wooden gun rack with simulated deer antlers, gold colored identification plate. Reported 20,000 made in 1976.
Issue Price: $325
Market Value: $1595

1976 Browning
Bicentennial 78

1977 Colt
Second Amendment
Commemorative

1977 Smith & Wesson
125th Anniversary

1977 Ithaca Ducks
Unlimited Commemorative

1978 Browning
Centennial Hi-Power

1977

COLT SECOND AMENDMENT COMMEMORATIVE

Peacemaker Buntline revolver; 22 rimfire; 7-1/2-inch barrel bears inscription "The Right To Keep And Bear Arms"; polished nickel-plated barrel, frame, ejector rod assembly, hammer, trigger; blued cylinder, backstrap, trigger guard; black pearlite stocks; fluted cylinder; specially serial numbered; marketed in special presentation case, carrying reproduction copy of Second Amendment to the Constitution. Reported 3000 made in 1977.
Issue Price: $194.95
Market Value: $650

ITHACA DUCKS UNLIMITED COMMEMORATIVE

Limited edition of Model 37 Featherlight pump action; commemorates DU 40th anniversary; 12-ga.; 30-inch Full choke barrel; vent rib; recoil pad; Raybar front sight; commemorative grip cap; receiver engraved with DU anniversary logo, banner commemorating occasion. Also made in high-grade custom version with more elaborate etching, hand-checkered full fancy American walnut stock, custom-fitted carrying case. Reported 5000 made in 1977.
Issue Price: Standard commemorative, $255; Custom model, $600.
Market Value: Standard: $500
Market Value: Custom: $700

MAG-NA-PORT CUSTOM SIX LIMITED EDITION

Revolver; built on Ruger Super Blackhawk; 44 Magnum; 6-inch barrel; same specs as Mag-na-port Mark V except yellow front sight insert, gold-outlined rear sight blade; gold inlay. 50 made in 1977.
Issue Price: $350
Market Value: $2250

MAG-NA-PORT TOMAHAWK LIMITED EDITION

Revolver; built on Ruger Blackhawk; 44 Magnum; Mag-na-ported 4-3/4-inch barrel; Metalife SS finish; smoothed trigger pull; red front sight insert; white outline rear sight; hammer engraved with Tomahawk

logo; topstrap engraved with Mag-na-port and Tomahawk logos; serial numbered 1 to 200; 200 made in 1977. Marketed in carrying case.
Issue Price: $495
Market Value: $2000

SMITH & WESSON 125TH ANNIVERSARY

Model 25 revolver; 45 Colt; 6-1/2-inch barrel; blued finish; Goncalo Alves stocks; "Smith & Wesson 125th Anniversary" gold-filled on barrel; sideplate has gold-filled anniversary seal; marketed in case bearing nickel-silver anniversary seal. Included is book, *125 Years With Smith & Wesson*. Reported 10,000 issued in 1977.
Market Value: $1095

SMITH & WESSON DELUXE EDITION 125TH ANNIVERSARY

Same specs as Smith & Wesson 125th Anniversary except Class A engraving; ivory stocks; anniversary medallion on box is sterling silver; book leather-bound. Reported 50 issued in 1977.
Market Value: $1695

WINCHESTER WELLS FARGO MODEL 94

Same specs as standard Model 94 except 30-30 only; antique silver-finish engraved receiver; nickel-silver stagecoach medallion inset in buttstock; checkered fancy American walnut stock forearm; curved buttplate. Reported 20,000 made in 1977.
Market Value: $1295

WINCHESTER CHEYENNE COMMEMORATIVE

Lever-action rifle; same specs as standard Model 94 carbine except 44-40; made specifically for the Canadian market. Reported 11,220 made in 1977.
Issue Price: $375
Market Value: $1295

1978

BROWNING CENTENNIAL HI-POWER

Commemorates Browning's centennial anniversary; same specs as standard 9mm Hi-Power except oil-

finished hand-checkered walnut stocks; Browning medallion inset on both sides; chrome finish; has centennial inscription with date hand-engraved on side; gold-plated trigger; fixed sights. Issued in fitted walnut case with red velvet lining. Only 3500 produced in 1978, with serial #1878D-0001 through 1878D-3500.
Issue Price: $495
Market Value: $895

COLT U.S. CAVALRY COMMEMORATIVE

Based on 1860 Army design; commemorates 200th anniversary of U.S. Cavalry, 1777 to 1977; blued barrel, hammer assembly, cylinder, backstrap, trigger; frame, hammer color case-hardened; brass trigger guard; one-piece walnut stocks; naval engagement scene roll marked on nonfluted cylinder; marketed with detachable walnut shoulder stock, accessories, in oiled American walnut presentation case. Reported 3000 units manufactured 1978.
Issue Price: $995
Market Value: $1450

WINCHESTER ANTLERED GAME COMMEMORATIVE

Built on Winchester 94 action but with polished 20-inch barrel; gold-colored inscription reading "Antlered Game;" gold-plated lever; tang and barrel bands match blue of receiver; 30-30 only. Total of 19,999 made in 1978.
Issue Price: $374.95
Market Value: $1350

WINCHESTER LEGENDARY LAWMAN

Model 94 Carbine; 30-30 only; same specs as standard model except 16-inch barrel; full-length tube magazine; antique silver-finish barrel bands; right side of barrel bears silver-colored inscription, "Legendary Lawman"; extended forearm, straight-grip stock; nickel-silver medallion set in buttstock features sheriff standing on Western street. Reported 20,000 manufactured in 1978.
Issue Price: $375
Market Value: $1495

1979 Winchester Set of 1000
Collector Issue

1979 Winchester Limited Edition II

1979 Winchester
Legendary Frontiersman

1979 Mag-Na-Port Bullseye
Limited Edition

1979 Mag-Na-Port Safari #1
Cape Buffalo

1979 Colt Ned Buntline Commemorative

1979

COLT NED BUNTLINE COMMEMORATIVE

Single Action Army revolver; 45 Colt; 12-inch barrel; built on New Frontier SAA frame; adjustable rear sight; nickel-plated; black composite rubber grips; marketed in custom presentation case with six nickel-plated 45 cartridges. Reported 3000 manufactured in 1979.
Issue Price: $900
Market Value: $1495

MAG-NA-PORT BACKPACKER LIMITED EDITION

Revolver; built on Charter Arms Bulldog; 44 Special; no front sight; Mag-na-ported 1.875-inch barrel; dehorned, anti-snag hammer; Pachmayr grips; Metalife SS finish; engraved with Mag-na-port logo and Backpacker 1 to 250 serial number; 250 made in 1979. Marketed in carrying case.
Issue Price: $295
Market Value: $400

MAG-NA-PORT BULLSEYE LIMITED EDITION

Semi-automatic; built on Ruger MKI Target Model; 22 LR; Mag-na-ported 5-1/2-inch barrel; gold-outlined rear sight; Clark target trigger; standard black Ruger grips; Metalife SS finish; Mag-na-port logo on end of bolt; lettering, logo gold inlaid; gold bullseye logo on receiver; serial numbered 001-200; 200 made in 1979. Marketed in wild poplar case.
Issue Price: $395
Market Value: $700

MAG-NA-PORT CLASSIC LIMITED EDITION

Revolver; built on Ruger Super Blackhawk; 44 Magnum; Mag-na-ported 7-1/2-inch barrel; yellow insert front sight, gold outline rear; satin nickel finish on backstrap, ejector rod; deluxe blued cylinder, frame, barrel; jeweled, gold-plated hammer, trigger; polished, gold-plated center pin release, ejector rod; "Mag-na-port Classic" engraved, gold inlaid on topstrap; other lettering, logos gold inlaid; carries Mag-na-port serial numbers 1 through 250; 250 made in 1979. Hammer, trigger were seal-locked to ensure unfired condition. Marketed in case of wild poplar with Mag-na-port logo.
Issue Price: $590
Market Value: $2500

MAG-NA-PORT SAFARI #1 CAPE BUFFALO

Revolver; built on Ruger Super Blackhawk; 44 Magnum; 6-inch barrel; Metalife finish; Mag-na-port vent process; yellow front insert on sight, Omega Maverick rear sight; smoothed action; Mag-na-port logo and serial numbers 001 through 200 engraved; stainless steel ejector rod housing; gold-plated hammer, trigger, center pin, center pin release, ejector rod and grip screws; antiqued factory grips inlaid with 44 Magnum case head; Cape buffalos engraved on cylinder. Only 200 made in 1979.
Issue Price: $995
Market Value: $1500

WINCHESTER LEGENDARY FRONTIERSMAN

Model 94 Carbine; receiver decorated with scenes of the old frontier; silver-plated finish on receiver; polished, blued barrel, finger lever, hammer and trigger; forearm and straight-grip stock of semi-fancy American walnut; cut checkering; "Legendary Frontiersman" in silver on right side of barrel. Reported 19,999 made in 1979
Issue Price: $549.95 each
Market Value: $1595

WINCHESTER LIMITED EDITION II

Rifle; built on standard Model 94 carbine action but with gold-plated receiver with etched game scenes on each side, gold-plated hammer, lever; rest of metal bright blued; top quality fancy walnut stock forend. Only 1500 made in 1979.
Issue Price: $1750
Market Value: $1895

WINCHESTER SET OF 1000 COLLECTOR ISSUE

Combines Model 94 in 30-30 and Model 9422 in 22 WMR; both with game scene engraved on receiver; levers, receivers, barrel bands are gold-plated. Marketed in red velvet-lined wooden case, with brass hardware, lock key. Only 1000 sets made in 1979.
Issue Price: $3000 per set
Market Value: $3000

1980 Wickliffe Big Game Commemorative

1980 Winchester Oliver Winchester Commemorative

1981 Winchester John Wayne Commemorative

1981 Browning Waterfowl/Mallard Limited Edition

1980

ITHACA MODEL 37 2500 SERIES CENTENNIAL
Pump-action shotgun; 12-ga. only; etched receiver; antiqued parts; deluxe walnut stock; silver-plated parts. Commemorated Ithaca's 100th anniversary. Unknown number made, 1977.
Market Value: $595

MAG-NA-PORT SAFARI #2 ELEPHANT
Revolver; built on Ruger Super Blackhawk; 44 Magnum; 7-1/2-inch barrel, with custom inverted crown; includes Mag-na-port venting, satin and bright nickel finish; jeweled and nickeled hammer, trigger; custom rosewood grips with inlaid ivory scrimshaw of elephant; engraved elephant on cylinder; scroll engraving at muzzle; Mag-na-port logo on topstrap; smoothed action; white outline rear sight, red front sight insert. Marketed in walnut presentation case inlaid with ivory elephant scrimshaw. Only 200 made in 1980.
Issue Price: $1395
Market Value: $1800

WICKLIFFE BIG GAME COMMEMORATIVE
Single shot; same specs as Wickliffe Model '76 except glossy stock finish; gold-filled receiver etchings, chambered for 338 Win. Magnum only. Only 200 made. Manufactured 1980 only.
Market Value: $750

WINCHESTER OLIVER WINCHESTER COMMEMORATIVE
Model 94; 38-55 Win. only; gold commemorative plaque featuring Oliver Winchester medallion inlaid in American walnut stock; gold-plated, engraved receiver, forend cap. Reported 19,999 made in 1980.
Issue Price: $595
Market Value: $1895

1981

BROWNING WATERFOWL/MALLARD LIMITED EDITION
Over/under; 12-ga.; 28-inch Modified/Full barrels; other specs same as Lightning Superposed model except each gun is inscribed in gold with the Latin scientific name for the mallard, has gold mallard inlaid in receiver, with two ducks on bottom, one on trigger guard; grayed, engraved receiver; French walnut stock forend; 24 lpi checkering; oil-finished hand-rubbed wood; marketed in velvet-lined black walnut case. Only 500 made in 1981.
Issue Price: $7000
Market Value: $5195

COLT JOHN M. BROWNING COMMEMORATIVE
Model 1911; 45 Auto; standard model to commemorate the 70th anniversary of the model's existence. Gold inlay on right side of slide announces the reason for manufacture, with eagle, scrollwork and Colt stallion; right side of slide also features extensive scrollwork; blued hammer and trigger, hand-checkered walnut grips. Reported 3000 made in 1981.
Issue Price: $1100
Market Value: $1095

MAG-NA-PORT SAFARI #3 LION
Revolver; built on Ruger Blackhawk; 44 Magnum; Mag-na-ported 5-1/2-inch barrel; highly polished blue-black finish; Omega Maverick rear sight, white front sight insert; silver inlay of Mag-na-port logo; custom grip with ivory scrimshaw of lion; lion engraving on cylinder and "Shumba" engraved on backstrap. Marketed in hand-crafted presentation case. Only 200 made in 1981.
Issue Price: $995
Market Value: $1550

REMINGTON 1981 DUCKS UNLIMITED SPECIAL
Model 1100 LT-20; 26-inch Improved Cylinder, vent-rib barrel; 2-3/4-inch chamber; left side of receiver panel carries words "Ducks Unlimited Special" in script lettering. Right receiver panel has DU mallard head logo with scrollwork. Right side of buttstock has laser-etched reproduction of DU crest. Only 2400 made in 1981, with serial numbers 0001-DU81 to 2400-DU81, for auction by DU.
Market Value: $695

REMINGTON 1981 CLASSIC
Bolt-action Model 700; 7mm Mauser only; 24-inch barrel; 44-1/2-inch overall length; cut-checkered American walnut stock of Classic design; satin finish

on wood; no sights; hinged floorplate; rubber recoil pad; sling swivel studs. Limited production in this caliber only in 1981.
Issue Price: $364.95
Market Value: $725

REMINGTON ATLANTIC DU COMMEMORATIVE
Model 1100 12-ga. magnum; 32-inch Full-choke, vent-rib barrel; right side of receiver is embossed with "Ducks Unlimited" and DU mallard head symbol; left side carries the words, "The Atlantic," surrounded by scroll markings. Made only in 1981; carries special DU serial numbers.
Issue Price: $552
Market Value: $695

REMINGTON CHESAPEAKE
Ducks Unlimited commemorative for 1981; Model 1100; 12-ga. magnum; 30-inch barrel; Full choke; select American walnut stock; cut checkering; recoil pad; gold-colored trigger; ivory bead front sight; left side of receiver decorated with plaque of flying duck scrollwork engraved gold-filled legend; furnished with foam-lined hard carrying case. Only 2400 made for DU auctions with opening bid of $950.
Market Value: $695

REMINGTON MODEL 1100 COLLECTORS EDITION
Same specs as standard Model 1100 except deep-relief etching, gold highlights, richly figured walnut stock positive cut checkering. Marketed with certificate showing serial number. Only 3000 made in 1981.
Market Value: $995

WINCHESTER JOHN WAYNE COMMEMORATIVE
Model 94 carbine; 32-40 Win. only; pewter-plated receiver; nickel-silver likeness of Wayne inlaid in American walnut stock; cut checkering; receiver engraved with cattle drive scene on one side, stagecoach under attack by Indians on other; scenes are edged with titles of Wayne's films. Reported 50,000 made in 1981, some marketed by U.S. Repeating Arms.
Issue Price: $600
Market Value: $1795

1982 Browning Waterfowl/Pintail Limited Edition

1980 Mag-Na-Port
Safari #2 Elephant

1981 Mag-Na-Port
Safari #3 Lion

1981 Remington
Atlantic DU Commemorative

1981 Colt John M. Browning
Commemorative

1981 Remington
1981 Ducks Unlimited Special

1981 Remington Chesapeake

1982 Remington
1982 Ducks Unlimited Special

1982 Colt
John Wayne Deluxe

1982 Colt
John Wayne
Presentation

1982 Colt John Wayne
Commemorative

1982

BROWNING WATERFOWL/PINTAIL LIMITED EDITION
Over/under; 12-ga.; 28-inch Modified/Full barrels; same specs as 1981 Mallard Limited Edition except hand-sculptured inlays of pintails in flight against background of cattails; gold-inlaid head of pintail on trigger; inscribed in gold are "American Pintail" and the scientific name, "Anas Acuta." Stock is of French walnut, with checkered butt. Marketed in velvet-lined black walnut case. Only 500 made in Belgium in 1982.
Issue Price: $8800
Market Value: $5195

COLT JOHN WAYNE COMMEMORATIVE
Single Action; 45 Colt; ivory grips; etched, gold-plated portrait of Wayne on cylinder, eagle and shield on barrel with name; gold-filled Wayne signature on backstrap; marketed in presentation case. Reported 3100 made.
Issue Price: $2995
Market Value: $2195

COLT JOHN WAYNE DELUXE
Same specs as John Wayne Commemorative except silver-plated, hand-engraved finish with 18-karat gold inlaid motif; two-piece ebony grips with ivory insert, gold-plated image of Wayne on horseback etched on right side of cylinder. Only 500 made.
Issue Price: $10,000
Market Value: $7700

COLT JOHN WAYNE PRESENTATION
Same specs as John Wayne Commemorative except blued finish, gold plating, 24-karat gold inlays, two-piece checkered ivory grips with gold inlay. Only 100 made.
Issue Price: $20,000
Market Value: $12,500

REMINGTON 1982 CLASSIC
Same specs as the 1981 Remington Classic except 257 Roberts; limited production of approximately 7000 in this caliber only in 1981.
Issue Price: $381.95
Market Value: $460

1983 Mag-Na-Port
Alaskan Series, Grizzly

1983 Mag-Na-Port
Alaskan Series, Moose

1983 Mag-Na-Port
Alaskan Series, Caribou

1983 Mag-Na-Port
Alaskan Series, Dall Sheep

1983 Colt Buffalo Bill
Wild West Show
Commemorative

1982 Winchester
Annie Oakley 22

1982 Ruger Model 1 Limited Edition

1982 Remington River
DU Commemorative

REMINGTON 1982 DU SPECIAL

Model 870; 20-ga. lightweight; 2-3/4-inch chamber, 26-inch Improved Cylinder barrel; decorated with gold-filled scrollwork inscribed with mallard logo, words, "Ducks Unlimited Special"; has gold-colored trigger, ivory bead front sight. Only 3000 made; serial numbers are 0001-DU82 to 3000-DU82.
Issue Price: $550
Market Value: $675

REMINGTON MODEL FOUR COLLECTORS EDITION

Same specs as standard Model Four semi-automatic except etched receiver; 24K gold inlays; all metal parts with high-luster finish; 30-06 only. Only 1500 made in 1982.
Market Value: $1195

REMINGTON RIVER DU COMMEMORATIVE

Model 670; 12-ga. magnum; 30-inch Full-choke, vent-rib barrel; dedicated to the Mississippi Flyway; left receiver panel has engraved bronze medallion of mallard duck flanked by script lettering of gun's model and commemorative title, "The River," set off by scroll markings filled in gold color. Special serial numbers are DU82-0001 to DU82-3000. Only 3000 made.
Issue Price: $425
Market Value: $695

RUGER MODEL I LIMITED EDITION

Mark I Target Model semi-automatic pistol of stainless steel introduced January 1, 1982, to mark the end of production of the standard model. Pistol was marketed in the same type of wooden case

and printed inner box in which the original Ruger auto was shipped at the beginning of production in 1949. Each pistol was accompanied by an exact reproduction of the original automatic pistol brochure. Barrel of each pistol was marked "1 of 5000" and the receiver roll marked with a replica of the signature of the inventor, William B. Ruger. Only 5000 made in 1982.
Issue Price: $435
Market Value: $695

WINCHESTER ANNIE OAKLEY 22

Rifle; 22 LR, 22 WMR; 20-1/2-inch barrel; based on Model 9422; barrel inscription gold inlaid; receiver roll engraved on right side with portrait of Annie Oakley, on left side with Oakley standing in saddle, shooting from moving horse; available with sling swivels, saddle ring on special order. Reported 6000 manufactured.
Issue Price: $699
Market Value: $1795

1983

BROWNING WATERFOWL/BLACK DUCK LIMITED EDITION

Over/under; 12-ga.; 28-inch Modified/Full barrels; same specs as 1981 Mallard Limited Edition except 24-karat black ducks inlaid in receiver; words, "Black Duck" and Latin designation "Anas Rubripes," engraved in gold within gold banners. Marketed in velvet-lined black walnut case. Only 500 made in Belgium in 1983.
Issue Price: $8800
Market Value: $5195

COLT BUFFALO BILL WILD WEST SHOW COMMEMORATIVE

Single Action Army; 45; 4-3/4-inch barrel etched with gold-plated figure of Colonel Cody on unfluted cylinder, cowboys, Indians and buffalo on barrel with commemorative inscription; two-piece walnut grips; blued finish, color case-hardened frame; marketed in cherry-stained hardwood case. Only 500 made.
Issue Price: $1349.95
Market Value: $2095

MAG-NA-PORT ALASKAN SERIES

Revolver; built on stainless steel Ruger Super Blackhawk; 44 Magnum; four variations in the series; rear sight is original Omega white outline; front sight is C-More by Magnum Sales, with different colored inserts; barrels are Mag-na-ported with Mag-na-port logo etched on each cylinder. "Alaskan Series" is etched into the barrel, "One of 200" into the topstrap, with appropriate animal's profile also etched into the cylinder; each gun was delivered with Mag-na-port seal as guarantee the hammer had never been in cocked position. Each gun marketed in walnut presentation case with appropriate animal's head branded into wood. Introduced, 1983.

MAG-NA-PORT ALASKAN GRIZZLY

Motif included 50 of the 200 guns in series; barrel had been cut to 4 5/8-inch and recrowned; C-More front sight carried a green insert.
Issue Price: $695
Market Value: $850

1983 Winchester Chief Crazy Horse Commemorative

1984 Winchester 9422 Eagle Scout Commemorative

1984 Texas Longhorn
South Texas Army Limited Edition

MAG-NA-PORT ALASKAN DALL SHEEP
Same as Grizzly with 50 guns issued except barrel cut to 5 1/2-inch, recrowned; replacement C-More front sight carries pink insert of high-contrast DuPont acetal.
Issue Price: $695
Market Value: $850

MAG-NA-PORT ALASKAN CARIBOU
Issue includes 50 guns with 6-1/2-inch recrowned barrel; insert of C-More sight is blaze orange in color.
Issue Price: $695
Market Value: $850

MAG-NA-PORT ALASKAN MOOSE
Comprises 50 guns with standard 7-1/2-inch Blackhawk barrel; C-More sight insert is bright yellow.
Issue Price: $695
Market Value: $850

MAG-NA-PORT SAFARI #4 RHINO
Revolver; built on stainless steel Ruger Super Blackhawk; 44 Magnum; 4-5/8-inch Mag-na-ported barrel; velvet hone finish; gold-plated hammer, trigger, ejector rod, center pin, center pin release; Omega white-outline rear sight, red insert front sight; rhino head hand-engraved on cylinder; Mag-na-port serial numbers 001 through 200 hand-engraved on frame. Marketed in walnut presentation case with overlay of African continent and hand-painted head of rhino. Only 200 made in 1983.
Issue Price: $895
Market Value: $1450

REMINGTON 1983 CLASSIC
Same specs as Classic limited issue of previous years except 300 H&H Magnum only. Approximately 3500 made in this caliber only in 1983.
Issue Price: $421.95
Market Value: $675

REMINGTON MISSISSIPPI DU COMMEMORATIVE
Model 870 12-ga. magnum; 32-inch Full-choke, vent-rib barrel; right side of receiver embossed with words, "Ducks Unlimited," DU mallard head symbol; left side of receiver carries title of gun, "The Mississippi," with scrollwork.
Issue Price: $454
Market Value: $650

WINCHESTER CHIEF CRAZY HORSE COMMEMORATIVE
Rifle; built on Model 94 action; 38-55 Win.; 24-inch barrel; stock decorated with brass tacks; medallion

in stock symbolizes united Sioux tribes; Chief Crazy Horse inscription engraved in barrel; receiver engraved, gold filled on both sides with Indian scenes, names of Sioux tribes in English, Lakota Sioux; saddle ring. Reported 19,999 made.
Issue Price: $600
Market Value: $1595

1984

AMERICA REMEMBERS BUFFALO BILL CENTENNIAL
Replica of Colt Model 1860 Army blackpowder 44 revolver; 8-inch barrel; extensive gold etching of Western scenes; bonded ivory stocks and powder flask; brass accessories; marketed in lined display case. Reported 2500 manufactured in Virginia gun factory, 1984.
Issue Price: $1950
Market Value: $895

AMERICAN HISTORICAL FOUNDATION KOREAN WAR COMMEMORATIVE THOMPSON
Semi-automatic; 45 ACP; same specs as standard Model 1927 Thompson except highly polished walnut buttstock, pistol grip, forend; gold-plated activator knob, Cutts compensator, rear sight base, trigger, sling swivels; commemorative medallions set in buttstock, pistol grip; special serial numbers, KW0001 through KW1500. Reported 1500 made by Auto Ordnance, 1984.
Issue Price: $1,195
Market Value: $1295

AMERICAN HISTORICAL FOUNDATION M1 GARAND WORLD WAR II COMMEMORATIVE
Reproduction of WWII combat rifle; select-grade walnut stock; highly blued finish; gold plating on smaller parts. Reported 2500 made by Springfield Armory in Illinois under special order; carried serial numbers WW0001 through WW2500. Marketed, 1984, with walnut display case.
Issue Price: $1695
Market Value: $1195

COLT KIT CARSON COMMEMORATIVE
Single action; 22 rimfire; based on Colt New Frontier model; 6-inch barrel; blued, color case-hardened frame; ivory-colored stocks; gold artwork in Western motif on barrel; marketed in custom cherry case with

hardbound copy of Kit Carson's Own Story; 950 made.
Issue Price: $549
Market Value: $650

COLT USA EDITION
Single Action Army revolver; 44-40; 7-1/2-inch barrel; fluted cylinder; checkered ivory stocks with fleur-de-lis pattern; gold inlaid frame borders, outline of state or capital city on recoil shield; gold-inlaid rampant colt on loading gate; gold-inlaid "USA" on left side of barrel; two gold-inlaid barrel bands; gold-inlaid ejector tube band; silver- and gold-inlaid stars; only 100 made.
Issue Price: $4995
Market Value: $5000

COLT THEODORE ROOSEVELT COMMEMORATIVE
Single action; based on Colt SAA; 7-1/2-inch barrel; 44-40; hand-fitted ivory stocks; backstrap bears gold TR monogram; barrel, cylinder hand engraved; marketed in oak presentation case; 500 made.
Issue Price: $1695
Market Value: $1995

REMINGTON 1984 CLASSIC
Same specs as earlier Classic Limited issues except 250-3000 Savage. Approximately 2500 made in this caliber in 1984.
Issue Price: $420.80
Market Value: $465

TEXAS LONGHORN SOUTH TEXAS ARMY LIMITED EDITION
Revolver; single action; all centerfire pistol calibers; 6-shot cylinder; 4-3/4-inch barrel; grooved topstrap rear sight, blade front; one-piece fancy walnut stocks; loading gate, ejector housing on left side of the gun; cylinder rotates to left; color case-hardened frame; high polish blue finish; music wire coil springs; hand made; "One of One Thousand" engraved on barrel; marketed in glass-covered display case. Only 1000 made.
Market Value: $1695

WEATHERBY 1984 MARK V OLYMPIC COMMEMORATIVE
Rifle; bolt-action; 300 Weatherby; same specs as standard Mark V except accents gold-plated; top-grade walnut stock with inlaid star. Reported 1000 made in Japan, 1984.
Issue Price: $2000
Market Value: $1100

1984 Winchester 9422 Boy Scout Commemorative

1984 Winchester Grouse Model

1985 Colt Texas Sesquicentennial

WINCHESTER 9422 EAGLE SCOUT COMMEMORATIVE

Same specs as Model 9422 XTR except receiver deep etched, plated in gold; left side has Boy Scout law, right side has Boy Scout oath; frame has "1910-1985" inscription; checkered stock, forend, high-luster finish; Eagle Scout medallion embedded in right side of stock; crescent steel buttplate; gold-plated forend cap; jeweled bolt. Marketed in oak presentation case; 1000 made.
Issue Price: $1710
Market Value: $3500

WINCHESTER 9422 BOY SCOUT COMMEMORATIVE

Same specs as Model 9422 except receiver roll-engraved, plated in antique pewter; frame carries "1910-1985" anniversary inscription, Boy Scout oath, law; lever has engraved frieze of scouting knots; "Boy Scouts of America" inscribed on barrel; medallion embedded in stock; 15,000 made.
Issue Price: $495
Market Value: $1195

WINCHESTER GROUSE MODEL

Limited edition over/under based on Model 101 configuration; custom built for the Ruffed Grouse Society; 20-ga. only; engraved scene of grouse on action; fancy walnut woodwork. Only 225 made in 1984.
Market Value: $1450

WINCHESTER/COLT 94 SET

Both guns 44-40 Win.; carbine with 20-inch barrel; tube magazine; 38-1/8-inch overall length; follows basic Model 94 specs except horse-and-rider trademark, WC monogram etched in gold on left side; gold-etched portrait of Oliver Winchester on right; right side of barrel has rendering of original Winchester factory; additional gold scrollwork; crescent buttplate; deep-cut spade checkering; semi-gloss finish on American walnut woodwork. Colt is Peacemaker SAA model with backstrap bearing Sam Colt signature in gold; WC monogram is gold-etched on left side of cylinder; barrel bears serpentine Colt logo in gold; right side of barrel has gold etching of original Colt factory; gold-plated scrollwork; oil-finished American walnut grips; 7-1/2-inch barrel; 4440 sets made.
Issue Price: $3995
Market Value: $2950

1985

AMERICAN HISTORICAL FOUNDATION WWII VICTORY SPECIAL EDITION M1 CARBINE

Semi-automatic; 30 Carbine; same specs as M1 Carbine standard military version except highly polished; American walnut stock; mirror-polished barrel, receiver; gold-plated rear sight, windage knob, front sight, trigger, magazine release, barrel bands, safety, slide stop; special serial numbers are WW0001 through WW2500. Reported 2,500 made under special contract by Iver Johnson Arms, 1985.
Issue Price: $695
Market Value: $595

COLT TEXAS SESQUICENTENNIAL

Single action; 45 Colt; built on SAA Sheriff's Model; 4-inch barrel; Texas legend, dates inlaid on barrel in gold; gold star in shield on cylinder; marketed in French-fitted oak presentation case; 1000 made.
Issue Price: $1836
Market Value: $1695

COLT SESQUICENTENNIAL PREMIER

Same specs as Texas Sesquicentennial; built on SAA design; 45 Colt; 4-3/4-inch barrel; 24-karat gold-plated trigger guard, backstrap; engraved gold-inlaid scenes of Texas history, including the Alamo; scrimshawed ivory grips; marketed in four-sided glass presentation case; 75 made.
Issue Price: $7995
Market Value: $5000

REMINGTON 1985 CLASSIC

Same specs as earlier versions except 350 Rem. Magnum. Approximately 6500 made in this caliber only in 1985.
Issue Price: $474.70
Market Value: $475

RUGER YR-25 CARBINE

Semi-automatic; 44 Magnum; same specs as the standard Ruger Model 44 except medallion in stock commemorating the 25th anniversary of the carbine's manufacture; the last year the model was made. Made only in 1985.
Market Value: $450

SIG MODEL 226 15TH ANNIVERSARY COMMEMORATIVE

Same specs as Model 226 except deep black non-reflective finish; ornately carved wooden grips; trigger, hammer, magazine release, decocking lever and slide stop all are gold-plated, all stampings on slide are gold-filled. Slide marking reads, "125 Jahre SIG Waffen 1860-1985"; marketed in leather presentation case. Only 200 imported into U.S. in 1985.
Issue Price: $2500
Market Value: $1195

WINCHESTER ATA HALL OF FAME COMMEMORATIVE

Combo trap set; 12-ga.; 34-inch single-barrel; 30-inch vent-rib over/under with Winchoke barrels; engraved with Amateur Trapshooting Assn. Hall of Fame logo; serial numbered HF1 through HF250; first 60 were auction items at 1985 Grand American; marketed in fitted luggage style case; only 250 made in 1985 in Japan by Winchester-Olin.
Issue Price: $2795
Market Value: $2750

1986

AMERICAN HISTORICAL FOUNDATION VIETNAM WAR COMMEMORATIVE THOMPSON

Semi-automatic; 45 ACP; basic specs of 1927 Thompson except highly polished blued finish; gold-plated rear sight, front sight and Cutts compensator, trigger, sling swivels; American walnut stock, forearm, with inset medallions; receiver carries gold-filled commemorative inscriptions, serial number, issuing organization, Thompson patent numbers. Reported 1500 made by Auto Ordnance Corp., on special order, 1986.
Issue Price: $1,295
Market Value: $1295

AMERICAN HISTORICAL FOUNDATION M1 GARAND KOREAN WAR COMMEMORATIVE

Semi-automatic; 30-06; same specs as M1 Garand military version except polished Fajen select American walnut stock; gold-plated front sight, rear sight base, trigger, windage knob, elevation knob, stacking swivel, sling swivels, safety; barrel, receiver and other metal parts mirror polished; gold-plated medallion inset in stock. Reported 2500 made, 1986, serial numbers KW0001 through KW2500.
Issue Price: $1895
Market Value: $1195

BROWNING BIG HORN SHEEP ISSUE

Same specs as standard Browning A-Bolt rifle except 270 Win. only; checkered stock is high-grade walnut with high-gloss finish; has brass spacers under grip cap, recoil pad; deep relief engraving; big horn displayed in 24-karat gold. Only 600 made in Japan. Introduced, 1986.
Market Value: $1250

BROWNING MODEL 1886 MONTANA CENTENNIAL

Same specs as 1886 High Grade lever-action rifle except different stock design; engraving on receiver reads "Montana Centennial". Only 1,000 made in Japan, 1986.
Issue Price: $995
Market Value: $1895

1986 Remington 1986 Classic

1986 Colt 150th Anniversary
Engraving Sampler

COLT 150TH ANNIVERSARY COMMEMORATIVE
Single Action Army revolver with 10-inch barrel, royal blue finish, authentic old-style frame with "B" engraving coverage, Goncalo Alves grips; anniversary logo is etched in 24K gold on backstrap, plus gold-etched signature panel. Marketed in an oak case with silver blue velvet lining; top of lid branded "1836-Colt-1986"; inside of the lid has inset 150th anniversary medallion; 1000 made with serial numbers AM-0001 through AM-1000. Made in 1986 only.
Issue Price: $1595
Market Value: $1995

COLT 150TH ANNIVERSARY ENGRAVING SAMPLER
Single Action Army; 4-3/4-inch barrel; blued or nickel finish; carries four styles of hand engraving; Henshaw, Nimschke, Helfricht and Colt Contemporary, with each style contained on one part of the gun; ivory grips are scrimshawed with the names of the four patterns. Made only in 1986.
Issue Price: Blued, $1612.95; Nickel, $1731.50
Market Value: $2500 to $3000 depending on finish, caliber and barrel length.

COLT 150TH ANNIVERSARY DOUBLE DIAMOND
Two-gun set of stainless steel, including the Python Ultimate with 6-inch barrel and a polished Officers Model 45 ACP automatic. Both guns carry matching serial numbers and rosewood grips as well as the Double Diamond logo. Marketed in a cherrywood presentation case with a framed glass lid; lining is black velvet. Serial numbers extend from 0001-DD through 1000-DD. Only 1000 sets made in 1986.
Issue Price: $1574.95
Market Value: $2000

COLT WHITETAILER II
King Cobra AA3080; 357 Magnum; 8-inch barrel, vented rib; red insert in front sight ramp, fully-adjustable white outline rear; rubber combat-style grips; transfer bar safety; brushed stainless steel finish; barrel marked on left side, "Whitetailer II"; furnished with 1-1/2-4x variable Burris scope, with brushed aluminum finish; Millett satin nickel mounts. Marketed in soft-sided custom carrying case. Produced in 1986; 1000 made.
Issue Price: $807.95
Market Value: $1595

KIMBER BROWNELL
Rifle; bolt-action; 22 rimfire; honors stockmaker Len Brownell. Has high-grade, full-length, Mannlicher-type stock. Reported 500 made, 1986.
Market Value: $1500

REMINGTON 1986 CLASSIC
No changes in the basic design except 264 Win. Magnum only.
Issue Price: $509.85
Market Value: $495

TEXAS LONGHORN SESQUICENTENNIAL MODEL
Revolver; single action; same specs as South Texas Army Limited Edition except with 3/4-coverage engraving, antique gold, nickel finish; one-piece ivory stocks. Marketed in hand-made walnut presentation case. Only 150 made in 1986.
Market Value: $2500

WINCHESTER 120TH ANNIVERSARY LIMITED EDITION
Model 94 carbine; 44-40 only; anniversary medallion in left side of receiver, with horse-and-rider trademark; right side of receiver carries gold-etched portrait of Oliver Winchester; signature is on the tang; right side of barrel has rendering of original Winchester factory; gold-plated scrollwork on barrel and receiver; magazine cap, front sight blade are gold-plated; has hoop-type lever, crescent buttplate. Only 1000 made in 1986. Serial numbers are WRA0001 to WRA1000.
Issue Price: $950
Market Value: $1895

WINCHESTER SILVER ANNIVERSARY MODEL 101
Special issue in 12-ga. only; 28-inch barrels, vent rib. Each gun marketed in a custom leather carrying case, complete with snap caps and silver initial plate. Only 101 made in 1986.
Issue Price: $5200
Market Value: $2995

1987

AMERICAN DERRINGER TEXAS COMMEMORATIVE
Same specs as Model 1 Derringer except solid brass frame; stainless steel barrel, stag grips. Made in 38 Special, 44-40, 44 American, 45 Colt. Produced in 1987.
Market Value: $295

AMERICAN HISTORICAL FOUNDATION GENERAL PATTON COMMEMORATIVE
Single Action Army revolver; 45 Colt; 4-3/4-inch barrel; same general specs as Colt Single Action Army but made in Italy by Uberti; all exposed metal silver-plated; engraved frame, cylinder, barrel; faux ivory grips with Patton initials. Serial numbered P0001 through P2500. Reported 2500 made, 1987.
Issue Price: $1495
Market Value: $1495

AMERICAN HISTORICAL FOUNDATION M14 VIETNAM COMMEMORATIVE
Semi-automatic rifle; 7.62mm NATO; version of maker's M1A; 22-inch barrel; highly polished blued metal; some gold-plated parts; select walnut stock. Reported 1500 in Army motif, 1500 in Marine motif made by Springfield Armoury, 1987.
Issue Price: $1600
Market Value: $1195

AMERICAN HISTORICAL FOUNDATION VIETNAM WAR COMMEMORATIVE THOMPSON
Semi-automatic; 45 ACP; polished lacquer American walnut stock; same general specs as standard Model 1927 except gold-plated small parts; roll-engraved; gold-filled legend on receiver. Reported 1500 made by Auto Ordnance with special serial numbers, 1987.

Issue Price: $1295
Market Value: $1295

BROWNING PRONGHORN ANTELOPE ISSUE
Same specs as standard Browning A-Bolt except 243 Win. only; extensive detailed engraving; pronghorn in gold on each side of receiver; stock has skip-line checkering, high-gloss finish, brass spacers under pistol-grip cap, recoil pad. Only 500 made in Japan. Introduced, 1987.
Market Value: $1100

F.I.E. YELLOW ROSE LIMITED EDITION
Same specs as the standard model except polymer grips scrimshawed with map of Texas, Texas state flag, yellow rose with green leaves; other scrimshawed depictions available. Marketed in French-fitted American walnut presentation case. Manufactured in 1987.
Market Value: $200

KIMBER CENTENNIAL
Bolt-action rifle commemorates the 100th anniversary of the 22 Long Rifle cartridge; tastefully engraved; match barrel; select walnut stock; skeleton buttplate. Reported 100 manufactured in 1987 with serial numbers C-1 through C-100.
Market Value: $2600

PARKER B GRADE LIMITED EDITION
Replica of Parker Bros. side-by-side shotgun; 12-, 20- and 28-ga.; extensive engraving follows original pattern. Reported 100 made in Japan, 1987, specifically for Parker Reproductions.
Issue Price: $3975
Market Value: $4800

REMINGTON 1987 CLASSIC
Same specs as other Model 700s in Classic Series except 338 Win. Magnum only. Approximately 3000 made in this chambering only in 1987.
Issue Price: $421
Market Value: $450

WALTHER 100TH YEAR COMMEMORATIVE
Semi-automatic; 9mm Para.; same basic specs as P-5 model except heavy engraving. Marketed in walnut presentation case. Number made, original price unknown. Introduced, 1987.
Market Value: $2350

WINCHESTER MODEL 70 XTR GOLDEN ANNIVERSARY
Similar to sporter magnum except select walnut classic-style stock old-style swivel bases, steel floorplate, grip cap, trigger guard; hand-engraving on barrel, receiver, magazine cover, trigger guard; inscription on barrel, "The Rifleman's Rifle 1937-1987"; hand engraved receiver, floor- plate, trigger guard, grip cap, crossbolt; chambered for 300 Win. Magnum only; 500 made.
Issue Price: $939
Market Value: $1350

1988 Colt Heirloom
Limited Edition

1988 American Historical Foundation M14
Vietnam Commemorative

1988 American Historical Foundation
Commemorative Texas Paterson

1988 American Historical Foundation
Teddy Roosevelt Commemorative

1988

AMERICA REMEMBERS U.S. CAVALRY MODEL
Limited edition blackpowder Colt Model 1860 replica; 44 blackpowder revolver; 8-inch barrel; gold-etched scene on cylinder; stag grips. Marketed in presentation case with replica brass cavalry buckle. Reported 2500 made in U.S., 1988.
Issue Price: $1650
Market Value: $895

AMERICAN HISTORICAL FOUNDATION AMERICAN ARMED FORCES UZI COMMEMORATIVE
Semi-automatic; 9mm Para.; basic specs of standard Uzi except highly polished blued finish; gold-plated magazine release, barrel ring nut, pistol-grip bushing, sear and trigger pivot pins, trigger, stock screws and nuts, sling keepers and cocking knob; furniture-finished woodstock carrying medallion with words, "The American Armed Forces Around The World." Marketed with gold-plated sight-adjustment tool. Reported 1500 made under special Israeli Military Industries contract, 1988.
Issue Price: $2195
Market Value: $1500

AMERICAN HISTORICAL FOUNDATION COMMEMORATIVE TEXAS PATERSON
Five-shot revolver; blackpowder; 36-caliber; part of Samuel Colt Golden Tribute Collection, commemorates 150th anniversary of gun's production; gold-plated, hand-engraved in Italy by Pedersoli; hand-fitted burled walnut grips; 9-inch octagonal barrel. Marketed with combination tool, extra cylinder. Reported 950 made, 1988.
Issue Price: $1495
Market Value: $1495

AMERICAN HISTORICAL FOUNDATION M14 VIETNAM COMMEMORATIVE
Semi-automatic; 7.62mm NATO; same specs as M14 military issue except high-quality Fajen stock; gold-plated components; patriotic inscriptions etched and gold-filled on operating rod and receiver. Made in two configurations, 500 Deluxe Museum Edition and 500 Collector Edition by Federal Arms under special contract, 1988, with special serial numbers.
Issue Price: Deluxe Museum Edition, $1,595; Collector Edition, $1,395
Deluxe Museum Edition
Market Value: $1195
Collector Edition
Market Value: $995

AMERICAN HISTORICAL FOUNDATION LAW ENFORCEMENT COMMEMORATIVE THOMPSON
Semi-automatic; 45 ACP; same specs as standard 1928 Thompson subgun except highly polished American walnut buttstock, grip and vertical foregrip; gold-plated frontsight, Cutts compensator; sling swivels. Receiver roll-engraved, gold-filled legend; police shield medallion in buttstock, rear grip carries medallion with police motto. Marketed with night stick carrying same serial number as gun. Reported 1500 made on special order by Auto Ordnance, 1988.
Issue Price: $1595
Market Value: $1295

AMERICAN HISTORICAL FOUNDATION TEDDY ROOSEVELT COMMEMORATIVE
Revolver; 45 Colt; same specs as Colt Single Action Army except 7-1/2-inch barrel; gold-plated ejector rod housing, trigger, hammer and cylinder; all other external metal parts sterling silver-plated; ivory/polymer grips, with buffalo head raised on right panel; TR monogram on left; extensively engraved in Nimaschke pattern of Roosevelt's original SAA. Reported 750 made in Italy by Uberti, 1988.
Issue Price: $1995
Market Value: $1495

AMERICAN HISTORICAL FOUNDATION U.S. ARMY COMMEMORATIVE
Semi-automatic; 45 ACP; same specs as standard Model 1911A1 except ten gold-plated parts; slide etched, gold-filled with U.S. Army seal, legend; Herrett burled walnut grips with Army medallion. Reported 1911 made on special order by Auto Ordnance, 1988.
Issue Price: $995
Market Value: $750

AMERICAN HISTORICAL FOUNDATION VIETNAM WAR M16 COMMEMORATIVE
Semi-automatic; 5.56mm; same basic specs as M16 military issue except high-gloss black finish; gold-plated flash suppressor, trigger, selector lever, bolt catch, rear sight windage knob, take-down pins, sling swivels; pistol grip and buttstock carry commemorative medallions. Marketed with adjustable black leather military-type sling. Reported 1,500 made by Colt on special order, 1988.
Issue Price: $1995
Market Value: $1795

BROWNING MODEL 12 LIMITED EDITION
Slide-action shotgun; 20-, 28-ga.; 2-3/4-inch chamber; 26-inch barrel; reproduction of the Winchester Model 12; has cut-checkered walnut stock; high-post floating rib, grooved sight plane; crossbolt safety in trigger guard; polished blue finish. Limited edition; 8500 Grade I, 4000 Grade V guns made in Japan in 1988. Imported by Browning.
Issue Price: Grade I, 20-ga., $734.95; Grade I, 28-ga., $771.95; Grade V, 20-ga., $1187; Grade V, 28-ga., $1246.
Mint Grade I
Market Value: $650
Mint Grade V
Market Value: $995

COLT HEIRLOOM LIMITED EDITION
Officers Model 1911A1; 45 ACP; produced in Colt Custom Shop on individual order, with serial numbers to order, combining numbers with family names or initials; full mirror finish; Combat Commander hammer; extended trigger; wide combat grip safety; ambidextrous safety; jeweled barrel, hammer and trigger; ivory grips; special grip medallion. Marketed in mahogany presentation case. Made in 1988-89.
Issue Price: $1500
Market Value: $1395

COLT U.S. MARSHALS BICENTENNIAL COMMEMORATIVE
Single Action Army revolver; 45 Colt; smooth walnut grips; 7-1/2-inch barrel; blued finish; U.S. Marshal medallion set in left grip panel; on left side of the barrel, marking is "U.S. Marshals Bicentennial 1789-1989"; on right side, legend reads "One of Five Hundred." Marketed in glass-topped case, with French blue velvet lining; U.S. Marshal's badge included. Produced for U.S. Marshals Foundation; 500 made in 1988.
Issue Price: $775
Market Value: $1495

KRICO 720 LIMITED EDITION
Bolt-action rifle; 270; 20-1/2-inch barrel; full-length Mannlicher-type stock; gold-plated trim and scrollwork on metal parts; serial number inlaid in gold. Made in Germany. Imported by Beeman Precision Arms, 1988.
Issue Price: $2375
Market Value: $2300

REMINGTON 1988 CLASSIC
Same specs as earlier rifles in the series except 35 Whelen. Approximately 7000 made in this caliber in 1988 only.
Issue Price: $440
Market Value: $495

1988 Browning Model 53 Limited Edition

1989 Mossberg National Wild Turkey Federation Limited Edition

1989 Colt Wyoming Centennial

1989 American Historical Foundation Browning Model 1885 Deerhunter Limited Edition

1989

AMERICAN HISTORICAL FOUNDATION BROWNING MODEL 1885 DEERHUNTER LIMITED EDITION
Lever-action; 45-70; same specs as original Winchester 1885 except has complete engraving coverage of receiver featuring a deer in a wreath; hand-finished walnut stock, forearm. Reported 100 made, 1989.
Issue Price: $2775
Market Value: $1750

AMERICAN HISTORICAL FOUNDATION VIETNAM WAR COMMEMORATIVE
Semi-automatic; 45 ACP; same specs as standard Model 1911A1 except gold-plated hammer, trigger, safety, slide stop, magazine catch, magazine catch lock and grip screws; slide engraved with Oriental dragons, carries bannered legend; American oak grips with medallion. Reported 2500 made by Auto Ordnance on special order, 1989.
Issue Price: $1095
Market Value: $795

BROWNING WYOMING CENTENNIAL
Model 1885 lever-action rifle; 25-06; same basic specs as standard model except tapered octagon barrel, No. 5 walnut stock, Wyoming state seal, centennial logo inlaid in gold. Reported 2000 made in 1989. Marketed by Sports, Inc.
Issue Price: $1200
Market Value: $1200

COLT BEVERLY HILLS POLICE COMMEMORATIVE
Colt Combat Government Model; 45 ACP; commemorates the 75th anniversary of California's Beverly Hills Police Department; gold-plated scene on both sides of slide includes city hall, police car, motorcycle officer foot patrolman; city insignia on rear of slide in gold; city seal inset in grips; gold-bannered commemorative buckle included; special serial numbers, BHPD001 to 150; 150 guns made in 1989. Marketed in red velvet-lined presentation case.
Issue Price: $785
Market Value: $950

COLT JOE FOSS LIMITED EDITION
Government Model auto; 45 ACP; blued finish; fixed sights; smooth walnut grips; left side of the slide covers Foss' life through WWII with gold-plated figures of farmhouse, Marine Corps seal, Marine aviator's wings, cannon and Grumman aircraft; at rear of the slide is bordered rampant colt. On the slide's right side, the gold-plated figures represent Foss' post-WWII career, including South Dakota capitol, a hunter, Mount Rushmore figures, and an F16 fighter aircraft, with words "A Tribute To Joe Foss." Serial numbers are JF0001 through JF2500; 2500 made in 1989. Marketed in walnut presentation case with red velvet lining. Included are brass plate and medallion.
Issue Price: $1375
Market Value: $995

COLT SNAKE EYES SET
Colt Python models; 357 Magnum; two guns in set; 2-1/2-inch barrels; one gun has blued finish, other is stainless steel; Snake Eyes name appears on left side of barrels; ivory-like grips with scrimshaw snake eyes dice on left side, royal flush poker hand on right; matching serial numbers EYES001 through EYES500 positioned on butt of each gun; glass-front presentation case is etched with gold letters, trim; interior of case is lined with green felt; interior lighting; Colt-marked poker chips, playing cards are French-fitted. 500 sets made in 1989.
Issue Price: $3500 per set
Market Value: $2700

COLT WYOMING CENTENNIAL
Single Action Army revolver; 45 Colt; 4-3/4-inch barrel; rosewood custom grips; gold-plated rampant colt medallion; left side of barrel carries roll-marked gold-washed logo with "1890 Wyoming Centennial." Unfluted cylinder carries gold-inlaid state seal on one side, centennial logo on the other. Only 200 made in 1989. Marketed in French-fitted walnut case with commemorative plate by Sports, Inc., Lewiston, Montana.
Issue Price: $1250
Market Value: $1395

MOSSBERG NATIONAL WILD TURKEY FEDERATION LIMITED EDITION
Same specs as standard Mossberg Model 835 Ulti-Mag 12-ga. pump-action shotgun, except camo finish; Wild Turkey Federation medallion inlaid in the stock. Marketed with a 10-pack of Federal 3-1/2-inch turkey-load shotshells. Made in 1989.
Issue Price: $477
Market Value: $295

REMINGTON 1989 CLASSIC
Same specs as earlier caliber chamberings in the series except 300 Weatherby Magnum. Approximately 6000 made in this caliber only.
Issue Price: $485
Market Value: $495

1990

AMERICA REMEMBERS FREDERICK REMINGTON MODEL 1886
Revolver; honors the famed Western artist's 100th anniversary as an associate of the National Academy of Design; 44 blackpowder 1886 Army replica; gold etching on 8-inch barrel, trigger, cylinder frame and gripstraps. Marketed with cased accessories. Reported 1000 made, 1990.
Issue Price: $1500
Market Value: $750

AMERICA REMEMBERS LIMITED EDITION TEXAS RANGER DRAGOON
Blackpowder 44 replica revolver; 8-inch barrel; silver-plating on gripstraps, trigger guard and cylinder; colorcase-hardened frame, loading lever; gold etched barrel, frame. Marketed in case with accessories. Reported 1000 made in U.S., 1990.
Issue Price: $1585
Market Value: $995

AMERICA REMEMBERS ROY ROGERS COWBOY EDITION
Single Action Army 45 Colt revolver; 4-3/4-inch barrel; gold-plated cylinder; gold etchings on barrel, gripstrap, frame; stag grips. Marketed in presentation case. Reported 2500 made, 1990.
Issue Price: $1550
Market Value: $1495

AMERICA REMEMBERS ROY ROGERS PREMIER EDITION
Same general specs as Roy Rogers Cowboy Edition except extensive inlays and heavy engraving. Reported 250 made, 1990.
Issue Price: $4500
Market Value: $2995

1991 American Historical Foundation WWII Commemorative Hi-Power

1991 Winchester 125th Anniversary Commemorative Model 94

1990 Winchester Wyoming Centennial Commemorative

AMERICA REMEMBERS ROYAL ARMORIES DRAGOON

Replica of 44 blackpowder 2nd Model Dragoon revolver made in England for Sam Colt; 7-1/2-inch barrel; hand-engraved case-hardened action; walnut grips with sterling silver plaque. Reported 1000 made, 1990.
Issue Price: $2450
Market Value: $1995

BROWNING MODEL 53 LIMITED EDITION

Rifle; 32-20; 7-shot half-length magazine; 22-inch round, tapered barrel; 39.5-inch overall length; weighs 6.8 lbs.; post bead front sight, open adjustable rear; cut-checkered select walnut stock, forend; metal grip cap; blued finish. Only 5000 produced in Japan. Based on Winchester Model 92 design. Introduced, 1990; dropped, 1991.
Issue Price: $675
Market Value: $595

COLT EL PRESIDENTE

Dressed-up version of the Colt Government Model 38 Super; highly polished Ultimate stainless finish; Pearlex grips; "El Presidente" and rampant colt are engraved on left side of the slide. Only 350 made in 1990 for Lew Horton Distributing. Marketed in special soft case with Colt logo.
Issue Price: $800
Market Value: $1695

KIMBER 10TH ANNIVERSARY ISSUE

Bolt-action rifle; 223 Remington; French walnut stock with shadow cheekpiece, slim forend; 22-inch barrel; round-top receiver; steel buttplate; scope mounts furnished. Introduced, 1990 in extremely limited numbers.
Market Value: $1600

REMINGTON 1990 CLASSIC

Same specs as previous 700 Classic models except 25-06 only; 4-shot magazine; 24-inch barrel. Made only in 1990.
Issue Price: $520
Market Value: $495

SMITH & WESSON MODEL 28 MAGNACLASSIC

Same specs as standard Model 29 except 7-1/2-inch full lug barrel; highly polished finish; target hammer, trigger; ergonomic Goncalo Alves grips with carnuba finish. Marketed in cherrywood case with gold-embossed leather lid, fitted velvet interior, black leather sight box, sight assortment, test target, certificate of authenticity; factory accurized; barrel laser-etched, "1 of 3000." 1550 were made in 1990.
Issue Price: $999
Market Value: $1200

SMITH & WESSON MODEL 629 MAGNACLASSIC

Same specs as Model 29 MagnaClassic except stainless steel; same markings; marketed with same accessory package. 1450 were made in 1990.
Issue Price: $999
Market Value: $1200

WINCHESTER WYOMING CENTENNIAL COMMEMORATIVE

Model 94-30-30; features coin-type finish on receiver, barrel bands; receiver engraved both sides with Wyoming scenes; left side carries engraved banners, "1890-1990" and "Wyoming Centennial"; 20-inch barrel; full buckhorn Marble sight; special serial numbers; only 999 made. Marketed exclusively by Cherry's.
Issue Price: $895
Market Value: $1395

1991

AMERICA REMEMBERS INTERPOL COLT SAA

Single Action Army revolver; 45 Colt; 4-3/4-inch barrel; engraving replica of that on Kornblath Interpol Model; silver-plated, with faux ivory grips; marketed in book-like leather case. Only 154 manufactured by Colt on special order, 1991.
Issue Price: $4500
Market Value: $2995

AMERICAN HISTORICAL FOUNDATION WWII COMMEMORATIVE HI-POWER

Semi-automatic; 9mm Para.; same specs as standard Hi-Power model except overall gold plating; carries deep-etched inscriptions, scrollwork; custom-finished walnut grips; inset with victory medallion. Marketed with extra magazine and cleaning rod, both gold-plated. Reported 500 made on special order by Browning 1991.
Issue Price: $1795
Market Value: $1295

GLOCK DESERT STORM COMMEMORATIVE

Built on the Glock 17 9mm Parabellum configuration; legend on the right side of the slide reads, "Operation Desert Storm January 16 - February 17, 1991"; on the left side is "New World Order" and the Glock 17 logo. On top of the slide are listed the 30 countries of the United Nations that took part in the campaign. Marketed with a field knife in a glass case bearing the Desert Storm shield. Only 1000 made in 1991.
Issue Price: $900
Market Value: $900

IVER JOHNSON 50TH ANNIVERSARY M-1 CARBINE

Semi-automatic; 30 U.S. Carbine; same specs as standard version except deluxe American walnut stock; red, white and blue American enameled flag embedded in stock; gold-filled, roll engraving with words "50th Anniversary 1941-1991" on slide; Parkerized finish. Introduced, 1991; still available.
Issue Price: $384.95
Market Value: $375

REMINGTON 1991 CLASSIC

Same Model 700 specs as other rifles in the annual series except 7mm Weatherby Magnum only; 4-shot magazine. Produced only in 1991.
Market Value: $495

REMINGTON 7400 175TH ANNIVERSARY RIFLE

Same specs as the standard Remington Model 7400 except receiver engraved with company's 175th Anniversary scroll design, American eagle; high-gloss American walnut stock; deep-cut checkering; 30-06 only. Introduced, 1991; dropped, 1992.
Market Value: $350

REMINGTON MODEL 11-87 175TH ANNIVERSARY COMMEMORATIVE

Same specs as the Model 11-87 Premier except engraved receiver carries anniversary design with American eagle; walnut stock, forend with high-gloss finish; 28-inch vent-rib barrel; 12-ga. only. Marketed with Rem Choke tubes. Made in 1991.
Issue Price: $618
Market Value: $450

SAVAGE MODEL 110WLE LIMITED EDITION

Same specs as Model 110G except 250-3000, 300 Savage, 7x57; high-luster fancy-grade American walnut stock, cut checkering, swivel studs, recoil pad, polished barrel; Savage logo is laser-etched on bolt. Marketed with gun lock, shooting glasses, ear plugs, sight-in target. Introduced, 1991; still available.
Market Value: $350

WINCHESTER 125TH ANNIVERSARY COMMEMORATIVE MODEL 84

Rifle; 30-30; features John Ulrich-style, full-coverage engraving; right side has 24-karat gold relief bull moose; left side has gold figures of buck and doe; 20-inch octagon barrel, lever are engraved, gold inlaid; full buckhorn rear sight; hand-checkered American walnut stock; marketed in French-fitted walnut presentation case exclusively by Cherry's. Only 125 made in 1991. **Issue Price:** $4995
Market Value: $5500

1992 Winchester
Kentucky Bicentennial
Commemorative

1992 Springfield Armory
Gulf Victory
Special Edition

1992

AMERICAN HISTORICAL FOUNDATION 40TH ANNIVERSARY RUGER COMMEMORATIVE

Semi-automatic; 22 LR; same specs as Ruger Mark II except faux ivory grips with red Ruger medallion inset in right grip, black medallion in left grip; gold-plated trigger, trigger pivot, hammer pivot, gripscrews, bolt handle, bolt stop, scrollwork; 40th Anniversary inset in barrel in gold. Reported 950 made, 1992.
Issue Price: $995
Market Value: $495

AMERICAN HISTORICAL FOUNDATION 50TH ANNIVERSARY WW II COLT

Semi-automatic; 45 ACP; same basic specs as Colt Model 1911A1; blued finish; faux ivory grips; issued in honor of six major battles in Pacific, six in Europe; explanatory legend etched in gold on slide; grips carry historical quotations, details of campaigns, rampant colt insignia. Reported 250 pistols made by Colt, 1992, for each of the twelve campaigns; guns numbered 001 through 250 with prefix appropriate to each campaign. Marketed in OD-lined presentation case with serially numbered Basic Field Manual.
Issue Price: $995
Market Value: $995

AMERICAN HISTORICAL SOCIETY SAMUEL COLT GOLDEN TRIBUTE BUNTLINE

Revolver; 45 Colt; same basic specs of Colt Single Action Army model except 12-inch barrel; all metal parts gold-plated; heavy engraving in Texas scroll pattern; hand-fitted walnut grips. Marketed in walnut wall display case with glass lid, brass hardware. Reported 950 made in Italy by Uberti, 1992.
Issue Price: $2195
Market Value: $1495

AMERICA REMEMBERS COWBOY HALL OF FAME REVOLVER

Single Action Army revolver; 45 Colt; 4-3/4-inch barrel; hand-fitted stag grips; blued steel barrel, trigger guard, gripstraps; gold-plated frame; gold-

etched scenes on cylinder. Marketed in velvet-lined display case with glass lid. Marketed in conjunction with the Cowboy Hall of Fame, Oklahoma City. Reported 1000 manufactured in 1992.
Issue Price: $1600
Market Value: $1600

AMERICA REMEMBERS EISENHOWER COMMEMORATIVE

Semi-automatic; 45 ACP; Springfield Armory-made Model 1911A1; 5-inch barrel; 7-shot magazine; checkered walnut grips with inset bronze medallions; blued slide carries gold decoration. Marketed in velvet-lined display case with Eisenhower's signature etched in walnut lid; framed photo of Ike autographed by his son, John. Reported 2500 made, 1992.
Issue Price: $1675
Market Value: $995

AMERICA REMEMBERS MEL TORME COLT SAA

Single Action Army revolver; 45 Colt; 5-1/2-inch barrel; mother of pearl grips; silver-inlaid engraving; gold-inlaid highlights. Marketed in leather-bound display case bearing gold-embossed signature of singer/gun fancier Torme. Reported 100 manufactured by Colt on special contract, 1992.
Issue Price: $4500
Market Value: $2995

AMERICA REMEMBERS RICHARD PETTY SILVER EDITION

Single Action Army revolver; 45 Colt; blued steel; sterling silver decoration; faux ivory grips with incised signature. Reported 1000 made by Colt in 1992.
Issue Price: $1495
Market Value: $1650 to $1700

SPRINGFIELD ARMORY GULF VICTORY SPECIAL EDITION

Semi-automatic; 45 ACP; same specs as Model 1911A1 except decoration; highly blued finish; gold plating on slide, small parts; marketed in padded, embroidered carrying case with jacket patch, window decal and medallion. Number made unknown.
Issue Price: $869
Market Value: $775

WINCHESTER ARAPAHO COMMEMORATIVE

Lever-action carbine; 30-30; same specs as standard Model 94 carbine except varnished select walnut stock, decoration; lever, receiver, barrel bands gold-plated, other metal parts blued; right side of the receiver etched with scene of Arapaho life, left side carries scene of buffalo hunt with a banner reading, "The Arapaho Commemorative." Reported 500 made exclusively for Cherry's by USRAC/Winchester, 1992.
Issue Price: $895
Market Value: $1295

WINCHESTER KENTUCKY BICENTENNIAL COMMEMORATIVE

Lever-action carbine; 30-30; same specs as standard Model 94 except receiver engraved in Italy, then bone charcoal case-colored; checkered stock, forearm. Banner on left side of receiver reads, "Kentucky Bicentennial 1792-1992"; racehorse etchings also featured. On right side is a Kentucky horse barn. Reported 500 made by USRA/Winchester exclusively for Cherry's, 1992.
Issue Price: $995
Market Value: $1295

WINCHESTER ONTARIO CONSERVATION COMMEMORATIVE

Lever-action carbine; 30-30; same specs as standard Model 94 except pewter finish of some parts; fancy walnut stock, decoration; right receiver panel carries Ontario game scene and portrait of conservation officer; left panel carries etching of moose, beavers in wilderness setting; replica of conservation officer's badge is set in stock. Reported 500 made by USRA/Winchester exclusively for Cherry's, 1992.
Issue Price: $795
Market Value: $1295

1994 American Historical Foundation
Limited Edition Colt Anaconda

1994 American Historical Foundation
Smith & Wesson Bank Note Limited Edition

1993 American Historical Foundation
Showcase Edition Colt M16

1994 American Historical Foundation
Colt Heritage Edition SAA

1993

AMERICA REMEMBERS AMERICAN EAGLE COLT

Semi-automatic; 45 ACP; Colt-made Model 1911A1; 5-inch barrel; blued finish; gold/silver bald eagle etched on each side; gold-plated safety, sights, hammer, grip screws. Marketed in blue velvet-lined walnutcase with American flag and brass identification plate. Reported 2500 made, 1993.
Issue Price: $1950
Market Value: $1950 to $2000

AMERICA REMEMBERS DON'T GIVE UP THE SHIP MODEL

Semi-autmatic; 45 ACP; Colt-made Model 1911A1; 4-inch barrel; blued finish; gold-etched on the slide are USS Constitution, USS Ticonderoga, plus appropriate legend; rosewood grips with Colt medallion. Reported 1997 made, 1993.
Issue Price: $1570
Market Value: $995

AMERICA REMEMBERS GEORGE JONES SAA

Single Action Army revolver; 45 Colt; blued steel finish, decorated with gold inlays of music scores; Jones' name on barrel; bonded pearl grips. Reported 950 made, 1993.
Issue Price: $1575
Market Value: $1495

AMERICA REMEMBERS HOPALONG CASSIDY COWBOY EDITION

Single Action Army revolver; 45 Colt; 5-1/2-inch barrel; grips of black water buffalo horn; blued finish; frame, barrel, cylinder decorated with sterling silver. Marketed in velvet-lined cherrywood display case. Reported 950 manufactured, 1993.
Issue Price: $1675
Market Value: $1650

AMERICA REMEMBERS HOPALONG PREMIERE EDITION

Same specs as Cowboy Edition except in addition to silver decoration it has deep engraving, gold inlays and a leather case embossed with William Boyd's monogram. Only 100 made, 1993.
Issue Price: $4500
Market Value: $2995

AMERICA REMEMBERS "WILL PENNY" CHARLTON HESTON TRIBUTE

Single Action Army revolver; 45 Colt; 5-1/2-inch barrel; blued steel; silver and gold decoration on metal, including cattledrive scene. Minted gold portrait medallion of Heston inset in single-piece walnut grips. Reported 500 manufactured in 1993.
Issue Price: $1850
Market Value: $995

AMERICAN HISTORICAL FOUNDATION GENERAL ROBERT E. LEE HENRY REPEATER

Lever-action rifle; 44-40; 44-inch overall length; same specs as original Henry repeating rifle except receiver scrolled with dogwood, cotton flowers, magnolias; high-gloss blued finish; gold-plated trigger, follower, front sight blade and lifter; oil-finished walnut stock; left side of receiver with gold-filled Confederate seal, right side with portrait of Lee and Confederate flag. Reported 250 made in Italy by Uberti, 1993.
Issue Price: $2495
Market Value: $1500

AMERICAN HISTORICAL FOUNDATION SHOWCASE EDITION COLT M16

Semi-auto; 5.56mm; same specs as standard Colt M16 military version except receiver, sights, barrel mirror polished or glass-beaded, then nickel-plated; plastic stock has heavily textured finish; sterling silver plaque inset in stock reads "The Showcase Edition Colt One of One Hundred"; same legend etched on magazine well, surrounding rampant colt. Reported 100 with special serial numbers made by Colt, 1993.
Issue Price: $1995
Market Value: $1795

AMERICAN HISTORICAL FOUNDATION SPECIAL EDITION M16 VIETNAM TRIBUTE

Semi-auto M16; 5.56mm; HBAR match configuration; heavy barrel; custom-textured buttstock, pistol grip and hand guard; gold-plated trigger, magazine release, safety, pivot pins, windage knob, elevation knob, flash suppressor, sling swivels; medallion in pistol grip displays Vietnam ribbon and legend. Reported 1500 made, 1993, on special order by Colt, serial numbers VI0001 through VI1500.
Issue Price: $1995
Market Value: $1795

AMERICAN HISTORICAL FOUNDATION SPECIAL EDITION S&W MODEL 629 HUNTER

Revolver; 44 Magnum; same specs as standard Model 629 except 6-inch Mag-Na-Ported barrel with integral scope base, variable underweight; heavily engraved; finger-grooved Goncalo Alves grips. Marketed with Tasco scope mounts, 2x Nikon pistol scope, S&W Performance Center shooting bag, Tasco shooting glasses, Silencio ear plugs. Only 50 made by S&W under special order, 1993.
Issue Price: $3795
Market Value: $1795

WINCHESTER NEZ PERCE COMMEMORATIVE

Lever-action carbine; 30-30; same specs as standard Model 94 except for decoration; nickel-finished receiver, lever, barrel bands; other parts blued; left side of the receiver etched with bust of Chief Joseph, map of tribe's travels; right side features Nez Perce encampment against mountain background. Reported 600 made by USRAC/Winchester on special order, 1993. Serial numbered NEZ001 through NEZ600.
Issue Price: $950
Market Value: $1295

1993 Winchester
Nez Perce
Commemorative

1993 Winchester Nez Perce
Commemorative Engraving

1993 American Historical Foundation Special Edition
S&W Model 629 Hunter

1994

AMERICA REMEMBERS AMERICAN INDIAN TRIBUTE CARBINE

Rifle; 45 Colt; same specs as Winchester Model 94 Wrangler except gold-plated loop-style lever; gold-plated barrel bands, action; right side of receiver with buffalo highlighted in nickel, Indian-head penny mounted ahead of ejection port; left side features buffalo hunt in nickel, with buffalo-head nickel adjoining. Reported 300 made by USRA, 1994.
Issue Price: $1295
Market Value: $1195

AMERICA REMEMBERS ARMY AIR FORCES TRIBUTE

Semi-automatic; 45 ACP; Colt-made Model 1911A1; decoration etched on left side of the slide, including Air Corps wings and Master of the Sky legend, nickel-plated; remainder of slide gold-plated; right side carries insignia of all sixteen Army Air combat units of the World War II era; gold-plated safety, sights and grip screws; rosewood custom grips inset with Colt medallion. Reported 500 made, 1994.
Issue Price: $1500
Market Value: $995

AMERICA REMEMBERS GETTYSBURG COMMEMORATIVE

Revolver; 44-caliber replica of Colt 1860 Army Model; 8-inch barrel; blued finish; select walnut grips; cylinder etched with panorama of Pickett's charge; barrel marked with gold, Gettysburg, Pennsylvania, July 1863 and line from Lincoln's address. Marketed in velvet-lined walnut display case; inset leather lid carries silhouette of a general, with "Gettysburg 1863" stamped in gold. Reported 1863 made, 1994.
Issue Price: $1350
Market Value: $995

AMERICA REMEMBERS JOHNNY CASH PATERSON

Revolver; 36-caliber blackpowder Colt Paterson replica; 12-1/2-inch overall length; bonded pearl grips; blued finish; decorated with 24-karat gold; titles of Cash's hit songs on barrel. Marketed in black-finished hardwood display case bearing Cash's signature. Included was a copy of Cash's biography. Reported 1000 made, 1994.
Issue Price: $1350
Market Value: $995

AMERICA REMEMBERS MARINE PACIFIC TRIBUTE

Semi-automatic; 45 ACP; Model 1911A1 design; 5-inch barrel; gold-plated slide, safety, grip screws, sights; slide etched with WWII battles on right side,

appropriate legend and Iwo Jima flag raising on left; custom rosewood grips with gold-plated Colt medallion; 500 made by Colt, 1994.
Issue Price: $1500
Market Value: $995

AMERICA REMEMBERS PACIFIC NAVY TRIBUTE

Semi-automatic; 45 ACP; Model 1911A1 design; 5-inch barrel; gold-plated slide, safety, grip screws; slide etched with appropriate inscriptions, classes of ships that participated in the Pacific in World War II; custom-checkered rosewood grips inset with U.S. Navy seal. Reported 500 made on special order by Auto Ordnance, 1944.
Issue Price: $1500
Market Value: $995

AMERICA REMEMBERS WWII GOLDEN ANNIVERSARY VICTORY TRIBUTE

Semi-automatic; Model 1911A1 design; 5-inch barrel, gold-plated slide, safety, sights, grip screws; slide etched with regimental badges of units under Eisenhower's command on D-Day; rosewood grips inset with gold commemorative medallion. Reported 500 made on special order by Colt, 1994.
Issue Price: $1500
Market Value: $1995

AMERICAN HISTORICAL FOUNDATION 2ND AMENDMENT BROWNING HI-POWER

Semi-automatic; 40 S&W; dedicated to the right to bear arms; same specs as standard Browning Hi-Power except silver plating overall, with gold-plated hammer, trigger, magazine release, safety, slide release, grip screws; scroll-etched frame, slide; polished rosewood grips, 2nd Amendment medallion inset in left grip. Reported 500 made on special order by Browning, 1994.
Issue Price: $1995
Market Value: $1295

AMERICAN HISTORICAL FOUNDATION COLT HERITAGE EDITION SAA

Revolver; 45 Colt; 4-3/4-inch barrel; honors Sam Colt and company history; same specs as standard Single Action Army model except heavy scroll engraving on frame barrel, cylinder, hammer; gold inlaid decoration, including rampant colt on recoil shield, company insignia on loading gate, bronc rider on frame, Colt 45 Single Action Army bannered in gold inlay on left side of barrel; walnut grips; Colt grip medallions. Marketed in stand-up glass/walnut case. Reported 250 made by Colt, 1995.
Issue Price: $2995
Market Value: $2995

AMERICAN HISTORICAL FOUNDATION LIMITED EDITION COLT ANACONDA

Double-action revolver; 44 Magnum; 8-inch barrel; same specs as standard Anaconda except major parts plated with black and gold titanium; identifying legend, rampant colt trademark etched in left side of barrel, gold-filled; polished rosewood grips inset with special Colt medallion. Reported 1000 made, 1995; serial numbers LE0001 through LE1000.
Issue Price: $1595
Market Value: $1675

AMERICAN HISTORICAL FOUNDATION SMITH & WESSON BANK NOTE LIMITED EDITION

Revolver; 45 ACP; stainless steel construction; same specs as S&W Model 625, underlug; left side of frame has "45" hand-cut, surrounded by Bank Note engraving pattern; right side hand-engraved, "Bank Note .45"; etched on right side of barrel ".45 Cal. Model of 1989"; custom Hogue Bill Jordan grips of patented synthetic. Reported 100 produced, 1995.
Issue Price: $2195
Market Value: $1495

MARLIN CENTURY LIMITED MODEL 1894

Lever-action rifle; 44-40; 12-shot tube magazine; 24-inch tapered octagonal barrel; 407/8-inch overall length; weighs 6-1/2 lbs.; checkered semi-fancy American black walnut stock, forearm; brass buttplate; carbine front sight, adjustable semi-buckhorn rear; lever, bolt, lever engraved in Italy. Commemorates 100th anniversary of model. Reported 2500 made, 1994.
Issue Price: $1087
Market Value: $1150

PEDERSOLI CREEDMORE COMMEMORATIVE

Single shot rifle; 45-70; 34-inch round/octagon barrel; hand-checkered American walnut stock; hand-fitted German silver forend cap; color case-hardened receiver, buttplate; tasteful engraving; hooded front sight, long Vernier tang rear; weighs 12 lbs., 2 oz. Reported 280 made on special order for Cherry's, 1995.
Issue Price: $1495
Market Value: $1795

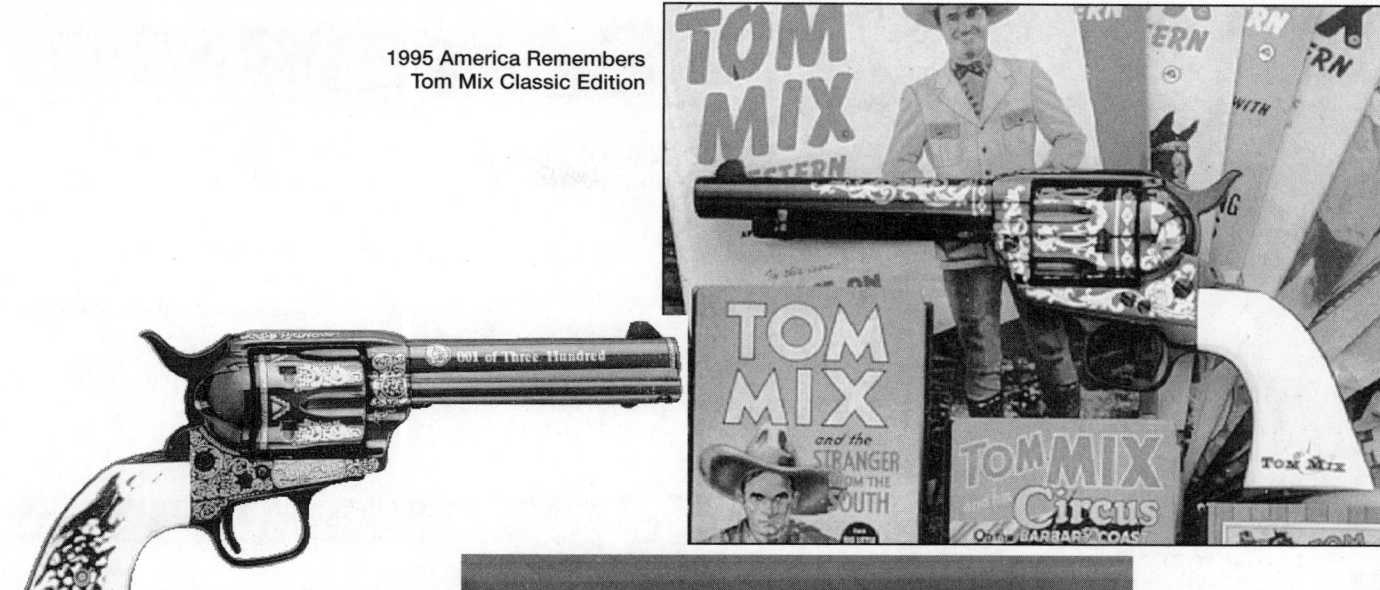

1995 America Remembers
Tom Mix Classic Edition

1995 America Remembers
American Indian Tribute

1995 America Remembers
Navajo Code Talkers Tribute

1995

AMERICA REMEMBERS
7TH CAVALRY TRIBUTE

Single Action Army revolver; 45 Colt; 7-1/2-inch barrel; blued finish; 24-karat gold etchings of crossed sabers on each side of barrel, unit designation, mixed cavalry and Indian symbols on cylinder; Custer portrait laser-carved in faux ivory grips. Marketed in walnut presentation case with replica cavalry belt buckle. Reported 500 made, 1995.
Issue Price: $1500
Market Value: $1495

AMERICA REMEMBERS
AMERICAN INDIAN TRIBUTE

Single Action Army revolver; 45 Colt; 4-3/4-inch barrel; genuine hand-fitted stag grips; blued finish; decorated with gold, nickel; left side of frame with Indian battle scene etched in gold; on right side etching of two bison. Individual edition number is stamped on right side of barrel, "The American Indian" on left. Marketed as a companion piece to 1994 issue American Indian Carbine in glass-topped cherrywood case, with brass plaque. Reported 300 made, 1995.
Issue Price: $1495
Market Value: $1495

AMERICA REMEMBERS
BUFFALO BILL SESQUICENTENNIAL

Single Action Army revolver; 45 Colt; 4-3/4-inch barrel; stag grips; blued finish; left side of frame with Buffalo Bill's Wild West etched in gold, right side carries American bison, Chief Scout Cody in Cheyenne territory; cylinder with gold-etched art of Cody's career. Issue commemorates 150th anniversary of his birth. Reported 500 made, 1995.
Issue Price: $1500
Market Value: $1495

AMERICA REMEMBERS
CHUCK YEAGER TRIBUTE

Semi-automatic; 45 ACP; 5-inch barrel; checkered rosewood grips; silver-plated with gold and blued decorations; left side carries etching of breaking the sound barrier and Yeager's signature; right side portrays subject as WWII fighter pilot with P-51 and Messerschmitt aircraft. Marketed in blue velvet-lined walnut case with signature laser-carved on lid. Reported 500 made on special order by Colt, 1995.
Issue Price: $1750
Market Value: $995

AMERICA REMEMBERS
NAVAJO CODE TALKERS TRIBUTE

Semi-automatic; 45 ACP; Colt-made Model 1911A1; 5-inch barrel; blued finish; stippled slide, with engraved Navajo Code Talkers Commemorative in banner; ironwood grips inlaid with silver, red coral and turquoise, silver figures of code talkers and Iwo Jima flag raising. Marketed in ironwood case with David Yellowhorse custom-made knife featuring stippled, gold-plated bolsters, handle of silver, turquoise, red coral and ironwood inlaid with flag-raising. Reported 300 sets made, 1995.
Issue Price: $3000
Market Value: $1500

AMERICA REMEMBERS
NORTH AMERICAN RODEO TRIBUTE

Lever-action carbine; 30-30; loop-style lever; 16-inch barrel; other specs the same as standard Model 94 Winchester except for gold-finished barrel bands, gold etching on trigger, trigger guard, hammer. On left side of receiver, "The Great North American Rodeo" in gold banner, steer wrestling and bronc riding in gold against a nickel background; right side has bull rider and barrel racer featured in gold, nickel. Reported 500 made by USRA/Winchester, 1995.
Issue Price: $1600
Market Value: $1495

AMERICA REMEMBERS
ROY ROGERS WINCHESTER
TRIBUTE

Lever-action rifle; 30-30; same specs as standard Model 94 Winchester except jeweled hammer and breechbolt, gold-plated lever, barrel bands and front sight hood; left side of receiver features portrait of Rogers in gold and nickel; right side with Rogers on rearing horse, six-guns leveled, also in nickel and gold. Reported 300 made on special order by USRA/Winchester, 1995.
Issue Price: $2100
Market Value: $1395

AMERICA REMEMBERS
TOM MIX CLASSIC EDITION

Single Action Army revolver; 45 Colt; blued finish; 5-1/2-inch barrel with TM brand in 24-karat gold; Mix brand also on each chamber of cylinder; gold signature on backstrap, portrait of Mix on recoil shield, repro of monument erected at the sight of his death on left; faux ivory grips carry Mix name, Stetson hat and TM brand. Marketed in walnut case with red velvet lining; included is Tom Mix comic book, circa 1948-1953. Reported 200 made by Uberti in Italy, 1995.
Issue Price: $1395
Market Value: $995

AMERICA REMEMBERS
TOM MIX PREMIER EDITION

Same specs as the Classic except barrel carries gold-filled edition numbers 1 through 50. Each gun also furnished with an original-edition Tom Mix Big Little Book of the 1930s. Fifty guns made by Colt, 1995.
Issue Price: $2595
Market Value: $1750

1995 America Remembers
North American Rodeo Tribute

1995 America Remembers
Marlin 1895 Century Limited

1995 America Remembers
Roy Rogers Tribute

1995 America Remembers
The Confederate Enfield Limited Edition

1995 America Remembers
Buffalo Bill Sesquicentennial

AMERICA REMEMBERS THE CONFEDERATE ENFIELD LIMITED EDITION

Single shot muzzle-loading rifle; 58 caliber; overall length, 55-inch; barrel length, 39-inch; European walnut stock; blued finish; gold-finished buttplate, hammer and lock, trigger guard, barrel bands, barrel design. Replica of Confederate belt buckle inlaid in right side of stock. Marketed in wall-mount display case with Confederate gray lining and uniform buttons of the eleven Rebel states as decoration. Reported 500 made, 1995.
Issue Price: $1695
Market Value: $1250

AMERICA REMEMBERS V-J DAY TRIBUTE

Semi-automatic; 45 ACP; Model 1911A1; 5-inch barrel; checkered rosewood grips inset with gold Colt medallion; blued finish, except for safety, hammer and grip screws; decoration on slide; top of slide carries engraved legend, gold seal; left side with gold portrait of Admiral Nimitz, with dive bomber, battleship; right side with Douglas MacArthur in victory wreath with his words at surrender ceremony. Reported 250 made, 1995.
Issue Price: $1495
Market Value: $995

AMERICAN HISTORICAL FOUNDATION LIMITED EDITION COLT GOLD CUP

Semi-automatic; 45 ACP; same specs as standard Colt Gold Cup but all exterior surfaces gold-plated, except backstrap. Banner carries legend, "Gold Cup Edition" and "One of 100". Reported 100 made, 1995.
Issue Price: $2195
Market Value: $1495

AMERICAN HISTORICAL FOUNDATION SECOND AMENDMENT S&W SIGMA

Semi-automatic; 40 S&W; 4-1/2-inch barrel; same specs as standard Sigma model except gold-filled etched scrollwork on slide, special commemorative medallion inset in grip; special serial numbers. Reported 250 made, 1995.
Issue Price: $1995
Market Value: $750

AMERICAN HISTORICAL FOUNDATION WORLD WAR II 50TH ANNIVERSARY THOMPSON

Semi-automatic; 45 ACP; gold-etched receiver follows military acorn motif; gold-plated trigger, rear sight base, Cutts compensator, actuator knob, sling swivels; American walnut stock inset with three medallions; special serial numbers. Reported 500 made by Auto Ordnance on special order, 1995.
Issue Price: $2495
Market Value: $1295

MARLIN 1895 CENTURY LIMITED

Lever-action; 45-70; commemorates company's 125th anniversary, 100th anniversary of model; same specs as original 1895 model except black walnut stock; French gray-finished receiver, etched with centennial dates; inletted steel buttplate. Unknown number made, 1995.
Issue Price: $1105
Market Value: $1195

MARLIN BAT MASTERSON COMMEMORATIVE

Lever-action carbine; 44 Special/44 Magnum; same specs as standard Marlin Model 1894 except decoration; receiver and bolt engraved in Italy; left receiver panel engraved with old Dodge City street scene with portrait of Masterson inset; right panel carries the names of towns where he enforced the law, with his derby, badge, a buffalo skull and other artwork; gold-plated action, other metal parts blued. Reported 500 made exclusively for Cherry's by Marlin, 1995.
Issue Price: $895
Market Value: $995

WINCHESTER FLORIDA SESQUICENTENNIAL COMMEMORATIVE

Lever-action carbine; same specs as standard Model 94 except decoration; lever, receiver, barrel bands gold-plated; barrel hammer, bolt, magazine tube deep-luster blued; left receiver panel engraved with state seal, state bird and Kennedy Space Center launch; right panel features Everglades with alligator, crane and airboat; checkered semi-fancy French walnut stock; special serial numbers FL001 through FL500. Reported 500 made exclusively for Cherry's, 1995.
Issue Price: $1195
Market Value: $1495

FIREARMS TRADE AND PROPRIETARY NAMES

A.A. Co.: Inexpensive pocket revolvers of unknown manufacture.

Acme: a) Trade name of the W.H. Davenport Firearms Company on shotguns. b) Trade name of the Hopkins and Allen Company on revolvers produced for the Merwin, Hulbert and Company and the Herman Boker Company of New York. c) Trade name of the Maltby, Henley and Company of New York on inexpensive pocket revolvers.

Acme Arms Company: Trade name of the J. Stevens Arms and Tool Company on pistols and shotguns produced for the Cornwall Hardware Company of New York.

Adams, N.R.: Trade name of the N. R. Davis and Company on shotguns.

Aetna: Trade name of the firm of Harrington and Richardson on inexpensive pocket revolvers.

Alaska: Trade name of the Hood Firearms Company on inexpensive pocket revolvers.

Alert: Trade name of the Hood Firearms Company on inexpensive pocket revolvers.

Alexander Gun Company: Trade name believed to have been E.K. Tryon of Philadelphia on imported shotguns.

Alexis: Trade name of the Hood Firearms Company on inexpensive pocket revolvers.

Allen 22: Trade name of the Hopkins and Allen Company on inexpensive pocket revolvers.

America: Trade name of the Crescent Firearms Company on inexpensive pocket revolvers.

American: Trade name of the Ely and Wray on inexpensive pocket revolvers.

American Barlock Wonder: Trade name of the H. & D. Folsom Arms Company on Shotguns made for the Sears, Roebuck Company of Chicago.

American Boy: Trade name used on firearms retailed by the Townley Metal and Hardware Company of Kansas City, Missouri.

American Bulldog: Trade name of the Iver Johnson Arms and Cycle Works on inexpensive pocket revolvers.

American Bulldog Revolver: Trade name of Harrington and Richardson Arms Company on an inexpensive pocket revolver.

American Eagle: Trade name of the Hopkins and Allen Company on inexpensive pocket revolvers.

American Gun Company: Trade name of H. & D. Folsom Arms Company on pistols and shotguns that firm retailed.

American Gun Barrel Company: Trade name of R. Avis of West Haven, Connecticut between 1916 and 1920.

American Nitro: Trade name of H. & D. Folsom Arms Co. on shotguns.

Americus: Trade name of the Hopkins and Allen Company on inexpensive pocket revolvers.

Angel: Trade name found on inexpensive pocket revolvers of unknown manufacture.

Arab, The: Trade name of the Harrington and Richardson Arms Company on shotguns.

Aristocrat: a) Trade name of the Hopkins and Allen Company on inexpensive pocket revolvers.

Armory Gun Company: Trade name of H. & D. Folsom Arms Co. on shotguns.

Aubrey Shotgun: Trade name found on shotguns made for the Sears, Roebuck and Company of Chicago by Albert Aubrey of Meriden, Connecticut.

Automatic: a) Trade name of the Forehand and Wadsworth Company on inexpensive pocket revolvers. b) Trade name of the Harrington and Richardson Arms Company on inexpensive pocket revolvers. c) Trade name of the Iver Johnson Arms and Cycle Works on inexpensive pocket revolvers.

Avenger: Trade name found on inexpensive pocket revolvers of unknown manufacture.

Baby Hammerless: Trade mark used successively by Henry Kolb and R. F. Sedgley on pocket revolvers. **Baby Russian:** Trade name of the American Arms Company on revolvers.

Baker Gun Company: Trade name of the H. & D. Folsom Arms Company on shotguns.

Baker Gun and Forging Company: Trade name of the H. & D. Folsom Arms Company on shotguns.

Bang: Trade name found on inexpensive pocket revolvers of unknown manufacture.

Bang Up: Trade name used on inexpensive pocket revolvers retailed by the Graham and Haines Company of New York.

Barker, T.: Trade name of the H. & D. Folsom Arms Company of New York on shotguns.

Bartlett Field: Trade name used on shotguns retailed by Hibbard, Spencer, Bartlett and Company of Chicago.

Batavia: Trade name used on shotguns produced by the Baker Gun Company.

Batavia Leader: Trade name used on shotguns produced by the Baker Gun Company.

Bay State: Trade name of the Harrington and Richardson Arms Company on both inexpensive pocket revolvers and shotguns.

Belknap: Trade name of the Belknap Hardware Company of Louisville, Kentucky on shotguns made by the Crescent Fire Arms Company, which.

Beilmore Gun Company: Trade name of the H. & D. Folsom Arms Company on shotguns made for them by the Crescent Fire Arms Company.

Berkshire: Trade name of the H. & D. Folsom Arms Company on shotguns made for the Shapleigh Hardware Company of St. Louis, Missouri.

Bicyle: Trade name used on firearms made by the Harrington and Richardson Arms Company.

Big All Right: Trade name used on shotguns manufactured by the Wright Arms Company.

Big Bonanza: Trade name found on inexpensive pocket revolvers of unknown manufacture.

Bismarck: Trade name found on inexpensive pocket revolvers of unknown manufacture.

Black Beauty: Trade name of the Sears, Roebuck and Company on imported shotguns.

Black Diamond: Trade name found on Belgian made shotguns retailed by an unknown American wholesaler.

Black Diana: Trade name of the Baker Gun Company or shotguns.

Blackfield: Trade name of the Hibbard, Spencer, Bartlet and Company of Chicago on shotguns.

Blackhawk: Trade name found on inexpensive pocket revolvers of unknown manufacture.

Black Prince: Trade name of the Hopkins and Allen Company on inexpensive pocket revolvers.

Bliss: Trade name believed to have been of the Norwich Arms Company.

Blood Hound: Trade name found on inexpensive pocket revolvers of unknown manufacture.

Bluefield: Trade name of the W.H. Davenport Firearms Company on shotguns.

Bluegrass: Trade name of the Belknap Hardware Company of Louisville, Kentucky on shotguns.

Bluegrass Arms Company: Trade name of shotguns made by H. & D. Folsom Arms Co. for Belknap Hardware of Louisville, KY.

Blue Jacket: Trade name of the Hopkins and Allen Company on inexpensive pocket revolvers they made for the Merwin, Hulbert and Company of New York.

Blue Leader: Trade name found on inexpensive pocket revolvers of unknown manufacture.

Blue Whistler: Trade name of the Hopkins and Allen Company on inexpensive pocket revolvers they made for the Merwin, Hulbert and Company of New York.

Bogardus Club Gun: Trade name found on Belgian made shotguns retailed by an unknown American wholesaler (possibly B. Kiftredge and Company of Cincinnati, Ohio).

Bonanza: Trade name of the Bacon Arms Company on inexpensive pocket revolvers.

Boom: Trade name of the Shattuck Arms Company on inexpensive pocket revolvers.

Boone Gun Company: Trade name of the Belknap Hardware Company of Louisville, Kentucky on firearms.

Boss: Trade name found on inexpensive pocket revolvers of unknown manufacture.

Boys Choice: Trade name of the Hood Firearms Company on inexpensive pocket revolvers.

Bride Black Prince: Trade name of H. & D. Folsom Arms Co. on shotguns.

Bridge Gun Company: Registered trade name of the Shapleigh Hardware Company, St. Louis, Missouri.

Bridgeport Arms Company: Trade name of H. & D. Folsom Arms Co. on shotguns.

Bright Arms Company: Trade name of H. & D. Folsom Arms Company

British Bulldog: Trade name found on inexpensive pocket revolvers of unknown American, Belgian and English manufacture (foreign makes bear extensive proofmarks).

Brownie: a) Trade name of the W.H. Davenport Firearms Company on shotguns. b) Trade name of the O.F. Mossberg Firearms Company on a four-shot pocket pistol.

Brutus: Trade name of the Hood Firearms Company on inexpensive pocket revolvers.

Buckeye: Trade name of the Hopkins and Allen Company on inexpensive pocket revolvers. a)Trade name of the Supplee - Biddle Hardware Company of Philadelphia.

Buffalo: Trade name of the Western Arms Company on an inexpensive pocket revolver.

Buffalo Bill: Trade name of the Iver Johnson Arms and Cycle Works on an inexpensive pocket revolver.

Bull Dog: Trade name of the Forehand and Wadsworth Company on inexpensive pocket revolvers.

Bull Dozer: a) Trade name of the Norwich Pistol Company on inexpensive pocket revolvers. b) Trade name of the Forehand and Wadsworth Company on inexpensive pocket revolvers. c) Trade name on Hammond Patent pistols made by the Connecticut Arms and Manufacturing Company.

Bull Frog: Trade name of the Hopkins and Allen Company on rifles.

Bulls Eye: Trade name of the Norwich Falls Pistol Company (O.A. Smith) on inexpensive pocket revolvers.

Burdick: Trade name of the H. & D. Folsom Arms Company on shotguns made for the Sears, Roebuck and Company of Chicago.

Butler, General: Trade name found on inexpensive pocket revolvers of unknown manufacture.

Cadet: Trade name of the Crescent Firearms Company on rifles.

Canadian Belle: Trade name of H. & D. Folsom Arms Co. on shotguns.

Cannon Breech: Trade name of the Hopkins and Allen Company on shotguns.

Carolina Arms Company: Trade name of the H. & D. Folsom Arms Company on shotguns produced for the Smith, Wadsworth Hardware Company of Charlotte, North Carolina.

Caroline Arms: Trade name of the H. & D. Folsom Arms Co.

Caruso: Trade name of the Crescent Firearms Company on shotguns made for the Hibbard, Spencer, Bartlett and Company of Chicago.

Centennial 1876: a) Trade name of the Deringer Pistol Company on inexpensive pocket revolvers. b) Trade name of the Hood Firearms Company on inexpensive pocket revolvers.

Central Arms Company: Trade name of the W. H. Davenport Firearms Company on shotguns made for the Shapleigh Hardware Company of St. Louis, Missouri.

Century Arms Company: Trade name of the W. H. Davenport Firearms Company on shotguns made for the Shapleigh Hardware Company of St. Louis, Missouri.

Challenge: a) Trade name found on inexpensive pocket revolvers of unknown manufacture. b) Trade name of the Sears, Roebuck and Company of Chicago on shotguns made by Albert Aubrey of Meriden, Connecticut.

Challenge Ejector: Trade name of the Sears, Roebuck and Company of Chicago on shotguns made by Albert Aubrey of Meriden, Connecticut.

Champion: a) Trade name of H.C. Squires on shotguns. b) Trade name of J.P. Lovell on shotguns. c) Trade name of the Iver Johnson Arms and Cycle Works on shotguns and inexpensive pocket revolvers. d) Trade name of the Norwich Arms Company on inexpensive pocket revolvers.

Chatham Arms Company: Trade name of H. & D. Folsom Arms Company used on shotguns.

Cherokee Arms Company: Trade name of the H. & D. Folsom Arms Company on shotguns made for C.M. Mclung and Company of Knoxville, Tennessee.

Chesapeake Gun Company: Trade name of the H. & D. Folsom Arms Company of New York.

Chicago: Trade name found on shotguns retailed by the Hibbard, Spencer, Bartlett and Company of Chicago.

Chicago Ledger: Trade name of the Chicago Firearms Company on inexpensive pocket revolvers.

Chicago Long Range Wonder: Trade name of the H. & D. Folsom Arms Company on shotguns made for the Sears, Roebuck and Company of Chicago.

Chicopee Arms Company: Trade name of the H. & D. Folsom Arms Company of New York.

Chieftain: Trade name found on inexpensive pocket revolvers of unknown manufacture.

Christian Protector: Trade name found on inexpensive pocket revolvers of unknown manufacture.

Climax XL: Trade name of Herman Boker and Company of New York on revolvers, rifles and shotguns.

Club Gun: Trade name of B. Kittredge and Company of Cincinnati, Ohio on shotguns.

Cock Robin: Trade name of the Hood Firearms Company on inexpensive pocket revolvers.

Colonial: Trade name of H. & D. Folsom Company on shotguns.

Colton Arms Company: Trade name of the Shapleigh Hardware Company of St. Louis, Missouri on imported shotguns.

Colton Firearms Company: Trade name of the Sears, Roebuck and Company of Chicago on shotguns.

Columbia: a) Trade name found on inexpensive pocket revolvers of unknown manufacture. b) Trade name of H.C. Squires on shotguns.

Columbia Arms Company: Registered trade name of Henry Keidel, Baltimore, Maryland.

Columbian: Trade name found on inexpensive pocket revolvers of unknown manufacture.

Columbian Firearms Company: a) Trade name of the Maltby, Henly and Company on inexpensive pocket revolvers. b) Trade name of the Crescent Firearms Company on shotguns.

Comet: Trade name of the Prescott Pistol Company on inexpensive pocket revolvers.

Commander: Trade name of the Norwich Arms Company on inexpensive pocket revolvers.

Commercial: Trade name of the Norwich Falls Pistol Company (O.A. Smith) on inexpensive pocket revolvers.

Compeer: Trade name of the H. & D. Folsom Arms Company on firearms made for the Van Camp Hardware and Iron Company of Indianapolis, Indiana.

Competition: Trade name of John Meunier of Milwaukee, Wisconsin on rifles.

Conestoga Rifle Works: Trade name of Henry Leman, Philadelphia, Pennsylvania.

Connecticut Arms Company: Trade name of H. & D. Folsom Arms Company on shotguns.

Continental: Trade name of the Great Western Gun Works of Pittsburgh, Pennsylvania on firearms.

Continental Arms Company: Trade name of the Marshall-Wells Company of Duluth, Minnesota on firearms.

Cotton King: Trade name found on inexpensive pocket revolvers of unknown manufacture.

Cowboy: Trade name of the Hibbard, Spencer, Bartlett and Company of Chicago on imported, inexpensive pocket revolvers.

Cowboy Ranger: Trade name of the Rohde Spencer Company of Chicago on inexpensive pocket revolvers.

Crack Shot: Trade name of the 3. Stevens Arms and Tool Company on rifles.

Crackerjack: Trade name of the J. Stevens Arms and Tool Company on pistols.

Creedmoore: a) Trade name of the Hopkins and Allen Company on inexpensive pocket revolvers. b) Trade name of the Chicago Firearms Company on inexpensive pocketrevolvers. c) Trade name of William Wunflein on rifles.

Creedmoore Armory: Trade name of A.D. McAusland of Omaha, Nebraska on rifles.

Creedmoore Arms Company: Trade name found on imported shotguns retailed by an unknown American wholesaler.

Crescent: Trade name of the Crescent Arms Company on inexpensive pocket revolvers and shotguns. Later bought by Savage Arms Co.

Crescent International IXL: Trade name of Herman Boker and Company of New York on shotguns.

Creve Coeur: Trade name of the Isaac Walker Hardware Company of Peoria, Illinois on imported shotguns.

Crown: Trade name of the Harrington and Richardson Arms Company on inexpensive pocket revolvers.

Crown Jewel: Trade name of the Norwich Arms Company on inexpensive pocket revolvers.

Cruso: Trade name of the H. & D. Folsom Arms Company on shotguns made for Hibbard, Spencer, Bartlett and Company of Chicago.

Cumberland Arms Company: Trade name of the H. & D. Folsom Arms Company on shotguns made for the Gray and Dudley Hardware Company of Nashville, Tennessee.

Czar: Trade name of the Hopkins and Allen Company on inexpensive pocket revolvers.

Daisy: a) Trade name of the Bacon Arms Company on inexpensive pocket revolvers. b) Registered proprietary trade name engraved on firearms made by the Winchester Repeating Arms Company for the F. Lassefter and Company, Limited of Sydney, Australia.

Daniel Boone Gun Company: Trade name of H. & D. Folsom Arms Company on shotguns made for Belknap Hardware Company of Louisville, Ky.

Daredevle: Trade name of Louis Eppinger of Detroit, Michigan on pistols.

Dash: Trade name found on inexpensive pocket revolvers of unknown manufacture.

Davis Guns: Trade names used successively by N.R. Davis, N.R. Davis & Sons, Davis-Warner and the Crescent - Davis Arms Company on various firearms. Later bought by Savage Arms Co.

Dead Shot: a) Trade name found on inexpensive pocket revolvers of unknown manufacture. b) Trade name of the Meriden Firearms Company on rifles.

Deer Slayer: Trade name of J. Henry and Son of Boulton, Pennsylvania on rifles.

Defender: a) Trade name of the Iver Johnson Arms and Cycle Works on inexpensive pocket revolvers. b) Trade name of the U.S. Small Arms Company on knife pistols.

Defiance: Trade name of the Norwich Arms Company on inexpensive pocket revolvers.

Delphian Arms Company: a) Trade name of the Supplee Biddle Hardware Company of Philadelphia, Pennsylvania on shotguns which were supplied by the H. & D. Folsom Company of New York. b) Trade name of the H. & D. Folsom Arms Company of New York on shotguns.

Delphian Manufacturing Company: Trade name of the H. & D. Folsom Arms Company of New York on shotguns.

Dexter: Trade name found on inexpensive pocket revolvers of unknown manufacture.

Diamond Arms Company: Trade name of the Shapleigh Hardware Company of St. Louis, Missouri on imported shotguns.

Dictator: Trade name of the Hopkins and Allen Company on inexpensive pocket revolvers.

Dominion Pistol: Trade name found on inexpensive pocket revolvers of unknown manufacture.

Double Header: Trade name of E.S. Renwick on Perry and Goddard Patent derringers.

Douglas Arms Company: Trade name of the Hopkins and Allen Company on shotguns.

Dreadnought: Trade name of the Hopkins and Allen Company on shotguns and inexpensive pocket revolvers.

Duchess: Trade name of the Hopkins and Allen Company on inexpensive pocket revolvers.

Duke: Trade name found on inexpensive pocket revolvers which may have been made by the Hopkins and Allen Company.

Dunlop Special: Trade name of the Davis Warner Arms Company on shotguns made for the Dunlop Hardware Company of Macon, Georgia.

Duplex: Trade name of the Osgood Gun Works of Norwich, Connecticut.

Eagle: Trade name of the Iver Johnson Arms and Cycle Works on inexpensive pocket revolvers.

Eagle Arms Company: Trade name of the Iver Johnson Arms and Cycle Works on inexpensive pocket revolvers.

Earlhood: Trade name of E.L. Dickinson on inexpensive pocket revolvers.

Earnest Companion: Trade name found on inexpensive pocket revolvers of unknown manufacture.

Earthquake: Trade name of E.L Dickinson on inexpensive pocket revolvers.

Eastern Arms Company: Trade name of the Sears, Roebuck and Company of Chicago on both shotguns and inexpensive revolvers made by the ver Johnson Arms and Cycle Works.

Eclipse: a) Trade name found on single shot derringers of unknown manufacture. b) Trade name of E.C. Meacham on imported shotguns.

Electric: Trade name found on inexpensive pocket revolvers of unknown manufacture.

Electric City Single Hammer: Trade name found on single shot shotguns retailed by the Wyeth Hardware and Manufacturing Company of St. Joseph, Missouri.

Elector: Trade name found on inexpensive pocket revolvers of unknown manufacture.

Elgin Arms Company: Trade name of the H. & D. Folsom Arms Company on shotguns made for the Strauss and Schram Company of Chicago.

Elita: Trade name of the W.H. Davenport Fire Arms Company on shotguns.

Empire: a) Trade name of the Rupertus Patented Pistol Manufacturing Company on inexpensive pocket revolvers. b) Trade name of the Cresent Firearms Company on shotguns.

Empire Arms Company: Trade name of the H. & D. Folsom Arms Company on firearms made for the Sears, Roebuck and Company of Chicago.

Enders Royal Shotgun: Trade name of the Crescent - Davis Firearms Company on shotguns made for the Simmons Hardware Company of St. Louis, Missouri.

Enders Special Service: Trade name of the Crescent Davis Firearms Company on shotguns made for the Simmons Hardware Company of St. Louis, Missouri.

Enterprise: Trade name of the Enterprise Gun Works on inexpensive pocket revolvers.

Essex Gun Works: Trade name of the Crescent - Davis Firearms Company on shotguns made for the Belknap Hardware Company of Louisville, Kentucky.

Eureka: Trade name of the Iver Johnson Arms and Cycle Works on inexpensive pocket revolvers.

Excel: Trade name of both the H. & D. Folsom Arms Company and the Iver Johnson Arms and Cycle Works on shotguns made for the Montgomery Ward and Company of Chicago.

Excelsior: a) Trade name found on inexpensive pocket revolvers of unknown manufacture b) Trade name of the Iver Johnson Arms and Cycle Works on shotguns.

Expert: a) Trade name found on single shot derringers of unknown manufacture. b) Trade name of the W.J. Davenport Firearms Company on shotguns made for the Witte Hardware Company of St. Louis, Missouri.

Express: Trade name of the Bacon Arms Company on inexpensive pocket revolvers.

Farwell Arms Company: Trade name of the Farwell, Ozmun, Kirk and Company of St. Paul, Minnesota on shotguns.

Fashion: Trade name found on inexpensive pocket revolvers of unknown manufacture.

Faultless: Trade name of the H. & D. Folsom Arms Company on shotguns made for the John M. Smythe Merchandise Company of Chicago.

Faultless Goose Gun: Trade name of the H. & D. Folsom Arms Company on shotguns made for the John M. Smythe Merchandise Company of Chicago.

Favorite: a) Trade name of the J. Stevens Arms and Tool Company on rifles. b) Trade name of the Iver Johnson Arms and Cycle Works on inexpensive pocket revolvers.

Favorite Navy: Trade name of the Iver Johnson Arms and Cycle Works on inexpensive pocket revolvers.

Featherlight: Trade name of the Sears, Roebuck and Company of Chicago on firearms.

Folks Gun Works: Trade name of William and Samuel Folk of Bryan, Ohio on rifles and shotguns.

Freemont Arms Company: Trade name found on shotguns distributed by an unknown retailer.

Frontier: Trade name of the Norwich Falls Pistol Company (O.A. Smith) on inexpensive pocket revolvers made for the firm of Maitby, Curtis and Company of New York.

Fulton: Trade name of the Hunter Arms Company on shotguns.

Fulton Arms Company: Trade name of the W. H. Davenport Firearms Company on shotguns.

Game Getter: Registered trade mark of the Marble Arms and Manufacturing Company on combination rifle shotguns.

Gem: a) Trade name of the J. Stevens Arms and Tool Company on single shot pocket pistols. b) Trade name of the Bacon Arms Company on inexpensive pocket revolvers.

General: Trade name of the Rupertus Patented Pistol Manufacturing Company on inexpensive pocket revolvers.

Gerrish: Trade name of G.W. Gerrish of Twin Falls, Idaho used on shotguns.

Gibralter: Trade name of Albert Aubrey on shotguns made for the Sears, Roebuck and Company of Chicago.

Gladiator: Trade name of Albert Aubrey on shotguns made for the Sears, Roebuck and Company of Chicago.

Gold Field: Trade name found on inexpensive pocket revolvers of unknown manufacture.

Gold Hibbard: Trade name of Hibbard, Spencer, Bartlett and Company of Chicago on firearms.

Gold Medal Wonder: Trade name of H. & D. Folsom Arms Co. on shotguns.

Governor: Trade name of the Bacon Arms Company on inexpensive pocket revolvers.

Guardian: Trade name of the Bacon Arms Company on inexpensive pocket revolvers.

Gut Buster: Trade name found on inexpensive pocket revolvers of unknown manufacture.

Gypsy: Trade name found on inexpensive pocket revolvers of unknown manufacture.

Half Breed: Trade name found on inexpensive pocket revolvers of unknown manufacture.

Hamilton Arms: Registered trade name of the Wiebusch and Hilger Company, New York.

Hammerless Auto Ejecting Revolver: Trade name of the Meriden Firearms Company used on revolvers made for the Sears, Roebuck and Company of New York.

Hanover Arms Co.: If no foreign proofmarks then trade name of H. & D. Folsom Arms Company.

Harrington, S.H.: If no foreign proofmarks then trade name of H. & D. Folsom Arms Company.

Frank Harrison Arms Company: Trade name of the Sickles and Preston Company of Davenport, Iowa on firearms.

Hart Arms Company: Trade name of a Cleveland, Ohio wholesaler (possibly the George Worthington Company).

Hartford Arms Company: Trade name of the H. & D. Folsom Arms on shotguns made for the Simmons Hardware Company of St. Louis, Missouri.

Harvard: Trade name of the H. & D. Folsom Arms Company on shotguns made for the George Worthington Company of Cleveland, Ohio.

Hercules: Trade name of the Iver Johnson Arms and Cycle Works on shotguns made for the Montgomery Ward and Company of Chicago.

Hermitage Arms Company: Trade name of the H. & D. Folsom Arms Company on shotguns made for the Gray and Dudley Hardware Company of Nashville, TN.

Hero: a) Trade name of the American Stand Tool Company on percussion pistols. b) Trade name of the Manhattan Firearms Manufacturing Company on percussion pistols.

Hexagon: Trade name of the Sears, Roebuck and Company of Chicago on shotguns.

Hinsdale: Trade name of the Hopkins and Allen Company on inexpensive pocket revolvers.

Holt Arms Company, S.: Trade name of the Sears, Roebuck and Company of Chicago on shotguns.

Hornet: Trade name of the Prescoft Pistol Company on inexpensive pocket revolvers.

Howard Arms Company: Trade name of the H. & D. Folsom Arms Company on shotguns they distributed.

Hudson: Trade name of the Hibbard, Spencer, Bartlett and Company of Chicago on shotguns.

Hunter: Trade name of the H. & D. Folsom Arms Company on shotguns made for the Belknap Hardware Company of Louisville, Kentucky.

The Hunter: Trade name of the Hunter Arms Company on shotguns.

Hurricane: Trade name found on inexpensive pocket revolvers of unknown manufacture.

Illinois Arms Company: Trade name of the Rohde, Spencer Company of Chicago on firearms.

Imperial: Trade name of the Lee Arms Company on inexpensive pocket revolvers.

Imperial Arms Company: Trade name of the Hopkins and \llen Company on inexpensive pocket revolvers.

Infallible: Trade name of the Lancaster Arms Company of Lancaster, Pennsylvania on shotguns.

Infallible Automatic Pistol: Trade name of the Kirtland Brothers Company of New York on inexpensive pistols.

International: a) Trade name found on inexpensive pocket revolvers of unknown manufacture. b) Trade name of E.C. Meacham on shotguns.

Interstate Arms Company: Trade name of the H. & D. Folsom Arms Company on shotguns made for the Townley Metal and Hardware Company of Kansas City, Missouri.

I.O.A.: Trade name of the Brown, Camp Hardware Company of Des Moines, Iowa on firearms.

Invincible: Trade name of the Iver Johnson Arms and Cycle Works on both shotguns and inexpensive pocket revolvers.

I.X.L.: a) Trade name of B.J. Hart on percussion revolvers. b) Trade name of the W.H. Davenport Firearms Company on shotguns made for the Witte Hardware Company of St. Louis, Missouri.

J.S.T. & Company: Trade name of the Iver Johnson Arms and Cycle Works on inexpensive pocket revolvers.

Jackson Arms Company: Trade name of the H. & D. Folsom Arms Company on shotguns made for C.M. Mclung and Company of Knoxville, Tennessee.

Jewel: Trade name of the Hood Fire Arms Company on inexpensive pocket revolvers.

Joker: Trade name of the Marlin Firearms Company on inexpensive pocket revolvers.

Joseph Arms Company (Norwich, Conn.): Trade name of H. & D. Folsom Arms Company.

Judge: Trade name found on inexpensive pocket revolvers of unknown manufacture.

KK: Trade name of the Hopkins and Allen Company on shotguns made for the Shapleigh Hardware Company of St. Louis, Missouri.

Keno: Trade name found on inexpensive pocket revolvers of unknown manufacture.

Kentucky: Trade name of the Iver Johnson Arms and Cycle Works on inexpensive pocket revolvers.

Keystone Arms Company: Trade name of the W.H. Davenport Firearms Company on shotguns made for the E.K. Tryon Company of Philadelphia, Pennsylvania.

Kill Buck: Trade name of the Enterprise Gun Works (James Bown), Pittsburgh, Pennsylvania.

Killdeer: Trade name of the Sears, Roebuck and Company of Chicago on firearms bearing their trade name Western Arms Company.

King Nitro: Trade name of the W.H. Davenport Firearm Company on shotguns made for the Shapleigh Hardware Company of St. Louis, Missouri.

King Pin: Trade name found on inexpensive single shot and volving pocket pistols.

Kingsland Gun Company: Trade name of the H. & D. Folsom Arms Company on shotguns made for the Geller, Ward and Hasner Company of St. Louis, Missouri.

Kirk Gun Company: Trade name of Farwell, Ozmun, and Kirk Company of St. Paul, Minnesota.

Knickerbocker: Trade name of the Crescent-Davis Firearms Company on shotguns.

Knickerbocker Club Gun: Trade name of Charles Godfrey of New York on imported shotguns he retailed. Knockabout: Trade name of the Montgomery Ward and Company of Chicago on shotguns.

Knox-All: Trade name of the Iver Johnson Arms and Cycle Works on firearms they made for the H. & D. Folsom Arms Company of New York.

Lakeside: Trade name of the H. & D. Folsom Arms Company on firearms they made for the Montgomery Ward and Company of Chicago.

Leader: a) Trade name of the Shattuck Arms Company on inexpensive pocket revolvers. b) Trade name of the Harrington and Richardson Arms Company on inexpensive pocket revolvers.

Leader Gun Company: Trade name of the H. & D. Folsom Arms Company on shotguns they made for the Charles Williams Stores, Inc. of New York.

Lees Hummer: Trade name of the H. & D. Folsom Arms Company on firearms they made for the Lee Hardware Company of Salina, Kansas.

Lees Special: Trade name of the H. & D. Folsom Arms Company on firearms they made for the Lee Hardware Company of Salina, Kansas.

Liberty: Trade name of the Norwich Falls Pistol Company (O.A. Smith) on inexpensive pocket revolvers.

Liege Gun Company: Trade name of the Hibbard, Spencer, Bartlett and Company of Chicago on imported shotguns.

Lion: Trade name of the Iver Johnson Arms and Cycle Works on inexpensive pocket revolvers.

Little Giant: Trade name of the Bacon Arms Company on inexpensive pocket revolvers.

Little John: Trade name of the Hood Firearms Company on inexpensive pocket revolvers.

Little Joker: Trade name found on inexpensive pocket revolvers of unknown manufacture.

Little Pal: Registered trade name for knife pistols made by L.E. Polhemus.

Little Pet: Trade name of the Sears, Roebuck and Company of Chicago on inexpensive pocket revolvers.

London Revolver: Trade name found on inexpensive pocket revolvers of unknown manufacture.

Lone Star: Trade name found on inexpensive pocket revolvers of unknown manufacture.

Long Range Winner: Trade name of the Sears, Roebuck and Company of Chicago on shotguns.

Long Range Wonder: Trade name of the Sears, Roebuck and Company of Chicago on shotguns.

Long Tom: Trade name of the Sears, Roebuck and Company of Chicago on shotguns.

Marshwood: Trade name of the H. and D. Folsom Arms Company on shotguns they made for the Charles Williams Stores Inc. of New York.

Marvel: Trade name of the J. Stevens Arms and Tool Company on various firearms.

Massachusetts Arms Company: Trade name of both the J. Stevens Arms and Tool Company and the H. & D. Folsom Arms Company on firearms made for the Blish, Mizet and Silliman Hardware Company of Atchinson, Kansas.

Maximum: Trade name found on inexpensive pocket revolvers of unknown manufacture.

Metropolitan: Trade name of the H. & D. Folsom Arms Company on firearms they made for the Siegal-Cooper Company of New York.

Metropolitan Police: a) Trade name of the Maitby, Curtiss and Company on inexpensive pocket revolvers. b) Trade name of the Rohde-Spencer Company of Chicago on inexpensive pocket revolvers.

Midget Hammerless: Trade name of the Rohde - Spencer Company of Chicago on inexpensive pocket revolvers.

Minnesota Arms Company: Trade name of the H. & D. Folsom Arms Company on shotguns they made for the Farwell, Ozmun, Kirk and Company of St. Paul, Minnesota.

Missaubi Arms Company: Trade name of the Hunter Arms Company, possibly for the Farwell, Ozmun, Kirk and Company of St. Paul, Minnesota.

Mississippi Arms Company: Trade name of the H. & D. Folsom Arms Company on firearms made for the Shapleigh Hardware Company of St. Louis, Missouri.

Mississippi Valley Arms Company: Trade name of the H. & D. Folsom Arms Company on firearms made for the Shapleigh Hardware Company of St. Louis, Missouri.

Mohawk: Trade name of the H. & D. Folsom Arms Company on firearms made for the Blish, Mizet and Silliman Hardware Company of Atchinson, Kansas.

Mohegan: Trade name of the Hood Firearms Company on inexpensive pocket revolvers.

Monarch: a) Trade name of the Hopkins and Allen Company on inexpensive pocket revolvers. b) Trade name of the Osgood Gun Works on Duplex revolvers.

Monitor: a) Trade name of the Whitneyville Armory on inexpensive pocket revolvers. b) Trade name of the H. & D. Folsom Arms Company on firearms made for the Paxton and Gallagher Company of Omaha, Nebraska.

Montgomery Arms Company: Trade name of the H. & D. Folsom Arms Company on a variety of firearms.

Mountain Eagle: Trade name of the Hopkins and Allen Company on inexpensive pocket revolvers.

Mount Vernon Arms Company: Trade name of the H. & D. Folsom Arms Company on firearms made for the Carlin, Hulifish Company of Alexandria, Virginia.

My Companion: Trade name found on inexpensive pocket revolvers of unknown manufacture.

My Friend: Trade name of James Reid of New York.

Napoleon: Trade name of the Thomas J. Ryan Pistol Manufacturing Company of Norwich, Connecticut on inexpensive pocket revolvers.

National Arms Company: Trade name of the H. & D. Folsom Arms Company on firearms made both for the May Hardware Company of Washington, D.C., and the Moskowitz and Herbach Company of Philadelphia, Pennsylvania.

Nevermiss: Trade name of the Marlin Firearms Company on single shot pocket pistols.

New Aubrey: Trade name of Albert Aubrey of Meriden, Connecticut on both revolvers and shotguns made for the Sears, Roebuck and Company of Chicago.

New Britain Arms Company: Trade name of H. & D. Folsom Arms Company. New Elgin Arms Company: Trade name of H. & D. Folsom Arms Company.

New Empire: Trade name of H. & D. Folsom Arms Co.

New England Arms Company: Trade name believed to have been of Charles Godfrey on shotguns made for the Rohde, Spencer Company of Chicago.

New Era Gun Works: Trade name of the Baker Gun Company on firearms made for an unknown retailer.

New Haven Arms Company: Trade name found on Belgian shotguns imported by either E.K.Tryon of Philadelphia or the Great Western Gun Works of Pittsburgh, Pennsylvania.

New Liberty: Trade name of the Sears, Roebuck and Company of Chicago on inexpensive pocket revolvers. New Rival: Trade name of the H. & O. Folsom Arms Company on firearms made for the Van Camp Hardware and Iron Company of Indianapolis, Indiana.

Newport: a) Trade name found on inexpensive pocket revolvers of unknown manufacture. b) Trade name of the H. & D. Folsom Arms Company on shotguns made for Hibbard, Spencer, Bartlett and Company of Chicago.

New Worcester: Trade name of the Torkalson Manufacturing Company of Worcester, Massachusetts.

New York Arms Company: Trade name of the H. & D. Folsom Arms Company on firearms made for the Garnet Carter Company of Chattanooga, Tennessee.

New York Gun Company: Trade name of the H. & O. Folsom Arms Company on firearms made for the Garnet Carter Company of Chattanooga, Tennessee.

New York Club: Trade name of the H. & O. Folsom Arms Company on rifles.

New York Machine Made: Trade name of the H. & D. Folsom Arms Company.

New York Pistol Company: Trade name of the Norwich Falls Pistol Company (O.A. Smith) on inexpensive pocket revolvers.

Nightingale: Trade name found on inexpensive pocket revolvers of unknown manufacture.

Nitro Bird: Trade name of the Richards and Conover Hardware Company of Kansas City, Missouri.

Nitro Hunter: Trade name of the H. & D. Folsom Arms Company on shotguns made for the Belknap Hardware Company of Louisville, Kentucky.

Nitro King: Trade name of the Sears, Roebuck and Company of Chicago on shotguns of unknown manufacture.

Nitro Special: Trade name of the J. Stevens Arms and Tool Company on shotguns.

Northfield Knife Company: Trade name of the Rome Revolver and Novelty Works of Rome, New York on inexpensive pocket revolvers.

Norwich Arms Company: a) Trade name of the Hood Firearms Company on inexpensive pocket revolvers. b) Trade name found on shotguns retailed by the Marshall, Wells Company of Duluth, Minnesota and Winnipeg, Manitoba, Canada.

Norwich Falls Pistol Company: Trade name of the O.A. Smith Company on inexpensive pocket revolvers made for Maltby, Curtis and Company of New York.

Norwich Lock Manufacturing Company: Trade name of.W. Hood Firearms Company on inexpensive pocket revolvers.

Not-Nac Manufacturing Company: Trade name of the H. & D. Folsom Arms Company on firearms made for the Canton Hardware Company of Canton, Ohio.

OK: a) Trade name of the Marlin Firearms Company on single shot pocket pistols. b) Trade name of Cowles and Son of Chicopee Falls, Massachusefts on single shot pocket pistols. c) Trade name found on inexpensive pocket revolvers of unknown manufacture.

Old Hickory: a) Trade name found on inexpensive pocket revolvers of unknown manufacture. b) Trade name of the Hibbard, Spencer, Bartleft and Company of Chicago on shotguns.

Old Reliable: Trade name of the Sharps Rifle Company.

Olympic: a) Trade name of the J. Stevens Arms and Tool Company on rifles and pistols. b) Trade name of the Morley and Murphy Hardware Company of Green Bay, Wisconsin on firearms (possibly made by the J. Stevens Arms and Tool Company).

Osprey: Trade name of Lou 3. Eppinger of Detroit, Michigan on firearms he made.

Our Lake: Trade name of E.L. and 3. Dickinson of Springfield, Massachusefts on inexpensive pocket revolvers.

Oxford Arms Company: Trade name of the H. & D. Folsom Arms Company on firearms made for the Belknap Hardware Company of Louisville, Kentucky.

Pagoma: Trade name of the H. & D. Folsom Arms Company on firearms made for the Paxton and Gallagher Company of Omaha, Nebraska.

Palmetto: Trade name of the Edward K. Tryon Company of Philadelphia, Pennsylvania on various types of firearms.

Panther: Trade name found on inexpensive pocket revolvers of jnknown manufacture.

Paragon: a) Trade name of the Prescoft Pistol Company on inexpensive pocket revolvers. b) Trade name of the Baker Gun Company on shotguns.

Parole: Trade name of the Bacon Arms Company on inexpensive pocket revolvers.

Path Finder: Trade name found on inexpensive pocket revolvers of unknown manufacture.

Patriot: Trade name found on inexpensive pocket revolvers of unknown manufacture.

Peace Maker: Trade name found on inexpensive pocket revolvers of unknown manufacture.

Peerless: Trade name of the Crescent-Davis Firearms Company on shotguns made for various wholesalers.

Pelican: Trade name of the Thomas, Ogilvie Hardware Company of Shreveport, Louisiana.

Penetrator: Trade name of the Norwich Arms Company on inexpensive pocket revolvers.

Peoria Chief: Trade name found on inexpensive pocket revolvers.

Perfect: Trade name of the Foehl and Weeks Firearms Manufacturing Company of Philadelphia, Pennsylvania on inexpensive pocket revolvers.

Perfection: a) Trade name of the H. & O. Folsom Arms Company on firearms made for the H.G. Lipscomb and Company of Nashville, Tennessee. b) Trade name of the John M. Smythe Merchandise Company of Chicago on firearms.

Pet: Trade name found on inexpensive pocket revolvers of unknown manufacture.

Petrel: Trade name found on inexpensive pocket revolvers of unknown manufacture.

Phenix: Trade name of J. Reid of New York on revolvers.

Phoenix: a) Trade name of J. Reid of New York on revolvers. b) Trade name of the Whitneyville Armory on percussion revolvers.

Piedmont: Trade name of the H. & O. Folsom Arms Company on firearms made for the Piedmont Hardware Company of Danville, Pennsylvania.

Pinafore: Trade name of the Norwich Falls Pistol Company (O.A. Smith) on inexpensive pocket revolvers.

Pioneer: Trade name found on inexpensive pocket revolvers of unknown manufacture.

Pioneer Arms Company: Trade name of the H. & O. Folsom Arms Company on firearms made for the Kruse and Baklmann Hardware Company of Cincinnati, Ohio.

Pittsfield: Trade name of the Hibbard, Spencer, Bartlett and Company of Chicago on firearms probably made by the H. & O. Folsom Arms Company.

Plug Ugly: Trade name found on inexpensive pocket revolvers of unknown manufacture.

Plymouth: Trade name of Spear and Company of Pittsburgh, Pennsylvania on firearms.

Pocahontas: Trade name found on inexpensive pocket revolvers of unknown manufacture.

Pointer: Trade name found on single shot pocket pistols of unknown manufacture.

Prairie Fire: Trade name found on inexpensive pocket revolversof unknown manufacture.

Prairie King: a) Trade name of the Bacon Arms Company on inexpensive pocket revolvers. b) Trade name of the H. & O. Folsom Arms company on inexpensive pocket revolvers.

Premier: a) Trade name of the Thomas E. Ryan Company on inexpensive pocket revolvers. b) Trade name of the Harrington and Richardson Arms Company on revolvers. c) Trade name of the Montgomery Ward Company of Chicago on firearms. d) Registered trade name of Edward K. Tryon and Company of Philadelphia, Pennsylvania.

Premium: Trade name of the Iver Johnson Arms and Cycle Works on inexpensive pocket revolvers.

Price, John W.: Trade name of the Belknap Hardware Company of Louisville, Kentucky on firearms.

Progress: Trade name of Charles J. Godfrey of New York on shotguns.

Protection: Trade name of the Whitneyville Armory on revolvers.

Protector: a) Trade name found on inexpensive pocket revolvers of unknown manufacture. b) Trade name of the Chicago Firearms company on inexpensive pocket revolvers.

Protector Arms Company: Trade name of the Rupertus Patented Pistol Manufacturing Company on inexpensive pocket revolvers.

Providence: Trade name found on inexpensive pocket revolvers of unknown manufacture.

Quail: Trade name of the Crescent-Davis Arms Company on shotguns.

Queen: a) Trade name of the Hood Firearms Company on inexpensive pocket revolvers. b) Trade name of the Hyde and Shattuck Company on inexpensive single shot pocket pistols.

Queen City: Trade name of the H. & O. Folsom Arms Company on firearms made for the Elmira Arms Company of Elmira, New York.

Ranger: a) Trade name found on inexpensive pocket revolvers of unknown manufacture. b) Trade name of Eastern Arms Company on various firearms made for Sears And Robuck and Co of Chicago. c) Trade name of the Sears, Roebuck and Company of Chicago on a wide variety of firearms marketed by that firm.

Reassurance: Trade name found on inexpensive pocket revolvers of unknown manufacture.

Red Chieftain: Trade name of the Supplee Biddle Hardware Company of Philadelphia, Pennsylvania on inexpensive pocket pistols.

Red Cloud: Trade name of the Ryan Pistol Manufacturing Company on inexpensive pocket revolvers.

Red Hot: Trade name found on inexpensive pocket revolvers of unknown manufacture.

Red Jacket: a) Trade name of the Lee Arms Company on inexpensive pocket revolvers. b) Trade name of the Hopkins and Allen Company on inexpensive pocket revolvers.

Reliable: Trade name found on inexpensive pocket revolvers of unknown manufacture.

Reliance: Trade name of John Meunier of Milwaukee, Wisconsin on rifles.

Rev-O-Noc: Trade name of the H. & O. Folsom Arms Company on firearms made for the Hibbard, Spencer, Bartlett and Company of Chicago; "Conover" spelled backward.

Rich-Con: Trade name of the H. & O. Folsom Arms Company for shotguns made for Richardson & Conover Hardware Company.

Richmond Arms Company: Trade name of the H. & O. Folsom Arms Company on firearms made for an unknown retailer.

Richter Company, Charles: Trade name of the H. & O. Folsom Arms Company on firearms made for the New York Sporting Goods Company of New York.

Rickard Arms Company: Trade name of the H. & O. Folsom Arms Company on firearms made for the J.A. Rickard Company of Schenectady, New York.

Rip Rap: Trade name of the Bacon Arms Company on inexpensive pocket revolvers.

Rival: Trade name of the H. & O. Folsom Arms Company on firearms made for the Van Camp Hardware and Iron Company of Indianapolis, Indiana.

Riverside Arms Company: Trade name of the J. Stevens Arms and Tool Company on various types of firearms.

Robin Hood: Trade name of the Hood Firearms Company on inexpensive pocket revolvers.

Rocky Hill: Trade name found on inexpensive cast iron percussion pocket pistols made in Rocky Hill, Connecticut.

Rodgers Arms Company: Trade name of the Hood Firearms Company on firearms made for an unknown retailer.

Royal Gun Company: Trade name of the Hollenbeck Gun Co. Wheeling West Virgina.

Royal Service: Trade name of the Shapleigh Hardware Company of St. Louis, Missouri on firearms.

Rummel Arms Company: Trade name of the H. & O. Folsom Arms Company on firearms made for the A.J. Rummel Arms Company of Toledo, Ohio.

Russel Arms Company: Registered trade name of the Wiebusch and Hilger Company of New York.

Russian Model: Trade name of the Forehand and Wadsworth Company on inexpensive pocket revolvers.

Safe Guard: Trade name found on inexpensive pocket revolvers of unknown manufacture.

Safety Police: Trade name of the Hopkins and Allen Company on inexpensive pocket revolvers.

St. Louis Arms Company: Trade name of the H. & O. Folsom Arms Company on firearms made for the Shapleigh Hardware Company of St. Louis, Missouri.

Scott: Trade name of the Hopkins and Allen Company on inexpensive pocket revolvers.

Secret Service Special: Trade name of the Rohde, Spencer Company of Chicago on inexpensive pocket revolvers.

Senator: Trade name found on inexpensive pocket revolvers of unknown manufacture.

Sentinel: Trade name found on inexpensive pocket revolvers of unknown manufacture.

Sheffield, The: Trade name of the A. Baldwin and Company, Limited of New Orleans, Louisiana on shotguns.

Sickels-Arms Company: Trade name of the Sickels and Preston Company of Davenport, Iowa on firearms.

Simson: Trade name of the Iver Johnson Arms and Cycle Works on firearms made for the Iver Johnson Sporting Goods Company of Boston, Massachusetts.

Sitting Bull: Trade name found on inexpensive pocket revolvers of unknown manufacture.

Skues Special: Trade name of Ira M. Skue of Hanover, Pennsylvania on shotguns.

Smoker: Trade name of the Iver Johnson Arms and Cycle Works on inexpensive pocket revolvers.

Smythe & Company, John M.: Trade name of H. & O. Folsom Arms Company for shotguns made for John M. Smythe Hardware Company of Chicago.

Southern Arms Company: Trade name of the H. & O. Folsom Arms Company on firearms made for an unknown retailer.

Southerner: a) Trade name of the Brown Manufacturing Company and the Merrimac Arms Manufacturing Company on single shot pocket pistols. b) Registered trade name of Asa Farr of New York on pistols.

Southron: Trade name found on inexpensive pocket pistols of unknown manufacture.

Special Service: Trade name of the Shapleigh Hardware Company of St. Louis, Missouri on inexpensive pocket revolvers.

Spencer Gun Company: Trade name of the H. & O. Folsom Arms Company. Splendor: Trade name found on inexpensive pocket revolvers of unknown manufacture.

Sportsman, The: Trade name of the H. & O. Folsom Arms Company on firearms made for the W. Bingham Company of Cleveland, Ohio.

Springfield Arms Company: Trade name of the J. Stevens Arms and Tool Company.

Spy: Trade name found on inexpensive pocket revolvers of unknown manufacture.

Square Deal: Trade name of the H. & O. Folsom Arms Company on firearms made for the Stratton, Warren Hardware Company of Memphis, Tennessee.

Stand: Trade name of the Marlin Firearms Company on revolvers.

Stanley Arms: Registered trade name of the Wiebusch and Hilger Company of New York on firearms.

Stanley Double Gun: Trade name of the H. & O. Folsom Arms Company on shotguns.

Star: a) Trade name found on inexpensive single shot pocket pistols of unknown manufacture. b) Trade name of the Prescott Pistol Company on inexpensive pocket revolvers.

State Arms Company: Trade name of the H. & O Folsom Arms Company on firearms made for the J. H. Lau and Company of New York.

Sterling: a) Trade name of E.L. and J. Dickinson of Springfield, Massachusetts on single shot pistols. b) Trade name of the H. & O. Folsom Arms Company on shotguns.

Stinger: Registered proprietary trade name engraved on firearms made by the Winchester Repeating Arms Company for the Perry Brothers Limited of Brisbane, Australia.

Stonewall: a) Trade name of the Marlin Firearms Company on single shot derringers. b) Trade name of T.F. Guion of Lycoming, Pennsylvania on single shot percussion pistols he retailed.

Striker: Trade name found on inexpensive pocket revolvers of unknown manufacture.

Sullivan Arms Company: Trade name of the H. & O. Folsom Arms Company on firearms made for the Sullivan Hardware Company of Anderson, South Carolina.

Superior: Trade name of the Paxton and Gallagher Company of Omaha, Nebraska on revolvers and shotguns.

Super Range: Trade name of the Sears, Roebuck and Company of Chicago on shotguns.

Sure Fire: Trade name found on inexpensive pocket revolvers of unknown manufacture.

Swamp Angel: Trade name of the Forehand and Wadsworth Company on inexpensive pocket revolvers.

Swift: Trade name of the Iver Johnson Arms and Cycle Works on firearms made for the John P. Lovell & Sons, Boston, Massachusetts.

Syco: Trade name of the Wyeth Hardware Company of St. Joseph, Missouri on firearms.

Ten Star: Trade name of the H. & D. Folsom Arms Company on firearms made for the Geller, Ward and Hasner Company of St. Louis, Missouri.

Terrier: Trade name of the Rupertus Pantented Pistol Maufacturing Company on inexpensive pocket revolvers.

Terror: Trade name of the Forehand and Wadsworth Company on inexpensive pocket revolvers.

Texas Ranger: Trade name of the Montgomery Ward and Company of Chicago on inexpensive pocket revolvers.

Thames Arms Company: Trade name of the Harrington and Richardson Arms Company on firearms they made for an unknown wholesaler.

Tiger: a) Trade name of the Iver Johnson Arms and Cycle Works on inexpensive pocket revolvers. b) Trade name of the J.H. Hall and Company of Nashville on shotguns.

Tobin Simplex: Trade name used on shotguns of unknown manufacture which were retailed by the G.B. Crandall Company, Limited of Woodstock, Ontario, Canada.

Toledo Firearms Company: a) Trade name of the Hopkins and Allen Company on inexpensive pocket revolvers. b) Trade name of E.L. and J. Dickinson on inexpensive pocket revolvers.

Toronto Belle: Trade name found on inexpensive pocket revolvers of unknown manufacture.

Townleys Pal and Townleys American Boy: Trade name of H. & D. Folsom Arms Company for shotguns made for Townley Metal and Hardware Company of Kansas City, Missouri.

Tramps Terror: Trade name of the Forehand and Wadsworth Company on inexpensive pocket revolvers.

Traps Best: Trade name believed to have been of the H. & D. Folsom Arms Company on firearms made for the Watkins, Coftrell Company of Richmond, Virginia.

Triumph: Trade name of the H. & D. Folsom Arms Company on shotguns.

Trojan: Trade name found on inexpensive pocket revolvers of unknown manufacture.

True Blue: Trade name found on inexpensive pocket revolvers of unknown manufacture.

Tryon Special: Trade name of the Edward K. Tryon Company of Philadelphia, Pennsylvania on shotguns.

Tycoon: Trade name of the Iver Johnson Arms and Cycle Works on inexpensive pocket revolvers.

Union: a) Trade name found on inexpensive single shot pocket pistols of unknown manufacture. b) Trade name of the Hood Firearms Company on inexpensive pocket revolvers. c) Trade name of the Prescott Pistol Company on inexpensive pocket revolvers.

Union Arms Company: Trade name of the H. & D. Folsom Arms Company on firearms made for the Bostwick, Braun Company of Toledo, Ohio.

Union Jack: Trade name found on inexpensive pocket revolvers of unknown manufacture.

Union N.Y.: Trade name of the Whitneyville Armory on inexpensive pocket revolvers.

Unique: Trade name of the C.S. Shattuck Arms Company on revolvers and four barrel pocket pistols.

United States Arms Company: Trade name of Norwich Falls Pistol Company (O.A. Smith) on inexpensive pocket revolvers.

U.S. Arms Company: Trade name used successively by the Alexander Waller and Company (1877), the Barton and Company (1878) and the H. & D. Folsom Arms Company (1879 forward) on a variety of firearms.

U.S. Revolver: Trade name of the Iver Johnson Arms and Cycle Works on inexpensive pocket revolvers.

U.S. Single Gun: Trade name of the Iver Johnson Arms and Cycle Works on single barrel shotguns.

Universal: Trade name of the Hopkins and Allen Company on inexpensive pocket revolvers.

Utica Firearms Company: Trade name of the Simmons Hardware Company of St. Louis, Missouri on firearms.

Valient: Trade name of the Spear and Company of Pittsburgh, Pennsylvania on firearms.

Veiled Prophet: Trade name of the T.E. Ryan Pistol Manufacturing Company on inexpensive pocket revolvers.

Venus: Trade name of the American Novelty Company of Chicago on inexpensive pocket revolvers.

Veteran: Trade name found on inexpensive pocket revolvers of unknown manufacture.

Veto: Trade name found on inexpensive pocket revolvers of unknown manufacture.

Victor: a) Trade name of the Marlin Firearms Company on single shot pocket pistols. b) Trade name of the Harrington and Richardson Arms Company on inexpensive pocket revolvers. c) Trade name of the H. & D. Folsom Arms Company on inexpensive pocket pistols and revolvers.

Victor Arms Company: Trade name of the H. & D. Folsom Arms Company on firearms made for the Hibbard, Spencer, Bartlett and Company of Chicago.

Victor Special: Trade name of the H. & D. Folsom Arms Company on firearms made for the Hibbard, Spencer, Bartleft and Company of Chicago.

Victoria: Trade name of the Hood Firearms Company on inexpensive pocket revolvers.

Virginia Arms Company: Trade name of the H. & D. Folsom Arms Company and later the Davis-Warner Arms Company on firearms made for the Virginia-Carolina Company of Richmond, Virginia.

Volunteer: Trade name of the H. & O. Folsom Arms Company on inexpensive pocket revolvers ade for the Belknap Hardware Company of Louisville, Kentucky.

Vulcan: Trade name of the H. & O. Folsom Arms Company on firearms made for the Edward K. Tryon Company of Philadelphia, Pennsylvania.

Walnut Hill: Trade name of the J. Stevens Arms and Tool Company on rifles.

Warner Arms Corporation: Trade name of the H. & O Folsom Arms Company on firearms made for the Kirtland Brothers, Inc. of New York.

Wasp: Trade name found on inexpensive pocket revolvers of unknown manufacture.

Wautauga: Trade name of the Whitaker, Holtsinger Hardware Company of Morristown, Tennessee on firearms.

Western: Trade name of the H. & O. Folsom Arms Company on firearms made for the Paxton and Gallagher Company of Omaha, Nebraska.

Western Arms Company: a) Trade name of the Bacon Arms on various types of firearms. b) Trade name of W.W. Marston on revolvers. c) Trade name of Henry Kolb and later R.F. Sedgly of Philadelphia, Pennsylvania on Baby Hammerless revolvers. d) Trade name of the Ithaca Gun Company on shotguns believed to have been made for the Montgomery Ward and Company of Chicago.

Western Field: Trade name of Montgomery Ward and Company of Chicago on shotguns of various makes.

Weston, J.J.: Trade name of the H. & O. Folsom Arms Company on shotguns.

Whippet: Trade name of the H. & O. Folsom Arms Company on firearms made for the Hibbard, Spencer, Bartleft and Company of Chicago.

Whistler: Trade name of the Hood Firearms Company on inexpensive pocket revolvers.

White Powder Wonder: Trade name of Albert Aubrey of Meriden, Connecticut on shotguns made for the Sears, Roebuck and Company of Chicago.

Wildwood: Trade name of the H. & O. Folsom Arms Company for shotguns made for Sears, Roebuck & Company.

Wilkinson Arms Company: Trade name of the H. & O. Folsom Arms Company on firearms made for the Richmond Hardware Company of Richmond, Virginia.

Wiltshire Arms Company: Trade name of the H. & O. Folsom Arms Company on firearms made for the Stauffer, Eshleman and Company of New Orleans, Louisiana.

Winfield Arms Company: Trade name of the H. & O. Folsom Arms Company on various types of firearms.

Winner: Trade name found on inexpensive pocket revolvers of-unknown manufacture.

Winoca Arms Company: Trade name of the H. & O. Folsom Arms Company on firearms made for the N. Jacobi Hardware Company of Wilmington, North Camlina.

Wittes Expert: Trade name of the Witte Hardware Company of St. Louis, Missouri on shotguns.

Wittes IXL: Trade name of the Wifte Hardware Company of St. Louis, Missouri on shotguns.

Wolverine Arms Company: Trade name of the H. & O. Folsom Arms Company on firearms made for the Fletcher Hardware Company of Wilmington, North Carolina.

Woodmaster: Trade name found on Belgian shotguns imported by an unknown wholesaler.

Worlds Fair: Trade name of the Hopkins and Allen Company on shotguns.

Worthington Arms Company: Trade name of the H. & O. Folsom Arms Company on various types of firearms.

Wyco: Trade name of the Wyeth Hardware and Manufacturing Company of St. Joseph, Missouri on firearms.

XL: a) Trade name of the Hopkins and Allen Company on inexpensive pocket revolvers. b) Trade name of the Marlin Firearms Company on single shot pocket pistols.

XPERT: a) Trade name of the Hopkins and Allen Company on inexpensive pocket revolvers. b) Trade name of the Iver Johnson Arms and Cycle Works on inexpensive single shot pocket pistols.

XXX Stand: Trade name of the Marlin Firearms Companyon revolvers.

Young America: Trade name of J.P. Lindsay of New York on superimposed - load percussion pistols.

Young American: Trade name of the Harrington and Richardson Arms Company on revolvers.

Firearms Trade and Proprietary Names
Used with Permission of Dave Fulton
Hoosier Gun Works
457 Park City - Bon Ayr Rd.
Park City, KY 42160
(270-749-2109)
www.HoosierGunWorks.com

UNITED STATES

ALABAMA

Alabama Gun Collectors Assn.
Secretary, P.O. Box 70965, Tuscaloosa, AL 35407

ALASKA

Alaska Gun Collectors Assn., Inc.
C.W. Floyd, Pres., 5240 Little Tree, Anchorage, AK 99507

ARIZONA

Arizona Arms Assn.
Don DeBusk, President, 4837 Bryce Ave., Glendale, AZ 85301

CALIFORNIA

California Cartridge Collectors Assn.
Rick Montgomery, 1729 Christina, Stockton, CA 95204/209-463-7216 evs.

California Waterfowl Assn.
4630 Northgate Blvd., #150, Sacramento, CA 95834

Greater Calif. Arms & Collectors Assn.
Donald L. Bullock, 8291 Carburton St., Long Beach, CA 90808-3302

Los Angeles Gun Ctg. Collectors Assn.
F.H. Ruffra, 20810 Amie Ave., Apt. #9, Torrance, CA 90503

Stock Gun Players Assn.
6038 Appian Way, Long Beach, CA, 90803

COLORADO

Colorado Gun Collectors Assn.
L.E.(Bud) Greenwald, 2553 S. Quitman St., Denver, CO 80219/303-935-3850

Rocky Mountain Cartridge Collectors Assn.
John Roth, P.O. Box 757, Conifer, CO 80433

CONNECTICUT

Ye Connecticut Gun Guild, Inc.
Dick Fraser, P.O. Box 425, Windsor, CT 06095

FLORIDA

Unified Sportsmen of Florida
P.O. Box 6565, Tallahassee, FL 32314

GEORGIA

Georgia Arms Collectors Assn., Inc.
Michael Kindberg, President, P.O. Box 277, Alpharetta, GA 30239-0277

ILLINOIS

Illinois State Rifle Assn.
P.O. Box 637, Chatsworth, IL 60921

Mississippi Valley Gun & Cartridge Coll. Assn.
Bob Filbert, P.O. Box 61, Port Byron, IL 61275/309-523-2593

Sauk Trail Gun Collectors
Gordell M. Matson, P.O. Box 1113, Milan, IL 61264

Wabash Valley Gun Collectors Assn., Inc.
Roger L. Dorsett, 2601 Willow Rd., Urbana, IL 61801/217-384-7302

INDIANA

Indiana State Rifle & Pistol Assn.
Thos. Glancy, P.O. Box 552, Chesterton, IN 46304

Southern Indiana Gun Collectors Assn., Inc.
Sheila McClary, 309 W. Monroe St., Boonville, IN 47601/812-897-3742

IOWA

Beaver Creek Plainsmen Inc.
Steve Murphy, Secy., P.O. Box 298, Bondurant, IA 50035

Central States Gun Collectors Assn.
Dennis Greischar, Box 841, Mason City, IA 50402-0841

KANSAS

Kansas Cartridge Collectors Assn.
Bob Linder, Box 84, Plainville, KS 67663

KENTUCKY

Kentuckiana Arms Collectors Assn.
Charles Billips, President, Box 1776, Louisville, KY 40201

Kentucky Gun Collectors Assn., Inc.
Ruth Johnson, Box 64, Owensboro, KY 42302/502-729-4197

LOUISIANA

Washitaw River Renegades
Sandra Rushing, P.O. Box 256, Main St., Grayson, LA 71435

MARYLAND

Baltimore Antique Arms Assn.
Mr. Cillo, 1034 Main St., Darlington, MD 21304

MASSACHUSETTS

Bay Colony Weapons Collectors, Inc.
John Brandt, Box 111, Hing-ham, MA 02043

Massachusetts Arms Collectors
Bruce E. Skinner, P.O. Box 31, No. Carver, MA 02355/508-866-5259

MICHIGAN

Association for the Study and Research of .22 Caliber Rimfire Cartridges
George Kass, 4512 Nakoma Dr., Okemos, MI 48864

MINNESOTA

Sioux Empire Cartridge Collectors Assn.
Bob Cameron, 14597 Glen-dale Ave. SE, Prior Lake, MN 55372

MISSISSIPPI

Mississippi Gun Collectors Assn.
Jack E. Swinney, P.O. Box 16323, Hattiesburg, MS 39402

MISSOURI

Greater St. Louis Cartridge Collectors Assn.
Don MacChesney, 634 Scottsdale Rd., Kirkwood, MO 63122-1109

Mineral Belt Gun Collectors Assn.
D.F. Saunders, 1110 Cleve-land Ave., Monett, MO 65708

Missouri Valley Arms Collectors Assn., Inc.
L.P Brammer II, Membership Secy., P.O. Box 33033, Kansas City, MO 64114

MONTANA

Montana Arms Collectors Assn.
Dean E. Yearout, Sr., Exec. Secy., 1516 21st Ave. S., Great Falls, MT 59405

Weapons Collectors Society of Montana
R.G. Schipf, Ex. Secy., 3100 Bancroft St., Missoula, MT 59801/406-728-2995

NEBRASKA

Nebraska Cartridge Collectors Club
Gary Muckel, P.O. Box 84442, Lincoln, NE 68501

NEW HAMPSHIRE

New Hampshire Arms Collectors, Inc.
James Stamatelos, Secy., P.O. Box 5, Cambridge, MA 02139

NEW JERSEY

Englishtown Benchrest Shooters Assn.
Michael Toth, 64 Cooke Ave., Carteret, NJ 07008

Jersey Shore Antique Arms Collectors
Joe Sisia, P.O. Box 100, Bayville, NJ 08721-0100

New Jersey Arms Collectors Club, Inc.
Angus Laidlaw, Vice Presi-dent, 230 Valley Rd., Montclair, NJ 07042/201-746-0939;
e-mail: acclaid-law@juno.com

NEW YORK

Iroquois Arms Collectors Assn.
Bonnie Robinson, Show Secy., P.O. Box 142, Ransomville, NY 14131/716-791-4096

Mid-State Arms Coll. & Shooters Club
Jack Ackerman, 24 S. Mountain Terr., Binghamton, NY 13903

NORTH CAROLINA

North Carolina Gun Collectors Assn.
Jerry Ledford, 3231-7th St. Dr. NE, Hickory, NC 28601

OHIO

Ohio Gun Collectors Assn.
P.O. Box 9007, Maumee, OH 43537-9007/419-897-0861; Fax:419-897-0860

Shotshell Historical and Collectors Society
Madeline Bruemmer, 3886 Dawley Rd., Ravenna, OH 44266

The Stark Gun Collectors, Inc.
William I. Gann, 5666 Waynesburg Dr., Waynesburg, OH 44688

OREGON

Oregon Arms Collectors Assn., Inc.
Phil Bailey, P.O. Box 13000-A, Portland, OR 97213-0017/503-281-6864; off.:503-281-0918

Oregon Cartridge Collectors Assn.
Boyd Northrup, P.O. Box 285, Rhododendron, OR 97049

PENNSYLVANIA

Presque Isle Gun Collectors Assn.
James Welch, 156 E. 37 St., Erie, PA 16504

SOUTH CAROLINA

Belton Gun Club, Inc.
Attn. Secretary
P.O. Box 126, Belton, SC 29627, (864) 369-6767

Gun Owners of South Carolina
Membership Div.: William Strozier, Secretary, P.O. Box 70, Johns Island, SC 29457-0070/803-762-3240; Fax:803-795-0711;
e-mail:76053.222@compuserve.com

SOUTH DAKOTA

Dakota Territory Gun Coll. Assn., Inc.
Curt Carter, Castlewood, SD 57223

TENNESSEE

Smoky Mountain Gun Coll. Assn., Inc.
Hugh W. Yabro, President, P.O. Box 23225, Knoxville, TN 37933

Tennessee Gun Collectors Assn., Inc.
M.H. Parks, 3556 Pleasant Valley Rd., Nashville, TN 37204-3419

TEXAS

Houston Gun Collectors Assn., Inc.
P.O. Box 741429, Houston, TX 77274-1429

Texas Cartridge Collectors Assn., Inc.
Robert Mellichamp, Memb. Contact, 907 Shirkmere, Houston, TX 77008/713-869-0558

Texas Gun Collectors Assn.
Bob Eder, Pres., P.O. Box 12067, El Paso, TX 79913/915-584-8183

Texas State Rifle Assn.
1131 Rockingham Dr., Suite 101, Richardson, TX 75080-4326

VIRGINIA

Virginia Gun Collectors Assn., Inc.
Addison Hurst, Secy., 38802 Charlestown Height, Water-ford, VA 20197/540-882-3543

WASHINGTON

Association of Cartridge Collectors on the Pacific Northwest
Robert Jardin, 14214 Mead-owlark Drive KPN, Gig Harbor, WA 98329

Washington Arms Collectors, Inc.
Joyce Boss, P.O. Box 389, Renton, WA, 98057-0389/206-255-8410

WISCONSIN

Great Lakes Arms Collectors Assn., Inc.
Edward C. Warnke, 2913 Woodridge Lane, Waukesha, WI 53188

Wisconsin Gun Collectors Assn., Inc.
Lulita Zellmer, P.O. Box 181, Sussex, WI 53089

WYOMING

Wyoming Weapons Collectors
P.O. Box 284, Laramie, WY 82073/307-745-4652 or 745-9530

NATIONAL ORGANIZATIONS

Amateur Trapshooting Assn.
David D. Bopp, Exec. Director, 601 W. National Rd., Vandalia, OH 45377/937-898-4638; Fax:937-898-5472

American Airgun Field Target Assn.
5911 Cherokee Ave., Tampa, FL 33604

American Coon Hunters Assn.
Opal Johnston, P.O. Cadet, Route 1, Box 492, Old Mines, MO 63630

American Custom Gunmakers Guild
Jan Billeb, Exec. Director, P.O. Box 812, Burlington, IA 52601-0812/319-752-6114 (Phone or Fax)

American Defense Preparedness Assn.
Two Colonial Place, 2101 Wilson Blvd., Suite 400, Arlington, VA 22201-3061

American Paintball League
P.O. Box 3561, Johnson City, TN 37602/800-541-9169

American Pistolsmiths Guild
Alex B. Hamilton, Pres., 1449 Blue Crest Lane, San Antonio, TX 78232/210-494-3063

American Police Pistol & Rifle Assn.
3801 Biscayne Blvd., Miami, FL 33137

American Single Shot Rifle Assn.
Gary Staup, Secy., 709 Car-olyn Dr., Delphos, OH 45833/419-692-3866. Web-site: www.assra.com

American Society of Arms Collectors
George E. Weatherly, P.O. Box 2567, Waxahachie, TX 75165

American Tactical Shooting Assn. (A.T.S.A.)
c/o Skip Gochenour, 2600 N. Third St., Harrisburg, PA 17110/717-233-0402; Fax:717-233-5340

Association of Firearm and Tool Mark Examiners
Lannie G. Emanuel, Secy., Southwest Institute of Forensic Sciences, P.O. Box 35728, Dallas, TX 75235/214-920-5979; Fax:214-920-5928; Membership Secy., Ann D. Jones, VA Div. of Forensic Science, P.O. Box 999, Richmond, VA 23208/804-786-4706; Fax:804-371-8328

Boone & Crockett Club
250 Station Dr., Missoula, MT 59801-2753

Browning Collectors Assn.
Secretary: Scherrie L. Bren-nac, 2749 Keith Dr., Villa Ridge, MO 63089/314-742-0571

Cast Bullet Assn., Inc., The
Ralland J. Fortier, Editor, 4103 Foxcraft Dr., Traverse City, MI 49684

Citizens Committee for the Right to Keep and Bear Arms
Natl. Hq., Liberty Park, 12500 NE Tenth Pl., Bellevue, WA 98005

Colt Collectors Assn.
25000 Highland Way, Los Gatos, CA 95030/408-353-2658.

Ducks Unlimited, Inc.
Natl. Headquarters, One Waterfowl Way, Memphis, TN 38120/901-758-3937

Fifty Caliber Shooters Assn.
PO Box 111, Monroe UT 84754-0111

Firearms Coalition/Neal Knox Associates
Box 6537, Silver Spring, MD 20906/301-871-3006

Firearms Engravers Guild of America
Rex C. Pedersen, Secy., 511 N. Rath Ave., Lundington, MI 49431/616-845-7695(Phone and Fax)

Foundation for North American Wild Sheep
720 Allen Ave., Cody, WY 82414-3402/web site: http://iigi.com/os/non/fnaws/ fnaw s.htm; e-mail: fnaws@ wyoming.com

Freedom Arms Collectors Assn.
P.O. Box 160302, Miami, FL 33116-0302

Garand Collectors Assn.
P.O. Box 181, Richmond, KY 40475

Golden Eagle Collectors Assn. (G.E.C.A.)
Chris Showler, 11144 Slate Creek Rd., Grass Valley, CA 95945

Gun Owners of America
8001 Forbes Place, Suite 102, Springfield, VA 22151/703-321-8585

Handgun Hunters International
J.D. Jones, Director, P.O. Box 357 MAG, Bloomingdale, OH 43910

Harrington & Richardson Gun Coll. Assn.
George L. Cardet, 330 S.W. 27th Ave., Suite 603, Miami, FL 33135

High Standard Collectors' Assn.
John J. Stimson, Jr., Pres., 540 W. 92nd St., Indianapolis, IN 46260

Hopkins & Allen Arms & Memorabilia Society (HAAMS)
P.O. Box 187, 1309 Pamela Circle, Delphos, OH 45833

International Ammunition Association, Inc.
C.R. Punnett, Secy., 8 Hillock Lane, Chadds Ford, PA 19317/610-358-1285; Fax:610-358-1560

International Benchrest Shooters
Joan Borden, RR1, Box 250BB, Springville, PA 18844/717-965-2366

International Blackpowder Hunting Assn.
P.O. Box 1180, Glenrock, WY 82637/307-436-9817

IHMSA (Intl. Handgun Metallic Silhouette Assn.)
PO Box 368, Burlington, IA 52601 Website: www.ihmsa.cor

International Society of Mauser Arms Collectors
Michael Kindberg, Pres., P.O. Box 277, Alpharetta, GA 30239-0277

Jews for the Preservation of Firearms Ownership (JPFO)
2872 S. Wentworth Ave., Milwaukee, WI 53207/414-769-0760; Fax:414-483-8435

Mannlicher Collectors Assn., The
Membership Office: P.O. Box1249, The Dalles, Oregon 97058

Marlin Firearms Collectors Assn., Ltd.
Dick Paterson, Secy., 407 Lincoln Bldg., 44 Main St., Champaign, IL 61820

Merwin Hulbert Association,
2503 Kentwood Ct., High Point, NC 27265

Miniature Arms Collectors/ Makers Society, Ltd.
Ralph Koebbeman, Pres., 4910 Kilburn Ave., Rockford, IL 61101/815-964-2569

M1 Carbine Collectors Assn. (M1-CCA)
623 Apaloosa Ln., Gardner-ville, NV 89410-7840

National Association of Buckskinners (NAB)
Territorial Dispatch—1800s Historical Publication, 4701 Marion St., Suite 324, Live-stock Exchange Bldg., Denver, CO 80216/303-297-9671

National Association of Derringer Collectors, The
P.O. Box 20572, San Jose, CA 95160

National Assn. of Federally Licensed Firearms Dealers
Andrew Molchan, 2455 E. Sunrise, Ft. Lauderdale, FL 33304

National Association to Keep and Bear Arms
P.O. Box 78336, Seattle, WA 98178

National Automatic Pistol Collectors Assn.
Tom Knox, P.O. Box 15738, Tower Grove Station, St. Louis, MO 63163

National Bench Rest Shooters Assn., Inc.
Pat Ferrell, 2835 Guilford Lane, Oklahoma City, OK 73120-4404/405-842-9585; Fax: 405-842-9575

National Muzzle Loading Rifle Assn.
Box 67, Friendship, IN 47021 / 812-667-5131. Website: www.nmlra@ nmlra.org

National Professional Paintball League (NPPL)
540 Main St., Mount Kisco, NY 10549/914-241-7400

National Reloading Manufacturers Assn.
One Centerpointe Dr., Suite 300, Lake Oswego, OR 97035

National Rifle Assn. of America
11250 Waples Mill Rd., Fair-fax, VA 22030 / 703-267-1000. Website: www.nra.org

National Shooting Sports Foundation, Inc.
Robert T. Delfay, President, Flintlock Ridge Office Center, 11 Mile Hill Rd., Newtown, CT 06470-2359/203-426-1320; FAX: 203-426-1087

National Skeet Shooting Assn.
Dan Snyuder, Director, 5931 Roft Road, San Antonio, TX 78253-9261/800-877-5338. Website: nssa-nsca.com

National Sporting Clays Association
Ann Myers, Director, 5931 Roft Road, San Antonio, TX 78253-9261/800-877-5338. Website: nssa-nsca.com

National Wild Turkey Federation, Inc.
P.O. Box 530, 770 Augusta Rd., Edgefield, SC 29824

North American Hunting Club
P.O. Box 3401, Minnetonka, MN 55343/612-936-9333; Fax: 612-936-9755

North American Paintball Referees Association (NAPRA)
584 Cestaric Dr., Milpitas, CA 95035

North-South Skirmish Assn., Inc.
Stevan F. Meserve, Exec. Secretary, 507 N. Brighton Court, Sterling, VA 20164-3919

Remington Society of America
Gordon Fosburg, Secretary, 11900 North Brinton Road, Lake, MI 48623

Rocky Mountain Elk Foundation
P.O. Box 8249, Missoula, MT 59807-8249/406-523-4500; Fax: 406-523-4581 Website: www.rmef.org

Ruger Collector's Assn., Inc.
P.O. Box 240, Greens Farms, CT 06436

Safari Club International
4800 W. Gates Pass Rd., Tucson, AZ 85745/520-620-1220

Sako Collectors Assn., Inc.
Jim Lutes, 202 N. Locust, Whitewater, KS 67154

Second Amendment Foundation
James Madison Building, 12500 NE 10th Pl., Bellevue, WA 98005

Single Action Shooting Society (SASS)
23255-A La Palma Avenue, Yorba Linda, CA 92887/714-694-1800; FAX: 714-694-1815/ email: sasseot@aol.com Web-site: www.sassnet.com

Smith & Wesson Collectors Assn.
Cally Pletl, Admin. Asst.,PO Box 444, Afton, NY 13730

Society of American Bayonet Collectors, The
P.O. Box 234, East Islip, NY 11730-0234

Southern California Schuetzen Society
Dean Lillard, 34657 Ave. E., Yucaipa, CA 92399

Sporting Arms and Ammunition Manufacturers' Institute (SAAMI)
Flintlock Ridge Office Center, 11 Mile Hill Rd., Newtown, CT 06470-2359/203-426-4358; FAX: 203-426-1087

Sporting Clays of America (SCA)
Ron L. Blosser, Pres., 9257 Buckeye Rd., Sugar Grove, OH 43155-9632/614-746-8334; Fax: 614-746-8605

Thompson/Center Assn., The
Joe Wright, President, Box 792, Northboro, MA 01532/508-845-6960

U.S. Practical Shooting Assn./IPSC
Dave Thomas, P.O. Box 811, Sedro Woolley, WA 98284/360-855-2245

U.S. Revolver Assn.
Brian J. Barer, 40 Larchmont Ave., Taunton, MA 02780/508-824-4836

U.S. Shooting Team
U.S. Olympic Shooting Center, One Olympic Plaza, Colorado Springs, CO 80909/719-578-4670

Varmint Hunters Assn., Inc., The
Box 759, Pierre, SD 57501/ Member Services 800-528-4868

Weatherby Collectors Assn., Inc.
P.O. Box 888, Ozark, MO 65721

Wildcatters, The
P.O. Box 170, Greenville, WI 54942

Winchester Arms Collectors Assn.
P.O. Box 230, Brownsboro, TX 75756/903-852-4027

The Women's Shooting Sports Foundation (WSSF)
4620 Edison Avenue, Ste. C, Colorado Springs, CO 80915/719-638-1299; FAX: 719-638-1271/e-mail: wssf@worldnet.att.net

ARGENTINA

Asociacion Argentina de Coleccionistas de Armes y Municiones
Castilla de Correos No. 28, Succursal I B, 1401 Buenos Aires, Republica Argentina

AUSTRALIA

Antique & Historical Arms Collectors of Australia
P.O. Box 5654, GCMC Queensland 9726, Australia

The Arms Collector's Guild of Queensland Inc.
Ian Skennerton, P.O. Box 433, Ashmore City 4214, Queensland, Australia

Australian Cartridge Collectors Assn., Inc.
Bob Bennett, 126 Landscape Dr., E. Doncaster 3109, Victoria, Ausrtalia

Sporting Shooters Assn. of Australia, Inc.
P.O. Box 2066, Kent Town, SA 5071, Australia

CANADA

ALBERTA

Canadian Historical Arms Society
P.O. Box 901, Edmonton, Alb., Canada T5J 2L8

National Firearms Assn.
Natl. Hq: P.O. Box 1779, Edmonton, Alb., Canada T5J 2P1

BRITISH COLUMBIA

The Historical Arms Collectors of B.C. (Canada)
Harry Moon, Pres., P.O. Box 50117, South Slope RPO, Burnaby, BC V5J 5G3, Can-ada/604-438-0950; Fax:604-277-3646

ONTARIO

Association of Canadian Cartridge Collectors
Monica Wright, RR 1, Mill-grove, ON, LOR IVO, Canada

Tri-County Antique Arms Fair
P.O. Box 122, RR #1, North Lancaster, Ont., Canada K0C 1Z0

EUROPE

BELGIUM

European Cartridge Research Assn.
Graham Irving, 21 Rue Schaltin, 4900 Spa, Bel-gium/32.87.77.43.40; Fax:32.87.77.27.51

CZECHOSLOVAKIA

Spolecnost Pro Studium Naboju (Czech Cartridge Research Assn.)
JUDr. Jaroslav Bubak, Pod Homolko 1439, 26601 Beroun 2, Czech Republic

DENMARK

Aquila Dansk Jagtpatron Historic Forening (Danish Historical Cartridge Collectors Club)
Steen Elgaard Møller, Ulriksdalsvej 7, 4840 Nr. Alslev, Denmark 10045-53846218; Fax:00455 384 6209

ENGLAND

Arms and Armour Society
Hon. Secretary A. Dove, P.O. Box 10232, London, 5W19 2ZD, England

Dutch Paintball Federation
Aceville Publ., Castle House 97 High Street, Colchester, Essex C01 1TH, England/011-44-206-564840

European Paintball Sports Foundation
c/o Aceville Publ., Castle House 97 High St., Colches-ter, Essex, C01 1TH, England

Historical Breechloading Smallarms Assn.
D.J. Penn M.A., Secy., P.O. Box 12778, London SE1 6BX, England. Journal and newsletter are $23 a yr., including airmail.

National Rifle Assn.
(Great Britain) Bisley Camp, Brookwood, Woking Surrey GU24 OPB, England/01483.797777; Fax: 014730686275

United Kingdom Cartridge Club
Ian Southgate, 20 Millfield, Elmley Castle, Nr. Pershore, Worcestershire, WR10 3HR, England

FRANCE

STAC-Western Co.
3 Ave. Paul Doumer (N.311); 78360 Montesson, France/01.30.53-43-65; Fax: 01.30.53.19.10

GERMANY

Bund Deutscher Sports-chüt-zen e.v. (BDS)
Borsigallee 10, 53125 Bonn 1, Germany

Deutscher Schützenbund
Lahnstrasse 120, 65195 Wiesbaden, Germany

SPAIN

Asociacion Espanola de Colleccionistas de Cartu-chos (A.E.C.C.)
Secretary: Apdo. Correos No. 1086, 2880-Alcala de Henares (Madrid), Spain. President: Apdo. Correos No. 682, 50080 Zaragoza, Spain

SWEDEN

Scandinavian Ammunition Research Assn.
Box 107, 77622 Hedemora, Sweden

NEW ZEALAND

New Zealand Cartridge Collectors Club
Terry Castle, 70 Tiraumea Dr., Pakuranga, Auckland, New Zealand

New Zealand Deerstalkers Assn.
P.O. Box 6514 TE ARO, Wellington, New Zealand

SOUTH AFRICA

Historical Firearms Soc. of South Africa
P.O. Box 145, 7725 Newlands, Republic of South Africa

Republic of South Africa Cartridge Collectors Assn.
Arno Klee, 20 Eugene St., Malanshof Randburg, Gauteng 2194, Republic of South Africa

S.A.A.C.A. (Southern Africa Arms and Ammunition Assn.)
Gauteng Office: P.O. Box 7597, Weltevreden Park, 1715, Republic of South Africa/011-679-1151; Fax: 011-679-1131; e-mail: saaaca@iafrica.com. Kwa-Zulu Natal office: P.O. Box 4065, Northway, Kwazulu-Natal 4065, Republic of South Africa

SAGA (S.A. Gunowners' Assn.)
P.O. Box 35203, Northway, Kwazulu-Natal 4065, Republic of South Africa

IMPORTANT NOTICE TO BOOK BUYERS

Books listed here may be bought from Ray Riling Arms Books Co., 6844 Gorsten St., P.O. Box 18925, Philadelphia, PA 19119, Phone 215/438-2456; FAX: 215-438-5395. E-Mail: sales@rayrilingarms-books.com. Joe Riling is the researcher and compiler of "The Arms Library" and a seller of gun books for over 32 years. The Riling stock includes books classic and modern, many hard-to-find items, and many not obtainable elsewhere. These pages list a portion of the current stock. They offer prompt, complete service, with delayed shipments occurring only on out-of-print or out-of-stock books.

Visit our web site at **www.rayrilingarmsbooks.com** and order all of your favorite titles on line from our secure site.

NOTICE FOR ALL CUSTOMERS: Remittance in U.S. funds must accompany all orders. For your convience we now accept Visa, Mastercard & American Express. For Shipments in the U.S. add $7.00 for the 1st book and $2.00 for each additional book for postage and insurance. Minimum order $10.00. International

Orders add $13.00 for the 1st book and $5.00 for each additional book. All International orders are shipped at the buyer's risk unless an additional $5 for insurance is included. USPS does not offer insurance to all countries unless shipped Air-Mail please e-mail or call for pricing.

Payments in excess of order or for "Backorders" are credited or fully refunded at request. Books "As-Ordered" are not returnable except by permission and a handling charge on these of 10% or $2.00 per book which ever is greater is deducted from refund or credit. Only Pennsylvania customers must include current sales tax.

A full variety of arms books also available from Rutgers Book Center, 127 Raritan Ave., Highland Park, NJ 08904/908-545-4344; FAX: 908-545-6686 or I.D.S.A. Books, 1324 Stratford Drive, Piqua, OH 45356/937-773-4203; FAX: 937-778-1922.

COLLECTORS

A Glossary of the Construction, Decoration and Use of Arms and Armor in All Countries and in All Times. By George Cameron Stone, Dover Publishing, New York 1999. Softcover. $39.95
> An exhaustive study of arms and armor in all countries through recorded history from the stone age up to the second world war. With over 4500 Black & White Illustrations. This Dover edition is an unabridged republication of the work originally published in 1934 by the Southworth Press, Portland MA. A new Introduction has been specially prepared for this edition.

Accoutrements of the United States Infantry, Riflemen, and Dragoons 1834-1839. by R.T. Huntington, Historical Arms Series No. 20. Canada: Museum Restoration. 58 pp. illus. Softcover. $8.95
> Although the 1841 edition of the U.S. Ordnance Manual provides ample information on the equipment that was in use during the 1840s, it is evident that the patterns of equipment that it describes were not introduced until 1838 or 1839. This guide is intended to fill this gap in our knowledge by providing an overview of what we now know about the accoutrements that were issued to the regular infantryman, rifleman, and dragoon, in the 1830's with excursions into earlier and later years.

Age of the Gunfighter; Men and Weapons on the Frontier 1840-1900. By Joseph G. Rosa, University of Oklahoma Press, Norman, OK, 1999. 192 pp., illustrated. Paper covers. $21.95
> Stories of gunfighters and their encounters and detailed descriptions of virtually every firearm used in the old West.

Air Guns. By Eldon G. Wolff, Duckett's Publishing Co., Tempe, AZ, 1997. 204 pp., illus Paper covers. $35.00
> Historical reference covering many makers, European and American guns, canes and more.

Allied and Enemy Aircraft: May 1918; Not to be Taken from the Front Lines, Historical Arms Series No. 27. Canada: Museum Restoration.
Softcover. $8.95
> The basis for this title is a very rare identification manual published by the French government in 1918 that illustrated 60 aircraft with three or more views: French, English American, German, Italian, and Belgian, which might have been seen over the trenches of France. Each is describe in a text translated from the original French. This is probably the most complete collection of illustrations of WW1 aircraft which has survived.

American Beauty; The Prewar Colt National Match Government Model Pistol. By Timothy J. Mullin, Collector Grade Publications, Cobourg, Ontario, Canada. 72 pp., illustrated. $34.95
> Includes over 150 serial numbers, and 20 spectacular color photos of factory engraved guns and other authenticated upgrades, including rare "double-carved" ivory grips.

American Military Saddle, 1776-1945, The. By R. Stephen Dorsey & Kenneth L. McPheeters, Collector's Library, Eugene, OR, 1999. 400 pp., illustrated. $59.95
> The most complete coverage of the subject ever written on the American Military Saddle. Nearly 1000 actual photos and official drawings, from the major public and private collections in the U.S. and Great Britain.

American Police Collectibles; Dark Lanterns and Other Curious Devices. By Matthew G. Forte, Turn of the Century Publishers, Upper Montclair, NJ, 1999. 248 pp., illustrated. $24.95
> For collectors of police memorabilia (handcuffs, police dark lanterns, mechanical and chain nippers, rattles, billy clubs and nightsticks) and police historians.

Ammunition; Small Arms, Grenades, and Projected Munitions. By Greenhill Publishing. 144 pp., Illustrated. $22.95 The best concise guide to modern ammunition available today. Covers ammo for small arms, grenades, and projected munitions. 144 pp., Illustrated. As NEW – Hardcover.

Antique Guns, the Collector's Guide, 2nd Edition, edited by John Traister, Stoeger Publishing Co., So. Hackensack, NJ, 1994. 320 pp., illus. Paper covers. **$19.95**
> Covers a vast spectrum of pre-1900 firearms: those manufactured by U.S. gunmakers as well as Canadian, French, German, Belgian, Spanish and other foreign firms.

Arming the Glorious Cause; Weapons of the Second War for Independence. By James B. Whisker, Daniel D. Hartzler and Larry W. Tantz, Old Bedford Village Press, Bedford, PA., 1998. 175 pp., illustrated. $45.00
> A photographic study of Confederate weapons.

Arms & Accoutrements of the Mounted Police 1873-1973. By Roger F. Phillips and Donald J. Klancher, Museum Restoration Service, Ont., Canada, 1982. 224 pp., illus. $49.95
> A definitive history of the revolvers, rifles, machine guns, cannons, ammunition, swords, etc. used by the NWMP, the RNWMP and the RCMP during the first 100 years of the Force.

Arms and Armor In Antiquity and The Middle Ages. By Charles Boutell, Combined Books Inc., PA 1996. 296 pp., w/ b/w illus. Also a descriptive Notice of Modern Weapons. Translated from the French of M.P. Lacombe, and with a Preface, Notes, and One Additional Chapter on Arms and Armour in England. $14.95

Arms and Armor in the Art Institute of Chicago. By Waltler J. Karcheski, Bulfinch, New York 1999. 128 pp., 103 color photos, 12 black & white illustrations. $50.00
> The George F. Harding Collection of arms and armor is the most visited installation at the Art Institute of Chicago - a testament to the enduring appeal of swords, muskets and the other paraphernalia of medieval and early modern war. Organized both chronologically and by type of weapon, this book captures the best of this astonishing collection in 115 striking photographs - most in color - accompanied by illuminating text. Here are intricately filigreed breastplates and ivory-handled crossbows, samurai katana and Toledo-steel scimitars, elaborately decorated maces and beautifully carved flintlocks - a treat for anyone who has ever been beguiled by arms, armor and the age of chivalry.

Arms and Armor in Colonial America 1526-1783. by Harold Peterson, Dover Publishing, New York, 2000. 350 pages with over 300 illustrations, index, bibliography & appendix. Softcover. $29.95
> Over 200 years of firearms, ammunition, equipment & edged weapons.

Arms and Armor: The Cleveland Museum of Art. By Stephen N. Fliegel, Abrams, New York, 1998. 172 color photos, 17 halftones. 181 pages. $49.50
> Intense look at the culture of the warrior and hunter, with an intriguing discussion of the decorative arts found on weapons and armor, set against the background of political and social history. Also provides information on the evolution of armor, together with manufacture and decoration, and weapons as technology and art.

Arms and Equipment of the Civil War. By Jack Coggins, Barnes & Noble, Rockleight, N.J., 1999. 160 pp., illustrated. $12.98
> This unique encyclopedia provides a new perspective on the war. It provides lively explanations of how ingenious new weapons spelled victory or defeat for both sides. Aided by more than 500 illustrations and on-the-scene comments by Union and Confederate soldiers.

Arms Makers of Colonial America. By James B. Whisker, Selinsgrove, PA:, 1992: Susquehanna University Press. 1st edition. 217 pages, illustrated. $45.00
> A comprehensively documented historical survey of the broad spectrum of arms makers in America who were active before 1783.

Arms Makers of Maryland. By Daniel D. Hartzler, George Shumway, York, PA, 1975. 200 pp., illus. $50.00
> A thorough study of the gunsmiths of Maryland who worked during the late 18th and early 19th centuries.

Arms Makers of Pennsylvania. By James B. Whisker, Selinsgrove, PA:: Susquehanna Univ. Press, 1990. 1st edition. 218 pages, illustrated in black and white and color. $45.00
> Concentrates primarily on the cottage industry gunsmiths & gun makers who worked in the Keystone State from it's early years through 1900.

Arms Makers of Western Pennsylvania. By James B. Whisker, Old Bedford Village Press. 1st edition. This deluxe hard bound edition has 176 pages, $45.00

Printed on fine coated paper, with many large photographs, and detailed text describing the period, lives, tools, and artistry of the Arms Makers of Western Pennsylvania.

Arsenal Of Freedom: The Springfield Armory 1890-1948. By Lt. Col. William Brophy, Andrew Mowbray, Inc., Lincoln, RI,1997. 20 pgs of photos. 400 pages. As New - Softcover. $29.95

A year by year account drawn from official records. Packed with reports, charts, tables, line drawings, and 20 page photo section.

Artistic Ingredients of the Longrifle. By George Shumway Publisher, 1989 102 pp., with 94 illus. $20.00

After a brief review of Pennsylvania-German folk art and architecture, to establish the artistic environment in which the longrifle was made, the author demonstrates that the sophisticated rococo decoration on the many of the finer longrifles is comparable to the best rococo work of Philadelphia cabinet makers and silversmiths.

Art of Gun Engraving, The. By Claude Gaier and Pietro Sabatti, Knickerbocker Press, N.Y., 1999. 160 pp., illustrated. $34.50

The richness and detail lavished on early firearms represents a craftsmanship nearly vanished. Beginning with crossbows in the 100's, hunting scenes, portraits, or mythological themes are intricately depicted within a few square inches of etched metal. The full-color photos contained herein recaptures this lost art with exquisite detail.

Astra Automatic Pistols. By Leonardo M. Antaris, FIRAC Publishing Co., Sterling, CO, 1989. 248 pp., illus. $55.00

Charts, tables, serial ranges, etc. The definitive work on Astra pistols.

Basic Documents on U.S. Martial Arms. Commentary. By Col. B. R. Lewis, reissue by Ray Riling, Phila., PA, 1956 and 1960. Rifle Musket Model 1855.

The first issue rifle of musket caliber, a muzzle loader equipped with the Maynard Primer, 32 pp. Rifle Musket Model 1863. The typical Union muzzle-loader of the Civil War, 26 pp. Breech-Loading Rifle Musket Model 1866. The first of our 50-caliber breechloading rifles, 12 pp. Remington Navy Rifle Model 1870. A commercial type breech-loader made at Springfield, 16 pp. Lee Straight Pull Navy Rifle Model 1895. A magazine cartridge arm of 6mm caliber. 23 pp. Breech-Loading Arms (five models) 27 pp. Ward-Burton Rifle Musket 1871-16 pp. Each $10.00.

Battle Weapons of the American Revolution. By George C. Neuman, Scurlock Publishing Co., Texarkana, TX, 2001. 400 pp. Illus. Softcovers. $34.95

The most extensive photographic collection of Revolutionary War weapons ever in one volume. More than 1,600 photos of over 500 muskets, rifles, swords, bayonets, knives and other arms used by both sides in America's War for Independence.

Bedford County Rifle and Its Makers, The. By George Shumway. 40pp. illustrated, Softcover. $10.00

The authors study of the graceful and distinctive muzzle-loading rifles made in Bedford County, Pennsylvania. Stands as a milestone on the long path to the understanding of America's longrifles.

Behold the Longrifle Again. By James B. Whisker, Old Bedford Village Press, Bedford, PA, 1997. 176 pp., illus. $45.00

Excellent reference work for the collector profusely illustrated with photographs of some of the finest Kentucky rifles showing front and back profiles and overall view.

Belgian Rattlesnake; The Lewis Automatic Machine Gun, The. By William M. Easterly, Collector Grade Publications, Cobourg, Ontario, Canada, 1998. 584 pp., illustrated. $79.95

The most complete account ever published on the life and times of Colonel Isaac Newton Lewis and his crowning invention, the Lewis Automatic machine gun.

Beretta Automatic Pistols. By J.B. Wood, Stackpole Books, Harrisburg, PA, 1985. 192 pp., illus. $24.95

Only English-language book devoted to the Beretta line. Includes all important models.

Big Guns, Civil War Siege, Seacoast, and Naval Cannon, The. By Edwin Olmstead, Wayne E. Stark, and Spencer C. Tucker, Museum Restoration Service, Bloomfield, Ontario, Canada, 1997. 360 pp., illustrated. $80.00

This book is designed to identify and record the heavy guns available to both sides by the end of the Civil War.

Birmingham Gunmakers. By Douglas Tate, Safari Press, Inc., Huntington Beach, CA, 1997. 300 pp., illus. $50.00

An invaluable work for anybody interested in the fine sporting arms crafted in this famous British gunmakers' city.

Blue Book of Gun Values, 22nd Edition. Edited by S.P. Fjestad, Blue Book Publications, Inc. Minneapolis, MN 2001. $34.95

This new 22nd Edition simply contains more firearms values and information than any other single publication. Expanded to over 1,600 pages featuring over 100,000 firearms prices, the new Blue Book of Gun Values also contains over _ million words of text – no other book is even close! Most of the information contained in this publication is simply not available anywhere else, for any price!

Blue Book of Modern Black Powder Values. By Dennis Adler, Blue Book Publications, Inc. Minneapolis, MN 2000. 200 pp., illustrated. 41 color photos. Softcover. $14.95

This new title contains more up-to-date black powder values and related information than any other single publication. With 120 pages, this new book will keep you up to date on modern black powder models and prices, including most makes & models introduced this year!

Blunderbuss 1500-1900, The. By James D. Forman, Historical Arms Series No. 32. Canada: Museum Restoration, 1994. An excellent and authoritative booklet giving tons of information on the Blunderbuss, a very neglected subject. 40 pages, illustrated. Softcover. $8.95

Boarders Away I: With Steel-Edged Weapons & Polearms. By William Gilkerson, Andrew Mowbray, Inc. Publishers, Lincoln, RI, 1993. 331 pp., illus. $48.00

Contains the essential 24 page chapter 'War at Sea' which sets the historical and practical context for the arms discussed. Includes chapters on, Early Naval Weapons, Boarding Axes, Cutlasses, Officers Fighting Swords and Dirks, and weapons at hand of Random Mayhem.

Boarders Away, Volume II: Firearms of the Age of Fighting Sail. By William Gilkerson, Andrew Mowbray, Inc. Publishers, Lincoln, RI, 1993. 331 pp., illus. $65.00

Covers the pistols, muskets, combustibles and small cannon used aboard American and European fighting ships, 1626-1826.

Book of Colt Firearms, The. By R. L. Wilson, Blue Book Publications, Inc, Minneapolis, MN, 1993. 616 pp., illus. $158.00

A complete Colt library in a single volume. In over 1,250.000 words, over 1,250 black and white and 67 color photographs, this mammoth work tells the Colt story from 1832 through the present.

Boothroyd's Revised Directory of British Gunmakers. By Geoffrey Boothroyd, Long Beach, CA: Safari Press, 2000. Revised edition. 412pp, photos. $39.95

Over a 30 year period Geoffrey Boothroyd has accumulated information on just about every sporting gun maker that ever has existed in the British Isles from 1850 onward. In this magnificent reference work he has placed all the gun makers he has found over the years (over 1000 entries) in an alphabetical listing with as much information as he has been able to unearth. One of the best reference sources on all British makers (including Wales, Scotland and Ireland) in which you can find data on the most obscure as well as the most famous. Contains starting date of the business, addresses, proprietors, what they made and how long they operated with other interesting details for the collector of fine British guns.

Boston's Gun Bible. By Boston T. Party, Ignacio, CO: Javelin Press, August 2000. Expanded Edition.Softcover. $28.00

This mammoth guide for gun owners everywhere is a completely updated and expanded edition (more than 500 new pages!) of Boston T. Party's classic Boston on Guns and Courage. Pulling no punches, Boston gives wise advice on which shoulder weapons and handguns to buy and why before exploring such topics as why you should consider not getting a concealed carry permit, what guns and gear will likely be outlawed next, how to spend within your budget, why you should go to a quality defensive shooting academy now, which guns and gadgets are inferior and why, how to stay off illegal government gun registration lists, how to spot an undercover agent trying to entrap law-abiding gun owners and much more.

Breech-Loading Carbines of the United States Civil War Period. By Brig. Gen. John Pitman, Armory Publications, Tacoma, WA, 1987. 94 pp., illus. $29.95

The first in a series of previously unpublished manuscripts originated by the late Brigadier General John Putnam. Exploded drawings showing parts actual size follow each sectioned illustration.

Breech-Loading Single-Shot Rifle, The. By Major Ned H. Roberts and Kenneth L. Waters, Wolfe Publishing Co., Prescott, AZ, 1995. 333 pp., illus. $28.50

A comprehensive and complete history of the evolution of the Schutzen and single-shot rifle.

Bren Gun Saga, The. By Thomas B. Dugelby, Collector Grade Publications, Cobourg, Ontario, Canada, 1999, revised and expanded edition. 406 pp., illustrated. $65.95

A modern, definitive book on the Bren in this revised expanded edition, which in terms of numbers of pages and illustrations is nearly twice the size of the original.

British Board of Ordnance Small Arms Contractors 1689-1840. By De Witt Bailey, Rhyl, England: W. S. Curtis, 2000. 150 pp. $18.00

Thirty years of research in the Archives of the Ordnance Board in London has identified more than 600 of these suppliers. The names of many can be found marking the regulation firearms of the period. In the study, the contractors are identified both alphabetically and under a combination of their date period together with their specialist trade.

British Enfield Rifles, Volume 1, The SMLE Mk I and Mk III Rifles, The. By Charles R. Stratton, North Cape Pub. Tustin, CA, 1997. 150 pp., illus. Paper covers. $16.95

A systematic and thorough examination on a part-by-part basis of the famous British battle rifle that endured for nearly 70 years as the British Army's number one battle rifle.

British Enfield Rifles, Volume 2, No.4 and No.5 Rifles. By Charles R. Stratton, North Cape Publications, Tustin, CA, 1999. 150 pp., illustrated. Paper covers. $16.95

The historical background for the development of both rifles describing each variation and an explanation of all the "marks", "numbers" and codes found on most parts.

British Enfield Rifles, Volume 4, The Pattern 1914 and U.S. Model 1917 Rifles. By Charles R. Stratton, North Cape Publications, Tustin, CA, 2000. Paper covers. $16.95

One of the lease know American and British collectible military rifles is analyzed on a part by part basis. All markings and codes, refurbishment procedures and WW 2 upgrade are included as are the various sniper rifle versions.

British Falling Block Breechloading Rifle from 1865, The. By Jonathan Kirton, Tom Rowe Books, Maynardsville, TN, 2nd edition, 1997. 380 pp., illus. $70.00

Expanded 2nd edition of a comprehensive work on the British falling block rifle.

British Gun Engraving. By Douglas Tate, Safari Press, Inc., Huntington Beach, CA, 1999. 240 pp., illustrated. Limited, signed and numbered edition, in a slipcase. $80.00

A historic and photographic record of the last two centuries.

British Service Rifles and Carbines 1888-1900. By Alan M. Petrillo, Excaliber Publications, Latham, NY, 1994. 72 pp., illus, Paper covers. $11.95

A complete review of the Lee-Metford and Lee-Enfield rifles and carbines.

British Single Shot Rifles, Volume 1, Alexander Henry. By Wal Winfer, Tom Rowe, Manardville, TN, 1998, 200 pp., illus. $50.00

Detailed Study of the single shot rifles made by Henry. Illustrated with hundreds of photographs and drawings.

British Single Shot Rifles Volume 2, George Gibbs. By Wal Winfer, Tom Rowe, Maynardville, TN, 1998. 177 pp., illus. $50.00

Detailed study of the Farquharson as made by Gibbs. Hundreds of photos.

British Single Shot Rifles, Volume 3, Jeffery. By Wal Winfer, Rowe Publications, Rochester, N.Y., 1999. 260 pp., illustrated. $60.00

The Farquharson as made by Jeffery and his competitors, Holland & Holland, Bland, Westley, Manton, etc. Large section on the development of nitro cartridges including the .600.

British Single Shot Rifles, Vol. 4; Westley Richards. By Wal Winfer, Rowe Publications, Rochester, N.Y., 2000. 265 pages, illustrated, photos. $60.00

In his 4th volume Winfer covers a detailed study of the Westley Richards single shot rifles, including Monkey Tails, Improved Martini, 1872,1873, 1878,1881, 1897 Falling Blocks. He also covers Westley Richards Cartridges, History and Reloading information.

British Small Arms Ammunition, 1864-1938 (Other than .303 inch). By Peter Labbett, Armory Publications, Seattle, WA. 1993, 358 pages, illus. Fourcolor dust jacket. $79.00

A study of British military rifle, handgun, machine gun, and aiming tube ammunition through 1 inch from 1864 to 1938. Photo-illustrated including the firearms that chambered the cartridges.

The British Soldier's Firearms from Smoothbore to Rifled Arms, 1850-1864. By Dr. C.H. Roads, R&R Books, Livonia, NY, 1994. 332 pp., illus. $49.00

A reprint of the classic text covering the development of British military hand and shoulder firearms in the crucial years between 1850 and 1864.

British Sporting Guns & Rifles. Compiled by George Hoyem, Armory Publications, Coeur d'Alene, ID, 1997. 1024 pp., illus. In two volumes. $250.00

Eighteen old sporting firearms trade catalogs and a rare book reproduced with their color covers in a limited, signed and numbered edition.

Browning Dates of Manufacture. Compiled by George Madis, Art and Reference House, Brownsboro, TX, 1989. 48 pp. $10.00

Gives the date codes and product codes for all models from 1824 to the present.

Browning Sporting Arms of Distinction 1903-1992. By Matt Eastman, Matt Eastman Publications, Fitzgerald, GA, 1995. 450 pp.; illus. $49.95

The most recognized publication on Browning sporting arms; covers all models.

Buffalo Bill's Wild West: An American Legend. By R.L. Wilson and Greg Martine, Random House, N.Y., 1999. 3,167 pp., illustrated. $60.00

Over 225 color plates and 160 black-and-white illustrations, with in-depth text and captions, the colorful arms, posters, photos, costumes, saddles, accoutrement are brought to life.

Bullard Arms. By G. Scott Jamieson, The Boston Mills Press, Ontario, Canada, 1989. 244 pp., illus. $35.00

The story of a mechanical genius whose rifles and cartridges were the equal to any made in America in the 1880s.

Burning Powder. Compiled by Major D.B. Wesson, Wolfe Publishing Company, Prescott, AZ, 1992. 110 pp. Soft cover. $10.95

A rare booklet from 1932 for Smith & Wesson collectors.

Burnside Breech Loading Carbines, The. By Edward A. Hull, Andrew Mowbray, Inc., Lincoln, RI, 1986. 95 pp., illus. $16.00

No. 1 in the "Man at Arms Monograph Series." A model-by-model historical/technical examination of one of the most widely used cavalry weapons of the American Civil War based upon important and previously unpublished research.

Camouflage Uniforms of European and NATO Armies; 1945 to the Present. By J. F. Borsarello, Atglen, PA: Schiffer Publications. Over 290 color and b/w photographs, 120 pages. Softcover. $29.95

This full-color book covers nearly all of the NATO, and other European armies' camouflaged uniforms, and not only shows and explains the many patterns, but also their efficacy of design. Described and illustrated are the variety of materials tested in over forty different armies, and includes the history of obsolete trial tests from 1945 to the present time. More than two hundred patterns have been manufactured since World War II using various landscapes and seasonal colors for their look. The Vietnam and Gulf Wars, African or South American events, as well as recent Yugoslavian independence wars have been used as experimental terrains to test a variety of patterns. This book provides a superb reference for the historian, re-enactor, designer, and modeler.

Camouflage Uniforms of the Waffen-SS A Photographic Reference. By Michael Beaver, Schiffer Publishing, Atglen, PA. Over 1,000 color and b/w photographs and illustrations, 296 pages. $69.95

Finally a book that unveils the shroud of mystery surrounding Waffen-SS camouflage clothing. Illustrated here, both in full color and in contemporary black and white photographs, this unparalleled look at Waffen-SS combat troops and their camouflage clothing will benefit both the historian and collector.

Canadian Gunsmiths from 1608: A Checklist of Tradesmen. By John Belton, Historical Arms Series No. 29. Canada: Museum Restoration, 1992. 40 pp., 17 illustrations. Softcover. $8.95

This Checklist is a greatly expanded version of HAS No. 14, listing the names, occupation, location, and dates of more than 1,500 men and women who worked as gunmakers, gunsmiths, armorers, gun merchants, gun patent holders, and a few other gun related trades. A collection of contemporary gunsmiths' letterhead have been provided to add color and depth to the study.

Cap Guns. By James Dundas, Schiffer Publishing, Atglen, PA, 1996. 160 pp., illus. Paper covers. $29.95

Over 600 full-color photos of cap guns and gun accessories with a current value guide.

Carbines of the Civil War. By John D. McAulay, Pioneer Press, Union City, TN, 1981. 123 pp., illus. Paper covers. $12.95

A guide for the student and collector of the colorful arms used by the Federal cavalry.

Carbines of the U.S. Cavalry 1861-1905. By John D. McAulay, Andrew Mowbray Publishers, Lincoln, RI, 1996. $35.00

Covers the crucial use of carbines from the beginning of the Civil War to the end of the cavalry carbine era in 1905.

Cartridge Carbines of the British Army. By Alan M. Petrillo, Excalibur Publications, Latham, NY, 1998. 72 pp., illustrated. Paper covers. $11.95

Begins with the Snider-Enfield which was the first regulation cartridge carbine introduced in 1866 and ends with the .303 caliber No.5, Mark 1 Enfield.

Cartridge Catalogues. Compiled by George Hoyem, Armory Publications, Coeur d'Alene, ID., 1997. 504 pp., illus. $125.00

Fourteen old ammunition makers' and designers' catalogs reproduced with their color covers in a limited, signed and numbered edition. Completely revised edition of the general purpose reference work for which collectors, police, scientists and laymen reach first for answers to cartridge identification questions. Available October, 1996.

Cartridge Reloading Tools of the Past. By R.H. Chamberlain and Tom Quigley, Tom Quigley, Castle Rock, WA, 1998. 167 pp., illustrated. Paper covers. $25.00

A detailed treatment of the extensive Winchester and Ideal lines of handloading tools and bulletmolds plus Remington, Marlin, Ballard, Browning and many others.

Cartridges for Collectors. By Fred Datig, Pioneer Press, Union City, TN, 1999. In three volumes of 176 pp. each. Vol.1 (Centerfire); Vol.2 (Rimfire and Misc.) types;

Vol.3 (Additional Rimfire, Centerfire, and Plastic.). All illustrations are shown in full-scale drawings. Volume 1, softcover only, $19.95. Volumes 2 & 3, Hardcover $19.95

Civil War Arms Makers and Their Contracts. Edited by Stuart C. Mowbray and Jennifer Heroux, Andrew Mowbray Publishing, Lincoln, RI, 1998. 595 pp. $39.50

A facsimile reprint of the Report by the Commissioner of Ordnance and Ordnance Stores, 1862.

Civil War Arms Purchases and Deliveries. Edited by Stuart C. Mowbray, Andrew Mowbray Publishing, Lincoln, RI, 1998. $39.50

A facsimile reprint of the master list of Civil War weapons purchases and deliveries including Small Arms, Cannon, Ordnance and Projectiles.

Civil War Breech Loading Rifles. By John D. McAulay, Andrew Mowbray, Inc., Lincoln, RI, 1991. 144 pp., illus. Paper covers. $15.00

All the major breech-loading rifles of the Civil War and most, if not all, of the obscure types are detailed, illustrated and set in their historical context.

Civil War Cartridge Boxes of the Union Infantryman. By Paul Johnson, Andrew Mowbray, Inc., Lincoln, RI, 1998. 352 pp., illustrated. $45.00

There were four patterns of infantry cartridge boxes used by Union forces during the Civil War. The author describes the development and subsequent pattern changes to these cartridge boxes.

Civil War Commanders. By Dean Thomas, Thomas Publications, Gettysburg, PA. 1998. 72 pages, illustrated, photos. Paper Covers. $9.95

138 photographs and capsule biographies of Union and Confederate officers. A convenient personalities reference guide.

Civil War Firearms. By Joseph G. Bilby, Combined Books, Conshohocken, PA, 1996. 252 pp., illus. $34.95

A unique work combining background data on each firearm including its battlefield use, and a guide to collecting and firing surviving relics and modern reproductions.

Civil War Guns. By William B. Edwards, Thomas Publications, Gettysburg, PA, 1997. 444 pp., illus. $40.00

The complete story of Federal and Confederate small arms; design, manufacture, identifications, procurement issue, employment, effectiveness, and postwar disposal by the recognized expert.

Civil War Infantryman: In Camp, On the March, And in Battle. By Dean Thomas, Thomas Publications, Gettysburg, PA. 1998. 72 pages, illustrated, Softcovers. $12.95

Uses first-hand accounts to shed some light on the "common soldier" of the Civil War from enlistment to muster-out, including camp, marching, rations, equipment, fighting, and more.

Civil War Pistols. By John D. McAulay, Andrew Mowbray Inc., Lincoln, RI, 1992. 166 pp., illus. $38.50

A survey of the handguns used during the American Civil War.

Civil War Sharps Carbines and Rifles. By Earl J. Coates and John D. McAulay, Thomas Publications, Gettysburg, PA, 1996. 108 pp., illus. Paper covers. $12.95

Traces the history and development of the firearms including short histories of specific serial numbers and the soldiers who received them.

Civil War Small Arms of the U.S. Navy and Marine Corps. By John D. McAulay, Mowbray Publishing, Lincoln, RI, 1999. 186 pp., illustrated. $39.00

The first reliable and comprehensive guide to the firearms and edged weapons of the Civil War Navy and Marine Corps.

Col. Burton's Spiller & Burr Revolver. By Matthew W. Norman, Mercer University Press, Macon, GA, 1997. 152 pp., illus. $22.95

A remarkable archival research project on the arm together with a comprehensive story of the establishment and running of the factory.

Collector's Guide to Colt .45 Service Pistols Models of 1911 and 1911A1. Enlarged and revised edition. Clawson Publications, Fort Wayne, IN, 1998. 130 pp., illustrated. $45.00

From 1911 to the end of production in 1945 with complete military identification including all contractors.

Collector's Guide to United States Combat Shotguns, A. By Bruce N. Canfield, Andrew Mowbray Inc., Lincoln, RI, 1992. 184 pp., illus. Paper covers. $24.00

This book provides full coverage of combat shotguns, from the earliest examples right up to the Gulf War and beyond.

Collector's Guide to Winchester in the Service, A. By Bruce N. Canfield, Andrew Mowbray, Inc., Lincoln, RI, 1991. 192 pp., illus. Paper covers. $22.00

The firearms produced by Winchester for the national defense. From Hotchkiss to the M14, each firearm is examined and illustrated.

Collector's Guide to the '03 Springfield, A. By Bruce N. Canfield, Andrew Mowbray Inc, Lincoln, RI, 1989. 160 pp., illus. Paper covers. $22.00

A comprehensive guide follows the '03 through its unparalleled tenure of service. Covers all of the interesting variations, modifications and accessories of this highly collectible military rifle.

Collector's Illustrated Encyclopedia of the American Revolution. By George C. Neumann and Frank J. Kravic, Rebel Publishing Co., Inc., Texarkana, TX, 1989. 286 pp., illus. $36.95

A showcase of more than 2,300 artifacts made, worn, and used by those who fought in the War for Independence.

Colonial Frontier Guns. By T.M. Hamilton, Pioneer Press, Union City, TN, 1988. 176 pp., illus. Paper covers. $17.50

A complete study of early flint muskets of this country.

Colt: An American Legend. By R.L. Wilson, Artabras, New York, 1997. 406 pages, fully illustrated, most in color. $60.00

A reprint of the commemorative album celebrates 150 years of the guns of Samuel Colt and the manufacturing empire he built, with expert discussion of every model ever produced, the innovations of each model and variants, updated model and serial number charts and magnificent photographic showcases of the weapons.

Colt Armory, The. By Ellsworth Grant, Manat-Arms Bookshelf, Lincoln, RI, 1996. 232 pp., illus. $35.00

A history of Colt's Manufacturing Company.

Colt Blackpowder Reproductions & Replica: A Collector's and Shooter's Guide. By Dennis Miller, Blue Book Publications, Minneapolis, MN, 1999. 288 pp., illustrated. Paper covers. $29.95

The first book on this important subject, and a must for the investor, collector, and shooter.

Colt Heritage. By R.L. Wilson, Simon & Schuster, 1979. 358 pp., illus. $75.00
The official history of Colt firearms 1836 to the present.

Colt Memorabilia Price Guide. By John Ogle, Krause Publications, Iola, WI, 1998. 256 pp., illus. Paper covers. $29.95
The first book ever compiled about the vast array of non-gun merchandise produced by Sam Colt's companies, and other companies using the Colt name.

Colt Model 1905 Automatic Pistol, The. By John Potocki, Andrew Mowbray Publishing, Lincoln, RI, 1998. 191 pp., illus. $28.00
Covers all aspects of the Colt Model 1905 Automatic Pistol, from its invention by the legendary John Browning to its numerous production variations.

Colt Peacemaker British Model. By Keith Cochran, Cochran Publishing Co., Rapid City, SD, 1989. 160 pp., illus. $35.00
Covers those revolvers Colt squeezed in while completing a large order of revolvers for the U.S. Cavalry in early 1874, to those magnificent cased target revolvers used in the pistol competitions at Bisley Commons in the 1890s.

Colt Peacemaker Encyclopedia. By Keith Cochran, Keith Cochran, Rapid City, SD, 1986. 434 pp., illus. $65.00
A must book for the Peacemaker collector.

Colt Peacemaker Encyclopedia, Volume 2. By Keith Cochran, Cochran Publishing Co., SD, 1992. 416 pp., illus. $60.00
Included in this volume are extensive notes on engraved, inscribed, historical and noted revolvers, as well as those revolvers used by outlaws, lawmen, movie and television stars.

Colt Percussion Accoutrements 1834-1873. By Robin Rapley, Robin Rapley, Newport Beach, CA, 1994. 432 pp., illus. Paper covers. $39.95
The complete collector's guide to the identification of Colt percussion accoutrements; including Colt conversions and their values.

Colt Pocket Hammerless Pistols. By Dr. John W. Brunner, Phillips Publications, Williamstown, NJ, 1998. 212 pp., illustrated. $59.95
You will never again have to question a .25, .32 or .380 with this well illustrated, definitive reference guide at hand.

Colt Revolvers and the Tower of London. By Joseph G. Rosa, Royal Armouries of the Tower of London, London, England, 1988. 72 pp., illus. Soft covers. $15.00
Details the story of Colt in London through the early cartridge period.

Colt Rifles and Muskets from 1847-1870. By Herbert Houze, Krause Publications, Iola, WI, 1996. 192 pp., illus. $34.95
Discover previously unknown Colt models along with an extensive list of production figures for all models.

Colt's SAA Post War Models. By George Garton, The Gun Room Press, Highland Park, NJ, 1995. 166 pp., illus. $39.95
Complete facts on the post-war Single Action Army revolvers. Information on calibers, production numbers and variations taken from factory records.

Colt Single Action Army Revolvers: The Legend, the Romance and the Rivals. By "Doc" O'Meara, Krause Publications, Iola, WI, 2000. 160 pp., illustrated with 250 photos in b&w and a 16 page color section. $34.95
Production figures, serial numbers by year, and rarities.

Colt Single Action Army Revolvers and Alterations. By C. Kenneth Moore, Mowbray Publishers, Lincoln, RI, 1999. 112 pp., illustrated. $35.00
A comprehensive history of the revolvers that collectors call "Artillery Models." These are the most historical of all S.A.A. Colts, and this new book covers all the details.

Colt Single Action Army Revolvers and the London Agency. By C. Kenneth Moore, Andrew Mowbray Publishers, Lincoln, RI, 1990. 144 pp., illus. $35.00
Drawing on vast documentary sources, this work chronicles the relationship between the London Agency and the Hartford home office.

Colt U.S. General Officers' Pistols, The. By Horace Greeley IV, Andrew Mowbray Inc., Lincoln, RI, 1990. 199 pp., illus. $38.00
These unique weapons, issued as a badge of rank to General Officers in the U.S. Army from WWII onward, remain highly personal artifacts of the military leaders who carried them. Includes serial numbers and dates of issue.

Colts from the William M. Locke Collection. By Frank Sellers, Andrew Mowbray Publishers, Lincoln, RI, 1996. 192 pp., illus. $55.00
This important book illustrates all of the famous Locke Colts, with captions by arms authority Frank Sellers.

Colt's Dates of Manufacture 1837-1978. By R.L. Wilson, published by Maurie Albert, Coburg, Australia; N.A. distributor I.D.S.A. Books, Hamilton, OH, 1983. 61 pp. $6.00
An invaluable pocket guide to the dates of manufacture of Colt firearms up to 1978.

Colt's 100th Anniversary Firearms Manual 1836-1936: A Century of Achievement. Wolfe Publishing Co., Prescott, AZ, 1992. 100 pp., illus. Paper covers. $12.95
Originally published by the Colt Patent Firearms Co., this booklet covers the history, manufacturing procedures and the guns of the first 100 years of the genius of Samuel Colt.

Colt's Pocket '49: Its Evolution Including the Baby Dragoon and Wells Fargo. By Robert Jordan and Darrow Watt, Privately Printed, Loma Mar, CA 2000. 304 pages, with 984 color photos, illus. Beautify bound in a deep blue leather like case. $125.00
Detailed information on all models and covers engraving, cases, accoutrements, holsters, fakes, and much more. Included is a summary booklet containing information such as serial numbers, production ranges & identifying photos. This book is a masterpiece on its subject.

Complete Guide to all United States Military Medals 1939 to Present. By Colonel Frank C. Foster, Medals of America Press, Fountain Inn, SC, 2000. 121 pp.,.illustrated, photos. $29.95
Complete criteria for every Army, Navy, Marines, Air Force, Coast Guard, and Merchant Marine awards since 1939. All decorations, service medals, and ribbons shown in full-color and accompanied by dates and campaigns as well as detailed descriptions on proper wear and display.

Complete Guide to the M1 Garand and the M1 Carbine. By Bruce N. Canfield, 2nd printing, Andrew Mowbray Inc., Lincoln, RI, 1999. 296 pp., illus. $39.50

Expanded and updated coverage of both the M1 Garand and the M1 Carbine, with more than twice as much information as the author's previous book on this topic.

Complete Guide to U.S. Infantry Weapons of the First War, The. By Bruce Canfield, Andrew Mowbray, Publisher, Lincoln, RI, 2000. 304 pp., illus. $39.95
The definitive study of the U.S. Infantry weapons used in WW1.

Complete Guide to U.S. Infantry Weapons of World War Two, The. By Bruce Canfield, Andrew Mowbray, Publisher, Lincoln, RI, 1995. 303 pp., illus. $39.95
A definitive work on the weapons used by the United States Armed Forces in WWII.

Concise Guide to the Artillery at Gettysburg, A. By Gregory Coco, Thomas Publications, Gettysburg, PA, 1998. 96 pp., illus. Paper Covers. $10.00
Coco's tenth book on Gettysburg is a beginner's guide to artillery and its use at the battle. It covers the artillery batteries describing the types of cannons, shells, fuses, etc.using interesting narrative and human interest stories.

Cooey Firearms, Made in Canada 1919-1979. By John A. Belton, Museum Restoration, Canada, 1998. 36pp., with 46 illus. Paper Covers. $8.95
More than 6 million rifles and at least 67 models, were made by this small Canadian riflemaker. They have been identified from the first 'Cooey Canuck' through the last variations made by the 'Winchester-Cooey'. Each is described and most are illustrated in this first book on The Cooey.

Cowboy Collectibles and Western Memorabilia. By Bob Bell and Edward Vebell, Schiffer Publishing, Atglen, PA, 1992. 160 pp., illus. Paper covers. $29.95
The exciting era of the cowboy and the wild west collectibles including rifles, pistols, gun rigs, etc.

Cowboy Culture: The Last Frontier of American Antiques. By Michael Friedman, Schiffer Publishing, Ltd., West Chester, PA, 1992. 300 pp., illustrated.
Covers the artful aspects of the old west, the antiques and collectibles. Illustrated with clear color plates of over 1,000 items such as spurs, boots, guns, saddles etc.

Cowboy and Gunfighter Collectible. By Bill Mackin, Mountain Press Publishing Co., Missoula, MT, 1995. 178 pp., illus. Paper covers. $25.00
A photographic encyclopedia with price guide and makers' index.

Cowboys and the Trappings of the Old West. By William Manns and Elizabeth Clair Flood, Zon International Publishing Co., Santa Fe, NM, 1997, 1st edition. 224 pp., illustrated. $45.00
A pictorial celebration of the cowboys dress and trappings.

Cowboy Hero Cap Pistols. By Rudy D'Angelo, Antique Trader Books, Dubuque, IA, 1998. 196 pp., illus. Paper covers. $34.95
Aimed at collectors of cap pistols created and named for famous film and television cowboy heroes, this in-depth guide hits all the marks. Current values are given.

Custom Firearms Engraving. By Tom Turpin, Krause Publications, Iola, WI, 1999. 208 pp., illustrated. $49.95
Over 200 four-color photos with more than 75 master engravers profiled. Engravers Directory with addresses in the U.S. and abroad.

Decorations, Medals, Ribbons, Badges and Insigna of the United States Army; World War 2 to Present, The. By Col. Frank C. Foster, Medals of America Press, Fountain Inn, SC. 2001. 145 pages, illustrated. $29.95
The most complete guide to United States Army medals, ribbons, rank, insignia had patches from WWII to the present day. Each medal and insignia shown in full color. Includes listing of respective criteria and campaigns.

Decorations, Medals, Ribbons, Badges and Insigna of the United States Navy; World War 2 to Present, The. By James G. Thompson, Medals of America Press, Fountain Inn, SC. 2000. 123 pages, illustrated. $29.95
The most complete guide to United States Navy medals, ribbons, rank, insignia had patches from WWII to the present day. Each medal and insignia shown in full color. Includes listing of respective criteria and campaigns.

Derringer in America, Volume 1, The Percussion Period, The. By R.L. Wilson and L.D. Eberhart, Andrew Mowbray Inc., Lincoln, RI, 1985. 271 pp., illus. $48.00
A long awaited book on the American percussion derringer.

Derringer in America, Volume 2, The Cartridge Period, The. By L.D. Eberhart and R.L. Wilson, Andrew Mowbray Inc., Publishers, Lincoln, RI, 1993. 284 pp., illus. $65.00
Comprehensive coverage of cartridge derringers organized alphabetically by maker. Includes all types of derringers known by the authors to have been offered to the American market.

Devil's Paintbrush: Sir Hiram Maxim's Gun, The. By Dolf Goldsmith, 3rd Edition, expanded and revised, Collector Grade Publications, Toronto, Canada, 2000. 384 pp., illus. $79.95
The classic work on the world's first true automatic machine gun.

Dr. Josephus Requa Civil War Dentist and the Billinghurst-Requa Volley Gun. By John M. Hyson, Jr., & Margaret Requa DeFrancisco, Museum Restoration Service, Bloomfield, Ont., Canada, 1999. 36 pp., illus. Paper covers. $8.95
The story of the inventor of the first practical rapid-fire gun to be used during the American Civil War.

Duck Stamp Story, The. By Eric Jay Dolin and Bob Dumaine, Krause Publications, Iola, WI, 2000. 208 pp., illustrated with color throughout. Paper covers. $29.95; Hardbound. $49.95
Detailed information on the value and rarity of every federal duck stamp. Outstanding art and illustrations.

Dutch Luger (Parabellum) A Complete History, The. By Bas J. Martens and Guus de Vries, Ironside International Publishers, Inc., Alexandria, VA, 1995. 268 pp., illus. $49.95
The history of the Luger in the Netherlands. An extensive description of the Dutch pistol and trials and the different models of the Luger in the Dutch service.

Eagle on U.S. Firearms, The. By John W. Jordan, Pioneer Press, Union City, TN, 1992. 140 pp., illus. Paper covers. $17.50
Stylized eagles have been stamped on government owned or manufactured firearms in the U.S. since the beginning of our country. This book lists and illustrates these various eagles in an informative and refreshing manner.

E. C. Prudhomme's Gun Engraving Review, The. By E. C. Prudhomme, R&R Books, Livonia, NY, 1994. 164 pp., illus. $60.00

As a source for engravers and collectors, this book is an indispensable guide to styles and techniques of the world's foremost engravers.

Encyclopedia of Rifles & Handguns; A Comprehensive Guide to Firearms. Edited by Sean Connolly, Chartwell Books, Inc., Edison, NJ., 1996. 160 pp., illustrated. $26.00
A lavishly illustrated book providing a comprehensive history of military and civilian personal firepower.

Eprouvettes: A Comprehensive Study of Early Devices for the Testing of Gunpowder. By R.T.W. Kempers, Royal Armouries Museum, Leeds, England, 1999. 352 pp., illustrated with 240 black & white and 28 color plates. $125.00
The first comprehensive study of eprouvettes ever attempted in a single volume.

European Firearms in Swedish Castles. By Kaa Wennberg, Bohuslaningens Boktryckeri AB, Uddevalla, Sweden, 1986. 156 pp., illus. $50.00
The famous collection of Count Keller, the Ettersburg Castle collection, and others. English text.

European Sporting Cartridges, Part 1. By W.B. Dixon, Armory Publications, Inc., Coeur d'Alene, ID, 1997. 250 pp., illus. $63.00
Photographs and drawings of over 550 centerfire cartridge case types in 1,300 illustrations produced in German and Austria from 1875 to 1995.

European Sporting Cartridges, Part 2. By W.B. Dixon, Armory Publications, Inc., Coeur d'Alene, ID, 2000. 240 pp., illus. $63.00
An illustrated history of centerfire hunting and target cartridges produced in Czechoslovakia, Switzerland, Norway, Sweden, Finland, Russia, Italy, Denmark, Belgium from 1875 to 1998. Adds 50 specimens to volume 1 (Germany-Austria). Also, illustrates 40 small arms magazine experiments during the late 19th Century, and includes the English-Language export ammunition catalogue of Kovo (Povaszke Strojarne), Prague, Czeck. from the, 1930's.

Fifteen Years in the Hawken Lode. By John D. Baird, The Gun Room Press, Highland Park, NJ, 1976. 120 pp., illus. $24.95
A collection of thoughts and observations gained from many years of intensive study of the guns from the shop of the Hawken brothers.

'51 Colt Navies. By Nathan L. Swayze, The Gun Room Press, Highland Park, NJ, 1993. 243 pp., illus. $59.95
The Model 1851 Colt Navy, its variations and markings.

Fighting Iron. By Art Gogan, Andrew Mowbray, Inc., Lincoln, R.I., 1999. 176 pp., illustrated. $28.00
The German K98k Rifle, 1934-1945: The Backbone of the Wehrmacht. By Richard D. Law, Collector Grade Publications, Toronto, Canada, 1993. 336 pp., illus. $69.95
The most comprehensive study ever published on the 14,000,000 bolt-action K98k rifles produced in Germany between 1934 and 1945.

German Machineguns. By Daniel D. Musgrave, Revised edition, Ironside International Publishers, Inc. Alexandria, VA, 1992. 586 pp., 650 illus. $49.95
The most definitive book ever written on German machineguns. Covers the introduction and development of machineguns in Germany from 1899 to the rearmament period after WWII.

German Military Rifles and Machine Pistols, 1871-1945. By Hans Dieter Gotz, Schiffer Publishing Co., West Chester, PA, 1990. 245 pp., illus. $35.00
This book portrays in words and pictures the development of the modern German weapons and their ammunition including the scarcely known experimental types.

German MP40 Maschinenpistole, The. By Frank Iannamico, Moose Lake Publishing, Harmony, ME, 1999. 185 pp., illustrated. Paper covers. $19.95
The history, development and use of this famous gun of World War 2.

German 7.9mm Military Ammunition, The. By Daniel W. Kent, Daniel W. Kent, Ann Arbor, MI, 1991. 244 pp., illus. $35.00
The long-awaited revised edition of a classic among books devoted to ammunition.

Golden Age of Remington, The. By Robert W.D. Ball, Krause publications, Iola, WI, 1995. 194 pp., illus. $29.95
For Remington collectors or firearms historians, this book provides a pictorial history of Remington through World War I. Includes value guide.

Government Models, The. By William H.D. Goddard, Andrew Mowbray Publishing, Lincoln, RI, 1998. 296 pp., illustrated. $58.50
The most authoritative source on the development of the Colt model of 1911.

Grasshoppers and Butterflies. By Adrian B. Caruana, Museum Restoration Service, Alexandria, Bay, N.Y., 1999. 32 pp., illustrated. Paper covers. $8.95
No.39 in the Historical Arms Series. The light 3 pounders of Pattison and Townsend.

Greener Story, The. By Graham Greener, Quiller Press, London, England, 2000. 256 pp., illustrated with 32 pages of color photos. $64.50
W.W. Greener, his family history, inventions, guns, patents, and more.

Guide to American Trade Catalogs 1744-1900, A. By Lawrence B. Romaine, Dover Publications, New York, NY. 422 pp., illus. Paper covers. $12.95

Guide to Ballard Breechloaders, A. By George J. Layman, Pioneer Press, Union City, TN, 1997. 261 pp., illus. Paper covers. $19.95
Documents the saga of this fine rifle from the first models made by Ball & Williams of Worchester, to its production by the Marlin Firearms Co, to the cessation of 19th century manufacture in 1891, and finally to the modern reproductions made in the 1990's.

Guide to the Maynard Breechloader, A. By George J. Layman, George J. Layman, Ayer, MA, 1993. 125 pp., illus. Paper covers. $11.95
The first book dedicated entirely to the Maynard family of breech-loading firearms. Coverage of the arms is given from the 1850s through the 1880s.

Guide to U. S. Army Dress Helmets 1872-1904, A. By Kasal and Moore, North Cape Publications, 2000. 88 pp., illus. Paper covers. $15.95
This thorough study provides a complete description of the Model 1872 & 1881 dress helmets worn by the U.S. Army. Including all components from bodies to plates to plumes & shoulder cords and tells how to differentiate the originals from reproductions. Extensively illustrated with photographs, '8 pages in full color' of complete helmets and their components.

Gun Collecting. By Geoffrey Boothroyd, Sportsman's Press, London, 1989. 208 pp., illus. $29.95
The most comprehensive list of 19th century British gunmakers and gunsmiths ever published.

Gunmakers of London 1350-1850. By Howard L. Blackmore, George Shumway Publisher, York, PA, 1986. 222 pp., illus. $35.00
A listing of all the known workmen of gun making in the first 500 years, plus a history of the guilds, cutlers, armourers, founders, blacksmiths, etc. 260 gunmarks are illustrated.

Gunmakers of London Supplement 1350-1850. By Howard L. Blackmore, Museum Restoration Service, Alexandria Bay, NY, 1999. 156 pp., illustrated. $60.00
Begins with an introductory chapter on "foreign" gunmakers followed by records of all the new information found about previously unidentified armourers, gunmakers and gunsmiths.

Guns that Won the West: Firearms of the American Frontier, 1865-1898, The. By John Walter, Stackpole Books, Inc., Mechanicsburg, PA.,1999. 256 pp., illustrated. $34.95
Here is the story of the wide range of firearms from pistols to rifles used by plainsmen and settlers, gamblers, native Americans and the U.S. Army.

Gunsmiths of Illinois. By Curtis L. Johnson, George Shumway Publishers, York, PA, 1995. 160 pp., illus. $50.00
Genealogical information is provided for nearly one thousand gunsmiths. Contains hundreds of illustrations of rifles and other guns, of handmade origin, from Illinois.

Gunsmiths of Manhattan, 1625-1900: A Checklist of Tradesmen, The. By Michael H. Lewis, Museum Restoration Service, Bloomfield, Ont., Canada, 1991. 40 pp., illus. Paper covers. $8.95
This listing of more than 700 men in the arms trade in New York City prior to about the end of the 19th century will provide a guide for identification and further research.

Guns of Dagenham: Lanchester, Patchett, Sterling, The. By Peter Laidler and David Howroyd, Collector Grade Publications, Inc., Cobourg, Ont., Canada, 1995. 310 pp., illus. $39.95
An in-depth history of the small arms made by the Sterling Company of Dagenham, Essex, England, from 1940 until Sterling was purchased by British Aerospace in 1989 and closed.

Guns of the Western Indian War. By R. Stephen Dorsey, Collector's Library, Eugene, OR, 1997. 220 pp., illus. Paper covers. $30.00
The full story of the guns and ammunition that made western history in the turbulent period of 1865-1890.

Gun Powder Cans & Kegs. By Ted & David Bacyk and Tom Rowe, Rowe Publications, Rochester, NY, 1999. 150 pp., illus. $63.00
The first book devoted to powder tins and kegs. All cans and kegs in full color. With a price guide and rarity scale.

Guns of Remington: Historic Firearms Spanning Two Centuries, The. Compiled by Howard M. Madaus, Biplane Productions, Publisher, in cooperation with Buffalo Bill Historical Center, Cody, WY, 1998. 352 pp., illustrated with over 800 color photos. $79.95
A complete catalog of the firearms in the exhibition, "It Never Failed Me: The Arms & Art of Remington Arms Company" at the Buffalo Bill Historical Center, Cody, Wyoming.

Gun Tools, Their History and Identification. By James B. Shaffer, Lee A. Rutledge and R. Stephen Dorsey, Collector's Library, Eugene, OR, 1992. 375 pp., illus. $30.00
Written history of foreign and domestic gun tools from the flintlock period to WWII.

Gun Tools, Their History and Identifications, Volume 2. By Stephen Dorsey and James B. Shaffer, Collectors' Library, Eugene, OR, 1997. 396 pp., illus. Paper covers. $30.00
Gun tools from the Royal Armouries Museum in England, Pattern Room, Royal Ordnance Reference Collection in Nottingham and from major private collections.

Gunsmiths of the Carolinas 1660-1870. By Daniel D. Hartzler and James B. Whisker, Old Bedford Village Press, Bedford, PA, 1998. 176 pp., illustrated. $40.00
This deluxe hard bound edition of 176 pages is printed on fine coated paper, with about 90 pages of large photographs of fine longrifles from the Carolinas, and about 90 pages of detailed research on the gunsmiths who created the highly prized and highly collectable longrifles. Dedicated to serious students of original Kentucky rifles, who may seldom encounter fine longrifles from the Carolinas.

Gunsmiths of Maryland. By Daniel D. Hartzler and James B. Whisker, Old Bedford Village Press, Bedford, PA, 1998. 208 pp., illustrated. $45.00
Covers firelock Colonial period through the breech-loading patent models. Featuring longrifles.

Gunsmiths of Virginia. By Daniel D. Hartzler and James B. Whisker, Old Bedford Village Press, Bedford, PA, 1992. 206 pp., illustrated. $45.00
A photographic study of American longrifles.

Gunsmiths of West Virginia. By Daniel D. Hartzler and James B. Whisker, Old Bedford Village Press, Bedford, PA, 1998. 176 pp., illustrated. $40.00
A photographic study of American longrifles.

Gunsmiths of York County, Pennsylvania. By Daniel D. Hartzler and James B. Whisker, Old Bedford Village Press, Bedford, PA, 1998. 160 pp., illustrated. $40.00
160 pages of photographs and research notes on the longrifles and gunsmiths of York County, Pennsylvania. Many longrifle collectors and gun builders have noticed that York County style rifles tend to be more formal in artistic decoration than some other schools of style. Patriotic themes, and folk art were popular design elements.

Hall's Military Breechloaders. By Peter A. Schmidt, Andrew Mowbray Publishers, Lincoln, RI, 1996. 232 pp., illus. $55.00
The whole story behind these bold and innovative firearms.

Handgun, The. By Geoffrey Boothroyd, David and Charles, North Pomfret, VT, 1989. 566 pp., illus. $60.00
Every chapter deals with an important period in handgun history from the 14th century to the present.

Handgun of Military Rifle Marks 1866-1950. By Richard A. Hoffman and Noel P. Schott, Mapleleaf Militaria Publishing, St. Louis, MO, 1999, second edition. 60 pp., illustrated. Paper covers. $20.00
An illustrated guide to identifying military rifle and marks.

Handguns & Rifles: The Finest Weapons from Around the World. By Ian Hogg, Random House Value Publishing, Inc., N.Y., 1999. 128 pp., illustrated. $18.98
The serious gun collector will welcome this fully illustrated examination of international handguns and rifles. Each entry covers the history of the weapon, what purpose it serves, and its advantages and disadvantages.

Hawken Rifle: Its Place in History, The. By Charles E. Hanson, Jr., The Fur Press, Chadron, NE, 1979. 104 pp., illus. Paper covers. $15.00
A definitive work on this famous rifle.

Hawken Rifles, The Mountain Man's Choice. By John D. Baird, The Gun Room Press, Highland Park, NJ, 1976. 95 pp., illus. $29.95
Covers the rifles developed for the Western fur trade. Numerous specimens are described and shown in photographs.

High Standard: A Collector's Guide to the Hamden & Hartford Target Pistols. By Tom Dance, Andrew Mowbray, Inc., Lincoln, RI, 1991. 192 pp., illus. Paper covers. $24.00
From Citation to Supermatic, all of the production models and specials made from 1951 to 1984 are covered according to model number or series.

Historic Pistols: The American Martial Flintlock 1760-1845. By Samuel E. Smith & Edwin W. Bitter, The Gun Room Press, Highland Park, NJ, 1986. 353 pp., illus. $45.00
Covers over 70 makers and 163 models of American martial arms.

Historical Hartford Hardware. By William W. Dalrymple, Colt Collector Press, Rapid City, SD, 1976. 42 pp., illus. Paper covers. $10.00
Historically associated Colt revolvers.

History and Development of Small Arms Ammunition, Volume 2, The. By George A. Hoyem, Armory Publications, Oceanside, CA, 1991. 303 pp., illus. $65.00
Covers the blackpowder military centerfire rifle, carbine, machine gun and volley gun ammunition used in 28 nations and dominions, together with the firearms that chambered them.

History and Development of Small Arms Ammunition, Volume 4, The. By George A. Hoyem, Armory Publications, Seattle, WA, 1998. 200 pp., illustrated $65.00
A comprehensive book on American black powder and early smokeless rifle cartridges.

History of Colt Firearms, The. By Dean Boorman, Lyons Press, New York, NY, 2001. 144 pp., illus. $29.95
Discover the fascinating story of the world's most famous revolver, complete with more than 150 stunning full-color photographs.

History of Modern U.S. Military Small Arms Ammunition. Volume 1, 1880-1939. Revised by F.W. Hackley, W.H. Woodin and E.L. Scranton, Thomas Publications, Gettysburg, PA, 1998. 328 pp., illus. $49.95
This revised edition incorporates all publicly available information concerning military small arms ammunition for the period 1880 through 1939 in a single volume.

History of Modern U.S. Military Small Arms Ammunition, Volume 2, 1940-1945. By F.W. Hackley, W.H. Woodin and E.L. Scranton. Gun Room Press, Highland Park, NJ. 300 + pages, illustrated. $39.95
Based on decades of original research conducted at the National Archives, numerous military, public and private museums and libraries, as well as individual collections, this edition incorporates all publicly available information concerning military small arms ammunition for the period 1940 through 1945.

History of Winchester Rifles, The. By Dean Boorman, Lyons Press, New York, NY, 2001. 144 pp., illus. $29.95
A captivating and wonderfully photographed history of one of the most legendary names in gun lore. 150 full-color photos.

History of Winchester Firearms 1866-1992, The. Sixth edition, updated, expanded, and revised by Thomas Henshaw, New Win Publishing, Clinton, NJ, 1993. 280 pp., illus. $27.95
This classic is the standard reference for all collectors and others seeking the facts about any Winchester firearm, old or new.

History of Winchester Repeating Arms Company. By Herbert G. Houze, Krause Publications, Iola, WI, 1994. 800 pp., illus. $50.00
The complete Winchester history from 1856-1981.

Honour Bound: The Chauchat Machine Rifle. By Gerard Demaison and Yves Buffetaut, Collector Grade Publications, Inc., Cobourg, Ont., Canada, 1995. $39.95
The story of the CSRG (Chauchat) machine rifle, the most manufactured automatic weapon of World War One.

Hopkins & Allen Revolvers & Pistols. By Charles E. Carder, Avil Onze Publishing, Delphos, OH, 1998, illustrated. Paper covers. $24.95
Covers over 165 photos, graphics and patent drawings.

How to Buy and Sell Used Guns. By John Traister, Stoeger Publishing Co., So. Hackensack, NJ, 1984. 192 pp., illus. Paper covers. $10.95
A new guide to buying and selling guns.

Hunting Weapons From the Middle Ages to the Twentieth Century. By Howard L. Blackmore, Dover Publications, Meneola, NY, 2000. 480 pp., illustrated. Paper covers. $16.95
Dealing mainly with the different classes of weapons used in sport—swords, spears, crossbows, guns, and rifles—from the Middle Ages until the present day.

Identification Manual on the .303 British Service Cartridge, No. 1-Ball Ammunition. By B.A. Temple, I.D.S.A. Books, Piqua, OH, 1986. 84 pp., 57 illus. $12.50

Identification Manual on the .303 British Service Cartridge, No. 2-Blank Ammunition. By B.A. Temple, I.D.S.A. Books, Piqua, OH, 1986. 95 pp., 59 illus. $12.50

Identification Manual on the .303 British Service Cartridge, No. 3-Special Purpose Ammunition. By B.A. Temple, I.D.S.A Books, Piqua, OH, 1987. 82 pp., 49 illus. $12.50

Identification Manual on the .303 British Service Cartridge, No. 4-Dummy Cartridges Henry 1869-c.1900. By B.A. Temple, I.D.S.A Books, Piqua, OH, 1988. 84 pp., 70 illus. $12.50

Identification Manual on the .303 British Service Cartridge, No. 5-Dummy Cartridges (2). By B.A. Temple, I.D.S.A. Books, Piqua, OH, 1994. 78 pp. $12.50

Illustrated Book of Guns, The. By David Miller, Salamander Books, N.Y., N.Y., 2000. 304 pp., illustrated in color. $34.95
An illustrated directory of over 1,000 military and sporting firearms.

Illustrated Encyclopedia of Civil War Collectibles, The. By Chuck Lawliss, Henry Holt and Co., New York, NY, 1997. 316 pp., illus. Paper covers. $22.95
A comprehensive guide to Union and Confederate arms, equipment, uniforms, and other memorabilia.

Illustrations of United States Military Arms 1776-1903 and Their Inspector's Marks. Compiled by Turner Kirkland, Pioneer Press, Union City, TN, 1988. 37 pp., illus. Paper covers. $7.00
Reprinted from the 1949 Bannerman catalog. Valuable information for both the advanced and beginning collector.

Indian War Cartridge Pouches, Boxes and Carbine Boots. By R. Stephen Dorsey, Collector's Library, Eugene, OR, 1993. 156 pp., illus. Paper Covers. $20.00
The key reference work to the cartridge pouches, boxes, carbine sockets and boots of the Indian War period 1865-1890.

Introduction to the Civil War Small Arms, An. By Earl J. Coates and Dean S. Thomas, Thomas Publishing Co., Gettysburg, PA, 1990. 96 pp., illus. Paper covers. $10.00
The small arms carried by the individual soldier during the Civil War.

Japanese Rifles of World War Two. By Duncan O. McCollum, Excalibur Publications, Latham, NY, 1996. 64 pp., illus. Paper covers. $18.95
A sweeping view of the rifles and carbines that made up Japan's arsenal during the conflict.

Kalashnikov Arms, compiled by Alexei Nedelin, Design Military Parade, Ltd., Moscow, Russia, 1997. 240 pp., illus. $49.95
Weapons versions stored in the St. Petersburg Military Historical Museum of Artillery, Engineer Troops and Communications and in the Izhmash JSC.

Kalashnikov "Machine Pistols, Assault Rifles, and Machine Guns, 1945 to the Present". By John Walter, Paladin Press, Boulder, CO, 1999, hardcover, photos, illus., 146 pp. $22.95
This exhaustive work published by Greenhill Military Manuals features a gun-by-gun directory of Kalashnikov variants. Technical specifications and illustrations are provided throughout, along with details of sights, bayonets, markings and ammunition. A must for the serious collector and historian.

Kentucky Pistol, The. By Roy Chandler and James Whisker, Old Bedford Village Press, Bedford, PA, 1997. 225 pp., illus. $60.00
A photographic study of Kentucky pistols from famous collections.

Kentucky Rifle, The. By Captain John G.W. Dillin, George Shumway Publisher, York, PA, 1993. 221 pp., illus. $50.00
This well-known book was the first attempt to tell the story of the American longrifle. This edition retains the original text and illustrations with supplemental footnotes provided by Dr. George Shumway.

Know Your Broomhandle Mausers. By R.J. Berger, Blacksmith Corp., Southport, CT, 1985. 96 pp., illus. Paper covers. $12.95
An interesting story on the big Mauser pistol and its variations.

Krag Rifles. By William S. Brophy, The Gun Room Press, Highland Park, NJ, 1980. 200 pp., illus. $35.00
The first comprehensive work detailing the evolution and various models, both military and civilian.

Krieghoff Parabellum, The. By Randall Gibson, Midland, TX, 1988. 279 pp., illus. $40.00
A comprehensive text pertaining to the Lugers manufactured by H. Krieghoff Waffenfabrik.

Las Pistolas Espanolas Tipo "Mauser,". By Artemio Mortera Perez, Quiron Ediciones, Valladolid, Spain, 1998. 71 pp., illustrated. Paper covers. $34.95
This book covers in detail Spanish machine pistols and C96 copies made in Spain. Covers all Astra "Mauser" pistol series and the complete line of Beistegui C96 type pistols. Spanish text.

Law Enforcement Memorabilia Price and Identification Guide. By Monty McCord, DBI Books a division of Krause Publications, Inc. Iola, WI, 1999. 208 pp., illustrated. Paper covers. $19.95
An invaluable reference to the growing wave of law enforcement collectors. Hundreds of items are covered from miniature vehicles to clothes, patches, and restraints.

Legendary Sporting Guns. By Eric Joly, Abbeville Press, New York, N.Y., 1999. 228 pp., illustrated. $65.00
A survey of hunting through the ages and relates how many different types of firearms were created and refined for use afield.

Legends and Reality of the AK. By Val Shilin and Charlie Cutshaw, Paladen Press, Boulder, CO, 2000. 192 pp., illustrated. Paper covers. $35.00
A behind-the-scenes look at history, design and impact of the Kalashnikov family of weapons.

LeMat, the Man, the Gun. By Valmore J. Forgett and Alain F. and Marie-Antoinette Serpette, Navy Arms Co., Ridgefield, NJ, 1996. 218 pp., illus. $49.95
The first definitive study of the Confederate revolvers invention, development and delivery by Francois Alexandre LeMat.

Les Pistolets Automatiques Francaise 1890-1990. By Jean Huon, Combined Books, Inc., Conshohocken, PA, 1997. 160 pp., illus. French text. $34.95
French automatic pistols from the earliest experiments through the World Wars and Indo-China to modern security forces.

Levine's Guide to Knives and Their Values, 4th Edition. By Bernard Levine, DBI Books, a division of Krause Publications, Iola, WI, 1997. 512 pp., illus. Paper covers. $27.95
All the basic tools for identifying, valuing and collecting folding and fixed blade knives.

Light 6-Pounder Battalion Gun of 1776, The. By Adrian Caruana, Museum Restoration Service, Bloomfield, Ontario, Canada, 2001. 76 pp., illus. Paper covers. $8.95

London Gun Trade, 1850-1920, The. By Joyce E. Gooding, Museum Restoration Service, Bloomfield, Ontario, Canada, 2001. 48 pp., illus. Paper covers. $8.95
Names, dates and locations of London gunmakers working between 1850 and 1920 are listed. Compiled from the original Kelly's Post Office Directories of the City of London.

London Gunmakers and the English Duelling Pistol, 1770-1830, The. By Keith R. Dill, Museum Restoration Service, Bloomfield, Ontario, Canada, 1997. 36 pp., illus. Paper covers. $8.95

Ten gunmakers made London one of the major gunmaking centers of the world. This book examines how the design and construction of their pistols contributed to that reputation and how these characteristics may be used to date flintlock arms.

Longrifles of North Carolina. By John Bivens, George Shumway Publisher, York, PA, 1988. 256 pp., illus. $50.00

Covers art and evolution of the rifle, immigration and trade movements. Committee of Safety gunsmiths, characteristics of the North Carolina rifle.

Longrifles of Pennsylvania, Volume 1, Jefferson, Clarion & Elk Counties. By Russel H. Harringer, George Shumway Publisher, York, PA, 1984. 200 pp., illus. $50.00

First in series that will treat in great detail the longrifles and gunsmiths of Pennsylvania.

Luger Handbook, The. By Aarron Davis, Krause Publications, Iola, WI, 1997. 112 pp., illus. Paper covers. $9.95

Quick reference to classify Luger models and variations with complete details including proofmarks.

Lugers at Random. By Charles Kenyon, Jr., Handgun Press, Glenview, IL, 1990. 420 pp., illus. $59.95

A new printing of this classic, comprehensive reference for all Luger collectors.

Luger Story, The. By John Walter, Stackpole Books, Mechanicsburg, PA, 2001. 256 pp., illus. Paper Covers $29.95

The standard history of the world's most famous handgun.

M1 Carbine. By Larry Ruth, Gunroom Press, Highland Park, NJ, 1987. 291 pp., illus. Paper $19.95

The origin, development, manufacture and use of this famous carbine of World War II.

M1 Carbine: Owner's Guide, The. By Scott A. Duff, Scott A. Duff, Export, PA, 1997. 126 pp., illus. Paper covers. $19.95

This book answers the questions M1 owners most often ask concerning maintenance activities not encounter by military users.

M1 Garand: Owner's Guide, The. By Scott A. Duff, Scott A. Duff, Export, PA, 1998. 132 pp., illus. Paper covers. $19.95

This book answers the questions M1 owners most often ask concerning maintenance activities not encounter by military users.

M1 Garand Serial Numbers and Data Sheets, The. By Scott A. Duff, Export, PA, 1995. 101 pp., illus. Paper covers. $11.95

Provides the reader with serial numbers related to dates of manufacture and a large sampling of data sheets to aid in identification or restoration.

M1 Garand 1936 to 1957, The. By Joe Poyer and Craig Riesch, North Cape Publications, Tustin, CA, 1996. 216 pp., illus. Paper covers. $19.95

Describes the entire range of M1 Garand production in text and quick-scan charts.

M1 Garand: Post World War, The. By Scott A. Duff, Scott A. Duff, Export, PA, 1990. 139 pp., illus. Soft covers. $19.95

A detailed account of the activities at Springfield Armory through this period. International Harvester, H&R, Korean War production and quantities delivered. Serial numbers.

M1 Garand: World War 2, The. By Scott A. Duff, Scott A. Duff, Export, PA, 1993. 210 pp., illus. Paper covers. $39.95

The most comprehensive study available to the collector and historian on the M1 Garand of World War II.

Maine Made Guns and Their Makers. By Dwight B. Demeritt Jr., Maine State Museum, Augusta, ME, 1998. 209 pp., illustrated. $55.00

An authoritative, biographical study of Maine gunsmiths.

Marlin Firearms: A History of the Guns and the Company That Made Them. By Lt. Col. William S. Brophy, USAR, Ret., Stackpole Books, Harrisburg, PA, 1989. 672 pp., illus. $75.00

The definitive book on the Marlin Firearms Co. and their products.

Martini-Henry .450 Rifles & Carbines. By Dennis Lewis, Excalibur Publications, Latham, NY, 1996. 72 pp., illus. Paper covers. $11.95

The stories of the rifles and carbines that were the mainstay of the British soldier through the Victorian wars.

Mauser Bolt Rifles. By Ludwig Olson, F. Brownell & Son, Inc., Montezuma, IA, 1999. 364 pp., illus. $59.95

The most complete, detailed, authoritative and comprehensive work ever done on Mauser bolt rifles. Completely revised deluxe 3rd edition.

Mauser Military Rifles of the World, 2nd Edition. By Robert Ball, Krause Publications, Iola, WI, 2000. 304 pp., illustrated with 1,000 b&w photos and a 48 page color section. $44.95

This 2nd edition brings more than 100 new photos of these historic rifles and the wars in which they were carried.

Mauser Smallbores Sporting, Target and Training Rifles. By Jon Speed, Collector Grade Publications, Cobourg, Ontario, Canada 1998. 349 pp., illustrated. $67.50

A history of all the smallbore sporting, target and training rifles produced by the legendary Mauser-Werke of Oberndorf Am Neckar.

Military Holsters of World War 2. By Eugene J. Bender, Rowe Publications, Rochester, NY, 1998. 200 pp., illustrated. $45.00

A revised edition with a new price guide of the most definitive book on this subject.

Military Pistols of Japan. By Fred L. Honeycutt, Jr., Julin Books, Palm Beach Gardens, FL, 1997. 168 pp., illus. $42.00

Covers every aspect of military pistol production in Japan through WWII.

Military Remington Rolling Block Rifle, The. By George Layman, Pioneer Press, TN, 1998. 146 pp., illus. Paper covers. $24.95

A standard reference for those with an interest in the Remington rolling block family of firearms.

Military Rifles of Japan, 5th Edition. By F.L. Honeycutt, Julin Books, Lake Park, FL, 1999. 208 pp., illus. $42.00

A new revised and updated edition. Includes the early Murata-period markings, etc.

Military Small Arms Data Book. By Ian V. Hogg, Stackpole Books, Mechanicsburg, PA, 1999. $44.95. 336 pp., illustrated.

Data on more than 1,500 weapons. Covers a vast range of weapons from pistols to anti-tank rifles. Essential data, 1870-2000, in one volume.

Modern Beretta Firearms. By Gene Gangarosa, Jr., Stoeger Publishing Co., So. Hackensack, NJ, 1994. 288 pp., illus. Paper covers. $16.95

Traces all models of modern Beretta pistols, rifles, machine guns and combat shotguns.

Modern Gun Values, The Gun Digest Book of, 10th Edition. By the Editors of Gun Digest, DBI Books, a division of Krause Publications, Iola, WI., 1996. 560 pp. illus. Paper covers. $21.95

Greatly updated and expanded edition describing and valuing over 7,000 firearms manufactured from 1900 to 1996. The standard for valuing modern firearms.

Modern Gun Identification & Value Guide, 13th Edition. By Russell and Steve Quertermous, Collector Books, Paducah, KY, 1998. 504 pp., illus. Paper covers. $14.95

Features current values for over 2,500 models of rifles, shotguns and handguns, with over 1,800 illustrations.

More Single Shot Rifles. By James C. Grant, The Gun Room Press, Highland Park, NJ, 1976. 324 pp., illus. $35.00

Details the guns made by Frank Wesson, Milt Farrow, Holden, Borchardt, Stevens, Remington, Winchester, Ballard and Peabody-Martini.

Mortimer, the Gunmakers, 1753-1923. By H. Lee Munson, Andrew Mowbray Inc., Lincoln, RI, 1992. 320 pp., illus. $65.00

Seen through a single, dominant, English gunmaking dynasty this fascinating study provides a window into the classical era of firearms artistry.

Mosin-Nagant Rifle, The. By Terence W. Lapin, North Cape Publications, Tustin, CA, 1998. 30 pp., illustrated. Paper covers. $19.95

The first ever complete book on the Mosin-Nagant rifle written in English. Covers every variation.

Navy Luger, The. By Joachim Gortz and John Walter, Handgun Press, Glenview, IL, 1988. 128 pp., illus. $24.95

The 9mm Pistol 1904 and the Imperial German Navy. A concise illustrated history.

New World of Russian Small Arms and Ammunition, The. By Charlie Cutshaw, Paladin Press, Boulder, CO, 1998. 160 pp., illustrated. $42.95

Detailed descriptions, specifications and first-class illustrations of the AN-94, PSS silent pistol, Bizon SMG, Saifa-12 tactical shotgun, the GP-25 grenade launcher and more cutting edge Russian weapons.

Number 5 Jungle Carbine, The. By Alan M. Petrillo, Excalibur Publications, Latham, NY, 1994. 32 pp., illus. Paper covers. $7.95

A comprehensive treatment of the rifle that collectors have come to call the "Jungle Carbine"—the Lee-Enfield Number 5, Mark 1.

'03 Era: When Smokeless Revolutionized U.S. Riflery, The. By Clark S. Campbell, Collector Grade Publications, Inc., Ontario, Canada, 1994. 334 pp., illus. $44.50

A much-expanded version of Campbell's The '03 Springfields, representing forty years of in-depth research into "all things '03."

Observations on Colt's Second Contract, November 2, 1847. By G. Maxwell Longfield and David T. Basnett, Museum Restoration Service, Bloomfield, Ontario, Canada, 1997. 36 pp., illus. Paper covers. $6.95

This study traces the history and the construction of the Second Model Colt Dragoon supplied in 1848 to the U.S. Cavalry.

Official Guide to Gunmarks, 3rd Edition. By Robert H. Balderson, House of Collectibles, New York, NY, 1996. 367 pp., illus. Paper covers. $15.00

Identifies manufacturers' marks that appear on American and foreign pistols, rifles and shotguns.

Official Price Guide to Gun Collecting. By R.L. Wilson, Ballantine/House of Collectibles, New York, NY, 1998. 450 pp., illus. Paper covers. $21.50

Covers more than 30,000 prices from Colt revolvers to Winchester rifles and shotguns to German Lugers and British sporting rifles and game guns.

Official Price Guide to Military Collectibles, 6th Edition. By Richard J. Austin, Random House, Inc., New York, NY, 1998. 200 pp., illus. Paper cover. $20.00

Covers weapons and other collectibles from wars of the distant and recent past. More than 4,000 prices are listed. Illustrated with 400 black & white photos plus a full-color insert.

Official Soviet SVD Manual, The. By Major James F. Gebhardt (Ret.) Paladin Press, Boulder, CO, 1999. 112 pp., illustrated. Paper covers. $15.00

Operating instructions for the 7.62mm Dragunov, the first Russian rifle developed from scratch specifically for sniping.

Old Gunsights: A Collector's Guide, 1850 to 2000. By Nicholas Stroebel, Krause Publications, Iola, WI, 1998. 320 pp., illus. Paper covers. $29.95

An in-depth and comprehensive examination of old gunsights and the rifles on which they were used to get accurate feel for prices in this expanding market.

Old Rifle scopes. By Nicholas Stroebel, Krause Publications, Iola, WI, 2000. 400 pp., illustrated. Paper covers. $31.95

This comprehensive collector's guide takes aim at more than 120 scope makers and 60 mount makers and features photos and current market values for 300 scopes and mounts manufactured from 1950-1985.

P-08 Parabellum Luger Automatic Pistol, The. Edited by J. David McFarland, Desert Publications, Cornville, AZ, 1982. 20 pp., illus. Paper covers. $11.95

Covers every facet of the Luger, plus a listing of all known Luger models.

Packing Iron. By Richard C. Rattenbury, Zon International Publishing, Millwood, NY, 1993. 216 pp., illus. $45.00

The best book yet produced on pistol holsters and rifle scabbards. Over 300 variations of holster and scabbards are illustrated in large, clear plates.

Parabellum: A Technical History of Swiss Lugers. By Vittorio Bobba, Priuli & Verlucca, Editori, Torino, Italy, 1996. Italian and English text. Illustrated. $100.00

Patents for Inventions, Class 119 (Small Arms), 1855-1930. British Patent Office, Armory Publications, Oceanside, CA, 1993. 7 volume set. $250.00

Contains 7980 abridged patent descriptions and their sectioned line drawings, plus a 37-page alphabetical index of the patentees.

Pattern Dates for British Ordnance Small Arms, 1718-1783. By DeWitt Bailey, Thomas Publications, Gettysburg, PA, 1997. 116 pp., illus. Paper covers. $20.00

The weapons discussed in this work are those carried by troops sent to North America between 1737 and 1783, or shipped to them as replacement arms while in America.

Pitman Notes on U.S. Martial Small Arms and Ammunition, 1776-1933, Volume 2, Revolvers and Automatic Pistols, The. By Brig. Gen. John Pitman, Thomas Publications, Gettysburg, PA, 1990. 192 pp., illus. $29.95
A most important primary source of information on United States military small arms and ammunition.

Plains Rifle, The. By Charles Hanson, Gun Room Press, Highland Park, NJ, 1989. 169 pp., illus. $35.00
All rifles that were made with the plainsman in mind, including pistols.

Powder and Ball Small Arms. By Martin Pegler, Windrow & Green, London, 1998. 128 pp., illus. $39.95
Part of the new "Live Firing Classic Weapons" series featuring full color photos of experienced shooters dressed in authentic costumes handling, loading and firing historic weapons.

Powder Flask Book, The. By Ray Riling, R&R Books, Livonia, NY, 1993. 514 pp., illus. $69.95.
The complete book on flasks of the 19th century. Exactly scaled pictures of 1,600 flasks are illustrated.

Proud Promise: French Autoloading Rifles, 1898-1979. By Jean Huon, Collector Grade Publications, Inc., Cobourg, Ont., Canada, 1995. 216 pp., illus. $39.95
The author has finally set the record straight about the importance of French contributions to modern arms design.

Purdey Gun and Rifle Makers: The Definitive History. By Donald Dallas, Quiller Press, London, 2000. 245 pp., illus. Color throughout. $100.00
A limited edition of 3,000 copies. Signed and Numbered. With a PURDEY book plate.

Reloading Tools, Sights and Telescopes for Single Shot Rifles. By Gerald O. Kelver, Brighton, CO, 1982. 163 pp., illus. Paper covers. $13.95
A listing of most of the famous makers of reloading tools, sights and telescopes with a brief description of the products they manufactured.

Remington-Lee Rifle, The. By Eugene F. Myszkowski, Excalibur Publications, Latham, NY, 1995. 100 pp., illus. Paper covers. $22.50
Features detailed descriptions, including serial number ranges, of each model from the first Lee Magazine Rifle produced for the U.S. Navy to the last Remington-Lee Small Bores shipped to the Cuban Rural Guard.

Revolvers of the British Services 1854-1954. By W.H.J. Chamberlain and A.W.F. Taylerson, Museum Restoration Service, Ottawa, Canada, 1989. 80 pp., illus. $27.50
Covers the types issued among many of the United Kingdom's naval, land or air services.

Rhode Island Arms Makers & Gunsmiths. By William O. Archibald, Andrew Mowbray, Inc., Lincoln, RI, 1990. 108 pp., illus. $16.50
A serious and informative study of an important area of American arms making.

Rifles of the World. By Oliver Achard, Chartwell Books, Inc., Edison, NJ, 141 pp., illus. $24.95
A unique insight into the world of long guns, not just rifles, but also shotguns, carbines and all the usual multi-barreled guns that once were so popular with European hunters, especially in Germany and Austria.

Rock Island '03, The. By C.S. Ferris, C.S. Ferris, Arvada, CO, 1993. 58 pp., illus. Paper covers. $12.50
A monograph of interest to the collector or historian concentrating on the U.S. M1903 rifle made by the less publicized of our two producing facilities.

Round Ball to Rimfire, Vol. 1. By Dean Thomas, Thomas Publications, Gettysburg, PA, 1997. 144 pp., illus. $40.00
The first of a two-volume set of the most complete history and guide for all small arms ammunition used in the Civil War. The information includes data from research and development that created it.

Ruger and his Guns. By R.L. Wilson, Simon & Schuster, New York, NY, 1996. 358 pp., illus. $65.00
A history of the man, the company and their firearms.

Russell M. Catron and His Pistols. By Warren H. Buxton, Ucross Books, Los Alamos, NM, 1998. 224 pp., illustrated. Paper covers. $49.50
An unknown American firearms inventor and manufacturer of the mid twentieth century. Military, commercial, ammunition.

SAFN-49 and The FAL, The. By Joe Poyer and Dr. Richard Feirman, North Cape Publications, Tustin, CA, 1998. 160 pp., illus. $14.95
The first complete overview of the SAFN-49 battle rifle, from its pre-World War 2 beginnings to its military service in countries as diverse as the Belgian Congo and Argentina. The FAL was "light" version of the SAFN-49 and it became the Free World's most adopted battle rifle.

Sam Colt's Own Record 1847. By John Parsons, Wolfe Publishing Co., Prescott, AZ, 1992. 167 pp., illus. $24.50
Chronologically presented, the correspondence published here completes the account of the manufacture, in 1847, of the Walker Model Colt revolver.

J. P. Sauer & Sohn, Sauer "Dein Waffenkamerad" Volume 2. By Cate & Krause, Walsworth Publishing, Chattanooga, TN, 2000. 440 pp., illus. $79.00
A historical study of Sauer automatic pistols. This new volume includes a great deal of new knowledge that has surfaced about the firm J.P. Sauer. You will find new photos, documentation, serial number ranges and historical facts which will expand the knowledge and interest in the oldest and best of the German firearms companies.

Scottish Firearms. By Claude Blair and Robert Woosnam-Savage, Museum Restoration Service, Bloomfield, Ont., Canada, 1995. 52 pp., illus. Paper covers. $8.95
This revision of the first book devoted entirely to Scottish firearms is supplemented by a register of surviving Scottish long guns.

Scottish Pistol, The. By Martin Kelvin. Fairleigh Dickinson University Press, Dist. By Associated University Presses, Cranbury, NJ, 1997. 256 pp., illus. $49.50
The Scottish pistol, its history, manufacture and design.

Sharps Firearms. By Frank Seller, Frank M. Seller, Denver, CO, 1998. 358 pp., illus. $55.00
Traces the development of Sharps firearms with full range of guns made including all martial variations.

Simeon North: First Official Pistol Maker of the United States. By S. North and R. North, The Gun Room Press, Highland Park, NJ, 1972. 207 pp., illus. $15.95
Reprint of the rare first edition.

SKS Carbine, The. By Steve Kehaya and Joe Poyer, North Cape Publications, Tustin, CA, 1997. 150 pp., illus. Paper covers. $16.95
The first comprehensive examination of a major historical firearm used through the Vietnam conflict to the diamond fields of Angola.

SKS Type 45 Carbines, The. By Duncan Long, Desert Publications, El Dorado, AZ, 1992. 110 pp., illus. Paper covers. $19.95
Covers the history and practical aspects of operating, maintaining and modifying this abundantly available rifle.

Smith & Wesson 1857-1945. By Robert J. Neal and Roy G. Jinks, R&R Books, Livonia, NY, 1996. 434 pp., illus. $50.00
The bible for all existing and aspiring Smith & Wesson collectors.

Sniper Variations of the German K98k Rifle. By Richard D. Law, Collector Grade Publications, Ontario, Canada, 1997. 240 pp., illus. $47.50
Volume 2 of "Backbone of the Wehrmacht" the author's in-depth study of the German K98k rifle. This volume concentrates on the telescopic-sighted rifle of choice for most German snipers during World War 2.

Southern Derringers of the Mississippi Valley. By Turner Kirkland, Pioneer Press, Tenn., 1971. 80 pp., illus., paper covers. $4.00
A guide for the collector, and a much-needed study.

Soviet Russian Postwar Military Pistols and Cartridges. By Fred A. Datig, Handgun Press, Glenview, IL, 1988. 152 pp., illus. $29.95
Thoroughly researched, this definitive sourcebook covers the development and adoption of the Makarov, Stechkin and the new PSM pistols. Also included in this source book is coverage on Russian clandestine weapons and pistol cartridges.

Soviet Russian Tokarev "TT" Pistols and Cartridges 1929-1953. By Fred Datig, Graphic Publishers, Santa Ana, CA, 1993. 168 pp., illus. $39.95
Details of rare arms and their accessories are shown in hundreds of photos. It also contains a complete bibliography and index.

Soviet Small-Arms and Ammunition. By David Bolotin, Handgun Press, Glenview, IL, 1996. 264 pp., illus. $49.95
An authoritative and complete book on Soviet small arms.

Sporting Collectibles. By Jim and Vivian Karsnitz, Schiffer Publishing Ltd., West Chester, PA, 1992. 160 pp., illus. Paper covers. $29.95
The fascinating world of hunting related collectibles presented in an informative text.

Springfield 1903 Rifles, The. By Lt. Col. William S. Brophy, USAR, Ret., Stackpole Books Inc., Harrisburg, PA, 1985. 608 pp., illus. $75.00
The illustrated, documented story of the design, development, and production of all the models, appendages, and accessories.

Springfield Armory Shoulder Weapons 1795-1968. By Robert W.D. Ball, Antique Trader Books, Dubuque, IA, 1998. 264 pp., illus. $34.95
This book documents the 255 basic models of rifles, including test and trial rifles, produced by the Springfield Armory. It features the entire history of rifles and carbines manufactured at the Armory, the development of each weapon with specific operating characteristics and procedures.

Springfield Model 1903 Service Rifle Production and Alteration, 1905-1910. By C.S. Ferris and John Beard, Arvada, CO, 1995. 66 pp., illus. Paper covers. $12.50
A highly recommended work for any serious student of the Springfield Model 1903 rifle.

Springfield Shoulder Arms 1795-1865. By Claud E. Fuller, S. & S. Firearms, Glendale, NY, 1996. 76 pp., illus. Paper covers. $17.95
Exact reprint of the scarce 1930 edition of one of the most definitive works on Springfield flintlock and percussion muskets ever published.

Standard Catalog of Firearms, 11th Edition. By Ned Schwing, Krause Publications, Iola, WI, 2001.1328 Pages, illustrated. 6,000+ b&w photos plus a 16-page color section. Paper covers. $32.95
This is the largest, most comprehensive and best-selling firearm book of all time! And this year's edition is a blockbuster for both shooters and firearm collectors. More than 12,000 firearms are listed and priced in up to six grades of condition. That's almost 80,000 prices! Gun enthusiasts will love the new full-color section of photos highlighting the finest firearms sold at auction this past year –including the new record for an American historical firearm: $684,000!

Standard Catalog of Winchester, 1st Edition, edited by David D. Kowalski, Krause Publications, Iola, WI, 2000. 704 pp., illustrated with 2,000 B&W photos and 75 color photos. Paper covers. $39.95
This book identifies and values more than 5,000 collectibles, including firearms, cartridges shotshells, fishing tackle, sporting goods and tools manufactured by Winchester Repeating Arms Co.

Steel Canvas: The Art of American Arms. By R.L. Wilson, Random House, NY, 1995, 384 pp., illus. $65.00
Presented here for the first time is the breathtaking panorama of America's extraordinary engravers and embellishers of arms, from the 1700s to modern times.

Stevens Pistols & Pocket Rifles. By K.L. Cope, Museum Restoration Service, Alexandria Bay, NY, 1992. 114 pp., illus. $24.50
This is the story of the guns and the man who designed them and the company which he founded to make them.

Study of Colt Conversions and Other Percussion Revolvers, A. By R. Bruce McDowell, Krause Publications, Iola, WI, 1997. 464 pp., illus. $39.95
The ultimate reference detailing Colt revolvers that have been converted from percussion to cartridge.

Sumptuous Flaske, The. By Herbert G. Houze, Andrew Mowbray, Inc., Lincoln, RI, 1989. 158 pp., illus. Soft covers. $35.00
Catalog of a recent show at the Buffalo Bill Historical Center bringing together some of the finest European and American powder flasks of the 16th to 19th centuries.

Swedish Mauser Rifles, The. By Steve Kehaya and Joe Poyer, North Cape Publications, Tustin, CA, 1999. 277 pp., illustrated. Paper covers. $19.95
Every known variation of the Swedish Mauser carbine and rifle is described including all match and target rifles and all sniper versions. Includes serial number and production data.

Televisions Cowboys, Gunfighters & Cap Pistols. By Rudy A. D'Angelo, Antique Trader Books, Norfolk, VA, 1999. 287 pp., illustrated in color and black and white. Paper covers. $31.95

Over 850 beautifully photographed color and black and white images of cap guns, actors, and the characters they portrayed in the "Golden Age of TV Westerns. With accurate descriptions and current values.

Thompson: The American Legend. By Tracie L. Hill, Collector Grade Publications, Ontario, Canada, 1996. 584 pp., illus. $85.00

The story of the first American submachine gun. All models are featured and discussed.

Toys That Shoot and Other Neat Stuff. By James Dundas, Schiffer Books, Atglen, PA, 1999. 112 pp., illustrated. Paper covers. $24.95

Shooting toys from the twentieth century, especially 1920's to 1960's, in over 420 color photographs of BB guns, cap shooters, marble shooters, squirt guns and more. Complete with a price guide.

Trapdoor Springfield, The. By M.D. Waite and B.D. Ernst, The Gun Room Press, Highland Park, NJ, 1983. 250 pp., illus. $39.95

The first comprehensive book on the famous standard military rifle of the 1873-92 period.

Treasures of the Moscow Kremlin: Arsenal of the Russian Tsars, A Royal Armories and the Moscow Kremlin Exhibition. HM Tower of London 13, June 1998 to 11 September, 1998. BAS Printers, Over Wallop, Hampshire, England. xxii plus 192 pp. over 180 color illustrations. Text in English and Russian. $65.00

For this exhibition catalog each of the 94 objects on display are photographed and described in detail to provide a most informative record of this important exhibition.

United States Martial Flintlocks. By Robert M. Reilly, Mowbray Publishing Co., Lincoln, RI, 1997. 264 pp., illus. $40.00

A comprehensive history of American flintlock longarms and handguns (mostly military) c. 1775 to c. 1840.

U.S. Breech-Loading Rifles and Carbines, Cal. 45. By Gen. John Pitman, Thomas Publications, Gettysburg, PA, 1992. 192 pp., illus. $29.95

The third volume in the Pitman Notes on U.S. Martial Small Arms and Ammunition, 1776-1933. This book centers on the "Trapdoor Springfield" models.

U.S. Handguns of World War 2: The Secondary Pistols and Revolvers. By Charles W. Pate, Andrew Mowbray, Inc., Lincoln, RI, 1998. 515 pp., illus. $39.00

This indispensable new book covers all of the American military handguns of World War 2 except for the M1911A1 Colt automatic.

U.S. Martial Single Shot Pistols. By Daniel D. Hartzler and James B. Whisker, Old Bedford Village Pess, Bedford, PA, 1998. 128 pp., illus. $45.00

A photographic chronicle of military and semi-martial pistols supplied to the U.S. Government and the several States.

U.S. Military Arms Dates of Manufacture from 1795. By George Madis, David Madis, Dallas, TX, 1989. 64 pp. Soft covers. $6.00

Lists all U.S. military arms of collector interest alphabetically, covering about 250 models.

U.S. Military Small Arms 1816-1865. By Robert M. Reilly, The Gun Room Press, Highland Park, NJ, 1983. 270 pp., illus. $39.95

Covers every known type of primary and secondary martial firearms used by Federal forces.

U.S. M1 Carbines: Wartime Production. By Craig Riesch, North Cape Publications, Tustin, CA, 1994. 72 pp., illus. Paper covers. $16.95

Presents only verifiable and accurate information. Each part of the M1 Carbine is discussed fully in its own section; including markings and finishes.

U.S. Naval Handguns, 1808-1911. By Fredrick R. Winter, Andrew Mowbray Publishers, Lincoln, RI, 1990. 128 pp., illus. $26.00

The story of U.S. Naval Handguns spans an entire century—included are sections on each of the important naval handguns within the period.

Walther: A German Legend. By Manfred Kersten, Safari Press, Inc., Huntington Beach, CA, 2000. 400 pp., illustrated. $85.00

This comprehensive book covers, in rich detail, all aspects of the company and its guns, including an illustrious and rich history, the WW2 years, all the pistols (models 1 through 9), the P-38, P-88, the long guns, .22 rifles, centerfires, Wehrmacht guns, and even a gun that could shoot around a corner.

Walther Pistols: Models 1 Through P99, Factory Variations and Copies. By Dieter H. Marschall, Ucross Books, Los Alamos, NM. 2000. 140 pages, with 140 b & w illustrations, index. Paper Covers. $19.95

This is the English translation, revised and updated, of the highly successful and widely acclaimed German language edition. This book provides the collector with a reference guide and overview of the entire line of the Walther military, police, and self-defense pistols from the very first to the very latest. Models 1-9, PP, PPK, MP, AP, HP, P.38, P1, P4, P38K, P5, P88, P99 and the Manurhin models. Variations, where issued, serial ranges, calibers, marks, proofs, logos, and design aspects in an astonishing quantity and variety are crammed into this very well researched and highly regarded work.

Walther Handgun Story: A Collector's and Shooter's Guide, The. By Gene Gangarosa, Steiger Publications, 1999. 300., illustrated. Paper covers. $21.95

Covers the entire history of the Walther empire. Illustrated with over 250 photos.

Walther P-38 Pistol. By Maj. George Nonte, Desert Publications, Cornville, AZ, 1982. 100 pp., illus. Paper covers. $11.95

Complete volume on one of the most famous handguns to come out of WWII. All models covered.

Walther Models PP & PPK, 1929-1945 – Volume 1. By James L. Rankin, Coral Gables, FL, 1974. 142 pp., illus. $40.00

Complete coverage on the subject as to finish, proofmarks and Nazi Party inscriptions.

Walther Volume II, Engraved, Presentation and Standard Models. By James L. Rankin, J.L. Rankin, Coral Gables, FL, 1977. 112 pp., illus. $40.00

The new Walther book on embellished versions and standard models. Has 88 photographs, including many color plates.

Walther, Volume III, 1908-1980. By James L. Rankin, Coral Gables, FL, 1981. 226 pp., illus. $40.00

Covers all models of Walther handguns from 1908 to date, includes holsters, grips and magazines.

W.F. Cody Buffalo Bill Collector's Guide with Values, The. By James W. Wojtowicz, Collector Books, Paducah, KY, 1998. 271 pp., illustrated. $24.95

A profusion of colorful collectibles including lithographs, programs, photographs, books, medals, sheet music, guns, etc. and today's values.

Winchester: An American Legend. By R.L. Wilson, Random House, New York, NY, 1991. 403 pp., illus. $65.00

The official history of Winchester firearms from 1849 to the present.

Winchester Bolt Action Military & Sporting Rifles 1877 to 1937. By Herbert G. Houze, Andrew Mowbray Publishing, Lincoln, RI, 1998. 295 pp., illus. $45.00

Winchester was the first American arms maker to commercially manufacture a bolt action repeating rifle, and this book tells the exciting story of these Winchester bolt actions.

Winchester Book, The. By George Madis, David Madis Gun Book Distributor, Dallas, TX, 1986. 650 pp., illus. $49.50

A new, revised 25th anniversary edition of this classic book on Winchester firearms. Complete serial ranges have been added.

Winchester Dates of Manufacture 1849-1984. By George Madis, Art & Reference House, Brownsboro, TX, 1984. 59 pp. $9.95

A most useful work, compiled from records of the Winchester factory.

Winchester Engraving. By R.L. Wilson, Beinfeld Books, Springs, CA, 1989. 500 pp., illus. $135.00

A classic reference work of value to all arms collectors.

Winchester Handbook, The. By George Madis, Art & Reference House, Lancaster, TX, 1982. 287 pp., illus. $24.95

The complete line of Winchester guns, with dates of manufacture, serial numbers, etc.

Winchester-Lee Rifle, The. By Eugene Myszkowski, Excalibur Publications, Tucson, AZ 2000. 96 pp., illustrated. Paper Covers. $22.95

The development of the Lee Straight Pull, the cartridge and the approval for military use. Covers details of the inventor and memorabilia of Winchester-Lee related material.

Winchester Lever Action Repeating Firearms, Vol. 1, The Models of 1866, 1873 and 1876. By Arthur Pirkle, North Cape Publications, Tustin, CA, 1995. 112 pp., illus. Paper covers. $19.95

Complete, part-by-part description, including dimensions, finishes, markings and variations throughout the production run of these fine, collectible guns.

Winchester Lever Action Repeating Rifles, Vol. 2, The Models of 1886 and 1892. By Arthur Pirkle, North Cape Publications, Tustin, CA, 1996. 150 pp., illus. Paper covers. $19.95

Describes each model on a part-by-part basis by serial number range complete with finishes, markings and changes.

Winchester Lever Action Repeating Rifles, Volume 3, The Model of 1894. By Arthur Pirkle, North Cape Publications, Tustin, CA, 1998. 150 pp., illus. Paper covers. $19.95

The first book ever to provide a detailed description of the Model 1894 rifle and carbine.

Winchester Lever Legacy, The. By Clyde "Snooky" Williamson, Buffalo Press, Zachary, LA, 1988. 664 pp., illustrated. $75.00

A book on reloading for the different calibers of the Winchester lever action rifle.

Winchester Model 94: The First 100 Years, The. By Robert C. Renneberg, Krause Publications, Iola, WI, 1991. 208 pp., illus. $34.95

Covers the design and evolution from the early years up to the many different editions that exist today.

Winchester Rarities. By Webster, Krause Publications, Iola, WI., 2000. 208 pp., with over 800 color photos, illus. $49.95

This book details the rarest of the rare; the one-of-a-kind items and the advertising pieces from years gone by. With nearly 800 full color photos and detailed pricing provided by experts in the field, this book gives collectors and enthusiasts everything they need.

Winchester Shotguns and Shotshells. By Ronald W. Stadt, Krause Publications, Iola, WI, 1995. 256 pp., illus. $34.95

The definitive book on collectible Winchester shotguns and shotshells manufactured through 1961.

Winchester Single-Shot- Volume 1; A History and Analysis, The. By John Campbell, Andrew Mowbray, Inc., Lincoln RI, 1995. 272 pp., illus. $55.00

Covers every important aspect of this highly-collectible firearm.

Winchester Single-Shot- Volume 2; Old Secrets and New Discoveries, The. By John Campbell, Andrew Mowbray, Inc., Lincoln RI, 2000. 280 pp., illus. $55.00

An exciting follow-up to the classic first volume.

Winchester Slide-Action Rifles, Volume 1: Model 1890 & 1906. By Ned Schwing, Krause Publications, Iola, WI, 1992. 352 pp., illus. $39.95

First book length treatment of models 1890 & 1906 with over 50 charts and tables showing significant new information about caliber style and rarity.

Winchester Slide-Action Rifles, Volume 2: Model 61 & Model 62. By Ned Schwing, Krause Publications, Iola, WI, 1993. 256 pp., illus. $34.95

A complete historic look into the Model 61 and the Model 62. These favorite slide-action guns receive a thorough presentation which takes you to the factory to explore receivers, barrels, markings, stocks, stampings and engraving in complete detail.

Winchester's North West Mounted Police Carbines and other Model 1876 Data. By Lewis E. Yearout, The author, Great Falls, MT, 1999. 224 pp., illustrated. Paper covers. $38.00

An impressive accumulation of the facts on the Model 1876, with particular emphasis on those purchased for the North West Mounted Police.

Worldwide Webley and the Harrington and Richardson Connection. By Stephen Cuthbertson, Ballista Publishing and Distributing Ltd., Gabriola Island, Canada, 1999. 259 pp., illus. $50.00

A masterpiece of scholarship. Over 350 photographs plus 75 original documents, patent drawings, and advertisements accompany the text.